THE

CAMBRIDGE DICTIONARY

OF

PHILOSOPHY

.

SECOND EDITION

Widely acclaimed as the most authoritative and accessible one-volume dictionary of philosophy available in English (and now with translations into Chinese, Italian, Korean, Russian, and Spanish forthcoming), this work is now in a second edition offering an even richer, more comprehensive, and more up-to-date survey of ideas and thinkers, written by an international team of 440 contributors.

Key features of this second edition:

- The most comprehensive entries on major philosophers
- 400 new entries including 50 on preeminent contemporary philosophers
- Extensive coverage of rapidly developing fields such as the philosophy of mind and applied ethics (bioethics and environmental, medical, and professional ethics)
- More entries on non-Western and non-European philosophy than any comparable volume, including African, Arabic, Islamic, Japanese, Jewish, Korean, and Latin American philosophy
- Broad coverage of Continental philosophy

Robert Audi is Charles J. Mach Distinguished Professor of Philosophy at the University of Nebraska, Lincoln.

THE
CAMBRIDGE
DICTIONARY
OF
PHILOSOPHY

SECOND EDITION

General Editor
ROBERT AUDI

CAMBRIDGE
UNIVERSITY PRESS

PUBLISHED BY THE PRESS SYNDICATE OF THE UNIVERSITY OF CAMBRIDGE
The Pitt Building, Trumpington Street, Cambridge, United Kingdom

CAMBRIDGE UNIVERSITY PRESS
The Edinburgh Building, Cambridge CB2 2RU, UK
40 West 20th Street, New York, NY 10011-4211, USA
10 Stamford Road, Oakleigh, VIC 3166, Australia
Ruiz de Alarcón 13, 28014 Madrid, Spain
Dock House, The Waterfront, Cape Town 8001, South Africa

http://www.cambridge.org

First published 1995
Reprinted 1996 (twice), 1997 (twice), 1998 (twice)
Second edition 1999
Reprinted 2000 (twice), 2001

Printed in the United States of America

Typefaces Meridien 9/11, with Optima   *System* QuarkXPress™   [PS]

A catalog record for this book is available from the British Library.

Library of Congress Cataloging in Publication Data
The Cambridge dictionary of philosophy / edited by Robert Audi. – 2nd
ed.
p. cm.
Includes index.
ISBN 0-521-63136-X (hb)
1. Philosophy – Dictionaries.   I. Audi, Robert, date–
II. Title: Dictionary of philosophy.
B41.C35   1999
103 – dc21   99–12920
                                                    CIP

ISBN 0 521 63136 X hardback
ISBN 0 521 63722 8 paperback

CONTENTS

CONTRIBUTORS

Mitchell Aboulafia (M.Ab.), *University of Houston, Clear Lake:* Mead

Frederick Adams (F.A.), *Central Michigan University:* algorithm, bit, cybernetics, Dretske, information theory, mathematical function, non-monotonic logic

Marilyn McCord Adams (M.M.A.), *Yale University:* Anselm, Ockham, Ockham's razor

Robert M. Adams (R.M.A.), *Yale University:* agape, possible worlds, theodicy, transcendence

Laird Addis (L.A.), *University of Iowa:* holism, Mannheim, methodological holism

James W. Allard (J.W.A.), *Montana State University:* absolute; Alexander; Bosanquet; Bradley; Caird; Ferguson; Glanvil; Green; McCosh; McTaggart; Mansel; Martineau; More, Thomas; Price; Rashdall; Wilson

David Allison (D.Al.), *State University of New York, Stony Brook:* Saussure, structuralism, Teilhard de Chardin

Claudio de Almeida (C.d.A.), *Pontífica Universidade Católica do Rio Grande do Sol:* Moore's paradox

William P. Alston (W.P.A.), *Syracuse University:* theory of appearing

Karl Ameriks (K.A.), *University of Notre Dame:* Kant

C. Anthony Anderson (C.A.A.), *University of California, Santa Barbara:* degree, intensional logic, substitutivity *salva veritate,* variable

David Leech Anderson (D.L.A.), *Illinois State University:* Putnam

Roger Ariew (R.Ar.), *Virginia Polytechnic Institute and State University:* crucial experiment, Duhem, Kuhn

David Armstrong (D.Ar.), *University of Texas, Austin:* Longinus, Lucretius, Marcus Aurelius

E. J. Ashworth (E.J.A.), *University of Waterloo:* Bruno, Campanella, Ficino, Fonseca, Gerson, Paracelsus, Pico della Mirandola

Margaret Atherton (M.At.), *University of Wisconsin, Milwaukee:* Astell; Cavendish; Cudworth, Damaris; Elizabeth of Bohemia; Shepherd; Wollstonecraft

Bruce Aune (B.A.), *University of Massachusetts, Amherst:* fallibilism, problem of other minds

Edward Wilson Averill (E.W.A.), *Texas Tech University:* qualities

Kent Bach (K.B.), *San Francisco State University:* action verb, criterion, metalanguage, speech act theory, type–token distinction

Lynne Rudder Baker (L.R.B.), *University of Massachusetts, Amherst:* functionalism

Thomas R. Baldwin (T.R.B.), *University of York:* Anscombe, Strawson

Jon Barwise (J.Ba.), *Indiana University:* compactness theorem, infinitary logic

George Bealer (G.B.), *University of Colorado:* property

William Bechtel (W.B.), *Washington University:* cognitive science, connectionism

Lawrence C. Becker (L.C.B.), *College of William and Mary:* meritarian, meritocracy, prisoner's dilemma, situation ethics

Mark A. Bedau (M.A.B.), *Reed College:* artificial life

Ernst Behler (E.Beh.), *University of Washington:* Novalis, Schlegel

José A. Benardete (J.A.B.), *Syracuse University:* infinity

Ermanno Bencivenga (E.Ben.), *University of California, Irvine:* existential generalization, existential instantiation, free logic

Jan Berg (J.Be.), *Technische Universität München:* Bolzano

Robert L. Bernasconi (R.L.B.), *University of Memphis:* Gadamer

Bernard Berofsky (B.B.), *Columbia University:* determinism, necessitarianism

Rod Bertolet (R.B.), *Purdue University:* presupposition, private language argument, theory of descriptions, token-reflexive, trope

Charles J. Beyer (C.J.B.), *State University of New York, Buffalo:* Montesquieu

Joseph Bien (J.Bi.), *University of Missouri, Columbia:* French personalism, Lukács, Ricoeur, Rousseau, Sorel

Joseph Bien (J.Bi.), *University of Missouri, Columbia;* and **Heinz Paetzold (H.P.),** *University of Hamburg:* Praxis school

Peg Birmingham (P.Bi.), *DePaul University:* Irigaray

Ivan Boh (I.Bo.), *Ohio State University: conditio sine qua non,* enthymeme, epicheirema, eristic, imposition, logical notation, obversion, Paul of Venice, Peter of Spain, polysyllogism, *pons asinorum,* Sheffer stroke, Sherwood, square of opposition, syllogism

James Bohman (J.Bo.), *St. Louis University:* Adorno, critical theory, *Erlebnis,* Frankfurt School, Habermas, hermeneutics, Horkheimer, Marcuse, Scheler, social action, *Verstehen,* Weber

Daniel Bonevac (D.Bo.), *University of Texas, Austin:* philosophy of logic

Laurence BonJour (L.B.), *University of Washington:* a priori, Broad, coherence theory of truth

William J. Bouwsma (W.J.B.), *University of California, Berkeley:* Calvin

Raymond D. Bradley (R.D.B.), *Simon Fraser University:* contingent, infinite regress argument, necessity

Myles Brand (M.B.), *Indiana University:* volition, wayward causal chain

Richard B. Brandt (R.B.B.), *University of Michigan:* Bentham, Ross

Michael E. Bratman (M.E.B.), *Stanford University:* intention

Stephen E. Braude (S.E.B.), *University of Maryland, Baltimore:* parapsychology

Daniel Breazeale (D.Br.), *University of Kentucky:* Fichte, Hölderlin, Jacobi, Reinhold, Schelling, Schiller

David O. Brink (D.O.B.), *University of California, San Diego:* emotivism, ethical constructivism, moral realism

Gordon G. Brittan, Jr. (G.G.B.), *Montana State University:* Enlightenment

Dan W. Brock (D.W.B.), *Brown University:* bioethics, utilitarianism

Anthony Brueckner (A.B.), *University of California, Santa Barbara:* lottery paradox, transcendental argument

Jeffrey Bub (J.Bub), *University of Maryland, College Park:* quantum logic

Ann E. Bumpus (A.E.B.), *Dartmouth College:* Thomson

Robert W. Burch (R.W.B.), *Texas A & M University:* antilogism, biconditional, conjunction, contraposition, contraries, contravalid, converse, disjunctive proposition, iff, inconsistent triad, logical product, negation, partition, sorites, truth table, truth-value

John Burgess (J.Bur.), *Princeton University:* forcing, independence results, tense logic

Arthur W. Burks (A.W.B.), *University of Michigan:* Babbage, computer theory, self-reproducing automaton, Turing machine, von Neumann

Panayot Butchvarov (P.Bu.), *University of Iowa:* conceptualism; first philosophy; Hartmann, N.; metaphysical realism; metaphysics; natural philosophy; substance; substantialism

Robert E. Butts (R.E.B.), *University of Western Ontario:* Bacon, Francis; Campbell; Eudoxus of Cnidus; functional dependence; Galileo; hypothetico-deductive method; incommensurability; Jevons; lawlike generalization; Priestley; Spencer; testability; theory-laden; Whewell

David Carr (D.C.), *Emory University:* philosophy of history

Noël Carroll (N.C.), *University of Wisconsin, Madison:* Carlyle, Danto

Edward S. Casey (E.S.C.), *State University of New York, Stony Brook:* Jung

Victor Caston (V.C.), *Brown University:* Alexander of Aphrodisias, *energeia, lekton, phantasia*

Victor Caston (V.C.), *Brown University;* and **Stephen A. White (S.A.W.)**, *University of Texas, Austin:* Andronicus of Rhodes, Antiochus of Ascalon

Albert Casullo (A.C.), *University of Nebraska, Lincoln:* bundle theory, compresence, identity of indiscernibles

Robert L. Causey (R.L.C.), *University of Texas, Austin:* magnitude, unity of science

Alan K. L. Chan (A.K.L.C.), *National University of Singapore:* Ch'ien-fu Lun, Ho Yen, *hsien*, Hsi K'ang, *hsing-ming*, Juan Chi, Ko Hung, Neo-Taoism, *Po-hu tung*

Deen K. Chatterjee (D.K.C.), *University of Utah:* abhinivesha, ahantā, ākāśa, anattāvāda, arādhya, avidya, dharma, samādhi, Vijñānavāda

Roderick M. Chisholm (R.M.C.), *Brown University:* Ducasse

Brian P. Copenhaver (B.P.C.), *University of California, Riverside:* hermetism

John Corcoran (J.Cor.), *State University of New York, Buffalo:* axiomatic method; borderline case; categoricity; Church; conditional; convention T; converse, outer and inner; corresponding conditional; degenerate case; De Morgan;

domain; ellipsis; laws of thought; limiting case; logical form; logical subject; material adequacy; mathematical analysis; omega; proof by recursion; recursive function; scheme; scope; Tarski; tautology; universe of discourse

John Cottingham (J.Cot.), *University of Reading: Cogito ergo sum*, Descartes

Roger Crisp (R.C.), *St. Anne's College, University of Oxford: agathon*, Anniceris, *aporia*, Arcesilaus of Pitane, *epagogé*, Eros, form, *logos, poiēsis*, rigorism

Frederick J. Crosson (F.J.C.), *University of Notre Dame:* Newman, noetic, preexistence

Antonio S. Cua (A.S.C.), *The Catholic University of America: chih*[1]; *chih-hsing ho-i; ch'üan; chün-tzu;* Hsün Tzu; *jung, ju; kung, szu; liang-chih; Li Chi; li-ch'i;* Lu Hsiang-shan; *pi; pien; sheng; t'ien-jen ho-i;* Wang Yang-ming

Phillip D. Cummins (P.D.C.), *University of Iowa:* Bayle

Martin Curd (M.C.), *Purdue University:* Boltzmann, energeticism, Maxwell, Schrödinger

Stephen L. Darwall (S.L.D.), *University of Michigan:* Butler, Frankena

Wayne A. Davis (W.A.D.), *Georgetown University:* analytic–synthetic distinction; counterfactuals; inferential knowledge; Lewis, D. K.

Timothy Joseph Day (T.J.D.), *University of Alabama, Birmingham:* logical indicator, operator theory of adverbs

John Deigh (J.D.), *Northwestern University:* ethics, motivational internalism

C. F. Delaney (C.F.D.), *University of Notre Dame:* Critical Realism, Dewey, hypostasis, instrumentalism, New Realism, personalism, wisdom

Daniel C. Dennett (D.C.D.), *Tufts University:* homunculus, intentionality, Mentalese, mentalism, topic-neutral

Michael R. DePaul (M.R.D.), *University of Notre Dame:* coherentism, reflective equilibrium

Michael Detlefsen (M.D.), *University of Notre Dame:* Brouwer, Gödel's incompleteness theorems, Hilbert, Hilbert's Program, metamathematics

Daniel Trent Devereux (D.T.D.), *University of Virginia:* eudaimonism, Socratic intellectualism

Philip E. Devine (P.E.D.), *Providence College:* euthanasia, principle of double effect

John M. Dillon (J.M.D.), *Trinity College, Dublin:* Alexandrian School, Ammonius Saccas, commentaries on Aristotle, commentaries on Plato, Damascius, Johannes Philoponus, Middle Platonism, Neoplatonism, Numenius of Apamea, Plotinus

Martin C. Dillon (M.C.D.), *Binghamton University:* Derrida, *différance*

Robert DiSalle (R.D.), *University of Western Ontario:* Helmholtz, relativity, space, space-time

Alan Donagan (A.D.), *California Institute of Technology:* Collingwood

Fred Dretske (F.D.), *Stanford University:* perception, sensibilia

Wilhelm Dupré (W.D.), *The Catholic University of the Netherlands:* Jaspers

Gerald Dworkin (G.D.), *University of California, Davis:* paternalism, positive and negative freedom

John Earman (J.Ea.) and **Richard M. Gale (R.M.Ga.)**, *University of Pittsburgh:* time

Ellery Eells (E.Ee.), *University of Wisconsin, Madison:* equiprobable, principle of indifference, probability, regression analysis

Catherine Z. Elgin (C.Z.E.), *Harvard University:* Goodman

Berent Enç (B.E.), *University of Wisconsin, Madison:* motivational explanation, paradigm, paradigm case argument, plurality of causes

Ronald P. Endicott (R.P.E.), *Arkansas State University:* Churchland, Patricia; Churchland, Paul

Edward Erwin (E.Er.), *University of Miami:* philosophy of psychology

John Etchemendy (J.Et.), *Stanford University:* logical consequence, paradox, satisfaction, semantic paradoxes, set-theoretic paradoxes

C. Stephen Evans (C.S.E.), *Calvin College: Angst,* Kierkegaard

Susan L. Feagin (S.L.F.), *University of Missouri, Kansas City:* aesthetic attitude, aesthetic property, aesthetics, beauty, expression theory of art, institutional theory of art, sublime

Solomon Feferman (S.Fe.), *Stanford University:* ordinal logic, reflection principles

Richard Feldman (R.Fe.), *University of Rochester:* epistemic privacy, evidence, knowledge by acquaintance, knowledge *de re*

Arthur Fine (A.F.), *Northwestern University:* Einstein, quantum mechanics

Maurice A. Finocchiaro (M.A.F.), *University of Nevada, Las Vegas:* Gramsci, Mosca

Richard E. Flathman (R.E.F.), *Johns Hopkins University:* Arendt, Oakeshott, political theory

Gvozden Flego (G.Fl.), *University of Zagreb:* Blondel, Fourier, Proudhon

Richard Foley (R.Fo.), *Rutgers University:* analysis, pragmatic contradiction, subjectivism, voluntarism

Graeme Forbes (G.Fo.), *Tulane University:* modal logic, operator, order, ordering, reality

Malcolm R. Forster (M.R.F.), *University of Wisconsin, Madison:* curve-fitting problem

Daniel Fouke (D.F.), *University of Dayton:* Pascal

Patrick Francken (P.F.), *Illinois State University:* time slice

Samuel Freeman (S.Fr.), *University of Pennsylvania:* Rawls

Elizabeth Fricker (E.F.), *Magdalen College, University of Oxford:* testimony

Miranda Fricker (M.F.), *Heythrop College, University of London:* feminist epistemology

Michael Friedman (M.F.), *Indiana University:* Hempel

Richard A. Fumerton (R.A.F.), *University of Iowa:* Ayer, logical positivism, phenomenalism, protocol statement

Alan Gabbey (A.G.), *Barnard College:* Boyle; Cambridge Platonists; More, Henry

Pieranna Garavaso (P.Gar.), *University of Minnesota, Morris:* Beccaria, Cajetan, Gentile, Gioberti, Joachim of Floris, Labriola, Marsilius of Padua, Medina, Pomponazzi, Rosmini-Serbati, Telesio, Valla, Vanini, Zabarella

Daniel Garber (D.Garb.), *University of Chicago:* Cordemoy, Geulincx, Goclenius, La Forge, mode, rationalism

Jorge L. A. Garcia (J.L.A.G.), *Rutgers University:* cardinal virtues, racism, virtue ethics

Don Garrett (D.Garr.), *University of North Carolina, Chapel Hill:* Spinoza

Philip Gasper (P.Gas.), *College of Notre Dame:* anti-realism, social constructivism

Berys Gaut (B.Ga.), *University of Saint Andrews:* consequentialism, depiction, fiction, intentional fallacy

Bernard Gert (B.Ge.), *Dartmouth College:* applied ethics, Hobbes, morality, rationality, supererogation

Roger F. Gibson (R.F.G.), *Washington University:* corners, indeterminacy of translation, oblique context, ontological commitment, quantifying in, Quine

Carl Ginet (C.G.), *Cornell University:* memory, paradox of analysis

Alan H. Goldman (A.H.G.), *University of Miami:* privileged access

Alvin I. Goldman (A.I.G.), *University of Arizona:* naturalistic epistemology, reliabilism, social epistemology

Alfonso Gömez-Lobo (A.G.-L.), *Georgetown University: hexis,* Peripatetic School

Lenn E. Goodman (L.E.G.), *Vanderbilt University:* al-Rāzī, Averroes, Avicenna, Ibn Daud, Maimonides, Miskawayh, Saadiah

Robert M. Gordon (R.M.G.), *University of Missouri, St. Louis:* emotion, empathy, James-Lange theory, simulation theory

Jorge J. E. Gracia (J.J.E.G.), *State University of New York, Buffalo:* Bañez, Gracián y Morales, individuation, John of Saint Thomas, Latin American philosophy, Mariana, Molina, Ortega y Gassett, *principium individuationis,* Soto, Suárez, Toletus, Unamuno, Vázquez, Vitoria

Daniel W. Graham (D.W.G.), *Brigham Young University:* Anaxagoras, Anaximander, Anaximenes of Miletus, ancient atomism, *apeiron,* Democritus, Empedocles, Heraclitus, Leucippus, Milesians, pre-Socratics, Thales

George A. Graham (G.A.G.), *University of Alabama, Birmingham:* associationism, attribution theory, behavior therapy, cognitive dissonance, conditioning, intervening variable, poverty of the stimulus, redintegration, sensorium, synaesthesia

Richard E. Grandy (R.E.G.), *Rice University:* Grice, Löwenheim-Skolem theorem, psycholinguistics

I. Grattan-Guinness (I.G.-G.), *Middlesex Polytechnic University:* calculus, Euclidean geometry, non-Euclidean geometry, Peano postulates

John Greco (J.G.), *Fordham University:* inference to the best explanation

Philip T. Grier (P.T.G.), *Dickinson College:* Il'in, Kropotkin, Shpet

Nicholas Griffin (N.G.), *McMaster University:* emotive conjugation, mnemic causation

Nicholas Griffin (N.G.), *McMaster University;* and **David B. Martens (D.B.M.)**, *Mount Royal College:* Russell

David A. Griffiths (D.A.G.), *University of Victoria:* Leroux

Paul J. Griffiths (P.J.G.), *University of Chicago:* abhidharma, ālaya-vijñāna, bhavaṅga, citta-mātra, dravyasat, jhāna, nirodha-samāpatti, samanantara-pratyaya, samatha, śūnyatā, vāsanā, vijñapti, vipassanā

Charles L. Griswold, Jr. (C.L.G.), *Boston University:* Smith

Charles B. Guignon (C.B.G.), *University of Vermont:* Heidegger

Pete A. Y. Gunter (P.A.Y.G.), *University of North Texas:* Bergson

Dimitri Gutas (D.Gu.), *Yale University:* Arabic philosophy, Ibn Khaldūn, *Sufism*

Gary Gutting (G.G.), *University of Notre Dame:* Bachelard; Canguilhem; Foucault; Lacan; MacIntyre; Rorty; Taylor, Charles; Voltaire

Paul Guyer (P.Gu.), *University of Pennsylvania:* Baumgarten, Cavell, Wolff

Kyame Gyekye (K.G.), *University of Ghana:* African philosophy

Oscar A. Haac (O.A.H.), *New York City:* Condillac, Constant, Cousin

Michael Hallett (M.H.), *McGill University:* Cantor, Dedekind, Skolem

Edward C. Halper (E.C.H.), *University of Georgia:* aitia, autarkia, dianoia, elenchus, *noûs*, one–many problem, one over many, *ousia, telos*

Jean Hampton (J. Ham.), *University of Arizona:* contractarianism, social contract

R. James Hankinson (R.J.H.), *University of Texas, Austin:* Galen, Hippocrates

K. R. Hanley (K.R.H.), *Le Moyne College:* Marcel

Russell Hardin (R.Har.), *New York University:* game theory, Pareto efficiency, voting paradox

Robert M. Harnish (R.M.H.), *University of Arizona:* Searle

William Harper (W.Har.), *University of Western Ontario:* natural kind

David Harrah (D.H.), *University of California, Riverside:* axiom of consistency, cut-elimination theorem, erotetic, fuzzy set, tonk

William Hasker (W.Has.), *Huntington College:* evidentialism, justification by faith, middle knowledge, self-referential incoherence

John Haugeland (J.Hau.), *University of Pittsburgh:* artificial intelligence

Roger Hausheer (R.Hau.), *University of Bradford:* Berlin

William Heald (W.He.), *University of Iowa:* Bergmann

Peter Heath (P.He.), *University of Virginia:* Austin, J. L.; Carroll

John Heil (J.F.H.), *Davidson College:* analytic philosophy, awareness, blindsight, Dennett, direct realism, doxastic, Kim, Molyneux question, ordinary language philosophy, power, preanalytic, pro attitude, prototype theory, pseudohallucination, reasons for belief, subdoxastic, Twin-Earth

Francis Heylighen (F.H.), *Free University of Brussels;* and **Cliff Joslyn (C.J.)**, *State University of New York, Binghamton:* systems theory

Kathleen Marie Higgins (K.M.H.), *University of Texas, Austin:* Schopenhauer

Risto Hilpinen (R.Hi.), *University of Miami and University of Turku:* epistemic logic, epistemic principle, KK-thesis, Peirce, tychism

Harold T. Hodes (H.T.H.), *Cornell University:* degree of unsolvability, hierarchy, lambda-calculus, logicism

Joshua Hoffman (J.Ho.) and **Gary Rosenkrantz (G.Ro.)**, *University of North Carolina, Greensboro:* Boscovich, life, mereology, organism, perdurance

Alan Holland (A.Ho.), *University of Lancaster:* environmental philosophy

Robert L. Holmes (R.L.H.), *University of Rochester:* Gandhi, just war theory, non-violence, pacifism, violence

Brad W. Hooker (B.W.H.), *University of Reading:* ascriptivism, Brandt, casuistry, descriptivism, Hare, justice, prescriptivism, sanction

Terence E. Horgan (T.E.H.), *University of Memphis:* folk psychology, supervenience

Tamara Horowitz (T.H.), *University of Pittsburgh:* entropy, stochastic process

Paul Horwich (P.Hor.), *Massachusetts Institute of Technology:* truth

Paul Hoβfeld (P.Hoβ.), *Albertus Magnus Institut:* Albertus Magnus

Anne Hudson (A.Hu.), *Lady Margaret Hall, University of Oxford:* Wyclif

Deal W. Hudson (D.W.H.), *Fordham University:* Gilson, Maritain, Mercier, Neo-Thomism

Carl A. Huffman (C.A.H.), *DePauw University:* Archytas, Philolaus, Pythagoras

David L. Hull (D.L.H.), *Northwestern University:* Darwinism, mechanistic explanation, Mendel, philosophy of biology, teleology

Patricia Huntington (P.Hu.), *Loyola University of Chicago:* Kristeva

Rosalind Hursthouse (R.Hu.), *Open University:* Foot

Ronald E. Hustwit (R.E.H.), *College of Wooster:* Bouwsma

Sarah Hutton (S.H.), *London:* Cockburn, Conway

Harry A. Ide (H.A.I.), *University of Nebraska, Lincoln:* Cynics, Cyrenaics, Sophists, thema

Philip J. Ivanhoe (P.J.I.), *University of Michigan:* Chang Hsüeh-ch'eng; Chang Tsai; Ch'eng Hao, Ch'eng Yi; *ch'i; ching;* Chou Tun-yi; *hsin²; hsü;* Huang-Lao; *I-Ching;* Kuo Hsiang; *li¹;* Shao Yung; *shen;* Tai Chen; Taoism; *tzu jan;* Wang Fu-chih; Wang Pi; Yen Yuan

Alfred L. Ivry (A.L.I.), *New York University:* al-Fārābī, al-Ghāzali, cabala, Ibn Gabirol, Jewish philosophy

Dale Jacquette (D.J.), *Pennsylvania State University:* abstract entity, act-object psychology, Brentano, extensionalism, haecceity, impredicative definition, Meinong, subject–object dichotomy, use–mention distinction

Richard Jeffrey (R.J.), *Princeton University:* Bayes's theorem, computability, decision theory, Ramsey

David Alan Johnson (D.A.J.), *Yeshiva University:* Bayesian rationality, doomsday argument, envelope paradox, grue paradox, qualitative predicate

Edward Johnson (E.J.), *University of New Orleans:* moral status, personhood

Mark D. Jordan (M.D.J.), *University of Notre Dame:* Ambrose, Augustine, Bernard of Chartres, Eckhart, Lull, patristic authors, Teresa of Ávila, William of Moerbeke

Hwa Yol Jung (H.Y.J.), *Moravian College:* Bakhtin, transversality

Robert Hillary Kane (R.H.K.), *University of Texas, Austin:* Arminius, Bloch, book of life, Lequier, *liberum arbitrium,* principle of insufficient reason, principle of plenitude, Renouvier, Socinianism

Tomis Kapitan (T.K.), *Northern Illinois University*: free will problem, guise theory, practition, quasi-indicator, self-determination

Jacquelyn Ann K. Kegley (J.A.K.K.), *California State University, Bakersfield:* Royce

James A. Keller (J.A.K.), *Wofford College:* process theology, thought experiment, unity in diversity

Ralph Kennedy (R.Ke.), *Wake Forest University:* Dutch book, Dutch book argument, Dutch book theorem, enantiamorphs, gambler's fallacy, homomorphism, problem of the speckled hen, self-presenting

Jaegwon Kim (J.K.), *Brown University:* causal law, causation, explanation

Yersu Kim (Y.K.), *Seoul National University:* Korean philosophy

Patricia Kitcher (P.K.), *Columbia University:* Beattie

Peter D. Klein (P.D.K.), *Rutgers University:* certainty, closure

E. D. Klemke (E.D.K.), *Iowa State University:* Moore

Virginia Klenk (V.K.), *Moorhead State University:* axiom of comprehension, comprehension, connected, copula, counterinstance, lexical ordering, normal form, order type omega, sentential connective

George L. Kline (G.L.K.), *Bryn Mawr College:* Bakunin, Berdyaev, Herzen, Russian nihilism, Russian philosophy, Solovyov

Simo Knuuttila (S.K.), *University of Helsinki:* future contingents

Joseph J. Kockelmans (J.J.K.), *Pennsylvania State University:* Continental philosophy, phenomenology

Konstantin Kolenda (K.K.), *Rice University:* humanism

Isaac Kramnick (I.K.), *Cornell University:* Burke

Richard Kraut (R.Kr.), *Northwestern University:* Plato, Socrates

Manfred Kuehn (M.K.), *Purdue University:* acosmism, Haeckel, Hamann, Hamilton, Herbart, Lambert, Maimon, Reimarus, Schulze, Tetens, Vaihinger

Steven T. Kuhn (S.T.K.), *Georgetown University:* decidability, deduction theorem, formalism, formalize, formal language, ideal language, is, Kripke semantics, sortal predicate, truth-value semantics

Henry E. Kyburg, Jr. (H.E.K.), *University of Rochester:* Carnap

John Lachs (J.La.), *Vanderbilt University:* Santayana

Stephen E. Lahey (S.E.L.), *Le Moyne College: insolubilia, obligationes, sophismata,* topics

Thomas H. Leahey (T.H.L.), *Virginia Commonwealth University:* Bain, camera obscura, faculty psychology, Fechner, Hartley, hologram, ideo-motor action, Köhler, Lewin, McDougall, Stout, Ward, Wundt

Joo Heung Lee (J.H.L.), *Wright College.:* Bataille

Keith Lehrer (K.L.), *University of Arizona:* Reid

Dorothy Leland (D.Le.), *Purdue University:* embodiment

Noah M. Lemos (N.M.L.), *De Pauw University:* false pleasure, Perry, value, value theory

Ernest LePore (E.L.), *Rutgers University:* Davidson, *de dicto,* holism, principle of verifiability, semantic holism, verificationism

Isaac Levi (I.L.), *Columbia University:* Bernoulli's theorem; Nagel, Ernest; reduction sentence; statistical explanation

Andrew Levine (A.L.), *University of Wisconsin, Madison:* Althusser

Alan E. Lewis (A.E.L.), *Austin Presbyterian Theological Seminary:* Arianism, Athanasius, Clement of Alexandria, henotheism, *homoousios*, Montanism, Pelagianism, Tertullian

Daniel E. Little (D.E.L.), *Bucknell University:* ethnography, ethnology, ethnomethodology, philosophy of the social sciences

Shu-hsien Liu (S.-h.L.), *Chinese University of Hong Kong:* Ch'en Hsien-chang; *ch'eng;* Chia Yi; *ch'ien, k'un;* Ch'ien Mu; Chinese philosophy; Chu Hsi; Fang; Fung Yu-lan; Han Yü; *hsing-erh-shang;* Hsiung Shih-li; Hsü Fu-kuan; Huang Tsung-hsi; Hu Hung; Hu Shih; K'ang Yu-wei; Liang Ch'i-ch'ao; Liang Sou-ming; Li Ao; *li-i-fen-shu;* Liu Shao-ch'i; Liu Tsung-chou; Mao Tse-tung; Mou Tsung-san; Neo-Confucianism; *shan, o;* Sun Yat-sen; *t'ai-chi;* T'ang Chün-i; T'an Ssu-tung; *tao-hsin, jen-hsin; tao-t'ung; t'i, yung; t'ien li, jen-yü;* Tung Chung-shu; Wang Ch'ung; Yang Hsiung; *yu, wu*

Shu-hsien Liu (S.-h.L.), *Chinese University of Hong Kong,* and Alan K. L. Chan (A.K.L.C.), *National University of Singapore:* Chiao Hung

Brian Loar (B.L.), *Rutgers University:* meaning

Lawrence B. Lombard (L.B.L.), *Wayne State University:* event

John Longeway (J.Lo.), *University of Wisconsin, Parkside:* Adelard of Bath, Albert of Saxony, Boehme, Erigena, Fludd, Gregory I, John of Damascus, Marsilius of Inghen, Nemesius of Emesa, Nicholas of Cusa, *Nihil ex nihilo fit, sensus communis,* terminist logic, William of Alnwick, William of Auvergne

Michael J. Loux (M.J.L.), *University of Notre Dame:* essentialism

E. J. Lowe (E.J.L.), *University of Durham:* Armstrong, Dummett

Steven Luper (S.L.), *Trinity University, San Antonio:* Nozick

Eugene C. Luschei (E.C.L.), *Brown University:* Kotarbiński, Leśniewski, Polish logic

William G. Lycan (W.G.L.), *University of North Carolina, Chapel Hill:* philosophy of language

David Lyons (D.Ly.), *Boston University:* Hart

William L. McBride (W.L.M.), *Purdue University:* existentialism, Marx, Marxism

Storrs McCall (S.Mc.), *McGill University:* Łukasiewicz

Hugh J. McCann (H.J.M.), *Texas A & M University:* action theory, practical reason, practical reasoning, reasons for action

Robert N. McCauley (R.N.Mc.), *Emory University:* evolutionary psychology

John J. McDermott (J.J.M.), *Texas A & M University:* Emerson, James, specious present

Scott MacDonald (S.Ma.), *Cornell University:* Boethius, Peter Lombard, transcendentals

Ralph McInerny (R.M.), *University of Notre Dame:* neo-Scholasticism, *philosophia perennis,* potency, synderesis

Thomas McKay (T.M.), *Syracuse University:* connotation, denotation, indirect discourse, propositional opacity, referentially transparent

Louis H. Mackey (L.H.M.), *University of Texas, Austin:* literary theory, philosophy of literature

Penelope Mackie (P.Mac.), *University of Birmingham:* compossible, counterpart theory, organic, organicism, process–product ambiguity

Michael McKinsey (M.M.), *Wayne State University:* anaphora, implicature, indexical

Brian P. McLaughlin (B.P.M.), *Rutgers University:* philosophy of mind

Ernan McMullin (E.M.), *University of Notre Dame:* Kepler, Mach, Poincaré

Edward H. Madden (E.H.M.), *University of Kentucky:* Thoreau, transcendentalism, Wright

Penelope Maddy (P.Mad.), *University of California, Irvine:* class, complementary class, continuum problem, maximal consistent set, Schröder-Bernstein theorem, set theory, transfinite number

G. B. Madison (G.B.M.), *McMaster University:* Merleau-Ponty

Bernd Magnus (B.M.), *University of California, Riverside:* postmodern

Rudolf A. Makkreel (R.A.M.), *Emory University:* Dilthey, *Einfühlung*

William E. Mann (W.E.M.), *University of Vermont:* accidentalism, Bernard of Clairvaux, *concursus dei, dictum de omni et nullo,* emanationism, eternal return, *infima species,* mystical experience, mysticism, *Nihil est in intellectu quod non prius fuerit in sensu,* paradoxes of omnipotence, Porphyry, soul, survival, tree of Porphyry

Peter Markie (P.Mar.), *University of Missouri, Columbia:* egocentric particular, egocentric predicament

Jean-Pierre Marquis (J.-P.M.), *University of Montreal:* category theory

A. Marras (A.M.), *University of Western Ontario:* behaviorism

Mike W. Martin (M.W.M.), *Chapman College:* bad faith, false consciousness, institution, professional ethics, self-deception, vital lie

A. P. Martinich (A.P.M.), *University of Texas, Austin:* distribution, *ens a se, ens rationis, ens realissimum, fundamentum divisionis, notum per se, obiectum quo,* pantheism, *Pantheismusstreit,* reism, *rerum natura, terminus a quo, theologia naturalis,* theosophy

Jack W. Meiland (J.W.M.), *University of Michigan:* category, category mistake, Ryle

Alfred R. Mele (A.R.M.), *Davidson College:* accidie, *akrasia,* control, extrinsic desire, motivation, rationalization, Socratic paradoxes, theoretical reason, toxin puzzle

Joseph R. Mendola (J.R.M.), *University of Nebraska, Lincoln:* informed consent, moral psychology, rational psychology

Christopher Menzel (C.M.), *Texas A & M University:* alethic modalities, type theory

Michael J. Meyer (M.J.M.), *Santa Clara University:* character, dignity, Percival

David W. Miller (D.W.M.), *University of Warwick:* demarcation, Popper

Robert N. Minor (R.N.Mi.), *University of Kansas:* ādhyātman, ahaṁkāra, ahiṁsā, akṣara, avatar, *bhakti, saṁsāra, sat/chit/ānanda,* Vishnu

Phillip Mitsis (P.Mi.), *Cornell University:* Cicero

James A. Montmarquet (J.A.M.), *Tennessee State University:* hedonism, perfectionism, *summum bonum,* virtue epistemology

Michael S. Moore (M.S.M.), *University of Pennsylvania:* basic norm, cheapest-cost avoider, critical legal studies, *mens rea,* M'Naghten rule, punishment, telishment

Donald R. Morrison (D.R.M.), *Rice University:* Xenophon

Stephen J. Morse (S.J.M.), *University of Pennsylvania:* diminished capacity

Paul K. Moser (P.K.M.), *Loyola University of Chicago:* belief, epistemic regress argument, epistemology, foundationalism, irrationality, metaphilosophy, pretheoretical

Alexander P. D. Mourelatos (A.P.D.M.), *University of Texas, Austin:* Abderites, Eleatic School, homoeomerous, hylozoism, Ionian philosophy, Melissus of Samos, Orphism, Parmenides, Xenophanes

Ian Mueller (I.M.), *University of Chicago:* Celsus, doxographers, Hypatia, Simplicius

James Bernard Murphy (J.B.M.), *Dartmouth College:* common good, semiosis, subsidiarity

Steven Nadler (S.N.), *University of Wisconsin, Madison:* Arnauld, Malebranche, occasionalism, *Port-Royal Logic*

Jan Narveson (J.Na.), *University of Waterloo:* social philosophy

Alan Nelson (A.N.), *University of California, Irvine:* Arrow's paradox; ideal market; Keynes; Mill, James; perfect competition; production theory; social choice theory

Jerome Neu (J.Ne.), *University of California, Santa Cruz:* Freud

Kai Nielsen (K.N.), *University of Calgary:* Engels, historicism

Ilkka Niiniluoto (I.N.), *University of Helsinki:* covering law model, truthlikeness, von Wright

Carlos G. Noreña (C.G.Nore.), *University of California, Santa Cruz:* Vives

Calvin G. Normore (C.G.Norm.), *University of Toronto:* Kilwardby, Scholasticism, Siger of Brabant

David Fate Norton (D.F.N.), *McGill University:* Hume

Donald Nute (D.N.), *University of Georgia:* default logic, defeasibility, intension

David S. Oderberg (D.S.O.), *University of Reading:* Geach

Steve Odin (S.O.), *University of Hawaii:* Japanese philosophy

Willard G. Oxtoby (W.G.O.), *University of Toronto:* Zoroastrianism

Heinz Paetzold (H.P.), *University of Hamburg:* Bodin, Erasmus, Helvétius

George S. Pappas (G.S.P.), *Ohio State University:* basing relation, Berkeley, idea, immaterialism

Anthony J. Parel (A.J.P.), *University of Calgary:* Machiavelli

R. P. Peerenboom (R.P.P.) and **Roger T. Ames (R.T.A.)**, *University of Hawaii:* Chinese Legalism; Hsü Hsing; *Huai Nan Tzu;* Hui Shih; Kuan Tzu; Lieh Tzu; *Lü-*

shih ch'un-ch'iu; Mohism; School of Names; Shang Yang; Shen Pu-Hai; Shen Tao; *shih*[1]; *shih*[2]; *shu*[1]; Sung Hsing; Tsou Yen; *wu-hsing;* Yang Chu; yin, yang

Francis Jeffry Pelletier (F.J.P.) and **István Berkeley (I.Be.)**, *University of Alberta:* vagueness

Adriaan T. Peperzak (A.T.P.), *Loyola University of Chicago:* Levinas

Philip Pettit (P.P.), *Australian National University:* Smart

Edmund L. Pincoffs (E.L.P.), *University of Texas, Austin:* Austin, John

Robert B. Pippin (R.B.P.), *University of Chicago:* Hegel

Alvin Plantinga (A.P.), *University of Notre Dame:* Alston

Louis P. Pojman (L.P.P.), *United States Military Academy, West Point:* agnoiology, agnosticism, apocatastasis, atheism, Basilides, Buchmanism, gnosticism, Gregory of Nyssa, meliorism, Origen, relativism, Valentinus, Westermarck

Richard H. Popkin (R.H.P.), *University of California, Los Angeles:* Charron, Ha-Levi, Mendelssohn, Montaigne, Sanches, Sextus Empiricus, Skeptics

John F. Post (J.F.P.), *Vanderbilt University:* naturalism

Carl J. Posy (C.J.P.), *Duke University:* choice sequence, mathematical intuitionism, philosophy of mathematics

William J. Prior (W.J.P.), *Santa Clara University:* ananke, divided line, *physis,* ring of Gyges, ship of Theseus, Socratic irony, *techne*

Richard Purtill (R.P.), *Western Washington University:* a fortiori argument, argument, *consequentia mirabilis,* equipollence, equivalence, Euler diagram, principle of bivalence, principle of contradiction, principle of excluded middle, Venn diagram

Philip L. Quinn (P.L.Q.), *University of Notre Dame:* divine command ethics, double truth, philosophy of religion, Swinburne, transubstantiation, Trinitarianism

Elizabeth S. Radcliffe (E.S.R.), *Santa Clara University:* Gay, Hutcheson, moral sense theory, sentimentalism, Shaftesbury, Wollaston

Diana Raffman (D.R.), *Ohio State University;* and **Walter Sinnott-Armstrong (W.S.-A.)**, *Dartmouth College:* Marcus

Gerard Raulet (G.Ra.), *Groupe de Recherche sur la Culture de Weimar, Paris:* Kleist, Lessing

Stephen L. Read (S.L.R.), *University of St. Andrews:* exponible, many-valued logic, pluralitive logic, relevance logic

Nicholas Rescher (N.R.), *University of Pittsburgh:* idealism

Henry S. Richardson (H.S.R.), *Georgetown University:* Nussbaum

Robert C. Richardson (R.C.R.), *University of Cincinnati:* black box, figure–ground, heuristics, modularity, split brain effects, Zeigarnik effect

Thomas Ricketts (T.R.), *University of Pennsylvania:* Frege

Mark Roberts (M.Ro.), *State University of New York, Stony Brook:* Barthes, signifier

Alexander Rosenberg (A.R.), *University of Georgia:* Coase theorem, philosophy of economics

William L. Rowe (W.L.R.), *Purdue University:* agent causation, antinomianism, *causa sui,* Clarke, immanence, prime mover, privation, theological naturalism

T. M. Rudavsky (T.M.R.), *Ohio State University:* Abrabanel, Isaac; Abrabanel, Judah; Crescas

Michael Ruse (M.Ru.), *University of Guelph:* creationism, evolutionary epistemology, social biology

Bruce Russell (B.R.), *Wayne State University:* definist, duty, egoism, good-making characteristic, intuition, self-evidence

Lilly-Marlene Russow (L.-M.R.), *Purdue University:* imagination

R. M. Sainsbury (R.M.S.), *King's College, University of London:* sorites paradox, unexpected examination paradox, Zeno's paradoxes

Nathan Salmon (N.S.), *University of California, Santa Barbara;* Kripke

Wesley C. Salmon (W.C.S.), *University of Pittsburgh:* confirmation, problem of induction, Reichenbach, theoretical term

David H. Sanford (D.H.S.), *Duke University:* circular reasoning, determinable, implication, indiscernibility of identicals, inference, Johnson

Marco Santambrogio (M.Sa.), *University of Cagliari:* Eco

David Sapire (D.S.), *University of The Witwatersrand:* disposition, propensity, state

Ruth A. Saunders (R.A.Sa.), *Wayne State University:* Piaget

Geoffrey Sayre-McCord (G.S.-M.), *University of North Carolina, Chapel Hill:* fact–value distinction

Charles Sayward (C.S.), *University of Nebraska, Lincoln:* conventionalism, deduction, diagonal procedure, formal semantics, open formula, propositional function, quantification

James P. Scanlan (J.P.Sc.), *Ohio State University:* Lenin, Plekhanov

Richard Schacht (R.Sc.), *University of Illinois, Urbana-Champaign:* Nietzsche, philosophical anthropology

Frederick F. Schmitt (F.F.S.), *University of Illinois, Urbana-Champaign:* Goldman

Jerome B. Schneewind (J.B.S.), *Johns Hopkins University:* classical republicanism, Crusius, Cumberland, du Vair, Filmer, Godwin, Grotius, human nature, natural law, Prichard, Pufendorf, Scottish common sense philosophy, Sidgwick, Stephen

Calvin O. Schrag (C.O.S.), *Purdue University:* pluralism, praxis, speculative philosophy

Alan D. Schrift (A.D.S.), *Grinnell College:* Lyotard

George F. Schumm (G.F.S.), *Ohio State University:* Boolean algebra, completeness, conditional proof, conjunction elimination, conjunction introduction, De Morgan's laws, dilemma, disjunction elimination, disjunction introduction, distributive laws, double negation, existential import, exportation, formal logic, Hintikka set, logical constant, logistic system, meaning postulate, *modus ponens, modus tollens,* paraconsistency, Peirce's law, *reductio ad absurdum,* relational logic, singular term, soundness, transformation rule, universal instantiation, valid, well-formed formula, Appendix of Special Symbols

Jean-Loup Seban (J.-L.S.), *Faculté Universitaire de Théologie Protestante de Bruxelles:* Brunschvicg, Cournot, Couturat, d'Ailly, d'Alembert, de Maistre, d'Holbach, Diderot, *Encyclopedia*, Fontenelle, Huygens, Jansenism, Laffitte, La Mettrie, La Peyrère, Luther, Saint-Simon, Swedenborgianism, synergism, Troeltsch, Valentinianism, Vauvenargues

David N. Sedley (D.N.S.), *Christ's College, University of Cambridge:* Epicureanism, Hellenistic philosophy, Stoicism

Kenneth Seeskin (K.See.), *Northwestern University:* Buber, Rosenzweig

Krister Segerberg (K.Seg.), *University of Uppsala:* dynamic logic

Charlene Haddock Seigfried (C.H.S.), *Purdue University:* Paine, pragmatism

Dennis M. Senchuk (D.M.S.), *Indiana University:* philosophy of education

James F. Sennett (J.F.S.), *McNeese State University:* Plantinga

William Lad Sessions (W.L.S.), *Washington and Lee University:* Tillich

Stewart Shapiro (S.Sha.), *Ohio State University:* effective procedure, mathematical structuralism, second-order logic

Donald W. Sherburne (D.W.S.), *Vanderbilt University:* Whitehead

Roger A. Shiner (R.A.Sh.), *University of Alberta:* Dworkin, jury nullification, legal realism, philosophy of law, responsibility

Sydney Shoemaker (S.Sho.), *Cornell University:* Malcolm, personal identity, physicalism, qualia, spatiotemporal continuity

Robert K. Shope (R.K.S.), *University of Massachusetts, Boston:* Lewis, C. I.

Kwong-loi Shun (K.-l.S.), *University of California, Berkeley: chih²*; Chuang Tzu; *chung, shu;* Confucianism; Confucius; Four Books; Han Fei Tzu; *hsing; jen;* Kao Tzu; *ko wu, chih chih; li³*; Mo Tzu; *wu wei; yi; yung*

Wilfried Sieg (W.S.), *Carnegie-Mellon University:* Church's thesis, consistency, formalization, proof theory

Marcus G. Singer (M.G.S.), *University of Wisconsin, Madison:* moral epistemology, polarity, universalizability

Georgette Sinkler (G.S.), *University of Illinois, Chicago:* Bacon, Roger; Gregory of Rimini; Grosseteste; John of Salisbury

Walter Sinnott-Armstrong (W.S.-A.), *Dartmouth College:* impartiality, moral dilemma, moral skepticism

Matti T. Sintonen (M.T.S.), *University of Helsinki:* Hintikka

Lawrence Sklar (L.S.), *University of Michigan:* philosophy of science

Brian Skyrms (B.Sk.), *University of California, Irvine:* induction, inductivism, mathematical induction, maximin strategy

Robert C. Sleigh (R.C.Sl.), *University of Massachusetts, Amherst:* Leibniz

Michael Anthony Slote (M.A.Sl.), *University of Maryland, College Park:* satisfice

Hans Sluga (H.S.), *University of California, Berkeley:* Wittgenstein

Barry Smith (B.Sm.), *State University of New York, Buffalo:* Ingarden

Michael Smith (M.Sm.), *Australian National University:* direction of fit, moral rationalism

Robin Smith (R.Sm.), *Texas A & M University:* dialectic

Robert Sokolowski (R.So.), *The Catholic University of America:* Husserl

Robert C. Solomon (R.C.So.), *University of Texas, Austin:* Camus, Sartre

Philip Soper (P.S.), *University of Michigan:* civil disobedience, jurisprudence, legal moralism, legal positivism, rule of law

Ernest Sosa (E.S.), *Brown University:* Chisholm, condition, justification, skepticism, state of affairs

Paul Vincent Spade (P.V.S.), *Indiana University: complexe significabile, genus generalissimum,* Heytesbury, Kilvington, *praedicamenta,* predicables, *proprietates terminorum, proprium, secundum quid, suppositio,* syncategoremata

T. L. S. Sprigge (T.L.S.S.), *University of Edinburgh:* ethical objectivism, panpsychism

Eric O. Springsted (E.O.S.), *Illinois College:* Weil

George J. Stack (G.J.S.), *State University of New York, Brockport:* Avenarius; Beneke; Czolbe; Hartmann, E. von; Lange; Spir; Steiner; Stirner; Teichmüller

Jason Stanley (J.Sta.), *Cornell University:* Chomsky

Sören Stenlund (S.St.), *Uppsala University:* combinatory logic

James P. Sterba (J.P.St.), *University of Notre Dame:* ideology, political philosophy

Josef Stern (J.Ste.), *University of Chicago:* Gersonides, Philo Judaeus

Matthias Steup (M.St.), *Saint Cloud State University:* Clifford, diallelon, epistemic deontologism, problem of the criterion

M. A. Stewart (M.A.St.), *University of Lancaster:* Fordyce, Ray, Stillingfleet, Turnbull

Frederick Suppe (F.S.), *University of Maryland, College Park:* abduction, eduction, modality, operationalism

Jere Paul Surber (J.P.Su.), *University of Denver: Erfahrung,* Feuerbach, Herder, Humboldt, Krause, *Lebensphilosophie,* Lotze

Zeno G. Swijtink (Z.G.S.), *Indiana University:* Beth's definability theorem, categorical theory, Craig's interpolation theorem, model theory, satisfiable, standard model

Richard Swinburne (R.Sw.), *Oriel College, University of Oxford:* miracle

Edith Dudley Sulla (E.D.S.), *North Carolina State University:* Oxford Calculators

Paul Teller (P.Te.), *University of California, Davis:* field theory, reduction

Larry S. Temkin (L.S.T.), *Rutgers University:* Parfit

H. S. Thayer (H.S.T.), *City University of New York:* Newton

Alan Thomas (A.T.), *University of Kent at Canterbury:* Williams

Terrence N. Tice (T.N.T.), *University of Michigan:* Schleiermacher

Paul Tidman (P.Ti.), *Mount Union College:* conceivability

Mark C. Timmons (M.C.T.), *University of Memphis:* constitution; ideal observer; Nagel, Thomas; objective rightness; resultance

William Tolhurst (W.T.), *Northern Illinois University:* externalism, free rider, slippery slope argument, vicious regress

James E. Tomberlin (J.E.T.), *California State University, Northridge:* Castañeda, deontic logic, deontic paradoxes

Rosemarie Tong (R.T.), *University of North Carolina, Charlotte:* feminist philosophy; Taylor, Harriet

J. D. Trout (J.D.T.), *Loyola University of Chicago:* alchemy, belief revision, empirical decision theory, scientific realism, uniformity of nature

Martin M. Tweedale (M.M.T.), *University of Alberta:* Abelard, Roscelin

Thomas Uebel (T.U.), *London School of Economics:* Vienna Circle

James Van Cleve (J.V.C.), *Brown University:* dependence

Harry van der Linden (H.v.d.L.), *Butler University:* Cohen, neo-Kantianism, Windelband

Peter van Inwagen (P.v.I.), *University of Notre Dame:* subsistence

Bryan W. Van Norden (B.W.V.N.), *Vassar College: cheng ming; ch'ing; Chung-yung; fa; hsiao; hsin*[1]*; Kung-sun Lung Tzu; Lao Tzu; li*[2]*; Mencius; ming; shang ti; Tahsüeh; tao; te; t'ien; wang, pa; yü*

Donald Phillip Verene (D.P.V.), *Emory University:* Cassirer, Croce, Vico

Thomas Vinci (T.V.), *Dalhousie University:* given; immediacy; Sellars, Wilfrid; solipsism

Donald Wayne Viney (D.W.V.), *Pittsburgh State University:* Hartshorne

Barbara Von Eckardt (B.V.E.), *University of Nebraska, Lincoln:* Fodor

Steven J. Wagner (S.J.W.), *University of Illinois, Urbana-Champaign:* accident, Cambridge change, identity, *per accidens,* proposition, relation

William J. Wainwright (W.J.Wa.), *University of Wisconsin, Milwaukee:* deism, demiurge, Edwards, natural religion, Paley

Paul E. Walker (P.E.W.), *University of Chicago:* al-Kindī, Ibn Bājja, Ibn Ṭufayl, Islamic Neoplatonism, *kalam*

Robert E. Wall (R.E.W.), *University of Texas, Austin:* donkey sentences, formal learnability theory, grammar, parsing

Craig Walton (C.Wa.), *University of Nevada, Las Vegas:* Ramus

Douglas Walton (D.W.), *University of Winnipeg:* informal fallacy, informal logic

Richard A. Watson (R.A.W.), *Washington University:* dualism, Gassendi, Mersenne

Michael V. Wedin (M.V.W.), *University of California, Davis:* Aristotle

Rudolph H. Weingartner (R.H.W.), *University of Pittsburgh:* Simmel

Paul Weirich (P.We.), *University of Missouri, Columbia:* Allais's paradox, bargaining theory, Bertrand's box paradox, Bertrand's paradox, Comte, Condorcet, Laplace, Newcomb's paradox, Saint Petersburg paradox

Paul J. Weithman (P.J.W.), *University of Notre Dame:* liberalism

Carl Wellman (C.We.), *Washington University:* Hohfeld, rights

Howard Wettstein (H.W.), *University of California, Riverside:* causal theory of proper names

Samuel C. Wheeler III (S.C.W.), *University of Connecticut:* deconstruction

Stephen A. White (S.A.W.), *University of Texas, Austin:* Lyceum, Megarians, myth of Er, Pyrrho of Elis, Strato of Lampsacus

Edward R. Wierenga (E.R.W.), *University of Rochester:* creation *ex nihilo,* disembodiment, divine attributes, divine foreknowledge, paradox of omniscience

Michael Williams (M.W.), *Northwestern University:* contextualism, logical construction

Fred Wilson (F.W.), *University of Toronto:* Mill, J. S.; Mill's methods

W. Kent Wilson (W.K.W.), *University of Illinois, Chicago:* ambiguity, count noun, equivocation, formal fallacy, linguistic relativity, open texture, theory of signs

Kenneth P. Winkler (K.P.W.), *Wellesley College:* Collier, sensationalism

John F. Wippel (J.F.W.), *The Catholic University of America:* Aquinas, Giles of Rome, Godfrey of Fontaines, Henry of Ghent, Thomism

Allan B. Wolter (A.B.W.), *The Catholic University of America:* Duns Scotus

Nicholas P. Wolterstorff (N.P.W.), *Yale University:* aesthetic formalism, empiricism, Locke, metaphor, mimesis

Rega Wood (R.W.), *New Haven, Conn.:* Alexander of Hales, Burley, Olivi, Richard Rufus, Wodeham

W. Jay Wood (W.J.Wo.), *Wheaton College:* Lewis, C. S.

Paul Woodruff (P.Wo.), *University of Texas, Austin:* Academy, *arete, dunamis,* entelechy, Gorgias, *hyle,* hylomorphism, Isocrates, New Academy, Thrasymachus

Takashi Yagisawa (T.Y.), *California State University, Northridge:* definiendum, definition, intensionality, logical syntax, rational reconstruction, Sapir-Whorf hypothesis

Yutaka Yamamoto (Y.Y.), *University of New Hampshire:* cognitive psychotherapy

Keith E. Yandell (K.E.Y.), *University of Wisconsin, Madison:* Advaita, *āgama, Ātman,* Bhagavad Gita, Brahman, Buddha, Buddhagosa, Buddhism, Cārvāka, Dharmakīrti, *dravya,* Dvaita Vedanta, Hinduism, Jainism, *kāla,* karma, Madhva, Mādhyamika, Mahāvīra, Manichaeanism, *māyā,* Mīmāmsā, Nāgārjuna, Nyāya-Vaishesika, Rāmānuja, Sakti, Sankhya-Yoga, Shankara, Siva, sutra, Upanishads, Vasubandhu, Vedanta, Vedas, Viśistadvaita Vedanta

Günter Zoller (G.Z.), *Ludwig Maximillian University, Munich:* Goethe

Jack A. Zupko (J.A.Z.), *San Diego State University:* Bonaventure, Buridan, Nicholas of Autrecourt, William of Auxerre

PREFACE TO THE FIRST EDITION

PHILOSOPHY HAS ALWAYS DONE extraordinary things with ordinary terms – 'believe' and 'know', 'cause' and 'explain', 'space' and 'time', 'justice' and 'goodness', 'language' and 'meaning', 'truth' and 'beauty', 'art', 'religion', 'science', 'mind', 'perception', 'reason', and countless others. The field has numerous technical terms that are also difficult to define, but it presents a dictionary maker with an even greater challenge because of what it does with our everyday vocabulary. I mean not only the kinds of common words just listed but many perhaps humbler-sounding terms like 'accident', 'action', 'grammar', 'set', and 'vague'. All of the everyday terms characterized in this volume are defined – in some manner – in standard dictionaries of the English language or covered in one or another encyclopedia. But many readers of philosophy – especially lay readers and those in other fields – need something quite different from both, a reference work much more specialized than the former and much less voluminous than the latter. However large they may be, ordinary dictionaries, even when accurate, are insufficiently informative to help readers who must look up terms for philosophical reasons; and, even when philosophically illuminating, encyclopedias and specialized reference books are often too lengthy, and sometimes too diffuse, to give readers a concise statement of what is philosophically central in the use of a term. This dictionary responds to the need for a comprehensive, multi-author philosophical reference work that is at once enormously wide in scope, intermediate in size, and authoritative in content. In far less space than is needed for comparable entries in an encyclopedia of philosophy or in a handbook devoted to a single subfield, this volume treats the multitude of subjects appropriate to a dictionary of philosophy with some of the depth made possible by specialist authors. It does this, so far as possible, in a way that makes many of its entries interesting reading for people simply curious about the intriguing concepts or the profound thinkers of the field.

In the first half of this century, the major philosophical dictionary published in English was James Mark Baldwin's *Dictionary of Philosophy and Psychology*, a multi-author work published by Peter Smith of Gloucester, Massachusetts; it appeared in 1901 in two volumes (followed by a bibliography in 1905) and was reprinted with revisions in 1925. In the second half of the century, dictionaries of philosophy in English have been much smaller than Baldwin's and either written by a single author or, occasionally, prepared by a group of writers rarely much larger than a dozen working within the confines of a small space. Few of the entries in these books are longer than 500 words; the most typical have been sketches of 150 words or less.

This dictionary, by contrast, is the work of an international team that includes 381 carefully selected contributors representing the major subfields of philosophy and many philosophical traditions. It contains substantial treatments of major philosophers, many of these entries running to several thousand words. It has hundreds of entries, often of 500 to 1,000 words, on other significant thinkers, and thousands of brief definitions of philosophically important terms. In addition, it provides detailed overviews, some more than 6,000 words, of the subfields of philosophy, such as epistemology, ethics, metaphysics, philosophy of mind, and philosophy of science. It supplies numerous cross-references to help readers in comprehending philosophical ideas, in understanding the terminology of the discipline, and in appreciating philosophers themselves. There are hundreds of entries on important terms and thinkers from non-Western philosophy, for instance from the Chinese, Indian, Japanese, and Korean traditions. The dictionary also covers a number of philosophically significant thinkers and terms from fields closely related to philosophy, including computer science, economics, law, linguistics, literature, mathematics, psychology and other behavioral sciences, and religion. The Appendix defines logical symbols and identifies other special symbols used in philosophy.

In an era that is producing a plethora of encyclopedias, companions, handbooks, and similar reference works, something more should be said about the need for a philosophical dictionary. These kinds of reference works differ significantly: a dictionary is definitional, though like this one it may be far more than that; encyclopedias, companions, and similar works sometimes do not define the terms that head their entries, and the main purposes of these works tend to be informational, historical, and bibliographical. There is no sharp distinction here; a definition may be informative, and the right kind of information about a topic can serve to define the concept in question. But in practice a good definition captures what is conceptually central to its target subject in a way that an encyclopedia or handbook article often does not (and need not) do at all, and quite commonly does not do in any brief, initial formulation.

A purist might think that a dictionary should exclude entries on thinkers altogether, on the ground that proper names do not admit of definition. Even if, strictly speaking, this should be true, it is perfectly intelligible to ask what Socrates, for instance, means to philosophers, or who he was, philosophically speaking. Such questions about thinkers are among the kinds appropriately treated in a philosophical dictionary and likely to interest general readers as well as many in the field of philosophy. Answering them does not require bibliography or extensive biography, and to include either of these would have meant a much longer and quite different volume. Primary texts are often cited in entries that focus on philosophers; but those entries are mainly devoted to central ideas of the thinkers in question. As compared, however, with the other, much smaller contemporary philosophical dictionaries in English, this one has more depth, particularly in entries on major philosophers, on subfields of philosophy, and on pivotal philosophical concepts.

Although the scope of this volume extends beyond Western philosophy and indeed beyond philosophy narrowly conceived, the central focus is on Western philosophers and Western thought. We have sought comprehensiveness, but make no pretense of completeness. Even with entries and subentries covering more than 4,000 concepts and philosophers, we could not include every philosophically significant term, or every thinker, that people interested in philosophy or reading philosophical literature might want to look up. This applies particularly to the areas where philosophy overlaps other fields, such as cognitive science, economic theory, feminist studies, linguistics, literary theory, mathematics, philosophy, and religion. We have, however, sought to include enough entries to assist readers both in approaching a great variety of "purely" philosophical texts and in comprehending a substantial range of interdisciplinary philosophical works.

To avoid distraction and interruptions of the text, internal cross-references (the "See also" ones) are supplied only at the ends of entries. The external cross-references (the "See" ones) are alphabetized along with the main entries and refer the reader to one or more entries that deal with the term or thinker in question. Internal cross-references are not generally used where it seems obvious what sorts of other entries might be consulted for supplementary or related information. The number of internal cross-references has also been kept small. This is in part to avoid diffusing the reader's efforts and in part because the Dictionary has entries that cover most of the philosophers discussed in the text and the vast majority of the philosophical terms the contributors use in their entries. Pursuing the cross-references that are supplied, however, will often lead to other useful ones and to a better understanding of the topic a reader originally looks up.

Many philosophers still living when the Dictionary went to press are cited in the Index of Names, which lists, for each name cited, one or more entries providing information about the person in question. The names included represent more than 600 philosophers and thinkers from all periods of philosophy who are not subjects of entries devoted entirely to their work. There are several reasons why the Dictionary does not contain entries focusing entirely on living figures. Above all, many who would have such entries, including most of the senior philosophers cited in the Index, are still producing philosophical work, and it should not be presumed that adequate portraits of them can be done at this time. The task of writing a description that is both sufficiently short for a volume like this and intellectually adequate is often impossible without a measure of historical distance. In many cases, readers will find helpful information through the Index, which lists hundreds of contemporary philosophers and many other thinkers (though by no means all of the numerous personal names mentioned in the main entries). There are, of course, many important figures in the field whom contributors unfortunately could not bring into the tight confines of their entries.

Some readers might be surprised to find that there is no entry simply on philosophy itself. This is partly because no short definition is adequate. It will not do to define 'philosophy' in the etymological way many have, as 'the love of wisdom': granting that it is natural for philosophers to love wisdom and for many lovers of wisdom to be inspired to pursue philosophy, a lover of wisdom can be quite unphilosophical, and even a good philosopher can be wise in at most a few domains of inquiry. Perhaps a great many philosophers (though certainly not all of them) would agree that philosophy is roughly the critical, normally systematic, study of an unlimited range of ideas and issues; but this characterization says nothing about what sorts of ideas and issues are central in philosophy or about its distinctive methods of studying them. In a way, this dictionary as a whole presents a conception of philosophy, one that is rich in content and widely representative of what has been, is, and perhaps will long continue to be, generally viewed as philosophical work. Those wanting a sense of what a good definition of 'philosophy' must encompass might fruitfully consider how one can define the concerns central to a number of major philosophers representing different periods, styles of philosophy, and cultures. One such list might include Plato, Aristotle, Aquinas, Descartes, Hume, Kant, Hegel, Mill, Peirce, Heidegger, and Wittgenstein. We might also try to construct a unifying characterization of some of the basic fields of philosophy – for instance epistemology, ethics, logic, and metaphysics – and beyond this, one should also consider what is central in such subfields as aesthetics, philosophy of history, philosophy of language, philosophy of logic, philosophy of mind, philosophy of religion, and philosophy of science. Reading the entries on these philosophers and fields will probably yield a much better indication of what philosophy is than we could expect from even a thousand-word entry.

Three features of the text may, for some readers, need comment. First, following a practice common among careful philosophical writers, we place single quotation marks around words or longer expressions when those expressions are named or directly referred to, as where one says that the term 'argument' may designate either the process of arguing or an argument presented therein. The second point concerns terms beginning with 'non', such as 'non-mental'. Except where such terms have a well-established use as words whose meaning is, like that of 'nonviolence' and 'noncombatant', not merely that of the negation of their basic, positive element, our practice is to place a hyphen after 'non'. An example should bring out the difference. Anything at all that is *not* a combatant – anything from ships and shoes and sealing wax to hills, brooks, standing lakes, and groves – is a *non*-combatant, but these things are not thereby noncombatants. Thus, 'noncombatant', 'nonviolence', 'nonstarter', and 'noncognitivism' appear as just written, whereas 'non-mental' and 'non-inferential' are hyphenated. This practice reflects a natural tendency of most philosophers and may be grounded partly in the sense that when used to form a complementary term, 'non' plays a special and very important role: more that of an operator on an established term than the role of a prefix creating a semantically distinctive term. The third point here concerns the substitution of an everyday word for a term often used by philosophers in a technical way. Both for brevity and to aid readers not familiar with the technical use of 'just in case', we have frequently used 'provided' instead of 'just in case' where the latter is equivalent to 'if and only if'. This substitution might have gone unnoticed by anyone other than the contributors affected by it, and no one consulted on the matter has judged that the substitution alters content; but I mention the change just in case anyone should be curious about it.

It is probably impossible to produce a work of this kind without errors, especially errors of omission. Comprehensiveness, of course, does not require completeness (supposing there is a clear notion of completeness for a work like this); nor is completeness even possible in a dictionary covering a dynamic and growing field. I would be happy to receive comments or corrections and will undertake to send them to the appropriate contributor(s) and to file them for possible future use. Two further comments may be in order here. First, although the length of the entries is not unrelated to the importance of their topics, other factors, such as the complexity of the concept in question, the degree of current or recent interest in it, and the style and wishes of the contributors, have also figured in determining length. Second, although authors were asked to strive for the highest level of accessibility appropriate to their topics, some entries are not intended to be fully intelligible to every reader (and, if they were, would ill serve those who need them). We trust that all of the entries have something of value for any interested reader; but some are intended to give specialized or technical information, and others proceed to specialized or technical matters shortly after an opening that is meant to provide what is likely to be essential for any reader consulting the entry.

ACKNOWLEDGMENTS

Special thanks are due to the Board of Advisors, who played a major part in determining the selection of entries. A number of them carefully studied long preliminary entry lists I sent them and also reviewed sample drafts of entries. For work far beyond the call of duty, I would particularly like to thank William P. Alston, Arthur W. Burks, Roderick M. Chisholm, Daniel Garber, Terence Irwin, Norman Kretzmann, John Lucas, John Perry, and Allen Wood, all of whom repeatedly provided comments and advice. I am also grateful for substantial help, during at least one stage, from the late Hector-Neri Castañeda and from Fred Dretske, Sally McConnell-Ginet, Michael Moore, Onora O'Neill, Richard Rorty, and Raimo Tuomela.

If there is any single person who stands out as a judicious, steady, and pervasive influence in the development of this dictionary, it is Terence Moore, Executive Editor at Cambridge University Press. He persuaded me to undertake the work of Editor-in-Chief in the first place, helped in the development of the volume at each formative stage, and provided editorial advice in every major phase. With a sharp critical eye, he attended to fine points of style and organization; he proposed authors, topics, and procedures; and he guided the design of both the text and its cover.

Many of the contributors provided indispensable advice along the way, and I am deeply grateful for their help. A large number of them revised their entries in the light of editorial comments, sometimes more than once. Many also spontaneously sent me updated versions or improvements during the years of the project. For my part, philosophical discussions with the contributors and the Editorial Board were a sustaining factor in a long and arduous task. These years of intensive work with a cross section of the world's best philosophers have given me a strong sense of the vitality and intellectual power of the profession of philosophy. I believe that a commitment to scholarship and truth prevails over fashion and idiosyncrasy and polemics.

The Dictionary has benefited from the advice of a number of experts in subfields of philosophy. Michael Detlefsen, drawing on his own long editorial experience in the field of logic, and George Schumm, who produced the Appendix of Special Symbols, were immensely helpful in determining and preparing a good portion of the hundreds of entries in logic and philosophy of mathematics. Kwong-loi Shun gave me advice at several points on the Chinese philosophy entries. Keith Yandell played a similar advisory role for the entries concerning Buddhism and Hinduism. Alexander Mourelatos provided excellent advice on some of the Greek philosophy entries. Comments and advice were also contributed by more people than I can name. They include James Allard, David Allison, Kent Bach, Lawrence Becker, Joseph Bien, Daniel Breazeale, Robert Butts, Victor Caston, James Childress, Wayne Davis, John Dillon, John Etchemendy, Bernard Gert, Lenn Goodman, Jorge Gracia, James Gustafson, Gary Cutting, John Heil, Robert Kane, George Kline, Joseph Kockelmans, Manfred Kuehn, Steven Kuhn, William McBride, William Mann, A. P. Martinich, Alfred Mele, Paul Moser, Donald Munro, Paul Pines, Louis Pojman, Carl Posy, William Rowe, Wesley Salmon, Richard Schacht, Jerome Schneewind, Calvin Schrag, Jean-Loup Seban, Hans Seigfried, Sydney Shoemaker, Ernest Sosa, M. A. Stewart, Elenore Stump, Paul Walker, Stephen White, Rega Wood, and, especially, Hugh McCann.

Technical and editorial assistance was provided by a number of people. W. M. Havighurst single-handedly did the copyediting for the Press and, with a keen eye and a deft hand, markedly improved the text at many points. His work required verifying large quantities of information, tracking thousands of details, and maintaining constant communication with me over nearly a year. Together we have tried to preserve both the contributors' content and, so far as possible in a volume of this kind, their style. I am also especially grateful to Allison Nespor for extensive help with the Index of Names, for proofreading of the entire volume, and for editorial advice at many points throughout the years of the project. I should add that the production schedule did not permit every contributor to read proofs, and some who read proofs did not read them for every entry they wrote. Errors that may have slipped through the several proofreadings may not be the responsibility of the contributors.

At the Press, I have received help and advice from Michael Agnes, Alan Gold, Kenneth Greenhall, Cathy Hennessy, Christine Murray, Alexis Ruda, and, especially, Sophia Prybylski, who painstakingly oversaw the entire process of correcting the proofs. My assistants in the Department of Philosophy at the University of Nebraska, Lincoln, have also been of help: Priscella Guerra, Nancy Slonneger, Michael Tonderum, Douglas Weber, and Xiaomei Yang. The support of the University of Nebraska and, especially, of my colleagues in the Philosophy Department, has been indispensable. I am also grateful for assistance from the Philosophy Department at Santa Clara University during my term as Fagothey Distinguished Professor in 1994.

I owe an incalculable debt to my family. Over the seven years of this project, my wife, Marie-Louise, gave me both advice on textual and literary matters and help with organization of files and some of the many mailings to authors. She and my children, Katherine, Evelyn, and Paul, also assisted with myriad editorial and clerical tasks and cheerfully tolerated the interruptions and problems that are inevitable in producing a work of this magnitude.

Robert Audi
Lincoln, Nebraska
February 1995

PREFACE TO THE SECOND EDITION

THE WIDESPREAD POSITIVE RECEPTION of the First Edition has been gratifying, and a number of translations are proceeding, into Chinese, Italian, Korean, Russian, and Spanish at this writing. The field of philosophy has expanded, however, and even apart from that I have become aware of several respects in which the Dictionary can better serve its readers. The result is a multitude of expansions in standing entries and the addition of some four hundred new entries. This extended coverage required sixty new authors, nearly half of them from outside North America.

The new entries range across the entire field of philosophy. We have made a special effort to increase our coverage of Continental philosophy and of subfields where growth is exceptionally rapid, such as ethics, philosophy of mind, and political philosophy. We have also added numerous cross-references. The cross-references are an element in the volume that many readers have said they found not only valuable in enhancing their initial understanding of an entry, but also welcome as a source of intriguing connections and as an invitation to browse.

In addition to citations of many living philosophers in the Index of Names, there is now selective coverage of a number of living philosophers in separate entries. With very few exceptions, this (quite small) group includes only thinkers in their mid-sixties or older. This constraint on inclusion is in part dictated by the difficulty of providing an adequate portrait of philosophers still actively advancing their positions, and it has required omitting a number of distinguished younger philosophers still making major changes in their views. Even with much older thinkers we do not presuppose that there will be no significant developments, but only a greater likelihood of discerning a rounded position that is unlikely to be abandoned.

In the difficult – and in a sense impossible – task of determining entries on living thinkers, advice was sought from both the Board and many other sources. We were also guided in part by the extent to which contributors to the First Edition relied on references to certain living thinkers. Given the Dictionary's overall purposes and its wide audience, which includes many readers outside philosophy, selection was weighted toward writers whom many *non-philosophers* may want to look up, and some weight was also given to considerations of diversity. In keeping with the overall purposes of the volume and the diversity of its readers, we have also decided not to undertake the large task of covering either living contributors to highly specialized subfields – such as logic or computer theory or much of philosophy of science – or philosophers whose main contributions are to the history of philosophy. There are, however, many important philosophers in these fields. A number are cited in the Index, which also lists many of the thinkers who are mentioned by one or more contributors but are not subjects of separate entries.

In taking account of the responses from readers of the First Edition, we have tried to do as much as possible without making the Dictionary too bulky for a single volume. So much of the response has been positive that although many standing entries have been revised, we have sought to make improvements in the book mainly by adding new ones. A few readers expressed puzzlement or disappointment that we do not have a bibliography at the end of each entry. We do generally have references to primary works by the thinker being portrayed or, in some cases, secondary works noteworthy in their own right. Our policy here is shaped partly by severe space constraints and, especially given those, by a desire to avoid directing readers to inadequately representative sources or works that may soon become obsolete. It is also based on a sense of the difference between a dictionary and an encyclopedia. Granting that this difference is not sharp, a dictionary is above all definitional, whereas encyclopedias are mainly informational, historical, and bibliographical. A dictionary clarifies basic concepts in a way encyclopedias need not. Indeed, some encyclopedias are best understood with the help of a good dictionary; some are even difficult to read without one.

As with the First Edition, I would be happy to receive comments or corrections and will undertake to file them and to send them to the appropriate author(s). Many of the Dictionary's contributors, as well as a number of careful readers, sent suggested corrections, and most of the suggestions have been followed or taken into account in preparing this edition. I should reiterate that, again as with the First Edition, these years of intensive work with a cross section of the world's best philosophers have given me a strong sense that the profession of philosophy has great vitality and intellectual strength. In both contributors and advisors, I have seen a steadfast commitment to scholarship, an abiding concern with accuracy and theoretical depth, an abundance of philosophical imagination, and a fidelity to high standards that prevails over the often alluring currents of schools or fashions or polemics. It is perhaps not appropriate for me to dedicate a collaborative volume of this kind, but if I were to do so, I would dedicate it to the contributors, in the hope that it may give to them and to all its readers some of the pleasure that the editing has given to me.

ACKNOWLEDGMENTS

In constructing this volume over a number of years, I have benefited from more comments and reactions than I can possibly remember, and I regret any omissions in the expressions of gratitude that follow.

The Board of Advisors deserves hearty thanks for a major part in the selection of new entries and new contributors. I would particularly like to thank William P. Alston, Arthur W. Burks, Fred Dretske, Terence Irwin, the late Norman Kretzmann, John Lucas, Sally McConnell-Ginet, Alexander Nehamas, Onora O'Neill, John Perry, Richard Rorty, John Searle, Raimo Tuomela, and Bas van Fraassen, many of whom repeatedly provided comments or advice. The editorial advice of Terence Moore, Executive Editor at the Press, and my regular discussions with him on matters of policy and design, have been incalculably valuable. Neither edition would have been possible without his contributions.

The Second Edition has benefited from the advice of many others, including a number who helped in preparing the First Edition. Among these are John

Corcoran, Gary Gutting, George Schumm, Kwong-loi Shun, and Keith Yandell, all of whom provided editorial advice and recommended adding certain entries in their areas of philosophical work or revising others. Corcoran deserves a great deal of credit for both identifying and filling gaps. Comments and advice were also contributed by more people than I can name. They include Margaret Atherton, Claudio de Almeida, Lynne Rudder Baker, Joseph Bien, Noël Carroll, Roger Crisp, Wayne Davis, Philip Gasper, Berys Gaut, Lenn Goodman, Paul Griffiths, Oscar Haac, Mike Harnish, John Heil, Brad Hooker, Patricia Huntington, Dale Jacquette, Robert Kane, George Kline, Manfred Kuehn, Steven Kuhn, Brian McLaughlin, William Mann, Ausonio Marras, Al Martinich, Alfred Mele, Joseph Mendola, David W. Miller, Paul Moser, James Murphy, Louis Pojman, William Prior, Wesley Salmon, Mark Sainsbury, Charles Sayward, Jerome Schneewind, Calvin Schrag, David Sedley, Roger Shiner, Marcus Singer, Brian Skyrms, M. A. Stewart, William Wainwright, Paul Weirich, and, especially, Hugh McCann, Ernest Sosa, and J. D. Trout.

Conscientious reviewers as well as colleagues and readers who contributed comments have been of help to me in expanding and revising the First Edition. Among the readers – mainly philosophers – I particularly want to thank Alasdair MacIntyre, Ruth Marcus, Dan Mueller, Eleonore Stump, and Mark van Roojen.

Editorial and technical assistance was provided by a number of people. At the Press, I have received help or advice from Michael Agnes, Janis Bolster – who oversaw the entire process of correcting the proofs – Alan Gold, Kenneth Greenhall, Cathy Hennessy, Nicholas Mirra, Christine Murray, Gwen Seznec, and others. W. M. Havighurst again served as the main copyeditor for the Press; his skillful and painstaking work has been of great help throughout. Allison Nespor and my assistants in the Department of Philosophy at the University of Nebraska, Lincoln, Jonathan Evans and Xiaomei Yang, have also contributed. The support of the University of Nebraska and my colleagues in the Philosophy Department has been indispensable. I am also grateful for assistance from the Philosophy Department at Santa Clara University during my term as Distinguished Professor of the College of Arts and Sciences in 1999.

As in the case of the First Edition, I owe an incalculable debt to my family. My wife, Marie-Louise, gave me both literary advice and help with organization of files and some of the many mailings. She and my children have also cheerfully tolerated the interruptions and problems that are inevitable in doing even a second edition of a work of this scope.

Robert Audi
Lincoln, Nebraska
June 1999

THE
CAMBRIDGE
DICTIONARY
OF
PHILOSOPHY

SECOND EDITION

A

Abailard, Pierre. See ABELARD.

Abdera, School of. See ABDERITES.

Abderites, the Greek philosophers Leucippus and Democritus, the two earliest exponents of atomism. Even though Abdera, in Thrace (northern Greece), was home to three pre-Socratics – Leucippus, Democritus, and Protagoras – the term 'Abderites' and the phrase 'School of Abdera' are applied only to Leucippus and Democritus. We can thus distinguish between early Greek atomism and Epicureanism, which is the later version of atomism developed by Epicurus of Athens. This modern usage is in one respect inapt: the corresponding Greek term, *Abderitēs, -ai,* was used in antiquity as a synonym of 'simpleton' – not in disparagement of any of the three philosophers of Abdera but as a regional slur. **See also** ANCIENT ATOMISM, PRE-SOCRATICS.

A.P.D.M.

abduction, canons of reasoning for the discovery, as opposed to the justification, of scientific hypotheses or theories.

Reichenbach distinguished the *context of justification* and the *context of discovery,* arguing that philosophy legitimately is concerned only with the former, which concerns verification and confirmation, whereas the latter is a matter for psychology. Thus he and other logical positivists claimed there are inductive logics of justification but not logics for discovery. Both hypothetico-deductive and Bayesian or other probabilistic inductive logics of justification have been proposed. Close examination of actual scientific practice increasingly reveals justificatory arguments and procedures that call into question the adequacy of such logics.

Norwood Russell Hanson distinguished the reasons for accepting a specific hypothesis from the reasons for suggesting that the correct hypothesis will be of a particular kind. For the latter he attempted to develop logics of *retroductive* or *abductive* reasoning that stressed analogical reasoning, but did not succeed in convincing many that these logics were different in kind from logics of justification. Today few regard the search for rigorous formal logics of discovery as promising. Rather, the search has turned to looking for "logics" in some weaker sense. Heuristic procedures, strategies for discovery, and the like are explored. Others have focused on investigating rationality in the growth of scientific knowledge, say, by exploring conditions under which research traditions or programs are progressive or degenerating. Some have explored recourse to techniques from cognitive science or artificial intelligence. Claims of success generally are controversial.

See also CONFIRMATION, INDUCTION, REICHENBACH.

F.S.

Abelard, Peter, in French, Pierre Abailard or Abélard (1079–1144), French theologian whose writings, particularly *Theologia Christiana,* constitute one of the more impressive attempts of the medieval period to use logical techniques to explicate Christian dogmas. He was born of a minor noble family in Brittany and studied logic and theology under some of the most notable teachers of the early twelfth century, including Roscelin, William of Champeaux, and Anselm of Laon. He rapidly eclipsed his teachers in logic and attracted students from all over Europe. His forays into theology were less enthusiastically received. Twice his views on the Trinity were condemned as heretical. Abelard led a dramatic life punctuated by bitter disputes with his opponents and a dangerous and celebrated love affair with Héloïse (c.1117). Much of this story is told in his autobiographical work, *Historia calamitatum.*

Abelard's two most important works in logic are his *Logica ingredientibus* and his *Dialectica.* In these treatises and others he is the first medieval Scholastic to make full use of Aristotle's *On Interpretation* and Boethius's commentaries on it to produce a sophisticated theory of the signification of words and sentences. The theory distinguishes the signification of an expression both from what the expression names and the idea in the mind of the speaker associated with the expression. Abelard allows a role for mental images in thinking, but he carefully avoids claiming that these are what words signify. In this he is very much aware of the pitfalls of subjectivist theories of meaning. His positive doctrines on what words signify tie in closely with his views on the signification of propositions and universals. For Abelard propositions are sentences that are either true or false; what they say (their *dicta*) is what they signify and these *dicta* are the primary bearers of truth and falsity. Abelard developed a genuinely propositional logic, the first since the Stoics. A universal, on the other hand, is a common noun or adjective, and what it means is what the verb phrase part of a proposition signifies. This is a sort of truncated *dictum,* which Abelard variously called a *status,* nature, or property. Neither *status* nor *dicta* are things, Abelard said, but they are mind-independent objects of thought. Abelard was particularly devastating in his attacks on realist theories of universals, but his view that universals are words was not meant to deny the objectivity of our knowledge of the world.

Abelard's theories in logic and ontology went far beyond the traditional ideas that had been handed down from Aristotle through the mediation of the late ancient commentators, Boethius in particular. They could have formed the basis of a fundamentally new synthesis in Western logic, but when more of the Aristotelian corpus became available in Western Europe during the twelfth century, concentration shifted to assimilating this already fully elaborated system of ideas. Consequently, Abelard's influence on later Scholastic thought, though noticeable, is not nearly as great as one might expect, given the acuteness and originality of his insights. **See also** BOETHIUS, ROSCELIN, SCHOLASTICISM.   M.M.T.

abhidharma, the analytical and systematic presentation of the major conceptual categories constituting Buddhist doctrine; used as a label for both the texts that contain such presentations and the content of what is presented. Early *abhidharma* texts (up to about the second century A.D.) are catechetical in form, defining key doctrinal terms schematically through question and answer; later works are more discursive, often containing extensive discussions of controverted metaphysical issues such as the existence of past objects or the nature of reference. The goal of *abhidharma* is to make a complete inventory of existents and of the relations that may hold among them. **See also** BUDDHISM.   P.J.G.

abhinivesha, Sanskrit word meaning 'self-love' or 'will to live'. In Indian philosophy in general and in the Sankhya-Yoga system in particular, *abhinivesha* was regarded as an aspect of *avidya*

(ignorance). Some other manifestations of *avidya* were said to be fear, attachment, and aversion, all of which were thought to generate karmic bondage and prevent one from attaining spiritual liberation. Lumped together with these, *abhinivesha* obviously has a negative connotation, even though in the Indian tradition it was not necessarily wrong, and even commendable at times, to exhibit self-love and a healthy will to live and prosper in the material world. So presumably the negative connotation of *abhinivesha* is an indication that what may be otherwise permissible can be improper or morally wrong if pursued in excess or for the wrong reason. **See also** AVIDYA.   D.K.C.

abortion. See MORAL STATUS.

Abrabanel, Isaac ben Judah (1437–1508), Spanish Jewish philosopher and statesman. On the periphery between late medieval Spanish philosophy and Renaissance humanism, Abrabanel concerned himself with traditional medieval Jewish subjects such as creation, prophecy, and theodicy. His works include biblical commentaries as well as philosophical and theological treatises; his most significant writings constitute his critique of Maimonides' *Guide of the Perplexed,* found in *Rosh Amanah* (1505) and *Mifalot Elohim* (1503). In his criticism of the Aristotelians, Abrabanel was influenced by Isaac Arama. Endorsing the rabbinic concept of prophecy, Abrabanel attacks Maimonides' naturalistic views of prophecy: he argues that Moses is not to be distinguished from the other prophets and that the knowledge of the prophets is not merely scientific and metaphysical, but miraculously produced by God. This emphasis upon the miraculous as opposed to the natural is developed in his theory of history and politics. His views about the ideal state reflect humanist leanings. While Abrabanel does see the civilized state of humans as a rebellion against God resulting from the fall, he is interested in the best kind of government under these circumstances. Accordingly, unity of society does not require a concentrated power but can be achieved through a collective will. This kind of government, Abrabanel claims, is advocated by the Torah and shown to be effective by the Italian republics of the period. With the coming of the Messiah, humankind will realize its spiritual potential, and when the corporeal universe vanishes, each soul will be able to contemplate eternally the essence of God. Abrabanel's political views influenced later Jewish messianic movements, and his biblical commentaries, translated into Latin, influenced later Christian humanist circles. **See also** ABRA-BANEL, JUDAH; MAIMONIDES.   T.M.R.

Abrabanel, Judah, also called Leone Ebreo or Leo Hebraeus (c.1460–c.1523), Spanish Jewish philosopher, poet, and physician. The oldest son of Isaac Abrabanel, Judah Abrabanel was, philosophically, a representative of Italian Platonism. He wrote his predominantly Neoplatonic philosophical work *Dialoghi d'Amore* (*Dialogues of Love*) in 1535. The original Italian manuscript was translated into French, Latin, Spanish, and Hebrew between 1551 and 1560. The interlocutors of this Platonic-style dialogue, Sophia and Philo, explore the nature of cosmic love. This love not only exists between God and creatures, but also operates in matter and form, the four elements, and the entire universe; it reflects both sensuous and intellectual beauty; in short it is transformed from a relation between God and the universe into a fundamental force around which all things are ordered. There is a mystical aspect to Abrabanel's account of love, and it is not surprising that reflections on mysticism, in addition to astrology, astronomy, and aesthetics, emerge throughout the work. Although primarily reflecting medieval Platonism and Neoplatonism, Abrabanel was also influenced by Marcilio Ficino, Pico della Mirandola, Maimonides, and Ibn Gabirol. His dialogue was read by many philosophers, including Giordano Bruno and Spinoza. His concept of love may be found in lyrical poetry of the period in Italy, France, and Spain, as well as in Michelangelo's *Sonnets* and Torquato Tasso's *Minturno*. **See also** ABRABANEL, ISAAC.   T.M.R.

absent qualia. See FUNCTIONALISM, PHILOSOPHY OF MIND.

absolute, the, term used by idealists to describe the one independent reality of which all things are an expression. Kant used the adjective 'absolute' to characterize what is unconditionally valid. He claimed that pure reason searched for absolute grounds of the understanding that were ideals only, but that practical reason postulated the real existence of such grounds as necessary for morality. This apparent inconsistency led his successors to attempt to systematize his view of reason. To do this, Schelling introduced the term 'the Absolute' for the unconditioned ground (and hence identity) of subject and object. Schelling was criticized by Hegel, who defined the Absolute as spirit: the logical neces-

sity that embodies itself in the world in order to achieve self-knowledge and freedom during the course of history. Many prominent nineteenth-century British and American idealists, including Bosanquet, Royce, and Bradley, defended the existence of a quasi-Hegelian absolute. **See also** HEGEL, IDEALISM, SCHELLING.   J.W.A.

absolute right. See RIGHTS.

absolute space. See SPACE.

Absolute Spirit. See HEGEL.

absolute threshold. See FECHNER.

absolute time. See TIME.

absolutism, ethical. See RELATIVISM.

abstract. See APPENDIX OF SPECIAL SYMBOLS.

abstracta. See ABSTRACT ENTITY, NATURALISM.

abstract entity, an object lacking spatiotemporal properties, but supposed to have being, to exist, or (in medieval Scholastic terminology) to subsist. Abstracta, sometimes collected under the category of universals, include mathematical objects, such as numbers, sets, and geometrical figures, propositions, properties, and relations. Abstract entities are said to be abstracted from particulars. The abstract triangle has only the properties common to all triangles, and none peculiar to any particular triangles; it has no definite color, size, or specific type, such as isosceles or scalene. Abstracta are admitted to an ontology by Quine's criterion if they must be supposed to exist (or subsist) in order to make the propositions of an accepted theory true. Properties and relations may be needed to account for resemblances among particulars, such as the redness shared by all red things. Propositions as the abstract contents or meanings of thoughts and expressions of thought are sometimes said to be necessary to explain translation between languages, and other semantic properties and relations.

Historically, abstract entities are associated with Plato's realist ontology of Ideas or Forms. For Plato, these are the abstract and only real entities, instantiated or participated in by spatiotemporal objects in the world of appearance or empirical phenomena. Aristotle denied the independent existence of abstract entities, and redefined a diluted sense of Plato's Forms as the secondary substances that inhere in primary substances or spatiotemporal particulars as the only genuine existents. The dispute persisted in medieval philosophy between realist metaphysicians, including Augustine and Aquinas, who accepted the existence of abstracta, and nominalists, such as Ockham, who maintained that similar objects may simply be referred to by the same name without participating in an abstract form. In modern philosophy, the problem of abstracta has been a point of contention between rationalism, which is generally committed to the existence of abstract entities, and empiricism, which rejects abstracta because they cannot be experienced by the senses. Berkeley and Hume argued against Locke's theory of abstract ideas by observing that introspection shows all ideas to be particular, from which they concluded that we can have no adequate concept of an abstract entity; instead, when we reason about what we call abstracta we are actually thinking about particular ideas delegated by the mind to represent an entire class of resemblant particulars, from which we may freely substitute others if we mistakenly draw conclusions peculiar to the example chosen. Abstract propositions were defended by Bolzano and Frege in the nineteenth century as the meanings of thought in language and logic. Dispute persists about the need for and nature of abstract entities, but many philosophers believe they are indispensable in metaphysics.

See also ARISTOTLE, BERKELEY, FREGE, METAPHYSICAL REALISM, OCKHAM, PLATO, PROPERTY.   D.J.

abstraction. See ABSTRACT ENTITY, BERKELEY.

abstraction, axiom of. See AXIOM OF COMPREHENSION.

abstraction, lambda-. See COMBINATORY LOGIC.

absurd. See CAMUS, EXISTENTIALISM.

absurdity. See CATEGORY MISTAKE, REDUCTIO AD ABSURDUM.

Abunaser. See AL-FĀRĀBĪ.

AC. See APPENDIX OF SPECIAL SYMBOLS.

Academic Skepticism. See SKEPTICISM, SKEPTICS.

Academy, the school established by Plato around 385 B.C. at his property outside Athens near the public park and gymnasium known by that name. Although it may not have maintained a continuous tradition, the many and varied philosophers of the Academy all considered themselves Plato's successors, and all of them celebrated and studied his work. The school survived in some form until A.D. 529, when it was dissolved, along with the other pagan schools, by the Eastern Roman emperor Justinian I. The history of the Academy is divided by some authorities into that of the Old Academy (Plato, Speusippus, Xenocrates, and their followers) and the New Academy (the Skeptical Academy of the third and second centuries B.C.). Others speak of five phases in its history: Old (as before), Middle (Arcesilaus), New (Carneades), Fourth (Philo of Larisa), and Fifth (Antiochus of Ascalon).

For most of its history the Academy was devoted to elucidating doctrines associated with Plato that were not entirely explicit in the dialogues. These "unwritten doctrines" were apparently passed down to his immediate successors and are known to us mainly through the work of Aristotle: there are two opposed first principles, the One and the Indefinite Dyad (Great and Small); these generate Forms or Ideas (which may be identified with numbers), from which in turn come intermediate mathematicals and, at the lowest level, perceptible things (Aristotle, *Metaphysics* I.6).

After Plato's death in 347, the Academy passed to his nephew Speusippus (c.407–339), who led the school until his death. Although his written works have perished, his views on certain main points, along with some quotations, were recorded by surviving authors. Under the influence of late Pythagoreans, Speusippus anticipated Plotinus by holding that the One transcends being, goodness, and even Intellect, and that the Dyad (which he identifies with matter) is the cause of all beings. To explain the gradations of beings, he posited gradations of matter, and this gave rise to Aristotle's charge that Speusippus saw the universe as a series of disjointed episodes. Speusippus abandoned the theory of Forms as ideal numbers, and gave heavier emphasis than other Platonists to the mathematicals.

Xenocrates (396–314), who once went with Plato to Sicily, succeeded Speusippus and led the Academy till his own death. Although he was a prolific author, Xenocrates' works have not survived, and he is known only through the work of other authors. He was induced by Aristotle's objections to reject Speusippus's views on some points, and he developed theories that were a major influence on Middle Platonism, as well as on Stoicism. In Xenocrates' theory the One is Intellect, and the Forms are ideas in the mind of this divine principle; the One is not transcendent, but it resides in an intellectual space above the heavens. While the One is good, the Dyad is evil, and the sublunary world is identified with Hades. Having taken Forms to be mathematical entities, he had no use for intermediate mathematicals. Forms he defined further as paradigmatic causes of regular natural phenomena, and soul as self-moving number.

Polemon (c.350–267) led the Academy from 314 to 267, and was chiefly known for his fine character, which set an example of self-control for his students. The Stoics probably derived their concept of *oikeiosis* (an accommodation to nature) from his teaching. After Polemon's death, his colleague Crates led the Academy until the accession of Arcesilaus.

The New Academy arose when Arcesilaus became the leader of the school in about 265 B.C. and turned the dialectical tradition of Plato to the Skeptical aim of suspending belief. The debate between the New Academy and Stoicism dominated philosophical discussion for the next century and a half. On the Academic side the most prominent spokesman was Carneades (c.213–129 B.C.).

In the early years of the first century B.C., Philo of Larisa attempted to reconcile the Old and the New Academy. His pupil, the former Skeptic Antiochus of Ascalon, was enraged by this and broke away to refound the Old Academy in about 87 B.C. This was the beginning of Middle Platonism (c.80 B.C.–A.D. 220). Antiochus's school was eclectic in combining elements of Platonism, Stoicism, and Aristotelian philosophy, and is known to us mainly through Cicero's *Academica*. Middle Platonism revived the main themes of Speusippus and Xenocrates, but often used Stoic or neo-Pythagorean concepts to explain them. The influence of the Stoic Posidonius (135–50/51 B.C.) was strongly felt on the Academy in this period, and Platonism flourished at centers other than the Academy in Athens, most notably in Alexandria, with Eudorus (first century B.C.) and Philo of Alexandria (fl. A.D. 39).

After the death of Philo, the center of interest returned to Athens, where Plutarch of Chaeronia (A.D. c.45–c.125) studied with Ammonius at the Academy, although Plutarch spent most of his career at his home in nearby Boeotia. His many philosophical treatises, which are rich sources for the history of philosophy, are gathered under the title *Moralia;* his interest in ethics and moral education led him to write the *Parallel Lives* (paired biographies of famous Romans and Athenians), for which he is best known.

After this period, the Academy ceased to be the name for a species of Platonic philosophy, although the school remained a center for Platonism, and was especially prominent under the leadership of the Neoplatonist Proclus (c.410–85).

See also MIDDLE PLATONISM, NEOPLATONISM, NEW ACADEMY, PLATO.   P.Wo.

accent, fallacy of. See INFORMAL FALLACY.

accessibility, epistemic. See EPISTEMOLOGY.

accessibility between two worlds. See POSSIBLE WORLDS.

accident, a feature or property of a substance (e.g., an organism or an artifact) without which the substance could still exist. According to a common essentialist view of persons, Socrates' size, color, and integrity are among his accidents, while his humanity is not. For Descartes, thinking is the essence of the soul, while any particular thought a soul entertains is an accident. According to a common theology, God has no accidents, since all truths about him flow by necessity from his nature. These examples suggest the diversity of traditional uses of the notion of accident. There is no uniform conception; but the Cartesian view, according to which the accidents are modes of (ways of specifying) the essence of a substance, is representative. An important ambiguity concerns the identity of accidents: if Plato and Aristotle have the same weight, is that weight one accident (say, the property of weighing precisely 70 kilograms) or two (one accident for Plato, one for Aristotle)? Different theorists give different answers (and some have changed their minds). Issues about accidents have become peripheral in this century because of the decline of traditional concerns about substance. But the more general questions about necessity and contingency are very much alive. **See also CONTINGENT, ESSENTIALISM, PROPERTY.**   S.J.W.

accident, fallacy of. See INFORMAL FALLACY.

accidental generalization. See LAWLIKE GENERALIZATION.

accidentalism, the metaphysical thesis that the occurrence of some events is either not necessitated or not causally determined or not predictable. Many determinists have maintained that although all events are caused, some nevertheless occur accidentally, if only because the causal laws determining them might have been different. Some philosophers have argued that even if determinism is true, some events, such as a discovery, could not have been predicted, on grounds that to *predict* a discovery is to *make* the discovery.

The term may also designate a theory of individuation: that individuals of the same kind or species are numerically distinct in virtue of possessing some different accidental properties. Two horses are the same in essence but numerically distinct because one of them is black, e.g., while the other is white. Accidentalism presupposes the identity of indiscernibles but goes beyond it by claiming that accidental properties *account for* numerical diversity within a species. Peter Abelard criticized a version of accidentalism espoused by his teacher, William of Champeaux, on the ground that accidental properties depend for their existence on the distinct individuals in which they inhere, and so the properties cannot account for the distinctness of the individuals. **See also DETERMINISM, IDENTITY OF INDISCERNIBLES.**　　　　　　　　　　　　W.E.M.

accidental property. See PROPERTY.

accidie (also acedia), apathy, listlessness, or ennui. This condition is problematic for the internalist thesis that, necessarily, any belief that one morally ought to do something is conceptually sufficient for having motivation to do it. Ann has long believed that she ought, morally, to assist her ailing mother, and she has dutifully acted accordingly. Seemingly, she may continue to believe this, even though, owing to a recent personal tragedy, she now suffers from accidie and is wholly lacking in motivation to assist her mother. **See also AKRASIA, MOTIVATIONAL INTERNALISM, SOCRATIC PARADOXES.**　　　　A.R.M.

accomplishment verb. See ACTION VERB.

achievement verb. See ACTION VERB.

Achilles paradox. See ZENO'S PARADOXES.

acosmism, a term formed in analogy to 'atheism,' meaning the denial of the ultimate reality of the world. Ernst Platner used it in 1776 to describe Spinoza's philosophy, arguing that Spinoza did not intend to deny "the existence of the God-

head, but the existence of the world." Maimon, Fichte, Hegel, and others make the same claim. By the time of Feuerbach it was also used to characterize a basic feature of Christianity: the denial of the world or worldliness. **See also FICHTE, HEGEL, SPINOZA.**　　　　　　　　　M.K.

acquaintance, knowledge by. See KNOWLEDGE BY ACQUAINTANCE.

acrasia. See AKRASIA.

act-content-object-psychology. See ACT-OBJECT PSYCHOLOGY.

act, propositional. See INTENTIONALITY.

act, voluntary. See ACTION THEORY.

action, basic. See PHILOSOPHY OF ACTION.

action, philosophy of. See ACTION THEORY.

action at a distance. See FIELD THEORY.

action theory, the study of the ontological structure of human action, the process by which it originates, and the ways in which it is explained. Most human actions are acts of *commission*: they constitute a class of events in which a subject (the agent) brings about some change or changes. Thus, in moving one's finger, one brings it about that one's finger moves. When the change brought about is an ongoing process (e.g., the continuing appearance of words on a page), the behavior is called an *activity* (writing). An action of *omission* occurs when an agent refrains from performing an action of commission. Since actions of commission are events, the question of their ontology is in part a matter of the general ontology of change. An important issue here is whether what occurs when an action is performed should be viewed as abstract or concrete. On the first approach, actions are understood either as proposition-like entities (e.g., Booth's moving a finger), or as a species of universal – namely, an *act-type* (moving a finger). What "occurred" when Booth moved his finger in Ford's Theater on April 14, 1865, is held to be the abstract entity in question, and the entity is viewed as repeatable: that is, precisely the same entity is held to have occurred on every other occasion of Booth's moving his finger. When actions are viewed as concrete, on the other hand, Booth's moving his finger in Ford's Theater is understood to be a non-repeatable particular, and the movement of the finger counts as an *act-token*, which instantiates the corresponding act-type. Concrete actions are time-bound: each belongs to a single behavioral episode, and other instantiations of the same act-type count as distinct events.

A second important ontological issue concerns the fact that by moving his finger, Booth also fired a gun, and killed Lincoln. It is common for more than one thing to be accomplished in a single exercise of agency, and how such doings are related is a matter of debate. If actions are understood as abstract entities, the answer is essentially foregone: there must be as many different actions on Booth's part as there are types exemplified. But if actions are viewed as particulars the same token can count as an instance of more than one type, and identity claims become possible. Here there is disagreement. *Fine-grained* theories of act individuation tend to confine identity claims to actions that differ only in ways describable through different modifications of the same main verb – e.g., where Placido both sings and sings loudly. Otherwise, different types are held to require different tokens: Booth's action of moving his finger is held to have generated or given rise to distinct actions of firing the gun and killing Lincoln, by virtue of having had as causal consequences the gun's discharge and Lincoln's death. The opposite, *coarse-grained* theory, however, views these causal relations as grounds for claiming Booth's acts were precisely identical. On this view, for Booth to kill Lincoln was simply for him to do something that caused Lincoln's death – which was in fact nothing more than to move his finger – and similarly for his firing the gun. There is also a compromise account, on which Booth's actions are related as part to whole, each consisting in a longer segment of the causal chain that terminates with Lincoln's death. The action of killing Lincoln consisted, on this view, in the entire sequence; but that of firing the gun terminated with the gun's discharge, and that of moving the finger with the finger's motion.

When, as in Booth's case, more than one thing is accomplished in a single exercise of agency, some are done *by* doing others. But if all actions were performed by performing others, an infinite regress would result. There must, then, be a class of *basic actions* – i.e., actions fundamental to the performance of all others, but not themselves done by doing something else. There is disagreement, however, on which actions are basic. Some theories treat bodily movements, such as Booth's moving his finger, as basic. Others point

out that it is possible to engage in action but to accomplish less than a bodily movement, as when one tries to move a limb that is restrained or paralyzed, and fails. According to these accounts, bodily actions arise out of a still more basic mental activity, usually called *volition* or willing, which is held to constitute the standard means for performing all overt actions.

The question of how bodily actions originate is closely associated with that of what distinguishes them from involuntary and reflex bodily events, as well as from events in the inanimate world. There is general agreement that the crucial difference concerns the mental states that attend action, and in particular the fact that voluntary actions typically arise out of states of intending on the part of the agent. But the nature of the relation is difficult, and there is the complicating factor that intention is sometimes held to reduce to other mental states, such as the agent's desires and beliefs. That issue aside, it would appear that unintentional actions arise out of more basic actions that are intentional, as when one unintentionally breaks a shoelace by intentionally tugging on it. But how intention is first translated into action is much more problematic, especially when bodily movements are viewed as basic actions. One cannot, e.g., count Booth's moving his finger as an intentional action simply because he intended to do so, or even on the ground (if it is true) that his intention caused his finger to move. The latter might have occurred through a strictly autonomic response had Booth been nervous enough, and then the moving of the finger would not have counted as an action at all, much less as intentional. Avoiding such "wayward causal chains" requires accounting for the agent's voluntary control over what occurs in genuinely intentional action – a difficult task when bodily actions are held to be basic. Volitional accounts have greater success here, since they can hold that movements are intentional only when the agent's intention is executed through volitional activity. But they must sidestep another threatened regress: if we call for an activity of willing to explain why Booth's moving his finger counts as intentional action, we cannot do the same for willing itself. Yet on most accounts volition does have the characteristics of intentional behavior. Volitional theories of action must, then, provide an alternative account of how mental activity can be intentional.

Actions are explained by invoking the agent's reasons for performing them. Characteristically, a reason may be understood to consist in a positive attitude of the agent toward one or another outcome, and a belief to the effect that the outcome may be achieved by performing the action in question. Thus Emily might spend the summer in France out of a desire to learn French, and a belief that spending time in France is the best way to do so. Disputed questions about reasons include how confident the agent must be that the action selected will in fact lead to the envisioned outcome, and whether obligation represents a source of motivation that can operate independently of the agent's desires.

Frequently, more than one course of action is available to an agent. *Deliberation* is the process of searching out and weighing the reasons for and against such alternatives. When successfully concluded, deliberation usually issues in a decision, by which an intention to undertake one of the contemplated actions is formed. The intention is then carried out when the time for action comes. Much debate has centered on the question of how reasons are related to decisions and actions. As with intention, an agent's simply having a reason is not enough for the reason to explain her behavior: her desire to learn French notwithstanding, Emily might have gone to France simply because she was transferred there. Only when an agent does something *for* a reason does the reason explain what is done. It is frequently claimed that this bespeaks a causal relation between the agent's strongest reason and her decision or action. This, however, suggests a determinist stance on the free will problem, leading some philosophers to balk. An alternative is to treat reason explanations as teleological explanations, wherein an action is held to be reasonable or justified in virtue of the goals toward which it was directed. But positions that treat reason explanations as non-causal require an alternative account of what it is to decide or act for one reason rather than another.

See also EVENT, FREE WILL PROBLEM, INTENTION, PRACTICAL REASONING, VOLITION.   H.J.M.

act(ion)-token. See ACTION THEORY.

act(ion)-type. See ACTION THEORY, TYPE THEORY.

action verb, a verb applied to an agent and describing an activity, an action, or an attempt at or a culmination of an action. Verbs applying to agents may be distinguished in two basic ways: by whether they can take the progressive (continuous) form and by whether or not there is a specific moment of occurrence/completion of the action named by the verb. An *activity verb* is

one describing something that goes on for a time but with no inherent endpoint, such as 'drive', 'laugh', or 'meditate'. One can stop doing such a thing but one cannot complete doing it. Indeed, one can be said to have done it as soon as one has begun doing it. An *accomplishment verb* is one describing something that goes on for a time toward an inherent endpoint, such as 'paint' (a fence), 'solve' (a problem), or 'climb' (a mountain). Such a thing takes a certain time to do, and one cannot be said to have done it until it has been completed. An *achievement verb* is one describing either the culmination of an activity, such as 'finish' (a job) or 'reach' (a goal); the effecting of a change, such as 'fire' (an employee) or 'drop' (an egg); or undergoing a change, such as 'hear' (an explosion) or 'forget' (a name). An achievement does not go on for a period of time but may be the culmination of something that does. Ryle singled out achievement verbs and state verbs (see below) partly in order to disabuse philosophers of the idea that what psychological verbs name must invariably be inner acts or activities modeled on bodily actions or activities. A *task verb* is an activity verb that implies attempting to do something named by an achievement verb. For example, to seek is to attempt to find, to sniff is to attempt to smell, and to treat is to attempt to cure. A *state* verb is a verb (not an action verb) describing a condition, disposition, or habit rather than something that goes on or takes place. Examples include 'own', 'weigh', 'want', 'hate', 'frequent', and 'teetotal'.

These differences were articulated by Zeno Vendler in *Linguistics and Philosophy* (1967). Taking them into account, linguists have classified verbs (and verb phrases) into four main aspectual classes, which they distinguish in respect to the availability and interpretation of the simple present tense, of the perfect tenses, of the progressive construction, and of various temporal adverbials, such as adverbs like 'yesterday', 'finally', and 'often', and prepositional phrases like 'for a long time' and 'in a while'. Many verbs belong to more than one category by virtue of having several related uses. For example, 'run' is both an activity and an accomplishment verb, and 'weigh' is both a state and an accomplishment verb. Linguists single out a class of *causative verbs*, such as 'force', 'inspire', and 'persuade', some of which are achievement and some accomplishment verbs. Such causative verbs as 'break', 'burn', and 'improve' have a correlative intransitive use, so that, e.g., to break something is to cause it to break.

See also PHILOSOPHY OF LANGUAGE, SPEECH ACT THEORY.   K.B.

active euthanasia. See EUTHANASIA.

active power. See POWER.

activity verb. See ACTION VERB.

act-object distinction. See BRENTANO, MEINONG.

act-object psychology, also called act-content-object psychology, a philosophical theory that identifies in every psychological state a mental act, a lived-through phenomenological content, such as a mental image or description of properties, and an intended object that the mental act is about or toward which it is directed by virtue of its content. The distinction between the act, content, and object of thought originated with Alois Höfler's *Logik* (1890), written in collaboration with Meinong. But the theory is historically most often associated with its development in Kazimierz Twardowski's *Zur Lehre vom Inhalt und Gegenstand der Vorstellung* ("On the Content and Object of Presentations," 1894), despite Twardowski's acknowledgment of his debt to Höfler.

Act-object psychology arose as a reaction to Franz Brentano's immanent intentionality thesis in his influential *Psychologie vom empirischen Standpunkt* ("Psychology from an Empirical Standpoint," 1874), in which Brentano maintains that intentionality is "the mark of the mental," by contrast with purely physical phenomena. Brentano requires that intended objects belong immanently to the mental acts that intend them – a philosophical commitment that laid Brentano open to charges of epistemological idealism and psychologism. Yet Brentano's followers, who accepted the intentionality of thought but resisted what they came to see as its detachable idealism and psychologism, responded by distinguishing the act-immanent phenomenological content of a psychological state from its act-transcendent intended object, arguing that Brentano had wrongly and unnecessarily conflated mental content with the external objects of thought.

Twardowski goes so far as to claim that content and object can never be identical, an exclusion in turn that is vigorously challenged by Husserl in his *Logische Untersuchungen* ("Logical Investigations," 1913, 1922), and by others in the phenomenological tradition who acknowledge the possibility that a self-reflexive thought can sometimes be about its own content as intended object, in which content and object are indistinguishable. Act-object psychology continues to be of interest to contemporary philosophy because of its relation to ongoing projects in phenomenology, and as a result of a resurgence of study of the concept of intentionality and qualia in philosophy of mind, cognitive psychology, and *Gegenstandstheorie*, or existent and non-existent intended object theory, in philosophical logic and semantics.

See also BRENTANO, HUSSERL, INTENTIONALITY, MEINONG, PHILOSOPHY OF MIND, POLISH LOGIC, QUALIA.   D.J.

act of commission. See ACTION THEORY.

act of omission. See ACTION THEORY.

actual infinite. See ARISTOTLE.

actualism. See GENTILE.

actualist. See MODAL LOGIC.

actuality. See POSSIBLE WORLDS.

actualization, first. See ARISTOTLE.

actualization, second. See ARISTOTLE.

actual occasion. See WHITEHEAD.

actual reality. See REALITY.

act utilitarianism. See UTILITARIANISM.

Adam de Wodeham. See WODEHAM.

adaptation. See DARWINISM.

adaptive system. See COMPUTER THEORY.

Adelard of Bath (c.1070–c.1145), English Benedictine monk notable for his contributions to the introduction of Arabic science in the West. After studying at Tours, he taught at Laon, then spent seven years traveling in Italy, possibly Spain, and Cilicia and Syria, before returning to England. In his dialogue *On the Same and the Different,* he remarks, concerning universals, that the names of individuals, species, and genera are imposed on the same essence regarded in different respects. He also wrote *Seventy-six Questions on Nature,* based on Arabic learning; works on the use of the abacus and the astrolabe; a work on falconry; and translations of Abu Ma'shar's Arabic

Shorter Introduction to Astronomy, al-Khwarizmi's (fl. c.830) astronomical tables, and *Euclid's Elements.*   J.Lo.

adequacy, analytic. See MATERIAL ADEQUACY.

adequacy, material. See MATERIAL ADEQUACY.

adequation. See HUSSERL.

ad hoc. See CURVE-FITTING PROBLEM.

ad hoc hypothesis. See CURVE-FITTING PROBLEM.

ādhyātman (Sanskrit, 'relating to or belonging to the self'), in early Hindu texts concerning such topics as knowledge of the self, meditating on that which appertains to the self, or spiritual exercise related to the self (*ādhyātma-yoga*). Later, it became a term for the Supreme Spirit, the Supreme Self, or the soul, which, in Indian thought, is other than the ego. In monistic systems, e.g. Advaita Vedanta, the *ādhyātman* is the one Self that is the impersonal Absolute (Brahman), a state of pure consciousness, ultimately the only Real. In dualist systems, e.g. Dvaita Vedanta, it is the true self or soul of each individual.   R.N.Mi.

adiaphora. See STOICISM.

adicity. See DEGREE.

adjunction. See CONJUNCTION INTRODUCTION.

Adorno, Theodor Wiesengrund (1903–69), German philosopher and aesthetic theorist, one of the main philosophers of the first generation of the Frankfurt School of critical theory. With Horkheimer, Adorno gave philosophical direction to the Frankfurt School and its research projects in its Institute for Social Research. An accomplished musician and composer, Adorno first focused on the theory of culture and art, working to develop a non-reductionist but materialist theory of art and music in many essays from the 1930s. Under the influence of Walter Benjamin, he turned toward developing a "micrological" account of cultural artifacts, viewing them as "constellations" of social and historical forces.

As his collaboration with Horkheimer increased, Adorno turned to the problem of a self-defeating dialectic of modern reason and freedom. Under the influence of the seemingly imminent victory of the Nazis in Europe, this analysis focused on the "entwinement of myth and Enlightenment." *The Dialectic of Enlightenment* (1941) argues that instrumental reason promises the subject autonomy from the forces of nature only to enslave it again by its own repression of its impulses and inclinations. The only way around this self-domination is "non-identity thinking," found in the unifying tendencies of a non-repressive reason. This self-defeating dialectic is represented by the striking image of Ulysses tied to the mast to survive his encounter with the Sirens. Adorno initially hoped for a positive analysis of the Enlightenment to overcome this genealogy of modern reason, but it is never developed. Instead, he turned to an increasingly pessimistic analysis of the growing reification of modern life and of the possibility of a "totally administered society."

Adorno held that "autonomous art" can open up established reality and negate the experience of reification. *Aesthetic Theory* (1970) develops this idea of autonomous art in terms of aesthetic form, or the capacity of the internal organization of art to restructure existing patterns of meaning. Authentic works of art have a "truth-value" in their capacity to bring to awareness social contradictions and antinomies. In *Negative Dialectics* (1966) Adorno provides a more general account of social criticism under the "fragmenting" conditions of modern rationalization and domination. These and other writings have had a large impact on cultural criticism, particularly through Adorno's analysis of popular culture and the "culture industry."

    See also CRITICAL THEORY, FRANKFURT SCHOOL.   J.Bo.

Advaita, also called Uttara Mīmāmsā, in Hinduism, the non-dualistic form of Vedanta. Advaita Vedanta makes an epistemological distinction (not a metaphysical one) between the level of appearance and the level of reality. This marks off how things appear versus how they are; there appear to be a multitude of distinct persons and physical objects, and a personal deity, whereas there is only ineffable Brahman. This doctrine, according to Advaita, is taught in the Upanishads and realized in an esoteric enlightenment experience called *moksha.* The opposing evidence provided by all experiences that (a) have a subject-consciousness-object structure (e.g., seeing a sunset) and evidence a distinction between what one experiences and oneself, or (b) have a subject/content structure (e.g., feeling pain) and evidence a distinction between oneself and one's states, is dismissed on the ground that these experiences involve "the making of distinctions." Critics claim that *moksha* itself, as an experience in which something allegedly is learned or grasped, also must involve "the making of distinctions." **See also** VEDANTA.   K.E.Y.

adventitious ideas. See IDEA.

adverbial theory. See PERCEPTION.

Aenesidemus. See SKEPTICISM, SKEPTICS.

aesthetic attitude, the appropriate attitude or frame of mind for approaching art (or nature or other objects or events) so that one might both appreciate its intrinsic perceptual qualities, and as a result have an aesthetic experience.

The aesthetic attitude has been construed in many ways: (1) as disinterested, so that one's experience of the work is not affected by any interest in its possible practical uses, (2) as a "distancing" of oneself from one's own personal concerns, (3) as the contemplation of an object, purely as an object of sensation, as it is in itself, for its own sake, in a way unaffected by any cognition or knowledge one may have of it. These different notions of aesthetic attitude have at times been combined within a single theory.

There is considerable doubt about whether there is such a thing as an aesthetic attitude. There is neither any special kind of action nor any special way of performing an ordinary action that ensures that we see a work as it "really is," and that results in our having an aesthetic experience. Furthermore, there are no *purely* sensory experiences, divorced from any cognitive content whatsoever. Criticisms of the notion of aesthetic attitude have reinforced attacks on aesthetics as a separate field of study within philosophy.

See also AESTHETIC PROPERTY, AESTHETICS, BEAUTY.   S.L.F.

aesthetic form. See AESTHETIC FORMALISM, AESTHETICS.

aesthetic formalism, the view that in our interactions with works of art, form should be given primacy. Rather than taking 'formalism' as the name of one specific theory in the arts, it is better and more typical to take it to name that *type* of theory which emphasizes the *form* of the artwork. Or, since emphasis on form is something that comes in degrees, it is best to think of theories of art as ranged on a continuum of *more for-*

malist and *less formalist*. It should be added that theories of art are typically complex, including definitions of art, recommendations concerning what we should attend to in art, analyses of the nature of the aesthetic, recommendations concerning the making of aesthetic evaluations, etc.; and each of these components may be more formalist or less so.

Those who use the concept of form mainly wish to contrast the artifact itself with its relations to entities outside itself – with its representing various things, its symbolizing various things, its being expressive of various things, its being the product of various intentions of the artist, its evoking various states in beholders, its standing in various relations of influence and similarity to preceding, succeeding, and contemporary works, etc. There have been some, however, who in emphasizing form have meant to emphasize not just the artifact but the perceptible form or design of the artifact. Kant, e.g., in his theory of aesthetic excellence, not only insisted that the only thing relevant to determining the beauty of an object is its appearance, but within the appearance, the *form,* the *design:* in visual art, not the colors but the design that the colors compose; in music, not the timbre of the individual sounds but the formal relationships among them.

It comes as no surprise that theories of music have tended to be much more formalist than theories of literature and drama, with theories of the visual arts located in between.

See also AESTHETICS.   N.P.W.

aesthetic property, a property or quality such as being dainty, garish, graceful, balanced, charming, majestic, trite, elegant, lifeless, ugly, or beautiful. By contrast, non-aesthetic properties are properties that require no special sensitivity or perceptiveness to perceive – such as a painting's being predominantly blue, its having a small red square in a corner or a kneeling figure in the foreground, or that the music becomes louder at a given point. Sometimes it is argued that a special perceptiveness or taste is needed to perceive a work's aesthetic qualities, and that this is a defining feature of a property's being aesthetic. A corollary of this view is that aesthetic qualities cannot be defined in terms of non-aesthetic qualities, though some have held that aesthetic qualities supervene on non-aesthetic qualities. **See also** AESTHETICS, BEAUTY, SUPERVENIENCE.   S.L.F.

aesthetics, the branch of philosophy that examines the nature of art and the character of our experience of art and of the natural environment. It emerged as a separate field of philosophical inquiry during the eighteenth century in England and on the Continent. Recognition of aesthetics as a separate branch of philosophy coincided with the development of theories of art that grouped together painting, poetry, sculpture, music, and dance (and often landscape gardening) as the same kind of thing, *les beaux arts*, or the fine arts. Baumgarten coined the term 'aesthetics' in his *Reflections on Poetry* (1735) as the name for one of the two branches of the study of knowledge, i.e., for the study of sensory experience coupled with feeling, which he argued provided a different type of knowledge from the distinct, abstract ideas studied by "logic." He derived it from the ancient Greek *aisthanomai* ('to perceive'), and "the aesthetic" has always been intimately connected with sensory experience and the kinds of feelings it arouses.

Questions specific to the field of aesthetics are: Is there a special attitude, the aesthetic attitude, which we should take toward works of art and the natural environment, and what is it like? Is there a distinctive type of experience, an aesthetic experience, and what is it? Is there a special object of attention that we can call the aesthetic object? Finally, is there a distinctive value, aesthetic value, comparable with moral, epistemic, and religious values? Some questions overlap with those in the philosophy of art, such as those concerning the nature of beauty, and whether there is a faculty of taste that is exercised in judging the aesthetic character and value of natural objects or works of art.

Aesthetics also encompasses the philosophy of art. The most central issue in the philosophy of art has been how to define 'art'. Not all cultures have, or have had, a concept of art that coincides with the one that emerged in Western Europe during the seventeenth and eighteenth centuries. What justifies our applying our concept to the things people in these other cultures have produced? There are also many pictures (including paintings), songs, buildings, and bits of writing, that are not art. What distinguishes those pictures, musical works, etc., that are art from those that are not? Various answers have been proposed that identify the distinguishing features of art in terms of form, expressiveness, intentions of the maker, and social roles or uses of the object.

Since the eighteenth century there have been debates about what kinds of things count as "art." Some have argued that architecture and ceramics are not art because their functions are primarily utilitarian, and novels were for a long time not listed among the "fine arts" because they are not embodied in a sensuous medium. Debates continue to arise over new media and what may be new art forms, such as film, video, photography, performance art, found art, furniture, posters, earthworks, and computer and electronic art. Sculptures these days may be made out of dirt, feces, or various discarded and mass-produced objects, rather than marble or bronze. There is often an explicit rejection of craft and technique by twentieth-century artists, and the subject matter has expanded to include the banal and everyday, and not merely mythological, historical, and religious subjects as in years past. All of these developments raise questions about the relevance of the category of "fine" or "high" art.

Another set of issues in philosophy of art concerns how artworks are to be interpreted, appreciated, and understood. Some views emphasize that artworks are products of individual efforts, so that a work should be understood in light of the producer's knowledge, skill, and intentions. Others see the meaning of a work as established by social conventions and practices of the artist's own time, but which may not be known or understood by the producer. Still others see meaning as established by the practices of the users, even if they were not in effect when the work was produced.

Are there objective criteria or standards for evaluating individual artworks? There has been much disagreement over whether value judgments have universal validity, or whether there can be no disputing about taste, if value judgments are relative to the tastes and interests of each individual (or to some group of individuals who share the same tastes and interests). A judgment such as "This is good" certainly seems to make a claim about the work itself, though such a claim is often based on the sort of feeling, understanding, or experience a person has obtained from the work. A work's aesthetic or artistic value is generally distinguished from simply liking it. But is it possible to establish what sort(s) of knowledge or experience(s) any given work should provide to any suitably prepared perceiver, and what would it be to be suitably prepared? It is a matter of contention whether a work's aesthetic and artistic values are independent of its moral, political, or epistemic stance or impact.

Philosophy of art has also dealt with the nature of taste, beauty, imagination, creativity, representation, expression, and expressiveness; style; whether artworks convey knowledge or truth; the nature of narrative and metaphor; the importance of genre; the ontological status of artworks; and the character of our emotional responses to art.

Work in the field has always been influenced by philosophical theories of language or meaning, and theories of knowledge and perception, and continues to be heavily influenced by psychological and cultural theory, including versions of semiotics, psychoanalysis, cognitive psychology, feminism, and Marxism. Some theorists in the late twentieth century have denied that the aesthetic and the "fine arts" can legitimately be separated out and understood as separate, autonomous human phenomena; they argue instead that these conceptual categories themselves manifest and reinforce certain kinds of cultural attitudes and power relationships. These theorists urge that aesthetics can and should be eliminated as a separate field of study, and that "the aesthetic" should not be conceived as a special kind of value. They favor instead a critique of the roles that images (not only painting, but film, photography, and advertising), sounds, narrative, and three-dimensional constructions have in expressing and shaping human attitudes and experiences.

See also AESTHETIC ATTITUDE, AESTHETIC PROPERTY, BEAUTY, EXPRESSION THEORY OF ART, INSTITUTIONAL THEORY OF ART.   S.L.F.

affirming the consequent. See FORMAL FALLACY.

a fortiori **argument**, an argument that moves from the premises that everything which possesses (a) certain characteristic(s) will possess some further characteristic(s) and that certain things possess the relevant characteristic(s) to an eminent degree to the conclusion that *a fortiori* (even more so) these things will possess the further characteristic(s). The second premise is often left implicit, so *a fortiori* arguments are often enthymemes. An example of an *a fortiori* argument can be found in Plato's *Crito:* We owe gratitude and respect to our parents and so should do nothing to harm them. Athenians owe even greater gratitude and respect to the laws of Athens and so *a fortiori* should do nothing to harm those laws. **See also ENTHYMEME, SYLLOGISM.**   R.P.

African philosophy, the philosophy produced by the preliterate cultures of Africa, distinctive in that African philosophy in the traditional setting is unwritten. For someone who is interested in studying, say, Chinese or Arabic philosophy, the written works of the individual thinkers are available; African philosophy, by contrast (with the exception of Ethiopian philosophy), has produced no written philosophical works.

The lack of written philosophical literature in Africa's cultural past is the outstanding reason for the persistent skepticism about the existence of African philosophy often entertained by scholars. There are some who would withhold the term 'philosophy' from African traditional thought and would reserve that term for the philosophical works being written by individual African philosophers today. There are others who, on the basis of (i) their own conception of the nature of philosophy, (ii) their sense of the history of the development of philosophical ideas in other cultures, (iii) their conviction about the importance of the universal character of the human capacity to wonder, or of the curiosity that leads some individuals in various cultures to raise fundamental questions about human life and experience, or (iv) their conviction that literacy is not a necessary condition for philosophizing, would apply 'philosophy' to African traditional thought, even though some of them would want to characterize it further as ethnophilosophy or folk philosophy. Two assumptions made about the character of African traditional thought have earned it those labels: one is the alleged communal (collective) subscription to a 'monolithic' set of ideas or beliefs; the other is the alleged lack of individualist elements in traditional thought. These assumptions have led some scholars to believe that African thought is a system of ideas or beliefs unanimously held by a whole tribe (*ethnos*), even though it may be argued that thought as such is always the product of an individual intellect. An individual may refine or build on the philosophical work of another individual, but the product will still be an individual intellectual enterprise.

What seems to have happened in Africa is that due to lack of a doxographic tradition, the ideas of unnamable (because unidentifiable) individuals that gained currency among the wider community became part of the pool of communal thought, as if they were the thought or a production of a whole *ethnos*, and expressed in its oral literature: in proverbs, myths and folk tales, rituals, religious beliefs, art symbols, customs, and traditions. These would, in fact, constitute the warp and woof of the fabric of traditional philosophy in Africa.

An extensive and profound critical evaluation

of concepts and values of traditional thought can be the starting point of modern African philosophy. The reason is that most of the traditional concepts, beliefs, and values have not relaxed their grip on modern African life and thought. But the modern African philosophy will also have to include the conceptual responses to the circumstances, experiences, and problems of modern African societies. This aspect of the philosophical enterprise will have to deal with the critical analysis, interpretation, and assessment of the changes that traditional values and ideas are going through in response to the pressures, both internal and external, weighing heavily on them through the ethos of contemporary life. Thus, African philosophy will not be a unique system, a windowless monad impervious to external influences. But it is conceivable – perhaps expected – that it will have some characteristics of its own.

As to the central themes of African philosophy, what one can appropriately do at this stage of its development is indicate some of the persistent assumptions, beliefs, and values embedded in African cultural and historical experiences. These would undoubtedly include: *supernaturalism* – ideas about God and other spiritual entities conceived in African ontologies, the dualistic or monistic perception of the external world, the (alleged) religiosity or spirituality of the African life, human destiny, and the moral life; *personhood and communitarianism* – social and humanistic ethics, notions of the community and the common good, the nature of the good life, the status of individuality in African socioethical thought; *political ideas* – chiefship and traditional political authority, traditional ideas of democracy, democratic thought in a communitarian framework, consensual politics and decision making, political legitimacy, corruption and political morality; and *tradition and modernity* – the notion of culture, ethnicity and nationhood, the nature and development of national culture and identity, the concept of development, technology, society, and values.

These themes and others have generated various ideas that must be critically analyzed and evaluated by contemporary African philosophers, who would in this way create a modern African philosophy with origins in the comprehensive culture and many-sided experiences of the African, yet aspects of which may be considered by other cultures to be worthwhile. Thanks to the literary culture they have inherited, contemporary African philosophers, through their own individual analyses and arguments, are in a position to contribute to the emergence of a modern African philosophy that would naturally comprise a multiplicity of individual philosophical ideas, arguments, and positions.   K.G.

āgama (Sanskrit, 'what has come down'), an authoritative religious text of an Indian sect. There are Hindu, Jain, and Buddhist *āgamas*. The Hindu *āgamas* fall into three main classes: Vaiṣṇava texts concerning the worship of Vishnu, Saiva texts dealing with worship of Siva, and Tantric texts regarding worship of Sakti. Saivism, e.g., has twenty-eight *āgamas*. An *āgama* may give instructions regarding making temples or idols, offer meditation techniques, teach philosophical doctrines, or commend methods of worship. The Mahayana Buddhist term for the basic teachings of the Theravada Buddhist tradition is '*āgama*'.   K.E.Y.

agape, unselfish love for all persons. An ethical theory according to which such love is the chief virtue, and actions are good to the extent that they express it, is sometimes called *agapism*. *Agape* is the Greek word most often used for love in the New Testament, and is often used in modern languages to signify whatever sort of love the writer takes to be idealized there. In New Testament Greek, however, it was probably a quite general word for love, so that any ethical ideal must be found in the text's substantive claims, rather than in the linguistic meaning of the word.   R.M.A.

agathon, Greek word meaning 'a good' or 'the good'. From Socrates onward, *agathon* was taken to be a central object of philosophical inquiry; it has frequently been assumed to be the goal of all rational action. Plato in the simile of the sun in the *Republic* identified it with the Form of the Good, the source of reality, truth, and intelligibility. Aristotle saw it as *eudaimonia*, intellectual or practical virtue, a view that found its way, via Stoicism and Neoplatonism, into Christianity. Modern theories of utility can be seen as concerned with essentially the same Socratic question.   R.C.

agent-based ethics. See VIRTUE ETHICS.

agent causation, the idea that the primary cause of an event is a substance; more specifically, causation by a substance, as opposed to an event. Thus a brick (a substance) may be said to be the cause of the breaking of the glass. The expression is also used more narrowly by Reid and others for the view that an action (or event) is caused by an exertion of power by some agent endowed with will and understanding. Thus, a person may be said to be the cause of her action of opening the door. In this restricted sense (Reid called it "the strict and proper sense"), an agent-cause must have the power to cause the action or event *and* the power not to cause it. Moreover, it must be "up to" the agent whether to cause the event or not to cause it. (It is not "up to" the brick whether to cause or not to cause the breaking of the glass.) The restricted sense of agent causation developed by Reid is closely tied to the view that the agent possesses free will.

Medieval philosophers distinguished the internal activity of the agent from the external event produced by that activity. The former was called "immanent causation" and the latter "transeunt causation." These terms have been adapted by Chisholm and others to mark the difference between agent causation and event causation. The idea is that the internal activity is agent-caused by the person whose activity it is; whereas the external event is event-caused by the internal activity of the agent.

See also CAUSATION, FREE WILL PROBLEM.

W.L.R.

agent-neutral. See UTILITARIANISM.

agent-relative. See UTILITARIANISM.

agnoiology (from Greek *agnoia*, 'ignorance'), the study of ignorance, its quality, and its conditions.

L.P.P.

agnosticism (from Greek *a-*, 'not', and *gnāstos*, 'known'), term invented by Thomas Henry Huxley in 1869 to denote the philosophical and religious attitude of those who claim that metaphysical ideas can be neither proved nor disproved. Huxley wrote, "I neither affirm nor deny the immortality of man. I see no reason for believing it, but on the other hand, I have no means of disproving it. I have no *a priori* objection to the doctrine."

Agnosticism is a form of skepticism applied to metaphysics, especially theism. The position is sometimes attributed to Kant, who held that we cannot have knowledge of God or immortality but must be content with faith. Agnosticism should not be confused with atheism, the belief that no god exists.

See also ATHEISM.

L.P.P.

agreement, method of. See MILL'S METHODS.

Agriculture School. See HSÜ HSING.

ahaṁkāra (Sanskrit, 'I-maker', 'I-crier'), in Hindu thought, the ego or faculty that gives the sense of 'I' or individual personality; by extension, egotism, pride, conceit. In the Sankhya and Yoga systems, it is the third element of ever-changing Nature evolving in creation. From it evolves the remainder of the phenomenal world. Other than Nature, which includes the individual intellect (*buddhi*), the faculty of perception (*manas*), the organs, and the senses, is the unchanging individual self (*puruṣa, Ātman*). The human predicament results from the ignorant identification of oneself with Nature rather than the true self. In earlier texts the cosmic sense of *ahaṁkāra* dominates as the means by which the Creator formulates Himself to create the world.

R.N.Mi.

ahantā, Sanskrit word meaning 'indestructible', 'unchangeable', 'eternal'. In traditional Hindu philosophical thought, the truly real was thought to be indestructible and eternal. Thus, because the Upanishadic Brahman and its subjective counterpart, the *Ātman,* were regarded as the truly real, they were thought to be unchangeable and eternal. The Hindu religious classic, the Bhagavad Gita (probably written between the fifth and the second century B.C.), made *ahantā* a well-known concept through the teachings of Krishna, who advised Arjuna that even though one's body may perish one's soul is eternal and indestructible, thus implying that the human soul contains the essence of the divine reality. See also BHAGAVAD GITA, BRAHMAN.

D.K.C.

ahiṁsā (Sanskrit), traditionally and literally, nonviolence to living creatures; for modern Indian thinkers, a positive sense of kindness to all creatures. To the Jains, *ahiṁsā* was a vow to injure no living being (*jiva*) in thought, word, or deed. Many Buddhists practice *ahiṁsā* as a precept that denies the existence of the ego, since injuring another is an assertion of egoism. With the modern period, particularly Gandhi, *ahiṁsā* was equated with self-sacrificial love for all beings. For Gandhi it was the first vow of the *satyāgrahi,* the one who "held onto Truth," the nonviolent resister. See also GANDHI, JAINISM.

R.N.Mi.

Ahura Mazda. See ZOROASTRIANISM.

Ailly, Pierre d'. See D'AILLY.

aisthesis. See ARISTOTLE.

aitia (Greek), cause. Originally referring to responsibility for a crime, this Greek term came to be used by philosophers to signify causality in a somewhat broader sense than the English 'cause' – the traditional rendering of *aitia* – can convey. An *aitia* is any answer to a why-question. According to Aristotle, how such questions ought to be answered is a philosophical issue addressed differently by different philosophers. He himself distinguishes four types of answers, and thus four *aitiai*, by distinguishing different types of questions: (1) Why is the statue heavy? Because it is made of bronze (material *aitia*). (2) Why did Persians invade Athens? Because the Athenians had raided their territory (moving or efficient *aitia*). (3) Why are the angles of a triangle equal to two right angles? Because of the triangle's nature (formal *aitia*). (4) Why did someone walk after dinner? Because (or for the sake) of his health (final *aitia*). Only the second of these would typically be called a cause in English. Though some render *aitia* as 'explanatory principle' or 'reason', these expressions inaptly suggest a merely mental existence; instead, an *aitia* is a thing or aspect of a thing. **See also ARISTOTLE, EXPLANATION.** E.C.H.

ākāśa, Sanskrit word translated as 'ether' or 'space'. Indian philosophical systems recognized various ontological categories, including that of substance. *Ākāśa* was thought of as a substance because it was believed to be the substratum of sound. Because *ākāśa* was understood to transmit sound waves, the term is better translated as 'ether' than 'space', but scholars are not unanimous on this. *Ākāśa*, though extended in space, was viewed as a non-material substance. It was thought of as all-pervading, infinite, indivisible and imperceivable, being inferred from the sensed quality of sound. D.K.C.

akrasia, also spelled *acrasia*, Greek term for weakness of will. *Akrasia* is a character flaw, also called incontinence, exhibited primarily in intentional behavior that conflicts with the agent's own values or principles. Its contrary is *enkrateia* (strength of will, continence, self-control). Both *akrasia* and *enkrateia*, Aristotle says, "are concerned with what is in excess of the state characteristic of most people; for the continent abide by their resolutions more, and the incontinent less, than most people can" (*Nicomachean Ethics* 1152a25–27). These resolutions may be viewed as judgments that it would be best to perform an action of a certain sort, or better to do one thing than another. *Enkrateia,* on that view, is the power (*kratos*) to act as one judges best in the face of competing motivation. *Akrasia* is a want or deficiency of such power. (Aristotle himself limited the sphere of both states more strictly than is now done, regarding both as concerned specifically with "pleasures and pains and appetites and aversions arising through touch and taste" [1150a9–10].)

Philosophers are generally more interested in incontinent and continent *actions* than in the corresponding states of character. Various species of incontinent or akratic behavior may be distinguished, including incontinent reasoning and akratic belief formation. The species of akratic behavior that has attracted most attention is uncompelled, intentional action that conflicts with a better or best judgment consciously held by the agent at the time of action. If, e.g., while judging it best not to eat a second piece of pie, you intentionally eat another piece, you act incontinently – provided that your so acting is uncompelled (e.g., your desire for the pie is not *irresistible*). Socrates denied that such action is possible, thereby creating one of the Socratic paradoxes.

In "unorthodox" instances of akratic action, a deed manifests weakness of will even though it *accords* with the agent's better judgment. A boy who decides, against his better judgment, to participate in a certain dangerous prank, might – owing to an avoidable failure of nerve – fail to execute his decision. In such a case, some would claim, his failure to act on his decision manifests weakness of will or *akrasia*. If, instead, he masters his fear, his participating in the prank might manifest *strength* of will, even though his so acting conflicts with his better judgment.

The occurrence of akratic actions seems to be a fact of life. Unlike many such (apparent) facts, this one has received considerable philosophical scrutiny for nearly two and a half millennia. A major source of the interest is clear: akratic action raises difficult questions about the connection between thought and action, a connection of paramount importance for most philosophical theories of the explanation of intentional behavior. Insofar as moral theory does not float free of evidence about the etiology of human behavior, the tough questions arise there as well. Ostensible akratic action, then, occupies a philosophical space in the intersection of the philosophy of mind and moral theory.

See also ACTION THEORY, INTENTION, PRACTICAL REASONING, VOLITION. A.R.M.

akṣara (Sanskrit, 'imperishable'), the highest reality in a variety of Hindu thought systems. From earliest times it also meant 'syllable', reflecting the search for the ultimate reality by Vedic priest-thinkers and the early primacy given to the sacred utterance as the support of the ritual order of the universe, later identified as the syllable *Om*. In later texts and the systematic thinkers it refers to the highest reality, which may be a personal supreme being or an impersonal absolute, such as the Highest Self (*paramātman*) of Shaṅkara (700–50). Non-technically, it can be used in any thought system of any entity believed to be imperishable.   R.N.Mi.

ālaya-vijñāna, Sanskrit term meaning literally 'storehouse consciousness', a category developed by Indian Buddhist metaphysicians to solve some specific philosophical problems, notably those of delayed karmic effect and causation at a temporal distance. The *ālaya-vijñāna* "stores," in unactualized but potential form, as "seeds," the results of an agent's volitional actions. These karmic "seeds" may come to fruition at a later time. Most Buddhists think of moments of consciousness (*vijñāna*) as intentional (having an object, being *of* something); the *ālaya-vijñāna* is an exception, allowing for the continuance of consciousness when the agent is apparently not conscious of anything (such as during dreamless sleep), and so also for the continuance of potential for future action during those times. **See also** BHAVAṄGA, VĀSANĀ.   P.J.G.

Albert of Saxony (1316–90), terminist logician from lower Saxony who taught in the arts faculty at Paris, 1351–62. He never finished his theology degree, as, under the influence of Buridan and Nicholas of Oresme, he turned to mathematics, physics, and logic. He was a founder of the University of Vienna in 1365 and was bishop of Halberstadt from 1366. His works on logic include *Logic, Questions on the Posterior Analytics, Sophismata, Treatise on Obligations,* and *Insolubilia*. He also wrote questions on Aristotle's physical works and on John of Sacrobosco's *De Sphaera*, and short treatises on squaring the circle and on the ratio of the diameter to the side of a square. His work is competent but rarely original. **See also** TERMINIST LOGIC.   J.Lo.

Albert the Great. See ALBERTUS MAGNUS.

Albertus Magnus, also called Albert the Great (c.1200–80), German Dominican philosopher-theologian. As a Parisian master of theology, he served on a commission that condemned the Talmud. He left Paris to found the first Dominican *studium generale* in Germany at Cologne in 1248. From 1252 until old age, Albert was repeatedly asked to be an arbiter and peacemaker. After serving briefly as bishop of Regensburg in 1260, he was ordered to preach the crusade of 1263–64 in Germany. He spent his last years writing in Cologne.

Albert contributed to philosophy chiefly as a commentator on Aristotle, although he occasionally reached different conclusions from Aristotle. Primarily, Albert was a theologian, as is evident from his extensive commentary on Peter Lombard's *Sentences* and his commentaries on the Old and New Testaments. As a theologian, he customarily developed his thought by commenting on traditional texts. For Albert, Aristotle offered knowledge ascertainable using reason, just as Scripture, based on God's word, tells of the supernatural. Albert saw Aristotle's works, many newly available, as an encyclopedic compendium of information on the natural universe; included here is the study of social and political conditions and ethical obligations, for Aristotelian "natural knowledge" deals with human nature as well as natural history. Aristotle is *the* Philosopher; however, unlike Holy Scripture, he must be corrected in places. Like Holy Scripture, though, Aristotle is occasionally obscure. To rectify these shortcomings one must rely on other authorities: in the case of Holy Scripture, reference is to the church fathers and established interpreters; in the case of Aristotle, to the Peripatetics. The term 'Peripatetics' extends to modern as well as ancient authors – al-Fārābī, Avicenna (Ibn-Sīnā), and Averroes (Ibn-Rushd), as well as Themistius and Alexander of Aphrodisias; even Seneca, Maimonides, and "our" Boethius are included.

For the most part, Albert saw Plato through the eyes of Aristotle and Averroes, since apart from the *Timaeus* very little of Plato's work was available in Latin. Albert considered the *Liber de causis* a work of Aristotle, supplemented by al-Fārābī, Avicenna, and al-Ghazālī and translated into Latin. When he commented on the *Liber de causis*, Albert was not aware that this Neoplatonic work – which speaks of the world emanating from the One as from a first cause – was based on Proclus and ultimately on Plotinus. But Albert's student, Aquinas, who had better translations of Aristotle, recognized that the *Liber de causis* was not an Aristotelian work.

Albert's metaphysics, which is expounded in his commentaries on Aristotle's *Metaphysics* and on the *Liber de causis*, contains profoundly contradictory elements. His inclination to synthesis led him to attempt to reconcile these elements – as on social and ecclesiastical questions he often sought peace through compromise. In his *Metaphysics* and *Physics* and in his *On the Heavens* and *On Generation and Corruption*, Aristotle presented the world as ever-changing and taught that an unmoved mover ("thought thinking itself") maintained everything in movement and animation by allowing its spiritual nature to be seen in all its cold, unapproachable beauty. The *Liber de causis*, on the other hand, develops the theory that the world emanates from the One, causing everything in the world in its pantheistic creativity, so that the caused world returns in mystic harmony to the One. Thus Albert's Aristotelian commentaries, begun in 1251–52, culminated in 1265 with his commentary on a work whose pseudo-Aristotelian character he was unable to recognize. Nevertheless, the Christian Neoplatonism that Albert placed on an Aristotelian basis was to exert an influence for centuries.

In natural philosophy, Albert often arrived at views independent of Aristotle. According to Aristotle's *Physics*, motion belongs to no single category; it is incomplete being. Following Avicenna and Averroes, Albert asks whether "becoming black," e.g. – which ceases when change ceases and blackness is finally achieved – differs from blackness essentially (*essentia*) or only in its being (*esse*). Albert establishes, contrary to Avicenna, that the distinction is only one of being.

In his discussions of place and space, stimulated by Avicenna, Albert also makes an original contribution. Only two dimensions – width and breadth – are essential to place, so that a fluid in a bottle is framed by the inner surface of the bottle. According to Albert, the significance of the third dimension, depth, is more modest, but nonetheless important. Consider a bucket of water: its base is the essential part, but its round walls maintain the cohesion of the water.

For Aristotle, time's material foundation is distinct from its formal definition. Materially, the movement of the fixed stars is basic, although time itself is neither movement nor change. Rather, just as before and after are continuous in space and there are earlier and later moments in movement as it proceeds through space, so time – being the number of motion – has earlier and later moments or "nows." The material of time consists of the uninterrupted flow of the indivisible nows, while time's form and essential expression is number. Following al-Fārābī and Avicenna, Albert's interpretation of these doctrines emphasizes not only the uninterrupted continuity of the flow of "nows," but also the quantity of time, i.e., the series of discrete, separate, and clearly distinct numbers. Albert's treatment of time did not lend itself well to later consideration of time as a dimension; his concept of time is therefore not well suited to accommodate our unified concept of space-time.

The use of the pseudo-Aristotelian *De proprietatibus elementorum* in *De causis proprietatum elementorum* gave Albert's worldview a strong astrological flavor. At issue here is how the planets influence the earth and mankind. Particularly important is the influence of Jupiter and Saturn on fire and the seas; when increased, it could produce fiery conflagrations, and when circumscribed, floods.

Albert was encyclopedic: a scientist and scholar as well as a philosopher and theologian. In addition to the works mentioned, he produced commentaries on Pseudo-Dionysius, a *Summa de creaturis*, a *Summa Theologica*, and many other treatises. Unlike other commentators, his exposition was continuous, an extensive paraphrase; he provided a complete Latin and Christian philosophy. Even in his lifetime, he was a named authority; according to Roger Bacon, his views were often given as much weight as those of Aristotle, Avicenna, and Averroes. His students or followers include Aquinas, Ulrich of Strassburg (d.1278?), Theodoric of Freiberg (d.1310?), Giles of Lessines (d.1304?), Meister Eckhart, Johannes Tauler (d.1361), Henry Suso (d.1366), and Jan van Ruysbroeck (d.1381).

See also ARISTOTLE, NEOPLATONISM, PETER LOMBARD.   P.Hoß.

Albinus. See COMMENTARIES ON PLATO, MIDDLE PLATONISM.

alchemy, a quasi-scientific practice and mystical art, mainly ancient and medieval, that had two broad aims: to change baser metals into gold and to develop the elixir of life, the means to immortality. Classical Western alchemy probably originated in Egypt in the first three centuries A.D. (with earlier Chinese and later Islamic and Indian variants) and was practiced in earnest in Europe by such figures as Paracelsus and Newton until the eighteenth century. Western alchemy addressed concerns of practical metallurgy, but its philosophical significance derived from an early Greek theory of the relations among the basic elements and from a religious-allegorical understanding of the alchemical transmutation of ores into gold, an understanding that treats this process as a spiritual ascent from human toward divine perfection. The purification of crude ores (worldly matter) into gold (material perfection) was thought to require a transmuting agent, the *philosopher's stone,* a mystical substance that, when mixed with alcohol and swallowed, was believed to produce immortality (spiritual perfection). The alchemical search for the philosopher's stone, though abortive, resulted in the development of ultimately useful experimental tools (e.g., the steam pump) and methods (e.g., distillation).   J.D.T.

Alcinous. See MIDDLE PLATONISM.

Alcmaeon of Croton. See PRE-SOCRATICS.

Alembert, Jean Le Rond d'. See D'ALEMBERT.

alethic modalities, historically, the four central ways or *modes* in which a given proposition might be true or false: necessity, contingency, possibility, and impossibility. (The term 'alethic' derives from Greek *aletheia,* 'truth'.) These modalities, and their logical interconnectedness, can be characterized as follows. A proposition that is *true but possibly false* is *contingently true* (e.g., that Aristotle taught Alexander); one that is *true and not-possibly (i.e., "impossibly") false* is *necessarily true* (e.g., that red things are colored). Likewise, a proposition that is *false but possibly true* is *contingently false* (e.g., that there are no tigers); and one that is *false and not-possibly true* is *necessarily false* (e.g., that seven and five are fourteen).

Though any one of the four modalities can be defined in terms of any other, necessity and possibility are generally taken to be the more fundamental notions, and most systems of alethic modal logic take one or the other as basic. Distinct modal systems differ chiefly in regard to their treatment of iterated modalities, as in the proposition *It is necessarily true that it is possibly true that it is possibly true that there are no tigers.* In the weakest of the most common systems, usually called T, every iterated modality is distinct from every other. In the stronger system S4, iterations of any given modality are redundant. So, e.g., the above proposition is equivalent to *It is necessarily true that it is possibly true that there are no tigers.* In the strongest and most widely accepted system S5, all iteration is redundant. Thus, the two propositions above are both equivalent simply to *It is possibly true that there are no tigers.*

See also CONTINGENT, MODAL LOGIC.   C.M.

Alexander, Samuel (1859–1938), Australian-born British philosopher. Born in Sydney, he was educated at Balliol College, Oxford, and taught for most of his career at the University of Manchester. His aim, which he most fully realized in *Space, Time, and Deity* (1920), was to provide a realistic account of the place of mind in nature. He described nature as a series of levels of existence where irreducible higher-level qualities emerge inexplicably when lower levels become sufficiently complex. At its lowest level reality consists of space-time, a process wherein points of space are redistributed at instants of time and which might also be called pure motion. From complexities in space-time matter arises, followed by secondary qualities, life, and mind. Alexander thought that the still-higher quality of deity, which characterizes the whole universe while satisfying religious sentiments, is now in the process of emerging from mind. **See also** PHILOSOPHY OF MIND.   J.W.A.

Alexander of Aphrodisias (fl. A.D. c.200), Greek philosopher, one of the foremost commentators on Aristotle in late antiquity. He exercised considerable influence on later Greek, Arabic, and Latin philosophy through to the Renaissance. On the problem of universals, Alexander endorses a brand of conceptualism: although several particulars may share a single, common nature, this nature does not exist *as a universal* except while abstracted in thought from the circumstances that accompany its particular instantiations. Regarding Aristotle's notorious distinction between the "agent" and "patient" intellects in *On the Soul* III.5, Alexander identifies the agent intellect with God, who, as the most intelligible entity, makes everything else intelligible. As its own self-subsistent object, this intellect alone is imperishable; the human intellect, in contrast, perishes at death. Of Alexander's many commentaries, only those on Aristotle's *Metaphysics* A–Δ, *Prior Analytics* I, *Topics, On the Senses,* and *Meterologics* are extant. We also have two polemical treatises, *On Fate* and *On Mixture,* directed against the Stoics; a psychological treatise, the *De anima* (based on Aristotle's); as well as an assortment of essays (including the *De intellectu*) and his *Problems and Solutions.* Nothing is known of Alexander's life apart from his appointment by the emperor Severus to a chair in Aristotelian philosophy between 198 and 209. **See also** ARISTOTLE, CONCEPTUALISM, STOICISM.   V.C.

Alexander of Hales (c.1185–1245), English Franciscan theologian, known as the *Doctor Irrefraga-*

bilis. The first to teach theology by lecturing on the *Sentences* of Peter Lombard, Alexander's emphasis on speculative theology initiated the golden age of Scholasticism. Alexander wrote commentaries on the Psalms and the Gospels; his chief works include his *Glossa in quattuor libros sententiarum, Quaestiones disputatatae antequam esset frater,* and *Quaestiones quodlibetales.* Alexander did not complete the *Summa fratris Alexandri;* Pope Alexander IV ordered the Franciscans to complete the *Summa Halesiana* in 1255.

Master of theology in 1222, Alexander played an important role in the history of the University of Paris, writing parts of Gregory IX's *Parens scientiarum* (1231). He also helped negotiate the peace between England and France in 1235–36. Later in 1236 he gave up his position as canon of Lichfield and archdeacon of Coventry to become a Franciscan, the first Franciscan master of theology; his was the original Franciscan chair of theology at Paris. Among the Franciscans, his most prominent disciples include St. Bonaventure, Richard Rufus of Cornwall, and John of La Rochelle, to whom he resigned his chair in theology near the end of his life.   R.W.

Alexandrian School, those Neoplatonic philosophers contemporary with and subsequent to Proclus (A.D. 412–85) who settled in Alexandria and taught there. They include Hermeias (fl. c.440), Proclus's fellow-student of Syrianus; Hermeias's son Ammonius (either 435–517 or 445–526); and Ammonius's three pupils, John Philoponus (c.490–575), Simplicius (writing after 532), and Asclepius (mid-sixth century). Later Alexandrians include Olympiodorus (495/505–after 565) and the Christians Elias (fl. c.540) and David (late sixth century). All these worked exclusively or primarily on the exegesis of Aristotle. Damascius (c.456–540) also took lectures from Ammonius at some time between 475 and 485, but in his doctrine he belongs much more to the Athenian tradition. Simplicius, on the other hand, while he moved to Athens to teach, remains more in the Alexandrian tradition.

Ever since Karl Praechter, who was influenced by a Hegelian view of historical development, the Alexandrian Platonists have been seen as professing a simpler form of metaphysics than the Athenian School, and deliberately avoiding controversy with the powerful Christian establishment in Alexandria by confining themselves largely to logic, mathematics, and the exegesis of Aristotle. There is a certain manifest truth in this picture, but modern scholarship (in particular Ilsetraut Hadot) has done much to show that even in Ammonius's commentaries on Aristotle there lurks distinctive Neoplatonic doctrine, so that the contrast with the Athenian School has become somewhat blurred. The School may be said to have come to an end with the departure of Stephanus to take up the chair of philosophy in Constantinople in about 610.

See also NEOPLATONISM.   J.M.D.

al-Fārābī, Abu Nasr, also called Abunaser, in Latin, Alpharabius (870–950), Islamic philosopher. Born in Turkestan, he studied and taught in Baghdad when it was the cultural capital of the Islamic world, responsive to the philosophical and scientific legacy of late antiquity. Al-Fārābī was highly instrumental in effecting a transition of Greek philosophy, last publicly known in its entirety in sixth-century Alexandria, into Islamic culture. Despite ongoing opposition because of philosophy's identification with pagan and Christian authors, al-Fārābī succeeded in naturalizing Western philosophy in the Islamic world, where it retained vitality for the next three hundred years. Al-Fārābī became known as "the second teacher," after Aristotle the main source of philosophical information. His summaries and interpretations of the teachings of Aristotle and Plato were widely read, and his attempt at synthesizing their views was very influential. Believing in the universal nature of truth and holding Plato and Aristotle in the highest esteem, he minimized their differences and adopted Neoplatonic teachings that incorporated elements of both traditions.

Unlike the first philosopher of the Islamic world, the ninth-century al-Kindī, al-Fārābī was in possession of full Arabic translations of many of the most important texts of classical times and of some major Hellenistic commentaries on them. His own commentaries and digests of the works of Plato and Aristotle made them more accessible to later generations of scholars, even as his relatively independent treatises established a high standard of logical rigor and subtlety for later Muslim and Jewish philosophers. Avicenna found his *Metaphysics* commentary indispensable for understanding Aristotle's text, while Maimonides recommended all his writings, calling them "pure flour." Medieval Scholastic thought, however, was more interested in Averroes and Avicenna than in al-Fārābī. Contemporary scholars such as Leo Strauss and Muhsin Mahdi have emphasized the esoteric nature of al-Fārābī's writings, seen as critical for understanding much of medieval Islamic and Jewish philosophy.

Al-Fārābī's main interests lay in logic and political theory. He understood that the *Organon* was just that, a universal instrument for understanding and improving reasoning and logical discourse. Against the traditional grammarians of Islam, he argued for the value-free and neutral nature of Greek logic, while against the theologians of Islam, the *mutakallimun,* he emphasized the difference between their dialectical type of discourse and the preferred demonstrative syllogism of the philosophers. Much of the responsibility for the separation between Islamic theology and philosophy may be attributed to al-Fārābī, who avoided engaging religious dogmas and specifically Muslim beliefs as much as possible. He was able to accommodate belief in prophecy and revelation to a general theory of emanation, though he made no special claims for the prophet of Islam. His general view of religion was that it was a popular and symbolic representation of philosophical ideas, often designed by philosophers. The influence of Plato's *Republic* in this and other areas of political philosophy is evident, though al-Fārābī's *Principles of the Views of the Citizens of the Best State* manages to give an Islamic coloration to Platonic teachings. Al-Fārābī's metaphysical beliefs are more problematical still, and he was reputed to have disowned his earlier belief in the immortality of the soul.

    See also ARABIC PHILOSOPHY.   A.L.I.

algebra, Boolean. See BOOLEAN ALGEBRA.

algebra, full subset. See BOOLEAN ALGEBRA.

al-Ghazālī, Abu Hamid (1058–1111). Islamic philosopher, theologian, jurist, and mystic. He was born in Khurasan and educated in Nishapur, then an intellectual center of eastern Islam. He was appointed the head of a seminary, the newly founded Nizamiyah of Baghdad, in which he taught law and theology with great success. Yet his exposure to logic and philosophy led him to seek a certainty in knowledge beyond that assumed by his profession. At first he attempted to address his problem academically, but after five years in Baghdad he resigned, left his family, and embarked on the mystic's solitary quest for *al-Haqq* (Arabic for 'the truth', 'the True One'). As a Sufi he wandered for ten years through many of Islam's major cities and centers of learning, finally returning to Nishapur and to teaching theology before his death.

    Al-Ghazālī's literary and intellectual legacy is particularly rich and multifaceted. In the catholicity of his work and the esteem in which he is held within Islam he may be compared to Aquinas and Maimonides in the Christian and Jewish traditions respectively. His *Revivification of the Religious Sciences* is considered to this day a major theological compendium. His mystical treatises also have retained their popularity, as has his much celebrated autobiography, *The Deliverance from Error.* This book chronicles his lifelong quest for truth and certainty, and his disappointment with the premises of dogmatic theology, both orthodox Sunni and heterodox Shiite thought, as well as with the teachings of the philosophers. The light of truth came to him, he believed, only through divine grace; he considered his senses and reasoning powers all susceptible to error.

    It was this pervasive sense of skepticism that led him, while still in Baghdad, to investigate philosophy's claims to knowledge. He first composed a summa of philosophical teachings, based primarily on the views of Avicenna, and called it *The Intentions of the Philosophers.* He later published a detailed and penetrating critique of these views, *The Incoherence of the Philosophers.* Averroes arose later in Muslim Spain to defend philosophy, particularly that of Aristotle, calling his book *The Incoherence of the Incoherence.* Averroes' work was more appreciated in the West, however, which also preferred al-Ghazālī's *Intentions* to his *Incoherence.* The former, shorn of its polemical purpose and thus appearing as a philosophical summa, was translated by Dominicus Gundissalinus as *Logica et Philosophia Algazelis,* giving al-Ghazālī a reputation in the West as at least a sometime advocate of philosophy. His attack upon the physics and metaphysics of his day, which was an amalgam of Aristotelian and Neoplatonic doctrines, was firmly rooted in Aristotelian logic, and anticipates Hume in understanding the non-necessary nature of causal relationships. For al-Ghazālī, the world as a whole proceeds not by any eternal or logical necessity, but by the will of God. That will is indefensible on philosophical grounds, he believed, as is the philosophers' notion of divine omniscience. Their god cannot on their terms be related to the world, and is ultimately redundant logically. What is regarded as miraculous becomes possible, once nature is understood to have no autonomy or necessary entailments.

    See also ARABIC PHILOSOPHY, SUFISM.

                                              A.L.I.

algorithm, a clerical or effective procedure that can be applied to any of a class of certain symbolic inputs and that will in a finite time and number of steps eventuate in a result in a corresponding symbolic output. A function for which an algorithm (sometimes more than one) can be given is an algorithmic function. The following are common examples: (a) given n, finding the nth prime number; (b) differentiating a polynomial; (c) finding the greatest common divisor of x and y (the Euclidean algorithm); and (d) given two numbers x, y, deciding whether x is a multiple of y. When an algorithm is used to calculate values of a numerical function, as in (a), (b), and (c), the function can also be described as algorithmically computable, effectively computable, or just computable. Algorithms are generally agreed to have the following properties – which made them essential to the theory of computation and the development of the Church-Turing thesis – (i) an algorithm can be given by a finite string of instructions, (ii) a computation device (or agent) can carry out or compute in accordance with the instructions, (iii) there will be provisions for computing, storing, and recalling steps in a computation, (iv) computations can be carried out in a discrete and stepwise fashion (in, say, a digital computer), and (v) computations can be carried out in a deterministic fashion (in, say, a deterministic version of a Turing machine).

See also CHURCH'S THESIS, COMPUTABILITY, COMPUTER THEORY.　　　　　　F.A.

algorithmic function. See ALGORITHM.

alienation. See MARX.

aliorelative. See RELATION.

al-Kindī, Abu Yusuf, in Latin, Alkindus (c.800–70), Arab philosopher who was an early and prominent supporter of philosophical studies among the Muslims. He combined a noble Arab lineage with an influential position in the caliphate during a critical period for the translation and propagation of Greek sciences in Arabic. Known as "the philosopher of the Arabs," he more than any other scholar of his generation was responsible, as a patron, book collector, editor, and writer, for the acceptance of philosophy, despite its foreign and non-Islamic Greek source. Later writers surpassed him in knowledge of philosophy, and his numerous epistles, treatises, and books were eventually left in limbo. Of the 250 titles recorded in his name on an unusual variety of subjects, most are lost. About forty survive in a poor state, full of uncertain readings and other textual problems. Nevertheless, al-Kindī's works provide ample evidence of his close interest in Aristotle and to an extent Plato.

Unlike later philosophers in the Islamic world, he firmly believed he could combine literal Koranic religious doctrines and Greek philosophical concepts. Among his best-known philosophical works is *On First Philosophy* (English translation by A. Ivry, 1974), whose theme is that the noblest part of philosophy is first philosophy, which is knowledge of the First Truth and the First Cause. Al-Kindī includes an extended demonstration of the finiteness of the universe, time, and motion and the consequent infinitude of a creator who was their cause, who is the pure unity that is the ultimate source of all else and yet who, in al-Kindī's mind, brings the world into being *ex nihilo*. In *On the Number of Aristotle's Books*, he separates prophetic knowledge from ordinary, discursive philosophy: prophets know intuitively without effort or time.

See also ARABIC PHILOSOPHY.　　　P.E.W.

Allais's paradox, a puzzle about rationality devised by Maurice Allais (b. 1911). Leonard Savage (1917–71) advanced the sure-thing principle, which states that a rational agent's ranking of a pair of gambles having the same consequence in a state S agrees with her ranking of any other pair of gambles the same as the first pair except for having some other common consequence in S. Allais devised an apparent counterexample with four gambles involving a 100-ticket lottery. The table lists prizes in units of $100,000.

Gambles	1	2 – 11	12 – 100
		Ticket Numbers	
A	5	5	5
B	0	25	5
C	5	5	0
D	0	25	0

Changing A's and B's common consequence for tickets 12–100 from 5 to 0 yields C and D respectively. Hence the sure-thing principle prohibits simultaneously preferring A to B, and D to C. Yet most people have these preferences, which seem coherent. This conflict generates the paradox.

Savage presented the sure-thing principle in *The Foundations of Statistics* (1954). Responding to preliminary drafts of that work, Allais formulated his counterexample in "The Foundations of a Positive Theory of Choice Involving Risk and a Criticism of the Postulates and Axioms of the American School" (1952).

See also DECISION THEORY, EMPIRICAL DECISION THEORY.　　　P.We.

allegory of the cave. See PLATO.

all-things-considered reason. See REASONS FOR ACTION.

Alnwick, William of. See WILLIAM OF ALNWICK.

Alpharabius. See AL-FĀRĀBĪ.

al-Rāzī, Abu Bakr, in Latin, Rhazes (c.854–925 or 932), Persian physician, philosopher, and chemist. He headed the hospital in Rayy, his birthplace, and later in Baghdad, often returning to Rayy, where he died. A learned Galenist and critic of Galen, he brought the same empirical, Hippocratic spirit to medicine that he had used in transmuting alchemy into a (Neoplatonically) naturalistic art. His medical works, including the first treatise on smallpox, drew on extensive (and compassionate) clinical experience and omnivorous reading – both reading and observation preserved in the twenty-five-volume *Ḥāwī*, translated in 1279 as the *Continens*. al-Rāzī's mildly ascetic ethics springs from hedonic prudential considerations and from his atomism. In keeping with the Epicureanism he might have imbibed from Galenic sources, he rejects special prophecy as imposture, arguing that reason, God's gift to all alike, is sufficient guidance. (Only differences of interest and application separate the subtle devices of artisans from those of intellectuals.) God, the world Soul, time, space, and matter are all eternal substances. Nature originates from Soul's irrational desire for embodiment, which is her only way of learning that her true homeland is the intellectual world. God's gift of intelligence gave order to the movements she stirred up at the creation, and allows her escape from a world in which pains outweigh pleasures and death is surcease. For one who engages in philosophy "creatively, diligently, and persistently" will inevitably surpass his predecessors; and anyone who thinks independently is assured of both progress and immortality.   L.E.G.

Alston, William P. (b.1921), American philosopher widely acknowledged as one of the most important contemporary epistemologists and one of the most important philosophers of religion of the twentieth century. He is particularly known for his argument that putative perception of God is epistemologically on all fours with putative perception of everyday material objects.

Alston graduated from Centenary College in 1942 and the U.S. Army in 1946. A fine musician, he had to choose between philosophy and music. Philosophy won out; he received his Ph.D. from the University of Chicago and began his philosophical career at the University of Michigan, where he taught for twenty-two years. Since 1980 he has taught at Syracuse University. Although his dissertation and some of his early work were on Whitehead, he soon turned to philosophy of language (*Philosophy of Language*, 1964). Since the early 1970s Alston has concentrated on epistemology and philosophy of religion.

In epistemology he has defended foundationalism (although not classical foundationalism), investigated epistemic justification with unusual depth and penetration, and called attention to important levels distinctions. His chief works here are *Epistemic Justification* (1989), a collection of essays; and *The Reliability of Sense Perception* (1993). His chief work in philosophy of religion is *Divine Nature and Human Language* (1989), a collection of essays on metaphysical and epistemological topics; and *Perceiving God* (1991). The latter is a magisterial argument for the conclusion that experiential awareness of God, more specifically perception of God, makes an important contribution to the grounds of religious belief. In addition to this scholarly work, Alston was a founder of the Society of Christian Philosophers, a professional society with more than 1,100 members, and the founding editor of *Faith and Philosophy*.

See also EPISTEMOLOGY, EVIDENTIALISM, FOUNDATIONALISM, JUSTIFICATION, PHILOSOPHY OF RELIGION.   A.P.

alternative, relevant. See CONTEXTUALISM.

alternative denial. See SHEFFER STROKE.

Althusser, Louis (1918–90), French Marxist philosopher whose publication in 1965 of two collections of essays, *Pour Marx* ("For Marx") and *Lire le Capital* ("Reading *Capital*"), made him a sensation in French intellectual circles and attracted a large international readership. The English translations of these texts in 1969 and 1970, respectively, helped shape the development of Marxist thought in the English-speaking world throughout the 1970s.

Drawing on the work of non-positivist French historians and philosophers of science, especially Bachelard, Althusser proclaimed the existence of an "epistemological break" in Marx's work, occurring in the mid-1840s. What preceded this break was, in Althusser's view, a prescientific theoretical humanism derived from Feuerbach and ultimately from Hegel. What followed it, Althusser maintained, was a science of history a development as monumental, potentially, as the rise of the new sciences of nature in the seventh century. Althusser argued that the nature and even the existence of this new kind of science had yet to be acknowledged, even by Marx himself. It therefore had to be reconstructed from Marx's writings, *Das Kapital* especially, and also discerned in the political practice of Lenin and other like-minded revolutionaries who implicitly understood what Marx intended. Althusser did little, however, to elaborate the content of this new science. Rather, he tirelessly defended it programmatically against rival construals of Marxism. In so doing, he took particular aim at neo-Hegelian and "humanistic" currents in the larger Marxist culture and (implicitly) in the French Communist Party, to which he belonged throughout his adult life.

After 1968, Althusser's influence in France faded. But he continued to teach at l'École Normale Superieure and to write, making important contributions to political theory and to understandings of "ideology" and related concepts. He also faced increasingly severe bouts of mania and depression. In 1980, in what the French courts deemed an episode of "temporary insanity," he strangled his wife. Althusser avoided prison, but spent much of the 1980s in mental institutions. During this period he wrote two extraordinary memoirs, *L'avenir dure longtemps* ("The Future Lasts Forever") and *Les faits* ("The Facts"), published posthumously in 1992.

See also BACHELARD, FEUERBACH, HEGEL, MARXISM, PHILOSOPHY OF HISTORY.   A.L.

altruism. See EGOISM.

ambiguity, a phonological (or orthographic) form having multiple meanings (senses, characters, semantic representations) assigned by the language system. A *lexical ambiguity* occurs when a lexical item (word) is assigned multiple meanings by the language. It includes (a) *homonymy,* i.e., distinct lexical items having the same sound or form but different senses – 'knight'/'night', 'lead' (n.)/'lead' (v.), 'bear' (n.)/'bear' (v.); and (b) *polysemy,* i.e., a single lexical item having multiple senses – 'lamb' (the animal)/'lamb' (the flesh), 'window' (glass)/'window' (opening). The distinction between homonymy and polysemy is problematic.

A *structural ambiguity* occurs when a phrase or sentence is correlated by the grammar of the language with distinct constituent structures (phrase markers or sequences of phrase markers). Example: 'Competent women and men

should apply' – '[$_{NP}$[$_{NP}$Competent women] and men] ...' vs. '[$_{NP}$Competent[$_{NP}$women and men]] ...', where 'NP' stands for 'noun phrase'.

A *scope ambiguity* is a structural ambiguity deriving from alternative interpretations of scopes of operators (see below). Examples: 'Walt will diet and exercise only if his doctor approves' – sentence operator scope: doctor's approval is a necessary condition for both diet and exercise (wide scope 'only if') vs. approval necessary for exercise but not for dieting (wide scope 'and'); 'Bertie has a theory about every occurrence' – quantifier scope: one grand theory explaining all occurrences ('a theory' having wide scope over 'every occurrence') vs. all occurrences explained by several theories together ('every occurrence' having wide scope). The *scope of an operator* is the shortest full subformula to which the operator is attached. Thus, in `(A & B) C`, the scope of '&' is '(A & B)'. For natural languages, the scope of an operator is what it C-commands. (X C-commands Y in a tree diagram provided the first branching node that dominates X also dominates Y.) An occurrence of an operator has *wide scope* relative to that of another operator provided the scope of the former properly includes scope of the latter. Examples: in '~(A & B)', '~' has wide scope over '&'; in '(∃x) (∀y) Fxy', the existential quantifier has wide scope over the universal quantifier.

A *pragmatic ambiguity* is duality of use resting on pragmatic principles such as those which underlie reference and conversational implicature; e.g., depending on contextual variables, 'I don't know that he's right' can express doubt or merely the denial of genuine knowledge.

See also IMPLICATURE, MEANING, PHILOSOPHY OF LANGUAGE, PRAGMATIC CONTRADICTION, SCOPE, VAGUENESS.   W.K.W.

ambiguity, elliptic. See ELLIPSIS.

Ambrose, Saint, known as Ambrose of Milan (c.339–97), Roman church leader and theologian. While bishop of Milan (374–97), he not only led the struggle against the Arian heresy and its political manifestations, but offered new models for preaching, for Scriptural exegesis, and for hymnody. His works also contributed to medieval Latin philosophy. Ambrose's appropriation of Neoplatonic doctrines was noteworthy in itself, and it worked powerfully on and through Augustine. Ambrose's commentary on the account of creation in Genesis, his *Hexaemeron,* preserved for medieval readers many pieces of ancient natural history and even some elements of physical explanation. Perhaps most importantly, Ambrose engaged ancient philosophical ethics in the search for moral lessons that marks his exegesis of Scripture; he also reworked Cicero's *De officiis* as a treatise on the virtues and duties of Christian living.   M.D.J.

Ammonius. See COMMENTARIES ON ARISTOTLE.

Ammonius Saccas (early third century A.D.), Platonist philosopher who taught in Alexandria. He apparently served early in the century as the teacher of the Christian philosopher Origen. He attracted the attention of Plotinus, who came to the city in 232 in search of philosophical enlightenment (Porphyry, *Life of Plotinus* 3). Ammonius (the epithet 'Saccas' seems to mean 'the bagman') was undoubtedly a charismatic figure, but it is not at all clear what, if any, were his distinctive doctrines, though he seems to have been influenced by Numenius. He wrote nothing, and may be thought of, in E. R. Dodds's words, as the Socrates of Neoplatonism. **See also** NEOPLATONISM.   J.M.D.

amoralist. See EMOTIVISM.

amphiboly. See INFORMAL FALLACY.

ampliatio. See PROPRIETATES TERMINORUM.

ampliative inference. See INDUCTION.

ampliative judgment. See KANT.

Analects. See CONFUCIUS.

analogical argument. See PHILOSOPHY OF RELIGION, PROBLEM OF OTHER MINDS.

analogical predication. See AQUINAS.

analogies of experience. See KANT.

analogy, argument from. See PHILOSOPHY OF RELIGION, PROBLEM OF OTHER MINDS.

analogy of proportion. See CAJETAN.

analysandum. See ANALYSIS, DEFINIENDUM.

analysans. See ANALYSIS, DEFINIENDUM.

analysis, the process of breaking up a concept, proposition, linguistic complex, or fact into its simple or ultimate constituents. That on which

the analysis is done is called the *analysandum*, and that which does the analysis is called the *analysans*. A number of the most important philosophers of the twentieth century, including Russell, Moore, and (the early) Wittgenstein, have argued that philosophical analysis is the proper method of philosophy. But the practitioners of analytic philosophy have disagreed about what kind of thing is to be analyzed. For example, Moore tried to analyze sense-data into their constituent parts. Here the analysandum is a complex psychological fact, the having of a sense-datum. More commonly, analytic philosophers have tried to analyze concepts or propositions. This is conceptual analysis. Still others have seen it as their task to give an analysis of various kinds of sentences – e.g., those involving proper names or definite descriptions. This is linguistic analysis. Each of these kinds of analysis faces a version of a puzzle that has come to be called the *paradox of analysis*. For linguistic analyses, the paradox can be expressed as follows: for an analysis to be adequate, the analysans must be synonymous with the analysandum; e.g., if 'male sibling' is to analyze 'brother', they must mean the same; but if they are synonymous, then 'a brother is a male sibling' is synonymous with 'a brother is a brother'; but the two sentences do not seem synonymous. Expressed as a dilemma, the paradox is that any proposed analysis would seem to be either inadequate (because the analysans and the analysandum are not synonymous) or uninformative (because they are synonymous). **See also** ANALYTIC PHILOSOPHY, DEFINITION, MATHEMATICAL ANALYSIS, MEANING, PARADOX OF ANALYSIS, RUSSELL.   R.Fo.

analysis, mathematical. See MATHEMATICAL ANALYSIS.

analysis, noematic. See HUSSERL.

analysis, noetic. See HUSSERL.

analysis, regression. See REGRESSION ANALYSIS.

analysis, standard. See MATHEMATICAL ANALYSIS.

analytic. See ANALYTIC–SYNTHETIC DISTINCTION.

analytic, transcendental. See KANT.

analytical definition. See DEFINITION.

analytical functionalism. See PHILOSOPHY OF MIND.

analytical jurisprudence. See JURISPRUDENCE.

analytical psychology. See JUNG.

analytic hierarchy. See HIERARCHY.

analytic jurisprudence. See JURISPRUDENCE.

analytic Marxism. See MARXISM.

analytic philosophy, an umbrella term currently used to cover a diverse assortment of philosophical techniques and tendencies. As in the case of chicken-sexing, it is relatively easy to identify analytic philosophy and philosophers, though difficult to say with any precision what the criteria are. Analytic philosophy is sometimes called Oxford philosophy or linguistic philosophy, but these labels are, at least, misleading. Whatever else it is, analytic philosophy is manifestly not a school, doctrine, or body of accepted propositions. Analytic philosophers tend largely, though not exclusively, to be English-speaking academics whose writings are directed, on the whole, to other English-speaking philosophers. They are the intellectual heirs of Russell, Moore, and Wittgenstein, philosophers who self-consciously pursued "philosophical analysis" in the early part of the twentieth century. Analysis, as practiced by Russell and Moore, concerned not language per se, but concepts and propositions. In their eyes, while it did not exhaust the domain of philosophy, *analysis* provided a vital tool for laying bare the logical form of reality. Wittgenstein, in the *Tractatus Logico-Philosophicus* (1921), contended, though obliquely, that the structure of language reveals the structure of the world; every meaningful sentence is analyzable into atomic constituents that designate the fine-grained constituents of reality. This "Tractarian" view was one Wittgenstein was to renounce in his later work, but it had considerable influence within the Vienna Circle in the 1920s, and in the subsequent development of logical positivism in the 1930s and 1940s. Carnap and Ayer, both exponents of positivism, held that the task of philosophy was not to uncover elusive metaphysical truths, but to provide analyses of scientific sentences. (Other sentences, those in ethics, for instance, were thought to lack "cognitive significance.") Their model was Russell's theory of descriptions, which provided a technique for analyzing away apparent commitments to suspicious entities. Meanwhile, a number of former proponents of analysis, influenced by Wittgenstein, had taken up what came to be called ordinary language philosophy. Philosophers of this persuasion focused on the role of words in the lives of ordinary speakers, hoping thereby to escape long-standing philosophical muddles. These muddles resulted, they thought, from a natural tendency, when pursuing philosophical theses, to be misled by the grammatical form of sentences in which those questions were posed. (A classic illustration might be Heidegger's supposition that 'nothing' must designate something, though a very peculiar something.)

Today, it is difficult to find much unanimity in the ranks of analytic philosophers. There is, perhaps, an implicit respect for argument and clarity, an evolving though informal agreement as to what problems are and are not tractable, and a conviction that philosophy is in some sense continuous with science. The practice of analytic philosophers to address one another rather than the broader public has led some to decry philosophy's "professionalization" and to call for a return to a pluralistic, community-oriented style of philosophizing. Analytic philosophers respond by pointing out that analytic techniques and standards have been well represented in the history of philosophy.

See also CONTINENTAL PHILOSOPHY, ORDINARY LANGUAGE PHILOSOPHY, PLURALISM, VIENNA CIRCLE.   J.F.H.

analytic–synthetic distinction, the distinction, made famous by Kant, according to which an affirmative subject-predicate statement (proposition, judgment) is called analytic if the predicate concept is contained in the subject concept, and synthetic otherwise. The statement 'All red roses are red' is analytic, since the concept 'red' is contained in the concept 'red roses'. 'All roses are red' is synthetic, since the concept 'red' is not contained in the concept 'roses'. The denial of an affirmative subject-predicate statement entails a contradiction if it is analytic. E.g., 'Not all red roses are red' entails 'Some roses are both red and not red'.

One concept may be contained in another, in Kant's sense, even though the terms used to express them are not related as part to whole. Since 'biped' means 'two-footed animal', the concept 'two-footed' is contained in the concept 'biped'. It is accordingly analytic that all bipeds are two-footed. The same analytic statement is expressed by the synonymous sentences 'All bipeds are two-footed' and 'All two-footed animals are two-footed'. Unlike statements, sentences cannot be classified as analytic or synthetic except relative to an interpretation.

Witness 'All Russian teachers are Russian', which in one sense expresses the analytic statement 'All teachers that are Russian are Russian', and in another the synthetic statement 'All teachers of Russian are Russian'.

Kant's innovation over Leibniz and Hume lay in separating the logicosemantic analytic–synthetic distinction from the epistemological a priori–a posteriori distinction and from the modal-metaphysical necessary–contingent distinction. It seems evident that any analytic statement is a priori (knowable without empirical evidence) and necessary (something that could not be false). The converse is highly controversial. Kant and his rationalist followers maintain that some a priori and necessary statements are synthetic, citing examples from logic ('Contradictions are impossible', 'The identity relation is transitive'), mathematics ('The sum of 7 and 5 is 12', 'The straight line between two points is the shortest'), and metaphysics ('Every event is caused'). Empiricists like J. S. Mill, Carnap, Ayer, and C. I. Lewis argue that such examples are either synthetic a posteriori or analytic a priori.

Philosophers since Kant have tried to clarify the analytic–synthetic distinction, and generalize it to all statements. On one definition, a sentence is analytic (on a given interpretation) provided it is "true solely in virtue of the meaning or definition of its terms." The truth of any sentence depends in part on the meanings of its terms. `All emeralds are green' would be false, e.g., if 'emerald' meant 'ruby'. What makes the sentence synthetic, it is claimed, is that its truth also depends on the properties of emeralds, namely, their being green. But the same holds for analytic sentences: the truth of 'All red roses are red' depends on the properties of red roses, namely, their being red. Neither is true solely in virtue of meaning.

A more adequate generalization defines an analytic statement as a formal logical truth: one "true in virtue of its logical form," so that all statements with the same form are true. In terms of sentences under an interpretation, an analytic truth is an explicit logical truth (one whose surface structure represents its logical form) or one that becomes an explicit logical truth when synonyms are substituted. The negative statement that tomorrow is not both Sunday and not Sunday is analytic by this definition, because all statements of the form $\int (p \, \& \sim p)$ are true. Kant's definition is obtained as a special case by stipulating that the predicate of an affirmative subject-predicate statement is contained in the subject provided the statement is logically true.

On a third generalization, 'analytic' denotes any statement whose denial entails a contradiction. Subject S contains predicate P provided being S entails being P. Whether this is broader or narrower than the second generalization depends on how 'entailment', 'logical form', and 'contradiction' are defined. On some construals, 'Red is a color' counts as analytic on the third generalization (its denial entails 'Something is and is not a color') but not on the second ('red' and 'colored' are logically unstructured), while the rulings are reversed for a counterfactual conditional like 'If this were a red rose it would be red'.

Following Quine, many have denied any distinction between analytic and synthetic statements. Some arguments presume the problematic "true by meaning" definition. Others are that: (1) the distinction cannot be defined without using related notions like 'meaning', 'concept', and 'statement', which are neither extensional nor definable in terms of behavior; (2) some statements (like 'All cats are animals') are hard to classify as analytic or synthetic; and (3) no statement (allegedly) is immune from rejection in the face of new empirical evidence. If these arguments were sound, however, the distinction between logical truths and others would seem equally dubious, a conclusion seldom embraced.

Some describe a priori truths, both synthetic and analytic, as conceptual truths, on the theory that they are all true in virtue of the nature of the concepts they contain. Conceptual truths are said to have no "factual content" because they are about concepts rather than things in the actual world. While it is natural to classify a priori truths together, the proffered theory is questionable. As indicated above, all truths hold in part because of the identity of their concepts, and in part because of the nature of the objects they are about. It is a fact that all emeralds are emeralds, and this proposition is about emeralds, not concepts.

See also A PRIORI, CONVENTIONALISM, NECESSITY, PHILOSOPHY OF LANGUAGE, QUINE.   W.A.D.

anamnesis. See FORM, PLATO.

ānanda. See SAT/CHIT/ĀNANDA.

ananke (Greek), necessity. The term was used by early Greek philosophers for a constraining or moving natural force. In Parmenides (frg. 8, line 30) *ananke* encompasses reality in limiting bonds; according to Diogenes Laertius, Democritus calls the vortex that generates the cosmos *ananke;* Plato (*Timaeus* 47e *ff.*) refers to *ananke* as the irrational element in nature, which reason orders in creating the physical world. As used by Aristotle (*Metaphysics* V.5), the basic meaning of 'necessary' is 'that which cannot be otherwise', a sense that includes logical necessity. He also distinguishes (*Physics* II.9) between simple and hypothetical necessity (conditions that must hold *if* something is to occur). **See also ARIS-TOTLE, PARMENIDES.**   W.J.P.

anaphor. See ANAPHORA.

anaphora, a device of reference or cross-reference in which a term (called an *anaphor*), typically a pronoun, has its semantic properties determined by a term or noun phrase (called the anaphor's *antecedent*) that occurs earlier. Sometimes the antecedent is a proper name or other independently referring expression, as in 'Jill went up the hill and then *she* came down again'. In such cases, the anaphor refers to the same object as its antecedent. In other cases, the anaphor seems to function as a variable bound by an antecedent quantifier, as in 'If any miner bought a donkey, *he* is penniless'. But anaphora is puzzling because not every example falls neatly into one of these two groups. Thus, in 'John owns some sheep and Harry vaccinates *them*' (an example due to Gareth Evans) the anaphor is arguably not bound by its antecedent 'some sheep'. And in 'Every miner who owns a donkey beats *it*' (a famous type of case discovered by Geach), the anaphor is arguably neither bound by 'a donkey' nor a uniquely referring expression. **See also QUANTIFICATION, THE-ORY OF DESCRIPTIONS.**   M.M.

anarchism. See KROPOTKIN, POLITICAL PHILOSOPHY.

anattāvāda, the Buddhist doctrine of no-soul, attributed to the Buddha (sixth century B.C.). The Buddha's idea of dependent origination (*pratītyasamutpāda*) leads to a process ontology of change where nothing is absolute, permanent, or substantive. Accordingly, the Buddha taught that a person's self consists of a bundle of fleeting impressions, analyzed into five groups (*skandhas*), rather than a substantive entity called the "soul." The Buddha's method of introspection to find out whether we can be aware of a soullike substance inside us is remarkably similar to David Hume's. The Hindu philosophical schools objected to *anattāvāda* because they

thought it could not satisfactorily explain such issues as personal identity, moral responsibility and karma, and rebirth.   D.K.C.

Anaxagoras (c.500–428 B.C.), Greek philosopher who was the first of the pre-Socratics to teach in Athens (c.480–450), where he influenced leading intellectuals such as Pericles and Euripides. He left Athens when he was prosecuted for impiety. Writing in response to Parmenides, he elaborated a theory of matter according to which nothing comes into being or perishes. The ultimate realities are stuffs such as water and earth, flesh and bone, but so are contraries such as hot and cold, likewise treated as stuffs. Every phenomenal substance has a portion of every elemental stuff, and there are no minimal parts of anything, but matter takes on the phenomenal properties of whatever predominates in the mixture. Anaxagoras posits an indefinite number of elemental stuffs, in contrast to his contemporary Empedocles, who requires only four elements; but Anaxagoras follows Parmenides more rigorously, allowing no properties or substances to emerge that were not already present in the cosmos as its constituents. Thus there is no ultimate gap between appearance and reality: everything we perceive is real. In Anaxagoras's cosmogony, an initial chaos of complete mixture gives way to an ordered world when *noûs* (mind) begins a vortex motion that separates cosmic masses of ether (the bright upper air), air, water, and earth. Mind is finer than the stuffs and is found in living things, but it does not mix with stuffs. Anaxagoras's theory of mind provides the first hint of a mind–matter dualism. Plato and Aristotle thought his assigning a cosmic role to mind made him sound like "a sober man" among his contemporaries, but they were disappointed that he did not exploit his idea to provide teleological explanations of natural phenomena. **See also PRE-SOCRATICS.**   D.W.G.

Anaximander (c.612–545 B.C.), Greek philosopher and cosmologist, reputedly the student and successor of Thales in the Milesian school. He described the cosmos as originating from *apeiron* (the boundless) by a process of separating off; a disk-shaped earth was formed, surrounded by concentric heavenly rings of fire enclosed in air. At "breathing holes" in the air we see jets of fire, which are the stars, moon, and sun. The earth stays in place because there is no reason for it to tend one way or another. The seasons arise from alternating periods where hot and dry or wet and cold powers predominate, governed by a temporal process (figuratively portrayed as the judgment of Time). Anaximander drew a map of the world and explained winds, rain, and lightning by naturalistic hypotheses. He also described the emergence of life in a way that prefigures the theory of evolution. Anaximander's interest in cosmology and cosmogony and his brilliant conjectures set the major questions for later pre-Socratics. **See also** APEIRON, MILESIANS.

D.W.G.

Anaximenes of Miletus (fl. c.545 B.C.), Greek philosopher, a pre-Socratic who, following in the tradition of the Milesians Thales and Anaximander, speculated about cosmology and meteorology. The source (*archē*) of the cosmos is air (*aēr*, originally mist), which by a process of rarefaction becomes fire, and by a process of condensation becomes wind, clouds, water, earth, and stones. Air is divine and causes life. The earth is flat and rides on a cushion of air, while a heavenly firmament revolves about it like a felt cap. Anaximenes also explained meteorological phenomena and earthquakes. Although less innovative than his predecessor Anaximander, he made progress in naturalistic explanations by appealing to a quantitative process of rarefaction and condensation rather than to mythical processes involving quasi-personal agents.

D.W.G.

ancestral (of a given relation R), the relation (also called the transitive closure of R) that relates one given individual to a second if and only if the first can be "reached" from the second by repeated "applications" of the given relation R. The ancestor relation is the *ancestral* of the parent relation since one person is an ancestor of a second if the first is a parent of the second or the first is a parent of a parent of the second or the first is a parent of a parent of a parent of the second, and so on. Frege discovered a simple method of giving a materially adequate and formally correct definition of the ancestral of a given relation in terms of the relation itself (plus logical concepts). This method is informally illustrated as follows: in order for one person A to be an ancestor of a second person B it is necessary and sufficient for A to have every property that belongs to every parent of B and that belongs to every parent of any person to whom it belongs. This and other similar methods made possible the reduction of all numerical concepts to those of zero and successor, which Frege then attempted to reduce to

concepts of pure logic. Frege's definition of the ancestral has become a paradigm in modern analytic philosophy as well as a historical benchmark of the watershed between traditional logic and modern logic. It demonstrates the exactness of modern logical analysis and, in comparison, the narrowness of traditional logic. **See also** FREGE, LOGICISM, RELATION.

J.Cor.

ancient atomism, the theory, originated by Leucippus and elaborated by Democritus, that the ultimate realities are atoms and the void. The theory was later used by Epicurus as the foundation for a philosophy stressing ethical concerns, Epicureanism. **See also** DEMOCRITUS, EPICUREANISM.

D.W.G.

Andronicus of Rhodes (first century B.C.), Greek philosopher, a leading member of the Lyceum who was largely responsible for establishing the canon of Aristotle's works still read today. He also edited the works of Theophrastus. At the time, Aristotle was known primarily for his philosophical dialogues, only fragments of which now survive; his more methodical treatises had stopped circulating soon after his death. By producing the first systematic edition of Aristotle's corpus, Andronicus revived study of the treatises, and the resulting critical debates dramatically affected the course of philosophy. Little is recorded about Andronicus's labors; but besides editing the texts and discussing titles, arrangement, and authenticity, he sought to explicate and assess Aristotle's thought. In so doing, he and his colleagues initiated the exegetical tradition of Aristotelian commentaries. Nothing he wrote survives; a summary account of emotions formerly ascribed to him is spurious. **See also** ARISTOTLE, COMMENTARIES ON ARISTOTLE, LYCEUM.

V.C. & S.A.W.

Anesidemus. See HELLENISTIC PHILOSOPHY, SKEPTICS.

Angst, German term for a special form of anxiety, an emotion seen by existentialists as both constituting and revealing the human condition. *Angst* plays a key role in the writings of Heidegger, whose concept is closely related to Kierkegaard's *angest* and Sartre's *angoisse*. The concept is first treated in this distinctive way in Kierkegaard's *The Concept of Anxiety* (1844), where anxiety is described as "the dizziness of freedom." Anxiety here represents freedom's self-awareness; it is the psychological precondition for the individual's attempt to become autonomous, a possibility that is seen as both alluring and disturbing. **See also** HEIDEGGER, KIERKEGAARD, SARTRE.

C.S.E.

anhomoeomerous. See HOMOEOMEROUS.

animal faith. See SANTAYANA.

Anniceraioi. See ANNICERIS.

Anniceris (fl. c.320–280 B.C.), Greek philosopher. A pupil of Antipater, he established a separate branch of the Cyrenaic school known as the *Anniceraioi*. He subscribed to typical Cyrenaic hedonism, arguing that the end of each action should be one's own pleasure, since we can know nothing of others' experiences. He tempered the implications of hedonism with the claim that a wise man attaches weight to respect for parents, patriotism, gratitude, and friendship, perhaps influencing Epicurus in this regard. Anniceris also played down the Cyrenaic stress on the intellect's role in hedonistic practical rationality, taking the Aristotelian view that cultivation of the right habits is indispensable. **See also** CYRENAICS.   R.C.

anomalism of the mental. See PHILOSOPHY OF MIND.

anomalous monism. See PHILOSOPHY OF MIND.

anomaly. See PARADIGM.

Anschauung. See KANT.

Anscombe, G(ertrude) E(lizabeth) M(argaret) (b. 1919), English philosopher who has held positions at Oxford and Cambridge, best known for her work in the philosophy of mind and for her editions and translations of Wittgenstein's later writings. Anscombe studied philosophy with Wittgenstein and became closely associated with him, writing *An Introduction to Wittgenstein's Tractatus* (1959). She is married to Peter Geach.

Anscombe's first major work was *Intention* (1957). She argues that the concept of intention is central to our understanding of ourselves as rational agents. The basic case is that of the intentions with which we act. These are identified by the reasons we give in answer to why-questions concerning our actions. Such reasons usually form a hierarchy that constitutes a practical syllogism of which action itself is the conclusion. Hence our intentions are a form of active practi-

cal knowledge that normally leads to action. Anscombe compares the direction of fit of this kind of knowledge with a shopping list's relation to one's purchases, and contrasts it with the direction of fit characteristic of a list of these purchases drawn up by an observer of the shopper. She maintains that the deep mistake of modern (i.e., post-medieval) philosophy has been to think that all knowledge is of this latter, observational, type.

This conception of active knowledge expressed through an agent's intentions conflicts with the passive conception of rationality characteristic of Hume and his followers, and Anscombe develops this challenge in papers critical of the is–ought distinction of Hume and his modern successors. In a famous paper, "Modern Moral Philosophy" (1958), she also argues that ought-statements make sense only in the context of a moral theology that grounds morality in divine commands. Since our culture rejects this theology, it is no surprise that "modern moral philosophers" cannot find much sense in them. We should therefore abandon them and return to the older conceptions of practical rationality and virtue. These conceptions, and the associated conception of natural law, provide the background to an uncompromising defense of traditional Catholic morality concerning sexuality, war, and the importance of the distinction between intention and foresight.

Anscombe has never been afraid of unpopular positions – philosophical and ethical. Her three volumes of *Collected Papers* (1981) include a defense of singular causation, an attack on the very idea of a subject of thought, and a critique of pacifism. She is one of the most original and distinctive English philosophers of her generation. **See also** ACTION THEORY, DIRECTION OF FIT, HUME, INTENTION, NATURAL LAW, WITTGENSTEIN.   T.R.B.

Anselm, Saint, called Anselm of Canterbury (1033–1109), Italian-born English philosophical theologian. A Benedictine monk and the second Norman archbishop of Canterbury, he is best known for his distinctive method – *fides quaerens intellectum;* his "ontological" argument for the existence of God in his treatise *Proslogion;* and his classic formulation of the satisfaction theory of the Atonement in the *Cur Deus homo.*

Like Augustine before him, Anselm is a Christian Platonist in metaphysics. He argues that the most accessible proofs of the existence of God are through value theory: in his treatise *Monologion,* he deploys a cosmological argument, showing the existence of a source of all goods, which is the Good per se and hence supremely good; that same thing exists per se and is the Supreme Being. In the *Proslogion*, Anselm begins with his conception of a being a greater than which cannot be conceived, and mounts his ontological argument that a being a greater than which cannot be conceived exists in the intellect, because even the fool understands the phrase when he hears it; but if it existed in the intellect alone, a greater could be conceived that existed in reality. This supremely valuable object is essentially whatever it is – other things being equal – that is better to be than not to be, and hence living, wise, powerful, true, just, blessed, immaterial, immutable, and eternal per se; even the paradigm of sensory goods – Beauty, Harmony, Sweetness, and Pleasant Texture, in its own ineffable manner. Nevertheless, God is supremely simple, not compounded of a plurality of excellences, but *"omne et unum, totum et solum bonum,"* a being a more delectable than which cannot be conceived.

Everything other than God has its being and its well-being through God as efficient cause. Moreover, God is the paradigm of all created natures, the latter ranking as better to the extent that they more perfectly resemble God. Thus, it is better to be human than to be horse, to be horse than to be wood, even though in comparison with God everything else is "almost nothing." For every created nature, there is a that-for-which-it-is-made (*ad quod factum est*). On the one hand, Anselm thinks of such teleology as part of the internal structure of the natures themselves: a creature of type *F* is a *true F* only insofar as it is/does/exemplifies that for which *F*'s were made; a defective *F*, to the extent that it does not. On the other hand, for Anselm, the *telos* of a created nature is that-for-which-*God*-made-it. Because God is personal and acts through reason and will, Anselm infers that prior (in the order of explanation) to creation, there was, in the reason of the maker, an exemplar, form, likeness, or rule of what he was going to make. In *De veritate* Anselm maintains that such teleology gives rise to obligation: since creatures *owe* their being and well-being to God as their cause, so they *owe* their being and well-being to God in the sense of having an obligation to praise him by being the best beings they can. Since every creature is of some nature or other, each can be its best by being that-for-which-God-made-it. Abstracting from impediments, non-rational natures fulfill

this obligation and "act rightly" by natural necessity; rational creatures, when they exercise their powers of reason and will to fulfill God's purpose in creating them. Thus, the goodness of a creature (how good a being it is) is a function of twin factors: its natural *telos* (i.e., what sort of imitation of divine nature it aims for), and its rightness (in exercising its natural powers to fulfill its *telos*). By contrast, God as absolutely independent owes no one anything and so has no obligations to creatures.

In *De casu diaboli*, Anselm underlines the optimism of his ontology, reasoning that since the Supreme Good and the Supreme Being are identical, every being is good and every good a being. Two further conclusions follow. First, evil is a privation of being, the absence of good in something that properly ought to have it (e.g., blindness in normally sighted animals, injustice in humans or angels). Second, since all genuine powers are given to enable a being to fulfill its natural *telos* and so to be the best being it can, all genuine (metaphysically basic) powers are optimific and essentially aim at goods, so that evils are merely incidental side effects of their operation, involving some lack of coordination among powers or between their exercise and the surrounding context. Thus, divine omnipotence does not, properly speaking, include corruptibility, passibility, or the ability to lie, because the latter are defects and/or powers in other things whose exercise obstructs the flourishing of the corruptible, passible, or potential liar.

Anselm's distinctive action theory begins teleologically with the observation that humans and angels were made for a happy immortality enjoying God, and to that end were given the powers of reason to make accurate value assessments and will to love accordingly. Anselm regards freedom and imputability of choice as essential and permanent features of all rational beings. But freedom cannot be defined as a power for opposites (the power to sin and the power not to sin), both because neither God nor the good angels have any power to sin, and because sin is an evil at which no metaphysically basic power can aim. Rather, freedom is the power to preserve justice for its own sake. Choices and actions are *imputable* to an agent only if they are spontaneous, from the agent itself. Creatures cannot act spontaneously by the necessity of their natures, because they do not have their natures from themselves but receive them from God. To give them the opportunity to become just of themselves, God furnishes them with two motivational drives toward the good: an affection for the advantageous (*affectio commodi*) or a tendency to will things for the sake of their benefit to the agent itself; and an affection for justice (*affectio justitiae*) or a tendency to will things because of their own intrinsic value. Creatures are able to align these drives (by letting the latter temper the former) or not. The good angels, who preserved justice by not willing some advantage possible for them but forbidden by God for that time, can no longer will more advantage than God wills for them, because he wills their maximum as a reward. By contrast, creatures, who sin by refusing to delay gratification in accordance with God's will, lose both uprightness of will and their affection for justice, and hence the ability to temper their pursuit of advantage or to will the best goods. Justice will never be restored to angels who desert it. But if animality makes human nature weaker, it also opens the possibility of redemption.

Anselm's argument for the necessity of the Incarnation plays out the dialectic of justice and mercy so characteristic of his prayers. He begins with the demands of justice: humans owe it to God to make all of their choices and actions conform to his will; failure to render what was owed insults God's honor and makes the offender liable to make satisfaction; because it is worse to dishonor God than for countless worlds to be destroyed, the satisfaction owed for any small sin is incommensurate with any created good; it would be maximally indecent for God to overlook such a great offense. Such calculations threaten certain ruin for the sinner, because God alone can do/be immeasurably deserving, and depriving the creature of its honor (through the eternal frustration of its *telos*) seems the only way to balance the scales. Yet, justice also forbids that God's purposes be thwarted through created resistance, and it was *divine mercy* that made humans for a beatific immortality with him. Likewise, humans come in families by virtue of their biological nature (which angels do not share), and justice allows an offense by one family member to be compensated by another. Assuming that all actual humans are descended from common first parents, Anselm claims that the human race can make satisfaction for sin, if God becomes human and renders to God what Adam's family owes.

When Anselm insists that humans were made for beatific intimacy with God and therefore are obliged to strive into God with all of their powers, he emphatically includes reason or intellect along with emotion and will. God, the controlling subject matter, is in part permanently inaccessible to us (because of the ontological incommensuration between God and creatures) and our progress is further hampered by the consequences of sin. Our powers will function best, and hence we have a duty to follow right order in their use: by submitting first to the holistic discipline of faith, which will focus our souls and point us in the right direction. Yet it is also a duty not to remain passive in our appreciation of authority, but rather for faith to seek to understand what it has believed. Anselm's works display a dialectical structure, full of questions, objections, and contrasting opinions, designed to stir up the mind. His quartet of teaching dialogues – *De grammatico, De veritate, De libertate arbitrii,* and *De casu diaboli* as well as his last philosophical treatise, *De concordia,* anticipate the genre of the Scholastic question (*quaestio*) so dominant in the thirteenth and fourteenth centuries. His discussions are likewise remarkable for their attention to modalities and proper-versus-improper linguistic usage.

  See also DIVINE ATTRIBUTES, FREE WILL PROBLEM, PHILOSOPHY OF RELIGION.

M.M.A.

An Sich. See HEGEL, KANT.

antecedent. See COUNTERFACTUALS.

antecedent, fallacy of denying the. See FORMAL FALLACY.

ante rem **realism.** See PROPERTY.

anthropology, philosophical. See PHILOSOPHICAL ANTHROPOLOGY.

anthroposophy. See STEINER.

antilogism, an inconsistent triad of propositions, two of which are the premises of a valid categorical syllogism and the third of which is the contradictory of the conclusion of this valid categorical syllogism. An antilogism is a special form of antilogy or self-contradiction. **See also** INCONSISTENT TRIAD.   R.W.B.

antinomianism, the view that one is not bound by moral law; specifically, the view that Christians are by grace set free from the need to observe moral laws. During the Reformation, antinomianism was believed by some (but not

Martin Luther) to follow from the Lutheran doctrine of justification by faith alone. **See also JUSTIFICATION BY FAITH, LUTHER.**   W.L.R.

antinomy. See KANT.

Antiochus of Ascalon (c.130–c.68 B.C.), Greek philosopher and the last prominent member of the New Academy. He played the major role in ending its two centuries of Skepticism and helped revive interest in doctrines from the Old Academy, as he called Plato, Aristotle, and their associates.

The impulse for this decisive shift came in epistemology, where the Skeptical Academy had long agreed with Stoicism that knowledge requires an infallible "criterion of truth" but disputed the Stoic claim to find this criterion in "cognitive perception." Antiochus's teacher, Philo of Larissa, broke with this tradition and proposed that perception need not be cognitive to qualify as knowledge. Rejecting this concession, Antiochus offered new arguments for the Stoic claim that some perception is cognitive, and hence knowledge. He also proposed a similar accommodation in ethics, where he agreed with the Stoics that virtue alone is sufficient for happiness but insisted with Aristotle that virtue is not the only good. These and similar attempts to mediate fundamental disputes have led some to label Antiochus an eclectic or syncretist; but some of his proposals, especially his appeal to the Old Academy, set the stage for Middle Platonism, which also sought to reconcile Plato and Aristotle. No works by Antiochus survive, but his students included many eminent Romans, most notably Cicero, who summarizes Antiochus's epistemology in the *Academica,* his critique of Stoic ethics in *De finibus* IV, and his purportedly Aristotelian ethics in *De finibus* V.

See also ACADEMY, ARISTOTLE, CICERO, MIDDLE PLATONISM, PLATO, STOICISM.
                                        V.C. & S.A.W.

Antipater. See STOICISM.

Antiphon. See SOPHISTS.

anti-razor. See OCKHAM'S RAZOR.

anti-realism, rejection, in one or another form or area of inquiry, of realism, the view that there are knowable mind-independent facts, objects, or properties. Metaphysical realists make the general claim that there is a world of mind-inde-

pendent objects. Realists in particular areas make more specific or limited claims. Thus moral realists hold that there are mind-independent moral properties, mathematical realists that there are mind-independent mathematical facts, scientific realists that scientific inquiry reveals the existence of previously unknown and unobservable mind-independent entities and properties. Anti-realists deny either that facts of the relevant sort are mind-independent or that knowledge of such facts is possible.

Berkeley's subjective idealism, which claims that the world consists only of minds and their contents, is a metaphysical anti-realism. Constructivist anti-realists, on the other hand, deny that the world consists only of mental phenomena, but claim that it is constituted by, or constructed from, our evidence or beliefs. Many philosophers find constructivism implausible or even incoherent as a metaphysical doctrine, but much more plausible when restricted to a particular domain, such as ethics or mathematics.

Debates between realists and anti-realists have been particularly intense in philosophy of science. Scientific realism has been rejected both by constructivists such as Kuhn, who hold that scientific facts are constructed by the scientific community, and by empiricists who hold that knowledge is limited to what can be observed. A sophisticated version of the latter doctrine is Bas van Fraassen's constructive empiricism, which allows scientists free rein in constructing scientific models, but claims that evidence for such models confirms only their observable implications.

See also CONSTRUCTIVISM, DIRECT REALISM, MORAL REALISM, SCIENTIFIC REALISM.
                                        P.Gas.

Antisthenes. See CYNICS.

antisymmetrical. See ORDERING, RELATION.

antithesis. See HEGEL.

apagoge. See ARISTOTLE.

apatheia. See STOICISM.

apeiron, Greek term meaning 'the boundless' or 'the unlimited', which evolved to signify 'the infinite'. Anaximander introduced the term to philosophy by saying that the source of all things was *apeiron.* There is some disagreement about whether he meant by this the spatially unbounded, the temporally unbounded, or the qualitatively indeterminate. It seems likely that he intended the term to convey the first meaning, but the other two senses also happen to apply to the spatially unbounded. After Anaximander, Anaximenes declared as his first principle that air is boundless, and Xenophanes made his flat earth extend downward without bounds, and probably outward horizontally without limit as well. Rejecting the tradition of boundless principles, Parmenides argued that "what-is" must be held within determinate boundaries. But his follower Melissus again argued that what-is must be boundless – in both time and space – for it can have no beginning or end. Another follower of Parmenides, Zeno of Elea, argued that if there are many substances, antinomies arise, including the consequences that substances are both limited and unlimited (*apeira*) in number, and that they are so small as not to have size and so large as to be unlimited in size. Rejecting monism, Anaxagoras argued for an indefinite number of elements that are each unlimited in size, and the Pythagorean Philolaus made limiters (*perainonta*) and unlimiteds (*apeira*) the principles from which all things are composed. The atomists Leucippus and Democritus conceived of a boundless universe, partly full (of an infinite number of atoms) and partly void; and in the universe are countless (*apeiroi*) worlds. Finally Aristotle arrived at an abstract understanding of the *apeiron* as "the infinite," claiming to settle paradoxes about the boundless by allowing for real quantities to be infinitely divisible potentially, but not actually (*Physics* III.4–8). The development of the notion of the *apeiron* shows how Greek philosophers evolved ever more abstract philosophical ideas from relatively concrete conceptions. **See also ARISTOTLE, PRE-SOCRATICS.**   D.W.G.

apellatio. See PROPRIETATES TERMINORUM.

apocatastasis (from Greek, 'reestablishment'), the restoration of all souls, including Satan's and his minions', in the kingdom of God. God's goodness will triumph over evil, and through a process of spiritual education souls will be brought to repentance and made fit for divine life. The theory originates with Origen but was also held by Gregory of Nyssa. In modern times F. D. Maurice (1805–72) and Karl Barth (1886–1968) held this position. **See also GREGORY OF NYSSA, ORIGEN.**   L.P.P.

apodictic. See HUSSERL, KANT.

apodosis. See COUNTERFACTUALS.

apophantic. See HUSSERL.

aporetic. See APORIA.

aporia (plural: *aporiai*), Greek term meaning 'puzzle', 'question for discussion', 'state of perplexity'. The *aporetic method* – the raising of puzzles without offering solutions – is typical of the elenchus in the early Socratic dialogues of Plato. These consist in the testing of definitions and often end with an *aporia*, e.g., that piety is both what is and what is not loved by the gods. Compare the paradoxes of Zeno, e.g., that motion is both possible and impossible.

In Aristotle's dialectic, the resolution of *aporiai* discovered in the views on a subject is an important source of philosophical understanding. The beliefs that one should love oneself most of all and that self-love is shameful, e.g., can be resolved with the right understanding of 'self'.

The possibility of argument for two inconsistent positions was an important factor in the development of Skepticism. In modern philosophy, the antinomies that Kant claimed reason would arrive at in attempting to prove the existence of objects corresponding to transcendental ideas may be seen as *aporiai*.
    See also ELENCHUS.   R.C.

a posteriori. See A PRIORI.

appearing, theory of. See THEORY OF APPEARING.

appellation. See SHERWOOD.

apperception. See KANT.

application (of a function). See COMBINATORY LOGIC.

applied ethics, the domain of ethics that includes professional ethics, such as business ethics, engineering ethics, and medical ethics, as well as practical ethics such as environmental ethics, which is applied, and thus practical as opposed to theoretical, but not focused on any one discipline. One of the major disputes among those who work in applied ethics is whether or not there is a general and universal account of morality applicable both to the ethical issues in the professions and to various practical problems. Some philosophers believe that each of the professions or each field of activity develops an ethical code for itself and that there need be no close relationship between (e.g.) business ethics, medical ethics, and environmental ethics. Others hold that the same moral system applies to all professions and fields. They claim that the appearance of different moral systems is simply due to certain problems being more salient for some professions and fields than for others.

The former position accepts the consequence that the ethical codes of different professions might conflict with one another, so that a physician in business might find that business ethics would require one action but medical ethics another. Engineers who have been promoted to management positions sometimes express concern over the tension between what they perceive to be their responsibility as engineers and their responsibility as managers in a business. Many lawyers seem to hold that there is similar tension between what common morality requires and what they must do as lawyers. Those who accept a universal morality hold that these tensions are all resolvable because there is only one common morality.

Underlying both positions is the pervasive but false view of common morality as providing a unique right answer to every moral problem. Those who hold that each profession or field has its own moral code do not realize that common morality allows for conflicts of duties. Most of those who put forward moral theories, e.g., utilitarians, Kantians, and contractarians, attempt to generate a universal moral system that solves all moral problems. This creates a situation that leads many in applied ethics to dismiss theoretical ethics as irrelevant to their concerns. An alternative view of a moral theory is to think of it on the model of a scientific theory, primarily concerned to describe common morality rather than generate a new improved version. On this model, it is clear that although morality rules out many alternatives as unacceptable, it does not provide unique right answers to every controversial moral question.

On this model, different fields and different professions may interpret the common moral system in somewhat different ways. For example, although deception is always immoral if not justified, what counts as deception is not the same in all professions. Not informing a patient of an alternative treatment counts as deceptive for a physician, but not telling a customer of an alternative to what she is about to buy does not count as deceptive for a salesperson. The professions also have considerable input into what special duties are incurred by becoming a member of their profession. Applied ethics is thus not the mechanical application of a common morality to a particular profession or field, but an independent discipline that clarifies and analyzes the practices in a field or profession so that common morality can be applied.

See also BIOETHICS, ETHICS, MORALITY, PRACTICAL REASON, RATIONALITY.   B.Ge.

a priori, prior to or independent of experience; contrasted with 'a posteriori' (empirical). These two terms are primarily used to mark a distinction between (1) two modes of epistemic justification, together with derivative distinctions between (2) kinds of propositions, (3) kinds of knowledge, and (4) kinds of argument. They are also used to indicate a distinction between (5) two ways in which a concept or idea may be acquired.

(1) A belief or claim is said to be justified a priori if its epistemic justification, the reason or warrant for thinking it to be true, does not depend at all on sensory or introspective or other sorts of *experience*; whereas if its justification does depend at least in part on such experience, it is said to be justified a posteriori or empirically. This specific distinction has to do only with the justification of the belief, and not at all with how the constituent concepts are acquired; thus it is no objection to a claim of a priori justificatory status for a particular belief that experience is required for the acquisition of some of the constituent concepts.

It is clear that the relevant notion of experience includes sensory and introspective experience, as well as such things as kinesthetic experience. Equally clearly, to construe experience in the broadest possible sense of, roughly, a conscious undergoing of any sort would be to destroy the point of the distinction, since even a priori justification presumably involves some sort of conscious process of awareness. The construal that is perhaps most faithful to the traditional usage is that which construes experience as any sort of cognitive input that derives, presumably causally, from features of the actual world that may not hold in other possible worlds. Thus, e.g., such things as clairvoyance or telepathy, if they were to exist, would count as forms of experience and any knowledge resulting therefrom as a posteriori; but the intuitive apprehension of properties or numbers or other sorts of abstract entities that are the same in all possible worlds, would not.

Understood in this way, the concept of a priori justification is an essentially negative concept, specifying as it does what the justification of the belief does *not* depend on, but saying nothing about what it does depend on. Historically, the main positive conception was that offered by proponents of rationalism (such as Plato, Descartes, Spinoza, and Leibniz), according to which a priori justification derives from the intuitive apprehension of necessary facts pertaining to universals and other abstract entities. (Although Kant is often regarded as a rationalist, his restriction of substantive a priori knowledge to the world of appearances represents a major departure from the main rationalist tradition.) In contrast, proponents of traditional empiricism, if they do not repudiate the concept of a priori justification altogether (as does Quine), typically attempt to account for such justification by appeal to linguistic or conceptual conventions. The most standard formulation of this empiricist view (a development of the view of Hume that all a priori knowledge pertains to "relations of ideas") is the claim (typical of logical positivism) that all a priori knowable claims or propositions are analytic. (A rationalist would claim in opposition that at least some a priori claims or propositions are synthetic.)

(2) A proposition that is the content of an a priori justified belief is often referred to as an a priori proposition (or an a priori truth). This usage is also often extended to include any proposition that is capable of being the content of such a belief, whether it actually has this status or not.

(3) If, in addition to being justified a priori or a posteriori, a belief is also true and satisfies whatever further conditions may be required for it to constitute knowledge, that knowledge is derivatively characterized as a priori or a posteriori (empirical), respectively. (Though a priori justification is often regarded as by itself guaranteeing truth, this should be regarded as a further substantive thesis, not as part of the very concept of a priori justification.) Examples of knowledge that have been classically regarded as a priori in this sense are mathematical knowledge, knowledge of logical truths, and knowledge of necessary entailments and exclusions of commonsense concepts ('Nothing can be red and green all over at the same time', 'If A is later than B and B is later than C, then A is later than C'); but many claims of metaphysics, ethics, and even theology have also been claimed to have this status.

(4) A deductively valid argument that also satisfies the further condition that each of the premises (or sometimes one or more particularly central premises) are justified a priori is referred to as an a priori argument. This label is also sometimes applied to arguments that are claimed to

have this status, even if the correctness of this claim is in question.

(5) In addition to the uses just catalogued that derive from the distinction between modes of justification, the terms 'a priori' and 'a posteriori' are also employed to distinguish two ways in which a concept or idea might be acquired by an individual person. An a posteriori or empirical concept or idea is one that is derived from experience, via a process of abstraction or ostensive definition. In contrast, an a priori concept or idea is one that is not derived from experience in this way and thus presumably does not require any particular experience to be realized (though the explicit realization of such a concept might still require experience as a "trigger"). The main historical account of such concepts, again held mainly by rationalists, construes them as innate, either implanted in the mind by God or, in the more contemporary version of the claim held by Chomsky, Fodor, and others, resulting from evolutionary development. Concepts typically regarded as having this sort of status include the concepts of substance, causation, God, necessity, infinity, and many others. Empiricists, in contrast, typically hold that all concepts are derived from experience.

See also ANALYTIC–SYNTHETIC DISTINCTION, NECESSITY, RATIONALISM.   L.B.

a priori argument. See A PRIORI.

a priori justification. See A PRIORI, JUSTIFICATION.

A-proposition. See SYLLOGISM.

Apuleius of Madaura. See MIDDLE PLATONISM.

Aquinas, Saint Thomas (1225–74), Italian philosopher-theologian, the most influential thinker of the medieval period. He produced a powerful philosophical synthesis that combined Aristotelian and Neoplatonic elements within a Christian context in an original and ingenious way.

Life and works. Thomas was born at Aquino castle in Roccasecca, Italy, and took early schooling at the Benedictine Abbey of Monte Cassino. He then studied liberal arts and philosophy at the University of Naples (1239–44) and joined the Dominican order. While going to Paris for further studies as a Dominican, he was detained by his family for about a year. Upon being released, he studied with the Dominicans at Paris, perhaps privately, until 1248, when he journeyed to

Cologne to work under Albertus Magnus. Thomas's own report (*reportatio*) of Albertus's lectures on the *Divine Names* of Dionysius and his notes on Albertus's lectures on Aristotle's *Ethics* date from this period. In 1252 Thomas returned to Paris to lecture there as a bachelor in theology. His resulting commentary on the *Sentences* of Peter Lombard dates from this period, as do two philosophical treatises, *On Being and Essence* (*De ente et essentia*) and *On the Principles of Nature* (*De principiis naturae*).

In 1256 he began lecturing as master of theology at Paris. From this period (1256–59) date a series of scriptural commentaries, the disputations *On Truth* (*De veritate*), Quodlibetal Questions VII–XI, and earlier parts of the *Summa against the Gentiles* (*Summa contra gentiles;* hereafter *SCG*). At different locations in Italy from 1259 to 1269, Thomas continued to write prodigiously, including, among other works, the completion of the *SCG;* a commentary on the *Divine Names;* disputations *On the Power of God* (*De potentia Dei*) and *On Evil* (*De malo*); and *Summa of Theology* (*Summa theologiae;* hereafter *ST*), Part I. In January 1269, he resumed teaching in Paris as regent master and wrote extensively until returning to Italy in 1272. From this second Parisian regency date the disputations *On the Soul* (*De anima*) and *On Virtues* (*De virtutibus*); continuation of *ST;* Quodlibets I–VI and XII; *On the Unity of the Intellect against the Averroists* (*De unitate intellectus contra Averroistas*); most if not all of his commentaries on Aristotle; a commentary on the *Book of Causes* (*Liber de causis*); and *On the Eternity of the World* (*De aeternitate mundi*). In 1272 Thomas returned to Italy where he lectured on theology at Naples and continued to write until December 6, 1273, when his scholarly work ceased. He died three months later en route to the Second Council of Lyons.

Doctrine. Aquinas was both a philosopher and a theologian. The greater part of his writings are theological, but there are many strictly philosophical works within his corpus, such as *On Being and Essence, On the Principles of Nature, On the Eternity of the World,* and the commentaries on Aristotle and on the *Book of Causes.* Also important are large sections of strictly philosophical writing incorporated into theological works such as the *SCG, ST,* and various disputations.

Aquinas clearly distinguishes between strictly philosophical investigation and theological investigation. If philosophy is based on the light of natural reason, theology (*sacra doctrina*) presupposes faith in divine revelation. While the natural light of reason is insufficient to discover things that can be made known to human beings only through revelation, e.g., belief in the Trinity, Thomas holds that it is impossible for those things revealed to us by God through faith to be opposed to those we can discover by using human reason. For then one or the other would have to be false; and since both come to us from God, God himself would be the author of falsity, something Thomas rejects as abhorrent. Hence it is appropriate for the theologian to use philosophical reasoning in theologizing.

Aquinas also distinguishes between the orders to be followed by the theologian and by the philosopher. In theology one reasons from belief in God and his revelation to the implications of this for created reality. In philosophy one begins with an investigation of created reality insofar as this can be understood by human reason and then seeks to arrive at some knowledge of divine reality viewed as the cause of created reality and the end or goal of one's philosophical inquiry (*SCG* II, c. 4). This means that the order Aquinas follows in his theological *Summae* (*SCG* and *ST*) is not the same as that which he prescribes for the philosopher (cf. Prooemium to Commentary on the *Metaphysics*). Also underlying much of Aquinas's thought is his acceptance of the difference between theoretical or speculative philosophy (including natural philosophy, mathematics, and metaphysics) and practical philosophy.

Being and analogy. For Aquinas the highest part of philosophy is metaphysics, the science of being as being. The subject of this science is not God, but *being,* viewed without restriction to any given kind of being, or simply as being (Prooemium to Commentary on *Metaphysics; In de trinitate,* qu. 5, a. 4). The metaphysician does not enjoy a direct vision of God in this life, but can reason to knowledge of him by moving from created effects to awareness of him as their uncreated cause. God is therefore not the subject of metaphysics, nor is he included in its subject. God can be studied by the metaphysician only indirectly, as the cause of the finite beings that fall under being as being, the subject of the science. In order to account for the human intellect's discovery of being as being, in contrast with being as mobile (studied by natural philosophy) or being as quantified (studied by mathematics), Thomas appeals to a special kind of intellectual operation, a negative judgment, technically named by him "separation." Through this operation one discovers that being, in order to be realized as such, need not be material and changing. Only as a result of this judgment is one justified in studying being as being.

Following Aristotle (and Averroes), Thomas is convinced that the term 'being' is used in various ways and with different meanings. Yet these different usages are not unrelated and do enjoy an underlying unity sufficient for being as being to be the subject of a single science. On the level of finite being Thomas adopts and adapts Aristotle's theory of unity by reference to a first order of being. For Thomas as for Aristotle this unity is guaranteed by the primary referent in our predication of being – substance. Other things are named being only because they are in some way ordered to and dependent on substance, the primary instance of being. Hence being is analogous. Since Thomas's application of analogy to the divine names presupposes the existence of God, we shall first examine his discussion of that issue.

The existence of God and the "five ways." Thomas holds that unaided human reason, i.e., philosophical reason, can demonstrate that God exists, that he is one, etc., by reasoning from effect to cause (*De trinitate*, qu. 2, a. 3; *SCG* I, c. 4). Best-known among his many presentations of argumentation for God's existence are the "five ways." Perhaps even more interesting for today's student of his metaphysics is a brief argument developed in one of his first writings, *On Being and Essence* (c.4). There he wishes to determine how essence is realized in what he terms "separate substances," i.e., the soul, intelligences (angels of the Christian tradition), and the first cause (God).

After criticizing the view that created separate substances are composed of matter and form, Aquinas counters that they are not entirely free from composition. They are composed of a form (or essence) and an act of existing (*esse*). He immediately develops a complex argument: (1) We can think of an essence or *quiddity* without knowing whether or not it actually exists. Therefore in such entities essence and act of existing differ unless (2) there is a thing whose quiddity and act of existing are identical. At best there can be only one such being, he continues, by eliminating multiplication of such an entity either through the addition of some difference or through the reception of its form in different instances of matter. Hence, any such being can only be separate and unreceived *esse*, whereas *esse* in all else is received in something else, i.e., essence. (3) Since *esse* in all other entities is therefore distinct from essence or quiddity, exis-

tence is communicated to such beings by something else, i.e., they are caused. Since that which exists through something else must be traced back to that which exists of itself, there must be some thing that causes the existence of everything else and that is identical with its act of existing. Otherwise one would regress to infinity in caused causes of existence, which Thomas here dismisses as unacceptable.

In qu. 2, a. 1 of *ST* I Thomas rejects the claim that God's existence is self-evident to us in this life, and in a. 2 maintains that God's existence can be demonstrated by reasoning from knowledge of an existing effect to knowledge of God as the cause required for that effect to exist.

The *first way* or argument (art. 3) rests upon the fact that various things in our world of sense experience are moved. But whatever is moved is moved by something else. To justify this, Thomas reasons that to be moved is to be reduced from potentiality to actuality, and that nothing can reduce itself from potency to act; for it would then have to be in potency (if it is to be moved) and in act at the same time and in the same respect. (This does not mean that a mover must formally possess the act it is to communicate to something else if it is to move the latter; it must at least possess it virtually, i.e., have the power to communicate it.) Whatever is moved, therefore, must be moved by something else. One cannot regress to infinity with moved movers, for then there would be no first mover and, consequently, no other mover; for second movers do not move unless they are moved by a first mover. One must, therefore, conclude to the existence of a first mover which is moved by nothing else, and this "everyone understands to be God."

The *second way* takes as its point of departure an ordering of efficient causes as indicated to us by our investigation of sensible things. By this Thomas means that we perceive in the world of sensible things that certain efficient causes cannot exercise their causal activity unless they are also caused by something else. But nothing can be the efficient cause of itself, since it would then have to be prior to itself. One cannot regress to infinity in ordered efficient causes. In ordered efficient causes, the first is the cause of the intermediary, and the intermediary is the cause of the last whether the intermediary is one or many. Hence if there were no first efficient cause, there would be no intermediary and no last cause. Thomas concludes from this that one must acknowledge the existence of a first efficient cause, "which everyone names God."

The *third way* consists of two major parts. Some

textual variants have complicated the proper interpretation of the first part. In brief, Aquinas appeals to the fact that certain things are subject to generation and corruption to show that they are "possible," i.e., capable of existing and not existing. Not all things can be of this kind (*revised text*), for that which has the possibility of not existing at some time does not exist. If, therefore, all things are capable of not existing, at some time there was nothing whatsoever. If that were so, even now there would be nothing, since what does not exist can only begin to exist through something else that exists. Therefore not all beings are capable of existing and not existing. There must be some necessary being. Since such a necessary, i.e., incorruptible, being might still be caused by something else, Thomas adds a second part to the argument. Every necessary being either depends on something else for its necessity or it does not. One cannot regress to infinity in necessary beings that depend on something else for their necessity. Therefore there must be some being that is necessary of itself and that does not depend on another cause for its necessity, i.e., God.

The statement in the first part to the effect that what has the possibility of not existing at some point does not exist has been subject to considerable dispute among commentators. Moreover, even if one grants this and supposes that every individual being is a "possible" and therefore has not existed at some point in the past, it does not easily follow from this that the totality of existing things will also have been nonexistent at some point in the past. Given this, some interpreters prefer to substitute for the third way the more satisfactory versions found in *SCG* I (ch. 15) and *SCG* II (ch. 15).

Thomas's *fourth way* is based on the varying degrees of perfection we discover among the beings we experience. Some are more or less good, more or less true, more or less noble, etc., than others. But the more and less are said of different things insofar as they approach in varying degrees something that is such to a maximum degree. Therefore there is something that is truest and best and noblest and hence that is also being to the maximum degree. To support this Thomas comments that those things that are true to the maximum degree also enjoy being to the maximum degree; in other words he appeals to the convertibility between being and truth (of being). In the second part of this argument Thomas argues that what is supremely such in a given genus is the cause of all other things in that genus. Therefore there is something that is the

cause of being, goodness, etc., for all other beings, and this we call God.

Much discussion has centered on Thomas's claim that the more and less are said of different things insofar as they approach something that is such to the maximum degree. Some find this insufficient to justify the conclusion that a maximum must exist, and would here insert an appeal to efficient causality and his theory of participation. If certan entities share or participate in such a perfection only to a limited degree, they must receive that perfection from something else. While more satisfactory from a philosophical perspective, such an insertion seems to change the argument of the fourth way significantly.

The *fifth way* is based on the way things in the universe are governed. Thomas observes that certain things that lack the ability to know, i.e., natural bodies, act for an end. This follows from the fact that they always or at least usually act in the same way to attain that which is best. For Thomas this indicates that they reach their ends by "intention" and not merely from chance. And this in turn implies that they are directed to their ends by some knowing and intelligent being. Hence some intelligent being exists that orders natural things to their ends. This argument rests on final causality and should not be confused with any based on order and design.

Aquinas's frequently repeated denial that in this life we can know what God is should here be recalled. If we can know that God exists and what he is not, we cannot know what he is (see, e.g., *SCG* I, c. 30). Even when we apply the names of pure perfections to God, we first discover such perfections in limited fashion in creatures. What the names of such perfections are intended to signify may indeed be free from all imperfection, but every such name carries with it some deficiency in the way in which it signifies. When a name such as 'goodness', for instance, is signified abstractly (e.g., 'God is goodness'), this abstract way of signifying suggests that goodness does not subsist in itself. When such a name is signified concretely (e.g., 'God is good'), this concrete way of signifying implies some kind of composition between God and his goodness. Hence while such names are to be affirmed of God as regards that which they signify, the way in which they signify is to be denied of him.

This final point sets the stage for Thomas to apply his theory of analogy to the divine names. Names of pure perfections such as 'good', 'true', 'being', etc., cannot be applied to God with exactly the same meaning they have when affirmed of creatures (univocally), nor with entirely different meanings (equivocally). Hence they are affirmed of God and of creatures by an analogy based on the relationship that obtains between a creature viewed as an effect and God its uncaused cause. Because some minimum degree of similarity must obtain between any effect and its cause, Thomas is convinced that in some way a caused perfection imitates and participates in God, its uncaused and unparticipated source. Because no caused effect can ever be equal to its uncreated cause, every perfection that we affirm of God is realized in him in a way different from the way we discover it in creatures. This dissimilarity is so great that we can never have quidditative knowledge of God in this life (know what God is). But the similarity is sufficient for us to conclude that what we understand by a perfection such as goodness in creatures is present in God in unrestricted fashion. Even though Thomas's identification of the kind of analogy to be used in predicating divine names underwent some development, in mature works such as *On the Power of God* (qu. 7, a. 7), *SCG* I (c.34), and *ST* I (qu. 13, a. 5), he identifies this as the analogy of "one to another," rather than as the analogy of "many to one." In none of these works does he propose using the analogy of "proportionality" that he had previously defended in *On Truth* (qu. 2, a. 11).

Theological virtues. While Aquinas is convinced that human reason can arrive at knowledge that God exists and at meaningful predication of the divine names, he does not think the majority of human beings will actually succeed in such an effort (*SCG* I, c. 4; *ST* II–IIae, qu. 2, a. 4). Hence he concludes that it was fitting for God to reveal such truths to mankind along with others that purely philosophical inquiry could never discover even in principle. Acceptance of the truth of divine revelation presupposes the gift of the theological virtue of faith in the believer. Faith is an infused virtue by reason of which we accept on God's authority what he has revealed to us. To believe is an act of the intellect that assents to divine truth as a result of a command on the part of the human will, a will that itself is moved by God through grace (*ST* II–IIae, qu. 2, a. 9).

For Thomas the theological virtues, having God (the ultimate end) as their object, are prior to all other virtues whether natural or infused. Because the ultimate end must be present in the intellect before it is present to the will, and

because the ultimate end is present in the will by reason of hope and charity (the other two theological virtues), in this respect faith is prior to hope and charity. Hope is the theological virtue through which we trust that with divine assistance we will attain the infinite good – eternal enjoyment of God (*ST* II–IIae, qu. 17, aa. 1–2). In the order of generation, hope is prior to charity; but in the order of perfection charity is prior both to hope and faith. While neither faith nor hope will remain in those who reach the eternal vision of God in the life to come, charity will endure in the blessed. It is a virtue or habitual form that is infused into the soul by God and that inclines us to love him for his own sake. If charity is more excellent than faith or hope (*ST* II–IIae, qu. 23, a. 6), through charity the acts of all other virtues are ordered to God, their ultimate end (qu. 23, a. 8).

See also ARISTOTLE, PHILOSOPHY OF RELIGION, THOMISM.   J.F.W.

Arabic philosophy, the philosophy produced in Arabic by philosophers of various ethnic and religious backgrounds who lived in societies in which Islamic civilization was dominant and who identified with its cultural values. (The appellation 'Islamic philosophy' is misleading, for it suggests a specific religious content that was not necessarily there – just as medieval Latin philosophy is not "Christian" philosophy.) In the historical evolution of Western philosophy it is the heir to post-Plotinian late Greek philosophy and the immediate precursor of later medieval philosophy, which it heavily influenced and to which it exhibits a parallel but independent development after Avicenna well into the twentieth century.

The philosophical curriculum of higher education that had spread among the Hellenized peoples of Egypt, the Middle East, and Iran in the sixth century followed the classification of the sciences current in Alexandria, a classification that had developed from that of Aristotle's works. Aristotle's *Organon*, including the *Rhetoric* and *Poetics*, and prefaced by Porphyry's *Isagoge*, constituted the canonical nine books on logic, the instrument of philosophy. Philosophy proper was then divided into theoretical and practical: theoretical philosophy was further subdivided into physics, mathematics, and metaphysics; and practical into ethics, economics (household management), and politics. Carriers of this higher education were primarily the Eastern churches and monastic centers in the Fertile Crescent. With the advent of Islam in the seventh century and the eventual spread of Arabic as the language of learning, the entire curriculum was translated upon demand into Arabic by Syriac-speaking Christians in the eighth through the tenth centuries. The demand from Arab intellectuals, who by the time of the translations had developed a significant scholarly tradition of their own and actively commissioned the translations. The entire corpus of Aristotle's writings, together with the complete range of commentaries from Alexander of Aphrodisias onward, constituted in Arabic the standard textbooks in logic, physics (including meteorology, the theory of the soul, and zoology), metaphysics, and ethics. Metaphysics was also studied as a rule in conjunction with or in the light of the pseudo-Aristotelian *Theologia Aristotelis* (selections from Plotinus's *Enneads*, Books 4–6) and the *Liber de causis*, along with other selections from Proclus's *Elements of Theology*. Mathematics included geometry (Euclid's *Elements*), astronomy (Ptolemy's *Almagest*), arithmetic (Nicomachus's *Introduction*), and music (Ptolemy's *Harmonics*). Economics was based almost exclusively on the neo-Pythagorean Bryson's *Oikonomikos,* while politics mainly drew on Plato's *Republic* and the *Laws* and especially on the pseudepigraphic correspondence between Aristotle and Alexander (Aristotle's *Politics* was known in Arabic in fragmentary form). In medicine, which was considered an applied science and as such remained outside this classification, Galen's entire works were translated. His abridgments of Plato and his Stoicizing logic formed the basic source of knowledge on these subjects in Arabic.

The early history of Arabic philosophy presents two independent lines of development. One is associated with the first philosopher and Arab polymath al-Kindī (d.873) and his followers, notably as-Sarakhsī (d.889), Abū-Zayd al-Balkhī (d.934), and al-ʿĀmirī (d.992). These philosophers, who appear to stand closer to the Neoplatonism of Athens than to the neo-Aristotelianism of Alexandria, sought in their works to present the various parts of philosophy to an Arab audience, integrate them into Islamic intellectual life, and solve the philosophical problems that arose in the process. The famous physician Rhazes (Abū-Bakr ar-Rāzī, d.925) may be tenuously related to this line, although he appears to be mostly an autodidact and his philosophy was decidedly more eclectic, leaving no following. The second is that of the Aristotelians of Baghdad, founded by the Nestorian scholar and translator Mattā Ibn Yānus (d.940). His Aristotelianism can be traced directly to the Alexandrian commentators and reaches beyond them to Alexander of Aphrodisias and Themistius. His students, al-Fārābī (d.950) and Yaḥyā Ibn ʿAdī (d.974), and the wide circle of disciples of the latter, prominent among whom are Abū-Sulaymān as-Sijistānī (d.c.985), ʿĪsā Ibn-Zurʿa (d.1008), Al-Ḥasan Ibn-Suwār (d.c.1030), and Abū-l-Faraj Ibn aṭ-Ṭayyib (d.1043), engaged in rigorous textual analysis and philosophical interpretation of Aristotle's works and composed independent monographs on all branches of philosophy. The Aristotelian line of Baghdad, and especially the work of al-Fārābī, was transmitted to Islamic Spain (al-Andalus) toward the end of the tenth century and formed the basis of the philosophical tradition there, whose major exponents were Ibn Bājja (Avempace, d.1139), Ibn Ṭufayl (d.1186), Averroes (Ibn Rushd, d.1198), and Maimonides (Ibn Maymūn, d.1204). This tradition came to an end with the *reconquista* of all Islamic Spain except Granada about two decades after the death of Ibn Tumlūs (d.1223), the last major Andalusian philosopher.

These two lines eventually merge in the work of Avicenna, who set himself the task of synthesizing, in the light of concerns valid in his time, the divergent tendencies of Aristotelian philosophy as it had developed throughout the ages. The Alexandrian schema of the classification of the sciences, which was adopted by Arabic philosophy, implicitly also presented, by means of the connections it established among the various subjects, a blueprint of a work that would encompass all philosophy. Philosophers prior to Avicenna, both the Greeks after Plotinus and the Arabs, failed to note its potential as an outline for a comprehensive work on all philosophy, and had worked on different parts of it. Avicenna was the first to perceive this and to create in his various writings an internally consistent system having mutually interdependent parts and based on the syllogistic logic of Aristotle. His philosophical summae thus mark the end of ancient and the beginning of Scholastic philosophy. In these works Avicenna paid relatively little attention to certain parts of philosophy, in particular the mathematical part of theoretical, and virtually the entirety of practical, philosophy. As a result, Arabic philosophy after him concentrated on three major fields – logic, physics, and metaphysics – which became the norm. Practical philosophy developed along different lines, to a large extent divorced from mainstream philosophy. The highly influential work by Miskawayh (d.1030) on ethics provided a model that was followed by later treatises, which constituted a separate genre of philosophical writings. As for mathematics, its different parts were pursued largely independently of the rest of philosophy.

After Avicenna, Arabic philosophy was dominated by his thought and developed along the lines of the reconstructed Peripateticism he established. In the first place, his powerful integrative systematization of philosophy elicited a reaction by certain philosophers toward a more pristine Aristotelianism, notably by Averroes, 'Abd-al-Laṭīf al-Baghdādī (d.1231), and the eighteenth-century Ottoman scholar Yanyali Esat (As'ad of Yanyā, d.1730), who even executed new Arabic translations from the Greek of some of Aristotle's physical works. Secondly, it generated among his followers, notable among whom are Naṣīr-ad-Dīn aṭ-Ṭūsī (d.1274) and Quṭb-ad-Dīn ar-Rāzī (d.1364), a long series of philosophically fecund commentaries and supercommentaries. Thirdly, it forced most theological writing to adopt logic as its method, and philosophical, rather than theological, analysis as the means of argumentation, a procedure established by al-Ghazālī (d.1111) and consolidated by Fakhr-ad-Dīn ar-Rāzī (d.1209). And fourthly, it formed the basis for the further development of his metaphysics (in particular the concepts of essence and existence and the schema of emanation) through the incorporation of the illuminationist philosophy of Suhrawardī of Aleppo (d.1193) and the mystical theories of Ibn 'Arabī (d.1240) in the works of Shiite philosophers active since Safavid times (sixteenth century). This movement, initiated by Mīr Dāmād (d.1632) and developed by his pupil Mullā Ṣadrā (d.1640), has continued after the latter's death among Iranian philosophers writing partly also in Persian.

The colonization of the Arab world by Western powers since the nineteenth century has resulted in the spread of modern European, and especially French, philosophy among Arab intellectuals. Modern Arab philosophical thought is now developing along these lines while at the same time efforts are being made to relate it to traditional Arabic philosophy.

See also AL-FĀRĀBĪ, AL-GHAZĀLĪ, AL-KINDĪ, ARISTOTLE, AVERROES, AVICENNA, ISLAMIC NEOPLATONISM.　　　　　　　　　　　D.Gu.

āradhya, Sanskrit word meaning 'object of worship or reverence'. In traditional Indian society, reverence was almost a way of life. Elders, especially one's parents and teachers, were held in godlike esteem. The Indians revered life in any form as sacred; hence, *ahiṁsā* (nonviolence) and vegetarianism were two important features of the ideal Indian life. In the Hindu polytheistic tradition, which continues even today, the countless Vedic deities, along with the later gods and goddesses in the Hindu pantheon, serve as *āradhya* objects. A popular form of *āradhya* in today's Hindu society is often a chosen deity worshiped in a household. **See also** AHIṀSĀ.

　　　　　　　　　　　　　　　　　　　D.K.C.

Arcesilaus of Pitane (c.315–242 B.C.), Greek Skeptic philosopher, founder of the Middle Academy. Influenced by Socratic elenchus, he claimed that, unlike Socrates, he was not even certain that he was certain of nothing. He shows the influence of Pyrrho in attacking the Stoic doctrine that the subjective certainty of the wise is the criterion of truth. At the theoretical level he advocated *epochē*, suspension of rational judgment; at the practical, he argued that *eulogon*, probability, can justify action – an early version of coherentism. His ethical views were not extreme; he held, e.g., that one should attend to one's own life rather than external objects. Though he wrote nothing except verse, he led the Academy into two hundred years of Skepticism.　　　　　　　　　　　　　　　R.C.

Archelaus of Athens. See PRE-SOCRATICS, SKEPTICS.

archetype. See JUNG.

Archimedian ordering. See LEXICAL ORDERING.

architecture, cognitive. See COGNITIVE SCIENCE.

Archytas (fl. 400–350 B.C.), Greek Pythagorean philosopher from Tarentum in southern Italy. He was elected general seven times and sent a ship to rescue Plato from Dionysius II of Syracuse in 361. He is famous for solutions to specific mathematical problems, such as the doubling of the cube, but little is known about his general philosophical principles. His proof that the numbers in a superparticular ratio have no mean proportional has relevance to music theory, as does his work with the arithmetic, geometric, and harmonic means. He gave mathematical accounts of the diatonic, enharmonic, and chromatic scales and developed a theory of acoustics. Fragments 1 and 2 and perhaps 3 are authentic, but most material preserved in his name is spurious. **See also** PYTHAGORAS.　　　　　　　　　　C.A.H.

Arendt, Hannah (1906–75), German-born American social and political theorist. She was educated in her native Germany, studying with Heidegger and Jaspers; fled to France in 1933; and emigrated in 1941 to the United States, where she taught at various universities. Her major works are *The Origins of Totalitarianism* (1951), *The Human Condition* (1958), *Between Past and Future* (1961), *On Revolution* (1963), *Crises of the Republic* (1972), and *The Life of the Mind* (1978).

In Arendt's view, for reasons established by Kant and deepened by Nietzsche, there is a breach between being and thinking, one that cannot be closed by thought. Understood as philosophizing or contemplation, thinking is a form of egoism that isolates us from one another and our world. Despite Kant, modernity remains mired in egoism, a condition compounded by the emergence of a "mass" that consists of bodies with needs temporarily met by producing and consuming and which demands governments that minister to these needs. In place of thinking, laboring, and the administration of things now called democracy, all of which are instrumental but futile as responses to the "thrown" quality of our condition, Arendt proposed to those capable of it a mode of being, *political action,* that she found in pronounced form in pre-Socratic Greece and briefly but gloriously at the founding of the Roman and American republics. Political action is initiation, the making of beginnings that can be explained neither causally nor teleologically. It is done in the space of appearances constituted by the presence of other political actors whose re-sponses – the telling of equally unpredictable stories concerning one another's actions – determine what actions are taken and give character to the acting participants. In addition to the refined discernments already implied, political action requires the courage to initiate one knows not what. Its outcome is power; not over other people or things but mutual empowerment to continue acting in concert and thereby to overcome egoism and achieve (positive) freedom and humanity.

See also KANT, NIETZSCHE, POLITICAL THEORY.   R.E.F.

aretaic. See ARETE.

arete, ancient Greek term meaning 'virtue' or 'excellence'. In philosophical contexts, the term was used mainly of virtues of human character; in broader contexts, *arete* was applicable to many different sorts of excellence. The cardinal virtues in the classical period were courage, wisdom, temperance (*sophrosune*), piety, and justice.

Sophists such as Protagoras claimed to teach such virtues, and Socrates challenged their credentials for doing so. Several early Platonic dialogues show Socrates asking after definitions of virtues, and Socrates investigates *arete* in other dialogues as well. Conventional views allowed that a person can have one virtue (such as courage) but lack another (such as wisdom), but Plato's *Protagoras* shows Socrates defending his thesis of the unity of *arete,* which implies that a person who has one *arete* has them all. Platonic accounts of the cardinal virtues (with the exception of piety) are given in Book IV of the *Republic.* Substantial parts of the *Nicomachean Ethics* of Aristotle are given over to discussions of *arete,* which he divides into virtues of character and virtues of intellect. This discussion is the ancestor of most modern theories of virtue ethics. **See also ARISTOTLE, VIRTUE ETHICS.**   P.Wo.

argument, a sequence of statements such that some of them (the *premises*) purport to give reason to accept another of them, the *conclusion.* Since we speak of bad arguments and weak arguments, the premises of an argument need not really support the conclusion, but they must give some appearance of doing so or the term 'argument' is misapplied. Logic is mainly concerned with the question of validity: whether *if* the premises are true we would have reason to accept the conclusion. A valid argument with true premises is called *sound.* A valid deductive argument is one such that if we accept the premises we are *logically* bound to accept the conclusion and if we reject the conclusion we are logically bound to reject one or more of the premises. Alternatively, the premises logically entail the conclusion.

A good inductive argument – some would reserve 'valid' for deductive arguments – is one such that if we accept the premises we are logically bound to regard the conclusion as probable, and, in addition, as more probable than it would be if the premises should be false. A few arguments have only one premise and/or more than one conclusion.

See also IMPLICATION, INDUCTION, LOGICAL CONSEQUENCE, MATHEMATICAL FUNCTION.   R.P.

argument, a priori. See A PRIORI.

argument, practical. See PRACTICAL REASONING.

argument from analogy. See PHILOSOPHY OF RELIGION, PROBLEM OF OTHER MINDS.

argument from authority. See INFORMAL FALLACY.

argument from design. See PHILOSOPHY OF RELIGION.

argument from evil. See PHILOSOPHY OF RELIGION.

argument from hallucination. See PERCEPTION.

argument from illusion. See PERCEPTION.

argument (of a function). See MATHEMATICAL FUNCTION.

argumentum ad baculum. See INFORMAL FALLACY.

argumentum ad hominem. See INFORMAL FALLACY.

argumentum ad ignorantium. See INFORMAL FALLACY.

argumentum ad judicium. See INFORMAL FALLACY.

argumentum ad misericordiam. See INFORMAL FALLACY.

argumentum ad populum. See INFORMAL FALLACY.

argumentum ad verecundiam. See INFORMAL FALLACY.

argumentum consensus. See INFORMAL FALLACY.

Arianism, diverse but related teachings in early Christianity that subordinated the Son to God the Father. In reaction the church developed its doctrine of the Trinity, whereby the Son (and Holy Spirit), though distinct persons (*hypostases*), share with the Father, as his ontological equals, the one being or substance (*ousia*) of God. Arius (c.250 – c.336) taught in Alexandria, where, on the hierarchical model of Middle Platonism, he sharply distinguished Scripture's transcendent God from the *Logos* or Son incarnate in Jesus. The latter, subject to suffering and humanly obedient to God, is inferior to the immutable Creator, the object of that obedience. God alone is eternal and ungenerated; the Son, divine not by nature but by God's choosing, is generated, with a beginning: the unique creature, through whom all else is made. The Council of Nicea, in 325, condemned Arius and favored his enemy Athanasius, affirming the Son's creatorhood and full deity, having the same being or substance (*homoousios*) as the Father. Arianism still flourished, evolving into the extreme view that the Son's being was neither the same as the Father's nor like it (*homoiousios*), but unlike it (*anomoios*). This too was anathematized, by the Council of 381 at Constantinople, which, ratifying what is commonly called the Nicene Creed, sealed orthodox Trinitarianism and the equality of the three persons against Arian subordinationism. **See also HOMOOUSIOS.** A.E.L.

Aristippus of Cyrene. See CYRENAICS.

Aristotle (384–322 B.C.), preeminent Greek philosopher born in Stagira, hence sometimes called the Stagirite. Aristotle came to Athens as a teenager and remained for two decades in Plato's Academy. Following Plato's death in 347, Aristotle traveled to Assos and to Lesbos, where he associated with Theophrastus and collected a wealth of biological data, and later to Macedonia, where he tutored Alexander the Great. In 335 he returned to Athens and founded his own philosophical school in the Lyceum. The site's colonnaded walk (*peripatos*) conferred on Aristotle and his group the name 'the Peripatetics'. Alexander's death in 323 unleashed anti-Macedonian forces in Athens. Charged with impiety, and mindful of the fate of Socrates, Aristotle withdrew to Chalcis, where he died.

Chiefly influenced by his association with Plato, Aristotle also makes wide use of the pre-Socratics. A number of works begin by criticizing and, ultimately, building on their views. The direction of Plato's influence is debated. Some scholars see Aristotle's career as a measured retreat from his teacher's doctrines. For others he began as a confirmed anti-Platonist but returned to the fold as he matured. More likely, Aristotle early on developed a keenly independent voice that expressed enduring puzzlement over such Platonic doctrines as the separate existence of Ideas and the construction of physical reality from two-dimensional triangles. Such unease was no doubt heightened by Aristotle's appreciation for the evidential value of observation as well as by his conviction that long-received and well-entrenched opinion is likely to contain at least part of the truth.

Aristotle reportedly wrote a few popular works for publication, some of which are dialogues. Of these we have only fragments and reports. Notably lost are also his lectures on the good and on the Ideas. Ancient cataloguers also list under Aristotle's name some 158 constitutions of Greek states. Of these, only the *Constitution of Athens* has survived, on a papyrus discovered in 1890. What remains is an enormous body of writing on virtually every topic of philosophical significance. Much of it consists of detailed lecture notes, working drafts, and accounts of his lectures written by others. Although efforts may have been under way in Aristotle's lifetime, Andronicus of Rhodes, in the first century B.C., is credited with giving the Aristotelian corpus its present organization. Virtually no extant manuscripts predate the ninth century A.D., so the corpus has been transmitted by a complex history of manuscript transcription. In 1831 the Berlin Academy published the first critical edition of Aristotle's work. Scholars still cite Aristotle by page, column, and line of this edition.

Logic and language. The writings on logic and language are concentrated in six early works: *Categories, On Interpretation, Prior Analytics, Posterior Analytics, Topics,* and *Sophistical Refutations.* Known since late antiquity as the *Organon,* these works share a concern with what is now called semantics. The *Categories* focuses on the relation between uncombined terms, such as 'white' or 'man', and the items they signify; *On Interpretation* offers an account of how terms combine to yield simple statements; *Prior Analytics* provides a systematic account of how three terms must be distributed in two categorical statements so as to yield logically a third such statement; *Posterior Analytics* specifies the conditions that categorical statements must meet to play a role in scientific explanation. The *Topics,* sometimes said to include *Sophistical Refutations,* is a handbook of "topics" and techniques for dialectical arguments concerning, principally, the four predicables: accident (what may or may not belong to a subject, as sitting belongs to Socrates); definition (what signifies a subject's essence, as rational animal is the essence of man); proprium (what is not in the essence of a subject but is unique to or counterpredicable of it, as all and only persons are risible); and genus (what is in the essence of subjects differing in species, as animal is in the essence of both men and oxen).

Categories treats the basic kinds of things that exist and their interrelations. Every uncombined term, says Aristotle, signifies essentially something in one of ten categories – a substance, a quantity, a quality, a relative, a place, a time, a position, a having, a doing, or a being affected. This doctrine underlies Aristotle's admonition that there are as many proper or per se senses of 'being' as there are categories. In order to isolate the things that exist primarily, namely, primary substances, from all other things and to give an account of their nature, two asymmetric relations of ontological dependence are employed. First, substance (*ousia*) is distinguished from the accidental categories by the fact that every accident is *present in* a substance and, therefore, cannot exist without a substance in which to inhere. Second, the category of substance itself is divided into ordinary individuals or primary substances, such as Socrates, and secondary substances, such as the species man and the genus animal. Secondary substances are *said of* primary substances and indicate what kind of thing the subject is. A mark of this is that both the name and the definition of the secondary substance can be predicated of the primary substance, as both *man* and *rational animal* can be predicated of Socrates. Universals in non-substance categories are also said of subjects, as color is said of white. Therefore, directly or indirectly, everything else is either present in or said of primary substances and without them nothing would exist. And because they are neither present in a subject nor said of a subject, primary substances depend on nothing else for their existence. So, in the *Categories,* the ordinary individual is ontologically basic.

On Interpretation offers an account of those meaningful expressions that are true or false, namely, statements or assertions. Following Plato's *Sophist,* a simple statement is composed of the semantically heterogeneous parts, name (*onoma*) and verb (*rhema*). In 'Socrates runs' the name has the strictly referential function of signifying the subject of attribution. The verb, on the other hand, is essentially predicative, signifying something holding of the subject. Verbs also indicate when something is asserted to hold and so make precise the statement's truth conditions. Simple statements also include general categorical statements. Since medieval times it has become customary to refer to the basic categoricals by letters: (A) Every man is white, (E) No man is white, (I) Some man is white, and (O) Not every man is white. *On Interpretation* outlines their logical relations in what is now called the square of opposition: A & E are contraries, A & O and E & I are contradictories, and A & I and E & O are superimplications. That A implies I reflects the no longer current view that all affirmative statements carry existential import.

One ambition of *On Interpretation* is a theory of the truth conditions for all statements that affirm or deny one thing or another. However, statements involving future contingencies pose a special problem. Consider Aristotle's notorious sea battle. Either it will or it will not happen tomorrow. If the first, then the statement 'There will be a sea battle tomorrow' is *now* true. Hence, it is now fixed that the sea battle occur tomorrow. If the second, then it is now fixed that the sea battle not occur tomorrow. Either way there can be no future contingencies. Although some hold that Aristotle would embrace the determinism they find implicit in this consequence, most argue either that he suspends the law of excluded middle for future contingencies or that he denies the principle of bivalence for future contingent statements. On the first option Aristotle gives up the claim that either the sea battle will happen tomorrow or not. On the second he keeps the claim but allows that future contingent statements are neither true nor false. Aristotle's evident attachment to the law of excluded middle, perhaps, favors the second option.

Prior Analytics marks the invention of logic as a formal discipline in that the work contains the first virtually complete system of logical inference, sometimes called *syllogistic*. The fact that the first chapter of the *Prior Analytics* reports that there is a syllogism whenever, certain things being stated, something else follows of necessity, might suggest that Aristotle intended to capture a general notion of logical consequence. However, the syllogisms that constitute the system of the *Prior Analytics* are restricted to the basic categorical statements introduced in *On Interpretation*. A syllogism consists of three different categorical statements: two premises and a conclusion. The *Prior Analytics* tells us which pairs of categoricals logically yield a third. The fourteen basic valid forms are divided into three figures and, within each figure, into moods. The system is foundational because second- and third-figure syllogisms are reducible to first-figure syllogisms, whose validity is self-evident. Although syllogisms are conveniently written as conditional sentences, the syllogistic proper is, perhaps, best seen as a system of valid deductive inferences rather than as a system of valid conditional sentences or sentence forms.

Posterior Analytics extends syllogistic to science and scientific explanation. A science is a deductively ordered body of knowledge about a definite genus or domain of nature. Scientific knowledge (*episteme*) consists not in knowing *that*, e.g., there is thunder in the clouds, but rather in knowing *why* there is thunder. So the theory of scientific knowledge is a theory of explanation and the vehicle of explanation is the first-figure syllogism *Barbara:* If (1) P belongs to all M and (2) M belongs to all S, then (3) P belongs to all S. To explain, e.g., why there is thunder, i.e., why there is noise in the clouds, we say: (3') Noise (P) belongs to the clouds (S) because (2') Quenching of fire (M) belongs to the clouds (S) and (1') Noise (P) belongs to quenching of fire (M). Because what is explained in science is invariant and holds of necessity, the premises of a scientific or *demonstrative syllogism* must be necessary. In requiring that the premises be prior to and more knowable than the conclusion, Aristotle embraces the view that explanation is asymmetrical: knowledge of the conclusion depends on knowledge of each premise, but each premise can be known independently of the conclusion. The premises must also give the causes of the conclusion. To inquire why P belongs to S is, in effect, to seek the middle term that gives the cause. Finally, the premises must be immediate and non-demonstrable. A premise is immediate just in case there is no middle term connecting its subject and predicate terms. Were P to belong to M because of a new middle, $M1$, then there would be a new, more basic premise, that is essential to the full explanation.

Ultimately, explanation of a received fact will consist in a chain of syllogisms terminating in primary premises that are immediate. These serve as axioms that define the science in question because they reflect the essential nature of the fact to be explained – as in (1') the essence of thunder lies in the quenching of fire. Because they are immediate, primary premises are not capable of syllogistic demonstration, yet they must be known if syllogisms containing them are to constitute knowledge of the conclusion. Moreover, were it necessary to know the primary premises syllogistically, demonstration would proceed infinitely or in a circle. The first alternative defeats the very possibility of explanation and the second undermines its asymmetric character. Thus, the primary premises must be known by the direct grasp of the mind (*noûs*). This just signals the appropriate way for the highest principles of a science to be known – even demonstrable propositions can be known directly, but they are explained only when located within the structure of the relevant science, i.e., only when demonstrated syllogistically. Although all sciences exhibit the same formal structure and use certain common principles, different sciences have different primary premises and, hence, different subject matters. This "one genus to one science" rule legislates that each science and its explanations be autonomous.

Aristotle recognizes three kinds of intellectual discipline. *Productive* disciplines, such as house building, concern the making of something external to the agent. *Practical* disciplines, such as ethics, concern the doing of something not separate from the agent, namely, action and choice. *Theoretical* disciplines are concerned with truth for its own sake. As such, they alone are sciences in the special sense of the *Posterior Analytics*. The three main kinds of special science are individuated by their objects – natural science by objects that are separate but not changeless, mathematics by objects that are changeless but not separate, and theology by separate and changeless objects. The mathematician studies the same objects as the natural scientist but in a quite different way. He takes an actual object, e.g. a chalk figure used in demonstration, and abstracts from or "thinks away" those of its properties, such as definiteness of size and imperfection of shape, that are irrelevant to its standing as a perfect exemplar of the purely mathematical properties under investigation. Mathematicians simply treat this abstracted circle, which is not separate from matter, as if it were separate. In this way the theorems they prove about the object can be taken as universal and necessary.

Physics. As the science of nature (*physis*), physics studies those things whose principles and causes of change and rest are internal. Aristotle's central treatise on nature, the *Physics,* analyzes the most general features of natural phenomena: cause, change, time, place, infinity, and continuity. The doctrine of the *four causes* is especially important in Aristotle's work. A cause (*aitia*) is something like an explanatory factor. The *material cause* of a house, for instance, is the matter (*hyle*) from which it is built; the moving or *efficient cause* is the builder, more exactly, the form in the builder's soul; the *formal cause* is its plan or form (*eidos*); and the *final cause* is its purpose or end (*telos*): provision of shelter. The complete explanation of the coming to be of a house will factor in all of these causes. In natural phenomena efficient, formal, and final causes often coincide. The form transmitted by the father is both the efficient cause and the form of the child, and the latter is glossed in terms of the child's end or complete development. This explains why Aris-

totle often simply contrasts matter and form. Although its objects are compounds of both, physics gives priority to the study of natural form. This accords with the *Posterior Analytics'* insistence that explanation proceed through causes that give the essence and reflects Aristotle's commitment to teleology. A natural process counts essentially as the development of, say, an oak or a man because its very identity depends on the complete form realized at its end. As with all things natural, the end is an internal governing principle of the process rather than an external goal.

All natural things are subject to change (*kinesis*). Defined as the actualization of the potential *qua* potential, a change is not an ontologically basic item. There is no category for changes. Rather, they are reductively explained in terms of more basic things – substances, properties, and potentialities. A pale man, e.g., has the potentiality to be or become tanned. If this potentiality is utterly unactualized, no change will ensue; if completely actualized, the change will have ended. So the potentiality must be actualized but not, so to speak, exhausted; i.e., it must be actualized *qua potentiality*. Designed for the ongoing operations of the natural world, the *Physics'* definition of change does not cover the generation and corruption of substantial items themselves. This sort of change, which involves matter and elemental change, receives extensive treatment in *On Generation and Corruption.*

Aristotle rejects the atomists' contention that the world consists of an infinite totality of indivisible atoms in various arrangements. Rather, his basic stuff is uniform elemental matter, any part of which is divisible into smaller such parts. Because nothing that is actually infinite can exist, it is only in principle that matter is always further dividable. So while countenancing the potential infinite, Aristotle squarely denies the *actual infinite*. This holds for the motions of the sublunary elemental bodies (earth, air, fire, and water) as well as for the circular motions of the heavenly bodies (composed of a fifth element, aether, whose natural motion is circular). These are discussed in *On the Heavens.* The four sublunary elements are further discussed in *Meteorology,* the fourth book of which might be described as an early treatise on chemical combination.

Psychology. Because the soul (*psyche*) is officially defined as the form of a body with the potentiality for life, psychology is a subfield of natural science. In effect, Aristotle applies the apparatus of form and matter to the traditional Greek view of the soul as the principle and cause of life. Although even the nutritive and reproductive powers of plants are effects of the soul, most of his attention is focused on topics that are psychological in the modern sense. *On the Soul* gives a general account of the nature and number of the soul's principal cognitive faculties. Subsequent works, chiefly those collected as the *Parva naturalia*, apply the general theory to a broad range of psychological phenomena from memory and recollection to dreaming, sleeping, and waking.

The soul is a complex of faculties. Faculties, at least those distinctive of persons, are capacities for cognitively grasping objects. Sight grasps colors, smell odors, hearing sounds, and the mind grasps universals. An organism's form is the particular organization of its material parts that enable it to exercise these characteristic functions. Because an infant, e.g., has the capacity to do geometry, Aristotle distinguishes two varieties of capacity or potentiality (*dynamis*) and actuality (*entelecheia*). The infant is a geometer *only* in potentiality. This *first potentiality* comes to him simply by belonging to the appropriate species, i.e., by coming into the world endowed with the potential to develop into a competent geometer. By actualizing, through experience and training, this first potentiality, he acquires a *first actualization.* This actualization is also a *second potentiality,* since it renders him a competent geometer able to exercise his knowledge at will. The exercise itself is a *second actualization* and amounts to active contemplation of a particular item of knowledge, e.g. the Pythagorean theorem. So the soul is further defined as the first actualization of a complex natural body.

Faculties, like sciences, are individuated by their objects. Objects of perception (*aisthesis*) fall into three general kinds. *Special* (proper) *sensibles,* such as colors and sounds, are directly perceived by one and only one sense and are immune to error. They demarcate the five special senses: sight, hearing, smell, taste, and touch. *Common sensibles,* such as movement and shape, are directly perceived by more than one special sense. Both special and common sensibles are proper objects of perception because they have a direct causal effect on the perceptual system. By contrast, the son of Diares is an *incidental sensible* because he is perceived not directly but as a consequence of directly perceiving something else that happens to be the son of Diares – e.g., a white thing.

Aristotle calls the mind (*noûs*) the place of forms because it is able to grasp objects apart from matter. These objects are nothing like Plato's separately existing Forms. As Aristotelian universals, their existence is entailed by and depends on their having instances. Thus, *On the Soul's* remark that universals are "somehow in the soul" only reflects their role in assuring the autonomy of thought. The mind has no organ because it is not the form or first actualization of any physical structure. So, unlike perceptual faculties, it is not strongly dependent on the body. However, the mind thinks its objects by way of images, which are something like internal representations, and these are physically based. Insofar as it thus depends on imagination (*phantasia*), the mind is weakly dependent on the body. This would be sufficient to establish the naturalized nature of Aristotle's mind were it not for what some consider an incurably dualist intrusion. In distinguishing something in the mind that makes all things from something that becomes all things, Aristotle introduces the notorious distinction between the active and passive intellects and may even suggest that the first is separable from the body. Opinion on the nature of the active intellect diverges widely, some even discounting it as an irrelevant insertion. But unlike perception, which depends on external objects, thinking is up to us. Therefore, it cannot simply be a matter of the mind's being affected. So Aristotle needs a mechanism that enables us to produce thoughts autonomously. In light of this functional role, the question of active intellect's ontological status is less pressing.

Biology. Aristotle's biological writings, which constitute about a quarter of the corpus, bring biological phenomena under the general framework of natural science: the four causes, form and matter, actuality and potentiality, and especially the teleological character of natural processes. If the *Physics* proceeds in an a priori style, the *History of Animals, Parts of Animals,* and *Generation of Animals* achieve an extraordinary synthesis of observation, theory, and general scientific principle. *History of Animals* is a comparative study of generic features of animals, including analogous parts, activities, and dispositions. Although its morphological and physiological descriptions show surprisingly little interest in teleology, *Parts of Animals* is squarely teleological. Animal parts, especially organs, are ultimately differentiated by function rather than morphology. The composition of, e.g., teeth and flesh is determined by their role in the overall functioning of the organism and, hence, requires teleology. *Generation of Animals* applies the form–matter and actuality–potentiality distinctions to animal reproduction, inheritance, and the development of accidental characteristics. The species form governs the development of an organism and determines what the organism is essentially. Although in the *Metaphysics* and elsewhere accidental characteristics, including inherited ones, are excluded from science, in the biological writings form has an expanded role and explains the inheritance of non-essential characteristics, such as eye color. The more fully the father's form is imposed on the minimally formed matter of the mother, the more completely the father's traits are passed on to the offspring. The extent to which matter resists imposition of form determines the extent to which traits of the mother emerge, or even those of more distant ancestors.

Aristotle shared the Platonists' interest in animal classification. Recent scholarship suggests that this is less an interest in elaborating a Linnean-style taxonomy of the animal kingdom than an interest in establishing the complex differentiae and genera central to definitions of living things. The biological works argue, moreover, that no single differentia could give the whole essence of a species and that the differentiae that do give the essence will fall into more than one division. If the second point rejects the method of dichotomous division favored by Plato and the Academy, the first counters Aristotle's own standard view that essence can be reduced to a single final differentia. The biological sciences are not, then, automatically accommodated by the *Posterior Analytics* model of explanation, where the essence or explanatory middle is conceived as a single causal property.

A number of themes discussed in this section are brought together in a relatively late work, *Motion of Animals*. Its psychophysical account of the mechanisms of animal movement stands at the juncture of physics, psychology, and biology.

Metaphysics. In Andronicus's edition, the fourteen books now known as the *Metaphysics* were placed after the *Physics*, whence comes the word 'metaphysics', whose literal meaning is 'what comes after the physics'. Aristotle himself prefers 'first philosophy' or 'wisdom' (*sophia*). The subject is defined as the theoretical science of the causes and principles of what is most knowable. This makes metaphysics a limiting case of Aristotle's broadly used distinction between what is better known to us and what is better known by nature. The genus animal, e.g.,

is better known by nature than the species man because it is further removed from the senses and because it can be known independently of the species. The first condition suggests that the most knowable objects would be the separately existing and thoroughly non-sensible objects of theology and, hence, that metaphysics is a special science. The second condition suggests that the most knowable objects are simply the most general notions that apply to things in general. This favors identifying metaphysics as the general science of being *qua* being. Special sciences study restricted modes of being. Physics, for instance, studies being *qua* having an internal principle of change and rest. A general science of being studies the principles and causes of things that are, simply insofar as they *are*. A good deal of the *Metaphysics* supports this conception of metaphysics. For example, Book IV, on the principle of non-contradiction, and Book X, on unity, similarity, and difference, treat notions that apply to anything whatever. So, too, for the discussion of form and actuality in the central books VII, VIII, and IX. Book XII, on the other hand, appears to regard metaphysics as the special science of theology.

Aristotle himself attempts to reconcile these two conceptions of metaphysics. Because it studies immovable substance, theology counts as first philosophy. However, it is also general precisely because it is first, and so it will include the study of being *qua* being. Scholars have found this solution as perplexing as the problem. Although Book XII proves the causal necessity for motion of an eternal substance that is an unmoved mover, this establishes no conceptual connection between the forms of sensible compounds and the pure form that is the unmoved mover. Yet such a connection is required, if a single science is to encompass both.

Problems of reconciliation aside, Aristotle had to face a prior difficulty concerning the very possibility of a general science of being. For the *Posterior Analytics* requires the existence of a genus for each science but the *Metaphysics* twice argues that being is not a genus. The latter claim, which Aristotle never relinquishes, is implicit in the *Categories*, where being falls directly into kinds, namely, the categories. Because these highest genera do not result from differentiation of a single genus, no univocal sense of being covers them. Although being is, therefore, ambiguous in as many ways as there are categories, a thread connects them. The ontological priority accorded primary substance in the *Categories* is made part of the very definition of non-substantial entities in the *Metaphysics:* to be an accident is by defini-tion to be an accident of some substance. Thus, the different senses of being all refer to the pri-mary kind of being, substance, in the way that exercise, diet, medicine, and climate are healthy by standing in some relation to the single thing health. The discovery of *focal meaning,* as this is sometimes called, introduces a new way of pro-viding a subject matter with the internal unity required for science. Accordingly, the *Metaphysics* modifies the strict "one genus to one science" rule of the *Posterior Analytics.* A single science may also include objects whose definitions are differ-ent so long as these definitions are related focally to one thing. So focal meaning makes possible the science of being *qua* being.

Focal meaning also makes substance the cen-tral object of investigation. The principles and causes of being in general can be illuminated by studying the principles and causes of the primary instance of being. Although the *Categories* distin-guishes primary substances from other things that are and indicates their salient characteristics (e.g., their ability to remain one and the same while taking contrary properties), it does not explain why it is that primary substances have such characteristics. The difficult central books of the *Metaphysics* – VII, VIII, and IX – investigate precisely this. In effect, they ask what, primarily, about the *Categories'* primary substances explains their nature. Their target, in short, is the *substance* of the primary substances of the *Categories.* As concrete empirical particulars, the latter are com-pounds of form and matter (the distinction is not explicit in the *Categories*) and so their substance must be sought among these internal structural features. Thus, *Metaphysics* VII considers form, matter, and the compound of form and matter, and quickly turns to form as the best candidate. In developing a conception of form that can play the required explanatory role, the notion of essence (*to ti en einai*) assumes center stage. The essence of a man, e.g., is the cause of certain mat-ter constituting a man, namely, the soul. So form in the sense of essence is the primary substance of the *Metaphysics.* This is obviously not the primary substance of the *Categories* and, although the same word (*eidos*) is used, neither is this form the species of the *Categories.* The latter is treated in the *Metaphysics* as a kind of universal compound abstracted from particular compounds and appears to be denied substantial status.

While there is broad, though not universal, agreement that in the *Metaphysics* form is primary substance, there is equally broad disagreement over whether this is particular form, the form belonging to a single individual, or species form, the form common to all individuals in the species. There is also lively discussion concerning the relation of the *Metaphysics* doctrine of pri-mary substance to the earlier doctrine of the *Cat-egories.* Although a few scholars see an outright contradiction here, most take the divergence as evidence of the development of Aristotle's views on substance. Finally, the role of the central books in the *Metaphysics* as a whole continues to be debated. Some see them as an entirely self-contained analysis of form, others as preparatory to Book XII's discussion of non-sensible form and the role of the unmoved mover as the final cause of motion.

Practical philosophy. Two of Aristotle's most heralded works, the *Nicomachean Ethics* and the *Politics,* are treatises in practical philosophy. Their aim is effective action in matters of conduct. So they deal with what is up to us and can be other-wise because in this domain lie choice and action. The practical nature of ethics lies mainly in the development of a certain kind of agent. The *Nicomachean Ethics* was written, Aristotle reminds us, "not in order to know what virtue is, but in order to become good." One becomes good by becoming a good chooser and doer. This is not simply a matter of choosing and doing right actions but of choosing or doing them in the right way. Aristotle assumes that, for the most part, agents know what ought to be done (the evil or vicious person is an exception). The *akratic* or morally weak agent desires to do other than what he knows ought to be done and acts on this desire against his better judgment. The *enkratic* or morally strong person shares the akratic agent's desire but acts in accordance with his better judg-ment. In neither kind of choice are desire and judgment in harmony. In the virtuous, on the other hand, desire and judgment agree. So their choices and actions will be free of the conflict and pain that inevitably accompany those of the akratic and enkratic agent. This is because the part of their soul that governs choice and action is so disposed that desire and right judgment coin-cide. Acquiring a stable disposition (*hexis*) of this sort amounts to acquiring moral virtue (*ethike arete*). The disposition is concerned with choices as would be determined by the person of practical wisdom (*phronesis*); these will be actions lying between extreme alternatives. They will lie in a mean – popularly called the "golden mean" – relative to the talents and stores of the agent. Choosing in this way is not easily done. It involves, for instance, feeling anger or extending generosity at the right time, toward the right people, in the right way, and for the right reasons. Intellectual virtues, such as excellence at mathematics, can be acquired by teaching, but moral virtue cannot. I may know what ought to be done and even perform virtuous acts without being able to act *virtuously*. Nonetheless, because moral virtue is a disposition concerning choice, deliberate performance of virtuous acts can, ultimately, instill a disposition to choose them in harmony and with pleasure and, hence, to act virtuously.

Aristotle rejected Plato's transcendental Form of the Good as irrelevant to the affairs of persons and, in general, had little sympathy with the notion of an absolute good. The goal of choice and action is the human good, namely, living well. This, however, is not simply a matter of possessing the requisite practical disposition. Practical wisdom, which is necessary for living well, involves skill at calculating the best means to achieve one's ends and this is an intellectual virtue. But the ends that are presupposed by deliberation are established by moral virtue. The end of all action, the good for man, is happiness (*eudaimonia*). Most things, such as wealth, are valued only as a means to a worthy end. Honor, pleasure, reason, and individual virtues, such as courage and generosity, are deemed worthy in their own right but they can also be sought for the sake of eudaimonia. Eudaimonia alone can be sought only for its own sake. Eudaimonia is not a static state of the soul but a kind of activity (*energeia*) of the soul – something like human flourishing. The happy person's life will be self-sufficient and complete in the highest measure. The good for man, then, is activity in accordance with virtue or the highest virtue, should there be one. Here 'virtue' means something like excellence and applies to much besides man. The excellence of an ax lies in its cutting, that of a horse in its equestrian qualities. In short, a thing's excellence is a matter of how well it performs its characteristic functions or, we might say, how well it realizes its nature.

The natural functions of persons reside in the exercise of their natural cognitive faculties, most importantly, the faculty of reason. So human happiness consists in activity in accordance with reason. However, persons can exercise reason in practical or in purely theoretical matters. The first suggests that happiness consists in the practical life of moral virtue, the second that it consists in the life of theoretical activity. Most of the *Nicomachean Ethics* is devoted to the moral virtues but the final book appears to favor theoretical activity (*theoria*) as the highest and most choice-

worthy end. It is man's closest approach to divine activity. Much recent scholarship is devoted to the relation between these two conceptions of the good, particularly, to whether they are of equal value and whether they exclude or include one another.

Ethics and politics are closely connected. Aristotle conceives of the state as a natural entity arising among persons to serve a natural function. This is not merely, e.g., provision for the common defense or promotion of trade. Rather, the state of the *Politics* also has eudaimonia as its goal, namely, fostering the complete and self-sufficient lives of its citizens. Aristotle produced a complex taxonomy of constitutions but reduced them, in effect, to three kinds: monarchy, aristocracy, and democracy. Which best serves the natural end of a state was, to some extent, a relative matter for Aristotle. Although he appears to have favored democracy, in some circumstances monarchy might be appropriate.

The standard ordering of Aristotle's works ends with the *Rhetoric* and the *Poetics*. The *Rhetoric*'s extensive discussion of oratory or the art of persuasion locates it between politics and literary theory. The relatively short *Poetics* is devoted chiefly to the analysis of tragedy. It has had an enormous historical influence on aesthetic theory in general as well as on the writing of drama.

See also AQUINAS, ESSENTIALISM, META-PHYSICS, PLATO, PRACTICAL REASONING, SOCRATES, SYLLOGISM, VIRTUE ETHICS.

M.V.W.

Aristotle, commentaries on. See COMMENTARIES ON ARISTOTLE.

arithmetic hierarchy. See HIERARCHY.

arity. See DEGREE.

Arius. See ARIANISM.

Arminianism. See ARMINIUS.

Arminius, Jacobus (1560–1609), Dutch theologian who, as a Dutch Reformed pastor and later professor at the University of Leiden, challenged Calvinist orthodoxy on predestination and free will. After his death, followers codified Arminius's views in a document asserting that God's grace is necessary for salvation, but not irresistible: the divine decree depends on human free choice. This became the basis for Arminianism, which was condemned by the Dutch Reformed synod but vigorously debated for centuries among Protestant theologians of different denominations. The term 'Arminian' is still occasionally applied to theologians who defend a free human response to divine grace against predestinationism.   R.H.K.

Armstrong, David M. (b.1926), Australian philosopher of mind and metaphysician, and until his retirement Challis Professor of Philosophy at Sydney, noted for his allegiance to a physicalist account of consciousness and to a realist view of properties conceived as universals. *A Materialist Theory of the Mind* (1968) develops a scientifically motivated version of the view that mental states are identical with physical states of the central nervous system. *Universals and Scientific Realism* (1978) and *What Is a Law of Nature?* (1983) argue that a scientifically adequate ontology must include universals in order to explain the status of natural laws. Armstrong contends that laws must be construed as expressing relations of necessitation between universals rather than mere regularities among particulars. However, he is only prepared to acknowledge the existence of such universals as are required for the purposes of scientific explanation. Moreover, he adopts an "immanent" or "Aristotelian" (as opposed to a "transcendent" or "Platonic") realism, refusing to accept the existence of uninstantiated universals and denying that universals somehow exist "outside" space and time.

More recently, Armstrong has integrated his scientifically inspired physicalism and property realism within the overall framework of an ontology of states of affairs, notably in *A World of States of Affairs* (1997). Here he advocates the truthmaker principle that every truth must be made true by some existing state of affairs and contends that states of affairs, rather than the universals and particulars that he regards as their constituents, are the basic building blocks of reality. Within this ontology, which in some ways resembles that of Wittgenstein's *Tractatus*, necessity and possibility are accommodated by appeal to combinatorial principles. As Armstrong explains in *A Combinatorial Theory of Possibility* (1989), this approach offers an ontologically economical alternative to the realist conception of possible worlds defended by David Lewis.

See also LAWLIKE GENERALIZATION, METAPHYSICAL REALISM, PHILOSOPHY OF SCIENCE, SCIENTIFIC REALISM.   E.J.L.

Arnauld, Antoine (1612–94), French theologian and philosopher, perhaps the most important and best-known intellectual associated with the Jansenist community at Port-Royal, as well as a staunch and orthodox champion of Cartesian philosophy. His theological writings defend the Augustinian doctrine of efficacious grace, according to which salvation is not earned by one's own acts, but granted by the irresistible grace of God. He also argues in favor of a strict contritionism, whereby one's absolution must be based on a true, heartfelt repentance, a love of God, rather than a selfish fear of God's punishment. These views brought him and Port-Royal to the center of religious controversy in seventeenth-century France, as Jansenism came to be perceived as a subversive extension of Protestant reform.

Arnauld was also constantly engaged in philosophical disputation, and was regarded as one of the sharpest and most philosophically acute thinkers of his time. His influence on several major philosophers of the period resulted mainly from his penetrating criticism of their systems. In 1641, Arnauld was asked to comment on Descartes's *Meditations*. The objections he sent – regarding, among other topics, the representational nature of ideas, the circularity of Descartes's proofs for the existence of God, and the apparent irreconcilability of Descartes's conception of material substance with the Catholic doctrine of Eucharistic transubstantiation – were considered by Descartes to be the most intelligent and serious of all. Arnauld offered his objections in a constructive spirit, and soon became an enthusiastic defender of Descartes's philosophy, regarding it as beneficial both to the advancement of human learning and to Christian piety. He insists, for example, that the immortality of the soul is well grounded in Cartesian mind–body dualism.

In 1662, Arnauld composed (with Pierre Nicole) the *Port-Royal Logic,* an influential treatise on language and reasoning. After several decades of theological polemic, during which he fled France to the Netherlands, Arnauld resumed his public philosophical activities with the publication in 1683 of *On True and False Ideas* and in 1685 of *Philosophical and Theological Reflections on the New System of Nature and Grace.* These two works, opening salvos in what would become a long debate, constitute a detailed attack on Malebranche's theology and its philosophical foundations. In the first, mainly philosophical treatise, Arnauld insists that ideas, or the mental representations that mediate human knowledge, are nothing but acts of the mind that put us in direct cognitive and perceptual contact with things in the world. (Malebranche, as Arnauld reads him, argues that ideas are immaterial but nonmental objects in God's understanding that we know and perceive instead of physical things. Thus, the debate is often characterized as between Arnauld's direct realism and Malebranche's representative theory.) Such mental acts also have representational content, or what Arnauld (following Descartes) calls "objective reality." This content explains the act's intentionality, or directedness toward an object. Arnauld would later argue with Pierre Bayle, who came to Malebranche's defense, over whether *all* mental phenomena have intentionality, as Arnauld believes, or, as Bayle asserts, certain events in the soul (e.g., pleasures and pains) are non-intentional.

This initial critique of Malebranche's epistemology and philosophy of mind, however, was intended by Arnauld only as a prolegomenon to the more important attack on his theology; in particular, on Malebranche's claim that God always acts by general volitions and never by particular volitions. This view, Arnauld argues, undermines the true Catholic system of divine providence and threatens the efficacy of God's will by removing God from direct governance of the world.

In 1686, Arnauld also entered into discussions with Leibniz regarding the latter's *Discourse on Metaphysics*. In the ensuing correspondence, Arnauld focuses his critique on Leibniz's concept of substance and on his causal theory, the preestablished harmony. In this exchange, like the one with Malebranche, Arnauld is concerned to preserve what he takes to be the proper way to conceive of God's freedom and providence; although his remarks on substance (in which he objects to Leibniz's reintroduction of "substantial forms") is also clearly motivated by his commitment to a strict Cartesian ontology – bodies are nothing more than extension, devoid of any spiritual element. Most of his philosophical activity in the latter half of the century, in fact, is a vigorous defense of Cartesianism, particularly on theological grounds (e.g., demonstrating the consistency between Cartesian metaphysics and the Catholic dogma of real presence in the Eucharist), as it became the object of condemnation in both Catholic and Protestant circles.

See also BAYLE, DESCARTES, LEIBNIZ, MALEBRANCHE.   S.N.

Arouet, François-Marie. See VOLTAIRE.

a round. See Appendix of Special Symbols.

arrow paradox. See ZENO'S PARADOXES.

Arrow's paradox, also called Arrow's (impossibility) theorem, a major result in social choice theory, named for its discoverer, economist Kenneth Arrow. It is intuitive to suppose that the preferences of individuals in a society can be expressed formally, and then aggregated into an expression of social preferences, a social choice function. Arrow's paradox is that individual preferences having certain well-behaved formalizations demonstrably cannot be aggregated into a similarly well-behaved social choice function satisfying four plausible formal conditions: (1) collective rationality – any set of individual orderings and alternatives must yield a social ordering; (2) Pareto optimality – if all individuals prefer one ordering to another, the social ordering must also agree; (3) non-dictatorship – the social ordering must not be identical to a particular individual's ordering; and (4) independence of irrelevant alternatives – the social ordering depends on no properties of the individual orderings other than the orders themselves, and for a given set of alternatives it depends only on the orderings of those particular alternatives.

Most attempts to resolve the paradox have focused on aspects of (1) and (4). Some argue that preferences can be rational even if they are intransitive. Others argue that cardinal orderings, and hence, interpersonal comparisons of preference intensity, are relevant.

See also DECISION THEORY, SOCIAL CHOICE THEORY.   A.N.

Arrow's theorem. See ARROW'S PARADOX.

art, philosophy of. See AESTHETICS.

art, representational theory of. See MIMESIS.

artifactuality. See INSTITUTIONAL THEORY OF ART.

artificial intelligence, also called AI, the scientific effort to design and build intelligent artifacts. Since the effort inevitably presupposes and tests theories about the nature of intelligence, it has implications for the philosophy of mind – perhaps even more than does empirical psychology. For one thing, actual construction amounts to a direct assault on the mind–body problem; should it succeed, some form of materialism would seem to be vindicated. For another, a working model, even a limited one, requires a more global conception of what intelligence is than do experiments to test specific hypotheses. In fact, psychology's own overview of its domain has been much influenced by fundamental concepts drawn from AI.

Although the idea of an intelligent artifact is old, serious scientific research dates only from the 1950s, and is associated with the development of programmable computers. Intelligence is understood as a *structural property* or capacity of an active system; i.e., it does not matter what the system is made of, as long as its parts and their interactions yield intelligent behavior overall. For instance, if solving logical problems, playing chess, or conversing in English manifests intelligence, then it is not important whether the "implementation" is electronic, biological, or mechanical, just as long as it solves, plays, or talks. Computers are relevant mainly because of their flexibility and economy: software systems are unmatched in achievable active complexity per invested effort.

Despite the generality of programmable structures and the variety of historical approaches to the mind, the bulk of AI research divides into two broad camps – which we can think of as *language*-oriented and *pattern*-oriented, respectively. Conspicuous by their absence are significant influences from the conditioned-response paradigm, the psychoanalytic tradition, the mental picture idea, empiricist (atomistic) associationism, and so on. Moreover, both AI camps tend to focus on cognitive issues, sometimes including perception and motor control. Notably omitted are such psychologically important topics as affect, personality, aesthetic and moral judgment, conceptual change, mental illness, etc. Perhaps such matters are beyond the purview of artificial *intelligence;* yet it is an unobvious substantive thesis that intellect can be cordoned off and realized independently of the rest of human life.

The two main AI paradigms emerged together in the 1950s (along with cybernetic and information-theoretic approaches, which turned out to be dead ends); and both are vigorous today. But for most of the sixties and seventies, the language-based orientation dominated attention and funding, for three signal reasons. First, computer data structures and processes themselves seemed languagelike: data were syntactically and semantically articulated, and processing was localized (serial). Second, twentieth-century linguistics and logic made it intelligible that and how such systems might work: automatic symbol manipulation made clear, powerful sense. Finally, the sorts of performance most amenable to the approach – explicit reasoning and "figuring out" – strike both popular and educated opin-

ion as particularly "intellectual"; hence, early successes were all the more impressive, while "trivial" stumbling blocks were easier to ignore.

The basic idea of the linguistic or *symbol manipulation* camp is that thinking is like talking – inner discourse – and, hence, that thoughts are like sentences. The suggestion is venerable; and Hobbes even linked it explicitly to computation. Yet, it was a major scientific achievement to turn the general idea into a serious theory. The account does not apply only, or even especially, to the sort of thinking that is accessible to conscious reflection. Nor is the "language of thought" supposed to be much like English, predicate logic, LISP, or any other familiar notation; rather, its detailed character is an empirical research problem. And, despite fictional stereotypes, the aim is not to build superlogical or inhumanly rational automata. Our human tendencies to take things for granted, make intuitive leaps, and resist implausible conclusions are not weaknesses that AI strives to overcome but abilities integral to real intelligence that AI aspires to share.

In what sense, then, is thought supposed to be languagelike? Three items are essential. First, thought tokens have a combinatorial syntactic structure; i.e., they are compounds of well-defined atomic constituents in well-defined (recursively specifiable) arrangements. So the constituents are analogous to words, and the arrangements are analogous to phrases and sentences; but there is no supposition that they should resemble any known words or grammar. Second, the contents of thought tokens, what they "mean," are a systematic function of their composition: the constituents and forms of combination have determinate significances that together determine the content of any well-formed compound. So this is like the meaning of a sentence being determined by its grammar and the meanings of its words. Third, the intelligent progress or sequence of thought is specifiable by rules expressed syntactically – they can be carried out by processes sensitive only to syntactic properties. Here the analogy is to proof theory: the formal validity of an argument is a matter of its according with rules expressed formally. But this analogy is particularly treacherous, because it immediately suggests the rigor of logical inference; but, if intelligence is specifiable by formal rules, these must be far more permissive, context-sensitive, and so on, than those of formal logic.

Syntax as such is perfectly neutral as to how the constituents are identified (by sound, by shape, by magnetic profile) and arranged (in time, in space, via address pointers). It is, in effect, a free parameter: whatever can serve as a bridge between the semantics and the processing. The account shares with many others the assumptions that thoughts are contentful (meaningful) and that the processes in which they occur can somehow be realized physically. It is distinguished by the two further theses that there must be some independent way of describing these thoughts that mediates between (simultaneously determines) their contents and how they are processed, and that, so described, they are combinatorially structured. Such a description is *syntactical*.

We can distinguish two principal phases in language-oriented AI, each lasting about twenty years. Very roughly, the first phase emphasized processing (search and reasoning), whereas the second has emphasized representation (knowledge). To see how this went, it is important to appreciate the intellectual breakthrough required to conceive AI at all. A machine, such as a computer, is a deterministic system, except for random elements. That is fine for perfectly constrained domains, like numerical calculation, sorting, and parsing, or for domains that are constrained except for prescribed randomness, such as statistical modeling. But, in the general case, intelligent behavior is neither perfectly constrained nor perfectly constrained with a little random variation thrown in. Rather, it is generally focused and sensible, yet also fallible and somewhat variable. Consider, e.g., chess playing (an early test bed for AI): listing all the legal moves for any given position is a perfectly constrained problem, and easy to program; but choosing the best move is not. Yet an intelligent player does not simply determine which moves would be legal and then choose one randomly; intelligence in chess play is to choose, if not always the best, at least usually a good move. This is something between perfect determinacy and randomness, a "between" that is not simply a mixture of the two. How is it achievable in a machine?

The crucial innovation that first made AI concretely and realistically conceivable is that of a *heuristic procedure*. (The term 'heuristic' derives from the Greek word for discovery, as in Archimedes' exclamation "Eureka!") The relevant point for AI is that discovery is a matter neither of following exact directions to a goal nor of dumb luck, but of looking around sensibly, being guided as much as possible by what you know in advance and what you find along the way. So a heuristic procedure is one for sensible discovery, a procedure for sensibly guided search. In chess, e.g., a player does well to bear in mind a number of rules of thumb: other things being equal, rooks are more valuable than knights, it is an asset to control the center of the board, and so on. Such guidelines, of course, are not valid in every situation; nor will they all be best satisfied by the same move. But, by following them while searching as far ahead through various scenarios as possible, a player can make generally sensible moves – much better than random – within the constraints of the game. This picture even accords fairly well with the introspective feel of choosing a move, particularly for less experienced players.

The essential insight for AI is that such rough-and-ready (*ceteris paribus*) rules can be deterministically programmed. It all depends on how you look at it. One and the same bit of computer program can be, from one point of view, a deterministic, infallible procedure for computing how a given move would change the relative balance of pieces, and from another, a generally sensible but fallible procedure for estimating how "good" that move would be. The substantive thesis about intelligence – human and artificial alike – then is that our powerful but fallible ability to form "intuitive" hunches, educated guesses, etc., is the result of (largely unconscious) search, guided by such heuristic rules.

The second phase of language-inspired AI, dating roughly from the mid-1970s, builds on the idea of heuristic procedure, but dramatically changes the emphasis. The earlier work was framed by a conception of intelligence as *finding* solutions to problems (good moves, e.g.). From such a perspective, the specification of the problem (the rules of the game plus the current position) and the provision of some heuristic guides (domain-specific rules of thumb) are merely a setting of the parameters; the real work, the real exercise of intelligence, lies in the intensive guided search undertaken in the specified terms. The later phase, impressed not so much by our problem-solving prowess as by how well we get along with "simple" common sense, has shifted the emphasis from search and reasoning to knowledge.

The motivation for this shift can be seen in the following two sentences:

> We gave the monkey the banana because it was ripe.
> We gave the monkey the banana because it was hungry.

The word 'it' is ambiguous, as the terminal adjectives make clear. Yet listeners effortlessly understand what is meant, to the point, usually, of not even noticing the ambiguity. The question is, how? Of course, it is "just common sense" that monkeys don't get ripe and bananas don't get hungry, so . . . But three further observations show that this is not so much an answer as a restatement of the issue. First, sentences that rely on common sense to avoid misunderstanding are anything but rare: conversation is rife with them. Second, just about any odd fact that "everybody knows" can be the bit of common sense that understanding the next sentence depends on; and the range of such knowledge is vast. Yet, third, dialogue proceeds in real time without a hitch, almost always. So the whole range of commonsense knowledge must be somehow at our mental fingertips all the time.

The underlying difficulty is not with speed or quantity alone, but with *relevance*. How does a system, given all that it knows about aardvarks, Alabama, and ax handles, "home in on" the pertinent fact that bananas don't get hungry, in the fraction of a second it can afford to spend on the pronoun 'it'? The answer proposed is both simple and powerful: common sense is not just randomly stored information, but is instead highly organized by topics, with lots of indexes, cross-references, tables, hierarchies, and so on. The words in the sentence itself trigger the "articles" on monkeys, bananas, hunger, and so on, and these quickly reveal that monkeys are mammals, hence animals, that bananas are fruit, hence from plants, that hunger is what animals feel when they need to eat – and that settles it. The amount of search and reasoning is minimal; the issue of relevance is solved instead by the antecedent *structure* in the stored knowledge itself. While this requires larger and more elaborate systems, the hope is that it will make them faster and more flexible.

The other main orientation toward artificial intelligence, the pattern-based approach – often called "connectionism" or "parallel distributed processing" – reemerged from the shadow of symbol processing only in the 1980s, and remains in many ways less developed. The basic inspiration comes not from language or any other psychological phenomenon (such as imagery or affect), but from the microstructure of the brain. The components of a connectionist system are relatively simple active nodes – *lots* of them – and relatively simple connections between those nodes – again, *lots* of them. One important type (and the easiest to visualize) has the nodes divided into layers, such that each node in layer A is connected to each node in layer B, each node in layer B is connected to each node in layer C, and so on. Each node has an activation level, which varies in response to the activations of other, connected nodes; and each connection has a weight, which determines how strongly (and in what direction) the activation of one node affects that of the other. The analogy with neurons and synapses, though imprecise, is intended.

So imagine a layered network with finely tuned connection weights and random (or zero) activation levels. Now suppose the activations of all the nodes in layer A are set in some particular way – some pattern is imposed on the activation state of this layer. These activations will propagate out along all the connections from layer A to layer B, and activate some pattern there. The activation of *each* node in layer B is a function of the activations of *all* the nodes in layer A, and of the weights of all the connections to it from those nodes. But since each node in layer B has its own connections from the nodes in layer A, it will respond in its own unique way to this pattern of activations in layer A. Thus, the *pattern* that results in layer B is a joint function of the pattern that was imposed on layer A and of the pattern of connection weights between the two layers. And a similar story can be told about layer B's influence on layer C, and so on, until some final pattern is induced in the last layer.

What are these patterns? They might be any number of things; but two general possibilities can be distinguished. They might be tantamount to (or substrata beneath) representations of some familiar sort, such as sentencelike structures or images; or they might be a kind (or kinds) of representation previously unknown. Now, people certainly do sometimes think in sentences (and probably images); so, to the extent that networks are taken as complete brain models, the first alternative must be at least partly right. But, to that extent, the models are also more physiological than psychological: it is rather the implemented sentences or images that directly model the mind. Thus, it is the possibility of a new genus of representation – sometimes called *distributed* representation – that is particularly exciting. On this alternative, the patterns in the mind represent in some way other than by mimetic imagery or articulate description. How?

An important feature of all network models is that there are two quite different categories of pattern. On the one hand, there are the relatively ephemeral patterns of activation in various groups of nodes; on the other, there are the relatively stable patterns of connection strength among the nodes. Since there are in general many more connections than nodes, the latter patterns are richer; and it is they that determine the capabilities of the network with regard to the former patterns. Many of the abilities most easily and "naturally" realized in networks can be subsumed under the heading *pattern completion:* the connection weights are adjusted – perhaps via a training regime – such that the network will *complete* any of the activation patterns from a predetermined group. So, suppose some fraction (say half) of the nodes in the net are clamped to the values they would have for one of those patterns (say P) while the remainder are given random (or default) activations. Then the network, when run, will reset the latter activations to the values belonging to P – thus "completing" it. If the unclamped activations are regarded as variations or deviations, pattern completion amounts to *normalization,* or grouping by *similarity.* If the initial or input nodes are always the same (as in layered networks), then we have pattern *association* (or transformation) from input to output. If the input pattern is a memory probe, pattern completion becomes access by *content.* If the output pattern is an identifier, then it is pattern *recognition.* And so on. Note that, although the operands are activation patterns, the "knowledge" about them, the ability to complete them, is contained in the connection patterns; hence, that ability or know-how is what the network represents.

There is no obvious upper bound on the possible refinement or intricacy of these pattern groupings and associations. If the input patterns are sensory stimuli and the output patterns are motor control, then we have a potential model of coordinated and even skillful behavior. In a system *also* capable of language, a network model (or component) might account for verbal recognition and content association, and even such "nonliteral" effects as trope and tone. Yet at least some sort of "symbol manipulation" seems essential for language use, regardless of how networklike the implementation is. One current speculation is that it might suffice to approximate a battery of symbolic processes as a special subsystem within a cognitive system that fundamentally works on quite different principles.

The attraction of the pattern-based approach is, at this point, not so much actual achievement as it is promise – on two grounds. In the first place, the space of possible models, not only network topologies but also ways of construing the patterns, is vast. Those built and tested so far have been, for practical reasons, rather small; so it is possible to hope beyond their present limitations to systems of significantly greater capability. But second, and perhaps even more attractive, those directions in which pattern-based systems show the most promise – skills, recognition, similarity, and the like – are among the areas of greatest frustration for language-based AI. Hence it remains possible, for a while at least, to overlook the fact that, to date, no connectionist network can perform long division, let alone play chess or solve symbolic logic problems.

See also COGNITIVE SCIENCE, COMPUTER THEORY, CONNECTIONISM, FORMAL LOGIC, GRAMMAR, PHILOSOPHY OF LANGUAGE, PHILOSOPHY OF MIND.   J.Hau.

artificial language. See FORMAL LANGUAGE, PHILOSOPHY OF LANGUAGE.

artificial life, an interdisciplinary science studying the most general character of the fundamental processes of life. These processes include self-organization, self-reproduction, learning, adaptation, and evolution. Artificial life (or ALife) is to theoretical biology roughly what artificial intelligence (AI) is to theoretical psychology – computer simulation is the methodology of choice. In fact, since the mind exhibits many of life's fundamental properties, AI could be considered a subfield of ALife. However, whereas most traditional AI models are serial systems with complicated, centralized controllers making decisions based on global state information, most natural systems exhibiting complex autonomous behavior are parallel, distributed networks of simple entities making decisions based solely on their local state information, so typical ALife models have a corresponding distributed architecture.

A computer simulation of evolving "bugs" can illustrate what ALife models are like. Moving around in a two-dimensional world periodically laden with heaps of "food," these bugs eat, reproduce, and sometimes perish from starvation. Each bug's movement is genetically determined by the quantities of food in its immediate neighborhood, and random mutations and crossovers modify these genomes during reproduction. Simulations started with random genes show spontaneous waves of highly adaptive genetic novelties continuously sweeping through the population at precisely quantifiable rates. See C. Langston et al., eds., *Artificial Life II* (1991).

ALife science raises and promises to inform many philosophical issues, such as: Is functionalism the right approach toward life? When, if ever, is a *simulation* of life *really alive?* When do systems exhibit the spontaneous emergence of properties?

See also ARTIFICIAL INTELLIGENCE, COMPUTER THEORY, CONNECTIONISM, FUNCTIONALISM.   M.A.B.

ascriptivism, the theory that to call an action voluntary is not to describe it as caused in a certain way by the agent who did it, but to express a commitment to hold the agent responsible for the action. Ascriptivism is thus a kind of noncognitivism as applied to judgments about the voluntariness of acts. Introduced by Hart in "Ascription of Rights and Responsibilities," *Proceedings of the Aristotelian Society* (1949), ascriptivism was given its name and attacked in Geach's "Ascriptivism," *Philosophical Review* (1960). Hart recanted in the Preface to his *Punishment and Responsibility* (1968). **See also** DESCRIPTIVISM.   B.W.H.

a se. See ENS A SE.

aseity. See DIVINE ATTRIBUTES, ENS A SE.

A-series. See TIME.

Aspasius. See COMMENTARIES ON ARISTOTLE.

aspectual action paradox. See DEONTIC PARADOXES.

assent, notional. See NEWMAN.

assent, real. See NEWMAN.

assertability, warranted. See DEWEY.

assertability conditions. See MEANING.

assertion. See PROPOSITION.

assertion sign. See Appendix of Special Symbols.

assertoric. See MODALITY.

assisted suicide. See BIOETHICS.

associationism, the psychological doctrine that association is the sole or primary basis of learning as well as of intelligent thought and behavior. Association occurs when one type of thought, idea, or behavior follows, or is contin-

gent upon, another thought, idea, or behavior or external event, and the second somehow bonds with the first. If the idea of eggs is paired with the idea of ham, then the two ideas may become associated. Associationists argue that complex states of mind and mental processes can be analyzed into associated elements. The complex may be novel, but the elements are products of past associations. Associationism often is combined with hedonism. Hedonism explains why events associate or bond: bonds are forged by pleasant experiences. If the pleasantness of eating eggs is combined with the pleasantness of eating ham, then ideas of ham and eggs associate. Bonding may also be explained by various non-hedonistic principles of association, as in Hume's theory of the association of ideas. One of these principles is contiguity in place or time.

Associationism contributes to the componential analysis of intelligent, rational activity into non-intelligent, non-rational, mechanical processes. People believe as they do, not because of rational connections among beliefs, but because beliefs associatively bond. Thus one may think of London when thinking of England, not because one possesses an inner logic of geographic beliefs from which one infers that London is in England. The two thoughts may co-occur because of contiguity or other principles.

Kinds of associationism occur in behaviorist models of classical and operant conditioning. Certain associationist ideas, if not associationism itself, appear in connectionist models of cognition, especially the principle that contiguities breed bonding.

Several philosophers and psychologists, including Hume, Hartley, and J. S. Mill among philosophers and E. L. Thorndike (1874–1949) and B. F. Skinner (1904–90) among psychologists, are associationists.

See also CONNECTIONISM; HARTLEY; HEDONISM; HUME; MILL, J. S.   G.A.G.

association of ideas. See ASSOCIATIONISM.

Astell, Mary (1666–1731), an early English feminist and author of *A Serious Proposal to the Ladies* (1694 and 1697) and *Some Reflections on Marriage* (1700). These works argue that women's shortcomings are not due to a lack of intellectual ability, since women have rational souls, and present an educational program to fit them rationally for their religious duties. Astell entered as well into the philosophical, theological, and political controversies of her day. Her *Letters Concerning the Love of God* (1695) is a correspondence with the

English Malebranchian, John Norris, over such issues as Norris's contention that our duty is to God only. Her most substantial work, *The Christian Religion, as Professed by a Daughter of the Church of England* (1705), lays out her views on the grounds and implications of natural and revealed religion. This work includes considerable critical attention to John Locke's ideas, and both this and the *Letters* called forth refutations from Locke's friend, Damaris Cudworth. **See also** CUDWORTH, DAMARIS; FEMINIST PHILOSOPHY; MALEBRANCHE.   M.At.

asymmetrical. See RELATION.

ataraxia. See EPICUREANISM, SEXTUS EMPIRICUS, SKEPTICS.

Athanasius (c.297–373), early Christian father, bishop in Alexandria (though frequently exiled), and a leading protagonist in the fourth-century disputes concerning Christ's relationship to God. Through major works like *On the Incarnation, Against the Arians,* and *Letters on the Holy Spirit,* Athanasius contributed greatly to the classical doctrines of the Incarnation and the Trinity. Opposing all forms of Arianism, which denied Christ's divinity and reduced him to a creature, Athanasius taught, in the language of the Nicene Creed, that Christ the Son, and likewise the Holy Spirit, were of the same being as God the Father (*homoousios*). Thus with terminology and concepts drawn from Greek philosophy, he helped to forge the distinctly Christian and un-Hellenistic doctrine of the eternal triune God, who became enfleshed in time and matter and restored humanity to immortality, forfeited through sin, by involvement in its condition of corruption and decay. **See also** ARIANISM.   A.E.L.

atheism (from Greek *a-,* 'not', and *theos,* 'god'), the view that there are no gods. A widely used sense denotes merely not believing in God and is consistent with agnosticism. A stricter sense denotes a belief that there is no God; this use has become the standard one. In the *Apology* Socrates is accused of atheism for not believing in the official Athenian gods. Some distinguish between *theoretical atheism* and *practical atheism.* A theoretical atheist is one who self-consciously denies the existence of a supreme being, whereas a practical atheist may believe that a supreme being exists but lives as though there were no god.   L.P.P.

Atheismusstreit. See FICHTE.

Athenian Academy. See DAMASCIUS.

Athenian School. See MIDDLE PLATONISM.

A-theory of time. See TIME.

Ātman, in Hindu thought, the individual, viewed by Advaita Vedanta as numerically identical to, and by other varieties of Vedanta as dependent on and capable of worship of, Brahman. Sometimes in Hinduism conceived as inherently conscious and possessed of intrinsic mental qualities, and sometimes viewed as having mental qualities only in the sense that the composite of *Ātman-embodied-in-a-physical-body* has this feature, *Ātman* beginninglessly transmigrates from life to life (or, for Advaita, appears to do so). It is embodied in successive bodies, accumulating karma and possibly achieving enlightenment with its consequent release from *saṃsāra,* the transmigratory wheel.   K.E.Y.

atomism, ancient. See ANCIENT ATOMISM.

atomism, logical. See RUSSELL.

atomism, semantic. See SEMANTIC HOLISM.

Atticus. See COMMENTARIES ON PLATO, MIDDLE PLATONISM.

attitude, phenomenological. See HUSSERL.

attitude, practical. See PRACTICAL REASONING.

attitude, propositional. See PROPOSITION, PHILOSOPHY OF MIND.

attitude, reactive. See STRAWSON.

attribute. See PROPERTY.

attribution theory, a theory in social psychology concerned with how and why ordinary people explain events. People explain by attributing causal powers to certain events rather than others. The theory attempts to describe and clarify everyday commonsense explanation, to identify criteria of explanatory success presupposed by common sense, and to compare and contrast commonsense explanation with scientific explanation. The heart of attribution theory is the thesis that people tend to attribute causal power to factors personally important to them, which they believe covary with alleged effects. For example, a woman may designate sexual discrimination as the cause of her not being promoted in a corporation. Being female is important to her and she believes that promotion and failure covary with gender. Males get promoted; females don't. Causal attributions tend to preserve self-esteem, reduce cognitive dissonance, and diminish the attributor's personal responsibility for misdeeds. When attributional styles or habits contribute to emotional ill-being, e.g. to chronic, inappropriate feelings of depression or guilt, attribution theory offers the following therapeutic recommendation: change attributions so as to reduce emotional ill-being and increase well-being. Hence if the woman blames herself for the failure, and if self-blame is part of her depressive attributional style, she would be encouraged to look outside herself, perhaps to sexual discrimination, for the explanation. **See also** EXPLANATION, MOTIVATIONAL EXPLANATION.   G.A.G.

attributive pluralism. See PLURALISM.

attributive use of descriptions. See THEORY OF DESCRIPTIONS.

Augustine, Saint, known as Augustine of Hippo (354–430), Christian philosopher and church father, one of the chief sources of Christian thought in the West; his importance for medieval and modern European philosophy is impossible to describe briefly or ever to circumscribe. Matters are made more difficult because Augustine wrote voluminously and dialectically as a Christian theologian, treating philosophical topics for the most part only as they were helpful to theology – or as corrected by it.

Augustine fashioned the narrative of the *Confessions* (397–400) out of the events of the first half of his life. He thus supplied later biographers with both a seductive selection of biographical detail and a compelling story of his successive conversions from adolescent sensuality, to the image-laden religion of the Manichaeans, to a version of Neoplatonism, and then to Christianity. The story is an unexcelled introduction to Augustine's views of philosophy. It shows, for instance, that Augustine received very little formal education in philosophy. He was trained as a rhetorician, and the only philosophical work that he mentions among his early reading is Cicero's (lost) *Hortensius,* an exercise in persuasion to the study of philosophy. Again, the narrative makes plain that Augustine finally rejected Manichaeanism because he came to see it as bad philosophy: a set of sophistical fantasies without rational coherence or explanatory force. More importantly, Augustine's final conversion to Christianity was prepared by his reading in "certain books of the Platonists" (*Confessions* 7.9.13). These Latin translations, which seem to have been anthologies or manuals of philosophic teaching, taught Augustine a form of Neoplatonism that enabled him to conceive of a cosmic hierarchy descending from an immaterial, eternal, and intelligible God. On Augustine's judgment, philosophy could do no more than that; it could not give him the power to order his own life so as to live happily and in a stable relation with the now-discovered God. Yet in his first years as a Christian, Augustine took time to write a number of works in philosophical genres. Best known among them are a refutation of Academic Skepticism (*Contra academicos,* 386), a theodicy (*De ordine,* 386), and a dialogue on the place of human choice within the providentially ordered hierarchy created by God (*De libero arbitrio,* 388/391–95).

Within the decade of his conversion, Augustine was drafted into the priesthood (391) and then consecrated bishop (395). The thirty-five years of his life after that consecration were consumed by labors on behalf of the church in northern Africa and through the Latin-speaking portions of the increasingly fragmented empire. Most of Augustine's episcopal writing was polemical both in origin and in form; he composed against authors or movements he judged heretical, especially the Donatists and Pelagians. But Augustine's sense of his authorship also led him to write works of fundamental theology conceived on a grand scale.

The most famous of these works, beyond the *Confessions,* are *On the Trinity* (399–412, 420), *On Genesis according to the Letter* (401–15), and *On the City of God* (413–26). *On the Trinity* elaborates in subtle detail the distinguishable "traces" of Father, Son, and Spirit in the created world and particularly in the human soul's triad of memory, intellect, and will. The commentary on Genesis 1–3, which is meant to be much more than a "literal" commentary in the modern sense, treats many topics in philosophical psychology and anthropology. It also teaches such cosmological doctrines as the "seed-reasons" (*rationes seminales*) by which creatures are given intelligible form. The *City of God* begins with a critique of the bankruptcy of pagan civic religion and its attendant philosophies, but it ends with the depiction of human history as a combat between forces of self-love, conceived as a diabolic city of earth, and the graced love of God, which founds that heavenly city within which alone peace is possible.

A number of other, discrete doctrines have been attached to Augustine, usually without the dialectical nuances he would have considered indispensable. One such doctrine concerns divine "illumination" of the human intellect, i.e., some active intervention by God in ordinary processes of human understanding. Another doctrine typically attributed to Augustine is the inability of the human will to do morally good actions without grace. A more authentically Augustinian teaching is that introspection or inwardness is the way of discovering the created hierarchies by which to ascend to God. Another authentic teaching would be that time, which is a distension of the divine "now," serves as the medium or narrative structure for the creation's return to God. But no list of doctrines or positions, however authentic or inauthentic, can serve as a faithful representation of Augustine's thought, which gives itself only through the carefully wrought rhetorical forms of his texts.

See also NEOPLATONISM, PATRISTIC AUTHORS, PHILOSOPHY OF RELIGION.   M.D.J.

Aurelius, Marcus. See MARCUS AURELIUS, STOICISM.

Austin, John (1790–1859), English legal philosopher known especially for his command theory of law. His career as a lawyer was unsuccessful but his reputation as a scholar was such that on the founding of University College, London, he was offered the chair of jurisprudence. In 1832 he published the first ten of his lectures, compressed into six as *The Province of Jurisprudence Determined.* Although he published a few papers, and his somewhat fragmentary *Lectures on Jurisprudence* (1863) was published posthumously, it is on the *Province* that his reputation rests. He and Bentham (his friend, London neighbor, and fellow utilitarian) were the foremost English legal philosophers of their time, and their influence on the course of legal philosophy endures.

Austin held that the first task of legal philosophy, one to which he bends most of his energy, is to make clear what laws are, and if possible to explain why they are what they are: their rationale. Until those matters are clear, legislative proposals and legal arguments can never be clear, since irrelevant considerations will inevitably creep in. The proper place for moral or theological considerations is in discussion of what the positive law ought to be, not of what it is. Theological considerations reduce to moral ones, since God can be assumed to be a good utilitarian. It is positive laws, "that is to say the laws which are

simply and strictly so called, . . . which form the appropriate matter of general and particular jurisprudence." They must also be distinguished from "laws metaphorical or figurative."

A *law in its most general sense* is "a rule laid down for the guidance of an intelligent being by an intelligent being having power over him." It is a command, however phrased. It is the commands of men to men, of political superiors, that form the body of positive law. General or comparative jurisprudence, the source of the rationale, if any, of particular laws, is possible because there are commands nearly universal that may be attributed to God or Nature, but they become positive law only when laid down by a ruler. The general model of an Austinian analytic jurisprudence built upon a framework of definitions has been widely followed, but cogent objections, especially by Hart, have undermined the command theory of law.

See also JURISPRUDENCE, PHILOSOPHY OF LAW.   E.L.P.

Austin, J(ohn) L(angshaw) (1911–60), English philosopher, a leading exponent of postwar "linguistic" philosophy. Educated primarily as a classicist at Shrewsbury and Balliol College, Oxford, he taught philosophy at Magdalen College. During World War II he served at a high level in military intelligence, which earned him the O.B.E., Croix de Guerre, and Legion of Merit. In 1952 he became White's Professor of Moral Philosophy at Oxford, and in 1955 and 1958 he held visiting appointments at Harvard and Berkeley, respectively. In his relatively brief career, Austin published only a few invited papers; his influence was exerted mainly through discussion with his colleagues, whom he dominated more by critical intelligence than by any preconceived view of what philosophy should be.

Unlike some others, Austin did not believe that philosophical problems all arise out of aberrations from "ordinary language," nor did he necessarily find solutions there; he dwelt, rather, on the authority of the vernacular as a source of nice and pregnant distinctions, and held that it deserves much closer attention than it commonly receives from philosophers. It is useless, he thought, to pontificate at large about knowledge, reality, or existence, for example, without first examining in detail how, and when, the words 'know', 'real', and 'exist' are employed in daily life. In *Sense and Sensibilia* (1962; compiled from lecture notes), the sense-datum theory comes under withering fire for its failings in this respect. Austin also provoked controversy with his well-known distinction between "performative" and "constative" utterances ('I promise' *makes* a promise, whereas 'he promised' merely reports one); he later recast this as a threefold differentiation of locutionary, illocutionary, and perlocutionary "forces" in utterance, corresponding (roughly) to the meaning, intention, and consequences of saying a thing, in one context or another. Though never very stable or fully worked out, these ideas have since found a place in the still-evolving study of speech acts. **See also** ORDINARY LANGUAGE PHILOSOPHY, SPEECH ACT THEORY.   P.He.

Australian materialism. See SMART.

autarkia, ancient Greek term meaning 'self-sufficiency'. *Autarkia* was widely regarded as a mark of the human good, happiness (*eudaimonia*). A life is self-sufficient when it is worthy of choice and lacks nothing. What makes a life self-sufficient – and thereby happy – was a matter of controversy. Stoics maintained that the mere possession of virtue would suffice; Aristotle and the Peripatetics insisted that virtue must be exercised and even, perhaps, accompanied by material goods. There was also a debate among later Greek thinkers over whether a self-sufficient life is solitary or whether only life in a community can be self-sufficient. **See also** ARISTOTLE, STOICISM.   E.C.H.

authenticity. See EXISTENTIALISM, HEIDEGGER.

autological. See SEMANTIC PARADOXES.

automata theory. See COMPUTER THEORY, SELF-REPRODUCING AUTOMATON.

automatism, conscious. See PHILOSOPHY OF MIND.

automaton. See COMPUTER THEORY, SELF-REPRODUCING AUTOMATON.

automaton, cellular. See SELF-REPRODUCING AUTOMATON.

automaton, finite. See COMPUTER THEORY, TURING MACHINE.

automaton, self-reproducing. See SELF-REPRODUCING AUTOMATON.

autonomy. See FREE WILL PROBLEM, KANT, POSITIVE AND NEGATIVE FREEDOM.

autonomy of biology. See UNITY OF SCIENCE.

autonomy of ethics. See ETHICS.

autonomy of psychology. See PHILOSOPHY OF PSYCHOLOGY.

avatar (from Sanskrit *avatāra*), in Hindu thought, any of the repeated "descents" of the Supreme Being into the physical world as an animal, human being, or combination thereof, to destroy evil and restore order. Predominately identified as the actions of the god Vishnu, these entrances into the world indicate that Vishnu as lord will adjust the cycle of karma. Its earliest reference is in the Bhagavad Gita (150 B.C.), where Krishna says that whenever dharma languishes he incarnates in age after age to destroy evildoers and promote the good. Later lists of avatars of Vishnu cite ten, twenty, or more, with Krishna and the Buddha as famous examples. The inclusion of prominent local deities in the list brought them under the influence of Vishnu devotees, and today even Jesus and Muhammad may be included. Modern philosophers such as Radhakrishnan (1888–1975) redefine the concept non-theistically, identifying an avatar as a human being who has attained enlightenment.   R.N.Mi.

Avempace. See IBN BĀJJA.

Avenarius, Richard (1843–96), German philosopher. He was born in Paris and educated at the University of Leipzig. He became a professor at Leipzig and succeeded Windelband at the University of Zürich in 1877. For a time he was editor of the *Zeitschrift für wissenschaftliche Philosophie*. His earliest work was *Über die beiden ersten Phasen des Spinozischen Pantheismus* (1868). His major work, *Kritik der reinen Erfahrung* (*Critique of Pure Experience,* 2 vols., 1888–90), was followed by his last study, *Der menschliche Weltbegriff* (1891).

In his post-Kantian *Kritik* Avenarius presented a radical positivism that sought to base philosophy on scientific principles. This "empirio-criticism" emphasized "pure experience" and descriptive and general definitions of experience. Metaphysical claims to transcend experience were rejected as mere creations of the mind. Like Hume, Avenarius denied the ontological validity of substance and causality. Seeking a scientific empiricism, he endeavored to delineate a descriptive determination of the form and content of pure experience. He thought that the subject–object dichotomy, the separation of inner and outer experiences, falsified reality. If we could avoid "introjecting" feeling, thought, and will into experience (and thereby splitting it into subject and object), we could attain the original "natural" view of the world.

Although Avenarius, in his *Critique of Pure Experience,* thought that changes in brain states parallel states of consciousness, he did not reduce sensations or states of consciousness to physiological changes in the brain. Because his theory of pure experience undermined dogmatic materialism, Lenin attacked his philosophy in *Materialism and Empirio-Criticism* (1952). His epistemology influenced Mach and his emphasis upon pure experience had considerable influence on James.

See also SUBJECT–OBJECT DICHOTOMY.
G.J.S.

Averroes, in Arabic, Ibn Rushd (1126–98), Islamic philosopher, jurist, and physician. Scion of a long line of *qāḍīs* (religious judges), he was born at Córdova and educated in Islamic law. Introduced to the Almohad ruler by Ibn Ṭufayl, author of the philosophical allegory *Ḥayy Ibn Yaqẓān,* he feigned ignorance of philosophy, only to learn that the leader of the dynasty so feared for its orthodoxy was thoroughly at home with philosophical issues. He was given a robe of honor and a mount and later invited to write his famous commentaries on Aristotle and made *qāḍī* of Seville, finally succeeding Ibn Ṭufayl as royal physician and becoming chief *qāḍī* of Córdova. He was persecuted when the sultan's successor needed orthodox support in his war with Christian Spain, but died in the calm of Marrakesh, the edicts against him rescinded.

His works, most often preserved in Hebrew or Latin translations ('Averroes' reflects efforts to Latinize 'Ibn Rushd'), include medical and astronomical writings; short, middle, and long commentaries on Aristotle ("his was the ultimate human mind"); a commentary on Plato's *Republic;* and spirited juridical and conceptual defenses of philosophy: *The Decisive Treatise* and *Incoherence of the Incoherence.* The former argues that philosophy, although restricted to the adept, is *mandated* by the Koranic (59:2) injunction to reflect on God's design. The latter answers al-Ghazālī's *Incoherence of the Philosophers,* defending naturalism and its presumed corollary, the world's eternity, but often cutting adrift the more Platonizing and original doctrines of Avicenna, al-Ghazālī's chief stalking horse. Thus Averroes rejects Avicenna's idea that the world itself is con-

tingent if it is necessitated by its causes, arguing that removing the necessity that is the hallmark of God's wisdom would leave us no way of inferring a wise Author of nature. Ultimately Averroes rejects emanation and seeks to return natural theology to the physics of matter and motion, discrediting Avicenna's metaphysical approach and locating God's act in the ordering of eternal matter. On bodily resurrection, individual providence, and miracles, he takes refuge in authority, fudge, and bluff; and even his defense of causal necessity smacks of a dogmatism expressive of the awkwardness of his position and the stiffening of Peripatetic thought. Yet he retains the idea that the intellect is immortal, indeed impersonal: since only matter differentiates individuals, all minds are ultimately one; they reach fulfillment and beatitude by making contact (*ittiṣāl;* cf. Plotinus's *aphe*) with the Active Intellect.

Many Jewish philosophers like Narboni and Albalag followed Averroes' arguments explicitly, reinterpreting Maimonides accordingly. But Averroes' efforts to accommodate rhetorical and dialectical along with philosophical discourse led to the branding of his Christian followers as exponents of a "double truth," although no text advances such a doctrine. Siger of Brabant, Boethius of Dacia, and Bernier of Nivelles were condemned for Averroistic heresies at Paris in the 1270s. But from the thirteenth to mid-seventeenth centuries Latin scholars regularly read Aristotle with Averroes' commentaries. His philosophic respondents include Ibn Taymiyya (d.1327), Gersonides, Albertus Magnus, and Aquinas. Spinoza's dogged eternalism links him vividly to Averroes.

See also ARABIC PHILOSOPHY.   L.E.G.

aversion therapy. See BEHAVIOR THERAPY.

Avicebron. See IBN GABIROL.

Avicenna, in Arabic, Ibn Sīnā (980–1037), Islamic philosopher and physician. Born near Bukhara, where his father served as a provincial governor, Avicenna came to manhood as the Persian Samanid dynasty was crumbling and spent much of his life fleeing from court to court to avoid the clutches of the rapacious conqueror Maḥmūd of Ghazna. His autobiography describes him as an intuitive student of philosophy and other Greek sciences who could not see the point of Aristotle's *Metaphysics,* until he read a tiny essay by al-Fārābī (870–950), who showed him what it means to seek the nature of being as such.

It was in metaphysics that Avicenna made his greatest contributions to philosophy, brilliantly synthesizing the rival approaches of the Aristotelian-Neoplatonic tradition with the creationist monotheism of Islamic dialectical theology (*kalām*). Where Aristotle sought and found being in its fullest sense in what was changeless in its nature (above all, in the species of things, the heavenly bodies, the cosmos as a whole), *kalām* understood being as the immediately given, allowing no inference beyond a single contingent datum to any necessary properties, correlatives, continuators, or successors. The result was a stringent atomist occasionalism resting ultimately on an early version of logical atomism. Avicenna preserved an Aristotelian naturalism alongside the Scriptural idea of the contingency of the world by arguing that any finite being is contingent in itself but necessary in relation to its causes. He adapted al-Fārābī's Neoplatonic emanationism to this schematization and naturalized in philosophy his own distinctive version of the *kalām* argument from contingency: any being must be either necessary or contingent, but if contingent, it requires a cause; since no infinite causal regress is possible, there must be a Necessary Being, which is therefore simple, the ultimate cause of all other things.

Avicenna found refuge at the court of one 'Alā al-Dawla, who bravely resisted the military pressures of Maḥmūd against his lands around Isfahan and made the philosopher and savant his vizier. Here Avicenna completed his famous philosophic work the *Shifā'* (known in Latin as the *Sufficientia*) and his *Qānūn fī Ṭibb*, the Galenic *Canon*, which remained in use as a medical textbook until finally brought down by the weight of criticisms during the Renaissance. Avicenna's philosophy was the central target of the polemical critique of the Muslim theologian al-Ghazālī (1058–1111) in his *Incoherence of the Philosophers*, mainly on the grounds that the philosopher's retention of the Aristotelian doctrine of the eternity of the world was inconsistent with his claim that God was the author of the world. Avicenna's related affirmations of the necessity of causation and universality of God's knowledge, al-Ghazālī argued, made miracles impossible and divine governance too impersonal to deserve the name. Yet Avicenna's philosophic works (numbering over a hundred in their Arabic and sometimes Persian originals) continued to exercise a major influence on Muslim and Jewish philosophers and (through Latin translations) on philosophers in the West.

See also ARABIC PHILOSOPHY.   L.E.G.

avidya, Sanskrit word meaning 'ignorance', 'lack of wisdom'. *Avidya* is a key concept in India's philosophical systems, which attempted to explain the reasons for karmic bondage leading to suffering and release from such bondage through spiritual liberation. The general idea was that karmic fetters arise because of *avidya*, which is ignorance of the true nature of reality. When wisdom dispels *avidya*, the individual is freed from bondage. There was intense speculation in Indian philosophy regarding the nature and the metaphysical status of *avidya*. If *avidya* causes bondage that traps the individual in the transmigratory cycle of life and death (*saṁsāra*), then where does *avidya* reside and how does it come into being?   D.K.C.

awareness, consciousness, a central feature of our lives that is notoriously difficult to characterize. You experience goings-on in the world, and, turning inward ("introspecting"), you experience your experiencing. Objects of awareness can be external or internal. Pressing your finger on the edge of a table, you can be aware of the table's edge, and aware of the feeling of pressure (though perhaps not simultaneously).

Philosophers from Locke to Nagel have insisted that our experiences have distinctive qualities: there is "something it is like" to have them. It would seem important, then, to distinguish qualities of objects of which you are aware from qualities of your awareness. Suppose you are aware of a round, red tomato. The tomato, but not your awareness, is round and red. What then are the qualities of your awareness? Here we encounter a deep puzzle that divides theorists into intransigent camps.

Some materialists, like Dennett, insist that awareness lacks qualities (or lacks qualities distinct from its objects: the qualities we attribute to experiences are really those of experienced objects). This opens the way to a dismissal of "phenomenal" qualities (qualia), qualities that seem to have no place in the material world. Others (T. Nagel, Ned Block) regard such qualities as patently genuine, preferring to dismiss any theory unable to accommodate them. Convinced that the qualities of awareness are ineliminable and irreducible to respectable material properties, some philosophers, following Frank Jackson, contend they are "epiphenomenal": real but causally inefficacious. Still others, including Searle, point to what they regard as a fundamental distinction between the "intrinsically subjective" character of awareness and the "objective," "public" character of material objects, but deny that this yields epiphenomenalism.

See also PHENOMENOLOGY, PHILOSOPHY OF MIND, QUALIA.   J.F.H.

axiology. See VALUE THEORY.

axiom. See AXIOMATIC METHOD.

axiomatic method, originally, a method for reorganizing the accepted propositions and concepts of an existent science in order to increase certainty in the propositions and clarity in the concepts. Application of this method was thought to require the identification of (1) the "universe of discourse" (domain, genus) of entities constituting the primary subject matter of the science, (2) the "primitive concepts" that can be grasped immediately without the use of definition, (3) the "primitive propositions" (or "axioms"), whose truth is knowable immediately, without the use of deduction, (4) an immediately acceptable "primitive definition" in terms of primitive concepts for each non-primitive concept, and (5) a deduction (constructed by chaining immediate, logically cogent inferences ultimately from primitive propositions and definitions) for each non-primitive accepted proposition. Prominent proponents of more or less modernized versions of the axiomatic method, e.g. Pascal, Nicod (1893–1924), and Tarski, emphasizing the critical and regulatory function of the axiomatic method, explicitly open the possibility that axiomatization of an existent, preaxiomatic science may lead to rejection or modification of propositions, concepts, and argumentations that had previously been accepted.

In many cases attempts to realize the ideal of an axiomatic science have resulted in discovery of "smuggled premises" and other previously unnoted presuppositions, leading in turn to recognition of the need for new axioms. Modern axiomatizations of geometry are much richer in detail than those produced in ancient Greece. The earliest extant axiomatic text is based on an axiomatization of geometry due to Euclid (fl. 300 B.C.), which itself was based on earlier, no-longer-extant texts. Archimedes (287–212 B.C.) was one of the earliest of a succession of post-Euclidean geometers, including Hilbert, Oswald Veblen (1880–1960), and Tarski, to propose modifications of axiomatizations of classical geometry. The traditional axiomatic method, often called the geometric method, made several presuppositions no longer widely accepted. The advent of non-Euclidean geometry was particularly important in this connection.

For some workers, the goal of reorganizing an existent science was joined to or replaced by a new goal: characterizing or giving implicit definition to the structure of the subject matter of the science. Moreover, subsequent innovations in logic and foundations of mathematics, especially development of syntactically precise formalized languages and effective systems of formal deductions, have substantially increased the degree of rigor attainable. In particular, critical axiomatic exposition of a body of scientific knowledge is now not thought to be fully adequate, however successful it may be in realizing the goals of the original axiomatic method, so long as it does not present the underlying logic (including language, semantics, and deduction system). For these and other reasons the expression 'axiomatic method' has undergone many "redefinitions," some of which have only the most tenuous connection with the original meaning.

See also CATEGORICITY, DEDUCTION, FORMALIZATION.   J.Cor.

axiomatic system. See AXIOMATIC METHOD, DEDUCTION.

axiom of abstraction. See AXIOM OF COMPREHENSION.

axiom of choice. See LÖWENHEIM-SKOLEM THEOREM, SET THEORY.

axiom of comprehension, also called axiom of abstraction, the axiom that for every property, there is a corresponding set of things having that property; i.e., $(\phi)\,(\exists A)\,(x)\,(x \in A \equiv \phi x)$, where ϕ is a property and A is a set. The axiom was used in Frege's formulation of set theory and is the axiom that yields Russell's paradox, discovered in 1901. If ϕx is instantiated as $x \notin x$, then the result that $A \in A \equiv A \notin A$ is easily obtained, which yields, in classical logic, the explicit contradiction $A \in A \,\&\, A \notin A$. The paradox can be avoided by modifying the comprehension axiom and using instead the separation axiom, $(\phi)\,(\exists A)$ $(x)\,(x \in A \equiv (\phi x \,\&\, x \in B))$. This yields only the result that $A \in A \equiv (A \notin A \,\&\, A \in B)$, which is not a contradiction. The paradox can also be avoided by retaining the comprehension axiom but restricting the symbolic language, so that '$x \in x$' is not a meaningful formula. Russell's type theory, presented in *Principia Mathematica*, uses this approach. **See also** FREGE, RUSSELL, SET THEORY, TYPE THEORY.   V.K.

axiom of consistency, an axiom stating that a given set of sentences is consistent. Let L be a formal language, D a deductive system for L, S any set of sentences of L, and C the statement 'S is consistent' (i.e., 'No contradiction is derivable from S via D'). For certain sets S (e.g., the theorems of D) it is interesting to ask: Can C be expressed in L? If so, can C be proved in D? If C can be expressed in L but not proved in D, can C be added (consistently) to D as a new axiom? Example (from Gödel): Let L and D be adequate for elementary number theory, and S be the axioms of D; then C can be expressed in L but not proved in D, but can be added as a new axiom to form a stronger system D'. Sometimes we can express in L an axiom of consistency in the semantic sense (i.e., 'There is a universe in which all the sentences in S are true'). Trivial example: suppose the only non-logical axiom in D is 'For any two sets B and B', there exists the union of B and B''. Then C might be 'There is a set U such that, for any sets B and B' in U, there exists in U the union of B and B''. **See also** CONSISTENCY, PROOF THEORY.   D.H.

axiom of extensionality. See SET THEORY.

axiom of infinity. See SET THEORY.

axiom of reducibility. See TYPE THEORY.

axiom of replacement. See SET THEORY.

axiom of separation. See AXIOM OF COMPREHENSION, SET THEORY.

axiom schema. See TRANSFORMATION RULE.

Ayer, A(lfred) J(ules) (1910–89), British philosopher, one of the most important of the British logical positivists. He continued to occupy a dominant place in analytic philosophy as he gradually modified his adherence to central tenets of the view. He was educated at Eton and Oxford, and, after a brief period at the University of Vienna, became a lecturer in philosophy at Christ Church in 1933. After the war he returned to Oxford as fellow and dean of Wadham College. He was Grote Professor of the Philosophy of Mind and Logic at the University of London (1946–59), Wykeham Professor of Logic in the University of Oxford and a fellow of New College (1959–78), and a fellow of Wolfson College, Oxford (1978–83). Ayer was knighted in 1973 and was a Chevalier de la Légion d'Honneur.

His early work clearly and forcefully developed the implications of the positivists' doctrines that all cognitive statements are either analytic and a priori, or synthetic, contingent, and a posteriori, and that empirically meaningful statements must be verifiable (must admit of confirmation or disconfirmation). In doing so he defended reductionist analyses of the self, the external world, and other minds. Value statements that fail the empiricist's criterion of meaning but defy naturalistic analysis were denied truth-value and assigned *emotive meaning.* Throughout his writings he maintained a foundationalist perspective in epistemology in which sense-data (later more neutrally described) occupied not only a privileged epistemic position but constituted the subject matter of the most basic statements to be used in reductive analyses. Although in later works he significantly modified many of his early views and abandoned much of their strict reductionism, he remained faithful to an empiricist's version of foundationalism and the basic idea behind the verifiability criterion of meaning. His books include *Language, Truth and Logic; The Foundations of Empirical Knowledge; The Problems of Knowledge; Philosophical Essays; The Concept of a Person; The Origins of Pragmatism; Metaphysics and Common Sense; Russell and Moore: The Analytical Heritage; The Central Questions of Philosophy; Probability and Evidence; Philosophy in the Twentieth Century; Russell; Hume; Freedom and Morality, Ludwig Wittgenstein;* and *Voltaire.*

See also EMOTIVISM, LOGICAL POSITIVISM.
R.A.F.

B

Babbage, Charles (1792–1871), English applied mathematician, inventor, and expert on machinery and manufacturing. His chief interest was in developing mechanical "engines" to compute tables of functions. Until the invention of the electronic computer, printed tables of functions were important aids to calculation.

Babbage invented the *difference engine*, a machine that consisted of a series of accumulators each of which, in turn, transmitted its contents to its successor, which added to them to its own contents. He built only a model, but George and Edvard Scheutz built difference engines that were actually used. Though tables of squares and cubes could be calculated by a difference engine, the more commonly used tables of logarithms and of trigonometric functions could not. To calculate these and other useful functions, Babbage conceived of the *analytical engine*, a machine for numerical analysis.

The analytical engine was to have a store (memory) and a mill (arithmetic unit). The store was to hold decimal numbers on toothed wheels, and to transmit them to the mill and back by means of wheels and toothed bars. The mill was to carry out the arithmetic operations of addition, subtraction, multiplication, and division mechanically, greatly extending the technology of small calculators. The operations of the mill were to be governed by pegged drums, derived from the music box.

A desired sequence of operations would be punched on cards, which would be strung together like the cards of a Jacquard loom and read by the machine. The control mechanisms could branch and execute a different sequence of cards when a designated quantity changed sign. Numbers would be entered from punched cards and the answers punched on cards. The answers might also be imprinted on metal sheets from which the calculated tables would be printed, thus avoiding the errors of proofreading.

Although Babbage formulated various partial plans for the analytical engine and built a few pieces of it, the machine was never realized. Given the limitations of mechanical computing technology, building an analytical engine would probably not have been an economical way to produce numerical tables.

The modern electronic computer was invented and developed completely independently of Babbage's pioneering work. Yet because of it, Babbage's work has been publicized and he has become famous.

See also COMPUTER THEORY. A.W.B.

Bachelard, Gaston (1884–1962), French philosopher of science and literary analyst. His philosophy of science (developed, e.g., in *The New Scientific Spirit*, 1934, and *Rational Materialism*, 1953) began from reflections on the relativistic and quantum revolutions in twentieth-century physics. Bachelard viewed science as developing through a series of discontinuous changes (epistemological breaks). Such breaks overcome *epistemological obstacles:* methodological and conceptual features of commonsense or outdated science that block the path of inquiry. Bachelard's emphasis on the discontinuity of scientific change strikingly anticipated Thomas Kuhn's focus, many years later, on revolutionary paradigm change. However, unlike Kuhn, Bachelard held to a strong notion of scientific progress across revolutionary discontinuities. Although each scientific framework rejects its predecessors as fundamentally erroneous, earlier frameworks may embody permanent achievements that will be preserved as special cases within subsequent frameworks. (Newton's laws of motion, e.g., are special limit-cases of relativity theory.)

Bachelard based his philosophy of science on a "non-Cartesian epistemology" that rejects Descartes's claim that knowledge must be founded on incorrigible intuitions of first truths. All knowledge claims are subject to revision in the light of further evidence. Similarly, he rejected a naive realism that defines reality in terms of givens of ordinary sense experience and ignores the ontological constructions of scientific concepts and instrumentation. He maintained, however, that denying this sort of realism did not entail accepting idealism, which makes only the mental ultimately real. Instead he argued for an "applied rationalism," which recognizes the active role of reason in constituting objects of knowledge while admitting that any constituting act of reason must be directed toward an antecedently given object.

Although Bachelard denied the objective reality of the perceptual and imaginative worlds, he emphasized their subjective and poetic significance. Complementing his writings on science are a series of books on imagination and poetic imagery (e.g., *The Psychoanalysis of Fire*, 1938; *The Poetics of Space*, 1957) which subtly unpack the meaning of archetypal (in Jung's sense) images. He put forward a "law of the four elements," according to which all images can be related to the earth, air, fire, and water posited by Empedocles as the fundamental forms of matter.

Together with Georges Canguilhem, his successor at the Sorbonne, Bachelard had an immense impact on several generations of French students of philosophy. He and Canguilhem offered an important alternative to the more fashionable and widely known phenomenology and existentialism and were major influences on (among others) Althusser and Foucault.

See also ALTHUSSER, FOUCAULT, FRANK-
FURT SCHOOL.   G.G.

backward causation. See CAUSATION.

Bacon, Francis (1561–1626), English philosopher, essayist, and scientific methodologist. In politics Bacon rose to the position of lord chancellor. In 1621 he retired to private life after conviction for taking bribes in his official capacity as judge.

Bacon championed the new empiricism resulting from the achievements of early modern science. He opposed alleged knowledge based on appeals to authority, and on the barrenness of Scholasticism. He thought that what is needed is a new attitude and methodology based strictly on scientific practices. The goal of acquiring knowledge is the good of mankind: knowledge is power. The social order that should result from applied science is portrayed in his *New Atlantis* (1627). The method of induction to be employed is worked out in detail in his *Novum Organum* (1620). This new logic is to replace that of Aristotle's syllogism, as well as induction by simple enumeration of instances. Neither of these older logics can produce knowledge of actual natural laws. Bacon thought that we must intervene in nature, manipulating it by means of experimental control leading to the invention of new technology.

There are well-known hindrances to acquisition of knowledge of causal laws. Such hindrances (false opinions, prejudices), which "anticipate" nature rather than explain it, Bacon calls idols (*idola*). Idols of the tribe (*idola tribus*) are natural mental tendencies, among which are the idle search for purposes in nature, and the impulse to read our own desires and needs into nature. *Idols of the cave* (*idola specus*) are predispositions of particular individuals. The individual is inclined to form opinions based on idiosyncrasies of education, social intercourse, reading, and favored authorities. *Idols of the marketplace* (*idola fori*) Bacon regards as the most potentially dangerous of all dispositions, because they arise from common uses of language that often result in verbal disputes. Many words, though thought to be meaningful, stand for nonexistent things; others, although they name actual things, are poorly defined or used in confused ways. *Idols of the theater* (*idola theatri*) depend upon the influence of received theories. The only authority possessed by such theories is that they are ingenious verbal constructions. The aim of acquiring genuine knowledge does not depend on superior skill in the use of words, but rather on the discovery of natural laws.

Once the idols are eliminated, the mind is free to seek knowledge of natural laws based on experimentation. Bacon held that nothing exists in nature except bodies (material objects) acting in conformity with fixed laws. These laws are "forms." For example, Bacon thought that the form or cause of heat is the motion of the tiny particles making up a body. This form is that on which the existence of heat depends. What induction seeks to show is that certain laws are perfectly general, universal in application. In every case of heat, there is a measurable change in the motion of the particles constituting the moving body.

Bacon thought that scientific induction proceeds as follows. First, we look for those cases where, given certain changes, certain others invariably follow. In his example, if certain changes in the form (motion of particles) take place, heat always follows. We seek to find all of the "positive instances" of the form that give rise to the effect of that form. Next, we investigate the "negative instances," cases where in the absence of the form, the qualitative change does not take place. In the operation of these methods it is important to try to produce experimentally "prerogative instances," particularly striking or typical examples of the phenomenon under investigation. Finally, in cases where the object under study is present to some greater or lesser degree, we must be able to take into account why these changes occur. In the example, quantitative changes in degrees of heat will be correlated to quantitative changes in the speed of the motion of the particles. This method implies that in many cases we can invent instruments to measure changes in degree. Such inventions are of course the hoped-for outcome of scientific inquiry, because their possession improves the lot of human beings.

Bacon's strikingly modern (but not entirely novel) empiricist methodology influenced nineteenth-century figures (e.g., Sir John Herschel and J. S. Mill) who generalized his results and used them as the basis for displaying new insights into scientific methodology.

See also INDUCTION; MILL, J. S.; WHEWELL.

R.E.B.

Bacon, Roger (c.1214–c.1293), English philosopher who earned the honorific title of *Doctor Mirabilis*. He was one of the first medievals in the Latin West to lecture and comment on newly recovered work by Aristotle in natural philosophy, physics, and metaphysics. Born in Somerset and educated at both Oxford University and the University of Paris, he became by 1273 a master of arts at Paris, where he taught for about ten years. In 1247 he resigned his teaching post to devote his energies to investigating and promoting topics he considered neglected but important insofar as they would lead to knowledge of God. The English "experimentalist" Grosseteste, the Frenchman Peter of Maricourt, who did pioneering work on magnetism, and the author of the pseudo-Aristotelian *Secretum secretorum* influenced Roger's new perspective. By 1257, however, partly from fatigue, Roger had put this work aside and entered the Franciscan order in England. To his dismay, he did not receive within the order the respect and freedom to write and teach he had expected.

During the early 1260s Roger's views about reforming the university curriculum reached Cardinal Guy le Gos de Foulques, who, upon becoming Pope Clement IV in 1265, demanded to see Roger's writings. In response, Roger produced the *Opus maius* (1267) – an encyclopedic work that argues, among other things, that (1) the study of Hebrew and Greek is indispensable for understanding the Bible, (2) the study of mathematics (encompassing geometry, astronomy, and astrology) is, with experimentation, the key to all the sciences and instrumental in theology, and (3) philosophy can serve theology by helping in the conversion of non-believers. Roger believed that although the Bible is the basis for human knowledge, we can use reason in the service of knowledge. It is not that rational argument can, on his view, provide full-blown proof of anything, but rather that with the aid of reason one can formulate hypotheses about nature that can be confirmed by experience. According to Roger, knowledge arrived at in this way will lead to knowledge of nature's creator. All philosophical, scientific, and linguistic endeavors are valuable ultimately for the service they can render to theology. Roger summarizes and develops his views on these matters in the *Opus minus* and the *Opus tertium,* produced within a year of the *Opus maius.*

Roger was altogether serious in advocating curricular change. He took every opportunity to rail against many of his celebrated contemporaries (e.g., Alexander of Hales, Bonaventure, Albertus Magnus, and Aquinas) for not being properly trained in philosophy and for contributing to the demise of theology by lecturing on Peter Lombard's *Sentences* instead of the Bible. He also wrote both Greek and Hebrew grammars, did important work in optics, and argued for calendar reform on the basis of his (admittedly derivative) astronomical research. One should not, however, think that Roger was a good mathematician or natural scientist. He apparently never produced a single theorem or proof in mathematics, he was not always a good judge of astronomical competence (he preferred al-Bitrūjī to Ptolemy), and he held alchemy in high regard, believing that base metals could be turned into silver and gold. Some have gone so far as to claim that Roger's renown in the history of science is vastly overrated, based in part on his being confusedly linked with the fourteenth-century Oxford Calculators, who do deserve credit for paving the way for certain developments in seventeenth-century science.

Roger's devotion to curricular reform eventually led to his imprisonment by Jerome of Ascoli (the future Pope Nicholas IV), probably between 1277 and 1279. Roger's teachings were said to have contained "suspect novelties." Judging from the date of his imprisonment, these novelties may have been any number of propositions condemned by the bishop of Paris, Étienne Tempier, in 1277. But his imprisonment may also have had something to do with the anger he undoubtedly provoked by constantly abusing the members of his order regarding their approach to education, or with his controversial Joachimite views about the apocalypse and the imminent coming of the Antichrist.

Given Roger's interest in educational reform and his knack for systematization, it is not unlikely that he was abreast of and had something to say about most of the central philosophical issues of the day. If so, his writings could be an important source of information about thirteenth-century Scholastic philosophy generally. In this connection, recent investigations have revealed, e.g., that he may well have played an important role in the development of logic and philosophy of language during the thirteenth and early fourteenth centuries. In the course of challenging the views of certain people (some of whom have been tentatively identified as Richard of Cornwall, Lambert of Auxerre, Siger of Brabant, Henry of Ghent, Boethius of Dacia, William Sherwood, and the Magister Abstractionum) on the nature of signs and how words function as signs, Roger develops and defends views that appear to be original. The pertinent texts include the *Sumule dialectices* (c.1250), the *De signis* (part of Part III of the *Opus maius*), and the *Compendium studii theologiae* (1292). E.g., in connection with the question whether Jesus could be called a man during the three-day entombment (and, thus, in connection with the related question whether man can be said to be animal when no man exists, and with the sophism 'This is a dead man, therefore this is a man'), Roger was not content to distinguish words from all other signs as had been the tradition. He distinguished between signs originating from nature and from the soul, and between natural signification and conventional (*ad placitum*) signification which results expressly or tacitly from the imposition of meaning by one or more individuals. He maintained that words signify existing and non-existing entities only equivocally, because words conventionally signify only presently existing things. On this view, therefore, 'man' is not used univocally when applied to an existing man and to a dead man.

See also ARISTOTLE, GROSSETESTE, PETER LOMBARD.   G.S.

Baden School. See NEO-KANTIANISM.

bad faith, (1) dishonest and blameworthy instances of self-deception; (2) inauthentic and self-deceptive refusal to admit to ourselves and others our full freedom, thereby avoiding anxiety in making decisions and evading responsibility for actions and attitudes (Sartre, *Being and Nothingness,* 1943); (3) hypocrisy or dishonesty in speech and conduct, as in making a promise without intending to keep it. One self-deceiving strategy identified by Sartre is to embrace other people's views in order to avoid having to form one's own; another is to disregard options so that one's life appears predetermined to move in a fixed direction. Occasionally Sartre used a narrower, fourth sense: self-deceptive beliefs held on the basis of insincere and unreasonable interpretations of evidence, as contrasted with the dishonesty of "sincerely" acknowledging one truth ("I am disposed to be a thief") in order to deny a deeper truth ("I am free to change"). **See also** FALSE CONSCIOUSNESS, SARTRE, VITAL LIE.   M.W.M.

Bain, Alexander (1818–1903), British philosopher and reformer, biographer of James Mill (1882) and J. S. Mill (1882) and founder of the first psychological journal, *Mind* (1876). In the development of psychology, Bain represents in England (alongside Continental thinkers such as Taine and Lotze) the final step toward the founding of psychology as a science. His significance stems from his wish to "unite psychology and physiology," fulfilled in *The Senses and the Intellect* (1855) and *The Emotions and the Will* (1859), abridged in one volume, *Mental and Moral Science* (1868). Neither Bain's psychology nor his physiology were particularly original. His psychology came from English empiricism and associationism, his physiology from Johannes Muller's (1801–58) *Elements of Physiology* (1842). Muller was an early advocate of the reflex, or sensorimotor, conception of the nervous system, holding that neurons conduct sensory information to the brain or motor commands from the brain, the brain connecting sensation with appropriate motor response. Like Hartley before him, Bain grounded the laws of mental association in the laws of neural connection. In opposition to faculty psychology, Bain rejected the existence of mental powers located in different parts of the brain (*On the Study of Character*, 1861). By combining associationism with modern physiology, he virtually completed the movement of philosophical psychology toward science. In philosophy, his most important concept was his analysis of belief as "a preparation to act." By thus entwining conception and action, he laid the foundation for pragmatism, and for the focus on adaptive behavior central to modern psychology. **See also** ASSOCIATIONISM.   T.H.L.

Bakhtin, Mikhail Mikhailovich (1895–1975), Russian philosopher and cultural theorist whose influence is pervasive in a wide range of academic disciplines – from literary hermeneutics to the epistemology of the human sciences, cultural theory, and feminism. He may legitimately be called a philosophical anthropologist in the venerable Continental tradition. Because of his seminal work on Rabelais and Dostoevsky's poetics, his influence has been greatest in literary hermeneutics.

Without question dialogism, or the construal of dialogue, is the hallmark of Bakhtin's thought. Dialogue marks the existential condition of humanity in which the self and the other are asymmetrical but double-binding. In his words, to exist means to communicate dialogically, and when the dialogue ends, everything else ends. Unlike Hegelian and Marxian dialectics but like the Chinese correlative logic of yin and yang, Bakhtin's dialogism is infinitely polyphonic, open-ended, and indeterminate, i.e., "unfinalizable" – to use his term. Dialogue means that there are neither first nor last words. The past and the future are interlocked and revolve around the axis of the present.

Bakhtin's dialogism is paradigmatic in a threefold sense. First, dialogue is never abstract but embodied. The lived body is the material condition of social existence as ongoing dialogue. Not only does the word become enfleshed, but dialogue is also the incorporation of the self and the other. Appropriately, therefore, Bakhtin's body politics may be called a Slavic version of Tantrism. Second, the Rabelaisian carnivalesque that Bakhtin's dialogism incorporates points to the "jesterly" politics of resistance and protest against the "priestly" establishment of officialdom. Third, the most distinguishing characteristic of Bakhtin's dialogism is the primacy of the other over the self, with a twofold consequence: one concerns ethics and the other epistemology. In modern philosophy, the discovery of "Thou" or the primacy of the other over the self in asymmetrical reciprocity is credited to Feuerbach. It is hailed as the "Copernican revolution" of mind, ethics, and social thought. Ethically, Bakhtin's dialogism, based on heteronomy, signals the birth of a new philosophy of responsibility that challenges and transgresses the Anglo-American tradition of "rights talk." Epistemologically, it lends our welcoming ears to the credence that the other may be right – the attitude that Gadamer calls the soul of dialogical hermeneutics.

See also BUBER, FEUERBACH, GADAMER, HERMENEUTICS, PHILOSOPHICAL ANTHROPOLOGY.   H.Y.J.

Bakunin, Mikhail (1814–76), Russian revolutionary anarchist. He lived in Western Europe in 1840–49 and again in 1861–76 after an intervening period in Western and Russian prisons and Siberian exile. Bakunin is best known for his vigorous if incoherent anarchist-socialist views. On the one hand, he claimed that the masses'

"instinct for freedom" would spark the social revolution; on the other, he claimed that the revolution would be the work of a conspiratorial elite of disciplined professionals. Still, Bakunin made two significant if limited philosophic contributions.

(1) In the early 1840s he spoke of the "incessant self-immolation of the positive in the pure flame of the negative," and came to see that "flame" as a necessary dialectical component of revolutionary action. His sharpest criticism was directed not at conservative attempts to defend the existing order but rather at (Hegelian) attempts to reconcile positive and negative and "liberal" efforts to find a "modest and harmless place" for the negative within the positive. For Bakunin the negative is absolutely justified in its "constructive" elimination of the positive. Writing in German (in 1842) he exploited both senses of the word *Lust,* namely "joy" and "urge," declaring that the *Lust* to destroy is at the same time a creative *Lust.*

(2) From 1861 until the end of his life Bakunin was committed to scientism, materialism, and atheism. But in the late 1860s he formulated a forceful critique of the political and social role of scientific elites and institutions. Individual life is concrete and particular; science is abstract and general and incapable of understanding or valuing living individuals. Instead, it tends to ignore or to exploit them. Bakunin, who had preached an anarchist revolt against church and state, now preached a "revolt of life against science, or rather against *government by science.*" This was related to his anarchist critique of Marx's statism and technicism; but it raised the more general question – one of continuing relevance and urgency – of the role of scientific experts in decisions about public policy.

See also POLITICAL PHILOSOPHY, RUSSIAN NIHILISM.   G.L.K.

Balguy, John. See HUTCHESON.

Bañez, Domingo (1528–1604), Spanish Dominican theologian and philosopher. Born in Valladolid, he studied at Salamanca, where he also taught for many years. As spiritual director of St. Teresa of Ávila, he exerted considerable influence on her views. He is known for his disputes with Molina concerning divine grace. Against Molina he held physical predetermination, the view that God physically determines the secondary causes of human action. This renders grace intrinsically efficacious and independent of human will and merits. He is also known for his understanding of the centrality of the act of existence (*esse*) in Thomistic metaphysics. Bañez's most important works are his commentaries on Aquinas's *Summa theologiae* and Aristotle's *On Generation and Corruption*. **See also AQUINAS, FREE WILL PROBLEM, METAPHYSICS, MOLINA.**

J.J.E.G.

Barbara. See ARISTOTLE, SYLLOGISM.

barber paradox. See PARADOX.

Barcan formula. See MODAL LOGIC.

bare particular. See METAPHYSICS.

bargaining theory, the branch of game theory that treats agreements, e.g., wage agreements between labor and management. In the simplest bargaining problems there are two bargainers. They can jointly realize various outcomes, including the outcome that occurs if they fail to reach an agreement. Each bargainer assigns a certain amount of utility to each outcome. The question is, what outcome will they realize if they are rational? Methods of solving bargaining problems are controversial. The best-known proposals are Nash's and Kalai and Smorodinsky's. Nash proposes maximizing the product of utility gains with respect to *the disagreement point.* Kalai and Smorodinsky propose maximizing utility gains with respect to the disagreement point, subject to the constraint that the ratio of utility gains equals the ratio of greatest possible gains. These methods of selecting an outcome have been axiomatically characterized. For each method, there are certain axioms of outcome selection such that that method alone satisfies the axioms. The axioms incorporate principles of rationality from *cooperative game theory.* They focus on features of outcomes rather than bargaining strategies. For example, one axiom requires that the outcome selected be *Pareto-optimal,* i.e., be an outcome such that no alternative is better for one of the bargainers and not worse for the other.

Bargaining problems may become more complicated in several ways. First, there may be more than two bargainers. If unanimity is not required for beneficial agreements, splinter groups or *coalitions* may form. Second, the protocol for offers, counteroffers, etc., may be relevant. Then principles of *non-cooperative game theory* concerning strategies are needed to justify solutions. Third, the context of a bargaining problem may be relevant. For instance, opportunities for *side payments,* differences in bargaining power, and interpersonal comparisons of utility may influence the solution. Fourth, simplifying assumptions, such as the assumption that bargainers have *complete information* about their bargaining situation, may be discarded.

Bargaining theory is part of the philosophical study of rationality. It is also important in ethics as a foundation for contractarian theories of morality and for certain theories of distributive justice.

See also DECISION THEORY, GAME THEORY.

P.We.

Barthes, Roland (1915–80), French post-structuralist literary critic and essayist. Born in Cherbourg, he suffered from numerous ailments as a child and spent much of his early life as a semi-invalid. After leaving the military, he took up several positions teaching subjects like classics, grammar, and philology. His interest in linguistics finally drew him to literature, and by the mid-1960s he had already published what would become a classic in structural analysis, *The Elements of Semiology.* Its principal message is that words are merely one kind of sign whose meaning lies in relations of difference between them. This concept was later amended to include the reading subject, and the structuring effect that the subject has on the literary work – a concept expressed later in his *S/Z* and *The Pleasure of the Text.* Barthes's most mature contributions to the post-structuralist movement were brilliant and witty interpretations of visual, tactile, and aural sign systems, culminating in the publication of several books and essays on photography, advertising, film, and cuisine. **See also POSTMODERN, SEMIOSIS, STRUCTURALISM.** M.Ro.

base, supervenience. See SUPERVENIENCE.

base clause. See MATHEMATICAL INDUCTION.

basic action. See ACTION THEORY.

basic belief. See BERKELEY, FOUNDATIONALISM, LOGICAL POSITIVISM, PLANTINGA.

basic norm, also called *Grundnorm,* in a legal system, the norm that determines the legal validity of all other norms. The content of such an ultimate norm may provide, e.g., that norms created by a legislature or by a court are legally valid. The validity of such an ultimate norm cannot be established as a matter of social fact (such as the social fact that the norm is accepted by some group within a society). Rather, the validity of the basic norm for any given legal system must be presupposed by the validity of the norms that it legitimates as laws. The idea of a basic norm is associated with the legal philosopher Hans Kelsen. **See also** JURISPRUDENCE, PHILOSOPHY OF LAW.   M.S.M.

basic particular. See STRAWSON.

basic proposition. See EPISTEMOLOGY.

basic sentence. See FOUNDATIONALISM.

basic statement. See FOUNDATIONALISM.

Basilides (A.D. c.120–40), Syrian Christian gnostic teacher in Alexandria who rivaled Valentinus. He improved on Valentinus's doctrine of emanations, positing 365 (the number of days in a year) levels of existence in the Pleroma (the fullness of the Godhead), all descending from the ineffable Father. He taught that the rival God was the God of the Jews (the God of the Old Testament), who created the material world. Redemption consists in the coming of the first begotten of the Father, *Noûs* (Mind), in human form in order to release the spiritual element imprisoned within human bodies. Like other gnostics he taught that we are saved by knowledge, not faith. He apparently held to the idea of reincarnation before the restoration of all things to the Pleroma. **See also** GNOSTICISM, VALENTINUS.   L.P.P.

basing relation, also called basis relation, the relation between a belief or item of knowledge and a second belief or item of knowledge when the latter is the ground (basis) of the first. It is clear that some knowledge is *indirect*, i.e., had or gained on the basis of some evidence, as opposed to direct knowledge, which (assuming there is any) is not so gained, or based. The same holds for justified belief. In one *broad* sense of the term, the basing relation is just the one connecting indirect knowledge or indirectly justified belief to the evidence: to give an account of either of the latter is to give an account of the basing relation.

There is a narrower view of the basing relation, perhaps implicit in the first. A person knows some proposition *P* on the basis of evidence or reasons only if her belief that *P* is based on the evidence or reasons, or perhaps on the possession of the evidence or reasons. The narrow basing relation is indicated by this question: where a belief that *P* constitutes indirect knowledge or

justification, what is it for that *belief* to be based on the evidence or reasons that support the knowledge or justification? The most widely favored view is that the relevant belief is based on evidence or reasons only if the belief is causally related to the belief or reasons. Proponents of this causal view differ concerning what, beyond this causal relationship, is needed by an account of the narrow basing relation.

See also COHERENTISM, FOUNDATIONALISM, INFERENTIAL KNOWLEDGE.   G.S.P.

basis clause. See MATHEMATICAL INDUCTION.

basis relation. See BASING RELATION.

Bataille, Georges (1897–1962), French philosopher and novelist with enormous influence on post-structuralist thought. By locating value in expenditure as opposed to accumulation, Bataille inaugurates the era of the death of the subject. He insists that individuals must transgress the limits imposed by subjectivity to escape isolation and communicate. Bataille's prewar philosophical contributions consist mainly of short essays, the most significant of which have been collected in *Visions of Excess*. These essays introduce the central idea that base matter disrupts rational subjectivity by attesting to the continuity in which individuals lose themselves. *Inner Experience* (1943), Bataille's first lengthy philosophical treatise, was followed by *Guilty* (1944) and *On Nietzsche* (1945). Together, these three works constitute Bataille's *Summa Atheologica*, which explores the play of the isolation and the dissolution of beings in terms of the experience of excess (laughter, tears, eroticism, death, sacrifice, poetry). *The Accursed Share* (1949), which he considered his most important work, is his most systematic account of the social and economic implications of expenditure. In *Erotism* (1957) and *The Tears of Eros* (1961), he focuses on the excesses of sex and death. Throughout his life, Bataille was concerned with the question of value. He located it in the excess that lacerates individuals and opens channels of communication. **See also** POSTMODERN, STRUCTURALISM.

J.H.L.

Baumgarten, Alexander Gottlieb (1714–62), German philosopher. Born in Berlin, he was educated in Halle and taught at Halle (1738–40) and Frankfurt an der Oder (1740–62). Baumgarten was brought up in the Pietist circle of A. H. Francke but adopted the anti-Pietist rationalism of Wolff. He wrote textbooks in metaphysics (*Metaphysica*, 1739) and ethics (*Ethica Philosophica*, 1740; *Initia Philosophiae Practicae Prima* ["First Elements of Practical Philosophy"], 1760) on which Kant lectured. For the most part, Baumgarten did not significantly depart from Wolff, although in metaphysics he was both further and yet closer to Leibniz than was Wolff: unlike Leibniz, he argued for real physical influx, but, unlike Wolff, he did not restrict preestablished harmony to the mind–body relationship alone, but (paradoxically) reextended it to include all relations of substances.

Baumgarten's claim to fame, however, rests on his introduction of the discipline of aesthetics into German philosophy, and indeed on his introduction of the term 'aesthetics' as well. Wolff had explained pleasure as the response to the perception of perfection by means of the senses, in turn understood as clear but confused perception. Baumgarten subtly but significantly departed from Wolff by redefining our response to beauty as pleasure in the perfection of sensory perception, i.e., in the unique potential of sensory as opposed to merely conceptual representation. This concept was first introduced in his dissertation *Meditationes Philosophicae de Nonnullis ad Poema Pertinentibus* ("Philosophical Meditations on some Matters pertaining to Poetry," 1735), which defined a poem as a "perfect sensate discourse," and then generalized in his two-volume (but still incomplete) *Aesthetica* (1750–58). One might describe Baumgarten's aesthetics as cognitivist but no longer rationalist: while in science or logic we must always prefer discursive clarity, in art we respond with pleasure to the maximally dense (or "confused") intimation of ideas. Baumgarten's theory had great influence on Lessing and Mendelssohn, on Kant's theory of aesthetic ideas, and even on the aesthetics of Hegel.

See also WOLFF.   P.Gu.

Bayesian. See BAYESIAN RATIONALITY, CONFIRMATION.

Bayesian rationality, minimally, a property a system of beliefs (or the believer) has in virtue of the system's "conforming to the probability calculus." "Bayesians" differ on what "rationality" requires, but most agree that (*i*) beliefs come in *degrees* (of firmness); (*ii*) these "degrees of belief" are (theoretically or ideally) *quantifiable*; (*iii*) such quantification can be understood in terms of person-relative, time-indexed "credence functions" from appropriate sets of objects of belief (propositions or sentences) – each set closed

under (at least) finite truth-functional combinations – into the set of real numbers; (*iv*) at any given time *t*, a person's credence function at *t* *ought* to be (usually: "on pain of a Dutch book argument") a *probability* function; that is, a mapping from the given set into the real numbers in such a way that the "probability" (the value) assigned to any given object *A* in the set is greater than or equal to zero, *and* is equal to unity (= 1) if *A* is a necessary truth, *and*, for any given objects *A* and *B* in the set, if *A* and *B* are incompatible (the negation of their conjunction is a necessary truth) then the probability assigned to their disjunction is equal to the sum of the probabilities assigned to each; so that the usual propositional probability axioms impose a sort of logic on degrees of belief. If a credence function is a probability function, then it (or the believer at the given time) is "coherent."

On these matters, on *conditional* degrees of belief, and on the further constraint on rationality many Bayesians impose (that change of belief ought to accord with "conditionalization"), the reader should consult John Earman, *Bayes or Bust? A Critical Examination of Bayesian Confirmation Theory* (1992); Colin Howson and Peter Urbach, *Scientific Reasoning: The Bayesian Approach* (1989); and Richard Jeffrey, *The Logic of Decision* (1965).

See also BAYES'S THEOREM, DECISION THEORY, DUTCH BOOK ARGUMENT, PROBABILITY, RATIONALITY.   D.A.J.

Bayes's rule. See BAYES'S THEOREM.

Bayes's theorem, any of several relationships between prior and posterior probabilities or odds, especially (1)–(3) below. All of these depend upon the basic relationship (0) between contemporaneous conditional and unconditional probabilities. Non-Bayesians think these useful only in narrow ranges of cases, generally because of skepticism about accessibility or significance of priors.

According to (1), posterior probability is prior

(0) $\mathrm{pr}(hyp_1 \mid data) = \mathrm{pr}(hyp_1 \; \& \; data)/\mathrm{P}(data)$

(1) $\mathrm{pr}(hyp_1 \mid data) = \mathrm{pr}(hyp_1) \times \dfrac{\mathrm{pr}(data \mid hyp_1)}{\mathrm{P}(data)}$

(2) $\dfrac{\mathrm{pr}(hyp_1 \mid data)}{\mathrm{pr}(hyp_2 \mid data)} = \dfrac{\mathrm{pr}(hyp_1)}{\mathrm{pr}(hyp_2)} \times \dfrac{\mathrm{pr}(data \mid hyp_1)}{\mathrm{pr}(data \mid hyp_2)}$

(3) $\mathrm{pr}(hyp_1 \mid data) = \dfrac{\mathrm{pr}(hyp_1) \times \mathrm{pr}(data \mid hyp_1)}{\Sigma_n \, \mathrm{pr}(hyp_n) \times \mathrm{pr}(data \mid hyp_n)}$

probability times the "relevance quotient" (Carnap's term). According to (2), posterior odds are prior odds times the "likelihood ratio" (R. A. Fisher's term). Relationship (3) comes from (1) by expanding P (*data*) via the law of total probability.

Bayes's *rule* (4) for updating probabilities has you set your new unconditional probabilities equal to your old conditional ones when fresh certainty about data leaves probabilities conditionally upon the data unchanged. The corresponding rule (5) has you do the same for odds. In decision theory the term is used differently, for the rule "Choose so as to maximize expectation of utility."

$$(4) \quad \text{new pr}(hyp_1) = \text{old pr}(hyp_1 \mid data)$$

$$(5) \quad \frac{\text{new pr}(hyp_1)}{\text{new pr}(hyp_2)} = \frac{\text{old pr}(hyp_1 \mid data)}{\text{old pr}(hyp_2 \mid data)}$$

See also DECISION THEORY, PROBABILITY.
R.J.

Bayle, Pierre (1647–1706), French philosopher who also pioneered in disinterested, critical history. A Calvinist forced into exile in 1681, Bayle nevertheless rejected the prevailing use of history as an instrument of partisan or sectarian interest. He achieved fame and notoriety with his multivolume *Dictionnaire historique et critique* (1695). For each subject covered, Bayle provided a biographical sketch and a dispassionate examination of the historical record and interpretive controversies. He also repeatedly probed the troubled and troubling boundary between reason and faith (philosophy and religion). In the article "David," the seemingly illicit conduct of God's purported agent yielded reflections on the morals of the elect and the autonomy of ethics. In "Pyrrho," Bayle argued that self-evidence, the most plausible candidate for the criterion of truth, is discredited by Christianity because some self-evident principles contradict essential Christian truths and are therefore false. Finally, provoking Leibniz's *Theodicy*, Bayle argued, most relentlessly in "Manichaeans" and "Paulicians," that there is no defensible rational solution to the problem of evil.

Bayle portrayed himself as a Christian skeptic, but others have seen instead an ironic critic of religion – a precursor of the French Enlightenment. Bayle's purely philosophical reflections support his self-assessment, since he consistently maintains that philosophy achieves not comprehension and contentment, but paradox and puzzlement. In making this case he proved to be a superb critic of philosophical systems. Some

examples are "Zeno of Elea" – on space, time, and motion; "Rorarius" – on mind and body and animal mechanism; and "Spinoza" – on the perils of monism. Bayle's skepticism concerning philosophy significantly influenced Berkeley and Hume. His other important works include *Pensées diverses de la comète de 1683* (1683); *Commentaire philosophique sur ces paroles de Jesus Christ: contrain les d'entrer* (1686); and *Réponse aux questions d'un provincial* (1704); and an early learned periodical, the *Nouvelles de la République des Lettres* (1684–87).

See also LEIBNIZ.
P.D.C.

Beattie, James (1735–1803), Scottish philosopher and poet who, in criticizing Hume, widened the latter's audience. A member of the Scottish school of common sense philosophy along with Oswald and Reid, Beattie's major work was *An Essay on the Nature and Immutability of Truth* (1771), in which he criticizes Hume for fostering skepticism and infidelity. His positive view was that the mind possesses a common sense, i.e., a power for perceiving self-evident truths. Common sense is instinctive, unalterable by education; truth is what common sense determines the mind to believe. Beattie cited Hume and then claimed that his views led to moral and religious evils. When Beattie's *Essay* was translated into German (1772), Kant could read Hume's discussions of personal identity and causation. Since these topics were not covered in Hume's *Inquiry Concerning Human Understanding*, Beattie provided Kant access to two issues in the *Treatises of Human Nature* critical to the development of transcendental idealism. See also HUME, SCOTTISH COMMON SENSE PHILOSOPHY.
P.K.

beauty, an aesthetic property commonly thought of as a species of aesthetic value. As such, it has been variously thought to be (1) a simple, indefinable property that cannot be defined in terms of any other properties; (2) a property or set of properties of an object that makes the object capable of producing a certain sort of pleasurable experience in any suitable perceiver; or (3) whatever produces a particular sort of pleasurable experience, even though what produces the experience may vary from individual to individual. It is in this last sense that beauty is thought to be "in the eye of the beholder."

If beauty is a simple, indefinable property, as in (1), then it cannot be defined conceptually and has to be apprehended by intuition or taste. Beauty, on this account, would be a particular sort of aesthetic property. If beauty is an object's capacity to produce a special sort of pleasurable experience, as in (2), then it is necessary to say what properties provide it with this capacity. The most favored candidates for these have been formal or structural properties, such as order, symmetry, and proportion. In the *Philebus* Plato argues that the form or essence of beauty is knowable, exact, rational, and measurable. He also holds that simple geometrical shapes, simple colors, and musical notes all have "intrinsic beauty," which arouses a pure, "unmixed" pleasure in the perceiver and is unaffected by context.

In the sixteenth and seventeenth centuries many treatises were written on individual art forms, each allegedly governed by its own rules. In the eighteenth century, Hutcheson held that 'beauty' refers to an "idea raised in us," and that any object that excites this idea is beautiful. He thought that the property of the object that excites this idea is "uniformity in variety."

Kant explained the nature of beauty by analyzing judgments that something is beautiful. Such judgments refer to an experience of the perceiver. But they are not merely expressions of personal experience; we claim that others should also have the same experience, and that they should make the same judgment (i.e., judgments that something is beautiful have "universal validity"). Such judgments are disinterested – determined not by any needs or wants on the part of the perceiver, but just by contemplating the mere appearance of the object. These are judgments about an object's *free beauty*, and making them requires using only those mental capacities that all humans have by virtue of their ability to communicate with one another. Hence the pleasures experienced in response to such beauty can in principle be shared by anyone.

Some have held, as in (3), that we apply the term 'beautiful' to things because of the pleasure they give us, and not on the basis of any specific qualities an object has. Archibald Alison held that it is impossible to find any properties common to all those things we call beautiful. Santayana believed beauty is "pleasure regarded as a quality of a thing," and made no pretense that certain qualities ought to produce that pleasure.

The Greek term *to kalon*, which is often translated as 'beauty', did not refer to a thing's autonomous aesthetic value, but rather to its "excellence," which is connected with its moral worth and/or usefulness. This concept is closer to Kant's notion of *dependent beauty*, possessed by an object judged as a particular kind of thing (such as a beautiful cat or a beautiful horse), than it is to free beauty, possessed by an object judged sim-

ply on the basis of its appearance and not in terms of any concept of use.

    See also AESTHETIC PROPERTY, AESTHETICS.   S.L.F.

Beauvoir, Simone de. See EXISTENTIALISM.

Beccaria, Cesare (1738–94), Italian criminologist and judicial and penal reformer. He studied in Parma and Pavia and taught political economy in Milan. Here, he met Pietro and Alessandro Verri and other Milanese intellectuals attempting to promote political, economical, and judiciary reforms. His major work, *Dei delitti e delle pene* ("On Crimes and Punishments," 1764), denounces the contemporary methods in the administration of justice and the treatment of criminals. Beccaria argues that the highest good is the greatest happiness shared by the greatest number of people; hence, actions against the state are the most serious crimes. Crimes against individuals and property are less serious, and crimes endangering public harmony are the least serious. The purposes of punishment are deterrence and the protection of society. However, the employment of torture to obtain confessions is unjust and useless: it results in acquittal of the strong and the ruthless and conviction of the weak and the innocent. Beccaria also rejects the death penalty as a war of the state against the individual. He claims that the duration and certainty of the punishment, not its intensity, most strongly affect criminals. Beccaria was influenced by Montesquieu, Rousseau, and Condillac. His major work was translated into many languages and set guidelines for revising the criminal and judicial systems of several European countries.   P.Gar.

becoming. See TIME.

becoming, temporal. See TIME.

Bedeutung. See FREGE.

begging the question. See CIRCULAR REASONING.

Begriff. See HEGEL.

behavioral equivalence. See TURING MACHINE.

behavioralism. See JURISPRUDENCE.

behaviorism, broadly, the view that behavior is fundamental in understanding mental phenomena. The term applies both to a scientific research program in psychology and to a philosophical doctrine. Accordingly, we distinguish between scientific (psychological, methodological) behaviorism and philosophical (logical, analytical) behaviorism.

Scientific behaviorism. First propounded by the American psychologist J. B. Watson (who introduced the term in 1913) and further developed especially by C. L. Hull, E. C. Tolman, and B. F. Skinner, it departed from the introspectionist tradition by redefining the proper task of psychology as the explanation and prediction of behavior – where to explain behavior is to provide a "functional analysis" of it, i.e., to specify the independent variables (stimuli) of which the behavior (response) is lawfully a function. It insisted that all variables – including behavior as the dependent variable – must be specifiable by the experimental procedures of the natural sciences: merely introspectible, internal states of consciousness are thus excluded from the proper domain of psychology. Although some behaviorists were prepared to admit internal neurophysiological conditions among the variables ("intervening variables"), others of more radical bent (e.g. Skinner) insisted on environmental variables alone, arguing that any relevant variations in the hypothetical inner states would themselves in general be a function of variations in (past and present) environmental conditions (as, e.g., thirst is a function of water deprivation). Although some basic responses are inherited reflexes, most are learned and integrated into complex patterns by a process of conditioning. In *classical (respondent) conditioning*, a response already under the control of a given stimulus will be elicited by new stimuli if these are repeatedly paired with the old stimulus: this is how we learn to respond to new situations. In *operant conditioning*, a response that has repeatedly been followed by a reinforcing stimulus (reward) will occur with greater frequency and will thus be "selected" over other possible responses: this is how we learn new responses. Conditioned responses can also be unlearned or "extinguished" by prolonged dissociation from the old eliciting stimuli or by repeated withholding of the reinforcing stimuli. To show how all human behavior, including "cognitive" or intelligent behavior, can be "shaped" by such processes of selective reinforcement and extinction of responses was the ultimate objective of scientific behaviorism. Grave difficulties in the way of the realization of this objective led to increasingly radical liberalization of the distinctive features of behaviorist methodology and eventually to its displacement by more cognitively oriented approaches (e.g. those inspired by information theory and by Chomsky's work in linguistics).

Philosophical behaviorism. A semantic thesis about the meaning of mentalistic expressions, it received its most sanguine formulation by the logical positivists (particularly Carnap, Hempel, and Ayer), who asserted that statements containing mentalistic expressions have the same meaning as, and are thus translatable into, some set of publicly verifiable (confirmable, testable) statements describing behavioral and bodily processes and dispositions (including verbal-behavioral dispositions). Because of the reductivist concerns expressed by the logical positivist thesis of physicalism and the unity of science, logical behaviorism (as some positivists preferred to call it) was a corollary of the thesis that psychology is ultimately (via a behavioristic analysis) reducible to physics, and that all of its statements, like those of physics, are expressible in a strictly extensional language.

Another influential formulation of philosophical behaviorism is due to Ryle (*The Concept of Mind*, 1949), whose classic critique of Cartesian dualism rests on the view that mental predicates are often used to ascribe dispositions to behave in characteristic ways: but such ascriptions, for Ryle, have the form of conditional, lawlike statements whose function is not to report the occurrence of inner states, physical or non-physical, of which behavior is the causal manifestation, but to license inferences about how the agent *would* behave *if* certain conditions obtained. To suppose that all declarative uses of mental language have a fact-stating or -reporting role at all is, for Ryle, to make a series of "category mistakes" – of which both Descartes and the logical positivists were equally guilty. Unlike the behaviorism of the positivists, Ryle's behaviorism required no physicalistic reduction of mental language, and relied instead on ordinary language descriptions of human behavior.

A further version of philosophical behaviorism can be traced to Wittgenstein (*Philosophical Investigations*, 1953), who argues that the epistemic criteria for the applicability of mentalistic terms cannot be private, introspectively accessible inner states but must instead be intersubjectively observable behavior. Unlike the previously mentioned versions of philosophical behaviorism, Wittgenstein's behaviorism seems to be consistent with metaphysical mind–body dualism, and is thus also non-reductivist.

Philosophical behaviorism underwent severe criticism in the 1950s and 1960s, especially by Chisholm, Charles Taylor, Putnam, and Fodor. Nonetheless it still lives on in more or less attenuated forms in the work of such diverse philosophers as Quine, Dennett, Armstrong, David Lewis, U. T. Place, and Dummett. Though current "functionalism" is often referred to as the natural heir to behaviorism, functionalism (especially of the Armstrong-Lewis variety) crucially differs from behaviorism in insisting that mental predicates, while definable in terms of behavior and behavioral dispositions, nonetheless designate *inner causal states* – states that are apt to cause certain characteristic behaviors.

See also COGNITIVE SCIENCE, FUNCTIONALISM, PHILOSOPHY OF MIND, PHILOSOPHY OF PSYCHOLOGY, RYLE, VERIFICATIONISM.

A.M.

behaviorism, supervenient. See PHILOSOPHY OF MIND.

behavior therapy, a spectrum of behavior modification techniques applied as therapy, such as aversion therapy, extinction, modeling, redintegration, operant conditioning, and desensitization. Unlike psychotherapy, which probes a client's recollected history, behavior therapy focuses on immediate behavior, and aims to eliminate undesired behavior and produce desired behavior through methods derived from the experimental analysis of behavior and from reinforcement theory. A chronic problem with psychotherapy is that the client's past is filtered through limited and biased recollection. Behavior therapy is more mechanical, creating systems of reinforcement and conditioning that may work independently of the client's long-term memory.

Collectively, behavior-therapeutic techniques compose a motley set. Some behavior therapists adapt techniques from psychotherapy, as in covert desensitization, where verbally induced mental images are employed as reinforcers. A persistent problem with behavior therapy is that it may require repeated application. Consider aversion therapy. It consists of pairing painful or punishing stimuli with unwelcome behavior. In the absence, after therapy, of the painful stimulus, the behavior may recur because association between behavior and punishment is broken. Critics charge that behavior therapy deals with immediate disturbances and overt behavior, to the neglect of underlying problems and irrationalities.

See also COGNITIVE PSYCHOTHERAPY.

G.A.G.

being. See HEIDEGGER, METAPHYSICS, TRANSCENDENTALS.

belief, a dispositional psychological state in virtue of which a person will assent to a proposition under certain conditions. Propositional knowledge, traditionally understood, entails belief.

A *behavioral view* implies that beliefs are just dispositions to behave in certain ways. Your believing that the stove is hot is just your being disposed to act in a manner appropriate to its being hot. The problem is that our beliefs, including their propositional content indicated by a "that"-clause, typically explain why we do what we do. You avoid touching the stove *because* you believe that it's dangerously hot. Explaining action via beliefs refers indispensably to propositional content, but the behavioral view does not accommodate this.

A *state-object view* implies that belief consists of a special relation between a psychological state and an object of belief, what is believed. The objects of belief, traditionally understood, are abstract propositions existing independently of anyone's thinking of them. The state of believing is a *propositional attitude* involving some degree of confidence toward a propositional object of belief. Such a view allows that two persons, even separated by a long period of time, can believe the same thing.

A state-object view allows that beliefs be dispositional rather than episodic, since they can exist while no action is occurring. Such a view grants, however, that one can have a disposition to act owing to believing something. Regarding mental action, a belief typically generates a disposition to *assent*, at least under appropriate circumstances, to the proposition believed. Given the central role of propositional content, however, a state-object view denies that beliefs are just dispositions to act. In addition, such a view should distinguish between dispositional believing and a mere disposition to believe. One can be merely disposed to believe many things that one does not actually believe, owing to one's lacking the appropriate psychological attitude to relevant propositional content.

Beliefs are either *occurrent* or *non-occurrent*. Occurrent belief, unlike non-occurrent belief, requires current assent to the proposition believed. If the assent is self-conscious, the belief is an *explicit* occurrent belief; if the assent is not self-conscious, the belief is an *implicit* occurrent belief. Non-occurrent beliefs permit that we do not cease to believe that $2 + 2 = 4$, for instance, merely because we now happen to be thinking of something else or nothing at all. **See also** ACT-OBJECT PSYCHOLOGY, BEHAVIORISM, DISPOSITION, PHILOSOPHY OF MIND.

P.K.M.

belief, basic. See BERKELEY, FOUNDATIONALISM, LOGICAL POSITIVISM.

belief, degree of. See BAYESIAN RATIONALITY.

belief, ethics of. See CLIFFORD.

belief, partial. See PROBABILITY.

belief, properly basic. See EVIDENTIALISM, PLANTINGA.

belief-desire model. See INTENTION.

belief revision, the process by which cognitive states change in light of new information. This topic looms large in discussions of Bayes's Theorem and other approaches in decision theory. The reasons prompting belief revision are characteristically epistemic; they concern such notions as quality of evidence and the tendency to yield truths. Many different rules have been proposed for updating one's belief set. In general, belief revision typically balances risk of error against information increase. Belief revision is widely thought to proceed either by expansion or by conceptual revision. Expansion occurs in virtue of new observations; a belief is changed, or a new belief established, when a hypothesis (or provisional belief) is supported by evidence whose probability is high enough to meet a favored criterion of epistemic warrant. The hypothesis then becomes part of the existing belief corpus, or is sufficient to prompt revision. Conceptual revision occurs when appropriate changes are made in theoretical assumptions – in accordance with such principles as simplicity and explanatory or predictive power – by which the corpus is organized. In actual cases, we tend to revise beliefs with an eye toward advancing the best comprehensive explanation in the relevant cognitive domain. **See also** BAYESIAN RATIONALITY, COHERENTISM, EPISTEMOLOGY, FOUNDATIONALISM, REFLECTIVE EQUILIBRIUM.

J.D.T.

Bell's theorem. See PHILOSOPHY OF SCIENCE, QUANTUM MECHANICS.

beneficence. See VIRTUE ETHICS.

Beneke, Friedrich Eduard (1798–1854), German philosopher who was influenced by Herbart and English empiricism and criticized rationalistic metaphysics. He taught at Berlin and published some eighteen books in philosophy. His major work was *Lehrbuch der Psychologie als Naturwissenschaft* (1833). He wrote a critical study of Kant's *Critique of Pure Reason* and another on his moral theory; other works included *Psychologie Skizzen* (1825), *Metaphysik und Religionphilosophie* (1840), and *Die neue Psychologie* (1845).

The "new psychology" developed by Beneke held that the hypostatization of "faculties" led to a mythical psychology. He proposed a method that would yield a natural science of the soul or, in effect, an associationist psychology. Influenced by the British empiricists, he conceived the elements of mental life as dynamic, active processes or impulses (*Trieben*). These "elementary faculties," originally activated by stimuli, generate the substantial unity of the nature of the psychic by their persistence as traces, as well as by their reciprocal adjustment in relation to the continuous production of new forces.

In what Beneke called "pragmatic psychology," the psyche is a bundle of impulses, forces, and functions. Psychological theory should rest on inductive analyses of the facts of inner perception. This, in turn, is the foundation of the philosophical disciplines of logic, ethics, metaphysics, and philosophy of religion. In this regard, Beneke held a psychologism. He agreed with Herbart that psychology must be based on inner experience and must eschew metaphysical speculation, but rejected Hebart's mathematical reductionism. Beneke sought to create a "pragmatic philosophy" based on his psychology. In his last years he contributed to pedagogic theory. **See also** ASSOCIATIONISM.

G.J.S.

benevolence. See VIRTUE ETHICS.

Bentham, Jeremy (1748–1832), British philosopher of ethics and political-legal theory. Born in London, he entered Queen's College, Oxford, at age 12, and after graduation entered Lincoln's Inn to study law. He was admitted to the bar in 1767 but never practiced. He spent his life writing, advocating changes along utilitarian lines (maximal happiness for everyone affected) of the whole legal system, especially the criminal law. He was a strong influence in changes of the British law of evidence; in abolition of laws permitting imprisonment for indebtedness; in the reform of Parliamentary representation; in the formation of a civil service recruited by examination; and in much else. His major work published during his lifetime was *An Introduction to the Principles of Morals and Legislation* (1789). He became head of a "radical" group including James Mill and J. S. Mill, and founded the *Westminster Review* and University College, London (where his embalmed body still reposes in a closet). He was a friend of Catherine of Russia and John Quincy Adams, and was made a citizen of France in 1792.

Pleasure, he said, is the only good, and pain the only evil: "else the words good and evil have no meaning." He gives a list of examples of what he means by 'pleasure': pleasures of taste, smell, or touch; of acquiring property; of learning that one has the goodwill of others; of power; of a view of the pleasures of those one cares about. Bentham was also a psychological hedonist: pleasures and pains determine what we do. Take pain. Your state of mind may be painful now (at the time just prior to action) because it includes the expectation of the pain (say) of being burned; the present pain (or the expectation of later pain – Bentham is undecided which) motivates action to prevent being burned. One of a person's pleasures, however, may be sympathetic enjoyment of the well-being of another. So it seems one can be motivated by the prospect of the happiness of another. His psychology here is not incompatible with altruistic motivation.

Bentham's critical utilitarianism lies in his claim that any action, or measure of government, *ought* to be taken if and only if it tends to augment the happiness of everyone affected – not at all a novel principle, historically. When "thus interpreted, the words *ought,* and *right* and *wrong* . . . have a meaning: when otherwise, they have none." Bentham evidently did not mean this statement as a purely linguistic point about the actual meaning of moral terms. Neither can this principle be *proved;* it is a first principle from which all proofs proceed. What kind of reason, then, can he offer in its support? At one point he says that the principle of utility, at least unconsciously, governs the judgment of "every thinking man . . . unavoidably." But his chief answer is his critique of a widely held principle that a person properly calls an act wrong if (when informed of the facts) he *disapproves* of it. (Bentham cites other language as coming to the same thesis: talk of a "moral sense," or common sense, or the understanding, or the law of nature, or right reason, or the "fitness of things.") He says that this is no principle at all, since a "principle is

something that points out some external consideration, as a means of warranting and guiding the internal sentiments of approbation. . . ." The alleged principle also allows for widespread disagreement about what is moral.

So far, Bentham's proposal has not told us exactly how to determine whether an action or social measure is right or wrong. Bentham suggests a hedonic calculus: in comparing two actions under consideration, we count up the pleasures or pains each will probably produce – how intense, how long-lasting, whether near or remote, including any derivative later pleasures or pains that may be caused, and sum them up for all persons who will be affected. Evidently these directions can provide at best only approximate results. We are in no position to decide whether one pleasure for one hour is greater than another pleasure for half an hour, even when they are both pleasures of one person who can compare them. How much more when the pleasures are of different persons? Still, we can make judgments important for the theory of punishment: whether a blow in the face with no lasting damage for one person is more or less painful than fifty lashes for his assailant!

Bentham has been much criticized because he thought that two pleasures are equal in value, if they are equally intense, enduring, etc. As he said, "Quantity of pleasure being equal, pushpin is as good as poetry." It has been thought (e.g., by J. S. Mill) that some pleasures, especially intellectual ones, are higher and deserve to count more. But it may be replied that the so-called higher pleasures are more enduring, are less likely to be followed by satiety, and open up new horizons of enjoyment; and when these facts are taken into account, it is not clear that there is need to accord higher status to intellectual pleasures as such.

A major goal of Bentham's was to apply to the criminal law his principle of maximizing the general utility. Bentham thought there should be no punishment of an offense if it is not injurious to someone. So how much punishment should there be? The least amount the effect of which will result in a greater degree of happiness, overall. The benefit of punishment is primarily deterrence, by attaching to the thought of a given act the thought of the painful sanction – which will deter both the past and prospective lawbreakers. The punishment, then, must be severe enough to outweigh the benefit of the offense to the agent, making allowance, by addition, for the uncertainty that the punishment will actually occur.

There are some harmful acts, however, that it is

not beneficial to punish. One is an act needful to produce a greater benefit, or avoid a serious evil, for the agent. Others are those which a penal prohibition could not deter: when the law is unpublished or the agent is insane or an infant. In some cases society need feel no alarm about the future actions of the agent. Thus, an act is criminal only if intentional, and the agent is excused if he acted on the basis of beliefs such that, were they true, the act would have caused no harm, unless these beliefs were culpable in the sense that they would not have been held by a person of ordinary prudence or benevolence. The propriety of punishing an act also depends somewhat on its motive, although no motive e.g., sexual desire, curiosity, wanting money, love of reputation – is bad in itself. Yet the propriety of punishment is affected by the presence of some motivations that enhance public security because it is unlikely that they – e.g., sympathetic concern or concern for reputation – will lead to bad intentional acts. When a given motive leads to a bad intention, it is usually because of the weakness of motives like sympathy, concern for avoiding punishment, or respect for law.

In general, the sanction of *moral* criticism should take lines roughly similar to those of the ideal law. But there are some forms of behavior, e.g., imprudence or fornication, which the law is hardly suited to punish, that can be sanctioned by morality.

The business of the moral philosopher is censorial: to say what the law, or morality, *ought* to be. To say what *is* the law is a different matter: what it is is the *commands* of the sovereign, defined as one whom the public, in general, habitually obeys. As consisting of commands, it is imperatival. The imperatives may be addressed to the public, as in "Let no one steal," or to judges: "Let a judge sentence anyone who steals to be hanged." It may be thought that there is a third part, an explanation, say, of what is a person's property; but this can be absorbed in the imperatival part, since the designations of property are just imperatives about who is to be free to do what. Why should anyone obey the actual laws? Bentham's answer is that one should do so if and only if it promises to maximize the general happiness. He eschews contract theories of political obligation: individuals now alive never contracted, and so how are they bound? He also opposes appeal to natural rights. If what are often mentioned as natural rights were taken seriously, no government could survive: it could not tax, require military service, etc. Nor does he accept appeal to "natural law," as if, once some law is

shown to be immoral, it can be said to be not really law. That would be absurd.

See also HEDONISM, PHILOSOPHY OF LAW, UTILITARIANISM.   R.B.B.

Berdyaev, Nicolas (1874–1948), Russian religious thinker. He began as a "Kantian Marxist" in epistemology, ethical theory, and philosophy of history, but soon turned away from Marxism (although he continued to accept Marx's critique of capitalism) toward a theistic philosophy of existence stressing the values of creativity and "meonic" freedom – a freedom allegedly prior to all being, including that of God. In exile after 1922, Berdyaev appears to have been the first to grasp clearly (in the early 1920s) that the Marxist view of historical time involves a morally unacceptable devaluing and instrumentalizing of the historical *present* (including living persons) for the sake of the remote *future* end of a perfected communist society. Berdyaev rejects the Marxist position on both Christian and Kantian grounds, as a violation of the intrinsic value of human persons. He sees the historical order as marked by inescapable tragedy, and welcomes the "end of history" as an "overcoming" of objective historical time by subjective "existential" time with its free, unobjectified creativity. For Berdyaev the "world of objects" – physical things, laws of nature, social institutions, and human roles and relationships – is a pervasive threat to "free spiritual creativity." Yet such creativity appears to be subject to inevitable frustration, since its outward embodiments are always "partial and fragmentary" and no "outward action" can escape ultimate "tragic failure." Russian Orthodox traditionalists condemned Berdyaev for claiming that all creation is a "divine-*human* process" and for denying God's omnipotence, but such Western process theologians as Hartshorne find Berdyaev's position highly congenial. **See also** RUSSIAN PHILOSOPHY.   G.L.K.

Bergmann, Gustav (1906–87), Austrian philosopher, the youngest member of the Vienna Circle. Born in Vienna, he received his doctorate in mathematics in 1928 from the University of Vienna. Originally influenced by logical positivism, he became a phenomenalist who also posited mental acts irreducible to sense-data (see his *The Metaphysics of Logical Positivism*, 1954). Although he eventually rejected phenomenalism, his ontology of material objects remained structurally phenomenalistic. Bergmann's world is one of momentary bare (i.e. natureless) particulars exemplifying (phenomenally) simple universals, relational as well as non-relational. Some of these universals are non-mental, such as color properties and spatial relations, while others, such as the "intentional characters" in virtue of which some particulars (mental acts) intend or represent the facts that are their "objects," are mental. Bergmann insisted that the world is independent of both our experience of it and our thought and discourse about it: he claimed that the connection of exemplification and even the propositional connectives and quantifiers are mind-independent. (See *Meaning and Existence*, 1959; *Logic and Reality*, 1964; and *Realism: A Critique of Brentano and Meinong*, 1967.)

Such extreme realism produced many criticisms of his philosophy that are only finally addressed in Bergmann's recently, and posthumously, published book, *New Foundations of Ontology* (1992), in which he concedes that his atomistic approach to ontology has inevitable limitations and proposes a way of squaring this insight with his thoroughgoing realism.

See also METAPHYSICS, VIENNA CIRCLE.

W.He.

Bergson, Henri Louis (1859–1941), French philosopher, the most influential of the first half of the twentieth century. Born in Paris and educated at the prestigious École Normale Supérieure, he began his teaching career at Clermont-Ferrand in 1884 and was called in 1900 to the Collège de France, where his lectures enjoyed unparalleled success until his retirement in 1921. Ideally placed in *la belle époque* of prewar Paris, his ideas influenced a broad spectrum of artistic, literary, social, and political movements. In 1918 he received the Légion d'honneur and was admitted into the French Academy. From 1922 through 1925 he participated in the League of Nations, presiding over the creation of what was later to become UNESCO. Forced by crippling arthritis into virtual seclusion during his later years, Bergson was awarded the Nobel Prize for literature in 1928.

Initially a disciple of Spencer, Bergson broke with him after a careful examination of Spencer's concept of time and mechanistic positivism. Following a deeply entrenched tradition in Western thought, Spencer treats time (on an analogy with space) as a series of discrete numerical units: instants, seconds, minutes. When confronted with experience, however – especially with that of our own psychological states – such concepts are, Bergson concludes, patently inadequate. Real duration, unlike clock time, is qualitative, dynamic, irreversible. It cannot be "spatialized"

without being deformed. It gives rise in us, moreover, to free acts, which, being qualitative and spontaneous, cannot be predicted.

Bergson's dramatic contrast of real duration and geometrical space, first developed in *Time and Free Will* (1890), was followed in 1896 by the mind–body theory of *Matter and Memory*. He argues here that the brain is not a locale for thought but a motor organ that, receiving stimuli from its environment, may respond with adaptive behavior. To his psychological and metaphysical distinction between duration and space Bergson adds, in *An Introduction to Metaphysics* (1903), an important epistemological distinction between intuition and analysis. Intuition probes the flow of duration in its concreteness; analysis breaks up duration into static, fragmentary concepts.

In *Creative Evolution* (1907), his best-known work, Bergson argues against both Lamarck and Darwin, urging that biological evolution is impelled by a vital impetus or *élan vital* that drives life to overcome the downward entropic drift of matter. Biological organisms, unlike dice, must compete and survive as they undergo permutations. Hence the unresolved dilemma of Darwinism. Either mutations occur one or a few at a time (in which case how can they be "saved up" to constitute new organs?) or they occur all at once (in which case one has a "miracle").

Bergson's vitalism, popular in literary circles, was not accepted by many scientists or philosophers. His most general contention, however – that biological evolution is not consistent with or even well served by a mechanistic philosophy – was broadly appreciated and to many seemed convincing. This aspect of Bergson's writings influenced thinkers as diverse as Lloyd Morgan, Alexis Carrel, Sewall Wright, Pierre Teilhard de Chardin, and A. N. Whitehead.

The contrasts in terms of which Bergson developed his thought (duration/space, intuition/analysis, life/entropy) are replaced in *The Two Sources of Morality and Religion* (1932) by a new duality, that of the "open" and the "closed." The Judeo-Christian tradition, he contends, if it has embraced in its history both the open society and the closed society, exhibits in its great saints and mystics a profound opening out of the human spirit toward all humanity. Bergson's distinction between the open and the closed society was popularized by Karl Popper in his *The Open Society and Its Enemies*.

While it has attracted serious criticism, Bergson's philosophy has also significantly affected subsequent thinkers. Novelists as diverse as

Nikos Kazantzakis, Marcel Proust, and William Faulkner; poets as unlike as Charles Péguy, ʰert Frost, and Antonio Machado; and psy- ⁻ists as dissimilar as Pierre Janet and Jean ⁻e to profit significantly from his explo- ⁻ duration, conceptualization, and ⁻th French existentialism and Amer- ⁻ss philosophy bear the imprint of his

⊃ SPENCER, TIME, WHITEHEAD.

P.A.Y.G.

ge (1685–1753), Irish philoso- ⁻ in the Anglican Church of Ire- ⁻e three great British empiricists ⁻e and Hume. He developed novel ⁻iews on the visual perception of ⁻e, and an idealist metaphysical ⁻efended partly on the seemingly ⁻nd that it was the best defense ⁻e and safeguard against skepti-

⁻died at Trinity College, Dublin, ⁻e graduated at nineteen. He was ⁻lowship at Trinity in 1707, and did the bulk of his philosophical writing between that year and 1713. He was made dean of Derry in 1724, following extensive traveling on the Continent; he spent the years 1728–32 in Rhode Island, waiting in vain for promised Crown funds to establish a college in Bermuda. He was made bishop of Cloyne, Ireland, in 1734, and he remained there as a cleric for nearly the remainder of his life.

Berkeley's first major publication, the *Essay Towards a New Theory of Vision* (1709), is principally a work in the psychology of vision, though it has important philosophical presuppositions and implications. Berkeley's theory of vision became something like the received view on the topic for nearly two hundred years and is a landmark work in the history of psychology. The work is devoted to three connected matters: how do we see, or visually estimate, the distances of objects from ourselves, the situation or place at which objects are located, and the magnitude of such objects?

Earlier views, such as those of Descartes, Malebranche, and Molyneux, are rejected on the ground that their answers to the above questions allow that a person can see the distance of an object without having first learned to correlate visual and other cues. This was supposedly done by a kind of natural geometry, a computation of the distance by determining the altitude of a triangle formed by light rays from the object and angle formed by light rays from the object and the line extending from one retina to the other. On the contrary, Berkeley holds that it is clear that seeing distance is something one learns to do through trial and error, mainly by correlating cues that suggest distance: the distinctness or confusion of the visual appearance; the feelings received when the eyes turn; and the sensations attending the straining of the eyes. None of these bears any necessary connection to distance.

Berkeley infers from this account that a person born blind and later given sight would not be able to tell by sight alone the distances objects were from her, nor tell the difference between a sphere and a cube. He also argues that in visually estimating distance, one is really estimating which tangible ideas one would likely experience if one were to take steps to approach the object. Not that these tangible ideas are themselves necessarily connected to the visual appearances. Instead, Berkeley holds that tangible and visual ideas are entirely heterogeneous, i.e., they are numerically and specifically distinct. The latter is a philosophical consequence of Berkeley's theory of vision, which is sharply at odds with a central doctrine of Locke's *Essay*, namely, that some ideas are common to both sight and touch.

Locke's doctrines also receive a great deal of attention in the *Principles of Human Knowledge* (1710). Here Berkeley considers the doctrine of abstract general ideas, which he finds in Book III of Locke's *Essay*. He argues against such ideas partly on the ground that we cannot engage in the process of abstraction, partly on the ground that some abstract ideas are impossible objects, and also on the ground that such ideas are not needed for either language learning or language use. These arguments are of fundamental importance for Berkeley, since he thinks that the doctrine of abstract ideas helps to support metaphysical realism, absolute space, absolute motion, and absolute time (*Principles*, 5, 100, 110–11), as well as the view that some ideas are common to sight and touch (*New Theory*, 123). All of these doctrines Berkeley holds to be mistaken, and the first is in direct conflict with his idealism. Hence, it is important for him to undermine any support these doctrines might receive from the abstract ideas thesis.

Berkeleyan idealism is the view that the only existing entities are finite and infinite perceivers each of which is a spirit or mental substance, and entities that are perceived. Such a thesis implies that ordinary physical objects exist if and only if they are perceived, something Berkeley encapsulates in the *esse est percipi* principle: for all sensible objects, i.e., objects capable of being perceived, their being is to be perceived. He gives essentially two arguments for this thesis. First, he holds that every physical object is just a collection of sensible qualities, and that every sensible quality is an idea. So, physical objects are just collections of sensible ideas. No *idea* can exist unperceived, something everyone in the period would have granted. Hence, no physical object can exist unperceived. The second argument is the so-called master argument of *Principles* 22–24. There Berkeley argues that one cannot conceive a sensible object existing unperceived, because if one attempts to do this one must thereby conceive that very object. He concludes from this that no such object can exist "without the mind," that is, wholly unperceived.

Many of Berkeley's opponents would have held instead that a physical object is best analyzed as a material *substratum*, in which some sensible qualities inhere. So Berkeley spends some effort arguing against material substrata or what he sometimes calls matter. His principal argument is that a sensible quality cannot inhere in matter, because a sensible quality is an idea, and surely an idea cannot exist except in a mind. This argument would be decisive if it were true that each sensible quality is an idea. Unfortunately, Berkeley gives no argument whatever for this contention in the *Principles,* and for that reason Berkeleyan idealism is not there well founded. Nor does the master argument fare much better, for there Berkeley seems to require a premise asserting that if an object is *conceived,* then that object is *perceived.* Yet such a premise is highly dubious.

Probably Berkeley realized that his case for idealism had not been successful, and certainly he was stung by the poor reception of the *Principles.* His next book, *Three Dialogues Between Hylas and Philonous* (1713), is aimed at rectifying these matters. There he argues at length for the thesis that each sensible quality is an idea. The master argument is repeated, but it is unnecessary if every sensible quality is an idea.

In the *Dialogues* Berkeley is also much concerned to combat skepticism and defend common sense. He argues that *representative realism* as held by Locke leads to skepticism regarding the external world and this, Berkeley thinks, helps to support atheism and free thinking in religion. He also argues, more directly, that representative realism is false. Such a thesis incorporates the claim that *some* sensible ideas represent real qualities in objects, the so-called primary qualities. But Berkeley argues that a sensible idea can be *like* nothing but another idea, and so ideas cannot represent qualities in objects. In this way, Berkeley eliminates one main support of skepticism, and to that extent helps to support the commonsensical idea that we gain knowledge of the existence and nature of ordinary physical objects by means of perception.

Berkeley's positive views in epistemology are usually interpreted as a version of foundationalism. That is, he is generally thought to have defended the view that beliefs about currently perceived ideas are basic beliefs, beliefs that are immediately and non-inferentially justified or that count as pieces of immediate knowledge, and that all other justified beliefs in contingent propositions are justified by being somehow based upon the basic beliefs. Indeed, such a foundationalist doctrine is often taken to help define empiricism, held in common by Locke, Berkeley, and Hume. But whatever the merits of such a view as an interpretation of Locke or Hume, it is not Berkeley's theory. This is because he allows that perceivers often have immediate and non-inferential justified beliefs, and knowledge, about physical objects. Hence, Berkeley accepts a version of foundationalism that allows for basic beliefs quite different from just beliefs about one's currently perceived ideas. Indeed, he goes so far as to maintain that such physical object beliefs are often certain, something neither Locke nor Hume would accept.

In arguing against the existence of matter, Berkeley also maintains that we literally have no coherent concept of such stuff because we cannot have any sensible idea of it. Parity of reasoning would seem to dictate that Berkeley should reject mental substance as well, thereby threatening his idealism from another quarter. Berkeley is sensitive to this line of reasoning, and replies that while we have no idea of the self, we do have some *notion* of the self, that is, some less-than-complete concept. He argues that a person gains some immediate knowledge of the existence and nature of herself in a *reflex act;* that is, when she is perceiving something she is also conscious that something is engaging in this perception, and this is sufficient for knowledge of that perceiving entity.

To complement his idealism, Berkeley worked out a version of scientific instrumentalism, both in the *Principles* and in a later Latin work, *De Motu* (1721), a doctrine that anticipates the views of Mach. In the *Dialogues* he tries to show how his idealism is consistent with the biblical account of the creation, and consistent as well with common sense.

Three later works of Berkeley's gained him an enormous amount of attention. *Alciphron* (1734) was written while Berkeley was in Rhode Island, and is a philosophical defense of Christian doctrine. It also contains some additional comments on perception, supplementing earlier work on that topic. *The Analyst* (1734) contains trenchant criticism of the method of fluxions in differential calculus, and it set off a flurry of pamphlet replies to Berkeley's criticisms, to which Berkeley responded in his *A Defense of Free Thinking in Mathematics. Siris* (1744) contains a detailed account of the medicinal values of tar-water, water boiled with the bark of certain trees. This book also contains a defense of a sort of corpuscularian philosophy that seems to be at odds with the idealism elaborated in the earlier works for which Berkeley is now famous.

In the years 1707–08, the youthful Berkeley kept a series of notebooks in which he worked out his ideas in philosophy and mathematics. These books, now known as the *Philosophical Commentaries,* provide the student of Berkeley with the rare opportunity to see a great philosopher's thought in development.

   See also HUME, IDEALISM, LOCKE, PERCEPTION, PHENOMENALISM.   G.S.P.

Berlin, Isaiah (1909–97), British philosopher and historian of ideas. He is widely acclaimed for his doctrine of radical objective pluralism; his writings on liberty; his modification, refinement, and defense of traditional liberalism against the totalitarian doctrines of the twentieth century (not least Marxism-Leninism); and his brilliant and illuminating studies in the history of ideas from Machiavelli and Vico to Marx and Sorel. A founding father with Austin, Ayer, and others of Oxford philosophy in the 1930s, he published several influential papers in its general spirit, but, without abandoning its empirical approach, he came increasingly to dissent from what seemed to him its unduly barren, doctrinaire, and truth-denying tendencies. From the 1950s onward he broke away to devote himself principally to social and political philosophy and to the study of general ideas.

His two most important contributions in social and political theory, brought together with two other valuable essays in *Four Essays on Liberty* (1969), are "Historical Inevitability" (1954) and his 1958 inaugural lecture as Chichele Professor of Social and Political Theory at Oxford, "Two Concepts of Liberty." The first is a bold and decisive attack on historical determinism and moral relativism and subjectivism and a ringing endorsement of the role of free will and responsibility in human history. The second contains Berlin's enormously influential attempt to distinguish clearly between "negative" and "positive" liberty. Negative liberty, foreshadowed by such thinkers as J. S. Mill, Constant, and above all Herzen, consists in making minimal assumptions about the ultimate nature and needs of the subject, in ensuring a minimum of external interference by authority of any provenance, and in leaving open as large a field for free individual choice as is consonant with a minimum of social organization and order. Positive liberty, associated with monist and voluntarist thinkers of all kinds, not least Hegel, the German Idealists, and their historical progeny, begins with the notion of self-mastery and proceeds to make dogmatic and far-reaching metaphysical assumptions about the essence of the subject. It then deduces from these the proper paths to freedom, and, finally, seeks to drive flesh-and-blood individuals down these preordained paths, whether they wish it or not, within the framework of a tight-knit centralized state under the irrefragable rule of rational experts, thus perverting what begins as a legitimate human ideal, i.e. positive self-direction and self-mastery, into a tyranny. "Two Concepts of Liberty" also sets out to disentangle liberty in either of these senses from other ends, such as the craving for recognition, the need to belong, or human solidarity, fraternity, or equality.

Berlin's work in the history of ideas is of a piece with his other writings. *Vico and Herder* (1976) presents the emergence of that historicism and pluralism which shook the two-thousand-year-old monist rationalist faith in a unified body of truth regarding all questions of fact and principle in all fields of human knowledge. From this profound intellectual overturn Berlin traces in subsequent volumes of essays, such as *Against the Current* (1979), *The Crooked Timber of Humanity* (1990), and *The Sense of Reality* (1996), the growth of some of the principal intellectual movements that mark our era, among them nationalism, fascism, relativism, subjectivism, nihilism, voluntarism, and existentialism. He also presents with persuasiveness and clarity that peculiar objective pluralism which he identified and made his own. There is an irreducible plurality of objective human values, many of which are incompatible with one another; hence the ineluctable need for absolute choices by individuals and groups, a need that confers supreme value upon, and forms one of the major justifications of, his conception of negative liberty;

hence, too, his insistence that utopia, namely a world where all valid human ends and objective values are simultaneously realized in an ultimate synthesis, is a conceptual impossibility.

While not himself founder of any definable school or movement, Berlin's influence as a philosopher and as a human being has been immense, not least on a variety of distinguished thinkers such as Stuart Hampshire, Charles Taylor, Bernard Williams, Richard Wollheim, Gerry Cohen, Steven Lukes, David Pears, and many others. His general intellectual and moral impact on the life of the twentieth century as writer, diplomat, patron of music and the arts, international academic elder statesman, loved and trusted friend to the great and the humble, and dazzling lecturer, conversationalist, and *animateur des idées*, will furnish inexhaustible material to future historians.

See also FREE WILL PROBLEM, LIBERALISM, POLITICAL PHILOSOPHY, POSITIVE AND NEGATIVE FREEDOM.   R.Hau.

Bernard of Chartres (fl. 1114–26), French philosopher. He was first a teacher (1114–19) and later chancellor (1119–26) of the cathedral school at Chartres, which was then an active center of learning in the liberal arts and philosophy. Bernard himself was renowned as a grammarian, i.e., as an expositor of difficult texts, and as a teacher of Plato. None of his works has survived whole, and only three fragments are preserved in works by others. He is now best known for an image recorded both by his student, John of Salisbury, and by William of Conches. In Bernard's image, he and all his medieval contemporaries were in relation to the ancient authors like "dwarfs sitting on the shoulders of giants." John of Salisbury takes the image to mean both that the medievals could see more and further than the ancients, and that they could do so only because they had been lifted up by such powerful predecessors.   M.D.J.

Bernard of Clairvaux, Saint (1090–1153), French Cistercian monk, mystic, and religious leader. He is most noted for his doctrine of Christian humility and his depiction of the mystical experience, which exerted considerable influence on later Christian mystics. Educated in France, he entered the monastery at Cîteaux in 1112, and three years later founded a daughter monastery at Clairvaux.

According to Bernard, honest self-knowledge should reveal the extent to which we fail to be what we should be in the eyes of God. That self-knowledge should lead us to curb our pride and so become more humble. Humility is necessary for spiritual purification, which in turn is necessary for contemplation of God, the highest form of which is union with God. Consistent with orthodox Christian doctrine, Bernard maintains that mystical union does not entail identity. One does not become God; rather, one's will and God's will come into complete conformity.

See also MYSTICISM.   W.E.M.

Bernoulli's theorem, also called the (weak) law of large numbers, the principle that if a series of trials is repeated n times where (a) there are two possible outcomes, 0 and 1, on each trial, (b) the probability p of 0 is the same on each trial, and (c) this probability is independent of the outcome of other trials, then, for arbitrary positive ε, as the number n of trials is increased, the probability that the absolute value $|r/n - p|$ of the difference between the relative frequency r/n of 0's in the n trials and p is less than ε approaches 1. The first proof of this theorem was given by Jakob Bernoulli in Part IV of his posthumously published *Ars Conjectandi* of 1713. Simplifications were later constructed and his result has been generalized in a series of "weak laws of large numbers." Although Bernoulli's theorem derives a conclusion about the probability of the relative frequency r/n of 0's for large n of trials given the value of p, in *Ars Conjectandi* and correspondence with Leibniz, Bernoulli thought it could be used to reason from information about r/n to the value of p when the latter is unknown. Speculation persists as to whether Bernoulli anticipated the inverse inference of Bayes, the confidence interval estimation of Peirce, J. Neyman, and E. S. Pearson, or the fiducial argument of R. A. Fisher. See also PROBABILITY.   I.L.

Berry's paradox. See SEMANTIC PARADOXES.

Bertrand's box paradox, a puzzle concerning conditional probability. Imagine three boxes with two drawers apiece. Each drawer of the first box contains a gold medal. Each drawer of the second contains a silver medal. One drawer of the third contains a gold medal, and the other a silver medal. At random, a box is selected and one of its drawers is opened. If a gold medal appears, what is the probability that the third box was selected? The probability seems to be ½, because the box is either the first or the third, and they seem equally probable. But a gold medal is less probable from the third box than from the first, so the third box is actually less probable than the first. By Bayes's theorem its probability is $^1/_3$. Joseph Bertrand, a French mathematician, published the paradox in *Calcul des probabilités* (*Calculus of Probabilities*, 1889). **See also BAYES'S THEOREM, PROBABILITY.**   P.We.

Bertrand's paradox, an inconsistency arising from the classical definition of an event's probability as the number of favorable cases divided by the number of possible cases. Given a circle, a chord is selected at random. What is the probability that the chord is longer than a side of an equilateral triangle inscribed in the circle? The event has these characterizations: (1) the apex angle of an isosceles triangle inscribed in the circle and having the chord as a leg is less than 60°, (2) the chord intersects the diameter perpendicular to it less than ½ a radius from the circle's center, and (3) the chord's midpoint lies within a circle concentric with the original and of ¼ its area. The definition thus suggests that the event's probability is $^1/_3$, $^1/_2$, and also ¼. Joseph Bertrand, a French mathematician, published the paradox in *Calcul des probabilités* (1889). **See also PROBABILITY.**   P.We.

Beth's definability theorem, a theorem for first-order logic. A theory defines a term τ implicitly if and only if an explicit definition of the term, on the basis of the other primitive concepts, is entailed by the theory. A theory defines a term implicitly if any two models of the theory with the same domain and the same extension for the other primitive terms are identical, i.e., also have the same extension for the term. An explicit definition of a term is a sentence that states necessary and sufficient conditions for the term's applicability. Beth's theorem was implicit in a method to show independence of a term that was first used by the Italian logician Alessandro Padoa (1868–1937). Padoa suggested, in 1900, that independence of a primitive algebraic term from the other terms occurring in a set of axioms can be established by two true interpretations of the axioms that differ only in the interpretation of the term whose independence has to be proven. He claimed, without proof, that the existence of two such models is not only sufficient for, but also implied by, independence.

Tarski first gave a proof of Beth's theorem in 1926 for the logic of the *Principia Mathematica* of Whitehead and Russell, but the result was only obtained for first-order logic in 1953 by the Dutch logician Evert Beth (1908–64). In modern expositions Beth's theorem is a direct implication of Craig's interpolation theorem. In a variation on Padoa's method, Karel de Bouvère described in 1959 a one-model method to show indefinability: if the set of logical consequences of a theory formulated in terms of the remaining vocabulary cannot be extended to a model of the full theory, a term is not explicitly definable in terms of the remaining vocabulary. In the philosophy of science literature this is called a failure of Ramsey-eliminability of the term.

See also MODEL THEORY.   Z.G.S.

Bhagavad Gita (from Sanskrit *Bhagavadgītā,* 'song of the blessed one/exalted lord'), Hindu devotional poem composed and edited between the fifth century B.C. and the second century A.D. It contains eighteen chapters and seven hundred verses, and forms the sixth book (Chapters 23–40) of the Indian epic Mahabharata. In its narrative, the warrior Arjuna, reluctantly waiting to wage war, receives a revelation from the Lord Krishna that emphasizes selfless deeds and *bhakti,* or devotion. Strictly classified as *smṛti* or fallible tradition, the Gita is typically treated as *shruti* or infallible revelation. Such major thinkers as Shaṅkara, Rāmānuja, and Madhva wrote commentaries on this beloved book. Shaṅkara reads it as teaching that enlightenment comes through right (Advaita Vedanta) knowledge alone even without performance of religious duties. Rāmānuja takes it to hold that enlightenment comes through performance of religious duties, particularly devotion to God for whose sake alone all other duties must be performed if one's sins are to be washed away. Such devotion leads to (or at its zenith includes) self-knowledge and knowledge of personal Brahman. Madhva sees the Gita as emphasizing divine uniqueness and the necessity of love and attachment to God and not to oneself or the consequences of one's deeds.   K.E.Y.

bhakti (Sanskrit), in Hindu theistic thought systems, devotion. *Bhakti* includes the ideas of faith, surrender, love, affection, and attachment. Its most common form of expression is worship by means of offerings, *pūjā.* Theistic thinkers such as Rāmānuja and Madhva argue that devotion is the key element that solves the human predicament. As a result the deity responds with grace or kindness (*prasādam*) and thereby causes the devotee to prosper or attain *moksha.* The *Bhakti Sūtras* (twelfth century A.D.) distinguish "lower *bhakti,"* i.e., devotion with personal goals in mind, from "higher *bhakti,"* i.e., selfless devotion practiced only to please the deity. The latter is liberation. Modern Hindu philosophers, following Shaṅkara and the modern Hindu apologist Swami Vivekānanda (1862–1902), often relegate *bhakti* to a lower path than knowledge (*jñāna*) for those who are unable to follow philosophy, but in the philosophical systems of many theists it is defended as the highest path with the main obstacle as unbelief, not ignorance. **See also** HINDUISM.   R.N.Mi.

bhavaṅga, a subliminal mode of consciousness, according to Theravada Buddhist philosophers, in which no mental activity occurs. The continued existence of the *bhavaṅga*-mind in states where there is no intentional mental activity (e.g., dreamless sleep) is what guarantees the continuance of a particular mental continuum in such states. It operates also in ordinary events of sensation and conceptualization, being connected with such intentional mental events in complex ways, and is appealed to as an explanatory category in the accounts of the process leading from death to rebirth. Some Buddhists also use it as a soteriological category, identifying the *bhavaṅga*-mind with mind in its pure state, mind as luminous and radiant. **See also** ĀLAYA-VIJÑĀNA, NIRODHA-SAMĀPATTI.   P.J.G.

biconditional, the logical operator, usually written with a triple-bar sign (≡) or a double-headed arrow (↔), used to indicate that two propositions have the same truth-value: that either both are true or else both are false. The term also designates a proposition having this sign, or a natural language expression of it, as its main connective; e.g., *P* if and only if *Q*. The truth table for the biconditional is

P	Q	P-biconditional-Q
T	T	T
T	F	F
F	T	F
F	F	T

The biconditional is so called because its application is logically equivalent to the conjunction '(*P*-conditional-*Q*)-and-(*Q*-conditional-*P*)'. **See also** TRUTH TABLE.   R.W.B.

biconditional, Tarskian. See TARSKI.

bilateral reduction sentence. See REDUCTION SENTENCE.

binary quantifier. See PLURALITIVE LOGIC.

bioethics, the subfield of ethics that concerns the ethical issues arising in medicine and from advances in biological science. One central area of bioethics is the ethical issues that arise in relations between health care professionals and patients. A second area focuses on broader issues of social justice in health care. A third area concerns the ethical issues raised by new biological knowledge or technology.

In relations between health care professionals and patients, a fundamental issue is the appropriate role of each in decision making about patient care. More traditional views assigning principal decision-making authority to physicians have largely been replaced with ideals of shared decision making that assign a more active role to patients. Shared decision making is thought to reflect better the importance of patients' self-determination in controlling their care. This increased role for patients is reflected in the ethical and legal doctrine of informed consent, which requires that health care not be rendered without the informed and voluntary consent of a competent patient. The requirement that consent be informed places a positive responsibility on health care professionals to provide their patients with the information they need to make informed decisions about care. The requirement that consent be voluntary requires that treatment not be forced, nor that patients' decisions be coerced or manipulated. If patients lack the capacity to make competent health care decisions, e.g. young children or cognitively impaired adults, a surrogate, typically a parent in the case of children or a close family member in the case of adults, must decide for them. Surrogates' decisions should follow the patient's advance directive if one exists, be the decision the patient would have made in the circumstances if competent, or follow the patient's best interests if the patient has never been competent or his or her wishes are not known.

A major focus in bioethics generally, and treatment decision making in particular, is care at or near the end of life. It is now widely agreed that patients are entitled to decide about and to refuse, according to their own values, any life-sustaining treatment. They are also entitled to have desired treatments that may shorten their lives, such as high doses of pain medications necessary to relieve severe pain from cancer, although in practice pain treatment remains inadequate for many patients. Much more controversial is whether more active means to end life such as physician-assisted suicide and voluntary euthanasia are morally permissible in individual cases or justified as public policy; both remain illegal except in a very few jurisdictions.

Several other moral principles have been central to defining professional–patient relationships in health care. A principle of truth telling requires that professionals not lie to patients. Whereas in the past it was common, especially with patients with terminal cancers, not to inform patients fully about their diagnosis and prognosis, studies have shown that practice has changed substantially and that fully informing patients does not have the bad effects for patients that had been feared in the past. Principles of privacy and confidentiality require that information gathered in the professional–patient relationship not be disclosed to third parties without patients' consent. Especially with highly personal information in mental health care, or information that may lead to discrimination, such as a diagnosis of AIDS, assurance of confidentiality is fundamental to the trust necessary to a well-functioning professional–patient relationship. Nevertheless, exceptions to confidentiality to prevent imminent and serious harm to others are well recognized ethically and legally.

More recently, work in bioethics has focused on justice in the allocation of health care. Whereas nearly all developed countries treat health care as a moral and legal right, and ensure it to all their citizens through some form of national health care system, in the United States about 15 percent of the population remains without any form of health insurance. This has fed debates about whether health care is a right or privilege, a public or individual responsibility. Most bioethicists have supported a right to health care because of health care's fundamental impact on people's well-being, opportunity, ability to plan their lives, and even lives themselves. Even if there is a moral right to health care, however, few defend an unlimited right to all beneficial health care, no matter how small the benefit and how high the cost. Consequently, it is necessary to prioritize or ration health care services to reflect limited budgets for health care, and both the standards and procedures for doing so are ethically controversial. Utilitarians and defenders of cost-effectiveness analysis in health policy support using limited resources to maximize aggregate health benefits for the population. Their critics argue that this ignores concerns about equity, concerns about how health care resources and health are distributed. For example, some have argued that equity requires giving priority to treating the worst-off or sickest, even at a sacrifice in aggregate health benefits;

moreover, taking account in prioritization of differences in costs of different treatments can lead to ethically problematic results, such as giving higher priority to providing very small benefits to many persons than very large but individually more expensive benefits, including life-saving interventions, to a few persons, as the state of Oregon found in its initial widely publicized prioritization program. In the face of controversy over standards for rationing care, it is natural to rely on fair procedures to make rationing decisions.

Other bioethics issues arise from dramatic advances in biological knowledge and technology. Perhaps the most prominent example is new knowledge of human genetics, propelled in substantial part by the worldwide Human Genome Project, which seeks to map the entire human genome. This project and related research will enable the prevention of genetically transmitted diseases, but already raises questions about which conditions to prevent in offspring and which should be accepted and lived with, particularly when the means of preventing the condition is by abortion of the fetus with the condition.

Looking further into the future, new genetic knowledge and technology will likely enable us to enhance normal capacities, not just prevent or cure disease, and to manipulate the genes of future children, raising profoundly difficult questions about what kinds of persons to create and the degree to which deliberate human design should replace "nature" in the creation of our offspring. A dramatic example of new abilities to create offspring, though now limited to the animal realm, was the cloning in Scotland in 1997 of a sheep from a single cell of an adult sheep; this event raised the very controversial future prospect of cloning human beings. Finally, new reproductive technologies, such as oocyte (egg) donation, and practices such as surrogate motherhood, raise deep issues about the meaning and nature of parenthood and families.

    See also DIGNITY, ETHICS, EUTHANASIA, INFORMED CONSENT.   D.W.B.

biological naturalism. See SEARLE.

biology, autonomy of. See UNITY OF SCIENCE.

biology, philosophy of. See PHILOSOPHY OF BIOLOGY.

biology, social. See SOCIAL BIOLOGY.

Birkhoff–von Neumann logic. See QUANTUM LOGIC.

bit (from *bi*nary digi*t*), a unit or measure of information. Suggested by John W. Tukey, a bit is both an amount of information (a reduction of eight equally likely possibilities to one generates three bits [= $\log_2$ 8] of information) and a system of representing that quantity. The binary system uses 1's and 0's. **See also INFORMATION THEORY.** F.A.

bivalence, principle of. See PRINCIPLE OF BIVALENCE.

black box, a hypothetical unit specified only by functional role, in order to explain some effect or behavior. The term may refer to a single entity with an unknown structure, or unknown internal organization, which realizes some known function, or to any one of a system of such entities, whose organization and functions are inferred from the behavior of an organism or entity of which they are constituents.

Within behaviorism and classical learning theory, the basic functions were taken to be generalized mechanisms governing the relationship of stimulus to response, including reinforcement, inhibition, extinction, and arousal. The organism was treated as a black box realizing these functions. Within cybernetics, though there are no simple input–output rules describing the organism, there is an emphasis on functional organization and feedback in controlling behavior. The components within a cybernetic system are treated as black boxes. In both cases, the details of underlying structure, mechanism, and dynamics are either unknown or regarded as unimportant.

See also BEHAVIORISM, PHILOSOPHY OF MIND, THEORETICAL TERM. R.C.R.

bleen. See GRUE PARADOX.

blindsight, a residual visual capacity resulting from lesions in certain areas of the brain (the striate cortex, area 17). Under routine clinical testing, persons suffering such lesions appear to be densely blind in particular regions of the visual field. Researchers have long recognized that, in primates, comparable lesions do not result in similar deficits. It has seemed unlikely that this disparity could be due to differences in brain function, however. And, indeed, when human subjects are tested in the way non-human subjects are tested, the disparity vanishes. Although subjects report that they can detect nothing in the blind field, when required to "guess" at properties of items situated there, they perform

remarkably well. They seem to "know" the contents of the blind field while remaining unaware that they know, often expressing astonishment on being told the results of testing in the blind field. **See also PERCEPTION.** J.F.H.

Bloch, Ernst (1885–1977), German philosopher. Influenced by Marxism, his views went beyond Marxism as he matured. He fled Germany in the 1930s, but returned after World War II to a professorship in East Germany, where his increasingly unorthodox ideas were eventually censured by the Communist authorities, forcing a move to West Germany in the 1960s. His major work, *The Principle of Hope* (1954–59), is influenced by German idealism, Jewish mysticism, Neoplatonism, utopianism, and numerous other sources besides Marxism. Humans are essentially unfinished, moved by a cosmic impulse, "hope," a tendency in them to strive for the as-yet-unrealized, which manifests itself as utopia, or vision of future possibilities. Despite his atheism, Bloch wished to retrieve the sense of self-transcending that he saw in the religious and mythical traditions of humankind. His ideas have consequently influenced theology as well as philosophy, e.g. the "theology of hope" of Jurgen Moltmann.

R.H.K.

Blondel, Maurice (1861–1949), French Christian philosopher who discovered the deist background of human action. In his main work, *Action* (1893, 2d rev. ed. 1950), Blondel held that action is part of the very nature of human beings and as such becomes an object of philosophy; through philosophy, action should find its meaning, i.e. realize itself rationally. An appropriate phenomenology of action through phenomenological description uncovers the phenomenal level of action but points beyond it. Such a supraphenomenal sense of action provides it a metaphysical status. This phenomenology of action rests on an immanent dialectics of action: a gap between the aim of the action and its realization. This gap, while dissatisfying to the actor, also drives him toward new activities. The only immanent solution of this dialectics and its consequences is a transcendent one. We have to realize that we, like other humans, cannot grasp our own activities and must accept our limitations and our finitude as well as the insufficiency of our philosophy, which is now understood as a philosophy of insufficiency and points toward the existence of the supernatural element in every human act, namely God. Human activity is the outcome of divine grace. Through action one touches the existence of God, something not possible by logical argumentation.

In the later phase of his development Blondel deserted his early "anti-intellectualism" and stressed the close relation between thought and action, now understood as inseparable and mutually interrelated. He came to see philosophy as a rational instrument of understanding one's actions as well as one's insufficiency.

G.Fl.

bodily continuity. See PERSONAL IDENTITY.

Bodin, Jean (c.1529–96), French political philosopher whose philosophy centers on the concept of sovereignty. His *Six livres de la république* (1577) defines a state as constituted by common public interests, families, and the sovereign. The sovereign is the lawgiver, who stands beyond the absolute rights he possesses; he must, however, follow the law of God, natural law, and the constitution. The ideal state was for Bodin a monarchy that uses aristocratic and democratic structures of government for the sake of the common good. In order to achieve a broader empirical picture of politics Bodin used historical comparisons. This is methodologically reflected in his *Methodus ad facilem historiarum cognitionem* (1566).

Bodin was clearly a theorist of absolutism. As a member of the *Politique* group he played a practical role in emancipating the state from the church. His thinking was influenced by his experience of civil war. In his *Heptaplomeres* (posthumous) he pleaded for tolerance with respect to all religions, including Islam and Judaism. As a public prosecutor, however, he wrote a manual for judges in witchcraft trials (*De la démonomanie des sorciers,* 1580). By stressing the peacemaking role of a strong state Bodin was a forerunner of Hobbes.

See also HOBBES, POLITICAL PHILOSOPHY.

H.P.

body, objective. See EMBODIMENT.

body, phenomenal. See EMBODIMENT.

Boehme, Jakob (1575–1624), German Protestant speculative mystic. Influenced especially by Paracelsus, Boehme received little formal education, but was successful enough as a shoemaker to devote himself to his writing, explicating his religious experiences. He published little in his lifetime, though enough to attract charges of heresy from local clergy. He did gather followers, and his works were published after his death. His writings are elaborately symbolic rather than argumentative, but respond deeply to fundamental problems in the Christian worldview. He holds that the Godhead, omnipotent will, is as nothing to us, since we can in no way grasp it. The *Mysterium Magnum,* the ideal world, is conceived in God's mind through an impulse to self-revelation. The actual world, separate from God, is created through His will, and seeks to return to the peace of the Godhead. The world is good, as God is, but its goodness falls away, and is restored at the end of history, though not entirely, for some souls are damned eternally. Human beings enjoy free will, and create themselves through rebirth in faith. The Fall is necessary for the self-knowledge gained in recovery from it. Recognition of one's hidden, free self is a recognition of God manifested in the world, so that human salvation completes God's act of self-revelation. It is also a recognition of evil rooted in the blind will underlying all individual existence, without which there would be nothing except the Godhead. Boehme's works influenced Hegel and the later Schelling. **See also** MYSTICISM, PARACELSUS.

J.Lo.

Boethius, Anicius Manlius Severinus (c.480–525), Roman philosopher and Aristotelian translator and commentator. He was born into a wealthy patrician family in Rome and had a distinguished political career under the Ostrogothic king Theodoric before being arrested and executed on charges of treason. His logic and philosophical theology contain important contributions to the philosophy of the late classical and early medieval periods, and his translations of and commentaries on Aristotle profoundly influenced the history of philosophy, particularly in the medieval Latin West.

His most famous work, *The Consolation of Philosophy,* composed during his imprisonment, is a moving reflection on the nature of human happiness and the problem of evil and contains classic discussions of providence, fate, chance, and the apparent incompatibility of divine foreknowledge and human free choice. He was known during his own lifetime, however, as a brilliant scholar whose knowledge of the Greek language and ancient Greek philosophy set him apart from his Latin contemporaries. He conceived his scholarly career as devoted to preserving and making accessible to the Latin West the great philosophical achievement of ancient Greece. To this end he announced an ambitious plan to translate into Latin and write commentaries on all of Plato and Aristotle, but it seems that he achieved this goal only for Aristotle's *Organon*. His extant translations include Porphyry's *Isagoge* (an introduction to Aristotle's *Categories*) and Aristotle's *Categories, On Interpretation, Prior Analytics, Topics,* and *Sophistical Refutations.* He wrote two commentaries on the *Isagoge* and *On Interpretation* and one on the *Categories,* and we have what appear to be his notes for a commentary on the *Prior Analytics.* His translation of the *Posterior Analytics* and his commentary on the *Topics* are lost. He also commented on Cicero's *Topica* and wrote his own treatises on logic, including *De syllogismis hypotheticis, De syllogismis categoricis, Introductio in categoricos syllogismos, De divisione,* and *De topicis differentiis,* in which he elaborates and supplements Aristotelian logic.

Boethius shared the common Neoplatonist view that the Platonist and Aristotelian systems could be harmonized by following Aristotle in logic and natural philosophy and Plato in metaphysics and theology. This plan for harmonization rests on a distinction between two kinds of forms: (1) forms that are conjoined with matter to constitute bodies – these, which he calls "images" (*imagines*), correspond to the forms in Aristotle's hylomorphic account of corporeal substances; and (2) forms that are pure and entirely separate from matter, corresponding to Plato's ontologically separate Forms. He calls these "true forms" and "the forms themselves." He holds that the former, "enmattered" forms depend for their being on the latter, pure forms. Boethius takes these three sorts of entities – bodies, enmattered forms, and separate forms – to be the respective objects of three different cognitive activities, which constitute the three branches of speculative philosophy. Natural philosophy is concerned with enmattered forms as enmattered, mathematics with enmattered forms considered apart from their matter (though they cannot be separated from matter in actuality), and theology with the pure and separate forms. He thinks that the mental abstraction characteristic of mathematics is important for understanding the Peripatetic account of universals: the enmattered, particular forms found in sensible things can be considered as universal when they are considered apart from the matter in which they inhere (though they cannot actually exist apart from matter). But he stops short of endorsing this moderately realist Aristotelian account of universals. His commitment to an ontology that includes not just Aristotelian natural forms but also Platonist Forms existing apart from matter implies a strong realist view of universals.

With the exception of *De fide catholica,* which is a straightforward credal statement, Boethius's theological treatises (*De Trinitate, Utrum Pater et Filius, Quomodo substantiae,* and *Contra Euthychen et Nestorium*) show his commitment to using logic and metaphysics, particularly the Aristotelian doctrines of the categories and predicables, to clarify and resolve issues in Christian theology. *De Trinitate,* e.g., includes a historically influential discussion of the Aristotelian categories and the applicability of various kinds of predicates to God. Running through these treatises is his view that predicates in the category of relation are unique by virtue of not always requiring for their applicability an ontological ground in the subjects to which they apply, a doctrine that gave rise to the common medieval distinction between so-called real and non-real relations.

Regardless of the intrinsic significance of Boethius's philosophical ideas, he stands as a monumental figure in the history of medieval philosophy rivaled in importance only by Aristotle and Augustine. Until the recovery of the works of Aristotle in the mid-twelfth century, medieval philosophers depended almost entirely on Boethius's translations and commentaries for their knowledge of pagan ancient philosophy, and his treatises on logic continued to be influential throughout the Middle Ages. The preoccupation of early medieval philosophers with logic and with the problem of universals in particular is due largely to their having been tutored by Boethius and Boethius's Aristotle. The theological treatises also received wide attention in the Middle Ages, giving rise to a commentary tradition extending from the ninth century through the Renaissance and shaping discussion of central theological doctrines such as the Trinity and Incarnation.

See also ARISTOTLE, COMMENTARIES ON ARISTOTLE, FUTURE CONTINGENTS, PHILOSOPHY OF RELIGION, PLATO.   S.Ma.

Boltzmann, Ludwig (1844–1906), Austrian physicist who was a spirited advocate of the atomic theory and a pioneer in developing the kinetic theory of gases and statistical mechanics. Boltzmann's most famous achievements were the transport equation, the H-theorem, and the probabilistic interpretation of entropy. This work is summarized in his *Vorlesungen über Gastheorie* ("Lectures on the Theory of Gases," 1896–98). He held chairs in physics at the universities of Graz, Vienna, Munich, and Leipzig before returning to Vienna as professor of theoretical physics in 1902. In 1903 he succeeded Mach at

Vienna and lectured on the philosophy of science.

In the 1890s the atomic-kinetic theory was attacked by Mach and by the energeticists led by Wilhelm Ostwald. Boltzmann's counterattack can be found in his *Populäre Schriften* ("Popular Writings," 1905). Boltzmann agreed with his critics that many of his mechanical models of gas molecules could not be true but, like Maxwell, defended models as invaluable heuristic tools. Boltzmann also insisted that it was futile to try to eliminate all metaphysical pictures from theories in favor of bare equations. For Boltzmann, the goal of physics is not merely the discovery of equations but the construction of a coherent picture of reality. Boltzmann defended his H-theorem against the reversibility objection of Loschmidt and the recurrence objection of Zermelo by conceding that a spontaneous decrease in entropy was possible but extremely unlikely. Boltzmann's views that irreversibility depends on the probability of initial conditions and that entropy increase determines the direction of time are defended by Reichenbach in *The Direction of Time* (1956).

See also ENTROPY, MACH, MAXWELL, PHILOSOPHY OF SCIENCE, REICHENBACH.   M.C.

Bolzano, Bernard (1781–1848), Austrian philosopher. He studied philosophy, mathematics, physics, and theology in Prague; received the Ph.D.; was ordained a priest (1805); was appointed to a chair in religion at Charles University in 1806; and, owing to his criticism of the Austrian constitution, was dismissed in 1819. He composed his two main works from 1823 through 1841: the *Wissenschaftslehre* (4 vols., 1837) and the posthumous *Grössenlehre*. His ontology and logical semantics influenced Husserl and, indirectly, Łukasiewicz, Tarski, and others of the Warsaw School. His conception of ethics and social philosophy affected both the cultural life of Bohemia and the Austrian system of education.

Bolzano recognized a profound distinction between the actual thoughts and judgments (*Urteile*) of human beings, their linguistic expressions, and the abstract propositions (*Sätze an sich*) and their parts which exist independently of those thoughts, judgments, and expressions. A proposition in Bolzano's sense is a preexistent sequence of ideas-as-such (*Vorstellungen an sich*). Only propositions containing finite ideas-as-such are accessible to the mind. Real things existing concretely in space and time have subsistence (*Dasein*) whereas abstract objects such as propositions have only logical existence. Adherences, i.e., forces, applied to certain concrete substances give rise to subjective ideas, thoughts, or judgments. A subjective idea is a part of a judgment that is not itself a judgment. The set of judgments is ordered by a causal relation.

Bolzano's abstract world is constituted of sets, ideas-as-such, certain properties (*Beschaffenheiten*), and objects constructed from these. Thus, sentence shapes are a kind of ideas-as-such, and certain complexes of ideas-as-such constitute propositions. Ideas-as-such can be generated from expressions of a language by postulates for the relation of being an object of something. Analogously, properties can be generated by postulates for the relation of something being applied to an object.

Bolzano's notion of religion is based on his distinction between propositions and judgments. His *Lehrbuch der Religionswissenschaft* (4 vols., 1834) distinguishes between religion in the objective and subjective senses. The former is a set of religious propositions, whereas the latter is the set of religious views of a single person. Hence, a subjective religion can contain an objective one. By defining a religious proposition as being moral and imperatives the rules of utilitarianism, Bolzano integrated his notion of religion within his ontology.

In the *Grössenlehre* Bolzano intended to give a detailed, well-founded exposition of contemporary mathematics and also to inaugurate new domains of research. Natural numbers are defined, half a century before Frege, as properties of "bijective" sets (the members of which can be put in one-to-one correspondence), and real numbers are conceived as properties of sets of certain infinite sequences of rational numbers. The analysis of infinite sets brought him to reject the Euclidean doctrine that the whole is always greater than any of its parts and, hence, to the insight that a set is infinite if and only if it is bijective to a proper subset of itself. This anticipates Peirce and Dedekind. Bolzano's extension of the linear continuum of finite numbers by infinitesimals implies a relatively constructive approach to nonstandard analysis. In the development of standard analysis the most remarkable result of the *Grössenlehre* is the anticipation of Weirstrass's discovery that there exist nowhere differentiable continuous functions.

The *Wissenschaftslehre* was intended to lay the logical and epistemological foundations of Bolzano's mathematics. A theory of science in Bolzano's sense is a collection of rules for delimiting the set of scientific textbooks. Whether a class of true propositions is a worthwhile object of representation in a scientific textbook is an ethical question decidable on utilitarian principles.

Bolzano proceeded from an expanded and standardized ordinary language through which he could describe propositions and their parts. He defined the semantic notion of truth and introduced the function corresponding to a "replacement" operation on propositions. One of his major achievements was his definition of logical derivability (*logische Ableitbarkeit*) between sets of propositions: *B* is logically derivable from *A* if and only if all elements of the sum of *A* and *B* are simultaneously true for some replacement of their non-logical ideas-as-such and if all elements of *B* are true for any such replacement that makes all elements of *A* true. In addition to this notion, which is similar to Tarski's concept of consequence of 1936, Bolzano introduced a notion corresponding to Gentzen's concept of consequence. A proposition is universally valid (*allgemeingültig*) if it is derivable from the null class. In his proof theory Bolzano formulated counterparts to Gentzen's cut rule.

Bolzano introduced a notion of inductive probability as a generalization of derivability in a limited domain. This notion has the formal properties of conditional probability. These features and Bolzano's characterization of probability density by the technique of variation are reminiscent of Wittgenstein's inductive logic and Carnap's theory of regular confirmation functions.

The replacement of conceptual complexes in propositions would, if applied to a formalized language, correspond closely to a substitution-semantic conception of quantification. His own philosophical language was based on a kind of free logic. In essence, Bolzano characterized a substitution-semantic notion of consequence with a finite number of antecedents. His quantification over individual and general concepts amounts to the introduction of a non-elementary logic of lowest order containing a quantification theory of predicate variables but no set-theoretical principles such as choice axioms. His conception of universal validity and of the semantic superstructure of logic leads to a semantically adequate extension of the predicate-logical version of Lewis's system S5 of modal logic without paradoxes. It is also possible to simulate Bolzano's theory of probability in a substitution-semantically constructed theory of probability functions. Hence, by means of an ontologically parsimonious superstructure without possible-worlds metaphysics, Bolzano was able to delimit essentially the realms of classical logical truth and additive probability spaces.

In geometry Bolzano created a new foundation from a topological point of view. He defined the notion of an isolated point of a set in a way reminiscent of the notion of a point at which a set is well-dimensional in the sense of Urysohn and Menger. On this basis he introduced his topological notion of a continuum and formulated a recursive definition of the dimensionality of non-empty subsets of the Euclidean 3-space, which is closely related to the inductive dimension concept of Urysohn and Menger. In a remarkable paragraph of an unfinished late manuscript on geometry he stated the celebrated curve theorem of Jordan.

See also FREE LOGIC, MODAL LOGIC, PHILOSOPHY OF MATHEMATICS, PROBABILITY, SET THEORY, TARSKI.   J.Be.

Bonaventure, Saint (c.1221–74), Italian theologian. Born John of Fidanza in Bagnorea, Tuscany, he was educated at Paris, earning a master's degree in arts and a doctorate in theology. He joined the Franciscans about 1243, while still a student, and was elected minister general of the order in 1257. Made cardinal bishop of Albano by Pope Gregory X in 1274, Bonaventure helped organize the Second Ecumenical Council of Lyons, during the course of which he died, in July 1274. He was canonized in 1482 and named a doctor of the church in 1587.

Bonaventure wrote and preached extensively on the relation between philosophy and theology, the role of reason in spiritual and religious life, and the extent to which knowledge in God is obtainable by the "wayfarer." His basic position is nicely expressed in *De reductione artium ad theologiam* ("On the Reduction of the Arts to Theology"): "the manifold wisdom of God, which is clearly revealed in sacred scripture, lies hidden in all knowledge and in all nature." He adds, "all divisions of knowledge are handmaids of theology." But he is critical of those theologians who wish to sever the connection between faith and reason. As he argues in another famous work, *Itinerarium mentis ad deum* ("The Mind's Journey unto God," 1259), "since, relative to our life on earth, the world is itself a ladder for ascending to God, we find here certain traces, certain images" of the divine hand, in which God himself is mirrored.

Although Bonaventure's own philosophical outlook is Augustinian, he was also influenced by Aristotle, whose newly available works he both read and appreciated. Thus, while upholding the Aristotelian ideas that knowledge of the external world is based on the senses and that the mind comes into existence as a *tabula rasa*, he also contends that divine illumination is necessary to explain both the acquisition of universal concepts from sense images, and the certainty of intellectual judgment. His own illuminationist epistemology seeks a middle ground between, on the one hand, those who maintain that the eternal light is the sole reason for human knowing, providing the human intellect with its archetypal and intelligible objects, and, on the other, those holding that the eternal light merely influences human knowing, helping guide it toward truth. He holds that our intellect has certain knowledge when stable; eternal archetypes are "contuited by us [*a nobis contuita*]," together with intelligible species produced by its own fallible powers.

In metaphysics, Bonaventure defends exemplarism, the doctrine that all creation is patterned after exemplar causes or ideas in the mind of God. Like Aquinas, but unlike Duns Scotus, he argues that it is through such ideas that God knows all creatures. He also adopts the emanationist principle that creation proceeds from God's goodness, which is self-diffusive, but differs from other emanationists, such as al-Fārābī, Avicenna, and Averroes, in arguing that divine emanation is neither necessary nor indirect (i.e., accomplished by secondary agents or intelligences). Indeed, he sees the views of these Islamic philosophers as typical of the errors bound to follow once Aristotelian rationalism is taken to its extreme. He is also well known for his anti-Aristotelian argument that the eternity of the world – something even Aquinas (following Maimonides) concedes as a theoretical possibility – is demonstrably false.

Bonaventure also subscribes to several other doctrines characteristic of medieval Augustinianism: universal hylomorphism, the thesis, defended by Ibn Gabirol and Avicenna (among others), that everything other than God is composed of matter and form; the plurality of forms, the view that subjects and predicates in the category of substance are ordered in terms of their metaphysical priority; and the ontological view of truth, according to which truth is a kind of rightness perceived by the mind. In a similar vein, Bonaventure argues that knowledge ultimately consists in perceiving truth directly, without argument or demonstration.

Bonaventure also wrote several classic works in the tradition of mystical theology. His best-known and most popular mystical work is the aforementioned *Itinerarium*, written in 1259 on a pilgrimage to La Verna, during which he beheld the six-winged seraph that had also appeared to Francis of Assisi when Francis received the stigmata. Bonaventure outlines a seven-stage spiritual journey, in which our mind moves from first considering God's traces in the perfections of irrational creatures, to a final state of peaceful repose, in which our affections are "transferred and transformed into God." Central to his writings on spiritual life is the theme of the "three ways": the purgative way, inspired by conscience, which expels sin; the illuminative way, inspired by the intellect, which imitates Christ; and the unitive way, inspired by wisdom, which unites us to God through love.

Bonaventure's writings most immediately influenced the work of other medieval Augustinians, such as Matthew of Aquasparta and John Peckham, and later, followers of Duns Scotus. But his modern reputation rests on his profound contributions to philosophical theology, Franciscan spirituality, and mystical thought, in all three of which he remains an authoritative source.

See also ARISTOTLE, AUGUSTINE.   J.A.Z.

boo-hurrah theory. See EMOTIVISM.

Book of Changes. See I-CHING.

book of life, expression found in Hebrew and Christian scriptures signifying a record kept by the Lord of those destined for eternal happiness (Exodus 32:32; Psalms 68; Malachi 3:16; Daniel 12:1; Philippians 4:3; Revelation 3:5, 17:8, 20:12, 21:27). Medieval philosophers often referred to the book of life when discussing issues of predestination, divine omniscience, foreknowledge, and free will. Figures like Augustine and Aquinas asked whether it represented God's unerring foreknowledge or predestination, or whether some names could be added or deleted from it. The term is used by some contemporary philosophers to mean a record of all the events in a person's life. **See also FREE WILL PROBLEM.**

R.H.K.

Boole, George. See BOOLEAN ALGEBRA, LOGICAL FORM.

Boolean algebra, (1) an ordered triple $(\mathbf{B}, -, \cap)$, where $\mathbf{B}$ is a set containing at least two elements and $-$ and $\cap$ are unary and binary operations in $\mathbf{B}$ such that (i) $a \cap b = b \cap a$, (ii) $a \cap (b \cap c) = (a \cap b) \cap c$, (iii) $a \cap -a = b \cap -b$, and (iv) $a \cap b = a$ if and only if $a \cap -b = a \cap -a$; (2) the theory of such algebras. Such structures are modern descendants of algebras published by the mathematician G. Boole in 1847 and representing the first successful algebraic treatment of logic. (Interpreting − and ∩ as negation and conjunction, respectively, makes Boolean algebra a calculus of propositions. Likewise, if **B** = {T,F} and − and ∩ are the truth-functions for negation and conjunction, then (**B**,−,∩) – the truth table for those two connectives – forms a two-element Boolean algebra.) Picturing a Boolean algebra is simple. (**B**,−,∩) is a *full subset algebra* if **B** is the set of all subsets of a given set and − and ∩ are set complementation and intersection, respectively. Then every finite Boolean algebra is isomorphic to a full subset algebra, while every infinite Boolean algebra is isomorphic to a subalgebra of such an algebra. It is for this reason that Boolean algebra is often characterized as the *calculus of classes.* **See also** SET THEORY, TRUTH TABLE.   G.F.S.

borderline case, in the logical sense, a case that falls within the "gray area" or "twilight zone" associated with a vague concept; in the pragmatic sense, a doubtful, disputed, or arguable case. These two senses are not mutually exclusive, of course. A moment of time near sunrise or sunset may be a borderline case of daytime or nighttime in the logical sense, but not in the pragmatic sense. A sufficiently freshly fertilized ovum may be a borderline case of a person in both senses. Fermat's hypothesis, or any of a large number of other disputed mathematical propositions, may be a borderline case in the pragmatic sense but not in the logical sense. A borderline case per se in either sense need not be a limiting case or a degenerate case. **See also** DEGENERATE CASE, LIMITING CASE, VAGUENESS.   J.Cor.

Born interpretation. See QUANTUM MECHANICS.

Bosanquet, Bernard (1848–1923), British philosopher, the most systematic British absolute idealist and, with F. H. Bradley, the leading British defender of absolute idealism. Although he derived his name from Huguenot ancestors, Bosanquet was thoroughly English. Born at Altwick and educated at Harrow and Balliol College, Oxford, he was for eleven years a fellow of University College, Oxford. The death of his father in 1880 and the resulting inheritance enabled Bosanquet to leave Oxford for London and a career as a writer and social activist. While writing, he taught courses for the London Ethical Society's Center for University Extension and

donated time to the Charity Organization Society. In 1895 he married his coworker in the Charity Organization Society, Helen Dendy, who was also the translator of Christoph Sigwart's *Logic.* Bosanquet was professor of moral philosophy at St. Andrews from 1903 to 1908. He gave the Gifford Lectures in 1911 and 1912. Otherwise he lived in London until his death.

Bosanquet's most comprehensive work, his two-volume Gifford Lectures, *The Principle of Individuality and Value* and *The Value and Destiny of the Individual,* covers most aspects of his philosophy. In *The Principle of Individuality and Value* he argues that the search for truth proceeds by eliminating contradictions in experience. (For Bosanquet a contradiction arises when there are incompatible interpretations of the same fact.) This involves making distinctions that harmonize the incompatible interpretations in a larger body of knowledge. Bosanquet thought there was no way to arrest this process short of recognizing that all human experience forms a comprehensive whole which is reality. Bosanquet called this totality "the Absolute." Just as conflicting interpretations of the same fact find harmonious places in the Absolute, so conflicting desires are also included. The Absolute thus satisfies all desires and provides Bosanquet's standard for evaluating other objects. This is because in his view the value of an object is determined by its ability to satisfy desires. From this Bosanquet concluded that human beings, as fragments of the Absolute, acquire greater value as they realize themselves by partaking more fully in the Absolute. In *The Value and Destiny of the Individual* Bosanquet explained how human beings could do this. As finite, human beings face obstacles they cannot overcome; yet they desire the good (i.e., the Absolute) which for Bosanquet overcomes all obstacles and satisfies all desires. Humans can best realize a desire for the good, Bosanquet thinks, by surrendering their private desires for the sake of the good. This attitude of surrender, which Bosanquet calls the religious consciousness, relates human beings to what is permanently valuable in reality and increases their own value and satisfaction accordingly.

Bosanquet's defense of this metaphysical vision rests heavily on his first major work, *Logic or the Morphology of Knowledge* (1888; 2d ed., 1911). As the subtitle indicates, Bosanquet took the subject matter of *Logic* to be the structure of knowledge. Like Hegel, who was in many ways his inspiration, Bosanquet thought that the nature of knowledge was defined by structures repeated in different parts of knowledge. He called these structures forms of judgment and tried to show that simple judgments are dependent on increasingly complex ones and finally on an all-inclusive judgment that defines reality. For example, the simplest element of knowledge is a demonstrative judgment like "This is hot." But making such a judgment presupposes understanding the contrast between 'this' and 'that'. Demonstrative judgments thus depend on comparative judgments like "This is hotter than that." Since these judgments are less dependent on other judgments, they more fully embody human knowledge. Bosanquet claimed that the series of increasingly complex judgments are not arranged in a simple linear order but develop along different branches finally uniting in disjunctive judgments that attribute to reality an exhaustive set of mutually exclusive alternatives which are themselves judgments. When one contained judgment is asserted on the basis of another, a judgment containing both is an *inference*. For Bosanquet inferences are mediated judgments that assert their conclusions based on grounds. When these grounds are made fully explicit in a judgment containing them, that judgment embodies the nature of inference: that one must accept the conclusion or reject the whole of knowledge. Since for Bosanquet the difference between any judgment and the reality it represents is that a judgment is composed of ideas that abstract from reality, a fully comprehensive judgment includes all aspects of reality. It is thus identical to reality. By locating all judgments within this one, Bosanquet claimed to have described the morphology of knowledge as well as to have shown that thought is identical to reality.

Bosanquet removed an objection to this identification in *History of Aesthetics* (1892), where he traces the development of the philosophy of the beautiful from its inception through absolute idealism. According to Plato and Aristotle beauty is found in imitations of reality, while in objective idealism it *is* reality in sensuous form. Drawing heavily on Kant, Bosanquet saw this process as an overcoming of the opposition between sense and reason by showing how a pleasurable feeling can partake of reason. He thought that absolute idealism explained this by showing that we experience objects as beautiful because their sensible qualities exhibit the unifying activity of reason.

Bosanquet treated the political implications of absolute idealism in his *Philosophical Theory of the State* (1898; 3d ed., 1920), where he argues that humans achieve their ends only in communities. According to Bosanquet, all humans rationally will their own ends. Because their ends differ from moment to moment, the ends they rationally will are those that harmonize their desires at particular moments. Similarly, because the ends of different individuals overlap and conflict, what they rationally will are ends that harmonize their desires, which are the ends of humans in communities. They are willed by the general will, the realization of which is self-rule or liberty. This provides the rational ground of political obligation, since the most comprehensive system of modern life is the state, the end of which is the realization of the best life for its citizens.

See also HEGEL, IDEALISM.   J.W.A.

Boscovich, Roger Joseph, or Rudjer Josip Bošković (1711–87), Croatian physicist and philosopher. Born of Serbian and Italian parents, he was a Jesuit and polymath best known for his *A Theory of Natural Philosophy Reduced to a Single Law of the Actions Existing in Nature*. This work attempts to explain all physical phenomena in terms of the attractions and repulsions of point particles (*puncta*) that are indistinguishable in their intrinsic qualitative properties. According to Boscovich's single law, *puncta* at a certain distance attract, until upon approaching one another they reach a point at which they repel, and eventually reach equilibrium. Thus, Boscovich defends a form of dynamism, or the theory that nature is to be understood in terms of force and not mass (where forces are functions of time and distance). By dispensing with extended substance, Boscovich avoided epistemological difficulties facing Locke's natural philosophy and anticipated developments in modern physics. Among those influenced by Boscovich were Kant (who defended a version of dynamism), Faraday, James Clerk Maxwell, and Lord Kelvin.

Boscovich's theory has proved to be empirically inadequate to account for phenomena such as light. A philosophical difficulty for Boscovich's *puncta*, which are physical substances, arises out of their zero-dimensionality. It is plausible that any power must have a basis in an object's intrinsic properties, and *puncta* appear to lack such support for their powers. However, it is extensional properties that *puncta* lack, and Boscovich could argue that the categorial property of being an unextended spatial substance provides the needed basis.   J.Ho. & G.Ro.

bottom-up. See COGNITIVE SCIENCE.

bound variable. See ONTOLOGICAL COMMITMENT, VARIABLE.

Bouwsma, O(ets) K(olk) (1898–1978), American philosopher, a practitioner of ordinary language philosophy and celebrated teacher. Through work on Moore and contact with students such as Norman Malcolm and Morris Lazerowitz, whom he sent from Nebraska to work with Moore, Bouwsma discovered Wittgenstein. He became known for conveying an understanding of Wittgenstein's techniques of philosophical analysis through his own often humorous grasp of sense and nonsense. Focusing on a particular pivotal sentence in an argument, he provided imaginative surroundings for it, showing how, in the philosopher's mouth, the sentence lacked sense. He sometimes described this as "the method of failure." In connection with Descartes's evil genius, e.g., Bouwsma invents an elaborate story in which the evil genius tries but fails to permanently deceive by means of a totally paper world. Our inability to imagine such a deception undermines the sense of the evil genius argument. His writings are replete with similar stories, analogies, and teases of sense and nonsense for such philosophical standards as Berkeley's idealism, Moore's theory of sense-data, and Anselm's ontological argument.

Bouwsma did not advocate theories nor put forward refutations of other philosophers' views. His talent lay rather in exposing some central sentence in an argument as disguised nonsense. In this, he went beyond Wittgenstein, working out the details of the latter's insights into language. In addition to this appropriation of Wittgenstein, Bouwsma also appropriated Kierkegaard, understanding him too as one who dispelled philosophical illusions – those arising from the attempt to understand Christianity. The ordinary language of religious philosophy was that of scriptures. He drew upon this language in his many essays on religious themes. His religious dimension made whole this person who gave no quarter to traditional metaphysics. His papers are published under the titles *Philosophical Essays, Toward a New Sensibility, Without Proof or Evidence*, and *Wittgenstein Conversations 1949–51*. His philosophical notebooks are housed at the Humanities Research Center in Austin, Texas. **See also ORDINARY LANGUAGE PHILOSOPHY, WITTGENSTEIN.**   R.E.H.

Boyle, Robert (1627–91), British chemist and physicist who was a major figure in seventeenth-century natural philosophy. To his contemporaries he was "the restorer" in England of the mechanical philosophy. His program was to replace the vacuous explanations characteristic of Peripateticism (the "quality of whiteness" in snow explains why it dazzles the eyes) by explanations employing the "two grand and most catholic principles of bodies, matter and motion," matter being composed of corpuscles, with motion "the grand agent of all that happens in nature." Boyle wrote influentially on scientific methodology, emphasizing experimentation (a Baconian influence), experimental precision, and the importance of devising "good and excellent" hypotheses. The dispute with Spinoza on the validation of explanatory hypotheses contrasted Boyle's experimental way with Spinoza's way of rational analysis. The 1670s dispute with Henry More on the ontological grounds of corporeal activity confronted More's "Spirit of Nature" with the "essential modifications" (motion and the "seminal principle" of activity) with which Boyle claimed God had directly endowed matter. As a champion of the corpuscularian philosophy, Boyle was an important link in the development before Locke of the distinction between primary and secondary qualities. A leading advocate of natural theology, he provided in his will for the establishment of the Boyle Lectures to defend Protestant Christianity against atheism and materialism. **See also MECHANISTIC EXPLANATION, PHILOSOPHY OF SCIENCE, SPINOZA.**   A.G.

bracketing. See HUSSERL, PHENOMENOLOGY.

Bradley, F(rancis) H(erbert) (1846–1924), the most original and influential nineteenth-century British idealist. Born at Clapham, he was the fourth son of an evangelical minister. His younger brother A. C. Bradley was a well-known Shakespearean critic. From 1870 until his death Bradley was a fellow of Merton College, Oxford. A kidney ailment, which first occurred in 1871, compelled him to lead a retiring life. This, combined with his forceful literary style, his love of irony, the dedication of three of his books to an unknown woman, and acclaim as the greatest British idealist since Berkeley, has lent an aura of mystery to his personal life.

The aim of Bradley's first important work, *Ethical Studies* (1876), is not to offer guidance for dealing with practical moral problems (Bradley condemned this as casuistry), but rather to explain what makes morality as embodied in the consciousness of individuals and in social institutions possible. Bradley thought it was the fact that moral agents take morality as an end in itself which involves identifying their wills with an ideal (provided in part by their stations in society) and then transferring that ideal to reality through action. Bradley called this process "self-realization." He thought that moral agents could realize their good selves only by suppressing their bad selves, from which he concluded that morality could never be completely realized, since realizing a good self requires having a bad one. For this reason Bradley believed that the moral consciousness would develop into religious consciousness which, in his secularized version of Christianity, required dying to one's natural self through faith in the actual existence of the moral ideal.

In *Ethical Studies* Bradley admitted that a full defense of his ethics would require a metaphysical system, something he did not then have. Much of Bradley's remaining work was an attempt to provide the outline of such a system by solving what he called "the great problem of the relation between thought and reality." He first confronted this problem in *The Principles of Logic* (1883), which is his description of thought. He took thought to be embodied in judgments, which are distinguished from other mental activities by being true or false. This is made possible by the fact that their contents, which Bradley called ideas, represent reality. A problem arises because ideas are universals and so represent kinds of things, while the things themselves are all individuals. Bradley solves this problem by distinguishing between the logical and grammatical forms of a judgment and arguing that all judgments have the logical form of conditionals. They assert that universal connections between qualities obtain in reality. The qualities are universals, the connections between them are conditional, while reality is one individual whole that we have contact with in immediate experience. All judgments, in his view, are abstractions from a diverse but non-relational immediate experience. Since judgments are inescapably relational, they fail to represent accurately non-relational reality and so fail to reach truth, which is the goal of thought. From this Bradley concluded that, contrary to what some of his more Hegelian contemporaries were saying, thought is not identical to reality and is never more than partially true.

Appearance and Reality (1893) is Bradley's description of reality: it is experience, all of it, all at once, blended in a harmonious way. Bradley defended this view by means of his criterion for reality. Reality, he proclaimed, does not contradict itself; anything that does is merely appearance. In Part I of *Appearance and Reality* Bradley relied on an infinite regress argument, now called *Bradley's regress*, to contend that relations and all

relational phenomena, including thought, are contradictory. They are appearance, not reality. In Part II he claimed that appearances are contradictory because they are abstracted by thought from the immediate experience of which they are a part. Appearances constitute the content of this whole, which in Bradley's view is experience. In other words, reality is experience in its totality. Bradley called this unified, consistent all-inclusive reality "the Absolute."

Today Bradley is mainly remembered for his argument against the reality of relations, and as the philosopher who provoked Russell's and Moore's revolution in philosophy. He would be better remembered as a founder of twentieth-century philosophy who based metaphysical conclusions on his account of the logical forms of judgments.

See also BOSANQUET, IDEALISM.   J.W.A.

Bradwardine, Thomas. See OXFORD CALCULATORS.

Brahma. See BRAHMAN.

Brahman, in Hinduism, the ultimate reality, possessed of being, consciousness, and bliss, dependent on nothing else for existence. Brahman is conceived as a personal deity (Brahma) in Viśistadvaita and Dvaita Vedanta and as apersonal and qualityless in Advaita Vedanta, in which "being, consciousness, and bliss" are interpreted negatively. While Brahman is conceived as *saguna* or "with qualities" in Viśistadvaita and Dvaita, for Advaita Brahman is *nirguna* or qualityless. For Viśistadvaita, 'Brahman' secondarily refers to the world dependent on Brahman strictly so called, namely all minds and material things that constitute Brahman's body. For Advaita, each apparently individual mind (or other thing) is identical to Brahman; Dvaita does not construe the world, or anything else, as Brahman's body. Enlightenment, or *moksha*, with its consequent escape from the cycle of rebirths, for Advaita involves recognizing one's identity with *nirguna* Brahman, and for Dvaita and Viśistadvaita involves repenting and forsaking one's sins and trusting a gracious Brahman for salvation. **See also** HINDUISM.   K.E.Y.

Brahmanism. See BRAHMAN.

brain in a vat. See PUTNAM, SKEPTICISM.

Brandt, Richard B. (1910–97), American moral philosopher, most closely associated with rule utilitarianism (which term he coined). Brandt earned degrees from Denison College and Cambridge University, and obtained a Ph.D. from Yale in 1936. He taught at Swarthmore College from 1937 to 1964 and at the University of Michigan from 1964 to 1981. His six books and nearly one hundred articles included work on philosophy of religion, epistemology, philosophy of mind, philosophy of action, political philosophy, and philosophy of law. His greatest contributions were in moral philosophy. He first defended rule utilitarianism in his textbook *Ethical Theory* (1959), but greatly refined his view in the 1960s in a series of articles, which were widely discussed and reprinted and eventually collected together in *Morality, Utilitarianism, and Rights* (1992). Further refinements appear in his *A Theory of the Good and the Right* (1979) and *Facts, Values, and Morality* (1996).

Brandt famously argued for a "reforming definition" of 'rational person'. He proposed that we use it to designate someone whose desires would survive exposure to all relevant empirical facts and to correct logical reasoning. He also proposed a "reforming definition" of 'morally right' that assigns it the descriptive meaning 'would be permitted by any moral code that all (or nearly all) rational people would publicly favor for the agent's society if they expected to spend a lifetime in that society'. In his view, rational choice between moral codes is determined not by prior moral commitments but by expected consequences. Brandt admitted that different rational people may favor different codes, since different rational people may have different levels of natural benevolence. But he also contended that most rational people would favor a rule-utilitarian code.

See also COGNITIVE PSYCHOTHERAPY, ETHICS, UTILITARIANISM.   B.W.H.

Brentano, Franz (1838–1917), German philosopher, one of the most intellectually influential and personally charismatic of his time. He is known especially for his distinction between psychological and physical phenomena on the basis of intentionality or internal object-directedness of thought, his revival of Aristotelianism and empirical methods in philosophy and psychology, and his value theory and ethics supported by the concept of correct pro- and anti-emotions or love and hate attitudes. Brentano made noted contributions to the theory of metaphysical categories, phenomenology, epistemology, syllogistic logic, and philosophy of religion. His teaching made a profound impact on his students in Würzburg and Vienna, many of whom became internationally respected thinkers in their fields, including Meinong, Husserl, Twardowski, Christian von Ehrenfels, Anton Marty, and Freud.

Brentano began his study of philosophy at the Aschaffenburg Royal Bavarian Gymnasium; in 1856–58 he attended the universities of Munich and Würzburg, and then enrolled at the University of Berlin, where he undertook his first investigations of Aristotle's metaphysics under the supervision of F. A. Trendelenburg. In 1859–60, he attended the Academy in Münster, reading intensively in the medieval Aristotelians; in 1862 he received the doctorate in philosophy *in absentia* from the University of Tübingen. He was ordained a Catholic priest in 1864, and was later involved in a controversy over the doctrine of papal infallibility, eventually leaving the church in 1873. He taught first as *Privatdozent* in the Philosophical Faculty of the University of Würzburg (1866–74), and then accepted a professorship at the University of Vienna. In 1880 he decided to marry, temporarily resigning his position to acquire Saxon citizenship, in order to avoid legal difficulties in Austria, where marriages of former priests were not officially recognized. Brentano was promised restoration of his position after his circumvention of these restrictions, but although he was later reinstated as lecturer, his appeals for reappointment as professor were answered only with delay and equivocation. He left Vienna in 1895, retiring to Italy, his family's country of origin. At last he moved to Zürich, Switzerland, shortly before Italy entered World War I. Here he remained active both in philosophy and psychology, despite his ensuing blindness, writing and revising numerous books and articles, frequently meeting with former students and colleagues, and maintaining an extensive philosophical-literary correspondence, until his death.

In *Psychologie vom empirischen Standpunkt* ("Psychology from an Empirical Standpoint," 1874), Brentano argued that intentionality is the mark of the mental, that every psychological experience contains an intended object – also called an intentional object – which the thought is about or toward which the thought is directed. Thus, *in* desire, something is desired. According to the immanent intentionality thesis, this means that the desired object is literally contained within the psychological experience of desire. Brentano claims that this is uniquely true of mental as opposed to physical or non-psychological phenomena, so that the intentionality of the psychological distinguishes mental from physical states. The immanent intentionality thesis provides a framework in which Brentano identifies three categories of psychological phenomena: thoughts (*Vorstellungen*), judgments, and emotive phenomena. He further maintains that every thought is also self-consciously reflected back onto itself as a secondary intended object in what he called the *eigentümliche Verfleckung.*

From 1905 through 1911, with the publication in that year of *Von der Klassifikation der psychischen Phänomene,* Brentano gradually abandoned the immanent intentionality thesis in favor of his later philosophy of reism, according to which only individuals exist, excluding putative nonexistent *irrealia,* such as lacks, absences, and mere possibilities. In the meantime, his students Twardowski, Meinong, and Husserl, reacting negatively to the idealism, psychologism, and related philosophical problems apparent in the early immanent intentionality thesis, developed alternative non-immanence approaches to intentionality, leading, in the case of Twardowski and Meinong and his students in the Graz school of phenomenological psychology, to the construction of *Gegenstandstheorie,* the theory of (transcendent existent and nonexistent intended) objects, and to Husserl's later transcendental phenomenology. The intentionality of the mental in Brentano's revival of the medieval Aristotelian doctrine is one of his most important contributions to contemporary non-mechanistic theories of mind, meaning, and expression. Brentano's immanent intentionality thesis was, however, rejected by philosophers who otherwise agreed with his underlying claim that thought is essentially object-directed.

Brentano's value theory (*Werttheorie*) offers a pluralistic account of value, permitting many different kinds of things to be valuable – although, in keeping with his later reism, he denies the existence of an abstract realm of values. Intrinsic value is objective rather than subjective, in the sense that he believes the pro- and anti-emotions we may have toward an act or situation are objectively correct if they present themselves to emotional preference with the same *apodicity* or unquestionable sense of rightness as other self-evident matters of non-ethical judgment. Among the controversial consequences of Brentano's value theory is the conclusion that there can be no such thing as absolute evil. The implication follows from Brentano's observation, first, that evil requires evil consciousness, and that consciousness of any kind, even the worst imaginable malice or malevolent ill will, is (considered merely as consciousness) intrinsically good. This means that necessarily there is always a mixture of intrinsic

good even in the most malicious possible states of mind, by virtue alone of being consciously experienced, so that pure evil never obtains. Brentano's value theory admits of no defense against those who happen not to share the same "correct" emotional attitudes toward the situations he describes. If it is objected that to another person's emotional preferences only good consciousness is intrinsically good, while infinitely bad consciousness despite being a state of consciousness appears instead to contain no intrinsic good and is absolutely evil, there is no recourse within Brentano's ethics except to acknowledge that this contrary emotive attitude toward infinitely bad consciousness may also be correct, even though it contradicts his evaluations.

Brentano's empirical psychology and articulation of the intentionality thesis, his moral philosophy and value theory, his investigations of Aristotle's metaphysics at a time when Aristotelian realism was little appreciated in the prevailing climate of post-Kantian idealism, his epistemic theory of evident judgment, his suggestions for the reform of syllogistic logic, his treatment of the principle of sufficient reason and existence of God, his interpretation of a four-stage cycle of successive trends in the history of philosophy, together with his teaching and personal moral example, continue to inspire a variety of divergent philosophical traditions.

See also ARISTOTLE, HUSSERL, INTENTIONALITY, MEINONG, PHENOMENOLOGY, VALUE.

D.J.

Brentano's thesis. See INTENTIONALITY.

bridge law. See REDUCTION.

British empiricists. See RATIONALISM.

Broad, C(harlie) D(unbar) (1887–1971), English epistemologist, metaphysician, moral philosopher, and philosopher of science. He was educated at Trinity College, Cambridge, taught at several universities in Scotland, and then returned to Trinity, first as lecturer in moral science and eventually as Knightbridge Professor of Moral Philosophy. His philosophical views are in the broadly realist tradition of Moore and Russell, though with substantial influence also from his teachers at Cambridge, McTaggart and W. E. Johnson. Broad wrote voluminously and incisively on an extremely wide range of philosophical topics, including most prominently the nature of perception, a priori knowledge and concepts, the problem of induction, the mind–

body problem, the free will problem, various topics in moral philosophy, the nature and philosophical significance of psychical research, the nature of philosophy itself, and various historical figures such as Leibniz, Kant, and McTaggart.

Broad's work in the philosophy of perception centers on the nature of sense-data (or *sensa*, as he calls them) and their relation to physical objects. He defends a rather cautious, tentative version of the causal theory of perception. With regard to a priori knowledge, Broad rejects the empiricist view that all such knowledge is of analytic propositions, claiming instead that reason can intuit necessary and universal connections between properties or characteristics; his view of concept acquisition is that while most concepts are abstracted from experience, some are a priori, though not necessarily innate. Broad holds that the rationality of inductive inference depends on a further general premise about the world, a more complicated version of the thesis that nature is uniform, which is difficult to state precisely and even more difficult to justify.

Broad's view of the mind–body problem is a version of dualism, though one that places primary emphasis on individual mental events, is much more uncertain about the existence and nature of the mind as a substance, and is quite sympathetic to epiphenomenalism. His main contribution to the free will problem consists in an elaborate analysis of the libertarian conception of freedom, which he holds to be both impossible to realize and at the same time quite possibly an essential precondition of the ordinary conception of obligation. Broad's work in ethics is diverse and difficult to summarize, but much of it centers on the issue of whether ethical judgments are genuinely cognitive in character.

Broad was one of the few philosophers to take psychical research seriously. He served as president of the Society for Psychical Research and was an occasional observer of experiments in this area. His philosophical writings on this subject, while not uncritical, are in the main sympathetic and are largely concerned to defend concepts like precognition against charges of incoherence and also to draw out their implications for more familiar philosophical issues.

As regards the nature of philosophy, Broad distinguishes between "critical" and "speculative" philosophy. Critical philosophy is analysis of the basic concepts of ordinary life and of science, roughly in the tradition of Moore and Russell. A very high proportion of Broad's own work consists of such analyses, often amazingly detailed and meticulous in character. But he is also sympathetic to the speculative attempt to arrive at an overall conception of the nature of the universe and the position of human beings therein, while at the same time expressing doubts that anything even remotely approaching demonstration is possible in such endeavors.

The foregoing catalog of views reveals something of the range of Broad's philosophical thought, but it fails to bring out what is most strikingly valuable about it. Broad's positions on various issues do not form anything like a system (he himself is reported to have said that there is nothing that answers to the description "Broad's philosophy"). While his views are invariably subtle, thoughtful, and critically penetrating, they rarely have the sort of one-sided novelty that has come to be so highly valued in philosophy. What they do have is exceptional clarity, dialectical insight, and even-handedness. Broad's skill at uncovering and displaying the precise shape of a philosophical issue, clarifying the relevant arguments and objections, and cataloging in detail the merits and demerits of the opposing positions has rarely been equaled. One who seeks a clear-cut resolution of an issue is likely to be impatient and disappointed with Broad's careful, measured discussions, in which unusual effort is made to accord all positions and arguments their due. But one who seeks a comprehensive and balanced understanding of the issue in question is unlikely to find a more trustworthy guide.

See also PARAPSYCHOLOGY, PHILOSOPHY OF MIND.   L.B

Brouwer, Luitzgen Egbertus Jan (1881–1966), Dutch mathematician and philosopher and founder of the intuitionist school in the philosophy of mathematics. Educated at the Municipal University of Amsterdam, where he received his doctorate in 1907, he remained there for his entire professional career, as *Privaat-Docent* (1909–12) and then professor (1912–55). He was among the preeminent topologists of his time, proving several important results. Philosophically, he was also unique in his strongly held conviction that philosophical ideas and arguments concerning the nature of mathematics ought to affect and be reflected in its practice.

His general orientation in the philosophy of mathematics was Kantian. This was manifested in his radical critique of the role accorded to logical reasoning by classical mathematics; a role that Brouwer, following Kant, believed to be incompatible with the role that intuition must properly play in mathematical reasoning. The best-known, if not the most fundamental, part of his critique of the role accorded to logic by classical mathematics was his attack on the principle of the excluded middle and related principles of classical logic. He challenged their reliability, arguing that their unrestricted use leads to results that, intuitionistically speaking, are not true.

However, in its fundaments, Brouwer's critique was not so much an attack on particular principles of classical logic as a criticism of the general role that classical mathematics grants to logical reasoning. He believed that logical structure (and hence logical inference) is a product of the linguistic representation of mathematical thought and not a feature of that thought itself. He stated this view in the so-called First Act of Intuitionism, which contains not only the chief critical idea of Brouwer's position, but also its core positive element. This positive element says, with Kant, that mathematics is an essentially languageless activity of the mind. (Brouwer went on to say something with which Kant would only have partially agreed: that this activity has its origin in the perception of a move of time.) The critical element complements this by saying that mathematics is thus to be kept wholly distinct from mathematical language and the phenomena of language described by logic.

The so-called Second Act of Intuitionism then extends the positive part of the First Act by stating that the "self-unfolding" of the primordial intuition of a move of time is the basis not only of the construction of the natural numbers but also of the (intuitionistic) continuum. Together, these two ideas form the basis of Brouwer's philosophy of mathematics – a philosophy that is radically at odds with most of twentieth-century philosophy of mathematics.

See also PHILOSOPHY OF MATHEMATICS.

M.D.

Bruno, Giordano (1548–1600), Italian speculative philosopher. He was born in Naples, where he entered the Dominican order in 1565. In 1576 he was suspected of heresy and abandoned his order. He studied and taught in Geneva, but left because of difficulties with the Calvinists. Thereafter he studied and taught in Toulouse, Paris, England, various German universities, and Prague. In 1591 he rashly returned to Venice, and was arrested by the Venetian Inquisition in 1592. In 1593 he was handed over to the Roman Inquisition, which burned him to death as a heretic.

Because of his unhappy end, his support for the Copernican heliocentric hypothesis, and his pronounced anti-Aristotelianism, Bruno has been mistakenly seen as the proponent of a sci-entific worldview against medieval obscurantism. In fact, he should be interpreted in the context of Renaissance hermetism. Indeed, Bruno was so impressed by the hermetic corpus, a body of writings attributed to the mythical Egyptian sage Hermes Trismegistus, that he called for a return to the magical religion of the Egyptians. He was also strongly influenced by Lull, Nicholas of Cusa, Ficino, and Agrippa von Nettesheim, an early sixteenth-century author of an influential treatise on magic. Several of Bruno's works were devoted to magic, and it plays an important role in his books on the art of memory. Techniques for improving the memory had long been a subject of discussion, but he linked them with the notion that one could so imprint images of the universe on the mind as to achieve special knowledge of divine realities and the magic powers associated with such knowledge. He emphasized the importance of the imagination as a cognitive power, since it brings us into contact with the divine. Nonetheless, he also held that human ideas are mere shadows of divine ideas, and that God is transcendent and hence incomprehensible.

Bruno's best-known works are the Italian dialogues he wrote while in England, including the following, all published in 1584: *The Ash Wednesday Supper; On Cause, Principle and Unity; The Expulsion of the Triumphant Beast;* and *On the Infinite Universe and Worlds*. He presents a vision of the universe as a living and infinitely extended unity containing innumerable worlds, each of which is like a great animal with a life of its own. He maintained the unity of matter with universal form or the World-Soul, thus suggesting a kind of pantheism attractive to later German idealists, such as Schelling. However, he never identified the World-Soul with God, who remained separate from matter and form. He combined his speculative philosophy of nature with the recommendation of a new naturalistic ethics. Bruno's support of Copernicus in *The Ash Wednesday Supper* was related to his belief that a living earth must move, and he specifically rejected any appeal to mere mathematics to prove cosmological hypotheses. In later work he described the monad as a living version of the Democritean atom. Despite some obvious parallels with both Spinoza and Leibniz, he seems not to have had much direct influence on seventeenth-century thinkers.   E.J.A.

Brunschvicg, Léon (1869–1944), French philosopher, an influential professor at the Sorbonne and the École Normale Supérieure of Paris, and a founder of the *Revue de Métaphysique et de Morale* (1893) and the Société Française de

Philosophie (1901). In 1940 he was forced by the Nazis to leave Paris and sought refuge in the non-occupied zone, where he died. A monistic idealist, Brunschvicg unfolded a philosophy of mind (*Introduction to the Life of the Mind*, 1900). His epistemology highlights judgment. Thinking is judging and judging is acting. He defined philosophy as "the mind's methodical self-reflection." Philosophy investigates man's growing self-understanding. The mind's recesses, or metaphysical truth, are accessible through analysis of the mind's timely manifestations. His major works therefore describe the progress of science as progress of consciousness: *The Stages of Mathematical Philosophy* (1912), *Human Experience and Physical Causality* (1922), *The Progress of Conscience in Western Philosophy* (1927), and *Ages of Intelligence* (1934). An heir of Renouvier, Cournot, and Revaisson, Brunschvicg advocated a moral and spiritual conception of science and attempted to reconcile idealism and positivism.   J.-L.S.

B-series. See TIME.

B-theory of time. See TIME.

Buber, Martin (1878–1965), German Jewish philosopher, theologian, and political leader. Buber's early influences include Hasidism and neo-Kantianism. Eventually he broke with the latter and became known as a leading religious existentialist. His chief philosophic works include his most famous book, *Ich und du* ("I and Thou," 1923); *Moses* (1946); *Between Man and Man* (1947); and *Eclipse of God* (1952).

The crux of Buber's thought is his conception of two primary relationships: I-Thou and I-It. I-Thou is characterized by openness, reciprocity, and a deep sense of personal involvement. The I confronts its Thou not as something to be studied, measured, or manipulated, but as a unique presence that responds to the I in its individuality. I-It is characterized by the tendency to treat something as an impersonal object governed by causal, social, or economic forces. Buber rejects the idea that people are isolated, autonomous agents operating according to abstract rules. Instead, reality arises *between* agents as they encounter and transform each other. In a word, reality is dialogical. Buber describes God as the ultimate Thou, the Thou who can never become an It. Thus God is reached not by inference but by a willingness to respond to the concrete reality of the divine presence.

See also EXISTENTIALISM, JEWISH PHILOSOPHY.   K.See.

Buchmanism, also called the Moral Rearmament Movement, a non-creedal international movement that sought to bring about universal brotherhood through a commitment to an objectivist moral system derived largely from the Gospels. It was founded by Frank Buchman (1878–1961), an American Lutheran minister who resigned from his church in 1908 in order to expand his ministry. To promote the movement, Buchman founded the Oxford Group at Oxford University in 1921.   L.P.P.

Buddha (from Sanskrit, 'the enlightened one'), a title (but not a name) of Siddhārta Gotama (c.563–c.483 B.C.), the historical founder of Buddhism, and of any of his later representations. 'Buddha' can also mean anyone who has attained the state of enlightenment (Buddhahood) sought in Buddhism. The *Pali Canon* mentions twenty-four Buddhas.

Siddhārta Gotama was the son of the ruler of a small state in what is now Nepal. Tradition says that he left home at the age of twenty-nine to seek enlightenment, achieved it at the age of thirty-five, and was a wandering teacher until his death at eighty. He found ready-made in Indian culture the ideas of karma ('fruits of action') and *saṁsāra* ('wheel of rebirth') as well as the view that escape from the wheel is the highest good, and offered his own Buddhist way of escape.

See also BUDDHISM.   K.E.Y.

Buddhagosa (fourth–fifth century A.D.), Theravada Buddhist philosopher whose major work was the *Visuddhimagga* ("Path of Purification"). He accepted the typical Buddhist doctrine that everything that exists (Nirvana aside) is impermanent and momentary. A mind at a moment is only a momentary collection of momentary states; over time it is a series of such collections; similarly for a physical object. He held that, through sensory perception, physical objects are known to exist mind-independently. To the objection that perception of an object cannot occur in a moment since perception requires memory, attention, recognition, examination, and the like, he theorized that there is physical time and there is mental time; a single physical moment passes while distinct mental moments mount to sixteen in number. Hence a complex perceptual process can occur within a series of mental moments while a single material moment passes. Critics (e.g., Buddhist Yogācāra philosophers) saw in this a denial of impermanence. **See also** BUDDHISM.   K.E.Y.

Buddhism, a religion of eastern and central Asia founded by Siddhārta Gotama Buddha. The Buddha found ready-made in Indian culture the ideas of karma ('fruits of action') and *saṁsāra* ('wheel of rebirth'), as well as the view that escape from the wheel is the highest good. Buddhist doctrine, like that of other Indian religions, offers its distinctive way to achieve that end. It teaches that at the core of the problem is desire or craving – for wealth, pleasure, power, continued existence – which fuels the flame of continued life. It adds that the solution is the snuffing out of craving by following the *Eightfold Path* (right speech, action, livelihood, effort, mindfulness, concentration, views, and intentions). The idea is that intuitive wisdom follows upon moral conduct and mental discipline in accord with Buddhist precepts. This involves accepting these claims: all existence is unsatisfactory (*dukkha*); all existence is impermanent (*anicca*); and there is no permanent self (*anatta*). Along with these claims go the doctrines of momentariness (everything that exists is transitory, lasting only a moment) and codependent origination (everything that exists does so dependently on other things).

Since God is typically conceived in monotheistic religions as existing independently and as either eternal or everlasting, there is no room within a Buddhist perspective for monotheism. Save for a heretical school, Buddhist traditions also reject all belief in substances. A substance, in this sense, is something that has properties, is not itself a property or a collection of properties, and endures through time. The obvious contrast to the Buddhist perspective is the notion of a self in Hinduism and Jainism, which is beginningless and endless, an indestructible entity sometimes conceived as inherently self-conscious and sometimes viewed as conscious only when embodied. But even the notion of a substance that endured but had a beginning or end or both, or a substance that existed dependently and endured so long as its sustaining conditions obtained, would run deep against the grain of typical Buddhist teaching.

The Buddha is said to have offered no opinion, and to have found no profit in speculation, on certain questions: whether the world is or is not eternal, whether the world is or is not infinite, and whether the soul is different from or identical to the body. The religious reason given for this indifference is that reflection on such matters does not lead to enlightenment. A philosophical reason sometimes given is that if, as Buddhism claims, there is no world of substances, whether minds or bodies, then these questions have no straightforward answer. They are like the question, What does the horn of the hare weigh? Hares have no horns to be heavy or light. Seen in the context of the assumptions common in the culture in which they were asked, the questions would suggest that there are substantival minds and bodies and a world made up of them, and to answer these questions, even negatively, would have involved at least implicitly sanctioning that suggestion.

Broadly, Indian Buddhism divides into *Theravada* ("Doctrine of the Elders," namely those who heard and followed the Buddha; this school is also called *Hinayana,* or "Lesser Vehicle") and *Mahayana* ("Greater Vehicle"). The Sautrāntika and Vaibhāsika schools belong to Theravada and the Mādhyamika and Yogācāra schools are Mahayana.

The Theravada schools. The Sautrāntika school holds that while sensory experience justifies belief in the existence of mind-independent objects, the justification it provides requires us to infer from our sensory experience physical objects that we do not directly experience; it embraces *representative realism.* Thus, while our seeming to experience mind-independent objects is no illusion, our knowledge that it is not illusory rests as much on inference as on perception. The explanation of the fact that we cannot perceive as we wish – that we see and taste but rice and water though we would prefer meat and wine – is that what we see depends on what there is to be represented and what the conditions are under which we do our perceiving.

The Vaibhāsika (followers of the *Vaibhāsha* commentary) school defends direct realism, contending that if sensory perception does not justify us in claiming actually to sense objects there is no way in which we can infer their existence. If what we directly experience are alleged representations or copies of objects we never see, from which we must then infer the objects copied, we have no reason to think that the copies *are* copies of anything. We do not determine the content of our perception because it typically is determined for us by the objects that we see. The very distinctions between dreams and waking perceptions, or veridical perceptions and illusions, to which idealists appeal, depend for their appropriateness to the idealist's purpose on our being able to tell that some perceptual experiences are reliable and some are not; but then the idealist cannot successfully use them. For both Theravada schools, there is no need to correct our belief in physical objects, or in minds, beyond our viewing both minds and objects as collections of (different sorts of) momentary states.

The Mahayana schools. The Mādhyamika school holds out for a more radical revision. Our experience of physical objects is reliable only if the beliefs that we properly base on it are true – only if things are as they sensorily seem. These beliefs are true only if we can sensorily distinguish between individual objects. But everything exists dependently, and nothing that exists dependently is an individual. So there are no individuals and we cannot distinguish between individual objects. So our sensory experience is not reliable, but rather is systematically illusory. Mādhyamika then adds the doctrine of an ineffable ultimate reality hidden behind our ordinary experience and descriptions, which is accessible only in esoteric enlightenment experience. In this respect it is like Advaita Vedanta, which it probably influenced. One result of the overall Mādhyamika teaching described here is that Nirvana and *saṁsāra,* the goal and ordinary life, are identified; roughly *saṁsāra* is how Nirvana seems to the unenlightened (as roughly, for Advaita, the world of dependent things is how qualityless Brahman appears to the unenlightened).

The Yogācāra (perhaps "Yoga" because it used meditation to remove belief in mind-independent physical objects) school of Mahayana Buddhism contends for a more ambitious revision of our beliefs about objects than does Sautrāntika or Vaibhāsika, but a less radical one than the Mādhyamika. Against the latter, it contends that if mind itself is empty of essence and if all there is is an ineffable reality, then there is no one to see the truth and no reliable way to discover it. Against the direct physical-object realism of the Vaibhāsika and the representational realism of the Sautrāntika, the Yogācāra philosophers argue that dream experience seems to be of objects that exist mind-independently and in a public space, and yet there are no such objects and there is no such space. What we have experiential evidence for is the existence of (non-substantival) minds and the experiences that those minds have. There are no substances at all and no physical states; there are only mental states that compose minds. Yogācāra philosophers too had to explain why our perceptual content is not something we can decide by whim, and its explanation came in terms of the theory that each collection of momentary states, and hence each series or stream of such collections, contains impressions that represent past experiences.

These impressions become potent under certain circumstances and determine the content of one's explicit or conscious perception. The stream, or substream, of representative impressions is a storehouse of memories and plays a role in Yogācāra theory analogous to that of the *Ātman* or *Jīva* in some of the schools of Hinduism. Critics suspected it of being a thin surrogate for a substantival self. AsaṄga, Dignāga, and especially Vasubandhu were leading Yogācāra philosophers. Further, critics of the Yogācāra idealism argued that while the view contends that there are minds other than one's own, it provided no way in which that belief could be justified.

Our discussion has dealt with Indian Buddhism. Buddhism largely died out in India around the thirteenth century. It thrived in other places, especially China, Tibet, and Japan. Japanese Pure Land Buddhism resembles monotheism more than do any of the traditions that we have discussed. *Zen* is a form of Mahayana that developed in China in the sixth and seventh centuries A.D. and spread to Japan. It involves esoteric teachings outside the sacred writings, following which is believed to lead to realization of Buddhahood.

The metaphysical and epistemological issues briefly discussed here demonstrate that the Buddhist tradition found it natural to trace the consequences of views about the nature of objects and persons, and about what experience teaches, beyond the scope of what Buddhism as a religion might strictly require. There are direct realists, representational realists, and idealists, and the question arises as to whether idealism slides into solipsism. There is no way of telling what a particular religious doctrine may or may not be related to. Arguably, certain Buddhist doctrines are incompatible with certain views in contemporary physics (and Buddhist apologists have claimed that contemporary physics provides some sort of confirmation of basic Buddhist categories). There is no a priori way to limit the relationships that may come to light between apparently very diverse, and quite unrelated, issues and doctrines.

See also CHINESE PHILOSOPHY, JAPANESE PHILOSOPHY, KOREAN PHILOSOPHY, METAPHYSICS, PHILOSOPHY OF RELIGION.   K.E.Y.

Buddhism, Hinayana. See BUDDHISM.

Buddhism, *Kyo-hak.* See KOREAN PHILOSOPHY.

Buddhism, Mahayana. See BUDDHISM.

Buddhism, *Son*. See KOREAN PHILOSOPHY.

Buddhism, Theravada. See BUDDHISM.

Buddhism, Zen. See BUDDHISM.

bundle theory, a view that accepts the idea that concrete objects consist of properties but denies the need for introducing substrata to account for their diversity. By contrast, one traditional view of concrete particular objects is that they are complexes consisting of two more fundamental kinds of entities: properties that can be exemplified by many different objects and a substratum that exemplifies those properties belonging to a particular object. Properties account for the *qualitative identity* of such objects while substrata account for their *numerical diversity.*

The bundle theory is usually glossed as the view that a concrete object is nothing but a bundle of properties. This gloss, however, is inadequate. For if a "bundle" of properties is, e.g., a *set* of properties, then bundles of properties differ in significant ways from concrete objects. For sets of properties are *necessary* and *eternal* while concrete objects are *contingent* and *perishing.*

A more adequate statement of the theory holds that a concrete object is a complex of properties which all stand in a fundamental contingent relation, call it *co-instantiation,* to one another. On this account, complexes of properties are neither necessary nor eternal. Critics of the theory, however, maintain that such complexes have all their properties *essentially* and cannot change properties, whereas concrete objects have some of their properties *accidentally* and undergo change. This objection fails to recognize that there are two distinct problems addressed by the bundle theory: (a) individuation and (b) identity through time. The first problem arises for *all* objects, both momentary and enduring. The second, however, arises only for enduring objects. The bundle theory typically offers two different solutions to these problems. An *enduring* concrete object is analyzed as a series of momentary objects which stand in some contingent relation R. Different versions of the theory offer differing accounts of the relation. For example, Hume holds that the self is a series of co-instantiated impressions and ideas, whose members are related to one another by causation and resemblance (this is his bundle theory of the self). A *momentary* object, however, is analyzed as a complex of properties all of which stand in the relation of co-instantiation to one another. Consequently, even if one grants that a momentary complex of properties has all of its members essentially, it does not follow that an enduring object, which contains the complex as a temporal part, has those properties essentially unless one endorses the controversial thesis that an enduring object has its temporal parts essentially. Similarly, even if one grants that a momentary complex of properties cannot change in its properties, it does not follow that an enduring object, which consists of such complexes, cannot change its properties.

Critics of the bundle theory argue that its analysis of momentary objects is also problematic. For it appears possible that two *different momentary objects* have all properties in common, yet there cannot be two *different complexes* with all properties in common. There are two responses available to a proponent of the theory. The first is to distinguish between a strong and a weak version of the theory. On the strong version, the thesis that a momentary object is a complex of co-instantiated properties is a *necessary truth,* while on the weak version it is a *contingent* truth. The *possibility* of two momentary objects with all properties in common impugns only the strong version of the theory. The second is to challenge the basis of the claim that it is possible for two momentary objects to have all their properties in common. Although critics allege that such a state of affairs is conceivable, proponents argue that investigation into the nature of conceivability does not underwrite this claim.

See also ESSENTIALISM, IDENTITY OF INDIS-CERNIBLES, METAPHYSICS, PHENOMENALISM, SUBSTANCE, TIME SLICE. A.C.

bundle theory of the self. See BUNDLE THEORY.

Burali-Forte paradox. See SET-THEORETIC PARADOXES, SET THEORY.

Buridan, Jean (c.1300–after 1358), French philosopher. He was born in Béthune and educated at the University of Paris. Unlike most philosophers of his time, Buridan spent his academic career as a master in the faculty of arts, without seeking an advanced degree in theology. He was also unusual in being a secular cleric rather than a member of a religious order.

Buridan wrote extensively on logic and natural philosophy, although only a few of his works have appeared in modern editions. The most important on logic are the *Summulae de dialectica* ("Sum of Dialectic"), an introduction to logic conceived as a revision of, and extended commentary on, the *Summulae logicales* of Peter of Spain, a widely used logic textbook of the period; and the *Tractatus de consequentiis,* a treatise on modes of inference. Most of Buridan's other writings are short literal commentaries (*expositiones*) and longer critical studies (*quaestiones*) of Aristotle's works.

Like most medieval nominalists, Buridan argued that universals have no real existence, except as concepts by which the mind "conceives of many things indifferently." Likewise, he included only particular substances and qualities in his basic ontology. But his nominalist program is distinctive in its implementation. He differs, e.g., from Ockham in his accounts of motion, time, and quantity (appealing, in the latter case, to quantitative forms to explain the impenetrability of bodies). In natural philosophy, Buridan is best known for introducing to the West the non-Aristotelian concept of impetus, or impressed force, to explain projectile motion. Although asses appear often in his examples, the particular example that has come (via Spinoza and others) to be known as "Buridan's ass," an ass starving to death between two equidistant and equally tempting piles of hay, is unknown in Buridan's writings. It may, however, have originated as a caricature of Buridan's theory of action, which attempts to find a middle ground between Aristotelian intellectualism and Franciscan voluntarism by arguing that the will's freedom to act consists primarily in its ability to defer choice in the absence of a compelling reason to act one way or the other.

Buridan's intellectual legacy was considerable. His works continued to be read and discussed in universities for centuries after his death. Three of his students and disciples, Albert of Saxony, Marsilius of Inghen, and Nicole Oresme, went on to become distinguished philosophers in their own right.

See also METAPHYSICS, OCKHAM.   J.A.Z.

Buridan's ass. See BURIDAN.

Burke, Edmund (1729–97), British statesman and one of the eighteenth century's greatest political writers. Born in Dublin, he moved to London to study law, then undertook a literary and political career. He sat in the House of Commons from 1765 to 1794. In speeches and pamphlets during these years he offered an ideological perspective on politics that endures to this day as the fountain of conservative wisdom.

The philosophical stance that pervades Burke's parliamentary career and writings is skepticism, a profound distrust of political rationalism, i.e., the achievement in the political realm of abstract and rational structures, ideals, and objectives. Burkean skeptics are profoundly anti-ideological, detesting what they consider the complex, mysterious, and existential givens of political life distorted, criticized, or planned from a perspective of abstract, generalized, and rational categories.

The seminal expression of Burke's skeptical conservatism is found in the *Reflections on the Revolution in France* (1790). The conservatism of the *Reflections* was earlier displayed, however, in Burke's response to radical demands in England for democratic reform of Parliament in the early 1780s. The English radicals assumed that legislators could remake governments, when all wise men knew that "a prescriptive government never was made upon any foregone theory." How ridiculous, then, to put governments on Procrustean beds and make them fit "the theories which learned and speculative men have made." Such prideful presumption required much more rational capacity than could be found among ordinary mortals.

One victim of Burke's skepticism is the vaunted liberal idea of the social contract. Commonwealths were neither constructed nor ought they to be renovated according to a priori principles. The concept of an original act of contract is just such a principle. The only contract in politics is the agreement that binds generations past, present, and future, one that "is but a clause in the great primeval contract of an eternal society." Burke rejects the voluntaristic quality of rationalist liberal contractualism. Individuals are not free to create their own political institutions. Political society and law are not "subject to the will of those who, by an obligation above them, and infinitely superior, are bound to submit their will to that law." Men and groups "are not morally at liberty, at their pleasure, and on their speculations of a contingent improvement" to rip apart their communities and dissolve them into an "unsocial, uncivil, unconnected chaos."

Burke saw our stock of reason as small; despite this people still fled their basic limitations in flights of ideological fancy. They recognized no barrier to their powers and sought in politics to make reality match their speculative visions. Burke devoutly wished that people would appreciate their weakness, their "subordinate rank in the creation." God has "subjected us to act the part which belongs to the place assigned us." And that place is to know the limits of one's rational and speculative faculties.

Instead of relying on their own meager supply of reason, politicians should avail themselves "of the general bank and capital of nations and of ages." Because people forget this they weave rational schemes of reform far beyond their power to implement.

Burke stands as the champion of political skepticism in revolt against Enlightenment rationalism and its "smugness of adulterated metaphysics," which produced the "revolution of doctrine and theoretic dogma." The sins of the French were produced by the "clumsy subtlety of their political metaphysics." The "faith in the dogmatism of philosophers" led them to rely on reason and abstract ideas, on speculation and a priori principles of natural right, freedom, and equality as the basis for reforming governments. Englishmen, like Burke, had no such illusions; they understood the complexity and fragility of human nature and human institutions, they were not "the converts of Rousseau . . . the disciples of Voltaire; Helvetius [had] made no progress amongst [them]."

See also POLITICAL PHILOSOPHY.   I.K.

Burley, Walter (c.1275–c.1344), English philosopher who taught philosophy at Oxford and theology at Paris. An orthodox Aristotelian and a realist, he attacked Ockham's logic and his interpretation of the Aristotelian categories. Burley commented on almost of all of Aristotle's works in logic, natural philosophy, and moral philosophy.

An early Oxford Calculator, Burley began his work as a fellow of Merton College in 1301. By 1310, he was at Paris. A student of Thomas Wilton, he probably incepted before 1322; by 1324 he was a fellow of the Sorbonne. His commentary on Peter Lombard's *Sentences* has been lost. After leaving Paris, Burley was associated with the household of Richard of Bury and the court of Edward III, who sent him as an envoy to the papal curia in 1327. *De vita et moribus philosophorum* ("On the Life and Manners of Philosophers"), an influential, popular account of the lives of the philosophers, has often been attributed to Burley, but modern scholarship suggests that the attribution is incorrect.

Many of Burley's independent works dealt with problems in natural philosophy, notably *De intensione et remissione formarum* ("On the Intension and Remission of Forms"), *De potentiis animae* ("On the Faculties of the Soul"), and *De substantia orbis*. *De primo et ultimo instanti* ("On First and Last Instants") discusses which temporal processes have intrinsic, which extrinsic limits. In his *Tractatus de formis* Burley attacks Ockham's theory of quantity. Similarly, Burley's theory of motion opposed Ockham's views. Ockham restricts the account of motion to the thing moving, and the quality, quantity, and place acquired by motion. By contrast, Burley emphasizes the process of motion and the quantitative measurement of that process. Burley attacks the view that the forms successively acquired in motion are included in the form finally acquired. He ridicules the view that contrary qualities (hot and cold) could simultaneously inhere in the same subject producing intermediate qualities (warmth).

Burley emphasized the formal character of logic in his *De puritate artis logicae* ("On the Purity of the Art of Logic"), one of the great medieval treatises on logic. Ockham attacked a preliminary version of *De puritate* in his *Summa logicae;* Burley called Ockham a beginner in logic. In *De puritate artis logicae,* Burley makes syllogistics a subdivision of consequences. His treatment of negation is particularly interesting for his views on double negation and the restrictions on the rule that not-not-*p* implies *p*. Burley distinguished between analogous words and analogous concepts and natures. His theory of analogy deserves detailed discussion. These views, like the views expressed in most of Burley's works, have seldom been carefully studied by modern philosophers.

See also OCKHAM, PETER LOMBARD.   R.W.

business ethics. See ETHICS.

Butler, Joseph (1692–1752), English theologian and Anglican bishop who made important contributions to moral philosophy, to the understanding of moral agency, and to the development of deontological ethics. Better known in his own time for *The Analogy of Religion* (1736), a defense, along broadly empiricist lines, of orthodox, "revealed" Christian doctrine against deist criticism, Butler's main philosophical legacy was a series of highly influential arguments and theses contained in a collection of *Sermons* (1725) and in two "Dissertations" appended to *The Analogy* – one on virtue and the other on personal identity. The analytical method of these essays ("everything is what it is and not another thing") provided a model for much of English-speaking moral philosophy to follow. For example, Butler is often credited with refuting *psychological hedonism,* the view that all motives can be reduced to the desire for pleasure or happiness. The sources of human motivation are complex and structurally various, he argued. Appetites and passions seek their own peculiar objects, and pleasure must itself be understood as involving an intrinsic positive regard for a particular object. Other philosophers had maintained, like Butler, that we can desire, e.g., the happiness of others intrinsically, and not just as a means to our own happiness. And others had argued that the person who aims singlemindedly at his own happiness is unlikely to attain it. Butler's distinctive contribution was to demonstrate that happiness and pleasure themselves require completion by specific objects for which we have an intrinsic positive regard. Self-love, the desire for our own happiness, is a *reflective* desire for, roughly, the satisfaction of our other desires. But self-love is not our only reflective desire; we also have "a settled reasonable principle of benevolence." We can consider the goods of others and come on reflection to desire their welfare more or less independently of particular emotional involvement such as compassion.

In morals, Butler equally opposed attempts to reduce virtue to benevolence, even of the most universal and impartial sort. Benevolence seeks the good or happiness of others, whereas the regulative principle of virtue is conscience, the faculty of moral approval or disapproval of conduct and character. Moral agency requires, he argued, the capacities to reflect disinterestedly on action, motive, and character, to judge these in distinctively moral terms (and not just in terms of their relation to the non-moral good of happiness), and to guide conduct by such judgments. Butler's views about the centrality of conscience in the moral life were important in the development of deontological ethics as well as in the working out of an associated account of moral agency. Along the first lines, he argued in the "Dissertation" that what it is right for a person to do depends, not just on the (non-morally) good or bad consequences of an action, but on such other morally relevant features as the relationships the agent bears to affected others (e.g., friend or beneficiary), or whether fraud, injustice, treachery, or violence is involved. Butler thus distinguished analytically between distinctively moral evaluation of action and assessing an act's relation to such non-moral values as happiness. And he provided succeeding deontological theorists with a litany of examples where the right thing to do is apparently not what would have the best consequences.

Butler believed God instills a "principle of reflection" or conscience in us through which we intrinsically disapprove of such actions as fraud and injustice. But he also believed that God, being omniscient and benevolent, fitted us with these moral attitudes because "He foresaw this constitution of our nature would produce more happiness, than forming us with a temper of mere general benevolence." This points, however, toward a kind of anti-deontological or consequentialist view, sometimes called *indirect conse-*

quentialism, which readily acknowledges that what it is right to do does not depend on which *act* will have the best consequences. It is entirely appropriate, according to indirect consequentialism, that conscience approve or disapprove of acts on grounds other than a calculation of consequences precisely because its doing so has the best consequences. Here we have a version of the sort of view later to be found, for example, in Mill's defense of utilitarianism against the objection that it conflicts with justice and rights. Morality is a system of social control that demands allegiance to considerations other than utility, e.g., justice and honesty. But it is justifiable only to the extent that the system itself has utility.

This sets up something of a tension. From the conscientious perspective an agent must distinguish between the question of which action would have the best consequences and the question of what he should do. And from that perspective, Butler thinks, one will necessarily regard one's answer to the second question as authoritative for conduct. Conscience necessarily implicitly asserts its own authority, Butler famously claimed. Thus, insofar as agents come to regard their conscience as simply a method of social control with good consequences, they will come to be alienated from the inherent authority their conscience implicitly claims. A similar issue arises concerning the relation between conscience and self-love. Butler says that both self-love and conscience are "superior principles in the nature of man" in that an action will be unsuitable to a person's nature if it is contrary to either. This makes conscience's authority conditional on its not conflicting with self-love (and vice versa). Some scholars, moreover, read other passages as implying that no agent could reasonably follow conscience unless doing so was in the agent's interest. But again, it would seem that an agent who internalized such a view would be alienated from the authority that, if Butler is right, conscience implicitly claims. For Butler, conscience or the principle of reflection is uniquely the faculty of practical *judgment.* Unlike either self-love or benevolence, even when these are added to the powers of inference and empirical cognition, only conscience makes moral agency possible. Only a creature with conscience can accord with or violate his own judgment of what he ought to do, and thereby be a "law to himself." This suggests a view that, like Kant's, seeks to link deontology to a conception of autonomous moral agency.

See also EGOISM, ETHICS, HEDONISM, UTILITARIANISM.   S.L.D.

C

cabala (from Hebrew *qabbala,* 'tradition'), a system of Jewish mysticism and theosophy practiced from the thirteenth to the eighteenth century; loosely, all forms of Jewish mysticism. Believed by its adherents to be a tradition communicated to Moses at Sinai, the main body of cabalistic writing, the *Zohar,* is thought to be the work primarily of Moses de León of Guadalajara, in the thirteenth century, though he attributed it to the second-century rabbi Simon bar Yohai. The *Zohar* builds on earlier Jewish mysticism, and is replete with gnostic and Neoplatonic themes. It offers the initiated access to the mysteries of God's being, human destiny, and the meaning of the commandments. The transcendent and strictly unitary God of rabbinic Judaism here encounters ten apparently real divine powers, called *sefirot,* which together represent God's being and appearance in the cosmos and include male and female principles. Evil in the world is seen as a reflection of a cosmic rupture in this system, and redemption on earth entails restoration of the divine order. Mankind can assist in this task through knowledge, piety, and observance of the law.

Isaac Luria in the sixteenth century developed these themes with graphic descriptions of the dramas of creation, cosmic rupture, and restoration, the latter process requiring human assistance more than ever.   A.L.I.

Caird, Edward (1835–1908), Scottish philosopher, a leading absolute idealist. Influential as both a writer and a teacher, Caird was professor of moral philosophy at Glasgow and master of Balliol College, Oxford. His aim in philosophy was to overcome intellectual oppositions. In his main work, *The Critical Philosophy of Kant* (1889), he argued that Kant had done this by using reason to synthesize rationalism and empiricism while reconciling science and religion. In Caird's view, Kant unfortunately treated reason as subjective, thereby retaining an opposition between self and world. Loosely following Hegel, Caird claimed that objective reason, or the Absolute, was a larger whole in which both self and world were fragments. In his *Evolution of Religion* (1893) Caird argued that religion progressively understands God as the Absolute and hence as what reconciles self and world. This allowed him to defend Christianity as the highest evolutionary stage of religion without defending the literal truth of Scripture. **See also IDEALISM, PHILOSOPHY OF RELIGION.**   J.W.A.

Cajetan, original name, Tommaso de Vio (c.1469–1534), Italian prelate and theologian. Born in Gaeta (from which he took his name), he entered the Dominican order in 1484 and studied philosophy and theology at Naples, Bologna, and Padua. He became a cardinal in 1517; during the following two years he traveled to Germany, where he engaged in a theological controversy with Luther. His major work is a *Commentary on St. Thomas' Summa of Theology* (1508), which promoted a renewal of interest in Scholastic and Thomistic philosophy during the sixteenth century. In agreement with Aquinas, Cajetan places the origin of human knowledge in sense perception. In contrast with Aquinas, he denies that the immortality of the soul and the existence of God as our creator can be proved. Cajetan's work in logic was based on traditional Aristotelian syllogistic logic but is original in its discussion of the notion of analogy. Cajetan distinguishes three types: analogy of inequality, analogy of attribution, and analogy of proportion. Whereas he rejected the first two types as improper, he regarded the last as the basic type of analogy and appealed to it in explaining how humans come to know God and how analogical reasoning applied to God and God's creatures avoids being equivocal. **See also THOMISM.**   P.Gar.

calculi of relations. See RELATIONAL LOGIC.

calculus, a central branch of mathematics, originally conceived in connection with the determination of the tangent (or normal) to a curve and of the area between it and some fixed axis; but it also embraced the calculation of volumes and of areas of curved surfaces, the lengths of curved lines, and so on. *Mathematical analysis* is a still broader branch that subsumed the calculus under its rubric (see below), together with the theories of functions and of infinite series. Still more general and/or abstract versions of analysis have been developed during the twentieth century, with applications to other branches of mathematics, such as probability theory.

The origins of the calculus go back to Greek mathematics, usually in problems of determining the slope of a tangent to a curve and the area enclosed underneath it by some fixed axes or by a closed curve; sometimes related questions such as the length of an arc of a curve, or the area of a curved surface, were considered. The subject flourished in the seventeenth century when the analytical geometry of Descartes gave algebraic means to extend the procedures. It developed further when the problems of slope and area were seen to require the finding of new functions, and that the pertaining processes were seen to be inverse. Newton and Leibniz had these insights in the late seventeenth century, independently and in different forms.

In the Leibnizian *differential calculus* the differential dx was proposed as an infinitesimal increment on x, and of the same dimension as x; the slope of the tangent to a curve with y as a function of x was the *ratio dy/dx*. The *integral, $\int x$,* was infinitely large and of the dimension of x; thus for linear variables x and y the area $\int y\,dx$ was the sum of the areas of rectangles y high and dx wide. All these quantities were variable, and so could admit higher-order differentials and integrals (ddx, $\int\int x$, and so on). This theory was extended during the eighteenth century, especially by Euler, to functions of several independent variables, and with the creation of the calculus of variations. The chief motivation was to solve differential equations: they were motivated largely by problems in mechanics, which was then the single largest branch of mathematics.

Newton's less successful *fluxional calculus* used limits in its basic definitions, thereby changing dimensions for the defined terms. The fluxion was the rate of change of a variable quantity relative to "time"; conversely, that variable was the "fluent" of its fluxion. These quantities were also variable; fluxions and fluents of higher orders could be defined from them.

A third tradition was developed during the late eighteenth century by J. L. Lagrange. For him the "derived functions" of a function $f(x)$ were definable by purely algebraic means from its Taylorian power-series expansion about any value of x. By these means it was hoped to avoid the use of both infinitesimals and limits, which exhibited conceptual difficulties, the former due to their unclear ontology as values greater than zero but smaller than any orthodox quantity, the latter because of the naive theories of their deployment.

In the early nineteenth century the Newtonian tradition died away, and Lagrange's did not gain general conviction; however, the Leibniz-Euler line kept some of its health, for its utility in physical applications. But all these theories gradually became eclipsed by the mathematical analysis of A. L. Cauchy. As with Newton's calculus, the theory of limits was central, but they were handled in a much more sophisticated way. He replaced the usual practice of defining the integral as (more or less) *automatically* the inverse of the differential (or fluxion or whatever) by giving *independent* definitions of the derivative and the integral; thus for the first time the fundamental "theorem" of the calculus, stating their inverse relationship, became a genuine theorem, requiring sufficient conditions upon the function to ensure its truth. Indeed, Cauchy pioneered the routine specification of necessary and/or sufficient conditions for truth of theorems in analysis. His discipline also incorporated the theory of (dis)continuous functions and the convergence or divergence of infinite series. Again, general definitions were proffered and conditions sought for properties to hold.

Cauchy's discipline was refined and extended in the second half of the nineteenth century by K. Weierstrass and his followers at Berlin. The study of existence theorems (as for irrational numbers), and also technical questions largely concerned with trigonometric series, led to the emergence of set topology. In addition, special attention was given to processes involving several variables changing in value together, and as a result the importance of quantifiers was recognized – for example, reversing their order from 'there is a y such that for all x . . .' to 'for all x, there is a y . . .'. This developed later into general set theory, and then to mathematical logic: Cantor was the major figure in the first aspect, while G. Peano pioneered much for the second.

Under this regime of "rigor," infinitesimals such as dx became unacceptable as mathematical objects. However, they always kept an unofficial place because of their utility when applying the calculus, and since World War II theories have been put forward in which the established level of rigor and generality are preserved (and even improved) but in which infinitesimals are reinstated. The best-known of these theories, the non-standard analysis of A. Robinson, makes use of model theory by defining infinitesimals as arithmetical inverses of the transfinite integers generated by a "non-standard model" of Peano's postulates for the natural numbers.

See also MATHEMATICAL ANALYSIS, PHIL-
OSOPHY OF MATHEMATICS, SET THEORY.
                                                    I.G.-G.

calculus, fluxional. See CALCULUS.

calculus, lambda-. See COMBINATORY LOGIC,
LAMBDA-CALCULUS.

calculus, propositional. See FORMAL LOGIC.

calculus, sentential. See FORMAL LOGIC.

calculus, sequential. See CUT-ELIMINATION THEO-
REM.

calculus of classes. See BOOLEAN ALGEBRA.

calculus of individuals. See MEREOLOGY.

calculus ratiocinator. See LEIBNIZ.

Calvin, John (1509–64), French theologian and
church reformer, a major figure in the Protestant
Reformation. He was especially important for the
so-called Reformed churches in France, Switzerland, the Netherlands, Germany, Scotland, and
England. Calvin was a theologian in the humanist tradition rather than a philosopher. He valued
philosophy as "a noble gift of God" and cited
philosophers (especially Plato) when it suited his
purposes; but he rejected philosophical speculation about "higher things" and despised –
though sometimes exploiting its resources – the
dominant (Scholastic) philosophy of his time, to
which he had been introduced at the University
of Paris. His eclectic culture also included a variety of philosophical ideas, of whose source he
was often unaware, that inevitably helped to
shape his thought. His *Christianae religionis institutio* (first ed. 1536 but repeatedly enlarged; in
English generally cited as *Institutes*), his theological treatises, his massive biblical commentaries,
and his letters, all of which were translated into
most European languages, thus helped to transmit various philosophical motifs and attitudes in
an unsystematic form both to contemporaries
and to posterity. He passed on to his followers
impulses derived from both the *antiqui* and the
moderni.

From the former he inherited an intellectualist anthropology that conceived of the personality as a hierarchy of faculties properly subordinated to reason, which was at odds with his
evangelical theology; and, though he professed

to scorn Stoicism, a moralism often more Stoic
than evangelical. He also relied occasionally on
the Scholastic *quaestio,* and regularly treated sub-
stantives, like the *antiqui,* as real entities. These
elements in his thought also found expression in
tendencies to a natural theology based on an
innate and universal religious instinct that can
discern evidences of the existence and attributes
of God everywhere in nature, and a conception
of the Diety as immutable and intelligible. This
side of Calvinism eventually found expression in
Unitarianism and universalism.

It was, however, in uneasy tension with other
tendencies in his thought that reflect both his
biblicism and a nominalist and Scotist sense of
the extreme transcendence of God. Like other
humanists, therefore, he was also profoundly
skeptical about the capacity of the human mind
to grasp ultimate truth, an attitude that rested,
for him, on both the consequences of original sin
and the merely conventional origins of language.
Corollaries of this were his sense of the contingency of all human intellectual constructions
and a tendency to emphasize the utility rather
than the truth even of such major elements in his
theology as the doctrine of predestination. It may
well be no accident, therefore, that later skepticism and pragmatism have been conspicuous in
thinkers nurtured by later Calvinism, such as
Bayle, Hume, and James.

See also HUMANISM, PHILOSOPHY OF RELI-
GION, TRANSCENDENCE.   W.J.B.

Cambridge change, a non-genuine change. If I
turn pale, I am changing, whereas your turning
pale is only a Cambridge change in me. When I
acquire the property of being such that you are
pale, *I* do not change. In general, an object's
acquiring a new property is not a sufficient condition for that object to change (although some
other object may genuinely change). Thus also,
my being such that you are pale counts only as a
Cambridge property of me, a property such that my
gaining or losing it is only a Cambridge change.
Cambridge properties are a proper subclass of
extrinsic properties: being south of Chicago is
considered an extrinsic property of me, but since
my moving to Canada would be a genuine
change, being south of Chicago cannot, for me,
be a Cambridge property.

The concept of a Cambridge change reflects a
way of thinking entrenched in common sense,
but it is difficult to clarify, and its philosophical
value is controversial. Neither science nor formal
semantics, e.g., supports this viewpoint. Perhaps

Cambridge changes and properties are, for better or worse, inseparable from a vague, intuitive metaphysics.

See also PROPERTY, TIME.   S.J.W.

Cambridge Platonists, a group of seventeenth-century philosopher-theologians at the University of Cambridge, principally including Benjamin Whichcote (1609–83), often designated the father of the Cambridge Platonists; Henry More; Ralph Cudworth (1617–88); and John Smith (1616–52). Whichcote, Cudworth, and Smith received their university education in or were at some time fellows of Emmanuel College, a stronghold of the Calvinism in which they were nurtured and against which they rebelled under mainly Erasmian, Arminian, and Neoplatonic influences. Other Cambridge men who shared their ideas and attitudes to varying degrees were Nathanael Culverwel (1618?–51), Peter Sterry (1613–72), George Rust (d.1670), John Worthington (1618–71), and Simon Patrick (1625–1707).

As a generic label, 'Cambridge Platonists' is a handy umbrella term rather than a dependable signal of doctrinal unity or affiliation. The Cambridge Platonists were not a self-constituted group articled to an explicit manifesto; no two of them shared quite the same set of doctrines or values. Their Platonism was not exclusively the pristine teaching of Plato, but was formed rather from Platonic ideas supposedly prefigured in Hermes Trismegistus, in the Chaldean Oracles, and in Pythagoras, and which they found in Origen and other church fathers, in the Neoplatonism of Plotinus and Proclus, and in the Florentine Neoplatonism of Ficino. They took contrasting and changing positions on the important belief (originating in Florence with Giovanni Pico della Mirandola) that Pythagoras and Plato derived their wisdom ultimately from Moses and the cabala. They were not equally committed to philosophical pursuits, nor were they equally versed in the new philosophies and scientific advances of the time.

The Cambridge Platonists' concerns were ultimately religious and theological rather than primarily philosophical. They philosophized as theologians, making eclectic use of philosophical doctrines (whether Platonic or not) for apologetic purposes. They wanted to defend "true religion," namely, their latitudinarian vision of Anglican Christianity, against a variety of enemies: the Calvinist doctrine of predestination; sectarianism; religious enthusiasm; fanaticism; the "hide-bound, strait-laced spirit" of Interregnum Puritanism; the "narrow, persecuting spirit" that followed the Restoration; atheism; and the impieties incipient in certain trends in contemporary science and philosophy. Notable among the latter were the doctrines of the mechanical philosophers, especially the materialism and mechanical determinism of Hobbes and the mechanistic pretensions of the Cartesians.

The existence of God, the existence, immortality, and dignity of the human soul, the existence of spirit activating the natural world, human free will, and the primacy of reason are among the principal teachings of the Cambridge Platonists. They emphasized the positive role of reason in all aspects of philosophy, religion, and ethics, insisting in particular that it is *irrational*-ity that endangers the Christian life. Human reason and understanding was "the Candle of the Lord" (Whichcote's phrase), perhaps their most cherished image. In Whichcote's words, "To go against Reason, is to go against God . . . Reason is the Divine Governor of Man's Life; it is the very Voice of God." Accordingly, "there is no real clashing at all betwixt any genuine point of Christianity and what true Philosophy and right Reason does determine or allow" (More). Reason directs us to the self-evidence of first principles, which "must be seen in their own light, and are perceived by an inward power of nature." Yet in keeping with the Plotinian mystical tenor of their thought, they found within the human soul the "Divine Sagacity" (More's term), which is the prime cause of human reason and therefore superior to it. Denying the Calvinist doctrine that revelation is the only source of spiritual light, they taught that the "natural light" enables us to know God and interpret the Scriptures.

Cambridge Platonism was uncompromisingly innatist. Human reason has inherited immutable intellectual, moral, and religious notions, "anticipations of the soul," which negate the claims of empiricism. The Cambridge Platonists were skeptical with regard to certain kinds of knowledge, and recognized the role of skepticism as a critical instrument in epistemology. But they were dismissive of the idea that Pyrrhonism be taken seriously in the practical affairs of the philosopher at work, and especially of the Christian soul in its quest for divine knowledge and understanding. Truth is not compromised by our inability to devise apodictic demonstrations. Indeed Whichcote passed a moral censure on those who pretend "the doubtfulness and uncertainty of reason."

Innatism and the natural light of reason shaped the Cambridge Platonists' moral philosophy. The unchangeable and eternal ideas of good and evil in the divine mind are the exemplars of ethical axioms or noemata that enable the human mind to make moral judgments. More argued for a "boniform faculty," a faculty higher than reason by which the soul rejoices in reason's judgment of the good.

The most philosophically committed and systematic of the group were More, Cudworth, and Culverwel. Smith, perhaps the most intellectually gifted and certainly the most promising (note his dates), defended Whichcote's Christian teaching, insisting that theology is more "a Divine Life than a Divine Science." More exclusively theological in their leanings were Whichcote, who wrote little of solid philosophical interest, Rust, who followed Cudworth's moral philosophy, and Sterry. Only Patrick, More, and Cudworth (all fellows of the Royal Society) were sufficiently attracted to the new science (especially the work of Descartes) to discuss it in any detail or to turn it to philosophical and theological advantage. Though often described as a Platonist, Culverwel was really a neo-Aristotelian with Platonic embellishments and, like Sterry, a Calvinist. He denied innate ideas and supported the *tabula rasa* doctrine, commending "the Platonists ... that they lookt upon the spirit of a man as the Candle of the Lord, though they were deceived in the time when 'twas lighted."

The Cambridge Platonists were influential as latitudinarians, as advocates of rational theology, as severe critics of unbridled mechanism and materialism, and as the initiators, in England, of the intuitionist ethical tradition. In the England of Locke they are a striking counterinstance of innatism and non-empirical philosophy.

See also MORE, HENRY; NEOPLATONISM; PHILOSOPHY OF RELIGION; PLATO.   A.G.

Cambridge property. See CAMBRIDGE CHANGE.

camera obscura, a darkened enclosure that focuses light from an external object by a pinpoint hole instead of a lens, creating an inverted, reversed image on the opposite wall. The adoption of the camera obscura as a model for the eye revolutionized the study of visual perception by rendering obsolete previous speculative philosophical theories, in particular the emanation theory, which explained perception as due to emanated copy-images of objects entering the eye, and theories that located the image of perception in the lens rather than the retina. By shifting the location of sensation to a projection on the retina, the camera obscura doctrine helped support the distinction of primary and secondary sense qualities, undermining the medieval realist view of perception and moving toward the idea that consciousness is radically split off from the world. **See also PERCEPTION.**

T.H.L.

Campanella, Tommaso (1568–1639), Italian theologian, philosopher, and poet. He joined the Dominican order in 1582. Most of the years between 1592 and 1634 he spent in prison for heresy and for conspiring to replace Spanish rule in southern Italy with a utopian republic. He fled to France in 1634 and spent his last years in freedom. Some of his best poetry was written while he was chained in a dungeon; and during less rigorous confinement he managed to write over a hundred books, not all of which survive. His best-known work, *The City of the Sun* (1602; published 1623), describes a community governed in accordance with astrological principles, with a priest as head of state. In later political writings, Campanella attacked Machiavelli and called for either a universal Spanish monarchy with the pope as spiritual head or a universal theocracy with the pope as both spiritual and temporal leader. His first publication was *Philosophy Demonstrated by the Senses* (1591), which supported the theories of Telesio and initiated his lifelong attack on Aristotelianism. He hoped to found a new Christian philosophy based on the two books of nature and Scripture, both of which are manifestations of God. While he appealed to sense experience, he was not a straightforward empiricist, for he saw the natural world as alive and sentient, and he thought of magic as a tool for utilizing natural processes. In this he was strongly influenced by Ficino. Despite his own difficulties with Rome, he wrote in support of Galileo. **See also FICINO, TELESIO.**   E.J.A.

Campbell, Norman Robert (1880–1949), British physicist and philosopher of science. A successful experimental physicist, Campbell (with A. Wood) discovered the radioactivity of potassium. His analysis of science depended on a sharp distinction between experimental laws and theories. Experimental laws are generalizations established by observations. A theory has the following structure. First, it requires a (largely arbitrary) hypothesis, which in itself is untestable. To render it testable, the theory requires a "dictionary" of propositions linking the hypothesis to scientific laws, which can be established experimentally. But theories are not merely logical relations between hypotheses and experimental laws; they also require concrete analogies or models. Indeed, the models suggest the nature of the propositions in the dictionary. The analogies are essential components of the theory, and, for Campbell, are nearly always mechanical. His theory of science greatly influenced Nagel's *The Structure of Science* (1961). **See also PHILOSOPHY OF SCIENCE, THEORETICAL TERM.**   R.E.B.

Camus, Albert (1913–60), French philosophical novelist and essayist who was also a prose poet and the conscience of his times. He was born and raised in Algeria, and his experiences as a fatherless, tubercular youth, as a young playwright and journalist in Algiers, and later in the anti-German resistance in Paris during World War II informed everything he wrote. His best-known writings are not overtly political; his most famous works, the novel *The Stranger* (written in 1940, published in 1942) and his book-length essay *The Myth of Sisyphus* (written in 1941, published in 1943) explore the notion of "the absurd," which Camus alternatively describes as the human condition and as "a widespread sensitivity of our times." The absurd, briefly defined, is the confrontation between ourselves – with our demands for rationality and justice – and an "indifferent universe." Sisyphus, who was condemned by the gods to the endless, futile task of rolling a rock up a mountain (whence it would roll back down of its own weight), thus becomes an exemplar of the human condition, struggling hopelessly and pointlessly to achieve something. The odd antihero of *The Stranger*, on the other hand, unconsciously accepts the absurdity of life. He makes no judgments, accepts the most repulsive characters as his friends and neighbors, and remains unmoved by the death of his mother and his own killing of a man. Facing execution for his crime, he "opens his heart to the benign indifference of the universe."

But such stoic acceptance is not the message of Camus's philosophy. Sisyphus thrives (he is even "happy") by virtue of his scorn and defiance of the gods, and by virtue of a "rebellion" that refuses to give in to despair. This same theme motivates Camus's later novel, *The Plague* (1947), and his long essay *The Rebel* (1951). In his last work, however, a novel called *The Fall* published in 1956, the year before he won the Nobel prize for literature, Camus presents an unforgettably perverse character named Jean-Baptiste Clamence, who exemplifies all the bitterness and despair rejected by his previous characters and in his earlier essays. Clamence, like the character in *The Stranger*, refuses to judge people, but whereas Meursault (the "stranger") is incapable of judgment, Clamence (who was once a lawyer) makes it a matter of philosophical principle, "for who among us is innocent?" It is unclear where Camus's thinking was heading when he was killed in an automobile accident (with his publisher, Gallimard, who survived).
      See also EXISTENTIALISM, SARTRE.

                                                          R.C.So.

Canguilhem, Georges (1904–96), French historian and philosopher of science. Canguilhem succeeded Gaston Bachelard as director of the Institut d'Histoire des Sciences et des Techniques at the University of Paris. He developed and sometimes revised Bachelard's view of science, extending it to issues in the biological and medical sciences, where he focused particularly on the concepts of the normal and the pathological (*The Normal and the Pathological*, 1966). On his account norms are not objective in the sense of being derived from value-neutral scientific inquiry, but are rooted in the biological reality of the organisms that they regulate.

Canguilhem also introduced an important methodological distinction between concepts and theories. Rejecting the common view that scientific concepts are simply functions of the theories in which they are embedded, he argued that the use of concepts to interpret data is quite distinct from the use of theories to explain the data. Consequently, the same concepts may occur in very different theoretical contexts. Canguilhem made particularly effective use of this distinction in tracing the origin of the concept of reflex action.
      See also BACHELARD, PHILOSOPHY OF THE SOCIAL SCIENCES, PSYCHOPATHOLOGY.

                                                            G.G.

Cantor, Georg (1845–1918), German mathematician, one of a number of late nineteenth-century mathematicians and philosophers (including Frege, Dedekind, Peano, Russell, and Hilbert) who transformed both mathematics and the study of its philosophical foundations. The philosophical import of Cantor's work is three-fold. First, it was primarily Cantor who turned arbitrary collections into objects of mathematical study, sets. Second, he created a coherent *mathematical* theory of the infinite, in particular a theory of transfinite numbers. Third, linking these, he was the first to indicate that it might be possible to present mathematics as nothing but the theory of sets, thus making set theory foundational for mathematics. This contributed to the view that the foundations of mathematics should itself become an object of mathematical study. Cantor also held to a form of principle of plenitude, the belief that all the infinities given in his theory of transfinite numbers are represented not just in mathematical (or "immanent" reality), but also in the "transient" reality of God's created world.

Cantor's main, direct achievement is his theory of transfinite numbers and infinity. He characterized (as did Frege) sameness of size in terms of one-to-one correspondence, thus accepting the paradoxical results known to Galileo and others, e.g., that the collection of *all* natural numbers has the same cardinality or size as that of all *even* numbers. He added to these surprising results by showing (1874) that there is the same number of algebraic (and thus rational) numbers as there are natural numbers, but that there are *more* points on a continuous line than there are natural (or rational or algebraic) numbers, thus revealing that there are at least two different kinds of infinity present in ordinary mathematics, and consequently demonstrating the need for a mathematical treatment of these infinities. This latter result is often expressed by saying that the continuum is *uncountable*. *Cantor's theorem* of 1892 is a generalization of part of this, for it says that the set of all subsets (the *power-set*) of a given set must be cardinally greater than that set, thus giving rise to the possibility of indefinitely many different infinities. (The collection of all real numbers has the same size as the power-set of natural numbers.) Cantor's theory of transfinite numbers (1880–97) was his developed mathematical theory of infinity, with the infinite cardinal numbers (the $\aleph$-, or aleph-, numbers) based on the infinite ordinal numbers that he introduced in 1880 and 1883. The $\aleph$-numbers are in effect the cardinalities of infinite *well-ordered* sets. The theory thus generates two famous questions, whether *all* sets (in particular the continuum) can be well ordered, and if so which of the $\aleph$-numbers represents the cardinality of the continuum. The former question was answered positively by Zermelo in 1904, though at the expense of postulating one of the most controversial principles in the history of mathematics, the axiom of choice. The latter question is the celebrated *continuum problem*. Cantor's famous *continuum hypothesis* (CH) is his conjecture that the cardinality of the continuum is represented by $\aleph_1$, the second aleph. CH was shown to be independent of the usual assumptions of set theory by Gödel (1938) and Cohen (1963). Extensions of

Cohen's methods show that it is consistent to assume that the cardinality of the continuum is given by almost any of the vast array of $\aleph$-numbers. The continuum problem is now widely considered insoluble.

Cantor's conception of set is often taken to admit the whole universe of sets as a set, thus engendering contradiction, in particular in the form of *Cantor's paradox*. For Cantor's theorem would say that the power-set of the universe must be bigger than it, while, since this power-set is a set of sets, it must be *contained* in the universal set, and thus can be no bigger. However, it follows from Cantor's early (1883) considerations of what he called the "absolute infinite" that none of the collections discovered later to be at the base of the paradoxes can be proper sets. Moreover, correspondence with Hilbert in 1897 and Dedekind in 1899 (see Cantor, *Gesammelte Abhandlungen mathematischen und philosophischen Inhalts*, 1932) shows clearly that Cantor was well aware that contradictions will arise if such collections *are* treated as ordinary sets.

See also CONTINUUM PROBLEM, SET-THEORETIC PARADOXES, SET THEORY.   M.H.

Cantor's paradox. See SET-THEORETIC PARADOXES.

Cantor's theorem. See CANTOR, CONTINUUM PROBLEM.

capacity, diminished. See DIMINISHED CAPACITY.

capacity responsibility. See RESPONSIBILITY.

cardinality. See SET-THEORETIC PARADOXES.

cardinal utility. See UTILITARIANISM.

cardinal virtues, prudence (practical wisdom), courage, temperance, and justice. Medievals deemed them cardinal (from Latin *cardo,* 'hinge') because of their important or pivotal role in human flourishing. In Plato's *Republic,* Socrates explains them through a doctrine of the three parts of the soul, suggesting that a person is *prudent* when knowledge of how to live (wisdom) informs her *reason, courageous* when informed reason governs her *capacity for wrath,* temperate when it also governs her *appetites,* and *just* when each part performs its proper task with informed reason in control. Development of thought on the cardinal virtues was closely tied to the doctrine of the unity of the virtues, i.e., that a person possessing one virtue will have them all. **See also** VIRTUE ETHICS.   J.L.A.G.

Carlyle, Thomas (1795–1881), Scottish-born essayist, historian, and social critic, one of the most popular writers and lecturers in nineteenth-century Britain. His works include literary criticism, history, and cultural criticism. With respect to philosophy, his views on the theory of history are his most significant contributions. According to Carlyle, great personages are the most important causal factor in history. *On Heroes, Hero-Worship and the Heroic in History* (1841) asserts, "Universal History, the history of what man has accomplished in this world, is at bottom the History of the Great Men who have worked here. They were the leaders of men, these great ones; the modellers, patterns, and in a wide sense creators, of whatsoever the general mass of men contrived to do or to attain; all things that we see standing accomplished in the world are properly the outer material result, the practical realisation and embodiment, of Thoughts that dwelt in the Great Men sent into the world: the soul of the whole world's history, it may justly be considered, were the history of these."

Carlyle's doctrine has been challenged from many different directions. Hegelian and Marxist philosophers maintain that the so-called great men of history are not really the engine of history, but merely reflections of deeper forces, such as economic ones, while contemporary historians emphasize the priority of "history from below" – the social history of everyday people – as far more representative of the historical process.

See also PHILOSOPHY OF HISTORY.   N.C.

Carnap, Rudolf (1891–1970), German-born American philosopher, one of the leaders of the Vienna Circle, a movement loosely called logical positivism or logical empiricism. He made fundamental contributions to semantics and the philosophy of science, as well as to the foundations of probability and inductive logic. He was a staunch advocate of, and active in, the unity of science movement.

Carnap received his Ph.D. in philosophy from the University of Jena in 1921. His first major work was *Die Logische Aufbau der Welt* (1928), in which he sought to apply the new logic recently developed by Frege and by Russell and Whitehead to problems in the philosophy of science. Although influential, it was not translated until 1967, when it appeared as *The Logical Structure of the World*. It was important as one of the first clear and unambiguous statements that the important work of philosophy concerned logical structure: that language and its logic were to be the focus of attention. In 1935 Carnap left his native Ger-

many for the United States, where he taught at the University of Chicago and then at UCLA.

Die Logiche Syntax der Sprach (1934) was rapidly translated into English, appearing as *The Logical Syntax of Language* (1937). This was followed in 1941 by *Introduction to Semantics,* and in 1942 by *The Formalization of Logic.* In 1947 *Meaning and Necessity* appeared; it provided the groundwork for a modal logic that would mirror the meticulous semantic development of first-order logic in the first two volumes. One of the most important concepts introduced in these volumes was that of a *state description.* A state description is the linguistic counterpart of a possible world: in a given language, the most complete description of the world that can be given.

Carnap then turned to one of the most pervasive and important problems to arise in both the philosophy of science and the theory of meaning. To say that the meaning of a sentence is given by the conditions under which it would be verified (as the early positivists did) or that a scientific theory is verified by predictions that turn out to be true, is clearly to speak loosely. Absolute verification does not occur. To carry out the program of scientific philosophy in a realistic way, we must be able to speak of the support given by inconclusive evidence, either in providing epistemological justification for scientific knowledge, or in characterizing the meanings of many of the terms of our scientific language. This calls for an understanding of probability, or as Carnap preferred to call it, degree of confirmation. We must distinguish between two senses of probability: what he called probability$_1$, corresponding to credibility, and probability$_2$, corresponding to the frequency or empirical conception of probability defended by Reichenbach and von Mises. 'Degree of confirmation' was to be the formal concept corresponding to credibility.

The first book on this subject, written from the same point of view as the works on semantics, was *The Logical Foundations of Probability* (1950). The goal was a logical definition of '$c(h,e)$': the degree of confirmation of a hypothesis h, relative to a body of evidence e, or the degree of rational belief that one whose total evidence was e should commit to h. Of course we must first settle on a formal language in which to express the hypothesis and the evidence; for this Carnap chooses a first-order language based on a finite number of one-place predicates, and a countable number of individual constants. Against this background, we perform the following reductions: '$c(h,e)$' represents a conditional probability; thus it can be represented as the ratio of the absolute probability of h & e to the absolute probability of e. Absolute probabilities are represented by the value of a measure function m, defined for sentences of the language. The problem is to define m. But every sentence in Carnap's languages is equivalent to a disjunction of state descriptions; the measure to be assigned to it must, according to the probability calculus, be the sum of the measures assigned to its constituent state descriptions. Now the problem is to define m for state descriptions. (Recall that state descriptions were part of the machinery Carnap developed earlier.) The function $c\dagger$ is a confirmation function based on the assignment of equal measures to each state description. It is inadequate, because if h is not entailed by e, $c\dagger(h,e) = m\dagger(h)$, the a priori measure assigned to h. We cannot "learn from experience." A measure that does not have that drawback is m^*, which is based on the assignment of equal measures to each structure description. A structure description is a set of state descriptions; two state descriptions belong to the same structure description just in case one can be obtained from the other by a permutation of individual constants. Within the structure description, equal values are assigned to each state description.

In the next book, *The Continuum of Inductive Methods*, Carnap takes the rate at which we learn from experience to be a fundamental parameter of his assignments of probability. Like measures on state descriptions, the values of the probability of the singular predictive inference determine all other probabilities. The "singular predictive inference" is the inference from the observation that individual 1 has one set of properties, individual 2 has another set of properties, etc., to the conclusion: individual j will have property k.

Finally, in the last works (*Studies in Inductive Logic and Probability*, vols. I [1971] and II [1980], edited with Richard Jeffrey) Carnap offered two long articles constituting his *Basic System of Inductive Logic*. This system is built around a language having families of attributes (e.g., color or sound) that can be captured by predicates. The basic structure is still monadic, and the logic still lacks identity, but there are more parameters. There is a parameter λ that reflects the "rate of learning from experience"; a parameter η that reflects an inductive relation between values of attributes belonging to families. With the introduction of arbitrary parameters, Carnap was edging toward a subjective or personalistic view of probability. How far he was willing to go down the subjectivist garden path is open to question; that he discovered more to be relevant

to inductive logic than the "language" of science seems clear.

Carnap's work on probability measures on formal languages is destined to live for a long time. So too is his work on formal semantics. He was a staunch advocate of the fruitfulness of formal studies in philosophy, of being clear and explicit, and of offering concrete examples. Beyond the particular philosophical doctrines he advocated, these commitments characterize his contribution to philosophy.

See also CONFIRMATION, PHILOSOPHY OF SCIENCE, PROBABILITY, VIENNA CIRCLE.

H.E.K.

Carneades. See ACADEMY.

Carroll, Lewis, pen name of Charles Lutwidge Dodgson (1832–98), English writer and mathematician. The eldest son of a large clerical family, he was educated at Rugby and Christ Church, Oxford, where he remained for the rest of his uneventful life, as mathematical lecturer (until 1881) and curator of the senior commonroom. His mathematical writings (under his own name) are more numerous than important. He was, however, the only Oxonian of his day to contribute to symbolic logic, and is remembered for his syllogistic diagrams, for his methods for constructing and solving elaborate sorites problems, for his early interest in logical paradoxes, and for the many amusing examples that continue to reappear in modern textbooks. Fame descended upon him almost by accident, as the author of *Alice's Adventures in Wonderland* (1865), *Through the Looking Glass* (1872), *The Hunting of the Snark* (1876), and *Sylvie and Bruno* (1889–93); saving the last, the only children's books to bring no blush of embarrassment to an adult reader's cheek.

Dodgson took deacon's orders in 1861, and though pastorally inactive, was in many ways an archetype of the prim Victorian clergyman. His religious opinions were carefully thought out, but not of great philosophic interest. The Oxford movement passed him by; he worried about sin (though rejecting the doctrine of eternal punishment), abhorred profanity, and fussed over Sunday observance, but was oddly tolerant of theatergoing, a lifelong habit of his own. Apart from the sentimental messages later inserted in them, the *Alice* books and *Snark* are blessedly devoid of religious or moral concern. Full of rudeness, aggression, and quarrelsome, if fallacious, argument, they have, on the other hand, a natural attraction for philosophers, who pillage them freely for illustrations. Humpty-Dumpty, the various Kings and Queens, the Mad Hatter, the Caterpillar, the White Rabbit, the Cheshire Cat, the Unicorn, the Tweedle brothers, the Bellman, the Baker, and the Snark make fleeting appearances in the pages of Russell, Moore, Broad, Quine, Nagel, Austin, Ayer, Ryle, Blanshard, and even Wittgenstein (an unlikely admirer of the Mock Turtle). The first such allusion (to the March Hare) is in Venn's *Symbolic Logic* (1881). The usual reasons for quotation are to make some point about meaning, stipulative definition, the logic of negation, time reversal, dream consciousness, the reification of fictions and nonentities, or the absurdities that arise from taking "ordinary language" too literally. (For exponents of word processing, the effect of running *Jabberwocky* through a spell-checker is to extinguish all hope for the future of Artificial Intelligence.)

Though himself no philosopher, Carroll's unique sense of philosophic humor keeps him (and his illustrator, Sir John Tenniel) effortlessly alive in the modern age. *Alice* has been translated into seventy-five languages; new editions and critical studies appear every year; imitations, parodies, cartoons, quotations, and ephemera proliferate beyond number; and Carroll societies flourish in several countries, notably Britain and the United States.   P.He.

Cartesian circle. See DESCARTES.

Cartesian demon. See DESCARTES.

Cartesian dualism. See DUALISM, PHILOSOPHY OF MIND.

Cartesian interactionism. See PHILOSOPHY OF MIND.

Cartesianism. See DESCARTES.

Cartesian product. See SET THEORY.

Cārvāka, Indian materialism. Its varieties share the view that the mind is simply the body and its capacities, but differ as to whether every mental property is simply a physical property under some psychological description (reductive materialism) or there are emergent irreducibly mental properties that are caused by physical properties and themselves have no causal impact (epiphenomenalism). Some Cārvāka epistemologists, at least according to their critics, accept only perception as a reliable source of knowledge, but in its most sophisticated form Cārvāka, not unlike logical

positivism, allows inference at least to conclusions that concern perceptually accessible states of affairs. **See also** HINDUISM.   K.E.Y.

Cassirer, Ernst (1874–1945), German philosopher and intellectual historian. He was born in the German city of Breslau (now Wroclaw, Poland) and educated at various German universities. He completed his studies in 1899 at Marburg under Hermann Cohen, founder of the Marburg School of neo-Kantianism. Cassirer lectured at the University of Berlin from 1906 to 1919, then accepted a professorship at the newly founded University of Hamburg. With the rise of Nazism he left Germany in 1933, going first to a visiting appointment at All Souls College, Oxford (1933–35) and then to a professorship at the University of Göteborg, Sweden (1935–41). In 1941 he went to the United States; he taught first at Yale (1941–44) and then at Columbia (1944–45).

Cassirer's works may be divided into those in the history of philosophy and culture and those that present his own systematic thought. The former include major editions of Leibniz and Kant; his four-volume study *The Problem of Knowledge* (vols. 1–3, 1906–20; vol. 4, 1950), which traces the subject from Nicholas of Cusa to the twentieth century; and individual works on Descartes, Leibniz, Kant, Rousseau, Goethe, the Renaissance, the Enlightenment, and English Platonism. The latter include his multivolume *The Philosophy of Symbolic Forms* (1923–29), which presents a philosophy of human culture based on types of symbolism found in myth, language, and mathematical science; and individual works concerned with problems in such fields as logic, psychology, aesthetics, linguistics, and concept formation in the humanities. Two of his best-known works are *An Essay on Man* (1944) and *The Myth of the State* (1946).

Cassirer did not consider his systematic philosophy and his historical studies as separate endeavors; each grounded the other. Because of his involvement with the Marburg School, his philosophical position is frequently but mistakenly typed as neo-Kantian. Kant is an important influence on him, but so are Hegel, Herder, Wilhelm von Humboldt, Goethe, Leibniz, and Vico. Cassirer derives his principal philosophical concept, *symbolic form,* most directly from Heinrich Hertz's conception of notation in mechanics and the conception of the symbol in art of the Hegelian aesthetician, Friedrich Theodor Vischer. In a wider sense his conception of symbolic form is a transformation of "idea" and "form" within the whole tradition of philosophical idealism. Cassirer's conception of symbolic form is not based on a distinction between the symbolic and the literal. In his view all human knowledge depends on the power to form experience through some type of symbolism. The forms of human knowledge are coextensive with forms of human culture. Those he most often analyzes are myth and religion, art, language, history, and science. These forms of symbolism constitute a total system of human knowledge and culture that is the subject matter of philosophy.

Cassirer's influence is most evident in the aesthetics of Susanne Langer (1895–1985), but his conception of the symbol has entered into theoretical anthropology, psychology, structural linguistics, literary criticism, myth theory, aesthetics, and phenomenology. His studies of the Renaissance and the Enlightenment still stand as groundbreaking works in intellectual history.

See also HEGEL, LEIBNIZ, NEO-KANTIANISM, VICO.   D.P.V.

Castañeda, Hector-Neri (1924–91), American analytical philosopher. Heavily influenced by his own critical reaction to Quine, Chisholm, and his teacher Wilfrid Sellars, Castañeda published four books and more than 175 essays. His work combines originality, rigor, and penetration, together with an unusual comprehensiveness – his network of theory and criticism reaches into nearly every area of philosophy, including action theory; deontic logic and practical reason; ethics; history of philosophy; metaphysics and ontology; philosophical methodology; philosophy of language, mind, and perception; and the theory of knowledge. His principal contributions are to metaphysics and ontology, indexical reference, and deontic logic and practical reasoning.

In metaphysics and ontology, Castañeda's chief work is guise theory, first articulated in a 1974 essay, a complex and global account of language, mind, ontology, and predication. By holding that ordinary concrete individuals, properties, and propositions all break down or separate into their various aspects or guises, he theorizes that thinking and reference are directed toward the latter. Each guise is a genuine item in the ontological inventory, having properties internally and externally. In addition, guises are related by standing in various sameness relations, only one of which is the familiar relation of strict identity. Since every guise enjoys bona fide ontological standing, whereas only some of these actually exist, Castañeda's ontology and semantics are Meinongian. With its intricate account of predication, guise theory affords a unified treatment of a wide range of philosophical problems concerning reference to nonexistents, negative existentials, intentional identity, referential opacity, and other matters.

Castañeda also played a pivotal role in emphasizing the significance of indexical reference. If, e.g., Paul assertively utters 'I prefer Chardonnay', it would obviously be incorrect for Bob to report 'Paul says that I prefer Chardonnay', since the last statement expresses (Bob's) speaker's reference, not Paul's. At the same time, Castañeda contends, it is likewise incorrect for Bob to report Paul's saying as either 'Paul says that Paul prefers Chardonnay' or 'Paul says that Al's luncheon guest prefers Chardonnay' (when Paul *is* Al's only luncheon guest), since each of these fail to represent the essentially indexical element of Paul's assertion. Instead, Bob may correctly report 'Paul says that he himself prefers Chardonnay', where 'he himself' is a quasi-indicator, serving to depict Paul's reference to himself *qua* self. For Castañeda (and others), quasi-indicators are a person's irreducible, essential means for describing the thoughts and experiences of others. A complete account of his view of indexicals, together with a full articulation of guise theory and his unorthodox theories of definite descriptions and proper names, is contained in *Thinking, Language, and Experience* (1989).

Castañeda's main views on practical reason and deontic logic turn on his fundamental practition–proposition distinction. A number of valuable essays on these views, together with his important replies, are collected in James E. Tomberlin, ed., *Agent, Language, and the Structure of the World* (1983), and Tomberlin, ed., *Hector-Neri Castañeda* (1986). The latter also includes Castañeda's revealing intellectual autobiography.

See also DEONTIC LOGIC, GUISE THEORY, MEINONG, PRACTICAL REASONING, PRACTITION, QUASI-INDICATOR.   J.E.T.

casuistry, the case-analysis approach to the interpretation of general moral rules. Casuistry starts with paradigm cases of how and when a given general moral rule should be applied, and then reasons by analogy to cases in which the proper application of the rule is less obvious – e.g., a case in which lying is the only way for a priest not to betray a secret revealed in confession. The point of considering the series of cases is to ascertain the morally relevant similarities and differences between cases. Casuistry's heyday was the first half of the seventeenth century. Reacting against casuistry's popularity with the Jesuits and against its tendency to qualify general moral rules, Pascal penned a polemic against casuistry from which the term never recovered (see his *Provincial Letters,* 1656). But the kind of reasoning to which the term refers is flourishing in contemporary practical ethics.   B.W.H.

categorematic. See SYNCATEGOREMATA.

categorematica. See SYNCATEGOREMATA.

categorical grammar. See GRAMMAR.

categorical imperative. See KANT.

categorical-in-power. See CATEGORICAL THEORY.

categorical proposition. See SYLLOGISM.

categorical theory, a theory all of whose models are isomorphic. Because of its weak expressive power, in first-order logic with identity only theories with a finite model can be categorical; without identity no theories are categorical. A more interesting property, therefore, is being categorical in power: a theory is categorical in power α when the theory has, up to isomorphism, only one model with a domain of cardinality α. Categoricity in power shows the capacity to characterize a structure completely, only limited by cardinality. For example, the first-order theory of dense order without endpoints is categorical in power ω the cardinality of the natural numbers. The first-order theory of simple discrete orderings with initial element, the ordering of the natural numbers, is not categorical in power ω. There are countable discrete orders, not isomorphic to the natural numbers, that are elementary equivalent to it, i.e., have the same elementary, first-order theory. In first-order logic categorical theories are complete. This is not necessarily true for extensions of first-order logic for which no completeness theorem holds. In such a logic a set of axioms may be categorical without providing an informative characterization of the theory of its unique model. The term 'elementary equivalence' was introduced around 1936 by Tarski for the property of being indistinguishable by elementary means. According to Oswald Veblen, who first used the term 'categorical' in 1904, in a discussion of the foundations of geometry, that term was suggested to him by the American pragmatist John Dewey. **See also** COMPLETENESS, MODEL THEORY.   Z.G.S.

categoricity, the semantic property belonging to a set of sentences, a "postulate set," that implicitly defines (completely describes, or characterizes up to isomorphism) the structure of its intended interpretation or *standard model.* The best-known categorical set of sentences is the postulate set for number theory attributed to Peano, which completely characterizes the structure of an arithmetic progression. This structure is exemplified by the system of natural numbers with zero as distinguished element and successor (addition of one) as distinguished function. Other exemplifications of this structure are obtained by taking as distinguished element an arbitrary integer, taking as distinguished function the process of adding an arbitrary positive or negative integer and taking as universe of discourse (or domain) the result of repeated application of the distinguished function to the distinguished element. (See, e.g., Russell's *Introduction to the Mathematical Philosophy,* 1918.)

More precisely, a postulate set is defined to be *categorical* if every two of its models (satisfying interpretations or realizations) are isomorphic (to each other), where, of course, two interpretations are *isomorphic* if between their respective universes of discourse there exists a one-to-one correspondence by which the distinguished elements, functions, relations, etc., of the one are mapped exactly onto those of the other. The importance of the analytic geometry of Descartes involves the fact that the system of points of a geometrical line with the "left-of relation" distinguished is isomorphic to the system of real numbers with the "less-than" relation distinguished. Categoricity, the ideal limit of success for the axiomatic method considered as a method for characterizing subject matter rather than for reorganizing a science, is known to be impossible with respect to certain subject matters using certain formal languages. The concept of categoricity can be traced back at least as far as Dedekind; the word is due to Dewey.

   See also AXIOMATIC METHOD, LÖWENHEIM-SKOLEM THEOREM, MATHEMATICAL ANALYSIS, MODEL THEORY.   J.COR.

categories, table of. See KANT.

categories of the understanding. See KANT.

category, an ultimate class. Categories are the highest genera of entities in the world. They may contain species but are not themselves species of any higher genera. Aristotle, the first philosopher to discuss categories systematically, listed ten, including substance, quality, quantity, relation, place, and time. If a set of categories is complete, then each entity in the world will belong to a category and no entity will belong to more than one category. A prominent example of a set of categories is Descartes's dualistic classification of mind and matter. This example brings out clearly another feature of categories: an attribute that can belong to entities in one category cannot be an attribute of entities in any other category. Thus, entities in the category of matter have extension and color while no entity in the category of mind can have extension or color. **See also** ARISTOTLE, GENUS GENERALISSIMUM, RYLE.   J.W.M.

category mistake, the placing of an entity in the wrong category. In one of Ryle's examples, to place the activity of exhibiting team spirit in the same class with the activities of pitching, batting, and catching is to make a category mistake; exhibiting team spirit is not a special function like pitching or batting but instead a way those special functions are performed. A second use of 'category mistake' is to refer to the attribution to an entity of a property which that entity cannot have (not merely does not happen to have), as in 'This memory is violet' or, to use an example from Carnap, 'Caesar is a prime number'. These two kinds of category mistake may seem different, but both involve misunderstandings of the natures of the things being talked about. It is thought that they go beyond simple error or ordinary mistakes, as when one attributes a property to a thing which that thing could have but does not have, since category mistakes involve attributions of properties (e.g., being a special function) to things (e.g., team spirit) that those things cannot have. According to Ryle, the test for category differences depends on whether replacement of one expression for another in the same sentence results in a type of unintelligibility that he calls "absurdity." **See also** RYLE.   J.W.M.

category-preserving. See LOGICAL FORM.

category theory, a mathematical theory that studies the universal properties of structures via their relationships with one another. A category C consists of two collections Ob_C and Mor_C, the *objects* and the *morphisms* of C, satisfying the following conditions: (i) for each pair (a, b) of objects there is associated a collection $Mor_C (a, b)$ of morphisms such that each member of Mor_C belongs to one of these collections; (ii) for each

object a of Ob_C, there is a morphism id_a, called the *identity* on a; (iii) a composition law associating with each morphism $f: a \rightarrow b$ and each morphism $g: b \rightarrow c$ a morphism $gf:a \rightarrow c$, called the *composite* of f and g; (iv) for morphisms $f: a \rightarrow b$, $g: b \rightarrow c$, and $h: c \rightarrow d$, the equation $h(gf) = (hg)f$ holds; (v) for any morphism $f: a \rightarrow b$, we have $id_b f = f$ and $f id_a = f$. Sets with specific structures together with a collection of mappings preserving these structures are categories. Examples: (1) sets with functions between them; (2) groups with group homomorphisms; (3) topological spaces with continuous functions; (4) sets with surjections instead of arbitrary maps constitute a different category. But a category need not be composed of sets and set-theoretical maps. Examples: (5) a collection of propositions linked by the relation of logical entailment is a category and so is any preordered set; (6) a monoid taken as the unique object and its elements as the morphisms is a category. The properties of an object of a category are determined by the morphisms that are coming out of and going in this object. Objects with a universal property occupy a key position. Thus, a terminal object a is characterized by the following universal property: for any object b there is a unique morphism from b to a. A singleton set is a terminal object in the category of sets. The Cartesian product of sets, the product of groups, and the conjunction of propositions are all terminal objects in appropriate categories. Thus category theory unifies concepts and sheds a new light on the notion of universality. **See also** PHILOSOPHY OF MATHEMATICS.   J.-P.M.

causal chain. See CAUSATION.

causal closure. See DAVIDSON.

causal decision theory. See DECISION THEORY.

causal dependence. See DEPENDENCE.

causal determinism. See DETERMINISM.

causal-historical theory of reference. See PHILOSOPHY OF LANGUAGE.

causal immediacy. See IMMEDIACY.

causal law, a statement describing a regular and invariant connection between types of events or states, where the connections involved are causal in some sense. When one speaks of causal laws as distinguished from laws that are not causal, the intended distinction may vary. Sometimes, a law is said to be causal if it relates events or states occurring at successive times, also called a *law of succession:* e.g., 'Ingestion of strychnine leads to death.' A causal law in this sense contrasts with a *law of coexistence,* which connects events or states occurring at the same time (e.g., the Wiedemann-Franz law relating thermal and electric conductivity in metals).

One important kind of causal law is the *deterministic law.* Causal laws of this kind state exceptionless connections between events, while probabilistic or statistical laws specify probability relationships between events. For any system governed by a set of deterministic laws, given the state of a system at a time, as characterized by a set of state variables, these laws will yield a unique state of the system for any later time (or, perhaps, at any time, earlier or later). Probabilistic laws will yield, for a given antecedent state of a system, only a probability value for the occurrence of a certain state at a later time. The laws of classical mechanics are often thought to be paradigmatic examples of causal laws in this sense, whereas the laws of quantum mechanics are claimed to be essentially probabilistic.

Causal laws are sometimes taken to be laws that explicitly specify certain events as causes of certain other events. Simple laws of this kind will have the form 'Events of kind *F* cause events of kind *G*'; e.g., 'Heating causes metals to expand'. A weaker related concept is this: a causal law is one that states a regularity between events which in fact are related as cause to effect, although the statement of the law itself does not say so (laws of motion expressed by differential equations are perhaps causal laws in this sense). These senses of 'causal law' presuppose a prior concept of causation.

Finally, causal laws may be contrasted with *teleological laws,* laws that supposedly describe how certain systems, in particular biological organisms, behave so as to achieve certain "goals" or "end states." Such laws are sometimes claimed to embody the idea that a future state that does not as yet exist can exert an influence on the present behavior of a system. Just what form such laws take and exactly how they differ from ordinary laws have not been made wholly clear, however.

See also CAUSATION, DETERMINISM, LAWLIKE GENERALIZATION.   J.K.

causal overdetermination. See CAUSATION.

causal relation, singular. See PHILOSOPHY OF MIND.

causal responsibility. See RESPONSIBILITY.

causal statement, singular. See CAUSATION.

causal theory of knowledge. See EPISTEMOLOGY, NATURALISTIC EPISTEMOLOGY.

causal theory of mental content. See SKEPTICISM.

causal theory of mind. See FUNCTIONALISM.

causal theory of perception. See PERCEPTION.

causal theory of proper names, the view that proper names designate what they name by virtue of a kind of causal connection to it. This view is a special case, and in some instances an unwarranted interpretation, of a *direct reference view* of names. On this approach, proper names, e.g., 'Machiavelli', are, as J. S. Mill wrote, "purely denotative. . . . they denote the individuals who are called by them; but they do not indicate or imply any attributes as belonging to those individuals" (*A System of Logic,* 1879). Proper names may *suggest* certain properties to many competent speakers, but any such associated information is no part of the definition of the name. Names, on this view, have no definitions. What connects a name to what it names is not the latter's satisfying some condition specified in the name's definition. Names, instead, are simply attached to things, applied as labels, as it were. A proper name, once attached, becomes a socially available device for making the relevant name bearer a subject of discourse.

On the other leading view, the *descriptivist view,* a proper name is associated with something like a definition. 'Aristotle', on this view, applies by definition to whoever satisfies the relevant properties – e.g., is 'the teacher of Alexander the Great, who wrote the *Nicomachean Ethics*'. Russell, e.g., maintained that ordinary proper names (which he contrasted with logically proper or genuine names) have definitions, that they are abbreviated definite descriptions. Frege held that names have sense, a view whose proper interpretation remains in dispute, but is often supposed to be closely related to Russell's approach. Others, most notably Searle, have defended descendants of the descriptivist view. An important variant, sometimes attributed to Frege, denies that names have articulable definitions, but nevertheless associates them with senses. And the bearer will still be, by definition (as it were), the unique thing to satisfy the relevant mode of presentation.

The direct reference approach is sometimes misleadingly called the causal theory of names. But the key idea need have nothing to do with causation: a proper name functions as a tag or label for its bearer, not as a surrogate for a descriptive expression. Whence the (allegedly) misleading term 'causal theory of names'? Contemporary defenders of Mill's conception like Keith Donnellan and Kripke felt the need to expand upon Mill's brief remarks. What connects a present use of a name with a referent? Here Donnellan and Kripke introduce the notion of a "historical chains of communication." As Kripke tells the story, a baby is baptized with a proper name. The name is used, first by those present at the baptism, subsequently by those who pick up the name in conversation, reading, and so on. The name is thus propagated, spread by usage "from link to link as if by a chain" (*Naming and Necessity,* 1980). There emerges a historical chain of uses of the name that, according to Donnellan and Kripke, bridges the gap between a present use of the name and the individual so named.

This "historical chain of communication" is occasionally referred to as a "casual chain of communication." The idea is that one's use of the name can be thought of as a causal factor in one's listener's ability to use the name to refer to the same individual. However, although Kripke in *Naming and Necessity* does occasionally refer to the chain of communication as *causal,* he more often simply speaks of the chain of communication, or of the fact that the name has been passed "by tradition from link to link" (p. 106). The causal aspect is not one that Kripke underscores. In more recent writings on the topic, as well as in lectures, Kripke never mentions causation in this connection, and Donnellan questions whether the chain of communication should be thought of as a causal chain.

This is not to suggest that there is no view properly called a "causal theory of names." There is such a view, but it is not the view of Kripke and Donnellan. The causal theory of names is a view propounded by physicalistically minded philosophers who desire to "reduce" the notion of "reference" to something more physicalistically acceptable, such as the notion of a causal chain running from "baptism" to later use. This is a view whose motivation is explicitly rejected by Kripke, and should be sharply distinguished from the more popular anti-Fregean approach sketched above.

See also MEANING, THEORY OF DESCRIPTIONS.   H.W.

causal theory of reference. See PHILOSOPHY OF LANGUAGE.

causation, the relation between cause and effect, or the act of bringing about an effect, which may be an event, a state, or an object (say, a statue). The concept of causation has long been recognized as one of fundamental philosophical importance. Hume called it "the cement of the universe": causation is the relation that connects events and objects of this world in significant relationships. The concept of causation seems pervasively present in human discourse. It is expressed by not only 'cause' and its cognates but by many other terms, such as 'produce', 'bring about', 'issue', 'generate', 'result', 'effect', 'determine', and countless others. Moreover, many common transitive verbs ("causatives"), such as 'kill', 'break', and 'move', tacitly contain causal relations (e.g., killing involves causing to die). The concept of action, or doing, involves the idea that the agent (intentionally) causes a change in some object or other; similarly, the concept of perception involves the idea that the object perceived causes in the perceiver an appropriate perceptual experience. The physical concept of force, too, appears to involve causation as an essential ingredient: force is the causal agent of changes in motion. Further, causation is intimately related to *explanation:* to ask for an explanation of an event is, often, to ask for its cause. It is sometimes thought that our ability to make predictions, and inductive inference in general, depends on our knowledge of causal connections (or the assumption that such connections are present): the knowledge that water quenches thirst warrants the predictive inference from 'X is swallowing water' to 'X's thirst will be quenched'. More generally, the identification and systematic description of causal relations that hold in the natural world have been claimed to be the preeminent aim of science. Finally, causal concepts play a crucial role in moral and legal reasoning, e.g., in the assessment of responsibilities and liabilities.

Event causation is the causation of one event by another. A sequence of causally connected events is called a causal chain. *Agent causation* refers to the act of an agent (person, object) in bringing about a change; thus, my opening the window (i.e., my causing the window to open) is an instance of agent causation. There is a controversy as to whether agent causation is reducible to event causation. My opening the window seems reducible to event causation since in reality a certain motion of my arms, an event, causes the window to open. Some philosophers, however, have claimed that not all cases of agent causation are so reducible. *Substantival causation* is the creation of a genuinely new substance, or object, rather than causing changes in preexisting substances, or merely rearranging them. The possibility of substantival causation, at least in the natural world, has been disputed by some philosophers. Event causation, however, has been the primary focus of philosophical discussion in the modern and contemporary period.

The analysis of event causation has been controversial. The following four approaches have been prominent: the regularity analysis, the counterfactual analysis, the manipulation analysis, and the probabilistic analysis. The heart of the *regularity* (or *nomological*) *analysis,* associated with Hume and J. S. Mill, is the idea that causally connected events must instantiate a general regularity between like kinds of events. More precisely: if *c* is a cause of *e,* there must be types or kinds of events, *F* and *G*, such that *c* is of kind *F, e* is of kind *G*, and events of kind *F* are regularly followed by events of kind *G*. Some take the regularity involved to be merely de facto "constant conjunction" of the two event types involved; a more popular view is that the regularity must hold as a matter of "nomological necessity" – i.e., it must be a "law." An even stronger view is that the regularity must represent a causal law. A law that does this job of subsuming causally connected events is called a "covering" or "subsumptive" law, and versions of the regularity analysis that call for such laws are often referred to as the "covering-law" or "nomic-subsumptive" model of causality.

The regularity analysis appears to give a satisfactory account of some aspects of our causal concepts: for example, causal claims are often tested by re-creating the event or situation claimed to be a cause and then observing whether a similar effect occurs. In other respects, however, the regularity account does not seem to fare so well: e.g., it has difficulty explaining the apparent fact that we can have knowledge of causal relations without knowledge of general laws. It seems possible to know, for instance, that someone's contraction of the flu was caused by her exposure to a patient with the disease, although we know of no regularity between such exposures and contraction of the disease (it may well be that only a very small fraction of persons who have been exposed to flu patients contract the disease). Do I need to know general regularities about itchings and scratchings to know that the itchy sensation on my left elbow caused me to scratch it? Further, not all

regularities seem to represent causal connections (e.g., Reid's example of the succession of day and night; two successive symptoms of a disease). Distinguishing causal from non-causal regularities is one of the main problems confronting the regularity theorist.

According to the *counterfactual analysis,* what makes an event a cause of another is the fact that if the cause event had not occurred the effect event would not have. This accords with the idea that cause is a condition that is *sine qua non* for the occurrence of the effect. The view that a cause is a necessary condition for the effect is based on a similar idea. The precise form of the counterfactual account depends on how counterfactuals are understood (e.g., if counterfactuals are explained in terms of laws, the counterfactual analysis may turn into a form of the regularity analysis).

The counterfactual approach, too, seems to encounter various difficulties. It is true that on the basis of the fact that if Larry had watered my plants, as he had promised, my plants would not have died, I could claim that Larry's not watering my plants caused them to die. But it is also true that if George Bush had watered my plants, they would not have died; but does that license the claim that Bush's not watering my plants caused them to die? Also, there appear to be many cases of dependencies expressed by counterfactuals that, however, are not cases of causal dependence: e.g., if Socrates had not died, Xanthippe would not have become a widow; if I had not raised my hand, I would not have signaled. The question, then, is whether these non-causal counterfactuals can be distinguished from causal counterfactuals without the use of causal concepts. There are also questions about how we could verify counterfactuals – in particular, whether our knowledge of causal counterfactuals is ultimately dependent on knowledge of causal laws and regularities.

Some have attempted to explain causation in terms of action, and this is the *manipulation analysis:* the cause is an event or state that we can produce at will, or otherwise manipulate, to produce a certain other event as an effect. Thus, an event is a cause of another provided that by bringing about the first event we can bring about the second. This account exploits the close connection noted earlier between the concepts of action and cause, and highlights the important role that knowledge of causal connections plays in our control of natural events. However, as an analysis of the concept of cause, it may well have things backward: the concept of action seems to be a richer and more complex concept that presupposes the concept of cause, and an analysis of cause in terms of action could be accused of circularity.

The reason we think that someone's exposure to a flu patient was the cause of her catching the disease, notwithstanding the absence of an appropriate regularity (even one of high probability), may be this: exposure to flu patients increases the probability of contracting the disease. Thus, an event, X, may be said to be a *probabilistic cause* of an event, Y, provided that the probability of the occurrence of Y, given that X has occurred, is greater than the antecedent probability of Y. To meet certain obvious difficulties, this rough definition must be further elaborated (e.g., to eliminate the possibility that X and Y are collateral effects of a common cause). There is also the question whether probabilistic causation is to be taken as an analysis of the general concept of causation, or as a special kind of causal relation, or perhaps only as evidence indicating the presence of a causal relationship. Probabilistic causation has of late been receiving increasing attention from philosophers.

When an effect is brought about by two independent causes either of which alone would have sufficed, one speaks of *causal overdetermination*. Thus, a house fire might have been caused by both a short circuit and a simultaneous lightning strike; either event alone would have caused the fire, and the fire, therefore, was causally overdetermined. Whether there are actual instances of overdetermination has been questioned; one could argue that the fire that would have been caused by the short circuit alone would not have been the same fire, and similarly for the fire that would have been caused by the lightning alone.

The steady buildup of pressure in a boiler would have caused it to explode but for the fact that a bomb was detonated seconds before, leading to a similar effect. In such a case, one speaks of *preemptive,* or *superseding, cause.* We are apt to speak of causes in regard to changes; however, "unchanges," e.g., this table's standing here through some period of time, can also have causes: the table continues to stand here because it is supported by a rigid floor. The presence of the floor, therefore, can be called a *sustaining cause* of the table's continuing to stand.

A cause is usually thought to precede its effect in time; however, some have argued that we must allow for the possibility of a cause that is temporally posterior to its effect – *backward causation* (sometimes called *retrocausation*). And there is no universal agreement as to whether a cause can be simultaneous with its effect – *concurrent causation.* Nor is there a general agreement as to whether cause and effect must, as a matter of conceptual necessity, be "contiguous" in time and space, either directly or through a causal chain of contiguous events – *contiguous causation.*

The attempt to "analyze" causation seems to have reached an impasse; the proposals on hand seem so widely divergent that one wonders whether they are all analyses of one and the same concept. But each of them seems to address some important aspect of the variegated notion that we express by the term 'cause', and it may be doubted whether there is a unitary concept of causation that can be captured in an enlightening philosophical analysis. On the other hand, the centrality of the concept, both to ordinary practical discourse and to the scientific description of the world, is difficult to deny. This has encouraged some philosophers to view causation as a primitive, one that cannot be further analyzed. There are others who advocate the extreme view (causal nihilism) that causal concepts play no role whatever in the advanced sciences, such as fundamental physical theories of space-time and matter, and that the very notion of cause is an anthropocentric projection deriving from our confused ideas of action and power.

See also AGENT CAUSATION, EXPLANATION, PHILOSOPHY OF SCIENCE.   J.K.

causation, backward. See CAUSATION.

causation, counterfactual analysis of. See CAUSATION.

causation, immanent. See AGENT CAUSATION.

causation, manipulation analysis of. See CAUSATION.

causation, probabilistic. See CAUSATION.

causation, regularity theory of. See CAUSATION.

causation, substance. See AGENT CAUSATION.

causation, transeunt. See AGENT CAUSATION.

causative verb. See ACTION VERB.

cause, efficient. See ARISTOTLE.

cause, final. See ARISTOTLE.

cause, formal. See ARISTOTLE.

cause, material. See ARISTOTLE.

cause, preemptive. See CAUSATION.

cause, superseding. See CAUSATION.

cause, sustaining. See CAUSATION.

causes, the four. See ARISTOTLE.

causa sui (Latin, 'cause of itself'), an expression applied to God to mean in part that God owes his existence to nothing other than himself. It does not mean that God somehow brought himself into existence. The idea is that the very nature of God logically requires that he exists. What accounts for the existence of a being that is *causa sui* is its own nature. **See also PHILOSOPHY OF RELIGION.**   W.L.R.

cave, allegory of the. See PLATO.

Cavell, Stanley Louis (b.1926), American philosopher whose work has explored skepticism and its consequences. He was Walter M. Cabot Professor of Aesthetics and General Value Theory at Harvard from 1963 until 1997. Central to Cavell's thought is the view that skepticism is not a theoretical position to be refuted by philosophical theory or dismissed as a mere misuse of ordinary language; it is a reflection of the fundamental limits of human knowledge of the self, of others, and of the external world, limits that must be accepted – in his term "acknowledged" – because the refusal to do so results in illusion and risks tragedy.

Cavell's work defends J. L. Austin from both positivism and deconstructionism (*Must We Mean What We Say?*, 1969, and *The Pitch of Philosophy*, 1994), but not because Cavell is an "ordinary language" philosopher. Rather, his defense of Austin has combined with his response to skepticism to make him a philosopher of the ordinary: he explores the conditions of the possibility and limits of ordinary language, ordinary knowledge, ordinary action, and ordinary human relationships. He uses both the resources of ordinary language and the discourse of philosophers, such as Wittgenstein, Heidegger, Thoreau, and Emerson, and of the arts. Cavell has explored the ineliminability of skepticism in *Must We Mean What We Say?*, notably in its essay on *King Lear*, and has developed his analysis in his 1979 magnum opus, *The Claim of Reason*. He has examined the

benefits of acknowledging the limits of human self-understanding, and the costs of refusing to do so, in a broad range of contexts from film (*The World Viewed*, 1971; *Pursuits of Happiness*, 1981; and *Contesting Tears*, 1996) to American philosophy (*The Senses of Walden*, 1972; and the chapters on Emerson in *This New Yet Unapproachable America*, 1989, and *Conditions Handsome and Unhandsome*, 1990).

A central argument in *The Claim of Reason* develops Cavell's approach by looking at Wittgenstein's notion of criteria. Criteria are not rules for the use of our words that can guarantee the correctness of the claims we make by them; rather, criteria bring out what we claim by using the words we do. More generally, in making claims to knowledge, undertaking actions, and forming interpersonal relationships, we always risk failure, but it is also precisely in that room for risk that we find the possibility of freedom. This argument is indebted not only to Wittgenstein but also to Kant, especially in the *Critique of Judgment*.

Cavell has used his view as a key to understanding classics of the theater and film. Regarding such tragic figures as Lear, he argues that their tragedies result from their refusal to accept the limits of human knowledge and human love, and their insistence on an illusory absolute and pure love. *The World Viewed* argues for a realistic approach to film, meaning that we should acknowledge that our cognitive and emotional responses to films are responses to the realities of the human condition portrayed in them. This "ontology of film" prepared the way for Cavell's treatment of the genre of comedies of remarriage in *Pursuits of Happiness*. It also grounds his treatment of melodrama in *Contesting Tears*, which argues that human beings must remain tragically unknown to each other if the limits to our knowledge of each other are not acknowledged.

In *The Claim of Reason* and later works Cavell has also contributed to moral philosophy by his defense – against Rawls's critique of "moral perfectionism" – of "Emersonian perfectionism": the view that no general principles of conduct, no matter how well established, can ever be employed in practice without the ongoing but never completed perfection of knowledge of oneself and of the others on and with whom one acts. Cavell's Emersonian perfectionism is thus another application of his Wittgensteinian and Kantian recognition that rules must always be supplemented by the capacity for judgment.

See also AUSTIN, J. L.; EMERSON; KANT;

ORDINARY LANGUAGE PHILOSOPHY; WITT-
GENSTEIN.   P.Gu.

Cavendish, Margaret, Duchess of Newcastle (1623–1673), English author of some dozen works in a variety of forms. Her central philosophical interest was the developments in natural science of her day. Her earliest works endorsed a kind of atomism, but her settled view, in *Philosophical Letters* (1664), *Observations upon Experimental Philosophy* (1666), and *Grounds of Natural Philosophy* (1668), was a kind of organic materialism. Cavendish argues for a hierarchy of increasingly fine matter, capable of self-motion. *Philosophical Letters*, among other matters, raises problems for the notion of inert matter found in Descartes, and *Observations upon Experimental Philosophy* criticizes microscopists such as Hooke for committing a double error, first of preferring the distortions introduced by instruments to unaided vision and second of preferring sense to reason. **See also** ORGANISM.   M.At.

cellular automaton. See SELF-REPRODUCING AUTOMATON.

Celsus (late second century A.D.?), anti-Christian writer known only as the author of a work called *The True Doctrine* (*Alethēs Logos*), which is quoted extensively by Origen of Alexandria in his response, *Against Celsus* (written in the late 240s). *The True Doctrine* is mainly important because it is the first anti-Christian polemic of which we have significant knowledge. Origen considers Celsus to be an Epicurean, but he is uncertain about this. There are no traces of Epicureanism in Origen's quotations from Celsus, which indicate instead that he is an eclectic Middle Platonist of no great originality, a polytheist whose conception of the "unnameable" first deity transcending being and knowable only by "synthesis, analysis, or analogy" is based on Plato's description of the Good in *Republic* VI. In accordance with the *Timaeus*, Celsus believes that God created "immortal things" and turned the creation of "mortal things" over to them. According to him, the universe has a providential organization in which humans hold no special place, and its history is one of eternally repeating sequences of events separated by catastrophes. **See also** MIDDLE PLATONISM, ORIGEN.   I.M.

central state materialism. See PHILOSOPHY OF MIND.

certainty, the property of being certain, which is either a psychological property of persons or an epistemic feature of proposition-like objects (e.g., beliefs, utterances, statements). We can say that a person, S, is *psychologically certain* that *p* (where '*p*' stands for a proposition) provided S has no doubt whatsoever that *p* is true. Thus, a person can be certain regardless of the degree of epistemic warrant for a proposition. In general, philosophers have not found this an interesting property to explore. The exception is Peter Unger, who argued for skepticism, claiming that (1) psychological certainty is required for knowledge and (2) no person is ever certain of anything or hardly anything. As applied to propositions, 'certain' has no univocal use. For example, some authors (e.g., Chisholm) may hold that a proposition is *epistemically certain* provided no proposition is more warranted than it. Given that account, it is possible that a proposition is certain, yet there are legitimate reasons for doubting it just as long as there are equally good grounds for doubting every equally warranted proposition. Other philosophers have adopted a Cartesian account of certainty in which a proposition is epistemically certain provided it is warranted and there are no legitimate grounds whatsoever for doubting it.

Both Chisholm's and the Cartesian characterizations of epistemic certainty can be employed to provide a basis for skepticism. If knowledge entails certainty, then it can be argued that very little, if anything, is known. For, the argument continues, only tautologies or propositions like 'I exist' or 'I have beliefs' are such that either nothing is more warranted or there are absolutely no grounds for doubt. Thus, hardly anything is known. Most philosophers have responded either by denying that 'certainty' is an absolute term, i.e., admitting of no degrees, or by denying that knowledge requires certainty (Dewey, Chisholm, Wittgenstein, and Lehrer). Others have agreed that knowledge does entail absolute certainty, but have argued that absolute certainty is possible (e.g., Moore).

Sometimes 'certain' is modified by other expressions, as in 'morally certain' or 'metaphysically certain' or 'logically certain'. Once again, there is no universally accepted account of these terms. Typically, however, they are used to indicate degrees of warrant for a proposition, and often that degree of warrant is taken to be a function of the *type* of proposition under consideration. For example, the proposition that smoking causes cancer is *morally certain* provided its warrant is sufficient to justify acting as though it were true. The evidence for such a proposition may, of necessity, depend upon recognizing particular features of the world. On the other hand, in order for a proposition, say that every event has a cause, to be *metaphysically certain*, the evidence for it must not depend upon recognizing particular features of the world but rather upon recognizing what must be true in order for our world to be the kind of world it is – i.e., one having causal connections. Finally, a proposition, say that every effect has a cause, may be *logically certain* if it is derivable from "truths of logic" that do not depend in any way upon recognizing anything about our world. Since other taxonomies for these terms are employed by philosophers, it is crucial to examine the use of the terms in their contexts.

　　See also EPISTEMOLOGY, JUSTIFICATION, SKEPTICISM.　　　　　　　　　　　　　　P.D.K.

ceteris paribus clause. See PHILOSOPHY OF SCIENCE.

CH. See Appendix of Special Symbols.

chance. See DETERMINISM.

change. See EVENT, TIME.

change, Cambridge. See CAMBRIDGE CHANGE.

Chang Hsüeh-ch'eng (1738–1801), Chinese historian and philosopher who devised a dialectical theory of civilization in which beliefs, practices, institutions, and arts developed in response to natural necessities. This process reached its zenith several centuries before Confucius, who is unique in being the sage destined to record this moment. Chang's teaching, "the Six Classics are all history," means the classics are not theoretical statements *about* the *tao* (Way) but traces of it in operation. In the ideal age, a unity of *chih* (government) and *chiao* (teaching) prevailed; there were no private disciplines or schools of learning and all writing was anonymous, being tied to some official function. Later history has meandered around this ideal, dominated by successive ages of philosophy, philology, and literature.　　　　　　　　　　　　　　　　　　P.J.I.

Chang Tsai (1020–1077), Chinese philosopher, a major Neo-Confucian figure whose *Hsi-ming* ("Western Inscription") provided much of the metaphysical basis for Neo-Confucian ethics. It argues that the cosmos arose from a single source, the *t'ai chi* (Supreme Ultimate), as undifferentiated *ch'i* (ether) took shape out of an inchoate, primordial state, *t'ai-hsü* (the supremely tenuous). Thus the universe is fundamentally one. The sage "realizes his oneness with the universe" but, appreciating his particular place and role in the greater scheme, expresses his love for it in a graded fashion. Impure endowments of *ch'i* prevent most people from seeing the true nature of the world. They act "selfishly" but through ritual practice and learning can overcome this and achieve sagehood.　　　　　　　　　　　　　　　　　　P.J.I.

chaos theory. See PHILOSOPHY OF SCIENCE.

chaotic system. See PHILOSOPHY OF SCIENCE.

character, the comprehensive set of ethical and intellectual dispositions of a person. Intellectual virtues – like carefulness in the evaluation of evidence – promote, for one, the practice of seeking truth. Moral or ethical virtues – including traits like courage and generosity – dispose persons not only to choices and actions but also to attitudes and emotions. Such dispositions are generally considered relatively stable and responsive to reasons.

　　Appraisal of character transcends direct evaluation of particular actions in favor of examination of some set of virtues or the admirable human life as a whole. On some views this admirable life grounds the goodness of particular actions. This suggests seeking guidance from role models, and their practices, rather than relying exclusively on rules. Role models will, at times, simply perceive the salient features of a situation and act accordingly. Being guided by role models requires some recognition of just who should be a role model. One may act out of character, since dispositions do not automatically produce particular actions in specific cases. One may also have a conflicted character if the virtues one's character comprises contain internal tensions (between, say, tendencies to impartiality and to friendship). The importance of formative education to the building of character introduces some good fortune into the acquisition of character. One can have a good character with a disagreeable personality or have a fine personality with a bad character because personality is not typically a normative notion, whereas character is.

　　See also CARDINAL VIRTUES, ETHICS, PERSONAL IDENTITY, EPISTEMOLOGY, VIRTUE ETHICS.　　　　　　　　　　　　　　　　M.J.M.

character, semantic. See INDEXICAL.

characteristica universalis. See COMPUTER THEORY, LEIBNIZ.

charity, principle of. See MEANING.

Charron, Pierre (1541–1603), French Catholic theologian who became the principal expositor of Montaigne's ideas, presenting them in didactic form. His first work, *The Three Truths* (1595), presented a negative argument for Catholicism by offering a skeptical challenge to atheism, non-Christian religions, and Calvinism. He argued that we cannot know or understand God because of His infinitude and the weakness of our faculties. We can have no good reasons for rejecting Christianity or Catholicism. Therefore, we should accept it on faith alone. His second work, *On Wisdom* (1603), is a systematic presentation of Pyrrhonian skepticism coupled with a fideistic defense of Catholicism. The skepticism of Montaigne and the Greek skeptics is used to show that we cannot know anything unless God reveals it to us. This is followed by offering an ethics to live by, an undogmatic version of Stoicism. This is the first modern presentation of a morality apart from any religious considerations. Charron's *On Wisdom* was extremely popular in France and England. It was read and used by many philosophers and theologians during the seventeenth century. Some claimed that his skepticism opened his defense of Catholicism to question, and suggested that he was insincere in his fideism. He was defended by important figures in the French Catholic church. **See also MONTAIGNE.**   R.H.P.

cheapest-cost avoider, in the economic analysis of law, the party in a dispute that could have prevented the dispute, or minimized the losses arising from it, with the lowest loss to itself. The term encompasses several types of behavior. As the lowest-cost accident avoider, it is the party that could have prevented the accident at the lowest cost. As the lowest-cost insurer, it is the party that could been have insured against the losses arising from the dispute. This could be the party that could have purchased insurance at the lowest cost or self-insured, or the party best able to appraise the expected losses and the probability of the occurrence. As the lowest-cost briber, it is the party least subject to transaction costs. This party is the one best able to correct any legal errors in the assignment of the entitlement by purchasing the entitlement from the other party. As the lowest-cost information gatherer, it is the party best able to make an informed judgment as to the likely benefits and costs of an action. **See also COASE THEOREM, PHILOSOPHY OF ECONOMICS.**   M.S.M.

Ch'en Hsien-chang (1428–1500), Chinese poet-philosopher. In the early Ming dynasty Chu Hsi's *li-hsüeh* (learning of principles) had been firmly established as the orthodoxy and became somewhat fossilized. Ch'en opposed this trend and emphasized "self-attained learning" by digging deep into the self to find meaning in life. He did not care for book learning and conceptualization, and chose to express his ideas and feelings through poems. Primarily a Confucian, he also drew from Buddhism and Taoism. He was credited with being the first to realize the depth and subtlety of *hsin-hsüeh* (learning of the mind), later developed into a comprehensive philosophy by Wang Yang-ming. **See also CHU HSI, NEO-CONFUCIANISM, WANG YANG-MING.**

S.-h.L.

ch'eng, Chinese term meaning 'sincerity'. It means much more than just a psychological attitude. Mencius barely touched upon the subject; it was in the Confucian *Doctrine of the Mean* that the idea was greatly elaborated. The ultimate metaphysical principle is characterized by *ch'eng,* as it is true, real, totally beyond illusion and delusion. According to the classic, sincerity is the Way of Heaven; to think how to be sincere is the Way of man; and only those who can be absolutely sincere can fully develop their nature, after which they can assist in the transforming and nourishing process of Heaven and Earth. **See also MENCIUS.**   S.-H.L.

Ch'eng Hao (1032–85), **Ch'eng Yi** (1033–1107), Chinese philosophers, brothers who established mature Neo-Confucianism. They elevated the notion of *li* (pattern) to preeminence and systematically linked their metaphysics to central ethical notions, e.g. *hsing* (nature) and *hsin* (heart/mind).

Ch'eng Hao was more mystical and a stronger intuitionist. He emphasized a universal, creative spirit of life, *jen* (benevolence), which permeates all things, just as *ch'i* (ether/vital force) permeates one's body, and likened an "unfeeling" (i.e., unbenevolent) person to an "unfeeling" (i.e., paralyzed) person. Both fail to realize a unifying "oneness."

Ch'eng Yi presented a more detailed and developed philosophical system in which the *li* (pattern) in the mind was awakened by perceiving the *li* in the world, particularly as revealed in the classics, and by *t'ui* (extending/inferring) their interconnections. If one studies with *ching* (reverential attentiveness), one can gain both cognitively accurate and affectively appropriate "real knowledge," which Ch'eng Yi illustrates with an allegory about those who "know" (i.e., have heard that) tigers are dangerous and those who "know" because they have been mauled.

The two brothers differ most in their views on self-cultivation. For Ch'eng Hao, it is more an inner affair: setting oneself right by bringing into full play one's moral intuition. For Ch'eng Yi, self-cultivation was more external: *chih chih* (extending knowledge) through *ko wu* (investigating things). Here lie the beginnings of the major schools of Neo-Confucianism: the Lu–Wang and Ch'eng–Chu schools. **See also** LI[1], NEO-CONFUCIANISM.   P.J.I.

cheng ming, also called Rectification of Names, a Confucian program of language reform advocating a return to traditional language. There is a brief reference to *cheng ming* in *Analects* 13:3, but Hsün Tzu presents the most detailed discussion of it. While admitting that new words (*ming*) will sometimes have to be created, Hsün Tzu fears the proliferation of words, dialects, and idiolects will endanger effective communication. He is also concerned that new ways of speaking may lend themselves to sophistry or fail to serve such purposes as accurately distinguishing the noble from the base. **See also** CONFUCIANISM.   B.W.V.N.

Cheng-shih hsüan-hsüeh. See NEO-TAOISM.

ch'i, Chinese term for ether, air, corporeal vital energy, and the "atmosphere" of a season, person, event, or work. *Ch'i* can be dense/impure or limpid/pure, warm/rising/active or cool/settling/still. The brave brim with *ch'i;* a coward lacks it. *Ch'i* rises with excitement or health and sinks with depression or illness. *Ch'i* became a concept coordinate with *li* (pattern), being the medium in which *li* is embedded and through which it can be experienced. *Ch'i* serves a role akin to 'matter' in Western thought, but being "lively" and "flowing," it generated a distinct and different set of questions.   P.J.I.

Chiao Hung (1540?–1620), Chinese historian and philosopher affiliated with the T'ai-chou school, often referred to as the left wing of Wang Yang-ming's *hsin-hsüeh* (learning of the mind). However, he did not repudiate book learning; he was very erudite, and became a forerunner of evidential research. He believed in the unity of the teachings of Confucianism, Buddhism, and Taoism. In opposition to Chu Hsi's orthodoxy he made use of insights of Ch'an (Zen) Buddhism to

give new interpretations to the classics. Learning for him is primarily and ultimately a process of realization in consciousness of one's innate moral nature. **See also** BUDDHISM, CHU HSI, NEO-CONFUCIANISM, WANG YANG-MING.
     S.-h.L. & A.K.L.C.

Chia Yi (200–168 B.C.), Chinese scholar who attempted to synthesize Legalist, Confucian, and Taoist ideas. The Ch'in dynasty (221–206 B.C.) used the Legalist practice to unify China, but unlimited use of cruel punishment also caused its quick downfall; hence the Confucian system of *li* (propriety) had to be established, and the emperor had to delegate his power to able ministers to take care of the welfare of the people. The ultimate Way for Chia Yi is *hsü* (emptiness), a Taoist idea, but he interpreted it in such a way that it is totally compatible with the practice of *li* and the development of culture. **See also** CONFUCIANISM, TAOISM.   S.-h.L.

ch'ien, k'un, in traditional Chinese cosmology, the names of the two most important trigrams in the system of *I-Ching* (the *Book of Changes*). *Ch'ien* (☰) is composed of three undivided lines, the symbol of yang, and *k'un* (☷) three divided lines, the symbol of yin. *Ch'ien* means Heaven, the father, creativity; *k'un* means Earth, the mother, endurance. The two are complementary; they work together to form the whole cosmic order. In the system of *I-Ching*, there are eight trigrams, the doubling up of two trigrams forms a hexagram, and there are a total of sixty-four hexagrams. The first two hexagrams are also named *ch'ien* (䷀) and *k'un* (䷁). **See also** T'AI-CHI.   S.-h.L.

chien ai. See MOHISM.

Ch'ien-fu Lun, Chinese title of *Comments of a Recluse* (second century A.D.), a Confucian political and cosmological work by Wang Fu. Divided into thirty-six essays, it gives a vivid picture of the sociopolitical world of later Han China and prescribes practical measures to overcome corruption and other problems confronting the state. There are discussions on cosmology affirming the belief that the world is constituted by vital energy (*ch'i*). The pivotal role of human beings in shaping the world is emphasized. A person may be favorably endowed, but education remains crucial. Several essays address the perceived excesses in religious practices. Above all, the author targets for criticism the system of official appointment that privileges family background and reputation at the expense of moral worth and ability. Largely Confucian in outlook, the work reflects strong utilitarian interest reminiscent of Hsün Tzu. **See also** CH'I, CONFUCIANISM.   A.K.L.C.

Ch'ien Mu (1895–1990), Chinese historian, a leading contemporary New Confucian scholar and cofounder (with T'ang Chün-i) of New Asia College in Hong Kong (1949). Early in his career he was respected for his effort to date the ancient Chinese philosophers and for his study of Confucian thought in the Han dynasty (206 B.C.–A.D. 220). During World War II he wrote the *Outline of Chinese History,* in which he developed a nationalist historical viewpoint stressing the vitality of traditional Chinese culture. Late in his career he published his monumental study of Chu Hsi (1130–1200). He firmly believed the spirit of Confucius and Chu Hsi should be revived today. **See also** CHINESE PHILOSOPHY, CHU HSI, T'ANG CHÜN-I.   S.-h.L.

chih[1], Chinese term roughly corresponding to 'knowledge'. A concise explanation is found in the *Hsün Tzu:* "That in man by which he knows is called *chih;* the *chih* that accords with actuality is called wisdom (*chih*)." This definition suggests a distinction between intelligence or the ability to know and its achievement or wisdom, often indicated by its homophone. The later Mohists provide more technical definitions, stressing especially the connection between names and objects. Confucians for the most part are interested in the ethical significance of *chih.* Thus *chih,* in the *Analects* of Confucius, is often used as a verb in the sense 'to realize', conveying understanding and appreciation of ethical learning, in addition to the use of *chih* in the sense of acquiring information. And one of the basic problems in Confucian ethics pertains to *chih-hsing ho-i* (the unity of knowledge and action). **See also** CONFUCIANISM, MOHISM.   A.S.C.

chih[2], Chinese term often translated as 'will'. It refers to general goals in life as well as to more specific aims and intentions. *Chih* is supposed to pertain to the heart/mind (*hsin*) and to be something that can be set up and attained. It is sometimes compared in Chinese philosophical texts to aiming in archery, and is explained by some commentators as "directions of the heart/mind." Confucians emphasize the need to set up the proper *chih* to guide one's behavior and way of life generally, while Taoists advocate letting oneself respond spontaneously to situations one is confronted with, free from direction by *chih.* **See also** CONFUCIANISM.   K.-l.S.

chih-hsing ho-i, Chinese term for the Confucian doctrine, propounded by Wang Yang-ming, of the unity of knowledge and action. The doctrine is sometimes expressed in terms of the unity of moral learning and action. A recent interpretation focuses on the non-contingent connection between prospective and retrospective moral knowledge or achievement. Noteworthy is the role of desire, intention, will, and motive in the mediation of knowledge and action as informed by practical reasonableness in reflection that responds to changing circumstances. Wang's doctrine is best construed as an attempt to articulate the concrete significance of *jen,* the Neo-Confucian ideal of the universe as a moral community.   A.S.C.

Chillington, Richard. See KILVINGTON.

Chinese Legalism, the collective views of the Chinese "school of laws" theorists, so called in recognition of the importance given to strict application of laws in the work of Shang Yang (390–338 B.C.) and his most prominent successor, Han Fei Tzu (d. 223 B.C.). The Legalists were political realists who believed that success in the context of Warring States China (403–221 B.C.) depended on organizing the state into a military camp, and that failure meant nothing less than political extinction. Although they challenged the viability of the Confucian model of ritually constituted community with their call to law and order, they sidestepped the need to dispute the ritual-versus-law positions by claiming that different periods had different problems, and different problems required new and innovative solutions.

Shang Yang believed that the fundamental and complementary occupations of the state, agriculture and warfare, could be prosecuted most successfully by insisting on adherence to clearly articulated laws and by enforcing strict punishments for even minor violations. There was an assumed antagonism between the interests of the individual and the interests of the state. By manipulating rewards and punishments and controlling the "handles of life and death," the ruler could subjugate his people and bring them into compliance with the national purpose. Law would replace morality and function as the exclusive standard of good. Fastidious application of the law, with severe punishments for infractions, was believed to be a policy that would arrest criminality and quickly make punishment unnecessary.

Given that the law served the state as an objective and impartial standard, the goal was to minimize any reliance upon subjective interpretation. The Legalists thus conceived of the machinery of state as operating automatically on the basis of self-regulating and self-perpetuating "systems." They advocated techniques of statecraft (*shu*) such as "accountability" (*hsing-ming*), the demand for absolute congruency between stipulated duties and actual performance in office, and "doing nothing" (*wu-wei*), the ruler residing beyond the laws of the state to reformulate them when necessary, but to resist reinterpreting them to accommodate particular cases.

Han Fei Tzu, the last and most influential spokesperson of Legalism, adapted the military precept of strategic advantage (*shih*) to the rule of government. The ruler, without the prestige and influence of his position, was most often a rather ordinary person. He had a choice: he could rely on his personal attributes and pit his character against the collective strength of his people, or he could tap the collective strength of the empire by using his position and his exclusive power over life and death as a fulcrum to ensure that his will was carried out. What was strategic advantage in warfare became political purchase in the government of the state. Only the ruler with the astuteness and the resolve to hoard and maximize all of the advantages available to him could guarantee continuation in power. Han Fei believed that the closer one was to the seat of power, the greater threat one posed to the ruler. Hence, all nobler virtues and sentiments – benevolence, trust, honor, mercy – were repudiated as means for conspiring ministers and would-be usurpers to undermine the absolute authority of the throne. Survival was dependent upon total and unflagging distrust.

See also FA, HAN FEI TZU, SHANG YANG.

R.P.P. & R.T.A.

Chinese philosophy, philosophy produced in China from the sixth century B.C. to the present.

Traditional Chinese philosophy. Its history may be divided into six periods:

(1) Pre-Ch'in, before 221 B.C.
   Spring and Autumn, 722–481 B.C.
   Warring States, 403–222 B.C.
(2) Han, 206 B.C.–A.D. 220
   Western (Former) Han, 206 B.C.–A.D. 8
   Hsin, A.D. 9–23
   Eastern (Later) Han, A.D. 25–220

(3) Wei-Chin, 220–420
   Wei, 220–65
   Western Chin, 265–317
   Eastern Chin, 317–420
(4) Sui-Tang, 581–907
   Sui, 581–618
   Tang, 618–907
   Five Dynasties, 907–60
(5) Sung-(Yüan)-Ming, 960–1644
   Northern Sung, 960–1126
   Southern Sung, 1127–1279
   Yuan (Mongol), 1271–1368
   Ming, 1368–1644
(6) Ch'ing (Manchu), 1644–1912

In the late Chou dynasty (1111–249 B.C.), before Ch'in (221–206 B.C.) unified the country, China entered the so-called Spring and Autumn period and the Warring States period, and Chou culture was in decline. The so-called hundred schools of thought were contending with one another; among them six were philosophically significant:

(a) *Ju-chia* (Confucianism), represented by Confucius (551–479 B.C.), Mencius (371–289 B.C.?), and Hsün Tzu (fl. 298–238 B.C.)
(b) *Tao-chia* (Taoism), represented by Lao Tzu (sixth or fourth century B.C.) and Chuang Tzu (between 399 and 295 B.C.)
(c) *Mo-chia* (Mohism), represented by Mo Tzu (fl. 479–438 B.C.)
(d) *Ming-chia* (Logicians), represented by Hui Shih (380–305 B.C.), Kung-sun Lung (b.380 B.C.?)
(e) *Yin-yang-chia* (Yin–yang school), represented by Tsou Yen (305–240 B.C.?)
(f) *Fa-chia* (Legalism), represented by Han Fei (d. 233 B.C.)

Thus, China enjoyed her first golden period of philosophy in the Pre-Ch'in period. As most Chinese philosophies were giving responses to existential problems then, it is no wonder Chinese philosophy had a predominantly practical character. It has never developed the purely theoretical attitude characteristic of Greek philosophy.

During the Han dynasty, in 136 B.C., Confucianism was established as the state ideology. But it was blended with ideas of Taoism, Legalism, and the Yin–yang school. An organic view of the universe was developed; creative thinking was replaced by study of the so-called Five Classics: *Book of Poetry, Book of History, Book of Changes, Book of Rites,* and *Spring and Autumn Annals.* As the First Emperor of Ch'in burned the Classics except for the *I-Ching*, in the early Han scholars were asked to write down the texts they had memorized in modern script. Later some texts in ancient script were discovered, but were rejected as spurious by modern-script supporters. Hence there were constant disputes between the modern-script school and the ancient-script school.

Wei-Chin scholars were fed up with studies of the Classics in trivial detail. They also showed a tendency to step over the bounds of rites. Their interest turned to something more metaphysical; the *Lao Tzu*, the *Chuang Tzu*, and the *I-Ching* were their favorite readings. Especially influential were Hsiang Hsiu's (fl. A.D. 250) and Kuo Hsiang's (d. A.D. 312) *Commentaries* on the *Chuang Tzu*, and Wang Pi's (226–49) *Commentaries* on the *Lao Tzu* and *I-Ching*. Although Wang's perspective was predominantly Taoist, he was the first to brush aside the *hsiang-shu* (forms and numbers) approach to the study of the *I-Ching* and concentrate on *i-li* (meanings and principles) alone. Sung philosophers continued the *i-li* approach, but they reinterpreted the Classics from a Confucian perspective.

Although Buddhism was imported into China in the late Han period, it took several hundred years for the Chinese to absorb Buddhist insights and ways of thinking. First the Chinese had to rely on *ko-i* (matching the concepts) by using Taoist ideas to transmit Buddhist messages. After the Chinese learned a great deal from Buddhism by translating Buddhist texts into Chinese, they attempted to develop the Chinese versions of Buddhism in the Sui–Tang period. On the whole they favored Mahayana over Hinayana (Theravada) Buddhism, and they developed a much more life-affirming attitude through Hua-yen and T'ien-tai Buddhism, which they believed to represent Buddha's mature thought. Ch'an went even further, seeking sudden enlightenment instead of scripture studies. Ch'an, exported to Japan, has become Zen, a better-known term in the West.

In response to the Buddhist challenge, the Neo-Confucian thinkers gave a totally new interpretation of Confucian philosophy by going back to insights implicit in Confucius's so-called Four Books: the *Analects*, the *Mencius*, *The Great Learning*, and the *Doctrine of the Mean* (the latter two were chapters taken from the *Book of Rites*). They were also fascinated by the *I-Ching*. They borrowed ideas from Buddhism and Taoism to develop a new Confucian cosmology and moral metaphysics. Sung–Ming Neo-Confucianism brought Chinese philosophy to a new height; some consider the period the Chinese Renais-

sance. The movement started with Chou Tun-i (1017–73), but the real founders of Neo-Confucianism were the Ch'eng brothers: Ch'eng Hao (1032–85) and Ch'eng Yi (1033–1107). Then came Chu Hsi (1130–1200), a great synthesizer often compared with Thomas Aquinas or Kant in the West, who further developed Ch'eng Yi's ideas into a systematic philosophy and originated the so-called Ch'eng–Chu school. But he was opposed by his younger contemporary Lu Hsiang-shan (1139–93). During the Ming dynasty, Wang Yang-ming (1472–1529) reacted against Chu Hsi by reviving the insight of Lu Hsiang-shan, hence the so-called Lu–Wang school.

During the Ch'ing dynasty, under the rule of the Manchus, scholars turned to historical scholarship and showed little interest in philosophical speculation. In the late Ch'ing, K'ang Yu-wei (1858–1927) revived the modern-script school, pushed for radical reform, but failed miserably in his attempt.

Contemporary Chinese philosophy. Three important trends can be discerned, intertwined with one another: the importation of Western philosophy, the dominance of Marxism on Mainland China, and the development of contemporary New Confucian philosophy. During the early twentieth century China awoke to the fact that traditional Chinese culture could not provide all the means for China to enter into the modern era in competition with the Western powers. Hence the first urgent task was to learn from the West.

Almost all philosophical movements had their exponents, but they were soon totally eclipsed by Marxism, which was established as the official ideology in China after the Communist takeover in 1949. Mao Tse-tung (1893–1976) succeeded in the line of Marx, Engels, Lenin, and Stalin. The Communist regime was intolerant of all opposing views. The Cultural Revolution was launched in 1967, and for a whole decade China closed her doors to the outside world. Almost all the intellectuals inside or outside of the Communist party were purged or suppressed. After the Cultural Revolution was over, universities were reopened in 1978. From 1979 to 1989, intellectuals enjoyed unprecedented freedom. One editorial in *People's Daily News* said that Marx's ideas were the product of the nineteenth century and did not provide all the answers for problems at the present time, and hence it was desirable to develop Marxism further. Such a message was interpreted by scholars in different ways. Although the thoughts set forth by scholars lacked depth, the lively atmosphere could be compared to the May Fourth New Culture Movement in 1919. Unfortunately, however, violent suppression of demonstrators in Peking's Tiananmen Square in 1989 put a stop to all this. Control of ideology became much stricter for the time being, although the doors to the outside world were not completely closed.

As for the Nationalist government, which had fled to Taiwan in 1949, the control of ideology under its jurisdiction was never total on the island; liberalism has been strong among the intellectuals. Analytic philosophy, existentialism, and hermeneutics all have their followers; today even radicalism has its attraction for certain young scholars.

Even though mainstream Chinese thought in the twentieth century has condemned the Chinese tradition altogether, that tradition has never completely died out. In fact the most creative talents were found in the contemporary New Confucian movement, which sought to bring about a synthesis between East and West. Among those who stayed on the mainland, Fung Yu-lan (1895–1990) and Ho Lin (1902–92) changed their earlier views after the Communist takeover, but Liang Sou-ming (1893–1988) and Hsiung Shih-li (1885–1968) kept some of their beliefs. Ch'ien Mu (1895–1990) and Tang Chün-i (1909–78) moved to Hong Kong and Thomé H. Fang (1899–1976), Hsü Fu-kuan (1903–82), and Mou Tsung-san (1909–95) moved to Taiwan, where they exerted profound influence on younger scholars. Today contemporary New Confucianism is still a vital intellectual movement in Hong Kong, Taiwan, and overseas; it is even studied in Mainland China. The New Confucians urge a revival of the traditional spirit of *jen* (humanity) and *sheng* (creativity); at the same time they turn to the West, arguing for the incorporation of modern science and democracy into Chinese culture.

The New Confucian philosophical movement in the narrower sense derived inspiration from Hsiung Shih-li. Among his disciples the most original thinker is Mou Tsung-san, who has developed his own system of philosophy. He maintains that the three major Chinese traditions – Confucian, Taoist, and Buddhist – agree in asserting that humans have the endowment for intellectual intuition, meaning personal participation in *tao* (the Way). But the so-called third generation has a much broader scope; it includes scholars with varied backgrounds such as Yu Ying-shih (b. 1930), Liu Shu-hsien (b. 1934), and Tu Wei-ming (b.1940), whose ideas have

impact on intellectuals at large and whose selected writings have recently been allowed to be published on the mainland. The future of Chinese philosophy will still depend on the interactions of imported Western thought, Chinese Marxism, and New Confucianism.

   See also BUDDHISM, CHU HSI, CONFUCIANISM, HSIUNG SHIH-LI, NEO-CONFUCIANISM, TAOISM, WANG YANG-MING.   S.-h.L.

Chinese room argument. See SEARLE.

ching, Chinese term meaning 'reverence', 'seriousness', 'attentiveness', 'composure'. In early texts, *ching* is the appropriate attitude toward spirits, one's parents, and the ruler; it was originally interchangeable with another term, *kung* (respect). Among Neo-Confucians, these terms are distinguished: *ching* reserved for the inner state of mind and *kung* for its outer manifestations. This distinction was part of the Neo-Confucian response to the quietistic goal of meditative calm advocated by many Taoists and Buddhists. Neo-Confucians sought to maintain an imperturbable state of "reverential attentiveness" not only in meditation but throughout all activity. This sense of *ching* is best understood as a Neo-Confucian appropriation of the Ch'an (Zen) ideal of *yi-hsing san-mei* (universal *samādhi*), prominent in texts such as the *Platform Sutra*.   P.J.I.

ch'ing, Chinese term meaning (1) 'essence', 'essential'; (2) 'emotion', 'passions'. Originally, the *ch'ing* of *x* was the properties without which *x* would cease to be the kind of thing that it is. In this sense it contrasts with the nature (*hsing*) of *x:* the properties *x* has if it is a *flourishing* instance of its kind. By the time of Hsün Tzu, though, *ch'ing* comes to refer to human emotions or passions. A list of "the six emotions" (*liu ch'ing*) soon became fairly standard: fondness (*hao*), dislike (*wu*), delight (*hsi*), anger (*nu*), sadness (*ai*), and joy (*le*).   B.W.V.N.

Chisholm, Roderick Milton (1916–99), influential American philosopher whose publications spanned the field, including ethics and the history of philosophy. He is mainly known as an epistemologist, metaphysician, and philosopher of mind. In early opposition to powerful forms of reductionism, such as phenomenalism, extensionalism, and physicalism, Chisholm developed an original philosophy of his own. Educated at Brown and Harvard (Ph.D., 1942), he spent nearly his entire career at Brown.

He is known chiefly for the following contributions. (a) Together with his teacher and later his colleague at Brown, C. J. Ducasse, he developed and long defended an adverbial account of sensory experience, set against the sense-datum act-object account then dominant. (b) Based on deeply probing analysis of the free will problematic, he defended a libertarian position, again in opposition to the compatibilism long orthodox in analytic circles. His libertarianism had, moreover, an unusual account of agency, based on distinguishing transeunt (event) causation from immanent (agent) causation. (c) In opposition to the celebrated linguistic turn of linguistic philosophy, he defended the primacy of intentionality, a defense made famous not only through important papers, but also through his extensive and eventually published correspondence with Wilfrid Sellars. (d) Quick to recognize the importance and distinctiveness of the *de se*, he welcomed it as a basis for much *de re* thought. (e) His realist ontology is developed through an intentional concept of "entailment," used to define key concepts of his system, and to provide criteria of identity for occupants of fundamental categories. (f) In epistemology, he famously defended forms of foundationalism and internalism, and offered a delicately argued (dis)solution of the ancient problem of the criterion.

The principles of Chisholm's epistemology and metaphysics are not laid down antecedently as hard-and-fast axioms. Lacking any inviolable antecedent privilege, they must pass muster in the light of their consequences and by comparison with whatever else we may find plausible. In this regard he sharply contrasts with such epistemologists as Popper, with the skepticism of justification attendant on his deductivism, and Quine, whose stranded naturalism drives so much of his radical epistemology and metaphysics. By contrast, Chisholm has no antecedently set epistemic or metaphysical principles. His philosophical views develop rather dialectically, with sensitivity to whatever considerations, examples, or counterexamples reflection may reveal as relevant. This makes for a demanding complexity of elaboration, relieved, however, by a powerful drive for ontological and conceptual economy.

See also EPISTEMOLOGY, FOUNDATIONALISM, FREE WILL PROBLEM, KNOWLEDGE DE SE, PROBLEM OF THE CRITERION, SKEPTICISM.

E.S.

chit. See SAT/CHIT/ĀNANDA.

choice, axiom of. See LÖWENHEIM-SKOLEM THEOREM, SET THEORY.

choice sequence, a variety of infinite sequence introduced by L. E. J. Brouwer to express the non-classical properties of the continuum (the set of real numbers) within intuitionism. A choice sequence is determined by a finite initial segment together with a "rule" for continuing the sequence. The rule, however, may allow some freedom in choosing each subsequent element. Thus the sequence might start with the rational numbers 0 and then ½, and the rule might require the $n + 1$st element to be some rational number within $(½)^n$ of the nth choice, without any further restriction. The sequence of rationals thus generated must converge to a real number, r. But r's definition leaves open its exact location in the continuum. Speaking intuitionistically, r violates the classical *law of trichotomy*: given any pair of real numbers (e.g., r and ½), the first is either less than, equal to, or greater than the second.

From the 1940s Brouwer got this non-classical effect without appealing to the apparently non-mathematical notion of free choice. Instead he used sequences generated by the activity of an idealized mathematician (the creating subject), together with propositions that he took to be undecided. Given such a proposition, P – e.g. Fermat's last theorem (that for $n > 2$ there is no general method of finding triplets of numbers with the property that the sum of each of the first two raised to the nth power is equal to the result of raising the third to the nth power) or Goldbach's conjecture (that every even number is the sum of two prime numbers) – we can modify the definition of r: The $n + 1$st element is ½ if at the nth stage of research P remains undecided. That element and all its successors are $½ + (½)^n$ if by that stage P is proved; they are $½ - (½)^n$ if P is refuted. Since he held that there is an endless supply of such propositions, Brouwer believed that we can always use this method to refute classical laws.

In the early 1960s Stephen Kleene and Richard Vesley reproduced some main parts of Brouwer's theory of the continuum in a formal system based on Kleene's earlier recursion-theoretic interpretation of intuitionism and of choice sequences. At about the same time – but in a different and occasionally incompatible vein – Saul Kripke formally captured the power of Brouwer's counterexamples without recourse to recursive functions and without invoking either the creating subject or the notion of free choice.

Subsequently Georg Kreisel, A. N. Troelstra, Dirk Van Dalen, and others produced formal systems that analyze Brouwer's basic assumptions about open-futured objects like choice sequences.

See also MATHEMATICAL INTUITIONISM, PHILOSOPHY OF MATHEMATICS.   C.J.P.

Chomsky, Noam (b.1928), preeminent American linguist, philosopher, and political activist who has spent his professional career at the Massachusetts Institute of Technology. Chomsky's best-known scientific achievement is the establishment of a rigorous and philosophically compelling foundation for the scientific study of the grammar of natural language. With the use of tools from the study of formal languages, he gave a far more precise and explanatory account of natural language grammar than had previously been given (*Syntactic Structures*, 1957). He has since developed a number of highly influential frameworks for the study of natural language grammar (e.g., *Aspects of the Theory of Syntax*, 1965; *Lectures on Government and Binding*, 1981; *The Minimalist Program*, 1995). Though there are significant differences in detail, there are also common themes that underlie these approaches. Perhaps the most central is that there is an innate set of linguistic principles shared by all humans, and the purpose of linguistic inquiry is to describe the initial state of the language learner, and account for linguistic variation via the most general possible mechanisms.

On Chomsky's conception of linguistics, languages are structures in the brains of individual speakers, described at a certain level of abstraction within the theory. These structures occur within the language faculty, a hypothesized module of the human brain. Universal Grammar is the set of principles hard-wired into the language faculty that determine the class of possible human languages. This conception of linguistics involves several influential and controversial theses. First, the hypothesis of a Universal Grammar entails the existence of innate linguistic principles. Secondly, the hypothesis of a language faculty entails that our linguistic abilities, at least so far as grammar is concerned, are not a product of general reasoning processes. Finally, and perhaps most controversially, since having one of these structures is an intrinsic property of a speaker, properties of languages so conceived are determined solely by states of the speaker. On this individualistic conception of language, there is no room in scientific linguistics for the social entities determined by linguistic communities

that are languages according to previous anthropological conceptions of the discipline.

Many of Chomsky's most significant contributions to philosophy, such as his influential rejection of behaviorism ("Review of Skinner's *Verbal Behavior*," *Language*, 1959), stem from his elaborations and defenses of the above consequences (cf. also *Cartesian Linguistics*, 1966; *Reflections on Language*, 1975; *Rules and Representations*, 1980; *Knowledge of Language*, 1986). Chomsky's philosophical writings are characterized by an adherence to methodological naturalism, the view that the mind should be studied like any other natural phenomenon. In recent years, he has also argued that reference, in the sense in which it is used in the philosophy of language, plays no role in a scientific theory of language ("Language and Nature," *Mind*, 1995).

See also FORMAL LEARNABILITY THEORY, GRAMMAR, MEANING, PHILOSOPHY OF LANGUAGE, PSYCHOLINGUISTICS.   J.Sta.

Chomsky hierarchy of languages. See PHILOSOPHY OF LANGUAGE.

chora. See KRISTEVA.

Chou Tun-yi (1017–73), Chinese Neo-Confucian philosopher. His most important work, the *T'ai-chi t'u-shuo* ("Explanations of the Diagram of the Supreme Ultimate"), consists of a chart, depicting the constituents, structure, and evolutionary process of the cosmos, along with an explanatory commentary. This work, together with his *T'ung-shu* ("Penetrating the *I-Ching*"), introduced many of the fundamental ideas of Neo-Confucian metaphysics. Consequently, heated debates arose concerning Chou's diagram, some claiming it described the universe as arising out of *wu* (non-being) and thus was inspired by and supported Taoism. Chou's primary interest was always cosmological; he never systematically related his metaphysics to ethical concerns. **See also T'AI-CHI.**   P.J.I.

Chrysippus. See STOICISM.

Chrysorrhoas. See JOHN OF DAMASCUS.

ch'üan, Chinese term for a key Confucian concept that may be rendered as meaning 'weighing of circumstances', 'exigency', or 'moral discretion'. A metaphorical extension of the basic sense of a steelyard for measuring weight, *ch'üan* essentially pertains to assessment of the importance of moral considerations to a current matter of concern. Alternatively, the exercise of *ch'üan* consists in a judgment of the comparative importance of competing options answering to a current problematic situation. The judgment must accord with *li* (principle, reason), i.e., be a principled or reasoned judgment. In the sense of exigency, *ch'üan* is a hard case, i.e., one falling outside the normal scope of the operation of standards of conduct. In the sense of 'moral discretion', *ch'üan* must conform to the requirement of *i* (rightness). **See also CONFUCIANISM.**

A.S.C.

Chuang Tzu, also called Chuang Chou (4th century B.C.), Chinese Taoist philosopher. According to many scholars, ideas in the inner chapters (chapters 1 to 7) of the text *Chuang Tzu* may be ascribed to the person Chuang Tzu, while the other chapters contain ideas related to his thought and later developments of his ideas. The inner chapters contain dialogues, stories, verses, sayings, and brief essays geared toward inducing an altered perspective on life. A realization that there is no neutral ground for adjudicating between opposing judgments made from different perspectives is supposed to lead to a relaxation of the importance one attaches to such judgments and to such distinctions as those between right and wrong, life and death, and self and others. The way of life advocated is subject to different interpretations. Parts of the text seem to advocate a way of life not radically different from the conventional one, though with a lessened emotional involvement. Other parts seem to advocate a more radical change; one is supposed to react spontaneously to situations one is confronted with, with no preconceived goals or preconceptions of what is right or proper, and to view all occurrences, including changes in oneself, as part of the transformation process of the natural order. **See also TAOISM.** K.-l.S.

Chu Hsi (1130–1200), Neo-Confucian scholar of the Sung dynasty (960–1279), commonly regarded as the greatest Chinese philosopher after Confucius and Mencius. His mentor was Ch'eng Yi (1033–1107), hence the so-called Ch'eng–Chu School. Chu Hsi developed Ch'eng Yi's ideas into a comprehensive metaphysics of *li* (principle) and *ch'i* (material force). *Li* is incorporeal, one, eternal, and unchanging, always good; *ch'i* is physical, many, transitory, and changeable, involving both good and evil. They are not to be mixed or separated. Things are composed of both *li* and *ch'i*. Chu identifies *hsing* (human nature) as *li*, *ch'ing* (feelings and emotions) as *ch'i*, and *hsin* (mind/heart) as *ch'i* of the subtlest kind, comprising principles. He interprets *ko-wu* in the *Great Learning* to mean the investigation of principles inherent in things, and *chih-chih* to mean the extension of knowledge. He was opposed by Lu Hsiang-shan (1139–93) and Wang Yang-ming (1472–1529), who argued that mind is principle. Mou Tsung-san thinks that Lu's and Wang's position was closer to Mencius's philosophy, which was honored as orthodoxy. But Ch'eng and Chu's commentaries on the Four Books were used as the basis for civil service examinations from 1313 until the system was abolished in 1905. **See also CH'IEN MU, CHINESE PHILOSOPHY, CONFUCIUS, FUNG YU-LAN, MENCIUS, WANG YANG-MING.** S.-h.L.

chung, shu, Chinese philosophical terms important in Confucianism, meaning 'loyalty' or 'commitment', and 'consideration' or 'reciprocity', respectively. In the *Analects,* Confucius observes that there is one thread running through his way of life, and a disciple describes the one thread as constituted by *chung* and *shu*. *Shu* is explained in the text as not doing to another what one would not have wished done to oneself, but *chung* is not explicitly explained. Scholars interpret *chung* variously as a commitment to having one's behavior guided by *shu*, as a commitment to observing the norms of *li* (rites) (to be supplemented by *shu*, which humanizes and adds a flexibility to the observance of such norms), or as a strictness in observing one's duties toward superiors or equals (to be supplemented by *shu*, which involves considerateness toward inferiors or equals, thereby humanizing and adding a flexibility to the application of rules governing one's treatment of them). The pair of terms continued to be used by later Confucians to refer to supplementary aspects of the ethical ideal or self-cultivation process; e.g., some used *chung* to refer to a full manifestation of one's originally good heart/mind (*hsin*), and *shu* to refer to the extension of that heart/mind to others. **See also CONFUCIANISM.** K.-l.S.

Chung-yung, a portion of the Chinese Confucian classic *Book of Rites.* The standard English title of the *Chung-yung* (composed in the third or second century B.C.) is *The Doctrine of the Mean,* but *Centrality and Commonality* is more accurate. Although frequently treated as an independent classic from quite early in its history, it did not receive canonical status until Chu Hsi made it one of the Four Books. The text is a collection of aphorisms and short essays unified by common themes. Portions of the text outline a virtue ethic, stressing flexible response to changing contexts, and identifying human flourishing with complete development of the capacities present in one's nature (*hsing*), which is given by Heaven (*t'ien*). As is typical of Confucianism, virtue in the family parallels political virtue. **See also** CH'ENG, TA-HSÜEH.   B.W.V.N.

chün-tzu, Chinese term meaning 'gentleman', 'superior man', 'noble person', or 'exemplary individual'. *Chün-tzu* is Confucius's practically attainable ideal of ethical excellence. A *chün-tzu*, unlike a *sheng* (sage), is one who exemplifies in his life and conduct a concern for *jen* (humanity), *li* (propriety), and *i* (rightness/righteousness). *Jen* pertains to affectionate regard to the well-being of one's fellows in the community; *li* to ritual propriety conformable to traditional rules of proper behavior; and *i* to one's sense of rightness, especially in dealing with changing circumstances. A *chün-tzu* is marked by a catholic and neutral attitude toward preconceived moral opinions and established moral practices, a concern with harmony of words and deeds. These salient features enable the *chün-tzu* to cope with novel and exigent circumstances, while at the same time heeding the importance of moral tradition as a guide to conduct.   A.S.C.

Church, Alonzo (1903–95), American logician, mathematician, and philosopher, known in pure logic for his discovery and application of the Church lambda operator, one of the central ideas of the Church lambda calculus, and for his rigorous formalizations of the theory of types, a higher-order underlying logic originally formulated in a flawed form by Whitehead and Russell. The lambda operator enables direct, unambiguous, symbolic representation of a range of philosophically and mathematically important expressions previously representable only ambiguously or after elaborate paraphrasing. In philosophy, Church advocated rigorous analytic methods based on symbolic logic. His philosophy was characterized by his own version of logicism, the view that mathematics is reducible to logic, and by his unhesitating acceptance of higher-order logics. Higher-order logics, including second-order, are ontologically rich systems that involve quantification of higher-order variables, variables that range over properties, relations, and so on. Higher-order logics were routinely used in foundational work by Frege, Peano, Hilbert, Gödel, Tarski, and others until around World War II, when they suddenly lost favor. In regard to both his logicism and his acceptance of higher-order logics, Church countered trends, increasingly dominant in the third quarter of the twentieth century, against reduction of mathematics to logic and against the so-called "ontological excesses" of higher-order logic. In the 1970s, although admired for his high standards of rigor and for his achievements, Church was regarded as conservative or perhaps even reactionary. Opinions have softened in recent years.

On the computational and epistemological sides of logic Church made two major contributions. He was the first to articulate the now widely accepted principle known as Church's thesis, that every effectively calculable arithmetic function is recursive. At first highly controversial, this principle connects intuitive, epistemic, extrinsic, and operational aspects of arithmetic with its formal, ontic, intrinsic, and abstract aspects. Church's thesis sets a purely arithmetic outer limit on what is computationally achievable. Church's further work on Hilbert's "decision problem" led to the discovery and proof of Church's theorem – basically that there is no computational procedure for determining, of a finite-premised first-order argument, whether it is valid or invalid. This result contrasts sharply with the previously known result that the computational truth-table method suffices to determine the validity of a finite-premised truth-functional argument. Church's thesis at once highlights the vast difference between propositional logic and first-order logic and sets an outer limit on what is achievable by "automated reasoning."

Church's mathematical and philosophical writings are influenced by Frege, especially by Frege's semantic distinction between sense and reference, his emphasis on purely syntactical treatment of proof, and his doctrine that sentences denote (are names of) their truth-values.

See also CHURCH'S THESIS, COMPUTABILITY, FORMALIZATION, HILBERT, HILBERT'S PROGRAM, LOGICISM, RECURSIVE FUNCTION THEORY, SECOND-ORDER LOGIC, TRUTH TABLE, TYPE THEORY.   J.Cor.

church fathers. See PATRISTIC AUTHORS.

Churchland, Patricia Smith (b.1943), Canadian-born American philosopher and advocate of neurophilosophy. She received her B.Phil. from Oxford in 1969 and held positions at the University of Manitoba and the Institute for Advanced Studies at Princeton, settling at the University of California, San Diego, with appointments in philosophy and the Institute for Neural Computation.

Skeptical of philosophy's a priori specification of mental categories and dissatisfied with computational psychology's purely top-down approach to their function, Churchland began studying the brain at the University of Manitoba medical school. The result was a unique merger of science and philosophy, a "neurophilosophy" that challenged the prevailing methodology of mind. Thus, in a series of articles that includes "Fodor on Language Learning" (1978) and "A Perspective on Mind-Brain Research" (1980), she outlines a new neurobiologically based paradigm. It subsumes simple non-linguistic structures and organisms, since the brain is an evolved organ; but it preserves functionalism, since a cognitive system's mental states are explained via high-level neurofunctional theories. It is a strategy of cooperation between psychology and neuroscience, a "co-evolutionary" process eloquently described in *Neurophilosophy* (1986) with the prediction that genuine cognitive phenomena will be reduced, some as conceptualized within the commonsense framework, others as transformed through the sciences.

The same intellectual confluence is displayed through Churchland's various collaborations: with psychologist and computational neurobiologist Terrence Sejnowski in *The Computational Brain* (1992); with neuroscientist Rodolfo Llinas in *The Mind-Brain Continuum* (1996); and with philosopher and husband Paul Churchland in *On the Contrary* (1998) (she and Paul Churchland are jointly appraised in R. McCauley, *The Churchlands and Their Critics*, 1996). From the viewpoint of neurophilosophy, interdisciplinary cooperation is essential for advancing knowledge, for the truth lies in the intertheoretic details.

See also PHILOSOPHY OF LANGUAGE, PHILOSOPHY OF MIND, PHILOSOPHY OF SCIENCE.

R.P.E.

Churchland, Paul M. (b.1942), Canadian-born American philosopher, leading proponent of eliminative materialism. He received his Ph.D. from the University of Pittsburgh in 1969 and held positions at the Universities of Toronto, Manitoba, and the Institute for Advanced Studies at Princeton. He is professor of philosophy and member of the Institute for Neural Computation at the University of California, San Diego.

Churchland's literary corpus constitutes a lucidly written, scientifically informed narrative where his neurocomputational philosophy unfolds. *Scientific Realism and the Plasticity of Mind* (1979) maintains that, though science is best construed realistically, perception is conceptually driven, with no observational given, while language is holistic, with meaning fixed by networks of associated usage. Moreover, regarding the structure of science, higher-level theories should be reduced by, incorporated into, or eliminated in favor of more basic theories from natural science, and, in the specific case, commonsense psychology is a largely false empirical theory, to be replaced by a non-sentential, neuroscientific framework. This skepticism regarding "sentential" approaches is a common thread, present in earlier papers, and taken up again in "Eliminative Materialism and the Propositional Attitudes" (1981).

When fully developed, the non-sentential, neuroscientific framework takes the form of connectionist network or parallel distributed processing models. Thus, with essays in *A Neurocomputational Perspective* (1989), Churchland adds that genuine psychological processes are sequences of activation patterns over neuronal networks. Scientific theories, likewise, are learned vectors in the space of possible activation patterns, with scientific explanation being prototypical activation of a preferred vector. Classical epistemology, too, should be neurocomputationally naturalized. Indeed, Churchland suggests a semantic view whereby synonymy, or the sharing of concepts, is a similarity between patterns in neuronal state-space. Even moral knowledge is analyzed as stored prototypes of social reality that are elicited when an individual navigates through other neurocomputational systems. The entire picture is expressed in *The Engine of Reason, the Seat of the Soul* (1996) and, with his wife Patricia Churchland, by the essays in *On the Contrary* (1998). What has emerged is a neurocomputational embodiment of the naturalist program, a panphilosophy that promises to capture science, epistemology, language, and morals in one broad sweep of its connectionist net.

See also CONNECTIONISM, MEANING, PHILOSOPHY OF MIND, PHILOSOPHY OF SCIENCE.

R.P.E.

Church's theorem. See CHURCH'S THESIS.

Church's thesis, the thesis, proposed by Alonzo Church at a meeting of the American Mathematical Society in April 1935, "that the notion of an effectively calculable function of positive integers should be identified with that of a recursive function. . . ." This proposal has been called Church's thesis ever since Kleene used that name in his *Introduction to Metamathematics* (1952). The informal notion of an effectively calculable function (effective procedure, or algorithm) had been used in mathematics and logic to indicate that a class of problems is solvable in a "mechanical fashion" by following fixed elementary rules. Underlying epistemological concerns came to the fore when modern logic moved in the late nineteenth century from axiomatic to formal presentations of theories. Hilbert suggested in 1904 that such formally presented theories be taken as objects of mathematical study, and metamathematics has been pursued vigorously and systematically since the 1920s. In its pursuit, concrete issues arose that required for their resolution a delimitation of the class of effective procedures. Hilbert's important *Entscheidungsproblem*, the decision problem for predicate logic, was one such issue. It was solved negatively by Church and Turing – relative to the precise notion of recursiveness; the result was obtained independently by Church and Turing, but is usually called *Church's theorem*. A second significant issue was the general formulation of the incompleteness theorems as applying to *all* formal theories (satisfying the usual representability and derivability conditions), not just to specific formal systems like that of *Principia Mathematica*.

According to Kleene, Church proposed in 1933 the identification of effective calculability with λ-definability. That proposal was not published at the time, but in 1934 Church mentioned it in conversation to Gödel, who judged it to be "thoroughly unsatisfactory." In his Princeton Lectures of 1934, Gödel defined the concept of a recursive function, but he was not convinced that all effectively calculable functions would fall under it. The proof of the equivalence between λ-definability and recursiveness (by Church and Kleene) led to Church's first published formulation of the thesis as quoted above. The thesis was reiterated in Church's "An Unsolvable Problem of Elementary Number Theory" (1936). Turing introduced, in "On Computable Numbers, with an Application to the *Entscheidungsproblem*" (1936), a notion of computability by machines and maintained that it captures effective calculability exactly. Post's paper "Finite Combinatory Processes, Formulation 1" (1936) contains a model of computation that is strikingly similar to Turing's. However, Post did not provide any analysis; he suggested considering the identification of effective calculability with his concept as a working hypothesis that should be verified by investigating ever wider formulations and reducing them to his basic formulation. (The classic papers of Gödel, Church, Turing, Post, and Kleene are all reprinted in Davis, ed., *The Undecidable*, 1965.)

In his 1936 paper Church gave one central reason for the proposed identification, namely that other plausible explications of the informal notion lead to mathematical concepts weaker than or equivalent to recursiveness. Two paradigmatic explications, calculability of a function via algorithms or in a logic, were considered by Church. In either case, the steps taken in determining function values have to be effective; and if the effectiveness of steps is, as Church put it, interpreted to mean recursiveness, then the function is recursive. The fundamental interpretative difficulty in Church's "step-by-step argument" (which was turned into one of the "recursiveness conditions" Hilbert and Bernays used in their 1939 characterization of functions that can be evaluated according to rules) was bypassed by Turing. Analyzing human mechanical computations, Turing was led to finiteness conditions that are motivated by the human computer's sensory limitations, but are ultimately based on memory limitations. Then he showed that any function calculable by a human computer satisfying these conditions is also computable by one of his machines. Both Church and Gödel found Turing's analysis convincing; indeed, Church wrote in a 1937 review of Turing's paper that Turing's notion makes "the identification with effectiveness in the ordinary (not explicitly defined) sense evident immediately."

This reflective work of partly philosophical and partly mathematical character provides one of the fundamental notions in mathematical logic. Indeed, its proper understanding is crucial for (judging) the philosophical significance of central metamathematical results – like Gödel's incompleteness theorems or Church's theorem. The work is also crucial for computer science, artificial intelligence, and cognitive psychology, providing in these fields a basic theoretical notion. For example, Church's thesis is *the* cornerstone for Newell and Simon's delimitation of the class of physical symbol systems, i.e. universal machines with a particular architecture; see Newell's *Physical Symbol Systems* (1980). Newell views the delimitation "as the most fundamental contribution of artificial intelligence and computer science to the joint enterprise of cognitive science." In a turn that had been taken by Turing in "Intelligent Machinery" (1948) and "Computing Machinery and Intelligence" (1950), Newell points out the basic role physical symbol systems take on in the study of the human mind: "the hypothesis is that humans are instances of physical symbol systems, and, by virtue of this, mind enters into the physical universe.... this hypothesis sets the terms on which we search for a scientific theory of mind."

See also COMPUTER THEORY, GÖDEL'S IN-COMPLETENESS THEOREMS, PROOF THEORY, RECURSIVE FUNCTION THEORY.   W.S.

Church-Turing thesis. See PHILOSOPHY OF MIND.

Cicero, Marcus Tullius (106–43 B.C.), Roman statesman, orator, essayist, and letter writer. He was important not so much for formulating individual philosophical arguments as for expositions of the doctrines of the major schools of Hellenistic philosophy, and for, as he put it, "teaching philosophy to speak Latin." The significance of the latter can hardly be overestimated. Cicero's coinages helped shape the philosophical vocabulary of the Latin-speaking West well into the early modern period.

The most characteristic feature of Cicero's thought is his attempt to unify philosophy and rhetoric. His first major trilogy, *On the Orator, On the Republic,* and *On the Laws,* presents a vision of wise statesmen-philosophers whose greatest achievement is guiding political affairs through rhetorical persuasion rather than violence. Philosophy, Cicero argues, needs rhetoric to effect its most important practical goals, while rhetoric is useless without the psychological, moral, and logical justification provided by philosophy. This combination of eloquence and philosophy constitutes what he calls *humanitas* – a coinage whose enduring influence is attested in later revivals of humanism – and it alone provides the foundation for constitutional governments; it is acquired, moreover, only through broad training in those subjects worthy of free citizens (*artes liberales*). In philosophy of education, this Ciceronian conception of a humane education encompassing poetry, rhetoric, history, morals, and politics endured as an ideal, especially for those convinced that instruction in the liberal disciplines is essential for citizens if their rational autonomy is to be expressed in ways that are culturally and politically beneficial.

A major aim of Cicero's earlier works is to appropriate for Roman high culture one of Greece's most distinctive products, philosophical theory, and to demonstrate Roman superiority. He thus insists that Rome's laws and political

institutions successfully embody the best in Greek political theory, whereas the Greeks themselves were inadequate to the crucial task of putting their theories into practice. Taking over the Stoic conception of the universe as a rational whole, governed by divine reason, he argues that human societies must be grounded in natural law. For Cicero, nature's law possesses the characteristics of a legal code; in particular, it is formulable in a comparatively extended set of rules against which existing societal institutions can be measured. Indeed, since they so closely mirror the requirements of nature, Roman laws and institutions furnish a nearly perfect paradigm for human societies. Cicero's overall theory, if not its particular details, established a lasting framework for anti-positivist theories of law and morality, including those of Aquinas, Grotius, Suárez, and Locke.

The final two years of his life saw the creation of a series of dialogue-treatises that provide an encyclopedic survey of Hellenistic philosophy. Cicero himself follows the moderate fallibilism of Philo of Larissa and the New Academy. Holding that philosophy is a method and not a set of dogmas, he endorses an attitude of systematic doubt. However, unlike Cartesian doubt, Cicero's does not extend to the real world behind phenomena, since he does not envision the possibility of strict phenomenalism. Nor does he believe that systematic doubt leads to radical skepticism about knowledge. Although no infallible criterion for distinguishing true from false impressions is available, some impressions, he argues, are more "persuasive" (*probabile*) and can be relied on to guide action.

In *Academics* he offers detailed accounts of Hellenistic epistemological debates, steering a middle course between dogmatism and radical skepticism. A similar strategy governs the rest of his later writings. Cicero presents the views of the major schools, submits them to criticism, and tentatively supports any positions he finds "persuasive." Three connected works, *On Divination, On Fate,* and *On the Nature of the Gods,* survey Epicurean, Stoic, and Academic arguments about theology and natural philosophy. Much of the treatment of religious thought and practice is cool, witty, and skeptically detached – much in the manner of eighteenth-century *philosophes* who, along with Hume, found much in Cicero to emulate. However, he concedes that Stoic arguments for providence are "persuasive." So too in ethics, he criticizes Epicurean, Stoic, and Peripatetic doctrines in *On Ends* (45) and their views on death, pain, irrational emotions, and happiness in *Tusculan Disputations* (45). Yet, a final work, *On Duties,* offers a practical ethical system based on Stoic principles. Although sometimes dismissed as the eclecticism of an amateur, Cicero's method of selectively choosing from what had become authoritative professional systems often displays considerable reflectiveness and originality.

See also HELLENISTIC PHILOSOPHY, NATURAL LAW, NEW ACADEMY, STOICISM.   P.Mi.

circularity. See CIRCULAR REASONING, DEFINITION, DIALLELON.

circular reasoning, reasoning that, when traced backward from its conclusion, returns to that starting point, as one returns to a starting point when tracing a circle. The discussion of this topic by Richard Whatley (1787–1863) in his *Logic* (1826) sets a high standard of clarity and penetration. Logic textbooks often quote the following example from Whatley:

> To allow every man an unbounded freedom of speech must always be, on the whole, advantageous to the State; for it is highly conducive to the interests of the Community, that each individual should enjoy a liberty perfectly unlimited, of expressing his sentiments.

This passage illustrates how circular reasoning is less obvious in a language, such as English, that, in Whatley's words, is "abounding in synonymous expressions, which have no resemblance in sound, and no connection in etymology." The premise and conclusion do not consist of just the same words in the same order, nor can logical or grammatical principles transform one into the other. Rather, they have the same propositional content: they say the same thing in different words. That is why appealing to one of them to provide reason for believing the other amounts to giving something as a reason for itself.

Circular reasoning is often said to *beg the question.* 'Begging the question' and *petitio principii* are translations of a phrase in Aristotle connected with a game of formal disputation played in antiquity but not in recent times. The meanings of 'question' and 'begging' do not in any clear way determine the meaning of 'question begging'.

There is no simple argument form that all and only circular arguments have. It is not logic, in Whatley's example above, that determines the identity of content between the premise and the conclusion. Some theorists propose rather more complicated formal or syntactic accounts of circularity. Others believe that any account of circular reasoning must refer to the beliefs of those who reason. Whether or not the following argument about articles in this dictionary is circular depends on why the first premise should be accepted:

(1) The article on inference contains no split infinitives.
(2) The other articles contain no split infinitives.
Therefore,
(3) No article contains split infinitives.

Consider two cases. Case I: Although (2) supports (1) inductively, both (1) and (2) have solid outside support independent of any prior acceptance of (3). This reasoning is not circular. Case II: Someone who advances the argument accepts (1) or (2) or both, only because he believes (3). Such reasoning is circular, even though neither premise expresses just the same proposition as the conclusion. The question remains controversial whether, in explaining circularity, we should refer to the beliefs of individual reasoners or only to the surrounding circumstances.

One purpose of reasoning is to increase the degree of reasonable confidence that one has in the truth of a conclusion. Presuming the truth of a conclusion in support of a premise thwarts this purpose, because the initial degree of reasonable confidence in the premise cannot then exceed the initial degree of reasonable confidence in the conclusion.

See also INFORMAL FALLACY, JUSTIFICATION.   D.H.S.

citta-mātra, the Yogācāra Buddhist doctrine that there are no extramental entities, given classical expression by Vasubandhu in the fourth or fifth century A.D. The classical form of this doctrine is a variety of idealism that claims (1) that a coherent explanation of the facts of experience can be provided without appeal to anything extramental; (2) that no coherent account of what extramental entities are like is possible; and (3) that therefore the doctrine that there is nothing but mind is to be preferred to its realistic competitors. The claim and the argument were and are controversial among Buddhist metaphysicians. **See also** VIJÑAPTI.   P.J.G.

civic humanism. See CLASSICAL REPUBLICANISM.

civil disobedience, a deliberate violation of the law, committed in order to draw attention to or rectify perceived injustices in the law or policies of a state. Illustrative questions raised by the topic include: how are such acts justified, how should the legal system respond to such acts when justified, and must such acts be done publicly, nonviolently, and/or with a willingness to accept attendant legal sanctions? **See also NON-VIOLENCE, POLITICAL PHILOSOPHY.**   P.S.

civil rights. See RIGHTS.

claim right. See HOHFELD, RIGHTS.

clairvoyance. See PARAPSYCHOLOGY.

Clarke, Samuel (1675–1729), English philosopher, preacher, and theologian. Born in Norwich, he was educated at Cambridge, where he came under the influence of Newton. Upon graduation Clarke entered the established church, serving for a time as chaplain to Queen Anne. He spent the last twenty years of his life as rector of St. James, Westminster.

Clarke wrote extensively on controversial theological and philosophical issues – the nature of space and time, proofs of the existence of God, the doctrine of the Trinity, the incorporeality and natural immortality of the soul, freedom of the will, the nature of morality, etc. His most philosophical works are his Boyle lectures of 1704 and 1705, in which he developed a forceful version of the cosmological argument for the existence and nature of God and attacked the views of Hobbes, Spinoza, and some proponents of deism; his correspondence with Leibniz (1715–16), in which he defended Newton's views of space and time and charged Leibniz with holding views inconsistent with free will; and his writings against Anthony Collins, in which he defended a libertarian view of the agent as the undetermined cause of free actions and attacked Collins's arguments for a materialistic view of the mind. In these works Clarke maintains a position of extreme rationalism, contending that the existence and nature of God can be conclusively demonstrated, that the basic principles of morality are necessarily true and immediately knowable, and that the existence of a future state of rewards and punishments is assured by our knowledge that God will reward the morally just and punish the morally wicked.

See also HOBBES, LEIBNIZ, PHILOSOPHY OF RELIGION, SPINOZA.   W.L.R.

class, term sometimes used as a synonym for 'set'. When the two are distinguished, a class is understood as a collection in the logical sense, i.e., as the extension of a concept (e.g. the class of red objects). By contrast, sets, i.e., collections in the mathematical sense, are understood as occurring in stages, where each stage consists of the sets that can be formed from the non-sets and the sets already formed at previous stages. When a set is formed at a given stage, only the non-sets and the previously formed sets are even candidates for membership, but absolutely anything can gain membership in a class simply by falling under the appropriate concept. Thus, it is classes, not sets, that figure in the inconsistent principle of unlimited comprehension. In set theory, *proper classes* are collections of sets that are never formed at any stage, e.g., the class of all sets (since new sets are formed at each stage, there is no stage at which all sets are available to be collected into a set). **See also SET THEORY.**   P.Mad.

class, equivalence. See PARTITION, RELATION.

class, proper. See CLASS.

class, reference. See PROBABILITY.

classical conditioning. See CONDITIONING.

classical liberalism. See LIBERALISM.

classical republicanism, also known as civic humanism, a political outlook developed by Machiavelli in Renaissance Italy and by James Harrington (1611–77) in seventeenth-century England, modified by eighteenth-century British and Continental writers and important for the thought of the American founding fathers.

Drawing on Roman historians, Machiavelli argued that a state could hope for security from the blows of fortune only if its (male) citizens were devoted to its well-being. They should take turns ruling and being ruled, be always prepared to fight for the republic, and limit their private possessions. Such men would possess a wholly secular *virtù* appropriate to political beings. Corruption, in the form of excessive attachment to private interest, would then be the most serious threat to the republic. Harrington's utopian *Oceana* (1656) portrayed England governed under such a system. Opposing the authoritarian views of Hobbes, it described a system in which the well-to-do male citizens would elect some of their number to govern for limited terms. Those governing would propose state policies; the others would vote on the acceptability of the proposals. Agriculture was the basis of economics, but the size of estates was to be strictly controlled. Harringtonianism helped form the views of the political party opposing the dominance of the king and court. Montesquieu in France drew on classical sources in discussing the importance of civic virtue and devotion to the republic.

All these views were well known to Jefferson, Adams, and other American colonial and revolutionary thinkers; and some contemporary communitarian critics of American culture return to classical republican ideas.

See also MACHIAVELLI, POLITICAL PHILOSOPHY.   J.B.S.

class paradox. See UNEXPECTED EXAMINATION PARADOX.

Cleanthes. See STOICISM.

clear and distinct idea. See DESCARTES.

Clement of Alexandria (A.D. c.150–c.215), formative teacher in the early Christian church who, as a "Christian gnostic," combined enthusiasm for Greek philosophy with a defense of the church's faith. He espoused spiritual and intellectual ascent toward that complete but hidden knowledge or *gnosis* reserved for the truly enlightened. Clement's school did not practice strict fidelity to the authorities, and possibly the teachings, of the institutional church, drawing upon the Hellenistic traditions of Alexandria, including Philo and Middle Platonism. As with the law among the Jews, so, for Clement, philosophy among the pagans was a pedagogical preparation for Christ, in whom *logos*, reason, had become enfleshed. Philosophers now should rise above their inferior understanding to the perfect knowledge revealed in Christ. Though hostile to gnosticism and its speculations, Clement was thoroughly Hellenized in outlook and sometimes guilty of Docetism, not least in his reluctance to concede the utter humanness of Jesus. **See also** GNOSTICISM. A.E.L.

Clifford, W(illiam) K(ingdon) (1845–79), British mathematician and philosopher. Educated at King's College, London, and Trinity College, Cambridge, he began giving public lectures in 1868, when he was appointed a fellow of Trinity, and in 1870 became professor of applied mathematics at University College, London. His academic career ended prematurely when he died of tuberculosis. Clifford is best known for his rigorous view on the relation between belief and evidence, which, in "The Ethics of Belief," he summarized thus: "It is wrong always, everywhere, and for anyone, to believe anything on insufficient evidence." He gives this example. Imagine a shipowner who sends to sea an emigrant ship, although the evidence raises strong suspicions as to the vessel's seaworthiness. Ignoring this evidence, he convinces himself that the ship's condition is good enough and, after it sinks and all the passengers die, collects his insurance money without a trace of guilt. Clifford maintains that the owner had no *right* to believe in the soundness of the ship. "He had acquired his belief not by honestly earning it in patient investigation, but by stifling his doubts." The right Clifford is alluding to is *moral,* for what one believes is not a private but a public affair and may have grave consequences for others. He regards us as morally obliged to investigate the evidence thoroughly on any occasion, and to withhold belief if evidential support is lacking. This obligation must be fulfilled however trivial and insignificant a belief may seem, for a violation of it may "leave its stamp upon our character forever." Clifford thus rejected Catholicism, to which he had subscribed originally, and became an agnostic. James's famous essay "The Will to Believe" criticizes Clifford's view. According to James, insufficient evidence need not stand in the way of religious belief, for we have a right to hold beliefs that go beyond the evidence provided they serve the pursuit of a legitimate goal. **See also** EPISTEMOLOGY, EVIDENTIALISM. M.St.

closed formula. See WELL-FORMED FORMULA.

closed loop. See CYBERNETICS.

closed sentence. See OPEN FORMULA.

closure. A set of objects, O, is said to exhibit *closure* or to be *closed* under a given operation, R, provided that for every object, x, if x is a member of O and x is R-related to any object, y, then y is a member of O. For example, the set of propositions is *closed under deduction,* for if p is a proposition and p entails q, i.e., q is deducible from p, then q is a proposition (simply because only propositions can be entailed by propositions). In addition, many subsets of the set of propositions are also closed under deduction. For example, the set of true propositions is closed under deduction or entailment. Others are not. Under most accounts of belief, we may fail to believe what is entailed by what we do, in fact, believe. Thus, if knowledge is some form of true, justified belief, knowledge is not closed under deduction, for we may fail to believe a proposition entailed by a known proposition. Nevertheless, there is a related issue that has been the subject of much debate, namely: Is the set of justified propositions closed under deduction? Aside from the obvious importance of the answer to that question in developing an account of justification, there are two important issues in epistemology that also depend on the answer.

Subtleties aside, the so-called Gettier problem depends in large part upon an affirmative answer to that question. For, assuming that a proposition can be justified and false, it is possible to construct cases in which a proposition, say *p*, is justified, false, but believed. Now, consider a true proposition, *q*, which is believed and entailed by *p*. If justification is closed under deduction, then *q* is justified, true, and believed. But if the *only* basis for believing *q* is *p*, it is clear that *q* is not known. Thus, true, justified belief is not sufficient for knowledge. What response is appropriate to this problem has been a central issue in epistemology since E. Gettier's publication of "Is Justified True Belief Knowledge?" (*Analysis*, 1963).

Whether justification is closed under deduction is also crucial when evaluating a common, traditional argument for skepticism. Consider any person, S, and let *p* be any proposition ordinarily thought to be knowable, e.g., that there is a table before S. The argument for skepticism goes like this:

(1) If *p* is justified for S, then, since *p* entails *q*, where *q* is 'there is no evil genius making S falsely believe that *p*', *q* is justified for S.
(2) S is not justified in believing *q*.
    Therefore, S is not justified in believing *p*.

The first premise depends upon justification being closed under deduction.
   See also EPISTEMIC LOGIC, EPISTEMOLOGY, JUSTIFICATION, SKEPTICISM.   P.D.K.

closure, causal. See DAVIDSON.

Coase theorem, a non-formal insight by Ronald Coase (Nobel Prize in Economics, 1991): assuming that there are no (transaction) costs involved in exchanging rights for money, then no matter how rights are initially distributed, rational agents will buy and sell them so as to maximize individual returns. In jurisprudence this proposition has been the basis for a claim about how

rights should be distributed even when (as is usual) transaction costs are high: the law should confer rights on those who would purchase them were they for sale on markets without transaction costs; e.g., the right to an indivisible, unsharable resource should be conferred on the agent willing to pay the highest price for it. **See also PHILOSOPHY OF ECONOMICS.**   A.R.

Cockburn, Catherine (Trotter) (1679–1749), English philosopher and playwright who made a significant contribution to the debates on ethical rationalism sparked by Clarke's Boyle lectures (1704–05). The major theme of her writings is the nature of moral obligation. Cockburn displays a consistent, non-doctrinaire philosophical position, arguing that moral duty is to be rationally deduced from the "nature and fitness of things" (*Remarks*, 1747) and is not founded primarily in externally imposed sanctions. Her writings, published anonymously, take the form of philosophical debates with others, including Samuel Rutherforth, William Warburton, Isaac Watts, Francis Hutcheson, and Lord Shaftesbury. Her best-known intervention in contemporary philosophical debate was her able defense of Locke's *Essay* in 1702.   S.H.

coercion. See FREE WILL PROBLEM.

cogito argument. See DESCARTES.

Cogito ergo sum (Latin, 'I think, therefore I am'), the starting point of Descartes's system of knowledge. In his *Discourse on the Method* (1637), he observes that the proposition 'I am thinking, therefore I exist' (*je pense, donc je suis*) is "so firm and sure that the most extravagant suppositions of the skeptics were incapable of shaking it." The celebrated phrase, in its better-known Latin version, also occurs in the *Principles of Philosophy* (1644), but is not to be found in the *Meditations* (1641), though the latter contains the fullest statement of the reasoning behind Descartes's certainty of his own existence. **See also DESCARTES.**   J.C.O.

cognitive architecture. See COGNITIVE SCIENCE.

cognitive dissonance, mental discomfort arising from conflicting beliefs or attitudes held simultaneously. Leon Festinger, who originated the theory of cognitive dissonance in a book of that title (1957), suggested that cognitive dissonance has motivational characteristics. Suppose a person is contemplating moving to a new city. She is considering both Birmingham and Boston. She cannot move to both, so she must choose. Dissonance is experienced by the person if in choosing, say, Birmingham, she acquires knowledge of bad or unwelcome features of Birmingham and of good or welcome aspects of Boston. The amount of dissonance depends on the relative intensities of dissonant elements. Hence, if the only dissonant factor is her learning that Boston is cooler than Birmingham, and she does not regard climate as important, she will experience little dissonance. Dissonance may occur in several sorts of psychological states or processes, although the bulk of research in cognitive dissonance theory has been on dissonance in choice and on the justification and psychological aftereffects of choice. Cognitive dissonance may be involved in two phenomena of interest to philosophers, namely, self-deception and weakness of will. Why do self-deceivers try to get themselves to believe something that, in some sense, they know to be false? One may resort to self-deception when knowledge causes dissonance. Why do the weak-willed perform actions they know to be wrong? One may become weak-willed when dissonance arises from the expected consequences of doing the right thing.   G.A.G.

cognitive meaning. See MEANING.

cognitive psychology. See COGNITIVE SCIENCE.

cognitive psychotherapy, an expression introduced by Brandt in *A Theory of the Good and the Right* (1979) to refer to a process of assessing and adjusting one's desires, aversions, or pleasures (henceforth, "attitudes"). This process is central to Brandt's analysis of rationality, and ultimately, to his view on the justification of morality.

Cognitive psychotherapy consists of the agent's criticizing his attitudes by repeatedly representing to himself, in an ideally vivid way and at appropriate times, all relevant available information. Brandt characterizes the key definiens as follows: (1) *available information* is "propositions accepted by the science of the agent's day, plus factual propositions justified by publicly accessible evidence (including testimony of others about themselves) and the principles of logic"; (2) information is *relevant* provided, if the agent were to reflect repeatedly on it, "it would make a difference," i.e., would affect the attitude in question, and the effect would be a function of its content, not an accidental byproduct; (3) rel-

evant information is represented in an *ideally vivid* way when the agent focuses on it with maximal clarity and detail and with no hesitation or doubt about its truth; and (4) *repeatedly* and *at appropriate times* refer, respectively, to the frequency and occasions that would result in the information's having the maximal attitudinal impact. Suppose Mary's desire to smoke were extinguished by her bringing to the focus of her attention, whenever she was about to inhale smoke, some justified beliefs, say that smoking is hazardous to one's health and may cause lung cancer; Mary's desire would have been removed by cognitive psychotherapy.

According to Brandt, an attitude is rational for a person provided it is one that would survive, or be produced by, cognitive psychotherapy; otherwise it is irrational. Rational attitudes, in this sense, provide a basis for moral norms. Roughly, the correct moral norms are those of a moral code that persons would opt for if (i) they were motivated by attitudes that survive the process of cognitive psychotherapy; and (ii) at the time of opting for a moral code, they were fully aware of, and vividly attentive to, all available information relevant to choosing a moral code (for a society in which they are to live for the rest of their lives). In this way, Brandt seeks a value-free justification for moral norms – one that avoids the problems of other theories such as those that make an appeal to intuitions.

See also ETHICS, INSTRUMENTALISM, INTUITION, RATIONALITY.   Y.Y.

cognitive science, an interdisciplinary research cluster that seeks to account for intelligent activity, whether exhibited by living organisms (especially adult humans) or machines. Hence, cognitive psychology and artificial intelligence constitute its core. A number of other disciplines, including neuroscience, linguistics, anthropology, and philosophy, as well as other fields of psychology (e.g., developmental psychology), are more peripheral contributors. The quintessential cognitive scientist is someone who employs computer modeling techniques (developing computer programs for the purpose of simulating particular human cognitive activities), but the broad range of disciplines that are at least peripherally constitutive of cognitive science have lent a variety of research strategies to the enterprise. While there are a few common institutions that seek to unify cognitive science (e.g., departments, journals, and societies), the problems investigated and the methods of investigation often are limited to a single contributing discipline. Thus, it is more appropriate to view cognitive science as a cross-disciplinary enterprise than as itself a new discipline.

While interest in cognitive phenomena has historically played a central role in the various disciplines contributing to cognitive science, the term properly applies to cross-disciplinary activities that emerged in the 1970s. During the preceding two decades each of the disciplines that became part of cogntive science gradually broke free of positivistic and behavioristic proscriptions that barred systematic inquiry into the operation of the mind. One of the primary factors that catalyzed new investigations of cognitive activities was Chomsky's generative grammar, which he advanced not only as an abstract theory of the structure of language, but also as an account of language users' mental knowledge of language (their linguistic *competence*). A more fundamental factor was the development of approaches for theorizing about information in an abstract manner, and the introduction of machines (computers) that could manipulate information. This gave rise to the idea that one might program a computer to process information so as to exhibit behavior that would, if performed by a human, require intelligence.

If one tried to formulate a unifying question guiding cognitive science research, it would probably be: How does the cognitive system work? But even this common question is interpreted quite differently in different disciplines. We can appreciate these differences by looking just at language. While psycholinguists (generally psychologists) seek to identify the processing activities in the mind that underlie language use, most linguists focus on the *products* of this internal processing, seeking to articulate the abstract structure of language. A frequent goal of computer scientists, in contrast, has been to develop computer programs to parse natural language input and produce appropriate syntactic and semantic representations.

These differences in objectives among the cognitive science disciplines correlate with different methodologies. The following represent some of the major methodological approaches of the contributing disciplines and some of the problems each encounters.

Artificial intelligence. If the human cognition system is viewed as computational, a natural goal is to simulate its performance. This typically requires formats for representing information as well as procedures for searching and manipulating it. Some of the earliest AI programs drew heavily on the resources of first-order predicate calculus, representing information in propositional formats and manipulating it according to logical principles. For many modeling endeavors, however, it proved important to represent information in larger-scale structures, such as frames (Marvin Minsky), schemata (David Rumelhart), or scripts (Roger Schank), in which different pieces of information associated with an object or activity would be stored together. Such structures generally employed default values for specific slots (specifying, e.g., that deer live in forests) that would be part of the representation unless overridden by new information (e.g., that a particular deer lives in the San Diego Zoo). A very influential alternative approach, developed by Allen Newell, replaces declarative representations of information with procedural representations, known as *productions*. These productions take the form of conditionals that specify actions to be performed (e.g., copying an expression into working memory) if certain conditions are satisfied (e.g., the expression matches another expression).

Psychology. While some psychologists develop computer simulations, a more characteristic activity is to acquire detailed data from human subjects that can reveal the cognitive system's actual operation. This is a challenging endeavor. While cognitive activities transpire within us, they frequently do so in such a smooth and rapid fashion that we are unaware of them. For example, we have little awareness of what occurs when we recognize an object as a chair or remember the name of a client. Some cognitive functions, though, seem to be transparent to consciousness. For example, we might approach a logic problem systematically, enumerating possible solutions and evaluating them serially. Allen Newell and Herbert Simon have refined methods for exploiting verbal protocols obtained from subjects as they solve such problems. These methods have been quite fruitful, but their limitations must be respected. In many cases in which we think we know how we performed a cognitive task, Richard Nisbett and Timothy Wilson have argued that we are misled, relying on folk theories to describe how our minds work rather than reporting directly on their operation. In most cases cognitive psychologists cannot rely on conscious awareness of cognitive processes, but must proceed as do physiologists trying to understand metabolism: they must devise experiments that reveal the underlying processes operative in cognition. One approach is to seek clues in the errors to which the cognitive system is prone. Such errors might be more easily accounted for by one kind of underlying process than by another. Speech errors, such as substituting 'bat cad' for 'bad cat', may be diagnostic of the mechanisms used to construct speech. This approach is often combined with strategies that seek to overload or disrupt the system's normal operation. A common technique is to have a subject perform two tasks at once – e.g., read a passage while watching for a colored spot. Cognitive psychologists may also rely on the ability to dissociate two phenomena (e.g., obliterate one while maintaining the other) to establish their independence. Other types of data widely used to make inferences about the cognitive system include patterns of reaction times, error rates, and priming effects (in which activation of one item facilitates access to related items). Finally, developmental psychologists have brought a variety of kinds of data to bear on cognitive science issues. For example, patterns of acquisition times have been used in a manner similar to reaction time patterns, and accounts of the origin and development of systems constrain and elucidate mature systems.

Linguistics. Since linguists focus on a product of cognition rather than the processes that produce the product, they tend to test their analyses directly against our shared knowledge of that product. Generative linguists in the tradition of Chomsky, for instance, develop grammars that they test by probing whether they generate the sentences of the language and no others. While grammars are certainly germane to developing processing models, they do not directly determine the structure of processing models. Hence, the central task of linguistics is not central to cognitive science. However, Chomsky has augmented his work on grammatical description with a number of controversial claims that are psycholinguistic in nature (e.g., his nativism and his notion of linguistic competence). Further, an alternative approach to incorporating psycholinguistic concerns, the *cognitive linguistics* of Lakoff and Langacker, has achieved prominence as a contributor to cognitive science.

Neuroscience. Cognitive scientists have generally assumed that the processes they study are carried out, in humans, by the brain. Until recently, however, neuroscience has been relatively peripheral to cognitive science. In part this is because neuroscientists have been chiefly concerned with the *implementation* of processes, rather than the processes themselves, and in part

because the techniques available to neuroscientists (such as single-cell recording) have been most suitable for studying the neural implementation of lower-order processes such as sensation. A prominent exception was the classical studies of brain lesions initiated by Broca and Wernicke, which seemed to show that the location of lesions correlated with deficits in production versus comprehension of speech. (More recent data suggest that lesions in Broca's area impair certain kinds of syntactic processing.) However, other developments in neuroscience promise to make its data more relevant to cognitive modeling in the future. These include studies of simple nervous systems, such as that of the aplysia (a genus of marine mollusk) by Eric Kandel, and the development of a variety of techniques for determining the brain activities involved in the performance of cognitive tasks (e.g., recording of evoked response potentials over larger brain structures, and imaging techniques such as positron emission tomography). While in the future neuroscience is likely to offer much richer information that will guide the development and constrain the character of cognitive models, neuroscience will probably not become central to cognitive science. It is itself a rich, multidisciplinary research cluster whose contributing disciplines employ a host of complicated research tools. Moreover, the focus of cognitive science can be expected to remain on cognition, not on its implementation.

So far cognitive science has been characterized in terms of its modes of inquiry. One can also focus on the domains of cognitive phenomena that have been explored. Language represents one such domain. Syntax was one of the first domains to attract wide attention in cognitive science. For example, shortly after Chomsky introduced his transformational grammar, psychologists such as George Miller sought evidence that transformations figured directly in human language processing. From this beginning, a more complex but enduring relationship among linguists, psychologists, and computer scientists has formed a leading edge for much cognitive science research. Psycholinguistics has matured; sophisticated computer models of natural language processing have been developed; and cognitive linguists have offered a particular synthesis that emphasizes semantics, pragmatics, and cognitive foundations of language.

Thinking and reasoning. These constitute an important domain of cognitive science that is closely linked to philosophical interests. Problem solving, such as that which figures in solving puzzles, playing games, or serving as an expert in a domain, has provided a prototype for thinking. Newell and Simon's influential work construed problem solving as a search through a problem space and introduced the idea of *heuristics* – generally reliable but fallible simplifying devices to facilitate the search. One arena for problem solving, scientific reasoning and discovery, has particularly interested philosophers. Artificial intelligence researchers such as Simon and Patrick Langley, as well as philosophers such as Paul Thagard and Lindley Darden, have developed computer programs that can utilize the same data as that available to historical scientists to develop and evaluate theories and plan future experiments. Cognitive scientists have also sought to study the cognitive processes underlying the sorts of logical reasoning (both deductive and inductive) whose normative dimensions have been a concern of philosophers. Philip Johnson-Laird, for example, has sought to account for human performance in dealing with syllogistic reasoning by describing a processing of constructing and manipulating *mental models*. Finally, the process of constructing and using analogies is another aspect of reasoning that has been extensively studied by traditional philosophers as well as cognitive scientists.

Memory, attention, and learning. Cognitive scientists have differentiated a variety of types of memory. The distinction between long- and short-term memory was very influential in the information-processing models of the 1970s. Short-term memory was characterized by limited capacity, such as that exhibited by the ability to retain a seven-digit telephone number for a short period. In much cognitive science work, the notion of *working memory* has superseded *short-term memory*, but many theorists are reluctant to construe this as a separate memory system (as opposed to a part of long-term memory that is activated at a given time). Endel Tulving introduced a distinction between semantic memory (general knowledge that is not specific to a time or place) and episodic memory (memory for particular episodes or occurrences). More recently, Daniel Schacter proposed a related distinction that emphasizes consciousness: implicit memory (access without awareness) versus explicit memory (which does involve awareness and is similar to episodic memory). One of the interesting results of cognitive research is the dissociation between different kinds of memory: a person might have severely impaired memory of

recent events while having largely unimpaired implicit memory. More generally, memory research has shown that human memory does not simply store away information as in a file cabinet. Rather, information is organized according to preexisting structures such as scripts, and can be influenced by events subsequent to the initial storage. Exactly what gets stored and retrieved is partly determined by *attention*, and psychologists in the information-processing tradition have sought to construct general cognitive models that emphasize memory and attention. Finally, the topic of learning has once again become prominent. Extensively studied by the behaviorists of the precognitive era, learning was superseded by memory and attention as a research focus in the 1970s. In the 1980s, artificial intelligence researchers developed a growing interest in designing systems that can learn; machine learning is now a major problem area in AI. During the same period, connectionism arose to offer an alternative kind of learning model.

Perception and motor control. Perceptual and motor systems provide the inputs and outputs to cognitive systems. An important aspect of perception is the recognition of something as a particular *kind* of object or event; this requires accessing knowledge of objects and events. One of the central issues concerning perception questions the extent to which perceptual processes are influenced by higher-level cognitive information (top-down processing) versus how much they are driven purely by incoming sensory information (bottom-up processing). A related issue concerns the claim that visual imagery is a distinct cognitive process and is closely related to visual perception, perhaps relying on the same brain processes. A number of cognitive science inquiries (e.g., by Roger Shepard and Stephen Kosslyn) have focused on how people use images in problem solving and have sought evidence that people solve problems by rotating images or scanning them. This research has been extremely controversial, as other investigators have argued against the use of images and have tried to account for the performance data that have been generated in terms of the use of propositionally represented information. Finally, a distinction recently has been proposed between the *What* and *Where* systems. All of the foregoing issues concern the *What* system (which recognizes and represents objects as exemplars of categories). The *Where* system, in contrast, concerns objects in their environment, and is particularly adapted to the dynamics of movement. Gibson's ecological psychology is a long-standing inquiry into this aspect of perception, and work on the neural substrates is now attracting the interest of cognitive scientists as well.

Recent developments. The breadth of cognitive science has been expanding in recent years. In the 1970s, cognitive science inquiries tended to focus on processing activities of adult humans or on computer models of intelligent performance; the best work often combined these approaches. Subsequently, investigators examined in much greater detail how cognitive systems develop, and developmental psychologists have increasingly contributed to cognitive science. One of the surprising findings has been that, contrary to the claims of William James, infants do not seem to confront the world as a "blooming, buzzing confusion," but rather recognize objects and events quite early in life. Cognitive science has also expanded along a different dimension. Until recently many cognitive studies focused on what humans could accomplish in laboratory settings in which they performed tasks isolated from real-life contexts. The motivation for this was the assumption that cognitive processes were generic and not limited to specific contexts. However, a variety of influences, including Gibsonian ecological psychology (especially as interpreted and developed by Ulric Neisser) and Soviet activity theory, have advanced the view that cognition is much more dynamic and situated in real-world tasks and environmental contexts; hence, it is necessary to study cognitive activities in an ecologically valid manner.

Another form of expansion has resulted from a challenge to what has been the dominant architecture for modeling cognition. An *architecture* defines the basic processing capacities of the cognitive system. The dominant cognitive architecture has assumed that the mind possesses a capacity for storing and manipulating symbols. These symbols can be composed into larger structures according to syntactic rules that can then be operated upon by formal rules that recognize that structure. Jerry Fodor has referred to this view of the cognitive system as the "language of thought hypothesis" and clearly construes it as a modern heir of rationalism. One of the basic arguments for it, due to Fodor and Zenon Pylyshyn, is that thoughts, like language, exhibit productivity (the unlimited capacity to generate new thoughts) and systematicity (exhibited by the inherent relation between thoughts such as 'Joan loves the florist' and 'The

florist loves Joan'). They argue that only if the architecture of cognition has languagelike compositional structure would productivity and systematicity be generic properties and hence not require special case-by-case accounts. The challenge to this architecture has arisen with the development of an alternative architecture, known as *connectionism, parallel distributed processing,* or *neural network modeling,* which proposes that the cognitive system consists of vast numbers of neuronlike units that excite or inhibit each other. Knowledge is stored in these systems by the adjustment of connection strengths between processing units; consequently, connectionism is a modern descendant of associationism. Connectionist networks provide a natural account of certain cognitive phenomena that have proven challenging for the symbolic architecture, including pattern recognition, reasoning with soft constraints, and learning. Whether they also can account for productivity and systematicity has been the subject of debate.

Philosophical theorizing about the mind has often provided a starting point for the modeling and empirical investigations of modern cognitive science. The ascent of cognitive science has not meant that philosophers have ceased to play a role in examining cognition. Indeed, a number of philosophers have pursued their inquiries as contributors to cognitive science, focusing on such issues as the possible reduction of cognitive theories to those of neuroscience, the status of folk psychology relative to emerging scientific theories of mind, the merits of rationalism versus empiricism, and strategies for accounting for the intentionality of mental states. The interaction between philosophers and other cognitive scientists, however, is bidirectional, and a number of developments in cognitive science promise to challenge or modify traditional philosophical views of cognition. For example, studies by cognitive and social psychologists have challenged the assumption that human thinking tends to accord with the norms of logic and decision theory. On a variety of tasks humans seem to follow procedures (heuristics) that violate normative canons, raising questions about how philosophers should characterize rationality. Another area of empirical study that has challenged philosophical assumptions has been the study of concepts and categorization. Philosophers since Plato have widely assumed that concepts of ordinary language, such as *red, bird,* and *justice,* should be definable by necessary and sufficient conditions. But celebrated studies by

Eleanor Rosch and her colleagues indicated that many ordinary-language concepts had a *prototype structure* instead. On this view, the categories employed in human thinking are characterized by prototypes (the clearest exemplars) and a metric that grades exemplars according to their degree of typicality. Recent investigations have also pointed to significant instability in conceptual structure and to the role of theoretical beliefs in organizing categories. This alternative conception of concepts has profound implications for philosophical methodologies that portray philosophy's task to be the analysis of concepts.

See also ARTIFICIAL INTELLIGENCE, INTENTIONALITY, PHILOSOPHY OF LANGUAGE, PHILOSOPHY OF MIND.   W.B.

cognitive value. See FREGE.

Cohen, Hermann (1842–1918), German Jewish philosopher who originated and led, with Paul Natorp (1854–1924), the Marburg School of neo-Kantianism. He taught at Marburg from 1876 to 1912. Cohen wrote commentaries on Kant's *Critiques* prior to publishing *System der Philosophie* (1902–12), which consisted of parts on logic, ethics, and aesthetics. He developed a Kantian idealism of the natural sciences, arguing that a transcendental analysis of these sciences shows that "pure thought" (his system of Kantian a priori principles) "constructs" their "reality." He also developed Kant's ethics as a democratic socialist ethics. He ended his career at a rabbinical seminary in Berlin, writing his influential *Religion der Vernunft aus den Quellen des Judentums* ("Religion of Reason out of the Sources of Judaism," 1919), which explicated Judaism on the basis of his own Kantian ethical idealism. Cohen's ethical-political views were adopted by Kurt Eisner (1867–1919), leader of the Munich revolution of 1918, and also had an impact on the revisionism (of orthodox Marxism) of the German Social Democratic Party, while his philosophical writings greatly influenced Cassirer. See also CASSIRER, KANT, NEO-KANTIANISM.   H.v.d.L.

coherence theory of justification. See COHERENTISM.

coherence theory of knowledge. See COHERENTISM.

coherence theory of truth, the view that either the nature of truth or the sole criterion for determining truth is constituted by a relation of coherence between the belief (or judgment) being assessed and other beliefs (or judgments).

As a view of the nature of truth, the coherence theory represents an alternative to the correspondence theory of truth. Whereas the correspondence theory holds that a belief is true provided it corresponds to independent reality, the coherence theory holds that it is true provided it stands in a suitably strong relation of coherence to other beliefs, so that the believer's total system of beliefs forms a highly or perhaps perfectly coherent system. Since, on such a characterization, truth depends entirely on the internal relations within the system of beliefs, such a conception of truth seems to lead at once to idealism as regards the nature of reality, and its main advocates have been proponents of absolute idealism (mainly Bradley, Bosanquet, and Brand Blanshard). A less explicitly metaphysical version of the coherence theory was also held by certain members of the school of logical positivism (mainly Otto Neurath and Carl Hempel).

The nature of the intended relation of coherence, often characterized metaphorically in terms of the beliefs in question fitting together or dovetailing with each other, has been and continues to be a matter of uncertainty and controversy. Despite occasional misconceptions to the contrary, it is clear that coherence is intended to be a substantially more demanding relation than mere consistency, involving such things as inferential and explanatory relations within the system of beliefs. Perfect or ideal coherence is sometimes described as requiring that every belief in the system of beliefs entails all the others (though it must be remembered that those offering such a characterization do not restrict entailments to those that are formal or analytic in character). Since actual human systems of belief seem inevitably to fall short of perfect coherence, however that is understood, their truth is usually held to be only approximate at best, thus leading to the absolute idealist view that truth admits of degrees.

As a view of the criterion of truth, the coherence theory of truth holds that the sole criterion or standard for determining whether a belief is true is its coherence with other beliefs or judgments, with the degree of justification varying with the degree of coherence. Such a view amounts to a coherence theory of epistemic justification. It was held by most of the proponents of the coherence theory of the nature of truth, though usually without distinguishing the two views very clearly.

For philosophers who hold both of these

views, the thesis that coherence is the sole criterion of truth is usually logically prior, and the coherence theory of the nature of truth is adopted as a consequence, the clearest argument being that only the view that perfect or ideal coherence is the nature of truth can make sense of the appeal to degrees of coherence as a criterion of truth.

See also COHERENTISM, IDEALISM, TRUTH.

L.B.

coherentism, in epistemology, a theory of the structure of knowledge or justified beliefs according to which all beliefs representing knowledge are known or justified in virtue of their relations to other beliefs, specifically, in virtue of belonging to a coherent system of beliefs. Assuming that the orthodox account of knowledge is correct at least in maintaining that justified true belief is necessary for knowledge, we can identify two kinds of coherence theories of knowledge: those that are coherentist merely in virtue of incorporating a coherence theory of justification, and those that are doubly coherentist because they account for both justification and truth in terms of coherence. What follows will focus on coherence theories of justification.

Historically, coherentism is the most significant alternative to foundationalism. The latter holds that some beliefs, basic or foundational beliefs, are justified apart from their relations to other beliefs, while all other beliefs derive their justification from that of foundational beliefs. Foundationalism portrays justification as having a structure like that of a building, with certain beliefs serving as the foundations and all other beliefs supported by them. Coherentism rejects this image and pictures justification as having the structure of a raft. Justified beliefs, like the planks that make up a raft, mutually support one another. This picture of the coherence theory is due to the positivist Otto Neurath. Among the positivists, Hempel shared Neurath's sympathy for coherentism. Other defenders of coherentism from the late nineteenth and early twentieth centuries were idealists, e.g., Bradley, Bosanquet, and Brand Blanshard. (Idealists often held the sort of double coherence theory mentioned above.)

The contrast between foundationalism and coherentism is commonly developed in terms of the regress argument. If we are asked what justifies one of our beliefs, we characteristically answer by citing some other belief that supports it, e.g., logically or probabilistically. If we are asked about this second belief, we are likely to cite a third belief, and so on. There are three shapes such an evidential chain might have: it could go on forever, if could eventually end in some belief, or it could loop back upon itself, i.e., eventually contain again a belief that had occurred "higher up" on the chain. Assuming that infinite chains are not really possible, we are left with a choice between chains that end and circular chains. According to foundationalists, evidential chains must eventually end with a foundational belief that is justified, if the belief at the beginning of the chain is to be justified. Coherentists are then portrayed as holding that circular chains can yield justified beliefs.

This portrayal is, in a way, correct. But it is also misleading since it suggests that the disagreement between coherentism and foundationalism is best understood as concerning only the structure of evidential chains. Talk of evidential chains in which beliefs that are further down on the chain are responsible for beliefs that are higher up naturally suggests the idea that just as real chains transfer forces, evidential chains transfer justification. Foundationalism then sounds like a real possibility. Foundational beliefs already have justification, and evidential chains serve to pass the justification along to other beliefs. But coherentism seems to be a nonstarter, for if no belief in the chain is justified to begin with, there is nothing to pass along. Altering the metaphor, we might say that coherentism seems about as likely to succeed as a bucket brigade that does not end at a well, but simply moves around in a circle.

The coherentist seeks to dispel this appearance by pointing out that the primary function of evidential chains is not to transfer epistemic status, such as justification, from belief to belief. Indeed, beliefs are not the primary locus of justification. Rather, it is whole systems of belief that are justified or not in the primary sense; individual beliefs are justified in virtue of their membership in an appropriately structured system of beliefs. Accordingly, what the coherentist claims is that the appropriate sorts of evidential chains, which will be circular – indeed, will likely contain numerous circles – constitute justified systems of belief. The individual beliefs within such a system are themselves justified in virtue of their place in the entire system and not because this status is passed on to them from beliefs further down some evidential chain in which they figure. One can, therefore, view coherentism with considerable accuracy as a version of foundationalism that holds all beliefs to be foundational. From this perspective, the difference between coherentism and traditional foundationalism has to do with what accounts for the epistemic status of foundational beliefs, with traditional foundationalism holding that such beliefs can be justified in various ways, e.g., by perception or reason, while coherentism insists that the only way such beliefs can be justified is by being a member of an appropriately structured system of beliefs.

One outstanding problem the coherentist faces is to specify exactly what constitutes a coherent system of beliefs. Coherence clearly must involve much more than mere absence of mutually contradictory beliefs. One way in which beliefs can be logically consistent is by concerning completely unrelated matters, but such a consistent system of beliefs would not embody the sort of mutual support that constitutes the core idea of coherentism. Moreover, one might question whether logical consistency is even necessary for coherence, e.g., on the basis of the preface paradox. Similar points can be made regarding efforts to begin an account of coherence with the idea that beliefs and degrees of belief must correspond to the probability calculus. So although it is difficult to avoid thinking that such formal features as logical and probabilistic consistency are significantly involved in coherence, it is not clear exactly how they are involved. An account of coherence can be drawn more directly from the following intuitive idea: a coherent system of belief is one in which each belief is epistemically supported by the others, where various types of epistemic support are recognized, e.g., deductive or inductive arguments, or inferences to the best explanation. There are, however, at least two problems this suggestion does not address. First, since very small sets of beliefs can be mutually supporting, the coherentist needs to say something about the scope a system of beliefs must have to exhibit the sort of coherence required for justification. Second, given the possibility of small sets of mutually supportive beliefs, it is apparently possible to build a system of very broad scope out of such small sets of mutually supportive beliefs by mere conjunction, i.e., without forging any significant support relations among them. Yet, since the interrelatedness of all truths does not seem discoverable by analyzing the concept of justification, the coherentist cannot rule out epistemically isolated subsystems of belief entirely. So the coherentist must say what sorts of isolated subsystems of belief are compatible with coherence.

The difficulties involved in specifying a more precise concept of coherence should not be pressed too vigorously against the coherentist. For one thing, most foundationalists have been forced to grant coherence a significant role within their accounts of justification, so no dialectical advantage can be gained by pressing them. Moreover, only a little reflection is needed to see that nearly all the difficulties involved in specifying coherence are manifestations within a specific context of quite general philosophical problems concerning such matters as induction, explanation, theory choice, the nature of epistemic support, etc. They are, then, problems that are faced by logicians, philosophers of science, and epistemologists quite generally, regardless of whether they are sympathetic to coherentism.

Coherentism faces a number of serious objections. Since according to coherentism justification is determined solely by the relations among beliefs, it does not seem to be capable of taking us outside the circle of our beliefs. This fact gives rise to complaints that coherentism cannot allow for any input from external reality, e.g., via perception, and that it can neither guarantee nor even claim that it is likely that coherent systems of belief will make contact with such reality or contain true beliefs. And while it is widely granted that justified false beliefs are possible, it is just as widely accepted that there is an important connection between justification and truth, a connection that rules out accounts according to which justification is not truth-conducive. These abstractly formulated complaints can be made more vivid, in the case of the former, by imagining a person with a coherent system of beliefs that becomes frozen, and fails to change in the face of ongoing sensory experience; and in the case of the latter, by pointing out that, barring an unexpected account of coherence, it seems that a wide variety of coherent systems of belief are possible, systems that are largely disjoint or even incompatible.

See also COHERENCE THEORY OF TRUTH, EPISTEMOLOGY, FOUNDATIONALISM, JUSTIFICATION.   M.R.D.

Coimbra commentaries. See FONSECA.

collective unconscious. See JUNG.

collectivity. See DISTRIBUTION.

Collier, Arthur (1680–1732), English philosopher, a Wiltshire parish priest whose *Clavis Universalis* (1713) defends a version of immaterialism closely akin to Berkeley's. Matter, Collier contends, "exists in, or in dependence on mind." He emphatically affirms the existence of bodies, and, like Berkeley, defends immaterialism as the only alternative to skepticism. Collier grants that bodies seem to be external, but their "quasi-externeity" is only the effect of God's will. In Part I of the *Clavis* Collier argues (as Berkeley had in his *New Theory of Vision*, 1709) that the visible world is not external. In Part II he argues (as Berkeley had in the *Principles*, 1710, and *Three Dialogues*, 1713) that the external world "is a being utterly impossible." Two of Collier's arguments for the "intrinsic repugnancy" of the external world resemble Kant's first and second antinomies. Collier argues, e.g., that the material world is both finite and infinite; the contradiction can be avoided, he suggests, only by denying its external existence.

Some scholars suspect that Collier deliberately concealed his debt to Berkeley; most accept his report that he arrived at his views ten years before he published them. Collier first refers to Berkeley in letters written in 1714–15. In *A Specimen of True Philosophy* (1730), where he offers an immaterialist interpretation of the opening verse of Genesis, Collier writes that "except a single passage or two" in Berkeley's *Dialogues*, there is no other book "which I ever heard of" on the same subject as the *Clavis*. This is a puzzling remark on several counts, one being that in the Preface to the *Dialogues*, Berkeley describes his earlier books. Collier's biographer reports seeing among his papers (now lost) an outline, dated 1708, on "the question of the visible world being without us or not," but he says no more about it. The biographer concludes that Collier's independence cannot reasonably be doubted; perhaps the outline would, if unearthed, establish this.

See also BERKELEY.   K.P.W.

colligation. See WHEWELL.

Collingwood, R(obin) G(eorge) (1889–1943), English philosopher and historian. His father, W. G. Collingwood, John Ruskin's friend, secretary, and biographer, at first educated him at home in Coniston and later sent him to Rugby School and then Oxford. Immediately upon graduating in 1912, he was elected to a fellowship at Pembroke College; except for service with admiralty intelligence during World War I, he remained at Oxford until 1941, when illness compelled him to retire. Although his *Autobiography* expresses strong disapproval of the lines on which, during his lifetime, philosophy at Oxford developed, he was a university "insider." In 1934 he was elected to the Waynflete Professorship, the first to become vacant after he had done enough work to be a serious candidate. He was also a leading archaeologist of Roman Britain.

Although as a student Collingwood was deeply influenced by the "realist" teaching of John Cook Wilson, he studied not only the British idealists, but also Hegel and the contemporary Italian post-Hegelians. At twenty-three, he published a translation of Croce's book on Vico's philosophy. *Religion and Philosophy* (1916), the first of his attempts to present orthodox Christianity as philosophically acceptable, has both idealist and Cook Wilsonian elements. Thereafter the Cook Wilsonian element steadily diminished. In *Speculum Mentis* (1924), he investigated the nature and ultimate unity of the four special 'forms of experience' – art, religion, natural science, and history – and their relation to a fifth comprehensive form – philosophy. While all four, he contended, are necessary to a full human life now, each is a form of error that is corrected by its less erroneous successor. Philosophy is error-free but has no content of its own: "The truth is not some perfect system of philosophy: it is simply the way in which all systems, however perfect, collapse into nothingness on the discovery that they are only systems." Some critics dismissed this enterprise as idealist (a description Collingwood accepted when he wrote), but even those who favored it were disturbed by the apparent skepticism of its result. A year later, he amplified his views about art in *Outlines of a Philosophy of Art*.

Since much of what Collingwood went on to write about philosophy has never been published, and some of it has been negligently destroyed, his thought after *Speculum Mentis* is hard to trace. It will not be definitively established until the more than 3,000 pages of his surviving unpublished manuscripts (deposited in the Bodleian Library in 1978) have been thoroughly studied. They were not available to the scholars who published studies of his philosophy as a whole up to 1990.

Three trends in how his philosophy developed, however, are discernible. The first is that as he continued to investigate the four special forms of experience, he came to consider each valid in its own right, and not a form of error. As early as 1928, he abandoned the conception of the historical past in *Speculum Mentis* as simply a spectacle, alien to the historian's mind; he now proposed a theory of it as thoughts explaining past actions that, although occurring in the past, can be rethought in the present. Not only can the identical thought "enacted" at a definite time in the past be "reenacted" any number of times after, but it can be known to be so reenacted if physical evidence survives that can be shown to be incompatible with other proposed reenactments. In 1933–34 he wrote a series of lectures (posthumously published as *The Idea of Nature*) in which he renounced his skepticism about whether the quantitative material world can be known, and inquired why the three constructive periods he recognized in European scientific thought, the Greek, the Renaissance, and the modern, could each advance our knowledge of it as they did. Finally, in 1937, returning to the philosophy of art and taking full account of Croce's later work, he showed that imagination expresses emotion and becomes false when it counterfeits emotion that is not felt; thus he transformed his earlier theory of art as purely imaginative. His later theories of art and of history remain alive; and his theory of nature, although corrected by research since his death, was an advance when published.

The second trend was that his conception of philosophy changed as his treatment of the special forms of experience became less skeptical. In his beautifully written *Essay on Philosophical Method* (1933), he argued that philosophy has an object – the *ens realissimum* as the one, the true, and the good – of which the objects of the special forms of experience are appearances; but that implies what he had ceased to believe, that the special forms of experience are forms of error. In his *Principles of Art* (1938) and *New Leviathan* (1942) he denounced the idealist principle of *Speculum Mentis* that to abstract is to falsify. Then, in his *Essay on Metaphysics* (1940), he denied that metaphysics is the science of being *qua* being, and identified it with the investigation of the "absolute presuppositions" of the special forms of experience at definite historical periods.

A third trend, which came to dominate his thought as World War II approached, was to see serious philosophy as practical, and so as having political implications. He had been, like Ruskin, a radical Tory, opposed less to liberal or even some socialist measures than to the bourgeois ethos from which they sprang. Recognizing European fascism as the barbarism it was, and detesting anti-Semitism, he advocated an anti-fascist foreign policy and intervention in the Spanish civil war in support of the republic. His last major publication, *The New Leviathan*, impressively defends what he called civilization against what he called barbarism; and although it was neglected by political theorists after the war was won, the collapse of Communism and the rise of Islamic states are winning it new readers.

See also CROCE, HEGEL, IDEALISM, PHILOSOPHY OF HISTORY, WILSON. A.D.

color realism. See QUALITIES.

combinatory logic, a branch of formal logic that deals with formal systems designed for the study of certain basic operations for constructing and manipulating functions as rules, i.e. as rules of calculation expressed by definitions.

The notion of a function was fundamental in the development of modern formal (or mathematical) logic that was initiated by Frege, Peano, Russell, Hilbert, and others. Frege was the first to introduce a generalization of the mathematical notion of a function to include propositional functions, and he used the general notion for formally representing logical notions such as those of a concept, object, relation, generality, and judgment. Frege's proposal to replace the traditional logical notions of subject and predicate by argument and function, and thus to conceive predication as functional application, marks a turning point in the history of formal logic. In most modern logical systems, the notation used to express functions, including propositional functions, is essentially that used in ordinary mathematics. As in ordinary mathematics, certain basic notions are taken for granted, such as the use of variables to indicate processes of substitution.

Like the original systems for modern formal logic, the systems of combinatory logic were designed to give a foundation for mathematics. But combinatory logic arose as an effort to carry the foundational aims further and deeper. It undertook an analysis of notions taken for granted in the original systems, in particular of the notions of substitution and of the use of variables. In this respect combinatory logic was conceived by one of its founders, H. B. Curry, to be concerned with the ultimate foundations and with notions that constitute a "prelogic." It was hoped that an analysis of this prelogic would disclose the true source of the difficulties connected with the logical paradoxes.

The operation of applying a function to one of its arguments, called *application,* is a primitive operation in all systems of combinatory logic. If f is a function and x a possible argument, then the result of the application operation is denoted (fx). In mathematics this is usually written $f(x)$, but the notation (fx) is more convenient in combinatory logic. The German logician M. Schönfinkel, who started combinatory logic in 1924, observed that it is not necessary to introduce functions of more than one variable, provided that the idea of a function is enlarged so that functions can be arguments as well as values of other functions. A function $F(x,y)$ is represented with the function f, which when applied to the argument x has, as a value, the function (fx), which, when applied to y, yields $F(x,y)$, i.e. $((fx)y) = F(x,y)$. It is therefore convenient to omit parentheses with association to the left so that $fx_1 \ldots x_n$ is used for $((\ldots (fx_1 \ldots) x_n)$. Schönfinkel's main result was to show how to make the class of functions studied closed under explicit definition by introducing two specific primitive functions, the *combinators* **S** and **K**, with the rules $\mathbf{K}xy = x$, and $\mathbf{S}xyz = xz(yz)$. (To illustrate the effect of **S** in ordinary mathematical notation, let f and g be functions of two and one arguments, respectively; then $\mathbf{S}fg$ is the function such that $\mathbf{S}fgx = f(x,g(x))$.) Generally, if $a(x_1, \ldots, x_n)$ is an expression built up from constants and the variables shown by means of the application operation, then there is a function F constructed out of constants (including the combinators **S** and **K**), such that $Fx_1 \ldots x_n = a(x_1, \ldots, x_n)$. This is essentially the meaning of the *combinatory completeness* of the theory of combinators in the terminology of H. B. Curry and R. Feys, *Combinatory Logic* (1958); and H. B. Curry, J. R. Hindley, and J. P. Seldin, *Combinatory Logic*, vol. II (1972).

The system of combinatory logic with **S** and **K** as the only primitive functions is the simplest equation calculus that is essentially undecidable. It is a type-free theory that allows the formation of the term ff, i.e. self-application, which has given rise to problems of interpretation. There are also type theories based on combinatory logic. The systems obtained by extending the theory of combinators with functions representing more familiar logical notions such as negation, implication, and generality, or by adding a device for expressing inclusion in logical categories, are studied in *illative combinatory logic*.

The theory of combinators exists in another, equivalent form, namely as the type-free λ-*calculus* created by Church in 1932. Like the theory of combinators, it was designed as a formalism for representing functions as rules of calculation, and it was originally part of a more general system of functions intended as a foundation for mathematics. The λ-calculus has application as a primitive operation, but instead of building up new functions from some primitive ones by application, new functions are here obtained by *functional abstraction*. If $a(x)$ is an expression built up by means of application from constants and the variable x, then $a(x)$ is considered to define a

function denoted $\lambda x.a\,(x)$, whose value for the argument b is $a(b)$, i.e. $(\lambda x.a\,(x))b = a(b)$. The function $\lambda x.a(x)$ is obtained from $a(x)$ by functional abstraction. The property of combinatory completeness or closure under explicit definition is postulated in the form of functional abstraction. The combinators can be defined using functional abstraction (i.e., $\mathbf{K} = \lambda x.\lambda y.x$ and $\mathbf{S} = \lambda x.\lambda y.\lambda z.xz(yz)$), and conversely, in the theory of combinators, functional abstraction can be defined. A detailed presentation of the λ-calculus is found in H. Barendregt, *The Lambda Calculus, Its Syntax and Semantics* (1981).

It is possible to represent the series of natural numbers by a sequence of closed terms in the λ-calculus. Certain expressions in the λ-calculus will then represent functions on the natural numbers, and these λ-*definable* functions are exactly the general recursive functions or the Turing computable functions. The equivalence of λ-definability and general recursiveness was one of the arguments used by Church for what is known as Church's thesis, i.e., the identification of the effectively computable functions and the recursive functions. The first problem about recursive undecidability was expressed by Church as a problem about expressions in the λ calculus.

The λ-calculus thus played a historically important role in the original development of recursion theory. Due to the emphasis in combinatory logic on the computational aspect of functions, it is natural that its method has been found useful in proof theory and in the development of systems of constructive mathematics. For the same reason it has found several applications in computer science in the construction and analysis of programming languages. The techniques of combinatory logic have also been applied in theoretical linguistics, e.g. in so-called Montague grammar.

In recent decades combinatory logic, like other domains of mathematical logic, has developed into a specialized branch of mathematics, in which the original philosophical and foundational aims and motives are of little and often no importance. One reason for this is the discovery of the new technical applications, which were not intended originally, and which have turned the interest toward several new mathematical problems. Thus, the original motives are often felt to be less urgent and only of historical significance. Another reason for the decline of the original philosophical and foundational aims may be a growing awareness in the philosophy of mathematics of the limitations of formal and mathematical methods as tools for conceptual clarification, as tools for reaching "ultimate foundations."

See also CHURCH'S THESIS, COMPUTABILITY, PROOF THEORY, RECURSIVE FUNCTION THEORY.   S.St.

command theory of law. See PHILOSOPHY OF LAW.

commentaries on Aristotle, the term commonly used for the Greek commentaries on Aristotle that take up about 15,000 pages in the Berlin *Commentaria in Aristotelem Graeca* (1882–1909), still the basic edition of them. Only in the 1980s did a project begin, under the editorship of Richard Sorabji, of King's College, London, to translate at least the most significant portions of them into English. They had remained the largest corpus of Greek philosophy not translated into any modern language.

Most of these works, especially the later, Neoplatonic ones, are much more than simple commentaries on Aristotle. They are also a mode of doing philosophy, the favored one at this stage of intellectual history. They are therefore important not only for the understanding of Aristotle, but also for both the study of the pre-Socratics and the Hellenistic philosophers, particularly the Stoics, of whom they preserve many fragments, and lastly for the study of Neoplatonism itself – and, in the case of John Philoponus, for studying the innovations he introduces in the process of trying to reconcile Platonism with Christianity.

The commentaries may be divided into three main groups.

(1) The first group of commentaries are those by Peripatetic scholars of the second to fourth centuries A.D., most notably Alexander of Aphrodisias (fl. c.200), but also the paraphraser Themistius (fl. c.360). We must not omit, however, to note Alexander's predecessor Aspasius, author of the earliest surviving commentary, one on the *Nicomachean Ethics* – a work not commented on again until the late Byzantine period. Commentaries by Alexander survive on the *Prior Analytics, Topics, Metaphysics* I–V, *On the Senses,* and *Meteorologics,* and his now lost ones on the *Categories, On the Soul,* and *Physics* had enormous influence in later times, particularly on Simplicius.

(2) By far the largest group is that of the Neoplatonists up to the sixth century A.D. Most important of the earlier commentators is Porphyry (232–c.309), of whom only a short commentary on the *Categories* survives, together with an introduction (*Isagoge*) to Aristotle's logical works, which provoked many commentaries

itself, and proved most influential in both the East and (through Boethius) in the Latin West. The reconciling of Plato and Aristotle is largely his work. His big commentary on the *Categories* was of great importance in later times, and many fragments are preserved in that of Simplicius. His follower Iamblichus was also influential, but his commentaries are likewise lost. The Athenian School of Syrianus (c.375–437) and Proclus (410–85) also commented on Aristotle, but all that survives is a commentary of Syrianus on Books III, IV, XIII, and XIV of the *Metaphysics.*

It is the early sixth century, however, that produces the bulk of our surviving commentaries, originating from the Alexandrian school of Ammonius, son of Hermeias (c.435–520), but composed both in Alexandria, by the Christian John Philoponus (c.490–575), and in (or at least *from*) Athens by Simplicius (writing after 532). Main commentaries of Philoponus are on *Categories, Prior Analytics, Posterior Analytics, On Generation and Corruption, On the Soul* I–II, and *Physics;* of Simplicius on *Categories, Physics, On the Heavens,* and (perhaps) *On the Soul.*

The tradition is carried on in Alexandria by Olympiodorus (c.495–565) and the Christians Elias (fl. c.540) and David (an Armenian, nicknamed the Invincible, fl. c.575), and finally by Stephanus, who was brought by the emperor to take the chair of philosophy in Constantinople in about 610. These scholars comment chiefly on the *Categories* and other introductory material, but Olympiodorus produced a commentary on the *Meteorologics.*

Characteristic of the Neoplatonists is a desire to reconcile Aristotle with Platonism (arguing, e.g., that Aristotle was not dismissing the Platonic theory of Forms), and to systematize his thought, thus reconciling him with himself. They are responding to a long tradition of criticism, during which difficulties were raised about incoherences and contradictions in Aristotle's thought, and they are concerned to solve these, drawing on their comprehensive knowledge of his writings. Only Philoponus, as a Christian, dares to criticize him, in particular on the eternity of the world, but also on the concept of infinity (on which he produces an ingenious argument, picked up, via the Arabs, by Bonaventure in the thirteenth century). The *Categories* proves a particularly fruitful battleground, and much of the later debate between realism and nominalism stems from arguments about the proper subject matter of that work.

The format of these commentaries is mostly that adopted by scholars ever since, that of taking one passage, or *lemma*, after another of the source work and discussing it from every angle, but there are variations. Sometimes the general subject matter is discussed first, and then details of the text are examined; alternatively, the *lemma* is taken in subdivisions without any such distinction. The commentary can also proceed explicitly by answering problems, or *aporiai*, which have been raised by previous authorities. Some commentaries, such as the short one of Porphyry on the *Categories*, and that of Iamblichus's pupil Dexippus on the same work, have a "catechetical" form, proceeding by question and answer. In some cases (as with Wittgenstein in modern times) the commentaries are simply transcriptions by pupils of the lectures of a teacher. This is the case, for example, with the surviving "commentaries" of Ammonius. One may also indulge in simple paraphrase, as does Themistius on *Posterior Analysis, Physics, On the Soul,* and *On the Heavens,* but even here a good deal of interpretation is involved, and his works remain interesting.

An important offshoot of all this activity in the Latin West is the figure of Boethius (c.480–524). It is he who first transmitted a knowledge of Aristotelian logic to the West, to become an integral part of medieval Scholasticism. He translated Porphyry's *Isagoge,* and the whole of Aristotle's logical works. He wrote a double commentary on the *Isagoge,* and commentaries on the *Categories* and *On Interpretation.* He is dependent ultimately on Porphyry, but more immediately, it would seem, on a source in the school of Proclus.

(3) The third major group of commentaries dates from the late Byzantine period, and seems mainly to emanate from a circle of scholars grouped around the princess Anna Comnena in the twelfth century. The most important figures here are Eustratius (c.1050–1120) and Michael of Ephesus (originally dated c.1040, but now fixed at c.1130). Michael in particular seems concerned to comment on areas of Aristotle's works that had hitherto escaped commentary. He therefore comments widely, for example, on the biological works, but also on the *Sophistical Refutations.* He and Eustratius, and perhaps others, seem to have cooperated also on a composite commentary on the *Nicomachean Ethics,* neglected since Aspasius. There is also evidence of lost commentaries on the *Politics* and the *Rhetoric.*

The composite commentary on the *Ethics* was translated into Latin in the next century, in England, by Robert Grosseteste, but earlier than this translations of the various logical commentaries

had been made by James of Venice (fl. c.1130), who may have even made the acquaintance of Michael of Ephesus in Constantinople. Later in that century other commentaries were being translated from Arabic versions by Gerard of Cremona (d.1187). The influence of the Greek commentary tradition in the West thus resumed after the long break since Boethius in the sixth century, but only now, it seems fair to say, is the full significance of this enormous body of work becoming properly appreciated.

See also ARISTOTLE, BOETHIUS, NEOPLATONISM, PORPHYRY. J.M.D.

commentaries on Plato, a term designating the works in the tradition of commentary (*hypomnema*) on Plato that may go back to the Old Academy (Crantor is attested by Proclus to have been the first to have "commented" on the *Timaeus*). More probably, the tradition arises in the first century B.C. in Alexandria, where we find Eudorus commenting, again, on the *Timaeus,* but possibly also (if the scholars who attribute to him the *Anonymous Theaetetus Commentary* are correct) on the *Theaetetus.* It seems also as if the Stoic Posidonius composed a commentary of some sort on the *Timaeus.* The commentary form (such as we can observe in the biblical commentaries of Philo of Alexandria) owes much to the Stoic tradition of commentary on Homer, as practiced by the second-century B.C. School of Pergamum. It was normal to select (usually consecutive) portions of text (*lemmata*) for general, and then detailed, comment, raising and answering "problems" (*aporiai*), refuting one's predecessors, and dealing with points of both doctrine and philology.

By the second century A.D. the tradition of Platonic commentary was firmly established. We have evidence of commentaries by the Middle Platonists Gaius, Albinus, Atticus, Numenius, and Cronius, mainly on the *Timaeus,* but also on at least parts of the *Republic,* as well as a work by Atticus's pupil Herpocration of Argos, in twenty-four books, on Plato's work as a whole. These works are all lost, but in the surviving works of Plutarch we find exegesis of parts of Plato's works, such as the creation of the soul in the *Timaeus* (35a–36d). The Latin commentary of Calcidius (fourth century A.D.) is also basically Middle Platonic.

In the Neoplatonic period (after Plotinus, who did not indulge in formal commentary, though many of his essays are in fact informal commentaries), we have evidence of much more comprehensive exegetic activity. Porphyry initiated the tradition with commentaries on the *Phaedo,*

Cratylus, Sophist, Philebus, Parmenides (of which the surviving anonymous fragment of commentary is probably a part), and the *Timaeus*. He also commented on the myth of Er in the *Republic*. It seems to have been Porphyry who is responsible for introducing the allegorical interpretation of the introductory portions of the dialogues, though it was only his follower Iamblichus (who also commented on all the above dialogues, as well as the *Alcibiades* and the *Phaedrus*) who introduced the principle that each dialogue should have only one central theme, or *skopos*. The tradition was carried on in the Athenian School by Syrianus and his pupils Hermeias (on the *Phaedrus* – surviving) and Proclus (*Alcibiades, Cratylus, Timaeus, Parmenides* – all surviving, at least in part), and continued in later times by Damascius (*Phaedo, Philebus, Parmenides*) and Olympiodorus (*Alcibiades, Phaedo, Gorgias* – also surviving, though sometimes only in the form of pupils' notes).

These commentaries are not now to be valued primarily as expositions of Plato's thought (though they do contain useful insights, and much valuable information); they are best regarded as original philosophical treatises presented in the mode of commentary, as is so much of later Greek philosophy, where it is not originality but rather faithfulness to an inspired master and a great tradition that is being striven for.

See also MIDDLE PLATONISM, NEOPLATONISM, PLATO.   J.M.D.

commission. See ACTION THEORY.

commissive. See SPEECH ACT THEORY.

common-consent arguments for the existence of God. See MARTINEAU.

common effects. See CAUSATION.

common good, a normative standard in Thomistic and Neo-Thomistic ethics for evaluating the justice of social, legal, and political arrangements, referring to those arrangements that promote the full flourishing of everyone in the community. Every good can be regarded as both a goal to be sought and, when achieved, a source of human fulfillment. A common good is any good sought by and/or enjoyed by two or more persons (as friendship is a good common to the friends); *the* common good is the good of a "perfect" (i.e., complete and politically organized) human community – a good that is the common goal of all who promote the justice of that community, as

well as the common source of fulfillment of all who share in those just arrangements.

'Common' is an analogical term referring to kinds and degrees of sharing ranging from mere similarity to a deep ontological communion. Thus, any good that is a genuine perfection of our common human nature is a common good, as opposed to merely idiosyncratic or illusory goods. But goods are common in a deeper sense when the degree of sharing is more than merely coincidental: two children engaged in parallel play enjoy a good in common, but they realize a common good more fully by engaging each other in one game; similarly, if each in a group watches the same good movie alone at home, they have enjoyed a good in common but they realize this good at a deeper level when they watch the movie together in a theater and discuss it afterward. In short, common good includes aggregates of private, individual goods but transcends these aggregates by the unique fulfillment afforded by mutuality, shared activity, and communion of persons.

As to the sources in Thomistic ethics for this emphasis on what is deeply shared over what merely coincides, the first is Aristotle's understanding of us as social and political animals: many aspects of human perfection, on this view, can be achieved only through shared activities in communities, especially the political community. The second is Christian Trinitarian theology, in which the single Godhead involves the mysterious communion of three divine "persons," the very exemplar of a common good; human personhood, by analogy, is similarly perfected only in a relationship of social communion.

The achievement of such intimately shared goods requires very complex and delicate arrangements of coordination to prevent the exploitation and injustice that plague shared endeavors. The establishment and maintenance of these social, legal, and political arrangements is "the" common good of a political society, because the enjoyment of all goods is so dependent upon the quality and the justice of those arrangements. The common good of the political community includes, but is not limited to, public goods: goods characterized by non-rivalry and non-excludability and which, therefore, must generally be provided by public institutions. By the principle of subsidiarity, the common good is best promoted by, in addition to the state, many lower-level non-public societies, associations, and individuals. Thus, religiously affiliated schools educating non-religious minority children might promote the common good without being public goods.

See also AQUINAS, JUSTICE, POLITICAL PHILOSOPHY, SOCIAL PHILOSOPHY, SUBSIDIARITY.
J.B.M.

common notions. See STOICISM.

common sense philosophy. See SCOTTISH COMMON SENSE PHILOSOPHY.

common sensibles. See ARISTOTLE, SENSUS COMMUNIS.

common sensism. See SCOTTISH COMMON SENSE PHILOSOPHY.

communication theory. See INFORMATION THEORY.

communism. See POLITICAL PHILOSOPHY.

communitarianism. See POLITICAL PHILOSOPHY.

commutative justice. See JUSTICE.

compactness. See DEDUCTION.

compactness theorem, a theorem for first-order logic: if every finite subset of a given infinite theory *T* is consistent, then the whole theory is consistent. The result is an immediate consequence of the completeness theorem, for if the theory were not consistent, a contradiction, say 'P and not-P', would be provable from it. But the proof, being a finitary object, would use only finitely many axioms from *T*, so this finite subset of *T* would be inconsistent.

This proof of the compactness theorem is very general, showing that any language that has a sound and complete system of inference, where each rule allows only finitely many premises, satisfies the theorem. This is important because the theorem immediately implies that many familiar mathematical notions are not expressible in the language in question, notions like those of a finite set or a well-ordering relation.

The compactness theorem is important for other reasons as well. It is the most frequently applied result in the study of first-order model theory and has inspired interesting developments within set theory and its foundations by generating a search for infinitary languages that obey some analog of the theorem.

See also INFINITARY LOGIC.
J.Ba.

compatibilism. See FREE WILL PROBLEM.

competence, linguistic. See PHILOSOPHY OF LANGUAGE.

complement. See RELATION.

complementarity. See PHILOSOPHY OF SCIENCE, QUANTUM MECHANICS.

complementary class, the class of all things not in a given class. For example, if *C* is the class of all red things, then its complementary class is the class containing everything that is not red. This latter class includes even non-colored things, like numbers and the class *C* itself. Often, the context will determine a less inclusive complementary class. If $B \subseteq A$, then the *complement of **B** with respect to **A*** is $A - B$. For example, if *A* is the class of physical objects, and *B* is the class of red physical objects, then the complement of *B* with respect to *A* is the class of non-red physical objects. **See also** SET THEORY.
P.Mad.

complementary term. See CONTRAPOSITION.

complementation. See NEGATION.

complete negation. See NECESSITY, PHILOSOPHY OF MIND.

completeness, a property that something – typically, a set of axioms, a logic, a theory, a set of well-formed formulas, a language, or a set of connectives – has when it is strong enough in some desirable respect.

(1) A set of axioms is *complete for the logic L* if every theorem of *L* is provable using those axioms.

(2) A logic *L* has *weak semantical completeness* if every valid sentence of the language of *L* is a theorem of *L*. *L* has *strong semantical completeness* (or is *deductively complete*) if for every set Γ of sentences, every logical consequence of Γ is deducible from Γ using *L*. A propositional logic *L* is *Halldén-complete* if whenever *A* ∨ *B* is a theorem of *L*, where *A* and *B* share no variables, either *A* or *B* is a theorem of *L*. And *L* is *Post-complete* if *L* is consistent but no stronger logic for the same language is consistent. Reference to the "completeness" of a logic, without further qualification, is almost invariably to either weak or strong semantical completeness. One curious exception: second-order logic is often said to be "incomplete," where what is meant is that it is not axiomatizable.

(3) A theory *T* is *negation-complete* (often simply *complete*) if for every sentence *A* of the lan-

guage of T, either A or its negation is provable in T. And T is *omega-complete* if whenever it is provable in T that a property ϕ holds of each natural number 0, 1, ... , it is also provable that every number has ϕ. (Generalizing on this, any set Γ of well-formed formulas might be called omega complete if $(v)A[v]$ is deducible from Γ whenever $A[t]$ is deducible from Γ for all terms t, where $A[t]$ is the result of replacing all free occurrences of v in $A[v]$ by t.)

(4) A language L is *expressively complete* if each of a given class of items is expressible in L. Usually, the class in question is the class of (two-valued) truth-functions. The propositional language whose sole connectives are $\sim$ and $\vee$ is thus said to be expressively (or *functionally*) complete, while that built up using $\vee$ alone is not, since classical negation is not expressible therein. Here one might also say that the set $\{\sim, \vee\}$ is expressively (or functionally) complete, while $\{\vee\}$ is not.

See also GÖDEL'S INCOMPLETENESS THEOREMS, SECOND-ORDER LOGIC, SHEFFER STROKE.   G.F.S.

completeness, combinatory. See COMBINATORY LOGIC.

completeness theorem. See SATISFIABLE.

complete symbol. See SYNCATEGOREMATA.

complexe significabile (plural: *complexe significabilia*), also called *complexum significabile*, in medieval philosophy, what is signified only by a *complexum* (a statement or declarative sentence), by a that-clause, or by a *dictum* (an accusative + infinitive construction, as in: 'I want him to go'). It is analogous to the modern proposition. The doctrine seems to have originated with Adam de Wodeham in the early fourteenth century, but is usually associated with Gregory of Rimini slightly later. *Complexe significabilia* do not fall under any of the Aristotelian categories, and so do not "exist" in the ordinary way. Still, they are somehow real. For before creation nothing existed except God, but even then God knew that the world was going to exist. The object of this knowledge cannot have been God himself (since God is necessary, but the world's existence is contingent), and yet did not "exist" before creation. Nevertheless, it was real enough to be an object of knowledge. Some authors who maintained such a view held that these entities were not only signifiable in a complex way by a statement, but were themselves complex in their inner structure; the term '*complexum significabile*' is unique to their theories. The theory of *complexe significabilia* was vehemently criticized by late medieval nominalists. See also ABSTRACT ENTITY, PROPOSITION.   P.V.S.

***complexum significabile*.** See COMPLEXE SIGNIFICABILE.

composition, fallacy of. See INFORMAL FALLACY.

compositional intention. See LEWIS, DAVID.

compositionality. See COGNITIVE SCIENCE, PHILOSOPHY OF LANGUAGE.

compossible, capable of existing or occurring together. E.g., two individuals are compossible provided the existence of one of them is compatible with the existence of the other. In terms of possible worlds, things are compossible provided there is some possible world to which all of them belong; otherwise they are incompossible. Not all possibilities are compossible. E.g., the extinction of life on earth by the year 3000 is possible; so is its continuation until the year 10,000; but since it is impossible that *both* of these things should happen, they are not compossible. Leibniz held that any non-actualized possibility must be incompossible with what is actual. See also PRINCIPLE OF PLENITUDE.
                                                    P.Mac.

comprehension, as applied to a term, the set of attributes implied by a term. The comprehension of 'square', e.g., includes being four-sided, having equal sides, and being a plane figure, among other attributes. The comprehension of a term is contrasted with its extension, which is the set of individuals to which the term applies. The distinction between the extension and the comprehension of a term was introduced in the *Port-Royal Logic* by Arnauld and Pierre Nicole in 1662. Current practice is to use the expression 'intension' rather than 'comprehension'. Both expressions, however, are inherently somewhat vague. See also AXIOM OF COMPREHENSION.
                                                    V.K.

comprehension, axiom of. See AXIOM OF COMPREHENSION.

comprehension, principle of. See SET THEORY.

comprehension schema. See SET-THEORETIC PARADOXES.

comprescence, an unanalyzable relation in terms of which Russell, in his later writings (especially in *Human Knowledge: Its Scope and Limits,* 1948), took concrete particular objects to be analyzable. Concrete particular objects are analyzable in terms of complexes of qualities all of whose members are *compresent.* Although this relation can be defined only ostensively, Russell states that it appears in psychology as "simultaneity in one experience" and in physics as "overlapping in space-time." *Complete complexes of compresence* are complexes of qualities having the following two properties: (1) all members of the complex are compresent; (2) given anything not a member of the complex, there is at least one member of the complex with which it is not compresent. He argues that there is strong empirical evidence that no two complete complexes have all their qualities in common. Finally, space-time point-instants are analyzed as complete complexes of compresence. Concrete particulars, on the other hand, are analyzed as series of *incomplete* complexes of compresence related by certain causal laws. **See also** BUNDLE THEORY, RUSSELL.

A.C.

computability, roughly, the possibility of computation on a Turing machine. The first convincing general definition, A. N. Turing's (1936), has been proved equivalent to the known plausible alternatives, so that the concept of computability is generally recognized as an absolute one. Turing's definition referred to computations by imaginary tape-processing machines that we now know to be capable of computing the same functions (whether simple sums and products or highly complex, esoteric functions) that modern digital computing machines could compute if provided with sufficient storage capacity. In the form 'Any function that is computable at all is computable on a Turing machine', this absoluteness claim is called *Turing's thesis.* A comparable claim for Alonzo Church's (1935) concept of λ-computability is called *Church's thesis.* Similar theses are enunciated for Markov algorithms, for S. C. Kleene's notion of general recursiveness, etc. It has been proved that the same functions are computable in all of these ways. There is no hope of proving any of those theses, for such a proof would require a definition of 'computable' – a definition that would simply be a further item in the list, the subject of a further thesis. But since computations of new kinds might be recognizable as genuine *in particular cases,* Turing's thesis and its equivalents, if false, might be decisively refuted by discovery of a particular function, a way of computing it, and a proof that no Turing machine can compute it.

The *halting problem* for (say) Turing machines is the problem of devising a Turing machine that computes the function $h(m, n) = 1$ or 0 depending on whether or not Turing machine number m ever halts, once started with the number n on its tape. This problem is unsolvable, for a machine that computed h could be modified to compute a function $g(n)$, which is undefined (the machine goes into an endless loop) when $h(n, n) = 1$, and otherwise agrees with $h(n, n)$. But this modified machine – Turing machine number k, say – would have contradictory properties: started with k on its tape, it would eventually halt if and only if it does not. Turing proved unsolvability of the *decision problem* for logic (the problem of devising a Turing machine that, applied to argument number n in logical notation, correctly classifies it as valid or invalid) by *reducing* the halting problem to the decision problem, i.e., showing how any solution to the latter could be used to solve the former problem, which we know to be unsolvable.

See also CHURCH'S THESIS, COMPUTER THEORY, TURING MACHINE.   R.J.

computability, algorithmic. See ALGORITHM.

computable. See EFFECTIVE PROCEDURE.

computational. See COMPUTER THEORY.

computational theories of mind. See COGNITIVE SCIENCE.

computer modeling. See COMPUTER THEORY.

computer program. See COMPUTER THEORY.

computer theory, the theory of the design, uses, powers, and limits of modern electronic digital computers. It has important bearings on philosophy, as may be seen from the many philosophical references herein.

Modern computers are a radically new kind of machine, for they are active physical realizations of formal languages of logic and arithmetic. Computers employ sophisticated languages, and they have reasoning powers many orders of magnitude greater than those of any prior machines. Because they are far superior to humans in many important tasks, they have produced a revolution in society that is as profound as the industrial revolution and is advancing much more rapidly. Furthermore, computers themselves are evolving rapidly.

When a computer is augmented with devices for sensing and acting, it becomes a powerful control system, or a robot. To understand the implications of computers for philosophy, one should imagine a robot that has basic goals and volitions built into it, including conflicting goals and competing desires. This concept first appeared in Karel Čapek's play *Rossum's Universal Robots* (1920), where the word 'robot' originated.

A computer has two aspects, *hardware* and *programming languages*. The theory of each is relevant to philosophy.

The software and hardware aspects of a computer are somewhat analogous to the human mind and body. This analogy is especially strong if we follow Peirce and consider all information processing in nature and in human organisms, not just the conscious use of language. Evolution has produced a succession of levels of sign usage and information processing: self-copying chemicals, self-reproducing cells, genetic programs directing the production of organic forms, chemical and neuronal signals in organisms, unconscious human information processing, ordinary languages, and technical languages. But each level evolved gradually from its predecessors, so that the line between body and mind is vague.

The hardware of a computer is typically organized into three general blocks: *memory, processor* (arithmetic unit and control), and various *input-output* devices for communication between machine and environment. The memory stores the *data* to be processed as well as the *program* that directs the processing. The processor has an *arithmetic-logic unit* for transforming data, and a *control* for executing the program. Memory, processor, and input-output communicate to each other through a fast switching system.

The memory and processor are constructed from registers, adders, switches, cables, and various other building blocks. These in turn are composed of electronic components: transistors, resistors, and wires. The input and output devices employ mechanical and electromechanical technologies as well as electronics. Some input-output devices also serve as auxiliary memories; floppy disks and magnetic tapes are examples. For theoretical purposes it is useful to imagine that the computer has an indefinitely expandable storage tape. So imagined, a computer is a physical realization of a Turing machine. The idea of an indefinitely expandable

memory is similar to the logician's concept of an axiomatic formal language that has an unlimited number of proofs and theorems.

The software of a modern electronic computer is written in a hierarchy of programming languages. The higher-level languages are designed for use by human programmers, operators, and maintenance personnel. The "machine language" is the basic hardware language, interpreted and executed by the control. Its words are sequences of binary digits or *bits*. Programs written in intermediate-level languages are used by the computer to translate the languages employed by human users into the machine language for execution.

A *programming language* has instructional means for carrying out three kinds of operations: data operations and transfers, transfers of control from one part of the program to the other, and program self-modification. Von Neumann designed the first modern programming language.

A programming language is general purpose, and an electronic computer that executes it can in principle carry out any algorithm or effective procedure, including the simulation of any other computer. Thus the modern electronic computer is a practical realization of the abstract concept of a universal Turing machine. What can actually be computed in practice depends, of course, on the state of computer technology and its resources.

It is common for computers at many different spatial locations to be interconnected into complex networks by telephone, radio, and satellite communication systems. Insofar as users in one part of the network can control other parts, either legitimately or illegitimately (e.g., by means of a "computer virus"), a global network of computers is really a global computer. Such vast computers greatly increase societal interdependence, a fact of importance for social philosophy.

The theory of computers has two branches, corresponding to the hardware and software aspects of computers.

The fundamental concept of hardware theory is that of a *finite automaton*, which may be expressed either as an idealized logical network of simple computer primitives, or as the corresponding temporal system of input, output, and internal states.

A finite automaton may be specified as a logical net of truth-functional switches and simple memory elements, connected to one another by idealized wires. These elements function synchronously, each wire being in a binary state (0 or 1) at each moment of time $t = 0, 1, 2, \ldots$. Each switching element (or "gate") executes a simple truth-functional operation (not, or, and, nor, not-and, etc.) and is imagined to operate instantaneously (compare the notions of sentential connective and truth table). A memory element (flip-flop, binary counter, unit delay line) preserves its input bit for one or more time-steps.

A well-formed net of switches and memory elements may not have cycles through switches only, but it typically has feedback cycles through memory elements. The wires of a logical net are of three kinds: input, internal, and output. Correspondingly, at each moment of time a logical net has an input state, an internal state, and an output state. A logical net or automaton need not have any input wires, in which case it is a closed system.

The complete history of a logical net is described by a deterministic law: at each moment of time t, the input and internal states of the net determine its output state and its next internal state. This leads to the second definition of 'finite automaton': it is a deterministic finite-state system characterized by two tables. The transition table gives the next internal state produced by each pair of input and internal states. The output table gives the output state produced by each input state and internal state.

The state analysis approach to computer hardware is of practical value only for systems with a few elements (e.g., a binary-coded decimal counter), because the number of states increases as a *power* of the number of elements. Such a rapid rate of increase of complexity with size is called the combinatorial explosion, and it applies to many discrete systems. However, the state approach to finite automata does yield abstract models of law-governed systems that are of interest to logic and philosophy. A correctly operating digital computer is a finite automaton. Alan Turing defined the finite part of what we now call a Turing machine in terms of states. It seems doubtful that a human organism has more computing power than a finite automaton.

A closed finite automaton illustrates Nietzsche's law of eternal return. Since a finite automaton has a finite number of internal states, at least one of its internal states must occur infinitely many times in any infinite state history. And since a closed finite automaton is deterministic and has no inputs, a repeated state must be followed by the same sequence of states each time it occurs. Hence the history of a closed finite automaton is periodic, as in the law of eternal return.

Idealized neurons are sometimes used as the primitive elements of logical nets, and it is plausible that for any brain and central nervous system there is a logical network that behaves the same and performs the same functions. This shows the close relation of finite automata to the brain and central nervous system. The switches and memory elements of a finite automaton may be made probabilistic, yielding a *probabilistic automaton*. These automata are models of indeterministic systems.

Von Neumann showed how to extend deterministic logical nets to systems that contain self-reproducing automata. This is a very basic logical design relevant to the nature of life.

The part of computer programming theory most relevant to philosophy contains the answer to Leibniz's conjecture concerning his *characteristica universalis* and calculus ratiocinator. He held that "all our reasoning is nothing but the joining and substitution of characters, whether these characters be words or symbols or pictures." He thought therefore that one could construct a universal, arithmetic language with two properties of great philosophical importance. First, every atomic concept would be represented by a prime number. Second, the truth-value of any logically true-or-false statement expressed in the *characteristica universalis* could be calculated arithmetically, and so any rational dispute could be resolved by calculation. Leibniz expected to do the computation by hand with the help of a calculating machine; today we would do it on an electronic computer. However, we know now that Leibniz's proposed language cannot exist, for no computer (or computer program) can calculate the truth-value of every logically true-or-false statement given to it. This fact follows from a logical theorem about the limits of what computer programs can do. Let E be a modern electronic computer with an indefinitely expandable memory, so that E has the power of a universal Turing machine. And let L be any formal language in which every arithmetic statement can be expressed, and which is consistent. Leibniz's proposed *characteristica universalis* would be such a language. Now a computer that is operating correctly is an active formal language, carrying out the instructions of its program deductively. Accordingly, Gödel's incompleteness theorems for formal arithmetic apply to computer E. It follows from these theorems that no program can enable computer E to decide of an arbitrary statement of *L* whether or not that statement is true. More strongly, there cannot even be a program that will enable *E* to enumerate the truths of language *L* one after another. Therefore Leibniz's *characteristica universalis* cannot exist.

Electronic computers are the first active or "live" mathematical systems. They are the latest addition to a long historical series of mathematical tools for inquiry: geometry, algebra, calculus and differential equations, probability and statistics, and modern mathematics.

The most effective use of computer programs is to instruct computers in tasks for which they are superior to humans. Computers are being designed and programmed to cooperate with humans so that the calculation, storage, and judgment capabilities of the two are synthesized. The powers of such *human–computer combines* will increase at an exponential rate as computers continue to become faster, more powerful, and easier to use, while at the same time becoming smaller and cheaper. The social implications of this are very important.

The modern electronic computer is a new tool for the logic of discovery (Peirce's abduction). An inquirer (or inquirers) operating a computer interactively can use it as a *universal simulator*, dynamically modeling systems that are too complex to study by traditional mathematical methods, including non-linear systems. Simulation is used to explain known empirical results, and also to develop new hypotheses to be tested by observation. Computer models and simulations are unique in several ways: complexity, dynamism, controllability, and visual presentability. These properties make them important new tools for modeling and thereby relevant to some important philosophical problems.

A human–computer combine is especially suited for the study of complex holistic and hierarchical systems with feedback (cf. cybernetics), including adaptive goal-directed systems. A hierarchical-feedback system is a dynamic structure organized into several levels, with the compounds of one level being the atoms or building blocks of the next higher level, and with cyclic paths of influence operating both on and between levels. For example, a complex human institution has several levels, and the people in it are themselves hierarchical organizations of self-copying chemicals, cells, organs, and such systems as the pulmonary and the central nervous system.

The behaviors of these systems are in general much more complex than, e.g., the behaviors of traditional systems of mechanics. Contrast an organism, society, or ecology with our planetary system as characterized by Kepler and Newton. Simple formulas (ellipses) describe the orbits of the planets. More basically, the planetary system is stable in the sense that a small perturbation of it produces a relatively small variation in its subsequent history. In contrast, a small change in the state of a holistic hierarchical feedback system often amplifies into a very large difference in behavior, a concern of *chaos theory*. For this reason it is helpful to model such systems on a computer and run sample histories. The operator searches for representative cases, interesting phenomena, and general principles of operation.

The human–computer method of inquiry should be a useful tool for the study of biological evolution, the actual historical development of complex adaptive goal-directed systems. Evolution is a logical and communication process as well as a physical and chemical process. But evolution is statistical rather than deterministic, because a single temporal state of the system results in a probabilistic distribution of histories, rather than in a single history. The genetic operators of mutation and crossover, e.g., are probabilistic operators. But though it is stochastic, evolution cannot be understood in terms of limiting relative frequencies, for the important developments are the repeated emergence of new phenomena, and there may be no evolutionary convergence toward a final state or limit. Rather, to understand evolution the investigator must simulate the statistical spectra of histories covering critical stages of the process.

Many important evolutionary phenomena should be studied by using simulation along with observation and experiment. Evolution has produced a succession of levels of organization: self-copying chemicals, self-reproducing cells, communities of cells, simple organisms, haploid sexual reproduction, diploid sexuality with genetic dominance and recessiveness, organisms composed of organs, societies of organisms, humans, and societies of humans. Most of these systems are complex hierarchical feedback systems, and it is of interest to understand how they emerged from earlier systems. Also, the interaction of competition and cooperation at all stages of evolution is an important subject, of relevance to social philosophy and ethics.

Some basic epistemological and metaphysical concepts enter into computer modeling. A *model* is a well-developed concept of its object, representing characteristics like structure and function. A model is similar to its object in important respects, but simpler; in mathematical terminology, a model is homomorphic to its object but not isomorphic to it. However, it is often useful to think of a model as isomorphic to an *embedded subsystem* of the system it models. For example, a gas is a complicated system of microstates of particles, but these microstates can be grouped into macrostates, each with a pressure, volume, and temperature satisfying the gas law $PV = kT$. The derivation of this law from the detailed mechanics of the gas is a *reduction* of the embedded subsystem to the underlying system. In many cases it is adequate to work with the simpler embedded subsystem, but in other cases one must work with the more complex but complete *underlying system*.

The law of an embedded subsystem may be different in kind from the law of the underlying system. Consider, e.g., a machine tossing a coin randomly. The sequence of tosses obeys a simple probability law, while the complex underlying mechanical system is deterministic. The random sequence of tosses is a probabilistic system embedded in a deterministic system, and a mathematical account of this embedding relation constitutes a reduction of the probabilistic system to a deterministic system. Compare the compatibilist's claim that free choice can be embedded in a deterministic system. Compare also a *pseudo-random* sequence, which is a deterministic sequence with adequate randomness for a given (finite) simulation. Note finally that the probabilistic system of quantum mechanics underlies the deterministic system of mechanics.

The ways in which models are used by goal-directed systems to solve problems and adapt to their environments are currently being modeled by human–computer combines. Since computer software can be converted into hardware, successful simulations of adaptive uses of models could be incorporated into the design of a robot. Human intentionality involves the use of a model of oneself in relation to others and the environment. A problem-solving robot using such a model would constitute an important step toward a robot with full human powers.

These considerations lead to the central thesis of the *philosophy of logical mechanism:* a finite deterministic automaton can perform all human functions. This seems plausible in principle (and is treated in detail in Merrilee Salmon, ed., *The Philosophy of Logical Mechanism: Essays in Honor of Arthur W. Burks*, 1990). A digital computer has reasoning and memory powers. Robots have sensory inputs for collecting information from the environment, and they have moving and acting devices. To obtain a robot with human powers, one would need to put these abilities under the direction of a system of desires, purposes, and goals. Logical mechanism is a form of mechanism or materialism, but differs from traditional forms of these doctrines in its reliance on the logical powers of computers and the logical nature of evolution and its products. The modern computer is a kind of complex hierarchical physical system, a system with memory, processor, and control that employs a hierarchy of programming languages. Humans are complex hierarchical systems designed by evolution – with structural levels of chemicals, cells, organs, and systems (e.g., circulatory, neural, immune) and linguistic levels of genes, enzymes, neural signals, and immune recognition. Traditional materialists did not have this model of a computer nor the contemporary understanding of evolution, and never gave an adequate account of logic and reasoning and such phenomena as goal-directedness and self-modeling.

See also ARTIFICIAL INTELLIGENCE, CYBERNETICS, DETERMINISM, GÖDEL'S INCOMPLETENESS THEOREMS, SELF-REPRODUCING AUTOMATON, TURING MACHINE. A.W.B.

Comte, Auguste (1798–1857), French philosopher and sociologist, the founder of positivism. He was educated in Paris at l'École Polytechnique, where he briefly taught mathematics. He suffered from a mental illness that occasionally interrupted his work.

In conformity with empiricism, Comte held that knowledge of the world arises from observation. He went beyond many empiricists, however, in denying the possibility of knowledge of unobservable physical objects. He conceived of positivism as a method of study based on observation and restricted to the observable. He applied positivism chiefly to science. He claimed that the goal of science is prediction, to be accomplished using laws of succession. Explanation insofar as attainable has the same structure as prediction. It subsumes events under laws of succession; it is not causal. Influenced by Kant, he held that the causes of phenomena and the nature of things-in-themselves are not knowable. He criticized metaphysics for ungrounded speculation about such matters; he accused it of not keeping imagination subordinate to observation. He advanced positivism for all the sciences but held that each science has additional special methods, and has laws not derivable by human intelligence from laws of other sciences. He corresponded extensively with J. S. Mill, who encouraged his work and discussed it in *Auguste Comte and Positivism* (1865). Twentieth-century logical positivism was inspired by Comte's ideas.

Comte was a founder of sociology, which he also called social physics. He divided the science into two branches – statics and dynamics dealing respectively with social organization and social development. He advocated a historical method of study for both branches. As a law of social development, he proposed that all societies pass through three intellectual stages, first interpreting phenomena theologically, then metaphysically, and finally positivistically. The general idea that societies develop according to laws of nature was adopted by Marx.

Comte's most important work is his six-volume *Cours de philosophie positive* (*Course in Positive Philosophy*, 1830–42). It is an encyclopedic treatment of the sciences that expounds positivism and culminates in the introduction of sociology. **See also** EMPIRICISM, LOGICAL POSITIVISM.

P.We.

conative. See VOLITION.

conceivability, capability of being conceived or imagined. Thus, golden mountains are conceivable; round squares, inconceivable. As Descartes pointed out, the sort of imaginability required is not the ability to form mental images. Chiliagons, Cartesian minds, and God are all conceivable, though none of these can be pictured "in the mind's eye." Historical references include Anselm's definition of God as "a being than which none greater can be conceived" and Descartes's argument for dualism from the conceivability of disembodied existence. Several of Hume's arguments rest upon the maxim that whatever is conceivable is possible. He argued, e.g., that an event can occur without a cause, since this is conceivable, and his critique of induction relies on the inference from the conceivability of a change in the course of nature to its possibility. In response, Reid maintained that to conceive is merely to understand the meaning of a proposition. Reid argued that impossibilities are conceivable, since we must be able to understand falsehoods. Many simply equate conceivability with possibility, so that to say something is conceivable (or inconceivable) just is to say that it is possible (or impossible). Such usage is controversial, since conceivability is broadly an epistemological notion concerning what can be thought, whereas possibility is a metaphysical notion concerning how things can be.

The same controversy can arise regarding the compossible, or co-possible, where two states of affairs are compossible provided it is possible that they both obtain, and two propositions are compossible provided their conjunction is possible. Alternatively, two things are compossible if and only if there is a possible world containing both. Leibniz held that two things are compossible provided they can be ascribed to the same possible world without contradiction. "There are many possible universes, each collection of compossibles making one of them." Others have argued that non-contradiction is sufficient for neither possibility nor compossibility.

The claim that something is inconceivable is usually meant to suggest more than merely an inability to conceive. It is to say that trying to conceive results in a phenomenally distinctive mental repugnance, e.g. when one attempts to conceive of an object that is red and green all over at once. On this usage the inconceivable might be equated with what one can "just see" to be impossible. There are two related usages of 'conceivable': (1) not inconceivable in the sense just described; and (2) such that one can "just see" that the thing in question is possible. Goldbach's conjecture would seem a clear example of something conceivable in the first sense, but not the second. **See also** LEIBNIZ, NECESSITY, POSSIBLE WORLDS.

P.Ti.

concept. See CONCEPTUALISM.

concept, denoting. See RUSSELL.

concept, theoretical. See THEORETICAL TERM.

conceptual analysis. See ANALYSIS.

conceptual immediacy. See IMMEDIACY.

conceptualism, the view that there are no universals and that the supposed classificatory function of universals is actually served by particular *concepts* in the mind. A universal is a property that can be instantiated by more than one individual thing (or particular) at the same time; e.g., the shape of this page, if identical with the shape of the next page, will be one property instantiated by two distinct individual things at the same time. If viewed as located where the pages are, then it would be *immanent*. If viewed as not having spatiotemporal location itself, but only bearing a connection, usually called *instantiation* or *exemplification*, to things that have such location, then the shape of this page would be *transcendent* and presumably would exist even if exemplified by nothing, as Plato seems to have held. The conceptualist rejects both views by holding that universals are merely concepts. Most generally, a concept may be understood as a principle of classification, something that can guide us in determining whether an entity belongs in a given class or does not. Of course, properties understood as universals satisfy, trivially, this definition and thus may be called concepts, as indeed they were by Frege. But the conceptualistic substantive views of concepts are that concepts are (1) *mental representations*, often called *ideas*, serving their classificatory function presumably by resembling the entities to be classified; or (2) brain states that serve the same function but presumably not by resemblance; or (3) general words (adjectives, common nouns, verbs) or uses of such words, an entity's belonging to a certain class being determined by the applicability to the entity of the appropriate word; or (4) abilities to classify correctly, whether or not with the aid of an item belonging under (1), (2), or (3). The traditional conceptualist holds (1). Defenders of (3) would be more properly called nominalists. In whichever way concepts are understood, and regardless of whether conceptualism is true, they are obviously essential to our understanding and knowledge of anything, even at the most basic level of cognition, namely, recognition. The classic work on the topic is *Thinking and Experience* (1954) by H. H. Price, who held (4). **See also** METAPHYSICS, PLATO, PROPERTY.   P.Bu.

conceptual polarity. See POLARITY.

conceptual priority. See DEPENDENCE.

conceptual role semantics. See MEANING, PHILOSOPHY OF MIND.

conceptual role theory of meaning. See MEANING.

conceptual truth. See ANALYTIC–SYNTHETIC DISTINCTION.

conciliarism. See GERSON.

concilience. See WHEWELL.

conclusive evidence. See EVIDENCE.

conclusive justification. See JUSTIFICATION.

concomitant variation, method of. See MILL'S METHODS.

concrescence. See WHITEHEAD.

concrete universal. See HEGEL.

concretion, principle of. See WHITEHEAD.

concretism. See REISM.

concurrent cause. See CAUSATION.

concursus dei, God's concurrence. The notion derives from a theory from medieval philosophical theology, according to which any case of causation involving created substances requires both the exercise of genuine causal powers inherent in creatures and the exercise of God's causal activity. In particular, a person's actions are the result of the person's causal powers, often including the powers of deliberation and choice, and God's causal endorsement. Divine concurrence maintains that the nature of God's activity is more determinate than simply conserving the created world in existence. Although divine concurrence agrees with occasionalism in holding God's power to be necessary for any event to occur, it diverges from occasionalism insofar as it regards creatures as causally active. **See also** OCCASIONALISM.   W.E.M.

Condillac, Étienne Bonnot de (1714–80), French philosopher, an empiricist who was considered the great analytical mind of his generation. Close to Rousseau and Diderot, he stayed within the church. He is closely (perhaps excessively) identified with the image of the statue that, in the *Traité des sensations* (*Treatise on Sense Perception*, 1754), he endows with the five senses to explain how perceptions are assimilated and produce understanding (cf. also his *Treatise on the Origins of Human Knowledge*, 1746). He maintains a critical distance from precursors: he adopts Locke's *tabula rasa* but from his first work to *Logique* (*Logic*, 1780) insists on the creative role of the mind as it analyzes and compares sense impressions. His *Traité des animaux* (*Treatise on Animals*, 1755), which includes a proof of the existence of God, considers sensate creatures rather than Descartes's *animaux machines* and sees God only as a final cause. He reshapes Leibniz's monads in the *Monadologie* (*Monadology*, 1748, rediscovered in 1980). In the *Langue des calculs* (*Language of Numbers*, 1798) he proposes mathematics as a model of clear analysis.

The origin of language and creation of symbols eventually became his major concern. His break with metaphysics in the *Traité des systèmes* (*Trea-*

tise on Systems, 1749) has been overemphasized, but Condillac does replace rational constructs with sense experience and reflection. His empiricism has been mistaken for materialism, his clear analysis for simplicity. The "ideologues," Destutt de Tracy and Laromiguière, found Locke in his writings. Jefferson admired him. Maine de Biran, while critical, was indebted to him for concepts of perception and the self; Cousin disliked him; Saussure saw him as a forerunner in the study of the origins of language.

See also LEIBNIZ, LOCKE, SENSATIONALISM.
O.A.H.

condition, a state of affairs or "way things are," most commonly referred to in relation to something that implies or is implied by it. Let *p, q,* and *r* be schematic letters for declarative sentences; and let *P, Q,* and *R* be corresponding nominalizations; e.g., if *p* is 'snow is white', then *P* would be 'snow's being white'. *P* can be a necessary or sufficient condition of *Q* in any of several senses. In the weakest sense *P* is a sufficient condition of *Q* iff (if and only if): if *p* then *q* (or if *P* is actual then *Q* is actual) – where the conditional is to be read as "material," as amounting merely to not-(*p &* not-*q*). At the same time *Q* is a necessary condition of *P* iff: if not-*q* then not-*p*. It follows that *P* is a sufficient condition of *Q* iff *Q* is a necessary condition of *P*. Stronger senses of sufficiency and of necessity are definable, in terms of this basic sense, as follows: *P* is *nomologically sufficient* (necessary) for *Q* iff it follows from the laws of nature, but not without them, that if *p* then *q* (that if *q* then *p*). *P* is *alethically or metaphysically* sufficient (necessary) for *Q* iff it is alethically or metaphysically necessary that if *p* then *q* (that if *q* then *p*). However, it is perhaps most common of all to interpret conditions in terms of subjunctive conditionals, in such a way that *P* is a sufficient condition of *Q* iff *P* would not occur unless *Q* occurred, or: if *P* should occur, *Q* would; and *P* is a necessary condition of *Q* iff *Q* would not occur unless *P* occurred, or: if *Q* should occur, *P* would. See also CAUSATION, PROPERTY, STATE OF AFFAIRS.   E.S.

conditional, a compound sentence, such as 'if Abe calls, then Ben answers,' in which one sentence, the antecedent, is connected to a second, the consequent, by the connective 'if ... then'. Propositions (statements, etc.) expressed by conditionals are called *conditional propositions (statements,* etc.) and, by ellipsis, simply *conditionals.* The ambiguity of the expression 'if ... then' gives rise to a semantic classification of condi-

tionals into material conditionals, causal conditionals, counterfactual conditionals, and so on. In traditional logic, conditionals are called hypotheticals, and in some areas of mathematical logic conditionals are called implications. Faithful analysis of the meanings of conditionals continues to be investigated and intensely disputed. **See also** CORRESPONDING CONDITIONAL, COUNTERFACTUALS, IMPLICATION, PROPOSITION, TRUTH TABLE.   J.Cor.

conditional, material. See COUNTERFACTUALS, IMPLICATION.

conditional, strict. See COUNTERFACTUALS, IMPLICATION.

conditional probability. See PROBABILITY.

conditional proof. (1) The argument form '*B* follows from *A;* therefore, if *A* then *B*' and arguments of this form. (2) The rule of inference that permits one to infer a conditional given a derivation of its consequent from its antecedent. This is also known as the *rule of conditional proof* or ⊃-*introduction.*   G.F.S.

conditional proposition. See CONDITIONAL, CONVERSE, COUNTERFACTUALS.

conditioning, a form of associative learning that occurs when changes in thought or behavior are produced by temporal relations among events. It is common to distinguish between two types of conditioning; one, *classical* or Pavlovian, in which behavior change results from events that occur before behavior; the other, *operant* or instrumental, in which behavior change occurs because of events after behavior. Roughly, classically and operantly conditioned behavior correspond to the everyday, folk-psychological distinction between involuntary and voluntary or goal-directed behavior. In classical conditioning, stimuli or events elicit a response (e.g., salivation); neutral stimuli (e.g., a dinner bell) gain control over behavior when paired with stimuli that already elicit behavior (e.g., the appearance of dinner). The behavior is involuntary. In operant conditioning, stimuli or events reinforce behavior after behavior occurs; neutral stimuli gain power to reinforce by being paired with actual reinforcers. Here, occasions in which behavior is reinforced serve as discriminative stimuli-evoking behavior. Operant behavior is goal-directed, if not consciously or deliberately, then through the bond between behavior and reinforcement.

Thus, the arrangement of condiments at dinner may serve as the discriminative stimulus evoking the request "Please pass the salt," whereas saying "Thank you" may reinforce the behavior of passing the salt.

It is not easy to integrate conditioning phenomena into a unified theory of conditioning. Some theorists contend that operant conditioning is really classical conditioning veiled by subtle temporal relations among events. Other theorists contend that operant conditioning requires mental representations of reinforcers and discriminative stimuli. B. F. Skinner (1904–90) argued in *Walden Two* (1948) that astute, benevolent behavioral engineers can and should use conditioning to create a social utopia.

See also REDINTEGRATION. G.A.G.

conditio sine qua non (Latin, 'a condition without which not'), a necessary condition; something without which something else could not be or could not occur. For example, being a plane figure is a *conditio sine qua non* for being a triangle. Sometimes the phrase is used emphatically as a synonym for an unconditioned presupposition, be it for an action to start or an argument to get going. I.Bo.

Condorcet, Marquis de, title of Marie-Jean-Antoine-Nicolas de Caritat (1743–94), French philosopher and political theorist who contributed to the *Encyclopedia* and pioneered the mathematical analysis of social institutions. Although prominent in the Revolutionary government, he was denounced for his political views and died in prison.

Condorcet discovered the voting paradox, which shows that majoritarian voting can produce cyclical group preferences. Suppose, for instance, that voters A, B, and C rank proposals x, y, and z as follows: A: xyz, B: yzx, and C: zxy. Then in majoritarian voting x beats y and y beats z, but z in turn beats x. So the resulting group preferences are cyclical. The discovery of this problem helped initiate social choice theory, which evaluates voting systems. Condorcet argued that any satisfactory voting system must guarantee selection of a proposal that beats all rivals in majoritarian competition. Such a proposal is called a *Condorcet winner*. His *jury theorem* says that if voters register their opinions about some matter, such as whether a defendant is guilty, and the probabilities that individual voters are right are greater than ½, equal, and independent, then the majority vote is more likely to be correct than any individual's or minority's vote.

Condorcet's main works are *Essai sur l'application de l'analyse à la probabilité des décisions rendues à la pluralité des voix* (*Essay on the Application of Analysis to the Probability of Decisions Reached by a Majority of Votes*, 1785); and a posthumous treatise on social issues, *Esquisse d'un tableau historique des progrès de l'esprit humain* (*Sketch for a Historical Picture of the Progress of the Human Mind*, 1795).

See also PROBABILITY, SOCIAL CHOICE THEORY, VOTING PARADOX. P.We.

Condorcet winner. See CONDORCET.

confirmation, an evidential relation between evidence and any statement (especially a scientific hypothesis) that this evidence supports. It is essential to distinguish two distinct, and fundamentally different, meanings of the term: (1) the *incremental* sense, in which a piece of evidence contributes at least some degree of support to the hypothesis in question – e.g., finding a fingerprint of the suspect at the scene of the crime lends some weight to the hypothesis that the suspect is guilty; and (2) the *absolute* sense, in which a body of evidence provides strong support for the hypothesis in question – e.g., a case presented by a prosecutor making it practically certain that the suspect is guilty. If one thinks of confirmation in terms of probability, then evidence that *increases* the probability of a hypothesis confirms it incrementally, whereas evidence that renders a hypothesis *highly probable* confirms it absolutely.

In each of the two foregoing senses one can distinguish three types of confirmation: (i) *qualitative*, (ii) *quantitative*, and (iii) *comparative*. (i) Both examples in the preceding paragraph illustrate qualitative confirmation, for no numerical values of the degree of confirmation were mentioned. (ii) If a gambler, upon learning that an opponent holds a certain card, asserts that her chance of winning has increased from $2/3$ to $3/4$, the claim is an instance of quantitative incremental confirmation. If a physician states that, on the basis of an X-ray, the probability that the patient has tuberculosis is .95, that claim exemplifies quantitative absolute confirmation. In the incremental sense, any case of quantitative confirmation involves a *difference* between two probability values; in the absolute sense, any case of quantitative confirmation involves *only one* probability value. (iii) Comparative confirmation in the incremental sense would be illustrated if an investigator said that possession of the murder weapon weighs more heavily against the suspect than does the fingerprint found at the scene of the crime. Comparative confirmation in the absolute sense would occur if a prosecutor claimed to have strong cases against two suspects thought to be involved in a crime, but that the case against one is stronger than that against the other.

Even given recognition of the foregoing six varieties of confirmation, there is still considerable controversy regarding its analysis. Some authors claim that quantitative confirmation does not exist; only qualitative and/or comparative confirmation are possible. Some authors maintain that confirmation has nothing to do with probability, whereas others – known as Bayesians – analyze confirmation explicitly in terms of Bayes's theorem in the mathematical calculus of probability. Among those who offer probabilistic analyses there are differences as to which interpretation of probability is suitable in this context. Popper advocates a concept of corroboration that differs fundamentally from confirmation.

Many (real or apparent) paradoxes of confirmation have been posed; the most famous is the *paradox of the ravens*. It is plausible to suppose that 'All ravens are black' can be incrementally confirmed by the observation of one of its instances, namely, a black crow. However, 'All ravens are black' is logically equivalent to 'All non-black things are non-ravens.' By parity of reasoning, an instance of this statement, namely, any non-black non-raven (e.g., a white shoe), should incrementally confirm it. Moreover, the *equivalence condition* – whatever confirms a hypothesis must equally confirm any statement logically equivalent to it – seems eminently reasonable. The result appears to facilitate indoor ornithology, for the observation of a white shoe would seem to confirm incrementally the hypothesis that all ravens are black. Many attempted resolutions of this paradox can be found in the literature.

See also TESTABILITY, VERIFICATIONISM.

W.C.S.

confirmation, degree of. See CARNAP.

confirmation, paradoxes of. See CONFIRMATION.

confirmational holism. See PHILOSOPHY OF SCIENCE.

Confucianism, a Chinese school of thought and set of moral, ethical, and political teachings usually considered to be founded by Confucius. Before the time of Confucius (sixth–fifth century

B.C.), a social group, the *Ju* (literally, 'weaklings' or 'foundlings'), existed whose members were ritualists and sometimes also teachers by profession. Confucius belonged to this group; but although he retained the interest in rituals, he was also concerned with the then chaotic social and political situation and with the search for remedies, which he believed to lie in the restoration and maintenance of certain traditional values and norms. Later thinkers who professed to be followers of Confucius shared such concern and belief and, although they interpreted and developed Confucius's teachings in different ways, they are often regarded as belonging to the same school of thought, traditionally referred to by Chinese scholars as *Ju-chia*, or the school of the *Ju*. The term 'Confucianism' is used to refer to some or all of the range of phenomena including the way of life of the *Ju* as a group of ritualists, the school of thought referred to as *Ju-chia*, the ethical, social, and political ideals advocated by this school of thought (which include but go well beyond the practice of rituals), and the influence of such ideals on the actual social and political order and the life of the Chinese.

As a school of thought, Confucianism is characterized by a common ethical ideal which includes an affective concern for all living things, varying in degree and nature depending on how such things relate to oneself; a reverential attitude toward others manifested in the observance of formal rules of conduct such as the way to receive guests; an ability to determine the proper course of conduct, whether this calls for observance of traditional norms or departure from such norms; and a firm commitment to proper conduct so that one is not swayed by adverse circumstances such as poverty or death. Everyone is supposed to have the ability to attain this ideal, and people are urged to exercise constant vigilance over their character so that they can transform themselves to embody this ideal fully. In the political realm, a ruler who embodies the ideal will care about and provide for the people, who will be attracted to him; the moral example he sets will have a transforming effect on the people.

Different Confucian thinkers have different conceptions of the way the ethical ideal may be justified and attained. Mencius (fourth century B.C.) regarded the ideal as a full realization of certain incipient moral inclinations shared by human beings, and emphasized the need to reflect on and fully develop such inclinations. Hsün Tzu (third century B.C.) regarded it as a way of optimizing the satisfaction of presocial human desires, and emphasized the need to learn the norms governing social distinctions and let them transform and regulate the pursuit of satisfaction of such desires. Different kinds of Confucian thought continued to evolve, yielding such major thinkers as Tung Chung-shu (second century B.C.) and Han Yü (A.D. 768–824). Han Yü regarded Mencius as the true transmitter of Confucius's teachings, and this view became generally accepted, largely through the efforts of Chu Hsi (1130–1200). The Mencian form of Confucian thought continued to be developed in different ways by such major thinkers as Chu Hsi, Wang Yang-ming (1472–1529), and Tai Chen (1723–77), who differed concerning the way to attain the Confucian ideal and the metaphysics undergirding it. Despite these divergent developments, Confucius continued to be revered within this tradition of thought as its first and most important thinker, and the Confucian school of thought continued to exert great influence on Chinese life and on the social and political order down to the present century.

See also CHU HSI, MENCIUS, WANG YANG-MING.   K.-l.S.

Confucius, also known as K'ung Ch'iu, K'ung Tzu, Kung Fu-tzu (sixth–fifth century B.C.), Chinese thinker usually regarded as founder of the Confucian school of thought. His teachings are recorded in the *Lun Yü* or *Analects*, a collection of sayings by him and by disciples, and of conversations between him and his disciples. His highest ethical ideal is *jen* (humanity, goodness), which includes an affective concern for the well-being of others, desirable attributes (e.g. filial piety) within familial, social, and political institutions, and other desirable attributes such as *yung* (courage, bravery). An important part of the ideal is the general observance of *li* (rites), the traditional norms governing conduct between people related by their different social positions, along with a critical reflection on such norms and a preparedness to adapt them to present circumstances. Human conduct should not be dictated by fixed rules, but should be sensitive to relevant considerations and should accord with *yi* (rightness, duty). Other important concepts include *shu* (consideration, reciprocity), which involves not doing to another what one would not have wished done to oneself, and *chung* (loyalty, commitment), interpreted variously as a commitment to the exercise of *shu*, to the norms of *li*, or to one's duties toward superiors and equals. The ideal of *jen* is within the reach of all, and one should constantly reflect on one's

character and correct one's deficiencies. *Jen* has transformative powers that should ideally be the basis of government; a ruler with *jen* will care about and provide for the people, who will be attracted to him, and the moral example he sets will inspire people to reform themselves. **See also** CONFUCIANISM, JEN, LI[2].   K.-l.S.

congruence. See LEWIS, C. I.

conjecture. See POPPER.

conjunction, the logical operation on a pair of propositions that is typically indicated by the coordinating conjunction 'and'. The truth table for conjunction is

P	Q	P-and-Q
T	T	T
T	F	F
F	T	F
F	F	F

Besides 'and', other coordinating conjunctions, including 'but', 'however', 'moreover', and 'although', can indicate logical conjunction, as can the semicolon ';' and the comma ','. **See also** TRUTH TABLE.   R.W.B.

conjunction elimination. (1) The argument form 'A and B; therefore, A (or B)' and arguments of this form. (2) The rule of inference that permits one to infer either conjunct from a conjunction. This is also known as the *rule of simplification* or $\wedge$-*elimination*. **See also** CONJUNCTION.   G.F.S.

conjunction introduction. (1) The argument form 'A, B; therefore, A and B' and arguments of this form. (2) The rule of inference that permits one to infer a conjunction from its two conjuncts. This is also known as the *rule of conjunction introduction,* $\wedge$-*introduction,* or *adjunction.* **See also** CONJUNCTION.   G.F.S.

conjunctive normal form. See NORMAL FORM.

connected, said of a relation R where, for any two *distinct* elements x and y of the domain, either xRy or yRx. R is said to be *strongly* connected if, for *any* two elements x and y, either xRy or yRx, even if x and y are identical. Given the domain of positive integers, for instance, the relation $<$ is connected, since for any two distinct numbers a and b, either $a < b$ or $b < a$. $<$ is *not* strongly connected, however, since if $a = b$ we do not have either $a < b$ or $b < a$. The relation $\leq$, however, is strongly connected, since either $a \leqslant b$ or $b \leqslant a$ for any two numbers, including the case where $a = b$. An example of a relation that is not connected is the subset relation $\subseteq$, since it is not true that for any two sets A and B, either $A \subseteq B$ or $B \subseteq A$. **See also** RELATION.   V.K.

connectionism, an approach to modeling cognitive systems which utilizes networks of simple processing units that are inspired by the basic structure of the nervous system. Other names for this approach are *neural network modeling* and *parallel distributed processing*. Connectionism was pioneered in the period 1940–65 by researchers such as Frank Rosenblatt and Oliver Selfridge. Interest in using such networks diminished during the 1970s because of limitations encountered by existing networks and the growing attractiveness of the computer model of the mind (according to which the mind stores symbols in memory and registers and performs computations upon them). Connectionist models enjoyed a renaissance in the 1980s, partly as the result of the discovery of means of overcoming earlier limitations (e.g., development of the back-propagation learning algorithm by David Rumelhart, Geoffrey Hinton, and Ronald Williams, and of the Boltzmann-machine learning algorithm by David Ackley, Geoffrey Hinton, and Terrence Sejnowski), and partly as limitations encountered with the computer model rekindled interest in alternatives. Researchers employing connectionist-type nets are found in a variety of disciplines including psychology, artificial intelligence, neuroscience, and physics. There are often major differences in the endeavors of these researchers: psychologists and artificial intelligence researchers are interested in using these nets to model cognitive behavior, whereas neuroscientists often use them to model processing in particular neural systems.

A connectionist system consists of a set of processing units that can take on activation values. These units are connected so that particular units can excite or inhibit others. The activation of any particular unit will be determined by one or more of the following: inputs from outside the system, the excitations or inhibitions supplied by other units, and the previous activation of the unit. There are a variety of different architectures invoked in connectionist systems. In *feedforward nets* units are clustered into layers and connections pass activations in a unidirectional manner from a layer of input units to a layer of output units, possibly passing through one or more layers of hidden units along the way. In these systems processing requires one pass of processing through the network. *Interactive nets* exhibit no directionality of processing: a given unit may excite or inhibit another unit, and it, or another unit influenced by it, might excite or inhibit the first unit. A number of processing cycles will ensue after an input has been given to some or all of the units until eventually the network settles into one state, or cycles through a small set of such states.

One of the most attractive features of connectionist networks is their ability to learn. This is accomplished by adjusting the weights connecting the various units of the system, thereby altering the manner in which the network responds to inputs. To illustrate the basic process of connectionist learning, consider a feedforward network with just two layers of units and one layer of connections. One learning procedure (commonly referred to as the *delta rule*) first requires the network to respond, using current weights, to an input. The activations on the units of the second layer are then compared to a set of target activations, and detected differences are used to adjust the weights coming from active input units. Such a procedure gradually reduces the difference between the actual response and the target response.

In order to construe such networks as cognitive models it is necessary to interpret the input and output units. *Localist* interpretations treat individual input and output units as representing concepts such as those found in natural language. *Distributed* interpretations correlate only patterns of activation of a number of units with ordinary language concepts. Sometimes (but not always) distributed models will interpret individual units as corresponding to microfeatures. In one interesting variation on distributed representation, known as *coarse coding*, each symbol will be assigned to a different subset of the units of the system, and the symbol will be viewed as active only if a predefined number of the assigned units are active.

A number of features of connectionist nets make them particularly attractive for modeling cognitive phenomena in addition to their ability to learn from experience. They are extremely efficient at pattern-recognition tasks and often generalize very well from training inputs to similar test inputs. They can often recover complete patterns from partial inputs, making them good models for content-addressable memory. Interactive networks are particularly useful in modeling cognitive tasks in which multiple constraints must be satisfied simultaneously, or in which the goal is to satisfy competing constraints as well as possible. In a natural manner they can override some constraints on a problem when it is not possible to satisfy all, thus treating the constraints as *soft*. While the cognitive connectionist models are not intended to model actual neural processing, they suggest how cognitive processes can be realized in neural hardware. They also exhibit a feature demonstrated by the brain but difficult to achieve in symbolic systems: their performance degrades gracefully as units or connections are disabled or the capacity of the network is exceeded, rather than crashing.

Serious challenges have been raised to the usefulness of connectionism as a tool for modeling cognition. Many of these challenges have come from theorists who have focused on the complexities of language, especially the systematicity exhibited in language. Jerry Fodor and Zenon Pylyshyn, for example, have emphasized the manner in which the meaning of complex sentences is built up compositionally from the meaning of components, and argue both that compositionality applies to thought generally and that it requires a symbolic system. Therefore, they maintain, while cognitive systems might be implemented in connectionist nets, these nets do not characterize the architecture of the cognitive system itself, which must have capacities for symbol storage and manipulation. Connectionists have developed a variety of responses to these objections, including emphasizing the importance of cognitive functions such as pattern recognition, which have not been as successfully modeled by symbolic systems; challenging the need for symbol processing in accounting for linguistic behavior; and designing more complex connectionist architectures, such as recurrent networks, capable of responding to or producing systematic structures.

See also ARTIFICIAL INTELLIGENCE, COGNITIVE SCIENCE, PHILOSOPHY OF MIND.   W.B.

connective, propositional. See SENTENTIAL CONNECTIVE.

connective, sentential. See SENTENTIAL CONNECTIVE.

connotation. (1) The ideas and associations brought to mind by an expression (used in contrast with 'denotation' and 'meaning'). (2) In a technical use, the properties jointly necessary and sufficient for the correct application of the expression in question. **See also** DENOTATION, MEANING.   T.M.

conscience. See BUTLER, SYNDERESIS.

consciousness. See PHILOSOPHY OF MIND.

consent, informed. See INFORMED CONSENT.

consent, tacit. See SOCIAL CONTRACT.

consequence. See FORMAL SEMANTICS.

consequence, logical. See LOGICAL CONSEQUENCE.

consequence, semantic. See MODAL LOGIC.

consequence argument. See FREE WILL PROBLEM.

consequence relation. See FORMAL SEMANTICS, LOGICAL CONSEQUENCE.

consequent. See COUNTERFACTUALS.

consequentialism, the doctrine that the moral rightness of an act is determined solely by the goodness of the act's consequences. Prominent consequentialists include J. S. Mill, Moore, and Sidgwick. Maximizing versions of consequentialism – the most common sort – hold that an act is morally right if and only if it produces the *best* consequences of those acts available to the agent. Satisficing consequentialism holds that an act is morally right if and only if it produces *enough* good consequences on balance. Consequentialist theories are often contrasted with deontological ones, such as Kant's, which hold that the rightness of an act is determined at least in part by something other than the goodness of the act's consequences.

A few versions of consequentialism are agent-relative: that is, they give each agent different aims, so that different agents' aims may conflict. For instance, egoistic consequentialism holds that the moral rightness of an act for an agent depends solely on the goodness of its consequences for him or her. However, the vast majority of consequentialist theories have been agent-neutral (and consequentialism is often defined in a more restrictive way so that agent-relative versions do not count as consequentialist). A doctrine is agent-neutral when it gives to each agent the same ultimate aims, so that different agents' aims cannot conflict. For instance, utilitarianism holds that an act is morally right if and only if it produces more happiness for the sentient beings it affects than any other act available to the agent. This gives each agent the same ultimate aim, and so is agent-neutral.

Consequentialist theories differ over what features of acts they hold to determine their goodness. Utilitarian versions hold that the only consequences of an act relevant to its goodness are its effects on the happiness of sentient beings. But some consequentialists hold that the promotion of other things matters too – achievement, autonomy, knowledge, or fairness, for instance. Thus utilitarianism, as a maximizing, agent-neutral, happiness-based view is only one of a broad range of consequentialist theories.

See also ETHICS; MILL, J. S.; MOORE; SIDGWICK; UTILITARIANISM.   B.Ga.

consequentialism, indirect. See BUTLER.

consequential property. See SUPERVENIENCE.

consequentia mirabilis, the logical principle that if a statement follows from its own negation it must be true. *Strict consequentia mirabilis* is the principle that if a statement follows logically from its own negation it is logically true. The principle is often connected with the paradoxes of strict implication, according to which any statement follows from a contradiction. Since the negation of a tautology is a contradiction, every tautology follows from its own negation. However, if every expression of the form 'if p then q' implies 'not-p or q' (they need not be equivalent), then from 'if not-p then p' we can derive 'not-not-p or p' and (by the principles of double negation and repetition) derive p. Since all of these rules are unexceptionable the principle of *consequentia mirabilis* is also unexceptionable. It is, however, somewhat counterintuitive, hence the name ('the astonishing implication'), which goes back to its medieval discoverers (or rediscoverers). **See also IMPLICATION.**
R.P.

conservation. See PHILOSOPHY OF SCIENCE.

conservation principle. See PHILOSOPHY OF SCIENCE.

consilience. See WHEWELL.

consistency, in traditional Aristotelian logic, a semantic notion: two or more statements are called consistent if they are simultaneously true under some interpretation (cf., e.g., W. S. Jevons, *Elementary Lessons in Logic,* 1870). In modern logic there is a syntactic definition that also fits complex (e.g., mathematical) theories developed since Frege's *Begriffsschrift* (1879): a set of statements is called consistent with respect to a certain logical calculus, if no formula 'P & $-P$' is derivable from those statements by the rules of the calculus; i.e., the theory is free from contradictions. If these definitions are equivalent for a logic, we have a significant fact, as the equivalence amounts to the completeness of its system of rules. The first such completeness theorem was obtained for sentential or propositional logic by Paul Bernays in 1918 (in his *Habilitationsschrift* that was partially published as *Axiomatische Untersuchung des Aussagen-Kalküls der "Principia Mathematica,"* 1926) and, independently, by Emil Post (in *Introduction to a General Theory of Elementary Propositions,* 1921); the completeness of predicate logic was proved by Gödel (in *Die Vollständigkeit der Axiome des logischen Funktionenkalküls,* 1930). The crucial step in such proofs shows that syntactic consistency implies semantic consistency.

Cantor applied the notion of consistency to sets. In a well-known letter to Dedekind (1899) he distinguished between an inconsistent and a consistent multiplicity; the former is such "that the assumption that all of its elements 'are together' leads to a contradiction," whereas the elements of the latter "can be thought of without contradiction as 'being together.' " Cantor had conveyed these distinctions and their motivation by letter to Hilbert in 1897 (see W. Purkert and H. J. Ilgauds, *Georg Cantor,* 1987). Hilbert pointed out explicitly in 1904 that Cantor had not given a rigorous criterion for distinguishing between consistent and inconsistent multiplicities. Already in his *Über den Zahlbegriff* (1899) Hilbert had suggested a remedy by giving consistency proofs for suitable axiomatic systems; e.g., to give the proof of the "existence of the totality of real numbers or – in the terminology of G. Cantor – the proof of the fact that the system of real numbers is a consistent (complete) set" by establishing the consistency of an axiomatic characterization of the reals – in modern terminology, of the theory of complete, ordered fields. And he claimed, somewhat indeterminately, that this could be done "by a suitable modification of familiar methods."

After 1904, Hilbert pursued a new way of giving consistency proofs. This novel way of proceeding, still aiming for the same goal, was to make use of the formalization of the theory at hand. However, in the formulation of Hilbert's Program during the 1920s the point of consistency proofs was no longer to guarantee the existence of suitable sets, but rather to establish the instrumental usefulness of strong mathematical theories **T**, like axiomatic set theory, relative to finitist mathematics. That focus rested on the observation that the statement formulating the syntactic consistency of **T** is equivalent to the reflection principle $\text{Pr}(a, \,'s') \rightarrow s$; here Pr is the finitist proof predicate for **T**, s is a finitistically meaningful statement, and 's' its translation into the language of **T**. If one could establish finitistically the consistency of **T**, one could be sure – on finitist grounds – that **T** is a reliable instrument for the proof of finitist statements.

There are many examples of significant relative consistency proofs: (i) non-Euclidean geometry relative to Euclidean, Euclidean geometry relative to analysis; (ii) set theory with the axiom of choice relative to set theory (without the axiom of choice), set theory with the negation of the axiom of choice relative to set theory; (iii) classical arithmetic relative to intuitionistic arithmetic, subsystems of classical analysis relative to intuitionistic theories of constructive ordinals. The mathematical significance of relative consistency proofs is often brought out by sharpening them to establish conservative extension results; the latter may then ensure, e.g., that the theories have the same class of provably total functions. The initial motivation for such arguments is, however, frequently philosophical: one wants to guarantee the coherence of the original theory on an epistemologically distinguished basis.

See also CANTOR, COMPLETENESS, GÖDEL'S INCOMPLETENESS THEOREMS, HILBERT'S PROGRAM, PROOF THEORY.   W.S.

consistency, axiom of. See AXIOM OF CONSISTENCY.

consistency, semantic. See CONSISTENCY.

consistency, syntactic. See CONSISTENCY.

Constant, Benjamin, in full, Henri-Benjamin Constant de Rebecque (1767–1830), Swiss-born defender of liberalism and passionate analyst of French and European politics. He welcomed the French Revolution but not the Reign of Terror, the violence of which he avoided by accepting a lowly diplomatic post in Braunschweig (1787–94). In 1795 he returned to Paris with Madame de Staël and intervened in parliamentary debates. His pamphlets opposed both extremes, the Jacobin and the Bonapartist. Impressed by Rousseau's *Social Contract,* he came to fear that like Napoleon's dictatorship, the "general will" could threaten civil rights. He had first welcomed Napoleon, but turned against his autocracy. He favored parliamentary democracy, separation of church and state, and a bill of rights. The high point of his political career came with membership in the *Tribunat* (1800–02), a consultative chamber appointed by the Senate.

His centrist position is evident in the *Principes de politique* (1806–10). Had not republican terror been as destructive as the Empire? In chapters 16–17, Constant opposes the liberty of the ancients and that of the moderns. He assumes that the Greek world was given to war, and therefore strengthened "political liberty" that favors the state over the individual (the liberty of the ancients). Fundamentally optimistic, he believed that war was a thing of the past, and that the modern world needs to protect "civil liberty," i.e. the liberty of the individual (the liberty of the moderns). The great merit of Constant's comparison is the analysis of historical forces, the theory that governments must support current needs and do not depend on deterministic factors such as the size of the state, its form of government, geography, climate, and race. Here he contradicts Montesquieu.

The opposition between ancient and modern liberty expresses a radical liberalism that did not seem to fit French politics. However, it was the beginning of the liberal tradition, contrasting political liberty in the service of the state with the civil liberty of the citizen (cf. Mill's *On Liberty,* 1859, and Berlin's *Two Concepts of Liberty,* 1958). *Principes* remained in manuscript until 1861; the scholarly editions of Étienne Hofmann (1980) are far more recent. Hofmann calls *Principes* the essential text between Montesquieu and Tocqueville. It was translated into English as *Constant, Political Writings* (ed. Biancamaria Fontana, 1988 and 1997).

Forced into retirement by Napoleon, Constant wrote his literary masterpieces, *Adolphe* and the diaries. He completed the *Principes,* then turned to *De la religion* (6 vols.), which he considered his supreme achievement.

See also MONTESQUIEU, POLITICAL PHILOSOPHY, POSITIVE AND NEGATIVE FREEDOM.   O.A.H.

constant, logical. See LOGICAL CONSTANT.

constant conjunction. See CAUSATION, HUME.

constant sum game. See GAME THEORY.

constative. See SPEECH ACT THEORY.

constitution, a relation between concrete particulars (including objects and events) and their parts, according to which at some time *t*, a concrete particular is said to be constituted by the sum of its parts without necessarily being identical with that sum. For instance, at some specific time *t*, Mt. Everest is constituted by the various chunks of rock and other matter that form Everest at *t*, though at *t* Everest would still have been Everest even if, contrary to fact, some particular rock that is part of the sum had been absent. Hence, although Mt. Everest is not identical to the sum of its material parts at *t*, it is constituted by them. The relation of constitution figures importantly in recent attempts to articulate and defend metaphysical physicalism (naturalism). To capture the idea that all that exists is ultimately physical, we may say that at the lowest level of reality, there are only microphysical phenomena, governed by the laws of microphysics, and that all other objects and events are ultimately constituted by objects and events at the microphysical level. **See also** IDENTITY, MORAL REALISM, NATURALISM, PHYSICALISM, REDUCTION.   M.C.T.

constitutive principle. See KANT.

construct. See LOGICAL CONSTRUCTION, OPERATIONALISM.

construct, hypothetical. See OPERATIONALISM.

constructionism, social. See SOCIAL CONSTRUCTIVISM.

constructive dilemma. See DILEMMA.

constructive empiricism. See SOCIAL CONSTRUCTIVISM.

constructivism, ethical. See ETHICAL CONSTRUCTIVISM.

constructivism, mathematical. See PHILOSOPHY OF MATHEMATICS.

constructivism, social. See SOCIAL CONSTRUCTIVISM.

consubstantiation. See TRANSUBSTANTIATION.

containment. See KANT.

content. See INDEXICAL, PHILOSOPHY OF MIND.

content, factual. See ANALYTIC–SYNTHETIC DISTINCTION.

content, latent. See FREUD.

content, manifest. See FREUD.

content, narrow. See PHILOSOPHY OF MIND.

content, propositional. See CIRCULAR REASONING.

content, wide. See PHILOSOPHY OF MIND.

content externalism. See PHILOSOPHY OF MIND.

context principle. See FREGE.

contextual definition. See DEFINITION.

contextualism, the view that inferential justification always takes place against a background of beliefs that are themselves in no way evidentially supported. The view has not often been defended by name, but Dewey, Popper, Austin, and Wittgenstein are arguably among its notable exponents. As this list perhaps suggests, contextualism is closely related to the "relevant alternatives" conception of justification, according to which claims to knowledge are justified not by ruling out any and every logically possible way in which what is asserted might be false or inadequately grounded, but by excluding certain especially relevant alternatives or epistemic shortcomings, these varying from one context of inquiry to another.

Formally, contextualism resembles foundationalism. But it differs from traditional, or substantive, foundationalism in two crucial respects. First, foundationalism insists that basic beliefs be self-justifying or intrinsically credible. True, for contemporary foundationalists, this intrinsic credibility need not amount to incorrigibility, as earlier theorists tended to suppose: but some degree of intrinsic credibility is indispensable for basic beliefs. Second, substantive foundational theories confine intrinsic credibility, hence the status of being epistemologically basic, to beliefs of some fairly narrowly specified kind(s). By contrast, contextualists reject all forms of the doctrine of intrinsic credibility, and in consequence place no restrictions on the kinds of beliefs that can, in appropriate circumstances, function as *contextually* basic. They regard this as a strength of their position, since explaining and defending attributions of intrinsic credibility has always been the foundationalist's main problem.

Contextualism is also distinct from the coherence theory of justification, foundationalism's traditional rival. Coherence theorists are as suspicious as contextualists of the foundationalist's specified kinds of basic beliefs. But coherentists react by proposing a radically holistic model of inferential justification, according to which a belief becomes justified through incorporation into a suitably coherent overall system of beliefs or "total view." There are many well-known problems with this approach: the criteria of coherence have never been very clearly articulated; it is not clear what satisfying such criteria has to do with making our beliefs likely to be true; and since it is doubtful whether anyone has a very clear picture of his system of beliefs as a whole, to insist that justification involves comparing the merits of competing total views seems to subject ordinary justificatory practices to severe idealization. Contextualism, in virtue of its formal affinity with foundationalism, claims to avoid all such problems.

Foundationalists and coherentists are apt to respond that contextualism reaps these benefits by failing to show how genuinely epistemic justification is possible. Contextualism, they charge, is finally indistinguishable from the skeptical view that "justification" depends on unwarranted assumptions. Even if, in context, these are pragmatically acceptable, epistemically speaking they are still just assumptions.

This objection raises the question whether contextualists mean to answer the same questions as more traditional theorists, or answer them in the same way. Traditional theories of justification are framed so as to respond to highly general skeptical questions – e.g., are we justified in any of our beliefs about the external world? It may be that contextualist theories are (or should be) advanced, not as direct answers to skepticism, but in conjunction with attempts to diagnose or dissolve traditional skeptical problems. Contextualists need to show how and why traditional demands for "global" justification misfire, if they do. If traditional skeptical problems are taken at face value, it is doubtful whether contextualism can answer them.

See also COHERENTISM, EPISTEMOLOGY, FOUNDATIONALISM, JUSTIFICATION.   M.W.

contiguity. See ASSOCIATIONISM.

continence. See AKRASIA.

Continental philosophy, the gradually changing spectrum of philosophical views that in the twentieth century developed in Continental Europe and that are notably different from the various forms of analytic philosophy that during the same period flourished in the Anglo-American world. Immediately after World War II the expression was more or less synonymous with 'phenomenology'. The latter term, already used earlier in German idealism, received a completely new meaning in the work of Husserl. Later on the term was also applied, often with substantial changes in meaning, to the thought of a great number of other Continental philosophers such as Scheler, Alexander Pfander, Hedwig Conrad-Martius, Nicolai Hartmann, and most philosophers mentioned below. For Husserl the aim of philosophy is to prepare humankind for a genuinely philosophical form of life, in and through which each human being gives him- or herself a rule through reason. Since the Renaissance, many philosophers have tried in vain to materialize this aim. In Husserl's view, the reason was that philosophers failed to use the proper philosophical method. Husserl's phenomenology was meant to provide philosophy with the method needed.

Among those deeply influenced by Husserl's ideas the so-called existentialists must be mentioned first. If 'existentialism' is construed strictly, it refers mainly to the philosophy of Sartre and Beauvoir. In a very broad sense it refers to the ideas of an entire group of thinkers influenced methodologically by Husserl and in content by Marcel, Heidegger, Sartre, or Merleau-Ponty. In this case one often speaks of *existential phenomenology.*

When Heidegger's philosophy became better known in the Anglo-American world, 'Continental philosophy' received again a new meaning. From Heidegger's first publication, *Being and Time* (1927), it was clear that his conception of phenomenology differs from that of Husserl in several important respects. That is why he qualified the term and spoke of *hermeneutic phenomenology* and clarified the expression by examining the "original" meaning of the Greek words from which the term was formed. In his view phenomenology must try "to let that which shows itself be seen from itself in the very way in which it shows itself from itself." Heidegger applied the method first to the mode of being of man with the aim of approaching the question concerning the meaning of being itself through this phenomenological interpretation. Of those who took their point of departure from Heidegger, but also tried to go beyond him, Gadamer and Ricoeur must be mentioned.

The structuralist movement in France added another connotation to 'Continental philosophy'. The term *structuralism* above all refers to an activity, a way of knowing, speaking, and acting that extends over a number of distinguished domains of human activity: linguistics, aesthetics, anthropology, psychology, psychoanalysis, mathematics, philosophy of science, and philosophy itself. Structuralism, which became a fashion in Paris and later in Western Europe generally, reached its high point on the Continent between 1950 and 1970. It was inspired by ideas first formulated by Russian formalism (1916–26) and Czech structuralism (1926–40), but also by ideas derived from the works of Marx and Freud. In France Foucault, Barthes, Althusser, and Derrida were the leading figures. Structuralism is not a new philosophical movement; it must be characterized by structuralist activity, which is meant to evoke ever new objects. This can be done in a constructive and a reconstructive manner, but these two ways of evoking objects can never be separated. One finds the constructive aspect primarily in structuralist aesthetics and linguistics, whereas the reconstructive aspect is more apparent in philosophical reflections upon the structuralist activity. Influenced by Nietzschean ideas, structuralism later developed in a number of directions, including poststructuralism; in this context the works of Gilles Deleuze, Lyotard, Irigaray, and Kristeva must be mentioned.

After 1970 'Continental philosophy' received again a new connotation: *deconstruction*. At first deconstruction presented itself as a reaction against philosophical hermeneutics, even though both deconstruction and hermeneutics claim their origin in Heidegger's reinterpretation of Husserl's phenomenology. The leading philosopher of the movement is Derrida, who at first tried to think along phenomenological and structuralist lines. Derrida formulated his "final" view in a linguistic form that is both complex and suggestive. It is not easy in a few sentences to state what deconstruction is. Generally speaking one can say that what is being deconstructed is texts; they are deconstructed to show that there are conflicting conceptions of meaning and implication in every text so that it is never possible definitively to show what a text really means. Derrida's own deconstructive work is concerned mainly with philosophical texts, whereas others apply the "method" predominantly to literary texts. What according to Derrida distinguished philosophy is its reluctance to face the fact that it, too, is a product of linguistic and rhetorical figures. Deconstruction is here that process of close reading that focuses on those elements where philosophers in their work try to erase all knowledge of its own linguistic and rhetorical dimensions. It has been said that if construction typifies modern thinking, then deconstruction is the mode of thinking that radically tries to overcome modernity. Yet this view is simplistic, since one also deconstructs Plato and many other thinkers and philosophers of the premodern age.

People concerned with social and political philosophy who have sought affiliation with Continental philosophy often appeal to the so-called critical theory of the Frankfurt School in general, and to Habermas's theory of communicative action in particular. Habermas's view, like the position of the Frankfurt School in general, is philosophically eclectic. It tries to bring into harmony ideas derived from Kant, German idealism, and Marx, as well as ideas from the sociology of knowledge and the social sciences. Habermas believes that his theory makes it possible to develop a communication community without alienation that is guided by reason in such a way that the community can stand freely in regard to the objectively given reality. Critics have pointed out that in order to make this theory work Habermas must substantiate a number of assumptions that until now he has not been able to justify.

See also ANALYTIC PHILOSOPHY, DECONSTRUCTION, EXISTENTIALISM, PHENOMENOLOGY, SARTRE, STRUCTURALISM.   J.J.K.

Continental rationalism. See RATIONALISM.

contingent, neither impossible nor necessary; i.e., both possible and non-necessary. The modal property of being contingent is attributable to a proposition, state of affairs, event, or – more debatably – an object. Muddles about the relationship between this and other modal properties have abounded ever since Aristotle, who initially conflated contingency with possibility but later realized that something that is possible may also be necessary, whereas something that is contingent cannot be necessary. Even today many philosophers are not clear about the "opposition" between contingency and necessity, mistakenly supposing them to be contradictory notions (probably because within the domain of *true* propositions the contingent and the necessary are indeed both exclusive and exhaustive of one another). But the contradictory of 'necessary' is 'non-necessary'; that of 'contingent' is 'non-contingent', as the following extended modal square of opposition shows:

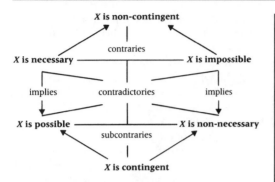

These logicosyntactical relationships are pre-served through various semantical interpreta-tions, such as those involving: (a) the logical modalities (proposition *P* is logically contingent just when *P* is neither a logical truth nor a logi-cal falsehood); (b) the causal or physical modal-ities (state of affairs or event *E* is physically contingent just when *E* is neither physically nec-essary nor physically impossible); and (c) the deontic modalities (act *A* is morally indetermi-nate just when *A* is neither morally obligatory nor morally forbidden).

In none of these cases does 'contingent' mean 'dependent,' as in the phrase 'is contingent upon'. Yet just such a notion of contingency seems to fea-ture prominently in certain formulations of the cosmological argument, all created objects being said to be contingent beings and God alone to be a necessary or non-contingent being. Conceptual clarity is not furthered by assimilating this sense of 'contingent' to the others.

See also MODAL LOGIC, NECESSITY.   R.D.B.

contingent being. See PHILOSOPHY OF RELIGION.

contingent liar. See SEMANTIC PARADOXES.

contingents, future. See FUTURE CONTINGENTS.

continuant. See TIME SLICE.

continuity, bodily. See PERSONAL IDENTITY.

continuity, psychological. See PERSONAL IDENTITY.

continuity, spatiotemporal. See SPATIOTEMPORAL CONTINUITY.

continuum hypothesis. See CANTOR, CONTINUUM PROBLEM.

continuum problem, an open question that arose in Cantor's theory of infinite cardinal numbers. By definition, two sets have the same *cardinal*

number if there is a one-to-one correspondence between them. For example, the function that sends 0 to 0, 1 to 2, 2 to 4, etc., shows that the set of even natural numbers has the same cardi-nal number as the set of all natural numbers, namely $\aleph_0$. That $\aleph_0$ is not the only infinite cardi-nal follows from *Cantor's theorem:* the *power set* of any set (i.e., the set of all its subsets) has a greater cardinality than the set itself. So, e.g., the power set of the natural numbers, i.e., the set of all sets of natural numbers, has a cardinal number greater than $\aleph_0$. The first infinite number greater than $\aleph_0$ is $\aleph_1$; the next after that is $\aleph_2$, and so on.

When arithmetical operations are extended into the infinite, the cardinal number of the power set of the natural numbers turns out to be $2^{\aleph_0}$. By Cantor's theorem, $2^{\aleph_0}$ must be greater than $\aleph_0$; the conjecture that it is equal to $\aleph_1$ is *Cantor's continuum hypothesis* (in symbols, CH or $2^{\aleph_0} = \aleph_1$). Since $2^{\aleph_0}$ is also the cardinality of the set of points on a continuous line, CH can also be stated in this form: any infinite set of points on a line can be brought into one-to-one correspon-dence either with the set of natural numbers or with the set of all points on the line.

Cantor and others attempted to prove CH, without success. It later became clear, due to the work of Gödel and Cohen, that their failure was inevitable: the continuum hypothesis can neither be proved nor disproved from the axioms of set theory (ZFC). The question of its truth or false-hood – the continuum problem – remains open.

See also CANTOR, INFINITY, SET THEORY.

P.Mad.

contractarianism, a family of moral and political theories that make use of the idea of a social con-tract. Traditionally philosophers (such as Hobbes and Locke) used the social contract idea to jus-tify certain conceptions of the state. In the twen-tieth century philosophers such as John Rawls have used the social contract notion to define and defend moral conceptions (both conceptions of political justice and individual morality), often (but not always) doing so in addition to devel-oping social contract theories of the state. The term 'contractarian' most often applies to this second type of theory.

There are two kinds of moral argument that the contract image has spawned, the first rooted in Hobbes and the second rooted in Kant. Hobbesians start by insisting that what is valuable is what a person desires or prefers, not what he ought to desire or prefer (for no such prescrip-tively powerful object exists); and rational action is action that achieves or maximizes the satisfaction of desires or preferences. They go on to insist that moral action is rational for a person to perform if and only if such action advances the satisfaction of his desires or preferences. And they argue that because moral action leads to peaceful and harmonious living conducive to the satisfaction of almost everyone's desires or preferences, moral actions are rational for almost everyone and thus "mutually agreeable." But Hobbesians believe that, to ensure that no cooperative person becomes the prey of immoral aggressors, moral actions must be the conventional norms in a community, so that each person can expect that if she behaves cooperatively, others will do so too. These conventions constitute the institution of morality in a society.

So the Hobbesian moral theory is committed to the idea that morality is a human-made institution, which is justified only to the extent that it effectively furthers human interests. Hobbesians explain the existence of morality in society by appealing to the convention-creating activities of human beings, while arguing that the *justification* of morality in any human society depends upon how well its moral conventions serve individuals' desires or preferences. By considering "what we *could* agree to" if we reappraised and redid the cooperative conventions in our society, we can determine the extent to which our present conventions are "mutually agreeable" and so rational for us to accept and act on. Thus, Hobbesians invoke both actual agreements (or rather, conventions) and hypothetical agreements (which involve considering what conventions would be "mutually agreeable") at different points in their theory; the former are what they believe our moral life consists in; the latter are what they believe our moral life *should* consist in – i.e., what our actual moral life should model. So the notion of the contract does not do justificational work *by itself* in the Hobbesian moral theory: this term is used only metaphorically. What we "could agree to" has moral force for the Hobbesians not because make-believe promises in hypothetical worlds have any binding force but because this sort of agreement is a device that (merely) reveals how the agreed-upon outcome is rational for all of us. In particular, thinking about "what we could all agree to" allows us to construct a deduction of practical reason to determine what policies are mutually advantageous.

The second kind of contractarian theory is derived from the moral theorizing of Kant. In his later writings Kant proposed that the "idea" of the "Original Contract" could be used to determine what policies for a society would be just.

When Kant asks "What could people agree to?," he is not trying to justify actions or policies by invoking, in any literal sense, the consent of the people. Only the consent of *real* people can be legitimating, and Kant talks about hypothetical agreements made by hypothetical people. But he does believe these make-believe agreements have moral force for us because the process by which these people reach agreement is morally revealing.

Kant's contracting process has been further developed by subsequent philosophers, such as Rawls, who concentrates on defining the hypothetical people who are supposed to make this agreement so that their reasoning will not be tarnished by immorality, injustice, or prejudice, thus ensuring that the outcome of their joint deliberations will be morally sound. Those contractarians who disagree with Rawls define the contracting parties in different ways, thereby getting different results. The Kantians' social contract is therefore a *device* used in their theorizing to *reveal* what is just or what is moral. So like Hobbesians, their contract talk is really just a way of reasoning that allows us to work out conceptual answers to moral problems. But whereas the Hobbesians' use of contract language expresses the fact that, on their view, morality is a human invention which (if it is well invented) ought to be mutually advantageous, the Kantians' use of the contract language is meant to show that moral principles and conceptions are provable theorems derived from a morally revealing and authoritative reasoning process or "moral proof procedure" that makes use of the social contract idea.

Both kinds of contractarian theory are individualistic, in the sense that they assume that moral and political policies must be justified with respect to, and answer the needs of, individuals. Accordingly, these theories have been criticized by communitarian philosophers, who argue that moral and political policies can and should be decided on the basis of what is best for a community. They are also attacked by utilitarian theorists, whose criterion of morality is the maximization of the utility of the community, and not the mutual satisfaction of the needs or preferences of individuals. Contractarians respond that whereas utilitarianism fails to take seriously the distinction between persons, contractarian theories make moral and political policies answerable to the legitimate interests and needs of individuals, which, contra the communitarians, they take to be the starting point of moral theorizing.

See also KANT, POLITICAL PHILOSOPHY, SOCIAL CONTRACT, SOCIAL PHILOSOPHY.

J.Ham.

contradiction. See TRUTH TABLE.

contradiction, pragmatic. See PRAGMATIC CONTRADICTION.

contradiction, principle of. See PRINCIPLE OF CONTRADICTION.

contradictories. See SQUARE OF OPPOSITION.

contraposition, the immediate logical operation on any categorical proposition that is accomplished by first forming the complements of both the subject term and the predicate term of that proposition and then interchanging these complemented terms. Thus, contraposition applied to the categorical proposition 'All cats are felines' yields 'All non-felines are non-cats', where 'non-feline' and 'non-cat' are, respectively, the complements (or complementary terms) of 'feline' and 'cat'. The result of applying contraposition to a categorical proposition is said to be the contrapositive of that proposition. **See also SQUARE OF OPPOSITION, SYLLOGISM.**   R.W.B.

contrapositive. See CONTRAPOSITION.

contraries, any pair of propositions that cannot both be true but can both be false; derivatively, any pair of properties that cannot both apply to a thing but that can both fail to apply to a thing. Thus the propositions 'This object is red all over' and 'This object is green all over' are contraries, as are the properties of being red all over and being green all over. Traditionally, it was considered that the categorical A-proposition 'All S's are P's' and the categorical E-proposition 'No S's are P's' were contraries; but according to De Morgan and most subsequent logicians, these two propositions are both true when there are no S's at all, so that modern logicians do not usually regard the categorical A- and E-propositions as being true contraries. **See also EXISTENTIAL IMPORT, SQUARE OF OPPOSITION, SYLLOGISM.**   R.W.B.

contrary-to-duty imperative. See DEONTIC PARADOXES.

contrary-to-fact conditional. See COUNTERFACTUALS.

contravalid, designating a proposition P in a log-

ical system such that every proposition in the system is a consequence of P. In most of the typical and familiar logical systems, contravalidity coincides with self-contradictoriness. **See also** IMPLICATION.   R.W.B.

contributive value. See VALUE.

contributory value. See VALUE.

control, an apparently causal phenomenon closely akin to power and important for such topics as intentional action, freedom, and moral responsibility. Depending upon the control you had over the event, your finding a friend's stolen car may or may not be an intentional action, a free action, or an action for which you deserve moral credit. Control seems to be a causal phenomenon. Try to imagine controlling a car, say, without causing anything. If you cause nothing, you have no effect on the car, and one does not control a thing on which one has no effect. But control need not be causally deterministic. Even if a genuine randomizer in your car's steering mechanism gives you only a 99 percent chance of making turns you try to make, you still have considerable control in that sphere. Some philosophers claim that we have no control over anything if causal determinism is true. That claim is false. When you drive your car, you normally are in control of its speed and direction, even if our world happens to be deterministic. **See also DETERMINISM, FREE WILL PROBLEM, POWER.**   A.R.M.

convention. See LEWIS, DAVID.

conventional implicature. See IMPLICATURE.

conventionalism, the philosophical doctrine that logical truth and mathematical truth are created by our choices, not dictated or imposed on us by the world. The doctrine is a more specific version of the linguistic theory of logical and mathematical truth, according to which the statements of logic and mathematics are true because of the way people use language. Of course, any statement owes its truth to some extent to facts about linguistic usage. For example, 'Snow is white' is true (in English) because of the facts that (1) 'snow' denotes snow, (2) 'is white' is true of white things, and (3) snow is white. What the linguistic theory asserts is that statements of logic and mathematics owe their truth *entirely* to the way people use language. Extralinguistic facts such as (3) are not relevant to the truth of such statements. Which aspects of linguistic usage produce logical truth and mathematical truth? The conventionalist answer is: certain linguistic conventions. These conventions are said to include rules of inference, axioms, and definitions.

The idea that geometrical truth is truth we create by adopting certain conventions received support by the discovery of non-Euclidean geometries. Prior to this discovery, Euclidean geometry had been seen as a paradigm of a priori knowledge. The further discovery that these alternative systems are consistent made Euclidean geometry seem rejectable without violating rationality. Whether we adopt the Euclidean system or a non-Euclidean system seems to be a matter of our choice based on such pragmatic considerations as simplicity and convenience.

Moving to number theory, conventionalism received a prima facie setback by the discovery that arithmetic is incomplete if consistent. For let S be an *undecidable* sentence, i.e., a sentence for which there is neither proof nor disproof. Suppose S is true. In what conventions does its truth consist? Not axioms, rules of inference, and definitions. For if its truth consisted in these items it would be provable. Suppose S is not true. Then its negation must be true. In what conventions does *its* truth consist? Again, no answer. It appears that if S is true or its negation is true and if neither S nor its negation is provable, then not all arithmetic truth is truth by convention. A response the conventionalist could give is that neither S nor its negation is true if S is undecidable. That is, the conventionalist could claim that arithmetic has truth-value gaps.

As to logic, all truths of classical logic are provable and, unlike the case of number theory and geometry, axioms are dispensable. Rules of inference suffice. As with geometry, there are alternatives to classical logic. The intuitionist, e.g., does not accept the rule 'From not-not-A infer A'. Even detachment – 'From A, if A then B, infer B' – is rejected in some multivalued systems of logic. These facts support the conventionalist doctrine that adopting any set of rules of inference is a matter of our choice based on pragmatic considerations. But (the anti-conventionalist might respond) consider a simple logical truth such as 'If Tom is tall, then Tom is tall'. Granted that this is provable by rules of inference from the empty set of premises, why does it follow that its truth is not imposed on us by extralinguistic facts about Tom? If Tom is tall the sentence is true because its consequent is true. If Tom is not tall the sentence is true because its antecedent is false. In either case the sentence owes its truth to facts about Tom.

See also MANY-VALUED LOGIC, PHILOSO-PHY OF LOGIC, PHILOSOPHY OF MATHEMATICS, POINCARÉ.   C.S.

conventionalism, ethical. See RELATIVISM.

conventionalism, geometric. See POINCARÉ.

conventional sign. See THEORY OF SIGNS.

convention T, a criterion of material adequacy (of proposed truth definitions) discovered, formally articulated, adopted, and so named by Tarski in connection with his 1929 definition of the concept of truth in a formalized language. Convention T is one of the most important of several independent proposals Tarski made concerning philosophically sound and logically precise treatment of the concept of truth. Various of these proposals have been criticized, but convention T has remained virtually unchallenged and is regarded almost as an axiom of analytic philosophy. To say that a proposed definition of an established concept is materially adequate is to say that it is "neither too broad nor too narrow," i.e., that the concept it characterizes is coextensive with the established concept. Since, as Tarski emphasized, for many formalized languages there are no criteria of truth, it would seem that there can be no general criterion of material adequacy of truth definitions. But Tarski brilliantly finessed this obstacle by discovering a specification that is fulfilled by the established correspondence concept of truth and that has the further property that any two concepts fulfilling it are necessarily coextensive. Basically, convention T requires that to be materially adequate a proposed truth definition must imply all of the infinitely many relevant Tarskian biconditionals; e.g., the sentence 'Some perfect number is odd' is true if and only if some perfect number is odd. Loosely speaking, a Tarskian biconditional for English is a sentence obtained from the form 'The sentence ——— is true if and only if ——' by filling the right blank with a sentence and filling the left blank with a name of the sentence. Tarski called these biconditionals "equivalences of the form T" and referred to the form as a "scheme." Later writers also refer to the form as "schema T." *See also* FORMAL SEMANTICS, GÖDEL'S INCOMPLETENESS THEOREMS, MATERIAL ADEQUACY, SATISFACTION, TARSKI, TRUTH.   J.Cor.

convergence. See PHILOSOPHY OF SCIENCE.

conversational implicature. See IMPLICATURE.

converse. (1) Narrowly, the result of the immediate logical operation called *conversion* on any categorical proposition, accomplished by interchanging the subject term and the predicate term of that proposition. Thus, the converse of the categorical proposition 'All cats are felines' is 'All felines are cats'. (2) More broadly, the proposition obtained from a given 'if . . . then . . .' (conditional) proposition by interchanging the antecedent and the consequent clauses, i.e., the propositions following the 'if' and the 'then', respectively; also, the argument obtained from an argument of the form '*P*; therefore *Q*' by interchanging the premise and the conclusion. **See also** RELATION.   R.W.B.

converse, outer and inner, respectively, the result of "converting" the two "terms" *or* the relation verb of a relational sentence. The outer converse of 'Abe helps Ben' is 'Ben helps Abe' and the inner converse is 'Abe is helped by Ben'. In simple, or atomic, sentences the outer and inner converses express logically equivalent propositions, and thus in these cases no informational ambiguity arises from the adjunction of 'and conversely' or 'but not conversely', despite the fact that such adjunction does not indicate which, if either, of the two converses intended is meant. However, in complex, or quantified, relational sentences such as 'Every integer precedes some integer' genuine informational ambiguity is produced. Under normal interpretations of the respective sentences, the outer converse expresses the false proposition that some integer precedes every integer, the inner converse expresses the true proposition that every integer is preceded by some integer. More complicated considerations apply in cases of quantified doubly relational sentences such as 'Every integer precedes every integer exceeding it'. The concept of scope explains such structural ambiguity: in the sentence 'Every integer precedes some integer and conversely', 'conversely' taken in the outer sense has wide scope, whereas taken in the inner sense it has narrow scope. **See also** AMBIGUITY, CONVERSE, RELATION, SCOPE.   J. Cor.

converse domain. See RELATION.

converse relation. See RELATION.

conversion. See CONVERSE.

Conway, Anne (c.1630–79), English philosopher whose *Principia philosophiae antiquissimae et recentissimae* (1690; English translation, *The Principles*

of the Most Ancient and Modern Philosophy, 1692) proposes a monistic ontology in which all created things are modes of one spiritual substance emanating from God. This substance is made up of an infinite number of hierarchically arranged spirits, which she calls monads. Matter is congealed spirit. Motion is conceived not dynamically but vitally. Lady Conway's scheme entails a moral explanation of pain and the possibility of universal salvation. She repudiates the dualism of both Descartes and her teacher, Henry More, as well as the materialism of Hobbes and Spinoza. The work shows the influence of cabalism and affinities with the thought of the mentor of her last years, Francis Mercurius van Helmont, through whom her philosophy became known to Leibniz.   S.H.

Cook Wilson, John. See WILSON.

coordination problem. See SOCIAL CHOICE THEORY.

coordinative definition. See DEFINITION.

Copernican revolution. See KANT.

copula, in logic, a form of the verb 'to be' that joins subject and predicate in singular and categorical propositions. In 'George is wealthy' and 'Swans are beautiful', e.g., 'is' and 'are', respectively, are copulas. Not all occurrences of forms of 'be' count as copulas. In sentences such as 'There are 51 states', 'are' is not a copula, since it does not join a subject and a predicate, but occurs simply as a part of the quantifier term 'there are'. **See also** DEFINITION, INTENSION, MEANING.
                                                V.K.

copulatio. See PROPRIETATES TERMINORUM.

Cordemoy, Géraud de (1626–84), French philosopher and member of the Cartesian school. His most important work is his *Le discernement du corps et de l'âme en six discours,* published in 1666 and reprinted (under slightly different titles) a number of times thereafter. Also important are the *Discours physique de la parole* (1668), a Cartesian theory of language and communication; and *Une lettre écrite à un sçavant religieux* (1668), a defense of Descartes's orthodoxy on certain questions in natural philosophy. Cordemoy also wrote a history of France, left incomplete at his death.

Like Descartes, Cordemoy advocated a mechanistic physics explaining physical phenomena in terms of size, shape, and local motion, and held that minds are incorporeal thinking substances. Like most Cartesians, Cordemoy also advocated a version of occasionalism. But unlike other Cartesians, he argued for atomism and admitted the void. These innovations were not welcomed by other members of the Cartesian school. But Cordemoy is often cited by later thinkers, such as Leibniz, as an important seventeenth-century advocate of atomism. **See also** OCCASIONALISM.   D.Garb.

corner quotes. See CORNERS.

corners, also called corner quotes, quasi-quotes, a notational device ($\ulcorner \urcorner$) introduced by Quine (*Mathematical Logic,* 1940) to provide a conveniently brief way of speaking generally about unspecified expressions of such and such kind. For example, a logician might want a conveniently brief way of saying in the metalanguage that the result of writing a wedge ' $\vee$ ' (the dyadic logical connective for a truth-functional use of 'or') between any two well-formed formulas (wffs) in the object language is itself a wff. Supposing the Greek letters ' ϕ ' and ' ψ ' available in the metalanguage as variables ranging over wffs in the object language, it is tempting to think that the formation rule stated above can be succinctly expressed simply by saying that if ϕ and ψ are wffs, then ' $\phi \vee \psi$ ' is a wff. But this will not do, for ' $\phi \vee \psi$ ' is not a wff. Rather, it is a hybrid expression of two variables of the metalanguage and a dyadic logical connective of the object language. The problem is that putting quotation marks around the Greek letters merely results in designating those letters themselves, not, as desired, in designating the context of the unspecified wffs. Quine's device of corners allows one to transcend this limitation of straight quotation since quasi-quotation, e.g., $\ulcorner \phi \vee \psi \urcorner$, amounts to quoting the constant contextual background, '# $\vee$ #', and imagining the unspecified expressions ϕ and ψ written in the blanks. **See also** USE–MENTION DISTINCTION.   R.F.G.

corrective justice. See JUSTICE.

correlativity. See POLARITY, RIGHTS.

correspondence theory of truth. See TRUTH.

corresponding conditional (of a given argument), any conditional whose antecedent is a (logical) conjunction of all of the premises of the argument and whose consequent is the conclusion. The two conditionals, 'if Abe is Ben and Ben is

wise, then Abe is wise' and 'if Ben is wise and Abe is Ben, then Abe is wise', are the two corresponding conditionals of the argument whose premises are 'Abe is Ben' and 'Ben is wise' and whose conclusion is 'Abe is wise'. For a one-premise argument, the corresponding conditional is the conditional whose antecedent is the premise and whose consequent is the conclusion. The limiting cases of the empty and infinite premise sets are treated in different ways by different logicians; one simple treatment considers such arguments as lacking corresponding conditionals.

   The *principle of corresponding conditionals* is that in order for an argument to be valid it is necessary and sufficient for all its corresponding conditionals to be tautological. The commonly used expression 'the corresponding conditional of an argument' is also used when two further stipulations are in force: first, that an argument is construed as having an (ordered) sequence of premises rather than an (unordered) set of premises; second, that conjunction is construed as a polyadic operation that produces in a unique way a single premise from a sequence of premises rather than as a dyadic operation that combines premises two by two. Under these stipulations the *principle of the corresponding conditional* is that in order for an argument to be valid it is necessary and sufficient for its corresponding conditional to be valid. These principles are closely related to *modus ponens,* to conditional proof, and to the so-called deduction theorem.
   See also ARGUMENT, CONDITIONAL, CONDITIONAL PROOF, LIMITING CASE, MODUS PONENS, PROPOSITION, TAUTOLOGY.   J.Cor.

corrigibility. See PRIVILEGED ACCESS.

cosmological argument. See PHILOSOPHY OF RELIGION.

cosmology. See METAPHYSICS.

cost–benefit analysis. See DECISION THEORY.

countable. See SET THEORY.

counterdomain. See RELATION.

counterexample. See COUNTERINSTANCE.

counterfactual analysis of causation. See CAUSATION.

counterfactuals, also called contrary-to-fact conditionals, subjunctive conditionals that presuppose the falsity of their antecedents, such as 'If Hitler had invaded England, Germany would have won' and 'If I were you, I'd run'.

Conditionals (or hypothetical statements) are compound statements of the form 'If p, (then) q', or equivalently 'q if p'. Component p is described as the antecedent (protasis) and q as the consequent (apodosis). A conditional like 'If Oswald *did not* kill Kennedy, then someone else *did*' is called indicative, because both the antecedent and consequent are in the indicative mood. One like 'If Oswald *had not* killed Kennedy, then someone else *would have*' is subjunctive. Many subjunctive and all indicative conditionals are *open*, presupposing nothing about the antecedent. Unlike 'If Bob had won, he'd be rich', neither 'If Bob should have won, he would be rich' nor 'If Bob won, he is rich' implies that Bob did not win. Counterfactuals presuppose, rather than assert, the falsity of their antecedents. 'If Reagan had been president, he would have been famous' seems inappropriate and out of place, but not false, given that Reagan was president. The difference between counterfactual and open subjunctives is less important logically than that between subjunctives and indicatives. Whereas the indicative conditional about Kennedy is true, the subjunctive is probably false. Replace 'someone' with 'no one' and the truth-values reverse.

The most interesting logical feature of counterfactuals is that they are not truth-functional. A truth-functional compound is one whose truth-value is completely determined in every possible case by the truth-values of its components. For example, the falsity of 'The President is a grandmother' and 'The President is childless' logically entails the falsity of 'The President is a grandmother and childless': *all* conjunctions with false conjuncts are false. But whereas 'If the President were a grandmother, the President would be childless' is false, other counterfactuals with equally false components are true, such as 'If the President were a grandmother, the President would be a mother'. The truth-value of a counterfactual is determined in part by the specific *content* of its components. This property is shared by indicative and subjunctive conditionals generally, as can be seen by varying the wording of the example. In marked contrast, the material conditional, $p \supset q$, of modern logic, defined as meaning that either p is false or q is true, is completely truth-functional. 'The President is a grandmother $\supset$ The President is childless' is just as true as 'The President is a grandmother $\supset$ The President is a mother'.

While stronger than the material conditional, the counterfactual is weaker than the strict conditional, $p \rightarrow q$, of modern modal logic, which says that $p \supset q$ is *necessarily* true. 'If the switch had been flipped, the light would be on' may in fact be true even though it is possible for the switch to have been flipped without the light's being on because the bulb could have burned out.

The fact that counterfactuals are neither strict nor material conditionals generated the *problem of counterfactual conditionals* (raised by Chisholm and Goodman): What are the truth conditions of a counterfactual, and how are they determined by its components? According to the "metalinguistic" approach, which resembles the deductive-nomological model of explanation, a counterfactual is true when its antecedent conjoined with *laws of nature* and statements of *background conditions* logically entails its consequent. On this account, 'If the switch had been flipped the light would be on' is true because the statement that the switch was flipped, plus the laws of electricity and statements describing the condition and arrangement of the circuitry, entail that the light is on. The main problem is to specify *which* facts are "fixed" for any given counterfactual and context. The background conditions cannot include the denials of the antecedent or the consequent, even though they are true, nor anything else that would not be true if the antecedent were. Counteridenticals, whose antecedents assert identities, highlight the difficulty: the background for 'If I were you, I'd run' must include facts about my character and your situation, but not vice versa. Counterlegals like 'Newton's laws would fail if planets had rectangular orbits', whose antecedents deny laws of nature, show that even the set of laws cannot be all-inclusive.

Another leading approach (pioneered by Robert C. Stalnaker and David K. Lewis) extends the possible worlds semantics developed for modal logic, saying that a counterfactual is true when its consequent is true in the *nearest possible world* in which the antecedent is true. The counterfactual about the switch is true on this account provided a world in which the switch was flipped and the light is on is closer to the actual world than one in which the switch was flipped but the light is not on. The main problem is to specify which world is nearest for any given counterfactual and context. The difference between indicative and subjunctive conditionals can be accounted for in terms of either a different set of background conditions or a different measure of nearness.

Counterfactuals turn up in a variety of philosophical contexts. To distinguish *laws* like 'All copper conducts' from equally true generalizations like 'Everything in my pocket conducts', some have observed that while anything *would* conduct if it *were* copper, not everything would conduct if it were in my pocket. And to have a *disposition* like solubility, it does not suffice to be either dissolving or not in water: it must in addition be true that the object would dissolve if it were in water. It has similarly been suggested that one event is the *cause* of another only if the latter would not have occurred if the former had not; that an action is *free* only if the agent could or would have done otherwise if he had wanted to; that a person is in a particular *mental state* only if he would behave in certain ways given certain stimuli; and that an action is *right* only if a completely rational and fully informed agent would choose it.

See also CAUSATION, POSSIBLE WORLDS.
W.A.D.

counteridenticals. See COUNTERFACTUALS.

counterinstance, also called counterexample. (1) A particular instance of an argument form that has all true premises but a false conclusion, thereby showing that the form is not universally valid. The argument form '$p \lor q, \sim p \mathrel{/} \therefore \sim q$', for example, is shown to be invalid by the counterinstance 'Grass is either red or green; Grass is not red; Therefore, grass is not green'. (2) A particular false instance of a statement form, which demonstrates that the form is not a logical truth. A counterinstance to the form '$(p \lor q) \supset p$', for example, would be the statement 'If grass is either red or green, then grass is red'. (3) A particular example that demonstrates that a universal generalization is false. The universal statement 'All large cities in the United States are east of the Mississippi' is shown to be false by the counterinstance of San Francisco, which is a large city in the United States that is not east of the Mississippi.
V.K.

counterpart theory, a theory that analyzes statements about what is possible and impossible for individuals (statements of *de re* modality) in terms of what holds of *counterparts* of those individuals in other possible worlds, a thing's counterparts being individuals that resemble it without being identical with it. (The name 'counterpart theory' was coined by David Lewis, the theory's principal exponent.) Whereas some theories analyze 'Mrs. Simpson might have been queen of England' as 'In some possible world,

Mrs. Simpson is queen of England', counterpart theory analyzes it as 'In some possible world, a counterpart of Mrs. Simpson is queen of (a counterpart of) England'. The chief motivation for counterpart theory is a combination of two views: (a) *de re* modality should be given a possible worlds analysis, and (b) each actual individual exists only in the actual world, and hence cannot exist with different properties in other possible worlds. Counterpart theory provides an analysis that allows 'Mrs. Simpson might have been queen' to be true compatibly with (a) and (b). For Mrs. Simpson's counterparts in other possible worlds, in those worlds where she herself does not exist, may have regal properties that the actual Mrs. Simpson lacks. Counterpart theory is perhaps prefigured in Leibniz's theory of possibility. **See also** COUNTERFACTUALS, POSSIBLE WORLDS.
P.Mac.

count noun, a noun that can occur syntactically (a) with quantifiers 'each', 'every', 'many', 'few', 'several', and numerals; (b) with the indefinite article, 'a(n)'; and (c) in the plural form. The following are examples of count nouns (CNs), paired with semantically similar mass nouns (MNs): 'each dollar / silver', 'one composition / music', 'a bed / furniture', 'instructions / advice'. MNs but not CNs can occur with the quantifiers 'much' and 'little': 'much poetry / poem(s)', 'little bread / loaf'. Both CNs and MNs may occur with 'all', 'most', and 'some'. Semantically, CNs but not MNs refer distributively, providing a counting criterion. It makes sense to ask how many CNs?: 'How many coins / gold?' MNs but not CNs refer collectively. It makes sense to ask how much MN?: 'How much gold / coins?'

One problem is that these syntactic and semantic criteria yield different classifications; another problem is to provide logical forms and truth conditions for sentences containing mass nouns.

See also DISTRIBUTION, MEANING, SORTAL PREDICATE.
W.K.W.

courage. See CARDINAL VIRTUES.

Cournot, Antoine-Augustin (1801–77), French mathematician and economist. A critical realist in scientific and philosophical matters, he was a conservative in religion and politics. His *Researches into the Mathematical Principles of the Theory of Wealth* (1838), though a fiasco at the time, pioneered mathematical economics. Cournot upheld a position midway between science and metaphysics. His philosophy rests on three basic concepts: order, chance, and probability. The *Exposition of the Theory of Chances and Probabilities* (1843) focuses on the calculus of probability, unfolds a theory of chance occurrences, and distinguishes among objective, subjective, and philosophical probability. The *Essay on the Foundations of Knowledge* (1861) defines science as logically organized knowledge. Cournot developed a probabilist epistemology, showed the relevance of probabilism to the scientific study of human acts, and further assumed the existence of a providential and complex order undergirding the universe. *Materialism, Vitalism, Rationalism* (1875) acknowledges transrationalism and makes room for finality, purpose, and God.

J.L.S.

Cousin, Victor (1792–1867), French philosopher who set out to merge the French psychological tradition with the pragmatism of Locke and Condillac and the inspiration of the Scottish (Reid, Stewart) and German idealists (Kant, Hegel). His early courses at the Sorbonne (1815–18), on "absolute" values that might overcome materialism and skepticism, aroused immense enthusiasm. The course of 1818, *Du Vrai, du Beau et du Bien* (*Of the True, the Beautiful, and the Good*), is preserved in the Adolphe Garnier edition of student notes (1836); other early texts appeared in the *Fragments philosophiques* (*Philosophical Fragments,* 1826). Dismissed from his teaching post as a liberal (1820), arrested in Germany at the request of the French police and detained in Berlin, he was released after Hegel intervened (1824); he was not reinstated until 1828. Under Louis-Philippe, he rose to highest honors, became minister of education, and introduced philosophy into the curriculum. His eclecticism, transformed into a spiritualism and cult of the "*juste milieu,*" became the official philosophy. Cousin rewrote his work accordingly and even succeeded in having *Du Vrai* (third edition, 1853) removed from the papal index. In 1848 he was forced to retire. He is noted for his educational reforms, as a historian of philosophy, and for his translations (Proclus, Plato), editions (Descartes), and portraits of ladies of seventeenth-century society.

O.A.H.

Couturat, Louis (1868–1914), French philosopher and logician who wrote on the history of philosophy, logic, philosophy of mathematics, and the possibility of a universal language. Couturat refuted Renouvier's finitism and advocated an actual infinite in *The Mathematical Infinite* (1896). He argued that the assumption of

infinite numbers was indispensable to maintain the continuity of magnitudes. He saw a precursor of modern logistic in Leibniz, basing his interpretation of Leibniz on the *Discourse on Metaphysics* and Leibniz's correspondence with Arnauld. His epoch-making *Leibniz's Logic* (1901) describes Leibniz's metaphysics as *panlogism.* Couturat published a study on Kant's mathematical philosophy (*Revue de Métaphysique,* 1904), and defended Peano's logic, Whitehead's algebra, and Russell's logistic in *The Algebra of Logic* (1905). He also contributed to André Lalande's *Vocabulaire technique et critique de la philosophie* (1926).

J.-L.S.

covering law model, the view of scientific explanation as a deductive argument which contains non-vacuously at least one universal law among its premises. The names of this view include 'Hempel's model', 'Hempel-Oppenheim (HO) model', 'Popper-Hempel model', 'deductive-nomological (D-N) model', and the 'subsumption theory' of explanation. The term 'covering law model of explanation' was proposed by William Dray.

The theory of scientific explanation was first developed by Aristotle. He suggested that science proceeds from mere knowing *that* to deeper knowing *why* by giving understanding of different things by the four types of causes. Answers to why-questions are given by scientific syllogisms, i.e., by deductive arguments with premises that are necessarily true and causes of their consequences. Typical examples are the "subsumptive" arguments that can be expressed by the Barbara syllogism:

> All ravens are black.
> Jack is a raven.
> Therefore, Jack is black.

> Plants containing chlorophyll are green.
> Grass contains chlorophyll.
> Therefore, grass is green.

In modern logical notation,

$$\frac{\forall x\,(Fx \rightarrow Gx)}{Ga}$$
$$Fa$$

$$\frac{\forall x\,(Fx \rightarrow Gx)}{\forall x\,(Hx \rightarrow Gx).}$$
$$\forall x\,(Hx \rightarrow Fx)$$

An explanatory argument was later called in Greek *synthesis*, in Latin *compositio* or *demonstratio propter quid.* After the seventeenth century, the terms 'explication' and 'explanation' became commonly used.

The nineteenth-century empiricists accepted Hume's criticism of Aristotelian essences and necessities: a law of nature is an extensional statement that expresses a uniformity, i.e., a constant conjunction between properties ('All swans are white') or types of events ('Lightning is always followed by thunder'). Still, they accepted the subsumption theory of explanation: "An individual fact is said to be explained by pointing out its cause, that is, by stating the law or laws of causation, of which its production is an instance," and "a law or uniformity in nature is said to be explained when another law or laws are pointed out, of which that law itself is but a case, and from which it could be deduced" (J. S. Mill). A general model of probabilistic explanation, with deductive explanation as a specific case, was given by Peirce in 1883.

A modern formulation of the subsumption theory was given by Hempel and Paul Oppenheim in 1948 by the following schema of D-N explanation:

$$
\begin{array}{l}
\left.\begin{array}{l}
\left.\begin{array}{l}
C_1, C_2, \ldots, C_k \\
\text{(statements of antecedent conditions)} \\
L_1, L_2, \ldots, L_r \\
\text{(general laws or lawlike sentences)}
\end{array}\right\} \text{Explanans}
\end{array}\right. \\
\underline{} \\
E \quad \text{description of the empirical} \quad \left.\begin{array}{l}\end{array}\right\} \text{Explanandum} \\
 \quad \text{phenomenon to be explained}
\end{array}
$$

logical deduction

Explanandum E is here a sentence that describes a known particular event or fact (singular explanation) or uniformity (explanation of laws). Explanation is an argument that answers an explanation-seeking why-question 'Why E?' by showing that E is nomically expectable on the basis of general laws ($r \geq 1$) and antecedent conditions. The relation between the explanans and the explanandum is logical deduction. Explanation is distinguished from other kinds of scientific systematization (prediction, postdiction) that share its logical characteristics – a view often called the *symmetry thesis* regarding explanation and prediction – by the presupposition that the phenomenon E is already known. This also separates explanations from reason-seeking arguments that answer questions of the form 'What reasons are there for believing that E?' Hempel and Oppenheim required that the explanans have empirical content, i.e., be testable by experiment or observation, and it must be true. If the strong condition of truth is dropped, we speak of *potential* explanation.

Dispositional explanations, for non-probabilis-

tic dispositions, can be formulated in the D-N model. For example, let Hx = 'x is hit by hammer', Bx = 'x breaks', and Dx = 'x is fragile'. Then the explanation why a piece of glass was broken may refer to its fragility and its being hit:

$$
\begin{array}{l}
\forall x \, (Hx \rightarrow (Dx \rightarrow Bx)) \\
\underline{Ha \ \& \ Da} \\
Ba
\end{array}
$$

It is easy to find examples of HO explanations that are not satisfactory: self-explanations ('Grass is green, because grass is green'), explanations with too weak premises ('John died, because he had a heart attack or his plane crashed'), and explanations with irrelevant information ('This stuff dissolves in water, because it is sugar produced in Finland'). Attempts at finding necessary and sufficient conditions in syntactic and semantic terms for acceptable explanations have not led to any agreement. The HO model also needs the additional Aristotelian condition that causal explanation is directed from causes to effects. This is shown by Sylvain Bromberger's flagpole example: the length of a flagpole explains the length of its shadow, but not vice versa. Michael Scriven has argued against Hempel that explanations of particular events should be given by singular causal statements 'E because C'. However, a regularity theory (Humean or stronger than Humean) of causality implies that the truth of such a singular causal statement presupposes a universal law of the form 'Events of type C are universally followed by events of type E'.

The HO version of the covering law model can be generalized in several directions. The explanans may contain probabilistic or statistical laws. The explanans-explanandum relation may be inductive (in this case the explanation itself is inductive). This gives us four types of explanations: *deductive-universal* (i.e., D-N), *deductive-probabilistic*, *inductive-universal*, and *inductive-probabilistic* (I-P). Hempel's 1962 model for I-P explanation contains a probabilistic covering law $P(G/F) = r$, where r is the statistical probability of G given F, and r in brackets is the inductive probability of the explanandum given the explanans:

$$
\begin{array}{l}
P(G/F) = r \\
\underline{\underline{Fa}} \\
Ga [r]
\end{array}
$$

The explanation-seeking question may be weakened from 'Why necessarily E?' to 'How possibly E?'. In a *corrective explanation*, the explanatory answer points out that the explanandum sentence *E* is not strictly true. This is the case in *approximate explanation* (e.g., Newton's theory entails a corrected form of Galileo's and Kepler's laws).

See also CAUSATION, EXPLANATION, GRUE PARADOX, PHILOSOPHY OF SCIENCE.   I.N.

Craig reduct. See CRAIG'S INTERPOLATION THEOREM.

Craig's interpolation theorem, a theorem for first-order logic: if a sentence ψ of first-order logic entails a sentence θ there is an "interpolant," a sentence Φ in the vocabulary common to θ and ψ that entails θ and is entailed by ψ. Originally, William Craig proved his theorem in 1957 as a lemma, to give a simpler proof of Beth's definability theorem, but the result now stands on its own. In abstract model theory, logics for which an interpolation theorem holds are said to have the Craig interpolation property. Craig's interpolation theorem shows that first-order logic is closed under implicit definability, so that the concepts embodied in first-order logic are all given explicitly.

In the philosophy of science literature 'Craig's theorem' usually refers to another result of Craig's: that any recursively enumerable set of sentences of first-order logic can be axiomatized. This has been used to argue that theoretical terms are in principle eliminable from empirical theories. Assuming that an empirical theory can be axiomatized in first-order logic, i.e., that there is a recursive set of first-order sentences from which all theorems of the theory can be proven, it follows that the set of consequences of the axioms in an "observational" sublanguage is a recursively enumerable set. Thus, by Craig's theorem, there is a set of axioms for this subtheory, the Craig-reduct, that contains only observation terms. Interestingly, the Craig-reduct theory may be semantically weaker, in the sense that it may have models that cannot be extended to a model of the full theory. The existence of such a model would prove that the theoretical terms cannot all be defined on the basis of the observational vocabulary only, a result related to Beth's definability theorem.

See also BETH'S DEFINABILITY THEOREM, PROOF THEORY.   Z.G.S.

Craig's theorem. See CRAIG'S INTERPOLATION THEOREM.

Crates of Thebes. See CYNICS.

Crates the Cynic. See CYNICS.

Cratylus of Athens. See HERACLITUS.

Cratylus Zeyl. See PRE-SOCRATICS.

creation *ex nihilo*, the act of bringing something into existence from nothing. According to traditional Christian theology, God created the world *ex nihilo*. To say that the world was created from nothing does not mean that there was a prior non-existent substance out of which it was fashioned, but rather that there was not anything out of which God brought it into being. However, some of the patristics influenced by Plotinus, such as Gregory of Nyssa, apparently understood creation *ex nihilo* to be an *emanation* from God according to which what is created comes, not from nothing, but from God himself. Not everything that God makes need be created *ex nihilo*; or if, as in Genesis 2: 7, 19, God made a human being and animals from the ground, a previously existing material, God did not create them from nothing. Regardless of how bodies are made, orthodox theology holds that human souls are created *ex nihilo*; the opposing view, *traducianism*, holds that souls are propagated along with bodies. See also GREGORY OF NYSSA, PHILOSOPHY OF RELIGION, PLOTINUS.   E.R.W.

creationism, acceptance of the early chapters of Genesis taken literally. Genesis claims that the universe and all of its living creatures including humans were created by God in the space of six days. The need to find some way of reconciling this story with the claims of science intensified in the nineteenth century, with the publication of Darwin's *Origin of Species* (1859). In the Southern states of the United States, the indigenous form of evangelical Protestant Christianity declared total opposition to evolutionism, refusing any attempt at reconciliation, and affirming total commitment to a literal "creationist" reading of the Bible. Because of this, certain states passed laws banning the teaching of evolutionism. More recently, literalists have argued that the Bible can be given full scientific backing, and they have therefore argued that "Creation science" may properly be taught in state-supported schools in the United States without violation of the constitutional separation of church and state. This claim was challenged in the state of Arkansas in 1981, and ultimately rejected by the U.S. Supreme Court.

The creationism dispute has raised some issues of philosophical interest and importance. Most obviously, there is the question of what constitutes a genuine science. Is there an adequate *cri*-

terion of demarcation between science and non-science, and will it put evolutionism on the one side and creationism on the other? Some philosophers, arguing in the spirit of Karl Popper, think that such a criterion can be found. Others are not so sure; and yet others think that some such criterion can be found, but shows creationism to be genuine science, albeit already proven false.

Philosophers of education have also taken an interest in creationism and what it represents. If one grants that even the most orthodox science may contain a value component, reflecting and influencing its practitioners' culture, then teaching a subject like biology almost certainly is not a normatively neutral enterprise. In that case, without necessarily conceding to the creationist anything about the true nature of science or values, perhaps one must agree that science with its teaching is not something that can and should be set apart from the rest of society, as an entirely distinct phenomenon.

See also DARWINISM, PHILOSOPHY OF BIOL-OGY, PHILOSOPHY OF RELIGION, PHILOSOPHY OF SCIENCE, TESTABILITY.   M.Ru.

creationism, theological. See PREEXISTENCE.

credibility. See CARNAP.

Crescas, Hasdai (d.1412), Spanish Jewish philosopher, theologian, and statesman. He was a well-known representative of the Jewish community in both Barcelona and Saragossa. Following the death of his son in the anti-Jewish riots of 1391, he wrote a chronicle of the massacres (published as an appendix to Ibn Verga, *Shevet Yehudah*, ed. M. Wiener, 1855). Crescas's devotion to protecting Spanish Jewry in a time when conversion was encouraged is documented in one extant work, the *Refutation of Christian Dogmas* (1397–98), found in the 1451 Hebrew translation of Joseph ibn Shem Tov (*Bittul 'Iqqarey ha-Nosrim*). His major philosophical work, *Or Adonai* (*The Light of the Lord*), was intended as the first of a two-part project that was to include his own more extensive systematization of *halakh*a (Jewish law) as well as a critique of Maimonides' work. But this second part, "Lamp of the Divine Commandment," was never written.

Or Adonai is a philosophico-dogmatic response to and attack on the Aristotelian doctrines that Crescas saw as a threat to the Jewish faith, doctrines concerning the nature of God, space, time, place, free will, and infinity. For theological rea-

sons he attempts to refute basic tenets in Aristotelian physics. He offers, e.g., a critique of Aristotle's arguments against the existence of a vacuum. The Aristotelian view of time is rejected as well. Time, like space, is thought by Crescas to be infinite. Furthermore, it is not an accident of motion, but rather exists only in the soul. In defending the fundamental doctrines of the Torah, Crescas must address the question discussed by his predecessors Maimonides and Gersonides, namely that of reconciling divine foreknowledge with human freedom. Unlike these two thinkers, Crescas adopts a form of determinism, arguing that God knows both the possible and what will necessarily take place. An act is contingent with respect to itself, and necessary with respect to its causes and God's knowledge. To be willed freely, then, is not for an act to be absolutely contingent, but rather for it to be "willed internally" as opposed to "willed externally."

Reactions to Crescas's doctrines were mixed. Isaac Abrabanel, despite his respect for Crescas's piety, rejected his views as either "unintelligible" or "simple-minded." On the other hand, Giovanni Pico della Mirandola appeals to Crescas's critique of Aristotelian physics; Judah Abrabanel's *Dialogues of Love* may be seen as accommodating Crescas's metaphysical views; and Spinoza's notions of necessity, freedom, and extension may well be influenced by the doctrines of *Or Adonai*.

See also GERSONIDES, MAIMONIDES.
                                          T.M.R.

criteriological connection. See CRITERION.

criteriology. See MERCIER.

criterion, broadly, a sufficient condition for the presence of a certain property or for the truth of a certain proposition. Generally, a criterion need be sufficient merely in normal circumstances rather than absolutely sufficient. Typically, a criterion is salient in some way, often by virtue of being a necessary condition as well as a sufficient one. The plural form, 'criteria', is commonly used for a set of singly necessary and jointly sufficient conditions. A set of truth conditions is said to be criterial for the truth of propositions of a certain form. A conceptual analysis of a philosophically important concept may take the form of a proposed set of truth conditions for paradigmatic propositions containing the concept in question. Philosophers have proposed criteria for such notions as meaningfulness, intentionality, knowledge, justification, justice, rightness, and identity (including personal identity and event identity), among many others.

There is a special use of the term in connection with Wittgenstein's well-known remark that "an 'inner process' stands in need of outward criteria," e.g., moans and groans for aches and pains. The suggestion is that a *criteriological connection* is needed to forge a conceptual link between items of a sort that are intelligible and knowable to items of a sort that, but for the connection, would not be intelligible or knowable. A mere *symptom* cannot provide such a connection, for establishing a correlation between a symptom and that for which it is a symptom presupposes that the latter is intelligible and knowable. One objection to a criteriological view, whether about aches or quarks, is that it clashes with realism about entities of the sort in question and lapses into, as the case may be, behaviorism or instrumentalism. For it seems that to posit a criteriological connection is to suppose that the nature and existence of entities of a given sort can depend on the conditions for their intelligibility or knowability, and that is to put the epistemological cart before the ontological horse.

See also PROBLEM OF THE CRITERION.

K.B.

criterion, problem of the. See PROBLEM OF THE CRITERION.

Critical idealism. See KANT.

critical legal studies, a loose assemblage of legal writings and thinkers in the United States and Great Britain since the mid-1970s that aspire to a jurisprudence and a political ideology. Like the American legal realists of the 1920s and 1930s, the jurisprudential program is largely negative, consisting in the discovery of supposed contradictions within both the law as a whole and areas of law such as contracts and criminal law. The jurisprudential implication derived from such supposed contradictions within the law is that any decision in any case can be defended as following logically from some authoritative propositions of law, making the law completely without guidance in particular cases. Also like the American legal realists, the political ideology of critical legal studies is vaguely leftist, embracing the communitarian critique of liberalism. Communitarians fault liberalism for its alleged overemphasis on individual rights and individual welfare at the expense of the intrinsic value of certain collective goods. Given the cognitive rel-

ativism of many of its practitioners, critical legal studies tends not to aspire to have anything that could be called a theory of either law or of politics. **See also JURISPRUDENCE, PHILOSOPHY OF LAW, POLITICAL PHILOSOPHY.** M.S.M.

critical philosophy. See BROAD, KANT.

Critical Realism, a philosophy that at the highest level of generality purports to integrate the positive insights of both New Realism and idealism. New Realism was the first wave of realistic reaction to the dominant idealism of the nineteenth century. It was a version of immediate and direct realism. In its attempt to avoid any representationalism that would lead to idealism, this tradition identified the immediate data of consciousness with objects in the physical world. There is no intermediary between the knower and the known. This heroic tour de force foundered on the phenomena of error, illusion, and perceptual variation, and gave rise to a successor realism – Critical Realism – that acknowledged the mediation of "the mental" in our cognitive grasp of the physical world.

'Critical Realism' was the title of a work in epistemology by Roy Wood Sellars (1916), but its more general use to designate the broader movement derives from the 1920 cooperative volume, *Essays in Critical Realism: A Cooperative Study of the Problem of Knowledge*, containing position papers by Durant Drake, A. O. Lovejoy, J. B. Pratt, A. K. Rogers, C. A. Strong, George Santayana, and Roy Wood Sellars. With New Realism, Critical Realism maintains that the primary object of knowledge is the independent physical world, and that what is immediately present to consciousness is not the physical object as such, but some corresponding mental state broadly construed. Whereas both New Realism and idealism grew out of the conviction that any such mediated account of knowledge is untenable, the Critical Realists felt that only if knowledge of the external world is explained in terms of a process of mental mediation, can error, illusion, and perceptual variation be accommodated. One could fashion an account of mental mediation that did not involve the pitfalls of Lockean representationalism by carefully distinguishing between the object known and the mental state through which it is known.

The Critical Realists differed among themselves both epistemologically and metaphysically. The mediating elements in cognition were variously construed as essences, ideas, or sense-data, and the precise role of these items in cognition was again variously construed. Metaphysically, some were dualists who saw knowledge as unexplainable in terms of physical processes, whereas others (principally Santayana and Sellars) were materialists who saw cognition as simply a function of conscious biological systems. The position of most lasting influence was probably that of Sellars because that torch was taken up by his son, Wilfrid, whose very sophisticated development of it was quite influential.

See also IDEALISM; METAPHYSICAL REALISM; NEW REALISM; PERCEPTION; SELLARS, WILFRID.   C.F.D.

critical theory, any social theory that is at the same time explanatory, normative, practical, and self-reflexive. The term was first developed by Horkheimer as a self-description of the Frankfurt School and its revision of Marxism. It now has a wider significance to include any critical, theoretical approach, including feminism and liberation philosophy. When they make claims to be scientific, such approaches attempt to give rigorous explanations of the causes of oppression, such as ideological beliefs or economic dependence; these explanations must in turn be verified by empirical evidence and employ the best available social and economic theories. Such explanations are also normative and critical, since they imply negative evaluations of current social practices. The explanations are also practical, in that they provide a better self-understanding for agents who may want to improve the social conditions that the theory negatively evaluates. Such change generally aims at "emancipation," and theoretical insight empowers agents to remove limits to human freedom and the causes of human suffering. Finally, these theories must also be self-reflexive: they must account for their own conditions of possibility and for their potentially transformative effects. These requirements contradict the standard account of scientific theories and explanations, particularly positivism and its separation of fact and value. For this reason, the methodological writings of critical theorists often attack positivism and empiricism and attempt to construct alternative epistemologies. Critical theorists also reject relativism, since the cultural relativity of norms would undermine the basis of critical evaluation of social practices and emancipatory change.

The difference between critical and non-critical theories can be illustrated by contrasting the Marxian and Mannheimian theories of ideology. Whereas Mannheim's theory merely describes relations between ideas of social conditions,

Marx's theory tries to show how certain social practices require false beliefs about them by their participants. Marx's theory not only explains why this is so, it also negatively evaluates those practices; it is practical in that by disillusioning participants, it makes them capable of transformative action. It is also self-reflexive, since it shows why some practices require illusions and others do not, and also why social crises and conflicts will lead agents to change their circumstances. It is scientific, in that it appeals to historical evidence and can be revised in light of better theories of social action, language, and rationality. Marx also claimed that his theory was superior for its special "dialectical method," but this is now disputed by most critical theorists, who incorporate many different theories and methods. This broader definition of critical theory, however, leaves a gap between theory and practice and places an extra burden on critics to justify their critical theories without appeal to such notions as inevitable historical progress. This problem has made critical theories more philosophical and concerned with questions of justification.

See also FRANKFURT SCHOOL, LOGICAL POSITIVISM, MANNHEIM, RELATIVISM.   J.Bo.

Croce, Benedetto (1866–1952), Italian philosopher. He was born at Pescasseroli, in the Abruzzi, and after 1886 lived in Naples. He briefly attended the University of Rome and was led to study Herbart's philosophy. In 1904 he founded the influential journal *La critica*. In 1910 he was made life member of the Italian senate. Early in his career he befriended Giovanni Gentile, but this friendship was breached by Gentile's Fascism. During the Fascist period and World War II Croce lived in isolation as the chief anti-fascist thinker in Italy. He later became a leader of the Liberal party and at the age of eighty founded the Institute for Historical Studies.

Croce was a literary and historical scholar who joined his great interest in these fields to philosophy. His best-known work in the English-speaking world is *Aesthetic as Science of Expression and General Linguistic* (1902). This was the first part of his "Philosophy of Spirit"; the second was his *Logic* (1905), the third his theory of the *Practical* (1909), and the fourth his *Historiography* (1917). Croce was influenced by Hegel and the Hegelian aesthetician Francesco De Sanctis (1817–83) and by Vico's conceptions of knowledge, history, and society. He wrote *The Philosophy of Giambattista Vico* (1911) and a famous commentary on Hegel, *What Is Living and What Is*

Dead in the Philosophy of Hegel (1907), in which he advanced his conception of the "dialectic of distincts" as more fundamental than the Hegelian dialectic of opposites.

Croce held that philosophy always springs from the occasion, a view perhaps rooted in his concrete studies of history. He accepted the general Hegelian identification of philosophy with the history of philosophy. His philosophy originates from his conception of aesthetics. Central to his aesthetics is his view of intuition, which evolved through various stages during his career. He regards aesthetic experience as a primitive type of cognition. Intuition involves an awareness of a particular image, which constitutes a non-conceptual form of knowledge. Art is the expression of emotion but not simply for its own sake. The expression of emotion can produce cognitive awareness in the sense that the particular intuited as an image can have a cosmic aspect, so that in it the universal human spirit is perceived. Such perception is present especially in the masterpieces of world literature. Croce's conception of aesthetic has connections with Kant's "intuition" (*Anschauung*) and to an extent with Vico's conception of a primordial form of thought based in imagination (*fantasia*).

Croce's philosophical idealism includes fully developed conceptions of logic, science, law, history, politics, and ethics. His influence to date has been largely in the field of aesthetics and in historicist conceptions of knowledge and culture. His revival of Vico has inspired a whole school of Vico scholarship. Croce's conception of a "Philosophy of Spirit" showed it was possible to develop a post-Hegelian philosophy that, with Hegel, takes "the true to be the whole" but which does not simply imitate Hegel.

See also AESTHETICS, HEGEL, KANT, VICO.

D.P.V.

crucial experiment, a means of deciding between rival theories that, providing parallel explanations of large classes of phenomena, come to be placed at issue by a single fact. For example, the Newtonian emission theory predicts that light travels faster in water than in air; according to the wave theory, light travels slower in water than in air. Dominique François Arago proposed a crucial experiment comparing the respective velocities. Léon Foucault then devised an apparatus to measure the speed of light in various media and found a lower velocity in water than in air. Arago and Foucault concluded for the wave theory, believing that the experiment refuted the emission theory. Other examples include Galileo's discovery of the phases of Venus (Ptolemaic versus Copernican astronomy), Pascal's Puy-de-Dôme experiment with the barometer (vacuists versus plenists), Fresnel's prediction of a spot of light in circular shadows (particle versus wave optics), and Eddington's measurement of the gravitational bending of light rays during a solar eclipse (Newtonian versus Einsteinian gravitation). At issue in crucial experiments is usually a novel prediction.

The notion seems to derive from Francis Bacon, whose *New Organon* (1620) discusses the "Instance of the Fingerpost (*Instantia* – later *experimentum – crucis*)," a term borrowed from the post set up at crossroads to indicate several directions. Crucial experiments were emphasized in early nineteenth-century scientific methodology – e.g., in John F. Herschel's *A Preliminary Discourse on the Study of Natural Philosophy* (1830). Duhem argued that crucial experiments resemble false dilemmas: hypotheses in physics do not come in pairs, so that crucial experiments cannot transform one of the two into a demonstrated truth. Discussing Foucault's experiment, Duhem asks whether we dare assert that no other hypothesis is imaginable and suggests that instead of light being either a simple particle or wave, light might be something else, perhaps a disturbance propagated within a dielectric medium, as theorized by Maxwell. In the twentieth century, crucial experiments and novel predictions figured prominently in the work of Imre Lakatos (1922–74). Agreeing that crucial experiments are unable to overthrow theories, Lakatos accepted them as retroactive indications of the fertility or progress of research programs.

See also BACON, FRANCIS; CONFIRMATION; DUHEM; PHILOSOPHY OF SCIENCE.   R.Ar.

Crusius, Christian August (1715–75), German philosopher, theologian, and a devout Lutheran pastor who believed that religion was endangered by the rationalist views especially of Wolff. He devoted his considerable philosophical powers to working out acute and often deep criticisms of Wolff and developing a comprehensive alternative to the Wolffian system. His main philosophical works were published in the 1740s. In his understanding of epistemology and logic Crusius broke with many of the assumptions that allowed Wolff to argue from how we think of things to how things are. For instance, Crusius tried to show that the necessity in causal connection is not the same as logical necessity. He rejected the Leibnizian view that this world is probably the best possible world, and he criticized the Wolffian view of freedom of the will as merely a concealed spiritual mechanism.

His ethics stressed our dependence on God and his commands, as did the natural law theory of Pufendorf, but he developed the view in some strikingly original ways. Rejecting voluntarism, Crusius held that God's commands take the form of innate principles of the will (not the understanding). Everyone alike can know what they are, so (contra Wolff) there is no need for moral experts. And they carry their own motivational force with them, so there is no need for external sanctions. We have obligations of prudence to do what will forward our own ends; but true obligation, the obligation of virtue, arises only when we act simply to comply with God's law, regardless of any ends of our own. In this distinction between two kinds of obligation, as in many of his other views, Crusius plainly anticipated much that Kant came to think. Kant when young read and admired his work, and it is mainly for this reason that Crusius is now remembered.

See also KANT, NATURAL LAW, PUFENDORF.

J.B.S.

Cudworth, Damaris, Lady Masham (1659–1708), English philosopher and author of two treatises on religion, *A Discourse Concerning the Love of God* (1690) and *Occasional Thoughts in Reference to a Virtuous Christian Life* (1705). The first argues against the views of the English Malebranchian, John Norris; the second, ostensibly about the importance of education for women, argues for the need to establish natural religion on rational principles and explores the place of revealed religion within a rational framework. Cudworth's reputation is founded on her long friendship with John Locke. Her correspondence with him is almost entirely personal; she also entered into a brief but philosophically interesting exchange of letters with Leibniz. **See also** LOCKE, MALEBRANCHE.   M.At.

Cudworth, Ralph. See CAMBRIDGE PLATONISTS, HYLOZOISM.

cultural relativism. See RELATIVISM.

Culverwel, Nathaniel. See CAMBRIDGE PLATONISTS.

Cumberland, Richard (1631–1718), English philosopher and bishop. He wrote a Latin *Treatise of the Laws of Nature* (1672), translated twice into English and once into French. Admiring Grotius, Cumberland hoped to refute Hobbes in the interests of defending Christian morality and religion.

He refused to appeal to innate ideas and a priori arguments because he thought Hobbes must be attacked on his own ground. Hence he offered a reductive and naturalistic account of natural law. The one basic moral law of nature is that the pursuit of the good of all rational beings is the best path to the agent's own good. This is true because God made nature so that actions aiding others are followed by beneficial consequences to the agent, while those harmful to others harm the agent. Since the natural consequences of actions provide sanctions that, once we know them, will make us act for the good of others, we can conclude that there is a divine law by which we are obligated to act for the common good. And all the other laws of nature follow from the basic law. Cumberland refused to discuss free will, thereby suggesting a view of human action as fully determined by natural causes. If on his theory it is a blessing that God made nature (including humans) to work as it does, the religious reader must wonder if there is any role left for God concerning morality. Cumberland is generally viewed as a major forerunner of utilitarianism. **See also** GROTIUS, HOBBES, NATURAL LAW.

J.B.S.

cum hoc ergo propter hoc. **See** INFORMAL FALLACY.

Cursus Coninbricensis. See FONSECA.

curve-fitting problem, the problem of making predictions from past observations by fitting curves to the data. Curve fitting has two steps: first, select a family of curves; then, find the best-fitting curve by some statistical criterion such as the method of least squares (e.g., choose the curve that has the least sum of squared deviations between the curve and data). The method was first proposed by Adrian Marie Legendre (1752–1833) and Carl Friedrich Gauss (1777–1855) in the early nineteenth century as a way of inferring planetary trajectories from noisy data.

More generally, curve fitting may be used to construct low-level empirical generalizations. For example, suppose that the ideal gas law, $P = nkT$, is chosen as the *form* of the law governing the dependence of the pressure P on the equilibrium temperature T of a fixed volume of gas, where n is the molecular number per unit volume and k is Boltzmann's constant (a universal constant equal to 1.3804×10^{-16} erg°C^{-1}. When the parameter nk is adjustable, the law specifies a *family* of curves – one for each numerical value of the parameter. Curve fitting may be used to determine the best-fitting member of the family, thereby effecting a measurement of the theoretical parameter, *nk*.

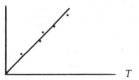

Best-fitting straight line passing through the origin

The philosophically vexing problem is how to justify the initial choice of the form of the law. On the one hand, one might choose a very large, complex family of curves, which would ensure excellent fit with *any* data set. The problem with this option is that the best-fitting curve may *over*-fit the data. If too much attention is paid to the random elements of the data, then the predictively useful trends and regularities will be missed. If it looks too good to be true, it probably is. On the other hand, simpler families run a greater risk of making grossly false assumptions about the true *form* of the law. Intuitively, the solution is to choose a *simple* family of curves that maintains a reasonable degree of fit. The simplicity of a family of curves is measured by the paucity of parameters. The problem is to say how and why such a trade-off between simplicity and goodness of fit should be made.

When a theory can accommodate recalcitrant data only by the ad hoc – i.e., improperly motivated – addition of new terms and parameters, students of science have long felt that the subsequent increase in the degree of fit should not count in the theory's favor, and such additions are sometimes called ad hoc hypotheses. The best-known example of this sort of ad hoc hypothesizing is the addition of epicycles upon epicycles in the planetary astronomy of Ptolemy and Copernicus. This is an example in which a gain in fit need not compensate for the loss of simplicity.

Contemporary philosophers sometimes formulate the curve-fitting problem differently. They often assume that there is no noise in the data, and speak of the problem of choosing among different curves that fit the data *exactly*. Then the problem is to choose the simplest curve from among all those curves that pass through every data point. The problem is that there is no universally accepted way of defining the simplicity of *single* curves.

No matter how the problem is formulated, it is widely agreed that simplicity should play some role in theory choice. Rationalists have championed the curve-fitting problem as exemplifying the underdetermination of theory from data and the need to make a priori assumptions about the simplicity of nature. Those philosophers who think that we have no such a priori knowledge still need to account for the relevance of simplicity to science.

Whewell described curve fitting as the colligation of facts in the quantitative sciences, and the agreement in the measured parameters (coefficients) obtained by different colligations of facts as the consilience of inductions. Different colligations of facts (say on the same gas at different volume or for other gases) may yield good agreement among independently measured values of parameters (like the molecular density of the gas and Boltzmann's constant). By identifying different parameters found to agree, we constrain the form of the law without appealing to a priori knowledge (good news for empiricism). But the accompanying increase in unification also worsens the overall degree of fit. Thus, there is also the problem of how and why we should trade off unification with total degree of fit.

Statisticians often refer to a family of hypotheses as a *model*. A rapidly growing literature in statistics on model selection has not yet produced any universally accepted formula for trading off simplicity with degree of fit. However, there is wide agreement among statisticians that the paucity of parameters is the appropriate way of measuring simplicity.

See also EXPLANATION, PHILOSOPHY OF SCIENCE, WHEWELL.   M.R.F.

Cusa. See NICHOLAS OF CUSA.

Cusanus. See NICHOLAS OF CUSA.

cut, Dedekind. See DEDEKIND.

cut-elimination theorem, a theorem stating that a certain type of inference rule (including a rule that corresponds to *modus ponens*) is not needed in classical logic. The idea was anticipated by J. Herbrand; the theorem was proved by G. Gentzen and generalized by S. Kleene. Gentzen formulated a sequent calculus – i.e., a deductive system with rules for statements about derivability. It includes a rule that we here express as 'From $(C \vdash D,M)$ and $(M,C \vdash D)$, infer $(C \vdash D)$' or 'Given that C yields D or M, and that C plus M yields D, we may infer that C yields D'.

This is called the *cut rule* because it cuts out the middle formula M. Gentzen showed that his sequent calculus is an adequate formalization of the predicate logic, and that the cut rule can be eliminated; anything provable with it can be proved without it. One important consequence of this is that, if a formula F is provable, then there is a proof of F that consists solely of sub-formulas of F. This fact simplifies the study of provability. Gentzen's methodology applies directly to classical logic but can be adapted to many nonclassical logics, including some intu-itionistic logics. It has led to some important the-orems about consistency, and has illuminated the role of auxiliary assumptions in the deriva-tion of consequences from a theory. **See also** **CONSISTENCY, PROOF THEORY.**   D.H.

cybernetics (coined by Norbert Wiener in 1947 from Greek *kubernētēs*, 'helmsman'), the study of the communication and manipulation of infor-mation in service of the control and guidance of biological, physical, or chemical energy systems. Historically, cybernetics has been intertwined with mathematical theories of information (communication) and computation. To describe the cybernetic properties of systems or processes requires ways to describe and measure informa-tion (reduce uncertainty) about events within the system and its environment. Feedback and feedforward, the basic ingredients of cybernetic processes, involve information – as what is fed forward or backward – and are basic to processes such as homeostasis in biological systems, automation in industry, and guidance systems. Of course, their most comprehensive applica-tion is to the purposive behavior (thought) of cognitively goal-directed systems such as our-selves.

Feedback occurs in closed-loop, as opposed to open-loop, systems. Actually, 'open-loop' is a misnomer (involving no loop), but it has become entrenched. The standard example of an open-loop system is that of placing a heater with con-stant output in a closed room and leaving it switched on. Room temperature may acciden-tally reach, but may also dramatically exceed, the temperature desired by the occupants. Such a heating system has no means of controlling itself to adapt to required conditions.

In contrast, the standard closed-loop system incorporates a feedback component. At the heart of cybernetics is the concept of control. A con-trolled process is one in which an end state that is reached depends essentially on the behavior of the controlling system and not merely on its external environment. That is, control involves partial independence for the system. A control system may be pictured as having both an inner and outer environment. The inner environment consists of the internal events that make up the system; the outer environment consists of events that causally impinge on the system, threatening disruption and loss of system integrity and stability. For a system to maintain its independence and identity in the face of fluc-tuations in its external environment, it must be able to detect information about those changes in the external environment. Information must pass through the interface between inner and outer environments, and the system must be able to compensate for fluctuations of the outer environment by adjusting its own inner envi-ronmental variables. Otherwise, disturbances in the outer environment will overcome the sys-tem – bringing its inner states into equilibrium with the outer states, thereby losing its identity as a distinct, independent system. This is nowhere more certain than with the homeosta-tic systems of the body (for temperature or blood sugar levels).

Control in the attainment of goals is accom-plished by minimizing error. *Negative feedback,* or information about error, is the difference between activity a system actually performs (output) and that activity which is its goal to per-form (input). The standard example of control incorporating negative feedback is the thermo-statically controlled heating system. The actual room temperature (system output) carries infor-mation to the thermostat that can be compared (via goal-state comparator) to the desired tem-perature for the room (input) as embodied in the set-point on the thermostat; a correction can then be made to minimize the difference (error) – the furnace turns on or off.

Positive feedback tends to amplify the value of the output of a system (or of a system distur-bance) by adding the value of the output to the system input quantity. Thus, the system accen-tuates disturbances and, if unchecked, will even-tually pass the brink of instability. Suppose that as room temperature rises it causes the thermo-static set-point to rise in direct proportion to the rise in temperature. This would cause the fur-nace to continue to output heat (possibly with disastrous consequences). Many biological mal-adies have just this characteristic. For example, severe loss of blood causes inability of the heart to pump effectively, which causes loss of arterial pressure, which, in turn, causes reduced flow of blood to the heart, reducing pumping efficiency.

Cognitively goal-directed systems are also cybernetic systems. Purposive attainment of a goal by a goal-directed system must have (at least): (1) an internal representation of the goal state of the system (a detector for whether the desired state is actual); (2) a feedback loop by which information about the present state of the system can be compared with the goal state as internally represented and by means of which an error correction can be made to minimize any difference; and (3) a causal dependency of system output upon the error-correction process of condition (2) (to distinguish goal success from fortuitous goal satisfaction).

See also COMPUTER THEORY, INFORMATION THEORY, SYSTEMS THEORY.   F.A.

Cynics, a classical Greek philosophical school characterized by asceticism and emphasis on the sufficiency of virtue for happiness (*eudaimonia*), boldness in speech, and shamelessness in action. The Cynics were strongly influenced by Socrates and were themselves an important influence on Stoic ethics.

An ancient tradition links the Cynics to Antisthenes (c.445–c.360 B.C.), an Athenian. He fought bravely in the battle of Tanagra and claimed that he would not have been so courageous if he had been born of two Athenians instead of an Athenian and a Thracian slave. He studied with Gorgias, but later became a close companion of Socrates and was present at Socrates' death. Antisthenes was proudest of his wealth, although he had no money, because he was satisfied with what he had and he could live in whatever circumstances he found himself. Here he follows Socrates in three respects. First, Socrates himself lived with a disregard for pleasure and pain – e.g., walking barefoot in snow. Second, Socrates thinks that in every circumstance a virtuous person is better off than a nonvirtuous one; Antisthenes anticipates the Stoic development of this to the view that virtue is sufficient for happiness, because the virtuous person uses properly whatever is present. Third, both Socrates and Antisthenes stress that the soul is more important than the body, and neglect the body for the soul. Unlike the later Cynics, however, both Socrates and Antisthenes do accept pleasure when it is available. Antisthenes also does not focus exclusively on ethics; he wrote on other topics, including logic. (He supposedly told Plato that he could see a horse but not horseness, to which Plato replied that he had not acquired the means to see horseness.) Diogenes of Sinope (c.400–c.325 B.C.) contin-

ued the emphasis on self-sufficiency and on the soul, but took the disregard for pleasure to asceticism. (According to one story, Plato called Diogenes "Socrates gone mad.") He came to Athens after being exiled from Sinope, perhaps because the coinage was defaced, either by himself or by others, under his father's direction. He took 'deface the coinage!' as a motto, meaning that the current standards were corrupt and should be marked as corrupt by being defaced; his refusal to live by them was his defacing them. For example, he lived in a wine cask, ate whatever scraps he came across, and wrote approvingly of cannibalism and incest. One story reports that he carried a lighted lamp in broad daylight looking for an honest human, probably intending to suggest that the people he did see were so corrupted that they were no longer really people. He apparently wanted to replace the debased standards of custom with the genuine standards of nature – but nature in the sense of what was minimally required for human life, which an individual human could achieve, without society. Because of this, he was called a Cynic, from the Greek word *kuon* (dog), because he was as shameless as a dog.

Diogenes' most famous successor was Crates (fl. c.328–325 B.C.). He was a Boeotian, from Thebes, and renounced his wealth to become a Cynic. He seems to have been more pleasant than Diogenes; according to some reports, every Athenian house was open to him, and he was even regarded by them as a household god. Perhaps the most famous incident involving Crates is his marriage to Hipparchia, who took up the Cynic way of life despite her family's opposition and insisted that educating herself was preferable to working a loom. Like Diogenes, Crates emphasized that happiness is self-sufficiency, and claimed that asceticism is required for self-sufficiency; e.g., he advises us not to prefer oysters to lentils. He argues that no one is happy if happiness is measured by the balance of pleasure and pain, since in each period of our lives there is more pain than pleasure.

Cynicism continued to be active through the third century B.C., and returned to prominence in the second century A.D. after an apparent decline.

See also EUDAIMONISM, SOCRATES, STOICISM, VIRTUE ETHICS.   H.A.I.

Cyrenaics, a classical Greek philosophical school that began shortly after Socrates and lasted for several centuries, noted especially for hedonism. Ancient writers trace the Cyrenaics back to Aristippus of Cyrene (fifth-fourth century B.C.), an associate of Socrates. Aristippus came to Athens because of Socrates' fame and later greatly enjoyed the luxury of court life in Sicily. (Some people ascribe the founding of the school to his grandchild Aristippus, because of an ancient report that the elder Aristippus said nothing clear about the human end.) The Cyrenaics include Aristippus's child Arete, her child Aristippus (taught by Arete), Hegesius, Anniceris, and Theodorus. The school seems to have been superseded by the Epicureans. No Cyrenaic writings survive, and the reports we do have are sketchy.

The Cyrenaics avoid mathematics and natural philosophy, preferring ethics because of its utility. (According to them, not only will studying nature not make us virtuous, it also won't make us stronger or richer.) Some reports claim that they also avoid logic and epistemology. But this is not true of all the Cyrenaics: according to other reports, they think logic and epistemology are useful, consider arguments (and also causes) as topics to be covered in ethics, and have an epistemology. Their epistemology is skeptical. We can know only how we are affected; we can know, e.g., that we are whitening, but not that whatever is causing this sensation is itself white. This differs from Protagoras's theory; unlike Protagoras the Cyrenaics draw no inferences about the things that affect us, claiming only that external things have a nature that we cannot know. But, like Protagoras, the Cyrenaics base their theory on the problem of conflicting appearances. Given their epistemology, if humans ought to aim at something that is not a way of being affected (i.e., something that is immediately perceived according to them), we can never know anything about it. Unsurprisingly, then, they claim that the end is a way of being affected; in particular, they are hedonists. The end of good actions is particular pleasures (smooth changes), and the end of bad actions is particular pains (rough changes). There is also an intermediate class, which aims at neither pleasure nor pain. Mere absence of pain is in this intermediate class, since the absence of pain may be merely a static state. Pleasure for Aristippus seems to be the sensation of pleasure, not including related psychic states. We should aim at pleasure (although not everyone does), as is clear from our naturally seeking it as children, before we consciously choose to. Happiness, which is the sum of the particular pleasures someone experiences, is choiceworthy only for the particular pleasures that constitute it, while particular pleasures are choiceworthy for themselves. Cyrenaics, then, are not concerned with maximizing total pleasure over a lifetime, but only with particular pleasures, and so they should not choose to give up particular pleasures on the chance of increasing the total.

Later Cyrenaics diverge in important respects from the original Cyrenaic hedonism, perhaps in response to the development of Epicurus's views. Hegesias claims that happiness is impossible because of the pains associated with the body, and so thinks of happiness as total pleasure minus total pain. He emphasizes that wise people act for themselves, and denies that people actually act for someone else. Anniceris, on the other hand, claims that wise people are happy even if they have few pleasures, and so seems to think of happiness as the sum of pleasures, and not as the excess of pleasures over pains. Anniceris also begins considering psychic pleasures: he insists that friends should be valued not only for their utility, but also for our feelings toward them. We should even accept losing pleasure because of a friend, even though pleasure is the end. Theodorus goes a step beyond Anniceris. He claims that the end of good actions is joy and that of bad actions is grief. (Surprisingly, he denies that friendship is reasonable, since fools have friends only for utility and wise people need no friends.) He even regards pleasure as intermediate between practical wisdom and its opposite. This seems to involve regarding happiness as the end, not particular pleasures, and may involve losing particular pleasures for long-term happiness.

See also EUDAIMONISM, HEDONISM, SOCRATES.   H.A.I.

Czolbe, Heinrich (1819–73), German philosopher. He was born in Danzig and trained in theology and medicine. His main works are *Neue Darstellung des Sensualismus* ("New Exposition of Sensualism," 1855), *Entstehung des Selbstbewusstseins* ("Origin of Self-Consciousness," 1856), *Die Grenzen und der Ursprung der menschlichen Erkenntnis* ("The Limits and Origin of Human Knowledge," 1865), and a posthumously published study, *Grundzüge der extensionalen Erkenntnistheorie* (1875).

Czolbe proposed a sensualistic theory of knowledge: knowledge is a copy of the actual, and spatial extension is ascribed even to ideas. Space is the support of all attributes. His later work defended a non-reductive materialism. Czolbe made the rejection of the supersensuous a central principle and defended a radical "sensationalism." Despite this, he did not present a dogmatic materialism, but cast his philosophy in hypothetical form.

In his study of the origin of self-consciousness Czolbe held that dissatisfaction with the actual world generates supersensuous ideas and branded this attitude as "immoral." He excluded supernatural phenomena on the basis not of physiological or scientific studies but of a "moral feeling of duty towards the natural world-order and contentment with it." The same valuation led him to postulate the eternality of terrestrial life. Nietzsche was familiar with Czolbe's works and incorporated some of his themes into his philosophy.

See also SENSATIONALISM.   G.J.S.

D

d'Ailly, Pierre (1350–1420), French Ockhamist philosopher, prelate, and writer. Educated at the Collège de Navarre, he was promoted to doctor in the Sorbonne in 1380, appointed chancellor of Paris University in 1389, consecrated bishop in 1395, and made a cardinal in 1411. He was influenced by John of Mirecourt's nominalism. He taught Gerson. At the Council of Constance (1414–18), which condemned Huss's teachings, d'Ailly upheld the superiority of the council over the pope (conciliarism). The relation of astrology to history and theology figures among his primary interests. His 1414 *Tractatus de Concordia astronomicae* predicted the 1789 French Revolution. He composed a *De anima*, a commentary on Boethius's *Consolation of Philosophy*, and another on Peter Lombard's *Sentences*. His early logical work, *Concepts and Insolubles* (c.1472), was particularly influential. In epistemology, d'Ailly contradistinguished "natural light" (indubitable knowledge) from reason (relative knowledge), and emphasized thereafter the uncertainty of experimental knowledge and the mere probability of the classical "proofs" of God's existence. His doctrine of God differentiates God's absolute power (*potentia absoluta*) from God's ordained power on earth (*potentia ordinata*). His theology anticipated fideism (*Deum esse sola fide tenetur*), his ethics the spirit of Protestantism, and his sacramentology Lutheranism.   J.-L.S.

d'Alembert, Jean Le Rond (1717–83), French mathematician, philosopher, and Encyclopedist. According to Grimm, d'Alembert was the prime luminary of the philosophic party. An abandoned, illegitimate child, he nonetheless received an outstanding education at the Jansenist Collège des Quatre-Nations in Paris. He read law for a while, tried medicine, and settled on mathematics. In 1743, he published an acclaimed *Treatise of Dynamics*. Subsequently, he joined the Paris Academy of Sciences and contributed decisive works on mathematics and physics. In 1754, he was elected to the French Academy, of which he later became permanent secretary. In association with Diderot, he launched the *Encyclopedia*, for which he wrote the epoch-making *Discours préliminaire* (1751) and numerous entries on science. Unwilling to compromise with the censorship, he resigned as coeditor in 1758.

In the *Discours préliminaire*, d'Alembert specified the divisions of the philosophical discourse on man: pneumatology, logic, and ethics. Contrary to Christian philosophies, he limited pneumatology to the investigation of the human soul. Prefiguring positivism, his *Essay on the Elements of Philosophy* (1759) defines philosophy as a comparative examination of physical phenomena. Influenced by Bacon, Locke, and Newton, d'Alembert's epistemology associates Cartesian psychology with the sensory origin of ideas. Though assuming the universe to be rationally ordered, he discarded metaphysical questions as inconclusive. The substance, or the essence, of soul and matter, is unknowable. Agnosticism ineluctably arises from his empirically based naturalism. D'Alembert is prominently featured in *D'Alembert's Dream* (1769), Diderot's dialogical apology for materialism.

See also ENCYCLOPEDIA.   J.-L.S.

Damascene, John. See JOHN OF DAMASCUS.

Damascius (c.462–c.550), Greek Neoplatonist philosopher, last head of the Athenian Academy before its closure by Justinian in A.D. 529. Born probably in Damascus, he studied first in Alexandria, and then moved to Athens shortly before Proclus's death in 485. He returned to Alexandria, where he attended the lectures of Ammonius, but came back again to Athens in around 515, to assume the headship of the Academy. After the closure, he retired briefly with some other philosophers, including Simplicius, to Persia, but left after about a year, probably for Syria, where he died.

He composed many works, including a life of his master Isidorus, which survives in truncated form; commentaries on Aristotle's *Categories, On the Heavens*, and *Meteorologics* I (all lost); commentaries on Plato's *Alcibiades, Phaedo, Philebus*, and *Parmenides*, which survive; and a surviving treatise *On First Principles*. His philosophical system is a further elaboration of the scholastic Neoplatonism of Proclus, exhibiting a great proliferation of metaphysical entities.

See also NEOPLATONISM.   J.M.D.

Danto, Arthur Coleman (b.1924), American philosopher of art and art history who has also contributed to the philosophies of history, action, knowledge, science, and metaphilosophy. Among his influential studies in the history of philosophy are books on Nietzsche, Sartre, and Indian thought.

Danto arrives at his philosophy of art through his "method of indiscernibles," which has greatly influenced contemporary philosophical aesthetics. According to his metaphilosophy, genuine philosophical questions arise when there is a theoretical need to differentiate two things that are perceptually indiscernible – such as prudential actions versus moral actions (Kant), causal chains versus constant conjunctions (Hume), and perfect dreams versus reality (Descartes). Applying the method to the philosophy of art, Danto asks what distinguishes an artwork, such as Warhol's *Brillo Box*, from its perceptually indiscernible, real-world counterparts, such as Brillo boxes by Proctor and Gamble. His answer – his partial definition of art – is that *x* is a work of art only if (1) *x* is about something and (2) *x* embodies its meaning (i.e., discovers a mode of presentation intended to be appropriate to whatever subject *x* is about). These two necessary conditions, Danto claims, enable us to distinguish between artworks and real things – between Warhol's *Brillo Box* and Proctor and Gamble's.

However, critics have pointed out that these conditions fail, since real Brillo boxes are about something (Brillo) about which they embody or convey meanings through their mode of presentation (viz., that Brillo is clean, fresh, and dynamic). Moreover, this is not an isolated example. Danto's theory of art confronts systematic difficulties in differentiating real cultural artifacts, such as industrial packages, from artworks proper.

In addition to his philosophy of art, Danto proposes a philosophy of art history. Like Hegel, Danto maintains that art history – as a developmental, progressive process – has ended. Danto believes that modern art has been primarily reflexive (i.e., about itself); it has attempted to use its own forms and strategies to disclose the essential nature of art. Cubism and abstract expressionism, for example, exhibit saliently the two-dimensional nature of painting. With each experiment, modern art has gotten closer to disclosing its own essence. But, Danto argues, with works such as Warhol's *Brillo Box*, artists have taken the philosophical project of self-definition as far as they can, since once an artist like Warhol has *shown* that artworks can be perceptually indiscernible from "real things" and, therefore,

can *look like anything*, there is nothing further that the artist qua artist can *show* through the medium of appearances about the nature of art. The task of defining art must be reassigned to philosophers to be treated discursively, and art history – as the developmental, progressive narrative of self-definition – ends.

Since that turn of events was putatively precipitated by Warhol in the 1960s, Danto calls the present period of art making "post-historical." As an art critic for *The Nation*, he has been chronicling its vicissitudes for a decade and a half. Some dissenters, nevertheless, have been unhappy with Danto's claim that art history has ended because, they maintain, he has failed to demonstrate that the only prospects for a developmental, progressive history of art reside in the project of the self-definition of art.

See also AESTHETICS.   N.C.

Darwin, Charles. See DARWINISM.

Darwinism, the view that biological species evolve primarily by means of chance variation and natural selection. Although several important scientists prior to Charles Darwin (1809–82) had suggested that species evolve and had provided mechanisms for that evolution, Darwin was the first to set out his mechanism in sufficient detail and provide adequate empirical grounding. Even though Darwin preferred to talk about descent with modification, the term that rapidly came to characterize his theory was *evolution*. According to Darwin, organisms vary with respect to their characteristics. In a litter of puppies, some will be bigger, some will have longer hair, some will be more resistant to disease, etc. Darwin termed these variations chance, not because he thought that they were in any sense "uncaused," but to reject any general correlation between the variations that an organism might need and those it gets, as Lamarck had proposed. Instead, successive generations of organisms become adapted to their environments in a more roundabout way. Variations occur in all directions. The organisms that happen to possess the characteristics necessary to survive and reproduce proliferate. Those that do not either die or leave fewer offspring.

Before Darwin, an adaptation was any trait that fits an organism to its environment. After Darwin, the term came to be limited to just those useful traits that arose through natural selection. For example, the sutures in the skulls of mammals make parturition easier, but they are not adaptations in an evolutionary sense because they arose in ancestors that did not give birth to live young, as is indicated by these same sutures appearing in the skulls of egg-laying birds. Because organisms are integrated systems, Darwin thought that adaptations had to arise through the accumulation of numerous, small variations. As a result, evolution is gradual. Darwin himself was unsure about how progressive biological evolution is. Organisms certainly become better adapted to their environments through successive generations, but as fast as organisms adapt to their environments, their environments are likely to change. Thus, Darwinian evolution may be goal-directed, but different species pursue different goals, and these goals keep changing.

Because heredity was so important to his theory of evolution, Darwin supplemented it with a theory of heredity – *pangenesis*. According to this theory, the cells throughout the body of an organism produce numerous tiny gemmules that find their way to the reproductive organs of the organism to be transmitted in reproduction. An offspring receives variable numbers of gemmules from each of its parents for each of its characteristics. For instance, the male parent might contribute 214 gemmules for length of hair to one offspring, 121 to another, etc., while the female parent might contribute 54 gemmules for length of hair to the first offspring and 89 to the second. As a result, characters tend to blend. Darwin even thought that gemmules themselves might merge, but he did not think that the merging of gemmules was an important factor in the blending of characters. Numerous objections were raised to Darwin's theory in his day, and one of the most telling stemmed from his adopting a blending theory of inheritance. As fast as natural selection biases evolution in a particular direction, blending inheritance neutralizes its effects. Darwin's opponents argued that each species had its own range of variation. Natural selection might bias the organisms belonging to a species in a particular direction, but as a species approached its limits of variation, additional change would become more difficult. Some special mechanism was needed to leap over the deep, though possibly narrow, chasms that separate species.

Because a belief in biological evolution became widespread within a decade or so after the publication of Darwin's *Origin of Species* in 1859, the tendency is to think that it was Darwin's view of evolution that became popular. Nothing could be further from the truth. Darwin's contemporaries found his theory too materialistic and haphazard because no supernatural or teleological force influenced evolutionary development. Darwin's contemporaries were willing to accept evolution, but not the sort advocated by Darwin. Although Darwin viewed the evolution of species on the model of individual development, he did not think that it was directed by some internal force or induced in a Lamarckian fashion by the environment. Most Darwinians adopted just such a position. They also argued that species arise in the space of a single generation so that the boundaries between species remained as discrete as the creationists had maintained. Ideal morphologists even eliminated any genuine temporal dimension to evolution. Instead they viewed the evolution of species in the same atemporal way that mathematicians view the transformation of an ellipse into a circle. The revolution that Darwin instigated was in most respects non-Darwinian. By the turn of the century, Darwinism had gone into a decided eclipse.

Darwin himself remained fairly open with respect to the mechanisms of evolution. For example, he was willing to accept a minor role for Lamarckian forms of inheritance, and he acknowledged that on occasion a new species might arise quite rapidly on the model of the Ancon sheep. Several of his followers were less flexible, rejecting all forms of Lamarckian inheritance and insisting that evolutionary change is always gradual. Eventually Darwinism became identified with the views of these neo-Darwinians. Thus, when Mendelian genetics burst on the scene at the turn of the century, opponents of Darwinism interpreted this new particulate theory of inheritance as being incompatible with Darwin's blending theory. The difference between Darwin's theory of pangenesis and Mendelian genetics, however, did not concern the existence of hereditary particles. Gemmules were as particulate as genes. The difference lay in numbers. According to early Mendelians, each character is controlled by a single pair of genes. Instead of receiving a variable number of gemmules from each parent for each character, each offspring gets a single gene from each parent, and these genes do not in any sense blend with each other. Blue eyes remain as blue as ever from generation to generation, even when the gene for blue eyes resides opposite the gene for brown eyes.

As the nature of heredity was gradually worked out, biologists began to realize that a Darwinian view of evolution could be combined with Mendelian genetics. Initially, the founders of this later stage in the development of neo-Darwinism exhibited considerable variation in their beliefs about the evolutionary process, but as they strove to produce a single, synthetic theory, they tended to become more Darwinian than Darwin had been. Although they acknowledged that other factors, such as the effects of small numbers, might influence evolution, they emphasized that natural selection is the sole directive force in evolution. It alone could explain the complex adaptations exhibited by organisms. New species might arise through the isolation of a few founder organisms, but from a populational perspective, evolution was still gradual. New species do not arise in the space of a single generation by means of "hopeful monsters" or any other developmental means. Nor was evolution in any sense directional or progressive. Certain lineages might become more complex for a while, but at this same time, others would become simpler. Because biological evolution is so opportunistic, the tree of life is highly irregular. But the united front presented by the neo-Darwinians was in part an illusion. Differences of opinion persisted, for instance over how heterogeneous species should be.

No sooner did neo-Darwinism become the dominant view among evolutionary biologists than voices of dissent were raised. Currently, almost every aspect of the neo-Darwinian paradigm is being challenged. No one proposes to reject naturalism, but those who view themselves as opponents of neo-Darwinism urge more important roles for factors treated as only minor by the neo-Darwinians. For example, neo-Darwinians view selection as being extremely sharp-sighted. Any inferior organism, no matter how slightly inferior, is sure to be eliminated. Nearly all variations are deleterious. Currently evolutionists, even those who consider themselves Darwinians, acknowledge that a high percentage of changes at the molecular level may be neutral with respect to survival or reproduction. On current estimates, over 95 percent of an organism's genes may have no function at all. Disagreement also exists about the level of organization at which selection can operate. Some evolutionary biologists insist that selection occurs primarily at the level of single genes, while others think that it can have effects at higher levels of organization, certainly at the organismic level, possibly at the level of entire species. Some biologists emphasize the effects of developmental constraints on the evolutionary process, while others have discovered unexpected mechanisms such as molecular drive. How much of this conceptual variation will become incorporated into Darwinism remains to be seen.

See also MECHANISTIC EXPLANATION, MENDEL, PHILOSOPHY OF BIOLOGY, TELEOLOGY.   D.L.H.

Darwinism, social. See SOCIAL BIOLOGY.

Dasein. See HEIDEGGER.

David. See COMMENTARIES ON ARISTOTLE.

Davidson, Donald (b.1917), American metaphysician and philosopher of mind and language. His views on the relationship between our conceptions of ourselves as persons and as complex physical objects have had an enormous impact on contemporary philosophy. Davidson regards the mind–body problem as the problem of the relation between mental and physical events; his discussions of explanation assume that the entities explained are events; causation is a relation between events; and action is a species of events, so that events are the very subject matter of action theory. His central claim concerning events is that they are concrete particulars – unrepeatable entities located in space and time. He does not take for granted that events exist, but argues for their existence and for specific claims as to their nature.

In "The Individuation of Events" (in *Essays on Actions and Events*, 1980), Davidson argues that a satisfactory theory of action must recognize that we talk of the same action under different descriptions. We must therefore assume the existence of actions. His strongest argument for the existence of events derives from his most original contribution to metaphysics, the semantic method of truth (*Essays on Actions and Events*, pp. 105–80; *Essays on Truth and Interpretation*, 1984, pp. 199–214). The argument is based on a distinctive trait of the English language (one not obviously shared by signal systems in lower animals), namely, its productivity of combinations. We learn modes of composition as well as words and are thus prepared to produce and respond to complex expressions never before encountered. Davidson argues, from such considerations, that our very understanding of English requires assuming the existence of events.

To understand Davidson's rather complicated views about the relationships between mind and body, consider the following claims:

(1) The mental and the physical are distinct.
(2) The mental and the physical causally interact.
(3) The physical is causally closed.

(1) says that no mental event is a physical event; (2), that some mental events cause physical events and vice versa; and (3), that all the causes of physical events are physical events. If mental events are distinct from physical events and sometimes cause them, then the physical is not causally closed. The dilemma posed by the plausibility of each of these claims and by their apparent incompatibility just is the traditional mind–body problem.

Davidson's resolution consists of three theses:

(4) There are no strict psychological or psychophysical laws; in fact, all strict laws are expressible in purely physical vocabulary.

(5) Mental events causally interact with physical events.

(6) Event c causes event e only if some strict causal law subsumes c and e.

It is commonly held that a property expressed by M is reducible to a property expressed by P (where M and P are not logically connected) only if some exceptionless law links them. So, given (4), mental and physical properties are distinct. (6) says that c causes e only if there are singular descriptions, D of c and D' of e, and a "strict" causal law, L, such that L and 'D occurred' entail 'D caused D''. (6) and the second part of (4) entail that physical events have only physical causes and that all event causation is physically grounded.

Given the parallel between (1)–(3) and (4)–(6), it may seem that the latter, too, are incompatible. But Davidson shows that they all can be true if (and only if) mental events are identical to physical events. Let us say that an event e is a physical event if and only if e satisfies a basic physical predicate (that is, a physical predicate appearing in a "strict" law). Since only physical predicates (or predicates expressing properties reducible to basic physical properties) appear in "strict" laws, every event that enters into causal relations satisfies a basic physical predicate. So, those mental events which enter into causal relations are also physical events. Still, the anomalous monist is committed only to a partial endorsement of (1). The mental and physical are distinct insofar as they are not linked by strict law – but they are not distinct insofar as mental events are in fact physical events.

See also ACTION THEORY, CAUSAL LAW, EVENT, PHILOSOPHY OF MIND, SUPERVENIENCE TRUTH.   E.L.

de Beauvoir, Simone. See EXISTENTIALISM.

decidability, as a property of sets, the existence of an effective procedure (a "decision procedure") which, when applied to any object, determines whether or not the object belongs to the set. A theory or logic is decidable if and only if the set of its theorems is. Decidability is proved by describing a decision procedure and showing that it works. The truth table method, for example, establishes that classical propositional logic is decidable. To prove that something is not decidable requires a more precise characterization of the notion of effective procedure. Using one such characterization (for which there is ample evidence), Church proved that classical predicate logic is not decidable. **See also CHURCH'S THESIS, TRUTH TABLE, TURING MACHINE.**

S.T.K.

decidable. See DECIDABILITY.

decision theory, the theory of rational decision, often called "rational choice theory" in political science and other social sciences. The basic idea (probably Pascal's) was published at the end of Arnaud's *Port-Royal Logic* (1662): "To judge what one must do to obtain a good or avoid an evil one must consider not only the good and the evil in itself but also the probability of its happening or not happening, and view geometrically the proportion that all these things have together."

Where goods and evils are monetary, Daniel Bernoulli (1738) spelled the idea out in terms of expected *utilities* as figures of merit for actions, holding that "in the absence of the unusual, the utility resulting from a fixed small increase in wealth will be inversely proportional to the quantity of goods previously possessed." This was meant to solve the *St. Petersburg paradox*:

> Peter tosses a coin ... until it should land "heads" [on toss n]. . . . He agrees to give Paul one ducat if he gets "heads" on the very first throw [and] with each additional throw the number of ducats he must pay is doubled. . . . Although the standard calculation shows that the value of Paul's expectation [of *gain*] is infinitely great [i.e., the sum of all possible gains $\times$ probabilities, $2^n/2 \times \frac{1}{2}^n$], it has . . . to be admitted that any fairly reasonable man would sell his chance, with great pleasure, for twenty ducats.

In this case Paul's expectation of utility is indeed finite on Bernoulli's assumption of inverse proportionality; but as Karl Menger observed (1934), Bernoulli's solution fails if payoffs are so large that *utilities* are inversely proportional to probabilities; then only boundedness of utility scales resolves the paradox.

Bernoulli's idea of diminishing marginal utility of wealth survived in the neoclassical texts of W. S. Jevons (1871), Alfred Marshall (1890), and A. C. Pigou (1920), where personal utility judgment was understood to cause preference. But in the 1930s, operationalistic arguments of John Hicks and R. G. D. Allen persuaded economists that on the contrary, (1) utility is no cause but a description, in which (2) the numbers indicate preference order but not intensity. In their *Theory of Games and Economic Behavior* (1946), John von Neumann and Oskar Morgenstern undid (2) by pushing (1) further: ordinal preferences among *risky* prospects were now seen to be describable on "interval" scales of subjective utility (like the Fahrenheit and Celsius scales for temperature), so that once utilities, e.g., 0 and 1, are assigned to any prospect and any preferred one, utilities of all prospects are determined by overall preferences among gambles, i.e., probability distributions over prospects. Thus, the utility midpoint between two prospects is marked by the distribution assigning probability ½ to each.

In fact, Ramsey had done that and more in a little-noticed essay ("Truth and Probability," 1931) teasing subjective probabilities as well as utilities out of ordinal preferences among gambles. In a form independently invented by L. J. Savage (*Foundations of Statistics,* 1954), this approach is now widely accepted as a basis for rational *decision analysis*. The 1968 book of that title by Howard Raiffa became a theoretical centerpiece of M.B.A. curricula, whose graduates diffused it through industry, government, and the military in a simplified format for defensible decision making, namely, "cost–benefit analyses," substituting expected numbers of dollars, deaths, etc., for preference-based expected utilities.

Social choice and group decision form the native ground of interpersonal comparison of personal utilities. Thus, John C. Harsanyi (1955) proved that if (1) individual and social preferences all satisfy the von Neumann-Morgenstern axioms, and (2) society is indifferent between two prospects whenever all individuals are, and (3) society prefers one prospect to another whenever someone does and nobody has the opposite preference, then social utilities are expressible as sums of individual utilities on interval scales obtained by stretching or compressing the individual scales by amounts determined by the social preferences. Arguably, the theorem shows how to derive interpersonal comparisons of individual preference intensities from social preference orderings that are thought to treat individual preferences on a par. Somewhat earlier, Kenneth Arrow had written that "interpersonal comparison of utilities has no meaning and, in fact, there is no meaning relevant to welfare economics in the measurability of individual utility" (*Social Choice and Individual Values,* 1951) – a position later abandoned (P. Laslett and W. G. Runciman, eds., *Philosophy, Politics and Society,* 1967). Arrow's "impossibility theorem" is illustrated by cyclic preferences (observed by Condorcet in 1785) among candidates A, B, C of voters 1, 2, 3, who rank them ABC, BCA, CAB, respectively, in decreasing order of preference, so that majority rule yields intransitive preferences for the group of three, of whom two (1, 3) prefer A to B and two (1, 2) prefer B to C but two (2, 3) prefer C to A. In general, the theorem denies existence of technically democratic schemes for forming social preferences from citizens' preferences. A clause tendentiously called "independence of irrelevant alternatives" in the definition of 'democratic' rules out appeal to preferences among non-candidates as a way to form social preferences among candidates, thus ruling out the preferences among gambles used in Harsanyi's theorem. (See John Broome, *Weighing Goods,* 1991, for further information and references.)

Savage derived the agent's probabilities for states as well as utilities for consequences from preferences among abstract acts, represented by deterministic assignments of consequences to states. An act's place in the preference ordering is then reflected by its *expected utility,* a probability-weighted average of the utilities of its consequences in the various states. Savage's states and consequences formed distinct sets, with every assignment of consequences to states constituting an act. While Ramsey had also taken acts to be functions from states to consequences, he took consequences to be propositions (sets of states), and assigned utilities to states, not consequences. A further step in that direction represents acts, too, by propositions (see Ethan Bolker, *Functions Resembling Quotients of Measures,* University Microfilms, 1965; and Richard Jeffrey, *The Logic of Decision,* 1965, 1990). Bolker's representation theorem states conditions under which preferences between truth of propositions determine probabilities and utilities nearly enough to make the position of a proposition in one's preference ranking reflect its "desirability," i.e., one's expectation of utility conditionally on it.

Alongside such basic properties as transitivity and connexity, a workhorse among Savage's assumptions was the "sure-thing principle":

> Preferences among acts having the same consequences in certain states are unaffected by arbitrary changes in those consequences.

This implies that agents see states as probabilistically independent of acts, and therefore implies that an act cannot be preferred to one that *dominates* it in the sense that the dominant act's consequences in each state have utilities at least as great as the other's. Unlike the sure thing principle, the principle 'Choose so as to maximize CEU (conditional expectation of utility)' rationalizes action aiming to enhance probabilities of preferred states of nature, as in quitting cigarettes to increase life expectancy. But as Nozick pointed out in 1969, there are problems in which choiceworthiness goes by dominance rather than CEU, as when the smoker (like R. A. Fisher in 1959) believes that the statistical association between smoking and lung cancer is due to a genetic allele, possessors of which are more likely than others to smoke and to contract lung cancer, although among them smokers are not especially likely to contract lung cancer. In such ("Newcomb") problems choices are ineffectual signs of conditions that agents would promote or prevent if they could. *Causal decision theories* modify the CEU formula to obtain figures of merit distinguishing causal efficacy from evidentiary significance – e.g., replacing conditional probabilities by probabilities of counterfactual conditionals; or forming a weighted average of CEU's under all hypotheses about causes, with agents' unconditional probabilities of hypotheses as weights; etc.

Mathematical statisticians leery of subjective probability have cultivated Abraham Wald's *Theory of Statistical Decision Functions* (1950), treating statistical estimation, experimental design, and hypothesis testing as zero-sum "games against nature." For an account of the opposite assimilation, of game theory to probabilistic decision theory, see Skyrms, *Dynamics of Rational Deliberation* (1990).

The "preference logics" of Sören Halldén, *The Logic of 'Better'* (1957), and G. H. von Wright, *The Logic of Preference* (1963), sidestep probability. Thus, Halldén holds that when truth of p is preferred to truth of q, falsity of q must be preferred to falsity of p, and von Wright (with Aristotle) holds that "this is more choiceworthy than that if this is choiceworthy without that, but that is not choiceworthy without this" (*Topics* III, 118a).

Both principles fail in the absence of special probabilistic assumptions, e.g., equiprobability of p with q.

Received wisdom counts decision theory clearly false as a description of human behavior, seeing its proper status as normative. But some, notably Davidson, see the theory as constitutive of the very concept of preference, so that, e.g., preferences can no more be intransitive than propositions can be at once true and false.

See also EMPIRICAL DECISION THEORY, GAME THEORY, RATIONALITY, SOCIAL CHOICE THEORY.   R.J.

decision tree. See DECISION THEORY.

declining marginal utility. See UTILITARIANISM.

decomposability. See MODULARITY.

deconstruction, a demonstration of the incompleteness or incoherence of a philosophical position using concepts and principles of argument whose meaning and use is legitimated only by that philosophical position. A deconstruction is thus a kind of internal conceptual critique in which the critic implicitly and provisionally adheres to the position criticized. The early work of Derrida is the source of the term and provides paradigm cases of its referent.

That deconstruction remains within the position being discussed follows from a fundamental deconstructive argument about the nature of language and thought. Derrida's earliest deconstructions argue against the possibility of an interior "language" of thought and intention such that the senses and referents of terms are determined by their very nature. Such terms are "meanings" or *logoi*. Derrida calls accounts that presuppose such magical thought-terms "logocentric." He claims, following Heidegger, that the conception of such *logoi* is basic to the concepts of Western metaphysics, and that Western metaphysics is fundamental to our cultural practices and languages. Thus there is no "ordinary language" uncontaminated by philosophy. *Logoi* ground all our accounts of intention, meaning, truth, and logical connection. Versions of *logoi* in the history of philosophy range from Plato's Forms through the self-interpreting ideas of the empiricists to Husserl's intentional entities.

Thus Derrida's fullest deconstructions are of texts that give explicit accounts of *logoi*, especially his discussion of Husserl in *Speech and Phenomena*. There, Derrida argues that meanings that are fully present to consciousness are in principle impossible. The idea of a meaning is the idea of a repeatable ideality. But "repeatability" is not a feature that can be present. So meanings, as such, cannot be fully before the mind. Self-interpreting *logoi* are an incoherent supposition.

Without *logoi*, thought and intention are merely wordlike and have no intrinsic connection to a sense or a referent. Thus "meaning" rests on connections of all kinds among pieces of language and among our linguistic interactions with the world. Without *logoi*, no special class of connections is specifically "logical." Roughly speaking, Derrida agrees with Quine both on the nature of meaning and on the related view that "our theory" cannot be abandoned all at once. Thus a philosopher must by and large think about a logocentric philosophical theory that has shaped our language in the very logocentric terms that that theory has shaped. Thus deconstruction is not an excision of criticized doctrines, but a much more complicated, self-referential relationship.

Deconstructive arguments work out the consequences of there being nothing helpfully better than words, i.e., of thoroughgoing nominalism. According to Derrida, without *logoi* fundamental philosophical contrasts lose their principled foundations, since such contrasts implicitly posit one term as a *logos* relative to which the other side is defective. Without *logos*, many contrasts cannot be made to function as principles of the sort of theory philosophy has sought. Thus the contrasts between metaphorical and literal, rhetoric and logic, and other central notions of philosophy are shown not to have the foundation that their use presupposes.

See also HEIDEGGER, HUSSERL, MEANING, PHILOSOPHY OF LANGUAGE.   S.C.W.

Dedekind, Richard (1831–1916), German mathematician, one of the most important figures in the mathematical analysis of foundational questions that took place in the late nineteenth century. Philosophically, three things are interesting about Dedekind's work: (1) the insistence that the fundamental numerical systems of mathematics must be developed independently of spatiotemporal or geometrical notions; (2) the insistence that the numbers systems rely on certain mental capacities fundamental to thought, in particular on the capacity of the mind to "create"; and (3) the recognition that this "creation" is "creation" according to certain key properties, properties that careful mathematical analysis reveals as essential to the subject matter. (1) is a concern Dedekind shared with Bolzano, Cantor,

Frege, and Hilbert; (2) sets Dedekind apart from Frege; and (3) represents a distinctive shift toward the later axiomatic position of Hilbert and somewhat away from the concern with the individual nature of the central abstract mathematical objects which is a central concern of Frege. Much of Dedekind's position is sketched in the *Habilitationsrede* of 1854, the procedure there being applied in outline to the extension of the positive whole numbers to the integers, and then to the rational field. However, the two works best known to philosophers are the monographs on irrational numbers (*Stetigkeit und irrationale Zahlen*, 1872) and on natural numbers (*Was sind und was sollen die Zahlen?*, 1888), both of which pursue the procedure advocated in 1854. In both we find an "analysis" designed to uncover the essential properties involved, followed by a "synthesis" designed to show that there can be such systems, this then followed by a "creation" of objects possessing the properties and nothing more.

In the 1872 work, Dedekind suggests that the essence of continuity in the reals is that whenever the line is divided into two halves by a *cut*, i.e., into two subsets A_1 and A_2 such that if $p \in A_1$ and $q \in A_2$, then $p < q$ and, if $p \in A_1$ and $q < p$, then $q \in A_1$, and if $p \in A_2$ and $q > p$, then $q \in A_2$ as well, then there is real number r which "produces" this cut, i.e., such that $A_1 = \{p; p < r\}$, and $A_2 = \{p: r \leq p\}$. The task is then to characterize the real numbers so that this is indeed true of them. Dedekind shows that, whereas the rationals themselves do not have this property, the collection of all *cuts* in the rationals does. Dedekind then "defines" the irrationals through this observation, not directly as the cuts in the rationals themselves, as was done later, but rather through the "creation" of "new (irrational) numbers" to correspond to those rational cuts not hitherto "produced" by a number.

The 1888 work starts from the notion of a "mapping" of one object onto another, which for Dedekind is necessary for all exact thought. Dedekind then develops the notion of a one-to-one into mapping, which is then used to characterize infinity ("Dedekind infinity"). Using the fundamental notion of a chain, Dedekind characterizes the notion of a "simply infinite system," thus one that is isomorphic to the natural number sequence. Thus, he succeeds in the goal set out in the 1854 lecture: isolating *precisely* the characteristic properties of the natural number system. But do simply infinite systems, in particular the natural number system, exist? Dedekind now argues: Any infinite system must contain a simply infinite system (Theorem 72). Correspondingly, Dedekind sets out to prove that there are infinite systems (Theorem 66), for which he uses an infamous argument (reminiscent of Bolzano's from thirty years earlier) involving "my thought-world," etc. It is generally agreed that the argument does not work, although it is important to remember Dedekind's wish to demonstrate that since the numbers are to be free creations of the human mind, his proofs should rely only on the properties of the mental. The specific act of "creation," however, comes in when Dedekind, starting from any simply infinite system, abstracts from the "particular properties" of this, claiming that what results is the simply infinite system of the natural numbers.

See also CANTOR, CONTINUUM PROBLEM, PHILOSOPHY OF MATHEMATICS.   M.H.

Dedekind cut. See DEDEKIND.

de dicto, of what is said (or of the proposition), as opposed to *de re,* of the thing. Many philosophers believe the following ambiguous, depending on whether they are interpreted *de dicto* or *de re:*

(1) It is possible that the number of U.S. states is even.
(2) Galileo believes that the earth moves.

Assume for illustrative purposes that there are propositions and properties. If (1) is interpreted as *de dicto,* it asserts that the proposition that the number of U.S. states is even is a possible truth – something true, since there are in fact fifty states. If (1) is interpreted as *de re,* it asserts that the actual number of states (fifty) has the property of being possibly even – something essentialism takes to be true. Similarly for (2); it may mean that Galileo's belief has a certain content – that the earth moves – or that Galileo believes, *of* the earth, that it moves.

More recently, largely due to Castañeda and John Perry, many philosophers have come to believe in *de se* ("of oneself") ascriptions, distinct from *de dicto* and *de re.* Suppose, while drinking with others, I notice that someone is spilling beer. Later I come to realize that it is I. I believed at the outset that someone was spilling beer, but didn't believe that *I* was. Once I did, I straightened my glass. The distinction between *de se* and *de dicto* attributions is supposed to be supported by the fact that while *de dicto* propositions must be either true or false, there is no *true* proposition embeddable within 'I believe that . . .' that correctly ascribes to me the belief that I myself am

spilling beer. The sentence 'I am spilling beer' will not do, because it employs an "essential" indexical, 'I'. Were I, e.g., to designate myself other than by using 'I' in attributing the relevant belief to myself, there would be no explanation of my straightening my glass. Even if I believed *de re* that LePore is spilling beer, this still does not account for why I lift my glass. For I might not know I am LePore. On the basis of such data, some philosophers infer that *de se* attributions are irreducible to *de re* or *de dicto* attributions.

See also KNOWLEDGE DE RE, TOKEN-REFLEXIVE.   E.L.

de dicto necessity. See NECESSITY.

deducibility relation. See DEDUCTION, Appendix of Special Symbols.

deduction, a finite sequence of sentences whose last sentence is a conclusion of the sequence (the one said to be deduced) and which is such that each sentence in the sequence is an axiom or a premise or follows from preceding sentences in the sequence by a rule of inference. A synonym is 'derivation'. Deduction is a system-relative concept. It makes sense to say something is a deduction only relative to a particular system of axioms and rules of inference. The very same sequence of sentences might be a deduction relative to one such system but not relative to another.

The concept of deduction is a generalization of the concept of proof. A proof is a finite sequence of sentences each of which is an axiom or follows from preceding sentences in the sequence by a rule of inference. The last sentence in the sequence is a theorem. Given that the system of axioms and rules of inference are effectively specifiable, there is an effective procedure for determining, whenever a finite sequence of sentences is given, whether it is a proof relative to that system. The notion of theorem is not in general effective (decidable). For there may be no method by which we can always find a proof of a given sentence or determine that none exists.

The concepts of deduction and consequence are distinct. The first is a syntactical; the second is semantical. It was a discovery that, relative to the axioms and rules of inference of classical logic, a sentence S is deducible from a set of sentences K provided that S is a consequence of K. Compactness is an important consequence of this discovery. It is trivial that sentence S is deducible from K just in case S is deducible from some finite subset of K. It is not trivial that S is a consequence of K just in case S is a consequence of some finite subset of K. This compactness property had to be shown.

A system of natural deduction is axiomless. Proofs of theorems within a system are generally easier with natural deduction. Proofs of theorems about a system, such as the results mentioned in the previous paragraph, are generally easier if the system has axioms.

In a secondary sense, 'deduction' refers to an inference in which a speaker claims the conclusion follows necessarily from the premises.

See also AXIOMATIC METHOD, COMPACTNESS THEOREM, EFFECTIVE PROCEDURE, FORMAL SEMANTICS, PROOF THEORY.   C.S.

deduction, natural. See DEDUCTION.

deduction, transcendental. See KANT.

deduction of the categories. See KANT.

deduction theorem, a result about certain systems of formal logic relating derivability and the conditional. It states that if a formula B is derivable from A (and possibly other assumptions), then the formula $A \rightarrow B$ is derivable without the assumption of A: in symbols, if $\Gamma \cup \{A\} \vdash B$ then $\Gamma \vdash A \rightarrow B$. The thought is that, for example, if *Socrates is mortal* is derivable from the assumptions *All men are mortal* and *Socrates is a man*, then *If Socrates is a man he is mortal* is derivable from *All men are mortal*. Likewise, *If all men are mortal then Socrates is mortal* is derivable from *Socrates is a man*. In general, the deduction theorem is a significant result only for axiomatic or Hilbert-style formulations of logic. In most natural deduction formulations a rule of conditional proof explicitly licenses derivations of $A \rightarrow B$ from $\Gamma \cup \{A\}$, and so there is nothing to prove. **See also** DEDUCTION.
                                                        S.T.K.

deductive closure. See CLOSURE.

deductive completeness. See COMPLETENESS.

deductive explanation. See COVERING LAW MODEL.

deductive justification. See JUSTIFICATION.

deductive-nomological model. See COVERING LAW MODEL.

deep structure. See GRAMMAR, PHILOSOPHY OF LANGUAGE, TRANSFORMATION RULE.

default logic, a formal system for reasoning with defaults, developed by Raymond Reiter in 1980. Reiter's defaults have the form '$P:MQ_1 , \ldots , MQ_n/R$', read 'If P is believed and $Q_1 \ldots Q_n$ are consistent with one's beliefs, then R may be believed'. Whether a proposition is consistent with one's beliefs depends on what defaults have already been applied. Given the defaults $P:MQ/Q$ and $R:M{\sim}Q/{\sim}Q$, and the facts P and R, applying the first default yields Q while applying the second default yields ${\sim}Q$. So applying either default blocks the other. Consequently, a default theory may have several default extensions.

Normal defaults having the form $P:MQ/Q$, useful for representing simple cases of nonmonotonic reasoning, are inadequate for more complex cases. Reiter produces a reasonably clean proof theory for normal default theories and proves that every normal default theory has an extension.

See also DEFEASIBILITY, NON-MONOTONIC LOGIC.   D.N.

defeasibility, a property that rules, principles, arguments, or bits of reasoning have when they might be *defeated* by some competitor. For example, the epistemic principle 'Objects normally have the properties they appear to have' or the normative principle 'One should not lie' are defeated, respectively, when perception occurs under unusual circumstances (e.g., under colored lights) or when there is some overriding moral consideration (e.g., to prevent murder). Apparently declarative sentences such as 'Birds typically fly' can be taken in part as expressing defeasible rules: take something's being a bird as evidence that it flies. Defeasible arguments and reasoning inherit their defeasibility from the use of defeasible rules or principles.

Recent analyses of defeasibility include circumscription and default logic, which belong to the broader category of non-monotonic logic. The rules in several of these formal systems contain special antecedent conditions and are not truly defeasible since they apply whenever their conditions are satisfied. Rules and arguments in other non-monotonic systems justify their conclusions only when they are not defeated by some other fact, rule, or argument. John Pollock distinguishes between *rebutting* and *undercutting* defeaters. 'Snow is not normally red' rebuts (in appropriate circumstances) the principle 'Things that look red normally are red', while 'If the available light is red, do not use the principle that things that look red normally are red' only undercuts the embedded rule. Pollock has influenced most other work on formal systems for defeasible reasoning.

See also DEFAULT LOGIC, EPISTEMOLOGY, NON-MONOTONIC LOGIC.   D.N.

defeat of reasons. See EPISTEMOLOGY, JUSTIFICATION.

definiendum (plural: definienda), the expression that is defined in a definition. The expression that gives the definition is the definiens (plural: definientia). In the definition

father, male parent,

'father' is the definiendum and 'male parent' is the definiens. In the definition 'A human being is a rational animal', 'human being' is the definiendum and 'rational animal' is the definiens. Similar terms are used in the case of conceptual analyses, whether they are meant to provide synonyms or not; 'definiendum' for 'analysandum' and 'definiens' for 'analysans'. In 'x knows that p if and only if it is true that p, x believes that p, and x's belief that p is properly justified', 'x knows that p' is the analysandum and 'it is true that p, x believes that p, and x's belief that p is properly justified' is the analysans. **See also** ANALYSIS, DEFINITION, MEANING.   T.Y.

definiens. See DEFINIENDUM.

definist, someone who holds that moral terms, such as 'right', and evaluative terms, such as 'good' – in short, *normative* terms – are definable in non-moral, non-evaluative (i.e., non-normative) terms. William Frankena offers a broader account of a definist as one who holds that ethical terms are definable in non-ethical terms. This would allow that they are definable in non-ethical but evaluative terms – say, 'right' in terms of what is non-morally intrinsically good. Definists who are also naturalists hold that moral terms can be defined by terms that denote natural properties, i.e., properties whose presence or absence can be determined by observational means. They might define 'good' as 'what conduces to pleasure'. Definists who are not naturalists will hold that the terms that do the defining do not denote natural properties, e.g., that 'right' means 'what is commanded by God'. **See also** ETHICS, MOORE, NATURALISM.   B.R.

definist fallacy. See MOORE.

definite description. See THEORY OF DESCRIPTIONS.

definite description operator. See Appendix of Special Symbols.

definition, specification of the meaning or, alternatively, conceptual content, of an expression. For example, 'period of fourteen days' is a definition of 'fortnight'. Definitions have traditionally been judged by rules like the following:

(1) A definition should not be too narrow. 'Unmarried adult male psychiatrist' is too narrow a definition for 'bachelor', for some bachelors are not psychiatrists. 'Having vertebrae and a liver' is too narrow for 'vertebrate', for, even though all actual vertebrate things have vertebrae and a liver, it is possible for a vertebrate thing to lack a liver.

(2) A definition should not be too broad. 'Unmarried adult' is too broad a definition for 'bachelor', for not all unmarried adults are bachelors. 'Featherless biped' is too broad for 'human being', for even though all actual featherless bipeds are human beings, it is possible for a featherless biped to be non-human.

(3) The defining expression in a definition should (ideally) exactly match the degree of vagueness of the expression being defined (except in a precising definition). 'Adult female' for 'woman' does not violate this rule, but 'female at least eighteen years old' for 'woman' does.

(4) A definition should not be circular. If 'desirable' defines 'good' and 'good' defines 'desirable', these definitions are circular.

Definitions fall into at least the following kinds:

analytical definition: definition whose corresponding biconditional is analytic or gives an analysis of the *definiendum*: e.g., 'female fox' for 'vixen', where the corresponding biconditional 'For any x, x is a vixen if and only if x is a female fox' is analytic; 'true in all possible worlds' for 'necessarily true', where the corresponding biconditional 'For any P, P is necessarily true if and only if P is true in all possible worlds' gives an analysis of the *definiendum*.

contextual definition: definition of an expression as it occurs in a larger expression: e.g., 'If it is not the case that Q, then P' contextually defines 'unless' as it occurs in 'P unless Q'; 'There is at least one entity that is F and is identical with any entity that is F' contextually defines 'exactly one' as it occurs in 'There is exactly one F'. Recursive definitions (see below) are an important variety of contextual definition. Another important application of contextual definition is Russell's theory of descriptions, which defines 'the' as it occurs in contexts of the form 'The so-and-so is such-and-such'.

coordinative definition: definition of a theoretical term by non-theoretical terms: e.g., 'the forty-millionth part of the circumference of the earth' for 'meter'.

definition by genus and species: When an expression is said to be applicable to some but not all entities of a certain type and inapplicable to all entities not of that type, the type in question is the genus, and the subtype of all and only those entities to which the expression is applicable is the species: e.g., in the definition 'rational animal' for 'human', the type *animal* is the genus and the subtype *human* is the species. Each species is distinguished from any other of the same genus by a property called the *differentia*.

definition in use: specification of how an expression is used or what it is used to express: e.g., 'uttered to express astonishment' for 'my goodness'. Wittgenstein emphasized the importance of definition in use in his use theory of meaning.

definition per genus et differentiam: definition by genus and difference; same as definition by genus and species.

explicit definition: definition that makes it clear that it is a definition and identifies the expression being defined as such: e.g., 'Father' means 'male parent'; 'For any *x, x* is a father by definition if and only if *x* is a male parent'.

implicit definition: definition that is not an explicit definition.

lexical definition: definition of the kind commonly thought appropriate for dictionary definitions of natural language terms, namely, a specification of their conventional meaning.

nominal definition: definition of a noun (usually a common noun), giving its linguistic meaning. Typically it is in terms of macrosensible characteristics: e.g., 'yellow malleable metal' for 'gold'. Locke spoke of nominal essence and contrasted it with real essence.

ostensive definition: definition by an example in which the referent is specified by pointing

or showing in some way: e.g., " 'Red' is *that* color," where the word 'that' is accompanied with a gesture pointing to a patch of colored cloth; " 'Pain' means *this*," where *'this'* is accompanied with an insertion of a pin through the hearer's skin; " 'Kangaroo' applies to all and only animals like *that*," where *'that'* is accompanied by pointing to a particular kangaroo.

persuasive definition: definition designed to affect or appeal to the psychological states of the party to whom the definition is given, so that a claim will appear more plausible to the party than it is: e.g., 'self-serving manipulator' for 'politician', where the claim in question is that all politicians are immoral.

precising definition: definition of a vague expression intended to reduce its vagueness: e.g., 'snake longer than half a meter and shorter than two meters' for 'snake of average length'; 'having assets ten thousand times the median figure' for 'wealthy'.

prescriptive definition: stipulative definition that, in a recommendatory way, gives a new meaning to an expression with a previously established meaning: e.g., 'male whose primary sexual preference is for other males' for 'gay'.

real definition: specification of the metaphysically necessary and sufficient condition for being the kind of thing a noun (usually a common noun) designates: e.g., 'element with atomic number 79' for 'gold'. Locke spoke of real essence and contrasted it with nominal essence.

recursive definition (also called inductive definition and definition by recursion): definition in three clauses in which (1) the expression defined is applied to certain particular items (the base clause); (2) a rule is given for reaching further items to which the expression applies (the recursive, or inductive, clause); and (3) it is stated that the expression applies to nothing else (the closure clause). E.g., 'John's parents are John's *ancestors;* any parent of John's ancestor is John's ancestor; nothing else is John's ancestor'. By the base clause, John's mother and father are John's ancestors. Then by the recursive clause, John's mother's parents and John's father's parents are John's ancestors; so are their parents, and so on. Finally, by the last (closure) clause, these people exhaust John's ancestors. The following defines multiplication in terms of addition: '$0 \times n = 0$. $(m + 1) \times n = (m \times n)$ $+ n$. Nothing else is the result of multiplying integers'. The base clause tells us, e.g., that $0 \times 4 = 0$. The recursive clause tells us, e.g., that $(0 + 1) \times 4 = (0 \times 4) + 4$. We then know that $1 \times 4 = 0 + 4 = 4$. Likewise, e.g., $2 \times 4 = (1 + 1) \times 4 = (1 \times 4) + 4 = 4 + 4 = 8$.

stipulative definition: definition regardless of the ordinary or usual conceptual content of the expression defined. It postulates a content, rather than aiming to capture the content already associated with the expression. Any explicit definition that introduces a new expression into the language is a stipulative definition: e.g., "For the purpose of our discussion 'existent' means 'perceivable' "; "By 'zoobeedoobah' we shall mean 'vain millionaire who is addicted to alcohol'."

synonymous definition: definition of a word (or other linguistic expression) by another word synonymous with it: e.g., 'buy' for 'purchase'; 'madness' for 'insanity'.

See also ANALYSIS, ESSENTIALISM, MEANING, PHILOSOPHY OF LANGUAGE, THEORY OF DESCRIPTIONS.   T.Y.

definition, contextual. See DEFINITION.

definition, explicit. See BETH'S DEFINABILITY THEOREM, DEFINITION.

definition, implicit. See BETH'S DEFINABILITY THEOREM.

definition in use. See DEFINITION, LOGICAL CONSTRUCTION.

deflationary theory of truth. See PHILOSOPHY OF LANGUAGE, TRUTH.

degenerate case, an expression used more or less loosely to indicate an individual or class that falls outside of a given background class to which it is otherwise very closely related, often in virtue of an ordering of a more comprehensive class. A degenerate case of one class is often a limiting case of a more comprehensive class. Rest (zero velocity) is a degenerate case of motion (positive velocity) while being a limiting case of velocity. The circle is a degenerate case of an equilateral and equiangular polygon. In technical or scientific contexts, the conventional term for the background class is often "stretched" to cover otherwise degenerate cases. A figure composed of two intersecting lines is a degenerate case of hyperbola in the sense of synthetic geometry, but it is a limiting case of hyperbola in the sense of analytic geometry. The null set is a degenerate case of set in an older sense but a limiting case of set in a modern sense. A line segment is a degenerate case of rectangle when rectangles are ordered by ratio of length to width, but it is not a limiting case under these conditions. **See also** BORDERLINE CASE, LIMITING CASE.   J.Cor.

degree, also called arity, adicity, in formal languages, a property of predicate and function expressions that determines the number of terms with which the expression is correctly combined to yield a well-formed expression. If an expression combines with a single term to form a well-formed expression, it is of *degree one* (*monadic, singulary*). Expressions that combine with two terms are of *degree two* (*dyadic, binary*), and so on. Expressions of degree greater than or equal to two are *polyadic*. The formation rules of a formalized language must effectively specify the degrees of its primitive expressions as part of the effective determination of the class of well-formed formulas. Degree is commonly indicated by an attached superscript consisting of an Arabic numeral. Formalized languages have been studied that contain expressions having *variable degree* (or *variable adicity*) and that can thus combine with any finite number of terms. An abstract relation that would be appropriate as extension of a predicate expression is subject to the same terminology, and likewise for function expressions and their associated functions. **See also** FORMAL LANGUAGE, MATHEMATICAL FUNCTION, PROPERTY.   C.A.A.

degree of belief. See BAYESIAN RATIONALITY.

degree of belief. See PROBABILITY.

degree of confirmation. See CARNAP.

degree of unsolvability, a maximal set of equally complex sets of natural numbers, with comparative complexity of sets of natural numbers construed as recursion-theoretic reducibility ordering. Recursion theorists investigate various notions of reducibility between sets of natural numbers, i.e., various ways of filling in the following schematic definition. For sets A and B of natural numbers: A is reducible to B iff (if and only if) there is an algorithm whereby each membership question about A (e.g., '$17 \in A$?') could be answered allowing consultation of an "oracle" that would correctly answer each membership question about B. This does not presuppose that there is a "real" oracle for B; the motivating idea is counterfactual: A is reducible to B iff: if membership questions about B were decidable then membership questions about A would also be decidable. On the other hand, the mathematical definitions of notions of reducibility involve no subjunctive conditionals or other intensional constructions. The notion of reducibility is determined by constraints on how the algorithm could use the oracle. Imposing no constraints yields *T-reducibility* ('T' for Turing), the most important and most studied notion of reducibility.

Fixing a notion r of reducibility: A is r-equivalent to B iff A is r-reducible to B and B is r-reducible to A. If r-reducibility is transitive, r-equivalence is an equivalence relation on the class of sets of natural numbers, one reflecting a notion of equal complexity for sets of natural numbers. A degree of unsolvability relative to r (an r-degree) is an equivalence class under that equivalence relation, i.e., a maximal class of sets of natural numbers any two members of which are r-equivalent, i.e., a maximal class of equally complex (in the sense of r-reducibility) sets of natural numbers. The r-reducibility-ordering of sets of natural numbers transfers to the r-degrees: for d and d' r-degrees, let $d \leq, d'$ iff for some $A \in d$ and $B \in d'$ A is r-reducible to B. The study of r-degrees is the study of them under this ordering.

The degrees generated by T-reducibility are the Turing degrees. Without qualification, 'degree of unsolvability' means 'Turing degree'. The least T-degree is the set of all recursive (i.e., using Church's thesis, solvable) sets of natural numbers. So the phrase 'degree of *un*solvability' is slightly misleading: the least such degree is "solvability."

By effectively coding functions from natural numbers to natural numbers as sets of natural numbers, we may think of such a function as belonging to a degree: that of its coding set.

Recursion theorists have extended the notions of reducibility and degree of unsolvability to other domains, e.g. transfinite ordinals and higher types taken over the natural numbers. **See also CHURCH'S THESIS, PHILOSOPHY OF MATHEMATICS, RECURSIVE FUNCTION THEORY.**   H.T.H.

deism, the view that true religion is natural religion. Some self-styled Christian deists accepted revelation although they argued that its content is essentially the same as natural religion. Most deists dismissed revealed religion as a fiction. God wants his creatures to be happy and has ordained virtue as the means to it. Since God's benevolence is disinterested, he will ensure that the knowledge needed for happiness is universally accessible. Salvation cannot, then, depend on special revelation. True religion is an expression of a universal human nature whose essence is reason and is the same in all times and places. Religious traditions such as Christianity and Islam originate in credulity, political tyranny, and priestcraft, which corrupt reason and overlay natural religion with impurities. Deism is largely a seventeenth- and eighteenth-century phenomenon and was most prominent in England. Among the more important English deists were John Toland (1670–1722), Anthony Collins (1676–1729), Herbert of Cherbury (1583–1648), Matthew Tindal (1657–1733), and Thomas Chubb (1679–1747). Continental deists included Voltaire and Reimarus. Thomas Paine and Elihu Palmer (1764–1806) were prominent American deists. Orthodox writers in this period use 'deism' as a vague term of abuse. By the late eighteenth century, the term came to mean belief in an "absentee God" who creates the world, ordains its laws, and then leaves it to its own devices. **See also PHILOSOPHY OF RELIGION.**   W.J.Wa.

de la Ramée, Pierre. See RAMUS.

deliberation. See ACTION THEORY, PRACTICAL REASONING.

de Maistre, Joseph-Marie (1753–1821), French political theorist, diplomat, and Roman Catholic exponent of theocracy. He was educated by the Jesuits in Turin. His counterrevolutionary political philosophy aimed at restoring the foundations of morality, the family, society, and the state in postrevolutionary Europe. Against Enlightenment ideals, he reclaimed Thomism, defended the hereditary and absolute monarchy, and championed ultramontanism (*The Pope*, 1821). *Considerations on France* (1796) argues that the decline of moral and religious values was responsible for the "satanic" 1789 revolution. Hence Christianity and Enlightenment philosophy were engaged in a fight to the death that he claimed the church would eventually win. Deeply pessimistic about human nature, the *Essay on the Generating Principle of Political Constitutions* (1810) traces the origin of authority in the human craving for order and discipline. *Saint*

Petersburg Evenings (1821) urges philosophy to surrender to religion and reason to faith.   J.-L.S.

demarcation, the line separating empirical science from mathematics and logic, from metaphysics, and from pseudoscience. Science traditionally was supposed to rely on induction, the formal disciplines (including metaphysics) on deduction. In the verifiability criterion, the logical positivists identified the demarcation of empirical science from metaphysics with the demarcation of the cognitively meaningful from the meaningless, classifying metaphysics as gibberish, and logic and mathematics, more charitably, as without sense. Noting that, because induction is invalid, the theories of empirical science are unverifiable, Popper proposed falsifiability as their distinguishing characteristic, and remarked that some metaphysical doctrines, such as atomism, are obviously meaningful. It is now recognized that science is suffused with metaphysical ideas, and Popper's criterion is therefore perhaps a (rather rough) criterion of demarcation of the empirical from the non-empirical rather than of the scientific from the non-scientific. It repudiates the unnecessary task of demarcating the cognitively meaningful from the cognitively meaningless. **See also FALSIFIABILITY, INDUCTION, MEANING, METAPHYSICS, POPPER, VERIFIABILITY.**   D.W.M.

demiurge (from Greek *dēmiourgos*, 'artisan', 'craftsman'), a deity who shapes the material world from the preexisting chaos. Plato introduces the demiurge in his *Timaeus*. Because he is perfectly good, the demiurge wishes to communicate his own goodness. Using the Forms as a model, he shapes the initial chaos into the best possible image of these eternal and immutable archetypes. The visible world is the result. Although the demiurge is the highest god and the best of causes, he should not be identified with the God of theism. His ontological and axiological status is lower than that of the Forms, especially the Form of the Good. He is also limited. The material he employs is not created by him. Furthermore, it is disorderly and indeterminate, and thus partially resists his rational ordering.

In gnosticism, the demiurge is the ignorant, weak, and evil or else morally limited cause of the cosmos. In the modern era the term has occasionally been used for a deity who is limited in power or knowledge. Its first occurrence in this sense appears to be in J. S. Mill's *Theism* (1874).

See also GNOSTICISM, PHILOSOPHY OF RELIGION, PLATO.   W.J.Wa.

democracy. See POLITICAL PHILOSOPHY.

Democritus (c.460–c.370 B.C.), Greek pre-Socratic philosopher. He was born at Abdera, in Thrace. Building on Leucippus and his atomism, he developed the atomic theory in *The Little World-system* and numerous other writings. In response to the Eleatics' argument that the impossibility of not-being entailed that there is no change, the atomists posited the existence of a plurality of tiny indivisible beings – the atoms – and not-being – the void, or empty space. Atoms do not come into being or perish, but they do move in the void, making possible the existence of a world, and indeed of many worlds. For the void is infinite in extent, and filled with an infinite number of atoms that move and collide with one another. Under the right conditions a concentration of atoms can begin a vortex motion that draws in other atoms and forms a spherical heaven enclosing a world. In our world there is a flat earth surrounded by heavenly bodies carried by a vortex motion. Other worlds like ours are born, flourish, and die, but their astronomical configurations may be different from ours and they need not have living creatures in them.

The atoms are solid bodies with countless shapes and sizes, apparently having weight or mass, and capable of motion. All other properties are in some way derivative of these basic properties. The cosmic vortex motion causes a sifting that tends to separate similar atoms as the sea arranges pebbles on the shore. For instance heavier atoms sink to the center of the vortex, and lighter atoms such as those of fire rise upward. Compound bodies can grow by the aggregations of atoms that become entangled with one another. Living things, including humans, originally emerged out of slime. Life is caused by fine, spherical soul atoms, and living things die when these atoms are lost. Human culture gradually evolved through chance discoveries and imitations of nature.

Because the atoms are invisible and the only real properties are properties of atoms, we cannot have direct knowledge of anything. Tastes, temperatures, and colors we know only "by convention." In general the senses cannot give us anything but "bastard" knowledge; but there is a "legitimate" knowledge based on reason, which takes over where the senses leave off – presumably demonstrating that there are atoms that the senses cannot testify of. Democritus offers a causal theory of perception – sometimes called the theory of effluxes – accounting for tastes in terms of certain shapes of atoms and for sight in terms of "effluences" or moving films of atoms that impinge on the eye.

Drawing on both atomic theory and conventional wisdom, Democritus develops an ethics of moderation. The aim of life is equanimity (*euthumiê*), a state of balance achieved by moderation and proportionate pleasures. Envy and ambition are incompatible with the good life.

Although Democritus was one of the most prolific writers of antiquity, his works were all lost. Yet we can still identify his atomic theory as the most fully worked out of pre-Socratic philosophies. His theory of matter influenced Plato's *Timaeus,* and his naturalist anthropology became the prototype for liberal social theories. Democritus had no immediate successors, but a century later Epicurus transformed his ethics into a philosophy of consolation founded on atomism. Epicureanism thus became the vehicle through which atomic theory was transmitted to the early modern period.

See also PRE-SOCRATICS.   D.W.G.

demonstration. See PROOF THEORY.

demonstrative. See INDEXICAL.

demonstrative inference. See INFERENCE.

demonstrative reasoning. See INFERENCE.

demonstrative syllogism. See ARISTOTLE.

De Morgan, Augustus (1806–71), prolific British mathematician, logician, and philosopher of mathematics and logic. He is remembered chiefly for several lasting contributions to logic and philosophy of logic, including discovery and deployment of the concept of universe of discourse, the cofounding of relational logic, adaptation of what are now known as De Morgan's laws, and several terminological innovations including the expression 'mathematical induction'. His main logical works, the monograph *Formal Logic* (1847) and the series of articles "On the Syllogism" (1846–62), demonstrate wide historical and philosophical learning, synoptic vision, penetrating originality, and disarming objectivity. His relational logic treated a wide variety of inferences involving propositions whose logical forms were significantly more complex than those treated in the traditional framework stemming from Aristotle, e.g. 'If every doctor is a teacher, then every ancestor of a doctor is an ancestor of a teacher'. De Morgan's conception of the infinite variety of logical forms of propositions vastly

widens that of his predecessors and even that of his able contemporaries such as Boole, Hamilton, Mill, and Whately. De Morgan did as much as any of his contemporaries toward the creation of modern mathematical logic. **See also** DE MORGAN'S LAWS, LOGICAL FORM, RELATIONAL LOGIC, UNIVERSE OF DISCOURSE.   J.Cor.

De Morgan's laws, the logical principles

$$\sim (A \wedge B) \equiv \sim A \vee \sim B,$$

$$\sim (A \vee B) \equiv \sim A \wedge \sim B,$$

$$\sim (\sim A \wedge \sim B) \equiv A \vee B,$$

and

$$\sim (\sim A \vee \sim B) \equiv A \wedge B,$$

though the term is occasionally used to cover only the first two. **See also** DISTRIBUTIVE LAWS.
                                                         G.F.S.

denial, alternative. See SHEFFER STROKE.

Dennett, Daniel C(lement) (b.1942), American philosopher, author of books on topics in the philosophy of mind, free will, and evolutionary biology, and tireless advocate of the importance of philosophy for empirical work on evolution and on the nature of the mind.

Dennett is perhaps best known for arguing that a creature (or, more generally, a system), *S,* possesses states of mind if and only if the ascription of such states to *S* facilitates explanation and prediction of *S*'s behavior (*The Intentional Stance,* 1987). (*S* might be a human being, a chimpanzee, a desktop computer, or a thermostat.) In ascribing beliefs and desires to *S* we take up an attitude toward *S,* the *intentional stance.* We could just as well (although for different purposes) take up other stances: the *design stance* (we understand *S* as a kind of engineered system) or the *physical stance* (we regard *S* as a purely physical system).

It might seem that, although we often enough ascribe beliefs and desires to desktop computers and thermostats, we do not mean to do so literally – as with people. Dennett's contention, however, is that there is nothing more (nor less) to having beliefs, desires, and other states of mind than being explicable by reference to such things. This, he holds, is not to demean beliefs, but only to affirm that to have a belief is to be describable in this particular way. If you are so describable, then it is true, literally true, that you have beliefs. Dennett extends this approach to consciousness, which he views not as an inwardly observable performance taking place in a "Cartesian Theater," but as a story we tell about ourselves, the compilation of "multiple drafts" concocted by neural subsystems (see *Conciousness Explained*, 1991). Elsewhere (*Darwin's Dangerous Idea*, 1995) Dennett has argued that principles of Darwinian selection apply to diverse domains including cosmology and human culture, and offered a compatibilist account of free will with an emphasis on agents' control over their actions (*Elbow Room*, 1984).

See also DARWINISM, FREE WILL PROBLEM, FUNCTIONALISM, INTENTIONALITY, PHILOSOPHY OF MIND.   J.F.H.

denotation, the thing or things that an expression applies to; extension. The term is used in contrast with 'meaning' and 'connotation'. A pair of expressions may apply to the same things, i.e., have the same denotation, yet differ in meaning: 'triangle', 'trilateral'; 'creature with a heart', 'creature with a kidney'; 'bird', 'feathered earthling'; 'present capital of France', 'City of Light'. If a term does not apply to anything, some will call it denotationless, while others would say that it denotes the empty set. Such terms may differ in meaning: 'unicorn', 'centaur', 'square root of pi'. Expressions may apply to the same thing(s), yet bring to mind different associations, i.e., have different connotations: 'persistent', 'stubborn', 'pigheaded'; 'white-collar employee', 'office worker', 'professional paper-pusher'; 'Lewis Carroll', 'Reverend Dodgson'. There can be confusion about the denotation-connotation terminology, because this pair is used to make other contrasts. Sometimes the term 'connotation' is used more broadly, so that any difference of either meaning or association is considered a difference of connotation. Then 'creature with a heart' and 'creature with a liver' might be said to denote the same individuals (or sets) but to connote different properties.

In a second use, denotation is the semantic value of an expression. Sometimes the denotation of a general term is said to be a property, rather than the thing(s) having the property. This occurs when the denotation-connotation terminology is used to contrast the property expressed with the connotation. Thus 'persistent' and 'pig-headed' might be said to denote the same property but differ in connotation.

See also CONNOTATION, EXTENSIONALISM, INTENSION, MEANING, PHILOSOPHY OF LANGUAGE.   T.M.

denotative meaning. See MEANING.

denoting concept. See RUSSELL.

dense ordering. See ORDERING.

denumerable. See INFINITY.

denying the antecedent. See FORMAL FALLACY.

Deodorus Cronos. See MEGARIANS.

deontic logic, the logic of obligation and permission. There are three principal types of formal deontic systems.

(1) *Standard deontic logic,* or SDL, results from adding a pair of monadic deontic operators O and P, read as "it ought to be that" and "it is permissible that," respectively, to the classical propositional calculus. SDL contains the following axioms: tautologies of propositional logic, $OA \equiv \sim P \sim A$, $OA \supset O \sim A$, $O(A \supset B) \supset (OA \supset OB)$, and OT, where T stands for any tautology. Rules of inference are *modus ponens* and substitution. (See the survey of SDL by Dagfinn Follesdal and Risto Hilpinin in R. Hilpinin, ed., *Deontic Logic,* 1971.)

(2) *Dyadic deontic logic* is obtained by adding a pair of dyadic deontic operators $O(/)$ and $P(/)$, to be read as "it ought to be that ... , given that ..." and "it is permissible that ..., given that ...," respectively. The SDL monadic operator O is defined as $OA \equiv O(A/T)$; i.e., a statement of absolute obligation OA becomes an obligation conditional on tautologous conditions. A statement of conditional obligation $O(A/B)$ is true provided that some value realized at some B-world where A holds is better than any value realized at any B-world where A does not hold. This *axiological* construal of obligation is typically accompanied by these axioms and rules of inference: tautologies of propositional logic, *modus ponens*, and substitution, $P(A/C) \equiv \sim O(\sim A/C)$, $O(A \& B/C) \equiv [O(A/C) \& O(B/C)]$, $O(A/C) \supset P(A/C)$, $O(T/C) \supset O(C/C)$, $O(T/C) \supset O(T/B \vee C)$, $[O(A/B) \& O(A/C)] \supset O(A/B \vee C)$, $[P(B/B \vee C) \& O(A/B \vee C)] \supset O(A/B)$, and $[P(\bot/C) \& O(A/B \vee C)] \supset O(A/B)$, where $\bot$ is the negation of any tautology. (See the comparison of alternative dyadic systems in Lennart Aqvist, *Introduction to Deontic Logic and the Theory of Normative Systems,* 1987.)

(3) *Two-sorted deontic logic,* due to Castañeda (*Thinking and Doing,* 1975), pivotally distinguishes between *propositions,* the bearers of truth-values, and *practitions,* the contents of commands, imperatives, requests, and such. Deontic operators apply to practitions, yielding propositions. The deontic operators Oi, Pi, Wi, and li are read as "it is obligatory i that," "it is permissible i that," "it is wrong i that," and "it is optional i

that," respectively, where *i* stands for any of the various types of obligation, permission, and so on. Let *p* stand for indicatives, where these express propositions; let *A* and *B* stand for practitives, understood to express practitions; and allow *p** to stand for both indicatives and practitives. For deontic definition there are $PiA \equiv\ \sim Oi \sim A$, $WiA \equiv Oi \sim A$, and $LiA \equiv (\sim OiA\ \&\ \sim Oi \sim A)$. Axioms and rules of inference include *p**, if *p** has the form of a truth-table tautology, $OiA \supset \sim Oi \sim A$, $O1A \supset A$, where *O1* represents *overriding obligation*, *modus ponens* for both indicatives and practitives, and the rule that if $(p\ \&\ A1\ \&\ \dots\ \&\ An) \supset B$ is a theorem, so too is $(p\ \&\ OiA1\ \&\ \dots\ \&\ OiAn) \supset OiB$.

See also DEONTIC PARADOXES, FORMAL LOGIC, MODAL LOGIC. 　　　　J.E.T.

deontic operator. See DEONTIC LOGIC.

deontic paradoxes, the paradoxes of deontic logic, which typically arise as follows: a certain set of English sentences about obligation or permission appears logically consistent, but when these same sentences are represented in a proposed system of deontic logic the result is a formally inconsistent set. To illustrate, a formulation is provided below of how two of these paradoxes beset standard deontic logic.

The *contrary-to-duty imperative paradox,* made famous by Chisholm (*Analysis,* 1963), arises from juxtaposing two apparent truths: first, some of us sometimes do what we should not do; and second, when such wrongful doings occur it is obligatory that the best (or a better) be made of an unfortunate situation. Consider this scenario. Art and Bill share an apartment. For no good reason Art develops a strong animosity toward Bill. One evening Art's animosity takes over, and he steals Bill's valuable lithographs. Art is later found out, apprehended, and brought before Sue, the duly elected local punishment-and-awards official. An inquiry reveals that Art is a habitual thief with a history of unremitting parole violation. In this situation, it seems that (1)–(4) are all true (and hence mutually consistent):

(1) Art steals from Bill.
(2) If Art steals from Bill, Sue ought to punish Art for stealing from Bill.
(3) It is obligatory that if Art does not steal from Bill, Sue does not punish him for stealing from Bill.
(4) Art ought not to steal from Bill.

Turning to *standard deontic logic,* or SDL, let *s* stand for 'Art steals from Bill' and let *p* stand for 'Sue

punishes Art for stealing from Bill'. Then (1)–(4) are most naturally represented in SDL as follows:

(1a) *s*.
(2a) $s \supset Op$.
(3a) $O(\sim s \supset \sim p)$.
(4a) $O \sim s$.

Of these, (1a) and (2a) entail *Op* by propositional logic; next, given the SDL axiom $O(A \supset B) \supset (OA \supset OB)$, (3a) implies $O \sim s \supset O \sim p$; but the latter, taken in conjunction with (4a), entails $O \sim p$ by propositional logic. In the combination of *Op*, $O \sim p$, and the axiom $OA \supset \sim O \sim A$, of course, we have a formally inconsistent set.

The *paradox of the knower,* first presented by Lennart Åqvist (*Noûs,* 1967), is generated by these apparent truths: first, some of us sometimes do what we should not do; and second, there are those who are obligated to know that such wrongful doings occur. Consider the following scenario. Jones works as a security guard at a local store. One evening, while Jones is on duty, Smith, a disgruntled former employee out for revenge, sets the store on fire just a few yards away from Jones's work station. Here it seems that (1)–(3) are all true (and thus jointly consistent):

(1) Smith set the store on fire while Jones was on duty.
(2) If Smith set the store on fire while Jones was on duty, it is obligatory that Jones knows that Smith set the store on fire.
(3) Smith ought not set the store on fire.

Independently, as a consequence of the concept of knowledge, there is the epistemic theorem that

(4) The statement that Jones knows that Smith set the store on fire entails the statement that Smith set the store on fire.

Next, within SDL (1) and (2) surely appear to imply:

(5) It is obligatory that Jones knows that Smith set the store on fire.

But (4) and (5) together yield

(6) Smith ought to set the store on fire,

given the SDL theorem that if $A \supset B$ is a theorem, so is $OA \supset OB$. And therein resides the paradox: not only does (6) appear false, the conjunction of (6) and (3) is formally inconsistent with the SDL axiom $OA \supset \sim O \sim A$.

The overwhelming verdict among deontic logicians is that SDL genuinely succumbs to the deontic paradoxes. But it is controversial what other approach is best followed to resolve these puzzles. Two of the most attractive proposals are Castañeda's two-sorted system (*Thinking and Doing*, 1975), and the agent-and-time relativized approach of Fred Feldman (*Philosophical Perspectives*, 1990).

See also DEONTIC LOGIC, FORMAL LOGIC, MORAL DILEMMA, SET-THEORETIC PARADOXES.   J.E.T.

deontological ethics. See ETHICS.

deontologism, epistemic. See EPISTEMIC DEONTOLOGISM.

dependence, in philosophy, a relation of one of three main types: epistemic dependence, or dependence in the order of knowing; conceptual dependence, or dependence in the order of understanding; and ontological dependence, or dependence in the order of being. When a relation of dependence runs in one direction only, we have a relation of *priority*. For example, if wholes are ontologically dependent on their parts, but the latter in turn are not ontologically dependent on the former, one may say that parts are ontologically prior to wholes. The phrase 'logical priority' usually refers to priority of one of the three varieties to be discussed here.

Epistemic dependence. To say that the facts in some class *B* are epistemically dependent on the facts in some other class *A* is to say this: one cannot know any fact in *B* unless one knows some fact in *A* that serves as one's evidence for the fact in *B*. For example, it might be held that to know any fact about one's physical environment (e.g., that there is a fire in the stove), one must know (as evidence) some facts about the character of one's own sensory experience (e.g., that one is feeling warm and seeing flames). This would be to maintain that facts about the physical world are epistemically dependent on facts about sensory experience. If one held in addition that the dependence is not reciprocal – that one can know facts about one's sensory experience without knowing as evidence any facts about the physical world – one would be maintaining that the former facts are epistemically prior to the latter facts. Other plausible (though sometimes disputed) examples of epistemic priority are the following: facts about the behavior of others are epistemically prior to facts about their mental states; facts about observable objects are epistemically prior to facts about the invisible parti-

cles postulated by physics; and singular facts (e.g., this crow is black) are epistemically prior to general facts (e.g., all crows are black).

Is there a class of facts on which all others epistemically depend and that depend on no further facts in turn – a bottom story in the edifice of knowledge? Some foundationalists say yes, positing a level of basic or foundational facts that are epistemically prior to all others. Empiricists are usually foundationalists who maintain that the basic level consists of facts about immediate sensory experience. Coherentists deny the need for a privileged stratum of facts to ground the knowledge of all others; in effect, they deny that any facts are epistemically prior to any others. Instead, all facts are on a par, and each is known in virtue of the way in which it fits in with all the rest.

Sometimes it appears that two propositions or classes of them each epistemically depend on the other in a vicious way – to know *A*, you must first know *B*, and to know *B*, you must first know *A*. Whenever this is genuinely the case, we are in a skeptical predicament and cannot know either proposition. For example, Descartes believed that he could not be assured of the reliability of his own cognitions until he knew that God exists and is not a deceiver; yet how could he ever come to know anything about God except by relying on his own cognitions? This is the famous problem of the Cartesian circle. Another example is the problem of induction as set forth by Hume: to know that induction is a legitimate mode of inference, one would first have to know that the future will resemble the past; but since the latter fact is establishable only by induction, one could know it only if one already knew that induction is legitimate. Solutions to these problems must show that contrary to first appearances, there is a way of knowing one of the problematic propositions independently of the other.

Conceptual dependence. To say that *B*'s are conceptually dependent on *A*'s means that to understand what a *B* is, you must understand what an *A* is, or that the concept of a *B* can be explained or understood only through the concept of an *A*. For example, it could plausibly be claimed that the concept *uncle* can be understood only in terms of the concept *male*. Empiricists typically maintain that we understand what an external thing like a tree or a table is only by knowing what experiences it would induce in us, so that the concepts we apply to physical things depend on the concepts we apply to our experiences. They typically also maintain that this dependence is not reciprocal, so that experiential concepts are conceptually prior to physical concepts.

Some empiricists argue from the thesis of conceptual priority just cited to the corresponding thesis of epistemic priority – that facts about experiences are epistemically prior to facts about external objects. Turning the tables, some foes of empiricism maintain that the conceptual priority is the other way about: that we can describe and understand what kind of experience we are undergoing only by specifying what kind of object typically causes it ("it's a smell like that of pine mulch"). Sometimes they offer this as a reason for denying that facts about experiences are epistemically prior to facts about physical objects. Both sides in this dispute assume that a relation of conceptual priority in one direction excludes a relation of epistemic priority in the opposite direction. But why couldn't it be the case *both* that facts about experiences are epistemically prior to facts about physical objects *and* that concepts of physical objects are conceptually prior to concepts of experiences? How the various kinds of priority and dependence are connected (e.g., whether conceptual priority implies epistemic priority) is a matter in need of further study.

Ontological dependence. To say that entities of one sort (the *B*'s) are ontologically dependent on entities of another sort (the *A*'s) means this: no *B* can exist unless some *A* exists; i.e., it is logically or metaphysically necessary that if any *B* exists, some *A* also exists. Ontological dependence may be either specific (the existence of any *B* depending on the existence of a particular *A*) or generic (the existence of any *B* depending merely on the existence of some *A* or other). If *B*'s are ontologically dependent on *A*'s, but not conversely, we may say that *A*'s are ontologically prior to *B*'s. The traditional notion of substance is often defined in terms of ontological priority – substances can exist without other things, as Aristotle said, but the others cannot exist without them.

Leibniz believed that composite entities are ontologically dependent on simple (i.e., partless) entities – that any composite object exists only because it has certain simple elements that are arranged in a certain way. Berkeley, J. S. Mill, and other phenomenalists have believed that physical objects are ontologically dependent on sensory experiences – that the existence of a table or a tree consists in the occurrence of sensory experiences in certain orderly patterns. Spinoza believed that all finite beings are onto-

logically dependent on God and that God is ontologically dependent on nothing further; thus God, being ontologically prior to everything else, is in Spinoza's view the only substance.

Sometimes there are disputes about the direction in which a relationship of ontological priority runs. Some philosophers hold that extensionless points are prior to extended solids, others that solids are prior to points; some say that things are prior to events, others that events are prior to things. In the face of such disagreement, still other philosophers (such as Goodman) have suggested that nothing is inherently or absolutely prior to anything else: *A*'s may be prior to *B*'s in one conceptual scheme, *B*'s to *A*'s in another, and there may be no saying which scheme is correct. Whether relationships of priority hold absolutely or only relative to conceptual schemes is one issue dividing realists and anti-realists.

See also FOUNDATIONALISM, IDEALISM, METAPHYSICAL REALISM, PHENOMENALISM, SUBSTANCE, SUPERVENIENCE.   J.V.C.

dependence, causal. See CAUSATION.

dependence, epistemic. See DEPENDENCE.

dependence, ontological. See DEPENDENCE.

dependent beauty. See BEAUTY.

depiction, pictorial representation, also sometimes called "iconic representation." Linguistic representation is conventional: it is only by virtue of a convention that the word 'cats' refers to cats. A picture of a cat, however, seems to refer to cats by other than conventional means; for viewers can correctly interpret pictures without special training, whereas people need special training to learn languages. Though some philosophers, such as Goodman (*Languages of Art*), deny that depiction involves a non-conventional element, most are concerned to give an account of what this non-conventional element consists in. Some hold that it consists in resemblance: pictures refer to their objects partly by resembling them. Objections to this are that anything resembles anything else to some degree; and that resemblance is a symmetric and reflexive relation, whereas depiction is not. Other philosophers avoid direct appeal to resemblance: Richard Wollheim (*Painting as an Art*) argues that depiction holds by virtue of the intentional deployment of the natural human capacity to see objects in marked surfaces; and

Kendall Walton (*Mimesis as Make-Believe*) argues that depiction holds by virtue of objects serving as props in reasonably rich and vivid visual games of make-believe. **See also MIMESIS, PEIRCE.**   B.Ga.

de re. See DE DICTO.

de re necessity. See NECESSITY.

derivation. See DEDUCTION.

derivational logicism. See LOGICISM.

Derrida, Jacques (b.1930), French philosopher, author of deconstructionism, and leading figure in the postmodern movement. Postmodern thought seeks to move beyond modernism by revealing inconsistencies or aporias within the Western European tradition from Descartes to the present. These aporias are largely associated with onto-theology, a term coined by Heidegger to characterize a manner of thinking about being and truth that ultimately grounds itself in a conception of divinity. Deconstruction is the methodology of revelation: it typically involves seeking out binary oppositions defined interdependently by mutual exclusion, such as good and evil or true and false, which function as founding terms for modern thought. The onto-theological metaphysics underlying modernism is a metaphysics of presence: to be is to be present, finally to be absolutely present to the absolute, that is, to the divinity whose own being is conceived as presence to itself, as the coincidence of being and knowing in the Being that knows all things and knows itself as the reason for the being of all that is. Divinity thus functions as the measure of truth. The aporia here, revealed by deconstruction, is that this modernist measure of truth cannot meet its own measure: the coincidence of what is and what is known is an impossibility for finite intellects.

Major influences on Derrida include Hegel, Freud, Heidegger, Sartre, Saussure, and structuralist thinkers such as Lévi-Strauss, but it was his early critique of Husserl, in *Introduction à "L'Origine de la géometrie" de Husserl* (1962), that gained him recognition as a critic of the phenomenological tradition and set the conceptual framework for his later work. Derrida sought to demonstrate that the origin of geometry, conceived by Husserl as the guiding paradigm for Western thought, was a supratemporal ideal of perfect knowing that serves as the goal of human knowledge. Thus the origin of geometry is insep-

arable from its end or *telos*, a thought that Derrida later generalizes in his deconstruction of the notion of origin as such. He argues that this ideal cannot be realized in time, hence cannot be grounded in lived experience, hence cannot meet the "principle of principles" Husserl designated as the prime criterion for phenomenology, the principle that all knowing must ground itself in consciousness of an object that is coincidentally conscious of itself. This revelation of the aporia at the core of phenomenology in particular and Western thought in general was not yet labeled as a deconstruction, but it established the formal structure that guided Derrida's later deconstructive revelations of the metaphysics of presence underlying the modernism in which Western thought culminates.

See also DECONSTRUCTION, HEIDEGGER, PHENOMENOLOGY, POSTMODERN.   M.C.D.

Descartes, René (1596–1650), French philosopher and mathematician, a founder of the "modern age" and perhaps the most important figure in the intellectual revolution of the seventeenth century in which the traditional systems of understanding based on Aristotle were challenged and, ultimately, overthrown. His conception of philosophy was all-embracing: it encompassed mathematics and the physical sciences as well as psychology and ethics, and it was based on what he claimed to be absolutely firm and reliable metaphysical foundations. His approach to the problems of knowledge, certainty, and the nature of the human mind played a major part in shaping the subsequent development of philosophy.

Life and works. Descartes was born in a small town near Tours that now bears his name. He was brought up by his maternal grandmother (his mother having died soon after his birth), and at the age of ten he was sent to the recently founded Jesuit college of La Flèche in Anjou, where he remained as a boarding pupil for nine years. At La Flèche he studied classical literature and traditional classics-based subjects such as history and rhetoric as well as natural philosophy (based on the Aristotelian system) and theology. He later wrote of La Flèche that he considered it "one of the best schools in Europe," but that, as regards the philosophy he had learned there, he saw that "despite being cultivated for many centuries by the best minds, it contained no point which was not disputed and hence doubtful."

At age twenty-two (having taken a law degree

at Poitiers), Descartes set out on a series of travels in Europe, "resolving," as he later put it, "to seek no knowledge other than that which could be found either in myself or the great book of the world." The most important influence of this early period was Descartes's friendship with the Dutchman Isaac Beeckman, who awakened his lifelong interest in mathematics – a science in which he discerned precision and certainty of the kind that truly merited the title of *scientia* (Descartes's term for genuine systematic knowledge based on reliable principles). A considerable portion of Descartes's energies as a young man was devoted to pure mathematics: his essay on *Geometry* (published in 1637) incorporated results discovered during the 1620s. But he also saw mathematics as the key to making progress in the applied sciences; his earliest work, the *Compendium Musicae*, written in 1618 and dedicated to Beeckman, applied quantitative principles to the study of musical harmony and dissonance. More generally, Descartes saw mathematics as a kind of paradigm for all human understanding: "those long chains composed of very simple and easy reasonings, which geometers customarily use to arrive at their most difficult demonstrations, gave me occasion to suppose that all the things which fall within the scope of human knowledge are interconnected in the same way" (*Discourse on the Method*, Part II).

In the course of his travels, Descartes found himself closeted, on November 10, 1619, in a "stove-heated room" in a town in southern Germany, where after a day of intense meditation, he had a series of vivid dreams that convinced him of his mission to found a new scientific and philosophical system. After returning to Paris for a time, he emigrated to Holland in 1628, where he was to live (though with frequent changes of address) for most of the rest of his life. By 1633 he had ready a treatise on cosmology and physics, *Le Monde;* but he cautiously withdrew the work from publication when he heard of the condemnation of Galileo by the Inquisition for rejecting (as Descartes himself did) the traditional geocentric theory of the universe. But in 1637 Descartes released for publication, in French, a sample of his scientific work: three essays entitled the *Optics, Meteorology,* and *Geometry.* Prefaced to that selection was an autobiographical introduction entitled *Discourse on the Method of rightly conducting one's reason and reaching the truth in the sciences.* This work, which includes discussion of a number of scientific issues such as the circulation of the blood, contains (in Part IV) a summary of Descartes's views on knowledge, certainty, and the metaphysical foundations of science. Criticisms of his arguments here led Descartes to compose his philosophical masterpiece, the *Meditations on First Philosophy,* published in Latin in 1641 – a dramatic account of the voyage of discovery from universal doubt to certainty of one's own existence, and the subsequent struggle to establish the existence of God, the nature and existence of the external world, and the relation between mind and body. The *Meditations* aroused enormous interest among Descartes's contemporaries, and six sets of objections by celebrated philosophers and theologians (including Mersenne, Hobbes, Arnauld, and Gassendi) were published in the same volume as the first edition (a seventh set, by the Jesuit Pierre Bourdin, was included in the second edition of 1642).

A few years later, Descartes published, in Latin, a mammoth compendium of his metaphysical and scientific views, the *Principles of Philosophy,* which he hoped would become a university textbook to rival the standard texts based on Aristotle. In the later 1640s, Descartes became interested in questions of ethics and psychology, partly as a result of acute questions about the implications of his system raised by Princess Elizabeth of Bohemia in a long and fruitful correspondence. The fruits of this interest were published in 1649 in a lengthy French treatise entitled *The Passions of the Soul.* The same year, Descartes accepted (after much hesitation) an invitation to go to Stockholm to give philosophical instruction to Queen Christina of Sweden. He was required to provide tutorials at the royal palace at five o'clock in the morning, and the strain of this break in his habits (he had maintained the lifelong custom of lying in bed late into the morning) led to his catching pneumonia. He died just short of his fifty-fourth birthday.

The Cartesian system. In a celebrated simile, Descartes described the whole of philosophy as like a tree: the roots are metaphysics, the trunk physics, and the branches are the various particular sciences, including mechanics, medicine, and morals. The analogy captures at least three important features of the Cartesian system. The first is its insistence on the essential unity of knowledge, which contrasts strongly with the Aristotelian conception of the sciences as a series of separate disciplines, each with its own methods and standards of precision. The sciences, as Descartes put it in an early notebook, are all "linked together" in a sequence that is in principle as simple and straightforward as the series of numbers. The second point conveyed by the tree simile is the utility of philosophy for ordinary living: the tree is valued for its fruits, and these are gathered, Descartes points out, "not from the roots or the trunk but from the ends of the branches" – the practical sciences. Descartes frequently stresses that his principal motivation is not abstract theorizing for its own sake: in place of the "speculative philosophy taught in the Schools," we can and should achieve knowledge that is "useful in life" and that will one day make us "masters and possessors of nature." Third, the likening of metaphysics or "first philosophy" to the roots of the tree nicely captures the Cartesian belief in what has come to be known as foundationalism – the view that knowledge must be constructed from the bottom up, and that nothing can be taken as established until we have gone back to first principles.

Doubt and the foundations of belief. In Descartes's central work of metaphysics, the *Meditations*, he begins his construction project by observing that many of the preconceived opinions he has accepted since childhood have turned out to be unreliable; so it is necessary, "once in a lifetime" to "demolish everything and start again, right from the foundations." Descartes proceeds, in other words, by applying what is sometimes called his method of doubt, which is explained in the earlier *Discourse on the Method*: "Since I now wished to devote myself solely to the search for truth, I thought it necessary to . . . reject as if absolutely false everything in which one could imagine the least doubt, in order to see if I was left believing anything that was entirely indubitable." In the *Meditations* we find this method applied to produce a systematic critique of previous beliefs, as follows. Anything based on the senses is potentially suspect, since "I have found by experience that the senses sometimes deceive, and it is prudent never to trust completely those who have deceived us even once." Even such seemingly straightforward judgments as "I am sitting here by the fire" may be false, since there is no guarantee that my present experience is not a dream. The *dream argument* (as it has come to be called) leaves intact the truths of mathematics, since "whether I am awake or asleep two and three make five"; but Descartes now proceeds to introduce an even more radical argument for doubt based on the following dilemma. If there is an omnipotent God, he could presumably cause me to go wrong every time I count two and three; if, on the other

hand, there is no God, then I owe my origins not to a powerful and intelligent creator, but to some random series of imperfect causes, and in this case there is even less reason to suppose that my basic intuitions about mathematics are reliable.

By the end of the First Meditation, Descartes finds himself in a morass of wholesale doubt, which he dramatizes by introducing an imaginary demon "of the utmost power and cunning" who is systematically deceiving him in every possible way. Everything I believe in – "the sky, the earth and all external things" – might be illusions that the demon has devised in order to trick me. Yet this very extremity of doubt, when pushed as far as it will go, yields the first indubitable truth in the Cartesian quest for knowledge – the existence of the thinking subject. "Let the demon deceive me as much as he may, he can never bring it about that I am nothing, so long as I think I am something. . . . I am, I exist, is certain, as often as it is put forward by me or conceived in the mind." Elsewhere, Descartes expresses this *cogito* argument in the famous phrase "*Cogito ergo sum*" ("I am thinking, therefore I exist").

Having established his own existence, Descartes proceeds in the Third Meditation to make an inventory of the ideas he finds within him, among which he identifies the idea of a supremely perfect being. In a much criticized causal argument he reasons that the representational content (or "objective reality") of this idea is so great that it cannot have originated from inside his own (imperfect) mind, but must have been planted in him by an actual perfect being – God. The importance of God in the Cartesian system can scarcely be overstressed. Once the deity's existence is established, Descartes can proceed to reinstate his belief in the world around him: since God is perfect, and hence would not systematically deceive, the strong propensity he has given us to believe that many of our ideas come from external objects must, in general, be sound; and hence the external world exists (Sixth Meditation). More important still, Descartes uses the deity to set up a reliable method for the pursuit of truth. Human beings, since they are finite and imperfect, often go wrong; in particular, the data supplied by the senses is often, as Descartes puts it, "obscure and confused." But each of us can nonetheless avoid error, provided we remember to withhold judgment in such doubtful cases and confine ourselves to the "clear and distinct" perceptions of the pure intellect. A reliable intellect was God's gift to man, and if we use it with the greatest possible care, we can be sure of avoiding error (Fourth Meditation).

In this central part of his philosophy, Descartes follows in a long tradition going back to Augustine (with its ultimate roots in Plato) that in the first place is skeptical about the evidence of the senses as against the more reliable abstract perceptions of the intellect, and in the second place sees such intellectual knowledge as a kind of illumination derived from a higher source than man's own mind. Descartes frequently uses the ancient metaphor of the "natural light" or "light of reason" to convey this notion that the fundamental intuitions of the intellect are inherently reliable. The label 'rationalist', which is often applied to Descartes in this connection, can be misleading, since he certainly does not rely on reason *alone:* in the development of his scientific theories he allows a considerable role to empirical observation in the testing of hypotheses and in the understanding of the mechanisms of nature (his "vortex theory" of planetary revolutions is based on observations of the behavior of whirlpools).

What is true, nonetheless, is that the fundamental building blocks of Cartesian science are the innate ideas (chiefly those of mathematics) whose reliability Descartes takes as guaranteed by their having been implanted in the mind by God. But this in turn gives rise to a major problem for the Cartesian system, which was first underlined by some of Descartes's contemporaries (notably Mersenne and Arnauld), and which has come to be known as the *Cartesian circle.* If the reliability of the clear and distinct perceptions of the intellect depends on our knowledge of God, then how can that knowledge be established in the first place? If the answer is that we can prove God's existence from premises that we clearly and distinctly perceive, then this seems circular; for how are we entitled, at this stage, to assume that our clear and distinct perceptions are reliable? Descartes's attempts to deal with this problem are not entirely satisfactory, but his general answer seems to be that there are some propositions that are so simple and transparent that, so long as we focus on them, we can be sure of their truth even without a divine guarantee.

Cartesian science and dualism. The scientific system that Descartes had worked on before he wrote the *Meditations* and that he elaborated in his later work, the *Principles of Philosophy,* attempts wherever possible to reduce natural phenomena to the quantitative descriptions of arithmetic and geometry: "my consideration of matter in corporeal things," he says in the *Principles,* "involves absolutely nothing apart from divisions, shapes and motions." This connects with his metaphysical commitment to relying only on clear and distinct ideas. In place of the elaborate apparatus of the Scholastics, with its plethora of "substantial forms" and "real qualities," Descartes proposes to mathematicize science. The material world is simply an indefinite series of variations in the shape, size, and motion of the single, simple, homogeneous matter that he terms *res extensa* ("extended substance"). Under this category he includes all physical and biological events, even complex animal behavior, which he regards as simply the result of purely mechanical processes (for non-human animals as mechanical automata, see *Discourse,* Part V).

But there is one class of phenomena that cannot, on Descartes's view, be handled in this way, namely conscious experience. Thought, he frequently asserts, is completely alien to, and incompatible with, extension: it occupies no space, is unextended and indivisible. Hence Descartes puts forward a dualistic theory of substance: in addition to the *res extensa* that makes up the material universe, there is *res cogitans,* or thinking substance, which is entirely independent of matter. And each conscious individual is a unique thinking substance: "This 'I' – that is, the soul, by which I am what I am, is entirely distinct from the body, and would not fail to be what it is even if the body did not exist."

Descartes's arguments for the incorporeality of the soul were challenged by his contemporaries and have been heavily criticized by subsequent commentators. In the *Discourse* and the Second Meditation, he lays great stress on his ability to form a conception of himself as an existing subject, while at the same time doubting the existence of any physical thing; but this, as the critics pointed out, seems inadequate to establish the conclusion that he is a *res cogitans* – a being whose whole essence consists simply in thought. I may be able to imagine myself without a body, but this hardly proves that I could in reality exist without one (see further the Synopsis to the *Meditations*). A further problem is that our everyday experience testifies to the fact that we are not incorporeal beings, but very much creatures of flesh and blood. "Nature teaches me by the sensations of pain, hunger, thirst and so on," Descartes admits in the Sixth Meditation, "that I am not merely present in my body as a sailor is present in a ship, but that I am very closely joined and as it were intermingled with it." Yet how can an incorporeal soul interact with the body in this way? In his later writings, Descartes speaks of the "union of soul and body" as a "primitive notion" (see letters to Elizabeth of May 21 and June 28, 1643); by this he seems to have meant that, just as there are properties (such as length) that belong to body alone, and properties (such as understanding) that belong to mind alone, so there are items such as sensations that are irreducibly psychophysical, and that belong to me insofar as I am an *embodied* consciousness. The explanation of such psychophysical events was the task Descartes set himself in his last work, *The Passions of the Soul;* here he developed his theory that the pineal gland in the brain was the "seat of the soul," where data from the senses were received (via the nervous system), and where bodily movements were initiated. But despite the wealth of physiological detail Descartes provides, the central philosophical problems associated with his dualistic account of humans as hybrid entities made up of physical body and immaterial soul are, by common consent, not properly sorted out.

Influence. Despite the philosophical difficulties that beset the Cartesian system, Descartes's vision of a unified understanding of reality has retained a powerful hold on scientists and philosophers ever since. His insistence that the path to progress in science lay in the direction of quantitative explanations has been substantially vindicated. His attempt to construct a system of knowledge by starting from the subjective awareness of the conscious self has been equally important, if only because so much of the epistemology of our own time has been a reaction against the autocentric perspective from which Descartes starts out. As for the Cartesian theory of the mind, it is probably fair to say that the dualistic approach is now widely regarded as raising more problems than it solves. But Descartes's insistence that the phenomena of conscious experience are recalcitrant to explanation in purely physical terms remains deeply influential, and the cluster of profound problems that he raised about the nature of the human mind and its relation to the material world are still very far from being adequately resolved.

See also COGITO ERGO SUM, FOUNDATIONALISM, PHILOSOPHY OF MIND, RATIONALISM.

J.COT.

description, definite. See THEORY OF DESCRIPTIONS.

description, knowledge by. See KNOWLEDGE BY ACQUAINTANCE.

description, state. See CARNAP.

description, structure. See CARNAP.

descriptions, theory of. See THEORY OF DESCRIPTIONS.

descriptive emergence. See METHODOLOGICAL HOLISM.

descriptive emergentism. See HOLISM.

descriptive individualism. See HOLISM.

descriptive meaning. See EMOTIVISM, MEANING.

descriptive metaphysics. See METAPHYSICS.

descriptive relativism. See RELATIVISM.

descriptivism, the thesis that the meaning of any evaluative statement is purely descriptive or factual, i.e., determined, apart from its syntactical features, entirely by its truth conditions. Nondescriptivism (of which emotivism and prescriptivism are the main varieties) is the view that the meaning of full-blooded evaluative statements is such that they *necessarily* express the speaker's sentiments or commitments. Nonnaturalism, naturalism, and supernaturalism are descriptivist views about the nature of the properties to which the meaning rules refer. Descriptivism is related to cognitivism and moral realism. **See also EMOTIVISM, ETHICS.**

B.W.H.

descriptivist theory of names. See CAUSAL THEORY OF PROPER NAMES.

de se. See DE DICTO, KNOWLEDGE DE RE.

desert. See MERITARIAN.

design, argument from. See PHILOSOPHY OF RELIGION.

designator, rigid. See MEANING.

desire, extrinsic. See EXTRINSIC DESIRE.

desire, intrinsic. See EXTRINSIC DESIRE.

desire-belief model. See INTENTION, MOTIVATION.

destructive dilemma. See DILEMMA.

detachment, rule of. See LOTTERY PARADOX, MODUS PONENS.

determinable, a general characteristic or property analogous to a genus except that while a property independent of a genus differentiates a species that falls under the genus, no such independent property differentiates a determinate that falls under the determinable. The color blue, e.g., is a determinate with respect of the determinable color: there is no property *F* independent of color such that a color is blue if and only if it is *F*. In contrast, there is a property, *having equal sides,* such that a rectangle is a square if and only if it has this property. *Square* is a properly differentiated species of the genus *rectangle.*

W. E. Johnson introduces the terms 'determinate' and 'determinable' in his *Logic,* Part I, Chapter 11. His account of this distinction does not closely resemble the current understanding sketched above. Johnson wants to explain the differences between the superficially similar 'Red is a color' and 'Plato is a man'. He concludes that the latter really predicates something, humanity, of Plato; while the former does not really predicate anything of red. Color is not really a property (or adjective, as Johnson puts it). The determinates red, blue, and yellow are grouped together not because of a property they have in common but because of the ways they differ from each other. Determinates under the same determinable are related to each other (and are thus comparable) in ways in which they are not related to determinates under other determinables. Determinates belonging to different determinables, such as color and shape, are incomparable.

'More determinate' is often used interchangeably with 'more specific'. Many philosophers, including Johnson, hold that the characters of things are absolutely determinate or specific. Spelling out what this claim means leads to another problem in analyzing the relation between determinate and determinable. By what principle can we exclude *red and round* as a determinate of *red* and *red* as a determinate of *red or round?*

See also JOHNSON, PROPERTY.   D.H.S.

determinate. See DETERMINABLE.

determinism, the view that every event or state of affairs is brought about by antecedent events or states of affairs in accordance with universal causal laws that govern the world. Thus, the state of the world at any instant determines a unique future, and that knowledge of all the positions of things and the prevailing natural forces would permit an intelligence to predict the future state of the world with absolute precision. This view was advanced by Laplace in the early nineteenth century; he was inspired by Newton's success at integrating our physical knowledge of the world.

Contemporary determinists do not believe that Newtonian physics is the supreme theory. Some do not even believe that all theories will someday be integrated into a unified theory. They do believe that, for each event, no matter how precisely described, there is some theory or system of laws such that the occurrence of that event under that description is derivable from those laws together with information about the prior state of the system. Some determinists formulate the doctrine somewhat differently: (a) every event has a sufficient cause; (b) at any given time, given the past, only one future is possible; (c) given knowledge of all antecedent conditions and all laws of nature, an agent could predict at any given time the precise subsequent history of the universe. Thus, determinists deny the existence of chance, although they concede that our ignorance of the laws or all relevant antecedent conditions makes certain events unexpected and, therefore, apparently happen "by chance."

The term 'determinism' is also used in a more general way as the name for any metaphysical doctrine implying that there is only one possible history of the world. The doctrine described above is really *scientific* or *causal determinism,* for it grounds this implication on a general fact about the natural order, namely, its governance by universal causal law. But there is also *theological determinism,* which holds that God determines everything that happens or that, since God has perfect knowledge about the universe, only the course of events that he knows will happen can happen. And there is *logical determinism,* which grounds the necessity of the historical order on the logical truth that all propositions, including ones about the future, are either true or false. Fatalism, the view that there are forces (e.g., the stars or the fates) that determine all outcomes independently of human efforts or wishes, is claimed by some to be a version of determinism. But others deny this on the ground that determinists do not reject the efficacy of human effort or desire; they simply believe that efforts and desires, which are sometimes effective, are themselves determined by antecedent factors (as in a causal chain of events).

m is a universal doctrine, it
actions and choices. But if
ces are determined, then some
free will is an illusion. For the
ce is an inevitable product of
ctors that rendered alternatives
ven if the agent had deliberated
. An omniscient agent could have
e action or choice beforehand. This
erates the problem of free will and
nism.

See also COMPUTER THEORY, FREE WILL
OBLEM, PHILOSOPHY OF SCIENCE.   B.B.

determinism, hard. See FREE WILL PROBLEM.

determinism, historical. See MARXISM.

determinism, linguistic. See LINGUISTIC RELATIVITY.

determinism, principle of. See MILL'S METHODS.

determinism, soft. See FREE WILL PROBLEM.

deterministic automaton. See COMPUTER THEORY.

deterministic law. See CAUSAL LAW.

deterrence. See JUST WAR THEORY, PUNISHMENT.

deviant causal chain. See WAYWARD CAUSAL CHAIN.

deviant logic. See PHILOSOPHY OF LOGIC.

Dewey, John (1859–1952), American philosopher, social critic, and theorist of education. During an era when philosophy was becoming thoroughly professionalized, Dewey remained a public philosopher having a profound international influence on politics and education. His career began inauspiciously in his student days at the University of Vermont and then as a high school teacher before he went on to study philosophy at the newly formed Johns Hopkins University. There he studied with Peirce, G. S. Hall, and G. S. Morris, and was profoundly influenced by the version of Hegelian idealism propounded by Morris. After receiving his doctorate in 1884, Dewey moved to the University of Michigan where he rejoined Morris, who had relocated there. At Michigan he had as a colleague the young social psychologist G. H. Mead, and during this period Dewey himself concentrated his writing in the general area of psychology. In 1894 he accepted an appointment as chair of the Department of Philosophy, Psychology, and Edu-

cation at the University of Chicago, bringing Mead with him. At Chicago Dewey was instrumental in founding the famous laboratory school, and some of his most important writings on education grew out of his work in that experimental school. In 1904 he left Chicago for Columbia University, where he joined F. J. E. Woodbridge, founder of *The Journal of Philosophy*. He retired from Columbia in 1930 but remained active in both philosophy and public affairs until his death in 1952. Over his long career he was a prolific speaker and writer, as evidenced by a literary output of forty books and over seven hundred articles.

Philosophy. At the highest level of generality Dewey's philosophical orientation can be characterized as a kind of *naturalistic empiricism*, and the two most fundamental notions in his philosophy can be gleaned from the title of his most substantial book, *Experience and Nature* (1925). His concept of experience had its origin in his Hegelian background, but Dewey divested it of most of its speculative excesses. He clearly conceived of himself as an empiricist but was careful to distinguish his notion of experience both from that of the idealist tradition and from the empiricism of the classical British variety. The idealists had so stressed the cognitive dimension of experience that they overlooked the non-cognitive, whereas he saw the British variety as inappropriately atomistic and subjectivist. In contrast to these Dewey fashioned a notion of experience wherein action, enjoyment, and what he called "undergoing" were integrated and equally fundamental. The felt immediacy of experience (what he generally characterized as its aesthetic quality) was basic and irreducible. He then situated cognitive experience against this broader background as arising from and conditioned by this more basic experience. Cognitive experience was the result of inquiry, which was viewed as a process arising from a felt difficulty within our experience, proceeding through the stage of conceptual elaboration of possible resolutions, to a final reconstruction of the experience wherein the initial fragmented situation is transformed into a unified whole. Cognitive inquiry is this mediating process from experience to experience, and knowledge is what makes possible the final more integrated experience, which Dewey termed a "consummation."

On this view knowing is a kind of doing, and the criterion of knowledge is "warranted assertability." On the first point, Dewey felt that one of the cardinal errors of philosophy from Plato to the modern period was what he called "the spectator theory of knowledge." Knowledge had been viewed as a kind of passive recording of facts in the world and success was seen as a matter of the correspondence of our beliefs to these antecedent facts. To the contrary, Dewey viewed knowing as a constructive conceptual activity that anticipated and guided our adjustment to future experiential interactions with our environment. It was with this constructive and purposive view of thinking in mind that Dewey dubbed his general philosophical orientation instrumentalism. Concepts are instruments for dealing with our experienced world. The fundamental categories of knowledge are to be functionally understood, and the classical dualisms of philosophy (mind–body, means–end, fact–value) are ultimately to be overcome.

The purpose of knowing is to effect some alteration in the experiential situation, and for this purpose some cognitive proposals are more effective than others. This is the context in which "truth" is normally invoked, and in its stead Dewey proposed "warranted assertability." He eschewed the notion of truth (even in its less dangerous adjectival and adverbial forms, 'true' and 'truly') because he saw it as too suggestive of a static and finalized correspondence between two separate orders. Successful cognition was really a more dynamic matter of a present resolution of a problematic situation resulting in a reconstructed experience or consummation. "Warranted assertability" was the success characterization, having the appropriately normative connotation without the excess metaphysical baggage.

Dewey's notion of experience is intimately tied to his notion of nature. He did not conceive of nature as "the-world-as-it-would-be-independent-of-human-experience" but rather as a developing system of natural transactions admitting of a tripartite distinction between the physicochemical level, the psychophysical level, and the level of human experience with the understanding that this categorization was not to be construed as implying any sharp discontinuities. Experience itself, then, is one of the levels of transaction in nature and is not reducible to the other forms. The more austere, "scientific" representations of nature as, e.g., a purely mechanical system, Dewey construed as merely useful conceptualizations for specific cognitive purposes. This enabled him to distinguish his "naturalism," which he saw as a kind of non-reductive empiricism, from "materialism," which he saw as a kind of reductive rationalism.

Dewey and Santayana had an ongoing dialogue on precisely this point.

Dewey's view was also naturalistic to the degree that it advocated the universal scope of scientific method. Influenced in this regard by Peirce, he saw scientific method not as restricted to a specific sphere but simply as the way we ought to think. The structure of all reflective thought is future-oriented and involves a movement from the recognition and articulation of a felt difficulty, through the elaboration of hypotheses as possible resolutions of the difficulty, to the stage of verification or falsification. The specific sciences (physics, biology, psychology) investigate the different levels of transactions in nature, but the scientific manner of investigation is simply a generalized sophistication of the structure of common sense and has no intrinsic restriction.

Dewey construed nature as an organic unity not marked by any radical discontinuities that would require the introduction of non-natural categories or new methodological strategies. The sharp dualisms of mind and body, the individual and the social, the secular and the religious, and most importantly, fact and value, he viewed as conceptual constructs that have far outlived their usefulness. The inherited dualisms had to be overcome, particularly the one between fact and value inasmuch as it functioned to block the use of reason as the guide for human action. On his view people naturally have values as well as beliefs. Given human nature, there are certain activities and states of affairs that we naturally prize, enjoy, and value. The human problem is that these are not always easy to come by nor are they always compatible. We are forced to deal with the problem of what we really want and what we ought to pursue. Dewey advocated the extension of scientific method to these domains. The deliberative process culminating in a practical judgment is not unlike the deliberative process culminating in factual belief. Both kinds of judgment can be responsible or irresponsible, right or wrong. This deliberative sense of evaluation as a process presupposes the more basic sense of evaluation concerning those dimensions of human experience we prize and find fulfilling. Here too there is a dimension of appropriateness, one grounded in the kind of beings we are, where the 'we' includes our social history and development. On this issue Dewey had a very Greek view, albeit one transposed into a modern evolutionary perspective. Fundamental questions of value and human fulfillment ultimately bear on our conception of the human community, and this in turn leads him to the issues of democracy and education.

Society and education. The ideal social order for Dewey is a structure that allows maximum self-development of all individuals. It fosters the free exchange of ideas and decides on policies in a manner that acknowledges each person's capacity effectively to participate in and contribute to the direction of social life. The respect accorded to the dignity of each contributes to the common welfare of all. Dewey found the closest approximation to this ideal in democracy, but he did not identify contemporary democracies with this ideal. He was not content to employ old forms of democracy to deal with new problems. Consistent with instrumentalism, he maintained that we should be constantly rethinking and reworking our democratic institutions in order to make them ever more responsive to changing times. This constant rethinking placed a considerable premium on intelligence, and this underscored the importance of education for democracy.

Dewey is probably best known for his views on education, but the centrality of his theory of education to his overall philosophy is not always appreciated. The fundamental aim of education for him is not to convey information but to develop critical methods of thought. Education is future-oriented and the future is uncertain; hence, it is paramount to develop those habits of mind that enable us adequately to assess new situations and to formulate strategies for dealing with the problematic dimensions of them. This is not to suggest that we should turn our backs on the past, because what we as a people have already learned provides our only guide for future activity. But the past is not to be valued for its own sake but for its role in developing and guiding those critical capacities that will enable us to deal with our ever-changing world effectively and responsibly.

With the advent of the analytic tradition as the dominant style of philosophizing in America, Dewey's thought fell out of favor. About the only arenas in which it continued to flourish were schools of education. However, with the recent revival of a general pragmatic orientation in the persons of Quine, Putnam, and Rorty, among others, the spirit of Dewey's philosophy is frequently invoked. Holism, anti-foundationalism, contextualism, functionalism, the blurring of the lines between science and philosophy and between the theoretical and the practical – all central themes in Dewey's philosophy – have become fashionable. Neo-pragmatism is a contemporary catchphrase. Dewey is, however, more frequently invoked than read, and even the Dewey that is invoked is a truncated version of the historical figure who constructed a comprehensive philosophical vision.

See also INSTRUMENTALISM, PEIRCE, PRAGMATISM.   C.F.D.

dharma, in Hinduism and especially in the early literature of the Vedas, a cosmic rule giving things their nature or essence, or in the human context, a set of duties and rules to be performed or followed to maintain social order, promote general well-being, and be righteous. Pursuit of dharma was considered one of the four fundamental pursuits of life, the three others being those of wealth (*artha*), pleasure (*kāma*), and spiritual liberation (*moksha*). In the Bhagavad Gita, dharma was made famous as *svadharma*, meaning one's assigned duties based on one's nature and abilities rather than on birth. The Hindu lawgiver Manu (who probably lived between the third century B.C. and the first century A.D.) codified the dharmic duties based on a fourfold order of society and provided concrete guidance to people in discharging their social obligations based on their roles and stations in life. Even though Manu, like the Gita, held that one's duties and obligations should fit one's nature rather than be determined by birth, the dharma-oriented Hindu society was eventually characterized by a rigid caste structure and a limited role for women. See also BHAGAVAD GITA.
D.K.C.

Dharmakīrti (seventh century A.D.), Indian Yogācāra Buddhist philosopher and logician. His works include *Pramānavārttika* ("Explanation of the Touchstones"), a major work in logic and epistemology; and *Nyāyabindu,* an introduction to his views. In *Santānāntara-siddhi* ("Establishment of the Existence of Other Minds") he defends his perceptual idealism against the charge of solipsism, claiming that he may as legitimately use the argument from analogy for the existence of others (drawing inferences from apparently intelligent behaviors to intelligences that cause them) as his perceptual realist opponents. He criticized Nyāya theistic arguments. He exercised a strong influence on later Indian work in logic.   K.E.Y.

d'Holbach, Paul-Henri-Dietrich, Baron (1723–89), French philosopher, a leading materialist and prolific contributor to the *Encyclopedia*. He was born in the Rhenish Palatinate, settled in France at an early age, and read law at Leiden. After inheriting an uncle's wealth and title, he became a solicitor at the Paris "Parlement" and a regular host of philosophical dinners attended by the Encyclopedists and visitors of renown (Gibbon, Hume, Smith, Sterne, Priestley, Beccaria, Franklin). Knowledgeable in chemistry and mineralogy and fluent in several languages, he translated German scientific works and English anti-Christian pamphlets into French.

Basically, d'Holbach was a synthetic thinker, powerful though not original, who systematized and radicalized Diderot's naturalism. Also drawing on Hobbes, Spinoza, Locke, Hume, Buffon, Helvétius, and La Mettrie, his treatises were so irreligious and anticlerical that they were published abroad anonymously or pseudonymously: *Christianity Unveiled* (1756), *The Sacred Contagion* (1768), *Critical History of Jesus* (1770), *The Social System* (1773), and *Universal Moral* (1776). His masterpiece, the *System of Nature* (1770), a "Lucretian" compendium of eighteenth-century materialism, even shocked Voltaire. D'Holbach derived everything from matter and motion, and upheld universal necessity. The self-sustaining laws of nature are normative. Material reality is therefore contrasted to metaphysical delusion, self-interest to alienation, and earthly happiness to otherworldly optimism. More vindictive than Toland's, d'Holbach's unmitigated critique of Christianity anticipated Feuerbach, Strauss, Marx, and Nietzsche. He discredited supernatural revelation, theism, deism, and pantheism as mythological, censured Christian virtues as unnatural, branded piety as fanatical, and stigmatized clerical ignorance, immorality, and despotism. Assuming that science liberates man from religious hegemony, he advocated sensory and experimental knowledge. Believing that society and education form man, he unfolded a mechanistic anthropology, a eudaimonistic morality, and a secular, utilitarian social and political program.

See also ENCYCLOPEDIA, PHILOSOPHY OF MIND.   J.-L.S.

diagonalization. See DIAGONAL PROCEDURE.

diagonal procedure, a method, originated by Cantor, for showing that there are infinite sets that cannot be put in one-to-one correspondence with the set of natural numbers (i.e., enumerated). For example, the method can be used to show that the set of real numbers x in the interval $0 < x \leq 1$ is not enumerable. Suppose $x_0, x_1, x_2, \ldots$ were such an enumeration (x_0 is the real correlated with 0; x_1, the real correlated with 1; and so on). Then consider the list formed by replacing each real in the enumeration with the unique non-terminating decimal fraction representing it:

$$. \quad x_{00} \quad x_{01} \quad x_{02} \quad \cdots$$
$$. \quad x_{10} \quad x_{11} \quad x_{12} \quad \cdots$$
$$. \quad x_{20} \quad x_{21} \quad x_{22} \quad \cdots$$
$$\cdots$$

(The first decimal fraction represents x_0; the second, x_1; and so on.) By diagonalization we select the decimal fraction shown by the arrows:

$$. \quad x_{00} \quad x_{01} \quad x_{02} \quad \cdots$$
$$. \quad x_{10} \quad x_{11} \quad x_{12} \quad \cdots$$
$$. \quad x_{20} \quad x_{21} \quad x_{22} \quad \cdots$$
$$\cdots$$

and change each digit x_{nn}, taking care to avoid a terminating decimal. This fraction

$$. \quad x^*{}_{00} \quad x^*{}_{11} \quad x^*{}_{22} \quad \cdots$$

is not on our list. For it differs from the first in the tenths place, from the second in the hundredths place, and from the third in the thousandths place, and so on. Thus the real it represents is not in the supposed enumeration. This contradicts the original assumption.

The idea can be put more elegantly. Let f be any function such that, for each natural number n, $f(n)$ is a set of natural numbers. Then there is a set S of natural numbers such that $n \in S \equiv n \notin f(n)$. It is obvious that, for each n, $f(n) \neq S$.

See also CANTOR, INFINITY, PHILOSOPHY OF MATHEMATICS.   C.S.

dialectic, an argumentative exchange involving contradiction or a technique or method connected with such exchanges. The word's origin is the Greek *dialegein*, 'to argue' or 'converse'; in Aristotle and others, this often has the sense 'argue for a conclusion', 'establish by argument'. By Plato's time, if not earlier, it had acquired a technical sense: a form of argumentation through question and answer. The adjective *dialektikos*, 'dialectical', would mean 'concerned with *dialegein*' or (of persons) 'skilled in *dialegein*'; the feminine *dialektikē* is then 'the art of *dialegein*'.

Aristotle says that Zeno of Elea invented

dialectic. He apparently had in mind Zeno's paradoxical arguments against motion and multiplicity, which Aristotle saw as dialectical because they rested on premises his adversaries conceded and deduced contradictory consequences from them. A first definition of dialectical argument might then be: 'argument conducted by question and answer, resting on an opponent's concessions, and aiming at refuting the opponent by deriving contradictory consequences'. This roughly fits the style of argument Socrates is shown engaging in by Plato. So construed, dialectic is primarily an art of refutation. Plato, however, came to apply 'dialectic' to the method by which philosophers attain knowledge of Forms. His understanding of that method appears to vary from one dialogue to another and is difficult to interpret. In *Republic* VI–VII, dialectic is a method that somehow establishes "non-hypothetical" conclusions; in the *Sophist*, it is a method of discovering definitions by successive divisions of genera into their species.

Aristotle's concept of dialectical argument comes closer to Socrates and Zeno: it proceeds by question and answer, normally aims at refutation, and cannot scientifically or philosophically establish anything. Aristotle differentiates dialectical arguments from *demonstration* (*apodeixis*), or scientific arguments, on the basis of their premises: demonstrations must have "true and primary" premises, dialectical arguments premises that are "apparent," "reputable," or "accepted" (these are alternative, and disputed, renderings of the term *endoxos*). However, dialectical arguments must be valid, unlike *eristic* or *sophistical* arguments. The *Topics*, which Aristotle says is the first art of dialectic, is organized as a handbook for dialectical debates; Book VIII clearly presupposes a rule-directed, formalized style of disputation presumably practiced in the Academy.

This use of 'dialectic' reappears in the early Middle Ages in Europe, though as Aristotle's works became better known after the twelfth century dialectic was increasingly associated with the formalized disputations practiced in the universities (recalling once again the formalized practice presupposed by Aristotle's *Topics*). In his *Critique of Pure Reason*, Kant declared that the ancient meaning of 'dialectic' was 'the logic of illusion' and proposed a "Transcendental Dialectic" that analyzed the "antinomies" (deductions of contradictory conclusions) to which pure reason is inevitably led when it extends beyond its proper sphere. This concept was further developed by Fichte and Schelling into a

traidic notion of *thesis*, opposing *antithesis*, and resultant *synthesis*. Hegel transformed the notion of contradiction from a logical to a metaphysical one, making dialectic into a theory not simply of arguments but of historical processes within the development of "spirit"; Marx transformed this still further by replacing 'spirit' with 'matter'.

See also ACADEMY, ARISTOTLE, HEGEL, MARX, PLATO, SOCRATES, TOPICS.   R.Sm.

dialectical argument. See DIALECTIC.

dialectical materialism. See MARX, PLEKHANOV.

dialecticians. See SCHOOL OF NAMES.

diallelon (from ancient Greek *di allēlon*, 'through one another'), a circular definition. A definition is circular provided either the *definiendum* occurs in the *definiens*, as in 'Law is a lawful command', or a first term is defined by means of a second term, which in turn is defined by the first term, as in 'Law is the expressed wish of a ruler, and a ruler is one who establishes laws.'

A *diallelus* is a circular argument: an attempt to establish a conclusion by a premise that cannot be known unless the conclusion is known in the first place. Descartes, e.g., argued: I clearly and distinctly perceive that God exists, and what I clearly and distinctly perceive is true. Therefore, God exists. To justify the premise that clear and distinct perceptions are true, however, he appealed to his knowledge of God's existence.

See also CIRCULAR REASONING, DEFINITION.   M.St.

diallelus. See DIALLELON.

dialogism. See BAKHTIN.

dianoia, Greek term for the faculty of thought, specifically of drawing conclusions from assumptions and of constructing and following arguments. The term may also designate the thought that results from using this faculty. We would use *dianoia* to construct a mathematical proof; in contrast, a being – if there is such a being it would be a god – that could simply intuit the truth of the theorem would use the faculty of intellectual intuition, *noûs*. In contrast with *noûs*, *dianoia* is the distinctly human faculty of reason. Plato uses *noûs* and *dianoia* to designate, respectively, the highest and second levels of the faculties represented on the divided line (*Republic* 511d–e). **See also** PLATO.   E.C.H.

dichotomy paradox. See ZENO'S PARADOXES.

dici de omni et nullo. See DICTUM DE OMNI ET NULLO.

dictum. See ABELARD, COMPLEXE SIGNIFICABILE.

dictum de omni et nullo, also *dici de omni et nullo* (Latin, 'said of all and none'), two principles that were supposed by medieval logicians to underlie all valid syllogisms. *Dictum de omni* applies most naturally to universal affirmative propositions, maintaining that in such a proposition, whatever falls under the subject term also falls under the predicate term. Thus, in 'Every whale is a mammal', whatever is included under 'whale' is included under 'mammal'. *Dictum de nullo* applies to universal negative propositions, such as 'No whale is a lizard', maintaining that whatever falls under the subject term does not fall under the predicate term. **See also SYLLOGISM.**   W.E.M.

Diderot, Denis (1713–84), French philosopher, Encyclopedist, dramatist, novelist, and art critic, a champion of Enlightenment values. He is known primarily as general editor of the *Encyclopedia* (1747–73), an analytical and interpretive compendium of eighteenth-century science and technology. A friend of Rousseau and Condillac, Diderot translated Shaftesbury's *Inquiry Concerning Virtue* (1745) into French. Revealing Lucretian affinities (*Philosophical Thoughts,* 1746), he assailed Christianity in *The Skeptics' Walk* (1747) and argued for a materialistic and evolutionary universe (*Letter on the Blind,* 1749); this led to a short imprisonment.

Diderot wrote mediocre bourgeois comedies; some bleak fiction (*The Nun,* 1760); and two satirical dialogues, *Rameau's Nephew* (1767) and *Jacques the Fatalist* (1765–84), his masterpieces. He innovatively theorized on drama (*Discourse on Dramatic Poetry,* 1758) and elevated art criticism to a literary genre (*Salons* in Grimm's *Literary Correspondence*). At Catherine II's invitation, Diderot visited Saint Petersburg in 1773 and planned the creation of a Russian university.

Promoting science, especially biology and chemistry, Diderot unfolded a philosophy of nature inclined toward monism. His works include physiological investigations, *Letter on the Deaf and Dumb* (1751) and *Elements of Physiology* (1774–80); a sensationalistic epistemology, *On the Interpretation of Nature* (1745); an aesthetic, *Essays on Painting* (1765); a materialistic philosophy of science, *D'Alembert's Dream* (1769); an anthropology, *Supplement to the Voyage of*

Bougainville (1772); and an anti-behavioristic *Refutation of Helvétius' Work "On Man"* (1773–80).
See also ENCYCLOPEDIA.   J.-L.S.

différance, a French coinage deployed by Derrida in *De la Grammatologie* (1967), where he defines it as "an economic concept designating the production of differing/deferring." *Différance* is polysemic, but its key function is to name the prime condition for the functioning of all language and thought: differing, the differentiation of signs from each other that allows us to differentiate things from each other. Deferring is the process by which signs refer to each other, thus constituting the self-reference essential to language, without ever capturing the being or presence that is the transcendent entity toward which it is aimed. Without the concepts or idealities generated by the iteration of signs, we could never identify a dog as a dog, could not perceive a dog (or any other thing) as such. Perception presupposes language, which, in turn, presupposes the ideality generated by the repetition of signs. Thus there can be no perceptual origin for language; language depends upon an "original repetition," a deliberate oxymoron that Derrida employs to signal the impossibility of conceiving an origin of language from within the linguistic framework in which we find ourselves. *Différance* is the condition for language, and language is the condition for experience: whatever meaning we may find in the world is attributed to the differing/deferring play of signifiers.

The notion of *différance* and the correlative thesis that meaning is language-dependent have been appropriated by radical thinkers in the attempt to demonstrate that political inequalities are grounded in nothing other than the conventions of sign systems governing differing cultures.
See also DECONSTRUCTION, DERRIDA, PERCEPTION, POSTMODERN.   M.C.D.

difference. See SET THEORY.

difference, method of. See MILL'S METHODS.

difference principle. See RAWLS.

différend. See LYOTARD.

differentia. See DEFINITION, TOPICS.

dignity, a moral worth or status usually attributed to human persons. Persons are said to have dignity as well as to express it. Persons are typically thought to have (1) "human dignity" (an intrinsic moral worth, a basic moral status, or both, which is had equally by all persons); and (2) a "sense of dignity" (an awareness of one's dignity inclining toward the expression of one's dignity and the avoidance of humiliation). Persons can lack a sense of dignity without consequent loss of their human dignity.

In Kant's influential account of the equal dignity of all persons, human dignity is grounded in the capacity for practical rationality, especially the capacity for autonomous self-legislation under the categorical imperative. Kant holds that dignity contrasts with price and that there is nothing – not pleasure nor communal welfare nor other good consequences – for which it is morally acceptable to sacrifice human dignity. Kant's categorical rejection of the use of persons as mere means suggests a now-common link between the possession of human dignity and human rights (see, e.g., the United Nations' *Universal Declaration of Human Rights*). One now widespread discussion of dignity concerns "dying with dignity" and the right to conditions conducive thereto.

See also KANT, MORAL STATUS, RIGHTS, VALUE.   M.J.M.

dilemma, an argument or argument form in which one of the premises is a disjunction. *Constructive dilemmas* take the form 'If *A* and *B*, if *C* then *D*, *A* or *C*; therefore *B* or *D*' and are instances of *modus ponens* in the special case where *A* is *C* and *B* is *D*; *destructive dilemmas* are of the form 'If *A* then *B*, if *C* then *D*, not-*B* or not-*D*; therefore not-*A* or not-*C*' and are likewise instances of *modus tollens* in that special case. A dilemma in which the disjunctive premise is false is commonly known as a *false dilemma*. **See also** MORAL DILEMMA.   G.F.S.

dilemma, moral. See MORAL DILEMMA.

Dilthey, Wilhelm (1833–1911), German philosopher and historian whose main project was to establish the conditions of historical knowledge, much as Kant's *Critique of Pure Reason* had for our knowledge of nature. He studied theology, history, and philosophy at Heidelberg and Berlin and in 1882 accepted the chair earlier held by Hegel at the University of Berlin.

Dilthey's first attempt at a critique of historical reason is found in the *Introduction to the Human Sciences* (1883), the last in the *Formation of the Historical World in the Human Sciences* (1910). He is also a recognized contributor to hermeneutics, literary criticism, and worldview theory. His *Life*

of Schleiermacher and essays on the Renaissance, Enlightenment, and Hegel are model works of *Geistesgeschichte*, in which philosophical ideas are analyzed in relation to their social and cultural milieu.

Dilthey holds that life is the ultimate nexus of reality behind which we cannot go. Life is viewed, not primarily in biological terms as in Nietzsche and Bergson, but as the historical totality of human experience. The basic categories whereby we reflect on life provide the background for the epistemological categories of the sciences. According to Dilthey, Aristotle's category of acting and suffering is rooted in prescientific experience, which is then explicated as the category of efficacy or influence (*Wirkung*) in the human sciences and as the category of cause (*Ursache*) in the natural sciences. Our understanding of influence in the human sciences is less removed from the full reality of life than are the causal explanations arrived at in the natural sciences. To this extent the human sciences can claim a priority over the natural sciences. Whereas we have direct access to the real elements of the historical world (psychophysical human beings), the elements of the natural world are merely hypothetical entities such as atoms. The natural sciences deal with outer experiences, while the human sciences are based on inner experience. Inner experience is reflexive and implicitly self-aware, but need not be introspective or explicitly self-conscious. In fact, we often have inner experiences of the same objects that outer experience is about. An outer experience of an object focuses on its physical properties; an inner experience of it on our felt responses to it. A lived experience (*Erlebnis*) of it includes both.

The distinction between the natural and the human sciences is also related to the methodological difference between explanation and understanding. The natural sciences seek causal explanations of nature – connecting the discrete representations of outer experience through hypothetical generalizations. The human sciences aim at an understanding (*Verstehen*) that articulates the typical structures of life given in lived experience. Finding lived experience to be inherently connected and meaningful, Dilthey opposed traditional atomistic and associationist psychologies and developed a descriptive psychology that Husserl recognized as anticipating phenomenological psychology.

In *Ideas* (1894) Dilthey argued that descriptive psychology could provide a neutral foundation for the other human sciences, but in his later hermeneutical writings, which influenced Heidegger and Hans-Georg Gadamer, he rejected the possibility of a foundational discipline or method. In the *Formation*, he asserted that all the human sciences are interpretive and mutually dependent. Hermeneutically conceived, understanding is a process of interpreting the "objectifications of life," the external expressions of human experience and activity. The understanding of others is mediated by these common objectifications and not immediately available through empathy (*Einfühlung*). Moreover, to fully understand myself I must interpret the expressions of my life just as I interpret the expressions of others.

Whereas the natural sciences aim at ever broader generalizations, the human sciences place equal weight on understanding individuality and universality. Dilthey regarded individuals as points of intersection of the social and cultural systems in which they participate. Any psychological contribution to understanding human life must be integrated into this more public framework. Although universal laws of history are rejected, particular human sciences can establish uniformities limited to specific social and cultural systems.

In a set of sketches (1911) supplementing the *Formation*, Dilthey further developed the categories of life in relation to the human sciences. After analyzing formal categories such as the part–whole relation shared by all the sciences, he distinguished the real categories of the human sciences from those of the natural sciences. The most important human science categories are value, purpose, and meaning, but they by no means exhaust the concepts needed to reflect on the ultimate sense of our existence. Such reflection receives its fullest expression in a worldview (*Weltanschauung*), such as the worldviews developed in religion, art, and philosophy. A worldview constitutes an overall perspective on life that sums up what we know about the world, how we evaluate it emotionally, and how we respond to it volitionally. Since Dilthey distinguished three exclusive and recurrent types of worldview naturalism (e.g., Democritus, Hume), the idealism of freedom (e.g., Socrates, Kant), and objective idealism (e.g., Parmenides, Hegel) – he is often regarded as a relativist. But Dilthey thought that both the natural and the human sciences could in their separate ways attain objective truth through a proper sense of method. Metaphysical formulations of worldviews are relative only because they attempt an impossible synthesis of all truth.

See also EINFÜHLUNG, ERLEBNIS, HEGEL, HERMENEUTICS, NIETZSCHE, PHILOSOPHY OF HISTORY.   R.A.M.

diminished capacity, a legal defense to criminal liability that exists in two distinct forms: (1) the *mens rea* variant, in which a defendant uses evidence of mental abnormality to cast doubt on the prosecution's assertion that, at the time of the crime, the defendant possessed the mental state criteria, the *mens rea*, required by the legal definition of the offense charged; and (2) the partial responsibility variant, in which a defendant uses evidence of mental abnormality to support a claim that, even if the defendant's mental state satisfied the *mens rea* criteria for the offense, the defendant's responsibility for the crime is diminished and thus the defendant should be convicted of a lesser crime and/or a lesser sentence should be imposed. The mental abnormality may be produced by mental disorder, intoxication, trauma, or other causes. The *mens rea* variant is not a distinct excuse: a defendant is simply arguing that the prosecution cannot prove the definitional, mental state criteria for the crime. Partial responsibility is an excuse, but unlike the similar, complete excuse of legal insanity, partial responsibility does not produce total acquittal; rather, a defendant's claim is for reduced punishment. A defendant may raise either or both variants of diminished capacity and the insanity defense in the same case.

For example, a common definition of first-degree murder requires the prosecution to prove that a defendant intended to kill and did so after premeditation. A defendant charged with this crime might raise both variants as follows. To deny the allegation of premeditation, a defendant might claim that the killing occurred instantaneously in response to a "command hallucination." If believed, a defendant cannot be convicted of *premeditated* homicide, but can be convicted of the lesser crime of second-degree murder, which typically requires only intent. And even a defendant who killed intentionally and premeditatedly might claim partial responsibility because the psychotic mental state rendered the agent's reasons for action nonculpably irrational. In this case, either the degree of crime might be reduced by operation of the partial excuse, rather than by negation of definitional *mens rea*, or a defendant might be convicted of first-degree murder but given a lesser penalty.

In the United States the *mens rea* variant exists in about half the jurisdictions, although its scope

is usually limited in various ways, primarily to avoid a defendant's being acquitted and freed if mental abnormality negated *all* the definitional mental state criteria of the crime charged. In English law, the *mens rea* variant exists but is limited by the type of evidence usable to support it. No American jurisdiction has adopted a distinct, straightforward partial responsibility variant, but various analogous doctrines and procedures are widely accepted. For example, partial responsibility grounds both the doctrine that intentional killing should be reduced from murder to voluntary manslaughter if a defendant acted "in the heat of passion" upon legally adequate provocation, and the sentencing judge's discretion to award a decreased sentence based on a defendant's mental abnormality. In addition to such partial responsibility analogues, England, Wales, and Scotland have directly adopted the partial responsibility variant, termed "diminished responsibility," but it applies only to prosecutions for murder. "Diminished responsibility" reduces a conviction to a lesser crime, such as manslaughter or culpable homicide, for behavior that would otherwise constitute murder.
See also FREE WILL PROBLEM, MENS REA, PHILOSOPHY OF LAW.   S.J.M.

diminished responsibility. See DIMINISHED CAPACITY.

Ding an sich. See KANT.

Diodoros Cronos. See MEGARIANS.

Diogenes Laertius. See DOXOGRAPHERS, VAGUENESS.

Diogenes of Apollonia. See PRE-SOCRATICS.

Diogenes of Ionoanda. See EPICUREANISM.

Diogenes the Cynic. See CYNICS.

direct discourse. See INDIRECT DISCOURSE.

direct intention. See INTENTION.

direction of fit, a metaphor that derives from a story in Anscombe's *Intention* (1957) about a detective who follows a shopper around town making a list of the things that the shopper buys. As Anscombe notes, whereas the detective's list has to match the way the world is (each of the things the shopper buys must be on the detective's list), the shopper's list is such that the world

has to fit with it (each of the things on the list are things that he must buy). The metaphor is now standardly used to describe the difference between kinds of speech act (assertions versus commands) and mental states (beliefs versus desires). For example, beliefs are said to have the world-to-mind direction of fit because it is in the nature of beliefs that their contents are supposed to match the world: false beliefs are to be abandoned. Desires are said to have the opposite mind-to-world direction of fit because it is in the nature of desires that the world is supposed to match their contents. This is so at least to the extent that the role of an unsatisfied desire that the world be a certain way is to prompt behavior aimed at making the world that way. **See also** ANSCOMBE, BELIEF, MOTIVATION.   M.Sm.

direct knowledge. See BASING RELATION.

direct passions. See HUME.

direct realism, the theory that perceiving is epistemically direct, unmediated by conscious or unconscious inference. Direct realism is distinguished, on the one hand, from indirect, or representative, realism, the view that perceptual awareness of material objects is mediated by an awareness of sensory representations, and, on the other hand, from forms of phenomenalism that identify material objects with states of mind. It might be thought that direct realism is incompatible with causal theories of perception. Such theories invoke causal chains leading from objects perceived (causes) to perceptual states of perceivers (effects). Since effects must be distinct from causes, the relation between an instance of perceiving and an object perceived, it would seem, cannot be direct. This, however, confuses *epistemic* directness with *causal* directness. A direct realist need only be committed to the former. In perceiving a tomato to be red, the content of my perceptual awareness is the tomato's being red. I enter this state as a result of a complex causal process, perhaps. But my perception may be direct in the sense that it is unmediated by an awareness of a representational sensory state from which I am led to an awareness of the tomato. Perceptual error, and more particularly, hallucinations and illusions, are usually thought to pose special difficulties for direct realists. My hallucinating a red tomato, for instance, is not my being directly aware of a red tomato, since I may hallucinate the tomato even when none is present. Perhaps, then, my hallucinating a red tomato is partly a matter of my being directly aware of a round, red sensory representation. And if my awareness in this case is indistinguishable from my perception of an actual red tomato, why not suppose that I am aware of a sensory representation in the veridical case as well? A direct realist may respond by denying that hallucinations are in fact indistinguishable from veridical perceivings or by calling into question the claim that, if sensory representations are required to explain hallucinations, they need be postulated in the veridical case. **See also PER-CEPTION, PHENOMENALISM.**   J.F.H.

direct reference. See CAUSAL THEORY OF PROPER NAMES.

direct sense. See OBLIQUE CONTEXT.

discourse ethics. See HABERMAS.

discrete time. See TIME.

disembodiment, the immaterial state of existence of a person who previously had a body. Disembodiment is thus to be distinguished from non-embodiment or immateriality. God and angels, if they exist, are non-embodied, or immaterial. By contrast, if human beings continue to exist after their bodies die, then they are disembodied. As this example suggests, disembodiment is typically discussed in the context of immortality or survival of death. It presupposes a view according to which persons are souls or some sort of immaterial entity that is capable of existing apart from a body. Whether it is possible for a person to become disembodied is a matter of controversy. Most philosophers who believe that this is possible assume that a disembodied person is conscious, but it is not obvious that this should be the case. **See also PERSONAL IDENTITY, PHILOSOPHY OF MIND, PLATO, SURVIVAL.**

E.R.W.

disjoint. See SET THEORY.

disjunction. See DISJUNCTIVE PROPOSITION, SYLLOGISM.

disjunction elimination. (1) The argument form 'A or B, if A then C, if B then C; therefore, C' and arguments of this form. (2) The rule of inference that permits one to infer C from a disjunction together with derivations of C from each of the disjuncts separately. This is also known as the *rule of disjunctive elimination* or V-*elimination.* **See also DISJUNCTIVE PROPOSITION.**   G.F.S.

disjunction introduction. (1) The argument form 'A (or B); therefore, A or B' and arguments of this form. (2) The rule of inference that permits one to infer a disjunction from either of its disjuncts. This is also known as the *rule of addition* or V-*introduction.* **See also DISJUNCTIVE PROPOSITION.**   G.F.S.

disjunctive normal form. See NORMAL FORM.

disjunctive proposition, a proposition whose main propositional operator (main connective) is the disjunction operator, i.e., the logical operator that represents 'and/or'. Thus, '(P-and/or-Q)-and-R' is not a disjunctive proposition because its main connective is the conjunction operation, but 'P-and/or-(Q-and-R)' is disjunctive.   R.W.B.

disjunctive syllogism. See SYLLOGISM.

disposition, a tendency of an object or system to act or react in characteristic ways in certain situations. Fragility, solubility, and radioactivity are typical physical dispositions; generosity and irritability are typical dispositions of persons. For behaviorism, functionalism, and some forms of materialism, mental events, such as the occurrence of an idea, and states such as beliefs, are also dispositions. Hypothetical or conditional statements are implied by dispositional claims and capture their basic meaning: the glass would shatter if suitably struck; left undisturbed, a radium atom will probably decay in a certain time; etc. These are usually taken as subjunctive rather than material conditionals (to avoid problems like having to count as soluble anything not immersed in water). The characteristic mode of action or reaction – shattering, decaying, etc. – is termed the disposition's *manifestation* or *display.* But it need not be observable. Fragility is a *regular* or *universal* disposition; a suitably struck glass invariably shatters. Radioactivity is *variable* or *probabilistic;* radium may or may not decay in a certain situation. Dispositions may also be *multi-track* or *multiply manifested,* rather than *single-track* or *singly manifested:* like hardness or elasticity, they may have different manifestations in different situations.

In *The Concept of Mind* (1949) Ryle argued that there is nothing more to dispositional claims than their associated conditionals: dispositional properties are not *occurrent;* to possess a dispositional property is not to undergo any episode or occurrence, or to be in a particular state. (Coupled with a positivist rejection of unobservables,

238

and a conception of mental episodes and states as dispositions, this supports the view of behaviorism that such episodes and states are nothing but dispositions to observable behavior.) By contrast, realism holds that dispositional talk is also about actual or occurrent properties or states, possibly unknown or unobservable. In particular, it is about the bases of dispositions in intrinsic properties or states: fragility is based in molecular structure, radioactivity in nuclear structure. A disposition's basis is viewed as at least partly the cause of its manifestation. Some philosophers hold that the bases are categorical, not dispositional (D. M. Armstrong, *A Materialist Theory of Mind,* 1968). Others, notably Popper, hold that all properties are dispositional.

See also BEHAVIORISM, COUNTERFACTU-ALS, PHILOSOPHY OF MIND, PHILOSOPHY OF SCIENCE, PROPENSITY, STATE.   D.S.

dispositional belief. See BELIEF.

dispositional state. See STATE.

dispositional theory of meaning. See MEANING.

dispositional theory of memory. See MEMORY.

disposition to believe. See BELIEF.

disquotation theory of truth. See TRUTH.

distinction, formal. See FUNDAMENTUM DIVISIONIS.

distinction, mental. See FUNDAMENTUM DIVISIONIS.

distinction, real. See FUNDAMENTUM DIVISIONIS.

distribution, the property of standing for every individual designated by a term. The Latin term *distributio* originated in the twelfth century; it was applied to terms as part of a theory of reference, and it may have simply indicated the property of a term prefixed by a universal quantifier. The term 'dog' in 'Every dog has his day' is distributed, because it supposedly refers to every dog. In contrast, the same term in 'A dog bit the mailman' is not distributed because it refers to only one dog. In time, the idea of distribution came to be used only as a heuristic device for determining the validity of categorical syllogisms: (1) every term that is distributed in a premise must be distributed in the conclusion; (2) the middle term must be distributed at least once.

Most explanations of distribution in logic text-books are perfunctory; and it is stipulated that the subject terms of universal propositions and the predicate terms of negative propositions are distributed. This is intuitive for A-propositions, e.g., 'All humans are mortal'; the property of being mortal is distributed over each human. The idea of distribution is not intuitive for, say, the predicate term of O-propositions. According to the doctrine, the sentence 'Some humans are not selfish' says in effect that if all the selfish things are compared with some select human (one that is not selfish), the relation of identity does not hold between that human and *any* of the selfish things. Notice that the idea of distribution is not mentioned in this explanation. The idea of distribution is currently disreputable, mostly because of the criticisms of Geach in *Reference and Generality* (1968) and its irrelevance to standard semantic theories.

The related term 'distributively' means 'in a manner designating every item in a group individually', and is used in contrast with 'collectively'. The sentence 'The rocks weighed 100 pounds' is ambiguous. If 'rocks' is taken distributively, then the sentence means that each rock weighed 100 pounds. If 'rocks' is taken collectively, then the sentence means that the total weight of the rocks was 100 pounds.

See also SYLLOGISM.   A.P.M.

distributive justice. See JUSTICE.

distributive laws, the logical principles

$$A \wedge (B \vee C) \equiv (A \wedge B) \vee (A \vee C)$$

and

$$A \vee (B \wedge C) \equiv (A \vee B) \wedge (A \vee C).$$

Conjunction is thus said to distribute over disjunction and disjunction over conjunction. **See also** DE MORGAN'S LAWS.   G.F.S.

distributively. See DISTRIBUTION.

divided line, one of three analogies (with the sun and cave) offered in Plato's *Republic* (VI, 509d–511e) as a partial explanation of the Good. Socrates divides a line into two unequal segments: the longer represents the intelligible world and the shorter the sensible world. Then each of the segments is divided in the same proportion. Socrates associates four mental states with the four resulting segments (beginning with the shortest): *eikasia,* illusion or the apprehension of images; *pistis,* belief in ordinary physical objects; *dianoia,* the sort of hypothetical reasoning engaged in by mathematicians; and *noesis*, rational ascent to the first principle of the Good by means of dialectic. **See also** PLATO, SOCRATES.   W.J.P.

divine attributes, properties of God; especially, those properties that are essential and unique to God. Among properties traditionally taken to be attributes of God, omnipotence, omniscience, and omnibenevolence are naturally taken to mean having, respectively, power, knowledge, and moral goodness to the maximum degree. Here God is understood as an eternal (or everlasting) being of immense power, knowledge, and goodness, who is the creator and sustainer of the universe and is worthy of human worship.

Omnipotence is maximal power. Some philosophers, notably Descartes, have thought that omnipotence requires the ability to do absolutely anything, including the logically impossible. Most classical theists, however, understood omnipotence as involving vast powers, while nevertheless being subject to a range of limitations of ability, including the inability to do what is logically impossible, the inability to change the past or to do things incompatible with what has happened, and the inability to do things that cannot be done by a being who has other divine attributes, e.g., to sin or to lie.

Omniscience is unlimited knowledge. According to the most straightforward account, omniscience is knowledge of all true propositions. But there may be reasons for recognizing a limitation on the class of true propositions that a being must know in order to be omniscient. For example, if there are true propositions about the future, omniscience would then include foreknowledge. But some philosophers have thought that foreknowledge of human actions is incompatible with those actions being free. This has led some to deny that there are truths about the future and others to deny that such truths are knowable. In the latter case, omniscience might be taken to be knowledge of all *knowable* truths. Or if God is eternal and if there are certain tensed or temporally indexical propositions that can be known only by someone who is in time, then omniscience presumably does not extend to such propositions. It is a matter of controversy whether omniscience includes middle knowledge, i.e., knowledge of what an agent would do if other, counterfactual, conditions were to obtain. Since recent critics of middle knowledge (in contrast to Báñez and other sixteenth-century Dominican opponents of Molina) usually

deny that the relevant counterfactual conditionals alleged to be the object of such knowledge are true, denying the possibility of middle knowledge need not restrict the class of true propositions a being must know in order to be omniscient. Finally, although the concept of omniscience might not itself constrain how an omniscient being acquires its knowledge, it is usually held that God's knowledge is neither inferential (i.e., derived from premises or evidence) nor dependent upon causal processes.

Omnibenevolence is, literally, complete desire for good; less strictly, perfect moral goodness. Traditionally it has been thought that God does not merely happen to be good but that he must be so and that he is unable to do what is wrong. According to the former claim God is *essentially* good; according to the latter he is *impeccable*. It is a matter of controversy whether God is perfectly good in virtue of complying with an external moral standard or whether he himself sets the standard for goodness.

Divine sovereignty is God's rule over all of creation. According to this doctrine God did not merely create the world and then let it run on its own; he continues to govern it in complete detail according to his good plan. Sovereignty is thus related to divine providence. A difficult question is how to reconcile a robust view of God's control of the world with libertarian free will.

Aseity (or *perseity*) is complete independence. In a straightforward sense, God is not dependent on anyone or anything for his existence. According to stronger interpretation of aseity, God is completely independent of everything else, including his properties. This view supports a doctrine of divine simplicity according to which God is not distinct from his properties.

Simplicity is the property of having no parts of any kind. According to the doctrine of divine simplicity, God not only has no spatial or temporal parts, but there is no distinction between God and his essence, between his various attributes (in him omniscience and omnipotence, e.g., are identical), and between God and his attributes. Attributing simplicity to God was standard in medieval theology, but the doctrine has seemed to many contemporary philosophers to be baffling, if not incoherent.

See also DESCARTES, DIVINE FOREKNOWLEDGE, MIDDLE KNOWLEDGE, MOLINA, PHILOSOPHY OF RELIGION.   E.R.W.

divine command ethics, an ethical theory according to which part or all of morality depends upon the will of God as promulgated by divine commands. This theory has an important place in the history of Christian ethics. Divine command theories are prominent in the Franciscan ethics developed by John Duns Scotus and William Ockham; they are also endorsed by disciples of Ockham such as d'Ailly, Gerson, and Gabriel Biel; both Luther and Calvin adopt divine command ethics; and in modern British thought, important divine command theorists include Locke, Berkeley, and Paley. Divine command theories are typically offered as accounts of the deontological part of morality, which consists of moral requirements (obligation), permissions (rightness), and prohibitions (wrongness). On a divine command conception, actions forbidden by God are morally wrong because they are thus forbidden, actions not forbidden by God are morally right because they are not thus forbidden, and actions commanded by God are morally obligatory because they are thus commanded.

Many Christians find divine command ethics attractive because the ethics of love advocated in the Gospels makes love the subject of a command. Matthew 22:37–40 records Jesus as saying that we are commanded to love God and the neighbor. According to Kierkegaard, there are two reasons to suppose that Christian love of neighbor must be an obligation imposed by divine command: first, only an obligatory love can be sufficiently extensive to embrace everyone, even one's enemies; second, only an obligatory love can be invulnerable to changes in its objects, a love that alters not when it alteration finds.

The chief objection to the theory is that dependence on divine commands would make morality unacceptably arbitrary. According to divine command ethics, murder would not be wrong if God did not exist or existed but failed to forbid it. Perhaps the strongest reply to this objection appeals to the doctrines of God's necessary existence and essential goodness. God could not fail to exist and be good, and so God could not fail to forbid murder. In short, divine commands are not arbitrary fiats.

See also ETHICS, LOCKE, OCKHAM.   P.L.Q.

divine command theory. See DIVINE COMMAND ETHICS, ETHICS.

divine foreknowledge, God's knowledge of the future. It appears to be a straightforward consequence of God's omniscience that he has knowl-
edge of the future, for presumably omniscience includes knowledge of all truths and there are truths about the future. Moreover, divine foreknowledge seems to be required by orthodox religious commitment to divine prophecy and divine providence. In the former case, God could not reliably reveal what will happen if he does know what will happen. And in the latter case, it is difficult to see how God could have a plan for what happens without knowing what that will be. A problem arises, however, in that it has seemed to many that divine foreknowledge is incompatible with human free action. Some philosophers (notably Boethius) have reasoned as follows: If God knows that a person will do a certain action, then the person must perform that action, but if a person must perform an action, the person does not perform the action freely. So if God knows that a person will perform an action, the person does not perform the action freely. This reason for thinking that divine foreknowledge is incompatible with human free action commits a simple modal fallacy. What must be the case is the conditional that if God knows that a person will perform an action then the person will in fact perform the action. But what is required to derive the conclusion is the implausible claim that from the assumption that God knows that a person will perform an action it follows not simply that the person *will* perform the action but that the person *must* perform it. Perhaps other attempts to demonstrate the incompatibility, however, are not as easily dismissed. One response to the apparent dilemma is to say that there really are no such truths about the future, either none at all or none about events, like future free actions, that are not causally necessitated by present conditions. Another response is to concede that there are truths about the future but to deny that truths about future free actions are knowable. In this case omniscience may be understood as knowledge, not of all truths, but of all knowable truths. A third, and historically important, response is to hold that God is eternal and that from his perspective everything is present and thus not future. These responses implicitly agree that divine foreknowledge is incompatible with human freedom, but they provide different accounts of omniscience according to which it does not include foreknowledge, or, at any rate, not foreknowledge of future free actions. **See also DIVINE ATTRIBUTES, FREE WILL PROBLEM, MIDDLE KNOWLEDGE, PHILOSOPHY OF RELIGION.**   E.R.W.

divine sovereignty. See DIVINE ATTRIBUTES.

division, fallacy of. See INFORMAL FALLACY.

D-N model. See COVERING LAW MODEL.

Doctor Irrefragabilis. See ALEXANDER OF HALES.

Doctor Mirabilis. See BACON, ROGER.

doctrine of infinite analysis. See LEIBNIZ.

doctrine of minute perceptions. See LEIBNIZ.

doctrine of the mean. See ARISTOTLE, CHUNG-YUNG.

Dodgson, Charles Lutwidge. See CARROLL.

dogmatism. See SKEPTICS.

domain, of a science, the class of individuals that constitute its subject matter. Zoology, number theory, and plane geometry have as their respective domains the class of animals, the class of natural numbers, and the class of plane figures. In *Posterior Analytics* 76b10, Aristotle observes that each science presupposes its domain, its basic concepts, and its basic principles. In modern formalizations of a science using a standard first-order formal language, the domain of the science is often, but not always, taken as the universe of the intended interpretation or intended model, i.e. as the range of values of the individual variables. **See also** AXIOMATIC METHOD, FORMAL-IZATION, FORMAL LOGIC, MODEL THEORY, ONTOLOGICAL COMMITMENT, UNIVERSE OF DISCOURSE, VARIABLE. J.Cor.

dominance, principle of. See NEWCOMB'S PARADOX.

dominate. See SCHRÖDER-BERNSTEIN THEOREM.

donkey sentences, sentences exemplified by 'Every man who owns a donkey beats it', 'If a man owns a donkey, he beats it', and similar forms, which have posed logical puzzles since medieval times but were noted more recently by Geach. At issue is the logical form of such sentences – specifically, the correct construal of the pronoun 'it' and the indefinite noun phrase 'a donkey'. Translations into predicate logic by the usual strategy of rendering the indefinite as existential quantification and the pronoun as a bound variable (cf. 'John owns a donkey and beats it' $\rightarrow$ ($\exists x$) (x is a donkey & John owns x &

John beats x)) are either ill-formed or have the wrong truth conditions. With a universal quantifier, the logical form carries the controversial implication that every donkey-owning man beats every donkey he owns. Efforts to resolve these issues have spawned much significant research in logic and linguistic semantics. **See also** LOGICAL FORM. R.E.W.

doomsday argument, an argument (associated chiefly with the mathematician Brandon Carter and the philosopher John Leslie) purporting to show, by appeal to Bayes's theorem (and Bayes's rule), that whatever antecedent probability we may have assigned to the hypothesis that human life will end relatively soon is magnified, perhaps greatly, upon our learning (or noticing) that we are among the first few score thousands of millions of human beings to exist. See Leslie's *The End of the World: The Science and Ethics of Human Extinction* (1996).

The argument is based on an allegedly close analogy between the question of the probability of imminent human extinction given our ordinal location in the temporal swath of humanity and the fact that the reader's name being among the first few drawn randomly from an urn may greatly enhance for the reader the probability that the urn contains fairly few names rather than very many.

See also BAYESIAN RATIONALITY, BAYES'S THEOREM, PROBABILITY. D.A.J.

dot notation. See LOGICAL NOTATION.

double aspect theory. See PHILOSOPHY OF MIND.

double effect, principle of. See PRINCIPLE OF DOUBLE EFFECT.

double negation. (1) The principle, also called the law of double negation, that every proposition is logically equivalent to its double negation. Thus, the proposition that Roger is a rabbit is equivalent to the proposition that Roger is not not a rabbit. The law holds in classical logic but not for certain non-classical concepts of negation. In intuitionist logic, for example, a proposition implies, but need not be implied by, its double negation. (2) The rule of inference, also called the rule of double negation, that permits one to infer the double negation of A from A, and vice versa. **See also** FORMAL LOGIC. G.F.S.

double negation, law of. See DOUBLE NEGATION.

double truth, the theory that a thing can be true in philosophy or according to reason while its opposite is true in theology or according to faith. It serves as a response to conflicts between reason and faith. For example, on one interpretation of Aristotle, there is only one rational human soul, whereas, according to Christian theology, there are many rational human souls. The theory of double truth was attributed to Averroes and to Latin Averroists such as Siger of Brabant and Boethius of Dacia by their opponents, but it is doubtful that they actually held it. Averroes seems to have held that a single truth is scientifically formulated in philosophy and allegorically expressed in theology. Latin Averroists apparently thought that philosophy concerns what would have been true by natural necessity absent special divine intervention, and theology deals with what is actually true by virtue of such intervention. On this view, there would have been only one rational human soul if God had not miraculously intervened to multiply what by nature could not be multiplied. No one clearly endorsed the view that rational human souls are both only one and also many in number. **See also AVERROES, SIGER OF BRABANT.**   P.L.Q.

doubt, methodic. See DESCARTES.

downward saturated set. See HINTIKKA SET.

doxa. See DOXASTIC.

doxastic (from Greek *doxa,* 'belief'), of or pertaining to belief. A doxastic mental state, for instance, is or incorporates a belief. Doxastic states of mind are to be distinguished, on the one hand, from such non-doxastic states as desires, sensations, and emotions, and, on the other hand, from subdoxastic states. By extension, a doxastic principle is a principle governing belief. A doxastic principle might set out conditions under which an agent's forming or abandoning a belief is justified (epistemically or otherwise). **See also REASONS FOR BELIEF.**   J.F.H.

doxastic holism. See HOLISM.

doxastic voluntarism. See VOLUNTARISM.

doxographers, compilers of and commentators on the opinions of ancient Greek philosophers. 'Doxographers' is an English translation of the modern Latin term coined by Hermann Diels for the title of his work *Doxographi Graeci* (1879).

Here Diels assembled a series of Greek texts in which the views of Greek philosophers from the archaic to the Hellenistic era are set out in a relatively schematic way. In a lengthy introduction Diels reconstructed the history of the writing of these opinions, the doxography; this reconstruction is now a standard part of the historiography of ancient philosophy. The doxography itself is important both as a source of information for early Greek philosophy and also because later writers, ancient, medieval, and modern, often relied on it rather than primary materials. The crucial text for Diels's reconstruction was the book *Physical Opinions of the Philosophers* (*Placita Philosophorum*), traditionally ascribed to Plutarch but no longer thought to be by him. The work lists the views of various philosophers and schools under subject headings such as "What Is Nature?" and "On the Rainbow." Out of this work and others Diels reconstructed a *Collection of Opinions* that he ascribed to Aetius (A.D. c.100), a person mentioned by Theodoret (fifth century) as the author of such a work. Diels took Aetius's ultimate source to be Theophrastus, who wrote a more discursive *Physical Opinions*. Because Aetius mentions the views of Hellenistic philosophers writing after Theophrastus, Diels postulated an intermediate source, which he called the *Vetusta Placita* (c.100 B.C.). The most accessible doxographical material is in the *Lives and Opinions of Eminent Philosophers* by Diogenes Laertius (A.D. c.200), who is, however, mainly interested in biography. He arranges philosophers by schools and treats each school chronologically.   I.M.

dravya, in Indian philosophies, substance. In Nyāya-Vaishesika all living and non-living things are substances, possessors of qualities (*gunas*) and causes of effects. Substances come in nine varieties: earth, air, fire, water, ether, time, space, minds, and bodies. For Jainism, there are six types of substances: the principles of motion and rest, space, time, minds, and bodies. Each (except time) is extended and each (except bodies) is immaterial. Viśistadvaita, claiming six sorts of substance, includes God as a substance, as does Dvaita, on which all other substances depend for existence. Typically, schools of Buddhism deny that there are any substances, holding that what appear to be such are only bundles of events or states.   K.E.Y.

dravyasat (Sanskrit, 'existence as a thing' or, more loosely, 'primary existence'), a category used by Indian Buddhist scholars to label the most basic kind of existence that entities can have. It was usually opposed to *prajñaptisat*, 'existence as a designation' or 'secondary existence'. According to most varieties of Buddhist metaphysics, anything that can be an object of thought or designation must exist in some sense; but some things exist primarily, really, in their own right (*dravya-sat*), while others exist only as objects of linguistic reference (*prajñapti-sat*). An example of the first kind would be a moment of physical form; an example of the second kind would be an ordinary object such as a pot, since this is composed of a series of existents of the first kind.   P.J.G.

dream argument. See DESCARTES.

Dretske, Fred (b.1932), American philosopher best known for his externalistic representational naturalism about experience, belief, perception, and knowledge. Educated at Purdue University and the University of Minnesota, he has taught at the University of Wisconsin (1960–88) and Stanford University (1988–98).

In *Seeing and Knowing* (1969) Dretske develops an account of *non-epistemic seeing*, denying that seeing is believing – that for a subject S to see a dog, say, S must apply a concept to it (dog, animal, furry). The dog must look some way to S (S must visually differentiate the dog, but need not conceptually categorize it). This contrasts with *epistemic seeing*, where for S to *see that* a dog is before him, S would have to believe that it is a dog.

In *Knowledge and the Flow of Information* (1981), a mind-independent objective sense of 'information' is applied to propositional knowledge and belief content. "Information" replaced Dretske's earlier notion of a "conclusive reason" (1971). Knowing that p requires having a true belief caused or causally sustained by an event that carries the information that p. Also, the semantic content of a belief is identified with the most specific digitally encoded piece of information to which it becomes selectively sensitive during a period of learning.

In *Explaining Behavior* (1988), Dretske's account of representation (and misrepresentation) takes on a teleological flavor. The semantic meaning of a structure is now identified with its indicator function. A structure recruited for a causal role of indicating F's, and sustained in that causal role by this ability, comes to mean F – thereby providing a causal role for the content of cognitive states, and avoiding epiphenomenalism about semantic content.

In *Naturalizing the Mind* (1995), Dretske's the-

ory of meaning is applied to the problems of consciousness and qualia. He argues that the empirically significant features of conscious experience are exhausted by their functional (and hence representational) roles of indicating external sensible properties. He rejects the views that consciousness is composed of a higher-order hierarchy of mental states and that qualia are due to intrinsic, non-representational features of the underlying physical systems.

Dretske is also known for his contributions on the nature of contrastive statements, laws of nature, causation, and epistemic non-closure, among other topics.

See also INFORMATION THEORY, NATURALISM, PHILOSOPHY OF MIND, QUALIA.   F.A.

dual-aspect theory. See PHILOSOPHY OF MIND.

dual-attribute theory. See PHILOSOPHY OF MIND.

dualism, the view that reality consists of two disparate parts. The crux of dualism is an apparently unbridgeable gap between two incommensurable orders of being that must be reconciled if our assumption that there is a comprehensible universe is to be justified. Dualism is exhibited in the pre-Socratic division between appearance and reality; Plato's realm of being containing eternal Ideas and realm of becoming containing changing things; the medieval division between finite man and infinite God; Descartes's substance dualism of thinking mind and extended matter; Hume's separation of fact from value; Kant's division between empirical phenomena and transcendental noumena; the epistemological double-aspect theory of James and Russell, who postulate a neutral substance that can be understood in separate ways either as mind or brain; and Heidegger's separation of being and time that inspired Sartre's contrast of being and nothingness. The doctrine of two truths, the sacred and the profane or the religious and the secular, is a dualistic response to the conflict between religion and science.

Descartes's dualism is taken to be the source of the mind–body problem. If the mind is active unextended thinking and the body is passive unthinking extension, how can these essentially unlike and independently existing substances interact causally, and how can mental ideas represent material things? How, in other words, can the mind know and influence the body, and how can the body affect the mind? Descartes said mind and body interact and that ideas represent material things without resembling them, but could not explain how, and concluded merely that God makes these things happen. Proposed dualist solutions to the mind–body problem are Malebranche's occasionalism (mind and body do not interact but God makes them appear to); Leibniz's preestablished harmony among non-interacting monads; and Spinoza's property dualism of mutually exclusive but parallel attributes expressing the one substance God. Recent mind–body dualists are Popper and John C. Eccles. Monistic alternatives to dualism include Hobbes's view that the mental is merely the epiphenomena of the material; Berkeley's view that material things are collections of mental ideas; and the contemporary materialist view of Smart, Armstrong, and Paul and Patricia Churchland that the mind is the brain. A classic treatment of these matters is Arthur O. Lovejoy's *The Revolt Against Dualism*.

Dualism is related to binary thinking, i.e., to systems of thought that are two-valued, such as logic in which theorems are valid or invalid, epistemology in which knowledge claims are true or false, and ethics in which individuals are good or bad and their actions are right or wrong. In *The Quest for Certainty*, Dewey finds that all modern problems of philosophy derive from dualistic oppositions, particularly between spirit and nature. Like Hegel, he proposes a synthesis of oppositions seen as theses versus antitheses. Recent attacks on the view that dualistic divisions can be explicitly described or maintained have been made by Wittgenstein, who offers instead a classification scheme based on overlapping family resemblances; by Quine, who casts doubt on the division between analytic or formal truths based on meanings and synthetic or empirical truths based on facts; and by Derrida, who challenges our ability to distinguish between the subjective and the objective. But despite the extremely difficult problems posed by ontological dualism, and despite the cogency of many arguments against dualistic thinking, Western philosophy continues to be predominantly dualistic, as witnessed by the indispensable use of two-valued matrixes in logic and ethics and by the intractable problem of rendering mental intentions in terms of material mechanisms or vice versa.

See also METAPHYSICS, PHILOSOPHY OF MIND. R.A.W.

dualism, Cartesian. See DUALISM, PHILOSOPHY OF MIND.

dualism, ethical. See ZOROASTRIANISM.

Ducasse, C(urt) J(ohn) (1881–1969), French-born American philosopher of mind and aesthetician. He arrived in the United States in 1900, received his Ph.D. from Harvard (1912), and taught at the University of Washington (1912–26) and Brown University (1926–58).

His most important work is *Nature, Mind and Death* (1951). The key to his general theory is a non-Humean view of causation: the relation of causing is triadic, involving (i) an initial event, (ii) the set of conditions under which it occurs, and (iii) a resulting event; the initial event is the cause, the resulting event is the effect. On the basis of this view he constructed a theory of categories – an explication of such concepts as those of substance, property, mind, matter, and body. Among the theses he defended were that minds are substances, that they causally interact with bodies, and that human beings are free despite every event's having a cause.

In *A Critical Examination of the Belief in a Life after Death* (1961), he concluded that "the balance of the evidence so far obtained is on the side of . . . survival." Like Schopenhauer, whom he admired, Ducasse was receptive to the religious and philosophical writings of the Far East. He wrote with remarkable objectivity on the philosophical problems associated with so-called paranormal phenomena.

Ducasse's epistemological views are developed in *Truth, Knowledge and Causation* (1968). He sets forth a realistic theory of perception (he says, about sense-qualities, "Berkeley is right and the realists are wrong" and, of material things, "the realists are right and Berkeley is wrong"). He provides the classical formulation of the "adverbial theory" or sense-qualities, according to which such qualities are not *objects* of experience or awareness but *ways* of experiencing or of being aware. One does not perceive a red material object by sensing a red sense-datum; for then perceiving would involve *three* entities – (i) the perceiving subject, (ii) the red sense-datum, and (iii) the red material object. But one may perceive a red material object by sensing redly; then the only entities involved are (i) the perceiving subject and (ii) the material object. Ducasse observes that, analogously, although it may be natural to say "dancing a waltz," it would be more accurate to speak of "dancing waltzily."

See also PERCEPTION, PHILOSOPHY OF MIND. R.M.C.

duck–rabbit. See FIGURE–GROUND.

Duhem, Pierre-Maurice-Marie (1861–1916),

French physicist who wrote extensively on the history and philosophy of science. Like Georg Helm, Wilhelm Ostwald, and others, he was an energeticist, believing generalized thermodynamics to be the foundation of all of physics and chemistry. Duhem spent his whole scientific life advancing energetics, from his failed dissertation in physics (a version of which was accepted as a dissertation in mathematics), published as *Le potentiel thermodynamique* (1886), to his mature treatise, *Traité d'énergétique* (1911). His scientific legacy includes the Gibbs-Duhem and Duhem-Margules equations. Possibly because his work was considered threatening by the Parisian scientific establishment or because of his right-wing politics and fervent Catholicism, he never obtained the position he merited in the intellectual world of Paris. He taught at the provincial universities of Lille, Rennes, and, finally, Bordeaux.

Duhem's work in the history and philosophy of science can be viewed as a defense of the aims and methods of energetics; whatever Duhem's initial motivation, his historical and philosophical work took on a life of its own. Topics of interest to him included the relation between history of science and philosophy of science, the nature of conceptual change, the historical structure of scientific knowledge, and the relation between science and religion. Duhem was an anti-atomist (or anti-Cartesian); in the contemporary debates about light and magnetism, Duhem's anti-atomist stance was also directed against the work of Maxwell. According to Duhem, atomists resolve the bodies perceived by the senses into smaller, imperceptible bodies. The explanation of observable phenomena is then referred to these imperceptible bodies and their motions, suitably combined. Duhem's rejection of atomism was based on his instrumentalism (or fictionalism): physical theories are not explanations but representations; they do not reveal the true nature of matter, but give general rules of which laws are particular cases; theoretical propositions are not true or false, but convenient or inconvenient. An important reason for treating physics as non-explanatory was Duhem's claim that there is general consensus in physics and none in metaphysics – thus his insistence on the autonomy of physics from metaphysics. But he also thought that scientific representations become more complete over time until they gain the status of a natural classification. Accordingly, Duhem attacked the use of models by some scientists, e.g. Faraday and Maxwell. Duhem's rejection of atomism was

coupled with a rejection of *inductivism*, the doctrine that the only physical principles are general laws known through induction, based on observation of facts. Duhem's rejection forms a series of theses collectively known as the *Duhem thesis:* experiments in physics are observations of phenomena accompanied by interpretations; physicists therefore do not submit single hypotheses, but whole groups of them, to the control of experiment; thus, experimental evidence alone cannot conclusively falsify hypotheses. For similar reasons, Duhem rejected the possibility of a crucial experiment. In his historical studies, Duhem argued that there were no abrupt discontinuities between medieval and early modern science – the so-called *continuity thesis;* that religion played a positive role in the development of science in the Latin West; and that the history of physics could be seen as a cumulative whole, defining the direction in which progress could be expected.

Duhem's philosophical works were discussed by the founders of twentieth-century philosophy of science, including Mach, Poincaré, the members of the Vienna Circle, and Popper. A revival of interest in Duhem's philosophy began with Quine's reference in 1953 to the Duhem thesis (also known as the *Duhem-Quine thesis*). As a result, Duhem's philosophical works were translated into English – as *The Aim and Structure of Physical Theory* (1954) and *To Save the Phenomena* (1969). By contrast, few of Duhem's extensive historical works – *Les origines de la statique* (2 vols., 1906–08), *Études sur Léonard de Vinci* (3 vols., 1906–13), and *Système du monde* (10 vols., 1913–59), e.g. – have been translated, with five volumes of the *Système du monde* actually remaining in manuscript form until 1954–59. Unlike his philosophical work, Duhem's historical work was not sympathetically received by his influential contemporaries, notably George Sarton. His supposed main conclusions were rejected by the next generation of historians of science, who presented modern science as discontinuous with that of the Middle Ages. This view was echoed by historically oriented philosophers of science who, from the early 1960s, emphasized discontinuities as a recurrent feature of change in science – e.g. Kuhn in *The Structure of Scientific Revolutions* (1962).

See also CRUCIAL EXPERIMENT, MACH, PHILOSOPHY OF SCIENCE, QUINE, VIENNA CIRCLE.
R.Ar.

Duhem-Quine thesis. See DUHEM.

Duhem thesis. See DUHEM.

Dummett, Michael A. E. (b.1925), British philosopher of language, logic, and mathematics, noted for his sympathy for metaphysical anti-realism and for his exposition of the philosophy of Frege. Dummett regards allegiance to the principle of bivalence as the hallmark of a realist attitude toward any field of discourse. This is the principle that any meaningful assertoric sentence must be determinately either true or else false, independently of anyone's ability to ascertain its truth-value by recourse to appropriate empirical evidence or methods of proof. According to Dummett, the sentences of any learnable language cannot have verification-transcendent truth conditions and consequently we should query the intelligibility of certain statements that realists regard as meaningful. On these grounds, he calls into question realism about the past and realism in the philosophy of mathematics in several of the papers in two collections of his essays, *Truth and Other Enigmas* (1978) and *The Seas of Language* (1993).

In *The Logical Basis of Metaphysics* (1991), Dummett makes clear his view that the fundamental questions of metaphysics have to be approached through the philosophy of language, and more specifically through the theory of meaning. Here his philosophical debts to Frege and Wittgenstein are manifest. Dummett has been the world's foremost expositor and champion of Frege's philosophy, above all in two highly influential books, *Frege: Philosophy of Language* (1973) and *Frege: Philosophy of Mathematics* (1991). This is despite the fact that Frege himself advocated a form of Platonism in semantics and the philosophy of mathematics that is quite at odds with Dummett's own anti-realist inclinations. It would appear, however, from what Dummett says in *Origins of Analytical Philosophy* (1993), that he regards Frege's great achievement as that of having presaged the "linguistic turn" in philosophy that was to see its most valuable fruit in the later work of Wittgenstein. Wittgenstein's principle that grasp of the meaning of a linguistic expression must be exhaustively manifested by the use of that expression is one that underlies Dummett's own approach to meaning and his anti-realist leanings. In logic and the philosophy of mathematics this is shown in Dummett's sympathy for the intuitionistic approach of Brouwer and Heyting, which involves a repudiation of the law of excluded middle, as set forth in Dummett's own

book on the subject, *Elements of Intuitionism* (1977).

See also BROUWER, MATHEMATICAL INTU-ITIONISM, METAPHYSICAL REALISM, WITTGEN-STEIN.   E.J.L.

dunamis, also *dynamis* (Greek, 'power', 'capacity'), as used by pre-Socratics such as Anaximander and Anaxagoras, one of the elementary character-powers, such as the hot or the cold, from which they believed the world was constructed. Plato's early theory of Forms borrowed from the concept of character-powers as causes present in things; courage, e.g., is treated in the *Laches* as a power in the soul. Aristotle also used the word in this sense to explain the origins of the elements. In the *Metaphysics* (especially Book IX), Aristotle used *dunamis* in a different sense to mean 'potentiality' in contrast to 'actuality' (*energeia* or *entelecheia*). In the earlier sense of *dunamis,* matter is treated as potentiality, in that it has the potential to receive form and so be actualized as a concrete substance. In the later Aristotelian sense of *dunamis,* dormant abilities are treated as potentialities, and *dunamis* is to *energeia* as sleeping is to waking, or having sight to seeing. **See also** ARISTOTLE, ENERGEIA.

P.Wo.

Duns Scotus, John (1266–1308), Scottish Franciscan metaphysician and philosophical theologian. He lectured at Oxford, Paris, and Cologne, where he died and his remains are still venerated.

Modifying Avicenna's conception of metaphysics as the science of being *qua* being, but univocally conceived, Duns Scotus showed its goal was to demonstrate God as the Infinite Being (revealed to Moses as the "I am who am"), whose creative will is the source of the world's contingency. Out of love God fashioned each creature with a unique "haecceity" or particularity formally distinct from its individualized nature. Descriptively identical with others of its kind, this nature, conceived in abstraction from haecceity, is both objectively real and potentially universal, and provides the basis for scientific knowledge that Peirce calls "Scotistic realism."

Duns Scotus brought many of Augustine's insights, treasured by his Franciscan predecessors, into the mainstream of the Aristotelianism of his day. Their notion of the will's "supersufficient potentiality" for self-determination he showed can be reconciled with Aristotle's notion of an "active potency," if one rejects the controversial principle that "whatever is moved is moved by another." Paradoxically, Aristotle's criteria for rational and non-rational potencies prove the rationality of the will, not the intellect, for he claimed that only rational faculties are able to act in opposite ways and are thus the source of creativity in the arts. If so, then intellect, with but one mode of acting determined by objective evidence, is non-rational, and so is classed with active potencies called collectively "nature." Only the will, acting "with reason," is free to will or nill this or that. Thus "nature" and "will" represent Duns Scotus's primary division of active potencies, corresponding roughly to Aristotle's dichotomy of non-rational and rational. Original too is his development of Anselm's distinction of the will's twofold inclination or "affection": one for the advantageous, the other for justice. The first endows the will with an "intellectual appetite" for happiness and actualization of self or species; the second supplies the will's specific difference from other natural appetites, giving it an innate desire to love goods objectively according to their intrinsic worth. Guided by right reason, this "affection for justice" inclines the will to act ethically, giving it a congenital freedom from the need always to seek the advantageous. Both natural affections can be supernaturalized, the "affection for justice" by charity, inclining us to love God above all and for his own sake; the affection for the advantageous by the virtue of hope, inclining us to love God as our ultimate good and future source of beatitude.

Another influential psychological theory is that of intuitive intellectual cognition, or the simple, non-judgmental awareness of a here-and-now existential situation. First developed as a necessary theological condition for the face-to-face vision of God in the next life, intellectual intuition is needed to explain our certainty of primary contingent truths, such as "I think," "I choose," etc., and our awareness of existence. Unlike Ockham, Duns Scotus never made intellectual intuition the basis for his epistemology, nor believed it puts one in direct contact with any extramental substance material or spiritual, for in this life, at least, our intellect works through the sensory imagination. Intellectual intuition seems to be that indistinct peripheral aura associated with each direct sensory-intellectual cognition. We know of it explicitly only in retrospect when we consider the necessary conditions for intellectual memory. It continued to be a topic of discussion and dispute down to the time of Calvin, who, influenced by the Sco-

tist John Major, used an auditory rather than a visual sense model of intellectual intuition to explain our "experience of God."

See also AUGUSTINE, AVICENNA, OCKHAM.

A.B.W.

Dutch book, a bet or combination of bets whereby the bettor is bound to suffer a net loss regardless of the outcome. A simple example would be a bet on a proposition p at odds of $3 : 2$ combined with a bet on not-p at the same odds, the total amount of money at stake in each bet being five dollars. Under this arrangement, if p turned out to be true one would win two dollars by the first bet but lose three dollars by the second, and if p turned out to be false one would win two dollars by the second bet but lose three dollars by the first. Hence, whatever happened, one would lose a dollar. **See also PROBABILITY.**

R.Ke.

Dutch book argument, the argument that a rational person's degrees of belief must conform to the axioms of the probability calculus, since otherwise, by the Dutch book theorem, he would be vulnerable to a Dutch book.   R.Ke.

Dutch book theorem, the proposition that anyone who (a) counts a bet on a proposition p as fair if the odds correspond to his degree of belief that p is true and who (b) is willing to make any combination of bets he would regard individually as fair will be vulnerable to a Dutch book provided his degrees of belief do not conform to the axioms of the probability calculus. Thus, anyone of whom (a) and (b) are true and whose degree of belief in a disjunction of two incompatible propositions is not equal to the sum of his degrees of belief in the two propositions taken individually would be vulnerable to a Dutch book.   R.Ke.

duty, what a person is obligated or required to do. Duties can be moral, legal, parental, occupational, etc., depending on their foundations or grounds. Because a duty can have several different grounds, it can be, say, both moral and legal, though it need not be of more than one type. *Natural duties* are moral duties people have simply in virtue of being persons, i.e., simply in virtue of their nature. There is a *prima facie duty* to do something if and only if there is an appropriate basis for doing that thing. For instance, a prima facie moral duty will be one for which there is a moral basis, i.e., some moral grounds. This contrasts with an all-things-considered duty, which is a duty one has if the appropriate grounds that support it outweigh any that count against it.

Negative duties are duties not to do certain things, such as to kill or harm, while *positive duties* are duties to act in certain ways, such as to relieve suffering or bring aid. While the question of precisely how to draw the distinction between negative and positive duties is disputed, it is generally thought that the violation of a negative duty involves an agent's causing some state of affairs that is the basis of the action's wrongness (e.g., harm, death, or the breaking of a trust), whereas the violation of a positive duty involves an agent's allowing those states of affairs to occur or be brought about.

Imperfect duties are, in Kant's words, "duties which allow leeway in the interest of inclination," i.e., that permit one to choose among several possible ways of fulfilling them. *Perfect duties* do not allow that leeway. Thus, the duty to help those in need is an imperfect duty since it can be fulfilled by helping the sick, the starving, the oppressed, etc., and if one chooses to help, say, the sick, one can choose which of the sick to help. However, the duty to keep one's promises and the duty not to harm others are perfect duties since they do not allow one to choose which promises to keep or which people not to harm. Most positive duties are imperfect; most negative ones, perfect.

See also DEONTIC LOGIC, KANT, RIGHTS, ROSS.   B.R.

du Vair, Guillaume (1556–1621), French philosopher, bishop, and political figure. Du Vair and Justus Lipsius were the two most influential propagators of neo-Stoicism in early modern Europe. Du Vair's *Sainte Philosophie* ("Holy Philosophy," 1584) and his shorter *Philosophie morale des Stoïques* ("Moral Philosophy of the Stoics," 1585), were translated and frequently reprinted. The latter presents Epictetus in a form usable by ordinary people in troubled times. We are to follow nature and live according to reason; we are not to be upset by what we cannot control; virtue is the good. Du Vair inserts, moreover, a distinctly religious note. We must be pious, accept our lot as God's will, and consider morality obedience to his command. Du Vair thus Christianized Stoicism, making it widely acceptable. By teaching that reason alone enables us to know how we ought to live, he became a founder of modern rationalism in ethics. **See also** ETHICS, HUMAN NATURE, STOICISM.   J.B.S.

Dvaita Vedanta, a variety of Hinduism according to which Brahman is an independently existing, omnipotent, omniscient personal deity. In Dvaita Vedanta, Brahman everlastingly sustains in existence a world of minds and physical things without their being properly viewed as the body of Brahman, since this would mistakenly suggest that Brahman is limited and can be affected in ways analogous to those in which human beings are limited and can be affected by their bodies. The Upanishadic texts concerning the individual *Āman*'s identity to Brahman, and all things being in Brahman, are understood as asserting dependence on Brahman and resemblance to Brahman rather than numerical identity with Brahman. Each person is held to have his or her own essence (cf. the medieval Scholastic notion of a *haecceity*) and accordingly some are destined for enlightenment, some for endless transmigration, and some for misery.   K.E.Y.

Dworkin, Ronald M. (b.1931), American jurist, political philosopher, and a central contributor to recent legal and political theory. He has served as professor of jurisprudence, University of Oxford (1969–98), professor of law, New York University (1975–), and Quain Professor of Jurisprudence, University College, London (1998–). He was the first significant critic of Hart's positivist analysis of law as based on a determinable set of social rules. Dworkin argues that the law contains legal principles as well as legal rules. Legal principles are standards phrased generally (e.g., 'No one shall profit from his own wrong'); they do not have a formal "pedigree," but are requirements of morality. Nonetheless, courts are obliged to apply such principles, and thus have no lawmaking discretion. Judicially enforceable legal rights must derive from antecedent political rights. Dworkin characterizes rights as political "trumps" – hence his title *Taking Rights Seriously* (2d ed., 1978), which collects the papers that defend the views sketched.

Dworkin postulates an idealized judge, Hercules, who can invariably determine what rights are legally enforceable. Dworkin denies any metaphysical commitments thereby, and emphasizes instead the constructive and interpretive nature of both adjudication and legal theory. These arguments are made in papers collected in *A Matter of Principle* (1985). *Law's Empire* (1986) systematizes his view. He presents there a theory of "law as integrity." The court's obligation is to make the community's law the best it can be by finding decisions that best fit both institutional history and moral principle. Hercules always best determines the best fit.

Dworkin has also contributed to substantive political theory. He defends a form of liberalism that makes equality as prominent as liberty. His account of equality is found in a number of independent papers; see, e.g., "Foundations of Liberal Equality," *Tanner Lectures on Human Values XI* (1990). Dworkin has applied his liberal theory in two ways. He has continually acted as a critical watchdog of the U.S. Supreme Court, assessing decisions for their adherence to the ideals of principle, respect for equality, and achievement of best fit. Some of these essays are in the two collections mentioned; the most recent are in *Freedom's Law* (1996). *Life's Dominion* (1993) derives from these ideals an account of abortion and euthanasia.

Dworkin's philosophizing has a conceptual richness and rhetorical fire that, when not wholly under control, give his theoretical positions a protean quality at the level of detail. Nonetheless, the ideas that adjudication should be principled and enforce rights, and that we all deserve equal dignity and respect, exercise a powerful fascination.

See also EUTHANASIA, HART, JURISPRU-DENCE, LEGAL POSITIVISM, MORAL STATUS, NATURAL LAW, POLITICAL PHILOSOPHY, RIGHTS.   R.A.Sh.

Dyad. See ACADEMY.

dynamic logic, a branch of logic in which, in addition to the usual category of formulas interpretable as propositions, there is a category of expressions interpretable as actions. Dynamic logic (originally called the modal logic of programs) emerged in the late 1970s as one step in a long tradition within theoretical computer science aimed at providing a way to formalize the analysis of programs and their action. A particular concern here was program verification: what can be said of the effect of a program if started at a certain point? To this end operators [α] and <α> were introduced with the following intuitive readings: [α]*A* to mean '*after every* terminating computation according to α it is the case that *A*' and <α>*A* to mean '*after some* terminating computation according to α it is the case that *A*'. The logic of these operators may be seen as a generalization of ordinary modal logic: where modal logic has one box operator □ and one diamond operator ◊, dynamic logic has one box operator [α] and one diamond operator <α> for every program expression α in the language.

In possible worlds semantics for modal logic a model is a triple (U, R, V) where U is a universe of points, R a binary relation, and V a valuation assigning to each atomic formula a subset of U. In dynamic logic, a model is a triple (U, R, V) where U and V are as before but R is a family of binary relations $R(\alpha)$, one for every program expression α in the language. Writing '⊨x *A*', where x is a point in U, for '*A* is true at x' (in the model in question), we have the following characteristic truth conditions (truth-functional compounds are evaluated by truth tables, as in modal logic):

⊨x *P* if and only if x is a point in $V(P)$, where P is an atomic formula,

⊨x[α]*A* if and only if, for *all y*, if x is $R(\alpha)$-related to y then ⊨y *A*,

⊨x <α> if and only if, for *some y*, x is $R(\alpha)$-related to y and ⊨y *A*.

Traditionally, dynamic logic will contain machinery for rendering the three regular operators on programs: '+' (sum), ';' (composition), and '*' (Kleene's star operation), as well as the test operator '?', which, operating on a proposition, will yield a program. The action α + β consists in carrying out α or carrying out β; the action α;β in first carrying out α, then carrying out β; the action α* in carrying out α some finite number of times (not excluding 0); the action ?*A* in verifying that *A*. Only standard models reflect these intuitions:

$$R(\alpha + \beta) = R(\alpha) \cup R(\beta),$$

$$R(\alpha;\beta) = R(\alpha) \mid R(\beta),$$

$$R(\alpha^*) = (R(\alpha))^*,$$

$$R(?A) = \{(x,x) : ⊨x A\}$$

(where '*' is the ancestral star)

The smallest propositional dynamic logic (PDL) is the set of formulas true at every point in every standard model. Note that dynamic logic analyzes non-deterministic action – this is evident at the level of atomic programs π where $R(\pi)$ is a relation, not necessarily a function, and also in the definitions of $R(\alpha + \beta)$ and $R(\alpha^*)$.

Dynamic logic has been extended in various ways, e.g., to first- and second-order predicate logic. Furthermore, just as deontic logic, tense logic, etc., are referred to as modal logic in the wide sense, so extensions of dynamic logic in the narrow sense such as process logic are often loosely referred to as dynamic logic in the wide sense.

The philosophical interest in dynamic logic rests with the expectation that it will prove a fruitful instrument for analyzing the concept of action in general: a successful analysis would be valuable in itself and would also be relevant to other disciplines such as deontic logic and the logic of imperatives.

See also COMPUTER THEORY, DEONTIC LOGIC, MODAL LOGIC.   K.Seg.

dynamis. See DUNAMIS, ENERGEIA.

dynamism. See BOSCOVICH.

E

Eckhart, Johannes, called Meister Eckhart (c.1260–1328), German mystic, theologian, and preacher. Eckhart entered the Dominican order early and began an academic circuit that took him several times to Paris as a student and master of theology and that initiated him into ways of thinking much influenced by Albertus Magnus and Thomas Aquinas. At Paris, Eckhart wrote the required commentary on the *Sentences* of Peter Lombard and finished for publication at least three formal disputations. But he had already held office within the Dominicans, and he continued to alternate work as administrator and as teacher. Eckhart preached throughout these years, and he continued to write spiritual treatises in the vernacular, of which the most important is the *Book of Divine Consolation* (1313/1322). Only about a third of Eckhart's main project in Latin, the *Opus tripartitum*, seems ever to have been completed.

Beginning in the early 1320s, questions were raised about Eckhart's orthodoxy. The questions centered on what was characteristic of his teaching, namely the emphasis on the soul's attaining "emptiness" so as to "give birth to God." The soul is ennobled by its emptying, and it can begin to "labor" with God to deliver a spark that enacts the miraculous union-and-difference of their love. After being acquitted of heresy once, Eckhart was condemned on 108 propositions drawn from his writings by a commission at Cologne. The condemnation was appealed to the Holy See, but in 1329 Eckhart was there judged "probably heretical" on 17 of 28 propositions drawn from both his academic and popular works. The condemnation clearly limited Eckhart's explicit influence in theology, though he was deeply appropriated not only by mystics such as Johannes Tauler and Henry Suso, but by church figures such as Nicholas of Cusa and Martin Luther. He has since been taken up by thinkers as different as Hegel, Fichte, and Heidegger.

See also ALBERTUS MAGNUS, AQUINAS, PETER LOMBARD. M.D.J.

eclecticism. See COUSIN.

Eco, Umberto (b.1932), Italian philosopher, intellectual historian, and novelist. A leading figure in the field of semiotics, the general theory of signs. Eco has devoted most of his vast production to the notion of interpretation and its role in communication.

In the 1960s, building on the idea that an active process of interpretation is required to take any sign as a sign, he pioneered reader-oriented criticism (*The Open Work*, 1962, 1976; *The Role of the Reader*, 1979) and championed a holistic view of meaning, holding that all of the interpreter's beliefs, i.e., his encyclopedia, are potentially relevant to word meaning. In the 1970s, equally influenced by Peirce and the French structuralists, he offered a unified theory of signs (*A Theory of Semiotics*, 1976), aiming at grounding the study of communication in general. He opposed the idea of communication as a natural process, steering a middle way between realism and idealism, particularly of the Sapir-Whorf variety. The issue of realism looms large also in his recent work. In *The Limits of Interpretation* (1990) and *Interpretation and Overinterpretation* (1992), he attacks deconstructionism. *Kant and the Platypus* (1997) defends a "contractarian" form of realism, holding that the reader's interpretation, driven by the Peircean regulative idea of objectivity and collaborating with the speaker's underdetermined intentions, is needed to fix reference.

In his historical essays, ranging from medieval aesthetics (*The Aesthetics of Thomas Aquinas*, 1956) to the attempts at constructing artificial and "perfect" languages (*The Search for the Perfect Language*, 1993) to medieval semiotics, he traces the origins of some central notions in contemporary philosophy of language (e.g., meaning, symbol, denotation) and such recent concerns as the language of mind and translation, to larger issues in the history of philosophy.

All his novels are pervaded by philosophical queries, such as Is the world an ordered whole? (*The Name of the Rose*, 1980), and How much interpretation can one tolerate without falling prey to some conspiracy syndrome? (*Foucault's Pendulum*, 1988). Everywhere, he engages the reader in the game of (controlled) interpretations.

See also DECONSTRUCTION, MEANING, SEMIOSIS, STRUCTURALISM. M.Sa.

ecofeminism. See ENVIRONMENTAL PHILOSOPHY.

economics, philosophy of. See PHILOSOPHY OF ECO-
NOMICS.

economics, welfare. See PHILOSOPHY OF ECONOM-
ICS.

education, philosophy of. See PHILOSOPHY OF EDU-
CATION.

eduction, the process of initial clarification, as of
a phenomenon, text, or argument, that normally
takes place prior to logical analysis. Out of the
flux of vague and confused experiences certain
characteristics are drawn into some kind of order
or intelligibility in order that attention can be
focused on them (Aristotle, *Physics* I). These characteristics often are latent, hidden, or implicit.
The notion often is used with reference to texts
as well as experience. Thus it becomes closely
related to exegesis and hermeneutics, tending to
be reserved for the sorts of clarification that precede formal or logical analyses. **See also**
HERMENEUTICS.   F.S.

Edwards, Jonathan (1703–58), American philosopher and theologian. He was educated at
Yale, preached in New York City, and in 1729
assumed a Congregational pastorate in North-
ampton, Massachusetts, where he became a
leader in the Great Awakening. Because of a dispute with his parishioners over qualifications for
communion, he was forced to leave in 1750. In
1751, he took charge of congregations in Stock-
bridge, a frontier town sixty miles to the west. He
was elected third president of Princeton in 1757
(but died shortly after inauguration).

The doctrine of God's absolute sovereignty is
explicated by occasionalism, a subjective idealism similar to Berkeley's, and phenomenalism.
According to Edwards, what are "vulgarly"
called causal relations are mere constant conjunctions. *True* causes necessitate their effects.
Since God's will alone meets this condition, God
is the only true cause. He is also the only true
substance. Physical objects are collections of
ideas of color, shape, and other "corporeal" qualities. Finite minds are series of "thoughts" or
"perceptions." Any substance underlying perceptions, thoughts, and "corporeal ideas" must
be something that "subsists by itself, stands
underneath, and keeps up" physical and mental
qualities. As the only thing that does so, God is
the only real substance. As the only true cause
and the only real substance, God is "in effect
being in general."

God creates to communicate his glory. Since
God's internal glory is constituted by his infinite
knowledge of, love of, and delight in himself as
the highest good, his "communication *ad extra*"
consists in the knowledge of, love of, and joy in
himself which he bestows upon creatures. The
essence of God's internal and external glory is
"holiness" or "true benevolence," a disinterested
love of being in general (i.e., of God and the
beings dependent on him). Holiness constitutes
"true beauty," a divine splendor or radiance of
which "secondary" (ordinary) beauty is an
imperfect image. God is thus supremely beautiful and the world is suffused with his loveliness.

Vindications of Calvinist conceptions of sin
and grace are found in *Freedom of the Will* (1754)
and *Original Sin* (1758). The former includes
sophisticated defenses of theological determinism and compatibilism. The latter contains arguments for occasionalism and interesting discussions of identity. Edwards thinks that natural
laws determine kinds or species, and kinds or
species determine criteria of identity. Since the
laws of nature depend on God's "arbitrary" decision, God establishes criteria of identity. He can
thus, e.g., constitute Adam and his posterity as
"one thing."

Edwards's religious epistemology is developed
in *A Treatise Concerning Religious Affections* (1746)
and *On the Nature of True Virtue* (1765). The conversion experience involves the acquisition of a
"new sense of the heart." Its core is the mind's
apprehension of a "new simple idea," the idea of
"true beauty." This idea is needed to properly
understand theological truths.

True Virtue also provides the fullest account of
Edwards's ethics – a moral sense theory that
identifies virtue with benevolence. Although
indebted to contemporaries like Hutcheson,
Edwards criticizes their attempts to construct
ethics on secular foundations. True benevolence

Edwards deeply influenced Congregational
and Presbyterian theology in America for over a
century, but had little impact on philosophy.
Interest in him revived in the middle of the
twentieth century, first among literary scholars
and theologians and later among philosophers.
While most of Edwards's published work defends
the Puritan version of Calvinist orthodoxy, his
notebooks reveal an interest in philosophical
problems for their own sake. Although he was
indebted to Continental rationalists like Malebranche, to the Cambridge Platonists, and especially to Locke, his own contributions are
sophisticated and original.

embraces being in general. Since God is, in effect, being in general, its essence is the love of God. A love restricted to family, nation, humanity, or other "private systems" is a form of self-love.

See also BERKELEY, CALVIN, FREE WILL PROBLEM, MORAL SENSE THEORY, OCCASIONALISM.   W.J.Wa.

effective procedure, a step-by-step recipe for computing the values of a function. It determines what is to be done at each step, without requiring any ingenuity of anyone (or any machine) executing it. The input and output of the procedure consist of items that can be processed mechanically. Idealizing a little, inputs and outputs are often taken to be strings on a finite alphabet. It is customary to extend the notion to procedures for manipulating natural numbers, via a canonical notation. Each number is associated with a string, its numeral. Typical examples of effective procedures are the standard grade school procedures for addition, multiplication, etc. One can execute the procedures without knowing anything about the natural numbers. The term 'mechanical procedure' or 'algorithm' is sometimes also used. A function f is computable if there is an effective procedure A that computes f. For every m in the domain of f, if A were given m as input, it would produce $f(m)$ as output. Turing machines are mathematical models of effective procedures. Church's thesis, or Turing's thesis, is that a function is computable provided there is a Turing machine that computes it. In other words, for every effective procedure, there is a Turing machine that computes the same function. **See also CHURCH'S THESIS, COMPUTER THEORY, TURING MACHINE.**
           S.Sha.

efficacious grace. See ARNAULD.

efficient cause. See ARISTOTLE.

effluences. See DEMOCRITUS.

effluxes, theory of. See DEMOCRITUS.

ego. See FREUD.

ego, empirical. See KANT.

ego, transcendental. See KANT.

egocentric particular, a word whose denotation is determined by identity of the speaker and/or the time, place, and audience of his utterance. Examples are generally thought to include 'I,' 'you', 'here', 'there', 'this', 'that', 'now', 'past', 'present', and 'future'. The term 'egocentric particular' was introduced by Russell in *An Inquiry into Meaning and Truth* (1940). In an earlier work, "The Philosophy of Logical Atomism" (*Monist*, 1918–19), Russell called such words "emphatic particulars."

Some important questions arise regarding egocentric particulars. Are some egocentric particulars more basic than others so that the rest can be correctly defined in terms of them but they cannot be correctly defined in terms of the rest? Russell thought all egocentric particulars can be defined by 'this'; 'I', for example, has the same meaning as 'the biography to which this belongs', where 'this' denotes a sense-datum experienced by the speaker. Yet, at the same time, 'this' can be defined by the combination 'what I-now notice'. Must we use at least some egocentric particulars to give a complete description of the world? Our ability to describe the world from a speaker-neutral perspective, so that the denotations of the terms in our description are independent of when, where, and by whom they are used, depends on our ability to describe the world without using egocentric particulars. Russell held that egocentric particulars are not needed in any part of the description of the world.

See also CAUSAL THEORY OF PROPER NAMES, INDEXICAL, TOKEN-REFLEXIVE.
           P.Mar.

egocentric predicament, each person's apparently problematic position as an experiencing subject, assuming that all our experiences are private in that no one else can have them. Two problems concern our ability to gain empirical knowledge. First, it is hard to see how we gain empirical knowledge of what others experience, if all experience is private. We cannot have their experience to see what it is like, for any experience we have is our experience and so not theirs. Second, it is hard to see how we gain empirical knowledge of how the external world is, independently of our experience. All our empirically justified beliefs seem to rest ultimately on what is given in experience, and if the empirically given is private, it seems it can only support justified beliefs about the world as we experience it. A third major problem concerns our ability to communicate with others. It is hard to see how we describe the world in a language others understand. We give meaning to some of our words by defining them by other words that already have meaning, and this process of definition appears to end with words we define ostensively; i.e., we use them to name something given in experience. If experiences are private, no one else can grasp the meaning of our ostensively defined words or any words we use them to define. No one else can understand our attempts to describe the world. **See also** PRIVATE LANGUAGE ARGUMENT, PROBLEM OF OTHER MINDS.   P.Mar.

egoism, any view that, in a certain way, makes the self central. There are several different versions of egoism, all of which have to do with how actions relate to the self. *Ethical egoism* is the view that people ought to do what is in their own self-interest. *Psychological egoism* is a view about people's motives, inclinations, or dispositions. One statement of psychological egoism says that, as a matter of fact, people always do what they believe is in their self-interest and, human nature being what it is, they cannot do otherwise. Another says that people never desire anything for its own sake except what they believe is in their own self-interest.

Altruism is the opposite of egoism. Any ethical view that implies that people sometimes ought to do what is in the interest of others and not in their self-interest can be considered a form of ethical altruism. The view that, human nature being what it is, people can do what they do not believe to be in their self-interest might be called *psychological altruism*. Different species of ethical and psychological egoism result from different interpretations of self-interest and of acting from self-interest, respectively. Some people have a broad conception of acting from self-interest such that people acting from a desire to help others can be said to be acting out of self-interest, provided they think doing so will not, on balance, take away from their own good. Others have a narrower conception of acting from self-interest such that one acts from self-interest only if one acts from the desire to further one's own happiness or good. Butler identified self-love with the desire to further one's own happiness or good and self-interested action with action performed from that desire alone. Since we obviously have other particular desires, such as the desires for honor, for power, for revenge, and to promote the good of others, he concluded that psychological egoism was false. People with a broader conception of acting from self-interest would ask whether anyone with those particular desires would act on them if they believed that, on balance, acting on them would result in a loss of happiness or good for themselves. If some

would, then psychological egoism is false, but if, given human nature as it is, no one would, it is true even if self-love is not the only source of motivation in human beings.

Just as there are broader and narrower conceptions of acting from self-interest, there are broader and narrower conceptions of self-interest itself, as well as subjective and objective conceptions of self-interest. Subjective conceptions relate a person's self-interest solely to the satisfaction of his desires or to what that person believes will make his life go best for him. Objective conceptions see self-interest, at least in part, as independent of the person's desires and beliefs. Some conceptions of self-interest are narrower than others, allowing that the satisfaction of only certain desires is in a person's self-interest, e.g., desires whose satisfaction makes that person's life go better for her. And some conceptions of self-interest count only the satisfaction of idealized desires, ones that someone would have after reflection about the nature of those desires and what they typically lead to, as furthering a person's self-interest.

See also BUTLER, ETHICS, MOTIVATIONAL INTERNALISM, REASONS FOR ACTION.   B.R.

egoistic consequentialism. See CONSEQUENTIALISM.

eidetic intuition. See HUSSERL.

eidos. See ARISTOTLE, HUSSERL.

Eightfold Path. See BUDDHISM.

eikasia. See DIVIDED LINE.

Einfühlung (German, 'feeling into'), empathy. In contrast to sympathy, where one's identity is preserved in feeling with or for the other, in empathy or *Einfühlung* one tends to lose oneself in the other. The concept of *Einfühlung* received its classical formulation in the work of Theodor Lipps, who characterized it as a process of involuntary, inner imitation whereby a subject identifies through feeling with the movement of another body, whether it be the real leap of a dancer or the illusory upward lift of an architectural column. Complete empathy is considered to be aesthetic, providing a non-representational access to beauty.

Husserl used a phenomenologically purified concept of *Einfühlung* to account for the way the self directly recognizes the other. Husserl's student Edith Stein described *Einfühlung* as a blind mode of knowledge that reaches the experience of the other without possessing it.

Einfühlung is not to be equated with *Verstehen* or human understanding, which, as Dilthey pointed out, requires the use of all one's mental powers, and cannot be reduced to a mere mode of feeling. To understand is not to apprehend something empathetically as the projected locus of an actual experience, but to apperceive the meaning of expressions of experience in relation to their context. Whereas understanding is reflective, empathy is prereflective.

See also DILTHEY, HUSSERL, VERSTEHEN.

R.A.M.

Einstein, Albert (1879–1955), German-born American physicist, founder of the special and general theories of relativity and a fundamental contributor to several branches of physics and to the philosophical analysis and critique of modern physics, notably of relativity and the quantum theory. Einstein was awarded the Nobel Prize for physics in 1922, "especially for his discovery of the law of the photoelectric effect."

Born in Ulm in the German state of Württemberg, Einstein studied physics at the Polytechnic in Zürich, Switzerland. He was called to Berlin as director of the Kaiser Wilhelm Institute for Physics (1914) at the peak of the German ultranationalism that surrounded World War I. His reaction was to circulate an internationalist "Manifesto to Europeans" and to pursue Zionist and pacifist programs. Following the dramatic confirmation of the general theory of relativity (1919) Einstein became an international celebrity. This fame also made him the frequent target of German anti-Semites, who, during one notable episode, described the theory of relativity as "a Jewish fraud." In 1933 Einstein left Germany for the Institute for Advanced Study in Princeton. Although his life was always centered on science, he was also engaged in the politics and culture of his times. He carried on an extensive correspondence (whose publication will run to over forty volumes) with both famous and ordinary people, including significant philosophical correspondence with Cassirer, Reichenbach, Moritz Schlick, and others. Despite reservations over logical positivism, he was something of a patron of the movement, helping to secure academic positions for several of its leading figures. In 1939 Einstein signed a letter drafted by the nuclear physicist Leo Szilard informing President Roosevelt about the prospects for harnessing atomic energy and warning of the German efforts to make a bomb. Einstein did not further participate in the development of atomic weapons, and later was influential in the movement against them. In 1952 he was offered, and declined, the presidency of Israel. He died still working on a unified field theory, and just as the founders of the Pugwash movement for nuclear disarmament adopted a manifesto he had cosigned with Russell.

Einstein's philosophical thinking was influenced by early exposure to Kant and later study of Hume and Mach, whose impact shows in the operationalism used to treat time in his famous 1905 paper on special relativity. That work also displays a passion for unity in science characteristic of nearly all his physical thinking, and that may relate to the monism of Spinoza, a philosopher whom he read and reread. Einstein's own understanding of relativity stressed the invariance of the space-time interval and promoted realism with regard to the structure of space-time. Realism also shows up in Einstein's work on Brownian motion (1905), which was explicitly motivated by his long-standing interest in demonstrating the reality of molecules (and atoms), and in the realist treatment of light quanta in his analysis (1905) of the photoelectric effect. While he pioneered the development of statistical physics, especially in his seminal investigations of quantum phenomena (1905–25), he never broke with his belief in determinism as the only truly fundamental approach to physical processes. Here again one sees an affinity with Spinoza. Realism and determinism brought Einstein into conflict with the new quantum theory (1925–26), whose observer dependence and "flight into statistics" convinced him that it could not constitute genuinely fundamental physics. Although influential in its development, he became the theory's foremost critic, never contributing to its refinement but turning instead to the program of unifying the electromagnetic and gravitational fields into one grand, deterministic synthesis that would somehow make room for quantum effects as limiting or singular cases. It is generally agreed that his unified field program was not successful, although his vision continues to inspire other unification programs, and his critical assessments of quantum mechanics still challenge the instrumentalism associated with the theory.

Einstein's philosophical reflections constitute an important chapter in twentieth-century thought. He understood realism as less a metaphysical doctrine than a motivational program, and he argued that determinism was a feature of theories rather than an aspect of the world directly. Along with the unity of science, other central themes in his thinking include his rejection of inductivism and his espousal of holism and constructivism (or conventionalism), emphasizing that meanings, concepts, and theories are free creations, not logically derivable from experience but subject rather to overall criteria of comprehensibility, empirical adequacy, and logical simplicity. Holism is also apparent in his acute analysis of the testability of geometry and his rejection of Poincaré's geometric conventionalism.

See also DETERMINISM, FIELD THEORY, QUANTUM MECHANICS, RELATIVITY, UNITY OF SCIENCE.   A.F.

élan vital. See BERGSON.

Eleatic School, strictly, two fifth-century B.C. Greek philosophers, Parmenides and Zeno of Elea. (The Ionian Greek colony of Elea or Hyele in southern Italy became Velia in Roman times and retains that name today.) A playful remark by Plato in *Sophist* 242d gave rise to the notion that Xenophanes of Colophon, who was active in southern Italy and Sicily, was Parmenides' teacher, had anticipated Parmenides' views, and founded the Eleatic School. Moreover, Melissus of Samos and (according to some ancient sources) even the atomist philosopher Leucippus of Abdera came to be regarded as "Eleatics," in the sense of sharing fundamental views with Parmenides and Zeno. In the broad and traditional use of the term, the Eleatic School characteristically holds that "all is one" and that change and plurality are unreal. So stated, the School's position is represented best by Melissus. **See also** MELISSUS OF SAMOS, PARMENIDES, XENOPHANES.   A.P.D.M.

elementary equivalence. See CATEGORICAL THEORY.

elementary quantification theory. See FORMAL LOGIC.

elenchus, a cross-examination or refutation. Typically in Plato's early dialogues, Socrates has a conversation with someone who claims to have some sort of knowledge, and Socrates refutes this claim by showing the interlocutor that what he thinks he knows is inconsistent with his other opinions. This refutation is called an elenchus. It is not entirely negative, for awareness of his own ignorance is supposed to spur the interlocutor to further inquiry, and the concepts and assumptions employed in the refutations serve as the

basis for positive Platonic treatments of the same topic. In contrast, sophistic elenchi are merely eristic: they aim simply at the refutation of an opponent by any means. Thus, Aristotle calls fallacies that only appear to be refutations "sophistical elenchi." **See also** SOCRATES.   E.C.H.

Elias. See COMMENTARIES ON ARISTOTLE.

eliminability, Ramsey. See BETH'S DEFINABILITY THEOREM.

eliminative induction. See INDUCTION.

eliminative materialism. See PHILOSOPHY OF MIND.

eliminativism. See FOLK PSYCHOLOGY.

Elizabeth of Bohemia (1618–80), German Princess whose philosophical reputation rests on her correspondence with Descartes. The most heavily discussed portion of this correspondence focuses on the relationship between the mind and the body and on Descartes's claim that the mind-body union is a simple notion. Her discussions of free will and of the nature of the sovereign good also have philosophical interest. **See also** DESCARTES, PHILOSOPHY OF MIND.   M.At.

ellipsis, an expression (spoken or written) from which semantically or syntactically essential material has been deleted, usually for conciseness. Elliptical sentences are often used to answer questions without repeating material occurring in the questions. For example, the word 'Lincoln' may be an answer to the question of the authorship of the Gettysburg Address or to the question of the birthplace of George Boole. The single word 'Lincoln' can be seen as an elliptical name when used as an ellipsis of 'Abraham Lincoln', and it can be seen as an elliptical sentence when used as an ellipsis for 'Abraham Lincoln wrote the Gettysburg Address'. Other typical elliptical sentences are: 'Abe is a father of two [children]', 'Ben arrives at twelve [noon]'. A typical ellipsis that occurs in discussion of ellipses involves citing the elliptical sentences with the deleted material added in brackets (often with 'sc.' or '*scilicet*') instead of also presenting the complete sentence. Ellipsis also occurs above the sentential level, e.g. where well-known premises are omitted in the course of argumentation. The word 'enthymeme' designates an elliptical argument expression from which one or more premise-expressions have been deleted. The expression 'elliptic ambiguity' designates ambiguity arising from ellipsis. **See also** AMBIGUITY, ARGUMENT, LOGICAL FORM.   J. Cor.

emanationism, a doctrine about the origin and ontological structure of the world, most frequently associated with Plotinus and other Neoplatonists, according to which everything else that exists is an emanation from a primordial unity, called by Plotinus "the One." The first product of emanation from the One is Intelligence (*noûs*), a realm resembling Plato's world of Forms. From Intelligence emanates Soul (*psuchē*), conceived as an active principle that imposes, insofar as that is possible, the rational structure of Intelligence on the matter that emanates from Soul. The process of emanation is typically conceived to be necessary and timeless: although Soul, for instance, proceeds from Intelligence, the notion of procession is one of logical dependence rather than temporal sequence. The One remains unaffected and undiminished by emanation: Plotinus likens the One to the sun, which necessarily emits light from its naturally infinite abundance without suffering change or loss of its own substance. Although emanationism influenced some Jewish, Christian, and Islamic thinkers, it was incompatible with those theistic doctrines of divine activity that maintained that God's creative choice and the world thus created were contingent, and that God can, if he chooses, interact directly with individual creatures. **See also** PLOTINUS.   W.E.M.

embodiment, the bodily aspects of human subjectivity. Embodiment is the central theme in European phenomenology, with its most extensive treatment in the works of Maurice Merleau-Ponty. Merleau-Ponty's account of embodiment distinguishes between "the objective body," which is the body regarded as a physiological entity, and "the phenomenal body," which is not just *some* body, some particular physiological entity, but *my* (or your) body as I (or you) experience it. Of course, it is possible to experience one's own body as a physiological entity. But this is not typically the case. Typically, I experience my body (tacitly) as a unified potential or capacity for doing this and that – typing this sentence, scratching that itch, etc. Moreover, this sense that I have of my own motor capacities (expressed, say, as a kind of bodily confidence) does not depend on an understanding of the physiological processes involved in performing the action in question.

The distinction between the objective and phenomenal body is central to understanding the phenomenological treatment of embodiment. Embodiment is not a concept that pertains to the body grasped as a physiological entity. Rather it pertains to the phenomenal body and to the role it plays in our object-directed experiences.

See also MERLEAU-PONTY, PHENOMENOLOGY.   D.Le.

emergence. See METHODOLOGICAL HOLISM.

emergentism, descriptive. See HOLISM.

emergent materialism. See PHILOSOPHY OF MIND.

Emersonian perfectionism. See CAVELL.

Emerson, Ralph Waldo (1803–82), American philosophical essayist, lecturer, and poet, a leading figure in the transcendentalist movement. He was born in Boston and educated at Harvard. As a young man he taught school and served as a Unitarian minister (1826–32). After he resigned his pastorate in 1832, he traveled to Europe to visit Coleridge, Carlyle, and Wordsworth. Upon his return, he settled in Concord, Massachusetts, and began anew as a public lecturer, essayist, and cultural critic. All the while he maintained a voluminous correspondence and kept a detailed, evocative journal. Most of this material has been published, and it casts considerable light on the depth of his thought, at times more so than his public presentations and books.

His life was pockmarked by personal tragedies, notably the death of his father when Emerson was eight; the death of his first wife, Ellen, after two years of marriage; and the death of his oldest son, Waldo, at the age of five. Such afflictions belie the commonly held assumption that Emerson was a thinker who did not face the intractable problem of evil. To the contrary, his writings should be read as a continuing struggle to render the richest possible version of our situation, given that "things are in the saddle and ride mankind."

Although Emerson did not write a systematic work in philosophy, he unquestionably bequeathed an important philosophical vision and countless philosophical pieces. Beginning with his concentration on the motif of nature, its embracing quality, and the rhythms of our inextricable presence within its activities, Emerson details the "compensatory" ebb and flow of the human journey. The human soul and nature are related as "print" to "seal," and yet nature is not always beneficent. In his essay "Compensation,"

Emerson writes that "the value of the universe continues to throw itself into every point. If the good is there, so is the evil; if the affinity, so the repulsion, if the force, so the limitation."

After the acclaim given the publication of Emerson's first book, *Nature* (1836), he began to gather his public lectures, a presentational medium at which he was riveting, convincing, and inspiring. In 1841 Emerson published his *Essays – First Series*, which included the lovely piece "Circles," wherein he follows the blunt maxim "we grizzle every day" with the healing affirmation that "life is a series of surprises." This volume also contains "Self-Reliance," which furnished a motto for the self-proclaiming intrepidity of nineteenth-century American individualism.

The enthusiastic response to Emerson's essays enabled him to publish three additional collections within the decade: *Essays – Second Series* (1844), *Nature, Addresses and Lectures* (1849), and *Representative Men* (1850). These books and their successors contained lectures, orations, poems, and addresses over a wide range of topics, philosophical, personal, characterological, travel, historical, and literary. Emerson's prose is swift, clear, and epigrammatic, like a series of written stochastic probes, resulting in a Yankee crazy quilt, munificent of shape and color. Emerson spoke to be heard and wrote to be read, especially by the often denigrated "common" person. In fact, during Emerson's European lecture tour in 1848, a letter to a London newspaper requested lowering the admission price so that poorer people could attend, for "to miss him is to lose an important part of the Nineteenth Century."

Emerson's deeply democratic attitude had a reflective philosophical base. He believed that ordinary experience was epiphanic if we but open ourselves to its virtually infinite messages. Despite his Brahmanic appearance and demeanor, Emerson was in continuous touch with ordinary things. He wrote, "Our chief experiences have been casual." His belief in the explosive and pedagogical character of ordinary experience is especially present in his influential oration "The American Scholar." After criticizing American thought as thoroughly derivative, he plots the influences necessary to generate a genuine scholar, paramount among them nature and the learning of the past, though he cautions us not to be trapped in excessive retrospection at the expense of "an original relation to the universe." It is his discussion of "action" as the third influence on the scholar that enables him to project his clearest statement of his underlying philosophical commitment. Without action, "thought can never ripen into truth," moreover, "thinking is a partial act," whereas living is a "total act." Expressly opposed to any form of psychological, religious, philosophical, or behavioral dualism, he counsels us that the spiritual is not set apart, beyond reach of those who toil in the everyday. Rather, the most profound meanings of the human condition, "lurk" in the "common," the "low," the "familiar," the "today."

The influence of the thought of Emerson reaches across class, caste, genre, and persuasion. Thinkers as diverse as James, Nietzsche, Whitman, Proust, Gertrude Stein, Robert Frost, Frank Lloyd Wright, Frederick Law Olmsted, and Wallace Stevens are among those deeply indebted to Emerson. Yet, it was Dewey who best caught the enduring bequest of Emerson, writing of "the final word of Emerson's philosophy, [as] the identity of Being, unqualified and immutable, with character."

See also TRANSCENDENTALISM.   J.J.M.

emotion, as conceived by philosophers and psychologists, any of several general types of mental states, approximately those that had been called "passions" by earlier philosophers, such as Descartes and Hume. Anger, e.g., is one emotion, fear a second, and joy a third. An emotion may also be a content-specific type, e.g., fear of an earthquake, or a token of an emotion type, e.g., Mary's present fear that an earthquake is imminent.

The various states typically classified as emotions appear to be linked together only by overlapping family resemblances rather than by a set of necessary and sufficient conditions. Thus an adequate philosophical or psychological "theory of emotion" should probably be a *family* of theories. Even to label these states "emotions" wrongly suggests that they are all marked by *emotion*, in the older sense of mental agitation (a metaphorical extension of the original sense, agitated motion). A person who is, e.g., pleased or sad about something is not typically agitated. To speak of anger, fear, joy, sadness, etc., collectively as "the emotions" fosters the assumption (which James said he took for granted) that these are just qualitatively distinct *feelings of mental agitation*. This exaggerates the importance of agitation and neglects the characteristic differences, noted by Aristotle, Spinoza, and others, in the types of situations that evoke the various emotions.

One important feature of most emotions is captured by the older category of passions, in the sense of 'ways of being acted upon'. In many languages nearly all emotion adjectives are derived from participles: e.g., the English words 'amused', 'annoyed', 'ashamed', 'astonished', 'delighted', 'embarrassed', 'excited', 'frightened', 'horrified', 'irritated', 'pleased', 'terrified', 'surprised', 'upset', and 'worried'. When we are, e.g., embarrassed, something acts on us, i.e., *embarrasses* us: typically, some situation or fact of which we are aware, such as our having on unmatched shoes. To call embarrassment a passion in the sense of a way of being acted upon does not imply that we are "passive" with respect to it, i.e., have no control over whether a given situation embarrasses us and thus no responsibility for our embarrassment.

Not only situations and facts but also *persons* may "do" something to us, as in love and hate, and mere *possibilities* may have an effect on us, as in fear and hope. The possibility emotions are sometimes characterized as "forward-looking," and emotions that are responses to actual situations or facts are said to be "backward-looking." These temporal characterizations are inaccurate and misleading. One may be fearful or hopeful that a certain event occurred in the past, provided one is not certain as to whether it occurred; and one may be, e.g., embarrassed about what is going to occur, provided one is certain it will occur.

In various passions the effect on us may include involuntary physiological changes, feelings of agitation due to arousal of the autonomic nervous system, characteristic facial expressions, and inclinations toward intentional action (or inaction) that arise independently of any rational warrant. Phenomenologically, however, these effects do not appear to us to be alien and non-rational, like muscular spasms. Rather they seem an integral part of our perception of the situation as, e.g., an embarrassing situation, or one that warrants our embarrassment.

See also JAMES-LANGE THEORY, PHILOSOPHY OF MIND.   R.M.G.

emotions, the seven. See KOREAN PHILOSOPHY.

emotions, the six. See CH'ING.

emotive conjugation, a humorous verbal conjugation, designed to expose and mock first-person bias, in which ostensibly the same action is described in successively more pejorative terms through the first, second, and third persons (e.g., "I am firm, You are stubborn, He is a pig-headed fool").

This example was used by Russell in the course of a BBC Radio "Brains' Trust" discussion in 1948. It was popularized later that year when *The New Statesman* ran a competition for other examples. An "unprecedented response" brought in 2,000 entries, including: "I am well informed, You listen to gossip, He believes what he reads in the paper"; and "I went to Oxford, You went to Cambridge, He went to the London School of Economics" (Russell was educated at Cambridge and later taught there).

See also RUSSELL.   N.G.

emotive meaning. See EMOTIVISM, MEANING.

emotivism, a noncognitivist metaethical view opposed to cognitivism, which holds that moral judgments should be construed as assertions about the moral properties of actions, persons, policies, and other objects of moral assessment, that moral predicates purport to refer to properties of such objects, that moral judgments (or the propositions that they express) can be true or false, and that cognizers can have the cognitive attitude of belief toward the propositions that moral judgments express. Noncognitivism denies these claims; it holds that moral judgments do not make assertions or express propositions. If moral judgments do not express propositions, the former can be neither true nor false, and moral belief and moral knowledge are not possible. The emotivist is a noncognitivist who claims that moral judgments, in their primary sense, express the appraiser's attitudes – approval or disapproval – toward the object of evaluation, rather than make assertions about the properties of that object.

Because emotivism treats moral judgments as the expressions of the appraiser's pro and con attitudes, it is sometimes referred to as the boo-hurrah theory of ethics. Emotivists distinguish their thesis that moral judgments express the appraiser's attitudes from the subjectivist claim that they state or report the appraiser's attitudes (the latter view is a form of cognitivism). Some versions of emotivism distinguish between this primary, emotive meaning of moral judgments and a secondary, descriptive meaning. In its primary, emotive meaning, a moral judgment expresses the appraiser's attitudes toward the object of evaluation rather than ascribing properties to that object. But secondarily, moral judgments refer to those non-moral properties of the object of evaluation in virtue of which the appraiser has and expresses her attitudes. So if I judge that your act of torture is wrong, my judgment has two components. Its primary, emotive sense is to express my disapproval of your act. Its secondary, descriptive sense is to denote those non-moral properties of your act upon which I base my disapproval. These are presumably the very properties that make it an act of torture – roughly, a causing of intense pain in order to punish, coerce, or afford sadistic pleasure.

By making emotive meaning primary, emotivists claim to preserve the univocity of moral language between speakers who employ different criteria of application for their moral terms. Also, by stressing the intimate connection between moral judgment and the agent's non-cognitive attitudes, emotivists claim to capture the motivational properties of moral judgment. Some emotivists have also attempted to account for ascriptions of truth to moral judgments by accepting the redundancy account of ascriptions of truth as expressions of agreement with the original judgment. The emotivist must think that such ascriptions of truth to moral judgments merely reflect the ascriber's agreement in non-cognitive attitude with the attitude expressed by the original judgment.

Critics of emotivism challenge these alleged virtues. They claim that moral agreement need not track agreement in attitude; there can be moral disagreement without disagreement in attitude (between moralists with different moral views), and disagreement in attitude without moral disagreement (between moralists and immoralists). By distinguishing between the meaning of moral terms and speakers' beliefs about the extension of those terms, critics claim that we can account for the univocity of moral terms in spite of moral disagreement without introducing a primary emotive sense for moral terms. Critics also allege that the emotivist analysis of moral judgments as the expression of the appraiser's attitudes precludes recognizing the possibility of moral judgments that do not engage or reflect the attitudes of the appraiser. For instance, it is not clear how emotivism can accommodate the amoralist – one who recognizes moral requirements but is indifferent to them. Critics also charge emotivism with failure to capture the cognitive aspects of moral discourse. Because emotivism is a theory about moral judgment or assertion, it is difficult for the emotivist to give a semantic analysis of moral predicates in unasserted contexts, such as in the antecedents of conditional moral judgments (e.g., "If he did *wrong*, then he ought to be punished"). Finally, one might want to recognize the *truth* of some moral judgments, perhaps in order to make room for the possibility of moral mis-

takes. If so, then one may not be satisfied with the emotivist's appeal to redundancy or disquotational accounts of the *ascription of truth*.

Emotivism was introduced by Ayer in *Language, Truth, and Logic* (2d ed., 1946) and refined by C. L. Stevenson in *Facts and Values* (1963) and *Ethics and Language* (1944).

See also COGNITIVISM, ETHICAL OBJECTIVISM, METAETHICS, MORAL SKEPTICISM, NIHILISM, NONCOGNITIVISM, PRESCRIPTIVISM.

D.O.B.

empathic solipsism. See SOLIPSISM.

empathy, imaginative projection into another person's situation, especially for vicarious capture of its emotional and motivational qualities. The term is an English rendering (by the Anglo-American psychologist E. G. Titchener, 1867–1927) of the German *Einfühlung*, made popular by Theodore Lipps (1851–1914), which also covered imaginative identification with inanimate objects of aesthetic contemplation. Under 'sympathy', many aspects were earlier discussed by Hume, Adam Smith, and other Scottish philosophers. Empathy has been considered a precondition of ethical thinking and a major contributor to social bonding and altruism, mental state attribution, language use, and translation.

The relevant spectrum of phenomena includes automatic and often subliminal motor mimicry of the expressions or manifestations of another's real or feigned emotion, pain, or pleasure; emotional contagion, by which one "catches" another's apparent emotion, often unconsciously and without reference to its cause or "object"; conscious and unconscious mimicry of direction of gaze, with consequent transfer of attention from the other's response to its cause; and conscious or unconscious role-taking, which reconstructs in imagination (with or without imagery) aspects of the other's situation as the other "perceives" it.

See also EINFÜHLUNG, EMOTION, EXPRESSION THEORY OF ART, HUME, PROBLEM OF OTHER MINDS, SIMULATION THEORY, SMITH, VERSTEHEN.   R.M.G.

Empedocles (c.495–c.435 B.C.), Greek pre-Socratic philosopher who created a physical theory in response to Parmenides while incorporating Pythagorean ideas of the soul into his philosophy. Following Parmenides in his rejection of coming-to-be and perishing, he accounted for phenomenal change by positing four elements (his "roots," *rizomata*), earth, water, air, and fire. When they mix together in set proportions they create compound substances such as blood and bone. Two forces act on the elements, Love and Strife, the former joining the different elements, the latter separating them. In his cyclical cosmogony the four elements combine to form the Sphere, a completely homogeneous spherical body permeated by Love, which, shattered by Strife, grows into a cosmos with the elements forming distinct cosmic masses of earth, water (the seas), air, and fire. There is controversy over whether Empedocles posits one or two periods when living things exist in the cycle. (On one view there are two periods, between which intervenes a stage of complete separation of the elements.) Empedocles accepts the Pythagorean view of reincarnation of souls, seeing life as punishment for an original sin and requiring the expiation of a pious and philosophical life. Thus the exile and return of the individual soul reflects in the microcosm the cosmic movement from harmony to division to harmony. Empedocles' four elements became standard in natural philosophy down to the early modern era, and Aristotle recognized his Love and Strife as an early expression of the efficient cause. **See also** PYTHAGORAS.   D.W.G.

empirical. See A PRIORI.

empirical decision theory, the scientific study of human judgment and decision making. A growing body of empirical research has described the actual limitations on inductive reasoning. By contrast, traditional decision theory is normative; the theory proposes ideal procedures for solving some class of problems.

The descriptive study of decision making was pioneered by figures including Amos Tversky, Daniel Kahneman, Richard Nisbett, and Lee Ross, and their empirical research has documented the limitations and biases of various heuristics, or simple rules of thumb, routinely used in reasoning. The representativeness heuristic is a rule of thumb used to judge probabilities based on the degree to which one class represents (or resembles) another class. For example, we assume that basketball players have a "hot hand" during a particular game – producing an uninterrupted string of successful shots – because we underestimate the relative frequency with which such successful runs occur in the entire population of that player's record. The availability heuristic is a rule of thumb that uses the ease with which an instance comes to mind as an index of the probability of an event.

Such a rule is unreliable when salience in memory misleads; for example, most people (incorrectly) rate death by shark attack as more probable than death by falling airplane parts. (For an overview, see D. Kahneman, P. Slovic, and A. Tversky, eds., *Judgment Under Uncertainty: Heuristics and Biases,* 1982.)

These biases, found in laypeople and statistical experts alike, have a natural explanation on accounts such as Herbert Simon's (1957) concept of "bounded rationality." According to this view, the limitations on our decision making are fixed in part by specific features of our psychological architecture. This architecture places constraints on such factors as processing speed and information capacity, and this in turn produces predictable, systematic errors in performance. Thus, rather than proposing highly idealized rules appropriate to an omniscient Laplacean genius – more characteristic of traditional normative approaches to decision theory – empirical decision theory attempts to formulate a descriptively accurate, and thus psychologically realistic, account of rationality.

Even if certain simple rules can, in particular settings, outperform other strategies, it is still important to understand the causes of the systematic errors we make on tasks perfectly representative of routine decision making. Once the context is specified, empirical decision-making research allows us to study both descriptive decision rules that we follow spontaneously and normative rules that we ought to follow upon reflection.

See also BAYESIAN RATIONALITY, DECISION THEORY, HEURISTICS.   J.D.T.

empirical ego. See KANT.

empirical meaning. See MEANING.

empirical probability. See PROBABILITY.

empiricism (from *empiric,* 'doctor who relies on practical experience', ultimately from Greek *empeiria,* 'experience'), a type of theory in epistemology, the basic idea behind all examples of the type being that experience has primacy in human knowledge and justified belief. Because empiricism is not a single view but a type of view with many different examples, it is appropriate to speak not just of empiricism but of empiricism*s.* Perhaps the most fundamental distinction to be drawn among the various empiricisms is that between those consisting of some claim about concepts and those consisting of some claim about beliefs – call these, respectively, *con-cept-empiricisms* and *belief-empiricisms*.

Concept-empiricisms all begin by singling out those concepts that apply to some experience or other; the concept of dizziness, e.g., applies to the experience of dizziness. And what is then claimed is that all concepts that human beings do and can possess either apply to some experience that someone has had, or have been derived from such concepts by someone's performing on those concepts one or another such mental oper-ation as combination, distinction, and abstrac-tion. How exactly *my* concepts are and must be related to *my* experience and to *my* performance of those mental operations are matters on which concept-empiricists differ; most if not all would grant we each acquire many concepts by learn-ing language, and it does not seem plausible to hold that each concept thus acquired either applies to some experience that one has oneself had or has been derived from such by oneself. But though concept-empiricists disagree con-cerning the conditions for linguistic acquisition or transmission of a concept, what unites them, to repeat, is the claim that all human concepts either apply to some experience that someone has actually had or they have been derived from such by someone's actually performing on those the mental operations of combination, distinc-tion, and abstraction. Most concept-empiricists will also say something more: that the experi-ence must have *evoked* the concept in the person having the experience, or that the person having the experience must have *recognized* that the con-cept applies to his or her experience, or some-thing of that sort.

What unites all *belief*-empiricists is the claim that for one's beliefs to possess one or another truth-relevant merit, they must be related in one or another way to someone's experience. Belief-empiricisms differ from each other, for one thing, with respect to the merit concerning which the claim is made. Some belief-empiricists claim that a belief does not have the status of *knowledge* unless it has the requisite relation to experience; some claim that a belief lacks *warrant* unless it has that relation; others claim that a belief is not *permissibly held* unless it stands in that relation; and yet others claim that it is not a *properly scien-tific* belief unless it stands in that relation. And not even this list exhausts the possibilities.

Belief-empiricisms also differ with respect to the specific relation to experience that is said to be necessary for the merit in question to be pres-ent. Some belief-empiricists hold, for example, that a belief is permissibly held only if its propo-sitional content is either a report of the person's present or remembered experience, or the belief is held on the basis of such beliefs and is proba-ble with respect to the beliefs on the basis of which it is held. Kant, by contrast, held the rather different view that if a belief is to consti-tute (empirical) *knowledge*, it must in some way *be about* experience.

Third, belief-empiricisms differ from each other with respect to the person to whose expe-rience a belief must stand in the relation speci-fied if it is to possess the merit specified. It need not always be an experience of the person whose belief is being considered. It might be an experi-ence of someone giving testimony about it.

It should be obvious that a philosopher might well accept one kind of empiricism while reject-ing others. Thus to ask philosophers whether they are empiricists is a question void for vague-ness. It is regularly said of Locke that he was an empiricist; and indeed, he was a concept-empiri-cist of a certain sort. But he embraced no version whatsoever of belief-empiricism.

Up to this point, 'experience' has been used without explanation. But anyone acquainted with the history of philosophy will be aware that different philosophers pick out different phe-nomena with the word; and even when they pick out the same phenomenon, they have dif-ferent views as to the structure of the phenome-non that they call 'experience.' The differences on these matters reflect yet more distinctions among empiricisms than have been delineated above.

See also EPISTEMOLOGY, LOGICAL POSI-TIVISM, RATIONALISM.   N.P.W.

empiricism, constructive. See SOCIAL CONSTRUC-TIVISM.

empiricism, British. See RATIONALISM.

empiricism, logical. See LOGICAL POSITIVISM.

enantiamorphs (from Greek *enantios*, 'opposite', and *morphe*, 'form'), objects whose shapes differ as do those of a right and left hand. One of a pair of enantiamorphs can be made to look identical in shape to the other by viewing it in a mirror but not merely by changing its spatial orientation. Enantiamorphs figure prominently in the work of Kant, who argued that the existence of enan-tiamorphic pairs entailed that Leibnizian rela-tional theories of space were to be rejected in favor of Newtonian absolutist theories, that some facts about space could be apprehended only by "pure intuition," and that space was mind-dependent. **See also** KANT, LEIBNIZ.

R.Ke.

encrateia. See AKRASIA.

Encyclopedia, in French, *Encyclopédie;* full English title: *Encyclopedia, or a Descriptive Dictionary of the Sciences, Arts and Trades.* Launched in 1747 by the Parisian publisher Le Breton, who had secured d'Alembert's and Diderot's editorship, the *Encyclopedia* was gradually released from 1751 to 1772, despite a temporary revocation of its royal privilege. Comprising seventeen folio volumes of 17,818 articles and eleven folio volumes of 2,885 plates, the work required a staff of 272 contributors, writers, and engravers. It incorporated the accumulated knowledge and rationalist, secularist views of the French Enlightenment and prescribed economic, social, and political reforms. Enormously successful, the work was reprinted with revisions five times before 1789.

Contributions were made by the *philosophes* Voltaire, Rousseau, Montesquieu, d'Holbach, Naigeon, and Saint-Lambert; the writers Duclos and Marmontel; the theologians Morellet and Malet; enlightened clerics, e.g. Raynal; explorers, e.g. La Condamine; natural scientists, e.g. Daubenton; physicians, e.g. Bouillet; the economists Turgot and Quesnay; engineers, e.g. Perronet; horologists, e.g. Berthoud; and scores of other experts.

"The purpose of an Encyclopedia," wrote Diderot, "is to collect the knowledge dispersed on the surface of the earth, and to unfold its general system" ("Encyclopedia," Vol. 5, 1755). The *Encyclopedia* offered the educated reader a comprehensive, systematic, and descriptive repository of contemporary liberal and mechanical arts. D'Alembert and Diderot developed a sensationalist epistemology ("Preliminary Discourse") under the influence of Locke and Condillac. They compiled and rationally classified existing knowledge according to the noetic process (memory, imagination, and reason). Based on the assumption of the unity of theory and praxis, their approach was positivistic and utilitarian.

The Encyclopedists vindicated experimental reason and the rule of nature, fostered the practice of criticism, and stimulated the development of new sciences. In religious matters, they cultivated ambiguity to escape censorship. Whereas most contributors held either conciliatory or orthodox positions, d'Alembert, Diderot, and d'Holbach barely concealed their naturalistic and atheistic opinions. Their radicalism was pervasive. Supernaturalism, obscurantism, and fanaticism were among the Encyclopedists' favorite targets. They identified religion with superstition and theology with black magic; asserted the superiority of natural morality over theological ethics; demanded religious toleration; and championed human rights. They innovatively retraced the historical conditions of the development of modern philosophy. They furthermore pioneered ideas on trade and industry and anticipated the relevance of historiography, sociology, economics, and linguistics.

As the most ambitious and expansive reference work of its time, the *Encyclopedia* crystallized the confidence of the eighteenth-century bourgeoisie in the capacity of reason to dispel the shadows of ignorance and improve society.

See also D'ALEMBERT, D'HOLBACH, DIDEROT, VOLTAIRE.

J.-L.S.

Encyclopedists. See ENCYCLOPEDIA.

end in itself. See KANT.

endurance. See PERDURANCE.

energeia, Greek term coined by Aristotle and often translated as 'activity', 'actuality', and even 'act', but more literally rendered '(a state of) functioning'. Since for Aristotle the function of an object is its *telos* or aim, *energeia* can also be described as an *entelecheia* or realization (another coined term he uses interchangeably with *energeia*). So understood, it can denote either (a) something's being functional, though not in use at the moment, and (b) something's actually functioning, which Aristotle describes as a "first realization" and "second realization" respectively (*On the Soul* II.5). In general, every *energeia* is correlative to some *dunamis,* a capability or power to function in a certain way, and in the central books of the *Metaphysics* Aristotle uses the linkage between these two concepts to explain the relation of form to matter. He also distinguishes between *energeia* and *kinēsis* (change or motion) (*Metaphysics* IX.6; *Nicomachean Ethics* X.4). A *kinēsis* is defined by reference to its terminus (e.g., learning *how to multiply*) and is thus incomplete at any point before reaching its conclusion. An *energeia,* in contrast, is a state complete in itself (e.g., seeing). Thus, Aristotle says that at any time that I am seeing, it is also true that I have seen; but it is not true that at any time I am learning that I have learned. In Greek, this difference is not so much one of tense as of aspect: the perfect tense marks a "perfect" or complete state, and not necessarily prior activity. **See also** ARISTOTLE.   V.C.

energeticism, also called energetism or energism, the doctrine that energy is the fundamental substance underlying all change. Its most prominent champion was the physical chemist Wilhelm Ostwald (1853–1932). In his address "Die Überwindung des wissenschaftlichen Materialismus" ("The Conquest of Scientific Materialism"), delivered at Lübeck in 1895, Ostwald chastised the atomic-kinetic theory as lacking progress and claimed that a unified science, energetics, could be based solely on the concept of energy. Many of Ostwald's criticisms of materialism and mechanistic reductionism derived from Mach. Ostwald's attempts to deduce the fundamental equations of thermodynamics and mechanics from the principles of energy conservation and transformation were indebted to the writings of Georg Helm (1874–1919), especially *Die Lehre von Energie* ("The Laws of Energy," 1887) and *Die Energetik* ("Energetics," 1898). Ostwald defended Helm's factorization thesis that all changes in energy can be analyzed as a product of intensity and capacity factors. The factorization thesis and the attempt to derive mechanics and thermodynamics from the principles of energetics were subjected to devastating criticisms by Boltzmann and Max Planck. Boltzmann also criticized the dogmatism of Ostwald's rejection of the atomic-kinetic theory. Ostwald's program to unify the sciences under the banner of energetics withered in the face of these criticisms. **See also** BOLTZMANN, MACH, PHILOSOPHY OF SCIENCE. M.C.

energetism, energism. See ENERGETICISM.

Engels, Friedrich (1820–95), German socialist and economist who, with Marx, was the founder of what later was called Marxism. Whether there are significant differences between Marx and Engels is a question much in dispute among scholars of Marxism. Certainly there are differences in emphasis, but there was also a division of labor between them. Engels, and not Marx, presented a Marxist account of natural science and integrated Darwinian elements in Marxian theory. But they also coauthored major works, including *The Holy Family, The German Ideology* (1845), and *The Communist Manifesto* (1848). Engels thought of himself as the junior partner in their lifelong collaboration. That judgment is correct, but Engels's work is both significant and more accessible than Marx's. He gave popular articulations of their common views in such books as *Socialism: Utopian and Scientific* and *Anti-Dühring* (1878). His work, more than Marx's, was taken by the Second International and many subsequent Marxist militants to be definitive of Marxism. Only much later with some Western Marxist theoreticians did his influence decline.

Engels's first major work, *The Condition of the Working Class in England* (1845), vividly depicted workers' lives, misery, and systematic exploitation. But he also saw the working class as a new force created by the industrial revolution, and he developed an account of how this new force would lead to the revolutionary transformation of society, including collective ownership and control of the means of production and a rational ordering of social life; all this would supersede the waste and disparity of human conditions that he took to be inescapable under capitalism.

The German Ideology, jointly authored with Marx, first articulated what was later called historical materialism, a conception central to Marxist theory. It is the view that the economic structure of society is the foundation of society; as the productive forces develop, the economic structure changes and with that political, legal, moral, religious, and philosophical ideas change accordingly. Until the consolidation of socialism, societies are divided into antagonistic classes, a person's class being determined by her relationship to the means of production. The dominant ideas of a society will be strongly conditioned by the economic structure of the society and serve the class interests of the dominant class. The social consciousness (the ruling ideology) will be that which answers to the interests of the dominant class.

From the 1850s on, Engels took an increasing interest in connecting historical materialism with developments in natural science. This work took definitive form in his *Anti-Dühring,* the first general account of Marxism, and in his posthumously published *Dialectics of Nature.* (*Anti-Dühring* also contains his most extensive discussion of morality.) It was in these works that Engels articulated the dialectical method and a systematic communist worldview that sought to establish that there were not only social laws expressing empirical regularities in society but also universal laws of nature and thought. These dialectical laws, Engels believed, reveal that both nature and society are in a continuous process of evolutionary though conflict-laden development.

Engels should not be considered primarily, if at all, a speculative philosopher. Like Marx, he was critical of and ironical about speculative philosophy and was a central figure in the socialist movement. While always concerned that his account be warrantedly assertible, Engels sought to make it not only true, but also a finely tuned instrument of working-class emancipation which would lead to a world without classes.

See also MARXISM, POLITICAL PHILOSOPHY.
K.N.

Enlightenment, a late eighteenth-century international movement in thought, with important social and political ramifications. The Enlightenment is at once a style, an attitude, a temper – critical, secular, skeptical, empirical, and practical. It is also characterized by core beliefs in human rationality, in what it took to be "nature," and in the "natural feelings" of mankind. Four of its most prominent exemplars are Hume, Thomas Jefferson, Kant, and Voltaire.

The Enlightenment belief in human rationality had several aspects. (1) Human beings are free to the extent that their actions are carried out for a reason. Actions prompted by traditional authority, whether religious or political, are therefore not free; liberation requires weakening if not also overthrow of this authority. (2) Human rationality is universal, requiring only education for its development. In virtue of their common rationality, all human beings have certain rights, among them the right to choose and shape their individual destinies. (3) A final aspect of the belief in human rationality was that the true forms of all things could be discovered, whether of the universe (Newton's laws), of the mind (associationist psychology), of good government (the U.S. Constitution), of a happy life (which, like good government, was "balanced"), or of beautiful architecture (Palladio's principles). The Enlightenment was preeminently a "formalist" age, and prose, not poetry, was its primary means of expression.

The Enlightenment thought of itself as a return to the classical ideas of the Greeks and (more especially) the Romans. But in fact it provided one source of the revolutions that shook Europe and America at the end of the eighteenth century, and it laid the intellectual foundations for both the generally scientific worldview and the liberal democratic society, which, despite the many attacks made on them, continue to function as cultural ideals.

See also HUME, KANT, LIBERALISM, LOCKE, VOLTAIRE.   G.G.B.

ens a se (Latin, 'a being from itself'), a being that

is completely independent and self-sufficient. Since every creature depends at least upon God for its existence, only God could be *ens a se*. In fact, only God is, and he must be. For if God depended on any other being, he would be dependent and hence not self-sufficient. To the extent that the ontological argument is plausible, it depends on conceiving of God as *ens a se*. In other words, God as *ens a se* is the greatest conceivable being. The idea of *ens a se* is very important in the *Monologion* and *Proslogion* of Anselm, in various works of Duns Scotus, and later Scholastic thought.

Ens a se should be distinguished from *ens ex se*, according to Anselm in *Monologion*. *Ens a se* is from itself and not "out of itself." In other words, *ens a se* does not depend upon itself for its own existence, because it is supposed to be dependent on absolutely nothing. Further, if *ens a se* depended upon itself, it would cause itself to exist, and that is impossible, according to medieval and Scholastic philosophers, who took causality to be irreflexive. (It is also transitive and asymmetric.) Hence, the medieval idea of *ens a se* should not be confused with Spinoza's idea of *causa sui*.

Later Scholastics often coined abstract terms to designate the property or entity that makes something to be what it is, in analogy with forming, say, 'rigidity' from 'rigid'. The Latin term '*aseitas*' is formed from the prepositional phrase in '*ens a se*' in this way; '*aseitas*' is translated into English as 'aseity'. A better-known example of forming an abstract noun from a concrete word is '*haecceitas*' (thisness) from '*haec*' (this).

See also ANSELM, DIVINE ATTRIBUTES, DUNS SCOTUS, PHILOSOPHY OF RELIGION.
A.P.M.

ens ex se. See ENS A SE.

en soi. See SARTRE.

ens per accidens. See PER ACCIDENS.

ens perfectissimo. See ENS REALISSIMUM.

ens rationis (Latin, 'a being of reason'), a thing dependent for its existence upon reason or thought; sometimes known as an intentional being. *Ens rationis* is the contrasting term for a real being (*res* or *ens in re extra animam*), such as an individual animal. Real beings exist independently of thought and are the foundation for truth. A being of reason depends upon thought or reason for its existence and is an invention of the mind, even if it has a foundation in some real being. (This conception requires the idea that there are degrees of being.) Two kinds of *entia rationis* are distinguished: those with a foundation in reality and those without one. The objects of logic, which include genera and species, e.g., animal and human, respectively, are *entia rationis* that have a foundation in reality, but are abstracted from it. In contrast, mythic and fictional objects, such as a chimera or Pegasus, have no foundation in reality. Blindness and deafness are also sometimes called *entia rationis*. **See also** AQUINAS, SUÁREZ.   A.P.M.

ens realissimum (Latin, 'most real being'), an informal term for God that occurs rarely in Scholastic philosophers. Within Kant's philosophy, it has a technical sense. It is an extension of Baumgarten's idea of *ens perfectissimum* (most perfect being), a being that has the greatest number of possible perfections to the greatest degree. Since *ens perfectissimum* refers to God as the sum of all possibilities and since actuality is greater than possibility, according to Kant, the idea of God as the sum of all actualities, that is, *ens realissimum*, is a preferable term for God.

Kant thinks that human knowledge is "constrained" to posit the idea of a necessary being. The necessary being that has the best claim to necessity is one that is completely unconditioned, that is, dependent on nothing; this is *ens realissimum*. He sometimes explicates it in three ways: as the substratum of all realities, as the ground of all realities, and as the sum of all realities. *Ens realissimum* is nonetheless empirically invalid, since it cannot be experienced by humans. It is something ideal for reason, not real in experience.

According to Kant, the ontological argument begins with the concept of *ens realissimum* and concludes that an existing object falls under that concept (*Critique of Pure Reason*, Book II, chapter 3).
See also BAUMGARTEN, KANT.   A.P.M.

entailment. See IMPLICATION.

entelechy (from Greek *entelecheia*), actuality. Aristotle, who coined both terms, treats *entelecheia* as a near synonym of *energeia* when it is used in this sense. *Entelecheia* figures in Aristotle's definition of the soul as the first actuality of the natural body (*On the Soul* II.1). This is explained by analogy with knowledge: first actuality is to knowledge as second actuality is to the active use of knowledge.

'Entelechy' is also a technical term in Leibniz for the primitive active force in every monad, which is combined with primary matter, and from which the active force, *vis viva*, is somehow derived.

The vitalist philosopher Hans Driesch used the Aristotelian term in his account of biology. Life, he held, is an entelechy; and an entelechy is a substantial entity, rather like a mind, that controls organic processes.
See also ENERGEIA, PHILOSOPHY OF BIOLOGY.   P.Wo.

enthymeme, an incompletely stated syllogism, with one premise, or even the conclusion, omitted. The term sometimes designates incompletely stated arguments of other kinds. We are expected to supply the missing premise or draw the conclusion if it is not stated. The result is supposed to be a syllogistic inference. For example: 'He will eventually get caught, for he is a thief'; or 'He will eventually be caught, for all habitual thieves get caught'. This notion of enthymeme as an incompletely stated syllogism has a long tradition and does not seem inconsistent with Aristotle's own characterization of it. Thus, Peter of Spain openly declares that an enthymeme is an argument with a single premise that needs to be reduced to syllogism. But Peter also points out that Aristotle spoke of enthymeme as "being of *ycos* and *signum*," and he explains that *ycos* here means 'probable proposition' while *signum* expresses the necessity of inference. '*P*, therefore *Q*' is an *ycos* in the sense of a proposition that appears to be true to all or to many; but insofar as *P* has virtually a double power, that of itself and of the proposition understood along with it, it is both probable and demonstrative, albeit from a different point of view. **See also** SYLLOGISM.   I.Bo.

entity, abstract. See ABSTRACT ENTITY.

entity, theoretical. See THEORETICAL TERM.

entrenchment. See GOODMAN.

entropy, in physics, a measure of disorder; in information theory, a measure of "information" in a technical sense.

In statistical physics the number of microstates accessible to the various particles of a large system of particles such as a cabbage or the air in a room is represented as Ω. Accessible microstates might be, for instance, energy levels the various particles can reach. One can greatly simplify the statement of certain laws of nature by introducing a logarithmic measure of these accessible microstates. This measure, called entropy, is defined by the formula: S(Entropy) = df. $k(ln\Omega)$, where k is Boltzmann's constant. When the entropy of a system increases, the system becomes more random and disordered, in the sense that a larger number of microstates become available for the system's particles to enter.

If a large physical system within which exchanges of energy occur is isolated, exchanging no energy with its environment, the entropy of the system tends to increase and never decreases. This result of statistical physics is part of the second law of thermodynamics. In real, evolving physical systems effectively isolated from their environments, entropy increases and thus aspects of the system's organization that depend upon there being only a limited range of accessible microstates are altered. For example, a cabbage totally isolated in a container would decay as complicated organic molecules eventually became unstructured in the course of ongoing exchanges of energy and attendant entropy increases.

In information theory, a state or event is said to contain more information than a second state or event if the former state is less probable and thus in a sense more surprising than the latter. Other plausible constraints suggest a logarithmic measure of information content. Suppose X is a set of alternative possible states, x_i, and $p(x_i)$ is the probability of each $x_i \in X$. If state x_i has occurred the information content of that occurrence is taken to be $-\log_2 p(x_i)$. This function increases as the probability of x_i decreases. If it is unknown which x_i will occur, it is reasonable to represent the expected information content of X as the sum of the information contents of the alternative states x_i weighted in each case by the probability of the state, giving:

$$- \sum_{x_i \in X} p(x_i)\log_2 p(x_i).$$

This is called the Shannon entropy.

Both Shannon entropy and physical entropy can be thought of as logarithmic measures of disarray. But this statement trades on a broad understanding of 'disarray'. A close relationship between the two concepts of entropy should not be assumed.

See also INFORMATION THEORY, PHILOSOPHY OF SCIENCE.   T.H.

envelope paradox, an apparent paradox in decision theory that runs as follows. You are shown two envelopes, M and N, and are reliably informed that each contains some finite positive amount of money, that the amount in one unspecified envelope is twice the amount in the unspecified other, and that you may choose only one. Call the amount in M 'm' and that in N 'n'. It might seem that: there is a half chance that $m = 2n$ and a half chance that $m = n/2$, so that the "expected value" of m is $(\frac{1}{2})(2n) + (\frac{1}{2})(n/2) = 1.25n$, so that you should prefer envelope M. But by similar reasoning it might seem that the expected value of n is $1.25m$, so that you should prefer envelope N. **See also** DECISION THEORY.

D.A.J.

environmental ethics. See ENVIRONMENTAL PHILOSOPHY.

environmental philosophy, the critical study of concepts defining relations between human beings and their non-human environment. Environmental ethics, a major component of environmental philosophy, addresses the normative significance of these relations. The relevance of ecological relations to human affairs has been recognized at least since Darwin, but the growing sense of human responsibility for their deterioration, reflected in books such as Rachel Carson's *Silent Spring* (1962) and Peter Singer's *Animal Liberation* (1975), has prompted the recent upsurge of interest.

Environmental philosophers have adduced a wide variety of human attitudes and practices to account for the perceived deterioration, including religious and scientific attitudes, social institutions, and industrial technology. Proposed remedies typically urge a reorientation or new "ethic" that recognizes "intrinsic value" in the natural world. Examples include the "land ethic" of Aldo Leopold (1887–1948), which pictures humans as belonging to, rather than owning, the biotic community ("the land"); deep ecology, a stance articulated by the Norwegian philosopher Arne Naess (b.1912), which advocates forms of identification with the non-human world; and ecofeminism, which rejects prevailing attitudes to the natural world that are perceived as patriarchal.

At the heart of environmental ethics lies the attempt to articulate the basis of concern for the natural world. It encompasses global as well as local issues, and considers the longer-term ecological, and even evolutionary, fate of the human and non-human world. Many of its practitioners question the anthropocentric claim that human beings are the exclusive or even central focus of ethical concern. In thus extending both the scope and the grounds of concern, it presents a challenge to the stance of conventional interhuman ethics. It debates how to balance the claims of present and future, human and non-human, sentient and non-sentient, individuals and wholes. It investigates the prospects for a sustainable relationship between economic and ecological systems, and pursues the implications of this relationship with respect to social justice and political institutions. Besides also engaging metaethical questions about, for example, the objectivity and commensurability of values, environmental philosophers are led to consider the nature and significance of environmental change and the ontological status of collective entities such as species and ecosystems. In a more traditional vein, environmental philosophy revives metaphysical debates surrounding the perennial question of "man's place in nature," and finds both precedent and inspiration in earlier philosophies and cultures.

See also APPLIED ETHICS, ETHICS, FEMINISM, NATURALISM, VALUE.   A.Ho.

epapogē, Greek term for 'induction'. Especially in the logic of Aristotle, *epagogē* is opposed to argument by syllogism. Aristotle describes it as "a move from particulars to the universal." E.g., premises that the skilled navigator is the best navigator, the skilled charioteer the best charioteer, and the skilled philosopher the best philosopher may support the conclusion by *epagogē* that those skilled in something are usually the best at it. Aristotle thought it more persuasive and clearer than the syllogistic method, since it relies on the senses and is available to all humans. The term was later applied to dialectical arguments intended to trap opponents.   R.C.

epicheirema, a polysyllogism in which each premise represents an enthymematic argument; e.g., 'A lie creates disbelief, because it is an assertion that does not correspond to truth; flattery is a lie, because it is a conscious distortion of truth; therefore, flattery creates disbelief'. Each premise constitutes an enthymematic syllogism. Thus, the first premise could be expanded into the following full-fledged syllogism: 'Every assertion that does not correspond to truth creates disbelief; a lie is an assertion that does not correspond to truth; therefore a lie creates disbelief'. We could likewise expand the second premise and offer a complete argument for it. Epicheirema can thus be a powerful tool in oral polemics, especially when one argues regressively, first

stating the conclusion with a sketch of support in terms of enthymemes, and then – if challenged to do so – expanding any or all of these enthymemes into standard categorical syllogisms. **See also** SYLLOGISM.   I.Bo.

Epictetus. See STOICISM.

Epicureanism, one of the three leading movements constituting Hellenistic philosophy. It was founded by Epicurus (341–271 B.C.), together with his close colleagues Metrodorus (c.331–278), Hermarchus (Epicurus's successor as head of the Athenian school), and Polyaenus (d. 278). He set up Epicurean communities at Mytilene, Lampsacus, and finally Athens (306 B.C.), where his school the Garden became synonymous with Epicureanism. These groups set out to live the ideal Epicurean life, detached from political society without actively opposing it, and devoting themselves to philosophical discussion and the cult of friendship. Their correspondence was anthologized and studied as a model of the philosophical life by later Epicureans, for whom the writings of Epicurus and his three cofounders, known collectively as "the Men," held a virtually biblical status.

Epicurus wrote voluminously, but all that survives are three brief epitomes (the *Letter to Herodotus* on physics, the *Letter to Pythocles* on astronomy, etc., and the *Letter to Menoeceus* on ethics), a group of maxims, and papyrus fragments of his magnum opus *On Nature*. Otherwise, we are almost entirely dependent on secondary citations, doxography, and the writings of his later followers.

The Epicurean physical theory is atomistic, developed out of the fifth-century system of Democritus. Per se existents are divided into bodies and space, each of them infinite in quantity. Space is, or includes, absolute void, without which motion would be impossible, while body is constituted out of physically indivisible particles, "atoms." Atoms are themselves further analyzable as sets of absolute "minima," the ultimate quanta of magnitude, posited by Epicurus to circumvent the paradoxes that Zeno of Elea had derived from the hypothesis of infinite divisibility. Atoms themselves have only the primary properties of shape, size, and weight. All secondary properties, e.g. color, are generated out of atomic compounds; given their dependent status, they cannot be added to the list of per se existents, but it does not follow, as the skeptical tradition in atomism had held, that they are not real either. Atoms are in constant rapid motion, at equal speed (since in the pure void there is nothing to slow them down). Stability emerges as an overall property of compounds, which large groups of atoms form by settling into regular patterns of complex motion, governed by the three motive principles of weight, collisions, and a minimal random movement, the "swerve," which initiates new patterns of motion and blocks the danger of determinism. Our world itself, like the countless other worlds, is such a compound, accidentally generated and of finite duration. There is no divine mind behind it, or behind the evolution of life and society: the gods are to be viewed as ideal beings, models of the Epicurean good life, and therefore blissfully detached from our affairs.

Canonic, the Epicurean theory of knowledge, rests on the principle that "all sensations are true." Denial of empirical cognition is argued to amount to skepticism, which is in turn rejected as a self-refuting position. Sensations are representationally (not propositionally) true. In the paradigm case of sight, thin films of atoms (Greek *eidola,* Latin *simulacra*) constantly flood off bodies, and our eyes mechanically report those that reach them, neither embroidering nor interpreting. Inference from these guaranteed (photographic, as it were) data to the nature of external objects themselves involves judgment, and there alone error can occur. Sensations thus constitute one of the three "criteria of truth," along with feelings, a criterion of values and introspective information, and *prolepseis,* or naturally acquired generic conceptions. On the basis of sense evidence, we are entitled to infer the nature of microscopic or remote phenomena. Celestial phenomena, e.g., cannot be regarded as divinely engineered (which would conflict with the *prolepsis* of the gods as tranquil), and experience supplies plenty of models that would account for them naturalistically. Such grounds amount to consistency with directly observed phenomena, and are called *ouk antimarturesis* ("lack of counterevidence"). Paradoxically, when several alternative explanations of the same phenomenon pass this test, all must be accepted: although only one of them can be true for each token phenomenon, the others, given their intrinsic possibility and the spatial and temporal infinity of the universe, must be true for tokens of the same type elsewhere. Fortunately, when it comes to the basic tenets of physics, it is held that only one theory passes this test of consistency with phenomena.

Epicurean ethics is hedonistic. Pleasure is our innate natural goal, to which all other values, including virtue, are subordinated. Pain is the only evil, and there is no intermediate state. Philosophy's task is to show how pleasure can be maximized, as follows: Bodily pleasure becomes more secure if we adopt a simple way of life that satisfies only our natural and necessary desires, with the support of like-minded friends. Bodily pain, when inevitable, can be outweighed by mental pleasure, which exceeds it because it can range over past, present, and future. The highest pleasure, whether of soul or body, is a satisfied state, "katastematic pleasure." The pleasures of stimulation ("kinetic pleasures"), including those resulting from luxuries, can vary this state, but have no incremental value: striving to accumulate them does not increase overall pleasure, but does increase our vulnerability to fortune. Our primary aim should instead be to minimize pain. This is achieved for the body through a simple way of life, and for the soul through the study of physics, which achieves the ultimate katastematic pleasure, "freedom from disturbance" (*ataraxia*), by eliminating the two main sources of human anguish, the fears of the gods and of death. It teaches us (a) that cosmic phenomena do not convey divine threats, (b) that death is mere disintegration of the soul, with hell an illusion. To fear our own future non-existence is as irrational as to regret the non-existence we enjoyed before we were born. Physics also teaches us how to evade determinism, which would turn moral agents into mindless fatalists: the swerve doctrine secures indeterminism, as does the logical doctrine that future-tensed propositions may be neither true nor false. The Epicureans were the first explicit defenders of free will, although we lack the details of their positive explanation of it. Finally, although Epicurean groups sought to opt out of public life, they took a keen and respectful interest in civic justice, which they analyzed not as an absolute value, but as a contract between humans to refrain from harmful activity on grounds of utility, perpetually subject to revision in the light of changing circumstances.

Epicureanism enjoyed widespread popularity, but unlike its great rival Stoicism it never entered the intellectual bloodstream of the ancient world. Its stances were dismissed by many as philistine, especially its rejection of all cultural activities not geared to the Epicurean good life. It was also increasingly viewed as atheistic, and its ascetic hedonism was misrepresented as crude sensualism (hence the modern use of 'epicure'). The school nevertheless continued to flourish down to and well beyond the end of the Hellenistic age. In the first century B.C. its exponents included Philodemus, whose fragmentarily surviving treatise *On Signs* attests to sophisticated debates on induction between Stoics and Epicureans, and Lucretius, the Roman author of the great Epicurean didactic poem *On the Nature of Things*. In the second century A.D. another Epicurean, Diogenes of Oenoanda, had his philosophical writings engraved on stone in a public colonnade, and passages have survived. Thereafter Epicureanism's prominence declined. Serious interest in it was revived by Renaissance humanists, and its atomism was an important influence on early modern physics, especially through Gassendi.

See also DOXOGRAPHERS, HELLENISTIC PHILOSOPHY.   D.N.S.

Epicurus. See EPICUREANISM.

Epimenides paradox. See SEMANTIC PARADOXES.

epiphenomenalism. See PHILOSOPHY OF MIND.

episodic. See DISPOSITION.

episteme. See ARISTOTLE.

epistemic. See PERCEPTION.

epistemic accessibility. See EPISTEMOLOGY.

epistemic certainty. See CERTAINTY.

epistemic deontologism, a duty-based view of the nature of epistemic justification. A central concern of epistemology is to account for the distinction between justified and unjustified beliefs. According to epistemic deontologism, the concept of justification may be analyzed by using, in a specific sense relevant to the pursuit of knowledge, terms such as 'ought', 'obligatory', 'permissible', and 'forbidden'. A subject S is justified in believing that p provided S does not violate any epistemic obligations – those that arise from the goal of believing what is true and not believing what is false. Equivalently, S is justified in believing that p provided believing p is – from the point of view taken in the pursuit of truth – permissible for S. Among contemporary epistemologists, this view is held by Chisholm, Laurence BonJour, and Carl Ginet. Its significance is twofold. If justification is a function of meeting obligations, then it is, contrary to some versions of naturalistic epistemology, *normative*. Second, if the normativity of justification is deontological, the factors that determine whether a belief is justified must

be internal to the subject's mind. Critics of epistemic deontologism, most conspicuously Alston, contend that belief is involuntary and thus cannot be a proper object of obligations. If, e.g., one is looking out the window and notices that it is raining, one is psychologically forced to believe that it is raining. Deontologists can reply to this objection by rejecting its underlying premise: epistemic obligations require that belief be voluntary. Alternatively, they may insist that belief is voluntary after all, and thus subject to epistemic obligations, for there is a means by which one can avoid believing what one ought not to believe: *weighing the evidence*, or *deliberation*. **See also** EPISTEMOLOGY, JUSTIFICATION.   M.St.

epistemic dependence. See DEPENDENCE.

epistemic holism. See HOLISM.

epistemic immediacy. See IMMEDIACY.

epistemic justification. See EPISTEMOLOGY.

epistemic logic, the logical investigation of epistemic concepts and statements. Epistemic concepts include the concepts of knowledge, reasonable belief, justification, evidence, certainty, and related notions. Epistemic logic is usually taken to include the logic of belief or *doxastic* logic.

Much of the recent work on epistemic logic is based on the view that it is a branch of modal logic. In the early 1950s von Wright observed that the epistemic notions *verified* (known to be true), *undecided,* and *falsified* are related to each other in the same way as the alethic modalities *necessary, contingent,* and *impossible,* and behave logically in analogous ways. This analogy is not surprising in view of the fact that the meaning of modal concepts is often explained epistemically. For example, in the 1890s Peirce defined *informational possibility* as that "which in a given (state of) information is not perfectly known not to be true," and called *informationally necessary* "that which is perfectly known to be true."

The modal logic of epistemic and doxastic concepts was studied systematically by Hintikka in his pioneering *Knowledge and Belief* (1962), which applied to the concepts of knowledge and belief the semantical method (the method of modal sets) that he had used earlier for the investigation of modal logic. In this approach, the truth of the proposition that a knows that p (briefly $K_a p$) in a possible world (or situation) u is taken to mean that p holds in all epistemic alternatives of

u; these are understood as worlds compatible with what a knows at u. If the relation of epistemic alternativeness is reflexive, the principle '$K_a p \rightarrow p$' (only what is the case can be known) is valid, and the assumption that the alternativeness relation is transitive validates the so-called KK-thesis, '$K_a p \rightarrow K_a K_a p$' (if a knows that p, a knows that a knows that p); these two assumptions together make the logic of knowledge similar to an S4-type modal logic. If the knowledge operator K_a and the corresponding epistemic possibility operator P_a are added to quantification theory with identity, it becomes possible to study the interplay between quantifiers and epistemic operators and the behavior of individual terms in epistemic contexts, and analyze such locutions as 'a knows who (what) b (some F) is'. The problems of epistemic logic in this area are part of the general problem of giving a coherent semantical account of propositional attitudes.

If a proposition p is true in all epistemic alternatives of a given world, so are all logical consequences of p; thus the possible-worlds semantics of epistemic concepts outlined above leads to the result that a person knows all logical consequences of what he knows. This is a paradoxical conclusion; it is called the problem of logical omniscience. The solution of this problem requires a distinction between different levels of knowledge – for example, between tacit and explicit knowledge. A more realistic model of knowledge can be obtained by supplementing the basic possible-worlds account by an analysis of the processes by which the implicit knowledge can be activated and made explicit.

Modal epistemic logics have found fruitful applications in the recent work on knowledge representation and in the logic and semantics of questions and answers in which questions are interpreted as requests for knowledge or "epistemic imperatives."

See also EPISTEMOLOGY, KK-THESIS, MODAL LOGIC.   R.Hi.

epistemic operator. See OPERATOR.

epistemic permissibility. See EPISTEMOLOGY.

epistemic possibility. See EPISTEMIC LOGIC.

epistemic principle, a principle of rationality applicable to such concepts as knowledge, justification, and reasonable belief. Epistemic principles include the principles of epistemic logic and principles that relate different epistemic concepts to one another, or epistemic concepts to non-epistemic ones (e.g., semantic concepts). Epistemic concepts include the concepts of knowledge, reasonable belief, justification, (epistemic) probability, and other concepts that are used for the purpose of assessing the reasonableness of beliefs and knowledge claims. Epistemic principles can be formulated as principles concerning *belief systems* or *information systems*, i.e., systems that characterize a person's possible *doxastic state* at a given time; a belief system may be construed as a set of (accepted) propositions or as a system of *degrees* of belief. It is possible to distinguish two kinds of epistemic principles: (a) principles concerning the rationality of a single belief system, and (b) principles concerning the rational *changes* of belief. The former include the requirements of coherence and consistency for beliefs (and for probabilities); such principles may be said to concern the *statics* of belief systems. The latter principles include various principles of belief revision and adjustment, i.e., principles concerning the *dynamics* of belief systems. **See also** CLOSURE, KK-THESIS.   R.Hi.

epistemic priority. See DEPENDENCE.

epistemic privacy, the relation a person has to a proposition when only that person can have direct or non-inferential knowledge of the proposition. It is widely thought that people have epistemic privacy with respect to propositions about certain of their own mental states. According to this view, a person can know directly that he has certain thoughts or feelings or sensory experiences. Perhaps others can also know that the person has these thoughts, feelings, or experiences, but if they can it is only as a result of inference from propositions about the person's behavior or physical condition. **See also** INFERENTIAL KNOWLEDGE, PRIVILEGED ACCESS.   R.Fe.

epistemic probability. See PROBABILITY.

epistemic rationality. See IRRATIONALITY.

epistemic regress argument, an argument, originating in Aristotle's *Posterior Analytics,* aiming to show that knowledge and epistemic justification have a two-tier structure as described by epistemic foundationalism. It lends itself to the following outline regarding justification. If you have any justified belief, this belief occurs in an evidential chain including at least two links: the supporting link (i.e., the evidence) and the supported link (i.e., the justified belief). This does not mean, however, that all evidence consists of beliefs. Evidential chains might come in any of four kinds: circular chains, endless chains, chains ending in unjustified beliefs, and chains anchored in foundational beliefs that do not derive their justification from other beliefs. Only the fourth, foundationalist kind is defensible as grounding knowledge and epistemic justification.

Could all justification be inferential? A belief, *B1*, is *inferentially* justified when it owes its justification, at least in part, to some other belief, *B2*. Whence the justification for *B2?* If *B2* owes its justification to *B1*, we have a troublesome circle. How can *B2* yield justification (or evidence) for *B1*, if *B2* owes its evidential status to *B1?* On the other hand, if *B2* owes its justification to another belief, *B3*, and *B3* owes its justification to yet another belief, *B4*, and so on ad infinitum, we have a troublesome endless regress of justification. Such a regress seems to deliver not actual justification, but at best merely potential justification, for the belief at its head. Actual finite humans, furthermore, seem not to be able to comprehend, or to possess, all the steps of an infinite regress of justification. Finally, if *B2* is itself unjustified, it evidently will be unable to provide justification for *B1*. It seems, then, that the structure of inferential justification does not consist of either circular justification, endless regresses of justification, or unjustified starter-beliefs.

We have foundationalism, then, as the most viable account of evidential chains, so long as we understand it as the structural view that some beliefs are justified non-inferentially (i.e., without deriving justification from other beliefs), but can nonetheless provide justification for other beliefs. More precisely, if we have any justified beliefs, we have some foundational, non-inferentially justified beliefs. This regress argument needs some refinement before its full force can be appreciated. With suitable refinement, however, it can seriously challenge such alternatives to foundationalism as coherentism and contextualism. The regress argument has been a key motivation for foundationalism in the history of epistemology.

See also COHERENTISM, EPISTEMOLOGY, FOUNDATIONALISM.   P.K.M.

epistemics. See GOLDMAN.

epistemic virtue. See VIRTUE EPISTEMOLOGY.

epistemology (from Greek *episteme*, 'knowledge', and *logos*, 'explanation'), the study of the nature of knowledge and justification; specifically, the study of (a) the defining features, (b) the substantive conditions or sources, and (c) the limits of knowledge and justification. The latter three categories are represented by traditional philosophical controversy over the analysis of knowledge and justification, the sources of knowledge and justification (e.g., rationalism versus empiricism), and the viability of skepticism about knowledge and justification.

Kinds of knowledge. Knowledge can be either explicit or tacit. Explicit knowledge is self-conscious in that the knower is aware of the relevant state of knowledge, whereas tacit knowledge is implicit, hidden from self-consciousness. Much of our knowledge is tacit: it is genuine but we are unaware of the relevant states of knowledge, even if we can achieve awareness upon suitable reflection. In this regard, knowledge resembles many of our psychological states. The existence of a psychological state in a person does not require the person's awareness of that state, although it may require the person's awareness of an object of that state (such as what is sensed or perceived).

Philosophers have identified various species of knowledge: for example, propositional knowledge (*that* something is so), non-propositional knowledge *of* something (e.g., knowledge by acquaintance, or by direct awareness), empirical (a posteriori) propositional knowledge, non-empirical (a priori) propositional knowledge, and knowledge of how to do something. Philosophical controversy has arisen over distinctions between such species, for example, over (i) the relations between some of these species (e.g., does knowing-how reduce to knowledge-that?), and (ii) the viability of some of these species (e.g., is there really such a thing as, or even a coherent notion of, a priori knowledge?). A primary concern of classical modern philosophy, in the seventeenth and eighteenth centuries, was the extent of our a priori knowledge relative to the extent of our a posteriori knowledge. Such rationalists as Descartes, Leibniz, and Spinoza contended that all genuine knowledge of the real world is a priori, whereas such empiricists as Locke, Berkeley, and Hume argued that all such knowledge is a posteriori. In his *Critique of Pure Reason* (1781), Kant sought a grand reconciliation, aiming to preserve the key lessons of both rationalism and empiricism.

Since the seventeenth and eighteenth centuries, a posteriori knowledge has been widely regarded as knowledge that depends for its supporting ground on some specific sensory or perceptual experience; and a priori knowledge has been widely regarded as knowledge that does not depend for its supporting ground on such experience. Kant and others have held that the supporting ground for a priori knowledge comes solely from purely intellectual processes called "pure reason" or "pure understanding." Knowledge of logical and mathematical truths typically serves as a standard case of a priori knowledge, whereas knowledge of the existence or presence of physical objects typically serves as a standard case of a posteriori knowledge. A major task for an account of a priori knowledge is the explanation of what the relevant purely intellectual processes are, and of how they contribute to non-empirical knowledge. An analogous task for an account of a posteriori knowledge is the explanation of what sensory or perceptual experience is and how it contributes to empirical knowledge. More fundamentally, epistemologists have sought an account of propositional knowledge *in general,* i.e., an account of what is common to a priori and a posteriori knowledge.

Ever since Plato's *Meno* and *Theaetetus* (c.400 B.C.), epistemologists have tried to identify the essential, defining components of knowledge. Identifying these components will yield an analysis of knowledge. A prominent traditional view, suggested by Plato and Kant among others, is that propositional knowledge (*that* something is so) has three individually necessary and jointly sufficient components: justification, truth, and belief. On this view, propositional knowledge is, by definition, justified true belief. This is the tripartite definition that has come to be called the *standard analysis.* We can clarify it by attending briefly to each of its three conditions.

The belief condition. This requires that anyone who knows that p (where 'p' stands for any proposition or statement) must believe that p. If, therefore, you do not believe that minds are brains (say, because you have not considered the matter at all), then you do not know that minds are brains. A knower must be psychologically related somehow to a proposition that is an object of knowledge for that knower. Proponents of the standard analysis hold that only belief can provide the needed psychological relation. Philosophers do not share a uniform account of belief, but some considerations supply common ground. Beliefs are not actions of assenting to a proposition; they rather are dispositional psychological states that can exist even when unmanifested. (You do not cease believing that

$2 + 2 = 4$, for example, whenever your attention leaves arithmetic.) Our believing that p seems to require that we have a *tendency* to assent to p in certain situations, but it seems also to be more than just such a tendency. What else believing requires remains highly controversial among philosophers.

Some philosophers have opposed the belief condition of the standard analysis on the ground that we can accept, or assent to, a known proposition without actually believing it. They contend that we can accept a proposition even if we fail to acquire a tendency, required by believing, to accept that proposition in certain situations. On this view, acceptance is a psychological act that does not entail any dispositional psychological state, and such acceptance is sufficient to relate a knower psychologically to a known proposition. However this view fares, one underlying assumption of the standard analysis seems correct: our concept of knowledge requires that a knower be psychologically related somehow to a known proposition. Barring that requirement, we shall be hard put to explain how knowers *psychologically possess* their knowledge of known propositions.

Even if knowledge requires belief, belief that p does not require knowledge that p, since belief can typically be false. This observation, familiar from Plato's *Theaetetus,* assumes that knowledge has a truth condition. On the standard analysis, if you know that p, then it is true that p. If, therefore, it is false that minds are brains, then you do not know that minds are brains. It is thus misleading to say, e.g., that astronomers before Copernicus knew that the earth is flat; at best, they justifiably believed that they knew this.

The truth condition. This condition of the standard analysis has not attracted any serious challenge. Controversy over it has focused instead on Pilate's vexing question: What is truth? This question concerns what truth *consists in,* not our ways of *finding out* what is true. Influential answers come from at least three approaches: truth as correspondence (i.e., agreement, of some specified sort, between a proposition and an actual situation); truth as coherence (i.e., interconnectedness of a proposition with a specified system of propositions); and truth as pragmatic cognitive value (i.e., usefulness of a proposition in achieving certain intellectual goals). Without assessing these prominent approaches, we should recognize, in accord with the standard analysis, that our concept of knowledge seems to have a factual requirement: we genuinely know that p only if *it is the case that p*. The pertinent notion of "its being the case" seems equivalent to the notion of "how reality is" or "how things really are." The latter notion seems essential to our notion of knowledge, but is open to controversy over its explication.

The justification condition. Knowledge is not simply true belief. Some true beliefs are supported only by lucky guesswork and hence do not qualify as knowledge. Knowledge requires that the satisfaction of its belief condition be "appropriately related" to the satisfaction of its truth condition. This is one broad way of understanding the justification condition of the standard analysis. More specifically, we might say that a knower must have *adequate indication* that a known proposition is true. If we understand such adequate indication as a sort of *evidence* indicating that a proposition is true, we have reached the traditional general view of the justification condition: justification as evidence. Questions about justification attract the lion's share of attention in contemporary epistemology. Controversy focuses on the meaning of 'justification' as well as on the substantive conditions for a belief's being justified in a way appropriate to knowledge.

Current debates about the meaning of 'justification' revolve around the question whether, and if so how, the concept of epistemic (knowledge-relevant) justification is normative. Since the 1950s Chisholm has defended the following deontological (obligation-oriented) notion of justification: the claim that a proposition, p, is epistemically justified for you *means* that it is false that you ought to refrain from accepting p. In other terms, to say that p is epistemically justified is to say that accepting p is *epistemically permissible* – at least in the sense that accepting p is consistent with a certain set of epistemic rules. This deontological construal enjoys wide representation in contemporary epistemology. A normative construal of justification need not be deontological; it need not use the notions of obligation and permission. Alston, for instance, has introduced a non-deontological normative concept of justification that relies mainly on the notion of what is *epistemically good* from the viewpoint of maximizing truth and minimizing falsity. Alston links epistemic goodness to a belief's being based on adequate grounds in the absence of overriding reasons to the contrary.

Some epistemologists shun normative construals of justification as superfluous. One noteworthy view is that 'epistemic justification' means simply 'evidential support' of a certain sort. To say that p is epistemically justifiable to some extent for you is, on this view, just to say that p is supportable to some extent by your overall evidential reasons. This construal will be non-normative so long as the notions of supportability and an evidential reason are non-normative. Some philosophers have tried to explicate the latter notions without relying on talk of epistemic permissibility or epistemic goodness. We can understand the relevant notion of "support" in terms of non-normative notions of entailment and explanation (or, answering why-questions). We can understand the notion of an "evidential reason" via the notion of a psychological state that can stand in a certain truth-indicating support relation to propositions. For instance, we might regard non-doxastic states of "seeming to perceive" something (e.g., seeming to see a dictionary here) as foundational truth indicators for certain physical-object propositions (e.g., the proposition that there is a dictionary here), in virtue of those states being best explained by those propositions. If anything resembling this approach succeeds, we can get by without the aforementioned normative notions of epistemic justification.

Foundationalism versus coherentism. Talk of foundational truth indicators brings us to a key controversy over justification: Does epistemic justification, and thus knowledge, have foundations, and if so, in what sense? This question can be clarified as the issue whether some beliefs can not only (a) have their epistemic justification *non-inferentially* (i.e., apart from evidential support from any other beliefs), but also (b) provide epistemic justification for all justified beliefs that lack such non-inferential justification. Foundationalism gives an affirmative answer to this issue, and is represented in varying ways by, e.g., Aristotle, Descartes, Russell, C. I. Lewis, and Chisholm.

Foundationalists do not share a uniform account of non-inferential justification. Some construe non-inferential justification as *self*-justification. Others reject literal self-justification for beliefs, and argue that foundational beliefs have their non-inferential justification in virtue of evidential support from the deliverances of *non*-belief psychological states, e.g., perception ("seem-ing-to-perceive" states), sensation ("seem-ing-to-sense" states), or memory ("seeming-to-remember" states). Still others understand non-inferential justification in terms of a belief's being "reliably produced," i.e., caused and sustained by some non-belief belief-producing process or source (e.g., perception, memory, introspection) that tends to produce true rather than false beliefs. This last view takes the causal source of a belief to be crucial to its justification. Unlike Descartes, contemporary foundationalists clearly separate claims to non-inferential, foundational justification from claims to certainty. They typically settle for a *modest* foundationalism implying that foundational beliefs need not be indubitable or infallible. This contrasts with the radical foundationalism of Descartes.

The traditional competitor to foundationalism is the coherence theory of justification, i.e., epistemic coherentism. This is not the coherence definition of truth; it rather is the view that the *justification* of any belief depends on that belief's having evidential support from some other belief via coherence relations such as entailment or explanatory relations. Notable proponents include Hegel, Bosanquet, and Sellars. A prominent contemporary version of epistemic coherentism states that evidential coherence relations among beliefs are typically explanatory relations. The rough idea is that a belief is justified for you so long as it either best explains, or is best explained by, some member of the system of beliefs that has maximal explanatory power for you. Contemporary coherentism is uniformly systemic or holistic; it finds the ultimate source of justification in a *system* of interconnected beliefs or potential beliefs.

One problem has troubled all versions of coherentism that aim to explain empirical justification: the *isolation argument*. According to this argument, coherentism entails that you can be epistemically justified in accepting an empirical proposition that is incompatible with, or at least improbable given, your total empirical evidence. The key assumption of this argument is that your total empirical evidence includes *non*-belief sensory and perceptual awareness-states, such as your feeling pain or your seeming to see something. These are not belief-states. Epistemic coherentism, by definition, makes justification a function solely of coherence relations between propositions, such as propositions one believes or accepts. Thus, such coherentism seems to isolate justification from the evidential import of non-belief awareness-states. Coherentists have tried to handle this problem, but no resolution enjoys wide acceptance.

Causal and contextualist theories. Some contemporary epistemologists endorse contextual-

ism regarding epistemic justification, a view suggested by Dewey, Wittgenstein, and Kuhn, among others. On this view, all justified beliefs depend for their evidential support on some unjustified beliefs that need no justification. In any context of inquiry, people simply assume (the acceptability of) some propositions as starting points for inquiry, and these "contextually basic" propositions, though lacking evidential support, can serve as evidential support for other propositions. Contextualists stress that contextually basic propositions can vary from context to context (e.g., from theological inquiry to biological inquiry) and from social group to social group. The main problem for contextualists comes from their view that *un*justified assumptions can provide epistemic justification for other propositions. We need a precise explanation of how an unjustified assumption can yield evidential support, how a non-probable belief can make another belief probable. Contextualists have not given a uniform explanation here.

Recently some epistemologists have recommended that we give up the traditional evidence condition for knowledge. They recommend that we construe the justification condition as a *causal* condition. Roughly, the idea is that you know that *p* if and only if (a) you believe that *p*, (b) *p* is true, and (c) your believing that *p* is causally produced and sustained by the fact that makes *p* true. This is the basis of *the causal theory of knowing*, which comes with varying details. Any such causal theory faces serious problems from our knowledge of universal propositions. Evidently, we know, for instance, that all dictionaries are produced by people, but our believing that this is so seems not to be causally supported by the fact that all dictionaries are humanly produced. It is not clear that the latter fact causally produces *any* beliefs.

Another problem is that causal theories typically neglect what seems to be crucial to any account of the justification condition: the requirement that justificational support for a belief be *accessible*, in some sense, to the believer. The rough idea is that one must be able to access, or bring to awareness, the justification underlying one's beliefs. The causal origins of a belief are, of course, often very complex and inaccessible to a believer. Causal theories thus face problems from an accessibility requirement on justification. *Internalism* regarding justification preserves an accessibility requirement on what confers justification, whereas epistemic *externalism* rejects this requirement. Debates over internalism and externalism abound in current epistemology, but internalists do not yet share a uniform detailed account of accessibility.

The Gettier problem. The standard analysis of knowledge, however elaborated, faces a devastating challenge that initially gave rise to causal theories of knowledge: the *Gettier problem*. In 1963 Edmund Gettier published a highly influential challenge to the view that if you have a justified true belief that *p*, then you know that *p*. Here is one of Gettier's counterexamples to this view: Smith is justified in believing the false proposition that (i) Jones owns a Ford. On the basis of (i), Smith infers, and thus is justified in believing, that (ii) either Jones owns a Ford or Brown is in Barcelona. As it happens, Brown is in Barcelona, and so (ii) is true. So, although Smith is justified in believing the true proposition (ii), Smith does not know (ii).

Gettier-style counterexamples are cases where a person has justified true belief that *p* but lacks knowledge that *p*. The Gettier problem is the problem of finding a modification of, or an alternative to, the standard analysis that avoids difficulties from Gettier-style counterexamples. The controversy over the Gettier problem is highly complex and still unsettled. Many epistemologists take the lesson of Gettier-style counterexamples to be that propositional knowledge requires a *fourth condition*, beyond the justification, truth, and belief conditions. No specific fourth condition has received overwhelming acceptance, but some proposals have become prominent. The so-called defeasibility condition, e.g., requires that the justification appropriate to knowledge be "undefeated" in the general sense that some appropriate subjunctive conditional concerning defeaters of justification be true of that justification. For instance, one simple defeasibility fourth condition requires of Smith's knowing that *p* that there be no true proposition, *q*, such that if *q* became justified for Smith, *p* would no longer be justified for Smith. So if Smith knows, on the basis of his visual perception, that Mary removed books from the library, then Smith's coming to believe the true proposition that Mary's identical twin removed books from the library would not undermine the justification for Smith's belief concerning Mary herself. A different approach shuns subjunctive conditionals of that sort, and contends that propositional knowledge requires justified true belief that is sustained by the collective totality of actual truths. This approach requires a detailed account of when justification is undermined and restored.

The Gettier problem is epistemologically important. One branch of epistemology seeks a precise understanding of the nature (e.g., the essential components) of propositional knowledge. Our having a precise understanding of propositional knowledge requires our having a Gettier-proof analysis of such knowledge. Epistemologists thus need a defensible solution to the Gettier problem, however complex that solution is.

Skepticism. Epistemologists debate the limits, or scope, of knowledge. The more restricted we take the limits of knowledge to be, the more skeptical we are. Two influential types of skepticism are *knowledge skepticism* and *justification skepticism*. Unrestricted knowledge skepticism implies that no one knows anything, whereas unrestricted justification skepticism implies the more extreme view that no one is even justified in believing anything. Some forms of skepticism are stronger than others. Knowledge skepticism in its strongest form implies that it is *impossible* for anyone to know anything. A weaker form would deny the actuality of our having knowledge, but leave open its possibility. Many skeptics have restricted their skepticism to a particular domain of supposed knowledge: e.g., knowledge of the external world, knowledge of other minds, knowledge of the past or the future, or knowledge of unperceived items. Such limited skepticism is more common than unrestricted skepticism in the history of epistemology.

Arguments supporting skepticism come in many forms. One of the most difficult is the *problem of the criterion*, a version of which has been stated by the sixteenth-century skeptic Montaigne: "To adjudicate [between the true and the false] among the appearances of things, we need to have a distinguishing method; to validate this method, we need to have a justifying argument; but to validate this justifying argument, we need the very method at issue. And there we are, going round on the wheel." This line of skeptical argument originated in ancient Greece, with epistemology itself. It forces us to face this question: How can we specify *what* we know without having specified *how* we know, and how can we specify *how* we know without having specified *what* we know? Is there any reasonable way out of this threatening circle? This is one of the most difficult epistemological problems, and a cogent epistemology must offer a defensible solution to it. Contemporary epistemology still lacks a widely accepted reply to this urgent problem.

See also A PRIORI, COHERENTISM, FOUNDATIONALISM, JUSTIFICATION, PERCEPTION, SKEPTICISM, TRUTH.   P.K.M.

epistemology, evolutionary. See EVOLUTIONARY EPISTEMOLOGY.

epistemology, genetic. See PIAGET.

epistemology, naturalistic. See NATURALISTIC EPISTEMOLOGY.

episyllogism. See POLYSYLLOGISM.

epoché. See HUSSERL, PHENOMENOLOGY.

E-proposition. See SYLLOGISM.

epsilon. See Appendix of Special Symbols.

equipollence, term used by Sextus Empiricus to express the view that there are arguments of equal strength on all sides of any question and that therefore we should suspend judgment on every question that can be raised. **See also** SEXTUS EMPIRICUS.   R.P.

equipossible. See EQUIPROBABLE.

equiprobable, having the same probability. Sometimes used in the same way as 'equipossible', the term is associated with Laplace's (the "classical") interpretation of probability, where the probability of an event is the ratio of the number of equipossibilities favorable to the event to the total number of equipossibilities. For example, the probability of rolling an even number with a "fair" six-sided die is ½ – there being *three* equipossibilities (2, 4, 6) favorable to even, and *six* equipossibilities (1, 2, 3, 4, 5, 6) in all (and $^3/_6 = ½$). The concept is now generally thought not to be widely applicable to the interpretation of probability, since natural equipossibilities are not always at hand (as in assessing the probability of a thermonuclear war tomorrow). **See also** PROBABILITY.   E.Ee.

equivalence, mutual inferability. The following are main kinds: two statements are materially equivalent provided they have the same truth-value, and logically equivalent provided each can be deduced from the other; two sentences or words are equivalent in meaning provided they can be substituted for each other in any context without altering the meaning of that context. In truth-functional logic, two statements are logically equivalent if they can never have truth-values different from each other. In this sense of 'logically equivalent' all tautologies are equivalent to each other and all contradictions are equivalent to each other. Similarly, in extensional set theory, two classes are equivalent provided they have the same numbers, so that all empty classes are regarded as equivalent. In a non-extensional set theory, classes would be equivalent only if their conditions of membership were logically equivalent or equivalent in meaning.   R.P.

equivalence, behavioral. See TURING MACHINE.

equivalence class. See PARTITION, RELATION.

equivalence condition. See CONFIRMATION.

equivalence relation. See PARTITION, RELATION.

equivocation, the use of an expression in two or more different senses in a single context. For example, in 'The end of anything is its perfection. But the end of life is death; so death is the perfection of life', the expression 'end' is first used in the sense of 'goal or purpose,' but in its second occurrence 'end' means 'termination.' The use of the two senses in this context is an equivocation. Where the context in which the expression used is an argument, the fallacy of equivocation may be committed. **See also** INFORMAL FALLACY.   W.K.W.

equivocation, fallacy of. See INFORMAL FALLACY.

Er, myth of. See MYTH OF ER.

Erasmus, Desiderius (1466?–1536), Dutch scholar and philosopher who played an important role in Renaissance humanism. Like his Italian forerunners Petrarch, Coluccio Salutati, Lorenzo Valla, Leonardo Bruni, and others, Erasmus stressed within philosophy and theology the function of philological precision, grammatical correctness, and rhetorical elegance. But for Erasmus the virtues of *bonae literarae* which are cultivated by the study of authors of Latin and Greek antiquity must be decisively linked with Christian spirituality. Erasmus has been called (by Huizinga) the first modern intellectual because he tried to influence and reform the mentality of society by working within the shadow of ecclesiastical and political leaders. He became one of the first humanists to make efficient use of the then new medium of printing. His writings embrace various forms, including diatribe, oration, locution, comment, dialogue, and letter.

After studying in Christian schools and living for a time in the monastery of Steyn near Gouda in the Netherlands, Erasmus worked for different patrons. He gained a post as secretary to the bishop of Kamerijk, during which time he wrote his first published book, the *Adagia* (first edition 1500), a collection of annotated Latin adages. Erasmus was an adviser to the Emperor Charles V, to whom he dedicated his *Institutio principii christiani* (1516). After studies at the University of Paris, where he attended lectures by the humanist Faber Stapulensis, Erasmus was put in touch by his patron Lord Mountjoy with the British humanists John Colet and Thomas More. Erasmus led a restless life, residing in several European cities including London, Louvain, Basel, Freiburg, Bologna, Turin (where he was awarded a doctorate of theology in 1506), and Rome.

By using the means of modern philology, which led to the ideal of the *bonae literarae*, Erasmus tried to reform the Christian-influenced mentality of his times. Inspired by Valla's *Annotationes* to the New Testament, he completed a new Latin translation of the New Testament, edited the writings of the early church fathers, especially St. Hieronymus, and wrote several commentaries on psalms. He tried to regenerate the spirit of early Christianity by laying bare its original sense against the background of scholastic interpretation. In his view, the rituals of the existing church blocked the development of an authentic Christian spirituality. Though Erasmus shared with Luther a critical approach toward the existing church, he did not side with the Reformation. His *Diatribe de libero arbitrio* (1524), in which he pleaded for the free will of man, was answered by Luther's *De servo arbitrio*.

The historically most influential books of Erasmus were *Enchirion militis christiani* (1503), in which he attacked hirelings and soldiers; the *Encomium moriae id est Laus stultitiae* (1511), a satire on modern life and the ecclesiastical pillars of society; and the sketches of human life, the *Colloquia* (first published in 1518, often enlarged until 1553). In the small book *Querela pacis* (1517), he rejected the ideology of justified wars propounded by Augustine and Aquinas. Against the madness of war Erasmus appealed to the virtues of tolerance, friendliness, and gentleness. All these virtues were for him the essence of Christianity.

See also HUMANISM; MORE, THOMAS.   H.P.

Erfahrung, German term translated into English, especially since Kant, as 'experience'. Kant does not use it as a technical term; rather, it indicates that which requires explanation through more precisely drawn technical distinctions such as those among 'sensibility', 'understanding', and 'reason'. In the early twentieth century, Husserl sometimes distinguishes between *Erfahrung* and *Erlebnis,* the former indicating experience as capable of being thematized and methodically described or analyzed, the latter experience as "lived through" and never fully available to analysis. Such a distinction occasionally reappears in later texts of phenomenology and existentialism. **See also** ERLEBNIS.   J.P.Su.

Erigena, John Scotus, also called John the Scot, Eriugena, and Scottigena (c.810–77), Irish-born scholar and theologian. He taught grammar and dialectics at the court of Charles the Bald near Laon from 845 on. In a controversy in 851, John argued that there was only one predestination, to good, since evil was strictly nothing. Thus no one is compelled to evil by God's foreknowledge, since, strictly speaking, God has no foreknowledge of what is not. But his reliance on dialectic, his Origenist conception of the world as a place of education repairing the damage done by sin, his interest in cosmology, and his perceived Pelagian tendencies excited opposition. Attacked by Prudentius of Troyes and Flores of Lyons, he was condemned at the councils of Valencia (855) and Langres (859). Charles commissioned him to translate the works of Pseudo-Dionysius and the *Ambigua* of Maximus the Confessor from the Greek. These works opened up a new world, and John followed his translations with commentaries on the Gospel of John and Pseudo-Dionysius, and then his chief work, the *Division of Nature* or *Periphyseon* (826–66), in the Neoplatonic tradition. He treats the universe as a procession from God, everything real in nature being a trace of God, and then a return to God through the presence of nature in human reason and man's union with God. John held that the nature of man is not destroyed by union with God, though it is deified. He was condemned for pantheism at Paris in 1210.   J.Lo.

eristic, the art of controversy, often involving fallacious but persuasive reasoning. The ancient Sophists brought this art to a high level to achieve their personal goal. They may have found their material in the "encounters" in the law courts as well as in daily life. To enhance persuasion they endorsed the use of unsound principles such as hasty generalizations, faulty analogies, illegitimate appeal to authority, the *post hoc ergo propter hoc* (i.e., "after this, therefore because of this") and other presumed principles. Aristotle exposed eristic argumentation in his *Sophistical Refutations*, which itself draws examples from Plato's *Euthydemus*. From this latter work comes the famous example: 'That dog is a father and that dog is his, therefore that dog is his father'. What is perhaps worse than its obvious invalidity is that the argument is superficially similar to a sound argument such as 'This is a table and this is brown, therefore this is a brown table'. In the *Sophistical Refutations* Aristotle undertakes to find procedures for detection of bad arguments and to propose rules for constructing sound arguments. **See also** DIALECTIC, INFORMAL FALLACY, SYLLOGISM.   I.Bo.

Erklärung. See VERSTEHEN.

Erlebnis, German term for experience used in late nineteenth- and early twentieth-century German philosophy. *Erlebnis* denotes experience in all its direct immediacy and lived fullness. It contrasts with the more typical German word *Erfahrung*, denoting ordinary experience as mediated through intellectual and constructive elements. As immediate, *Erlebnis* eludes conceptualization, in both the lived present and the interiority of experience. As direct, *Erlebnis* is also disclosive and extraordinary: it reveals something real that otherwise escapes thinking. Typical examples include art, religion, and love, all of which also show the anti-rationalist and polemical uses of the concept. It is especially popular among the Romantic mystics like Novalis and the anti-rationalists Nietzsche and Bergson, as well as in phenomenology, *Lebensphilosophie*, and existentialism.

As used in post-Hegelian German philosophy, the term describes two aspects of subjectivity. The first concerns the epistemology of the human sciences and of phenomenology. Against naturalism and objectivism, philosophers appeal to the ineliminable, subjective qualities of experience to argue that interpreters must understand "what it is like to be" some experiencing subject, from the inside. The second use of the term is to denote extraordinary and interior experiences like art, religion, freedom, and vital energy. In both cases, it is unclear how such experience could be identified or known in its immediacy, and much recent German thought,

such as Heidegger and hermeneutics, rejects the concept.
See also ERFAHRUNG, EXISTENTIALISM, PHENOMENOLOGY.   J.Bo.

Eros, the Greek god of erotic love. Eros came to be symbolic of various aspects of love, first appearing in Hesiod in opposition to reason. In general, however, Eros was seen by Greeks (e.g., Parmenides) as a unifying force. In Empedocles, it is one of two external forces explaining the history of the cosmos, the other being Strife. These forces resemble the "hidden harmony" of Heraclitus.

The *Symposium* of Plato is the best-known ancient discussion of Eros, containing speeches from various standpoints – mythical, sophistic, etc. Socrates says he has learned from the priestess Diotima of a nobler form of Eros in which sexual desire can be developed into the pursuit of understanding the Form of beauty.

The contrast between agape and Eros is found first in Democritus. This became important in Christian accounts of love. In Neoplatonism, Eros referred to the mystical union with Being sought by philosophers. Eros has become important recently in the work of Continental writers.
See also AGAPE.   R.C.

erotetic, in the strict sense, pertaining to questions. Erotetic logic is the logic of questions. Different conceptions of questions yield different kinds of erotetic logic. A Platonistic approach holds that questions exist independently of interrogatives. For P. Tichý, a question is a function on possible worlds, the right answer being the value of the function at the actual world. Erotetic logic is the logic of such functions. In the epistemic-imperative approach (of L. Åqvist, Hintikka, et al.), one begins with a system for epistemic sentences and embeds this in a system for imperative sentences, thus obtaining sentences of the form 'make it the case that I know . . .' and complex compounds of such sentences. Certain ones of these are defined to be interrogatives. Then erotetic logic is the logic of epistemic imperatives and the conditions for satisfaction of these imperatives. In the abstract interrogative approach (of N. Belnap, T. Kubiński, and many others), one chooses certain types of expression to serve as interrogatives, and, for each type, specifies what expressions count as answers of various kinds (direct, partial, . . .). On this approach we may say that interrogatives express questions, or we may identify questions with interrogatives, in which case the only meaning that an interrogative has is that it has the answers that it does. Either way, the emphasis is on interrogatives, and erotetic logic is the logic of systems that provide interrogatives and specify answers to them.

In the broad sense, 'erotetic' designates what pertains to utterance-and-response. In this sense erotetic logic is the logic of the relations between (1) sentences of many kinds and (2) the expressions that count as appropriate replies to them. This includes not only the relations between question and answer but also, e.g., between assertion and agreement or denial, command and report of compliance or refusal, and (for many types of sentence *S*) between *S* and various corrective replies to *S* (e.g., denial of the presupposition of *S*). Erotetic logics may differ in the class of sentences treated, the types of response counted as appropriate, the assignment of other content (presupposition, projection, etc.), and other details. **See also** DEONTIC LOGIC, EPISTEMIC LOGIC, MODAL LOGIC.   D.H.

error theory. See MORAL REALISM.

***Esprit* movement.** See FRENCH PERSONALISM.

Esse est percipi. See BERKELEY.

essence. See ESSENTIALISM.

essence, nominal. See ESSENTIALISM.

essence, real. See ESSENTIALISM.

essentialism, a metaphysical theory that objects have essences and that there is a distinction between essential and non-essential or accidental predications. Different issues have, however, been central in debates about essences and essential predication in different periods in the history of philosophy. In our own day, it is commitment to the notion of *de re* modality that is generally taken to render a theory essentialist; but in the essentialist tradition stemming from Aristotle, discussions of essence and essential predication focus on the distinction between *what* an object is and *how* it is. According to Aristotle, the universals that an ordinary object instantiates include some that mark it out as what it is and others that characterize it in some way but do not figure in an account of what it is. In the *Categories,* he tells us that while the former are *said of* the object, the latter are merely *present in* it; and in other writings, he distinguishes between what he calls *kath hauto* or per se predications (where these include the predication of what-universals) and *kata sumbebekos* or *per accidens* predications (where these include the predication of how-universals). He concedes that universals predicated of an object *kath hauto* are necessary to that object; but he construes the necessity here as derivative. It is because a universal marks out an entity, *x*, as what *x* is and hence underlies its being the thing that it is that the universal is necessarily predicated of *x*.

The concept of definition is critically involved in Aristotle's essentialism. First, it is the kind – *infima species* – under which an object falls or one of the items (genus or differentia) included in the definition of that kind that is predicated of the object *kath hauto*. But, second, Aristotle's notion of an essence just is the notion of the ontological correlate of a definition. The term in his writings we translate as 'essence' is the expression *to ti ein einai* (the what it is to be). Typically, the expression is followed by a substantival expression in the dative case, so that the expressions denoting essences are phrases like 'the what it is to be for a horse' and 'the what it is to be for an oak tree'; and Aristotle tells us that, for any kind, *K*, the what it is to be for a *K* just is that which we identify when we provide a complete and accurate definition of *K*.

Now, Aristotle holds that there is definition only of universals; and this commits him to the view that there are no individual essences. Although he concedes that we can provide definitions of universals from any of his list of ten categories, he gives pride of place to the essences of universals from the category of substance. Substance-universals can be identified without reference to essences from other categories, but the essences of qualities, quantities, and other non-substances can be defined only by reference to the essences of substances. In his early writings, Aristotle took the familiar particulars of common sense (things like the individual man and horse of *Categories* V) to be the primary substances; and in these writings it is the essences we isolate by defining the kinds or species under which familiar particulars fall that are construed as the basic or paradigmatic essences. However, in later writings, where ordinary particulars are taken to be complexes of matter and form, it is the substantial forms of familiar particulars that are the primary substances, so their essences are the primary or basic essences; and a central theme in Aristotle's most mature writings is the idea that the primary substances and their essences are necessarily one and the same in number.

The conception of essence as the ontological correlate of a definition – often called quiddity – persists throughout the medieval tradition; and in early modern philosophy, the idea that the identity of an object is constituted by what it is plays an important role in Continental rationalist thinkers. Indeed, in the writings of Leibniz, we find the most extreme version of traditional essentialism. Whereas Aristotle had held that essences are invariably general, Leibniz insisted that each individual has an essence peculiar to it. He called the essence associated with an entity its complete individual concept; and he maintained that the individual concept somehow entails all the properties exemplified by the relevant individual. Accordingly, Leibniz believed that an omniscient being could, for each possible world and each possible individual, infer from the individual concept of that individual the whole range of properties exemplified by that individual in that possible world. But, then, from the perspective of an omniscient being, all of the propositions identifying the properties the individual actually exhibits would express what Aristotle called *kath hauto* predications. Leibniz, of course, denied that our perspective is that of an omniscient being; we fail to grasp individual essences in their fullness, so from our perspective, the distinction between essential and accidental predications holds.

While classical rationalists espoused a thoroughgoing essentialism, the Aristotlelian conceptions of essence and definition were the repeated targets of attacks by classical British empiricists. Hobbes, e.g., found the notion of essence philosophically useless and insisted that definition merely displays the meanings conventionally associated with linguistic expressions. Locke, on the other hand, continued to speak of essences; but he distinguished between real and nominal essences. As he saw it, the familiar objects of common sense are collections of copresent sensible ideas to which we attach a single name like 'man' or 'horse'. Identifying the ideas constitutive of the relevant collection gives us the nominal essence of a man or a horse. Locke did not deny that real essences might underlie such collections, but he insisted that it is nominal rather than real essences to which we have epistemic access. Hume, in turn, endorsed the idea that familiar objects are collections of sensible ideas, but rejected the idea of some underlying real essence to which we have no access; and he implicitly reinforced the Hobbesian critique of Aristotelian essences with his attack on the idea of *de re* necessities. So definition merely expresses the meanings we conventionally associate with words, and the only necessity associated with definition is linguistic or verbal necessity.

From its origins, the twentieth-century analytic tradition endorsed the classical empiricist critique of essences and the Humean view that necessity is merely linguistic. Indeed, even the Humean concession that there is a special class of statements true in virtue of their meanings came into question in the forties and fifties, when philosophers like Quine argued that it is impossible to provide a noncircular criterion for distinguishing analytic and synthetic statements. So by the late 1950s, it had become the conventional wisdom of philosophers in the Anglo-American tradition that both the notion of a real essence and the derivative idea that some among the properties true of an object are essential to that object are philosophical dead ends. But over the past three decades, developments in the semantics of modal logic have called into question traditional empiricist skepticism about essence and modality and have given rise to a rebirth of essentialism. In the late fifties and early sixties, logicians (like Kripke, Hintikka, and Richard Montague) showed how formal techniques that have as their intuitive core the Leibnizian idea that necessity is truth in all possible worlds enable us to provide completeness proofs for a whole range of nonequivalent modal logics. Metaphysicians seized on the intuitions underlying these formal methods. They proposed that we take the picture of alternative possible worlds seriously and claimed that attributions of *de dicto* modality (necessity and possibility as they apply to propositions) can be understood to involve quantification over possible worlds. Thus, to say that a proposition, *p*, is necessary is to say that for every possible world, *W*, *p* is true in *W*; and to say that *p* is possible is to say that there is at least one possible world, *W*, such that *p* is true in *W*.

These metaphysicians went on to claim that the framework of possible worlds enables us to make sense of *de re* modality. Whereas *de dicto* modality attaches to propositions taken as a whole, an ascription of *de re* modality identifies the modal status of an object's exemplification of an attribute. Thus, we speak of Socrates as being necessarily or essentially rational, but only contingently snub-nosed. Intuitively, the essential properties of an object are those it could not have lacked; whereas its contingent properties are properties it exemplifies but could have failed to exemplify. The "friends of possible worlds" insisted that we can make perfectly good sense of this intuitive distinction if we say that an object,

x, exhibits a property, P, essentially just in case x exhibits P in the actual world and in every possible world in which x exists and that x exhibits P merely contingently just in case x exhibits P in the actual world, but there is at least one possible world, W, such that x exists in W and fails to exhibit P in W.

Not only have these neo-essentialists invoked the Leibnizian conception of alternative possible worlds in characterizing the *de re* modalities, many have endorsed Leibniz's idea that each object has an individual essence or what is sometimes called a *haecceity*. As we have seen, the intuitive idea of an individual essence is the idea of a property an object exhibits essentially and that no other object could possibly exhibit; and contemporary essentialists have fleshed out this intuitive notion by saying that a property, P, is the haecceity or individual essence of an object, x, just in case (1) x exhibits P in the actual world and in all worlds in which x exists and (2) there is no possible world where an object distinct from x exhibits P. And some defenders of individual essences (like Plantinga) have followed Leibniz in holding that the haecceity of an object provides a complete concept of that object, a property such that it entails, for every possible world, W, and every property, P, either the proposition that the object in question has P in W or the proposition that it fails to have P in W. Accordingly, they agree that an omniscient being could infer from the individual essence of an object a complete account of the history of that object in each possible world in which it exists.

See also ARISTOTLE, DEFINITION, HAECCEITY, MODAL LOGIC, NECESSITY, POSSIBLE WORLDS.   M.J.L.

essentialism, mereological. See HAECCEITY, MEREOLOGY.

essential property. See PROPERTY.

eternal recurrence. See ETERNAL RETURN.

eternal return, the doctrine that the same events, occurring in the same sequence and involving the same things, have occurred infinitely many times in the past and will occur infinitely many times in the future. Attributed most notably to the Stoics and Nietzsche, the doctrine is antithetical to philosophical and religious viewpoints that claim that the world order is unique, contingent in part, and directed toward some goal. The Stoics interpret eternal return as the consequence of perpetual divine activity imposing exceptionless causal principles on the world in a supremely rational, providential way. The world, being the best possible, can only be repeated endlessly. The Stoics do not explain why the best world cannot be everlasting, making repetition unnecessary. It is not clear whether Nietzsche asserted eternal return as a cosmological doctrine or only as a thought experiment designed to confront one with the authenticity of one's life: would one affirm that life even if one were consigned to live it over again without end? On either interpretation, Nietzsche's version, like the Stoic version, stresses the inexorability and necessary interconnectedness of all things and events, although unlike the Stoic version, it rejects divine providence. **See also** NIETZSCHE, STOICISM.

W.E.M.

eternal return, law of. See COMPUTER THEORY.

eternity. See DIVINE ATTRIBUTES.

ethical absolutism. See RELATIVISM.

ethical constructivism, a form of anti-realism about ethics which holds that there are moral facts and truths, but insists that these facts and truths are in some way constituted by or dependent on our moral beliefs, reactions, or attitudes. For instance, an ideal observer theory that represents the moral rightness and wrongness of an act in terms of the moral approval and disapproval that an appraiser would have under suitably idealized conditions can be understood as a form of ethical constructivism. Another form of constructivism identifies the truth of a moral belief with its being part of the appropriate system of beliefs, e.g., of a system of moral and nonmoral beliefs that is internally coherent. Such a view would maintain a coherence theory of moral truth. Moral relativism is a constructivist view that allows for a plurality of moral facts and truths. Thus, if the idealizing conditions appealed to in an ideal observer theory allow that different appraisers can have different reactions to the same actions under ideal conditions, then that ideal observer theory will be a version of moral relativism as well as of ethical constructivism. Or, if different systems of moral beliefs satisfy the appropriate epistemic conditions (e.g. are equally coherent), then the truth or falsity of particular moral beliefs will have to be relativized to different moral systems or codes. **See also** ETHICAL OBJECTIVISM, ETHICS, IDEAL OBSERVER, RELATIVISM.   D.O.B.

ethical conventionalism. See RELATIVISM.

ethical dualism. See ZOROASTRIANISM.

ethical egoism. See EGOISM.

ethical eudaimonism. See EUDAIMONISM.

ethical hedonism. See HEDONISM.

ethical intuitionism. See ETHICS.

ethical naturalism. See ETHICS, MORAL REALISM, NATURALISM.

ethical nihilism. See RELATIVISM.

ethical objectivism, the view that the objects of the most basic concepts of ethics (which may be supposed to be values, obligations, duties, oughts, rights, or what not) exist, or that facts about them hold, objectively and that similarly worded ethical statements by different persons make the same factual claims (and thus do not concern merely the speaker's feelings). To say that a fact is objective, or that something has objective existence, is usually to say that its holding or existence is not derivative from its being thought to hold or exist. (In the Scholastic terminology still current in the seventeenth century 'objective' had the more or less contrary meaning of having status only as an object of thought.) In contrast, fact, or a thing's existence, is subjective if it holds or exists only in the sense that it is thought to hold or exist, or that it is merely a convenient human posit for practical purposes. A fact holds, or an object exists, *intersubjectively* if somehow its acknowledgment is binding on all thinking subjects (or all subjects in some specified group), although it does not hold or exist independently of their thinking about it. Some thinkers suppose that intersubjectivity is all that can ever properly be meant by objectivity.

Objectivism may be naturalist or non-naturalist. The naturalist objectivist believes that values, duties, or whatever are natural phenomena detectable by introspection, perception, or scientific inference. Thus values may be identified with certain empirical qualities of (anybody's) experience, or duties with empirical facts about the effects of action, e.g. as promoting or hindering social cohesion. The non-naturalist objectivist (eschewing what Moore called the *naturalistic fallacy*) believes that values or obligations (or whatever items he thinks most basic in ethics) exist independently of any belief about them, but that their existence is not a matter of any ordinary fact detectable in the above ways but can be revealed to ethical intuition as standing in a necessary (but not analytic) relation to natural phenomena.

'Ethical subjectivism' usually means the doctrine that ethical statements are simply reports on the speaker's feelings (though, confusingly enough, such statements may be objectively true or false). Perhaps it ought to mean the doctrine that nothing is good or bad but thinking makes it so. Attitude theories of morality, for which such statements express, rather than report upon, the speaker's feelings, are also, despite the objections of their proponents, sometimes called subjectivist.

In a more popular usage an objective matter of fact is one on which all reasonable persons can be expected to agree, while a matter is subjective if various alternative opinions can be accepted as reasonable. What is subjective in this sense may be quite objective in the more philosophical sense in question above.

See also ETHICS, MOORE, MORAL REALISM.
T.L.S.S.

ethical pragmatism. See MORAL EPISTEMOLOGY.

ethical relativism. See RELATIVISM.

ethical skepticism. See RELATIVISM.

ethics, the philosophical study of morality. The word is also commonly used interchangeably with 'morality' to mean the subject matter of this study; and sometimes it is used more narrowly to mean the moral principles of a particular tradition, group, or individual. Christian ethics and Albert Schweitzer's ethics are examples. In this article the word will be used exclusively to mean the philosophical study.

Ethics, along with logic, metaphysics, and epistemology, is one of the main branches of philosophy. It corresponds, in the traditional division of the field into formal, natural, and moral philosophy, to the last of these disciplines. It can in turn be divided into the general study of goodness, the general study of right action, applied ethics, metaethics, moral psychology, and the metaphysics of moral responsibility. These divisions are not sharp, and many important studies in ethics, particularly those that examine or develop whole systems of ethics, are interdivisional. Nonetheless, they facilitate the identification of different problems, movements, and schools within the discipline.

The first two, the general study of goodness and the general study of right action, constitute the main business of ethics. Correlatively, its principal substantive questions are what ends we ought, as fully rational human beings, to choose and pursue and what moral principles should govern our choices and pursuits. How these questions are related is the discipline's principal structural question, and structural differences among systems of ethics reflect different answers to this question. In contemporary ethics, the study of structure has come increasingly to the fore, especially as a preliminary to the general study of right action. In the natural order of exposition, however, the substantive questions come first.

Goodness and the question of ends. Philosophers have typically treated the question of the ends we ought to pursue in one of two ways: either as a question about the components of a good life or as a question about what sorts of things are good in themselves. On the first way of treating the question, it is assumed that we naturally seek a good life; hence, determining its components amounts to determining, relative to our desire for such a life, what ends we ought to pursue. On the second way, no such assumption about human nature is made; rather it is assumed that whatever is good in itself is worth choosing or pursuing. The first way of treating the question leads directly to the theory of human well-being. The second way leads directly to the theory of intrinsic value.

The first theory originated in ancient ethics, and *eudaimonia* was the Greek word for its subject, a word usually translated 'happiness,' but sometimes translated 'flourishing' in order to make the question of human well-being seem more a matter of how well a person is doing than how good he is feeling. These alternatives reflect the different conceptions of human well-being that inform the two major views within the theory: the view that feeling good or pleasure is the essence of human well-being and the view that doing well or excelling at things worth doing is its essence. The first view is hedonism in its classical form. Its most famous exponent among the ancients was Epicurus. The second view is perfectionism, a view that is common to several schools of ancient ethics. Its adherents include Plato, Aristotle, and the Stoics. Among the moderns, the best-known defenders of classical hedonism and perfectionism are respectively J. S. Mill and Nietzsche.

Although these two views differ on the question of what human well-being essentially consists in, neither thereby denies that the other's answer has a place in a good human life. Indeed, mature statements of each typically assign the other's answer an ancillary place. Thus, hedonism, as expounded by Epicurus, takes excelling at things worth doing – exercising one's intellectual powers and moral virtues in exemplary and fruitful ways, e.g. – as the tried and true means to experiencing life's most satisfying pleasures. And perfectionism, as developed in Aristotle's ethics, underscores the importance of pleasure – the deep satisfaction that comes from doing an important job well, e.g. – as a natural concomitant of achieving excellence in things that matter. The two views, as expressed in these mature statements, differ not so much in the kinds of activities they take to be central to a good life as in the ways they explain the goodness of such a life. The chief difference between them, then, is philosophical rather than prescriptive.

The second theory, the theory of intrinsic value, also has roots in ancient ethics, specifically, Plato's theory of Forms. But unlike Plato's theory, the basic tenets of which include certain doctrines about the reality and transcendence of value, the theory of intrinsic value neither contains nor presupposes any metaphysical theses. At issue in the theory is what things are good in themselves, and one can take a position on this issue without committing oneself to any thesis about the reality or unreality of goodness or about its transcendence or immanence. A list of the different things philosophers have considered good in themselves would include life, happiness, pleasure, knowledge, virtue, friendship, beauty, and harmony. The list could easily be extended.

An interest in what constitutes the goodness of the various items on the list has brought philosophers to focus primarily on the question of whether something unites them. The opposing views on this question are monism and pluralism. Monists affirm the list's unity; pluralists deny it. Plato, for instance, was a monist. He held that the goodness of everything good in itself consisted in harmony and therefore each such thing owed its goodness to its being harmonious. Alternatively, some philosophers have proposed pleasure as the sole constituent of goodness. Indeed, conceiving of pleasure as a particular kind of experience or state of consciousness, they have proposed this kind of experience as the only thing good in itself and characterized all other good things as instrumentally good, as owing their goodness to their being sources of pleasure. Thus, hedonism too can be a species of monism.

In this case, though, one must distinguish between the view that it is one's own experiences of pleasure that are intrinsically good and the view that anyone's experiences of pleasure, indeed, any sentient being's experiences of pleasure, are intrinsically good. The former is called (by Sidgwick) egoistic hedonism, the latter universal hedonism. This distinction can be made general, as a distinction between egoistic and universal views of what is good in itself or, as philosophers now commonly say, between agent-relative and agent-neutral value. As such, it indicates a significant point of disagreement in the theory of intrinsic value, a disagreement in which the seeming arbitrariness and blindness of egoism make it harder to defend. In drawing this conclusion, however, one must be careful not to mistake these egoistic views for views in the theory of human well-being, for each set of views represents a set of alternative answers to a different question. One must be careful, in other words, not to infer from the greater defensibility of universalism vis-à-vis egoism that universalism is the predominant view in the general study of goodness.

Right action. The general study of right action concerns the principles of right and wrong that govern our choices and pursuits. In modern ethics these principles are typically given a jural conception. Accordingly, they are understood to constitute a moral code that defines the duties of men and women who live together in fellowship. This conception of moral principles is chiefly due to the influence of Christianity in the West, though some of its elements were already present in Stoic ethics. Its ascendancy in the general study of right action puts the theory of duty at the center of that study.

The theory has two parts: the systematic exposition of the moral code that defines our duties; and its justification. The first part, when fully developed, presents complete formulations of the fundamental principles of right and wrong and shows how they yield all moral duties. The standard model is an axiomatic system in mathematics, though some philosophers have proposed a technical system of an applied science, such as medicine or strategy, as an alternative. The second part, if successful, establishes the authority of the principles and so validates the code. Various methods and criteria of justification are commonly used; no single one is canonical. Success in establishing the principles'

authority depends on the soundness of the argument that proceeds from whatever method or criterion is used.

One traditional criterion is implicit in the idea of an axiomatic system. On this criterion, the fundamental principles of right and wrong are authoritative in virtue of being self-evident truths. That is, they are regarded as comparable to axioms not only in being the first principles of a deductive system but also in being principles whose truth can be seen immediately upon reflection. Use of this criterion to establish the principles' authority is the hallmark of *intuitionism*. Once one of the dominant views in ethics, its position in the discipline has now been seriously eroded by a strong, twentieth-century tide of skepticism about all claims of self-evidence.

Currently, the most influential method of justification consistent with using the model of an axiomatic system to expound the morality of right and wrong draws on the jural conception of its principles. On this method, the principles are interpreted as expressions of a legislative will, and accordingly their authority derives from the sovereignty of the person or collective whose will they are taken to express. The oldest example of the method's use is the *divine command theory*. On this theory, moral principles are taken to be laws issued by God to humanity, and their authority thus derives from God's supremacy. The theory is the original Christian source of the principles' jural conception. The rise of secular thought since the Enlightenment has, however, limited its appeal. Later examples, which continue to attract broad interest and discussion, are formalism and contractarianism.

Formalism is best exemplified in Kant's ethics. It takes a moral principle to be a precept that satisfies the formal criteria of a universal law, and it takes formal criteria to be the marks of pure reason. Consequently, moral principles are laws that issue from reason. As Kant puts it, they are laws that we, as rational beings, give to ourselves and that regulate our conduct insofar as we engage each other's rational nature. They are laws for a republic of reason or, as Kant says, a kingdom of ends whose legislature comprises all rational beings. Through this ideal, Kant makes intelligible and forceful the otherwise obscure notion that moral principles derive their authority from the sovereignty of reason.

Contractarianism also draws inspiration from Kant's ethics as well as from the social contract theories of Locke and Rousseau. Its fullest and most influential statement appears in the work of Rawls. On this view, moral principles represent the ideal terms of social cooperation for people who live together in fellowship and regard each other as equals. Specifically, they are taken to be the conditions of an ideal agreement among such people, an agreement that they would adopt if they met as an assembly of equals to decide collectively on the social arrangements governing their relations and reached their decision as a result of open debate and rational deliberation. The authority of moral principles derives, then, from the fairness of the procedures by which the terms of social cooperation would be arrived at in this hypothetical constitutional convention and the assumption that any rational individual who wanted to live peaceably with others and who imagined himself a party to this convention would, in view of the fairness of its procedures, assent to its results. It derives, that is, from the hypothetical consent of the governed.

Philosophers who think of a moral code on the model of a technical system of an applied science use an entirely different method of justification. In their view, just as the principles of medicine represent knowledge about how best to promote health, so the principles of right and wrong represent knowledge about how best to promote the ends of morality. These philosophers, then, have a teleological conception of the code. Our fundamental duty is to promote certain ends, and the principles of right and wrong organize and direct our efforts in this regard. What justifies the principles, on this view, is that the ends they serve are the right ones to promote and the actions they prescribe are the best ways to promote them. The principles are authoritative, in other words, in virtue of the wisdom of their prescriptions.

Different teleological views in the theory of duty correspond to different answers to the question of what the right ends to promote are. The most common answer is happiness; and the main division among the corresponding views mirrors the distinction in the theory of intrinsic value between egoism and universalism. Thus, egoism and universalism in the theory of duty hold, respectively, that the fundamental duty of morality is to promote, as best as one can, one's own happiness and that it is to promote, as best as one can, the happiness of humanity. The former is ethical egoism and is based on the ideal of rational self-love. The latter is *utilitarianism* and is based on the ideal of rational benevolence. Ethical egoism's most famous exponents in modern philosophy are Hobbes and Spinoza. It has had few distinguished defenders since their time. Bentham and J. S. Mill head the list of distin-

guished defenders of utilitarianism. The view continues to be enormously influential.

On these teleological views, answers to questions about the ends we ought to pursue determine the principles of right and wrong. Put differently, the general study of right action, on these views, is subordinate to the general study of goodness. This is one of the two leading answers to the structural question about how the two studies are related. The other is that the general study of right action is to some extent independent of the general study of goodness. On views that represent this answer, some principles of right and wrong, notably principles of justice and honesty, prescribe actions even though more evil than good would result from doing them. These views are deontological. *Fiat justitia ruat coelum* captures their spirit. The opposition between teleology and deontology in ethics underlies many of the disputes in the general study of right action.

The principal substantive and structural questions of ethics arise not only with respect to the conduct of human life generally but also with respect to specific walks of life such as medicine, law, journalism, engineering, and business. The examination of these questions in relation to the common practices and traditional codes of such professions and occupations has resulted in the special studies of *applied ethics*. In these studies, ideas and theories from the general studies of goodness and right action are applied to particular circumstances and problems of some profession or occupation, and standard philosophical techniques are used to define, clarify, and organize the ethical issues found in its domain. In medicine, in particular, where rapid advances in technology create, overnight, novel ethical problems on matters of life and death, the study of biomedical ethics has generated substantial interest among practitioners and scholars alike.

Metaethics. To a large extent, the general studies of goodness and right action and the special studies of applied ethics consist in systematizing, deepening, and revising our beliefs about how we ought to conduct our lives. At the same time, it is characteristic of philosophers, when reflecting on such systems of belief, to examine the nature and grounds of these beliefs. These questions, when asked about ethical beliefs, define the field of *metaethics*. The relation of this field to the other studies is commonly represented by taking the other studies to constitute the field of ethics proper and then taking metaethics to be the study of the concepts, methods of justification, and ontological assumptions of the field of ethics proper.

Accordingly, metaethics can proceed from either an interest in the epistemology of ethics or an interest in its metaphysics. On the first approach, the study focuses on questions about the character of ethical knowledge. Typically, it concentrates on the simplest ethical beliefs, such as 'Stealing is wrong' and 'It is better to give than to receive', and proceeds by analyzing the concepts in virtue of which these beliefs are ethical and examining their logical basis. On the second approach, the study focuses on questions about the existence and character of ethical properties. Typically, it concentrates on the most general ethical predicates such as goodness and wrongfulness and considers whether there truly are ethical properties represented by these predicates and, if so, whether and how they are interwoven into the natural world. The two approaches are complementary. Neither dominates the other.

The epistemological approach is comparative. It looks to the most successful branches of knowledge, the natural sciences and pure mathematics, for paradigms. The former supplies the paradigm of knowledge that is based on observation of natural phenomena; the latter supplies the paradigm of knowledge that seemingly results from the sheer exercise of reason. Under the influence of these paradigms, three distinct views have emerged: naturalism, rationalism, and noncognitivism.

Naturalism takes ethical knowledge to be empirical and accordingly models it on the paradigm of the natural sciences. Ethical concepts, on this view, concern natural phenomena. Rationalism takes ethical knowledge to be a priori and accordingly models it on the paradigm of pure mathematics. Ethical concepts, on this view, concern morality understood as something completely distinct from, though applicable to, natural phenomena, something whose content and structure can be apprehended by reason independently of sensory inputs. Noncognitivism, in opposition to these other views, denies that ethics is a genuine branch of knowledge or takes it to be a branch of knowledge only in a qualified sense. In either case, it denies that ethics is properly modeled on science or mathematics. On the most extreme form of noncognitivism, there are no genuine ethical concepts; words like 'right', 'wrong', 'good', and 'evil' have no cognitive meaning but rather serve to vent feelings and emotions, to express decisions and commitments, or to influence attitudes and dispositions. On less extreme forms, these words are taken to have some cognitive meaning, but conveying that meaning is held to be decidedly secondary to the purposes of venting feelings, expressing decisions, or influencing attitudes. Naturalism is well represented in the work of Mill; rationalism in the works of Kant and the intuitionists. And noncognitivism, which did not emerge as a distinctive view until the twentieth century, is most powerfully expounded in the works of C. L. Stevenson and Hare. Its central tenets, however, were anticipated by Hume, whose skeptical attacks on rationalism set the agenda for subsequent work in metaethics.

The metaphysical approach is centered on the question of objectivity, the question of whether ethical predicates represent real properties of an external world or merely apparent or invented properties, properties that owe their existence to the perception, feeling, or thought of those who ascribe them. Two views dominate this approach. The first, *moral realism*, affirms the real existence of ethical properties. It takes them to inhere in the external world and thus to exist independently of their being perceived. For moral realism, ethics is an objective discipline, a discipline that promises discovery and confirmation of objective truths. At the same time, moral realists differ fundamentally on the question of the character of ethical properties. Some, such as Plato and Moore, regard them as purely intellective and thus irreducibly distinct from empirical properties. Others, such as Aristotle and Mill, regard them as empirical and either reducible to or at least supervenient on other empirical properties. The second view, *moral subjectivism*, denies the real existence of ethical properties. On this view, to predicate, say, goodness of a person is to impose some feeling, impulse, or other state of mind onto the world, much as one projects an emotion onto one's circumstances when one describes them as delightful or sad. On the assumption of moral subjectivism, ethics is not a source of objective truth. In ancient philosophy, moral subjectivism was advanced by some of the Sophists, notably Protagoras. In modern philosophy, Hume expounded it in the eighteenth century and Sartre in the twentieth century.

Regardless of approach, one (and perhaps the central) problem of metaethics is how value is related to fact. On the epistemological approach, this problem is commonly posed as the question of whether judgments of value are derivable from statements of fact. Or, to be more exact, can there be a logically valid argument whose conclusion is a judgment of value and all of whose premises are statements of fact? On the metaphysical approach, the problem is commonly posed as the question of whether moral predicates represent properties that are explicable as complexes of empirical properties. At issue, in either case, is whether ethics is an autonomous discipline, whether the study of moral values and principles is to some degree independent of the study of observable properties and events. A negative answer to these questions affirms the autonomy of ethics; a positive answer denies ethics' autonomy and implies that it is a branch of the natural sciences.

Moral psychology. Even those who affirm the autonomy of ethics recognize that some facts, particularly facts of human psychology, bear on the general studies of goodness and right action. No one maintains that these studies float free of all conception of human appetite and passion or that they presuppose no account of the human capacity for voluntary action. It is generally recognized that an adequate understanding of desire, emotion, deliberation, choice, volition, character, and personality is indispensable to the theoretical treatment of human well-being, intrinsic value, and duty. Investigations into the nature of these psychological phenomena are therefore an essential, though auxiliary, part of ethics. They constitute the adjunct field of *moral psychology*.

One area of particular interest within this field is the study of those capacities by virtue of which men and women qualify as moral agents, beings who are responsible for their actions. This study is especially important to the theory of duty since that theory, in modern philosophy, characteristically assumes a strong doctrine of individual responsibility. That is, it assumes principles of culpability for wrongdoing that require, as conditions of justified blame, that the act of wrongdoing be one's own and that it not be done innocently. Only moral agents are capable of meeting these conditions. And the presumption is that normal, adult human beings qualify as moral agents whereas small children and nonhuman animals do not. The study then focuses on those capacities that distinguish the former from the latter as responsible beings.

The main issue is whether the power of reason alone accounts for these capacities. On one side of the issue are philosophers like Kant who hold that it does. Reason, in their view, is both the pilot and the engine of moral agency. It not only guides one toward actions in conformity with one's duty, but it also produces the desire to do one's duty and can invest that desire with enough strength to overrule conflicting impulses of appetite and passion. On the other side are philosophers, such as Hume and Mill, who take reason to be one of several capacities that constitute moral agency. On their view, reason works strictly in the service of natural and sublimated desires, fears, and aversions to produce intelligent action, to guide its possessor toward the objects of those desires and away from the objects of those fears. It cannot, however, by itself originate any desire or fear. Thus, the desire to act rightly, the aversion to acting wrongly, which are constituents of moral agency, are not products of reason but are instead acquired through some mechanical process of socialization by which their objects become associated with the objects of natural desires and aversions. On one view, then, moral agency consists in the power of reason to govern behavior, and being rational is thus sufficient for being responsible for one's actions. On the other view, moral agency consists in several things including reason, but also including a desire to act rightly and an aversion to acting wrongly that originate in natural desires and aversions. On this view, to be responsible for one's actions, one must not only be rational but also have certain desires and aversions whose acquisition is not guaranteed by the maturation of reason. Within moral psychology, one cardinal test of these views is how well they can accommodate and explain such common experiences of moral agency as conscience, weakness, and moral dilemma.

At some point, however, the views must be tested by questions about freedom. For one cannot be responsible for one's actions if one is incapable of acting freely, which is to say, of one's own free will. The capacity for free action is thus essential to moral agency, and how this capacity is to be explained, whether it fits within a deterministic universe, and if not, whether the notion of moral responsibility should be jettisoned, are among the deepest questions that the student of moral agency must face. What is more, they are not questions to which moral psychology can furnish answers. At this point, ethics descends into metaphysics.

See also BIOETHICS, CONTRACTARIANISM, HEDONISM, JUSTICE, MORALITY, NATURALISM, PERFECTIONISM, UTILITARIANISM.   J.D.

ethics, autonomy of. See ETHICS.

ethics, deontological. See ETHICS.

ethics, divine command. See DIVINE COMMAND ETHICS.

ethics, environmental. See ENVIRONMENTAL PHILOSOPHY.

ethics, evolutionary. See PHILOSOPHY OF BIOLOGY.

ethics, teleological. See ETHICS.

ethics of belief. See CLIFFORD.

ethics of love. See DIVINE COMMAND ETHICS.

ethnography, an open-ended family of techniques through which anthropologists investigate cultures; also, the organized descriptions of other cultures that result from this method. Cultural anthropology – *ethnology* – is based primarily on fieldwork through which anthropologists immerse themselves in the life of a local culture (village, neighborhood) and attempt to describe and interpret aspects of the culture. Careful observation is one central tool of investigation. Through it the anthropologist can observe and record various features of social life, e.g. trading practices, farming techniques, or marriage arrangements. A second central tool is the interview, through which the researcher explores the beliefs and values of members of the local culture. Tools of historical research, including particularly oral history, are also of use in ethnography, since the cultural practices of interest often derive from a remote point in time. **See also ETHNOLOGY.**   D.E.L.

ethnology, the comparative and analytical study of cultures; cultural anthroplogy. Anthropologists aim to describe and interpret aspects of the culture of various social groups – e.g., the hunter-gatherers of the Kalahari, rice villages of the Chinese Canton Delta, or a community of physicists at Livermore Laboratory. Topics of particular interest include religious beliefs, linguistic practices, kinship arrangements, marriage patterns, farming technology, dietary practices, gender relations, and power relations. Cultural anthropology is generally conceived as an empirical science, and this raises several methodological and conceptual difficulties. First is the role of the observer. The injection of an alien observer into the local culture unavoidably disturbs that culture. Second, there is the problem of intelligibility across cultural systems – *radical translation*. One goal of ethnographic research is to arrive at an interpretation of a set of beliefs and values

that are thought to be radically different from the researcher's own beliefs and values; but if this is so, then it is questionable whether they can be accurately translated into the researcher's conceptual scheme. Third, there is the problem of empirical testing of ethnographic interpretations. To what extent do empirical procedures constrain the construction of an interpretation of a given cultural milieu? Finally, there is the problem of generalizability. To what extent does fieldwork in one location permit anthropologists to generalize to a larger context – other villages, the dispersed ethnic group represented by this village, or this village at other times? **See also ETHNOGRAPHY, PHILOSOPHY OF THE SOCIAL SCIENCES.**   D.E.L.

ethnomethodology, a phenomenological approach to interpreting everyday action and speech in various social contexts. Derived from phenomenological sociology and introduced by Harold Garfinkel, the method aims to guide research into meaningful social practices as experienced by participants. A major objective of the method is to interpret the rules that underlie everyday activity and thus constitute part of the normative basis of a given social order. Research from this perspective generally focuses on mundane social activities – e.g., psychiatrists evaluating patients' files, jurors deliberating on defendants' culpability, or coroners judging causes of death. The investigator then attempts to reconstruct an underlying set of rules and ad hoc procedures that may be taken to have guided the observed activity. The approach emphasizes the *contextuality* of social practice – the richness of unspoken shared understandings that guide and orient participants' actions in a given practice or activity. **See also VERSTEHEN.**   D.E.L.

Eucken, Rudolf. See LEBENSPHILOSOPHIE.

Euclid. See EUCLIDEAN GEOMETRY.

Euclidean geometry, the version of geometry that includes among its axioms the parallel axiom, which asserts that, given a line L in a plane, there exists just one line in the plane that passes through a point not on L but never meets L. The phrase 'Euclidean geometry' refers both to the doctrine of geometry to be found in Euclid's *Elements* (fourth century B.C.) and to the mathematical discipline that was built on this basis afterward. In order to present properties of rectilinear and curvilinear curves in the plane and solids in space, Euclid sought definitions, axioms, and postulates to ground the reasoning. Some of his assumptions belonged more to the underlying logic than to the geometry itself. Of the specifically geometrical axioms, the least self-evident stated that only one line passes through a point in a plane parallel to a non-coincident line within it, and many efforts were made to prove it from the other axioms. Notable forays were made by G. Saccheri, J. Playfair, and A. M. Legendre, among others, to put forward results logically contradictory to the parallel axiom (e.g., that the sum of the angles between the sides of a triangle is greater than 180°) and thus standing as candidates for falsehood; however, none of them led to paradox. Nor did logically equivalent axioms (such as that the angle sum equals 180°) seem to be more or less evident than the axiom itself. The next stages of this line of reasoning led to non-Euclidean geometry.

From the point of view of logic and rigor, Euclid was thought to be an apotheosis of certainty in human knowledge; indeed, 'Euclidean' was also used to suggest certainty, without any particular concern with geometry. Ironically, investigations undertaken in the late nineteenth century showed that, quite apart from the question of the parallel axiom, Euclid's system actually depended on more axioms than he had realized, and that filling all the gaps would be a formidable task. Pioneering work done especially by M. Pasch and G. Peano was brought to a climax in 1899 by Hilbert, who produced what was hoped to be a complete axiom system. (Even then the axiom of continuity had to wait for the second edition!) The endeavor had consequences beyond the Euclidean remit; it was an important example of the growth of axiomatization in mathematics as a whole, and it led Hilbert himself to see that questions like the consistency and completeness of a mathematical theory must be asked at another level, which he called metamathematics. It also gave his work a formalist character; he said that his axiomatic talk of points, lines, and planes could be of other objects.

Within the Euclidean realm, attention has fallen in recent decades upon "neo-Euclidean" geometries, in which the parallel axiom is upheld but a different metric is proposed. For example, given a planar triangle *ABC*, the Euclidean distance between *A* and *B* is the hypotenuse *AB;* but the "rectangular distance" *AC* + *CB* also satisfies the properties of a metric, and a geometry working with it is very useful in, e.g., economic geography, as anyone who drives around a city will readily understand.

See also NON-EUCLIDEAN GEOMETRY, PHILOSOPHY OF MATHEMATICS.   I.G.-G.

eudaimonia. See ARISTOTLE, EUDAIMONISM.

eudaimonism (from Greek *eudaimonia,* 'happiness', 'flourishing'), the ethical doctrine that happiness is the ultimate justification for morality. The ancient Greek philosophers typically begin their ethical treatises with an account of happiness, and then argue that the best way to achieve a happy life is through the cultivation and exercise of virtue. Most of them make virtue or virtuous activity a constituent of the happy life; the Epicureans, however, construe happiness in terms of pleasure, and treat virtue as a means to the end of pleasant living. Ethical eudaimonism is sometimes combined with psychological eudaimonism – i.e., the view that all free, intentional action is aimed ultimately at the agent's happiness. A common feature of ancient discussions of ethics, and one distinguishing them from most modern discussions, is the view that an agent would not be rationally justified in a course of action that promised less happiness than some alternative open to him. Hence it seems that most of the ancient theories are forms of egosim. But the ancient theories differ from modern versions of egoism since, according to the ancients, at least some of the virtues are dispositions to act from primarily other-regarding motives: although the agent's happiness is the ultimate justification of virtuous action, it is not necessarily what motivates such action. Since happiness is regarded by most of the ancients as the ultimate *end* that justifies our actions, their ethical theories seem teleological; i.e., right or virtuous action is construed as action that contributes to or maximizes the good. But appearances are again misleading, for the ancients typically regard virtuous action as also valuable for its own sake and hence *constitutive* of the agent's happiness. **See also** EGOISM, ETHICS, HEDONISM, UTILITARIANISM.   D.T.D.

Eudoxus of Cnidus (c.408–c.355 B.C.), Greek astronomer and mathematician, a student of Plato. He created a test of the equality of two ratios, invented the method of exhaustion for calculating areas and volumes within curved boundaries, and introduced an astronomical system consisting of homocentric celestial spheres. This system views the visible universe as a set of twenty-seven spheres contained one inside the other and each concentric to the earth. Every celestial body is located on the equator of an ideal sphere that revolves with uniform speed on its axis. The poles are embedded in the surface of another sphere, which also revolves uniformly around an axis inclined at a constant angle to that of the first sphere. In this way enough spheres are introduced to capture the apparent motions of all heavenly bodies. Aristotle adopted the system of homocentric spheres and provided a physical interpretation for it in his cosmology.

R.E.B.

Euler diagram, a logic diagram invented by the mathematician Euler that represents standard form statements in syllogistic logic by two circles and a syllogism by three circles. In modern adaptations of Euler diagrams, distributed terms are represented by complete circles and undistributed terms by partial circles (circle segments or circles made with dotted lines):

Euler diagrams are more perspicuous ways of showing validity and invalidity of syllogisms than Venn diagrams, but less useful as a mechanical test of validity since there may be several choices of ways to represent a syllogism in Euler diagrams, only one of which will show that the syllogism is invalid. **See also** SYLLOGISM, VENN DIAGRAM.

R.P.

Eurytus of Croton. See PRE-SOCRATICS.

euthanasia, broadly, the beneficent timing or negotiation of the death of a sick person; more narrowly, the killing of a human being on the grounds that he is better off dead. In an extended sense, the word 'euthanasia' is used to refer to the painless killing of non-human animals, in our interests at least as much as in theirs.

Active euthanasia is the taking of steps to end a person's – especially a patient's – life. Passive euthanasia is the omission or termination of means of prolonging life, on the grounds that the person is better off without them. The distinction between active and passive euthanasia is a rough guide for applying the more fundamental distinction between intending the patient's death and pursuing other goals, such as the relief of her pain, with the expectation that she will die sooner rather than later as a result.

Voluntary euthanasia is euthanasia with the patient's consent, or at his request. Involuntary euthanasia is euthanasia over the patient's objections. Non-voluntary euthanasia is the killing of a person deemed incompetent with the consent of someone – say a parent – authorized to speak on his behalf. Since candidates for euthanasia are frequently in no condition to make major decisions, the question whether there is a difference between involuntary and non-voluntary euthanasia is of great importance.

Few moralists hold that life must be prolonged whatever the cost. Traditional morality forbids directly intended euthanasia: human life belongs to God and may be taken only by him. The most important arguments for euthanasia are the pain and indignity suffered by those with incurable diseases, the burden imposed by persons unable to take part in normal human activities, and the supposed right of persons to dispose of their lives however they please. Non-theological arguments against euthanasia include the danger of expanding the principle of euthanasia to an ever-widening range of persons and the opacity of death and its consequent incommensurability with life, so that we cannot safely judge that a person is better off dead.

See also BIOETHICS, ETHICS, INFORMED CONSENT.

P.E.D.

event, anything that happens; an occurrence. Two fundamental questions about events, which philosophers have usually treated together, are: (1) Are there events?, and (2) If so, what is their nature? Some philosophers simply assume that there are events. Others argue for that, typically through finding semantic theories for ordinary claims that apparently concern the fact that some agent has done something or that some thing has changed.

Most philosophers presume that the events whose existence is proved by such arguments are abstract particulars, "particulars" in the sense that they are non-repeatable and spatially locatable, "abstract" in the sense that more than one event can occur simultaneously in the same place. The theories of events espoused by Davidson (in his causal view), Kim (though his view may be unstable in this respect), Jonathan Bennett, and Lawrence Lombard take them to be abstract particulars. However, Chisholm takes events to be abstract universals; and Quine and Davidson (in his later view) take them to be concrete particulars.

Some philosophers who think of events as abstract particulars tend to associate the concept of an event with the concept of *change*; an event is a change in some object or other (though some philosophers have doubts about this and others have denied it outright). The time at which an event, construed as a particular, occurs can be associated with the (shortest) time at which the object, which is the subject of that event, changes from the having of one property to the having of another, contrary property. Events inherit whatever spatial locations they have from the spatial locations, if any, of the things that those events are changes in. Thus, an event that is a change in an object, *x*, from being *F* to being *G*, is located wherever *x* is at the time it changes from being *F* to being *G*.

Some events are those of which another event is composed (e.g., the sinking of a ship seems composed of the sinkings of its parts). However, it also seems clear that not every group of events comprises another; there just is no event composed of a certain explosion on Venus and my birth.

Any adequate theory about the nature of events must address the question of what properties, if any, such things have essentially. One issue is whether the causes (or effects) of events are essential to those events. A second is whether it is essential to each event that it be a change in the entity it is in fact a change in. A third is whether it is essential to each event that it occur at the time at which it in fact occurs.

A chief component of a theory of events is a *criterion of identity*, a principle giving conditions necessary and sufficient for an event *e* and an event *e'* to be one and the same event. Quine holds that events may be identified with the temporal parts of physical objects, and that events and physical objects would thus share the same condition of identity: sameness of spatiotemporal location. Davidson once proposed that events are identical provided they have the same causes and effects. More recently, Davidson abandoned this position in favor of Quine's.

Kim takes an event to be the exemplification of a property (or relation) by an object (or objects) at a time. This idea has led to his view that an event *e* is the same as an event *e'* if and only if *e* and *e'* are the exemplifications of the same property by the same object(s) at the same time. Lombard's view is a variation on this account, and is derived from the idea of events

as the changes that physical objects undergo when they alter.

See also CAUSATION, DAVIDSON, META-PHYSICS, PERDURANCE, QUINE.   L.B.L.

event causation. See CAUSATION.

everlasting. See DIVINE ATTRIBUTES.

evidence, information bearing on the truth or falsity of a proposition. In philosophical discussions, a person's evidence is generally taken to be all the information a person has, positive or negative, relevant to a proposition. The notion of evidence used in philosophy thus differs from the ordinary notion according to which physical objects, such as a strand of hair or a drop of blood, counts as evidence. One's information about such objects could be evidence in the philosophical sense.

The concept of evidence plays a central role in our understanding of knowledge and rationality. According to a traditional and widely held view, one has knowledge only when one has a true belief based on very strong evidence. Rational belief is belief based on adequate evidence, even if that evidence falls short of what is needed for knowledge. Many traditional philosophical debates, such as those about our knowledge of the external world, the rationality of religious belief, and the rational basis for moral judgments, are largely about whether the evidence we have in these areas is sufficient to yield knowledge or rational belief.

The senses are a primary source of evidence. Thus, for most, if not all, of our beliefs, ultimately our evidence traces back to sensory experience. Other sources of evidence include memory and the testimony of others. Of course, both of these sources rely on the senses in one way or another. According to rationalist views, we can also get evidence for some propositions through mere reason or reflection, and so reason is an additional source of evidence.

The evidence one has for a belief may be conclusive or inconclusive. Conclusive evidence is so strong as to rule out all possibility of error. The discussions of skepticism show clearly that we lack conclusive evidence for our beliefs about the external world, about the past, about other minds, and about nearly any other topic. Thus, an individual's perceptual experiences provide only inconclusive evidence for beliefs about the external world since such experiences can be deceptive or hallucinatory. Inconclusive, or prima facie, evidence can always be defeated or overridden by subsequently acquired evidence, as, e.g., when testimonial evidence in favor of a proposition is overridden by the evidence provided by subsequent experiences.

See also EPISTEMOLOGY, SKEPTICISM.   R.Fe.

evidence of the senses. See EVIDENCE.

evidentialism, in the philosophy of religion, the view that religious beliefs can be rationally accepted only if they are supported by one's "total evidence," understood to mean all the other propositions one knows or justifiably believes to be true. Evidentialists typically add that, in order to be rational, one's degree of belief should be proportioned to the strength of the evidential support. Evidentialism was formulated by Locke as a weapon against the sectarians of his day and has since been used by Clifford (among many others) to attack religious belief in general. A milder form of evidentialism is found in Aquinas, who, unlike Clifford, thinks religion can meet the evidentialist challenge.

A contrasting view is *fideism,* best understood as the claim that one's fundamental religious convictions are not subject to independent rational assessment. A reason often given for this is that devotion to God should be one's "ultimate concern," and to subject faith to the judgment of reason is to place reason above God and make of it an idol. Proponents of fideism include Tertullian, Kierkegaard, Karl Barth, and some Wittgensteinians.

A third view, which as yet lacks a generally accepted label, may be termed *experientialism;* it asserts that some religious beliefs are directly justified by religious experience. Experientialism differs from evidentialism in holding that religious beliefs can be rational without being supported by inferences from other beliefs one holds; thus theistic arguments are superfluous, whether or not there are any sound ones available. But experientialism is not fideism; it holds that religious beliefs may be directly grounded in religious experience wtihout the mediation of other beliefs, and may be rationally warranted on that account, just as perceptual beliefs are directly grounded in perceptual experience. Recent examples of experientialism are found in Plantinga's "Reformed Epistemology," which asserts that religious beliefs grounded in experience can be "properly basic," and in the contention of Alston that in religious experience the subject may be "perceiving God."

See also PHILOSOPHY OF RELIGION.

W.Has.

evidential reason. See EPISTEMOLOGY.

evil, moral. See PHILOSOPHY OF RELIGION.

evil, natural. See PHILOSOPHY OF RELIGION.

evil, problem of. See PHILOSOPHY OF RELIGION.

evolution. See DARWINISM.

evolutionary epistemology, a theory of knowledge inspired by and derived from the fact and processes of organic evolution (the term was coined by the social psychologist Donald Campbell). Most evolutionary epistemologists subscribe to the theory of evolution through natural selection, as presented by Darwin in the *Origin of Species* (1859). However, one does find variants, especially one based on some kind of neo-Lamarckism, where the inheritance of acquired characters is central (Spencer endorsed this view) and another based on some kind of jerky or "saltationary" evolutionism (Thomas Kuhn, at the end of *The Structure of Scientific Revolutions,* accepts this idea).

There are two approaches to evolutionary epistemology. First, one can think of the transformation of organisms and the processes driving such change as an *analogy* for the growth of knowledge, particularly scientific knowledge. "Darwin's bulldog," T. H. Huxley, was one of the first to propose this idea. He argued that just as between organisms we have a struggle for existence, leading to the selection of the fittest, so between scientific ideas we have a struggle leading to a selection of the fittest. Notable exponents of this view today include Stephen Toulmin, who has worked through the analogy in some detail, and David Hull, who brings a sensitive sociological perspective to bear on the position. Karl Popper identifies with this form of evolutionary epistemology, arguing that the selection of ideas is his view of science as bold conjecture and rigorous attempt at refutation by another name.

The problem with this analogical type of evolutionary epistemology lies in the disanalogy between the raw variants of biology (mutations), which are random, and the raw variants of science (new hypotheses), which are very rarely random. This difference probably accounts for the fact that whereas Darwinian evolution is not genuinely progressive, science is (or seems to be) the paradigm of a progressive enterprise. Because of this problem, a second set of epistemologists inspired by evolution insist that one must take the biology *literally.* This group, which includes Darwin, who speculated in this way even in his earliest notebooks, claims that evolution predisposes us to think in certain fixed adaptive patterns. The laws of logic, e.g., as well as mathematics and the methodological dictates of science, have their foundations in the fact that those of our would-be ancestors who took them seriously survived and reproduced, and those that did not did not. No one claims that we have innate knowledge of the kind demolished by Locke. Rather, our thinking is channeled in certain directions by our biology. In an update of the biogenetic law, therefore, one might say that whereas a claim like $5 + 7 = 12$ is phylogenetically a posteriori, it is ontogenetically a priori.

A major division in this school is between the continental evolutionists, most notably the late Konrad Lorenz, and the Anglo-Saxon supporters, e.g. Michael Ruse. The former think that their evolutionary epistemology simply updates the critical philosophy of Kant, and that biology both explains the necessity of the synthetic a priori and makes reasonable belief in the thing-in-itself. The latter deny that one can ever get that necessity, certainly not from biology, or that evolution makes reasonable a belief in an objectively real world, independent of our knowing. Historically, these epistemologists look to Hume and in some respects to the American pragmatists, especially William James. Today, they acknowledge a strong family resemblance to such naturalized epistemologists as Quine, who has endorsed a kind of evolutionary epistemology.

Critics of this position, e.g. Philip Kitcher, usually strike at what they see as the soft scientific underbelly. They argue that the belief that the mind is constructed according to various innate adaptive channels is without warrant. It is but one more manifestation of today's Darwinians illicitly seeing adaptation everywhere. It is better and more reasonable to think knowledge is rooted in culture, if it is person-dependent at all.

A mark of a good philosophy, like a good science, is that it opens up new avenues for research. Although evolutionary epistemology is not favored by conventional philosophers, who sneer at the crudities of its (frequently non-philosophically trained) proselytizers, its supporters feel convinced that they are contributing to a forward-moving philosophical research program. As evolutionists, they are used to things taking time to succeed.

See also DARWINISM, EPISTEMOLOGY, PHILOSOPHY OF BIOLOGY, SOCIAL BIOLOGY.

M.Ru.

evolutionary ethics. See PHILOSOPHY OF BIOLOGY.

evolutionary psychology, the subfield of psychology that explains human behavior and cultural arrangements by employing evolutionary biology and cognitive psychology to discover, catalog, and analyze psychological mechanisms. Human minds allegedly possess many innate, special-purpose, domain-specific psychological mechanisms (modules) whose development requires minimal input and whose operations are context-sensitive, mostly automatic, and independent of one another and of general intelligence. (Disagreements persist about the functional isolation and innateness of these modules.) Some evolutionary psychologists compare the mind – with its specialized modules – to a Swiss army knife. Different modules substantially constrain behavior and cognition associated with language, sociality, face recognition, and so on.

Evolutionary psychologists emphasize that psychological phenomena reflect the influence of biological evolution. These modules and associated behavior patterns assumed their forms during the Pleistocene. An evolutionary perspective identifies adaptive problems and features of the Pleistocene environment that constrained possible solutions. Adaptive problems often have cognitive dimensions. For example, an evolutionary imperative to aid kin presumes the ability to detect kin. Evolutionary psychologists propose models to meet the requisite cognitive demands. Plausible models should produce adaptive behaviors and avoid maladaptive ones – e.g., generating too many false positives when identifying kin. Experimental psychological evidence and social scientific field observations aid assessment of these proposals.

These modules have changed little. Modern humans manage with primitive hunter-gatherers' cognitive equipment amid the rapid cultural change that equipment produces. The pace of that change outstrips the ability of biological evolution to keep up. Evolutionary psychologists hold, consequently, that: (1) contrary to sociobiology, which appeals to biological evolution directly, exclusively evolutionary explanations of human behavior will not suffice; (2) contrary to theories of cultural evolution, which appeal to biological evolution analogically, it is at least possible that no cultural arrangement has ever been adaptive; and (3) contrary to social scientists, who appeal to some general conception of learning or socialization to explain cultural transmission, specialized psychological mechanisms contribute substantially to that process.

See also COGNITIVE SCIENCE, DARWINISM, MODULARITY, PHILOSOPHY OF THE SOCIAL SCIENCES, SOCIAL BIOLOGY.   R.N.Mc.

exact similarity. See IDENTITY.

examination, paradox of the. See UNEXPECTED EXAMINATION PARADOX.

exciting reason. See HUTCHESON.

excluded middle, principle of. See PRINCIPLE OF EXCLUDED MIDDLE.

exclusionary reason. See JURISPRUDENCE.

exclusive disjunction. See DISJUNCTIVE PROPOSITION.

excuse. See JUSTIFICATION.

exemplarism. See BONAVENTURE.

exemplification. See CONCEPTUALISM.

existence. See SUBSISTENCE.

existence, 'is' of. See IS.

existential. See HEIDEGGER.

existential generalization, a rule of inference admissible in classical quantification theory. It allows one to infer an existentially quantified statement $\exists xA$ from any instance A (a/x) of it. (Intuitively, it allows one to infer 'There exists a liar' from 'Epimenides is a liar'.) It is equivalent to universal instantiation – the rule that allows one to infer any instance A (a/x) of a universally quantified statement $\forall xA$ from $\forall xA$. (Intuitively, it allows one to infer 'My car is valuable' from 'Everything is valuable'.) Both rules can also have equivalent formulations as axioms; then they are called specification $(\forall xA \supset A$ $(a/x))$ and particularization $((A(a/x) \supset \exists xA))$. All of these equivalent principles are denied by free logic, which only admits weakened versions of them. In the case of existential generalization, the weakened version is: infer $\exists xA$ from $A(a/x)$ & E!a. (Intuitively: infer 'There exists a liar' from 'Epimenides is a liar and Epimenides exists'.) **See also** EXISTENTIAL INSTANTIATION, FORMAL LOGIC, FREE LOGIC, UNIVERSAL INSTANTIATION.   E.Ben.

existential graph. See PEIRCE.

existential import, a commitment to the existence of something implied by a sentence, statement, or proposition. For example, in Aristotelian logic (though not in modern quantification theory), any sentence of the form 'All F's are G's' implies 'There is an F that is a G' and is thus said to have as existential import a commitment to the existence of an F that is a G. According to Russell's theory of descriptions, sentences containing definite descriptions can likewise have existential import since 'The F is a G' implies 'There is an F'. The presence of singular terms is also often claimed to give rise to existential commitment. Underlying this notion of existential import is the idea – long stressed by W. V. Quine – that ontological commitment is measured by *existential sentences* (*statements, propositions*) of the form $(\exists v)$ ϕ. **See also** ONTOLOGICAL COMMITMENT.   G.F.S.

existential instantiation, a rule of inference admissible in classical quantification theory. It allows one to infer a statement A from an existentially quantified statement $\exists xB$ if A can be inferred from an instance $B(a/x)$ of $\exists xB$, provided that a does not occur in either A or B or any other premise of the argument (if there are any). (Intuitively, it allows one to infer a contradiction C from 'There exists a highest prime' if C can be inferred from 'a is a highest prime' and a does not occur in C.) Free logic allows for a stronger form of this rule: with the same provisions as above, A can be inferred from $\exists xB$ if it can be inferred from $B(a/x)$ & E!a. (Intuitively, it is enough to infer 'There is a highest natural number' from 'a is a highest prime and a exists'.) **See also** FORMAL LOGIC, FREE LOGIC.   E.Ben.

existentialism, a philosophical and literary movement that came to prominence in Europe, particularly in France, immediately after World War II, and that focused on the uniqueness of each human individual as distinguished from abstract universal human qualities. Historians differ as to antecedents. Some see an existentialist precursor in Pascal, whose aphoristically expressed Catholic fideism questioned the power of rationalist thought and preferred the God of Scripture to the abstract "God of the philosophers." Many agree that Kierkegaard, whose fundamentally similar but Protestant fideism was based on a profound unwillingness to situate either God or any individual's relationship with God within a systematic philosophy, as Hegel had done, should be considered the first modern existentialist, though he too lived long before the term emerged. Others find a proto-existentialist in Nietzsche, because of the aphoristic and anti-systematic nature of his writings, and on the literary side, in Dostoevsky. (A number of twentieth-century novelists, such as Franz Kafka, have been labeled existentialists.)

A strong existentialist strain is to be found in certain other theist philosophers who have written since Kierkegaard, such as Lequier, Berdyaev, Marcel, Jaspers, and Buber, but Marcel later decided to reject the label 'existentialist', which he had previously employed. This reflects its increasing identification with the atheistic existentialism of Sartre, whose successes, as in the novel *Nausea*, and the philosophical work *Being and Nothingness*, did most to popularize the word. A mass-audience lecture, "Existentialism Is a Humanism," which Sartre (to his later regret) allowed to be published, provided the occasion for Heidegger, whose early thought had greatly influenced Sartre's evolution, to take his distance from Sartre's existentialism, in particular for its self-conscious concentration on human reality over Being. Heidegger's *Letter on Humanism*, written in reply to a French admirer, signals an important turn in his thinking. Nevertheless, many historians continue to classify Heidegger as an existentialist – quite reasonably, given his early emphasis on existential categories and ideas such as anxiety in the presence of death, our sense of being "thrown" into existence, and our temptation to choose anonymity over authenticity in our conduct. This illustrates the difficulty of fixing the term 'existentialism'. Other French thinkers of the time, all acquaintances of Sartre's, who are often classified as existentialists, are Camus, Simone de Beauvoir, and, though with less reason, Merleau-Ponty.

Camus's novels, such as *The Stranger* and *The Plague*, are cited along with *Nausea* as epitomizing the uniqueness of the existentialist antihero who acts out of authenticity, i.e., in freedom from any conventional expectations about what so-called human nature (a concept rejected by Sartre) supposedly requires in a given situation, and with a sense of personal responsibility and absolute lucidity that precludes the "bad faith" or lying to oneself that characterizes most conventional human behavior. Good scholarship prescribes caution, however, about superimposing too many Sartrean categories on Camus. In fact the latter, in his brief philosophical essays, notably *The Myth of Sisyphus*, distinguishes existentialist writers and philosophers, such as Kierkegaard, from *absurdist* thinkers and heroes, whom he regards more highly, and of whom the mythical Sisyphus (condemned eternally by the gods to roll a huge boulder up a hill before being forced, just before reaching the summit, to start anew) is the epitome. Camus focuses on the concept of the *absurd*, which Kierkegaard had used to characterize the object of his religious faith (an incarnate God). But for Camus existential absurdity lies in the fact, as he sees it, that there is always at best an imperfect fit between human reasoning and its intended objects, hence an impossibility of achieving certitude. Kierkegaard's leap of faith is, for Camus, one more pseudo-solution to this hard, absurdist reality.

Almost alone among those named besides Sartre (who himself concentrated more on social and political thought and became indebted to Marxism in his later years), Simone de Beauvoir (1908–86) unqualifiedly accepted the existentialist label. In *The Ethics of Ambiguity*, she attempted, using categories familiar in Sartre, to produce an existentialist ethics based on the recognition of radical human freedom as "projected" toward an open future, the rejection of inauthenticity, and a condemnation of the "spirit of seriousness" (akin to the "spirit of gravity" criticized by Nietzsche) whereby individuals identify themselves wholly with certain fixed qualities, values, tenets, or prejudices. Her feminist masterpiece, *The Second Sex*, relies heavily on the distinction, part existentialist and part Hegelian in inspiration, between a life of immanence, or passive acceptance of the role into which one has been socialized, and one of transcendence, actively and freely testing one's possibilities with a view to redefining one's future. Historically, women have been consigned to the sphere of immanence, says de Beauvoir, but in fact a woman in the traditional sense is not something that one is *made*, without appeal, but rather something that one *becomes*.

The Sartrean ontology of *Being and Nothingness*, according to which there are two fundamental asymmetrical "regions of being," being-in-itself and being-for-itself, the latter having no definable essence and hence, as "nothing" in itself, serving as the ground for freedom, creativity, and action, serves well as a theoretical framework for an existentialist approach to human existence. (*Being and Nothingness* also names a third ontological region, being-for-others, but that may be disregarded here.) However, it would be a mistake to treat even Sartre's existentialist insights, much less those of others, as dependent on this ontology, to which he himself made little direct reference in his later works. Rather, it is the implications of the common central claim that we human beings exist without justification (hence "absurdly") in a world into which we are "thrown," condemned to assume full responsibility for our free actions and for the very values according to which we act, that make existentialism a continuing philosophical challenge, particularly to ethicists who believe right choices to be dictated by our alleged human essence or nature.

See also CAMUS, EVIDENTIALISM, HEIDEGGER, KIERKEGAARD, SARTRE.   W.L.M.

existential polarity. See POLARITY.

existential proposition. See EXISTENTIAL IMPORT.

existential quantifier. See FORMAL LOGIC.

Existenz **philosophy**. See JASPERS.

ex nihilo. See CREATION EX NIHILO.

expected return. See SAINT PETERSBURG PARADOX.

expected utility. See NEWCOMB'S PARADOX, SAINT PETERSBURG PARADOX.

experientialism. See EVIDENTIALISM.

experimentum crusis. See CRUCIAL EXPERIMENT.

explaining reason. See REASONS FOR ACTION, REASONS FOR BELIEF.

explanandum. See EXPLANATION.

explanans. See EXPLANATION.

explanation, an act of making something intelligible or understandable, as when we explain an event by showing why or how it occurred. Just about anything can be the object of explanation: a concept, a rule, the meaning of a word, the point of a chess move, the structure of a novel. However, there are two sorts of things whose explanation has been intensively discussed in philosophy: events and human actions.

Individual events, say the collapse of a bridge, are usually explained by specifying their cause: the bridge collapsed because of the pressure of the flood water and its weakened structure. This is an example of causal explanation. There usually are indefinitely many causal factors responsible for the occurrence of an event, and the choice of a particular factor as "the cause" appears to depend primarily on contextual considerations. Thus, one explanation of an automobile accident may cite the icy road condition; another the inexperienced driver; and still another the defective brakes. Context may determine which of these and other possible explanations is the appropriate one. These explanations of *why* an event occurred are sometimes contrasted with explanations of *how* an event occurred. A "how" explanation of an event consists in an informative description of the process that has led to the occurrence of the event, and such descriptions are likely to involve descriptions of causal processes.

The *covering law model* is an influential attempt to represent the general form of such explanations: an explanation of an event consists in "subsuming," or "covering," it under a law. When the covering law is deterministic, the explanation is thought to take the form of a deductive argument: a statement – the explanandum – describing the event to be explained is logically derived from the explanans – the law together with statements of antecedent conditions. Thus, we might explain why a given rod expanded by offering this argument: 'All metals expand when heated; this rod is metallic and it was heated; therefore, it expanded'. Such an explanation is called a *deductive-nomological explanation*. On the other hand, probabilistic or statistical laws are thought to yield *statistical explanations* of individual events. Thus, the explanation of the contraction of a contagious disease on the basis of exposure to a patient with the disease may take the form of a statistical explanation. Details of the statistical model have been a matter of much controversy. It is sometimes claimed that although explanations, whether in ordinary life or in the sciences, seldom conform fully to the covering law model, the model nevertheless represents an ideal that all explanations must strive to attain. The covering law model, though influential, is not universally accepted.

Human actions are often explained by being "rationalized' – i.e., by citing the agent's beliefs and desires (and other "intentional" mental states such as emotions, hopes, and expectations) that constitute a reason for doing what was done. You opened the window because you wanted some fresh air and believed that by opening the window you could secure this result. It has been a controversial issue whether such rationalizing explanations are causal; i.e., whether they invoke beliefs and desires as a cause of the action. Another issue is whether these "rationalizing" explanations must conform to the covering law model, and if so, what laws might underwrite such explanations.

See also CAUSATION, COVERING LAW MODEL, PHILOSOPHY OF SCIENCE.   J.K.

explanation, covering law. See COVERING LAW MODEL.

explanation, deductive. See COVERING LAW MODEL.

explanation, inductive. See COVERING LAW MODEL.

explanation, purposive. See PHILOSOPHY OF MIND.

explanation, subsumption theory of. See COVERING LAW MODEL.

explanation, teleological. See TELEOLOGY.

explanatory emergence. See METHODOLOGICAL HOLISM.

explanatory reductionism. See METHODOLOGICAL HOLISM.

explicit definition. See BETH'S DEFINABILITY THEOREM, DEFINITION.

exponible. In medieval logic, exponible propositions were those that needed to be expounded, i.e., elaborated in order to make clear their true logical form. A modern example might be: 'Giorgione was so called because of his size', which has a misleading form, suggesting a simple predication, whereas it really means, 'Giorgione was called "Giorgione" because of his size'. Medieval examples were: 'Every man except Socrates is running', expounded as 'Socrates is not running and every man other than Socrates is running'; and 'Only Socrates says something true', uttered by, say, Plato, which Albert of Saxony claims should be expounded not only as 'Socrates says something true and no one other than Socrates says something true', but needs a third clause, 'Plato says something false'.

This last example brings out an important aspect of exponible propositions, namely, their use in sophisms. Sophismatic treatises were a common medieval genre in which metaphysical and logical issues were approached dialectically by their application in solving puzzle cases. Another important ingredient of exponible propositions was their containing a particular term, sometimes called the exponible term; attention on such terms was focused in the study of syncategorematic expressions, especially in the thirteenth century. However, note that such exponible terms could only be expounded in context, not by an explicit definition. Syncategorematic terms that produced exponible propositions were terms such as 'twice', 'except', 'begins' and 'ceases', and 'insofar as' (e.g. 'Socrates insofar as he is rational is risible').

See also SYNCATEGOREMATA.   S.L.R.

exportation (1) In classical logic, the principle that $(A \land B) \supset C$ is logically equivalent to $A \supset (B \supset C)$. (2) The principle $((A \land B) \rightarrow C) \rightarrow (A \rightarrow (B \rightarrow C))$, which relevance logicians hold to be fallacious when '$\rightarrow$' is read as 'entails'. (3) In discussions of propositional attitude verbs, the principle that from 'a Vs that b is a(n) ϕ' one may infer 'a Vs ϕ-hood of b', where V has its relational (transparent) sense. For example, exportation (in sense 3) takes one from 'Ralph believes that Ortcutt is a spy' to 'Ralph believes spyhood of Ortcutt', wherein 'Ortcutt' can now be replaced by a bound variable to yield '$(\exists x)$ (Ralph believes spyhood of x)'. **See also** QUANTIFYING IN, RELEVANCE LOGIC.   G.F.S.

expressibility logicism. See LOGICISM.

expressionism. See EXPRESSION THEORY OF ART.

expression theory of art, a theory that defines art as the expression of feelings or emotion (sometimes called expressionism in art). Such theories first acquired major importance in the nineteenth century in connection with the rise of Romanticism. Expression theories are as various as the different views about what counts as expressing emotion. There are four main variants.

(1) *Expression as communication*. This requires that the artist actually have the feelings that are expressed, when they are initially expressed. They are "embodied" in some external form, and thereby transmitted to the perceiver. Leo Tolstoy (1828–1910) held a view of this sort.

(2) *Expression as intuition*. An intuition is the apprehension of the unity and individuality of something. An intuition is "in the mind," and hence the artwork is also. Croce held this view, and in his later work argued that the unity of an intuition is established by feeling.

(3) *Expression as clarification*. An artist starts out with vague, undefined feelings, and expression is a process of coming to clarify, articulate, and understand them. This view retains Croce's idea that expression is in the artist's mind, as well as

his view that we are all artists to the degree that we articulate, clarify, and come to understand our own feelings. Collingwood held this view.

(4) *Expression as a property of the object.* For an artwork to be an expression of emotion is for it to have a given structure or form. Suzanne K. Langer (1895–1985) argued that music and the other arts "presented" or exhibited structures or forms of feeling in general.

See also AESTHETICS, INSTITUTIONAL THE-ORY OF ART.   S.L.F.

expressive completeness. See COMPLETENESS.

expressive meaning. See MEANING.

extension. See INTENSION.

extensionalism, a family of ontologies and semantic theories restricted to existent entities. Extensionalist ontology denies that the domain of any true theory needs to include non-existents, such as fictional, imaginary, and impossible objects like Pegasus the winged horse or round squares. Extensionalist semantics reduces meaning and truth to set-theoretical relations between terms in a language and the existent objects, standardly spatiotemporal and abstract entities, that belong to the term's extension. The extension of a name is the particular existent denoted by the name; the extension of a predicate is the set of existent objects that have the property represented by the predicate. The sentence 'All whales are mammals' is true in extensionalist semantics provided there are no whales that are not mammals, no existent objects in the extension of the predicate 'whale' that are not also in the extension of 'mammal'. Linguistic contexts are extensional if: (i) they make reference only to existent objects; (ii) they support substitution of codesignative terms (referring to the same thing), or of logically equivalent propositions, *salva veritate* (without loss of truth-value); and (iii) it is logically valid to existentially quantify (conclude that *There exists an object such that* . . . etc.) objects referred to within the context. Contexts that do not meet these requirements are intensional, non-extensional, or referentially opaque.

The implications of extensionalism, associated with the work of Frege, Russell, Quine, and mainstream analytic philosophy, are to limit its explanations of mind and meaning to existent objects and material-mechanical properties and relations describable in an exclusively exten-

sional idiom. Extensionalist semantics must try to analyze away apparent references to non-existent objects, or, as in Russell's extensionalist theory of definite descriptions, to classify all such predications as false. Extensionalist ontology in the philosophy of mind must eliminate or reduce propositional attitudes or *de dicto* mental states, expressed in an intensional idiom, such as 'believes that ———', 'fears that ———', and the like, usually in favor of extensional characterizations of neurophysiological states. Whether extensionalist philosophy can satisfy these explanatory obligations, as the thesis of extensionality maintains, is controversial.

See also ABSTRACT ENTITY, INTENSIONALITY, PHILOSOPHY OF LANGUAGE, RUSSELL, THEORY OF DESCRIPTIONS, TRUTH.   D.J.

extensionality, axiom of. See SET THEORY.

extensionality thesis. See EXTENSIONALISM.

extensive abstraction. See WHITEHEAD.

extensive magnitude. See MAGNITUDE.

externalism, the view that there are objective reasons for action that are not dependent on the agent's desires, and in that sense external to the agent. Internalism (about reasons) is the view that reasons for action must be internal in the sense that they are grounded in motivational facts about the agent, e.g. her desires and goals. Classic internalists such as Hume deny that there are objective reasons for action. For instance, whether the fact that an action would promote health is a reason to do it depends on whether one has a desire to be healthy. It may be a reason for some and not for others. The doctrine is hence a version of relativism; a fact is a reason only insofar as it is so connected to an agent's psychological states that it can motivate the agent. By contrast, externalists hold that not all reasons depend on the internal states of particular agents. Thus an externalist could hold that promoting health is objectively good and that the fact that an action would promote one's health is a reason to perform it regardless of whether one desires health.

This dispute is closely tied to the debate over motivational internalism, which may be conceived as the view that moral beliefs (for instance) are, by virtue of entailing motivation, internal reasons for action. Those who reject motivational internalism must either deny that (sound) moral beliefs always provide reasons for action or hold that they provide external reasons.

See also ETHICS, MOTIVATIONAL INTERNALISM, RELATIVISM.   W.T.

externalism, content. See PHILOSOPHY OF MIND.

externalism, epistemological. See EPISTEMOLOGY.

externalism, motivational. See MOTIVATIONAL INTERNALISM.

external negation. See NEGATION.

external reason. See EXTERNALISM.

external relation. See RELATION.

exteroception. See PERCEPTION.

extrasensory perception. See PARAPSYCHOLOGY.

extrinsic desire, a desire of something for its conduciveness to something else that one desires. Extrinsic desires are distinguished from *intrinsic* desires, desires of items for their own sake, or as ends. Thus, an individual might desire financial security extrinsically, as a means to her happiness, and desire happiness intrinsically, as an end. Some desires are *mixed:* their objects are desired both for themselves and for their conduciveness to something else. Jacques may desire to jog, e.g., both for its own sake (as an end) and for the sake of his health. A desire is *strictly intrinsic* if and only if its object is desired for itself alone. A desire is *strictly extrinsic* if and only if its object is not desired, even partly, for its own sake. (Desires for "good news" – e.g., a desire to hear that one's child has survived a car accident – are sometimes classified as extrinsic desires, even if the information is desired only because of what it indicates and not for any instrumental value that it may have.)

Desires of each kind help to explain action. Owing partly to a mixed desire to entertain a friend, Martha might acquire a variety of extrinsic desires for actions conducive to that goal. Less happily, intrinsically desiring to be rid of his toothache, George might extrinsically desire to schedule a dental appointment. If all goes well for Martha and George, their desires will be satisfied, and that will be due in part to the effects of the desires upon their behavior.

See also ACTION THEORY, INTENTION, MOTIVATIONAL EXPLANATION, VALUE.

A.R.M.

extrinsic property. See RELATION.

extrinsic relation. See RELATION.

F

fa, Chinese term for (1) a standard, model, paradigm, or exemplar; (2) proper procedure, behavior, or technique; (3) a rule or law; (4) dharma. A mental image (*yi*) of a circle, a compass, and a particular circle can each serve as a *fa* for identifying circles. The sage-kings, their institutions, and their behavior are all *fa* for rulers to emulate. Methods of governing (e.g., by reward and punishment) are *fa*. Explicit laws or bureaucratic rules are also *fa*. (See *Mo Tzu*, "Dialectical Chapters," and *Kuan Tzu*, chapter 6, "Seven Standards.") After the introduction of Buddhism to China, *fa* is used to translate 'dharma'. **See also BUDDHISM, DHARMA, MO TZU.** B.W.V.N.

fa-chia. See CHINESE LEGALISM.

fact. See STATE OF AFFAIRS.

facticity. See HEIDEGGER, SARTRE.

factual content. See ANALYTIC–SYNTHETIC DISTINCTION.

fact–value distinction, the apparently fundamental difference between how things are and how they should be. That people obey the law (or act honestly or desire money) is one thing; that they should is quite another. The first is a matter of fact, the second a matter of value.

Hume is usually credited with drawing the distinction when he noticed that one cannot uncontroversially infer an 'ought' from an 'is' (the is–ought gap). From the fact, say, that an action would maximize overall happiness, we cannot legitimately infer that it ought to be done – without the introduction of some (so far suppressed) evaluative premise. We could secure the inference by assuming that one ought always to do what maximizes overall happiness. But that assumption is evidently evaluative. And any other premise that might link the non-evaluative premises to an evaluative conclusion would look equally evaluative. No matter how detailed and extensive the non-evaluative premises, it seems no evaluative conclusion follows (directly and as a matter of logic). Some have replied that at least a few non-evaluative claims do entail evaluative ones. To take one popular example, from the fact that some promise was made, we might (it appears) legitimately infer that it ought to be kept, other things equal – and this without the introduction of an evaluative premise. Yet many argue that the inference fails, or that the premise is actually evaluative, or that the conclusion is not.

Hume himself was both bold and brief about the gap's significance, claiming simply that paying attention to it "wou'd subvert all the vulgar systems of morality, and let us see, that the distinction of vice and virtue is not founded merely on the relations of objects, nor is perceiv'd by reason" (*Treatise of Human Nature*). Others have been more expansive. Moore, for instance, in effect relied upon the gap to establish (via the open question argument) that any attempt to define evaluative terms using non-evaluative ones would commit the naturalistic fallacy. Moore's main target was the suggestion that 'good' *means* "pleasant" and the fallacy, in this context, is supposed to be misidentifying an evaluative property, being good, with a natural property, being pleasant. Assuming that evaluative terms have meaning, Moore held that some could be defined using others (he thought, e.g., that 'right' could be defined as "productive of the greatest possible good") and that the rest, though meaningful, must be indefinable terms denoting simple, non-natural, properties. Accepting Moore's use of the open question argument but rejecting both his non-naturalism and his assumption that evaluative terms must have (descriptive) meaning, emotivists and prescriptivists (e.g. Ayer, C. L. Stevenson, and Hare) argued that evaluative terms have a role in language other than to denote properties. According to them, the primary role of evaluative language is not to describe, but to prescribe. The logical gap between 'is' and 'ought', they argue, establishes both the difference between fact and value and the difference between describing (how things are) and recommending (how they might be). Some naturalists, though, acknowledge the gap and yet maintain that the evaluative claims nonetheless do refer to natural properties. In the process they deny the ontological force of the open question argument and treat evaluative claims as describing a special class of facts.

See also ETHICS, MOORE, MORAL REALISM.

G.S.-M.

faculty psychology, the view that the mind is a collection of departments responsible for distinct psychological functions. Related to faculty psychology is the doctrine of localization of function, wherein each faculty has a specific brain location. Faculty psychologies oppose theories of mind as a unity with one function (e.g., those of Descartes and associationism) or as a unity with various capabilities (e.g., that of Ockham), and oppose the related holistic distributionist or mass-action theory of the brain. Faculty psychology began with Aristotle, who divided the human soul into five *special senses*, three *inner senses* (*common sense, imagination, memory*) and *active* and *passive mind*. In the Middle Ages (e.g., Aquinas) Aristotle's three inner senses were subdivied, creating more elaborate lists of five to seven *inward wits*. Islamic physician-philosophers such as Avicenna integrated Aristotelian faculty psychology with Galenic medicine by proposing brain locations for the faculties.

Two important developments in faculty psychology occurred during the eighteenth century. First, Scottish philosophers led by Reid developed a version of faculty psychology opposed to the empiricist and associationist psychologies of Locke and Hume. The Scots proposed that humans were endowed by God with a set of faculties permitting knowledge of the world and morality. The Scottish system exerted considerable influence in the United States, where it was widely taught as a moral, character-building discipline, and in the nineteenth century this "Old Psychology" opposed the experimental "New Psychology." Second, despite then being called a charlatan, Franz Joseph Gall (1758–1828) laid the foundation for modern neuropsychology in his work on localization of function. Gall rejected existing faculty psychologies as philosophical, unbiological, and incapable of accounting for everyday behavior. Gall proposed an innovative behavioral and biological list of faculties and brain localizations based on comparative anatomy, behavior study, and measurements of the human skull. Today, faculty psychology survives in trait and instinct theories of personality, Fodor's theory that mental functions are implemented by neurologically "encapsulated" organs, and localizationist theories of the brain.

See also ARISTOTLE, PHILOSOPHY OF MIND, PHILOSOPHY OF PSYCHOLOGY.   T.H.L.

faith. See BAD FAITH, PHILOSOPHY OF RELIGION.

fallacy. See FORMAL FALLACY, INFORMAL FALLACY.

fallacy of accent. See INFORMAL FALLACY.

fallacy of accident. See INFORMAL FALLACY.

fallacy of affirming the consequent. See FORMAL FALLACY.

fallacy of composition. See INFORMAL FALLACY.

fallacy of denying the antecedent. See FORMAL FALLACY.

fallacy of division. See INFORMAL FALLACY.

fallacy of equivocation. See INFORMAL FALLACY.

fallacy of false cause. See INFORMAL FALLACY.

fallacy of four terms. See SYLLOGISM.

fallacy of hasty generalization. See INFORMAL FALLACY.

fallacy of irrelevant conclusion. See INFORMAL FALLACY.

fallacy of many questions. See INFORMAL FALLACY.

fallacy of misplaced concreteness. See WHITEHEAD.

fallacy of *secundum quid*. See INFORMAL FALLACY.

fallibilism, the doctrine, relative to some significant class of beliefs or propositions, that they are inherently uncertain and possibly mistaken. The most extreme form of the doctrine attributes uncertainty to every belief; more restricted forms attribute it to all empirical beliefs or to beliefs concerning the past, the future, other minds, or the external world. Most contemporary philosophers reject the doctrine in its extreme form, holding that beliefs about such things as elementary logical principles and the character of one's current feelings cannot possibly be mistaken.

Philosophers who reject fallibilism in some form generally insist that certain beliefs are analytically true, self-evident, or intuitively obvious. These means of supporting the infallibility of some beliefs are now generally discredited. W. V. Quine has cast serious doubt on the very notion of analytic truth, and the appeal to self-evidence or intuitive obviousness is open to the charge that those who officially accept it do not always agree on what is thus evident or obvious (there is no objective way of identifying it), and that beliefs said to be self-evident have sometimes been proved false, the causal principle and the axiom of abstraction (in set theory) being striking examples. In addition to emphasizing the evolution of logical and mathematical principles, fallibilists have supported their position mainly by arguing that the existence and nature of mind-independent objects can legitimately be ascertained only be experimental methods and that such methods can yield conclusions that are, at best, probable rather than certain.   B.A.

false cause, fallacy of. See INFORMAL FALLACY.

false consciousness, (1) lack of clear awareness of the source and significance of one's beliefs and attitudes concerning society, religion, or values; (2) objectionable forms of ignorance and false belief; (3) dishonest forms of self-deception. Marxists (if not Marx) use the expression to explain and condemn illusions generated by unfair economic relationships. Thus, workers who are unaware of their alienation, and "happy homemakers" who only dimly sense their dependency and quiet desperation, are molded in their attitudes by economic power relationships that make the status quo seem natural, thereby eclipsing their long-term best interests. Again, religion is construed as an economically driven ideology that functions as an "opiate" blocking clear awareness of human needs. Collingwood interprets false consciousness as self-corrupting untruthfulness in disowning one's emotions and ideas (*The Principles of Art*, 1938). **See also BAD FAITH, EXISTENTIALISM.**
M.W.M.

false dilemma. See DILEMMA.

false pleasure, pleasure taken in something false. If it is false that Jones is honest, but Smith believes Jones is honest and is pleased that Jones is honest, then Smith's pleasure is false. If pleasure is construed as an intentional attitude, then the truth or falsity of a pleasure is a function of whether its intentional object obtains. On this view, S's being pleased that p is a true pleasure if an only if S is pleased that p and p is true. S's being pleased that p is a false pleasure if and only if S is

pleased that p and p is false. Alternatively, Plato uses the expression 'false pleasure' to refer to things such as the cessation of pain or neutral states that are neither pleasant nor painful that a subject confuses with genuine or true pleasures. Thus, being released from tight shackles might mistakenly be thought pleasant when it is merely the cessation of a pain. **See also HEDONISM, VALUE.**   N.M.L.

falsifiability. See POPPER, TESTABILITY.

falsification. See POPPER.

falsum. See Appendix of Special Symbols.

family resemblance. See WITTGENSTEIN.

Fang, Thomé H. (1899–1976), Chinese philosopher of culture. Educated at the University of Nanking and the University of Wisconsin, he had an early interest in Dewey's pragmatism, but returned to the ideals of Chinese philosophy during World War II. He had a grand philosophical scheme, always discussing issues from a comparative viewpoint through perspectives of ancient Greek, modern European, Chinese, and Indian thought. He exerted a profound influence on younger philosophers in Taiwan after 1949. **See also CHINESE PHILOSOPHY.**   S.-h.L.

Fārābī, al-. See AL-FĀRĀBĪ.

fascism. See POLITICAL PHILOSOPHY.

fatalism. See FREE WILL PROBLEM.

feature-placing discourse. See STRAWSON.

Fechner, Gustav Theodor (1801–87), German physicist and philosopher whose *Elemente der Psychophysik* (1860; English translation, 1966) inaugurated experimental psychology. Obsessed with the mind–body problem, Fechner advanced an identity theory in which every object is both mental and physical, and in support invented psychophysics – the "exact science of the functional relations ... between mind and body." Fechner began with the concept of the *limen*, or sensory threshold. The *absolute threshold* is the stimulus strength (R, *Reiz*) needed to create a conscious sensation (S), and the *relative threshold* is the strength that must be added to a stimulus for a *just noticeable difference* (*jnd*) to be perceived. E. H. Weber (1795–1878) had shown that a constant ratio held between relative threshold and stimulus magnitude, Weber's law: $\Delta R/R = k$. By experimentally determining *jnd*'s for pairs of stimulus magnitudes (such as weights), Fechner formulated his "functional relation," $S = \text{k} \log R$, Fechner's law, an identity equation of mind and matter. Later psychophysicists replaced it with a power law, $R = kS^n$, where n depends on the kind of stimulus. The importance of psychophysics to psychology consisted in its showing that quantification of experience was possible, and its providing a general paradigm for psychological experimentation in which controlled stimulus conditions are systematically varied and effects observed. In his later years, Fechner brought the experimental method to bear on aesthetics (*Vorschule der Aesthetik*, 1876).   T.H.L.

Fechner's law. See FECHNER.

feedback. See CYBERNETICS.

feedforward. See CYBERNETICS.

felicific calculus. See BENTHAM.

felicity conditions. See SPEECH ACT THEORY.

feminist epistemology, epistemology from a feminist perspective. It investigates the relevance that the gender of the inquirer/knower has to epistemic practices, including the theoretical practice of epistemology. It is typified both by themes that are exclusively feminist in that they could arise only from a critical attention to gender, and by themes that are non-exclusively feminist in that they might arise from other politicizing theoretical perspectives besides feminism.

A central, exclusively feminist theme is the relation between philosophical conceptions of reason and cultural conceptions of masculinity. Here a historicist stance must be adopted, so that philosophy is conceived as the product of historically and culturally situated (hence gendered) authors. This stance brings certain patterns of intellectual association into view – patterns, perhaps, of alignment between philosophical conceptions of reason as contrasted with emotion or intuition, and cultural conceptions of masculinity as contrasted with femininity.

A central, non-exclusively feminist theme might be called "social-ism" in epistemology. It has two main tributaries: political philosophy, in the form of Marx's historical materialism; and philosophy of science, in the form of either Quinean naturalism or Kuhnian historicism. The first has resulted in feminist standpoint theory, which adapts and develops the Marxian idea that different social groups have different epistemic standpoints, where the material positioning of one of the groups is said to bestow an epistemic privilege. The second has resulted in feminist work in philosophy of science which tries to show that not only epistemic values but also non-epistemic (e.g. gendered) values are of necessity sometimes an influence in the generation of scientific theories. If this can be shown, then an important feminist project suggests itself: to work out a rationale for regulating the influence of these values so that science may be more self-transparent and more responsible.

By attempting to reveal the epistemological implications of the fact that knowers are diversely situated in social relations of identity and power, feminist epistemology represents a radicalizing innovation in the analytic tradition, which has typically assumed an asocial conception of the epistemic subject, and of the philosopher.

   See also EPISTEMOLOGY, FEMINIST PHILOSOPHY, KUHN, MARXISM, QUINE.   M.F.

feminist philosophy, a discussion of philosophical concerns that refuses to identify the human experience with the male experience. Writing from a variety of perspectives, feminist philosophers challenge several areas of traditional philosophy on the grounds that they fail (1) to take seriously women's interests, identities, and issues; and (2) to recognize women's ways of being, thinking, and doing as valuable as those of men.

Feminist philosophers fault traditional metaphysics for splitting the self from the other and the mind from the body; for wondering whether "other minds" exist and whether personal identity depends more on memories or on physical characteristics. Because feminist philosophers reject all forms of ontological dualism, they stress the ways in which individuals interpenetrate each other's psyches through empathy, and the ways in which the mind and body coconstitute each other.

Because Western culture has associated rationality with "masculinity" and emotionality with "femininity," traditional epistemologists have often concluded that women are less human than men. For this reason, feminist philosophers argue that reason and emotion are symbiotically related, coequal sources of knowledge. Feminist philosophers also argue that Cartesian knowledge, for all its certainty and clarity, is very limited. People want to know more than that they exist; they want to know what other people are thinking and feeling.

Feminist philosophers also observe that traditional philosophy of science is not as objective as it claims to be. Whereas traditional philosophers of science often associate scientific success with scientists' ability to control, rule, and otherwise dominate nature, feminist philosophers of science associate scientific success with scientists' ability to listen to nature's self-revelations. Since it willingly yields abstract theory to the testimony of concrete fact, a science that listens to what nature says is probably more objective than one that does not.

Feminist philosophers also criticize traditional ethics and traditional social and political philosophy. Rules and principles have dominated traditional ethics. Whether agents seek to maximize utility for the aggregate or do their duty for the sake of duty, they measure their conduct against a set of universal, abstract, and impersonal norms. Feminist philosophers often call this traditional view of ethics a "justice" perspective, contrasting it with a "care" perspective that stresses responsibilities and relationships rather than rights and rules, and that attends more to a moral situation's particular features than to its general implications.

Feminist social and political philosophy focus on the political institutions and social practices that perpetuate women's subordination. The goals of feminist social and political philosophy are (1) to explain why women are suppressed, repressed, and/or oppressed in ways that men are not; and (2) to suggest morally desirable and politically feasible ways to give women the same justice, freedom, and equality that men have. Liberal feminists believe that because women have the same rights as men do, society must provide women with the same educational and occupational opportunities that men have. Marxist feminists believe that women cannot be men's equals until women enter the work force en masse and domestic work and child care are socialized. Radical feminists believe that the fundamental causes of women's oppression are sexual. It is women's reproductive role and/or their sexual role that causes their subordination. Unless women set their own reproductive goals (childlessness is a legitimate alternative to motherhood) and their own sexual agendas (lesbianism, autoeroticism, and celibacy are alternatives to heterosexuality), women will remain less than free. Psychoanalytic feminists believe that women's subordination is the result of early-childhood experiences that cause them to overdevelop their abilities to relate to other people on the one hand and to underdevelop their abilities to assert themselves as autonomous agents on the other. Women's greatest strength, a capacity for deep relationships, may also be their greatest weakness: a tendency to be controlled by the needs and wants of others. Finally, existentialist feminists claim that the ultimate cause of women's subordination is ontological. Women are the Other; men are the Self. Until women define themselves in terms of themselves, they will continue to be defined in terms of what they are not: men.

Recently, socialist feminists have attempted to weave these distinctive strands of feminist social and political thought into a theoretical whole. They argue that women's condition is overdetermined by the structures of production, reproduction and sexuality, and the socialization of children. Women's status and function in *all* of these structures must change if they are to achieve full liberation. Furthermore, women's psyches must also be transformed. Only then will women be liberated from the kind of patriarchal thoughts that undermine their self-concept and make them always the Other.

Interestingly, the socialist feminist effort to establish a specifically feminist standpoint that represents how women see the world has not gone without challenge. Postmodern feminists regard this effort as an instantiation of the kind of typically male thinking that tells only one story about reality, truth, knowledge, ethics, and politics. For postmodern feminists, such a story is neither feasible nor desirable. It is not feasible because women's experiences differ across class, racial, and cultural lines. It is not desirable because the "One" and the "True" are philosophical myths that traditional philosophy uses to silence the voices of the many. Feminist philosophy must be many and not One because women are many and not One. The more feminist thoughts, the better. By refusing to center, congeal, and cement separate thoughts into a unified and inflexible truth, feminist philosophers can avoid the pitfalls of traditional philosophy.

As attractive as the postmodern feminist approach to philosophy may be, some feminist philosophers worry that an overemphasis on difference and a rejection of unity may lead to intellectual as well as political disintegration. If feminist philosophy is to be without any standpoint whatsoever, it becomes difficult to ground claims about what is *good* for women in particular and for human beings in general. It is a major challenge to contemporary feminist philosophy, therefore, to reconcile the pressures for diversity and difference with those for integration and commonality.

See also ETHICS, EXISTENTIALISM, MARXISM, POLITICAL PHILOSOPHY, POSTMODERN.

R.T.

Ferguson, Adam (1723–1816), Scottish philosopher and historian. His main theme was the rise and fall of virtue in individuals and societies. In his most important work, *An Essay on the History of Civil Society* (1766), he argued that human happiness (of which virtue is a constituent) is found in pursuing social goods rather than private ends. Ferguson thought that ignoring social goods not only prevented social progress but led to moral corruption and political despotism. To support this he used classical texts and travelers' writings to reconstruct the history of society from "rude nations" through barbarism to civilization. This allowed him to express his concern for the danger of corruption inherent in the increasing self-interest manifested in the incipient commercial civilization of his day. He attempted to systematize his moral philosophy in *The Principles of Moral and Social Science* (1792).   J.W.A.

Fermat's last theorem. See CHOICE SEQUENCE.

Feuerbach, Ludwig Andreas (1804–72), German materialist philosopher and critic of religion. He provided the major link between Hegel's absolute idealism and such later theories of historical materialism as those of Marx and other "young (or new) Hegelians." Feuerbach was born in Bavaria and studied theology, first at Heidelberg and then Berlin, where he came under the philosophical influence of Hegel. He received his doctorate in 1828 and, after an early publication severely critical of Christianity, retired from official German academic life. In the years between 1836 and 1846, he produced some of his most influential works, which include "Towards a Critique of Hegel's Philosophy" (1839), *The Essence of Christianity* (1841), *Principles of the Philosophy of the Future* (1843), and *The Essence of Religion* (1846). After a brief collaboration with Marx, he emerged as a popular champion of political liberalism in the revolutionary period of 1848. During the reaction that followed, he again left public life and died dependent upon the support of friends.

Feuerbach was pivotal in the intellectual history of the nineteenth century in several respects. First, after a half-century of metaphysical system construction by the German idealists, Feuerbach revived, in a new form, the original Kantian project of philosophical critique. However, whereas Kant had tried "to limit reason in order to make room for faith," Feuerbach sought to demystify both faith and reason in favor of the concrete and situated existence of embodied human consciousness. Second, his "method" of "transformatory criticism" – directed, in the first instance, at Hegel's philosophical pronouncements – was adopted by Marx and has retained its philosophical appeal. Briefly, it suggested that "Hegel be stood on his feet" by "inverting" the subject and predicate in Hegel's idealistic pronouncements. One should, e.g., rewrite "The individual is a function of the Absolute" as "The Absolute is a function of the individual." Third, Feuerbach asserted that the philosophy of German idealism was ultimately an extenuation of theology, and that theology was merely religious consciousness systematized. But since religion itself proves to be merely a "dream of the human mind," metaphysics, theology, and religion can be reduced to "anthropology," the study of concrete embodied human consciousness and its cultural products.

The philosophical influence of Feuerbach flows through Marx into virtually all later historical materialist positions; anticipates the existentialist concern with concrete embodied human existence; and serves as a paradigm for all later approaches to religion on the part of the social sciences.

See also HEGEL, KANT, MARX, MARXISM.

J.P.Su.

Fichte, Johann Gottlieb (1762–1814), German philosopher. He was a proponent of an uncompromising system of transcendental idealism, the *Wissenschaftslehre*, which played a key role in the development of post-Kantian philosophy. Born in Saxony, Fichte studied at Jena and Leipzig. The writings of Kant led him to abandon metaphysical determinism and to embrace transcendental idealism as "the first system of human freedom." His first book, *Versuch einer Kritik aller Offenbarung* ("Attempt at a Critique of all Revelations," 1792), earned him a reputation as a brilliant exponent of Kantianism, while his early political writings secured him a reputation as a Jacobin.

Inspired by Reinhold, Jacobi, Maimon, and Schulze, Fichte rejected the "letter" of Kantianism and, in the lectures and writings he produced at Jena (1794–99), advanced a new, rigorously systematic presentation of what he took to be its "spirit." He dispensed with Kant's things-in-themselves, the original duality of faculties, and the distinction between the transcendental aesthetic and the transcendental analytic. By emphasizing the unity of theoretical and practical reason in a way consistent with "the primacy of practical reason," Fichte sought to establish the unity of the critical philosophy as well as of human experience.

In *Ueber den Begriff der Wissenschaftslehre* ("On the Concept of the *Wissenschaftslehre*," 1794) he explained his conception of philosophy as "the science of science," to be presented in a deductive system based on a self-evident first principle. The basic "foundations" of this system, which Fichte called *Wissenschaftslehre* (theory of science), were outlined in his *Grundlage der gesamten Wissenschaftslehre* ("Foundations of the Entire *Wissenschaftslehre*," 1794–95) and *Grundriß der Eigentümlichen der Wissenschaftslehre in Rücksicht auf das theoretische Vermögen* ("Outline of the Distinctive Character of the *Wissenschaftslehre* with respect to the Theoretical Faculty," 1795) and then, substantially revised, in his lectures on *Wissenschaftslehre nova methodo* (1796–99).

The "foundational" portion of the *Wissenschaftslehre* links our affirmation of freedom to our experience of natural necessity. Beginning with the former ("the I simply posits itself"), it then demonstrates how a freely self-positing subject must be conscious not only of itself, but also of "representations accompanied by a feeling of necessity" and hence of an objective world. Fichte insisted that the essence of selfhood lies in an active positing of its own self-identity and hence that self-consciousness is an auto-productive *activity:* a *Tathandlung* or "fact/act." However, the I can posit itself only as *limited;* in order for the originally posited act of "sheer self-positing" to occur, certain other mental acts must occur as well, acts through which the I posits for itself an objective, spatiotemporal world, as well as a moral realm of free, rational beings. The I first posits its own limited condition in the form of "feeling" (occasioned by an inexplicable *Anstoß* or "check" upon its own practical striving), then as a "sensation," then as an "intuition" of a thing, and finally as a "concept." The distinction between the I and the not-I arises only in these reiterated acts of self-positing, a complete description of which thus amounts to a "genetic deduction" of the necessary conditions of experience. Freedom is thereby shown to be possible only in the context of natural necessity, where it is limited and finite. At the same time "our freedom is a theoretical determining principle of our world."

Though it must posit its freedom "absolutely" – i.e., *schlechthin* or "for no reason" – a genuinely free agent can exist only as a finite individual endlessly striving to overcome its own limits.

After establishing its "foundations," Fichte extended his *Wissenschaftslehre* into social and political philosophy and ethics. Subjectivity itself is essentially *intersubjective,* inasmuch as one can be empirically conscious of oneself only as one *individual* among many and must thus posit the freedom of others in order to posit one's own freedom. But for this to occur, the freedom of each individual must be limited; indeed, "the concept of right or justice (*Recht*) is nothing other than the concept of the coexistence of the freedom of several rational/sensuous beings." The *Grundlage des Naturrechts* ("Foundations of Natural Right," 1796–97) examines how individual freedom must be externally limited if a community of free individuals is to be possible, and demonstrates that a just political order is a demand of reason itself, since "the concept of justice or right is a condition of self-consciousness." "Natural rights" are thus entirely independent of moral duties. Unlike political philosophy, which purely concerns the public realm, ethics, which is the subject of *Das System der Sittenlehre* ("The System of Ethical Theory," 1798), concerns the inner realm of conscience. It views objects not as *given* to consciousness but as *produced* by free action, and concerns not what *is,* but what *ought* to be. The task of ethics is to indicate the particular duties that follow from the general obligation to determine oneself freely (the categorical imperative).

Before Fichte could extend the *Wissenschaftslehre* into the philosophy of religion, he was accused of atheism and forced to leave Jena. The celebrated controversy over his alleged atheism (the *Atheismusstreit*) was provoked by "Ueber den Grund unseres Glaubens in einer göttliche Weltregierung" ("On the Basis of our Belief in a Divine Governance of the World," 1798), in which he sharply distinguished between philosophical and religious questions. While defending our right to posit a "moral world order," Fichte insisted that this order does not require a personal deity or "moral lawgiver."

After moving to Berlin, Fichte's first concern was to rebut the charge of atheism and to reply to the indictment of philosophy as "nihilism" advanced in Jacobi's *Open Letter to Fichte* (1799). This was the task of *Die Bestimmung des Menschen* ("The Vocation of Man," 1800). During the French occupation, he delivered *Reden an die deutsche Nation* ("Addresses to the German

Nation," 1808), which proposed a program of national education and attempted to kindle German patriotism. The other publications of his Berlin years include a foray into political economy, *Der geschlossene Handelstaat* ("The Closed Commercial State," 1800); a speculative interpretation of human history, *Die Grundzüge des gegenwärtiges Zeitalters* ("The Characteristics of the Present Age," 1806); and a mystically tinged treatise on salvation, *Die Anweisung zum seligen Leben* ("Guide to the Blessed Life," 1806). In unpublished private lectures he continued to develop radically new versions of the *Wissenschaftslehre*.

Fichte's substantial influence was not limited to his well-known influence on Schelling and Hegel (both of whom criticized the "subjectivism" of the early *Wissenschaftslehre*). He is also important in the history of German nationalism and profoundly influenced the early Romantics, especially Novalis and Schlegel. Recent decades have seen renewed interest in Fichte's transcendental philosophy, expecially the later, unpublished versions of the *Wissenschaftslehre*. This century's most significant contribution to Fichte studies, however, is the ongoing publication of the first critical edition of his complete works.

    See also HEGEL, IDEALISM, KANT.   D.Br.

Ficino, Marsilio (1433–99), Italian Neoplatonic philosopher who played a leading role in the cultural life of Florence. Ordained a priest in 1473, he hoped to draw people to Christ by means of Platonism. It was through Ficino's translation and commentaries that the works of Plato first became accessible to the Latin-speaking West, but the impact of Plato's work was considerably affected by Ficino's other interests. He accepted Neoplatonic interpretations of Plato, including those of Plotinus, whom he translated; and he saw Plato as the heir of Hermes Trismegistus, a mythical Egyptian sage and supposed author of the hermetic corpus, which he translated early in his career. He embraced the notion of a *prisca theologia*, an ancient wisdom that encapsulated philosophic and religious truth, was handed on to Plato, and was later validated by the Christian revelation. The most popular of his original works was *Three Books on Life* (1489), which contains the fullest Renaissance exposition of a theory of magic, based mainly on Neoplatonic sources. He postulated a living cosmos in which the World-Soul is linked to the world-body by spirit. This relationship is mirrored in man, whose spirit (or astral body) links his body and soul, and the resulting correspondence between

microcosm and macrocosm allows both man's control of natural objects through magic and his ascent to knowledge of God. Other popular works were his commentary on Plato's *Symposium* (1469), which presents a theory of Platonic love; and his *Platonic Theology* (1474), in which he argues for the immortality of the soul. **See also** NEOPLATONISM.   E.J.A.

fiction, in the widest usage, whatever contrasts with what is a matter of fact. As applied to works of fiction, however, this is not the appropriate contrast. For a work of fiction, such as a historical novel, might turn out to be true regarding its historical subject, without ceasing to be fiction. The correct contrast of fiction is to non-fiction. If a work of fiction might turn out to be true, how is 'fiction' best defined? According to some philosophers, such as Searle, the writer of non-fiction performs illocutionary speech acts, such as asserting that such-and-such occurred, whereas the writer of fiction characteristically only *pretends* to perform these illocutionary acts. Others hold that the core idea to which appeal should be made is that of making-believe or imagining certain states of affairs. Kendall Walton (*Mimesis as Make-Believe*, 1990), for instance, holds that a work of fiction is to be construed in terms of a prop whose function is to serve in games of make-believe. Both kinds of theory allow for the possibility that a work of fiction might turn out to be true. **See also** AESTHETICS, IMAGINATION, PHILOSOPHY OF LITERATURE, SPEECH ACT THEORY.   B.Ga.

fiction, logical. See LOGICAL CONSTRUCTION.

fictionalism. See DUHEM.

fideism. See EVIDENTIALISM.

"Fido" – Fido theory of meaning. See MEANING.

field (of a relation). See RELATION.

field theory, a theory that proceeds by assigning values of physical quantities to the points of space, or of space-time, and then lays down laws relating these values. For example, a field theory might suppose a value for matter density, or a temperature for each space-time point, and then relate these values, usually in terms of differential equations. In these examples there is at least the tacit assumption of a physical substance that fills the relevant region of space-time. But no such assumption need be made. For instance, in

Maxwell's theory of the electromagnetic field, each point of space-time carries a value for an electric and a magnetic field, and these values are then governed by Maxwell's equations. In general relativity, the geometry (e.g., the curvature) of space-time is itself treated as a field, with law-like connections with the distribution of energy and matter.

Formulation in terms of a field theory resolves the problem of action at a distance that so exercised Newton and his contemporaries. We often take causal connection to require spatial contiguity. That is, for one entity to act causally on another, the two entities need to be contiguous. But in Newton's description gravitational attraction acts across spatial distances. Similarly, in electrostatics the mutual repulsion of electric charges is described as acting across spatial distances. In the times of both Newton and Maxwell numerous efforts to understand such action at a distance in terms of some space-filling mediating substance produced no viable theory. Field theories resolve the perplexity. By attributing values of physical quantities directly to the space-time points one can describe gravitation, electrical and magnetic forces, and other interactions without action at a distance or any intervening physical medium. One describes the values of physical quantities, attributed directly to the space-time points, as influencing only the values at immediately neighboring points. In this way the influences propagate through space-time, rather than act instantaneously across distances or through a medium.

Of course there is a metaphysical price: on such a description the space-time points themselves take on the role of a kind of dematerialized ether. Indeed, some have argued that the pervasive role of field theory in contemporary physics and the need for space-time points for a field-theoretic description constitute a strong argument for the existence of the space-time points. This conclusion contradicts "relationalism," which claims that there are only spatiotemporal relations, but no space-time points or regions thought of as particulars.

Quantum field theory appears to take on a particularly abstract form of field theory, since it associates a quantum mechanical operator with each space-time point. However, since operators correspond to physical magnitudes rather than to values of such magnitudes, it is better to think of the field-theoretic aspect of quantum field theory in terms of the quantum mechanical amplitudes that it also associates with the space-time points.

See also EINSTEIN, NEWTON, PHILOSOPHY OF SCIENCE, QUANTUM MECHANICS, SPACE-TIME.   P.Te.

figure. See SYLLOGISM.

figure–ground, the discrimination of an object or figure from the context or background against which it is set. Even when a connected region is grouped together properly, as in the famous figure that can be seen either as a pair of faces or as a vase, it is possible to interpret the region alternately as figure and as ground. This fact was originally elaborated in 1921 by Edgar Rubin (1886–1951). Figure–ground effects and the existence of other ambiguous figures such as the Necker cube and the duck–rabbit challenged the prevailing assumption in classical theories of perception – maintained, e.g., by J. S. Mill and H. von Helmholtz – that complex perceptions could be understood in terms of primitive sensations constituting them.

The underdetermination of perception by the visual stimulus, noted by Berkeley in his *Essay* of 1709, takes account of the fact that the retinal image is impoverished with respect to three-dimensional information. Identical stimulation at the retina can result from radically different distal sources. Within Gestalt psychology, the *Gestalt,* or pattern, was recognized to be underdetermined by constituent parts available in proximal stimuli. M. Wertheimer (1880–1943) observed in 1912 that apparent motion could be induced by viewing a series of still pictures in rapid succession. He concluded that perception of the whole, as involving movement, was fundamentally different from the perception of the static images of which it is composed. W. Köhler

An example of visual reversal from Edgar Rubin: the object depicted can be seen alternately as a vase or as a pair of faces. The reversal occurs whether there is a black ground and white figure or white figure and black ground.

(1887–1967) observed that there was no figure–ground articulation in the retinal image, and concluded that inherently ambiguous stimuli required some autonomous selective principles of perceptual organization. As subsequently developed by Gestalt psychologists, form is taken as the primitive unit of perception. In philosophical treatments, figure–ground effects are used to enforce the conclusion that interpretation is central to perception, and that perceptions are no more than hypotheses based on sensory data.
 See also KÖHLER, PERCEPTION.   R.C.R.

Filmer, Robert (1588–1653), English political writer who produced, most importantly, the posthumous *Patriarcha* (1680). It is remembered because Locke attacked it in the first of his *Two Treatises of Government* (1690). Filmer argued that God gave complete authority over the world to Adam, and that from him it descended to his eldest son when he became the head of the family. Thereafter only fathers directly descended from Adam could properly be rulers. Just as Adam's rule was not derived from the consent of his family, so the king's inherited authority is not dependent on popular consent. He rightly makes laws and imposes taxes at his own good pleasure, though like a good father he has the welfare of his subjects in view. Filmer's patriarchalism, intended to bolster the absolute power of the king, is the classic English statement of the doctrine. **See also POLITICAL PHILOSOPHY.**
               J.B.S.

final cause. See ARISTOTLE.

finitary proof. See HILBERT'S PROGRAM.

finite automaton. See COMPUTER THEORY, TURING MACHINE.

finitism. See HILBERT, PHILOSOPHY OF MATHEMATICS.

first actualization. See ARISTOTLE.

first cause. See PRIME MOVER.

first cause argument. See PHILOSOPHY OF RELIGION.

first imposition. See IMPOSITION.

first intention. See IMPOSITION.

first law of thermodynamics. See ENTROPY.

first limit theorem. See PROBABILITY.

first mover. See PRIME MOVER.

firstness. See PEIRCE.

first-order. See ORDER.

first-order logic. See FORMAL LOGIC, ORDER, SECOND-ORDER LOGIC.

first philosophy, in Aristotle's *Metaphysics,* the study of being *qua* being, including the study of theology (as understood by him), since the divine is being *par excellence.* Descartes's *Meditations on First Philosophy* was concerned chiefly with the existence of God, the immortality of the soul, and the nature of matter and of the mind. **See also METAPHYSICS.**   P.Bu.

first potentiality. See ARISTOTLE.

fitness. See PHILOSOPHY OF BIOLOGY.

five phases. See WU-HSING.

Five Ways. See AQUINAS.

Fludd, Robert (1574–1637), English physician and writer. Influenced by Paracelsus, hermetism, and the cabala, Fludd defended a Neoplatonic worldview on the eve of its supersession by the new mechanistic philosophy. He produced improvements in the manufacture of steel and invented a thermometer, though he also used magnets to cure disease and devised a salve to be applied to a weapon to cure the wound it had inflicted. He held that science got its ideas from Scripture allegorically interpreted, when they were of any value. His works combine theology with an occult, Neoplatonic reading of the Bible, and contain numerous fine diagrams illustrating the mutual sympathy of human beings, the natural world, and the supernatural world, each reflecting the others in parallel harmonic structures. In controversy with Kepler, Fludd claimed to uncover essential natural processes rooted in natural sympathies and the operation of God's light, rather than merely describing the external movements of the heavens. Creation is the extension of divine light into matter. Evil arises from a darkness in God, his failure to will. Matter is uncreated, but this poses no problem for orthodoxy, since matter is nothing, a mere possibility without the least actuality, not *something*

coeternal with the Creator. **See also** NEOPLA-
TONISM.   J.Lo.

fluxion. See CALCULUS.

flying arrow paradox. See ZENO'S PARADOXES.

focal meaning. See ARISTOTLE.

Fodor, Jerry A. (b.1935), influential contemporary American philosopher of psychology,
known for his energetic (and often witty)
defense of intensional realism, a computational-
representational model of thought, and an atomistic, externalist theory of content determination
for mental states. Fodor's philosophical writings
fall under three headings. First, he has defended
the theory of mind implicit in contemporary cognitive psychology, that the cognitive mind-brain
is both a representational/computational device
and, ultimately, physical. He has taken on behaviorists (Ryle), psychologists in the tradition of
J. J. Gibson, and eliminative materialists (P. A.
Churchland). Second, he has engaged in various
theoretical disputes within cognitive psychology,
arguing for the modularity of the perceptual and
language systems (roughly, the view that they
are domain-specific, mandatory, limited-access,
innately specified, hardwired, and informationally encapsulated) (*The Modularity of Mind*, 1983);
for a strong form of nativism (that virtually all of
our concepts are innate); and for the existence of
a "language of thought" (*The Language of Thought*,
1975). The latter has led him to argue against
connectionism as a psychological theory (as
opposed to an implementation theory).

Finally, he has defended the views of ordinary
propositional attitude psychology that our mental states (1) are semantically evaluable (intentional), (2) have causal powers, and (3) are such
that the implicit generalizations of folk psychology are largely true of them. His defense is
twofold. Folk psychology is unsurpassed in
explanatory power; furthermore, it is vindicated
by contemporary cognitive psychology insofar as
ordinary propositional attitude states can be
identified with information-processing states,
those that consist in a computational relation to
a representation. The representational component of such states allows us to explain the
semantic evaluability of the attitudes; the computational component, their causal efficacy. Both
sorts of accounts raise difficulties. The first is satisfactory only if supplemented by a naturalistic
account of representational content. Here Fodor
has argued for an atomistic, externalist causal

theory (*Psychosemantics*, 1987) and against holism
(the view that no mental representation has content unless many other non-synonymous mental representations also have content) (*Holism: A
Shopper's Guide*, 1992), against conceptual role
theories (the view that the content of a representation is determined by its conceptual role)
(Ned Block, Brian Loar), and against teleofunc-
tional theories (teleofunctionalism is the view
that the content of a representation is determined, at least in part, by the biological functions
of the representations themselves or systems that
produce or use those representations) (Ruth Millikan, David Papineau). The second sort is satisfactory only if it does not imply epiphenomenalism with respect to content properties. To
avoid such epiphenomenalism, Fodor has
argued that not only strict laws but also *ceteris
paribus* laws can be causal. In addition, he has
sought to reconcile his externalism vis-à-vis content with the view that causal efficacy requires an
individualistic individuation of states. Two solutions have been explored: the supplementation
of broad (externally determined) content with
narrow content, where the latter supervenes on
what is "in the head" (*Psychosemantics*, 1987), and
its supplementation with modes of presentation
identical to sentences of the language of thought
(*The Elm and the Expert*, 1995).

   See also COGNITIVE SCIENCE, CONNECTION-
ISM, FOLK PSYCHOLOGY, HOLISM, LANGUAGE
OF THOUGHT, MEANING, PHILOSOPHY OF
MIND.   B.V.E.

folk psychology, in one sense, a putative network
of principles constituting a commonsense theory
that allegedly underlies everyday explanations of
human behavior; the theory assigns a central
role to mental states like belief, desire, and intention. Consider an example of an everyday commonsense psychological explanation: Jane went
to the refrigerator because she wanted a beer and
she believed there was beer in the refrigerator.
Like many such explanations, this adverts to a
so-called propositional attitude – a mental state,
expressed by a verb ('believe') plus a that-clause,
whose intentional content is propositional. It
also adverts to a mental state, expressed by a verb
('want') plus a direct-object phrase, whose
intentional content appears *not* to be propositional.

   In another, related sense, folk psychology is a
network of social practices that includes ascribing such mental states to ourselves and others,
and proffering explanations of human behavior
that advert to these states. The two senses need

distinguishing because some philosophers who acknowledge the existence of folk psychology in the second sense hold that commonsense psychological explanations do not employ empirical generalizations, and hence that there is no such *theory* as folk psychology. (Henceforth, 'FP' will abbreviate 'folk psychology' in the first sense; the unabbreviated phrase will be used in the second sense.)

Eliminativism in philosophy of mind asserts that FP is an empirical theory; that FP is therefore subject to potential scientific falsification; and that mature science very probably will establish that FP is so radically false that humans simply do not undergo mental states like beliefs, desires, and intentions. One kind of eliminativist argument first sets forth certain methodological strictures about how FP would have to integrate with mature science in order to be true (e.g., being smoothly reducible to neuroscience, or being absorbed into mature cognitive science), and then contends that these strictures are unlikely to be met. Another kind of argument first claims that FP embodies certain strong empirical commitments (e.g., to mental representations with languagelike syntactic structure), and then contends that such empirical presuppositions are likely to turn out false.

One influential version of folk psychological realism largely agrees with eliminativism about what is required to vindicate folk psychology, but also holds that mature science is likely to provide such vindication. Realists of this persuasion typically argue, for instance, that mature cognitive science will very likely incorporate FP, and also will very likely treat beliefs, desires, and other propositional attitudes as states with languagelike syntactic structure. Other versions of folk-psychological realism take issue, in one way or another, with either (i) the eliminativists' claims about FP's empirical commitments, or (ii) the eliminativists' strictures about how FP must mesh with mature science in order to be true, or both. Concerning (i), for instance, some philosophers maintain that FP per se is not committed to the existence of languagelike mental representations. If mature cognitive science turns out not to posit a "language of thought," they contend, this would not necessarily show that FP is radically false; instead it might only show that propositional attitudes are subserved in some other way than via languagelike representational structures.

Concerning (ii), some philosophers hold that FP can be true without being as tightly connected to mature scientific theories as the eliminativists

require. For instance, the demand that the special sciences be smoothly reducible to the fundamental natural sciences is widely considered an excessively stringent criterion of intertheoretic compatibility; so perhaps FP could be true without being smoothly reducible to neuroscience. Similarly, the demand that FP be directly absorbable into empirical cognitive science is sometimes considered too stringent as a criterion either of FP's truth, or of the soundness of its ontology of beliefs, desires, and other propositional attitudes, or of the legitimacy of FP-based explanations of behavior. Perhaps FP is a true theory, and explanatorily legitimate, even if it is not destined to become a part of science. Even if FP's ontological categories are not scientific natural kinds, perhaps its generalizations are like generalizations about clothing: true, explanatorily usable, and ontologically sound. (No one doubts the existence of hats, coats, or scarves. No one doubts the truth or explanatory utility of generalizations like 'Coats made of heavy material tend to keep the body warm in cold weather', even though these generalizations are not laws of any science.)

Yet another approach to folk psychology, often wedded to realism about beliefs and desires (although sometimes wedded to instrumentalism), maintains that folk psychology does not employ empirical generalizations, and hence is not a *theory* at all. One variant denies that folk psychology employs *any* generalizations, empirical or otherwise. Another variant concedes that there are folk-psychological generalizations, but denies that they are empirical; instead they are held to be analytic truths, or norms of rationality, or both at once. Advocates of non-theory views typically regard folk psychology as a hermeneutic, or interpretive, enterprise. They often claim too that the attribution of propositional attitudes, and also the proffering and grasping of folk-psychological explanations, is a matter of imaginatively projecting oneself into another person's situation, and then experiencing a kind of empathic understanding, or *Verstehen*, of the person's actions and the motives behind them. A more recent, hi-tech, formulation of this idea is that the interpreter "runs a cognitive simulation" of the person whose actions are to be explained.

Philosophers who defend folk-psychological realism, in one or another of the ways just canvassed, also sometimes employ arguments based on the allegedly self-stultifying nature of eliminativism. One such argument begins from the premise that the notion of action is folk-psychological – that a behavioral event counts as an action only if it is caused by propositional attitudes that rationalize it (under some suitable act-description). If so, and if humans never really undergo propositional attitudes, then they never really *act* either. In particular, they never really *assert* anything, or *argue* for anything (since asserting and arguing are species of action). So if eliminativism is true, the argument concludes, then eliminativists can neither assert it nor argue for it – an allegedly intolerable pragmatic paradox. Eliminativists generally react to such arguments with breathtaking equanimity. A typical reply is that although our present concept of action might well be folk-psychological, this does not preclude the possibility of a future successor concept, purged of any commitment to beliefs and desires, that could inherit much of the role of our current, folk-psychologically tainted, concept of action.

See also COGNITIVE SCIENCE, PHILOSOPHY OF MIND, REDUCTION, SIMULATION THEORY.

T.E.H.

Fonseca, Pedro da (1528–99), Portuguese philosopher and logician. He entered the Jesuit order in 1548. Apart from a period (1572–82) in Rome, he lived in Portugal, teaching philosophy and theology at the universities of Evora and Coimbra and performing various administrative duties for his order. He was responsible for the idea of a published course on Aristotelian philosophy, and the resulting series of Coimbra commentaries, the *Cursus Conimbricensis*, was widely used in the seventeenth century. His own logic text, the *Institutes of Dialectic* (1564), went into many editions. It is a good example of Renaissance Aristotelianism, with its emphasis on Aristotle's syllogistic, but it retains some material on medieval developments, notably consequences, exponibles, and supposition theory. Fonseca also wrote a commentary on Aristotle's *Metaphysics* (published in parts from 1577 on), which contains the Greek text, a corrected Latin translation, comments on textual matters, and an extensive exploration of selected philosophical problems. He cites a wide range of medieval philosophers, both Christian and Arab, as well as the newly published Greek commentators on Aristotle. His own position is sympathetic to Aquinas, but generally independent. Fonseca is important not so much for any particular doctrines, though he did hold original views on such matters as analogy, but for his provision of fully documented, carefully written and carefully argued books that, along with others in the

same tradition, were read at universities, both Catholic and Protestant, well into the seventeenth century. He represents what is often called the Second Scholasticism.　　　E.J.A.

Fontenelle, Bernard Le Bovier de (1657–1757), French writer who heralded the age of the *philosophes*. A product of Jesuit education, he was a versatile freethinker with skeptical inclinations. *Dialogues of the Dead* (1683) showed off his analytical mind and elegant style. In 1699, he was appointed secretary of the Academy of Sciences. He composed famous eulogies of scientists; defended the superiority of modern science over tradition in *Digression on Ancients and Moderns* (1688); popularized Copernican astronomy in *Conversations on the Plurality of Worlds* (1686) – famous for postulating the inhabitation of planets; stigmatized superstition and credulity in *History of Oracles* (1687) and *The Origin of Fables* (1724); promoted Cartesian physics in *The Theory of Cartesian Vortices* (1752); and wrote *Elements of Infinitesimal Calculus* (1727) in the wake of Newton and Leibniz.　　　J.-L.S.

Foot, Philippa (b.1920), British philosopher who exerted a lasting influence on the development of moral philosophy in the second half of the twentieth century. Her persisting, intertwined themes are opposition to all forms of subjectivism in ethics, the significance of the virtues and vices, and the connection between morality and rationality. In her earlier papers, particularly "Moral Beliefs" (1958) and "Goodness and Choice" (1961), reprinted in *Virtues and Vices* (1978), she undermines the subjectivist accounts of moral "judgment" derived from C. L. Stevenson and Hare by arguing for many logical or conceptual connections between evaluations and the factual statements on which they must be based. Lately she has developed this kind of thought into the naturalistic claim that moral evaluations are determined by facts about our life and our nature, as evaluations of features of plants and animals (as good or defective specimens of their kind) are determined by facts about their nature and their life.

Foot's opposition to subjectivism has remained constant, but her views on the virtues in relation to rationality have undergone several changes. In "Moral Beliefs" she relates them to self-interest, maintaining that a virtue must benefit its possessor; in the (subsequently repudiated) "Morality as a System of Hypothetical Imperatives" (1972) she went as far as to deny that there was necessarily anything contrary to reason in being uncharitable or unjust. In "Does Moral Subjectivism Rest on a Mistake?" (*Oxford Journal of Legal Studies,* 1995) the virtues themselves appear as forms of practical rationality. Her most recent work, soon to be published as *The Grammar of Goodness,* preserves and develops the latter claim and reinstates ancient connections between virtue, rationality, and happiness.

See also ETHICS, HARE, VIRTUE ETHICS.

R.Hu.

force, illocutionary. See PHILOSOPHY OF LANGUAGE, SPEECH ACT THEORY.

forcing, a method introduced by Paul J. Cohen – see his *Set Theory and the Continuum Hypothesis* (1966) – to prove independence results in Zermelo-Fraenkel set theory (ZF). Cohen proved the independence of the axiom of choice (AC) from ZF, and of the continuum hypothesis (CH) from ZF + AC. The consistency of AC with ZF and of CH with ZF + AC had previously been proved by Gödel by the method of constructible sets. A model of ZF consists of layers, with the elements of a set at one layer always belonging to lower layers. Starting with a model M, Cohen's method produces an "outer model" N with no more levels but with more sets at each level (whereas Gödel's method produces an 'inner model' L): much of what will become true in N can be "forced" from within M. The method is applicable only to hypotheses in the more "abstract" branches of mathematics (infinitary combinatorics, general topology, measure theory, universal algebra, model theory, etc.); but there it is ubiquitous. Applications include the proof by Robert M. Solovay of the consistency of the measurability of all sets (of all projective sets) with ZF (with ZF + AC); also the proof by Solovay and Donald A. Martin of the consistency of Martin's axiom (MA) plus the negation of the continuum hypothesis ($\sim$CH) with ZF + AC. (CH implies MA; and of known consequences of CH about half are implied by MA, about half refutable by MA + $\sim$CH.) Numerous simplifications, extensions, and variants (e.g. Boolean-valued models) of Cohen's method have been introduced. See also INDEPENDENCE RESULTS, SET THEORY.

J.Bur.

Fordyce, David (1711–51), Scottish philosopher and educational theorist whose writings were influential in the eighteenth century. His lectures formed the basis of his *Elements of Moral Philosophy,* written originally for *The Preceptor* (1748), later translated into German and French, and

abridged for the articles on moral philosophy in the first *Encylopaedia Britannica* (1771). Fordyce combines the preacher's appeal to the heart in the advocacy of virtue with a moral "scientist's" appraisal of human psychology. He claims to derive our duties experimentally from a study of the prerequisites of human happiness.

M.A.St.

foreknowledge, divine. See DIVINE FOREKNOWLEDGE.

form, in metaphysics, especially Plato's and Aristotle's, the structure or essence of a thing as contrasted with its matter.

(1) Plato's *theory of Forms* is a realistic ontology of universals. In his elenchus, Socrates sought what is common to, e.g., all chairs. Plato believed there must be an essence – or Form – common to everything falling under one concept, which makes anything what it is. A chair is a chair because it "participates in" the Form of Chair. The Forms are ideal "patterns," unchanging, timeless, and perfect. They exist in a world of their own (cf. the Kantian noumenal realm). Plato speaks of them as self-predicating: the Form of Beauty is perfectly beautiful. This led, as he realized, to the *Third Man argument* that there must be an infinite number of Forms. The only true understanding is of the Forms. This we attain through *anamnesis,* "recollection."

(2) Aristotle agreed that forms are closely tied to intelligibility, but denied their separate existence. Aristotle explains change and generation through a distinction between the form and matter of substances. A lump of bronze (matter) becomes a statue through its being molded into a certain shape (form). In his earlier metaphysics, Aristotle identified primary substance with the composite of matter and form, e.g. Socrates. Later, he suggests that primary substance is form – what makes Socrates what he is (the form here is his soul). This notion of forms as essences has obvious similarities with the Platonic view. They became the "substantial forms" of Scholasticism, accepted until the seventeenth century.

(3) Kant saw form as the a priori aspect of experience. We are presented with phenomenological "matter," which has no meaning until the mind imposes some form upon it.

See also ARISTOTLE, KANT, METAPHYSICS, PLATO.

R.C.

form, aesthetic. See AESTHETIC FORMALISM, AESTHETICS.

form, grammatical. See LOGICAL FORM.

form, logical. See LOGICAL FORM.

form, Platonic. See FORM, PLATO.

form, schematic. See LOGICAL FORM.

form, substantial. See FORM, HYLOMORPHISM.

formal cause. See ARISTOTLE.

formal distinction. See FUNDAMENTUM DIVISIONIS.

formal fallacy, an invalid inference pattern that is described in terms of a formal logic. There are three main cases: (1) an invalid (or otherwise unacceptable) argument identified solely by its form or structure, with no reference to the content of the premises and conclusion (such as equivocation) or to other features, generally of a pragmatic character, of the argumentative discourse (such as unsuitability of the argument for the purposes for which it is given, failure to satisfy inductive standards for acceptable argument, etc.; the latter conditions of argument evaluation fall into the purview of informal fallacy); (2) a formal rule of inference, or an argument form, that is not valid (in the logical system on which the evaluation is made), instances of which are sufficiently frequent, familiar, or deceptive to merit giving a name to the rule or form; and (3) an argument that is an instance of a fallacious rule of inference or of a fallacious argument form and that is not itself valid.

The criterion of satisfactory argument typically taken as relevant in discussing formal fallacies is validity. In this regard, it is important to observe that rules of inference and argument forms that are not valid may have instances (which may be another rule or argument form, or may be a specific argument) that *are* valid. Thus, whereas the argument form

(i) *P, Q;* therefore *R*

(a form that every argument, including every valid argument, consisting of two premises shares) is not valid, the argument form (ii), obtained from (i) by substituting *P&Q* for *R,* is a valid instance of (i):

(ii) *P, Q;* therefore *P&Q.*

Since (ii) is not invalid, (ii) is not a formal fallacy though it is an instance of (i). Thus, some instances of formally fallacious rules of inference or argument-forms may be valid and therefore not be formal fallacies. Examples of formal fallacies follow below, presented according to the system of logic appropriate to the level of description of the fallacy. There are no standard names for some of the fallacies listed below.

Fallacies of sentential (propositional) logic.

Affirming the consequent: If *p* then *q; q /* ∴ *p.*

'If Richard had his nephews murdered, then Richard was an evil man; Richard was an evil man. Therefore, Richard had his nephews murdered.'

Denying the antecedent: If *p* then *q;* not-*p /* ∴ not-*q.*

'If North was found guilty by the courts, then North committed the crimes charged of him; North was not found guilty by the courts. Therefore, North did not commit the crimes charged of him.'

Commutation of conditionals: If *p* then *q /* ∴ If *q* then *p.*

'If Reagan was a great leader, then so was Thatcher. Therefore, if Thatcher was a great leader, then so was Reagan."

Improper transposition: If *p* then *q /* ∴ If not-*p* then not-*q.*

'If the nations of the Middle East disarm, there will be peace in the region. Therefore, if the nations of the Middle East do not disarm, there will not be peace in the region.'

Improper disjunctive syllogism (affirming one disjunct): p or *q; p /* ∴, not-*q.*

'Either John is an alderman or a ward committeeman; John is an alderman. Therefore, John is not a ward committeeman.' (This rule of inference would be valid if 'or' were interpreted exclusively, where '*p* or $_{EX}q$' is true if exactly one constituent is true and is false otherwise. In standard systems of logic, however, 'or' is interpreted inclusively.)

Fallacies of syllogistic logic.

Fallacies of distribution (where *M* is the middle term, *P* is the major term, and *S* is the minor term).

Undistributed middle term: the middle term is not distributed in either premise (roughly, nothing is said of all members of the class it designates), as in

Some *P* are *M*	'Some politicians are crooks.
Some *M* are *S*	Some crooks are thieves.
∴Some *S* are *P*.	∴Some politicians are thieves.'

Illicit major (undistributed major term): the major term is distributed in the conclusion but not in the major premise, as in

All *M* are *P*	'All radicals are communists.
No *S* are *M*	No socialists are radicals.
∴Some *S* are not *P*.	∴Some socialists are not communists.'

Illicit minor (undistributed minor term): the minor term is distributed in the conclusion but not in the minor premise, as in

All *P* are *M*	'All neo-Nazis are radicals.
All *M* are *S*	All radicals are terrorists.
∴All *S* are *P*.	∴All terrorists are neo-Nazis.'

Fallacies of negation.

Two negative premises (exclusive premises): the syllogism has two negative premises, as in

No *M* are *P*	'No racist is just.
Some *M* are not *S*	Some racists are not police.
∴Some *S* are not *P*.	∴Some police are not just.'

Illicit negative/affirmative: the syllogism has a negative premise (conclusion) but no negative conclusion (premise), as in

All *M* are *P*	'All liars are deceivers.
Some *M* are not *S*	Some liars are not aldermen.
∴Some *S* are *P*.	∴Some aldermen are deceivers.'

and

All *P* are *M*	'All vampires are monsters.
All *M* are *S*	All monsters are creatures.
∴Some *S* are not *P*.	∴Some creatures are not vampires.'

Fallacy of existential import: the syllogism has two universal premises and a particular conclusion, as in

All *P* are *M*	'All horses are animals.
No *S* are *M*	No unicorns are animals.

∴Some *S* are not *P*.	∴Some unicorns are not horses.'

A syllogism can commit more than one fallacy. For example, the syllogism

Some *P* are *M*
Some *M* are *S*
∴No *S* are *P*

commits the fallacies of undistributed middle, illicit minor, illicit major, and illicit negative/affirmative.

Fallacies of predicate logic.

Illicit quantifier shift: inferring from a universally quantified existential proposition to an existentially quantified universal proposition, as in

(∀*x*) (∃*y*) F*xy* / ∴ (∃*y*) (∀*x*) F*xy*
'Everyone is irrational at some time (or other) /∴ At some time, everyone is irrational.'

Some are/some are not (unwarranted contrast): inferring from 'Some *S* are *P*' that 'Some *S* are not *P*' or inferring from 'Some *S* are not *P*' that 'Some *S* are *P*', as in

(∃*x*) (*Sx* & *Px*) / ∴ (∃*x*) (*Sx* & ~*Px*)
'Some people are left-handed / ∴ Some people are not left-handed.'

Illicit substitution of identicals: where φ is an opaque (oblique) context and α and β are singular terms, to infer from φα; α = β / ∴ φβ, as in

'The Inspector believes Hyde is Hyde; Hyde is Jekyll / ∴ The Inspector believes Hyde is Jekyll.'

See also EXISTENTIAL IMPORT, LOGICAL FORM, MODAL LOGIC, SYLLOGISM.   W.K.W.

formalism, the view that mathematics concerns manipulations of symbols according to prescribed structural rules. It is cousin to nominalism, the older and more general metaphysical view that denies the existence of all abstract objects and is often contrasted with Platonism, which takes mathematics to be the study of a special class of non-linguistic, non-mental objects, and intuitionism, which takes it to be the study of certain mental constructions. In sophisticated versions, mathematical activity can comprise the study of possible formal manipulations within a system as well as the manipulations themselves, and the "symbols" need not be regarded as either linguistic or concrete. Formalism is often associated with the mathematician

David Hilbert. But Hilbert held that the "finitary" part of mathematics, including, for example, simple truths of arithmetic, describes indubitable facts about real objects and that the "ideal" objects that feature elsewhere in mathematics are introduced to facilitate research about the real objects. Hilbert's formalism is the view that the *foundations* of mathematics can be secured by proving the consistency of formal systems to which mathematical theories are reduced. Gödel's two incompleteness theorems establish important limitations on the success of such a project. **See also** ABSTRACT ENTITY, AESTHETIC FORMALISM, HILBERT'S PROGRAM, MATHEMATICAL INTUITIONISM, PHILOSOPHY OF MATHEMATICS.   S.T.K.

formalism, aesthetic. See AESTHETIC FORMALISM.

formalism, ethical. See ETHICS.

formalism, jurisprudential. See JURISPRUDENCE.

formalism, legal. See JURISPRUDENCE.

formalization, an abstract representation of a theory that must satisfy requirements sharper than those imposed on the structure of theories by the axiomatic-deductive method. That method can be traced back to Euclid's *Elements*. The crucial additional requirement is the regimentation of inferential steps in proofs: not only do axioms have to be given in advance, but the rules representing argumentative steps must also be taken from a predetermined list. To avoid a regress in the definition of proof and to achieve intersubjectivity on a minimal basis, the rules are to be "formal" or "mechanical" and must take into account only the form of statements. Thus, to exclude any ambiguity, a precise and effectively described language is needed to formalize particular theories. The general kind of requirements was clear to Aristotle and explicit in Leibniz; but it was only Frege who, in his *Begriffsschrift* (1879), presented, in addition to an expressively rich language with relations and quantifiers, an adequate logical calculus. Indeed, Frege's calculus, when restricted to the language of predicate logic, turned out to be semantically complete. He provided for the first time the means to formalize mathematical proofs.

Frege pursued a clear philosophical aim, namely, to recognize the "epistemological nature" of theorems. In the introduction to his *Grundgesetze der Arithmetik* (1893), Frege wrote: "By insisting that the chains of inference do not

have any gaps we succeed in bringing to light every axiom, assumption, hypothesis or whatever else you want to call it on which a proof rests; in this way we obtain a basis for judging the epistemological nature of the theorem." The Fregean frame was used in the later development of mathematical logic, in particular, in proof theory. Gödel established through his incompleteness theorems fundamental limits of formalizations of particular theories, like the system of *Principia Mathematica* or axiomatic set theories. The general notion of formal theory emerged from the subsequent investigations of Church and Turing clarifying the concept of 'mechanical procedure' or 'algorithm.' Only then was it possible to state and prove the incompleteness theorems for all formal theories satisfying certain very basic representability and derivability conditions. Gödel emphasized repeatedly that these results do not establish "any bounds for the powers of human reason, but rather for the potentialities of pure formalism in mathematics."

See also CHURCH'S THESIS, FREGE, GÖDEL'S INCOMPLETENESS THEOREMS, PROOF THEORY.
                                                                W.S.

formalize, narrowly construed, to formulate a subject as a theory in first-order predicate logic; broadly construed, to describe the essentials of the subject in some formal language for which a notion of consequence is defined. For Hilbert, formalizing mathematics requires at least that there be finite means of checking purported proofs. **See also** FORMALIZATION, PROOF THEORY.   S.T.K.

formal justice. See JUSTICE.

formal language, a language in which an expression's grammaticality and interpretation (if any) are determined by precisely defined rules that appeal only to the form or shape of the symbols that constitute it (rather than, for example, to the intention of the speaker). It is usually understood that the rules are finite and effective (so that there is an algorithm for determining whether an expression is a formula) and that the grammatical expressions are *uniquely readable,* i.e., they are generated by the rules in only one way. A paradigm example is the language of first-order predicate logic, deriving principally from the *Begriffsschrift* of Frege. The grammatical formulas of this language can be delineated by an inductive definition: (1) a capital letter 'F', 'G', or 'H', with or without a numerical subscript, followed by a string of lowercase letters '*a*', '*b*', or '*c*', with or without numerical subscripts, is a formula; (2) if *A* is a formula, so is ~*A*; (3) if *A* and *B* are formulas, so are (*A* & *B*), (*A* → *B*), and (*A* ∨ *B*); (4) if *A* is a formula and *v* is a lowercase letter '*x*', '*y*', or '*z*', with or without numerical subscripts, then ∃*vA*' *and* ∀*vA*' are formulas where *A*' is obtained by replacing one or more occurrences of some lowercase letter in *A* (together with its subscripts if any) by *v*; (5) nothing is a formula unless it can be shown to be one by finitely many applications of the clauses 1–4. The definition uses the device of metalinguistic variables: clauses with '*A*' and '*B*' are to be regarded as abbreviations of all the clauses that would result by replacing these letters uniformly by names of expressions. It also uses several naming conventions: a string of symbols is named by enclosing it within single quotes and also by replacing each symbol in the string by its name; the symbols '∨', '(',')', '&', '→', '~' are considered names of themselves. The interpretation of predicate logic is spelled out by a similar inductive definition of truth in a model. With appropriate conventions and stipulations, alternative definitions of formulas can be given that make expressions like '(*P* ∨ *Q*)' the names of formulas rather than formulas themselves. On this approach, formulas need not be written symbols at all and form cannot be identified with shape in any narrow sense. For Tarski, Carnap, and others a formal language also included rules of "transformation" specifying when one expression can be regarded as a consequence of others. Today it is more common to view the language and its consequence relation as distinct. Formal languages are often contrasted with natural languages, like English or Swahili. Richard Montague, however, has tried to show that English is itself a formal language, whose rules of grammar and interpretation are similar to – though much more complex than – predicate logic. **See also FORMAL LOGIC.**   S.T.K.

formal learnability theory, the study of human language learning through explicit formal models typically employing artifical languages and simplified learning strategies. The fundamental problem is how a learner is able to arrive at a grammar of a language on the basis of a finite sample of presented sentences (and perhaps other kinds of information as well). The seminal work is by E. Gold (1967), who showed, roughly, that learnability of certain types of grammars from the Chomsky hierarchy by an unbiased learner required the presentation of ungram-

matical strings, identified as such, along with grammatical strings. Recent studies have concentrated on other types of grammar (e.g., generative transformational grammars), modes of presentation, and assumptions about learning strategies in an attempt to approximate the actual situation more closely. **See also GRAMMAR.**   R.E.W.

formal logic, the science of correct reasoning, going back to Aristotle's *Prior Analytics,* based upon the premise that the validity of an argument is a function of its structure or logical form. The modern embodiment of formal logic is *symbolic (mathematical) logic.* This is the study of valid inference in artificial, precisely formulated languages, the grammatical structure of whose sentences or well-formed formulas is intended to mirror, or be a regimentation of, the logical forms of their natural language counterparts. These *formal languages* can thus be viewed as (mathematical) models of fragments of natural language. Like models generally, these models are idealizations, typically leaving out of account such phenomena as vagueness, ambiguity, and tense. But the idea underlying symbolic logic is that to the extent that they reflect certain structural features of natural language arguments, the study of valid inference in formal languages can yield insight into the workings of those arguments.

The standard course of study for anyone interested in symbolic logic begins with the (classical) *propositional calculus (sentential calculus),* or PC. Here one constructs a theory of valid inference for a formal language built up from a stock of propositional variables (sentence letters) and an expressively complete set of connectives. In the propositional calculus, one is therefore concerned with arguments whose validity turns upon the presence of (two-valued) truth-functional sentence-forming operators on sentences such as (classical) negation, conjunction, disjunction, and the like. The next step is the *predicate calculus (lower functional calculus, first-order logic, elementary quantification theory),* the study of valid inference in first-order languages. These are languages built up from an expressively complete set of connectives, first-order universal or existential quantifiers, individual variables, names, predicates (relational symbols), and perhaps function symbols.

Further, and more specialized, work in symbolic logic might involve looking at fragments of the language of the propositional or predicate calculus, changing the semantics that the language is standardly given (e.g., by allowing truth-value gaps or more than two truth-values), further embellishing the language (e.g., by adding modal or other non-truth-functional connectives, or higher-order quantifiers), or liberalizing the grammar or syntax of the language (e.g., by permitting infinitely long well-formed formulas). In some of these cases, of course, symbolic logic remains only marginally connected with natural language arguments as the interest shades off into one in formal languages for their own sake, a mark of the most advanced work being done in formal logic today.

See also DEONTIC LOGIC, EPISTEMIC LOGIC, FREE LOGIC, INFINITARY LOGIC, MANY-VALUED LOGIC, MATHEMATICAL INTUITIONISM, MODAL LOGIC, RELEVANCE LOGIC, SECOND-ORDER LOGIC.   G.F.S.

formal mode. See METALANGUAGE.

formal reality. See REALITY.

formal semantics, the study of the interpretations of formal languages. A formal language can be defined apart from any interpretation of it. This is done by specifying a set of its symbols and a set of formation rules that determine which strings of symbols are grammatical or well formed. When rules of inference (transformation rules) are added and/or certain sentences are designated as axioms a logical system (also known as a logistic system) is formed. An interpretation of a formal language is (roughly) an assignment of meanings to its symbols and truth conditions to its sentences.

Typically a distinction is made between a standard interpretation of a formal language and a non-standard interpretation. Consider a formal language in which arithmetic is formulable. In addition to the symbols of logic (variables, quantifiers, brackets, and connectives), this language will contain '0', '+', '•', and 's'. A standard interpretation of it assigns the set of natural numbers as the domain of discourse, zero to '0', addition to '+', multiplication to '•', and the successor function to 's'. Other standard interpretations are isomorphic to the one just given. In particular, standard interpretations are numeral-complete in that they correlate the numerals one-to-one with the domain elements. A result due to Gödel and Rosser is that there are universal quantifications $(x)A(x)$ that are not deducible from the Peano axioms (if those axioms are consistent) even though each $A(n)$ is provable. The Peano axioms (if consistent) are true on each standard interpretation. Thus each $A(n)$ is true

on such an interpretation. Thus $(x)A(x)$ is true on such an interpretation since a standard interpretation is numeral-complete. However, there are non-standard interpretations that do not correlate the numerals one-to-one with domain elements. On some of these interpretations each $A(n)$ is true but $(x)A(x)$ is false.

In constructing and interpreting a formal language we use a language already known to us, say, English. English then becomes our metalanguage, which we use to talk about the formal language, which is our object language. Theorems proven within the object language must be distinguished from those proven in the metalanguage. The latter are metatheorems.

One goal of a semantical theory of a formal language is to characterize the consequence relation as expressed in that language and prove semantical metatheorems about that relation. A sentence S is said to be a consequence of a set of sentences K provided S is true on every interpretation on which each sentence in K is true. This notion has to be kept distinct from the notion of deduction. The latter concept can be defined only by reference to a logical system associated with a formal language. Consequence, however, can be characterized independently of a logical system, as was just done.

See also DEDUCTION, LOGICAL SYNTAX, METALANGUAGE, PROOF THEORY, TRANSFORMATION RULE.   C.S.

formal sign. See SEMIOSIS.

formation rule. See WELL-FORMED FORMULA.

form of life. See WITTGENSTEIN.

Forms, theory of. See PLATO.

formula. See WELL-FORMED FORMULA.

formula, closed. See OPEN FORMULA, WELL-FORMED FORMULA.

formula, open. See OPEN FORMULA, WELL-FORMED FORMULA.

Foucault, Michel (1926–84), French philosopher and historian of thought. Foucault's earliest writings (e.g., *Maladie mentale et personnalité* ["Mental Illness and Personality"], 1954) focused on psychology and developed within the frameworks of Marxism and existential phenomenology. He soon moved beyond these frameworks, in directions suggested by two fundamental influences:

history and philosophy of science, as practiced by Bachelard and (especially) Canguilhem, and the modernist literature of, e.g., Raymond Roussel, Bataille, and Maurice Blanchot. In studies of psychiatry (*Histoire de la folie* ["History of Madness in the Classical Age"], 1961), clinical medicine (*The Birth of the Clinic*, 1963), and the social sciences (*The Order of Things*, 1966), Foucault developed an approach to intellectual history, "the archaeology of knowledge," that treated systems of thought as "discursive formations" independent of the beliefs and intentions of individual thinkers. Like Canguilhem's history of science and like modernist literature, Foucault's archaeology displaced the human subject from the central role it played in the humanism dominant in our culture since Kant. He reflected on the historical and philosophical significance of his archaeological method in *The Archaeology of Knowledge* (1969).

Foucault recognized that archaeology provided no account of transitions from one system to another. Accordingly, he introduced a "genealogical" approach, which does not replace archaeology but goes beyond it to explain changes in systems of discourse by connecting them to changes in the non-discursive practices of social power structures. Foucault's genealogy admitted the standard economic, social, and political causes but, in a non-standard, Nietzschean vein, refused any unified teleological explanatory scheme (e.g., Whig or Marxist histories). New systems of thought are seen as contingent products of many small, unrelated causes, not fulfillments of grand historical designs. Foucault's geneaological studies emphasize the essential connection of knowledge and power. Bodies of knowledge are not autonomous intellectual structures that happen to be employed as Baconian instruments of power. Rather, precisely as bodies of knowledge, they are tied (but not reducible) to systems of social control. This essential connection of power and knowledge reflects Foucault's later view that power is not merely repressive but a creative, if always dangerous, source of positive values.

Discipline and Punish (1975) showed how prisons constitute criminals as objects of disciplinary knowledge. The first volume of the *History of Sexuality* (1976) sketched a project for seeing how, through modern biological and psychological sciences of sexuality, individuals are controlled by their own knowledge as self-scrutinizing and self-forming subjects. The second volume was projected as a study of the origins of the modern notion of a subject in practices of Christian con-

fession. Foucault wrote such a study (*The Confessions of the Flesh*) but did not publish it because he decided that a proper understanding of the Christian development required a comparison with ancient conceptions of the ethical self. This led to two volumes (1984) on Greek and Roman sexuality: *The Use of Pleasure* and *The Care of the Self*. These final writings make explicit the ethical project that in fact informs all of Foucault's work: the liberation of human beings from contingent conceptual constraints masked as unsurpassable a priori limits and the adumbration of alternative forms of existence.

See also BACHELARD, CANGUILHEM, NIETZSCHE.   G.G.

foundationalism, the view that knowledge and epistemic (knowledge-relevant) justification have a two-tier structure: some instances of knowledge and justification are non-inferential, or foundational; and all other instances thereof are inferential, or non-foundational, in that they derive ultimately from foundational knowledge or justification. This structural view originates in Aristotle's *Posterior Analytics* (at least regarding knowledge), receives an extreme formulation in Descartes's *Meditations*, and flourishes, with varying details, in the works of such twentieth-century philosophers as Russell, C. I. Lewis, and Chisholm. Versions of foundationalism differ on two main projects: (a) the precise explanation of the nature of non-inferential, or foundational, knowledge and justification, and (b) the specific explanation of how foundational knowledge and justification can be transmitted to non-foundational beliefs. Foundationalism allows for differences on these projects, since it is essentially a view about the *structure* of knowledge and epistemic justification.

The question whether knowledge has foundations is essentially the question whether the sort of justification pertinent to knowledge has a two-tier structure. Some philosophers have construed the former question as asking whether knowledge depends on beliefs that are certain in some sense (e.g., indubitable or infallible). This construal bears, however, on only one species of foundationalism: *radical* foundationalism. Such foundationalism, represented primarily by Descartes, requires that foundational beliefs be certain and able to guarantee the certainty of the non-foundational beliefs they support. Radical foundationalism is currently unpopular for two main reasons. First, very few, if any, of our perceptual beliefs are certain (i.e., indubitable); and, second, those of our beliefs that might be candidates for certainty (e.g., the belief that I am thinking) lack sufficient substance to guarantee the certainty of our rich, highly inferential knowledge of the external world (e.g., our knowledge of physics, chemistry, and biology).

Contemporary foundationalists typically endorse *modest* foundationalism, the view that non-inferentially justified, foundational beliefs need not possess or provide certainty and need not deductively support justified non-foundational beliefs. Foundational beliefs (or statements) are often called *basic* beliefs (or statements), but the precise understanding of 'basic' here is controversial among foundationalists. Foundationalists agree, however, in their general understanding of non-inferentially justified, foundational beliefs as beliefs whose *justification* does not derive from other beliefs, although they leave open whether the *causal basis* of foundational beliefs includes other beliefs. (Epistemic justification comes in degrees, but for simplicity we can restrict discussion to justification sufficient for satisfaction of the justification condition for knowledge; we can also restrict discussion to what it takes for a belief to *have* justification, omitting issues of what it takes to *show* that a belief has it.)

Three prominent accounts of non-inferential justification are available to modest foundationalists: (a) self-justification, (b) justification by non-belief, non-propositional experiences, and (c) justification by a non-belief reliable origin of a belief. Proponents of self-justification (including, at one time, Ducasse and Chisholm) contend that foundational beliefs can justify themselves, with no evidential support elsewhere. Proponents of foundational justification by non-belief experiences shun literal self-justification; they hold, following C. I. Lewis, that foundational perceptual beliefs can be justified by non-belief sensory or perceptual experiences (e.g., seeming to see a dictionary) that make true, are best explained by, or otherwise support, those beliefs (e.g., the belief that there is, or at least appears to be, a dictionary here). Proponents of foundational justification by reliable origins find the basis of non-inferential justification in belief-forming processes (e.g., perception, memory, introspection) that are truth-conducive, i.e., that tend to produce true rather than false beliefs. This view thus appeals to the reliability of a belief's non-belief origin, whereas the previous view appeals to the particular sensory or perceptual experiences that correspond to (e.g., make true or are best explained by) a foundational belief.

Despite disagreements over the basis of foundational justification, modest foundationalists typically agree that foundational justification is characterized by *defeasibility*, i.e., can be defeated, undermined, or overridden by a certain sort of expansion of one's evidence or justified beliefs. For instance, your belief that there is a blue dictionary before you could lose its justification (e.g., the justification from your current perceptual experiences) if you acquired new evidence that there is a blue light shining on the dictionary before you. Foundational justification, therefore, can vary over time if accompanied by relevant changes in one's perceptual evidence. It does not follow, however, that foundational justification positively depends, i.e., is based, on grounds for denying that there are defeaters. The relevant dependence can be regarded as negative in that there need only be an absence of genuine defeaters. Critics of foundationalism sometimes neglect that latter distinction regarding epistemic dependence.

The second big task for foundationalists is to explain how justification transmits from foundational beliefs to inferentially justified, non-foundational beliefs. Radical foundationalists insist, for such transmission, on entailment relations that guarantee the truth or the certainty of non-foundational beliefs. Modest foundationalists are more flexible, allowing for merely probabilistic inferential connections that transmit justification. For instance, a modest foundationalist can appeal to explanatory inferential connections, as when a foundational belief (e.g., I seem to feel wet) is best explained for a person by a particular physical-object belief (e.g., the belief that the air conditioner overhead is leaking on me). Various other forms of probabilistic inference are available to modest foundationalists; and nothing in principle requires that they restrict foundational beliefs to what one "seems" to sense or to perceive.

The traditional motivation for foundationalism comes largely from an eliminative regress argument, outlined originally (regarding knowledge) in Aristotle's *Posterior Analytics*. The argument, in shortest form, is that foundationalism is a correct account of the structure of justification since the alternative accounts all fail. *Inferential* justification is justification wherein one belief, *B1*, is justified on the basis of another belief, *B2*. How, if at all, is *B2*, the supporting belief, itself justified? Obviously, Aristotle suggests, we cannot have a circle here, where *B2* is justified by *B1*; nor can we allow the chain of support to extend endlessly, with no ultimate basis for justification. We cannot, moreover, allow *B2* to remain unjustified, lest it lack what it takes to support *B1*. If this is right, the structure of justification does not involve circles, endless regresses, or unjustified starter-beliefs. That is, this structure is evidently foundationalist. This is, in skeletal form, the regress argument for foundationalism. Given appropriate flesh, and due attention to skepticism about justification, this argument poses a serious challenge to non-foundationalist accounts of the structure of epistemic justification, such as epistemic coherentism. More significantly, foundationalism will then show forth as one of the most compelling accounts of the structure of knowledge and justification. This explains, at least in part, why foundationalism has been very prominent historically and is still widely held in contemporary epistemology.

See also COHERENTISM, EPISTEMOLOGY, JUSTIFICATION.   P.K.M.

foundation axiom. See SET THEORY.

Four Books, a group of Confucian texts including the *Ta-hsüeh* (*Great Learning*), *Chung-Yung* (*Doctrine of the Mean*), *Lun Yü* (*Analects*), and *Meng Tzu* (*Book of Mencius*), the latter two containing respectively the teachings of Confucius (sixth–fifth century B.C.) and Mencius (fourth century B.C.), and the former two being chapters from the *Li-Chi* (*Book of Rites*). Chu Hsi (1130–1200) selected the texts as basic ones for Confucian education, and wrote influential commentaries on them. The texts served as the basis of civil service examinations from 1313 to 1905; as a result, they exerted great influence both on the development of Confucian thought and on Chinese life in general.   K.-l.S.

four causes. See ARISTOTLE.

four elements. See EMPEDOCLES.

four humors. See GALEN.

Fourier, François-Marie-Charles (1772–1837), French social theorist and radical critic, often called a utopian socialist. His main works were *The Theory of Universal Unity* (1822) and *The New Industrial and Societal World* (1829).

He argued that since each person has, not an integral soul but only a partial one, personal integrity is possible only in unity with others. Fourier thought that all existing societies were antagonistic. (Following Edenism, he believed societies developed through stages of savagery, patriarchalism, barbarianism, and civilization.)

He believed this antagonism could be transcended only in Harmony. It would be based on twelve kinds of passions. (Five were sensual, four affective, and three distributive; and these in turn encouraged the passion for unity.) The basic social unit would be a phalanx containing 300–400 families (about 1,600–1,800 people) of scientifically blended characters. As a place of production but also of maximal satisfaction of the passions of every member, Harmony should make labor attractive and pleasurable. The main occupations of its members should be gastronomy, opera, and horticulture. It should also establish a new world of love (a form of polygamy) where men and women would be equal in rights. Fourier believed that phalanxes would attract members of all other social systems, even the less civilized, and bring about this new world system.

Fourier's vision of cooperation (both in theory and experimental practice) influenced some anarchists, syndicalists, and the cooperationist movement. His radical social critique was important for the development of political and social thought in France, Europe, and North America.

See also POLITICAL PHILOSOPHY.   G.Fl.

fourth condition. See EPISTEMOLOGY.

fourth condition problem. See EPISTEMOLOGY.

frame. See COGNITIVE SCIENCE.

Frankena, William K. (1908–94), American moral philosopher who wrote a series of influential articles and a text, *Ethics* (1963), which was translated into eight languages and remains in use today. Frankena taught at the University of Michigan (1937–78), where he and his colleagues Charles Stevenson (1908–79), a leading noncognitivist, and Richard Brandt, an important ethical naturalist, formed for many years one of the most formidable faculties in moral philosophy in the world.

Frankena was known for analytical rigor and sharp insight, qualities already evident in his first essay, "The Naturalistic Fallacy" (1939), which refuted Moore's influential claim that ethical naturalism (or any other reductionist ethical theory) could be convicted of logical error. At best, Frankena showed, reductionists could be said to conflate or misidentify ethical properties with properties of some other kind. Even put this way, such assertions were question-begging, Frankena argued. Where Moore claimed to see properties of two different kinds, naturalists and other reductionists claimed to be able to see only one.

Many of Frankena's most important papers concerned similarly fundamental issues about value and normative judgment. "Obligation and Motivation in Recent Moral Philosophy" (1958), for example, is a classic treatment of the debate between internalism, which holds that motivation is essential to obligation or to the belief or perception that one is obligated, and externalism, which holds that motivation is only contingently related to these. In addition to metaethics, Frankena's published works ranged broadly over normative ethical theory, virtue ethics, moral psychology, religious ethics, moral education, and the philosophy of education. Although relatively few of his works were devoted exclusively to the area, Frankena was also known as the preeminent historian of ethics of his day. More usually, Frankena used the history of ethics as a framework within which to discuss issues of perennial interest.

It was, however, for *Ethics,* one of the most widely used and frequently cited philosophical ethics textbooks of the twentieth century, that Frankena was perhaps best known. *Ethics* continues to provide an unparalleled introduction to the subject, as useful in a first undergraduate course as it is to graduate students and professional philosophers looking for perspicuous ways to frame issues and categorize alternative solutions. For example, when in the 1970s philosophers came to systematically investigate normative ethical theories, it was Frankena's distinction in *Ethics* between deontological and teleological theories to which they referred.

See also ETHICS, MORAL PSYCHOLOGY, MOTIVATIONAL INTERNALISM, NATURALISM.

S.L.D.

Frankfurt School, a group of philosophers, cultural critics, and social scientists associated with the Institute for Social Research, which was founded in Frankfurt in 1929. Its prominent members included, among others, the philosophers Horkheimer, Adorno, and Marcuse, as well as the psychoanalyst Erich Fromm (1900–80) and the literary critic Walter Benjamin (1892–1940). Habermas is the leading representative of its second generation. The Frankfurt School is less known for particular theories or doctrines than for its program of a "critical theory of society." Critical theory represents a sophisticated effort to continue Marx's transformation of moral philosophy into social and political critique, while rejecting orthodox Marxism as a

dogma. Critical theory is primarily a way of doing philosophy, integrating the normative aspects of philosophical reflection with the explanatory achievements of the social sciences. The ultimate goal of its program is to link theory and practice, to provide insight, and to empower subjects to change their oppressive circumstances and achieve human emancipation, a rational society that satisfies human needs and powers.

The first generation of the Frankfurt School went through three phases of development. The first, lasting from the beginning of the Institute until the end of the 1930s, can be called "interdisciplinary historical materialism" and is best represented in Horkheimer's programmatic writings. Horkheimer argued that a revised version of historical materialism could organize the results of social research and give it a critical perspective. The second, "critical theory" phase saw the abandonment of Marxism for a more generalized notion of critique. However, with the near-victory of the Nazis in the early 1940s, Horkheimer and Adorno entered the third phase of the School, "the critique of instrumental reason." In their *Dialectic of Enlightenment* (1941) as well as in Marcuse's *One Dimensional Man* (1964), the process of instrumentally dominating nature leads to dehumanization and the domination of human beings. In their writings after World War II, Adorno and Horkheimer became increasingly pessimistic, seeing around them a "totally administered society" and a manipulated, commodity culture.

Horkheimer's most important essays are from the first phase and focus on the relation of philosophy and social science. Besides providing a clear definition and program for critical social science, he proposes that the normative orientation of philosophy should be combined with the empirical research in the social sciences. This metaphilosophical orientation distinguishes a "critical," as opposed to "traditional," theory. For example, such a program demands rethinking the relation of epistemology to the sociology of science. A critical theory seeks to show how the norm of truth is historical and practical, without falling into the skepticism or relativism of traditional sociologies of knowledge such as Mannheim's.

Adorno's major writings belong primarily to the second and third phases of the development of the Frankfurt School. As the possibilities for criticism appeared to him increasingly narrow, Adorno sought to discover them in aesthetic experience and the mimetic relation to nature. Adorno's approach was motivated by his view that modern society is a "false totality." His diagnosis of the causes traced this trend back to the spread of a one-sided, instrumental reason, based on the domination of nature and other human beings. For this reason, he sought a non-instrumental and non-dominating relation to nature and to others, and found it in diverse and fragmentary experiences. Primarily, it is art that preserves this possibility in contemporary society, since in art there is a possibility of mimesis, or the "non-identical" relation to the object. Adorno's influential attempt to avoid "the logic of identity" gives his posthumous *Aesthetic Theory* (1970) and other later works a paradoxical character.

It was in reaction to the third phase that the second generation of the Frankfurt School recast the idea of a critical theory. Habermas argued for a new emphasis on normative foundations as well as a return to an interdisciplinary research program in the social sciences. After first developing such a foundation in a theory of cognitive interests (technical, practical, and emancipatory), Habermas turned to a theory of the unavoidable presuppositions of communicative action and an ethics of discourse. The potential for emancipatory change lies in communicative, or discursive, rationality and practices that embody it, such as the democratic public sphere. Habermas's analysis of communication seeks to provide norms for non-dominating relations to others and a broader notion of reason.

See also ADORNO, CONTINENTAL PHILOSOPHY, CRITICAL THEORY, MARXISM, PHILOSOPHY OF THE SOCIAL SCIENCES, PRAXIS, WEBER.
J.Bo.

Frankfurt-style case. See FREE WILL PROBLEM.

free beauty. See BEAUTY.

freedom, negative. See POSITIVE AND NEGATIVE FREEDOM.

freedom, positive. See POSITIVE AND NEGATIVE FREEDOM.

freedom, practical. See FREE WILL PROBLEM.

free logic, a system of quantification theory, with or without identity, that allows for non-denoting singular terms. In classical quantification theory, all singular terms (free variables and individual constants) are assigned a denotation in all models. But this condition appears counterintuitive when such systems are applied to natural language, where many singular terms seem to be non-denoting ('Pegasus', 'Sherlock Holmes', and the like). Various solutions of this problem have been proposed, ranging from Frege's *chosen object theory* (assign an arbitrary denotation to each non-denoting singular term) to Russell's *description theory* (deny singular term status to most expressions used as such in natural language, and eliminate them from the "logical form" of that language) to a weakening of the quantifiers' "existential import," which allows for denotations to be possible, but not necessarily actual, objects. All these solutions preserve the structure of classical quantification theory and make adjustments at the level of application.

Free logic is a more radical solution: it allows for legitimate singular terms to be denotationless, maintains the quantifiers' existential import, but modifies both the proof theory and the semantics of first-order logic. Within proof theory, the main modification consists of eliminating the rule of existential generalization, which allows one to infer 'There exists a flying horse' from 'Pegasus is a flying horse'. Within semantics, the main problem is giving truth conditions for sentences containing non-denoting singular terms, and there are various ways of accomplishing this. *Conventional* semantics assigns truth-values to atomic sentences containing non-denoting singular terms by convention, and then determines the truth-values of complex sentences as usual. *Outer domain* semantics divides the domain of interpretation into an inner and an outer part, using the inner part as the range of quantifiers and the outer part to provide for "denotations" for non-denoting singular terms (which are then not literally denotationless, but rather left without an *existing* denotation). *Supervaluational* semantics, when considering a sentence A, assigns all possible combinations of truth-values to the atomic components of A containing non-denoting singular terms, evaluates A on the basis of each of those combinations, and then assigns to A the logical product of all such evaluations. (Thus both 'Pegasus flies' and 'Pegasus does not fly' turn out truth-valueless, but 'Pegasus flies or Pegasus does not fly' turns out true since whatever truth-value is assigned to its atomic component 'Pegasus flies' the truth-value for the whole sentence is true.) A free logic is *inclusive* if it allows for the possibility that the range of quantifiers be empty (that there exists nothing at all); it is *exclusive* otherwise.

See also FORMAL SEMANTICS, PROOF THEORY, QUANTIFICATION.   E.Ben.

free rider, a person who benefits from a social arrangement without bearing an appropriate share of the burdens of maintaining that arrangement, e.g. one who benefits from government services without paying one's taxes that support them. The arrangements from which a free rider benefits may be either formal or informal. Cooperative arrangements that permit free riders are likely to be unstable; parties to the arrangement are unlikely to continue to bear the burdens of maintaining it if others are able to benefit without doing their part. As a result, it is common for cooperative arrangements to include mechanisms to discourage free riders, e.g. legal punishment, or in cases of informal conventions the mere disapproval of one's peers. It is a matter of some controversy as to whether it is always morally wrong to benefit from an arrangement without contributing to its maintenance. **See also** JUSTICE, SOCIAL CHOICE THEORY, UTILITARIANISM.								W.T.

free variable. See VARIABLE.

free will defense. See PHILOSOPHY OF RELIGION.

free will problem, the problem of the nature of free agency and its relation to the origins and conditions of responsible behavior. For those who contrast 'free' with 'determined', a central question is whether humans are free in what they do or determined by external events beyond their control. A related concern is whether an agent's responsibility for an action requires that the agent, the act, or the relevant decision be free. This, in turn, directs attention to action, motivation, deliberation, choice, and intention, and to the exact sense, if any, in which our actions are under our control. Use of 'free will' is a matter of traditional nomenclature; it is debated whether freedom is properly ascribed to the will or the agent, or to actions, choices, deliberations, etc.

Controversy over conditions of responsible behavior forms the predominant historical and conceptual background of the free will problem. Most who ascribe moral responsibility acknowledge some sense in which agents must be free in acting as they do; we are not responsible for what we were forced to do or were unable to avoid no matter how hard we tried. But there are differing accounts of moral responsibility and disagreements about the nature and extent of such *practical freedom* (a notion also important in Kant). Accordingly, the free will problem centers on these questions: Does moral responsibility

require any sort of practical freedom? If so, what sort? Are people practically free? Is practical freedom consistent with the antecedent determination of actions, thoughts, and character? There is vivid debate about this last question. Consider a woman deliberating about whom to vote for. From her first-person perspective, she feels free to vote for any candidate and is convinced that the selection is up to her regardless of prior influences. But viewing her eventual behavior as a segment of larger natural and historical processes, many would argue that there are underlying causes determining her choice. With this contrast of intuitions, any attempt to decide whether the voter is free depends on the precise meanings associated with terms like 'free', 'determine', and 'up to her'.

One thing (event, situation) *determines* another if the latter is a consequence of it, or necessitated by it, e.g., the voter's hand movements by her intention. As usually understood, determinism holds that whatever happens is determined by antecedent conditions, where determination is standardly conceived as causation by antecedent events and circumstances. So construed, determinism implies that at any time the future is already fixed and unique, with no possibility of alternative development. Logical versions of determinism declare each future event to be determined by what is already true, specifically, by the truth that it will occur then. Typical theological variants accept the *predestination* of all circumstances and events inasmuch as a divine being knows in advance (or even from eternity) that they will obtain.

Two elements are common to most interpretations of 'free'. First, freedom requires an absence of determination or certain sorts of determination, and second, one acts and chooses freely only if these endeavors are, properly speaking, one's *own*. From here, accounts diverge. Some take freedom (liberty) of indifference or the contingency of alternative courses of action to be critical. Thus, for the woman deliberating about which candidate to select, each choice is an open alternative inasmuch as it is possible but not yet necessitated. Indifference is also construed as motivational equilibrium, a condition some find essential to the idea that a free choice must be rational. Others focus on freedom (liberty) of spontaneity, where the voter is free if she votes as she chooses or desires, a reading that reflects the popular equation of freedom with "doing what you want." Associated with both analyses is a third by which the woman acts freely if she exercises her control, implying responsiveness to intent as well as both abilities to perform an act and to refrain. A fourth view identifies freedom with autonomy, the voter being autonomous to the extent that her selection is self-determined, e.g., by her character, deeper self, higher values, or informed reason. Though distinct, these conceptions are not incompatible, and many accounts of practical freedom include elements of each.

Determinism poses problems if practical freedom requires contingency (alternate possibilities of action). *Incompatibilism* maintains that determinism precludes freedom, though incompatibilists differ whether everything *is* determined. Those who accept determinism thereby endorse *hard determinism* (associated with eighteenth-century thinkers like d'Holbach and, recently, certain behaviorists), according to which freedom is an illusion since behavior is brought about by environmental and genetic factors. Some hard determinists also deny the existence of moral responsibility. At the opposite extreme, *metaphysical libertarianism* asserts that people are free and responsible and, *a fortiori*, that the past does not determine a unique future – a position some find enhanced by developments in quantum physics. Among adherents of this sort of incompatibilism are those who advocate a freedom of indifference by describing responsible choices as those that are undetermined by antecedent circumstances (Epicureans). To rebut the charge that choices, so construed, are random and not really one's "own," it has been suggested that several elements, including an agent's reasons, delimit the range of possibilities and influence choices without necessitating them (a view held by Leibniz and, recently, by Robert Kane). Libertarians who espouse agency causation, on the other hand, blend contingency with autonomy in characterizing a free choice as one that is determined by the agent who, in turn, is not caused to make it (a view found in Carneades and Reid).

Unwilling to abandon practical freedom yet unable to understand how a lack of determination could be either necessary or desirable for responsibility, many philosophers take practical freedom and responsibility to be consistent with determinism, thereby endorsing *compatibilism*. Those who also accept determinism advocate what James called *soft determinism*. Its supporters include some who identify freedom with autonomy (the Stoics, Spinoza) and others who champion freedom of spontaneity (Hobbes, Locke, Hume). The latter speak of *liberty* as the power of doing or refraining from an action according to

what one wills, so that by choosing otherwise one would have done otherwise. An agent fails to have liberty when constrained, that is, when either prevented from acting as one chooses or compelled to act in a manner contrary to what one wills. Extending this model, liberty is also diminished when one is caused to act in a way one would not otherwise prefer, either to avoid a greater danger (*coercion*) or because there is deliberate interference with the envisioning of alternatives (*manipulation*).

Compatibilists have shown considerable ingenuity in responding to criticisms that they have ignored freedom of choice or the need for open alternatives. Some apply the spontaneity, control, or autonomy models to decisions, so that the voter chooses freely if her decision accords with her desires, is under her control, or conforms to her higher values, deeper character, or informed reason. Others challenge the idea that responsibility requires alternative possibilities of action. The so-called *Frankfurt-style cases* (developed by Harry G. Frankfurt) are situations where an agent acts in accord with his desires and choices, but because of the presence of a counterfactual intervener – a mechanism that would have prevented the agent from doing any alternative action had he shown signs of acting differently – the agent could not have done otherwise. Frankfurt's intuition is that the agent is as responsible as he would have been if there were no intervener, and thus that responsible action does not require alternative possibilities. Critics have challenged the details of the Frankfurt-style cases in attempting to undermine the appeal of the intuition.

A different compatibilist tactic recognizes the need for open alternatives and employs versions of the indifference model in describing practical freedom. Choices are free if they are contingent relative to certain subsets of circumstances, e.g. those the agent is or claims to be cognizant of, with the openness of alternatives grounded in what one can choose "for all one knows."

Opponents of compatibilism charge that since these refinements leave agents subject to external determination, even by hidden controllers, compatibilism continues to face an insurmountable challenge. Their objections are sometimes summarized by the *consequence argument* (so called by Peter van Inwagen, who has prominently defended it): if everything were determined by factors beyond one's control, then one's acts, choices, and character would also be beyond one's control, and consequently, agents would never be free and there would be nothing for which they are responsible. Such reasoning usually employs principles asserting the closure of the *practical modalities* (ability, control, avoidability, inevitability, etc.) under consequence relations. However, there is a reason to suppose that the sort of ability and control required by responsibility involve the agent's *sense* of what can be accomplished. Since cognitive states are typically not closed under consequence, the closure principles underlying the consequence argument are disputable.

See also ACTION THEORY, CLOSURE, DETER-MINISM, DIMINISHED CAPACITY, MIDDLE KNOWLEDGE, RESPONSIBILITY.   T.K.

Frege, Gottlob (1848–1925), German mathematician and philosopher. A founder of modern mathematical logic, an advocate of logicism, and a major source of twentieth-century analytic philosophy, he directly influenced Russell, Wittgenstein, and Carnap. Frege's distinction between the sense and the reference of linguistic expressions continues to be debated.

His first publication in logic was his strikingly original 1879 *Begriffsschrift* (*Concept-notation*). Here he devised a formal language whose central innovation is the quantifier-variable notation to express generality; he set forth in this language a version of second-order quantificational logic that he used to develop a logical definition of the ancestral of a relation. Frege invented his *Begriffs-schrift* in order to circumvent drawbacks of the use of colloquial language to state proofs. Colloquial language is irregular, unperspicuous, and ambiguous in its expression of logical relationships. Moreover, logically crucial features of the content of statements may remain tacit and unspoken. It is thus impossible to determine exhaustively the premises on which the conclusion of any proof conducted within ordinary language depends. Frege's *Begriffsschrift* is to force the explicit statement of the logically relevant features of any assertion. Proofs in the system are limited to what can be obtained from a body of evidently true logical axioms by means of a small number of truth-preserving notational manipulations (inference rules). Here is the first hallmark of Frege's view of logic: his formulation of logic as a formal system and the ideal of explicitness and rigor that this presentation subserves. Although the formal exactitude with which he formulates logic makes possible the metamathematical investigation of formalized theories, he showed almost no interest in metamathematical questions. He intended the *Begriffsschrift* to be used.

How though does Frege conceive of the subject matter of logic? His orientation in logic is shaped by his *anti-psychologism*, his conviction that psychology has nothing to do with logic. He took his notation to be a full-fledged language in its own right. The logical axioms do not mention objects or properties whose investigation pertains to some special science; and Frege's quantifiers are unrestricted. Laws of logic are, as he says, the laws of truth, and these are the most general truths. He envisioned the supplementation of the logical vocabulary of the *Begriffsschrift* with the basic vocabulary of the special sciences. In this way the *Begriffsschrift* affords a framework for the completely rigorous deductive development of any science whatsoever. This resolutely nonpsychological universalist view of logic as the most general science is the second hallmark of Frege's view of logic. This universalist view distinguishes his approach sharply from the coeval algebra of logic approach of George Boole and Ernst Schröder. Wittgenstein, both in the *Tractatus Logico-Philosophicus* (1921) and in later writings, is very critical of Frege's universalist view. Logical positivism – most notably Carnap in *The Logical Syntax of Language* (1934) – rejected it as well. Frege's universalist view is also distinct from more contemporary views. With his view of quantifiers as intrinsically unrestricted, he saw little point in talking of varying interpretations of a language, believing that such talk is a confused way of getting at what is properly said by means of second-order generalizations. In particular, the semantical conception of logical consequences that becomes prominent in logic after Kurt Gödel's and Tarski's work is foreign to Frege.

Frege's work in logic was prompted by an inquiry after the ultimate foundation for arithmetic truths. He criticized J. S. Mill's empiricist attempt to ground knowledge of the arithmetic of the positive integers inductively in our manipulations of small collections of things. He also rejected crudely formalist views that take pure mathematics to be a sort of notational game. In contrast to these views and Kant's, he hoped to use his *Begriffsschrift* to define explicitly the basic notions of arithmetic in logical terms and to deduce the basic principles of arithmetic from logical axioms and these definitions. The explicitness and rigor of his formulation of logic will guarantee that there are no implicit extralogical premises on which the arithmetical conclusions depend. Such proofs, he believed, would show arithmetic to be analytic, not synthetic as Kant had claimed. However, Frege redefined 'analytic' to mean 'provable from logical laws' (in his rather un-Kantian sense of 'logic') and definitions.

Frege's strategy for these proofs rests on an analysis of the concept of cardinal number that he presented in his nontechnical 1884 book, *The Foundations of Arithmetic*. Frege, attending to the use of numerals in statements like 'Mars has two moons', argued that it contains an assertion about a concept, that it asserts that there are exactly two things falling under the concept 'Martian moon'. He also noted that both numerals in these statements and those of pure arithmetic play the logical role of singular terms, his proper names. He concluded that numbers are objects so that a definition of the concept of number must then specify what objects numbers are. He observed that

(1) the number of F = the number of G just in case there is a one-to-one correspondence between the objects that are F and those that are G.

The right-hand side of (1) is statable in purely logical terms. As Frege recognized, thanks to the definition of the ancestral of a relation, (1) suffices in the second-order setting of the *Begriffsschrift* for the derivation of elementary arithmetic. The vindication of his logicism requires, however, the logical definition of the expression 'the number of'. He sharply criticized the use in mathematics of any notion of set or collection that views a set as built up from its elements. However, he assumed that, corresponding to each concept, there is an object, the extension of the concept. He took the notion of an extension to be a logical one, although one to which the notion of a concept is prior. He adopted as a fundamental logical principle the ill-fated biconditional: the extension of F = the extension of G just in case every F is G, and vice versa. If this principle were valid, he could exploit the equivalence relation over concepts that figures in the right-hand side of (1) to identify the number of F with a certain extension and thus obtain (1) as a theorem. In *The Basic Laws of Arithmetic* (vol. 1, 1893; vol. 2, 1903) he formalized putative proofs of basic arithmetical laws within a modified version of the *Begriffsschrift* that included a generalization of the law of extensions. However, Frege's law of extensions, in the context of his logic, is inconsistent, leading to Russell's paradox, as Russell communicated to Frege in 1902. Frege's attempt to establish logicism was thus, on its own terms, unsuccessful.

In *Begriffsschrift* Frege rejected the thesis that every uncompound sentence is logically seg-

mented into a subject and a predicate. Subsequently, he said that his approach in logic was distinctive in starting not from the synthesis of concepts into judgments, but with the notion of truth and that to which this notion is applicable, the judgeable contents or thoughts that are expressed by statements. Although he said that truth is the goal of logic, he did not think that we have a grasp of the notion of truth that is independent of logic. He eschewed a correspondence theory of truth, embracing instead a redundancy view of the truth-predicate. For Frege, to call truth the goal of logic points toward logic's concern with inference, with the recognition-of-the-truth (judging) of one thought on the basis of the recognition-of-the-truth of another. This recognition-of-the-truth-of is not verbally expressed by a predicate, but rather in the assertive force with which a sentence is uttered. The starting point for logic is then reflection on elementary inference patterns that analyze thoughts and reveal a logical segmentation in language.

This starting point, and the fusion of logical and ontological categories it engenders, is arguably what Frege is pointing toward by his enigmatic *context principle* in *Foundations*: only in the context of a sentence does a word have a meaning. He views sentences as having a function-argument segmentation like that manifest in the terms of arithmetic, e.g., $(3 \times 4) + 2$. Truth-functional inference patterns, like *modus ponens*, isolate sentences as logical units in compound sentences. Leibniz's law – the substitution of one name for another in a sentence on the basis of an equation – isolates proper names. Proper names designate objects. Predicates, obtainable by removing proper names from sentences, designate concepts. The removal of a predicate from a sentence leaves a higher level predicate that signifies a second-level concept under which first-level concepts fall. An example is the universal quantifier over objects: it designates a second-level concept under which a first-level concept falls, if every object falls under it. Frege takes each first-level concept to be determinately true or false of each object. Vague predicates, like 'is bald', thus fail to signify concepts. This requirement of concept determinacy is a product of Frege's construal of quantification over objects as intrinsically unrestricted. Thus, concept determinacy is simply a form of the law of the excluded middle: for any concept F and any object x, either x is F or x is not F.

Frege elaborates and modifies his basic logical ideas in three seminal papers from 1891–92, "Function and Concept," "On Concept and

Object," and "On Sense and Meaning." In "Function and Concept," Frege sharpens his conception of the function-argument structure of language. He introduces the two truth-values, the True and the False, and maintains that sentences are proper names of these objects. Concepts become functions that map objects to either the True or the False. The course-of-values of a function is introduced as a generalization of the notion of an extension. Generally then, an object is anything that might be designated by a proper name. There is nothing more basic to be said by way of elucidating what an object is. Similarly, first-level functions are what are designated by the expressions that result from removing names from compound proper names. Frege calls functions *unsaturated* or incomplete, in contrast to objects, which are saturated. Proper names and function names are not intersubstitutable so that the distinction between objects and functions is a type-theoretic, categorial distinction. No function is an object; no function name designates an object; there are no quantifiers that simultaneously generalize over both functions and concepts.

Just here Frege's exposition of his views, if not the views themselves, encounter a difficulty. In explaining his views, he uses proper names of the form 'the concept *F*' to talk about concepts; and in contrasting unsaturated functions with saturated objects, apepars to generalize over both with a single quantifier. Benno Kerry, a contemporary of Frege, charged Frege's views with inconsistency. Since the phrase 'the concept *horse*' is a proper name, it must designate an object. On Frege's view, it follows that the concept 'horse' is not a concept, but an object, an apparent inconsistency. Frege responded to Kerry's criticism in "On Concept and Object." He embraced Kerry's paradox, denying that it represents a genuine inconsistency, while admitting that his remarks about the function–object distinction are, as the result of an unavoidable awkwardness of language, misleading. Frege maintained that the distinction between function and object is logically simple and so cannot be properly defined. His remarks on the distinction are informal handwaving designed to elucidate what is captured within the *Begriffsschrift* by the difference between proper names and function names together with their associated distinct quantifiers. Frege's handling of the function-object distinction is a likely source for Wittgenstein's say–show distinction in the *Tractatus*.

At the beginning of "On Sense and Meaning," Frege distinguishes between the reference or meaning (*Bedeutung*) of a proper name and its sense (*Sinn*). He observes that the sentence 'The Morning Star is identical with the Morning Star' is a trivial instance of the principle of identity. In contrast, the sentence 'The Morning Star is identical with the Evening Star' expresses a substantive astronomical discovery. The two sentences thus differ in what Frege called their *cognitive value:* someone who understood both might believe the first and doubt the second. This difference cannot be explained in terms of any difference in reference between names in these sentences. Frege explained it in terms of a difference between the senses expressed by 'the Morning Star' and 'the Evening Star'. In posthumously published writings, he indicated that the sense–reference distinction extends to function names as well. In this distinction, Frege extends to names the notion of the judgeable content expressed by a sentence: the sense of a name is the contribution that the name makes to the thought expressed by sentences in which it occurs. Simultaneously, in classifying sentences as proper names of truth-values, he applies to sentences the notion of a name's referring to something. Frege's function-argument view of logical segmentation constrains his view of both the meaning and the sense of compound names: the substitution for any name occurring in a compound expression of a name with the same reference (sense) yields a new compound expression with the same reference (sense) as the original.

Frege advances several theses about sense that individually and collectively have been a source of debate in philosophy of language. First, the sense of an expression is what is grasped by anyone who understands it. Despite the connection between understanding and sense, Frege provides no account of synonymy, no identity criteria for senses. Second, the sense of an expression is not something psychological. Senses are objective. They exist independently of anyone's grasping them; their availability to different thinkers is a presupposition for communication in science. Third, the sense expressed by a name is a mode of presentation of the name's reference. Here Frege's views contrast with Russell's. Corresponding to Frege's thoughts are Russell's propositions. In *The Principles of Mathematics* (1903), Russell maintained that the meaningful words in a sentence designate things, properties, and relations that are themselves constituents of the proposition expressed by the sentence. For Frege, our access through judgment to objects and functions is via the senses that are expressed by names that mean these items. These senses, not the items they present, occur in thoughts. Names expressing different senses may refer to the same item; and some names, while expressing a sense, refer to nothing. Any compound name containing a name that has a sense, but lacks a reference, itself lacks a meaning. A person may fully understand an expression without knowing whether it means anything and without knowing whether it designates what another understood name does. Fourth, the sense ordinarily expressed by a name is the reference of the name, when the name occurs in indirect discourse. Although the Morning Star is identical with the Evening Star, the inference from the sentence 'Smith believes that the Morning Star is a planet' to 'Smith believes that the Evening Star is a planet' is not sound. Frege, however, accepts Leibniz's law without restriction. He accordingly takes such seeming failures of Leibniz's law to expose a pervasive ambiguity in colloquial language: names in indirect discourse do not designate what they designate outside of indirect discourse. The fourth thesis is offered as an explanation of this ambiguity.

See also LOGICISM, MEANING, RUSSELL, SET-THEORETIC PARADOXES, SET THEORY.

T.R.

Frege-Geach point. See GEACH.

frequency theory of probability. See PROBABILITY.

French personalism, a Christian socialism stressing social activism and personal responsibility, the theoretical basis for the Christian workers' *Esprit* movement begun in the 1930s by Emmanuel Mounier (1905–50), a Christian philosopher and activist. Influenced by both the religious existentialism of Kierkegaard and the radical social action called for by Marx and in part taking direction from the earlier work of Charles Péguy, the movement strongly opposed fascism and called for worker solidarity during the 1930s and 1940s. It also urged a more humane treatment of France's colonies. Personalism allowed for a Christian socialism independent of both more conservative Christian groups and the Communist labor unions and party. Its most important single book is Mounier's *Personalism*. The quarterly journal *Esprit* has regularly published contributions of leading French and international thinkers. Such well-known Christian philosophers as Henry Duméry, Marcel, Maritain, and Ricoeur were attracted to the movement. See also MARCEL, MARITAIN, PERSONALISM, RICOEUR.   J.Bi.

Freud, Sigmund (1856–1939), Austrian neurologist and psychologist, the founder of psychoanalysis. Starting with the study of hysteria in late nineteenth-century Vienna, Freud developed a theory of the mind that has come to dominate modern thought. His notions of the unconscious, of a mind divided against itself, of the meaningfulness of apparently meaningless activity, of the displacement and transference of feelings, of stages of psychosexual development, of the pervasiveness and importance of sexual motivation, as well as of much else, have helped shape modern consciousness. His language (and that of his translators), whether specifying divisions of the mind (e.g. id, ego, and superego), types of disorder (e.g. obsessional neurosis), or the structure of experience (e.g. Oedipus complex, narcissism), has become the language in which we describe and understand ourselves and others. As the poet W. H. Auden wrote on the occasion of Freud's death, "if often he was wrong and, at times, absurd, / to us he is no more a person / now but a whole climate of opinion / under whom we conduct our different lives. . . ."

Hysteria is a disorder involving organic symptoms with no apparent organic cause. Following early work in neurophysiology, Freud (in collaboration with Josef Breuer) came to the view that "hysterics suffer mainly from reminiscences," in particular buried memories of traumatic experiences, the strangulated affect of which emerged (in conversion hysteria) in the distorted form of physical symptoms. Treatment involved the recovery of the repressed memories to allow the cathartic discharge or abreaction of the previously displaced and strangulated affect. This provided the background for Freud's *seduction theory,* which traced hysterical symptoms to traumatic prepubertal sexual assaults (typically by fathers). But Freud later abandoned the seduction theory because the energy assumptions were problematic (e.g., if the only energy involved was strangulated affect from long-past external trauma, why didn't the symptom successfully use up that energy and so clear itself up?) and because he came to see that fantasy could have the same effects as memory of actual events: "psychical reality was of more importance than material reality." What was repressed was not memories, but desires. He came to see the repetition of symptoms as fueled by internal, in particular sexual, energy.

While it is certainly true that Freud saw the

working of sexuality almost everywhere, it is not true that he explained everything in terms of sexuality alone. Psychoanalysis is a theory of internal psychic conflict, and conflict requires at least two parties. Despite developments and changes, Freud's *instinct theory* was determinedly dualistic from beginning to end – at the beginning, *libido* versus *ego* or self-preservative instincts, and at the end *Eros* versus *Thanatos*, life against death. Freud's instinct theory (not to be confused with standard biological notions of hereditary behavior patterns in animals) places instincts on the borderland between the mental and physical and insists that they are internally complex. In particular, the sexual instinct must be understood as made up of components that vary along a number of dimensions (source, aim, and object). Otherwise, as Freud argues in his *Three Essays on the Theory of Sexuality* (1905), it would be difficult to understand how the various perversions are recognized as "sexual" despite their distance from the "normal" conception of sexuality (heterosexual genital intercourse between adults). His broadened concept of sexuality makes intelligible sexual preferences emphasizing different sources (erotogenic zones or bodily centers of arousal), aims (acts, such as intercourse and looking, designed to achieve pleasure and satisfaction), and objects (whether of the same or different gender, or even other than whole living persons). It also allows for the recognition of infantile sexuality. Phenomena that might not on the surface appear sexual (e.g. childhood thumbsucking) share essential characteristics with obviously sexual activity (infantile sensual sucking involves pleasurable stimulation of the same erotogenic zone, the mouth, stimulated in adult sexual activities such as kissing), and can be understood as earlier stages in the development of the same underlying instinct that expresses itself in such various forms in adult sexuality. The standard developmental stages are oral, anal, phallic, and genital.

Neuroses, which Freud saw as "the *negative* of perversions" (i.e., the same desires that might in some lead to perverse activity, when repressed, result in neurosis), could often be traced to struggles with the Oedipus complex: the "nucleus of the neuroses." The Oedipus complex, which in its positive form postulates sexual feelings toward the parent of the opposite sex and ambivalently hostile feelings toward the parent of the same sex, suggests that the universal shape of the human condition is a triangle. The conflict reaches its peak between the ages of three and five, during the phallic stage of psychosexual development. The fundamental structuring of emotions has its roots in the prolonged dependency of the human infant, leading to attachment – a primary form of love – to the primary caregiver, who (partly for biological reasons such as lactation) is most often the mother, and the experience of others as rivals for the time, attention, and concern of the primary caregiver. Freud's views of the Oedipus complex should not be oversimplified. The sexual desires involved, e.g., are typically unconscious and necessarily infantile, and infantile sexuality and its associated desires are not expressed in the same form as mature genital sexuality. His efforts to explain the distinctive features of female psychosexual development in particular led to some of his most controversial views, including the postulation of penis envy to explain why girls but not boys standardly experience a shift in gender of their primary love object (both starting with the mother as the object). Later love objects, including psychoanalysts as the objects of transference feelings (in the analytic setting, the analyst functions as a blank screen onto which the patient projects feelings), are the results of displacement or transference from earlier objects: "The finding of an object is in fact a refinding of it."

Freud used the same structure of explanation for symptoms and for more normal phenomena, such as dreams, jokes, and slips of the tongue. All can be seen as compromise formations between forces pressing for expression (localized by Freud's structural theory in the *id*, understood as a reservoir of unconscious instinct) and forces of repression (some also unconscious, seeking to meet the constraints of morality and reality). On Freud's underlying model, the fundamental process of psychic functioning, the *primary process*, leads to the uninhibited discharge of psychic energy. Such discharge is experienced as pleasurable, hence the governing principle of the fundamental process is called the *pleasure principle*. Increase of tension is experienced as unpleasure, and the psychic apparatus aims at a state of equilibrium or constancy (sometimes Freud writes as if the state aimed at is one of zero tension, hence the *Nirvana principle* associated with the death instinct in Freud's *Beyond the Pleasure Principle* [1920]). But since pleasure can in fact only be achieved under specific conditions, which sometimes require arrangement, planning, and delay, individuals must learn to inhibit discharge, and this *secondary process* thinking is governed by what Freud came to call the *reality principle*. The aim is still satisfaction, but the "exigencies of life" require attention, reasoning, and judgment to avoid falling into the fantasy wish-fulfillment of the primary process. Sometimes *defense mechanisms* designed to avoid increased tension or unpleasure can fail, leading to neurosis (in general, under the theory, a *neurosis* is a psychological disorder rooted in unconscious conflict – particular neuroses being correlated with particular phases of development and particular mechanisms of defense). *Repression,* involving the confining of psychic representations to the unconscious, is the most important of the defense mechanisms. It should be understood that unlike preconscious ideas, which are merely descriptively unconscious (though one may not be aware of them at the moment, they are readily accessible to consciousness), unconscious ideas in the strict sense are kept from awareness by forces of repression, they are dynamically unconscious – as evidenced by the resistance to making the unconscious conscious in therapy. Freud's deep division of the mind between unconscious and conscious goes beyond neurotic symptoms to help make sense of familiar forms of irrationality (such as self-deception, ambivalence, and weakness of the will) that are highly problematical on Cartesian models of an indivisible unitary consciousness. Perhaps the best example of the primary process thinking that characterizes the unconscious (unconstrained by the realities of time, contradiction, causation, etc.) can be found in dreaming.

Freud regarded dreams as "the royal road to a knowledge of the unconscious." Dreams are the disguised fulfillment of unconscious wishes. In extracting the meaning of dreams through a process of interpretation, Freud relied on a central distinction between the *manifest content* (the dream as dreamt or as remembered on waking) and the *latent content* (the unconscious dream-thoughts). Freud held that interpretation via association to particular elements of the manifest content reversed the process of dream construction, the *dream-work* in which various mechanisms of distortion operated on the day's residues (perceptions and thoughts stemming from the day before the dream was dreamt) and the latent dream-thoughts to produce the manifest dream. Prominent among the mechanisms are the condensation (in which many meanings are represented by a single idea) and displacement (in which there is a shift of affect from a significant and intense idea to an associated but otherwise insignificant one) also typical of neurotic symptoms, as well as considerations of representability and secondary revision more specific to dream

formation. Symbolism is less prominent in Freud's theory of dreams than is often thought; indeed, the section on symbols appeared only as a later addition to *The Interpretation of Dreams* (1900). Freud explicitly rejected the ancient "dream book" mode of interpretation in terms of fixed symbols, and believed one had to recover the hidden meaning of a dream through the dreamer's (not the interpreter's) associations to particular elements. Such associations are a part of the process of free association, in which a patient is obliged to report to the analyst all thoughts without censorship of any kind. The process is crucial to *psychoanalysis,* which is both a technique of psychotherapy and a method of investigation of the workings of the mind.

Freud used the results of his investigations to speculate about the origins of morality, religion, and political authority. He tended to find their historical and psychological roots in early stages of the development of the individual. Morality in particular he traced to the internalization (as one part of the resolution of the Oedpius complex) of parental prohibitions and demands, producing a conscience or *superego* (which is also the locus of self-observation and the ego-ideal). Such identification by incorporation – introjection – plays an important role in character formation in general. The instinctual renunciation demanded by morality and often achieved by repression Freud regarded as essential to the order society needs to conduct its business. Civilization gets the energy for the achievements of art and science by sublimation of the same instinctual drives. But the costs of society and civilization to the individual in frustration, unhappiness, and neurosis can be too high. Freud's individual therapy was meant to lead to the liberation of repressed energies (which would not by itself guarantee happiness); he hoped it might also provide energy to transform the world and moderate its excess demands for restraint. But just as his individual psychology was founded on the inevitability of internal conflict, in his social thought he saw some limits (especially on aggression – the death instinct turned outward) as necessary and he remained pessimistic about the apparently endless struggle reason must wage (*Civilization and Its Discontents,* 1930).

See also JUNG, PHILOSOPHY OF MIND, PHILOSOPHY OF PSYCHOLOGY, SELF-DECEPTION.

J.Ne.

Fries, Jakob Friedrich. See NEO-KANTIANISM.

full subset algebra. See BOOLEAN ALGEBRA.

function, mathematical. See ALGORITHM, MATHEMATICAL FUNCTION.

function, probability. See BAYESIAN RATIONALITY.

function, state. See QUANTUM MECHANICS.

function, teleological. See TELEOLOGY.

functional. See RELATION.

functional abstraction. See COMBINATORY LOGIC.

functional calculus, lower. See FORMAL LOGIC.

functional completeness. See COMPLETENESS.

functional dependence, a relationship between variable magnitudes (especially physical magnitudes) and certain properties or processes. In modern physical science there are two types of laws stating such relationships.

(1) There are numerical laws stating concomitant variation of certain quantities, where a variation in any one is accompanied by variations in the others. An example is the law for ideal gases: $pV = aT$, where p is the pressure of the gas, V its volume, T its absolute temperature, and a a constant derived from the mass and the nature of the gas. Such laws say nothing about the temporal order of the variations, and tests of the laws can involve variation of any of the relevant magnitudes. Concomitant variation, not causal sequence, is what is tested for.

(2) Other numerical laws state variations of physical magnitudes correlated with times. Galileo's law of free fall asserts that the change in the unit time of a freely falling body (in a vacuum) in the direction of the earth is equal to gt, where g is a constant and t is the time of the fall, and where the rate of time changes of g is correlative with the temporal interval t. The law is true of any body in a state of free fall and for any duration. Such laws are also called "dynamical" because they refer to temporal processes usually explained by the postulation of forces acting on the objects in question.   R.E.B.

functional explanation. See PHILOSOPHY OF THE SOCIAL SCIENCES.

functionalism, the view that mental states are defined by their causes and effects. As a metaphysical thesis about the nature of mental states, functionalism holds that what makes an inner state mental is not an intrinsic property of the state, but rather its *relations* to sensory stimulation (input), to other inner states, and to behavior (output). For example, what makes an inner state a pain is its being a type of state (typically) caused by pinpricks, sunburns, and so on, a type that causes other mental states (e.g., worry), and a type that causes behavior (e.g., saying "ouch"). Propositional attitudes also are identified with functional states: an inner state is a desire for water partly in virtue of its causing a person to pick up a glass and drink its contents when the person believes that the glass contains water.

The basic distinction needed for functionalism is that between *role* (in terms of which a type of mental state is defined) and *occupant* (the particular thing that occupies a role). Functional states exhibit *multiple realizability:* in different kinds of beings (humans, computers, Martians), a particular kind of causal role may have different occupants – e.g., the causal role definitive of a belief that p, say, may be occupied by a neural state in a human, but occupied (perhaps) by a hydraulic state in a Martian. Functionalism, like behaviorism, thus entails that mental states may be shared by physically dissimilar systems. Although functionalism does not automatically rule out the existence of immaterial souls, its motivation has been to provide a materialistic account of mentality.

The advent of the computer gave impetus to functionalism. First, the distinction between software and hardware suggested the distinction between role (function) and occupant (structure). Second, since computers are automated, they demonstrate how inner states can be causes of output in the absence of a homunculus (i.e., a "little person" intelligently directing output). Third, the Turing machine provided a model for one of the earliest versions of functionalism. A Turing machine is defined by a table that specifies transitions from current state and input to next state (or to output). According to Turing machine functionalism, any being with pscychological states has a unique best description, and each psychological state is identical to a machine table state relative to that description. To be in mental state type M is to instantiate or realize Turing machine T in state S.

Turing machine functionalism, developed largely by Putnam, has been criticized by Putnam, Ned Block, and Fodor. To cite just one serious problem: two machine table states – and hence, according to Turing machine functionalism, two psychological states – are distinct if they are followed by different states or by different outputs. So, if a pinprick causes A to say "Ouch" and causes B to say "Oh," then, if Turing machine functionalism were true, A's and B's states of pain would be different psychological states. But we do not individuate psychological states so finely, nor should we: such fine-grained individuation would be unsuitable for psychology. Moreover, if we assume that there is a path from any state to any other state, Turing machine functionalism has the unacceptable consequence that no two systems have any of their states in common unless they have all their states in common.

Perhaps the most prominent version of functionalism is the *causal theory of mind*. Whereas Turing machine functionalism is based on a technical computational or psychological theory, the causal theory of mind relies on commonsense understanding: according to the causal theory of mind, the concept of a mental state is the concept of a state apt for bringing about certain kinds of behavior (Armstrong). Mental state terms are defined by the commonsense platitudes in which they appear (David Lewis). Philosophers can determine a priori what mental states are (by conceptual analysis or by definition). Then scientists determine what physical states occupy the causal roles definitive of mental states. If it turned out that there was no physical state that occupied the causal role of, say, pain (i.e., was caused by pinpricks, etc., and caused worry, etc.), it would follow, on the causal theory, that pain does not exist. To be in mental state type M is to be in a physical state N that occupies causal role R.

A third version is teleological or "homuncular" functionalism, associated with William G. Lycan and early Dennett. According to homuncular functionalism, a human being is analogous to a large corporation, made up of cooperating departments, each with its own job to perform; these departments interpret stimuli and produce behavioral responses. Each department (at the highest subpersonal level) is in turn constituted by further units (at a sub-subpersonal level) and so on down until the neurological level is reached. The role–occupant distinction is thus relativized to level: an occupant at one level is a role at the next level down. On this view, to be in a mental state type M is to have a sub-...sub-personal ϕ-er that is in its characteristic state $S(\phi)$.

All versions of functionalism face problems about the qualitative nature of mental states. The difficulty is that functionalism individuates states in purely relational terms, but the acrid odor of, say, a paper mill seems to have a non-relational, qualitative character that functionalism misses altogether. If two people, on seeing a ripe banana, are in states with the same causes and effects, then, by functionalist definition, they are in the same mental state – say, having a sensation of yellow. But it seems possible that one has an "inverted spectrum" relative to the other, and hence that their states are qualitatively different. Imagine that, on seeing the banana, one of the two is in a state qualitatively indistinguishable from the state that the other would be in on seeing a ripe tomato. Despite widespread intuitions that such inverted spectra are possible, according to functionalism, they are not. A related problem is that of "absent qualia." The population of China, or even the economy of Bolivia, could be functionally equivalent to a human brain – i.e., there could be a function that mapped the relations between inputs, outputs, and internal states of the population of China onto those of a human brain; yet the population of China, no matter how its members interact with one another and with other nations, intuitively does not have mental states. The status of these arguments remains controversial.

See also BEHAVIORISM, INTENTIONALITY, PHILOSOPHY OF MIND, TURING MACHINE.

L.R.B.

functionalism, analytical. See PHILOSOPHY OF MIND.

functionalism, machine state. See PHILOSOPHY OF MIND.

functionalism, Turing machine. See FUNCTIONALISM.

functional jurisprudence. See JURISPRUDENCE.

functor. See FORMAL LOGIC.

fundamentum divisionis (Latin, 'foundation of a division'), term in Scholastic logic and ontology meaning 'grounds for a distinction'. Some distinctions categorize separately existing things, such as men and beasts. This is a *real* distinction, and the *fundamentum divisionis* exists in reality. Some distinctions categorize things that cannot exist separately but can be distinguished mentally, such as the difference between being a human being and having a sense of humor, or the difference between a soul and one of its powers, say, the power of thinking. A *mental* distinction is also called a *formal* distinction. Duns Scotus is well known for the idea of *formalis distinctio cum fundamento ex parte rei* (a formal distinction with a foundation in the thing), primarily in order to handle logical problems with the Christian concept of God. God is supposed to be absolutely simple; i.e., there can be no multiplicity of composition in him. Yet, according to traditional theology, many properties can be truly attributed to him. He is wise, good, and powerful. In order to preserve the simplicity of God, Duns Scotus claimed that the difference between wisdom, goodness, and power was only formal but still had some foundation in God's own being.   A.P.M.

Fung Yu-lan (1895–1990), Chinese philosopher. He was educated at Peking University and earned his Ph.D. from Columbia University. His *History of Chinese Philosophy* was the first such complete history of high quality by a contemporary scholar. During World War II he attempted to reconstruct Chu Hsi's philosophy in terms of the New Realism that he had learned from the West, and developed his own system of thought, a new philosophy of *li* (principle). After the Communist takeover in 1949, he gave up his earlier thought, denouncing Confucian philosophy during the Cultural Revolution. After the Cultural Revolution he changed his position again and rewrote his *History of Chinese Philosophy* in seven volumes. **See also CHINESE PHILOSOPHY, CHU HSI.**   S.-h.L.

future contingents, singular events or states of affairs that may come to pass, and also may not come to pass, in the future. There are three traditional problems involving future contingents: the question of universal validity of the principle of bivalence, the question of free will and determinism, and the question of foreknowledge.

The debate about future contingents in modern philosophical logic was revived by Łukasiewicz's work on three-valued logic. He thought that in order to avoid fatalistic consequences, we must admit that the principle of bivalence (for any proposition, p, either p is true or not-p is true) does not hold good for propositions about future contingents. Many authors have considered this view confused. According to von Wright, e.g., when propositions are said to be true or false and 'is' in 'it is true that' is tenseless or atemporal, the illusion of determinism does not arise. It has its roots in a tacit oscillation between a temporal and an atemporal reading of the phrase 'it is true'. In a temporalized reading, or in its tensed variants such as 'it was/will be/is already true', one can substitute, for 'true', other words like 'certain', 'fixed', or 'necessary'. Applying this diachronic necessity to atemporal

predications of truth yields the idea of logical determinism.

In contemporary discussions of tense and modality, future contingents are often treated with the help of a model of time as a line that breaks up into branches as it moves from left to right (i.e., from past to future). Although the conception of truth at a moment has been found philosophically problematic, the model of historical modalities and branching time as such is much used in works on freedom and determination.

Aristotle's *On Interpretation* IX contains a classic discussion of future contingents with the famous example of tomorrow's sea battle. Because of various ambiguities in the text and in Aristotle's modal conceptions in general, the meaning of the passage is in dispute. In the *Metaphysics* VI.3 and in the *Niocmachean Ethics* III.5, Aristotle tries to show that not all things are predetermined. The Stoics represented a causally deterministic worldview; an ancient example of logical determinism is Diodorus Cronus's famous master argument against contingency.

Boethius thought that Aristotle's view can be formulated as follows: the principle of bivalence is universally valid, but propositions about future contingents, unlike those about past and present things, do not obey the stronger principle according to which each proposition is either determinately true or determinately false. A proposition is indeterminately true as long as the conditions that make it true are not yet fixed. This was the standard Latin doctrine from Abelard to Aquinas. Similar discussions occurred in Arabic commentaries on *On Interpretation*.

In the fourteenth century, many thinkers held that Aristotle abandoned bivalence for future contingent propositions. This restriction was usually refuted, but it found some adherents like Peter Aureoli. Duns Scotus and Ockham heavily criticized the Boethian-Thomistic view that God can know future contingents only because the flux of time is present to divine eternity. According to them, God contingently foreknows free acts. Explaining this proved to be a very cumbersome task. Luis de Molina (1535–1600) suggested that God knows what possible creatures would do in any possible situation. This "middle knowledge" theory about counterfactuals of freedom has remained a living theme in philosophy of religion; analogous questions are treated in theories of subjunctive reasoning.

See also ARISTOTLE, BOETHIUS, FREE WILL PROBLEM, MANY-VALUED LOGIC, TENSE LOGIC, VAGUENESS.   S.K.

fuzzy logic. See FUZZY SET, VAGUENESS.

fuzzy set, a set in which membership is a matter of degree. In classical set theory, for every set S and thing x, either x is a member of S or x is not. In fuzzy set theory, things x can be members of sets S to any degree between 0 and 1, inclusive. Degree 1 corresponds to 'is a member of' and 0 corresponds to 'is not'; the intermediate degrees are degrees of vagueness or uncertainty. (Example: Let S be the set of men who are bald at age forty.) L. A. Zadeh developed a logic of fuzzy sets as the basis for a logic of vague predicates. A fuzzy set can be represented mathematically as a function from a given universe into the interval $[0, 1]$. **See also** SET THEORY, VAGUENESS.

D.H.

G

Gadamer, Hans-Georg (b.1900), German philosopher, the leading proponent of hermeneutics in the second half of the twentieth century. He studied at Marburg in the 1920s with Natorp and Heidegger. His first book, *Plato's Dialectical Ethics* (1931), bears their imprint and reflects his abiding interest in Greek philosophy. *Truth and Method* (1960) established Gadamer as an original thinker and had an impact on a variety of disciplines outside philosophy, including theology, legal theory, and literary criticism.

The three parts of *Truth and Method* combine to displace the scientific conceptions of truth and method as the model for understanding in the human sciences. In the first part, which presents itself as a critique of the abstraction inherent in aesthetic consciousness, Gadamer argues that artworks make a claim to truth. Later Gadamer draws on the play of art in the experience of the beautiful to offer an analogy to how a text draws its readers into the event of truth by making a claim on them. In the central portion of the book Gadamer presents tradition as a condition of understanding. Tradition is not for him an object of historical knowledge, but part of one's very being. The final section of *Truth and Method* is concerned with language as the site of tradition. Gadamer sought to shift the focus of hermeneutics from the problems of obscurity and misunderstanding to the community of understanding that the participants in a dialogue share through language.

Gadamer was involved in three debates that define his philosophical contribution. The first was an ongoing debate with Heidegger reflected throughout Gadamer's corpus. Gadamer did not accept all of the innovations that Heidegger introduced into his thinking in the 1930s, particularly his reconstruction of the history of philosophy as the history of being. Gadamer also rejected Heidegger's elevation of Hölderlin to the status of an authority. Gadamer's greater accessibility led Habermas to characterize Gadamer's contribution as that of having "urbanized the Heideggerian province." The second debate was with Habermas himself. Habermas criticized Gadamer's rejection of the Enlightenment's "prejudice against prejudice." Whereas Habermas objected to the conservatism inherent in

Gadamer's rehabilitation of prejudice, Gadamer explained that he was only setting out the conditions for understanding, conditions that did not exclude the possibility of radical change. The third debate, which formed the basis of *Dialogue and Deconstruction* (1989), was with Derrida. Derridean deconstruction is indebted to Heidegger's later philosophy and so this debate was in part about the direction philosophy should take after Heidegger. However, many observers concluded that there was no real engagement between Gadamer and Derrida. To some it seemed that Derrida, by refusing to accept the terms on which Gadamer insisted dialogue should take place, had exposed the limits imposed by hermeneutics. To others it was confirmation that any attempt to circumvent the conditions of dialogue specified by Gadamerian hermeneutics is self-defeating.

See also DERRIDA, HEIDEGGER, HERMENEUTICS. R.L.B.

Gaius. See COMMENTARIES ON PLATO, MIDDLE PLATONISM.

Galen (A.D. 129–c.215), physician and philosopher from Greek Asia Minor. He traveled extensively in the Greco-Roman world before settling in Rome and becoming court physician to Marcus Aurelius. His philosophical interests lay mainly in the philosophy of science (*On the Therapeutic Method*) and nature (*On the Function of Parts*), and in logic (*Introduction to Logic*, in which he develops a crude but pioneering treatment of the logic of relations). Galen espoused an extreme form of directed teleology in natural explanation, and sought to develop a syncretist picture of cause and explanation drawing on Plato, Aristotle, the Stoics, and preceding medical writers, notably Hippocrates, whose views he attempted to harmonize with those of Plato (*On the Doctrines of Hippocrates and Plato*). He wrote on philosophical psychology (*On the Passions and Errors of the Soul*); his materialist account of mind (*Mental Characteristics Are Caused by Bodily Conditions*) is notable for its caution in approaching issues (such as the actual nature of the substance of the soul and the age and structure of the universe) that he regarded as undecidable. In physiology, he adopted a version of the four-humor theory, that health consists in an appropriate balance of four basic bodily constituents (blood, black bile, yellow bile, and phlegm), and disease in a corresponding imbalance (a view owed ultimately to Hippocrates). He sided with the rationalist physicians against the empiricists, holding that it was possible to elaborate and to support theories concerning the fundamentals of the human body; but he stressed the importance of observation and experiment, in particular in anatomy (he discovered the function of the recurrent laryngeal nerve by dissection and ligation). Via the Arabic tradition, Galen became the most influential doctor of the ancient world; his influence persisted, in spite of the discoveries of the seventeenth century, until the end of the nineteenth century. He also wrote extensively on semantics, but these texts are lost.   R.J.H.

Galileo Galilei (1564–1642), Italian astronomer, natural philosopher, and physicist. His *Dialogue concerning the Two Chief World Systems* (1632) defended Copernicus by arguing against the major tenets of the Aristotelian cosmology. On his view, one kind of motion replaces the multiple distinct celestial and terrestrial motions of Aristotle; mathematics is applicable to the real world; and explanation of natural events appeals to efficient causes alone, not to hypothesized natural ends. Galileo was called before the Inquisition, was made to recant his Copernican views, and spent the last years of his life under house arrest. *Discourse concerning Two New Sciences* (1638) created the modern science of mechanics: it proved the laws of free fall, thus making it possible to study accelerated motions; asserted the principle of the independence of forces; and proposed a theory of parabolic ballistics. His work was developed by Huygens and Newton.

Galileo's scientific and technological achievements were prodigious. He invented an air thermoscope, a device for raising water, and a computer for calculating quantities in geometry and ballistics. His discoveries in pure science included the isochronism of the pendulum and the hydrostatic balance. His telescopic observations led to the discovery of four of Jupiter's satellites (the Medicean Stars), the moon's mountains, sunspots, the moon's libration, and the nature of the Milky Way. In methodology Galileo accepted the ancient Greek ideal of demonstrative science, and employed the method of retroductive inference, whereby the phenomena under investigation are attributed to remote causes. Much of his work utilizes the hypothetico-deductive method.   R.E.B.

gambler's fallacy, also called Monte Carlo fallacy, the fallacy of supposing, of a sequence of independent events, that the probabilities of later outcomes must increase or decrease to "compensate" for earlier outcomes. For example, since (by Bernoulli's theorem) in a long run of tosses of a fair coin it is very probable that the coin will come up heads roughly half the time, one might think that a coin that has not come up heads recently must be "due" to come up heads – must have a probability greater than one-half of doing so. But this is a misunderstanding of the law of large numbers, which requires no such compensating tendencies of the coin. The probability of heads remains one-half for each toss despite the preponderance, so far, of tails. In the sufficiently long run what "compensates" for the presence of improbably long subsequences in which, say, tails strongly predominate, is simply that such subsequences occur rarely and therefore have only a slight effect on the statistical character of the whole. **See also** BERNOULLI'S THEOREM, PROBABILITY.   R.Ke.

game theory, the theory of the structure of, and the rational strategies for performing in, games or gamelike human interactions. Although there were forerunners, game theory was virtually invented by the mathematician John von Neumann and the economist Oskar Morgenstern in the early 1940s. Its most striking feature is its compact representation of interactions of two or more choosers, or players. For example, two players may face two choices each, and in combination these choices produce four possible outcomes. Actual choices are of strategies, not of outcomes, although it is assessments of outcomes that recommend strategies. To do well in a game, even for all choosers to do well, as is often possible, generally requires taking all other players' positions and interests into account. Hence, to evaluate strategies directly, without reference to the outcomes they might produce in interaction with others, is conspicuously perverse. It is not surprising, therefore, that in ethics, game theory has been preeminently applied to utilitarian moral theory.

As the numbers of players and strategies rise, the complexity of games increases geometrically. If two players have two strategies each and each ranks the four possible outcomes without ties, there are already seventy-eight strategically distinct games. Even minor real-life interactions may have astronomically greater complexity. One might complain that this makes game theory useless. Alternatively, one can note that this makes it realistic and helps us understand why real-life choices are at least as complex as they sometimes seem. To complicate matters further, players can choose over probabilistic combinations of their "pure" strategies. Hence, the original four outcomes in a simple 2×2 game define a continuum of potential outcomes.

After noting the structure of games, one might then be struck by an immediate implication of this mere description. A rational individual may be supposed to attempt to maximize her potential or expected outcome in a game. But if there are two or more choosers in a game, in general they cannot all maximize simultaneously over their expected outcomes while assuming that all others are doing likewise. This is a mathematical principle: in general, we cannot maximize over two functions simultaneously. For example, the general notion of the greatest good of the greatest number is incoherent. Hence, in interactive choice contexts, the simple notion of economic rationality is incoherent. Virtually all of early game theory was dedicated to finding an alternative principle for resolving game interactions. There are now many so-called *solution theories*, most of which are about outcomes rather than strategies (they stipulate which outcomes or range of outcomes is game-theoretically rational). There is little consensus on how to generalize from the ordinary rationality of merely choosing more rather than less (and of displaying consistent preferences) to the general choice of strategies in games.

Payoffs in early game theory were almost always represented in cardinal, transferable utilities. Transferable utility is an odd notion that was evidently introduced to avoid the disdain with which economists then treated interpersonal comparisons of utility. It seems to be analogous to money. In the language of contemporary law and economics, one could say the theory is one of wealth maximization. In the early theory, the rationality conditions were as follows. (1) In general, if the sums of the payoffs to all players in various outcomes differ, it is assumed that rational players will manage to divide the largest possible payoff among themselves. (2) No individual will accept a payoff below the "security level" obtainable even if all the other players form a coalition against the individual. (3) Finally, sometimes it is also assumed that no group of players will rationally accept less than it could get as its group

security level – but in some games, no outcome can meet this condition. This is an odd combination of individual and collective elements. The collective elements are plausibly thought of as merely predictive: if we individually wish to do well, we should combine efforts to help us do best as a group. But what we want is a theory that converts individual preferences into collective results. Unfortunately, to put a move doing just this in the foundations of the theory is question-begging. Our fundamental burden is to determine whether a theory of individual rationality can produce collectively good results, not to stipulate that it must.

In the theory with cardinal, additive payoffs, we can divide games into *constant sum* games, in which the sum of all players' payoffs in each outcome is a constant, and *variable sum* games. *Zero-sum* games are a special case of constant sum games. Two-person constant sum games are games of pure conflict, because each player's gain is the other's loss. In constant sum games with more than two players and in all variable sum games, there is generally reason for coalition formation to improve payoffs to members of the coalition (hence, the appeal of assumptions 1 and 3 above). Games without transferable utility, such as games in which players have only ordinal preferences, may be characterized as games of pure conflict or of pure coordination when players' preference orderings over outcomes are opposite or identical, respectively, or as games of mixed motive when their orderings are partly the same and partly reversed. Mathematical analysis of such games is evidently less tractable than that of games with cardinal, additive utility, and their theory is only beginning to be extensively developed.

Despite the apparent circularity of the rationality assumptions of early game theory, it is the game theorists' prisoner's dilemma that makes clear that compelling individual principles of choice can produce collectively deficient outcomes. This game was discovered about 1950 and later given its catchy but inapt name. If they play it in isolation from any other interaction between them, two players in this game can each do what seems individually best and reach an outcome that both consider inferior to the outcome that results from making opposite strategy choices. Even with the knowledge that this is the problem they face, the players still have incentive to choose the strategies that jointly produce the inferior outcome. Prisoner's dilemma involves both coordination and conflict. It has played a central role in contemporary discussions of moral and political philosophy. Games that predominantly involve coordination, such as when we coordinate in all driving on the right or all on the left, have a similarly central role. The understanding of both classes of games has been read into the political philosophies of Hobbes and Hume and into mutual advantage theories of justice.

See also DECISION THEORY, PRISONER'S DILEMMA, UTILITARIANISM.					R.Har.

Gandhi, Mohandas Karamchand, called Mahatma (1869–1948), Indian nationalist leader, an advocate of nonviolent mass political action who opposed racial discrimination in South Africa (1893–1914) and British colonial rule in India. He called his approach *Satyagraha* (Sanskrit *satya,* 'truth', and *agraha,* 'force'), considering it a science whose end is truth (which he identified with God) and method nonviolence (*ahiṁsā*). He emphasized constructive resolution, rather than elimination, of conflict, the interrelatedness of means and ends (precluding evil means to good ends), and the importance of enduring suffering oneself rather than inflicting it upon adversaries.

Gandhi believed limited knowledge of truth deprives us of a warrant to use violence. He took nonviolence to be more than mere abstention from violence and to call for courage, discipline, and love of an opponent. Ordinary persons can practice it without full understanding of Satyagraha, which he himself disclaimed. He came to distinguish Satyagraha from passive resistance, a weapon of the weak that can turn to violence when faced with failure. Satyagraha requires strength and consistency and cannot be used in an unjust cause. Not an absolutist, Gandhi said that though nonviolence is always preferable, when forced to choose between violence and cowardice one might better choose violence. He was a man of practice more than a theoretician and claimed the superiority of Satyagraha to violence could be proven only be demonstration, not argument. He saw his work as an experiment with truth. He was influenced particularly by the Bhagavad Gita from Hindu thought, the Sermon on the Mount from Christianity, and the writings of Tolstoy, Ruskin, Emerson, and Thoreau.

See also BHAGAVAD GITA, NONVIOLENCE, PACIFISM.					R.L.H.

Gassendi, Pierre (1592–1655), French philosopher and scientist who advocated a *via media* to scientific knowledge about the empirically observable material world that avoids both the dogmatism of Cartesians, who claimed to have certain knowledge, and the skepticism of Montaigne and Charron, who doubted that we have knowledge about anything. Gassendi presented Epicurean atomism as a model for explaining how bodies are structured and interact. He advanced a hypothetico-deductive method by proposing that experiments should be used to test mechanistic hypotheses. Like the ancient Pyrrhonian Skeptics, he did not challenge the immediate reports of our senses; but unlike them he argued that while we cannot have knowledge of the inner essences of things, we can develop a reliable science of the world of appearances. In this he exemplified the mitigated skepticism of modern science that is always open to revision on the basis of empirical evidence.

Gassendi's first book, *Exercitationes Paradoxicae Adversis Aristoteleos* (1624), is an attack on Aristotle. He is best known as the author of the fifth set of objections to Descartes's *Meditations* (1641), in which Gassendi proposed that even clear and distinct ideas may represent no objects outside our minds, a possibility that Descartes called the objection of objections, but dismissed as destructive of all reason. Gassendi's *Syntagma Philosophiae Epicuri* (1649) contains his development of Epicurean philosophy and science. His elaboration of the mechanistic atomic model and his advocacy of experimental testing of hypotheses were crucially important in the rise of modern science.

Gassendi's career as a Catholic priest, Epicurean atomist, mitigated skeptic, and mechanistic scientist presents a puzzle – as do the careers of several other philosopher-priests in the seventeenth century – concerning his true beliefs. On the one hand, he professed faith and set aside Christian doctrine as not open to challenge. On the other hand, he utilized an arsenal of skeptical arguments that was beginning to undermine and would eventually destroy the rational foundations of the church. Gassendi thus appears to be of a type almost unknown today, a thinker indifferent to the apparent discrepancy between his belief in Christian doctrine and his advocacy of materialist science.

See also DESCARTES, EPICUREANISM, SKEPTICS.					R.A.W.

Gauss, Carl Friedrich. See NON-EUCLIDEAN GEOMETRY.

Gay, John (1699–1745), British moralist who tried to reconcile divine command theory and utilitarianism. The son of a minister, Gay was elected a fellow of Sidney Sussex College, Cambridge, where he taught church history, Hebrew, and Greek. His one philosophical essay, "Dissertation Concerning the Fundamental Principle of Virtue or Morality" (1731), argues that obligation is founded on the will of God, which, because people are destined to be happy, directs us to act to promote the general happiness. Gay offers an associationist psychology according to which we pursue objects that have come to be associated with happiness (e.g. money), regardless of whether they now make us happy, and argues, contra Hutcheson, that our moral sense is conditioned rather than natural. Gay's blend of utilitarianism with associationist psychology gave David Hartley the basis for his moral psychology, which later influenced Bentham in his formulation of classical utilitarianism. **See also HARTLEY, HUTCHESON, MORAL SENSE THEORY.**   E.S.R.

GCH. See Appendix of Special Symbols.

Geach, Peter (b.1916), English philosopher and logician whose main work has been in logic and philosophy of language. A great admirer of McTaggart, he has published a sympathetic exposition of the latter's work (*Truth, Love and Immortality*, 1979), and has always aimed to emulate what he sees as the clarity and rigor of the Scottish idealist's thought. Greatly influenced by Frege and Wittgenstein, Geach is particularly noted for his powerful use of what he calls "the Frege point," better called "the Frege-Geach point," that the same thought may occur as asserted or unasserted and yet retain the same truth-value. The point has been used by Geach to refute ascriptivist theories of responsibility, and can be employed against noncognitivist theories of ethics, which are said to face the Frege-Geach problem of accounting for the sense of moral ascriptions in contexts like 'If he did wrong, he will be punished'. He is also noted for helping to bring Frege to the English-speaking world, through co-translations with Max Black (1909– 88). In logic he is known for proving, independently of Quine, a contradiction in Frege's way out of Russell's paradox (*Mind*, 1956), and for his defense of modern Fregean-Russellian logic against traditional Aristotelian-Scholastic logic. He also has a deep admiration for the Polish logicians.

In metaphysics, Geach is known for his defense of *relative identity*, the thesis that an object *a* can be the same *F* (where *F* is a kind-term) as an object *b* while not being the same *G*, even though *a* and *b* are both *G*'s. His spirited defense of the thesis has been met by equally vigorous attacks, and it has not received wide acceptance. An obvious application of the thesis is to the defense of the doctrine of the Trinity (e.g., the Father is the same god as the Son but not the same person), which has caught the attention of some philosophers of religion.

Geach's main works include *Mental Acts* (1958), which attacks dispositional theories of mind, *Reference and Generality* (1962), which contains much important work on logic, and the collection *Logic Matters* (1972). A notable defender of Catholicism (despite his animadversions against Scholastic logic), his religious views find their greatest exposure in *God and the Soul* (1969), *Providence and Evil* (1977), and *The Virtues* (1977). He is married to the philosopher Elizabeth Anscombe.

See also ASCRIPTIVISM, FREGE, IDENTITY, MCTAGGART, RUSSELL, WITTGENSTEIN.

D.S.O.

Gegenstandstheorie. See ACT-OBJECT PSYCHOLOGY.

Geist. See HEGEL.

Geisteswissenschaften. See WEBER.

Gemeinschaft. See SOCIAL PHILOSOPHY.

gender theory. See POSTMODERN.

genealogy. See FOUCAULT, NIETZSCHE.

generality. See VAGUENESS.

generalizability. See UNIVERSALIZABILITY.

generalization, existential. See EXISTENTIAL GENERALIZATION.

generalization, universal. See UNIVERSALIZABILITY.

generalization argument. See UNIVERSALIZABILITY.

generalization principle. See UNIVERSALIZABILITY.

generalized continuum hypothesis. See Appendix of Special Symbols.

generalized quantifier. See FORMAL LOGIC.

general jurisprudence. See JURISPRUDENCE, PHILOSOPHY OF LAW.

general relativity. See RELATIVITY.

general systems theory. See SYSTEMS THEORY.

general term. See SINGULAR TERM.

general will. See ROUSSEAU.

generative grammar. See GRAMMAR.

generic consistency, principle of. See UNIVERSALIZABILITY.

generic sentence. See PHILOSOPHY OF LANGUAGE.

genetic epistemology. See PIAGET.

genetic fallacy. See INFORMAL FALLACY.

genotext. See KRISTEVA.

Gentile, Giovanni (1875–1944), Italian idealist philosopher and educational reformer. He taught at the universities of Palermo, Pisa, and Rome, and became minister of education in the first years of Mussolini's government (1922–24). He was the most influential intellectual of the Fascist regime and promoted a radical transformation of the Italian school system, most of which did not survive that era.

Gentile rejected Hegel's dialectics as the process of an objectified thought. His *actualism* (or actual idealism) claims that only the pure act of thinking or the Transcendental Subject can undergo a dialectical process. All reality, such as nature, God, good, and evil, is immanent in the dialectics of the Transcendental Subject, which is distinct from Empirical Subjects. Among his major works are *La teoria generale dello spirito come atto puro* (1916; translated as *The Theory of Mind as Pure Act*, 1922) and *Sistema di logica come teoria del conoscere* ("System of Logic as a Theory of Knowledge," 1917).

Gentile's pedagogical views were also influenced by actualism. Education is an act that overcomes the difficulties of intersubjective communication and realizes the unity of the pupil and the teacher within the Transcendental Subject (*Sommario di pedagogia come scienza filosofica*, "Summary of Pedagogy as a Philosophical Science," 1913–14). Actualism was influential in Italy during Gentile's life. With Croce's historicism, it influenced British idealists like Bosanquet and Collingwood.

See also IDEALISM.   P.Gar.

genus. See DEFINITION.

genus, summum. See GENUS GENERALISSIMUM.

genus generalissimum (Latin, 'most general genus'), a genus that is not a species of some higher genus; a broadest natural kind. One of the ten Aristotelian categories, it is also called *summum genus* (highest genus). For Aristotle and many of his followers, the ten categories are not species of some higher all-inclusive genus – say, being. Otherwise, that all-inclusive genus would wholly include its differences, and would be universally predicable of them. But no genus is predicable of its differences in this manner. Few authors explained this reasoning clearly, but some pointed out that if the difference 'rational' just meant 'rational animal', then to define 'man' as 'rational animal' would be to define him as 'rational animal animal', which is ill formed. So too generally: no genus can include its differences in this way. Thus there is no all-inclusive genus; the ten categories are the most general genera. **See also** DEFINITION, PRAEDICAMENTA, PREDICABLES.   P.V.S.

geometric conventionalism. See POINCARÉ.

geometry, Euclidean. See EUCLIDEAN GEOMETRY.

geometry, non-Euclidean. See NON-EUCLIDEAN GEOMETRY.

Gerson, Jean de, original name, Jean Charlier (1363–1429), French theologian, philosopher, and ecclesiastic. He studied in Paris, and succeeded the nominalist Pierre d'Ailly as chancellor of the university in 1395. Both d'Ailly and Gerson played a prominent part in the work of the Council of Constance (1414–18). Much of Gerson's influence on later thinkers arose from his *conciliarism*, the view that the church is a political society and that a general council, acting on behalf of the church, has the power to depose a pope who fails to promote the church's welfare, for it seemed that similar arguments could apply to other forms of political society. Gerson's conciliarism was not constitutionalism in the modern sense, for he appealed to corporate and hierarchical ideas of church government, and did not rest his case on any principle of individual rights. His main writings dealt with mystical theology, which, he thought, brings the believer closer to the beatific vision of God than do other forms of theology. He was influenced by

St. Bonaventure and Albertus Magnus, but especially by Pseudo-Dionysius, whom he saw as a
disciple of St. Paul and not as a Platonist. He was
thus able to adopt an anti-Platonic position in his
attacks on the mystic Ruysbroeck and on contemporary followers of Duns Scotus, such as
Jean de Ripa. In dismissing Scotist realism, he
made use of nominalist positions, particularly
those that emphasized divine freedom. He
warned theologians against being misled by
pride into supposing that natural reason alone
could solve metaphysical problems; and he
emphasized the importance of a priest's pastoral
duties. Despite his early prominence, he spent
the last years of his life in relative obscurity.

E.J.A.

Gersonides, also called Levi ben Gershom
(1288–1344), French Jewish philosopher and
mathematician, the leading Jewish Aristotelian
after Maimonides. Gersonides was also a distinguished Talmudist, Bible commentator, and
astronomer. His philosophical writings include
supercommentaries on most of Averroes' commentaries on Aristotle (1319–24); *On the Correct
Syllogism* (1319), a treatise on the modal syllogism; and a major Scholastic treatise, *The Wars of
the Lord* (1317–29). In addition, his biblical commentaries rank among the best examples of
philosophical scriptural exegesis; especially noteworthy is his interpretation of the Song of Songs
as an allegory describing the ascent of the human
intellect to the agent intellect.

Gersonides' mentors in the Aristotelian tradition were Maimonides and Averroes. However,
more than either of them, Gersonides held philosophical truth and revealed truth to be coextensive: he acknowledged neither the conflict that
Averroes saw between reason and revelation nor
Maimonides' critical view of the limitations of
the human intellect. Furthermore, while remaining within the Aristotelian framework, Gersonides was not uncritical of it; his independence
can be illustrated by two of his most distinctive
positions. First, against Maimonides, Gersonides
claimed that it is possible to demonstrate *both* the
falsity of the Aristotelian theory of the eternity of
the world (Averroes' position) and the absurdity
of creation *ex nihilo,* the traditional rabbinic view
that Maimonides adopted, though for non-
demonstrative reasons. Instead Gersonides
advocated the Platonic theory of temporal creation from primordial matter. Second, unlike
Maimonides and Averroes, who both held that
the alleged contradiction between divine foreknowledge of future contingent particulars and

human freedom is spurious, Gersonides took the
dilemma to be real. In defense of human freedom, he then argued that it is logically impossible even for God to have knowledge of
particulars *as particulars,* since his knowledge is
only of general laws. At the same time, by
redefining 'omniscience' as knowing everything
that is knowable, he showed that this impossibility is no deficiency in God's knowledge.

Although Gersonides' biblical commentaries
received wide immediate acceptance, subsequent medieval Jewish philosophers, e.g., Hasdai
Crescas, by and large reacted negatively to his
rigorously rationalistic positions. Especially with
the decline of Aristotelianism within the philosophical world, both Jewish and Christian, he
was either criticized sharply or simply ignored.

See also ARISTOTLE, AVERROES, JEWISH
PHILOSOPHY, MAIMONIDES, PHILOSOPHY OF
RELIGION.   J.Ste.

Gesellschaft. See SOCIAL PHILOSOPHY.

Gestalt. See FIGURE–GROUND, KÖHLER.

Gestalt psychology. See KÖHLER.

Gettier problem. See EPISTEMOLOGY.

Gettier-style example. See EPISTEMOLOGY.

Geulincx, Arnold (1624–69), Dutch philosopher.
Born in Antwerp, he was educated at Louvain
and there became professor of philosophy (1646)
and dean (1654). In 1657 he was forced out of
Louvain, perhaps for his Jansenist or Cartesian
tendencies, and in 1658 he moved to Leyden and
became a Protestant. Though he taught there
until his death, he never attained a regular professorship at the university. His main philosophical work is his *Ethica* (1675), only Part I of which
appeared during his lifetime as *De virtute et primis
ejus proprietatibus* (1665). Also published during
his lifetime were the *Questiones quodlibeticae*
(1652; later editions published as *Saturnalia*), a
Logica (1661), and a *Methodus inveniendi argu-
menta* (1665). His most important works,
though, were published posthumously; in addition to the *Ethica,* there is the *Physica vera* (1688),
the *Physica peripatetica* (1690), the *Metaphysica
vera* (1691), and the *Metaphysica ad mentem peri-
pateticam* (1691). There are also two posthumous
commentaries on Descartes's *Principia Philosophiae* (1690 and 1691).

Geulincx was deeply influenced by Descartes,
and had many ideas that closely resemble those

of the later Cartesians as well as those of more independent thinkers like Spinoza and Leibniz. Though his grounds were original, like many later Cartesians, Geulincx upheld a version of occasionalism; he argued that someone or something can only do what it knows how to do, inferring from that that we cannot be the genuine causes of our own bodily movements. In discussing the mind–body relation, Geulincx used a clock analogy similar to one Leibniz used in connection with his preestablished harmony. Geulincx also held a view of mental and material substance reminiscent of that of Spinoza. Finally, he proposed a system of ethics grounded in the idea of a virtuous will. Despite the evident similarities between Geulincx's views and the views of his more renowned contemporaries, it is very difficult to determine exactly what influence Geulincx may have had on them, and they may have had on him.

See also DESCARTES, LEIBNIZ, OCCASIONALISM.   D.Garb.

Ghazālī, al-. See AL-GHAZĀLĪ.

ghost in the machine. See RYLE.

Giles of Rome, original name, Egidio Colonna (c.1243–1316), Italian theologian and ecclesiastic. A member of the order of the Hermits of St. Augustine, he studied arts at Augustinian house and theology at the University in Paris (1260–72) but was censured by the theology faculty (1277) and denied a license to teach as master. Owing to the intervention of Pope Honorius IV, he later returned from Italy to Paris to teach theology (1285–91), was appointed general of his order (1292), and became archbishop of Bourges (1295).

Giles both defended and criticized views of Aquinas. He held that essence and existence are really distinct in creatures, but described them as "things"; that prime matter cannot exist without some substantial form; and, early in his career, that an eternally created world is possible. He defended only one substantial form in composites, including man. He supported Pope Boniface VIII in his quarrel with Philip IV of France.

J.F.W.

Gilson, Étienne (1884–1978), French Catholic philosopher, historian, cofounder of the Pontifical Institute of Medieval Studies in Toronto, and a major figure in Neo-Thomism. Gilson discovered medieval philosophy through his pioneering work on Descartes's Scholastic

background. As a historian, he argued that early modern philosophy was incomprehensible without medieval thought, and that medieval philosophy itself did not represent the unified theory of reality that some Thomists had supposed. His studies of Duns Scotus, Augustine, Bernard, Aquinas, Bonaventure, Dante, and Abelard and Héloïse explore this diversity. But in his Gifford lectures (1931–32), *The Spirit of Medieval Philosophy,* Gilson attempted a broad synthesis of medieval teaching on philosophy, metaphysics, ethics, and epistemology, and employed it in his critique of modern philosophy, *The Unity of Philosophical Experience* (1937). Most of all, Gilson attempted to reestablish Aquinas's distinction between essence and existence in created being, as in *Being and Some Philosophers* (1949). **See also** NEO-THOMISM, THOMISM.   D.W.H.

Gioberti, Vincenzo (1801–52), Italian philosopher and statesman. He was an ordained priest, was imprisoned and exiled for advocating Italian unification, and became a central political figure during the Risorgimento.

His major political work, *Del primato morale e civile degli Italiani* ("On the Moral and Civil Primacy of Italians," 1843), argues for a federation of the Italian states with the pope as its leader. Gioberti's philosophical theory, *ontologism,* in contrast to Hegel's idealism, identifies the dialectics of Being with God's creation. He condensed his theory in the formula: "Being creates the existent." The dialectics of Being, which is the only necessary substance, is a *palingenesis,* or a return to its origin, in which the existent first departs from and imitates its creator (*mimesis*), and then returns to its creator (*methexis*). By intuition, the human mind comes in contact with God and discovers truth by retracing the dialectics of Being. However, knowledge of supernatural truths is given only by God's revelation (*Teorica del soprannaturale* ["Theory of the Supernatural," 1838] and *Introduzione allo studio della filosofia* ["Introduction to the Study of Philosophy," 1841]). Gioberti criticized modern philosophers such as Descartes for their psychologism – seeking truth from the human subject instead of from Being itself and its revelation. His thought is still influential in Italy, especially in Christian spiritualism.   P.Gar.

given, in epistemology, the "brute fact" element to be found or postulated as a component of perceptual experience. Some theorists who endorse the existence of a given element in experience think that we can find this element by careful introspection of what we experience (Moore, H. H. Price). Such theorists generally distinguish between those components of ordinary perceptual awareness that constitute what we believe or know about the objects we perceive and those components that we strictly perceive. For example, if we analyze introspectively what we are aware of when we see an apple we find that what we believe of the apple is that it is a three-dimensional object with a soft, white interior; what we see of it, strictly speaking, is just a red-shaped expanse of one of its facing sides. This latter is what is "given" in the intended sense.

Other theorists treat the given as postulated rather than introspectively found. For example, some theorists treat cognition as an activity imposing form on some material given in conscious experience. On this view, often attributed to Kant, the given and the conceptual are inter-defined and logically inseparable. Sometimes this interdependence is seen as rendering a description of the given as impossible; in this case the given is said to be ineffable (C. I. Lewis, *Mind and the World Order,* 1929).

On some theories of knowledge (foundationalism) the first variant of the given – that which is "found" rather than "postulated" – provides the empirical foundations of what we might know or justifiably believe. Thus, if I believe on good evidence that there is a red apple in front of me, the evidence is the non-cognitive part of my perceptual awareness of the red apple-shaped expanse. Epistemologies postulating the first kind of givenness thus require a single entity-type to explain the sensorial nature of perception and to provide immediate epistemic foundations for empirical knowledge. This requirement is now widely regarded as impossible to satisfy; hence Wilfred Sellars describes the discredited view as the myth of the given.

See also PERCEPTION; PHENOMENALISM; SELLARS, WILFRID.   T.V.

given, myth of the. See SELLARS, WILFRID.

Glanvill, Joseph (1636–80), English philosopher and Anglican minister who defended the Royal Society against Scholasticism. Glanvill believed that certainty was possible in mathematics and theology, but not in empirical knowledge. In his most important philosophical work, *The Vanity of Dogmatizing* (1661), he claimed that the human corruption that resulted from Adam's fall precludes dogmatic knowledge of nature. Using traditional skeptical arguments as well as an analysis of causality that partially anticipated

Hume, Glanvill argued that all empirical knowledge is the probabilistic variety acquired by piecemeal investigation. Despite his skepticism he argued for the existence of witches in *Witches and Witchcraft* (1668).   J.W.A.

Gleason's theorem. See QUANTUM LOGIC.

global supervenience. See SUPERVENIENCE.

gnosticism, a dualistic religious and philosophical movement in the early centuries of the Christian church, especially important in the second century under the leadership of Valentinus and Basilides. They taught that matter was evil, the result of a cosmic disruption in which an evil *archon* (often associated with the god of the Old Testament, Yahweh) rebelled against the heavenly *pleroma* (the complete spiritual world). In the process divine sparks were unleashed from the pleroma and lodged in material human bodies. Jesus was a high-ranking archon (*Logos*) sent to restore those souls with divine sparks to the pleroma by imparting esoteric knowledge (*gnosis*) to them.

Gnosticism influenced and threatened the orthodox church from within and without. Non-Christian gnostic sects rivaled Christianity, and Christian gnostics threatened orthodoxy by emphasizing salvation by knowledge rather than by faith. Theologians like Clement of Alexandria and his pupil Origen held that there were two roads to salvation, the way of faith for the masses and the way of esoteric or mystical knowledge for the philosophers.

Gnosticism profoundly influenced the early church, causing it to define its scriptural canon and to develop a set of creeds and an episcopal organization.

See also CLEMENT OF ALEXANDRIA, ORIGEN.   L.P.P.

goal-directed system. See COMPUTER THEORY, CYBERNETICS.

Göckel, Rudolph. See GOCLENIUS.

Goclenius, Rudolphus, in Germany, Rudolf Göckel (1547–1628), German philosopher. After holding some minor posts elsewhere, Goclenius became professor at the University of Marburg in 1581, where he remained until his death, teaching physics, logic, mathematics, and ethics. Though he was well read and knowledgeable of later trends in these disciplines, his basic sympathies were Aristotelian. Goclenius was very well regarded by his contemporaries, who called him the Plato of Marburg, the Christian Aristotle, and the Light of Europe, among other things. He published an unusually large number of books, including the *Psychologia, hoc est de hominis perfectione* ... (1590), the *Conciliator philosophicus* (1609), the *Controversiae logicae et philosophicae* (1609), and numerous other works on logic, rhetoric, physics, metaphysics, and the Latin language. But his most lasting work was his *Lexicon Philosophicum* (1613), together with its companion, the *Lexicon Philosophicum Graecum* (1615). These lexicons provide clear definitions of the philosophical terminology of late Scholastic philosophy, and are still useful as reference works for sixteenth- and early seventeenth-century thought.   D.Garb.

God. See DIVINE ATTRIBUTES, PHILOSOPHY OF RELIGION.

God, arguments for the existence of. See DIVINE ATTRIBUTES, ENS A SE, PHILOSOPHY OF RELIGION.

Gödel, Kurt. See GÖDEL'S INCOMPLETENESS THEOREMS.

Gödel numbering. See GÖDEL'S INCOMPLETENESS THEOREMS.

Gödel's incompleteness theorems, two theorems formulated and proved by the Austrian logician Kurt Gödel (1906–78) in his famous 1931 paper "Über formal unentscheidbare Sätze der *Principia Mathematica* und vervandter Systeme I," probably the most celebrated results in the whole of logic. They are aptly referred to as "incompleteness" theorems since each shows, for any member of a certain class of formal systems, that there is a sentence formulable in its language that it cannot prove, but that it would be desirable for it to prove. In the case of the first theorem (G1), what cannot be proved is a true sentence of the language of the given theory. G1 is thus a disappointment to any theory constructor who wants his theory to tell the whole truth about its subject. In the case of the second theorem (G2), what cannot be proved is a sentence of the theory that "expresses" its consistency. G2 is thus a disappointment to those who desire a straightforward execution of Hilbert's Program.

The proofs of the incompleteness theorems can be seen as based on three main ideas. The first is that of a *Gödel numbering*, i.e., an assignment of natural numbers to each of the various objects (i.e., the terms, formulas, axioms, proofs, etc.) belonging to the various syntactical categories of the given formal system T (referred to here as the "represented theory") whose metamathematics is under consideration. The second is that of a *representational scheme*. This includes (i) the use of the Gödel numbering to develop number-theoretic codifications of various of the metamathematical properties pertaining to the represented theory, and (ii) the selection of a theory S (hereafter, the "representing theory") and a family of formulas from that theory (the "representing formulas") in terms of which to register as theorems various of the facts concerning the metamathematical properties of the represented theory thus encoded. The basic result of this representational scheme is the weak representation of the set of (Gödel numbers of) theorems of T, where a set Λ of numbers is said to be weakly represented in S by a formula '$L(x)$' of S just in case for every number v, $v \in \Lambda$ if and only if '$L([v])$' is a theorem of S, where '$[v]$' is the standard term of S that, under the intended interpretation of S, designates the number n. Since the set of (Gödel numbers of) theorems of the represented theory T will typically be recursively enumerable, and the representing theory S must be capable of weakly representing this set, the basic strength requirement on S is that it be capable of weakly representing the recursively enumerable sets of natural numbers. Because basic systems of arithmetic (e.g. Robinson's arithmetic and Peano arithmetic) all have this capacity, Gödel's theorems are often stated using containment of a fragment of arithmetic as the basic strength requirement governing the capacities of the representing theory (which, of course, is also often the represented theory). More on this point below.

The third main idea behind the incompleteness theorems is that of a *diagonal* or *fixed point* construction within S for the notion of unprovability-in-T; i.e., the formulation of a sentence *Gödel* of S which, under the given Gödel numbering of T, the given representation of T's metamathematical notions in S, and the intended interpretation of the language of S, says of itself that it is not provable-in-T. *Gödel* is thus false if provable and unprovable if true. More specifically, if '$\text{Prov}_T(x)$' is a formula of S that weakly represents the set of (Gödel numbers of) theorems of T in S, then *Gödel* can be any formula of S that is provably equivalent in S to the formula '$\sim \text{Prov}_T([Gödel])$'.

Given this background, G1 can be stated as follows: If (a) the representing theory S is any subtheory of the represented theory T (up to and including the represented theory itself), (b) the representing theory S is consistent, (c) the formula 'Prov$_T$ (x)' weakly represents the set of (Gödel numbers of) theorems of the represented theory T in the representing theory S, and (d) *Gödel* is any sentence provably equivalent in the representing theory S to 'Prov$_T$ ([*Gödel*])', then neither *Gödel* nor ~*Gödel* is a theorem of the representing theory S.

The proof proceeds in two parts. In the first part it is shown that, for any representing theory S (up to and including the case where $S = T$), if S is consistent, then ~*Gödel* is not a theorem of S. To obtain this in its strongest form, we pick the strongest subtheory S of T possible, namely $S = T$, and construct a *reductio*. Thus, suppose that (1) ~*Gödel* is a theorem of T. From (1) and (d) it follows that (2) 'Prov$_T$([*Gödel*])' is a theorem of T. And from (2) and (c) (in the "if" direction) it follows that (3) *Gödel* is a theorem of T. But (1) and (3) together imply that the representing theory T is inconsistent. Hence, if T is consistent, ~*Gödel* cannot be a theorem of T.

In the second part of the proof it is argued that if the representing theory S is consistent, then *Gödel* is not a theorem of it. Again, to obtain the strongest result, we let S be the strongest subtheory of T possible (namely T itself) and, as before, argue by *reductio*. Thus we suppose that (A) *Gödel* is a theorem of S ($= T$). From this assumption and condition (d) it follows that (B) '~Prov$_r$ ([*Gödel*])' is a theorem of S ($= T$). By (A) and (c) (in the "only if" direction) it follows that (C) 'Prov$_T$ ([*Gödel*])' is a theorem of S ($= T$). But from (B) and (C) it follows that S ($= T$) is inconsistent. Hence, *Gödel* is not provable in any consistent representing theory S up to and including T itself.

The above statement of G1 is, of course, not the usual one. The usual statement suppresses the distinction stressed above between the representing and represented theories and collaterally replaces our condition (c) with a clause to the effect that T is a recursively axiomatizable extension of some suitably weak system of arithmetic (e.g. Robinson's arithmetic, primitive recursive arithmetic, or Peano arithmetic). This puts into a single clause what, metamathematically speaking, are two separate conditions – one pertaining to the representing theory, the other to the represented theory. The requirement that T be an extension of the selected weak arithmetic addresses the question of T's adequacy as a representing theory, since the crucial fact about extensions of the weak arithmetic chosen is that they are capable of weakly representing all

recursively enumerable sets. This constraint on T's capabilities as a representing theory is in partnership with the usual requirement that, in its capacity as a represented theory, T be recursively axiomatizable. For T's recursive axiomatizability ensures (under ordinary choices of logic for T) that its set of theorems will be recursively enumerable – and hence weakly representable in the kind of representing theory that it itself (by virtue of its being an extension of the weak arithmetic specified) is.

G1 can, however, be extended to certain theories whose sets of (Gödel numbers of) theorems are *not* recursively enumerable. When this is done, the basic capacity required of the representing theory is no longer merely that the recursively enumerable sets of natural numbers be representable in it, but that it also be capable of representing various non-recursively enumerable sets, and hence that it go beyond the weak arithmetics mentioned earlier.

G2 is a more demanding result that G1 in that it puts significantly stronger demands on the formula 'Prov$_T$ (x)' used to express the notion of provability for the represented theory T. In proving G1 all that is required of 'Prov$_T$ (x)' is that it weakly represent θ (= the set of Gödel numbers of theorems of T); i.e., that it yield an extensionally accurate registry of the theorems of the represented theory in the representing theory. G2 places additional conditions on 'Prov$_T$ (x)'; conditions which result from the fact that, to prove G2, we must codify the second part of the proof of G1 in T itself. To do this, 'Prov$_T$ (x)' must be a *provability predicate* for T. That is, it must satisfy the following constraints, commonly referred to as the Derivability Conditions (for 'Prov$_T$ (x)'):

(I) If A is a theorem of the represented theory, then 'Prov$_T$ ([A])' must be a theorem of the representing theory.

(II) Every instance of the formula 'Prov$_T$ ([$A \rightarrow B$]) $\rightarrow$ (Prov$_T$ ([A]) $\rightarrow$ Prov$_T$ ([B]))' must be a theorem of T.

(III) Every instance of the formula 'Prov$_T$ ([A]) $\rightarrow$ Prov$_T$ ([Prov$_T$ ([A])])' must be a theorem of T.

(I), of course, is just part of the requirement that 'Prov$_T$ ([A])' weakly represent T's theorem-set in T. So it does not go beyond what is required for the proof of G1. (II) and (III), however, do. They make it possible to "formalize" the second part of the proof of G1 in T itself. (II) captures, in terms of 'Prov$_T$ (X)', the *modus ponens* inference by which (B) is derived from (A), and (III) codifies in T the appeal to (c) used in deriving (C) from (A).

The result of this "formalization" process is a proof within T of the formula 'Con$_T \to$ Gödel' (where Con$_T$ is a formula of the form '$\sim$ Prov$_T$ ([#])', with 'Prov$_T$ (x)' a provability predicate for T and '[#]' the standard numeral denoting the Gödel number # of some formula refutable in T). From this, and the proof of the second part of G1 itself (in which the first Derivability Condition, which is just the "only if" direction of (c), figures prominently), we arrive at the following result, which is a generalized form of G2: If S is any consistent representing theory up to and including the represented theory T itself, 'Prov$_T$ (x)' any provability predicate for T, and Con$_T$ any formula of T of the form '$\sim$ Prov$_T$ ([#])', then Con$_T$ is not a theorem of S. To the extent that, in being a provability predicate for T, 'Prov$_T$ (x)' "expresses" the notion of provability of the represented theory T, it seems fair to say that Con$_T$ expresses its consistency. And to the extent that this is true, it is sensible to read G2 as saying that for any representing theory S and any represented theory T extending S, if S is consistent, then the consistency of T is not provable in S.

See also COMPUTER THEORY, CONSISTENCY, HILBERT'S PROGRAM, PROOF THEORY.　　M.D.

Godfrey of Fontaines (probably before 1250–1306 or 1309), French philosopher. He taught theology at Paris (1285–c.1299; 1303–04). Among his major writings are fifteen Quodlibetal Questions and other disputations. He was strongly Aristotelian in philosophy, with Neoplatonic influences in metaphysics. He defended identity of essence and existence in creatures against theories of their real or intentional distinction, and argued for the possibility of demonstrating God's existence and of some quidditative knowledge of God. He admitted divine ideas for species but not for individuals within species. He made wide applications of Aristotelian act-potency theory – e.g., to the distinction between the soul and its powers, to the explanation of intellection and volition, to the general theory of substance and accident, and in unusual fashion to essence-existence "composition" of creatures.
　　　　　　　　　　　　　　　　　　J.F.W.

Godwin, William (1756–1836), English philosopher, novelist, and political writer. Godwin's main philosophical treatise, *Enquiry concerning Political Justice* (1793), aroused heated debate. He argued for radical forms of determinism, anarchism, and utilitarianism. Government corrupts everyone by encouraging stereotyped thinking that prevents us from seeing each other as unique individuals. Godwin's novel *Caleb Williams* (1794) portrays a good man corrupted by prejudice. Once we remove prejudice and artificial inequality we will see that our acts are wholly determined. This makes punishment pointless. Only in small, anarchic societies can people see others as they really are and thus come to feel sympathetic concern for their well-being. Only so can we be virtuous, because virtue is acting from sympathetic feelings to bring the greatest happiness to all affected.

Godwin took this principle quite literally, and accepted all its consequences. Truthfulness has no claim on us other than the happiness it brings. If keeping a promise causes less good than breaking it, there is no reason at all to keep it. If one must choose between saving the life either of a major human benefactor or of one's mother, one must choose the benefactor. Ideally we would need no rules in morals at all. They prevent us from seeing others properly, thereby impairing the sympathetic feelings that constitute virtue. Rights are pointless since sympathetic people will act to help others. Later utilitarians like Bentham had difficulty in separating their positions from Godwin's notorious views.

See also BENTHAM.　　　　　　　　　　　　J.B.S.

Goethe, Johann Wolfgang von (1749–1832), German writer whose career spans as well as trancends the periods of *Sturm und Drang* (Storm and Stress), neo-classicism, and romanticism. He wrote lyric poetry, dramas, and fictional, essayistic, and aphoristic prose as well as works in various natural sciences, including anatomy, botany, and optics. A lawyer by training, for most of his life Goethe was a government official at the provincial court of Saxony-Weimar. In his numerous contributions to world literature, such as the novels *The Sorrows of Young Werther* (1774), *Wilhelm Meister's Years of Apprenticeship* (1795/96), *Elective Affinities* (1809), and *Wilhelm Meister's Years of Pilgrimage* (1821/29), and the two-part tragedy *Faust* (1808/32), Goethe represented the tensions between individual and society as well as between culture and nature, with increased recognition of their tragic opposition and the need to cultivate a resigned self-discipline in artistic and social matters. In his poetic and scientific treatment of nature he was influenced by Spinoza's pantheist identification of nature and God and maintained that everything in nature is animate and expressive of divine presence. In his theory and practice of science he opposed the quantitative and experimental method and insisted on a description of the phenomena that was to include the intuitive grasp of the archetypal forms or shapes underlying all development in nature. **See also** PANTHEISM, SPINOZA.   G.Z.

Goldbach's conjecture. See CHOICE SEQUENCE.

golden mean. See ARISTOTLE.

Goldman, Alvin I(ra) (b.1938), American philosopher who has made notable contributions to action theory, naturalistic and social epistemology, philosophy of mind, and cognitive science. He has persistently urged the relevance of cognitive and social science to problems in epistemology, metaphysics, the philosophy of mind, and ethics. *A Theory of Human Action* (1970) proposes a causal theory of action, describes the generative structure of basic and non-basic action, and argues for the compatibility of free will and determinism. In "Epistemics: The Regulative Theory of Cognition" (1978), he argued that traditional epistemology should be replaced by 'epistemics', which differs from traditional epistemology in characterizing knowledge, justified belief, and rational belief in light of empirical cognitive science. Traditional epistemology has used a coarse-grained notion of belief, taken too restrictive a view of cognitive methods, offered advice for ideal cognizers rather than for human beings with limited cognitive resources, and ignored flaws in our cognitive system that must be recognized if cognition is to be improved. Epistemologists must attend to the results of cognitive science if they are to remedy these deficiencies in traditional epistemology. Goldman later developed epistemics in *Epistemology and Cognition* (1986), in which he developed a historical, reliabilist theory of knowledge and epistemic justification and employed empirical cognitive science to characterize knowledge, evaluate skepticism, and assess human cognitive resources. In *Liaisons: Philosophy Meets the Cognitive and Social Sciences* (1992) and in *Knowledge in a Social World* (1999), he defended and elaborated a veritistic (i.e., truth-oriented) evaluation of communal belief-profiles, social institutions, and social practices (e.g., the practice of restricting evidence admissible in a jury trial). He has opposed the widely accepted view that mental states are functional states ("The Psychology of Folk Psychology," *Behavioral and Brain Sciences*, 1993) and defended a simulation theory of mental state attribution, on which one attributes mental states to another

by imagining what mental state one would be in if one were in the other's situation ("In Defense of the Simulation Theory," 1992). He has also argued that cognitive science bears on ethics by providing information relevant to the nature of moral evaluation, moral choice, and hedonic states associated with the good (e.g., happiness) ("Ethics and Cognitive Science," 1993). **See also** ACTION THEORY, COGNITIVE SCIENCE, EPISTEMOLOGY, RELIABILISM, SIMULATION THEORY, SOCIAL EPISTEMOLOGY.   F.F.S.

good. See ETHICS.

good, common. See COMMON GOOD.

good-making characteristic, a characteristic that makes whatever is intrinsically or inherently good, good. Hedonists hold that pleasure and conducing to pleasure are the sole good-making characteristics. Pluralists hold that those characteristics are only some among many other good-making characteristics, which include, for instance, knowledge, friendship, beauty, and acting from a sense of duty. **See also** ETHICS, HEDONISM.   B.R.

Goodman, Nelson (1906–98), American philosopher who made seminal contributions to metaphysics, epistemology, and aesthetics. Like Quine, Goodman repudiates analyticity and kindred notions. Goodman's work can be read as a series of investigations into how to do philosophy without them. A central concern is how symbols structure facts and our understanding of them. *The Structure of Appearance* (1952) presents Goodman's constructionalism. Pretheoretical beliefs are vague and mutually inconsistent. By devising an interpreted formal system that derives them from or explicates them in terms of suitable primitives, we bring them into logical contact, eliminate inconsistencies, and disclose unanticipated logical and theoretical connections. Multiple, divergent systems do justice to the same pretheoretical beliefs. All systems satisfying our criteria of adequacy are equally acceptable. Nothing favors any one of them over the others. *Ways of Worldmaking* (1978) provides a less formal treatment of the same themes. Category schemes dictate criteria of identity for their objects. So mutually irreducible category schemes do not treat of the same things. Since a world consists of the things it comprises, irreducible schemes mark out different worlds. There are, Goodman concludes, many worlds if any. Inasmuch as the categories that define identity conditions on objects are human constructs, we make worlds.

Languages of Art (1968) argues that art, like science, makes and reveals worlds. Aesthetics is the branch of epistemology that investigates art's cognitive functions. Goodman analyzes the syntactic and semantic structures of symbol systems, both literal and figurative, and shows how they advance understanding in art and elsewhere. *Fact, Fiction, and Forecast* (1954) poses the new riddle of induction. An item is *grue* if and only if it is examined before future time *t* and found to be green or is not so examined and is blue. All hitherto examined emeralds are both green and grue. What justifies our expecting future emeralds to be green, not grue? Inductive validity, the riddle demonstrates, depends on the characterization as well as the classification of the evidence class. 'Green' is preferable, Goodman maintains, because it is entrenched in inductive practice. This does not guarantee that inferences using 'green' will yield truths. Nothing guarantees that. But entrenched predicates are pragmatically advantageous, because they mesh with our habits of thought and other cognitive resources. Goodman's other works include *Problems and Projects* (1972), *Of Mind and Other Matters* (1984), and *Reconceptions* (1988), written with Catherine Z. Elgin.

See also AESTHETICS, ANALYTIC–SYNTHETIC DISTINCTION, GRUE PARADOX.   C.Z.E.

Gorgias (c.483–c.376 B.C.), Greek Sophist. A teacher of rhetoric from Leontini in Syracuse, Gorgias came to Athens in 427 B.C. as an ambassador from his city and caused a sensation with his artful oratory. He is known through references and short quotations in later writers, and through a few surviving texts – two speeches and a philosophical treatise. He taught a rhetorical style much imitated in antiquity, by delivering model speeches to paying audiences. Unlike other Sophists he did not give formal instruction in other topics, nor prepare a formal rhetorical manual.

He was known to have had views on language, on the nature of reality, and on virtue. Gorgias's style was remarkable for its use of poetic devices such as rhyme, meter, and elegant words, as well as for its dependence on artificial parallelism and balanced antithesis. His surviving speeches, defenses of Helen and Palamedes, display a range of arguments that rely heavily on what the ancients called *eikos* ('likelihood' or 'probability'). Gorgias maintained in his "Helen" that a speech can compel its audience to action; else-where he remarked that in the theater it is wiser to be deceived than not.

Gorgias's short book *On Nature* (or *On What Is Not*) survives in two paraphrases, one by Sextus Empiricus and the other (now considered more reliable) in an Aristotelian work, *On Melissus, Xenophanes, and Gorgias*. Gorgias argued for three theses: that nothing exists; that even if it did, it could not be known; and that even if it could be known, it could not be communicated. Although this may be in part a parody, most scholars now take it to be a serious philosophical argument in its own right. In ethics, Plato reports that Gorgias thought there were different virtues for men and for women, a thesis Aristotle defends in the *Politics*.

See also SOPHISTS.   P.Wo.

Göttingen School. See NEO-KANTIANISM.

grace, efficacious. See ARNAULD.

Gracián y Morales, Baltasar (1601–58), Spanish writer, moralist, and a leading literary theorist of the Spanish baroque. Born in Belmonte, he entered the Jesuit order in 1619 and became rector of the Jesuit College at Tarragona and a favorite of King Philip III. Gracián's most important works are *Agudeza y arte de ingenio* ("The Art of Worldly Wisdom," 1642–48) and *El criticón* ("The Critic," 1651–57). The first provides philosophical support for *conceptismo*, a Spanish literary movement that sought to create new concepts through the development of an elaborate style, characterized by subtlety (*agudeza*) and ingenious literary artifices. *El criticón*, written in the conceptist style, is a philosophical novel that pessimistically criticizes the evils of civilization. Gracián anticipates Rousseau's noble savage in claiming that, although human beings are fundamentally good in the state of nature, they are corrupted by civilization. Echoing a common theme of Spanish thought at the time, he attributes the nefarious influence of civilization to the confusion it creates between appearance and reality. But Gracián's pessimism is tempered by faith: man has hope in the afterlife, when reality is finally revealed.

Gracián wrote several other influential books. In *El héroe* ("The Hero," 1637) and *El político* ("The Politician," 1640), he follows Machiavelli in discussing the attributes of the ideal prince; *El discreto* ("The Man of Discretion," 1646) explores the ideal gentleman, as judged by Spanish society. Most of Gracián's books were published under pseudonyms to avoid censure by his order.

Among authors outside Spain who used his ideas are Nietzsche, Schopenhauer, Voltaire, and Rousseau.   J.J.E.G.

grammar, a system of rules specifying a language. The term has often been used synonymously with 'syntax', the principles governing the construction of sentences from words (perhaps also including the systems of word derivation and inflection – case markings, verbal tense markers, and the like). In modern linguistic usage the term more often encompasses other components of the language system such as phonology and semantics as well as syntax. Traditional grammars that we may have encountered in our school days, e.g., the grammars of Latin or English, were typically fragmentary and often *prescriptive* – basically a selective catalog of forms and sentence patterns, together with constructions to be avoided. Contemporary linguistic grammars, on the other hand, aim to be *descriptive,* and even *explanatory,* i.e., embedded within a general theory that offers principled reasons for why natural languages are the way they are. This is in accord with the generally accepted view of linguistics as a science that regards human language as a natural phenomenon to be understood, just as physicists attempt to make sense of the world of physical objects.

Since the publication of *Syntactic Structures* (1957) and *Aspects of the Theory of Syntax* (1965) by Noam Chomsky, grammars have been almost universally conceived of as *generative* devices, i.e., precisely formulated deductive systems – commonly called generative grammars – specifying all and only the well-formed sentences of a language together with a specification of their relevant structural properties. On this view, a grammar of English has the character of a *theory* of the English language, with the grammatical sentences (and their structures) as its theorems and the grammar rules playing the role of the rules of inference. Like any empirical theory, it is subject to disconfirmation if its predictions do not agree with the facts – if, e.g., the grammar implies that 'white or snow the is' is a well-formed sentence or that 'The snow is white' is not.

The object of this theory construction is to model the system of knowledge possessed by those who are able to speak and understand an unlimited number of novel sentences of the language specified. Thus, a grammar in this sense is a psychological entity – a component of the human mind – and the task of linguistics (avowedly a mentalistic discipline) is to determine exactly of what this knowledge consists. Like other mental phenomena, it is not observable directly but only through its effects. Thus, underlying linguistic *competence* is to be distinguished from actual linguistic *performance,* which forms part of the evidence for the former but is not necessarily an accurate reflection of it, containing, as it does, errors, false starts, etc. A central problem is how this competence arises in the individual, i.e., how a grammar is inferred by a child on the basis of a finite, variable, and imperfect sample of utterances encountered in the course of normal development. Many sorts of observations strongly suggest that grammars are not constructed *de novo* entirely on the basis of experience, and the view is widely held that the child brings to the task a significant, genetically determined predisposition to construct grammars according to a well-defined pattern. If this is so, and since apparently no one language has an advantage over any other in the learning process, this inborn component of linguistic competence can be correctly termed a *universal grammar.* It represents whatever the grammars of all natural languages, actual or potential, necessarily have in common because of the innate linguistic competence of human beings. The apparent diversity of natural languages has often led to a serious underestimation of the scope of universal grammar.

One of the most influential proposals concerning the nature of universal grammar was Chomsky's theory of *transformational grammar.* In this framework the syntactic structure of a sentence is given not by a single object (e.g., a parse tree, as in *phrase structure grammar*), but rather by a sequence of trees connected by operations called *transformations.* The initial tree in such a sequence is specified (generated) by a phrase structure grammar, together with a lexicon, and is known as the *deep structure.* The final tree in the sequence, the *surface structure,* contains the morphemes (meaningful units) of the sentence in the order in which they are written or pronounced. For example, the English sentences 'John hit the ball' and its passive counterpart 'The ball was hit by John' might be derived from the same deep structure (in this case a tree looking very much like the surface structure for the active sentence) except that the optional transformational rule of passivization has been applied in the derivation of the latter sentence. This rule rearranges the constituents of the tree in such a way that, among other changes, the direct object ('the ball') in deep structure becomes the surface-structure subject of the passive sentence. It is thus an important feature of this theory that grammatical relations such as subject, object, etc., of a sentence are not absolute but are relative to the level of structure. This accounts for the fact that many sentences that appear superficially similar in structure (e.g., 'John is easy to please', 'John is eager to please') are nonetheless perceived as having different underlying (deep-structure) grammatical relations. Indeed, it was argued that any theory of grammar that failed to make a deep-structure/surface-structure distinction could not be adequate.

Contemporary linguistic theories have, nonetheless, tended toward minimizing the importance of the transformational rules with corresponding elaboration of the role of the lexicon and the principles that govern the operation of grammars generally. Theories such as generalized phrase-structure grammar and lexical function grammar postulate no transformational rules at all and capture the relatedness of pairs such as active and passive sentences in other ways. Chomsky's principles and parameters approach (1981) reduces the transformational component to a single general movement operation that is controlled by the simultaneous interaction of a number of principles or subtheories: binding, government, control, etc. The universal component of the grammar is thus enlarged and the contribution of language-specific rules is correspondingly diminished. Proponents point to the advantages this would allow in language acquisition. Presumably a considerable portion of the task of grammar construction would consist merely in setting the values of a small number of parameters that could be readily determined on the basis of a small number of instances of grammatical sentences.

A rather different approach that has been influential has arisen from the work of Richard Montague, who applied to natural languages the same techniques of model theory developed for logical languages such as the predicate calculus. This so-called *Montague grammar* uses a *categorial grammar* as its syntactic component. In this form of grammar, complex lexical and phrasal categories can be of the form A/B. Typically such categories combine by a kind of "cancellation" rule: $A/B + B \rightarrow A$ (something of category A/B combines with something of category B to yield something of category A). In addition, there is a close correspondence between the syntactic category of an expression and its semantic type; e.g., common nouns such as 'book' and 'girl' are of type e/t, and their semantic values are functions from individuals (entities, or e-type things) to truth-values (T-type things), or equivalently, sets

of individuals. The result is an explicit, interlocking syntax and semantics specifying not only the syntactic structure of grammatical sentences but also their truth conditions. Montague's work was embedded in his own view of universal grammar, which has not, by and large, proven persuasive to linguists. A great deal of attention has been given in recent years to merging the undoubted virtues of Montague grammar with a linguistically more palatable view of universal grammar.

See also CHOMSKY, LOGICAL FORM, PARSING, PHILOSOPHY OF LANGUAGE.   R.E.W.

grammar, categorial. See GRAMMAR.

grammar, Montague. See GRAMMAR.

grammar, transformational. See GRAMMAR.

grammar, universal. See GRAMMAR.

grammatical form. See LOGICAL FORM.

grammaticality intuitions. See INTUITION.

grammatical predicate. See LOGICAL SUBJECT.

grammatical subject. See LOGICAL SUBJECT.

Gramsci, Antonio (1891–1937), Italian political leader whose imprisonment by the Fascists for his involvement with the Italian Communist Party had the ironical result of sparing him from Stalinism and enabling him to better articulate his distinctive political philosophy. In 1917 he welcomed the Bolshevik Revolution as a "revolution against *Capital*" rather than against capitalism: as a revolution refuting the deterministic Marxism according to which socialism could arise only by the gradual evolution of capitalism, and confirming the possibility of the radical transformation of social institutions. In 1921 he supported creation of the Italian Communist Party; as its general secretary from 1924, he tried to reorganize it along more democratic lines. In 1926 the Fascists outlawed all opposition parties. Gramsci spent the rest of his life in various prisons, where he wrote more than a thousand pages of notes ranging from a few lines to chapter-length essays. These *Prison Notebooks* pose a major interpretive challenge, but they reveal a keen, insightful, and open mind grappling with important social and political problems.

The most common interpretation stems from Palmiro Togliatti, Gramsci's successor as leader of the Italian Communists. After the fall of Fascism and the end of World War II, Togliatti read into Gramsci the so-called Italian road to socialism: a strategy for attaining the traditional Marxist goals of the classless society and the nationalization of the means of production by cultural means, such as education and persuasion. In contrast to Bolshevism, one had to first conquer social institutions, and then their control would yield the desired economic and political changes. This democratic theory of Marxist revolution was long regarded by many as especially relevant to Western industrial societies, and so for this and other reasons Gramsci is a key figure of Western Marxism. The same theory is often called Gramsci's theory of hegemony, referring to a relationship between two political units where one dominates the other with the consent of that other.

This interpretation was a political reconstruction, based primarily on Gramsci's Communist involvement and on highly selective passages from the *Notebooks*. It was also based on exaggerating the influence on Gramsci of Marx, Engels, Lenin, and Gentile, and minimizing influences like Croce, Mosca, Machiavelli, and Hegel. No new consensus has emerged yet; it would have to be based on analytical and historical spadework barely begun. One main interpretive issue is whether Gramsci, besides questioning the means, was also led to question the ends of traditional Marxism. In one view, his commitment to rational persuasion, political realism, methodological fallibilism, democracy, and pluralism is much deeper than his inclinations toward the classless society, the abolition of private property, the bureaucratically centralized party, and the like; in particular, his pluralism is an aspect of his commitment to the dialectic as a way of thinking, a concept he adapted from Hegel through Croce.

See also MARXISM.   M.A.F.

great chain of being. See PRINCIPLE OF PLENITUDE.

greatest happiness principle. See UTILITARIANISM.

Great Learning. See TA-HSÜEH.

Greek Skepticism. See SKEPTICS.

Green, T(homas) H(ill) (1836–82), British absolute idealist and social philosopher. The son of a clergyman, Green studied and taught at Oxford. His central concern was to resolve what he saw as the spiritual crisis of his age by analyz-

ing knowledge and morality in ways inspired by Kant and Hegel. In his lengthy introduction to Hume's *Treatise,* he argued that Hume had shown knowledge and morality to be impossible on empiricist principles. In his major work, *Prolegomena to Ethics* (1883), Green contended that thought imposed relations on sensory feelings and impulses (whose source was an eternal consciousness) to constitute objects of knowledge and of desire. Furthermore, in acting on desires, rational agents seek the satisfaction of a self that is realized through their own actions. This requires rational agents to live in harmony among themselves and hence to act morally. In *Lectures on the Principles of Political Obligation* (1885) Green transformed classical liberalism by arguing that even though the state has no intrinsic value, its intervention in society is necessary to provide the conditions that enable rational beings to achieve self-satisfaction. **See also** HUME, IDEALISM, POLITICAL PHILOSOPHY.

J.W.A.

Gregory I, Saint, called Gregory the Great (c.540–604), a pope and Roman political leader. Born a patrician, he was educated for public office and became prefect of Rome in 570. In 579, he was appointed papal representative in Constantinople, returning to Rome as counselor to Pope Pelagius II in 586. He was elected Pope Gregory I in 590. When the Lombards attacked Rome in 594, Gregory bought them off. Constantinople would neither cede nor defend Italy, and Gregory stepped in as secular ruler of what became the Papal States. He asserted the universal jurisdiction of the bishop of Rome, and claimed patriarchy of the West. His writings include important letters; the *Moralia,* an exposition of the Book of Job summarizing Christian theology; *Pastoral Care,* which defined the duties of the clergy for the Middle Ages; and *Dialogues,* which deals chiefly with the immortality of the soul, holding it could enter heaven immediately without awaiting the Last Judgment. His thought, largely Augustinian, is unoriginal, but was much quoted in the Middle Ages. **See also** AUGUSTINE.   J.Lo.

Gregory of Nyssa, Saint (335–98), Greek theologian and mystic who tried to reconcile Platonism with Christianity. As bishop of Cappadocia in eastern Asia Minor, he championed orthodoxy and was prominent at the First Council of Constantinople. He related the doctrine of the Trinity to Plato's ideas of the One and the Many. He followed Origen in believing that man's material nature was due to the fall and in believing in the *Apocatastasis*, the universal restoration of all souls, including Satan's, in the kingdom of God. **See also** APOCATASTASIS, ORIGEN.   L.P.P.

Gregory of Rimini (c.1300–58), Italian philosopher and monk. He studied in Italy, England, and France, and taught at the universities of Bologna, Padua, Perugia, and Paris before becoming prior general of the Hermits of St. Augustine in his native city of Rimini, about eighteen months before he died.

Gregory earned the honorific title "the Authentic Doctor" because he was considered by many of his contemporaries to be a faithful interpreter of Augustine, and thus a defender of tradition, in the midst of the skepticism of Ockham and his disciples regarding what could be known in natural philosophy and theology. Thus, in his commentary on Books I and II of Peter Lombard's *Sentences*, Gregory rejected the view that because of God's omnipotence he can do anything and is therefore unknowable in his nature and in his ways. Gregory also maintained that after Adam's fall from righteousness, men need, in conjunction with their free will, God's help (grace) to perform morally good actions.

In non-religious matters Gregory is usually associated with the theory of the *complexe significabile*, according to which the object of knowledge acquired by scientific proof is neither an object existing outside the mind, nor a word (*simplex*) or a proposition (*complexum*), but rather the *complexe significabile*, that which is totally and adequately signified by the proposition expressed in the conclusion of the proof in question. **See also** COMPLEXE SIGNIFICABILE.   G.S.

Grelling's paradox. See SET-THEORETIC PARADOXES.

Grice, H. P(aul) (1913–88), English philosopher whose early work concerned perception and philosophy of language, and whose most influential contribution was the concept of a conversational implicature and the associated theoretical machinery of conversational postulates. The concept of a conversational implicature was first used in his 1961 paper on the causal theory of reference. Grice distinguished between the meaning of the words used in a sentence and what is implied by the speaker's choice of words. If someone says "It looks as if there is a mailbox in front of me," the choice of words implies that there is some doubt about the mailbox. But, Grice argued, that is a matter of word choice and the sentence itself does not imply that there is doubt.

The term 'conversational implicature' was introduced in Grice's William James lectures in 1968 (published in 1988) and used to defend the use of the material conditional as a logical translation of 'if-then'.

With Strawson ("In Defence of Dogma"), Grice gave a spirited defense of the analytic–synthetic distinction against Quine's criticisms. In subsequent systematic papers Grice attempted, among other things, to give a theoretical grounding of the distinction.

Though Grice's earlier work was part of the Oxford ordinary language tradition, in 1968 he moved to Berkeley, and his later work was more formal and theoretical. In his last decade, he concentrated more on metaphysics, especially the concept of absolute value. **See also** ANALYTIC–SYNTHETIC DISTINCTION, IMPLICATURE, ORDINARY LANGUAGE PHILOSOPHY.   R.E.G.

Groot, Huigh de. See GROTIUS.

Grosseteste, Robert (c.1168–1253), English theologian who began life on the bottom rung of feudal society in Suffolk and became one of the most influential philosophers in pre-Reformation England. He studied at Oxford, becoming a master of arts between 1186 and 1189. Sometime after this period he joined the household of William de Vere, bishop of Hereford. Grosseteste may have been associated with the local cathedral school in Hereford, several of whose members were part of a relatively advanced scientific tradition. It was a center for the study of natural science and astrology as well as liberal arts and theology. If so, this would explain, at least in part, his lifelong interest in work in natural philosophy. Between 1209 and 1214 Grosseteste became a master of theology, probably in Paris. In 1221 he became the first chancellor of Oxford. From 1229 to 1235 he was secular lecturer in theology to the recently established Franciscan order at Oxford. It was during his tenure with the Franciscans that he studied Greek – an unusual endeavor for a medieval schoolman. He spent the last eighteen years of his life as bishop of Lincoln.

As a university scholar, Grosseteste was an original thinker who used Aristotelian and Augustinian theses as points of departure. He believed, with Aristotle, that sense knowledge is the basis of all knowledge, and that the basis for sense knowledge is our discovery of the cause of what is experienced or revealed by experiment. He also believed, with Augustine, that light plays an important role in creation. Thus he maintained that God produced the world by first creating prime matter from which issued a point of light (*lux*), the first corporeal form or power, one of whose manifestations is visible light. The diffusion of this light resulted in extension or tridimensionality in the form of the nine concentric celestial spheres and the four terrestrial spheres of fire, air, water, and earth. According to Grosseteste, the diffusion of light takes place in accordance with laws of mathematical proportionality (geometry). Everything, therefore, is a manifestation of light, and mathematics is consequently indispensable to science and knowledge generally. The principles Grosseteste employs to support his views are presented in, e.g., his commentary on Aristotle's *Posterior Analytics*, the *De luce* ("Of Light"), and the *De lineis, angulis et figuris* ("Of Lines, Angles, and Figures"). He worked in areas as seemingly disparate as optics and angelology.

Grosseteste was one of the first to take an interest in and introduce into the Oxford curriculum newly recovered Aristotelian texts – some of which he translated, along with Greek commentaries on them. His work and interest in natural philosophy, mathematics, the Bible, and languages profoundly influenced his younger contemporary, Roger Bacon, and the educational goals of the Franciscan order. It also helped to stimulate work in these areas during the fourteenth century.

See also COMMENTARIES ON ARISTOTLE.
G.S.

Grotius, Hugo, in Dutch, Huigh de Groot (1583–1645), Dutch humanist, a founder of modern views of international law and a major theorist of natural law. A lawyer and Latinist, Grotius developed a new view of the law of nature in order to combat moral skepticism and to show how there could be rational settlement of moral disputes despite religious disagreements. He argued in *The Law of War and Peace* (1625) that humans are naturally both competitive and sociable. The laws of nature show us how we can live together despite our propensity to conflict. They can be derived from observation of our nature and situation. These laws reflect the fact that each individual possesses rights, which delimit the social space within which we are free to pursue our own goals. Legitimate government arises when we give up some rights in order to save or improve our lives. The obligations that the laws of nature impose would bind us, Grotius notoriously said, even if God did not exist; but he

held that God does enforce the laws. They set the limits on the laws that governments may legitimately impose. The laws of nature reflect our possession of both precise perfect rights of justice, which can be protected by force, and imperfect rights, which are not enforceable, nor even statable very precisely. Grotius's views on our combative but sociable nature, on the function of the law of nature, and on perfect and imperfect rights were of central importance in later discussions of morality and law. See also NATURAL LAW, RIGHTS.   J.B.S.

ground rule. See THEMA.

grue paradox, a paradox in the theory of induction, according to which *every* intuitively acceptable inductive argument, A, may be mimicked by indefinitely many other inductive arguments – each seemingly quite analogous to A and therefore seemingly as acceptable, yet each nonetheless intuitively unacceptable, and each yielding a conclusion contradictory to that of A, given the assumption that sufficiently many and varied of the sort of things induced upon exist as yet unexamined (which is the only circumstance in which A is of interest). Suppose the following is an intuitively acceptable inductive argument: (A_1) All hitherto observed emeralds are green; therefore, all emeralds are green. Now introduce the color-predicate 'grue', where (for some given, as yet wholly future, temporal interval T) an object is grue provided it has the property of being either green and first examined before T, or blue and not first examined before T. Then consider the following inductive argument: (A_2) All hitherto observed emeralds are grue; therefore, all emeralds are grue. The premise is true, and A_2 is formally analogous to A_1. But A_2 is intuitively unacceptable; if there are emeralds unexamined before T, then the conclusion of A_2 says that these emeralds are blue, whereas the conclusion of A_1 says that they are green.

Other counterintuitive competing arguments could be given, e.g.: (A_3) All hitherto observed emeralds are grellow; therefore, all emeralds are grellow (where an object is grellow provided it is green and located on the earth, or yellow otherwise).

It would seem, therefore, that some *restriction* on induction is required. The new riddle of induction offers two challenges. First, *state* the restriction – i.e., *demarcate* the intuitively acceptable inductions from the unacceptable ones, in some general way, without constant appeal to intuition. Second, *justify* our preference for the one group of inductions over the other. (These two parts of the new riddle are often conflated. But it is at least conceivable that one might solve the analytical, demarcative part without solving the justificatory part, and, perhaps, vice versa.)

It will not do to rule out, a priori, "gruelike" (now commonly called "gruesome") variances in nature. Water (pure H_2O) varies in its physical state along the parameter of temperature. If so, why might not emeralds vary in color along the parameter of time of first examination?

One approach to the problem of restriction is to focus on the *conclusions* of inductive arguments (e.g., All emeralds are green, All emeralds are grue) and to distinguish those which may legitimately so serve (called "projectible hypotheses") from those which may not. The question then arises whether *only* non-gruesome hypotheses (those which do not contain gruesome predicates) are projectible. Aside from the task of defining 'gruesome predicate' (which could be done structurally relative to a preferred language), the answer is *no*. The English predicate 'solid and less than 0°C, or liquid and more than 0°C but less than 100°C, or gaseous and more than 100°C' is gruesome on any plausible structural account of gruesomeness (note the similarity to the English 'grue' equivalent: green and first examined before *T*, or blue and not first examined before *T*). Nevertheless, where *non-transitional* water is pure H_2O at one atmosphere of pressure (save that which is in a transitional state, i.e., melting/freezing or boiling/condensing, i.e., at 0°C or 100°C), we happily project the hypothesis that all non-transitional water falls under the above gruesome predicate.

Perhaps this is because, if we rewrite the projection about non-transitional water as a conjunction of non-gruesome hypotheses – (i) All water at less than 0°C is solid, (ii) All water at more than 0°C but less than 100°C is liquid, and (iii) All water at more than 100°C is gaseous – we note that (i)–(iii) are all supported (there are known positive instances); whereas if we rewrite the gruesome projection about emeralds as a conjunction of non-gruesome hypotheses – (i*) All emeralds first examined before *T* are green, and (ii*) All emeralds not first examined before *T* are blue – we note that (ii*) is as yet unsupported.

It would seem that, whereas a non-gruesome hypothesis is projectible provided it is unviolated and supported, a gruesome hypothesis is projectible provided it is unviolated and equivalent to a conjunction of non-gruesome hypotheses, each of which is supported.

The grue paradox was discovered by Nelson Goodman. It is most fully stated in his *Fact, Fiction and Forecast* (1955).

See also PROBLEM OF INDUCTION, QUALITATIVE PREDICATE.   D.A.J.

Grundnorm. See BASIC NORM.

guise theory, a system developed by Castañeda to resolve a number of issues concerning the content of thought and experience, including reference, identity statements, intensional contexts, predication, existential claims, perception, and fictional discourse. For example, since (i) Oedipus believed that he killed the man at the crossroads, and (ii) the man at the crossroads was his (Oedipus's) father, it might seem that (iii) Oedipus believed that he killed his father. Guise theory blocks this derivation by taking 'was' in (ii) to express, not genuine identity, but a contingent sameness relation betweeen the distinct referents of the descriptions. Definite descriptions are typically treated as referential, contrary to Russell's theory of descriptions, and their referents are identical in both direct and indirect discourse, contrary to Frege's semantics.

To support this solution, guise theory offers unique accounts of predication and singular referents. The latter are *individual guises*, which, like Fregean senses and Meinong's incomplete objects, are thinly individuated aspects or "slices" of ordinary objects at best. Every guise is a structure $c\{F_1 \ldots, F_n\}$ where c is an operator expressed by 'the' in English – transforming a set of properties $\{F_1, \ldots, F_n\}$ into a distinct concrete individual, each property being an *internal* property of the guise. Guises have external properties by standing in various sameness relations to other guises that have these properties internally. There are four such relations, besides genuine identity, each an equivalence relation in its field. If the oldest philosopher happens to be wise, e.g., wisdom is factually predicated of the guise 'the oldest philosopher' because it is *consubstantiated* with 'the oldest wise philosopher'. Other sameness relations account for fictional predication (*consociation*) and necessary external predication (*conflation*). Existence is self-consubstantiation. An ordinary physical object is, at any moment, a cluster of consubstantiated (hence, existing) guises, while continuants are formed through the *transubstantiation* of guises within temporally distinct clusters. There are no substrates, and while every guise "subsists," not all exist, e.g., the Norse God of Thunder. The position thus permits a unified account of singular reference.

One task for guise theory is to explain how a "concretized" set of properties differs internally from a mere set. Perhaps guises are *façons de penser* whose core sets are concretized if their component properties are conceived as coinstan-

tiated, with non-existents analyzable in terms of the failure of the conceived properties to actually be coinstantiated. However, it is questionable whether this approach can achieve all that Castañeda demands of guise theory.

See also CASTAÑEDA, PRACTITION.   T.K.

H

Habermas, Jürgen (b.1929), German philosopher and social theorist, a leading representative of the second generation of the Frankfurt School of critical theory. His work has consistently returned to the problem of the normative foundations of social criticism and critical social inquiry not supplied in traditional Marxism and other forms of critical theory, such as postmodernism. His habilitation, *The Structural Transformation of the Public Sphere* (1961), is an influential historical analysis of the emergence of the ideal of a public sphere in the eighteenth century and its subsequent decline. Habermas turned then to the problems of the foundations and methodology of the social sciences, developing a criticism of positivism and his own interpretive explanatory approach in *The Logic of the Social Sciences* (1963) and his first major systematic work, *Knowledge and Human Interests* (1967).

Rejecting the unity of method typical of positivism, Habermas argues that social inquiry is guided by three distinct interests: in control, in understanding, and in emancipation. He is especially concerned to use emancipatory interest to overcome the limitations of the model of inquiry based on understanding and argues against "universality of hermeneutics" (defended by hermeneuticists such as Gadamer) and for the need to supplement interpretations with explanations in the social sciences. As he came to reject the psychoanalytic vocabulary in which he formulated the interest in emancipation, he turned to finding the basis for understanding and social inquiry in a theory of rationality more generally.

In the next phase of his career he developed a comprehensive social theory, culminating in his two-volume *The Theory of Communicative Action* (1982). The goal of this theory is to develop a "critical theory of modernity," on the basis of a comprehensive theory of communicative (as opposed to instrumental) rationality. The first volume develops a theory of communicative rationality based on "discourse," or second-order communication that takes place both in everyday interaction and in institutionalized practices of argumentation in science, law, and criticism. This theory of rationality emerges from a universal or "formal" pragmatics, a speech act theory based on making explicit the rules and norms of the competence to communicate in linguistic interaction. The second volume develops a diagnosis of modern society as suffering from "one-sided rationalization," leading to disruptions of the communicative lifeworld by "systems" such as markets and bureaucracies.

Finally, Habermas applies his conception of rationality to issues of normative theory, including ethics, politics, and the law. "Discourse Ethics: Notes on a Program of Moral Justification" (1982) argues for an intersubjective notion of practical reason and discursive procedure for the justification of universal norms. This "discourse principle" provides a dialogical version of Kant's idea of universalization; a norm is justified if and only if it can meet with the reasoned agreement of all those affected. *Between Facts and Norms* (1992) combines his social and normative theories to give a systematic account of law and democracy. His contribution here is an account of deliberative democracy appropriate to the complexity of modern society. His work in all of these phases provides a systematic defense and critique of modern institutions and a vindication of the universal claims of public practical reason.

See also CRITICAL THEORY, FRANKFURT SCHOOL, HERMENEUTICS.   J.B.

haecceity (from Latin *haec*, 'this'), (1) loosely, thisness; more specifically, an irreducible category of being, the fundamental actuality of an existent entity; or (2) an individual essence, a property an object has necessarily, without which it would not be or would cease to exist as the individual it is, and which, necessarily, no other object has. There are in the history of philosophy two distinct concepts of haecceity. The idea originated with the work of the thirteenth-century philosopher Duns Scotus, and was discussed in the same period by Aquinas, as a positive perfection that serves as a primitive existence and individuation principle for concrete existents. In the seventeenth century Leibniz transformed the concept of haecceity, which Duns Scotus had explicitly denied to be a form or universal, into the notion of an individual essence, a distinctive nature or set of necessary characteristics uniquely identifying it under the principle of the identity of indiscernibles.

Duns Scotus's *haecceitas* applies only to the being of contingently existent entities in the actual world, but Leibniz extends the principle to individuate particular things not only through the changes they may undergo in the actual world, but in any alternative logically possible world. Leibniz admitted as a consequence the controversial thesis that every object by virtue of its haecceity has each of its properties essentially or necessarily, so that only the counterparts of individuals can inhabit distinct logically possible worlds. A further corollary – since the possession of particular parts in a particular arrangement is also a property and hence involved in the individual essence of any complex object – is the doctrine of *mereological essentialism:* every composite is necessarily constituted by a particular configuration of particular proper parts, and loses its self-identity if any parts are removed or replaced. **See also** DUNS SCOTUS, ESSENTIALISM, IDENTITY OF INDISCERNIBLES, METAPHYSICS.   D.J.

Haeckel, Ernst (1834–1919), German zoologist, an impassioned adherent of Darwin's theory of evolution. His popular work *Die Welträtsel* (*The Riddle of the Universe*, 1899) became a best-seller and was very influential in its time. Lenin is said to have admired it. Haeckel's philosophy, which he called monism, is characterized negatively by his rejection of free will, immortality, and theism, as well as his criticisms of the traditional forms of materialism and idealism. Positively it is distinguished by passionate arguments for the fundamental unity of organic and inorganic nature and a form of pantheism.

M.K.

Ha-Levi, Judah (c.1075–1141), Spanish Jewish philosopher and poet. Born in Toledo, he studied biblical and rabbinical literature as well as philosophy. His poetry introduces Arabic forms in Hebrew religious expression. He was traveling to Jerusalem on a pilgrimage when he died. His most important philosophical work is *Kuzari: The Book of Proof and Argument of the Despised Faith,* which purports to be a discussion of a Christian, a Muslim, and a Jew, each offering the king of the Khazars (in southern Russia) reasons for adopting his faith. Around 740 the historical king and most of his people converted to Judaism. Ha-Levi presents the Christian and the Muslim as Aristotelian thinkers, who fail to convince the king. The Jewish spokesman begins by asserting his belief in the God of Abraham, Isaac, and Jacob, the God of history who is continuously active in history, rather than the God of the philosophers. Jewish history is the inner core of world history. From the revelation at Sinai, the most witnessed divine event claimed by any religion, the Providential history of the Jews is the way God has chosen to make his message clear to all humankind. Ha-Levi's view is the classical expression of Jewish particularism and nationalism. His ideas have been influential in Judaism and were early printed in Latin and Spanish. **See also** JEWISH PHILOSOPHY.   R.H.P.

Halldén-complete. See COMPLETENESS.

hallucination. See PSEUDOHALLUCINATION.

hallucination, argument from. See PERCEPTION.

halting problem. See COMPUTABILITY.

Hamann, Johann Georg (1730–88), German philosopher. Born and educated in Königsberg, Hamann, known as the Magus of the North, was one of the most important Christian thinkers in Germany during the second half of the eighteenth century. Advocating an irrationalistic theory of faith (inspired by Hume), he opposed the prevailing Enlightenment philosophy. He was a mentor of the *Sturm und Drang* literary movement and had a significant influence on Jacobi, Hegel, and Kierkegaard. As a close acquaintance of Kant, he also had a great impact on the development of Kant's critical philosophy through his Hume translations. Hamann's most important works, criticized and admired for their difficult and obscure style, were the *Socratic Memorabilia* (1759), *Aesthetica in nuce* ("Aesthetics in a Nutshell," 1762), and several works on language. He suppressed his "metacritical" writings out of respect for Kant. However, they were published after his death and now constitute the best-known part of his work.   M.K.

Hamilton, William (1788–1856), Scottish philosopher and logician. Born in Glasgow and educated at Glasgow, Edinburgh, and Oxford, he was for most of his life professor at the University of Edinburgh (1821–56). Though hardly an orthodox or uncritical follower of Reid and Stewart, he became one of the most important members of the school of Scottish common sense philosophy. His "philosophy of the conditioned" has a somewhat Kantian flavor. Like Kant, he held that we can have knowledge only of "the relative manifestations of an existence, which in itself it is our highest wisdom to recognize as beyond the reach of philosophy." Unlike Kant, however, he argued for the position of a "natural realism" in the Reidian tradition. The doctrine of the relativity of knowledge has seemed to many – including J. S. Mill – contradictory to his realism. For Hamilton, the two are held together by a kind of intuitionism that emphasizes certain facts of consciousness that are both primitive and incomprehensible. They are, though constitutive of knowledge, "less forms of cognitions than of beliefs." In logic he argued for a doctrine involving quantification of predicates and the view that propositions can be reduced to equations. **See also SCOTTISH COMMON SENSE PHILOSOPHY.**   M.K.

Han Fei Tzu, also called Master Han Fei (third century B.C.), Chinese Legalist political theorist. He was a prince of the state of Han and a student of Hsün Tzu. His thought, recorded in the text *Han Fei Tzu,* mainly concerned the method of government and was addressed primarily to rulers. Han Fei Tzu believed that human beings are self-seeking by nature, and that they can rarely be transformed by education and moral examples. Accordingly, the ruler should institute a precisely formulated and clearly propagated system of laws (*fa*) to regulate their behavior, and enforce it with punishment. Officials, in addition to being governed by laws, are to be rewarded and punished according to whether their performance coincides with their official duties and proposed plans. The ruler should enforce this system strictly without favoritism, should shun contact with subordinates to avoid breeding familiarity, and should conceal his personal likes and dislikes to avoid their being exploited. Having properly set up the machinary of government, the government will run smoothly with minimal intervention by the ruler. **See also CHINESE LEGALISM.**   K.-l.S.

Han Yü (768–824), Chinese poet and essayist who, though his thoughts lacked philosophical depth, was the first to emphasize "correct transmission" of the Way from the sage-emperors to Confucius and Mencius. His views later profoundly influenced Neo-Confucian philosophers in the Sung dynasty. He vigorously defended Confucianism against Buddhism and Taoism on cultural grounds: the monks and nuns were parasites on society. He also formulated a threefold theory on which human nature has superior, medium, and inferior grades. **See also CONFUCIANISM, CONFUCIUS, MENCIUS, NEO-CONFUCIANISM, TAO-T'UNG.**   S.-h.L.

happiness. See ARISTOTLE, HEDONISM, UTILITARIANISM.

hard determinism. See FREE WILL PROBLEM.

Hardenberg, Friedrich von. See NOVALIS.

hardware. See COMPUTER THEORY.

Hare, R(ichard) M(ervyn) (b.1919), English philosopher who is one of the most influential moral philosophers of the twentieth century and the developer of prescriptivism in metaethics.

Hare was educated at Rugby and Oxford, then served in the British army during World War II and spent years as a prisoner of war in Burma. In 1947 he took a position at Balliol College and was appointed White's Professor of Moral Philosophy at the University of Oxford in 1966. On retirement from Oxford, he became Graduate Research Professor at the University of Florida (1983–93). His major books are *Language of Morals* (1953), *Freedom and Reason* (1963), *Moral Thinking* (1981), and *Sorting Out Ethics* (1997). Many collections of his essays have also appeared, and a collection of other leading philosophers' articles on his work was published in 1988 (*Hare and Critics,* eds. Seanor and Fotion).

According to Hare, a careful exploration of the nature of our moral concepts reveals that (nonironic) judgments about what one morally ought to do are expressions of the will, or commitments to act, that are subject to certain logical constraints. Because moral judgments are *prescriptive,* we cannot sincerely subscribe to them while refusing to comply with them in the relevant circumstances. Because moral judgments are *universal* prescriptions, we cannot sincerely subscribe to them unless we are willing for them to be followed were we in other people's positions with their preferences. Hare later contended that vividly to imagine ourselves completely in other people's positions involves our acquiring preferences about what should happen to us in those positions that mirror exactly what those people now want for themselves. So, ideally, we decide on a universal prescription on the basis of not only our existing preferences about the actual situation but also the new preferences we would have if we were wholly in other people's positions. What we can prescribe universally is what maximizes net satisfaction of this amalgamated set of preferences. Hence, Hare concluded that his theory of moral judgment leads to preference-satisfaction act utilitarianism. However, like most other utilitarians, he argued that the best way to maximize utility is to have, and generally to act on, certain not directly utilitarian dispositions – such as dispositions not to hurt others or steal, to keep promises and tell the truth, to take special responsibility for one's own family, and so on.

See also EMOTIVISM, ETHICS, PRESCRIP-TIVISM, UTILITARIANISM.   B.W.H.

harmony, preestablished. See LEIBNIZ.

harmony of the spheres. See PYTHAGORAS.

Hart, H(erbert) L(ionel) A(dolphus) (1907–92), English philosopher principally responsible for the revival of legal and political philosophy after World War II. After wartime work with military intelligence, Hart gave up a flourishing law practice to join the Oxford faculty, where he was a brilliant lecturer, a sympathetic and insightful critic, and a generous mentor to many scholars.

Like the earlier "legal positivists" Bentham and John Austin, Hart accepted the "separation of law and morals": moral standards can deliberately be incorporated in law, but there is no automatic or necessary connection between law and sound moral principles. In *The Concept of Law* (1961) he critiqued the Bentham-Austin notion that laws are orders backed by threats from a political community's "sovereign" – some person or persons who enjoy habitual obedience and are habitually obedient to no other human – and developed the more complex idea that law is a "union of primary and secondary rules." Hart agreed that a legal system must contain some "obligation-imposing" "primary" rules, restricting freedom. But he showed that law also includes independent "power-conferring" rules that facilitate choice, and he demonstrated that a legal system requires "secondary" rules that create public offices and authorize official action, such as legislation and adjudication, as well as "rules of recognition" that determine which other rules are valid in the system.

Hart held that rules of law are "open-textured," with a core of determinate meaning and a fringe of indeterminate meaning, and thus capable of answering some but not all legal questions that can arise. He doubted courts' claims to discover law's meaning when reasonable competing interpretations are available, and held that courts decide such "hard cases" by first performing the important "legislative" function of filling gaps in the law.

Hart's first book was an influential study (with A. M. Honoré) of *Causation in the Law* (1959). His inaugural lecture as Professor of Jurisprudence, "Definition and Theory in Jurisprudence" (1953), initiated a career-long study of rights, reflected also in *Essays on Bentham: Studies in Jurisprudence and Political Theory* (1982) and in *Essays in Jurisprudence and Philosophy* (1983).

He defended liberal public policies. In *Law, Liberty and Morality* (1963) he refuted Lord Devlin's contention that a society justifiably enforces the code of its moral majority, whatever it might be. In *The Morality of the Criminal Law* (1965) and in *Punishment and Responsibility* (1968), Hart contributed substantially to both analytic and normative theories of crime and punishment.

See also LIBERALISM, PHILOSOPHY OF LAW, POLITICAL PHILOSOPHY, RIGHTS.   D.Ly.

Hartley, David (1705–57), British physician and philosopher. Although the notion of association of ideas is ancient, he is generally regarded as the founder of associationism as a self-sufficient psychology. Despite similarities between his association psychology and Hume's, Hartley developed his system independently, acknowledging only the writings of clergyman John Gay (1699–1745). Hartley was one of many Enlightenment thinkers aspiring to be "Newtons of the mind," in Peter Gay's phrase. In Hartley, this took the form of uniting association philosophy with physiology, a project later brought to fruition by Bain. His major work, *Observations on Man* (1749), pictured mental events and neural events as operating on parallel tracks in which neural events cause mental events. On the mental side, Hartley distinguished (like Hume) between sensation and idea. On the physiological side, Hartley adopted Newton's conception of nervous transmission by vibrations of a fine granular substance within nerve-tubes. Vibrations within sensory nerves peripheral to the brain corresponded to the sensations they caused, while small vibrations in the brain, *vibratiuncles*, corresponded to ideas. Hartley proposed a single law of association, contiguity modified by frequency, which took two forms, one for the mental side and one for the neural: ideas, or vibratiuncles, occurring together regularly become associated. Hartley distinguished between *simultaneous association*, the link between ideas that occur at the same

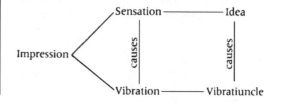

moment, and *successive association,* between ideas that closely succeed one another. Successive associations occur only in a forward direction; there are no backward associations, a thesis generating much controversy in the later experimental study of memory. **See also** ASSOCIATIONISM. T.H.L.

Hartmann, Eduard von (1842–1906), German philosopher who sought to synthesize the thought of Schelling, Hegel, and Schopenhauer. The most important of his fifteen books was *Philosophie des Unbewussten* (*Philosophy of the Unconscious,* 1869). For Hartmann both will and idea are interrelated and are expressions of an absolute "thing-in-itself," the unconscious. The unconscious is the active essence in natural and psychic processes and is the teleological dynamic in organic life. Paradoxically, he claimed that the teleology immanent in the world order and the life process leads to insight into the irrationality of the "will-to-live." The maturation of rational consciousness would, he held, lead to the negation of the total volitional process and the entire world process would cease. Ideas indicate the "what" of existence and constitute, along with will and the unconscious, the three modes of being. Despite its pessimism, this work enjoyed considerable popularity.

Hartmann was an unusual combination of speculative idealist and philosopher of science (defending vitalism and attacking mechanistic materialism); his pessimistic ethics was part of a cosmic drama of redemption. Some of his later works dealt with a critical form of Darwinism that led him to adopt a positive evolutionary stance that undermined his earlier pessimism. His general philosophical position was self-described as "transcendental realism." His *Philosophy of the Unconscious* was translated into English by W. C. Coupland in three volumes in 1884. There is little doubt that his metaphysics of the unconscious prepared the way for Freud's later theory of the unconscious mind. **See also** FREUD, HEGEL, SCHELLING, SCHOPENHAUER. G.J.S.

Hartmann, Nicolai (1882–1950), Latvian-born German philosopher. He taught at the universities of Marburg, Cologne, Berlin, and Göttingen, and wrote more than a dozen major works on the history of philosophy, ontology, epistemology, ethics, and aesthetics. A realist in epistemology and ontology, Hartmann held that cognition is the apprehension of something independent of the act of apprehension or any other

mental events. An accurate phenomenology, such as Husserl's, would acknowledge, according to him, that we apprehend not only particular, spatiotemporal objects, but also "ideal objects," "essences," which Hartmann explicitly identified with Platonic Forms. Among these are ethical values and the objects of mathematics and logic. Our apprehension of values is emotional in character, as Scheler had held. This point is compatible with their objectivity and their mind-independence, since the emotions are just another mode of apprehension. The point applies, however, only to ethical values. Aesthetic values are essentially subjective; they exist only for the subject experiencing them. The number of ethical values is far greater than usually supposed, nor are they derivable from a single fundamental value. At best we only glimpse some of them, and even these may not be simultaneously realizable. This explains and to some extent justifies the existence of moral disagreement, between persons as well as between whole cultures.

Hartmann was most obviously influenced by Plato, Husserl, and Scheler. But he was a major, original philosopher in his own right. He has received less recognition than he deserves probably because his views were quite different from those dominant in recent Anglo-American philosophy or in recent Continental philosophy. What is perhaps his most important work, *Ethics,* was published in German in 1926, one year before Heidegger's *Being and Time,* and appeared in English in 1932. **See also** A PRIORI, HUSSERL, MORAL REALISM, PLATO, SCHELER. P.B.u

Hartshorne, Charles (b.1897), chief American exponent of process philosophy and theology in the late twentieth century. After receiving the Ph.D. at Harvard in 1923 he came under the influence of Whitehead, and later, with Paul Weiss, edited *The Collected Papers of C. S. Peirce* (1931–35). In *The Philosophy and Psychology of Sensation* (1934) Hartshorne argued that all sensations are feelings on an *affective continuum.* These ideas were later incorporated into a *neoclassical metaphysic* that is panpsychist, indeterministic, and theistic. Nature is a theater of interactions among ephemeral centers of creative activity, each of which becomes objectively immortal in the memory of God.

In *Man's Vision of God* (1941) Hartshorne chastised philosophers for being insufficiently attentive to the varieties of theism. His alternative, called *dipolar theism,* also defended in *The Divine*

Relativity (1948), pictures God as supremely related to and perfectly responding to every actuality. The universe is God's body. The divine is, in different respects, infinite and finite, eternal and temporal, necessary and contingent. Establishing God's existence is a metaphysical project, which Hartshorne characterizes in *Creative Synthesis* (1970) as the search for necessary truths about existence. The central element in his cumulative case for God's existence, called the *global argument,* is a modal version of the ontological argument, which Hartshorne was instrumental in rehabilitating in *The Logic of Perfection* (1962) and *Anselm's Discovery* (1965).

Creative Synthesis also articulated the theory that aesthetic values are the most universal and that beauty is a mean between the twin extremes of order/disorder and simplicity/complexity. *The Zero Fallacy* (1997), Hartshorne's twentieth book, summarized his assessment of the history of philosophy – also found in *Insights and Oversights of Great Thinkers* (1983) and *Creativity in American Philosophy* (1984) – and introduced important refinements of his metaphysics.

See also PANPSYCHISM, PHILOSOPHY OF RELIGION, PROCESS PHILOSOPHY, WHITE-HEAD.   D.W.V.

hasty generalization, fallacy of. See INFORMAL FALLACY.

heap paradox. See SORITES PARADOX.

heart. See HSIN[1].

Heaven. See T'IEN.

hedonic calculus. See BENTHAM.

hedonism, the view that pleasure (including the absence of pain) is the sole intrinsic good in life. The hedonist may hold that, questions of morality aside, persons inevitably do seek pleasure (psychological hedonism); that, questions of psychology aside, morally we should seek pleasure (ethical hedonism); or that we inevitably do, and ought to, seek pleasure (ethical and psychological hedonism combined).

Psychological hedonism itself admits of a variety of possible forms. One may hold, e.g., that all motivation is based on the prospect of present or future pleasure. More plausibly, some philosophers have held that all choices of future actions are based on one's presently taking greater pleasure in the *thought* of doing one act rather than another. Still a third type of hedonism – with roots in empirical psychology – is that the attainment of pleasure is the primary drive of a wide range of organisms (including human beings) and is responsible, through some form of conditioning, for all acquired motivations.

Ethical hedonists may, but need not, appeal to some form of psychological hedonism to buttress their case. For, at worst, the truth of some form of psychological hedonism makes ethical hedonism empty or inescapable – but not false. As a value theory (a theory of what is ultimately good), ethical hedonism has typically led to one or the other of two conceptions of morally correct action. Both of these are expressions of moral consequentialism in that they judge actions strictly by their consequences. On standard formulations of utilitarianism, actions are judged by the amount of pleasure they produce for all (sentient beings); on some formulations of egoist views, actions are judged by their consequences for one's *own* pleasure. Neither egoism nor utilitarianism, however, must be wedded to a hedonistic value theory.

A hedonistic value theory admits of a variety of claims about the characteristic sources and types of pleasure. One contentious issue has been what activities yield the greatest *quantity* of pleasure – with prominent candidates including philosophical and other forms of intellectual discourse, the contemplation of beauty, and activities productive of "the pleasures of the senses." (Most philosophical hedonists, despite the popular associations of the word, have not espoused sensual pleasure.) Another issue, famously raised by J. S. Mill, is whether such different varieties of pleasure admit of differences of *quality* (as well as quantity). Even supposing them to be equal in quantity, can we say, e.g., that the pleasures of intellectual activity are superior in quality to those of watching sports on television? And if we do say such things, are we departing from strict hedonism by introducing a value distinction not really based on pleasure at all?

Most philosophers have found hedonism – both psychological and ethical – exaggerated in its claims. One difficulty for both sorts of hedonism is the *hedonistic paradox,* which may be put as follows. Many of the deepest and best pleasures of life (of love, of child rearing, of work) seem to come most often to those who are engaging in an activity for reasons other than pleasure seeking. Hence, not only is it dubious that we always in fact seek (or value only) pleasure, but also dubious that the best way to achieve pleasure is to seek it.

Another area of difficulty concerns happiness – and its relation to pleasure. In the tradition of Aristotle, happiness is broadly understood as something like well-being and has been viewed, not implausibly, as a kind of natural end of all human activities. But 'happiness' in this sense is broader than 'pleasure', insofar as the latter designates a particular kind of feeling, whereas 'well-being' does not. Attributions of happiness, moreover, appear to be normative in a way in which attributions of pleasure are not. It is thought that a truly happy person has achieved, is achieving, or stands to achieve, certain things respecting the "truly important" concerns of human life. Of course, such achievements will characteristically produce pleasant feelings; but, just as characteristically, they will involve states of active enjoyment of activities – where, as Aristotle first pointed out, there are no distinctive feelings of pleasure apart from the doing of the activity itself. In short, the Aristotelian thesis that happiness is the natural end of all human activities, even if it is true, does not seem to lend much support to hedonism – psychological or ethical.

See also ARISTOTLE, ETHICS, EUDAIMONISM, UTILITARIANISM, VALUE.   J.A.M.

hedonistic paradox. See HEDONISM.

Hegel, Georg Wilhelm Friedrich (1770–1831), one of the most influential and systematic of the German idealists, also well known for his philosophy of history and philosophy of religion.

Life and works. Hegel, the eldest of three children, was born in Stuttgart, the son of a minor financial official in the court of the Duchy of Württemberg. His mother died when he was eleven. At eighteen, he began attending the theology seminary or *Stift* attached to the University at Tübingen; he studied theology and classical languages and literature and became friendly with his future colleague and adversary, Schelling, as well as the great genius of German Romantic poetry, Hölderlin. In 1793, upon graduation, he accepted a job as a tutor for a family in Bern, and moved to Frankfurt in 1797 for a similar post. In 1799 his father bequeathed him a modest income and the freedom to resign his tutoring job, pursue his own work, and attempt to establish himself in a university position. In 1801, with the help of Schelling, he moved to the university town of Jena, already widely known as the home of Schiller, Fichte, and the Schlegel brothers. After lecturing for a few years, he became a professor in 1805.

Prior to the move to Jena, Hegel's essays had been chiefly concerned with problems in morality, the theory of culture, and the philosophy of religion. Hegel shared with Rousseau and the German Romantics many doubts about the political and moral implications of the European Enlightenment and modern philosophy in general, even while he still enthusiastically championed what he termed the *principle of modernity,* "absolute freedom." Like many, he feared that the modern attack on feudal political and religious authority would merely issue in the reformulation of new internalized and still repressive forms of authority. And he was among that legion of German intellectuals infatuated with ancient Greece and the superiority of their supposedly harmonious social life, compared with the authoritarian and legalistic character of the Jewish and later Christian religions.

At Jena, however, he coedited a journal with Schelling, *The Critical Journal of Philosophy,* and came to work much more on the philosophic issues created by the critical philosophy or "transcendental idealism" of Kant, and its legacy in the work of Rheinhold, Fichte, and Schelling. His written work became much more influenced by these theoretical projects and their attempt to extend Kant's search for the basic categories necessary for experience to be discriminated and evaluated, and for a theory of the subject that, in some non-empirical way, was responsible for such categories. Problems concerning the completeness, interrelation, and ontological status of such a categorial structure were quite prominent, along with a continuing interest in the relation between a free, self-determining agent and the supposed constraints of moral principles and other agents.

In his early years at Jena (especially before Schelling left in 1803), he was particularly preoccupied with this problem of a systematic philosophy, a way of accounting for the basic categories of the natural world and for human practical activity that would ground all such categories on commonly presupposed and logically interrelated, even interdeducible, principles. (In Hegel's terms, this was the problem of the relation between a "Logic" and a "Philosophy of Nature" and "Philosophy of Spirit.") After 1803, however, while he was preparing his own systematic philosophy for publication, what had been planned as a short introduction to this system took on a life of its own and grew into one of Hegel's most provocative and influential books. Working at a furious pace, he finished what would be eventually called *The Phenomenology of Spirit* in a period of great personal and political turmoil. During the final writing of the book, he had learned that Christina Burkhard would give birth to his illegitimate son. (Ludwig was born in February 1807.) And he is supposed to have completed the text on October 13, 1807, the day Napoleon's armies captured Jena.

It was certainly an unprecedented work. In conception, it is about the human race itself as a developing, progressively more self-conscious subject, but its content seems to take in a vast, heterogeneous range of topics, from technical issues in empiricist epistemology to the significance of burial rituals. Its range is so heterogeneous that there is controversy to this day about whether it has any overall unity, or whether it was pieced together at the last minute. Adding to the interpretive problem, Hegel often invented his own striking language of "inverted worlds," "struggles to the death for recognition," "unhappy consciousness," "spiritual animal kingdoms," and "beautiful souls."

Continuing his university career at Jena in those times looked out of the question, so Hegel accepted a job at Bamberg editing a newspaper, and in the following year began an eight-year stint (1808–16) as headmaster and philosophy teacher at a Gymnasium (or secondary school) at Nürnberg. During this period, at forty-one, he married the twenty-year-old Marie von Tucher. He also wrote what is easily his most difficult work, and the one he often referred to as his most important, a magisterial two-volume *Science of Logic,* which attempts to be a philosophical account of the concepts necessary in all possible kinds of account-givings.

Finally, in 1816, Hegel was offered a chair in philosophy at the University of Heidelberg, where he published the first of several versions of his *Encyclopedia of the Philosophical Sciences,* his own systematic account of the relation between the "logic" of human thought and the "real" expression of such interrelated categories in our understanding of the natural world and in our understanding and evaluation of our own activities. In 1818, he accepted the much more prestigious post in philosophy at Berlin, where he remained until his death in 1831. Soon after his arrival in Berlin, he began to exert a powerful influence over German letters and intellectual life. In 1821, in the midst of a growing political and nationalist crisis in Prussia, he published his controversial book on political philosophy, *The Philosophy of Right.* His lectures at the university were later published as his philosophy of history,

of aesthetics, and of religion, and as his history of philosophy.

Philosophy. Hegel's most important ideas were formed gradually, in response to a number of issues in philosophy and often in response to historical events. Moreover, his language and approach were so heterodox that he has inspired as much controversy about the meaning of his position as about its adequacy. Hence any summary will be as much a summary of the controversies as of the basic position.

His dissatisfactions with the absence of a public realm, or any forms of genuine social solidarity in the German states and in modernity generally, and his distaste with what he called the "positivity" of the orthodox religions of the day (their reliance on law, scripture, and abstract claims to authority), led him to various attempts to make use of the Greek polis and classical art, as well as the early Christian understanding of love and a renewed "folk religion," as critical foils to such tendencies. For some time, he also regarded much traditional and modern philosophy as itself a kind of lifeless classifying that only contributed to contemporary fragmentation, myopia, and confusion.

These concerns remained with him throughout his life, and he is thus rightly known as one of the first modern thinkers to argue that what had come to be accepted as the central problem of modern social and political life, the legitimacy of state power, had been too narrowly conceived. There are now all sorts of circumstances, he argued, in which people might satisfy the modern criterion of legitimacy and "consent" to the use of some power, but not fully understand the terms within which such issues are posed, or assent in an attenuated, resentful, manipulated, or confused way. In such cases they would experience no connection between their individual will and the actual content of the institutions they are supposed to have sanctioned. The modern problem is as much *alienation (Entfremdung)* as sovereignty, an exercise of will in which the product of one's will appears "strange" or "alien," "other," and which results in much of modern life, however chosen or willed, being fundamentally unsatisfying.

However, during the Jena years, his views on this issue changed. Most importantly, philosophical issues moved closer to center stage in the Hegelian drama. He no longer regarded philosophy as some sort of self-undermining activity that merely prepared one for some leap into genuine "speculation" (roughly Schelling's position) and began to champion a unique kind of comprehensive, very determinate reflection on the interrelations among all the various classical alternatives in philosophy. Much more controversially, he also attempted to understand the way in which such relations and transitions were also reflected in the history of the art, politics, and religions of various historical communities. He thus came to think that philosophy should be some sort of recollection of its past history, a realization of the mere partiality, rather than falsity, of its past attempts at a comprehensive teaching, and an account of the centrality of these continuously developing attempts in the development of other human practices. Through understanding the "logic" of such a development, a reconciliation of sorts with the implications of such a rational process in contemporary life, or at least with the potentialities inherent in contemporary life, would be possible.

In all such influences and developments, one revolutionary aspect of Hegel's position became clearer. For while Hegel still frequently argued that the subject matter of philosophy was "reason," or "the Absolute," the unconditioned presupposition of all human account-giving and evaluation, and thereby an understanding of the "whole" within which the natural world and human deeds were "parts," he also always construed this claim to mean that the subject matter of philosophy was the history of human experience itself. Philosophy was about the real world of human change and development, understood by Hegel to be the collective self-education of the human species about itself. It could be this, and satisfy the more traditional ideals because, in one of his most famous phrases, "what is actual is rational," or because some full account could be given of the logic or teleological order, even the necessity, for the great conceptual and political changes in human history. We could thereby finally reassure ourselves that the way our species had come to conceptualize and evaluate is not finite or contingent, but is "identical" with "what there is, in truth." This *identity theory* or *Absolute Knowledge* means that we will then be able to be "at home" in the world and so will have understood what philosophers have always tried to understand, "how things in the broadest possible sense of the term hang together in the broadest possible sense of the term." The way it all hangs together is, finally, "due to us," in some collective and historical and "logical" sense. (In a much disputed passage in his *Philosophy of Religion* lectures, Hegel even suggested that with such an understanding, history itself would be over.)

Several elements in this general position have inspired a good deal of excitement and controversy. To advance claims such as these Hegel had to argue against a powerful, deeply influential assumption in modern thought: the priority of the individual, self-conscious subject. Such an assumption means, for example, that almost all social relations, almost all our bonds to other human beings, exist because and only because they are made, willed into existence by individuals otherwise naturally unattached to each other. With respect to knowledge claims, while there may be many beliefs in a common tradition that we unreflectively share with others, such shared beliefs are also taken primarily to be the *result* of individuals continuously affirming such beliefs, however implicitly or unreflectively. Their being shared is simply a consequence of their being simultaneously affirmed or assented to by individuals.

Hegel's account requires a different picture, an insistence on the priority of some kind of collective subject, which he called human "spirit" or *Geist*. His general theory of conceptual and historical change requires the assumption of such a collective subject, one that even can be said to be "coming to self-consciousness" about itself, and this required that he argue against the view that so much could be understood as the result of individual will and reflection. Rather, he tried in many different ways to show that the formation of what might appear to an individual to be his or her own particular intention or desire or belief already reflected a complex social inheritance that could itself be said to be evolving, even evolving progressively, with a "logic" of its own. The completion of such collective attempts at self-knowledge resulted in what Hegel called the realization of *Absolute Spirit*, by which he either meant the absolute completion of the human attempt to know itself, or the realization in human affairs of some sort of extrahuman transcendence, or full expression of an infinite God.

Hegel tried to advance all such claims about social subjectivity without in some way hypostatizing or reifying such a subject, as if it existed independently of the actions and thoughts of individuals. This claim about the deep dependence of individuals on one another (even for their very identity), even while they maintain their independence, is one of the best-known examples of Hegel's attempt at a *dialectical* resolution of many of the traditional oppositions and antinomies of past thought. Hegel often argued that what appeared to be contraries in philosophy, such as mind/body, freedom/determinism, idealism/materialism, universal/particular, the state/the individual, or even God/man, appeared such incompatible alternatives only because of the undeveloped and so incomplete perspective within which the oppositions were formulated.

So, in one of his more famous attacks on such dualisms, human freedom according to Hegel could not be understood coherently as some purely rational self-determination, independent of heteronomous impulses, nor the human being as a perpetual opposition between reason and sensibility. In his moral theory, Kant had argued for the latter view and Hegel regularly returned to such Kantian claims about the opposition of duty and inclination as deeply typical of modern dualism. Hegel claimed that Kant's version of a rational principle, the "categorical imperative," was so formal and devoid of content as not to be action-guiding (it could not coherently rule in or rule out the appropriate actions), and that the "moral point of view" rigoristically demanded a pure or dutiful motivation to which no human agent could conform. By contrast, Hegel claimed that the dualisms of morality could be overcome in *ethical life* (*Sittlichkeit*), those modern social institutions which, it was claimed, provided the content or true "objects" of a rational will. These institutions, the family, civil society, and the state, did not require duties in potential conflict with our own substantive ends, but were rather experienced as the "realization" of our individual free will. It has remained controversial what for Hegel a truly free, rational self-determination, continuous with, rather than constraining, our desire for happiness and self-actualization, amounted to. Many commentators have noted that, among modern philosophers, only Spinoza, whom Hegel greatly admired, was as insistent on such a thoroughgoing *compatibilism,* and on a refusal to adopt the Christian view of human beings as permanently divided against themselves.

In his most ambitious analysis of such oppositions Hegel went so far as to claim that, not only could alternatives be shown to be ultimately compatible when thought together within some higher-order "Notion" (*Begriff*) that resolved or "sublated" the opposition, but that one term in such opposition could actually be said to imply or require its contrary, that a "positing" of such a notion would, to maintain consistency, require its own "negating," and that it was this sort of dialectical opposition that could be shown to require a sublation, or *Aufhebung* (a term of art in Hegel that simultaneously means in German 'to cancel', 'to preserve', and 'to raise up').

This claim for a dialectical development of our fundamental notions has been the most severely criticized in Hegel's philosophy. Many critics have doubted that so much basic conceptual change can be accounted for by an internal critique, one that merely develops the presuppositions inherent in the affirmation of some notion or position or related practice. This issue has especially attracted critics of Hegel's *Science of Logic,* where he tries first to show that the attempt to categorize anything that is, simply and immediately, as "Being," is an attempt that both "negates itself," or ends up categorizing everything as "Nothing," and then that this self-negation requires a resolution in the higher-order category of "Becoming." This analysis continues into an extended argument that purports to show that any attempt to categorize anything at all must ultimately make use of the distinctions of "essence" and "appearance," and elements of syllogistic and finally Hegel's own dialectical logic, and both the details and the grand design of that project have been the subject of a good deal of controversy. (Unfortunately, much of this controversy has been greatly confused by the popular association of the terms "thesis," "antithesis," and "synthesis" with Hegel's theory of dialectic. These crude, mechanical notions were invented in 1837 by a less-than-sensitive Hegel expositor, Heinrich Moritz Chalybäus, and were never used as terms of art by Hegel.)

Others have argued that the tensions Hegel does identify in various positions and practices require a much broader analysis of the historical, especially economic, context within which positions are formulated and become important, or some more detailed attention to the empirical discoveries or paradoxes that, at the very least, contribute to basic conceptual change.

Those worried about the latter problem have also raised questions about the logical relation between universal and particular implied in Hegel's account. Hegel, following Fichte, radicalizes a Kantian claim about the inaccessibility of pure particularity in sensations (Kant had written that "intuitions without concepts are blind"). Hegel charges that Kant did not draw sufficiently radical conclusions from such an antiempiricist claim, that he should have completely rethought the traditional distinction between "what was given to the mind" and "what the mind did with the given." By contrast Hegel is confident that he has a theory of a "concrete universal," concepts that cannot be understood as pale generalizations or abstract representations of given particulars, because they are required for particulars to be apprehended in the first place. They are not originally dependent on an immediate acquaintance with particulars; there is no such acquaintance. Critics wonder if Hegel has much of a theory of particularity left, if he does not claim rather that particulars, or whatever now corresponds to them, are only interrelations of concepts, and in which the actual details of the organization of the natural world and human history are deduced as conceptual necessities in Hegel's *Encyclopedia*. (This interpretation of Hegel, that he believes all entities are really the thoughts, expressions, or modes of a single underlying mental substance, and that this mind develops and posits itself with some sort of conceptual necessity, has been termed a *panlogicism*, a term of art coined by Hermann Glockner, a Hegel commentator in the first half of the twentieth century. It is a much-disputed reading.)

Such critics are especially concerned with the implications of this issue in Hegel's political theory, where the great modern opposition between the state and the individual seems subjected to this same logic, and the individual's true individuality is said to reside in and only in the political universal, the State. Thus, on the one hand, Hegel's political philosophy is often praised for its early identification and analysis of a fundamental, new aspect of contemporary life – the categorically distinct realm of *political* life in modernity, or the independence of the "State" from the social world of private individuals engaged in competition and private association ("civil society"). But, on the other hand, his attempt to argue for a completion of these domains in the State, or that individuals could only be said to be free in allegiance to a State, has been, at least since Marx, one of the most criticized aspects of his philosophy.

Finally, criticisms also frequently target the underlying intention behind such claims: Hegel's career-long insistence on finding some basic unity among the many fragmented spheres of modern thought and existence, and his demand that this unity be articulated in a discursive account, that it not be merely felt, or gestured at, or celebrated in edifying speculation. Post-Hegelian thinkers have tended to be suspicious of any such intimations of a whole for modern experience, and have argued that, with the destruction of the premodern world, we simply have to content ourselves with the disconnected, autonomous spheres of modern interests.

In his lecture courses these basic themes are treated in wide-ranging accounts of the basic institutions of cultural history. History itself is treated as fundamentally political history, and, in typically Hegelian fashion, the major epochs of political history are claimed to be as they were because of the internal inadequacies of past epochs, all until some final political semiconsciousness is achieved and realized. Art is treated equally developmentally, evolving from symbolic, through "classical," to the most intensely self-conscious form of aesthetic subjectivity, romantic art. The *Lectures on the Philosophy of Religion* embody these themes in some of the most controversial ways, since Hegel often treats religion and its development as a kind of picture or accessible "representation" of his own views about the relation of thought to being, the proper understanding of human finitude and "infinity," and the essentially social or communal nature of religious life. This has inspired a characteristic debate among Hegel scholars, with some arguing that Hegel's appropriation of religion shows that his own themes are essentially religious (if an odd, pantheistic version of Christianity), while others argue that he has so Hegelianized religious issues that there is little distinctively religious left.

Influence. This last debate is typical of that prominent in the post-Hegelian tradition. Although, in the decades following his death, there was a great deal of work by self-described Hegelians on the history of law, on political philosophy, and on aesthetics, most of the prominent academic defenders of Hegel were interested in theology, and many of these were interested in defending an interpretation of Hegel consistent with traditional Christian views of a personal God and personal immortality. This began to change with the work of "young Hegelians" such as D. F. Strauss (1808–74), Feuerbach (1804–72), Bruno Bauer (1809–82), and Arnold Ruge (1803–80), who emphasized the humanistic and historical dimensions of Hegel's account of religion, rejected the Old Hegelian tendencies toward a reconciliation with contemporary political life, and began to reinterpret and expand Hegel's account of the productive activity of human spirit (eventually focusing on labor rather than intellectual and cultural life). Strauss himself characterized the fight as between "left," "center," and "right" Hegelians, depending on whether one was critical or conservative politically, or had a theistic or a humanistic view of Hegelian *Geist*. The most famous young or left Hegelian was Marx, especially during his days in Paris as coeditor, with Ruge, of the *Deutsch-französischen Jahrbücher* (1844).

In Great Britain, with its long skeptical, empiricist, and utilitarian tradition, Hegel's work had little influence until the latter part of the nineteenth century, when philosophers such as Green and Caird took up some of the holistic themes in Hegel and developed a neo-Hegelian reading of issues in politics and religion that began to have influence in the academy. The most prominent of the British neo-Hegelians of the next generation were Bosanquet, Mc-Taggart, and especially Bradley, all of whom were interested in many of the metaphysical implications of Hegel's idealism, what they took to be a Hegelian claim for the "internally related" interconnection of all particulars within one single, ideal or mental, substance. Moore and Russell waged a hugely successful counterattack in the name of traditional empiricism and what would be called "analytic philosophy" against such an enterprise and in this tradition largely finished off the influence of Hegel (or what was left of the historical Hegel in these neo-Hegelian versions).

In Germany, Hegel has continued to influence a number of different schools of neo-Marxism, sometimes itself simply called "Hegelian Marxism," especially the Frankfurt School, or "critical theory" group (especially Adorno, Horkheimer, and Marcuse). And he has been extremely influential in France, particularly thanks to the lectures of a brilliant if idiosyncratic Russian émigré, Alexander Kojève, who taught Hegel in the 1930s at the École Pratique des Hautes Études to the likes of Merleau-Ponty and Lacan. Kojève was as much influenced by Marx and Heidegger as Hegel, but his lectures inspired many thinkers to turn again to Hegel's account of human self-definition in time and to the historicity of all institutions and practices and so forged an unusual link between Hegel and postwar existentialism.

Hegelian themes continue to resurface in contemporary hermeneutics, in "communitarianism" in ethics, and in the increasing attention given to conceptual change and history in the philosophy of science. This has meant for many that Hegel should now be regarded not only as the origin of a distinctive tradition in European philosophy that emphasizes the historical and social nature of human existence, but as a potential contributor to many new and often interdisciplinary approaches to philosophy.

See also FRANKFURT SCHOOL, IDEALISM, KANT, PHILOSOPHY OF HISTORY.   R.B.P.

Hegelians, Young. See HEGEL.

Hegesias. See CYRENAICS.

Heidegger, Martin (1889–1976), German philosopher whose early works contributed to phenomenology and existentialism (e.g., Sartre) and whose later works paved the way to hermeneutics (Gadamer) and post-structuralism (Derrida and Foucault). Born in Messkirch in the Black Forest region, Heidegger first trained to be a Jesuit, but switched to mathematics and philosophy in 1911. As an instructor at Freiburg University, he worked with the founder of phenomenology, Husserl. His masterwork, *Sein und Zeit* (*Being and Time*, 1927), was published while he was teaching at Marburg University. This work, in opposition to the preoccupation with epistemology dominant at the time, focused on the traditional question of metaphysics: What is the being of entities in general? Rejecting abstract theoretical approaches to this question, Heidegger drew on Kierkegaard's religious individualism and the influential movement called life-philosophy – *Lebensphilosophie*, then identified with Nietzsche, Bergson, and Dilthey – to develop a highly original account of humans as embedded in concrete situations of action. Heidegger accepted Husserl's chair at Freiburg in 1928; in 1933, having been elected rector of the University, he joined the Nazi party. Although he stepped down as rector one year later, new evidence suggests complicity with the Nazis until the end of the war. Starting in the late thirties, his writings started to shift toward the "antihumanist" and "poetic" form of thinking referred to as "later Heidegger."

Heidegger's lifelong project was to answer the "question of being" (*Seinsfrage*). This question asks, concerning things in general (rocks, tools, people, etc.), what is it to be an entity of these sorts? It is the question of ontology first posed by ancient Greek philosophers from Anaximander to Aristotle. Heidegger holds, however, that philosophers starting with Plato have gone astray in trying to answer this question because they have tended to think of being as a property or essence enduringly present in things. In other words, they have fallen into the "metaphysics of presence," which thinks of being as substance. What is overlooked in traditional metaphysics is the background conditions that enable entities to show up as counting or mattering in some specific way in the first place. In his early works, Heidegger tries to bring this concealed dimension of things to light by recasting the question of being: What is the *meaning* of being? Or, put differently, how do entities come to show up as *intelligible* to us in some determinate way? And this question calls for an analysis of the entity that has some prior understanding of things: human existence or *Dasein* (the German word for "existence" or "being-there," used to refer to the structures of humans that make possible an understanding of being). Heidegger's claim is that *Dasein*'s pretheoretical (or "preontological") understanding of being, embodied in its everyday practices, opens a "clearing" in which entities can show up *as*, say, tools, protons, numbers, mental events, and so on. This historically unfolding clearing is what the metaphysical tradition has overlooked.

In order to clarify the conditions that make possible an understanding of being, then, *Being and Time* begins with an analytic of *Dasein*. But Heidegger notes that traditional interpretations of human existence have been one-sided to the extent that they concentrate on our ways of existing when we are engaged in theorizing and detached reflection. It is this narrow focus on the spectator attitude that leads to the picture, found in Descartes, of the self as a mind or subject representing material objects – the so-called subject-object model. In order to bypass this traditional picture, Heidegger sets out to describe *Dasein*'s "average everydayness," i.e., our ordinary, prereflective agency when we are caught up in the midst of practical affairs. The "phenomenology of everydayness" is supposed to lead us to see the totality of human existence, including our moods, our capacity for authentic individuality, and our full range of involvements with the world and with others. The analytic of *Dasein* is also an ontological hermeneutics to the extent that it provides an account of how understanding in general is possible. The result of the analytic is a portrayal of human existence that is in accord with what Heidegger regards as the earliest Greek experience of being as an emerging-into-presence (*physis*): to be human is to be a temporal event of self-manifestation that lets other sorts of entities first come to "emerge and abide" in the world. From the standpoint of this description, the traditional concept of substance – whether mental or physical – simply has no role to play in grasping humans. Heidegger's brilliant diagnoses or "de-structurings" of the tradition suggest that the idea of substance arises only when the conditions making entities possible are forgotten or concealed.

Heidegger holds that there is no pregiven human essence. Instead, humans, as self-interpreting beings, just are what they make of themselves in the course of their active lives. Thus, as everyday agency, *Dasein* is not an object with

properties, but is rather the "happening" of a life course "stretched out between birth and death." Understood as the "historicity" of a temporal movement or "becoming," *Dasein* is found to have three main "existentials" or basic structures shared by every "existentiell" (i.e., specific and local) way of living. First, *Dasein* finds itself *thrown* into a world not of its choosing, already delivered over to the task of living out its life in a concrete context. This "facticity" of our lives is revealed in the moods that let things matter to us in some way or other – e.g., the burdensome feelings of concern that accompany being a parent in our culture. Second, as *projection, Dasein* is always already taking some stand on its life by acting in the world. Understood as agency, human existence is "ahead of itself" in two senses: (1) our competent dealings with familiar situations sketch out a range of possibilities for how things may turn out in the future, and (2) each of our actions is contributing to shaping our lives as people of specific sorts. *Dasein* is future-directed in the sense that the ongoing fulfillment of possibilities in the course of one's active life constitutes one's identity (or being). To say that *Dasein* is "being-toward-death" is to say that the stands we take (our "understanding") define our being as a totality. Thus, my actual ways of treating my children throughout my life define my *being* as a parent in the end, regardless of what good intentions I might have. Finally, *Dasein* is *discourse* in the sense that we are always articulating – or "addressing and discussing" – the entities that show up in our concernful absorption in current situations. These three existentials define human existence as a temporal unfolding. The unity of these dimensions – being already in a world, ahead of itself, and engaged with things – Heidegger calls *care*. This is what it means to say that humans are the entities whose being is *at issue* for them. Taking a stand on our own being, we constitute our identity through what we do.

The formal structure of *Dasein* as temporality is made concrete through one's specific involvements in the world (where 'world' is used in the life-world sense in which we talk about the business world or the world of academia). *Dasein* is the unitary phenomenon of being-in-the-world. A core component of Heidegger's early works is his description of how *Dasein*'s practical dealings with equipment define the *being* of the entities that show up in the world. In hammering in a workshop, e.g., what ordinarily shows up for us is not a hammer-thing with properties, but rather a web of significance relations shaped by our projects. Hammering is "in order to" join boards, which is "for" building a bookcase, which is "for the sake of" being a person with a neat study. The hammer is encountered in terms of its place in this holistic context of functionality – the "ready-to-hand." In other words, the *being* of the equipment – its "ontological definition" – consists of its relations to other equipment and its actual use within the entire practical context. Seen from this standpoint, the brute, meaningless objects assumed to be basic by the metaphysical tradition – the "present-at-hand" – can show up only when there is a *breakdown* in our ordinary dealings with things, e.g., when the hammer breaks or is missing. In this sense, the ready-to-hand is said to be more primordial than the material objects treated as basic by the natural sciences.

It follows, then, that the being of entities in the world is constituted by the framework of intelligibility or "disclosedness" opened by *Dasein*'s practices. This clearing is truth in the original meaning of the Greek word *aletheia*, which Heidegger renders as 'un-concealment'. But it would be wrong to think that what is claimed here is that humans are initially just given, and that they then go on to create a clearing. For, in Heidegger's view, our *own* being as agents of specific types is defined by the world into which we are thrown: in my workshop, I can be a craftsman or an amateur, but not a samurai paying court to a daimyo. Our identity as agents is made possible by the context of shared forms of life and linguistic practices of a public life-world. For the most part, we exist as the "they" (*das Man*), participants in the historically constituted "co-happening of a people" (*Volk*).

The embeddedness of our existence in a cultural context explains our inveterate tendency toward inauthenticity. As we become initiated into the practices of our community, we are inclined to drift along with the crowd, doing what "one" does, enacting stereotyped roles, and thereby losing our ability to seize on and define our own lives. Such *falling* into public preoccupations Heidegger sees as a sign that we are fleeing from the fact that we are finite beings who stand before death (understood as the culmination of our possibilities). When, through anxiety and hearing the call of conscience, we face up to our being-toward-death, our lives can be transformed. To be authentic is to clear-sightedly face up to one's responsibility for what one's life is adding up to as a whole. And because our lives are inseparable from our community's existence, authenticity involves seizing on the possibilities

circulating in our shared "heritage" in order to realize a communal "destiny."

Heidegger's ideal of resolute "taking action" in the current historical situation no doubt contributed to his leap into politics in the 1930s. According to his writings of that period, the ancient Greeks inaugurated a "first beginning" for Western civilization, but centuries of forgetfulness (beginning with the Latinization of Greek words) have torn us away from the primal experience of being rooted in that initial setting. Heidegger hoped that, guided by the insights embodied in great works of art (especially Hölderlin's poetry), National Socialism would help bring about a world-rejuvenating "new beginning" comparable to the first beginning in ancient Greece.

Heidegger's later writings attempt to fully escape the subjectivism he sees dominating Western thought from its inception up to Nietzsche. "The Origin of the Work of Art" (1935), for example, shows how a great work of art such as a Greek temple, by shaping the world in which a people live, constitutes the kinds of people that can live in that world. *An Introduction to Metaphysics* (1935) tries to recover the Greek experience of humans as beings whose activities of gathering and naming (*logos*) are above all a *response* to what is more than human. The later writings emphasize that which resists all human mastery and comprehension. Such terms as 'nothingness', 'earth', and 'mystery' suggest that what shows itself to us always depends on a background of what does not show itself, what remains concealed. Language comes to be understood as the medium through which anything, including the human, first becomes accessible and intelligible. Because language is the source of all intelligibility, Heidegger says that humans do not speak, but rather language speaks us – an idea that became central to post-structuralist theories.

In his writings after the war, Heidegger replaces the notions of resoluteness and political activism with a new ideal of letting-be or releasement (*Gelassenheit*), a stance characterized by meditative thinking, thankfulness for the "gift" of being, and openness to the silent "call" of language. The technological "enframing" (*Gestell*) of our age – encountering everything as a standing reserve on hand for our use – is treated not as something humans do, but instead as a manifestation of being itself. The "anti-humanism" of these later works is seen in the description of technology (the mobilization of everything for the sole purpose of greater efficiency) as an epochal event in the "history of being," a way things have come-into-their-own (*Ereignis*) rather than as a human accomplishment. The history or "sending" (*Geschick*) of being consists of epochs that have all gone increasingly astray from the original beginning inaugurated by the pre-Socratics. Since human willpower alone cannot bring about a new epoch, technology cannot be ended by our efforts. But a non-technological way of encountering things is hinted at in a description of a jug as *fourfold* of earth, sky, mortals, and gods, and Heidegger reflects on forms of poetry that point to a new, non-metaphysical way of experiencing being. Through a transformed relation to language and art, and by abandoning "onto-theology" (the attempt to ground all entities in one supreme entity), we might prepare ourselves for a transformed way of understanding being.

See also CONTINENTAL PHILOSOPHY, EXISTENTIALISM, HERMENEUTICS, HUSSERL, LEBENSPHILOSOPHIE, POSTMODERN.　　　C.B.G.

Heidelberg School. See NEO-KANTIANISM.

Heisenberg indeterminacy principle. See QUANTUM MECHANICS.

Heisenberg uncertainty principle. See QUANTUM MECHANICS.

Hellenistic philosophy, the philosophical systems of the Hellenistic age (323–30 B.C., although 311–87 B.C. better defines it as a philosophical era), notably Epicureanism, Stoicism, and Skepticism. These all emerged in the generation after Aristotle's death (322 B.C.), and dominated philosophical debate until the first century B.C., during which there were revivals of traditional Platonism and of Aristotelianism. The age was one in which much of the eastern Mediterranean world absorbed Greek culture (was "Hellenized," hence "Hellenistic"), and recruits to philosophy flocked from this region to Athens, which remained the center of philosophical activity until 87 B.C. Then the Roman sack of Athens drove many philosophers into exile, and neither the schools nor the styles of philosophy that had grown up there ever fully recovered.

Very few philosophical writings survive intact from the period. Our knowledge of Hellenistic philosophers depends mainly on later doxography, on the Roman writers Lucretius and Cicero (both mid-first century B.C.), and on what we learn from the schools' critics in later centuries, e.g. Sextus Empiricus and Plutarch.

'Skeptic', a term not actually current before the very end of the Hellenistic age, serves as a convenient label to characterize two philosophical movements. The first is the New Academy: the school founded by Plato, the Academy, became in this period a largely dialectical one, conducting searching critiques of other schools' doctrines without declaring any of its own, beyond perhaps the assertion (however guarded) that nothing could be known and the accompanying recommendation of "suspension of judgment" (*epoche*). The nature and vivacity of Stoicism owed much to its prolonged debates with the New Academy. The founder of this Academic phase was Arcesilaus (school head c.268–c.241); its most revered and influential protagonist was Carneades (school head in the mid-second century); and its most prestigious voice was that of Cicero (106–43 B.C.), whose highly influential philosophical works were written mainly from a New Academic stance. But by the early first century B.C. the Academy was drifting back to a more doctrinal stance, and in the later part of the century it was largely eclipsed by a second "skeptic" movement, Pyrrhonism. This was founded by Aenesidemus, a pioneering skeptic despite his claim to be merely reviving the philosophy of Pyrrho, a philosophical guru of the early Hellenistic period. His neo-Pyrrhonism survives today mainly through the writings of Sextus Empiricus (second century A.D.), an adherent of the school who, strictly speaking, represents its post-Hellenistic phase.

The Peripatos, Aristotle's school, officially survived throughout the era, but it is not regarded as a distinctively "Hellenistic" movement. Despite the eminence of Aristotle's first successor, Theophrastus (school head 322–287), it thereafter fell from prominence, its fortunes only reviving around the mid-first century B.C. It is disputed how far the other Hellenistic philosophers were even aware of Aristotle's treatises, which should not in any case be regarded as a primary influence on them.

Each school had a location in Athens to which it could draw pupils. The Epicurean school was a relatively private institution, its "Garden" outside the city walls housing a close-knit philosophical community. The Stoics took their name from the Stoa Poikile, the "Painted Colonnade" in central Athens where they gathered. The Academics were based in the Academy, a public grove just outside the city. Philosophers were public figures, a familiar sight around town. Each school's philosophical identity was further clarified by its absolute loyalty to the name of its founder – respectively Epicurus, Zeno of Citium, and Plato – and by the polarities that developed in interschool debates. Epicureanism is diametrically opposed on most issues to Stoicism. Academic Skepticism provides another antithesis to Stoicism, not through any positions of its own (it had none), but through its unflagging critical campaign against every Stoic thesis.

It is often said that in this age the old Greek political institution of the city-state had broken down, and that the Hellenistic philosophies were an answer to the resulting crisis of values. Whether or not there is any truth in this, it remains clear that moral concerns were now much less confined to the individual city-state than previously, and that at an extreme the boundaries had been pushed back to include all mankind within the scope of an individual's moral obligations. Our "affinity" (*oikeiosis*) to all mankind is an originally Stoic doctrine that acquired increasing currency with other schools. This attitude partly reflects the weakening of national and cultural boundaries in the Hellenistic period, as also in the Roman imperial period that followed it.

The three recognized divisions of philosophy were ethics, logic, and physics. In ethics, the central objective was to state and defend an account of the "end" (*telos*), the moral goal to which all activity was subordinated: the Epicureans named pleasure, the Stoics conformity with nature. Much debate centered on the semimythical figure of the wise man, whose conduct in every conceivable circumstance was debated by all schools. Logic in its modern sense was primarily a Stoic concern, rejected as irrelevant by the Epicureans. But Hellenistic logic included epistemology, where the primary focus of interest was the "criterion of truth," the ultimate yardstick against which all judgments could be reliably tested. Empiricism was a surprisingly uncontroversial feature of Hellenistic theories: there was little interest in the Platonic-Aristotelian idea that knowledge in the strict sense is non-sensory, and the debate between dogmatists and Skeptics was more concerned with the question whether any proposed sensory criterion was adequate. Both Stoics and Epicureans attached especial importance to *prolepsis*, the generic notion of a thing, held to be either innate or naturally acquired in a way that gave it a guaranteed veridical status. Physics saw an opposition between Epicurean atomism, with its denial of divine providence, and the Stoic world-continuum, imbued with divine rationality. The issue of determinism was also placed on the philo-sophical map: Epicurean morality depends on the denial of (both physical and logical) determinism, whereas Stoic morality is compatible with, indeed actually requires, the deterministic causal nexus through which providence operates.

See also DOXOGRAPHERS, EPICUREANISM, SKEPTICS, STOICISM.   D.N.S.

Helmholtz, Hermann von (1821–94), German physiologist and physicist known for ground-breaking work in physics, physiological optics, perceptual psychology, and the philosophy of geometry. Formally trained as a physician, he distinguished himself in physics in 1848 as a codiscoverer of the law of conservation of energy, and by the end of his life was perhaps the most influential figure in German physical research. Philosophically, his most important influence was on the study of space. Intuitionist psychologists held that the geometrical structure of three-dimensional space was given directly in sensation by innate physiological mechanisms; Helmholtz brought this theory to severe empirical trials and argued, on the contrary, that our knowledge of space consists of inferences from accumulated experience. On the mathematical side, he attacked Kant's view that Euclidean geometry is the a priori form of outer intuition by showing that it is possible to have visual experience of non-Euclidean space ("On the Origins and Meaning of Geometrical Axioms," 1870). His crucial insight was that empirical geometry depends on physical assumptions about the behavior of measuring instruments. This inspired the view of Poincaré and logical empiricism that the empirical content of geometry is fixed by physical definitions, and made possible Einstein's use of non-Euclidean geometry in physics. **See also** PHILOSOPHY OF MATHEMATICS, POINCARÉ.   R.D.

Helvétius, Claude Adrien (1715–71), French philosopher prominent in the formative phases of eighteenth-century materialism in France. His *De l'esprit* (1758) was widely discussed internationally, but condemned by the University of Paris and burned by the government. Helvétius attempted to clarify his doctrine in his posthumously published *De l'homme*.

Following Locke's criticism of the innate ideas, Helvétius stressed the function of experience in our acquisition of knowledge. In accord with the doctrines of d'Holbach, Condillac, and La Mettrie, the materialist Helvétius regarded the sensations as the basis of all our knowledge. Only by comparison, abstraction, and combination of sensations do we reach the level of concepts. Peculiar to Helvétius, however, is the stress on the social determinations of our knowledge. Specific interests and passions are the starting point of all our striving for knowledge. Egoism is the spring of our desires and actions. The civil laws of the enlightened state enabled egoism to be transformed into social competition and thereby diverted toward public benefits.

Like his materialist contemporary d'Holbach and later Condorcet, Helvétius sharply criticized the social function of the church. Priests, he claimed, provided society with wrong moral ideas. He demanded a thorough reform of the educational system for the purpose of individual and social emancipation. In contrast to the teachings of Rousseau, Helvétius praised the further development of science, art, and industry as instruments for the historical progress of mankind. The ideal society consists of enlightened because well-educated citizens living in comfortable and even moderately luxurious circumstances. All people should participate in the search for truth, by means of public debates and discussions. Truth is equated with the moral good. Helvétius had some influence on Marxist historical materialism.   H.P.

Hempel, Carl G(ustav) (1905–97), eminent philosopher of science associated with the Vienna Circle of logical empiricist philosophers in the early 1930s, before his emigration to the United States; thereafter he became one of the most influential philosophers of science of his time, largely through groundbreaking work on the logical analysis of the concepts of confirmation and scientific explanation. Hempel received his doctorate under Reichenbach at the University of Berlin in 1934 with a dissertation on the logical analysis of probability. He studied with Carnap at the University of Vienna in 1929–30, where he participated in the "protocol-sentence debate" concerning the observational basis of scientific knowledge raging within the Vienna Circle between Moritz Schlick (1882–1936) and Otto Neurath (1882–1945).

Hempel was attracted to the "radical physicalism" articulated by Neurath and Carnap, which denied the foundational role of immediate experience and asserted that all statements of the total language of science (including observation reports or protocol-sentences) can be revised as science progresses. This led to Hempel's first major publication, "On the Logical Positivists' Theory of Truth" (1935). He moved to the United States to work with Carnap at the University of Chicago in 1937–38. He also taught at Queens College and Yale before his long career at Princeton (1955–1975). In the 1940s he collaborated with his friends Olaf Helmer and Paul Oppenheim on a celebrated series of papers, the most influential of which are "Studies in the Logic of Confirmation" (1945) and "Studies in the Logic of Explanation" (1948, coauthored with Oppenheim). The latter paper articulated the deductive-nomological model, which characterizes scientific explanations as deductively valid arguments proceeding from general laws and initial conditions to the fact to be explained, and served as the basis for all future work on the subject.

Hempel's papers on explanation and confirmation (and also related topics such as concept formation, criteria of meaningfulness, and scientific theories) were collected together in *Aspects of Scientific Explanation* (1965), one of the most important works in postwar philosophy of science. He also published a more popular, but extremely influential introduction to the field, *Philosophy of Natural Science* (1966). Hempel and Kuhn became colleagues at Princeton in the 1960s. Another fruitful collaboration ensued, as a result of which Hempel moved away from the Carnapian tradition of logical analysis toward a more naturalistic and pragmatic conception of science in his later work. As he himself explains, however, this later turn can also be seen as a return to a similarly naturalistic conception Neurath had earlier defended within the Vienna Circle.

See also CARNAP, COVERING LAW MODEL, EXPLANATION, PHILOSOPHY OF SCIENCE, VIENNA CIRCLE.   M.F.

Hempel-Oppenheim model. See COVERING LAW MODEL.

Henkin semantics. See SECOND-ORDER LOGIC.

henotheism, allegiance to one supreme deity while conceding existence to others; also described as monolatry, incipient monotheism, or practical monotheism. It occupies a middle ground between polytheism and radical monotheism, which denies reality to all gods save one. It has been claimed that early Judaism passed through a henotheistic phase, acknowledging other Middle Eastern deities (albeit condemning their worship), en route to exclusive recognition of Yahweh. But the concept of progress from polytheism through henotheism to monotheism is a rationalizing construct, and cannot be supposed to capture the complex development of any historical religion, including that of ancient Israel.   A.E.L.

Henry of Ghent (c.1217–93), Belgian theologian and philosopher. After serving as a church official at Tournai and Brugge, he taught theology at Paris from 1276. His major writings were *Summa quaestionum ordinariarum* (*Summa of Ordinary Questions*) and *Quodlibeta* (*Quodlibetal Questions*). He was the leading representative of the neo-Augustinian movement at Paris in the final quarter of the thirteenth century. His theory of knowledge combines Aristotelian elements with Augustinian illuminationism. Heavily dependent on Avicenna for his view of the reality enjoyed by essences of creatures (*esse essentiae*) from eternity, he rejected both real distinction and real identity of essence and existence in creatures, and defended their intentional distinction. He also rejected a real distinction between the soul and its powers and rejected the purely potential character of prime matter. He defended the duality of substantial form in man, the unicity of form in other material substances, and the primacy of will in the act of choice.   J.F.W.

Hentisberi, Hentisberus. See HEYTESBURY.

Heraclitus (fl. c.500 B.C.), Greek philosopher. A transition figure between the Milesian philosophers and the later pluralists, Heraclitus stressed unity in the world of change. He follows the Milesians in positing a series of cyclical transformations of basic stuffs of the world; for instance, he holds that fire changes to water and earth in turn. Moreover, he seems to endorse a single source or *archē* of natural substances, namely fire. But he also observes that natural transformations necessarily involve contraries such as hot and cold, wet and dry. Indeed, without the one contrary the other would not exist, and without contraries the cosmos would not exist. Hence strife is justice, and war is the father and king of all. In the conflict of opposites there is a hidden harmony that sustains the world, symbolized by the tension of a bow or the attunement of a lyre. Scholars disagree about whether Heraclitus's chief view is that there is a one in the many or that process is reality. Clearly the underlying unity of phenomena is important for him. But he also stresses the transience of physical substances and the importance of processes and qualities. Moreover, his underlying source of unity seems to be a law of process and opposi-

tion; thus he seems to affirm both the unity of phenomena and the reality of process.

Criticizing his predecessors such as Pythagoras and Xenophanes for doing research without insight, Heraclitus claims that we should listen to the *logos*, which teaches that all things are one. The *logos*, a principle of order and knowledge, is common to all, but the many remain ignorant of it, like sleepwalkers unaware of the reality around them. All things come to pass according to the *logos*; hence it is the law of change, or at least its expression.

Heraclitus wrote a single book, perhaps organized into sections on cosmology, politics and ethics, and theology. Apparently, however, he did not provide a continuous argument but a series of epigrammatic remarks meant to reveal the nature of reality through oracular and riddling language. Although he seems to have been a recluse without immediate disciples, he may have stirred Parmenides to his reaction against contraries. In the late fifth century B.C. Cratylus of Athens preached a radical Heraclitean doctrine according to which everything is in flux and there is accordingly no knowledge of the world. This version of Heracliteanism influenced Plato's view of the sensible world and caused Plato and Aristotle to attribute a radical doctrine of flux to Heraclitus. Democritus imitated Heraclitus's ethical sayings, and in Hellenistic times the Stoics appealed to him for their basic principles.

See also LOGOS, WHITEHEAD.   D.W.G.

Herbart, Johann Friedrich (1776–1841), German philosopher who significantly contributed to psychology and the theory of education. Rejecting the idealism of Fichte and Hegel, he attempted to establish a form of psychology founded on experience. The task of philosophy is the analysis of concepts given in ordinary experience. Logic must clarify these concepts, Metaphysics should correct them, while Aesthetics and Ethics are to complement them by an analysis of values. Herbart advocated a form of determinism in psychology and ethics. The laws that govern psychological processes are identical with those that govern the heavens. He subordinated ethics to aesthetics, arguing that our moral values originate from certain immediate and involuntary judgments of like and dislike. The five basic ideas of morality are inner freedom, perfection, benevolence, law, and justice or equity. Herbart's view of education – that it should aim at producing individuals who possess inner freedom and strength of character – was highly influential in nineteenth-century Germany.   M.K.

Herder, Johann Gottfried von (1744–1803), German philosopher, an intellectual and literary figure central to the transition from the German Enlightenment to Romanticism. He was born in East Prussia and received an early classical education. About 1762, while studying theology at the University of Königsberg, he came under the influence of Kant. He also began a lifelong friendship with Hamann, who especially stimulated his interests in the interrelations among language, culture, and history. After ordination as a Lutheran minister in 1765, he began his association with the Berlin Academy, earning its prestigious "prize" for his "Essay on the Origin of Language" (1772). In 1776 he was appointed *Generalsuperintendent* of the Lutheran clergy at Weimar through the intercession of Goethe. He was then able to focus his intellectual and literary powers on most of the major issues of his time. Of particular note are his contributions to psychology in *Of the Cognition and Sensation of the Human Soul* (1778); to the philosophy of history and culture in *Ideas for the Philosophy of the History of Mankind* (1784–91), perhaps his most influential work; and to philosophy in *Understanding and Experience* (1799), which contains his extensive *Metakritik* of Kant's *Critique of Pure Reason*.

Herder was an intellectual maverick and provocateur, writing when the Enlightenment conception of reason was in decline but before its limited defense by Kant or its total rejection by Romanticism had become entrenched in the German-speaking world. Rejecting any rational system, Herder's thought is best viewed as a mosaic of certain ideas that reemerge in various guises throughout his writings. Because of these features, Herder's thought has been compared with that of Rousseau.

Herder's philosophy can be described as involving elements of naturalism, organicism, and vitalism. He rejected philosophical explanations, appealing to the supernatural or divine, such as the concept of the "immortal soul" in psychology, a "divine origin" of language, or "providence" in history. He sought to discern an underlying primordial force to account for the psychological unity of the various "faculties." He viewed this natural tendency toward "organic formation" as also operative in language and culture, and as ultimately manifested in the dynamic development of the various cultures in the form of a universal history. Finally, he often wrote in a way that suggested the dynamic process of life itself as the basic metaphor undergirding his thought.

His influence can be traced through Humboldt into later linguistics and through Schelling and Hegel in the philosophy of history and later German historicism. He anticipated elements of vitalism in Schopenhauer and Bergson.

See also NATURALISM, ORGANICISM, PHILOSOPHY OF BIOLOGY.   J.P.Su.

hereditary property. See RELATION.

Hermarchus. See EPICUREANISM.

hermeneutic circle. See HERMENEUTICS.

hermeneutics, the art or theory of interpretation, as well as a type of philosophy that starts with questions of interpretation. Originally concerned more narrowly with interpreting sacred texts, the term acquired a much broader significance in its historical development and finally became a philosophical position in twentieth-century German philosophy. There are two competing positions in hermeneutics: whereas the first follows Dilthey and sees interpretation or *Verstehen* as a method for the historical and human sciences, the second follows Heidegger and sees it as an "ontological event," an interaction between interpreter and text that is part of the history of what is understood. Providing rules or criteria for understanding what an author or native "really" meant is a typical problem for the first approach. The interpretation of the law provides an example for the second view, since the process of applying the law inevitably transforms it. In general, hermeneutics is the analysis of this process and its conditions of possibility. It has typically focused on the interpretation of ancient texts and distant peoples, cases where the unproblematic everyday understanding and communication cannot be assumed.

Schleiermacher's analysis of understanding and expression related to texts and speech marks the beginning of hermeneutics in the modern sense of a scientific methodology. This emphasis on methodology continues in nineteenth-century historicism and culminates in Dilthey's attempt to ground the human sciences in a theory of interpretation, understood as the imaginative but publicly verifiable reenactment of the subjective experiences of others. Such a method of interpretation reveals the possibility of an objective knowledge of human beings not accessible to empiricist inquiry and thus of a distinct methodology for the human sciences. One result of the analysis of interpretation in the nineteenth century was the recognition of "the hermeneutic circle," first developed by Schleiermacher. The circularity of interpretation concerns the relation of parts to the whole: the interpretation of each part is dependent on the interpretation of the whole. But interpretation is circular in a stronger sense: if every interpretation is itself based on interpretation, then the circle of interpretation, even if it is not vicious, cannot be escaped.

Twentieth-century hermeneutics advanced by Heidegger and Gadamer radicalize this notion of the hermeneutic circle, seeing it as a feature of all knowledge and activity. Hermeneutics is then no longer the method of the human sciences but "universal," and interpretation is part of the finite and situated character of all human knowing. "Philosophical hermeneutics" therefore criticizes Cartesian foundationalism in epistemology and Enlightenment universalism in ethics, seeing science as a cultural practice and prejudices (or prejudgments) as ineliminable in all judgments. Positively, it emphasizes understanding as continuing a historical tradition, as well as dialogical openness, in which prejudices are challenged and horizons broadened.

See also GADAMER, HEIDEGGER, HISTORICISM, SCHLEIERMACHER, VERSTEHEN.   J.Bo.

hermeticism. See HERMETISM.

hermetism, also hermeticism, a philosophical theology whose basic impulse was the gnostic conviction that human salvation depends on revealed knowledge (*gnōsis*) of God and of the human and natural creations. Texts ascribed to Hermes Trismegistus, a Greco-Egyptian version of the Egyptian god Thoth, may have appeared as early as the fourth century B.C., but the surviving Corpus Hermeticum in Greek and Latin is a product of the second and third centuries A.D. Fragments of the same literature exist in Greek, Armenian, and Coptic as well; the Coptic versions are part of a discovery made at Nag Hammadi after World War II. All these Hermetica record hermetism as just described. Other Hermetica traceable to the same period but surviving in later Arabic or Latin versions deal with astrology, alchemy, magic, and other kinds of occultism. Lactantius, Augustine, and other early Christians cited Hermes but disagreed on his value; before Iamblichus, pagan philosophers showed little interest. Muslims connected Hermes with a Koranic figure, Idris, and thereby enlarged the medieval hermetic tradition, which had its first large effects in the Latin West among the twelfth-century Platonists of Chartres. The only ancient hermetic text then available in the West was the Latin *Asclepius,* but in 1463 Ficino interrupted his epochal translation of Plato to Latinize fourteen of the seventeen Greek discourses in the main body of the Corpus Hermeticum (as distinct from the many Greek fragments preserved by Stobaeus but unknown to Ficino).

Ficino was willing to move so quickly to Hermes because he believed that this Egyptian deity stood at the head of the "ancient theology" (*prisca theologia*), a tradition of pagan revelation that ran parallel to Christian scripture, culminated with Plato, and continued through Plotinus and the later Neoplatonists. Ficino's Hermes translation, which he called the *Pimander,* shows no interest in the magic and astrology about which he theorized later in his career. Trinitarian theology was his original motivation. The *Pimander* was enormously influential in the later Renaissance, when Giovanni Pico della Mirandola, Lodovico Lazzarelli, Jacques Lefèvre d'Etaples, Symphorien Champier, Francesco Giorgi, Agostino Steuco, Francesco Patrizi, and others enriched Western appreciation of Hermes. The first printed Greek Hermetica was the 1554 edition of Adrien Turnebus. The last before the nineteenth century appeared in 1630, a textual hiatus that reflected a decline in the reputation of Hermes after Isaac Casaubon proved philologically in 1614 that the Greek Hermetica had to be post-Christian, not the remains of primeval Egyptian wisdom. After Casaubon, hermetic ideas fell out of fashion with most Western philosophers of the current canon, but the historiography of the ancient theology remained influential for Newton and for lesser figures even later. The content of the Hermetica was out of tune with the new science, so Casaubon's redating left Hermes to the theosophical heirs of Robert Fludd, whose opponents (Kepler, Mersenne, Gassendi) turned away from the Hermetica and similar fascinations of Renaissance humanist culture. By the nineteenth century, only theosophists took Hermes seriously as a prophet of pagan wisdom, but he was then rediscovered by German students of Christianity and Hellenistic religions, especially Richard Reitzenstein, who published his *Poimandres* in 1904. The ancient Hermetica are now read in the 1946–54 edition of A. D. Nock and A. J. Festugière.

See also FICINO.   B.P.C.

Herzen, Alexander (1812–70), Russian editor, memoirist, and social philosopher, in exile in Western Europe from 1847. Herzen moved in his philosophy of history from an early Hegelian rationalism to a "philosophy of contingency," stressing the "whirlwind of chances" in nature and in human life and the "tousled improvisation" of the historical process. He rejected determinism, emphasizing the "phenomenological fact" of the experienced "sense of freedom." Anticipating the Dostoevsky of the "Legend of the Grand Inquisitor," he offered an original analysis of the "escape from freedom" and the cleaving to moral and political authority, and sketched a curiously contemporary-sounding "emotivist" ethical theory. After 1848, disillusioned with "bourgeois" Europe and its "self-enclosed individualism," but equally disillusioned with what he had come to see as the bourgeois ideal of many European socialists, Herzen turned to the Russian peasant and the peasant village commune as offering the best hope for a humane development of society. In this "Russian socialism" he anticipated a central doctrine of the Russian populists of the 1870s.

Herzen stood alone in resisting the common tendency of such otherwise different thinkers as Feuerbach, Marx, and J. S. Mill to undervalue the historical present, to overvalue the historical future, and to treat actual persons as means in the service of remote, merely possible historical ends. Herzen's own central emphasis fell powerfully and consistently on the freedom, independence, and non-instrumentalizable value of living persons. And he saw more clearly than any of his contemporaries that there are no future persons, that it is only in the present that free human individuals live and move and have their being.

See also RUSSIAN PHILOSOPHY. G.L.K.

heterological. See SET-THEORETIC PARADOXES.

heteronomy. See KANT.

heuristics, a rule or solution adopted to reduce the complexity of computational tasks, thereby reducing demands on resources such as time, memory, and attention. If an algorithm is a procedure yielding a correct solution to a problem, then a *heuristic* procedure may not reach a solution even if there is one, or may provide an incorrect answer. The reliability of heuristics varies between domains; the resulting biases are predictable, and provide information about system design. Chess, for example, is a finite game with a finite number of possible positions, but there is no known algorithm for finding the optimal move. Computers and humans both employ heuristics in evaluating intermediate moves,

relying on a few significant cues to game quality, such as safety of the king, material balance, and center control. The use of these criteria simplifies the problem, making it computationally tractable. They are heuristic guides, reliable but limited in success. There is no guarantee that the result will be the best move or even good. They are nonetheless satisfactory for competent chess.

Work on human judgment indicates a similar moral. Examples of judgmental infelicities support the view that human reasoning systematically violates standards for statistical reasoning, ignoring base rates, sample size, and correlations. Experimental results suggest that humans utilize judgmental heuristics in gauging probabilities, such as *representativeness,* or the degree to which an individual or event resembles a prototypical member of a category. Such heuristics produce reasonable judgments in many cases, but are of limited validity when measured by a Bayesian standard. Judgmental heuristics are biased and subject to systemic errors. Experimental support for the importance of these heuristics depends on cases in which subjects deviate from the normative standard.

See also BAYESIAN RATIONALITY, EMPIRICAL DECISION THEORY. R.C.R.

hexis (Greek, from *hexo,* 'to have', 'to be disposed'), a (good or bad) condition, disposition, or state. The traditional rendering, 'habit' (Latin *habitus*), is misleading, for it tends to suggest the idea of an involuntary and merely repetitious pattern of behavior. A *hexis* is rather a state of character or of mind that disposes us to deliberately choose to act or to think in a certain way. The term acquired a quasi-technical status after Aristotle advanced the view that *hexis* is the genus of virtue, both moral and intellectual. In the *Nicomachean Ethics* he distinguishes *hexeis* from passions (*pathē*) and faculties (*dunamis*) of the soul. If a man fighting in the front ranks feels afraid when he sees the enemy approaching, he is undergoing an involuntary passion. His capacity to be affected by fear on this or other occasions is part of his makeup, one of his faculties. If he chooses to stay where his commanders placed him, this is due to the *hexis* or state of character we call courage. Likewise, one who is consistently good at identifying what is best for oneself can be said to possess a *hexis* called prudence. Not all states and dispositions are commendable. Cowardice and stupidity are also *hexeis.* Both in the sense of 'state' and of 'possession' *hexis* plays a role in Aristotle's *Categories.* **See also** ARISTOTLE, VIRTUE ETHICS. A.G.-L.

Heytesbury, William, also called Hentisberus, Hentisberi, Tisberi (before 1313–c.1372), English philosopher and chancellor of Oxford University. He wrote *Sophismata* ("Sophisms"), *Regulae solvendi sophismata* ("Rules for Solving Sophisms"), and *De sensu composito et diviso* ("On the Composite and Divided Sense"). Other works are doubtfully attributed to him. Heytesbury belonged to the generation immediately after Thomas Bradwardine and Kilvington, and was among the most significant members of the Oxford Calculators, important in the early developemnt of physics. Unlike Kilvington but like Bradwardine, he appealed to mathematical calculations in addition to logical and conceptual analysis in the treatment of change, motion, acceleration, and other physical notions. His *Regulae* includes perhaps the most influential treatment of the liar paradox in the Middle Ages. Heytesbury's work makes widespread use of "imaginary" thought experiments assuming physical impossibilities that are yet logically consistent. His influence was especially strong in Italy in the fifteenth century, where his works were studied widely and commented on many times. **See also OXFORD CALCULATORS.**   P.V.S.

hidden variable. See PHILOSOPHY OF SCIENCE, QUANTUM MECHANICS.

hierarchical system. See COMPUTER THEORY.

hierarchy, a division of mathematical objects into subclasses in accordance with an ordering that reflects their complexity. Around the turn of the century, analysts interested in the "descriptive set theory" of the real numbers defined and studied two systems of classification for sets of reals, the Borel (due to Emil Borel) and the G hierarchies. In the 1940s, logicians interested in recursion and definability (most importantly, Stephen Kleene) introduced and studied other hierarchies (the arithmetic, the hyperarithmetic, and the analytical hierarchies) of reals (identified with sets of natural numbers) and of sets of reals; the relations between this work and the earlier work were made explicit in the 1950s by J. Addison. Other sorts of hierarchies have been introduced in other corners of logic. All these so-called hierarchies have at least this in common: they divide a class of mathematical objects into subclasses subject to a natural well-founded ordering (e.g., by subsethood) that reflects the complexity (in a sense specific to the hierarchy under consideration) of the objects they contain. What follows describes several hierarchies from the study of definability. (For more historical and mathematical information see *Descriptive Set Theory* by Y. Moschovakis, North-Holland Publishing Co., 1980.)

(1) Hierarchies of formulas. Consider a formal language L with quantifiers '$\forall$' and '$\exists$'. Given a set B of formulas in L, we inductively define a hierarchy that treats the members of B as "basic." Set $\Pi_0 = \Sigma_0 = B$. Suppose sets Π_n and Σ_n of formulas have been defined. Let Π_{n+1} = the set of all formulas of the form $Q_1 v_1 \ldots Q_m v_m \varphi$ when $v_1, \ldots, v_m$ are distinct variables, $Q_1, \ldots, Q_m$ are all '$\forall$', $m \geq 1$, and $\varphi \in \Sigma_n$. Let Σ_{n+1} = the set of all formulas of that form for $Q_1, \ldots, Q_m$ all '$\exists$', and $\varphi \in \Pi_n$.

Here are two such hierarchies for languages of arithmetic. Take the logical constants to be truth-functions, '$\forall$' and '$\exists$'.

(i) Let L^0 = the first-order language of arithmetic, based on '$=$', a two-place predicate-constant '$<$', an individual-constant for 0, function-constants for successor, addition, and multiplication; 'first-order' means that bound variables are all first-order (ranging over individuals); we'll allow free second-order variables (ranging over properties or sets of individuals). Let B = the set of bounded formulas, i.e. those formed from atomic formulas using connectives and bounded quantification: if φ is bounded so are $\forall v(v < \tau \supset \varphi)$ and $\exists v(v < \tau \& \varphi)$.

(ii) Let L^1 = the second-order language of arithmetic (formed from L^0 by allowing bound second-order variables); let B = the set of formulas in which no second-order variable is bound, and take all $v_1, \ldots, v_m$ as above to be second-order variables.

(2) Hierarchies of definable sets. (i) The Arithmetic Hierarchy. For a set of natural numbers (call such a thing 'a real') $A : A \in \Pi_n^0$ [or Σ_n^0] if and only if A is defined over the standard model of arithmetic (i.e., with the constant for 0 assigned to 0, etc., and with the first-order variables ranging over the natural numbers) by a formula of L^0 in P_n [respectively Σ_n] as described in (1.i). Set $\Delta_n^0 = \Pi_n^0$ Thus:

$$\Pi_0^0 = \Sigma_0^0 \subseteq \Delta_1^0 \begin{array}{c} \subsetneq \Pi_1^0 \subsetneq \\ \subsetneq \Sigma_1^0 \subsetneq \end{array} \Delta_2^0 \begin{array}{c} \subsetneq \Pi_2^0 \subsetneq \\ \subsetneq \Sigma_2^0 \subsetneq \end{array} \Delta_3^0 \ldots$$

In fact, all these inclusions are proper. This hierarchy classifies the reals simple enough to be defined by arithmetic formulas. Example: '$\exists y \, x = y + y'$ defines the set *even* of even natural numbers; the formula $\in \Sigma_1$, so *even* $\in \Sigma_1^0$; *even* is also defined by a formula in Π_1; so *even* $\in \Pi_1^0$, giving *even* $\in \Delta_1^0$. In fact, $\Sigma_1^0 =$ the class of recursively enumerable reals, and $\Delta_1^0 =$ the class of recursive reals. The classification of reals under the arithmetic hierarchy reflects complexity of defining formulas; it differs from classification in terms of a notion of *degree of unsolvability,* that reflecting a notion of comparative computational complexity; but there are connections between these classifications.

The Arithmetic Hierarchy extends to sets of reals (using a free second-order variable in defining sentences). Example: '$\exists x \, (Xx \,\&\, \exists y \, y = x + x)$' $\in \Sigma_1$ and defines the set of those reals with an even number; so that set $\in \Sigma_1^0$.

(ii) The Analytical Hierarchy. Given a real A : $A \in \Pi_n^1 \, [\Sigma_n^1]$ if and only if A is defined (over the standard model of arithmetic with second-order variables ranging over all sets of natural numbers) by a formula of L^1 in Π_n (respectively Σ_n) as described in (1.ii); $\Delta_n^1 = \Pi_n^1 \cap \Sigma_n^1$. Similarly for a set of reals. The inclusions pictured above carry over, replacing superscripted 0's by 1's. This classifies all reals and sets of reals simple enough to have analytical (i.e., second-order arithmetic) definitions.

The subscripted 'n' in 'Π_n^0', etc., ranged over natural numbers. But the Arithmetic Hierarchy is extended "upward" into the transfinite by the ramified-analytical hierarchy. Let $R_0 =$ the class of all arithmetical reals. For an ordinal α let $R_{\alpha+1}$ $=$ the class of all sets of reals definable by formulas of L^1 in which second-order variables range only over reals in R_α – this constraint imposes ramification. For a limit-ordinal λ, let R_λ $= U_{\alpha<\lambda} R_\alpha$. Each R_α for $\alpha > 0$ is further "hierarchized" using the classification of defining formulas given above in (2.i). This process stops yielding new reals at a countable ordinal called β_0. All reals classified by this hierarchy turn out to be in Σ_2^1. The initial segment of this hierarchy for which the ordinals are recursive (i.e., constructive) is the hyperarithmetic hierarchy; reals it classifies turn out to be exactly the Δ_1^1 reals.

The above hierarchies arise in arithmetic. Similar hierarchies arise in pure set theory; e.g. by transferring the "process" that produced the ramified analytical hierarchy to pure set theory we obtain the constructible hierarchy, defined by Gödel in his 1939 monograph on the continuum hypothesis.

See also DEGREE OF UNSOLVABILITY, MATHEMATICAL ANALYSIS, SET THEORY.   H.T.H.

higher order. See ORDER.

higher-order logic. See FORMAL LOGIC, PHILOSOPHY OF LOGIC, SECOND-ORDER LOGIC.

Hilbert, David (1862–1943), German mathematician and philosopher of mathematics. Born in Königsberg, he also studied and served on the faculty there, accepting Weber's chair in mathematics at Göttingen in 1895. He made important contributions to many different areas of mathematics and was renowned for his grasp of the entire discipline. His more philosophical work was divided into two parts. The focus of the first, which occupied approximately ten years beginning in the early 1890s, was the foundations of geometry and culminated in his celebrated *Grundlagen der Geometrie* (1899). This is a rich and complex work that pursues a variety of different projects simultaneously. Prominent among these is one whose aim is to determine the role played in geometrical reasoning by principles of continuity. Hilbert's interest in this project was rooted in Kantian concerns, as is confirmed by the inscription, in the *Grundlagen,* of Kant's synopsis of his critical philosophy: "Thus all human knowledge begins with intuition, goes from there to concepts and ends with ideas."

Kant believed that the continuous could not be represented in intuition and must therefore be regarded as an idea of pure reason – i.e., as a device playing a purely regulative role in the development of our geometrical knowledge (i.e., our knowledge of the spatial manifold of sensory experience). Hilbert was deeply influenced by this view of Kant's and his work in the foundations of geometry can be seen, in large part, as an attempt to test it by determining whether (or to what extent) pure geometry can be developed without appeal to principles concerning the nature of the continuous. To a considerable extent, Hilbert's work confirmed Kant's view – showing, in a manner more precise than any Kant had managed, that appeals to the continuous can indeed be eliminated from much of our geometrical reasoning.

The same basic Kantian orientation also governed the second phase of Hilbert's foundational work, where the focus was changed from geometry to arithmetic and analysis. This is the phase during which *Hilbert's Program* was developed. This project began to take shape in the 1917 essay "Axiomatisches Denken." (The 1904 paper "Über die Grundlagen der Logik und Arithmetik," which turned away from geometry and toward arithmetic, does not yet contain more than a glimmer of the ideas that would later become central to Hilbert's proof theory.) It reached its philosophically most mature form in the 1925 essay "Über das Unendliche," the 1926 address "Die Grundlagen der Mathematik," and the somewhat more popular 1930 paper "Naturerkennen und Logik." (From a technical as opposed to a philosophical vantage, the classical statement is probably the 1922 essay "Neubegründung der Mathematik. Erste Mitteilung.") The key elements of the program are (i) a distinction between *real* and *ideal* propositions and methods of proof or derivation; (ii) the idea that the so-called ideal methods, though, again, playing the role of Kantian regulative devices (as Hilbert explicitly and emphatically declared in the 1925 paper), are nonetheless indispensable for a reasonably efficient development of our mathematical knowledge; and (iii) the demand that the reliability of the ideal methods be established by real (or finitary) means.

As is well known, Hilbert's Program soon came under heavy attack from Gödel's incompleteness theorems (especially the second), which have commonly been regarded as showing that the third element of Hilbert's Program (i.e., the one calling for a finitary proof of the reliability of the ideal systems of classical mathematics) cannot be carried out.

See also GÖDEL'S INCOMPLETENESS THEOREMS, HILBERT'S PROGRAM, PROOF THEORY.

M.D.

Hilbert's Program, a proposal in the foundations of mathematics, named for its developer, the German mathematician-philosopher David Hilbert, who first formulated it fully in the 1920s. Its aim was to justify classical mathematics (in particular, classical analysis and set theory), though only as a Kantian regulative device and not as descriptive science. The justification thus presupposed a division of classical mathematics into two parts: the part (termed *real* mathematics by Hilbert) to be regulated, and the part (termed *ideal* mathematics by Hilbert) serving as regulator.

Real mathematics was taken to consist of the meaningful, true propositions of mathematics and their justifying proofs. These proofs – commonly known as finitary proofs – were taken to be of an especially elementary epistemic character, reducing, ultimately, to quasi-perceptual intuitions concerning finite assemblages of perceptually intuitable signs regarded from the point of view of their shapes and sequential arrangement. Ideal mathematics, on the other hand, was taken to consist of sentences that do not express genuine propositions and derivations that do not

constitute genuine proofs or justifications. The epistemic utility of ideal sentences (typically referred to as ideal propositions, though, as noted above, they do not express genuine propositions at all) and proofs was taken to derive not from their meaning and/or evidentness, but rather from the role they play in some formal algebraic or calculary scheme intended to identify or locate the real truths. It is thus a metatheoretic function of the formal or algebraic properties induced on those propositions and proofs by their positions in a larger derivational scheme. Hilbert's ideal mathematics was thus intended to bear the same relation to his real mathematics as Kant's faculty of pure reason was intended to bear to his faculty of understanding. It was to be a regulative device whose proper function is to guide and facilitate the development of our system of real judgments. Indeed, in his 1925 essay "Über das Unendliche," Hilbert made just this point, noting that ideal elements do not correspond to anything in reality but serve only as *ideas* "if, following Kant's terminology, one understands as an idea a concept of reason which transcends all experience and by means of which the concrete is to be completed into a totality."

The structure of Hilbert's scheme, however, involves more than just the division of classical mathematics into real and ideal propositions and proofs. It uses, in addition, a subdivision of the real propositions into the problematic and the unproblematic. Indeed, it is this subdivision of the reals that is at bottom responsible for the introduction of the ideals. Unproblematic real propositions, described by Hilbert as the basic equalities and inequalities of arithmetic (e.g., '3 > 2', '2 < 3', '2 + 3 = 3 + 2') together with their sentential (and certain of their bounded quantificational) compounds, are the evidentially most basic judgments of mathematics. They are immediately intelligible and decidable by finitary intuition. More importantly, they can be logically manipulated in all the ways that classical logic allows without leading outside the class of real propositions. The characteristic feature of the problematic reals, on the other hand, is that they cannot be so manipulated.

Hilbert gave two kinds of examples of problematic real propositions. One consisted of universal generalizations like 'for any non-negative integer a, $a + 1 = 1 + a$', which Hilbert termed hypothetical judgments. Such propositions are problematic because their denials do not bound the search for counterexamples. Hence, the instance of the (classical) law of excluded middle that is obtained by disjoining it with its denial is not itself a real proposition. Consequently, it cannot be manipulated in all the ways permitted by classical logic without going outside the class of real propositions. Similarly for the other kind of problematic real discussed by Hilbert, which was a bounded existential quantification. Every such sentence has as one of its classical consequents an unbounded existential quantification of the same matrix. Hence, since the latter is not a real proposition, the former is not a real proposition that can be fully manipulated by classical logical means without going outside the class of real propositions. It is therefore "problematic."

The question why full classical logical manipulability should be given such weight points up an important element in Hilbert's thinking: namely, that classical logic is regarded as the preferred logic of human thinking – the logic of the optimally functioning human epistemic engine, the logic according to which the human mind most naturally and efficiently conducts its inferential affairs. It therefore has a special psychological status and it is because of this that the right to its continued use must be preserved. As just indicated, however, preservation of this right requires addition of ideal propositions and proofs to their real counterparts, since applying classical logic to the truths of real mathematics leads to a system that contains ideal as well as real elements.

Hilbert believed that to justify such an addition, all that was necessary was to show it to be consistent with real mathematics (i.e., to show that it proves no real proposition that is itself refutable by real means). Moreover, Hilbert believed that this must be done by finitary means. The proof of Gödel's second incompleteness theorem in 1931 brought considerable pressure to bear on this part of Hilbert's Program even though it may not have demonstrated its unattainability.

See also BROUWER, GÖDEL'S INCOMPLETENESS THEOREMS, HILBERT, PHILOSOPHY OF MATHEMATICS.   M.D.

Hinayana Buddhism. See BUDDHISM.

Hinduism, the group of religious and philosophical traditions of India that accept the doctrinal authority of the Vedas and Upanishads, comprising the schools Mīmāmsā, Sankhya-Yoga, Nyāya-Vaishesika, and Vedanta (six in number, with the connection within pairs of schools, indicated by hyphenation, based on historical and conceptual linkages). Most of the standard issues in Greco-European philosophy receive independent discussion in classical Indian thought. Perhaps the closest Indian term to 'philosophy' is *darśana* (seeing); the goal of philosophy is typically taken to be not simply understanding, but enlightenment (*moksha*), which involves escape from the reincarnation cycle and from karma. All of the orthodox schools formally accept the doctrines that the individual Ātman beginninglessly transmigrates from body to body unless it attains enlightenment and that in each lifetime the Ātman acts and hence accumulates consequences of its actions that will accrue to it in future lifetimes (karma), though some schools (notably Advaita Vedanta) hold metaphysical views that radically alter any meaning that the doctrines of transmigration and karma can have.

The "seeing" typically involves embracing the content of the sacred texts and being transformed by it. In the same general cultural and intellectual context as Hinduism, Cārvāka rejects any such notion of philosophy, and Jainism, Buddhism, and some varieties of Hinduism reject monotheism though all but Cārvāka accept some sort of religious perspective and center on some notion of enlightenment.

Metaphysics, epistemology, logic, and ethics are richly represented in Hinduism. As is typical in Greco-European philosophy, apart from (e.g.) some of the medieval Scholastics and contemporary symbolic logicians, study of deductive inference and probability is not sharply distinguished from epistemology, though in Hinduism it is typically marked off from psychological considerations.

There are debates about the success of natural theology, with versions (e.g.) of teleological and contingency arguments and discussions of the problem of evil, the latter typically being related to a consideration of justice and karma. Monotheistic views typically regard the world as everlastingly dependent on Brahman rather than as having been created after a period in which nothing dependent existed or as a condition of there being time at all. Typically, the universe is seen as oscillating between states in which atoms have come together into bodies that provide embodiment for transmigrating souls and states in which atoms come apart and souls remain inactive.

Disputes occur concerning the nature of persons and personal identity, pluralism versus monism, and a personal Deity versus an Absolute. Advaita Vedanta apparently holds that it is logically impossible for *B* to depend upon *A* and for *B* also to be an individual distinct from *A*, whereas the other varieties of Vedanta hold (in different ways) that dependence does not rule out distinct individuality. The former assumption is compatible with (though it does not entail) monism and the latter allows for (but does not require) monotheism. There are pluralistic (thus non-monistic) schools that are not monotheistic. Schools differ about whether the variety of conscious and self-conscious states belongs intrinsically to souls or only to soul-body composites; those holding the former view think of persons or minds as transmigrating from life to life, whereas those holding the latter view have a thinner notion of the traveler. There are debates among schools of Hinduism, Buddhism, and Jainism over whether a substantival or an event or state account of persons and objects is more defensible. For some schools, immaterial souls and material atoms exist both beginninglessly and independently. For others they exist beginninglessly and dependently. For still others, no such things exist at all.

Epistemology, logic, and philosophy of language flourish. Questions concerning evidence are discussed along the lines of what counts as a valid source of knowledge (e.g., perception, inference, testimony). Indian grammarians developed techniques of reducing complex expressions to simple ones and developed a use–mention distinction. Mīmāmsa philosophers were concerned with the logical analysis of prescriptions. Vaishesika thinkers were concerned to classify the meanings of words, offering the categories of substance, quality, action, universal, ultimate difference, inherence, and absence, and found the result of both logical and ontological significance.

Ethics is also richly represented, typically within a perspective in which the highest good (*moksha*, enlightenment) is viewed as escape from the beginningless cycle of rebirth and the clutches of karma, with the content of the highest good being very diversely conceived. Sometimes enlightenment is conceived as involving retention of personal identity, sometimes as involving loss thereof; sometimes a view is held that denies that there is anything to preserve. Thus moral philosophy is typically done in the light of explicitly religious, or at least metaphysical, doctrines. The Cārvāka perspectives, at least as interpreted by their opponents, either accept hedonism or eschew ethics entirely. For some metaphysical and religious views, morality has to do only with those activities that one must engage in or refuse to engage in to achieve an enlightenment that contains no moral component and perhaps involves nothing along the lines of one's identity as a person; in such contexts, moral values serve religious values that themselves contain no moral element. In other perspectives, the status of persons is such that their continued existence as distinct persons is required in order for enlightenment to occur and moral elements enter intrinsically into the nature of the highest good.

The classical Hindu philosopher typically in effect accepts some such proposition as the following: The Hindu scriptures contain the truth about the nature of what is ultimately real, about the nature of the human self, and about how to obtain the highest good. Some critics – including Indian unorthodox materialists – argue that there cannot be any genuine philosophy in Hinduism. (Similar questions are raised concerning Jewish, Christian, and Muslim medieval philosophers.) The acceptance of the indicated proposition does not tell one what the truth about ultimate reality, the self, or the highest good is; various quite different accounts of these matters are presented within the Hindu scriptures. This creates a problem: since the texts are authoritative their teachings must be true. Inconsistent propositions cannot be true; showing that your opponent's views are self-contradictory is a refutation within philosophical Hinduism as much as in Anglo-American analytic circles. Hence the teachings of the texts must be consistent, and so not everything in them can be read literally. In sum, it is not obvious what in the authoritative texts is to be read literally and what non-literally, but since patently contradictory doctrines are offered if one reads everything literally, something must be read non-literally (or as provisional, the best that some people can understand until they become more capable). Thus if one accepts the indicated proposition one must decide which of the textual accounts is the right one – the one *ex hypothesi* intended by the texts to be taken as their literal doctrine. Deciding this typically is not a matter of simple exegesis. Thus one must decide what grounds are required in order to establish that it is one rather than another of these views that is intended literally. Often the de facto answer is that the intended view is the *true* view, with the issue as to which view is true being decided in substantial part by reference to reason and experience and by "how the argument goes." Further, the views presented in the authoritative text, once one has decided what they literally are, will likely have various philosophical implications. (For example, perhaps surprisingly, Rāmānuja's theory of perceptual error relates intimately to his views on the divine attributes.) Some of these implications may seem false, and if this happens there is a *modus tollens* consideration that leads to asking again what the text really means. But even if no such consideration arises, the philosophical implications of a position are likely themselves to need explication if they are to be clearly understood.

In Hinduism philosophy typically is done in a commentarial setting, though (as in European medieval contexts) once the commentator is doing philosophy he often goes on to topics very far indeed from the views discussed in the texts. Of course, the more wide-ranging a commentary is, the less unnatural it is that a commentary on that commentary be even more wide-ranging; thus a relatively independent philosophical tradition arises. The result is a very considerable body of philosophical literature and tradition in India that can be approached without assuming anything about the indicated proposition, one way or another.

See also ĀTMAN, BRAHMAN, KARMA, UPAN-ISHADS, VEDAS.   K.E.Y.

Hintikka, Jaakko (b.1929), Finnish philosopher with contributions to logic, philosophy of mathematics, epistemology, linguistics and philosophy of language, philosophy of science, and history of philosophy. His work on distributive normal forms and model set techniques yielded an improved inductive logic. Model sets differ from Carnap's state-descriptions in being partial and not complete descriptions of "possible worlds." The techniques simplified metatheoretical proofs and led to new results in e.g. probability theory and the semantic theory of information. Their main philosophical import nevertheless is in bridging the gap between proof theory and model theory.

Model sets that describe several possible "alternative" worlds lead to the possible worlds semantics for modal and intensional logics. Hintikka has used them as a foundation for the logic of propositional attitudes (epistemic logic and the logic of perception), and in studies on individuation, identification, and intentionality. Epistemic logic also provides a basis for Hintikka's logic of questions, in which conclusiveness conditions for answers can be defined. This has resulted in an interrogative model of inquiry in which knowledge-seeking is viewed as a pursuit of conclusive answers to initial "big" questions by strategically organized series of "small" questions (put to nature or to another source of information). The applications include scientific

discovery and explanation. Hintikka's independence-friendly logic gives the various applications a unified basis.

Hintikka's background philosophy and approach to formal semantics and its applications is broadly Kantian with emphasis on seeking-and-finding methods and the constitutive activity of the inquirer. Apart from a series of studies inspired by Kant, he has written extensively on Aristotle, Plato, Descartes, Leibniz, Frege, and Wittgenstein. Hintikka's academic career has been not only in Finland, chiefly at the University of Helsinki, but (especially) in the United States, where he has held professorships at Stanford, Florida State, and (currently) Boston University. His students and co-workers in the Finnish school of inductive logic and in other areas include Leila Haaparanta (b.1954), Risto Hilpinen (b.1943), Simo Knuuttila (b.1946), Martin Kusch (b.1959), Ilkka Niiniluoto (b.1946), Juhani Pietarinen (b.1938), Veikko Rantala (b.1933), Gabriel Sandu (b.1954), Matti Sintonen (b.1951), and Raimo Tuomela (b.1940).

See also EROTETIC LOGIC, HINTIKKA SET, INDUCTIVE LOGIC, MODEL THEORY, POSSIBLE WORLDS, PROOF THEORY.   M.T.S.

Hintikka set, also called *model set, downward saturated set,* a set (of a certain sort) of well-formed formulas that are all true under a single interpretation of their non-logical symbols (named after Jaakko Hintikka). Such a set can be thought of as a (partial) description of a logically possible state of affairs, or possible world, full enough to make evident that the world described is indeed possible. Thus it is required of a Hintikka set Γ that it contain no atomic formula and its negation, that $A, B \in \Gamma$ if $A \wedge B \in \Gamma$, that $A \in \Gamma$ or $B \in \Gamma$ if $A \vee B \in \Gamma$, and so forth, for each logical constant. See also POSSIBLE WORLDS, SET THEORY.   G.F.S.

Hippias of Elis. See SOPHISTS.

Hippocrates (fifth century B.C.), semilegendary Greek physician from Cos. Some sixty treatises survive under his name, but it is doubtful whether he was the author of any of them. The Hippocratic corpus contains material from a wide variety of standpoints, ranging from an extreme empiricism that rejected all grand theory (*On Ancient Medicine*) to highly speculative theoretical physiology (*On the Nature of Man, On Regimen*). Many treatises were concerned with the accurate observation and classification of diseases (*Epi-*

demics) rather than treatment. Some texts (*On the Art*) defended the claims of medicine to scientific status against those who pointed to its inaccuracies and conjectural status; others (*Oath, On Decorum*) sketch a code of professional ethics. Almost all his treatises were notable for their materialism and rejection of supernatural "explanations"; their emphasis on observation; and their concern with the isolation of causal factors. A large number of texts are devoted to gynecology. The Hippocratic corpus became the standard against which later doctors measured themselves; and, via Galen's rehabilitation and extension of Hippocratic method, it became the basis for Western medicine for two millennia.

R.J.H.

historical determinism. See MARXISM.

historicality. See PHILOSOPHY OF HISTORY.

historical jurisprudence. See JURISPRUDENCE.

historical materialism. See ENGELS.

historical theory of reference. See PHILOSOPHY OF LANGUAGE.

historicism, the doctrine that knowledge of human affairs has an irreducibly historical character and that there can be no ahistorical perspective for an understanding of human nature and society. What is needed instead is a philosophical explication of historical knowledge that will yield the rationale for all sound knowledge of human activities.

So construed, historicism is a philosophical doctrine originating in the methodological and epistemological presuppositions of critical historiography. In the mid-nineteenth century certain German thinkers (Dilthey most centrally), reacting against positivist ideals of science and knowledge, rejected scientistic models of knowledge, replacing them with historical ones. They applied this not only to the discipline of history but to economics, law, political theory, and large areas of philosophy. Initially concerned with methodological issues in particular disciplines, historicism, as it developed, sought to work out a common philosophical doctrine that would inform all these disciplines. What is essential to achieve knowledge in the human sciences is to employ the ways of understanding used in historical studies. There should in the human sciences be no search for natural laws; knowledge there will be interpretive and rooted in concrete historical occurrences. As such it will be inescapably perspectival and contextual (contextualism). This raises the issue of whether historicism is a form of historical relativism. Historicism appears to be committed to the thesis that what for a given people is warrantedly assertible is determined by the distinctive historical perspective in which they view life and society. The stress on uniqueness and concrete specificity and the rejection of any appeal to universal laws of human development reinforce that. But the emphasis on cumulative development into larger contexts of our historical knowledge puts in doubt an identification of historicism and historical relativism.

The above account of historicism is that of its main proponents: Meinecke, Croce, Collingwood, Ortega y Gasset, and Mannheim. But in the twentieth century, with Popper and Hayek, a very different conception of historicism gained some currency. For them, to be a historicist is to believe that there are "historical laws," indeed even a "law of historical development," such that history has a pattern and even an end, that it is the central task of social science to discover it, and that these laws should determine the direction of political action and social policy. They attributed (incorrectly) this doctrine to Marx but rightly denounced it as pseudo-science. However, some later Marxists (Lukács, Korsch, and Gramsci) were historicists in the original non-Popperian sense as was the critical theorist Adorno and hermeneuticists such as Gadamer.

See also COLLINGWOOD, CROCE, DILTHEY, ENGELS, PHILOSOPHY OF HISTORY.   K.N.

historicity. See PHILOSOPHY OF HISTORY.

history, philosophy of. See PHILOSOPHY OF HISTORY.

Hobbes, Thomas (1588–1679), English philosopher whose writings, especially the English version of *Leviathan* (1651), strongly influenced all of subsequent English moral and political philosophy. He also wrote a trilogy comprising *De Cive* (1642; English version, *Philosophical Rudiments Concerning Government and Society*, 1651), *De Corpore* (*On the Body*, 1655), and *De Homine* (*On Man*, 1658). Together with *Leviathan* (the revised Latin version of which was published in 1668), these are his major philosophical works. However, an early draft of his thoughts, *The Elements of Law, Natural and Political* (also known as *Human Nature* and *De Corpore Politico*), was published without permission in 1650. Many of the misinterpretations of Hobbes's views on human nature come from mistaking this early work as representing his mature views.

Hobbes was influential not only in England, but also on the Continent. He is the author of the third set of objections to Descartes's *Meditations*. Spinoza's *Tractatus Theologico-politicus* was deeply influenced by Hobbes, not only in its political views but also in the way it dealt with Scripture. Hobbes was not merely a philosopher; he was mathematical tutor to Charles II and also a classical scholar. His first published work was a translation of Thucydides (1628), and among his latest, about a half-century later, were translations of Homer's *Iliad* and *Odyssey*.

Hobbes's philosophical views have a remarkably contemporary sound. In metaphysics, he holds a strong materialist view, sometimes viewing mental phenomena as epiphenomenal, but later moving toward a reductive or eliminative view. In epistemology he held a sophisticated empiricism, which emphasized the importance of language for knowledge. If not the originator of the contemporary compatibilist view of the relationship between free will and determinism (see *The Questions Concerning Liberty, Necessity and Chance*, 1656), he was one of the primary influences. He also was one of the most important philosophers of language, explicitly noting that language is used not only to describe the world but to express attitudes and, performatively, to make promises and contracts.

One of Hobbes's outstanding characteristics is his intellectual honesty. Though he may have been timid (he himself claims that he was, explaining that his mother gave birth to him because of fright over the coming of the Spanish Armada), his writing shows no trace of it. During more than half his long lifetime he engaged in many philosophical controversies, which required considerably more courage in Hobbes's day than at present. Both the Roman Catholic church and Oxford University banned the reading of his books and there was talk not only of burning his books but of burning Hobbes himself.

An adequate interpretation of Hobbes requires careful attention to his accounts of human nature, reason, morality, and law. Although he was not completely consistent, his moral and political philosophy is remarkably coherent. His political theory is often thought to require an egoistic psychology, whereas it actually requires only that most persons be concerned with their own self-interest, especially their own preservation. It does not require that most not be concerned with other persons as well. All that Hobbes denies is an undifferentiated natural

benevolence: "For if by nature one man should love another (that is) as man, there could no reason be returned why every man should not equally love every man, as being equally man." His argument is that limited benevolence is not an adequate foundation upon which to build a state.

Hobbes's political theory does not require the denial of limited benevolence, he indeed includes benevolence in his list of the passions in *Leviathan*: "*Desire* of good to another, BENEVOLENCE, GOOD WILL, CHARITY. If to man generally, GOOD NATURE." Psychological egoism not only denies benevolent action, it also denies action done from a moral sense, i.e., action done because one believes it is the morally right thing to do. But Hobbes denies neither kind of action.

> But when the words ['just' and 'unjust'] are applied to persons, to be just signifies as much as to be delighted in just dealing, to study how to do righteousness, or to endeavor in all things to do that which is just; and to be unjust is to neglect righteous dealing, or to think it is to be measured not according to my contract, but some present benefit.

Hobbes's pessimism about the number of just people is primarily due to his awareness of the strength of the passions and his conviction that most people have not been properly educated and disciplined.

Hobbes is one of the few philosophers to realize that to talk of that part of human nature which involves the passions is to talk about human populations. He says, "though the wicked were fewer than the righteous, yet because we cannot distinguish them, there is a necessity of suspecting, heeding, anticipating, subjugating, self-defending, ever incident to the most honest and fairest conditioned." Though we may be aware of small communities in which mutual trust and respect make law enforcement unnecessary, this is never the case when we are dealing with a large group of people. Hobbes's point is that if a large group of people are to live together, there must be a common power set up to enforce the rules of the society. That there is not now, nor has there ever been, any large group of people living together without such a common power is sufficient to establish his point.

Often overlooked is Hobbes's distinction between people considered as if they were simply animals, not modified in any way by education or discipline, and civilized people. Though obviously an abstraction, people as animals are fairly well exemplified by children. "Unless you give children all they ask for, they are peevish, and cry, aye and strike their parents sometimes; and all this they have from nature." In the state of nature, people have no education or training, so there is "continual fear, and danger of violent death, and the life of man, [is] solitary, poor, nasty, brutish, and short." But real people have been brought up in families; they are, at least to some degree, civilized persons, and how they will behave depends on how they are brought up. Hobbes does not say that society is a collection of misfits and that this is why we have all the trouble that we do – a position congenial to the psychological egoist. But he does acknowledge that "many also (perhaps most men) either through defect of mind, or want of education, remain unfit during the whole course of their lives; yet have they, infants as well as those of riper years, a human nature; wherefore man is made fit for society not by nature, but by education." Education and training may change people so that they act out of genuine moral motives. That is why it is one of the most important functions of the sovereign to provide for the proper training and education of the citizens. In the current debate between nature and nurture, on the question of behavior Hobbes would come down strongly on the side of nurture.

Hobbes's concept of reason has more in common with the classical philosophical tradition stemming from Plato and Aristotle, where reason sets the ends of behavior, than with the modern tradition stemming from Hume where the only function of reason is to discover the best means to ends set by the passions. For Hobbes, reason is very complex; it has a goal, lasting self-preservation, and it seeks the way to this goal. It also discovers the means to ends set by the passions, but it governs the passions, or tries to, so that its own goal is not threatened. Since its goal is the same in all people, it is the source of rules applying to all people. All of this is surprisingly close to the generally accepted account of rationality. We generally agree that those who follow their passions when they threaten their life are acting irrationally. We also believe that everyone always ought to act rationally, though we know that few always do so. Perhaps it was just the closeness of Hobbes's account of reason to the ordinary view of the matter that has led to its being so completely overlooked.

The failure to recognize that the avoidance of violent death is the primary goal of reason has distorted almost all accounts of Hobbes's moral and political philosophy, yet it is a point on which Hobbes is completely clear and consistent.

He explicitly says that reason "teaches every man to fly a contra-natural dissolution [*mortem violentam*] as the greatest mischief that can arrive to nature." He continually points out that it is a dictate of right reason to seek peace when possible because people cannot "expect any lasting preservation continuing thus in the state of nature, that is, of war." And he calls temperance and fortitude precepts of reason because they tend to one's preservation.

It has not generally been recognized that Hobbes regarded it as an end of reason to avoid violent death because he often talks of the avoidance of death in a way that makes it seem merely an object of a passion. But it is reason that dictates that one take all those measures necessary for one's preservation; peace if possible, if not, defense. Reason's dictates are categorical; it would be a travesty of Hobbes's view to regard the dictates of reason as hypothetical judgments addressed to those whose desire for their own preservation happens to be greater than any conflicting desire. He explicitly deplores the power of the irrational appetites and expressly declares that it is a dictate of reason that one not scorn others because "most men would rather lose their lives (that I say not, their peace) than suffer slander." He does not say if you would rather die than suffer slander, it is rational to do so.

Hobbes, following Aristotle, regards morality as concerned with character traits or habits. Since morality is objective, it is only those habits that are called good by reason that are moral virtues. "Reason declaring peace to be good, it follows by the same reason, that all the necessary means to peace be good also; and therefore that modesty, equity, trust, humanity, mercy (which we have demonstrated to be necessary to peace), are good manners or habits, that is, virtues." Moral virtues are those habits of acting that the reason of all people must praise. It is interesting to note that it is only in *De Homine* that Hobbes explicitly acknowledges that on this account, prudence, temperance, and courage are not moral virtues. In *De Cive* he distinguishes temperance and fortitude from the other virtues and does not call them moral, but he does not explicitly deny that they are moral virtues. But in *De Homine,* he explicitly points out that one should not "demand that the courage and prudence of the private man, if useful only to himself, be praised or held as a virtue by states or by any other men whatsoever to whom these same are not useful."

That morality is determined by reason and that reason has as its goal self-preservation seems to lead to the conclusion that morality also has as its goal self-preservation. But it is not the self-preservation of an individual person that is the goal of morality, but of people as citizens of a state. That is, moral virtues are those habits of persons that make it rational for all other people to praise them. These habits are not those that merely lead to an individual's own preservation, but to the preservation of all; i.e., to peace and a stable society. Thus, "Good dispositions are those that are suitable for entering into civil society; and good manners (that is, moral virtues) are those whereby what was entered upon can be best preserved." And in *De Cive*, when talking of morality, he says, "The goodness of actions consist[s] in this, that it [is] in order to peace, and the evil in this, that it [is] related to discord."

The nature of morality is a complex and vexing question. If, like Hobbes, we regard morality as applying primarily to those manners or habits that lead to peace, then his view seems satisfactory. It yields, as he notes, all of the moral virtues that are ordinarily considered such, and further, it allows one to distinguish courage, prudence, and temperance from the moral virtues. Perhaps most important, it provides, in almost self-evident fashion, the justification of morality. For what is it to justify morality but to show that reason favors it? Reason, seeking self-preservation, must favor morality, which seeks peace and a stable society. For reason knows that peace and a stable society are essential for lasting preservation. This simple and elegant justification of morality does not reduce morality to prudence; rather it is an attempt, in a great philosophical tradition stemming from Plato, to reconcile reason or rational self-interest and morality.

In the state of nature every person is and ought to be governed only by their own reason. Reason dictates that they seek peace, which yields the laws of nature, but it also allows them to use any means they believe will best preserve themselves, which is what Hobbes calls *The Right of Nature*. Hobbes's insight is to see that, except when one is in clear and present danger, in which case one has an inalienable right to defend oneself, the best way to guarantee one's long-term preservation is to give up one's right to act on one's own decisions about what is the best way to guarantee one's long-term preservation and agree to act on the decisions of that single person or group who is the sovereign. If all individuals and groups are allowed to act on the decisions they regard as best, not accepting the commands of the sovereign, i.e., the laws, as the overriding guide for their actions, the result is anarchy and civil war. Except in rare and unusual cases, uniformity of action following the decision of the sovereign is more likely to lead to long-term preservation than diverse actions following diverse decisions. And this is true even if each one of the diverse decisions, if accepted by the sovereign as its decision, would have been more likely to lead to long-term preservation than the actual decision that the sovereign made.

This argument explains why Hobbes holds that sovereigns cannot commit injustice. Only injustice can properly be punished. Hobbes does not deny that sovereigns can be immoral, but he does deny that the immorality of sovereigns can properly be punished. This is important, for otherwise any immoral act by the sovereign would serve as a pretext for punishing the sovereign, i.e., for civil war. What is just and unjust is determined by the laws of the state, what is moral and immoral is not. Morality is a wider concept than that of justice and is determined by what leads to peace and stability. However, to let justice be determined by what the reason of the people takes to lead to peace and stability, rather than by what the reason of the sovereign decides, would be to invite discord and civil war, which is contrary to the goal of morality: a stable society and peace. One can create an air of paradox by saying that for Hobbes it is immoral to attempt to punish some immoral acts, namely, those of the sovereign. Hobbes is willing to accept this seeming paradox for he never loses sight of the goal of morality, which is peace.

To summarize Hobbes's system: people, insofar as they are rational, want to live out their natural lives in peace and security. To do this, they must come together into cities or states of sufficient size to deter attack by any group. But when people come together in such a large group there will always be some that cannot be trusted, and thus it is necessary to set up a government with the power to make and enforce laws. This government, which gets both its right to govern and its power to do so from the consent of the governed, has as its primary duty the people's safety. As long as the government provides this safety the citizens are obliged to obey the laws of the state in all things. Thus, the rationality of seeking lasting preservation requires seeking peace; this in turn requires setting up a state with sufficient power to keep the peace. Anything that threatens the stability of the state is to be avoided.

As a practical matter, Hobbes took God and religion very seriously, for he thought they provided some of the strongest motives for action. Half of *Leviathan* is devoted to trying to show that his moral and political views are supported by Scripture, and to discredit those religious views that may lead to civil strife. But accepting the sincerity of Hobbes's religious views does not require holding that Hobbes regarded God as the foundation of morality. He explicitly denies that atheists and deists are subject to the commands of God, but he never denies that they are subject to the laws of nature or of the civil state. Once one recognizes that, for Hobbes, reason itself provides a guide to conduct to be followed by all people, there is absolutely no need to bring in God. For in his moral and political theory there is nothing that God can do that is not already done by reason.

See also CONTRACTARIANISM, NATURAL LAW, POLITICAL PHILOSOPHY.   B.Ge.

Hohenheim, Theophrastus Bombastus von. See PARACELSUS.

Hohfeld, Wesley Newcomb (1879–1918), American jurist who taught at Stanford and Yale. His main contribution to legal and moral theory was his identification of eight fundamental legal conceptions:

One person X has a legal *duty* to a second person Y to do some act A when the law requires X to do A for Y.

X has a legal *privilege* (or liberty) in face of Y to do A when X has no legal duty to Y not to do A.

X has a legal *right* (or claim) against Y that Y do A when Y has a legal duty to X to do A.

X has a legal *no-right* against Y that Y not do A when Y has a legal liberty in face of X to do A.

X has a legal *power* over Y to effect some legal consequence C for Y when there is some voluntary action of X that will bring about C for Y.

X has a legal *disability* in face of Y to effect C when there is no action X can perform that will bring about C for Y.

X has a legal *liability* in face of Y to effect C when Y has a legal power to effect C for X.

X has a legal *immunity* against Y from C when Y has no legal power over X to effect C.

Moral philosophers have adapted Hohfeld's terminology to express analogous moral conceptions.

In jurisprudence or ethics, these fundamental conceptions provide something like atoms into which all more complex legal or moral relationships can be analyzed. In logic, these conceptions reveal pairs of correlatives, such as a claim of X against Y and a duty of Y to X, each of which implies the other, and pairs of opposites, such as a duty of X to Y and a liberty of Y in face of X, which are contradictories. In the theory of rights, his distinctions between liberties, claims, powers, and immunities are often used to reveal ambiguities in the language of rights or to classify species of rights.

See also DUTY, ETHICS, RIGHTS.   C.We.

Holbach, Paul-Henri-Dietrich d'. See D'HOLBACH.

Hölderlin, Johann Christian Friedrich (1770–1843), German poet, novelist, and dramatist. He studied at Tübingen, where he befriended Schelling and Hegel, and at Jena, where he met Schiller and Fichte. Since Hölderlin never held an academic position or published any of his philosophical writings, his influence on philosophy was primarily through his personality, conversations, and letters. He is widely viewed as the author of the so-called "Oldest System-Program of German Idealism," a fragment that culminates in an exaltation of poetry and a call for a new "mythology of reason." This theme is illustrated in the novel *Hyperion* (1797/99), which criticizes the subjective heroism of ethical idealism, emphasizes the sacred character of nature, and attempts to conflate religion and art as "overseers of reason."

In his veneration of nature and objections to Fichte's treatment of the "Not-I," Hölderlin echoed Schelling's Naturphilosophie. In his Hellenism and his critique of the "philosophy of reflection" (see *Ueber Sein und Urteil* ["On Being and Judgment"]) he anticipated and influenced Hegel. In Hölderlin's exaltation of art as alone capable of revealing the nature of reality, he betrayed a debt to Schiller and anticipated Romanticism. However, his view of the poet possesses a tragic dimension quite foreign to Schelling and the younger Romantics. The artist, as the interpreter of divine nature, mediates between the gods and men, but for this very reason is estranged from his fellows. This aspect of Hölderlin's thought influenced Heidegger.

                                     D.Br.

holism, any of a wide variety of theses that in one way or another affirm the equal or greater reality or the explanatory necessity of the whole of some system in relation to its parts. In philosophy, the issues of holism (the word is more reasonably, but less often, spelled 'wholism') have appeared traditionally in the philosophy of biology, of psychology, and especially of the human sciences. In the context of description, holism with respect to some system maintains that the whole has some properties that its parts lack. This doctrine will ordinarily be trivially true unless it is further held, in the thesis of *descriptive emergentism,* that these properties of the whole cannot be defined by properties of the parts. The view that all properties of the wholes in question can be so defined is *descriptive individualism.* In the context of explanation, holism with respect to some object or system maintains either (1) that the laws of the more complex cases in it are *not* deducible by way of any composition laws or laws of coexistence from the laws of the less complex cases (e.g., that the laws of the behavior of people in groups are not deducible by composition laws or laws of coexistence from the laws of solitary behavior), or (2) that all the variables that constitute the system interact with each other. This denial of deducibility is known also as *metaphysical* or *methodological holism,* whereas affirming the deducibility is *methodological individualism.* In a special case of explanatory holism that presupposes descriptive emergentism, holism is sometimes understood as the thesis that with respect to some system the whole has properties that interact "back" with the properties of its parts. In the philosophy of biology, any of these forms of holism may be known as *vitalism,* while in the philosophy of psychology they have been called *Gestalt* doctrine.

In the philosophy of the social sciences, where 'holism' has had its most common use in philosophy, the many issues have often been reduced to that of metaphysical holism versus methodological individualism. This terminology reflected the positivists' belief that holism was non-empirical in postulating social "wholes" or the reality of society beyond individual persons and their properties and relations (as in Durkheim and other, mostly Continental, thinkers), while individualism was non-metaphysical (i.e., empirical) in relying ultimately only on observable properties in describing and explaining social phenomena.

More recently, 'holism' has acquired additional uses in philosophy, especially in epistemology and philosophy of language. *Doxastic* or *epistemic holism* are theses about the "web of belief," usually something to the effect that a person's beliefs are so connected that their change on any topic may affect their content on any other topic or, perhaps, that the beliefs of a rational person are so connected. *Semantic* or *meaning holism* have both been used to denote either the thesis that the meanings of all terms (or sentences) in a language are so connected that any change of meaning in one of them *may* change any other meaning, or the thesis that changes of belief entail changes of meaning.

See also KÖHLER, METHODOLOGICAL HOLISM, PHILOSOPHY OF BIOLOGY, PHILOSOPHY OF THE SOCIAL SCIENCES, SEMANTIC HOLISM.   L.A.

holism, confirmational. See PHILOSOPHY OF SCIENCE.

holism, doxastic. See HOLISM.

holism, epistemic. See HOLISM.

holism, methodological. See METHODOLOGICAL HOLISM.

holism, semantic. See SEMANTIC HOLISM.

holistic system. See COMPUTER THEORY.

hologram, the image of an object in three dimensions created and reproduced by the use of lasers. Holography is a method for recording and reproducing such images. Holograms are remarkable in that, unlike normal photographs, every part of them contains the complete image but in reduced detail. Thus a small square cut from a hologram can still be laser-illuminated to reveal the whole scene originally holographed, albeit with loss of resolution. This feature made the hologram attractive to proponents of the thesis of distribution of function in the brain, who argued that memories are like holograms, not being located in a single precise engram – as claimed by advocates of localization of function – but distributed across perhaps all of the cortex. Although intriguing, the holographic model of memory storage failed to gain acceptance. Current views favor D. O. Hebb's "cell assembly" concept, in which memories are stored in the connections between a group of neurons. **See also** CONNECTIONISM, PERCEPTION.   T.H.L.

homoeomerity. See HOMOEOMEROUS.

homoeomerous (from Greek *homoiomerēs,* 'of like parts'), having parts, no matter how small, that share the constitutive properties of the whole. The derivative abstract noun is 'homoeomery'. The Greek forms of the adjective and of its corresponding privative 'anhomoeomerous' are used by Aristotle to distinguish between (a) non-uniform parts of living things, e.g., limbs and organs, and (b) biological stuffs, e.g., blood, bone, sap. In spite of being composed of the four elements, each of the biological stuffs, when taken individually and without admixtures, is through-and-through F, where F represents the cluster of the constitutive properties of that stuff. Thus, if a certain physical volume qualifies as blood, all its mathematically possible subvolumes, regardless of size, also qualify as blood. Blood is thus homoeomerous. By contrast, a face or a stomach or a leaf are anhomoeomerous: the parts of a face are not a face, etc. In Aristotle's system, the homoeomery of the biological stuffs is tied to his doctrine of the infinite divisibility of matter. The distinction is prefigured in Plato (*Protagoras* 329d).

The term 'homoeomerous' is stricter in its application than the ordinary terms 'homogeneous' and 'uniform'. For we may speak of a homogeneous entity even if the properties at issue are identically present only in samples that fall above a certain size: the color of the sea can be homogeneously or uniformly blue; but it is not homoeomerously blue.

The adjective *homoiomerēs, -es,* and the noun *homoiomereia* also occur – probably tendentiously, under the influence of Aristotle's usage – in our ancient sources for a pre-Aristotelian philosopher, Anaxagoras of Clazomenae, with reference to the constituent "things" (*chrēmata*) involved in the latter's scheme of universal mixture. Moreover, the concept of homoeomery has played a significant role outside ancient Greek philosophy, notably in twentieth-century accounts of the contrast between mass terms and count terms or sortals.

See also ANAXAGORAS, ARISTOTLE, COUNT NOUN, SORTAL PREDICATE.   A.P.D.M.

homoeomery. See HOMOEOMEROUS.

homoiousian. See HOMOOUSIOS.

homological. See SET-THEORETIC PARADOXES.

homomorphism, in model theory, a structure-preserving mapping from one structure to another. A structure consists of a domain of objects together with a function specifying interpretations, with respect to that domain, of the relation symbols, function symbols, and individual symbols of a given language. Relations, functions, and individuals in different structures for a

language L *correspond* to one another if they are interpretations of the same symbol of L. To call a mapping "structure-preserving" is to say (1) that if objects in the first structure bear a certain relation to one another, then their images in the second structure (under the mapping) bear the corresponding relation to one another, (2) that the value of a function for a given object (or n-tuple of objects) in the first structure has as its image under the mapping the value of the corresponding function for the image of the object (or n-tuple of images) in the second structure, and (3) that the image in the second structure of an object in the first is the corresponding object. An *isomorphism* is a homomorphism that is one-to-one and whose inverse is also a homomorphism. **See also** MODEL THEORY.   R.Ke.

homonymy. See AMBIGUITY.

homoousian. See HOMOOUSIOS.

homoousios (Greek, 'of the same substance'), a concept central to the Christian doctrine of the Trinity, enshrined in the Nicene Creed of A.D. 381. It attests that God the Son (and by extension the Spirit) is of one and the same being or substance (*ousia*) as the Father. Reflecting the insistence of Athanasius against Arianism that Christ is God's eternal, coequal Son and not a creature, the Nicene *homoousios* is also to be differentiated from a rival formula, *homoiousios* (Greek, 'of similar substance'), which affirms merely the Son's likeness in being to God. Though notoriously and superficially an argument over one Greek iota, the issue was philosophically profound and theologically crucial whether or not Jesus of Nazareth incarnated God's own being, revealed God's own truth, and mediated God's own salvation. **See also** TRINITARIANISM.   A.E.L.

homuncular functionalism. See FUNCTIONALISM.

homunculus (from Latin, 'little man'), a miniature adult held to inhabit the brain (or some other organ) who perceives all the inputs to the sense organs and initiates all the commands to the muscles. Any theory that posits such an internal agent risks an infinite regress (sometimes called the *homunculus fallacy*), since we can ask whether there is a little man in the little man's head, responsible for his perception and action, and so on. Many familiar views of the mind and its activities seem to require a homunculus. For instance, models of visual perception that posit an inner picture as its product apparently require a homunculus to look at the picture, and models of action that treat intentions as commands to the muscles apparently require a homunculus to issue the commands. It is never an easy matter to determine whether a theory is committed to the existence of a homunculus that vitiates the theory, and in some circumstances, homunculi can be legitimately posited at intermediate levels of theory: "Homunculi are *bogeymen* only if they duplicate *entire* the talents they are rung in to explain. If one can get a team or committee of *relatively* ignorant, narrow-minded, blind homunculi to produce the intelligent behavior of the whole, this is progress" (Dennett, *Brainstorms*, 1978). Theories (in philosophy of mind or artificial intelligence or cognitive science) that posit such teams of homunculi have been called *homuncular functionalism* by William Lycan.   D.C.D.

Horkheimer, Max (1895–1973), German philosopher, the leading theorist of the first generation of the Frankfurt School of critical theory. Both as director of the Institute for Social Research and in his early philosophical essays published in the *Zeitschrift für Sozialforschung*, Horkheimer set the agenda for the collaborative work of the Frankfurt School in the social sciences, including analyses of the developments of state capitalism, the family, modern culture, and fascism. His programmatic essays on the relation of philosophy and the social sciences long provided the philosophical basis for Frankfurt School social criticism and research and have profoundly influenced Habermas's reformulation of Frankfurt School critical theory. In these essays, such as "The Present Situation of Social Philosophy and the Tasks of an Institute for Social Research" (1931), Horkheimer elaborated a cooperative relation between philosophy and the social sciences through an interdisciplinary historical materialism. His "Traditional and Critical Theory" (1937) develops the distinction between "critical" and "traditional" theories in terms of basic goals: critical theories aim at emancipating human beings rather than describing reality as it is now.

In the darkest days of World War II Horkheimer began collaborating with Adorno on *The Dialectic of Enlightenment* (1941), in which they see the origins of modern reason and autonomy in the domination of nature and the inner self. This genealogy of modern reason argues that myth and enlightenment are inseparably "entwined," a view proposed primarily to explain the catastrophe in which Europe found

itself. While Horkheimer thought that a revised notion of Hegelian dialectics might lead beyond this impasse, he never completed this positive project. Instead, he further developed the critique of instrumental reason in such works as *Eclipse of Reason* (1947), where he argues that modern institutions, including democracy, are under the sway of formal and instrumental rationality and the imperatives of self-preservation. While he did little new work after this period, he turned at the end of his life to a philosophical reinterpretation of religion and the content of religious experience and concepts, developing a negative theology of the "completely Other." His most enduring influence is his clear formulation of the epistemology of practical and critical social inquiry oriented to human emancipation.

See also CRITICAL THEORY, FRANKFURT SCHOOL.   J.Bo.

hormic psychology. See MCDOUGALL.

Ho Yen (d.A.D. 249), Chinese philosopher, an early leader of the Neo-Taoist movement. Ho Yen brought into currency the idea of "non-being" (*wu*) in explaining the *tao* and the origin of being. Without limit and inexhaustible, the *tao* constitutes the totality of all there is. Formless and nameless, it is a creative vital energy (*ch'i*) that through a process of differentiation produces heaven and earth and the myriad creatures. Ho Yen is also famous for his view that the sage does not have emotions (*ch'ing*). This is because the sage is exceptionally endowed with pure *ch'i*-energy, which precludes emotional disturbance. Ethically, this further translates into a critique of hypocrisy and the abuse of power that Ho Yen considered the bane of Chinese society. **See also** CH'ING, NEO-TAOISM.   A.K.L.C.

hsiao, Chinese team meaning 'filial piety'. *Hsiao* refers both to a virtue and to acts manifesting that virtue. Originally, *hsiao* had to do with the proper performance of one's parents' funeral rituals and sacrifices to one's ancestors. Later, *hsiao* came to encompass the proper treatment of one's parents while they are alive. *Hsiao* is fundamental to Confucianism in that showing proper respect for one's parents is thought to be related to respect for legitimate political authority. **See also** CONFUCIANISM, LI².   B.W.V.N.

hsien, in Chinese philosophy, divine "immortals" or "transcendents" – spiritual beings who have attained the *tao* and are characterized by transcendence and immortality; a central ideal in religious Taoism. The idea has its roots in ancient Chinese religion; in its mature form, it signifies a being constituted by the purest and most potent form of vital energy (*ch'i*), which renders him/her beyond the limitations of mundane life. Thus, *hsien* are often characterized by the power of flight. In poetry and philosophic discourse, *hsien* evokes fulfillment and freedom, especially from desire and the vagaries of human striving. In religious Taoism, there is an important debate whether immortality can be achieved through effort. Various methods that fall under the general rubrics of "internal alchemy" (*nei-tan*) and "external alchemy" (*wai-tan*) have been devised to bring about the perfected state. **See also** CH'I, TAOISM.   A.K.L.C.

Hsi K'ang (A.D.223–62), Chinese philosopher, a key representative of Neo-Taoism. Hsi K'ang's philosophy centers on the concept of *tzu-jan* – naturalness or, literally, what is of itself so – which depicts the inherent order of the Taoist universe. Nature conforms to "necessary principles" (*pi-jan chih li*); individuals receive an energy endowment (*ch'i*) at birth of varying richness that defines their nature and capacity. While endowment is inborn, self-cultivation directed at dispelling self-interest can substantially enhance one's physical and spiritual well-being. In ethics and politics, Hsi K'ang thus advocates going beyond the orthodox teachings of Confucianism (*ming-chiao*), which emphasize learning, conformity, and tradition. Hsi is also famous for his musical theory that "sounds do not have sorrow or joy" (*sheng wu ai-lo*): while sounds are naturally produced, emotions involve subjective and cognitive reactions. **See also** CH'I, NEO-TAOISM.   A.K.L.C.

hsin¹, Chinese term meaning 'heart', 'mind', 'feeling'. Generally, the *hsin* is both the physical organ we call the heart, and the faculty of appetition, cognition, and emotion, but the precise nature and proper role of *hsin* is one of the fundamental issues dividing Chinese philosophers. Mencius speaks of "four hearts," associating a particular virtue and set of emotional and cognitive capacities with each. Chuang Tzu suggests that we "fast" (*chai*), rather than cultivate, the *hsin*, letting ourselves be guided instead by the *ch'i*. Hsün Tzu holds that the *hsin* should control and sublimate the desires. In Neo-Confucianism, the *hsin* is conceived as a fully developed moral sense, present in every human, whose proper functioning is obscured by selfish desires. Neo-Confucians differ over whether *hsin* is identical

with principle (*li*) and nature (*hsing*). **See also** CONFUCIANISM, LI¹, MENCIUS, NEO-CONFUCIANISM.   B.W.V.N.

hsin², Chinese term meaning 'trust', 'faith', 'trustworthiness', 'honest'. In early texts, *hsin* is the mutual trust of sincerity between worshiper and spirit. The Chinese character for this word consists of two elements representing 'person' and 'speech', and this provides a reliable guide to its root sense: being true to one's word. *Hsin* became one of the cardinal Confucian virtues: trustworthiness or honesty (but only in service to what is right). In Buddhist contexts, *hsin* can mean 'faith' in the religious sense, e.g., the Pure Land School's practice of faith in Amitābha Buddha. This influenced Neo-Confucianism and is manifested in their faith in a perfect, innate moral faculty. **See also** CHINESE PHILOSOPHY, NEO-CONFUCIANISM.   P.J.I.

hsing, Chinese philosophical term generally agreed to be derived from '*sheng*' (life, growth), and usually translated as 'nature'. In its earliest use as a term distinct from '*sheng*', it probably referred to the tendency or direction of development that a thing will realize if unobstructed (e.g. it is the *hsing* of a sprout to grow into a full-grown plant and the *hsing* of water to flow downward), and the *hsing* of human beings is also supposed to be their proper course of development. The concept *hsing* probably entered philosophical discourse with the development of the school of thought associated with Yang Chu (fifth–fourth century B.C.), which regarded the *hsing* of human beings as the tendency to live a life of a certain span in good health and with sensory desires appropriately satisfied. It subsequently became a central concept in Confucian thought, though understood differently by different Confucian thinkers. Mencius (fourth century B.C.) regarded the moral way of life as a full realization of the *hsing* of human beings, which is constituted by the direction of development indicated by certain incipient moral inclinations of the heart/mind (*hsin*); *hsing* is good in that it has a moral direction. Hsün Tzu (third century B.C.) regarded the moral way of life as a transformation of the *hsing* of human beings, which comprises primarily self-regarding desires human beings have by birth; *hsing* is evil in that unregulated pursuit of satisfaction of such desires leads to strife and disorder. Different views of *hsing* continued to evolve; but ever since the view that Mencius was the true transmitter of Confucius's teachings became established, largely through the efforts of Chu Hsi (1130–1200), the idea that the *hsing* of human beings is good has been a central tenet of Confucian thought. **See also** CONFUCIANISM.   K.-l.S.

hsing-erh-shang, in Chinese philosophy, formless or metaphysical. In part one of the *I-Ching* (the *Book of Changes*) there is a statement that what is *hsing-erh-shang* is called *tao* (the Way), and what is *hsing-er-hsia* (with form) is called *ch'i*, a concrete thing. In the Chinese way of thinking, *tao* and *ch'i* are understood to be inseparable from each other; as *tao* is both transcendent and immanent, it permeates things, and things must not be cut off and alienated from their metaphysical origin. **See also** CHINESE PHILOSOPHY.
S.-h.L.

hsing-ming, in Chinese philosophy, "forms and names," an important philosophical concept associated with Legalism and the Huang–Lao School (the school of the Yellow Emperor and Lao Tzu), which flourished during the Warring States period and the early Han dynasty (third–second century B.C.). The narrower meaning of the term has to do with a system of law and punishment, designed especially to keep state officials in check. More broadly, *hsing-ming* points to a vision of order, in which all "names" (*ming*) should correspond to their underlying "form" (*hsing*) or reality. Applied to politics, this suggests that the ruler must discern the workings of the cosmos, ensure that officials perform their assigned duties, and allow the people to prosper in the perceived natural order of things. **See also** CHINESE LEGALISM.   A.K.L.C.

Hsiung Shih-li (1885–1968), Chinese contemporary New Confucian philosopher. He was a revolutionary when young and later studied *Wei-shih* (*Vijnanavada*, 'Consciousness-Only') philosophy at the China Buddhist Institute under Ou-yang Ching-wu (1871–1943). But, dissatisfied, he developed his New *Wei-shih* philosophy of creativity based on the insights he derived from the *I-Ching*. He became influential and had Mou Tsung-san, T'ang Chün-i, and Hsü Fu-kuan among his disciples. After the Communist takeover in 1949, he still rejected materialism, but embraced a radical social philosophy that was not shared by most of his former disciples. **See also** CHINESE PHILOSOPHY, HSÜ FU-KUAN, I-CHING, T'ANG CHÜN-I.   S.-h.L.

hsü, Chinese term meaning 'void', 'vacuity', 'the tenuous'. *Hsü* is not the absence of all things but a state in which things lack distinctions. For Chuang Tzu, *hsü* is the ideal state of mind, in which the mind is receptive to all things, perceives clearly, and responds effortlessly, as a clean mirror reflects the images before it. Hsün Tzu develops this ideal, characterizing a mind that is *hsü* (tenuous), unified and still. Extending later Taoist views, Neo-Confucians regard *hsü* as the original, inchoate state of the cosmos, out of which all things continually emerge and into which they eventually dissolve. Neo-Confucians distinguish *hsü* from the Buddhist concept *k'ung* (emptiness), which they see as denying the ultimate reality of the world. **See also** NEO-CONFUCIANISM.   P.J.I.

Hsü Fu-kuan (1903–82), Chinese intellectual and historian who served directly under Chiang Kai-shek at one time, but became a critic of the Nationalist government after it moved to Taiwan in 1949. He founded *Democratic Review*, the influential magazine that spread the ideas of contemporary New Confucians. He also started the Department of Chinese at Tunghai University in 1955 and invited Mou Tsung-san to join the staff to form another center of New Confucianism other than New Asia College in Hong Kong. He characterized his own position as between academic studies and politics, and between historical scholarship and philosophical understanding. His magnum opus was the three-volume *History of Han Thought;* his works on Chinese literature and art were also widely quoted. **See also** CH'IEN MU, HSIUNG SHIH-LI, T'ANG CHÜN-I.
S.-h.L.

Hsü Hsing (c.315 B.C.), Chinese philosopher, a member of the Tillers or Agriculture School (*Nung Chia*). The Tillers believed that in antiquity Shen Nung, the Divine Farmer, had ruled without reward, punishment, or administration over a decentralized utopia of small communities where all, including the ruler, lived by their own labor. Accordingly, Hsü Hsing attacked contemporary rulers who did not plow the fields but rather lived off the labor of others. He also sought to stabilize grain prices by controlling supply: grain would be stored in good years and distributed in bad ones.   R.P.P. & R.T.A.

Hsün Tzu (third century B.C.), a tough-minded Confucian philosopher best known for his opposition to Mencius's conception of the inherent goodness of human nature. For Hsün Tzu, the essential nature of human beings is bad in the sense of possessing a problematical motivational structure: every human seeks to satisfy his/her desires; unless guided by *li* (propriety) and *i* (rightness), these desires inevitably lead to conflict especially in view of the scarcity of goods and the native human tendency toward partiality for one's own benefits and for those of one's close relations. Significantly, the *li* or rules of proper behavior perform three basic functions: delimiting, supportive, and ennobling. The first draws the boundaries of proper conduct; the second provides channels for satisfaction of desires within these boundaries; and the third provides sources for ennobling personal character in accordance with *jen* (benevolence) and *i* (rightness). Hsün Tzu is also noted for emphasizing law as a supplement to *li* (rules of proper conduct); the need of argumentation to resolve ethical disagreement; the importance of clarity of mind, as opposed to *pi* (obscuration) in the pursuit of ethical knowledge; and the importance of Confucian classics in character education. **See also** MENCIUS.   A.S.C.

Huai Nan Tzu, an ancient Chinese syncretic compendium of knowledge. It was compiled by an academy of scholars residing under the patronage of one of the most prominent literary figures of the age, Liu An, Prince of Huai Nan, and presented to the imperial court of Emperor Wu in about 140 B.C. The twenty treatises that make up the text include technical tracts on astronomy, topography, and calendrics, as well as original reconfigurations of the ideas and beliefs that flourished in the formative period of classical Chinese philosophy. In many ways, it is a Han dynasty (206 B.C.–A.D. 220) summary of existing knowledge, and like most Chinese documents it is practical and prescriptive. As a political document, it is syncretic, blending Confucian, Legalist, and Taoist precepts to recommend a kind of practicable Taoist alternative to political centralism.   R.P.P. & R.T.A.

Huang–Lao (Chinese, 'School of the Yellow Emperor and Lao Tzu'), an eclectic school (c. third century B.C.) purportedly based on the teachings of the mythic Yellow Emperor and Lao Tzu, advocating a kind of *Realpolitik* Taoism stressing reliance on methods of ruling (e.g., rewards and punishments) and the power of political and social structures. Huang–Lao sought to establish a perfectly organized state, which *tzu jan* (naturally) runs smoothly, in which the ruler reigns (not rules) through *wu wei* (non-action). Huang–Lao's mystical side concerns its claim that only the ruler can attain the

unifying vision needed for such organization and that this vision is achieved through the practice of stillness and *hsü* (tenuousness).   P.J.I.

Huang Tsung-hsi (1610–95), Chinese philosopher and historian. A student of Liu Tsung-chou (1578–1645), the last great Neo-Confucian philosopher in the Ming dynasty, he compiled *Ming-ju-hsüeh-an* and *Sung-Yüan-hsüeh-an*, important anthologies and critical accounts of the Neo-Confucianists of the Ming dynasty and Sung and Yüan dynasties. He also wrote *Ming-i-tai-fang-lu* ("Waiting for the Dawn: A Plan for the Prince"), in which he denounced the system of government working only for the selfish interest of the ruler. This work exerted great influence in the last days of the Chinese empire. **See also** CHINESE PHILOSOPHY, CHU HSI, WANG YANG-MING.   S.-h.L.

Hu Hung, also called Wu-feng (1100–55), Chinese Neo-Confucian philosopher and an important figure in the Hunan School. According to him, *hsin* (mind/heart) is the outward manifestation of *hsing* (human nature); one must first understand the nature of *jen* (humanity) before one can practice moral cultivation. Professor Mou Tsung-san believed that Hu Hung succeeded Chou Tun-yi, Chang Tsai, and Ch'eng Hao, representing a third line of thought other than those of Ch'eng–Chu and Lu–Wang. **See also** CHANG TSAI, CH'ENG HAO, CHOU TUN-YI, CHU HSI, NEO-CONFUCIANISM.   S.-h.L.

Hui Shih (c.380–305 B.C.), Chinese philosopher, prime minister of the state of Wei, and a leading member of the School of Names (*ming chia*, also referred to as *pien che*, the Dialecticians or Sophists). As a friend and debating partner of the Taoist philosopher Chuang Tzu, Hui Shih parried Chuang Tzu's poetic, rhapsodic, and meditation-based intuitions with sophisticated logic and analytic rigor. An advocate of the Mohist idea of impartial concern for others (*chien ai*) and an opponent of war, he is most famous for his Ten Paradoxes, collected in the *Chuang Tzu*. Though Hui Shih's explanations are no longer extant, paradoxes such as "I go to Yüeh today but arrived yesterday" and "The south has no limit yet has a limit" raise issues of relativity and perspectivism with respect to language, values, and concepts such as space and time. **See also** CHUANG TZU.   R.P.P. & R.T.A.

humanism, a set of presuppositions that assigns to human beings a special position in the scheme of things. Not just a school of thought or a collection of specific beliefs or doctrines, humanism is rather a general perspective from which the world is viewed. That perspective received a gradual yet persistent articulation during different historical periods and continues to furnish a central leitmotif of Western civilization. It comes into focus when it is compared with two competing positions. On the one hand, it can be contrasted with the emphasis on the supernatural, transcendent domain, which considers humanity to be radically dependent on divine order. On the other hand, it resists the tendency to treat humanity scientifically as part of the natural order, on a par with other living organisms. Occupying the middle position, humanism discerns in human beings unique capacities and abilities, to be cultivated and celebrated for their own sake.

The word 'humanism' came into general use only in the nineteenth century but was applied to intellectual and cultural developments in previous eras. A teacher of classical languages and literatures in Renaissance Italy was described as *umanista* (contrasted with *legista*, teacher of law), and what we today call "the humanities," in the fifteenth century was called *studia humanitatis*, which stood for grammar, rhetoric, history, literature, and moral philosophy. The inspiration for these studies came from the rediscovery of ancient Greek and Latin texts; Plato's complete works were translated for the first time, and Aristotle's philosophy was studied in more accurate versions than those available during the Middle Ages.

The unashamedly humanistic flavor of classical writings had a tremendous impact on Renaissance scholars. Here, one felt no weight of the supernatural pressing on the human mind, demanding homage and allegiance. Humanity – with all its distinct capacities, talents, worries, problems, possibilities – was the center of interest. It has been said that medieval thinkers philosophized on their knees, but, bolstered by the new studies, they dared to stand up and to rise to full stature. Instead of devotional Church Latin, the medium of expression was the people's own language – Italian, French, German, English. Poetical, lyrical self-expression gained momentum, affecting all areas of life. New paintings showed great interest in human form. Even while depicting religious scenes, Michelangelo celebrated the human body, investing it with instrinsic value and dignity. The details of daily life – food, clothing, musical instruments – as well as nature and landscape – domestic and exotic – were lovingly examined in paintings and poetry. Imagination was stirred by stories brought home by the discoverers of new lands and continents, enlarging the scope of human possibilities as exhibited in the customs and the natural environments of strange, remote peoples.

The humanist mode of thinking deepened and widened its tradition with the advent of eighteenth-century thinkers. They included French *philosophes* like Voltaire, Diderot, and Rousseau, and other European and American figures – Bentham, Hume, Lessing, Kant, Franklin, and Jefferson. Not always agreeing with one another, these thinkers nevertheless formed a family united in support of such values as freedom, equality, tolerance, secularism, and cosmopolitanism. Although they championed untrammeled use of the mind, they also wanted it to be applied in social and political reform, encouraging individual creativity and exalting the active over the contemplative life. They believed in the perfectibility of human nature, the moral sense and responsibility, and the possibility of progress.

The optimistic motif of perfectibility endured in the thinking of nineteenth- and twentieth-century humanists, even though the accelerating pace of industrialization, the growth of urban populations, and the rise in crime, nationalistic squabbles, and ideological strife leading to large-scale inhumane warfare often put in question the efficacy of humanistic ideals. But even the depressing run of human experience highlighted the appeal of those ideals, reinforcing the humanistic faith in the values of endurance, nobility, intelligence, moderation, flexibility, sympathy, and love.

Humanists attribute crucial importance to education, conceiving of it as an all-around development of personality and individual talents, marrying science to poetry and culture to democracy. They champion freedom of thought and opinion, the use of intelligence and pragmatic research in science and technology, and social and political systems governed by representative institutions. Believing that it is possible to live confidently without metaphysical or religious certainty and that all opinions are open to revision and correction, they see human flourishing as dependent on open communication, discussion, criticism, and unforced consensus.

See also ENCYCLOPEDIA, POLITICAL PHILOSOPHY, SOCIAL PHILOSOPHY.   K.K.

humanism, civic. See CLASSICAL REPUBLICANISM.

human nature, a quality or group of qualities, belonging to all and only humans, that explains the kind of being we are. We are all two-footed and featherless, but 'featherless biped' does not explain our socially significant characteristics. We are also all both animals and rational beings (at least potentially), and 'rational animal' might explain the special features we have that other kinds of beings, such as angels, do not.

The belief that there is a human nature is part of the wider thesis that all natural kinds have essences. Acceptance of this position is compatible with many views about the specific qualities that constitute human nature. In addition to rationality and embodiment, philosophers have said that it is part of our nature to be wholly self-interested, benevolent, envious, sociable, fearful of others, able to speak and to laugh, and desirous of immortality.

Philosophers disagree about how we are to discover our nature. Some think metaphysical insight into eternal forms or truths is required, others that we can learn it from observation of biology or of behavior. Most have assumed that only males display human nature fully, and that females, even at their best, are imperfect or incomplete exemplars.

Philosophers also disagree on whether human nature determines morality. Some think that by noting our distinctive features we can infer what God wills us to do. Others think that our nature shows at most the limits of what morality can require, since it would plainly be pointless to direct us to ways of living that our nature makes impossible.

Some philosophers have argued that human nature is plastic and can be shaped in different ways. Others hold that it is not helpful to think in terms of human nature. They think that although we share features as members of a biological species, our other qualities are socially constructed. If the differences between male and female reflect cultural patterns of child rearing, work, and the distribution of power, our biologically common features do not explain our important characteristics and so do not constitute a nature.

See also EMBODIMENT, ESSENTIALISM, PHILOSOPHY OF MIND.   J.B.S.

human rights. See RIGHTS.

human sciences. See WEBER.

Humboldt, Wilhelm von (1767–1835), German statesman, scholar, and educator, often regarded as the father of comparative linguistics. Born in Potsdam, Wilhelm, with his younger brother Alexander, was educated by private tutors in the "enlightened" style thought suitable for future Prussian diplomats. This included classical languages, history, philosophy, and political economy. After his university studies in law at Frankfurt an der Oder and Göttingen, his career was divided among assorted diplomatic posts, writing on a broad range of topics, and (his first love) the study of languages. His broad-ranging works reveal the important influences of Herder in his conception of history and culture, Kant and Fichte in philosophy, and the French "Ideologues" in linguistics. His most enduring work has proved to be the Introduction (published in 1836) to his massive study of the Kawi language spoken on Java.

Humboldt maintained that language, as a vital and dynamic "organism," is the key to understanding both the operations of the human mind and the distinctive differences characteristic of various national cultures. Every language possesses a distinctive *inner form* that shapes, in a way reminiscent of Kant's more general categories, the subjective experiences, the worldview, and ultimately the institutions of a given nation and its culture. While all later comparative linguists are indebted to both his empirical studies and his theoretical insights, such philosophers of culture as Dilthey and Cassirer acknowledge him as establishing language as a central concern for the human sciences.   J.P.Su.

Hume, David (1711–76), Scottish philosopher and historian who may be aptly considered the leading neo-skeptic of the early modern period. Many of Hume's immediate predecessors (Descartes, Bayle, and Berkeley) had grappled with important elements of skepticism. Hume consciously incorporated many of these same elements into a philosophical system that manages to be both skeptical and constructive.

Born and educated in Edinburgh, Hume spent three years (1734–37) in France writing the penultimate draft of *A Treatise of Human Nature*. In middle life, in addition to writing a wide-ranging set of essays and short treatises and a long *History of England,* he served briefly as companion to a mad nobleman, then as a military attaché, before becoming librarian of the Advocates Library in Edinburgh. In 1763 he served as private secretary to Lord Hertford, the British ambassador in Paris; in 1765 he became secretary to the embassy there and then served as chargé d'affaires. In 1767–68 he served in London as under-secretary of state for the Northern Department. He retired to Edinburgh in 1769 and died there.

Hume's early care was chiefly in the hands of his widowed mother, who reported that young David was "uncommon wake-minded" (i.e., uncommonly acute, in the local dialect of the period). His earliest surviving letter, written in 1727, indicates that even at sixteen he was engaged in the study that resulted in the publication (1739) of the first two volumes of *A Treatise of Human Nature*. By the time he left college (c.1726) he had a thorough grounding in classical authors, especially Cicero and the major Latin poets; in natural philosophy (particularly that of Boyle) and mathematics; in logic or theory of knowledge, metaphysics, and moral philosophy; and in history. His early reading included many of the major English and French poets and essayists of the period. He reports that in the three years ending about March 1734, he read "most of the celebrated Books in Latin, French & English," and also learned Italian. Thus, although Hume's views are often supposed to result from his engagement with only one or two philosophers (with either Locke and Berkeley, or Hutcheson or Newton), the breadth of his reading suggests that no single writer or philosophical tradition provides the comprehensive key to his thought.

Hume's most often cited works include *A Treatise of Human Nature* (three volumes, 1739–40); an *Abstract* (1740) of volumes 1 and 2 of the *Treatise*; a collection of approximately forty essays (*Essays Moral, Political, and Literary*, first published, for the most part, between 1741 and 1752); *An Enquiry concerning Human Understanding* (1748); *An Enquiry concerning the Principles of Morals* (1751); *The Natural History of Religion* (1757); a six-volume *History of England* from Roman times to 1688 (1754–62); a brief autobiography, *My Own Life* (1777); and *Dialogues concerning Natural Religion* (1778).

Hume's neo-skeptical stance manifests itself in each of these works. He insists that philosophy "cannot go beyond experience; and any hypothesis, that pretends to discover the ultimate original qualities of human nature, ought at first to be rejected as presumptuous and chimerical." He says of the *Treatise* that it "is very sceptical, and tends to give us a notion of the imperfections and narrow limits of the human understanding." But he goes well beyond the conventional recognition of human limitations; from his skeptical starting place he projects an observationally based science of human nature, and produces a comprehensive and constructive account of human nature and experience.

Hume begins the *Treatise* with a discussion of the "elements" of his philosophy. Arguing that it is natural philosophers (scientists) who should explain how sensation works, he focuses on those entities that are the immediate and *only* objects present to the mind. These he calls "perceptions" and distinguishes into two kinds, "impressions" and "ideas." Hume initially suggests that impressions (of which there are two kinds: of sensation and of reflection) are more forceful or vivacious than ideas, but some ideas (those of memory, e.g.) do sometimes take on enough force and vivacity to be called impressions, and belief also adds sufficient force and vivacity to ideas to make them practically indistinguishable from impressions. In the end we find that impressions are clearly distinguished from ideas only insofar as ideas are always causally dependent on impressions.

Thomas Reid charged that the allegedly representative theory of perception found in Descartes and Locke had served as a philosophical Trojan horse leading directly to skeptical despair. Hume was fully aware of the skeptical implications of this theory. He knew well those sections of Bayle and Locke that reveal the inadequacy of Descartes's attempts to prove that there is an external world, and also appreciated the force of the objections brought by Bayle and Berkeley against the primary–secondary quality distinction championed by Locke. Hume adopted the view that the immediate objects of the mind are always "perceptions" because he thought it correct, and in spite of the fact that it leads to skepticism about the external world. Satisfied that the battle to establish absolutely reliable links between thought and reality had been fought and lost, Hume made no attempt to explain how our impressions of sensation are linked to their entirely "unknown causes." He instead focused exclusively on perceptions *qua* objects of mind:

As to those *impressions*, which arise from the *senses*, their ultimate cause is, in my opinion, perfectly inexplicable by human reason, and 'twill always be impossible to decide with certainty, whether they arise immediately from the object, or are produc'd by the creative power of the mind, or are deriv'd from the author of our being. Nor is such a question any way material to our present purpose. We may draw inferences from the coherence of our perceptions, whether they be true or false; whether they represent nature justly, or be mere illusions of the senses.

Book I of the *Treatise* is an effort to show how our perceptions cohere to form certain fundamental notions (those of space and time, causal connection, external and independent existence, and mind) in which, skeptical doubts notwithstanding, we repose belief and on which "life and action entirely depend."

According to Hume, we have no direct impressions of space and time, and yet the ideas of space and time are essential to our existence. This he explains by tracing our idea of space to a "manner of appearance": by means of two senses, sight and touch, we have impressions that array themselves as so many points on a contrasting background; the imagination transforms these particulars of experience into a "compound impression, which represents extension" or the abstract idea of space itself. Our idea of time is, *mutatis mutandis,* accounted for in the same way: "As 'tis from the disposition of visible and tangible objects we receive the idea of space, so from the succession of ideas and impressions we form the idea of time." The abstract idea of time, like all other abstract ideas, is represented in the imagination by a "particular individual idea of a determinate quantity and quality" joined to a term, 'time', that has general reference.

Hume is often credited with denying there is physical necessity and that we have any idea of necessary connection. This interpretation significantly distorts his intent. Hume was convinced by the Cartesians, and especially by Malebranche, that neither the senses nor reason can establish that one object (a cause) is connected together with another object (an effect) in such a way that the presence of the one entails the existence of the other. Experience reveals only that objects thought to be causally related are contiguous in time and space, that the cause is prior to the effect, and that similar objects have been constantly associated in this way. These are the defining, perceptible features of the causal relation. And yet there seems to be more to the matter. "There is," he says, a "NECESSARY CONNECTION to be taken into consideration," and our belief in that relation must be explained. Despite our demonstrated inability to see or prove that there are necessary causal connections, we continue to think and act as if we had knowledge of them. We act, for example, as though the future will necessarily resemble the past, and "wou'd appear ridiculous" if we were to say "that 'tis only probable the sun will rise to-morrow, or

that all men must dye." To explain this phenomenon Hume asks us to imagine what life would have been like for Adam, suddenly brought to life in the midst of the world. Adam would have been unable to make even the simplest predictions about the future behavior of objects. He would not have been able to predict that one moving billiard ball, striking a second, would cause the second to move. And yet we, endowed with the same faculties, can not only make, but are unable to resist making, this and countless other such predictions.

What is the difference between ourselves and this putative Adam? Experience. We have experienced the constant conjunction (the invariant succession of paired objects or events) of particular causes and effects and, although our experience never includes even a glimpse of a causal connection, it does arouse in us an expectation that a particular event (a "cause") will be followed by another event (an "effect") previously and constantly associated with it. Regularities of experience give rise to these feelings, and thus determine the mind to transfer its attention from a present impression to the idea of an absent but associated object. The idea of necessary connection is copied from these feelings. The idea has its foundation in the mind and is projected onto the world, but there is nonetheless such an idea. That there is an objective physical necessity to which this idea corresponds is an untestable hypothesis, nor would demonstrating that such necessary connections had held in the past guarantee that they will hold in the future. Thus, while not denying that there may be physical necessity or that there is an idea of necessary connection, Hume remains a skeptic about causal necessity.

Hume's account of our *belief* in future effects or absent causes – of the process of mind that enables us to plan effectively – is a part of this same explanation. Such belief involves an idea or conception of the entity believed in, but is clearly different from mere conception without belief. This difference cannot be explained by supposing that some further idea, an idea of belief itself, is present when we believe, but absent when we merely conceive. There is no such idea. Moreover, given the mind's ability to freely join together any two consistent ideas, if such an idea were available we by an act of will could, contrary to experience, combine the idea of belief with any other idea, and by so doing cause ourselves to believe anything. Consequently, Hume concludes that belief can only be a "different MANNER of conceiving an object"; it is a livelier, firmer, more vivid and intense conception. Belief in certain "matters of fact" – the belief that because some event or object is now being experienced, some other event or object not yet available to experience *will in the future* be experienced – is brought about by previous experience of the constant conjunction of two impressions. These two impressions have been associated together in such a way that the experience of one of them automatically gives rise to an idea of the other, and has the effect of transferring the force or liveliness of the impression to the associated idea, thereby causing this idea to be believed or to take on the lively character of an impression.

Our beliefs in continuing and independently existing objects and in our own continuing selves are, on Hume's account, beliefs in "fictions," or in entities entirely beyond all experience. We have impressions that we naturally but mistakenly suppose to be continuing, external objects, but analysis quickly reveals that these impressions are by their very nature fleeting and observer-dependent. Moreover, none of our impressions provides us with a distinctive mark or evidence of an external origin. Similarly, when we focus on our own minds, we experience only a sequence of impressions and ideas, and never encounter the mind or self in which these perceptions are supposed to inhere. To ourselves we appear to be merely "a bundle or collection of different perceptions, which succeed each other with an inconceivable rapidity, and are in a perpetual flux and movement." How do we, then, come to believe in external objects or our own selves and self-identity? Neither reason nor the senses, working with impressions and ideas, provide anything like compelling proof of the existence of continuing, external objects, or of a continuing, unified self. Indeed, these two faculties cannot so much as account for our *belief* in objects or selves. If we had only reason and the senses, the faculties championed by, respectively, the rationalists and empiricists, we would be mired in a debilitating and destructive uncertainty. So unfortunate an outcome is avoided only by the operation of an apparently unreliable third faculty, the imagination. It, by means of what appear to be a series of outright mistakes and trivial suggestions, leads us to believe in our own selves and in independently existing objects. The skepticism of the philosophers is in this way both confirmed (we can provide no arguments, e.g., proving the existence of the external world) and shown to be of little practical import. An irrational faculty, the imagination, saves us from the excesses of philosophy: "Phi-

losophy wou'd render us entirely *Pyrrhonian*," says Hume, were not nature, in the form of the imagination, too strong for it.

Books II and III of the *Treatise* and the *Enquiry concerning the Principles of Morals* reveal Hume's concern to explain our moral behavior and judgments in a manner that is consistent with his science of human nature, but which nonetheless recognizes the irreducible moral content of these judgments. Thus he attempted to rescue the passions from the ad hoc explanations and negative assessments of his predecessors. From the time of Plato and the Stoics the passions had often been characterized as irrational and unnatural animal elements that, given their head, would undermine humankind's true, rational nature. Hume's most famous remark on the subject of the passions, "Reason is, and ought only to be, the slave of the passions," will be better understood if read in this context (and if it is remembered that he also claims that reason can and does extinguish some passions). In contrast to the long-standing orthodoxy, Hume assumes that the passions constitute an integral and legitimate part of human nature, a part that can be explained without recourse to physical or metaphysical speculation. The passions can be treated as of a piece with other perceptions: they are secondary impressions ("impressions of reflection") that derive from prior impressions and ideas. Some passions (pride and humility, love and hatred) may be characterized as *indirect*; i.e., they arise as the result of a double relation of impressions and ideas that gives them one form of intentional character. These passions have both assignable *causes* (typically, the qualities of some person or some object belonging to a person) and a kind of indirect *object* (the person with the qualities or objects just mentioned); the object of pride or humility is always oneself, while the object of love or hatred is always another. The *direct* passions (desire, aversion, hope, fear, etc.) are feelings *caused* immediately by pleasure or pain, or the prospect thereof, and take entities or events as their intentional objects.

In his account of the will Hume claims that while all human actions are caused, they are nonetheless free. He argues that our ascriptions of causal connection have all the same foundation, namely, the observation of a "uniform and regular conjunction" of one object with another. Given that in the course of human affairs we observe "the same uniformity and regular operation of natural principles" found in the physical world, and that this uniformity results in an expectation of exactly the sort produced by physical regularities, it follows that there is no "negation of necessity and causes," or no *liberty of indifference*. The will, that *"internal impression we feel and are conscious of when we knowingly give rise to"* any action or thought, is an effect always linked (by constant conjunction and the resulting feeling of expectation) to some prior cause. But, insofar as our actions are not forcibly constrained or hindered, we do remain free in another sense: we retain a *liberty of spontaneity*. Moreover, only freedom in this latter sense is consistent with morality. A liberty of indifference, the possibility of uncaused actions, would undercut moral assessment, for such assessments presuppose that actions are causally linked to motives.

Morality is for Hume an entirely human affair founded on human nature and the circumstances of human life (one form of naturalism). We as a species possess several notable dispositions that, over time, have given rise to morality. These include a disposition to form bonded family groups, a disposition (sympathy) to communicate and thus share feelings, a disposition – the moral sense – to feel approbation and disapprobation in response to the actions of others, and a disposition to form general rules. Our disposition to form family groups results in small social units in which a natural generosity operates. The fact that such generosity is possible shows that the egoists are mistaken, and provides a foundation for the distinction between virtue and vice. The fact that the moral sense responds differently to distinctive motivations – we feel approbation in response to well-intended actions, disapprobation in response to ill-intended ones – means that our moral assessments have an affective but nonetheless cognitive foundation. To claim that Nero was vicious is to make a judgment about Nero's motives or character in consequence of an observation of him that has caused an impartial observer to feel a unique sentiment of disapprobation. That our moral judgments have this affective foundation accounts for the practical and motivational character of morality. Reason is "perfectly inert," and hence our practical, action-guiding moral distinctions must derive from the sentiments or feelings provided by our moral sense.

Hume distinguishes, however, between the "natural virtues" (generosity, benevolence, e.g.) and the "artificial virtues" (justice, allegiance, e.g.). These differ in that the former not only produce good on each occasion of their practice, but are also on every occasion approved. In contrast, any particular instantiation of justice may be "contrary to the public good" and be approved

only insofar as it is entailed by "a general scheme or system of action, which is advantageous." The artificial virtues differ also in being the result of contrivance arising from "the circumstances and necessities of life." In our original condition we did not need the artificial virtues because our natural dispositions and responses were adequate to maintain the order of small, kinship-based units. But as human numbers increased, so too did the scarcity of some material goods lead to an increase in the possibility of conflict, particularly over property, between these units. As a consequence, and out of self-interest, our ancestors were gradually led to establish conventions governing property and its exchange. In the early stages of this necessary development our disposition to form general rules was an indispensable component; at later stages, sympathy enables many individuals to pursue the artificial virtues from a combination of self-interest and a concern for others, thus giving the fully developed artificial virtues a foundation in two kinds of motivation.

Hume's *Enquiry concerning Human Understanding* and his *Enquiry concerning the Principles of Morals* represent his effort to "recast" important aspects of the *Treatise* into more accessible form. His *Essays* extend his human-centered philosophical analysis to political institutions, economics, and literary criticism. His best-selling *History of England* provides, among much else, an extended historical analysis of competing Whig and Tory claims about the origin and nature of the British constitution.

Hume's trenchant critique of religion is found principally in his *Enquiry concerning Human Understanding, Natural History of Religion,* and *Dialogues*. In an effort to curb the excesses of religious dogmatism, Hume focuses his attention on miracles, on the argument from design, and on the origin of the idea of monotheism. Miracles are putative facts used to justify a commitment to certain creeds. Such commitments are often maintained with a mind-numbing tenacity and a disruptive intolerance toward contrary views. Hume argues that the widely held view of miracles as violations of a law of nature is incoherent, that the evidence for even the most likely miracle will always be counterbalanced by the evidence establishing the law of nature that the miracle allegedly violates, and that the evidence supporting any given miracle is necessarily suspect. His argument leaves open the possibility that violations of the laws of nature may have occurred, but shows that beliefs about such events lack the force of evidence needed to justify the arrogance and intolerance that characterizes so many of the religious.

Hume's critique of the argument from design has a similar effect. This argument purports to show that our well-ordered universe must be the effect of a supremely intelligent cause, that each aspect of this divine creation is well designed to fulfill some beneficial end, and that these effects show us that the Deity is caring and benevolent. Hume shows that these conclusions go well beyond the available evidence. The pleasant and well-designed features of the world are balanced by a good measure of the unpleasant and the plainly botched. Our knowledge of causal connections depends on the experience of constant conjunctions. Such connections cause the vivacity of a present impression to be transferred to the idea associated with it, and leave us believing in that idea. But in this case the effect to be explained, the universe, is unique, and its cause unknown. Consequently, we cannot possibly have experiential grounds for any kind of inference about this cause. On experiential grounds the most we can say is that there is a massive, mixed effect, and, as we have through experience come to believe that effects have causes commensurate to them, this effect probably does have a commensurately large and mixed cause. Furthermore, as the effect is remotely like the products of human manufacture, we can say *"that the cause or causes of order in the universe probably bear some remote analogy to human intelligence."* There is indeed an inference to be drawn from the unique effect in question (the universe) to the cause of that effect, but it is not the "argument" of the theologians nor does it in any way support sectarian pretension or intolerance.

The *Natural History of Religion* focuses on the question of the origin of religion in human nature, and delivers a thoroughly naturalistic answer: the widespread but not universal belief in invisible and intelligent power can be traced to derivative and easily perverted principles of our nature. Primitive peoples found physical nature not an orderly whole produced by a beneficent designer, but arbitrary and fearsome, and they came to understand the activities of nature as the effect of petty powers that could, through propitiating worship, be influenced to ameliorate their lives. Subsequently, the same fears and perceptions transformed polytheism into monotheism, the view that a single, omnipotent being created and still controls the world and all that transpires in it. From this conclusion Hume goes on to argue that monotheism, apparently the more sophisticated position,

is morally retrograde. Monotheism tends naturally toward zeal and intolerance, encourages debasing, "monkish virtues," and proves itself a danger to society: it is a source of violence and a cause of immorality. In contrast, polytheism, which Hume here regards as a form of atheism, is tolerant of diversity and encourages genuine virtues that improve humankind. From a moral point of view, at least this one form of atheism is superior to theism.

See also BUNDLE THEORY, CAUSATION, EMPIRICISM, ETHICS, PHILOSOPHY OF RELIGION, PROBLEM OF INDUCTION, SKEPTICISM.

D.F.N.

humors. See GALEN.

Hu Shih (1891–1962), Chinese philosopher and historian and a famous liberal intellectual in contemporary China. He studied at Columbia University under Dewey, and brought pragmatism to China. He was the Chinese ambassador to the United States during World War II and later headed the Academia Sinica in Taipei. A versatile writer, he helped to initiate the vernacular movement in Chinese literature; published his *Ancient History of Chinese Philosophy* in 1919, the first history of Chinese philosophy written from a modern point of view; and advocated wholesale Westernization or modernization of China. A reformist committed to the democratic ideal, he remained an anti-Communist throughout his life. **See also** CHINESE PHILOSOPHY, LIANG SOU-MING.

S.-h.L.

Husserl, Edmund (1859–1938), German philosopher and founder of phenomenology. Born in Prossnits (now Prostějov in the Czech Republic), he studied science and philosophy at Leipzig, mathematics and philosophy at Berlin, and philosophy and psychology at Vienna and Halle. He taught at Halle (1887–1901), Göttingen (1901–16), and Freiburg (1916–28). Husserl and Frege were the founders of the two major twentieth-century trends. Through his work and his influence on Russell, Wittgenstein, and others, Frege inspired the movement known as analytic philosophy, while Husserl, through his work and his influence on Heidegger, Sartre, Merleau-Ponty, and others, established the movement known as phenomenology.

Husserl began his academic life as a mathematician. He studied at Berlin with Kronecker and Weierstrass and wrote a dissertation in mathematics at Vienna. There, influenced by Brentano, his interests turned toward philosophy and psychology but remained related to mathematics. His habilitation, written at Halle, was a psychological-philosophical study of the concept of number and led to his first book, *The Philosophy of Arithmetic* (1891). Husserl distinguishes between numbers given intuitively and those symbolically intended. The former are given as the objective correlates of acts of counting; when we count things set out before us, we constitute groups, and these groups can be compared with each other as more and less. In this way the first few numbers in the number series can be intuitively presented. Although most numbers are only symbolically intended, their sense as numbers is derived from those that are intuitively given.

During 1890–1900 Husserl expanded his philosophical concerns from mathematics to logic and the general theory of knowledge, and his reflections culminated in his *Logical Investigations* (1900–01). The work is made up of six investigations preceded by a volume of prolegomena. The prolegomena are a sustained and effective critique of *psychologism*, the doctrine that reduces logical entities, such as propositions, universals, and numbers, to mental states or mental activities. Husserl insists on the objectivity of such targets of consciousness and shows the incoherence of reducing them to the activities of mind. The rest of the work examines signs and words, abstraction, parts and wholes, logical grammar, the notion of presentation, and truth and evidence. His earlier distinction between intuitive presentation and symbolic intention is now expanded from our awareness of numbers to the awareness of all sorts of objects of consciousness. The contrast between empty intention and fulfillment or intuition is applied to perceptual objects, and it is also applied to what he calls *categorial objects:* states of affairs, relationships, causal connections, and the like. Husserl claims that we can have an intellectual intuition of such things and he describes this intuition; it occurs when we articulate an object as having certain features or relationships. The formal structure of categorial objects is elegantly related to the grammatical parts of language. As regards simple material objects, Husserl observes that we can intend them either emptily or intuitively, but even when they are intuitively given, they retain sides that are absent and only cointended by us, so perception itself is a mixture of empty and filled intentions.

The term 'intentionality' refers to both empty and filled, or signitive and intuitive, intentions. It names the relationship consciousness has toward things, whether those things are directly given or meant only in their absence. Husserl also shows that the identity of things is given to us when we see that the object we once intended emptily is the same as what is actually given to us now. Such identities are given even in perceptual experience, as the various sides and aspects of things continue to present one and the same object, but identities are given even more explicitly in categorial intuition, when we recognize the partial identity between a thing and its features, or when we directly focus on the identity a thing has with itself. These phenomena are described under the general rubric of identity-synthesis.

A weakness in the first edition of *Logical Investigations* was the fact that Husserl remained somewhat Kantian in it and distinguished sharply between the thing as it is given to us and the thing-in-itself; he claimed that in his phenomenology he described only the thing as it is given to us. In the decade 1900–10, through deeper reflection on our experience of time, on memory, and on the nature of philosophical thinking, he overcame this Kantian distinction and claimed that the thing-in-itself can be intuitively given to us as the identity presented in a manifold of appearances. His new position was expressed in *Ideas Pertaining to a Pure Phenomenology and Phenomenological Philosophy* (1913). The book was misinterpreted by many as adopting a traditional idealism, and many thinkers who admired Husserl's earlier work distanced themselves from what he now taught.

Husserl published three more books. *Formal and Transcendental Logic* (1929) was written right after his retirement; *Cartesian Meditations* (1931), which appeared in French translation, was an elaboration of some lectures he gave in Paris. In addition, some earlier manuscripts on the experience of time were assembled by Edith Stein and edited by Heidegger in 1928 as *Lectures on the Phenomenology of Inner Time-Consciousness*. Thus, Husserl published only six books, but he amassed a huge amount of manuscripts, lecture notes, and working papers. He always retained the spirit of a scientist and did his philosophical work in the manner of tentative experiments. Many of his books can be seen as compilations of such experiments rather than as systematic treatises. Because of its exploratory and developmental character, his thinking does not lend itself to doctrinal summary. Husserl was of Jewish ancestry, and after his death his papers were in danger from the Nazi regime; they were covertly taken out of Germany by a Belgian scholar, Herman

Leo Van Breda, who, after World War II, established the Husserl Archives at Louvain. This institution, with centers at Cologne, Freiburg, Paris, and New York, has since supervised the critical edition of many volumes of Husserl's writings in the series *Husserliana*.

Husserl believes that things are presented to us in various ways, and that philosophy should be engaged in precise description of these appearances. It should avoid constructing large-scale theories and defending ideologies. It should analyze, e.g., how visual objects are perceived and how they depend on our cognitive activity of seeing, focusing, moving about, on the correlation of seeing with touching and grasping, and so on. Philosophy should describe the different ways in which such "regions of being" as material objects, living things, other persons, and cultural objects are given, how the past and the present are intended, how speech, numbers, time and space, and our own bodies are given to us, and so on. Husserl carries out many such analyses himself and in all of them distinguishes between the object given and the subjective conscious activity we must perform to let it be given. The phenomenological description of the object is called *noematic analysis* and that of the subjective intentions is called *noetic analysis*. The *noema* is the object as described phenomenologically, the *noesis* is the corresponding mental activity, also as described by phenomenology. The objective and the subjective are correlative but never reducible to one another.

In working out such descriptions we must get to the essential structures of things. We do so not by just generalizing over instances we have experienced, but by a process he calls "free variation" or "imaginative variation." We attempt in our imagination to remove various features from the target of our analysis; the removal of some features would leave the object intact, but the removal of other features would destroy the object; hence, when we come upon the latter we know we have hit on something essential to the thing. The method of imaginative variation thus leads to *eidetic intuition*, the insight that this or that feature belongs to the *eidos*, the essence, of the thing in question. Eidetic intuition is directed not only toward objects but also toward the various forms of intentionality, as we try to determine the essence of perception, memory, judging, and the like.

Husserl thinks that the eidetic analysis of intentionality and its objects yields apodictic truths, truths that can be seen to be necessary. Examples might be that human beings could not

be without a past and future, and that each material perceptual object has sides and aspects other than those presented at any moment. Husserl admits that the objects of perceptual experience, material things, are not given apodictically to perception because they contain parts that are only emptily intended, but he insists that the phenomenological reflection on perceptual experience, the reflection that yields the statement that perception involves a mixture of empty and filled intentions, can be apodictic: we know apodictically that perception must have a mixture of empty and filled intentions. Husserl did admit in the 1920s that although phenomenological experience and statements could be apodictic, they would never be adequate to what they describe, i.e., further clarifications of what they signify could always be carried out. This would mean, e.g., that we can be apodictically sure that human beings could not be what they are if they did not have a sense of past and future, but what it is to have a past and future always needs deeper clarification.

Husserl has much to say about philosophical thinking. He distinguishes between the "natural attitude," our straightforward involvement with things and the world, and the "phenomenological attitude," the reflective point of view from which we carry out philosophical analysis of the intentions exercised in the natural attitude and the objective correlates of these intentions. When we enter the phenomenological attitude, we put out of action or suspend all the intentions and convictions of the natural attitude; this does not mean that we doubt or negate them, only that we take a distance from them and contemplate their structure. Husserl calls this suspension the phenomenological *epoché*. In our human life we begin, of course, in the natural attitude, and the name for the processs by which we move to the phenomenological attitude is called the phenomenological reduction, a "leading back" from natural beliefs to the reflective consideration of intentions and their objects. In the phenomenological attitude we look at the intentions that we normally look through, those that function anonymously in our straightforward involvement with the world. Throughout his career, Husserl essayed various "ways to reduction" or arguments to establish philosophy. At times he tried to model the argument on Descartes's methodical doubt; at times he tried to show that the world-directed sciences need the further supplement of phenomenological reflection if they are to be truly scientific.

One of the special features of the natural attitude is that it simply accepts the world as a background or horizon for all our more particular experiences and beliefs. The world is not a large thing nor is it the sum total of things; it is the horizon or matrix for all particular things and states of affairs. The world as noema is correlated to our world-belief or world-doxa as noesis. In the phenomenological attitude we take a distance even toward our natural being in the world and we describe what it is to have a world. Husserl thinks that this sort of radical reflection and radical questioning is necessary for beginning philosophy and entering into what he calls pure or transcendental phenomenology; so long as we fail to question our world-belief and the world as such, we fail to reach philosophical purity and our analyses will in fact become parts of worldly sciences (such as psychology) and will not be philosophical.

Husserl distinguishes between the apophantic and the ontological domains. The apophantic is the domain of senses and propositions, while the ontological is the domain of things, states of affairs, relations, and the like. Husserl calls "apophantic analytics" the science that examines the formal, logical structures of the apophantic domain and "formal ontology" the science that examines the formal structures of the ontological domain. The movement between focusing on the ontological domain and focusing on the apophantic domain occurs within the natural attitude, but it is described from the phenomenological attitude. This movement establishes the difference between propositions and states of affairs, and it permits scientific verification; science is established in the zigzag motion between focusing on things and focusing on propositions, which are then verified or falsified when they are confirmed or disconfirmed by the way things appear. Evidence is the activity of either having a thing in its direct presence or experiencing the conformity or disconformity between an empty intention and the intuition that is to fulfill it. There are degrees of evidence; things can be given more or less fully and more or less distinctly. *Adequation* occurs when an intuition fully satisfies an empty intention.

Husserl also makes a helpful distinction between the passive, thoughtless repetition of words and the activity of explicit judging, in which we distinctly make judgments on our own. Explicit thinking can itself fall back into passivity or become "sedimented" as people take it for granted and go on to build further thinking upon it. Such sedimented thought must be reactivated and its meanings revived. Passive thinking may harbor contradictions and incoherences; the application of formal logic presumes judgments that are distinctly executed.

In our reflective phenomenological analyses we describe various intentional acts, but we also discover the ego as the owner or agent behind these acts. Husserl distinguishes between the *psychological ego*, the ego taken as a part of the world, and the *transcendental ego*, the ego taken as that which has a world and is engaged in truth, and hence to some extent transcends the world. He often comments on the remarkable ambiguity of the ego, which is both a part of the world (as a human being) and yet transcends the world (as a cognitive center that possesses or intends the world). The transcendental ego is not separable from individuals; it is a dimension of every human being. We each have a transcendental ego, since we are all intentional and rational beings. Husserl also devoted much effort to analyzing intersubjectivity and tried to show how other egos and other minds, other centers of conscious and rational awareness, can be presented and intended. The role of the body, the role of speech and other modes of communication, and the fact that we all share things and a world in common are important elements in these analyses.

The transcendental ego, the source of all intentional acts, is constituted through time: it has its own identity, which is different from that of the identity of things or states of affairs. The identity of the ego is built up through the flow of experiences and through memory and anticipation. One of Husserl's major contributions is his analysis of time-consciousness and its relation to the identity of the self, a topic to which he often returns. He distinguishes among the objective time of the world, the inner time of the flow of our experiences (such as acts of perception, judgments, and memories), and a third, still deeper level that he calls "the consciousness of inner time." It is this third, deepest level, the consciousness of inner time, that permits even our mental acts to be experienced as temporal. This deepest level also provides the ultimate context in which the identity of the ego is constituted. In one way, we achieve our conscious identity through the memories that we store and recall, but these memories themselves have to be stitched together by the deepest level of temporality in order to be recoverable as belonging to one and the same self. Husserl observes that on this deepest level of the consciousness of inner time, we never have a simple atomic present: what we come to as ultimate is a moving form that has a retention of the immediate past, a pro-tention of that which is coming, and a central core. This form of inner time-consciousness, the form of what Husserl calls "the living present," is prior even to the ego and is a kind of apex reached by his philosophical analysis.

One of the important themes that Husserl developed in the last decade of his work is that of the life-world or *Lebenswelt*. He claims that scientific and mathematical abstraction has roots in the prescientific world, the world in which we live. This world has its own structures of appearance, identification, evidence, and truth, and the scientific world is established on its basis. One of the tasks of phenomenology is to show how the idealized entities of science draw their sense from the life-world. Husserl claims, e.g., that geometrical forms have their roots in the activity of measuring and in the idealization of the volumes, surfaces, edges, and intersections we experience in the life-world. The sense of the scientific world and its entities should not be placed in opposition to the life-world, but should be shown, by phenomenological analysis, to be a development of appearances found in it. In addition, the structures and evidences of the life-world itself must be philosophically described.

Husserl's influence in philosophy has been very great during the entire twentieth century, especially in Continental Europe. His concept of intentionality is understood as a way of overcoming the Cartesian dualism between mind and world, and his study of signs, formal systems, and parts and wholes has been valuable in structuralism and literary theory. His concept of the life-world has been used as a way of integrating science with wider forms of human activity, and his concepts of time and personal identity have been useful in psychoanalytic theory and existentialism. He has inspired work in the social sciences and recently his ideas have proved helpful to scholars in cognitive science and artificial intelligence.

See also BRENTANO, INTENTIONALITY, KANT, PHENOMENOLOGY.   R.So.

Hutcheson, Francis (1694–1746), Scottish philosopher who was the chief exponent of the early modern moral sense theory and of a similar theory postulating a sense of beauty. He was born in Drumalig, Ireland, and completed his theological training in 1717 at the University of Glasgow, where he later taught moral philosophy. He was a Presbyterian minister and founded an academy for Presbyterian youth in Dublin.

Sparked by Hobbes's thesis, in *Leviathan*

(1651), that human beings always act out of self-interest, moral debate in the eighteenth century was preoccupied with the possibility of a genuine benevolence. Hutcheson characterized his first work, *An Inquiry into the Original of our Ideas of Beauty and Virtue* (1725), as a defense of the non-egoistic moral sense theory of his more immediate predecessor, Shaftesbury, against the egoism of Bernard Mandeville (1670–1733). His second work, *An Essay on the Nature and Conduct of the Passions and Affections with Illustrations on the Moral Sense* (1728), explores the psychology of human action, apparently influenced by Butler's classification of the passions (in his *Sermons*, 1726).

Hutcheson asserts the existence of several "internal" senses – i.e., capacities for perceptual responses to concepts (such as one's idea of Nero's character), as opposed to perceptions of physical objects. Among these internal senses are those of honor, sympathy, morality, and beauty. Only the latter two, however, are discussed in detail by Hutcheson, who develops his account of each within the framework of Locke's empiricist epistemology. For Hutcheson, the idea of beauty is produced in us when we experience pleasure upon thinking of certain natural objects or artifacts, just as our idea of moral goodness is occasioned by the approval we feel toward an agent when we think of her actions, even if they in no way benefit us. Beauty and goodness (and their opposites) are analogous to Lockean secondary qualities, such as colors, tastes, smells, and sounds, in that their existence depends somehow on the minds of perceivers. The quality the sense of beauty consistently finds pleasurable is a pattern of "uniformity amidst variety," while the quality the moral sense invariably approves is benevolence.

A principal reason for thinking we possess a moral sense, according to Hutcheson, is that we approve of many actions unrelated or even contrary to our interests – a fact that suggests not all approval is reason-based. Further, he argues that attempts to explain our feelings of approval or disapproval without referring to a moral sense are futile: our reasons are ultimately grounded in the fact that we simply are constituted to care about others and take pleasure in benevolence (the quality of being concerned about others for their own sakes). For instance, we approve of temperance because overindulgence signifies selfishness, and selfishness is contrary to benevolence. Hutcheson also finds that the ends promoted by the benevolent person have a tendency to produce the greatest happiness for the greatest number. Thus, since he regards being motivated by benevolence as what makes actions morally good, Hutcheson's theory is a version of motive utilitarianism.

On Hutcheson's moral psychology, we are motivated, ultimately, not by reason alone, but by desires that arise in us at the prospect of our own or others' pleasure. Hutcheson formulates several quantitative maxims that purport to relate the strength of motivating desires to the degrees of good, or benefit, projected for different actions – an analysis that anticipates Bentham's hedonic calculus. Hutcheson was also one of the first philosophers to recognize and make use of the distinction between exciting, or motivating, reasons and justifying reasons. *Exciting reasons* are affections, or desires, ascribed to an agent as motives that explain particular actions. *Justifying reasons* derive from the approval of the moral sense and serve to indicate why a certain action is morally good. The connection between these two kinds of reasons has been a source of considerable debate.

Contemporary critics included John Balguy (1686–1748), who charged that Hutcheson's moral theory renders virtue arbitrary, since it depends on whatever human nature God happened to give us, which could just as well have been such as to make us delight in malice. Hutcheson discussed his views in correspondence with Hume, who later sent Hutcheson the unpublished manuscript of his own account of moral sentiment (Book III of *A Treatise of Human Nature*). As a teacher of Adam Smith, Hutcheson helped shape Smith's widely influential economic and moral theories. Hutcheson's major works also include *A Short Introduction to Moral Philosophy* (originally published in Latin in 1742) and *A System of Moral Philosophy* (1755).

See also BENTHAM, HUME, MORAL SENSE THEORY, SMITH.   E.S.R.

Huygens, Christiaan (1629–95), Dutch physicist and astronomer who ranked among the leading experimental scientists of his time and influenced many other thinkers, including Leibniz. He wrote on physics and astronomy in Latin (*Horologium Oscillatorium*, 1673; *De Vi Centrifuga*, 1703) and in French for the *Journal des Scavans*. He became a founding member of the French Academy of Sciences. Huygens ground lenses, built telescopes, discovered the rings of Saturn, and invented the pendulum clock. His most popular composition, *Cosmotheoros* (1699), inspired by Fontenelle, praises a divine architect and conjectures the possible existence of rational beings on other planets.   J.-L.S.

Hwajaeng-non. See KOREAN PHILOSOPHY.

hyle, ancient Greek term for matter. Aristotle brought the word into use in philosophy by contrast with the term for form, and as designating one of the four causes. By *hyle* Aristotle usually means 'that out of which something has been made', but he can also mean by it 'that which has form'. In Aristotelian philosophy *hyle* is sometimes also identified with potentiality and with substrate. Neoplatonists identified *hyle* with the receptacle of Plato. **See also** ARISTOTLE, FORM, HYLOMORPHISM, METAPHYSICS, SUBSTANCE.

P.Wo.

hylomorphism, the doctrine, first taught by Aristotle, that concrete substance consists of form in matter (*hyle*). The details of this theory are explored in the central books of Aristotle's *Metaphysics* (Zeta, Eta, and Theta). **See also** ARISTOTLE, FORM, HYLE, SUBSTANCE.   P.Wo.

hylozoism (from Greek *hylē*, 'matter', and *zōē*, 'life'), the doctrine that matter is intrinsically alive, or that all bodies, from the world as a whole down to the smallest corpuscle, have some degree or some kind of life. It differs from panpsychism though the distinction is sometimes blurred – in upholding the universal presence of life per se, rather than of soul or of psychic attributes. Inasmuch as it may also hold that there are no living entities not constituted of matter, hylozoism is often criticized by theistic philosophers as a form of atheism. The term was introduced polemically by Ralph Cudworth, the seventeenth-century Cambridge Platonist, to help define a position that is significantly in contrast to soul–body dualism (Pythagoras, Plato, Descartes), reductive materialism (Democritus, Hobbes), and Aristotelian hylomorphism. So understood, hylozoism had many advocates in the eighteenth and nineteenth centuries, among both scientists and naturalistically minded philosophers. In the twentieth century, the term has come to be used, rather unhelpfully, to characterize the animistic and naive-vitalist views of the early Greek philosophers, especially Thales, Anaximenes, Heraclitus, and Empedocles – who could hardly count as hylozoists in Cudworth's sophisticated sense. **See also** ARTIFICIAL LIFE, CAMBRIDGE PLATONISTS, HYLOMORPHISM, PANPSYCHISM.   A.P.D.M.

Hypatia (c.370–415), Greek Neoplatonist philosopher who lived and taught in Alexandria. She was brutally murdered by a Christian mob because of her associations with the city's prefect, who was in conflict with its aggressive archbishop, Cyril. She is said to have written commentaries on certain mathematical works, but the only certain trace of her literary activity is in her father Theon's commentary on book 3 of Ptolemy's *Almagest*, which Theon says is Hypatia's redaction. Hypatia appears to have been a very popular philosophy teacher. She presumably professed a standard Neoplatonist curriculum, using mathematics as a ladder to the intelligible world. A good sense of her views can be gained from the essays, hymns, and letters of her pupil Synesius, bishop of Ptolemais and an eclectic man of letters. Hypatia's modern fame can be traced back to the anticlericalism of the Enlightenment; see, e.g., chapter 47 of Edward Gibbon's *History of the Decline and Fall of the Roman Empire* (1778). The most influential representation of her appeared in Charles Kingsley's didactic historical novel *Hypatia or New Foes with an Old Face* (1853). The facts that – according to ancient report – Hypatia was not only a brilliant person, but a beautiful one who aroused the erotic passion of (at least) one student, and that she was stripped naked before being slaughtered, seem to have contributed to the revival of interest in her. **See also** NEOPLATONISM.   I.M.

hypostasis (from Latin, 'substance'), the process of regarding a concept or abstraction as an independent or real entity. The verb forms 'hypostatize' and 'reify' designate the acts of positing objects of a certain sort for the purposes of one's theory. It is sometimes implied that a fallacy is involved in so describing these processes or acts, as in 'Plato was guilty of the reification of universals'. The issue turns largely on criteria of ontological commitment. **See also** METAPHYSICS, ONTOLOGICAL COMMITMENT.   C.F.D.

hypostatize. See HYPOSTASIS.

hypothetical consent. See CONTRACTARIANISM.

hypothetical construct. See OPERATIONALISM.

hypothetical imperative. See KANT.

hypothetical syllogism. See SYLLOGISM.

hypothetico-deductive method, a method of testing hypotheses. Thought to be preferable to the method of enumerative induction, whose limitations had been decisively demonstrated by Hume, the hypothetico-deductive (H-D) method has been viewed by many as the ideal scientific method. It is applied by introducing an explanatory hypothesis resulting from earlier inductions, a guess, or an act of creative imagination. The hypothesis is logically conjoined with a statement of initial conditions. The purely deductive consequences of this conjunction are derived as predictions, and the statements asserting them are subjected to experimental or observational test. More formally, given $(H \cdot A) \rightarrow O$, H is the hypothesis, A a statement of initial conditions, and O one of the testable consequences of $(H \cdot A)$. If the hypothesis is 'all lead is malleable', and 'this piece of lead is now being hammered' states the initial conditions, it follows deductively that 'this piece of lead will change shape'. In deductive logic the schema

$$\frac{(H \cdot A) \rightarrow O}{O}{(H \cdot A)}$$

is formally invalid, committing the logical fallacy of affirming the consequent. But repeated occurrences of O can be said to confirm the conjunction of H and A, or to render it more probable. On the other hand, the schema

$$\frac{(H \cdot A) \rightarrow O}{\text{not-}O}{\text{not-}(H \cdot A)}$$

is deductively valid (the argument form *modus tollens*). For this reason, Karl Popper and his followers think that the H-D method is best employed in seeking falsifications of theoretical hypotheses. Criticisms of the method point out that infinitely many hypotheses can explain, in the H-D mode, a given body of data, so that successful predictions are not probative, and that (following Duhem) it is impossible to test isolated singular hypotheses because they are always contained in complex theories any one of whose parts is eliminable in the face of negative evidence. **See also** CURVE-FITTING PROBLEM, DUHEM, TESTABILITY.   R.E.B.

I

Iamblichus. See COMMENTARIES ON PLATO, NEOPLATONISM.

Ibn Bājja, Abu Bakr, in Latin, Avempace (d.1139), Spanish Islamic philosopher who was exceptionally well regarded by later Arabic authorities. During a career as a government official and vizier he wrote important treatises on philosophy but appears to have left most of them unfinished. One of them provides an important theory of the conjunction of the intellect with the human, based in part on notions of progressive abstraction of specific forms and the universality of the Active Intellect. Another offers a political philosophy grounded in assumptions about a representative of the virtuous city who exists within a hostile, erring city as a solitary or aberrant "weed." P.E.W.

Ibn Daud, Abraham, also called Rabad (c.1110–80), Spanish Jewish historian and astronomer, a philosophic precursor of Maimonides. Born in Córdova and schooled by a beloved uncle, Baruch Albalia, in Jewish and Greco-Arabic learning, he fled the Almohad invasion of 1146, settling in Christian Toledo, where he was martyred. His *Sefer ha-Qabbalah* (1161; translated by Gerson Cohen as *The Book of Tradition*, 1967) finds providential continuity in Jewish intellectual history. His *Emunah Ramah* (1161; translated by Norbert Samuelson as *The Exalted Faith*, 1986) was written in Arabic but preserved in Hebrew. It anchors Jewish natural theology and ethics in Avicennan metaphysics, mitigated by a voluntaristic account of emanation and by the assertion that God created matter. Ibn Daud saves human freedom by holding that God knows undetermined events as possible. He defends prophecy as an outpouring of the Active Intellect – or of God – on those whose natures and circumstances permit their inspiration. Prophetic miracles are perfectly natural alterations of the familiar characters of things. **See also AVICENNA.** L.E.G.

Ibn Gabirol, Solomon, in Latin, Avicebron (c.1020–c.1057), Spanish Jewish philosopher and poet, the author (in Arabic) of *The Source of Life*, a classic of Neoplatonic thought. This work was written without any explicit Jewish associations, and was preserved only in a twelfth-century Latin translation, the *Fons vitae*. Consequently, its author was assumed until the last century to be Muslim or Christian. Jewish Neoplatonists and mystics until the Renaissance were familiar with the work and its author, and its influence was felt in Christian Scholastic circles as well. Ibn Gabirol's philosophy is also reflected in his epic Hebrew poem "The Royal Crown," which merges the personal and religious feelings of the poet with a verse summary of his metaphysical and astronomical beliefs.

The *Fons vitae* is a prolix and often inconsistent treatise, but exhibits radical creativity. The influence of Proclus and of the first Jewish Neoplatonist, the tenth-century Isaac Israeli, is also evident. Ibn Gabirol superimposes on the traditional Neoplatonic triad of universal substances, the Intellect, Soul, and Nature, another set of creative and more fundamental hypostases, the One, Divine Will, and Form and Matter. In one of his most radical formulations, this primordial Form and Matter are thought to suffuse not only the entire world that proceeds from them, but to be found within the One itself, Matter being identified with the divine essence, Form with Divine Will. Matter here emerges as prior and more essential to the divine being than Form; God by implication is identified primarily with potentiality and becoming, a point not lost upon the mystics.

See also JEWISH PHILOSOPHY. A.L.I.

Ibn Khaldūn, 'Abdurrahmān (1332–1406), Arab historian, scholar, and politician, the first thinker to articulate a comprehensive theory of historiography and philosophy of history in his *Muqaddima* (final revision 1402), the introductory volume to his *Universal History* (*Kitāb al-'ibar*, 1377–82). Born and raised in Tunis, he spent the politically active first part of his life in northwestern Africa and Muslim Spain. He moved to Cairo in 1382 to pursue a career as professor of Mālikī law and judge.

Ibn Khaldūn created in the *Muqaddima* (English translation by F. Rosenthal, 1967) what he called an "entirely original science." He established a scientific methodology for historiography by providing a theory of the basic laws operating in history so that not only could the occurrences of the past be registered but also "the how and why of events" could be understood. Historiography is based on the criticism of sources; the criteria to be used are inherent probability of the historical reports (*khabar;* plural: *akhbār*) – to be judged on the basis of an understanding of significant political, economic, and cultural factors – and their conformity with reality and the nature of the historical process. The latter he analyzed as the cyclical (every three generations, c.120 years) rise and decline of human societies (*'umrān*) insofar as they exhibit a political cohesiveness (*'aṣabīya*) in accepting the authority of a dynastic head of state. Ibn Khaldūn's sources were the actual course of Islamic history and the injunctions about political and social behavior found in the Greek/Persian/Arab mirrors for princes and wisdom literature, welded together by an Aristotelian teleological realism/empiricism; by contrast, he was critical of the metaphysical Platonic utopias of thinkers like al-Fārābī. His influence is to be felt in later Arab authors and in particular in Ottoman historiography. In the West, where he has been intensely studied since the eighteenth century, he has been variously seen as the founder of sociology, economic history, and other modern theories of state. (See A. Al-Azmeh, *Ibn Khaldūn*, 1989.)

  See also ARABIC PHILOSOPHY.   D.Gu.

Ibn Rushd. See AVERROES.

Ibn Sīnā. See AVICENNA.

Ibn Ṭufayl, Abu Bakr (d.1186), Spanish Islamic philosopher who played an important role in promoting the philosophical career of Averroes. His own contribution, however, is a famous philosophical fantasy, *Hayy ibn Yaqzan* – an account of a solitary autodidact who grows up on a deserted island yet discovers by his own unaided efforts a philosophical (Aristotelian) explanation of the world and of divine truths. Later, having finally come in contact with human civilization, this character also recognizes the necessity of religious law and regulation for that other, essentially imperfect, society, although he holds himself personally above this requirement. The work attracted considerable attention in late seventeenth-century Europe following its publication in 1671. **See also ARABIC PHILOSOPHY.**
                                           P.E.W.

I-Ching ("Book of Changes"), a Chinese divination manual that may have existed in some form as early as the seventh century B.C. It was not philosophically significant until augmented by a group of appendices, the "Ten Wings," around 200 B.C. The book has tremendously influenced Chinese thought since the Han dynasty, for at least two reasons. First, it provided a cosmology that systematically grounded certain ideas, particularly Confucian ethical claims, in the nature of the cosmos. Second, it presented this cosmology through a system of loosely described symbols that provided virtually limitless interpretive possibilities. In order to "read" the text properly, one needed to *be* a certain kind of person. In this way, the *I-Ching* accommodated both intuitionism and self-cultivationism, two prominent characteristics of early Chinese thought. At the same time, the text's endless interpretive possibilities allowed it to be used in widely different ways by a variety of thinkers. **See also CHINESE PHILOSOPHY, CONFUCIANISM.**
                                           P.J.I.

icon. See PEIRCE.

id. See FREUD.

idea, in the seventeenth and eighteenth centuries, whatever is immediately before the mind when one thinks. The notion of thinking was taken in a very broad sense; it included perception, memory, and imagination, in addition to thinking narrowly construed.

  In connection with perception, ideas were often (though not always – Berkeley is the exception) held to be representational images, i.e., images *of* something. In other contexts, ideas were taken to be concepts, such as the concept of a horse or of an infinite quantity, though concepts of these sorts certainly do not appear to be images.

  An *innate idea* was either a concept or a general truth, such as 'Equals added to equals yield equals', that was allegedly not learned but was in some sense always in the mind. Sometimes, as in Descartes, innate ideas were taken to be cognitive capacities rather than concepts or general truths, but these capacities, too, were held to be inborn.

  An *adventitious idea*, either an image or a concept, was an idea accompanied by a judgment concerning the non-mental cause of that idea. So, a visual image was an adventitious idea provided one judged of that idea that it was caused by something outside one's mind, presumably by the object being seen.

See also BERKELEY, DESCARTES, HUME, LOCKE, PERCEPTION.   G.S.P.

idea, clear and distinct. See DESCARTES.

idea, innate. See IDEA.

idealism, the philosophical doctrine that reality is somehow mind-correlative or mind-coordinated – that the real objects constituting the "external world" are not independent of cognizing minds, but exist only as in some way correlative to mental operations. The doctrine centers on the conception that reality as we understand it reflects the workings of mind. Perhaps its most radical version is the ancient Oriental spiritualistic or panpsychistic idea, renewed in Christian Science, that minds and their thoughts are all there is – that reality is simply the sum total of the visions (or dreams?) of one or more minds.

A dispute has long raged within the idealist camp over whether "the mind" at issue in such idealistic formulas was a mind emplaced outside of or behind nature (*absolute* idealism), or a nature-pervasive power of rationality of some sort (*cosmic* idealism), or the collective impersonal social mind of people in general (*social* idealism), or simply the distributive collection of individual minds (*personal* idealism). Over the years, the less grandiose versions of the theory came increasingly to the fore, and in recent times virtually all idealists have construed "the minds" at issue in their theory as separate individual minds equipped with socially engendered resources.

There are certainly versions of idealism short of the spiritualistic position of an ontological idealism that (as Kant puts it at *Prolegomena*, section 13, n. 2) holds that "there are none but thinking beings." Idealism need certainly not go so far as to affirm that mind *makes* or *constitutes* matter; it is quite enough to maintain (e.g.) that all of the characterizing properties of physical existents resemble phenomenal sensory properties in representing dispositions to affect mind-endowed creatures in a certain sort of way, so that these properties have no standing without reference to minds. Weaker still is an explanatory idealism which merely holds that an adequate *explanation* of the real always requires some recourse to the operations of mind.

Historically, positions of the generally idealistic type have been espoused by numerous thinkers. For example, Berkeley maintained that "to be [real] is to be perceived" (*esse est percipi*). And while this does not seem particularly plausible because of its inherent commitment to omniscience, it seems more sensible to adopt "to be is to be perceivable" (*esse est percipile esse*). For Berkeley, of course, this was a distinction without a difference: if something is perceivable at all, then God perceives it. But if we forgo philosophical reliance on God, the matter looks different, and pivots on the question of what is perceivable for perceivers who are *physically realizable* in "the real world," so that *physical* existence could be seen – not so implausibly – as tantamount to observability-in-principle.

The three positions to the effect that real things just exactly are things as philosophy or as science or as "common sense" takes them to be – positions generally designated as *Scholastic, scientific,* and *naive* realism, respectively – are in fact versions of epistemic idealism exactly because they see reals as inherently knowable and do not contemplate mind-transcendence for the real. Thus, the thesis of naive ("commonsense") realism that 'External things exist exactly as we know them' sounds realistic or idealistic according as one stresses the first three words of the dictum or the last four.

Any theory of natural teleology that regards the real as explicable in terms of value could to this extent be counted as idealistic, in that valuing is by nature a mental process. To be sure, the good of a creature or species of creatures (e.g., their well-being or survival) need not be something mind-represented. But nevertheless, goods count as such precisely because if the creatures at issue *could* think about it, they *would* adopt them as purposes. It is this circumstance that renders any sort of teleological explanation at least conceptually idealistic in nature. Doctrines of this sort have been the stock-in-trade of philosophy from the days of Plato (think of the Socrates of the *Phaedo*) to those of Leibniz, with his insistence that the real world must be the best possible. And this line of thought has recently surfaced once more in the controversial "anthropic principle" espoused by some theoretical physicists.

Then too it is possible to contemplate a position along the lines envisioned in Fichte's *Wissenschaftslehre* (*The Science of Knowledge*), which sees the ideal as providing the determining factor for the real. On such a view, the real is not characterized by the science we actually have but by the ideal science that is the *telos* of our scientific efforts. On this approach, which Wilhelm Wundt characterized as "ideal-realism" (*Idealrealismus;* see his *Logik*, vol. 1, 2d ed., 1895), the knowledge that achieves adequation to the real (*adaequatio ad rem*) by adequately characterizing the true facts in scientific matters is not the knowledge actually afforded by present-day science, but only that of an ideal or perfected science.

Over the years, many objections to idealism have been advanced. Samuel Johnson thought to refute Berkeley's phenomenalism by kicking a stone. He conveniently forgot that Berkeley goes to great lengths to provide for stones – even to the point of invoking the aid of God on their behalf. Moore pointed to the human hand as an undeniably mind-external material object. He overlooked that, gesticulate as he would, he would do no more than induce people to accept the presence of a hand on the basis of the hand-orientation of their *experience*. Peirce's "Harvard Experiment" of letting go of a stone held aloft was supposed to establish Scholastic realism because his audience could not control their expectation of the stone's falling to earth. But an uncontrollable expectation is still an expectation, and the realism at issue is no more than a realistic thought-exposure.

Kant's famous "Refutation of Idealism" argues that our conception of ourselves as mind-endowed beings presupposes material objects because we view our mind-endowed selves as existing in an objective temporal order, and such an order requires the existence of periodic physical processes (clocks, pendula, planetary regularities) for its establishment. At most, however, this argument succeeds in showing that such physical processes have to be assumed by minds, the issue of their actual mind-independent existence remaining unaddressed. (Kantian realism is an intraexperiential "empirical" realism.)

It is sometimes said that idealism confuses objects with our knowledge of them and conflates the real with our thought about it. But this charge misses the point. The only reality with which we inquirers can have any cognitive commerce is reality as we conceive it to be. Our only information about reality is via the operation of mind – our only cognitive access to reality is through the mediation of mind-devised models of it.

Perhaps the most common objection to idealism turns on the supposed mind-independence of the real: "Surely things in nature would remain substantially unchanged if there were no minds." This is perfectly plausible in one sense, namely the *causal* one – which is why causal idealism has its problems. But it is certainly not true *conceptually*. The objector has to specify just exactly what would remain the same. "Surely

roses would smell just as sweet in a mind-denuded world!" Well . . . yes and no. To be sure, the absence of minds would not *change* roses. But roses and rose fragrance and sweetness – and even the *size* of roses – are all factors whose determination hinges on such mental operations as smelling, scanning, measuring, and the like. Mind-requiring processes are needed for something in the world to be discriminated as a rose and determined to bear certain features. Identification, classification, property attribution are all required and by their very nature are all mental operations. To be sure, the role of mind is here hypothetical. ("If certain interactions with duly constituted observers took place, then certain outcomes would be noted.") But the fact remains that nothing could be discriminated or characterized as a rose in a context where the prospect of performing suitable mental operations (measuring, smelling, etc.) is not presupposed.

Perhaps the strongest argument favoring idealism is that any characterization of the real that we can devise is bound to be a mind-constructed one: *our* only access to information about what the real is is through the mediation of mind. What seems right about idealism is inherent in the fact that in investigating the real we are clearly constrained to use our own concepts to address our own issues – that we can learn about the real only in our own terms of reference. But what seems right about realism is that the answers to the questions we put to the real are provided by reality itself – whatever the answers may be, they are substantially what they are because it is reality itself that determines them to be that way.

See also BERKELEY, FICHTE, HEGEL, KANT, METAPHYSICS.   N.R.

idealism, Critical. See KANT.

idealism, transcendental. See KANT.

ideal language, a system of notation that would correct perceived deficiencies of ordinary language by requiring the structure of expressions to mirror the structure of that which they represent. The notion that conceptual errors can be corrected and philosophical problems solved (or dissolved) by properly representing them in some such system figured prominently in the writings of Leibniz, Carnap, Russell, Wittgenstein, and Frege, among others. For Russell, the ideal, or "logically perfect," language is one in which grammatical form coincides with logical form, there are no vague or ambiguous expressions, and no proper names that fail to denote. Frege's *Begriffsschrift* is perhaps the most thorough and successful execution of the ideal language project. Deductions represented within this system (or its modern descendants) can be effectively checked for correctness. **See also** CARNAP, FORMAL LANGUAGE, LOGICAL FORM, RUSSELL.   S.T.K.

ideal market, a hypothetical market, used as a tool of economic analysis, in which all relevant agents are perfectly informed of the price of the good in question and the cost of its production, and all economic transactions can be undertaken with no cost. A specific case is a market exemplifying perfect competition. The term is sometimes extended to apply to an entire economy consisting of ideal markets for every good. **See also** PERFECT COMPETITION, PHILOSOPHY OF ECONOMICS.   A.N.

ideal mathematics. See HILBERT'S PROGRAM.

ideal observer, a hypothetical being, possessed of various qualities and traits, whose moral reactions (judgments or attitudes) to actions, persons, and states of affairs figure centrally in certain theories of ethics. There are two main versions of ideal observer theory: (a) those that take the reactions of ideal observers as a standard of the *correctness* of moral judgments, and (b) those that analyze the *meanings* of moral judgments in terms of the reactions of ideal observers.

Theories of the first sort – ideal observer theories of correctness – hold, e.g., that judgments like 'John's lying to Brenda about her father's death was wrong (bad)' are correct provided any ideal observer would have a negative attitude toward John's action. Similarly, 'Alison's refusal to divulge confidential information about her patient was right (good)' is correct provided any ideal observer would have a positive attitude toward that action. This version of the theory can be traced to Adam Smith, who is usually credited with introducing the concept of an ideal observer into philosophy, though he used the expression 'impartial spectator' to refer to the concept. Regarding the correctness of moral judgments, Smith wrote: "That precise and distinct measure can be found nowhere but in the sympathetic feelings of the impartial and well-informed spectator" (*A Theory of Moral Sentiments*, 1759).

Theories of a second sort – ideal observer theories of meaning – take the concept of an ideal observer as part of the very meaning of ordinary moral judgments. Thus, according to Roderick Firth ("Ethical Absolutism and the Ideal Observer," *Philosophy and Phenomenological Research,* 1952), moral judgments of the form '*x* is good (bad)', on this view, mean 'All ideal observers would feel moral approval (disapproval) toward *x*', and similarly for other moral judgments (where such approvals and disapprovals are characterized as felt desires having a "demand quality").

Different conceptions of an ideal observer result from variously specifying those qualities and traits that characterize such beings. Smith's characterization includes being well informed and impartial. However, according to Firth, an ideal observer must be omniscient; omnipercipient, i.e., having the ability to imagine vividly any possible events or states of affairs, including the experiences and subjective states of others; disinterested, i.e., having no interests or desires that involve essential reference to any particular individuals or things; dispassionate; consistent; and otherwise a "normal" human being. Both versions of the theory face a dilemma: on the one hand, if ideal observers are richly characterized as impartial, disinterested, and normal, then since these terms appear to be moral-evaluative terms, appeal to the reactions of ideal observers (either as a standard of correctness or as an analysis of meaning) is circular. On the other hand, if ideal observers receive an impoverished characterization in purely non-evaluative terms, then since there is no reason to suppose that such ideal observers will often all agree in their reactions to actions, people, and states of affairs, most moral judgments will turn out to be incorrect. **See also** ETHICAL OBJECTIVISM, ETHICS, RELATIVISM.   M.C.T.

ideal proposition. See HILBERT'S PROGRAM.

ideal type. See MOSCA, WEBER.

ideal utilitarianism. See RASHDALL, UTILITARIANISM.

ideas of practical reason. See KANT.

ideas of pure reason. See KANT.

ideas of reflection. See LOCKE.

ideas of sensation. See LOCKE.

idea theory of meaning. See MEANING.

ideational theory of meaning. See PHILOSOPHY OF LANGUAGE.

Identity proper is *numerical identity*, to be distinguished from *exact similarity* (*qualitative identity*). Intuitively, two exactly similar objects are "copies" of each other; still they are two, hence not identical. One way to express this is via the notions of *extrinsic* and *intrinsic properties:* exactly similar objects differ in respect of the former only. But we can best explain 'instrinsic property' by saying that a thing's intrinsic properties are those it shares with its copies. These notions appear virtually interdefinable. (Note that the concept of an extrinsic property must be relativized to a class or kind of things. Not being in San Francisco is an extrinsic property of persons but arguably an intrinsic property of cities.) While qualitative identity is a familiar notion, its theoretical utility is unclear. The absolute notion of qualitative identity should, however, be distinguished from an unproblematic relative notion: if some list of salient properties is fixed in a given context (say, in mechanics or normative ethics), then the exactly similar things, relative to that context, are those that agree on the properties listed.

Both the identity of indiscernibles and (less frequently) the indiscernibility of identicals are sometimes called *Leibniz's law*. Neither attribution is apt. Although Leibniz would have accepted the former principle, his distinctive claim was the impossibility of exactly similar objects: numerically distinct individuals cannot even share all intrinsic properties. Moreover, this was not, for him, simply a law of identity but rather an application of his principle of sufficient ordinary material body to its constituent matter may suggest that the logician's analysis of identity does not cleanly capture our everyday notion(s).

Consider a bronze statue. Although the statue may seem to be nothing besides its matter, reflection on change over time suggests a distinction. The statue may be melted down, hence destroyed, while the bronze persists, perhaps simply as a mass or perhaps as a new statue formed from the same bronze. Alternatively, the statue may persist even as some of its bronze is dissolved in acid. So the statue seems to be one thing and the bronze another. Yet what is the bronze besides a statue? Surely we do not have *two* statues (or statuelike objects) in one place? Some authors feel that variants of the identity relation may permit a perspicuous description of the relation of statue and bronze:

(1) *tensed identity:* Assume a class of time-bound properties – roughly, properties an object can have at a time regardless of what properties it has at other times. (E.g., a statue's shape, location, or elegance.) Then $a = {}_t b$ provided a and b share all time-bound properties at time t. Thus, the statue and the bronze may be identical at time t_1 but not at t_2.

(2) *relative identity:* a and b may be identical relative to one concept (or predicate) but not to another. Thus, the statue may be held to be the same *lump of matter* as the bronze but not the same *object of art*.

(3) If objects *a* and *b* have all their *non-relational qualitative* properties in common, then *a* and *b* are identical.

Two questions regarding these principles are raised: Which, if any, are true? If any are true, are they necessarily true?

Discussions of the identity of indiscernibles typically restrict the scope of the principle to concrete objects. Although the notions of qualitative and non-relational properties play a prominent role in these discussions, they are notoriously difficult to define. Intuitively, a qualitative property is one that can be instantiated by more than one object and does not involve being related to another *particular* object. It does not follow that all qualitative properties are non-relational, since some relational properties, such as *being on top of a brown desk,* do not involve being related to some *particular* object.

(1) is generally regarded as necessarily true but trivial, since if *a* and *b* have *all* properties in common then *a* has the property of being identical with *b* and *b* has the property of being identical with *a*. Hence, most discussions focus on (2) and (3). (3) is generally regarded as, at best, a contingent truth since it appears possible to conceive of two distinct red balls of the same size, shade of color, and composition. Some have argued that elementary scientific particles, such as electrons,

describe someone else's political views which one regards as unsound. This use derives from Marx's employment of the term to signify a false consciousness shared by the members of a particular social class. For example, according to Marx, members of the capitalist class share the ideology that the laws of the competitive market are natural and impersonal, that workers in a competitive market are paid all that they can be paid, and that the institutions of private property in the means of production are natural and justified. **See also MARXISM, POLITICAL PHILOSOPHY.**   J.P.St.

ideo-motor action, a theory of the will according to which "every representation of a movement awakens in some degree the actual movement which is its object" (William James). Proposed by physiologist W. B. Carpenter, and taught by Lotze and Renouvier, ideo-motor action was developed by James. He rejected the regnant analysis of voluntary behavior, which held that will operates by reinstating "feelings of innervation" (Wundt) in the efferent nerves. Deploying introspection and physiology, James showed that feelings of innervation do not exist. James advanced ideo-motor action as the psychological basis of volition: actions tend to occur automatically when thought, unless inhibited by a contrary idea. Will consists in fixing attention on a desired idea until it dominates consciousness, the execution of movement following automatically. James also rejected Bain's associationist thesis that pleasure or pain is the necessary spring of action, since according to ideo-motor theory thought of an action by itself produces it. James's analysis became dogma, but was effectively attacked by psychologist E. L. Thorndike (1874–1949), who proposed in its place the behavioristic doctrine that ideas have no power to cause behavior, and argued that belief in ideo-motor action amounted to belief in sympathetic magic. Thus did will leave the vocabulary of psychology. **See also JAMES, VOLITION.**   T.H.L.

idols of the cave. See BACON, FRANCIS.

idols of the marketplace. See BACON, FRANCIS.

idols of the mind. See BACON, FRANCIS.

idols of the theater. See BACON, FRANCIS.

idols of the tribe. See BACON, FRANCIS.

iff, an abbreviation for 'if and only if' that is used as if it were a single propositional operator (connective). Another synonym for 'iff' is 'just in case'. The justification for treating 'iff' as if it were a single propositional connective is that 'P if and only if Q' is elliptical for 'P if Q, and P only if Q', and this assertion is logically equivalent to 'P biconditional Q'. **See also BICONDITIONAL.**
      R.W.B.

ignoratio elenchi. See INFORMAL FALLACY.

Il'in, Ivan Aleksandrovich (1883–1954), Russian philosopher and conservative legal and political theorist. He authored an important two-volume commentary on Hegel (1918), plus extensive writings in ethics, political theory, aesthetics, and spirituality. Exiled in 1922, he was known for his passionate opposition to Bolshevism, his extensive proposals for rebuilding a radically reformed Russian state, church, and society in a post-Communist future, and his devout Russian Orthodox spirituality. He is widely regarded as a master of Russian language and a penetrating interpreter of the history of Russian culture. His collected works are currently being published in Moscow. **See also RUSSIAN PHILOSOPHY.**   P.T.G.

illation. See INDUCTION.

illative. See INDUCTION.

illative sense. See NEWMAN.

illicit process of the major. See SYLLOGISM.

illicit process of the minor. See SYLLOGISM.

illocutionary act. See SPEECH ACT THEORY.

illocutionary force. See PHILOSOPHY OF LANGUAGE, SPEECH ACT THEORY.

illocutionary force potential. See SPEECH ACT THEORY.

illusion, argument from. See PERCEPTION.

image theory of meaning. See MEANING.

image theory of memory. See MEMORY.

imagination, the mental faculty sometimes thought to encompass all acts of thinking about something novel, contrary to fact, or not currently perceived; thus: "Imagine that Lincoln had not been assassinated," or "Use your imagination to create a new design for roller skates." 'Imagination' also denotes an important perception-like aspect of some such thoughts, so that to imagine something is to bring to mind what it would be like to perceive it.

Philosophical theories of imagination must explain its apparent intentionality: when we imagine, we always imagine *something*. Imagination is always directed toward an object, even though the object may not exist. Moreover, imagination, like perception, is often seen as involving qualia, or special subjective properties that are sometimes thought to discredit materialist, especially functionalist, theories of mind.

The intentionality of imagination and its perceptual character lead some theories to equate imagination with "imaging": being conscious of or perceiving a mental image. However, because the ontological status of such images and the nature of their properties are obscure, many philosophers have rejected mental images in favor of an adverbial theory on which to imagine something red is best analyzed as imagining "redly." Such theories avoid the difficulties associated with mental images, but must offer some other way to account for the apparent intentionality of imagination as well as its perceptual character.

Imagination, in the hands of Husserl and Sartre, becomes a particularly apt subject for phenomenology. It is also cited as a faculty that separates human thought from any form of artificial intelligence. Finally, imagination often figures prominently in debates about possibility, in that what is imaginable is often taken to be coextensive with what is possible. **See also** CONCEIVABILITY, IDEA, INTENTIONALITY, PERCEPTION, PHILOSOPHY OF MIND.   L.-M.R.

imaging. See IMAGINATION.

immanence, a term most often used in contrast to 'transcendence' to express the way in which God is thought to be present in the world. The most extreme form of immanence is expressed in pantheism, which identifies God's substance either partly or wholly with the world. In contrast to pantheism, Judaism and Christianity hold God to be a totally separate substance from the world. In Christianity, the separateness of God's substance from that of the world is guaranteed by the doctrine of creation *ex nihilo.* Aquinas held that God is in the world as an efficient cause is present to that on which it acts. Thus, God is present in the world by continuously acting on it to preserve it in existence. Perhaps the weakest notion of immanence is expressed in eighteenth- and nineteenth-century deism, in which God initially creates the world and institutes its universal laws, but is basically an absentee landlord, exercising no providential activity over its continuing history. **See also** DEISM, NATURAL RELIGION, PHILOSOPHY OF RELIGION, TRANSCENDENCE.
                                                                W.L.R.

immanent causation. See AGENT CAUSATION.

immaterial. See DISEMBODIMENT.

immaterialism, the view that objects are best characterized as mere collections of qualities: "a certain colour, taste, smell, figure and consistence having been observed to go together, are accounted one distinct thing, signified by the name *apple*" (Berkeley, *Principles,* 1). So construed, immaterialism anticipates by some two hundred years a doctrine defended in the early twentieth century by Russell. The negative side of the doctrine comes in the denial of material substance or matter. Some philosophers had held that ordinary objects are individual material substances in which qualities inhere. The account is mistaken because, according to immaterialism, there is no such thing as material substance, and so qualities do not inhere in it.

Immaterialism should not be confused with Berkeley's idealism. The latter, but not the former, implies that objects and their qualities exist if and only if they are perceived.
     See also BERKELEY, IDEALISM, PHENOMENALISM.   G.S.P.

immediacy, presence to the mind without intermediaries. The term 'immediate' and its cognates have been used extensively throughout the history of philosophy, generally without much explanation. Descartes, e.g., explains his notion of thought thus: "I use this term to include everything that is within us in a way that we are immediately aware of it" (*Second Replies*). He offers no explanation of immediate awareness. However, when used as a primitive in this way, the term may simply mean that thoughts are the immediate objects of perception because thoughts are the only things perceived in the strict and proper sense that no perception of an intermediary is required for the person's awareness of them.
     Sometimes 'immediate' means 'not mediated'. (1) An inference from a premise to a conclusion can exhibit logical immediacy because it does not depend on other premises. This is a technical usage of proof theory to describe the form of a certain class of inference rules. (2) A concept can exhibit conceptual immediacy because it is definitionally primitive, as in the Berkeleian doctrine that perception of qualities is immediate, and perception of objects is defined by the perception of their qualities, which is directly understood. (3) Our perception of something can exhibit causal immediacy because it is not caused by intervening acts of perception or cognition, as with seeing someone immediately in the flesh rather than through images on a movie screen. (4) A belief-formation process can possess psychological immediacy because it contains no subprocess of reasoning and in that sense has no psychological mediator. (5) Our knowledge of something can exhibit epistemic immediacy because it is justified without inference from another proposition, as in intuitive knowledge of the existence of the self, which has no epistemic mediator.
     A noteworthy special application of immediacy is to be found in Russell's notion of knowledge by acquaintance. This notion is a development of the venerable doctrine originating with Plato, and also found in Augustine, that understanding the nature of some object requires that we can gain immediate cognitive access to that object. Thus, for Plato, to understand the nature

of beauty requires acquaintance with beauty itself. This view contrasts with one in which understanding the nature of beauty requires *linguistic competence* in the use of the word 'beauty' or, alternatively, with one that requires having a *mental representation* of beauty. Russell offers sense-data and universals as examples of things known by acquaintance.

To these senses of immediacy we may add another category whose members have acquired special meanings within certain philosophical traditions. For example, in Hegel's philosophy if (*per impossibile*) an object were encountered "as existing in simple immediacy" it would be encountered as it is in itself, unchanged by conceptualization. In phenomenology "immediate" experience is, roughly, *bracketed* experience.

See also BERKELEY, EPISTEMOLOGY, IDEA, INFERENTIAL KNOWLEDGE, PERCEPTION, PHILOSOPHY OF MIND.   T.V.

immediate inference. See INFERENCE.

immortality. See DISEMBODIMENT, SOUL.

impartiality, a state or disposition achieved to the degree that one's actions or attitudes are not influenced in a relevant respect by which members of a relevant group are benefited or harmed by one's actions or by the object of one's attitudes. For example, a basketball referee and that referee's calls are impartial when the referee's applications of the rules are not affected by whether the calls help one team or the other. A fan's approval of a call lacks impartiality if that attitude results from the fan's preference for one team over the other.

Impartiality in this general sense does not exclude arbitrariness or guarantee fairness; nor does it require neutrality among values, for a judge can be impartial between parties while favoring liberty and equality for all. Different situations might call for impartiality in different respects toward different groups, so disagreements arise, for example, about when morality requires or allows partiality toward friends or family or country. Moral philosophers have proposed various tests of the kind of impartiality required by morality, including role reversibility (Kurt Baier), universalizability (Hare), a veil of ignorance (Rawls), and a restriction to beliefs shared by all rational people (Bernard Gert).

See also ETHICS, HARE, RAWLS, UNIVERSALIZABILITY.   W.S.-A.

imperative, categorical. See KANT.

imperative, hypothetical. See KANT.

imperfect duty. See DUTY, KANT.

imperfect rights. See GROTIUS.

implication, a relation that holds between two statements when the truth of the first ensures the truth of the second. A number of statements together imply Q if their joint truth ensures the truth of Q. An argument is deductively valid exactly when its premises imply its conclusion. Expressions of the following forms are often interchanged one for the other: 'P implies Q', 'Q follows from P', and 'P entails Q'. ('Entailment' also has a more restricted meaning.)

In ordinary discourse, 'implication' has wider meanings that are important for understanding reasoning and communication of all kinds. The sentence 'Last Tuesday, the editor remained sober throughout lunch' does not imply that the editor is not always sober. But one who asserted the sentence typically would imply this. The theory of *conversational implicature* explains how speakers often imply more than their sentences imply.

The term 'implication' also applies to conditional statements. A *material implication* of the form 'if P, then Q' (often symbolized '$P \rightarrow Q$' or '$P \supset Q$') is true so long as either the if-clause P is false or the main clause Q is true; it is false only if P is true and Q is false. A *strict implication* of the form 'if P, then Q' (often symbolized '$P \rightarrow Q$') is true exactly when the corresponding material implication is necessarily true; i.e., when it is impossible for P to be true when Q is false. The following valid forms of argument are called *paradoxes of material implication:*

Q. Therefore, $P \supset Q$.

Not-P. Therefore, $P \supset Q$.

The appearance of paradox here is due to using 'implication' as a name both for a relation between statements and for statements of conditional form. A conditional statement can be true even though there is no relation between its components. Consider the following valid inference:

Butter floats in milk. Therefore, fish sleep at night $\supset$ butter floats in milk.

Since the simple premise is true, the conditional conclusion is also true despite the fact that the nocturnal activities of fish and the comparative densities of milk and butter are completely unrelated. The statement 'Fish sleep at night' does not imply that butter floats in milk. It is better to call a conditional statement that is true just so long as it does not have a true if-clause and a false main clause a *material conditional* rather than a material implication.

Strict conditional is similarly preferable to 'strict implication'. Respecting this distinction, however, does not dissolve all the puzzlement of the so-called *paradoxes of strict implication:*

> *Necessarily Q.* Therefore, $P \rightarrow Q$.

> *Impossible that P.* Therefore, $P \rightarrow Q$.

Here is an example of the first pattern:

> Necessarily, all rectangles are rectangles. Therefore, fish sleep at night $\rightarrow$ all rectangles are rectangles.

'All rectangles are rectangles' is an example of a vacuous truth, so called because it is devoid of content. 'All squares are rectangles' and '5 is greater than 3' are not so obviously vacuous truths, although they are necessary truths. Vacuity is not a sharply defined notion.

Here is an example of the second pattern:

> It is impossible that butter always floats in milk yet sometimes does not float in milk. Therefore, butter always floats in milk yet sometimes does not float in milk $\rightarrow$ fish sleep at night.

Does the if-clause of the conclusion imply (or entail) the main clause? On one hand, what butter does in milk is, as before, irrelevant to whether fish sleep at night. On this ground, relevance logic denies there is a relation of implication or entailment. On the other hand, it is impossible for the if-clause to be true when the main clause is false, because it is impossible for the if-clause to be true in any circumstances whatever.

See also COUNTERFACTUALS, FORMAL LOGIC, IMPLICATURE, PRESUPPOSITION, RELEVANCE LOGIC.   D.H.S.

implication, paradoxes of. See IMPLICATION.

implication, strict. See IMPLICATION.

implicature, a pragmatic relation different from, but easily confused with, the semantic relation of entailment. This concept was first identified, explained, and used by H. P. Grice (*Studies in the Way of Words,* 1989). Grice identified two main types of implicature, *conventional* and *conversa-*

tional. A speaker is said to conversationally implicate a proposition *P* in uttering a given sentence, provided that, although *P* is not logically implied by what the speaker says, the assumption that the speaker is attempting cooperative communication warrants inferring that the speaker believes *p.* If B says, "There is a garage around the corner" in response to A's saying, "I am out of gas," B conversationally implicates that the garage is open and has gas to sell.

Grice identifies several conversational maxims to which cooperative speakers may be expected to conform, and which justify inferences about speakers' implicatures. In the above example, the implicatures are due to the Maxim of Relevance. Another important maxim is that of Quantity ("Make your contribution as informative as is required"). Among implicatures due to the Maxim of Quantity are *scalar implicatures,* wherein the sentence uttered contains an element that is part of a quantitative scale. Utterance of such a sentence conversationally implicates that the speaker does not believe related propositions higher on the scale of informativeness. For instance, speakers who say, "*Some* of the zoo animals escaped," implicate that they do not believe that *most* of the zoo animals escaped, or that *all* of the zoo animals escaped.

Unlike conversational implicatures, *conventional* implicatures are due solely to the meaning of the sentence uttered. A sentence utterance is said by Grice to conventionally implicate a proposition, *p,* if the meaning of the sentence commits the speaker to *p,* even though what the sentence says does not entail *p.* Thus, uttering "She was poor but she was honest" implicates, but does not *say,* that there is a contrast between poverty and honesty.

See also PRESUPPOSITION.   M.M.

implicit definition. See BETH'S DEFINABILITY THEOREM, DEFINITION.

imposition, a property of terms resulting from a linguistic convention to designate something. Terms are not mere noises but significant sounds. Those designating extralinguistic entities, such as 'tree', 'stone', 'blue', and the like, were classified by the tradition since Boethius as terms of first imposition; those designating other terms or other linguistic items, such as 'noun', 'declension', and the like, were classified as terms of second imposition. The distinction between terms of first and second imposition belongs to the realm of written and spoken language, while the parallel distinction between terms of first and second intention belongs to the realm of mental language: first intentions are, broadly, thoughts about trees, stones, colors, etc.; second intentions are thoughts about first intentions. **See also** INTENTIONALITY, METALANGUAGE.

I.Bo.

impredicative definition, the definition of a concept in terms of the totality to which it belongs. Russell, in the second (1925) edition of *Principia Mathematica*, introduced the term 'impredicative', prohibiting this kind of definition from the conceptual foundations of mathematics, on the grounds that they imply formal logical paradoxes. The impredicative definition of the set *R* of all sets that are not members of themselves in Russell's paradox leads to the self-contradictory conclusion that *R* is a member of itself if and only if it is not a member of itself. To avoid antinomies of this kind in the formalization of logic, Russell first implemented in his ramified type theory the vicious circle principle, that no whole may contain parts that are definable only in terms of that whole. The limitation of ramified type theory is that without use of impredicative definitions it is impossible to quantify over all mathematical objects, but only over all mathematical objects of a certain order or type. Without being able to quantify over all real numbers generally, many of the most important definitions and theorems of classical real number theory cannot be formulated. Russell for this reason later abandoned ramified in favor of simple type theory, which avoids the logical paradoxes without outlawing impredicative definition by forbidding the predication of terms of any type (object, property and relation, higher-order properties and relations of properties and relations, etc.) to terms of the same type. **See also** DEFINITION, PHILOSOPHY OF MATHEMATICS, QUANTIFICATION, SET-THEORETIC PARADOXES, TYPE THEORY.   D.J.

impredicative property. See TYPE THEORY.

impression. See HUME.

improper symbol. See SYNCATEGOREMATA.

inclusive disjunction. See DISJUNCTIVE PROPOSITION.

incoherence, self-referential. See SELF-REFERENTIAL INCOHERENCE.

incommensurability, in the philosophy of science, the property exhibited by two scientific theories provided that, even though they may not logically contradict one another, they have reference to no common body of data. Positivist and logical empiricist philosophers of science like Carnap had long sought an adequate account of a theory-neutral language to serve as the basis for testing competing theories. The predicates of this language were thought to refer to observables; the observation language described the observable world or (in the case of theoretical terms) could do so in principle. This view is alleged to suffer from two major defects. First, observation is infected with theory – what else could specify the meanings of observation terms except the relevant theory? Even to perceive is to interpret, to conceptualize, what is perceived. And what about observations made by instruments? Are these not completely constrained by theory? Second, studies by Kuhn, Paul Feyerabend, and others argued that in periods of revolutionary change in science the adoption of a new theory includes acceptance of a completely new conceptual scheme that is incommensurable with the older, now rejected, theory. The two theories are incommensurable because their constituent terms cannot have reference to a theory-neutral set of observations; there is no overlap of observational meaning between the competitor theories; even the data to be explained are different. Thus, when Galileo overthrew the physics of Aristotle he replaced his conceptual scheme – his "paradigm" – with one that is not logically incompatible with Aristotle's, but is incommensurable with it because in a sense it is about a different world (or the world conceived entirely differently). Aristotle's account of the motion of bodies relied upon occult qualities like natural tendencies; Galileo's relied heavily upon contrived experimental situations in which variable factors could be mathematically calculated. Feyerabend's even more radical view is that unless scientists introduce new theories incommensurable with older ones, science cannot possibly progress, because falsehoods will never be uncovered. It is an important implication of these views about incommensurability that acceptance of theories has to do not only with observable evidence, but also with subjective factors, social pressures, and expectations of the scientific community. Such acceptance appears to threaten the very possibility of developing a coherent methodology for science. **See also** PARADIGM, PHILOSOPHY OF SCIENCE, THEORETICAL TERM.

R.E.B.

incompatibilism. See FREE WILL PROBLEM.

incompleteness. See COMPLETENESS.

incompleteness theorem. See GÖDEL'S INCOMPLETENESS THEOREMS.

incomplete symbol. See LOGICAL CONSTRUCTION, RUSSELL, SYNCATEGOREMATA, THEORY OF DESCRIPTIONS.

incompossible. See COMPOSSIBLE.

inconsistent triad, (1) most generally, any three propositions such that it cannot be the case that all three of them are true; (2) more narrowly, any three categorical propositions such that it cannot be the case that all three of them are true. A categorical syllogism is valid provided the three propositions that are its two premises and the negation (contradiction) of its conclusion are an inconsistent triad; this fact underlies various tests for the validity of categorical syllogisms, which tests are often called "methods of" inconsistent triads. **See also ANTILOGISM, SYLLOGISM.**

R.W.B.

incontinence. See AKRASIA.

incorrigibility. See PRIVILEGED ACCESS.

indenumerable. See INFINITY.

independence. See DEPENDENCE.

independence, logical. See INDEPENDENCE RESULTS.

independence, probabilistic. See PROBABILITY.

independence, statistical. See PROBABILITY.

independence results, proofs of non-deducibility. Any of the following equivalent conditions may be called independence: (1) A is not deducible from B; (2) its negation $\sim A$ is consistent with B; (3) there is a model of B that is not a model of A; e.g., the question of the non-deducibility of the parallel axiom from the other Euclidean axioms is equivalent to that of the consistency of its negation with them, i.e. of non-Euclidean geometry. Independence results may be not absolute but relative, of the form: *if* B is consistent (or has a model), *then* B together with $\sim A$ is (or does); e.g. models of non-Euclidean geometry are built within Euclidean geometry. In another sense, a set B is said to be independent if it is *irredundant*, i.e., each hypothesis in B is independent of the others; in yet another sense, A is said to be inde-

pendent of B if it is undecidable by B, i.e., *both* independent of *and* consistent with B.

The incompleteness theorems of Gödel are independence results, prototypes for many further proofs of undecidability by subsystems of classical mathematics, or by classical mathematics as a whole, as formalized in Zermelo-Fraenkel set theory with the axiom of choice (ZF + AC or ZFC). Most famous is the undecidability of the continuum hypothesis, proved consistent relative to ZFC by Gödel, using his method of constructible sets, and independent relative to ZFC by Paul J. Cohen, using his method of forcing. Rather than build models from scratch by such methods, independence (consistency) for A can also be established by showing A implies (is implied by) some A^* already known independent (consistent). Many suitable A^* (Jensen's Diamond, Martin's Axiom, etc.) are now available. Philosophically, formalism takes A's undecidability by ZFC to show the question of A's truth meaningless; Platonism takes it to establish the need for new axioms, such as those of large cardinals. (Considerations related to the incompleteness theorems show that there is no hope even of a relative consistency proof for these axioms, yet they imply, by way of determinacy axioms, many important consequences about real numbers that are independent of ZFC.)

With non-classical logics, e.g. second-order logic, (1)–(3) above may not be equivalent, so several senses of independence become distinguishable. The question of independence of one axiom from others may be raised also for formalizations of logic itself, where many-valued logics provide models.

See also FORCING, GÖDEL'S INCOMPLETENESS THEOREMS, SET THEORY.   J.Bur.

indeterminacy argument. See SKEPTICISM.

indeterminacy of translation, a pair of theses derived, originally, from a thought experiment regarding radical translation first propounded by Quine in *Word and Object* (1960) and developed in his *Ontological Relativity* (1969), *Theories and Things* (1981), and *Pursuit of Truth* (1990). *Radical translation* is an imaginary context in which a field linguist is faced with the challenge of translating a hitherto unknown language. Furthermore, it is stipulated that the linguist has no access to bilinguals and that the language to be translated is historically unrelated to that of the linguist. Presumably, the only data the linguist has to go on are the observable behaviors of native speakers amid the publicly observable objects of their environment.

(1) The *strong thesis of indeterminacy,* indeterminacy of translation of theoretical sentences as wholes, is the claim that in the context of radical translation a linguist (or linguists) could construct a number of manuals for translating the (natives') source language into the (linguists') target language such that each manual could be consistent with all possible behavior data and yet the manuals could diverge with one another in countless places in assigning different target-language sentences (holophrastically construed) as translations of the same source-language sentences (holophrastically construed), diverge even to the point where the sentences assigned have conflicting truth-values; *and* no further data, physical or mental, could single out one such translation manual as being the uniquely correct one. *All* such manuals, which are consistent with all the possible behavioral data, are correct.

(2) The *weak thesis of indeterminacy,* indeterminacy of reference (or inscrutability of reference), is the claim that given all possible behavior data, divergent target-language interpretations of words within a source-language sentence could offset one another so as to sustain different target-language translations of the same source-language sentence; *and* no further data, physical or mental, could single out one such interpretation as the uniquely correct one. *All* such interpretations, which are consistent with all the possible behavioral data, are correct. This weaker sort of indeterminacy takes two forms: an ontic form and a syntactic form. Quine's famous example where the source-language term 'gavagai' could be construed either as 'rabbit', 'undetached rabbit part', 'rabbithood', etc. (see *Word and Object*), and his proxy function argument where different ontologies could be mapped onto one another (see *Ontological Relativity, Theories and Things,* and *Pursuit of Truth*), both exemplify the ontic form of indeterminacy of reference. On the other hand, his example of the Japanese classifier, where a particular three-word construction of Japanese can be translated into English such that the third word of the construction can be construed with equal justification either as a term of divided reference or as a mass term (see *Ontological Relativity* and *Pursuit of Truth*), exemplifies the syntactic form of indeterminacy of reference.

See also MEANING, PHILOSOPHY OF LANGUAGE, PHILOSOPHY OF MIND.   R.F.G.

indeterminacy principle. See QUANTUM MECHANICS.

indeterminate. See VAGUENESS.

index. See PEIRCE.

indexical, a type of expression whose semantic value is in part determined by features of the context of utterance, and hence may vary with that context. Among indexicals are the personal pronouns, such as 'I', 'you', 'he', 'she', and 'it'; demonstratives, such as 'this' and 'that'; temporal expressions, such as 'now', 'today', 'yesterday'; and locative expressions, such as 'here', 'there', etc. Although classical logic ignored indexicality, many recent practitioners, following Richard Montague, have provided rigorous theories of indexicals in the context of formal semantics. Perhaps the most plausible and thorough treatment of indexicals is by David Kaplan (b.1933; a prominent American philosopher of language and logic whose long-unpublished "Demonstratives" was especially influential; it eventually appeared in J. Almog, J. Perry, and H. Wettstein, eds., *Themes from Kaplan,* 1988). Kaplan argues persuasively that indexical singular terms are directly referential and a species of rigid designator. He also forcefully brings out a crucial lesson to be learned from indexicals, namely, that there are two types of meaning, which Kaplan calls "content" and "character." A sentence containing an indexical, such as 'I am hungry', can be used to say different things in different contexts, in part because of the different semantic contributions made by 'I' in these contexts. Kaplan calls a term's contribution to what is said in a context the term's *content.* Though the content of an indexical like 'I' varies with its context, it will nevertheless have a single meaning in the language, which Kaplan calls the indexical's *character.* This character may be conceived as a rule of function that assigns different contents to the indexical in different contexts. **See also PHILOSOPHY OF LANGUAGE, TOKEN-REFLEXIVE.**   M.M.

Indian philosophy. See BUDDHISM, HINDUISM, JAINISM.

indicator, logical. See LOGICAL INDICATOR.

indicator word. See LOGICAL INDICATOR.

indifference, liberty of. See FREE WILL PROBLEM, HUME.

indifference, principle of. See PRINCIPLE OF INDIFFERENCE.

indirect consequentialism. See BUTLER.

indirect discourse, also called *oratio obliqua,* the use of words to report what others say, but without direct quotation. When one says "John said, 'Not every doctor is honest,' " one uses the words in one's quotation directly – one uses *direct discourse* to make an assertion about what John said. Accurate direct discourse must get the exact words. But in *indirect discourse* one can use other words than John does to report what he said, e.g., "John said that some physicians are not honest." The words quoted here capture the sense of John's assertion (the proposition he asserted).

By extension, 'indirect discourse' designates the use of words in reporting beliefs. One uses words to characterize the proposition believed rather than to make a direct assertion. When Alice says, "John believes that some doctors are not honest," she uses the words 'some doctors are not honest' to present the proposition that John believes. She does not assert the proposition. By contrast, direct discourse, also called *oratio recta,* is the ordinary use of words to make assertions.

See also INTENSIONALITY, QUANTIFYING IN, REFERENTIALLY TRANSPARENT.   T.M.

indirect intention. See INTENTION.

indirect knowledge. See BASING RELATION.

indirect passions. See HUME.

indirect proof. See REDUCTIO AD ABSURDUM.

indirect sense. See OBLIQUE CONTEXT.

indirect speech act. See SPEECH ACT THEORY.

indiscernibility of identicals, the principle that if *A* and *B* are identical, there is no difference between *A* and *B:* everything true of *A* is true of *B,* and everything true of *B* is true of *A; A* and *B* have just the same properties; there is no property such that *A* has it while *B* lacks it, or *B* has it while *A* lacks it. A tempting formulation of this principle, 'Any two things that are identical have all their properties in common', verges on nonsense; for two things are never identical. '*A* is numerically identical with *B*' means that *A* and *B* are one and the same. *A* and *B* have just the same properties because *A,* that is, *B,* has just the properties that it has. This principle is sometimes called Leibniz's law. It should be distinguished

from its converse, Leibniz's more controversial principle of the identity of indiscernibles.

A contraposed form of the indiscernibility of identicals – call it the distinctness of discernibles – reveals its point in philosophic dialectic. If something is true of *A* that is not true of *B,* or (to say the same thing differently) if something is true of *B* that is not true of *A,* then *A* and *B* are *not* identical; they are distinct. One uses this principle to attack identity claims. Classical arguments for dualism attempt to find something true of the mind that is not true of anything physical. For example, the mind, unlike everything physical, is indivisible. Also, the existence of the mind, unlike the existence of everything physical, cannot be doubted. This last argument shows that the distinctness of discernibles requires great care of application in intentional contexts.

See also IDENTITY, INTENSIONALITY.

D.H.S.

individual. See METAPHYSICS.

individualism. See POLITICAL PHILOSOPHY.

individualism, descriptive. See HOLISM.

individualism, methodological. See METHODOLOGICAL HOLISM.

individuation, (1) in metaphysics, a process whereby a universal, e.g., *cat,* becomes instantiated in an individual – also called a particular e.g., *Minina;* (2) in epistemology, a process whereby a knower discerns an individual, e.g., someone discerns Minina. The double understanding of individuation raises two distinct problems: identifying the causes of metaphysical individuation, and of epistemological individuation. In both cases the causes are referred to as the *principle of individuation.* Attempts to settle the metaphysical and epistemological problems of individuation presuppose an understanding of the nature of *individuality.* Individuality has been variously interpreted as involving one or more of the following: indivisibility, difference, division within a species, identity through time, impredicability, and non-instantiability. In general, theories of individuation try to account variously for one or more of these.

Individuation may apply to both substances (e.g., Minina) and their features (e.g., Minina's fur color), generating two different sorts of theories. The theories of the metaphysical individuation of substances most often proposed identify six types of principles: a bundle of features (Russell); space and/or time (Boethius); matter (Aristotle); form (Averroes); a decharacterized, *sui generis* component called bare particular (Bergmann) or haecceity (Duns Scotus); and existence (Avicenna). Sometimes several principles are combined. For example, for Aquinas the principle of individuation is matter under dimensions (*materia signata*). Two sorts of objections are often brought against these views of the metaphysical individuation of substances. One points out that some of these theories violate the *principle of acquaintance*, since they identify as individuators entities for which there is no empirical evidence. The second argues that some of these theories explain the individuation of substances in terms of accidents, thus contradicting the ontological precedence of substance over accident.

The two most common theories of the epistemological individuation of substances identify spatiotemporal location and/or the features of substances as their individuators; we know a thing as an individual by its location in space and time or by its features. The objections that are brought to bear against these theories are generally based on the ineffectiveness of those principles in all situations to account for the discernment of all types of individuals.

The theories of the metaphysical individuation of the features of substances fall into two groups. Some identify the substance itself as the principle of individuation; others identify some feature(s) of the substance as individuator(s). Most accounts of the epistemological individuation of the features of substances are similar to these views.

The most common objections to the metaphysical theories of the individuation of features attempt to show that these theories are either incomplete or circular. It is argued, e.g., that an account of the individuation of features in terms of substance is incomplete because the individuation of the substance must also be accounted for: How would one know what tree one sees, apart from its features? However, if the substance is individuated by its features, one falls into a vicious circle. Similar points are made with respect to the epistemological theories of the individuation of features.

Apart from the views mentioned, some philosophers hold that individuals are individual essentially (per se), and therefore that they do not undergo individuation. Under those conditions either there is no need for a metaphysical principle of individuation (Ockham), or else the principle of individuation is identified as the individual entity itself (Suárez).

See also BUNDLE THEORY, IDENTITY, METAPHYSICS, PRINCIPIUM INDIVIDUATIONIS.

J.J.E.G.

indubitability. See PRIVILEGED ACCESS.

induction, (1) in the narrow sense, inference to a generalization from its instances; (2) in the broad sense, any *ampliative inference* – i.e., any inference where the claim made by the conclusion goes beyond the claim jointly made by the premises. Induction in the broad sense includes, as cases of particular interest: argument by analogy, predictive inference, inference to causes from signs and symptoms, and confirmation of scientific laws and theories. The narrow sense covers one extreme case that is not ampliative. That is the case of *mathematical induction*, where the premises of the argument necessarily imply the generalization that is its conclusion.

Inductive logic can be conceived most generally as the theory of the evaluation of ampliative inference. In this sense, much of probability theory, theoretical statistics, and the theory of computability are parts of inductive logic. In addition, studies of scientific method can be seen as addressing in a less formal way the question of the logic of inductive inference. The name 'inductive logic' has also, however, become associated with a specific approach to these issues deriving from the work of Bayes, Laplace, De Morgan, and Carnap. On this approach, one's prior probabilities in a state of ignorance are determined or constrained by some principle for the quantification of ignorance and one learns by conditioning on the evidence. A recurrent difficulty with this line of attack is that the way in which ignorance is quantified depends on how the problem is described, with different logically equivalent descriptions leading to different prior probabilities.

Carnap laid down as a postulate for the application of his inductive logic that one should always condition on one's total evidence. This *rule of total evidence* is usually taken for granted, but what justification is there for it? Good pointed out that the standard Bayesian analysis of the expected value of new information provides such a justification. Pure cost-free information always has non-negative expected value, and if there is positive probability that it will affect a decision, its expected value is positive. Ramsey made the same point in an unpublished manuscript. The proof generalizes to various models of learning uncertain evidence.

A deductive account is sometimes presented

where induction proceeds by *elimination* of possibilities that would make the conclusion false. Thus Mill's methods of experimental inquiry are sometimes analyzed as proceeding by elimination of alternative possibilities. In a more general setting, the hypothetico-deductive account of science holds that theories are confirmed by their observational consequences – i.e., by elimination of the possibilities that this experiment or that observation falsifies the theory. *Induction by elimination* is sometimes put forth as an alternative to probabilistic accounts of induction, but at least one version of it is consistent with – and indeed a consequence of – probabilistic accounts. It is an elementary fact of probability that if F, the potential falsifier, is inconsistent with T and both have probability strictly between 0 and 1, then the probability of T conditional on not-F is higher than the unconditional probability of T.

In a certain sense, inductive support of a universal generalization by its instances may be a special case of the foregoing, but this point must be treated with some care. In the first place, the universal generalization must have positive prior probability. (It is worth noting that Carnap's systems of inductive logic do not satisfy this condition, although systems of Hintikka and Niiniluoto do.) In the second place, the notion of instance must be construed so the "instances" of a universal generalization are in fact logical consequences of it. Thus 'If A is a swan then A is white' is an instance of 'All swans are white' in the appropriate sense, but 'A is a white swan' is not. The latter statement is logically stronger than 'If A is a swan then A is white' and a complete report on species, weight, color, sex, etc., of individual A would be stronger still. Such statements are not logical consequences of the universal generalization, and the theorem does not hold for them. For example, the report of a man 7 feet 11¾ inches tall might actually reduce the probability of the generalization that all men are under 8 feet tall.

Residual queasiness about the foregoing may be dispelled by a point made by Carnap apropos of Hempel's discussion of paradoxes of confirmation. 'Confirmation' is ambiguous. 'E confirms H' may mean that the probability of H conditional on E is greater than the unconditional probability of H, in which case deductive consequences of H confirm H under the conditions set forth above. Or 'E confirms H' may mean that the probability of H conditional on E is high (e.g., greater than .95), in which case if E confirms H, then E confirms every logical consequence of H. Conflation of the two senses can lead one to the

paradoxical conclusion that E confirms E & P and thus P for any statement, P.

See also CONFIRMATION, MATHEMATICAL INDUCTION, MILL'S METHODS, PROBLEM OF INDUCTION.   B.Sk.

induction, eliminative. See INDUCTION.

induction, intuitive. See ROSS.

induction, mathematical. See MATHEMATICAL INDUCTION.

induction, new riddle of. See GRUE PARADOX.

induction, problem of. See PROBLEM OF INDUCTION.

inductive clause. See MATHEMATICAL INDUCTION.

inductive definition. See DEFINITION.

inductive explanation. See COVERING LAW MODEL.

inductive justification. See JUSTIFICATION.

inductive probability. See PROBABILITY.

inductivism, a philosophy of science invented by Popper and P. K. Feyerabend as a foil for their own views. According to inductivism, a unique a priori inductive logic enables one to construct an algorithm that will compute from any input of data the best scientific theory accounting for that data. **See also** ALGORITHM, DUHEM, PHILOSOPHY OF SCIENCE.   B.Sk.

infallibility. See PRIVILEGED ACCESS.

inference, the process of drawing a conclusion from premises or assumptions, or, loosely, the conclusion so drawn. An *argument* can be merely a number of statements of which one is designated the conclusion and the rest are designated premises. Whether the premises imply the conclusion is thus independent of anyone's actual beliefs in either of them. Belief, however, is essential to inference. Inference occurs only if someone, owing to believing the premises, begins to believe the conclusion or continues to believe the conclusion with greater confidence than before. Because inference requires a subject who has beliefs, some requirements of (an ideally) acceptable inference do not apply to abstract arguments: one must believe the premises; one must believe that the premises support the conclusion; neither of these beliefs may be based on one's prior belief in the conclusion. W. E. Johnson called these the epistemic conditions of inference. In a *reductio ad absurdum* argument that deduces a self-contradiction from certain premises, not all steps of the argument will correspond to steps of inference. No one deliberately infers a contradiction. What one infers, in such an argument, is that certain premises are inconsistent.

Acceptable inferences can fall short of being *ideally* acceptable according to the above requirements. Relevant beliefs are sometimes indefinite. Infants and children infer despite having no grasp of the sophisticated notion of support. One function of idealization is to set standards for that which falls short. It is possible to judge how nearly inexplicit, automatic, unreflective, less-than-ideal inferences meet ideal requirements.

In ordinary speech, 'infer' often functions as a synonym of 'imply', as in 'The new tax law infers that we have to calculate the value of our shrubbery'. Careful philosophical writing avoids this usage. Implication is, and inference is not, a relation between statements.

Valid deductive inference corresponds to a valid deductive argument: it is logically impossible for all the premises to be true when the conclusion is false. That is, the conjunction of all the premises and the negation of the conclusion is inconsistent. Whenever a conjunction is inconsistent, there is a valid argument for the negation of any conjunct from the other conjuncts. (Relevance logic imposes restrictions on validity to avoid this.) Whenever one argument is deductively valid, so is another argument that goes in a different direction. (1) 'Stacy left her slippers in the kitchen' implies (2) 'Stacy had some slippers'. Should one acquainted with Stacy and the kitchen infer (2) from (1), or infer not-(1) from not-(2), or make neither inference? Formal logic tells us about implication and deductive validity, but it cannot tell us when or what to infer. Reasonable inference depends on comparative degrees of reasonable belief.

An inference in which every premise and every step is beyond question is a demonstrative inference. (Similarly, reasoning for which this condition holds is demonstrative reasoning.) Just as what is beyond question can vary from one situation to another, so can what counts as demonstrative. The term presumably derives from Aristotle's *Posterior Analytics*. Understanding Aristotle's views on demonstration requires understanding his general scheme for classifying inferences.

Not all inferences are deductive. In an induc-

tive inference, one infers from an observed combination of characteristics to some similar unobserved combination.

'Reasoning' like 'painting', and 'frosting', and many other words, has a process–product ambiguity. Reasoning can be a process that occurs in time or it can be a result or product. A letter to the editor can both contain reasoning and be the result of reasoning. It is often unclear whether a word such as 'statistical' that modifies the words 'inference' or 'reasoning' applies primarily to stages in the process or to the content of the product.

One view, attractive for its simplicity, is that the stages of the process of reasoning correspond closely to the parts of the product. Examples that confirm this view are scarce. Testing alternatives, discarding and reviving, revising and transposing, and so on, are as common to the process of reasoning as to other creative activities. A product seldom reflects the exact history of its production.

In *An Examination of Sir William Hamilton's Philosophy*, J. S. Mill says that reasoning is a source from which we derive new truths (Chapter 14). This is a useful saying so long as we remember that not all reasoning is inference.

See also DEDUCTION, IMPLICATION, INDUCTION.   D.H.S.

inference rule. See LOGISTIC SYSTEM.

inference to the best explanation, an inference by which one concludes that something is the case on the grounds that this best explains something else one believes to be the case. Paradigm examples of this kind of inference are found in the natural sciences, where a hypothesis is accepted on the grounds that it best explains relevant observations. For example, the hypothesis that material substances have atomic structures best explains a range of observations concerning how such substances interact. Inferences to the best explanation occur in everyday life as well. Upon walking into your house you observe that a lamp is lying broken on the floor, and on the basis of this you infer that the cat has knocked it over. This is plausibly analyzed as an inference to the best explanation; you believe that the cat has knocked over the lamp because this is the best explanation for the lamp's lying broken on the floor.

The nature of inference to the best explanation and the extent of its use are both controversial. Positions that have been taken include: (a) that it is a distinctive kind of inductive reasoning; (b) that all good inductive inferences involve inference to the best explanation; and (c) that it is not a distinctive kind of inference at all, but is rather a special case of enumerative induction. Another controversy concerns the criteria for what makes an explanation best. Simplicity, cognitive fit, and explanatory power have all been suggested as relevant merits, but none of these notions is well understood. Finally, a skeptical problem arises: inference to the best explanation is plausibly involved in both scientific and commonsense knowledge, but it is not clear why the best explanation that occurs to a person is likely to be true.

See also ABDUCTION, EXPLANATION, INDUCTION, INFERENCE, PHILOSOPHY OF SCIENCE.   J.G.

inferential justification. See FOUNDATIONALISM.

inferential knowledge, a kind of "indirect" knowledge, namely, knowledge based on or resulting from inference. Assuming that knowledge is at least true, justified belief, inferential knowledge is constituted by a belief that is justified because it is inferred from certain other beliefs. The knowledge that 7 equals 7 seems non-inferential. We do not infer from anything that 7 equals 7 – it is obvious and self-evident. The knowledge that 7 is the cube root of 343, in contrast, seems inferential. We cannot know this without inferring it from something else, such as the result obtained when multiplying 7 times 7 times 7.

Two sorts of inferential relations may be distinguished. 'I inferred that someone died because the flag is at half-mast' may be true because yesterday I acquired the belief about the flag, which caused me to acquire the further belief that someone died. 'I inferentially believe that someone died because the flag is at half-mast' may be true now because I retain the belief that someone died and it remains based on my belief about the flag. My belief that someone died is thus either *episodically* or *structurally inferential.* The episodic process is an occurrent, causal relation among belief acquisitions. The structural basing relation may involve the retention of beliefs, and need not be occurrent. (Some reserve 'inference' for the episodic relation.) An inferential belief acquired on one basis may later be held on a different basis, as when I forget I saw a flag at half-mast but continue to believe someone died because of news reports.

That "How do you know?" and "Prove it!" always seem pertinent suggests that all knowledge is inferential, a version of the coherence theory. The well-known regress argument seems to show, however, that not all knowledge can be inferential, which is a version of foundationalism. For if S knows something inferentially, S must infer it correctly from premises S knows to be true. The question whether those premises are also known inferentially begins either an infinite regress of inferences (which is humanly impossible) or a circle of justification (which could not constitute good reasoning).

Which sources of knowledge are non-inferential remains an issue even assuming foundationalism. When we see that an apple is red, e.g., our knowledge is based in some manner on the way the apple looks. "How do you know it is red?" can be answered: "By the way it looks." This answer seems correct, moreover, only if an inference from the way the apple looks to its being red would be warranted. Nevertheless, perceptual beliefs are formed so automatically that talk of inference seems inappropriate. In addition, inference as a process whereby beliefs are acquired as a result of holding other beliefs may be distinguished from inference as a state in which one belief is sustained on the basis of others. Knowledge that is inferential in one way need not be inferential in the other.

See also FOUNDATIONALISM, INFERENCE, PRACTICAL REASONING.   W.A.D.

infima species (Latin, 'lowest species'), a species that is not a genus of any other species. According to the theory of classification, division, and definition that is part of traditional or Aristotelian logic, every individual is a specimen of some *infima species.* An *infima species* is a member of a genus that may in turn be a species of a more inclusive genus, and so on, until one reaches a *summum genus,* a genus that is not a species of a more inclusive genus. Socrates and Plato are specimens of the *infima specis* human being (mortal rational animal), which is a species of the genus rational animal, which is a species of the genus animal, and so on, up to the *summum genus* substance. Whereas two specimens of animal – e.g., an individual human and an individual horse – can differ partly in their essential characteristics, no two specimens of the *infima species* human being can differ in essence. **See also** ARISTOTLE, ESSENTIALISM, GENUS GENERALISSIMUM, TREE OF PORPHYRY.   W.E.M.

infinitary logic, the logic of expressions of infinite length. Quine has advanced the claim that first-order logic (FOL) is *the* language of science, a position accepted by many of his followers. However, many important notions of mathematics and science are not expressible in FOL. The notion of finiteness, e.g., is central in mathematics but cannot be expressed within FOL. There is no way to express such a simple, precise claim as 'There are only finitely many stars' in FOL. This and related expressive limitations in FOL seriously hamper its applicability to the study of mathematics and have led to the study of stronger logics.

There have been various approaches to getting around the limitations by the study of so-called strong logics, including second-order logic (where one quantifies over sets or properties, not just individuals), generalized quantifiers (where one adds quantifiers in addition to the usual 'for all' and 'there exists'), and branching quantifiers (where notions of independence of variables is introduced). One of the most fruitful methods has been the introduction of idealized "infinitely long" statements. For example, the above statement about the stars would be formalized as an infinite disjunction: there is at most one star, or there are at most two stars, or there are at most three stars, etc. Each of these disjuncts is expressible in FOL.

The expressive limitations in FOL are closely linked with Gödel's famous completeness and incompleteness theorems. These results show, among other things, that any attempt to systematize the laws of logic is going to be inadequate, one way or another. Either it will be confined to a language with expressive limitations, so that these notions cannot even be expressed, or else, if they can be expressed, then an attempt at giving an effective listing of axioms and rules of inference for the language will fall short. In infinitary logic, the rules of inference can have infinitely many premises, and so are not effectively presentable.

Early work in infinitary logic used cardinality as a guide: whether or not a disjunction, conjunction, or quantifier string was permitted had to do only with the cardinality of the set in question. It turned out that the most fruitful of these logics was the language with countable conjunctions and finite strings of first-order quantifiers. This language had further refinements to so-called admissible languages, where more refined set-theoretic considerations play a role in determining what counts as a formula.

Infinitary languages are also connected with strong axioms of infinity, statements that do not follow from the usual axioms of set theory but for which one has other evidence that they might well be true, or at least consistent. In particular, compact cardinals are infinite cardinal numbers where the analogue of the compactness theorem of FOL generalizes to the associated infinitary language. These cardinals have proven to be very important in modern set theory.

During the 1990s, some infinitary logics played a surprising role in computer science. By allowing arbitrarily long conjunctions and disjunctions, but only finitely many variables (free or bound) in any formula, languages with attractive closure properties were found that allowed the kinds of inductive procedures of computer science, procedures not expressible in FOL.

See also COMPACTNESS THEOREM, COMPLETENESS, GÖDEL'S INCOMPLETENESS THEOREMS, INFINITY, SECOND-ORDER LOGIC.

J.Ba.

infinite, actual. See ARISTOTLE.

infinite analysis, doctrine of. See LEIBNIZ.

infinite regress argument, a distinctively philosophical kind of argument purporting to show that a thesis is defective because it generates an infinite series when either (form A) no such series exists or (form B) were it to exist, the thesis would lack the role (e.g., of justification) that it is supposed to play.

The mere generation of an infinite series is not objectionable. It is misleading therefore to use 'infinite regress' (or 'regress') and 'infinite series' equivalently. For instance, both of the following claims generate an infinite series: (1) every natural number has a successor that itself is a natural number, and (2) every event has a causal predecessor that itself is an event. Yet (1) is true (arguably, necessarily true), and (2) may be true for all that logic can say about the matter. Likewise, there is nothing contrary to logic about any of the infinite series generated by the suppositions that (3) every free act is the consequence of a free act of choice; (4) every intelligent operation is the result of an intelligent mental operation; (5) whenever individuals x and y share a property F there exists a third individual z which paradigmatically has F and to which x and y are somehow related (as copies, by participation, or whatnot); or (6) every generalization from experience is inductively inferable from experience by appeal to some other generalization from experience.

What Locke (in the *Essay concerning Human Understanding*) objects to about the theory of free will embodied in (3) and Ryle (in *The Concept of Mind*) objects to about the "intellectualist legend" embodied in (4) can therefore be only that it is just plain false as a matter of fact that we perform an infinite number of acts of choice or operations of the requisite kinds. In effect their infinite regress arguments are of form A: they argue that the theories concerned must be rejected because they falsely imply that such infinite series exist.

Arguably the infinite regress arguments employed by Plato (in the *Parmenides*) regarding his own theory of Forms and by Popper (in the *Logic of Scientific Discovery*) regarding the principle of induction proposed by Mill, are best construed as having form B, their objections being less to (5) or (6) than to their epistemic versions: (5*) that we can *understand* how x and y can share a property F only if we understand that there exists a third individual (the "Form" z) which paradigmatically has F and to which x and y are related; and (6*) that since the principle of induction must itself be a generalization from experience, we are *justified* in accepting it only if it can be inferred from experience by appeal to a higher-order, and justified, inductive principle. They are arguing that because the series generated by (5) and (6) are infinite, the epistemic enlightenment promised by (5*) and (6*) will forever elude us.

When successful, infinite regress arguments can show us that certain sorts of explanation, understanding, or justification are will-o'-the-wisps. As Passmore has observed (in *Philosophical Reasoning*) there is an important sense of 'explain' in which it is impossible to explain predication. We cannot explain x's and y's possession of the common property F by saying that they *are called by the same name* (nominalism) or *fall under the same concept* (conceptualism) any more than we can by saying that they *are related to the same form* (Platonic realism), since each of these is itself a property that x and y are supposed to have in common. Likewise, it makes no sense to try to explain why anything at all exists by invoking the existence of something else (such as the theist's God). The general truths that things exist, and that things may have properties in common, are "brute facts" about the way the world is.

Some infinite regress objections fail because they are directed at "straw men." Bradley's regress argument against the pluralist's "arrangement of given facts into relations and qualities," from which he concludes that monism is true, is a case in point. He correctly argues that if one posits the existence of two or more things, then there must be relations of some sort between them, and then (given his covert assumption that these relations are things) concludes that there must be further relations between these relations ad infinitum. Bradley's regress misfires because a pluralist would reject his assumption. Again, some regress arguments fail because they presume that any infinite series is vicious. Aquinas's regress objection to an infinite series of movers, from which he concludes that there must be a prime mover, involves this sort of confusion.

See also EPISTEMIC REGRESS ARGUMENT, INFINITY, VICIOUS REGRESS. R.D.B.

infinity, in set theory, the property of a set whereby it has a *proper subset* whose members can be placed in one-to-one correspondence with all the members of the set, as the even integers can be so arranged in respect to the natural numbers by the function $f(x) = x/2$, namely:

$$
\begin{array}{cccc}
2 & 4 & 6 & 8 \quad \ldots \\
\downarrow & \downarrow & \downarrow & \downarrow \\
1 & 2 & 3 & 4 \quad \ldots
\end{array}
$$

Devised by Richard Dedekind in defiance of the age-old intuition that no part of a thing can be as large as the thing, this set-theoretical definition of 'infinity', having been much acclaimed by philosophers like Russell as a model of conceptual analysis that philosophers were urged to emulate, can elucidate the putative infinity of space, time, and even God, his power, wisdom, etc.

If a set's being *denumerable* – i.e., capable of having its members placed in one-to-one correspondence with the natural numbers – can well appear to define much more simply what the infinity of an infinite set is, Cantor exhibited the real numbers (as expressed by unending decimal expansions) as a counterexample, showing them to be indenumerable by means of his famous diagonal argument. Suppose all the real numbers between 0 and 1 are placed in one-to-one correspondence with the natural numbers, thus:

$$
\begin{array}{rcl}
1 & \leftarrow & .8632 \quad \ldots \\
2 & \leftarrow & .3476 \quad \ldots \\
3 & \leftarrow & .9832 \quad \ldots \\
\cdot & & \cdot \\
\cdot & & \cdot \\
\cdot & & \cdot
\end{array}
$$

Going down the principal diagonal, we can construct a new real number, e.g., .954 ... , not found in the infinite "square array." The most important result in set theory, Cantor's theorem, is denied its full force by the maverick followers of Skolem, who appeal to the fact that, though the real numbers constructible in any standard axiomatic system will be indenumerable relative to the resources of the system, they can be seen to be denumerable when viewed from outside it. Refusing to accept the absolute indenumerability of any set, the Skolemites, in relativizing the notion to some system, provide one further instance of the allure of relativism.

More radical still are the nominalists who, rejecting all abstract entities and sets in particular, might be supposed to have no use for Cantor's theorem. Not so. Assume with Democritus that there are infinitely many of his atoms, made of adamant. Corresponding to each infinite subset of these *atoms* will be their *mereological sum* or "fusion," namely a certain quantity of adamant. Concrete entities acceptable to the nominalist, these quantities can be readily shown to be indenumerable. Whether Cantor's still higher infinities beyond $\aleph_1$ admit of any such nominalistic realization remains a largely unexplored area. Aleph-zero or $\aleph_0$ being taken to be the transfinite number of the natural numbers, there are then $\aleph_1$ real numbers (assuming the continuum hypothesis), while the power set of the reals has $\aleph_2$ members, and the power set of that $\aleph_3$ members, etc. In general, K_2 will be said to have a greater number (finite or transfinite) of members than K_1 provided the members of K_1 can be put in one-to-one correspondence with some proper subset of K_2 but not vice versa.

Skepticism regarding the higher infinities can trickle down even to $\aleph_0$, and if both Aristotle and Kant, the former in his critique of Zeno's paradoxes, the latter in his treatment of cosmological antinomies, reject any actual, i.e. completed, infinite, in our time Dummett's return to verificationism, as associated with the mathematical intuitionism of Brouwer, poses the keenest challenge. Recognition-transcendent sentences like 'The total number of stars is infinite' are charged with violating the intersubjective conditions required for a speaker of a language to manifest a grasp of their meaning.

See also CONTINUUM PROBLEM, SET THEORY.   J.A.B.

infinity, axiom of. See SET THEORY.

informal fallacy, an error of reasoning or tactic of argument that can be used to persuade someone with whom you are reasoning that your argument is correct when really it is not. The standard treatment of the informal fallacies in logic textbooks draws heavily on Aristotle's list, but there are many variants, and new fallacies have often been added, some of which have gained strong footholds in the textbooks. The word 'informal' indicates that these fallacies are not simply localized faults or failures in the given propositions (premises and conclusion) of an argument to conform to a standard of semantic correctness (like that of deductive logic), but are misuses of the argument in relation to a context of reasoning or type of dialogue that an arguer is supposed to be engaged in. *Informal logic* is the subfield of logical inquiry that deals with these fallacies. Typically, informal fallacies have a pragmatic (practical) aspect relating to how an argument is being used, and also a dialectical aspect, pertaining to a context of dialogue – normally an exchange between two participants in a discussion. Both aspects are major concerns of informal logic.

Logic textbooks classify informal fallacies in various ways, but no clear and widely accepted system of classification has yet become established. Some textbooks are very inventive and prolific, citing many different fallacies, including novel and exotic ones. Others are more conservative, sticking with the twenty or so mainly featured in or derived from Aristotle's original treatment, with a few widely accepted additions. The paragraphs below cover most of these "major" or widely featured fallacies, the ones most likely to be encountered by name in the language of everyday educated conversation.

The *genetic fallacy* is the error of drawing an inappropriate conclusion about the goodness or badness of some property of a thing from the goodness or badness of some property of the origin of that thing. For example, 'This medication was derived from a plant that is poisonous; therefore, even though my physician advises me to take it, I conclude that it would be very bad for me if I took it.' The error is inappropriately arguing from the origin of the medication to the conclusion that it must be poisonous in any form or situation. The genetic fallacy is often construed very broadly making it coextensive with the personal attack type of argument (see the description of *argumentum ad hominem* below) that condemns a prior argument by condemning its source or proponent.

Argumentum ad populum (argument to the people) is a kind of argument that uses appeal to popular sentiments to support a conclusion. Sometimes called "appeal to the gallery" or "appeal to popular pieties" or even "mob appeal," this kind of argument has traditionally been portrayed as fallacious. However, there need be nothing wrong with appealing to popular sentiments in argument, so long as their evidential value is not exaggerated. Even so, such a tactic can be fallacious when the attempt to arouse mass enthusiasms is used as a substitute to cover for a failure to bring forward the kind of evidence that is properly required to support one's conclusion.

Argumentum ad misericordiam (argument to pity) is a kind of argument that uses an appeal to pity, sympathy, or compassion to support its conclusion. Such arguments can have a legitimate place in some discussions – e.g., in appeals for charitable donations. But they can also put emotional pressure on a respondent in argument to try to cover up a weak case. For example, a student who does not have a legitimate reason for a late assignment might argue that if he doesn't get a high grade, his disappointed mother might have a heart attack.

The *fallacy of composition* is the error of arguing from a property of parts of a whole to a property of the whole – e.g., 'The important parts of this machine are light; therefore this machine is light.' But a property of the parts cannot always be transferred to the whole. In some cases, examples of the fallacy of composition are arguments from *all* the parts to a whole, e.g. 'Everybody in the country pays her debts. Therefore the country pays its debts.' The *fallacy of division* is the converse of that of composition: the error of arguing from a property of the whole to a property of its parts – e.g., 'This machine is heavy; therefore all the parts of this machine are heavy.' The problem is that the property possessed by the whole need not transfer to the parts.

The *fallacy of false cause*, sometimes called *post hoc, ergo propter hoc* (after this, therefore because of this), is the error of arguing that because two events are correlated with one another, especially when they vary together, the one is the cause of the other. For example, there might be a genuine correlation between the stork population in certain areas of Europe and the human birth rate. But it would be an error to conclude, on that basis alone, that the presence of storks causes babies to be born. In general, however, correlation is good, if sometimes weak, evidence for causation. The problem comes in when the evidential strength of the correlation is exaggerated as causal evidence. The apparent connection could just be coincidence, or due to other factors that have not been taken into account, e.g., some third factor that causes both the events that are correlated with each other.

The *fallacy of secundum quid* (neglecting qualifications) occurs where someone is arguing from a general rule to a particular case, or vice versa. One version of it is arguing from a general rule while overlooking or suppressing legitimate exceptions. This kind of error has also often been called the *fallacy of accident*. An example would be the argument 'Everyone has the right to freedom of speech; therefore it is my right to shout "Fire" in this crowded theater if I want to.' The other version of *secundum quid*, sometimes also called the *fallacy of converse accident,* or the *fallacy of hasty generalization,* is the error of trying to argue from a particular case to a general rule that does not properly fit that case. An example would be the argument 'Tweetie [an ostrich] is a bird that does not fly; therefore birds do not fly'. The fault is the failure to recognize or acknowledge that Tweetie is not a typical bird with respect to flying.

Argumentum consensus gentium (argument from the consensus of the nations) is a kind that appeals to the common consent of mankind to support a conclusion. Numerous philosophers and theologians in the past have appealed to this kind of argument to support conclusions like the existence of God and the binding character of moral principles. For example, 'Belief in God is practically universal among human beings past and present; therefore there is a practical weight of presumption in favor of the truth of the proposition that God exists'. A version of the *consensus gentium* argument represented by this example has sometimes been put forward in logic textbooks as an instance of the *argumentum ad populum* (described above) called the argument from popularity: 'Everybody believes (accepts) *P* as true; therefore *P* is true'. If interpreted as applicable in all cases, the argument from popularity is not generally sound, and may be regarded as a fallacy. However, if regarded as a presumptive inference that only applies in some cases, and as subject to withdrawal where evidence to the contrary exists, it can sometimes be regarded as a weak but plausible argument, useful to serve as a provisional guide to prudent action or reasoned commitment.

Argumentum ad hominem (literally, argument against the man) is a kind of argument that uses a personal attack against an arguer to refute her argument. In the abusive or personal variant, the character of the arguer (especially character for veracity) is attacked; e.g., 'You can't believe what Smith says – he is a liar'. In evaluating testimony (e.g., in legal cross-examination), attacking an arguer's character can be legitimate in some cases. Also in political debate, character can be a legitimate issue. However, *ad hominem* arguments are commonly used fallaciously in attacking an opponent unfairly – e.g., where the attack is not merited, or where it is used to distract an audience from more relevant lines of argument. In the circumstantial variant, an arguer's personal circumstances are claimed to be in conflict with his argument, implying that the arguer is either confused or insincere; e.g., 'You don't practice what you preach'. For example, a politician who has once advocated not raising taxes may be accused of "flip-flopping" if he himself subsequently favors legislation to raise taxes. This type of argument is not inherently fallacious, but it can go badly wrong, or be used in a fallacious way, for example if circumstances changed, or if the alleged conflict was less serious than the attacker claimed. Another variant is the "poisoning the well" type of *ad hominem* argument, where an arguer is said to have shown no regard for the truth, the implication being that nothing he says henceforth can ever be trusted as reliable.

Yet another variant of the *ad hominem* argument often cited in logic textbooks is the *tu quoque* (you-too reply), where the arguer attacked by an *ad hominem* argument turns around and says, "What about you? Haven't you ever lied before? You're just as bad." Still another variant is the bias type of *ad hominem* argument, where one party in an argument charges the other with not being honest or impartial or with having hidden motivations or personal interests at stake.

Argumentum ad baculum (argument to the club) is a kind of argument that appeals to a threat or to fear in order to support a conclusion, or to intimidate a respondent into accepting it. *Ad baculum* arguments often take an indirect form; e.g., 'If you don't do this, harmful consequences to you might follow'. In such cases the utterance can often be taken as a threat. *Ad baculum* arguments are not inherently fallacious, because appeals to threatening or fearsome sanctions – e.g., harsh penalties for drunken driving – are not necessarily failures of critical argumentation. But because *ad baculum* arguments are powerful in eliciting emotions, they are often used persuasively as sophistical tactics in argumentation to avoid fulfilling the proper requirements of a burden of proof.

Argument from authority is a kind of argument that uses expert opinion (de facto authority) or the pronouncement of someone invested with an institutional office or title (de jure authority) to support a conclusion. As a practical but fallible method of steering discussion toward a pre-

sumptive conclusion, the argument from authority can be a reasonable way of shifting a burden of proof. However, if pressed too hard in a discussion or portrayed as a better justification for a conclusion than the evidence warrants, it can become a fallacious *argumentum ad verecundiam* (see below). It should be noted, however, that arguments based on expert opinions are widely accepted both in artificial intelligence and everyday argumentation as legitimate and sound under the right conditions. Although arguments from authority have been strongly condemned during some historical periods as inherently fallacious, the current climate of opinion is to think of them as acceptable in some cases, even if they are fallible arguments that can easily go wrong or be misused by sophistical persuaders.

Argumentum ad judicium represents a kind of knowledge-based argumentation that is empirical, as opposed to being based on an arguer's personal opinion or viewpoint. In modern terminology, it apparently refers to an argument based on objective evidence, as opposed to somebody's subjective opinion. The term appears to have been invented by Locke to contrast three commonly used kinds of arguments and a fourth special type of argument. The first three types of argument are based on premises that the respondent of the argument is taken to have already accepted. Thus these can all be called "personal" in nature. The fourth kind of argument – *argumentum ad judicium* – does not have to be based on what some person accepts, and so could perhaps be called "impersonal." Locke writes that the first three kinds of arguments can dispose a person for the reception of truth, but cannot help that person to the truth. Only the *argumentum ad judicium* can do that. The first three types of arguments come from "my shamefacedness, ignorance or error," whereas the *argumentum ad judicium* "comes from proofs and arguments and light arising from the nature of things themselves." The first three types of arguments have only a preparatory function in finding the truth of a matter, whereas the *argumentum ad judicium* is more directly instrumental in helping us to find the truth.

Argumentum ad verecundiam (argument to reverence or respect) is the fallacious use of expert opinion in argumentation to try to persuade someone to accept a conclusion. In the *Essay concerning Human Understanding* (1690) Locke describes such arguments as tactics of trying to prevail on the assent of someone by portraying him as irreverent or immodest if he does not readily yield to the authority of some learned opinion cited. Locke does not claim, however, that all appeals to expert authority in argument are fallacious. They can be reasonable if used judiciously.

Argumentum ad ignorantiam (argument to ignorance) takes the following form: a proposition *a* is not known or proved to be true (false); therefore *A* is false (true). It is a negative type of knowledge-based or presumptive reasoning, generally not conclusive, but it is nevertheless often non-fallacious in balance-of-consideration cases where the evidence is inconclusive to resolve a disputed question. In such cases it is a kind of presumption-based argumentation used to advocate adopting a conclusion provisionally, in the absence of hard knowledge that would determine whether the conclusion is true or false. An example would be: Smith has not been heard from for over seven years, and there is no evidence that he is alive; therefore it may be presumed (for the purpose of settling Smith's estate) that he is dead. Arguments from ignorance ought not to be pressed too hard or used with too strong a degree of confidence. An example comes from the U.S. Senate hearings in 1950, in which Senator Joseph McCarthy used case histories to argue that certain persons in the State Department should be considered Communists. Of one case he said, "I do not have much information on this except the general statement of the agency that there is nothing in the files to disprove his Communist connections." The strength of any argument from ignorance depends on the thoroughness of the search made. The argument from ignorance can be used to shift a burden of proof merely on the basis of rumor, innuendo, or false accusations, instead of real evidence.

Ignoratio elenchi (ignorance of refutation) is the traditional name, following Aristotle, for the fault of failing to keep to the point in an argument. The fallacy is also called *irrelevant conclusion* or *missing the point*. Such a failure of relevance is essentially a failure to keep closely enough to the issue under discussion. Suppose that during a criminal trial, the prosecutor displays the victim's bloody shirt and argues at length that murder is a horrible crime. The digression may be ruled irrelevant to the question at issue of whether the defendant is guilty of murder. Alleged failures of this type in argumentation are sometimes quite difficult to judge fairly, and a ruling should depend on the type of discussion the participants are supposed to be engaged in. In some cases, conventions or institutional rules of procedure – e.g. in a criminal

trial – are aids to determining whether a line of argumentation should be judged relevant or not.

Petitio principii (asking to be granted the "principle" or issue of the discussion to be proved), also called *begging the question*, is the fallacy of improperly arguing in a circle. Circular reasoning should not be presumed to be inherently fallacious, but can be fallacious where the circular argument has been used to disguise or cover up a failure to fulfill a burden of proof. The problem arises where the conclusion that was supposed to be proved is presumed within the premises to be granted by the respondent of the argument. Suppose I ask you to prove that this bicycle (the ownership of which is subject to dispute) belongs to Hector, and you reply, "All the bicycles around here belong to Hector." The problem is that without independent evidence that shows otherwise, the premise that all the bicycles belong to Hector takes for granted that this bicycle belongs to Hector, instead of proving it by properly fulfilling the burden of proof.

The *fallacy of many questions* (also called the *fallacy of complex question*) is the tactic of packing unwarranted presuppositions into a question so that any direct answer given by the respondent will trap her into conceding these presuppositions. The classical case is the question, "Have you stopped beating your spouse?" No matter how the respondent answers, yes or no, she concedes the presuppositions that (a) she has a spouse, and (b) she has beaten that spouse at some time. Where one or both of these presumptions are unwarranted in the given case, the use of this question is an instance of the fallacy of many questions.

The *fallacy of equivocation* occurs where an ambiguous word has been used more than once in an argument in such a way that it is plausible to interpret it in one way in one instance of its use and in another way in another instance. Such an argument may seem persuasive if the shift in the context of use of the word makes these differing interpretations plausible. Equivocation, however, is generally seriously deceptive only in longer sequences of argument where the meaning of a word or phrase shifts subtly but significantly. A simplistic example will illustrate the gist of the fallacy: 'The news media should present all the facts on anything that is in the public interest; the public interest in lives of movie stars is intense; therefore the news media should present all the facts on the private lives of movie stars'. This argument goes from plausible premises to an implausible conclusion by trading on the ambiguity of 'public interest'. In one sense it means 'public benefit' while in another sense it refers to something more akin to curiosity.

Amphiboly (double arrangement) is a type of traditional fallacy (derived from Aristotle's list of fallacies) that refers to the use of syntactically ambiguous sentences like 'Save soap and waste paper'. Although the logic textbooks often cite examples of such sentences as fallacies, they have never made clear how they could be used to deceive in a serious discussion. Indeed, the example cited is not even an argument, but simply an ambiguous sentence. In cases of some advertisements like 'Two pizzas for one special price', however, one can see how the amphiboly seriously misleads readers into thinking they are being offered two pizzas for the regular price of one. *Accent* is the use of shifting stress or emphasis in speech as a means of deception. For example, if a speaker puts stress on the word 'created' in 'All men were created equal' it suggests (by implicature) the opposite proposition to 'All men are equal', namely 'Not all men are (now) equal'. The oral stress allows the speaker to covertly suggest an inference the hearer is likely to draw, and to escape commitment to the conclusion suggested by later denying he said it.

The *slippery slope argument,* in one form, counsels against some contemplated action (or inaction) on the ground that, once taken, it will be a first step in a sequence of events that will be difficult to resist and will (or may or must) lead to some dangerous (or undesirable or disastrous) outcome in the end. It is often argued, e.g., that once you allow euthanasia in any form, such as the withdrawal of heroic treatments of dying patients in hospitals, then (through erosion of respect for human life), you will eventually wind up with a totalitarian state where old, feeble, or politically troublesome individuals are routinely eliminated. Some slippery slope arguments can be reasonable, but they should not be put forward in an exaggerated way, supported with insufficient evidence, or used as a scare tactic. **See also CIRCULAR REASONING, FORMAL FALLACY, IMPLICATURE, INFORMAL LOGIC, PRAGMATIC CONTRADICTION, VALID.**   D.W.

informal logic, also called practical logic, the use of logic to identify, analyze, and evaluate arguments as they occur in contexts of discourse in everyday conversations. In informal logic, arguments are assessed on a case-by-case basis, relative to how the argument was used in a given context to persuade someone to accept the conclusion, or at least to give some reason relevant to accepting the conclusion. **See also CIRCULAR**

REASONING, FORMAL FALLACY, IMPLICATURE, INFORMAL FALLACY, PRAGMATIC CONTRADICTION, VALID.   D.W.

information-theoretic semantics. See PHILOSOPHY OF MIND.

information theory, also called communication theory, a primarily mathematical theory of communication. Prime movers in its development include Claude Shannon, H. Nyquist, R. V. L. Hartley, Norbert Wiener, Boltzmann, and Szilard. Original interests in the theory were largely theoretical or applied to telegraphy and telephony, and early development clustered around engineering problems in such domains. Philosophers (Bar-Hillel, Dretske, and Sayre, among others) are mainly interested in information theory as a source for developing a semantic theory of information and meaning. The mathematical theory has been less concerned with the details of how a message acquires meaning and more concerned with what Shannon called the "fundamental problem of communication" – reproducing at one point either exactly or approximately a message (that already has a meaning) selected at another point. Therefore, the two interests in information – the mathematical and the philosophical – have remained largely orthogonal.

Information is an objective (mind-independent) entity. It can be generated or carried by messages (words, sentences) or other products of cognizers (interpreters). Indeed, communication theory focuses primarily on conditions involved in the generation and transmission of coded (linguistic) messages. However, almost any event can (and usually does) generate information capable of being encoded or transmitted. For example, Colleen's acquiring red spots can contain information about Colleen's having the measles and graying hair can carry information about her grandfather's aging. This information can be encoded into messages about measles or aging (respectively) and transmitted, but the information would exist independently of its encoding or transmission. That is, this information would be generated (under the right conditions) by occurrence of the measles-induced spots and the age-induced graying themselves – regardless of anyone's actually noticing.

This objective feature of information explains its potential for epistemic and semantic development by philosophers and cognitive scientists. For example, in its epistemic dimension, a single (event, message, or Colleen's spots) that contains (carries) the information that Colleen has the measles is something from which one (mom, doctor) can come to know that Colleen has the measles. Generally, an event (signal) that contains the information that p is something from which one can come to know that p is the case – provided that one's knowledge is indeed based on the information that p. Since information is objective, it can generate what we want from knowledge – a fix on the way the world objectively is configured. In its semantic dimension, information can have intentionality or aboutness. What is happening at one place (thermometer reading rising in Colleen's mouth) can carry information about what is happening at another place (Colleen's body temperature rising). The fact that messages (or mental states, for that matter) can contain information about what is happening elsewhere, suggests an exciting prospect of tracing the meaning of a message (or of a thought) to its informational origins in the environment. To do this in detail is what a semantic theory of information is about.

The mathematical theory of information is purely concerned with information in its quantitative dimension. It deals with how to measure and transmit amounts of information and leaves to others the work of saying what (how) meaning or content comes to be associated with a signal or message. In regard to amounts of information, we need a way to measure how much information is generated by an event (or message) and how to represent that amount. Information theory provides the answer.

Since information is an objective entity, the amount of information associated with an event is related to the objective probability (likelihood) of the event. Events that are less likely to occur generate more information than those more likely to occur. Thus, to discover that the toss of a fair coin came up heads contains more information than to discover this about the toss of a coin biased (.8) toward heads. Or, to discover that a lie was knowingly broadcast by a censored, state-run radio station, contains less information than that a lie was knowingly broadcast by a non-censored, free radio station (say, the BBC). A (perhaps surprising) consequence of associating amounts of information with objective likelihoods of events is that some events generate no information at all. That is, that $5^5 = 3125$ or that water freezes at $0°C$. (on a specific occasion) generates no information at all – since these things cannot be otherwise (their probability of being otherwise is zero). Thus, their occurrence generates zero information.

Shannon was seeking to measure the amount of information generated by a message and the amount transmitted by its reception (or about average amounts transmissible over a channel). Since his work, it has become standard to think of the measure of information in terms of reductions of uncertainty. Information is identified with the reduction of uncertainty or elimination of possibilities represented by the occurrence of an event or state of affairs. The amount of information is identified with how many possibilities are eliminated. Although other measures are possible, the most convenient and intuitive way that this quantity is standardly represented is as a logarithm (to the base 2) and measured in bits (short for how many *bi*nary dig*its* needed to represent binary decisions involved in the reduction or elimination of possibilities. If person A chooses a message to send to person B, from among 16 equally likely alternative messages (say, which number came up in a fair drawing from 16 numbers), the choice of one message would represent 4 bits of information ($16 = 2^4$ or $\log_2 16 = 4$).

Thus, to calculate the amount of information generated by a selection from equally likely messages (signals, events), the amount of information I of the message s is calculated

$$I(s) = \log_n.$$

If there is a range of messages ($s1 \ldots sN$) not all of which are equally likely (letting ($p(si) =$ the probability of any si's occurrence), the amount of information generated by the selection of any message si is calculated

$$I(si) = \log 1/p(si)$$
$$= -\log p(si) \ [\log 1/x = -\log x]$$

While each of these formulas says how much information is generated by the selection of a specific message, communication theory is seldom primarily interested in these measures. Philosophers are interested, however. For if knowledge that p requires receiving the information that p occurred, and if p's occurrence represents 4 bits of information, then S would know that p occurred only if S received information equal to (at least) 4 bits. This may not be sufficient for S to know p – for S must receive the right amount of information in a non-deviant causal way and S must be able to extract the content of the information – but this seems clearly necessary.

Other measures of information of interest in communication theory include the average information, or *entropy,* of a source,

$$I(s) = \Sigma p(si) \times I(si),$$

a measure for *noise* (the amount of information that person B receives that was *not* sent by person A), and for equivocation (the amount of information A wanted or tried to send to B that B did not receive). These concepts from information theory and the formulas for measuring these quantities of information (and others) provide a rich source of tools for communication applications as well as philosophical applications. **See also** COMPUTER THEORY, EPISTEMOLOGY, PERCEPTION.   F.A.

informed consent, voluntary agreement in the light of relevant information, especially by a patient to a medical procedure. An example would be consent to a specific medical procedure by a competent adult patient who has an adequate understanding of all the relevant treatment options and their risks. It is widely held that both morality and law require that no medical procedures be performed on competent adults without their informed consent. This doctrine of informed consent has been featured in case laws since the 1950s, and has been a focus of much discussion in medical ethics. Underwritten by a concern to protect patients' rights to self-determination and also by a concern with patients' well-being, the doctrine was introduced in an attempt to delineate physicians' duties to inform patients of the risks and benefits of medical alternatives and to obtain their consent to a particular course of treatment or diagnosis. Interpretation of the legitimate scope of the doctrine has focused on a variety of issues concerning what range of patients is competent to give consent and hence from which ones informed consent must be required; concerning how much, how detailed, and what sort of information must be given to patients to yield informed consent; and concerning what sorts of conditions are required to ensure both that there is proper understanding of the information and that consent is truly voluntary rather than unduly influenced by the institutional authority of the physician. **See also** ETHICS.   J.R.M.

Ingarden, Roman Witold (1893–1970), the leading Polish phenomenologist, who taught in Lvov and Cracow and became prominent in the English-speaking world above all through his work in aesthetics and philosophy of literature. His *Literary Work of Art* (German 1931, English 1973) presents an ontological account of the literary work as a stratified structure, including word

sounds and meanings, represented objects and aspects, and associated metaphysical and aesthetic qualities.

The work forms part of a larger ontological project of combating the transcendental idealism of his teacher Husserl, and seeks to establish the essential difference in structure between mind-dependent 'intentional' objects and objects in reality. Ingarden's ontological investigations are set out in his *The Controversy over the Existence of the World* (Polish 1947/48, German 1964–74, partial English translation as *Time and Modes of Being*, 1964). The work rests on a tripartite division of formal, material, and existential ontology and contains extensive analyses of the ontological structures of individual things, events, processes, states of affairs, properties and relations. It culminates in an attempted refutation of idealism on the basis of an exhaustive account of the possible relations between consciousness and reality. **See also** PHENOMENOLOGY.   B.Sm.

inherent value. See VALUE.

innate idea. See IDEA.

innatism. See CAMBRIDGE PLATONISTS.

inner converse. See CONVERSE, OUTER AND INNER.

***in rebus* realism.** See METAPHYSICAL REALISM.

inscrutability of reference. See INDETERMINACY OF TRANSLATION.

insolubilia, sentences embodying a semantic antinomy such as the liar paradox. *Insolubilia* were used by late medieval logicians to analyze self-nullifying sentences, the possibility that all sentences imply that they are true, and the relation between spoken, written, and mental language. At first, theorists focused on nullification to explicate a sentence like 'I am lying', which, when spoken, entails that the speaker "says nothing." Bradwardine suggested that such sentences signify that they are at once true and false, prompting Burley to argue that all sentences imply that they are true. Roger Swineshead used *insolubilia* to distinguish between truth and correspondence to reality; while 'This sentence is false' is itself false, it corresponds to reality, while its contradiction, 'This sentence is not false,' does not, although the latter is also false. Later, Wyclif used *insolubilia* to describe the senses in which a sentence can be true, which led to his belief in the reality of logical beings or entities of reason, a central tenet of his realism. Pierre d'Ailly used *insolubilia* to explain how mental language differs from spoken and written language, holding that there are no mental language insolubles, but that spoken and written language lend themselves to the phenomenon by admitting a single sentence corresponding to two distinct mental sentences. **See also BURLEY, D'AILLY, OXFORD CALCULATORS, SEMANTIC PARADOXES, WYCLIF.** S.E.L.

instantiation. See PROPERTY.

instantiation, universal. See UNIVERSAL INSTANTIATION.

institution. (1) An organization such as a corporation or college. (2) A social practice such as marriage or making promises. (3) A system of rules defining a possible form of social organization, such as capitalist versus Communist principles of economic exchange.

In light of the power of institutions to shape societies and individual lives, writers in professional ethics have explored four main issues. First, what political and legal institutions are feasible, just, and otherwise desirable (Plato, *Republic*; Rawls, *A Theory of Justice*)? Second, how are values embedded in institutions through the constitutive rules that define them (for example, "To promise is to undertake an obligation"), as well as through regulatory rules imposed on them from outside, such that to participate in institutions is a value-laden activity (Searle, *Speech Acts*, 1969)? Third, do institutions have collective responsibilities or are the only responsibilities those of individuals, and in general how are the responsibilities of individuals, institutions, and communities related? Fourth, at a more practical level, how can we prevent institutions from becoming corrupted by undue regard for money and power (MacIntyre, *After Virtue*, 1981) and by patriarchal prejudices (Susan Moller Okin, *Justice, Gender, and the Family*, 1989)?

See also PHILOSOPHY OF LAW, PROFESSIONAL ETHICS, RESPONSIBILITY. M.W.M.

institutional theory of art, the view that something becomes an artwork by virtue of occupying a certain position within the context of a set of institutions.

George Dickie originated this theory of art (*Art and the Aesthetic*, 1974), which was derived loosely from Arthur Danto's "The Artworld" (*Journal of Philosophy*, 1964). In its original form

it was the view that a work of art is an artifact that has the status of candidate for appreciation conferred upon it by some person acting on behalf of the art world. That is, there are institutions – such as museums, galleries, and journals and newspapers that publish reviews and criticism – and there are individuals who work within those institutions – curators, directors, dealers, performers, critics – who decide, by accepting objects or events for discussion and display, what is art and what is not. The concept of artifactuality may be extended to include found art, conceptual art, and other works that do not involve altering some preexisting material, by holding that a use, or context for display, is sufficient to make something into an artifact.

This definition of art raises certain questions. What determines – independently of such notions as a concern with *art* – whether an institution is a member of the art world? That is, is the definition ultimately circular? What is it to accept something as a candidate for appreciation? Might not this concept also threaten circularity, since there could be not only artistic but also other kinds of appreciation?

See also AESTHETICS, EXPRESSION THEORY OF ART. S.L.F.

instrumental conditioning. See CONDITIONING.

instrumentalism, in its most common meaning, a kind of anti-realistic view of scientific theories wherein theories are construed as calculating devices or instruments for conveniently moving from a given set of observations to a predicted set of observations. As such the theoretical statements are not candidates for truth or reference, and the theories have no ontological import. This view of theories is grounded in a positive distinction between observation statements and theoretical statements, and the according of privileged epistemic status to the former. The view was fashionable during the era of positivism but then faded; it was recently revived, in large measure owing to the genuinely perplexing character of quantum theories in physics.

'Instrumentalism' has a different and much more general meaning associated with the pragmatic epistemology of Dewey. Deweyan instrumentalism is a general functional account of all concepts (scientific ones included) wherein the epistemic status of concepts and the rationality status of actions are seen as a function of their role in integrating, predicting, and controlling our concrete interactions with our experienced world. There is no positivistic distinction between observation and theory, and truth and reference give way to "warranted assertability."

See also DEWEY, METAPHYSICAL REALISM, PHILOSOPHY OF SCIENCE, THEORETICAL TERM.
C.F.D.

instrumental rationality. See RATIONALITY.

instrumental sign. See SEMIOSIS.

instrumental value. See VALUE.

insufficient reason. See PRINCIPLE OF INSUFFICIENT REASON.

intelligible world. See KANT.

intension, the meaning or connotation of an expression, as opposed to its extension or denotation, which consists of those things signified by the expression. The intension of a declarative sentence is often taken to be a proposition and the intension of a predicate expression (common noun, adjective) is often taken to be a concept. For Frege, a predicate expression refers to a concept and the intension or *Sinn* ("sense") of a predicate expression is a mode of presentation distinct from the concept. Objects like propositions or concepts that can be the intension of terms are called intensional objects. (Note that 'intensional' is not the same word as 'intentional', although the two are related.) The extension of a declarative sentence is often taken to be a state of affairs and that of a predicate expression to be the set of objects that fall under the concept which is the intension of the term. Extension is not the same as reference. For example, the term 'red' may be said to refer to the property redness but to have as its extension the set of all red things. Alternatively properties and relations are sometimes taken to be intensional objects, but the property redness is never taken to be part of the extension of the adjective 'red'. See also EXTENSIONALISM, INTENSIONALITY, INTENSIONAL LOGIC, MEANING.   D.N.

intension, compositional. See LEWIS, DAVID.

intensionality, failure of extensionality. A linguistic context is extensional if and only if the extension of the expression obtained by placing any subexpression in that context is the same as the extension of the expression obtained by placing in that context any subexpression with the same extension as the first subexpression. Modal, intentional, and direct quotational con-

texts are main instances of intensional contexts. Take, e.g., sentential contexts. The extension of a sentence is its truth or falsity (truth-value). The extension of a definite description is what it is true of: 'the husband of Xanthippe' and 'the teacher of Plato' have the same extension, for they are true of the same man, Socrates. Given this, it is easy to see that 'Necessarily, . . . was married to Xanthippe' is intensional, for 'Necessarily, the husband of Xanthippe was married to Xanthippe' is true, but 'Necessarily, the teacher of Plato was married to Xanthippe' is not. Other modal terms that generate intensional contexts include 'possibly', 'impossibly', 'essentially', 'contingently', etc. Assume that Smith has heard of Xanthippe but not Plato. 'Smith believes that . . . was married to Xanthippe' is intensional, for 'Smith believes that the husband of Xanthippe was married to Xanthippe' is true, but 'Smith believes that the teacher of Plato was married to Xanthippe' is not. Other intentional verbs that generate intensional contexts include 'know', 'doubt', 'wonder', 'fear', 'intend', 'state', and 'want'. 'The fourth word in ". . . " has nine letters' is intensional, for 'The fourth word in "the husband of Xanthippe" has nine letters' is true but 'the fourth word in "the teacher of Plato" has nine letters' is not. See also EXTENSIONALISM, MEANING, QUANTIFYING IN, REFERENTIALLY TRANSPARENT.   T.Y.

intensional logic, that part of deductive logic which treats arguments whose validity or invalidity depends on strict difference, or identity, of meaning. The denotation of a singular term (i.e., a proper name or definite description), the class of things of which a predicate is true, and the truth or falsity (the truth-value) of a sentence may be called the *extensions* of these respective linguistic expressions. Their *intensions* are their meanings strictly so called: the (individual) concept conveyed by the singular term, the property expressed by the predicate, and the proposition asserted by the sentence. The most extensively studied part of formal logic deals largely with inferences turning only on extensions. One principle of extensional logic is that if two singular terms have identical denotations, the truth-values of corresponding sentences containing the terms are identical. Thus the inference from 'Bern is the capital of Switzerland' to 'You are in Bern if and only if you are in the capital of Switzerland' is valid. But this is invalid: 'Bern is the capital of Switzerland. Therefore, you believe that you are in Bern if and only if you believe that you are in the capital of Switzerland.' For one may lack the belief that Bern is the capital of Switzerland. It seems that we should distinguish between the intensional meanings of 'Bern' and of 'the capital of Switzerland'. One supposes that only a strict identity of intension would license interchange in such a context, in which they are in the scope of a propositional attitude. It has been questioned whether the idea of an intension really applies to proper names, but parallel examples are easily constructed that make similar use of the differences in the meanings of predicates or of whole sentences. Quite generally, then, the principle that expressions with the same extension may be interchanged with preservation of extension of the containing expression, seems to fail for such "intensional contexts."

The range of expressions producing such sensitive contexts includes psychological verbs like 'know', 'believe', 'suppose', 'assert', 'desire', 'allege', 'wonders whether'; expressions conveying modal ideas such as necessity, possibility, and impossibility; some adverbs, e.g. 'intentionally'; and a large number of other expressions – 'prove', 'imply', 'make probable', etc. Although reasoning involving some of these is well understood, there is not yet general agreement on the best methods for dealing with arguments involving many of these notions.

See also MODAL LOGIC.   C.A.A.

intensive magnitude. See MAGNITUDE.

intention, (1) a characteristic of action, as when one acts *intentionally* or *with a certain intention;* (2) a feature of one's mind, as when one *intends (has an intention)* to act in a certain way now or in the future. Betty, e.g., intentionally walks across the room, does so with the intention of getting a drink, and now intends to leave the party later that night. An important question is: how are (1) and (2) related? (See Anscombe, *Intention,* 1963, for a groundbreaking treatment of these and other basic problems concerning intention.)

Some philosophers see acting with an intention as basic and as subject to a three-part analysis. For Betty to walk across the room with the intention of getting a drink is for Betty's walking across the room to be explainable (in the appropriate way) by her desire or (as is sometimes said) pro-attitude in favor of getting a drink and her belief that walking across the room is a way of getting one. On this *desire-belief model* (or want-belief model) the main elements of acting with an intention are (a) the action, (b) appropriate desires (pro-attitudes) and beliefs, and (c) an appropriate explanatory relation between (a)

and (b). (See Davidson, "Actions, Reasons, and Causes" in *Essays on Actions and Events,* 1980.) In explaining (a) in terms of (b) we give an explanation of the action in terms of the agent's purposes or reasons for so acting. This raises the fundamental question of what kind of explanation this is, and how it is related to explanation of Betty's movements by appeal to their physical causes.

What about intentions to act in the future? Consider Betty's intention to leave the party later. Though the intended action is later, this intention may nevertheless help explain some of Betty's planning and acting between now and then. Some philosophers try to fit such future-directed intentions directly into the desire-belief model. John Austin, e.g., would identify Betty's intention with her belief that she will leave later because of her desire to leave (*Lectures on Jurisprudence,* vol. I, 1873). Others see future-directed intentions as distinctive attitudes, not to be reduced to desires and/or beliefs.

How is belief related to intention? One question here is whether an intention to *A* requires a belief that one will *A*. A second question is whether a belief that one will *A* in executing some intention ensures that one intends to *A*. Suppose that Betty believes that by walking across the room she will interrupt Bob's conversation. Though she has no desire to interrupt, she still proceeds across the room. Does she intend to interrupt the conversation? Or is there a coherent distinction between what one intends and what one merely expects to bring about as a result of doing what one intends? One way of talking about such cases, due to Bentham (*An Introduction to the Principles of Morals and Legislation,* 1789), is to say that Betty's walking across the room is "directly intentional," whereas her interrupting the conversation is only "obliquely intentional" (or indirectly intentional).

See also ACTION THEORY, PRINCIPLE OF DOUBLE EFFECT.   M.E.B.

intention, direct. See INTENTION.

intention, first. See IMPOSITION.

intention, indirect. See INTENTION.

intention, oblique. See INTENTION.

intention, second. See IMPOSITION.

intentional fallacy, the (purported) fallacy of holding that the meaning of a work of art is fixed by the artist's intentions. (Wimsatt and Beardsley, who introduced the term, also used it to name the [purported] fallacy that the artist's aims are relevant to determining the success of a work of art; however, this distinct usage has not gained general currency.) Wimsatt and Beardsley were formalists; they held that interpretation should focus purely on the work of art itself and should exclude appeal to biographical information about the artist, other than information concerning the private meanings the artist attached to his words.

Whether the intentional fallacy is in fact a fallacy is a much discussed issue within aesthetics. Intentionalists deny that it is: they hold that the meaning of a work of art is fixed by some set of the artist's intentions. For instance, Richard Wollheim (*Painting as an Art*) holds that the meaning of a painting is fixed by the artist's fulfilled intentions in making it. Other intentionalists appeal not to the actual artist's intentions, but to the intentions of the implied or postulated artist, a construct of criticism, rather than a real person.

See also AESTHETIC FORMALISM, AESTHETICS, INTENTION.   B.Ga.

intentionality, aboutness. Things that are about other things exhibit intentionality. Beliefs and other mental states exhibit intentionality, but so, in a derived way, do sentences and books, maps and pictures, and other representations. The adjective 'intentional' in this philosophical sense is a technical term not to be confused with the more familiar sense, characterizing something done on purpose. Hopes and fears, for instance, are not things we do, not intentional acts in the latter, familiar sense, but they are intentional phenomena in the technical sense: hopes and fears are *about* various things.

The term was coined by the Scholastics in the Middle Ages, and derives from the Latin verb *intendo*, 'to point (at)' or 'aim (at)' or 'extend (toward)'. Phenomena with intentionality thus point outside of themselves to something else: whatever they are of or about. The term was revived by the nineteenth-century philosopher and psychologist Franz Brentano, who claimed that intentionality defines the distinction between the mental and the physical; all and only mental phenomena exhibit intentionality. Since intentionality is an irreducible feature of mental phenomena, and since no physical phenomena could exhibit it, mental phenomena could not be a species of physical phenomena. This claim, often called the Brentano thesis or Brentano's irreducibility thesis, has often been cited to support the view that the mind cannot

be the brain, but this is by no means generally accepted today.

There was a second revival of the term in the 1960s and 1970s by analytic philosophers, in particular Chisholm, Sellars, and Quine. Chisholm attempted to clarify the concept by shifting to a logical definition of intentional *idioms*, the terms used to speak of mental states and events, rather than attempting to define the intentionality of the states and events themselves. Intentional idioms include the familiar "mentalistic" terms of folk psychology, but also their technical counterparts in theories and discussions in cognitive science, 'X believes that *p*,' and 'X desires that *q*' are paradigmatic intentional idioms, but according to Chisholm's logical definition, in terms of referential opacity (the failure of substitutivity of coextensive terms *salva veritate*), so are such less familiar idioms as 'X stores the information that *p*' and 'X gives high priority to achieving the state of affairs that *q*'.

Although there continue to be deep divisions among philosophers about the proper definition or treatment of the concept of intentionality, there is fairly widespread agreement that it marks a feature – aboutness or content – that is central to mental phenomena, and hence a central, and difficult, problem that any theory of mind must solve.

See also BRENTANO, FOLK PSYCHOLOGY, QUANTIFYING IN, REFERENTIALLY TRANSPARENT.   D.C.D.

intentional object. See BRENTANO.

intentional species. See AQUINAS, ARISTOTLE.

interchangeability *salva veritate*. See SUBSTITUTIVITY SALVA VERITATE.

internalism, epistemological. See EPISTEMOLOGY.

internalism, motivational. See MOTIVATIONAL INTERNALISM.

internalism, reasons. See EXTERNALISM.

internal necessity. See NECESSITY.

internal negation. See NEGATION.

internal realism. See PHILOSOPHY OF SCIENCE.

internal reason. See EXTERNALISM.

internal relation. See RELATION.

interoception. See PERCEPTION.

interpersonal utility. See UTILITARIANISM.

interpretant. See PEIRCE.

interpretation. See MODAL LOGIC.

interpretation, non-standard. See FORMAL SEMANTICS.

interpretation, standard. See FORMAL SEMANTICS.

interpretive system. See OPERATIONALISM.

intersection. See SET THEORY.

intersubjectivity. See MERLEAU-PONTY.

intersubstitutivity *salva veritate.* See SUBSTITUTIVITY SALVA VERITATE.

interval scale. See MAGNITUDE.

intervening variable, in psychology, a state of an organism or person postulated to explain behavior and defined in terms of its causes and effects rather than its intrinsic properties. A food drive, conceived as an intervening variable, may be defined in terms of the number of hours without food (causes) and the strength or robustness of efforts to secure it (effects) rather than in terms of hungry feeling (intrinsic property). There are at least three reasons for postulating intervening variables. First, time lapse between stimulus and behavior may be large, as when an animal eats food found hours earlier. Why didn't the animal eat when it first discovered food? Perhaps at the time of discovery, it had already eaten, so food drive was reduced. Second, the same animal or person may act differently in the same sort of situation, as when we eat at noon one day but delay until 3 p.m. the next. Again, this may be because of variation in food drive. Third, behavior may occur in the absence of external stimulation, as when an animal forages for food. This, too, may be explained by the strength of the food drive. Intervening variables have been viewed, depending on the background theory, as convenient fictions or as psychologically real states. **See also THEORETICAL TERM.**   G.A.G.

intrapersonal utility. See UTILITARIANISM.

intrinsic desire. See EXTRINSIC DESIRE.

intrinsic property. See RELATION.

intrinsic relation. See RELATION.

intrinsic value. See VALUE.

introjection. See FREUD.

introspection. See AWARENESS.

intuition, a non-inferential knowledge or grasp, as of a proposition, concept, or entity, that is not based on perception, memory, or introspection; also, the capacity in virtue of which such cognition is possible. A person might know that $1 + 1 = 2$ intuitively, i.e., not on the basis of inferring it from other propositions. And one might know intuitively what yellow is, i.e., might understand the concept, even though 'yellow' is not definable. Or one might have intuitive awareness of God or some other entity. Certain mystics hold that there can be intuitive, or immediate, apprehension of God. Ethical intuitionists hold both that we can have intuitive knowledge of certain moral concepts that are indefinable, and that certain propositions, such as that pleasure is intrinsically good, are knowable through intuition. Self-evident propositions are those that can be seen (non-inferentially) to be true once one fully understands them. It is often held that all and only self-evident propositions are knowable through intuition, which is here identified with a certain kind of intellectual or rational insight. Intuitive knowledge of moral or other philosophical propositions or concepts has been compared to the intuitive knowledge of grammaticality possessed by competent users of a language. Such language users can know immediately whether certain sentences are grammatical or not without recourse to any conscious reasoning. **See also A PRIORI, EPISTEMOLOGY.**
                                                    B.R.

intuition, eidetic. See HUSSERL.

intuition, sensible. See KANT.

intuitionism, ethical. See ETHICS.

intuitionism, mathematical. See MATHEMATICAL INTUITIONISM.

intuitionism, Oxford school of. See PRICHARD.

intuitionist logic. See FORMAL LOGIC, PHILOSOPHY OF LOGIC.

intuitions. See PREANALYTIC.

intuitive induction. See ROSS.

inversion, spectrum. See QUALIA.

inverted qualia. See PHILOSOPHY OF MIND, QUALIA.

invisible hand. See SMITH, SOCIAL PHILOSOPHY.

involuntary euthanasia. See EUTHANASIA.

inwardness. See TAYLOR, CHARLES.

Ionian philosophy, the characteristically naturalist and rationalist thought of Greek philosophers of the sixth and fifth centuries B.C. who were active in Ionia, the region of ancient Greek colonies on the coast of Asia Minor and adjacent islands. First of the Ionian philosophers were the three Milesians. **See also MILESIANS, PRE-SOCRATICS.**   A.P.D.M.

iota operator. See Appendix of Special Symbols.

I-proposition. See SYLLOGISM.

Irigaray, Luce (b.1930), French feminist philosopher and psychoanalyst. Her earliest work was in psychoanalysis and linguistics, focusing on the role of negation in the language of schizophrenics (*Languages,* 1966). A trained analyst with a private practice, she attended Lacan's seminars at the École Normale Supérieure and for several years taught a course in the psychoanalysis department at Vincennes. With the publication of *Speculum, De l'autre femme* (*Speculum of the Other Woman*) in 1974 she was dismissed from Vincennes. She argues that psychoanalysis, specifically its attitude toward women, is historically and culturally determined and that its phallocentric bias is treated as universal truth.

With the publication of *Speculum* and *Ce Sexe qui n'en est pas un* (*This Sex Which Is Not One*) in 1977, her work extends beyond psychoanalysis and begins a critical examination of philosophy. Influenced primarily by Hegel, Nietzsche, and Heidegger, her work is a critique of the fundamental categories of philosophical thought: one/many, identity/difference, being/non-being, rational/irrational, mind/body, form/matter, transcendental/sensible. She sets out to show the concealed aspect of metaphysical constructions and what they depend on, namely, the unacknowledged mother. In *Speculum,* the mirror figures as interpretation and criticism of the enclosure of the Western subject within the mirror's frame, constituted solely through the masculine imaginary. Her project is one of constituting the world – and not only the specular world – of the other as woman. This engagement with the history of philosophy emphasizes the historical and sexual determinants of philosophical discourse, and insists on bringing the transcendental back to the elements of the earth and embodiment.

Her major contribution to philosophy is the notion of sexual difference. *An Ethics of Sexual Difference* (1984) claims that the central contemporary philosophical task is to think through sexual difference. Although her notion of sexual difference is sometimes taken to be an essentialist view of the feminine, in fact it is an articulation of the difference between the sexes that calls into question an understanding of either the feminine or masculine as possessing a rigid gender identity. Instead, sexual difference is the erotic desire for otherness. Insofar as it is an origin that is continuously differentiating itself from itself, it challenges Aristotle's understanding of the *arche* as solid ground or *hypokeimenon*. As *aition* or first cause, sexual difference is responsible for something coming into being and is that to which things are indebted for their being. This indebtedness allows Irigaray to formulate an ethics of sexual difference.

Her latest work continues to rethink the foundations of ethics. Both *Towards a Culture of Difference* (1990) and *I Love To You* (1995) claim that there is no civil identity proper to women and therefore no possibility of equivalent social and political status for men and women. She argues for a legal basis to ground the reciprocity between the sexes; that there is no living universal, that is, a universal that reflects sexual difference; and that this lack of a living universal leads to an absence of rights and responsibilities which reflects both men and women. She claims, therefore, that it is necessary to "sexuate" rights. These latest works continue to make explicit the erotic and ethical project that informs all her work: to think through the dimension of sexual difference that opens up access to the alliances between living beings who are engendered and not fabricated, and who refuse to sacrifice desire for death, power, or money.

See also FREUD, HEGEL, HEIDEGGER, NIETZSCHE, POSTMODERN.   P.Bi.

irrationality, unreasonableness. Whatever it entails, irrationality can characterize belief, desire, intention, and action.

Irrationality is often explained in instrumental, or goal-oriented, terms. You are irrational if you (knowingly) fail to do your best, or at least to do what you appropriately think adequate, to achieve your goals. If ultimate goals are rationally assessable, as Aristotelian and Kantian traditions hold, then rationality and irrationality are not purely instrumental. The latter traditions regard certain specific (kinds of) goals, such as human well-being, as essential to rationality. This substantialist approach lost popularity with the rise of modern decision theory, which implies that, in satisfying certain consistency and completeness requirements, one's preferences toward the possible outcomes of available actions determine what actions are rational and irrational for one by determining the personal utility of their outcomes. Various theorists have faulted modern decision theory on two grounds: human beings typically lack the consistent preferences and reasoning power required by standard decision theory but are not thereby irrational, and rationality requires goods exceeding maximally efficient goal satisfaction.

When relevant goals concern the acquisition of truth and the avoidance of falsehood, *epistemic* rationality and irrationality are at issue. Otherwise, some species of non-epistemic rationality or irrationality is under consideration. Species of non-epistemic rationality and irrationality correspond to the kind of relevant goal: moral, prudential, political, economic, aesthetic, or some other. A comprehensive account of irrationality will elucidate epistemic and non-epistemic irrationality as well as such sources of irrationality as weakness of will and ungrounded belief.

See also DECISION THEORY, JUSTIFICATION, RATIONALITY.   P.K.M.

irredundant. See INDEPENDENCE RESULTS.

irreflexive. See RELATION.

irrelevant conclusion, fallacy of. See INFORMAL FALLACY.

is, third person singular form of the verb 'be', with at least three fundamental senses that philosophers distinguish according to the resources required for a proper logical representation. The 'is' of existence (*There is a unicorn in the garden*: $\exists x\ (Ux \wedge Gx)$) uses the existential quantifier. The 'is' of identity (*Hesperus is Phosphorus*: $j = k$) employs the predicate of identity. The 'is' of predication (*Samson is strong*: Sj)

merely juxtaposes predicate symbol and proper name.

Some controversy attends the first sense. Some (notably Meinong) maintain that 'is' applies more broadly than 'exists,' the former producing truths when combined with 'deer' and 'unicorn' and the latter producing truths when combined with 'deer' but not 'unicorn'. Others (like Aquinas) take 'being' (*esse*) to denote some special activity that every existing object necessarily performs, which would seem to imply that with 'is' they attribute more to an object than we do with 'exists'.

Other issues arise in connection with the second sense. Does *Hesperus is Phosphorus*, for example, attribute anything more to the heavenly body than its identity with itself? Consideration of such a question led Frege to conclude that names (and other meaningful expressions) of ordinary language have a "sense" or "mode of presenting" the object to which they refer that representations within our standard, extensional logical systems fail to expose. The distinction between the 'is' of identity and the 'is' of predication parallels Frege's distinction between object and concept: words signifying objects stand to the right of the 'is' of identity and those signifying concepts stand to the right of the 'is' of predication. Although it seems remarkable that so many deep and difficult philosophical concepts should link to a single short and commonplace word, we should perhaps not read too much into that observation. Some languages divide the various roles played by English's compact copula among several constructions, and others use the corresponding word for other purposes.

See also EXISTENTIAL IMPORT, IDENTITY, QUALITIES.   S.T.K.

Isaac Israeli. See JEWISH PHILOSOPHY.

Isagoge. See PORPHYRY.

Islamic Neoplatonism, a Neoplatonism constituting one of several philosophical tendencies adopted by Muslim philosophers. Aristotle was well known and thoroughly studied among those thinkers in the Islamic world specifically influenced by ancient Greek philosophy; Plato less so. In part both were understood in Neoplatonic terms. But, because the *Enneads* came to be labeled mistakenly the *Theology of Aristotle*, the name of 'Plotinus' had no significance. A similar situation befell the other ancient Neoplatonists. The *Theology* and other important sources of Neoplatonic thinking were, therefore, often seen as merely the "theological" speculations of the two major Greek philosophical authorities – mainly Aristotle: all of this material being roughly equivalent to something Islamic Neoplatonists called the "divine Plato." For a few Islamic philosophers, moreover, such as the critically important al-Fārābī, Neoplatonism had little impact. They followed a tradition of philosophical studies based solely on an accurate knowledge of Aristotle plus the political teachings of Plato without this "theology." In the works of less avowedly "philosophical" thinkers, however, a collection of falsely labeled remnants of ancient Neoplatonism – bits of the *Enneads*, pieces of Proclus's *Elements of Theology* (notably the Arabic version of the famous *Liber de causis*), and various pseudo-epigraphic doxographies full of Neoplatonic ideas – gave rise to a true Islamic Neoplatonism.

This development followed two distinct paths. The first and more direct route encompassed a number of tenth-century authors who were attracted to Neoplatonic theories about God's or the One's complete and ineffable transcendence, about intellect's unity and universality, and about soul as a hypostatic substance having continual existence in a universal as well as a particular being, the latter being the individual human soul. These doctrines held appeal as much for their religious as for their philosophical utility. A second form of Neoplatonism arose in the intellectual elements of Islamic mysticism, i.e., Sufism. There, the influence of Plotinus's concept of the ecstatic confrontation and ultimate union with the One found a clear, although unacknowledged, echo. In later periods, too, the "divine Plato" enjoyed a revival of importance via a number of influential philosophers, such as Suhrawardī of Aleppo (twelfth century) and Mullā Ṣadrā (seventeenth century), who were interested in escaping the narrow restrictions of Peripatetic thought.

See also ARABIC PHILOSOPHY, NEOPLATONISM, SUFISM.   P.E.W.

Islamic philosophy. See ARABIC PHILOSOPHY.

Isocrates (436–338 B.C.), Greek rhetorician and teacher who was seen as the chief contemporary rival of Plato. A pupil of Socrates and also of Gorgias, he founded a school in about 392 that attracted many foreign students to Athens and earned him a sizable income. Many of his works touch on his theories of education; *Against the Sophists* and *On the Antidosis* are most important in this respect. The latter stands to Isocrates as the *Apology* of Plato stands to Socrates, a defense of his life's work against an attack not on his life, but on his property. The aim of his teaching was good judgment in practical affairs, and he believed his contribution to Greece through education more valuable than legislation could possibly be. He repudiated instruction in theoretical philosophy, and insisted on distinguishing his teaching of rhetoric from the sophistry that gives clever speakers an unfair advantage. In politics he was a Panhellenic patriot, and urged the warring Greek city-states to unite under strong leadership and take arms against the Persian Empire. His most famous work, and the one in which he took the greatest pride, was the *Panegyricus*, a speech in praise of Athens. In general, he supported democracy in Athens, but toward the end of his life complained bitterly of abuses of the system.   P.Wo.

isolation argument. See EPISTEMOLOGY.

isomorphism. See CATEGORICITY, HOMOMORPHISM, KÖHLER.

is–ought distinction. See FACT–VALUE DISTINCTION.

is–ought problem. See FACT–VALUE DISTINCTION.

Israeli, Isaac. See JEWISH PHILOSOPHY.

iterated modality. See ALETHIC MODALITIES.

iterative hierarchy. See SET THEORY.

I-Thou relationship. See BUBER.

J

Jacobi, Friedrich Heinrich (1743–1819), German man of letters, popular novelist, and author of several influential philosophical works. His *Ueber die Lehre des Spinoza* (1785) precipitated a dispute with Mendelssohn on Lessing's alleged pantheism. The ensuing *Pantheismusstreit* (pantheism controversy) focused attention on the apparent conflict between human freedom and any systematic, philosophical interpretation of reality. In the appendix to his *David Hume über den Glauben, oder Idealismus und Realismus* ("David Hume on Belief, or Idealism and Realism," 1787), Jacobi scrutinized the new transcendental philosophy of Kant, and subjected Kant's remarks concerning "things-in-themselves" to devastating criticism, observing that, though one could not enter the critical philosophy without presupposing the existence of things-in-themselves, such a belief is incompatible with the tenets of that philosophy. This criticism deeply influenced the efforts of post-Kantians (e.g., Fichte) to improve transcendental idealism. In 1799, in an "open letter" to Fichte, Jacobi criticized philosophy in general and transcendental idealism in particular as "nihilism." Jacobi espoused a fideistic variety of direct realism and characterized his own standpoint as one of "non-knowing." Employing the arguments of "Humean skepticism," he defended the necessity of a "leap of faith," not merely in morality and religion, but in every area of human life. Jacobi's criticisms of reason and of science profoundly influenced German Romanticism. Near the end of his career he entered bitter public controversies with Hegel and Schelling concerning the relationship between faith and knowledge. **See also KANT.**   D.Br.

Jainism, an Indian religious and philosophical tradition established by Mahāvīra, a contemporary of the historical Buddha, in the latter half of the sixth and the beginning of the fifth century B.C. The tradition holds that each person (*jiva*) is everlasting and indestructible, a self-conscious identity surviving as a person even in a state of final enlightenment. It accepts personal immortality without embracing any variety of monotheism. On the basis of sensory experience it holds that there exist mind-independent physical objects, and it regards introspective experience as establishing the existence of enduring selves. It accepts the doctrines of rebirth and karma and conceives the ultimate good as escape from the wheel of rebirth. It rejects all violence as incompatible with achieving enlightenment. **See also BUDDHISM.**   K.E.Y.

James, William (1842–1910), American philosopher, psychologist, and one of the founders of pragmatism. He was born in New York City, the oldest of five children and elder brother of the novelist Henry James and diarist Alice James. Their father, Henry James, Sr., was an unorthodox religious philosopher, deeply influenced by the thought of Swedenborg, some of which seeped into William's later fascination with psychical research.

The James family relocated to Cambridge, Massachusetts, but the father insisted on his children obtaining a European education, and prolonged trips to England and the Continent were routine, a procedure that made William multilingual and extraordinarily cosmopolitan. In fact, a pervasive theme in James's personal and creative life was his deep split between things American and European: he felt like a bigamist "coquetting with too many countries."

As a person, James was extraordinarily sensitive to psychological and bodily experiences. He could be described as "neurasthenic" – afflicted with constant psychosomatic symptoms such as dyspepsia, vision problems, and clinical depression. In 1868 he recorded a profound personal experience, a "horrible fear of my own existence." In two 1870 diary entries, James first contemplates suicide and then pronounces his belief in free will and his resolve to act on that belief in "doing, suffering and creating."

Under the influence of the then burgeoning work in experimental psychology, James attempted to sustain, on empirical grounds, his belief in the self as Promethean, as self-making rather than as a playing out of inheritance or the influence of social context. This bold and extreme doctrine of individuality is bolstered by his attack on both the neo-Hegelian and associationist doctrines. He held that both approaches miss the empirical reality of relations as affectively experienced and the reality of consciousness as a "stream," rather than an aspect of an Absolute or simply a box holding a chain of concepts corresponding to single sense impressions.

In 1890, James published his masterpiece, *The Principles of Psychology*, which established him as the premier psychologist of the Euro-American world. It was a massive compendium and critique of virtually all of the psychology literature then extant, but it also claimed that the discipline was in its infancy. James believed that the problems he had unearthed could only be understood by a philosophical approach.

James held only one academic degree, an M.D. from Harvard, and his early teaching at Harvard was in anatomy and physiology. He subsequently became a professor of psychology, but during the writing of the *Principles*, he began to teach philosophy as a colleague of Royce and Santayana. From 1890 forward James saw the fundamental issues as at bottom philosophical and he undertook an intense inquiry into matters epistemological and metaphysical; in particular, "the religious question" absorbed him.

The Will to Believe and Other Essays in Popular Philosophy was published in 1897. The lead essay, "The Will to Believe," had been widely misunderstood, partly because it rested on unpublished metaphysical assumptions and partly because it ran aggressively counter to the reigning dogmas of social Darwinism and neo-Hegelian absolutism, both of which denigrated the personal power of the individual. For James, one cannot draw a conclusion, fix a belief, or hold to a moral or religious maxim unless all suggestions of an alternative position are explored. Further, some alternatives will be revealed only if one steps beyond one's frame of reference, seeks novelty, and "wills to believe" in possibilities beyond present sight.

The risk taking in such an approach to human living is further detailed in James's essays "The Dilemma of Determinism" and "The Moral Philosopher and the Moral Life," both of which stress the irreducibility of ambiguity, the presence of chance, and the desirability of tentativeness in our judgments.

After presenting the Gifford Lectures in 1901–02, James published his classic work, *The Varieties of Religious Experience*, which coalesced his interest in psychic states both healthy and sick and afforded him the opportunity to present again his firm belief that human life is characterized by a vast array of personal, cultural, and religious approaches that cannot and should not be reduced one to the other. For James, the "actual peculiarities of the world" must be central to any philosophical discussion of truth. In his Hibbert Lectures of 1909, published as *A Pluralistic Universe*, James was to represent this sense of plurality, openness, and the variety of human experience on a wider canvas, the vast reach of consciousness, cosmologically understood.

Unknown to all but a few philosophical correspondents, James had been assiduously filling notebooks with reflections on the mind–body problem and the relationship between meaning and truth and with a philosophical exploration and extension of his doctrine of relations as found earlier in the *Principles*. In 1904–05 James published a series of essays, gathered posthumously in 1912, on the meaning of experience and the problem of knowledge. In a letter to François Pillon in 1904, he writes: "My philosophy is what I call a radical empiricism, a pluralism, a 'tychism,' which represents order as being gradually won and always in the making." Following his 1889 essay "On Some Omissions of Introspective Psychology" and his chapter on "The Stream of Thought" in the *Principles*, James takes as given that relations between things are equivalently experienced as the things themselves. Consequently, "the only meaning of essence is teleological, and that classification and conception are purely teleological weapons of the mind."

The description of consciousness as a stream having a fringe as well as a focus, and being selective all the while, enables him to take the next step, the formulation of his pragmatic epistemology, one that was influenced by, but is different from, that of Peirce. Published in 1907, *Pragmatism* generated a transatlantic furor, for in it James unabashedly states that "Truth *happens* to be an idea. It *becomes* true, is *made* true by events." He also introduces the philosophically notorious claim that "theories" must be found that will "work." Actually, he means that a proposition cannot be judged as true independently of its consequences as judged by experience.

James's prose, especially in *Pragmatism*, alternates between scintillating and limpid. This quality led to both obfuscation of his intention and a lulling of his reader into a false sense of simplicity. He does not deny the standard definition of truth as a propositional claim about an existent, for he writes "woe to him whose beliefs play fast and loose with the order which realities follow in his experience; they will lead him nowhere or else make false connexions." Yet he regards this structure as but a prologue to the creative activity of the human mind. Also in *Pragmatism,* speaking of the world as "really malleable," he argues that man engenders truths upon reality. This tension between James as a radical empiricist with the affirmation of the blunt, obdurate relational manifold given to us in our experience and James as a pragmatic idealist holding to the constructing, engendering power of the Promethean self to create its own personal world, courses throughout all of his work.

James was chagrined and irritated by the quantity, quality, and ferocity of the criticism leveled at *Pragmatism.* He attempted to answer those critics in a book of disparate essays, *The Meaning of Truth* (1909). The book did little to persuade his critics; since most of them were unaware of his radically empirical metaphysics and certainly of his unpublished papers, James's pragmatism remained misunderstood until the publication of Perry's magisterial two-volume study, *The Thought and Character of William James* (1935).

By 1910, James's heart disease had worsened; he traveled to Europe in search of some remedy, knowing full well that it was a farewell journey. Shortly after returning to his summer home in Chocorua, New Hampshire, he died. One month earlier he had said of a manuscript (posthumously published in 1911 as *Some Problems in Philosophy*), "say that by it I hoped to round out my system, which is now too much like an arch only on one side." Even if he had lived much longer, it is arguable that the other side of the arch would not have appeared, for his philosophy was ineluctably geared to seeking out the novel, the surprise, the tychistic, and the plural, and to denying the finality of all conclusions. He warned us that "experience itself, taken at large, can grow by its edges" and no matter how laudable or seductive our personal goal, "life is in the transitions."

The *Works of William James,* including his unpublished manuscripts, have been collected in a massive nineteen-volume critical edition by Harvard University Press (1975–88). His work can be seen as an imaginative vestibule into the twentieth century. His ideas resonate in the work of Royce, Unamuno, Niels Bohr, Husserl, M. Montessori, Dewey, and Wittgenstein.

See also DEWEY, PEIRCE, PRAGMATISM.

J.J.M.

James-Lange theory, the theory, put forward by William James and independently by C. Lange, a Danish anatomist, that an emotion is the felt awareness of bodily reactions to something perceived or thought (James) or just the bodily reac-

tions themselves (Lange). According to the more influential version (James, "What Is an Emotion?" *Mind,* 1884), "our natural way of thinking" mistakenly supposes that the perception or thought causes the emotion, e.g., fear or anger, which in turn causes the bodily reactions, e.g., rapid heartbeat, weeping, trembling, grimacing, and actions such as running and striking. In reality, however, the fear or anger consists in the bodily sensations *caused by* these reactions.

In support of this theory, James proposed a thought experiment: Imagine feeling some "strong" emotion, one with a pronounced "wave of bodily disturbance," and then subtract in imagination the felt awareness of this disturbance. All that remains, James found, is "a cold and neutral state of intellectual perception," a cognition lacking in emotional coloration. Consequently, it is our bodily feelings that emotionalize consciousness, imbuing our perceptions and thoughts with emotional qualities and endowing each type of emotion, such as fear, anger, and joy, with its special feeling quality. But this does not warrant James's radical conclusion that emotions or emotional states are effects rather than causes of bodily reactions. That conclusion requires the further assumption, which James shared with many of his contemporaries, that the various emotions are nothing but particular feeling qualities.

Historically, the James-Lange theory led to further inquiries into the physiological and cognitive causes of emotional feelings and helped transform the psychology of emotions from a descriptive study relying on introspection to a broader naturalistic inquiry.

See also EMOTION.   R.M.G.

Jansenism, a set of doctrines advanced by European Roman Catholic reformers, clergy, and scholars in the seventeenth and eighteenth centuries, characterized by a predestinarianism that emphasized Adam's fall, irresistible efficacious grace, limited atonement, election, and reprobation. Addressing the issue of free will and grace left open by the Council of Trent (1545–63), a Flemish bishop, Cornelius Jansen (1585–1638), crystallized the seventeenth-century Augustinian revival, producing a compilation of Augustine's anti-Pelagian teachings (*Augustinus*). Propagated by Saint Cyran and Antoine Arnauld (*On Frequent Communion,* 1643), adopted by the nuns of Port-Royal, and defended against Jesuit attacks by Pascal (*Provincial Letters,* 1656–57), Jansenism pervaded Roman Catholicism from Utrecht to Rome for over 150 years. Condemned by Pope Innocent X (*Cum Occasione*, 1653) and crushed by Louis XIV and the French clergy (the 1661 formulary), it survived outside France and rearmed for a counteroffensive. Pasquier Quesnel's (1634–1719) "second Jansenism," condemned by Pope Clement XI (*Unigenitus*, 1713), was less Augustinian, more rigorist, and advocated Presbyterianism and Gallicanism.　　J.-L.S.

Japanese philosophy, philosophy in Japan, beginning with Buddhist thought and proceeding to academic "philosophy" (*tetsugaku*), which emerged in Japan only during the Meiji Restoration period beginning in 1868. Among representatives of traditional Japanese Buddhist philosophical thought should be mentioned Saichō (767–822) of Tendai; Kūkai (774–835) of Shingon; Shinran (1173–1262) of Jōdo Shinshū; Dōgen (1200–53) of Sōtō Zen; and Nichiren (1222–82) of Nichiren Buddhism. During the medieval period a duty-based warrior ethic of loyalty and self-sacrifice emerged from within the *Bushidō* tradition of the Samurai, developed out of influences from Confucianism and Zen. Also, the Zen-influenced path of *Geidō* or way of the artist produced an important religio-aesthetic tradition with ideas of beauty like *aware* (sad beauty), *yūgen* (profundity), *ma* (interval), *wabi* (poverty), *sabi* (solitariness), and *shibui* (understatement). While each sect developed its own characteristics, a general feature of traditional Japanese Buddhist philosophy is its emphasis on "impermanence" (*mujō*), the transitoriness of all non-substantial phenomena as expressed through the aesthetic of perishability in *Geidō* and the constant remembrance of death in the warrior ethic of *Bushidō*.

Much of twentieth-century Japanese philosophy centers around the development of, and critical reaction against, the thought of Nishida Kitarō (1870–1945) and the "Kyoto School" running through Tanabe Hajime, Nishitani Keiji, Hisamatsu Shin'ichi, Takeuchi Yoshinori, Ueda Shizuteru, Abe Masao, and, more peripherally, Watsuji Tetsurō, Kuki Shūzō, and D. T. Suzuki. The thought of Nishida is characterized by the effort to articulate an East-West philosophy and interfaith dialogue within a Buddhist framework of "emptiness" (*kū*) or "nothingness" (*mu*). In his maiden work, *A Study of Good* (1911), Nishida elaborates a theory of "pure experience" (*junsui keiken*) influenced especially by William James. Like James, Nishida articulates "pure experience" as an immediate awareness in the stream of consciousness emerging prior to subject–object dualism. Yet it is widely agreed that

Nishida reformulates "pure experience" in light of his own study of Zen Buddhism.

Throughout his career Nishida continuously reworked the idea of "pure experience" in terms of such notions as "self-awareness," "absolute will," "acting intuition," "absolute nothingness," and the "social-historical world." *From the Acting to the Seeing* (1927) signifies a turning point in Nishida's thought in that it introduces his new concept of *basho*, the "place" of "absolute Nothingness" wherein the "true self" arises as a "self-identity of absolute contradictions." Nishida's penultimate essay, "The Logic of Place and a Religious Worldview" (1945), articulates a theory of religious experience based upon the "self-negation" of both self and God in the place of Nothingness. In this context he formulates an interfaith dialogue between the Christian *kenōsis* (self-emptying) and Buddhist *śūnyatā* (emptiness) traditions.

In *Religion and Nothingness* (1982), Nishitani Keiji develops Nishida's philosophy in terms of a Zen logic wherein all things at the eternalistic standpoint of Being are emptied in the nihilistic standpoint of Relative Nothingness, which in turn is emptied into the middle way standpoint of Emptiness or Absolute Nothingness represented by both Buddhist *śūnyatā* and Christian *kenōsis*. For Nishitani, this shift from Relative to Absolute Nothingness is the strategy for overcoming nihilism as described by Nietzsche. Hisamatsu Shin'ichi interprets Japanese aesthetics in terms of Nishida's Self of Absolute Nothingness in *Zen and the Fine Arts* (1971).

The encounter of Western philosophy with Zen Nothingness is further developed by Abe Masao in *Zen and Western Thought* (1985). Whereas thinkers like Nishida, Nishitani, Hisamatsu, Ueda, and Abe develop a Zen approach based upon the immediate experience of Absolute Nothingness through the "self-power" (*jiriki*) of intuition, *Philosophy as Metanoetics* (1986) by Tanabe Hajime instead takes up the stance of Shinran's Pure Land Buddhism, according to which Nothingness is the transforming grace of absolute "Other-power" (*tariki*) operating through faith.

Watsuji Tetsurō's *Ethics* (1937), the premier work in modern Japanese moral theory, develops a communitarian ethics in terms of the "betweenness" (*aidagara*) of persons based on the Japanese notion of self as *ningen*, whose two characters reveal the double structure of personhood as both individual and social. Kuki Shūzō's *The Structure of Iki* (1930), often regarded as the most creative work in modern Japanese aesthetics, analyzes the Edo ideal of *iki* or "chic" as having a threefold structure representing the fusion of the "amorousness" (*bitai*) of the Geisha, the "valor" (*ikuji*) of the Samurai, and the "resignation" (*akirame*) of the Buddhist priest. Marxist thinkers like Tosaka Jun (1900–45) have developed strong ideological critiques of the philosophy articulated by Nishida and the Kyoto School. In summary, the outstanding contribution of modern Japanese philosophy has been the effort to forge a synthesis of Eastern and Western values within the overall framework of an Asian worldview.

See also BUDDHISM, CONFUCIANISM.   S.O.

Jaspers, Karl Theodor (1883–1969), German psychologist and philosopher, one of the main representatives of the existentialist movement (although he rejected 'existentialism' as a distortion of the philosophy of existence). From 1901 until 1908 Jaspers studied law and medicine at the universities of Heidelberg, Munich, Berlin, and Göttingen. He concluded his studies with an M.D. (*Homesickness and Crime*) from the University of Heidelberg (where he stayed until 1948). From 1908 until 1915 he worked as a voluntary assistant in the psychiatric clinic, and published his first major work (*Allgemeine Psychopathologie*, 1913; *General Psychopathology*, 1965). After his habilitation in psychology (1913) Jaspers lectured as *Privatdocent*. In 1919 he published *Psychologie der Weltanschauung* ("Psychology of Worldviews"). Two years later he became professor in philosophy. Because of his personal convictions and marriage with Gertrud Mayer (who was Jewish) the Nazi government took away his professorship in 1937 and suppressed all publications. He and his wife were saved from deportation because the American army liberated Heidelberg a few days before the fixed date of April 14, 1945. In 1948 he accepted a professorship from the University of Basel.

As a student, Jaspers felt a strong aversion to academic philosophy. However, as he gained insights in the fields of psychiatry and psychology, he realized that both the study of human beings and the meaning of scientific research pointed to questions and problems that demanded their own thoughts and reflections. Jaspers gave a systematic account of them in his three-volume *Philosophie* (1931; with postscript, 1956; *Philosophy*, 1969–71), and in the 1,100 pages of *Von der Wahrheit* (*On Truth*, 1947). In the first volume ("Philosophical World-orientation") he discusses the place and meaning of philosophy with regard to the human situation in gen-

eral and scientific disciplines in particular. In the second ("Clarification of Existence"), he contrasts the compelling modes of objective (scientific) knowledge with the possible (and in essence non-objective) awareness of being in self-relation, communication, and historicity, both as being oneself presents itself in freedom, necessity, and transcendence, and as existence encounters its unconditionality in limit situations (of death, suffering, struggle, guilt) and the polar intertwining of subjectivity and objectivity. In the third volume ("Metaphysics") he concentrates on the meaning of transcendence as it becomes translucent in appealing ciphers (of nature, history, consciousness, art, etc.) to possible existence under and against the impact of stranding.

His *Von der Wahrheit* is the first volume of a projected work on philosophical logic (cf. *Nachlaß zur philosophischen Logik*, ed. H. Saner and M. Hänggi, 1991) in which he develops the more formal aspects of his philosophy as "periechontology" (ontology of the encompassing, *des Umgreifenden*, with its modes of being there, consciousness, mind, existence, world, transcendence, reason) and clarification of origins. In both works Jaspers focuses on "existential philosophy" as "that kind of thinking through which man tries to become himself both as thinking makes use of all real knowledge and as it transcends this knowledge. This thinking does not recognize objects, but clarifies and enacts at once the being of the one who thinks in this way" (*Philosophische Autobiographie*, 1953).

In his search for authentic existence in connection with the elaboration of "philosophical faith" in reason and truth, Jaspers had to achieve a thorough understanding of philosophical, political, and religious history as well as an adequate assessment of the present situation. His aim became a world philosophy as a possible contribution to universal peace out of the spirit of free and limitless communication, unrestricted open-mindedness, and unrelenting truthfulness. Besides a comprehensive history of philosophy (*Die großen Philosophen I*, 1957; II and III, 1981; *The Great Philosophers*, 2 vols., 1962, 1966) and numerous monographs (on Cusanus, Descartes, Leonardo da Vinci, Schelling, Nietzsche, Strindberg, van Gogh, Weber) he wrote on subjects such as the university (*Die Idee der Universität*, 1946; *The Idea of the University*, 1959), the spiritual situation of the age (*Die geistige Situation der Zeit*, 1931; *Man in the Modern Age*, 1933), the meaning of history (*Vom Ursprung und Ziel der Geschichte*, 1949; *The Origin and Goal of History*,

1953, in which he developed the idea of an "axial period"), the guilt question (*Die Schuldfrage*, 1946; *The Question of German Guilt*, 1947), the atomic bomb (*Die Atombombe und die Zukunft des Menschen*, 1958; *The Future of Mankind*, 1961), German politics (*Wohin treibt die Bundesrepublik?* 1966; *The Future of Germany*, 1967). He also wrote on theology and religious issues (*Die Frage der Entymythologisierung. Eine Diskussion mit Rudolf Bultmann*, 1954; *Myth and Christianity*, 1958; *Der philosophische Glaube angesichts der Offenbarung*, 1962; *Philosophical Faith and Revelation*, 1967).

See also EXISTENTIALISM, METAPHYSICS.

W.D.

Jean Poinsot. See JOHN OF SAINT THOMAS.

jen, Chinese philosophical term, important in Confucianism, variously translated as 'kindness', 'humanity', or 'benevolence'. Scholars disagree as to whether it has the basic meaning of an attribute distinctive of certain aristocratic clans, or the basic meaning of kindness, especially kindness of a ruler to his subjects. In Confucian thought, it is used to refer both to an all-encompassing ethical ideal for human beings (when so used, it is often translated as 'humanity', 'humaneness', or 'goodness'), and more specifically to the desirable attribute of an emotional concern for all living things, the degree and nature of such concern varying according to one's relation to such things (when so used, it is often translated as 'benevolence'). Later Confucians explain *jen* in terms of one's being of one body with all things, and hence one's being sensitive and responsive to their well-being. In the political realm, Confucians regard *jen* as ideally the basis of government. A ruler with *jen* will care about and provide for the people, and people will be attracted to the ruler and be inspired to reform themselves. Such a ruler will succeed in bringing order and be without rivals, and will become a true king (*wang*). See also CONFUCIANISM.

K.-l.S.

jen hsin. See TAO-HSIN, JEN-HSIN.

jen-yü. See T'IEN LI, JEN-YÜ.

Jevons, William Stanley (1835–82), British economist, logician, and philosopher of science. In economics, he clarified the idea of value, arguing that it is a function of utility. Later theorists imitated his use of the calculus and other mathematical tools to reach theoretical results. His approach anticipated the idea of marginal utility, a notion basic in modern economics. Jevons regarded J. S. Mill's logic as inadequate, preferring the new symbolic logic of Boole. One permanent contribution was his introduction of the concept of inclusive 'or', with 'or' meaning 'either or, or both'. To aid in teaching the new logic of classes and propositions, Jevons invented his "logical piano." In opposition to the confidence in induction of Mill and Whewell, both of whom thought, for different reasons, that induction can arrive at exact and necessary truths, Jevons argued that science yields only approximations, and that any perfect fit between theory and observation must be grounds for suspicion that we are wrong, not for confidence that we are right. Jevons introduced probability theory to show how rival hypotheses are evaluated. He was a subjectivist, holding that probability is a measure of what a perfectly rational person would believe given the available evidence. See also INDUCTION, PROBABILITY, UTILITARIANISM.

R.E.B.

Jewish philosophy. The subject begins with Philo Judaeus (c.20 B.C.–A.D. 40) of Alexandria. Applying Stoic techniques of allegory, he developed a philosophical hermeneutic that transformed biblical persons and places into universal symbols and virtues; retaining the Hebrew Bible's view of a transcendent God, Philo identified Plato's world of ideas with the mind or word of God, construing it as the creative intermediary to the world. This *logos* doctrine influenced Christian theology strongly, but had little effect upon Jewish thought. Rabbinic Judaism was indifferent and probably hostile to all expressions of Greek philosophy, Philo's writings included.

The tradition of philosophical theology that can be traced to Philo took hold in Judaism only in the ninth century, and only after it became accepted in the Islamic world, which Jews then inhabited. Saadiah Gaon (882–942) modeled his philosophical work *The Book of Critically Chosen Beliefs and Convictions* on theological treatises written by Muslim free will theologians. Unlike them, however, and in opposition to Jewish Karaites, Saadiah rejected atomistic occasionalism and accepted the philosophers' view of a natural order, though one created by God. Saadiah's knowledge of Greek philosophy was imperfect and eclectic, yet he argued impressively against the notion of infinite duration, in order to affirm the necessity of believing in a created universe and hence in a Creator. Saadiah accepted the historicity of revelation at Sinai and the validity of Jewish law on more dogmatic grounds, though he developed a classification of the commandments that distinguished between them on grounds of greater and lesser rationality.

Isaac Israeli (850–950), while a contemporary of Saadiah's, was as different from him as East (Baghdad for Saadiah) is from West (for Israeli, Qayrawan, North Africa). Israeli showed no interest in theology, and was attracted to Neoplatonism and the ideas advanced by the first Muslim philosopher, al-Kindī. The strictly philosophical and essentially Neoplatonic approach in Jewish philosophy reached a high point with the *Fons Vitae* of Solomon Ibn Gabirol (1020–57). He followed Israeli in emphasizing form and matter's priority over that of the universal mind or *noûs*. This heralds the growing dominance of Aristotelian concepts in medieval Jewish philosophy, in all but political thought, a dominance first fully expressed, in Spain, in *The Exalted Faith* of Abraham Ibn Daud (c.1110–80). Many of the themes and perspectives of Neoplatonism are here retained, particularly that of emanation and the return of the soul to its source via intellectual conjunction, as well as the notion of the unknowable and strict unity of God; but the specific structures of Neoplatonic thought give way to those of Aristotle and his commentators. This mix of approaches was perfected by the Muslim *falāsifa* al-Fārābī (872–950) and Avicenna (980–1037), who became the main authorities for most Jewish philosophers through the twelfth century, competing afterward with Averroes (1126–98) for the minds of Jewish philosophers.

Judah Ha-Levi (1075–1141), in *The Kuzari*, also written in Spain, fought this attraction to philosophy with an informed critique of its Aristotelian premises. But Moses Maimonides (1138–1204), in his *Guide to the Perplexed*, written in Egypt and destined to become the major work of medieval Jewish philosophy, found little reason to fault the philosophers other than for accepting an eternal universe. His reservations on this subject, and his reticence in discussing some other tenets of Jewish faith, led many to suspect his orthodoxy and to seek esoteric meanings in all his philosophical views, a practice that continues today. Whatever his philosophical allegiance, Maimonides viewed Judaism as the paradigmatic philosophical religion, and saw the ideal philosopher as one who contributes to the welfare of his community, however much personal happiness is to be found ultimately only in contemplation of God. Gersonides (1288–1344), living in Provence, responded fully to both Maimonides' and Averroes' teachings, and in his *Wars of the Lord* denied the personal providence of

popular faith. These sorts of assertions led Hasdai Crescas (1340–1410) to attack the philosophers on their own premises, and to offer a model of divine love instead of intelligence as the controlling concept for understanding oneself and God.

Modern Jewish philosophy begins in Germany with Moses Mendelssohn (1729–86), who attempted philosophically to remove from Judaism its theocratic and politically compelling dimensions. Hermann Cohen (1842–1918) further emphasized, under the influence of Kant and Hegel, what he perceived as the essentially ethical and universal rational teachings of Judaism. Martin Buber (1878–1965) dramatically introduced an existential personalism into this ethicist reading of Judaism, while Franz Rosenzweig (1886–1929) attempted to balance existential imperatives and ahistorical interpretations of Judaism with an appreciation for the phenomenological efficacy of its traditional beliefs and practices. The optimistic and universal orientation of these philosophies was severely tested in World War II, and Jewish thinkers emerged after that conflict with more assertive national philosophies.

See also BUBER, CRESCAS, GERSONIDES, MAIMONIDES, PHILO JUDAEUS, SAADIAH.

A.L.I.

jhāna, a term used by Theravada Buddhists meaning 'pondering' or 'contemplation' and often translated into English as 'meditation'. This is one of many terms used to describe both techniques of meditation and the states of consciousness that result from the use of such techniques. *Jhāna* has a specific technical use: it denotes a hierarchically ordered series of four (or sometimes five) states of consciousness, states produced by a gradual reduction in the range of affective experience. The first of these states is said to include five mental factors, which are various kinds of affect and cognitive function, while the last consists only of equanimity, a condition altogether free from affect. **See also** SAMATHA, VIPASSANĀ.

P.J.G.

Joachim of Floris (c.1132/35–1202), Italian mystic who traveled to the Holy Land and, upon his return, became a Cistercian monk and abbot. He later retired to Calabria, in southern Italy, where he founded the order of San Giovanni in Fiore. He devoted the rest of his life to meditation and the recording of his prophetic visions. In his major works *Liber concordiae Novi ac Veteri Testamenti* ("Book of the Concordances between the New and the Old Testament," 1519), *Expositio* *in Apocalypsim* (1527), and *Psalterium decem chordarum* (1527), Joachim illustrates the deep meaning of history as he perceived it in his visions. History develops in coexisting patterns of twos and threes. The two testaments represent history as divided in two phases ending in the First and Second Advent, respectively. History progresses also through stages corresponding to the Holy Trinity. The age of the Father is that of the law; the age of the Son is that of grace, ending approximately in 1260; the age of the Spirit will produce a spiritualized church. Some monastic orders like the Franciscans and Dominicans saw themselves as already belonging to this final era of spirituality and interpreted Joachim's prophecies as suggesting the overthrow of the contemporary ecclesiastical institutions. Some of his views were condemned by the Lateran Council in 1215.   P.Gar.

Johannes Philoponus (c.490–575), Greek philosopher and theologian, who worked in Alexandria (*philoponus*, 'workaholic', just a nickname). A Christian from birth, he was a pupil of the Platonist Ammonius, and is the first Christian Aristotelian. As such, he challenged Aristotle on many points where he conflicted with Christian doctrine, e.g. the eternity of the world, the need for an infinite force, the definition of place, the impossibility of a vacuum, and the necessity for a fifth element to be the substance of the heavens. Johannes composed commentaries on Aristotle's *Categories, Prior* and *Posterior Analytics, Meteorologics*, and *On the Soul;* and a treatise *Against Proclus: On the Eternity of the World.* There is dispute as to whether the commentaries exhibit a change of mind (away from orthodox Aristotelianism) on these questions.   J.M.D.

John Damascene. See JOHN OF DAMASCUS.

John of Damascus, Saint, also called John Damascene and Chrysorrhoas (Golden Speaker) (c.675–c.750), Greek theologian and Eastern church doctor. Born of a well-to-do family in Damascus, he was educated in Greek, Arabic, and Islamic thought. He attained a high position in government but resigned under the anti-Christian Caliph Abdul Malek and became a monk about 700, living outside Jerusalem. He left extensive writings, most little more than compilations of older texts. The Iconoclastic Synod of 754 condemned his arguments in support of the veneration of images in the three *Discourses against the Iconoclasts* (726–30), but his orthodoxy was confirmed in 787 at the Second

Council of Nicaea. His *Sources of Knowledge* consists of a *Dialectic,* a history of heresies, and an exposition of orthodoxy. Considered a saint from the end of the eighth century, he was much respected in the East and was regarded as an important witness to Eastern Orthodox thought by the West in the Middle Ages.   J.Lo.

John of Saint Thomas, also known as John Poinsot (1589–1644), Portuguese theologian and philosopher. Born in Lisbon, he studied at Coimbra and Louvain, entered the Dominican order (1610), and taught at Alcalá de Henares, Piacenza, and Madrid. His most important works are the *Cursus philosophicus* ("Course of Philosophy," 1632–36), a work on logic and natural philosophy; and the *Cursus theologicus* ("Course of Theology," 1637–44), a commentary on Aquinas's *Summa theologiae.*

John considered himself a Thomist, but he modified Aquinas's views in important ways. The "Ars Logica," the first part of the *Cursus philosophicus,* is the source of much subsequent Catholic teaching in logic. It is divided into two parts: the first deals with formal logic and presents a comprehensive theory of terms, propositions, and reasoning; the second discusses topics in material logic, such as predicables, categories, and demonstration. An important contribution in the first is a comprehensive theory of signs that has attracted considerable attention in the twentieth century among such philosophers as Maritain, Yves Simon, John Wild, and others. An important contribution in the second part is the division of knowledge according to physical, mathematical, and metaphysical degrees, which was later adopted by Maritain. John dealt with metaphysical problems in the second part of the *Cursus philosophicus* and in the *Cursus theologicus.* His views are modifications of Aquinas's. For example, Aquinas held that the principle of individuation is matter designated by quantity; John interpreted this as matter radically determined by dimensions, where the dimensions are indeterminate.

In contrast to other major figures of the Spanish Scholasticism of the times, John did not write much in political and legal theory. He considered ethics and political philosophy to be speculative rather than practical sciences, and adopted a form of probabilism. Moreover, when in doubt about a course of action, one may simply adopt any pertinent view proposed by a prudent moralist.

See also AQUINAS, PEIRCE, SEMIOSIS.
                                                    J.J.E.G.

John of Salisbury (c.1120–80), English prelate and humanist scholar. Between 1135 and 1141 he studied dialectic with Peter Abelard and theology with Gilbert of Poitiers in Paris. It is possible that during this time he also studied grammar, rhetoric, and part of the *quadrivium* with William of Conches at the Cathedral School of Chartres. After 1147 he was for a time a member of the Roman Curia, secretary to Theobald, archbishop of Canterbury, and friend of Thomas Becket. For his role in Becket's canonization, Louis VII of France rewarded him with the bishopric of Chartres in 1176.

Although John was a dedicated student of philosophy, it would be misleading to call him a philosopher. In his letters, biographies of Anselm and Becket, and *Memoirs of the Papal Court* (1148–52), he provides, in perhaps the best medieval imitation of classical Latin style, an account of some of the most important ideas, events, and personalities of his time. Neither these works nor his *Polycraticus* and *Metalogicon,* for which he is most celebrated, are systematic philosophical treatises. The *Polycraticus* is, however, considered one of the first medieval treatises to take up political theory in any extended way. In it John maintains that if a ruler does not legislate in accordance with natural moral law, legitimate resistance to him can include his assassination. In the *Metalogicon,* on the other hand, John discusses, in a humanist spirit, the benefits for a civilized world of philosophical training based on Aristotle's logic. He also presents current views on the nature of universals, and, not surprisingly, endorses an Aristotelian view of them as neither extramental entities nor mere words, but mental concepts that nevertheless have a basis in reality insofar as they are the result of the mind's abstracting from extramental entities what those entities have in common.   G.S.

Johnson, W(illiam) E(rnest) (1858–1931), British philosopher who lectured on psychology and logic at Cambridge University. His *Logic* was published in three parts: Part I (1921); Part II, *Demonstrative Inference: Deductive and Inductive* (1922); and Part III, *The Logical Foundations of Science* (1924). He did not complete Part IV on probability, but in 1932 *Mind* published three of its intended chapters. Johnson's other philosophical publications, all in *Mind,* were not abundant. The discussion note "On Feeling as Indifference" (1888) deals with problems of classification. "The Logical Calculus" (three parts, 1892) anticipates the "Cambridge" style of logic while continuing the tradition of Jevons and Venn; the same is true of treatments of formal logic in *Logic.* "Analysis of Thinking" (two parts, 1918) advances an adverbial theory of experience. Johnson's philosophic influence at Cambridge exceeded the influence of these publications, as one can see from the references to him by John Neville Keynes in *Studies and Exercises in Formal Logic* and by his son John Maynard Keynes in *A Treatise on Probability.*

Logic contains original and distinctive treatments of induction, metaphysics, the philosophy of mind, and philosophical logic. Johnson's theory of inference proposes a treatment of implication that is an alternative to the view of Russell and Whitehead in *Principia Mathematica.* He coined the term 'ostensive definition' and introduced the distinction between determinates and determinables.

See also DETERMINABLE, INFERENCE.

D.H.S.

John the Scot. See ERIGENA.

joint method of agreement and difference. See MILL'S METHODS.

ju. See CONFUCIANISM.

Juan Chi (210–63), Chinese Neo-Taoist philosopher. Among his extant writings the most important are *Ta-Chuang lun* ("Discourse on the *Chuang Tzu*") and *Ta-jen hsien-sheng chuan* ("Biography of Master Great Man"). The concept of naturalness (*tzu-jan*) underpins Juan's philosophy. The "great man" is devoid of self-interest, completely at ease with his own nature and the natural order at large. In contrast, orthodox tradition (*ming-chiao*) suppresses openness and sincerity to secure benefit. Politically *tzu-jan* envisages a self-governing pristine state, a Taoist version of anarchism. However, the "great man" furnishes a powerful symbol not because he plots to overthrow the monarchy or withdraws from the world to realize his own ambition, but because he is able to initiate a process of healing that would revitalize the rule of the *tao.* **See also** NEO-TAOISM.   A.K.L.C.

judgment. See AKRASIA, FACULTY PSYCHOLOGY, KANT.

Jung, Carl Gustav (1875–1961), Swiss psychologist and founder of analytical psychology, a form of psychoanalysis that differs from Freud's chiefly by an emphasis on the collective character of the unconscious and on archetypes as its privileged contents. Jung, like Freud, was deeply influenced by philosophy in his early years. Before his immersion in psychiatry, he wrote several essays of explicitly philosophical purport. Kant was doubtless the philosopher who mattered most to Jung, for whom archetypes were conceived as a priori structures of the human psyche. Plato and Neoplatonists, Schopenhauer and especially Nietzsche (to whose *Zarathustra* he devoted a seminar of several years' duration) were also of critical importance. Jung was a close reader of James, and his *Psychological Types* (1921) – in addition to an extended discussion of nominalism versus realism – contains a detailed treatment of Jamesian typologies of the self.

Jung considered the self to be an amalgamation of an "ectopsyche" – consisting of four functions (intuition, sensation, feeling, and thinking) that surround an ego construed not as a singular entity but as a "complex" of ideas and emotions – and an "endosphere" (i.e., consciousness turned inward in memory, affect, etc.). The personal unconscious, which preoccupied Freud, underlies the endosphere and its "invasions," but it is in turn grounded in the collective unconscious shared by all humankind. The collective unconscious was induced by Jung from his analysis of dream symbols and psychopathological symptoms. It is an inherited archive of archaic-mythic forms and figures that appear repeatedly in the most diverse cultures and historical epochs. Such forms and figures – also called archetypes – are considered "primordial images" preceding the "ideas" that articulate rational thought. As a consequence, the self, rather than being autonomous, is embedded in a prepersonal and prehistoric background from which there is no effective escape. However, through prolonged psychotherapeutically guided "individuation," a slow assimilation of the collective unconscious into daily living can occur, leading to an enriched and expanded sense of experience and selfhood.

See also FREUD, JAMES, NIETZSCHE. E.S.C.

jung, ju, Chinese terms that express the Confucian distinction between honor and shame or disgrace. The *locus classicus* of the discussion is found in Hsün Tzu's works. While the distinction between *jung* (honor) and *ju* (disgrace, shame) pertains to the normal, human conditions of security and danger, harm and benefit, it is crucial to distinguish honor as derived from mere external recognition and honor justly deserved, and to distinguish shame or disgrace due to circumstance, as in poverty, from that due to one's own ethical misconduct. The *chün-tzu* (paradig-

matic individual) should be content with the shame due to circumstance but not with shame justly deserved because of misconduct. The key issue is shame or honor justly deserved from the point of view of *jen* (benevolence) and *yi* (rightness), and not shame or honor resting on contingencies beyond one's control. **See also HSÜN TZU.** A.S.C.

jurisprudence, the science or knowledge of law; thus, in its widest sense, the study of the legal doctrines, rules, and principles of any legal system. More commonly, however, the term designates the study not of the actual laws of particular legal systems, but of the general concepts and principles that underlie a legal system or that are common to all such systems (general jurisprudence). Jurisprudence in this sense, sometimes also called the philosophy of law, may be further subdivided according to the major focus of a particular study. Examples include historical jurisprudence (a study of the development of legal principles over time, often emphasizing the origin of law in custom or tradition rather than in enacted rules), sociological jurisprudence (an examination of the relationship between legal rules and the behavior of individuals, groups, or institutions), functional jurisprudence (an inquiry into the relationship between legal norms and underlying social interests or needs), and analytical jurisprudence (an investigation into the meaning of, and conceptual connections among, legal concepts).

Within analytical jurisprudence the most substantial body of thought focuses on the meaning of the concept of law itself (legal theory) and the relationship between that concept and the concept of morality. *Legal positivism,* the view that there is no necessary connection between law and morality, opposes the natural law view that no sharp distinction between these concepts can be drawn. The former view is sometimes thought to be a consequence of positivism's insistence that legal validity is determined ultimately by reference to certain basic social facts: "the command of the sovereign" (John Austin), the *Grundnorm* (Hans Kelsen), or "the rule of recognition" (H. L. A. Hart). These different positivist characterizations of the basic, law-determining fact yield different claims about the normative character of law, with classical positivists (e.g., John Austin) insisting that legal systems are essentially coercive, whereas modern positivists (e.g., Hans Kelsen) maintain that they are normative.

Disputes within legal theory often generate or arise out of disputes about theories of adjudication, or how judges do or should decide cases. Mechanical jurisprudence, or *formalism,* the theory that all cases can be decided solely by analyzing legal concepts, is thought by many to have characterized judicial decisions and legal reasoning in the nineteenth century; that theory became an easy target in the twentieth century for various forms of *legal realism,* the view that law is better determined by observing what courts and citizens actually do than by analyzing stated legal rules and concepts.

Recent developments in the natural law tradition also focus on the process of adjudication and the normative claims that accompany the judicial declaration of legal rights and obligations. These normative claims, natural law theorists argue, show that legal rights are a species of political or moral rights. In consequence, one must either revise prevailing theories of adjudication and abandon the social-fact theory of law (Ronald Dworkin), or explore the connection between legal theory and the classical question of political theory: Under what conditions do legal obligations, even if determined by social facts, create genuine political obligations (e.g., the obligation to obey the law)? Other jurisprudential notions that overlap topics in political theory include rule of law, legal moralism, and civil disobedience.

The disputes within legal theory about the connection between law and morality should not be confused with discussions of "natural law" within moral theory. In moral theory, the term denotes a particular view about the objective status of moral norms that has produced a considerable literature, extending from ancient Greek and Roman thought, through medieval theological writings, to contemporary ethical thought. Though the claim that one cannot sharply separate law and morality is often made as part of a general natural law moral theory, the referents of the term 'natural law' in legal and moral theory do not share any obvious logical relationship. A moral theorist could conclude that there is no necessary connection between law and morality, thus endorsing a positivist view of law, while consistently advocating a natural law view of morality itself; conversely, a natural law legal theorist, in accepting the view that there is a connection between law and morality, might nonetheless endorse a substantive moral theory different from that implied by a natural law moral theory.

See also LEGAL REALISM, NATURAL LAW, PHILOSOPHY OF LAW, POLITICAL PHILOSOPHY, RIGHTS.   P.S.

jury nullification, a jury's ability, or the exercise of that ability, to acquit a criminal defendant despite finding facts that leave no reasonable doubt about violation of a criminal statute. This ability is not a right, but an artifact of criminal procedure. In the common law, the jury has sole authority to determine the facts, and the judge to determine the law. The jury's findings of fact cannot be reviewed.

The term 'nullification' suggests that jury nullification is opposed to the rule of law. This thought would be sound only if an extreme legal positivism were true – that the law is nothing but the written law and the written law covers every possible fact situation. Jury nullification is better conceived as a form of equity, a rectification of the inherent limits of written law. In nullifying, juries make law. To make jury nullification a right, then, raises problems of democratic legitimacy, such as whether a small, randomly chosen group of citizens has authority to make law.

See also JURISPRUDENCE, LEGAL POSITIVISM, NATURAL LAW, POLITICAL PHILOSOPHY.   R.A.Sh.

jury theorem. See CONDORCET.

jus ad bellum. See JUST WAR THEORY.

jus in bello. See JUST WAR THEORY.

justice, each getting what he or she is due. *Formal* justice is the impartial and consistent application of principles, whether or not the principles themselves are just. *Substantive* justice is closely associated with rights, i.e., with what individuals can legitimately demand of one another or what they can legitimately demand of their government (e.g., with respect to the protection of liberty or the promotion of equality).

Retributive justice concerns when and why punishment is justified. Debate continues over whether punishment is justified as retribution for past wrongdoing or because it deters future wrongdoing. Those who stress retribution as the justification for punishment usually believe human beings have libertarian free will, while those who stress deterrence usually accept determinism.

At least since Aristotle, justice has commonly been identified both with obeying law and with treating everyone with fairness. But if law is, and justice is not, entirely a matter of convention, then justice cannot be identified with obeying law. The literature on legal positivism and natural law theory contains much debate about whether there are moral limits on what conventions could count as law.

Corrective justice concerns the fairness of demands for civil damages. *Commutative* justice concerns the fairness of wages, prices, and exchanges. *Distributive* justice concerns the fairness of the distribution of resources. Commutative justice and distributive justice are related, since people's wages influence how much resources they have. But the distinction is important because it may be just to pay A more than B (because A is more productive than B) but just that B is left with more after-tax resources (because B has more children to feed than A does). In modern philosophy, however, the debate about just wages and prices has been overshadowed by the larger question of what constitutes a just distribution of resources. Some (e.g., Marx) have advocated distributing resources in accordance with needs. Others have advocated their distribution in whatever way maximizes utility in the long run. Others have argued that the fair distribution is one that, in some sense, is to everyone's advantage. Still others have maintained that a just distribution is whatever results from the free market. Some theorists combine these and other approaches.

See also ETHICS, KANT, RIGHTS, UTILITARIANISM.   B.W.H.

justice as fairness. See RAWLS.

justification, a concept of broad scope that spans epistemology and ethics and has as special cases the concepts of apt belief and right action. The concept has, however, highly varied application. Many things, of many different sorts, can be justified. Prominent among them are beliefs and actions. To say that X is justified is to say something *positive* about X. Other things being equal, it is better that X be justified than otherwise. However, not all good entities are *justified*. The storm's abating may be good since it spares some lives, but it is not thereby justified. What we can view as justified or unjustified is what we can relate appropriately to someone's faculties or choice. (Believers might hence view the storm's abating as justified after all, if they were inclined to judge divine providence.)

Just as in epistemology we need to distinguish justification from truth, since either of these might apply to a belief in the absence of the other, so in ethics we must distinguish justification from utility: an action might be optimific but not justified, and justified but not optimific. What is distinctive of justification is then the implied evaluation of an agent (thus the connection, however remote, with faculties of choice). To say that a belief is (epistemically) justified (apt) or to say that an action is (ethically) justified ("right" – in one sense) is to make or imply a judgment on the subject and how he or she has arrived at that action or belief.

Often a much narrower concept of justification is used, one according to which X is justified only if X has been or at least can be justified through adducing reasons. Such adducing of reasons can be viewed as the giving of an argument of any of several sorts: e.g., conclusive, *prima facie*, inductive, or deductive.

A conclusive justification or argument adduces conclusive reasons for the possible (object of) action or belief that figures in the conclusion. In turn, such reasons are *conclusive* if and only if they raise the status of the conclusion action or belief so high that the subject concerned would be well advised to *conclude* deliberation or inquiry.

A prima facie justification or argument adduces a prima facie reason R (or more than one) in favor of the possible (object of) action or belief O that figures in the conclusion. In turn, R is a prima facie reason for O if and only if R specifies an advantage or positive consideration in favor of O, one that puts O in a better light than otherwise. Even if R is a prima facie reason for O, however, R can be outweighed, overridden, or defeated by contrary considerations R'. Thus my returning a knife that I promised to return to its rightful owner has in its favor the prima facie reason that it is my legal obligation and the fulfillment of a promise, but if the owner has gone raving mad, then there may be reasons against returning the knife that override, outweigh, or defeat. (And there may also be reasons that *defeat* a positive prima facie reason without amounting to reasons *for* the opposite course. Thus it may emerge that the promise to return the knife was extracted under duress.)

A (valid) deductive argument for a certain conclusion C is a sequence of thoughts or statements whose last member is C (not necessarily last temporally, but last in the sequence) and each member of which is either an assumption or premise of the argument or is based on earlier members of the sequence in accordance with a sound principle of necessary inference, such as *simplification:* from (P & Q) to P; or *addition:* from P to (P or Q); or *modus ponens:* from P and (P only if Q) to Q. Whereas the premises of a deductive argument necessarily entail the conclusion, which cannot possibly fail to be true when the premises are all true, the premises of an inductive argument do not thus entail its conclusion but offer considerations that only make the conclusion in some sense more probable than it would be otherwise. From the premises that it rains and that if it rains the streets are wet, one may deductively derive the conclusion that the streets *are* wet. However, the premise that I have tried to start my car on many, many winter mornings during the two years since I bought it and that it has always started, right up to and including yesterday, does not deductively imply that it will start when I try today. Here the conclusion does not follow deductively. Though here the reason provided by the premise is only an inductive reason for believing the conclusion, and indeed a prima facie and defeasible reason, nevertheless it might well be in our sense a *conclusive* reason. For it might enable us rightfully to conclude inquiry and/or deliberation and proceed to (action or, in this case) belief, while turning our attention to other matters (such as driving to our destination).

    See also EPISTEMOLOGY, ETHICS, SKEPTICISM.   E.S.

justification, conclusive. See JUSTIFICATION.

justification, deductive. See JUSTIFICATION.

justification, epistemic. See EPISTEMOLGY.

justification, inductive. See JUSTIFICATION.

justification, inferential. See FOUNDATIONALISM.

justification, propositional. See EPISTEMOLOGY.

justification by faith, the characteristic doctrine of the Protestant Reformation that sinful human beings can be justified before God through faith in Jesus Christ. 'Being justified' is understood in forensic terms: before the court of divine justice humans are not considered guilty because of their sins, but rather are declared by God to be holy and righteous in virtue of the righteousness of Christ, which God counts on their behalf. Justification is received by faith, which is not merely belief in Christian doctrine but includes a sincere and heartfelt trust and commitment to God in Christ for one's salvation. Such faith, if genuine, leads to the reception of the transforming influences of God's grace and to a life of love, obedience, and service to God. These consequences of faith, however, are considered under the heading of *sanctification* rather than justification.

The rival Roman Catholic doctrine of justification – often mislabeled by Protestants as "justification by works" – understands key terms differently. 'Being just' is understood not primarily in forensic terms but rather as a comprehensive state of being rightly related to God, including the forgiveness of sins, the reception of divine grace, and inner transformation. Justification is a work of God initially accomplished at baptism; among the human "predispositions" for justification are faith (understood as believing the truths God has revealed), awareness of one's sinfulness, hope in God's mercy, and a resolve to do what God requires. Salvation is a gift of God that is not deserved by human beings, but the measure of grace bestowed depends to some extent on the sincere efforts of the sinner who is seeking salvation. The Protestant and Catholic doctrines are not fully consistent with each other, but neither are they the polar opposites they are often made to appear by the caricatures each side offers of the other.

    See also PHILOSOPHY OF RELIGION.

                          W.Has.

justification by works. See JUSTIFICATION BY FAITH.

justifying reason. See HUTCHESON.

just in case. See IFF.

just war theory, a set of conditions justifying the resort to war (*jus ad bellum*) and prescribing how war may permissibly be conducted (*jus in bello*). The theory is a Western approach to the moral assessment of war that grew out of the Christian tradition beginning with Augustine, later taking both religious and secular (including legalist) forms.

    Proposed conditions for a just war vary in both number and interpretation. Accounts of *jus ad bellum* typically require: (1) just cause: an actual or imminent wrong against the state, usually a violation of rights, but sometimes provided by the need to protect innocents, defend human rights, or safeguard the way of life of one's own or other peoples; (2) competent authority: limiting the undertaking of war to a state's legitimate rulers; (3) right intention: aiming only at peace and the ends of the just cause (and not war's attendant suffering, death, and destruction); (4) proportionality: ensuring that anticipated good not be outweighed by bad; (5) last resort: exhausting peaceful alternatives before going to war; and (6) probability of success: a reasonable prospect that war will succeed. *Jus in bello* requires: (7) proportionality: ensuring that the means used in war befit the ends of the just cause and that their resultant good and bad, when individuated, be proportionate in the sense of (4); and (8) discrimination: prohibiting the killing of noncombatants and/or innocents. Sometimes conditions (4), (5), and (6) are included in (1). The conditions are usually considered individually necessary and jointly sufficient for a fully just war. But sometimes strength of just cause is taken to offset some lack of proportion in means, and sometimes absence of right intention is taken to render a war evil though not necessarily unjust. Most just war theorists take *jus ad bellum* to warrant only defensive wars. But some follow earlier literature and allow for just offensive wars.

Early theorists deal primarily with *jus ad bellum*, later writers with both *jus ad bellum* and *jus in bello*. Recent writers stress *jus in bello*, with particular attention to deterrence: the attempt, by instilling fear of retaliation, to induce an adversary to refrain from attack. Some believe that even though large-scale use of nuclear weapons would violate requirements of proportionality and discrimination, the threatened use of such weapons can maintain peace, and hence justify a system of nuclear deterrence.

See also POLITICAL PHILOSOPHY.   R.L.H.

K

kabala. See CABALA.

kāla, in Indian thought, time. The universe frequently is seen as forever oscillating between order and chaos. Thus the goal of human existence, religiously conceived, tends to involve escape from time. Jainism views time as immaterial, beginningless, and continuous (without parts), distinguishing between time as perceived (in divisions of units of our temporal measurement) and time as it inherently is (unitless). For Sankhya-Yoga, there is no time distinct from atoms, and the minimum temporal unit is the duration of an atom's transverse of its own spatial unit. For Nyāya-Vaishesika, time is a particular substance that exists independently and appears to have parts only because we perceive it through noticing distinct changes. Advaita Vedanta takes time to be only phenomenal and apparent. Viśistadvaita Vedanta takes time to be an inert substance dependent on Brahman, coordinate with *prakṛti* (material stuff), and beginningless. K.E.Y.

kalam, an Arabic term denoting a form of religious and theological discourse. The word itself literally means 'argue' or 'discuss'; although often translated as 'theology' or 'dialectical theology', the Muslim usage does not correspond exactly. In origin *kalam* was an argumentative reaction to certain perceived doctrinal deviations on key issues – e.g., the status of the sinner, the justice of God, attributes of God. Thus themes and content in *kalam* were normally historically specific and not generally speculative. Later, in a formal confrontation with philosophy, the predominantly dialectical mode of reasoning employed until the twelfth century was replaced by full use of syllogistic methods. Ultimately, the range of speculation grew until, in the sophisticated compendiums of the major authorities, *kalam* became intellectually speculative as well as doctrinally defensive.

In a major development, one school of *kalam* – the Ash'arites – adopted an atomistic theory that rejected the necessity of immediate or proximate causation, arguing instead that patterns perceived in nature are merely the habitual actions of God as he constantly re-creates and refashions the universe.

See also ARABIC PHILOSOPHY. P.E.W.

K'ang Yu-wei (1858–1927), Chinese scholar who pushed for radical reforms under Emperor Kuan-hsü and was forced into exile. He belonged to the modern-script school with respect to studies of the *Spring and Autumn Annals,* and believed that Confucius was only borrowing the names and authority of the ancient sage-emperors to push for reform in his own days. K'ang gave expression to utopian ideals in his book *Ta-tung* (*Great Unity*). Among his disciples were T'an Ssu-t'ung (1865–98) and Liang Ch'i-ch'ao (1873–1929). He became a reactionary in his old age and refused to accept the fact that China had become a republic. **See also** CONFUCIUS, LIANG CH'I-CH'AO. S.-h.L.

Kant, Immanuel (1724–1804), preeminent German philosopher whose distinctive concern was to vindicate the authority of reason. He believed that by a critical examination of its own powers, reason can distinguish unjustifiable traditional metaphysical claims from the principles that are required by our theoretical need to determine ourselves within spatiotemporal experience and by our practical need to legislate consistently with all other rational wills. Because these principles are necessary and discoverable, they defeat empiricism and skepticism, and because they are disclosed as simply the conditions of orienting ourselves coherently within experience, they contrast with traditional rationalism and dogmatism.

Kant was born and raised in the eastern Prussian university town of Königsberg (today Kaliningrad), where, except for a short period during which he worked as a tutor in the nearby countryside, he spent his life as student and teacher. He was trained by Pietists and followers of Leibniz and Wolff, but he was also heavily influenced by Newton and Rousseau.

In the 1750s his theoretical philosophy began attempting to show how metaphysics must accommodate as certain the fundamental principles underlying modern science; in the 1760s his practical philosophy began attempting to show (in unpublished form) how our moral life must be based on a rational and universally accessible self-legislation analogous to Rousseau's political principles. The breakthrough to his own distinctive philosophy came in the 1770s, when he insisted on treating epistemology as first philosophy. After arguing in his Inaugural Dissertation (*On the Form and Principles of the Sensible and Intelligible World*, 1770) both that our spatiotemporal knowledge applies only to appearances and that we can still make legitimate metaphysical claims about "intelligible" or non-spatiotemporal features of reality (e.g., that there is one world of substances interconnected by the action of God), there followed a "silent decade" of preparation for his major work, the epoch-making *Critique of Pure Reason* (first or "A" edition, 1781; second or "B" edition, with many revisions, 1787; Kant's initial reaction to objections to the first edition dominate his short review, *Prolegomena to any Future Metaphysics*, 1783; the full title of which means 'preliminary investigations for any future metaphysics that will be able to present itself as a science', i.e., as a body of certain truths). This work resulted in his mature doctrine of *transcendental idealism*, namely, that all our theoretical knowledge is restricted to the systematization of what are mere spatiotemporal appearances. This position is also called *formal* or *Critical idealism*, because it criticizes theories and claims beyond the realm of experience, while it also insists that although the form of experience is ideal, or relative to us, this is not to deny the reality of something independent of this form. Kant's earlier works are usually called *pre-Critical* not just because they precede his *Critique* but also because they do not include a full commitment to this idealism.

Kant supplemented his "first *Critique*" (often cited just as "the" *Critique*) with several equally influential works in practical philosophy – *Groundwork of the Metaphysics of Morals* (1785), *Critique of Practical Reason* (the "second *Critique*," 1788), and *Metaphysics of Morals* (consisting of "Doctrine of Justice" and "Doctrine of Virtue," 1797). Kant's philosophy culminated in arguments advancing a purely moral foundation for traditional theological claims (the existence of God, immortality, and a transcendent reward or penalty proportionate to our goodness), and thus was characterized as "denying knowledge in order to make room for faith." To be more precise, Kant's Critical project was to restrict theoretical knowledge in such a way as to make it possible for practical knowledge to reveal how pure rational faith has an absolute claim on us. This position was reiterated in the *Critique of Judgment* (the "third *Critique*," 1790), which also extended Kant's philosophy to aesthetics and scientific methodology by arguing for a priori but limited principles in each of these domains. Kant was followed by radical idealists (Fichte, Schelling), but he regarded himself as a philosopher of the Enlightenment, and in numerous shorter works he elaborated his belief that everything must submit to the "test of criticism," that human reason must face the responsibility of determining the sources, extent, and bounds of its own principles.

The *Critique* concerns pure reason because Kant believes all these determinations can be made a priori, i.e., such that their justification does not depend on any particular course of experience ('pure' and 'a priori' are thus usually interchangeable). For Kant 'pure reason' often signifies just pure theoretical reason, which determines the realm of nature and of what is, but Kant also believes there is *pure practical reason* (or *Wille*), which determines a priori and independently of sensibility the realm of freedom and of what ought to be. Practical reason in general is defined as that which determines rules for the faculty of desire and will, as opposed to the faculties of cognition and of feeling. On Kant's mature view, however, the practical realm is necessarily understood in relation to moral considerations, and these in turn in terms of laws taken to have an unconditional imperative force whose validity requires presuming that they are addressed to a being with absolute freedom, the faculty to choose (*Willkür*) to will or not to will to act for their sake.

Kant also argues that no evidence of human freedom is forthcoming from empirical knowledge of the self as part of spatiotemporal nature, and that the belief in our freedom, and thus the moral laws that presuppose it, would have to be given up if we thought that our reality is determined by the laws of spatiotemporal appearances alone. Hence, to maintain the crucial practical component of his philosophy it was necessary for Kant first to employ his theoretical philosophy to show that it is at least possible that the spatiotemporal realm does not exhaust reality, so that there can be a non-empirical and free side to the self. Therefore Kant's first *Critique* is a theoretical foundation for his entire system, which is devoted to establishing not just (i) what the most general necessary principles for the spatiotemporal domain are – a project that has been called his "metaphysics of experience" – but also (ii) that this domain cannot without contradiction define ultimate reality (hence his transcendental idealism). The first of these claims involves Kant's primary use of the term 'transcendental', namely in the context of what he calls a *transcendental deduction,* which is an argument or "exposition" that establishes a necessary role for an a priori principle in our experience. As Kant explains, while mathematical principles are a priori and are necessary for experience, the mathematical proof of these principles is not itself transcendental; what is transcendental is rather the philosophical argument that these principles necessarily apply in experience. While in this way some transcendental arguments may presume propositions from an established science (e.g., geometry), others can begin with more modest assumptions – typically the proposition that there is experience or empirical knowledge at all – and then move on from there to uncover a priori principles that appear required for specific features of that knowledge.

Kant begins by connecting metaphysics with the problem of synthetic a priori judgment. As necessary, metaphysical claims must have an a priori status, for we cannot determine that they are necessary by mere a posteriori means. As objective rather than merely formal, metaphysical judgments (unlike those of logic) are also said to be synthetic. This synthetic a priori character is claimed by Kant to be mysterious and yet shared by a large number of propositions that were undisputed in his time. The mystery is how a proposition can be known as necessary and yet be objective or "ampliative" or not merely "analytic." For Kant an analytic proposition is one whose predicate is "contained in the subject." He does not mean this "containment" relation to be understood psychologically, for he stresses that we can be psychologically and even epistemically bound to affirm non-analytic propositions. The containment is rather determined simply by what is contained in the concepts of the subject term and the predicate term. However, Kant also denies that we have ready real definitions for empirical or a priori concepts, so it is unclear how one determines what is really contained in a subject or predicate term. He seems to rely on intuitive procedures for saying when it is that one necessarily connects a subject and predicate without relying on a hidden conceptual relation. Thus he proposes that mathematical constructions, and not mere conceptual elucidations, are what warrant necessary judgments about trian-

gles. In calling such judgments *ampliative,* Kant does not mean that they merely add to what we may have explicitly seen or implicitly known about the subject, for he also grants that complex analytic judgments may be quite informative, and thus "new" in a psychological or epistemic sense.

While Kant stresses that non-analytic or synthetic judgments rest on "intuition" (*Anschauung*), this is not part of their definition. If a proposition could be known through its concepts alone, it must be analytic, but if it is not knowable in this way it follows only that we need something other than concepts. Kant presumed that this something must be intuition, but others have suggested other possibilities, such as postulation. Intuition is a technical notion of Kant, meant for those representations that have an immediate relation to their object. Human intuitions are also all sensible (or sensuous) or passive, and have a singular rather than general object, but these are less basic features of intuition, since Kant stresses the possibility of (non-human) non-sensible or "intellectual" intuition, and he implies that singularity of reference can be achieved by non-intuitive means (e.g., in the definition of God). The immediacy of intuition is crucial because it is what sets them off from concepts, which are essentially representations of representations, i.e., rules expressing what is common to a set of representations.

Kant claims that mathematics, and metaphysical expositions of our notions of space and time, can reveal several evident synthetic a priori propositions, e.g., that there is one infinite space. In asking what could underlie the belief that propositions like this are certain, Kant came to his *Copernican revolution.* This consists in considering not how our representations may necessarily conform to objects as such, but rather how objects may necessarily conform to our representations. On a "pre-Copernican" view, objects are considered just by themselves, i.e., as "things-in-themselves" (*Dinge an sich*) totally apart from any intrinsic cognitive relation to our representations, and thus it is mysterious how we could ever determine them a priori. If we begin, however, with our own faculties of representation we might find something in them that determines how objects must be – at least when considered just as *phenomena* (singular: *phenomenon*), i.e., as objects of experience rather than as *noumena* (singular: *noumenon*), i.e., things-in-themselves specified negatively as unknown and beyond our experience, or positively as knowable in some absolute non-sensible way – which

Kant insists is theoretically impossible for sensible beings like us. For example, Kant claims that when we consider our faculty for receiving impressions, or sensibility, we can find not only contingent contents but also two necessary forms or "pure forms of intuition": space, which structures all outer representations given us, and time, which structures all inner representations. These forms can explain how the synthetic a priori propositions of mathematics will apply with certainty to all the objects of our experience. That is, if we suppose that in intuiting these propositions we are gaining a priori insight into the forms of our representation that must govern all that can come to our sensible awareness, it becomes understandable that all objects in our experience will have to conform with these propositions.

Kant presented his transcendental idealism as preferable to all the alternative explanations that he knew for the possibility of mathematical knowledge and the metaphysical status of space and time. Unlike empiricism, it allowed necessary claims in this domain; unlike rationalism, it freed the development of this knowledge from the procedures of mere conceptual analysis; and unlike the Newtonians it did all this without giving space and time a mysterious status as an absolute thing or predicate of God. With proper qualifications, Kant's doctrine of the transcendental ideality of space and time can be understood as a radicalization of the modern idea of primary and secondary qualities. Just as others had contended that sensible color and sound qualities, e.g., can be intersubjectively valid and even objectively based while existing only as relative to our sensibility and not as ascribable to objects in themselves, so Kant proposed that the same should be said of spatiotemporal predicates. Kant's doctrine, however, is distinctive in that it is not an empirical hypothesis that leaves accessible to us other theoretical and non-ideal predicates for explaining particular experiences. It is rather a metaphysical thesis that enriches empirical explanations with an a priori framework, but begs off any explanation for that framework itself other than the statement that it lies in the "constitution" of human sensibility as such.

This "Copernican" hypothesis is not a clear proof that spatiotemporal features could not apply to objects apart from our forms of intuition, but more support for this stronger claim is given in Kant's discussion of the "antinomies" of rational cosmology. An *antinomy* is a conflict between two a priori arguments arising from reason when, in its distinctive work as a higher log-

ical faculty connecting strings of judgments, it posits a real unconditioned item at the origin of various hypothetical syllogisms. There are antinomies of quantity, quality, relation, and modality, and they each proceed by pairs of dogmatic arguments which suppose that since one kind of unconditioned item cannot be found, e.g., an absolutely first event, another kind must be posited, e.g., a complete infinite series of past events. For most of the other antinomies, Kant indicates that contradiction can be avoided by allowing endless series in experience (e.g., of chains of causality, of series of dependent beings), series that are compatible with – but apparently do not require – unconditioned items (uncaused causes, necessary beings) outside experience. For the antinomy of quantity, however, he argues that the only solution is to drop the common dogmatic assumption that the set of spatiotemporal objects constitutes a determinate whole, either absolutely finite or infinite. He takes this to show that spatiotemporality must be transcendentally ideal, only an indeterminate feature of our experience and not a characteristic of things-in-themselves.

Even when structured by the pure forms of space and time, sensible representations do not yield knowledge until they are grasped in concepts and these concepts are combined in a judgment. Otherwise, we are left with mere impressions, scattered in an unintelligible "multiplicity" or *manifold;* in Kant's words, "thoughts without content are empty, intuitions without concepts are blind." Judgment requires both concepts and intuitions; it is not just any relation of concepts, but a bringing together of them in a particular way, an "objective" unity, so that one concept is predicated of another – e.g., "all bodies are divisible" – and the latter "applies to certain appearances that present themselves to us," i.e., are intuited. Because any judgment involves a unity of thought that can be prefixed by the phrase 'I think', Kant speaks of all representations, to the extent that they can be judged by us, as subject to a necessary unity of *apperception.* This term originally signified self-consciousness in contrast to direct consciousness or perception, but Kant uses it primarily to contrast with 'inner sense', the precognitive manifold of temporal representations as they are merely given in the mind. Kant also contrasts the *empirical ego,* i.e., the self as it is known contingently in experience, with the *transcendental ego,* i.e., the self thought of as the subject of structures of intuiting and thinking that are necessary throughout experience.

The fundamental need for concepts and judgments suggests that our "constitution" may require not just intuitive but also conceptual *forms*, i.e., "pure concepts of the understanding," or "categories." The proof that our experience does require such forms comes in the "deduction of the objective validity of the pure concepts of the understanding," also called the transcendental *deduction of the categories,* or just *the deduction.* This most notorious of all Kantian arguments appears to be in one way harder and in one way easier than the transcendental argument for pure intuitions. Those intuitions were held to be necessary for our experience because as structures of our sensibility nothing could even be imagined to be given to us without them. Yet, as Kant notes, it might seem that once representations are given in this way we can still imagine that they need not then be combined in terms of such pure concepts as causality. On the other hand, Kant proposed that a list of putative categories could be derived from a list of the necessary forms of the logical table of judgments, and since these forms would be required for any finite understanding, whatever its mode of sensibility is like, it can seem that the validity of pure concepts is even more inescapable than that of pure intuitions. That there is nonetheless a special difficulty in the transcendental argument for the categories becomes evident as soon as one considers the specifics of Kant's list. The logical table of judgments is an a priori collection of all possible judgment forms organized under four headings, with three subforms each: quantity (universal, particular, singular), quality (affirmative, negative, infinite), relation (categorical, hypothetical, disjunctive), and modality (problematic, assertoric, apodictic). This list does not map exactly onto any one of the logic textbooks of Kant's day, but it has many similarities with them; thus *problematic* judgments are simply those that express logical possibility, and *apodictic* ones are those that express logical necessity.

The table serves Kant as a clue to the "metaphysical deduction" of the categories, which claims to show that there is an origin for these concepts that is genuinely a priori, and, on the premise that the table is proper, that the derived concepts can be claimed to be fundamental and complete. But by itself the list does not show exactly what categories follow from, i.e., are necessarily used with, the various forms of judgment, let alone what their specific meaning is for our mode of experience. Above all, even when it is argued that each experience and every judgment requires at least one of the four general

forms, and that the use of any form of judgment does involve a matching pure concept (listed in the table of categories: reality, negation, limitation; unity, plurality, totality; inherence and subsistence, causality and dependence, community; possibility – impossibility, existence – non-existence, and necessity – contingency) applying to the objects judged about, this does not show that the complex relational forms and their corresponding categories of causality and community are necessary unless it is shown that these specific forms of judgment are *each* necessary for our experience. Precisely because this is initially not evident, it can appear, as Kant himself noted, that the validity of controversial categories such as causality cannot be established as easily as that of the forms of intuition. Moreover, Kant does not even try to prove the objectivity of the traditional modal categories but treats the principles that use them as mere definitions relative to experience. Thus a problematic judgment, i.e., one in which "affirmation or negation is taken as merely possible," is used when something is said to be possible in the sense that it "agrees with the formal conditions of experience, i.e., with the conditions of intuition and of concepts."

A clue for rescuing the relational categories is given near the end of the Transcendental Deduction (B version), where Kant notes that the a priori all-inclusiveness and unity of space and time that is claimed in the treatment of sensibility must, like all cognitive unity, ultimately have a foundation in judgment. Kant expands on this point by devoting a key section called the *analogies of experience* to arguing that the possibility of our judging objects to be determined in an objective position in the unity of time (and, indirectly, space) requires three a priori principles (each called an "Analogy") that employ precisely the relational categories that seemed especially questionable. Since these categories are established as needed just for the determination of time and space, which themselves have already been argued to be transcendentally ideal, Kant can conclude that for us even a priori claims using pure concepts of the understanding provide what are only transcendentally ideal claims. Thus we cannot make determinate theoretical claims about categories such as substance, cause, and community in an absolute sense that goes beyond our experience, but we can establish principles for their spatiotemporal specifications, called *schemata,* namely, the three Analogies: "in all change of appearance substance is permanent," "all alterations take place in conformity with the law of the connection of cause and effect," and "all substances, insofar as they can be perceived to coexist in space, are in thoroughgoing reciprocity." Kant initially calls these regulative principles of experience, since they are required for organizing all objects of our empirical knowledge within a unity, and, unlike the constitutive principles for the categories of quantity and quality (namely: "all intuitions [for us] are extensive magnitudes," and "in all appearances the real that is an object of sensation has intensive magnitude, that is, a degree"), they do not characterize any individual item by itself but rather only by its real relation to other objects of experience. Nonetheless, in comparison to mere heuristic or methodological principles (e.g., seek simple or teleological explanations), these Analogies are held by Kant to be objectively necessary for experience, and for this reason can also be called constitutive in a broader sense.

The remainder of the *Critique* exposes the "original" or "transcendental" ideas of pure reason that pretend to be constitutive or theoretically warranted but involve unconditional components that wholly transcend the realm of experience. These include not just the antinomic cosmological ideas noted above (of these Kant stresses the idea of transcendental freedom, i.e., of uncaused causing), but also the rational psychological ideas of the soul as an immortal substance and the rational theological idea of God as a necessary and perfect being. Just as the pure concepts of the understanding have an origin in the necessary forms of judgments, these ideas are said to originate in the various syllogistic forms of reason: the idea of a soul-substance is the correlate of an unconditioned first term of a categorical syllogism (i.e., a subject that can never be the predicate of something else), and the idea of God is the correlate of the complete sum of possible predicates that underlies the unconditioned first term of the disjunctive syllogism used to give a complete determination of a thing's properties. Despite the a priori origin of these notions, Kant claims we cannot theoretically establish their validity, even though they do have regulative value in organizing our notion of a human or divine spiritual substance. Thus, even if, as Kant argues, traditional proofs of immortality, and the teleological, cosmological, and ontological arguments for God's existence, are invalid, the notions they involve can be affirmed as long as there is, as he believes, a sufficient non-theoretical, i.e., moral argument for them. When interpreted on the basis of such an argument, they are transformed into ideas of practical reason, ideas that, like perfect virtue, may not be verified or

realized in sensible experience, but have a rational warrant in pure practical considerations.

Although Kant's pure practical philosophy culminates in religious hope, it is primarily a doctrine of obligation. Moral value is determined ultimately by the nature of the intention of the agent, which in turn is determined by the nature of what Kant calls the general maxim or subjective principle underlying a person's action. One follows a *hypothetical imperative* when one's maxim does not presume an unconditional end, a goal (like the fulfillment of duty) that one should have irrespective of all sensible desires, but rather a "material end" dependent on contingent inclinations (e.g., the directive "get this food," in order to feel happy). In contrast, a *categorical imperative* is a directive saying what ought to be done from the perspective of pure reason alone; it is categorical because what this perspective commands is not contingent on sensible circumstances and it always carries overriding value. The general formula of the categorical imperative is to act only according to those maxims that can be consistently willed as a universal law – something said to be impossible for maxims aimed merely at material ends. In accepting this imperative, we are doubly self-determined, for we are not only determining our action freely, as Kant believes humans do in all exercises of the faculty of choice; we are also accepting a principle whose content is determined by that which is absolutely essential to us as agents, namely our pure practical reason. We thus are following our own law and so have *autonomy* when we accept the categorical imperative; otherwise we fall into *heteronomy*, or the (free) acceptance of principles whose content is determined independently of the essential nature of our own ultimate being, which is rational.

Given the metaphysics of his transcendental idealism, Kant can say that the categorical imperative reveals a supersensible power of freedom in us such that we must regard ourselves as part of an intelligible world, i.e., a domain determined ultimately not by natural laws but rather by laws of reason. As such a rational being, an agent is an end in itself, i.e., something whose value is not dependent on external material ends, which are contingent and valued only as means to the end of happiness – which is itself only a conditional value (since the satisfaction of an evil will would be improper). Kant regards accepting the categorical imperative as tantamount to respecting rational nature as an end in itself, and to willing as if we were legislating a kingdom of ends. This is to will that the world become a "systematic union of different rational beings through common laws," i.e., laws that respect and fulfill the freedom of all rational beings. Although there is only one fundamental principle of morality, there are still different types of specific duties. One basic distinction is between strict duty and imperfect duty. Duties of justice, of respecting in action the rights of others, or the duty not to violate the dignity of persons as rational agents, are strict because they allow no exception for one's inclination. A perfect duty is one that requires a specific action (e.g. keeping a promise), whereas an imperfect duty, such as the duty to perfect oneself or to help others, cannot be completely discharged or demanded by right by someone else, and so one has considerable latitude in deciding when and how it is to be respected. A meritorious duty involves going beyond what is strictly demanded and thereby generating an obligation in others, as when one is extraordinarily helpful to others and "merits" their gratitude.

See also EPISTEMOLOGY, ETHICS, IDEALISM, METAPHYSICS, RATIONALISM, TRANSCENDENTAL ARGUMENT.   K.A.

Kao Tzu (fifth–fourth century B.C.), Chinese thinker and philosophical adversary of Mencius (4th century B.C.). He is referred to in the *Meng Tzu* (*Book of Mencius*). A figure of the same name appeared in the *Mo Tzu* as a (probably younger) contemporary of Mo Tzu (fifth century B.C.), but it is unclear if the two were the same individual. As presented in the *Meng Tzu*, Kao Tzu held that human nature (*hsing*) is morally neutral, and that living morally requires learning rightness (*yi*) from sources (such as philosophical doctrines) outside the heart/mind (*hsin*), and shaping one's way of life accordingly. These ideas are opposed to Mencius's belief that the heart/mind has incipient moral inclinations from which rightness can be derived, and that living morally involves one's fully developing such inclinations. Ever since the view that Mencius was the true transmitter of Confucius's teachings became established, largely through the efforts of Chu Hsi (1130–1200), Confucians have distanced themselves from Kao Tzu's position and even criticized philosophical opponents for holding positions similar to Kao Tzu's. **See also** CONFUCIANISM, MENCIUS.   K.-l.S.

karma, in Indian thought, the force whereby right and wrong actions bring benefits and punishments in this or a future existence. This occurs not arbitrarily, but by law. The conditions of birth

(one's sex, caste, circumstances of life) are profoundly affected by one's karmic "bank account." A typical Buddhist perspective is that the state of the non-conscious world at any given time is largely determined by the total karmic situation that then holds.

For all of the Indian perspectives that accept the karma-and-transmigration perspective, religious enlightenment, the highest good, includes escape from karma. Were it *absolutely* impossible to act without karmic consequences, obviously such escape would be impossible. (Suicide is viewed as merely ending the life of one's current body, and typically is viewed as wrong, so that the cosmic effect of one's suicide will be more punishment.) Thus non-theistic views hold that one who has achieved a pre-enlightenment status – typically reached by meditation, alms-giving, ascetic discipline, or the achieving of esoteric knowledge – can act so as to maintain life without collecting karmic consequences so long as one's actions are not morally wrong and are done disinterestedly. In theistic perspectives, where moral wrongdoing is sin and acting rightly is obedience to God, karma is the justice of Brahman in action and Brahman may pardon a repentant sinner from the results of wrong actions and place the forgiven sinner in a relation to Brahman that, at death, releases him or her from transmigratory wheel.

See also BRAHMAN, BUDDHISM.   K.E.Y.

karmic. See KARMA.

katastematic pleasure. See EPICUREANISM.

Kepler, Johannes (1571–1630), German mathematical astronomer, speculative metaphysician, and natural philosopher. He was born in Weil der Stadt, near Stuttgart. He studied astronomy with Michael Maestlin at the University of Tübingen, and then began the regular course of theological studies that prepared him to become a Lutheran pastor. Shortly before completing these studies he accepted the post of mathematician at Graz. "Mathematics" was still construed as including astronomy and astrology. There he published the *Mysterium cosmographicum* (1596), the first mjaor astronomical work to utilize the Copernican system since Copernicus's own *De revolutionibus* half a century before. The Copernican shift of the sun to the center allowed Kepler to propose an explanation for the spacing of the planets (the Creator inscribed the successive planetary orbits in the five regular polyhedra) and for their motions (a sun-centered driving force diminishing with distance from the sun). In this way, he could claim to have overcome the traditional prohibition against the mathematical astronomer's claiming reality for the motion he postulates. Ability to *explain* had always been the mark of the philosopher.

Kepler, a staunch Lutheran, was forced to leave Catholic Graz as bitter religious and political disputes engulfed much of northern Europe. He took refuge in the imperial capital, Prague, where Tycho Brahe, the greatest observational astronomer of the day, had established an observatory. Tycho asked Kepler to compose a defense of Tycho's astronomy against a critic, Nicolaus Ursus, who had charged that it was "mere hypothesis." The resulting *Apologia* (1600) remained unpublished; it contains a perceptive analysis of the nature of astronomical hypothesis. Merely saving the phenomena, Kepler argues, is in general not sufficient to separate two mathematical systems like those of Ptolemy and Copernicus. Other more properly explanatory "physical" criteria will be needed.

Kepler was allowed to begin work on the orbit of Mars, using the mass of data Tycho had accumulated. But shortly afterward, Tycho died suddenly (1601). Kepler succeeded to Tycho's post as Imperial Mathematician; more important, he was entrusted with Tycho's precious data. Years of labor led to the publication of the *Astronomia nova* (1609), which announced the discovery of the elliptical orbit of Mars. One distinctive feature of Kepler's long quest for the true shape of the orbit was his emphasis on finding a possible *physical* evaluation for any planetary motion he postulated before concluding that it was the true motion. Making the sun's force magnetic allowed him to suppose that its effect on the earth would vary as the earth's magnetic axis altered its orientation to the sun, thus perhaps explaining the varying distances and speeds of the earth in its elliptical orbit. The full title of his book makes his ambition clear: *A New Astronomy Based on Causes, or A Physics of the Sky.*

Trouble in Prague once more forced Kepler to move. He eventually found a place in Linz (1612), where he continued his exploration of cosmic harmonies, drawing on theology and philosophy as well as on music and mathematics. The *Harmonia mundi* (1618) was his favorite among his books: "It can wait a century for a reader, as God himself has waited six thousand years for a witness." The discovery of what later became known as his third law, relating the periodic times of any two planets as the ratio of the $^3/_2$ power of their mean distances, served to con-

firm his long-standing conviction that the universe is fashioned according to ideal harmonic relationships.

In the *Epitome astronomiae Copernicanae* (1612), he continued his search for causes "either natural or archetypal," not only for the planetary motions, but for such details as the size of the sun and the densities of the planets. He was more convinced than ever that a physics of the heavens had to rest upon its ability to explain (and not just to predict) the peculiarities of the planetary and lunar motions. What prevented him from moving even further than he did toward a new physics was that he had not grasped what later came to be called the principle of inertia. Thus he was compelled to postulate not only an attractive force between planet and sun but also a second force to urge the planet onward. It was Newton who showed that the second force is unnecessary, and who finally constructed the "physics of the sky" that had been Kepler's ambition. But he could not have done it without Kepler's notion of a quantifiable force operating between planet and sun, an unorthodox notion shaped in the first place by an imagination steeped in Neoplatonic metaphysics and the theology of the Holy Spirit.

See also NEWTON.   E.M.

Kerry's paradox. See FREGE.

Keynes, John Maynard (1883–1946), English economist and public servant who revolutionized economic theory and the application of economic theory in government policy. His most philosophically important works were *The General Theory of Employment, Interest and Money* (1936) and *A Treatise on Probability* (1921). Keynes was also active in English philosophical life, being well acquainted with such thinkers as Moore and Ramsey.

In the philosophy of probability, Keynes pioneered the treatment of propositions as the bearers of probability assignments. Unlike classical subjectivists, he treated probabilities as objective evidential relations among propositions. These relations were to be directly epistemically accessible to an intuitive faculty. An idiosyncratic feature of Keynes's system is that different probability assignments cannot always be compared (ordered as equal, less than, or greater than one another).

Keynesian economics is still presented in introductory textbooks and it has permanently affected both theory and practice. Keynes's economic thought had a number of philosophically important dimensions. While his theorizing was in the capitalistic tradition, he rejected Smith's notion of an invisible hand that would optimize the performance of an economy without any intentional direction by individuals or by the government. This involved rejection of the economic policy of laissez-faire, according to which government intervention in the economy's operation is useless, or worse. Keynes argued that natural forces could deflect an economy from a course of optimal growth and keep it permanently out of equilibria. In the *General Theory* he proposed a number of mechanisms for adjusting its performance. He advocated programs of government taxation and spending, not primarily as a means of providing public goods, but as a means of increasing prosperity and avoiding unemployment. Political philosophers are thereby provided with another means for justifying the existence of strong governments.

One of the important ways that Keynes's theory still directs much economic theorizing is its deep division between microeconomics and macroeconomics. Keynes argued, in effect, that microeconomic analysis with its emphasis on ideal individual rationality and perfect competition was inadequate as a tool for understanding such important macrophenomena as employment, interest, and money. He tried to show how human psychological foibles and market frictions required a qualitatively different kind of analysis at the macro level. Much current economic theorizing is concerned with understanding the connections between micro- and macrophenomena and micro- and macroeconomics in an attempt to dissolve or blur the division. This issue is a philosophically important instance of a potential theoretical reduction.

See also PHILOSOPHY OF ECONOMICS, PROBABILITY.   A.N.

Kierkegaard, Søren Aabye (1813–55), Danish writer whose "literature," as he called it, includes philosophy, psychology, theology and devotional literature, fiction, and literary criticism. Born to a well-to-do middle class family, he consumed his inheritance while writing a large corpus of books in a remarkably short time. His life was marked by an intense relationship with a devout but melancholy father, from whom he inherited his own bent to melancholy, with which he constantly struggled. A decisive event was his broken engagement from Regine Olsen, which precipitated the beginning of his authorship; his first books are partly an attempt to explain, in a covert and symbolic way, the reasons why he felt

he could not marry. Later Kierkegaard was involved in a controversy in which he was mercilessly attacked by a popular satirical periodical; this experience deepened his understanding of the significance of suffering and the necessity for an authentic individual to stand alone if necessary against "the crowd." This caused him to abandon his plans to take a pastorate, a post for which his theological education had prepared him. At the end of his life, he waged a lonely, public campaign in the popular press and in a magazine he founded himself, against the Danish state church. He collapsed on the street with the final issue of this magazine, *The Instant*, ready for the printer, and was carried to a hospital. He died a few weeks later, affirming a strong Christian faith, but refusing to take communion from the hands of a priest of the official church.

Though some writers have questioned whether Kierkegaard's writings admit of a unified interpretation, he himself saw his literature as serving Christianity; he saw himself as a "missionary" whose task was to "reintroduce Christianity into Christendom." However, much of this literature does not address Christianity directly, but rather concerns itself with an analysis of human existence. Kierkegaard saw this as necessary, because Christianity is first and foremost a way of existing. He saw much of the confusion about Christian faith as rooted in confusion about the nature of existence; hence to clear up the former, the latter must be carefully analyzed. The great misfortune of "Christendom" and "the present age" is that people "have forgotten what it means to exist," and Kierkegaard sees himself as a modern Socrates sent to "remind" others of what they know but have forgotten. It is not surprising that the analyses of human existence he provides have been of great interest to non-Christian writers as well.

Kierkegaard frequently uses the verb 'to exist' (*at existere*) in a special sense, to refer to human existence. In this sense God is said not to *exist*, even though God has eternal reality. Kierkegaard describes human existence as an unfinished process, in which "the individual" (a key concept in his thought) must take responsibility for achieving an identity as a self through free choices. Such a choice is described as a *leap*, to highlight Kierkegaard's view that intellectual reflection alone can never motivate action. A decision to end the process of reflection is necessary and such a decision must be generated by passion. The passions that shape a person's self are referred to by Kierkegaard as the individual's "inwardness" or "subjectivity." The most significant passions, such as love and faith, do not merely happen; they must be cultivated and formed.

The process by which the individual becomes a self is described by Kierkegaard as ideally moving through three stages, termed the "stages on life's way." Since human development occurs by freedom and not automatically, however, the individual can become fixated in any of these stages. Thus the stages also confront each other as rival views of life, or "spheres of existence." The three stages or spheres are the aesthetic, the ethical, and the religious. A distinctive feature of Kierkegaard's literature is that these three life-views are represented by pseudonymous "characters" who actually "author" some of the books; this leads to interpretive difficulties, since it is not always clear what to attribute to Kierkegaard himself and what to the pseudonymous character. Fortunately, he also wrote many devotional and religious works under his own name, where this problem does not arise.

The aesthetic life is described by Kierkegaard as lived for and in "the moment." It is a life governed by "immediacy," or the satisfaction of one's immediate desires, though it is capable of a kind of development in which one learns to enjoy life reflectively, as in the arts. What the aesthetic person lacks is commitment, which is the key to the ethical life, a life that attempts to achieve a unified self through commitment to ideals with enduring validity, rather than simply momentary appeal. The religious life emerges from the ethical life when the individual realizes both the transcendent character of the true ideals and also how far short of realizing those ideals the person is.

In *Concluding Unscientific Postscript* two forms of the religious life are distinguished: a "natural" religiosity (religiousness "A") in which the person attempts to relate to the divine and resolve the problem of guilt, relying solely on one's natural "immanent" idea of the divine; and Christianity (religiousness "B"), in which God becomes incarnate as a human being in order to establish a relation with humans. Christianity can be accepted only through the "leap of faith." It is a religion not of "immanence" but of "transcendence," since it is based on a revelation. This revelation cannot be rationally demonstrated, since the incarnation is a paradox that transcends human reason. Reason can, however, when the passion of faith is present, come to understand the appropriateness of recognizing its own limits and accepting the paradoxical incarnation of God in the form of Jesus Christ.

The true Christian is not merely an admirer of Jesus, but one who believes by becoming a follower.

The irreducibility of the religious life to the ethical life is illustrated for Kierkegaard in the biblical story of Abraham's willingness to sacrifice his son Isaac to obey the command of God. In *Fear and Trembling* Kierkegaard (through his pseudonym Johannes de Silentio) analyzes this act of Abraham's as involving a "teleological suspension of the ethical." Abraham's act cannot be understood merely in ethical terms as a conflict of duties in which one rationally comprehensible duty is superseded by a higher one. Rather, Abraham seems to be willing to "suspend" the ethical as a whole in favor of a higher religious duty. Thus, if one admires Abraham as "the father of faith," one admires a quality that cannot be reduced to simply moral virtue. Some have read this as a claim that religious faith may require immoral behavior; others argue that what is relativized by the teleological suspension of the ethical is not an eternally valid set of moral requirements, but rather ethical obligations as these are embedded in human social institutions. Thus, in arguing that "the ethical" is not the highest element in existence, Kierkegaard leaves open the possibility that our social institutions, and the ethical ideals that they embody, do not deserve our absolute and unqualified allegiance, an idea with important political implications.

In accord with his claim that existence cannot be reduced to intellectual thought, Kierkegaard devotes much attention to emotions and passions. Anxiety is particularly important, since it reflects human freedom. Anxiety involves a "sympathetic antipathy and an antipathetic sympathy"; it is the psychological state that precedes the basic human fall into sin, but it does not explain this "leap," since no final explanation of a free choice can be given. Such negative emotions as despair and guilt are also important for Kierkegaard; they reveal the emptiness of the aesthetic and the ultimately unsatisfactory character of the ethical, driving individuals on toward the religious life. Irony and humor are also seen as important "boundary zones" for the stages of existence. The person who has discovered his or her own "eternal validity" can look ironically at the relative values that capture most people, who live their lives aesthetically. Similarly, the "existential humorist" who has seen the incongruities that necessarily pervade our ethical human projects is on the border of the religious life.

Kierkegaard also analyzes the passions of faith

and love. Faith is ultimately understood as a "willing to be oneself" that is made possible by a transparent, trusting relationship to the "power that created the self." Kierkegaard distinguishes various forms of love, stressing that Christian love must be understood as neighbor love, a love that is combined and is not rooted in any natural relationship to the self, such as friendship or kinship, but ultimately is grounded in the fact that all humans share a relationship to their creator.

Kierkegaard is well known for his critique of Hegel's absolute idealism. Hegel's claim to have written "the system" is ridiculed for its pretensions of finality. From the Dane's perspective, though reality may be a system for God, it cannot be so for any existing thinker, since both reality and the thinker are incomplete and system implies completeness. Hegelians are also criticized for pretending to have found a presuppositionless or absolute starting point; for Kierkegaard, philosophy begins not with doubt but with wonder. Reflection is potentially infinite; the doubt that leads to skepticism cannot be ended by thought alone but only by a resolution of the will. Kierkegaard also defends traditional Aristotelian logic and the principle of non-contradiction against the Hegelian introduction of "movement" into logic. Kierkegaard is particularly disturbed by the Hegelian tendency to see God as immanent in society; he thought it important to understand God as "wholly other," the "absolutely different" who can never be exhaustively embodied in human achievement or institutions. To stand before God one must stand as an individual, in "fear and trembling," conscious that this may require a break with the given social order.

Kierkegaard is often characterized as the father of existentialism. There are reasons for this; he does indeed philosophize existentially, and he undoubtedly exercised a deep influence on many twentieth-century existentialists such as Sartre and Camus. But the characterization is anachronistic, since existentialism as a movement is a twentieth-century phenomenon, and the differences between Kierkegaard and those existentialists are also profound. If existentialism is defined as the denial that there is such a thing as a human essence or nature, it is unlikely that Kierkegaard is an existentialist. More recently, the Dane has also been seen as a precursor of postmodernism. His rejection of classical foundationalist epistemologies and employment of elusive literary techniques such as his pseudonyms again make such associations somewhat plausible. However, despite his rejection of the

system and criticism of human claims to finality and certitude, Kierkegaard does not appear to espouse any form of relativism or have much sympathy for "anti-realism." He has the kind of passion for clarity and delight in making sharp distinctions that are usually associated with contemporary "analytic" philosophy. In the end he must be seen as his own person, a unique Christian presence with sensibilities that are in many ways Greek and premodern rather than postmodern. He has been joyfully embraced and fervently criticized by thinkers of all stripes. He remains "the individual" he wrote about, and to whom he dedicated many of his works.

See also CAMUS, EXISTENTIALISM, HEGEL, POSTMODERN, SARTRE.   C.S.E.

Kilvington, Richard, surname also spelled Kilmington, Chillington (1302/05–61), English philosopher, theologian, and ecclesiastic. He was a scholar associated with the household of Richard de Bury and an early member of the Oxford Calculators, important in the early development of physics. Kilvington's *Sophismata* (early 1320s) is the only work of his studied extensively to date. It is an investigation of puzzles regarding change, velocity and acceleration, motive power, beginning and ceasing, the continuum, infinity, knowing and doubting, and the liar and related paradoxes. His approach is peculiar insofar as all these are treated in a purely logical or conceptual way, in contrast to the mathematical "calculations" used by Bradwardine, Heytesbury, and other later Oxford Calculators to handle problems in physics. Kilvington also wrote a commentary on Peter Lombard's *Sentences* and questions on Aristotle's *On Generation and Corruption, Physics,* and *Nicomachean Ethics.* **See also** OXFORD CALCULATORS.   P.V.S.

Kilwardby, Robert (d.1279), English philosopher and theologian. He apparently studied and perhaps taught at the University of Paris, later joining the Dominicans and perhaps lecturing at Oxford. He became archbishop of Canterbury in 1272 and in 1277 condemned thirty propositions, among them Aquinas's position that there is a single substantial form in a human being. Kilwardby resigned his archbishopric in 1278 and was appointed to the bishopric of Santa Rufina in Italy, where he died.

Kilwardby wrote extensively and had considerable medieval influence, especially in philosophy of language; but it is now unusually difficult to determine which works are authentically his. *De Ortu Scientiarum* advanced a sophisticated account of how names are imposed and a detailed account of the nature and role of logic. In metaphysics he insisted that things are individual and that universality arises from operations of the soul. He wrote extensively on happiness and was concerned to show that some happiness is possible in this life. In psychology he argued that freedom of decision is a disposition arising from the cooperation of the intellect and the will.   C.G.Norm.

Kim, Jaegwon (b.1934), Korean-American philosopher, writing in the analytic tradition, author of important works in metaphysics and the philosophy of mind.

Kim has defended a "fine-grained" conception of events according to which an event is the possessing of a property by an object at a time (see "Causation, Nomic Subsumption, and the Concept of Event," 1973; this and other papers referred to here are collected in *Supervenience and Mind*, 1993). This view has been a prominent rival of the "coarse-grained" account of events associated with Davidson.

Kim's work on the concept of supervenience has been widely influential, especially in the philosophy of mind (see "Supervenience as a Philosophical Concept," 1990). He regards supervenience (or, as he now prefers, "property covariation") as a relation holding between property families (mental properties and physical properties, for instance). If *A*-properties supervene on *B*-properties, then, necessarily, for any *A*-property, *a*, if an object, *o*, has *a*, there is some *B*-property, *b*, such that *o* has *b*, and (necessarily) anything that has *b* has *a*. Stronger or weaker versions of supervenience result from varying the modal strength of the parenthetical 'necessarily', or omitting it entirely.

Although the notion of supervenience has been embraced by philosophers who favor some form of "non-reductive physicalism" (the view that the mental depends on, but is not reducible to, the physical), Kim himself has expressed doubts that physicalism can avoid reduction ("The Myth of Nonreductive Materialism," 1989). If mental properties supervene on, but are distinct from, physical properties, then it is hard to see how mental properties could have a part in the production of physical effects – or mental effects, given the dependence of the mental on the physical.

More recently, Kim has developed an account of "functional reduction" according to which supervenient properties are causally efficacious if and only if they are functionally reducible to properties antecedently accepted as causally efficacious (*Mind in a Physical World,* 1998). Properties, including properties of conscious experiences, not so reducible are "epiphenomenal."

See also DAVIDSON, EVENT, PHILOSOPHY OF MIND, REDUCTION, SUPERVENIENCE.   J.F.H.

Kindī, al-. See AL-KINDĪ.

kinesis. See ARISTOTLE.

kinetic pleasure. See EPICUREANISM.

kingdom of ends. See KANT.

KK-thesis, the thesis that knowing entails knowing that one knows, symbolized in propositional epistemic logic as $Kp \rightarrow KKp$, where 'K' stands for knowing. According to the KK-thesis, the (propositional) logic of knowledge resembles the modal system S4. The KK-thesis was introduced into epistemological discussion by Hintikka in *Knowledge and Belief* (1962). He calls the KK-thesis a "virtual implication," a conditional whose negation is "indefensible." A tacit or an explicit acceptance of the thesis has been part of many philosophers' views about knowledge since Plato and Aristotle. If the thesis is formalized as $K_a p \rightarrow K_a K_a p$, where '$K_a$' is read as '*a* knows that', it holds only if the person *a* knows that he is referred to by '*a*'; this qualification is automatically satisfied for the first-person case. The validity of the thesis seems sensitive to variations in the sense of 'know'; it has sometimes been thought to characterize a strong concept of knowledge, e.g., knowledge based on (factually) conclusive reasons, or *active* as opposed to implicit knowledge. If knowledge is regarded as true belief based on conclusive evidence, the KK-thesis entails that a person knows that *p* only if his evidence for *p* is also sufficient to justify the claim that he knows that *p*; the epistemic claim should not require additional evidence. **See also** EPISTEMOLOGY.   R.Hi.

Kleist, Heinrich von (1771–1811), German philosopher and literary figure whose entire work is based on the antinomy of reason and sentiment, one as impotent as the other, and reflects the *Aufklärung* crisis at the turn of the century. In 1799 he resigned from the Prussian army. Following a reading of Kant, he lost faith in a "life's plan" as inspired by Leibniz's, Wolff's, and Shaftesbury's rationalism. He looked for salvation in Rousseau but concluded that sentiment revealed itself just as untrustworthy as reason as soon as man left the state of original grace and realized himself to be neither a puppet nor a god (see *Essay on the Puppet Theater*, 1810).

The Schroffenstein Family, Kleist's first play (1802), repeats the Shakespearian theme of two young people who love each other but belong to warring families. One already finds in it the major elements of Kleist's universe: the incapacity of the individual to master his fate, the theme of the tragic error, and the importance of the juridical. In 1803, Kleist returned to philosophy and literature and realized in *Amphitryon* (1806) the impossibility of the individual knowing himself and the world and acting deliberately in it. The divine order that is the norm of tragic art collapses, and with it, the principle of identity. Kleistian characters, "modern" individuals, illustrate this normative chaos. *The Broken Jug* (a comedy written in 1806) shows Kleist's interest in law. In his two parallel plays, *Penthesilea* and *The Young Catherine of Heilbronn*, Kleist presents an alternative: either "the marvelous order of the world" and the theodicy that carries Catherine's fate, or the sublime and apocryphal mission of the Christlike individual who must redeem the corrupt order. Before his suicide in 1811, Kleist looked toward the renaissance of the German nation for a historical way out of this metaphysical conflict.

See also LEIBNIZ, SHAFTESBURY, WOLFF.

G.Ra.

knower, paradox of the. See DEONTIC PARADOXES.

knowledge, tacit. See EPISTEMOLOGY.

knowledge, causal theory of. See EPISTEMOLOGY, NATURALISTIC EPISTEMOLOGY.

knowledge, direct. See BASING RELATION.

knowledge, indirect. See BASING RELATION.

knowledge, inferential. See INFERENTIAL KNOWLEDGE.

knowledge, propositional. See EPISTEMOLOGY.

knowledge, relativity of. See MANNHEIM.

knowledge by acquaintance, knowledge of objects by means of direct awareness of them. The notion of knowledge by acquaintance is primarily associated with Russell (*The Problems of Philosophy*, 1912). Russell first distinguishes knowledge

of truths from knowledge of things. He then distinguishes two kinds of knowledge of things: knowledge by acquaintance and knowledge by description. Ordinary speech suggests that we are acquainted with the people and the physical objects in our immediate environments. On Russell's view, however, our contact with these things is indirect, being mediated by our mental representations of them. He holds that the only things we know by acquaintance are the content of our minds, abstract universals, and, perhaps, ourselves.

Russell says that knowledge by description is indirect knowledge of objects, our knowledge being mediated by other objects and truths. He suggests that we know external objects, such as tables and other people, only by description (e.g., the cause of my present experience). Russell's discussion of this topic is quite puzzling. The considerations that lead him to say that we lack acquaintance with external objects also lead him to say that, strictly speaking, we lack knowledge of such things. This seems to amount to the claim that what he has called "knowledge by description" is not, strictly speaking, a kind of knowledge at all.

Russell also holds that every proposition that a person understands must be composed entirely of elements with which the person is acquainted. This leads him to propose analyses of familiar propositions in terms of mental objects with which we are acquainted.

See also PERCEPTION, RUSSELL.   R.Fe.

knowledge by description. See KNOWLEDGE BY ACQUAINTANCE.

knowledge *de dicto*. See KNOWLEDGE DE RE.

knowledge *de re*, knowledge, with respect to some object, that it has a particular property, or knowledge, of a group of objects, that they stand in some relation. Knowledge *de re* is typically contrasted with knowledge *de dicto*, which is knowledge of facts or propositions. If persons A and B know that a winner has been declared in an election, but only B knows which candidate has won, then both have *de dicto* knowledge that someone has won, but only B has *de re* knowledge about some candidate that she is the winner. Person B can knowingly attribute the property of being the winner to one of the candidates. It is generally held that to have *de re* knowledge about an object one must at least be in some sense familiar with or causally connected to the object.

A related concept is knowledge *de se*. This is self-knowledge, of the sort expressed by 'I am —— '. Knowledge *de se* is not simply *de re* knowledge about oneself. A person might see a group of people in a mirror and notice that one of the people has a red spot on his nose. He then has *de dicto* knowledge that someone in the group has a red spot on his nose. On most accounts, he also has *de re* knowledge with respect to that individual that he has a spot. But if he has failed to recognize that he himself is the one with the spot, then he lacks *de se* knowledge. He doesn't know (or believe) what he would express by saying "I have a red spot." So, according to this view, knowledge *de se* is not merely knowledge *de re* about oneself.

See also DE DICTO.   R.Fe.

knowledge *de se*. See KNOWLEDGE DE RE.

knowledge, tacit. See EPISTEMOLOGY.

Köhler, Wolfgang (1887–1967), German and American (after 1935) psychologist who, with Wertheimer and Koffka, founded Gestalt psychology. Köhler made two distinctive contributions to Gestalt doctrine, one empirical, one theoretical. The empirical contribution was his study of animal thinking, performed on Tenerife Island from 1913 to 1920 (*The Mentality of Apes*, 1925). The then dominant theory of problem solving was E. L. Thorndike's (1874–1949) associationist trial-and-error learning theory, maintaining that animals attack problems by trying out a series of behaviors, one of which is gradually "stamped in" by success. Köhler argued that trial-and-error behavior occurred only when, as in Thorndike's experiments, part of the problem situation was hidden. He arranged more open puzzles, such as getting bananas hanging from a ceiling, requiring the ape to get a (visible) box to stand on. His apes showed *insight* – suddenly arriving at the correct solution. Although he demonstrated the existence of insight, its nature remains elusive, and trial-and-error learning remains the focus of research.

Köhler's theoretical contribution was the concept of *isomorphism*, Gestalt psychology's theory of psychological representation. He held an identity theory of mind and body, and isomorphism claims that a topological mapping exists between the behavioral field in which an organism is acting (cf. Lewin) and fields of electrical currents in the brain (not the "mind"). Such currents have not been discovered. Important works by Köhler include *Gestalt Psychology* (1929), *The Place of Value*

in a World of Facts (1938), *Dynamics in Psychology* (1940), and *Selected Papers* (1971, ed. M. Henle).
See also FIGURE–GROUND.   T.H.L.

Ko Hung (fourth century A.D.), Chinese Taoist philosopher, also known as the Master Who Embraced Simplicity (Pao-p'u tzu). Ko Hung is a pivotal figure in the development of Taoism. His major work, the *Pao-p'u tzu*, emphasizes the importance of moral cultivation as a necessary step to spiritual liberation. In this Ko is often said to have synthesized Confucian concerns with Taoist aspirations. He champions the use of special drugs that would purify the body and spirit in the quest for Taoist transcendence. A firm believer in the existence of immortals (*hsien*) and the possibility of joining the ranks of the perfected, Ko experimented with different methods that fall under the rubric of "external alchemy" (*wai-tan*), which merits attention also in the history of Chinese science. **See also** HSIEN.

A.K.L.C.

Korean philosophy, philosophy in traditional Korea. Situated on the eastern periphery of the Asian mainland and cut off by water on three sides from other potential countervailing influences, Korea, with its more than two millennia of recorded history and a long tradition of philosophical reflection, was exposed from early on to the pervasive influence of China. The influences and borrowings from China – among the most pervasive of which have been the three major religiophilosophic systems of the East, Taoism, Buddhism, and Confucianism – were, in time, to leave their indelible marks on the philosophical, cultural, religious, linguistic, and social forms of Korean life. These influences from the Asian continent, which began to infiltrate Korean culture during the Three Kingdoms era (57 B.C. to A.D. 558), did not, however, operate in a vacuum. Even in the face of powerful and pervasive exogenous influences, shamanism – an animistic view of man and nature – remained the strong substratum of Korean culture, influencing and modifying the more sophisticated religions, philosophies, and ideologies that found entry into Korea during the last two thousand years.

Originally a philosophical formula for personal salvation through the renunciation of worldly desire, Buddhism, in the course of propagation from its point of origin, had absorbed enough esoteric deities and forms of worship to constitute a new school, Mahayana, and it was this type of Buddhism that found ready acceptance in Korea. Its beliefs were, at the plebeian level, further mixed with native shamanism and integrated into a shamanistic polytheism. The syncretic nature of Korean Buddhism manifests itself at the philosophical level in a tendency toward a reconciliatory synthesis of opposing doctrines. Korean Buddhism produced a number of monk-philosophers, whose philosophical writings were influential beyond the boundaries of Korea. Wonhyo (617–86) of Silla and Pojo Chinul (1158–1210) of Koryo may be singled out as the most original and representative of those Buddhist philosophers.

As Buddhism became more entrenched, a number of doctrinal problems and disputes began to surface. The most basic and serious was the dispute between the Madhyamika and Vijnaptimatrata-vadin schools of thought within Mahayana Buddhism. At the metaphysical level the former tended to negate existence, while the latter affirmed existence. An epistemological corollary of this ontological dispute was a dispute concerning the possibility of secular truth as opposed to transcendental truth. The former school denied its possibility, while the latter affirmed it. No mediation between these two schools of thought, either in their country of origin, India, or Korea, seemed possible.

It was to this task of reconciling these two opposed schools that Wonhyo dedicated himself. In a series of annotations and interpretations of the Buddhist scriptures, particularly of the *Taeseung Kishin-non* ("The Awakening of Faith in Mahayana"), he worked out a position that became subsequently known as *Hwajaeng-non* – a theory of reconciliation of dispute. It consisted in essence of seeing the two opposed schools as two different aspects of one mind. Wonhyo's *Hwajaeng-non*, as the first full-scale attempt to reconcile the opposing doctrines in Mahayana Buddhism, was referred to frequently in both Chinese and Japanese Buddhist exegetical writings.

The same spirit of reconciliation is also manifest later during the Koryo dynasty (918–1392) in Chinul's *Junghae-ssangsu*, in which the founder of Korean *Son* Buddhism attempts a reconciliation between *Kyo-hak* (Scriptural school of Buddhism) and *Son-ga* (Meditation school of Buddhism), which were engaged in a serious confrontation with each other. Although many of its teachings were derivations from Mahayana Buddhist metaphysics, the *Son* school of Buddhism emphasized the realization of enlightenment without depending upon scriptural teachings, while the Scriptural school of Buddhism emphasized a gradual process of enlight-

enment through faith and the practice of understanding scriptures. Himself a *Son* master, Chinul provided a philosophical foundation for Korean *Son* by incorporating the doctrines of Scriptural Buddhism as the philosophical basis for the practices of *Son*. Chinul's successful synthesis of *Kyo* and *Son* served as the basis for the development of an indigenous form of *Son* Buddhism in Korea. It is primarily this form of Buddhism that is meant when one speaks of Korean Buddhism today.

Ethical self-cultivation stands at the core of Confucianism. Confucian theories of government and social relationships are founded upon it, and the metaphysical speculations have their place in Confucianism insofar as they are related to this overriding concern. The establishment in A.D. 372 of *Taehak*, a state-oriented Confucian institute of higher learning in the kingdom of Kokuryo, points to a well-established tradition of Confucian learning already in existence on the Korean peninsula during the Three Kingdoms era. Although Buddhism was the state religion of the Unified Silla period (668–918), Confucianism formed its philosophical and structural backbone. From 682, when a national academy was established in the Unified Silla kingdom as a training ground for high-level officials, the content of formal education in Korea consisted primarily of Confucian and other related Chinese classics; this lasted well into the nineteenth century. The preeminence of Confucianism in Korean history was further enhanced by its adoption by the founders of the Choson dynasty (1392–1910) as the national ideology.

The Confucianism that flourished during the Choson period was Neo-Confucianism, a philosophical synthesis of original Confucianism, Buddhism, and Taoism achieved by the Chinese philosopher Chu Hsi in the twelfth century. During the five hundred years of Neo-Confucian orthodoxy, a number of Korean scholars succeeded in bringing Neo-Confucian philosophical speculation to new heights of originality and influence both at home and abroad. Yi Hwang (better known by his pen name T'oegye, 1501–70) and his adversary Yi I (Yulgok, 1536–84) deserve special mention.

T'oegye interpreted the origin of the four cardinal virtues (benevolence, righteousness, propriety, and knowledge) and the seven emotions (pleasure, anger, sorrow, joy, love, hate, and desire) in such a way as to accord priority to the principle of reason *I* over the principle of material force *Ki*. T'oegye went a step further than his Sung mentor Chu Hsi by claiming that the principle of reason includes within itself the generative power for matter. This theory was criticized by Yulgok, who claimed that the source of generative power in the universe lay in the matter of material force itself. The philosophical debate carried on by these men and its implications for ethics and statecraft are generally considered richer in insight and more intricate in argumentation than that in China. T'oegye's ideas in particular were influential in spreading Neo-Confucianism in Japan.

Neo-Confucian philosophical speculation in the hands of those lesser scholars who followed T'oegye and Yulgok, however, became overly speculative and impractical. It evolved, moreover, into a rigid national orthodoxy by the middle of the seventeenth century. Dissatisfaction with this intellectual orthodoxy was further deepened by Korea's early encounter with Christianity and Western science, which had been reaching Korea by way of China since the beginning of the seventeenth century. Coupled with the pressing need for administrative and economic reforms subsequent to the Japanese invasion (1592–97), these tendencies gave rise to a group of illustrious Confucian scholars who, despite the fact that their individual lives spanned a 300-year period from 1550 to 1850, were subsequently and collectively given the name *Silhak*. Despite their diverse interests and orientations, these scholars were bound by their devotion to the spirit of practicality and utility as well as to seeking facts grounded in evidence in all scholarly endeavors, under the banner of returning to the spirit of the original Confucianism. Chong Yag-yong (1762–1836), who may be said to be the culmination of the *Silhak* movement, was able to transform these elements and tendencies into a new Confucian synthesis.

See also BUDDHISM, CHINESE PHILOSOPHY, CONFUCIANISM, JAPANESE PHILOSOPHY, NEO-CONFUCIANISM.   Y.K.

Kotarbiński, Tadeusz (1886–1981), Polish philosopher, cofounder, with Łukasiewicz and Leśniewski, of the Warsaw Center of Logical Research. His broad philosophical interests and humanistic concerns, probity, scholarship, and clarity in argument, consequent persuasiveness, and steadfast championship of human rights made him heir to their common mentor Kasimir Twardowski, father of modern Polish philosophy. In philosophical, historical, and methodological works like his influential *Elements of Theory of Knowledge, Formal Logic, and Scientific Methodology* (1929; mistitled *Gnosiology* in English transla-

tion), he popularized the more technical contributions of his colleagues, and carried on Twardowski's objectivist and "anti-irrationalist" critical tradition, insisting on accuracy and clarity, holding that philosophy has no distinctive method beyond the logical and analytical methods of the empirical and deductive sciences. As a free-thinking liberal humanist socialist, resolved to be "a true compass, not a weathervane," he defended autonomous ethics against authoritarianism, left *or* right. His lifelong concern with community and social practice led him to develop *praxiology* as a theory of efficacious action.

Following Leśniewsi's "refutation" of Twardowski's Platonism, Kotarbiński insisted on translating abstractions into more concrete terms. The principal tenets of his "reist, radical realist, and imitationist" rejection of Platonism, phenomenalism, and introspectionism are (1) *pansomatism* or *ontological reism* as modernized monistic materialism: whatever is anything at all (even a soul) is *a body* – i.e., a concrete individual object, resistant and spatiotemporally extended, enduring at least a while; (2) consequent *radical realism:* no object is a "property," "relation," "event," "fact," or "abstract entity" of any other kind, nor "sense-datum," "phenomenon," or essentially "private mental act" or "fact" accessible only to "introspection"; (3) *concretism* or *semantic reism* and *imitationism* as a concomitant "nominalist" *program* – thus, abstract terms that, hypostatized, might appear to name "abstract entities" are *pseudo-names* or *onomatoids* to be eliminated by philosophical analysis and elucidatory paraphrase. Hypostatizations that might appear to imply existence of such Platonic universals are translatable into equivalent generalizations characterizing only bodies. Psychological propositions are likewise reducible, ultimately to the basic form: Individual So-and-so experiences thus; Such-and-such is so. Only as thus reduced can such potentially misleading expressions be rightly understood and judged true or false.

See also POLISH LOGIC.   E.C.L.

ko wu, chih chih, Chinese philosophical terms used in the *Ta-hsüeh* (*Great Learning*) to refer to two related stages or aspects of the self-cultivation process, subsequently given different interpretations by later Confucian thinkers. '*Ko*' can mean 'correct', 'arrive at' or 'oppose'; '*wu*' means 'things'. The first '*chih*' can mean 'expand' or 'reach out'; the second '*chih*' means 'knowledge'. Chu Hsi (1130–1200) took '*ko wu*' to mean arriving at *li* (principle, pattern) in human affairs and *'chih chih'* to mean the expansion of knowledge; an important part of the self-cultivation process involves expanding one's moral knowledge by examining daily affairs and studying classics and historical documents. Wang Yang-ming (1472–1529) took *'ko wu'* to mean correcting the activities of one's heart/mind (*hsin*), and *'chih chih'* the reaching out of one's innate knowledge (*liang chih*); an important part of the self-cultivation process involves making fully manifest one's innate knowledge by constantly watching out for and eliminating distortive desires.   K.-l.S.

Krause, Karl Christian Friedrich (1781–1832), German philosopher representative of a tendency to develop Kant's views in the direction of pantheism and mysticism. Educated at Jena, he came under the influence of Fichte and Schelling. Taking his philosophical starting point as Fichte's analysis of self-consciousness, and adopting as his project a "spiritualized" systematic elaboration of the philosophy of Spinoza (somewhat like the young Schelling), he arrived at a position that he called *panentheism*. According to this, although nature and human consciousness are part of God or Absolute Being, the Absolute is neither exhausted in nor identical with them. To some extent, he anticipated Hegel in invoking an "end of history" in which the finite realm of human affairs would reunite with the infinite essence in a universal moral and "spiritual" order. **See also** FICHTE, PANTHEISM, SCHELLING.   J.P.Su.

Krebs. See NICHOLAS OF CUSA.

Kripke, Saul A(aron) (b.1940), American mathematician and philosopher, considered one of the most deeply influential contemporary figures in logic and philosophy. While a teenager, he formulated a semantics for modal logic (the logic of necessity and possibility) based on Leibniz's notion of a possible world, and, using the apparatus, proved completeness for a variety of systems (1959, 1963). Possible world semantics (due in part also to Carnap and others) has proved to be one of the most fruitful developments in logic and philosophy.

Kripke's 1970 Princeton lectures, *Naming and Necessity* (1980), were a watershed. The work primarily concerns proper names of individuals (e.g., 'Aristotle') and, by extension, terms for natural kinds ('water') and similar expressions. Kripke uses his thesis that any such term is a *rigid designator* – i.e., designates the same thing with respect to every possible world in which that thing exists (and does not designate anything else with respect to worlds in which it does not exist) – to argue, contrary to the received Fregean view, that the designation of a proper name is not semantically secured by means of a description that gives the sense of the name. On the contrary, the description associated with a particular use of a name will frequently designate something else entirely. Kripke derives putative examples of necessary a posteriori truths, as well as contingent a priori truths. In addition, he defends *essentialism* – the doctrine that some properties of things are properties that those things could not fail to have (except by not existing) – and uses it, together with his account of natural-kind terms, to argue against the identification of mental entities with their physical manifestations (e.g., sensations with specific neural events). In a sequel, "A Puzzle about Belief" (1979), Kripke addresses the problem of substitution failure in sentential contexts attributing belief or other propositional attitudes. Kripke's interpretation of the later Wittgenstein as a semantic skeptic has also had a profound impact (*Wittgenstein on Rules and Private Language*, 1980, 1982).

His semantic theory of truth ("Outline of a Theory of Truth," 1975) has sparked renewed interest in the liar paradox ('This statement is false') and related paradoxes, and in the development of non-classical languages containing their own truth predicates as possible models for natural language. In logic, he is also known for his work in intuitionism and on his theory of transfinite recursion on admissible ordinals. Kripke, McCosh Professor of Philosophy (emeritus) at Princeton, frequently lectures on numerous further significant results in logic and philosophy, but those results have remained unpublished.

See also A PRIORI, CAUSAL THEORY OF PROPER NAMES, MEANING, PHILOSOPHY OF LANGUAGE, WITTGENSTEIN.   N.S.

Kripke semantics, a type of formal semantics for languages with operators $\square$ and $\lozenge$ for necessity and possibility ('possible worlds semantics' and 'relational semantics' are sometimes used for the same notion); also, a similar semantics for intuitionistic logic. In a basic version a *frame* for a sentential language with $\square$ and $\lozenge$ is a pair (W,R) where W is a non-empty set (the "possible worlds") and R is a binary relation on W – the relation of "relative possibility" or "accessibility." A *model* on the frame (W,R) is a triple (W,R,V), where V is a function (the "valuation function") that assigns truth-values to sentence letters at worlds. If $w \in W$ then a sentence $\Box A$ is *true at world w in the model* (W,R,V) if A is true at all worlds $v \in W$ for which wRv. Informally, $\Box A$ is true at world w if A is true at all the worlds that would be possible if w were actual. This is a generalization of the doctrine commonly attributed to Leibniz that necessity is truth in all possible worlds. A is valid in the model (W,R,V) if it is true at all worlds $w \in W$ in that model. It is valid in the frame (W,R) if it is valid in all models on that frame. It is valid if it is valid in all frames. In predicate logic versions, a frame may include another component D, that assigns a non-empty set Dw of objects (*the existents at w*) to each possible world w. Terms and quantifiers may be treated either as *objectual* (denoting and ranging over individuals) or *conceptual* (denoting and ranging over functions from possible worlds to individuals) and either as *actualist* or *possibilist* (denoting and ranging over either existents or possible existents). On some of these treatments there may arise further choices about whether and how truth-values should be assigned to sentences that assert relations among non-existents.

The development of Kripke semantics marks a watershed in the modern study of modal systems. In the 1930s, 1940s, and 1950s a number of axiomatizations for necessity and possibility were proposed and investigated. Carnap showed that for the simplest of these systems, C. I. Lewis's S5, $\Box A$ can be interpreted as saying that A is true in all "state descriptions." Answering even the most basic questions about the other systems, however, required effort and ingenuity. In the late fifties and early sixties Stig Kanger, Richard Montague, Saul Kripke, and Jaakko Hintikka each formulated interpretations for such systems that generalized Carnap's semantics by using something like the accessibility relation described above. Kripke's semantics was more natural than the others in that accessibility was taken to be a relation among mathematically primitive "possible worlds," and, in a series of papers, Kripke demonstrated that versions of it provide characteristic interpretations for a number of modal systems. For these reasons Kripke's formulation has become standard. Relational semantics provided simple solutions to some older problems about the distinctness and relative strength of the various systems. It also opened new areas of investigation, facilitating *general* results (establishing decidability and other properties for infinite classes of modal systems), *incompleteness* results (exhibiting systems not determined by any class of frames), and *correspondence* results (showing that the frames verifying certain modal formulas were exactly the frames meeting certain conditions on R). It suggested parallel interpretations for notions whose patterns of inference were known to be similar to that of necessity and possibility, including obligation and permission, epistemic necessity and possibility, provability and consistency, and, more recently, the notion of a computation's inevitably or possibly terminating in a particular state. It inspired similar semantics for nonclassical conditionals and the more general neighborhood or functional variety of possible worlds semantics.

The philosophical utility of Kripke semantics is more difficult to assess. Since the accessibility relation is often explained in terms of the modal operators, it is difficult to maintain that the semantics provides an explicit analysis of the modalities it interprets. Furthermore, questions about which version of the semantics is correct (particularly for quantified modal systems) are themselves tied to substantive questions about the nature of things and worlds. The semantics does impose important constraints on the meaning of modalities, and it provides a means for many philosophical questions to be posed more clearly and starkly.

See also FORMAL SEMANTICS, MODAL LOGIC, NECESSITY, POSSIBLE WORLDS.   S.T.K.

Kristeva, Julia (b.1941), Bulgarian-born French linguist, practicing psychoanalyst, widely influential social theorist, and novelist. The centerpiece of Kristeva's semiotic theory has two correlative moments: a focus on the speaking subject as embodying unconscious motivations (and not simply the conscious intentionality of a Husserlian transcendental ego) and an articulation of the signifying phenomenon as a dynamic, productive process (not a static sign-system).

Kristeva's most systematic philosophical work, *La Révolution du langage poétique* (1974), brings her semiotics to mature expression through an effective integration of psychoanalysis (Freud and Lacan), elements of linguistic models (from Roman Jakobson to Chomskyan generative grammar) and semiology (from Saussure to Peirce and Louis Hjelmslev), and a literary approach to text (influenced by Bakhtin). Together the symbolic and the semiotic, two dialectical and irreconcilable modalities of meaning, constitute the signifying process. The symbolic designates the systematic rules governing denotative and propositional speech, while the semiotic isolates an archaic layer of meaning that is neither representational nor based on relations among signs. The concept of the *chora* combines the semiotic, translinguistic layer of meaning (genotext) with a psychoanalytic, drive-based model of unconscious sound production, dream logic, and fantasy life that defy full symbolic articulation. Drawing on Plato's non-unified notion of the maternal receptacle (*Timaeus*), the *chora* constitutes the space where subjectivity is generated. Drives become "ordered" in rhythmic patterns during the pre-Oedipal phase before the infant achieves reflexive capacity, develops spatial intuition and time consciousness, and posits itself as an enunciating subject. Ordered, but not according to symbolic laws, semiotic functions arise when the infant forms associations between its vocal gesticulations and sensorimotor development, and patterns these associations after the mother's corporeal modulations. The semiotic *chora,* while partly repressed in identity formation, links the subject's preverbal yet functional affective life to signification.

All literary forms – epic narrative, metalanguage, contemplation or *theoria* and text-practice – combine two different registers of meaning, phenotext and genotext. Yet they do so in different ways and none encompasses both registers in totality. The phenotext refers to language in its function "to communicate" and can be analyzed in terms of syntax and semantics. Though not itself linguistic, the genotext reveals itself in the way that "phonematic" and "melodic devices" and "syntactic and logical" features establish "semantic" fields. The genotext isolates the specific mode in which a text sublimates drives; it denotes the "process" by which a literary form generates a particular type of subjectivity. Poetic language is unique in that it largely reveals the genotext.

This linkage between semiotic processes, genotext, and poetic language fulfills the early linguistic project (1967–73) and engenders a novel post-Hegelian social theory. Synthesizing semiotics and the destructive death drive's attack against stasis artfully restores permanence to Hegelian negativity. Poetic mimesis, because it transgresses grammatical rules while sustaining signification, reactivates the irreducible negativity and heterogeneity of drive processes. So effectuating anamnesis, poetry reveals the subject's constitution within language and, by holding open rather than normalizing its repressed desire, promotes critical analysis of symbolic and institutionalized values. Later works like *Pouvoirs de l'horreur* (1980), *Etrangers à nous-mêmes*

(1989), *Histoires d'amour* (1983), and *Les Nouvelles maladies de l'âme* (1993) shift away from collective political agency to a localized, culturally therapeutic focus. Examining xenophobic social formations, abjection and societal violence, romantic love, grief, women's melancholic poison in patriarchy, and a crisis of moral values in the postmetaphysical age, they harbor forceful implications for ethics and social theory.

See also BAKHTIN, FEMINISM, FREUD, POSTMODERN, SEMIOTICS, STRUCTURALISM.

P.Hu.

Kropotkin, Petr Alekseevich (1842–1921), Russian geographer, geologist, naturalist, and philosopher, best remembered for his anarchism and his defense of mutual aid as a factor of evolution. Traveling extensively in Siberia on scientific expeditions (1862–67), he was stimulated by Darwin's newly published theory of evolution and sought, in the Siberian landscape, confirmation of Darwin's Malthusian principle of the struggle for survival. Instead Kropotkin found that *under*population was the rule, that climate was the main obstacle to survival, and that mutual aid was a far more common phenomenon than Darwin recognized. He soon generalized these findings to social theory, opposing social Darwinism, and also began to espouse anarchist theory. See also ANARCHISM, DARWINISM, RUSSIAN PHILOSOPHY.   P.T.G.

Kuan Tzu, also called Kuan Chung (d.645 B.C.), Chinese statesman who was prime minister of Ch'i and considered a forefather of Legalism. He was traditionally albeit spuriously associated with the *Kuan Tzu,* an eclectic work containing Legalist, Confucian, Taoist, five phases, and Huang–Lao ideas from the fourth to the second centuries B.C. As minister, Kuan Tzu achieved peace and social order through the hegemonic system (*pa*), wherein the ruling Chou king ratified a collective power-sharing arrangement with the most powerful feudal lords.

R.P.P. & R.T.A.

Kuhn, Thomas S(amuel) (1922–96), American historian and philosopher of science. Kuhn studied at Harvard, where he received degrees in physics (1943, 1946) and a doctorate in the history of science (1949). He then taught history of science or philosophy of science at Harvard (1951–56), Berkeley (1956–64), Princeton (1964–79), and M.I.T. (1979–91). Kuhn traced his shift from physics to the history and philosophy of science to a moment in 1947 when he was asked to teach some science to humanities majors. Searching for a case study to illuminate the development of Newtonian mechanics, Kuhn opened Aristotle's *Physics* and was astonished at how "simply wrong" it was. After a while, Kuhn came to "think like an Aristotelian physicist" and to realize that Aristotle's basic concepts were totally unlike Newton's, and that, understood on its own terms, Aristotle's *Physics* was not bad Newtonian mechanics. This new perspective resulted in *The Copernican Revolution* (1957), a study of the transformation of the Aristotelian geocentric image of the world to the modern heliocentric one.

Pondering the structure of these changes, Kuhn produced his immensely influential second book, *The Structure of Scientific Revolutions* (1962). He argued that scientific thought is defined by "paradigms," variously describing these as disciplinary matrixes or exemplars, i.e., conceptual world-views consisting of beliefs, values, and techniques shared by members of a given community, or an element in that constellation: concrete achievements used as models for research. According to Kuhn, scientists accept a prevailing paradigm in "normal science" and attempt to articulate it by refining its theories and laws, solving various puzzles, and establishing more accurate measurements of constants. Eventually, however, their efforts may generate anomalies; these emerge only with difficulty, against a background of expectations provided by the paradigm. The accumulation of anomalies triggers a crisis that is sometimes resolved by a revolution that replaces the old paradigm with a new one. One need only look to the displacement of Aristotelian physics and geocentric astronomy by Newtonian mechanics and heliocentrism for instances of such paradigm shifts. In this way, Kuhn challenged the traditional conception of scientific progress as gradual, cumulative acquisition of knowledge. He elaborated upon these themes and extended his historical inquiries in his later works, *The Essential Tension* (1977) and *Black-Body Theory and the Quantum Discontinuity* (1978).

See also PARADIGM, PHILOSOPHY OF SCIENCE.   R.Ar.

k'un. See CH'IEN, K'UN.

kung, szu, a Chinese distinction corresponding to the opposition between "public" and "private" interests, a key feature of Confucian and Legalist ethics. The distinction is sometimes expressed by other terms suggestive of distinction between impartiality and partiality, as in the *Mo Tzu,* or the Neo-Confucian distinction between Heavenly principle (*t'ien-li*) and selfish desires. For the Confucians, private and personal concerns are acceptable only insofar as they do not conflict with the rules of propriety (*li*) and righteousness (*i*). Partiality toward one's personal relationships is also acceptable provided that such partiality admits of reasonable justification, especially when such a concern is not incompatible with *jen* or the ideal of humanity. This view contrasts with egoism, altruism, and utilitarianism. **See also** CHINESE LEGALISM, CONFUCIANISM.   A.S.C.

K'ung Ch'iu. See CONFUCIUS.

Kung Fu-tzu. See CONFUCIUS.

Kung-sun Lung Tzu (fl. 300 B.C.), Chinese philosopher best known for his dialogue defending the claim "A white horse is not a horse." Kung-sun probably regarded his paradox only as an entertaining exercise in disputation (*pien*), and not as philosophically illuminating. Nonetheless, it may have had the serious effect of helping to bring disputation into disrepute in China. Numerous interpretations of the "white horse" dialogue have been proposed. One recent theory is that Kung-sun Lung Tzu is assuming that 'white horse' refers to two things (an equine shape and a color) while 'horse' refers only to the shape, and then simply observing that the whole (shape and color) is not identical with one of its parts (the shape). **See also** PIEN.   B.W.V.N.

K'ung Tzu. See CONFUCIUS.

Kuo Hsiang (died A.D. 312), Chinese thinker of the *Hsüan Hsüeh* (Mysterious Learning) School. He is described, along with thinkers like Wang Pi, as a Neo-Taoist. Kuo helped develop the notion of *li* (pattern) as the underlying structure of the cosmos, of which each thing receives an individual *fen* (allotment). All things are "one" in having such "natural" roles to play, and by being *tzu jan* (spontaneous), can attain a mystical oneness with all things. For Kuo, the *fen* of human beings included standard Confucian virtues. Kuo is credited with editing the current edition of the *Chuang Tzu* and composing what is now the oldest extant commentary on it. **See also** NEO-TAOISM.   P.J.I.

***Kyo-hak* Buddhism**. See KOREAN PHILOSOPHY.

Kyoto School. See JAPANESE PHILOSOPHY.

L

Labriola, Antonio (1843–1904), Italian Marxist philosopher who studied Hegel and corresponded with Engels for several years (*Lettere a Engels*, 1949). His essays on Marxism appeared first in French in the collection *Essais sur la conception matérialiste de l'histoire* ("Essays on the Materialist Conception of History," 1897). Another influential work, *Discorrendo di socialismo e di filosofia* ("Talks about Socialism and Philosophy," 1897), collects ten letters to Georges Sorel on Marxism. Labriola did not intend to develop an original Marxist theory but only to give an accurate exposition of Marx's thought. He believed that socialism would inevitably ensue from the inner contradictions of capitalist society and defended Marx's views as objective scientific truths. He criticized revisionism and defended the need to maintain the orthodoxy of Marxist thought. His views and works were publicized by two of his students, Sorel in France and Croce in Italy. In the 1950s Antonio Gramsci brought new attention to Labriola as an example of pure and independent Marxism. **See also MARXISM, SOREL.** P.Gar.

Lacan, Jacques (1901–81), French practitioner and theorist of psychoanalysis. Lacan developed and transformed Freudian theory and practice on the basis of the structuralist linguistics originated by Saussure. According to Lacan, the unconscious is not a congeries of biological instincts and drives, but rather a system of linguistic signifiers. He construes, e.g., the fundamental Freudian processes of condensation and displacement as instances of metaphor and metonymy. Lacan proposed a Freudianism in which any traces of the substantial Cartesian self are replaced by a system of symbolic functions. Contrary to standard views, the ego is an imaginary projection, not our access to the real (which, for Lacan, is the unattainable and inexpressible limit of language). In accord with his theoretical position, Lacan developed a new form of psychoanalytic practice that tried to avoid rather than achieve the "transference" whereby the analysand identifies with the mature ego of the analyst. Lacan's writings (e.g., *Écrits* and the numerous volumes of his *Séminaires*) are of legendary difficulty, offering idiosyncratic networks of allusion, word play, and paradox, which some find rich and stimulating and others irresponsibly obscure. Beyond psychoanalysis, Lacan has been particularly influential on literary theorists and on post-structuralist philosophers such as Foucault, Derrida, and Deleuze. **See also FOUCAULT, FREUD.** G.G.

Laffitte, Pierre (1823–1903), French positivist philosopher, a disciple of Comte and founder (1878) of the *Revue Occidentale*. Laffitte spread positivism by adopting Comte's format of "popular" courses. He faithfully acknowledged Comte's objective method and religion of humanity. Laffitte wrote *Great Types of Humanity* (1875–76). In *Positive Ethics* (1881), he distinguishes between theoretical and practical ethics. His *Lectures on First Philosophy* (1889–95) sets forth a metaphysics, or a body of general and abstract laws, that attempts to complete positivism, to resolve the conflict between the subjective and the objective, and to avert materialism. **See also COMTE, LOGICAL POSITIVISM.** J.-L.S.

La Forge, Louis de (1632–66), French philosopher and member of the Cartesian school. La Forge seems to have become passionately interested in Descartes's philosophy in about 1650, and grew to become one of its most visible and energetic advocates. La Forge (together with Gérard van Gutschoven) illustrated the 1664 edition of Descartes's *L'homme* and provided an extensive commentary; both illustrations and commentary were often reprinted with the text. His main work, though, is the *Traité de l'esprit de l'homme* (1665): though not a commentary on Descartes, it is "in accordance with the principles of René Descartes," according to its subtitle. It attempts to continue Descartes's program in *L'homme*, left incomplete at his death, by discussing the mind and its union with the body.

In many ways La Forge's work is quite orthodox; he carefully follows Descartes's opinions on the nature of body, the nature of soul, etc., as they appear in the extant writings to which he had access. But with others in the Cartesian school, La Forge's work contributed to the establishment of the doctrine of occasionalism as

Cartesian orthodoxy, a doctrine not explicitly found in Descartes's writings.

See also DESCARTES, OCCASIONALISM.

D.Garb.

Lambda-abstraction. See COMBINATORY LOGIC, LAMBDA-CALCULUS.

lambda-calculus, also λ-calculus, a theory of mathematical functions that is (a) "logic-free," i.e. contains no logical constants (formula-connectives or quantifier-expressions), and (b) equational, i.e. '=' is its sole predicate (though its metatheory refers to relations of reducibility between terms). There are two species, untyped and typed, each with various subspecies.

Termhood is always inductively defined (as is being a type-expression, if the calculus is typed). A definition of being a term will contain at least these clauses: take infinitely many variables (of each type if the calculus is typed) to be terms; for any terms τ and σ (of appropriate type if the calculus is typed), $(\tau\sigma)$ is a term (of type determined by that of τ and σ if the calculus is typed); for any term τ and a variable υ (perhaps meeting certain conditions), $(\lambda\upsilon\tau)$ is a term ("of" type determined by that of τ and υ if the calculus is typed). $(\tau\sigma)$ is an application-term; $(\lambda\upsilon\tau)$ is a λ-term, the λ-abstraction of τ, and its λ-prefix binds all free occurrences of υ in τ. Relative to any assignment a of values (of appropriate type if the calculus is typed) to its free variables, each term denotes a unique entity. Given a term $(\tau\sigma)$, τ denotes a function and $(\tau\sigma)$ denotes the output of that function when it is applied to the denotatum of σ, all relative to a. $(\lambda\upsilon\tau)$ denotes relative to a that function which when applied to any entity x (of appropriate type if the calculus is typed) outputs the denotatum of τ relative to the variant of a obtained by assigning υ to the given x.

Alonzo Church introduced the untyped λ-calculus around 1932 as the basis for a foundation for mathematics that took all mathematical objects to be functions. It characterizes a universe of functions, each with that universe as its domain and each yielding values in that universe. It turned out to be almost a notational variant of combinatory logic, first presented by Moses Schonfinkel (1920, written up and published by Behmann in 1924).

Church presented the simplest typed λ calculus in 1940. Such a calculus characterizes a domain of objects and functions, each "of" a unique type, so that the type of any given function determines two further types, one being the type of all and only those entities in the domain of that function, the other being the type of all those entities output by that function.

In 1972 Jean-Yves Girard presented the first second-order (or polymorphic) typed λ-calculus. It uses additional type-expressions themselves constructed by second-order λ-abstraction, and also more complicated terms constructed by λ-abstracting with respect to certain type-variables, and by applying such terms to type-expressions.

The study of λ-calculi has deepened our understanding of constructivity in mathematics. They are of interest in proof theory, in category theory, and in computer science.

See also CATEGORY THEORY, COMBINATORY LOGIC, PROOF THEORY.

H.T.H.

lambda-operator. See LAMBDA-CALCULUS.

lambda-term. See COMBINATORY LOGIC, LAMBDA-CALCULUS.

Lambert, Johann Heinrich (1728–77), German natural philosopher, logician, mathematician, and astronomer. Born in Mulhouse (Alsace), he was an autodidact who became a prominent member of the Munich Academy (1759) and the Berlin Academy (1764). He made significant discoveries in physics and mathematics. His most important philosophical works were *Neues Organon* ("New Organon, or Thoughts on the Investigation and Induction of Truth and the Distinction Between Error and Appearances," 1764) and *Anlage zur Architectonic* ("Plan of an Architectonic, or Theory of the Simple and Primary Elements in Philosophical and Mathematical Knowledge," 1771). Lambert attempted to revise metaphysics. Arguing against both German rationalism and British empiricism, he opted for a form of phenomenalism similar to that of Kant and Tetens. Like his two contemporaries, he believed that the mind contains a number of basic concepts and principles that make knowledge possible. The philosopher's task is twofold: first, these fundamental concepts and principles have to be analyzed; second, the truths of science have to be derived from them. In his own attempt at accomplishing this, Lambert tended more toward Leibniz than Locke.

M.K.

La Mettrie, Julien Offroy de (1707–51), French philosopher who was his generation's most notorious materialist, atheist, and hedonist. Raised in Brittany, he was trained at Leiden by Hermann Boerhaave, an iatromechanist, whose works he translated into French. As a Lockean sensationalist who read Gassendi and followed the Swiss physiologist Haller, La Mettrie took nature to be life's dynamic and ultimate principle. In 1745 he published *Natural History of the Soul*, which attacked Cartesian dualism and dispensed with God.

Drawing from Descartes's animal-machine, his masterpiece, *Man the Machine* (1747), argued that the organization of matter alone explains man's physical and intellectual faculties. Assimilating psychology to mechanistic physiology, La Mettrie integrated man into nature and proposed a materialistic monism. An Epicurean and a libertine, he denied any religious or rational morality in *Anti-Seneca* (1748) and instead accommodated human behavior to natural laws. Anticipating Sade's nihilism, his *Art of Enjoying Pleasures* and *Metaphysical Venus* (1751) eulogized physical passions. Helvétius, d'Holbach, Marx, Plekhanov, and Lenin all acknowledged a debt to his belief that "to write as a philosopher is to teach materialism."   J.-L.S.

Lange, Friedrich Albert (1828–75), German philosopher and social scientist. Born at Wald near Solingen, he became a university instructor at Bonn in 1851, professor of inductive logic at Zürich in 1870, and professor at Marburg in 1873, establishing neo-Kantian studies there. He published three books in 1865: *Die Arbeiterfrage* (*The Problem of the Worker*), *Die Grundlegung der mathematischen Psychologie* (*The Foundation of Mathematical Psychology*), and *J. S. Mills Ansichten über die sociale Frage und die angebliche Umwälzung der Socialwissenschaftlichen durch Carey* (*J. S. Mill's Views of the Social Question and Carey's Supposed Social-Scientific Revolution*). Lange's most important work, however, *Geschichte des Materialismus* (*History of Materialism*), was published in 1866. An expanded second edition in two volumes appeared in 1873–75 and in three later editions.

The *History of Materialism* is a rich, detailed study not only of the development of materialism but of then-recent work in physical theory, biological theory, and political economy; it includes a commentary on Kant's analysis of knowledge. Lange adopts a restricted positivistic approach to scientific interpretations of man and the natural world and a conventionalism in regard to scientific theory, and also encourages the projection of aesthetic interpretations of "the All" from "the standpoint of the ideal." Rejecting reductive materialism, Lange argues that a strict analysis of materialism leads to ineliminable idealist theoretical issues, and he adopts a form of materio-idealism. In his *Geschichte* are anticipations of instrumental fictionalism, pragmatism,

conventionalism, and psychological egoism. Following the skepticism of the scientists he discusses, Lange adopts an agnosticism about the ultimate constituents of actuality and a radical phenomenalism. His major work was much admired by Russell and significantly influenced the thought of Nietzsche.

History of Materialism predicted coming sociopolitical "earthquakes" because of the rise of science, the decline of religion, and the increasing tensions of "the social problem." *Die Arbeiterfrage* explores the impact of industrialization and technology on the "social problem" and predicts a coming social "struggle for survival" in terms already recognizable as Social Darwinism. Both theoretically and practically, Lange was a champion of workers and favored a form of democratic socialism. His study of J. S. Mill and the economist Henry Carey was a valuable contribution to social science and political economic theory.

See also JAMES-LANGE THEORY, NEO-KANTIANISM.   G.J.S.

language, artificial. See FORMAL LANGUAGE, PHILOSOPHY OF LANGUAGE.

language, natural. See FORMAL LANGUAGE, PHILOSOPHY OF LANGUAGE.

language, philosophy of. See PHILOSOPHY OF LANGUAGE.

language game. See WITTGENSTEIN.

language of thought. See MEANING, MENTALESE, PHILOSOPHY OF LANGUAGE.

Lao Tzu (sixth century B.C.), Chinese philosopher traditionally thought to be a contemporary of Confucius and the author of the *Tao Te Ching* ("Classic of *tao* and *te*"). Most contemporary scholars hold that "Lao Tzu" is a composite of legendary early sages, and that the *Tao Te Ching* is an anthology, a version of which existed no earlier than the third century B.C. The *Tao Te Ching* combines paradoxical mysticism with hardheaded political advice (Han Fei Tzu wrote a commentary on it) and a call to return to a primitive utopia, without the corrupting accoutrements of civilization, such as ritual (*li*), luxury items, and even writing. In its exaltation of spontaneous action and denigration of Confucian virtues such as *jen*, the text is reminiscent of Chuang Tzu, but it is distinctive both for its style (which is lapidary to the point of obscurity) and its political orientation. Translations of the *Tao Te Ching* are based on either the Wang Pi text or the recently discovered *Ma-wang-tui* text. **See also** NEO-TAO-ISM, TAOISM.   B.W.V.N.

La Peyrère, Isaac (1596–1676), French religious writer, a Calvinist of probable Marrano extraction and a Catholic convert whose messianic and anthropological work (*Men Before Adam*, 1656) scandalized Jews, Catholics, and Protestants alike. Anticipating both ecumenism and Zionism, *The Recall of the Jews* (1643) claims that, together, converted Jews and Christians will usher in universal redemption. A threefold "salvation history" undergirds La Peyrère's "Marrano theology": (1) election of the Jews; (2) their rejection and the election of the Christians; (3) the recall of the Jews.   J.-L.S.

Laplace, Pierre Simon de (1749–1827), French mathematician and astronomer who produced the definitive formulation of the classical theory of probability. He taught at various schools in Paris, including the École Militaire; one of his students was Napoleon, to whom he dedicated his work on probability.

According to Laplace, probabilities arise from our ignorance. The world is deterministic, so the probability of a possible event depends on our limited information about it rather than on the causal forces that determine whether it shall occur. Our chief means of calculating probabilities is the principle of insufficient reason, or the principle of indifference. It says that if there is no reason to believe that one of n mutually exclusive and jointly exhaustive possible cases will obtain rather than some other, so that the cases are equally possible, then the probability of each case is $1/n$. In addition, the probability of a possible event equivalent to a disjunction of cases is the number of cases favorable to the event divided by the total number of cases. For instance, the probability that the top card of a well-shuffled deck is a diamond is $13/52$. Laplace's chief work on probability is *Théorie analytique des probabilités* (*Analytic Theory of Probabilities*, 1812).

    See also PROBABILITY.   P.We.

La Ramée, Pierre. See RAMUS.

large numbers, law of. See BERNOULLI'S THEOREM.

latent content. See FREUD.

Latin American philosophy, the philosophy of Latin America, which is European in origin and constitutes a chapter in the history of Western philosophy. Pre-Columbian indigenous cultures had developed ideas about the world that have been interpreted by some scholars as philosophical, but there is no evidence that any of those ideas were incorporated into the philosophy later practiced in Latin America. It is difficult to characterize Latin American philosophy in a way applicable to all of its 500-year history. The most one can say is that, in contrast with European and Anglo-American philosophy, it has maintained a strong human and social interest, has been consistently affected by Scholastic and Catholic thought, and has significantly affected the social and political institutions in the region. Latin American philosophers tend to be active in the educational, political, and social lives of their countries and deeply concerned with their own cultural identity.

The history of philosophy in Latin America can be divided into four periods: colonial, independentist, positivist, and contemporary.

Colonial period (c.1550–c.1750). This period was dominated by the type of Scholasticism officially practiced in the Iberian peninsula. The texts studied were those of medieval Scholastics, primarily Aquinas and Duns Scotus, and of their Iberian commentators, Vitoria, Soto, Fonseca, and, above all, Suárez. The university curriculum was modeled on that of major Iberian universities (Salamanca, Alcalá, Coimbra), and instructors produced both systematic treatises and commentaries on classical, medieval, and contemporary texts. The philosophical concerns in the colonies were those prevalent in Spain and Portugal and centered on logical and metaphysical issues inherited from the Middle Ages and on political and legal questions raised by the discovery and colonization of America. Among the former were issues involving the logic of terms and propositions and the problems of universals and individuation; among the latter were questions concerning the rights of Indians and the relations of the natives with the conquerors.

The main philosophical center during the early colonial period was Mexico; Peru became important in the seventeenth century. Between 1700 and 1750 other centers developed, but by that time Scholasticism had begun to decline. The founding of the Royal and Pontifical University of Mexico in 1553 inaugurated Scholastic instruction in the New World. The first teacher of philosophy at the university was Alonso de la Vera Cruz (c.1504–84), an Augustinian and disciple of Soto. He composed several didactic treatises on logic, metaphysics, and science, including *Recognitio summularum* ("Introductory Logic," 1554), *Dialectica resolutio* ("Advanced Logic," 1554), and *Physica speculatio* ("Physics," 1557). He also wrote a theologico-legal work, the *Speculum conjugiorum* ("On Marriage," 1572), concerned with the status of precolonial Indian marriages. Alonso's works are eclectic and didactic and show the influence of Aristotle, Peter of Spain, and Vitoria in particular. Another important Scholastic figure in Mexico was the Dominican Tomás de Mercado (c.1530–75). He produced commentaries on the logical works of Peter of Spain and Aristotle and a treatise on international commerce, *Summa de tratos y contratos* ("On Contracts," 1569). His other sources are Porphyry and Aquinas. Perhaps the most important figure of the period was Antonio Rubio (1548–1615), author of the most celebrated Scholastic book written in the New World, *Logica mexicana* ("Mexican Logic," 1605). It underwent seven editions in Europe and became a logic textbook in Alcalá. Rubio's sources are Aristotle, Porphyry, and Aquinas, but he presents original treatments of several logical topics. Rubio also commented on several of Aristotle's other works.

In Peru, two authors merit mention. Juan Pérez Menacho (1565–1626) was a prolific writer, but only a moral treatise, *Theologia et moralis tractatus* ("Treatise on Theology and Morals"), and a commentary on Aquinas's *Summa theologiae* remain. The Chilean-born Franciscan, Alfonso Briceño (c.1587–1669), worked in Nicaragua and Venezuela, but the center of his activities was Lima. In contrast with the Aristotelian-Thomistic flavor of the philosophy of most of his contemporaries, Briceño was a Scotistic Augustinian. This is evident in *Celebriores controversias in primum sententiarum Scoti* ("On Scotus's First Book of the Sentences," 1638) and *Apologia de vita et doctrina Joannis Scotti* ("Apology for John Scotus," 1642).

Although Scholasticism dominated the intellectual life of colonial Latin America, some authors were also influenced by humanism. Among the most important in Mexico were Juan de Zumárraga (c.1468–1548); the celebrated defender of the Indians, Bartolomé de Las Casas (1474–1566); Carlos Sigüenza y Góngora (1645–1700); and Sor Juana Inés de La Cruz (1651–95). The last one is a famous poet, now considered a precursor of the feminist movement. In Peru, Nicolás de Olea (1635–1705) stands out. Most of these authors were trained in Scholasticism but incorporated the concerns and ideas of humanists into their work.

Independentist period (c.1750–c.1850). Just before and immediately after independence, leading Latin American intellectuals lost interest in Scholastic issues and became interested in social and political questions, although they did not completely abandon Scholastic sources. Indeed, the theories of natural law they inherited from Vitoria and Suárez played a significant role in forming their ideas. But they also absorbed non-Scholastic European authors. The rationalism of Descartes and other Continental philosophers, together with the empiricism of Locke, the social ideas of Rousseau, the ethical views of Bentham, the skepticism of Voltaire and other Encyclopedists, the political views of Condorcet and Montesquieu, the eclecticism of Cousin, and the ideology of Destutt de Tracy, all contributed to the development of liberal ideas that were a background to the independentist movement. Most of the intellectual leaders of this movement were men of action who used ideas for practical ends, and their views have limited theoretical value. They made reason a measure of legitimacy in social and governmental matters, and found the justification for revolutionary ideas in natural law. Moreover, they criticized authority; some, regarding religion as superstitious, opposed ecclesiastical power. These ideas paved the way for the later development of positivism.

The period begins with the weakening hold of Scholasticism on Latin American intellectuals and the growing influence of early modern philosophy, particularly Descartes. Among the first authors to turn to modern philosophy was Juan Benito Díaz de Gamarra y Dávalos (1745–83) in Mexico who wrote *Errores del entendimiento humano* ("Errors of Human Understanding," 1781) and *Academias filosóficas* ("Philosophical Academies," 1774). Also in Mexico was Francisco Javier Clavijero (1731–87), author of a book on physics and a general history of Mexico. In Brazil the turn away from Scholasticism took longer. One of the first authors to show the influence of modern philosophy was Francisco de Mont'Alverne (1784–1858) in *Compêndio de filosofia* (1883). These first departures from Scholasticism were followed by the more consistent efforts of those directly involved in the independentist movement. Among these were Simón Bolívar (1783–1830), leader of the rebellion against Spain in the Andean countries of South America, and the Mexicans Miguel Hidalgo y Costilla (1753–1811), José María Morelos y Pavón (1765–1815), and José Joaquín Fernández de Lizardi

(1776–1827). In Argentina, Mariano Moreno (1778–1811), Juan Crisóstomo Lafinur (d. 1823), and Diego Alcorta (d. 1808), among others, spread the liberal ideas that served as a background for independence.

Positivist period (c.1850–c.1910). During this time, positivism became not only the most popular philosophy in Latin America but also the official philosophy of some countries. After 1910, however, positivism declined drastically. Latin American positivism was eclectic, influenced by a variety of thinkers, including Comte, Spencer, and Haeckel. Positivists emphasized the explicative value of empirical science while rejecting metaphysics. According to them, all knowledge is based on experience rather than theoretical speculation, and its value lies in its practical applications. Their motto, preserved on the Brazilian flag, was "Order and Progress." This positivism left little room for freedom and values; the universe moved inexorably according to mechanistic laws.

Positivism was a natural extension of the ideas of the independentists. It was, in part, a response to the needs of the newly liberated countries of Latin America. After independence, the concerns of Latin American intellectuals shifted from political liberation to order, justice, and progress. The beginning of positivism can be traced to the time when Latin America, responding to these concerns, turned to the views of French socialists such as Saint-Simon and Fourier. The Argentinians Esteban Echevarría (1805–51) and Juan Bautista Alberdi (1812–84) were influenced by them. Echevarría's *Dogma socialista* ("Socialist Dogma," 1846) combines socialist ideas with eighteenth-century rationalism and literary Romanticism, and Alberdi follows suit, although he eventually turned toward Comte. Alberdi is, moreover, the first Latin American philosopher to worry about developing a philosophy adequate to the needs of Latin America. In *Ideas* (1842), he stated that philosophy in Latin America should be compatible with the economic, political, and social requirements of the region.

Another transitional thinker, influenced by both Scottish philosophy and British empiricism, was the Venezuelan Andrés Bello (1781–1865). A prolific writer, he is the most important Latin American philosopher of the nineteenth century. His *Filosofía del entendimiento* ("Philosophy of Understanding," 1881) reduces metaphysics to psychology. Bello also developed original ideas about language and history. After 1829, he worked in Chile, where his influence was strongly felt.

The generation of Latin American philosophers after Alberdi and Bello was mostly positivistic. Positivism's heyday was the second half of the nineteenth century, but two of its most distinguished advocates, the Argentinian José Ingenieros (1877–1925) and the Cuban Enrique José Varona (1849–1933), worked well into the twentieth century. Both modified positivism in important ways. Ingenieros left room for metaphysics, which, according to him, deals in the realm of the "yet-to-be-experienced." Among his most important books are *Hacia una moral sin dogmas* ("Toward a Morality without Dogmas," 1917), where the influence of Emerson is evident, *Principios de psicología* ("Principles of Psychology," 1911), where he adopts a reductionist approach to psychology, and *El hombre mediocre* ("The Mediocre Man," 1913), an inspirational book popular among Latin American youths. In *Conferencias filosóficas* ("Philosophical Lectures," 1880–88), Varona went beyond the mechanistic explanations of behavior common among positivists.

In Mexico the first and leading positivist was Gabino Barreda (1818–81), who reorganized Mexican education under President Juárez. An ardent follower of Comte, Barreda made positivism the basis of his educational reforms. He was followed by Justo Sierra (1848–1912), who turned toward Spencer and Darwin and away from Comte, criticizing Barreda's dogmatism.

Positivism was introduced in Brazil by Tobias Barreto (1839–89) and Silvio Romero (1851–1914) in Pernambuco, around 1869. In 1875 Benjamin Constant (1836–91) founded the Positivist Society in Rio de Janeiro. The two most influential exponents of positivism in the country were Miguel Lemos (1854–1916) and Raimundo Teixeira Mendes (1855–1927), both orthodox followers of Comte. Positivism was more than a technical philosophy in Brazil. Its ideas spread widely, as is evident from the inclusion of positivist ideas in the first republican constitution.

The most prominent Chilean positivists were José Victorino Lastarria (1817–88) and Valentín Letelier (1852–1919). More dogmatic adherents to the movement were the Lagarrigue brothers, Jorge (d. 1894), Juan Enrique (d. 1927), and Luis (d. 1953), who promoted positivism in Chile well after it had died everywhere else in Latin America.

Contemporary period (c.1910–present). Contemporary Latin American philosophy began with the demise of positivism. The first part of the period was dominated by thinkers who rebelled against positivism. The principal figures, called the Founders by Francisco Romero, were Alejandro Korn (1860–1936) in Argentina, Alejandro Octavio Deústua (1849–1945) in Peru, José Vasconcelos (1882–1959) and Antonio Caso (1883–1946) in Mexico, Enrique Molina (1871–1964) in Chile, Carlos Vaz Ferreira (1872–1958) in Uruguay, and Raimundo de Farias Brito (1862–1917) in Brazil. In spite of little evidence of interaction among these philosophers, their aims and concerns were similar. Trained as positivists, they became dissatisfied with positivism's dogmatic intransigence, mechanistic determinism, and emphasis on pragmatic values. Deústua mounted a detailed criticism of positivistic determinism in *Las ideas de orden y de libertad en la historia del pensamiento humano* ("The Ideas of Order and Freedom in the History of Human Thought," 1917–19). About the same time, Caso presented his view of man as a spiritual reality that surpasses nature in *La existencia como economía, como desinterés y como caridad* ("Existence as Economy, Disinterestedness, and Charity," 1916). Following in Caso's footsteps and inspired by Pythagoras and the Neoplatonists, Vasconcelos developed a metaphysical system with aesthetic roots in *El monismo estético* ("Aesthetic Monism," 1918).

An even earlier criticism of positivism is found in Vaz Ferreira's *Lógica viva* ("Living Logic," 1910), which contrasts the abstract, scientific logic favored by positivists with a logic of life based on experience, which captures reality's dynamic character. The earliest attempt at developing an alternative to positivism, however, is found in Farias Brito. Between 1895 and 1905 he published a trilogy, *Finalidade do mundo* ("The World's Goal"), in which he conceived the world as an intellectual activity which he identified with God's thought, and thus as essentially spiritual. The intellect unites and reflects reality but the will divides it.

Positivism was superseded by the Founders with the help of ideas imported first from France and later from Germany. The process began with the influence of Étienne Boutroux (1845–1921) and Bergson and of French vitalism and intuitionism, but it was cemented when Ortega y Gasset introduced into Latin America the thought of Scheler, Nicolai Hartmann, and other German philosophers during his visit to Argentina in 1916. The influence of Bergson was present in most of the founders, particularly

Molina, who in 1916 wrote *La filosofía de Bergson* ("The Philosophy of Bergson"). Korn was exceptional in turning to Kant in his search for an alternative to positivism. In *La libertad creadora* ("Creative Freedom," 1920–22), he defends a creative concept of freedom. In *Axiología* ("Axiology," 1930), his most important work, he defends a subjectivist position.

The impact of German philosophy, including Hegel, Marx, Schopenhauer, Nietzsche, and the neo-Kantians, and of Ortega's philosophical perspectivism and historicism, were strongly felt in the generation after the founders. The Mexican Samuel Ramos (1897–1959), the Argentinians Francisco Romero (1891–1962) and Carlos Astrada (1894–1970), the Brazilian Alceu Amoroso Lima (1893–1982), the Peruvian José Carlos Mariátegui (1895–1930), and others followed the Founders' course, attacking positivism and favoring, in many instances, a philosophical style that contrasted with its scientistic emphasis. The most important of these figures was Romero, whose *Theory of Man* (1952) developed a systematic philosophical anthropology in the context of a metaphysics of transcendence. Reality is arranged according to degrees of transcendence, the lowest of which is the physical and the highest the spiritual. The bases of Ramos's thought are found in Ortega as well as in Scheler and N. Hartmann. Ramos appropriated Ortega's perspectivism and set out to characterize the Mexican situation in *Profile of Man and Culture in Mexico* (1962). Some precedent existed for the interest in the culturally idiosyncratic in Vasconcelos's *Raza cósmica* ("Cosmic Race," 1925), but Ramos opened the doors to a philosophical awareness of Latin American culture that has been popular ever since. Ramos's most traditional work, *Hacia un nuevo humanismo* ("Toward a New Humanism," 1940), presents a philosophical anthropology of Orteguean inspiration.

Astrada studied in Germany and adopted existential and phenomenological ideas in *El juego existencial* ("The Existential Game," 1933), while criticizing Scheler's axiology. Later, he turned toward Hegel and Marx in *Existencialismo y crisis de la filosofía* ("Existentialism and the Crisis of Philosophy," 1963). Amoroso Lima worked in the Catholic tradition and his writings show the influence of Maritain. His *O espírito e o mundo* ("Spirit and World," 1936) and *Idade, sexo e tempo* ("Age, Sex, and Time," 1938) present a spiritual view of human beings, which he contrasted with Marxist and existentialist views. Mariátegui is the most distinguished representative of Marxism in Latin America. His *Siete ensayos de inter-pretación de la realidad peruana* ("Seven Essays on the Interpretation of Peruvian Reality," 1928) contains an important statement of social philosophy, in which he uses Marxist ideas freely to analyze the Peruvian sociopolitical situation.

In the late 1930s and 1940s, as a consequence of the political upheaval created by the Spanish Civil War, a substantial group of peninsular philosophers settled in Latin America. Among the most influential were Joaquín Xirau (1895–1946), Eduardo Nicol (b.1907), Luis Recaséns Siches (b.1903), Juan D. García Bacca (b.1901), and, perhaps most of all, José Gaos (1900–69). Gaos, like Caso, was a consummate teacher, inspiring many students. Apart from the European ideas they brought, these immigrants introduced methodologically more sophisticated ways of doing philosophy, including the practice of studying philosophical sources in the original languages. Moreover, they helped to promote Pan-American communication. The conception of *hispanidad* they had inherited from Unamuno and Ortega helped the process. Their influence was felt particularly by the generation born around 1910. With this generation, Latin American philosophy established itself as a professional and reputable discipline, and philosophical organizations, research centers, and journals sprang up. The core of this generation worked in the German tradition. Risieri Frondizi (Argentina, 1910–83), Eduardo García Máynez (Mexico, b.1908), Juan Llambías de Azevedo (Uruguay, 1907–72), and Miguel Reale (Brazil, b.1910) were all influenced by Scheler and N. Hartmann and concerned themselves with axiology and philosophical anthropology. Frondizi, who was also influenced by Anglo-American philosophy, defended a functional view of the self in *Substancia y función en el problema del yo* ("The Nature of the Self," 1952) and of value as a Gestalt quality in *Qué son los valores?* ("What is Value?" 1958). Apart from these thinkers, there were representatives of other traditions in this generation. Following Ramos, Leopoldo Zea (Mexico, b.1912) stimulated the study of the history of ideas in Mexico and initiated a controversy that still rages concerning the identity and possibility of a truly Latin American philosophy. Representing existentialism was Vicente Ferreira da Silva (Brazil, b.1916), who did not write much but presented a vigorous criticism of what he regarded as Hegelian and Marxist subjectivism in *Ensaios filosóficos* ("Philosophical Essays," 1948). Before he became interested in existentialism, he

had been interested in logic, publishing the first textbook of mathematical logic written in Latin America – *Elementos de lógica matemática* ("Elements of Mathematical Logic," 1940). A philosopher whose interest in mathematical logic moved him away from phenomenology is Francisco Miró Quesada (Peru, b.1918). He explored rationality and eventually the perspective of analytic philosophy.

Owing to the influence of Maritain, several members of this generation adopted a Neo-Thomistic or Scholastic approach. The main figures to do so were Oswaldo Robles (b.1904) in Mexico, Octavio Nicolás Derisi (b.1907) in Argentina, Alberto Wagner de Reyna (b.1915) in Peru, and Clarence Finlayson (1913–54) in Chile and Colombia. Even those authors who worked in this tradition addressed issues of axiology and philosophical anthropology. There was, therefore, considerable thematic unity in Latin American philosophy between 1940 and 1960. The overall orientation was not drastically different from the preceding period. The Founders used French vitalism against positivism, and the following generation, with Ortega's help, took over the process, incorporating German spiritualism and the new ideas introduced by phenomenology and existentialism to continue in a similar direction. As a result, the phenomenology of Scheler and N. Hartmann and the existentialism of Heidegger and Sartre dominated philosophy in Latin America between 1940 and 1960. To this must be added the renewed impetus of neo-Scholasticism. Few philosophers worked outside these philosophical currents, and those who did had no institutional power. Among these were sympathizers of philosophical analysis, and those who contributed to the continuing development of Marxism.

This situation has begun to change since 1960, substantially as a result of a renewed interest in Marxism, the progressive influence of analytic philosophy, and the development of a new philosophical current called the philosophy of liberation. Moreover, the question raised by Zea in the 1940s concerning the identity and possibility of a Latin American philosophy remains a focus of attention and controversy. And, more recently, there has been interest in such Continental philosophers as Foucault, Habermas, and Derrida, in neopragmatists like Rorty, and in feminist philosophy. Socialist thought is not new to Latin America. In this century, Emilio Frugoni (1880–1969) in Uruguay and Mariátegui in Peru, among others, adopted a Marxist perspective, although a heterodox one. But only in the last three decades has Marxism been taken seriously in Latin American academic circles. Indeed, until recently Marxism was a marginal philosophical movement in Latin America. The popularity of the Marxist perspective has made possible its increasing institutionalization. Among its most important thinkers are Adolfo Sánchez Vázquez (Spain, b.1915), Vicente Lombardo Toledano (b.1894) and Eli de Gortari (b.1918) in Mexico, and Caio Prado Júnior (1909–86) in Brazil.

In contrast to Marxism, philosophical analysis arrived late in Latin America and, owing to its technical and academic character, has not yet influenced more than a relatively small number of Latin American philosophers. Nonetheless, and thanks in part to its high theoretical caliber, analysis has become one of the most forceful philosophical currents in the region. The publication of journals with an analytic bent such as *Crítica* in Mexico, *Análisis Filosófico* in Argentina, and *Manuscrito* in Brazil, the foundation of the Sociedad Argentina de Análisis Filosófico (SADAF) in Argentina and the Sociedad Filosófica Iberoamericana (SOFIA) in Mexico, and the growth of analytic publications in high-profile journals of neutral philosophical orientation, such as *Revista Latinoamericana de Filosofía*, indicate that philosophical analysis is well established in Latin America. The main centers of analytic activity are Buenos Aires, Mexico City, and Campinas and São Paulo in Brazil. The interests of Latin American analysts center on questions of ethical and legal philosophy, the philosophy of science, and more recently cognitive science. Among its most important proponents are Genaro R. Carrió (b.1922), Gregorio Klimovsky (b.1922), and Tomás Moro Simpson (b.1929) in Argentina; Luis Villoro (Spain, b. 1922) in Mexico; Francisco Miró Quesada in Peru; Roberto Torretti (Chile, b.1930) in Puerto Rico; Mario Bunge (Argentina, b.1919), who works in Canada; and Héctor-Neri Castañeda (Guatemala, 1924–91).

The *philosophy of liberation* is an autochthonous Latin American movement that mixes an emphasis on Latin American intellectual independence with Catholic and Marxist ideas. The historicist perspective of Leopoldo Zea, the movement known as the *theology of liberation*, and some elements from the national-popular Peronist ideology prepared the ground for it. The movement started in the early 1970s with a group of Argentinian philosophers, who, owing to the military repression of 1976–83 in Argentina, went into exile in various countries of Latin America. This early diaspora created permanent splits in the movement and spread its ideas throughout the region. Although proponents of this viewpoint do not always agree on their goals, they share the notion of liberation as a fundamental concept: the liberation from the slavery imposed on Latin America by imported ideologies and the development of a genuinely autochthonous thought resulting from reflection on the Latin American reality. As such, their views are an extension of the thought of Ramos and others who earlier in the century initiated the discussion of the cultural identity of Latin America.   J.J.E.G.

lattice theory. See BOOLEAN ALGEBRA.

law, bridge. See REDUCTION.

law, natural. See NATURAL LAW.

law, philosophy of. See PHILOSOPHY OF LAW.

lawlike generalization, also called nomological (or nomic), a generalization that, unlike an *accidental generalization*, possesses nomic necessity or counterfactual force. Compare (1) 'All specimens of gold have a melting point of 1,063° C' with (2) 'All the rocks in my garden are sedimentary'. (2) may be true, but its generality is restricted to rocks in my garden. Its truth is accidental; it does not state what *must* be the case. (1) is true without restriction. If we write (1) as the conditional 'For any x and for any time t, if x is a specimen of gold subjected to a temperature of 1,063° C, then x will melt', we see that the generalization states what must be the case. (1) supports the hypothetical counterfactual assertion 'For any specimen of gold x and for any time t, if x were subjected to a temperature of 1,063° C, then x would melt', which means that we accept (1) as nomically necessary: it remains true even if no further specimens of gold are subjected to the required temperature. This is not true of (2), for we know that at some future time an igneous rock might appear in my garden. Statements like (2) are not lawlike; they do not possess the unrestricted necessity we require of lawlike statements. Ernest Nagel has claimed that a nomological statement must satisfy two other conditions: it must deductively entail or be deductively entailed by other laws, and its scope of prediction must exceed the known evidence for it. **See also CAUSAL LAW.**   R.E.B.

lawlike statement. See LAWLIKE GENERALIZATION.

law of double negation. See DOUBLE NEGATION.

law of eternal return. See COMPUTER THEORY.

law of identity. See IDENTITY.

law of large numbers. See BERNOULLI'S THEOREM.

law of nature. See NATURAL LAW, PHILOSOPHY OF SCIENCE.

law of succession. See CAUSAL LAW.

law of trichotomy. See CHOICE SEQUENCE, RELATION.

laws of thought, laws by which or in accordance with which valid thought proceeds, or that justify valid inference, or to which all valid deduction is reducible. Laws of thought are rules that apply without exception to any subject matter of thought, etc.; sometimes they are said to be the object of logic. The term, rarely used in exactly the same sense by different authors, has long been associated with three equally ambiguous expressions: the law of identity (ID), the law of contradiction (or non-contradiction; NC), and the law of excluded middle (EM).

Sometimes these three expressions are taken as propositions of formal ontology having the widest possible subject matter, propositions that apply to entities per se: (ID) every thing is (i.e., is identical to) itself; (NC) no thing having a given quality also has the negative of that quality (e.g., no even number is non-even); (EM) every thing either has a given quality or has the negative of that quality (e.g., every number is either even or non-even). Equally common in older works is use of these expressions for principles of metalogic about propositions: (ID) every proposition implies itself; (NC) no proposition is both true and false; (EM) every proposition is either true or false. Beginning in the middle to late 1800s these expressions have been used to denote propositions of Boolean Algebra about classes: (ID) every class includes itself; (NC) every class is such that its intersection ("product") with its own complement is the null class; (EM) every class is such that its union ("sum") with its own complement is the universal class. More recently the last two of the three expressions have been used in connection with the classical propositional logic and with the so-called *prototetic* or quantified propositional logic; in both cases the law of non-contradiction involves the negation of the conjunction ('and')

of something with its own negation and the law of excluded middle involves the disjunction ('or') of something with its own negation. In the case of propositional logic the "something" is a schematic letter serving as a place-holder, whereas in the case of prototetic logic the "something" is a genuine variable. The expressions 'law of non-contradiction' and 'law of excluded middle' are also used for semantic principles of model theory concerning sentences and interpretations: (NC) under no interpretation is a given sentence both true and false; (EM) under any interpretation, a given sentence is either true or false.

The expressions mentioned above all have been used in many other ways. Many other propositions have also been mentioned as laws of thought, including the *dictum de omni et nullo* attributed to Aristotle, the substitutivity of identicals (or equals) attributed to Euclid, the so-called identity of indiscernibles attributed to Leibniz, and other "logical truths." The expression "laws of thought" gained added prominence through its use by Boole (1815–64) to denote theorems of his "algebra of logic"; in fact, he named his second logic book *An Investigation of the Laws of Thought* (1854). Modern logicians, in almost unanimous disagreement with Boole, take this expression to be a misnomer; none of the above propositions classed under 'laws of thought' are explicitly about thought per se, a mental phenomenon studied by psychology, nor do they involve explicit reference to a thinker or knower as would be the case in pragmatics or in epistemology. The distinction between psychology (as a study of mental phenomena) and logic (as a study of valid inference) is widely accepted.

See also CONVENTIONALISM, DICTUM DE OMNI ET NULLO, PHILOSOPHY OF LOGIC, SET THEORY.   J.Cor.

leap of faith. See KIERKEGAARD.

least squares method. See REGRESSION ANALYSIS.

Lebensphilosophie, German term, translated as 'philosophy of life', that became current in a variety of popular and philosophical inflections during the second half of the nineteenth century. Such philosophers as Dilthey and Eucken (1846–1926) frequently applied it to a general philosophical approach or attitude that distinguished itself, on the one hand, from the construction of comprehensive systems by Hegel and his followers and, on the other, from the tendency of empiricism and early positivism to reduce human experience to epistemological questions about sensations or impressions. Rather, a *Lebensphilosophie* should begin from a recognition of the variety and complexity of concrete and already meaningful human experience as it is "lived"; it should acknowledge that all human beings, including the philosopher, are always immersed in historical processes and forms of organization; and it should seek to understand, describe, and sometimes even alter these and their various patterns of interrelation without abstraction or reduction. Such "philosophies of life" as those of Dilthey and Eucken provided much of the philosophical background for the conception of the social sciences as interpretive rather than explanatory disciplines. They also anticipated some central ideas of phenomenology, in particular the notion of the Life-World in Husserl, and certain closely related themes in Heidegger's version of existentialism. **See also** DILTHEY, HUSSERL, VERSTEHEN.   J.P.Su.

Lebenswelt. See HUSSERL.

legal disability. See HOHFELD.

legal duty. See HOHFELD.

legal ethics. See ETHICS.

legal formalism. See JURISPRUDENCE.

legal immunity. See HOHFELD.

Legalism, Chinese. See CHINESE LEGALISM.

legal liability. See HOHFELD.

legal moralism, the view (defended in this century by, e.g., Lord Patrick Devlin) that law may properly be used to enforce morality, including notably "sexual morality." Contemporary critics of the view (e.g., Hart) expand on the argument of Mill that law should only be used to prevent harm to others. **See also** MILL, J. S.; PHILOSOPHY OF LAW; POLITICAL PHILOSOPHY.   P.S.

legal no-right. See HOHFELD.

legal positivism, a theory about the nature of law, commonly thought to be characterized by two major tenets: (1) that there is no necessary connection between law and morality; and (2) that legal validity is determined ultimately by reference to certain basic social facts, e.g., the com-

mand of the sovereign (John Austin), the *Grundnorm* (Hans Kelsen), or the rule of recognition (Hart). These different descriptions of the basic law-determining facts lead to different claims about the normative character of law, with classical positivists (e.g., John Austin) insisting that law is essentially coercive, and modern positivists (e.g., Hans Kelsen) maintaining that it is normative. The traditional opponent of the legal positivist is the natural law theorist, who holds that no sharp distinction can be drawn between law and morality, thus challenging positivism's first tenet. Whether that tenet follows from positivism's second tenet is a question of current interest and leads inevitably to the classical question of political theory: Under what conditions might legal obligations, even if determined by social facts, create genuine political obligations (e.g., the obligation to obey the law)? **See also** JURISPRUDENCE, PHILOSOPHY OF LAW.   P.S.

legal power. See HOHFELD.

legal principle. See DWORKIN.

legal privilege. See HOHFELD.

legal realism, a theory in philosophy of law or jurisprudence broadly characterized by the claim that the nature of law is better understood by observing what courts and citizens actually do than by analyzing stated legal rules and legal concepts. The theory is also associated with the thoughts that legal rules are disguised predictions of what courts will do, and that only the actual decisions of courts constitute law.

There are two important traditions of legal realism, in Scandinavia and in the United States. Both began in the early part of the century, and both focus on the reality (hence the name 'legal realism') of the actual legal system, rather than on law's official image of itself. The Scandinavian tradition is more theoretical and presents its views as philosophical accounts of the normativity of law based on skeptical methodology – the normative force of law consists in nothing but the feelings of citizens or officials or both about or their beliefs in that normative force. The older, U.S. tradition is more empirical or sociological or instrumentalist, focusing on how legislation is actually enacted, how rules are actually applied, how courts' decisions are actually taken, and so forth. U.S. legal realism in its contemporary form is known as *critical legal studies*. Its argumentation is both empirical (law as experienced to be and as being oppressive by gender, race, and class) and theoretical (law as essentially indeterminate, or interpretative – properties that prime law for its role in political manipulation).

See also CRITICAL LEGAL STUDIES, JURISPRUDENCE, LEGAL POSITIVISM, PHILOSOPHY OF LAW.   R.A.Sh.

legal right. See HOHFELD, RIGHTS.

legal rule. See DWORKIN.

legisign. See PEIRCE.

Leibniz, Gottfried Wilhelm (1646–1716), German rationalist philosopher who made seminal contributions in geology, linguistics, historiography, mathematics, and physics, as well as philosophy. He was born in Leipzig and died in Hanover. Trained in the law, he earned a living as a councilor, diplomat, librarian, and historian, primarily in the court of Hanover. His contributions in mathematics, physics, and philosophy were known and appreciated among his educated contemporaries in virtue of his publication in Europe's leading scholarly journals and his vast correspondence with intellectuals in a variety of fields. He was best known in his lifetime for his contributions to mathematics, especially to the development of the calculus, where a debate raged over whether Newton or Leibniz should be credited with priority for its discovery. Current scholarly opinion seems to have settled on this: each discovered the basic foundations of the calculus independently; Newton's discovery preceded that of Leibniz; Leibniz's publication of the basic theory of the calculus preceded that of Newton.

Leibniz's contributions to philosophy were known to his contemporaries through articles published in learned journals, correspondence, and one book published in his lifetime, the *Theodicy* (1710). He wrote a book-length study of Locke's philosophy, *New Essays on Human Understanding*, but decided not to publish it when he learned of Locke's death. Examination of Leibniz's papers after his own death revealed that what he published during his lifetime was but the tip of the iceberg.

Perhaps the most complete formulation of Leibniz's mature metaphysics occurs in his correspondence (1698–1706) with Burcher De Volder, a professor of philosophy at the University of Leyden. Leibniz therein formulated his basic ontological thesis:

Considering matters accurately, it must be said that there is nothing in things except simple substances, and, in them, nothing but perception and appetite. Moreover, matter and motion are not so much substances or things as they are the phenomena of percipient beings, the reality of which is located in the harmony of each percipient with itself (with respect to different times) and with other percipients.

In this passage Leibniz asserts that the basic individuals of an acceptable ontology are all *monads,* i.e., immaterial entities lacking spatial parts, whose basic properties are a function of their perceptions and appetites. He held that each monad perceives all the other monads with varying degrees of clarity, except for God, who perceives all monads with utter clarity. Leibniz's main theses concerning causality among the created monads are these: God creates, conserves, and concurs in the actions of each created monad. Each state of a created monad is a causal consequence of its preceding state, except for its state at creation and any of its states due to miraculous divine causality. Intrasubstantial causality is the rule with respect to created monads, which are precluded from intersubstantial causality, a mode of operation of which God alone is capable.

Leibniz was aware that elements of this monadology may seem counterintuitive, that, e.g., there appear to be extended entities composed of parts, existing in space and time, causally interacting with each other. In the second sentence of the quoted passage Leibniz set out some of the ingredients of his theory of the *preestablished harmony,* one point of which is to save those appearances that are sufficiently well-founded to deserve saving. In the case of material objects, Leibniz formulated a version of phenomenalism, based on harmony among the perceptions of the monads. In the case of apparent intersubstantial causal relations among created monads, Leibniz proposed an analysis according to which the underlying reality is an increase in the clarity of relevant perceptions of the apparent causal agent, combined with a corresponding decrease in the clarity of the relevant perceptions of the apparent patient.

Leibniz treated material objects and intersubstantial causal relations among created entities as well-founded phenomena. By contrast, he treated space and time as ideal entities. Leibniz's mature metaphysics includes a threefold classification of entities that must be accorded some degree of reality: ideal entities, well-founded phenomena, and actual existents, i.e., the monads with their perceptions and appetites. In the passage quoted above Leibniz set out to distinguish the actual entities, the monads, from material entities, which he regarded as well-founded phenomena. In the following passage from another letter to De Volder he formulated the distinction between actual and ideal entities:

> In actual entities there is nothing but discrete quantity, namely, the multitude of monads, i.e., simple substances. . . . But continuous quantity is something ideal, which pertains to possibles, and to actuals, insofar as they are possible. Indeed, a continuum involves indeterminate parts, whereas, by contrast, there is nothing indefinite in actual entities, in which every division that can be made, is made. Actual things are composed in the manner that a number is composed of unities, ideal things are composed in the manner that a number is composed of fractions. The parts are actual in the real whole, but not in the ideal. By confusing ideal things with real substances when we seek actual parts in the order of possibles and indeterminate parts in the aggregate of actual things, we entangle ourselves in the labyrinth of the continuum and in inexplicable contradictions.

The labyrinth of the continuum was one of two labyrinths that, according to Leibniz, vex the philosophical mind. His views about the proper course to take in unraveling the labyrinth of the continuum are one source of his monadology. Ultimately, he concluded that whatever may be infinitely divided without reaching indivisible entities is not something that belongs in the basic ontological category. His investigations of the nature of individuation and identity over time provided premises from which he concluded that only indivisible entities are ultimately real, and that an individual persists over time only if its subsequent states are causal consequences of its preceding states. In refining the metaphysical insights that yielded the monadology, Leibniz formulated and defended various important metaphysical theses, e.g.: the *identity of indiscernibles* – that individual substances differ with respect to their intrinsic, non-relational properties; and the doctrine of *minute perceptions* – that each created substance has some perceptions of which it lacks awareness.

In the process of providing what he took to be an acceptable account of well-founded phenom-

ena, Leibniz formulated various theses counter to the then prevailing Cartesian orthodoxy, concerning the nature of material objects. In particular, Leibniz argued that a correct application of Galileo's discoveries concerning acceleration of freely falling bodies of the phenomena of impact indicates that force is not to be identified with quantity of motion, i.e., mass times velocity, as Descartes held, but is to be measured by mass times the square of the velocity. Moreover, Leibniz argued that it is force, measured as mass times the square of the velocity, that is conserved in nature, not quantity of motion. From these results Leibniz drew some important metaphysical conclusions. He argued that force, unlike quantity of motion, cannot be reduced to a conjunction of modifications of extension. But force is a central property of material objects. Hence, he concluded that Descartes was mistaken in attempting to reduce matter to extension and its modifications. Leibniz concluded that each material substance must have a substantial form that accounts for its active force. These conclusions have to do with entities that Leibniz viewed as phenomenal. He drew analogous conclusions concerning the entities he regarded as ultimately real, i.e., the monads. Thus, although Leibniz held that each monad is absolutely simple, i.e., without parts, he also held that the matter–form distinction has an application to each created monad. In a letter to De Volder he wrote:

> Therefore, I distinguish (1) the primitive entelechy or soul, (2) primary matter, i.e., primitive passive power, (3) monads completed from these two, (4) mass, i.e., second matter . . . in which innumerable subordinate monads come together, (5) the animal, i.e., corporeal substance, which a dominating monad makes into one machine.

The second labyrinth vexing the philosophical mind, according to Leibniz, is the labyrinth of freedom. It is fair to say that for Leibniz the labyrinth of freedom is fundamentally a matter of how it is possible that some states of affairs obtain contingently, i.e., how it is possible that some propositions are true that might have been false. There are two distinct sources of the problem of contingency in Leibniz's philosophy, one theological, and the other metaphysical. Each source may be grasped by considering an argument that appears to have premises to which Leibniz was predisposed and the conclusion that every state of affairs that obtains, obtains necessarily, and hence that there are no contingent propositions.

The metaphysical argument is centered on some of Leibniz's theses about the nature of truth. He held that the truth-value of all propositions is settled once truth-values have been assigned to the elementary propositions, i.e., those expressed by sentences in subject-predicate form. And he held that a sentence in subject-predicate form expresses a true proposition if and only if the concept of its predicate is included in the concept of its subject. But this makes it sound as if Leibniz were committed to the view that an elementary proposition is true if and only if it is conceptually true, from which it seems to follow that an elementary proposition is true if and only if it is necessarily true. Leibniz's views concerning the relation of the truth-value of non-elementary propositions to the truth-value of elementary propositions, then, seem to entail that there are no contingent propositions. He rejected this conclusion in virtue of rejecting the thesis that if an elementary proposition is conceptually true then it is necessarily true. The materials for his rejection of this thesis are located in theses connected with his program for a universal science (*scientia universalis*). This program had two parts: a universal notation (*characteristica universalis*), whose purpose was to provide a method for recording scientific facts as perspicuous as algebraic notation, and a formal system of reasoning (*calculus ratiocinator*) for reasoning about the facts recorded. Supporting Leibniz's belief in the possibility and utility of the *characteristica universalis* and the *calculus ratiocinator* is his thesis that all concepts arise from simple primitive concepts via concept conjunction and concept complementation. In virtue of this thesis, he held that all concepts may be analyzed into their simple, primitive components, with this proviso: in some cases there is no finite analysis of a concept into its primitive components; but there is an analysis that converges on the primitive components without ever reaching them. This is the *doctrine of infinite analysis,* which Leibniz applied to ward off the threat to contingency apparently posed by his account of truth. He held that an elementary proposition is necessarily true if and only if there is a finite analysis that reveals that its predicate concept is included in its subject concept. By contrast, an elementary proposition is contingently true if and only if there is no such finite analysis, but there is an analysis of its predicate concept that converges on a component of its subject concept.

The theological argument may be put this way. There would be no world were God not to choose to create a world. As with every choice, as,

indeed, with every state of affairs that obtains, there must be a sufficient reason for that choice, for the obtaining of that state of affairs – this is what the *principle of sufficient reason* amounts to, according to Leibniz. The reason for God's choice of a world to create must be located in God's power and his moral character. But God is all-powerful and morally perfect, both of which attributes he has of necessity. Hence, of necessity, God chose to create the best possible world. Whatever possible world is the best possible world, is so of necessity. Hence, whatever possible world is actual, is so of necessity. A possible world is defined with respect to the states of affairs that obtain in it. Hence, whatever states of affairs obtain, do so of necessity. Therefore, there are no contingent propositions.

Leibniz's options here were limited. He was committed to the thesis that the principle of sufficient reason, when applied to God's choice of a world to create, given God's attributes, yields the conclusion that this is the best possible world – a fundamental component of his solution to the problem of evil. He considered two ways of avoiding the conclusion of the argument noted above. The first consists in claiming that although God is metaphysically perfect of necessity, i.e., has every simple, positive perfection of necessity, and although God is morally perfect, nonetheless he is not morally perfect of necessity, but rather by choice. The second consists in denying that whatever possible world is the best, is so of necessity, relying on the idea that the claim that a given possible world is the best involves a comparison with infinitely many other possible worlds, and hence, if true, is only contingently true. Once again the doctrine of infinite analysis served as the centerpiece of Leibniz's efforts to establish that, contrary to appearances, his views do not lead to necessitarianism, i.e., to the thesis that there is no genuine contingency.

Much of Leibniz's work in philosophical theology had as a central motivation an effort to formulate a sound philosophical and theological basis for various church reunion projects – especially reunion between Lutherans and Calvinists on the Protestant side, and ultimately, reunion between Protestants and Catholics. He thought that most of the classical arguments for the existence of God, if formulated with care, i.e., in the way in which Leibniz formulated them, succeeded in proving what they set out to prove. For example, Leibniz thought that Descartes's version of the ontological argument established the existence of a perfect being, with one crucial proviso: that an absolutely perfect being is possible.

Leibniz believed that none of his predecessors had established this premise, so he set out to do so. The basic idea of his purported proof is this. A perfection is a simple, positive property. Hence, there can be no demonstration that there is a formal inconsistency in asserting that various collections of them are instantiated by the same being. But if there is no such demonstration, then it is possible that something has them all. Hence, a perfect being is possible.

Leibniz did not consider in detail many of the fundamental epistemological issues that so moved Descartes and the British empiricists. Nonetheless, Leibniz made significant contributions to the theory of knowledge. His account of our knowledge of contingent truths is much like what we would expect of an empiricist's epistemology. He claimed that our knowledge of particular contingent truths has its basis in sense perception. He argued that simple enumerative induction cannot account for all our knowledge of universal contingent truths; it must be supplemented by what he called the a priori conjectural method, a precursor of the hypothetico-deductive method. He made contributions to developing a formal theory of probability, which he regarded as essential for an adequate account of our knowledge of contingent truths.

Leibniz's rationalism is evident in his account of our a priori knowledge, which for him amounted to our knowledge of necessary truths. Leibniz thought that Locke's empiricism did not provide an acceptable account of a priori knowledge, because it attempted to locate all the materials of justification as deriving from sensory experience, thus overlooking what Leibniz took to be the primary source of our a priori knowledge, i.e., what is innate in the mind. He summarized his debate with Locke on these matters thus:

> Our differences are on matters of some importance. It is a matter of knowing if the soul in itself is entirely empty like a writing tablet on which nothing has as yet been written (*tabula rasa*), ... and if everything inscribed there comes solely from the senses and experience, or if the soul contains originally the sources of various concepts and doctrines that external objects merely reveal on occasion.

The idea that some concepts and doctrines are innate in the mind is central not only to Leibniz's theory of knowledge, but also to his metaphysics, because he held that the most basic metaphysical concepts, e.g., the concepts of the self, substance, and causation, are innate.

Leibniz utilized the ideas behind the *characteristica universalis* in order to formulate a system of formal logic that is a genuine alternative to Aristotelian syllogistic logic and to contemporary quantification theory. Assuming that propositions are, in some fashion, composed of concepts and that all composite concepts are, in some fashion, composed of primitive simple concepts, Leibniz formulated a logic based on the idea of assigning numbers to concepts according to certain rules. The entire program turns on his concept containment account of truth previously mentioned. In connection with the metatheory of this logic Leibniz formulated the principle: *"eadem sunt quorum unum alteri substitui potest salva veritate"* ("Those things are the same of which one may be substituted for the other preserving truth-value"). The proper interpretation of this principle turns in part on exactly what "things" he had in mind. It is likely that he intended to formulate a criterion of concept identity. Hence, it is likely that this principle is distinct from the identity of indiscernibles, previously mentioned, and also from what has come to be called *Leibniz's law,* i.e., the thesis that if x and y are the same individual then whatever is true of x is true of y and vice versa.

The account outlined above concentrates on Leibniz's mature views in metaphysics, epistemology, and logic. The evolution of his thought in these areas is worthy of close study, which cannot be brought to a definitive state until all of his philosophical work has been published in the edition of the Akademie der Wissenschaften in Berlin.

See also DESCARTES, IDENTITY OF INDISCERNIBLES, LOCKE, POSSIBLE WORLDS, RATIONALISM, SPINOZA.   R.C.Sl.

Leibniz's law. See IDENTITY, LEIBNIZ.

lekton (Greek, 'what can be said'), a Stoic term sometimes translated as 'the meaning of an utterance'. *Lekta* differ from utterances in being what utterances *signify:* they are said to be what the Greek grasps and the non-Greek speaker does not when Greek is spoken. Moreover, *lekta* are incorporeal, which for the Stoics means they do not, strictly speaking, exist, but only "subsist," and so cannot act or be acted upon. They constitute the content of our mental states: they are what we assent to and endeavor toward and they "correspond" to the presentations given to rational animals. The Stoics acknowledged *lekta* for predicates as well as for sentences (including questions, oaths, and imperatives); *axiomata* or propositions are *lekta* that can be assented to and may be true or false (although being essentially tensed, their truth-values may change). The Stoics' theory of reference suggests that they also acknowledged singular propositions, which "perish" when the referent ceases to exist. **See also** PHILOSOPHY OF LANGUAGE, PROPOSITION, STOICISM.   V.C.

lemmata. See COMMENTARIES ON PLATO.

Lenin, Vladimir Ilich (1870–1924), Russian political leader and Marxist theorist, a principal creator of Soviet dialectical materialism. In *Materialism and Empirio-Criticism* (1909), he attacked Russian contemporaries who sought to interpret Marx's philosophy in the spirit of the phenomenalistic positivism of Avenarius and Mach. Rejecting their position as idealist, Lenin argues that matter is not a construct from sensations but an objective reality independent of consciousness; because our sensations directly copy this reality, objective truth is possible. The dialectical dimension of Lenin's outlook is best elaborated in his posthumous *Philosophical Notebooks* (written 1914–16), a collection of reading notes and fragments in which he gives close attention to the Hegelian dialectic and displays warm sympathy toward it, though he argues that the dialectic should be interpreted materialistically rather than idealistically. Some of Lenin's most original theorizing, presented in *Imperialism as the Highest Stage of Capitalism* (1916) and *State and Revolution* (1918), is devoted to analyzing the connection between monopoly capitalism and imperialism and to describing the coming violent replacement of bourgeois rule by, first, the "dictatorship of the proletariat" and, later, stateless communism. Lenin regarded all philosophy as a partisan weapon in the class struggle, and he wielded his own philosophy polemically in the interests of Communist revolution.

As a result of the victory of the Bolsheviks in November 1917, Lenin's ideas were enshrined as the cornerstone of Soviet intellectual culture and were considered above criticism until the advent of *glasnost* in the late 1980s. With the end of Communist rule following the dissolution of the Soviet Union in 1991, his influence declined precipitously.

See also MARXISM, RUSSIAN PHILOSOPHY.
                                                      J.P.Sc.

Leopold, Friedrich. See NOVALIS.

Lequier, Jules (1814–62), French philosopher, educated in Paris, whose works were not published in his lifetime. He influenced Renouvier, who regarded Lequier as his "master in philosophy." Through Renouvier, he came to the attention of James, who called Lequier a "philosopher of genius." Central to Lequier's philosophy is the idea of freedom understood as the power to "create," or add novelty to the world. Such freedom involves an element of arbitrariness and is incompatible with determinism. Anticipating James, Lequier argued that determinism, consistently affirmed, leads to skepticism about truth and values. Though a devout Roman Catholic, his theological views were unorthodox for his time. God cannot know future free actions until they occur and therefore cannot be wholly immutable and eternal. Lequier's views anticipate in striking ways some views of James, Bergson, Alexander, and Peirce, and the process philosophies and process theologies of Whitehead and Hartshorne.   R.H.K.

Leroux, Pierre (1797–1871), French philosopher reputed to have introduced the word *socialisme* in France (c.1834). He claimed to be the first to use *solidarité* as a sociological concept (in his memoirs, *La Grève de Samarez* [*The Beach at Samarez*], 1863).

The son of a Parisian café owner, Leroux centered his life work on journalism, both as a printer (patenting an advanced procedure for typesetting) and as founder of a number of significant serial publications. The *Encyclopédie Nouvelle* (*New Encyclopedia*, 1833–48, incomplete), which he launched with Jean Reynaud (1806–63), was conceived and written in the spirit of Diderot's magnum opus. It aspired to be the platform for republican and democratic thought during the July Monarchy (1830–48). The reformer's influence on contemporaries such as Hugo, Belinsky, J. Michelet, and Heine was considerable.

Leroux fervently believed in Progress, unlimited and divinely inspired. This doctrine he took to be eighteenth-century France's particular contribution to the Enlightenment. Progress must make its way between twin perils: the "follies of illuminism" or "foolish spiritualism" and the "abject orgies of materialism." Accordingly, Leroux blamed Condillac for having "drawn up the code of materialism" by excluding an innate Subject from his sensationalism ("Condillac," *Encyclopédie Nouvelle*). Cousin's eclecticism, state doctrine under the July Monarchy and synonym for immobility ("Philosophy requires no further development; it is complete as is," Leroux wrote sarcastically in 1838, echoing Cousin), was a constant target of his polemics. Having abandoned traditional Christian beliefs, Leroux viewed immortality as an infinite succession of rebirths on earth, our sense of personal identity being preserved throughout by Platonic "reminiscences" (*De l'Humanité* [*Concerning Humanity*], 1840).

See also CONDILLAC, COUSIN, ENLIGHTENMENT.   D.A.G.

Leśniewski, Stanisław (1886–1939), Polish philosopher-logician, cofounder, with Łukasiewicz and Kotarbiński, of the Warsaw Center of Logical Research. He perfected the logical reconstruction of classical mathematics by Frege, Schröder, Whitehead, and Russell in his synthesis of mathematical with modernized Aristotelian logic. A pioneer in scientific semantics whose insights inspired Tarski, Leśniewski distinguished genuine antinomies of belief, in theories intended as true mathematical sciences, from mere formal inconsistencies in uninterpreted calculi. Like Frege an acute critic of formalism, he sought to perfect *one* comprehensive, logically true instrument of scientific investigation. Demonstrably consistent, relative to classical elementary logic, and distinguished by its philosophical motivation and logical economy, his system integrates his central achievements. Other contributions include his ideographic notation, his method of natural deduction from suppositions and his demonstrations of inconsistency of other systems, even Frege's revised foundations of arithmetic. Fundamental were (1) his 1913 refutation of Twardowski's Platonistic theory of abstraction, which motivated his "constructive nominalism"; and (2) his deep analyses of Russell's paradox, which led him to distinguish *distributive* from *collective* predication and (as generalized to subsume Grelling and Nelson's paradox of self-reference) *logical* from *semantic* paradoxes, and so (years before Ramsey and Gödel) to differentiate, not just the correlatives object language and metalanguage, but *any* such correlative linguistic stages, and thus to relativize semantic concepts to successive hierarchical strata in metalinguistic stratification.

His system of logic and foundations of mathematics comprise a hierarchy of three axiomatic deductive theories: prototethic, ontology, and mereology. Each can be variously based on just one axiom introducing a single undefined term. His protetheses are basic to *any* further theory. Ontology, applying them, complements protothetic to form his logic. Leśniewski's ontology develops his logic of predication, beginning (e.g.)

with singular predication characterizing the individual so-and-so as being one (of the one or more) such-and-such, without needing class-abstraction operators, dispensable here as in Russell's "no-class theory of classes." But this, his logic of nouns, nominal or predicational functions, etc., synthesizing formulations by Aristotle, Leibniz, Boole, Schröder, and Whitehead, also represents a universal theory of being and beings, beginning with related individuals and their characteristics, kinds, or classes *distributively* understood to include individuals as singletons or "one-member classes."

Leśniewski's directives of definition and logical grammar for his systems of protothetic and ontology provide for the unbounded hierarchies of "open," functional expressions. Systematic conventions of contextual determinacy, exploiting dependence of meaning on context, permit unequivocal use of the same *forms* of expression to bring out systematic analogies between homonyms as analogues in Aristotle's and Russell's sense, *systematically* ambiguous, differing in semantic category and hence significance. Simple distinctions of semantic category within the object language of the system itself, together with the metalinguistic stratification to relativize semantic concepts, prevent logical and semantic paradoxes as effectively as Russell's ramified theory of types.

Leśniewski's system of logic, though expressively rich enough to permit Platonist interpretation in terms of universals, is yet "metaphysically neutral" in being free from ontic commitments. It neither postulates, presupposes, nor implies existence of either individuals or abstractions, but relies instead on equivalences without existential import that merely introduce and explicate new terms. In his "nominalist" construction of the endless Platonic ladder of abstraction, logical principles can be elevated step by step, from any level to the next, by definitions making abstractions eliminable, translatable by definition into generalizations characterizing related individuals. In this sense it is "constructively nominalist," as a developing language always open to introduction of new terms and categories, without appeal to "convenient fictions."

Leśniewski's system, completely designed by 1922, was logically and chronologically in advance of Russell's 1925 revision of *Principia Mathematica* to accommodate Ramsey's simplification of Russell's theory of types. Yet Leśniewski's premature death, the ensuing disruption of war, which destroyed his manuscripts and dispersed survivors such as Sobociński and Lejewski, and the relative inaccessibility of publications delayed by Leśniewski's own perfectionism have retarded understanding of his work.

See also POLISH LOGIC.   E.C.L.

Lessing, Gotthold Ephraim (1729–81), German philosopher, critic, and literary figure whose philosophical and theological work aimed to replace the so-called possession of truth by a search for truth through public debate. The son of a Protestant minister, he studied theology but gave it up to take part in the literary debate between Gottsched and the Swiss Bodmer and Breitinger, which dealt with French classicism (Boileau) and English influences (Shakespeare for theater and Milton for poetry). His literary criticism (*Briefe, die neueste Literatur betreffend* ["Letters on the New Literature"], 1759–65), his own dramatic works, and his theological-philosophical reflections were united in his conception of a practical *Aufklärung*, which opposed all philosophical or religious dogmatism. Lessing's creation and direction of the National German Theater of Hamburg (1767–70) helped to form a sense of German national identity.

In 1750 Lessing published *Thoughts on the Moravian Brothers*, which contrasted religion as lived by this pietist community with the ecclesiastical institution. In 1753–54 he wrote a series of "rehabilitations" (*Rettugen*) to show that the opposition between dogmas and heresies, between "truth" and "error," was incompatible with living religious thought. This position had the seeds of a historical conception of religion that Lessing developed during his last years. In 1754 he again attempted a deductive formulation, inspired by Spinoza, of the fundamental truths of Christianity. Lessing rejected this rationalism, as substituting a dogma of reason for one of religion. To provoke public debate on the issue, be published H. S. Reimarus's *Fragments of an Anonymous Author* (1774–78), which the Protestant hierarchy considered atheistic. The relativism and soft deism to which his arguments seemed to lead were transformed in his *Education of Mankind* (1780) into a historical theory of truth.

In Lessing's view, all religions have an equal dignity, for none possesses "the" truth; they represent only *ethical* and *practical* moments in the history of mankind. Revelation is assimilated into an education of mankind and God is compared to a teacher who reveals to man only what he is able to assimilate. This secularization of the history of salvation, in which God becomes immanent in the world, is called pantheism ("the quarrel of pantheism"). For Lessing, Judaism and Christianity are the preliminary stages of a third gospel, the "Gospel of Reason." *The Masonic Dialogues* (1778) introduced this historical and practical conception of truth as a progress from "thinking by oneself" to dialogue ("thinking aloud with a friend").

In the literary domain Lessing broke with the culture of the baroque: against the giants and martyrs of baroque tragedy, he offered the tragedy of the bourgeois, with whom any spectator must be able to identify. After a poor first play in 1755 – *Miss Sara Sampson* – which only reflected the sentimentalism of the time, Lessing produced a model of the genre with *Emilia Galotti* (1781). *The Hamburg Dramaturgy* (1767–68) was supposed to be influenced by Aristotle, but its union of fear and pity was greatly influenced by Moses Mendelssohn's theory of "mixed sensations." Lessing's entire aesthetics was based not on permanent ontological, religious, or moral rules, but on the spectator's interest. In *Laokoon* (1766) he associated this aesthetics of reception with one of artistic production, i.e., a reflection on the means through which poetry and the plastic arts create this interest: the plastic arts by natural signs and poetry through the arbitrary signs that overcome their artificiality through the imitation not of nature but of action. Much like Winckelmann's aesthetics, which influenced German classicism for a considerable time, Lessing's aesthetics opposed the baroque, but for a theory of ideal beauty inspired by Plato it substituted a foundation of the beautiful in the agreement between producer and receptor.

See also MENDELSSOHN.   G.Ra.

Leucippus (fl. c.440 B.C.), Greek pre-Socratic philosopher credited with founding atomism, expounded in a work titled *The Great World-system*. Positing the existence of atoms and the void, he answered Eleatic arguments against change by allowing change of place. The arrangements and rearrangements of groups of atoms could account for macroscopic changes in the world, and indeed for the world itself. Little else is known of Leucippus. It is difficult to distinguish his contributions from those of his prolific follower Democritus. **See also ANCIENT ATOMISM.**

D.W.G.

level. See TYPE THEORY.

Levi ben Gershom. See GERSONIDES.

Levinas, Emmanuel (1906–95), Lithuanian-born French philosopher. Educated as an orthodox Jew and a Russian citizen, he studied philosophy at Strasbourg (1924–29) and Freiburg (1928–29), introduced the work of Husserl and Heidegger in France, taught philosophy at a Jewish school in Paris, spent four years in a German labor camp (1940–44), and was a professor at the universities of Poitiers, Nanterre, and the Sorbonne.

To the impersonal totality of being reduced to "the same" by the Western tradition (including Hegel's and Husserl's idealism and Heidegger's ontology), Levinas opposes the irreducible otherness of the human other, death, time, God, etc. In *Totalité et Infini: Essai sur l'extériorité* (1961), he shows how the other's facing and speaking urge philosophy to transcend the horizons of comprehension, while *Autrement qu'être ou au-delà de l'essence* (1974) concentrates on the self of "me" as one-for-the-other. Appealing to Plato's form of the Good and Descartes's idea of the infinite, Levinas describes the asymmetrical relation between the other's "highness" or "infinity" and me, whose self-enjoyment is thus interrupted by a basic imperative: Do not kill me, but help me to live! The fact of the other's existence immediately reveals the basic "ought" of ethics; it awakens me to a responsibility that I have never been able to choose or to refuse. My radical "passivity," thus revealed, shows the anachronic character of human temporality. It also refers to the immemorial past of "Him" whose "illeity" is still otherwise other than the human other: God, or the Good itself, who is neither an object nor a you. Religion and ethics coincide because the only way to meet with God is to practice one's responsibility for the human other, who is "in the trace of God."

Comprehensive thematization and systematic objectification, though always in danger of reducing all otherness, have their own relative and subordinate truth, especially with regard to the economic and political conditions of universal justice toward all individuals whom I cannot encounter personally. With and through the other I meet *all* humans. In this experience lies the origin of equality and human rights. Similarly, theoretical thematization has a positive role if it remains aware of its ancillary or angelic role with regard to concern for the other. What is said in philosophy betrays the saying by which it is communicated. It must therefore be unsaid in a return to the saying. More than desire for theoretical wisdom, philosophy is the wisdom of love.

See also HEIDEGGER, HUSSERL.   A.T.P.

Lewin, Kurt (1890–1947), German and American (after 1932) psychologist, perhaps the most influential of the Gestalt psychologists in the United States. Believing traditional psychology was stuck in an "Aristotelian" class-logic stage of theorizing, Lewin proposed advancing to a "Galilean" stage of field theory. His central field concept was the "*life space*, containing the person and his psychological environment." Primarily concerned with motivation, he explained locomotion as caused by life-space objects' *valences*, psychological vectors of force acting on people as physical vectors of force act on physical objects. Objects with positive valence exert attractive force; objects with negative valence exert repulsive force; ambivalent objects exert both. To attain theoretical rigor, Lewin borrowed from mathematical topology, mapping life spaces as diagrams. For example, this represented the motivational conflict involved in choosing between pizza and hamburger:

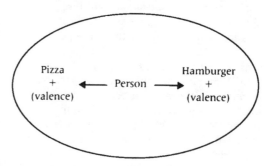

Life spaces frequently contain psychological barriers (e.g., no money) blocking movement toward or away from a valenced object. Lewin also created the important field of group dynamics in 1939, carrying out innovative studies on children and adults, focusing on group cohesion and effects of leadership style. His main works are *A Dynamic Theory of Personality* (1935), *Principles of Topological Psychology* (1936), and *Field Theory in Social Science* (1951). **See also KÖHLER, MOTIVATIONAL EXPLANATION.**   T.H.L.

Lewis, C(larence) I(rving) (1883–1964), American philosopher who advocated a version of pragmatism and empiricism, but was nonetheless strongly influenced by Kant. Lewis was born in Massachusetts, educated at Harvard, and taught at the University of California (1911–20) and Harvard (1920–53). He wrote in logic (*A Survey of Symbolic Logic*, 1918; *Symbolic Logic*, 1932, coauthored with C. H. Langford), in epistemology (*Mind and the World Order*, 1929; *An Analysis of Knowledge and Valuation*, 1946), and in ethical theory (*The Ground and Nature of the Right*, 1965; *Our Social Inheritance*, 1957).

General views. Use of the senses involves "presentations" of sense experiences that signalize external objects. Reflection upon the relations of sense experiences to psychological "intensions" permits our thoughts to refer to aspects of objective reality. Consequently, we can experience those non-presented objective conditions. Intensions, which include the mind's categories, are meanings in one ordinary sense, and concepts in a philosophical sense. When judging counts as knowing, it has the future-oriented function and sole value of guiding action in pursuit of what one evaluates as good. Intensions do not fundamentally depend upon being formulated in those linguistic phrases that may express them and thereby acquire meaning. *Pace* Kant, our categories are replaceable when pragmatically unsuccessful, and are sometimes invented, although typically socially instilled. Kant also failed to realize that any a priori knowledge concerns only what is expressed by an "analytic truth," i.e., what is knowable with certainty via reflection upon intensions and permits reference to the necessary inclusion (and exclusion) relations between objective properties. Such inclusion/exclusion relationships are "entailments" expressible by a use of "if . . . then . . ." different from material implication.

The degree of justification of an empirical judgment about objective reality (e.g., that there is a doorknob before one) and of any beliefs in consequences that are probable given the judgment, approximates to certainty when the judgment stands in a relationship of "congruence" to a collection of justified judgments (e.g., a collection including the judgments that one remembers seeing a doorknob a moment before, and that one has not just turned around).

Lewis's empiricism involves one type of phenomenalism. Although he treats external conditions as metaphysically distinct from passages of sense experience, he maintains that the process of learning about the former does not involve more than learning about the latter. Accordingly, he speaks of the "sense meaning" of an intension, referring to an objective condition. It concerns what one intends to count as a process that verifies that the particular intension applies to the objective world. Sense meanings of a statement may be conceived as additional "entailments" of it, and are expressible by conjunctions of an infinite number of statements each of which is "the general form of a specific terminat-

ing judgment" (as defined below). Lewis wants his treatment of sense meaning to rule out Berkeley's view that objects exist only when perceived.

Verification of an objective judgment, as Kant realized, is largely specified by a non-social process expressed by a rule to act in imaginable ways in response to imaginable present sense experiences (e.g. seeing a doorknob) and thereupon to have imaginable future sense experiences (e.g. feeling a doorknob). Actual instances of such passages of sense experience raise the probability of an objective judgment, whose verification is always partial. Apprehensions of sense experiences are judgments that are not reached by basing them on grounds in a way that might conceivably produce errors. Such apprehensions are "certain." The latter term may be employed by Lewis in more than one sense, but here it at least implies that the judgment is rationally credible and in the above sense not capable of being in error. So such an apprehension is "datal," i.e., rationally employed in judging other matters, and "immediate," i.e., formed noninferentially in response to a presentation. These presentations make up "the (sensory) given." Sense experience is what remains after everything that is less than certain in one's experience of an objective condition is set aside. Lewis thought some version of the epistemic regress argument to be correct, and defended the Cartesian view that without something certain as a foundation no judgment has any degree of justification.

Technical terminology.

Presentation: something involved in experience, e.g. a visual impression, in virtue of which one possesses a non-inferential judgment that it is involved.

The given: those presentations that have the content that they do independently of one's intending or deciding that they have it.

Terminating: decisively and completely verifiable or falsifiable in principle. (E.g., where *S* affirms a present sense experience, *A* affirms an experience of seeming to initiate an action, and *E* affirms a future instance of sense experience, the judgment '*S* and if *A* then *E*' is terminating.)

The general form of the terminating judgment that S and if A then E: the conditional that if *S* then (in all probability) *E*, if *A*. (An actual judgment expressed by this conditional is based on remembering passages of sense experience of type *S/A/E* and is justified thanks to the principle of induction and the principle that seeming to remember an event makes the judgment that the event occurred justified at least to some degree. These statements concern a connection that holds independently of whether anyone is thinking and underlies the rationality of relying to any degree upon what is not part of one's self.)

Congruence: the relationship among statements in a collection when the following conditional is true: If each had some degree of justification independently of the remaining ones, then each would be made more justified by the conjoint truth of the remaining ones. (When the antecedent of this conditional is true, and a statement in the collection is such that it is highly improbable that the remaining ones all be true unless it is true, then it is made very highly justified.)

Pragmatic a priori: those judgments that are not based on the use of the senses but on employing a set of intensions, and yet are susceptible of being reasonably set aside because of a shift to a different set of intensions whose employment is pragmatically more useful (roughly, more useful for the attainment of what has intrinsic value).

Valuation: the appraising of something as having value or being morally right. (What has some value that is not due to its consequences is what has intrinsic value, e.g., enjoyable experiences of self-realization in living rationally. Other evaluations of what is good are empirical judgments concerning what may be involved in actions leading to what is intrinsically good. Rational reflection permits awareness of various moral principles.)

See also ANALYTIC–SYNTHETIC DISTINCTION; A PRIORI; CERTAINTY; FOUNDATIONALISM; PHENOMENALISM; PRAGMATISM; SELLARS, WILFRID.   R.K.S.

Lewis, C(live) S(taples) (1898–1963), English literary critic, novelist, and Christian apologist. Born in Belfast, Lewis took three first-class degrees at Oxford, became a tutor at its Magdalen College in 1925, and assumed the chair of medieval and Renaissance studies at Cambridge in 1954. While his tremendous output includes important works on medieval literature and literary criticism, he is best known for his fiction and Christian apologetics. Lewis combined a poetic sense and appreciation of argument that allowed him to communicate complex philosophical and theological material to lay audiences.

His popular writings in the philosophy of religion range over a variety of topics, including the nature and existence of God (*Mere Christianity,* 1952), miracles (*Miracles,* 1947), hell (*The Great Divorce,* 1945), and the problem of evil (*The Problem of Pain,* 1940). His own conversion to Christianity as an adult is chronicled in his autobiography (*Surprised by Joy,* 1955). In defending theism Lewis employed arguments from natural theology (most notably versions of the moral and teleological arguments) and arguments from religious experience. Also of philosophical interest is his defense of moral absolutism in *The Abolition of Man* (1943).

See also PHILOSOPHY OF RELIGION.

W.J.Wo.

Lewis, David K. (b.1941), American philosopher influential in many areas. Lewis received the B.A. in philosophy from Swarthmore in 1962 and the Ph.D. in philosophy from Harvard in 1967. He has been a member of the philosophy department at U.C.L.A. (1966–70) and Princeton (1970–).

In philosophy of mind, Lewis is known principally for "An Argument for the Identity Theory" (1966), "Psychophysical and Theoretical Identifications" (1972), and "Mad Pain and Martian Pain" (1980). He argues for the functionalist thesis that mental states are defined by their typical causal roles, and the materialist thesis that the causal roles definitive of mental states are occupied by physical states. Lewis develops the view that theoretical definitions in general are functionally defined, applying the formal concept of a Ramsey sentence. And he suggests that the platitudes of commonsense or folk psychology constitute the theory implicitly defining psychological concepts.

In philosophy of language and linguistics, Lewis is known principally for *Convention* (1969), "General Semantics" (1970), and "Languages and Language" (1975). His theory of convention had its source in the theory of games of pure coordination developed by von Neumann and Morgenstern. Roughly, conventions are arbitrary solutions to coordination problems that perpetuate themselves once a precedent is set because they serve a common interest. Lewis requires it to be common knowledge that people prefer to conform to a conventional regularity given that others do. He treats linguistic meanings as compositional intensions. The basic intensions for lexical constituents are functions assigning extensions to indices, which include contextual factors and a possible world. An analytic sentence is one true at every index. Languages are functions from sentences to meanings, and the language of a population is the one in which they have a convention of truthfulness and trust.

In metaphysics and modal logic, Lewis is known principally for "Counterpart Theory and Quantified Modal Logic" (1968) and *On the Plurality of Worlds* (1986). Based on its theoretical benefits, Lewis argues for modal realism: other possible worlds and the objects in them are just as real as the actual world and its inhabitants. Lewis develops a non-standard form of modal logic in which objects exist in at most one possible world, and for which the necessity of identity fails. Properties are identified with the set of objects that have them in any possible world, and propositions as the set of worlds in which they are true. He also develops a finergrained concept of structured properties and propositions.

In philosophical logic and philosophy of science, Lewis is best known for *Counterfactuals* (1973), "Causation" (1973), and "Probabilities of Conditionals and Conditional Probabilities" (1976). He developed a formal semantics for counterfactual conditionals that matches their truth conditions and logic much more adequately than the previously available material or strict conditional analyses. Roughly, a counterfactual is true if its consequent is true in every possible world in which its antecedent is true that is as similar overall to the actual world as the truth of the antecedent will allow. Lewis then defended an analysis of causation in terms of counterfactuals: *c* caused *e* if *e* would not have occurred if *c* had not occurred or if there is a chain of events leading from *e* to *c* each member of which is counterfactually dependent on the next. He presents a reductio ad absurdum argument to show that conditional probabilities could not be identified with the probabilities of any sort of conditional.

Lewis has also written on visual experience, events, holes, parts of classes, time travel, survival and identity, subjective and objective probability, desire as belief, attitudes *de se*, deontic logic, decision theory, the prisoner's dilemma and the Newcomb problem, utilitarianism, dispositional theories of value, nuclear deterrence, punishment, and academic ethics.

See also CAUSATION, CONDITIONAL, FUNCTIONALISM, MEANING, POSSIBLE WORLDS.

W.A.D.

lexical ambiguity. See AMBIGUITY.

lexical ordering, also called lexicographic order-

ing, a method, given a finite ordered set of symbols, such as the letters of the alphabet, of ordering all finite *sequences* of those symbols. All finite sequences of letters, e.g., can be ordered as follows: first list all *single* letters in alphabetical order; then list all *pairs* of letters in the order *aa, ab, . . . az; ba . . . bz; . . . ; za . . . zz*. Here pairs are first grouped and alphabetized according to the first letter of the pair, and then within these groups are alphabetized according to the second letter of the pair. All sequences of three letters, four letters, etc., are then listed in order by an analogous process. In this way every sequence of *n* letters, for any *n*, is listed.

Lexical ordering differs from alphabetical ordering, although it makes use of it, because all sequences with *n* letters come before any sequence with *n* + 1 letters; thus, *zzt* will come before *aaab*. One use of lexical ordering is to show that the set of all finite sequences of symbols, and thus the set of all words, is at most denumerably infinite.

See also INFINITY. V.K.

*li*¹, Chinese term meaning 'pattern', 'principle', 'good order', 'inherent order', or 'to put in order'. During the Han dynasty, *li* described not only the pattern of a given thing, event, or process, but the underlying grand pattern of everything, the deep structure of the cosmos. Later, Hua-yen Buddhists, working from the Mahayana doctrine that all things are conditioned and related through past causal relationships, claimed that each thing reflects the *li* of all things. This influenced Neo-Confucians, who developed a metaphysics of *li* and *ch'i* (ether), in which all things possess all *li* (and hence they are "one" in some deep sense), but because of the differing quality of their *ch'i*, things manifest different and distinct characteristics. The *hsin* (heart/mind) contains all *li* (some insist it *is li*) but is obscured by "impure" *ch'i*; hence we understand *some* things and can learn others. Through self-cultivation, one can purify one's *ch'i* and achieve complete and perfect understanding. **See also NEO-CONFUCIANISM, TAOISM.** P.J.I.

*li*², Chinese term meaning 'rite', 'ritual', 'etiquette', 'ritual propriety'. In its earliest use, *li* refers to politico-religious rituals such as sacrifices to ancestors or funerals. Soon the term came to encompass matters of etiquette, such as the proper way to greet a guest. In some texts the *li* include even matters of morality or natural law. Mencius refers to *li* as a virtue, but it is unclear how it is distinct from his other cardinal virtues. Emphasis upon *li* is one of the distinctive features of Confucianism. Critics charge that this emphasis is a conflation of the natural with the conventional or simply naive traditionalism. Others claim that the notion of *li* draws attention to the subtle interdependence of morality and convention, and points the way to creating genuine communities by treating "the secular as sacred." **See also CONFUCIANISM, MOHISM, TAOISM.**

B.W.V.N.

li³, Chinese term meaning 'profit' or 'benefit', and probably with the basic meaning of 'smooth' or 'unimpeded'. Mo Tzu (fourth century B.C.) regarded what brings *li* (benefit) to the public as the criterion of *yi* (rightness), and certain other classical Chinese texts also describe *yi* as the basis for producing *li*. Confucians tend to use '*li*' pejoratively to refer to what profits oneself or social groups (e.g., one's family) to which one belongs, and contrast *li* with *yi*. According to them, one should ideally be guided by *yi* rather than *li*, and in the political realm, a preoccupation with *li* will lead to strife and disorder. **See also CONFUCIANISM, MOHISM.**

K.-l.S.

liability responsibility. See RESPONSIBILITY.

Liang Ch'i-ch'ao (1873–1929), Chinese scholar and writer. A disciple of K'ang Yu-wei, the young Liang was a reformist unsympathetic to Sun Yat-sen's revolutionary activities. But after the republic was founded, he embraced the democratic ideal. He was eager to introduce ideas from the West to reform the Chinese people. But after a tour of Europe he had great reservations about Western civilization. His unfavorable impressions touched off a debate between science and metaphysics in 1923. His scholarly works include studies of Buddhism and of Chinese thought in the last three hundred years. **See also CHINESE PHILOSOPHY, K'ANG YU-WEI, SUN YAT-SEN.**

S.-h.L.

liang-chih, Chinese term commonly rendered as 'innate knowledge of the good', although that translation is quite inadequate to the term's range of meanings. The term first occurs in *Mencius* but becomes a key concept in Wang Yang-ming's philosophy. A coherent explication of *liang-chih* must attend to the following features. (1) Mencius's *liang-chih* (sense of right and wrong) is the ability to distinguish right from wrong conduct. For Wang "this sense of right and wrong is nothing but the love [of good] and the

hate [of evil]." (2) Wang's *liang-chih* is a moral consciousness informed by a vision of *jen* or "forming one body" with all things in the universe. (3) The exercise of *liang-chih* involves deliberation in coping with changing circumstances. (4) The extension of *liang-chih* is indispensable to the pursuit of *jen*. **See also MENCIUS.**

A.S.C.

Liang Sou-ming (1893–1988), Chinese philosopher branded as the last Confucian. He actually believed, however, that Buddhist philosophy was more profound than Confucian philosophy. Against those advocating Westernization, Liang pointed out that Western and Indian cultures went to two extremes; only the Chinese culture took a middle course. But it was immature, and must learn first from the West, then from India. After the Communist takeover, he refused to denounce traditional Chinese culture. He valued human-heartedness, which he felt was neglected by Western science and Marxism. He was admired overseas for his courage in standing up to Mao Tse-tung. **See also CHINESE PHILOSOPHY, HU SHIH, MAO TSE-TUNG.** S.-h.L.

Li Ao (fl. A.D. 798), Chinese philosopher who learned Buddhist dialects and developed a theory of human nature (*hsing*) and feelings (*ch'ing*) more sophisticated than that of Han Yü, his teacher. He wrote a famous article, "*Fu-hsing shu*" ("Essay on returning to Nature"), which exerted profound influence on Sung-Ming Neo-Confucian philosophers. According to him, there are seven feelings: joy, anger, pity, fear, love, hate, and desire. These feelings tend to obscure one's nature. Only when the feelings do not operate can one's nature gain its fulfillment. The sage does possess the feelings, but he remains immovable; hence in a sense he also has never had such feelings. **See also HAN YÜ, NEO-CONFUCIANISM.** S.-h.L.

liar cycle. See SEMANTIC PARADOXES.

liar paradox. See SEMANTIC PARADOXES.

liberalism, a political philosophy first formulated during the Enlightenment in response to the growth of modern nation-states, which centralize governmental functions and claim sole authority to exercise coercive power within their boundaries. One of its central theses has long been that a government's claim to this authority is justified only if the government can show those who live under it that it secures their liberty. A central thesis of contemporary liberalism is that government must be neutral in debates about the good human life.

John Locke, one of the founders of liberalism, tried to show that constitutional monarchy secures liberty by arguing that free and equal persons in a state of nature, concerned to protect their freedom and property, would agree with one another to live under such a regime. *Classical liberalism*, which attaches great value to economic liberty, traces its ancestry to Locke's argument that government must safeguard property. Locke's use of an agreement or *social contract* laid the basis for the form of liberalism championed by Rousseau and most deeply indebted to Kant. According to Kant, the sort of liberty that should be most highly valued is *autonomy*. Agents enjoy autonomy, Kant said, when they live according to laws they would give to themselves. Rawls's *A Theory of Justice* (1971) set the main themes of the chapter of liberal thought now being written. Rawls asked what principles of justice citizens would agree to in a contract situation he called "the original position." He argued that they would agree to principles guaranteeing adequate basic liberties and fair equality of opportunity, and requiring that economic inequalities benefit the least advantaged. A government that respects these principles secures the autonomy of its citizens by operating in accord with principles citizens would give themselves in the original position. Because of the conditions of the original position, citizens would not choose principles based on a controversial conception of the good life. Neutrality among such conceptions is therefore built into the foundations of Rawls's theory.

Some critics argue that liberalism's emphasis on autonomy and neutrality leaves it unable to account for the values of tradition, community, or political participation, and unable to limit individual liberty when limits are needed. Others argue that autonomy is not the notion of freedom needed to explain why common forms of oppression like sexism are wrong. Still others argue that liberalism's focus on Western democracies leaves it unable to address the most pressing problems of contemporary politics. Recent work in liberal theory has therefore asked whether liberalism can accommodate the political demands of religious and ethnic communities, ground an adequate conception of democracy, capture feminist critiques of extant power structures, or guide nation-building in the face of secessionist, nationalist, and fundamentalist claims.

See also KANT, LOCKE, POLITICAL PHILOSOPHY, RAWLS, ROUSSEAU, SOCIAL CONTRACT.
                                                P.J.W.

liberal theory of the state. See LOCKE, POLITICAL PHILOSOPHY.

libertarianism, metaphysical. See FREE WILL PROBLEM.

libertarianism, political. See POLITICAL PHILOSOPHY.

liberty. See FREE WILL PROBLEM, HOHFELD, JURISPRUDENCE, POLITICAL PHILOSOPHY.

liberty of indifference. See FREE WILL PROBLEM, HUME.

liberty of spontaneity. See FREE WILL PROBLEM, HUME.

liberty of the ancients. See CONSTANT.

liberty of the moderns. See CONSTANT.

liberty right. See RIGHTS.

liberum arbitrium, Latin expression meaning 'free judgment', often used to refer to medieval doctrines of free choice or free will. It appears in the title of Augustine's seminal work *De libero arbitrio voluntatis* (usually translated 'On the Free Choice of the Will') and in many other medieval writings (e.g., Aquinas, in *Summa theologiae* I, asks "whether man has free choice [*liberum arbitrium*]"). For medieval thinkers, a judgment (*arbitrium*) "of the will" was a conclusion of practical reasoning – "I *will* do this" (hence, a choice or decision) – in contrast to a judgment "of the intellect" ("This is the case"), which concludes theoretical reasoning. **See also FREE WILL PROBLEM, PRACTICAL REASONING.**
                                                R.H.K.

Li Chi ("Record of Rites"), Chinese Confucian treatise, one of the three classics of *li* (rites, rules of proper conduct). For Confucian ethics, the treatise is important for its focus on the reasoned justification of *li,* the role of virtues in human relationships, and the connection between personal cultivation and the significance of the rites of mourning and sacrifices. Perhaps even more important, the *Li Chi* contains two of the basic Four Books of Confucian ethics: *The Great Learning* (*Ta Hsüeh*) and *The Doctrine of the Mean* (*Chung Yung*). It also contains a brief essay on learning that stresses its interaction with ethical teaching. **See also** CONFUCIANISM.   A.S.C.

li-ch'i, technical term in Chinese Neo-Confucianism primarily used in the context of speculative cosmology, metaphysics, and ontology for accounting for changing phenomena and their ethical significance. *Li* is often rendered as 'principle', 'order', 'pattern', or 'reason'; *ch'i* as 'material force', 'ether', or 'energy'. Recent Neo-Confucian scholarship provides no clear guide to the *li-ch'i* distinction. In ethical contexts, however, the distinction is used to explain the origin of human good and evil. In its pure state, *ch'i* is inseparable from *li*, in the sense of compliance with the Confucian ethical norm that can be reasonably justified. In its impure state, *ch'i* presumably explains the existence of human evils. This perplexing distinction remains a subject of scholarly inquiry. **See also** CH'I, LI¹, NEO-CONFUCIANISM.   A.S.C.

Lieh Tzu, also called Lieh Yu-K'ou (440?–360? B.C.), Chinese Taoist philosopher whose name serves as the title of a work of disputed date. The *Lieh Tzu,* parts (perhaps most) of which were written as late as the third or fourth century A.D., is primarily a Taoist work but contains one chapter reflecting ideas associated with Yang Chu. However, whereas the original teachings of Yang Chu emphasized one's duty to preserve bodily integrity, health, and longevity, a task that may require exercise and discipline, the Yang Chu chapter advocates hedonism as the means to nourish life. The primary Taoist teaching of the *Lieh Tzu* is that destiny trumps will, fate conquers effort.   R.P.P. & R.T.A.

life, the characteristic property of living substances or things; it is associated with either a capacity for mental activities such as perception and thought (*mental life*) or physical activities such as absorption, excretion, metabolism, synthesis, and reproduction (*physical life*). *Biological* or *carbon-based life* is a natural kind of physical life that essentially involves a highly complex, self-regulating system of carbon-based macromolecules and water molecules. *Silicon-based life* is wholly speculative natural kind of physical life that essentially involves a highly complex, self-regulating system of silicon-based macromolecules. This kind of life might be possible, since at high temperatures silicon forms macromolecules with chemical properties somewhat similar to those of carbon-based macromolecules. Living

organisms have a high degree of functional organization, with a regulating or controlling master part, e.g., a dog's nervous system, or the DNA or nucleus of a single-celled organism. Mental life is usually thought to be dependent or supervenient upon physical life, but some philosophers have argued for the possibility at least of purely spiritual mental life, i.e., souls. The above characterization of biological life appropriately implies that viruses are not living things, since they lack the characteristic activities of living things, with the exception of an attenuated form of reproduction. **See also** ARTIFICIAL LIFE, ORGANISM.   J.Ho. & G.Ro.

life space. See LEWIN.

life world. See HUSSERL.

light of nature. See DESCARTES.

li-i-fen-shu, a Chinese phrase meaning 'Principle is one while duties or manifestations are many'. Chang Tsai (1020–77) wrote the essay "The Western Inscription" in which he said that all people were his brothers and sisters. Ch'eng Yi's (1033–1107) disciple Yang Shih (1053–1135) suspected Chang Tsai of teaching the Mohist doctrine of universal love. Ch'eng Yi then coined the phrase to clarify the situation: Chang Tsai was really teaching the Confucian doctrine of graded love – while principle (*li*) is one, duties are many. Chu Hsi (1130–1200) further developed the idea into a metaphysics by maintaining that principle is one while manifestations are many, just as the same moon shines over different rivers. **See also** CHINESE PHILOSOPHY, CHU HSI.   S.-h.L.

limited variety, principle of. See MILL'S METHODS.

limiting case, an individual or subclass of a given background class that is maximally remote from "typical" or "paradigm" members of the class with respect to some ordering that is not always explicitly mentioned. The number zero is a limiting case of cardinal number. A triangle is a limiting case of polygon. A square is a limiting case of rectangle when rectangles are ordered by the ratio of length to width. Certainty is a limiting case of belief when beliefs are ordered according to "strength of subjective conviction." Knowledge is a limiting case of belief when beliefs are ordered according "adequacy of objective grounds." A limiting case is necessarily a case (member) of the background class; in contrast a borderline case need not be a case and a degenerate case may clearly fail to be a case at all. **See also BORDERLINE CASE, DEGENERATE CASE.**

J.Cor.

linear order. See RELATION.

linguistic analysis. See ANALYSIS.

linguistic competence. See PHILOSOPHY OF LANGUAGE.

linguistic determinism. See LINGUISTIC RELATIVITY.

linguistic performance. See PHILOSOPHY OF LANGUAGE.

linguistic philosophy. See ANALYTIC PHILOSOPHY.

linguistic relativity, the thesis that at least some distinctions found in one language are found in no other language (a version of the Sapir-Whorf hypothesis); more generally, the thesis that different languages utilize different representational systems that are at least in some degree informationally incommensurable and hence non-equivalent. The differences arise from the arbitrary features of languages resulting in each language encoding lexically or grammatically some distinctions not found in other languages.

The thesis of *linguistic determinism* holds that the ways people perceive or think about the world, especially with respect to their classificatory systems, are causally determined or influenced by their linguistic systems or by the structures common to all human languages. Specifically, implicit or explicit linguistic categorization determines or influences aspects of nonlinguistic categorization, memory, perception, or cognition in general. Its strongest form (probably a straw-man position) holds that linguistically unencoded concepts are unthinkable. Weaker forms hold that concepts that are linguistically encoded are more accessible to thought and easier to remember than those that are not. This thesis is independent of that of linguistic relativity. Linguistic determinism plus linguistic relativity as defined here implies the Sapir-Whorf hypothesis.

See also SAPIR-WHORF HYPOTHESIS.

W.K.W.

linguistics, philosophy of. See PHILOSOPHY OF LANGUAGE.

linguistic semantics. See PHILOSOPHY OF LANGUAGE.

linguistic theory of logical truth. See CONVENTIONALISM.

literal meaning. See MEANING.

literary theory, a reasoned account of the nature of the literary artifact, its causes, effects, and distinguishing features. So understood, literary theory is part of the systematic study of literature covered by the term 'criticism', which also includes interpretation of literary works, philology, literary history, and the evaluation of particular works or bodies of work. Because it attempts to provide the conceptual foundations for practical criticism, literary theory has also been called "critical theory." However, since the latter term has been appropriated by neo-Marxists affiliated with the Frankfurt School to designate their own kind of social critique, 'literary theory' is less open to misunderstanding. Because of its concern with the ways in which literary productions differ from other verbal artifacts and from other works of art, literary theory overlaps extensively with philosophy, psychology, linguistics, and the other human sciences.

The first *ex professo* theory of literature in the West, for centuries taken as normative, was Aristotle's *Poetics*. On Aristotle's view, poetry is a verbal imitation of the forms of human life and action in language made vivid by metaphor. It stimulates its audience to reflect on the human condition, enriches their understanding, and thereby occasions the pleasure that comes from the exercise of the cognitive faculty. The first real paradigm shift in literary theory was introduced by the Romantics of the nineteenth century. The *Biographia Literaria* (1817) of Samuel Taylor Coleridge, recounting the author's conversion from Humean empiricism to a form of German idealism, defines poetry not as a representation of objective structures, but as the imaginative self-expression of the creative subject. Its emphasis is not on the poem as a source of pleasure but on poetry as a heightened form of spiritual activity. The standard work on the transition from classical (imitation) theory to Romantic (expression) theory is M. H. Abrams's *The Mirror and the Lamp* (1953).

In the present century theory has assumed a place of prominence in literary studies. In the first half of the century the works of I. A. Richards – from his early positivist account of poetry in books like *Science and Poetry* (1926) to his later idealist views in books like *The Philosophy of Rhetoric* (1936) – sponsored the practice of the American New Critics. The most influential theorist of the period is Northrop Frye, whose formalist manifesto, *Anatomy of Criticism* (1957), proposed to make criticism the "science of literature." The introduction of Continental thought to the English-speaking critical establishment in the 1960s and after spawned a bewildering variety of competing theories of literature: e.g., Russian formalism, structuralism, deconstruction, new historicism, Marxism, Freudianism, feminism, and even the anti-theoretical movement called the "new pragmatism." The best summary account of these developments is Frank Lentricchia's *After the New Criticism* (1980).

Given the present near-chaos in criticism, the future of literary theory is unpredictable. But the chaos itself offers ample opportunities for philosophical analysis and calls for the kind of conceptual discrimination such analysis can offer. Conversely, the study of literary theory can provide philosophers with a better understanding of the textuality of philosophy and of the ways in which philosophical content is determined by the literary form of philosophical texts.

See also AESTHETICS, PHILOSOPHY OF LITERATURE.   L.H.M.

literature, philosophy of. See PHILOSOPHY OF LITERATURE.

Liu Shao-ch'i (1898–1969), Chinese Communist leader. A close ally of Mao Tse-tung, he was purged near the end of his life when he refused to follow Mao's radical approach during the Cultural Revolution, became an ally of the practical Teng Hsiao-ping, and was branded the biggest Capitalist Roader in China. In 1939 he delivered in Yenan the influential speech "How to Be a Good Communist," published in 1943 and widely studied by Chinese Communists. As he emphasized self-discipline, there appeared to be a Confucian dimension in his thought. The article was banned during the Cultural Revolution, and he was accused of teaching reactionary Confucianism in the revolutionary camp. He was later rehabilitated. See also MAO TSE-TUNG.   S.-h.L.

Liu Tsung-chou, also called Ch'i-shan (1578–1645), Chinese philosopher commonly regarded as the last major figure in Sung–Ming Neo-Confucianism. He opposed all sorts of dualist thoughts, including Chu Hsi's philosophy. He was also not happy with some of Wang Yang-ming's followers who claimed that men in the streets were all sages. He shifted the emphasis from rectification of the mind to sincerity of the will, and he gave a new interpretation to "watchful over the self" in the *Doctrine of the Mean.* Among his disciples was the great intellectual historian Huang Tsung-hsi. **See also** CHU HSI, HUANG TSUNG-HSI, HU HUNG, NEO-CONFUCIANISM, WANG YANG-MING.   S.-h.L.

Llull, Ramon. See LULL.

Lobachevsky, Nikolai. See NON-EUCLIDEAN GEOMETRY.

locality assumption. See QUANTUM MECHANICS.

Locke, John (1632–1704), English philosopher and proponent of empiricism, famous especially for his *Essay concerning Human Understanding* (1689) and for his *Second Treatise of Government,* also published in 1689, though anonymously. He came from a middle-class Puritan family in Somerset, and became acquainted with Scholastic philosophy in his studies at Oxford. Not finding a career in church or university attractive, he trained for a while as a physician, and developed contacts with many members of the newly formed Royal Society; the chemist Robert Boyle and the physicist Isaac Newton were close acquaintances. In 1667 he joined the London households of the then Lord Ashley, later first Earl of Shaftesbury; there he became intimately involved in discussions surrounding the politics of resistance to the Catholic king, Charles II. In 1683 he fled England for the Netherlands, where he wrote out the final draft of his *Essay.* He returned to England in 1689, a year after the accession to the English throne of the Protestant William of Orange. In his last years he was the most famous intellectual in England, perhaps in Europe generally. Locke was not a university professor immersed in the discussions of the philosophy of "the schools" but was instead intensely engaged in the social and cultural issues of his day; his writings were addressed not to professional philosophers but to the educated public in general.

The *Essay*. The initial impulse for the line of thought that culminated in the *Essay* occurred early in 1671, in a discussion Locke had with some friends in Lord Shaftesbury's apartments in

London on matters of morality and revealed religion. In his Epistle to the Reader at the beginning of the *Essay* Locke says that the discussants

> found themselves quickly at a stand by the difficulties that arose on every side. After we had awhile puzzled ourselves, without coming any nearer a resolution of those doubts which perplexed us, it came into my thoughts that we took a wrong course, and that before we set ourselves upon enquiries of that nature it was necessary to examine our own abilities, and see what objects our understandings were or were not fitted to deal with.

Locke was well aware that for a thousand years European humanity had consulted its textual inheritance for the resolution of its moral and religious quandaries; elaborate strategies of interpretation, distinction, etc., had been developed for extracting from those disparate sources a unified, highly complex, body of truth. He was equally well aware that by his time, more than a hundred years after the beginning of the Reformation, the moral and religious tradition of Europe had broken up into warring and contradictory fragments. Accordingly he warns his readers over and over against basing their convictions merely on say-so, on unexamined tradition. As he puts it in a short late book of his, *The Conduct of the Understanding*, "We should not judge of things by men's opinions, but of opinions by things." We should look to "the things themselves," as he sometimes puts it. But to know how to get at the things themselves it is necessary, so Locke thought, "to examine our own abilities." Hence the project of the *Essay*.

The *Essay* comes in four books, Book IV being the culmination. Fundamental to understanding Locke's thought in Book IV is the realization that knowledge, as he thinks of it, is a fundamentally different phenomenon from belief. Locke holds, indeed, that knowledge is typically *accompanied* by belief; it is not, though, to be identified with it. Knowledge, as he thinks of it, is direct awareness of some fact – in his own words, perception of some agreement or disagreement among things. Belief, by contrast, consists of *taking* some proposition to be true – whether or not one is directly aware of the corresponding fact. The question then arises: Of what sorts of facts do we human beings have direct awareness? Locke's answer is: Only of facts that consist of relationships among our "ideas." Exactly what Locke had in mind when he spoke of *ideas* is a vexed topic; the traditional view, for which there is a great

deal to be said, is that he regarded ideas as *mental objects*. Furthermore, he clearly regarded some ideas as being *representations* of other entities; his own view was that we can think about non-mental entities only by being aware of mental entities that represent those non-mental realities.

Locke argued that knowledge, thus understood, is "short and scanty" – much too short and scanty for the living of life. Life requires the formation of beliefs on matters where knowledge is not available. Now what strikes anyone who surveys human beliefs is that many of them are false. What also strikes any perceptive observer of the scene is that often we can – or could have – done something about this. We can, to use Locke's language, "regulate" and "govern" our belief-forming capacities with the goal in mind of getting things right. Locke was persuaded that not only *can* we thus regulate and govern our belief-forming capacities; we *ought* to do so. It is a God-given obligation that rests upon all of us. Specifically, for each human being there are some matters of such "concernment," as Locke calls it, as to place the person under obligation to try his or her best to get things right. For all of us there will be many issues that are not of such concernment; for those cases, it will be acceptable to form our beliefs in whatever way nature or custom has taught us to form them. But for each of us there will be certain practical matters concerning which we are obligated to try our best – these differing from person to person. And certain matters of ethics and religion are of such concern to everybody that we are all obligated to try our best, on these matters, to get in touch with reality.

What does trying our best consist of, when knowledge – perception, awareness, insight – is not available? One can think of the practice Locke recommends as having three steps. First one collects whatever evidence one can find for and against the proposition in question. This evidence must consist of things that one *knows;* otherwise we are just wandering in darkness. And the totality of the evidence must be a reliable indicator of the probability of the proposition that one is considering. Second, one analyzes the evidence to determine the probability of the proposition in question, on that evidence. And last, one places a level of confidence in the proposition that is proportioned to its probability on that satisfactory evidence. If the proposition is highly probable on that evidence, one believes it very firmly; if it only is quite probable, one believes it rather weakly; etc. The main thrust of the latter half of Book IV of the *Essay* is Locke's exhortation to his readers to adopt this practice in the forming of beliefs on matters of high concernment – and in particular, on matters of morality and religion. It was his view that the new science being developed by his friends Boyle and Newton and others was using exactly this method.

Though Book IV was clearly seen by Locke as the culmination of the *Essay*, it by no means constitutes the bulk of it. Book I launches a famous attack on innate ideas and innate knowledge; he argues that all our ideas and knowledge can be accounted for by tracing the way in which the mind uses its innate capacities to work on material presented to it by sensation and reflection (i.e., self-awareness). Book II then undertakes to account for all our ideas, on the assumption that the only "input" is ideas of sensation and reflection, and that the mind, which at birth is a *tabula rasa* (or blank tablet), works on these by such operations as combination, division, generalization, and abstraction. And then in Book III Locke discusses the various ways in which words hinder us in our attempt to get to the things themselves.

Along with many other thinkers of the time, Locke distinguished between what he called *natural* theology and what he called *revealed* theology. It was his view that a compelling, demonstrative argument could be given for the existence of God, and thus that we could have *knowledge* of God's existence; the existence of God is a condition of our own existence. In addition, he believed firmly that God had revealed things to human beings. As he saw the situation, however, we can at most have *beliefs*, not *knowledge*, concerning what God has revealed. For we can never just "see" that a certain episode in human affairs is a case of divine revelation. Accordingly, we must apply the practice outlined above, beginning by assembling satisfactory evidence for the conclusion that a certain episode really is a case of divine revelation. In Locke's view, the occurrence of miracles provides the required evidence. An implication of these theses concerning natural and revealed religion is that it is never right for a human being to believe something about God without having evidence for its truth, with the evidence consisting ultimately of things that one "sees" immediately to be true.

Locke held to a divine command theory of moral obligation; to be morally obligated to do something is for God to require of one that one

do that. And since a great deal of what Jesus taught, as Locke saw it, was a code of moral obligation, it follows that once we have evidence for the revelatory status of what Jesus said, we automatically have evidence that what Jesus taught as our moral obligation really is that. Locke was firmly persuaded, however, that revelation is not our only mode of access to moral obligation. Most if not all of our moral obligations can also be arrived at by the use of our natural capacities, unaided by revelation. To that part of our moral obligations which can in principle be arrived at by the use of our natural capacities, Locke (in traditional fashion) gave the title of *natural law*. Locke's own view was that morality could in principle be established as a deductive science, on analogy to mathematics: one would first argue for God's existence and for our status as creatures of God; one would then argue that God was good, and cared for the happiness of God's creatures. Then one would argue that such a good God would lay down commands to his creatures, aimed at their overall happiness. From there, one would proceed to reflect on what does in fact conduce to human happiness. And so forth. Locke never worked out the details of such a deductive system of ethics; late in his life he concluded that it was beyond his capacities. But he never gave up on the ideal.

The *Second Treatise* and other writings. Locke's theory of natural law entered intimately into the theory of civil obedience that he developed in the *Second Treatise of Government*. Imagine, he said, a group of human beings living in what he called a *state of nature* – i.e., a condition in which there is no governmental authority and no private property. They would still be under divine obligation; and much (if not all) of that obligation would be accessible to them by the use of their natural capacities. There would be for them a natural law. In this state of nature they would have title to their own persons and labor; natural law tells us that these are inherently our "possessions." But there would be no possessions beyond that. The physical world would be like a gigantic English commons, given by God to humanity as a whole. Locke then addresses himself to two questions: How can we account for the emergence of political obligation from such a situation, and how can we account for the emergence of private property? As to the former, his answer is that we in effect make a contract with one another to institute a government for the elimination of certain deficiencies in the state of nature, and then to obey that government, provided it does what we have contracted with one another it should do and does not exceed that. Among the deficiencies of the state of nature that a government can be expected to correct is the sinful tendency of human beings to transgress on other persons' properties, and the equally sinful tendency to punish such transgressions more severely than the law of nature allows. As to the emergence of private property, something from the world at large becomes a given person's property when that person "mixes" his or her labor with it. For though God gave the world as a whole to all of us together, natural law tells us that each person's labor belongs to that person himself or herself – unless he or she freely contracts it to someone else. Locke's *Second Treatise* is thus an articulate statement of the so-called liberal theory of the state; it remains one of the greatest of such, and proved enormously influential. It should be seen as supplemented by the *Letters concerning Toleration* (1689, 1690, 1692) that Locke wrote on religious toleration, in which he argued that all theists who have not pledged civil allegiance to some foreign power should be granted equal toleration.

Some letters that Locke wrote to a friend concerning the education of the friend's son should also be seen as supplementing the grand vision. If we survey the way in which beliefs are actually formed in human beings, we see that passion, the partisanship of distinct traditions, early training, etc., play important obstructive roles. It is impossible to weed out entirely from one's life the influence of such factors. When it comes to matters of high "concernment," however, it is our obligation to do so; it is our obligation to implement the three-step practice outlined above, which Locke defends as doing one's best. But Locke did not think that the cultural reform he had in mind, represented by the appropriate use of this new practice, could be expected to come about as the result just of writing books and delivering exhortations. Training in the new practice was required; in particular, training of small children, before bad habits had been ingrained. Accordingly, Locke proposes in *Some Thoughts concerning Education* (1693) an educational program aimed at training children in when and how to collect satisfactory evidence, appraise the probabilities of propositions on such evidence, and place levels of confidence in those propositions proportioned to their probability on that evidence.

See also BERKELEY, EPISTEMOLOGY, ETHICS, EVIDENTIALISM, HUME, POLITICAL PHILOSOPHY.   N.P.W.

locutionary act. See SPEECH ACT THEORY.

logic, combinatory. See COMBINATORY LOGIC.

logic, default. See DEFAULT LOGIC.

logic, deontic. See DEONTIC LOGIC.

logic, deviant. See PHILOSOPHY OF LOGIC.

logic, dynamic. See DYNAMIC LOGIC.

logic, epistemic. See EPISTEMIC LOGIC.

logic, erotetic. See EROTETIC.

logic, formal. See FORMAL LOGIC.

logic, free. See FREE LOGIC.

logic, higher-order. See FORMAL LOGIC, PHILOSOPHY OF LOGIC, SECOND-ORDER LOGIC.

logic, infinitary. See INFINITARY LOGIC.

logic, informal. See INFORMAL FALLACY, INFORMAL LOGIC.

logic, intensional. See INTENSIONAL LOGIC.

logic, many-valued. See MANY-VALUED LOGIC.

logic, mathematical. See FORMAL LOGIC.

logic, modal. See MODAL LOGIC.

logic, non-monotonic. See NON-MONOTONIC LOGIC.

logic, ordinal. See ORDINAL LOGIC.

logic, philosophy of. See PHILOSOPHY OF LOGIC.

logic, pluralitive. See PLURALITIVE LOGIC.

logic, Polish. See POLISH LOGIC.

logic, predicate. See FORMAL LOGIC.

logic, quantum. See QUANTUM LOGIC.

logic, relational. See RELATIONAL LOGIC.

logic, second-order. See SECOND-ORDER LOGIC.

logic, symbolic. See FORMAL LOGIC.

logic, tense. See TENSE LOGIC.

logic, terminist. See TERMINIST LOGIC.

logic, three-valued. See MANY-VALUED LOGIC.

logical atomism. See RUSSELL.

logical behaviorism. See BEHAVIORISM, PHILOSOPHY OF MIND.

logical certainty. See CERTAINTY.

logical consequence, a proposition, sentence, or other piece of information that follows logically from one or more other propositions, sentences, or pieces of information. A proposition C is said to follow logically from, or to be a logical consequence of, propositions $P_1, P_2, \ldots$, if it must be the case that, on the assumption that $P_1, P_2, \ldots$, P_n are all true, the proposition C is true as well. For example, the proposition 'Smith is corrupt' is a logical consequence of the two propositions 'All politicians are corrupt' and 'Smith is a politician', since it must be the case that on the assumption that 'All politicians are corrupt' and 'Smith is a politician' are both true, 'Smith is corrupt' is also true.

Notice that proposition C can be a logical consequence of propositions $P_1, P_2, \ldots, P_n$, even if $P_1, P_2, \ldots, P_n$ are not actually all true. Indeed this is the case in our example. 'All politicians are corrupt' is not, in fact, true: there are some honest politicians. But if it were true, and if Smith were a politician, then 'Smith is corrupt' would have to be true. Because of this, it is said to be a logical consequence of those two propositions.

The logical consequence relation is often written using the symbol ⊨, called the double turnstile. Thus to indicate that C is a logical consequence of $P_1, P_2, \ldots, P_n$, we would write:

$$P_1, P_2, \ldots, P_n \models C$$
or:
$$\mathbf{P} \models C$$

where P stands for the set containing the propositions $p_1, p_2, \ldots, p_n$.

The term 'logical consequence' is sometimes reserved for cases in which C follows from $P_1, P_2, \ldots, P_n$ solely in virtue of the meanings of the so-called logical expressions (e.g., 'some', 'all', 'or', 'and', 'not') contained by these propositions. In this more restricted sense, 'Smith is not a politician' is not a logical consequence of the proposition 'All politicians are corrupt' and 'Smith is honest', since to recognize the consequence relation here we must also understand the specific meanings of the non-logical expressions 'corrupt' and 'honest'.

See also DEDUCTION, IMPLICATION, LOGICAL FORM, PROOF THEORY.   J.Et.

logical constant, a symbol, such as the connectives ~, ∧, ⊃, or ≡ or the quantifiers ∃ or ∀ of elementary quantification theory, that represents logical form. The contrast here is with expressions such as terms, predicates, and function symbols, which are supposed to represent the "content" of a sentence or proposition. Beyond this, there is little consensus on how to understand logical constancy. It is sometimes said, e.g., that a symbol is a logical constant if its interpretation is fixed across admissible valuations, though there is disagreement over exactly how to construe this "fixity" constraint. This account seems to make logical form a mere artifact of one's choice of a model theory. More generally, it has been questioned whether there are any objective grounds for classifying some expressions as logical and others not, or whether such a distinction is (wholly or in part) conventional. Other philosophers have suggested that logical constancy is less a semantic notion than an epistemic one: roughly, that α is a logical constant if the semantic behavior of certain other expressions together with the semantic contribution of α determine a priori (or in some other epistemically privileged fashion) the extensions of complex expressions in which a occurs. There is also considerable debate over whether particular symbols, such as the identity sign, modal operators, and quantifiers other than ∃ and ∀, are, or should be treated as, logical constants. See also LOGICAL FORM, MODEL THEORY.
                                                                      G.F.S.

logical construction, something built by logical operations from certain elements. Suppose that any sentence, S, containing terms apparently referring to objects of type F can be paraphrased without any essential loss of content into some (possibly much more complicated) sentence, S_p, containing only terms referring to objects of type G (distinct from F): in this case, objects of type F may be said to be logical constructions out of objects of type G. The notion originates with Russell's concept of an "incomplete symbol," which he introduced in connection with his theory of descriptions. According to Russell, a definite description – i.e., a descriptive phrase, such as 'the present king of France', apparently picking out a unique object – cannot be taken at face value as a genuinely referential term. One reason for this is that the existence of the objects seemingly referred to by such phrases can be meaningfully denied. We can say, "The present king of France does not exist," and it is hard to see how this could be if 'the present king of France', to be meaningful, has to refer to the present king of France. One solution, advocated by Meinong, is to claim that the referents required by what ordinary grammar suggests are singular terms must have some kind of "being," even though this need not amount to actual existence; but this solution offended Russell's "robust sense of reality." According to Russell, then, 'The F is G' is to be understood as equivalent to (something like) 'One and only one thing Fs and that thing is G'. (The phrase 'one and only one' can itself be paraphrased away in terms of quantifiers and identity.) The crucial feature of this analysis is that it does not define the problematic phrases by providing synonyms: rather, it provides a rule, which Russell called "a definition in use," for paraphrasing whole sentences in which they occur into whole sentences in which they do not. This is why definite descriptions are "incomplete symbols": we do not specify objects that are their meanings; we lay down a rule that explains the meaning of whole sentences in which they occur. Thus definite descriptions disappear under analysis, and with them the shadowy occupants of Meinong's realm of being.

Russell thought that the kind of analysis represented by the theory of descriptions gives the clue to the proper method for philosophy: solve metaphysical and epistemological problems by reducing ontological commitments. The task of philosophy is to substitute, wherever possible, logical constructions for inferred entities. Thus in the philosophy of mathematics, Russell attempted to eliminate numbers, as a distinct category of objects, by showing how mathematical statements can be translated into (what he took to be) purely logical statements. But what really gave Russell's program its bite was his thought that we can refer only to objects with which we are directly acquainted. This committed him to holding that all terms apparently referring to objects that cannot be regarded as objects of acquaintance should be given contextual definitions along the lines of the theory of descriptions: i.e., to treating everything beyond the scope of acquaintance as a logical construction (or a "logical fiction"). Most notably, Russell regarded physical objects as logical constructions out of sense-data, taking this to resolve the skeptical problem about our knowledge of the external world.

The project of showing how physical objects can be treated as logical constructions out of sense-data was a major concern of analytical philosophers in the interwar period, Carnap's *Der Logische Aufbau der Welt* ("The Logical Structure of the World," 1928) standing as perhaps its major monument. However, the project was not a success. Even Carnap's construction involves a system of space-time coordinates that is not analyzed in sense-datum terms and today few, if any, philosophers believe that such ambitious projects can be carried through.

See also DEFINITION, REDUCTION, RUSSELL, SOCIAL CONSTRUCTIVISM, THEORY OF DESCRIPTIONS.   M.W.

logical dependence. See DEPENDENCE.

logical empiricism. See LOGICAL POSITIVISM.

logical fiction. See LOGICAL CONSTRUCTION.

logical form, the form obtained from a proposition, a set of propositions, or an argument by abstracting from the subject matter of its content terms or by regarding the content terms as mere placeholders or blanks in a form. In a logically perfect language the logical form of a proposition, a set of propositions, or an argument is determined by the grammatical form of the sentence, the set of sentences, or the argument-text expressing it. Two sentences, sets of sentences, or argument-texts are said to have the same grammatical form, in this sense, if a uniform one-to-one substitution of content words transforms the one exactly into the other. The sentence 'Abe properly respects every agent who respects himself' may be regarded as having the same grammatical form as the sentence 'Ben generously assists every patient who assists himself'. Substitutions used to determine sameness of grammatical form cannot involve change of form words such as 'every', 'no', 'some', 'is', etc., and they must be category-preserving, i.e., they must put a proper name for a proper name, an adverb for an adverb, a transitive verb for a transitive verb, and so on. Two sentences having the same grammatical form have exactly the same form words distributed in exactly the same pattern; and although they of course need not, and usually do not, have the same content words, they do have exactly the same number of content words. The most distinctive feature of form words, which are also called syncategorematic terms or logical terms, is their *topic neutrality*; the form words in a sentence are entirely independent of and are in no way indicative of its content or topic.

Modern formal languages used in formal axiomatizations of mathematical sciences are often taken as examples of logically perfect languages. Pioneering work on logically perfect languages was done by George Boole (1815–64), Frege, Giuseppe Peano (1858–1952), Russell, and Church. According to the principle of logical form, an argument is (formally) valid or invalid in virtue of logical form. More explicitly, every two arguments in the same form are both valid or both invalid. Thus, every argument in the same form as a valid argument is valid and every argument in the same form as an invalid argument is invalid. The argument form that a given argument fits (or has) is not determined solely by the logical forms of its constituent propositions; the arrangement of those propositions is critical because the process of interchanging a premise with the conclusion of a valid argument can result in an invalid argument.

The principle of logical form, from which formal logic gets its name, is commonly used in establishing invalidity of arguments and consistency of sets of propositions. In order to show that a given argument is invalid it is sufficient to exhibit another argument as being in the same logical form and as having all true premises and a false conclusion. In order to show that a given set of propositions is consistent it is sufficient to exhibit another set of propositions as being in the same logical form and as being composed exclusively of true propositions. The history of these methods traces back through non-Cantorian set theory, non-Euclidean geometry, and medieval logicians (especially Anselm) to Aristotle. These methods must be used with extreme caution in languages such as English that fail to be logically perfect as a result of ellipsis, amphiboly, ambiguity, etc. For example, 'This is a male dog' implies 'This is a dog' but 'This is a brass monkey' does not imply 'This is a monkey', as would be required in a logically perfect language. Likewise, of two propositions commonly expressed by the ambiguous sentence 'Ann and Ben are married' one does and one does not imply the proposition that Ann is married to Ben.

Quine and other logicians are careful to distinguish, in effect, the (unique) logical form of a proposition from its (many) *schematic forms*. The proposition (A) 'If Abe is Ben, then if Ben is wise Abe is wise' has exactly one logical form, which it shares with (B) 'If Carl is Dan, then if Dan is kind Carl is kind', whereas it has all of the following schematic forms: (1) If P then if Q then R; (2) If P then Q; (3) P. The principle of form for propositions is that every two propositions in the same logical form are both tautological (logically necessary) or both non-tautological. Thus, although propositions A and B are tautological there are non-tautological propositions that fit the three schematic forms just mentioned.

Failure to distinguish logical form from schematic form has led to fallacies. According to the principle of logical form quoted above every argument in the same logical form as an invalid argument is invalid, but it is not the case that every argument sharing a schematic form with an invalid argument is invalid. Contrary to what would be fallaciously thought, the conclusion 'Abe is Ben' *is* logically implied by the following two propositions taken together, 'If Abe is Ben, then Ben is Abe' and 'Ben is Abe', even though the argument shares a schematic form with invalid arguments "committing" the fallacy of affirming the consequent.

See also AMBIGUITY, FORMAL LOGIC, LAWS OF THOUGHT, LOGICAL SYNTAX, TAUTOLOGY.

                                         J.Cor.

logical form, principle of. See LOGICAL FORM.

logical grammar. See GRAMMAR.

logical graph. See PEIRCE.

logical immediacy. See IMMEDIACY.

logical implication. See IMPLICATION.

logical independence. See INDEPENDENCE RESULTS.

logical indicator, also called indicator word, an expression that provides some help in identifying the conclusion of an argument or the premises offered in support of a conclusion. Common premise indicators include 'for', 'because', and 'since'. Common conclusion indicators include 'so', 'it follows that', 'hence', 'thus', and 'therefore'.

> Since Tom sat in the back of the room, he could not hear the performance clearly. Therefore, he could not write a proper review.

'Since' makes clear that Tom's seat location is offered as a reason to explain his inability to hear the performance. 'Therefore' indicates that the proposition that Tom could not write a proper review is the conclusion of the argument. T.J.D.

logically perfect language. See LOGICAL FORM, SCOPE.

logically proper name. See RUSSELL.

logical mechanism. See COMPUTER THEORY.

logical necessity. See NECESSITY.

logical notation, symbols designed to achieve unambiguous formulation of principles and inferences in deductive logic. Such notations involve some regimentation of words, word order, etc., of natural language. Some schematization was attempted even in ancient times by Aristotle, the Megarians, the Stoics, Boethius, and the medievals. But Leibniz's vision of a universal logical language began to be realized only in the past 150 years.

The notation is not yet standardized, but the following varieties of logical operators in propositional and predicate calculus may be noted. Given that 'p', 'q', 'r', etc., are propositional variables, or propositions, we find, in the contexts of their application, the following variety of operators (called truth-functional connectives).

Negation: '$\sim p$', '$\neg p$', '$\bar{p}$', 'p''.
Conjunction: '$p \cdot q$', '$p \,\&\, q$', '$p \wedge q$'.
Weak or inclusive disjunction: '$p \vee q$'.
Strong or exclusive disjunction: '$p \,\dot{\vee}\, q$', '$p + q$', '$p \veebar q$'.
Material conditional (sometimes called *material implication*): '$p \supset q$', '$p \rightarrow q$'.
Material biconditional (sometimes called *material equivalence*): '$p \equiv q$', '$p \leftrightarrow q$'.

And, given that 'x', 'y', 'z', etc., are individual variables and 'F', 'G', 'H', etc., are predicate letters, we find in the predicate calculus two quantifiers, a universal and an existential quantifier:

Universal quantification: '$(x)Fx$', '$(\forall x)Fx$', '$\wedge xFx$'.
Existential quantification: '$(Ex)Fx$', '$(\exists x)Fx$', '$\vee xFx$'.

The formation principle in all the schemata involving dyadic or binary operators (connectives) is that the logical operator is placed between the propositional variables (or propositional constants) connected by it. But there exists a notation, the so-called *Polish notation*, based on the formation rule stipulating that all operators, and not only negation and quantifiers, be placed in front of the schemata over which they are ranging. The following representations are the result of application of that rule:

Negation: 'Np'.
Conjunction: 'Kpq'.
Weak or inclusive disjunction: 'Apq'.
Strong or exclusive disjunction: 'Jpq'.
Conditional: 'Cpq'.
Biconditional: 'Epq'.
Sheffer stroke: 'Dpq'.
Universal quantification: 'ΠxFx'.
Existential quantifications: 'ΣxFx'.

Remembering that 'K', 'A', 'J', 'C', 'E', and 'D' are dyadic functors, we expect them to be followed by two propositional signs, each of which may itself be simple or compound, but no parentheses are needed to prevent ambiguity. Moreover, this notation makes it very perspicuous as to what kind of proposition a given compound proposition is: all we need to do is to look at the leftmost operator. To illustrate, '$p \vee (q \,\&\, r)$' is a disjunction of 'p' with the conjunction 'Kqr', i.e., '$ApKqr$', while '$(p \vee q) \,\&\, r$' is a conjunction of a disjunction 'Apq' with 'r', i.e., '$KApqr$'. '$\sim p \rightarrow q$' is written as '$CNpq$', i.e., 'if Np, then q', while negation of the whole conditional, '$\sim(p \rightarrow q)$', becomes '$NCpq$'. A logical thesis such as '$((p \,\&\, q) \rightarrow r) \rightarrow ((s \rightarrow p) \rightarrow (s \,\&\, q) \rightarrow r))$' is written concisely as '$CCKpqrCCspCKsqr$'. The general proposition '$(\forall x)(Fx \rightarrow Gx)$' is written as '$\Pi xCFxGx$', while a truth-function of quantified propositions '$(\forall x)Fx \rightarrow (\exists y)Gy$' is written as '$C\Pi xFx\Sigma yGy$'. An equivalence such as '$(\forall x) Fx \leftrightarrow \sim (\exists x) \sim Fx$' becomes '$E\Pi xFxN\Sigma xNFx$', etc.

Dot notation is way of using dots to construct well-formed formulas that is more thrifty with punctuation marks than the use of parentheses with their progressive strengths of scope. But dot notation is less thrifty than the parenthesis-free Polish notation, which secures well-formed expressions entirely on the basis of the order of logical operators relative to truth-functional compounds. Various dot notations have been devised. The convention most commonly adopted is that punctuation dots always operate away from the connective symbol that they flank. It is best to explain dot punctuation by examples:

(1) '$p \vee (q \sim r)$' becomes '$p \vee .q \rightarrow \sim r$';
(2) '$(p \vee q) \rightarrow \sim r$' becomes '$p \vee q . \rightarrow \sim r$';
(3) '$(p \rightarrow (q \leftrightarrow r)) \vee (p \vee r)$' becomes '$p \rightarrow . q \leftrightarrow r: \vee . p \vee r$';
(4) '$(\sim p \leftrightarrow q) \cdot (r \rightarrow s)$' becomes '$\sim p \leftrightarrow q . r \leftrightarrow s$'.

Note that here the dot is used as conjunction dot and is not flanked by punctuation dots, although in some contexts additional punctuation dots may have to be added, e.g., $'p.((q . r) \rightarrow s)'$, which is rewritten as $'p : q.r. \rightarrow s'$. The scope of a group of n dots extends to the group of n or more dots.

(5) $'\sim p \leftrightarrow (q.(r \rightarrow s))'$ becomes $'\sim p. \leftrightarrow : q.r \rightarrow s'$;

(6) $'\sim p \leftrightarrow ((q . r) \rightarrow s)'$ becomes $'\sim p. \leftrightarrow : q.r. \rightarrow s'$;

(7) $'(\sim p \leftrightarrow (q . r)) \rightarrow s'$ becomes $'\sim p \leftrightarrow. q.r: \rightarrow s'$.

The notation for modal propositions made popular by C. I. Lewis consisted of the use of '◊' to express the idea of possibility, in terms of which other alethic modal notions were defined. Thus, starting with '◊ p' for 'It is *possible* that p' we get '$\sim$ ◊ p' for 'It is not possible that p' (i.e., 'It is *impossible* that p'), '$\sim$ ◊ $\sim p$' for 'It is not possible that not p' (i.e., 'It is *necessary* that p'), and '◊ $\sim p$' for 'It is possible that not p' (i.e., 'It is *contingent* that p' in the sense of 'It is not necessary that p', i.e., 'It is possible that not p'). Given this primitive or undefined notion of possibility, Lewis proceeded to introduce the notion of strict implication, represented by '$\rightarrow$' and defined as follows: '$p \rightarrow q . = . \sim$ ◊ $(p . \sim q)$'. More recent tradition finds it convenient to use '□', either as a defined or as a primitive symbol of necessity. In the parenthesis-free Polish notation the letter 'M' is usually added as the sign of possibility and sometimes the letter 'L' is used as the sign of necessity. No inconvenience results from adopting these letters, as long as they do not coincide with any of the existing truth-functional operators 'N', 'K', 'A', 'J', 'C', 'E', 'D'. Thus we can express symbolically the sentences 'If p is necessary, then p is possible' as '$CNMNpMp$' or as '$CLpMp$'; 'It is necessary that whatever is F is G' as '$NMN\Pi xCFxGx$' or as '$L\Pi xCFxGx$'; and 'Whatever is F is necessarily G' as '$\Pi xCFxNMNGx$' or as $\Pi xCFxLGx$; etc.

See also IMPLICATION, MODAL LOGIC, WELL-FORMED FORMULA, **Appendix of Special Symbols.**   I.Bo.

logical paradoxes. See SET-THEORETIC PARADOXES.

logical positivism, also called positivism, a philosophical movement inspired by empiricism and verificationism; it began in the 1920s and flourished for about twenty or thirty years. While there are still philosophers who would identify themselves with some of the logical positivists' theses, many of the central docrines of the theory have come under considerable attack in the last half of this century. In some ways logical positivism can be seen as a natural outgrowth of radical or British empiricism and logical atomism. The driving force of positivism may well have been adherence to the verifiability criterion for the meaningfulness of cognitive statements. Acceptance of this principle led positivists to reject as problematic many assertions of religion, morality, and the kind of philosophy they described as metaphysics.

The verifiability criterion of meaning. The radical empiricists took genuine ideas to be composed of simple ideas traceable to elements in experience. If this is true and if thoughts about the empirical world are "made up" out of ideas, it would seem to follow that all genuine thoughts about the world must have as constituents thoughts that denote items of experience. While not all positivists tied meaning so clearly to the sort of experiences the empiricists had in mind, they were convinced that a genuine contingent assertion about the world must be verifiable through experience or observation.

Questions immediately arose concerning the relevant sense of 'verify'. Extreme versions of the theory interpret verification in terms of experiences or observations that entail the truth of the proposition in question. Thus for my assertion that there is a table before me to be meaningful, it must be in principle possible for me to accumulate evidence or justification that would guarantee the existence of the table, which would make it impossible for the table not to exist. Even this statement of the view is ambiguous, however, for the impossibility of error could be interpreted as logical or conceptual, or something much weaker, say, causal. Either way, extreme verificationism seems vulnerable to objections. Universal statements, such as 'All metal expands when heated', are meaningful, but it is doubtful that any observations could ever conclusively verify them. One might modify the criterion to include as meaningful only statements that can be *either* conclusively confirmed *or* conclusively disconfirmed. It is doubtful, however, that even ordinary statements about the physical world satisfy the extreme positivist insistence that they admit of conclusive verification or falsification. If the evidence we have for believing what we do about the physical world consists of knowledge of fleeting and subjective sensation, the possibility of hallucination or deception by a malevolent, powerful being seems to preclude the possibility of any finite sequence of sensations conclusively establishing the existence or absence of a physical object.

Faced with these difficulties, at least some positivists retreated to a more modest form of verificationism which insisted only that if a proposition is to be meaningful it must be possible to find evidence or justification that bears on the *likelihood* of the proposition's being true. It is, of course, much more difficult to find counterexamples to this weaker form of verificationism, but by the same token it is more difficult to see how the principle will do the work the positivists hoped it would do of weeding out allegedly problematic assertions.

Necessary truth. Another central tenet of logical positivism is that all meaningful statements fall into two categories: necessary truths that are analytic and knowable a priori, and contingent truths that are synthetic and knowable only a posteriori. If a meaningful statement is not a contingent, empirical statement verifiable through experience, then it is either a formal tautology or is analytic, i.e., reducible to a formal tautology through substitution of synonymous expressions. According to the positivist, tautologies and analytic truths that do not describe the world are made true (if true) or false (if false) by some fact about the rules of language. '*P* or not-*P*' is made true by rules we have for the use of the connectives 'or' and 'not' and for the assignments of the predicates 'true' and 'false'.

Again there are notorious problems for logical positivism. It is difficult to reduce the following apparently necessary truths to formal tautologies through the substitution of synonymous expressions: (1) Everything that is blue (all over) is not red (all over). (2) All equilateral triangles are equiangular triangles. (3) No proposition is both true and false. Ironically, the positivists had a great deal of trouble categorizing the very theses that defined their view, such as the claims about meaningfulness and verifiability and the claims about the analytic–synthetic distinction.

Reductionism. Most of the logical positivists were committed to a foundationalist epistemology according to which all justified belief rests ultimately on beliefs that are non-inferentially justified. These non-inferentially justified beliefs were sometimes described as basic, and the truths known in such manner were often referred to as self-evident, or as *protocol statements*. Partly because the positivists disagreed as to how to understand the notion of a basic belief or a protocol statement, and even disagreed as to what would be good examples, positivism was by no means a monolithic movement. Still, the ver-

ifiability criterion of meaning, together with certain beliefs about where the foundations of justification lie and beliefs about what constitutes legitimate reasoning, drove many positivists to embrace extreme forms of reductionism. Briefly, most of them implicitly recognized only deduction and (reluctantly) induction as legitimate modes of reasoning. Given such a view, difficult epistemological gaps arise between available evidence and the commonsense conclusions we want to reach about the world around us. The problem was particularly acute for empiricists who recognized as genuine empirical foundations only propositions describing perceptions or subjective sensations. Such philosophers faced an enormous difficulty explaining how what we know about sensations could confirm for us assertions about an objective physical world. Clearly we cannot deduce any truths about the physical world from what we know about sensations (remember the possibility of hallucination). Nor does it seem that we could inductively establish sensation as evidence for the existence of the physical world when all we have to rely on ultimately is our awareness of sensations. Faced with the possibility that all of our commonplace assertions about the physical world might fail the verifiability test for meaningfulness, many of the positivists took the bold step of arguing that statements about the physical world could really be viewed as reducible to (equivalent in meaning to) very complicated statements about sensations. Phenomenalists, as these philosophers were called, thought that asserting that a given table exists is equivalent in meaning to a complex assertion about what sensations or sequences of sensations a subject would have were he to have certain other sensations.

The gap between sensation and the physical world is just one of the epistemic gaps threatening the meaningfulness of commonplace assertions about the world. If all we know about the mental states of others is inferred from their physical behavior, we must still explain how such inference is justified. Thus logical positivists who took protocol statements to include ordinary assertions about the physical world were comfortable reducing talk about the mental states of others to talk about their behavior; this is logical behaviorism. Even some of those positivists who thought empirical propositions had to be reduced ultimately to talk about sensations were prepared to translate talk about the mental states of others into talk about their behavior, which, ironically, would in turn get translated right back into talk about sensation.

Many of the positivists were primarily concerned with the hypotheses of theoretical physics, which seemed to go far beyond anything that could be observed. In the context of philosophy of science, some positivists seemed to take as unproblematic ordinary statements about the macrophysical world but were still determined either to reduce theoretical statements in science to complex statements about the observable world, or to view theoretical entities as a kind of convenient fiction, description of which lacks any literal truth-value. The limits of a positivist's willingness to embrace reductionism are tested, however, when he comes to grips with knowledge of the past. It seems that propositions describing memory experiences (if such "experiences" really exist) do not entail any truths about the past, nor does it seem possible to establish memory inductively as a reliable indicator of the past. (How could one establish the past correlations without relying on memory?) The truly hard-core reductionists actually toyed with the possibility of reducing talk about the past to talk about the present and future, but it is perhaps an understatement to suggest that at this point the plausibility of the reductionist program was severely strained.

See also ANALYTIC–SYNTHETIC DISTINCTION, BEHAVIORISM, EMPIRICISM, FOUNDATIONALISM, PHILOSOPHY OF SCIENCE, VERIFICATIONISM, VIENNA CIRCLE.   R.A.F.

logical predicate. See LOGICAL SUBJECT.

logical priority. See DEPENDENCE.

logical probability. See PROBABILITY.

logical product, a conjunction of propositions or predicates. The term 'product' derives from an analogy that conjunction bears to arithmetic multiplication, and that appears very explicitly in an algebraic logic such as a Boolean algebra. In the same way, 'logical sum' usually means the disjunction of propositions or predicates, and the term 'sum' derives from an analogy that disjunction bears with arithmetic addition. In the logical literature of the nineteenth century, e.g. in the works of Peirce, 'logical product' and 'logical sum' often refer to the relative product and relative sum, respectively. In the work of George Boole, 'logical sum' indicates an operation that corresponds not to disjunction but rather to the exclusive 'or'. The use of 'logical sum' in its contemporary sense was introduced by John Venn and then adopted and promulgated by Peirce.

'Relative product' was introduced by Augustus De Morgan and also adopted and promulgated by Peirce.   R.W.B.

logical reconstruction. See RATIONAL RECONSTRUCTION.

logical subject, in Aristotelian and traditional logic, the common noun, or sometimes the intension or the extension of the common noun, that follows the initial quantifier word ('every', 'some', 'no', etc.) of a sentence, as opposed to the grammatical subject, which is the entire noun phrase including the quantifier and the noun, and in some usages, any modifiers that may apply. The grammatical subject of 'Every number exceeding zero is positive' is 'every number', or in some usages, 'every number exceeding zero', whereas the logical subject is 'number', or the intension or the extension of 'number'. Similar distinctions are made between the logical predicate and the grammatical predicate: in the above example, 'is positive' is the grammatical predicate, whereas the logical predicate is the adjective 'positive', or sometimes the property of being positive or even the extension of the word 'positive'. In standard first-order logic the logical subject of a sentence under a given interpretation is the entire universe of discourse of the interpretation. **See also** GRAMMAR, LOGICAL FORM, SUBJECT, UNIVERSE OF DISCOURSE.
                J.Cor.

logical sum. See LOGICAL PRODUCT.

logical syntax, description of the forms of the expressions of a language in virtue of which the expressions stand in logical relations to one another. Implicit in the idea of logical syntax is the assumption that all – or at least most – logical relations hold in virtue of form: e.g., that 'If snow is white, then snow has color' and 'Snow is white' jointly entail 'Snow has color' in virtue of their respective forms, 'If P, then Q', 'P', and 'Q'. The form assigned to an expression in logical syntax is its logical form.

Logical form may not be immediately apparent from the surface form of an expression. Both (1) 'Every individual is physical' and (2) 'Some individual is physical' apparently share the subject-predicate form. But this surface form is not the form in virtue of which these sentences (or the propositions they might be said to express) stand in logical relations to other sentences (or propositions), for if it were, (1) and (2) would have the same logical relations to all sentences (or propositions), but they do not; (1) and (3) 'Aristotle is an individual' jointly entail (4) 'Aristotle is physical', whereas (2) and (3) do not jointly entail (4). So (1) and (2) differ in logical form. The contemporary logical syntax, devised largely by Frege, assigns very different logical forms to (1) and (2), namely: 'For every x, if x is an individual, then x is physical' and 'For some x, x is an individual and x is physical', respectively. Another example: (5) 'The satellite of the moon has water' seems to entail 'There is at least one thing that orbits the moon' and 'There is no more than one thing that orbits the moon'. In view of this, Russell assigned to (5) the logical form 'For some x, x orbits the moon, and for every y, if y orbits the moon, then y is identical with x, and for every y, if y orbits the moon, then y has water'.

See also GRAMMAR, LOGICAL FORM, THEORY OF DESCRIPTIONS.   T.Y.

logical system. See FORMAL SEMANTICS, LOGISTIC SYSTEM.

logical table of judgments. See KANT.

logical truth, linguistic theory of. See CONVENTIONALISM.

logicism, the thesis that mathematics, or at least some significant portion thereof, is part of logic. Modifying Carnap's suggestion (in "The Logicist Foundation for Mathematics," first published in *Erkenntnis*, 1931), this thesis is the conjunction of two theses: *expressibility logicism:* mathematical propositions are (or are alternative expressions of) purely logical propositions; and *derivational logicism:* the axioms and theorems of mathematics can be derived from pure logic.

Here is a motivating example from the arithmetic of the natural numbers. Let the cardinality-quantifiers be those expressible in the form 'there are exactly . . . many xs such that', which we abbreviate $\ulcorner(\ldots x)\urcorner$ with '. . .' replaced by an Arabic numeral. These quantifiers are expressible with the resources of first-order logic with identity; e.g. '$(2x)Px$' is equivalent to '$\exists x \exists y (x \neq y$ & $\forall z[Pz \equiv (z = x \lor z = y)])$', the latter involving no numerals or other specifically mathematical vocabulary. Now $2 + 3 = 5$ is surely a mathematical truth. We might take it to express the following: if we take two things and then another three things we have five things, which is a validity of second-order logic involving no mathematical vocabulary:

$$\forall X \forall Y \ ([(2x) \ Xx \ \& \ (3x) \ Yx \ \& \ \neg\exists x(Xx \ \& \ Yx)] \supset (5x) \ (Xx \lor Yx)).$$

Furthermore, this is provable in any formalized fragment of second-order logic that includes all of first-order logic with identity and second-order '$\forall$'-introduction.

But what counts as logic? As a derivation? As a derivation from pure logic? Such unclarities keep alive the issue of whether some version or modification of logicism is true.

The "classical" presentations of logicism were Frege's *Grundgesetze der Arithmetik* and Russell and Whitehead's *Principia Mathematica.* Frege took logic to be a formalized fragment of second-order logic supplemented by an operator forming singular terms from "incomplete" expressions, such a term standing for an extension of the "incomplete" expression standing for a concept of level 1 (i.e. type 1). Axiom 5 of *Grundgesetze* served as a comprehension-axiom implying the existence of extensions for arbitrary Fregean concepts of level 1. In his famous letter of 1901 Russell showed that axiom to be inconsistent, thus derailing Frege's original program.

Russell and Whitehead took logic to be a formalized fragment of a ramified full finite-order (i.e. type ω) logic, with higher-order variables ranging over appropriate propositional functions. The *Principia* and their other writings left the latter notion somewhat obscure. As a defense of expressibility logicism, *Principia* had this peculiarity: it postulated typical ambiguity where naive mathematics seemed unambiguous; e.g., each type had its own system of natural numbers two types up. As a defense of derivational logicism, *Principia* was flawed by virtue of its reliance on three axioms, a version of the Axiom of Choice, and the axioms of Reducibility and Infinity, whose truth was controversial. Reducibility could be avoided by eliminating the ramification of the logic (as suggested by Ramsey). But even then, even the arithmetic of the natural numbers required use of Infinity, which in effect asserted that there are infinitely many individuals (i.e., entities of type 0). Though Infinity was "purely logical," i.e., contained only logical expressions, in his *Introduction to Mathematical Philosophy* (p. 141) Russell admits that it "cannot be asserted by logic to be true." Russell then (pp. 194–95) forgets this: "If there are still those who do not admit the identity of logic and mathematics, we may challenge them to indicate at what point in the successive definitions and deductions of *Principia Mathematica* they consider that logic ends and mathematics begins. It will then be obvious that any answer is arbitrary." The answer, "Section 120, in which Infinity is first assumed!," is not arbitrary. In *Principia* Russell and Whitehead say of Infinity that they "prefer to keep it as a hypothesis" (Vol. 2, p. 203). Perhaps then they did not really take logicism to assert the above identity, but rather a correspondence: to each sentence φ of mathematics there corresponds a conditional sentence of logic whose antecedent is the Axiom of Infinity and whose consequent is a purely logical reformulation of φ.

In spite of the problems with the "classical" versions of logicism, if we count so-called higher-order (at least second-order) logic as logic, and if we reformulate the thesis to read 'Each area of mathematics is, or is part of, *a* logic', logicism remains alive and well.

See also FREGE, GÖDEL'S INCOMPLETENESS THEOREMS, PHILOSOPHY OF MATHEMATICS, SET THEORY.   H.T.H.

logic of discovery. See ABDUCTION.

logic of validation. See ABDUCTION.

logistic system, a formal language together with a set of axioms and rules of inference, or what many today would call a "logic." The original idea behind the notion of a logistic system was that the language, axioms, rules, and attendant concepts of proof and theorem were to be specified in a mathematically precise fashion, thus enabling one to make the study of deductive reasoning an exact science. One was to begin with an effective specification of the primitive symbols of the language and of which (finite) sequences of symbols were to count as sentences or well-formed formulas. Next, certain sentences were to be singled out effectively as axioms. The rules of inference were also to be given in such a manner that there would be an effective procedure for telling which rules are rules of the system and what inferences they license. A proof was then defined as any finite sequence of sentences, each of which is either an axiom or follows from some earlier line(s) by one of the rules, with a theorem being the last line of a proof. With the subsequent development of logic, the requirement of effectiveness has sometimes been dropped, as has the requirement that sentences and proofs be finite in length. See also ALGORITHM, INFINITARY LOGIC, PROOF THEORY.   G.F.S.

logocentric. See DECONSTRUCTION.

logoi. See DECONSTRUCTION, LOGOS.

logos (plural: *logoi*) (Greek, 'word', 'speech', 'reason'), term with the following main philosophi-

cal senses. (1) Rule, principle, law. E.g., in Stoicism the *logos* is the divine order and in Neoplatonism the intelligible regulating forces displayed in the sensible world. The term came thus to refer, in Christianity, to the Word of God, to the instantiation of his agency in creation, and, in the New Testament, to the person of Christ. (2) Proposition, account, explanation, thesis, argument. E.g., Aristotle presents a *logos* from first principles. (3) Reason, reasoning, the rational faculty, abstract theory (as opposed to experience), discursive reasoning (as opposed to intuition). E.g., Plato's *Republic* uses the term to refer to the intellectual part of the soul. (4) Measure, relation, proportion, ratio. E.g., Aristotle speaks of the *logoi* of the musical scales. (5) Value, worth. E.g., Heraclitus speaks of the man whose *logos* is greater than that of others.   R.C.

Lombard, Peter. See PETER LOMBARD.

Longinus (late first century A.D.), Greek literary critic, author of a treatise *On the Sublime* (*Peri hypsous*). The work is ascribed to "Dionysius or Longinus" in the manuscript and is now tentatively dated to the end of the first century A.D. The author argues for five sources of sublimity in literature: (a) grandeur of thought and (b) deep emotion, both products of the writer's "nature"; (c) figures of speech, (d) nobility and originality in word use, and (e) rhythm and euphony in diction, products of technical artistry. The passage on emotion is missing from the text. The treatise, with Aristotelian but enthusiastic spirit, throws light on the emotional effect of many great passages of Greek literature; noteworthy are its comments on Homer (ch. 9). Its nostalgic plea for an almost romantic independence and greatness of character and imagination in the poet and orator in an age of dictatorial government and somnolent peace is unique and memorable. See also AESTHETICS, ARISTOTLE.   D.Ar.

loop, closed. See CYBERNETICS.

loop, open. See CYBERNETICS.

lottery paradox, a paradox involving two plausible assumptions about justification which yield the conclusion that a fully rational thinker may justifiably believe a pair of contradictory propositions. The unattractiveness of this conclusion has led philosophers to deny one or the other of the assumptions in question. The paradox, which is due to Henry Kyburg, is generated as follows. Suppose I am contemplating a fair lottery involving n tickets (for some suitably large n), and I justifiably believe that exactly one ticket will win. Assume that if the probability of p, relative to one's evidence, meets some given high threshold less than 1, then one has justification for believing that p (and not merely justification for believing that p is highly probable). This is sometimes called a *rule of detachment* for inductive hypotheses. Then supposing that the number n of tickets is large enough, the rule implies that I have justification for believing (T_1) that the first ticket will lose (since the probability of T_1 (= ($n - 1$)/n) will exceed the given high threshold if n is large enough). By similar reasoning, I will also have justification for believing (T_2) that the second ticket will lose, and similarly for each remaining ticket. Assume that if one has justification for believing that p and justification for believing that q, then one has justification for believing that p and q. This is a consequence of what is sometimes called "deductive closure for justification," according to which one has justification for believing the deductive consequences of what one justifiably believes. Closure, then, implies that I have justification for believing that T_1 and T_2 and ... T_n. But this conjunctive proposition is equivalent to the proposition that no ticket will win, and we began with the assumption that I have justification for believing that exactly one ticket will win. **See also** CLOSURE, JUSTIFICATION.   A.B.

Lotze, Rudolf Hermann (1817–81), German philosopher and influential representative of post-Hegelian German metaphysics. Lotze was born in Bautzen and studied medicine, mathematics, physics, and philosophy at Leipzig, where he became instructor, first in medicine and later in philosophy. His early views, expressed in his *Metaphysik* (1841) and *Logik* (1843), were influenced by C. H. Weisse, a former student of Hegel's. He succeeded J. F. Herbart as professor of philosophy at Göttingen, where he served from 1844 until shortly before his death. Between 1856 and 1864, he published, in three volumes, his best-known work, *Mikrocosmus*. *Logik* (1874) and *Metaphysik* (1879) were published as the first two parts of his unfinished three-volume *System der Philosophie*.

While Lotze shared the metaphysical and systematic appetites of his German idealist predecessors, he rejected their intellectualism, favoring an emphasis on the primacy of feeling; believed that metaphysics must fully respect the methods, results, and "mechanistic" assumptions of the empirical sciences; and saw philoso-

phy as the never completed attempt to raise and resolve questions arising from the inevitable pluralism of methods and interests involved in science, ethics, and the arts. A strong personalism is manifested in his assertion that feeling discloses to us a relation to a personal deity and its teleological workings in nature. His most enduring influences can be traced, in America, through Royce, Santayana, B. P. Bowne, and James, and, in England, through Bosanquet and Bradley.

See also IDEALISM, PERSONALISM.   J.P.Su.

love, ethics of. See DIVINE COMMAND ETHICS.

Löwenheim-Skolem theorem, the result that for any set of sentences of standard predicate logic, if there is any interpretation in which they are all true, there there is also an interpretation whose domain consists of natural numbers and in which they are all true.

Leopold Löwenheim proved in 1915 that for finite sets of sentences of standard predicate logic, if there is any interpretation in which they are true, there is also an interpretation that makes them true and where the domain is a subset of the domain of the first interpretation, and the new domain can be mapped one-to-one onto a set of natural numbers. Löwenheim's proof contained some gaps and made essential but implicit use of the *axiom of choice*, a principle of set theory whose truth was, and is, a matter of debate. In fact, the Löwenheim-Skolem theorem is equivalent to the axiom of choice. Thoralf Skolem, in 1920, gave a more detailed proof that made explicit the appeal to the axiom of choice and that extended the scope of the theorem to include infinite sets of sentences. In 1922 he gave an essentially different proof that did not depend on the axiom of choice and in which the domain consisted of natural numbers rather than being of the same size as a set of natural numbers. In most contemporary texts, Skolem's result is proved by methods later devised by Gödel, Herbrand, or Henkin for proving other results. If the language does not include an identity predicate, then Skolem's result is that the second domain consists of the entire set of natural numbers; if the language includes an identity predicate, then the second domain may be a proper subset of the natural numbers. (See van Heijenoort, *From Frege to Gödel: A Source Book in Mathematical Logic 1879–1931*, 1967, for translations of the original papers.)

The original results were of interest because they showed that in many cases unexpected interpretations with smaller infinite domains than those of the initially given interpretation could be constructed. It was later shown – and this is the Upward Löwenheim-Skolem theorem – that interpretations with larger domains could also be constructed that rendered true the same set of sentences. Hence the theorem as stated initially is sometimes referred to as the Downward Löwenheim-Skolem theorem.

The theorem was surprising because it was believed that certain sets of axioms characterized domains, such as the continuum of real numbers, that were larger than the set of natural numbers. This surprise is called *Skolem's paradox*, but it is to be emphasized that this is a philosophical puzzle rather than a formal contradiction. Two main lines of response to the paradox developed early. The realist, who believes that the continuum exists independently of our knowledge or description of it, takes the theorem to show either that the full truth about the structure of the continuum is ineffable or at least that means other than standard first-order predicate logic are required. The constructivist, who believes that the continuum is in some sense our creation, takes the theorem to show that size comparisons among infinite sets is not an absolute matter, but relative to the particular descriptions given. Both positions have received various more sophisticated formulations that differ in details, but they remain the two main lines of development.

See also SET THEORY.   R.E.G.

lower functional calculus. See FORMAL LOGIC.

Lucretius (99 or 94–55 B.C.), Roman poet, author of *On the Nature of Things* (*De rerum natura*), an epic poem in six books. Lucretius's emphasis, as an orthodox Epicurean, is on the role of even the most technical aspects of physics and philosophy in helping to attain emotional peace and dismiss the terrors of popular religion. Each book studies some aspect of the school's theories, while purporting to offer elementary instruction to its addressee, Memmius. Each begins with an ornamental proem and ends with a passage of heightened emotional impact; the argumentation is adorned with illustrations from personal observation, frequently of the contemporary Roman and Italian scene. Book 1 demonstrates that nothing exists but an infinity of atoms moving in an infinity of void. Opening with a proem on the love of Venus and Mars (an allegory of the Roman peace), it ends with an image of Epicurus as conqueror, throwing the javelin of war outside the finite universe of the geocentric astronomers. Book 2 proves the mortality of all finite worlds; Book 3, after proving the mortality of the human soul, ends with a hymn on the theme that there is nothing to feel or fear in death. The discussion of sensation and thought in Book 4 leads to a diatribe against the torments of sexual desire. The shape and contents of the visible world are discussed in Book 5, which ends with an account of the origins of civilization. Book 6, about the forces that govern meteorological, seismic, and related phenomena, ends with a frightening picture of the plague of 429 B.C. at Athens. The unexpectedly gloomy end suggests the poem is incomplete (also the absence of two great Epicurean themes, friendship and the gods). **See also** EPICURE-ANISM.   D.Ar.

Lu Hsiang-shan (1139–93), Chinese Neo-Confucian philosopher, an opponent of Chu Hsi's metaphysics. For Lu the mind is quite sufficient for realizing the Confucian vision of the unity and harmony of man and nature (*t'ien-jen ho-i*). While Chu Hsi focused on "following the path of study and inquiry," Lu stressed "honoring the moral nature (of humans)." Lu is a sort of metaphysical idealist, as evident in his statement, "The affairs of the universe are my own affairs," and in his attitude toward the Confucian classics: "If in our study we know the fundamentals, then all the Six Classics [the *Book of Odes, Book of History, Book of Rites, Book of Changes*, the *Chou-li*, and the *Spring and Autumn Annals*] are my footnotes." The realization of Confucian vision is ultimately a matter of self-realization, anticipating a key feature of Wang Yang-ming's philosophy. **See also** NEO-CONFUCIANISM.   A.S.C.

Luis de Molina. See MOLINA.

Lukács, Georg (1885–1971), Hungarian Marxist philosopher best known for his *History and Class Consciousness: Studies in Marxist Dialectics* (1923). In 1918 he joined the Hungarian Communist Party and for much of the remainder of his career had a controversial relationship with it. For several months in 1919 he was People's Commissar for Education in Béla Kun's government, until he fled to Vienna and later moved to Berlin. In 1933 he fled Hitler and moved to Moscow, remaining there until the end of World War II, when he returned to Budapest as a university professor. In 1956 he was Minister of Culture in Imre Nagy's short-lived government. This led to a brief exile in Rumania. In his later years he returned to teaching in Budapest and was much celebrated by the Hungarian government. His *Collected Works* are forthcoming in both German and Hungarian. He is equally celebrated for his literary criticism and his reconstruction of the young Marx's thought.

For convenience his work is often divided into three periods: the pre-Marxist, the Stalinist, and the post-Stalinist. What unifies these periods and remains constant in his work are the problems of dialectics and the concept of totality. He stressed the Marxist claim of the possibility of a dialectical unity of subject and object. This was to be obtained through the proletariat's realization of itself and the concomitant destruction of economic alienation in society, with the understanding that truth was a still-to-be-realized totality. (In the post–World War II period this theme was taken up by the Yugoslavian praxis theorists.) The young neo-Kantian Lukács presented an aesthetics stressing the subjectivity of human experience and the emptiness of social experience. This led several French philosophers to claim that he was the first major existentialist of the twentieth century; he strongly denied it. Later he asserted that realism is the only correct way to understand literary criticism, arguing that since humanity is at the core of any social discussion, form depends on content and the content of politics is central to all historical social interpretations of literature.

Historically Lukács's greatest claim to fame within Marxist circles came from his realization that Marx's materialist theory of history and the resultant domination of the economic could be fully understood only if it allowed for both necessity and species freedom. In *History and Class Consciousness* he stressed Marx's debt to Hegelian dialectics years before the discovery of Marx's *Economic and Philosophical Manuscripts of 1844*. Lukács stresses his Hegelian Marxism as the correct orthodox version over and against the established Engels-inspired Soviet version of a dialectics of nature. His claim to be returning to Marx's methodology emphasizes the primacy of the concept of totality. It is through Marx's use of the dialectic that capitalist society can be seen as essentially reified and the proletariat viewed as the true subject of history and the only possible salvation of humanity. All truth is to be seen in relation to the proletariat's historical mission. Marx's materialist conception of history itself must be examined in light of proletarian knowledge. Truth is no longer given but must be understood in terms of relative moments in the process of the unfolding of the real union of theory and praxis: the totality of social relations. This union is not to be realized as some statistical understanding, but rather grasped through proletarian consciousness and directed party action in which subject and object are one. (Karl Mannheim included a modified version of this theory of social-historical relativism in his work on the sociology of knowledge.) In Europe and America this led to Western Marxism. In Eastern Europe and the Soviet Union it led to condemnation. If both the known and the knower are moments of the same thing, then there is a two-directional dialectical relationship, and Marxism cannot be understood from Engels's one-way movement of the dialectic of nature.

The Communist attack on Lukács was so extreme that he felt it necessary to write an apologetic essay on Lenin's established views. In *The Young Hegel: Studies in the Relations between Dialectics and Economics* (1938), Lukács modified his views but still stressed the dialectical commonality of Hegel and Marx. In Lukács's last years he unsuccessfully tried to develop a comprehensive ethical theory. The positive result was over two thousand pages of a preliminary study on social ontology.

See also MARXISM, PRAXIS.   J.Bi.

Łukasiewicz, Jan (1878–1956), Polish philosopher and logician, the most renowned member of the Warsaw School. The work for which he is best known is the discovery of many-valued logics, but he also invented bracket-free Polish notation; obtained original consistency, completeness, independence, and axiom-shortening results for sentential calculi; rescued Stoic logic from the misinterpretation and incomprehension of earlier historians and restored it to its rightful place as the first formulation of the theory of deduction; and finally incorporated Aristotle's syllogisms, both assertoric and modal, into a deductive system in his work *Aristotle's Syllogistic from the Standpoint of Modern Formal Logic*.

Reflection on Aristotle's discussion of future contingency in *On Interpretation* led Łukasiewicz in 1918 to posit a third truth-value, *possible*, in addition to *true* and *false*, and to construct a formal three-valued logic. Where in his notation *Cpq* denotes 'if p then q', *Np* 'not p', *Apq* 'either p or q', and *Kpq* 'both p and q', the system is defined by the following matrices (½ is the third truth-value):

C	1	$\frac{1}{2}$	O	N
* 1	1	$\frac{1}{2}$	O	O
$\frac{1}{2}$	1	1	$\frac{1}{2}$	$\frac{1}{2}$
O	1	1	1	1

Apq is defined as *CCpqq*, and *Kpq* as *NANpNq*. The system was axiomatized by Wajsberg in 1931. Łukasiewicz's motivation in constructing a formal system of three-valued logic was to break the grip of the idea of universal determinism on the imagination of philosophers and scientists. For him, there was *causal* determinism (shortly to be undermined by quantum theory), but there was also *logical* determinism, which in accordance with the principle of bivalence decreed that the statement that J.L. would be in Warsaw at noon on December 21 next year was either true or false now, and indeed had been either true or false for all time. In three-valued logic this statement would take the value ½, thus avoiding any apparent threat to free will posed by the law of bivalence.

See also MANY-VALUED LOGIC, POLISH LOGIC.   S.Mc.

Lull, Raymond, also spelled Raymond Lully, Ramon Llull (c.1232–1316), Catalan Christian mystic and missionary. A polemicist against Islam, a social novelist, and a constructor of schemes for international unification, Lull is best known in the history of philosophy for his quasi-algebraic or combinatorial treatment of metaphysical principles. His logic of divine and creaturely attributes is set forth first in an *Ars compendiosa inveniendi veritatem* (1274), next in an *Ars demonstrativa* (1283–89), then in reworkings of both of these and in the *Tree of Knowledge,* and finally in the *Ars brevis* and the *Ars generalis ultima* (1309–16). Each of these contains tables and diagrams that permit the reader to calculate the interactions of the various principles. Although his dates place him in the period of mature Scholasticism, the vernacular language and the Islamic or Judaic construction of Lull's works relegate him to the margin of Scholastic debates. His influence is to be sought rather in late medieval and Renaissance cabalistic or hermetic traditions. **See also** CABALA, SCHOLASTICISM.
                                                        M.D.J.

lumen naturale. See DESCARTES.

Lun Yu. See CONFUCIUS.

Lü-shih ch'un-ch'iu, a Chinese anthology of late Warring States (403–221 B.C.) philosophical writings. It was compiled by a patron, Lü Pu-wei, who became chancellor of the state of Ch'in in about 240 B.C. As the earliest example of the encyclopedic genre, and often associated with the later *Huai Nan Tzu,* it includes the full spectrum of philosophical schools, and covers topics from competing positions on human nature to contemporary farming procedures. An important feature of this work is its development of correlative yin–yang and five-phases vocabulary for organizing the natural and human processes of the world, positing relations among the various seasons, celestial bodies, tastes, smells, materials, colors, geographical directions, and so on. **See also** HUAI NAN TZU; WU-HSING; YIN, YANG.
                                                R.P.P. & R.T.A.

Luther, Martin (1483–1546), German religious reformer and leader of the Protestant Reformation. He was an Augustinian friar and unsystematic theologian from Saxony, schooled in nominalism (Ockham, Biel, Staupitz) and trained in biblical languages. Luther initially taught philosophy and subsequently Scripture (Romans, Galatians, Hebrews) at Wittenberg University. His career as a church reformer began with his public denunciation, in the 95 theses, of the sale of indulgences in October 1517. Luther produced three incendiary tracts: *Appeal to the Nobility, The Babylonian Captivity of the Church,* and *The Freedom of a Christian Man* (1520), which prompted his excommunication. At the 1521 Diet of Worms he claimed: "I am bound by the Scripture I have quoted and my conscience is captive to the Word of God. I cannot and will not retract anything since it is neither safe nor right to go against my conscience. Here I stand, may God help me."

Despite his modernist stance on the primacy of conscience over tradition, the reformer broke with Erasmus over free will (*De servo Arbitrio,* 1525), championing an Augustinian, anti-humanist position. His crowning achievement, the translation of the Bible into German (1534/45), shaped the modern German language. On the strength of a biblical-Christocentric, anti-philosophical theology, he proclaimed justification by faith alone and the priesthood of all believers. He unfolded a *theologia crucis,* reformed the Mass, acknowledged only two sacraments (baptism and the Eucharist), advocated consubstantiation instead of transubstantiation, and propounded the Two Kingdoms theory in church–state relations.

See also JUSTIFICATION BY FAITH, TRAN-
SUBSTANTIATION.   J.-L.S.

Lyceum, (1) an extensive ancient sanctuary of
Apollo just east of Athens, the site of public ath-
letic facilities where Aristotle taught during the
last decade of his life; (2) a center for philosophy
and systematic research in science and history
organized there by Aristotle and his associates; it
began as an informal group and lacked any legal
status until Theophrastus, Aristotle's colleague
and principal heir, acquired land and buildings
there c.315 B.C. By a principle of metonymy
common in philosophy (cf. 'Academy', 'Oxford',
'Vienna'), the name 'Lyceum' came to refer collectively to members of the school and their
methods and ideas, although the school
remained relatively non-doctrinaire. Another
ancient label for adherents of the school and
their ideas, apparently derived from Aristotle's
habit of lecturing in a portico (*peripatos*) at the
Lyceum, is 'Peripatetic'.

The school had its heyday in its first decades,
when members included Eudemus, author of
lost histories of mathematics; Aristoxenus, a prolific writer, principally on music (large parts of
two treatises survive); Dicaearchus, a polymath
who ranged from ethics and politics to psychology and geography; Meno, who compiled a history of medicine; and Demetrius of Phaleron, a
dashing intellect who wrote extensively and
ruled Athens on behalf of foreign dynasts from
317 to 307. Under Theophrastus and his successor Strato, the school produced original work,
especially in natural science. But by the mid-
third century B.C., the Lyceum had lost its initial
vigor. To judge from meager evidence, it offered
sound education but few new ideas; some members enjoyed political influence, but for nearly
two centuries, rigorous theorizing was displaced
by intellectual history and popular moralizing. In
the first century B.C., the school enjoyed a modest renaissance when Andronicus oversaw the
first methodical edition of Aristotle's works and
began the exegetical tradition that culminated in
the monumental commentaries of Alexander of
Aphrodisias (fl. A.D. 200).

See also ACADEMY, ANDRONICUS OF
RHODES, ARISTOTLE, COMMENTARIES ON
ARISTOTLE, STRATO OF LAMPSACUS.   S.A.W.

Lyotard, Jean-François (1924–98), French philosopher, a leading representative of the movement known in the English-speaking world as
post-structuralism. Among major post-structuralist theorists (Gilles Deleuze [1925–97], Derrida, Foucault), Lyotard is most closely associated
with postmodernism. With roots in phenomenology (a student of Merleau-Ponty, his first
book, *Phenomenology* [1954], engages phenomenology's history and engages phenomenology
with history) and Marxism (in the 1960s Lyotard
was associated with the Marxist group Socialisme ou Barbarie, founded by Cornelius Castori-
adis [1922–97] and Claude Lefort [b.1924]),
Lyotard's work has centered on questions of art,
language, and politics.

His first major work, *Discours, figure* (1971),
expressed dissatisfaction with structuralism and,
more generally, any theoretical approach that
sought to escape history through appeal to a
timeless, universal structure of language divorced from our experiences. *Libidinal Economy*
(1974) reflects the passion and enthusiasm of the
events of May 1968 along with a disappointment
with the Marxist response to those events. *The
Postmodern Condition: A Report on Knowledge*
(1979), an occasional text written at the request
of the Quebec government, catapulted Lyotard
to the forefront of critical debate. Here he introduced his definition of the postmodern as
"incredulity toward metanarratives": the postmodern names not a specific epoch but an anti-
foundationalist attitude that exceeds the
legitimating orthodoxy of the moment. Postmodernity, then, resides constantly at the heart
of the modern, challenging those totalizing and
comprehensive master narratives (e.g., the
Enlightenment narrative of the emancipation of
the rational subject) that serve to legitimate its
practices. Lyotard suggests we replace these narratives by less ambitious, "little narratives" that
refrain from totalizing claims in favor of recognizing the specificity and singularity of events.

Many, including Lyotard, regard *The Differend*
(1983) as his most original and important work.
Drawing on Wittgenstein's *Philosophical Investigations* and Kant's *Critique of Judgment,* it reflects on
how to make judgments (political as well as aesthetic) where there is no rule of judgment to
which one can appeal. This is the *différend,* a dispute between (at least) two parties in which the
parties operate within radically heterogeneous
language games so incommensurate that no consensus can be reached on principles or rules that
could govern how their dispute might be settled.
In contrast to litigations, where disputing parties
share a language with rules of judgment to consult to resolve their dispute, *différends* defy resolution (an example might be the conflicting

claims to land rights by aboriginal peoples and current residents). At best, we can express *différends* by posing the dispute in a way that avoids delegitimating either party's claim. In other words, our political task, if we are to be just, is to phrase the dispute in a way that respects the difference between the competing claims.

In the years following *The Differend,* Lyotard published several works on aesthetics, politics, and postmodernism; the most important may well be his reading of Kant's third *Critique* in *Lessons on the Analytic of the Sublime* (1991).

See also DERRIDA, FOUCAULT, POSTMODERN, STRUCTURALISM.   A.D.S.

M

McCosh, James (1811–94), Scottish philosopher, a common sense realist who attempted to reconcile Christianity with evolution. A prolific writer, McCosh was a pastor in Scotland and a professor at Queen's College, Belfast, before becoming president of the College of New Jersey (now Princeton University). In *The Intuitions of the Mind* (1860) he argued that while acts of intelligence begin with immediate knowledge of the self or of external objects, they also exhibit intuitions in the spontaneous formation of self-evident convictions about objects. In opposition to Kant and Hamilton, McCosh treated intuitions not as forms imposed by minds on objects, but as inductively ascertainable rules that minds follow in forming convictions after perceiving objects. In his *Examination of Mr. J. S. Mill's Philosophy* (1866) McCosh criticized Mill for denying the existence of intuitions while assuming their operation. In *The Religious Aspects of Evolution* (1885) McCosh defended the design argument by equating Darwin's chance variations with supernatural design. J.W.A.

McDougall, William (1871–1938), British and American (after 1920) psychologist. He was probably the first to define psychology as the science of behavior (*Physiological Psychology*, 1905; *Psychology: The Science of Behavior*, 1912) and he invented *hormic* (purposive) psychology. By the early twentieth century, as psychology strove to become scientific, *purpose* had become a suspect concept, but following Stout, McDougall argued that organisms possess an "intrinsic power of self-determination," making goal seeking the essential and defining feature of behavior. In opposition to mechanistic and intellectualistic psychologies, McDougall, again following Stout, proposed that innate *instincts* (later, *propensities*) directly or indirectly motivate all behavior (*Introduction to Social Psychology*, 1908). Unlike more familiar psychoanalytic instincts, however, many of McDougall's instincts were social in nature (e.g. gregariousness, deference). Moreover, McDougall never regarded a person as merely an assemblage of unconnected and quarreling motives, since people are "integrated unities" guided by one supreme motive around which others are organized. McDougall's stress on behavior's inherent purposiveness influenced the behaviorist E. C. Tolman, but was otherwise roundly rejected by more mechanistic behaviorists and empiricistically inclined sociologists. In his later years, McDougall moved farther from mainstream thought by championing Lamarckism and sponsoring research in parapsychology. Active in social causes, McDougall was an advocate of eugenics (*Is America Safe for Democracy?*, 1921). T.H.L.

Mach, Ernst (1838–1916), Austrian physicist and influential philosopher of science. He was born in Turas, Moravia, now part of the Czech Republic, and studied physics at the University of Vienna. Appointed professor of mathematics at Graz in 1864, he moved in 1867 to the chair of physics at Prague, where he came to be recognized as one of the leading scientists in Europe, contributing not only to a variety of fields of physics (optics, electricity, mechanics, acoustics) but also to the new field of psychophysics, particularly in the field of perception. He returned to Vienna in 1895 to a chair in philosophy, designated for a new academic discipline, the history and theory of inductive science. His writings on the philosophy of science profoundly affected the founders of the Vienna Circle, leading Mach to be regarded as a progenitor of logical positivism.

His best-known work, *The Science of Mechanics* (1883), epitomized the main themes of his philosophy. He set out to extract the logical structure of mechanics from an examination of its history and procedures. Mechanics fulfills the human need to abridge the facts about motion in the most economical way. It rests on "sensations" (akin to the "ideas" or "sense impressions" of classical empiricism); indeed, the world may be said to *consist* of sensations (a thesis that later led Lenin in a famous polemic to accuse Mach of idealism). Mechanics is inductive, not demonstrative; it has no a priori element of any sort. The divisions between the sciences must be recognized to be arbitrary, a matter of convenience only. The sciences must be regarded as descriptive, not as explanatory. Theories may *appear* to explain, but the underlying entities they postulate, like atoms, for example, are no more than aids to prediction. To suppose them to represent reality would be metaphysical and therefore idle. Mach's most enduring legacy to philosophy is his enduring suspicion of anything "metaphysical."

See also LOGICAL POSITIVISM, VIENNA CIRCLE.   E.M.

Machiavelli, Niccolò (1469–1527), the Italian political theorist commonly considered the most influential political thinker of the Renaissance. Born in Florence, he was educated in the civic humanist tradition. From 1498 to 1512, he was secretary to the second chancery of the republic of Florence, with responsibilities for foreign affairs and the revival of the domestic civic militia. His duties involved numerous diplomatic missions both in and outside Italy. With the fall of the republic in 1512, he was dismissed by the returning Medici regime. From 1513 to 1527 he lived in enforced retirement, relieved by writing and occasional appointment to minor posts.

Machiavelli's writings fall into two genetically connected categories: chancery writings (reports, memoranda, diplomatic writings) and formal books, the chief among them *The Prince* (1513), the *Discourses* (1517), the *Art of War* (1520), *Florentine Histories* (1525), and the comic drama *Mandragola* (1518). With Machiavelli a new vision emerges of politics as autonomous activity leading to the creation of free and powerful states. This vision derives its norms from what humans do rather than from what they ought to do. As a result, the problem of evil arises as a central issue: the political actor reserves the right "to enter into evil when necessitated." The requirement of classical, medieval, and civic humanist political philosophies that politics must be practiced within the bounds of virtue is met by redefining the meaning of virtue itself. Machiavellian *virtù* is the ability to achieve "effective truth" regardless of moral, philosophical, and theological restraints. He recognizes two limits on *virtù*: (1) *fortuna*, understood as either chance or as a goddess symbolizing the alleged causal powers of the heavenly bodies; and (2) the agent's own temperament, bodily humors, and the quality of the times. Thus, a premodern astrological cosmology and the anthropology and cyclical theory of history derived from it underlie his political philosophy. History is seen as the conjoint product of human activity and the alleged activity of the heavens, understood as the "general cause" of all human motions in the sublunar world. There is no room here for the sovereignty of the Good, nor the ruling Mind, nor Providence. Kingdoms, republics, and religions follow a naturalistic pattern of birth, growth, and decline. But, depending on the outcome of the struggle between *virtù* and *fortuna*, there is the possibility of political renewal; and Machiavelli saw himself as the philosopher of political renewal.

Historically, Machiavelli's philosophy came to be identified with Machiavellianism (also spelled Machiavellism), the doctrine that the reason of state recognizes no moral superior and that, in its pursuit, everything is permitted. Although Machiavelli himself does not use the phrase 'reason of state', his principles have been and continue to be invoked in its defense.

See also POLITICAL PHILOSOPHY, SOCIAL PHILOSOPHY.   A.J.P.

Machiavellianism. See MACHIAVELLI.

machine state. See PHILOSOPHY OF MIND.

machine state functionalism. See PHILOSOPHY OF MIND.

Mach's principle. See PHILOSOPHY OF SCIENCE.

MacIntyre, Alasdair (b.1929), British-American philosopher and eminent contemporary representative of Aristotelian ethics. He was born in Scotland, educated in England, and has taught at universities in both England and (mainly) the United States. His early work included perceptive critical discussions of Marx and Freud as well as his influential *A Short History of Ethics*. His most discussed work, however, has been *After Virtue* (1981), an analysis and critique of modern ethical views from the standpoint of an Aristotelian virtue ethics.

MacIntyre begins with the striking unresolvability of modern ethical disagreements, which he diagnoses as due to a lack of any shared substantive conception of the ethical good. This lack is itself due to the modern denial of a human nature that would provide a meaning and goal for human life. In the wake of the Enlightenment, MacIntyre maintains, human beings are regarded as merely atomistic individuals, employing a purely formal reason to seek fulfillment of their contingent desires. Modern moral theory tries to derive moral values from this conception of human reality. Utilitarians start from desires, arguing that they must be fulfilled in such a way as to provide the greatest happiness (utility). Kantians start from reason, arguing that our commitment to rationality requires recognizing the rights of others to the same goods that we desire for ourselves. MacIntyre, however, maintains that the modern notions of utility and of rights are fictions: there is no way to argue from individual desires to an interest in making others happy or to inviolable rights of all persons. He concludes that Enlightenment liberalism cannot construct a coherent ethics and that therefore our only alternatives are to accept a Nietzschean reduction of morality to will-to-power or to return to an Aristotelian ethics grounded in a substantive conception of human nature.

MacIntyre's positive philosophical project is to formulate and defend an Aristotelian ethics of the virtues (based particularly on the thought of Aquinas), where virtues are understood as the moral qualities needed to fulfill the potential of human nature. His aim is not the mere revival of Aristotelian thought but a reformulation and, in some cases, revision of that thought in light of its history over the last 2,500 years.

MacIntyre pays particular attention to formulating concepts of practice (communal action directed toward a intrinsic good), virtue (a habit needed to engage successfully in a practice), and tradition (a historically extended community in which practices relevant to the fulfillment of human nature can be carried out). His conception of tradition is particularly noteworthy. His an effort to provide Aristotelianism with a historical orientation that Aristotle himself never countenanced; and, in contrast to Burke, it makes tradition the locus of rational reflection on and revision of past practices, rather than a merely emotional attachment to them. MacIntyre has also devoted considerable attention to the problem of rationally adjudicating the claims of rival traditions (especially in *Whose Justice? Which Rationality?,* 1988) and to making the case for the Aristotelian tradition as opposed to that of the Enlightenment and that of Nietzscheanism (especially in *Three Rival Versions of Moral Inquiry,* 1990).

See also AQUINAS, ARISTOTLE, ETHICS, KANT, LIBERALISM, VIRTUE ETHICS.   G.G.

McTaggart, John McTaggart Ellis (1866–1925), English philosopher, the leading British personal idealist. Aside from his childhood and two extended visits to New Zealand, McTaggart lived in Cambridge as a student and fellow of Trinity College. His influence on others at Trinity, including Russell and Moore, was at times great, but he had no permanent disciples. He began formulating and defending his views by critically examining Hegel. In *Studies in the Hegelian Dialectic* (1896) he argued that Hegel's dialectic is valid but subjective, since the Absolute Idea Hegel used it to derive contains nothing corresponding to the dialectic. In *Studies in Hegelian Cosmology* (1901) he applied the dialectic to such topics as sin, punishment, God, and immortality. In his *Commentary on Hegel's Logic* (1910) he concluded that the task of philosophy is to rethink the nature of reality using a method resembling Hegel's dialectic.

McTaggart attempted to do this in his major work, *The Nature of Existence* (two volumes, 1921 and 1927). In the first volume he tried to deduce the nature of reality from self-evident truths using only two empirical premises, that something exists and that it has parts. He argued that substances exist, that they are related to each other, that they have an infinite number of substances as parts, and that each substance has a sufficient description, one that applies only to it and not to any other substance. He then claimed that these conclusions are inconsistent unless the sufficient descriptions of substances entail the descriptions of their parts, a situation that requires substances to stand to their parts in the relation he called determining correspondence. In the second volume he applied these results to the empirical world, arguing that matter is unreal, since its parts cannot be determined by determining correspondence. In the most celebrated part of his philosophy, he argued that time is unreal by claiming that time presupposes a series of positions, each having the incompatible qualities of past, present, and future. He thought that attempts to remove the incompatibility generate a vicious infinite regress. From these and other considerations he concluded that selves are real, since their parts can be determined by determining correspondence, and that reality is a community of eternal, perceiving selves. He denied that there is an inclusive self or God in this community, but he affirmed that love between the selves unites the community producing a satisfaction beyond human understanding.

See also HEGEL, IDEALISM.   J.W.A.

Madhva (1238–1317), Indian philosopher who founded Dvaita Vedanta. His major works are the *Brahma-Sūtra-Bhaṣya* (his commentary, competitive with Shankara's and Rāmānuja's, on the *Brahma-Sūtras* of Bādarāyana); the *Gītā-Bhāṣya* and *Gitatatparya* (commentaries on the Bhagavad Gita); the *Anu-Vyākhyāna* (an extension of the *Brahma-Sūtra-Bhāṣya* including a general critique of Advaita Vedanta); the *Pramāṇa Laksana,* an account of his epistemology; and the *Tattva-Saṃkhyāna,* a presentation of his ontology. He distinguishes between an independent Brahman and a dependent world of persons and bodies and holds that each person has a distinct individual essence. **See also** ADVAITA, VEDANTA.

K.E.Y.

Mādhyamika (Sanskrit, 'middle way'), a variety of Mahayana Buddhism that is a middle way in the sense that it neither claims that nothing at all exists nor does it embrace the view that there is a plurality of distinct things. It embraces the position in the debate about the nature of things that holds that all things are "empty." Mādhyamika offers an account of why the Buddha rejected the question of whether the enlightened one survives death, saying that none of the four answers (affirmative, negative, affirmative and negative, neither affirmative nor negative) applies.

The typically Buddhist doctrine of codependent arising asserts that everything that exists depends for its existence on something else; nothing (nirvana aside) at any time does or can exist on its own. From this doctrine, together with the view that if *A* cannot exist independent of *B*, *A* cannot be an individual distinct from *B*, Mādhyamika concludes that in offering causal descriptions (or spatial or temporal descriptions) we assume that we can distinguish between individual items. If everything exists dependently, and nothing that exists dependently is an individual, there are no individuals. Thus we cannot distinguish between individual items. Hence the assumption on which we offer causal (or spatial or temporal) descriptions is false, and thus those descriptions are radically defective.

Mādhyamika then adds the doctrine of an ineffable ultimate reality hidden behind our ordinary experience and descriptions and accessible only in esoteric enlightenment experience. The Buddha rejected all four answers because the question is raised in a context that assumes individuation among items of ordinary experience, and since that assumption is false, all of the answers are misleading; each answer assumes a distinction between the enlightened one and other things. The Mādhyamika seems, then, to hold that to be real is to exist independently; the apparent objects of ordinary experience are *śūnya* (empty, void); they lack any essence or character of their own. As such, they are only apparently knowable, and the real is seamless.

Critics (e.g., Yogācāra Mahayana Buddhist philosophers) deny that this view is coherent, or even that there is any view here at all. In one sense, the Mādhyamika philosopher Nāgārjuna himself denies that there is any position taken, maintaining that his critical arguments are simply reductions to absurdity of views that his opponents hold and that he has no view of his own. Still, it seems clear in Nāgārjuna's writings, and plain in the tradition that follows him, that there is supposed to be something the realization of which is essential to becoming enlightened, and the Mādhyamika philosopher must walk the (perhaps non-existent) line between saying two things: first, that final truth concerns an ineffable reality and that this itself is not a view, and second, that this represents what the Buddha taught and hence is something different both from other Buddhist perspectives that offer a mistaken account of the Buddha's message and from non-Buddhist alternatives.

See also BUDDHISM, NĀGĀRJUNA.   K.E.Y.

magnitude, extent or size of a thing with respect to some attribute; technically, a quantity or dimension. A *quantity* is an attribute that admits of several or an infinite number of degrees, in contrast to a *quality* (e.g., triangularity), which an object either has or does not have.

Measurement is assignment of numbers to objects in such a way that these numbers correspond to the degree or amount of some quantity possessed by their objects. The theory of measurement investigates the conditions for, and uniqueness of, such numerical assignments. Let D be a domain of objects (e.g., a set of physical bodies) and L be a relation on this domain; i.e., Lab may mean that if a and b are put on opposite pans of a balance, the pan with a does not rest lower than the other pan. Let $\circ$ be the operation of weighing two objects together in the same pan of a balance. We then have an empirical relational system $\mathbf{E} = \langle D, L, \circ \rangle$. One can prove that, if $\mathbf{E}$ satisfies specified conditions, then there exists a *measurement function* mapping D to a set *Num* of real numbers, in such a way that the L and $\circ$ relations between objects in D correspond to the $\leq$ and $+$ relations between their numerical values. Such an existence theorem for a measurement function from an empirical relational system $\mathbf{E}$ to a numerical relational system, $\mathbf{N} = \langle Num, \leq + \rangle$, is called a *representation theorem*.

Measurement functions are not unique, but a *uniqueness theorem* characterizes all such functions for a specified kind of empirical relational system and specified type of numerical image. For example, suppose that for any measurement functions f, g for $\mathbf{E}$ there exists real number $\alpha > 0$ such that for any x in D, $f(x) = \alpha g(x)$. Then it is said that the measurement is on a *ratio scale*, and the function $\sigma(x) = \alpha x$, for x in the real numbers, is the *scale transformation*. For some empirical systems, one can prove that any two measurement functions are related by $f = \alpha g + \beta$, where $\alpha > 0$ and β are real numbers. Then the measurement is on an *interval scale*, with the scale transformation $\sigma(x) = \alpha x + \beta$; e.g., measurement of temperature without an absolute zero is on an interval scale. In addition to ratio and interval scales, other *scale types* are defined in terms of various scale transformations; many relational systems have been mathematically analyzed for possible applications in the behavioral sciences. Measurement with weak scale types may provide only an ordering of the objects, so quantitative measurement and comparative orderings can be treated by the same general methods.

The older literature on measurement often distinguishes *extensive* from *intensive* magnitudes. In the former case, there is supposed to be an empirical operation (like ∘ above) that in some sense directly corresponds to addition on numbers. An intensive magnitude supposedly has no such empirical operation. It is sometimes claimed that genuine quantities must be extensive, whereas an intensive magnitude is a quality. This *extensive* versus *intensive* distinction (and its use in distinguishing quantities from qualities) is imprecise and has been supplanted by the theory of scale types sketched above.

    See also OPERATIONALISM, PHILOSOPHY OF SCIENCE.   R.L.C.

Mahabharata. See BHAGAVAD GITA.

Mahāvīra, title ('Great Hero') of Vardhamāna Jnātṛputra (sixth century B.C.), Indian religious leader who founded Jainism. He is viewed within Jainism as the twenty-fourth and most recent of a series of *Tīrthankaras* or religious "ford-makers" and conquerors (over ignorance) and as the establisher of the Jain community. His enlightenment is described in the *Jaina Sutras* as involving release of his inherently immortal soul from reincarnation and karma and as including his omniscience. According to Jaina tradition, Vardhamāna Jnātṛputra was born into a warrior class and at age thirty became a wandering ascetic seeking enlightenment, which he achieved at age forty-two. **See also JAINISM.**
                              K.E.Y.

Mahayana Buddhism. See BUDDHISM.

maieutic. See SOCRATES.

Maimon, Salomon (1753–1800), Lithuanian-born German Jewish philosopher who became the friend and protégé of Moses Mendelssohn and was an acute early critic and follower of Kant. His most important works were the *Versuch über die Transzendentalphilosophie. Mit einem Anhang über die symbolische Erkenntnis* ("Essay on Transcendental Philosophy. With an Appendix on Symbolic Cognition," 1790), the *Philosophisches Wörterbuch* ("Philosophical Dictionary," 1791) and the *Versuch einer neuen Logik oder Theorie des Denkens* ("Attempt at a New Logic or Theory of Thought," 1794). Maimon argued against the "thing-in-itself" as it was conceived by Karl Leonhard Reinhold and Gottlieb Ernst Schulze. For Maimon, the thing-in-itself was merely a limiting concept, not a real object "behind" the phenomena. While he thought that Kant's system was sufficient as a refutation of rationalism or "dogmatism," he did not think that it had – or could – successfully dispose of skepticism. Indeed, he advanced what can be called a skeptical interpretation of Kant. On the other hand, he also argued against Kant's sharp distinction between sensibility and understanding and for the necessity of assuming the idea of an "infinite mind." In this way, he prepared the way for Fichte and Hegel. However, in many ways his own theory is more similar to that of the neo-Kantian Hermann Cohen. **See also JEWISH PHILOSOPHY, NEO-KANTIANISM.**   M.K.

Maimonides, Latinized name of Moses ben Maimon (1135–1204), Spanish-born Jewish philosopher, physician, and jurist. Born in Córdova, Maimonides and his family fled the forced conversions of the Almohad invasion in 1148, living anonymously in Fez before finding refuge in 1165 in Cairo. There Maimonides served as physician to the vizier of Saladin, who overthrew the Fāṭimid dynasty in 1171. He wrote ten medical treatises, but three works secured his position among the greatest rabbinic jurists: his *Book of the Commandments,* cataloguing the 613 biblical laws; his *Commentary on the Mishnah,* expounding the rational purposes of the ancient rabbinic code; and the fourteen-volume *Mishneh Torah,* a codification of Talmudic law that retains almost canonical authority.

His Arabic philosophic masterpiece *The Guide to the Perplexed* mediates between the Scriptural and philosophic idioms, deriving a sophisticated negative theology by subtly decoding biblical anthropomorphisms. It defends divine creation against al-Fārābī's and Avicenna's eternalism, while rejecting efforts to demonstrate creation apodictically. The radical occasionalism of Arabic dialectical theology (*kalām*) that results from such attempts, Maimonides argues, renders nature unintelligible and divine governance irrational: if God creates each particular event, natural causes are otiose, and much of creation is in vain. But Aristotle, who taught us the very principles of demonstration, well understood, as his resort to persuasive language reveals, that his arguments for eternity were not demonstrative. They project, metaphysically, an analysis of time, matter, and potentiality as they are now and ignore the possibility that at its origin a thing had a very different nature. We could allegorize biblical creation if it were demonstrated to be false. But since it is not, we argue that creation is more plausible conceptually and preferable theologically to its alternative: more plausible, because a free creative act allows differentiation of the world's multiplicity from divine simplicity, as the seemingly mechanical necessitation of emanation, strictly construed, cannot do; preferable, because Avicennan claims that God is author of the world and determiner of its contingency are undercut by the assertion that at no time was nature other than it is now.

Maimonides read the biblical commandments thematically, as serving to inform human character and understanding. He followed al-Fārābī's Platonizing reading of Scripture as a symbolic elaboration of themes best known to the philosopher. Thus he argued that prophets learn nothing new from revelation; the ignorant remain ignorant, but the gift of imagination in the wise, if they are disciplined by the moral virtues, especially courage and contentment, gives wing to ideas, rendering them accessible to the masses and setting them into practice. In principle, any philosopher of character and imagination might be a prophet; but in practice the legislative, ethical, and mythopoeic imagination that serves philosophy finds fullest articulation in one tradition. Its highest phase, where imagination yields to pure intellectual communion, was unique to Moses, elaborated in Judaism and its daughter religions. Maimonides' philosophy was pivotal for later Jewish thinkers, highly valued by Aquinas and other Scholastics, studied by Spinoza in Hebrew translation, and annotated by Leibniz in Buxtorf's 1629 rendering, *Doctor Perplexorum*.

See also JEWISH PHILOSOPHY.   L.E.G.

Maistre, Joseph-Marie de. See DE MAISTRE.

major premise. See SYLLOGISM.

major term. See SYLLOGISM.

Malcolm, Norman (1911–90), American philosopher who was a prominent figure in post–World War II analytic philosophy and perhaps the foremost American interpreter and advocate of Wittgenstein. His association with Wittgenstein (vividly described in his *Ludwig Wittgenstein, A Memoir*, 1958) began when he was a student at Cambridge (1938–40). Other influences were Bouwsma, Malcolm's undergraduate teacher at the University of Nebraska, and Moore, whom he knew at Cambridge. Malcolm taught for over thirty years at Cornell, and after his retirement in 1978 was associated with King's College, London.

Malcolm's earliest papers (e.g., "The Verification Argument," 1950, and "Knowledge and Belief," 1952) dealt with issues of knowledge and skepticism, and two dealt with Moore. "Moore and Ordinary Language" (1942) interpreted Moore's defense of common sense as a defense of ordinary language, but "Defending Common Sense" (1949) argued that Moore's "two hands" proof of the external world involved a misuse of 'know'. Moore's proof was the topic of extended discussions between Malcolm and Wittgenstein during the latter's 1949 visit in Ithaca, New York, and these provided the stimulus for Wittgenstein's *On Certainty*.

Malcolm's "Wittgenstein's Philosophical Investigations" (1954) was a highly influential discussion of Wittgenstein's later philosophy, and especially of his "private language argument." Two other works of that period were Malcolm's *Dreaming* (1958), which argued that dreams do not have genuine duration or temporal location, and do not entail having genuine experiences, and "Anselm's Ontological Arguments" (1960), which defended a version of the ontological argument.

Malcolm wrote extensively on memory, first in his "Three Lectures on Memory," published in his *Knowledge and Certainty* (1963), and then in his *Memory and Mind* (1976). In the latter he criticized both philosophical and psychological theories of memory, and argued that the notion of a memory trace "is not a scientific discovery . . . [but] a product of philosophical thinking, of a sort that is natural and enormously tempting, yet thoroughly muddled."

A recurrent theme in Malcolm's thought was that philosophical understanding requires getting to the root of the temptations to advance some philosophical doctrine, and that once we do so we will see the philosophical doctrines as confused or nonsensical. Although he was convinced that dualism and other Cartesian views about the mind were thoroughly confused, he thought no better of contemporary materialist and functionalist views, and of current theorizing in psychology and linguistics (one paper is entitled "The Myth of Cognitive Processes and Structures"). He shared with Wittgenstein both an antipathy to scientism and a respect for religion. He shared with Moore an antipathy to obscurantism and a respect for common sense.

Malcolm's last published book, *Nothing Is Hidden* (1986), examines the relations between Wittgenstein's earlier and later philosophies. His other books include *Problems of Mind* (1971), *Thought and Knowledge* (1977), and *Consciousness and Causality* (1984), the latter coauthored with Armstrong. His writings are marked by an exceptionally lucid, direct, and vivid style.

See also BOUWSMA, MOORE, ORDINARY LANGUAGE PHILOSOPHY, WITTGENSTEIN.

S.Sho.

Malebranche, Nicolas (1638–1715), French philosopher and theologian, an important but unorthodox proponent of Cartesian philosophy. Malebranche was a priest of the Oratory, a religious order founded in 1611 by Cardinal Bérulle, who was favorably inclined toward Descartes. Malebranche himself became a Cartesian after reading Descartes's physiological *Treatise on Man* in 1664, although he ultimately introduced crucial modifications into Cartesian ontology, epistemology, and physics.

Malebranche's most important philosophical work is *The Search After Truth* (1674), in which he presents his two most famous doctrines: the vision in God and occasionalism. He agrees with Descartes and other philosophers that ideas, or immaterial representations present to the mind, play an essential role in knowledge and perception. But whereas Descartes's ideas are mental entities, or modifications of the soul, Malebranche argues that the ideas that function in human cognition are in God – they just are the essences and ideal archetypes that exist in the divine understanding. As such, they are eternal and independent of finite minds, and make possible the clear and distinct apprehension of objective, neccessary truth. Malebranche presents the vision in God as the proper Augustinian view, albeit modified in the light of Descartes's epistemological distinction between understanding and sensation. The theory explains both our apprehension of universals and mathematical and moral principles, as well

as the conceptual element that, he argues, necessarily informs our perceptual acquaintance with the world. Like Descartes's theory of ideas, Malebranche's doctrine is at least partly motivated by an antiskepticism, since God's ideas cannot fail to reveal either eternal truths or the essences of things in the world created by God. The vision in God, however, quickly became the object of criticism by Locke, Arnauld, Foucher, and others, who thought it led to a visionary and skeptical idealism, with the mind forever enclosed by a veil of divine ideas.

Malebranche is also the best-known proponent of occasionalism, the doctrine that finite created beings have no causal efficacy and that God alone is a true causal agent. Starting from Cartesian premises about matter, motion, and causation – according to which the essence of body consists in extension alone, motion is a mode of body, and a causal relation is a logically necessary relation between cause and effect – Malebranche argues that bodies and minds cannot be genuine causes of either physical events or mental states. Extended bodies, he claims, are essentially inert and passive, and thus cannot possess any motive force or power to cause and sustain motion. Moreover, there is no necessary connection between any mental state (e.g. a volition) or physical event and the bodily motions that usually follow it. Such necessity is found only between the will of an omnipotent being and its effects. Thus, all phenomena are directly and immediately brought about by God, although he always acts in a lawlike way and on the proper occasion.

Malebranche's theory of ideas and his occasionalism, as presented in the *Search* and the later *Dialogues on Metaphysics* (1688), were influential in the development of Berkeley's thought; and his arguments for the causal theory foreshadow many of the considerations regarding causation and induction later presented by Hume. In addition to these innovations in Cartesian metaphysics and epistemology, Malebranche also modified elements of Descartes's physics, most notably in his account of the hardness of bodies and of the laws of motion.

In his other major work, the *Treatise on Nature and Grace* (1680), Malebranche presents a theodicy, an explanation of how God's wisdom, goodness, and power are to be reconciled with the apparent imperfections and evils in the world. In his account, elements of which Leibniz borrows, Malebranche claims that God could have created a more perfect world, one without the defects that plague this world, but that this would have involved greater complexity in the divine ways. God always acts in the simplest way possible, and only by means of lawlike general volitions; God never acts by "particular" or ad hoc volitions. But this means that while on any particular occasion God could intervene and forestall an apparent evil that is about to occur by the ordinary courses of the laws of nature (e.g. a drought), God would not do so, for this would compromise the simplicity of God's means. The perfection or goodness of the world per se is thus relativized to the simplicity of the laws of that world (or, which is the same thing, to the generality of the divine volitions that, on the occasionalist view, govern it). Taken together, the laws and the phenomena of the world form a whole that is most worthy of God's nature – in fact, the best combination possible. Malebranche then extends this analysis to explain the apparent injustice in the distribution of grace among humankind. It is just this extension that initiated Arnauld's attack and drew Malebranche into a long philosophical and theological debate that would last until the end of the century.

See also ARNAULD, BERKELEY, OCCASIONALISM.   S.N.

Mani. See MANICHAEANISM.

Manichaeanism, also Manichaeism, a syncretistic religion founded by the Babylonian prophet Mani (A.D. 216–77), who claimed a revelation from God and saw himself as a member of a line that included the Buddha, Zoroaster, and Jesus. In dramatic myths, Manichaeanism posited the good kingdom of God, associated with light, and the evil kingdom of Satan, associated with darkness. Awareness of light caused greed, hate, and envy in the darkness; this provoked an attack of darkness on light. In response the Father sent Primal Man, who lost the fight so that light and darkness were mixed. The Primal Man appealed for help, and the Living Spirit came to win a battle, making heaven and earth out of the corpses of darkness and freeing some capured light. A Third Messenger was sent; in response the power of darkness created Adam and Eve, who contained the light that still remained under his sway. Then Jesus was sent to a still innocent Adam who nonetheless sinned, setting in motion the reproductive series that yields humanity.

This is the mythological background to the Manichaean account of the basic religious problem: the human soul is a bit of captured light, and the problem is to free the soul from darkness through asceticism and esoteric knowledge. Manichaeanism denies that Jesus was crucified, and Augustine, himself a sometime Manichaean, viewed the religion as a Docetic heresy that denies the incarnation of the second person of the Trinity in a real human body. The religion exhibits the pattern of escape from embodiment as a condition of salvation, also seen in Hinduism and Buddhism.

See also AUGUSTINE, BUDDHISM, HINDUISM.
                                                                                        K.E.Y.

manifest content. See FREUD.

manifold. See KANT.

Mannheim, Karl (1893–1947), Hungarian-born German social scientist best known for his sociology of knowledge. Born in Budapest, where he took a university degree in philosophy, he settled in Heidelberg in 1919 as a private scholar until his call to Frankfurt as professor of sociology in 1928. Suspended as a Jew and as foreign-born by the Nazis in 1933, he accepted an invitation from the London School of Economics, where he was a lecturer for a decade. In 1943, Mannheim became the first professor of sociology of education at the University of London, a position he held until his death.

Trained in the Hegelian tradition, Mannheim defies easy categorization: his mature politics became those of a liberal committed to social planning; with his many studies in the sociology of culture, of political ideologies, of social organization, of education, and of knowledge, among others, he founded several subdisciplines in sociology and political science. While his *Man and Society in an Age of Reconstruction* (1940) expressed his own commitment to social planning, his most famous work, *Ideology and Utopia* (original German edition, 1929; revised English edition, 1936), established *sociology of knowledge* as a scientific enterprise and simultaneously cast doubt on the possibility of the very scientific knowledge on which social planning was to proceed. As developed by Mannheim, sociology of knowledge attempts to find the social *causes* of beliefs as contrasted with the *reasons* people have for them. Mannheim seemed to believe that this investigation both presupposes and demonstrates the impossibility of "objective" knowledge of society, a theme that relates sociology of knowledge to its roots in German philosophy and social theory (especially Marxism) and earlier in the thought of the *idéologues* of the immediate post–French Revolution decades.   L.A.

Mansel, Henry Longueville (1820–71), British philosopher and clergyman, a prominent defender of Scottish common sense philosophy. Mansel was a professor of philosophy and ecclesiastical history at Oxford, and the dean of St. Paul's Cathedral. Much of his philosophy was derived from Kant as interpreted by Hamilton. In *Prolegomena Logica* (1851) he defined logic as the science of the laws of thought, while in *Metaphysics* (1860) he argued that human faculties are not suited to know the ultimate nature of things. He drew the religious implications of these views in his most influential work, *The Limits of Religious Thought* (1858), by arguing that God is rationally inconceivable and that the only available conception of God is an analogical one derived from revelation. From this he concluded that religious dogma is immune from rational criticism. In the ensuing controversy Mansel was criticized by Spenser, Thomas Henry Huxley (1825–95), and J. S. Mill.   J.W.A.

many questions, fallacy of. See INFORMAL FALLACY.

many-valued logic, a logic that rejects the principle of bivalence: every proposition is true or false. However, there are two forms of rejection: the truth-functional mode (many-valued logic proper), where propositions may take many values beyond simple truth and falsity, values functionally determined by the values of their components; and the truth-value gap mode, in which the only values are truth and falsity, but propositions may have neither. What value they do or do not have is not determined by the values or lack of values of their constituents.

Many-valued logic has its origins in the work of Łukasiewicz and (independently) Post around 1920, in the first development of truth tables and semantic methods. Łukasiewicz's philosophical motivation for his three-valued calculus was to deal with propositions whose truth-value was open or "possible" – e.g., propositions about the future. He proposed they might take a third value. Let 1 represent truth, 0 falsity, and the third value be, say, ½. We take $\neg$ (not) and $\rightarrow$ (implication) as primitive, letting $v(\neg A) = 1 - v(A)$ and $v(A \rightarrow B) = \min(1, 1 - v(A) + v(B))$. These valuations may be displayed:

$\rightarrow$	0	$\frac{1}{2}$	1	$\neg$
0	1	1	1	1
$\frac{1}{2}$	$\frac{1}{2}$	1	1	$\frac{1}{2}$
1	0	$\frac{1}{2}$	1	0

Łukasiewicz generalized the idea in 1922, to allow first any finite number of values, and finally infinitely, even continuum-many values (between 0 and 1). One can then no longer represent the functionality by a matrix; however, the formulas given above can still be applied. Wajsberg axiomatized Łukasiewicz's calculus in 1931. In 1953 Łukasiewicz published a four-valued extensional modal logic.

In 1921, Post presented an m-valued calculus, with values 0 (truth), . . . , $m - 1$ (falsity), and matrices defined on $\neg$ and v (or): $v(\neg A) = 1 + v(A)$ (modulo m) and $v(A v B) = \min(v(A), v(B))$. Translating this for comparison into the same framework as above, we obtain the matrices (with 1 for truth and 0 for falsity):

$\rightarrow$	0	$\frac{1}{2}$	1	$\neg$
0	1	1	1	1
$\frac{1}{2}$	0	$\frac{1}{2}$	1	0
1	$\frac{1}{2}$	$\frac{1}{2}$	1	$\frac{1}{2}$

The strange cyclic character of $\neg$ makes Post's system difficult to interpret – though he did give one in terms of sequences of classical propositions. A different motivation led to a system with three values developed by Bochvar in 1939, namely, to find a solution to the logical paradoxes. (Łukasiewicz had noted that his three-valued system was free of antinomies.) The third value is indeterminate (so arguably Bochvar's system is actually one of gaps), and any combination of values one of which is indeterminate is indeterminate; otherwise, on the determinate values, the matrices are classical. Thus we obtain for $\neg$ and $\rightarrow$, using 1, ½, and 0 as above:

$\rightarrow$	0	$\frac{1}{2}$	1	$\neg$
0	1	$\frac{1}{2}$	1	1
$\frac{1}{2}$	$\frac{1}{2}$	$\frac{1}{2}$	$\frac{1}{2}$	$\frac{1}{2}$
1	0	$\frac{1}{2}$	1	0

In order to develop a logic of many values, one needs to characterize the notion of a *thesis*, or logical truth. The standard way to do this in many-valued logic is to separate the values into designated and undesignated. Effectively, this is to reintroduce bivalence, now in the form: Every proposition is either designated or undesignated. Thus in Łukasiewicz's scheme, 1 (truth) is the only designated value; in Post's, any initial segment 0, . . . , $n - 1$, where $n < m$ (0 as truth). In general, one can think of the various designated values as types of truth, or ways a proposition may be true, and the undesignated ones as ways it can be false. Then a proposition is a thesis if and only if it takes only designated values. For example, $p \rightarrow p$ is, but $p \lor \neg p$ is not, a Łukasiewicz thesis.

However, certain matrices may generate no logical truths by this method, e.g., the Bochvar matrices give ½ for every formula any of whose variables is indeterminate. If both 1 and ½ were designated, all theses of classical logic would be theses; if only 1, no theses result. So the distinction from classical logic is lost. Bochvar's solution was to add an external assertion and negation. But this in turn runs the risk of undercutting the whole philosophical motivation, if the external negation is used in a Russell-type paradox.

One alternative is to concentrate on consequence: A is a consequence of a set of formulas X if for every assignment of values either no member of X is designated or A is. Bochvar's consequence relation (with only 1 designated) results from restricting classical consequence so that every variable in A occurs in some member of X.

There is little technical difficulty in extending many-valued logic to the logic of predicates and quantifiers. For example, in Łukasiewicz's logic, $v(\forall xA) = \min \{v(A(a/x)): a \in D\}$, where D is, say, some set of constants whose assignments exhaust the domain. This interprets the universal quantifier as an "infinite" conjunction.

In 1965, Zadeh introduced the idea of *fuzzy sets*, whose membership relation allows indeterminacies: it is a function into the unit interval [0,1], where 1 means definitely in, 0 definitely out. One philosophical application is to the sorites paradox, that of the heap. Instead of insisting that there be a sharp cutoff in number of grains between a heap and a non-heap, or between red and, say, yellow, one can introduce a spectrum of indeterminacy, as definite applications of a concept shade off into less clear ones.

Nonetheless, many have found the idea of assigning further definite values, beyond truth and falsity, unintuitive, and have instead looked to develop a scheme that encompasses truth-value gaps. One application of this idea is found in Kleene's strong and weak matrices of 1938. Kleene's motivation was to develop a logic of partial functions. For certain arguments, these give no definite value; but the function may later be extended so that in such cases a definite value is given. Kleene's constraint, therefore, was that the matrices be regular: no combination is given a definite value that might later be changed; moreover, on the definite values the matrices must be classical. The weak matrices are as for Bochvar. The strong matrices yield (1 for truth, 0 for falsity, and u for indeterminacy):

$\rightarrow$	0	u	1		$\neg$
0	1	1	1		1
u	u	u	1		u
1	0	u	1		0

An alternative approach to truth-value gaps was presented by Bas van Fraassen in the 1960s. Suppose $v(A)$ is undefined if $v(B)$ is undefined for any subformula B of A. Let a classical extension of a truth-value assignment v be any assignment that matches v on 0 and 1 and assigns either 0 or 1 whenever v assigns no value. Then we can define a *supervaluation* w over v: $w(A) = 1$ if the value of A on all classical extensions of v is 1, 0 if it is 0 and undefined otherwise. A is valid if $w(A) = 1$ for all supervaluations w (over arbitrary valuations). By this method, excluded middle, e.g., comes out valid, since it takes 1 in all classical extensions of any partial valuation. Van Fraassen presented several applications of the supervaluation technique. One is to free logic, logic in which empty terms are admitted.

See also FREE LOGIC, VAGUENESS.   S.L.R.

Mao Tse-tung (1893–1976), Chinese Communist leader, founder of the People's Republic of China in 1949. He believed that Marxist ideas must be adapted to China. Contrary to the Marxist orthodoxy, which emphasized workers, Mao organized peasants in the countryside. His philosophical writings include *On Practice* (1937) and *On Contradiction* (1937), synthesizing dialectical materialism and traditional Chinese philosophy. In his later years he departed from the gradual strategy of his *On New Democracy* (1940) and adopted increasingly radical means to change China. Finally he started the Cultural Revolution in 1967 and plunged China into disaster. **See also** CHINESE PHILOSOPHY, LIANG SOU-MING, LIU SHAO-CH'I.   S.-h.L.

Marburg School. See NEO-KANTIANISM.

Marcel, Gabriel (1889–1973), French philosopher and playwright, a major representative of French existential thought. He was a member of the Academy of Political and Social Science of the Institute of France. Musician, drama critic, and lecturer of international renown, he authored thirty plays and as many philosophic essays. He considered his principal contribution to be that of a philosopher-dramatist. Together, his dramatic and philosophic works cut a path for the reasoned exercise of freedom to enhance the dignity of human life. The conflicts and challenges of his own life he brought to the light of the theater; his philosophic works followed as efforts to discern critically through rigorous, reasoned analyses the alternative options life offers.

His dramatic masterpiece, *The Broken World,* compassionately portrayed the devastating sense of emptiness, superficial activities, and fractured relationships that plague the modern era. This play cleared a way for Marcel to transcend nineteenth-century British and German idealism, articulate his distinction between problem and mystery, and evolve an existential approach that reflectively clarified mysteries that can provide depth and meaningfulness to human life. In the essay "On the Ontological Mystery," a philosophic sequel to *The Broken World,* Marcel confronted the questions "Who am I? – Is Being empty or full?" He explored the regions of body or incarnate being, intersubjectivity, and transcendence. His research focused principally on intersubjectivity clarifying the requisite attitudes and essential characteristics of I-Thou encounters, interpersonal relations, commitment and creative fidelity – notions he also developed in *Homo Viator* (1945) and *Creative Fidelity* (1940).

Marcel's thought balanced despair and hope, infidelity and fidelity, self-deception and a spirit of truth. He recognized both the role of freedom and the role of fundamental attitudes or prephilosophic dispositions, as these influence one's way of being and the interpretation of life's meaning.

Concern for the presence of loved ones who have died appears in both Marcel's dramatic and philosophic works, notably in *Presence and Immortality.* This concern, coupled with his reflections on intersubjectivity, led him to explore how a human subject can experience the presence of God or the presence of loved ones from beyond death. Through personal experience, dramatic imagination, and philosophic investigation, he discovered that such presence can be experienced principally by way of inwardness and depth. "Presence" is a spiritual influx that profoundly affects one's being, uplifting it and enriching one's personal resources. While it does depend on a person's being open and permeable, presence is not something that the person can summon forth. A conferral or presence is always a gratuitous gift, coauthored and marked by its signal benefit, an incitement to create. So Marcel's reflection on interpersonal communion enabled him to conceive philosophically how God can be present to a person as a life-giving and personalizing force whose benefit is always an incitement to create.

See also BUBER, EXISTENTIALISM, PHILOSOPHY OF LITERATURE.   K.R.H.

Marcus, Ruth Barcan (b.1921), American philosopher best known for her seminal work in philosophical logic. In 1946 she published the first systematic treatment of quantified modal logic, thereby turning aside Quine's famous attack on the coherence of combining quantifiers with alethic operators. She later extended the first-order formalization to second order with identity (1947) and to modalized set theory (1963). Marcus's writings in logic either inaugurated or brought to the fore many issues that have loomed large in subsequent philosophical theorizing. Of particular significance are the Barcan formula (1946), the theorem about the necessity of identity (1963), a flexible notion of extensionality (1960, 1961), and the view that ordinary proper names are contentless directly referential tags (1961). This last laid the groundwork for the theory of direct reference later advanced by Kripke, Keith Donnellan, David Kaplan, and others.

No less a revolutionary in moral theory, Marcus undermined the entire structure of standard deontic logic in her paper on iterated deontic modalities (1966). She later (1980) argued against some theorists that moral dilemmas are real, and against others that moral dilemmas need neither derive from inconsistent rules nor imply moral anti-realism.

In her series of papers on belief (1981, 1983, 1990), Marcus repudiates theories that identify beliefs with attitudes to linguistic or quasi-linguistic items. She argues instead that for an agent *A* to believe that *p* is for *A* to be disposed to behave as if *p* obtains (where *p* is a possible state of affairs). Her analysis mobilizes a conception of rational agents as seeking to maintain global coherence among the verbal and non-verbal indicators of their beliefs.

During much of Marcus's career she served as Reuben Post Halleck Professor of Philosophy at Yale University. She has also served as chair of the Board of Officers of the American Philosophical Association and president of its Central Division, president of the Association of Symbolic Logic, and president of the Institut International de Philosophie.

See also BELIEF, CAUSAL THEORY OF PROPER NAMES, MODAL LOGIC, MORAL DILEMMA, PHILOSOPHY OF LANGUAGE, PHILOSOPHY OF LOGIC, QUINE.   D.R. & W.S.-A.

Marcus Aurelius (A.D. 121–80), Roman emperor (from 161) and philosopher. Author of twelve books of *Meditations* (Greek title, *To Himself*), Marcus Aurelius is principally interesting in the history of Stoic philosophy (of which he was a diligent student) for his ethical self-portrait. Except for the first book, detailing his gratitude to his family, friends, and teachers, the aphorisms are arranged in no order; many were written in camp during military campaigns. They reflect both the Old Stoa and the more eclectic views of Posidonius, with whom he holds that involvement in public affairs is a moral duty. Marcus, in accord with Stoicism, considers immortality doubtful; happiness lies in patient acceptance of the will of the panentheistic Stoic God, the material soul of a material universe. Anger, like all emotions, is forbidden the Stoic emperor: he exhorts himself to compassion for the weak and evil among his subjects. "Do not be turned into 'Caesar,' or dyed by the purple: for that happens" (6.30). "It is the privilege of a human being to love even those who stumble" (7.22). Sayings like these, rather than technical arguments, give the book its place in literary history. **See also** HELLENISTIC PHILOSOPHY, STOICISM.   D.Ar.

Marcuse, Herbert (1898–1979). German-born American political philosopher who reinterpreted the ideas of Marx and Freud. Marcuse's work is among the most systematic and philosophical of the Frankfurt School theorists. After an initial attempt to unify Hegel, Marx, and Heidegger in an ontology of historicity in his habilitation on *Hegel's Ontology and the Theory of Historicity* (1932), Marcuse was occupied during the 1930s with the problem of truth in a critical historical social theory, defending a context-independent notion of truth against relativizing tendencies of the sociology of knowledge. Marcuse thought Hegel's "dialectics" provided an alternative to relativism, empiricism, and positivism and even developed a revolutionary interpretation of the Hegelian legacy in *Reason and Revolution* (1941) opposed to Popper's totalitarian one.

After World War II, Marcuse appropriated Freud in the same way that he had appropriated Hegel before the war, using his basic concepts for a critical theory of the repressive character of civilization in *Eros and Civilization* (1955). In many respects, this book comes closer to presenting a positive conception of reason and Enlightenment than any other work of the Frankfurt School. Marcuse argued that civilization has been antagonistic to happiness and freedom through its constant struggle against basic human instincts. According to Marcuse, human existence is grounded in Eros, but these impulses depend upon and are shaped by labor. By synthesizing Marx and Freud, Marcuse holds out the utopian possibility of happiness and freedom in the unity of Eros and labor, which at the very least points toward the reduction of "surplus repression" as the goal of a rational economy and emancipatory social criticism.

This was also the goal of his aesthetic theory as developed in *The Aesthetic Dimension* (1978). In *One Dimensional Man* (1964) and other writings, Marcuse provides an analysis of why the potential for a free and rational society has never been realized: in the irrationality of the current social totality, its creation and manipulation of false needs (or "repressive desublimation"), and hostility toward nature. Perhaps no other Frankfurt School philosopher has had as much popular influence as Marcuse, as evidenced by his reception in the student and ecology movements.

See also CRITICAL THEORY, FRANKFURT SCHOOL.   J.Bo.

marginal utility. See UTILITARIANISM.

Mariana, Juan de (1536–1624), Spanish Jesuit historian and political philosopher. Born in Talavera de la Reina, he studied at Alcalá de Henares and taught at Rome, Sicily, and Paris. His political ideas are contained in *De rege et regis institutione* ("On Kingship," 1599) and *De monetae mutatione* ("On Currency," 1609). Mariana held that political power rests on the community of citizens, and the power of the monarch derives from the people. The natural state of humanity did not include, as Vitoria held, government and other political institutions. The state of nature was one of justice in which all possessions were held in common, and cooperation characterized human relations. Private property is the result of technological advances that produced jealousy and strife. Antedating both Hobbes and Rousseau, Mariana argued that humans made a contract and delegated their political power to leaders in order to eliminate injustice and strife. However, only the people have the right to change the law. A monarch who does not follow the law and ceases to act for the citizens' welfare may be forcibly removed. Tyrannicide is thus justifiable under some circumstances. **See also** CONTRACTARIANISM, POLITICAL PHILOSOPHY.   J.J.E.G.

Maritain, Jacques (1882–1973), French Catholic philosopher whose innovative interpretation of Aquinas's philosophy made him a central figure in Neo-Thomism. Bergson's teaching saved him from metaphysical despair and a suicide pact with his fiancée. After his discovery of Aquinas, he rejected Bergsonism for a realistic account of the concept and a unified theory of knowledge, aligning the empirical sciences with the philosophy of nature, metaphysics, theology, and mysticism in *Distinguish to Unite or The Degrees of Knowledge* (1932). Maritain opposed the skepticism and idealism that severed the mind from sensibility, typified by the "angelism" of Descartes's intuitionism. Maritain traced the practical effects of angelism in art, politics, and religion. His *Art and Scholasticism* (1920) employs ancient and medieval notions of art as a virtue and beauty as a transcendental aspect of being. In politics, especially *Man and the State* (1961), Maritain stressed the distinction between the *person* and the *individual,* the ontological foundation of natural rights, the religious origins of the democratic ideal, and the importance of the common good. He also argued for the possibility of philosophy informed by the data of revelation without compromising its integrity, and an *Integral Humanism* (1936) that affirms the political order while upholding the eternal destiny of the human person. **See also AQUINAS, NEO-THOMISM.** D.W.H.

Markov process. See STOCHASTIC PROCESS.

Marsilio dei Mainardine. See MARSILIUS OF PADUA.

Marsilius of Inghen (c.1330–96), Dutch philosopher and theologian. Born near Nijmegen, Marsilius studied under Buridan, taught at Paris for thirty years, then, in 1383, moved to the newly founded University of Heidelberg, where he and Albert of Saxony established nominalism in Germany. In logic, he produced an Ockhamist revision of the *Tractatus* of Peter of Spain, often published as *Textus dialectices* in early sixteenth-century Germany, and a commentary on Aristotle's *Prior Analytics.* He developed Buridan's theory of impetus in his own way, accepted Bradwardine's account of the proportions of velocities, and adopted Nicholas of Oresme's doctrine of intension and remission of forms, applying the new physics in his commentaries on Aristotle's physical works. In theology he followed Ockham's skeptical emphasis on faith, allowing that one might prove the existence of God along Scotistic lines, but insisting that, since

natural philosophy could not accommodate the creation of the universe *ex nihilo,* God's omnipotence was known only through faith. J.Lo.

Marsilius of Padua, in Italian, Marsilio dei Mainardini (1275/80–1342), Italian political theorist. He served as rector of the University of Paris between 1312 and 1313; his anti-papal views forced him to flee Paris (1326) for Nuremberg, where he was political and ecclesiastic adviser of Louis of Bavaria.

His major work, *Defensor pacis* ("Defender of Peace," 1324), attacks the doctrine of the supremacy of the pope and argues that the authority of a secular ruler elected to represent the people is superior to the authority of the papacy and priesthood in both temporal and spiritual affairs. Three basic claims of Marsilius's theory are that reason, not instinct or God, allows us to know what is just and conduces to the flourishing of human society; that governments need to enforce obedience to the laws by coercive measures; and that political power ultimately resides in the people. He was influenced by Aristotle's ideal of the state as necessary to foster human flourishing. His thought is regarded as a major step in the history of political philosophy and one of the first defenses of republicanism. P.Gar.

Martineau, James (1805–1900), English philosopher of religion and ethical intuitionist. As a minister and a professor, Martineau defended Unitarianism and opposed pantheism. In *A Study of Religion* (1888) Martineau agreed with Kant that reality as we experience it is the work of the mind, but he saw no reason to doubt his intuitive conviction that the phenomenal world corresponds to a real world of enduring, causally related objects. He believed that the only intelligible notion of causation is given by willing and concluded that reality is the expression of a divine will that is also the source of moral authority. In *Types of Ethical Theory* (1885) he claimed that the fundamental fact of ethics is the human tendency to approve and disapprove of the motives leading to voluntary actions, actions in which there are two motives present to consciousness. After freely choosing one of the motives, the agent can determine which action best expresses it. Since Martineau thought that agents intuitively know through conscience which motive is higher, the core of his ethical theory is a ranking of the thirteen principal motives, the highest of which is reverence. **See also INTUITIONISM.** J.W.A.

Marx, Karl (1818–83), German social philosopher, economic theorist, and revolutionary. He lived and worked as a journalist in Cologne, Paris, and Brussels. After the unsuccessful 1848 revolutions in Europe, he settled in London, doing research and writing and earning some money as correspondent for the *New York Tribune*.

In early writings, he articulated his critique of the religiously and politically conservative implications of the then-reigning philosophy of Hegel, finding there an acceptance of existing private property relationships and of the alienation generated by them. Marx understood alienation as a state of radical disharmony (1) among individuals, (2) between them and their own life activity, or labor, and (3) between individuals and their system of production. Later, in his masterwork *Capital* (1867, 1885, 1894), Marx employed Hegel's method of dialectic to generate an internal critique of the theory and practice of capitalism, showing that, under assumptions (notably that human labor is the source of economic value) found in such earlier theorists as Adam Smith, this system must undergo increasingly severe crises, resulting in the eventual seizure of control of the increasingly centralized means of production (factories, large farms, etc.) from the relatively small class of capitalist proprietors by the previously impoverished non-owners (the *proletariat*) in the interest of a thenceforth classless society.

Marx's early writings, somewhat utopian in tone, most never published during his lifetime, emphasize social ethics and ontology. In them, he characterizes his position as a "humanism" and a "naturalism." In the *Theses on Feuerbach*, he charts a middle path between Hegel's idealist account of the nature of history as the self-unfolding of spirit and what Marx regards as the ahistorical, mechanistic, and passive materialist philosophy of Feuerbach; Marx proposes a conception of history as forged by human activity, or praxis, within determinate material conditions that vary by time and place. In later Marxism, this general position is often labeled *dialectical materialism*.

Marx began radically to question the nature of philosophy, coming to view it as *ideology*, i.e., a thought system parading as autonomous but in fact dependent on the material conditions of the society in which it is produced. The tone of *Capital* is therefore on the whole less philosophical and moralistic, more social scientific and tending toward historical determinism, than that of the earlier writings, but punctuated by bursts of indignation against the baneful effects of capitalism's profit orientation and references to the "society of associated producers" (socialism or communism) that would, or could, replace capitalist society. His enthusiastic predictions of immanent worldwide revolutionary changes, in various letters, articles, and the famous *Communist Manifesto* (1848; jointly authored with his close collaborator, Friedrich Engels), depart from the generally more hypothetical character of the text of *Capital* itself.

The linchpin that perhaps best connects Marx's earlier and later thought and guarantees his enduring relevance as a social philosopher is his analysis of the role of human labor power as a peculiar type of *commodity* within a system of commodity exchange (his *theory of surplus value*). Labor's peculiarity, according to him, lies in its capacity actively to generate more *exchange value* than it itself costs employers as subsistence wages. But to treat human beings as profit-generating commodities risks neglecting to treat them as human beings.

See also MARXISM, POLITICAL PHILOSOPHY, PRAXIS.   W.L.M.

Marxism, the philosophy of Karl Marx, or any of several systems of thought or approaches to social criticism derived from Marx. The term is also applied, incorrectly, to certain sociopolitical structures created by dominant Communist parties during the mid-twentieth century.

Karl Marx himself, apprised of the ideas of certain French critics who invoked his name, remarked that he knew at least that he was not a Marxist. The fact that his collaborator, Friedrich Engels, a popularizer with a greater interest than Marx in the natural sciences, outlived him and wrote, among other things, a "dialectics of nature" that purported to discover certain universal natural laws, added to the confusion. Lenin, the leading Russian Communist revolutionary, near the end of his life discovered previously unacknowledged connections between Marx's *Capital* (1867) and Hegel's *Science of Logic* (1812–16) and concluded (in his *Philosophical Notebooks*) that Marxists for a half-century had not understood Marx. Specific political agendas of, among others, the Marxist faction within the turn-of-the-century German Social Democratic Party, the Bolshevik faction of Russian socialists led by Lenin, and later governments and parties claiming allegiance to "Marxist-Leninist principles" have contributed to reinterpretations. For several decades in the Soviet Union and countries allied with it, a broad agreement concerning fundamental Marxist doctrines was established and politically enforced, resulting in a doctrinaire version labeled "orthodox Marxism" and virtually ensuring the widespread, wholesale rejection of Marxism as such when dissidents taught to accept this version as authentic Marxism came to power.

Marx never wrote a systematic exposition of his thought, which in any case drastically changed emphases across time and included elements of history, economics, and sociology as well as more traditional philosophical concerns. In one letter he specifically warns against regarding his historical account of Western capitalism as a transcendental analysis of the supposedly necessary historical development of any and all societies at a certain time. It is thus somewhat paradoxical that Marxism is often identified as a "totalizing" if not "totalitarian" system by postmodernist philosophers who reject global theories or "grand narratives" as inherently invalid. However, the evolution of Marxism since Marx's time helps explain this identification.

That "orthodox" Marxism would place heavy emphasis on historical determinism – the inevitability of a certain general sequence of events leading to the replacement of capitalism by a socialist economic system (in which, according to a formula in Marx's *Critique of the Gotha Program*, each person would be remunerated according to his/her work) and eventually by a communist one (remuneration in accordance with individual *needs*) – was foreshadowed by Plekhanov. In *The Role of the Individual in History*, he portrayed individual idiosyncrasies as accidental: e.g., had Napoleon not existed the general course of history would not have turned out differently. In *Materialism and Empiriocriticism*, Lenin offered epistemological reinforcement for the notion that Marxism is the uniquely true worldview by defending a "copy" or "reflection" theory of knowledge according to which true concepts simply mirror objective reality, like photographs. Elsewhere, however, he argued against "economism," the inference that the historical inevitability of communism's victory obviated political activism. Lenin instead maintained that, at least under the repressive political conditions of czarist Russia, only a clandestine party of professional revolutionaries, acting as the vanguard of the working class and in its interests, could produce fundamental change. Later, during the long political reign of Josef Stalin, the hegemonic Communist Party of the USSR was identified as the supreme interpreter of these interests, thus justifying totalitarian rule.

So-called Western Marxism opposed this "orthodox" version, although the writings of one of its foremost early representatives, Georg Lukacs, who brilliantly perceived the close connection between Hegel's philosophy and the early thought of Marx before the unpublished manuscripts proving this connection had been retrieved from archives, actually tended to reinforce both the view that the party incarnated the ideal interests of the proletariat (see his *History and Class Consciousness*) and an aesthetics favoring the art of "socialist realism" over more experimental forms. His contemporary, Karl Korsch, in *Marxism as Philosophy*, instead saw Marxism as above all a heuristic method, pointing to salient phenomena (e.g., social class, material conditioning) generally neglected by other philosophies. His counsel was in effect followed by the Frankfurt School of critical theory, including Walter Benjamin in the area of aesthetics, Theodor Adorno in social criticism, and Wilhelm Reich in psychology. A spate of "new Marxisms" – the relative degrees of their fidelity to Marx's original thought cannot be weighed here – developed, especially in the wake of the gradual rediscovery of Marx's more ethically oriented, less deterministic early writings. Among the names meriting special mention in this context are Ernst Bloch, who explored Marxism's connection with utopian thinking; Herbert Marcuse, critic of the "one-dimensionality" of industrial society; the Praxis school (after the name of their journal and in view of their concern with analyzing social practices) of Yugoslav philosophers; and the later Jean-Paul Sartre. Also worthy of note are the writings, many of them composed in prison under Mussolini's Italian Fascist rule, of Antonio Gramsci, who stressed the role of cultural factors in determining what is dominant politically and ideologically at any given time.

Simultaneous with the decline and fall of regimes in which "orthodox Marxism" was officially privileged has been the recent development of new approaches, loosely connected by virtue of their utilization of techniques favored by British and American philosophers, collectively known as analytic Marxism. Problems of justice, theories of history, and the questionable nature of Marx's theory of surplus value have been special concerns to these writers. This development suggests that the current unfashionableness of Marxism in many circles, due largely to its understandable but misleading identification with the aforementioned regimes, is itself only a temporary phenomenon, even if future Marxisms are likely to range even further from Marx's own specific concerns while still sharing his commitment to identifying, explaining, and criticizing hierarchies of dominance and subordination, particularly those of an economic order, in human society.

See also CRITICAL THEORY, FRANKFURT SCHOOL, LUKACS, MARX, PRAXIS, PRAXIS SCHOOL.   W.L.M.

mass noun. See COUNT NOUN.

master argument. See MEGARIANS.

material adequacy, the property that belongs to a formal definition of a concept when that definition characterizes or "captures" the extension (or material) of the concept. Intuitively, a formal definition of a concept is materially adequate if and only if it is neither too broad nor too narrow. Tarski advanced the state of philosophical semantics by discovering the criterion of material adequacy of truth definitions contained in his convention T. Material adequacy contrasts with analytic adequacy, which belongs to definitions that provide a faithful analysis. Defining an integer to be even if and only if it is not the sum of two consecutive integers would be materially adequate but not analytically adequate, whereas defining an integer to be even if and only if it is a multiple of 2 would be both materially and analytically adequate. See also CONVENTION T, DEFINITION, FORMAL SEMANTICS, TARSKI, TRUTH.   J. Cor.

material cause. See ARISTOTLE.

material conditional. See COUNTERFACTUALS, IMPLICATION.

material equivalence. See EQUIVALENCE.

material implication. See IMPLICATION.

material implication, paradoxes of. See IMPLICATION.

materialism. See METAPHYSICS, PHILOSOPHY OF MIND.

materialism, Australian. See SMART.

materialism, central state. See PHILOSOPHY OF MIND.

materialism, dialectical. See MARX, PLEKHANOV.

materialism, emergent. See PHILOSOPHY OF MIND.

materialism, historical. See ENGELS.

materialism, non-reductive. See PHILOSOPHY OF MIND.

material mode. See METALANGUAGE.

material supposition. See SUPPOSITIO.

mathematical analysis, also called standard analysis, the area of mathematics pertaining to the so-called real number system, i.e. the area that can be based on an axiom set whose intended interpretation (standard model) has the set of real numbers as its domain (universe of discourse). Thus analysis includes, among its many subbranches, elementary algebra, differential and integral calculus, differential equations, the calculus of variations, and measure theory. Analytic geometry involves the application of analysis to geometry. Analysis contains a large part of the mathematics used in mathematical physics. The real numbers, which are representable by the ending and unending decimals, are usefully construed as (or as corresponding to) distances measured, relative to an arbitrary unit length, positively to the right and negatively to the left of an arbitrarily fixed zero point along a geometrical straight line. In particular, the class of *real numbers* includes as increasingly comprehensive proper subclasses the natural numbers, the integers (positive, negative, and zero), the rational numbers (or fractions), and the algebraic numbers (such as the square root of two). Especially important is the presence in the class of real numbers of non-algebraic (or transcendental) irrational numbers such as pi. The set of real numbers includes arbitrarily small and arbitrarily large, finite quantities, while excluding infinitesimal and infinite quantities.

Analysis, often conceived as the mathematics of continuous magnitude, contrasts with arithmetic (natural number theory), which is regarded as the mathematics of discrete magnitude. Analysis is often construed as involving not just the real numbers but also the imaginary (complex) numbers. Traditionally analysis is expressed in a second-order or higher-order language wherein its axiom set has categoricity; each of its models is isomorphic to (has the same structure as) the standard model. When analysis is carried out in a first-order language, as has been increasingly the case since the 1950s, categoricity is impossible and it has nonstandard models in addition to its standard model. A *non-standard model* of analysis is an interpretation not isomorphic to the standard model but nevertheless satisfying the axiom set. Some of the non-standard models involve objects reminiscent of the much-despised "infinitesimals" that were essential to the Leibniz approach to calculus and that were subject to intense criticism by Berkeley and other philosophers and philosophically sensitive mathematicians. These non-standard models give rise to a new area of mathematics, non-standard analysis, within which the fallacious arguments used by Leibniz and other early analysts form the heuristic basis of new and entirely rigorous proofs.

See also CALCULUS, CATEGORICITY, PHILOSOPHY OF MATHEMATICS.   J.Cor.

mathematical constructivism. See PHILOSOPHY OF MATHEMATICS.

mathematical function, an operation that, when applied to an entity (set of entities) called its argument(s), yields an entity known as the value of the function for that argument(s). This operation can be expressed by a functional equation of the form $y = f(x)$ such that a variable y is said to be a function of a variable x if corresponding to each value of x there is one and only one value of y. The x is called the independent variable (or argument of the function) and the y the dependent variable (or value of the function). (Some definitions consider the relation to be the function, not the dependent variable, and some definitions permit more than one value of y to correspond to a given value of x, as in $x^2 + y^2 = 4$.) More abstractly, a function can be considered to be simply a special kind of relation (set of ordered pairs) that to any element in its domain relates exactly one element in its range. Such a function is said to be a *one-to-one correspondence* if and only if the set $\{x,y\}$ elements of S and $\{z,y\}$ elements of S jointly imply $x = z$. Consider, e.g., the function $\{(1,1), (2,4), (3,9), (4,16), (5,25), (6,36)\}$, each of whose members is of the form (x,x^2) – the squaring function. Or consider the function $\{(0,1), (1,0)\}$ – which we can call the negation function. In contrast, consider the function for exclusive alternation (as in you may have a beer or glass of wine, but not both). It is not a one-to-one correspondence. For, 0 is the value of $(0,1)$ and of $(1,0)$, and 1 is the value of $(0,0)$ and of $(1,1)$.

If we think of a function as defined on the natural numbers – functions from N^n to N for various n (most commonly $n = 1$ or 2) – a *partial function* is a function from N^n to N whose domain is not necessarily the whole of N^n (e.g., not defined for all of the natural numbers). A *total function* from N^n to N is a function whose domain is the whole of N^n (e.g., all of the natural numbers).

See also FUNCTIONALISM, TELEOLOGY.   F.A.

mathematical induction, a method of definition and a method of proof. A collection of objects can be defined inductively. All members of such a collection can be shown to have a property by an inductive proof. The natural numbers and the set of well-formed formulas of a formal language are familiar examples of sets given by inductive definition. Thus, the set of *natural numbers* is inductively defined as the smallest set, N, such that: (B) 0 is in N and (I) for any x in N the successor of x is in N. (B) is the *basic clause* and (I) the *inductive clause* of this definition. Or consider a propositional language built on negation and conjunction. We start with a denumerable class of atomic sentence symbols ATOM = {A1, A2, . . .}. Then we can define the set of well-formed formulas, WFF, as the smallest set of expressions such that: (B) every member of ATOM is in WFF and (I) if x is in WFF then $(\sim x)$ is in WFF and if x and y are in WFF then $(x \,\&\, y)$ is in WFF. We show that all members of an inductively defined set have a property by showing that the members specified by the basis have that property and that the property is preserved by the induction. For example, we show that all WFFs have an even number of parentheses by showing (i) that all ATOMs have an even number of parentheses and (ii) that if x and y have an even number of parentheses then so do $(\sim x)$ and $(x \,\&\, y)$. This shows that the set of WFFs with an even number of parentheses satisfies (B) and (I). The set of WFFs with an even number of parentheses must then be identical to WFF, since – by definition – WFF is the smallest set that satisfies (B) and (I).

Ordinary proof by mathematical induction shows that all the natural numbers, or all members of some set with the order type of the natural numbers, share a property. Proof by *transfinite induction,* a more general form of proof by mathematical induction, shows that all members of some well-ordered set have a certain property. A set is well-ordered if and only if every non-empty subset of it has a least element. The natural numbers are well-ordered. It is a consequence of the axiom of choice that every set can be well-ordered. Suppose that a set, X, is well-ordered and that P is the subset of X whose members have the property of interest. Suppose that it can be shown for any element x of X, if all members of X less that x are in P, then so is x. Then it follows by transfinite induction that all members of X have the property, that $X = P$. For if X did not coincide with P, then the set of elements of x not in P would be non-empty. Since X is well-ordered, this set would have a least element, x^*. But then by definition, all members of X less than x^* are in P, and by hypothesis x^* must be in P after all.

See also INDUCTION, PHILOSOPHY OF MATHEMATICS, PROOF THEORY.   B.Sk.

mathematical intuitionism, a twentieth-century movement that reconstructs mathematics in accordance with an epistemological idealism and a Kantian metaphysics. Specifically, Brouwer, its founder, held that there are no unexperienced truths and that mathematical objects stem from the a priori form of those conscious acts which generate empirical objects. Unlike Kant, however, Brouwer rejected the apriority of space and based mathematics solely on a refined conception of the intuition of time.

Intuitionistic mathematics. According to Brouwer, the simplest mathematical act is to distinguish between two diverse elements in the flow of consciousness. By repeating and concatenating such acts we generate each of the natural numbers, the standard arithmetical operations, and thus the rational numbers with their operations as well. Unfortunately, these simple, terminating processes cannot produce the convergent infinite sequences of rational numbers that are needed to generate the continuum (the non-denumerable set of real numbers, or of points on the line). Some "proto-intuitionists" admitted infinite sequences whose elements are determined by finitely describable rules. However, the set of all such algorithmic sequences is denumerable and thus can scarcely generate the continuum. Brouwer's first attempt to circumvent this – by postulating a single intuition of an ever growing continuum – mirrored Aristotle's picture of the continuum as a dynamic whole composed of inseparable parts. But this approach was incompatible with the set-theoretic framework that Brouwer accepted, and by 1918 he had replaced it with the concept of an infinite choice sequence. A choice sequence of rational numbers is, to be sure, generated by a "rule," but the rule may leave room for some degree of freedom in choosing the successive elements. It might, e.g., simply require that the $n + 1$st choice be a

rational number that lies within $1/n$ of the nth choice. The set of real numbers generated by such semideterminate sequences is demonstrably non-denumerable. Following his epistemological beliefs, Brouwer admitted only those properties of a choice sequence which are determined by its rule and by a finite number of actual choices. He incorporated this restriction into his version of set theory and obtained a series of results that conflict with standard (classical) mathematics. Most famously, he proved that every function that is fully defined over an interval of real numbers is uniformly continuous. (Pictorially, the graph of the function has no gaps or jumps.) Interestingly, one corollary of this theorem is that the set of real numbers cannot be divided into mutually exclusive subsets, a property that rigorously recovers the Aristotelian picture of the continuum.

The clash with classical mathematics. Unlike his disciple Arend Heyting, who considered intuitionistic and classical mathematics as separate and therefore compatible subjects, Brouwer viewed them as incompatible treatments of a single subject matter. He even occasionally accused classical mathematics of inconsistency at the places where it differed from intuitionism. This clash concerns the basic concept of what counts as a mathematical object. Intuitionism allows, and classical mathematics rejects, objects that may be indeterminate with respect to some of their properties.

Logic and language. Because he believed that mathematical constructions occur in prelinguistic consciousness, Brouwer refused to limit mathematics by the expressive capacity of any language. Logic, he claimed, merely codifies already completed stages of mathematical reasoning. For instance, the principle of the excluded middle stems from an "observational period" during which mankind catalogued finite phenomena (with decidable properties); and he derided classical mathematics for inappropriately applying this principle to infinitary aspects of mathematics.

Formalization. Brouwer's views notwithstanding, in 1930 Heyting produced formal systems for intuitionistic logic (IL) and number theory. These inspired further formalizations (even of the theory of choice sequences) and a series of proof-theoretic, semantic, and algebraic studies that related intuitionistic and classical formal systems. Stephen Kleene, e.g., interpreted IL and other intuitionistic formal systems using the classical theory of recursive functions. Gödel, who showed that IL cannot coincide with any finite many-valued logic, demonstrated its relation to the modal logic, S4; and Kripke provided a formal semantics for IL similar to the possible worlds semantics for S4. For a while the study of intuitionistic formal systems used strongly classical methods, but since the 1970s intuitionistic methods have been employed as well.

Meaning. Heyting's formalization reflected a theory of meaning implicit in Brouwer's epistemology and metaphysics, a theory that replaces the traditional correspondence notion of truth with the notion of constructive proof. More recently Michael Dummett has extended this to a warranted assertability theory of meaning for areas of discourse outside of mathematics. He has shown how assertabilism provides a strategy for combating realism about such things as physical objects, mental objects, and the past.

See also BROUWER, CHOICE SEQUENCE, PHILOSOPHY OF MATHEMATICS, SET THEORY.

C.J.P.

mathematical logic. See FORMAL LOGIC.

mathematical space. See SPACE.

mathematical structuralism, the view that the subject of any branch of mathematics is a structure or structures. The slogan is that mathematics is the science of structure. Define a "natural number system" to be a countably infinite collection of objects with one designated initial object and a successor relation that satisfies the principle of mathematical induction. Examples of natural number systems are the Arabic numerals and an infinite sequence of distinct moments of time. According to structuralism, arithmetic is about the form or structure common to natural number systems. Accordingly, a natural number is something like an office in an organization or a place in a pattern. Similarly, real analysis is about the real number structure, the form common to complete ordered fields. The philosophical issues concerning structuralism concern the nature of structures and their places. Since a structure is a one-over-many of sorts, it is something like a universal. Structuralists have defended analogues of some of the traditional positions on universals, such as realism and nominalism. See also MATHEMATICAL INDUCTION, PEANO POSTULATES, PHILOSOPHY OF MATHEMATICS.

S.Sha.

mathematics, philosophy of. See PHILOSOPHY OF MATHEMATICS.

matrix mechanics. See QUANTUM MECHANICS.

matter. See METAPHYSICS.

matter, prime. See HYLOMORPHISM.

matter, principle of the conservation of. See PHILOSOPHY OF SCIENCE.

maxim. See KANT.

maximal consistent set, in formal logic, any set of sentences S that is consistent – i.e., no contradiction is provable from S – and maximally so – i.e., if T is consistent and $S \subseteq T$, then $S = T$. It can be shown that if S is maximally consistent and s is a sentence in the same language, then either σ or $\sim \sigma$ (the negation of σ) is in S. Thus, a maximally consistent set is complete: it settles every question that can be raised in the language. See also COMPLETENESS, SET THEORY. P.Mad.

maximal proposition. See TOPICS.

maximin strategy, a strategy that maximizes an agent's minimum gain, or equivalently, minimizes his maximum loss. Writers who work in terms of loss thus call such a strategy a *minimax strategy*. The term 'security strategy', which avoids potential confusions, is now widely used. For each action, its security level is its payoff under the worst-case scenario. A security strategy is one with maximal security level.

An agent's security strategy maximizes his expected utility if and only if (1) he is certain that "nature" has his worst interests at heart and (2) he is certain that nature will be certain of his strategy when choosing hers. The first condition is satisfied in the case of a two-person zero-sum game where the payoff structure is commonly known. In this situation, "nature" is the other player, and her gain is equal to the first player's loss. Obviously, these conditions do not hold for all decision problems.

See also DECISION THEORY, GAME THEORY.

B.Sk.

Maxwell, James Clerk (1831–79), Scottish physicist who made pioneering contributions to the theory of electromagnetism, the kinetic theory of gases, and the theory of color vision. His work on electromagnetism is summarized in his *Treatise on Electricity and Magnetism* (1873). In 1871 he became Cambridge University's first professor of experimental physics and founded the Cavendish Laboratory, which he directed until his death.

Maxwell's most important achievements were his field theory of electromagnetism and the discovery of the equations that bear his name. The field theory unified the laws of electricity and magnetism, identified light as a transverse vibration of the electromagnetic ether, and predicted the existence of radio waves. The fact that Maxwell's equations are Lorentz-invariant and contain the speed of light as a constant played a major role in the genesis of the special theory of relativity. He arrived at his theory by searching for a "consistent representation" of the ether, i.e., a model of its inner workings consistent with the laws of mechanics. His search for a consistent representation was unsuccessful, but his papers used mechanical models and analogies to guide his thinking. Like Boltzmann, Maxwell advocated the heuristic value of model building.

Maxwell was also a pioneer in statistical physics. His derivation of the laws governing the macroscopic behavior of gases from assumptions about the random collisions of gas molecules led directly to Boltzmann's transport equation and the statistical analysis of irreversibility. To show that the second law of thermodynamics is probabilistic, Maxwell imagined a "neat-fingered" demon who could cause the entropy of a gas to decrease by separating the faster-moving gas molecules from the slower-moving ones.

See also PHILOSOPHY OF SCIENCE, RELATIVITY.   M.C.

māyā, a term with various uses in Indian thought; it expresses the concept of Brahman's power to act. One type of Brahmanic action is the assuming of material forms whose appearance can be changed at will. Demons as well as gods are said to have *māyā*, understood as power to do things not within a standard human repertoire. A deeper sense refers to the idea that Brahman has and exercises the power to sustain everlastingly the entire world of conscious and non-conscious things.

Monotheistically conceived, *māyā* is the power of an omnipotent and omniscient deity to produce the world of dependent things. This power typically is conceived as feminine (Sakti) and various representations of the deity are conceived as male with female consorts, as with Vishnu and Siva. Without Sakti, Brahman would be masculine and passive and no created world would exist. By association, *māyā* is the product of created activity. The created world is conceived as dependent, both a manifestation of divine power and a veil between Brahman and the devotee. Monistically conceived, *māyā* expresses the notion that there only seems to be a world composed of distinct conscious and non-conscious things, and rather than this seeming multiplicity there exists only ineffable Brahman. Brahman is conceived as somehow producing the illusion of there being a plurality of persons and objects, and enlightenment (*moksha*) is conceived as seeing through the illusion. Monotheists, who ask who, on the monistic view, has the qualities requisite to produce illusion and how an illusion can see through itself, regard enlightenment (*moksha*) as a matter of devotion to the Brahman whom the created universe partially manifests, but also veils, whose nature is also revealed in religious experience.

See also BRAHMAN.   K.E.Y.

Mead, George Herbert (1863–1931), American philosopher, social theorist, and social reformer. He was a member of the Chicago school of pragmatism, which included figures such as James Hayden Tufts and John Dewey. Whitehead agreed with Dewey's assessment of Mead: "a seminal mind of the very first order." Mead was raised in a household with deep roots in New England puritanism, but he eventually became a confirmed naturalist, convinced that modern science could make the processes of nature intelligible. On his path to naturalism he studied with the idealist Josiah Royce at Harvard. The German idealist tradition of Fichte, Schelling, and Hegel (who were portrayed by Mead as Romantic philosophers in *Movements of Thought in the Nineteenth Century*) had a lasting influence on his thought, even though he became a confirmed empiricist.

Mead is considered the progenitor of the school of symbolic interaction in sociology, and is best known for his explanation of the genesis of the mind and the self in terms of language development and role playing. A close friend of Jane Addams (1860–1935), he viewed his theoretical work in this area as lending weight to his progressive political convictions. Mead is often referred to as a *social behaviorist*. He employed the categories of stimulus and response in order to explain behavior, but contra behaviorists such as John B. Watson, Mead did not dismiss conduct that was not observed by others. He examined the nature of self-consciousness, whose development is depicted in *Mind, Self, and Society, from the Standpoint of a Social Behaviorist*. He also addressed behavior in terms of the phases of an organism's adjustment to its environment in *The Philosophy of the Act*.

His reputation as a theorist of the social development of the self has tended to eclipse his original work in other areas of concern to philosophers, e.g., ethics, epistemology, metaphysics, and the philosophy of science. Influenced by Darwin, Mead sought to understand nature, as well as social relationships, in terms of the process of emergence. He emphasized that qualitatively new forms of life arise through natural and intelligible processes. When novel events occur the past is transformed, for the past has now given rise to the qualitatively new, and it must be seen from a different perspective. Between the arrival of the new order – which the novel event instigates – and the old order, there is a phase of readjustment, a stage that Mead describes as one of *sociality*. Mead's views on these and related matters are discussed in *The Philosophy of the Present*. Mead never published a book-length work in philosophy. His unpublished manuscripts and students' notes were edited and published as the books cited above.

See also PHILOSOPHY OF THE SOCIAL SCIENCES, PRAGMATISM.   M.Ab.

mean, doctrine of the. See ARISTOTLE, CHUNG-YUNG.

meaning, the conventional, common, or standard sense of an expression, construction, or sentence in a given language, or of a non-linguistic signal or symbol. *Literal meaning* is the non-figurative, strict meaning an expression or sentence has in a language by virtue of the dictionary meaning of its words and the import of its syntactic constructions. *Synonymy* is sameness of literal meaning: 'prestidigitator' means 'expert at sleight of hand'. It is said that meaning is what a good translation preserves, and this may or may not be literal: in French *'Où sont les neiges d'antan?'* literally means 'Where are the snows of yesteryear?' and figuratively means 'nothing lasts'. Signal-types and symbols have non-linguistic conventional meaning: the white flag means truce; the lion means St. Mark.

In another sense, *meaning* is what a person intends to communicate by a particular utterance – utterer's meaning, as Grice called it, or *speaker's meaning*, in Stephen Schiffer's term. A speaker's meaning may or may not coincide with the literal meaning of what is uttered, and it may be non-linguistic. Non-literal: in saying "we will soon be in our tropical paradise," Jane meant that they would soon be in Antarctica. Literal: in

saying "that's deciduous," she meant that the tree loses its leaves every year. Non-linguistic: by shrugging, she meant that she agreed.

The literal meaning of a sentence typically does not determine exactly what a speaker says in making a literal utterance: the meaning of 'she is praising me' leaves open what John says in uttering it, e.g. that Jane praises John at 12:00 p.m., Dec. 21, 1991. A not uncommon – but theoretically loaded – way of accommodating this is to count the context-specific things that speakers say as *propositions*, entities that can be expressed in different languages and that are (on certain theories) the content of what is said, believed, desired, and so on. On that assumption, a sentence's literal meaning is a context-independent rule, or function, that determines a certain proposition (the content of what the speaker says) given the context of utterance. David Kaplan has called such a rule or function a sentence's "character."

A sentence's literal meaning also includes its potential for performing certain *illocutionary acts*, in J. L. Austin's term. The meaning of an imperative sentence determines what orders, requests, and the like can literally be expressed: 'sit down there' can be uttered literally by Jane to request (or order or urge) John to sit down at 11:59 a.m. on a certain bench in Santa Monica. Thus a sentence's literal meaning involves both its character and a constraint on illocutionary acts: it maps contexts onto illocutionary acts that have (something like) determinate propositional contents. A context includes the identity of speaker, hearer, time of utterance, and also aspects of the speaker's intentions.

In ethics the distinction has flourished between the *expressive* or *emotive meaning* of a word or sentence and its *cognitive meaning*. The emotive meaning of an utterance or a term is the attitude it expresses, the pejorative meaning of 'chiseler', say. An emotivist in ethics, e.g. C. L. Stevenson (1908–79), holds that the literal meaning of 'it is good' is identical with its emotive meaning, the positive attitude it expresses. On Hare's theory, the literal meaning of 'ought' is its *prescriptive meaning*, the imperative force it gives to certain sentences that contain it. Such "noncognitivist" theories can allow that a term like 'good' also has non-literal *descriptive meaning*, implying non-evaluative properties of an object. By contrast, cognitivists take the literal meaning of an ethical term to be its *cognitive meaning*: 'good' stands for an objective property, and in asserting "it is good" one literally expresses, not an attitude, but a true or false judgment.

'Cognitive meaning' serves as well as any other term to capture what has been central in the theory of meaning beyond ethics, the "factual" element in meaning that remains when we abstract from its illocutionary and emotive aspects. It is what is shared by 'there will be an eclipse tomorrow' and 'will there be an eclipse tomorrow?'. This common element is often identified with a proposition (or a "character"), but, once again, that is theoretically loaded. Although cognitive meaning has been the preoccupation of the theory of meaning in the twentieth century, it is difficult to define precisely in non-theoretical terms. Suppose we say that the cognitive meaning of a sentence is 'that aspect of its meaning which is capable of being true or false': there are non-truth-conditional theories of meaning (see below) on which this would not capture the essentials. Suppose we say it is 'what is capable of being asserted': an emotivist might allow that one can assert that a thing is good. Still many philosophers have taken for granted that they know cognitive meaning (under that name or not) well enough to theorize about what it consists in, and it is the focus of what follows.

The oldest theories of meaning in modern philosophy are the seventeenth-to-nineteenth-century *idea theory* (also called the ideational theory) and *image theory* of meaning, according to which the meaning of words in public language derives from the ideas or mental images that words are used to express. As for what constitutes the representational properties of ideas, Descartes held it to be a basic property of the mind, inexplicable, and Locke a matter of resemblance (in some sense) between ideas and things. Contemporary analytic philosophy speaks more of propositional attitudes – thoughts, beliefs, intentions – than of ideas and images; and it speaks of the *contents* of such attitudes: if Jane believes that there are lions in Africa, that belief has as its content that there are lions in Africa. Virtually all philosophers agree that propositional attitudes have some crucial connection with meaning.

A fundamental element of a theory of meaning is where it locates the basis of meaning, in thought, in individual speech, or in social practices. (i) Meaning may be held to derive entirely from the content of thoughts or propositional attitudes, that mental content itself being constituted independently of public linguistic meaning. ('Constituted independently of' does not imply 'unshaped by'.) (ii) It may be held that the contents of beliefs and communicative intentions themselves derive in part from the meaning of overt speech, or even from social practices.

Then meaning would be jointly constituted by both individual psychological and social linguistic facts.

Theories of the first sort include those in the style of Grice, according to which sentences' meanings are determined by practices or implicit conventions that govern *what speakers mean* when they use the relevant words and constructions. A speaker's meaning is explained in terms of certain propositional attitudes, namely the speaker's intentions to produce certain effects in hearers. To mean that it is raining is to utter or to do something (not necessarily linguistic) with the intention (very roughly) of getting one's hearer to believe that it is raining. Theories of speaker's meaning have been elaborated by Grice and by Schiffer. David Lewis has proposed that linguistic meaning is constituted by implicit conventions that systematically associate sentences with speakers' beliefs rather than with communicative intentions.

The contents of thought might be held to be constitutive of linguistic meaning independently of communication. Russell, and Wittgenstein in his early writings, wrote about meaning as if the key thing is the propositional content of the belief or thought that a sentence (somehow) expresses; they apparently regarded this as holding on an individual basis and not essentially as deriving from communication intentions or social practices. And Chomsky speaks of the point of language as being "the free expression of thought." Such views suggest that 'linguistic meaning' may stand for two properties, one involving communication intentions and practices, the other more intimately related to thinking and conceiving.

By contrast, the content of propositional attitudes and the meaning of overt speech might be regarded as coordinate facts neither of which can obtain independently: to interpret other people one must assign both content to their beliefs/intentions and meaning to their utterances. This is explicit in Davidson's truth-conditional theory (see below); perhaps it is present also in the post-Wittgensteinian notion of meaning as assertability conditions – e.g., in the writings of Dummett.

On still other accounts, linguistic meaning is essentially social. Wittgenstein is interpreted by Kripke as holding in his later writings that social rules are essential to meaning, on the grounds that they alone explain the *normative* aspect of meaning, explain the fact that an expression's meaning determines that some uses are correct or others incorrect. Another way in which meaning may be essentially social is Putnam's "division of linguistic labor": the meanings of some terms, say in botany or cabinetmaking, are set for the rest of us by specialists. The point might extend to quite non-technical words, like 'red': a person's use of it may be socially deferential, in that the rule which determines what 'red' means in his mouth is determined, not by his individual usage, but by the usage of some social group to which he semantically defers. This has been argued by Tyler Burge to imply that the contents of thoughts themselves are in part a matter of social facts.

Let us suppose there is a language L that contains no indexical terms, such as 'now', 'I', or demonstrative pronouns, but contains only proper names, common nouns, adjectives, verbs, adverbs, logical words. (No natural language is like this; but the supposition simplifies what follows.) Theories of meaning differ considerably in how they would specify the meaning of a sentence S of L. Here are the main contenders. (i) Specify S's *truth conditions:* S is true if and only if some swans are black. (ii) Specify the *proposition* that S expresses: S means (the proposition) that some swans are black. (iii) Specify S's *assertability conditions:* S is assertable if and only if black-swan-sightings occur or black-swan-reports come in, etc. (iv) Translate S into that sentence of our language which has the same *use* as S or the same *conceptual role.*

Certain theories, especially those that specify meanings in ways (i) and (ii), take the *compositionality of meaning* as basic. Here is an elementary fact: a sentence's meaning is a function of the meanings of its component words and constructions, and as a result we can utter and understand new sentences – old words and constructions, new sentences. Frege's theory of *Bedeutung* or reference, especially his use of the notions of function and object, is about compositionality. In the *Tractatus,* Wittgenstein explains compositionality in his *picture theory* of meaning and theory of truth-functions. According to Wittgenstein, a sentence or proposition is a picture of a (possible) state of affairs; terms correspond to non-linguistic elements, and those terms' arrangements in sentences have the same form as arrangements of elements in the states of affairs the sentences stand for.

The leading *truth-conditional theory* of meaning is the one advocated by Davidson, drawing on the work of Tarski. Tarski showed that, for certain formalized languages, we can construct a finite set of rules that entails, for each sentence S of the infinitely many sentences of such a lan-

guage, something of the form 'S is true if and only if . . .'. Those finitely statable rules, which taken together are sometimes called a *truth theory* of the language, might entail ' "(x) $(Rx \rightarrow Bx)$" is true if and only if every raven is black'. They would do this by having separately assigned interpretations to 'R', 'B', '$\rightarrow$', and '(x)'. Truth conditions are compositionally determined in analogous ways for sentences, however complex.

Davidson proposes that Tarski's device is applicable to natural languages and that it explains, moreover, what meaning is, given the following setting. Interpretation involves a *principle of charity:* interpreting a person N means making the best possible sense of N, and this means assigning meanings so as to maximize the overall truth of N's utterances. A systematic interpretation of N's language can be taken to be a Tarski-style truth theory that (roughly) maximizes the truth of N's utterances. If such a truth theory implies that a sentence S is true in N's language if and only if some swans are black, then that tells us the meaning of S in N's language.

A *propositional theory* of meaning would accommodate compositionality thus: a finite set of rules, which govern the terms and constructions of L, assigns (derivatively) a proposition (putting aside ambiguity) to each sentence S of L by virtue of S's terms and constructions. If L contains indexicals, then such rules assign to each sentence not a fully specific proposition but a 'character' in the above sense. Propositions may be conceived in two ways: (a) as sets of possible circumstances or "worlds" – then 'Hesperus is hot' in English is assigned the set of possible worlds in which Hesperus is hot; and (b) as structured combinations of elements – then 'Hesperus is hot' is assigned a certain ordered pair of elements $<M1,M2>$. There are two theories about M1 and M2. They may be the *senses* of 'Hesperus' and '(is) hot', and then the ordered pair is a "Fregean" proposition. They may be the *references* of 'Hesperus' and '(is) hot', and then the ordered pair is a "Russellian" proposition. This difference reflects a fundamental dispute in twentieth-century philosophy of language.

The *connotation* or *sense* of a term is its "mode of presentation," the way it presents its *denotation* or reference. Terms with the same reference or denotation may present their references differently and so differ in sense or connotation. This is unproblematic for complex terms like 'the capital of Italy' and 'the city on the Tiber', which refer to Rome via different connotations. Controversy arises over simple terms, such as proper names and common nouns. Frege distinguished sense and reference for all expressions; the proper names 'Phosphorus' and 'Hesperus' express descriptive senses according to how we understand them – [that bright starlike object visible before dawn in the eastern sky . . .], [that bright starlike object visible after sunset in the western sky . . .]; and they refer to Venus by virtue of those senses. Russell held that ordinary proper names, such as 'Romulus', abbreviate definite descriptions, and in this respect his view resembles Frege's. But Russell also held that, for those simple terms (not 'Romulus') into which statements are analyzable, sense and reference are not distinct, and meanings are "Russellian" propositions. (But Russell's view of their constituents differs from present-day views.)

Kripke rejected the "Frege-Russell" view of ordinary proper names, arguing that the reference of a proper name is determined, not by a descriptive condition, but typically by a causal chain that links name and reference – in the case of 'Hesperus' a partially perceptual relation perhaps, in the case of 'Aristotle' a causal-historical relation. A proper name is rather a *rigid designator:* any sentence of the form 'Aristotle is . . . ' expresses a proposition that is true in a given possible world (or set of circumstances) if and only if our (actual) Aristotle satisfies, in that world, the condition ' . . . '. The "Frege-Russell" view by contrast incorporates in the proposition, not the actual referent, but a descriptive condition connotated by 'Aristotle' (the author of the *Metaphysics,* or the like), so that the name's reference differs in different worlds even when the descriptive connotation is constant. (Someone else could have written the *Metaphysics.*)

Some recent philosophers have taken the rigid designator view to motivate the stark thesis that meanings are Russellian propositions (or characters that map contexts onto such propositions): in the above proposition/meaning <M1,M2>, M1 is simply the referent – the planet Venus – itself. This would be a *referential theory of meaning,* one that equates meaning with reference. But we must emphasize that the rigid designator view does not directly entail a referential theory of meaning.

What about the meanings of predicates? What sort of entity is M2 above? Putnam and Kripke also argue an anti-descriptive point about *natural kind terms,* predicates like '(is) gold', '(is a) tiger', '(is) hot'. These are not equivalent to descriptions – 'gold' does not mean 'metal that is yellow, malleable, etc.' – but are rigid designators of underlying natural kinds whose identities are discovered by science. On a referential theory of meanings as Russellian propositions, the meaning of 'gold' is then a natural kind. (A complication arises: the property or kind that 'widow' stands for seems a good candidate for being the sense or connotation of 'widow', for what one understands by it. The distinction between Russellian and Fregean propositions is not then firm at every point.)

On the standard sense-theory of meanings as Fregean propositions, M1 and M2 are pure descriptive senses. But a certain "neo-Fregean" view, suggested but not held by Gareth Evans, would count M1 and M2 as *object-dependent senses.* For example, 'Hesperus' and 'Phosphorus' would rigidly designate the same object but have distinct senses that cannot be specified without mention of that object. Note that, if proper names or natural kind terms have meanings of either sort, their meanings vary from speaker to speaker.

A propositional account of meaning (or the corresponding account of "character") may be part of a broader theory of meaning; for example: (a) a Grice-type theory involving implicit conventions; (b) a theory that meaning derives from an intimate connection of language and thought; (c) a theory that invokes a principle of charity or the like in interpreting an individual's speech; (d) a social theory on which meaning cannot derive entirely from the independently constituted contents of individuals' thoughts or uses.

A central tradition in twentieth-century theory of meaning identifies meaning with factors other than propositions (in the foregoing senses) and truth-conditions. The meaning of a sentence is what one understands by it; and understanding a sentence is knowing how to use it – knowing how to verify it and when to assert it, or being able to think with it and to use it in inferences and practical reasoning. There are competing theories here.

In the 1930s, proponents of logical positivism held a *verification theory of meaning,* whereby a sentence's or statement's meaning consists in the conditions under which it can be verified, certified as acceptable. This was motivated by the positivists' empiricism together with their view of truth as a metaphysical or non-empirical notion. A descendant of verificationism is the thesis, influenced by the later Wittgenstein, that the meaning of a sentence consists in its *assertability conditions,* the circumstances under which one is justified in asserting the sentence. If justification and truth can diverge, as they appear to, then a sentence's assertability conditions can be distinct from (what non-verificationists see as) its truth conditions. Dummett has argued that assertability conditions are the basis of meaning and that truth-conditional semantics rests on a mistake (and hence also propositional semantics in sense [a] above). A problem with assertability theories is that, as is generally acknowledged, *compositional* theories of the assertability conditions of sentences are not easily constructed.

A *conceptual role theory of meaning* (also called conceptual role semantics) typically presupposes that we think in a language of thought (an idea championed by Fodor), a system of internal states structured like a language that may or may not be closely related to one's natural language. The conceptual role of a term is a matter of how thoughts that contain the term are dispositionally related to other thoughts, to sensory states, and to behavior. Hartry Field has pointed out that our Fregean intuitions about 'Hesperus' and 'Phosphorus' are explained by those terms' having distinct conceptual roles, without appeal to Fregean descriptive senses or the like, and that this is compatible with those terms' rigidly designating the same object. This combination can be articulated in two ways. Gilbert Harman proposes that meaning is "wide" conceptual role, so that conceptual role incorporates not just inferential factors, etc., but also Kripke-Putnam external reference relations. But there are also two-factor theories of meaning, as proposed by Field among others, which recognize two strata of meaning, one corresponding to how a person understands a term – its narrow conceptual role, the other involving references, Russellian propositions, or truth-conditions.

As the language-of-thought view indicates, some concerns about meaning have been taken over by theories of the *content* of thoughts or propositional attitudes. A distinction is often made between the *narrow content* of a thought and its *wide content*. If psychological explanation invokes only "what is in the head," and if thought contents are essential to psychological explanation, there must be narrow content. Theories have appealed to the "syntax" or conceptual roles or "characters" of internal sentences, as well as to images and stereotypes. A thought's wide content may then be regarded (as motivated by the Kripke-Putnam arguments) as a Russellian proposition. The naturalistic reference-relations that determine the elements of such propositions are the focus of causal, "informational" and "teleological" theories by Fodor, Dretske, and Ruth Millikan.

Assertability theories and conceptual role theories have been called *use theories of meaning* in a broad sense that marks a contrast with truth-conditional theories. On a use theory in this broad sense, understanding meaning consists in *knowing how* to use a term or sentence, or being disposed to use a term or sentence in response to certain external or conceptual factors. But 'use theory' also refers to the doctrine of the later writings of Wittgenstein, by whom theories of meaning that abstract from the very large variety of interpersonal uses of language are declared a philosopher's mistake. The meanings of terms and sentences are a matter of the *language games* in which they play roles; these are too various to have a common structure that can be captured in a philosopher's theory of meaning.

Conceptual role theories tend toward *meaning holism*, the thesis that a term's meaning cannot be abstracted from the entirety of its conceptual connections. On a holistic view any belief or inferential connection involving a term is as much a candidate for determining its meaning as any other. This could be avoided by affirming the analytic–synthetic distinction, according to which some of a term's conceptual connections are constitutive of its meaning and others only incidental. ('Bachelors are unmarried' versus 'Bachelors have a tax advantage'.) But many philosophers follow Quine in his skepticism about that distinction. The implications of holism are drastic, for it strictly implies that different people's words cannot mean the same. In the philosophy of science, meaning holism has been held to imply the incommensurability of theories, according to which a scientific theory that replaces an earlier theory cannot be held to contradict it and hence not to correct or to improve on it – for the two theories' apparently common terms would be equivocal. Remedies might include, again, maintaining some sort of analytic–synthetic distinction for scientific terms, or holding that conceptual role theories and hence holism itself, as Field proposes, hold only intrapersonally, while taking interpersonal and intertheoretic meaning comparisons to be referential and truth-conditional. Even this, however, leads to difficult questions about the interpretation of scientific theories. A radical position, associated with Quine, identifies the meaning of a theory as a whole with its *empirical meaning*, that is, the set of actual and possible sensory or perceptual situations that would count as verifying the theory as a whole. This can be seen as a successor to the verificationist theory, with theory replacing statement or sentence. Articulations of meaning internal to a theory would then be spurious, as would virtually all ordinary intuitions about meaning. This fits well Quine's skepticism about meaning, his thesis of the *indeterminacy of translation,* according to which no objective facts distinguish a favored translation of another language into ours from every apparently incorrect translation. Many constructive theories of meaning may be seen as replies to this and other skepticisms about the objective status of semantic facts.

See also FORMAL SEMANTICS, PHILOSOPHY OF LANGUAGE, PHILOSOPHY OF MIND, SEMANTIC HOLISM, SPEECH ACT THEORY, VERIFICATIONISM.   B.L.

meaning, conceptual role theory of. See MEANING.

meaning, descriptive. See EMOTIVISM, MEANING.

meaning, dispositional theory of. See MEANING.

meaning, emotive. See EMOTIVISM, MEANING.

meaning, focal. See ARISTOTLE.

meaning, idea theory of. See MEANING.

meaning, ideational theory of. See PHILOSOPHY OF LANGUAGE.

meaning, image theory of. See MEANING.

meaning, picture theory of. See MEANING, WITTGENSTEIN.

meaning, referential theory of. See MEANING, PHILOSOPHY OF LANGUAGE.

meaning, speaker's. See MEANING.

meaning, truth-conditional theory of. See MEANING.

meaning, use theory of. See MEANING, PHILOSOPHY OF LANGUAGE.

meaning, verifiability theory of. See MEANING, PHILOSOPHY OF LANGUAGE, VERIFICATIONISM.

meaning holism. See HOLISM.

meaning postulate, a sentence that specifies part or all of the meaning of a predicate. Meaning postulates would thus include explicit, contextual, and recursive definitions, reduction sentences for dispositional predicates, and, more generally, any sentences stating how the extensions of predicates are interrelated by virtue of the meanings of those predicates. For example, any reduction sentence of the form (x) $(x$ has ϕ $\supset$ $(x$ is malleable $\equiv x$ has $\psi))$ could be a meaning postulate for the predicate 'is malleable'. The notion of a meaning postulate was introduced by Carnap, whose original interest stemmed from a desire to explicate sentences that are analytic ("true by virtue of meaning") but not logically true. Where Γ is a set of such postulates, one could say that A is analytic with respect to Γ if and only if A is a logical consequence of Γ. On this account, e.g., the sentence 'Jake is not a married bachelor' is analytic with respect to {'All bachelors are unmarried'}. **See also** ANALYTIC–SYNTHETIC DISTINCTION, MEANING, REDUCTION SENTENCE.   G.F.S.

measurement. See MAGNITUDE.

measurement, theory of. See MAGNITUDE.

mechanical jurisprudence. See JURISPRUDENCE.

mechanism, logical. See COMPUTER THEORY.

mechanistic explanation, a kind of explanation countenanced by views that range from the extreme position that all natural phenomena can be explained entirely in terms of masses in motion of the sort postulated in Newtonian mechanics, to little more than a commitment to naturalistic explanations. Mechanism in its extreme form is clearly false because numerous physical phenomena of the most ordinary sort cannot be explained entirely in terms of masses in motion. Mechanics is only one small part of physics. Historically, explanations were designated as mechanistic to indicate that they included no reference to final causes or vital forces. In this weak sense, all present-day scientific explanations are mechanistic. The adequacy of mechanistic explanation is usually raised in connection with living creatures, especially those capable of deliberate action. For example, chromosomes lining up opposite their partners in preparation for meiosis looks like anything but a purely mechanical process, and yet the more we discover about the process, the more mechanistic it turns out to be. The mechanisms responsible for meiosis arose through variation and selection and cannot be totally understood without reference to the evolutionary process, but meiosis as it takes place at any one time appears to be a purely mechanistic physicochemical process. Intentional behavior is the phenomenon that is most resistant to explanation entirely in physicochemical terms. The problem is not that we do not know enough about the functioning of the central nervous system but that no matter how it turns out to work, we will be disinclined to explain human action entirely in terms of physicochemical processes. The justification for this disinclination tends to turn on what we mean when we describe people as behaving intentionally. Even so, we may simply be mistaken to ascribe more to human action than can be explained in terms of purely physicochemical processes. See also BEHAVIORISM, EXPLANATION, PHILOSOPHY OF MIND.

D.L.H.

mediate inference. See INFERENCE.

medical ethics. See ETHICS.

Medina, Bartolomeo (1527–80), Spanish Dominican theologian who taught theology at Alcalá and then at Salamanca. His major works are commentaries on Aquinas's *Summa theologica*. Medina is often called the father of probabilism but scholars disagree on the legitimacy of this attribution. Support for it is contained in Medina's commentary on Aquinas's *Prima secundae* (1577). Medina denies that it is sufficient for an opinion to be probable that there are apparent reasons in its favor and that it is supported by many people. For then all errors would be probable. Rather, an opinion is probable if it can be followed without censure and reproof, as when wise persons state and support it with excellent reasons. Medina suggests the use of these criteria in decisions concerning moral dilemmas (*Suma de casos morales* ["Summa of Moral Questions"], 1580). P.Gar.

Megarians, also called Megarics, a loose-knit group of Greek philosophers active in the fourth and early third centuries B.C., whose work in logic profoundly influenced the course of ancient philosophy. The name derives from that of Megara, the hometown of Euclid (died c.365 B.C.; unrelated to the later mathematician), who was an avid companion of Socrates and author of (lost) Socratic dialogues. Little is recorded about his views, and his legacy rests with his philosophical heirs. Most prominent of these was Eubulides, a contemporary and critic of Aristotle; he devised a host of logical paradoxes, including the liar and the sorites or heap paradoxes. To many this ingenuity seemed sheer eristic, a label

some applied to him. One of his associates, Alexinus, was a leading critic of Zeno, the founder of Stoicism, whose arguments he twitted in incisive parodies. Stilpo (c.380–c.300 B.C.), a native of Megara, was also famous for disputation but best known for his *apatheia* (impassivity). Rivaling the Cynics as a preacher of self-reliance, he once insisted, after his city and home were plundered, that he lost nothing of his own since he retained his knowledge and virtue. Zeno the Stoic was one of many followers he attracted.

Most brilliant of the Megarians was Diodorus, nicknamed Cronus or "Old Fogey" (fl. 300 B.C.), who had an enormous impact on Stoicism and the skeptical Academy. Among the first explorers of propositional logic, he and his associates were called "the dialecticians," a label that referred not to an organized school or set of doctrines but simply to their highly original forms of reasoning. Diodorus defined *the possible* narrowly as what either is or will be true, and *the necessary* broadly as what is true and will not be false. Against his associate Philo, the first proponent of *material implication,* he maintained that a *conditional* is true if and only if it is *never* the case that its antecedent is true and its consequent false. He argued that matter is atomic and that time and motion are likewise discrete. With an exhibitionist's flair, he demonstrated that meaning is conventional by naming his servants "But" and "However." Most celebrated is his Master (or Ruling) Argument, which turns on three propositions: (1) Every truth about the past is *necessary;* (2) nothing *impossible* follows from something *possible;* and (3) some things are *possible* that neither are nor will be true. His aim was apparently to establish his definition of possibility by showing that its negation in (3) is inconsistent with (1) and (2), which he regarded as obvious. Various Stoics, objecting to the implication of determinism here, sought to uphold a wider form of possibility by overturning (1) or (2). Diodorus's fame made him a target of satire by eminent poets, and it is said that he expired from shame after failing to solve on the spot a puzzle Stilpo posed at a party.

See also ACADEMY, ARISTOTLE, CYNICS, SOCRATES, SORITES PARADOX, STOICISM.

S.A.W.

Meinong, Alexius (1853–1920), Austrian philosopher and psychologist, founder of *Gegenstandstheorie,* the theory of (existent and non-existent intended) objects. He was the target of Russell's criticisms of the idea of non-existent objects in his landmark essay "On Denoting" (1905).

Meinong, after eight years at the Vienna Gymnasium, enrolled in the University of Vienna in 1870, studying German philology and history and completing a dissertation (1874) on Arnold von Brescia. After this period he became interested in philosophy as a result of his critical self-directed reading of Kant. At the suggestion of his teacher Franz Brentano, he undertook a systematic investigation of Hume's empiricism, culminating in his first publications in philosophy, the *Hume-Studien* I, II (1878 and 1882). In 1882, Meinong was appointed Professor Extraordinarius at the University of Graz (receiving promotion to Ordinarius in 1889), where he remained until his death. At Graz he established the first laboratory for experimental psychology in Austria, and was occupied with psychological as well as philosophical problems throughout his career. The Graz school of phenomenological psychology and philosophical semantics, which centered on Meinong and his students, made important contributions to object theory in philosophical semantics, metaphysics, ontology, value theory, epistemology, theory of evidence, possibility and probability, and the analysis of emotion, imagination, and abstraction.

Meinong's object theory is based on a version of Brentano's immanent intentionality thesis, that every psychological state contains an intended object toward which the mental event (or, in a less common terminology, a *mental act*) is semantically directed. Meinong, however, rejects Brentano's early view of the immanence of the intentional, maintaining that thought is directed toward transcendent mind-independent existent or non-existent objects. Meinong distinguishes between judgments about the being (*Sein*) of intended objects of thought, and judgments about their "so-being," character, or nature (*Sosein*). He claims that every thought is intentionally directed toward the transcendent mind-independent object the thought purports to be "about," which entails that in at least some cases contingently non-existent and even impossible objects, for instance Berkeley's golden mountain and the round square, must be included as non-existent intended objects in the object theory semantic domain. Meinong further maintains that an intended object's *Sosein* is independent of its *Sein* or ontological status, of whether or not the object happens to exist. This means, contrary to what many philosophers have supposed, that non-existent objects can truly possess the constitutive properties predicated of them in thought.

Meinong's object theory evolved over a period of years, and underwent many additions and revisions. In its mature form, the theory includes the following principles: (1) Thought can freely (even if falsely) assume the existence of any describable object (principle of unrestricted free assumption, or *unbeschränkten Annahmefreiheit* thesis); (2) Every thought is intentionally directed toward a transcendent, mind-independent intended object (modified intentionality thesis); (3) Every intended object has a nature, character, *Sosein*, "how-it-is," "so-being," or "being thus-and-so," regardless of its ontological status (independence of *Sosein* from *Sein* thesis); (4) Being or non-being is not part of the *Sosein* of any intended object, nor of an object considered in itself (indifference thesis, or doctrine of the *Aussersein* of the homeless pure object); (5) There are two modes of being or *Sein* for intended objects: (a) spatiotemporal existence and (b) Platonic subsistence (*Existenz/Bestand* thesis); (6) There are some intended objects that do not have *Sein* at all, but neither exist nor subsist (objects of which it is true that there are no such objects).

Object theory, unlike extensionalist semantics, makes it possible, as in much of ordinary and scientific thought and language, to refer to and truly predicate properties of non-existent objects. There are many misconceptions about Meinong's theory, such as that reflected in the objection that Meinong is a super-Platonist who inflates ontology with non-existent objects that nevertheless have being in some sense, that object theory tolerates outright logical inconsistency rather than mere incompatibility of properties in the *Soseine* of impossible intended objects. Russell, in his reviews of Meinong's theory in 1904–05, raises the problem of the existent round square, which seems to be existent by virtue of the independence of *Sosein* from *Sein*, and to be non-existent by virtue of being globally and simultaneously both round and square. Meinong's response involves several complex distinctions, but it has been observed that to avoid the difficulty he need only appeal to the distinction between *konstitutorisch* or nuclear and *ausserkonstitutorisch* or extranuclear properties, adopted from a suggestion by his student Ernst Mally (1878–1944), according to which only ordinary nuclear properties like being red, round, or ten centimeters tall are part of the *Sosein* of any object, to the exclusion of categorical or extranuclear properties like being existent, determinate, possible, or impossible. This avoids counterexamples like the existent round square, because it limits the independence of *Sosein* from *Sein* exclusively to nuclear properties, implying that neither the existent nor the non-existent round square can possibly have the (extranuclear) property of being existent or non-existent in their respective *Soseine,* and cannot be said truly to have the properties of being existent or non-existent merely by free assumption and the independence of *Sosein* from *Sein.*

See also BRENTANO, EXTENSIONALISM, FORMAL SEMANTICS, INTENTIONALITY, META-PHYSICS.   D.J.

Meister Eckhart. See ECKHART.

Melanchthon, Philip. See SYNERGISM.

meliorism (from Latin *melior,* 'better'), the view that the world is neither completely good nor completely bad, and that incremental progress or regress depend on human actions. By creative intelligence and education we can improve the environment and social conditions. The position is first attributed to George Eliot and William James. Whitehead suggested that meliorism applies to God, who can both improve the world and draw sustenance from human efforts to improve the world. See also JAMES, WHITE-HEAD.   L.P.P.

Melissus of Samos (fl. mid-fifth century B.C.), Greek philosopher, traditionally classified as a member of the Eleatic School. He was also famous as the victorious commander in a pre-emptive attack by the Samians on an Athenian naval force (441 B.C.). Like Parmenides – who must have influenced Melissus, even though there is no evidence the two ever met – Melissus argues that "what-is" or "the real" cannot come into being out of nothing, cannot perish into nothing, is homogeneous, and is unchanging. Indeed, he argues explicitly (whereas Parmenides only implies) that there is only one such entity, that there is no void, and that even spatial rearrangement (*metakosmēsis*) must be ruled out. But unlike Parmenides, Melissus deduces that what-is is temporally infinite (in significant contrast to Parmenides, regardless as to whether the latter held that what-is exists strictly in the "now" or that it exists non-temporally). More-over, Melissus argues that what-is is spatially infinite (whereas Parmenides spoke of "bounds" and compared what-is to a well-made ball). Sig-nificantly, Melissus repeatedly speaks of "the One." It is, then, in Melissus, more than in Par-menides or in Zeno, that we find the emphasis on monism. In a corollary to his main argument, Melissus argues that "if there were many things,"

each would have to be – *per impossibile* – exactly like "the One." This remark has been interpreted as issuing the challenge that was taken up by the atomists. But it is more reasonable to read it as a philosophical strategist's preemptive strike: Melissus anticipates the move made in the plu-ralist systems of the second half of the fifth cen-tury, viz., positing a plurality of eternal and unchanging elements that undergo only spatial rearrangement. See also ELEATIC SCHOOL, PARMENIDES, PRE-SOCRATICS.   A.P.D.M.

memory, the retention of, or the capacity to retain, past experience or previously acquired information. There are two main philosophical questions about memory: (1) In what does memory consist? and (2) What constitutes knowing a fact on the basis of memory? Not all memory is remembering facts: there is remem-bering one's perceiving or feeling or acting in a certain way – which, while it entails remember-ing the fact that one did experience in that way, must be more than that. And not all remember-ing of facts is knowledge of facts: an extremely hesitant attempt to remember an address, if one gets it right, counts as remembering the address even if one is too uncertain for this to count as *knowing* it.

(1) Answers to the first question agree on some obvious points: that memory requires (a) a pres-ent and (b) a past state of, or event in, the sub-ject, and (c) the right sort of internal and causal relations between the two. Also, we must distin-guish between memory *states* (remembering for many years the name of one's first-grade teacher) and memory *occurrences* (recalling the name when asked). A memory state is usually taken to be a disposition to display an appropri-ate memory occurrence given a suitable stimu-lus. But philosophers disagree about further specifics. On one theory (held by many empiri-cists from Hume to Russell, among others, but now largely discredited), occurrent memory consists in images of past experience (which have a special quality marking them as memory images) and that memory of facts is read off such image memory. This overlooks the point that people commonly remember facts without remembering when or how they learned them. A more sophisticated theory of factual memory (popular nowadays) holds that an occurrent memory of a fact requires, besides a past learn-ing of it, (i) some sort of present mental repre-sentation of it (perhaps a linguistic one) and (ii) continuous storage between then and now of a representation of it. But condition (i) may not be

conceptually necessary: a disposition to dial the right number when one wants to call home constitutes remembering the number (provided it is appropriately linked causally to past learning of the number) and manifesting that disposition is occurrently remembering the fact as to what the number is even if one does not in the process mentally represent that fact. Condition (ii) may also be too strong: it seems at least conceptually possible that a causal link sufficient for memory should be secured by a relation that does not involve anything continuous between the relevant past and present occurrences (in *The Analysis of Mind,* Russell countenanced this possibility and called it "mnemic causation").

(2) What must be added to remembering that *p* to get a case of knowing it because one remembers it? We saw that one must not be uncertain that *p*. Must one also have grounds for trusting one's memory impression (its seeming to one that one remembers) that *p*? How could one have such grounds except by knowing them on the basis of memory? The facts one can know *not* on the basis of memory are limited at most to what one presently perceives and what one presently finds self-evident. If no memory belief qualifies as knowledge unless it is supported by memory knowledge of the reliability of one's memory, then the process of qualifying as memory knowledge cannot succeed: there would be an endless chain, or loop, of facts – this belief is memory knowledge if and only if this other belief is, which is if and only if this other one is, and so on – which never becomes a set that entails that any belief is memory knowledge. On the basis of such reasoning a skeptic might deny the possibility of memory knowledge. We may avoid this consequence without going to the lax extreme of allowing that any correct memory impression is knowledge; we can impose the (frequently satisfied) requirement that one *not have* reasons specific to the particular case for believing that one's memory impression might be unreliable. Finally, remembering that *p* becomes memory knowledge that *p* only if one believes that *p because* it seems to one that one remembers it. One might remember that *p* and confidently believe that *p*, but if one has no memory impression of having previously learned it, or one has such an impression but does not trust it and believes that *p* only for other reasons (or no reason), then one should not be counted as knowing that *p* on the basis of memory.

See also EPISTEMOLOGY, PERCEPTION, SKEPTICISM.   C.G.

memory, image theory of. See MEMORY.

memory, occurrent. See MEMORY.

memory, representational theory of. See MEMORY.

Mencius, also known as Meng-tzu, Meng K'o (fl. fourth century B.C.), Chinese Confucian philosopher, probably the single most influential philosopher in the Chinese tradition. His sayings, discussions, and debates were compiled by disciples in the book entitled *Meng-tzu.*

Mencius is best known for his assertion that human nature is good but it is unclear what he meant by this. At one point, he says he only means that a human can become good. Elsewhere, though, he says that human nature is good just as water flows downward, implying that humans will become good if only their natural development is unimpeded. Certainly, part of what is implied by the claim that human nature is good is Mencius's belief that all humans have what he describes as four "hearts" or "sprouts" – benevolence (*jen*), righteousness (*yi*), ritual propriety (*li*), and wisdom (*chih*). The term 'sprout' seems to refer to an incipient emotional or behavioral reaction of a virtuous nature. Mencius claims, e.g., that any human who saw a child about to fall into a well would have a spontaneous feeling of concern, which is the sprout of benevolence. Although all humans manifest the sprouts, "concentration" (*ssu*) is required in order to nurture them into mature virtues. Mencius is not specific about what concentration is, but it probably involves an ongoing awareness of, and delight in, the operation of the sprouts. The result of the concentration and consequent delight in the operation of the sprouts is the "extension" (*t'ui, ta, chi*) or "filling out" (*k'uo, ch'ung*) of the incipient reactions, so that benevolence, for instance, comes to be manifested to all suffering humans. Nonetheless, Mencius maintains the belief, typical of Confucianism, that we have greater moral responsibility for those tied to us because of particular relationships such as kinship. Mencius is also Confucian in his belief that the virtues first manifest themselves within the family.

Although Mencius is a self-cultivationist, he also believes that one's environment can positively or negatively affect one's moral development, and encourages rulers to produce social conditions conducive to virtue. He admits, however, that there are moral prodigies who have flourished despite deleterious circumstances.

Mencius's virtue ethic is like Aristotle's in combining antinomianism with a belief in the objectivity of specific moral judgments, but his de-emphasis of intellectual virtues and emphasis upon benevolence are reminiscent of Joseph Butler. Mencius differs from Butler, however, in that although he thinks the Confucian way is the most profitable, he condemns profit or self-love as a motivation. Mencius saw himself as defending the doctrines of Confucius against the philosophies of other thinkers, especially Mo Tzu and Yang Chu. In so doing, he often goes beyond what Confucius said.

See also CHUANG TZU, CONFUCIANISM, FOUR BOOKS, HSÜN TZU.   B.W.V.N.

Mendel, Gregor (1822–84), Austrian botanist and discoverer of what are now considered the basic principles of heredity. An Augustinian monk who conducted plant-breeding experiments in a monastery garden in Brünn (now Brno, Czech Republic), Mendel discovered that certain characters of a common variety of garden pea are transmitted in a strikingly regular way. The characters with which he dealt occur in two distinct states, e.g., pods that are smooth or ridged. In characters such as these, one state is dominant to its recessive partner, i.e., when varieties of each sort are crossed, all the offspring exhibit the dominant character. However, when the offspring of these crosses are themselves crossed, the result is a ratio of three dominants to one recessive. In modern terms, pairs of genes (alleles) separate at reproduction (segregation) and each offspring receives only one member of each pair. Of equal importance, the recessive character reappears unaffected by its temporary suppression. Alleles remain pure. Mendel also noted that the pairs of characters that he studied assort independently of each other, i.e., if two pairs of characters are followed through successive crosses, no statistical correlations in their transmission can be found. As genetics developed after the turn of the century, the simple "laws" that Mendel had set out were expanded and altered. Only a relatively few characters exhibit two distinct states, one dominant to the other. In many, the heterozygote exhibits an intermediate state. In addition, genes do not exist in isolation from each other but together on chromosomes. Only those genes that reside on different pairs of chromosomes assort in total independence of each other.

During his research, Mendel corresponded with Karl von Nägeli (1817–91), a major authority in plant hybridization. Von Nägeli urged Mendel to cross varieties of the common hawkweed. When Mendel took his advice, he failed to discover the hereditary patterns that he had found in garden peas. In 1871 Mendel ceased his research to take charge of his monastery. In 1900 Hugo de Vries (1848–1935) stumbled upon several instances of three-to-one ratios while developing his own theory of the origin of species. No sooner did he publish his results than two young biologists announced independent discovery of what came to be known as Mendel's laws. The founders of modern genetics abandoned attempts to work out the complexities of embryological development and concentrated just on transmission. As a result of several unfortunate misunderstandings, early Mendelian geneticists thought that their theory of genetics was incompatible with Darwin's theory of evolution. Eventually, however, the two theories were merged to form the synthetic theory of evolution. In the process, R. A. Fisher (1890–1962) questioned the veracity of Mendel's research, arguing that the only way that Mendel could have gotten data as good as he did was by sanitizing it.

Present-day historians view all of the preceding events in a very different light. The science of heredity that developed at the turn of the century was so different from anything that Mendel had in mind that Mendel hardly warrants being considered its father. The neglect of Mendel's work is made to seem so problematic only by reading later developments back into Mendel's original paper. Like de Vries, Mendel was interested primarily in developing a theory of the origin of species. The results of Mendel's research on the hawkweed brought into question the generalizability of the regularities that he had found in peas, but they supported his theory of species formation through hybridization. Similarly, the rediscovery of Mendel's laws can be viewed as an instance of multiple, simultaneous discovery only by ignoring important differences in the views expressed by these authors. Finally, Mendel certainly did not mindlessly organize and report his data, but the methods that he used can be construed as questionable only in contrast to an overly empirical, inductive view of science. Perhaps Mendel was no Mendelian, but he was not a fraud either.

See also DARWINISM.   D.L.H.

Mendelian genetics. See MENDEL.

Mendelssohn, Moses (1729–86), German philosopher known as "the Jewish Socrates." He began as a Bible and Talmud scholar. After moving to Berlin he learned Latin and German, and became a close friend of Lessing, who modeled the Jew in his play *Nathan the Wise* after him. Mendelssohn began writing on major philosophical topics of the day, and won a prize from the Berlin Academy in 1764. He was actively engaged in discussions about aesthetics, psychology, and religion, and offered an empirical, subjectivist view that was very popular at the time. His most famous writings are *Morgenstunden* (*Morning Hours, or Lectures on the Existence of God,* 1785), *Phaedon* (*Phaedo, or on the Immortality of the Soul,* 1767), and *Jerusalem* (1783).

He contended that one could prove the existence of God and the immortality of the soul. He accepted the ontological argument and the argument from design. In *Phaedo* he argued that since the soul is a simple substance it is indestructible. Kant criticized his arguments in the first *Critique.* Mendelssohn was pressed by the Swiss scientist Lavater to explain why he, as a reasonable man, did not accept Christianity. At first he ignored the challenge, but finally set forth his philosophical views about religion and Judaism in *Jerusalem,* where he insisted that Judaism is not a set of doctrines but a set of practices. Reasonable persons can accept that there is a universal religion of reason, and there are practices that God has ordained that the Jews follow. Mendelssohn was a strong advocate of religious toleration and separation of church and state. His views played an important part in the emancipation of the Jews, and in the Jewish Enlightenment that flowered in Germany at the beginning of the nineteenth century.

See also JEWISH PHILOSOPHY.   R.H.P.

Meng K'o. See MENCIUS.

Meng-tzu. See MENCIUS.

mens rea, literally, guilty mind, in law Latin. It is one of the two main prerequisites (along with *actus reus*) for prima facie liability to criminal punishment in Anglo-American legal systems. To be punishable in such systems, one must not only have performed a legally prohibited action, such as killing another human being; one must have done so with a culpable state of mind, or *mens rea.* Such culpable mental states are of three kinds: they are either motivational states of purpose, cognitive states of belief, or the non-mental state of negligence.

To illustrate each of these with respect to the act of killing: a killer may kill either having another's death as ultimate purpose, or as medi-

ate purpose on the way to achieving some further, ultimate end. Alternatively, the killer may act believing to a practical certainty that his act will result in another's death, even though such death is an unwanted side effect, or he may believe that there is a substantial and unjustified risk that his act will cause another's death. The actor may also be only negligent, which is to take an unreasonable risk of another's death even if the actor is not aware either of such risk or of the lack of justification for taking it.

Mens rea usually does not have to do with any awareness by the actor that the act done is either morally wrong or legally prohibited. Neither does *mens rea* have to do with any emotional state of guilt or remorse, either while one is acting or afterward. Sometimes in its older usages the term is taken to include the absence of excuses as well as the mental states necessary for prima facie liability; in such a usage, the requirement is helpfully labeled "general *mens rea,*" and the requirement above discussed is labeled "special *mens rea.*"

See also DIMINISHED CAPACITY, ETHICS, INTENTION.   M.S.M.

mental content, causal theory of. See SKEPTICISM.

mental distinction. See FUNDAMENTUM DIVISIONIS.

Mentalese, the language of thought (the title of a book by Fodor, 1975) or of "brain writing" (a term of Dennett's); specifically, a languagelike medium of representation in which the contents of mental events are supposedly expressed or recorded. (The term was probably coined by Wilfrid Sellars, with whose views it was first associated.) If what one believes are propositions, then it is tempting to propose that believing something is having the Mentalese expression of that proposition somehow written in the relevant place in one's mind or brain. Thinking a thought, at least on those occasions when we think "wordlessly" (without formulating our thoughts in sentences or phrases composed of words of a public language), thus appears to be a matter of creating a short-lived Mentalese expression in a special arena or work space in the mind. In a further application of the concept, the process of coming to understand a sentence of natural language can be viewed as one of translating the sentence into Mentalese. It has often been argued that this view of understanding only postpones the difficult questions of meaning, for it leaves unanswered the question of how Mentalese expressions come to have the meanings they do. There have been frequent attempts to develop versions of the hypothesis that mental activity is conducted in Mentalese, and just as frequent criticisms of these attempts. Some critics deny there is anything properly called representation in the mind or brain at all; others claim that the system of representation used by the brain is not enough like a natural language to be called a language. Even among defenders of Mentalese, it has seldom been claimed that all brains "speak" the same Mentalese. **See also** PHILOSOPHY OF LANGUAGE; PHILOSOPHY OF MIND; SELLARS, WILFRID.   D.C.D.

mentalism, any theory that posits explicitly mental events and processes, where 'mental' means exhibiting intentionality, not necessarily being immaterial or non-physical. A mentalistic theory is couched in terms of belief, desire, thinking, feeling, hoping, etc. A scrupulously non-mentalistic theory would be couched entirely in extensional terms: it would refer only to behavior or to neurophysiological states and events. The attack on mentalism by behaviorists was led by B. F. Skinner, whose criticisms did not all depend on the assumption that mentalists were dualists, and the subsequent rise of cognitive science has restored a sort of mentalism (a "thoroughly modern mentalism," as Fodor has called it) that is explicitly materialistic.

See also BEHAVIORISM, COGNITIVE SCIENCE, PHILOSOPHY OF MIND.   D.C.D.

mental representation. See COGNITIVE SCIENCE.

Mercier, Désiré-Joseph (1851–1926), Belgian Catholic philosopher, a formative figure in Neo-Thomism and founder of the Institut Supérieur de Philosophie (1889) at Louvain. Created at the request of Pope Leo XIII, Mercier's institute treated Aquinas as a subject of historical research and as a philosopher relevant to modern thought. His approach to Neo-Thomism was distinctive for its direct response to the epistemological challenges posed by idealism, rationalism, and positivism. Mercier's epistemology was termed a criteriology; it intended to defend the certitude of the intellect against skepticism by providing an account of the motives and rules that guide judgment. Truth is affirmed by intellectual judgment by conforming itself not to the thing-in-itself but to its abstract apprehension. Since the certitude of judgment is a state of the cognitive faculty in the human soul, Mercier considered criteriology as psychology; see *Critériologie générale ou Théorie générale de la certitude*

(1906), *Origins of Contemporary Psychology* (trans. 1918), and *Manual of Scholastic Philosophy* (trans. 1917–18). **See also** AQUINAS, NEO-THOMISM.
D.W.H.

mereological essentialism. See HAECCEITY.

mereological sum. See MEREOLOGY.

mereology (from Greek *meros*, 'part'), the mathematical theory of parts; specifically, Leśniewski's formal theory of parts. Typically, a mereological theory employs notions such as the following: proper part, improper part, overlapping (having a part in common), disjoint (not overlapping), mereological product (the "intersection" of overlapping objects), mereological sum (a collection of parts), mereological difference, the universal sum, mereological complement, and atom (that which has no proper parts).

Formal mereologies are axiomatic systems. Leśniewski's mereology and Goodman's formal mereology (which he calls the Calculus of Individuals) are compatible with nominalism, i.e., no reference is made to sets, properties, or other abstract entities. Leśniewski hoped that his mereology, with its many parallels to set theory, would provide an alternative to set theory as a foundation for mathematics.

Fundamental and controversial implications of Leśniewski's and Goodman's theories include their *extensionality* and *collectivism*. Extensional theories imply that for any individuals, x and y, $x = y$ provided x and y have the same proper parts. One reason extensionality is controversial is that it rules out an object's acquiring or losing a part, and therefore is inconsistent with commonsense beliefs such as that a car has a new tire or that a table has lost a sliver of wood. A second reason for controversy is that extensionality is incompatible with the belief that a statue and the piece of bronze of which it is made have the same parts and yet are diverse objects.

Collectivism implies that any individuals, no matter how scattered, have a mereological sum or constitute an object. Moreover, according to collectivism, assembling or disassembling parts does not affect the existence of things, i.e., nothing is created or destroyed by assembly or disassembly, respectively. Thus, collectivism is incompatible with commonsense beliefs such as that when a watch is disassembled, it is destroyed, or that when certain parts are assembled, a watch is created.

Because the aforementioned formal theories shun modality, they lack the resources to express the thesis that a whole has each of its parts *necessarily*. This thesis of mereological essentialism has recently been defended by Roderick Chisholm.

See also ESSENTIALISM, EXTENSIONALISM, METAPHYSICS, SET THEORY.   J.Ho. & G.Ro.

meritarian, one who asserts the relevance of individual merit, as an independent justificatory condition, in attempts to design social structures or distribute goods. 'Meritarianism' is a recently coined term in social and political philosophy, closely related to 'meritocracy', and used to identify a range of related concerns that supplement or oppose egalitarian, utilitarian, and contractarian principles and principles based on entitlement, right, interest, and need, among others. For example, one can have a pressing need for an Olympic medal but not merit it; one can have the money to buy a masterpiece but not be worthy of it; one can have the right to a certain benefit but not deserve it. Meritarians assert that considerations of desert are always relevant and sometimes decisive in such cases.

What counts as merit, and how important should it be in moral, social, and political decisions? Answers to these questions serve to distinguish one meritarian from another, and sometimes to blur the distinctions between the meritarian position and others. Merit may refer to any of these: comparative rank, capacities, abilities, effort, intention, or achievement. Moreover, there is a relevance condition to be met: to say that highest honors in a race should go to the most deserving is presumably to say that the honors should go to those with the relevant sort of merit – speed, e.g., rather than grace. Further, meritarians may differ about the strength of the merit principle, and how various political or social structures should be influenced by it.

See also ETHICS, JUSTICE.   L.C.B.

meritocracy, in ordinary usage, a system in which advancement is based on ability and achievement, or one in which leadership roles are held by talented achievers. The term may also refer to an elite group of talented achievers. In philosophical usage, the term's meaning is similar: a meritocracy is a scheme of social organization in which essential offices, and perhaps careers and jobs of all sorts are (a) open only to those who have the relevant qualifications for successful performance in them, or (b) awarded only to the candidates who are likely to perform the best, or (c) managed so that people advance in and retain their offices and jobs solely on the basis of the quality of their performance in them,

or (d) all of the above. **See also** JUSTICE, MERITARIAN.   L.C.B.

meritorious duty. See KANT.

Merleau-Ponty, Maurice (1908–61), French philosopher described by Paul Ricoeur as "the greatest of the French phenomenologists." Merleau-Ponty occupied the chair of child psychology and pedagogy at the Sorbonne and was later professor of philosophy at the Collège de France. His sudden death preceded completion of an important manuscript; this was later edited and published by Claude Lefort under the title *The Visible and the Invisible*. The relation between the late, unfinished work and his early *Phenomenology of Perception* (1945) has received much scholarly discussion. While some commentators see a significant shift in direction in his later thought, others insist on continuity throughout his work. Thus, the exact significance of his philosophy, which in his life was called both a philosophy *of* ambiguity and an *ambiguous* philosophy, retains to this day its essential ambiguity.

With his compatriot and friend, Sartre, Merleau-Ponty was responsible for introducing the phenomenology of Edmund Husserl into France. Impressed above all by the later Husserl and by Husserl's notion of the life-world (*Lebenswelt*), Merleau-Ponty combined Husserl's transcendental approach to epistemological issues with an existential orientation derived from Heidegger and Marcel. Going even further than Heidegger, who had himself sought to go beyond Husserl by "existentializing" Husserl's Transcendental Ego (referring to it as *Dasein*), Merleau-Ponty sought to emphasize not only the existential (worldly) nature of the human subject but, above all, its bodily nature. Thus his philosophy could be characterized as a philosophy of the lived body or the body subject (*le corps propre*). Although Nietzsche called attention to the all-importance of the body, it was Merleau-Ponty who first made the body the central theme of a detailed philosophical analysis. This provided an original perspective from which to rethink such perennial philosophical issues as the nature of knowledge, freedom, time (temporality), language, and intersubjectivity. Especially in his early work, Merleau-Ponty battled against absolutist thought ("*la pensée de l'absolu*"), stressing the insurmountable ambiguity and contingency of all meaning and truth. An archopponent of Cartesian rationalism, he was an early and ardent spokesman for that position now called antifoundationalism.

Merleau-Ponty's major early work, the *Phenomenology of Perception*, is best known for its central thesis concerning "the primacy of perception." In this lengthy study he argued that all the "higher" functions of consciousness (e.g., intellection, volition) are rooted in and depend upon the subject's prereflective, bodily existence, i.e., perception ("All consciousness is perceptual, even the consciousness of ourselves"). Merleau-Ponty maintained, however, that perception had never been adequately conceptualized by traditional philosophy. Thus the book was to a large extent a dialectical confrontation with what he took to be the two main forms of objective thinking – intellectualism and empiricism – both of which, he argued, ignored the *phenomenon* of perception. His principal goal was to get beyond the intellectual constructs of traditional philosophy (such as sense-data) and to effect "a return to the phenomena," to the world as we actually experience it as embodied subjects prior to all theorizing. His main argument (directed against mainline philosophy) was that the lived body is not an *object* in the world, distinct from the knowing subject (as in Descartes), but is the subject's own *point of view on the world;* the body is itself the original knowing *subject* (albeit a non- or prepersonal, "anonymous" subject), from which all other forms of knowledge derive, even that of geometry. As a phenomenological (or, as he also said, "archaeological") attempt to unearth the basic (corporeal) modalities of human existence, emphasizing the rootedness (*enracinement*) of the personal subject in the obscure and ambiguous life of the body and, in this way, the insurpassable contingency of all meaning, the *Phenomenology* was immediately and widely recognized as a major statement of French existentialism.

In his subsequent work in the late 1940s and the 1950s, in many shorter essays and articles, Merleau-Ponty spelled out in greater detail the philosophical consequences of "the primacy of perception." These writings sought to respond to widespread objections that by "grounding" all intellectual and cultural acquisitions in the prereflective and prepersonal life of the body, the *Phenomenology of Perception* results in a kind of reductionism and anti-intellectualism and teaches only a "bad ambiguity," i.e., completely undermines the notions of reason and truth. By shifting his attention from the phenomenon of perception to that of (creative) expression, his aim was to work out a "good ambiguity" by showing how "communication with others and thought take up and go beyond the realm of per-

ception which initiated us to the truth." His announced goal after the *Phenomenology* was "working out in a rigorous way the philosophical foundations" of a theory of truth and a theory of intersubjectivity (including a theory of history). No such large-scale work (a sequel, as it were, to the *Phenomenology*) ever saw the light of day, although in pursuing this project he reflected on subjects as diverse as painting, literary language, Saussurian linguistics, structuralist anthropology, politics, history, the human sciences, psychoanalysis, contemporary science (including biology), and the philosophy of nature.

Toward the end of his life, however, Merleau-Ponty did begin work on a projected large-scale manuscript, the remnants of which were published posthumously as *The Visible and the Invisible*. A remarkable feature of this work (as Claude Lefort has pointed out) is the resolute way in which Merleau-Ponty appears to be groping for a new philosophical language. His express concerns in this abortive manuscript are explicitly ontological (as opposed to the more limited phenomenological concerns of his early work), and he consistently tries to avoid the subject (consciousness)–object language of the philosophy of consciousness (inherited from Husserl's transcendental idealism) that characterized the *Phenomenology of Perception*. Although much of Merleau-Ponty's later thought was a response to the later Heidegger, Merleau-Ponty sets himself apart from Heidegger in this unfinished work by claiming that the only ontology possible is an indirect one that can have no direct access to Being itself. Indeed, had he completed it, Merleau-Ponty's new ontology would probably have been one in which, as Lefort has remarked, "the word Being would not have to be uttered." He was always keenly attuned to "the sensible world"; the key term in his ontological thinking is not so much 'Being' as it is 'the flesh', a term with no equivalent in the history of philosophy. What traditional philosophy referred to as "subject" and "object" were not two distinct sorts of reality, but merely *differentiations* of one sole and *massive* adhesion to Being [Nature] which is the flesh." By viewing the perceiving subject as "a coiling over of the visible upon the visible," Merleau-Ponty was attempting to overcome the subject–object dichotomy of modern philosophy, which raised the intractable problems of the external world and other minds. With the notion of the flesh he believed he could finally overcome the solipsism of modern philosophy and had discovered the basis for a genuine intersubjectivity (conceived of as basically an *intercorporeity*).

Does 'flesh' signify something significantly different from 'body' in Merleau-Ponty's earlier thought? Did his growing concern with ontology (and the question of nature) signal abandonment of his earlier phenomenology (to which the question of nature is foreign)? This has remained a principal subject of conflicting interpretations in Merleau-Ponty scholarship.

As illustrated by his last, unfinished work, Merleau-Ponty's oeuvre as a whole is fragmentary. He always insisted that true philosophy is the enemy of the system, and he disavowed closure and completion. While Heidegger has had numerous disciples and epigones, it is difficult to imagine what a "Merleau-Ponty school of philosophy" would be. This is not to deny that Merleau-Ponty's work has exerted considerable influence. Although he was relegated to a kind of intellectual purgatory in France almost immediately upon his death, the work of his poststructuralist successors such as Foucault and Jacques Derrida betrays a great debt to his previous struggles with philosophical modernity. And in Germany, Great Britain, and, above all, North America, Merleau-Ponty has continued to be a source of philosophical inspiration and the subject of extensive scholarship. Although his work does not presume to answer the key questions of existence, it is a salient model of philosophy conceived of as unremitting interrogation. It is this questioning ("zetetic") attitude, combined with a non-dogmatic humanism, that continues to speak not only to philosophers but also to a wide audience among practitioners of the human sciences (phenomenological psychology being a particularly noteworthy example).

See also CONTINENTAL PHILOSOPHY, EXISTENTIALISM, PHENOMENOLOGY, SUBJECT–OBJECT DICHOTOMY.   G.B.M.

Mersenne, Marin (1588–1648), French priest who compiled massive works on philosophy, mathematics, music, and natural science, and conducted an enormous correspondence with such figures as Galileo, Descartes, and Hobbes. He translated Galileo's *Mechanics* and Herbert of Cherbury's *De Veritate* and arranged for publication of Hobbes's *De Cive*. He is best known for gathering the objections published with Descartes's *Meditations*. Mersenne served a function in the rise of modern philosophy and science that is today served by professional journals and associations.

His works contain attacks on deists, atheists, libertines, and skeptics; but he also presents mitigated skepticism as a practical method for attaining scientific knowledge. He did not believe that we can attain knowledge of inner essences, but argued – by displaying it – that we have an immense amount of knowledge about the material world adequate to our needs.

Like Gassendi, Mersenne advocated mechanistic explanations in science, and following Galileo, he proposed mathematical models of material phenomena. Like the Epicureans, he believed that mechanism was adequate to save the phenomena. He thus rejected Aristotelian forms and occult powers. Mersenne was another of the great philosopher-priests of the seventeenth century who believed that to increase scientific knowledge is to know and serve God.

See also DESCARTES, EPICUREANISM.

R.A.W.

Merton School. See OXFORD CALCULATORS.

metaethical relativism. See RELATIVISM.

metaethics. See ETHICS.

metalanguage, in formal semantics, a language used to describe another language (*the object language*). The object language may be either a natural language or a formal language. The goal of a formal semantic theory is to provide an axiomatic or otherwise systematic theory of meaning for the object language. The metalanguage is used to specify the object language's symbols and formation rules, which determine its grammatical sentences or well-formed formulas, and to assign meanings or interpretations to these sentences or formulas. For example, in an *extensional semantics*, the metalanguage is used to assign denotations to the singular terms, extensions to the general terms, and truth conditions to sentences. The standard format for assigning truth conditions, as in Tarski's formulation of his "semantical conception of truth," is a T-sentence, which takes the form 'S is true if and only if p.' Davidson adapted this format to the purposes of his truth-theoretic account of meaning. Examples of T-sentences, with English as the metalanguage, are ' "*La neige est blanche*" is true if and only if snow is white', where the object langauge is French and the homophonic (Davidson) '"Snow is white" is true if and only if snow is white', where the object language is English as well.

Although for formal purposes the distinction between metalanguage and object language must be maintained, in practice one can use a langauge to talk about expressions in the very same language. One can, in Carnap's terms, shift from the *material mode* to the *formal mode,* e.g. from 'Every veterinarian is an animal doctor' to ' "Veterinarian" means "animal doctor".' This shift is important in discussions of synonymy and of the analytic–synthetic distinction. Carnap's distinction corresponds to the use–mention distinction. We are speaking in the formal mode – we are mentioning a linguistic expression – when we ascribe a property to a word or other expression type, such as its spelling, pronunciation, meaning, or grammatical category, or when we speak of an expression token as misspelled, mispronounced, or misused. We are speaking in the material mode when we say "Reims is hard to find" but in the formal mode when we say " 'Reims' is hard to pronounce."

See also PHILOSOPHY OF LANGUAGE, TYPE–TOKEN DISTINCTION, USE–MENTION DISTINCTION.   K.B.

metalogic. See PROOF THEORY.

metamathematics, the study and establishment, by restricted (and, in particular, finitary) means, of the consistency or reliability of the various systems of classical mathematics. The term was apparently introduced, with pejorative overtones relating it to 'metaphysics', in the 1870s in connection with the discussion of non-Euclidean geometries. It was introduced in the sense given here, shorn of negative connotations, by Hilbert (see his "Neubegründung der Mathematik. Erste Mitteilung," 1922), who also referred to it as *Beweistheorie* or proof theory. A few years later (specifically, in the 1930 papers "Über einige fundamentale Begriffe der Metamathematik" and "Fundamentale Begriffe der Methodologie der deduktiven Wissenschaften. I") Tarski fitted it with a somewhat broader, less restricted sense: broader in that the scope of its concerns was increased to include not only questions of consistency, but also a host of other questions (e.g. questions of independence, completeness and axiomatizability) pertaining to what Tarski referred to as the "methodology of the deductive sciences" (which was his synonym for 'metamathematics'); less restricted in that the standards of proof were relaxed so as to permit other than finitary – indeed, other than constructive – means.

On this broader conception of Tarski's, formalized deductive disciplines form the field of research of metamathematics roughly in the same sense in which spatial entities form the field of research in geometry or animals that of zoology. Disciplines, he said, are to be regarded as sets

of sentences to be investigated from the point of view of their consistency, axiomatizability (of various types), completeness, and categoricity or degree of categoricity, etc. Eventually (see the 1935 and 1936 papers "Grundzüge des Systemenkalkül, Erster Teil" and "Grundzüge der Systemenkalkül, Zweiter Teil") Tarski went on to include all manner of semantical questions among the concerns of metamathematics, thus diverging rather sharply from Hilbert's original syntactical focus. Today, the terms 'metatheory' and 'metalogic' are used to signify that broad set of interests, embracing both syntactical and semantical studies of formal languages and systems, which Tarski came to include under the general heading of metamathematics. Those having to do specifically with semantics belong to that more specialized branch of modern logic known as *model theory,* while those dealing with purely syntactical questions belong to what has come to be known as proof theory (where this latter is now, however, permitted to employ other than finitary methods in the proofs of its theorems).

See also CATEGORICITY, COMPLETENESS, CONSISTENCY, MODEL THEORY, PROOF THEORY.   M.D.

metaphilosophy, the theory of the nature of philosophy, especially its goals, methods, and fundamental assumptions. First-order philosophical inquiry includes such disciplines as epistemology, ontology, ethics, and value theory. It thus constitutes the main activity of philosophers, past and present. The philosophical study of first-order philosophical inquiry raises philosophical inquiry to a higher order. Such higher-order inquiry is metaphilosophy. The first-order philosophical discipline of (e.g.) epistemology has the nature of knowledge as its main focus, but that discipline can itself be the focus of higher-order philosophical inquiry. The latter focus yields a species of metaphilosophy called metaepistemology. Two other prominent species are metaethics and metaontology. Each such branch of metaphilosophy studies the goals, methods, and fundamental assumptions of a first-order philosophical discipline.

Typical metaphilosophical topics include (a) the conditions under which a claim is philosophical rather than non-philosophical, and (b) the conditions under which a first-order philosophical claim is either meaningful, true, or warranted. Metaepistemology, e.g., pursues not the nature of knowledge directly, but rather the conditions under which claims are genuinely epistemological and the conditions under which epistemological claims are either meaningful, or true, or warranted. The distinction between philosophy and metaphilosophy has an analogue in the familiar distinction between mathematics and metamathematics.

Questions about the autonomy, objectivity, relativity, and modal status of philosophical claims arise in metaphilosophy. Questions about autonomy concern the relationship of philosophy to such disciplines as those constituting the natural and social sciences. For instance, is philosophy methodologically independent of the natural sciences? Questions about objectivity and relativity concern the kind of truth and warrant available to philosophical claims. For instance, are philosophical truths characteristically, or ever, made true by mind-independent phenomena in the way that typical claims of the natural sciences supposedly are? Or, are philosophical truths unavoidably conventional, being fully determined by (and thus altogether relative to) linguistic conventions? Are they analytic rather than synthetic truths, and is knowledge of them a priori rather than a posteriori? Questions about modal status consider whether philosophical claims are necessary rather than contingent. Are philosophical claims necessarily true or false, in contrast to the contingent claims of the natural sciences? The foregoing questions identify major areas of controversy in contemporary metaphilosophy.

See also ANALYTIC–SYNTHETIC DISTINCTION, A PRIORI, EPISTEMOLOGY, MEANING.

P.K.M.

metaphor, a figure of speech (or a trope) in which a word or phrase that literally denotes one thing is used to denote another, thereby implicitly comparing the two things. In the normal use of the sentence 'The Mississippi is a river', 'river' is used literally – or as some would prefer to say, used in its literal sense. By contrast, if one assertively uttered "Time is a river," one would be using 'river' metaphorically – or be using it in a metaphorical sense.

Metaphor has been a topic of philosophical discussion since Aristotle; in fact, it has almost certainly been more discussed by philosophers than all the other tropes together. Two themes are prominent in the discussions up to the nineteenth century. One is that metaphors, along with all the other tropes, are *decorations* of speech; hence the phrase 'figures of speech'. Metaphors are adornments or figurations. They do not contribute to the cognitive meaning of the

discourse; instead they lend it color, vividness, emotional impact, etc. Thus it was characteristic of the Enlightenment and proto-Enlightenment philosophers – Hobbes and Locke are good examples – to insist that though philosophers may sometimes have good reason to communicate their thought with metaphors, they themselves should do their thinking entirely without metaphors. The other theme prominent in discussions of metaphor up to the nineteenth century is that metaphors are, so far as their cognitive force is concerned, elliptical similes. The cognitive force of 'Time is a river', when 'river' in that sentence is used metaphorically, is the same as 'Time is like a river'.

What characterizes almost all theories of metaphor from the time of the Romantics up through our own century is the rejection of both these traditional themes. Metaphors – so it has been argued – are not cognitively dispensable decorations. They contribute to the *cognitive* meaning of our discourse; and they are indispensable, not only to religious discourse, but to ordinary, and even scientific, discourse, not to mention poetic. Nietzsche, indeed, went so far as to argue that all speech is metaphorical. And though no consensus has yet emerged on how and what metaphors contribute to meaning, nor how we recognize what they contribute, near-consensus has emerged on the thesis that they do not work as elliptical similes.

See also MEANING, PHILOSOPHY OF LANGUAGE, TROPE.   N.P.W.

metaphysical certainty. See CERTAINTY.

metaphysical holism. See METHODOLOGICAL HOLISM.

metaphysical libertarianism. See FREE WILL PROBLEM.

metaphysical naturalism. See METAPHYSICS, NATURALISM.

metaphysical necessity. See NECESSITY, PHILOSOPHY OF MIND.

metaphysical realism, in the widest sense, the view that (a) there are real objects (usually the view is concerned with spatiotemporal objects), (b) they exist independently of our experience or our knowledge of them, and (c) they have properties and enter into relations independently of the concepts with which we understand them or of the language with which we describe them. *Anti-realism* is any view that rejects one or more of these three theses, though if (a) is rejected the rejection of (b) and (c) follows trivially. (If it merely denies the existence of material things, then its traditional name is 'idealism.')

Metaphysical realism, in all of its three parts, is shared by common sense, the sciences, and most philosophers. The chief objection to it is that we can form no conception of real objects, as understood by it, since any such conception must rest on the concepts we already have and on our language and experience. To accept the objection seems to imply that we can have no knowledge of real objects as they are in themselves, and that truth must not be understood as correspondence to such objects. But this itself has an even farther reaching consequence: either (i) we should accept the seemingly absurd view that there are no real objects (since the objection equally well applies to minds and their states, to concepts and words, to properties and relations, to experiences, etc.), for we should hardly believe in the reality of something of which we can form no conception at all; or (ii) we must face the seemingly hopeless task of a drastic change in what we mean by 'reality', 'concept', 'experience', 'knowledge', 'truth', and much else. On the other hand, the objection may be held to reduce to a mere tautology, amounting to 'We (can) know reality only as we (can) know it', and then it may be argued that no substantive thesis, which anti-realism claims to be, is derivable from a mere tautology. Yet even if the objection is a tautology, it serves to force us to avoid a simplistic view of our cognitive relationship to the world.

In discussions of universals, metaphysical realism is the view that there are universals, and usually is contrasted with nominalism. But this either precludes a standard third alternative, namely conceptualism, or simply presupposes that concepts are general words (adjectives, common nouns, verbs) or uses of such words. If this presupposition is accepted, then indeed conceptualism would be the same as nominalism, but this should be argued, not legislated verbally. Traditional conceptualism holds that concepts are particular mental entities, or at least mental dispositions, that serve the classificatory function that universals have been supposed to serve and also explain the classificatory function that general words undoubtedly also serve.

See also ARMSTRONG, CONCEPTUALISM, METAPHYSICS, MORAL REALISM, PROPERTY, SCIENTIFIC REALISM.   P.Bu.

metaphysical voluntarism. See VOLUNTARISM.

metaphysics, most generally, the philosophical investigation of the nature, constitution, and structure of reality. It is broader than science, e.g., physics and even cosmology (the science of the nature, structure, and origin of the universe as a whole), since one of its concerns is the existence of non-physical entities, e.g., God. It is also more fundamental, since it investigates questions science does not address but the answers to which it presupposes. Are there, for instance, physical objects at all, and does every event have a cause?

So understood, metaphysics was rejected by positivism on the ground that its statements are "cognitively meaningless" since they are not empirically verifiable. More recent philosophers, such as Quine, reject metaphysics on the ground that science alone provides genuine knowledge. In *The Metaphysics of Logical Positivism* (1954), Bergmann argued that logical positivism, and any view such as Quine's, presupposes a metaphysical theory. And the positivists' criterion of cognitive meaning was never formulated in a way satisfactory even to them. A successor of the positivist attitude toward metaphysics is P. F. Strawson's preference (especially in *Individuals*, 1959) for what he calls *descriptive metaphysics*, which is "content to describe the actual structure of our thought about the world," as contrasted with *revisionary metaphysics*, which is "concerned to produce a better structure."

The view, sometimes considered scientific (but an assumption rather than an argued theory), that all that there is, is spatiotemporal (a part of "nature") and is knowable only through the methods of the sciences, is itself a metaphysics, namely *metaphysical naturalism* (not to be confused with natural philosophy). It is not part of science itself.

In its most general sense, metaphysics may seem to coincide with philosophy as a whole, since anything philosophy investigates is presumably a part of reality, e.g., knowledge, values, and valid reasoning. But it is useful to reserve the investigation of such more specific topics for distinct branches of philosophy, e.g., epistemology, ethics, aesthetics, and logic, since they raise problems peculiar to themselves.

Perhaps the most familiar question in metaphysics is whether there are only material entities – *materialism* – or only mental entities, i.e., minds and their states – *idealism* – or both – *dualism*. Here 'entity' has its broadest sense: anything real. More specific questions of metaphysics concern the existence and nature of certain individuals – also called *particulars* – (e.g., God), or certain properties (e.g., are there properties that nothing exemplifies?) or relations (e.g., is there a relation of causation that is a necessary connection rather than a mere regular conjunction between events?). The nature of space and time is another important example of such a more specific topic. Are space and time peculiar individuals that "contain" ordinary individuals, or are they just systems of relations between individual things, such as being (spatially) higher or (temporally) prior. Whatever is the answer, space and time are what render a world out of the totality of entities that are parts of it. Since on any account of knowledge, our knowledge of the world is extremely limited, concerning both its spatial and temporal dimensions and its inner constitution, we must allow for an indefinite number of possible ways the world may be, might have been, or will be. And this thought gives rise to the idea of an indefinite number of possible worlds. This idea is useful in making vivid our understanding of the nature of necessary truth (a necessarily true proposition is one that is true in all possible worlds) and thus is commonly employed in modal logic. But the idea can also make possible worlds seem real, a highly controversial doctrine.

The notion of a spatiotemporal world is commonly that employed in discussions of the so-called issue of *realism* versus *anti-realism*, although this issue has also been raised with respect to universals, values, and numbers, which are not usually considered spatiotemporal. While there is no clear sense in asserting that nothing is real, there seems to be a clear sense in asserting that there is no spatiotemporal world, especially if it is added that there are minds and their ideas. This was Berkeley's view. But contemporary philosophers who raise questions about the reality of the spatiotemporal world are not comfortable with Berkeleyan minds and ideas and usually just somewhat vaguely speak of "ourselves" and our "representations." The latter are themselves often understood as material (states of our brains), a clearly inconsistent position for anyone denying the reality of the spatiotemporal world.

Usually, the contemporary anti-realist does not actually deny it but rather adopts a view resembling Kant's transcendental idealism. Our only conception of the world, the anti-realist would argue, rests on our perceptual and conceptual faculties, including our language. But then what reason do we have to think that this conception is true, that it corresponds to the world as the world is in itself? Had our faculties and language been different, surely we would have had very different conceptions of the world. And very different conceptions of it are possible even in terms of our present faculties, as seems to be shown by the fact that very different scientific theories can be supported by exactly the same data. So far, we do not have anti-realism proper. But it is only a short step to it! If our conception of an independent spatiotemporal world is necessarily subjective, then we have no good reason for supposing that there is such a world, especially since it seems self-contradictory to speak of a conception that is independent of our conceptual faculties. It is clear that this question, like almost all the questions of general metaphysics, is at least in part epistemological.

Metaphysics can also be understood in a more definite sense, suggested by Aristotle's notion (in his *Metaphysics,* the title of which was given by an early editor of his works, not by Aristotle himself) of "first philosophy," namely, the study of being *qua* being, i.e., of the most general and necessary characteristics that anything must have in order to count as a being, an entity (*ens*). Sometimes 'ontology' is used in this sense, but this is by no means common practice, 'ontology' being often used as a synonym of 'metaphysics'.

Examples of criteria (each of which is a major topic in metaphysics) that anything must meet in order to count as a being, an entity, are the following.

(A) Every entity must be either an individual thing (e.g., Socrates and this book), or a property (e.g., Socrates' color and the shape of this book), or a relation (e.g., marriage and the distance between two cities), or an event (e.g., Socrates' death), or a state of affairs (e.g., Socrates' having died), or a set (e.g., the set of Greek philosophers). These kinds of entities are usually called *categories,* and metaphysics is very much concerned with the question whether these are the only categories, or whether there are others, or whether some of them are not ultimate because they are reducible to others (e.g., events to states of affairs, or individual things to temporal series of events).

(B) The existence, or being, of a thing is what makes it an entity.

(C) Whatever has identity and is distinct from everything else is an entity.

(D) The nature of the "connection" between an entity and its properties and relations is what makes it an entity. Every entity must have properties and perhaps must enter into relations with at least some other entities.

(E) Every entity must be logically self-consistent. It is noteworthy that after announcing his project of first philosophy, Aristotle immediately embarked on a defense of the law of non-contradiction.

Concerning (A) we may ask (i) whether at least some individual things (particulars) are *substances*, in the Aristotelian sense, i.e., enduring through time and changes in their properties and relations, or whether all individual things are momentary. In that case, the individuals of common sense (e.g., this book) are really temporal series of momentary individuals, perhaps events such as the book's being on a table at a specific instant. We may also ask (ii) whether any entity has *essential properties*, i.e., properties without which it would not exist, or whether all properties are *accidental*, in the sense that the entity could exist even if it lost the property in question. We may ask (iii) whether properties and relations are *particulars* or *universals*, e.g., whether the color of this page and the color of the next page, which (let us assume) are exactly alike, are two distinct entities, each with its separate spatial location, or whether they are identical and thus one entity that is exemplified by, perhaps even located in, the two pages.

Concerning (B), we may ask whether existence is itself a property. If it is, how is it to be understood, and if it is not, how are we to understand '*x* exists' and '*x* does not exist', which seem crucial to everyday and scientific discourse, just as the thoughts they express seem crucial to everyday and scientific thinking? Should we countenance, as Meinong did, objects having no existence, e.g. golden mountains, even though we can talk and think about them? We can talk and think about a golden mountain and even claim that it is true that the mountain is golden, while knowing all along that what we are thinking and talking about does not exist. If we do not construe non-existent objects as something, then we are committed to the somewhat startling view that everything exists.

Concerning (C) we may ask how to construe informative identity statements, such as, to use Frege's example, 'The Evening Star is identical with the Morning Star'. This contrasts with trivial and perhaps degenerate statements, such as 'The Evening Star is identical with the Evening Star', which are almost never made in ordinary or scientific discourse. The former are essential to any coherent, systematic cognition (even to everyday recognition of persons and places). Yet they are puzzling. We cannot say that they assert of *two* things that they are *one*, even though ordinary language suggests precisely this. Neither can we just say that they assert that a certain thing is identical with itself, for this view would be obviously false if the statements are informative. The fact that Frege's example includes definite descriptions ('the Evening Star', 'the Morning Star') is irrelevant, contrary to Russell's view. Informative identity statements can also have as their subject terms proper names and even demonstrative pronouns (e.g., 'Hesperus is identical with Phosphorus' and 'This [the shape of this page] is identical with that [the shape of the next page]'), the reference of which is established not by description but ostensively, perhaps by actual pointing.

Concerning (D) we can ask about the nature of the relationship, usually called instantiation or exemplification, between an entity and its properties and relations. Surely, there is such a relationship. But it can hardly be like an ordinary relation such as marriage that connects things of the same kind. And we can ask what is the connection between that relation and the entities it relates, e.g., the individual thing on one hand and its properties and relations on the other. Raising this question seems to lead to an infinite regress, as Bradley held; for the supposed connection is yet another relation to be connected with something else. But how do we avoid the regress? Surely, an individual thing and its properties and relations are not unrelated items. They have a certain unity. But what is its character? Moreover, we can hardly identify the individual thing except by reference to its properties and relations. Yet if we say, as some have, that it is nothing but a bundle of its properties and relations, could there not be another bundle of exactly the same properties and relations, yet distinct from the first one? (This question concerns the so-called problem of individuation, as well as the principle of the identity of indiscernibles.) If an individual is something other than its properties and relations (e.g., what has been called a *bare particular*), it would seem to be unobservable and thus perhaps unknowable.

Concerning (E), virtually no philosopher has questioned the law of non-contradiction. But there are important questions about its status. Is it merely a linguistic convention? Some have held this, but it seems quite implausible. Is the law of non-contradiction a deep truth about being *qua* being? If it is, (E) connects closely with (B) and (C), for we can think of the concepts of self-consistency, identity, and existence as the most fundamental metaphysical concepts. They are also fundamental to logic, but logic, even if ultimately grounded in metaphysics, has a rich additional subject matter (sometimes merging with that of mathematics) and therefore is properly regarded as a separate branch of philosophy.

The word 'metaphysics' has also been used in at least two other senses: first, the investigation of entities and states of affairs "transcending" human experience, in particular, the existence of God, the immortality of the soul, and the freedom of the will (this was Kant's conception of the sort of metaphysics that, according to him, required "critique"); and second, the investigation of any alleged supernatural or occult phenomena, such as ghosts and telekinesis. The first sense is properly philosophical, though seldom occurring today. The second is strictly popular, since the relevant supernatural phenomena are most questionable on both philosophical and scientific grounds. They should not be confused with the subject matter of *philosophical theology*, which may be thought of as part of metaphysics in the general philosophical sense, though it was included by Aristotle in the subject matter of metaphysics in his sense of the study of being *qua* being.

See also BUNDLE THEORY, CAUSATION, NATURALISM, PHILOSOPHY OF RELIGION, PROPERTY, TIME.   P.Bu.

metaphysics of presence. See DERRIDA, POSTMODERN.

metatheorem. See FORMAL SEMANTICS.

metatheory. See PHILOSOPHY OF LOGIC.

metempsychosis. See PYTHAGORAS.

method, axiomatic. See AXIOMATIC METHOD.

methodic doubt. See DESCARTES.

methodism. See PROBLEM OF THE CRITERION.

method of agreement. See MILL'S METHODS.

method of difference. See MILL'S METHODS.

method of doubt. See DESCARTES.

method of residues. See MILL'S METHODS.

method of supervaluations. See VAGUENESS.

methodological conservatism. See PHILOSOPHY OF SCIENCE.

methodological holism, also called metaphysical holism, the thesis that with respect to some system there is *explanatory emergence*, i.e., the laws of the more complex situations in the system are *not* deducible by way of any composition laws or laws of coexistence from the laws of the simpler or simplest situation(s). Explanatory emergence may exist in a system for any of the following reasons: that at some more complex level a variable interacts that does not do so at simpler levels, that a property of the "whole" interacts with properties of the "parts," that the relevant variables interact by different laws at more complex levels owing to the complexity of the levels, or (the limiting case) that strict lawfulness breaks down at some more complex level. Thus, explanatory emergence does *not* presuppose *descriptive emergence*, the thesis that there are properties of "wholes" (or more complex situations) that cannot be defined through the properties of the "parts" (or simpler situations).

The opposite of methodological holism is *methodological individualism*, also called *explanatory reductionism*, according to which all laws of the "whole" (or more complex situations) can be deduced from a combination of the laws of the simpler or simplest situation(s) *and* either some composition laws or laws of coexistence (depending on whether or not there is descriptive emergence). Methodological individualists need not deny that there may be significant lawful connections among properties of the "whole," but must insist that all such properties are either definable through, or connected by laws of coexistence with, properties of the "parts."

See also HOLISM, PHILOSOPHY OF THE SOCIAL SCIENCES, REDUCTION.   L.A.

methodological individualism. See METHODOLOGICAL HOLISM.

methodological naturalism. See NATURALISM.

methodological skepticism. See SKEPTICISM.

methodological solipsism. See SOLIPSISM.

methodology. See PHILOSOPHY OF SCIENCE.

Metrodorus. See EPICUREANISM.

microreduction. See REDUCTION.

middle knowledge, knowledge of a particular kind of propositions, now usually called "counterfactuals of freedom," first attributed to God by the sixteenth-century Jesuit Luis de Molina. These propositions state, concerning each possible free creature God could create, what that creature would do in each situation of (libertarian) free choice in which it could possibly find itself. The claim that God knows these propositions offers important theological advantages; it helps in explaining both how God can have foreknowledge of free actions and how God can maintain close providential control over a world containing libertarian freedom. Opponents of middle knowledge typically argue that it is impossible for there to be true counterfactuals of freedom. **See also FREE WILL PROBLEM, MOLINA.**   W.Has.

Middle Platonism, the period of Platonism between Antiochus of Ascalon (c.130–68 B.C.) and Plotinus (A.D. 204–70), characterized by a rejection of the skeptical stance of the New Academy and by a gradual advance, with many individual variations, toward a comprehensive dogmatic position on metaphysical principles, while exhibiting a certain latitude, as between Stoicizing and Peripateticizing positions, in the sphere of ethics.

Antiochus himself was much influenced by Stoic materialism (though disagreeing with the Stoics in ethics), but in the next generation a neo-Pythagorean influence made itself felt, generating the mix of doctrines that one may most properly term Middle Platonic. From Eudorus of Alexandria (fl. c.25 B.C.) on, a transcendental, two-world metaphysic prevailed, featuring a supreme god, or Monad, a secondary creator god, and a world soul, with which came a significant change in ethics, substituting, as an 'end of goods' (*telos*), "likeness to God" (from Plato, *Theaetetus* 176b), for the Stoicizing "assimilation to nature" of Antiochus.

Our view of the period is hampered by a lack of surviving texts, but it is plain that, in the absence of a central validating authority (the Academy as an institution seems to have perished in the wake of the capture of Athens by Mithridates in 88 B.C.), a considerable variety of doctrine prevailed among individual Platonists and schools of Platonists, particularly in relation to a preference for Aristotelian or Stoic principles of ethics.

Most known activity occurred in the late first and second centuries A.D. Chief figures in this period are Plutarch of Chaeronea (c.45–125), Calvenus Taurus (fl. c.145), and Atticus (fl. c.175), whose activity centered on Athens (though Plutarch remained loyal to Chaeronea in Boeotia); Gaius (fl. c.100) and Albinus (fl. c.130) – not to be identified with "Alcinous," author of the *Didaskalikos;* the rhetorician Apuleius of Madaura (fl. c.150), who also composed a useful treatise on the life and doctrines of Plato; and the neo-Pythagoreans Moderatus of Gades (fl. c.90), Nicomachus of Gerasa (fl. c.140), and Numenius (fl. c.150), who do not, however, constitute a "school." Good evidence for an earlier stage of Middle Platonism is provided by the Jewish philosopher Philo of Alexandria (c.25 B.C.–A.D. 50).

Perhaps the single most important figure for the later Platonism of Plotinus and his successors is Numenius, of whose works we have only fragments. His speculations on the nature of the first principle, however, do seem to have been a stimulus to Plotinus in his postulation of a supraessential One. Plutarch is important as a literary figure, though most of his serious philosophical works are lost; and the handbooks of Alcinous and Apuleius are significant for our understanding of second-century Platonism. **See also COMMENTARIES ON PLATO, NEO-PLATONISM, PERIPATETIC SCHOOL, PLATO, STOICISM.**   J.M.D.

Middle Stoicism. See STOICISM.

middle term. See SYLLOGISM.

middle way. See MĀDHYAMIKA.

Milesians, the pre-Socratic philosophers of Miletus, a Greek city-state on the Ionian coast of Asia Minor. During the 6th century B.C. Thales, Anaximander, and Anaximenes produced the earliest Western philosophies, stressing an *archē* or material source from which the cosmos and all things in it were generated. **See also ANAXIMANDER, ANAXIMENES OF MILETUS, THALES OF MILETUS.**   D.W.G.

Mill, James (1773–1836), Scottish-born philosopher and social theorist. He applied the utilitarianism of his contemporary Bentham to such social matters as systems of education and government, law and penal systems, and colonial policy. He also advocated the associationism of Hume. Mill was an influential thinker in early nineteenth-century London, but his most important role in the history of philosophy was the influence he had on his son, J. S. Mill. He raised his more famous son as a living experiment in his associationist theory of education. His utilitarian views were developed and extended by J. S. Mill, while his associationism was also adopted by his son and became a precursor of the latter's phenomenalism. **See also** MILL, J. S.   A.N.

Mill, John Stuart (1806–73), British empiricist philosopher and utilitarian social reformer. He was the son of James Mill, a historian of British India, a leading defender of Bentham's utilitarianism, and an advocate of reforms based on that philosophy. The younger Mill was educated by his father in accordance with the principles of the associationist psychology adopted by the Benthamites and deriving from Hartley, and was raised with the expectation that he would become a defender of the principles of the Benthamite school. He began the study of Greek at three and Latin at eight, and later assisted his father in educating his younger brothers and sisters. At twenty he went to France to learn the language, and studied chemistry and mathematics at Montpellier. From 1824 to 1828 he wrote regularly for the *Westminster Review*, the Benthamite journal. In 1828 he underwent a mental crisis that lasted some months. This he later attributed to his rigid education; in any case he emerged from a period of deep depression still advocating utilitarianism but in a very much revised version. Mill visited Paris during the revolution of 1830, meeting Lafayette and other popular leaders, and was introduced to the writings of Saint-Simon and Comte. Also in 1830 he met Mrs. Harriet Taylor, to whom he immediately became devoted. They married only in 1851, when her husband died. He joined the India House headquarters of the East India Company in 1823, serving as an examiner until the company was dissolved in 1858 in the aftermath of the Indian Mutiny. Mill sat in Parliament from 1865 to 1868. Harriet Mill died in 1858, and was buried at Avignon, where Mill thereafter regularly resided for half of each year until his own death.

Mill's major works are his *System of Logic, Deductive and Inductive* (first edition, 1843), *Political Economy* (first edition, 1848), *On Liberty* (1860), *Utilitarianism* (first published in *Fraser's Magazine*, 1861), *The Subjection of Women* (1869), *An Examination of Sir William Hamilton's Philosophy* (1865), and the posthumous *Three Essays on Religion* (1874). His writing style is excellent, and his history of his own mental development, the *Autobiography* (1867), is a major Victorian literary text.

His main opponents philosophically were Whewell and Hamilton, and it is safe to say that after Mill their intuitionism in metaphysics, philosophy of science, and ethics could no longer be defended. Mill's own views were later to be eclipsed by those of T. H. Green, F. H. Bradley, and the other British idealists. In the present century his views in metaphysics and philosophy of science have been revived and defended by Russell and the logical positivists, while his utilitarian ethics has regained its status as one of the major ethical theories. His social philosophy deeply infuenced the Fabians and other groups on the British left; its impact continues.

Mill was brought up on the basis of, and to believe in, the strict utilitarianism of his father. His own development largely consisted in his attempts to broaden it, to include a larger and more sympathetic view of human nature, and to humanize its program to fit this broader view of human beings. In his own view, no doubt largely correct, he did not so much reject his father's principles as fill in the gaps and eliminate rigidities and crudities. He continued throughout his life his father's concern to propagate principles conceived as essential to promoting human happiness. These extended from moral principles to principles of political economy to principles of logic and metaphysics.

Psychology. Mill's vision of the human being was rooted in the psychological theories he defended. Arguing against the intuitionism of Reid and Whewell, he extended the associationism of his father. On this theory, ideas have their genetic antecedents in sensation, a complex idea being generated out of a unique set of simple, elementary ideas, through associations based on regular patterns in the presented sensations. Psychological analysis reveals the elementary parts of ideas and is thus the means for investigating the causal origins of our ideas. The elder Mill followed Locke in conceiving analysis on the model of definition, so that the psychological elements are present in the idea they compose and the idea is nothing but its associated elements. The younger Mill emerged from his mental crisis with the recognition that mental states are often more than the sum of the ideas that are their genetic antecedents. On the revised model of analysis, the analytical elements are not actually present in the idea, but are present only dispositionally, ready to be recovered by association under the analytical set. Moreover, it is words that are defined, not ideas, though words become general only by becoming associated with ideas.

Analysis thus became an empirical task, rather than something settled a priori according to one's metaphysical predispositions, as it had been for Mill's predecessors. The revised psychology allowed the younger Mill to account empirically in a much more subtle way than could the earlier associationists for the variations in our states of feeling. Thus, for example, the original motive to action is simple sensations of pleasure, but through association things originally desired as means become associated with pleasure and thereby become desirable as ends, as parts of one's pleasure. But these acquired motives are not merely the sum of the simple pleasures that make them up; they are more than the sum of those genetic antecedents. Thus, while Mill holds with his father that persons seek to maximize their pleasures, unlike his father he also holds that not all ends are selfish, and that pleasures are not only quantitatively but also qualitatively distinct.

Ethics. In ethics, then, Mill can hold with the intuitionists that our moral sentiments are qualitatively distinct from the lower pleasures, while denying the intuitionist conclusion that they are innate. Mill urges, with his father and Bentham, that the basic moral norm is the principle of utility, that an action is right provided it maximizes human welfare. Persons always act to maximize their own pleasure, but the general human welfare can be among the pleasures they seek. Mill's position thus does not have the problems that the apparently egoistic psychology of his father created. The only issue is whether a person *ought* to maximize human welfare, whether he *ought to be* the sort of person who is so motivated.

Mill's own ethics is that this is indeed what one ought to be, and he tries to bring this state of human being about in others by example, and by urging them to expand the range of their human sympathy through poetry like that of Wordsworth, through reading the great moral teachers such as Jesus and Socrates, and by other means of moral improvement.

Mill also offers an argument in defense of the principle of utility. Against those who, like Whewell, argue that there is no basic right to pleasure, he argues that as a matter of psychological fact, people seek only pleasure, and concludes that it is therefore pointless to suggest that they ought to do anything other than this. The test of experience thus excludes ends other than pleasure. This is a plausible argument. Less plausible is his further argument that since each seeks her own pleasure, the general good is the (ultimate) aim of all. This latter argument unfortunately presupposes the invalid premise that the law for a whole follows from laws about the individual parts of the whole.

Other moral rules can be justified by their utility and the test of experience. For example, such principles of justice as the rules of property and of promise keeping are justified by their role in serving certain fundamental human needs. Exceptions to such secondary rules can be justified by appeal to the principle of utility. But there is also utility in not requiring in every application a lengthy utilitarian calculation, which provides an objective justification for overlooking what might be, objectively considered in terms of the principle of utility, an exception to a secondary rule.

Logic and philosophy of science. The test of experience is also brought to bear on norms other than those of morality, e.g., those of logic and philosophy of science. Mill argues, against the rationalists, that science is not demonstrative from intuited premises. Reason in the sense of deductive logic is not a logic of proof but a logic of consistency. The basic axioms of any science are derived through generalization from experience. The axioms are generic and delimit a range of possible hypotheses about the specific subject matter to which they are applied. It is then the task of experiment and, more generally, observation to eliminate the false and determine which hypothesis is true. The axioms, the most generic of which is the law of the uniformity of nature, are arrived at not by this sort of process of elimination but by induction by simple enumeration: Mill argues plausibly that on the basis of experience this method becomes more reliable the more generic is the hypothesis that it is used to justify. But like Hume, Mill holds that for any generalization from experience the evidence can never be sufficient to eliminate all possibility of doubt.

Explanation for Mill, as for the logical positivists, is by subsumption under matter-of-fact generalizations. Causal generalizations that state sufficient or necessary and sufficient conditions are more desirable as explanations than mere regularities. Still more desirable is a law or body of laws that gives necessary and sufficient conditions for *any* state of a system, i.e., a body of laws for which there are no explanatory gaps. As for explanation of laws, this can proceed either by filling in gaps or by subsuming the law under a generic theory that unifies the laws of several areas.

Mill argues that in the social sciences the subject matter is too complex to apply the normal methods of experiment. But he also rejects the purely deductive method of the Benthamite political economists such as his father and David Ricardo. Rather, one must deduce the laws for wholes, i.e., the laws of economics and sociology, from the laws for the parts, i.e., the laws of psychology, and *then* test these derived laws against the accumulated data of history. Mill got the idea for this methodology of the social sciences from Comte, but unfortunately it is vitiated by the false idea, already noted, that one can deduce without any further premise the laws for wholes from the laws for the parts. Subsequent methodologists of the social sciences have come to substitute the more reasonable methods of statistics for this invalid method Mill proposes.

Mill's account of scientific method does work well for empirical sciences, such as the chemistry of his day. He was able to show, too, that it made good sense of a great deal of physics, though it is arguable that it cannot do justice to theories that explain the atomic and subatomic structure of matter – something Mill himself was prepared to acknowledge. He also attempted to apply his views to geometry, and even more implausibly, to arithmetic. In these areas, he was certainly bested by Whewell, and the world had to wait for the logical work of Russell and Whitehead before a reasonable empiricist account of these areas became available.

Metaphysics. The starting point of all inference is the sort of observation we make through our senses, and since we know by experience that we have no ideas that do not derive from sense experience, it follows that we cannot conceive a world beyond what we know by sense. To be sure, we can form generic concepts, such as that of an event, which enable us to form concepts of entities that we cannot experience, e.g., the concept of *the tiny speck of sand that stopped my watch* or the concept of *the event that is the cause of my present sensation.* Mill held that what we know of the laws of sensation is sufficient to make it reasonable to suppose that the immediate cause of one's present sensation is the state of one's nervous system. Our concept of an objective physical object is also of this sort; it is the set of events that jointly constitute a permanent possible cause of sensation. It is our inductive knowledge of laws that justifies our beliefs that there are entities that fall under these concepts. The point is that these entities, while unsensed, are

(we reasonably believe) part of the world we know by means of our senses.

The contrast is to such things as the substances and transcendent Ideas of rationalists, or the God of religious believers, entities that can be known only by means that go beyond sense and inductive inferences therefrom. Mill remained essentially pre-Darwinian, and was willing to allow the plausibility of the hypothesis that there is an intelligent designer for the perceived order in the universe. But this has the status of a scientific hypothesis rather than a belief in a substance or a personal God transcending the world of experience and time. Whewell, at once the defender of rationalist ideas for science and for ethics and the defender of established religion, is a special object for Mill's scorn.

Social and political thought. While Mill is respectful of the teachings of religious leaders such as Jesus, the institutions of religion, like those of government and of the economy, are all to be subjected to criticism based on the principle of utility: Do they contribute to human welfare? Are there any alternatives that could do better? Thus, Mill argues that a free-market economy has many benefits but that the defects, in terms of poverty for many, that result from private ownership of the means of production may imply that we should institute the alternative of socialism or public ownership of the means of production. He similarly argues for the utility of liberty as a social institution: under such a social order individuality will be encouraged, and this individuality in turn tends to produce innovations in knowledge, technology, and morality that contribute significantly to improving the general welfare. Conversely, institutions and traditions that stifle individuality, as religious institutions often do, should gradually be reformed. Similar considerations argue on the one hand for democratic representative government and on the other for a legal system of rights that can defend individuals from the tyranny of public opinion and of the majority.

Status of women. Among the things for which Mill campaigned were women's rights, women's suffrage, and equal access for women to education and to occupations. He could not escape his age and continued to hold that it was undesirable for a woman to work to help support her family. While he disagreed with his father and Bentham that all motives are egoistic and self-interested, he nonetheless held that in most affairs of economics and government such motives are dominant. He was therefore led to disagree with his father that votes for women are unnecessary since the male can speak for the family. Women's votes are needed precisely to check the pursuit of male self-interest. More generally, equality is essential if the interests of the family as such are to be served, rather than making the family serve male self-interest as had hitherto been the case. Changing the relation between men and women to one of equality will force both parties to curb their self-interest and broaden their social sympathies to include others. Women's suffrage is an essential step toward the moral improvement of humankind.

See also BENTHAM, EMPIRICISM, MILL'S METHODS, PHILOSOPHY OF THE SOCIAL SCIENCES, UTILITARIANISM, WHEWELL.   F.W.

millet paradox. See SORITES PARADOX.

Mill's methods, procedures for discovering necessary conditions, sufficient conditions, and necessary and sufficient conditions, where these terms are used as follows: if whenever A then B (e.g., whenever there is a fire then oxygen is present), then B is a *necessary (causal) condition* for A; and if whenever C then D (e.g., whenever sugar is in water, then it dissolves), then C is a *sufficient (causal) condition* for D.

Method of agreement. Given a pair of hypotheses about necessary conditions, e.g.,

(1) whenever A then B_1
whenever A then B_2,

then an observation of an individual that is A but not B_2 will eliminate the second alternative as false, enabling one to conclude that the uneliminated hypothesis is true. This method for discovering necessary conditions is called the method of agreement. To illustrate the method of agreement, suppose several people have all become ill upon eating potato salad at a restaurant, but have in other respects had quite different meals, some having meat, some vegetables, some desserts. Being ill and not eating meat eliminates the latter as the cause; being ill and not eating dessert eliminates the latter as cause; and so on. It is the condition in which the individuals who are ill agree that is not eliminated. We therefore conclude that this is the cause or necessary condition for the illness.

Method of difference. Similarly, with respect to the pair of hypotheses concerning sufficient conditions, e.g.,

(2) whenever C_1 then D
whenever C_2 then D,

an individual that is C_1 but not D will eliminate the first hypothesis and enable one to conclude that the second is true. This is the *method of difference*. A simple change will often yield an example of an inference to a sufficient condition by the method of difference. If something changes from C_1 to C_2, and also thereupon changes from not-D to D, one can conclude that C_2, in respect of which the instances differ, is the cause of D. Thus, Becquerel discovered that burns can be caused by radium, i.e., proximity to radium is a sufficient but not necessary condition for being burned, when he inferred that the radium he carried in a bottle in his pocket was the cause of a burn on his leg by noting that the presence of the radium was the only relevant causal difference between the time when the burn was present and the earlier time when it was not.

Clearly, both methods can be generalized to cover any finite number of hypotheses in the set of alternatives. The two methods can be combined in the *joint method of agreement and difference* to yield the discovery of conditions that are both necessary and sufficient.

Sometimes it is possible to eliminate an alternative, not on the basis of observation, but on the basis of previously inferred laws. If we know by previous inductions that no C_2 is D, then observation is not needed to eliminate the second hypothesis of (2), and we can infer that what remains, or the residue, gives us the sufficient condition for D. Where an alternative is eliminated by previous inductions, we are said to use the *method of residues*.

The methods may be generalized to cover quantitative laws. A cause of Q may be taken not to be a necessary and sufficient condition, but a factor P on whose magnitude the magnitude of Q functionally depends. If P varies when Q varies, then one can use methods of elimination to infer that P causes Q. This has been called the *method of concomitant variation*. More complicated methods are needed to infer what precisely is the function that correlates the two magnitudes.

Clearly, if we are to conclude that one of (1) is true on the basis of the given data, we need an additional premise to the effect that

there is at least one necessary condition for B and it is among the set consisting of A_1 and A_2.

The existence claim here is known as a *principle of determinism* and the delimited range of alternatives is known as a *principle of limited variety*. Similar principles are needed for the other methods. Such principles are clearly empirical, and must be given prior inductive support if the methods of elimination are to be conclusive. In practice, generic scientific theories provide these principles to guide the experimenter. Thus, on the basis of the observations that justified Kepler's laws, Newton was able to eliminate all hypotheses concerning the force that moved the planets about the sun save the inverse square law, provided that he also assumed as applying to this specific sort of system the generic theoretical framework established by his three laws of motion, which asserted that there exists a force accounting for the motion of the planets (determinism) and that this force satisfies certain conditions, e.g., the action-reaction law (limited variety).

The eliminative methods constitute the basic logic of the experimental method in science. They were first elaborated by Francis Bacon (see J. Weinberg, *Abstraction, Relation, and Induction*, 1965). They were restated by Hume, elaborated by J. F. W. Herschel, and located centrally in scientific methodology by J. S. Mill. Their structure was studied from the perspective of modern developments in logic by Keynes, W. E. Johnson, and especially Broad.

See also CAUSATION, CONFIRMATION, GRUE PARADOX, INDUCTION, PHILOSOPHY OF SCIENCE. F.W.

Mīmāmsā, also called Pūrva Mīmāmsā, an orthodox school within Hinduism that accepts the existence of everlasting souls or minds to which consciousness is not intrinsic, everlasting material atoms, and mind-independent physical objects caused by the natural mutual attraction of atoms. Atheistic, it accepts – in common with the other orthodox schools – the doctrines of the beginningless transmigration of souls and the operation of karma.

Mīmāmsā accepts perception, inference, and testimony (or authority) as reliable sources of knowledge. Testimony comes in two kinds, personal and impersonal. Personal testimony (someone's spoken or written word, giving knowledge if the person giving it is reliable) is descriptive. Impersonal testimony (the Vedas) is imperatival, giving commands that ritual actions be performed; properly understanding and following these commands is essential to achieving enlightenment. Reliable personal testimony presupposes reliable perception and inference; impersonal testimony does not.

Postulation is taken to be a fourth source of knowledge. If the postulation that event *A* occurred adequately explains that event *B* occurred, though *A* is unobserved and there is no necessary or universal connection between events like *A* and events like *B*, one can know that *A* occurred, but this knowledge is neither perceptual nor inferential. In effect, this distinguishes inference to best explanation (abduction) from inductive reasoning.

See also HINDUISM, KARMA. K.E.Y.

mimesis (from Greek *mimēsis*, 'imitation'), the modeling of one thing on another, or the presenting of one thing by another; imitation. The concept played a central role in the account formulated by Plato and Aristotle of what we would now call the fine arts. The poet, the dramatist, the painter, the musician, the sculptor, all compose a mimesis of reality. Though Plato, in his account of painting, definitely had in mind that the painter *imitates* physical reality, the general concept of mimesis used by Plato and Aristotle is usually better translated by 'representation' than by 'imitation': it belongs to the nature of the work of art to represent, to re-present, reality. This *representational* or *mimetic theory of art* remained far and away the dominant theory in the West until the rise of Romanticism – though by no means everyone agreed with Plato that it is concrete items of physical reality that the artist represents. The hold of the mimetic theory was broken by the insistence of the Romantics that, rather than the work of art being an imitation, it is the *artist* who, in his or her creative activity, imitates Nature or God by composing an autonomous object.

Few contemporary theorists of art would say that the essence of art is to represent; the mimetic theory is all but dead. In part this is a reflection of the power of the Romantic alternative to the mimetic theory; in part it is a reflection of the rise to prominence over the last century of nonobjective, abstract painting and sculpture and of "absolute" instrumental music. Nonetheless, the *phenomenon* of representation has not ceased to draw the attention of theorists. In recent years three quite different general theories of representation have appeared: Nelson Goodman's (*The Languages of Art*), Nicholas Wolterstorff's (*Works and Worlds of Art*), and Kendall Walton's (*Mimesis as Make-Believe*).

See also AESTHETICS. N.P.W.

mimetic theory of art. See MIMESIS.

mind. See HSIN¹, PHILOSOPHY OF MIND, PROBLEM OF OTHER MINDS.

mind, causal theory of. See FUNCTIONALISM.

mind, philosophy of. See PHILOSOPHY OF MIND.

mind–body problem. See PHILOSOPHY OF MIND.

ming, Chinese term meaning 'fate', 'mandate'. In general, *ming* is what is outside of human control. '*Ming*' is thus nearly synonymous with one use of '*t'ien*', as in the observation by Mencius: "That which is done when no one does it is due to *t'ien;* that which comes about when no one brings it about is due to *ming.*" *Ming* can also refer to the mandate to rule given by *t'ien* or the "moral endowment" of each human. **See also** CHUNG-YUNG, T'IEN.   B.W.V.N.

ming chia. See SCHOOL OF NAMES.

minimalist theory of truth. See TRUTH.

minimax strategy. See MAXIMIN STRATEGY.

Minkowski space-time. See RELATIVITY, SPACE-TIME.

minor premise. See SYLLOGISM.

minor term. See SYLLOGISM.

minute perceptions, doctrine of. See LEIBNIZ.

miracle, an extraordinary event brought about by God. In the medieval understanding of nature, objects have certain natural powers and tendencies to exercise those powers under certain circumstances. Stones have the power to fall to the ground, and the tendency to exercise that power when liberated from a height. A miracle is then an extraordinary event in that it is not brought about by any object exercising its natural powers – e.g., a liberated stone rising in the air – but brought about directly by God.

In the modern understanding of nature, there are just events (states of objects) and laws of nature that determine which events follow which other events. There is a law of nature that heavy bodies when liberated fall to the ground. A miracle is then a "violation" of a law of nature by God. We must understand by a law a princi-

ple that determines what happens unless there is intervention from outside the natural order, and by a "violation" such an intervention. There are then three problems in identifying a miracle. The first is to determine whether an event of some kind, if it occurred, would be a violation of a law of nature (beyond the natural power of objects to bring about). To know this we must know what are the laws of nature. The second problem is to find out whether such an event did occur on a particular occasion. Our own memories, the testimony of witnesses, and physical traces will be the historical evidence of this, but they can mislead. And the evidence from what happened on other occasions that some law L is a law of nature is evidence supporting the view that on the occasion in question L was operative, and so there was no violation. Hume claimed that in practice there has never been enough historical evidence for a miracle to outweigh the latter kind of counterevidence. Finally, it must be shown that God was the cause of the violation. For that we need grounds from natural theology for believing that there is a God and that this is the sort of occasion on which he is likely to intervene in nature.

   See also EVENT, LAWLIKE GENERALIZATION, PHILOSOPHY OF RELIGION.   R.Sw.

Miskawayh (936–c.1030), Persian courtier-statesman, historian, physician, and advocate of Greek and other ancient learning in Islam. His *On the Refinement of Character* (tr. Constantine Zurayk, 1968) has been called "the most influential work on philosophical ethics" in Islam. It transmutes Koranic command ethics into an Aristotelian virtue ethics whose goal is the disciplining (*ta'dib*, cf. the Greek *paideia*) of our natural irascibility, allowing our deeper unity to be expressed in love and fellowship. Miskawayh's system was copied widely – crucially, in al-Ghazālī's all-but-canonical treatment of virtue ethics – but denatured by al-Ghazālī's substitution of pietistic themes where Miskawayh seemed too secular or humanistic. **See also** AL-GHAZĀLĪ.   L.E.G.

misplaced concreteness, fallacy of. See WHITEHEAD.

Mitfreude. See VALUE.

mixed hypothetical syllogism. See SYLLOGISM.

M'Naghten rule, a rule in Anglo-American criminal law defining legal insanity for purposes of creating a defense to criminal liability: legal insanity is any defect of reason, due to disease of the mind, that causes an accused criminal either not to know the nature and quality of his act, or not to know that his act was morally or legally wrong. Adopted in the M'Naghten case in England in 1843, the rule harks back to the responsibility test for children, which was whether they were mature enough to know the difference between right and wrong. The rule is alternatively viewed today as being either a test of a human being's general status as a moral agent or a test of when an admitted moral agent is nonetheless excused because of either factual or moral/legal mistakes. On the first (or status) interpretation of the rule, the insane are exempted from criminal liability because they, like young children, lack the rational agency essential to moral personhood. On the second (or mistake) interpretation of the rule, the insane are exempted from criminal liability because they instantiate the accepted moral excuses of mistake or ignorance. **See also** DIMINISHED CAPACITY, RESPONSIBILITY.   M.S.M.

mnemic causation, a type of causation in which, in order to explain the proximate cause of an organism's behavior, it is necessary to specify not only the present state of the organism and the present stimuli operating upon it, but also the past experiences of the organism. The term was introduced by Russell in *The Analysis of Mind* (1921). **See also** MEMORY.   N.G.

modalities, alethic. See ALETHIC MODALITIES.

modality, the manner in which a proposition (or statement) describes or applies to its subject matter. Derivatively 'modality' refers to characteristics of entities or states of affairs described by modal propositions.

Modalities are classified as follows: *Assertoric* propositions are expressions of mere fact. *Alethic* modalities include necessity and possibility (the latter two sometimes are referred to respectively as the *apodictic* and *problematic* modalities). The *causal* modalities include causal (or empirical) necessity and possibility, whereas the *deontic* modalities include obligation and permittedness. There are *epistemic* modalities such as knowing *that* and *doxastic* ones such as believing *that*.

Following medieval logicians, propositions can be distinguished on the basis of whether the modality is introduced via adverbial modification of the copula or verb (*sensus divisus*) or via a modal operator that modifies the proposition

(*sensus compositus*). Today many deny the distinction or confine attention just to modal operators. Modal operators in non-assertoric propositions are said to produce referential opacity or oblique contexts in which truth is not preserved under substitution of extensionally equivalent expressions.

Modal and deontic logics provide formal analyses of various modalities. Intensional logics investigate the logic of oblique contexts. Modal logicians have produced possible worlds semantics interpretations wherein propositions *MP* with modal operator *M* are true provided *P* is true in all suitable (e.g., logically possible, causally possible, morally permissible, rationally acceptable) possible worlds. Modal realism grants ontological status to possible worlds other than the actual world or otherwise commits to objective modalities in nature or reality.

    See also INTENSIONAL LOGIC, MODAL LOGIC, QUANTIFYING IN.   F.S.

modality, iterated. See ALETHIC MODALITIES.

modality, practical. See FREE WILL PROBLEM.

modality, problematic. See MODALITY.

modality *de dicto*. See ESSENTIALISM.

modality *de re*. See ESSENTIALISM.

modal logic, the study of the logic of the operators 'it is possible that' and 'it is necessary that'. These operators are usually symbolized by ◊ and □ respectively, and each can be defined in terms of the other. To say that a proposition is possible, or possibly true, is to say that it is not necessarily false. Thus ◊ φ could be regarded as an abbreviation of ~□~φ. Equally, to say that a proposition is necessary, or necessarily true, is to deny that its negation is possible. Thus □φ could be regarded as an abbreviation of ~◊~φ. However, it aids comprehension to take both operators as primitive.

Systems of sentential modal logic are obtained by adding ◊ and □ to sentential logic; if the sentential logic is classical/intuitionist/minimal, so is the corresponding modal logic. We concentrate on the classical case here. As with any kind of logic, there are three components to a system of modal logic: a syntax, which determines the formal language $\mathcal{L}$ and the notion of well-formed formula (wff); a semantics, which determines the semantic consequence relation ⊨ on $\mathcal{L}$-wffs; and a system of inference, which determines the deductive consequence relation ⊢ on $\mathcal{L}$-wffs. The syntax of the modal operators is the same in every system: briefly, the modal operators are one-place connectives like negation. There are many different systems of modal logic, some of which can be generated by different ways of setting up the semantics. Each of the familiar ways of doing this can be associated with a sound and complete system of inference. Alternatively, a system of inference can be laid down first and we can search for a semantics for it relative to which it is sound and complete. Here we give primacy to the semantic viewpoint.

Semantic consequence is defined in modal logic in the usual classical way: a set of sentences Σ semantically entails a sentence σ, Σ ⊨ σ, if and only if no interpretation I makes all members of Σ true and σ false. The question is how to extend the notion of interpretation from sentential logic to accommodate the modal operators. In classical sentential logic, an interpretation is an assignment to each sentence letter of exactly one of the two truth-values ⊤ and ⊥, and the truth-value of a sentence in an interpretation is calculated by applying the truth-functions expressed, according to the semantics, by the connectives, to the sentence letters of the sentence. But we cannot extend this to modal logic by assigning some further truth-functions to the modal operators, since neither of these operators expresses a truth-function. For example, given just that ϕ is true, we cannot determine the truth-value of □ϕ, for if ϕ is a contingent truth ('Hume is a famous philosopher') then □ϕ is false, while if ϕ is necessary ('All famous philosophers are philosophers') then □ϕ is true.

The solution is to regard ◊ and □ as quantifiers over entities called *possible worlds*. A possible world is a complete way things might be or might have been; the actual world is a possible world and so is any other way things might have gone, e.g. one in which Hume was obscure. □ϕ is then interpreted as saying that ϕ is true in *all* possible worlds, while ◊ϕ is interpreted as saying that ϕ is true at *at least one* possible world. A statement is true if it is true at the actual world (usually denoted 'w^*'), and given some supply of possible worlds, the truth-value of any statement ϕ at the actual world can be calculated by applying these two rules for the modal operators (together with the truth-functions for the non-modal connectives). For example, □(B→◊(C & D)) is true at w^* if B → ◊(C & D) is true at every world w, which requires in turn that either B is false at w or else that at some world u, C and D are both true. Thus we can calculate the truth-value of □(B → ◊(C &

D)) provided we know the truth-values of the sentence letters B, C, and D at each world.

An interpretation should therefore contain a collection W of possible worlds (including one designated as w^*) and a specification, for each world w, of the truth-values of all sentence letters at w; in other words, a collection W of worlds that associates each w in W with an interpretation of the non-modal part of the language. However, there is also a third component. A world v may be said to be *possible relative to* a world u if no proposition necessarily true at u is false at v. The idea here is to accommodate the thought that what is necessary or possible may depend on how things actually are; thus, given the way things actually are, certain things may be possible that would not be possible if things had actually been different. Suppose that I might have originated from a different sperm, or a different egg, but not both, and suppose that at the actual world I originate from s_1 and e_1, so that there is a possible world u where I originate from s_1 and e_2 and a possible world v where I originate from s_2 and e_1. Then both u and v are possible relative to the actual world, but if it is true at every world that one could not have originated from a different sperm *and* egg, then u and v are each impossible relative to the other. The third component of an interpretation is therefore a stipulation of which worlds are possible relative to which. The stipulation takes the form of the specification of a two-place relation R on W. A two-place relation on a set is a collection of pairs of objects from the set; e.g., the relation 'immediately precedes' on the natural numbers is the set of pairs $<m,n>$ where $n = m + 1$. So to determine relative possibility in a model, we identify R with a collection of pairs of the form $<u,v>$ where each of u and v is in W. If a pair $<u,v>$ is in R, v is possible relative to u, and if $<u,v>$ is not in R, v is impossible relative to u. The relative possibility relation then enters into the rules for evaluating modal operators. For example, we do not want to say that at the actual world, it is possible for me to originate from a different sperm *and* egg, since the only worlds where this takes place are impossible relative to the actual world. So we have the rule that ◊ϕ is true at a world u if ϕ is true at some world v such that v is possible relative to u. Similarly, □ϕ is true at a world u if ϕ is true at every world v which is possible relative to u.

R may have simple first-order properties such as *reflexivity*, $(\forall x)Rxx$, *symmetry*, $(\forall x)(\forall y)(Rxy \rightarrow Ryx)$, and *transitivity*, $(\forall x)(\forall y)(\forall z)((Rxy \,\&\, Ryz) \rightarrow Rxz)$, and different modal systems can be obtained by imposing different combinations of these on R (other systems can be obtained from *higher-order* constraints). The least constrained system is the system K, in which no structural properties are put on R. In K we have $\Diamond$ (B & C) ⊨ $\Diamond$ B, since if $\Diamond$ (B & C) holds at w^* then (B & C) holds at some world w possible relative to w^*, and thus by the truth-function for &, B holds at w as well, so $\Diamond$ B holds at w^*. Hence any interpretation that makes $\Diamond$ (B & C) true (= true at w^*) also makes $\Diamond$ B true. Since there are no restrictions on R in K, we can expect $\Diamond$ (B & C) ⊨ $\Diamond$ B in every system of modal logic generated by constraining R. However, for K we also have C ⊭ $\Diamond$ C. For suppose C holds at w^*. $\Diamond$ C holds at w^* only if there is some world possible relative to w^* where C holds. But there need be no such world. In particular, since R need not be reflexive, w^* itself need not be possible relative to w^*. Concomitantly, in any system for which we stipulate a reflexive R, we will have C ⊨ $\Diamond$ C. The simplest such system is known as T, which has the same semantics as K except that R is stipulated to be reflexive in every interpretation. In other systems, further or different constraints are put on R. For example, in the system B, each interpretation must have an R that is reflexive and symmetric, and in the system S4, each interpretation must have an R that is reflexive and transitive. In B we have $\Diamond$ C ⊭ $\Diamond$ $\Diamond$ C, as can be shown by an interpretation with non-transitive R, while in S4 we have $\Diamond$ □C ⊭ C, as can be shown by an interpretation with non-symmetric R. Correspondingly, in S4, $\Diamond$ C ⊨ $\Diamond$ $\Diamond$ C, and in B, $\Diamond$ □C ⊨ C. The system in which R is reflexive, transitive, and symmetric is called S5, and in this system, R can be omitted. For if R has all three properties, R is an *equivalence* relation, i.e., it partitions W into mutually exclusive and jointly exhaustive equivalence classes. If C_u is the equivalence class to which u belongs, then the truth-value of a formula at u is independent of the truth-values of sentence letters at worlds not in C_u, so only the worlds in C_{w^*} are relevant to the truth-values of sentences in an S5 interpretation. But within C_{w^*} R is universal: every world is possible relative to every other. Consequently, in an S5 interpretation, we need not specify a relative possibility relation, and the evaluation rules for $\Diamond$ and □ need not mention relative possibility; e.g., we can say that $\Diamond$ ϕ is true at a world u if there is at least one world v at which ϕ is true. Note that by the characteristics of R, whenever Σ ⊨ σ in K, T, B, or S4, then Σ ⊨ σ in S5: the other systems are *contained in* S5. K is contained in all the systems we have mentioned, while T is contained in B and S4, neither of which is contained in the other.

Sentential modal logics give rise to quantified modal logics, of which quantified S5 is the best-known. Just as, in the sentential case, each world in an interpretation is associated with a valuation of sentence letters as in non-modal sentential logic, so in quantified modal logic, each world is associated with a valuation of the sort familiar in non-modal first-order logic. More specifically, in quantified S5, each world w is assigned a domain D_w – the things that exist at w – such that at least one D_w is non-empty, and each atomic n-place predicate of the language is assigned an extension Ext_w of n-tuples of objects that satisfy the predicate at w. So even restricting ourselves to just the one first-order extension of a sentential system, S5, various degrees of freedom are already evident. We discuss the following: (a) variability of domains, (b) interpretation of quantifiers, and (c) predication.

(a) Should all worlds have the same domain or may the domains of different worlds be different? The latter appears to be the more natural choice; e.g., if neither of of D_{w^*} and D_u are subsets of the other, this represents the intuitive idea that some things that exist might not have, and that there could have been things that do not actually exist (though formulating this latter claim requires adding an operator for 'actually' to the language). So we should distinguish two versions of S5, one with constant domains, S5C, and the other with variable domains, S5V. (b) Should the truth of $(\exists v)\phi$ at a world w require that ϕ is true at w of some object in D_w or merely of some object in D (D is the domain of all possible objects, $\cup_{w \in W} D_w$)? The former treatment is called the *actualist* reading of the quantifiers, the latter, the *possibilist* reading. In S5C there is no real choice, since for any w, $D = D_w$, but the issue is live in S5V. (c) Should we require that for any n-place atomic predicate F, an n-tuple of objects satisfies F at w only if every member of the n-tuple belongs to D_w, i.e., should we require that atomic predicates be existence-entailing?

If we abbreviate $(\exists y)$ $(y = x)$ by Ex (for 'x exists'), then in S5C, □$(\forall x)$□Ex is logically valid on the actualist reading of $\forall$ (=~$\exists$~) and on the possibilist. On the former, the formula says that at each world, anything that exists at that world exists at every world, which is true; while on the latter, using the definition of 'Ex', it says that at each world, anything that exists at some world or other is such that at every world, it exists at some world or other, which is also true; indeed, the formula stays valid in S5C with possibilist quantifiers even if we make E a primitive logical constant, stipulated to be true at every w of exactly the things that exist at w. But in S5V with actualist quantifiers, $\Box(\forall x)\Box Ex$ is invalid, as is $(\forall x)\Box Ex$ – consider an interpretation where for some u, D_u is a proper subset of D_{w^*}. However, in S5V with possibilist quantifiers, the status of the formula, if 'Ex' is defined, depends on whether identity is existence-entailing. If it is existence-entailing, then $\Box(\forall x)\Box Ex$ is invalid, since an object in D satisfies $(\exists y)(y = x)$ at w only if that object exists at w, while if identity is not existence-entailing, the formula is valid.

The interaction of the various options is also evident in the evaluation of two well-known schemata: the *Barcan formula*, $\Diamond\, (\exists x)\phi x \to (\exists x)\, \Diamond\, \phi x$; and its converse, $(\exists x)\, \Diamond\, \phi x \to \Diamond\, (\exists x)\phi x$. In S5C with '$Ex$' either defined or primitive, both schemata are valid, but in S5V with actualist quantifiers, they both fail. For the latter case, if we substitute $\sim E$ for ϕ in the converse Barcan formula we get a conditional whose antecedent holds at w^* if there is u with D_u a proper subset of D_{w^*}, but whose consequent is logically false. The Barcan formula fails when there is a world u with D_u not a subset of D_{w^*}, and the condition ϕ is true of some non-actual object at u and not of any actual object there. For then $\Diamond\, (\exists x)\phi$ holds at w^* while $(\exists x)\, \Diamond\, \phi x$ fails there. However, if we require atomic predicates to be existence-entailing, then instances of the converse Barcan formula with ϕ atomic are valid. In S5V with possibilist quantifiers, all instances of both schemata are valid, since the prefixes $(\exists x)\, \Diamond\,$ and $\Diamond\, (\exists x)$ correspond to $(\exists x)\, (\exists w)$ and $(\exists w)\, (\exists x)$, which are equivalent (with actualist quantifiers, the prefixes correspond to $(\exists x \in D_{w^*})$, and $(\exists w)$ $(\exists x \in D_w)$ which are non-equivalent if D_w and D_{w^*} need not be the same set).

Finally in S5V with actualist quantifiers, the standard quantifier introduction and elimination rules must be adjusted. Suppose c is a name for an object that does not actually exist; then $\sim Ec$ is true but $(\exists x) \sim Ex$ is false. The quantifier rules must be those of free logic: we require Ec & ϕc before we infer $(\exists v)\phi v$ and $Ec \to \phi c$, as well as the usual $\forall$I restrictions, before we infer $(\forall v)\phi v$.

See also CONTINGENT, ESSENTIALISM, MATHEMATICAL INTUITIONISM, POSSIBLE WORLDS, SECOND-ORDER LOGIC.   G.Fo.

modal logic of programs. See DYNAMIC LOGIC.

modal realism. See LEWIS, DAVID.

modal square of opposition. See CONTINGENT.

mode (from Latin *modus*, 'way', 'fashion'), a term used in many senses in philosophy. In Aristotelian logic, it refers either to the arrangement of universal, particular, affirmative, or negative propositions within a syllogism, only certain of which are valid (this is often translated as 'mood' in English), or to the property a proposition has by virtue of which it is necessary or contingent, possible or impossible. In Scholastic metaphysics, it was often used in a not altogether technical sense to mean that which characterizes a thing and distinguishes it from others. Micraelius (*Lexicon philosophicum*, 1653) writes that "a mode does not compose a thing, but distinguishes it and makes it determinate." It was also used in the context of the modal distinction in the theory of distinctions to designate the distinction that holds between a substance and its modes or between two modes of a single substance. The term 'mode' also appears in the technical vocabulary of medieval speculative grammar in connection with the notions of modes of signifying (*modi significandi*), modes of understanding (*modi intelligendi*), and modes of being (*modi essendi*).

The term 'mode' became especially important in the seventeenth century, when Descartes, Spinoza, and Locke each took it up, giving it three somewhat different special meanings within their respective systems. Descartes makes 'mode' a central notion in his metaphysics in his *Principia philosophiae*. For Descartes, each substance is characterized by a principal attribute, thought for mind and extension for body. Modes, then, are particular ways of being extended or thinking, i.e., particular sizes, shapes, etc., or particular thoughts, properties (in the broad sense) that individual things (substances) have. In this way, 'mode' occupies the role in Descartes's philosophy that 'accident' does in Aristotelian philosophy. But for Descartes, each mode must be connected with the principal attribute of a substance, a *way of being* extended or a *way* of thinking, whereas for the Aristotelian, accidents may or may not be connected with the essence of the substance in which they inhere.

Like Descartes, Spinoza recognizes three basic metaphysical terms, 'substance,' 'attribute', and 'mode'. Recalling Descartes, he defines 'mode' as "the affections of a substance, or that which is in another, and which is also conceived through another" (*Ethics* I). But for Spinoza, there is only one substance, which has all possible attributes. This makes it somewhat difficult to determine exactly what Spinoza means by 'modes', whether they are to be construed as being in some sense "properties" of God, the one infinite substance, or whether they are to be construed more broadly as simply individual things that depend for their existence on God, just as Cartesian modes depend on Cartesian substance. Spinoza also introduces somewhat obscure distinctions between infinite and finite modes, and between immediate and mediate infinite modes.

Locke uses 'mode' in a way that evidently derives from Descartes's usage, but that also differs from it. For Locke, modes are "such complex *Ideas,* which however compounded, contain not in them the supposition of subsisting by themselves, but are considered as Dependences on, or Affections of Substances" (*Essay* II). Modes are thus ideas that represent to us the complex properties of things, ideas derived from what Locke calls the simple ideas that come to us from experience. Locke distinguishes between simple modes like number, space, and infinity, which are supposed to be constructed by compounding the same idea many times, and mixed modes like obligation or theft, which are supposed to be compounded of many simple ideas of different sorts.

See also DESCARTES, LOCKE, METAPHYSICS, PROPERTY, SPINOZA.   D.Garb.

model. See COMPUTER THEORY, MODEL THEORY.

modeling, computer. See COMPUTER THEORY.

model set. See HINTIKKA SET.

model theory, a branch of mathematical logic that deals with the connection between a language and its interpretations or structures. Basic to it is the characterization of the conditions under which a sentence is true in structure. It is confusing that the term 'model' itself is used slightly differently: a model for a sentence is a structure for the language of the sentence in which it is true. Model theory was originally developed for explicitly constructed, formal languages, with the purpose of studying foundational questions of mathematics, but was later applied to the semantical analysis of empirical theories, a development initiated by the Dutch philosopher Evert Beth, and of natural languages, as in Montague grammar. More recently, in *situation theory,* we find a theory of semantics in which not the concept of truth in a structure, but that of information carried by a statement about a situation, is central.

The term 'model theory' came into use in the 1930s, with the work on first-order model theory by Tarski, but some of the most central results of the field date from before that time. The history of the field is complicated by the fact that in the 1910s and 1920s, when the first model-theoretic findings were obtained, the separation between first-order logic and its extensions was not yet completed. Thus, in 1915, there appeared an article by Leopold Löwenheim, containing the first version of what is now called the Löwenheim-Skolem theorem. Löwenheim proved that every satisfiable sentence has a countable model, but he did not yet work in first-order logic as we now understand it. One of the first who did so was the Norwegian logician Thoralf Skolem, who showed in 1920 that a set of first-order sentences that has a model, has a countable model, one form of the Löwenheim-Skolem theorem. Skolem argued that logic was first-order logic and that first-order logic was the proper basis for metamathematical investigations, fully accepting the relativity of set-theoretic notions in first-order logic. Within philosophy this thesis is still dominant, but in the end it has not prevailed in mathematical logic. In 1930 Kurt Gödel solved an open problem of Hilbert-Ackermann and proved a completeness theorem for first-order logic. This immediately led to another important model-theoretic result, the *compactness theorem:* if every finite subset of a set of sentences has a model then the set has a model. A good source for information about the model theory of first-order logic, or classical model theory, is still *Model Theory* by C. C. Chang and H. J. Keisler (1973).

When the separation between first-order logic and stronger logics had been completed and the model theory of first-order logic had become a mature field, logicians undertook in the late 1950s the study of extended model theory, the model theory of extensions of first-order logic: first of cardinality quantifiers, later of infinitary languages and of fragments of second-order logic. With so many examples of logics around – where sometimes classical theorems did generalize, sometimes not – Per Lindström showed in 1969 what sets first-order logic apart from its extensions: it is the strongest logic that is both compact and satisfies the Löwenheim-Skolem theorem. This work has been the beginning of a study of the relations between various properties logics may possess, the so-called abstract model.

See also FORMAL SEMANTICS, LÖWENHEIM-SKOLEM THEOREM, SATISFACTION.

Z.G.S.

modernism. See POSTMODERN.

modest foundationalism. See FOUNDATIONALISM.

modularity, the commitment to functionally independent and specialized cognitive systems in psychological organization, or, more generally, in the organization of any complex system. Modularity entails that behavior is the product of components with subordinate functions, that these functions are realized in discrete physical systems, and that the subsystems are minimally interactive. Modular organization varies from *simple decomposability* to what Herbert Simon calls *near decomposability*. In the former, component systems are independent, operating according to intrinsically determined principles; system behavior is an additive or aggregative function of these independent contributions. In the latter, the short-run behavior of components is independent of the behavior of other components; the system behavior is a relatively simple function of component contributions.

In the early nineteenth century, Franz Joseph Gall (1758–1828) defended a modular organization for the mind/brain, holding that the cerebral hemispheres consist of a variety of organs, or centers, each subserving specific intellectual and moral functions. This picture of the brain as a collection of relatively independent organs contrasts sharply with the traditional view that intellectual activity involves the exercise of a general faculty in a variety of domains, a view that was common to Descartes and Hume as well as Gall's major opponents such as Pierre Flourens (1794–1867). By the middle of the nineteenth century, the French physicians Jean-Baptiste Bouillaud (1796–1881) and Pierre-Paul Broca (1824–80) defended the view that language is controlled by localized structures in the left hemisphere and is relatively independent of other cognitive activities. It was later discovered by Karl Wernicke (1848–1905) that there are at least two centers for the control of language, one more posterior and one more anterior. On these views, there are discrete physical structures responsible for language, which are largely independent of one another and of structures responsible for other psychological functions. This is therefore a modular organization. This view of the neurophysiological organization of language continues to have advocates into the late twentieth century, though the precise characterization of the functions these two centers serve is controversial. Many more recent views have tended to limit modularity to more peripheral functions such as vision, hearing, and motor control and speech, but have excluded so-called higher cognitive processes.

See also COGNITIVE SCIENCE, PHILOSOPHY OF MIND.   R.C.R.

modus ponendo tollens. See SYLLOGISM.

modus ponens, in full, *modus ponendo ponens* (Latin, 'proposing method'), (1) the argument form 'If *A* then *B*; *A*; therefore, *B*', and arguments of this form (compare *fallacy of affirming the consequent*); (2) the rule of inference that permits one to infer the consequent of a conditional from that conditional and its antecedent. This is also known as the *rule of ⊃-elimination* or *rule of ⊃-detachment*. See also COUNTERFACTUALS, FORMAL FALLACY.   G.F.S.

modus tollendo ponens. See SYLLOGISM.

modus tollens, in full, *modus tollendo tollens* (Latin, 'removing method'), (1) the argument form 'If *A* then *B*; not-*B*; therefore, not-*A*', and arguments of this form (compare *fallacy of denying the antecedent*); (2) the rule of inference that permits one to infer the negation of the antecedent of a conditional from that conditional and the negation of its consequent. See also COUNTERFACTUALS, FORMAL FALLACY.   G.F.S.

Mohism, a school of classical Chinese thought founded by Mo Tzu (fl. 479–438 B.C.). Mo Tzu was the first major philosopher to challenge Confucius. Whereas Confucius believed a moral life was an end in itself, Mo Tzu advocated a form of utilitarianism wherein the test of moral rightness (*yi*) was the amount of benefit (*li*) to the gods, state, and people. Accordingly, Mo Tzu condemned war as harmful, criticized Confucians for their elaborate funerals and wasteful indulgence in music, and promoted a hierarchical meritocracy dominated by a powerful ruler as the most efficient way to unify the conflicting moral views and interests of the people, and thereby achieve social order. Mo Tzu also attacked fatalism, and unlike the agnostic Confucius, firmly believed in spirits and an anthropomorphic Heaven (*t'ien*) that rewarded those who benefited others and punished those who did not. He is most famous for his doctrine of *chien ai* or impartial concern (often translated as universal love). Whereas Confucius espoused a relational morality in which one's obligations varied depending on the status of the parties and the degree of closeness, Mo Tzu insisted that each person be treated equally as an object of moral concern.

During the Warring States period (403–221 B.C.), the Mohists split into three factions. The Later Mohist Canons, most of which were written as late as the third century B.C., are characterized by analytical reasoning and logical sophistication. Later Mohists sought to provide a rational rather than a religious basis for Mo Tzu's utilitarianism based upon logical (and causal) necessity (*pi*). Treating a wide variety of subjects from politics to optics to economics, the Canons are organized around four topics: discourse, or knowledge of the relation between names and objects; ethics, or knowledge of how to act; sciences, or knowledge of objects; and argumentation, or knowledge of names. As Confucianism emerged to become the state ideology, the Mohists disappeared sometime in the early Han dynasty (206 B.C.–A.D. 220), having been in important measure co-opted by the leading interpreter of Confucianism of the period, Hsün Tzu (c.298–238 B.C.).

See also CONFUCIANISM, LI³, MO TZU, YI.
R.P.P. & R.T.A.

Mohist School. See MOHISM, MO TZU.

moksha. See MĀYĀ.

Molina, Luis de (1535–1600), Spanish Jesuit theologian and philosopher. He studied and taught at Coimbra and Évora and also taught in Lisbon and Madrid. His most important works are the *Concordia liberi arbitrii cum gratiae donis* ("Free Will and Grace," 1588), *Commentaria in primam divi Thomae partem* ("Commentary on the First Part of Thomas's *Summa*," 1592), and *De justitia et jure* ("On Justice and Law," 1592–1613).

Molina is best known for his doctrine of middle knowledge (*scientia media*). Its aim was to preserve free will while maintaining the Christian doctrine of the efficacy of divine grace. It was opposed by Thomists such as Bañez, who maintained that God exercises physical predetermination over *secondary causes* of human action and, thus, that grace is intrinsically efficacious and independent of human will and merits. For Molina, although God has foreknowledge of what human beings will choose to do, neither that knowledge nor God's grace determine human will; the cooperation (*concursus*) of divine grace with human will does not determine the will to a particular action. This is made possible by God's middle knowledge, which is a knowledge in between the knowledge God has of what existed, exists, and will exist, and the knowledge God has of what has not existed, does not exist, and will not exist. Middle knowledge is God's knowledge of conditional future contingent events, namely, of what persons would do under any possible set of circumstances. Thanks to this knowledge, God can arrange for certain human acts to occur by prearranging the circumstances surrounding the choice without determining the human will. Thus, God's grace is concurrent with the act of the will and does not predetermine it, rendering the Thomistic distinction between sufficient and efficacious grace superfluous.

See also AQUINAS, FREE WILL PROBLEM, FUTURE CONTINGENTS, MIDDLE KNOWLEDGE.
J.J.E.G.

Molyneux question, also called Molyneux's problem, the question that, in correspondence with Locke, William Molyneux (or Molineux, 1656–98), a Dublin lawyer and member of the Irish Parliament, posed and Locke inserted in the second edition of his *Essay Concerning Human Understanding* (1694; book 2, chap. 9, section 8):

> Suppose a Man born blind, and now adult, and taught by his touch to distinguish a Cube, and a Sphere of the same metal, and nighly of the same bigness, so as to tell, when he felt one and t'other, which is the Cube, which the Sphere. Suppose then the Cube and Sphere placed on a Table, and the Blind Man to be made to see. Quære, Whether by his sight, before he touch'd them, he could now distinguish, and tell, which is the Globe, which the Cube.

Although it is tempting to regard Molyneux's question as straightforwardly empirical, attempts to gauge the abilities of newly sighted adults have yielded disappointing and ambiguous results. More interesting, perhaps, is the way in which different theories of perception answer the question. Thus, according to Locke, sensory modalities constitute discrete perceptual channels, the contents of which perceivers must *learn* to correlate. Such a theory answers the question in the negative (as did Molyneux himself). Other theories encourage different responses. **See also** PERCEPTION.
J.F.H.

monad. See LEIBNIZ.

monadology. See LEIBNIZ.

monism. See PHILOSOPHY OF MIND.

monism, anomalous. See PHILOSOPHY OF MIND.

monism, neutral. See PHILOSOPHY OF MIND, RUS-
SELL.

monotonic. See NON-MONOTONIC LOGIC.

Montague grammar. See GRAMMAR.

Montaigne, Michel de (1533–92), French essayist and philosopher who set forth the Renaissance version of Greek skepticism. Born and
raised in Bordeaux, he became its mayor, and
was an adviser to leaders of the Reformation
and Counter-Reformation. In 1568 he translated
the work of the Spanish rationalist theologian
Raimund Sebond on natural theology. Shortly
thereafter he began writing *essais,* attempts, as
the author said, to paint himself. These, the first
in this genre, are rambling, curious discussions of
various topics, suggesting tolerance and an
undogmatic Stoic morality. The longest *essai,* the
"Apology for Raimund Sebond," "defends"
Sebond's rationalism by arguing that since no
adequate reasons or evidence could be given to
support any point of view in theology, philosophy, or science, one should not blame Sebond for
his views. Montaigne then presents and develops
the skeptical arguments found in Sextus Empiricus and Cicero.

Montaigne related skeptical points to then-
current findings and problems. Data of explorers,
he argues, reinforce the cultural and ethical relativism of the ancient Skeptics. Disagreements
between Scholastics, Platonists, and Renaissance
naturalists on almost everything cast doubt on
whether any theory is correct. Scientists like
Copernicus and Paracelsus contradict previous
scientists, and will probably be contradicted by
future ones. Montaigne then offers the more theoretical objections of the Skeptics, about the
unreliability of sense experience and reasoning
and our inability to find an unquestionable criterion of true knowledge. Trying to know reality is
like trying to clutch water. What should we then
do? Montaigne advocates suspending judgment
on all theories that go beyond experience,
accepting experience undogmatically, living according to the dictates of nature, and following
the rules and customs of one's society. Therefore
one should remain in the religion in which one
was born, and accept only those principles that
God chooses to reveal to us.

Montaigne's skepticism greatly influenced
European thinkers in undermining confidence in
previous theories and forcing them to seek new
ways of grounding knowledge. His acceptance of
religion on custom and faith provided a way of
living with total skepticism. His presentation of
skepticism in a modern language shaped the
vocabulary and the problems of philosophy in
modern times.

See also SKEPTICISM, SKEPTICS.   R.H.P.

Montanism, a charismatic, schismatic movement
in early Christianity, originating in Phrygia in the
late second century. It rebuked the mainstream
church for laxity and apathy, and taught moral
purity, new, i.e. postbiblical, revelation, and the
imminent end of the world. Traditional accounts,
deriving from critics of the movement, contain
exaggerations and probably some fabrications.
Montanus himself, abetted by the prophetesses
Maximilla and Prisca, announced in ecstatic
speech a new, final age of prophecy. This fulfilled
the biblical promises that in the last days the Holy
Spirit would be poured out universally (Joel 2:
28ff.; Acts 2: 16ff.) and would teach "the whole
truth" (Jon. 14:26; 16:13). It also empowered the
Montanists to enjoin more rigorous discipline
than that required by Jesus. The sect denied that
forgiveness through baptism covered serious
subsequent sin; forbade remarriage for widows
and widowers; practiced fasting; and condemned
believers who evaded persecution. Some later
followers may have identified Montanus with
the Holy Spirit itself, though he claimed only to
be the Spirit's mouthpiece. The "new prophecy"
flourished for a generation, especially in North
Africa, gaining a famous convert in Tertullian.
But the church's bishops repudiated the movement's criticisms and innovations, and turned
more resolutely against postapostolic revelation,
apocalyptic expectation, and ascetic extremes.

A.E.L.

Montanus. See MONTANISM.

Monte Carlo fallacy. See GAMBLER'S FALLACY.

Montesquieu, Baron de La Brède et de, title of
Charles-Louis de Secondat (1689–1755), French
political philosopher, the political *philosophe* of
the Enlightenment. He was born at La Brède,
educated at the Oratorian Collège de Juilly
(1700–05), and received law degrees from the
University of Bordeaux (1708). From his uncle
he inherited the barony of Montesquieu (1716)
and the office of Président à Mortier at the Parliament of Guyenne at Bordeaux. Fame, national

and international, came suddenly (1721) with the *Lettres persanes* ("The Persian Letters"), published in Holland and France, a landmark of the Enlightenment. His *Réflexions sur la monarchie universelle en Europe,* written and printed (1734) to remind the authorities of his qualifications and availability, delivered the wrong message at the wrong time (anti-militarism, pacifism, free trade, while France supported Poland's King Stanislas, dethroned by Russia and Austria). Montesquieu withdrew the *Réflexions* before publication and substituted the *Considerations on the Romans:* the same thesis is expounded here, but in the exclusively classical context of ancient history. The stratagem succeeded: the Amsterdam edition was freely imported; the Paris edition appeared with a royal *privilège* (1734).

A few months after the appearance of the *Considerations,* he undertook *L'Esprit des lois,* the outline of a modern political science, conceived as the foundation of an effective governmental policy. His optimism was shaken by the disasters of the War of Austrian Succession (1740–48); the *Esprit des lois* underwent hurried changes that upset its original plan. During the very printing process, the author was discovering the true essence of his *philosophie pratique:* it would never culminate in a final, invariable program, but in an orientation, continuously, intelligently adapting to the unpredictable circumstances of historical time in the light of permanent values.

According to *L'Esprit des lois,* governments are either republics, monarchies, or despotisms. The principles, or motivational forces, of these types of government are, respectively, political virtue, honor, and fear. The type of government a people has depends on its character, history, and geographical situation. Only a constitutional government that separates its executive, legislative, and judicial powers preserves political liberty, taken as the power to do what one ought to will. A constitutional monarchy with separation of powers is the best form of government. Montesquieu influenced the authors of the U.S. Constitution and the political philosophers Burke and Rousseau.

See also BURKE, ENCYCLOPEDIA, POLITICAL PHILOSOPHY, ROUSSEAU.   C.J.B.

mood. See SYLLOGISM.

Moore, G(eorge) E(dward) (1873–1958), English philosopher who spearheaded the attack on idealism and was a major supporter of realism in all its forms: metaphysical, epistemological, and axiological. He was born in Upper Norwood, a sub-

urb of London; did his undergraduate work at Cambridge University; spent 1898–1904 as a fellow of Trinity College; returned to Cambridge in 1911 as a lecturer; and was granted a professorship there in 1925. He also served as editor of *Mind.*

The bulk of his work falls into four categories: metaphysics, epistemology, ethics, and philosophical methodology.

Metaphysics. In this area, Moore is mainly known for his attempted refutation of idealism and his defense thereby of realism. In his "The Refutation of Idealism" (1903), he argued that there is a crucial premise that is essential to *all* possible arguments for the idealistic conclusion that "All reality is mental (spiritual)." This premise is: "To be *is* to be perceived" (in the broad sense of 'perceive'). Moore argued that, under every possible interpretation of it, that premise is either a tautology or false; hence no significant conclusion can ever be inferred from it. His positive defense of realism had several prongs. One was to show that there are certain claims held by non-realist philosophers, both idealist ones and skeptical ones. Moore argued, in "A Defense of Common Sense" (1925), that these claims are either factually false or self-contradictory, or that in some cases there is no good reason to believe them. Among the claims that Moore attacked are these: "Propositions about (purported) material facts are false"; "No one has ever known any such propositions to be true"; "Every (purported) physical fact is logically dependent on some mental fact"; and "Every physical fact is causally dependent on some mental fact." Another major prong of Moore's defense of realism was to argue for the existence of an external world and later to give a "Proof of an External World" (1933).

Epistemology. Most of Moore's work in this area dealt with the various kinds of knowledge we have, why they must be distinguished, and the problem of perception and our knowledge of an external world. Because he had already argued for the existence of an external world in his metaphysics, he here focused on *how* we know it. In many papers and chapters (e.g., "The Nature and Reality of Objects of Perception," 1906) he examined and at times supported three main positions: naive or direct realism, representative or indirect realism, and phenomenalism. Although he seemed to favor direct realism at first, in the majority of his papers he found representative realism to be the most supportable position despite its problems. It should also be noted that, in connection with his leanings toward representative realism, Moore maintained the existence of sense-data and argued at length for an account of just how they are related to physical objects. That there are sense-data Moore never doubted. The question was, What is their (ontological) status?

With regard to the various kinds of knowledge (or ways of knowing), Moore made a distinction between dispositional (or non-actualized) and actualized knowledge. Within the latter Moore made distinctions between direct apprehension (often known as knowledge by acquaintance), indirect apprehension, and knowledge proper (or propositional knowledge). He devoted much of his work to finding the conditions for knowledge proper.

Ethics. In his major work in ethics, *Principia Ethica* (1903), Moore maintained that the central problem of ethics is, What is good? – meaning by this, not what things are good, but how 'good' is to be defined. He argued that there can be only one answer, one that may seem disappointing, namely: good is good, or, alternatively, 'good' is indefinable. Thus 'good' denotes a "unique, simple object of thought" that is indefinable and unanalyzable. His first argument on behalf of that claim consisted in showing that to identify good with some other object (i.e., to define 'good') is to commit the naturalistic fallacy. To commit this fallacy is to reduce ethical propositions to either psychological propositions or reportive definitions as to how people use words. In other words, what was meant to be an ethical proposition, that *X* is good, becomes a factual proposition about people's desires or their usage of words. Moore's second argument ran like this: Suppose 'good' were definable. Then the result would be even worse than that of reducing ethical propositions to non-ethical propositions – ethical propositions would be tautologies! For example, suppose you defined 'good' as 'pleasure'. Then suppose you maintained that pleasure is good. All you would be asserting is that pleasure is pleasure, a tautology. To avoid this conclusion 'good' *must* mean something other than 'pleasure'. Why is this the *naturalistic* fallacy? Because good is a non-natural property. But even if it were a natural one, there would still be a fallacy. Hence some have proposed calling it the *definist fallacy* – the fallacy of attempting to define 'good' by any means. This argument is often known as the open question argument because whatever purported definition of 'good' anyone offers, it would always be an open question whether whatever satisfies the definition

really is good. In the last part of *Principia Ethica* Moore turned to a discussion of what sorts of things are the greatest goods with which we are acquainted. He argued for the view that they are personal affection and aesthetic enjoyments.

Philosophical methodology. Moore's methodology in philosophy had many components, but two stand out: his appeal to and defense of common sense and his utilization of various methods of (philosophical/conceptual) analysis. "A Defense of Common Sense" argued for his claim that the commonsense view of the world is wholly true, and for the claim that any view which opposed that view is either factually false or self-contradictory. Throughout his writings Moore distinguished several kinds of analysis and made use of them extensively in dealing with philosophical problems. All of these may be found in the works cited above and other essays gathered into Moore's *Philosophical Studies* (1922) and *Philosophical Papers* (1959). These have been referred to as refutational analysis, with two subforms, showing contradictions and "translation into the concrete"; distinctional analysis; decompositional analysis (either definitional or divisional); and reductional analysis.

Moore was greatly revered as a teacher. Many of his students and colleagues have paid high tribute to him in very warm and grateful terms.

See also ANALYSIS, DEFINITION, EPISTEMOLOGY, ETHICS, MALCOLM, NATURALISM.

E.D.K.

Moore's paradox, as first discussed by G. E. Moore, the perplexity involving assertion of what is expressed by conjunctions such as 'It's raining, but I believe it isn't' and 'It's raining, but I don't believe it is'. The oddity of such present-tense first-person uses of 'to believe' seems peculiar to those conjunctions just because it is assumed both that, when asserting – roughly, representing as true – a conjunction, one also asserts its conjuncts, and that, *as a rule*, the assertor *believes* the asserted proposition. Thus, no perplexity arises from assertions of, for instance, 'It's raining today, but I (falsely) *believed* it wasn't until I came out to the porch' and 'If it's raining but I believe it isn't, I have been misled by the weather report'. However, there are reasons to think that, if we rely only on these assumptions and examples, our characterization of the problem is unduly narrow. First, assertion seems relevant only because we are interested in what the assertor *believes*. Secondly, those conjunctions are disturbing only insofar as they show that some of the assertor's beliefs, *though contingent, can only be irrationally held.* Thirdly, autobiographical reports that may justifiably be used to charge the reporter with irrationality need be neither about his belief system, nor conjunctive, nor true (e.g., 'I don't exist', 'I have no beliefs'), nor false (e.g., 'It's raining, but I have no evidence that it is'). So, Moore's paradox is best seen as the problem posed by *contingent* propositions that cannot be justifiably believed. Arguably, in forming a belief of those propositions, the believer acquires *non-overridable evidence* against believing them. A successful analysis of the problem along these lines may have important epistemological consequences. **See also** CONTINGENT, EPISTEMOLOGY, EVIDENCE, JUSTIFICATION, MOORE, PARADOX, PROPOSITION, RATIONALITY, REASONS FOR BELIEF.   C.d.A.

moral argument for God's existence. See PHILOSOPHY OF RELIGION.

moral certainty. See CERTAINTY.

moral dilemma. (1) Any problem where morality is relevant. This broad use includes not only conflicts among moral reasons but also conflicts between moral reasons and reasons of law, religion, or self-interest. In this sense, Abraham is in a moral dilemma when God commands him to sacrifice his son, even if he has no moral reason to obey. Similarly, I am in a moral dilemma if I cannot help a friend in trouble without forgoing a lucrative but morally neutral business opportunity.

'Moral dilemma' also often refers to (2) any topic area where it is not *known* what, if anything, is morally good or right. For example, when one asks whether abortion is immoral in any way, one could call the topic "the moral dilemma of abortion." This epistemic use does not imply that anything really is immoral at all.

Recently, moral philosophers have discussed a much narrower set of situations as "moral dilemmas." They usually define 'moral dilemma' as (3) a situation where an agent morally *ought* to do each of two acts but cannot do both. The best-known example is Sartre's student who morally ought to care for his mother in Paris but at the same time morally ought to go to England to join the Free French and fight the Nazis.

However, 'ought' covers ideal actions that are not morally required, such as when someone ought to give to a certain charity but is not required to do so. Since most common examples of moral dilemmas include moral obligations or

duties, or other requirements, it is more accurate to define 'moral dilemma' more narrowly as (4) a situation where an agent has a moral *requirement* to do each of two acts but cannot do both.

Some philosophers also refuse to call a situation a moral dilemma when one of the conflicting requirements is clearly overridden, such as when I must break a trivial promise in order to save a life. To exclude such resolvable conflicts, 'moral dilemma' can be defined as (5) a situation where an agent has a moral requirement to adopt each of two alternatives, and *neither* requirement is *overridden,* but the agent cannot fulfill both.

Another common move is to define 'moral dilemma' as (6) a situation where every alternative is morally *wrong.* This is equivalent to (4) or (5), respectively, if an act is morally wrong whenever it violates any moral requirement or any non-overridden moral requirement. However, we usually do not call an act wrong unless it violates an overriding moral requirement, and then (6) rules out moral dilemmas by definition, since overriding moral requirements clearly cannot conflict.

Although (5) thus seems preferable, some would object that (5) includes trivial requirements and conflicts, such as conflicts between trivial promises. To include only tragic situations, we could define 'moral dilemma' as (7) a situation where an agent has a *strong* moral obligation or requirement to adopt each of two alternatives, and neither is overridden, but the agent cannot adopt both alternatives. This definition is strong enough to raise the important controversies about moral dilemmas without being so strong as to rule out their possibility by definition.

See also DEONTIC LOGIC, DUTY, ETHICS.
    W.S.-A.

moral epistemology, the discipline, at the intersection of ethics and epistemology, that studies the epistemic status and relations of moral judgments and principles. It has developed out of an interest, common to both ethics and epistemology, in questions of justification and justifiability – in epistemology, of statements or beliefs, and in ethics, of actions as well as judgments of actions and also general principles of judgment. Its most prominent questions include the following. Can normative claims be true or false? If so, how can they be known to be true or false? If not, what status do they have, and are they capable of justification? If they are capable of justification, how can they be justified? Does the justification of normative claims differ with respect to particular claims and with respect to general principles?

In epistemology recent years have seen a tendency to accept as valid an account of knowledge as entailing justified true belief, a conception that requires an account not just of truth but also of justification and of justified belief. Thus, under what conditions is someone justified, epistemically, in believing something? Justification, of actions, of judgments, and of principles, has long been a central element in ethics. It is only recently that justification in ethics came to be thought of as an epistemological problem, hence 'moral epistemology', as an expression, is a fairly recent coinage, although its problems have a long lineage.

One long-standing linkage is provided by the challenge of skepticism. Skepticism in ethics can be about the existence of any genuine distinction between right and wrong, or it can focus on the possibility of attaining any knowledge of right and wrong, good or bad. Is there a right answer? is a question in the metaphysics of ethics. Can we know what the right answer is, and if so how? is one of moral epistemology. Problems of perception and observation and ones about observation statements or sense-data play an important role in epistemology. There is not any obvious parallel in moral epistemology, unless it is the role of prereflective moral judgments, or commonsense moral judgments – moral judgments unguided by any overt moral theory – which can be taken to provide the data of moral theory, and which need to be explained, systematized, coordinated, or revised to attain an appropriate relation between theory and data. This would be analogous to taking the data of epistemology to be provided, not by sense-data or observations but by judgments of perception or observation statements. Once this step is taken the parallel is very close. One source of moral skepticism is the apparent lack of any observational counterpart for moral predicates, which generates the question how moral judgments can be true if there is nothing for them to correspond to. Another source of moral skepticism is apparently constant disagreement and uncertainty, which would appear to be explained by the skeptical hypothesis denying the reality of moral distinctions. Noncognitivism in ethics maintains that moral judgments are not objects of knowledge, that they make no statements capable of truth or falsity, but are or are akin to expressions of attitudes.

Some other major differences among ethical theories are largely epistemological in character. Intuitionism maintains that basic moral propositions are knowable by intuition. Empiricism in ethics maintains that moral propositions can be established by empirical means or are complex forms of empirical statements. Ethical rationalism maintains that the fundamental principle(s) of morality can be established a priori as holding of necessity. This is exemplified by Kant's moral philosophy, in which the categorical imperative is regarded as synthetic a priori; more recently by what Alan Gewirth (b.1912) calls the "principle of generic consistency," which he claims it is self-contradictory to deny. Ethical empiricism is exemplified by classical utilitarianism, such as that of Bentham, which aspires to develop ethics as an empirical science. If the consequences of actions can be scientifically predicted and their utilities calculated, then ethics can be a science. Situationism is equivalent to concrete case intuitionism in maintaining that we can know immediately what ought to be done in specific cases, but most ethical theories maintain that what ought to be done is, in J. S. Mill's words, determined by "the application of a law to an individual case." Different theories differ on the epistemic status of these laws and on the process of application. Deductivists, either empiricistic or rationalistic, hold that the law is essentially unchanged in the application; non-deductivists hold that the law is modified in the process of application. (This distinction is explained in F. L. Will [1909–98], *Beyond Deduction*, 1988.) There is similar variation about what if anything is self-evident, Sidgwick maintaining that only certain highly abstract principles are self-evident, Ross that only general rules are, and Prichard that only concrete judgments are, "by an act of moral thinking."

Other problems in moral epistemology are provided by the fact–value distinction – and controversies about whether there is any such distinction – and the is–ought question, the question how a moral judgment can be derived from statements of fact alone. Naturalists affirm the possibility, non-naturalists deny it. Prescriptivists claim that moral judgments are prescriptions and cannot be deduced from descriptive statements alone. This question ultimately leads to the question how an ultimate principle can be justified. If it cannot be deduced from statements of fact, that route is out; if it must be deduced from some other moral principle, then the principle deduced cannot be ultimate and in any case this process is either circular or leads to an infinite regress. If the ultimate principle is self-evident, then the problem may have an answer. But if it is not it would appear to be arbitrary. The problem of the justification of an ultimate principle continues to be a leading one in moral epistemology.

Recently there has been much interest in the status and existence of "moral facts." Are there any, what are they, and how are they established as "facts"? This relates to questions about moral realism. Moral realism maintains that moral predicates are real and can be known to be so; anti-realists deny this. This denial links with the view that moral properties supervene on natural ones, and the problem of supervenience is another recent link between ethics and epistemology.

Pragmatism in ethics maintains that a moral problem is like any problem in that it is the occasion for inquiry and moral judgments are to be regarded as hypotheses to be tested by how well they resolve the problem. This amounts to an attempt to bypass the is–ought problem and all such "dualisms." So is constructivism, a development owing much to the work of Rawls, which contrasts with moral realism. Constructivism maintains that moral ideas are human constructs and the task is not epistemological or metaphysical but practical and theoretical – that of attaining reflective equilibrium between considered moral judgments and the principles that coordinate and explain them. On this view there are no moral facts. Opponents maintain that this only replaces a foundationalist view of ethics with a coherence conception.

The question whether questions of moral epistemology can in this way be bypassed can be regarded as itself a question of moral epistemology. And the question of the foundations of morality, and whether there are foundations, can still be regarded as a question of moral epistemology, as distinct from a question of the most convenient and efficient arrangement of our moral ideas.

See also ETHICAL CONSTRUCTIVISM, ETHICS, INTUITION, MORAL REALISM, REFLECTIVE EQUILIBRIUM.   M.G.S.

moral evil. See PHILOSOPHY OF RELIGION.

morality, an informal public system applying to all rational persons, governing behavior that affects others, having the lessening of evil or harm as its goal, and including what are commonly known as the moral rules, moral ideals, and moral virtues. To say that it is a public sys-tem means that all those to whom it applies must understand it and that it must not be irrational for them to use it in deciding what to do and in judging others to whom the system applies. Games are the paradigm cases of public systems; all games have a point and the rules of a game apply to all who play it. All players know the point of the game and its rules, and it is not irrational for them to be guided by the point and rules and to judge the behavior of other players by them.

To say that morality is informal means that there is no decision procedure or authority that can settle all its controversial questions. Morality thus resembles a backyard game of basketball more than a professional game. Although there is overwhelming agreement on most moral matters, certain controversial questions must be settled in an ad hoc fashion or not settled at all. For example, when, if ever, abortion is acceptable is an unresolvable moral matter, but each society and religion can adopt its own position. That morality has no one in a position of authority is one of the most important respects in which it differs from law and religion.

Although morality must include the commonly accepted moral rules such as those prohibiting killing and deceiving, different societies can interpret these rules somewhat differently. They can also differ in their views about the scope of morality, i.e., about whether morality protects newborns, fetuses, or non-human animals. Thus different societies can have somewhat different moralities, although this difference has limits. Also within each society, a person may have his own view about when it is justified to break one of the rules, e.g., about how much harm would have to be prevented in order to justify deceiving someone. Thus one person's morality may differ somewhat from another's, but both will agree on the overwhelming number of non-controversial cases.

A moral theory is an attempt to describe, explain, and if possible justify, morality. Unfortunately, most moral theories attempt to generate some simplified moral code, rather than to describe the complex moral system that is already in use. Morality does not resolve all disputes. Morality does not require one always to act so as to produce the best consequences or to act only in those ways that one would will everyone to act. Rather morality includes both moral rules that no one should transgress and moral ideals that all are encouraged to follow, but much of what one does will not be governed by morality.

See also APPLIED ETHICS, ETHICS, JUSTICE, MORALITY, UTILITARIANISM.   B.Ge.

morality, slave. See NIETZSCHE.

moral patient. See MORAL STATUS.

moral point of view. See ETHICS.

moral psychology, (1) the subfield of psychology that traces the development over time of moral reasoning and opinions in the lives of individuals (this subdiscipline includes work of Jean Piaget, Lawrence Kohlberg, and Carol Gilligan); (2) the part of philosophy where philosophy of mind and ethics overlap, which concerns all the psychological issues relevant to morality. There are many different psychological matters relevant to ethics, and each may be relevant in more than one way. Different ethical theories imply different sorts of connections. So moral psychology includes work of many and diverse kinds. But several traditional clusters of concern are evident.

Some elements of moral psychology consider the psychological matters relevant to metaethical issues, i.e., to issues about the general nature of moral truth, judgment, and knowledge. Different metaethical theories invoke mental phenomena in different ways: noncognitivism maintains that sentences expressing moral judgments do not function to report truths or falsehoods, but rather, e.g., to express certain emotions or to prescribe certain actions. So some forms of noncognitivism imply that an understanding of certain sorts of emotions, or of special activities like prescribing that may involve particular psychological elements, is crucial to a full understanding of how ethical sentences are meaningful. Certain forms of cognitivism, the view that moral (declarative) sentences do express truths or falsehoods, imply that moral facts consist of psychological facts, that for instance moral judgments consist of expressions of positive psychological attitudes of some particular kind toward the objects of those judgments. And an understanding of psychological phenomena like sentiment is crucial according to certain sorts of *projectivism,* which hold that the supposed moral properties of things are mere misleading projections of our sentiments onto the objects of those sentiments. Certain traditional moral sense theories and certain traditional forms of intuitionism have held that special psychological faculties are crucial for our epistemic access to moral truth.

Particular views in normative ethics, particular views about the moral status of acts, persons, and other targets of normative evaluation, also often suggest that an understanding of certain psychological matters is crucial to ethics. Actions, intentions, and character are some of the targets of evaluation of normative ethics, and their proper understanding involves many issues in philosophy of mind. Also, many normative theorists have maintained that there is a close connection between pleasure, happiness, or desire-satisfaction and a person's good, and these things are also a concern of philosophy of mind. In addition, the rightness of actions is often held to be closely connected to the motives, beliefs, and other psychological phenomena that lie behind those actions.

Various other traditional philosophical concerns link ethical and psychological issues: the nature of the patterns in the long-term development in individuals of moral opinions and reasoning, the appropriate form for moral education and punishment, the connections between obligation and motivation, i.e., between moral reasons and psychological causes, and the notion of free will and its relation to moral responsibility and autonomy. Some work in philosophy of mind also suggests that moral phenomena, or at least normative phenomena of some kind, play a crucial role in illuminating or constituting psychological phenomena of various kinds, but the traditional concern of moral psychology has been with the articulation of the sort of philosophy of mind that can be useful to ethics.

See also AKRASIA, ETHICS, PRACTICAL REASONING, SELF-DECEPTION.   J.R.M.

moral rationalism, the view that the substance of morality, usually in the form of general moral principles, can be known a priori. The view is defended by Kant in *Groundwork of the Metaphysic of Morals,* but it goes back at least to Plato. Both Plato and Kant thought that a priori moral knowledge could have an impact on what we do quite independently of any desire that we happen to have. This motivational view is also ordinarily associated with moral rationalism. It comes in two quite different forms. The first is that a priori moral knowledge consists in a sui generis mental state that is both belief-like and desire-like. This seems to have been Plato's view, for he held that the belief that something is good is itself a disposition to promote that thing. The second is that a priori moral knowledge consists in a belief that is capable of rationally producing a distinct desire.

Rationalists who make the first claim have had trouble accommodating the possibility of someone's believing that something is good but, through weakness of will, not mustering the desire to do it. Accordingly, they have been forced to assimilate weakness of will to ignorance of the good. Rationalists who make the second claim about reason's action-producing capacity face no such problem. For this reason, their view is often preferred. The best-known anti-rationalist about morality is Hume. His *Treatise of Human Nature* denies both that morality's substance can be known by reason alone and that reason alone is capable of producing action.

See also AKRASIA, ETHICS, HUME, KANT, MORAL SENSE THEORY, MOTIVATIONAL INTERNALISM, RATIONALISM.   M.Sm.

moral realism, a metaethical view committed to the objectivity of ethics. It has (1) metaphysical, (2) semantic, and (3) epistemological components.

(1) Its metaphysical component is the claim that there are moral facts and moral properties whose existence and nature are independent of people's beliefs and attitudes about what is right or wrong. In this claim, moral realism contrasts with an error theory and with other forms of nihilism that deny the existence of moral facts and properties. It contrasts as well with various versions of moral relativism and other forms of ethical constructivism that make moral facts consist in facts about people's moral beliefs and attitudes.

(2) Its semantic component is primarily cognitivist. Cognitivism holds that moral judgments should be construed as assertions about the moral properties of actions, persons, policies, and other objects of moral assessment, that moral predicates purport to refer to properties of such objects, that moral judgments (or the propositions that they express) can be true or false, and that cognizers can have the cognitive attitude of belief toward the propositions that moral judgments express. These cognitivist claims contrast with the noncognitive claims of emotivism and prescriptivism, according to which the primary purpose of moral judgments is to express the appraiser's attitudes or commitments, rather than to state facts or ascribe properties. Moral realism also holds that truth for moral judgments is non-epistemic; in this way it contrasts with moral relativism and other forms of ethical constructivism that make the truth of a moral judgment epistemic.

The metaphysical and semantic theses imply that there are some true moral propositions. An error theory accepts the cognitivist semantic claims but denies the realist metaphysical thesis. It holds that moral judgments should be construed as containing referring expressions and having truth-values, but insists that these referring expressions are empty, because there are no moral facts, and that no moral claims are true. Also on this theory, commonsense moral thought presupposes the existence of moral facts and properties, but is systematically in error. In this way, the error theory stands to moral realism much as atheism stands to theism in a world of theists. (J. L. Mackie introduced and defended the error theory in his *Ethics: Inventing Right and Wrong,* 1977.)

(3) Finally, if moral realism is to avoid skepticism it must claim that some moral beliefs are true, that there are methods for justifying moral beliefs, and that moral knowledge is possible.

While making these metaphysical, semantic, and epistemological claims, moral realism is compatible with a wide variety of other metaphysical, semantic, and epistemological principles and so can take many different forms. The moral realists in the early part of the twentieth century were generally intuitionists. Intuitionism combined a commitment to moral realism with a foundationalist moral epistemology according to which moral knowledge must rest on self-evident moral truths and with the non-naturalist claim that moral facts and properties are *sui generis* and not reducible to any natural facts or properties. Friends of noncognitivism found the metaphysical and epistemological commitments of intuitionism extravagant and so rejected moral realism. Later moral realists have generally sought to defend moral realism without the metaphysical and epistemological trappings of intuitionism. One such version of moral realism takes a naturalistic form. This form of ethical naturalism claims that our moral beliefs are justified when they form part of an explanatorily coherent system of beliefs with one another and with various non-moral beliefs, and insists that moral properties are just natural properties of the people, actions, and policies that instantiate them. Debate between realists and anti-realists and within the realist camp centers on such issues as the relation between moral judgment and action, the rational authority of morality, moral epistemology and methodology, the relation between moral and non-moral natural properties, the place of ethics in a naturalistic worldview, and the parity of ethics and the sciences.

See also EMOTIVISM, ETHICAL CONSTRUC-TIVISM, ETHICAL OBJECTIVISM, ETHICS, NATU-RALISM.   D.O.B.

Moral Rearmament Movement. See BUCHMAN-ISM.

moral sense theory, an ethical theory, developed by eighteenth-century British philosophers – notably Shaftesbury, Hutcheson, and Hume – according to which the pleasure or pain a person feels upon thinking about (or "observing") certain character traits is indicative of the virtue or vice, respectively, of those features. It is a theory of "moral perception," offered in response to moral rationalism, the view that moral distinctions are derived by reason alone, and combines Locke's empiricist doctrine that all ideas begin in experience with the belief, widely shared at the time, that feelings play a central role in moral evaluation and motivation. On this theory, our emotional responses to persons' characters are often "perceptions" of their morality, just as our experiences of an apple's redness and sweetness are perceptions of its color and taste. These ideas of morality are seen as products of an "internal" sense, because they are produced in the "observer" only after she forms a concept of the conduct or trait being observed (or contemplated) – as when a person realizes that she is seeing someone intentionally harm another and reacts with displeasure at what she sees. The moral sense is conceived as being analogous to, or possibly an aspect of, our capacity to recognize varying degrees of beauty in things, which modern writers call "the sense of beauty."

Rejecting the popular view that morality is based on the will of God, Shaftesbury maintains rather that morality depends on human nature, and he introduces the notion of a sense of right and wrong, possessed uniquely by human beings, who alone are capable of reflection. Hutcheson argues that to approve of a character is to regard it as virtuous. For him, reason, which discovers relations of inanimate objects to rational agents, is unable to arouse our approval in the absence of a moral sense. Ultimately, we can explain why, for example, we approve of someone's temperate character only by appealing to our natural tendency to feel pleasure (sometimes identified with approval) at the thought of characters that exhibit benevolence, the trait to which all other virtues can be traced. This dispo-

sition to feel approval (and disapproval) is what Hutcheson identifies as the moral sense.

Hume emphasizes that typical human beings make moral distinctions on the basis of their feelings only when those sentiments are experienced from a disinterested or "general" point of view. In other words, we turn our initial sentiments into moral judgments by compensating for the fact that we feel more strongly about those to whom we are emotionally close than those from whom we are more distant. On a widely held interpretation of Hume, the moral sense provides not only judgments, but also motives to act according to those judgments, since its feelings may be motivating passions or arouse such passions.

Roderick Firth's (1917–87) twentieth-century ideal observer theory, according to which moral good is designated by the projected reactions of a hypothetically omniscient, disinterested observer possessing other ideal traits, as well as Brandt's contemporary moral spectator theory, are direct descendants of the moral sense theory.

See also BUTLER, HUME, HUTCHESON, SHAFTESBURY.   E.S.R.

moral skepticism, any metaethical view that raises fundamental doubts about morality as a whole. Different kinds of doubts lead to different kinds of moral skepticism.

The primary kinds of moral skepticism are epistemological. *Moral justification skepticism* is the claim that nobody ever has (any or adequate) justification for believing any substantive moral claim. *Moral knowledge skepticism* is the claim that nobody ever knows that any substantive moral claim is true. If knowledge implies justification, as is often assumed, then moral justification skepticism implies moral knowledge skepticism. But even if knowledge requires justification, it requires more, so moral knowledge skepticism does not imply moral justification skepticism.

Another kind of skeptical view in metaethics rests on linguistic analysis. Some emotivists, expressivists, and prescriptivists argue that moral claims (like "Cheating is morally wrong") resemble expressions of emotion or desire (like "Boo, cheating") or prescriptions for action (like "Don't cheat"), which are neither true nor false, so moral claims themselves are neither true nor false. This *linguistic moral skepticism,* which is sometimes called noncognitivism, implies moral knowledge skepticism if knowledge implies truth.

Even if such linguistic analyses are rejected,

one can still hold that no moral properties or facts really exist. This *ontological moral skepticism* can be combined with the linguistic view that moral claims assert moral properties and facts to yield an error theory that all positive moral claims are false.

A different kind of doubt about morality is often raised by asking, "Why should I be moral?" *Practical moral skepticism* answers that there is not always any reason or any adequate reason to be moral or to do what is morally required. This view concerns reasons to act rather than reasons to believe.

Moral skepticism of all these kinds is often seen as immoral, but moral skeptics can act and be motivated and even hold moral beliefs in much the same way as non-skeptics. Moral skeptics just deny that their or anyone else's moral beliefs are justified or known or true, or that they have adequate reason to be moral.

See also EMOTIVISM, ETHICS, JUSTIFICA-TION, MORAL EPISTEMOLOGY, PRESCRIP-TIVISM, SKEPTICISM.   W.S.-A.

moral status, the suitability of a being to be viewed as an appropriate object of direct moral concern; the nature or degree of a being's ability to count as a ground of claims against moral agents; the moral standing, rank, or importance of a (kind of) being; the condition of being a moral patient; moral considerability.

Ordinary moral reflection involves considering others. But *which* others ought to be considered? And how are the various objects of moral consideration to be weighed against one another? Anything might be the topic of moral discussion, but not everything is thought to be an appropriate object of *direct* moral concern. If there are any ethical constraints on how we may treat a ceramic plate, these seem to derive from considerations about other beings, not from the interests or good or nature of the plate. The same applies, presumably, to a clod of earth. Many philosophers view a living but insentient being, such as a dandelion, in the same way; others have doubts. According to some, even sentient animal life is little more deserving of moral consideration than the clod or the dandelion. This tradition, which restricts significant moral status to humans, has come under vigorous and varied attack by defenders of animal liberation. This attack criticizes speciesism, and argues that "humanism" is analogous to theories that illegitimately base moral status on race, gender, or social class.

Some philosophers have referred to beings that *are* appropriate objects of direct moral concern as "moral patients." Moral *agents* are those beings whose actions are subject to moral evaluation; analogously, moral *patients* would be those beings whose suffering (in the sense of being the objects of the actions of moral agents) permits or demands moral evaluation. Others apply the label 'moral patients' more narrowly, just to those beings that are appropriate objects of direct moral concern but are *not* (also) moral agents.

The issue of moral status concerns not only whether beings count *at all* morally, but also to what degree they count. After all, beings who are moral patients might still have their claims outweighed by the preferred claims of other beings who possess some *special* moral status. We might, with Nozick, propose "utilitarianism for animals, Kantianism for people." Similarly, the bodily autonomy argument in defense of abortion, made famous by Thomson, does not deny that the fetus is a moral patient, but insists that her/his/its claims are limited by the pregnant woman's prior claim to control her bodily destiny.

It has often been thought that moral status should be tied to the condition of "personhood." The idea has been either that *only persons* are moral patients, or that persons possess a *special moral status* that makes them (morally) more important than nonpersons. Personhood, on such theories, is a minimal condition for moral patiency. Why? Moral patiency is said to be "correlative" with moral agency: a creature has both or neither. Alternatively, persons have been viewed not as the only moral patients, but as a specially privileged elite among moral patients, possessing *rights* as well as interests.

See also ETHICS, KANT, PERSONAL IDEN-TITY, PERSONHOOD, RIGHTS.   E.J.

moral subjectivism. See ETHICS.

More, Henry (1614–87), English philosopher, theologian, and poet, the most prolific of the Cambridge Platonists. In 1631 he entered Christ's College, where he spent the rest of his life after becoming Fellow in 1641. He was primarily an apologist of anti-Calvinist, latitudinarian stamp whose inalienable philosophico- theological purpose was to demonstrate the existence and immortality of the soul and to cure "two enormous distempers of the mind," atheism and "enthusiasm." He described himself as "a Fisher for Philosophers, desirous to draw them to or retain them in the Christian Faith." His eclectic method deployed Neoplatonism (notably Plotinus and Ficino), mystical theologies, cabalistic doctrines (as More misconceived them), empirical findings (including reports of witchcraft and ghosts), the new science, and the new philosophy, notably the philosophy of Descartes. Yet he rejected Descartes's beast-machine doctrine, his version of dualism, and the pretensions of Cartesian mechanical philosophy to explain all physical phenomena. Animals have souls; the universe is alive with souls. Body and spirit are spatially extended, the former being essentially impenetrable, inert, and *discerpible* (divisible into parts), the latter essentially penetrable, *indiscerpible*, active, and capable of a spiritual density, which More called essential *spissitude*, "the redoubling or contracting of substance into less space than it does sometimes occupy." Physical processes are activated and ordered by the *spirit of nature*, a *hylarchic principle* and "the vicarious power of God upon this great *automaton*, the world." More's writings on natural philosophy, especially his doctrine of infinite space, are thought to have influenced Newton. More attacked Hobbes's materialism and, in the 1660s and 1670s, the impieties of Dutch Cartesianism, including the perceived atheism of Spinoza and his circle. He regretted the "enthusiasm" for and conversion to Quakerism of Anne Conway, his "extramural" tutee and assiduous correspondent.

More had a partiality for coinages and linguistic exotica. We owe to him 'Cartesianism' (1662), coined a few years before the first appearance of the French equivalent, and the substantive 'materialist' (1668).

See also BOYLE, CAMBRIDGE PLATONISTS, DESCARTES, NEOPLATONISM.   A.G.

More, Sir **Thomas** (1477 or 1478–1535), English humanist, statesman, martyr, and saint. A lawyer by profession, he entered royal service in 1517 and became lord chancellor in 1529. After refusing to swear to the Act of Supremacy, which named Henry VIII the head of the English church, More was beheaded as a traitor.

Although his writings include biography, poetry, letters, and anti-heretical tracts, his only philosophical work, *Utopia* (published in Latin, 1516), is his masterpiece. Covering a wide variety of subjects including government, education, punishment, religion, family life, and euthanasia, *Utopia* contrasts European social institutions with their counterparts on the imaginary island of Utopia. Inspired in part by Plato's *Republic*, the Utopian communal system is designed to teach virtue and reward it with happiness. The absence of money, private property, and most social distinctions allows Utopians the leisure to

develop the faculties in which happiness consists. Because of More's love of irony, *Utopia* has been subject to quite different interpretations.
                                                                                                    J.W.A.

Mosca, Gaetano (1858–1941), Italian political scientist who made pioneering contributions to the theory of democratic elitism. Combining the life of a university professor with that of a politician, he taught such subjects as constitutional law, public law, political science, and history of political theory; at various times he was also an editor of the Parliamentary proceedings, an elected member of the Chamber of Deputies, an under-secretary for colonial affairs, a newspaper columnist, and a member of the Senate.

For Mosca 'elitism' refers to the empirical generalization that every society is ruled by an organized minority. His democratic commitment is embodied in what he calls juridical defense: the normative principle that political developments are to be judged by whether and how they prevent any one person, class, force, or institution from dominating the others. His third main contribution is a framework consisting of two intersecting distinctions that yield four possible *ideal types*, defined as follows: in autocracy, authority flows from the rulers to the ruled; in liberalism, from the ruled to the rulers; in democracy, the ruling class is open to renewal by members of other classes; in aristocracy it is not. He was influenced by, and in turn influenced, positivism, for the elitist thesis presumably constitutes the fundamental "law" of political "science." Even deeper is his connection with the tradition of Machiavelli's political realism. There is also no question that he practiced an empirical approach. In the tradition of elitism, he may be compared and contrasted with Pareto, Michels, and Schumpeter; and in the tradition of Italian political philosophy, to Croce, Gentile, and Gramsci.

See also CROCE, GENTILE, GRAMSCI, MACHIAVELLI, WEBER.   M.A.F.

Moses ben Maimon. See MAIMONIDES.

Mo Ti. See MO TZU.

motion. See NEWTON.

motivation, a property central in motivational explanations of intentional conduct. To assert that Ann is driving to Boston today because she wants to see the Red Sox play and believes that they are playing today in Boston is to offer a motivational explanation of this action. On a popular interpretation, the assertion mentions a pair of attitudes: a desire and a belief. Ann's desire is a paradigmatic motivational attitude in that it inclines her to bring about the satisfaction of that very attitude. The primary function of motivational attitudes is to bring about their own satisfaction by inducing the agent to undertake a suitable course of action, and, arguably, any attitude that has that function is, *ipso facto*, a motivational one. The related thesis that only attitudes having this function are motivational – or, more precisely, motivation-constituting – is implausible. Ann hopes that the Sox won yesterday. Plainly, her hope cannot bring about its own satisfaction, since Ann has no control over the past. Even so, the hope seemingly may motivate action (e.g., Ann's searching for sports news on her car radio), in which case the hope is motivation-constituting. Some philosophers have claimed that our beliefs that we are morally required to take a particular course of action are motivation-constituting, and such beliefs obviously do not have the function of bringing about their own satisfaction (i.e., their truth). However, the claim is controversial, as is the related claim that beliefs of this kind are "besires" – that is, not merely beliefs but desires as well. **See also** ACCIDIE, ACTION THEORY, MOTIVATIONAL EXPLANATION, MOTIVATIONAL INTERNALISM.

A.R.M.

motivational explanation, a type of explanation of goal-directed behavior where the explanans appeals to the motives of the agent. The explanation usually is in the following form: Smith swam hard in order to win the race. Here the description of what Smith did identifies the behavior to be explained, and the phrase that follows 'in order to' identifies the goal or the state of affairs the obtaining of which was the moving force behind the behavior. The general presumption is that the agent whose behavior is being explained is capable of deliberating and acting on the decisions reached as a result of the deliberation. Thus, it is dubious whether the explanation contained in 'The plant turned toward the sun in order to receive more light' is a motivational explanation.

Two problems are thought to surround motivational explanations. First, since the state of affairs set as the goal is, at the time of the action, non-existent, it can only act as the "moving force" by appearing as the intentional object of an inner psychological state of the agent. Thus,

motives are generally desires for specific objects or states of affairs on which the agent acts. So motivational explanation is basically the type of explanation provided in folk psychology, and as such it inherits all the alleged problems of the latter. And second, what counts as a motive for an action under one description usually fails to be a motive for the same action under a different description. My motive for saying "hello" may have been my desire to answer the phone, but my motive for saying "hello" loudly was to express my irritation at the person calling me so late at night.

See also ACTION THEORY, EXPLANATION, FOLK PSYCHOLOGY, PHILOSOPHY OF MIND.

B.E.

motivational internalism, the view that moral motivation is internal to moral duty (or the sense of duty). The view represents the contemporary understanding of Hume's thesis that morality is essentially practical. Hume went on to point out the apparent logical gap between statements of fact, which express theoretical judgments, and statements about what ought to be done, which express practical judgments. Motivational internalism offers one explanation for this gap. No motivation is internal to the recognition of facts.

The specific internal relation the view affirms is that of necessity. Thus, motivational internalists hold that if one sees that one has a duty to do a certain action or that it would be right to do it, then necessarily one has a motive to do it. For example, if one sees that it is one's duty to donate blood, then necessarily one has a motive to donate blood. Motivational externalism, the opposing view, denies this relation. Its adherents hold that it is possible for one to see that one has a duty to do a certain action or that it would be right to do it yet have no motive to do it. Motivational externalists typically, though not universally, deny any real gap between theoretical and practical judgments.

Motivational internalism takes either of two forms, rationalist and anti-rationalist. Rationalists, such as Plato and Kant, hold that the content or truth of a moral requirement guarantees in those who understand it a motive of compliance. Anti-rationalists, such as Hume, hold that moral judgment necessarily has some affective or volitional component that supplies a motive for the relevant action but that renders morality less a matter of reason and truth than of feeling or commitment. It is also possible in the abstract to draw an analogous distinction between two forms of motivational externalism, cognitivist and noncognitivist, but because the view springs from an interest in assimilating practical judgment to theoretical judgment, its only influential form has been cognitivist. **See also** EMOTIVISM, ETHICS, HUME.   J.D.

Mo Tzu, also known as Master Mo, Mo Ti (fifth century B.C.), Chinese philosopher and founder of the Mohist school of thought, which was a major rival to Confucianism in ancient China. The text *Mo Tzu* contains different versions of his teachings as well as subsequent developments of his thought. Mo Tzu regarded rightness (*yi*) as determined by what benefits (*li*) the public, where benefit is understood in terms of such things as order and increased resources in society. He opposed the musical activities and ritual practices of the Confucians on the ground that such practices are detrimental to the public good. He is probably best known for advocating the ideal of an equal concern to benefit and avoid harm to every human being. Practicing this ideal is to the public good, since strife and disorder stem from partiality toward oneself or one's family or social group. Also, it being the will of Heaven (*t'ien*) that people have equal concern for all, one will be rewarded or punished by Heaven according to whether one practices this ideal. In response to worries about the practicability of the ideal, Mo Tzu insisted that it was simple and easy to put the ideal into practice, leaving himself open to the charge that he neglected the complexities of emotional management. **See also** CONFUCIANISM, MOHISM.   K.-l.S.

Mou Tsung-san (1909–95), Chinese philosopher, perhaps the most original thinker among contemporary Neo-Confucians. Educated at Peking University, he first studied Western philosophy but was converted to Chinese philosophy under the influence of Hsiung Shih-li. He made a great breakthrough in his study of Sung–Ming Neo-Confucian philosophy, arguing that Chu Hsi was really a side branch that took the position of the orthodoxy. He maintained that all three major Chinese traditions, Confucian, Taoist, and Buddhist, assert that humans have the endowment for intellectual intuition, meaning personal participation in *tao* (the Way). **See also** CHINESE PHILOSOPHY, HSIUNG SHIH-LI, HSÜ FU-KUAN, NEO-CONFUCIANISM, T'ANG CHÜN-I.   S.-h.L.

moving rows paradox. See ZENO'S PARADOXES.

multiple realizability. See FUNCTIONALISM.

multiple-relation theory. See PERCEPTION.

mystical experience, an experience alleged to reveal some aspect of reality not normally accessible to sensory experience or cognition. The experience – typically characterized by its profound emotional impact on the one who experiences it, its transcendence of spatial and temporal distinctions, its transitoriness, and its ineffability – is often but not always associated with some religious tradition. In theistic religions, mystical experiences are claimed to be brought about by God or by some other superhuman agent. Theistic mystical experiences evoke feelings of worshipful awe. Their content can vary from something no more articulate than a feeling of closeness to God to something as specific as an item of revealed theology, such as, for a Christian mystic, a vision of the Trinity. Non-theistic mystical experiences are usually claimed to reveal the metaphysical unity of all things and to provide those who experience them with a sense of inner peace or bliss. **See also** MYSTICISM.   W.E.M.

mysticism, a doctrine or discipline maintaining that one can gain knowledge of reality that is not accessible to sense perception or to rational, conceptual thought. Generally associated with a religious tradition, mysticism can take a theistic form, as it has in Jewish, Christian, and Islamic traditions, or a non-theistic form, as it has in Buddhism and some varieties of Hinduism. Mystics claim that the mystical experience, the vehicle of mystical knowledge, is usually the result of spiritual training, involving some combination of prayer, meditation, fasting, bodily discipline, and renunciation of worldly concerns. Theistic varieties of mysticism describe the mystical experience as granted by God and thus not subject to the control of the mystic. Although theists claim to feel closeness to God during the mystical experience, they regard assertions of identity of the self with God as heretical. Non-theistic varieties are more apt to describe the experience as one that can be induced and controlled by the mystic and in which distinctions between the self and reality, or subject and object, are revealed to be illusory. Mystics claim that, although veridical, their experiences cannot be adequately described in language, because ordinary communication is based on sense experience and conceptual differentiation: mystical writings are thus characterized by metaphor and simile. It is controversial whether all mystical experiences are basically the same, and whether the apparent diversity among them is the result of interpretations influenced by different cultural traditions. **See also** MYSTICAL EXPERIENCE, PHILOSOPHY OF RELIGION.   W.E.M.

myth of Er, a tale at the end of Plato's *Republic* dramatizing the rewards of justice and philosophy by depicting the process of reincarnation. Complementing the main argument of the work, that it is intrinsically better to be just than unjust, this longest of Plato's myths blends traditional lore with speculative cosmology to show that justice also pays, usually in life and certainly in the afterlife. Er, a warrior who revived shortly after death, reports how judges assign the souls of the just to heaven but others to punishment in the underworld, and how most return after a thousand years to behold the celestial order, to choose their next lives, and to be born anew. **See also** PLATO.   S.A.W.

myth of the given. See SELLARS, WILFRID.

Nāgārjuna (fl. early second century A.D.), Indian Mahayana Buddhist philosopher, founder of the Mādhyamika view. The *Mūlanadhyamakārikā Prajñā* ("The Fundamental Verses on the Middle Way") and the *Sūnyātasaptati* ("The Septuagint on Emptiness") are perhaps his major works. He distinguishes between "two truths": a conditional truth, which is provisional and reflects the sort of distinctions we make in everyday speech and find in ordinary experience; and a final truth, which is that there exists only an ineffable independent reality. Overcoming acceptance of the conventional, conditional truth is requisite for seeing the final truth in enlightenment. **See also** MĀDHYAMIKA.   K.E.Y.

Nagel, Ernest (1901–85), Czech-born American philosopher, the preeminent American philosopher of science in the period from the mid-1930s to the 1960s. Arriving in New York as a ten-year-old immigrant, he earned his B.S. degree from the College of the City of New York and his Ph.D. from Columbia University in 1931. He was a member of the Philosophy Department at Columbia from 1930 to 1970. He coauthored the influential *An Introduction to Logic and Scientific Method* with his former teacher, M. R. Cohen. His many publications include two well-known classics: *Principles of the Theory of Probability* (1939) and *Structure of Science* (1960).

Nagel was sensitive to developments in logic, foundations of mathematics, and probability theory, and he shared with Russell and with members of the Vienna Circle like Carnap and Phillip Frank a respect for the relevance of scientific inquiry for philosophical reflection. But his writing also reveals the influences of M. R. Cohen and that strand in the thinking of the pragmatism of Peirce and Dewey which Nagel himself called "contextualist naturalism." He was a persuasive critic of Russell's views of the data of sensation as a source of non-inferential premises for knowledge and of cognate views expressed by some members of the Vienna Circle. Unlike Frege, Russell, Carnap, Popper, and others, he rejected the view that taking account of context in characterizing method threatened to taint philosophical reflection with an unacceptable psychologism. This stance subsequently allowed

him to oppose historicist and sociologist approaches to the philosophy of science.

Nagel's contextualism is reflected in his contention that ideas of determinism, probability, explanation, and reduction "can be significantly discussed only if they are directed to the *theories* or *formulations* of a science and not its subject matter" (*Principles of the Theory of Probability*, 1939). This attitude infused his influential discussions of covering law explanation, statistical explanation, functional explanation, and reduction of one theory to another, in both natural and social science. Similarly, his contention that participants in the debate between realism and instrumentalism should clarify the import of their differences for (context-sensitive) scientific methodology served as the core of his argument casting doubt on the significance of the dispute.

In addition to his extensive writings on scientific knowledge methodology, Nagel wrote influential essays on measurement, the history of mathematics, and the philosophy of law.

See also COVERING LAW MODEL, PHILOSOPHY OF SCIENCE, REDUCTION, VIENNA CIRCLE.
                                        I.L.

Nagel, Thomas (b.1937), American professor of philosophy and of law at New York University, known for his important contributions in the fields of metaphysics, epistemology, ethics, and political philosophy. Nagel's work in these areas is unified by a particular vision of perennial philosophical problems, according to which they emerge from a clash between two perspectives from which human beings can view themselves and the world. From an impersonal perspective, which results from detaching ourselves from our particular viewpoints, we strive to achieve an objective view of the world, whereas from a personal perspective, we see the world from our particular point of view. According to Nagel, dominance of the impersonal perspective in trying to understand reality leads to implausible philosophical views because it fails to accommodate facts about the self, minds, agency, and values that are revealed through engaged personal perspectives.

In the philosophy of mind, for instance, Nagel criticizes various reductive accounts of mentality resulting from taking an exclusively impersonal standpoint because they inevitably fail to account for the irreducibly subjective character of consciousness. In ethics, consequentialist moral theories (like utilitarianism), which feature strong impartialist demands that stem from taking a detached, impersonal perspective, find resistance from the personal perspective within which individual goals and motives are accorded an importance not found in strongly impartialist moral theories. An examination of such problems in metaphysics, epistemology, and ethics is found in his *Moral Questions* (1979) and *The View from Nowhere* (1986). In *Equality and Partiality* (1990) Nagel argues that the impersonal standpoint gives rise to an egalitarian form of impartial regard for all people that often clashes with the goals, concerns, and affections that individuals experience from a personal perspective. Quite generally, then, as Nagel sees it, one important philosophical task is to explore ways in which these two standpoints on both theoretical and practical matters might be integrated.

Nagel has also made important contributions regarding the nature and possibility of reason or rationality in both its theoretical and its practical uses. *The Possibility of Altruism* (1970) is an exploration of the structure of practical reason in which Nagel defends the rationality of prudence and altruism, arguing that the possibility of such behavior is connected with our capacities to view ourselves respectively persisting through time and recognizing the reality of other persons. *The Last Word* (1998) is a defense of reason against skeptical views, according to which reason is a merely contingent, locally conditioned feature of particular cultures and hence relative.

See also ETHICS, MORAL RATIONALISM, PHILOSOPHY OF MIND, PRACTICAL REASON.

M.C.T.

naive realism. See PERCEPTION.

name, logically proper. See RUSSELL.

names, causal theory of. See CAUSAL THEORY OF PROPER NAMES.

names, descriptivist theory of. See CAUSAL THEORY OF PROPER NAMES.

narrow content. See PHILOSOPHY OF MIND.

narrow reflective equilibrium. See REFLECTIVE EQUILIBRIUM.

nativism. See FODOR.

Natorp, Paul Gerhard. See NEO-KANTIANISM.

natural deduction. See DEDUCTION.

natural duty. See DUTY.

natural evil. See PHILOSOPHY OF RELIGION.

naturalism, the twofold view that (1) everything is composed of natural entities – those studied in the sciences (on some versions, the natural sciences) – whose properties determine all the properties of things, persons included (abstracta like possibilia and mathematical objects, if they exist, being constructed of such abstract entities as the sciences allow); and (2) acceptable methods of justification and explanation are continuous, in some sense, with those in science. Clause (1) is metaphysical or ontological, clause (2) methodological and/or epistemological. Often naturalism is formulated only for a specific subject matter or domain. Thus ethical naturalism holds that moral properties are equivalent to or at least determined by certain natural properties, so that moral judgments either form a subclass of, or are (non-reductively) determined by the factual or descriptive judgments, and the appropriate methods of moral justification and explanation are continuous with those in science.

Aristotle and Spinoza sometimes are counted among the ancestors of naturalism, as are Democritus, Epicurus, Lucretius, and Hobbes. But the major impetus to naturalism in the last two centuries comes from advances in science and the growing explanatory power they signify. By the 1850s, the synthesis of urea, reflections on the conservation of energy, work on "animal electricity," and discoveries in physiology suggested to Feuerbach, L. Buchner, and others that all aspects of human beings are explainable in purely natural terms. Darwin's theory had even greater impact, and by the end of the nineteenth century naturalist philosophies were making inroads where idealism once reigned unchallenged. Naturalism's ranks now included H. Spencer, J. Tyndall, T. H. Huxley, W. K. Clifford, and E. Haeckel. Early in the twentieth century, Santayana's naturalism strongly influenced a number of American philosophers, as did Dewey's. Still other versions of naturalism flourished in America in the 1930s and 1940s, including those of R. W. Sellars and M. Cohen. Today most American and other philosophers of mind are naturalists of some stripe, largely because of what they see as the lessons of continuing scientific advances, some of them spectacular, particularly in the brain sciences.

Nonetheless, twentieth-century philosophy has been largely anti-naturalist. Both phenomenology in the Husserlian tradition and analytic philosophy in the Fregean tradition, together with their descendants, have been united in rejecting psychologism, a species of naturalism according to which empirical discoveries about mental processes are crucial for understanding the nature of knowledge, language, and logic. In order to defend the autonomy of philosophy against inroads from descriptive science, many philosophers have tried to turn the tables by arguing for the priority of philosophy over science, hence over any of its alleged naturalist implications. Many continue to do so, often on the ground that philosophy alone can illuminate the normativity and intentionality involved in knowledge, language, and logic; or on the ground that philosophy can evaluate the normative and regulative presuppositions of scientific practice which science itself is either blind to or unequipped to analyze; or on the ground that philosophy understands how the language of science can no more be used to get outside itself than any other, hence can no more be known to be in touch with the world and ourselves than any other; or on the ground that would-be justifications of fundamental method, naturalist method certainly included, are necessarily circular because they must employ the very method at issue.

Naturalists may reply by arguing that naturalism's methodological clause (2) entails the opposite of dogmatism, requiring as it does an uncompromising fallibilism about philosophical matters that is continuous with the open, self-critical spirit of science. If evidence were to accumulate against naturalism's metaphysical clause (1), (1) would have to be revised or rejected, and there is no a priori reason such evidence could in principle never be found; indeed many naturalists reject the a priori altogether. Likewise, (2) itself might have to be revised or even rejected in light of adverse argument, so that in this respect (2) is self-referentially consistent. Until then, (2)'s having survived rigorous criticism to date is justification enough, as is the case with hypotheses in science, which often are deployed without circularity in the course of their own evaluation, whether positive or negative (H. I. Brown, "Circular Justifications," 1994). So too can language be used without circularity in expressing hypotheses about the relations between language and the prelinguistic world (as illustrated by R. Millikan's *Language, Thought and Other Biological Categories*, 1984; cf. Post, "Epistemology," 1996). As for normativity and intentionality, naturalism does not entail materialism or physicalism, according to which everything is composed of the entities or processes studied in physics, and the properties of these basic physical affairs determine all the properties of things (as in Quine). Some naturalists deny this, holding that more things than are dreamt of in physics are required to account for normativity and intentionality – and consciousness.

Nor need naturalism be reductive, in the sense of equating every property with some natural property. Indeed many physicalists themselves explain how the physical, hence natural, properties of things might determine other, non-natural properties without being equivalent to them (G. Hellman, T. Horgan, D. Lewis; see J. Post, *The Faces of Existence*, 1987). Often the determining physical properties are not all properties of the thing *x* that has the non-natural properties, but include properties of items separated from *x* in space and time or in some cases bearing no physical relation to *x* that does any work in determining *x*'s properties (Post, " 'Global' Supervenient Determination: Too Permissive?" 1995). Thus naturalism allows a high degree of holism and historicity, which opens the way for a non-reductive naturalist account of intentionality and normativity, such as Millikan's, that is immune to the usual objections, which are mostly objections to reduction. The alternative psychosemantic theories of Dretske and Fodor, being largely reductive, remain vulnerable to such objections.

In these and other ways non-reductive naturalism attempts to combine a monism of entities – the natural ones of which everything is composed – with a pluralism of properties, many of them irreducible or emergent. Not everything is nothing but a natural thing, nor need naturalism accord totalizing primacy to the natural face of existence. Indeed, some naturalists regard the universe as having religious and moral dimensions that enjoy a crucial kind of primacy; and some offer theologies that are more traditionally theist (as do H. N. Wieman, C. Hardwick, J. Post). So far from exhibiting "reptilian indifference" to humans and their fate, the universe can be an enchanted place of belonging.

See also A PRIORI, EMERGENCE, HOLISM, INTENTIONALITY, METAPHYSICS, PHILOSOPHY OF MIND, PHYSICALISM, PROPERTY, PSYCHOLOGISM, SUPERVENIENCE, THEOLOGICAL NATURALISM.   J.F.P.

naturalism, biological. See SEARLE.

naturalism, ethical. See ETHICS, MORAL REALISM.

naturalism, metaphysical. See METAPHYSICS, NATU-RALISM.

naturalism, methodological. See NATURALISM.

naturalism, reductive. See NATURALISM.

naturalism, theological. See THEOLOGICAL NATU-RALISM.

naturalistic epistemology, an approach to episte-mology that views the human subject as a nat-ural phenomenon and uses empirical science to study epistemic activity. The phrase was intro-duced by Quine ("Epistemology Naturalized," in *Ontological Relativity and Other Essays*, 1969), who proposed that epistemology should be a chapter of psychology. Quine construed classical episte-mology as Cartesian epistemology, an attempt to ground all knowledge in a firmly logical way on immediate experience. In its twentieth-century embodiment, it hoped to give a translation of all discourse and a deductive validation of all sci-ence in terms of sense experience, logic, and set theory. Repudiating this dream as forlorn, Quine urged that epistemology be abandoned and replaced by psychology. It would be a scientific study of how the subject takes sensory stimula-tions as input and delivers as output a theory of the three-dimensional world. This formulation appears to eliminate the normative mission of epistemology. In later writing, however, Quine has suggested that normative epistemology can be naturalized as a chapter of engineering: the technology of predicting experience, or sensory stimulations.

Some theories of knowledge are naturalistic in their depiction of knowers as physical systems in causal interaction with the environment. One such theory is the causal theory of knowing, which says that a person knows that p provided his belief that p has a suitable causal connection with a corresponding state of affairs. Another example is the information-theoretic approach developed by Dretske (*Knowledge and the Flow of Information*, 1981). This says that a person knows that p only if some signal "carries" this informa-tion (that p) to him, where information is con-strued as an objective commodity that can be processed and transmitted via instruments, gauges, neurons, and the like. Information is "carried" from one site to another when events located at those sites are connected by a suitable lawful dependence.

The normative concept of justification has also been the subject of naturalistic construals. Whereas many theories of justified belief focus on logical or probabilistic relations between evi-dence and hypothesis, naturalistic theories focus on the psychological processes causally responsi-ble for the belief. The logical status of a belief does not fix its justificational status. Belief in a tautol-ogy, for instance, is not justified if it is formed by blind trust in an ignorant guru. According to Goldman (*Epistemology and Cognition*, 1986), a belief qualifies as justified only if it is produced by reliable belief-forming processes, i.e., processes that generally have a high truth ratio. Goldman's larger program for naturalistic epistemology is called "epistemics," an interdisciplinary enter-prise in which cognitive science would play a major role. Epistemics would seek to identify the subset of cognitive operations available to the human cognizer that are best from a truth-bear-ing standpoint. Relevant truth-linked properties include problem-solving power and speed, i.e., the abilities to obtain correct answers to ques-tions of interest and to do so quickly.

Close connections between epistemology and artificial intelligence have been proposed by Clark Glymour, Gilbert Harman, John Pollock, and Paul Thagard. Harman stresses that princi-ples of good reasoning are not directly given by rules of logic. *Modus ponens*, e.g., does not tell you to infer q if you already believe p and 'if p then q'. In some cases it is better to subtract a belief in one of the premises rather than add a belief in q. Belief revision also requires attention to the stor-age and computational limitations of the mind. Limits of memory capacity, e.g., suggest a princi-ple of clutter avoidance: not filling one's mind with vast numbers of useless beliefs (Harman, *Change in View*, 1986).

Other conceptions of naturalistic epistemology focus on the history of science. Larry Laudan conceives of naturalistic epistemology as a scien-tific inquiry that gathers empirical evidence con-cerning the past track records of various scientific methodologies, with the aim of determining which of these methodologies can best advance the chosen cognitive ends.

Naturalistic epistemology need not confine its attention to individual epistemic agents; it can also study communities of agents. This perspec-tive invites contributions from sciences that address the social side of the knowledge-seeking enterprise. If naturalistic epistemology is a nor-mative inquiry, however, it must not simply describe social practices or social influences; it must analyze the impact of these factors on the attainment of cognitive ends. Philosophers such as David Hull, Nicholas Rescher, Philip Kitcher, and Alvin Goldman have sketched models inspired by population biology and economics to explore the epistemic consequences of alternative distributions of research activity and different ways that professional rewards might influence the course of research.

See also ARTIFICIAL INTELLIGENCE, EPISTEMOLOGY, NATURALISM, RELIABILISM.

A.I.G.

naturalistic fallacy. See MOORE.

natural kind, a category of entities classically conceived as having modal implications; e.g., if Socrates is a member of the natural kind *human being,* then he is necessarily a human being. The idea that nature fixes certain sortals, such as 'water' and 'human being', as correct classifications that appear to designate kinds of entities has roots going back at least to Plato and Aristotle. Anil Gupta has argued that sortals are to be distinguished from properties designated by such predicates as 'red' by including criteria for individuating the particulars (*bits* or *amounts* for mass nouns) that fall under them as well as criteria for sorting those particulars into the class.

Quine is salient among those who find the modal implications of natural kinds objectionable. He has argued that the idea of natural kinds is rooted in prescientific intuitive judgments of comparative similarity, and he has suggested that as these intuitive classifications are replaced by classifications based on scientific theories these modal implications drop away. Kripke and Putnam have argued that science in fact uses natural kind terms having the modal implications Quine finds so objectionable. They see an important role in scientific methodology for the capacity to refer demonstratively to such natural kinds by pointing out particulars that fall under them. Certain inferences within science – such as the inference to the charge for electrons generally from the measurement of the charge on one or a few electrons – seem to be additional aspects of a role for natural kind terms in scientific practice. Other roles in the methodology of science for natural kind concepts have been discussed in recent work by Ian Hacking and Thomas Kuhn.

See also COUNT NOUN, ESSENTIALISM, PHILOSOPHY OF SCIENCE, QUALITATIVE PREDICATE.

W.Har.

natural language. See FORMAL LANGUAGE, PHILOSOPHY OF LANGUAGE.

natural law, also called law of nature, in moral and political philosophy, an objective norm or set of objective norms governing human behavior, similar to the positive laws of a human ruler, but binding on all people alike and usually understood as involving a superhuman legislator.

Ancient Greek and Roman thought, particularly Stoicism, introduced ideas of eternal laws directing the actions of all rational beings and built into the very structure of the universe. Roman lawyers developed a doctrine of a law that all civilized peoples would recognize, and made some effort to explain it in terms of a natural law common to animals and humans. The most influential forms of natural law theory, however, arose from later efforts to use Stoic and legal language to work out a Christian theory of morality and politics. The aim was to show that the principles of morals could be known by reason alone, without revelation, so that the whole human race could know how to live properly. The law of nature applies, on this understanding, only to rational beings, who can obey or disobey it deliberately and freely. It is thus different in kind from the laws God laid down for the inanimate and irrational parts of creation. Natural law theorists often saw continuities and analogies between natural laws for humans and those for the rest of creation but did not confuse them.

The most enduringly influential natural law writer was Aquinas. On his view God's eternal reason ordains laws directing all things to act for the good of the community of the universe, the declaration of His own glory. Human reason can participate sufficiently in God's eternal reason to show us the good of the human community. The natural law is thus our sharing in the eternal law in a way appropriate to our human nature. God lays down certain other laws through revelation; these divine laws point us toward our eternal goal. The natural law concerns our earthly good, and needs to be supplemented by human laws. Such laws can vary from community to community, but to be binding they must always stay within the limits of the law of nature. God engraved the most basic principles of the natural law in the minds of all people alike, but their detailed application takes reasoning powers that not everyone may have.

Opponents of Aquinas – called voluntarists – argued that God's will, not his intellect, is the source of law, and that God could have laid down different natural laws for us. Hugo Grotius rejected their position, but unlike Aquinas he conceived of natural law as meant not to direct us to bring about some definite common good but to set the limits on the ways in which each of us could properly pursue our own personal aims. This Grotian outlook was developed by Hobbes, Pufendorf, and Locke along voluntarist lines. Thomistic views continued to be expounded by Protestant as well as Roman Catholic writers until the end of the seventeenth century. Thereafter, while natural law theory remained central to Catholic teaching, it ceased to attract major new non-Catholic proponents.

Natural law doctrine in both Thomistic and Grotian versions treats morality as basically a matter of compliance with law. Obligation and duty, obedience and disobedience, merit and guilt, reward and punishment, are central notions. Virtues are simply habits of following laws. Though the law is suited to our distinctive human nature and can be discovered by the proper use of reason, it is not a self-imposed law. In following it we are obeying God.

Since the early eighteenth century, philosophical discussions of whether or not there is an objective morality have largely ceased to center on natural law. The idea remains alive, however, in jurisprudence. Natural law theories are opposed to legal positivism, the view that the only binding laws are those imposed by human sovereigns, who cannot be subject to higher legal constraints. Legal theorists arguing that there are rational objective limits to the legislative power of rulers often think of these limits in terms of natural law, even when their theories do not invoke or imply any of the religious aspects of earlier natural law positions.

See also AQUINAS, GROTIUS, HOBBES, PHILOSOPHY OF LAW, PUFENDORF.   J.B.S.

natural light. See DESCARTES.

natural meaning. See MEANING.

naturalness. See JUAN CHI.

natural number. See MATHEMATICAL ANALYSIS, MATHEMATICAL INDUCTION.

natural philosophy, the study of nature or of the spatiotemporal world. This was regarded as a task for philosophy before the emergence of modern science, especially physics and astronomy, and the term is now only used with reference to premodern times. Philosophical questions about nature still remain, e.g., whether materialism is true, but they would usually be placed in metaphysics or in a branch of it that may be called *philosophy of nature*. Natural philosophy is not to be confused with *metaphysical naturalism*, which is the metaphysical view (no part of science itself) that all that there is is the spatiotemporal world and that the only way to study it is that of the empirical sciences. It is also not to be confused with natural theology, which also may be considered part of metaphysics. **See also** METAPHYSICS.   P.Bu.

natural religion, a term first occurring in the second half of the seventeenth century, used in three related senses, the most common being (1) a body of truths about God and our duty that can be discovered by natural reason. These truths are sufficient for salvation or (according to some orthodox Christians) would have been sufficient if Adam had not sinned. Natural religion in this sense should be distinguished from natural theology, which does not imply this. A natural religion may also be (2) one that has a human, as distinct from a divine, origin. It may also be (3) a religion of human nature as such, as distinguished from religious beliefs and practices that have been determined by local circumstances. Natural religion in the third sense is identified with humanity's original religion. In all three senses, natural religion includes a belief in God's existence, justice, benevolence, and providential government; in immortality; and in the dictates of common morality. While the concept is associated with deism, it is also sympathetically treated by Christian writers like Clarke, who argues that revealed religion simply restores natural religion to its original purity and adds inducements to compliance. **See also** CLARKE, PHILOSOPHY OF RELIGION.
                W.J.Wa.

natural right. See RIGHTS.

natural selection. See DARWINISM.

natural sign. See THEORY OF SIGNS.

natural theology. See PHILOSOPHY OF RELIGION, THEOLOGIA NATURALIS.

natura naturans. See SPINOZA.

natura naturata. See SPINOZA.

nature, law of. See NATURAL LAW, PHILOSOPHY OF SCIENCE.

nature, right of. See HOBBES.

nature, state of. See HOBBES.

Naturphilosophie. See SCHELLING.

Naturwissenschaften. See WEBER.

Néant. See SARTRE.

necessary. See CONTINGENT.

necessary condition. See CONDITION.

necessary truth. See NECESSITY.

necessitarianism, the doctrine that necessity is an objective feature of the world. Natural language permits speakers to express *modalities:* a state of affairs can be *actual* (Paris's being in France), merely *possible* (chlorophyll's making things blue), or *necessary* (2 + 2 = 4). Anti-necessitarians believe that these distinctions are not grounded in the nature of the world. Some of them claim that the distinctions are merely verbal. Others, e.g., Hume, believed that psychological facts, like our expectations of future events, explain the idea of necessity. Yet others contend that the modalities reflect epistemic considerations; necessity reflects the highest level of an inquirer's commitment. Some necessitarians believe there are different modes of metaphysical necessity, e.g., *causal* and *logical* necessity. Certain proponents of idealism believe that each fact is necessarily connected with every other fact so that the ultimate goal of scientific inquiry is the discovery of a completely rigorous mathematical system of the world. **See also** DETER-MINISM, FREE WILL PROBLEM. B.B.

necessity, a modal property attributable to a whole proposition (dictum) just when it is not possible that the proposition be false (the proposition being *de dicto* necessary). Narrowly construed, a proposition P is logically necessary provided P satisfies certain syntactic conditions, namely, that P's denial is formally self-contradictory. More broadly, P is logically necessary just when P satisfies certain semantic conditions, namely, that P's denial is false, and P true, in all possible worlds. These semantic conditions were first suggested by Leibniz, refined by Wittgenstein and Carnap, and fully developed as the possible worlds semantics of Kripke, Hintikka, et al., in the 1960s. Previously, philosophers had to rely largely on intuition to determine the acceptabil-

ity or otherwise of formulas involving the necessity operator, $\Box$, and were at a loss as to which of various axiomatic systems for modal logic, as developed in the 1930s by C. I. Lewis, best captured the notion of logical necessity. There was much debate, for instance, over the characteristic (NN) thesis of Lewis's system S4, namely, $\Box P \supset \Box \Box P$ (if P is necessary then it is necessarily necessary). But given a Leibnizian account of the truth conditions for a statement of the form $\Box \alpha$ namely (R1) that $\Box \alpha$ is true provided α is true in all possible worlds, and (R2) that $\Box \alpha$ is false provided there is at least one possible world in which α is false, a proof can be constructed by *reductio ad absurdum*. For suppose that $\Box P \supset \Box \Box P$ is false in some arbitrarily chosen world W. Then its antecedent will be true in W, and hence (by R1) it follows (a) that P will be true in all possible worlds. But equally its consequent will be false in W, and hence (by R2) $\Box P$ will be false in at least one possible world, from which (again by R2) it follows (b) that P will be false in at least one possible world, thus contradicting (a). A similar proof can be constructed for the characteristic thesis of S5, namely, $\sim \Box \sim P \supset \Box \sim \Box \sim P$ (if P is possibly true then it is necessarily possible).

Necessity is also attributable to a property F of an object O provided it is not possible that (there is no possible world in which) O exists and lacks $F - F$ being *de re* necessary, internal or essential to O. For instance, the non-repeatable (haecceitist) property of *being identical to O* is *de re* necessary (essential) to O, and arguably the repeatable property of *being extended* is *de re* necessary to all colored objects.

See also CONTINGENT, ESSENTIALISM, HAECCEITY, MODAL LOGIC, POSSIBLE WORLDS. R.D.B.

necessity, metaphysical. See NECESSITY, PHILOSOPHY OF MIND.

necessity, nomic. See LAWLIKE GENERALIZATION.

negation, the logical operation on propositions that is indicated, e.g., by the prefatory clause 'It is not the case that . . .'. Negation is standardly distinguished sharply from the operation on predicates that is called complementation and that is indicated by the prefix 'non-'. Because negation can also be indicated by the adverb 'not', a distinction is often drawn between external negation, which is indicated by attaching the prefatory 'It is not the case that . . .' to an assertion, and internal negation, which is indicated by inserting the adverb 'not' (along with, perhaps, grammatically necessary words like 'do' or 'does') into the assertion in such a way as to indicate that the adverb 'not' modifies the verb. In a number of cases, the question arises as to whether external and internal negation yield logically equivalent results. For example, 'It is not the case that Santa Claus exists' would seem obviously to be true, whereas 'Santa Claus does not exist' seems to some philosophers to presuppose what it denies, on the ground that nothing could be truly asserted of Santa Claus unless he existed. **See also** DOUBLE NEGATION, TRUTH TABLE.   R.W.B.

negation-complete. See COMPLETENESS.

negative duty. See DUTY.

negative feedback. See CYBERNETICS.

negative freedom. See POSITIVE AND NEGATIVE FREEDOM.

negative liberty. See POSITIVE AND NEGATIVE FREEDOM.

Nemesius of Emesa (fl. c.390–400), Greek Christian philosopher. His treatise on the soul, *On the Nature of Man,* translated from Greek into Latin by Alphanus of Salerno and Burgundio of Pisa (c.1160), was attributed to Gregory of Nyssa in the Middle Ages, and enjoyed some authority; the treatise rejects Plato for underplaying the unity of soul and body, and Aristotle for making the soul essentially corporeal. The soul is self-subsistent, incorporeal, and by nature immortal, but naturally suited for union with the body. Nemesius draws on Ammonius Saccas and Porphyry, as well as analogy to the union of divine and human nature in Christ, to explain the incorruptible soul's perfect union with the corruptible body. His review of the powers of the soul draws especially on Galen on the brain. His view that rational creatures possess free will in virtue of their rationality influenced Maximus the Confessor and John of Damascus.   J.Lo.

Neo-Confucianism, Confucianism as revived in China during the late tenth to mid-seventeenth centuries. It has also been called *Tao-hsüeh* (learning of the Way) or *Li-hsüeh* (learning of principles) in the broader sense. It is without any doubt Confucianism, since Sung–Ming Confucianists also found their ultimate commitment in *jen* (humanity or human-heartedness) and regulated their behavior by *li* (propriety). But it

acquired new features, since it was a movement in response to the challenges from Buddhism and Neo-Taoism. Therefore it developed sophisticated theories of human mind and nature and also cosmology and metaphysics far beyond the scope of Pre-Ch'in Confucianism. If the Confucian ideal may be characterized by *nei-sheng-wai-wang* (inward sageliness and outward kingliness), then the Neo-Confucianists certainly made greater contributions to the *nei-sheng* side, as they considered *wei-chi-chih-hsüeh* (learning for one's self) as their primary concern, and developed sophisticated discipline of the mind comparable to the kind of transcendental meditation practiced by Buddhists and Taoists. They put emphasis on finding resources within the self. Hence they moved away from the Han tradition of writing extensive commentaries on the Five Classics. Instead, they looked for guidance to the so-called Four Books: the *Analects*, the *Mencius, The Great Learning*, and *The Doctrine of the Mean*. They also believed that they should put what they had learned from the words of the sages and worthies into practice in order to make themselves better. This was to start a new trend in sharp contrast to the earlier Five Dynasties period (907–60), when moral standards had fallen to a new low.

According to Chu Hsi, the movement started with Chou Tun-yi (1017–73), who, along with Chang Tsai (1020–77), gave new interpretations to the *I-Ching* (the *Book of Changes*) and *The Doctrine of the Mean* in combination with the *Analects* and the *Mencius* so as to develop new cosmologies and metaphysics in response to the challenges from Buddhism and Taoism. The name of Shao Yung (1011–77), an expert on the *I-Ching,* was excluded, as his views were considered too Taoistic. But the true founders and leaders of the movement were the two Ch'eng brothers – Ch'eng Hao (1032–85) and Ch'eng Yi (1033–1107). Onetime pupils of Chou, they developed *li* (principle) into a philosophical concept. Even though Hua-yen Buddhism had used the term first, the Ch'eng brothers gave it a totally new interpretation from a Confucian perspective. Later scholars find that the thoughts of the two brothers differed both in style and in substance. Ch'eng Hao believed in *i-pen* (one foundation), while Ch'eng Yi developed a dualistic metaphysics of *li* (principle) and *ch'i* (material force). On the surface Chu Hsi was the follower of the Ch'eng brothers, but in fact he was only following the lead of Ch'eng Yi, and promoted the so-called *Li-hsüeh* (learning of principles) in the narrower sense. His younger contemporary

Lu Hsiang-shan (1139–93) objected to Chu's method of looking for principles among things. He urged us to realize principle within one's own mind, went back to Mencius's teaching to establish the greater part of the self first, and promoted the so-called *hsin-hsüeh* (learning of the mind). But Chu Hsi's commentaries on the Four Books were adopted as the basis of civil service examinations in the Yüan dynasty; Lu's views were largely ignored until there were revived in the Ming dynasty (1368–1644) by Wang Yang-ming (1472–1529), who identified the mind with principle and advocated that knowledge and action are one. Since Lu–Wang's thoughts were closer to Mencius, who was honored to have represented the orthodox line of transmission of the Way, Mou Tsung-san advanced the theory that Chu Hsi was the side branch taking over the orthodoxy; he also believed that Hu Hung (1100–55) and Liu Tsung-chou (1578–1645) developed a third branch of Neo-Confucianism in addition to that of Ch'eng and Chu and that of Lu and Wang. His views have generated many controversies. Sung–Ming Neo-Confucianism was hailed as creating the second golden period of Chinese philosophy since the late Chou. Huang Tsung-hsi (1610–95), a pupil of Liu Tsung-chou and the last important figure in Sung–Ming Neo-Confucianism, extensively studied the movement and wrote essential works on it.

    See also CHU HSI, CONFUCIANISM, CONFU-CIUS, HUANG TSUNG-HSI, LI CHI, MENCIUS, SHAO YUNG, WANG YANG-MING.   S.-h.L.

neo-Euclidean geometry. See EUCLIDEAN GEOMETRY.

neo-Friesian School. See NEO-KANTIANISM.

neo-Kantianism, the diverse Kantian movement that emerged within German philosophy in the 1860s, gained a strong academic foothold in the 1870s, reached its height during the three decades prior to World War I, and disappeared with the rise of Nazism. The movement was initially focused on renewed study and elaboration of Kant's epistemology in response to the growing epistemic authority of the natural sciences and as an alternative to both Hegelian and speculative idealism and the emerging materialism of, among others, Ludwig Büchner (1824–99). Later neo-Kantianism explored Kant's whole philosophy, applied his critical method to disciplines other than the natural sciences, and developed its own philosophical systems. Some

originators and/or early contributors were Kuno Fischer (1824–1907), Hermann von Helmholtz (1821–94), Friedrich Albert Lange (1828–75), Eduard Zeller (1814–1908), and Otto Liebmann (1840–1912), whose *Kant und die Epigonen* (1865) repeatedly stated what became a neo-Kantian motto, "Back to Kant!"

    Several forms of neo-Kantianism are to be distinguished. T. K. Oesterreich (1880–1949), in *Friedrich Ueberwegs Grundriss der Geschichte der Philosophie* ("F.U.'s Compendium of the History of Philosophy," 1923), developed the standard, somewhat chronological, classification:

(1) The physiological neo-Kantianism of Helmholtz and Lange, who claimed that physiology is "developed or corrected Kantianism."

(2) The metaphysical neo-Kantianism of the later Liebmann, who argued for a Kantian "critical metaphysics" (beyond epistemology) in the form of "hypotheses" about the essence of things.

(3) The realist neo-Kantianism of Alois Riehl (1844–1924), who emphasized the real existence of Kant's thing-in-itself.

(4) The logistic-methodological neo-Kantianism of the Marburg School of Hermann Cohen (1842–1918) and Paul Natorp (1854–1924).

(5) The axiological neo-Kantianism of the Baden or Southwest German School of Windelband (1848–1915) and Heinrich Rickert (1863–1936).

(6) The relativistic neo-Kantianism of Georg Simmel (1858–1918), who argued for Kantian categories relative to individuals and cultures.

(7) The psychological neo-Kantianism of Leonard Nelson (1882–1927), originator of the Göttingen School; also known as the neo-Friesian School, after Jakob Friedrich Fries (1773–1843), Nelson's self-proclaimed precursor. Like Fries, Nelson held that Kantian a priori principles cannot be transcendentally justified, but can be discovered only through introspection.

Oesterreich's classification has been narrowed or modified, partly because of conflicting views on how distinctly "Kantian" a philosopher must have been to be called "neo-Kantian." The very term 'neo-Kantianism' has even been called into question, as suggesting real intellectual commonality where little or none is to be found. There is, however, growing consensus that Marburg and Baden neo-Kantianism were the most important and influential.

Marburg School. Its founder, Cohen, developed its characteristic Kantian idealism of the natural sciences by arguing that physical objects are truly known only through the laws of these sciences and that these laws presuppose the application of Kantian a priori principles and concepts. Cohen elaborated this idealism by eliminating Kant's dualism of sensibility and understanding, claiming that space and time are construction methods of "pure thought" rather than a priori forms of perception and that the notion of any "given" (perceptual data) prior to the "activity" of "pure thought" is meaningless. Accordingly, Cohen reformulated Kant's thing-in-itself as the regulative idea that the mathematical description of the world can always be improved. Cohen also emphasized that "pure thought" refers not to individual consciousess – on his account Kant had not yet sufficiently left behind a "subject–object" epistemology – but rather to the content of his own system of a priori principles, which he saw as subject to change with the progress of science. Just as Cohen held that epistemology must be based on the "fact of science," he argued, in a decisive step beyond Kant, that ethics must transcendentally deduce both the moral law and the ideal moral subject from a humanistic science – more specifically, from jurisprudence's notion of the legal person. This analysis led to the view that the moral law demands that all institutions, including economic enterprises, become democratic – so that they display unified wills and intentions as transcendental conditions of the legal person – and that all individuals become co-legislators. Thus Cohen arrived at his frequently cited claim that Kant "is the true and real originator of German socialism." Other important Marburg Kantians were Cohen's colleague Natorp, best known for his studies on Plato and philosophy of education, and their students Karl Vorländer (1860–1928), who focused on Kantian socialist ethics as a corrective of orthodox Marxism, and Ernst Cassirer (1874–1945).

Baden School. The basic task of philosophy and its transcendental method is seen as identifying universal values that make possible culture in its varied expressions. This focus is evident in Windelband's influential insight that the natural sciences seek to formulate general laws – *nomothetic* knowledge – while the historical sciences seek to describe unique events – *idiographic* knowledge. This distinction is based on the val-

ues (interests) of mastery of nature and understanding and reliving the unique past in order to affirm our individuality. Windelband's view of the historical sciences as idiographic raised the problem of selection central to his successor Rickert's writings: How can historians objectively determine which individual events are historically significant? Rickert argued that this selection must be based on the values that are generally recognized within the cultures under investigation, not on the values of historians themselves. Rickert also developed the transcendental argument that the objectivity of the historical sciences necessitates the assumption that the generally recognized values of different cultures approximate in various degrees universally valid values. This argument was rejected by Weber, whose methodological work was greatly indebted to Rickert.

See also CASSIRER, COHEN, KANT, LANGE, TRANSCENDENTAL ARGUMENT, WINDELBAND.

H.v.d.L.

Neoplatonism, that period of Platonism following on the new impetus provided by the philosophical speculations of Plotinus (A.D. 204–69). It extends, as a minimum, to the closing of the Platonic School in Athens by Justinian in 529, but maximally through Byzantium, with such figures as Michael Psellus (1018–78) and Pletho (c.1360–1452), the Renaissance (Ficino, Pico, and the Florentine Academy), and the early modern period (the Cambridge Platonists, Thomas Taylor), to the advent of the "scientific" study of the works of Plato with Schleiermacher (1768–1834) at the beginning of the nineteenth century. The term was formerly also used to characterize the whole period from the Old Academy of Plato's immediate successors, Speusippus and Xenocrates, through what is now termed Middle Platonism (c.80 B.C.–A.D. 220), down to Plotinus. This account confines itself to the "minimum" interpretation.

Neoplatonism proper may be divided into three main periods: that of Plotinus and his immediate followers (third century); the "Syrian" School of Iamblichus and his followers (fourth century); and the "Athenian" School begun by Plutarch of Athens, and including Syrianus, Proclus, and their successors, down to Damascius (fifth–sixth centuries).

Plotinus and his school. Plotinus's innovations in Platonism (developed in his essays, the *Enneads*, collected and edited by his pupil Porphyry after his death), are mainly two: (a) above the traditional supreme principle of earlier Platonism (and Aristotelianism), a self-thinking intellect, which was also regarded as true being, he postulated a principle superior to intellect and being, totally unitary and simple ("the One"); (b) he saw reality as a series of levels (One, Intelligence, Soul), each higher one outflowing or radiating into the next lower, while still remaining unaffected in itself, and the lower ones fixing themselves in being by somehow "reflecting back" upon their priors. This eternal process gives the universe its existence and character. Intelligence operates in a state of non-temporal simultaneity, holding within itself the "forms" of all things. Soul, in turn, generates time, and receives the forms into itself as "reason principles" (*logoi*). Our physical three-dimensional world is the result of the lower aspect of Soul (nature) projecting itself upon a kind of negative field of force, which Plotinus calls "matter." Matter has no positive existence, but is simply the receptacle for the unfolding of Soul in its lowest aspect, which projects the forms in three-dimensional space. Plotinus often speaks of matter as "evil" (e.g. *Enneads* II.8), and of the Soul as suffering a "fall" (e.g. *Enneads* V.1, 1), but in fact he sees the whole cosmic process as an inevitable result of the superabundant productivity of the One, and thus "the best of all possible worlds."

Plotinus was himself a mystic, but he arrived at his philosophical conclusions by perfectly logical means, and he had not much use for either traditional religion or any of the more recent superstitions. His immediate pupils, Amelius (c.225–90) and Porphyry (234–c.305), while somewhat more hospitable to these, remained largely true to his philosophy (though Amelius had a weakness for triadic elaborations in metaphysics). Porphyry was to have wide influence, both in the Latin West (through such men as Marius Victorinus, Augustine, and Boethius), and in the Greek East (and even, through translations, on medieval Islam), as the founder of the Neoplatonic tradition of commentary on both Plato and Aristotle, but it is mainly as an expounder of Plotinus's philosophy that he is known. He added little that is distinctive, though that little is currently becoming better appreciated.

Iamblichus and the Syrian School. Iamblichus (c.245–325), descendant of an old Syrian noble family, was a pupil of Porphyry's, but dissented from him on various important issues. He set up his own school in Apamea in Syria, and attracted many pupils.

One chief point of dissent was the role of theurgy (really just magic, with philosophical underpinnings, but not unlike Christian sacramental theology). Iamblichus claimed, as against Porphyry, that philosophical reasoning alone could not attain the highest degree of enlightenment, without the aid of theurgic rites, and his view on this was followed by all later Platonists. He also produced a metaphysical scheme far more elaborate than Plotinus's, by a Scholastic filling in, normally with systems of triads, of gaps in the "chain of being" left by Plotinus's more fluid and dynamic approach to philosophy. For instance, he postulated two Ones, one completely transcendent, the other the source of all creation, thus "resolving" a tension in Plotinus's metaphysics.

Iamblichus was also concerned to fit as many of the traditional gods as possible into his system, which later attracted the attention of the Emperor Julian, who based himself on Iamblichus when attempting to set up a Hellenic religion to rival Christianity, a project which, however, died with him in 363.

The Athenian School. The precise links between the pupils of Iamblichus and Plutarch (d.432), founder of the Athenian School, remain obscure, but the Athenians always retained a great respect for the Syrian. Plutarch himself is a dim figure, but Syrianus (c.370–437), though little of his writings survives, can be seen from constant references to him by his pupil Proclus (412–85) to be a major figure, and the source of most of Proclus's metaphysical elaborations.

The Athenians essentially developed and systematized further the doctrines of Iamblichus, creating new levels of divinity (e.g. intelligible-intellectual gods, and "henads" in the realm of the One – though they rejected the two Ones), this process reaching its culmination in the thought of the last head of the Athenian Academy, Damascius (c.456–540).

The drive to systematize reality and to objectivize concepts, exhibited most dramatically in Proclus's *Elements of Theology*, is a lasting legacy of the later Neoplatonists, and had a significant influence on the thought, among others, of Hegel.

See also COMMENTARIES ON PLATO, ISLAMIC NEOPLATONISM.   J.M.D.

Neoplatonism, Islamic. See ISLAMIC NEOPLATONISM.

neo-Scholasticism, the movement given impetus

by Pope Leo XIII's encyclical *Aeterni Patris* (1879), which, while stressing Aquinas, was a general recommendation of the study of medieval Scholasticism as a source for the solution of vexing modern problems. Leo assumed that there was a doctrine common to Aquinas, Bonaventure, Albertus Magnus, and Duns Scotus, and that Aquinas was a preeminent spokesman of the common view. Maurice De Wulf employed the phrase 'perennial philosophy' to designate this common medieval core as well as what Scholasticism is relevant to later times. Historians like Mandonnet, Grabmann, and Gilson soon contested the idea that there was a single medieval doctrine and drew attention to the profound differences between the great medieval masters. The discussion of Christian philosophy precipitated by Brehier in 1931 generated a variety of suggestions as to what medieval thinkers and later Christian philosophers have in common, but this was quite different from the assumption of *Aeterni Patris*. The pedagogical directives of this and later encyclicals brought about a revival of Thomism rather than of Scholasticism, generally in seminaries, ecclesiastical colleges, and Catholic universities.

Louvain's Higher Institute of Philosophy under the direction of Cardinal Mercier and its *Revue de Philosophie Néoscolastique* were among the first fruits of the Thomistic revival. The *studia generalia* of the Dominican order continued at a new pace, the Saulchoir publishing the *Revue thomiste*. In graduate centers in Milan, Madrid, Latin America, Paris, and Rome, men were trained for the task of teaching in colleges and seminaries, and scholarly research began to flourish as well. The Leonine edition of the writings of Aquinas was soon joined by new critical editions of Bonaventure, Duns Scotus, and Ockham, as well as Albertus Magnus. Medieval studies in the broader sense gained from the quest for manuscripts and the growth of paleography and codicology.

Besides the historians mentioned above, Jacques Maritain (1882–1973), a layman and convert to Catholicism, did much both in his native France and in the United States to promote the study of Aquinas. The Pontifical Institute of Mediaeval Studies at Toronto, with Gilson regularly and Maritain frequently in residence, became a source of college and university teachers in Canada and the United States, as Louvain and, in Rome, the Jesuit Gregorianum and the Dominican Angelicum already were. In the 1940s Americans took doctorates in theology and philosophy at Laval in Quebec and soon the influence of Charles De Koninck was felt. Jesuits at St. Louis University began to publish *The Modern Schoolman*, Dominicans in Washington *The Thomist*, and the American Catholic Philosophical Association *The New Scholasticism*. The School of Philosophy at Catholic University, long the primary domestic source of professors and scholars, was complemented by graduate programs at St. Louis, Georgetown, Notre Dame, Fordham, and Marquette.

In the golden period of the Thomistic revival in the United States, from the 1930s until the end of the Vatican Council II in 1965, there were varieties of Thomism based on the variety of views on the relation between philosophy and science. By the 1960s Thomistic philosophy was a prominent part of the curriculum of all Catholic colleges and universities. By 1970, it had all but disappeared under the mistaken notion that this was the intent of Vatican II. This had the effect of releasing Aquinas into the wider philosophical world.

See also AQUINAS, NEO-THOMISM, SCHOLASTICISM.   R.M.

Neo-Taoism, in Chinese, *hsüan-hsüeh* ('Profound Learning', 'Mysterious Learning', or 'Dark Learning'), a broad, multifaceted revival of Taoist learning that dominated Chinese philosophy from the third to the sixth century A.D. Literally 'dark red', *hsüan* is used in the *Lao Tzu* (*Tao Te Ching*) to describe the sublime mystery of the *tao*. Historically, *hsüan-hsüeh* formed a major topic of "Pure Conversation" (*ch'ing-t'an*), where scholars in a time of political upheaval sought to arrest the perceived decline of the *tao*. When the Wei dynasty replaced the Han in A.D. 220, a first wave of Neo-Taoist philosophers represented by Ho Yen (c.190–249) and Wang Pi (226–49) radically reinterpreted the classical heritage to bring to light its profound meaning. The Confucian orthodoxy – as distinguished from the original teachings of Confucius – was deemed ineffectual and an obstacle to renewal. One of the most important debates in Profound Learning – the debate on "words and meaning" – criticizes Han scholarship for its literal imagination and confronts the question of interpretation. Words are necessary but not sufficient for understanding. The ancient sages had a unified view of the Tao, articulated most clearly in the *I-Ching, Lao Tzu,* and *Chuang Tzu,* but distorted by Han scholars. Most Neo-Taoists concentrated on these "Three Profound Treatises" (*san-hsüan*). Wang Pi is best known for his commentaries on the *I-Ching* and the *Lao Tzu;* and Kuo Hsiang (d.312), another leading Neo-Taoist, is arguably the most important *Chuang Tzu* commentator in Chinese history.

The *tao* is the source of all being, but against identifying the *tao* with a creator "heaven" or an original "vital energy" (*ch'i*), Wang Pi argues that being originates from "non-being" (*wu*). The concept of non-being, taken from the *Lao Tzu*, brings out the transcendence of the *tao*. Nameless and without form, the *tao* as such can be described only negatively as *wu*, literally "not having" any characteristics. In contrast, for Kuo Hsiang, non-being does not explain the origin of being because, as entirely conceptual, it cannot create anything. If non-being cannot bring forth being, and if the idea of a creator remains problematic, the only alternative is to regard the created order as coming into existence spontaneously. This implies that being is eternal. Particular beings can be traced to contingent causes, but ultimately the origin of being can be understood only in terms of a process of "self-transformation." Chinese sources often contrast Wang Pi's "valuing non-being" (*kuei-wu*) with Kuo Hsiang's "exaltation of being" (*ch'ung-yu*).

In ethics and politics, Wang stresses that the *tao* is manifest in nature as constant principles (*li*). This is what the classics mean by *tzu-jan*, naturalness or literally what is of itself so. The hierarchical structure of sociopolitical relations also has a basis in the order of nature. While Wang emphasizes unity, Kuo Hsiang champions diversity. The principle of nature dictates that everyone has a particular "share" of vital energy, the creative power of the *tao* that determines one's physical, intellectual, and moral capacity. Individual differences ought to be accepted, but do not warrant value discrimination. Each individual is in principle complete in his/her own way, and constitutes an indispensable part in a larger whole. Taoist ethics thus consists in being true to oneself, and nourishing one's nature. In government, naturalness finds expression in non-action (*wu-wei*), which may be contrasted with Legalist policies emphasizing punishment and control. For Wang Pi, *wu-wei* aims at preserving the natural order so that the myriad things can flourish. Practically, it involves the elimination of willful intervention and a return to "emptiness and quiescence"; i.e., freedom from the dictates of desire and a life of guileless simplicity. Not to be confused with total inaction, according to Kuo Hsiang, *wu-wei* signifies a mode of being that fully uses one's natural endowment. When one is guided by inherent moral principles, there is no place for artificiality or self-deception in the

Taoist way of life. Ethical purity does not entail renunciation. Though the sage finds himself along the corridors of power, he safeguards his nature and remains empty of desire. In government, the sage ruler naturally reduces arbitrary restrictions, adjusts policies to suit changing needs, identifies the right people for office, and generally creates an environment in which all under heaven can dwell in peace and realize their potential.

Ho Yen died a victim of political intrigue, at the close of the Cheng-shih reign period (240–49) of the Wei dynasty. Wang Pi died later in the same year. Historians refer to "Cheng-shih *hsüan-hsüeh*" to mark the first phase of Neo-Taoism. Later, political power was controlled by the Ssu-ma family, who eventually founded the Chin dynasty in A.D. 265. During the Wei–Chin transition, a group of intellectuals, the "Seven Worthies of the Bamboo Grove," came to represent the voice of Profound Learning. Among them, Hsi K'ang (223–62), Juan Chi (210–63), and Hsiang Hsiu (c.227–80) are of particular interest to philosophy. In different ways, they look to naturalness as a basis for renewal. Debates in Profound Learning often revolve around the relationship between "orthodox teachings" (*ming-chiao*) and *tzu-jan*. For Wang Pi and Kuo Hsiang, government and society should ideally conform to nature. Both Hsi K'ang and Juan Chi found *ming-chiao* impinging on naturalness. This also gave impetus to the development of a counterculture. Central to this is the place of emotion in the ethical life. Ho Yen is credited with the view that sages are without emotions (*ch'ing*), whose exceptional *ch'i*-endowment translates into a purity of being that excludes emotional disturbance. Hsi K'ang also values dispassion, and Hsiang Hsiu urges putting passion under the rule of ritual; but many appreciated strong emotion as a sign of authenticity, which often contravened orthodox teachings. As Pure Conversation gained currency, it became fashionable to give free rein to one's impulses; and many hoped to establish a reputation by opposing orthodoxy. The debate on naturalness raises the further question of talent or capacity (*ts'ai*) and its relationship to human nature (*hsing*). In Profound Learning, four distinct positions have been proposed: that talent and nature are identical (*t'ung*); different (*i*); harmonious (*ho*); and separate (*li*). This is important because the right talent must be identified to serve political ends.

In the early fourth century, the Chin dynasty had to flee its capital and rebuild in south China. As the literati resettled, they looked back to the time of Ho Yen and Wang Pi as the golden age of Profound Learning. Although Pure Conversation continued with undiminished vigor, it did not introduce many new ideas. As it entered its last phase, another Taoist work, the *Lieh-tzu*, came to rival the "Three Profound Treatises." Chang Chan (c.330–400) wrote an important commentary on the work, which not only recapitulated many of the ideas that spanned the spectrum of Neo-Taoist philosophy but also borrowed Buddhist ideas. From the fourth century onward, Buddhist masters frequently engaged in Pure Conversation and challenged *hsüan-hsüeh* scholars at their own game.

See also BUDDHISM, CHINESE LEGALISM, CHINESE PHILOSOPHY.   A.K.L.C.

Neo-Thomism, a philosophical-theological movement in the nineteenth and twentieth centuries manifesting a revival of interest in Aquinas. It was stimulated by Pope Leo XIII's encyclical *Aeterni Patris* (1879) calling for a renewed emphasis on the teaching of Thomistic principles to meet the intellectual and social challenges of modernity. The movement reached its peak in the 1950s, though its influence continues to be seen in organizations such as the American Catholic Philosophical Association. Among its major figures are Joseph Kleutgen, Désiré Mercier, Joseph Maréchal, Pierre Rousselot, Réginald Garrigou-LaGrange, Martin Grabmann, M.-D. Chenu, Jacques Maritain, Étienne Gilson, Yves R. Simon, Josef Pieper, Karl Rahner, Cornelio Fabro, Emerich Coreth, Bernard Lonergan, and W. Norris Clarke. Few, if any, of these figures have described themselves as Neo-Thomists; some explicitly rejected the designation. Neo-Thomists have little in common except their commitment to Aquinas and his relevance to the contemporary world. Their interest produced a more historically accurate understanding of Aquinas and his contribution to medieval thought (Grabmann, Gilson, Chenu), including a previously ignored use of the Platonic metaphysics of participation (Fabro). This richer understanding of Aquinas, as forging a creative synthesis in the midst of competing traditions, has made arguing for his relevance easier. Those Neo-Thomists who were suspicious of modernity produced fresh readings of Aquinas's texts applied to contemporary problems (Pieper, Gilson). Their influence can be seen in the revival of virtue theory and the work of Alasdair MacIntyre. Others sought to develop Aquinas's thought with the aid of later Thomists (Maritain, Simon) and incorporated the interpretations of

Counter-Reformation Thomists, such as Cajetan and Jean Poinsot, to produce more sophisticated, and controversial, accounts of the intelligence, intentionality, semiotics, and practical knowledge. Those Neo-Thomists willing to engage modern thought on its own terms interpreted modern philosophy sympathetically using the principles of Aquinas (Maréchal, Lonergan, Clarke), seeking dialogue rather than confrontation. However, some readings of Aquinas are so thoroughly integrated into modern philosophy that they can seem assimilated (Rahner, Coreth); their highly individualized metaphysics inspired as much by other philosophical influences, especially Heidegger, as Aquinas. Some of the labels currently used among Neo-Thomists suggest a division in the movement over critical, post-Kantian methodology. 'Existential Thomism' is used for those who emphasize both the real distinction between essence and existence and the role of the sensible in the mind's first grasp of being. 'Transcendental Thomism' applies to figures like Maréchal, Rousselot, Rahner, and Coreth who rely upon the inherent dynamism of the mind toward the real, rooted in Aquinas's theory of the active intellect, from which to deduce their metaphysics of being. See also AQUINAS, GILSON, MARITAIN, MERCIER, THOMISM.   D.W.H.

Neumann, John von. See VON NEUMANN.

neural net. See CONNECTIONISM.

neural network modeling. See CONNECTIONISM.

Neurath, Otto. See VIENNA CIRCLE.

neurophilosophy. See CHURCHLAND, PATRICIA.

neuroscience. See COGNITIVE SCIENCE.

neustic. See PRESCRIPTIVISM.

neutrality. See LIBERALISM.

neutral monism. See PHILOSOPHY OF MIND.

New Academy, the name given the Academy, the school founded by Plato in Athens, during the time it was controlled by Academic Skeptics after about 265 B.C. Its principal leaders in this period were Arcesilaus (315–242) and Carneades (219–129); our most accessible source for the New Academy is Cicero's *Academica*.

A master of logical techniques such as sorites

(which he learned from Diodorus), Arcesilaus attempted to revive the dialectic of Plato, using it to achieve the suspension of belief he learned to value from Pyrrho. Later, and especially under the leadership of Carneades, the New Academy developed a special relationship with Stoicism: as the Stoics found new ways to defend their doctrine of the criterion, Carneades found new ways to refute it in the Stoics' own terms. Carneades' visit to Rome in 155 B.C. with a Stoic and a Peripatetic marks the beginning of Rome's interest in Greek philosophy. His anti-Stoic arguments were recorded by his successor Clitomachus (d. c.110 B.C.), whose work is known to us through summaries in Cicero.

Clitomachus was succeeded by Philo of Larisa (c.160–79 B.C.), who was the teacher of Antiochus of Ascalon (c.130–c.67 B.C.). Philo later attempted to reconcile the Old and the New Academy by softening the Skepticism of the New and by fostering a Skeptical reading of Plato. Angered by this, Antiochus broke away in about 87 B.C. to found what *he* called the Old Academy, which is now considered to be the beginning of Middle Platonism. Probably about the same time, Aenesidemus (dates unknown) revived the strict Skepticism of Pyrrho and founded the school that is known to us through the work of Sextus Empiricus. Academic Skepticism differed from Pyrrhonism in its sharp focus on Stoic positions, and possibly in allowing for a weak assent (as opposed to belief, which they suspended) in what is probable; and Pyrrhonians accused Academic Skeptics of being dogmatic in their rejection of the possibility of knowledge. The New Academy had a major influence on the development of modern philosophy, most conspicuously through Hume, who considered that his brand of mitigated skepticism belonged to this school.

See also ACADEMY, ISLAMIC NEOPLATONISM, SKEPTICS.   P.Wo.

Newcomb's paradox, a conflict between two widely accepted principles of rational decision, arising in the following decision problem, known as *Newcomb's problem.* Two boxes are before you. The first contains either $1,000,000 or nothing. The second contains $1,000. You may take the first box alone or both boxes. Someone with uncanny foresight has predicted your choice and fixed the content of the first box according to his prediction. If he has predicted that you will take only the first box, he has put $1,000,000 in that box; and if he has predicted that you will take both boxes, he has left the first box empty. The expected utility of an option is commonly

obtained by multiplying the utility of its possible outcomes by their probabilities given the option, and then adding the products. Because the predictor is reliable, the probability that you receive $1,000,000 given that you take only the first box is high, whereas the probability that you receive $1,001,000 given that you take both boxes is low. Accordingly, the expected utility of taking only the first box is greater than the expected utility of taking both boxes. Therefore *the principle of maximizing expected utility* says to take only the first box. However, *the principle of dominance* says that if the states determining the outcomes of options are causally independent of the options, and there is one option that is better than the others in each state, then you should adopt it. Since your choice does not causally influence the contents of the first box, and since choosing both boxes yields $1,000 in addition to the contents of the first box whatever they are, the principle says to take both boxes.

Newcomb's paradox is named after its formulator, William Newcomb. Nozick publicized it in "Newcomb's Problem and Two Principles of Choice" (1969). Many theorists have responded to the paradox by changing the definition of the expected utility of an option so that it is sensitive to the causal influence of the option on the states that determine its outcome, but is insensitive to the evidential bearing of the option on those states.

See also DECISION THEORY, UTILITARIANISM.   P.We.

Newcomb's problem. See NEWCOMB'S PARADOX.

Newman, John Henry (1801–90), English prelate and philosopher of religion. As fellow at Oriel College, Oxford, he was a prominent member of the Anglican Oxford Movement. He became a Roman Catholic in 1845, took holy orders in 1847, and was made a cardinal in 1879.

His most important philosophical work is the *Grammar of Assent* (1870). Here Newman explored the difference between formal reasoning and the informal or natural movement of the mind in discerning the truth about the concrete and historical. Concrete reasoning in the mode of *natural inference* is implicit and unreflective; it deals not with general principles as such but with their employment in particular circumstances. Thus a scientist must judge whether the phenomenon he confronts is a novel significant datum, a coincidence, or merely an insignificant variation in the data.

The acquired capacity to make judgments of

this sort Newman called the *illative sense,* an intellectual skill shaped by experience and personal insight and generally limited for individuals to particular fields of endeavor. The illative sense makes possible a judgment of certitude about the matter considered, even though the formal argument that partially outlines the process possesses only objective probability for the novice. Hence probability is not necessarily opposed to certitude.

In becoming aware of its tacit dimension, Newman spoke of recognizing a mode of *informal inference*. He distinguished such reasoning, which, by virtue of the illative sense, culminates in a judgment of certitude about the way things are (real assent), from formal reasoning conditioned by the certainty or probability of the premises, which assents to the conclusion thus conditioned (notional assent). In real assent, the proposition functions to "image" the reality, to make its reality present.

In the *Development of Christian Doctrine* (1845), Newman analyzed the ways in which some ideas unfold themselves only through historical development, within a tradition of inquiry. He sought to delineate the common pattern of such development in politics, science, philosophy, and religion. Although his focal interest was in how religious doctrines develop, he emphasizes the general character of such a pattern of progressive articulation.   F.J.C.

New Realism, an early twentieth-century revival, both in England and in the United States, of various forms of realism in reaction to the dominant idealisms inherited from the nineteenth century. In America this revival took a cooperative form when six philosophers (Ralph Barton Perry, Edwin Holt, William Pepperell Montague, Walter Pitkin, Edward Spaulding, and Walter Marvin) published "A Program and First Platform of Six Realists" (1910), followed two years later by the cooperative volume *The New Realism,* in which each authored an essay. This volume gave rise to the designation 'New Realists' for these six philosophers.

Although they clearly disagreed on many particulars, they concurred on several matters of philosophical style and epistemological substance. Procedurally they endorsed a cooperative and piecemeal approach to philosophical problems, and they were constitutionally inclined to a closeness of analysis that would prepare the way for later philosophical tendencies. Substantively they agreed on several epistemological stances central to the refutation of idealism.

Among the doctrines in the New Realist platform were the rejection of the fundamental character of epistemology; the view that the entities investigated in logic, mathematics, and science are not "mental" in any ordinary sense; the view that the things known are not the products of the knowing relation nor in any fundamental sense conditioned by their being known; and the view that the objects known are immediately and directly present to consciousness while being independent of that relation. New Realism was a version of direct realism, which viewed the notions of mediation and representation in knowledge as opening gambits on the slippery slope to idealism.

Their refutation of idealism focused on pointing out the fallacy of moving from the truism that every object of knowledge is known to the claim that its being consists in its being known. That we are obviously at the center of what we know entails nothing about the nature of what we know. Perry dubbed this fact "the egocentric predicament," and supplemented this observation with arguments to the effect that the objects of knowledge are in fact independent of the knowing relation.

New Realism as a version of direct realism had as its primary conceptual obstacle "the facts of relativity," i.e., error, illusion, perceptual variation, and valuation. Dealing with these phenomena without invoking "mental intermediaries" proved to be the stumbling block, and New Realism soon gave way to a second cooperative venture by another group of American philosophers that came to be known as Critical Realism.

The term 'new realism' is also occasionally used with regard to those British philosophers (principal among them Moore and Russell) similarly involved in refuting idealism. Although individually more significant than the American group, theirs was not a cooperative effort, so the group term came to have primarily an American referent.

See also CRITICAL REALISM, IDEALISM, PERCEPTION.   C.F.D.

new riddle of induction. See GRUE PARADOX.

new theory of reference. See PUTNAM.

Newton, Sir Isaac (1642–1727), English physicist and mathematician, one of the greatest scientists of all time. Born in Woolsthorpe, Lincolnshire, he attended Cambridge University, receiving the B.A. in 1665; he became a fellow of Trinity in

1667 and Lucasian Professor of Mathematics in 1669. He was elected fellow of the Royal Society in 1671 and served as its president from 1703 until his death. In 1696 he was appointed warden of the mint. In his later years he was involved in political and governmental affairs rather than in active scientific work. A sensitive, secretive person, he was prone to irascibility – most notably in a dispute with Leibniz over priority of invention of the calculus. His unparalleled scientific accomplishments overshadow a deep and sustained interest in ancient chronology, biblical study, theology, and alchemy.

In his early twenties Newton's genius asserted itself in an astonishing period of mathematical and experimental creativity. In the years 1664–67, he discovered the binomial theorem; the "method of fluxions" (calculus); the principle of the composition of light; and fundamentals of his theory of universal gravitation.

Newton's masterpiece, *Philosophiae Naturalis Principia Mathematica* ("The Mathematical Principles of Natural Philosophy"), appeared in 1687. This work sets forth the mathematical laws of physics and "the system of the world." Its exposition is modeled on Euclidean geometry: propositions are demonstrated mathematically from definitions and mathematical axioms. The world system consists of material bodies (masses composed of hard particles) at rest or in motion and interacting according to three axioms or *laws of motion:*

(1) Every body continues in its state of rest or of uniform motion in a straight line unless it is compelled to change that state by forces impressed upon it.

(2) The change of motion is proportional to the motive force impressed and is made in the direction of the straight line in which that force is impressed. [Here, the impressed force equals mass times the rate of change of velocity, i.e., acceleration. Hence the familiar formula, $F = ma$.]

(3) To every action there is always opposed an equal reaction; or, the mutual action of two bodies upon each other is always equal and directed to contrary parts.

Newton's general law of gravitation (in modern restatement) is:

Every particle of matter attracts every other particle with a force varying directly as the product of their masses and inversely as the square of the distance between them.

The statement of the laws of motion is preceded by an equally famous scholium in which Newton enunciates the ultimate conditions of his universal system: absolute time, space, place, and motion. He speaks of these as independently existing "quantities" according to which true measurements of bodies and motions can be made as distinct from relative "sensible measures" and apparent observations. Newton seems to have thought that his system of mathematical principles presupposed and is validated by the absolute framework. The scholium has been the subject of much critical discussion. The main problem concerns the justification of the absolute framework. Newton commends adherence to experimental observation and induction for advancing scientific knowledge, and he rejects speculative hypotheses. But absolute time and space are not observable. (In the scholium Newton did offer a renowned experiment using a rotating pail of water as evidence for distinguishing true and apparent motions and proof of absolute motion.) It has been remarked that conflicting strains of a rationalism (anticipating Kant) and empiricism (anticipating Hume) are present in Newton's conception of science. Some of these issues are also evident in Newton's *Optics* (1704, especially the fourth edition, 1730), which includes a series of suggestive "Queries" on the nature of light, gravity, matter, scientific method, and God.

The triumphant reception given to Newton's *Principia* in England and on the Continent led to idealization of the man and his work. Thus Alexander Pope's famous epitaph:

Nature and Nature's laws lay hid in night;
God said, "Let Newton be!" and all was light.

The term 'Newtonian', then, denoted the view of nature as a universal system of mathematical reason and order divinely created and administered. The metaphor of a "universal machine" was frequently applied. The view is central in the eighteenth-century Enlightenment, inspiring a religion of reason and the scientific study of society and the human mind. More narrowly, 'Newtonian' suggests a reduction of any subject matter to an ontology of individual particles and the laws and basic terms of mechanics: mass, length, and time.

See also FIELD THEORY, PHILOSOPHY OF SCIENCE, QUANTUM MECHANICS, SPACE, TIME.
H.S.T.

Newtonian. See NEWTON.

Nicholas Kryfts. See NICHOLAS OF CUSA.

Nicholas of Autrecourt (c.1300–after 1350), French philosopher and theologian. Born in Autrecourt, he was educated at Paris and earned bachelor's degrees in theology and law and a master's degree in arts. After a list of propositions from his writings was condemned in 1346, he was sentenced to burn his works publicly and recant, which he did in Paris the following year. He was appointed dean of Metz cathedral in 1350.

Nicholas's ecclesiastical troubles arose partly from nine letters (two of which survive) which reduce to absurdity the view that appearances provide a sufficient basis for certain and evident knowledge. On the contrary, except for "certitude of the faith," we can be certain only of what is equivalent or reducible to the principle of non-contradiction. He accepts as a consequence of this that we can never validly infer the existence of one distinct thing from another, including the existence of substances from qualities, or causes from effects. Indeed, he finds that "in the whole of his natural philosophy and metaphysics, Aristotle had such [evident] certainty of scarcely two conclusions, and perhaps not even of one." Nicholas devotes another work, the *Exigit ordo executionis* (also known as *The Universal Treatise*), to an extended critique of Aristotelianism. It attacks what seemed to him the blind adherence given by his contemporaries to Aristotle and Averroes, showing that the opposite of many conclusions alleged to have been demonstrated by the Philosopher – e.g., on the divisibility of continua, the reality of motion, and the truth of appearances – are just as evident or apparent as those conclusions themselves.

Because so few of his writings are extant, however, it is difficult to ascertain just what Nicholas's own views were. Likewise, the reasons for his condemnation are not well understood, although recent studies have suggested that his troubles might have been due to a reaction to certain ideas that he appropriated from English theologians, such as Adam de Wodeham.

Nicholas's views elicited comment not only from church authorities, but also from other philosophers, including Buridan, Marsilius of Inghen, Albert of Saxony, and Nicholas of Oresme. Despite a few surface similarities, however, there is no evidence that his teachings on certainty or causality had any influence on modern philosophers, such as Descartes or Hume.

See also ARISTOTLE, OCKHAM, RATIONAL-ISM.   J.A.Z.

Nicholas of Cusa, also called Nicolaus Cusanus, Nicholas Kryfts (1401–64), German philosopher, an important Renaissance Platonist. Born in Kues on the Moselle, he earned a doctorate in canon law in 1423. He became known for his *De concordantia catholica,* written at the Council of Basel in 1432, a work defending the conciliarist position against the pope. Later, he decided that only the pope could provide unity for the church in its negotiations with the East, and allied himself with the papacy. In 1437–38, returning from a papal legation to Constantinople, he had his famous insight into the coincidence of opposites (*coincidentia oppositorum*) in the infinite, upon which his *On Learned Ignorance* is based. His unceasing labor was chiefly responsible for the Vienna Concordat with the Eastern church in 1448. He was made cardinal in 1449 as a reward for his efforts, and bishop of Brixen (Bressanone) in 1450. He traveled widely in Germany as a papal legate (1450–52) before settling down in his see.

Cusa's central insight was that all oppositions are united in their infinite measure, so that what would be logical contradictions for finite things coexist without contradiction in God, who is the measure of (i.e., is the form or essence of) all things, and identical to them inasmuch as he is identical with their reality, quiddity, or essence. Considered as it is contracted to the individual, a thing is only an image of its measure, not a reality in itself. His position drew on mathematical models, arguing, for instance, that an infinite straight line tangent to a circle is the measure of the curved circumference, since a circle of infinite diameter, containing all the being possible in a circle, would coincide with the tangent. In general, the measure of a thing must contain all the possible being of that sort of thing, and so is infinite, or unlimited, in its being. Cusa attacked Aristotelians for their unwillingness to give up the principle of non-contradiction. His epistemology is a form of Platonic skepticism. Our knowledge is never of reality, the infinite measure of things that is their essence, but only of finite images of reality corresponding to the finite copies with which we must deal. These images are constructed by our own minds, and do not represent an immediate grasp of any reality. Their highest form is found in mathematics, and it is only through mathematics that reason can understand the world. In relation to the infinite real, these images and the contracted realities they enable us to know have only an infinitesimal reality. Our knowledge is only a mass of conjectures, i.e., assertions that are true insofar as they capture some part of the truth, but never the whole truth, the infinite measure, as it really is in itself. Cusa was much read in the Renaissance, and is sometimes said to have had significant influence on German thought of the eighteenth century, in particular on Leibniz, and German idealism, but it is uncertain, despite the considerable intrinsic merit of his thought, if this is true.

See also PLATO.   J.Lo.

Nietzsche, Friedrich Wilhelm (1844–1900), German philosopher and cultural critic. Born in a small town in the Prussian province of Saxony, Nietzsche's early education emphasized religion and classical languages and literature. After a year at the university at Bonn he transferred to Leipzig, where he pursued classical studies. There he happened upon Schopenhauer's *The World as Will and Representation,* which profoundly influenced his subsequent concerns and early philosophical thinking. It was as a classical philologist, however, that he was appointed professor at the Swiss university at Basel, before he had even received his doctorate, at the astonishingly early age of twenty-four.

A mere twenty years of productive life remained to him, ending with a mental and physical collapse in January 1889, from which he never recovered. He held his position at Basel for a decade, resigning in 1879 owing to the deterioration of his health from illnesses he had contracted in 1870 as a volunteer medical orderly in the Franco-Prussian war. At Basel he lectured on a variety of subjects chiefly relating to classical studies, including Greek and Roman philosophy as well as literature. During his early years there he also became intensely involved with the composer Richard Wagner; and his fascination with Wagner was reflected in several of his early works – most notably his first book, *The Birth of Tragedy* (1872), and his subsequent essay *Richard Wagner in Bayreuth* (1876). His later break with Wagner, culminating in his polemic *The Case of Wagner* (1888), was both profound and painful to him. While at first regarding Wagner as a creative genius showing the way to a cultural and spiritual renewal, Nietzsche came to see him and his art as epitomizing and exacerbating the fundamental problem with which he became increasingly concerned.

This problem was the pervasive intellectual and cultural crisis Nietzsche later characterized in terms of the "death of God" and the advent of "nihilism." Traditional religious and metaphysical ways of thinking were on the wane, leaving a void that modern science could not fill, and endangering the health of civilization. The discovery of some life-affirming alternative to Schopenhauer's radically pessimistic response to this disillusionment became Nietzsche's primary concern. In *The Birth of Tragedy* he looked to the Greeks for clues and to Wagner for inspiration, believing that their art held the key to renewed human flourishing for a humanity bereft both of the consolations of religious faith and of confidence in reason and science as substitutes for it. In his subsequent series of *Untimely Meditations* (1873–76) he expanded upon his theme of the need to reorient human thought and endeavor to this end, and criticized a variety of tendencies detrimental to it that he discerned among his contemporaries.

Both the deterioration of Nietzsche's health and the shift of his interest away from his original discipline prevented retention of his position at Basel. In the first years after his retirement, he completed his transition from philologist to philosopher and published the several parts of *Human, All-Too-Human* (1878–90), *Daybreak* (1881), and the first four parts of *The Gay Science* (1882). These aphoristic writings sharpened and extended his analytical and critical assessment of various human tendencies and social, cultural, and intellectual phenomena. During this period his thinking became much more sophisticated; and he developed the philosophical styles and concerns that found mature expression in the writings of the final years of his brief active life, following the publication of the four parts of *Thus Spoke Zarathustra* (1883–85).

These last remarkably productive years saw the appearance of *Beyond Good and Evil* (1886), a fifth part of *The Gay Science, On the Genealogy of Morals* (1887), *The Case of Wagner* (1888), and a series of prefaces to his earlier works (1886–87), as well as the completion of several books published after his collapse – *Twilight of the Idols* (1889), *The Antichrist* (1895), and *Ecce Homo* (1908). He was also amassing a great deal of material in notebooks, of which a selection was later published under the title *The Will to Power.* (The status and significance of this mass of *Nachlass* material are matters of continuing controversy.)

In the early 1880s, when he wrote *Thus Spoke Zarathustra,* Nietzsche arrived at a conception of human life and possibility – and with it, of value and meaning – that he believed could overcome the Schopenhauerian pessimism and nihilism that he saw as outcomes of the collapse of traditional modes of religious and philosophical interpretation. He prophesied a period of nihilism in the aftermath of their decline and fall; but this prospect deeply distressed him. He was convinced of the untenability of the "God hypothesis," and indeed of all religious and metaphysical interpretations of the world and ourselves; and yet he was well aware that the very possibility of the affirmation of life was at stake, and required more than the mere abandonment of all such "lies" and "fictions." He took the basic challenge of philosophy now to be to reinterpret life and the world along more tenable lines that would also overcome nihilism.

What Nietzsche called "the death of God" was both a cultural event – the waning and impending demise of the "Christian-moral" interpretation of life and the world – and also a philosophical development: the abandonment of anything like the God-hypothesis (all demidivine absolutes included). As a cultural event it was a phenomenon to be reckoned with, and a source of profound concern; for he feared a "nihilistic rebound" in its wake, and worried about the consequences for human life and culture if no countermovement to it were forthcoming. As a philosophical development, on the other hand, it was his point of departure, which he took to call for a radical reconsideration of everything from life and the world and human existence and knowledge to value and morality. The "de-deification of nature," the "translation of man back into nature," the "revaluation of values," the tracing of the "genealogy of morals" and their critique, and the elaboration of "naturalistic" accounts of knowledge, value, morality, and our entire "spiritual" nature thus came to be his main tasks. His published and unpublished writings contain a wealth of remarks, observations, and suggestions contributing importantly to them.

It is a matter of controversy, even among those with a high regard for Nietzsche, whether he tried to work out positions on issues bearing any resemblance to those occupying other philosophers before and after him in the mainstream of the history of philosophy. He was harshly critical of most of his predecessors and contemporaries; and he broke fundamentally with them and their basic ideas and procedures. His own writings, moreover, bear little resemblance to those of most other philosophers. Those he himself published (as well as his reflections in his notebooks) do not systematically set out and develop views. Rather, they consist for the most part in collections of short paragraphs and sets of aphorisms, often only loosely if at all connected. Many deal

with philosophical topics, but in very unconventional ways; and because his remarks about these topics are scattered through many different works, they are all too easily taken in isolation and misunderstood. On some topics, moreover, much of what he wrote is found only in his very rough notebooks, which he filled with thoughts without indicating the extent of his reflected commitment to them. His language, furthermore, is by turns coolly analytical, heatedly polemical, sharply critical, and highly metaphorical; and he seldom indicates clearly the scope of his claims and what he means by his terms.

It is not surprising, therefore, that many philosophers have found it difficult to know what to make of him and to take him seriously – and that some have taken him to repudiate altogether the traditional philosophical enterprise of seeking reasoned conclusions with respect to questions of the kind with which philosophers have long been concerned, heralding the "death" not only of religious and metaphysical thinking, but also of philosophy itself. Others read him very differently, as having sought to effect a fundamental reorientation of philosophical thinking, and to indicate by both precept and example how philosophical inquiry might better be pursued. Those who regard Nietzsche in the former way take his criticisms of his philosophical predecessors and contemporaries to apply to any attempt to address such matters. They seize upon and construe some of his more sweeping negative pronouncements on truth and knowledge as indicating that he believed we can only produce fictions and merely expedient (or possibly creative) perspectival expressions of our needs and desires, as groups or as individuals. They thus take him as a radical nihilist, concerned to subvert the entire philosophical enterprise and replace it with a kind of thinking more akin to the literary exploration of human possibilities in the service of life – a kind of artistic play liberated from concern with truth and knowledge. Those who view him in the latter way, on the other hand, take seriously his concern to find a way of *overcoming* the nihilism he believed to result from traditional ways of thinking; his retention of recast notions of truth and knowledge; and his evident concern – especially in his later writings – to contribute to the comprehension of a broad range of phenomena. This way of understanding him, like the former, remains controversial; but it permits an interpretation of his writings that is philosophically more fruitful.

Nietzsche indisputably insisted upon the *inter-*

pretive character of all human thought; and he called for "new philosophers" who would follow him in engaging in more self-conscious and intellectually responsible attempts to assess and improve upon prevailing interpretations of human life. He also was deeply concerned with how these matters might better be *evaluated,* and with the *values* by which human beings live and might better do so. Thus he made much of the need for a *revaluation* of all received values, and for attention to the problems of the nature, status, and standards of value and evaluation. One form of inquiry he took to be of great utility in connection with both of these tasks is *genealogical* inquiry into the conditions under which various modes of interpretation and evaluation have arisen. It is only one of the kinds of inquiry he considered necessary in both cases, however, serving merely to prepare for others that must be brought to bear before any conclusions are warranted.

Nietzsche further emphasized the *perspectival* character of all thinking and the merely provisional character of all knowing, rejecting the idea of the very possibility of absolute knowledge transcending all perspectives. However, because he also rejected the idea that things (and values) have absolute existence "in themselves" apart from the relations in which he supposes their reality to consist, he held that, if viewed in the multiplicity of perspectives from which various of these relations come to light, they admit of a significant measure of comprehension. This *perspectivism* thus does not exclude the possibility of any sort of knowledge deserving of the name, but rather indicates how it is to be conceived and achieved. His kind of philosophy, which he characterizes as *fröhliche Wissenschaft* (cheerful science), proceeds by way of a variety of such "perspectival" approaches to the various matters with which he deals.

Thus for Nietzsche there is no "truth" in the sense of the correspondence of anything we might think or say to "being," and indeed no "true world of being" to which it may even be imagined to fail to correspond; no "knowledge" conceived in terms of any such truth and reality; and, further, no knowledge at all – even of ourselves and the world of which we are a part – that is absolute, non-perspectival, and certain. But that is not the end of the matter. There are, e.g., ways of thinking that may be more or less well warranted in relation to differing sorts of interest and practice, not only within the context of social life but also in our dealings with our environing world. Nietzsche's reflections on the

reconceptualization of truth and knowledge thus point in the direction of a naturalistic epistemology that he would have replace the conceptions of truth and knowledge of his predecessors, and fill the nihilistic void seemingly left by their bankruptcy. There is, moreover, a good deal about ourselves and our world that he became convinced we can comprehend. Our comprehension may be restricted to what life and the world show themselves to be and involve in our experience; but if they are the only kind of reality, there is no longer any reason to divorce the notions of truth, knowledge, and value from them. The question then becomes how best to interpret and assess what we find as we proceed to explore them. It is to these tasks of interpretation and "revaluation" that Nietzsche devoted his main efforts in his later writings.

In speaking of the death of God, Nietzsche had in mind not only the abandonment of the God-hypothesis (which he considered to be utterly "unworthy of belief," owing its invention and appeal entirely to naïveté, error, all-too-human need, and ulterior motivation), but also the demise of all metaphysical substitutes for it. He likewise criticized and rejected the related postulations of substantial "souls" and self-contained "things," taking both notions to be ontological fictions merely reflecting our artificial (though convenient) linguistic-conceptual shorthand for functionally unitary products, processes, and sets of relations. In place of this cluster of traditional ontological categories and interpretations, he conceived the world in terms of an interplay of forces without any inherent structure or final end. It ceaselessly organizes and reorganizes itself, as the fundamental disposition he called *will to power* gives rise to successive arrays of power relationships. "This world is the will to power – and nothing besides," he wrote; "and you yourselves are also this will to power – and nothing besides!"

Nietzsche's idea of the *eternal return* (or eternal recurrence) underscores this conception of a world without beginning or end, in which things happen repeatedly in the way they always have. He first introduced this idea as a test of one's ability to affirm one's own life and the general character of life in this world as they are, without reservation, qualification, or appeal to anything transcending them. He later entertained the thought that all events might actually recur eternally in exactly the same sequence, and experimented in his unpublished writings with arguments to this effect. For the most part, however, he restricted himself to less problematic uses of the idea that do not presuppose its literal truth in this radical form. His rhetorical embellishments and experimental elaborations of the idea may have been intended to make it more vivid and compelling; but he employed it chiefly to depict his conception of the radically non-linear character of events in this world and their fundamental homogeneity, and to provide a way of testing our ability to live with it. If we are sufficiently strong and well disposed to life to affirm it even on the supposition that it will only be the same sequence of events repeated eternally, we have what it takes to endure and flourish in the kind of world in which Nietzsche believed we find ourselves in the aftermath of disillusionment.

Nietzsche construed human nature and existence *naturalistically,* in terms of the will to power and its ramifications in the establishment and expression of the kinds of complex systems of dynamic quanta in which human beings consist. "The soul is only a word for something about the body," he has Zarathustra say; and the body is fundamentally a configuration of natural forces and processes. At the same time, he insisted on the importance of social arrangements and interactions in the development of human forms of awareness and activity. He also emphasized the possibility of the emergence of exceptional human beings capable of an independence and creativity elevating them above the level of the general human rule. So he stressed the difference between "higher men" and "the herd," and through Zarathustra proclaimed the *Übermensch* ('overman' or 'superman') to be "the meaning of the earth," employing this image to convey the ideal of the overcoming of the "all-too-human" and the fullest possible creative "enhancement of life." Far from seeking to diminish our humanity by stressing our animality, he sought to direct our efforts to the emergence of a "higher humanity" capable of endowing existence with a human redemption and justification, above all through the enrichment of cultural life.

Notwithstanding his frequent characterization as a nihilist, therefore, Nietzsche in fact sought to counter and overcome the nihilism he expected to prevail in the aftermath of the collapse and abandonment of traditional religious and metaphysical modes of interpretation and evaluation. While he was highly critical of the latter, it was not his intention merely to oppose them; for he further attempted to make out the possibility of forms of truth and knowledge to which philosophical interpreters of life and the world might

aspire, and espoused a "Dionysian value-standard" in place of all non-naturalistic modes of valuation. In keeping with his interpretation of life and the world in terms of his conception of will to power, Nietzsche framed this standard in terms of his interpretation of them. The only tenable alternative to nihilism must be based upon a recognition and affirmation of the world's fundamental character. This meant positing as a general standard of value the attainment of a kind of life in which the will to power as the creative transformation of existence is raised to its highest possible intensity and qualitative expression. This in turn led him to take the "enhancement of life" and creativity to be the guiding ideas of his revaluation of values and development of a naturalistic value theory.

This way of thinking carried over into Nietzsche's thinking about morality. Insisting that moralities as well as other traditional modes of valuation ought to be assessed "in the perspective of life," he argued that most of them were contrary to the enhancement of life, reflecting the all-too-human needs and weaknesses and fears of less favored human groups and types. Distinguishing between "master" and "slave" moralities, he found the latter to have become the dominant type of morality in the modern world. He regarded present-day morality as a "herd-animal morality," well suited to the requirements and vulnerabilities of the mediocre who are the human rule, but stultifying and detrimental to the development of potential exceptions to that rule. Accordingly, he drew attention to the origins and functions of this type of morality (as a social-control mechanism and device by which the weak defend and avenge and assert themselves against the actually or potentially stronger). He further suggested the desirability of a "higher morality" for the exceptions, in which the contrast of the basic "slave/herd morality" categories of "good and evil" would be replaced by categories more akin to the "good and bad" contrast characteristic of "master morality," with a revised (and variable) content better attuned to the conditions and attainable qualities of the enhanced forms of life such exceptional human beings can achieve.

The strongly creative flavor of Nietzsche's notions of such a "higher humanity" and associated "higher morality" reflects his linkage of both to his conception of art, to which he attached great importance. Art, for Nietzsche, is fundamentally creative (rather than cognitive), serving to prepare for the emergence of a sensibility and manner of life reflecting the highest potentiality of human beings. Art, as the creative transformation of the world as we find it (and of ourselves thereby) on a small scale and in particular media, affords a glimpse of a kind of life that would be lived more fully in this manner, and constitutes a step toward emergence. In this way, Nietzsche's mature thought thus expands upon the idea of the basic connection between art and the justification of life that was his general theme in his first major work, *The Birth of Tragedy.*

See also EXISTENTIALISM, HEGEL, KANT, SCHOPENHAUER.   R.Sc.

Nihil est in intellectu quod non prius fuerit in sensu (Latin, 'Nothing is in the understanding that had not previously been in the senses'), a principal tenet of empiricism. A weak interpretation of the principle maintains that all concepts are acquired from sensory experience; no concepts are innate or a priori. A stronger interpretation adds that all propositional knowledge is derived from sense experience. The weak interpretation was held by Aquinas and Locke, who thought nevertheless that we can know some propositions to be true in virtue of the relations between the concepts involved. The stronger interpretation was endorsed by J. S. Mill, who argued that even the truths of mathematics are inductively based on experience. See also EMPIRICISM.   W.E.M.

Nihil ex nihilo fit (Latin, 'Nothing arises from nothing'), an intuitive metaphysical principle first enunciated in the West by Parmenides, often held equivalent to the proposition that nothing arises without a cause. Creation *ex nihilo* is God's production of the world without any natural or material cause, but involves a supernatural cause, and so it would not violate the principle.   J.Lo.

nihilism, ethical. See RELATIVISM.

nihilism, philosophical. See NIETZSCHE, RUSSIAN NIHILISM.

nihilism, Russian. See RUSSIAN NIHILISM.

nihilism, semantic. See SEMANTIC HOLISM.

nirodha-samapātti, also known as *samjñā-vedayita-nirodha* (Sanskrit, 'attainment of cessation'), a term used by Indian Buddhists to denote a state produced by meditation in which no mental events of any kind occur. What ceases in *nirodha-samāpatti* is all the operations of the mind; all that remains is the mindless body. Some Buddhists took this state to have salvific significance, and so likened it to Nirvana. But its principal philosophical interest lies in the puzzle it produced for Buddhist theorists: What causal account can be given that will make sense of the reemergence of mental events from a continuum in which none exist, given the pan-Buddhist assumption that all existents are momentary?

P.J.G.

NN thesis. See NECESSITY.

noema. See HUSSERL, NOETIC.

noemata moralia. See MORE, THOMAS.

noematic analysis. See HUSSERL.

noesis. See DIVIDED LINE, HUSSERL.

noetic (from Greek *noētikos*, from *noētos*, 'perceiving'), of or relating to apprehension by the intellect. In a strict sense the term refers to nonsensuous data given to the cognitive faculty, which discloses their intelligible meaning as distinguished from their sensible apprehension. We hear a sentence spoken, but it becomes intelligible for us only when the sounds function as a foundation for noetic apprehension.

For Plato, the objects of such apprehension (*noetá*) are the Forms (*eide*) with respect to which the sensible phenomena are only occasions of manifestation: the Forms in themselves transcend the sensible and have their being in a realm apart. For empiricist thinkers, e.g., Locke, there is strictly speaking no distinct noetic aspect, since "ideas" are only faint sense impressions. In a looser sense, however, one may speak of ideas as independent of reference to particular sense impressions, i.e. independent of their origin, and then an idea can be taken to signify a class of objects.

Husserl uses the term to describe the intentionality or dyadic character of consciousness in general, i.e. including both eidetic or categorial and perceptual knowing. He speaks of the correlation of *noesis* or intending and *noema* or the intended object of awareness. The categorial or eidetic is the perceptual object as intellectually cognized; it is not a realm apart, but rather what is disclosed or made present ("constituted")

when the mode of appearance of the perceptual object is intended by a categorial noesis.
  See also HUSSERL, NOÛS.   F.J.C.

noetic analysis. See HUSSERL.

noise. See INFORMATION THEORY.

nomic. See LAWLIKE GENERALIZATION.

nomic necessity. See LAWLIKE GENERALIZATION.

nominal definition. See DEFINITION.

nominal essence. See ESSENTIALISM.

nominalism. See METAPHYSICAL REALISM, PROPERTY.

nominalization. See STATE OF AFFAIRS.

nominatum. See OBLIQUE CONTEXT.

nomological. See LAWLIKE GENERALIZATION.

nomothetic. See WINDELBAND.

non-action. See WU WEI.

non causa pro causa. See INFORMAL FALLACY.

noncognitivism. See EMOTIVISM, ETHICS.

non-contradiction, principle of. See PRINCIPLE OF CONTRADICTION.

non-duplication principle. See PHILOSOPHY OF MIND.

non-embodiment. See DISEMBODIMENT.

non-epistemic. See PERCEPTION.

non-Euclidean geometry, those axiomatized versions of geometry in which the parallel axiom of Euclidean geometry is rejected, after so many unsuccessful attempts to prove it. As in so many branches of mathematics, C. F. Gauss had thought out much of the matter first, but he kept most of his ideas to himself. As a result, credit is given to J. Bolyai and N. Lobachevsky, who worked independently from the late 1820s. Instead of assuming that just one line passes through a point in a plane parallel to a non-coincident coplanar line, they offered a geometry in which a line admits more than one parallel, and

the sum of the "angles" between the "sides" of a "triangle" lies below 180°. Then in mid-century G. F. B. Riemann conceived of a geometry in which lines always meet (so no parallels), and the sum of the "angles" exceeds 180°. In this connection he distinguished between the unboundedness of space as a property of its extent, and the special case of the infinite measure over which distance might be taken (which is dependent upon the curvature of that space).

  Pursuing the (published) insight of Gauss, that the curvature of a surface could be defined in terms only of properties dependent solely on the surface itself (and later called "intrinsic"), Riemann also defined the metric on a surface in a very general and intrinsic way, in terms of the differential arc length. Thereby he clarified the ideas of "distance" that his non-Euclidean precursors had introduced (drawing on trigonometric and hyperbolic functions); arc length was now understood geodesically as the shortest "distance" between two "points" on a surface, and was specified independent of any assumptions of a geometry within which the surface was embedded. Further properties, such as that pertaining to the "volume" of a three-"dimensional" solid, were also studied.

  The two main types of non-Euclidean geometry, and its Euclidean parent, may be summarized as follows:

Discoverer	Parallels	Curvature	Angle sum
[Euclidean]	One	Zero	= 180°
Bolyai, Lobachevsky	Two or more	Negative	< 180°
Riemann	Zero	Positive	> 180°

  Reaction to these geometries was slow to develop, but their impact gradually emerged. As mathematics, their legitimacy was doubted; but in 1868 E. Beltrami produced a model of a Bolyai-type two-dimensional space inside a planar circle. The importance of this model was to show that the consistency of this geometry depended upon that of the Euclidean version, thereby dispelling the fear that it was an inconsistent flash of the imagination. During the last thirty years of the nineteenth century a variety of variant geometries were proposed, and the relationships between them were studied, together with consequences for projective geometry.

  On the empirical side, these geometries, and especially Riemann's approach, affected the understanding of the relationship between geometry and space; in particular, it posed the question whether space is curved or not (the latter being the Euclidean answer). The geometries thus played a role in the emergence and articulation of relativity theory, especially the differential geometry and tensorial calculus within which its mathematical properties could be expressed.

Philosophically the new geometries stressed the hypothetical nature of axiomatizing, in contrast to the customary view of mathematical theories as true in some (usually) unclear sense. This feature led to the name 'metageometry' for them; it was intended (as an ironical proposal of opponents) to be in line with the hypothetical character of metaphysics in philosophy. They also helped to encourage conventionalist philosophy of science (with Poincaré, e.g.), and put fresh light on the age-old question of the (im)possibility of a priori knowledge.

See also EUCLIDEAN GEOMETRY, PHILOSOPHY OF MATHEMATICS.   I.G.-G.

non-monotonic logic, a logic that fails to be monotonic, i.e., in proof-theoretic terms, fails to meet the condition that for all statements $v_1, \ldots v_n, \phi, \psi$, if '$v_1, \ldots v_n \vdash \phi$', then, for any ψ, '$v_1, \ldots v_n, \psi \vdash \phi$'. (Equivalently, let Γ represent a collection of statements, $v_1 \ldots v_n$, and say that in monotonic logic, if '$\Gamma \vdash \phi$', then, for any ψ, '$\Gamma, \psi \vdash \phi$' and similarly in other cases.) A non-monotonic logic is any logic with the following property: For some Γ, ϕ, and ψ, '$\Gamma_{NML} \phi$ but '$\Gamma, \psi \not\vdash_{NML} \phi$'. This is a weak non-monotonic logic. In a strong non-monotonic logic, we might have, again for some Γ, ϕ, ψ, where Γ is consistent and $\Gamma \wedge \phi$ is consistent: '$\Gamma, \psi \vdash_{NML} \neg \phi$'.

A primary motivation (among AI researchers) for non-monotonic logic or defeasible reasoning, which is so evident in commonsense reasoning, is to produce a machine representation for default reasoning or defeasible reasoning. The interest in defeasible reasoning readily spreads to epistemology, logic, and ethics.

The exigencies of practical affairs requires leaping to conclusions, going beyond available evidence, making assumptions. In doing so, we often err and must leap back from our conclusions, undo our assumptions, revise our beliefs. In the literature's standard example, Tweety is a bird and all birds fly, except penguins and ostriches. Does Tweety fly? If pressed, we may need to form a belief about this matter. Upon discovering that Tweety is a penguin, we may have to retract our conclusion. Any representation of defeasible reasoning must capture the non-monotonicity of this reasoning. Non-monotonic logic is an attempt to do this within logic

itself – by adding rules of inference that do not preserve monotonicity.

Although practical affairs require us to reason defeasibly, the best way to achieve non-monotonicity may not be to add non-monotonic rules of inference to standard logic. What one gives up in such systems may well not be worth the cost: loss of the deduction theorem and of a coherent notion of consistency. Therefore, the challenge of non-monotonic logic (or defeasible reasoning, generally) is to develop a rigorous way to represent the structure of non-monotonic reasoning without losing or abandoning the historically hard-won properties of monotonic (standard) logic.

See also ARTIFICIAL INTELLIGENCE, DEFAULT LOGIC, DEFEASIBILITY.   F.A.

non-natural properties. See MOORE.

non-predicative property. See TYPE THEORY.

non-propositional knowledge. See EPISTEMOLOGY.

non-reductive materialism. See PHILOSOPHY OF MIND.

non-reductive physicalism. See KIM.

non-reflexive. See RELATION.

non-standard analysis. See MATHEMATICAL ANALYSIS.

non-standard interpretation. See FORMAL SEMANTICS.

non-standard model. See STANDARD MODEL.

non-standard semantics. See SECOND-ORDER LOGIC.

non-symmetric. See RELATION.

non-transitive. See RELATION.

nonviolence, the renunciation of violence in personal, social, or international affairs. It often includes a commitment (called active nonviolence or nonviolent direct action) actively to oppose violence (and usually evil or injustice as well) by nonviolent means.

Nonviolence may renounce physical violence alone or both physical and psychological violence. It may represent a purely personal commitment or be intended to be normative for others as well. When unconditional – *absolute nonviolence* – it renounces violence in all actual and hypothetical circumstances. When conditional – *conditional nonviolence* – it concedes the justifiability of violence in hypothetical circumstances but denies it in practice. Held on moral grounds (*principled nonviolence*), the commitment belongs to an ethics of conduct or an ethics of virtue. If the former, it will likely be expressed as a moral rule or principle (e.g., One ought always to act nonviolently) to guide action. If the latter, it will urge cultivating the traits and dispositions of a nonviolent character (which presumably then will be expressed in nonviolent action). As a principle, nonviolence may be considered either basic or derivative. Either way, its justification will be either utilitarian or deontological.

Held on non-moral grounds (*pragmatic nonviolence*), nonviolence is a means to specific social, political, economic, or other ends, themselves held on non-moral grounds. Its justification lies in its effectiveness for these limited purposes rather than as a way of life or a guide to conduct in general. An alternative source of power, it may then be used in the service of evil as well as good. Nonviolent social action, whether of a principled or pragmatic sort, may include non-cooperation, mass demonstrations, marches, strikes, boycotts, and civil disobedience – techniques explored extensively in the writings of Gene Sharp. Undertaken in defense of an entire nation or state, nonviolence provides an alternative to war. It seeks to deny an invading or occupying force the capacity to attain its objectives by withholding the cooperation of the populace needed for effective rule and by nonviolent direct action, including civil disobedience. It may also be used against oppressive domestic rule or on behalf of social justice. Gandhi's campaign against British rule in India, Scandinavian resistance to Nazi occupation during World War II, and Martin Luther King, Jr.'s actions on behalf of civil rights in the United States are illustrative.

Nonviolence has origins in Far Eastern thought, particularly Taoism and Jainism. It has strands in the Jewish Talmud, and many find it implied by the New Testament's Sermon on the Mount.

See also CIVIL DISOBEDIENCE, GANDHI, PACIFISM.   R.L.H.

norm. See BASIC NORM.

normal form, a formula equivalent to a given logical formula, but having special properties. The main varieties follow.

Conjunctive normal form. If $D_1 \ldots D_n$ are disjunctions of sentential variables or their negations, such as $(p \lor \sim q \lor r)$, then a formula F is in conjunctive normal form provided $F = D_1$ & D_2 & .. & D_n. The following are in conjunctive normal form: $(\sim p \lor q)$; $(p \lor q \lor r)$ & $(\sim p \lor \sim q \lor \sim r)$ & $(\sim q \lor r)$. Every formula of sentential logic has an equivalent conjunctive normal form; this fact can be used to prove the completeness of sentential logic.

Disjunctive normal form. If $C_1 \ldots C_n$ are conjunctions of sentential variables or their negations, such as p & $\sim q$ & $\sim r$, then a formula F is in disjunctive normal form provided $F = C_1 \lor C_2 \lor$ .. C_n. The following are thus in disjunctive normal form: $(p$ & $\sim q) \lor (\sim p$ & $q)$; $(p$ & q & $\sim r) \lor (\sim p$ & $\sim q$ & $\sim r)$. Every formula of sentential logic has an equivalent disjunctive normal form.

Prenex normal form. A formula of predicate logic is in prenex normal form if (1) all quantifiers occur at the beginning of the formula, (2) the scope of the quantifiers extends to the end of the formula, and (3) what follows the quantifiers contains at least one occurrence of every variable that appears in the set of quantifiers. Thus, $(\exists x)(\exists y)(Fx \supset Gy)$ and $(x)(\exists y)(z)((Fxy \lor Gyz) \supset Dxyz)$ are in prenex normal form. The formula may contain free variables; thus, $(\exists x)(y)(Fxyz \supset Gwyx)$ is also in prenex normal form. The following, however, are not in prenex normal form: $(x)(\exists y)(Fx \supset Gx)$; $(x)(y)Fxy \supset Gxy$. Every formula of predicate logic has an equivalent formula in prenex normal form.

Skolem normal form. A formula F in predicate logic is in Skolem normal form provided (1) F is in prenex normal form, (2) every existential quantifier precedes any universal quantifier, (3) F contains at least one existential quantifier, and (4) F contains no free variables. Thus, $(\exists x)(\exists y)(z)(Fxy \supset Gyz)$ and $(\exists x)(\exists y)(\exists z)(w)(Fxy \lor Fyz \lor Fzw)$ are in Skolem normal form; however, $(\exists x)(y)Fxyz$ and $(x)(y)(Fxy \lor Gyx)$ are not. Any formula has an equivalent Skolem normal form; this has implications for the completeness of predicate logic.

See also COMPLETENESS.   V.K.

normative. See DEFINIST.

normative ethics. See ETHICS.

normative reason. See REASONS FOR ACTION, REASONS FOR BELIEF.

normative relativism. See RELATIVISM.

notation, logical. See LOGICAL NOTATION.

notion. See BERKELEY.

notional assent. See NEWMAN.

notum per se (Latin, 'known through itself'), self-evident. This term corresponds roughly to the term 'analytic'. In Thomistic theology, there are two ways for a thing to be self-evident, *secundum se* (in itself) and *quoad nos* (to us). The proposition that God exists is self-evident in itself, because God's existence is identical with his essence; but it is not self-evident to us (humans), because humans are not directly acquainted with God's essence. See Aquinas's *Summa theologiae* I, q.2,a.1,c. **See also** ANALYTIC–SYNTHETIC DISTINCTION, AQUINAS, SELF-EVIDENCE.

A.P.M.

noumenal world. See KANT.

noumenon. See KANT.

noûs, Greek term for mind or the faculty of reason. *Noûs* is the highest type of thinking, the kind a god would do. Sometimes called the faculty of intellectual intuition, it is at work when someone understands definitions, concepts, and anything else that is grasped all at once. *Noûs* stands in contrast with another intellectual faculty, *dianoia*. When we work through the steps of an argument, we exercise *dianoia;* to be certain the conclusion is true without argument – to just "see" it, as, perhaps, a god might – is to exercise *noûs*. Just which objects could be apprehended by *noûs* was controversial. E.C.H.

Novalis, pseudonym of Friedrich von Hardenberg (1772–1801), German poet and philosopher of early German Romanticism. His starting point was Fichte's reflective type of transcendental philosophy; he attempted to complement Fichte's focus on philosophical speculation by including other forms of intellectual experience such as faith, love, poetry, and religion, and exhibit their equally autonomous status of existence. Of special importance in this regard is his analysis of the imagination in contrast to reason, of the poetic power in distinction from the reasonable faculties. Novalis insists on a complementary interaction between these two spheres, on a union of philosophy and poetry. Another important aspect of his speculation concerns the relation between the inner and the outer world, subject and object, the human being and nature. Novalis attempted to reveal the correspondence, even unity between these two realms and to present the world as a "universal trope" or a "symbolic image" of the human mind and vice versa. He expressed his philosophical thought mostly in fragments. **See also** FICHTE. E.Beh.

Nozick, Robert (b.1938), American philosopher currently at Harvard University, best known for *Anarchy, State, and Utopia* (1974), which defends the libertarian position that only a minimal state (limited to protecting rights) is just. Nozick argues that a minimal state, but not a more extensive state, could arise without violating rights. Drawing on Kant's dictum that people may not be used as mere means, Nozick says that people's rights are inviolable, no matter how useful violations might be to the state. He criticizes principles of redistributive justice on which theorists base defenses of extensive states, such as the principle of utility, and Rawls's principle that goods should be distributed in favor of the least well-off. Enforcing these principles requires eliminating the cumulative effects of free exchanges, which violates (permanent, bequeathable) property rights. Nozick's own entitlement theory says that a distribution of holdings is just if people under that distribution are entitled to what they hold. Entitlements, in turn, would be clarified using principles of justice in acquisition, transfer, and rectification.

Nozick's other works include *Philosophical Explanations* (1981), *The Examined Life* (1989), *The Nature of Rationality* (1993), and *Socratic Puzzles* (1997). These are contributions to rational choice theory, epistemology, metaphysics, philosophy of mind, philosophy of religion, and ethics. *Philosophical Explanations* features two especially important contributions. The first is Nozick's (reliabilist, causal) view that beliefs that constitute knowledge must *track the truth*. My belief that (say) a cat is on the mat tracks the truth only if (a) I would not believe this if a cat were not on the mat, and (b) I would believe this if a cat were there. The tracking account positions Nozick to reject the principle that people know all of the things they believe via deductions from things they know, and to reject versions of skepticism based on this principle of closure. The second is Nozick's closest continuer theory of identity, according to which *A*'s identity at a later time can depend on facts about other existing things, for it depends on (1) what continues *A* closely enough to be *A* and (2) what continues *A* more closely than any other existing thing. Nozick's 1969 essay "Newcomb's Problem and Two Principles of Choice" is another important contribution. It is the first discussion of Newcomb's problem, a problem in decision theory, and presents many positions prominent in subsequent debate.

See also CLOSURE, NEWCOMB'S PARADOX, POLITICAL PHILOSOPHY, RAWLS.   S.L.

n-tuple. See SET THEORY.

null class. See SET THEORY.

null relation. See RELATION.

number. See MATHEMATICAL ANALYSIS, PHILOSOPHY OF MATHEMATICS, QUALITIES.

number, natural. See MATHEMATICAL ANALYSIS, MATHEMATICAL INDUCTION.

number, rational. See MATHEMATICAL ANALYSIS.

number, real. See MATHEMATICAL ANALYSIS.

number, transcendental. See MATHEMATICAL ANALYSIS.

numbers, law of large. See BERNOULLI'S THEOREM.

number theory. See PHILOSOPHY OF MATHEMATICS.

Numenius of Apamea (fl. mid-second century A.D.), Greek Platonist philosopher of neo-Pythagorean tendencies. Very little is known of his life apart from his residence in Apamea, Syria, but his philosophical importance is considerable. His system of three levels of spiritual reality – a primal god (the Good, the Father), who is almost supra-intellectual; a secondary, creator god (the demiurge of Plato's *Timaeus*); and a world soul – largely anticipates that of Plotinus in the next century, though he was more strongly dualist than Plotinus in his attitude to the physical world and matter. He was much interested in the wisdom of the East, and in comparative religion. His most important work, fragments of which are preserved by Eusebius, is a dialogue *On the Good*, but he also wrote a polemic work *On the Divergence of the Academics from Plato*, which shows him to be a lively controversialist.   J.M.D.

numerical identity. See IDENTITY.

nung chia. See HSÜ HSING.

Nussbaum, Martha C(raven) (b.1947), American philosopher, classicist, and public intellectual with influential views on the human good, the emotions and their place in practical reasoning, and the rights of women and homosexuals. After training at Harvard in classical philology, she published a critical edition, with translation and commentary, of Aristotle's *Motion of Animals* (1978). Its essays formulated ideas that she has continued to articulate: that perception is trainable, imagination interpretive, and desire a reaching out for the good. Via provocative readings of Plato, Aristotle, Aeschylus, Sophocles, and Euripides, *The Fragility of Goodness* (1986) argues that many true goods succumb to fortune, lack any common measure, and demand fine-tuned discernment. The essays in *Love's Knowledge* (1990) – on Proust, Dickens, Beckett, Henry James, and others – explore the emotional implications of our fragility and the particularism of practical reasoning. They also undertake a brief against Plato's ancient criticism of the poets, an argument that Nussbaum carried on years later in debates with Judge Richard Posner. *The Therapy of Desire* (1994) dissects the Stoics' conviction that our vulnerability calls for philosophical therapy to extirpate the emotions. While Nussbaum holds that the Stoics were mistaken about the good, she has adopted and strengthened their view that emotions embody judgments – most notably in her Gifford Lectures of 1993, *Upheavals of Thought.*

A turning point in Nussbaum's career came in 1987, when she became a part-time research adviser at the United Nations–sponsored World Institute for Development Economics Research. She there adapted her Aristotelian account of the human good to help ground the "capabilities approach" that the economist and philosopher Amartya Sen was developing for policymakers to use in assessing individuals' well-being. Nussbaum spells out the human capabilities essential to leading a good life, integrating them within a nuanced liberalism of universalist appeal. This view has ramified: *Poetic Justice* (1996) argues that its legal realization must avoid the oversimplifications that utilitarianism and economics encourage and instead balance generality with emotionally sensitive imagination. *Sex and Social Justice* (1998) explores her view's implications for problems of sexual inequality, gay rights, and sexual objectification. *Feminist Internationalism*, her 1998 Seeley Lectures, argues that an effective international feminism must champion rights, eschew relativism, and study local traditions sufficiently closely to see their diversity.

See also AESTHETICS, ARISTOTLE, EMOTION, PRACTICAL REASONING, VIRTUE ETHICS.   H.S.R.

Nyāya-Vaishesika, one of the orthodox schools of Hinduism. It holds that earth, air, fire, and water are the four types of atoms. Space is a substance and a container of atoms. The atoms are everlasting and eternal, though their combinations are neither. Properties of complexes are explained in terms of the properties of their components. There are emergent properties the causation of which does not require that something come from nothing; one need only grant brute causal connections.

Nyāya is a monotheistic perspective and Nyāya philosopher Udana wrote a text – *Kusmāñjali* ("The Handful of Flowers") – in natural theology; this tenth-century work is an Indian classic on the subject. In addition to material things composed of atoms, there are immaterial persons. Each person is an enduring, substantial self whose nature is to be conscious and who is capable of love and aversion, of feeling pleasure and pain, and of making choices; selves differ from one another even when not embodied by virtue of being different centers of consciousness, not merely in terms of having had diverse transmigratory biographies. Nyāya-Vaishesika is the Hindu school most like Anglo-American philosophy, as evidenced in its studies of inference and perception.

See also HINDUISM.   K.E.Y.

Oakeshott, Michael (1900–91), British philosopher and political theorist trained at Cambridge and in Germany. He taught first at Cambridge and Oxford; from 1951 he was professor of political science at the London School of Economics and Political Science. His works include *Experience and Its Modes* (1933), *Rationalism in Politics* (1962), *On Human Conduct* (1975), and *On History* (1983).

Oakeshott's misleading general reputation, based on *Rationalism in Politics,* is as a conservative political thinker. *Experience and Its Modes* is a systematic work in the tradition of Hegel. Human experience is exclusively of a world of ideas intelligible insofar as it is coherent. This world divides into modes (historical, scientific, practical, and poetic experience), each being partly coherent and categorially distinct from all others. Philosophy is the never entirely successful attempt to articulate the coherence of the world of ideas and the place of modally specific experience within that whole.

His later works examine the postulates of historical and practical experience, particularly those of religion, morality, and politics. All conduct in the practical mode postulates freedom and is an "exhibition of intelligence" by agents who appropriate inherited languages and ideas to the generic activity of self-enactment. Some conduct pursues specific purposes and occurs in "enterprise associations" identified by goals shared among those who participate in them. The most estimable forms of conduct, exemplified by "conversation," have no such purpose and occur in "civil societies" under the purely "adverbial" considerations of morality and law. "Rationalists" illicitly use philosophy to dictate to practical experience and subordinate human conduct to some master purpose. Oakeshott's distinctive achievement is to have melded holistic idealism with a morality and politics radical in their affirmation of individuality.

See also POLITICAL THEORY.   R.E.F.

obiectum quo (Latin, 'object by which'), in medieval and Scholastic epistemology, the object by which an object is known. It should be understood in contrast with *obiectum quod,* which refers to the object that is known. For example, when a person knows what an apple is, the apple is the *obiectum quod* and his concept of the apple is the *obiectum quo.* That is, the concept is instrumental to knowing the apple, but is not itself what is known. Human beings need concepts in order to have knowledge, because their knowledge is receptive, in contrast with God's which is productive. (God creates what he knows.) Human knowledge is mediated; divine knowledge is immediate.

Scholastic philosophers believe that the distinction between *obiectum quod* and *obiectum quo* exposes the crucial mistake of idealism. According to idealists, the object of knowledge, i.e., what a person knows, is an idea. In contrast, the Scholastics maintain that idealists conflate the object of knowledge with the means by which human knowledge is made possible. Humans must be connected to the object of knowledge by something (*obiectum quo*), but what connects them is not that to which they are connected.

A.P.M.

object, intentional. See BRENTANO.

object, propositional. See PROPOSITION.

objective body. See EMBODIMENT.

objective probability. See PROBABILITY.

objective reality. See DESCARTES, REALITY.

objective reason. See REASONS FOR ACTION.

objective rightness. In ethics, an action is objectively right for a person to perform (on some occasion) if the agent's performing it (on that occasion) really *is* right, whether or not the agent, or anyone else, believes it is. An action is *subjectively* right for a person to perform (on some occasion) if the agent believes, or perhaps justifiably believes, of that action that it is (objectively) right. For example, according to a version of utilitarianism, an action is objectively right provided the action is optimific in the sense that the consequences that would result from its performance are at least as good as those that would result from any alternative action the agent could instead perform. Were this theory correct, then an action would be an objectively right action for an agent to perform (on some occasion) if and only if that action is in fact optimific. An action can be both objectively and subjectively right or neither. But an action can also be subjectively right, but fail to be objectively right, as where the action fails to be optimific (again assuming that a utilitarian theory is correct), yet the agent believes the action is objectively right. And an action can be objectively right but not subjectively right, where, despite the objective rightness of the action, the agent has no beliefs about its rightness or believes falsely that it is not objectively right.

This distinction is important in our moral assessments of agents and their actions. In cases where we judge a person's action to be objectively wrong, we often mitigate our judgment of the agent when we judge that the action was, for the agent, subjectively right. This same objective–subjective distinction applies to other ethical categories such as wrongness and obligatoriness, and some philosophers extend it to items other than actions, e.g., emotions.

See also ETHICAL OBJECTIVISM, SUBJECTIVISM, UTILITARIANISM.   M.C.T.

objectivism. See ETHICAL OBJECTIVISM.

object language. See METALANGUAGE.

objectual quantification. See QUANTIFICATION.

obligating reason. See REASONS FOR ACTION.

obligation. See DEONTIC LOGIC, ETHICS.

obligation, political. See POLITICAL PHILOSOPHY.

obligationes, the study of inferentially inescapable, yet logically odd arguments, used by late medieval logicians in analyzing inferential reasoning. In *Topics* VIII.3 Aristotle describes a respondent's task in a philosophical argument as providing answers so that, if they must defend the impossible, the impossibility lies in the nature of the position, and not in its logical defense. In *Prior Analytics* I.13 Aristotle argues that nothing impossible follows from the possible. Burley, whose logic exemplifies early fourteenth-century *obligationes* literature, described the resulting logical exercise as a contest

between interlocutor and respondent. The interlocutor must force the respondent into maintaining contradictory statements in defending a position, and the respondent must avoid this while avoiding maintaining the impossible, which can be either a position logically incompatible with the position defended or something impossible in itself. Especially interesting to Scholastic logicians were the paradoxes of disputation inherent in such disputes. Assuming that a respondent has successfully defended his position, the interlocutor may be able to propose a commonplace position that the respondent can neither accept nor reject, given the truth of the first, successfully defended position.

Roger Swineshead introduced a controversial innovation to *obligationes* reasoning, later rejected by Paul of Venice. In the traditional style of obligation, a premise was relevant to the argument only if it followed from or was inconsistent with either (a) the proposition defended or (b) all the premises consequent to the former and prior to the premise in question. By admitting any premise that was either consequent to or inconsistent with the proposition defended alone, without regard to intermediate premises, Swineshead eliminated concern with the order of sentences proposed by the interlocutor, making the respondent's task harder.

See also ARISTOTLE, BURLEY, KILVINGTON, OXFORD CALCULATORS, PAUL OF VENICE.
     S.E.L.

oblique context. As explained by Frege in "Über Sinn und Bedeutung" (1892), a linguistic context is oblique (*ungerade*) if and only if an expression (e.g., proper name, dependent clause, or sentence) in that context does not express its direct (customary) sense. For Frege, the sense of an expression is the mode of presentation of its nominatum, if any. Thus in direct speech, the direct (customary) sense of an expression designates its direct (customary) nominatum. For example, the context of the proper name 'Kepler' in

(1) Kepler died in misery.

is non-oblique (i.e., direct) since the proper name expresses its direct (customary) sense, say, the sense of 'the man who discovered the elliptical planetary orbits', thereby designating its direct (customary) nominatum, Kepler himself. Moreover, the entire sentence expresses its direct sense, namely, the proposition that Kepler died in misery, thereby designating its direct nominatum, a truth-value, namely, the *true*. By contrast, in indirect speech an expression neither expresses its direct sense nor, therefore, designates its direct nominatum. One such sort of oblique context is direct quotation, as in

(2) 'Kepler' has six letters.

The word appearing within the quotation marks neither expresses its direct (customary) sense nor, therefore, designates its direct (customary) nominatum, Kepler. Rather, it designates a word, a proper name. Another sort of oblique context is engendered by the verbs of propositional attitude. Thus, the context of the proper name 'Kepler' in

(3) Frege believed Kepler died in misery.

is oblique, since the proper name expresses its indirect sense, say, the sense of the words 'the man widely known as Kepler', thereby designating its indirect nominatum, namely, the sense of 'the man who discovered the elliptical planetary orbits'. Note that the indirect nominatum of 'Kepler' in (3) is the same as the direct sense of 'Kepler' in (1). Thus, while 'Kepler' in (1) designates the man Kepler, 'Kepler' in (3) designates the direct (customary) sense of the word 'Kepler' in (1). Similarly, in (3) the context of the dependent clause 'Kepler died in misery' is oblique since the dependent clause expresses its indirect sense, namely, the sense of the words 'the proposition that Kepler died in misery', thereby designating its indirect nominatum, namely, the proposition that Kepler died in misery. Note that the indirect nominatum of 'Kepler died in misery' in (3) is the same as the direct sense of 'Kepler died in misery' in (1). Thus, while 'Kepler died in misery' in (1) designates a truth-value, 'Kepler died in misery' in (3) designates a proposition, the direct (customary) sense of the words 'Kepler died in misery' in (1).

See also INDIRECT DISCOURSE, MEANING, QUANTIFYING IN.   R.F.G.

oblique intention. See INTENTION.

observation. See PHILOSOPHY OF SCIENCE.

observation language. See INCOMMENSURABILITY.

observation sentence. See PHILOSOPHY OF SCIENCE.

observation term. See PHILOSOPHY OF SCIENCE.

obversion, a sort of immediate inference that allows a transformation of affirmative categorical

A-propositions and I-propositions into the corresponding negative E-propositions and O-propositions, and of E- and O-propositions into the corresponding A- and I-propositions, keeping in each case the order of the subject and predicate terms, but changing the original predicate into its complement, i.e., into a negated term. For example, 'Every man is mortal' – 'No man is non-mortal'; 'Some students are happy' – 'Some students are not non-happy'; 'No dogs are jealous' – 'All dogs are non-jealous'; and 'Some bankers are not rich' – 'Some bankers are not non-rich'. **See also** SQUARE OF OPPOSITION, SYLLOGISM.   I.Bo.

obviousness. See SELF-EVIDENCE.

Occam, William. See OCKHAM.

occasionalism, a theory of causation held by a number of important seventeenth-century Cartesian philosophers, including Johannes Clauberg (1622–65), Géraud de Cordemoy (1626–84), Arnold Geulincx (1624–69), Louis de la Forge (1632–66), and Nicolas Malebranche (1638–1715). In its most extreme version, occasionalism is the doctrine that all finite created entities are devoid of causal efficacy, and that God is the only true causal agent. Bodies do not cause effects in other bodies nor in minds; and minds do not cause effects in bodies nor even within themselves. God is directly, immediately, and solely responsible for bringing about all phenomena. When a needle pricks the skin, the physical event is merely an occasion for God to cause the relevant mental state (pain); a volition in the soul to raise an arm or to think of something is only an occasion for God to cause the arm to rise or the ideas to be present to the mind; and the impact of one billiard ball upon another is an occasion for God to move the second ball. In all three contexts – mind–body, body–body, and mind alone – God's ubiquitous causal activity proceeds in accordance with certain general laws, and (except for miracles) he acts only when the requisite material or psychic conditions obtain. Less thoroughgoing forms of occasionalism limit divine causation (e.g., to mind–body or body–body alone). Far from being an ad hoc solution to a Cartesian mind–body problem, as it is often considered, occasionalism is argued for from general philosophical considerations regarding the nature of causal relations (considerations that later appear, modified, in Hume), from an analysis of the Cartesian concept of matter and of the necessary impotence of finite substance, and, perhaps most importantly, from theological premises about the essential ontological relation between an omnipotent God and the created world that he sustains in existence. Occasionalism can also be regarded as a way of providing a metaphysical foundation for explanations in mechanistic natural philosophy. Occasionalists are arguing that motion must ultimately be grounded in something higher than the passive, inert extension of Cartesian bodies (emptied of the substantial forms of the Scholastics); it needs a causal ground in an active power. But if a body consists in extension alone, motive force cannot be an inherent property of bodies. Occasionalists thus identify force with the will of God. In this way, they are simply drawing out the implications of Descartes's own metaphysics of matter and motion. **See also** CORDEMOY, GEULINCX, LEIBNIZ, MALEBRANCHE.   S.N.

occurrent. See DISPOSITION.

occurrent belief. See BELIEF.

occurrent memory. See MEMORY.

occurrent state. See STATE.

Ockham, William (c.1285–1347), also written William Occam, known as the More than Subtle Doctor, English Scholastic philosopher known equally as the father of nominalism and for his role in the Franciscan dispute with Pope John XXII over poverty. Born probably in the village of Ockham near London, William Ockham entered the Franciscan order at an early age and studied at Oxford, attaining the rank of *baccalarius formatus*. His brilliant but controversial career was cut short when John Lutterell, former chancellor of Oxford University, presented the pope with a list of fifty-six allegedly heretical theses extracted from Ockham's writings. The papal commission studied them for two years and found fifty-one open to censure, but none was formally condemned. While in Avignon, Ockham researched previous papal concessions to the Franciscans regarding collective poverty, eventually concluding that John XXII contradicted his predecessors and hence was "no true pope." After committing these charges to writing, Ockham fled with Michael of Cesena, then minister general of the order, first to Pisa and ultimately to Munich, where he lived until his death, writing many treatises about church–state relations. Although

departures from his eminent predecessors have combined with ecclesiastical difficulties to make Ockham unjustly notorious, his thought remains, by current lights, philosophically and theologically conservative.

On most metaphysical issues, Ockham fancied himself the true interpreter of Aristotle. Rejecting the doctrine that universals are real things other than names or concepts as "the worst error of philosophy," Ockham dismissed not only Platonism, but also "modern realist" doctrines according to which natures enjoy a double mode of existence and are universal in the intellect but numerically multiplied in particulars. He argues that everything real is individual and particular, while universality is a property pertaining only to names and that by virtue of their signification relations. Because Ockham understands the primary names to be mental (i.e., naturally significant concepts), his own theory of universals is best classified as a form of *conceptualism*.

Ockham rejects atomism, and defends Aristotelian hylomorphism in physics and metaphysics, complete with its distinction between substantial and accidental forms. Yet, he opposes the reifying tendency of the "moderns" (unnamed contemporary opponents), who posited a distinct kind of thing (*res*) for each of Aristotle's ten categories; he argues that – from a purely philosophical point of view – it is indefensible to posit anything besides particular substances and qualities. Ockham followed the Franciscan school in recognizing a plurality of substantial forms in living things (in humans, the forms of corporeity, sensory soul, and intellectual soul), but diverged from Duns Scotus in asserting a real, not a formal, distinction among them.

Aristotle had reached behind regular correlations in nature to posit substance-things and accident-things as primitive explanatory entities that essentially are or give rise to powers (*virtus*) that produce the regularities; similarly, Ockham distinguishes efficient causality properly speaking from *sine qua non* causality, depending on whether the correlation between A's and B's is produced by the power of A or by the will of another, and explicitly denies the existence of any *sine qua non* causation in nature. Further, Ockham insists, in Aristotelian fashion, that created substance- and accident-natures are essentially the causal powers they are in and of themselves and hence independently of their relations to anything else; so that not even God can make heat naturally a coolant. Yet, if God cannot change, He shares with created things the ability to obstruct such "Aristotelian" productive powers and prevent their normal operation. Ockham's nominalistic conceptualism about universals does not keep him from endorsing the uniformity of nature principle, because he holds that individual natures are powers and hence that co-specific things are maximally similar powers. Likewise, he is conventional in appealing to several other a priori causal principles: "Everything that is in motion is moved by something," "Being cannot come from non-being," "Whatever is produced by something is really conserved by something as long as it exists." He even recognizes a kind of necessary connection between created causes and effects – e.g., while God could act alone to produce any created effect, a particular created effect could not have had another created cause of the same species instead. Ockham's main innovation on the topic of causality is his attack on Duns Scotus's distinction between "essential" and "accidental" orders and contrary contention that every genuine efficient cause is an immediate cause of its effects.

Ockham is an Aristotelian reliabilist in epistemology, taking for granted as he does that human cognitive faculties (the senses and intellect) work always or for the most part. Ockham infers that since we have certain knowledge both of material things and of our own mental acts, there must be some distinctive species of acts of awareness (intuitive cognitions) that are the power to produce such evident judgments. Ockham is matter-of-fact both about the disruption of human cognitive functions by created obstacles (as in sensory illusion) and about divine power to intervene in many ways. Such facts carry no skeptical consequences for Ockham, because he defines certainty in terms of freedom from *actual* doubt and error, not from the *logical, metaphysical, or natural possibility* of error.

In action theory, Ockham defends the liberty of indifference or contingency for all rational beings, created or divine. Ockham shares Duns Scotus's understanding of the will as a self-determining power for opposites, but not his distaste for causal models. Thus, Ockham allows that (1) unfree acts of will may be necessitated, either by the agent's own nature, by its other acts, or by an external cause; and that (2) the efficient causes of free acts may include the agent's intellectual and sensory cognitions as well as the will itself. While recognizing innate motivational tendencies in the human agent – e.g., the inclination to seek sensory pleasure and avoid pain, the *affectio commodi* (tendency to seek its own advantage), and the *affectio iustitiae* (inclination

to love things for their own intrinsic worth) – he denies that these limit the will's scope. Thus, Ockham goes beyond Duns Scotus in assigning the will the power, with respect to any option, to will for it (*velle*), to will against it (*nolle*), or not to act at all. In particular, Ockham concludes that the will can will against (*nolle*) the good, whether ignorantly or perversely – by hating God or by willing against its own happiness, the good-in-general, the enjoyment of a clear vision of God, or its own ultimate end. The will can also will (*velle*) evils – the opposite of what right reason dictates, unjust deeds *qua* unjust, dishonest, and contrary to right reason, and evil under the aspect of evil.

Ockham enforces the traditional division of moral science into non-positive morality or ethics, which directs acts apart from any precept of a superior authority and draws its principles from reason and experience; and positive morality, which deals with laws that oblige us to pursue or avoid things, not because they are good or evil in themselves, but because some legitimate superior commands them. The notion that Ockham sponsors an unmodified divine command theory of ethics rests on conflation and confusion. Rather, in the area of non-positive morality, Ockham advances what we might label a "modified right reason theory," which begins with the Aristotelian ideal of rational self-government, according to which morally virtuous action involves the agent's free coordination of choice with right reason. He then observes that suitably informed right reason would dictate that God, as the infinite good, ought to be loved above all and for his own sake, and that such love ought to be expressed by the effort to please him in every way (among other things, by obeying all his commands). Thus, if right reason is the primary norm in ethics, divine commands are a secondary, derivative norm. Once again, Ockham is utterly unconcerned about the *logical possibility* opened by divine liberty of indifference, that these twin norms might conflict (say, if God commanded us to act contrary to right reason); for him, their de facto congruence suffices for the moral life. In the area of soteriological merit and demerit (a branch of positive morality), things are the other way around: divine will is the primary norm; yet because God includes following the dictates of right reason among the criteria for divine acceptance (thereby giving the moral life eternal significance), right reason becomes a secondary and derivative norm there.

See also ARISTOTLE, DIVINE COMMAND ETHICS, DUNS SCOTUS.   M.M.A.

Ockham's razor, also called the principle of par-simony, a methodological principle commending a bias toward simplicity in the construction of theories. The parameters whose simplicity is singled out for attention have varied considerably, from kinds of entities to the number of presupposed axioms to the nature of the curve drawn between data points. Found already in Aristotle, the tag "entities should not be multiplied beyond necessity" became associated with William Ockham (although he never states *that* version, and even if non-contradiction rather than parsimony is his favorite weapon in metaphysical disputes), perhaps because it characterized the spirit of his philosophical conclusions. Opponents, who thought parsimony was being carried too far, formulated an "anti-razor": where fewer entities do not suffice, posit more! **See also** CURVE-FITTING PROBLEM, OCKHAM.   M.M.A.

oligarchy. See POLITICAL PHILOSOPHY.

Olivi, Peter John (c.1247–98), French philosopher-theologian whose views on the theory and practice of Franciscan poverty led to a long series of investigations of his orthodoxy. Olivi's preference for humility, as well as the suspicion with which he was regarded, prevented his becoming a master of theology at Paris. After 1285, he was effectively vindicated and permitted to teach at Florence and Montpellier. But after his death, probably in part because his remains were venerated and his views were championed by the Franciscan Spirituals, his orthodoxy was again examined. The Council of Vienne (1311–12) condemned three unrelated tenets associated with Olivi. Finally, in 1326, Pope John XXII condemned a series of statements based on Olivi's Apocalypse commentary.

Olivi thought of himself chiefly as a theologian, writing copious biblical commentaries; his philosophy of history was influenced by Joachim of Fiore. His views on poverty inspired the leader of the Franciscan Observant reform movement, St. Bernardino of Siena. Apart from his views on poverty, Olivi is best known for his philosophical independence from Aristotle, whom he condemned as a materialist. Contrary to Aristotle's theory of projectile motion, Olivi advocated a theory of impetus. He undermined orthodox views on Aristotelian categories. His attack on the category of relation was thought to have dangerous implications in Trinitarian theology. Ockham's theory of quantity is in part a defense of views presented by Olivi. Olivi was critical of Augustinian as well as Aristotelian views; he

abandoned the theories of seminal reason and divine illumination. He also argued against positing impressed sensible and intelligible species, claiming that only the soul, not perceptual objects, played an active role in perception. Bold as his philosophical views were, he presented them tentatively.

A voluntarist, he emphasized the importance of will. He claimed that an act of understanding was not possible in the absence of an act of will. He provided an important experiential argument for the freedom of the will.

His treatises on contracts revealed a sophisticated understanding of economics. His treatise on evangelical poverty includes the first defense of a theory of papal infallibility.   R.W.

Olympiodorus. See NEOPLATONISM.

omega, the last letter of the Greek alphabet (ω). Following Cantor (1845–1911), it is used in lowercase as a proper name for the first infinite ordinal number, which is the ordinal of the natural ordering of the set of finite ordinals. By extension it is also used as a proper name for the set of finite ordinals itself or even for the set of natural numbers. Following Gödel (1906–78), it is used as a prefix in names of various logical properties of sets of sentences, most notably omega-completeness and omega-consistency.

Omega-completeness, in the original sense due to Tarski, is a syntactical property of sets of sentences in a formal arithmetic language involving a symbol '0' for the number zero and a symbol 's' for the so-called *successor function,* resulting in each natural number being named by an expression, called a numeral, in the following series: '0', 's0', 'ss0', and so on. For example, five is denoted by 'sssss0'. A set of sentences is said to be omega-complete if it (deductively) yields every universal sentence all of whose singular instances it yields. In this framework, as usual, every universal sentence, 'for every *n, n* has *P*' yields each and every one of its singular instances, '0 has *P*', 's0 has *P*', 'ss0 has *P*', etc. However, as had been known by logicians at least since the Middle Ages, the converse is not true, i.e., it is not in general the case that a universal sentence is deducible from the set of its singular instances. Thus one should not expect to find omega-completeness except in exceptional sets. The set of all true sentences of arithmetic is such an exceptional set; the reason is the semantic fact that every universal sentence (whether or not in arithmetic) is materially equivalent to the set of all its singular instances. A set of sentences that is not omega-complete is said to be omega-incomplete. The existence of omega-incomplete sets of sentences is a phenomenon at the core of the 1931 Gödel incompleteness result, which shows that every "effective" axiom set for arithmetic is omega-incomplete and thus has as theorems all singular instances of a universal sentence that is not one of its theorems. Although this is a remarkable fact, the existence of omega-incomplete sets per se is far from remarkable, as suggested above. In fact, the empty set and equivalently the set of all tautologies are omega-incomplete because each yields all singular instances of the non-tautological formal sentence, here called *FS,* that expresses the proposition that every number is either zero or a successor.

Omega-consistency belongs to a set that does not yield the negation of any universal sentence all of whose singular instances it yields. A set that is not omega-consistent is said to be omega-inconsistent. Omega-inconsistency of course implies consistency in the ordinary sense; but it is easy to find consistent sets that are not omega-consistent, e.g., the set whose only member is the negation of the formal sentence *FS* mentioned above. Corresponding to the syntactical properties just mentioned there are analogous semantic properties whose definitions are obtained by substituting '(semantically) implies' for '(deductively) yields'.

The Greek letter omega and its English name have many other uses in modern logic. Carnap introduced a non-effective, non-logical rule, called the *omega rule,* for "inferring" a universal sentence from its singular instances; adding the omega rule to a standard axiomatization of arithmetic produces a complete but non-effective axiomatization. An omega-valued logic is a many-valued logic whose set of truth-values is or is the same size as the set of natural numbers.

See also COMPLETENESS, CONSISTENCY, GÖDEL'S INCOMPLETENESS THEOREMS.

J.COR.

omega, order type. See ORDER TYPE OMEGA.

omega-complete. See COMPLETENESS, FORMAL LOGIC, OMEGA.

omega-consistent. See FORMAL LOGIC, OMEGA.

omega rule. See OMEGA.

omega-valued. See OMEGA.

omission. See ACTION THEORY.

omnibenevolence. See DIVINE ATTRIBUTES.

omnipotence. See DIVINE ATTRIBUTES, PARADOXES OF OMNIPOTENCE.

omnipotence, paradoxes of. See PARADOXES OF OMNIPOTENCE.

omniscience. See DIVINE ATTRIBUTES, PRIVILEGED ACCESS.

omniscience, logical. See DIVINE ATTRIBUTES.

one–many problem, also called one-and-many problem, the question whether all things are one or many. According to both Plato and Aristotle this was the central question for pre-Socratic philosophers. Those who answered "one," the monists, ascribed to all things a single nature such as water, air, or oneness itself. They appear not to have been troubled by the notion that numerically many things would have this one nature. The pluralists, on the other hand, distinguished many principles or many types of principles, though they also maintained the unity of each principle. Some monists understood the unity of all things as a denial of motion, and some pluralists advanced their view as a way of refuting this denial. To judge from our sources, early Greek metaphysics revolved around the problem of the one and the many. In the modern period the dispute between monists and pluralists centered on the question whether mind and matter constitute one or two substances and, if one, what its nature is. **See also PRE-SOCRATICS, SPINOZA.**   E.C.H.

one over many, a universal; especially, a Platonic Form. According to Plato, if there are, e.g., *many* large things, there must be some *one* largeness itself in respect of which they are large; this "one over many" (*hen epi pollōn*) is an intelligible entity, a Form, in contrast with the sensible many. Plato himself recognizes difficulties explaining how the one character can be present to the many and why the one and the many do not together constitute still another many (e.g., *Parmenides* 131a–133b). Aristotle's sustained critique of Plato's Forms (*Metaphysics* A 9, Z 13–15) includes these and other problems, and it is he, more than Plato, who regularly uses 'one over many' to refer to Platonic Forms. **See also ARISTOTLE, ONE–MANY PROBLEM, PLATO.**   E.C.H.

one-way reduction sentence. See REDUCTION SENTENCE.

ontological argument. See PHILOSOPHY OF RELIGION.

ontological commitment, the object or objects common to the ontology fulfilling some (regimented) theory (a term fashioned by Quine). The ontology of a (regimented) theory consists in the objects the theory assumes there to be. In order to show that a theory assumes a given object, or objects of a given class, we must show that the theory would be true only if that object existed, or if that class is not empty. This can be shown in two different but equivalent ways: if the notation of the theory contains the existential quantifier '(Ex)' of first-order predicate logic, then the theory is shown to assume a given object, or objects of a given class, provided that object is required among the values of the bound variables, or (additionally) is required among the values of the domain of a given predicate, in order for the theory to be true. Thus, if the theory entails the sentence '(Ex)(x is a dog)', then the values over which the bound variable 'x' ranges must include at least one dog, in order for the theory to be true. Alternatively, if the notation of the theory contains for each predicate a complementary predicate, then the theory assumes a given object, or objects of a given class, provided some predicate is required to be true of that object, in order for the theory to be true. Thus, if the theory contains the predicate 'is a dog', then the extension of 'is a dog' cannot be empty, if the theory is to be true. However, it is possible for different, even mutually exclusive, ontologies to fulfill a theory equally well. Thus, an ontology containing collies to the exclusion of spaniels and one containing spaniels to the exclusion of collies might each fulfill a theory that entails '(Ex) (x is a dog)'. It follows that some of the objects a theory assumes (in its ontology) may not be among those to which the theory is ontologically committed. A theory is ontologically committed to a given object only if that object is common to all of the ontologies fulfilling the theory. And the theory is ontologically committed to objects of a given class provided that class is not empty according to each of the ontologies fulfilling the theory. **See also QUANTIFICATION, THEORY OF DESCRIPTIONS.**   R.F.G.

ontological dependence. See DEPENDENCE.

ontological priority. See DEPENDENCE.

ontological solipsism. See SOLIPSISM.

ontologism. See GIOBERTI.

ontology. See METAPHYSICS.

onto-theology. See DERRIDA.

opacity. See QUANTIFYING IN, REFERENTIALLY TRANSPARENT.

opacity, referential. See REFERENTIALLY TRANSPARENT.

opaque construction. See QUANTIFYING IN.

opaque context. See QUANTIFYING IN.

open formula, also called open sentence, a sentence with a free occurrence of a variable. A closed sentence, sometimes called a statement, has no free occurrences of variables.

In a language whose only variable-binding operators are quantifiers, an occurrence of a variable in a formula is bound provided that occurrence either is *within* the scope of a quantifier employing that variable or *is* the occurrence in that quantifier. An occurrence of a variable in a formula is free provided it is not bound. The formula '$xy > 0$' is open because both 'x' and 'y' occur as free variables. In 'For some real number $y, xy > 0$', no occurrence of 'y' is free; but the occurrence of 'x' is free, so the formula is open. The sentence 'For every real number x, for some real number $y, xy > 0$' is closed, since none of the variables occur free.

Semantically, an open formula such as '$xy > 0$' is neither true nor false but rather *true of* or *false of* each assignment of values to its free-occurring variables. For example, '$xy > 0$' is true of each assignment of two positive or two negative real numbers to 'x' and to 'y' and it is false of each assignment of 0 to either and false at each assignment of a positive real to one of the variables and a negative to the other.

    See also QUANTIFICATION, SCOPE.   C.S.

open loop. See CYBERNETICS.

open question argument. See MOORE.

open sentence. See OPEN FORMULA.

open society. See POPPER.

open texture, the possibility of vagueness. Friedrich Waismann ("Verifiability," *Proceedings of the Aristotelian Society,* 1945) introduced the concept, claiming that open texture is a universal property of empirical terms. Waismann claimed that an inexhaustible source of vagueness remains even after measures are taken to make an expression precise. His grounds were, first, that there are an indefinite number of possibilities for which it is indeterminate whether the expression applies (i.e., for which the expression is vague). There is, e.g., no definite answer whether a catlike creature that repeatedly vanishes into thin air, then reappears, is a cat. Waismann's explanation is that when we define an empirical term, we frame criteria of its applicability only for foreseeable circumstances. Not all possible situations in which we may use the term, however, can be foreseen. Thus, in unanticipated circumstances, real or merely possible, a term's criteria of applicability may yield no definite answer to whether it applies. Second, even for terms such as 'gold', for which there are several precise criteria of application (specific gravity, X-ray spectrograph, solubility in *aqua regia*), applying different criteria can yield divergent verdicts, the result being vagueness.

Waismann uses the concept of open texture to explain why experiential statements are not conclusively verifiable, and why phenomenalist attempts to translate material object statements fail.

See also PHENOMENALISM, VAGUENESS, VERIFICATIONISM.   W.K.W.

operant conditioning. See CONDITIONING.

operational definition. See OPERATIONALISM.

operationalism, a program in philosophy of science that aims to interpret scientific concepts via experimental procedures and observational outcomes. P. W. Bridgman introduced the terminology when he required that theoretical concepts be identified with the operations used to measure them. Logical positivism's criteria of cognitive significance incorporated the notion: Bridgman's operationalism was assimilated to the positivistic requirement that theoretical terms T be *explicitly defined* via (logically equivalent to) directly observable conditions O. Explicit definitions failed to accommodate alternative measurement procedures for the same concept, and so were replaced by *reduction sentences* that partially defined individual concepts in observational terms via sentences such as 'Under observable circum-

stances C, x is T if and only if O'. Later this was weakened to allow ensembles of theoretical concepts to be partially defined via *interpretative systems* specifying collective observable effects of the concepts rather than effects peculiar to single concepts.

These cognitive significance notions were incorporated into various behaviorisms, although the term 'operational definition' is rarely used by scientists in Bridgman's or the explicit definition senses: *intervening variables* are theoretical concepts defined via reduction sentences and hypothetical constructs are definable by interpretative systems but not reduction sentences. In scientific contexts observable terms often are called *dependent* or *independent variables.*

When, as in science, the concepts in theoretical assertions are only partially defined, observational consequences do not exhaust their content, and so observational data *underdetermines* the truth of such assertions in the sense that more than one theoretical assertion will be compatible with maximal observational data.

See also BEHAVIORISM, REDUCTION, REDUCTION SENTENCE, THEORETICAL TERM.
                                                     F.S.

operator, a one-place sentential connective; i.e., an expression that may be prefixed to an open or closed sentence to produce, respectively, a new open or closed sentence. Thus 'it is not the case that' is a (truth-functional) operator. The most thoroughly investigated operators are the intensional ones; an intensional operator O, when prefixed to an open or closed sentence E, produces an open or closed sentence OE, whose extension is determined not by the extension of E but by some other property of E, which varies with the choice of O. For example, the extension of a closed sentence is its truth-value A, but if the modal operator 'it is necessary that' is prefixed to A, the extension of the result depends on whether A's extension belongs to it necessarily or contingently. This property of A is usually modeled by assigning to A a subset X of a domain of possible worlds W. If $X = W$ then 'it is necessary that A' is true, but if X is a proper subset of W, it is false. Another example involves the epistemic operator 'it is plausible that'. Since a true sentence may be either plausible or implausible, the truth-value of 'it is plausible that A' is not fixed by the truth-value of A, but rather by the body of evidence that supports A relative to a thinker in a given context. This may also be modeled in a possible worlds framework, by stipulating, for each world, which worlds, if any, are plausible relative to it. The topic of intensional operators is controversial, and it is even disputable whether standard examples really are operators at the correct level of logical form. For instance, it can be argued that 'it is necessary that', upon analysis, turns out to be a universal quantifier over possible worlds, or a predicate of expressions. On the former view, instead of 'it is necessary that A' we should write 'for every possible world w, $A(w)$', and, on the latter, 'A is necessarily true'. **See also** INTENSIONAL LOGIC, MODAL LOGIC, POSSIBLE WORLDS.   G.Fo.

operator, deontic. See DEONTIC LOGIC.

operator, propositional. See SENTENTIAL CONNECTIVE.

operator, scope of. See AMBIGUITY, SCOPE.

operator, sentential. See SENTENTIAL CONNECTIVE.

operator theory of adverbs, a theory that treats adverbs and other predicate modifiers as predicate-forming operators on predicates. The theory expands the syntax of first-order logic by adding operators of various degrees, and makes corresponding additions to the semantics. Romane Clark, Terence Parsons, and Richard Montague (with Hans Kamp) developed the theory independently in the early 1970s. For example: 'John runs quickly through the kitchen' contains a simple one-place predicate, 'runs' (applied to John); a zero-place operator, 'quickly', and a one-place operator, 'through ()' (with 'the kitchen' filling its place). The logical form of the sentence becomes

$$[O_1^1(a) [O_2^0 [P(b)]]],$$

which can be read:

[through (the kitchen) [quickly [runs (John)]]].

Semantically 'quickly' will be associated with an operation that takes us from the extension of 'runs' to a subset of that extension. 'John runs quickly' will imply 'John runs'. 'Through (the kitchen)' and other operators are handled similarly. The wide variety of predicate modifiers complicates the inferential conditions and semantics of the operators. 'John is finally done' implies 'John is done'. 'John is nearly done' implies 'John is not done'. Clark tries to distinguish various types of predicate modifiers and provides a different semantic analysis for opera-

tors of different sorts. The theory can easily characterize syntactic aspects of predicate modifier iteration. In addition, after being modified the original predicates remain as predicates, and maintain their original degree. Further, there is no need to force John's running into subject position as might be the case if we try to make 'quickly' an ordinary predicate.   T.J.D.

O-proposition. See SYLLOGISM.

oratio obliqua. See INDIRECT DISCOURSE.

order, the level of a logic as determined by the type of entity over which the free variables of that logic range. Entities of the lowest type, usually called type O, are known as individuals, and entities of higher type are constructed from entities of lower type. For example, type 1 entities are (i) functions from individuals or n-tuples of individuals to individuals, and (ii) n-place relations on individuals. First-order logic is that logic whose variables range over individuals, and a model for first-order logic includes a domain of individuals. The other logics are known as higher-order logics, and the first of these is second-order logic, in which there are variables that range over type 1 entities. In a model for second-order logic, the first-order domain determines the second-order domain. For every sentence to have a definite truth-value, only totally defined functions are allowed in the range of second-order function variables, so these variables range over the collection of total functions from n-tuples of individuals to individuals, for every value of n. The second-order predicate variables range over all subsets of n-tuples of individuals. Thus if D is the domain of individuals of a model, the type 1 entities are the union of the two sets $\{X: \exists n: X \subseteq D^n \times D\}$, $\{X: \exists n: X \subseteq D^n\}$. Quantifiers may bind second-order variables and are subject to introduction and elimination rules. Thus whereas in first-order logic one may infer 'Someone is wise, '$(\exists x)Wx$', from 'Socrates is wise', 'Ws', in second-order logic one may also infer 'there is something that Socrates is', '$(\exists X)Xs$'. The step from first- to second-order logic iterates: in general, type n entities are the domain of $n + 1$th–order variables in $n + 1$th–order logic, and the whole hierarchy is known as the theory of types. **See also** TYPE THEORY.
          G.Fo.

ordered n-tuple. See SET THEORY.

ordered pair. See SET THEORY.

ordering, an arrangement of the elements of a set so that some of them come before others. If X is a set, it is useful to identify an ordering R of X with a subset R of $X \times X$, the set of all ordered pairs with members in X. If $< x,y > \in R$ then x comes before y in the ordering of X by R, and if $< x,y > \notin R$ and $< y,x > \notin R$, then x and y are incomparable. Orders on X are therefore relations on X, since a relation on a set X is any subset of $X \times X$. Some minimal conditions a relation must meet to be an ordering are (i) reflexivity: $(\forall x) Rxx$; (ii) antisymmetry: $(\forall x)(\forall y)((Rxy \ \& \ Ryx) \supset x = y)$; and (iii) transitivity: $(\forall x)(\forall y)(\forall z)((Rxy \ \& \ Ryz) \supset Rxz)$. A relation meeting these three conditions is known as a *partial order* (also less commonly called a *semi-order*), and if reflexivity is replaced by irreflexivity, $(\forall x) \sim Rxx$, as a *strict partial order*.

Other orders are strengthenings of these. Thus a tree-ordering of X is a partial order with a distinguished root element α, i.e. $(\forall x) R \alpha x$, and that satisfies the backward linearity condition that from any element there is a unique path back to α: $(\forall x)(\forall y)(\forall z)((Ryx \ \& \ Rzx) \supset (Ryz \lor Rzy)$. A total order on X is a partial order satisfying the connectedness requirement: $(\forall x)(\forall y)(Rxy \lor Ryx)$. Total orderings are sometimes known as strict linear orderings, contrasting with weak linear orderings, in which the requirement of antisymmetry is dropped. The natural number line in its usual order is a strict linear order; a weak linear ordering of a set X is a strict linear order of levels on which various members of X may be found, while adding antisymmetry means that each level contains only one member.

Two other important orders are *dense* (partial or total) orders, in which, between any two elements, there is a third; and *well-orders*. A set X is said to be well-ordered by R if R is total and every non-empty subset of Y of X has an R-least member: $(\forall Y \subseteq X)[Y \neq \emptyset \supset (\exists z \in Y)(\forall w \in Y) Rzw]$. Well-ordering rules out infinite descending sequences, while a strict well-ordering, which is irreflexive rather than reflexive, rules out loops. The best-known example is the membership relation of axiomatic set theory, in which there are no loops such as $x \in y \in x$ or $x \in x$, and no infinite descending chains $\ldots x_2 \in x_1 \in x_0$.

See also RELATION, SET THEORY.   G.Fo.

ordering, Archimedian. See LEXICAL ORDERING.

order type omega, in mathematics, the order type of the infinite set of natural numbers. The last letter of the Greek alphabet, ω, is used to denote this order type; ω is thus the first infinite ordinal number. It can be defined as the set of all finite ordinal numbers ordered by magnitude; that is, $\omega = \{0,1,2,3 \ldots \}$. A set has order type ω provided it is denumerably infinite, has a first element but not a last element, has for each element a unique successor, and has just one element with no immediate predecessor. The set of even numbers ordered by magnitude, $\{2,4,6,8 \ldots \}$, is of order type ω. The set of natural numbers listing first all even numbers and then all odd numbers, $\{2,4,6,8 \ldots; 1,3,5,7 \ldots \}$, is not of order type ω, since it has two elements, 1 and 2, with no immediate predecessor. The set of negative integers ordered by magnitude, $\{ \ldots -3,-2,-1\}$, is also not of order type ω, since it has no first element.   V.K.

ordinal logic, any means of associating effectively and uniformly a logic (in the sense of a formal axiomatic system) S_a with each constructive ordinal notation a. This notion and term for it was introduced by Alan Turing in his paper "Systems of Logic Based on Ordinals" (1939). Turing's aim was to try to overcome the incompleteness of formal systems discovered by Gödel in 1931, by means of the transfinitely iterated, successive adjunction of unprovable but correct principles. For example, according to Gödel's second incompleteness theorem, for each effectively presented formal system S containing a modicum of elementary number theory, if S is consistent then S does not prove the purely universal arithmetical proposition Con_s expressing the consistency of S (via the Gödel-numbering of symbolic expressions), even though Con_s is correct. However, it may be that the result S' of adjoining Con_s to S is inconsistent. This will not happen if every purely existential statement provable in S is correct; call this condition $(E\text{-}C)$. Then if S satisfies $(E\text{-}C)$, so also does $S' = S + Con_s$; now S' is still incomplete by Gödel's theorem, though it is more complete than S. Clearly the passage from S to S' can be iterated any finite number of times, beginning with any S_0 satisfying $(E\text{-}C)$, to form $S_1 = S'_0$, $S_2 = S'_1$, etc. But this procedure can also be extended into the transfinite, by taking S_ω to be the union of the systems S_n for $n = 0, 1, 2 \ldots$ and then $S_{\omega+1} = S'_\omega$, $S_{\omega+2} = S'_{\omega+1}$, etc.; condition $(E\text{-}C)$ is preserved throughout.

To see how far this and other effective extension procedures of any effectively presented system S to another S' can be iterated into the transfinite, one needs the notion of the set O of constructive ordinal notations, due to Alonzo Church and Stephen C. Kleene in 1936. O is a set of natural numbers, and each a in O denotes an ordinal α, written as $|a|$. There is in O a notation for 0, and with each a in O is associated a notation $sc(a)$ in O with $|sc(a)| = |a| + 1$; finally, if f is a number of an effective function $\{f\}$ such that for each n, $\{f\}(n) = a_n$ is in O and $|a_n| < |a_{n+1}|$, then we have a notation $\ell(f)$ in O with $|\ell(f)| = \lim_n |a_n|$.

For quite general effective extension procedures of S to S' and for any given S_0, one can associate with each a in O a formal system S_a satisfying $S_{sc(a)} = S'_a$ and $S_{\ell(f)} =$ the union of the $S_{\{f\}(n)}$ for $n = 0, 1, 2. \ldots$ However, as there might be many notations for each constructive ordinal, this ordinal logic need not be invariant, in the sense that one need not have: if $|a| = |b|$ then S_a and S_b have the same consequences. Turing proved that an ordinal logic cannot be both complete for true purely universal statements and invariant. Using an extension procedure by certain proof-theoretic reflection principles, he constructed an ordinal logic that *is* complete for true purely universal statements, hence not invariant. (The history of this and later work on ordinal logics is traced by the undersigned in "Turing in the Land of $O(z)$," in *The Universal Turing Machine: A Half Century Survey*, edited by Rolf Herken [1988].)

See also GÖDEL'S INCOMPLETENESS THEOREMS, REFLECTION PRINCIPLES.   S.Fe.

ordinal utility. See UTILITARIANISM.

ordinary language philosophy, a loosely structured philosophical movement holding that the significance of concepts, including those central to traditional philosophy – e.g., the concepts of truth and knowledge – is fixed by linguistic practice. Philosophers, then, must be attuned to the actual *uses* of words associated with these concepts. The movement enjoyed considerable prominence chiefly among English-speaking philosophers between the mid-1940s and the early 1960s. It was initially inspired by the work of Wittgenstein, and later by John Wisdom, Gilbert Ryle, Norman Malcolm, and J. L. Austin, though its roots go back at least to Moore and arguably to Socrates. Ordinary language philosophers do not mean to suggest that, to discover what truth is, we are to poll our fellow speakers or consult dictionaries. Rather, we are to ask how the word 'truth' functions in everyday, nonphilosophical settings. A philosopher whose theory of truth is at odds with ordinary usage has simply misidentified the concept. Philosophical error, ironically, was thought by Wittgenstein to

arise from our "bewitchment" by language. When engaging in philosophy, we may easily be misled by superficial linguistic similarities. We suppose minds to be special sorts of entity, for instance, in part because of grammatical parallels between 'mind' and 'body'. When we fail to discover any entity that might plausibly count as a mind, we conclude that minds must be nonphysical entities. The cure requires that we remind ourselves how 'mind' and its cognates are actually used by ordinary speakers. **See also** ANALYTIC PHILOSOPHY; AUSTIN, J.   J.F.H.

organic, having parts that are organized and interrelated in a way that is the same as, or analogous to, the way in which the parts of a living animal or other biological organism are organized and interrelated. Thus, an organic unity or organic whole is a whole that is organic in the above sense. These terms are primarily used of entities that are not literally organisms but are supposedly analogous to them. Among the applications of the concept of an organic unity are: to works of art, to the state (e.g., by Hegel), and to the universe as a whole (e.g., in absolute idealism).

The principal element in the concept is perhaps the notion of an entity whose parts cannot be understood except by reference to their contribution to the whole entity. Thus to describe something as an organic unity is typically to imply that its properties cannot be given a reductive explanation in terms of those of its parts; rather, at least some of the properties of the parts must themselves be explained by reference to the properties of the whole. Hence it usually involves a form of holism. Other features sometimes attributed to organic unities include a mutual dependence between the existence of the parts and that of the whole and the need for a teleological explanation of properties of the parts in terms of some end or purpose associated with the whole. To what extent these characteristics belong to genuine biological organisms is disputed.

See also ORGANICISM, ORGANISM.
                                                       P.Mac.

organicism, a theory that applies the notion of an organic unity, especially to things that are not literally organisms.

G. E. Moore, in *Principia Ethica*, proposed a principle of organic unities, concerning intrinsic value: the (intrinsic) value of a whole need not be equivalent to the sum of the (intrinsic) values of its parts. Moore applies the principle in arguing that there is no systematic relation between the intrinsic value of an element of a complex whole and the difference that the presence of that element makes to the value of the whole. E.g., he holds that although a situation in which someone experiences pleasure in the contemplation of a beautiful object has far greater intrinsic goodness than a situation in which the person contemplates the same object without feeling pleasure, this does not mean that the pleasure itself has much intrinsic value.

See also HOLISM, REDUCTION, VALUE.

P.Mac.

organic unity. See ORGANIC.

organism, a carbon-based living thing or substance, e.g., a paramecium, a tree, or an ant. Alternatively, 'organism' can mean a hypothetical living thing of another natural kind, e.g., a silicon-based living thing. Defining conditions of a carbon-based living thing, x, are as follows. (1) x has a layer made of *m-molecules*, i.e., carbon-based macromolecules of repeated units that have a high capacity for selective reactions with other similar molecules. x can absorb and excrete through this layer. (2) x can metabolize m-molecules. (3) x can synthesize m-molecular parts of x by means of activities of a proper part of x that is a *nuclear molecule*, i.e., an m-molecule that can copy itself. (4) x can exercise the foregoing capacities in such a way that the corresponding activities are causally interrelated as follows: x's absorption and excretion causally contribute to x's metabolism; these processes jointly causally contribute to x's synthesizing; and x's synthesizing causally contributes to x's absorption, excretion, and metabolism. (5) x belongs to a natural kind of compound physical substance that can have a member, y, such that: y has a proper part, z; z is a nuclear molecule; and y reproduces by means of z's copying itself. (6) x is not possibly a proper part of something that satisfies (1)–(6). The last condition expresses the independence and autonomy of an organism. For example, a *part* of an organism, e.g., a heart cell, is not an organism. It also follows that a *colony* of organisms, e.g., a colony of ants, is not an organism.

See also LIFE, ORGANIC, ORGANICISM.

J.Ho. & G.Ro.

Organon. See ARISTOTLE.

Origen (A.D. 185–253), Christian theologian and biblical scholar in the Alexandrian church. Born in Egypt, he became head of the catechetical school in Alexandria. Like his mentor, Clement of Alexandria, he was influenced by Middle Platonism. His principal works were *Hexapla, On First Principles,* and *Contra Celsum.* The *Hexapla,* little of which survives, consisted of six Hebrew and two Greek versions of the Old Testament with Origen's commentary. *On First Principles* sets forth the most systematic Christian theology of the early church, including some doctrines subsequently declared heretical, such as the subordination of the Son ("a secondary god") and Spirit to the Father, preexisting human souls (but not their transmigration), and a premundane fall from grace of each human soul. The most famous of his views was the notion of apocatastasis, universal salvation, the universal restoration of all creation to God in which evil is defeated and the devil and his minions repent of their sins. He interpreted hell as a temporary purgatory in which impure souls were purified and made ready for heaven. His notion of subordination of the Son of God to the Father was condemned by the church in 533.

Origen's *Contra Celsum* is the first sustained work in Christian apologetics. It defends Christianity before the pagan world. Origen was a leading exponent of the allegorical interpretation of the Scriptures, holding that the text had three levels of meaning corresponding to the three parts of human nature: body, soul, and spirit. The first was the historical sense, sufficient for simple people; the second was the moral sense; and the third was the mystical sense, open only to the deepest souls.

L.P.P.

original position. See LIBERALISM, RAWLS.

Orpheus. See ORPHISM.

Orphism, a religious movement in ancient Greece that may have influenced Plato and some of the pre-Socratics. Neither the nature of the movement nor the scope of its influence is adequately understood: ancient sources and modern scholars tend to confuse Orphism with Pythagoreanism and with ancient mystery cults, especially the Bacchic or Dionysiac mysteries. "Orphic poems," i.e., poems attributed to Orpheus (a mythic figure), circulated as early as the mid-sixth century B.C. We have only indirect evidence of the early Orphic poems; but we do have a sizable body of fragments from poems composed in later antiquity. Central to both early and later versions is a theogonic-cosmogonic narrative that posits Night as the primal entity – ostensibly a revision of the account offered by Hesiod – and gives major emphasis to the birth, death through dismemberment, and rebirth of the god Dionysus. Plato gives us clear evidence of the existence in his time of itinerant religious teachers who, drawing on the "books of Orpheus," performed and taught rituals of initiation and purification intended to procure divine favor either in this life or in an afterlife. The extreme skepticism of such scholars as Ulrich von Wilamowitz-Moellendorff and I. M. Linforth concerning the importance of early Orphism for Greek religion and Greek philosophy has been undermined by archaeological findings in recent decades: the Derveni papyrus, which is a fragment of a philosophical commentary on an Orphic theogony; and inscriptions with Orphic instructions for the dead, from funerary sites in southern Italy, mainland Greece, and the Crimea.   A.P.D.M.

Ortega y Gasset, José (1883–1955), Spanish philosopher and essayist. Born in Madrid, he studied there and in Leipzig, Berlin, and Marburg. In 1910 he was named professor of metaphysics at the University of Madrid and taught there until 1936, when he was forced to leave because of his political involvement in and support for the Spanish Republic. He returned to Spain in 1945.

Ortega was a prolific writer whose works fill nine thick volumes. Among his most influential books are *Meditaciones del Quijote* ("Meditations on the Quixote," 1914), *El tema de nuestro tiempo* ("The Modern Theme," 1923), *La revolución de las masas* ("The Revolt of the Masses," 1932), *La deshumanización del arte* ("The Dehumanization of Art," 1925), *Historia como sistema* ("History as a System," 1941), and the posthumously published *El hombre y la gente* ("Man and People," 1957) and *La idea de principio en Leibniz* ("The Idea of Principle in Leibniz," 1958). His influence in Spain and Latin America was enormous, in part because of his brilliant style of writing and lecturing. He avoided jargon and rejected systematization; most of his works were first written as articles for newspapers and magazines. In 1923 he founded the *Revista de Occidente,* a cultural magazine that helped spread his ideas and introduced German thought into Spain and Latin America.

Ortega ventured into nearly every branch of philosophy, but the kernel of his views is his metaphysics of vital reason (*rasón vital*) and his perspectival epistemology. For Ortega, reality is identified with "my life"; something is real only insofar as it is rooted and appears in "my life." "My life" is further unpacked as "myself" and "my circumstances" (*"yo soy yo y mi circumstancia"*). The self is not an entity separate from what surrounds it; there is a dynamic interaction and interdependence of self and things. These and the self together constitute reality.

Because every life is the result of an interaction between self and circumstances, every self has a unique perspective. Truth, then, is perspectival, depending on the unique point of view from which it is determined, and no perspective is false except one that claims exclusivity. This doctrine is known as Ortega's *perspectivism.*   J.J.E.G.

ostensive definition. See DEFINITION.

Ostwald, Wilhelm. See ENERGETICISM.

other minds, problem of. See PROBLEM OF OTHER MINDS.

ought–is problem. See FACT–VALUE DISTINCTION.

ousia, ancient Greek term traditionally translated as 'substance'. Formed from the participle for 'being', the term *ousia* refers to the character of being, beingness, as if this were itself an entity. Just as redness is the character that red things have, so *ousia* is the character that beings have. Thus, the *ousia of something* is the character that makes it be, its nature. But *ousia* also refers to an entity that possesses being in its own right; for consider a case where the *ousia* of something is just the thing itself. Such a thing possesses being by virtue of itself; because its being depends on nothing else, it is self-subsistent and has a higher degree of being than things whose being depends on something else. Such a thing would be an *ousia.*

Just which entities meet the criteria for *ousia* is a question addressed by Aristotle. Something such as redness that exists only as an attribute would not have being in its own right. An individual person is an *ousia,* but Aristotle also argues that his form is more properly an *ousia;* and an unmoved mover is the highest type of *ousia.* The traditional rendering of the term into Latin as *substantia* and English as 'substance' is appropriate only in contexts like Aristotle's *Categories* where an *ousia* "stands under" attributes. In his *Metaphysics,* where Aristotle argues that being a substrate does not characterize *ousia,* and in other Greek writers, 'substance' is often not an apt translation.

See also SUBSTANCE.   E.C.H.

outer converse. See CONVERSE, OUTER AND INNER.

outer domain semantics. See FREE LOGIC.

overdetermination. See CAUSATION.

overman. See NIETZSCHE.

overriding reason. See REASONS FOR ACTION.

Oxford Calculators, a group of natural philosophers, mathematicians, and logicians who flourished at Oxford University in the second quarter of the fourteenth century. The name derives from the *Liber calculationum (Book of Calculations),* written some time before 1350. The author of this work, often called "Calculator" by later Continental authors, was probably named Richard Swineshead. The *Book of Calculations* discussed a number of issues related to the quantification or measurement of local motion, alteration, and augmentation (for a fuller description, see John Murdoch and Edith Sylla, "Swineshead, Richard," in *Dictionary of Scientific Biography,* Vol. 13, 1976). The *Book of Calculations* has been studied mainly by historians of science and grouped together with a number of other works discussing natural philosophical topics by such authors as Thomas Bradwardine, William Heytesbury, and John Dumbleton. In earlier histories many of the authors now referred to as Oxford Calculators are referred to as the Merton School, since many of them were fellows of Merton College. But since some authors whose work appears to fit into the same intellectual tradition (e.g., Richard Kilvington, whose *Sophismata* represents an earlier stage of the tradition later epitomized by William Heytesbury's *Sophismata*) have no known connection with Merton College, the name 'Oxford Calculators' would appear to be a more accurate appellation.

The works of the Oxford Calculators were produced in the context of education in the Oxford arts faculty (see Edith Sylla, "The Oxford Calculators," in Norman Kretzmann, Anthony Kenny, and Jan Pinborg, eds., *The Cambridge History of Later Medieval Philosophy,* 1982). In Oxford at this time logic was the centerpiece of the early years of undergraduate education. After logic, Oxford came to be known for its work in mathematics, astronomy, and natural philosophy. Students studying under the Oxford faculty of arts not only heard lectures on the liberal arts and on natural philosophy, moral philosophy, and metaphysics; they were also required to take part in disputations. William Heytesbury's *Regule solvendi sophismatum (Rules for Solving Sophismata)* explicitly and Swineshead's *Book of Calculations* implicitly are written to prepare students for these disputations.

The three influences most formative on the work of the Oxford Calculators were (1) the tradition of commentaries on the works of Aristotle; (2) the developments in logical theory, particularly the theories of categorematic and syncategorematic terms and the theory of logical supposition; and (3) developments in mathematics, particularly the theory of ratios as developed in Thomas Bradwardine's *De proportionibus velocitatum in motibus (On the Ratios of Velocities in Motions).* In addition to Richard Swineshead, Heytesbury, Bradwardine, Dumbleton, and Kilvington, other authors and works related to the work of the Oxford Calculators are Walter Burley, *De primo et ultimo instanti, Tractatus Primus (De formis accidentalibus), Tractatus Secundus (De intensione et remissione formarum);* Roger Swineshead, *Descriptiones motuum;* and John Bode, *A est unum calidum.* These and other works had a considerable later influence on the Continent.

See also BURLEY, COMMENTARIES ON ARISTOTLE, HEYTESBURY, KILVINGTON. E.D.S.

Oxford philosophy. See ANALYTIC PHILOSOPHY.

Oxford school of intuitionism. See PRICHARD.

P

PA. See APPENDIX OF SPECIAL SYMBOLS.

pa. See WANG, PA.

pacifism, (1) opposition to war, usually on moral or religious grounds, but sometimes on the practical ground (pragmatic pacifism) that it is wasteful and ineffective; (2) opposition to all killing and violence; (3) opposition only to war of a specified kind (e.g., nuclear pacifism).

Not to be confused with passivism, pacifism usually involves actively promoting peace, understood to imply cooperation and justice among peoples and not merely absence of war. But some (usually religious) pacifists accept military service so long as they do not carry weapons. Many pacifists subscribe to nonviolence. But some consider violence and/or killing permissible, say, in personal self-defense, law enforcement, abortion, or euthanasia. *Absolute pacifism* rejects war in all circumstances, hypothetical and actual. *Conditional pacifism* concedes war's permissibility in some hypothetical circumstances but maintains its wrongness in practice. If at least some hypothetical wars have better consequences than their alternative, absolute pacifism will almost inevitably be deontological in character, holding war intrinsically wrong or unexceptionably prohibited by moral principle or divine commandment. Conditional pacifism may be held on either deontological or utilitarian (teleological or sometimes consequentialist) grounds. If deontological, it may hold war at most prima facie wrong intrinsically but nonetheless virtually always impermissible in practice because of the absence of counterbalancing right-making features. If utilitarian, it will hold war wrong, not intrinsically, but solely because of its consequences. It may say either that every particular war has worse consequences than its avoidance (act utilitarianism) or that general acceptance of (or following or compliance with) a rule prohibiting war will have best consequences even if occasional particular wars have best consequences (rule utilitarianism).

See also NONVIOLENCE. R.L.H.

Paine, Thomas (1737–1809), American political philosopher, revolutionary defender of democracy and human rights, and champion of popular radicalism in three countries. Born in Thetford, England, he emigrated to the American colonies in 1774; he later moved to France, where he was made a French citizen in 1792. In 1802 he returned to the United States, where he was rebuffed by the public because of his support for the French Revolution. Paine was the best-known polemicist for the American Revolution. In many incendiary pamphlets, he called for a new, more democratic republicanism. His direct style and uncompromising egalitarianism had wide popular appeal.

In *Common Sense* (1776) Paine asserted that commoners were the equal of the landed aristocracy, thus helping to spur colonial resentments sufficiently to support independence from Britain. The sole basis of political legitimacy is universal, active consent; taxation without representation is unjust; and people have the right to resist when the contract between governor and governed is broken.

He defended the French Revolution in *The Rights of Man* (1791–92), arguing against concentrating power in any one individual and against a property qualification for suffrage. Since natural law and right reason as conformity to nature are accessible to all rational persons, sovereignty resides in human beings and is not bestowed by membership in class or nation. Opposed to the extremist Jacobins, he helped write, with Condorcet, a constitution to secure the Revolution.

The Age of Reason (1794), Paine's most misunderstood work, sought to secure the social cohesion necessary to a well-ordered society by grounding it in belief in a divinity. But in supporting deism and attacking established religion as a tool of enslavement, he alienated the very laboring classes he sought to enlighten. A lifelong adversary of slavery and supporter of universal male suffrage, Paine argued for redistributing property in *Agrarian Justice* (1797).

See also DEISM, POLITICAL PHILOSOPHY.

C.H.S.

Paley, William, (1743–1805), English moral philosopher and theologian. He was born in Peterborough and educated at Cambridge, where he lectured in moral philosophy, divinity, and Greek New Testament before assuming a series of posts in the Church of England, the last as archdeacon of Carlisle. *The Principles of Moral and Political Philosophy* (1785) first introduced utilitarianism to a wide public. Moral obligation is created by a divine command "coupled" with the expectation of everlasting rewards or punishments. While God's commands can be ascertained "from Scripture and the light of nature," Paley emphasizes the latter. Since God wills human welfare, the rightness or wrongness of actions is determined by their "tendency to promote or diminish the general happiness." *Horae Pauline: Or the Truth of the Scripture History of St Paul Evinced* appeared in 1790, *A View of the Evidences of Christianity* in 1794. The latter defends the authenticity of the Christian miracles against Hume. *Natural Theology* (1802) provides a design argument for God's existence and a demonstration of his attributes. Nature exhibits abundant contrivances whose "several parts are framed and put together for a purpose." These contrivances establish the existence of a powerful, wise, benevolent designer. They cannot show that its power and wisdom are unlimited, however, and "omnipotence" and "omniscience" are mere "superlatives." Paley's *Principles* and *Evidences* served as textbooks in England and America well into the nineteenth century. **See also** DIVINE ATTRIBUTES, HUME, MIRACLE, PHILOSOPHY OF RELIGION, UTILITARIANISM.   W.J.Wa.

Panaetius. See STOICISM.

panentheism. See KRAUSE, PANTHEISM.

panlogism. See HEGEL.

panpsychism, the doctrine that the physical world is pervasively psychical, sentient or conscious (understood as equivalent). The idea, usually, is that it is articulated into certain ultimate units or particles, momentary or enduring, each with its own distinct charge of sentience or consciousness, and that some more complex physical units possess a sentience emergent from the interaction between the charges of sentience pertaining to their parts, sometimes down through a series of levels of articulation into sentient units. Animal consciousness is the overall sentience pertaining to some substantial part or aspect of the brain, while each neuron may have its own individual charge of sentience, as may each included atom and subatomic particle. Else-

where the only sentient units may be at the atomic and subatomic level.

Two differently motivated versions of the doctrine should be distinguished. The first implies no particular view about the nature of matter, and regards the sentience pertaining to each unit as an extra to its physical nature. Its point is to explain animal and human consciousness as emerging from the interaction and perhaps fusion of more pervasive sentient units. The better motivated, second version holds that the inner essence of matter is unknown. We know only structural facts about the physical or facts about its effects on sentience like our own. Panpsychists hypothesize that the otherwise unknown inner essence of matter consists in sentience or consciousness articulated into the units we identify externally as fundamental particles, or as a supervening character pertaining to complexes of such or complexes of complexes, etc. Panpsychists can thus uniquely combine the idealist claim that there can be no reality without consciousness with rejection of any subjectivist reduction of the physical world to human experience of it.

Modern versions of panpsychism (e.g. of Whitehead, Hartshorne, and Sprigge) are only partly akin to hylozoism as it occurred in ancient thought. Note that neither version need claim that every physical object possesses consciousness; no one supposes that a team of conscious cricketers must itself be conscious.

See also HYLOZOISM, WHITEHEAD.   T.L.S.S.

pantheism, the view that God is identical with everything. It may be seen as the result of two tendencies: an intense religious spirit and the belief that all reality is in some way united. Pantheism should be distinguished from *panentheism*, the view that God is in all things. Just as water might saturate a sponge and in that way be in the entire sponge, but not be identical with the sponge, God might be in everything without being identical with everything.

Spinoza is the most distinguished pantheist in Western philosophy. He argued that since substance is completely self-sufficient, and only God is self-sufficient, God is the only substance. In other words, God is everything. Hegel is also sometimes considered a pantheist since he identifies God with the totality of being.

Many people think that pantheism is tantamount to atheism, because they believe that theism requires that God transcend ordinary, sensible reality at least to some degree. It is not obvious that theism requires a transcendent or personal notion of God; and one might claim that the belief that it does is the result of an anthropomorphic view of God. In Eastern philosophy, especially the Vedic tradition of Indian philosophy, pantheism is part of a rejection of polytheism. The apparent multiplicity of reality is illusion. What is ultimately real or divine is Brahman.

See also BRAHMAN, PANTHEISMUSSTREIT, PHILOSOPHY OF RELIGION.   A.P.M.

Pantheismusstreit (German, 'dispute over pantheism'), a debate primarily between the German philosophers Jacobi and Mendelssohn, although it also included Lessing, Kant, and Goethe. The basic issue concerned what pantheism is and whether all pantheists are atheists. In particular, it concerned whether Spinoza was a pantheist, and if so, whether he was an atheist; and how close Lessing's thought was to Spinoza's. The standard view, propounded by Bayle and Leibniz, was that Spinoza's pantheism was a thin veil for his atheism. Lessing and Goethe did not accept this harsh interpretation of him. They believed that his pantheism avoided the alienating transcendence of the standard Judeo-Christian concept of God. It was debated whether Lessing was a Spinozist or some form of theistic pantheist. Lessing was critical of dogmatic religions and denied that there was any revelation given to all people for rational acceptance. He may have told Jacobi that he was a Spinozist; but he may also have been speaking ironically or hypothetically. See also SPINOZA.   A.P.M.

Paracelsus, pseudonym of Theophrastus Bombastus von Hohenheim (1493–1541), Swiss chemist, physician, and natural philosopher. He pursued medical studies at various German and Austrian universities, probably completing them at Ferrara (1513–16). Thereafter he had little to do with the academic world, apart from a brief and stormy period as professor of medicine at Basle (1527–28). Instead, he worked first as a military surgeon and later as an itinerant physician in Germany, Austria, and Switzerland. His works were mainly in German rather than Latin, and only a few were published during his lifetime.

His importance for medical practice lay in his insistence on observation and experiment, and his use of chemical methods for preparing drugs. The success of Paracelsian medicine and chemistry in the later sixteenth and seventeenth centuries was, however, largely due to the theoretical background he provided. He firmly rejected the classical medical inheritance, particularly Galen's explanation of disease as an imbalance of humors; he drew on a combination of biblical sources, German mysticism, alchemy, and Neoplatonic magic as found in Ficino to present a unified view of humankind and the universe. He saw man as a microcosm, reflecting the nature of the divine world through his immortal soul, the sidereal world through his astral body or vital principle, and the terrestrial world through his visible body. Knowledge requires union with the object, but because elements of all the worlds are found in man, he can acquire knowledge of the universe and of God, as partially revealed in nature. The physician needs knowledge of vital principles (called *astra*) in order to heal. Disease is caused by external agents that can affect the human vital principle as well as the visible body. Chemical methods are employed to isolate the appropriate vital principles in minerals and herbs, and these are used as antidotes.

Paracelsus further held that matter contains three principles, sulfur, mercury, and salt. As a result, he thought it was possible to transform one metal into another by varying the proportions of the fundamental principles; and that such transformations could also be used in the production of drugs.

See also ALCHEMY, MYSTICISM.   E.J.A.

paraconsistency, the property of a logic in which one cannot derive all statements from a contradiction. What is objectionable about contradictions, from the standpoint of classical logic, is not just that they are false but that they imply any statement whatsoever: one who accepts a contradiction is thereby committed to accepting everything. In paraconsistent logics, however, such as relevance logics, contradictions are isolated inferentially and thus rendered relatively harmless. The interest in such logics stems from the fact that people sometimes continue to work in inconsistent theories even after the inconsistency has been exposed, and do so without inferring everything. Whether this phenomenon can be explained satisfactorily by the classical logician or shows instead that the underlying logic of, e.g., science and mathematics is some non-classical paraconsistent logic, is disputed. See also CONSISTENCY, RELEVANCE LOGIC.   G.F.S.

paradigm, as used by Thomas Kuhn (*The Structure of Scientific Revolutions,* 1962), a set of scientific and metaphysical beliefs that make up a theoretical framework within which scientific theories can be tested, evaluated, and if necessary revised. Kuhn's principal thesis, in which the notion of a paradigm plays a central role, is structured around an argument against the logical empiricist view of scientific theory change. Empiricists viewed theory change as an ongoing smooth and cumulative process in which empirical facts, discovered through observation or experimentation, forced revisions in our theories and thus added to our ever-increasing knowledge of the world. It was claimed that, combined with this process of revision, there existed a process of intertheoretic reduction that enabled us to understand the macro in terms of the micro, and that ultimately aimed at a unity of science. Kuhn maintains that this view is incompatible with what actually happens in case after case in the history of science. Scientific change occurs by "revolutions" in which an older paradigm is overthrown and is replaced by a framework incompatible or even incommensurate with it. Thus the alleged empirical "facts," which were adduced to support the older theory, become irrelevant to the new; the questions asked and answered in the new framework cut across those of the old; indeed the vocabularies of the two frameworks make up different languages, not easily intertranslatable. These episodes of revolution are separated by long periods of "normal science," during which the theories of a given paradigm are honed, refined, and elaborated. These periods are sometimes referred to as periods of "puzzle solving," because the changes are to be understood more as fiddling with the details of the theories to "save the phenomena" than as steps taking us closer to the truth.

A number of philosophers have complained that Kuhn's conception of a paradigm is too imprecise to do the work he intended for it. In fact, Kuhn, fifteen years later, admitted that at least two distinct ideas were exploited by the term: (i) the "shared elements [that] account for the relatively unproblematic character of professional communication and for the relative unanimity of professional judgment," and (ii) "concrete problem solutions, accepted by the group [of scientists] as, in a quite usual sense, paradigmatic" (Kuhn, "Second Thoughts on Paradigms," 1977). Kuhn offers the terms 'disciplinary matrix' and 'exemplar', respectively, for these two ideas.

    See also KUHN, LOGICAL POSITIVISM, PHILOSOPHY OF SCIENCE, REDUCTION, UNITY OF SCIENCE.   B.E.

paradigm case argument, an argument designed to yield an affirmative answer to the following general type of skeptically motivated question: Are *A*'s really *B*? E.g., Do material objects really exist? Are any of our actions really free? Does induction really provide reasonable grounds for one's beliefs? The structure of the argument is simple: in situations that are "typical," "exemplary," or "paradigmatic," standards for which are supplied by common sense, or ordinary language, part of what it is to be *B* essentially involves *A*. Hence it is absurd to doubt if *A*'s are ever *B*, or to doubt if *in general A*'s are *B*. (More commonly, the argument is encountered in the linguistic mode: part of what it *means* for something to be *B* is that, in paradigm cases, it be an *A*. Hence the question whether *A*'s are ever *B* is meaningless.)

    An example may be found in the application of the argument to the problem of induction. (See Strawson, *Introduction to Logical Theory,* 1952.) When one believes a generalization of the form 'All *F*'s are *G*' on the basis of good inductive evidence, i.e., evidence constituted by innumerable and varied instances of *F* all of which are *G*, one would *thereby* have good reasons for holding this belief. The argument for this claim is based on the content of the concepts of reasonableness and of strength of evidence. Thus according to Strawson, the following two propositions are analytic:

(1) It is reasonable to have a degree of belief in a proposition that is proportional to the strength of the evidence in its favor.
(2) The evidence for a generalization is strong in proportion as the number of instances, and the variety of circumstances in which they have been found, is great.

Hence, Strawson concludes, "to ask whether it is reasonable to place reliance on inductive procedures is like asking whether it is reasonable to proportion the degree of one's convictions to the strength of the evidence. Doing this is what 'being reasonable' *means* in such a context" (p. 257).

    In such arguments the role played by the appeal to paradigm cases is crucial. In Strawson's version, paradigm cases are constituted by "innumerable *and* varied instances." Without such an appeal the argument would fail completely, for it is clear that not all uses of induction *are* reasonable. Even when this appeal is made clear though, the argument remains questionable, for it fails to confront adequately the force of the word 'really' in the skeptical challenges.

See also ANALYTIC-SYNTHETIC DISTINC-
TION, PROBLEM OF INDUCTION.   B.E.

paradox, a seemingly sound piece of reasoning based on seemingly true assumptions that leads to a contradiction (or other obviously false conclusion). A paradox reveals that either the principles of reasoning or the assumptions on which it is based are faulty. It is said to be solved when the mistaken principles or assumptions are clearly identified and rejected. The philosophical interest in paradoxes arises from the fact that they sometimes reveal fundamentally mistaken assumptions or erroneous reasoning techniques.

Two groups of paradoxes have received a great deal of attention in modern philosophy. Known as the semantic paradoxes and the logical or set-theoretic paradoxes, they reveal serious difficulties in our intuitive understanding of the basic notions of semantics and set theory.

Other well-known paradoxes include the barber paradox and the prediction (or hangman or unexpected examination) paradox. The *barber paradox* is mainly useful as an example of a paradox that is easily resolved. Suppose we are told that there is an Oxford barber who shaves all and only the Oxford men who do not shave themselves. Using this description, we can apparently derive the contradiction that this barber both shaves and does not shave himself. (If he does not shave himself, then according to the description he must be one of the people he shaves; if he does shave himself, then according to the description he is one of the people he does not shave.) This paradox can be resolved in two ways. First, the original claim that such a barber exists can simply be rejected: perhaps no one satisfies the alleged description. Second, the described barber may exist, but not fall into the class of Oxford men: a woman barber, e.g., could shave all and only the Oxford men who do not shave themselves.

The *prediction paradox* takes a variety of forms. Suppose a teacher tells her students on Friday that the following week she will give a single quiz. But it will be a surprise: the students will not know the evening before that the quiz will take place the following day. They reason that she cannot give such a quiz. After all, she cannot wait until Friday to give it, since then they would know Thursday evening. That leaves Monday through Thursday as the only possible days for it. But then Thursday can be ruled out for the same reason: they would know on Wednesday evening. Wednesday, Tuesday, and Monday can be ruled out by similar reasoning. Convinced by

this seemingly correct reasoning, the students do not study for the quiz. On Wednesday morning, they are taken by surprise when the teacher distributes it. It has been pointed out that the students' reasoning has this peculiar feature: in order to rule out any of the days, they must assume that the quiz will be given and that it will be a surprise. But their alleged conclusion is that it cannot be given or else will not be a surprise, undermining that very assumption. Kaplan and Montague have argued (in "A Paradox Regained," *Notre Dame Journal of Formal Logic,* 1960) that at the core of this puzzle is what they call the knower paradox – a paradox that arises when intuitively plausible principles about knowledge (and its relation to logical consequence) are used in conjunction with knowledge claims whose content is, or entails, a denial of those very claims.

See also DEONTIC PARADOXES, PARADOXES OF OMNIPOTENCE, SEMANTIC PARADOXES, SET-THEORETIC PARADOXES, ZENO'S PARADOXES.   J.Et.

paradoxes, deontic. See DEONTIC PARADOXES.

paradoxes, logical. See SET-THEORETIC PARADOXES.

paradoxes, semantic. See SEMANTIC PARADOXES.

paradoxes, set-theoretic. See SET-THEORETIC PARADOXES.

paradoxes of confirmation. See CONFIRMATION.

paradoxes of material implication. See IMPLICATION.

paradoxes of omnipotence, a series of paradoxes in philosophical theology that maintain that God could not be omnipotent because the concept is inconsistent, alleged to result from the intuitive idea that if God is omnipotent, then God must be able to do anything.

(1) Can God perform logically contradictory tasks? If God can, then God should be able to make himself simultaneously omnipotent and not omnipotent, which is absurd. If God cannot, then it appears that there is something God cannot do. Many philosophers have sought to avoid this consequence by claiming that the notion of performing a logically contradictory task is empty, and that question (1) specifies no task that God can perform *or* fail to perform.

(2) Can God cease to be omnipotent? If God can and were to do so, then at any time there-

after, God would no longer be completely sovereign over all things. If God cannot, then God cannot do something that others can do, namely, impose limitations on one's own powers. A popular response to question (2) is to say that omnipotence is an essential attribute of a necessarily existing being. According to this response, although God cannot cease to be omnipotent any more than God can cease to exist, these features are not liabilities but rather the lack of liabilities in God.

(3) Can God create another being who is omnipotent? Is it logically possible for two beings to be omnipotent? It might seem that there could be, if they never disagreed in fact with each other. If, however, omnipotence requires control over all possible but counterfactual situations, there could be two omnipotent beings only if it were impossible for them to disagree.

(4) Can God create a stone too heavy for God to move? If God can, then there is something that God cannot do – move such a stone – and if God cannot, then there is something God cannot do – create such a stone. One reply is to maintain that 'God cannot create a stone too heavy for God to move' is a harmless consequence of 'God can create stones of any weight and God can move stones of any weight.'

See also DIVINE ATTRIBUTES, PHILOSOPHY OF RELIGION.   W.E.M.

paradoxes of self-reference. See RUSSELL, TYPE THEORY.

paradoxes of set theory. See SET-THEORETIC PARADOXES, SET THEORY.

paradoxes of strict implication. See IMPLICATION.

paradox of analysis, an argument that it is impossible for an analysis of a meaning to be informative for one who already understands the meaning. Consider: 'An F is a G' (e.g., 'A circle is a line all points on which are equidistant from some one point') gives a correct analysis of the meaning of 'F' only if 'G' means the same as 'F'; but then anyone who already understands both meanings must already know what the sentence says. Indeed, that will be the same as what the trivial 'An F is an F' says, since replacing one expression by another with the same meaning should preserve what the sentence says. The conclusion that 'An F is a G' cannot be informative (for one who already understands all its terms) is paradoxical only for cases where 'G' is not only synonymous with but more complex

than 'F', in such a way as to give an *analysis* of 'F'. ('A first cousin is an offspring of a parent's sibling' gives an analysis, but 'A dad is a father' does not and in fact could not be informative for one who already knows the meaning of all its words.) The paradox appears to fail to distinguish between different sorts of knowledge. Encountering for the first time (and understanding) a correct analysis of a meaning one already grasps brings one from merely *tacit* to *explicit* knowledge of its truth. One sees that it does capture the meaning and thereby sees a way of *articulating* the meaning one had not thought of before. **See also** ANALYSIS, DEFINITION, MEANING.   C.G.

paradox of omniscience, an objection to the possibility of omniscience, developed by Patrick Grim, that appeals to an application of Cantor's power set theorem. Omniscience requires knowing all truths; according to Grim, that means knowing every truth in the set of all truths. But there is no set of all truths. Suppose that there were a set **T** of all truths. Consider all the subsets of **T**, that is, all members of the power set $\mathscr{P}\mathbf{T}$. Take some truth $\mathbf{T_1}$. For each member of $\mathscr{P}\mathbf{T}$ either $\mathbf{T_1}$ is a member of that set or $\mathbf{T_1}$ is not a member of that set. There will thus correspond to each member of $\mathscr{P}\mathbf{T}$ a further truth specifying whether $\mathbf{T_1}$ is or is not a member of that set. Therefore there are at least as many truths as there are members of $\mathscr{P}\mathbf{T}$. By the power set theorem, there are more members of $\mathscr{P}\mathbf{T}$ than there are of **T**. So **T** is not the set of all truths. By a parallel argument, no other set is, either. So there is no set of all truths, after all, and therefore no one who knows every member of that set. The objection may be countered by denying that the claim 'for every proposition p, if p is true God knows that p' requires that there be a set of all true propositions. **See also** CANTOR, DIVINE ATTRIBUTES.   E.R.W.

paradox of self-deception. See SELF-DECEPTION.

paradox of the examination. See UNEXPECTED EXAMINATION PARADOX.

paradox of the heap. See SORITES PARADOX.

paradox of the knower. See DEONTIC PARADOXES.

paradox of the ravens. See CONFIRMATION.

paradox of the stone. See PARADOXES OF OMNIPOTENCE.

parallel distributed processing. See CONNECTION-ISM.

parallelism. See PHILOSOPHY OF MIND.

parallelism, psychophysical. See PHILOSOPHY OF MIND.

parapsychology, the study of certain anomalous phenomena and ostensible causal connections neither recognized nor clearly rejected by traditional science. Parapsychology's principal areas of investigation are *extrasensory perception* (ESP), *psychokinesis* (PK), and cases suggesting the *survival* of mental functioning following bodily death. The study of ESP has traditionally focused on two sorts of ostensible phenomena, *telepathy* (the apparent anomalous influence of one person's mental states on those of another, commonly identified with apparent communication between two minds by extrasensory means) and *clairvoyance* (the apparent anomalous influence of a physical state of affairs on a person's mental states, commonly identified with the supposed ability to perceive or know of objects or events not present to the senses). The forms of ESP may be viewed either as types of cognition (e.g., the anomalous knowledge of another person's mental states) or as merely a form of anomalous causal influence (e.g., a distant burning house causing one to have – possibly incongruous – thoughts about fire). The study of PK covers the apparent ability to produce various physical effects independently of familiar or recognized intermediate sorts of causal links. These effects include the ostensible movement of remote objects, materializations (the apparently instantaneous production of matter), apports (the apparently instantaneous relocation of an object), and (in laboratory experiments) statistically significant non-random behavior of normally random microscopic processes (such as radioactive decay). Survival research focuses on cases of ostensible *reincarnation* and mental *mediumship* (i.e., "channeling" of information from an apparently deceased communicator).

Cases of ostensible *precognition* may be viewed as types of telepathy and clairvoyance, and suggest the causal influence of some state of affairs on an earlier event (an agent's ostensible precognitive experience). However, those opposed to backward causation may interpret ostensible precognition either as a form of unconscious inference based on contemporaneous information acquired by ESP, or else as a form of PK (possibly in conjunction with telepathic influence) by which the precognizer brings about the events apparently precognized.

The data of parapsychology raise two particularly deep issues. The evidence suggesting survival poses a direct challenge to materialist theories of the mental. And the evidence for ESP and PK suggests the viability of a "magical" worldview associated usually with so-called primitive societies, according to which we have direct and intimate access to and influence on the thoughts and bodily states of others.

See also PHILOSOPHY OF MIND, PHILOSOPHY OF PSYCHOLOGY.   S.E.B.

Pareto efficiency, also called Pareto optimality, a state of affairs in which no one can be made better off without making someone worse off. The Italian economist Vilfredo Pareto (1848–1923) referred to optimality rather than efficiency, but usage has drifted toward the less normative term. Pareto supposed that utilitarian addition of welfare across individuals is meaningless. He concluded that the only useful aggregate measures of welfare must be ordinal. One state of affairs is Pareto-superior to another if we cannot move to the second state without making someone worse off. Although the Pareto criteria are generally thought to be positive rather than normative, they are often used as normative principles for justifying particular changes or refusals to make changes. For example, some economists and philosophers take the Pareto criteria as moral constraints and therefore oppose certain government policies. In market and voluntary exchange contexts, it makes sense to suppose every exchange will be Pareto-improving, at least for the direct parties to the exchange. If, however, we fail to account for external effects of our exchange on other people, it may not be Pareto-improving. Moreover, we may fail to provide collective benefits that require the cooperation or coordination of many individuals' efforts. Hence, even in markets, we cannot expect to achieve Pareto efficiency. We might therefore suppose we should invite government intervention to help us. But in typical social contexts, it is often hard to believe that significant policy changes can be Pareto-improving: there are sure to be losers from any change. **See also** PERFECT COMPETITION, SOCIAL CHOICE THEORY, UTILITARIANISM.
R.Har.

Pareto optimality. See PARETO EFFICIENCY.

Pareto-superior. See PARETO EFFICIENCY.

Parfit, Derek (b.1942), British philosopher internationally known for his major contributions to the metaphysics of persons, moral theory, and practical reasoning. Parfit first rose to prominence by challenging the prevalent view that personal identity is a "deep fact" that must be all or nothing and that matters greatly in rational and moral deliberations. Exploring puzzle cases involving fission and fusion, Parfit propounded a reductionist account of personal identity, arguing that what matters in survival are physical and psychological continuities. These are a matter of degree, and sometimes there may be no answer as to whether some future person would be me.

Parfit's magnum opus, *Reasons and Persons* (1984), is a strikingly original book brimming with startling conclusions that have significantly reshaped the philosophical agenda. Part One treats different theories of morality, rationality, and the good; blameless wrongdoing; moral immorality; rational irrationality; imperceptible harms and benefits; harmless torturers; and the self-defeatingness of certain theories. Part Two introduces a critical present-aim theory of individual rationality, and attacks the standard self-interest theory. It also discusses the rationality of different attitudes to time, such as caring more about the future than the past, and more about the near than the remote. Addressing the age-old conflict between self-interest and morality, Parfit illustrates that contrary to what the self-interest theory demands, it can be rational to care about certain other aims as much as, or more than, about our own future well-being. In addition, Parfit notes that the self-interest theory is a hybrid position, neutral with respect to time but partial with respect to persons. Thus, it can be challenged from one direction by morality, which is neutral with respect to both persons and time, and from the other by a present-aim theory, which is partial with respect to both persons and time. Part Three refines Parfit's views regarding personal identity and further criticizes the self-interest theory: personal identity is not what matters, hence reasons to be specially concerned about our future are not provided by the fact that it will be *our* future. Part Four presents puzzles regarding future generations and argues that the moral principles we need when considering future people must take an impersonal form. Parfit's arguments deeply challenge our understanding of moral ideals and, some believe, the possibility of comparing outcomes.

Parfit has three forthcoming manuscripts, tentatively titled *Rediscovering Reasons, The Metaphysics of the Self,* and *On What Matters.* His current focus is the normativity of reasons. A reductionist about persons, he is a non-reductionist about reasons. He believes in irreducibily normative beliefs that are in a strong sense true. A realist about reasons for acting and caring, he challenges the views of naturalists, noncognitivists, and constructivists. Parfit contends that internalists conflate normativity with motivating force, that contrary to the prevalent view that *all* reasons are provided by desires, *no* reasons are, and that Kant poses a greater threat to rationalism than Hume.

Parfit is Senior Research Fellow of All Souls College, Oxford, and a regular visiting professor at both Harvard and New York University. Legendary for monograph-length criticisms of book manuscripts, he is editor of the Oxford Ethics Series, whose goal is to make definite moral progress, a goal Parfit himself is widely believed to have attained.

See also ETHICS, EXTERNALISM, MORAL REALISM, MOTIVATIONAL INTERNALISM, PERSONAL IDENTITY, PRACTICAL REASON. L.S.T.

parity of reasons. See PRINCIPLE OF INDIFFERENCE.

Parmenides (early fifth century B.C.), Greek philosopher, the most influential of the pre-Socratics, active in Elea (Roman and modern Velia), an Ionian Greek colony in southern Italy. He was the first Greek thinker who can properly be called an ontologist or metaphysician. Plato refers to him as "venerable and awesome," as "having magnificent depth" (*Theaetetus* 183e–184a), and presents him in the dialogue *Parmenides* as a searching critic – in a fictional and dialectical transposition – of Plato's own theory of Forms.

Nearly 150 lines of a didactic poem by Parmenides have been preserved, assembled into about twenty fragments. The first part, "Truth," provides the earliest specimen in Greek intellectual history of a sustained deductive argument. Drawing on intuitions concerning thinking, knowing, and language, Parmenides argues that "the real" or "what-is" or "being" (*to eon*) must be ungenerable and imperishable, indivisible, and unchanging. According to a Plato-inspired tradition, Parmenides held that "all is one." But the phrase does not occur in the fragments; Parmenides does not even speak of "the One"; and it is possible that either a holistic One or a plurality of absolute monads might conform to Parmenides' deduction. Nonetheless, it is difficult to resist the impression that the argument converges on a unique entity, which may indifferently be referred to as Being, or the All, or the One.

Parmenides embraces fully the paradoxical consequence that the world of ordinary experience fails to qualify as "what-is." Nonetheless, in "Opinions," the second part of the poem, he expounds a dualist cosmology. It is unclear whether this is intended as candid phenomenology – a doctrine of appearances – or as an ironic foil to "Truth." It is noteworthy that Parmenides was probably a physician by profession. Ancient reports to this effect are borne out by fragments (from "Opinions") with embryological themes, as well as by archaeological findings at Velia that link the memory of Parmenides with Roman-period remains of a medical school at that site. Parmenides' own attitude notwithstanding, "Opinions" recorded four major scientific breakthroughs, some of which, doubtless, were Parmenides' own discoveries: that the earth is a sphere; that the two tropics and the Arctic and Antarctic circles divide the earth into five zones; that the moon gets its light from the sun; and that the morning star and the evening star are the same planet.

The term Eleatic School is misleading when it is used to suggest a common doctrine supposedly held by Parmenides, Zeno of Elea, Melissus of Samos, and (anticipating Parmenides) Xenophanes of Colophon. The fact is, many philosophical groups and movements, from the middle of the fifth century onward, were influenced, in different ways, by Parmenides, including the "pluralists," Empedocles, Anaxagoras, and Democritus. Parmenides' deductions, transformed by Zeno into a repertoire of full-blown paradoxes, provided the model both for the eristic of the Sophists and for Socrates' elenchus. Moreover, the Parmenidean criteria for "what-is" lie unmistakably in the background not only of Plato's theory of Forms but also of salient features of Aristotle's system, notably, the priority of actuality over potentiality, the unmoved mover, and the man-begets-man principle. Indeed, all philosophical and scientific systems that posit principles of conservation (of substance, of matter, of matter-energy) are inalienably the heirs to Parmenides' deduction.

See also ELEATIC SCHOOL, MELISSUS OF SAMOS, PRE-SOCRATICS.   A.P.D.M.

parousia. See PLATO.

parse tree. See PARSING.

parsimony, principle of. See OCKHAM'S RAZOR.

parsing, the process of determining the syntactic structure of a sentence according to the rules of a given grammar. This is to be distinguished from the generally simpler task of *recognition,* which is merely the determination of whether or not a given string is well-formed (grammatical). In general, many different parsing strategies can be employed for grammars of a particular type, and a great deal of attention has been given to the relative efficiencies of these techniques. The most thoroughly studied cases center on the context-free phrase structure grammars, which assign syntactic structures in the form of singly-rooted trees with a left-to-right ordering of "sister" nodes. Parsing procedures can then be broadly classified according to the sequence of steps by which the parse tree is constructed: top-down versus bottom-up; depth-first versus breadth-first; etc. In addition, there are various strategies for exploring alternatives (agendas, backtracking, parallel processing) and there are devices such as "charts" that eliminate needless repetitions of previous steps. Efficient parsing is of course important when language, whether natural or artificial (e.g., a programming language), is being processed by computer. Human beings also parse rapidly and with apparently little effort when they comprehend sentences of a natural language. Although little is known about the details of this process, psycholinguists hope that study of mechanical parsing techniques might provide insights. **See also** GRAMMAR.   R.E.W.

partial belief. See PROBABILITY.

partial function. See MATHEMATICAL FUNCTION.

partial order. See RELATION.

partial ordering. See ORDERING.

participation. See PLATO.

particular. See CONCEPTUALISM, INDIVIDUATION, METAPHYSICS.

particular, bare. See METAPHYSICS.

particular, basic. See STRAWSON.

particularism. See PROBLEM OF THE CRITERION.

particular proposition. See SYLLOGISM.

partition, division of a set into mutually exclusive and jointly exhaustive subsets. Derivatively, 'partition' can mean any set P whose members are mutually exclusive and jointly exhaustive subsets of set S. Each subset of a partition P is called a *partition class* of S with respect to P. Partitions are intimately associated with equivalence relations, i.e. with relations that are transitive, symmetric, and reflexive. Given an equivalence relation R defined on a set S, R induces a partition P of S in the following natural way: members s_1 and s_2 belong to the same partition class of P if and only if s_1 has the relation R to s_2. Conversely, given a partition P of a set S, P induces an equivalence relation R defined on S in the following natural way: members s_1 and s_2 are such that s_1 has the relation R to s_2 if and only if s_1 and s_2 belong to the same partition class of P. For obvious reasons, then, partition classes are also known as *equivalence classes*. **See also** RELATION, SET THEORY.   R.W.B.

Parva naturalia. See ARISTOTLE.

Pascal, Blaise (1623–62), French philosopher known for his brilliance as a mathematician, physicist, inventor, theologian, polemicist, and French prose stylist. Born at Clermont-Ferrand in the Auvergne, he was educated by his father, Étienne, and first gained note for his contribution to mathematics when at sixteen he produced, under the influence of Desargues, a work on the projective geometry of the cone. This was published in 1640 under the title *Essai pour les coniques* and includes what has since become known as Pascal's theorem. Pascal's other mathematical accomplishments include the original development of probability theory, worked out in correspondence with Fermat, and a method of infinitesimal analysis to which Leibniz gave credit for inspiring his own development of the calculus. Pascal's early scientific fame rests also on his work in physics, which includes a treatise on hydrostatics (*Traités de l'équilibre des liqueurs et de la pesanteur de la masse de l'air*) and his experiments with the barometer, which attempted to establish the possibility of a vacuum and the weight of air as the cause of the mercury's suspension.

Pascal's fame as a stylist rests primarily on his *Lettres provinciales* (1656–57), which were an anonymous contribution to a dispute between the Jansenists, headed by Arnauld, and the Jesuits. Jansenism was a Catholic religious movement that emphasized an Augustinian position on questions of grace and free will. Pascal, who was not himself a Jansenist, wrote a series of scathing satirical letters ridiculing both Jesuit casuistry and the persecution of the Jansenists for their purported adherence to five propositions in Jansen's *Augustinus*.

Pascal's philosophical contributions are found throughout his work, but primarily in his *Pensées* (1670), an intended apology for Christianity left incomplete and fragmentary at his death. The influence of the *Pensées* on religious thought and later existentialism has been profound because of their extraordinary insight, passion, and depth. At the time of Pascal's death some of the fragments were sewn together in clusters; many others were left unorganized, but recent scholarship has recovered much of the original plan of organization. The *Pensées* raise skeptical arguments that had become part of philosophical parlance since Montaigne. While these arguments were originally raised in order to deny the possibility of knowledge, Pascal, like Descartes in the *Meditations*, tries to utilize them toward a positive end. He argues that what skepticism shows us is not that knowledge is impossible, but that there is a certain paradox about human nature: we possess knowledge yet recognize that this knowledge cannot be rationally justified and that rational arguments can even be directed against it (fragments 109, 131, and 110). This peculiarity can be explained only through the Christian doctrine of the fall (e.g., fragment 117).

Pascal extends his skeptical considerations by undermining the possibility of demonstrative proof of God's existence. Such knowledge is impossible on philosophical grounds because such a proof could be successful only if an absurdity followed from denying God's existence, and nature furnishes us with no knowledge incompatible with unbelief (fragments 429 and 781). Furthermore, demonstrative proof of God's existence is incompatible with the epistemological claims of Christianity, which make God's personal agency essential to religious knowledge (fragments 460, 449). Pascal's use of skepticism and his refusal to admit proofs of God's existence have led some commentators, like Richard Popkin ("Fideism," 1967) and Terence Penelhum ("Skepticism and Fideism," 1983) to interpret Pascal as a fideist, i.e., one who denies that religious belief can be based on anything other than pragmatic reasons. But such an interpretation disregards Pascal's attempts to show that Christian belief is rational because of the explanatory power of its doctrines, particularly its doctrine of the fall (e.g., fragments 131, 137, 149, 431, 449, and 482). These purported demonstrations of the explanatory superiority of Christianity prepare the way for Pascal's famous "wager" (fragment 418).

The wager is among the fragments that Pascal had not classified at the time of his death, but textual evidence shows that it would have been included in Section 12, entitled "Commencement," after the demonstrations of the superior explanatory power of Christianity. The wager is a direct application of the principles developed in Pascal's earlier work on probability, where he discovered a calculus that could be used to determine the most rational action when faced with uncertainty about future events, or what is now known as decision theory. In this case the uncertainty is the truth of Christianity and its claims about afterlife; and the actions under consideration are whether to believe or not. The choice of the most rational action depends on what would now be called its "expected value." The expected value of an action is determined by (1) assigning a value, s, to each possible outcome of the action, (2) subtracting the cost of the action, c, from this value, and (3) multiplying the difference by the probability of the respective outcomes and adding these products together. Pascal invites the reader to consider Christian faith and unbelief as if they were acts of wagering on the truth of Christianity. If one believes, then there are two possible outcomes – either God exists or not. If God does exist, the stake to be gained is infinite life. If God does not exist, there are no winnings. Because the potential winnings are infinite, religious belief is more rational than unbelief because of its greater expected value.

The wager has been subjected to numerous criticisms. William James argued that it is indecisive, because it would apply with equal validity to any religion that offers a promise of infinite rewards (*The Will to Believe*, 1897). But this ignores Pascal's careful attempt to show that only Christianity has adequate explanatory power, so that the choice is intended to be between Christianity and unbelief. A stronger objection to the wager arises from contemporary work in decision theory that prohibits the introduction of infinite values because they have the counterintuitive result of making even the slightest risk irrational. But while these objections are valid, they do not refute Pascal's strategy in the *Pensées*, in which the proofs of Christianity's explanatory power and the wager have only the preliminary role of inducing the reader to seek the religious certainty that comes only from a saving religious experience which he calls "inspiration" (fragments 110, 381, 382, 588, 808).

See also DECISION THEORY, PHILOSOPHY OF RELIGION, PROBABILITY.   D.F.

Pascal's wager. See PASCAL.

passion. See EMOTION, HUME, PRACTICAL REASONING.

passions. See EMOTION.

passions, direct. See HUME.

passions, indirect. See HUME.

passive euthanasia. See EUTHANASIA.

passive power. See POWER.

paternalism, interference with the liberty or autonomy of another person, with justifications referring to the promotion of the person's good or the prevention of harm to the person. More precisely, P acts paternalistically toward Q if and only if (a) P acts with the intent of averting some harm or promoting some benefit for Q; (b) P acts contrary to (or is indifferent to) the current preferences, desires or values of Q; and (c) P's act is a limitation on Q's autonomy or liberty.

The presence of both autonomy and liberty in clause (c) is to allow for the fact that lying to someone is not clearly an interference with liberty. Notice that one can act paternalistically by telling people the truth (as when a doctor insists that a patient know the exact nature of her illness, contrary to her wishes). Note also that the definition does not settle any questions about the legitimacy or illegitimacy of paternalistic interventions.

Typical examples of paternalistic actions are (1) laws requiring motorcyclists to wear helmets; (2) court orders allowing physicians to transfuse Jehovah's Witnesses against their wishes; (3) deception of a patient by physicians to avoid upsetting the patient; (4) civil commitment of persons judged dangerous to themselves; and (5) laws forbidding swimming while lifeguards are not on duty.

Soft (weak) paternalism is the view that paternalism is justified only when a person is acting non-voluntarily *or* one needs time to determine whether the person is acting voluntarily or not. *Hard* (strong) paternalism is the view that paternalism is sometimes justified even when the person being interfered with is acting voluntarily.

The analysis of the term is relative to some set of problems. If one were interested in the organizational behavior of large corporations, one might adopt a different definition than if one were concerned with limits on the state's right to exercise coercion. The typical normative problems about paternalistic actions are whether, and to what extent, the welfare of individuals may outweigh the need to respect their desire to lead their own lives and make their own decisions (even when mistaken). J. S. Mill is the best example of a virtually absolute anti-paternalism, at least with respect to the right of the state to act paternalistically. He argued that unless we have reason to believe that a person is not acting voluntarily, as in the case of a man walking across a bridge that, unknown to him, is about to collapse, we ought to allow adults the freedom to act even if their acts are harmful to themselves.

See also FREE WILL PROBLEM; MILL, J. S.; POLITICAL PHILOSOPHY; POSITIVE AND NEGATIVE FREEDOM; RIGHTS.   G.D.

patriarchalism. See FILMER.

patristic authors, also called church fathers, a group of early Christian authors originally so named because they were considered the "fathers" (*patres*) of the orthodox Christian churches. The term is now used more broadly to designate the Christian writers, orthodox or heterodox, who were active in the first six centuries or so of the Christian era. The chronological division is quite flexible, and it is regularly moved several centuries later for particular purposes. Moreover, the study of these writers has traditionally been divided by languages, of which the principal ones are Greek, Latin, and Syriac. The often sharp divisions among patristic scholarships in the different languages are partly a reflection of the different histories of the regional churches, partly a reflection of the sociology of modern scholarship.

Greeks. The patristic period in Greek is usually taken as extending from the first writers after the New Testament to such figures as Maximus the Confessor (579/580–662) or John of Damascus (c.650–c.750). The period is traditionally divided around the Council of Nicea (325). Pre-Nicean Greek authors of importance to the history of philosophy include Irenaeus (130/140–after 198?), Clement of Alexandria (c.150–after 215), and Origen (c.180–c.254). Important Nicean and post-Nicean authors include Athanasius (c.295–373); the Cappadocians, i.e., Gregory of Nazianzus (c.330–90), Basil of Cesarea (c.330–79), and his brother, Gregory of Nyssa (335/340–c.394); and John Chrysostom (c.350–407).

Philosophical topics and practices are constantly engaged by these Greek authors. Justin Martyr (second century), e.g., describes his conversion to Christianity quite explicitly as a transit through lower forms of philosophy into the true philosophy. Clement of Alexandria, again, uses the philosophic genre of the protreptic and a host of ancient texts to persuade his pagan readers that they ought to come to Christianity as to the true wisdom. Origen devotes his *Against Celsus* to the detailed rebuttal of one pagan philosopher's attack on Christianity. More importantly, if more subtly, the major works of the Cappadocians appropriate and transform the teachings of any number of philosophic authors – Plato and the Neoplatonists in first place, but also Aristotle, the Stoics, and Galen.

Latins. The Latin churches came to count four post-Nicean authors as its chief teachers: Ambrose (337/339–97), Jerome (c.347–419), Augustine (354–430), and Gregory the Great (c.540–604). Other Latin authors of philosophical interest include Tertullian (fl. c.195–c.220), Lactantius (c.260–c.330), Marius Victorinus (280/285–before 386), and Hilary of Poitiers (fl. 356–64).

The Latin patristic period is typically counted from the second century to the fifth or sixth, i.e., roughly from Tertullian to Boethius. The Latin authors share with their Greek contemporaries a range of relations to the pagan philosophic schools, both as rival institutions and as sources of useful teaching. Tertullian's *Against the Nations* and *Apology,* for example, take up pagan accusations against Christianity and then counterattack a number of pagan beliefs, including philosophical ones. By contrast, the writings of Marius Victorinus, Ambrose, and Augustine enact transformations of philosophic teachings, especially from the Neoplatonists. Because philosophical erudition was generally not as great among the Latins as among the Greeks, they were both more eager to accept philosophical doctrines and freer in improvising variations on them.

See also AUGUSTINE, BOETHIUS, CLEMENT OF ALEXANDRIA, GREGORY OF NYSSA, TERTULLIAN.   M.D.J.

Paul of Venice (c.1368–1429), Italian philosopher and theologian. A Hermit of Saint Augustine (O.E.S.A.), he spent three years as a student in Oxford (1390–93) and taught at the University of Padua, where he became a doctor of arts and theology in 1408. He also held appointments at the universities of Parma, Siena, and Bologna. He was active in the administration of his order, holding various high offices. Paul of Venice wrote commentaries on several logical, ethical, and physical works of Aristotle, but his name is connected especially with an extremely popular textbook, *Logica parva* (over 150 manuscripts survive, and more than forty printed editions of it were made), and with a huge *Logica magna*. These Oxford-influenced works contributed to the favorable climate enjoyed by the English logic in northern Italian universities from the late fourteenth century through the fifteenth century.   I.Bo.

Peano, Giuseppe. See LOGICAL FORM, PEANO POSTULATES.

Peano postulates, also called Peano axioms, a list of assumptions from which the integers can be defined from some initial integer, equality, and successorship, and usually seen as defining progressions. The Peano postulates for arithmetic were produced by G. Peano in 1889. He took the set N of integers with a first term 1 and an equality relation between them, and assumed these nine axioms: 1 belongs to N; N has more than one member; equality is reflexive, symmetric, and associative, and closed over N; the successor of any integer in N also belongs to N, and is unique; and a principle of *mathematical induction* applying across the members of N, in that if 1 belongs to some subset M of N and so does the successor of any of its members, then in fact $M = N$. In some ways Peano's formulation was not clear. He had no explicit rules of inference, nor any guarantee of the legitimacy of inductive definitions (which Dedekind established shortly before him). Further, the four properties attached to equality were seen to belong to the underlying "logic" rather than to arithmetic itself; they are now detached.

It was realized (by Peano himself) that the postulates specified progressions rather than integers (e.g., 1, ½, ¼, ⅛, ... , would satisfy them, with suitable interpretations of the properties). But his work was significant in the axiomatization of arithmetic; still deeper foundations would lead with Russell and others to a major role for general set theory in the foundations of mathematics.

In addition, with O. Veblen, T. Skolem, and others, this insight led in the early twentieth century to "non-standard" models of the postulates being developed in set theory and mathematical analysis; one could go beyond the '. . .' in the sequence above and admit "further" objects, to produce valuable alternative models of the postulates. These procedures were of great significance also to model theory, in highlighting the property of the non-categoricity of an axiom system. A notable case was the "non-standard analysis" of A. Robinson, where infinitesimals were defined as arithmetical inverses of transfinite numbers without incurring the usual perils of rigor associated with them.

See also PHILOSOPHY OF MATHEMATICS.
                                                                I.G.-G.

Peirce, Charles S(anders) (1839–1914), American philosopher, scientist, and mathematician, the founder of the philosophical movement called pragmatism. Peirce was born in Cambridge, Massachusetts, the second son of Benjamin Peirce, who was professor of mathematics and astronomy at Harvard and one of America's leading mathematicians. Charles Peirce studied at Harvard University and in 1863 received a degree in chemistry. In 1861 he began work with the U.S. Coast and Geodetic Survey, and remained in this service for thirty years. Simultaneously with his professional career as a scientist, Peirce worked in logic and philosophy. He lectured on philosophy and logic at various universities and institutes, but was never able to obtain a permanent academic position as a teacher of philosophy. In 1887 he retired to Milford, Pennsylvania, and devoted the rest of his life to philosophical work. He earned a meager income from occasional lectures and by writing articles for periodicals and dictionaries. He spent his last years in extreme poverty and ill health.

Pragmatism. Peirce formulated the basic principles of pragmatism in two articles, "The Fixation of Belief" and "How to Make Our Ideas Clear" (1877–78). The title of the latter paper refers to Descartes's doctrine of *clear* and *distinct* ideas. According to Peirce, the criteria of clarity and distinctness must be supplemented by a third condition of meaningfulness, which states that the meaning of a proposition or an "intellectual conception" lies in its "practical consequences." In his paper "Pragmatism" (1905) he formulated the "Principle of Pragmatism" or the "Pragmatic Maxim" as follows:

In order to ascertain the meaning of an intellectual conception we should consider what practical consequences might conceivably result by necessity from the truth of that conception; and the sum of these consequences will constitute the entire meaning of the conception.

By "practical consequences" Peirce means conditional propositions of the form 'if p, then q', where the antecedent describes some action or experimental condition, and the consequent describes an observable phenomenon or a "sensible effect." According to the Pragmatic Maxim, the meaning of a proposition (or of an "intellectual conception") can be expressed as a conjunction of such "practical conditionals."

The Pragmatic Maxim might be criticized on the ground that many meaningful sentences (e.g., theoretical hypotheses) do not entail any "practical consequences" in themselves, but only in conjunction with other hypotheses. Peirce anticipated this objection by observing that "the maxim of pragmatism is that a conception can have no logical effect or import differing from that of a second conception except so far as, taken in connection with other conceptions and intentions, it might conceivably modify our practical conduct differently from that of the second conception" ("Pragmatism and Abduction," 1903).

Theory of inquiry and philosophy of science.
Peirce adopted Bain's definition of belief as "that which a man is prepared to act upon." Belief guides action, and as a content of belief a proposition can be regarded as a maxim of conduct. According to Peirce, belief is a satisfactory and desirable state, whereas the opposite of belief, the state of *doubt*, is an unsatisfactory state. The starting point of inquiry is usually some surprising phenomenon that is inconsistent with one's previously accepted beliefs, and that therefore creates a state of doubt. The purpose of inquiry is the replacement of this state by that of belief: "the sole aim of inquiry is the settlement of opinion." A successful inquiry leads to *stable* opinion, a state of belief that need not later be given up. Peirce regarded the ultimate stability of opinion as a *criterion* of truth and reality: "the real . . . is that which, sooner or later, information and reasoning would finally result in, and which is therefore independent of the vagaries of you and me." He accepted, however, an objectivist *conception* of truth and reality: the defining characteristic of reality is its independence of the opinions of individual persons.

In "The Fixation of Belief" Peirce argued that the scientific method, a method in which we let our beliefs be determined by external reality, "by something upon which our thinking has no effect," is the best way of settling opinion. Much of his philosophical work was devoted to the analysis of the various forms of inference and argument employed in science. He studied the concept of probability and probabilistic reasoning in science, criticized the subjectivist view of probability, and adopted an objectivist conception, according to which probability can be defined as a relative frequency in the long run.

Peirce distinguished between three main types of inference, which correspond to three stages of inquiry: (i) *abduction*, a tentative acceptance of an explanatory hypothesis which, if true, would make the phenomenon under investigation intelligible; (ii) *deduction*, the derivation of testable consequences from the explanatory hypothesis; and (iii) *induction*, the evaluation of the hypothesis in the light of these consequences. He called this method of inquiry the *inductive method;* in the contemporary philosophy of science it is usually called the *hypothetico-deductive method*. According to Peirce, the scientific method can be viewed as an application of the pragmatic maxim: the testable consequences derived from an explanatory hypothesis constitute its concrete "meaning" in the sense of the Pragmatic Maxim. Thus the Maxim determines the admissibility of a hypothesis as a possible (meaningful) explanation.

According to Peirce, inquiry is always dependent on beliefs that are not subject to doubt at the time of the inquiry, but such beliefs might be questioned on some other occasion. Our knowledge does not rest on indubitable "first premises," but all beliefs are dependent on other beliefs. According to Peirce's doctrine of *fallibilism*, the conclusions of science are always tentative. The rationality of the scientific method does not depend on the certainty of its conclusions, but on its *self-corrective* character: by continued application of the method science can detect and correct its own mistakes, and thus eventually lead to the discovery of truth.

Logic, the theory of signs, and the philosophy of language. In "The Logic of Relatives," published in 1883 in a collection of papers by himself and his students at the Johns Hopkins University (*Studies in Logic by Members of the Johns Hopkins University*), Peirce formalized relational statements by using subscript indices for individuals (individual variables), and construed the quantifiers 'some' and 'every' as variable binding operators; thus Peirce can be regarded (together with the German logician Frege) as one of the founders of quantification theory (predicate logic). In his paper "On the Algebra of Logic – A Contribution to the Philosophy of Notation" (1885) he interpreted propositional logic as a calculus of truth-values, and defined (logically) necessary truth (in propositional logic) as truth for all truth-value assignments to sentential letters. He studied the logic of modalities and in the 1890s he invented a system of *logical graphs* (called "existential graphs"), based on a diagrammatic representation of propositions, in which he anticipated some basic ideas of the possible worlds semantics of modal logic. Peirce's letters and notebooks contain significant logical and philosophical insights. For example, he examined three-valued truth tables ("Triadic Logic"), and discovered (in 1886) the possibility of representing the truth-functional connectives of propositional logic by electrical switching circuits.

Peirce regarded logic as a part of a more general area of inquiry, *the theory of signs*, which he also called *semeiotic* (nowadays usually spelled 'semiotic(s)'). According to Peirce, sign relations are triadic, involving the sign itself, its *object* (or what the sign stands for), and an *interpretant* which determines how the sign represents the object; the interpretant can be regarded as the *meaning* of the sign. The interpretant of a sign is another sign which in turn has its own interpretant (or interpretants); such a sequence of interpretants ends in an "ultimate logical interpretant," which is "a change of habit of conduct."

On the basis of the triadic character of the sign relation Peirce distinguished three divisions of signs. These divisions were based on (i) the character of the sign itself, (ii) the relation between the sign and its object, and (iii) the way in which the interpretant represents the object. These divisions reflect Peirce's system of three fundamental ontological categories, which he termed *Quality* or *Firstness*, *Relation* or *Secondness*, and *Representation* or *Thirdness*. Thus, according to the first division, a sign can be (a) a *qualisign*, a mere quality or appearance (a *First*); (b) a *sinsign* or *token*, an individual object, or event (a *Second*); or (c) a *legisign* or a general *type* (a *Third*). Secondly, signs can be divided into *icons, indices,* and *symbols* on the basis of their relations to their objects: an icon refers to an object on the basis of its similarity to the object (in some respect); an index stands in a dynamic or causal relation to its object; whereas a symbol functions as a sign of an object by virtue of a rule or habit of interpre-

tation. Peirce's third division divides signs into *rhemes* (predicative signs), *propositional signs* (propositions), and *arguments*. Some of the concepts and distinctions introduced by Peirce, e.g., the distinction between "types" and "tokens" and the division of signs into "icons," "indices," and "symbols," have become part of the standard conceptual repertoire of philosophy and semiotics. In his philosophy of language Peirce made a distinction between a proposition and an assertion, and studied the logical character of assertive speech acts.

Metaphysics. In spite of his critical attitude toward traditional metaphysics, Peirce believed that metaphysical questions can be discussed in a meaningful way. According to Peirce, metaphysics studies the most general traits of reality, and "kinds of phenomena with which every man's experience is so saturated that he usually pays no particular attention to them." The basic categories of *Firstness, Secondness,* and *Thirdness* mentioned above occupy a central position in Peirce's metaphysics. Especially in his later writings he emphasized the reality and metaphysical irreducibility of *Thirdness*, and defended the view that general phenomena (for example, general laws) cannot be regarded as mere conjunctions of their actual individual instances. This view was associated with Peirce's *synechism*, the doctrine that the world contains genuinely continuous phenomena. He regarded synechism as a new form of Scholastic realism. In the area of modalities Peirce's basic categories appear as *possibility, actuality,* and *necessity*. Here he argued that reality cannot be identified with existence (or actuality), but comprises real (objective) possibilities. This view was partly based on his realization that many conditional statements, for instance the "practical" conditionals expressing the empirical import of a proposition (in the sense of the Pragmatic Maxim), cannot be construed as material or truth-functional conditionals, but must be regarded as modal (subjunctive) conditionals. In his cosmology Peirce propounded the doctrine of tychism, according to which there is absolute chance in the universe, and the basic laws of nature are probabilistic and inexact.

Peirce's position in contemporary philosophy. Peirce had few disciples, but some of his students and colleagues became influential figures in American philosophy and science, e.g., the philosophers James, Royce, and Dewey and the economist Thorstein Veblen. Peirce's pragmatism became widely known through James's lectures and writings, but Peirce was dissatisfied with James's version of pragmatism, and renamed his own form of it 'pragmaticism', which term he considered to be "ugly enough to keep it safe from kidnappers." Pragmatism became an influential philosophical movement during the twentieth century through Dewey (philosophy of science and philosophy of education), C. I. Lewis (theory of knowledge), Ramsey, Ernest Nagel, and Quine (philosophy of science). Peirce's work in logic influenced, mainly through his contacts with the German logician Ernst Schröder, the model-theoretic tradition in twentieth-century logic.

There are three comprehensive collections of Peirce's papers: *Collected Papers of Charles Sanders Peirce* (1931–58), vols. 1–6 edited by Charles Hartshorne and Paul Weiss, vols. 7–8 edited by Arthur Burks; *The New Elements of Mathematics by Charles S. Peirce* (1976), edited by Carolyn Eisele; and *Writings of Charles S. Peirce: A Chronological Edition* (1982–).

See also DEWEY, JAMES, PHILOSOPHY OF SCIENCE, PRAGMATISM, TRUTH, TYCHISM.

R.Hi.

Peirce's law, the principle '$((A \rightarrow B) \rightarrow A) \rightarrow A$', which holds in classical logic but fails in the eyes of relevance logicians when ' $\rightarrow$' is read as 'entails'. **See also IMPLICATION, RELEVANCE LOGIC.**

G.F.S.

Pelagianism, the doctrine in Christian theology that, through the exercise of free will, human beings can attain moral perfection. A broad movement devoted to this proposition was only loosely associated with its eponymous leader. Pelagius (c.354–c.425), a lay theologian from Britain or Ireland, taught in Rome prior to its sacking in 410. He and his disciple Celestius found a forceful adversary in Augustine, whom they provoked to stiffen his stance on original sin, the bondage of the will, and humanity's total reliance upon God's grace and predestination for salvation. To Pelagius, this constituted fatalism and encouraged moral apathy. God would not demand perfection, as the Bible sometimes suggested, were that impossible to attain. Rather grace made the struggle easier for a sanctity that would not be unreachable even in its absence. Though in the habit of sinning, in consequence of the fall, we have not forfeited the capacity to overcome that habit nor been released from the imperative to do so. For all its moral earnestness this teaching seems to be in conflict with much

of the New Testament, especially as interpreted by Augustine, and it was condemned as heresy in 418. The bondage of the will has often been reaffirmed, perhaps most notably by Luther in dispute with Erasmus. Yet Christian theology and practice have always had their sympathizers with Pelagianism and with its reluctance to attest the loss of free will, the inevitability of sin, and the utter necessity of God's grace.

A.E.L.

Pelagius. See PELAGIANISM.

per accidens (Latin, 'by accident'), by, as, or being an accident or non-essential feature. A *per accidens predication* is one in which an accident is predicated of a substance. (The terminology is medieval. Note that the accident and substance themselves, not words standing for them, are the terms of the predication relation.) An *ens* (entity) *per accidens* is either an accident or the "accidental unity" of a substance and an accident (Descartes, e.g., insists that a person is *not* a *per accidens* union of body and mind.) **See also ACCIDENT, ESSENTIALISM, PROPERTY.** S.J.W.

percept. See PERCEPTION.

perception, the extraction and use of information about one's environment (exteroception) and one's own body (interoception). The various external senses – sight, hearing, touch, smell, and taste – though they overlap to some extent, are distinguished by the kind of information (e.g., about light, sound, temperature, pressure) they deliver. Proprioception, perception of the self, concerns stimuli arising within, and carrying information about, one's own body – e.g., acceleration, position, and orientation of the limbs.

There are distinguishable stages in the extraction and use of sensory information, one (an earlier stage) corresponding to our perception of objects (and events), the other, a later stage, to the perception of facts about these objects. We see, e.g., both the cat on the sofa (an object) and *that* the cat is on the sofa (a fact). Seeing an object (or event) – a cat on the sofa, a person on the street, or a vehicle's movement – does not require that the object (event) be identified or recognized in any particular way (perhaps, though this is controversial, in any way whatsoever). One can, e.g., see a cat on the sofa and mistake it for a rumpled sweater. Airplane lights are often misidentified as stars, and one can see the movement of an object either as the movement of oneself or (under some viewing conditions) as expansion (or contraction). Seeing objects and events is, in this sense, *non-epistemic:* one can see *O* without knowing (or believing) that it is *O* that one is seeing. Seeing facts, on the other hand, is *epistemic;* one cannot see *that* there is a cat on the sofa without, thereby, coming to know that there is a cat on the sofa. Seeing a fact is coming to know the fact in some visual way. One can see *objects* – the fly in one's soup, e.g., – without realizing that there is a fly in one's soup (thinking, perhaps, it is a bean or a crouton); but to see a fact, the fact *that* there is a fly in one's soup is, necessarily, to know it is a fly. This distinction applies to the other sense modalities as well. One can hear the telephone ringing without realizing that it is the telephone (perhaps it's the TV or the doorbell), but to hear a fact, *that* it is the telephone (that is ringing), is, of necessity, to know that it is the telephone that is ringing.

The other ways we have of describing what we perceive are primarily variations on these two fundamental themes. In seeing *where* (he went), *when* (he left), *who* (went with him), and *how* he was dressed, e.g., we are describing the perception of *some* fact of a certain sort without revealing exactly which fact it is. If Martha saw where he went, then Martha saw (hence, came to know) some fact having to do with where he went, some fact of the form 'he went *there*'. In speaking of states and conditions (the condition of his room, her injury), and properties (the color of his tie, the height of the building), we sometimes, as in the case of objects, mean to be describing a non-epistemic perceptual act, one that carries no implications for what (if anything) is known. In other cases, as with facts, we mean to be describing the acquisition of some piece of knowledge. One can see or hear a word without recognizing it as a word (it might be in a foreign language), but can one see a misprint and *not* know it is a misprint? It obviously depends on what one uses 'misprint' to refer to: an object (a word that is misprinted) or a fact (the fact that it is misprinted).

In examining and evaluating theories (whether philosophical or psychological) of perception it is essential to distinguish *fact perception* from *object perception.* For a theory might be a plausible theory about the perception of objects (e.g., psychological theories of "early vision") but not at all plausible about our perception of facts. Fact perception, involving, as it does, knowledge (and, hence, belief) brings into play the entire cognitive system (memory, concepts, etc.) in a way the former does not. Perceptual relativity – e.g., the idea that what we perceive is relative to

our language, our conceptual scheme, or the scientific theories we have available to "interpret" phenomena – is quite implausible as a theory about our perception of objects. A person lacking a word for, say, kumquats, lacking this concept, lacking a scientific way of classifying these objects (are they a fruit? a vegetable? an animal?), can still see, touch, smell, and taste kumquats. Perception of *objects* does not depend on, and is therefore not relative to, the observer's linguistic, conceptual, cognitive, and scientific assets or shortcomings. Fact perception, however, is another matter. Clearly one cannot see that there are kumquats in the basket (as opposed to seeing the objects, the kumquats, in the basket) if one has no idea of, no concept of, what a kumquat is. Seeing facts is much more sensitive (and, hence, relative) to the conceptual resources, the background knowledge and scientific theories, of the observer, and this difference must be kept in mind in evaluating claims about perceptual relativity. Though it does not make *objects* invisible, ignorance does tend to make facts perceptually inaccessible.

There are characteristic experiences associated with the different senses. Tasting a kumquat is not at all like seeing a kumquat although the same object is perceived (indeed, the same fact – that it is a kumquat – may be perceived). The difference, of course, is in the subjective experience one has in perceiving the kumquat. A *causal theory of perception* (of objects) holds that the perceptual object, what it is we see, taste, smell, or whatever, is that object that causes us to have this subjective experience. Perceiving an object is that object's causing (in the right way) one to have an experience of the appropriate sort. I see a bean in my soup if it is, in fact (whether I *know* it or not is irrelevant), a bean in my soup that is causing me to have this visual experience. I taste a bean if, in point of fact, it is a bean that is causing me to have the kind of taste experience I am now having. If it is (unknown to me) a bug, not a bean, that is causing these experiences, then I am (unwittingly) seeing and tasting a bug – perhaps a bug that looks and tastes like a bean. What *object* we see (taste, smell, etc.) is determined by the causal facts in question. What we know and believe, how we interpret the experience, is irrelevant, although it will, of course, determine what we *say* we see and taste. The same is to be said, with appropriate changes, for our perception of facts (the most significant change being the replacement of belief for experience). I see *that* there is a bug in my soup if the fact that there is a bug in my soup causes me to believe that there is a bug in my soup. I can *taste* that there is a bug in my soup when this fact causes me to have this belief via some taste sensation.

A causal theory of perception is more than the claim that the physical objects we perceive cause us to have experiences and beliefs. This much is fairly obvious. It is the claim that this causal relation is *constitutive* of perception, that *necessarily*, if S sees *O*, then *O* causes a certain sort of experience in S. It is, according to this theory, impossible, on conceptual grounds, to perceive something with which one has no causal contact. If, e.g., future events do not cause present events, if there is no backward causation, then we cannot perceive future events and objects. Whether or not future *facts* can be perceived (or known) depends on how liberally the causal condition on knowledge is interpreted.

Though conceding that there *is* a world of mind-independent objects (trees, stars, people) that cause us to have experiences, some philosophers – traditionally called *representative realists* – argue that we nonetheless do not directly perceive these external objects. What we directly perceive are the effects these objects have on us – an internal image, idea, or impression, a more or less (depending on conditions of observation) accurate representation of the external reality that helps produce it. This subjective, directly apprehended object has been called by various names: a sensation, percept, sense-datum, sensum, and sometimes, to emphasize its representational aspect, *Vorstellung* (German, 'representation'). Just as the images appearing on a television screen represent their remote causes (the events occurring at some distant concert hall or playing field), the images (visual, auditory, etc.) that occur in the mind, the sense-data of which we are directly aware in normal perception, represent (or sometimes, when things are not working right, *mis*represent) their external physical causes.

The representative realist typically invokes arguments from illusion, facts about hallucination, and temporal considerations to support his view. Hallucinations are supposed to illustrate the way we can have the same *kind* of experience we have when (as we commonly say) we see a real bug without there being a real bug (in our soup or anywhere else) causing us to have the experience. When we hallucinate, the bug we "see" is, in fact, a figment of our own imagination, an image (i.e., sense-datum) in the mind that, because it shares *some* of the properties of a real bug (shape, color, etc.), we might mistake for

a real bug. Since the subjective experiences can be indistinguishable from that which we have when (as we commonly say) we really see a bug, it is reasonable to infer (the representative realist argues) that in normal perception, when we take ourselves to be seeing a real bug, we are also directly aware of a buglike image in the mind. A hallucination differs from a normal perception, not in *what* we are aware of (in both cases it is a sense-datum) but in the cause of these experiences. In normal perception it is an actual bug; in hallucination it is, say, drugs in the bloodstream. In both cases, though, we are caused to have the same thing: an awareness of a buglike sense-datum, an object that, in normal perception, we naively take to be a real bug (thus saying, and encouraging our children to say, that we see a bug).

The argument from illusion points to the fact that our experience of an object changes even when the object that we perceive (or *say* we perceive) remains unchanged. Though the physical object (the bug or whatever) remains the same color, size, and shape, what we experience (according to this argument) changes color, shape, and size as we change the lighting, our viewing angle, and distance. Hence, it is concluded, what we experience cannot really be the physical object itself. Since it varies with changes in *both* object and viewing conditions, what we experience must be a causal result, an effect, of *both* the object we commonly say we see (the bug) *and* the conditions in which we view it. This internal effect, it is concluded, is a sense-datum.

Representative realists have also appealed to the fact that perceiving a physical object is a causal process that takes time. This temporal lag is most dramatic in the case of distant objects (e.g., stars), but it exists for every physical object (it takes time for a neural signal to be transmitted from receptor surfaces to the brain). Consequently, at the moment (a short time *after* light leaves the object's surface) we see a physical object, the object *could* no longer exist. It could have ceased to exist during the time light was being transmitted to the eye or during the time it takes the eye to communicate with the brain. Yet, even if the object ceases to exist before we become aware of anything (before a visual experience occurs), we are, or so it seems, aware of *something* when the causal process reaches its climax in the brain. This something of which we are aware, since it cannot be the physical object (*it* no longer exists), must be a sense-datum. The representationalist concludes in this "time-lag argument," therefore, that even when the physical object does not cease to exist (this, of course, is the normal situation), we are directly aware, not of it, but of its (slightly later-occurring) representation.

Representative realists differ among themselves about the question of how much (if at all) the sense-data of which we are aware resemble the external objects (of which we are not aware). Some take the external cause to have some of the properties (the so-called primary properties) of the datum (e.g., extension) and not others (the so-called secondary properties – e.g., color).

Direct (or *naive*) *realism* shares with representative realism a commitment to a world of independently existing objects. Both theories are forms of perceptual realism. It differs, however, in its view of how we are related to these objects in ordinary perception. Direct realists deny that we are aware of mental intermediaries (sense-data) when, as we ordinarily say, we see a tree or hear the telephone ring. Though direct realists differ in their degree of naïveté about how (and in what respect) perception is supposed to be direct, they need not be so naive (as sometimes depicted) as to deny the scientific facts about the causal processes underlying perception. Direct realists can easily admit, e.g., that physical objects cause us to have experiences of a particular kind, and that these experiences are private, subjective, or mental. They can even admit that it is this causal relationship (between object and experience) that constitutes our seeing and hearing physical objects. They need not, in other words, deny a causal theory of perception. What they must deny, if they are to remain *direct* realists, however, is an analysis of the subjective experience (that objects cause us to have) into an awareness *of* some object. For to understand this experience as an awareness of some object is, given the wholly subjective (mental) character of the experience itself, to interpose a mental entity (what the experience is an awareness of) between the perceiver and the physical object that causes him to have this experience, the physical object that is supposed to be *directly* perceived.

Direct realists, therefore, avoid analyzing a perceptual experience into an act (sensing, being aware of, being acquainted with) and an object (the sensum, sense-datum, sensation, mental representation). The experience we are caused to have when we perceive a physical object or event is, instead, to be understood in some other way. The *adverbial theory* is one such possibility. As the name suggests, this theory takes its cue from the way nouns and adjectives can some-

times be converted into adverbs without loss of descriptive content. So, for instance, it comes to pretty much the same thing whether we describe a conversation as animated (adjective) or say that we conversed animatedly (an adverb). So, also, according to an adverbialist, when, as we commonly say, we see a red ball, the red ball causes in us (a moment later) an experience, yes, but not (as the representative realist says) an awareness (mental act) of a sense-datum (mental object) that is red and circular (adjectives). The experience is better understood as one in which there is no object at all, as sensing redly and circularly (adverbs). The adverbial theorist insists that one can experience circularly and redly without there being, in the mind or anywhere else, red circles (this, in fact, is what the adverbialist thinks occurs in dreams and hallucinations of red circles). To experience redly is *not* to have a red experience; nor is it to experience redness (in the mind). It is, says the adverbialist, a *way* or a *manner* of perceiving ordinary objects (especially red ones seen in normal light). Just as dancing gracefully is not a thing we dance, so perceiving redly is not a thing – and certainly not a red thing in the mind – that we experience.

The adverbial theory is only one option the direct realist has of acknowledging the causal basis of perception while, at the same time, maintaining the directness of our perceptual relation with independently existing objects. What is important is not that the experience be construed adverbially, but that it *not* be interpreted, as representative realists interpret it, as awareness of some internal object. For a direct realist, the appearances, though they are subjective (mind-dependent) are *not* objects that interpose themselves between the conscious mind and the external world.

As classically understood, both naive and representative realism are theories about *object* perception. They differ about whether it is the external object or an internal object (an idea in the mind) that we (most directly) apprehend in ordinary sense perception. But they need not (although they usually do) differ in their analysis of our knowledge of the world around us, in their account of fact perception. A direct realist about object perception may, e.g., be an indirect realist about the facts that we know about these objects. To see, not only a red ball in front of one, but *that* there is a red ball in front of one, it may be necessary, even on a direct theory of (object) perception, to infer (or in some way derive) this fact from facts that are known more directly about one's experiences of the ball. Since, e.g., a direct theorist may be a causal theorist, may think that seeing a red ball is (in part) constituted by the having of certain sorts of experience, she may insist that knowledge of the cause of these experiences must be derived from knowledge of the experience itself. If one is an adverbialist, e.g., one might insist that knowledge of physical objects is derived from knowledge of how (redly? bluely? circularly? squarely?) one experiences these objects.

By the same token, a representative realist could adopt a direct theory of fact perception. Though the *objects* we directly see are mental, the facts we come to know *by* experiencing these subjective entities are facts about ordinary physical objects. We do not infer (at least at no conscious level) that there is a bug in our soup from facts (known more directly) about our own conscious experiences (from facts about the sensations the bug causes in us). Rather, our sensations cause us, directly, to have beliefs about our soup. There is no intermediate belief; hence, there is no intermediate knowledge; hence, no intermediate fact perception. Fact perception is, in this sense, direct. Or so a representative realist can maintain even though committed to the indirect perception of the objects (bug and soup) involved in this fact. This merely illustrates, once again, the necessity of distinguishing object perception from fact perception.

See also DIRECT REALISM, EPISTEMOLOGY, METAPHYSICAL REALISM, PHILOSOPHY OF MIND, SKEPTICISM, THEORY OF APPEARING.

F.D.

perceptual realism. See PERCEPTION.

perceptual relativity. See PERCEPTION.

Percival, Thomas (1740–1804), English physician and author of *Medical Ethics* (1803). He was central in bringing the Western traditions of medical ethics from prayers and oaths (e.g., the Hippocratic oath) toward more detailed, modern codes of proper professional conduct. His writing on the normative aspects of medical practice was part ethics, part prudential advice, part professional etiquette, and part jurisprudence. *Medical Ethics* treated standards for the professional conduct of physicians relative to surgeons and apothecaries (pharmacists and general practitioners), as well as hospitals, private practice, and the law. The issues Percival addressed include privacy, truth telling, rules for professional con-

sultation, human experimentation, public and private trust, compassion, sanity, suicide, abortion, capital punishment, and environmental nuisances. Percival had his greatest influence in England and America. At its founding in 1847, the American Medical Association used *Medical Ethics* to guide its own first code of medical ethics.

M.J.M.

perdurance, in one common philosophical use, the property of being temporally continuous and having temporal parts. There are at least two conflicting theories about temporally continuous substances. According to the first, temporally continuous substances have temporal parts (they *perdure*), while according to the second, they do not. In one ordinary philosophical use, *endurance* is the property of being temporally continuous and *not* having temporal parts. There are modal versions of the aforementioned two theories: for example, one version of the first theory is that *necessarily,* temporally continuous substances have temporal parts, while another version implies that *possibly,* they do not. Some versions of the first theory hold that a temporally continuous substance is composed of instantaneous temporal parts or "object-stages," while on other versions these object-stages are not *parts* but *boundaries.* **See also** IDENTITY, METAPHYSICS, PERSONAL IDENTITY. J.Ho. & G.Ro.

perfect competition, the state of an ideal market under the following conditions: (a) every consumer in the market is a perfectly rational maximizer of utility; (b) every producer is a perfect maximizer of profit; (c) there is a very large (ideally infinite) number of producers of the good in question, which ensures that no producer can set the price for its output (otherwise, an imperfect competitive state of oligopoly or monopoly obtains); and (d) every producer provides a product perfectly indistinguishable from that of other producers (if consumers could distinguish products to the point that there was no longer a very large number of producers for each distinguishable good, competition would again be imperfect).

Under these conditions, the market price is equal to the marginal cost of producing the last unit. This in turn determines the market supply of the good, since each producer will gain by increasing production when price exceeds marginal cost and will generally cut losses by decreasing production when marginal cost exceeds price. Perfect competition is sometimes thought to have normative implications for political philosophy, since it results in Pareto optimality.

The concept of perfect competition becomes extremely complicated when a market's evolution is considered. Producers who cannot equate marginal cost with the market price will have negative profit and must drop out of the market. If this happens very often, then the number of producers will no longer be large enough to sustain perfect competition, so new producers will need to enter the market.

See also PHILOSOPHY OF ECONOMICS, PRODUCTION THEORY.   A.N.

perfect duty. See DUTY, KANT.

perfectionism, an ethical view according to which individuals and their actions are judged by a maximal standard of achievement – specifically, the degree to which they approach ideals of aesthetic, intellectual, emotional, or physical "perfection." Perfectionism, then, may depart from, or even dispense with, standards of conventional morality in favor of standards based on what appear to be non-moral values. These standards reflect an admiration for certain very rare levels of human achievement. Perhaps the most characteristic of these standards are artistic and other forms of creativity; but they prominently include a variety of other activities and emotional states deemed "noble" – e.g., heroic endurance in the face of great suffering. The perfectionist, then, would also tend toward a rather non-egalitarian – even aristocratic – view of humankind. The rare genius, the inspired few, the suffering but courageous artist – these examples of human perfection are genuinely worthy of our estimation, according to this view.

Although no fully worked-out system of "perfectionist philosophy" has been attempted, aspects of all of these doctrines may be found in such philosophers as Nietzsche. Aristotle, as well, appears to endorse a perfectionist idea in his characterization of the human good. Just as the good lyre player not only exhibits the characteristic activities of this profession but achieves standards of excellence with respect to these, the good human being, for Aristotle, must achieve standards of excellence with respect to the virtue or virtues distinctive of human life in general.

See also ARISTOTLE, NIETZSCHE, VIRTUE ETHICS.   J.A.M.

perfectionism, Emersonian. See CAVELL.

perfect right. See GROTIUS, RIGHTS.

performance, linguistic. See PHILOSOPHY OF LANGUAGE.

performative. See SPEECH ACT THEORY.

performative fallacy. See INFORMAL FALLACY.

per genus et differentiam. See DEFINITION.

Peripatetic School, also called Peripatos, the philosophical community founded by Aristotle at a public gymnasium (the Lyceum) after his return to Athens in c.335 B.C. The derivation of 'Peripatetic' from the alleged Aristotelian custom of "walking about" (*peripatein*) is probably wrong. The name should be explained by reference to a "covered walking hall" (*peripatos*) among the school facilities. A scholarch or headmaster presided over roughly two classes of members: the *presbyteroi* or seniors, who probably had some teaching duties, and the *neaniskoi* or juniors. No evidence of female philosophers in the Lyceum has survived.

During Aristotle's lifetime his own lectures, whether for the inner circle of the school or for the city at large, were probably the key attraction and core activity; but given Aristotle's knack for organizing group research projects, we may assume that young and old Peripatetics spent much of their time working on their own specific assignments either at the library, where they could consult works of earlier writers, or at some kind of repository for specimens used in zoological and botanical investigations. As a resident alien, Aristotle could not own property in Athens and hence was not the legal owner of the school. Upon his final departure from Athens in 322, his longtime collaborator Theophrastus of Eresus in Lesbos (c.370–287) succeeded him as scholarch.

Theophrastus was an able Aristotelian who wrote extensively on metaphysics, psychology, physiology, botany, ethics, politics, and the history of philosophy. With the help of the Peripatetic dictator Demetrius of Phaleron, he was able to secure property rights over the physical facilities of the school. Under Theophrastus, the Peripatos continued to flourish and is said to have had 2,000 students, surely not all at the same time. His successor, Strato of Lampsakos (c.335–269), had narrower interests and abandoned key Aristotelian tenets. With him a progressive decline set in, to which the early loss of Aristotle's personal library, taken to Asia Minor by Neleus of Skepsis, certainly contributed. By the first century B.C. the Peripatos had ceased to exist. Philosophers of later periods sympathetic to Aristotle's views have also been called Peripatetics.

See also ARISTOTLE, LYCEUM.   A.G.-L.

Peripatos. See HELLENISTIC PHILOSOPHY, PERIPATETIC SCHOOL.

perlocutionary act. See SPEECH ACT THEORY.

permissibility. See DEONTIC LOGIC, EPISTEMOLOGY.

Perry, Ralph Barton (1876–1957), American philosopher who taught at Harvard University and wrote extensively in ethics, social philosophy, and the theory of knowledge. He received a Pulitzer Prize in 1936 for *The Thought and Character of William James,* a biography of his teacher and colleague. Perry's other major works include: *The Moral Economy* (1909), *General Theory of Value* (1926), *Puritanism and Democracy* (1944), and *Realms of Value* (1954). He is perhaps best known for his views on value. He writes in *General Theory of Value,* "Any object, whatever it be, acquires value when any interest, whatever it be, is taken in it; just as anything whatsoever becomes a target when anyone whosoever aims at it." Something's having value is nothing but its being the object of some interest, and to know whether it has value one need only know whether it is the object of someone's interest. Morality aims at the promotion of the moral good, which he defines as "harmonious happiness." This consists in the reconciliation, harmonizing, and fulfillment of all interests.

Perry's epistemological and metaphysical views were part of a revolt against idealism and dualism. Along with five other philosophers, he wrote *The New Realism* (1912). The "New Realists" held that the objects of perception and memory are directly presented to consciousness and are just what they appear to be; nothing intervenes between the knower and the external world. The view that the objects of perception and memory are presented by means of ideas leads, they argued, to idealism, skepticism, and absurdity. Perry is also known for having developed, along with E. B. Holt, the "specific response" theory, which is an attempt to construe belief and perception in terms of bodily adjustment and behavior.

See also NEW REALISM, VALUE.   N.M.L.

per se. See ESSENTIALISM, PER ACCIDENS.

perseity. See DIVINE ATTRIBUTES.

personal identity, the (numerical) identity over time of persons. The question of what personal identity consists in is the question of what it is (what the necessary and sufficient conditions are) for a person existing at one time and a person existing at another time to be one and the same person. Here there is no question of there being any entity that is the "identity" of a person; to say that a person's identity consists in such and such is just shorthand for saying that facts about personal identity, i.e., facts to the effect that someone existing at one time is the same as someone existing at another time, consist in such and such. (This should not be confused with the usage, common in ordinary speech and in psychology, in which persons are said to have identities, and, sometimes, to seek, lose, or regain their identities, where one's "identity" intimately involves a set of values and goals that structure one's life.)

The words 'identical' and 'same' mean nothing different in judgments about persons than in judgments about other things. The problem of personal identity is therefore not one of defining a special *sense* of 'identical,' and it is at least misleading to characterize it as defining a particular *kind* of identity. Applying Quine's slogan "no entity without identity," one might say that characterizing any sort of entity involves indicating what the identity conditions for entities of that sort are (so, e.g., part of the explanation of the concept of a set is that sets having the same members are identical), and that asking what the identity of persons consists in is just a way of asking what sorts of things persons are. But the main focus in traditional discussions of the topic has been on one kind of identity judgment about persons, namely those asserting "identity over time"; the question has been about what the persistence of persons over time consists in.

What has made the identity (persistence) of persons of special philosophical interest is partly its epistemology and partly its connections with moral and evaluative matters. The crucial epistemological fact is that persons have, in memory, an access to their own past histories that is unlike the access they have to the histories of other things (including other persons); when one remembers doing or experiencing something, one normally has no need to employ any criterion of identity in order to know that the subject of the remembered action or experience is (i.e., is identical with) oneself. The moral and evaluative matters include moral responsibility (someone can be held responsible for a past action only if he or she is identical to the person who did it) and our concern for our own survival and future well-being (since it seems, although this has been questioned, that what one wants in wanting to survive is that there should exist in the future someone who is identical to oneself).

The modern history of the topic of personal identity begins with Locke, who held that the identity of a person consists neither in the identity of an immaterial substance (as dualists might be expected to hold) nor in the identity of a material substance or "animal body" (as materialists might be expected to hold), and that it consists instead in "same consciousness." His view appears to have been that the persistence of a person through time consists in the fact that certain actions, thoughts, experiences, etc., occurring at different times, are somehow united in memory. Modern theories descended from Locke's take memory continuity to be a special case of something more general, psychological continuity, and hold that personal identity consists in this. This is sometimes put in terms of the notion of a "person-stage," i.e., a momentary "time slice" of the history of a person. A series of person-stages will be psychologically continuous if the psychological states (including memories) occurring in later members of the series grow out of, in certain characteristic ways, those occurring in earlier members of it; and according to the psychological continuity view of personal identity, person-stages occurring at different times are stages of the same person provided they belong to a single, non-branching, psychologically continuous series of person-stages.

Opponents of the Lockean and neo-Lockean (psychological continuity) view tend to fall into two camps. Some, following Butler and Reid, hold that personal identity is indefinable, and that nothing informative can be said about what it consists in. Others hold that the identity of a person consists in some sort of physical continuity – perhaps the identity of a living human organism, or the identity of a human brain.

In the actual cases we know about (putting aside issues about non-bodily survival of death), psychological continuity and physical continuity go together. Much of the debate between psychological continuity theories and physical continuity theories has centered on the interpretation of thought experiments involving brain transplants, brain-state transfers, etc., in which these come apart. Such examples make vivid the question of whether our fundamental criteria of personal identity are psychological, physical, or both.

Recently philosophical attention has shifted somewhat from the question of what personal identity consists in to questions about its importance. The consideration of hypothetical cases of "fission" (in which two persons at a later time are psychologically continuous with one person at an earlier time) has suggested to some that we can have survival – or at any rate what matters in survival – without personal identity, and that our self-interested concern for the future is really a concern for whatever future persons are psychologically continuous with us.

See also PHILOSOPHY OF MIND.   S.Sho.

personalism, a version of personal idealism that flourished in the United States (principally at Boston University) from the late nineteenth century to the mid-twentieth century. Its principal proponents were Borden Parker Bowne (1847–1910) and three of his students: Albert Knudson (1873–1953); Ralph Flewelling (1871–1960), who founded *The Personalist*; and, most importantly, Edgar Sheffield Brightman (1884–1953). Their personalism was both idealistic and theistic and was influential in philosophy and in theology. Personalism traced its philosophical lineage to Berkeley and Leibniz, and had as its foundational insight the view that all reality is ultimately personal. God is the transcendent person and the ground or creator of all other persons; nature is a system of objects either for or in the minds of persons.

Both Bowne and Brightman considered themselves empiricists in the tradition of Berkeley. Immediate experience is the starting point, but this experience involves a fundamental knowledge of the self as a personal being with changing states. Given this pluralism, the coherence, order, and intelligibility of the universe are seen to derive from God, the uncreated person. Bowne's God is the eternal and omnipotent being of classical theism, but Brightman argued that if God is a real person he must be construed as both temporal and finite. Given the fact of evil, God is seen as gradually gaining control over his created world, with regard to which his will is intrinsically limited.

Another version of personalism developed in France out of the neo-Scholastic tradition. E. Mounier (1905–50), Maritain, and Gilson identified themselves as personalists, inasmuch as they viewed the infinite person (God) and finite persons as the source and locus of intrinsic value. They did not, however, view the natural order as intrinsically personal.

See also IDEALISM, NEO-THOMISM.   C.F.D.

personality. See CHARACTER.

personal supposition. See SUPPOSITIO.

personhood, the condition or property of being a person, especially when this is considered to entail moral and/or metaphysical importance. Personhood has been thought to involve various traits, including (moral) *agency*; *reason* or rationality; *language*, or the cognitive skills language may support (such as *intentionality* and *self-consciousness*); and ability to enter into suitable *relations* with other persons (viewed as members of a self-defining group). Buber emphasized the difference between the I-It relationship holding between oneself and an *object*, and the I-Thou relationship, which holds between oneself and another *person* (who can be addressed). Dennett has construed persons in terms of the "intentional stance," which involves explaining another's behavior in terms of beliefs, desires, intentions, etc.

Questions about when personhood begins and when it ends have been central to debates about abortion, infanticide, and euthanasia, since personhood has often been viewed as the mark, if not the basis, of a being's possession of special moral status.

See also ETHICS, MORAL STATUS, PERSONAL IDENTITY, PHILOSOPHY OF MIND.   E.J.

person stage. See PERSONAL IDENTITY.

perspectivism. See NIETZSCHE, ORTEGA Y GASSET, TEICHMÜLLER.

persuasive definition. See DEFINITION.

Peter Abelard. See ABELARD.

Peter Lombard (c.1095–1160), Italian theologian and author of the *Book of Sentences* (*Liber sententiarum*), a renowned theological sourcebook in the later Middle Ages. Peter was educated at Bologna, Reims, and Paris before teaching in the school of Notre Dame in Paris. He became a canon at Notre Dame in 1144–45 and was elected bishop of Paris in 1159. His extant works include commentaries on the Psalms (written in the mid-1130s) and on the epistles of Paul (c.1139–41); a collection of sermons; and his one-volume summary of Christian doctrine, the *Sentences* (completed by 1158).

The *Sentences* consists of four books: Book I, *On the Trinity*; Book II, *On the Creation of Things*; Book III, *On the Incarnation*; and Book IV, *On the Doc-*

trine of Signs (or *Sacraments*). His discussion is organized around particular questions or issues e.g., "On Knowledge, Foreknowledge, and Providence" (Book I), "Is God the Cause of Evil and Sin?" (Book II). For a given issue Peter typically presents a brief summary, accompanied by short quotations, of main positions found in Scripture and in the writings of the church fathers and doctors, followed by his own determination or adjudication of the matter. Himself a theological conservative, Peter seems to have intended this sort of compilation of scriptural and ancient doctrinal teaching as a counter to the popularity, fueled by the recent recovery of important parts of Aristotle's logic, of the application of dialectic to theological matters.

The *Sentences* enjoyed wide circulation and admiration from the beginning, and within a century of its composition it became a standard text in the theology curriculum. From the mid-thirteenth through the mid-fourteenth century every student of theology was required, as the last stage in obtaining the highest academic degree, to lecture and comment on Peter's text. Later medieval thinkers often referred to Peter as "the Master" (*magister*), thereby testifying to the *Sentences'* preeminence in theological training. In lectures and commentaries, the greatest minds of this period used Peter's text as a framework in which to develop their own original positions and debate with their contemporaries. As a result the *Sentences*-commentary tradition is an extraordinarily rich repository of later medieval philosophical and theological thought.   S.Ma.

Peter of Spain. It is now thought that there were two Peters of Spain. The Spanish prelate and philosopher (c.1205–77) was born in Lisbon, studied at Paris, and taught medicine at Siena (1248–50). He served in various ecclesiastical posts in Portugal and Italy (1250–73) before being elected pope as John XXI in 1276. He wrote several books on philosophical psychology and compiled the famous medical work *Thesaurus pauperum*.

The second Peter of Spain was a Spanish Dominican who lived during the first half of the thirteenth century. His *Tractatus*, later called *Summulae logicales*, received over 166 printings during subsequent centuries. The *Tractatus* presents the essentials of Aristotelian logic (propositions, universals, categories, syllogism, dialectical topics, and the sophistical fallacies) and improves on the mnemonic verses of William Sherwood; he then introduces the subjects of the so-called *parva logicalia* (supposition, relatives, ampliation, appellation, restriction, distribution), all of which were extensively developed in the later Middle Ages. There is not sufficient evidence to claim that Peter wrote a special treatise on consequences, but his understanding of conditionals as assertions of necessary connection undoubtedly played an important role in the rules of simple, as opposed to as-of-now, consequences.

I.Bo.

petitio principii. See INFORMAL FALLACY.

phalanx. See FOURIER.

phantasia (Greek, 'appearance', 'imagination'), (1) the state we are in when something appears to us to be the case; (2) the capacity in virtue of which things appear to us. Although frequently used of conscious and imagistic experiences, '*phantasia*' is not limited to such states; in particular, it can be applied to any propositional attitude where something is taken to be the case. But just as the English 'appears' connotes that one has epistemic reservations about what is actually the case, so '*phantasia*' suggests the possibility of being misled by appearances and is thus often a subject of criticism. According to Plato, *phantasia* is a "mixture" of sensation and belief; in Aristotle, it is a distinct faculty that makes truth and falsehood possible. The Stoics take a *phantasia* to constitute one of the most basic mental states, in terms of which other mental states are to be explained, and in rational animals it bears the propositional content expressed in language. This last use becomes prominent in ancient literary and rhetorical theory to designate the ability of language to move us and convey subjects vividly as well as to range beyond the bounds of our immediate experience. Here lie the origins of the modern concept of imagination (although not the Romantic distinction between fancy and imagination). Later Neoplatonists, such as Proclus, take *phantasia* to be necessary for abstract studies such as geometry, by enabling us to envision spatial relations. **See also** IMAGINATION.   V.C.

phase space. See STATE.

phenomena. See KANT.

phenomenal body. See EMBODIMENT.

phenomenalism, the view that propositions asserting the existence of physical objects are equivalent in meaning to propositions asserting that subjects would have certain sequences of sensations were they to have certain others. The basic idea behind phenomenalism is compatible with a number of different analyses of the self or conscious subject. A phenomenalist might understand the self as a substance, a particular, or a construct out of actual and possible experience. The view also is compatible with any number of different analyses of the visual, tactile, auditory, olfactory, gustatory, and kinesthetic sensations described in the antecedents and consequents of the subjunctive conditionals that the phenomenalist uses to analyze physical object propositions (as illustrated in the last paragraph). Probably the most common analysis of sensations adopted by traditional phenomenalists is a *sense-datum theory,* with the sense-data construed as mind-dependent entities. But there is nothing to prevent a phenomenalist from accepting an adverbial theory or theory of appearing instead.

The origins of phenomenalism are difficult to trace, in part because early statements of the view were usually not careful. In his *Dialogues,* Berkeley hinted at phenomenalism when he had Philonous explain how he could reconcile an ontology containing only minds and ideas with the story of a creation that took place before the existence of people. Philonous imagines that if he had been present at the creation he should have seen things, i.e., had sensations, in the order described in the Bible. It can also be argued, however, that J. S. Mill in *An Examination of Sir William Hamilton's Philosophy* was the first to put forth a clearly phenomenalistic analysis when he identified matter with the "permanent possibility of sensation." When Mill explained what these permanent possibilities are, he typically used conditionals that describe the sensations one would have if one were placed in certain conditions.

The attraction of classical phenomenalism grew with the rise of logical positivism and its acceptance of the verifiability criterion of meaning. Phenomenalists were usually *foundationalists* who were convinced that justified belief in the physical world rested ultimately on our noninferentially justified beliefs about our sensations. Implicitly committed to the view that only deductive and inductive inferences are legitimate, and further assuming that to be justified in believing one proposition *P* on the basis of another *E,* one must be justified in believing both *E* and that *E* makes *P* probable, the phenomenalist saw an insuperable difficulty in justifying belief in ordinary statements about the physical world given prevalent conceptions of physical objects. If all we ultimately have as our evidence for believing in physical objects is what we know about the occurrence of sensation, how can we establish sensation as evidence for the existence of physical objects? We obviously cannot deduce the existence of physical objects from any finite sequence of sensations. The sensations could, e.g., be hallucinatory. Nor, it seems, can we observe a correlation between sensation and something else in order to generate the premises of an inductive argument for the conclusion that sensations are reliable indicators of physical objects. The key to solving this problem, the phenomenalist argues, is to reduce assertions about the physical world to complicated assertions about the sequences of sensations a subject would have were he to have certain others. The truth of such conditionals, e.g., that if I have the clear visual impression of a cat, then there is one before me, might be mind-independent in the way in which one wants the truth of assertions about the physical world to be mind-independent. And to the phenomenalist's great relief, it would seem that we could justify our belief in such conditional statements without having to correlate anything but sensations.

Many philosophers today reject some of the epistemological, ontological, and metaphilosophical presuppositions with which phenomenalists approached the problem of understanding our relation to the physical world through sensation. But the argument that was historically most decisive in convincing many philosophers to abandon phenomenalism was the argument from perceptual relativity first advanced by Chisholm in "The Problem of Perception." Chisholm offers a strategy for attacking any phenomenalistic analysis. The first move is to force the phenomenalist to state a conditional describing only sensations that is an alleged consequence of a physical object proposition. C. I. Lewis, e.g., in *An Analysis of Knowledge and Valuation,* claims that the assertion (*P*) that there is a doorknob before me and to the left entails (*C*) that if I were to seem to see a doorknob and seem to reach out and touch it then I would seem to feel it. Chisholm argues that if *P* really did entail *C* then there could be no assertion *R* that when conjoined with *P* did not entail *C*. There is, however, such an assertion: I am unable to move my limbs and my hands but am subject to delusions such that I think I am moving them; I often seem to be initiating a grasping motion but with no feeling of contacting anything. Chisholm argues, in effect, that what sensations one would have if one were to have certain others *always* depends

in part on the internal and external *physical* conditions of perception and that this fact dooms any attempt to find necessary and sufficient conditions for the truth of a physical object proposition couched in terms that describe only connections between sensations.

See also BERKELEY; LEWIS, C. I.; LOGICAL POSITIVISM; PERCEPTION.   R.A.F.

phenomenal property. See QUALIA.

phenomenal world. See KANT.

phenomenological attitude. See HUSSERL.

phenomenological reduction. See HUSSERL.

phenomenology, in the twentieth century, the philosophy developed by Husserl and some of his followers. The term has been used since the mid-eighteenth century and received a carefully defined technical meaning in the works of both Kant and Hegel, but it is not now used to refer to a homogeneous and systematically developed philosophical position. The question of what phenomenology is may suggest that phenomenology is one among the many contemporary philosophical conceptions that have a clearly delineated body of doctrines and whose essential characteristics can be expressed by a set of well-chosen statements. This notion is not correct, however. In contemporary philosophy there is no system or school called "phenomenology," characterized by a clearly defined body of teachings. Phenomenology is neither a school nor a trend in contemporary philosophy. It is rather a movement whose proponents, for various reasons, have propelled it in many distinct directions, with the result that today it means different things to different people.

While within the phenomenological movement as a whole there are several related currents, they, too, are by no means homogeneous. Though these currents have a common point of departure, they do not project toward the same destination. The thinking of most phenomenologists has changed so greatly that their respective views can be presented adequately only by showing them in their gradual development. This is true not only for Husserl, founder of the phenomenological movement, but also for such later phenomenologists as Scheler, N. Hartmann, Heidegger, Sartre, and Merleau-Ponty.

To anyone who studies the phenomenological movement without prejudice the differences among its many currents are obvious. It has been said that phenomenology consists in an analysis and description of consciousness; it has been claimed also that phenomenology simply blends with existentialism. Phenomenology is indeed the study of essences, but it also attempts to place essences back into existence. It is a transcendental philosophy interested only in what is "left behind" after the phenomenological reduction is performed, but it also considers the world to be already there before reflection begins. For some philosophers phenomenology is speculation on transcendental subjectivity, whereas for others it is a method for approaching concrete existence. Some use phenomenology as a search for a philosophy that accounts for space, time, and the world, just as we experience and "live" them. Finally, it has been said that phenomenology is an attempt to give a direct description of our experience as it is in itself without taking into account its psychological origin and its causal explanation; but Husserl speaks of a "genetic" as well as a "constitutive" phenomenology.

To some people, finding such an abundance of ideas about one and the same subject constitutes a strange situation; for others it is annoying to contemplate the "confusion"; and there will be those who conclude that a philosophy that cannot define its own scope does not deserve the discussion that has been carried on in its regard. In the opinion of many, not only is this latter attitude not justified, but precisely the opposite view defended by Thevenaz should be adopted. As the term 'phenomenology' signifies first and foremost a methodical conception, Thevenaz argues that because this method, originally developed for a very particular and limited end, has been able to branch out in so many varying forms, it manifests a latent truth and power of renewal that implies an exceptional fecundity.

Speaking of the great variety of conceptions within the phenomenological movement, Merleau-Ponty remarked that the responsible philosopher must recognize that phenomenology may be practiced and identified as a manner or a style of thinking, and that it existed as a movement before arriving at a complete awareness of itself as a philosophy. Rather than force a living movement into a system, then, it seems more in keeping with the ideal of the historian as well as the philosopher to follow the movement in its development, and attempt to describe and evaluate the many branches in and through which it has unfolded itself. In reality the picture is not as dark as it may seem at first sight. Notwithstanding the obvious differences, most phenomenologists share certain insights that are very important for their mutual philosophical conception as a whole. In this connection the following must be mentioned:

(1) Most phenomenologists admit a radical difference between the "natural" and the "philosophical" attitude. This leads necessarily to an equally radical difference between philosophy and science. In characterizing this difference some phenomenologists, in agreement with Husserl, stress only epistemological issues, whereas others, in agreement with Heidegger, focus their attention exclusively on ontological topics.

(2) Notwithstanding this radical difference, there is a complicated set of relationships between philosophy and science. Within the context of these relationships philosophy has in some sense a foundational task with respect to the sciences, whereas science offers to philosophy at least a substantial part of its philosophical problematic.

(3) To achieve its task philosophy must perform a certain reduction, or *epoche*, a radical change of attitude by which the philosopher turns from things to their meanings, from the ontic to the ontological, from the realm of the objectified meaning as found in the sciences to the realm of meaning as immediately experienced in the "life-world." In other words, although it remains true that the various phenomenologists differ in characterizing the reduction, no one seriously doubts its necessity.

(4) All phenomenologists subscribe to the doctrine of intentionality, though most elaborate this doctrine in their own way. For Husserl intentionality is a characteristic of conscious phenomena or acts; in a deeper sense, it is the characteristic of a finite consciousness that originally finds itself without a world. For Heidegger and most existentialists it is the human reality itself that is intentional; as Being-in-the-world its essence consists in its *ek-sistence*, i.e., in its standing out toward the world.

(5) All phenomenologists agree on the fundamental idea that the basic concern of philosophy is to answer the question concerning the "meaning and Being" of beings. All agree in addition that in trying to materialize this goal the philosopher should be primarily interested not in the ultimate cause of all finite beings, but in how the Being of beings and the Being of the world are to be constituted. Finally, all agree that in answering the question concerning the meaning of Being a privileged position is to be attributed to subjectivity, i.e., to that being which questions the Being of beings. Phenomenologists differ,

however, the moment they have to specify what is meant by subjectivity. As noted above, whereas Husserl conceives it as a worldless monad, Heidegger and most later phenomenologists conceive it as *being-in-the-world*. Referring to Heidegger's reinterpretation of his phenomenology, Husserl writes:

> one misinterprets my phenomenology backwards from a level which it was its very purpose to overcome, in other words, one has failed to understand the fundamental novelty of the phenomenological reduction and hence the progress from mundane subjectivity (i.e., man) to transcendental subjectivity; consequently one has remained stuck in an anthropology . . . which according to my doctrine has not yet reached the genuine philosophical level, and whose interpretation as philosophy means a lapse into "transcendental anthropologism," that is, "psychologism."

(6) All phenomenologists defend a certain form of intuitionism and subscribe to what Husserl calls the "principle of all principles": "whatever presents itself in 'intuition' in primordial form (as it were in its bodily reality), is simply to be accepted as it gives itself out to be, though only within the limits in which it then presents itself." Here again, however, each phenomenologist interprets this principle in keeping with his general conception of phenomenology as a whole.

Thus, while phenomenologists do share certain insights, the development of the movement has nevertheless been such that it is not possible to give a simple definition of what phenomenology is. The fact remains that there are many phenomenologists and many phenomenologies. Therefore, one can only faithfully report what one has experienced of phenomenology by reading the phenomenologists.

See also HEIDEGGER, HUSSERL, MERLEAU-PONTY, SARTRE, SCHELER.   J.J.K.

phenotext. See KRISTEVA.

Philodemus. See EPICUREANISM.

Philo Judaeus (c.20 B.C.–A.D. 40), Jewish Hellenistic philosopher of Alexandria who composed the bulk of his work in the form of commentaries and discourses on Scripture. He made the first known sustained attempt to synthesize its revealed teachings with the doctrines of classical philosophy. Although he was not the first to apply the methods of allegorical interpretation to Scripture, the number and variety of his interpretations make Philo unique. With this interpretive tool, he transformed biblical narratives into Platonic accounts of the soul's quest for God and its struggle against passion, and the Mosaic commandments into specific manifestations of general laws of nature.

Philo's most influential idea was his conception of God, which combines the personal, ethical deity of the Bible with the abstract, transcendentalist theology of Platonism and Pythagoreanism. The Philonic deity is both the loving, just God of the Hebrew Patriarchs and the eternal One whose essence is absolutely unknowable and who creates the material world by will from primordial matter which He creates *ex nihilo*. Besides the intelligible realm of ideas, which Philo is the earliest known philosopher to identify as God's thoughts, he posited an intermediate divine being which he called, adopting scriptural language, the *logos*. Although the exact nature of the *logos* is hard to pin down – Philo variously and, without any concern for consistency, called it the "first-begotten Son of the uncreated Father," "Second God," "idea of ideas," "archetype of human reason," and "pattern of creation" – its main functions are clear: to bridge the huge gulf between the transcendent deity and the lower world and to serve as the unifying law of the universe, the ground of its order and rationality. A philosophical eclectic, Philo was unknown to medieval Jewish philosophers but, beyond his anticipations of Neoplatonism, he had a lasting impact on Christianity through Clement of Alexandria, Origen, and Ambrose.

See also HELLENISTIC PHILOSOPHY.   J.Ste.

Philolaus (470?–390? B.C.), pre-Socratic Greek philosopher from Croton in southern Italy, the first Pythagorean to write a book. The surviving fragments of it are the earliest primary texts for Pythagoreanism, but numerous spurious fragments have also been preserved.

Philolaus's book begins with a cosmogony and includes astronomical, medical, and psychological doctrines. His major innovation was to argue that the cosmos and everything in it is a combination not just of *unlimiteds* (what is structured and ordered, e.g. material elements) but also of *limiters* (structural and ordering elements, e.g. shapes). These elements are held together in a *harmonia* (fitting together), which comes to be in accord with perspicuous mathematical relationships, such as the whole number ratios that correspond to the harmonic intervals (e.g. octave =

1 : 2). He argued that secure knowledge is possible insofar as we grasp the *number* in accordance with which things are put together. His astronomical system is famous as the first to make the earth a planet. Along with the sun, moon, fixed stars, five planets, and counter-earth (thus making the perfect number ten), the earth circles the central fire (a combination of the limiter "center" and the unlimited "fire"). Philolaus's influence is seen in Plato's *Philebus;* he is the primary source for Aristotle's account of Pythagoreanism.

See also PYTHAGORAS.   C.A.H.

Philo of Larisa. See ACADEMY.

Philoponus, John. See JOHANNES PHILOPONUS.

philosopher's stone. See ALCHEMY.

philosophes. See ENCYCLOPEDIA.

philosophia perennis (Latin, 'perennial philosophy'), a supposed body of truths that appear in the writings of the great philosophers, or the truths common to opposed philosophical viewpoints. The term is derived from the title of a book (*De perenni philosophia*) published by Agostino Steuco of Gubbio in 1540. It suggests that the differences between philosophers are inessential and superficial and that the common essential truth emerges, however partially, in the major philosophical schools. Aldous Huxley employed it as a title. L. Lavelle, N. Hartmann, and K. Jaspers also employ the phrase. M. De Wulf and many others use the phrase to characterize Neo-Thomism as the chosen vehicle of essential philosophical truths.   R.M.

philosophical anthropology, philosophical inquiry concerning human nature, often starting with the question of what generally characterizes human beings in contrast to other kinds of creatures and things. Thus broadly conceived, it is a kind of inquiry as old as philosophy itself, occupying philosophers from Socrates to Sartre; and it embraces philosophical psychology, the philosophy of mind, philosophy of action, and existentialism. Such inquiry presupposes no immutable "essence of man," but only the meaningfulness of distinguishing between what is "human" and what is not, and the possibility that philosophy as well as other disciplines may contribute to our self-comprehension. It leaves open the question of whether other kinds of naturally occurring or artificially produced entity may possess the hallmarks of our humanity, and countenances the possibility of the biologically evolved, historically developed, and socially and individually variable character of everything about our attained humanity.

More narrowly conceived, philosophical anthropology is a specific movement in recent European philosophy associated initially with Scheler and Helmuth Plessner, and subsequently with such figures as Arnold Gehlen, Cassirer, and the later Sartre. It initially emerged in the late 1920s in Germany, simultaneously with the existential philosophy of Heidegger and the critical social theory of the Frankfurt School, with which it competed as German philosophers turned their attention to the comprehension of human life. This movement was distinguished from the outset by its attempt to integrate the insights of phenomenological analysis with the perspectives attainable through attention to human and comparative biology, and subsequently to social inquiry as well. This turn to a more naturalistic approach to the understanding of ourselves, as a particular kind of living creature among others, is reflected in the titles of the two works published in 1928 that inaugurated the movement: Scheler's *Man's Place in Nature* and Plessner's *The Levels of the Organic and Man.* For both Scheler and Plessner, however, as for those who followed them, our nature must be understood by taking further account of the social, cultural, and intellectual dimensions of human life. Even those like Gehlen, whose *Der Mensch* (1940) exhibits a strongly biological orientation, devoted much attention to these dimensions, which our biological nature both constrains and makes possible. For all of them, the relation between the biological and the social and cultural dimensions of human life is a central concern and a key to comprehending our human nature.

One of the common themes of the later philosophical-anthropological literature – e.g., Cassirer's *An Essay on Man* (1945) and Sartre's *Critique of Dialectical Reason* (1960) as well as Plessner's *Contitio Humana* (1965) and Gehlen's *Early Man and Late Culture* (1963) – is the *plasticity* of human nature, made possible by our biological constitution, and the resulting great differences in the ways human beings live. Yet this is not taken to preclude saying anything meaningful about human nature generally; rather, it merely requires attention to the kinds of general features involved and reflected in human diversity and variability.

Critics of the very idea and possibility of a philosophical anthropology (e.g., Althusser and Foucault) typically either deny that there are any such general features or maintain that there are none outside the province of the biological sciences (to which philosophy can contribute nothing substantive). Both claims, however, are open to dispute; and the enterprise of a philosophical anthropology remains a viable and potentially significant one.

See also FRANKFURT SCHOOL, NIETZSCHE.

R.Sc.

philosophical behaviorism. See BEHAVIORISM.

philosophical psychology. See PHILOSOPHY OF MIND.

philosophical theology. See METAPHYSICS.

philosophy, critical. See BROAD, KANT.

philosophy, Latin American. See LATIN AMERICAN PHILOSOPHY.

philosophy, speculative. See SPECULATIVE PHILOSOPHY.

philosophy of action. See ACTION THEORY.

philosophy of art. See AESTHETICS.

philosophy of biology, the philosophy of science applied to biology. On a conservative view of the philosophy of science, the same principles apply throughout science. Biology supplies additional examples but does not provide any special problems or require new principles. For example, the reduction of Mendelian genetics to molecular biology exemplifies the same sort of relation as the reduction of thermodynamics to statistical mechanics, and the same general analysis of reduction applies equally to both. More radical philosophers argue that the subject matter of biology has certain unique features; hence, the philosophy of biology is itself unique. The three features of biology most often cited by those who maintain that philosophy of biology is unique are functional organization, embryological development, and the nature of selection. Organisms are functionally organized. They are capable of maintaining their overall organization in the face of fairly extensive variation in their environments. Organisms also undergo ontogenetic development resulting from extremely complex interactions between the genetic makeup of the organism and its successive environments. At each step, the course that an organism takes is determined by an interplay between its genetic makeup, its current state of development, and

the environment it happens to confront. The complexity of these interactions produces the nature–nurture problem. Except for human artifacts, similar organization does not occur in the non-living world.

The *species problem* is another classic issue in the philosophy of biology. Biological species have been a paradigm example of natural kinds since Aristotle. According to nearly all pre-Darwinian philosophers, species are part of the basic makeup of the universe, like gravity and gold. They were held to be as eternal, immutable, and discrete as these other examples of natural kinds. If Darwin was right, species are not eternal. They come and go, and once gone can no more reemerge than Aristotle can once again walk the streets of Athens. Nor are species immutable. A sample of lead can be transmuted into a sample of gold, but these elements as elements remain immutable in the face of such changes. However, Darwin insisted that species themselves, not merely their instances, evolved. Finally, because Darwin thought that species evolved gradually, the boundaries between species are not sharp, casting doubt on the essentialist doctrines so common in his day. In short, if species evolve, they have none of the traditional characteristics of species. Philosophers and biologists to this day are working out the consequences of this radical change in our worldview.

The topic that has received the greatest attention by philosophers of biology in the recent literature is the nature of evolutionary theory, in particular selection, adaptation, fitness, and the population structure of species. In order for selection to operate, variation is necessary, successive generations must be organized genealogically, and individuals must interact differentially with their environments. In the simplest case, genes pass on their structure largely intact. In addition, they provide the information necessary to produce organisms. Certain of these organisms are better able to cope with their environments and reproduce than are other organisms. As a result, genes are perpetuated differentially through successive generations. Those characteristics that help an organism cope with its environments are termed adaptations. In a more restricted sense, only those characteristics that arose through past selective advantage count as adaptations.

Just as the notion of IQ was devised as a single measure for a combination of the factors that influence our mental abilities, fitness is a measure of relative reproductive success. Claims about the tautological character of the principle of the survival of the fittest stem from the blunt assertion that fitness just *is* relative reproductive success, as if intelligence just *is* what IQ tests measure. Philosophers of biology have collaborated with biologists to analyze the notion of fitness. This literature has concentrated on the role that causation plays in selection and, hence, must play in any adequate explication of fitness. One important distinction that has emerged is between replication and differential interaction with the environment. Selection is a function of the interplay between these two processes. Because of the essential role of variation in selection, all the organisms that belong to the same species either at any one time or through time cannot possibly be essentially the same. Nor can species be treated adequately in terms of the statistical covariance of either characters or genes. The populational structure of species is crucial. For example, species that form numerous, partially isolated demes are much more likely to speciate than those that do not. One especially controversial question is whether species themselves can function in the evolutionary process rather than simply resulting from it.

Although philosophers of biology have played an increasingly important role in biology itself, they have also addressed more traditional philosophical questions, especially in connection with evolutionary epistemology and ethics. Advocates of *evolutionary epistemology* argue that knowledge can be understood in terms of the adaptive character of accurate knowledge. Those organisms that hold false beliefs about their environment, including other organisms, are less likely to reproduce themselves than those with more accurate beliefs. To the extent that this argument has any force at all, it applies only to human-sized entities and events. One common response to evolutionary epistemology is that sometimes people who hold manifestly false beliefs flourish at the expense of those who hold more realistic views of the world in which we live. On another version of evolutionary epistemology, knowledge acquisition is viewed as just one more instance of a selection process. The issue is not to justify our beliefs but to understand how they are generated and proliferated. Advocates of *evolutionary ethics* attempt to justify certain ethical principles in terms of their survival value. Any behavior that increases the likelihood of survival and reproduction is "good," and anything that detracts from these ends is "bad." The main objection to evolutionary ethics is that it violates the is–ought distinction. According to most ethical systems, we are asked to sacrifice ourselves

for the good of others. If these others were limited to our biological relatives, then the biological notion of inclusive fitness might be adequate to account for such altruistic behavior, but the scope of ethical systems extends past one's biological relatives. Advocates of evolutionary ethics are hard pressed to explain the full range of behavior that is traditionally considered as virtuous. Either biological evolution cannot provide an adequate justification for ethical behavior or else ethical systems must be drastically reduced in their scope.

See also DARWINISM, ESSENTIALISM, MECHANISTIC EXPLANATIONS, MENDEL, PHILOSOPHY OF SCIENCE.   D.L.H.

philosophy of economics, the study of methodological issues facing positive economic theory and normative problems on the intersection of welfare economics and political philosophy.

Methodological issues. Applying approaches and questions in the philosophy of science specifically to economics, the philosophy of economics explores epistemological and conceptual problems raised by the explanatory aims and strategy of economic theory: Do its assumptions about individual choice constitute laws, and do they explain its derived generalizations about markets and economies? Are these generalizations laws, and if so, how are they tested by observation of economic processes, and how are theories in the various compartments of economics – microeconomics, macroeconomics – related to one another and to econometrics? How are the various schools – neoclassical, institutional, Marxian, etc. – related to one another, and what sorts of tests might enable us to choose between their theories?

Historically, the chief issue of interest in the development of the philosophy of economics has been the empirical adequacy of the assumptions of rational "economic man": that all agents have complete and transitive cardinal or ordinal utility rankings or preference orders and that they always choose that available option which maximizes their utility or preferences. Since the actual behavior of agents appears to disconfirm these assumptions, the claim that they constitute causal laws governing economic behavior is difficult to sustain. On the other hand, the assumption of preference-maximizing behavior is indispensable to twentieth-century economics. These two considerations jointly undermine the claim that economic theory honors criteria on explanatory power and evidential probity drawn from physical science. Much work by economists and philosophers has been devoted therefore to disputing the claim that the assumptions of rational choice theory are false or to disputing the inference from this claim to the conclusion that the cognitive status of economic theory as empirical science is thereby undermined. Most frequently it has been held that the assumptions of rational choice are as harmless and as indispensable as idealizations are elsewhere in science. This view must deal with the allegation that unlike theories embodying idealization elsewhere in science, economic theory gains little more in predictive power from these assumptions about agents' calculations than it would secure without any assumptions about individual choice.

Normative issues. Both economists and political philosophers are concerned with identifying principles that will ensure just, fair, or equitable distributions of scarce goods. For this reason neoclassical economic theory shares a history with utilitarianism in moral philosophy. Contemporary welfare economics continues to explore the limits of utilitarian prescriptions that optimal economic and political arrangements should maximize and/or equalize utility, welfare, or some surrogate. It also examines the adequacy of alternatives to such utilitarian principles. Thus, economics shares an agenda of interests with political and moral philosophy. Utilitarianism in economics and philosophy has been constrained by an early realization that utilities are neither cardinally measurable nor interpersonally comparable. Therefore the prescription to maximize and/or equalize utility cannot be determinatively obeyed. Welfare theorists have nevertheless attempted to establish principles that will enable us to determine the equity, fairness, or justice of various economic arrangements, and that do not rely on interpersonal comparisons required to measure whether a distribution is maximal or equal in the utility it accords all agents. Inspired by philosophers who have surrendered utilitarianism for other principles of equality, fairness, or justice in distribution, welfare economists have explored Kantian, social contractarian, and communitarian alternatives in a research program that cuts clearly across both disciplines.

Political philosophy has also profited as much from innovations in economic theory as welfare economics has benefited from moral philosophy. Theorems from welfare economics that establish the efficiency of markets in securing distributions that meet minimal conditions of optimality and fairness have led moral philosophers to reexamine the moral status of free-market exchange. Moreover, philosophers have come to appreciate that coercive social institutions are sometimes best understood as devices for securing public goods – goods like police protection that cannot be provided to those who pay for them without also providing them to free riders who decline to do so. The recognition that everyone would be worse off, including free riders, were the coercion required to pay for these goods not imposed, is due to welfare economics and has led to a significant revival of interest in the work of Hobbes, who appears to have prefigured such arguments.

See also DECISION THEORY, PHILOSOPHY OF THE SOCIAL SCIENCES, POLITICAL PHILOSOPHY, SOCIAL CHOICE THEORY, UTILITARIANISM. A.R.

philosophy of education, a branch of philosophy concerned with virtually every aspect of the educational enterprise. It significantly overlaps other, more mainstream branches (especially epistemology and ethics, but even logic and metaphysics). The field might almost be construed as a "series of footnotes" to Plato's *Meno*, wherein are raised such fundamental issues as whether virtue can be taught; what virtue is; what knowledge is; what the relation between knowledge of virtue and being virtuous is; what the relation between knowledge and teaching is; and how and whether teaching is possible. While few people would subscribe to Plato's doctrine (or convenient fiction, perhaps) in *Meno* that learning by being taught is a process of recollection, the paradox of inquiry that prompts this doctrine is at once the root text of the perennial debate between rationalism and empiricism and a profoundly unsettling indication that teaching passeth understanding.

Mainstream philosophical topics considered within an educational context tend to take on a decidedly genetic cast. So, e.g., epistemology, which analytic philosophy has tended to view as a justificatory enterprise, becomes concerned if not with the historical origins of knowledge claims then with their genesis within the mental economy of persons generally – in consequence of their educations. And even when philosophers of education come to endorse something akin to Plato's classic account of knowledge as justified true belief, they are inclined to suggest, then, that the conveyance of knowledge via instruction must somehow provide the student with the justification along with the true belief – thereby reintroducing a genetic dimension to a topic long lacking one. Perhaps, indeed, analytic philosophy's general (though not universal) neglect of philosophy of education is traceable in some measure to the latter's almost inevitably genetic perspective, which the former tended to decry as armchair science and as a threat to the autonomy and integrity of proper philosophical inquiry. If this has been a basis for neglect, then philosophy's more recent, postanalytic turn toward naturalized inquiries that reject any dichotomy between empirical and philosophical investigations may make philosophy of education a more inviting area.

Alfred North Whitehead, himself a leading light in the philosophy of education, once remarked that we are living in the period of educational thought subject to the influence of Dewey, and there is still no denying the observation. Dewey's instrumentalism, his special brand of pragmatism, informs his extraordinarily comprehensive progressive philosophy of education; and he once went so far as to define all of philosophy as the general theory of education. He identifies the educative process with the growth of experience, with growing as developing – where experience is to be understood more in active terms, as involving doing things that change one's objective environment and internal conditions, than in the passive terms, say, of Locke's "impression" model of experience. Even traditionalistic philosophers of education, most notably Maritain, have acknowledged the wisdom of Deweyan educational means, and have, in the face of Dewey's commanding philosophical presence, reframed the debate with progressivists as one about appropriate educational ends – thereby insufficiently acknowledging Dewey's trenchant critique of the means–end distinction. And even some recent analytic philosophers of education, such as R. S. Peters, can be read as if translating Deweyan insights (e.g., about the aim of education) into an analytic idiom.

Analytic philosophy of education, as charted by Peters, Israel Scheffler, and others in the Anglo-American philosophical tradition, has used the tools of linguistic analysis on a wide variety of educational concepts (learning, teaching, training, conditioning, indoctrinating, etc.) and investigated their interconnections: Does teaching entail learning? Does teaching inevitably involve indoctrinating? etc. This careful, subtle, and philosophically sophisticated work has made possible a much-needed conceptual precision in educational debates, though the debaters who most influence public opinion and policy have rarely availed themselves of that precisification. Recent work in philosophy of education, however, has taken up some major educational objectives – moral and other values, critical and creative thinking – in a way that promises to have an impact on the actual conduct of education. Philosophy of education, long isolated (in schools of education) from the rest of the academic philosophical community, has also been somewhat estranged from the professional educational mainstream. Dewey would surely have approved of a change in this status quo.

See also DEWEY, EPISTEMOLOGY, PIAGET, PLATO, PRAGMATISM, VIRTUE ETHICS. D.M.S.

philosophy of history, the philosophical study of human history and of attempts to record and interpret it. 'History' in English (and its equivalent in most modern European languages) has two primary senses: (1) the temporal progression of large-scale human events and actions, primarily but not exclusively in the past; and (2) the discipline or inquiry in which knowledge of the human past is acquired or sought. This has led to two senses of 'philosophy of history', depending on which "history" has been the object of philosophers' attentions. Philosophy of history in the first sense is often called substantive (or speculative), and placed under metaphysics. Philosophy of history in the second sense is called critical (or analytic) and can be placed in epistemology.

Substantive philosophy of history. In the West, substantive philosophy of history is thought to begin only in the Christian era. In the *City of God*, Augustine wonders why Rome flourished while pagan, yet fell into disgrace after its conversion to Christiantity. Divine reward and punishment should apply to whole peoples, not just to individuals. The unfolding of events in history should exhibit a plan that is intelligible rationally, morally, and (for Augustine) theologically. As a believer Augustine is convinced that there is such a plan, though it may not always be evident. In the modern period, philosophers such as Vico and Herder also sought such intelligibility in history. They also believed in a long-term direction or purpose of history that is often opposed to and makes use of the purposes of individuals. The most elaborate and best-known example of this approach is found in Hegel, who thought that the gradual realization of human freedom could be discerned in history even if much slavery, tyranny, and suffering are necessary in the process. Marx, too, claimed to know the laws – in his case economic – according to which history unfolds. Similar searches for overall "meaning" in human history have been undertaken in the twentieth century, notably by Arnold Toynbee (1889–1975), author of the twelve-volume *Study of History*, and Oswald Spengler (1880–1936), author of *Decline of the West*. But the whole enterprise was denounced by the positivists and neo-Kantians of the late nineteenth century as irresponsible metaphysical speculation. This attitude was shared by twentieth-century neopositivists and some of their heirs in the analytic tradition. There is some irony in this, since positivism, explicitly in thinkers like Comte and implicitly in others, involves belief in progressively enlightened stages of human history crowned by the modern age of science.

Critical philosophy of history. The critical philosophy of history, i.e., the epistemology of historical knowledge, can be traced to the late nineteenth century and has been dominated by the paradigm of the natural sciences. Those in the positivist, neopositivist, and postpositivist tradition, in keeping with the idea of the unity of science, believe that to know the historical past is to *explain* events causally, and all causal explanation is ultimately of the same sort. To explain human events is to derive them from laws, which may be social, psychological, and perhaps ultimately biological and physical. Against this reductionism, the neo-Kantians and Dilthey argued that history, like other humanistic disciplines (*Geisteswissenschaften*), follows irreducible rules of its own. It is concerned with particular events or developments for their own sake, not as instances of general laws, and its aim is to understand, rather than explain, human actions. This debate was resurrected in the twentieth century in the English-speaking world. Philosophers like Hempel and Morton White (b.1917) elaborated on the notion of causal explanation in history, while Collingwood and William Dray (b.1921) described the "understanding" of historical agents as grasping the thought behind an action or discovering its *reasons* rather than its *causes*. The comparison with natural science, and the debate between reductionists and anti-reductionists, dominated other questions as well: Can or should history be objective and value-free, as science purportedly is? What is the significance of the fact that historians can never perceive the events that interest them, since they are in the past? Are they not limited by their point of view, their place in history, in a way scientists are not? Some positivists were inclined to exclude history from science, rather than make it into one, relegating it to "literature" because it could never meet the standards of objectivity and genuine explanation; it was often the anti-positivists who defended the cognitive legitimacy of our knowledge of the past.

In the non-reductionist tradition, philosophers have increasingly stressed the *narrative* character of history: to understand human actions generally, and past actions in particular, is to tell a coherent story about them. History, according to W. B. Gallie (b.1912), is a species of the genus Story. History does not thereby become fiction: narrative remains a "cognitive instrument" (Louis Mink, 1921–83) just as appropriate to its domain as theory construction is to science. Nevertheless, concepts previously associated with fictional narratives, such as plot structure and beginning-middle-end, are seen as applying to historical narratives as well. This tradition is carried further by Hayden White (b.1928), who analyzes classical nineteenth-century histories (and even substantive philosophies of history such as Hegel's) as instances of romance, comedy, tragedy, and satire. In White's work this mode of analysis leads him to some skepticism about history's capacity to "represent" the reality of the past: narratives seem to be imposed upon the data, often for ideological reasons, rather than drawn from them. To some extent White's view joins that of some positivists who believe that history's literary character excludes it from the realm of science. But for White this is hardly a defect. Some philosophers have criticized the emphasis on narrative in discussions of history, since it neglects search and discovery, deciphering and evaluating sources, etc., which is more important to historians than the way they "write up" their results. Furthermore, not all history is presented in narrative form. The debate between pro- and anti-narrativists among philosophers of history has its parallel in a similar debate among historians themselves. Academic history in recent times has seen a strong turn away from traditional political history toward social, cultural, and economic analyses of the human past. Narrative is associated with the supposedly outmoded focus on the doings of kings, popes, and generals. These are considered (e.g. by the French historian Fernand Braudel, 1902–85) merely surface ripples compared to the deeper-lying and slower-moving currents of social and economic change. It is the methods and concepts of the social sciences, not the art of the storyteller, on which the historian must draw. This debate has now lost some of its steam and narrative history has made something of a comeback among historians. Among philosophers Paul Ricoeur has tried to show that even ostensibly non-narrative history retains narrative features.

Historicity. Historicity (or historicality: *Geschichtlichkeit*) is a term used in the phenomenological and hermeneutic tradition (from Dilthey and Husserl through Heidegger and Gadamer) to indicate an essential feature of human existence. Persons are not merely *in* history; their past, including their social past, figures in their conception of themselves and their future possibilities. Some awareness of the past is thus constitutive of the self, prior to being formed into a cognitive discipline.

Modernism and the postmodern. It is possible to view some of the debates over the modern and postmodern in recent Continental philosophy as a new kind of philosophy of history. Philosophers like Lyotard and Foucault see the modern as the period from the Enlightenment and Romanticism to the present, characterized chiefly by belief in "grand narratives" of historical progress, whether capitalist, Marxist, or positivist, with "man" as the triumphant hero of the story. Such belief is now being (or should be) abandoned, bringing modernism to an end. In one sense this is like earlier attacks on the substantive philosophy of history, since it unmasks as unjustified moralizing certain beliefs about large-scale patterns in history. It goes even further than the earlier attack, since it finds these beliefs at work even where they are not explicitly expressed. In another sense this is a continuation of the substantive philosophy of history, since it makes its own grand claims about large-scale historical patterns. In this it joins hands with other philosophers of our day in a general historicization of knowledge (e.g., the philosophy of science merges with the history of science) and even of philosophy itself. Thus the later Heidegger – and more recently Richard Rorty – view philosophy itself as a large-scale episode in Western history that is nearing or has reached its end. Philosophy thus merges with the history of philosophy, but only thanks to a philosophical reflection on this history as part of history as a whole.

See also EXPLANATION, HEGEL, HISTORICISM, PHILOSOPHY OF THE SOCIAL SCIENCES, VERSTEHEN.   D.C.

philosophy of language, the philosophical study of natural language and its workings, particularly of linguistic meaning and the use of language. A *natural language* is any one of the thousands of various tongues that have developed historically among populations of human beings and have been used for everyday purposes – including English, Italian, Swahili, and Latin – as opposed to the formal and other artificial "languages" invented by mathematicians, logicians, and computer scientists, such as arithmetic, the predicate calculus, and LISP or COBOL. There are intermediate cases, e.g., Esperanto, Pig Latin, and the sort of "philosophese" that mixes English words with logical symbols. Contemporary philosophy of language centers on the theory of meaning, but also includes the theory of reference, the theory of truth, philosophical pragmatics, and the philosophy of linguistics.

The main question addressed by the theory of meaning is: In virtue of what are certain physical marks or noises meaningful linguistic expressions, and in virtue of what does any particular set of marks or noises have the distinctive meaning it does? A theory of meaning should also give a comprehensive account of the "meaning phenomena," or general semantic properties of sentences: synonymy, ambiguity, entailment, and the like. Some theorists have thought to express these questions and issues in terms of language-neutral items called propositions: 'In virtue of what does a particular set of marks or noises express the proposition it does?'; cf. ' "*La neige est blanche*" expresses the proposition that snow is white', and 'Synonymous sentences express the same proposition'. On this view, to *understand* a sentence is to "grasp" the proposition expressed by that sentence. But the explanatory role and even the existence of such entities are disputed.

It has often been maintained that certain special sentences are *true* solely in virtue of their meanings and/or the meanings of their component expressions, without regard to what the nonlinguistic world is like ('No bachelor is married'; 'If a thing is blue it is colored'). Such vacuously true sentences are called *analytic*. However, Quine and others have disputed whether there really is such a thing as analyticity.

Philosophers have offered a number of sharply competing hypotheses as to the nature of meaning, including: (1) the referential view that words mean by standing for things, and that a sentence means what it does because its parts correspond referentially to the elements of an actual or possible state of affairs in the world; (2) ideational or mentalist theories, according to which meanings are ideas or other psychological phenomena in people's minds; (3) "use" theories, inspired by Wittgenstein and to a lesser extent by J. L. Austin: a linguistic expression's "meaning" is its conventionally assigned role as a game-piece-like token used in one or more existing social practices; (4) Grice's hypothesis that a sentence's or word's meaning is a function of what audience response a typical speaker would intend to elicit in uttering it; (5) inferential role theories, as developed by Wilfrid Sellars out of Carnap's and Wittgenstein's views: a sentence's meaning is specified by the set of sentences from which it can correctly be inferred and the set of those which can be inferred from it (Sellars himself provided for "language-entry" and "language-exit" moves as partly constitutive of meaning, in addition to inferences); (6) verificationism, the view that a sentence's meaning is the set of possible experiences that would confirm it or provide evidence for its truth; (7) the truth-conditional theory: a sentence's meaning is the distinctive condition under which it *is* true, the situation or state of affairs that, if it obtained, would make the sentence true; (8) the null hypothesis, or eliminativist view, that "meaning" is a myth and there is no such thing – a radical claim that can stem either from Quine's doctrine of the indeterminacy of translation or from eliminative materialism in the philosophy of mind.

Following the original work of Carnap, Alonzo Church, Hintikka, and Richard Montague in the 1950s, the theory of meaning has made increasing use of "possible worlds"–based intensional logic as an analytical apparatus. Propositions (sentence meanings considered as entities), and truth conditions as in (7) above, are now commonly taken to be structured sets of possible worlds – e.g., the set of worlds *in which* Aristotle's maternal grandmother hates broccoli. And the structure imposed on such a set, corresponding to the intuitive constituent structure of a proposition (as the concepts 'grandmother' and 'hate' are constituents of the foregoing proposition), accounts for the meaning-properties of sentences that express the proposition.

Theories of meaning can also be called *semantics,* as in "Gricean semantics" or "Verificationist semantics," though the term is sometimes restricted to referential and/or truth-conditional theories, which posit meaning-constitutive relations between words and the nonlinguistic world. Semantics is often contrasted with *syntax,* the structure of grammatically permissible ordering relations between words and other words in well-formed sentences, and with *pragmatics,* the

rules governing the use of meaningful expressions in particular speech contexts; but linguists have found that semantic phenomena cannot be kept purely separate either from syntactic or from pragmatic phenomena.

In a still more specialized usage, *linguistic semantics* is the detailed study (typically within the truth-conditional format) of particular types of construction in particular natural languages, e.g., belief-clauses in English or adverbial phrases in Kwakiutl. Linguistic semantics in that sense is practiced by some philosophers of language, by some linguists, and occasionally by both working together. Montague grammar and situation semantics are common formats for such work, both based on intensional logic.

The *theory of reference* is pursued whether or not one accepts either the referential or the truth-conditional theory of meaning. Its main question is: In virtue of what does a linguistic expression designate one or more things in the world? (Prior to theorizing and defining of technical uses, 'designate', 'denote', and 'refer' are used interchangeably.) Denoting expressions are divided into *singular terms,* which purport to designate particular individual things, and *general terms,* which can apply to more than one thing at once. Singular terms include proper names ('Cindy', 'Bangladesh'), definite descriptions ('my brother', 'the first baby born in the New World'), and singular pronouns of various types ('this', 'you', 'she'). General terms include common nouns ('horse', 'trash can'), mass terms ('water', 'graphite'), and plural pronouns ('they', 'those').

The twentieth century's dominant theory of reference has been the *description theory,* the view that linguistic terms refer by expressing descriptive features or properties, the referent being the item or items that in fact possess those properties. For example, a definite description does that directly: 'My brother' denotes whatever person does have the property of being my brother. According to the description theory of proper names, defended most articulately by Russell, such names express identifying properties indirectly by abbreviating definite descriptions. A general term such as 'horse' was thought of as expressing a cluster of properties distinctive of horses; and so forth. But the description theory came under heavy attack in the late 1960s, from Keith Donnellan, Kripke, and Putnam, and was generally abandoned on each of several grounds, in favor of the *causal-historical theory* of reference. The causal-historical idea is that a particular use of a linguistic expression denotes by being etiologically grounded in the thing or group that is its referent; a historical causal chain of a certain shape leads backward in time from the act of referring to the referent(s). More recently, problems with the causal-historical theory as originally formulated have led researchers to backpedal somewhat and incorporate some features of the description theory. Other views of reference have been advocated as well, particularly analogues of some of the theories of meaning listed above – chiefly (2)–(6) and (8).

Modal and propositional-attitude contexts create special problems in the theory of reference, for referring expressions seem to alter their normal semantic behavior when they occur within such contexts. Much ink has been spilled over the question of why and how the substitution of a term for another term having exactly the same referent can change the truth-value of a containing modal or propositional-attitude sentence.

Interestingly, the theory of truth historically predates articulate study of meaning or of reference, for philosophers have always sought the nature of truth. It has often been thought that a *sentence* is true in virtue of expressing a true belief, truth being primarily a property of beliefs rather than of linguistic entities; but the main theories of truth have also been applied to sentences directly. The *correspondence theory* maintains that a sentence is true in virtue of its elements' mirroring a fact or actual state of affairs. The *coherence theory* instead identifies truth as a relation of the true sentence to other sentences, usually an epistemic relation. *Pragmatic* theories have it that truth is a matter either of practical utility or of idealized epistemic warrant. Deflationary views, such as the traditional *redundancy theory* and D. Grover, J. Camp, and N. D. Belnap's *prosentential theory,* deny that truth comes to anything more important or substantive than what is already codified in a recursive Tarskian truth-definition for a language.

Pragmatics studies the use of language in context, and the context-dependence of various aspects of linguistic interpretation. First, one and the same sentence can express different meanings or propositions from context to context, owing to ambiguity or to indexicality or both. An *ambiguous* sentence has more than one meaning, either because one of its component words has more than one meaning (as 'bank' has) or because the sentence admits of more than one possible syntactic analysis ('Visiting doctors can be tedious', 'The mouse tore up the street'). An *indexical* sentence can change in truth-value from context to context owing to the presence of an element whose reference fluctuates, such as a demonstrative pronoun ('She told him off yesterday', 'It's time for that meeting now'). One branch of pragmatics investigates how context determines a single propositional meaning for a sentence on a particular occasion of that sentence's use.

Speech act theory is a second branch of pragmatics that presumes the propositional or "locutionary" meanings of utterances and studies what J. L. Austin called the illocutionary forces of those utterances, the distinctive types of linguistic act that are performed by the speaker in making them. (E.g., in uttering 'I will be there tonight', a speaker might be issuing a warning, uttering a threat, making a promise, or merely offering a prediction, depending on conventional and other social features of the situation. A crude test of illocutionary force is the "hereby" criterion: one's utterance has the force of, say, a warning, if it could fairly have been paraphrased by the corresponding "explicitly performative" sentence beginning 'I hereby warn you that . . .'.) Speech act theory interacts to some extent with semantics, especially in the case of explicit performatives, and it has some fairly dramatic syntactic effects as well.

A third branch of pragmatics (not altogether separate from the second) is the *theory of conversation* or *theory of implicature,* founded in the 1960s by Grice. Grice noted that sentences, when uttered in particular contexts, often generate "implications" that are not logical consequences of those sentences ('Is Jones a good philosopher?' – 'He has very neat handwriting'). Such implications can usually be identified as what the speaker meant in uttering her sentence; thus (for that reason and others), what Grice calls utterer's meaning can diverge sharply from sentence-meaning or "timeless" meaning. To explain those non-logical implications, Grice offered a now widely accepted *theory of conversational implicature.* Conversational implicatures arise from the interaction of the sentence uttered with mutually shared background assumptions and certain principles of efficient and cooperative conversation.

The philosophy of linguistics studies the academic discipline of linguistics, particularly theoretical linguistics considered as a science or purported science; it examines methodology and fundamental assumptions, and also tries to incorporate linguists' findings into the rest of philosophy of language. Theoretical linguistics concentrates on syntax, and took its contemporary form in the 1950s under Zellig Harris and Chomsky: it seeks to describe each natural language in terms of a *generative grammar* for that language, i.e., a set of recursive rules for combining words that will generate all and only the "well-formed strings" or grammatical sentences of that language. The set must be finite and the rules recursive because, while our information-processing resources for recognizing grammatical strings as such are necessarily finite (being subagencies of our brains), there is no limit in any natural language either to the length of a single grammatical sentence or to the number of grammatical sentences; a small device must have infinite generative and parsing capacity. Many grammars work by generating simple "deep structures" (a kind of tree diagram), and then producing multiple "surface structures" as variants of those deep structures, by means of rules that rearrange their parts. The surface structures are syntactic parsings of natural-language sentences, and the deep structures from which they derive encode both basic grammatical relations between the sentences' major constituents and, on some theories, the sentences' main semantic properties as well; thus, sentences that share a deep structure will share some fundamental grammatical properties and all or most of their semantics.

As Paul Ziff and Davidson saw in the 1960s, the foregoing syntactic problem and its solution had semantic analogues. From small resources, human speakers *understand* – compute the meanings of – arbitrarily long and novel sentences without limit, and almost instantaneously. This ability seems to require semantic *compositionality,* the thesis that the meaning of a sentence is a function of the meanings of its semantic primitives or smallest meaningful parts, built up by way of syntactic compounding. Compositionality also seems to be required by learnability, since a normal child can learn an infinitely complex dialect in at most two years, but must learn semantic primitives one at a time.

A grammar for a natural language is commonly taken to be a piece of psychology, part of an explanation of speakers' verbal abilities and behavior. As such, however, it is a considerable idealization: it is a theory of speakers' linguistic "competence" rather than of their actual verbal performance. The latter distinction is required by the fact that speakers' considered, reflective judgments of grammatical correctness do not line up very well with the class of expressions that actually are uttered and understood unreflectively by those same speakers. Some gram-

matical sentences are too hard for speakers to parse quickly; some are too long to finish parsing at all; speakers commonly utter what they know to be formally ungrammatical strings; and real speech is usually fragmentary, interspersed with vocalizations, false starts, and the like. Actual departures from formal grammaticality are ascribed by linguists to "performance limitations," i.e., psychological factors such as memory failure, weak computational capacity, or heedlessness; thus, actual verbal behavior is to be explained as resulting from the perturbation of competence by performance limitations.

    See also GRAMMAR, MEANING, SPEECH ACT THEORY, THEORY OF DESCRIPTIONS, TRUTH.

                            W.G.L.

philosophy of law, also called general jurisprudence, the study of conceptual and theoretical problems concerning the nature of law as such, or common to any legal system.

    Problems in the philosophy of law fall roughly into two groups. The first contains problems internal to law and legal systems as such. These include (a) the nature of legal rules; the conditions under which they can be said to exist and to influence practice; their normative character, as mandatory or advisory; and the (in)determinacy of their language; (b) the structure and logical character of legal norms; the analysis of legal principles as a class of legal norms; and the relation between the normative force of law and coercion; (c) the identity conditions for legal systems; when a legal system exists; and when one legal system ends and another begins; (d) the nature of the reasoning used by courts in adjudicating cases; (e) the justification of legal decisions; whether legal justification is through a chain of inferences or by the coherence of norms and decisions; and the relation between intralegal and extralegal justification; (f) the nature of legal validity and of what makes a norm a valid law; the relation between validity and efficacy, the fact that the norms of a legal system are obeyed by the norm-subjects; (g) properties of legal systems, including comprehensiveness (the claim to regulate any behavior) and completeness (the absence of gaps in the law); (h) legal rights; under what conditions citizens possess them; and their analytical structure as protected normative positions; (i) legal interpretation; whether it is a pervasive feature of law or is found only in certain kinds of adjudication; its rationality or otherwise; and its essentially ideological character or otherwise.

    The second group of problems concerns the

relation between law as one particular social institution in a society and the wider political and moral life of that society: (a) the nature of legal obligation; whether there is an obligation, prima facie or final, to obey the law as such; whether there is an obligation to obey the law only when certain standards are met, and if so, what those standards might be; (b) the authority of law; and the conditions under which a legal system has political or moral authority or legitimacy; (c) the functions of law; whether there are functions performed by a legal system in a society that are internal to the design of law; and analyses from the perspective of political morality of the functioning of legal systems; (d) the legal concept of responsibility; its analysis and its relation to moral and political concepts of responsibility; in particular, the place of mental elements and causal elements in the assignment of responsibility, and the analysis of those elements; (e) the analysis and justification of legal punishment; (f) legal liberty, and the proper limits or otherwise of the intrusion of the legal system into individual liberty; the plausibility of legal moralism; (g) the relation between law and justice, and the role of a legal system in the maintenance of social justice; (h) the relation between legal rights and political or moral rights; (i) the status of legal reasoning as a species of practical reasoning; and the relation between law and practical reason; (j) law and economics; whether legal decision making in fact tracks, or otherwise ought to track, economic efficiency; (k) legal systems as sources of and embodiments of political power; and law as essentially gendered, or imbued with race or class biases, or otherwise.

Theoretical positions in the philosophy of law tend to group into three large kinds – legal positivism, natural law, and legal realism. Legal positivism concentrates on the first set of problems, and typically gives formal or content-independent solutions to such problems. For example, legal positivism tends to regard legal validity as a property of a legal rule that the rule derives merely from its formal relation to other legal rules; a morally iniquitous law is still for legal positivism a valid legal rule if it satisfies the required formal existence conditions. Legal rights exist as normative consequences of valid legal rules; no questions of the status of the right from the point of view of political morality arise. Legal positivism does not deny the importance of the second set of problems, but assigns the task of treating them to other disciplines – political philosophy, moral philosophy, sociology, psychology, and so forth. Questions of how society should design its legal institutions, for legal positivism, are not technically speaking problems in the philosophy of law, although many legal positivists have presented their theories about such questions.

Natural law theory and legal realism, by contrast, regard the sharp distinction between the two kinds of problem as an artifact of legal positivism itself. Their answers to the first set of problems tend to be substantive or content-dependent. Natural law theory, for example, would regard the question of whether a law was consonant with practical reason, or whether a legal system was morally and politically legitimate, as in whole or in part determinative of the issue of legal validity, or of whether a legal norm granted a legal right. The theory would regard the relation between a legal system and liberty or justice as in whole or in part determinative of the normative force and the justification for that system and its laws. Legal realism, especially in its contemporary politicized form, sees the claimed role of the law in legitimizing certain gender, race, or class interests as the prime salient property of law for theoretical analysis, and questions of the determinacy of legal rules or of legal interpretation or legal right as of value only in the service of the project of explaining the political power of law and legal systems.

See also DWORKIN, HART, JURISPRUDENCE, LEGAL MORALISM, LEGAL POSITIVISM, LEGAL REALISM, NATURAL LAW, POLITICAL PHILOSOPHY.   R.A.Sh.

philosophy of liberation. See LATIN AMERICAN PHILOSOPHY.

philosophy of linguistics. See PHILOSOPHY OF LANGUAGE.

philosophy of literature, literary theory. However, while the literary theorist, who is often a literary critic, is primarily interested in the conceptual foundations of practical criticism, philosophy of literature, usually done by philosophers, is more often concerned to place literature in the context of a philosophical system. Plato's dialogues have much to say about poetry, mostly by way of aligning it with Plato's metaphysical, epistemological, and ethico-political views. Aristotle's *Poetics*, the earliest example of literary theory in the West, is also an attempt to accommodate the practice of Greek poets to Aristotle's philosophical system as a whole. Drawing on the thought of philosophers like Kant and Schelling, Samuel Taylor Coleridge offers in his *Biographia*

Literaria a philosophy of literature that is to Romantic poetics what Aristotle's treatise is to classical poetics: a literary theory that is confirmed both by the poets whose work it legitimates and by the metaphysics that recommends it. Many philosophers, among them Hume, Schopenhauer, Heidegger, and Sartre, have tried to make room for literature in their philosophical edifices. Some philosophers, e.g., the German Romantics, have made literature (and the other arts) the cornerstone of philosophy itself. (See Philippe Lacoue-Labarthe and Jean-Luc Nancy, *The Literary Absolute,* 1988.)

Sometimes 'philosophy of literature' is understood in a second sense: philosophy *and* literature; i.e., philosophy and literature taken to be distinct and essentially autonomous activities that may nonetheless sustain determinate relations to each other. Philosophy of literature, understood in this way, is the attempt to identify the *differentiae* that distinguish philosophy from literature and to specify their relationships to each other. Sometimes the two are distinguished by their subject matter (e.g., philosophy deals with objective structures, literature with subjectivity), sometimes by their methods (philosophy is an act of reason, literature the product of imagination, inspiration, or the unconscious), sometimes by their effects (philosophy produces knowledge, literature produces emotional fulfillment or release), etc. Their relationships then tend to occupy the area(s) in which they are not essentially distinct. If their subject matters are distinct, their effects may be the same (philosophy and literature both produce understanding, the one of fact and the other of feeling); if their methods are distinct, they may be approaching the same subject matter in different ways; and so on. For Aquinas, e.g., philosophy and poetry may deal with the same objects, the one communicating truth about the object in syllogistic form, the other inspiring feelings about it through figurative language. For Heidegger, the philosopher investigates the meaning of being while the poet names the holy, but their preoccupations tend to converge at the deepest levels of thinking. For Sartre, literature is philosophy *engagé,* existential-political activity in the service of freedom.

'Philosophy of literature' may also be taken in a third sense: philosophy *in* literature, the attempt to discover matters of philosophical interest and value in literary texts. The philosopher may undertake to identify, examine, and evaluate the philosophical content of literary texts that contain expressions of philosophical ideas and discussions of philosophical prob-

lems – e.g., the debates on free will and theodicy in Fyodor Dostoevsky's *The Brothers Karamazov.* Many if not most college courses on philosophy of literature are taught from this point of view. Much interesting and important work has been done in this vein; e.g., Santayana's *Three Philosophical Poets* (1910), Cavell's essays on Emerson and Thoreau, and Nussbaum's *Love's Knowledge* (1989). It should be noted, however, that to approach the matter in this way presupposes that literature and philosophy are simply different forms of the same content: what philosophy expresses in the form of argument literature expresses in lyric, dramatic, or narrative form. The philosopher's treatment of literature implies that he is uniquely positioned to explicate the subject matter treated in both literary and philosophical texts, and that the language of philosophy gives optimal expression to a content less adequately expressed in the language of literature. The model for this approach may well be Hegel's *Phenomenology of Spirit,* which treats art (along with religion) as imperfect adumbrations of a truth that is fully and properly articulated only in the conceptual mode of philosophical dialectic.

Dissatisfaction with this presupposition (and its implicit privileging of philosophy over literature) has led to a different view of the relation between philosophy and literature and so to a different program for philosophy of literature. The self-consciously literary form of Kierkegaard's writing is an integral part of his polemic against the philosophical imperialism of the Hegelians. In this century, the work of philosophers like Derrida and the philosophers and critics who follow his lead suggests that it is mistaken to regard philosophy and literature as alternative expressions of an identical content, and seriously mistaken to think of philosophy as the master discourse, the "proper" expression of a content "improperly" expressed in literature. All texts, on this view, have a "literary" form, the texts of philosophers as well as the texts of novelists and poets, and their content is internally determined by their "means of expression." There is just as much "literature in philosophy" as there is "philosophy in literature." Consequently, the philosopher of literature may no longer be able simply to extract philosophical matter from literary form. Rather, the modes of literary expression confront the philosopher with problems that bear on the presuppositions of his own enterprise. E.g., fictional mimesis (especially in the works of postmodern writers) raises questions about the possibility and the presumed normativeness of factual representation, and in so doing tends to undermine the traditional hierarchy that elevates "fact" over "fiction."

Philosophers' perplexity over the truth-value of fictional statements is an example of the kind of problems the study of literature can create for the practice of philosophy (see Rorty, *Consequences of Pragmatism,* 1982, ch. 7). Or again, the self-reflexivity of contemporary literary texts can lead philosophers to reflect critically on their own undertaking and may seriously unsettle traditional notions of self-referentiality. When it is not regarded as another, attractive but perhaps inferior source of philosophical ideas, literature presents the philosopher with epistemological, metaphysical, and methodological problems not encountered in the course of "normal" philosophizing.

See also AESTHETICS, LITERARY THEORY, POSTMODERN.   L.H.M.

philosophy of logic, the arena of philosophy devoted to examining the scope and nature of logic. Aristotle considered logic an organon, or foundation, of knowledge. Certainly, inference is the source of much human knowledge. Logic judges inferences good or bad and tries to justify those that are good. One need not agree with Aristotle, therefore, to see logic as essential to epistemology. Philosophers such as Wittgenstein, additionally, have held that the structure of language reflects the structure of the world. Because inferences have elements that are themselves linguistic or are at least expressible in language, logic reveals general features of the structure of language. This makes it essential to linguistics, and, on a Wittgensteinian view, to metaphysics. Moreover, many philosophical battles have been fought with logical weaponry. For all these reasons, philosophers have tried to understand what logic is, what justifies it, and what it tells us about reason, language, and the world.

The nature of logic. Logic might be defined as the science of inference; inference, in turn, as the drawing of a conclusion from premises. A simple argument is a sequence, one element of which, the conclusion, the others are thought to support. A complex argument is a series of simple arguments. Logic, then, is primarily concerned with arguments. Already, however, several questions arise. (1) Who thinks that the premises support the conclusion? The speaker? The audience? Any competent speaker of the language? (2) What are the elements of arguments?

Thoughts? Propositions? Philosophers following Quine have found these answers unappealing for lack of clear identity criteria. Sentences are more concrete and more sharply individuated. But should we consider sentence tokens or sentence types? Context often affects interpretation, so it appears that we must consider tokens or types-in-context. Moreover, many sentences, even with contextual information supplied, are ambiguous. Is a sequence with an ambiguous sentence one argument (which may be good on some readings and bad on others) or several? For reasons that will become clear, the elements of arguments should be the primary bearers of truth and falsehood in one's general theory of language. (3) Finally, and perhaps most importantly, what does 'support' mean?

Logic evaluates inferences by distinguishing good from bad arguments. This raises issues about the status of logic, for many of its pronouncements are explicitly normative. The philosophy of logic thus includes problems of the nature and justification of norms akin to those arising in metaethics. The solutions, moreover, may vary with the logical system at hand. Some logicians attempt to characterize reasoning in natural language; others try to systematize reasoning in mathematics or other sciences. Still others try to devise an ideal system of reasoning that does not fully correspond to any of these. Logicians concerned with inference in natural, mathematical, or scientific languages tend to justify their norms by describing inferential practices in that language as actually used by those competent in it. These descriptions justify norms partly because the practices they describe include evaluations of inferences as well as inferences themselves.

The scope of logic. Logical systems meant to account for natural language inference raise issues of the scope of logic. How does logic differ from semantics, the science of meaning in general? Logicians have often treated only inferences turning on certain commonly used words, such as 'not', 'if', 'and', 'or', 'all', and 'some', taking them, or items in a symbolic language that correspond to them, as logical constants. They have neglected inferences that do not turn on them, such as

My brother is married.
Therefore, I have a sister-in-law.

Increasingly, however, semanticists have used 'logic' more broadly, speaking of the logic of belief, perception, abstraction, or even kinship.

Such uses seem to treat logic and semantics as coextensive. Philosophers who have sought to maintain a distinction between the semantics and logic of natural language have tried to develop non-arbitrary criteria of logical constancy.

An argument is valid provided the truth of its premises guarantees the truth of its conclusion. This definition relies on the notion of truth, which raises philosophical puzzles of its own. Furthermore, it is natural to ask what kind of connection must hold between the premises and conclusion. One answer specifies that an argument is valid provided replacing its simple constituents with items of similar categories while leaving logical constants intact could never produce true premises and a false conclusion. On this view, validity is a matter of form: an argument is valid if it instantiates a valid form. Logic thus becomes the theory of logical form. On another view, an argument is valid if its conclusion is true in every possible world or model in which its premises are true. This conception need not rely on the notion of a logical constant and so is compatible with the view that logic and semantics are coextensive.

Many issues in the philosophy of logic arise from the plethora of systems logicians have devised. Some of these are *deviant logics*, i.e., logics that differ from classical or standard logic while seeming to treat the same subject matter. Intuitionistic logic, for example, which interprets the connectives and quantifiers non-classically, rejecting the law of excluded middle and the interdefinability of the quantifiers, has been supported with both semantic and ontological arguments. Brouwer, Heyting, and others have defended it as the proper logic of the infinite; Dummett has defended it as the correct logic of natural language. Free logic allows non-denoting referring expressions but interprets the quantifiers as ranging only over existing objects. Many-valued logics use at least three truth-values, rejecting the classical assumption of bivalence – that every formula is either true or false.

Many logical systems attempt to extend classical logic to incorporate tense, modality, abstraction, higher-order quantification, propositional quantification, complement constructions, or the truth predicate. These projects raise important philosophical questions.

Modal and tense logics. Tense is a pervasive feature of natural language, and has become important to computer scientists interested in con-

current programs. Modalities of several sorts – alethic (possibility, necessity) and deontic (obligation, permission), for example – appear in natural language in various grammatical guises. Provability, treated as a modality, allows for revealing formalizations of metamathematics.

Logicians have usually treated modalities and tenses as sentential operators. C. I. Lewis and Langford pioneered such approaches for alethic modalities; von Wright, for deontic modalities; and Prior, for tense. In each area, many competing systems developed; by the late 1970s, there were over two hundred axiom systems in the literature for propositional alethic modal logic alone.

How might competing systems be evaluated? Kripke's semantics for modal logic has proved very helpful. Kripke semantics in effect treats modal operators as quantifiers over possible worlds. Necessarily *A*, e.g., is true at a world if and only if *A* is true in all worlds accessible from that world. Kripke showed that certain popular axiom systems result from imposing simple conditions on the accessibility relation. His work spawned a field, known as correspondence theory, devoted to studying the relations between modal axioms and conditions on models. It has helped philosophers and logicians to understand the issues at stake in choosing a modal logic and has raised the question of whether there is one true modal logic. Modal idioms may be ambiguous or indeterminate with respect to some properties of the accessibility relation. Possible worlds raise additional ontological and epistemological questions.

Modalities and tenses seem to be linked in natural language, but attempts to bring tense and modal logic together remain young. The sensitivity of tense to intra- and extralinguistic context has cast doubt on the project of using operators to represent tenses. Kamp, e.g., has represented tense and aspect in terms of event structure, building on earlier work by Reichenbach.

Truth. Tarski's theory of truth shows that it is possible to define truth recursively for certain languages. Languages that can refer to their own sentences, however, permit no such definition given Tarski's assumptions – for they allow the formulation of the liar and similar paradoxes. Tarski concluded that, in giving the semantics for such a language, we must ascend to a more powerful metalanguage. Kripke and others, however, have shown that it is possible for a language permitting self-reference to contain its own truth predicate by surrendering bivalence or taking the truth predicate indexically.

Higher-order logic. First-order predicate logic allows quantification only over individuals. Higher-order logics also permit quantification over predicate positions. Natural language seems to permit such quantification: 'Mary has every quality that John admires'. Mathematics, moreover, may be expressed elegantly in higher-order logic. Peano arithmetic and Zermelo-Fraenkel set theory, e.g., require infinite axiom sets in first-order logic but are finitely axiomatizable – and categorical, determining their models up to isomorphism – in second-order logic.

Because they quantify over properties and relations, higher-order logics seem committed to Platonism. Mathematics reduces to higher-order logic; Quine concludes that the latter is not logic. Its most natural semantics seems to presuppose a prior understanding of properties and relations. Also, on this semantics, it differs greatly from first-order logic. Like set theory, it is incomplete; it is not compact. This raises questions about the boundaries of logic. Must logic be axiomatizable? Must it be possible, i.e., to develop a logical system powerful enough to prove every valid argument valid? Could there be valid arguments with infinitely many premises, any finite fragment of which would be invalid?

With an operator for forming abstract terms from predicates, higher-order logics easily allow the formulation of paradoxes. Russell and Whitehead for this reason adopted type theory, which, like Tarski's theory of truth, uses an infinite hierarchy and corresponding syntactic restrictions to avoid paradox. Type-free theories avoid both the restrictions and the paradoxes, as with truth, by rejecting bivalence or by understanding abstraction indexically.

See also, FORMAL LOGIC, FREE LOGIC, MODAL LOGIC, RELEVANCE LOGIC, TENSE LOGIC, TYPE THEORY.   D.Bo.

philosophy of mathematics, the study of ontological and epistemological problems raised by the content and practice of mathematics. The present agenda in this field evolved from critical developments, notably the collapse of Pythagoreanism, the development of modern calculus, and an early twentieth-century foundational crisis, which forced mathematicians and philosophers to examine mathematical methods and presuppositions.

Greek mathematics. The Pythagoreans, who represented the height of early demonstrative Greek mathematics, believed that all scientific relations were measureable by natural numbers (1, 2, 3, etc.) or ratios of natural numbers, and thus they assumed discrete, atomic units for the measurement of space, time, and motion. The discovery of irrational magnitudes scotched the first of these beliefs. Zeno's paradoxes showed that the second was incompatible with the natural assumption that space and time are infinitely divisible. The Greek reaction, ultimately codified in Euclid's *Elements,* included Plato's separation of mathematics from empirical science and, within mathematics, distinguished *number theory* – a study of discretely ordered entities – from geometry, which concerns continua. Following Aristotle (and employing methods perfected by Eudoxus), Euclid's proofs used only "potentially infinite" geometric and arithmetic procedures. The *Elements'* axiomatic form and its constructive proofs set a standard for future mathematics. Moreover, its dependence on visual intuition (whose consequent deductive gaps were already noted by Archimedes), together with the challenge of Euclid's infamous fifth postulate (about parallel lines), and the famous unsolved problems of compass and straightedge construction, established an agenda for generations of mathematicians.

The calculus. The two millennia following Euclid saw new analytical tools (e.g., Descartes's geometry) that wedded arithmetic and geometric considerations and toyed with infinitesimally small quantities. These, together with the demands of physical application, tempted mathematicians to abandon the pristine Greek dichotomies. Matters came to a head with Newton's and Leibniz's (almost simultaneous) discovery of the powerful computational techniques of the calculus. While these unified physical science in an unprecedented way, their dependence on unclear notions of infinitesimal spatial and temporal increments emphasized their shaky philosophical foundation. Berkeley, for instance, condemned the calculus for its unintuitability. However, this time the power of the new methods inspired a decidedly conservative response. Kant, in particular, tried to anchor the new mathematics in intuition. Mathematicians, he claimed, construct their objects in the "pure intuitions" of space and time. And these mathematical objects are the a priori forms of transcendentally ideal empirical objects. For Kant this combination of epistemic empiricism and ontological idealism explained the physical applicability of mathematics and thus granted "objective validity" (i.e., scientific legitimacy) to mathematical procedures.

Two nineteenth-century developments undercut this Kantian constructivism in favor of a more abstract conceptual picture of mathematics. First, Jànos Bolyai, Carl F. Gauss, Bernhard Riemann, Nikolai Lobachevsky, and others produced consistent non-Euclidean geometries, which undid the Kantian picture of a single a priori science of space, and once again opened a rift between pure mathematics and its physical applications. Second, Cantor and Dedekind defined the real numbers (i.e., the elements of the continuum) as infinite sets of rational (and ultimately natural) numbers. Thus they founded mathematics on the concepts of infinite set and natural number. Cantor's set theory made the first concept rigorously mathematical; while Peano and Frege (both of whom advocated securing rigor by using formal languages) did that for the second. Peano axiomatized number theory, and Frege ontologically reduced the natural numbers to sets (indeed sets that are the extensions of purely logical concepts). Frege's Platonistic conception of numbers as unintuitable objects and his claim that mathematical truths follow analytically from purely logical definitions – the thesis of *logicism* – are both highly anti-Kantian.

Foundational crisis and movements. But anti-Kantianism had its own problems. For one thing, Leopold Kronecker, who (following Peter Dirichlet) wanted mathematics reduced to arithmetic and no further, attacked Cantor's abstract set theory on doctrinal grounds. Worse yet, the discovery of internal antinomies challenged the very consistency of abstract foundations. The most famous of these, Russell's paradox (the set of all sets that are not members of themselves both is and isn't a member of itself), undermined Frege's basic assumption that every well-formed concept has an extension. This was a full-scale crisis. To be sure, Russell himself (together with Whitehead) preserved the logicist foundational approach by organizing the universe of sets into a hierarchy of levels so that no set can be a member of itself. (This is type theory.) However, the crisis encouraged two explicitly Kantian foundational projects. The first, Hilbert's Program, attempted to secure the "ideal" (i.e., infinitary) parts of mathematics by formalizing them and then proving the resultant formal systems to be conservative (and hence consistent) extensions of finitary theories. Since the proof itself was to

use no reasoning more complicated than simple numerical calculations – *finitary reasoning* – the whole metamathematical project belonged to the untainted ("contentual") part of mathematics. Finitary reasoning was supposed to update Kant's intuition-based epistemology, and Hilbert's consistency proofs mimic Kant's notion of objective validity. The second project, Brouwer's intuitionism, rejected formalization, and was not only epistemologically Kantian (resting mathematical reasoning on the a priori intuition of time), but ontologically Kantian as well. For intuitionism generated both the natural and the real numbers by temporally ordered conscious acts. The reals, in particular, stem from choice sequences, which exploit Brouwer's epistemic assumptions about the open future.

These foundational movements ultimately failed. Type theory required ad hoc axioms to express the real numbers; Hilbert's Program foundered on Gödel's theorems; and intuitionism remained on the fringes because it rejected classical logic and standard mathematics. Nevertheless the legacy of these movements – their formal methods, indeed their philosophical agenda – still characterizes modern research on the ontology and epistemology of mathematics. Set theory, e.g. (despite recent challenges from category theory), is the lingua franca of modern mathematics. And formal languages with their precise semantics are ubiquitous in technical and philosophical discussions. Indeed, even intuitionistic mathematics has been formalized, and Michael Dummett has recast its ontological idealism as a semantic antirealism that defines truth as warranted assertability. In a similar semantic vein, Paul Benacerraf proposed that the philosophical problem with Hilbert's approach is inability to provide a uniform realistic (i.e., referential, non-epistemic) semantics for the allegedly ideal and contentual parts of mathematics; and the problem with Platonism is that its semantics makes its objects unknowable.

Ontological issues. From this modern perspective, the simplest realism is the outright Platonism that attributes a standard model consisting of "independent" objects to classical theories expressed in a first-order language (i.e., a language whose quantifiers range over objects but not properties). But in fact realism admits variations on each aspect. For one thing, the Löwenheim-Skolem theorem shows that formalized theories can have non-standard models. There are expansive non-standard models: Abraham Robinson, e.g., used infinitary non-standard models of Peano's axioms to rigorously reintroduce infinitesimals. (Roughly, an infinitesimal is the reciprocal of an infinite element in such a model.) And there are also "constructive" models, whose objects must be explicitly definable. Predicative theories (inspired by Poincaré and Hermann Weyl), whose stage-by-stage definitions refer only to previously defined objects, produce one variety of such models. Gödel's constructive universe, which uses less restricted definitions to model apparently non-constructive axioms like the axiom of choice, exemplifies another variety. But there are also views (various forms of structuralism) which deny that formal theories have unique standard models at all. These views – inspired by the fact, already sensed by Dedekind, that there are multiple equivalid realizations of formal arithmetic – allow a mathematical theory to characterize only a broad family of models and deny unique reference to mathematical terms. Finally, some realistic approaches advocate formalization in second-order languages, and some eschew ordinary semantics altogether in favor of substitutional quantification. (These latter are still realistic, for they still distinguish truth from knowledge.)

Strict *finitists* – inspired by Wittgenstein's more stringent epistemic constraints – reject even the open-futured objects admitted by Brouwer, and countenance only finite (or even only "feasible") objects. In the other direction, A. A. Markov and his school in Russia introduced a syntactic notion of algorithm from which they developed the field of "constructive analysis." And the American mathematician Errett Bishop, starting from a Brouwer-like disenchantment with mathematical realism and with strictly formal approaches, recovered large parts of classical analysis within a non-formal constructive framework.

All of these approaches assume abstract (i.e., causally isolated) mathematical objects, and thus they have difficulty explaining the wide applicability of mathematics (constructive or otherwise) within empirical science. One response, Quine's "indispensability" view, integrates mathematical theories into the general network of empirical science. For Quine, mathematical objects – just like ordinary physical objects – exist simply in virtue of being referents for terms in our best scientific theory. By contrast Hartry Field, who denies that any abstract objects exist, also denies that any purely mathematical assertions are literally true. Field attempts to recast physical science in a relational language without mathematical terms and then use Hilbert-style conservative extension results to explain the evident utility of abstract mathematics. Hilary Putnam and Charles Parsons have each suggested views according to which mathematics has no objects proper to itself, but rather concerns only the possibilities of physical constructions. Recently, Geoffrey Hellman has combined this modal approach with structuralism.

Epistemological issues. The equivalence (proved in the 1930s) of several different representations of computability to the reasoning representable in elementary formalized arithmetic led Alonzo Church to suggest that the notion of finitary reasoning had been precisely defined. Church's thesis (so named by Stephen Kleene) inspired Georg Kreisel's investigations (in the 1960s and 70s) of the general conditions for rigorously analyzing other informal philosophical notions like semantic consequence, Brouwerian choice sequences, and the very notion of a set. Solomon Feferman has suggested more recently that this sort of piecemeal conceptual analysis is already present in mathematics; and that this rather than any global foundation is the true role of foundational research. In this spirit, the relative consistency arguments of modern proof theory (a continuation of Hilbert's Program) provide information about the epistemic grounds of various mathematical theories. Thus, on the one hand, proofs that a seemingly problematic mathematical theory is a conservative extension of a more secure theory provide some epistemic support for the former. In the other direction, the fact that classical number theory is consistent relative to intuitionistic number theory shows (contra Hilbert) that his view of constructive reasoning must differ from that of the intuitionists.

Gödel, who did not believe that mathematics required any ties to empirical perception, suggested nevertheless that we have a special non-sensory faculty of mathematical intuition that, when properly cultivated, can help us decide among formally independent propositions of set theory and other branches of mathematics. Charles Parsons, in contrast, has examined the place of perception-like intuition in mathematical reasoning. Parsons himself has investigated models of arithmetic and of set theory composed of quasi-concrete objects (e.g., numerals and other signs). Others (consistent with some of Parsons's observations) have given a Husserl-style phenomenological analysis of mathematical intuition.

Frege's influence encouraged the logical positivists and other philosophers to view mathematical knowledge as analytic or conventional.

Poincaré responded that the principle of mathematical induction could not be analytic, and Wittgenstein also attacked this conventionalism. In recent years, various formal independence results and Quine's attack on analyticity have encouraged philosophers and historians of mathematics to focus on cases of mathematical knowledge that do not stem from conceptual analysis or strict formal provability. Some writers (notably Mark Steiner and Philip Kitcher) emphasize the analogies between empirical and mathematical discovery. They stress such things as conceptual evolution in mathematics and instances of mathematical generalizations supported by individual cases. Kitcher, in particular, discusses the analogy between axiomatization in mathematics and theoretical unification. Penelope Maddy has investigated the intramathematical grounds underlying the acceptance of various axioms of set theory. More generally, Imre Lakatos argued that most mathematical progress stems from a concept-stretching process of conjecture, refutation, and proof. This view has spawned a historical debate about whether critical developments such as those mentioned above represent Kuhn-style revolutions or even crises, or whether they are natural conceptual advances in a uniformly growing science.

See also CALCULUS, GÖDEL'S INCOMPLETENESS THEOREMS, HILBERT'S PROGRAM, LOGICISM, MATHEMATICAL INTUITIONISM, SET THEORY.   C.J.P.

philosophy of mind, the branch of philosophy that includes the philosophy of psychology, philosophical psychology, and the area of metaphysics concerned with the nature of mental phenomena and how they fit into the causal structure of reality. Philosophy of psychology, a branch of the philosophy of science, examines what psychology says about the nature of psychological phenomena; examines aspects of psychological theorizing such as the models used, explanations offered, and laws invoked; and examines how psychology fits with the social sciences and natural sciences. Philosophical psychology investigates folk psychology, a body of commonsensical, protoscientific views about mental phenomena. Such investigations attempt to articulate and refine views found in folk psychology about conceptualization, memory, perception, sensation, consciousness, belief, desire, intention, reasoning, action, and so on. The *mind–body problem,* a central metaphysical one in the philosophy of mind, is the problem of whether mental phenomena are physical and, if not, how they are related to physical phenomena. Other metaphysical problems in the philosophy of mind include the free will problem, the problem of personal identity, and the problem of how, if at all, irrational phenomena such as *akrasia* and self-deception are possible.

Mind–body dualism

Cartesian dualism. The doctrine that the soul is distinct from the body is found in Plato and discussed throughout the history of philosophy, but Descartes is considered the father of the modern mind–body problem. He maintained that the essence of the physical is extension in space. Minds are unextended substances and thus are distinct from any physical substances. The essence of a mental substance is to think. This twofold view is called *Cartesian dualism.* Descartes was well aware of an intimate relationship between mind and the brain. (There is no a priori reason to think that the mind is intimately related to the brain; Aristotle, e.g., did not associate them.) Descartes (mistakenly) thought the seat of the relationship was in the *pineal gland.* He maintained, however, that our minds are not our brains, lack spatial location, and can continue to exist after the death and destruction of our bodies.

Cartesian dualism invites the question: What connects the mind and brain? Causation is Descartes's answer: states of our minds causally interact with states of our brains. When bodily sensations such as aches, pains, itches, and tickles cause us to moan, wince, scratch, or laugh, they do so by causing brain states (events, processes), which in turn cause bodily movements. In deliberate action, we act on our desires, motives, and intentions to carry out our purposes; and acting on these mental states involves their causing brain states, which in turn cause our bodies to move, thereby causally influencing the physical world. The physical world, in turn, influences our minds through its influence on our brains. Perception of the physical world with five senses – sight, hearing, smell, taste, and touch – involves causal transactions from the physical to the mental: what we perceive (i.e., see, hear, etc.) causes a sense experience (i.e., a visual experience, aural experience, etc.). Thus, Descartes held that there is two-way psychophysical causal interaction: from the mental to the physical (as in action) and from the physical to the mental (as in perception). The conjunction of Cartesian dualism and the doctrine of two-way psychophysical causal interaction is called *Cartesian interactionism.*

Perhaps the most widely discussed difficulty for this view is how states of a non-spatial substance (a mind) can causally interact with states of a substance that is in space (a brain). Such interactions have seemed utterly mysterious to many philosophers. Mystery would remain even if an unextended mind is locatable at a point in space (say, the center of the pineal gland). For Cartesian interactionism would still have to maintain that causal transactions between mental states and brain states are fundamental, i.e., unmediated by any underlying mechanism. Brain states causally interact with mental states, but there is no answer to the question of how they do so. The interactions are brute facts. Many philosophers, including many of Descartes's contemporaries, have found that difficult to accept.

Parallelism. Malebranche and Leibniz, among others, rejected the possibility of psychophysical causal interaction. They espoused versions of *parallelism:* the view that the mental and physical realms run in parallel, in that types of mental phenomena co-occur with certain types of physical phenomena, but these co-occurrences never involve causal interactions. On all extant versions, the parallels hold because of God's creation. Leibniz's parallelism is *preestablished harmony:* the explanation of why mental types and certain physical types co-occur is that in the possible world God actualized (i.e., this world) they co-occur. In discussing the relation between the mental and physical realms, Leibniz used the analogy of two synchronized but unconnected clocks. The analogy is, however, somewhat misleading; suggesting causal mechanisms internal to each clock and intramental and intraphysical (causal) transactions. But Leibniz's monadology doctrine excludes the possibility of such transactions: mental and physical phenomena have no effects even within their own realms. Malebranche is associated with occasionalism, according to which only God, through his continuous activities, causes things to happen: non-divine phenomena never cause anything. Occasionalism differs from preestablished harmony in holding that God is continually engaged in acts of creation; each moment creating the world anew, in such a way that the correlations hold.

Both brands of parallelism face formidable difficulties. First, both rest on highly contentious, obscure theological hypotheses. The contention that God exists and the creation stories in question require extensive defense and explanation. God's relationship to the world can seem at least as mysterious as the relationship Descartes posits between minds and brains. Second, since parallelism denies the possibility of psychophysical interaction, its proponents must offer alternatives to the causal theory of perception and the causal theory of action or else deny that we can perceive and that we can act intentionally. Third, since parallelism rejects intramental causation, it must either deny that reasoning is possible or explain how it is possible without causal connections between thoughts. Fourth, since parallelism rejects physical transactions, it is hard to see how it can allow, e.g., that one physical thing ever moves another; for that would require causing a change in location. Perhaps none of these weighty difficulties is ultimately insuperable; in any case, parallelism has been abandoned.

Epiphenomenalism. Empirical research gives every indication that the occurrence of any brain state can, in principle, be causally explained by appeal solely to other physical states. To accommodate this, some philosophers espoused *epiphenomenalism,* the doctrine that physical states cause mental states, but mental states do not cause anything. (This thesis was discussed under the name 'conscious automatism' by Huxley and Hogeson in the late nineteenth century. William James was the first to use the term 'epiphenomena' to mean phenomena that lack causal efficacy. And James Ward coined the term 'epiphenomenalism' in 1903.) Epiphenomenalism implies that there is only one-way psychophysical action – from the physical to the mental. Since epiphenomenalism allows such causal action, it can embrace the causal theory of perception. However, when combined with Cartesian dualism, epiphenomenalism, like Cartesian interactionism, implies the problematic thesis that states of an extended substance can affect states of an unextended substance. An epiphenomenalist can avoid this problem by rejecting the view that the mind is an unextended substance while maintaining that mental states and events are nonetheless distinct from physical states and events. Still, formidable problems would remain. It is hard to see how epiphenomenalism can allow that we are ever intentional agents. For intentional agency requires acting on reasons, which, according to the causal theory of action, requires a causal connection between reasons and actions. Since epiphenomenalism denies that such causal connections are possible, it must either maintain that our sense of agency is illusory or offer an alternative to the causal theory of action. Similarly, it must explain how thinking is possible given that there are no causal connections between thoughts.

Monism

The dual-aspect theory.
Many philosophers reject Descartes's bifurcation of reality into mental and physical substances. Spinoza held a *dual-attribute theory* – also called the *dual-aspect theory* – according to which the mental and the physical are distinct modes of a single substance, God. The mental and the physical are only two of infinitely many modes of this one substance. Many philosophers opted for a thoroughgoing *monism,* according to which all of reality is really of one kind. Materialism, idealism, and neutral monism are three brands of monism. Hobbes, a contemporary of Descartes, espoused *materialism,* the brand of monism according to which everything is material or physical. Berkeley is associated with *idealism,* the brand of monism according to which everything is mental. He held that both mental and physical phenomena are perceptions in the mind of God. For Hegel's idealism, everything is part of the World Spirit. The early twentieth-century British philosophers Bradley and McTaggart also held a version of idealism. *Neutral monism* is the doctrine that all of reality is ultimately of one kind, which is neither mental nor physical. Hume was a neutral monist, maintaining that mental and physical substances are really just bundles of the neutral entities. Versions of neutral monism were later held by Mach and, for a short time, Russell. Russell called his neutral entities sensibilia and claimed that minds and physical objects are logical constructions out of them.

Phenomenalism. This view, espoused in the twentieth century by, among others, Ayer, argues that all empirical statements are synonymous with statements solely about phenomenal appearances. While the doctrine is about statements, phenomenalism is either a neutral monism or an idealism, depending on whether phenomenal appearances are claimed to be neither mental nor physical or, instead, mental. The required translations of physical statements into phenomenal ones proved not to be forthcoming, however. Chisholm offered a reason why they would not be: what appearances a physical state of affairs (e.g., objects arrayed in a room) has depends both on physical conditions of observation (e.g., lighting) and physical conditions of the perceiver (e.g., of the nervous system). At best, a statement solely about phenomenal appearances is equivalent to one about a physical state of affairs, only when certain physical conditions of observation and certain physical conditions of the perceiver obtain.

Materialism. Two problems face any monism: it must characterize the phenomena it takes as basic, and it must explain how the fundamental phenomena make up non-basic phenomena. The idealist and neutral monist theories proposed thus far have faltered on one or both counts. Largely because of scientific successes of the twentieth century, such as the rebirth of the atomic theory of matter, and the successes of quantum mechanics in explaining chemistry and of chemistry in turn in explaining much of biology, many philosophers today hold that materialism will ultimately succeed where idealism and neutral monism apparently failed. Materialism, however, comes in many different varieties and each faces formidable difficulties.

Logical behaviorism. Ryle ridiculed Cartesianism as the view that there is a ghost in the machine (the body). He claimed that the view that the mind is a substance rests on a category mistake: 'mind' is a noun, but does not name an object. Cartesianism confuses the logic of discourse about minds with the logic of discourse about bodies. To have a mind is not to possess a special sort of entity; it is simply to have certain capacities and dispositions. (Compare the thesis that to be alive is to possess not a certain entity, an entelechy or *élan vital,* but rather certain capacities and dispositions.) Ryle maintained, moreover, that it was a mistake to regard mental states such as belief, desire, and intention as internal causes of behavior. These states, he claimed, are dispositions to behave in overt ways.

In part in response to the dualist point that one can understand our ordinary psychological vocabulary ('belief', 'desire', 'pain', etc.) and know nothing about the physical states and events in the brain, *logical behaviorism* has been proposed as a materialist doctrine that explains this fact. On this view, talk of mental phenomena is shorthand for talk of actual and potential overt bodily behavior (i.e., dispositions to overt bodily behavior). Logical behaviorism was much discussed from roughly the 1930s until the early 1960s. (While Ryle is sometimes counted as a logical behaviorist, he was not committed to the thesis that all mental talk can be translated into behavioral talk.)

The translations promised by logical behaviorism appear unachievable. As Putnam and others pointed out, one can fake being in pain and one can be in pain and yet not behave or be disposed to behave as if one were in pain (e.g., one might be paralyzed or might be a "super-spartan"). Logical behaviorism faces similar difficulties in translating sentences about (what Russell called) *propositional attitudes* (i.e., beliefs that *p*, desires that *p*, hopes that *p*, intentions that *p*, and the like). Consider the following sample proposal (similar to one offered by Carnap): one believes that the cat is on the mat if and only if one is disposed to assent to 'The cat is on the mat'. First, the proposed translation meets the condition of being purely behavioral only if assenting is understandable in purely behavioral terms. That is doubtful. The proposal also fails to provide a sufficient or a necessary condition: someone may assent to 'The cat is on the mat' and yet not believe the cat is on the mat (for the person may be trying to deceive); and a belief that the cat is on the mat will dispose one to assent to 'The cat is on the mat' only if one understands what is being asked, wants to indicate that one believes the cat is on the mat, and so on. But none of these conditions is required for believing that the cat is on the mat. Moreover, to invoke any of these mentalistic conditions defeats the attempt to provide a purely behavioral translation of the belief sentence.

Although the project of translation has been abandoned, in recent years Dennett has defended a view in the spirit of logical behaviorism, *intentional systems theory:* belief-desire talk functions to characterize overall patterns of dispositions to overt behavior (in an environmental context) for the purposes of predicting overt behavior. The theory is sometimes characterized as *supervenient behaviorism* since it implies that whether an individual has beliefs, desires, intentions and the like supervenes on his dispositions to overt behavior: if two individuals are exactly alike in respect of their dispositions to overt behavior, the one has intentional states if and only if the other does. (This view allows, however, that the contents of an individual's intentional states – what the individual believes, desires, etc. – may depend on environmental factors. So it is not committed to the supervenience of the contents of intentional states on dispositions to overt behavior. See the discussion of content externalism below.) One objection to this view, due to Ned Block, is that it would mistakenly count as an intentional agent a giant look-up table – "a Blockhead" – that has the same dispositions to peripheral behavior as a genuine intentional agent. (A look-up table is a simple mechanical device that looks up preprogrammed responses.)

Identity theories. In the early 1950s, Herbert Feigl claimed that mental states are brain states. He pointed out that if mental properties or state types are merely nomologically correlated with physical properties or state types, the connecting laws would be "nomological danglers": irreducible to physical laws, and thus additional fundamental laws. According to the *identity theory*, the connecting laws are not fundamental laws (and so not nomological danglers) since they can be explained by identifying the mental and physical properties in question.

In the late 1950s and the early 1960s, the philosopher Smart and the psychologist U. T. Place defended the materialist view that sensations are identical with brain processes. Smart claimed that while mental terms differ in meaning from physical terms, scientific investigation reveals that they have the same referents as certain physical terms. (Compare the fact that while 'the Morning Star' and 'the Evening Star' differ in meaning empirical investigation reveals the same referent: Venus.) Smart and Place claimed that feeling pain, e.g., is some brain process, exactly which one to be determined by scientific investigation. Smart claimed that sensation talk is paraphraseable in *topic-neutral* terms; i.e., in terms that leave open whether sensational properties are mental or physical. 'I have an orange afterimage' is paraphraseable (roughly) as: 'There is something going on like what is going on when I have my eyes open, am awake, and there is an orange illuminated in good light in front of me, i.e., when I really see an orange'. The description is topic-neutral since it leaves open whether what is going on is mental or physical. Smart maintained that scientific investigation reveals that what in fact meets the topic-neutral description is a brain process. He held that psychophysical identity statements such as 'Pain is C-fiber firing' are contingent, likening these to, e.g., 'Lightning is electrical discharge', which is contingent and knowable only through empirical investigation.

Central state materialism. This brand of materialism was defended in the late 1960s and the early 1970s by Armstrong and others. On this view, mental states are states that are apt to produce a certain range of behavior. Central state materialists maintain that scientific investigation reveals that such states are states of the central nervous system, and thus that mental states are contingently identical with states of the central nervous system. Unlike logical behaviorism, central state materialism does not imply that mental sentences can be translated into physical sentences. Unlike both logical behaviorism and intentional systems theory, central state materialism implies that mental states are actual internal states with causal effects. And unlike Cartesian interactionism, it holds that psychophysical interaction is just physical causal interaction.

Some central state materialists held in addition that the mind is the brain. However, if the mind were the brain, every change in the brain would be a change in the mind; and that seems false: not every little brain change amounts to a change of mind. Indeed, the mind ceases to exist when brain death occurs, while the brain continues to exist. The moral that most materialists nowadays draw from such considerations is that the mind is not any physical substance, since it is not a substance of *any* sort. To have a mind is not to possess a special substance, but rather to have certain capacities – to think, feel, etc. To that extent, Ryle was right. However, central state materialists insist that the properly functioning brain is the material seat of mental capacities, that the exercise of mental capacities consists of brain processes, and that mental states are brain states that can produce behavior.

Epistemological objections have been raised to identity theories. As self-conscious beings, we have a kind of privileged access to our own mental states. The exact avenue of privileged access, whether it is introspection or not, is controversial. But it has seemed to many philosophers that our access to our own mental states is privileged in being open only to us, whereas we lack any privileged access to the states of our central nervous systems. We come to know about central nervous system states in the same way we come to know about the central nervous system states of others. So, against central state materialism and the identity theory, it is claimed that mental states cannot be states of our central nervous systems.

Taking privileged access to imply that we have incorrigible knowledge of our conscious mental states, and despairing of squaring privileged access so understood with materialism, Rorty advocated *eliminative materialism*, the thesis that there actually are no mental phenomena. A more common materialist response, however, is to deny that privileged access entails incorrigibility and to maintain that privileged access is compatible with materialism. Some materialists maintain that while certain types of mental states (e.g., sensations) are types of neurological states, it will be knowable only by empirical investigation that they are. Suppose pain is a neural state N. It will be only a posteriori knowable that pain

is N. Via the avenue of privileged access, one comes to believe that one is in a pain state, but not that one is in an N-state. One can believe one is in a pain state without believing that one is in an N-state because the concept of pain is different from the concept of N. Nevertheless, pain is N. (Compare the fact that while water is H_2O, the concept of water is different from that of H_2O. Thus, while water is H_2O, one can believe there is water in the glass without believing that there is H_2O in it. The avenue of privileged access presents N conceptualized as pain, but never as neurological state N. The avenue of privileged access involves the exercise of mental, but not neurophysiological, concepts. However, our mental concepts answer to – apply in virtue of – the same properties (state types) as do certain of our neurophysiological concepts.

The identity theory and central state materialism both hold that there are contingent psychophysical property and type identities. Some theorists in this tradition tried to distinguish a notion of theoretical identity from the notion of strict identity. They held that mental states are theoretically, but not strictly, identical with brain states. Against any such distinction, Kripke argued that identities are metaphysically necessary, i.e., hold in every possible world. If $A = B$, then necessarily $A = B$. Kripke acknowledged that there can be contingent statements of identity. But such statements, he argued, will employ at least one term that is not a *rigid designator*, i.e., a term that designates the same thing in every world in which it designates anything. Thus, since 'the inventor of bifocals' is a non-rigid designator, 'Benjamin Franklin is the inventor of bifocals' is contingent. While Franklin is the inventor of bifocals, he might not have been. However, statements of identity in which the identity sign is flanked by rigid designators are, if true, metaphysically necessary. Kripke held that proper names are rigid designators, and hence, the true identity statement 'Cicero is Tully' is metaphysically necessary. Nonetheless, a metaphysically necessary identity statement can be knowable only a posteriori. Indeed, 'Cicero is Tully' is knowable only a posteriori. Both 'water' and 'H_2O', he maintained, are rigid designators: each designates the same kind of stuff in every possible world. And he thus maintained that it is metaphysically necessary that water is H_2O, despite its not being a priori knowable that water is H_2O. On Kripke's view, any psychophysical identity statement that employs mental terms and physical terms that are rigid designators will also be metaphysically necessary, if true.

Central state materialists maintain that mental concepts are equivalent to concepts whose descriptive content is the state that is apt to produce such-and-such behavior in such-and-such circumstances. These defining descriptions for mental concepts are intended to be meaning-giving, not contingent reference-fixing descriptions; they are, moreover, not rigid designators. Thus, the central state materialists can concede that all identities are necessary, but maintain that psychophysical claims of identity are contingent claims of identity since the mental terms that figure in those statements are not rigid designators. However, Kripke maintained that our concepts of sensations and other qualitative states are not equivalent to the sorts of descriptions in question. The term 'pain', he maintained, is a rigid designator. This position might be refuted by a successful functional analysis of the concept of pain in physical and/or topic-neutral terms. However, no successful analysis of this sort has yet been produced. (See the section on consciousness below.)

A materialist can grant Kripke that 'pain' is a rigid designator and claim that a statement such as 'Pain is C-fiber firing' will be metaphysically necessary if true, but only a posteriori knowable. However, Kripke raised a formidable problem for this materialism. He pointed out that if a statement is metaphysically necessary but only a posteriori knowable, its appearance of contingency calls for explanation. Despite being metaphysically necessary, 'Water is H_2O' appears contingent. According to Kripke, we explain this appearance by noting that one can coherently imagine a world in which something has all the phenomenal properties of water, and so is an "epistemic counterpart" of it, yet is not H_2O. The fact that we can coherently imagine such epistemic counterparts explains why 'Water is H_2O' appears contingent. But no such explanation is available for (e.g.) 'Pain is C-fiber firing'. For an epistemic counterpart of pain, something with the phenomenal properties of pain – the feel of pain – *is* pain. Something can look, smell, taste, and feel like water yet not be water. But whatever feels like pain is pain: pain is a feeling. In contrast, we can explain the apparent contingency of claims like 'Water is H_2O' because water is not constituted by its phenomenal properties; our concept of water allows that it may have a "hidden essence," i.e., an essential microstructure. If Kripke is right, then anyone who maintains that a statement of identity concerning a type of bodily sensation and a type of physical state is metaphysically necessary yet a posteriori,

must explain the appearance of contingency in a way that differs from the way Kripke explains the appearance of contingency of 'Water is H_2O'. This is a formidable challenge. (The final section, on consciousness, sketches some materialist responses to it.)

The general issue of property and state type identity is controversial. The claim that water is H_2O despite the fact that the concept of water is distinct from the concept of H_2O seems plausible. However, property or state type identity is more controversial than the identity of types of substances. For properties or state types, there are no generally accepted "non-duplication principles" – to use a phrase of David Lewis's. (A non-duplication principle for A's will say that no two A's can be exactly alike in a certain respect; e.g., no two sets can have exactly the same members.) It is widely denied, for instance, that no two properties can be possessed by exactly the same things. Two properties, it is claimed, can be possessed by the same things; likewise, two state types can occur in the same space-time regions. Even assuming that mental concepts are distinct from physical concepts, the issue of whether mental state types are physical state types raises the controversial issue of the non-duplication principle for state types.

Token and type physicalisms. *Token physicalism* is the thesis that every particular is physical. *Type physicalism* is the thesis that every type or kind of entity is physical; thus, the identity thesis and central state materialism are type physicalist theses since they imply that types of mental states are types of physical states. Type physicalism implies token physicalism: given the former, every token falls under some physical type, and therefore is token-token identical with some token of a physical type. But token physicalism does not imply type physicalism; the former leaves open whether physical tokens fall under non-physical types. Some doctrines billed as materialist or physicalist embrace token epiphenomenalism, but reject type physicalism.

Non-reductive materialism. This form of materialism implies token physicalism, but denies type physicalism and, as well, that mental types (properties, etc.) are reducible to physical types. This doctrine has been discussed since at least the late nineteenth century and was widely discussed in the first third of the twentieth century. The British philosophers George Henry Lewes, Samuel Alexander, Lloyd Morgan, and C. D. Broad all held or thought plausible a certain version of non-reductive materialism. They held or sympathized with the view that every substance

either is or is wholly made up of physical particles, that the well-functioning brain is the material seat of mental capacities, and that token
mental states (events, processes, etc.) are token
neurophysiological states (events, processes,
etc.). However, they either held or thought plausible the view that mental capacities, properties,
etc., emerge from, and thus do not reduce to,
physical capacities, properties, etc. Lewes coined
the term 'emergence'; and Broad later labeled
the doctrine *emergent materialism.* Emergent
materialists maintain that laws correlating mental and physical properties are irreducible. (These
laws would be what Feigl called nomological
danglers.) Emergentists maintain that, despite
their untidiness, such laws must be accepted
with natural piety.

Davidson's doctrine of *anomalous monism* is a
current brand of non-reductive materialism. He
explicitly formulates this materialist thesis for
events; and his irreducibility thesis is restricted to
intentional mental types – e.g., believings, desir-
ings, and intendings. Anomalous monism says
that every event token is physical, but that intentional mental predicates and concepts (ones
expressing propositional attitudes) do not
reduce, by law or definition, to physical predicates or concepts. Davidson offers an original
argument for this irreducibility thesis. Mental
predicates and concepts are, he claims, governed
by constitutive principles of rationality, but physical predicates and concepts are not. This difference, he contends, excludes the possibility of
reduction of mental predicates and concepts to
physical ones. Davidson denies, moreover, that
there are strict psychological or psychophysical
laws. He calls the conjunction of this thesis and
his irreducibility thesis the principle of the
anomalism of the mental. His argument for
token physicalism (for events) appeals to the
principle of the anomalism of the mental and to
the principle of the nomological character of
causality: when two events are causally related,
they are subsumed by a strict law. He maintains
that all strict laws are physical. Given that claim,
and given the principle of the nomological character of causality, it follows that every event that
is a cause or effect is a physical event. On this
view, psychophysical causation is just causation
between physical events. Stephen Schiffer has
also maintained a non-reductive materialism,
one he calls *ontological physicalism and sentential
dualism:* every particular is physical, but mental
truths are irreducible to physical truths.

Non-reductive materialism presupposes that
mental state (event) tokens can fall under physical state types and, thereby, count as physical
state tokens. This presupposition is controversial;
no uncontroversial non-duplication principle for
state tokens settles the issue. Suppose, however,
that mental state tokens are physical state
tokens, despite mental state types not being
physical state types. The issue of how mental
state types and physical state types are related
remains. Suppose that some physical token x is
of a mental type M (say, a belief that the cat is on
the mat) and some other physical token y is not
of type M. There must, it seems, be some difference between x and y in virtue of which x is, and
y is not, of type M. Otherwise, it is simply a brute
fact that x is and y is not of type M. That, however, seems implausible. The claim that certain
physical state tokens fall under mental state
types simply as a matter of brute fact would leave
the difference in question utterly mysterious.
But if it is not a brute fact, then there is some
explanation of why a certain physical state is a
mental state of a certain sort. The non-reductive
materialist owes us an explanation that does not
imply psychophysical reduction.

Moreover, even though the non-reductive
materialist can claim that mental states are
causes because they are physical states with
physical effects, there is some question whether
mental state types are relevant to causal relations. Suppose every state is a physical state.
Given that physical states causally interact in
virtue of falling under physical types, it follows
that whenever states causally interact they do so
in virtue of falling under physical types. That
raises the issue of whether states are ever causes
in virtue of falling under mental types. *Type
epiphenomenalism* is the thesis that no state can
cause anything in virtue of falling under a mental type. *Token epiphenomenalism,* the thesis that
no mental state can cause anything, implies type
epiphenomenalism, but not conversely. Non-
reductive materialists are not committed to
token physicalism. However, token epiphenomenalism may be false but type epiphenomenalism true since mental states may be causes only
in virtue of falling under physical types, never in
virtue of falling under mental types. Broad raised
the issue of type epiphenomenalism and discussed whether emergent materialism is committed to it. Ted Honderich, Jaegwon Kim,
Ernest Sosa, and others have in recent years
raised the issue of whether non-reductive materialism is committed to type epiphenomenalism.
Brian McLaughlin has argued that the claim that
an event acts as a cause in virtue of falling under
a certain physical type is consistent with the

claim that it also acts as a cause in virtue of falling under a certain mental type, even when the mental type is not identical with the physical type. But even if this is so, the relationship between mental types and physical types must be addressed. Ernest LePore and Barry Loewer, Frank Jackson and Philip Pettit, Stephen Yablo, and others have attempted to characterize a relation between mental types and physical types that allows for the causal relevance of mental types. But whether there is a relation between mental and physical properties that is both adequate to secure the causal relevance of mental properties and available to non-reductive materialists remains an open question.

Davidson's anomalous monism may appear to be a kind of dual-aspect theory: there are events and they can have two sorts of autonomous aspects, mental and physical. However, while Davidson holds that mental properties (or types) do not reduce to physical ones, he also holds that the mental properties of an event depend on its physical properties in that the former supervene on the latter in this sense: no two events can be exactly alike in every physical respect and yet differ in some mental respect. This proposal introduced the notion of supervenience into contem- porary philosophy of mind. Often non-reductive materialists argue that mental properties (types) supervene on physical properties (types). Kim, however, has distinguished various supervenience relations, and argues that some are too weak to count as versions of materialism (as opposed to, say, dual-aspect theory), while other supervenience relations are too strong to use to formulate non-reductive materialism since they imply reducibility. According to Kim, non-reductive materialism is an unstable position.

Materialism as a supervenience thesis. Several philosophers have in recent years attempted to define the thesis of materialism using a *global supervenience thesis.* Their aim is not to formulate a brand of non-reductive materialism; they maintain that their supervenience thesis may well imply reducibility. Their aim is, rather, to formulate a thesis to which anyone who counts as a genuine materialist must subscribe. David Lewis has maintained that materialism is true if and only if any non-alien possible worlds that are physically indiscernible are mentally indiscernible as well. *Non-alien possible worlds* are worlds that have exactly the same *perfectly natural properties* as the actual world. Frank Jackson has offered this proposal: materialism is true if and only if any *minimal physical duplicate* of the

actual world is a duplicate simpliciter of the actual world. A world is a physical duplicate of the actual world if and only if it is exactly like the actual world in every physical respect (physical particular for physical particular, physical property for physical property, physical relation for physical relation, etc.); and a world is a duplicate simpliciter of the actual world if and only if it is exactly like the actual world in every respect. A minimal physical duplicate of the actual world is a physical duplicate that contains nothing else (by way of particulars, kinds, properties, etc.) than it must in order to be a physical duplicate of the actual world. Two questions arise for any formulation of the thesis of materialism. Is it adequate to materialism? And, if it is, is it true?

Functionalism. The nineteenth-century British philosopher George Henry Lewes maintained that while not every neurological event is mental, every mental event is neurological. He claimed that what makes certain neurological events mental events is their causal role in the organism. This is a very early version of functionalism, nowadays a leading approach to the mind–body problem.

Functionalism implies an answer to the question of what makes a state token a mental state of a certain kind M: namely, that it is an instance of some functional state type identical with M. There are two versions of this proposal. On one, a mental state type M of a system will be identical with the state type that plays a certain causal role R in the system. The description 'the state type that plays R in the system' will be a non-rigid designator; moreover, different state types may play R in different organisms, in which case the mental state is *multiply realizable*. On the second version, a mental state type M is identical with a second-order state type, the state of being in some first-order state that plays causal role R. More than one first-order state may play role R, and thus M may be multiply realizable. On either version, if the relevant causal roles are specifiable in physical or topic-neutral terms, then the functional definitions of mental state types will be, in principle, physically reductive. Since the roles would be specified partly in topic-neutral terms, there may well be possible worlds in which the mental states are realized by non-physical states; thus, functionalism does not imply token physicalism. However, functionalists typically maintain that, on the empirical evidence, mental states are realized (in our world) only by physical states. Functionalism comes in many varieties.

Smart's topic-neutral analysis of our talk of sensations is in the spirit of functionalism. And Armstrong's central state materialism counts as a kind of functionalism since it maintains that mental states are states apt to produce a certain range of behavior, and thus identifies states as mental states by their performing this causal role. However, functionalists today typically hold that the defining causal roles include causal roles vis-à-vis input state types, as well as output state types, and also vis-à-vis other internal state types of the system in question.

In the 1960s David Lewis proposed a functionalist theory, *analytical functionalism*, according to which definitions of mental predicates such as 'belief', 'desire', and the like (though not predicates such as 'believes that *p*' or 'desires that *q*') can be obtained by conjoining the platitudes of commonsense psychology and formulating the *Ramsey sentence* for the conjunction. The relevant Ramsey sentence is a second-order quantificational sentence that quantifies over the mental predicates in the conjunction of commonsense psychological platitudes, and from it one can derive definitions of the mental predicates. On this view, it will be analytic that a certain mental state (e.g., belief) is the state that plays a certain causal role vis-à-vis other states; and it is a matter of empirical investigation what state plays the role. Lewis claimed that such investigation reveals that the state types that play the roles in question are physical states.

In the early 1960s, Putnam proposed a version of scientific functionalism, *machine state functionalism:* according to this view, mental states are types of Turing machine table states. Turing machines are mechanical devices consisting of a tape with squares on it that either are blank or contain symbols, and an executive that can move one square to the left, or one square to the right, or stay where it is. And it can either write a symbol on a square, erase a symbol on a square, or leave the square as it is. (According to the Church-Turing thesis, every computable function can be computed by a Turing machine.) Now there are two functions specifying such a machine: one from input states to output states, the other from input states to input states. And these functions are expressible by counterfactuals (e.g., 'If the machine is in state s_1 and receives input I, it will emit output O and enter state s_2'). *Machine tables* are specified by the counterfactuals that express the functions in question. So the main idea of machine state functionalism is that any given mental type is definable as the state type that participates in certain counterfactual

relationships specified in terms of purely formal, and so not semantically interpreted, state types. Any system whose inputs, outputs, and internal states are counterfactually related in the way characterized by a machine table is a *realization* of that table. This version of machine state functionalism has been abandoned: no one maintains that the mind has the architecture of a Turing machine. However, computational psychology, a branch of cognitive psychology, presupposes a scientific functionalist view of cognitive states: it takes the mind to have a computational architecture. (See the section on cognitive psychology below.)

Functionalism – the view that what makes a state a realization of a mental state is its playing a certain causal role – remains a leading theory of mind. But functionalism faces formidable difficulties. Block has pinpointed one. On the one hand, if the input and output states that figure in the causal role alleged to define a certain mental state are specified in insufficient detail, the functional definition will be too liberal: it will mistakenly classify certain states as of that mental type. On the other hand, if the input and output states are specified in too much detail, the functional definition will be chauvinistic: it will fail to count certain states as instances of the mental state that are in fact such instances. Moreover, it has also been argued that functionalism cannot capture conscious states since types of conscious states do not admit of functional definitions.

Cognitive psychology, content, and consciousness

Cognitive psychology. Many claim that one aim of cognitive psychology is to provide explanations of intentional capacities, capacities to be in intentional states (e.g., believing) and to engage in intentional activities (e.g., reasoning). Fodor has argued that classical cognitive psychology postulates a cognitive architecture that includes a language of thought: a system of mental representation with a combinatorial syntax and semantics, and computational processes defined over these mental representations in virtue of their syntactic structures. On this view, cognition is rule-governed symbol manipulation. Mental symbols have meanings, but they participate in computational processes solely in virtue of their syntactic or formal properties. The mind is, so to speak, a syntactic engine. The view implies a kind of content parallelism: syntax-sensitive causal transitions between symbols will preserve semantic coherence. Fodor has maintained that, on this language-of-thought view of cognition (the classical view), being in a belief-that-*p* state can be understood as consisting in bearing a computational relation (one that is constitutive of belief) to a sentence in the language of thought that means that *p;* and similarly for desire, intention, and the like. The explanation of intentional capacities will be provided by a computational theory for mental sentences in conjunction with a *psychosemantic theory,* a theory of meaning for mental sentences.

A research program in cognitive science called *connectionism* postulates networks of neuron-like units. The units can be either on or off, or can have continuous levels of activation. Units are connected, the connections have various degrees of strength, and the connections can be either inhibitory or excitatory. Connectionism has provided fruitful models for studying how neural networks compute information. Moreover, connectionists have had much success in modeling pattern recognition tasks (e.g., facial recognition) and tasks consisting of learning categories from examples. Some connectionists maintain that connectionism will yield an alternative to the classical language-of-thought account of intentional states and capacities. However, some favor a mixed-models approach to cognition: some cognitive capacities are symbolic, some connectionist. And some hold that connectionism will yield an implementational architecture for a symbolic cognitive architecture, one that will help explain how a symbolic cognitive architecture is realized in the nervous system.

Content externalism. Many today hold that Twin-Earth thought experiments by Putnam and Tyler Burge show that the contents of a subject's mental states do not supervene on intrinsic properties of the subject: two individuals can be exactly alike in every intrinsic respect, yet be in mental states with different contents. (In response to Twin-Earth thought experiments, some philosophers have, however, attempted to characterize a notion of *narrow content,* a kind of content that supervenes on intrinsic properties of thinkers.) Content, externalists claim, depends on extrinsic-contextual factors. If externalism is correct, then a psychosemantic theory must examine the relation between mental symbols and the extrinsic, contextual factors that determine contents. Stephen Stich has argued that psychology should eschew psychosemantics and concern itself only with the syntactic properties of mental sentences. Such a psychology could not explain intentional capacities. But Stich urges that computational psychology also

eschew that explanatory goal. If, however, psychology is to explain intentional capacities, a psychosemantic theory is needed. Dretske, Fodor, Ruth Millikan, and David Papineau have each independently attempted to provide, in physicalistically respectable terms, foundations for a naturalized externalist theory of the content of mental sentences or internal physical states. Perhaps the leading problem for these theories of content is to explain how the physical and functional facts about a state determine a unique content for it. Appealing to work by Quine and by Kripke, some philosophers argue that such facts will not determine unique contents.

Both causal and epistemic concerns have been raised about externalist theories of content. Such theories invite the question whether the property of having a certain content is ever causally relevant. If content is a contextual property of a state that has it, can states have effects in virtue of their having a certain content? This is an important issue because intentional states figure in explanations not only in virtue of their intentional mode (whether they are beliefs, or desires, etc.) but also in virtue of their contents. Consider an everyday belief-desire explanation. The fact that the subject's belief was that there was milk in the refrigerator and the fact that the subject's desire was for milk are both essential to the belief and desire explaining why the subject went to the refrigerator. Dretske, who maintains that content depends on a causal-historical context, has attempted to explain how the property of having a certain content can be causally relevant even though the possession of the property depends on causal-historical factors. And various other philosophers have attempted to explain how the causal relevance of content can be squared with the fact that it fails to supervene on intrinsic properties of the subject. A further controversial question is whether externalism is consistent with our having privileged access to what we are thinking.

Consciousness. Conscious states such as pain states, visual experiences, and so on, are such that it is "like" something for the subject of the state to be in them. Such states have a qualitative aspect, a phenomenological character. The what-it-is-like aspects of experiences are called *qualia.* Qualia pose a serious difficulty for physicalism. Broad argued that one can know all the physical properties of a chemical and how it causally interacts with other physical phenomena and yet not know what it is like to smell it. He concluded that the smell of the chemical is not itself a physical property, but rather an irreducible emergent property. Frank Jackson has recently defended a version of the argument, which has been dubbed the knowledge argument. Jackson argues that a super-scientist, Mary, who knows all the physical and functional facts about color vision, light, and matter, but has never experienced redness since she has spent her entire life in a black and white room, would not know what it is like to visually experience red. He concludes that the physical and functional (topic-neutral) facts do not entail all the facts, and thus materialism is false. In response, Lawrence Nemirow, David Lewis, and others have argued that knowing what it is like to be in a certain conscious state is, in part, a matter of know-how (e.g., to be able to imagine oneself in the state) rather than factual knowledge, and that the failure of knowledge of the physical and functional facts to yield such know-how does not imply the falsity of materialism.

Functionalism seems unable to solve the problem of qualia since qualia seem not to be functionally definable. In the 1970s, Fodor and Ned Block argued that two states can have the same causal role, thereby realizing the same functional state, yet the qualia associated with each can be inverted. This is called the problem of *inverted qualia*. The color spectrum, e.g., might be inverted for two individuals (a possibility raised by Locke), despite their being in the same functional states. They further argued that two states might realize the same functional state, yet the one might have qualia associated with it and the other not. This is called the problem of *absent qualia*. Sydney Shoemaker has argued that the possibility of absent qualia can be ruled out on functionalist grounds. However, he has also refined the inverted qualia scenario and further articulated the problem it poses for functionalism. Whether functionalism or physicalism can avoid the problems of absent and inverted qualia remains an open question.

Thomas Nagel claims that conscious states are subjective: to fully understand them, one must understand what it is like to be in them, but one can do that only by taking up the experiential point of view of a subject in them. Physical states, in contrast, are objective. Physical science attempts to characterize the world in abstraction from the experiential point of view of any subject. According to Nagel, whether phenomenal mental states reduce to physical states turns on whether subjective states reduce to objective states; and, at present, he claims, we have no understanding of how they could. Nagel has suggested that consciousness may be explainable only by appeal to as yet undiscovered basic non-mental, non-physical properties – "proto-mental properties" – the idea being that experiential points of view might be constituted by proto-mental properties together with physical properties. He thus claims that *panphysicism* is worthy of serious consideration. Frank Jackson, James Van Cleve, and David Chalmers have argued that conscious properties are emergent, i.e., fundamental, irreducible macro-properties; and Chalmers sympathizes with a brand of panphysicism. Colin McGinn claims that while conscious properties are likely reductively explainable by brain properties, our minds seem conceptually closed to the explaining properties: we are unable to conceptualize them, just as a cat is unable to conceptualize a square root. Dennett attempts to explain consciousness in supervenient behaviorist terms. David Rosenthal argues that consciousness is a special case of intentionality – more specifically, that conscious states are just states we can come in a certain direct way to believe we are in. Dretske, William Lycan, and Michael Tye argue that conscious properties are intentional properties and physicalistically reducible. Patricia Churchland argues that conscious phenomena are reducible to neurological phenomena. Brian Loar contends that qualia are identical with either functional or neurological states of the brain; and Christopher Hill argues specifically that qualia are identical with neurological states. Loar and Hill attempt to explain away the appearance of contingency of psychophysical identity claims, but in a way different from the way Kripke attempts to explain the appearance of contingency of 'Water is H_2O', since they concede that that mode of explanation is unavailable. They appeal to differences in the conceptual roles of neurological and functional concepts by contrast with phenomenal concepts. They argue that while such concepts are different, they answer to the same properties. The nature of consciousness thus remains a matter of dispute.

See also ACTION THEORY, COGNITIVE SCIENCE, CONNECTIONISM, FOLK PSYCHOLOGY, INTENTIONALITY, MEANING, PHILOSOPHY OF LANGUAGE, PHILOSOPHY OF SCIENCE, PHYSICALISM.   B.P.M.

philosophy of organism. See WHITEHEAD.

philosophy of psychology, the philosophical study of psychology. Psychology began to separate from philosophy with the work of the nine-

teenth-century German experimentalists, especially Fechner (1801–87), Helmholtz (1821–
94), and Wundt (1832–1920). In the first half of
the twentieth century, the separation was completed in this country insofar as separate psychology departments were set up in most
universities, psychologists established their own
journals and professional associations, and experimental methods were widely employed, although not in every area of psychology (the first
experimental study of the effectiveness of a psychological therapy did not occur until 1963).
Despite this achievement of *autonomy*, however,
issues have remained about the nature of the
connections, if any, that should continue
between psychology and philosophy.

One radical view, that virtually all such connections should be severed, was defended by the
behaviorist John Watson in his seminal 1913
paper "Psychology as the Behaviorist Views It."
Watson criticizes psychologists, even the experimentalists, for relying on introspective methods
and for making consciousness the subject matter
of their discipline. He recommends that psychology be a purely objective experimental branch of
natural science, that its theoretical goal be to predict and control behavior, and that it discard all
reference to consciousness. In making behavior
the sole subject of psychological inquiry, we
avoid taking sides on "those time-honored relics
of philosophical speculation," namely competing
theories about the mind–body problem, such as
interactionism and parallelism. In a later work,
published in 1925, Watson claimed that the success of behaviorism threatened the very existence of philosophy: "With the behavioristic
point of view now becoming dominant, it is hard
to find a place for what has been called philosophy. Philosophy is passing – has all but passed,
and unless new issues arise which will give a
foundation for a new philosophy, the world has
seen its last great philosopher."

One new issue was the credibility of behaviorism. Watson gave no argument for his view that
prediction and control of behavior should be the
only theoretical goals of psychology. If the
attempt to explain behavior is also legitimate, as
some anti-behaviorists argue, then it would
seem to be an empirical question whether that
goal can be met without appealing to mentalistic
causes. Watson and his successors, such as B. F.
Skinner, cited no credible empirical evidence
that it could, but instead relied primarily on
philosophical arguments for banning postulation
of mentalistic causes. As a consequence, behaviorists virtually guaranteed that philosophers of

psychology would have at least one additional
task beyond wrestling with traditional mind–
body issues: the analysis and criticism of behaviorism itself.

Although behaviorism and the mind–body
problem were never the sole subjects of philosophy of psychology, a much richer set of topics
developed after 1950 when the so-called cognitive revolution occurred in American psychology. These topics include innate knowledge and
the acquisition of transformational grammars,
intentionality, the nature of mental representation, functionalism, mental imagery, the language of thought, and, more recently,
connectionism. Such topics are of interest to
many cognitive psychologists and those in other
disciplines, such as linguistics and artificial intelligence, who contributed to the emerging discipline known as cognitive science. Thus, after the
decline of various forms of behaviorism and the
consequent rise of cognitivism, many philosophers of psychology collaborated more closely
with psychologists. This increased cooperation
was probably due not only to a broadening of the
issues, but also to a methodological change in
philosophy. In the period roughly between 1945
and 1975, conceptual analysis dominated both
American and English philosophy of psychology
and the closely related discipline, the philosophy
of mind. Many philosophers took the position
that philosophy was essentially an a priori discipline. These philosophers rarely cited the empirical studies of psychologists. In recent decades,
however, philosophy of psychology has become
more empirical, at least in the sense that more
attention is being paid to the details of the empirical studies of psychologists. The result is more
interchanges between philosophers and psychologists.

Although interest in cognitive psychology appears to predominate in recent American philosophy of psychology, the new emphasis on
empirical studies is also reflected in philosophic
work on topics not directly related to cognitive
psychology. For example, philosophers of psychology have written books in recent years on
the clinical foundations of psychoanalysis, the
foundations of behavior therapy and behavior
modification, and self-deception. The emphasis
on empirical data has been taken one step further by naturalists, who argue that in epistemology, at least, and perhaps in all areas of philosophy, philosophical questions should either
be replaced by questions from empirical psychology or be answered by appeal to empirical
studies in psychology and related disciplines. It is

still too early to predict the fruitfulness of the naturalist approach, but this new trend might well have pleased Watson. Taken to an extreme, naturalism would make philosophy dependent on psychology instead of the reverse and thus would further enhance the autonomy of psychology that Watson desired.

See also BEHAVIORISM, COGNITIVE SCIENCE, NATURALISM, PHILOSOPHY OF MIND.   E.Er.

philosophy of religion, the subfield of philosophy devoted to the study of religious phenomena. Although religions are typically complex systems of theory and practice, including both myths and rituals, philosophers tend to concentrate on evaluating religious truth claims. In the major theistic traditions, Judaism, Christianity, and Islam, the most important of these claims concern the existence, nature, and activities of God. Such traditions commonly understand God to be something like a person who is disembodied, eternal, free, all-powerful, all-knowing, the creator and sustainer of the universe, and the proper object of human obedience and worship. One important question is whether this conception of the object of human religious activity is coherent; another is whether such a being actually exists. Philosophers of religion have sought rational answers to both questions.

The major theistic traditions draw a distinction between religious truths that can be discovered and even known by unaided human reason and those to which humans have access only through a special divine disclosure or revelation. According to Aquinas, e.g., the existence of God and some things about the divine nature can be proved by unaided human reason, but such distinctively Christian doctrines as the Trinity and Incarnation cannot be thus proved and are known to humans only because God has revealed them. Theists disagree about how such divine disclosures occur; the main candidates for vehicles of revelation include religious experience, the teachings of an inspired religious leader, the sacred scriptures of a religious community, and the traditions of a particular church. The religious doctrines Christian traditions take to be the content of revelation are often described as matters of faith. To be sure, such traditions typically affirm that faith goes beyond mere doctrinal belief to include an attitude of profound trust in God. On most accounts, however, faith involves doctrinal belief, and so there is a contrast within the religious domain itself between faith and reason. One way to spell out the contrast – though not the only way – is to

imagine that the content of revelation is divided into two parts. On the one hand, there are those doctrines, if any, that can be known by human reason but are also part of revelation; the existence of God is such a doctrine if it can be proved by human reason alone. Such doctrines might be accepted by some people on the basis of rational argument, while others, who lack rational proof, accept them on the authority of revelation. On the other hand, there are those doctrines that cannot be known by human reason and for which the authority of revelation is the sole basis. They are objects of faith rather than reason and are often described as mysteries of faith. Theists disagree about how such exclusive objects of faith are related to reason. One prominent view is that, although they go beyond reason, they are in harmony with it; another is that they are contrary to reason. Those who urge that such doctrines should be accepted despite the fact that, or even precisely because, they are contrary to reason are known as *fideists;* the famous slogan *credo quia absurdum* ('I believe because it is absurd') captures the flavor of extreme fideism. Many scholars regard Kierkegaard as a fideist on account of his emphasis on the paradoxical nature of the Christian doctrine that Jesus of Nazareth is God incarnate.

Modern philosophers of religion have, for the most part, confined their attention to topics treatable without presupposing the truth of any particular tradition's claims about revelation and have left the exploration of mysteries of faith to the theologians of various traditions. A great deal of philosophical work clarifying the concept of God has been prompted by puzzles that suggest some incoherence in the traditional concept. One kind of puzzle concerns the coherence of individual claims about the nature of God. Consider the traditional affirmation that God is all-powerful (omnipotent). Reflection on this doctrine raises a famous question: Can God make a stone so heavy that even God cannot lift it? No matter how this is answered, it seems that there is at least one thing that even God cannot do, i.e., make such a stone or lift such a stone, and so it appears that even God cannot be all-powerful. Such puzzles stimulate attempts by philosophers to analyze the concept of omnipotence in a way that specifies more precisely the scope of the powers coherently attributable to an omnipotent being. To the extent that such attempts succeed, they foster a deeper understanding of the concept of God and, if God exists, of the divine nature. Another sort of puzzle concerns the consistency of attributing two or more properties to

God. Consider the claim that God is both immutable and omniscient. An immutable being is one that cannot undergo internal change, and an omniscient being knows all truths, and believes no falsehoods. If God is omniscient, it seems that God must first know and hence believe that it is now Tuesday and not believe that it is now Wednesday and later know and hence believe that it is now Wednesday and not believe that it is now Tuesday. If so, God's beliefs change, and since change of belief is an internal change, God is not immutable. So it appears that God is not immutable if God is omniscient. A resolution of this puzzle would further contribute to enriching the philosophical understanding of the concept of God.

It is, of course, one thing to elaborate a coherent concept of God; it is quite another to know, apart from revelation, that such a being actually exists. A proof of the existence of God would yield such knowledge, and it is the task of *natural theology* to evaluate arguments that purport to be such proofs. As opposed to *revealed theology*, natural theology restricts the assumptions fit to serve as premises in its arguments to things naturally knowable by humans, i.e., knowable without special revelation from supernatural sources. Many people have hoped that such natural religious knowledge could be universally communicated and would justify a form of religious practice that would appeal to all humankind because of its rationality. Such a religion would be a natural religion. The history of natural theology has produced a bewildering variety of arguments for the existence of God. The four main types are these: ontological arguments, cosmological arguments, teleological arguments, and moral arguments.

The earliest and most famous version of the *ontological argument* was set forth by Anselm of Canterbury in chapter 2 of his *Proslogion*. It is a bold attempt to deduce the existence of God from the concept of God: we understand God to be a perfect being, something than which nothing greater can be conceived. Because we have this concept, God at least exists in our minds as an object of the understanding. Either God exists in the mind alone, or God exists both in the mind and as an extramental reality. But if God existed in the mind alone, then we could conceive of a being greater than that than which nothing greater can be conceived, namely, one that also existed in extramental reality. Since the concept of a being greater than that than which nothing greater be conceived is incoherent, God cannot exist in the mind alone. Hence God exists not only in the mind but also in extramental reality.

The most celebrated criticism of this form of the argument was Kant's, who claimed that existence is not a real predicate. For Kant, a real predicate contributes to determining the content of a concept and so serves as a part of its definition. But to say that something falling under a concept exists does not add to the content of a concept; there is, Kant said, no difference in conceptual content between a hundred real dollars and a hundred imaginary dollars. Hence whether or not there exists something that corresponds to a concept cannot be settled by definition. The existence of God cannot be deduced from the concept of a perfect being because existence is not contained in the concept or the definition of a perfect being.

Contemporary philosophical discussion has focused on a slightly different version of the ontological argument. In chapter 3 of *Proslogion* Anselm suggested that something than which nothing greater can be conceived cannot be conceived not to exist and so exists necessarily. Following this lead, such philosophers as Charles Hartshorne, Norman Malcolm, and Alvin Plantinga have contended that God cannot be a contingent being who exists in some possible worlds but not in others. The existence of a perfect being is either necessary, in which case God exists in every possible world, or impossible, in which case God exists in no possible worlds. On this view, if it is so much as possible that a perfect being exists, God exists in every possible world and hence in the actual world. The crucial premise in this form of the argument is the assumption that the existence of a perfect being is possible; it is not obviously true and could be rejected without irrationality. For this reason, Plantinga concedes that the argument does not prove or establish its conclusion, but maintains that it does make it rational to accept the existence of God.

The key premises of various *cosmological arguments* are statements of obvious facts of a general sort about the world. Thus, the argument to a first cause begins with the observation that there are now things undergoing change and things causing change. If something is a cause of such change only if it is itself caused to change by something else, then there is an infinitely long chain of causes of change. But, it is alleged, there cannot be a causal chain of infinite length. Therefore there is something that causes change, but is not caused to change by anything else, i.e., a first cause. Many critics of this form of the argument deny its assumption that there cannot be an infinite causal regress or chain of causes. This argument also fails to show that there is only one first cause and does not prove that a first cause must have such divine attributes as omniscience, omnipotence, and perfect goodness.

A version of the cosmological argument that has attracted more attention from contemporary philosophers is the argument from contingency to necessity. It starts with the observation that there are *contingent beings* – beings that could have failed to exist. Since contingent beings do not exist of logical necessity, a contingent being must be caused to exist by some other being, for otherwise there would be no explanation of why it exists rather than not doing so. Either the causal chain of contingent beings has a first member, a contingent being not caused by another contingent being, or it is infinitely long. If, on the one hand, the chain has a first member, then a necessary being exists and causes it. After all, being contingent, the first member must have a cause, but its cause cannot be another contingent being. Hence its cause has to be non-contingent, i.e., a being that could not fail to exist and so is necessary. If, on the other hand, the chain is infinitely long, then a necessary being exists and causes the chain as a whole. This is because the chain as a whole, being itself contingent, requires a cause that must be non-contingent since it is not part of the chain. In either case, if there are contingent beings, a necessary being exists. So, since contingent beings do exist, there is a necessary being that causes their existence. Critics of this argument attack its assumption that there must be an explanation for the existence of every contingent being. Rejecting the principle that there is a sufficient reason for the existence of each contingent thing, they argue that the existence of at least some contingent beings is an inexplicable brute fact. And even if the principle of sufficient reason is true, its truth is not obvious and so it would not be irrational to deny it. Accordingly, William Rowe (b.1931) concludes that this version of the cosmological argument does not prove the existence of God, but he leaves open the question of whether it shows that theistic belief is reasonable.

The starting point of *teleological arguments* is the phenomenon of goal-directedness in nature. Aquinas, e.g., begins with the claim that we see that things which lack intelligence act for an end so as to achieve the best result. Modern science has discredited this universal metaphysical teleology, but many biological systems do seem to display remarkable adaptations of means to ends. Thus, as William Paley (1743–1805) insisted, the eye is adapted to seeing and its parts cooperate in complex ways to produce sight. This suggests an analogy between such biological systems and human artifacts, which are known to be products of intelligent design. Spelled out in mechanical terms, the analogy grounds the claim that the world as a whole is like a vast machine composed of many smaller machines. Machines are contrived by intelligent human designers. Since like effects have like causes, the world as a whole and many of its parts are therefore probably products of design by an intelligence resembling the human but greater in proportion to the magnitude of its effects. Because this form of the argument rests on an analogy, it is known as the *analogical argument* for the existence of God; it is also known as the *design argument* since it concludes the existence of an intelligent designer of the world.

Hume subjected the design argument to sustained criticism in his *Dialogues Concerning Natural Religion*. If, as most scholars suppose, the character Philo speaks for Hume, Hume does not actually reject the argument. He does, however, think that it warrants only the very weak conclusion that the cause or causes of order in the universe probably bear some remote analogy to human intelligence. As this way of putting it indicates, the argument does not rule out polytheism; perhaps different minor deities designed lions and tigers. Moreover, the analogy with human artificers suggests that the designer or designers of the universe did not create it from nothing but merely imposed order on already existing matter. And on account of the mixture of good and evil in the universe, the argument does not show that the designer or designers are morally admirable enough to deserve obedience or worship. Since the time of Hume, the design argument has been further undermined by the emergence of Darwinian explanations of biological adaptations in terms of natural selection that give explanations of such adaptations in terms of intelligent design stiff competition.

Some *moral arguments* for the existence of God conform to the pattern of *inference to the best explanation*. It has been argued that the hypothesis that morality depends upon the will of God provides the best explanation of the objectivity of moral obligations. Kant's moral argument, which is probably the best-known specimen of this type, takes a different tack. According to Kant, the complete good consists of perfect virtue rewarded with perfect happiness, and virtue deserves to be rewarded with proportional happiness because it makes one worthy to be happy. If morality is to command the allegiance of reason, the complete good must be a real possibility, and so practical reason is entitled to postulate that the conditions necessary to guarantee its possibility obtain. As far as anyone can tell, nature and its laws do not furnish such a guarantee; in this world, apparently, the virtuous often suffer while the vicious flourish. And even if the operation of natural laws were to produce happiness in proportion to virtue, this would be merely coincidental, and hence finite moral agents would not have been made happy just because they had by their virtue made themselves worthy of happiness. So practical reason is justified in postulating a supernatural agent with sufficient goodness, knowledge, and power to ensure that finite agents receive the happiness they deserve as a reward for their virtue, though theoretical reason can know nothing of such a being. Critics of this argument have denied that we must postulate a systematic connection between virtue and happiness in order to have good reasons to be moral. Indeed, making such an assumption might actually tempt one to cultivate virtue for the sake of securing happiness rather than for its own sake.

It seems therefore that none of these arguments by itself conclusively proves the existence of God. However, some of them might contribute to a cumulative case for the existence of God. According to Richard Swinburne, cosmological, teleological, and moral arguments individually increase the probability of God's existence even though none of them makes it more probable than not. But when other evidence such as that deriving from providential occurrences and religious experiences is added to the balance, Swinburne concludes that theism becomes more probable than its negation. Whether or not he is right, it does appear to be entirely correct to judge the rationality of theistic belief in the light of our total evidence.

But there is a case to be made against theism too. Philosophers of religion are interested in arguments against the existence of God, and fairness does seem to require admitting that our total evidence contains much that bears negatively on the rationality of belief in God. The *problem of evil* is generally regarded as the strongest objection to theism. Two kinds of evil can be distinguished. *Moral evil* inheres in the wicked actions of moral agents and the bad consequences they produce. An example is torturing the innocent. When evil actions are considered

theologically as offenses against God, they are regarded as sins. *Natural evils* are bad consequences that apparently derive entirely from the operations of impersonal natural forces, e.g. the human and animal suffering produced by natural catastrophes such as earthquakes and epidemics. Both kinds of evil raise the question of what reasons an omniscient, omnipotent, and perfectly good being could have for permitting or allowing their existence. Theodicy is the enterprise of trying to answer this question and thereby to justify the ways of God to humans.

It is, of course, possible to deny the presuppositions of the question. Some thinkers have held that evil is unreal; others have maintained that the deity is limited and so lacks the power or knowledge to prevent the evils that occur. If one accepts the presuppositions of the question, the most promising strategy for theodicy seems to be to claim that each evil God permits is necessary for some greater good or to avoid some alternative to it that is at least as bad if not worse. The strongest form of this doctrine is the claim made by Leibniz that this is the best of all possible worlds. It is unlikely that humans, with their cognitive limitations, could ever understand all the details of the greater goods for which evils are necessary, assuming that such goods exist; however, we can understand how some evils contribute to achieving goods. According to the soul-making theodicy of John Hick (b.1922), which is rooted in a tradition going back to Irenaeus, admirable human qualities such as compassion could not exist except as responses to suffering, and so evil plays a necessary part in the formation of moral character. But this line of thought does not seem to provide a complete theodicy because much animal suffering occurs unnoticed by humans and child abuse often destroys rather than strengthens the moral character of its victims.

Recent philosophical discussion has often focused on the claim that the existence of an omniscient, omnipotent, and perfectly good being is logically inconsistent with the existence of evil or of a certain quantity of evil. This is the logical problem of evil, and the most successful response to it has been the *free will defense*. Unlike a theodicy, this defense does not speculate about God's reasons for permitting evil but merely argues that God's existence is consistent with the existence of evil. Its key idea is that moral good cannot exist apart from libertarian free actions that are not causally determined. If God aims to produce moral good, God must create free creatures upon whose cooperation he must depend, and so divine omnipotence is limited by the freedom God confers on creatures. Since such creatures are also free to do evil, it is possible that God could not have created a world containing moral good but no moral evil. Plantinga extends the defense from moral to natural evil by suggesting that it is also possible that all natural evil is due to the free actions of non-human persons such as Satan and his cohorts. Plantinga and Swinburne have also addressed the probabilistic problem of evil, which is the claim that the existence of evil disconfirms or renders improbable the hypothesis that God exists. Both of them argue for the conclusion that this is not the case.

Finally, it is worth mentioning three other topics on which contemporary philosophers of religion have worked to good effect. Important studies of the meaning and use of religious language were stimulated by the challenge of logical positivism's claim that theological language is *cognitively meaningless*. Defenses of such Christian doctrines as the Trinity, Incarnation, and Atonement against various philosophical objections have recently been offered by people committed to elaborating an explicitly Christian philosophy. And a growing appreciation of religious pluralism has both sharpened interest in questions about the cultural relativity of religious rationality and begun to encourage progress toward a comparative philosophy of religions. Such work helps to make philosophy of religion a lively and diverse field of inquiry.

See also AQUINAS, DIVINE ATTRIBUTES, DIVINE FOREKNOWLEDGE, FREE WILL PROBLEM, MYSTICISM, PARADOXES OF OMNIPOTENCE, THEODICY, THEOLOGICAL NATURALISM.   P.L.Q.

philosophy of science, the branch of philosophy that is centered on a critical examination of the sciences: their methods and their results. One branch of the philosophy of science, *methodology,* is closely related to the theory of knowledge. It explores the methods by which science arrives at its posited truths concerning the world and critically explores alleged rationales for these methods. Issues concerning the sense in which theories are accepted in science, the nature of the confirmation relation between evidence and hypothesis, the degree to which scientific claims can be falsified by observational data, and the like, are the concern of methodology. Other branches of the philosophy of science are concerned with the meaning and content of the posited scientific results and are closely related to metaphysics and the philosophy of language.

Typical problems examined are the nature of scientific laws, the cognitive content of scientific theories referring to unobservables, and the structure of scientific explanations. Finally, philosophy of science explores specific foundational questions arising out of the specific results of the sciences. Typical questions explored might be metaphysical presuppositions of space-time theories, the role of probability in statistical physics, the interpretation of measurement in quantum theory, the structure of explanations in evolutionary biology, and the like.

Concepts of the credibility of hypotheses. Some crucial concepts that arise when issues of the credibility of scientific hypotheses are in question are the following:

Inductivism is the view that hypotheses can receive evidential support from their predictive success with respect to particular cases falling under them.

If one takes the principle of inductive inference to be that the future will be like the past, one is subject to the skeptical objection that this rule is empty of content, and even self-contradictory, if any kind of "similarity" of cases is permitted. To restore content and consistency to the rule, and for other methodological purposes as well, it is frequently alleged that only *natural kinds,* a delimited set of "genuine" properties, should be allowed in the formulation of scientific hypotheses.

The view that theories are first arrived at as creative hypotheses of the scientist's imagination and only then confronted, for justificatory purposes, with the observational predictions deduced from them, is called the *hypothetico-deductive model* of science. This model is contrasted with the view that the very discovery of hypotheses is somehow "generated" out of accumulated observational data.

The view that hypotheses are confirmed to the degree that they provide the "best explanatory account" of the data is often called *abduction* and sometimes called *inference to the best explanation.*

The alleged relation that evidence bears to hypothesis, warranting its truth but not, generally, guaranteeing that truth, is called *confirmation.* Methodological accounts such as inductivism countenance such evidential warrant, frequently speaking of evidence as making a hypothesis probable but not establishing it with certainty.

Probability in the confirmational context is supposed to be a relationship holding between propositions that is quantitative and is described by the formal theory of probability. It is supposed to measure the "degree of support" that one proposition gives to another, e.g. the degree of support evidential statements give to a hypothesis allegedly supported by them.

Scientific methodologists often claim that science is characterized by *convergence*. This is the claim that scientific theories in their historical order are converging to an ultimate, final, and ideal theory. Sometimes this final theory is said to be true because it corresponds to the "real world," as in realist accounts of convergence. In pragmatist versions this ultimate theory is the defining standard of truth.

It is sometimes alleged that one ground for choosing the most plausible theory, over and above conformity of the theory with the observational data, is the *simplicity* of the theory. Many versions of this thesis exist, some emphasizing formal elements of the theory and others, e.g., emphasizing paucity of ontological commitment by the theory as the measure of simplicity.

It is sometimes alleged that in choosing which theory to believe, the scientific community opts for theories compatible with the data that make minimal changes in scientific belief necessary from those demanded by previously held theory. The believer in *methodological conservatism* may also try to defend such epistemic conservatism as normatively rational.

An experiment that can decisively show a scientific hypothesis to be false is called a *crucial experiment* for the hypothesis. It is a thesis of many philosophers that for hypotheses that function in theories and can only confront observational data when conjoined with other theoretical hypotheses, no absolutely decisive crucial experiment can exist.

Concepts of the structure of hypotheses. Here are some of the essential concepts encountered when it is the structure of scientific hypotheses that is being explored:

In its explanatory account of the world, science posits novel entities and properties. Frequently these are alleged to be not accessible to direct observation. A *theory* is a set of hypotheses positing such entities and properties. Some philosophers of science divide the logical consequences of a theory into those referring only to observable things and features and those referring to the unobservables as well. Various reductionist, eliminationist, and instrumentalist approaches to theory agree that the full cognitive content of a theory is exhausted by its observational consequences reported by its *observation*

sentences, a claim denied by those who espouse realist accounts of theories.

The view that the parts of a theory that do not directly relate observational consequences ought not to be taken as genuinely referential at all, but, rather, as a "mere linguistic instrument" allowing one to derive observational results from observationally specifiable posits, is called *instrumentalism*. From this point of view terms putatively referring to unobservables fail to have genuine reference and individual non-observational sentences containing such terms are not individually genuinely true or false.

Verificationism is the general name for the doctrine that, in one way or another, the semantic content of an assertion is exhausted by the conditions that count as warranting the acceptance or rejection of the assertion. There are many versions of verificationist doctrines that try to do justice both to the empiricist claim that the content of an assertion is its totality of empirical consequences and also to a wide variety of anti-reductionist intuitions about meaning.

The doctrine that theoretical sentences must be strictly translatable into sentences expressed solely in observational terms in order that the theoretical assertions have genuine cognitive content is sometimes called *operationalism*. The "operation" by which a magnitude is determined to have a specified value, characterized observationally, is taken to give the very meaning of attributing that magnitude to an object.

The doctrine that the meanings of terms in theories are fixed by the role the terms play in the theory as a whole is often called *semantic holism*. According to the semantic holist, definitions of theoretical terms by appeal to observational terms cannot be given, but all of the theoretical terms have their meaning given "as a group" by the structure of the theory as a whole. A related doctrine in confirmation theory is that confirmation accrues to whole theories, and not to their individual assertions one at a time. This is *confirmational holism*.

To see another conception of cognitive content, conjoin all the sentences of a theory together. Then replace each theoretical term in the sentence so obtained with a predicate variable and existentially quantify over all the predicate variables so introduced. This is the *Ramsey sentence* for a (finitely axiomatized) theory. This sentence has the same logical consequences framable in the observational vocabulary alone as did the original theory. It is often claimed that the Ramsey sentence for a theory exhausts the cognitive content of the theory. The Ramsey sentence is supposed to "define" the meaning of the theoretical terms of the original theory as well as have empirical consequences; yet by asserting the existence of the theoretical properties, it is sometimes alleged to remain a realist construal of the theory. The latter claim is made doubtful, however, by the existence of "merely representational" interpretations of the Ramsey sentence.

Theories are often said to be so related that one theory is reducible to another. The study of the relation theories bear to one another in this context is said to be the study of intertheoretic *reduction*. Such reductive claims can have philosophical origins, as in the alleged reduction of material objects to sense-data or of spatiotemporal relations to causal relations, or they can be scientific discoveries, as in the reduction of the theory of light waves to the theory of electromagnetic radiation. Numerous "models" of the reductive relation exist, appropriate for distinct kinds and cases of reduction.

The term *scientific realism* has many and varied uses. Among other things that have been asserted by those who describe themselves as scientific realists are the claims that "mature" scientific theories typically refer to real features of the world, that the history of past falsifications of accepted scientific theories does not provide good reason for persistent skepticism as to the truth claims of contemporary theories, and that the terms of theories that putatively refer to unobservables ought to be taken at their referential face value and not reinterpreted in some instrumentalistic manner.

Internal realism denies irrealist claims founded on the past falsification of accepted theories. Internal realists are, however, skeptical of "metaphysical" claims of "correspondence of true theories to the real world" or of any notion of truth that can be construed in radically non-epistemic terms. While theories may converge to some ultimate "true" theory, the notion of truth here must be understood in some version of a Peircian idea of truth as "ultimate warranted assertability."

The claim that any theory that makes reference to posited unobservable features of the world in its explanatory apparatus will always encounter rival theories incompatible with the original theory but equally compatible with all possible observational data that might be taken as confirmatory of the original theory is the claim of the *underdetermination thesis*.

A generalization taken to have "lawlike force" is called a *law of nature*. Some suggested criteria for generalizations having lawlike force are the ability of the generalization to back up the truth of claims expressed as counterfactual conditions; the ability of the generalization to be confirmed inductively on the basis of evidence that is only a proper subset of all the particular instances falling under the generality; and the generalization having an appropriate place in the simple, systematic hierarchy of generalizations important for fundamental scientific theories of the world.

The application of a scientific law to a given actual situation is usually hedged with the proviso that for the law's predictions to hold, "all other, unspecified, features of the situation are normal." Such a qualifying clause is called a *ceteris paribus* clause. Such "everything else being normal" claims cannot usually be "filled out," revealing important problems concerning the "open texture" of scientific claims.

The claim that the full specification of the state of the world at one time is sufficient, along with the laws of nature, to fix the full state of the world at any other time, is the claim of *determinism*. This is not to be confused with claims of total predictability, since even if determinism were true the full state of the world at a time might be, in principle, unavailable for knowledge.

Concepts of the foundations of physical theories. Here, finally, are a few concepts that are crucial in discussing the foundations of physical theories, in particular theories of space and time and quantum theory:

The doctrine that space and time must be thought of as a family of spatial and temporal relations holding among the material constituents of the universe is called *relationism*. Relationists deny that "space itself" should be considered an additional constituent of the world over and above the world's material contents. The doctrine that "space itself" must be posited as an additional constituent of the world over and above ordinary material things of the world is *substantivalism*.

Mach's principle is the demand that all physical phenomena, including the existence of inertial forces used by Newton to argue for a substantivalist position, be explainable in purely relationist terms. Mach speculated that Newton's explanation for the forces in terms of acceleration with respect to "space itself" could be replaced with an explanation resorting to the acceleration of the test object with respect to the remaining matter of the universe (the "fixed stars").

In quantum theory the claim that certain

"conjugate" quantities, such as position and momentum, cannot be simultaneously "determined" to arbitrary degrees of accuracy is the *uncertainty principle*. The issue of whether such a lack of simultaneous exact "determination" is merely a limitation on our knowledge of the system or is, instead, a limitation on the system's having simultaneous exact values of the conjugate quantities, is a fundamental one in the interpretation of quantum mechanics.

Bell's theorem is a mathematical result aimed at showing that the explanation of the statistical correlations that hold between causally noninteractive systems cannot always rely on the positing that when the systems did causally interact in the past independent values were fixed for some feature of each of the two systems that determined their future observational behavior. The existence of such "local hidden variables" would contradict the correlational predictions of quantum mechanics. The result shows that quantum mechanics has a profoundly "non-local" nature.

Can quantum probabilities and correlations be obtained as averages over variables at some deeper level than those specifying the quantum state of a system? If such quantities exist they are called *hidden variables*. Many different types of hidden variables have been proposed: deterministic, stochastic, local, non-local, etc. A number of proofs exist to the effect that positing certain types of hidden variables would force probabilistic results at the quantum level that contradict the predictions of quantum theory.

Complementarity was the term used by Niels Bohr to describe what he took to be a fundamental structure of the world revealed by quantum theory. Sometimes it is used to indicate the fact that magnitudes occur in conjugate pairs subject to the uncertainty relations. Sometimes it is used more broadly to describe such aspects as the ability to encompass some phenomena in a wave picture of the world and other phenomena in a particle picture, but implying that no one picture will do justice to all the experimental results.

The orthodox formalization of quantum theory posits two distinct ways in which the quantum state can evolve. When the system is "unobserved," the state evolves according to the deterministic Schrödinger equation. When "measured," however, the system suffers a discontinuous "collapse of the wave packet" into a new quantum state determined by the outcome of the measurement process. Understanding how to reconcile the measurement process with the laws of dynamic evolution of the system is the *measurement problem*.

Conservation and symmetry. A number of important physical principles stipulate that some physical quantity is conserved, i.e. that the quantity of it remains invariant over time. Early *conservation principles* were those of matter (mass), of energy, and of momentum. These became assimilated together in the relativistic principle of the conservation of momentum-energy. Other conservation laws (such as the conservation of baryon number) arose in the theory of elementary particles. A *symmetry* in physical theory expressed the invariance of some structural feature of the world under some transformation. Examples are translation and rotation invariance in space and the invariance under transformation from one uniformly moving reference frame to another. Such symmetries express the fact that systems related by symmetry transformations behave alike in their physical evolution. Some symmetries are connected with space-time, such as those noted above, whereas others (such as the symmetry of electromagnetism under so-called gauge transformations) are not. A very important result of the mathematician Emma Noether shows that each conservation law is derivable from the existence of an associated underlying symmetry.

Chaos theory and chaotic systems. In the history of the scientific study of deterministic systems, the paradigm of explanation has been the prediction of the future states of a system from a specification of its initial state. In order for such a prediction to be useful, however, nearby initial states must lead to future states that are close to one another. This is now known to hold only in exceptional cases. In general deterministic systems are *chaotic systems*, i.e., even initial states very close to one another will lead in short intervals of time to future states that diverge quickly from one another.

Chaos theory has been developed to provide a wide range of concepts useful for describing the structure of the dynamics of such chaotic systems. The theory studies the features of a system that will determine if its evolution is chaotic or non-chaotic and provides the necessary descriptive categories for characterizing types of chaotic motion.

Randomness. The intuitive distinction between a sequence that is random and one that is orderly plays a role in the foundations of probability theory and in the scientific study of dynamical systems. But what is a random sequence? Subjectivist definitions of randomness focus on the inability of an agent to determine, on the basis of his knowledge, the future occurrences in the sequence. Objectivist definitions of randomness seek to characterize it without reference to the knowledge of any agent. Some approaches to defining objective randomness are those that require probability to be the same in the original sequence and in subsequences "mechanically" selectable from it, and those that define a sequence as random if it passes every "effectively constructible" statistical test for randomness. Another important attempt to characterize objective randomness compares the length of a sequence to the length of a computer program used to generate the sequence. The basic idea is that a sequence is random if the computer programs needed to generate the sequence are as long as the sequence itself.

See also CONFIRMATION, DUHEM, EXPLANATION, HYPOTHETICO-DEDUCTIVE METHOD, LAWLIKE GENERALIZATION, PHILOSOPHY OF THE SOCIAL SCIENCES, SCIENTIFIC REALISM, THEORETICAL TERM.   L.S.

philosophy of the social sciences, the study of the logic and methods of the social sciences. Central questions include: What are the criteria of a good social explanation? How (if at all) are the social sciences distinct from the natural sciences? Is there a distinctive method for social research? Through what empirical procedures are social science assertions to be evaluated? Are there irreducible social laws? Are there causal relations among social phenomena? Do social facts and regularities require some form of reduction to facts about individuals? What is the role of theory in social explanation? The philosophy of social science aims to provide an interpretation of the social sciences that answers these questions.

The philosophy of social science, like that of natural science, has both a descriptive and a prescriptive side. On the one hand, the field is *about* the social sciences – the explanations, methods, empirical arguments, theories, hypotheses, etc., that actually occur in the social science literature. This means that the philosopher needs extensive knowledge of several areas of social science research in order to be able to formulate an analysis of the social sciences that corresponds appropriately to scientists' practice. On the other hand, the field is *epistemic:* it is concerned with the idea that scientific theories and hypotheses are put forward as *true* or probable, and are justified on *rational* grounds (empirical and theoretical). The philosopher aims to provide a critical evaluation of existing social science methods and practices insofar as these methods are found to be less truth-enhancing than they might be. These two aspects of the philosophical enterprise suggest that philosophy of social science should be construed as a rational reconstruction of existing social science practice – a reconstruction guided by existing practice but extending beyond that practice by identifying faulty assumptions, forms of reasoning, and explanatory frameworks.

Philosophers have disagreed over the relation between the social and natural sciences. One position is *naturalism,* according to which the methods of the social sciences should correspond closely to those of the natural sciences. This position is closely related to *physicalism,* the doctrine that all higher-level phenomena and regularities – including social phenomena – are ultimately reducible to physical entities and the laws that govern them. On the other side is the view that the social sciences are inherently distinct from the natural sciences. This perspective holds that social phenomena are metaphysically distinguishable from natural phenomena because they are *intentional* – they depend on the meaningful actions of individuals. On this view, natural phenomena admit of causal explanation, whereas social phenomena require intentional explanation. The anti-naturalist position also maintains that there is a corresponding difference between the methods appropriate to natural and social science. Advocates of the *Verstehen* method hold that there is a method of intuitive interpretation of human action that is radically distinct from methods of inquiry in the natural sciences.

One important school within the philosophy of social science takes its origin in this fact of the meaningfulness of human action. Interpretive sociology maintains that the goal of social inquiry is to provide interpretations of human conduct within the context of culturally specific meaningful arrangements. This approach draws an analogy between literary texts and social phenomena: both are complex systems of meaningful elements, and the goal of the interpreter is to provide an interpretation of the elements that makes sense of them. In this respect social science involves a *hermeneutic* inquiry: it requires that the interpreter should tease out the meanings underlying a particular complex of social behavior, much as a literary critic pieces together an interpretation of the meaning of a complex literary text. An example of this approach is Weber's treatment of the relation between capitalism and the Protestant ethic. Weber attempts to identify the elements of western European culture that shaped human action in this environment in such a way as to produce capitalism. On this account, both Calvinism and capitalism are historically specific complexes of values and meanings, and we can better understand the emergence of capitalism by seeing how it corresponds to the meaningful structures of Calvinism.

Interpretive sociologists often take the meaningfulness of social phenomena to imply that social phenomena do not admit of causal explanation. However, it is possible to accept the idea that social phenomena derive from the purposive actions of individuals without relinquishing the goal of providing causal explanations of social phenomena. For it is necessary to distinguish between the general idea of a causal relation between two events or conditions and the more specific idea of "causal determination through strict laws of nature." It is true that social phenomena rarely derive from strict laws of nature; wars do not result from antecedent political tensions in the way that earthquakes result from antecedent conditions in plate tectonics. However, since non-deterministic causal relations can derive from the choices of individual persons, it is evident that social phenomena admit of causal explanation, and in fact much social explanation depends on asserting causal relations between social events and processes – e.g., the claim that the administrative competence of the state is a crucial causal factor in determining the success or failure of a revolutionary movement. A central goal of causal explanation is to discover the conditions existing prior to the event that, given the law-governed regularities among phenomena of this sort, were sufficient to produce this event. To say that C is a cause of E is to assert that the occurrence of C, in the context of a field of social processes and mechanisms F, brought about E (or increased the likelihood of the occurrence of E). Central to causal arguments in the social sciences is the idea of a causal mechanism – a series of events or actions leading from cause to effect. Suppose it is held that the extension of a trolley line from the central city to the periphery caused the deterioration of public schools in the central city. In order to make out such a claim it is necessary to provide some account of the social and political mechanisms that join the antecedent condition to the consequent.

An important variety of causal explanation in social science is materialist explanation. This type of explanation attempts to explain a social feature in terms of features of the material environment in the context of which the social phenomenon occurs. Features of the environment that often appear in materialist explanations include topography and climate; thus it is sometimes maintained that banditry thrives in remote regions because the rugged terrain makes it more difficult for the state to repress bandits. But materialist explanations may also refer to the material needs of society – e.g., the need to produce food and other consumption goods to support the population. Thus Marx holds that it is the development of the "productive forces" (technology) that drives the development of property relations and political systems. In each case the materialist explanation must refer to the fact of human agency – the fact that human beings are capable of making deliberative choices on the basis of their wants and beliefs – in order to carry out the explanation; in the banditry example, the explanation depends on the fact that bandits are prudent enough to realize that their prospects for survival are better in the periphery than in the core. So materialist explanations too accept the point that social phenomena depend on the purposive actions of individuals.

A central issue in the philosophy of social science involves the relation between social regularities and facts about individuals. *Methodological individualism* is the position that asserts the primacy of facts about individuals over facts about social entities. This doctrine takes three forms: a claim about social entities, a claim about social concepts, and a claim about social regularities. The first version maintains that social entities are reducible to ensembles of individuals – as an insurance company might be reduced to the ensemble of employees, supervisors, managers, and owners whose actions constitute the company. Likewise, it is sometimes held that social concepts must be reducible to concepts involving only individuals – e.g., the concept of a social class might be defined in terms of concepts pertaining only to individuals and their behavior. Finally, it is sometimes held that social regularities must be derivable from regularities of individual behavior. There are several positions opposed to methodological individualism. At the extreme there is *methodological holism* – the doctrine that social entities, facts, and laws are autonomous and irreducible; for example, that social structures such as the state have dynamic properties independent of the beliefs and purposes of the particular persons who occupy positions within the structure. A third position intermediate between these two holds that every social explanation requires microfoundations – an account of the circumstances at the individual level that led individuals to behave in such ways as to bring about the observed social regularities. If we observe that an industrial strike is successful over an extended period of time, it is not sufficient to explain this circumstance by referring to the common interest that members of the union have in winning their demands. Rather, we need information about the circumstances of the individual union member that induce him or her to contribute to this public good. The microfoundations dictum does not require, however, that social explanations be couched in non-social concepts; instead, the circumstances of individual agents may be characterized in social terms.

Central to most theories of explanation is the idea that explanation depends on general laws governing the phenomena in question. Thus the discovery of the laws of electrodynamics permitted the explanation of a variety of electromagnetic phenomena. But social phenomena derive from the actions of purposive men and women; so what kinds of regularities are available on the basis of which to provide social explanations? A fruitful research framework in the social sciences is the idea that men and women are *rational,* so it is possible to explain their behavior as the outcome of a deliberation about means of achieving their individual ends. This fact in turn gives rise to a set of regularities about individual behavior that may be used as a ground for social explanation. We may explain some complex social phenomenon as the aggregate result of the actions of a large number of individual agents with a hypothesized set of goals within a structured environment of choice.

Social scientists have often been inclined to offer *functional explanations* of social phenomena. A functional explanation of a social feature is one that explains the presence and persistence of the feature in terms of the beneficial consequences the feature has for the ongoing working of the social system as a whole. It might be held, e.g., that sports clubs in working-class Britain exist because they give working-class people a way of expending energy that would otherwise go into struggles against an exploitative system, thus undermining social stability. Sports clubs are explained, then, in terms of their contribution to social stability. This type of explanation is based on an analogy between biology and sociology.

Biologists explain species traits in terms of their contribution to reproductive fitness, and sociologists sometimes explain social traits in terms of their contribution to "social" fitness. However, the analogy is misleading, because there is a general mechanism establishing functionality in the biological realm that is not present in the social realm. This is the mechanism of natural selection, through which a species arrives at a set of traits that are locally optimal. There is no analogous process at work in the social realm, however; so it is groundless to suppose that social traits exist *because* of their beneficial consequences for the good of society as a whole (or important subsystems within society). So functional explanations of social phenomena must be buttressed by specific accounts of the causal processes that underlie the postulated functional relationships.

See also CAUSATION, DECISION THEORY, EXPLANATION, PHILOSOPHY OF SCIENCE, VERSTEHEN.   D.E.L.

Philo the Megarian. See MEGARIANS.

phrase marker. See AMBIGUITY.

phrase structure. See PARSING.

phrastic. See PRESCRIPTIVISM.

phronesis. See ARISTOTLE.

physicalism, in the widest sense of the term, materialism applied to the question of the nature of mind. So construed, physicalism is the thesis – call it ontological physicalism – that whatever exists or occurs is ultimately constituted out of physical entities. But sometimes 'physicalism' is used to refer to the thesis that whatever exists or occurs can be completely described in the vocabulary of physics. Such a view goes with either reductionism or eliminativism about the mental. Here reductionism is the view that psychological explanations, including explanations in terms of "folk-psychological" concepts such as those of belief and desire, are reducible to explanations formulable in a physical vocabulary, which in turn would imply that entities referred to in psychological explanations can be fully described in physical terms; and elminativism is the view that nothing corresponds to the terms in psychological explanations, and that the only correct explanations are in physical terms.

The term 'physicalism' appears to have originated in the Vienna Circle, and the reductionist version initially favored there was a version of behaviorism: psychological statements were held to be translatable into behavioral statements, mainly hypothetical conditionals, expressible in a physical vocabulary. The psychophysical identity theory held by Herbert Feigl, Smart, and others, sometimes called type physicalism, is reductionist in a somewhat different sense. This holds that mental states and events are identical with neurophysiological states and events. While it denies that there can be analytic, meaning-preserving translations of mental statements into physicalistic ones, it holds that by means of synthetic "bridge laws," identifying mental types with physical ones, mental statements can in principle be translated into physicalistic ones with which they are at least nomologically equivalent (if the terms in the bridge laws are rigid designators, the equivalence will be necessary). The possibility of such a translation is typically denied by functionalist accounts of mind, on the grounds that the same mental state may have indefinitely many different physical realizations, and sometimes on the grounds that it is logically possible, even if it never happens, that mental states should be realized non-physically.

In his classic paper "The 'mental' and the 'physical' " (1958), Feigl distinguishes two senses of 'physical': 'physical$_1$' and 'physical$_2$'. 'Physical$_1$' is practically synonymous with 'scientific', applying to whatever is "an essential part of the coherent and adequate descriptive and explanatory account of the spatiotemporal world." 'Physical$_2$' refers to "the type of concepts and laws which suffice in principle for the explanation and prediction of inorganic processes." (It would seem that if Cartesian dualism were true, supposing that possible, then once an integrated science of the interaction of immaterial souls and material bodies had been developed, concepts for describing the former would count as physical$_1$.) Construed as an ontological doctrine, physicalism says that whatever exists or occurs is entirely constituted out of those entities that constitute inorganic things and processes. Construed as a reductionist or elminativist thesis about description and explanation, it is the claim that a vocabulary adequate for describing and explaining inorganic things and processes is adequate for describing and explaining whatever exists.

While the second of these theses seems to imply the first, the first does not imply the second. It can be questioned whether the notion of a "full" description of what exists makes sense. And many ontological physicalists (materialists)

hold that a reduction to explanations couched in the terminology of physics is impossible, not only in the case of psychological explanations but also in the case of explanations couched in the terminology of such special sciences as biology. Their objection to such reduction is not merely that a purely physical description of (e.g.) biological or psychological phenomena would be unwieldy; it is that such descriptions necessarily miss important laws and generalizations, ones that can only be formulated in terms of biological, psychological, etc., concepts.

If ontological physicalists (materialists) are not committed to the reducibility of psychology to physics, neither are they committed to any sort of identity theory claiming that entities picked out by mental or psychological descriptions are identical to entities fully characterizable by physical descriptions. As already noted, materialists who are functionalists deny that there are type-type identities between mental entities and physical ones. And some deny that materialists are even committed to token-token identities, claiming that any psychological event could have had a different physical composition and so is not identical to any event individuated in terms of a purely physical taxonomy.

See also NATURALISM, PHILOSOPHY OF MIND, REDUCTION, UNITY OF SCIENCE.

S.Sho.

physical realization. See REDUCTION.

physician-assisted suicide. See BIOETHICS.

physis, Greek term for nature, primarily used to refer to the nature or essence of a living thing (Aristotle, *Metaphysics* V.4). *Physis* is defined by Aristotle in *Physics* II.1 as a source of movement and rest that belongs to something in virtue of itself, and identified by him primarily with the form, rather than the matter, of the thing. The term is also used to refer to the natural world as a whole. *Physis* is often contrasted with *techne*, art; in ethics it is also contrasted with *nomos*, convention, e.g. by Callicles in Plato's *Gorgias* (482e *ff.*), who distinguishes natural from conventional justice. **See also** ARISTOTLE, PLATO, TECHNE.   W.J.P.

pi, Chinese term meaning 'screen', 'shelter', or 'cover'. *Pi* is Hsün Tzu's metaphor for an obscuration or blindness of mind. In this condition the mind is obstructed in its proper functioning, e.g., thinking, remembering, imagining, and judging. In short, a *pi* is anything that obstructs the mind's cognitive task. When the mind is in the state of *pi*, reason is, so to speak, not operating properly. The opposite of *pi* is clarity of mind, a precondition for the pursuit of knowledge.   A.S.C.

Piaget, Jean (1896–1980), Swiss psychologist and epistemologist who profoundly influenced questions, theories, and methods in the study of cognitive development. The philosophical interpretation and implications of his work, however, remain controversial. Piaget regarded himself as engaged in genetic epistemology, the study of what knowledge is through an empirical investigation of how our epistemic relations to objects are improved. Piaget hypothesized that our epistemic relations are constructed through the progressive organization of increasingly complex behavioral interactions with physical objects. The cognitive system of the adult is neither learned, in the Skinnerian sense, nor genetically preprogrammed. Rather, it results from the organization of specific interactions whose character is shaped both by the features of the objects interacted with (a process called *accommodation*) and by the current cognitive system of the child (a process called *assimilation*). The tendency toward *equilibrium* results in a change in the nature of the interaction as well as in the cognitive system. Of particular importance for the field of cognitive development were Piaget's detailed descriptions and categorizations of changes in the organization of the cognitive system from birth through adolescence. That work focused on changes in the child's understanding of such things as space, time, cause, number, length, weight, and morality. Among his major works are *The Child's Conception of Number* (1941), *Biology and Knowledge* (1967), *Genetic Epistemology* (1970), and *Psychology and Epistemology* (1970). **See also** EPISTEMOLOGY.   R.A.Sa.

Pico della Mirandola, Giovanni (1463–94), Italian philosopher who, in 1486, wrote a series of 900 theses which he hoped to dispute publicly in Rome. Thirteen of these were criticized by a papal commission. When Pico defended himself in his *Apology*, the pope condemned all 900 theses. Pico fled to France, but was briefly imprisoned there in 1488. On his release, he returned to Florence and devoted himself to private study. He hoped to write a *Concord of Plato and Aristotle*, but the only part he was able to complete was *On Being and the One* (1492), in which he uses Aquinas and Christianity to reconcile Plato's and Aristotle's views about God's being and unity.

He is often described as a syncretist, but in fact he made it clear that the truth of Christianity has priority over the *prisca theologia* or ancient wisdom found in the hermetic corpus and the cabala. Though he was interested in magic and astrology, he adopts a guarded attitude toward them in his *Heptaplus* (1489), which contains a mystical interpretation of Genesis; and in his *Disputations Against Astrology*, published posthumously, he rejects them both. The treatise is largely technical, and the question of human freedom is set aside as not directly relevant. This fact casts some doubt on the popular thesis that Pico's philosophy was a celebration of man's freedom and dignity. Great weight has been placed on Pico's most famous work, *On the Dignity of Man* (1486). This is a short oration intended as an introduction to the disputation of his 900 theses, and the title was invented after his death. Pico has been interpreted as saying that man is set apart from the rest of creation, and is completely free to form his own nature. In fact, as the *Heptaplus* shows, Pico saw man as a microcosm containing elements of the angelic, celestial, and elemental worlds. Man is thus firmly within the hierarchy of nature, and is a bond and link between the worlds. In the oration, the emphasis on freedom is a moral one: man is free to choose between good and evil.   E.J.A.

picture theory of meaning. See MEANING, WITTGENSTEIN.

pien, Chinese Mohist technical term for disputation, defined as 'contending over converse claims'. It involves discrimination between what does and does not "fit the facts." In Hsün Tzu, *pien* as discrimination pertains especially to the ability to distinguish mental states (such as anger, grief, love, hate, and desires) as well as proper objects of different senses. *Pien* is significantly used in the context of justification as a phase in ethical argumentation. Among other things, *pien* as justification pertains to projection of the significance of comparable past ethical experiences to present "hard cases" of human life.   A.S.C.

pien che. See SCHOOL OF NAMES.

Pierre d'Ailly. See D'AILLY.

pineal gland. See DESCARTES, PHILOSOPHY OF MIND.

pistis. See DIVIDED LINE.

Plantinga, Alvin (b.1932), one of the most important twentieth-century American philosophers of religion. His ideas have determined the direction of debate in many aspects of the discipline. He has also contributed substantially to analytic epistemology and the metaphysics of modality. Plantinga is currently director of the Center for Philosophy of Religion and John O'Brien Professor of Philosophy at the University of Notre Dame.

Plantinga's philosophy of religion has centered on the epistemology of religious belief. His *God and Other Minds* (1967) introduced a defining claim of his career – that belief in God may be rational even if it is not supported by successful arguments from natural theology. This claim was fully developed in a series of articles published in the 1980s, in which he argued for the position he calls "Reformed Epistemology." Borrowing from the work of theologians such as Calvin, Bavinck, and Barth, Plantinga reasoned that theistic belief is "properly basic," justified not by other beliefs but by immediate experience. This position was most thoroughly treated in his article "Reason and Belief in God" (Plantinga and Wolterstorff, eds., *Faith and Rationality*, 1983).

In early work Plantinga assumed an internalist view of epistemic justification. Later he moved to externalism, arguing that basic theistic belief would count as knowledge if true and appropriately produced. He developed this approach in "Justification and Theism" (*Faith and Philosophy*, 1987). These ideas led to the development of a full-scale externalist epistemological theory, first presented in his 1989 Gifford Lectures and later published in the two-volume set *Warrant: The Current Debate* and *Warrant and Proper Function* (1993). This theory has become the focal point of much contemporary debate in analytic epistemology.

Plantinga is also a leading theorist in the metaphysics of modality. *The Nature of Necessity* (1974) developed a possible worlds semantics that has become standard in the literature. His analysis of possible worlds as maximally consistent states of affairs offers a realist compromise between nominalist and extreme reificationist conceptions. In the last two chapters, Plantinga brings his modal metaphysics to bear on two classical topics in the philosophy of religion. He presented what many consider the definitive version of the free will defense against the argument from evil and a modal version of the ontological argument that may have produced more response than any version since Anselm's original offering.

See also EPISTEMOLOGY, EVIDENTIALISM, PHILOSOPHY OF RELIGION, POSSIBLE WORLDS.

J.F.S.

Plato (427–347 B.C.), preeminent Greek philosopher whose chief contribution consists in his conception of the observable world as an imperfect image of a realm of unobservable and unchanging "Forms," and his conception of the best life as one centered on the love of these divine objects.

Life and influences. Born in Athens to a politically powerful and aristocratic family, Plato came under the influence of Socrates during his youth and set aside his ambitions for a political career after Socrates was executed for impiety. His travels in southern Italy and Sicily brought him into closer contact with the followers of Pythagoras, whose research in mathematics played an important role in his intellectual development. He was also acquainted with Cratylus, a follower of Heraclitus, and was influenced by their doctrine that the world is in constant flux. He wrote in opposition to the relativism of Protagoras and the purely materialistic mode of explanation adopted by Democritus. At the urging of a devoted follower, Dion, he became involved in the politics of Syracuse, the wealthiest city of the Greek world, but his efforts to mold the ideas of its tyrant, Dionysius II, were unmitigated failures. These painful events are described in Plato's *Letters* (*Epistles*), the longest and most important of which is the Seventh Letter, and although the authenticity of the *Letters* is a matter of controversy, there is little doubt that the author was well acquainted with Plato's life. After returning from his first visit to Sicily in 387, Plato established the Academy, a fraternal association devoted to research and teaching, and named after the sacred site on the outskirts of Athens where it was located. As a center for political training, it rivaled the school of Isocrates, which concentrated entirely on rhetoric. The best-known student of the Academy was Aristotle, who joined at the age of seventeen (when Plato was sixty) and remained for twenty years.

Chronology of the works. Plato's works, many of which take the form of dialogues between Socrates and several other speakers, were composed over a period of about fifty years, and this has led scholars to seek some pattern of philosophical development in them. Increasingly sophisticated stylometric tests have been devised to calculate the linguistic similarities among the dialogues. Ancient sources indicate that the *Laws* was Plato's last work, and there is now consensus that many affinities exist between the style of this work and several others, which can therefore also be safely regarded as late works; these include the *Sophist, Statesman,* and *Philebus* (perhaps written in that order). Stylometric tests also support a rough division of Plato's other works into early and middle periods. For example, the *Apology, Charmides, Crito, Euthyphro, Hippias Minor, Ion, Laches,* and *Protagoras* (listed alphabetically) are widely thought to be early; while the *Phaedo, Symposium, Republic,* and *Phaedrus* (perhaps written in that order) are agreed to belong to his middle period. But in some cases it is difficult or impossible to tell which of two works belonging to the same general period preceded the other; this is especially true of the early dialogues. The most controversial chronological question concerns the *Timaeus:* stylometric tests often place it with the later dialogues, though some scholars think that its philosophical doctrines are discarded in the later dialogues, and they therefore assign it to Plato's middle period. The underlying issue is whether he abandoned some of the main doctrines of this middle period.

Early and middle dialogues. The early dialogues typically portray an encounter between Socrates and an interlocutor who complacently assumes that he understands a common evaluative concept like courage, piety, or beauty. For example, Euthyphro, in the dialogue that bears his name, denies that there is any impiety in prosecuting his father, but repeated questioning by Socrates shows that he cannot say what single thing all pious acts have in common by virtue of which they are rightly called pious. Socrates professes to have no answer to these "What is *X*?" questions, and this fits well with the claim he makes in the *Apology* that his peculiarly human form of wisdom consists in realizing how little he knows. In these early dialogues, Socrates seeks but fails to find a philosophically defensible theory that would ground our use of normative terms.

The *Meno* is similar to these early dialogues – it asks what virtue is, and fails to find an answer – but it goes beyond them and marks a transition in Plato's thinking. It raises for the first time a question about methodology: if one does not have knowledge, how is it possible to acquire it simply by raising the questions Socrates poses in the early dialogues? To show that it is possible, Plato demonstrates that even a slave ignorant of geometry can begin to learn the subject through questioning. The dialogue then proposes an explanation of our ability to learn in this way: the soul acquired knowledge before it entered the body, and when we learn we are really *recollecting* what we once knew and forgot. This bold

speculation about the soul and our ability to learn contrasts with the noncommittal position Socrates takes in the *Apology,* where he is undecided whether the dead lose all consciousness or continue their activities in Hades. The confidence in immortality evident in the *Meno* is bolstered by arguments given in the *Phaedo, Republic,* and *Phaedrus.* In these dialogues, Plato uses metaphysical considerations about the nature of the soul and its ability to learn to support a conception of what the good human life is. Whereas the Socrates of the early dialogues focuses almost exclusively on ethical questions and is pessimistic about the extent to which we can answer them, Plato, beginning with the *Meno* and continuing throughout the rest of his career, confidently asserts that we can answer Socratic questions if we pursue ethical and metaphysical inquiries together.

The Forms. The *Phaedo* is the first dialogue in which Plato decisively posits the existence of the abstract objects that he often called "Forms" or "Ideas." (The latter term should be used with caution, since these objects are not creations of a mind, but exist independently of thought; the singular Greek terms Plato often uses to name these abstract objects are *eidos* and *idea.*) These Forms are eternal, changeless, and incorporeal; since they are imperceptible, we can come to have knowledge of them only through thought. Plato insists that it would be an error to identify two equal sticks with what Equality itself is, or beautiful bodies with what Beauty itself is; after all, he says, we might mistakenly take two equal sticks to be unequal, but we would never suffer from the delusion that Equality itself is unequal. The unchanging and incorporeal Form is the sort of object that is presupposed by Socratic inquiry; what every pious act has in common with every other is that it bears a certain relationship – called "participation" – to one and the same thing, the Form of Piety. In this sense, what makes a pious act pious and a pair of equal sticks equal are the Forms Piety and Equality. When we call sticks equal or acts pious, we are implicitly appealing to a standard of equality or piety, just as someone appeals to a standard when she says that a painted portrait of someone is a man. Of course, the pigment on the canvas is not a man; rather, it is properly called a man because it bears a certain relationship to a very different sort of object. In precisely this way, Plato claims that the Forms are what many of our words refer to, even though they are radically different sorts of objects from the ones revealed to the senses.

Love. For Plato the Forms are not merely an unusual item to be added to our list of existing objects. Rather, they are a source of moral and religious inspiration, and their discovery is therefore a decisive turning point in one's life. This process is described by a fictional priestess named Diotima in the *Symposium,* a dialogue containing a series of speeches in praise of love and concluding with a remarkable description of the passionate response Socrates inspired in Alcibiades, his most notorious admirer. According to Diotima's account, those who are in love are searching for something they do not yet understand; whether they realize it or not, they seek the eternal possession of the good, and they can obtain it only through productive activity of some sort. Physical love perpetuates the species and achieves a lower form of immortality, but a more beautiful kind of offspring is produced by those who govern cities and shape the moral characteristics of future generations. Best of all is the kind of love that eventually attaches itself to the Form of Beauty, since this is the most beautiful of all objects and provides the greatest happiness to the lover. One develops a love for this Form by ascending through various stages of emotional attachment and understanding. Beginning with an attraction to the beauty of one person's body, one gradually develops an appreciation for the beauty present in all other beautiful bodies; then one's recognition of the beauty in people's souls takes on increasing strength, and leads to a deeper attachment to the beauty of customs, laws, and systems of knowledge; and this process of emotional growth and deepening insight eventually culminates in the discovery of the eternal and changeless beauty of Beauty itself.

Plato's theory of erotic passion does not endorse "Platonic love," if that phrase designates a purely spiritual relationship completely devoid of physical attraction or expression. What he insists on is that desires for physical contact be restrained so that they do not subvert the greater good that can be accomplished in human relationships. His sexual orientation (like that of many of his Athenian contemporaries) is clearly homosexual, and he values the moral growth that can occur when one man is physically attracted to another, but in Book I of the *Laws* he condemns genital activity when it is homosexual, on the ground that such activity should serve a purely procreative purpose.

Plato's thoughts about love are further developed in the *Phaedrus.* The lover's longing for and physical attraction to another make him disregard the norms of commonplace and dispassionate human relationships: love of the right sort is therefore one of four kinds of divine madness. This fourfold classificatory scheme is then used as a model of proper methodology. Starting with the *Phaedrus,* classification – what Plato calls the "collection and division of kinds" – becomes the principal method to be used by philosophers, and this approach is most fully employed in such late works as the *Sophist, Statesman,* and *Philebus.* Presumably it contributed to Aristotle's interest in categories and biological classification.

The *Republic.* The moral and metaphysical theory centered on the Forms is most fully developed in the *Republic,* a dialogue that tries to determine whether it is in one's own best interests to be a just person. It is commonly assumed that injustice pays if one can get away with it, and that just behavior merely serves the interests of others. Plato attempts to show that on the contrary justice, properly understood, is so great a good that it is worth any sacrifice. To support this astonishing thesis, he portrays an ideal political community: there we will see justice writ large, and so we will be better able to find justice in the individual soul. An ideal city, he argues, must make radical innovations. It should be ruled by specially trained philosophers, since their understanding of the Form of the Good will give them greater insight into everyday affairs. Their education is compared to that of a prisoner who, having once gazed upon nothing but shadows in the artificial light of a cave, is released from bondage, leaves the cave, eventually learns to see the sun, and is thereby equipped to return to the cave and see the images there for what they are. Everything in the rulers' lives is designed to promote their allegiance to the community: they are forbidden private possessions, their sexual lives are regulated by eugenic considerations, and they are not to know who their children are. Positions of political power are open to women, since the physical differences between them and men do not in all cases deprive them of the intellectual or moral capacities needed for political office. The works of poets are to be carefully regulated, for the false moral notions of the traditional poets have had a powerful and deleterious impact on the general public. Philosophical reflection is to replace popular poetry as the force that guides moral education.

What makes this city ideally just, according to Plato, is the dedication of each of its components to one task for which it is naturally suited and specially trained. The rulers are ideally equipped to rule; the soldiers are best able to enforce their commands; and the economic class, composed of farmers, craftsmen, builders, and so on, are content to do their work and to leave the tasks of making and enforcing the laws to others. Accordingly what makes the soul of a human being just is the same principle: each of its components must properly perform its own task. The part of us that is capable of understanding and reasoning is the part that must rule; the assertive part that makes us capable of anger and competitive spirit must give our understanding the force it needs; and our appetites for food and sex must be trained so that they seek only those objects that reason approves. It is not enough to educate someone's reason, for unless the emotions and appetites are properly trained they will overpower it. Just individuals are those who have fully integrated these elements of the soul. They do not unthinkingly follow a list of rules; rather, their just treatment of others flows from their own balanced psychological condition. And the paradigm of a just person is a philosopher, for reason rules when it becomes passionately attached to the most intelligible objects there are: the Forms. It emerges that justice pays because attachment to these supremely valuable objects is part of what true justice of the soul is. The worth of our lives depends on the worth of the objects to which we devote ourselves. Those who think that injustice pays assume that wealth, domination, or the pleasures of physical appetite are supremely valuable; their mistake lies in their limited conception of what sorts of objects are worth loving.

Late dialogues. The *Republic* does not contain Plato's last thoughts on moral or metaphysical matters. For example, although he continues to hold in his final work, the *Laws,* that the family and private wealth should ideally be abolished, he describes in great detail a second-best community that retains these and many other institutions of ordinary political life. The sovereignty of law in such a state is stressed continually; political offices are to be filled by elections and lots, and magistrates are subject to careful scrutiny and prosecution. Power is divided among several councils and offices, and philosophical training is not a prerequisite for political participation. This second-best state is still worlds apart from a modern liberal democracy – poetic works and many features of private life are carefully regulated, and atheism is punished with death – but it is remarkable that Plato, after having made no concessions to popular participation in the *Republic,*

devoted so much energy to finding a proper place for it in his final work.

Plato's thoughts about metaphysics also continued to evolve, and perhaps the most serious problem in interpreting his work as a whole is the problem of grasping the direction of these further developments. One notorious obstacle to understanding his later metaphysics is presented by the *Parmenides,* for here we find an unanswered series of criticisms of the theory of Forms. For example, it is said that if there is reason to posit one Form of Largeness (to select an arbitrary example) then there is an equally good reason to posit an unlimited number of Forms of this type. The "first" Form of Largeness must exist because according to Plato whenever a number of things are large, there is a Form of Largeness that makes them large; but now, the argument continues, if we consider this Form together with the other large things, we should recognize still another Form, which makes the large things and Largeness itself large. The argument can be pursued indefinitely, but it seems absurd that there should be an unlimited number of Forms of this one type. (In antiquity the argument was named *the Third Man,* because it claims that in addition to a second type of object called "man" – the Form of Man – there is even a third.)

What is Plato's response to this and other objections to his theory? He says in the *Parmenides* that we must continue to affirm the existence of such objects, for language and thought require them; but instead of responding directly to the criticisms, he embarks on a prolonged examination of the concept of unity, reaching apparently conflicting conclusions about it. Whether these contradictions are merely apparent and whether this treatment of unity contains a response to the earlier critique of the Forms are difficult matters of interpretation. But in any case it is clear that Plato continues to uphold the existence of unchanging realities; the real difficulty is whether and how he modifies his earlier views about them.

In the *Timaeus,* there seem to be no modifications at all – a fact that has led some scholars to believe, in spite of some stylometric evidence to the contrary, that this work was written before Plato composed the critique of the Forms in the *Parmenides.* This dialogue presents an account of how a divine but not omnipotent craftsman transformed the disorderly materials of the universe into a harmonious cosmos by looking to the unchanging Forms as paradigms and creating, to the best of his limited abilities, constantly fluctuating images of those paradigms. The created cosmos is viewed as a single living organism governed by its own divinely intelligent soul; time itself came into existence with the cosmos, being an image of the timeless nature of the Forms; space, however, is not created by the divine craftsman but is the characterless receptacle in which all change takes place. The basic ingredients of the universe are not earth, air, fire, and water, as some thinkers held; rather, these elements are composed of planes, which are in turn made out of elementary triangular shapes. The *Timaeus* is an attempt to show that although many other types of objects besides the Forms must be invoked in order to understand the orderly nature of the changing universe – souls, triangles, space – the best scientific explanations will portray the physical world as a purposeful and very good approximation to a perfect pattern inherent in these unchanging and eternal objects.

But Forms do not play as important a role in the *Philebus*, a late dialogue that contains Plato's fullest answer to the question, What is the good? He argues that neither pleasure not intelligence can by itself be identified with the good, since no one would be satisfied with a life that contained just one of these but totally lacked the other. Instead, goodness is identified with proportion, beauty, and truth; and intelligence is ranked a superior good to pleasure because of its greater kinship to these three. Here, as in the middle dialogues, Plato insists that a proper understanding of goodness requires a metaphysical grounding. To evaluate the role of pleasure in human life, we need a methodology that applies to all other areas of understanding. More specifically, we must recognize that everything can be placed in one of four categories: the limited, the unlimited, the mixture of these two, and the intelligent creation of this mixture. Where Forms are to be located in this scheme is unclear. Although metaphysics is invoked to answer practical questions, as in the *Republic*, it is not precisely the same metaphysics as before.

Though we naturally think of Plato primarily as a writer of philosophical works, he regards the written word as inferior to spoken interchange as an instrument for learning and teaching. The drawbacks inherent in written composition are most fully set forth in the *Phaedrus*. There is no doubt that in the Academy he participated fully in philosophical debate, and on at least one occasion he lectured to a general audience. We are told by Aristoxenus, a pupil of Aristotle, that many in Plato's audience were baffled and disappointed by a lecture in which he maintained that

Good is one. We can safely assume that in conversation Plato put forward important philosophical ideas that nonetheless did not find their way into his writings. Aristotle refers in *Physics* IV.2 to one of Plato's doctrines as unwritten, and the enigmatic positions he ascribes to Plato in *Metaphysics* I.6 – that the Forms are to be explained in terms of number, which are in turn generated from the One and the dyad of great and small – seem to have been expounded solely in discussion. Some scholars have put great weight on the statement in the Seventh Letter that the most fundamental philosophical matters must remain unwritten, and, using later testimony about Plato's unwritten doctrines, they read the dialogues as signs of a more profound but hidden truth. The authenticity of the Seventh Letter is a disputed question, however. In any case, since Aristotle himself treats the middle and late dialogues as undissembling accounts of Plato's philosophy, we are on firm ground in adopting the same approach.

See also ARISTOTLE, COMMENTARIES ON PLATO, NEOPLATONISM, SOCRATES.   R.Kr.

Plato, commentaries on. See COMMENTARIES ON PLATO.

Platonic form. See FORM, PLATO.

pleasure. See EPICUREANISM, HEDONISM.

pleasure, katastematic. See EPICUREANISM.

pleasure, kinetic. See EPICUREANISM.

pleasure principle. See FREUD.

Plekhanov, Georgy Valentinovich (1856–1918), a leading theoretician of the Russian revolutionary movement and the father of Russian Marxism. Exiled from his native Russia for most of his adult life, in 1883 he founded in Switzerland the first Russian Marxist association – the Emancipation of Labor, a forerunner of the Russian Social Democratic Workers' party. In philosophy he sought to systematize and disseminate the outlook of Marx and Engels, for which he popularized the name 'dialectical materialism'. For the most part an orthodox Marxist in his understanding of history, Plekhanov argued that historical developments cannot be diverted or accelerated at will; he believed that Russia was not ready for a proletarian revolution in the first decades of the twentieth century, and consequently he opposed the Bolshevik faction in the split (1903) of the Social Democratic party. At the same time he was not a simplistic economic determinist: he accepted the role of geographical, psychological, and other non-economic factors in historical change. In epistemology, Plekhanov agreed with Kant that we cannot know things in themselves, but he argued that our sensations may be conceived as "hieroglyphs," corresponding point by point to the elements of reality without resembling them. In ethics, too, Plekhanov sought to supplement Marx with Kant, tempering the class analysis of morality with the view that there are universally binding ethical principles, such as the principle that human beings should be treated as ends rather than means. Because in these and other respects Plekhanov's version of Marxism conflicted with Lenin's, his philosophy was scornfully rejected by doctrinaire Marxist-Leninists during the Stalin era. **See also** RUSSIAN PHILOSOPHY.   J.P.Sc.

plenitude, principle of. See PRINCIPLE OF PLENITUDE.

pleonetetic logic. See PLURALITIVE LOGIC.

Plotinus (A.D. 204–70), Greco-Roman Neoplatonist philosopher. Born in Egypt, though doubtless of Greek ancestry, he studied Platonic philosophy in Alexandria with Ammonius Saccas (232–43); then, after a brief adventure on the staff of the Emperor Gordian III on an unsuccessful expedition against the Persians, he came to Rome in 244 and continued teaching philosophy there until his death. He enjoyed the support of many prominent people, including even the Emperor Gallienus and his wife. His chief pupils were Amelius and Porphyry, the latter of whom collected and edited his philosophical essays, the *Enneads* (so called because arranged by Porphyry in six groups of nine). The first three groups concern the physical world and our relation to it, the fourth concerns Soul, the fifth Intelligence, and the sixth the One. Porphyry's arrangement is generally followed today, though a chronological sequence of tractates, which he also provides in his introductory *Life of Plotinus*, is perhaps preferable. The most important treatises are I.1; I.2; I.6; II.4; II.8; III.2–3; III.6; III.7; IV.3–4; V.1; V.3; VI.4–5; VI.7; VI.8; VI.9; and the group III.8, V.8, V.5, and II.9 (a single treatise, split up by Porphyry, that is a wide-ranging account of Plotinus's philosophical position, culminating in an attack on gnosticism).

Plotinus saw himself as a faithful exponent of Plato (see especially *Enneads* V.1), but he is far more than that. Platonism had developed considerably in the five centuries that separate Plato from Plotinus, taking on much from both Aristotelianism and Stoicism, and Plotinus is the heir to this process. He also adds much himself.

See also EMANATIONISM, NEOPLATONISM.

      J.M.D.

pluralism, a philosophical perspective on the world that emphasizes diversity rather than homogeneity, multiplicity rather than unity, difference rather than sameness. The philosophical consequences of pluralism were addressed by Greek antiquity in its preoccupation with the problem of the one and the many. The proponents of pluralism, represented principally by Empedocles, Anaxagoras, and the Atomists (Leucippus and Democritus), maintained that reality was made up of a multiplicity of entities. Adherence to this doctrine set them in opposition to the monism of the Eleatic School (Parmenides), which taught that reality was an impermeable unity and an unbroken solidarity. It was thus that pluralism came to be defined as a philosophical alternative to monism.

In the development of Occidental thought, pluralism came to be contrasted not only with monism but also with dualism, the philosophical doctrine that there are two, and only two, kinds of existents. Descartes, with his doctrine of two distinct substances – extended non-thinking substance versus non-extended thinking substance – is commonly regarded as having provided the clearest example of philosophical dualism. Pluralism thus needs to be understood as marking out philosophical alternatives to both monism and dualism.

Pluralism as a metaphysical doctrine requires that we distinguish substantival from attributive pluralism. *Substantival pluralism* views the world as containing a multiplicity of substances that remain irreducible to each other. *Attributive pluralism* finds the multiplicity of kinds not among the furniture of substances that make up the world but rather among a diversity of attributes and distinguishing properties. However, pluralism came to be defined not only as a metaphysical doctrine but also as a regulative principle of explanation that calls upon differing explanatory principles and conceptual schemes to account for the manifold events of nature and the varieties of human experience.

Recent philosophical thought has witnessed a resurgence of interest in pluralism. This was evident in the development of American pragmatism, where pluralism received piquant expression in James's *A Pluralistic Universe* (1909). More recently pluralism was given a voice in the thought of the later Wittgenstein, with its heavy accent on the plurality of language games displayed in our ordinary discourse. Also, in the current developments of philosophical postmodernism (Jean-François Lyotard), one finds an explicit pluralistic orientation. Here the emphasis falls on the multiplicity of signifiers, phrase regimens, genres of discourse, and narrational strategies. The alleged unities and totalities of thought, discourse, and action are subverted in the interests of reclaiming the diversified and heterogeneous world of human experience.

Pluralism in contemporary thought initiates a move into a postmetaphysical age. It is less concerned with traditional metaphysical and epistemological issues, seeking answers to questions about the nature and kinds of substances and attributes; and it is more attuned to the diversity of social practices and the multiple roles of language, discourse, and narrative in the panoply of human affairs.

See also DEWEY, POSTMODERN, PRAGMATISM, SPECULATIVE PHILOSOPHY.   C.O.S.

pluralitive logic, also called pleonetetic logic, the logic of 'many', 'most', 'few', and similar terms (including 'four out of five', 'over 45 percent' and so on). Consider

(1) 'Almost all F are G'
(2) 'Almost all F are not G'
(3) 'Most F are G'
(4) 'Most F are not G'
(5) 'Many F are G'
(6) 'Many F are not G'

(1) i.e., 'Few F are not G' and (6) are contradictory, as are (2) and (5) and (3) and (4). (1) and (2) cannot be true together (i.e., they are contraries), nor can (3) and (4), while (5) and (6) cannot be false together (i.e., they are subcontraries). Moreover, (1) entails (3) which entails (5), and (2) entails (4) which entails (6). Thus (1)–(6) form a generalized "square of opposition" (fitting inside the standard one).

Sometimes (3) is said to be true if more than half the F's are G, but this makes 'most' unnecessarily precise, for 'most' does not literally mean 'more than half'. Although many pluralitive terms are vague, their interrelations are logically precise. Again, one might define 'many' as 'There are at least n', for some fixed n, at least relative to context. But this not only erodes the vagueness, it also fails to work for arbitrarily large and infinite domains.

'Few', 'most', and 'many' are binary quantifiers, a type of generalized quantifier. A unary quantifier, such as the standard quantifiers 'some' and 'all', connotes a second-level property, e.g., 'Something is F' means 'F has an instance', and 'All F's are G' means 'F and not G has no instance'. A generalized quantifier connotes a second-level relation. 'Most F's are G' connotes a binary relation between F and G, one that cannot be reduced to any property of a truth-functional compound of F and G. In fact, none of the standard pluralitive terms can be defined in first-order logic.

See also FORMAL LOGIC, SQUARE OF OPPOSITION, VAGUENESS.   S.L.R.

plurality of causes, as used by J. S. Mill, more than one cause of a single effect; i.e., tokens of different event types causing different tokens of the same event type. Plurality of causes is distinct from overdetermination of an event by more than one actual or potential token cause. For example, an animal's death has a plurality of causes: it may die of starvation, of bleeding, of a blow to the head, and so on. Mill thought these cases were important because he saw that the existence of a plurality of causes creates problems for his four methods for determining causes. Mill's method of agreement is specifically vulnerable to the problem: the method fails to reveal the cause of an event when the event has more than one type of cause, because the method presumes that causes are necessary for their effects.

Actually, plurality of causes is a commonplace fact about the world because very few causes are necessary for their effects. Unless the background conditions are specified in great detail, or the identity of the effect type is defined very narrowly, almost all cases involve a plurality of causes. For example, flipping the light switch is a necessary cause of the light's going on, only if one assumes that there will be no short circuit across the switch, that the wiring will remain as it is, and so on, or if one assumes that by 'the light's going on' one means the light's going on *in the normal way*.

See also CAUSATION; MILL, J. S.; MILL'S METHODS; TYPE–TOKEN DISTINCTION.   B.E.

Plutarch of Athens. See NEOPLATONISM.

Plutarch of Chaeronea. See ACADEMY, MIDDLE PLATONISM.

PM. See APPENDIX OF SPECIAL SYMBOLS.

pneuma. See STOICISM.

Po-hu tung ("White Tiger Hall Consultations"), an important Chinese Confucian work of the later Han dynasty, resulting from discussions at the imperial palace in A.D. 79 on the classics and their commentaries. Divided into forty-three headings, the text sums up the dominant teachings of Confucianism by affirming the absolute position of the monarch, a cosmology and moral psychology based on the yin–yang theory, and a comprehensive social and political philosophy. While emphasizing benevolent government, it legitimizes the right of the ruler to use force to quell disorder. A system of "three bonds and six relationships" defines the hierarchical structure of society. Human nature, identified with the yang cosmic force, must be cultivated, while feelings (yin) are to be controlled especially by rituals and education. The Confucian orthodoxy affirmed also marks an end to the debate between the Old Text school and the New Text school that divided earlier Han scholars. **See also** CONFUCIANISM; YIN, YANG.   A.K.L.C.

poiēsis (Greek, 'production'), behavior aimed at an external end. In Aristotle, *poiēsis* is opposed to *praxis* (action). It is characteristic of crafts – e.g. building, the end of which is houses. It is thus a *kinēsis* (process). For Aristotle, exercising the virtues, since it must be undertaken for its own sake, cannot be *poiēsis*. The knowledge involved in virtue is therefore not the same as that involved in crafts.   R.C.

Poincaré, Jules Henri (1854–1912), French mathematician and influential philosopher of science. Born into a prominent family in Nancy, he showed extraordinary talent in mathematics from an early age. He studied at the École des Mines and worked as a mining engineer while completing his doctorate in mathematics (1879). In 1881, he was appointed professor at the University of Paris, where he lectured on mathematics, physics, and astronomy until his death. His original contributions to the theory of differential equations, algebraic topology, and number theory made him the leading mathematician of his day. He published almost five hundred technical papers as well as three widely read books on the philosophy of science: *Science and Hypothesis* (1902), *The Value of Science* (1905), and *Science and Method* (1908).

Poincaré's philosophy of science was shaped by his approach to mathematics. Geometric axioms are neither synthetic a priori nor empirical; they are more properly understood as *definitions*. Thus, when one set of axioms is preferred over another for use in physics, the choice is a matter of "convention"; it is governed by criteria of simplicity and economy of expression rather than by which geometry is "correct." Though Euclidean geometry is used to describe the motions of bodies in space, it makes no sense to ask whether physical space "really" is Euclidean. Discovery in mathematics resembles discovery in the physical sciences, but whereas the former is a construction of the human mind, the latter has to be fitted to an order of nature that is ultimately independent of mind.

Science provides an economic and fruitful way of expressing the relationships between classes of sensations, enabling reliable predictions to be made. These sensations reflect the world that causes them; the (limited) objectivity of science derives from this fact, but science does not purport to determine the nature of that underlying world. Conventions, choices that are not determinable by rule, enter into the physical sciences at all levels. Such principles as that of the conservation of energy may appear to be empirical, but are in fact postulates that scientists have chosen to treat as implicit definitions. The decision between alternative hypotheses also involves an element of convention: the choice of a particular curve to represent a finite set of data points, e.g., requires a judgment as to which is simpler.

Two kinds of hypotheses, in particular, must be distinguished. Inductive generalizations from observation ("real generalizations") are hypothetical in the limited sense that they are always capable of further precision. Then there are theories ("indifferent hypotheses") that postulate underlying entities or structures. These entities may seem explanatory, but strictly speaking are no more than devices useful in calculation. For atomic theory to *explain,* atoms would have to exist. But this cannot be established in the only way permissible for a scientific claim, i.e. directly by experiment. Shortly before he died, Poincaré finally allowed that Perrin's experimental verification of Einstein's predictions regarding Brownian motion, plus his careful marshaling of twelve other distinct experimental methods of calculating Avogadro's number, constituted the equivalent of an experimental proof of the existence of atoms: "One can say that we see them because we can count them. . . . The atom of the chemist is now a reality."

See also CONVENTIONALISM, PHILOSOPHY OF MATHEMATICS.   E.M.

polarity, the relation between distinct phenomena, terms, or concepts such that each inextricably requires, though it is opposed to, the other, as in the relation between the north and south poles of a magnet. In application to terms or concepts, polarity entails that the meaning of one involves the meaning of the other. This is *conceptual* polarity. Terms are *existentially* polar provided an instance of one cannot exist unless there exists an instance of the other. The second sense implies the first. *Supply* and *demand* and *good* and *evil* are instances of conceptual polarity. *North* and *south* and *buying* and *selling* are instances of existential polarity. Some polar concepts are opposites, such as *truth* and *falsity*. Some are *correlative*, such as question and answer: an answer is always an answer *to* a question; a question *calls for* an answer, but a question can be an answer, and an answer can be a question. The concept is not restricted to pairs and can be extended to generate mutual interdependence, multipolarity. **See also** MEANING, PHILOSOPHY OF LANGUAGE.   M.G.S.

Polish logic, logic as researched, elucidated, and taught in Poland, 1919–39. Between the two wars colleagues Jan Łukasiewicz, Tadeusz Kotarbiński, and Stanisław Leśniewski, assisted by students-become-collaborators such as Alfred Tarski, Jerzy Słupecki, Stanisław Jaskowski, and Bolesław Sobociński, together with mathematicians in Warsaw and philosophical colleagues elsewhere, like Kasimir Ajdukiewicz and Tadeusz Czeżowski, made Warsaw an internationally known center of research in logic, metalogic, semantics, and foundations of mathematics. The Warsaw "school" also dominated Polish philosophy, and made Poland the country that introduced modern logic even in secondary schools.

All three founders took their doctorates in Lvov under Kasimir Twardowski (1866–1938), mentor of leading thinkers of independent Poland between the wars. Arriving from Vienna to take the chair of philosophy at twenty-nine, Twardowski had to choose between concentrating on his own research and organizing the study of philosophy in Poland. Dedicating his life primarily to the community task, he became the founder of modern Polish philosophy.

Twardowski's informal distinction between distributive and collective conceptions influenced classification of philosophy and the sciences, and anticipated Leśniewski's formal axiomatizations in ontology and mereology, respectively. Another common inheritance important in Polish logic was Twardowski's stress on the process–product ambiguity. He applied this distinction to disambiguate 'meaning' and refine his teacher Brentano's account of mental acts as meaningful ("intentional") events, by differentiating (1) what is *meant* or "intended" by the act, its objective noema or noematic "intentional object," from (2) its corresponding noetic *meaning* or subjective "content," the correlated characteristic or structure by which it "intends" its "object" or "objective" – i.e., *means that:* such-and-such (is so).

Twardowski's teaching – especially this careful analysis of "contents" and "objects" of mental acts – contributed to Meinong's theory of objects, and linked it, Husserl's phenomenology, and Anton Marty's "philosophical grammar" with the "descriptive psychology" of their common teacher, the Aristotelian and Scholastic empiricist Brentano, and thus with sources of the analytic movements in Vienna and Cambridge. Twardowski's lectures on the philosophical logic of content and judgment prepared the ground for scientific semantics; his references to Boolean algebra opened the door to mathematical logic; and his phenomenological idea of a general theory of objects pointed toward Leśniewski's ontology. Twardowski's maieutic character, integrity, grounding in philosophical traditions, and arduous training (lectures began at six a.m.), together with his realist defense of the classical Aristotelian correspondence theory of truth against "irrationalism," dogmatism, skepticism, and psychologism, influenced his many pupils, who became leaders of Polish thought in diverse fields. But more influential than any doctrine was his rigorist ideal of philosophy as a strict scientific discipline of criticism and logical analysis, precise definition, and conceptual clarification. His was a school not of *doctrine* but of *method*. Maintaining this common methodological inheritance in their divergent ways, and encouraged to learn more mathematical logic than Twardowski himself knew, his students in logic were early influenced by Frege's and Husserl's critique of psychologism in logic, Husserl's logical investigations, and the logical reconstruction of classical mathematics by Frege, Schröder, Whitehead, and Russell.

As lecturer in Lvov from 1908 until his appointment to Warsaw in 1915, Łukasiewicz introduced mathematical logic into Poland. To Leśniewski, newly arrived from studies in Germany as an enthusiast for Marty's philosophy of language, Łukasiewicz's influential 1910 *Critique* of Aristotle's principle of contradiction was a "revelation" in 1911. Among other things it revealed paradoxes like Russell's, which preoccupied him for the next eleven years as, logically refuting Twardowski's Platonist theory of abstraction, he worked out his own solutions and, influenced also by Leon Chwistek, outgrew the influence of Hans Cornelius and Leon Petrażycki, and developed his own "constructively nominalist" foundations.

In 1919 Kotarbiśski and Leśniewski joined Łukasiewicz in Warsaw, where they attracted students like Tarski, Sobociński, and Słupecki in the first generation, and Andrzej Mostowski and Czesław Lejewski in the next. When the war came, the survivors were scattered and the metalogicians Morchaj Wajsberg, Moritz Presburger, and Adolf Lindenbaum were killed or "disappeared" by the Gestapo. Łukasiewicz concentrated increasingly on history of logic (especially in reconstructing the logic of Aristotle and the Stoics) and deductive problems concerning syllogistic and propositional logic. His idea of logical probability and development of three- or many-valued and modal calculi reflected his indeterminist sympathies in prewar exchanges with Kotarbiński and Leśniewski on the status of truths (eternal, sempiternal, or both?), especially as concerns future contingencies. Leśniewski concentrated on developing his *logical* systems. He left elaboration of many of his seminal metalogical and semantic insights to Tarski, who, despite a divergent inclination to simplify metamathematical deductions by expedient postulation, shared with Leśniewski, Łukasiewicz, and Ajdukiewicz the conviction that only formalized languages can be made logically consistent subjects *and* instruments of rigorous scientific investigation. Kotarbiński drew on Leśniewski's logic of predication to defend his "reism" (as *one* possible application of Leśniewski's ontology), to facilitate his "concretist" program for translating abstractions into more concrete terms, and to rationalize his "imitationist" account of mental acts or dispositions. Inheriting Twardowski's role as cultural leader and educator, Kotarbiński popularized the logical achievements of his colleagues in (e.g.) his substantial 1929 treatise on the theory of knowledge, formal logic, and scientific methodology; this work became required reading for serious students and, together with the lucid textbooks by Łukasiewicz and Ajdukiewicz, raised the level of philosophical discussion in Poland. Jaskowski published a system of "natural deduction" by the suppositional method practiced by Leśniewski since 1916. Ajdukiewicz based his syntax on Leśniewski's

logical grammar, and by his searching critiques influenced Kotarbiński's "reist" and "concretist" formulations.

Closest in Poland to the logical positivists of the Vienna Circle, Ajdukiewicz brought new sophistication to the philosophy of language and of science by his examination of the role of conventions and meaning postulates in scientific theory and language, distinguishing axiomatic, deductive, and empirical rules of meaning. His evolving and refined conventionalist analyses of theories, languages, "world perspectives," synonymy, translation, and analyticity, and his philosophical clarification by paraphrase anticipated views of Carnap, Feigl, and Quine. But the Polish thinkers, beyond their common methodological inheritance and general adherence to extensional logic, subscribed to little common doctrine, and in their exchanges with the Vienna positivists remained "too sober" (said Łukasiewicz) to join in sweeping antimetaphysical manifestos. Like Twardowski, they were critics of traditional formulations, who sought not to *proscribe* but to *reform* metaphysics, by reformulating issues clearly enough to advance understanding. Indeed, except for Chwistek, the mathematician Jan Ślezyński, and the historians I. M. Bocheński, Z. A. Jordan, and Jan Salamucha, in addition to the phenomenologist Roman Ingarden, the key figures in Polish logic were all philosophical descendants of Twardowski.

See also KOTARBIŃSKI, LEŚNIEWSKI, ŁUKASIEWICZ.   E.C.L.

Polish notation. See LOGICAL NOTATION.

political obligation. See POLITICAL PHILOSOPHY.

political philosophy, the study of the nature and justification of coercive institutions. Coercive institutions range in size from the family to the nation-state and world organizations like the United Nations. They are institutions that at least sometimes employ force or the threat of force to control the behavior of their members. Justifying such coercive institutions requires showing that the authorities within them have a right to be obeyed and that their members have a corresponding obligation to obey them, i.e., that these institutions have legitimate political authority over their members.

Classical political philosophers, like Plato and Aristotle, were primarily interested in providing a justification for city-states like Athens or Sparta. But historically, as larger coercive institutions became possible and desirable, political philosophers sought to justify them. After the seventeenth century, most political philosophers focused on providing a justification for nation-states whose claim to legitimate authority is restricted by both geography and nationality. But from time to time, and more frequently in the nineteenth and twentieth centuries, some political philosophers have sought to provide a justification for various forms of world government with even more extensive powers than those presently exercised by the United Nations. And quite recently, feminist political philosophers have raised important challenges to the authority of the family as it is presently constituted.

Anarchism (from Greek *an archos*, 'no government') rejects this central task of political philosophy. It maintains that no coercive institutions are justified. Proudhon, the first self-described anarchist, believed that coercive institutions should be replaced by social and economic organizations based on voluntary contractual agreement, and he advocated peaceful change toward anarchism. Others, notably Blanqui and Bakunin, advocated the use of violence to destroy the power of coercive institutions. Anarchism inspired the anarcho-syndicalist movement, Makhno and his followers during the Russian Civil War, the Spanish anarchists during the Spanish Civil War, and the anarchist *gauchistes* during the 1968 "May Events" in France.

Most political philosophers, however, have sought to justify coercive institutions; they have simply disagreed over what sort of coercive institutions are justified. Liberalism, which derives from the work of Locke, is the view that coercive institutions are justified when they promote liberty. For Locke, liberty requires a constitutional monarchy with parliamentary government. Over time, however, the ideal of liberty became subject to at least two interpretations. The view that seems closest to Locke's is *classical liberalism*, which is now more frequently called (political) *libertarianism*. This form of liberalism interprets constraints on liberty as positive acts (i.e., acts of commission) that prevent people from doing what they otherwise could do. According to this view, failing to help people in need does not restrict their liberty. Libertarians maintain that when liberty is so interpreted only a minimal or night-watchman state that protects against force, theft, and fraud can be justified. In contrast, in *welfare liberalism*, a form of liberalism that derives from the work of T. H. Green, constraints on liberty are interpreted to include, in addition, neg-

ative acts (i.e., acts of omission) that prevent people from doing what they otherwise could do. According to this view, failing to help people in need does restrict their liberty. Welfare liberals maintain that when liberty is interpreted in this fashion, coercive institutions of a welfare state requiring a guaranteed social minimum and equal opportunity are justified. While no one denies that when liberty is given a welfare liberal interpretation some form of welfare state is required, there is considerable debate over whether a minimal state is required when liberty is given a libertarian interpretation. At issue is whether the liberty of the poor is constrained when they are prevented from taking from the surplus possessions of the rich what they need for survival. If such prevention does constrain the liberty of the poor, it could be argued that their liberty should have priority over the liberty of the rich not to be interfered with when using their surplus possessions for luxury purposes. In this way, it could be shown that even when the ideal of liberty is given a libertarian interpretation, a welfare state, rather than a minimal state, is justified.

Both libertarianism and welfare liberalism are committed to *individualism*. This view takes the rights of individuals to be basic and justifies the actions of coercive institutions as promoting those rights. *Communitarianism*, which derives from the writings of Hegel, rejects individualism. It maintains that rights of individuals are not basic and that the collective can have rights that are independent of and even opposed to what liberals claim are the rights of individuals. According to communitarians, individuals are constituted by the institutions and practices of which they are a part, and their rights and obligations derive from those same institutions and practices. *Fascism* is an extreme form of communitarianism that advocates an authoritarian state with limited rights for individuals. In its National Socialism (Nazi) variety, fascism was also anti-Semitic and militarist.

In contrast to liberalism and communitarianism, *socialism* takes equality to be the basic ideal and justifies coercive institutions insofar as they promote equality. In capitalist societies where the means of production are owned and controlled by a relatively small number of people and used primarily for their benefit, socialists favor taking control of the means of production and redirecting their use to the general welfare. According to Marx, the principle of distribution for a socialist society is: from each according to ability, to each according to needs. Socialists disagree among themselves, however, over who should control the means of production in a socialist society. In the version of socialism favored by Lenin, those who control the means of production are to be an elite seemingly differing only in their ends from the capitalist elite they replaced. In other forms of socialism, the means of production are to be controlled democratically. In advanced capitalist societies, national defense, police and fire protection, income redistribution, and environmental protection are already under democratic control. Democracy or "government by the people" is thought to apply in these areas, and to require some form of representation. Socialists simply propose to extend the domain of democratic control to include control of the means of production, on the ground that the very same arguments that support democratic control in these recognized areas also support democratic control of the means of production. In addition, according to Marx, socialism will transform itself into communism when most of the work that people perform in society becomes its own reward, making differential monetary reward generally unnecessary. Then distribution in society can proceed according to the principle, from each according to ability, to each according to needs.

It so happens that all of the above political views have been interpreted in ways that deny that women have the same basic rights as men. By contrast, *feminism,* almost by definition, is the political view that women and men have the same basic rights. In recent years, most political philosophers have come to endorse equal basic rights for women and men, but rarely do they address questions that feminists consider of the utmost importance, e.g., how responsibilities and duties are to be assigned in family structures.

Each of these political views must be evaluated both internally and externally by comparison with the other views. Once this is done, their practical recommendations may not be so different. For example, if welfare liberals recognize that the basic rights of their view extend to distant peoples and future generations, they may end up endorsing the same degree of equality socialists defend.

Whatever their practical requirements, each of these political views justifies civil disobedience, even revolution, when certain of those requirements have not been met. Civil disobedience is an illegal action undertaken to draw attention to a failure by the relevant authorities to meet basic moral requirements, e.g., the refusal of Rosa Parks to give up her seat in a bus to a white man in accord with the local ordinance in Montgomery, Alabama, in 1955. Civil disobedience is justified when illegal action of this sort is the best way to get the relevant authorities to bring the law into better correspondence with basic moral requirements. By contrast, revolutionary action is justified when it is the only way to correct a radical failure of the relevant authorities to meet basic moral requirements. When revolutionary action is justified, people no longer have a political obligation to obey the relevant authorities; that is, they are no longer morally required to obey them, although they may still continue to do so, e.g. out of habit or fear.

Recent contemporary political philosophy has focused on the communitarian–liberal debate. In defense of the communitarian view, Alasdair MacIntyre has argued that virtually all forms of liberalism attempt to separate rules defining right action from conceptions of the human good. On this account, he contends, these forms of liberalism must fail because the rules defining right action cannot be adequately grounded apart from a conception of the good. Responding to this type of criticism, some liberals have openly conceded that their view is not grounded independently of some conception of the good. Rawls, e.g., has recently made clear that his liberalism requires a conception of the political good, although not a comprehensive conception of the good. It would seem, therefore, that the debate between communitarians and liberals must turn on a comparative evaluation of their competing conceptions of the good. Unfortunately, contemporary communitarians have not yet been very forthcoming about what particular conception of the good their view requires.

See also ETHICS, JUSTICE, LIBERALISM, POLITICAL THEORY, SOCIAL PHILOSOPHY.

J.P.St.

political theory, reflection concerning the empirical, normative, and conceptual dimensions of political life. There are no topics that all political theorists do or ought to address, no required procedures, no doctrines acknowledged to be authoritative. The meaning of 'political theory' resides in its fluctuating uses, not in any essential property. It is nevertheless possible to identify concerted tendencies among those who have practiced this activity over twenty-five centuries.

Since approximately the seventeenth century, a primary question has been how best to justify the political rule of some people over others. This question subordinated the issue that had directed and organized most previous political theory, namely, what constitutes the best form of political regime. Assuming political association to be a divinely ordained or naturally necessary feature of the human estate, earlier thinkers had asked what mode of political association contributes most to realizing the good for humankind. Signaling the variable but intimate relationship between political theory and political practice, the change in question reflected and helped to consolidate acceptance of the postulate of natural human equality, the denial of divinely or naturally given authority of some human beings over others. Only a small minority of post-seventeenth-century thinkers have entertained the possibility, perhaps suggested by this postulate, that no form of rule can be justified, but the shift in question altered the political theory agenda. Issues concerning consent, individual liberties and rights, various forms of equality as integral to justice, democratic and other controls on the authority and power of government – none of which were among the first concerns of ancient or medieval political thinkers – moved to the center of political theory.

Recurrent tendencies and tensions in political theory may also be discerned along dimensions that cross-cut historical divisions. In its most celebrated representations, political theory is integral to philosophy. Systematic thinkers such as Plato and Aristotle, Augustine and Aquinas, Hobbes and Hegel, present their political thoughts as supporting and supported by their ethics and theology, metaphysics and epistemology. Political argumentation must satisfy the same criteria of logic, truth, and justification as any other; a political doctrine must be grounded in the nature of reality. Other political theorists align themselves with empirical science rather than philosophy. Often focusing on questions of power, they aim to give accurate accounts and factually grounded assessments of government and politics in particular times and places. Books IV–VI of Aristotle's *Politics* inaugurate this conception of political theory; it is represented by Montesquieu, Marx, and much of utilitarianism, and it is the numerically predominant form of academic political theorizing in the twentieth century. Yet others, e.g., Socrates, Machiavelli, Rousseau, and twentieth-century thinkers such as Rawls, mix the previously mentioned modes but understand themselves as primarily pursuing the practical objective of improving their own political societies.

See also POLITICAL PHILOSOPHY, SOCIAL PHILOSOPHY.   R.E.F.

polyadic. See DEGREE.

Polyaenus. See EPICUREANISM.

polysemy. See AMBIGUITY.

polysyllogism, a series of syllogisms connected by the fact that the conclusion of one syllogism becomes a premise of another. The syllogism whose conclusion is used as a premise in another syllogism within the chain is called the prosyllogism; the syllogism is which the conclusion of another syllogism within the chain is used as a premise is called the episyllogism. To illustrate, take the standard form of the simplest polysyllogism:

(α)
(1) Every B is A
(2) Every C is B
(3) ∴ Every C is A

(β)
(4) Every C is A
(5) Every D is C
(6) ∴ Every D is A.

The first member (α) of this polysyllogism is the prosyllogism, since its conclusion, (3), occurs as a premise, (4), in the second argument. This second member, (β), is the episyllogism, since it employs as one of its premises (4) the conclusion (3) of the first syllogism. It should be noted that the terms 'prosyllogism' and 'episyllogism' are correlative terms. Moreover, a polysyllogism may have more than two members. **See also** SYLLOGISM.   I.Bo.

Pomponazzi, Pietro (1462–1525), Italian philosopher, an Aristotelian who taught at the universities of Padua and Bologna. In *De incantationibus* ("On Incantations," 1556), he regards the world as a system of natural causes that can explain apparently miraculous phenomena. Human beings are subject to the natural order of the world, yet divine predestination and human freedom are compatible (*De fato*, "On Fate," 1567). Furthermore, he distinguishes between what is proved by natural reason and what is accepted by faith, and claims that, since there are arguments for and against the immortality of the human individual soul, this belief is to be accepted solely on the basis of faith (*De immortalitate animae*, "On the Immortality of the Soul,"

1516). He defended his view of immortality in the *Apologia* (1518) and in the *Defensorium* (1519). These three works were reprinted as *Tractatus acutissimi* (1525).

Pomponazzi's work was influential until the seventeenth century, when Aristotelianism ceased to be the main philosophy taught at the universities. The eighteenth-century freethinkers showed new interest in his distinction between natural reason and faith.   P.Gar.

pons asinorum (Latin, 'asses' bridge'), a methodological device based upon Aristotle's description of the ways in which one finds a suitable middle term to demonstrate categorical propositions. Thus, to prove the universal affirmative, one should consider the characters that entail the predicate *P* and the characters entailed by the subject *S*. If we find in the two groups of characters a common member, we can use it as a middle term in the syllogistic proof of (say) 'All *S* are *P*'. Take 'All men are mortal' as the contemplated conclusion. We find that 'organism' is among the characters entailing the predicate 'mortal' and is also found in the group of characters entailed by the subject 'men', and thus it may be used in a syllogistic proof of 'All men are mortal'. To prove negative propositions we must, in addition, consider characters incompatible with the predicate, or incompatible with the subject. Finally, proofs of particular propositions require considering characters that entail the subject. **See also SYL-LOGISM.**   I.Bo.

Popper, Karl Raimund (1902–94), Austrian-born British philosopher best known for contributions to philosophy of science and to social and political philosophy. Educated at the University of Vienna (Ph.D., 1928), he taught philosophy in New Zealand for a decade before becoming a reader and then professor in logic and scientific method at the London School of Economics (1946–69). He was knighted in 1965, elected a fellow of the Royal Society in 1976, and appointed Companion of Honour in 1982 (see his autobiography, *Unended Quest*, 1976).

In opposition to logical positivism's verifiability criterion of cognitive significance, Popper proposes that science be characterized by its method: the criterion of demarcation of empirical science from pseudo-science and metaphysics is falsifiability (*Logik der Forschung*, 1934, translated as *The Logic of Scientific Discovery*, 1959). According to *falsificationism*, science grows, and may even approach the truth, not by amassing supporting

evidence, but through an unending cycle of problems, tentative solutions – unjustifiable *conjectures* – and error elimination; i.e., the vigorous testing of deductive consequences and the refutation of conjectures that fail (*Conjectures and Refutations*, 1963). Since conjectures are not inferences and refutations are not inductive, there is no inductive inference or inductive logic. More generally, criticism is installed as the hallmark of rationality, and the traditional justificationist insistence on proof, conclusive or inconclusive, on confirmation, and on positive argument, is repudiated.

Popper brings to the central problems of Kant's philosophy an uncompromising realism and objectivism, the tools of modern logic, and a Darwinian perspective on knowledge, thereby solving Hume's problem of induction without lapsing into irrationalism (*Objective Knowledge*, 1972). He made contributions of permanent importance also to the axiomatization of probability theory (*The Logic of Scientific Discovery*, 1959); to its interpretation, especially the propensity interpretation (*Postscript to The Logic of Scientific Discovery*, 3 vols. 1982–83); and to many other problems (*The Self and Its Brain*, with John C. Eccles, 1977).

Popper's social philosophy, like his epistemology, is anti-authoritarian. Since it is a historicist error to suppose that we can predict the future of mankind (*The Poverty of Historicism*, 1957), the prime task of social institutions in an *open society* – one that encourages criticism and allows rulers to be replaced without violence – must be not large-scale utopian planning but the minimization, through piecemeal reform, of avoidable suffering. This way alone permits proper assessment of success or failure, and thus of learning from experience (*The Open Society and Its Enemies*, 1945).

See also CONFIRMATION, DARWINISM, HISTORICISM, LOGICAL POSITIVISM, PHILOSOPHY OF SCIENCE, PROBABILITY, PROBLEM OF INDUCTION, RATIONALITY.   D.W.M.

Porphyry (c.232–c.304), Greek Neoplatonist philosopher, second to Plotinus in influence. He was born in Tyre, and is thus sometimes called Porphyry the Phoenician. As a young man he went to Athens, where he absorbed the Platonism of Cassius Longinus, who had in turn been influenced by Ammonius Saccas in Alexandria. Porphyry went to Rome in 263, where he became a disciple of Plotinus, who had also been influenced by Ammonius. Porphyry lived in Rome until 269, when, urged by Plotinus to travel as a cure for severe depression, he traveled to Sicily. He remained there for several years before returning to Rome to take over Plotinus's school. He apparently died in Rome.

Porphyry is not noted for original thought. He seems to have dedicated himself to explicating Aristotle's logic and defending Plotinus's version of Neoplatonism. During his years in Sicily, Porphyry wrote his two most famous works, the lengthy *Against the Christians,* of which only fragments survive, and the *Isagoge,* or "Introduction." The *Isagoge,* which purports to give an elementary exposition of the concepts necessary to understand Aristotle's *Categories,* was translated into Latin by Boethius and routinely published in the Middle Ages with Latin editions of Aristotle's *Organon,* or logical treatises. Its inclusion in that format arguably precipitated the discussion of the so-called problem of universals in the twelfth century. During his later years in Rome, Porphyry collected Plotinus's writings, editing and organizing them into a scheme of his own – not Plotinus's – design, six groups of nine treatises, thus called the *Enneads.* Porphyry prefaced his edition with an informative biography of Plotinus, written shortly before Porphyry's own death.

See also NEOPLATONISM, PLOTINUS, TREE OF PORPHYRY.   W.E.M.

Port-Royal Logic, originally entitled *La logique, ou L'art de penser,* a treatise on logic, language, and method composed by Antoine Arnauld and Pierre Nicole (1625–95), possibly with the help of Pascal, all of whom were *solitaires* associated with the convent at Port-Royal-des-Champs, the spiritual and intellectual center of French Jansenism. Originally written as an instruction manual for the son of the Duc de Luynes, the *Logic* was soon expanded and published (the first edition appeared in 1662, but it was constantly being modified, augmented, and rewritten by its authors; by 1685 six editions in French had appeared).

The work develops the linguistic theories presented by Arnauld and Claude Lancelot in the *Grammaire générale et raisonnée* (1660), and reflects the pedagogical principles embodied in the curriculum of the "little schools" run by Port-Royal. Its content is also permeated by the Cartesianism to which Arnauld was devoted. The *Logic*'s influence grew beyond Jansenist circles, and it soon became in seventeenth-century France a standard manual for rigorous thinking. Eventually, it was adopted as a textbook in French schools. The authors declare their goal to be to make thought more precise for better distinguishing truth from error – philosophical and theological – and to develop sound judgment. They are especially concerned to dispel the errors and confusions of the Scholastics. Logic is "the art of directing reason to a knowledge of things for the instruction of ourselves and others." This art consists in reflecting on the mind's four principal operations: conceiving, judging, reasoning, and ordering. Accordingly, the *Logic* is divided into four sections: on ideas and conception, on judgments, on reasoning, and on method.   S.N.

Posidonius. See ACADEMY, COMMENTARIES ON PLATO, STOICISM.

positional qualities. See QUALITIES.

positive and negative freedom, respectively, the area within which the individual is self-determining and the area within which the individual is left free from interference by others. More specifically, one is free in the positive sense to the extent that one has control over one's life, or rules oneself. In this sense the term is very close to that of 'autonomy'. The forces that can prevent this self-determination are usually thought of as internal, as desires or passions. This conception of freedom can be said to have originated with Plato, according to whom a person is free when the parts of the soul are rightly related to each other, i.e. the rational part of the soul rules the other parts. Other advocates of positive freedom include Spinoza, Rousseau, Kant, and Hegel.

One is free in the negative sense if one is not prevented from doing something by another person. One is prevented from doing something if another person makes it impossible for one to do something or uses coercion to prevent one from doing something. Hence persons are free in the negative sense if they are not made unfree in the negative sense. The term 'negative liberty' was coined by Bentham to mean the absence of coercion. Advocates of negative freedom include Hobbes, Locke, and Hume.

See also FREE WILL PROBLEM, KANT, POLITICAL PHILOSOPHY.   G.D.

positive duty. See DUTY.

positive feedback. See CYBERNETICS.

positive freedom. See POSITIVE AND NEGATIVE FREEDOM.

positive morality. See JURISPRUDENCE.

positivism, legal. See JURISPRUDENCE, LEGAL POSITIVISM.

positivism, logical. See COMTE, LOGICAL POSITIVISM.

possibilia. See NECESSITY, POSSIBLE WORLDS.

possibilist. See EPISTEMIC LOGIC.

possibility. See NECESSITY.

possibility, epistemic. See EPISTEMIC LOGIC.

possible worlds, alternative worlds in terms of which one may think of possibility. The idea of thinking about possibility in terms of such worlds has played an important part, both in Leibnizian philosophical theology and in the development of modal logic and philosophical reflection about it in recent decades. But there are important differences in the forms the idea has taken, and the uses to which it has been put, in the two contexts.

Leibniz used it in his account of creation. In his view God's mind necessarily and eternally contains the ideas of infinitely many worlds that God could have created, and God has chosen the best of these and made it actual, thus creating it. (Similar views are found in the thought of Leibniz's contemporary, Malebranche.) The possible worlds are thus the complete alternatives among which God chose. They are possible at least in the sense that they are logically consistent; whether something more is required in order for them to be coherent as worlds is a difficult question in Leibniz interpretation. They are complete in that they are possible totalities of creatures; each includes a whole (possible) universe, in its whole spatial extent and its whole temporal history (if it is spatially and temporally ordered). The temporal completeness deserves emphasis. If "the world of tomorrow" is "a better world" than "the world of today," it will still be part of the same "possible world" (the actual one); for the actual "world," in the relevant sense, includes whatever actually has happened or will happen throughout all time. The completeness extends to every detail, so that a milligram's difference in the weight of the smallest bird would make a different possible world. The completeness of possible worlds may be limited in one way, however. Leibniz speaks of worlds as aggregates of *finite* things. As alternatives for God's creation, they may well not be thought of as including God, or

at any rate, not every fact about God. For this and other reasons it is not clear that in Leibniz's thought the possible can be identified with what is true in some possible world, or the necessary with what is true in all possible worlds.

That identification is regularly assumed, however, in the recent development of what has become known as *possible worlds semantics* for modal logic (the logic of possibility and necessity, and of other conceptions, e.g. those pertaining to time and to morality, that have turned out to be formally analogous). The basic idea here is that such notions as those of validity, soundness, and completeness can be defined for modal logic in terms of models constructed from sets of alternative "worlds." Since the late 1950s many important results have been obtained by this method, whose best-known exponent is Saul Kripke. Some of the most interesting proofs depend on the idea of a relation of *accessibility* between worlds in the set. Intuitively, one world is accessible from another if and only if the former is possible in (or from the point of view of) the latter. Different systems of modal logic are appropriate depending on the properties of this relation (e.g., on whether it is or is not reflexive and/or transitive and/or symmetrical).

The purely formal results of these methods are well established. The application of possible worlds semantics to conceptions occurring in metaphysically richer discourse is more controversial, however. Some of the controversy is related to debates over the metaphysical reality of various sorts of possibility and necessity. Particularly controversial, and also a focus of much interest, have been attempts to understand modal claims *de re*, about particular individuals as such (e.g., that I could not have been a musical performance), in terms of the identity and nonidentity of individuals in different possible worlds.

Similarly, there is debate over the applicability of a related treatment of subjunctive conditionals, developed by Robert Stalnaker and David Lewis, though it is clear that it yields interesting formal results. What is required, on this approach, for the truth of 'If it were the case that *A*, then it would be the case that *B*', is that, among those possible worlds in which *A* is true, some world in which *B* is true be more similar, in the relevant respects, to the actual world than any world in which *B* is false.

One of the most controversial topics is the nature of possible worlds themselves. Mathematical logicians need not be concerned with this; a wide variety of sets of objects, real or fictitious, can be viewed as having the properties required of sets of "worlds" for their purposes. But if metaphysically robust issues of modality (e.g., whether there are more possible colors than we ever see) are to be understood in terms of possible worlds, the question of the nature of the worlds must be taken seriously. Some philosophers would deny any serious metaphysical role to the notion of possible worlds. At the other extreme, David Lewis has defended a view of possible worlds as concrete totalities, things of the same sort as the whole actual universe, made up of entities like planets, persons, and so forth. On his view, the actuality of the actual world consists only in its being *this* one, the one that *we* are in; apart from its relation to us or our linguistic acts, the actual is not metaphysically distinguished from the merely possible. Many philosophers find this result counterintuitive, and the infinity of concrete possible worlds an extravagant ontology; but Lewis argues that his view makes possible attractive reductions of modality (both logical and causal), and of such notions as that of a proposition, to more concrete notions. Other philosophers are prepared to say there are non-actual possible worlds, but that they are entities of a quite different sort from the actual concrete universe – sets of propositions, perhaps, or some other type of "abstract" object. Leibniz himself held a view of this kind, thinking of possible worlds as having their being only in God's mind, as intentional objects of God's thought.

See also COUNTERFACTUALS, KRIPKE SEMANTICS, MODAL LOGIC.   R.M.A.

possible worlds semantics. See KRIPKE SEMANTICS, POSSIBLE WORLDS.

postcard paradox. See SEMANTIC PARADOXES.

Post-complete. See COMPLETENESS.

post hoc, ergo propter hoc. See INFORMAL FALLACY.

postmodern, of or relating to a complex set of reactions to modern philosophy and its presuppositions, as opposed to the kind of agreement on substantive doctrines or philosophical questions that often characterizes a philosophical movement. Although there is little agreement on precisely what the presuppositions of modern philosophy are, and disagreement on which philosophers exemplify these presuppositions, postmodern philosophy typically opposes foundationalism, essentialism, and realism. For Rorty,

e.g., the presuppositions to be set aside are foundationalist assumptions shared by the leading sixteenth-, seventeenth-, and eighteenth-century philosophers. For Nietzsche, Heidegger, Foucault, and Derrida, the contested presuppositions to be set aside are as old as metaphysics itself, and are perhaps best exemplified by Plato. Postmodern philosophy has even been characterized, by Lyotard, as *preceding* modern philosophy, in the sense that the presuppositions of philosophical modernism emerge out of a disposition whose antecedent, unarticulated beliefs are already postmodern.

Postmodern philosophy is therefore usefully regarded as a complex cluster concept that includes the following elements: an anti- (or post-) epistemological standpoint; anti-essentialism; anti-realism; anti-foundationalism; opposition to transcendental arguments and transcendental standpoints; rejection of the picture of knowledge as accurate representation; rejection of truth as correspondence to reality; rejection of the very idea of canonical descriptions; rejection of final vocabularies, i.e., rejection of principles, distinctions, and descriptions that are thought to be unconditionally binding for all times, persons, and places; and a suspicion of grand narratives, metanarratives of the sort perhaps best illustrated by dialectical materialism.

In addition to these things postmodern philosophy is "against," it also opposes characterizing this menu of oppositions as relativism, skepticism, or nihilism, and it rejects as "the metaphysics of presence" the traditional, putatively impossible dream of a complete, unique, and closed explanatory system, an explanatory system typically fueled by binary oppositions. On the positive side, one often finds the following themes: its critique of the notion of the neutrality and sovereignty of reason – including insistence on its pervasively gendered, historical, and ethnocentric character; its conception of the social construction of word–world mappings; its tendency to embrace historicism; its critique of the ultimate status of a contrast between epistemology, on the one hand, and the sociology of knowledge, on the other hand; its dissolution of the notion of the autonomous, rational subject; its insistence on the artifactual status of divisions of labor in knowledge acquisition and production; and its ambivalence about the Enlightenment and its ideology.

Many of these elements or elective affinities were already surfacing in the growing opposition to the spectator theory of knowledge, in Europe and in the English-speaking world, long before the term 'postmodern' became a commonplace. In Anglophone philosophy this took the early form of Dewey's (and pragmatism's) opposition to positivism, early Kuhn's redescription of scientific practice, and Wittgenstein's insistence on the language-game character of representation; critiques of "the myth of the given" from Sellars to Davidson and Quine; the emergence of epistemology naturalized; and the putative description-dependent character of data, tethered to the theory dependence of descriptions (in Kuhn, Sellars, Quine, and Arthur Fine – perhaps in all constructivists in the philosophy of science).

In Europe, many of these elective affinities surfaced explicitly in and were identified with post-structuralism, although traces are clearly evident in Heidegger's (and later in Derrida's) attacks on Husserl's residual Cartesianism; the rejection of essential descriptions (*Wesensanschauungen*) in Husserl's sense; Saussure's and structuralism's attack on the autonomy and coherence of a transcendental signified standing over against a self-transparent subject; Derrida's deconstructing the metaphysics of presence; Foucault's redescriptions of *epistemes;* the convergence between French- and English-speaking social constructivists; attacks on the language of enabling conditions as reflected in worries about the purchase of necessary and sufficient conditions talk on both sides of the Atlantic; and Lyotard's many interventions, particularly those against grand narratives.

Many of these elective affinities that characterize postmodern philosophy can also be seen in the virtually universal challenges to moral philosophy as it has been understood traditionally in the West, not only in German and French philosophy, but in the reevaluation of "the morality of principles" in the work of MacIntyre, Williams, Nussbaum, John McDowell, and others. The force of postmodern critiques can perhaps best be seen in some of the challenges of feminist theory, as in the work of Judith Butler and Hélène Cixous, and gender theory generally. For it is in gender theory that the conception of "reason" itself as it has functioned in the shared philosophical tradition is redescribed as a conception that, it is often argued, is (en)gendered, patriarchal, homophobic, and deeply optional.

The term 'postmodern' is less clear in philosophy, its application more uncertain and divided than in some other fields, e.g., postmodern architecture. In architecture the concept is relatively clear. It displaces modernism in assignable ways, emerges as an oppositional force against architectural modernism, a rejection of the work and tradition inaugurated by Walter Gropius, Henri Le Corbusier, and Mies van der Rohe, especially the International Style. In postmodern architecture, the modernist principle of abstraction, of geometric purity and simplicity, is displaced by multivocity and pluralism, by renewed interest in buildings as signs and signifiers, interest in their referential potential and resources. The modernist's aspiration to buildings that are timeless in an important sense is itself read by postmodernists as an iconography that privileges the brave new world of science and technology, an aspiration that glorifies uncritically the industrial revolution of which it is itself a quintessential expression. This aspiration to timelessness is displaced in postmodern architecture by a direct and self-conscious openness to and engagement with history. It is this relative specificity of the concept postmodern architecture that enabled Charles Jencks to write that "Modern Architecture died in St. Louis Missouri on July 15, 1972 at 3:32 P.M." Unfortunately, no remotely similar sentence can be written about postmodern philosophy.

See also ANTI-REALISM, DECONSTRUCTION, FOUCAULT, FOUNDATIONALISM, LYOTARD, RORTY, SOCIAL CONSTRUCTIVISM, STRUCTURALISM. B.M.

post-structuralism. See CONTINENTAL PHILOSOPHY, LYOTARD, STRUCTURALISM.

potency, for Aristotle, a kind of capacity that is a correlative of action. We require no instruction to grasp the difference between 'X can do Y' and 'X is doing Y', the latter meaning that the deed is actually being done. That an agent has a potency to do something is not a pure prediction so much as a generalization from past performance of individual or kind. Aristotle uses the example of a builder, meaning someone able to build, and then confronts the Megaric objection that the builder can be called a builder only when he actually builds. Clearly one who is doing something can do it, but Aristotle insists that the napping carpenter has the potency to hammer and saw. A potency based on an acquired skill like carpentry derives from the potency shared by those who acquire and those who do not acquire the skill. An unskilled worker can be said to be a builder "in potency," not in the sense that he has the skill and can employ it, but in the sense that he can acquire the skill. In both acquisition and employment, 'potency' refers to the actual – either the actual acquisition of the skill or its actual use. These correlatives emerged from Aristotle's analysis of change and becoming. That which, from not having the skill, comes to have it is said to be "in potency" to that skill. From not having a certain shape, wood comes to have a certain shape. In the shaped wood, a potency is actualized. Potency must not be identified with the un-shaped, with what Aristotle calls privation. Privation is the negation of *P* in a subject capable of *P*. Parmenides' identification of privation and potency, according to Aristotle, led him to deny change. How can not-*P* become *P*? It is the subject of not-*P* to which the change is attributed and which survives the change that is in potency to *X*. **See also** ARISTOTLE.   R.M.

potentiality, first. See ARISTOTLE.

potentiality, second. See ARISTOTLE.

pour soi. See SARTRE.

poverty of the stimulus, a psychological phenomenon exhibited when behavior is stimulus-unbound, and hence the immediate stimulus characterized in straightforward physical terms does not completely control behavior. Human beings sort stimuli in various ways and hosts of influences seem to affect when, why, and how we respond – our background beliefs, facility with language, hypotheses about stimuli, etc. Suppose a person visiting a museum notices a painting she has never before seen. Pondering the unfamiliar painting, she says, "an ambitious visual synthesis of the music of Mahler and the poetry of Keats." If stimulus (painting) controls response, then her utterance is a product of earlier responses to similar stimuli. Given poverty of the stimulus, no such control is exerted by the stimulus (the painting). Of course, some influence of response must be conceded to the painting, for without it there would be no utterance. However, the utterance may well outstrip the visitor's conditioning and learning history. Perhaps she had never before talked of painting in terms of music and poetry. The linguist Noam Chomsky made poverty of the stimulus central to his criticism of B. F. Skinner's *Verbal Behavior* (1957). Chomsky argued that there is no predicting, and certainly no critical stimulus control of, much human behavior.   G.A.G.

power, a disposition; an ability or capacity to yield some outcome. One tradition (which includes Locke) distinguishes active and passive powers. A knife has the active power to slice an apple, which has the passive power to be sliced by the knife. The distinction seems largely grammatical, however. Powers act in concert: the power of a grain of salt to dissolve in water and the water's power to dissolve the salt are reciprocal and their manifestations mutual.

Powers or dispositions are sometimes thought to be relational properties of objects, properties possessed only in virtue of objects standing in appropriate relations to other objects. However, if we distinguish, as we must, between a power and its manifestation, and if we allow that an object could possess a power that it never manifested (a grain of salt remains soluble even if it never dissolves), it would seem that an object could possess a power even if appropriate reciprocal partners for its manifestation were altogether non-existent. This appears to have been Locke's view (*An Essay concerning Human Understanding*, 1690) of "secondary qualities" (colors, sounds, and the like), which he regarded as powers of objects to produce certain sorts of sensory experience in observers.

Philosophers who take powers seriously disagree over whether powers are intrinsic, "built into" properties (this view, defended by C. B. Martin, seems to have been Locke's), or whether the connection between properties and the powers they bestow is contingent, dependent perhaps upon contingent laws of nature (a position endorsed by Armstrong). Is the solubility of salt a characteristic built into the salt, or is it a "second-order" property possessed by the salt in virtue of (i) the salt's possession of some "first-order" property and (ii) the laws of nature?

Reductive analyses of powers, though influential, have not fared well. Suppose a grain of salt is soluble in water. Does this mean that if the salt were placed in water, it would dissolve? No. Imagine that were the salt placed in water, a technician would intervene, imposing an electromagnetic field, thereby preventing the salt from dissolving. Attempts to exclude "blocking" conditions – by appending "other things equal" clauses perhaps – face charges of circularity: in nailing down what other things must be equal we find ourselves appealing to powers. Powers evidently are fundamental features of our world. **See also** DISPOSITION, QUALITIES, RELATION, SUPERVENIENCE.   J.F.H.

power set. See SET THEORY.

practical argument. See PRACTICAL REASONING.

practical attitude. See PRACTICAL REASONING.

practical freedom. See FREE WILL PROBLEM.

practical judgment. See AKRASIA.

practical logic. See INFORMAL LOGIC.

practical modality. See FREE WILL PROBLEM.

practical rationality. See RATIONALITY.

practical reason, the capacity for argument or demonstrative inference, considered in its application to the task of prescribing or selecting behavior. Some philosophical concerns in this area pertain to the actual thought processes by which plans of action are formulated and carried out in practical situations. A second major issue is what role, if any, practical reason plays in determining norms of conduct. Here there are two fundamental positions.

Instrumentalism is typified by Hume's claim that reason is, and ought only to be, the slave of the passions. According to instrumentalism, reason by itself is incapable of influencing action directly. It may do so indirectly, by disclosing facts that arouse motivational impulses. And it fulfills an indispensable function in discerning means–end relations by which our objectives may be attained. But none of those objectives is *set* by reason. All are set by the *passions* – the desiderative and aversive impulses aroused in us by what our cognitive faculties apprehend. It does not follow from this alone that ethical motivation reduces to mere desire and aversion, based on the pleasure and pain different courses of action might afford. There might yet be a specifically ethical passion, or it might be that independently based moral injunctions have in themselves a special capacity to provoke ordinary desire and aversion. Nevertheless, instrumentalism is often associated with the view that pleasure and pain, happiness and unhappiness, are the sole objects of value and disvalue, and hence the only possible motivators of conduct. Hence, it is claimed, moral injunctions must be grounded in these motives, and practical reason is of interest only as subordinated to inclination.

The alternative to instrumentalism is the view championed by Kant, that practical reason is an *autonomous* source of normative principles, capable of motivating behavior independently of ordinary desire and aversion. On this view it is the passions that lack intrinsic moral import, and the function of practical reason is to limit their motivational role by formulating normative principles binding for all rational agents and founded in the operation of practical reason itself. Theories of this kind usually view moral principles as grounded in consistency, and an impartial respect for the autonomy of all rational agents. To be morally acceptable, principles of conduct must be universalizable, so that all rational agents could behave in the same way without their conduct either destroying itself or being inconsistently motivated.

There are advantages and disadvantages to each of these views. Instrumentalism offers a simpler account of both the function of practical reason and the sources of human motivation. But it introduces a strong subjective element by giving primacy to desire, thereby posing a problem of how moral principles can be universally binding. The Kantian approach offers more promise here, since it makes universalizability essential to any type of behavior being moral. But it is more complex, and the claim that the deliverances of practical reason carry intrinsic motivational force is open to challenge.

See also INSTRUMENTALISM, KANT, MOTI-VATIONAL INTERNALISM, PRACTICAL REA-SONING, RATIONALITY.   H.J.M.

practical reasoning, the inferential process by which considerations for or against envisioned courses of action are brought to bear on the formation and execution of intention. The content of a piece of practical reasoning is a *practical argument.* Practical arguments can be complex, but they are often summarized in syllogistic form. Important issues concerning practical reasoning include how it relates to theoretical reasoning, whether it is a causal process, and how it can be evaluated.

Theories of practical reasoning tend to divide into two basic categories. On one sort of view, the intrinsic features of practical reasoning exhibit little or no difference from those of theoretical reasoning. What makes practical reasoning practical is its subject matter and motivation. Hence the following could be a bona fide *practical syllogism:*

> Exercise would be good for me.
> Jogging is exercise.
> Therefore, jogging would be good for me.

This argument has practical subject matter, and if made with a view toward intention formation it would be practical in motivation also. But it consists entirely of propositions, which are appropriate contents for belief-states. In principle, therefore, an agent could accept its conclusion without intending or even desiring to jog. Intention formation requires a further step. But if the content of an intention cannot be a proposition, that step could not count in itself as practical reasoning unless such reasoning can employ the contents of strictly practical mental states. Hence many philosophers call for practical syllogisms such as:

> Would that I exercise.
> Jogging is exercise.
> Therefore, I shall go jogging.

Here the first premise is optative and understood to represent the content of a desire, and the conclusion is the content of a *decision* or act of intention formation. These contents are not true or false, and so are not propositions.

Theories that restrict the contents of practical reasoning to propositions have the advantage that they allow such reasoning to be evaluated in terms of familiar logical principles. Those that permit the inclusion of optative content entail a need for more complex modes of evaluation. However, they bring more of the process of intention formation under the aegis of reason; also, they can be extended to cover the execution of intentions, in terms of syllogisms that terminate in volition. Both accounts must deal with cases of self-deception, in which the considerations an agent cites to justify a decision are not those from which it sprang, and cases of *akrasia,* where the agent views one course of action as superior, yet carries out another.

Because mental content is always abstract, it cannot in itself be a nomic cause of behavior. But the states and events to which it belongs – desires, beliefs, etc. – can count as causes, and are so treated in deterministic explanations of action. Opponents of determinism reject this step, and seek to explain action solely through the teleological or justifying force carried by mental content.

Practical syllogisms often summarize very complex thought processes, in which multiple options are considered, each with its own positive and negative aspects. Some philosophers hold that when successfully concluded, this process issues in a judgment of what action would be best all things considered – i.e., in light of all relevant considerations. Practical reasoning can be evaluated in numerous ways. Some concern the reasoning process itself: whether it is timely and duly considers the relevant alternatives, as well as whether it is well structured log-

ically. Other concerns have to do with the products of practical reasoning. Decisions may be deemed irrational if they result in incompatible intentions, or conflict with the agent's beliefs regarding what is possible. They may also be criticized if they conflict with the agent's best interests. Finally, an agent's intentions can fail to accord with standards of morality. The relationship among these ways of evaluating intentions is important to the foundations of ethics.

See also ACTION THEORY, AKRASIA, INTUITION, PRACTITION, REASONS FOR ACTION, VOLITION.   H.J.M.

practical syllogism. See PRACTICAL REASONING.

practical wisdom. See ARISTOTLE.

practition, Castañeda's term for the characteristic content of practical thinking. Each practition represents an action as something to be done, say, as intended, commanded, recommended, etc., and not as an accomplishment or prediction. Thus, unlike propositions, practitions are not truth-valued, but they can be components of valid arguments and so possess values akin to truth; e.g., the command 'James, extinguish your cigar!' seems *legitimate* given that James is smoking a cigar in a crowded bus. Acknowledging practitions is directly relevant to many other fields. See also ACTION THEORY, CASTAÑEDA, DEONTIC LOGIC, FREE WILL PROBLEM, PRACTICAL REASONING.   T.K.

praedicabilia. See PREDICABLES.

praedicamenta (singular: *praedicamentum*), in medieval philosophy, the ten Aristotelian categories: substance, quantity, quality, relation, where, when, position (i.e., orientation – e.g., "upright"), having, action, and passivity. These were the ten most general of all genera. All of them except substance were regarded as accidental. It was disputed whether this tenfold classification was intended as a linguistic division among categorematic terms or as an ontological division among extralinguistic realities. Some authors held that the division was primarily linguistic, and that extralinguistic realities were divided according to some but not all the *praedicamenta.* Most authors held that everything in any way real belonged to one *praedicamentum* or another, although some made an exception for God. But authors who believed in *complexe significabile* usually regarded them as not belonging to any *praedicamentum*. **See also** ARISTOTLE, COMPLEXE SIGNIFICABILE, GENUS GENERALISSIMUM.   P.V.S.

pragmatic ambiguity. See AMBIGUITY.

pragmatic contradiction, a contradiction that is generated by pragmatic rather than logical implication. *A* logically implies *B* if it is impossible for *B* to be false if *A* is true, whereas *A* pragmatically implies *B* if in most (but not necessarily all) contexts, saying '*A*' can reasonably be taken as indicating that *B* is true. Thus, if I say, "It's raining," *what* I say does not logically imply that I believe that it is raining, since it is possible for it to be raining without my believing it is. Nor does *my saying* that it is raining logically imply that I believe that it is, since it is possible for me to say this without believing it. But my saying this does pragmatically imply that I believe that it is raining, since normally my saying this can reasonably be taken to indicate that I believe it. Accordingly, if I were to say, "It's raining but I don't believe that it's raining," the result would be a pragmatic contradiction. The first part ("It's raining") does not logically imply the negation of the second part ("I don't believe that it's raining") but my saying the first part does pragmatically imply the negation of the second part. **See also** IMPLICATURE, PRESUPPOSITION.   R.Fo.

pragmatic maxim. See PEIRCE.

pragmatics. See PHILOSOPHY OF LANGUAGE, SPEECH ACT THEORY, THEORY OF SIGNS.

pragmatic theory of truth. See PRAGMATISM, TRUTH.

pragmatism, a philosophy that stresses the relation of theory to praxis and takes the continuity of experience and nature as revealed through the outcome of directed action as the starting point for reflection. Experience is the ongoing transaction of organism and environment, i.e., both subject and object are constituted in the process. When intelligently ordered, initial conditions are deliberately transformed according to ends-in-view, i.e., intentionally, into a subsequent state of affairs thought to be more desirable. Knowledge is therefore guided by interests or values. Since the reality of objects cannot be known prior to experience, truth claims can be justified only as the fulfillment of conditions that are experimentally determined, i.e., the outcome of inquiry.

As a philosophic movement, pragmatism was first formulated by Peirce in the early 1870s in the Metaphysical Club in Cambridge, Massachusetts; it was announced as a distinctive position in James's 1898 address to the Philosophical Union at the University of California at Berkeley, and further elaborated according to the Chicago School, especially by Dewey, Mead, and Jane Addams (1860–1935). Emphasis on the reciprocity of theory and praxis, knowledge and action, facts and values, follows from its post-Darwinian understanding of human experience, including cognition, as a developmental, historically contingent, process. C. I. Lewis's pragmatic a priori and Quine's rejection of the analytic–synthetic distinction develop these insights further.

Knowledge is instrumental – a tool for organizing experience satisfactorily. Concepts are habits of belief or rules of action. Truth cannot be determined solely by epistemological criteria because the adequacy of these criteria cannot be determined apart from the goals sought and values instantiated. Values, which arise in historically specific cultural situations, are intelligently appropriated only to the extent that they satisfactorily resolve problems and are judged worth retaining. According to pragmatic theories of truth, truths are beliefs that are confirmed in the course of experience and are therefore fallible, subject to further revision. True beliefs for Peirce represent real objects as successively confirmed until they converge on a final determination; for James, leadings that are worthwhile; and according to Dewey's theory of inquiry, the transformation of an indeterminate situation into a determinate one that leads to warranted assertions.

Pragmatic ethics is naturalistic, pluralistic, developmental, and experimental. It reflects on the motivations influencing ethical systems, examines the individual developmental process wherein an individual's values are gradually distinguished from those of society, situates moral judgments within problematic situations irreducibly individual and social, and proposes as ultimate criteria for decision making the value for life as growth, determined by all those affected by the actual or projected outcomes.

The original interdisciplinary development of pragmatism continues in its influence on the humanities. Oliver Wendell Holmes, Jr., member of the Metaphysical Club, later justice of the U.S. Supreme Court, developed a pragmatic theory of law. Peirce's Principle of Pragmatism, by which meaning resides in conceivable practical effects, and his triadic theory of signs developed into the field of semiotics. James's *Principles of Psychology* (1890) not only established experimental psychology in North America, but shifted philosophical attention away from abstract analyses of rationality to the continuity of the biological and the mental. The reflex arc theory was reconstructed into an interactive loop of perception, feeling, thinking, and behavior, and joined with the selective interest of consciousness to become the basis of radical empiricism. Mead's theory of the emergence of self and mind in social acts and Dewey's analyses of the individual and society influenced the human sciences. Dewey's theory of education as community-oriented, based on the psychological developmental stages of growth, and directed toward full participation in a democratic society, was the philosophical basis of progressive education.

See also CONTEXTUALISM, DEWEY, JAMES, NATURALISM, PEIRCE.   C.H.S.

pragmatism, ethical. See MORAL EPISTEMOLOGY.

praxis (from Greek *prasso*, 'doing', 'acting'), in Aristotle, the sphere of thought and action that comprises the ethical and political life of man, contrasted with the theoretical designs of logic and epistemology (*theoria*). It was thus that 'praxis' acquired its general definition of 'practice' through a contrastive comparison with 'theory'.

Throughout the history of Western philosophy the concept of praxis found a place in a variety of philosophical vocabularies. Marx and the neo-Marxists linked the concept with a production paradigm in the interests of historical explanation. Within such a scheme of things the activities constituting the relations of production and exchange are seen as the dominant features of the socioeconomic history of humankind. Significations of 'praxis' are also discernible in the root meaning of *pragma* (deed, affair), which informed the development of American pragmatism. In more recent times the notion of praxis has played a prominent role in the formation of the school of critical theory, in which the performatives of praxis are seen to be more directly associated with the entwined phenomena of discourse, communication, and social practices.

The central philosophical issues addressed in the current literature on praxis have to do with the theory–practice relationship and the problems associated with a value-free science. The general thrust is that of undermining or subverting the traditional bifurcation of theory and practice via a recognition of praxis-oriented en-deavors that antedate both theory construction and the construal of practice as a mere application of theory. Both the project of "pure theory," which makes claims for a value-neutral standpoint, and the purely instrumentalist understanding of practice, as itself shorn of discernment and insight, are jettisoned. The consequent philosophical task becomes that of understanding human thought and action against the backdrop of the everyday communicative endeavors, habits, and skills, and social practices that make up our inheritance in the world.

See also CRITICAL THEORY, MARX, MARXISM.   C.O.S.

Praxis school, a school of philosophy originating in Zagreb and Belgrade which, from 1964 to 1974, published the international edition of the leading postwar Marxist journal *Praxis*. During the same period, it organized the Korcula Summer School, which attracted scholars from around the Western world. In a reduced form the school continues each spring with the Social Philosophy Course in Dubrovnik, Croatia. The founders of praxis philosophy include Gajo Petrovic (Zagreb), Milan Kangrga (Zagreb), and Mihailo Markovic (Belgrade). Another well-known member of the group is Svetozar Stojanovic (Belgrade), and a second-generation leader is Gvozden Flego (Zagreb).

The Praxis school emphasized the writings of the young Marx while subjecting dogmatic Marxism to one of its strongest criticisms. Distinguishing between Marx's and Engels's writings and emphasizing alienation and a dynamic concept of the human being, it contributed to a greater understanding of the interrelationship between the individual and society. Through its insistence on Marx's call for a "ruthless critique," the school stressed open inquiry and freedom of speech in both East and West.

Quite possibly the most important and original philosopher of the group, and certainly Croatia's leading twentieth-century philosopher, was Gajo Petrovic (1927–93). He called for (1) understanding philosophy as a radical critique of all existing things, and (2) understanding human beings as beings of praxis and creativity. This later led to a view of human beings as revolutionary by nature. At present he is probably best remembered for his *Marx in the Mid-Twentieth Century* and *Philosophie und Revolution*. Milan Kangrga (b.1923) also emphasizes human creativity while insisting that one should understand human beings as producers who humanize nature. An ethical problematic of humanity can be realized through a variety of disciplines that include aesthetics, philosophical anthropolgy, theory of knowledge, ontology, and social thought. Mihailo Markovic (b.1923), a member of the Belgrade Eight, is best known for his theory of meaning, which leads him to a theory of socialist humanism. His most widely read work in the West is *From Affluence to Praxis: Philosophy and Social Criticism.*

See also MARXISM, PRAXIS.   J.Bi. & H.P.

preanalytic, considered but naive; commonsensical; not tainted by prior explicit theorizing; said of judgments and, derivatively, of beliefs or intuitions underlying such judgments. Preanalytic judgments are often used to test philosophical theses. All things considered, we prefer theories that accord with preanalytic judgments to those that do not, although most theorists exhibit a willingness to revise preanalytic assessments in light of subsequent inquiry. Thus, a preanalytic judgment might be thought to constitute a starting point for the philosophical consideration of a given topic. Is justice giving every man his due? It may seem so, preanalytically. Attention to concrete examples, however, may lead us to a different view. It is doubtful, even in such cases, that we altogether abandon preanalytic judgments. Rather, we endeavor to reconcile apparently competing judgments, making adjustments in a way that optimizes overall coherence. **See also** PRETHEORETICAL, REFLECTIVE EQUILIBRIUM.   J.F.H.

precising definition. See DEFINITION.

precognition. See PARAPSYCHOLOGY.

preconscious. See FREUD.

pre-Critical. See KANT.

predestination. See FREE WILL PROBLEM.

predicables, also *praedicabilia,* sometimes called the *quinque voces* (five words), in medieval philosophy, genus, species, difference, *proprium,* and accident, the five main ways general predicates can be predicated. The list comes from Porphyry's *Isagoge.* It was debated whether it applies to linguistic predicates only or also to extralinguistic universals.

Things that have accidents can exist without them; other predicables belong necessarily to whatever has them. (The Aristotelian/Porphyrian notion of "inseparable accident" blurs this picture.) Genus and species are natural kinds; other predicables are not. A natural kind that is not a narrowest natural kind is a genus; one that is not a broadest natural kind is a species. (Some genera are also species.) A *proprium* is not a species, but is coextensive with one. A difference belongs necessarily to whatever has it, but is neither a natural kind nor coextensive with one.

See also ACCIDENT, DEFINITION, PRAEDICAMENTA, PROPRIUM.   P.V.S.

predicate. See GRAMMAR, LOGICAL SUBJECT.

predicate, projectible. See GRUE PARADOX.

predicate calculus. See FORMAL LOGIC.

predicate hierarchy. See HIERARCHY.

predicate logic. See FORMAL LOGIC.

predication. See QUALITIES.

predication, 'is' of. See IS.

predicative property. See TYPE THEORY.

prediction. See PHILOSOPHY OF SCIENCE.

prediction paradox. See PARADOX.

preemptive cause. See CAUSATION.

preestablished harmony. See LEIBNIZ, PHILOSOPHY OF MIND.

preexistence, existence of the individual soul or psyche prior to its current embodiment, when the soul or psyche is taken to be separable and capable of existing independently from its embodiment. The current embodiment is then often described as a reincarnation of the soul. Plato's Socrates refers to such a doctrine several times in the dialogues, notably in the myth of Er in Book X of the *Republic.* The doctrine is distinguished from two other teachings about the soul: creationism, which holds that the individual human soul is directly created by God, and traducianism, which held that just as body begets body in biological generation, so the soul of the new human being is begotten by the parental soul. In Hinduism, the cycle of reincarnations represents the period of estrangement and trial for the soul or *Ātman* before it achieves release (*moksha*).   F.J.C.

preface paradox. See SEMANTIC PARADOXES.

preference. See DECISION THEORY.

preference logics. See DECISION THEORY.

preference satisfaction utilitarianism. See HARE.

prehension. See WHITEHEAD.

premise. See ARGUMENT.

premise, major. See SYLLOGISM.

premise, minor. See SYLLOGISM.

prenex normal form. See NORMAL FORM.

prescriptive definition. See DEFINITION.

prescriptive meaning. See MEANING.

prescriptivism, the theory that evaluative judgments necessarily have prescriptive meaning. Associated with noncognitivism and moral antirealism, prescriptivism holds that moral language is such that, if you say that you think one ought to do a certain kind of act, and yet you are not committed to doing that kind of act in the relevant circumstances, then you either spoke insincerely or are using the word 'ought' in a less than full-blooded sense. Prescriptivism owes its stature to Hare. One of his innovations is the distinction between "secondarily evaluative" and "primarily evaluative" words. The prescriptive meaning of secondarily evaluative words, such as 'soft-hearted' or 'chaste', may vary significantly while their descriptive meanings stay relatively constant. Hare argues the reverse for the primarily evaluative words 'good', 'bad', 'right', 'wrong', 'ought', and 'must'. For example, some people assign to 'wrong' the descriptive meaning 'forbidden by God', others assign it the descriptive meaning 'causes social conflict', and others give it different descriptive meanings; but since all use 'wrong' with the same prescriptive meaning, they are using the same concept.

In part to show how moral judgments can be prescriptive and yet have the same logical relations as indicative sentences, Hare distinguished between phrastics and neustics. The *phrastic,* or content, can be the same in indicative and prescriptive sentences; e.g., 'Sam's leaving' is the phrastic not only of the indicative 'Sam will leave' but also of the prescription 'Sam ought to leave'. Hare's *Language of Morals* (1952) specified that the *neustic* indicates mood, i.e., whether the sentence is indicative, imperative, interrogative, etc. However, in an article in *Mind* (1989) and in *Sorting Out Ethics* (1997), he used 'neustic' to refer to the sign of subscription, and 'tropic' to refer to the sign of mood.

Prescriptivity is especially important if moral judgments are universalizable. For then we can employ golden rule–style moral reasoning.

   See also EMOTIVISM, ETHICS, HARE, UNIVERSALIZABILITY.   B.W.H.

present-aim theory. See PARFIT.

pre-Socratics, the early Greek philosophers who were not influenced by Socrates. (Generally they lived before Socrates, but some are contemporary with him or even younger.) The classification (though not the term) goes back to Aristotle, who saw Socrates' humanism and emphasis on ethical issues as a watershed in the history of philosophy. Aristotle rightly noted that philosophers prior to Socrates had stressed natural philosophy and cosmology rather than ethics. He credited them with discovering material principles and moving causes of natural events, but he criticized them for failing to stress structural elements of things (formal causes) and values or purposes (final causes).

Unfortunately, no writing of any pre-Socratic survives in more than a fragmentary form, and evidence of their views is thus often indirect, based on reports or criticisms of later writers. In order to reconstruct pre-Socratic thought, scholars have sought to collect testimonies of ancient sources and to identify quotations from the pre-Socratics in those sources. As modern research has revealed flaws in the interpretations of ancient witnesses, it has become a principle of exegesis to base reconstructions of their views on the actual words of the pre-Socratics themselves wherever possible. Because of the fragmentary and derivative nature of our evidence, even basic principles of a philosopher's system sometimes remain controversial; nevertheless, we can say that thanks to modern methods of historiography, there are many points we understand better than ancient witnesses who are our secondary sources.

Our best ancient secondary source is Aristotle, who lived soon after the pre-Socratics and had access to most of their writings. He interprets his predecessors from the standpoint of his own theory; but any historian must interpret philosophers in light of some theoretical background. Since we have extensive writings of Aristotle, we understand his system and can filter out his own prejudices. His colleague Theophrastus was the first professional historian of philosophy. Adopting Aristotle's general framework, he systematically discussed pre-Socratic theories. Unfortunately his work itself is lost, but many fragments and summaries of parts of it remain. Indeed, virtually all ancient witnesses writing after Theophrastus depend on him for their general understanding of the early philosophers, sometimes by way of digests of his work. When biography became an important genre in later antiquity, biographers collected facts, anecdotes, slanders, chronologies (often based on crude a priori assumptions), lists of book titles, and successions of school directors, which provide potentially valuable information.

By reconstructing ancient theories, we can trace the broad outlines of pre-Socratic development with some confidence. The first philosophers were the Milesians, philosophers of Miletus on the Ionian coast of Asia Minor, who in the sixth century B.C. broke away from mythological modes of explanation by accounting for all phenomena, even apparent prodigies of nature, by means of simple physical hypotheses. Aristotle saw the Milesians as material monists, positing a physical substrate – of water, or the *apeiron*, or air; but their material source was probably not a continuing substance that underlies all changes as Aristotle thought, but rather an original stuff that was transformed into different stuffs.

Pythagoras migrated from Ionia to southern Italy, founding a school of Pythagoreans who believed that souls transmigrated and that number was the basis of all reality. Because Pythagoras and his early followers did not publish anything, it is difficult to trace their development and influence in detail. Back in Ionia, Heraclitus criticized Milesian principles because he saw that if substances changed into one another, the process of transformation was more important than the substances that appeared in the cycle of changes. He thus chose the unstable substance fire as his material principle and stressed the unity of opposites. Parmenides and the Eleatic School criticized the notion of not-being that theories of physical transformations seemed to presuppose. One cannot even conceive of or talk of not-being; hence any conception that presupposes not-being must be ruled out. But the basic notions of coming-to-be, differentiation, and indeed change in general presuppose not-being, and thus must be rejected. Eleatic analysis leads to the further conclusion,

implicit in Parmenides, explicit in Melissus, that there is only one substance, what-is. Since this substance does not come into being or change in any way, nor does it have any internal differentiations, the world is just a single changeless, homogeneous individual.

Parmenides' argument seems to undermine the foundations of natural philosophy. After Parmenides philosophers who wished to continue natural philosophy felt compelled to grant that coming-to-be and internal differentiation of a given substance were impossible. But in order to accommodate natural processes, they posited a plurality of unchanging, homogeneous elements – the four elements of Empedocles, the elemental stuffs of Anaxagoras, the atoms of Democritus – that by arrangement and rearrangement could produce the cosmos and the things in it. There is no real coming-to-be and perishing in the world since the ultimate substances are everlasting; but some limited kind of change such as chemical combination or mixture or locomotion could account for changing phenomena in the world of experience. Thus the "pluralists" incorporated Eleatic principles into their systems while rejecting the more radical implications of the Eleatic critique.

Pre-Socratic philosophers developed more complex systems as a response to theoretical criticisms. They focused on cosmology and natural philosophy in general, championing reason and nature against mythological traditions. Yet the pre-Socratics have been criticized both for being too narrowly scientific in interest and for not being scientific (experimental) enough. While there is some justice in both criticisms, their interests showed breadth as well as narrowness, and they at least made significant conceptual progress in providing a framework for scientific and philosophical ideas. While they never developed sophisticated theories of ethics, logic, epistemology, or metaphysics, nor invented experimental methods of confirmation, they did introduce the concepts that ultimately became fundamental in modern theories of cosmic, biological, and cultural evolution, as well as in atomism, genetics, and social contract theory. Because the Socratic revolution turned philosophy in different directions, the pre-Socratic line died out. But the first philosophers supplied much inspiration for the sophisticated fourth-century systems of Plato and Aristotle as well as the basic principles of the great Hellenistic schools, Epicureanism, Stoicism, and Skepticism.

See also ELEATIC SCHOOL, IONIAN PHILOS-

OPHY, MILESIANS, PARMENIDES, PYTHAGO-
RAS.   D.W.G.

presupposition, (1) a relation between sentences
or statements, related to but distinct from entailment and assertion; (2) what a speaker takes to
be understood in making an assertion. The first
notion is semantic, the second pragmatic.

The semantic notion was introduced by Strawson in his attack on Russell's theory of descriptions, and perhaps anticipated by Frege.
Strawson argued that 'The present king of France
is bald' does not entail 'There is a present king of
France' as Russell held, but instead presupposes
it. Semantic presupposition can be defined thus:
a sentence or statement S presupposes a sentence
or statement S' provided S entails S' and the
negation of S also entails S'. S' is a condition of
the truth *or* falsity of S. Thus, since 'There is a
present king of France' is false, 'The present king
of France is bald' is argued to be neither true nor
false. So construed, presupposition is defined in
terms of, but is distinct from, entailment. It is also
distinct from assertion, since it is viewed as a
precondition of the truth or falsity of what is
asserted.

The pragmatic conception does not appeal to
truth conditions, but instead contrasts what a
speaker presupposes and what that speaker
asserts in making an utterance. Thus, someone
who utters 'The present king of France is bald'
presupposes – believes and believes that the
audience believes – that there is a present king of
France, and asserts that this king is bald. So conceived, presuppositions are beliefs that the
speaker takes for granted; if these beliefs are
false, the utterance will be inappropriate in some
way, but it does not follow that the sentence
uttered lacks a truth-value. These two notions of
presupposition are logically independent. On the
semantic characterization, presupposition is a
relation between sentences or statements requiring that there be truth-value gaps. On the pragmatic characterization, it is speakers rather than
sentences or statements that have presuppositions; no truth-value gaps are required. Many
philosophers and linguists have argued for treating what have been taken to be cases of semantic presupposition, including the one discussed
above, as pragmatic phenomena. Some have
denied that semantic presuppositions exist. If
not, intuitions about presupposition do not support the claims that natural languages have
truth-value gaps and that we need a three-valued logic to represent the semantics of natural
language adequately.

Presupposition is also distinct from implicature. If someone reports that he has just torn his
coat and you say, "There's a tailor shop around
the corner," you conversationally implicate that
the shop is open. This is not a semantic presupposition because if it is false that the shop is open,
there is no inclination to say that your assertion
was neither true nor false. It is not a pragmatic
presupposition because it is not something you
believe the hearer believes.

See also IMPLICATION, IMPLICATURE,
MANY-VALUED LOGIC.   R.B.

pretheoretical, independent of theory. More specifically, a proposition is pretheoretical, according
to some philosophers, if and only if it does not
depend for its plausibility or implausibility on
theoretical considerations or considerations of
theoretical analysis. The term 'preanalytic' is
often used synonymously with 'pretheoretical',
but the former is more properly paired with
analysis rather than with theory. Some philosophers characterize pretheoretical propositions as
"intuitively" plausible or implausible. Such
propositions, they hold, can regulate philosophical theorizing as follows: in general, an adequate
philosophical theory should not conflict with
intuitively plausible propositions (by implying
intuitively implausible propositions), and should
imply intuitively plausible propositions. Some
philosophers grant that theoretical considerations can override "intuitions" – in the sense of
intuitively plausible propositions – when overall
theoretical coherence (or reflective equilibrium)
is thereby enhanced. **See also** ANALYTIC PHI-
LOSOPHY, INTUITION, METAPHILOSOPHY,
ORDINARY LANGUAGE PHILOSOPHY, PREANA-
LYTIC, REFLECTIVE EQUILIBRIUM.   P.K.M.

Price, Richard (1723–91), Welsh Dissenting
minister, actuary, and moral philosopher. His
main work, *A Review of the Principal Question in
Morals* (1758), is a defense of rationalism in
ethics. He argued that the understanding immediately perceives simple, objective, moral qualities of actions. The resulting intuitive knowledge
of moral truths is accompanied by feelings of
approval and disapproval responsible for moral
motivation. He also wrote influential papers on
life expectancy, public finance, and annuities;
communicated to the Royal Society the paper by
his deceased friend Thomas Bayes containing
Bayes's theorem; and defended the American
and French revolutions. Burke's *Reflections on the
Revolution in France* is a response to one of Price's
sermons.   J.W.A.

Prichard, H(arold) A(rthur) (1871–1947), English philosopher and founder of the Oxford school of intuitionism. An Oxford fellow and professor, he published *Kant's Theory of Knowledge* (1909) and numerous essays, collected in *Moral Obligation* (1949, 1968) and in *Knowledge and Perception* (1950). Prichard was a realist in his theory of knowledge, following Cook Wilson. He held that through direct perception in concrete cases we obtain knowledge of universals and of necessary connections between them, and he elaborated a theory about our knowledge of material objects. In "Does Moral Philosophy Rest on a Mistake?" (1912) he argued powerfully that it is wrong to think that a general theory of obligation is possible. No single principle captures the various reasons why obligatory acts are obligatory. Only by direct perception in particular cases can we see what we ought to do. With this essay Prichard founded the Oxford school of intuitionism, carried on by, among others, Ross. **See also ETHICS, ROSS.**   J.B.S.

Priestley, Joseph (1733–1804), British experimental chemist, theologian, and philosopher. In 1774 he prepared oxygen by heating mercuric oxide. Although he continued to favor the phlogiston hypothesis, his work did much to discredit that idea. He discovered many gases, including ammonia, sulfur dioxide, carbon monoxide, and hydrochloric acid. While studying the layer of carbon dioxide over a brewing vat, he conceived the idea of dissolving it under pressure. The resulting "soda water" was famous throughout Europe.

His *Essay on Government* (1768) influenced Jefferson's ideas in the American Declaration of Independence. The essay also contributed to the utilitarianism of Bentham, supplying the phrase "the greatest happiness of the greatest number." Priestley modified the associationism of Locke, Hume, and Hartley, holding that a sharp distinction must be drawn between the results of association in forming natural propensities and its effects on the development of moral ideas. On the basis of this distinction, he argued, against Hume, that differences in individual moral sentiments are results of education, through the association of ideas, a view anticipated by Helvétius. Priestley served as minister to anti-Establishment congregations. His unpopular stress on individual freedom resulted in his move to Pennsylvania, where he spent his last years.   R.E.B.

prima facie duty. See DUTY, ROSS.

prima facie evidence. See EVIDENCE.

prima facie justification. See JUSTIFICATION.

prima facie right. See RIGHTS.

primarily valuative word. See PRESCRIPTIVISM.

primary process. See FREUD.

primary qualities. See QUALITIES.

primary rule. See HART.

primary substance. See ARISTOTLE.

prime matter. See HYLOMORPHISM.

prime mover, the original source and cause of motion (change) in the universe – an idea that was developed by Aristotle and became important in Judaic, Christian, and Islamic thought about God. According to Aristotle, something that is in motion (a process of change) is moving from a state of potentiality to a state of actuality. For example, water that is being heated is potentially hot and in the process of becoming actually hot. If a cause of change must itself actually be in the state that it is bringing about, then nothing can produce motion in itself; whatever is in motion is being moved by another. For otherwise something would be both potentially and actually in the same state. Thus, the water that is potentially hot can become hot only by being changed by something else (the fire) that is actually hot. The prime mover, the original cause of motion, must itself, therefore, not be in motion; it is an unmoved mover.

Aquinas and other theologians viewed God as the prime mover, the ultimate cause of all motion. Indeed, for these theologians the argument to establish the existence of a first mover, itself unmoved, was a principal argument used in their efforts to prove the existence of God on the basis of reason. Many modern thinkers question the argument for a first mover on the ground that it does not seem to be logically impossible that the motion of one thing be caused by a second thing whose motion in turn is caused by a third thing, and so on without end. Defenders of the argument claim that it presupposes a distinction between two different causal series, one temporal and one simultaneous, and argue that the objection succeeds only against a temporal causal series.

See also AGENT CAUSATION, AQUINAS, ARISTOTLE.   W.L.R.

primitive symbol. See LOGISTIC SYSTEM.

principium individuationis, the cause (or basis) of individuality in individuals; what makes something individual as opposed to universal, e.g., what makes the cat Minina individual and thus different from the universal, *cat*. Questions regarding the principle of individuation were first raised explicitly in the early Middle Ages. Classical authors largely ignored individuation; their ontological focus was on the problem of universals. The key texts that originated the discussion of the principle of individuation are found in Boethius. Between Boethius and 1150, individuation was always discussed in the context of more pressing issues, particularly the problem of universals. After 1150, individuation slowly emerged as a focus of attention, so that by the end of the thirteenth century it had become an independent subject of discussion, especially in Aquinas and Duns Scotus.

Most early modern philosophers conceived the problem of individuation epistemically rather than metaphysically; they focused on the discernibility of individuals rather than the cause of individuation (Descartes). With few exceptions (Karl Popper), the twentieth century has followed this epistemic approach (P. F. Strawson).

See also INDIVIDUATION, METAPHYSICS.
                                                                       J.J.E.G.

principle of bivalence, the principle that any (significant) statement is either true or false. It is often confused with the principle of excluded middle. Letting 'Tp' stand for 'p is true' and '$T{\sim}p$' for 'p is false' and otherwise using standard logical notation, bivalence is '$Tp \lor T{\sim}p$' and excluded middle is '$T(p \lor {\sim}p)$'. That they are different principles is shown by the fact that in probability theory, where 'Tp' can be expressed as '$\Pr(p) = 1$', bivalence '$(\Pr(p) = 1) \lor (\Pr(\sim p) = 1)$' is not true for all values of p – e.g. it is not true where 'p' stands for 'given a fair toss of a fair die, the result will be a six' (a statement with a probability of $^1/_6$, where $\sim p$ has a probability of $^5/_6$) – but excluded middle '$\Pr(p \lor \sim p) = 1$' is true for all definite values of p, including the probability case just given. If we allow that some (significant) statements have no truth-value *or* probability and distinguish external negation 'Tp' from internal negation '$T{\sim}p$', we can distin-

guish bivalence and excluded middle from the principle of non-contradiction, namely, '${\sim}(Tp \cdot T{\sim}p)$', which is equivalent to '${\sim}Tp \lor {\sim}T{\sim}p$'. Standard truth-functional logic sees no difference between 'p' and 'Tp', or '${\sim}Tp$' and '$T{\sim}p$', and thus is unable to distinguish the three principles. Some philosophers of logic deny there is such a difference. **See also** MANY-VALUED LOGIC, PHILOSOPHY OF LOGIC, VAGUENESS.
                                                                       R.P.

principle of charity. See MEANING.

principle of comprehension. See SET THEORY.

principle of concretion. See WHITEHEAD.

principle of conservation. See PHILOSOPHY OF SCIENCE.

principle of contradiction, also called principle of non-contradiction, the principle that a statement and its negation cannot both be true. It can be distinguished from the principle of bivalence, and given certain controversial assumptions, from the principle of excluded middle; but in truth-functional logic all three are regarded as equivalent. Outside of formal logic the principle of (non-)contradiction is best expressed as Aristotle expresses it: "Nothing can both be and not be at the same time in the same respect." **See also** LAWS OF THOUGHT, PRINCIPLE OF BIVALENCE.   R.P.

principle of determinism. See MILL'S METHODS.

principle of dominance. See NEWCOMB'S PARADOX.

principle of double effect, the view that there is a morally relevant difference between those consequences of our actions we intend and those we do not intend but do still foresee. According to the principle, if increased literacy means a higher suicide rate, those who work for education are not guilty of driving people to kill themselves. A physician may give a patient painkillers foreseeing that they will shorten his life, even though the use of outright poisons is forbidden and the physician does not intend to shorten the patient's life. An army attacking a legitimate military target may accept as inevitable, without intending to bring about, the deaths of a number of civilians.

Traditional moral theologians affirmed the existence of exceptionless prohibitions such as that against taking an innocent human life, while using the principle of double effect to resolve hard cases and avoid moral blind alleys. They held that one may produce a forbidden effect, provided (1) one's action also had a good effect, (2) one did not seek the bad effect as an end or as a means, (3) one did not produce the good effect through the bad effect, and (4) the good effect was important enough to outweigh the bad one.

Some contemporary philosophers and Roman Catholic theologians hold that a modified version of the principle of double effect is the sole justification of deadly deeds, even when the person killed is not innocent. They drop any restriction on the causal sequence, so that (e.g.) it is legitimate to cut off the head of an unborn child to save the mother's life. But they oppose capital punishment on the ground that those who inflict it require the death of the convict as part of their plan. They also play down the fourth requirement, on the ground that the weighing of incommensurable goods it requires is impossible.

Consequentialists deny the principle of double effect, as do those for whom the crucial distinction is between what we cause by our actions and what just happens. In the most plausible view, the principle does not presuppose exceptionless moral prohibitions, only something stronger than prima facie duties. It is easier to justify an oblique evasion of a moral requirement than a direct violation, even if direct violations are sometimes permissible. So understood, the principle is a guide to prudence rather than a substitute for it.

See also ETHICS, EUTHANASIA, INTENTION, JUST WAR THEORY.   P.E.D.

principle of excluded middle, the principle that the disjunction of any (significant) statement with its negation is always true; e.g., 'Either there is a tree over 500 feet tall or it is not the case that there is such a tree'. The principle is often confused with the principle of bivalence. See also PRINCIPLE OF BIVALENCE.   R.P.

principle of generic consistency. See UNIVERSALIZABILITY.

principle of indifference, a rule for assigning a probability to an event based on "parity of reasons." According to the principle, when the "weight of reasons" favoring one event is equal to the "weight of reasons" favoring another, the two events should be assigned the same probability. When there are n mutually exclusive and

collectively exhaustive events, and there is no reason to favor one over another, then we should be "indifferent" and the n events should each be assigned probability $1/n$ (the events are equiprobable), according to the principle. This principle is usually associated with the names Bernoulli (*Ars Conjectandi,* 1713) and Laplace (*Théorie analytique des probabilités,* 1812), and was so called by J. M. Keynes (*A Treatise on Probability,* 1921). The principle gives probability both a subjective ("degree of belief") and a logical ("partial logical entailment") interpretation. One rationale for the principle says that in ignorance, when no reasons favor one event over another, we should assign equal probabilities. It has been countered that *any* assignment of probabilities at all is a claim to *some* knowledge. Also, several seemingly natural applications of the principle, involving non-linearly related variables, have led to some mathematical contradictions, known as Bertrand's paradox, and pointed out by Keynes. See also BERTRAND'S PARADOX, EQUIPROBABLE, KEYNES, LAPLACE, PROBABILITY.   E.Ee.

principle of insufficient reason, the principle that if there is no sufficient reason (or explanation) for something's being (the case), then it will not be (the case). Since the rise of modern probability theory, many have identified the principle of insufficient reason with the principle of indifference (a rule for assigning a probability to an event based on "parity of reasons"). The two principles are closely related, but it is illuminating historically and logically to view the principle of insufficient reason as the general principle stated above (which is related to the principle of *sufficient* reason) and to view the principle of indifference as a special case of the principle of insufficient reason applying to probabilities. As Mach noted, the principle of insufficient reason, thus conceived, was used by Archimedes to argue that a lever with equal weights at equal distances from a central fulcrum would not move, since if there is no sufficient reason why it should move one way or the other, it would not move one way or the other. Philosophers from Anaximander to Leibniz used the same principle to argue for various metaphysical theses.

The principle of indifference can be seen to be a special case of this principle of insufficient reason applying to probabilities, if one reads the principle of indifference as follows: when there are N mutually exclusive and exhaustive events and there is no sufficient reason to believe that any one of them is more probable than any other, then no one of them is more probable than any other (they are equiprobable). The idea of "parity of reasons" associated with the principle of indifference is, in such manner, related to the idea that there is no sufficient reason for favoring one outcome over another. This is significant because the principle of insufficient reason is logically equivalent to the more familiar principle of sufficient reason (if something is [the case], then there is a sufficient reason for its being [the case]) – which means that the principle of indifference is a logical consequence of the principle of sufficient reason. If this is so, we can understand why so many were inclined to believe the principle of indifference was an a priori truth about probabilities, since it was an application to probabilities of that most fundamental of all alleged a priori principles of reasoning, the principle of sufficient reason. Nor should it surprise us that the alleged a priori truth of the principle of indifference was as controversial in probability theory as was the alleged a priori truth of the principle of sufficient reason in philosophy generally.

   See also PRINCIPLES OF INDIFFERENCE, PROBABILITY.   R.H.K.

principle of limited variety. See MILL'S METHODS.

principle of logical form. See LOGICAL FORM.

principle of maximizing expected utility. See NEWCOMB'S PARADOX.

principle of non-contradiction. See PRINCIPLE OF CONTRADICTION.

principle of parsimony. See OCKHAM'S RAZOR.

principle of perfection. See LEIBNIZ.

principle of plenitude, the principle that every genuine possibility is realized or actualized. This principle of the "fullness of being" was named by A. O. Lovejoy, who showed that it was commonly assumed throughout the history of Western science and philosophy, from Plato to Plotinus (who associated it with inexhaustible divine productivity), through Augustine and other medieval philosophers, to the modern rationalists (Spinoza and Leibniz) and the Enlightenment. Lovejoy connected plenitude to the great chain of being, the idea that the universe is a hierarchy of beings in which every possible form is actualized. In the eighteenth century, the principle was "temporalized": every

possible form of creature would be realized – not necessarily at all times – but at some stage "in the fullness of time." A clue about the significance of plenitude lies in its connection to the principle of sufficient reason (everything has a sufficient reason [cause or explanation] for being or not being). Plenitude says that if there is no sufficient reason for something's not being (i.e., if it is genuinely possible), then it exists – which is logically equivalent to the negative version of sufficient reason: if something does not exist, then there is a sufficient reason for its not being.   R.H.K.

principle of proportionality. See CAJETAN.

principle of self-determination. See SELF-DETERMINATION.

principle of subsidiarity. See SUBSIDIARITY.

principle of sufficient reason. See LEIBNIZ, PRINCIPLE OF INSUFFICIENT REASON.

principle of the anomalism of the mental. See PHILOSOPHY OF MIND.

principle of the conservation of matter. See PHILOSOPHY OF SCIENCE.

principle of uncertainty. See PHILOSOPHY OF SCIENCE, QUANTUM MECHANICS.

principle of universality. See UNIVERSALIZABILITY.

principle of universalizability. See UNIVERSALIZABILITY.

principle of unlimited comprehension. See SET THEORY.

principle of utility. See UTILITARIANISM.

principle of verifiability, a claim about what meaningfulness is: at its simplest, a sentence is meaningful provided there is a method for verifying it. Therefore, if a sentence has no such method, i.e., if it does not have associated with it a way of telling whether it is conclusively true or conclusively false, then it is meaningless. The purpose for which this verificationist principle was originally introduced was to demarcate sentences that are "apt to make a significant statement of fact" from "nonsensical" or "pseudo-" sentences. It is part of the emotive theory of content, e.g., that moral discourse is not (literally, cognitively) meaningful, and therefore, not factual. And, with the verifiability principle, the central European logical positivists of the 1920s hoped to strip "metaphysical discourse" of its pretensions of factuality. For them, whether there is a reality external to the mind, as the realists claim, or whether all reality is made up of "ideas" or "appearances," as idealists claim, is a "meaningless pseudo-problem."

The verifiability principle proved impossible to frame in a form that did not admit all metaphysical sentences as meaningful. (Further, it casts doubt on its own status. How was *it* to be verified?) So, e.g., in the first edition of *Language, Truth and Logic,* Ayer proposed that a sentence is verifiable, and consequently meaningful, if some observation sentence can be deduced from it in conjunction with certain other premises, without being deducible from those other premises alone. It follows that any metaphysical sentence M is meaningful since 'if M, then O' always is an appropriate premise, where O is an observation sentence. In the preface to the second edition, Ayer offered a more sophisticated account: M is directly verifiable provided it is an observation sentence or it entails, in conjunction with certain observation sentences, some observation sentence that does not follow from them alone. And M is indirectly verifiable provided it entails, in conjunction with certain other premises, some directly verifiable sentence that does not follow from those other premises alone and these additional premises are either analytic or directly verifiable (or are independently indirectly verifiable). The new verifiability principle is then that all and only sentences directly or indirectly verifiable are "literally meaningful." Unfortunately, Ayer's emendation admits every non-analytic sentence. Let M be any metaphysical sentence and O_1 and O_2 any pair of observation sentences logically independent of each other. Consider sentence A: 'either O_1 or (not-M and not-O_2)'. Conjoined with O_2, A entails O_1. But O_2 alone does not entail O_1. So A is directly verifiable. Therefore, since M conjoined with A entails O_1, which is not entailed by A alone, M is indirectly verifiable. Various repairs have been attempted; none has succeeded.

See also LOGICAL POSITIVISM, MEANING, VERIFICATIONISM, VIENNA CIRCLE.   E.L.

priority, conceptual. See DEPENDENCE.

prior probability. See BAYES'S THEOREM.

prisca theologica. See FICINO.

prisoner's dilemma, a problem in game theory, and more broadly the theory of rational choice, that takes its name from a familiar sort of plea-bargaining situation: Two prisoners (Robin and Carol) are interrogated separately and offered the same deal: If one of them confesses ("defects") and the other does not, the defector will be given immunity from prosecution and the other will get a stiff prison sentence. If both confess, both will get moderate prison terms. If both remain silent (cooperate with each other), both will get light prison terms for a lesser offense. There are thus four possible outcomes:

(1) Robin confesses and gets immunity, while Carol is silent and gets a stiff sentence.
(2) Both are silent and get light sentences.
(3) Both confess and get moderate sentences.
(4) Robin is silent and gets a stiff sentence, while Carol confesses and gets immunity.

Assume that for Robin, (1) would be the best outcome, followed by (2), (3), and (4), in that order. Assume that for Carol, the best outcome is (4), followed by (2), (3), and (1). Each prisoner then reasons as follows: "My confederate will either confess or remain silent. If she confesses, I must do likewise, in order to avoid the 'sucker's payoff' (immunity for her, a stiff sentence for me). If she remains silent, then I must confess in order to get immunity – the best outcome for me. Thus, no matter what my confederate does, I must confess." Under those conditions, both will confess, effectively preventing each other from achieving anything better than the option they both rank as only third-best, even though they agree that option (2) is second-best.

This illustrative story (attributed to A. W. Tucker) must not be allowed to obscure the fact that many sorts of social interactions have the same structure. In general, whenever any two parties must make simultaneous or independent choices over a range of options that has the ordinal payoff structure described in the plea bargaining story, they are in a prisoner's dilemma. Diplomats, negotiators, buyers, and sellers regularly find themselves in such situations. They are called *iterated* prisoner's dilemmas if the same parties repeatedly face the same choices with each other.

Moreover, there are analogous problems of cooperation and conflict at the level of many-person interactions: so-called *n*-person prisoner's diemmas or free rider problems. The provision of public goods provides an example. Suppose there is a public good, such as clean air, national defense, or public radio, which we all want. Suppose that is can be provided only by collective action, at some cost to each of the contributors, but that we do not have to have a contribution from everyone in order to get it. Assume that we all prefer having the good to not having it, and that the best outcome for each of us would be to have it without cost to ourselves. So each of us reasons as follows: "Other people will either contribute enough to produce the good by themselves, or they will not. If they do, then I can have it cost-free (the best option for me) and thus I should not contribute. But if others do not contribute enough to produce the good by themselves, and if the probability is very low that my costly contribution would make the difference between success and failure, once again I should not contribute." Obviously, if we all reason in this way, we will not get the public good we want. Such problems of collective action have been noticed by philosophers since Plato. Their current nomenclature, rigorous game-theoretic formulation, empirical study, and systematic philosophical development, however, has occurred since 1950.

See also GAME THEORY, SOCIAL CHOICE THEORY.   L.C.B.

privacy, epistemic. See EPISTEMIC PRIVACY.

private language argument, an argument designed to show that there cannot be a language that only one person can speak – a language that is essentially private, that no one else can in principle understand. In addition to its intrinsic interest, the private language argument is relevant to discussions of linguistic rules and linguistic meaning, behaviorism, solipsism, and phenomenalism. The argument is closely associated with Wittgenstein's *Philosophical Investigations* (1958). The exact structure of the argument is controversial; this account should be regarded as a standard one, but not beyond dispute.

The argument begins with the supposition that a person assigns signs to sensations, where these are taken to be private to the person who has them, and attempts to show that this supposition cannot be sustained because no standards for the correct or incorrect application of the same sign to a recurrence of the same sensation are possible. Thus Wittgenstein supposes that he undertakes to keep a diary about the recurrence of a certain sensation; he associates it with the sign '*S*', and marks '*S*' on a calendar every day he has that sensation. Wittgenstein finds the nature of

the association of the sign and sensation obscure, on the ground that '*S*' cannot be given an ordinary definition (this would make its meaning publicly accessible) or even an ostensive definition. He further argues that there is no difference between correct and incorrect entries of '*S*' on subsequent days. The initial sensation with which the sign '*S*' was associated is no longer present, and so it cannot be compared with a subsequent sensation taken to be of the same kind. He could at best claim to remember the nature of the initial sensation, and judge that it is of the same kind as today's. But since the memory cannot confirm its own accuracy, there is no possible test of whether he remembers the initial association of sign and sensation *right* today. Consequently there is no criterion for the correct reapplication of the sign '*S*'. Thus we cannot make sense of the notion of correctly reapplying '*S*', and cannot make sense of the notion of a private language.

The argument described appears to question only the claim that one could have terms for private mental occurrences, and may not seem to impugn a broader notion of a private language whose expressions are not restricted to signs for sensations. Advocates of Wittgenstein's argument would generalize it and claim that the focus on sensations simply highlights the absence of a distinction between correct and incorrect reapplications of words. A language with terms for publicly accessible objects would, if *private to its user*, still be claimed to lack criteria for the correct reapplication of such terms. This broader notion of a private language would thus be argued to be equally incoherent.

See also PHILOSOPHY OF LANGUAGE, PROBLEM OF OTHER MINDS, WITTGENSTEIN.   R.B.

privation, a lack of something that it is natural or good to possess. The term is closely associated with the idea that evil is itself only a lack of good, *privatio boni*. In traditional theistic religions everything other than God is created by God out of nothing, creation *ex nihilo*. Since, being perfect, God would create only what is good, the entire original creation and every creature from the most complex to the simplest are created entirely good. The original creation contains no evil whatever. What then is evil and how does it enter the world? The idea that evil is a privation of good does not mean, e.g., that a rock has some degree of evil because it lacks such good qualities as consciousness and courage. A thing has some degree of evil only if it lacks some good that is proper for that thing to possess. In the original creation each created thing possessed the goods proper to the sort of thing it was. According to Augustine, evil enters the world when creatures with free will abandon the good above themselves for some lower, inferior good. Human beings, e.g., become evil to the extent that they freely turn from the highest good (God) to their own private goods, becoming proud, selfish, and wicked, thus deserving the further evils of pain and punishment. One of the problems for this explanation of the origin of evil is to account for why an entirely good creature would use its freedom to turn from the highest good to a lesser good. **See also** PHILOSOPHY OF RELIGION.

W.L.R.

privileged access, special first-person awareness of the contents of one's own mind. Since Descartes, many philosophers have held that persons are aware of the occurrent states of their own minds in a way distinct from both their mode of awareness of physical objects and their mode of awareness of the mental states of others.

Cartesians view such apprehension as privileged in several ways. First, it is held to be immediate, both causally and epistemically. While knowledge of physical objects and their properties is acquired via spatially intermediate causes, knowledge of one's own mental states involves no such causal chains. And while beliefs about physical properties are justified by appeal to ways objects appear in sense experience, beliefs about the properties of one's own mental states are not justified by appeal to properties of a different sort. I justify my belief that the paper on which I write is white by pointing out that it appears white in apparently normal light. By contrast, my belief that white appears in my visual experience seems to be self-justifying.

Second, Cartesians hold that first-person apprehension of occurrent mental contents is epistemically privileged in being absolutely certain. Absolute certainty includes infallibility, incorrigibility, and indubitability. That a judgment is infallible means that it cannot be mistaken; its being believed entails its being true (even though judgments regarding occurrent mental contents are not necessary truths). That it is incorrigible means that it cannot be overridden or corrected by others or by the subject himself at a later time. That it is indubitable means that a subject can never have grounds for doubting it. Philosophers sometimes claim also that a subject is omniscient with regard to her own occurrent mental states:

if a property appears within her experience, then she knows this.

Subjects' privileged access to the immediate contents of their own minds can be held to be necessary or contingent. Regarding corrigibility, for example, proponents of the stronger view hold that first-person reports of occurrent mental states could never be overridden by conflicting evidence, such as conflicting readings of brain states presumed to be correlated with the mental states in question. They point out that knowledge of such correlations would itself depend on first-person reports of mental states. If a reading of my brain indicates that I am in pain, and I sincerely claim not to be, then the law linking brain states of that type with pains must be mistaken. Proponents of the weaker view hold that, while persons are currently the best authorities as to the occurrent contents of their own minds, evidence such as conflicting readings of brain states could eventually override such authority, despite the dependence of the evidence on earlier first-person reports.

Weaker views on privileged access may also deny infallibility on more general grounds. In judging anything, including an occurrent mental state, to have a particular property P, it seems that I must remember which property P is, and memory appears to be always fallible. Even if such judgments are always fallible, however, they may be more immediately justified than other sorts of judgments. Hence there may still be privileged access, but of a weaker sort.

In the twentieth century, Ryle attacked the idea of privileged access by analyzing introspection, awareness of what one is thinking or doing, in terms of behavioral dispositions, e.g. dispositions to give memory reports of one's mental states when asked to do so. But while behaviorist or functional analyses of some states of mind may be plausible, for instance analyses of cognitive states such as beliefs, accounts in these terms of occurrent states such as sensations or images are far less plausible. A more influential attack on stronger versions of privileged access was mounted by Wilfrid Sellars. According to him, we must be trained to report non-inferentially on properties of our sense experience by first learning to respond with whole systems of concepts to public, physical objects. Before I can learn to report a red sense impression, I must learn the system of color concepts and the logical relations among them by learning to respond to colored objects. Hence, knowledge of my own mental states cannot be the firm basis from which I progress to other knowledge.

Even if this order of concept acquisition is determined necessarily, it still may be that persons' access to their own mental states is privileged in some of the ways indicated, once the requisite concepts have been acquired. Beliefs about one's own occurrent states of mind may still be more immediately justified than beliefs about physical properties, for example.

See also CERTAINTY, FOUNDATIONALISM, IMMEDIACY, PERCEPTION.   A.H.G.

pro attitude, a favorable disposition toward an object or state of affairs. Although some philosophers equate pro attitudes with desires, the expression is more often intended to cover a wide range of conative states of mind including wants, feelings, wishes, values, and principles. My regarding a certain course of action open to me as morally required and my regarding it as a source of selfish satisfaction equally qualify as pro attitudes toward the object of that action. It is widely held that intentional action, or, more generally, acting for reasons, is necessarily based, in part, on one or more pro attitudes. If I go to the store in order to buy some turnips, then, in addition to my regarding my store-going as conducive to turnip buying, I must have some pro attitude toward turnip buying. **See also** ACTION THEORY, PRACTICAL REASONING.   J.F.H.

probabilism. See MEDINA.

probabilistic automaton. See COMPUTER THEORY, SELF-REPRODUCING AUTOMATON.

probabilistic causation. See CAUSATION.

probabilistic disposition. See DISPOSITION.

probabilistic independence. See PROBABILITY.

probabilistic law. See CAUSAL LAW.

probability, a numerical value that can attach to items of various kinds (e.g., propositions, events, and kinds of events) that is a measure of the degree to which they may or should be expected – or the degree to which they have "their own disposition," i.e., independently of our psychological expectations – to be true, to occur, or to be exemplified (depending on the kind of item the value attaches to). There are both multiple interpretations of probability and two main kinds of theories of probability: abstract formal calculi and interpretations of the calculi. An abstract formal calculus axiomatically

characterizes formal properties of probability functions, where the arguments of the function are often thought of as sets, or as elements of a Boolean algebra. In application, the nature of the arguments of a probability function, as well as the meaning of probability, are given by interpretations of probability.

The most famous axiomatization is Kolmogorov's (*Foundations of the Theory of Probability*, 1933). The three axioms for probability functions Pr are: (1) $Pr(X) \geq 0$ for all X; (2) $Pr(X) = 1$ if X is necessary (e.g., a tautology if a proposition, a necessary event if an event, and a "universal set" if a set); and (3) $Pr(X \lor Y) = Pr(X) + Pr(Y)$ (where '$\lor$' can mean, e.g., logical disjunction, or set-theoretical union) if X and Y are mutually exclusive ($X \& Y$ is a contradiction if they are propositions, they can't both happen if they are events, and their set-theoretical intersection is empty if they are sets). Axiom (3) is called finite additivity, which is sometimes generalized to countable additivity, involving infinite disjunctions of propositions, or infinite unions of sets. *Conditional probability*, $Pr(X/Y)$ (the probability of X "given" or "conditional on" Y), is defined as the quotient $Pr(X \& Y)/Pr(Y)$. An item X is said to be *positively* or *negatively statistically* (or *probabilistically*) *correlated with* an item Y according to whether $Pr(X/Y)$ is greater than or less than $Pr(X/\sim Y)$ (where $\sim Y$ is the negation of a proposition Y, or the non-occurrence of an event Y, or the set-theoretical complement of a set Y); in the case of equality, X is said to be *statistically* (or *probabilistically*) *independent* of Y. All three of these probabilistic relations are symmetric, and sometimes the term 'probabilistic relevance' is used instead of 'correlation'. From the axioms, familiar theorems can be proved: e.g., (4) $Pr(\sim X) = 1 - Pr(X)$; (5) $Pr(X \lor Y) = Pr(X) + Pr(Y) - Pr(X \& Y)$ (for all X and Y); and (6) (a simple version of Bayes's theorem) $Pr(X/Y) = Pr(Y/X)Pr(X)/Pr(Y)$. Thus, an abstract formal calculus of probability allows for calculation of the probabilities of some items from the probabilities of others.

The main interpretations of probability include the *classical, relative frequency, propensity, logical*, and *subjective* interpretations. According to the classical interpretation, the probability of an event, e.g. of heads on a coin toss, is equal to the ratio of the number of "equipossibilities" (or equiprobable events) favorable to the event in question to the total number of relevant equipossibilities. On the relative frequency interpretation, developed by Venn (*The Logic of Chance*, 1866) and Reichenbach (*The Theory of Probability*,

1935), probability attaches to sets of events within a "reference class." Where W is the reference class, and n is the number of events in W, and m is the number of events in (or of kind) X, within W, then the probability of X, relative to W, is m/n. For various conceptual and technical reasons, this kind of "actual finite relative frequency" interpretation has been refined into various infinite and hypothetical infinite relative frequency accounts, where probability is defined in terms of limits of series of relative frequencies in finite (nested) populations of increasing sizes, sometimes involving hypothetical infinite extensions of an actual population. The reasons for these developments involve, e.g.: the artificial restriction, for finite populations, of probabilities to values of the form i/n, where n is the size of the reference class; the possibility of "mere coincidence" in the actual world, where these may not reflect the true physical dispositions involved in the relevant events; and the fact that probability is often thought to attach to possibilities involving single events, while probabilities on the relative frequency account attach to sets of events (this is the "problem of the single case," also called the "problem of the reference class"). These problems also have inspired "propensity" accounts of probability, according to which probability is a more or less primitive idea that measures the physical propensity or disposition of a given kind of physical situation to yield an outcome of a given type, or to yield a "long-run" relative frequency of an outcome of a given type.

A theorem of probability proved by Jacob Bernoulli (*Ars Conjectandi*, 1713) and sometimes called *Bernoulli's theorem* or the weak law of large numbers, and also known as the first limit theorem, is important for appreciating the frequency interpretation. The theorem states, roughly, that in the long run, frequency settles down to probability. For example, suppose the probability of a certain coin's landing heads on any given toss is 0.5, and let e be any number greater than 0. Then the theorem implies that as the number of tosses grows without bound, the probability approaches 1 that the frequency of heads will be within e of 0.5. More generally, let p be the probability of an outcome O on a trial of an experiment, and assume that this probability remains constant as the experiment is repeated. After n trials, there will be a frequency, f_n, of trials yielding outcome O. The theorem says that for any numbers d and e greater than 0, there is an n such that the probability (P) that $|p-f_n| < e$ is within d of 1 ($P > 1-d$). Bernoulli also showed how to calculate such n for given values of d, e, and p. It is important to notice that the theorem concerns probabilities, and *not certainty*, for a long-run frequency. Notice also the assumption that the probability p of O remains constant as the experiment is repeated, so that the outcomes on trials are probabilistically independent of earlier outcomes.

The kinds of interpretations of probability just described are sometimes called "objective" or "statistical" or "empirical" since the value of a probability, on these accounts, depends on what actually happens, or on what actual given physical situations are disposed to produce – as opposed to depending only on logical relations between the relevant events (or propositions), or on what we should rationally expect to happen or what we should rationally believe. In contrast to these accounts, there are the "logical" and the "subjective" interpretations of probability. Carnap ("The Two Concepts of Probability," *Philosophy and Phenomenological Research*, 1945) has marked this kind of distinction by calling the second concept *probability*$_1$ and the first *probability*$_2$.

According to the logical interpretation, associated with Carnap (see also *Logical Foundations of Probability*, 1950; and *Continuum of Inductive Methods*, 1952), the probability of a proposition X given a proposition Y is the "degree to which Y logically entails X." Carnap developed an ingenious and elaborate set of systems of logical probability, including, e.g., separate systems depending on the degree to which one happens to be, logically and rationally, sensitive to new information in the reevaluation of probabilities. There is, of course, a connection between the ideas of logical probability, rationality, belief, and belief revision. It is natural to explicate the "logical-probabilistic" idea of the probability of X given Y as the degree to which a rational person would believe X having come to learn Y (taking account of background knowledge). Here, the idea of *belief* suggests a *subjective* (sometimes called *epistemic* or *partial belief* or *degree of belief*) interpretation of probability; and the idea of probability *revision* suggests the concept of *induction:* both the logical and the subjective interpretations of probability have been called "inductive probability" – a formal apparatus to characterize rational learning from experience.

The subjective interpretation of probability, according to which the probability of a proposition is a measure of one's degree of belief in it, was developed by, e.g., Ramsey ("Truth and Probability," in his *Foundations of Mathematics and Other Essays*, 1926); Definetti ("Foresight: Its Logical Laws, Its Subjective Sources," 1937, translated by H. Kyburg, Jr., in H. E. Smokler, *Studies in Subjective Probability,* 1964); and Savage (*The Foundations of Statistics,* 1954). Of course, subjective probability varies from person to person. Also, in order for this to be an interpretation of *probability,* so that the relevant axioms are satisfied, not all persons can count – only rational, or "coherent" persons should count. Some theorists have drawn a connection between rationality and probabilistic degrees of belief in terms of dispositions to set coherent betting odds (those that do not allow a "Dutch book" – an arrangement that forces the agent to lose come what may), while others have described the connection in more general decision-theoretic terms.

See also BAYES'S THEOREM, CARNAP, DUTCH BOOK, INDUCTION, PROPENSITY, REICHENBACH.   E.Ee.

probability, prior. See BAYES'S THEOREM.

probability function. See BAYESIAN RATIONALITY.

problematic judgment. See KANT.

problematic modality. See MODALITY.

problem of evil. See PHILOSOPHY OF RELIGION.

problem of induction. First stated by Hume, this problem concerns the logical basis of inferences from observed matters of fact to unobserved matters of fact. Although discussion often focuses upon predictions of future events (e.g., a solar eclipse), the question applies also to inferences to past facts (e.g., the extinction of dinosaurs) and to present occurrences beyond the range of direct observation (e.g., the motions of planets during daylight hours). Long before Hume the ancient Skeptics had recognized that such inferences cannot be made with *certainty;* they realized there can be no demonstrative (deductive) inference, say, from the past and present to the future. Hume, however, posed a more profound difficulty: Are we justified in placing *any* degree of confidence in the conclusions of such inferences? His question is whether there is any type of non-demonstrative or inductive inference in which we can be justified in placing any confidence at all.

According to Hume, our inferences from the observed to the unobserved are based on regularities found in nature. We believe, e.g., that the earth, sun, and moon move in regular patterns (according to Newtonian mechanics), and on that basis astronomers predict solar and lunar eclipses. Hume notes, however, that all of our evidence for such uniformities consists of past and present experience; in applying these uniformities to the future behavior of these bodies we are making an inference from the observed to the unobserved. This point holds in general. Whenever we make inferences from the observed to the unobserved we rely on the uniformity of nature. The basis for our belief that nature is reasonably uniform is our experience of such uniformity in the past. If we infer that nature will continue to be uniform in the future, we are making an inference from the observed to the unobserved – precisely the kind of inference for which we are seeking a justification. We are thus caught up in a circular argument.

Since, as Hume emphasized, much of our reasoning from the observed to the unobserved is based on causal relations, he analyzed causality to ascertain whether it could furnish a necessary connection between distinct events that could serve as a basis for such inferences. His conclusion was negative. We cannot establish any such connection a priori, for it is impossible to deduce the nature of an effect from its cause – e.g., we cannot deduce from the appearance of falling snow that it will cause a sensation of cold rather than heat. Likewise, we cannot deduce the nature of a cause from its effect – e.g., looking at a diamond, we cannot deduce that it was produced by great heat and pressure. All such knowledge is based on past experience. If we infer that future snow will feel cold or that future diamonds will be produced by great heat and pressure, we are again making inferences from the observed to the unobserved.

Furthermore, if we carefully observe cases in which we believe a cause–effect relation holds, we cannot perceive any necessary connection between cause and effect, or any power in the cause that brings about the effect. We observe only that an event of one type (e.g., drinking water) occurs prior to and contiguously with an event of another type (quenching thirst). Moreover, we notice that events of the two types have exhibited a constant conjunction; i.e., whenever an event of the first type has occurred in the past it has been followed by one of the second type. We cannot discover any necessary connection or causal power a posteriori; we can only establish priority, contiguity, and constant conjunction up to the present. If we infer that this constant conjunction will persist in future cases, we are making another inference from observed to unobserved cases. To use causality as a basis for justifying inference from the observed to the unobserved would again invovle a circular argument.

Hume concludes skeptically that there can be no rational or logical justification of inferences from the observed to the unobserved – i.e., inductive or non-demonstrative inference. Such inferences are based on custom and habit. Nature has endowed us with a proclivity to extrapolate from past cases to future cases of a similar kind. Having observed that events of one type have been regularly followed by events of another type, we experience, upon encountering a case of the first type, a psychological expectation that one of the second type will follow. Such an expectation does not constitute a rational justification.

Although Hume posed his problem in terms of homely examples, the issues he raises go to the heart of even the most sophisticated empirical sciences, for all of them involve inference from observed phenomena to unobserved facts. Although complex theories are often employed, Hume's problem still applies. Its force is by no means confined to induction by simple enumeration.

Philosophers have responded to the problem of induction in many different ways. Kant invoked synthetic a priori principles. Many twentieth-century philosophers have treated it as a pseudo-problem, based on linguistic confusion, that requires dissolution rather than solution. Carnap maintained that *inductive intuition* is indispensable. Reichenbach offered a *pragmatic vindication*. Goodman has recommended replacing Hume's "old riddle" with a new riddle of induction that he has posed. Popper, taking Hume's skeptical arguments as conclusive, advocates deductivism. He argues that induction is unjustifiable and dispensable. None of the many suggestions is widely accepted as correct.

See also CAUSATION, GRUE PARADOX, HUME, SKEPTICISM, UNIFORMITY OF NATURE.

                                W.C.S.

problem of other minds, the question of what rational basis a person can have for the belief that other persons are similarly conscious and have minds. Every person, by virtue of being conscious, is aware of her own state of consciousness and thus knows she has a mind; but the mental states of others are not similarly apparent to her.

An influential attempt to solve this problem was made by philosophical behaviorists. According to Ryle in *The Concept of Mind* (1949), a mind is not a ghost in the physical machine but (roughly speaking) an aggregate of dispositions to behave intelligently and to respond overtly to sensory stimulation. Since the behavior distinctive of these mentalistic dispositions is readily observable in other human beings, the so-called problem of other minds is easily solved: it arose from mere confusion about the concept of mind. Ryle's opponents were generally willing to concede that such dispositions provide proof that another person has a "mind" or is a sentient being, but they were not willing to admit that those dispositions provide proof that other people actually have feelings, thoughts, and sensory experiences. Their convictions on this last matter generated a revised version of the other-minds problem; it might be called the problem of other-person experiences.

Early efforts to solve the problem of other minds can be viewed as attempts to solve the problem of other-person experiences. According to J. S. Mill's *Examination of Sir William Hamilton's Philosophy* (1865), one can defend one's conviction that others have feelings and other subjective experiences by employing an argument from analogy. To develop that analogy one first attends to how one's own experiences are related to overt or publicly observable phenomena. One might observe that one feels pain when pricked by a pin and that one responds to the pain by wincing and saying "ouch." The next step is to attend to the behavior and circumstances of others. Since other people are physically very similar to oneself, it is reasonable to conclude that if they are pricked by a pin and respond by wincing and saying "ouch," they too have felt pain. Analogous inferences involving other sorts of mental states and other sorts of behavior and circumstances add strong support, Mill said, to one's belief in other-person experiences.

Although arguments from analogy are generally conceded to provide rationally acceptable evidence for unobserved phenomena, the analogical argument for other-person experiences was vigorously attacked in the 1960s by philosophers influenced by Wittgenstein's *Philosophical Investigations* (1953). Their central contention was that anyone employing the argument must assume that, solely from her own case, she knows what feelings and thoughts are. This assumption was refuted, they thought, by Wittgenstein's private language argument, which proved that we learn what feelings and thoughts are only in the process of learning a publicly understandable language containing an appropriate psychological vocabulary. To understand this latter vocabulary, these critics said, one must be able to use its ingredient words correctly in relation to others as well as to oneself; and this can be ascertained only because words like 'pain' and 'depression' are associated with behavioral criteria. When such criteria are satisfied by the behavior of others, one knows that the words are correctly applied to them and that one is justified in believing that they have the experiences in question. The supposed problem of other-person experiences is thus "dissolved" by a just appreciation of the preconditions for coherent thought about psychological states.

Wittgenstein's claim that, to be conceivable, "an inner process stands in need of external criteria," lost its hold on philosophers during the 1970s. An important consideration was this: if a feeling of pain is a genuine reality different from the behavior that typically accompanies it, then so-called pain behavior cannot be shown to provide adequate evidence for the presence of pain by a purely linguistic argument; some empirical inductive evidence is needed. Since, contrary to Wittgenstein, one knows what the feeling of pain is like only by having that feeling, one's belief that other people occasionally have feelings that are significantly like the pain one feels oneself apparently must be supported by an argument in which analogy plays a central role. No other strategy seems possible.

See also BEHAVIORISM, PHILOSOPHY OF MIND, PRIVATE LANGUAGE ARGUMENT, WITTGENSTEIN.   B.A.

problem of the criterion, a problem of epistemology, arising in the attempt both to formulate the *criteria* and to determine the *extent* of knowledge. Skeptical and non-skeptical philosophers disagree as to what, or how much, we know. Do we have knowledge of the external world, other minds, the past, and the future? Any answer depends on what the correct criteria of knowledge are. The problem is generated by the seeming plausibility of the following two propositions:

(1) In order to recognize instances, and thus to determine the extent, of knowledge, we must know the criteria for it.
(2) In order to know the criteria for knowledge (i.e., to distinguish between correct and incorrect criteria), we must already be able to recognize its instances.

According to an argument of ancient Greek Skepticism, we can know neither the extent nor the criteria of knowledge because (1) and (2) are both true. There are, however, three further possibilities. First, it might be that (2) is true but (1) false: we can recognize instances of knowledge

even if we do not know the criteria of knowledge. Second, it might be that (1) is true but (2) false: we can identify the criteria of knowledge without prior recognition of its instances. Finally, it might be that both (1) and (2) are false. We can know the extent of knowledge without knowing criteria, and vice versa. Chisholm, who has devoted particular attention to this problem, calls the first of these options *particularism,* and the second *methodism.* Hume, a skeptic about the extent of empirical knowledge, was a methodist. Reid and Moore were particularists; they rejected Hume's skepticism on the ground that it turns obvious cases of knowledge into cases of ignorance. Chisholm advocates particularism because he believes that, unless one knows to begin with what ought to count as an instance of knowledge, any choice of a criterion is ungrounded and thus arbitrary. Methodists turn this argument around: they reject as dogmatic any identification of instances of knowledge not based on a criterion. **See also SKEPTICISM.**

    M.St.

problem of the single case. See PROBABILITY, PROPENSITY.

problem of the speckled hen, a problem propounded by Ryle as an objection to Ayer's analysis of perception in terms of sense-data. It is implied by this analysis that, if I see a speckled hen (in a good light and so on), I do so by means of apprehending a speckled sense-datum. The analysis implies further that the sense-datum actually has just the number of speckles that I seem to see as I look at the hen, and that it is immediately evident to me just how many speckles this is. Thus, if I seem to see many speckles as I look at the hen, the sense-datum I apprehend must actually contain many speckles, and it must be immediately evident to me how many it does contain. Now suppose it seems to me that I see more than 100 speckles. Then the datum I am apprehending must contain more than 100 speckles. Perhaps it contains 132 of them. The analysis would then imply, absurdly, that it must be immediately evident to me that the number of speckles is exactly 132. One way to avoid this implication would be to deny that a sense-datum of mine could contain exactly 132 speckles – or any other large, determinate number of them – precisely on the ground that it could never seem to me that I was seeing exactly that many speckles. A possible drawback of this approach is that it involves committing oneself to the claim, which some philosophers have found self-contradictory, that a sense-datum may contain many speckles even if there is no large number n such that it contains n speckles. **See also** PERCEPTION, VAGUENESS.   R.Ke.

proceduralism. See JURISPRUDENCE.

process philosophy. See WHITEHEAD.

process–product ambiguity, an ambiguity that occurs when a noun can refer either to a process (or activity) or to the product of that process (or activity). E.g., 'The definition was difficult' could mean either that the activity of defining was a difficult one to perform, or that the definiens (the form of words proposed as equivalent to the term being defined) that the definer produced was difficult to understand. Again, 'The writing absorbed her attention' leaves it unclear whether it was the activity of writing or a product of that activity that she found engrossing. Philosophically significant terms that might be held to exhibit process–product ambiguity include: 'analysis', 'explanation', 'inference', 'thought'.
                                                   P.Mac.

process theology, any theology strongly influenced by the theistic metaphysics of Whitehead or Hartshorne; more generally, any theology that takes process or change as basic characteristics of all actual beings, including God. Those versions most influenced by Whitehead and Hartshorne share a core of convictions that constitute the most distinctive theses of process theology: God is constantly growing, though certain abstract features of God (e.g., being loving) remain constant; God is related to every other actual being and is affected by what happens to it; every actual being has some self-determination, and God's power is reconceived as the power to lure (attempt to persuade) each actual being to be what God wishes it to be. These theses represent significant differences from ideas of God common in the tradition of Western theism, according to which God is unchanging, is not really related to creatures because God is not affected by what happens to them, and has the power to do whatever it is logically possible for God to do (omnipotence). Process theologians also disagree with the idea that God knows the future in all its details, holding that God knows only those details of the future that are causally necessitated by past events. They claim these are only certain abstract features of a small class of events in the near future and of an even smaller class in the more distant future. Because of their under-standing of divine power and their affirmation of creaturely self-determination, they claim that they provide a more adequate theodicy. Their critics claim that their idea of God's power, if correct, would render God unworthy of worship; some also make this claim about their idea of God's knowledge, preferring a more traditional idea of omniscience.

Although Whitehead and Hartshorne were both philosophers rather than theologians, process theology has been more influential among theologians. It is a major current in contemporary American Protestant theology and has attracted the attention of some Roman Catholic theologians as well. It also has influenced some biblical scholars who are attempting to develop a distinctive *process hermeneutics*.
    See also PHILOSOPHY OF RELIGION, WHITEHEAD.   J.A.K.

Proclus. See COMMENTARIES ON PLATO, HELLENISTIC PHILOSOPHY, NEOPLATONISM.

Prodicus. See SOPHISTS.

production theory, the economic theory dealing with the conversion of factors of production into consumer goods. In capitalistic theories that assume ideal markets, firms produce goods from three kinds of factors: capital, labor, and raw materials. Production is subject to the constraint that profit (the difference between revenues and costs) be maximized. The firm is thereby faced with the following decisions: how much to produce, what price to charge for the product, what proportions to combine the three kinds of factors in, and what price to pay for the factors. In markets close to perfect competition, the firm will have little control over prices so the decision problem tends to reduce to the amounts of factors to use. The range of feasible factor combinations depends on the technologies available to firms. Interesting complications arise if not all firms have access to the same technologies, or if not all firms make accurate responses concerning technological changes. Also, if the scale of production affects the feasible technologies, the firms' decision process must be subtle. In each of these cases, imperfect competition will result.

Marxian economists think that the concepts used in this kind of production theory have a normative component. In reality, a large firm's capital tends to be owned by a rather small, privileged class of non-laborers and labor is treated as a commodity like any other factor. This might lead to the perception that profit results primarily from capital and, therefore, belongs to its owners. Marxians contend that labor is primarily responsible for profit and, consequently, that labor is entitled to more than the market wage.

See also PERFECT COMPETITION, PHILOSOPHY OF ECONOMICS.   A.N.

productive reason. See THEORETICAL REASON.

professional ethics, a term designating one or more of (1) the justified moral values that should govern the work of professionals; (2) the moral values that actually do guide groups of professionals, whether those values are identified as (a) principles in codes of ethics promulgated by professional societies or (b) actual beliefs and conduct of professionals; and (3) the study of professional ethics in the preceding senses, either (i) normative (philosophical) inquiries into the values desirable for professionals to embrace, or (ii) descriptive (scientific) studies of the actual beliefs and conduct of groups of professionals. Professional values include principles of obligation and rights, as well as virtues and personal moral ideals such as those manifested in the lives of Jane Addams, Albert Schweitzer, and Thurgood Marshall.

Professions are defined by advanced expertise, social organizations, society-granted monopolies over services, and especially by shared commitments to promote a distinctive public good such as health (medicine), justice (law), or learning (education). These shared commitments imply special duties to make services available, maintain confidentiality, secure informed consent for services, and be loyal to clients, employers, and others with whom one has fiduciary relationships. Both theoretical and practical issues surround these duties. The central theoretical issue is to understand how the justified moral values governing professionals are linked to wider values, such as human rights. Most practical dilemmas concern how to balance conflicting duties. For example, what should attorneys do when confidentiality requires keeping information secret that might save the life of an innocent third party? Other practical issues are problems of vagueness and uncertainty surrounding how to apply duties in particular contexts. For example, does respect for patients' autonomy forbid, permit, or require a physician to assist a terminally ill patient desiring suicide? Equally important is how to resolve conflicts of interest in which self-seeking places moral values at risk.

See also APPLIED ETHICS, BIOETHICS.
M.W.M.

programming language. See COMPUTER THEORY.

programs, modal logic of. See DYNAMIC LOGIC.

projectible predicate. See GRUE PARADOX.

projection. See HEIDEGGER.

projectivism. See MORAL PSYCHOLOGY.

prolepsis. See EPICUREANISM, HELLENISTIC PHILOSOPHY.

proof. See PROOF THEORY.

proof, finitary. See HILBERT'S PROGRAM.

proof, indirect. See REDUCTIO AD ABSURDUM.

proof by recursion, also called proof by mathematical induction, a method for conclusively demonstrating the truth of universal propositions about the natural numbers. The system of (natural) numbers is construed as an infinite sequence of elements beginning with the number 1 and such that each subsequent element is the (immediate) successor of the preceding element. The (immediate) successor of a number is the sum of that number with 1. In order to apply this method to show that every number has a certain chosen property it is necessary to demonstrate two subsidiary propositions often called respectively the basis step and the inductive step. The *basis step* is that the number 1 has the chosen property; the *inductive step* is that the successor of any number having the chosen property is also a number having the chosen property (in other words, for every number n, if n has the chosen property then the successor of n also has the chosen property). The inductive step is itself a universal proposition that may have been proved by recursion.

The most commonly used example of a theorem proved by recursion is the remarkable fact, known before the time of Plato, that the sum of the first n odd numbers is the square of n. This proposition, mentioned prominently by Leibniz as requiring and having demonstrative proof, is expressed in universal form as follows: for every number n, the sum of the first n odd numbers is n^2. $1 = 1^2$, $(1 + 3) = 2^2$, $(1 + 3 + 5) = 3^2$, and so on. Rigorous formulation of a proof by recursion often uses as a premise the proposition called, since the time of De Morgan, the principle of mathematical induction: every property belonging to 1 and belonging to the successor of every number to which it belongs is a property that belongs without exception to every number. Peano (1858–1932) took the principle of mathematical induction as an axiom in his 1889 axiomatization of arithmetic (or the theory of natural numbers). The first acceptable formulation of this principle is attributed to Pascal.

See also DE MORGAN, OMEGA, PHILOSOPHY OF MATHEMATICS.   J.Cor.

proof-theoretic reflection principles. See REFLECTION PRINCIPLES.

proof theory, a branch of mathematical logic founded by David Hilbert in the 1920s to pursue Hilbert's Program. The foundational problems underlying that program had been formulated around the turn of the century, e.g., in Hilbert's famous address to the International Congress of Mathematicians in Paris (1900). They were closely connected with investigations on the foundations of analysis carried out by Cantor and Dedekind; but they were also related to their conflict with Kronecker on the nature of mathematics and to the difficulties of a completely unrestricted notion of set or multiplicity. At that time, the central issue for Hilbert was the consistency of sets in Cantor's sense. He suggested that the existence of consistent sets (multiplicities), e.g., that of real numbers, could be secured by proving the consistency of a suitable, characterizing axiomatic system; but there were only the vaguest indications on how to do that. In a radical departure from standard practice and his earlier hints, Hilbert proposed four years later a novel way of attacking the consistency problem for theories in *Über die Grundlagen der Logik und der Arithmetik* (1904). This approach would require, first, a strict formalization of logic together with mathematics, then consideration of the finite syntactic configurations constituting the joint formalism as mathematical objects, and showing by mathematical arguments that contradictory formulas cannot be derived.

Though Hilbert lectured on issues concerning the foundations of mathematics during the subsequent years, the technical development and philosophical clarification of proof theory and its aims began only around 1920. That involved, first of all, a detailed description of logical calculi and the careful development of parts of mathematics in suitable systems. A record of the former

is found in Hilbert and Ackermann, *Grundzüge der theoretischen Logik* (1928); and of the latter in Supplement IV of Hilbert and Bernays, *Grundlagen der Mathematik II* (1939). This presupposes the clear distinction between metamathematics and mathematics introduced by Hilbert. For the purposes of the consistency program metamathematics was now taken to be a very weak part of arithmetic, so-called finitist mathematics, believed to correspond to the part of mathematics that was accepted by constructivists like Kronecker and Brouwer. Additional metamathematical issues concerned the completeness and decidability of theories. The crucial technical tool for the pursuit of the consistency problem was Hilbert's ϵ-calculus.

The metamathematical problems attracted the collaboration of young and quite brilliant mathematicians (with philosophical interests); among them were Paul Bernays, Wilhelm Ackermann, John von Neumann, Jacques Herbrand, Gerhard Gentzen, and Kurt Schütte. The results obtained in the 1920s were disappointing when measured against the hopes and ambitions: Ackermann, von Neumann, and Herbrand established essentially the consistency of arithmetic with a very restricted principle of induction. That limits of finitist considerations for consistency proofs had been reached became clear in 1931 through Gödel's incompleteness theorems. Also, special cases of the decision problem for predicate logic (Hilbert's *Entscheidungsproblem*) had been solved; its general solvability was made rather implausible by some of Gödel's results in his 1931 paper. The actual proof of unsolvability had to wait until 1936 for a conceptual clarification of 'mechanical procedure' or 'algorithm'; that was achieved through the work of Church and Turing.

The further development of proof theory is roughly characterized by two complementary tendencies: (1) the extension of the metamathematical frame relative to which "constructive" consistency proofs can be obtained, and (2) the refined formalization of parts of mathematics in theories much weaker than set theory or even full second-order arithmetic. The former tendency started with the work of Gödel and Gentzen in 1933 establishing the consistency of full classical arithmetic relative to intuitionistic arithmetic; it led in the 1970s and 1980s to consistency proofs of strong subsystems of second-order arithmetic relative to intuitionistic theories of constructive ordinals. The latter tendency reaches back to Weyl's book *Das Kontinuum* (1918) and culminated in the 1970s by showing that the classical results of mathematical analysis can be formally obtained in conservative extensions of first-order arithmetic. For the metamathematical work Gentzen's introduction of sequent calculi and the use of transfinite induction along constructive ordinals turned out to be very important, as well as Gödel's primitive recursive functionals of finite type. The methods and results of proof theory are playing, not surprisingly, a significant role in computer science.

Work in proof theory has been motivated by issues in the foundations of mathematics, with the explicit goal of achieving epistemological reductions of strong theories for mathematical practice (like set theory or second-order arithmetic) to weak, philosophically distinguished theories (like primitive recursive arithmetic). As the formalization of mathematics in strong theories is crucial for the metamathematical approach, and as the programmatic goal can be seen as a way of circumventing the philosophical issues surrounding strong theories, e.g., the nature of infinite sets in the case of set theory, Hilbert's philosophical position is often equated with formalism – in the sense of Frege in his *Über die Grundlagen der Geometrie* (1903–06) and also of Brouwer's inaugural address *Intuitionism and Formalism* (1912). Though such a view is not completely unsupported by some of Hilbert's polemical remarks during the 1920s, on balance, his philosophical views developed into a sophisticated instrumentalism, if that label is taken in Ernest Nagel's judicious sense (*The Structure of Science,* 1961). Hilbert's is an instrumentalism emphasizing the contentual motivation of mathematical theories; that is clearly expressed in the first chapter of Hilbert and Bernays's *Grundlagen der Mathematik I* (1934). A sustained philosophical analysis of proof-theoretic research in the context of broader issues in the philosophy of mathematics was provided by Bernays; his penetrating essays stretch over five decades and have been collected in *Abhandlungen zur Philosophie der Mathematik* (1976).

See also CONSISTENCY, FORMALIZATION, GÖDEL'S INCOMPLETENESS THEOREMS, HILBERT'S PROGRAM, METAMATHEMATICS. W.S.

propensity, an irregular or non-necessitating causal disposition of an object or system to produce some result or effect. Propensities are usually conceived as essentially probabilistic in nature. A die may be said to have a propensity of "strength" or magnitude $1/6$ to turn up a 3 if thrown from a dice box, of strength $1/3$ to turn up, say, a 3 or 4, etc. But propensity talk is arguably

appropriate only when determinism fails. Strength is often taken to vary from 0 to 1.

Popper regarded the propensity notion as a new physical or metaphysical hypothesis, akin to that of forces. Like Peirce, he deployed it to interpret probability claims about single cases: e.g., the probability of *this* radium atom's decaying in 1,600 years is $1/2$. On relative frequency interpretations, probability claims are about properties of large classes such as relative frequencies of outcomes in them, rather than about single cases. But single-case claims appear to be common in quantum theory. Popper advocated a propensity interpretation of quantum theory. Propensities also feature in theories of indeterministic or probabilistic causation.

Competing theories about propensities attribute them variously to complex systems such as chance or experimental set-ups or arrangements (a coin and tossing device), to entities within such set-ups (the coin itself), and to particular trials of such set-ups. *Long-run* theories construe propensities as dispositions to give rise to certain relative frequencies of, or probability distributions over, outcomes in long runs of trials, which are sometimes said to "manifest" or "display" the propensities. Here a propensity's strength is identical to some such frequency. By contrast, *single-case* theories construe propensities as dispositions of singular trials to bring about particular outcomes. Their existence, not their strength, is displayed by such an outcome. Here frequencies provide evidence about propensity strength. But the two can always differ; they converge with a limiting probability of 1 in an appropriate long run.

See also CAUSATION, DETERMINISM, DISPOSITION, PEIRCE, PROBABILITY, QUANTUM MECHANICS. D.S.

proper class. See CLASS.

properly basic relief. See EVIDENTIALISM, PLANTINGA.

proper names, causal theory of. See CAUSAL THEORY OF PROPER NAMES.

proper sensibles. See ARISTOTLE.

proper symbol. See SYNCATEGOREMATA.

properties of terms, doctrine of. See SHERWOOD.

property, roughly, an attribute, characteristic, feature, trait, or aspect.

Intensionality. There are two salient ways of talking about properties. First, as *predicables* or *instantiables*. For example, the property red is predicable of red objects; they are instances of it. Properties are said to be *intensional* entities in the sense that distinct properties can be truly predicated of (i.e., have as instances) exactly the same things: the property of being a creature with a kidney ≠ the property of being a creature with a heart, though these two sets have the same members. Properties thus differ from sets (collections, classes); for the latter satisfy a principle of *extensionality*: they are identical if they have the same elements. The second salient way of talking about properties is by means of *property abstracts* such as 'the property of being *F*'. Such linguistic expressions are said to be intensional in the following semantical (vs. ontological) sense: 'the property of being *F*' and 'the property of being *G*' can denote different properties even though the predicates '*F*' and '*G*' are true of exactly the same things. The standard explanation (Frege, Russell, Carnap, et al.) is that 'the property of being *F*' denotes the property that the predicate '*F*' expresses. Since predicates '*F*' and '*G*' can be true of the same things without being synonyms, the property abstracts 'being *F*' and 'being *G*' can denote different properties.

Identity criteria. Some philosophers believe that properties are identical if they necessarily have the same instances. Other philosophers hold that this criterion of identity holds only for a special subclass of properties – those that are purely qualitative – and that the properties for which this criterion does not hold are all "complex" (e.g., relational, disjunctive, conditional, or negative properties). On this theory, complex properties are identical if they have the same form and their purely qualitative constituents are identical.

Ontological status. Because properties are a kind of universal, each of the standard views on the ontological status of universals has been applied to properties as a special case. *Nominalism:* only particulars (and perhaps collections of particulars) exist; therefore, either properties do not exist or they are reducible (following Carnap et al.) to collections of particulars (including perhaps particulars that are not actual but only possible). *Conceptualism:* properties exist but are dependent on the mind. *Realism:* properties exist independently of the mind. Realism has two main versions. *In rebus* realism: a property exists only if it has instances. *Ante rem* realism: a property can exist even if it has no instances. For example, the property of being a man weighing over ton has no instances; however, it is plausible to hold that this property does exist. After all, this property seems to be what is expressed by the predicate 'is a man weighing over a ton'.

Essence and accident. The properties that a given entity has divide into two disjoint classes: those that are essential to the entity and those that are accidental to it. A property is essential to an entity if, necessarily, the entity cannot exist without being an instance of the property. A property is accidental to an individual if it is possible for the individual to exist without being an instance of the property. Being a number is an essential property of nine; being the number of the planets is an accidental property of nine. Some philosophers believe that all properties are either essential by nature or accidental by nature. A property is *essential by nature* if it can be an essential property of some entity and, necessarily, it is an essential property of each entity that is an instance of it. The property of being self-identical is thus essential by nature. However, it is controversial whether every property that is essential to something must be essential by nature. The following is a candidate counterexample. If this automobile backfires loudly on a given occasion, loudness would seem to be an essential property of the associated bang. That particular bang could not exist without being loud. If the automobile had backfired softly, that particular bang would not have existed; an altogether distinct bang – a soft bang – would have existed. By contrast, if a man is loud, loudness is only an accidental property of him; he could exist without being loud. Loudness thus appears to be a counterexample: although it is an essential property of certain particulars, it is not essential by nature. It might be replied (echoing Aristotle) that a loud bang and a loud man instantiate loudness in different ways and, more generally, that properties can be predicated (instantiated) in different ways. If so, then one should be specific about which kind of predication (instantiation) is intended in the definition of 'essential by nature' and 'accidental by nature'. When this is done, the counterexamples might well disappear. If there are indeed different ways of being predicated (instantiated), most of the foregoing remarks about intensionality, identity criteria, and the ontological status of properties should be refined accordingly.

See also ESSENTIALISM, INTENSIONALITY, RELATION.   G.B.

property, accidental. See RELATION.

property, Cambridge. See CAMBRIDGE CHANGE.

property, consequential. See SUPERVENIENCE.

property, extrinsic. See RELATION.

property, hereditary. See RELATION.

property, impredicative. See TYPE THEORY.

property, intrinsic. See RELATION.

property, non-predicative. See TYPE THEORY.

property, phenomenal. See QUALIA.

property, predicative. See TYPE THEORY.

proportionality, principle of. See CAJETAN.

proposition, an abstract object said to be that to which a person is related by a belief, desire, or other psychological attitude, typically expressed in language containing a psychological verb ('think', 'deny', 'doubt', etc.) followed by a that-clause. The psychological states in question are called propositional attitudes. When I believe that snow is white I stand in the relation of believing to the proposition that snow is white. When I hope that the protons will not decay, hope relates me to the proposition that the protons will not decay. A proposition can be a common object for various attitudes of various agents: that the protons will not decay can be the object of my belief, my hope, and your fear.

A sentence expressing an attitude is also taken to express the associated proposition. Because 'The protons will not decay' identifies my hope, it identifies the proposition to which my hope relates me. Thus the proposition can be the shared meaning of this sentence and all its synonyms, in English or elsewhere (e.g., *'die Protonen werden nicht zerfallen'*).

This, in sum, is the traditional doctrine of propositions. Although it seems indispensable in *some* form – for theorizing about thought and language, difficulties abound.

Some critics regard propositions as excess baggage in any account of meaning. But unless this is an expression of nominalism, it is confused. Any systematic theory of meaning, plus an apparatus of sets (or properties) will let us construct proposition-like objects. The proposition a sentence *S* expresses might, e.g., be identified with a certain set of features that determines *S*'s meaning. Other sentences with these same features would then express the same proposition. A natural way to associate propositions with sentences is to let the features in question be semantically significant features of the words from which sentences are built. Propositions then acquire the logical structures of sentences: they are atomic, conditional, existential, etc. But combining the view of propositions as meanings with the traditional idea of propositions as bearers of truth-values brings trouble. It is assumed that two sentences that express the same proposition have the same truth-value (indeed, that sentences have their truth-values *in virtue of* the propositions they express). Yet if propositions are also meanings, this principle fails for sentences with indexical elements: although 'I am pale' has a single meaning, two utterances of it can differ in truth-value. In response, one may suggest that the proposition a sentence *S* expresses depends both on the linguistic meaning of *S* and on the referents of *S*'s indexical elements. But this reveals that proposition is a quite technical concept – and one that is not motivated simply by a need to talk about meanings.

Related questions arise for propositions as the objects of (propositional) attitudes. My belief that I am pale may be true, yours that you are pale false. So our beliefs should take distinct propositional objects. Yet we would each use the same sentence, 'I am pale', to express our belief. Intuitively, your belief and mine also play similar cognitive roles. We may each choose the sun exposure, clothing, etc., that we take to be appropriate to a fair complexion. So our attitudes seem in an important sense to be the same – an identity that the assignment of distinct propositional objects hides. Apparently, the characterization of beliefs (e.g.) as being propositional attitudes is at best one component of a more refined, largely unknown account.

Quite apart from complications about indexicality, propositions inherit standard difficulties about meaning. Consider the beliefs that Hesperus is a planet and that Phosphorus is a planet. It seems that someone might have one but not the other, thus that they are attitudes toward distinct propositions. This difference apparently reflects the difference in meaning between the sentences 'Hesperus is a planet' and 'Phosphorus is a planet'. The principle would be that non-synonymous sentences express distinct propositions. But it is unclear what makes for a difference in meaning. Since the sentences agree in logico-grammatical structure and in the referents of their terms, their specific meanings must depend on some more subtle feature that has resisted definition. Hence our concept of proposition is also only partly defined. (Even the idea that the sentences here express the same proposition is not easily refuted.)

What such difficulties show is not that the concept of proposition is invalid but that it belongs to a still rudimentary descriptive scheme. It is too thoroughly enmeshed with the concepts of meaning and belief to be of use in solving their attendant problems. (This observation is what tends, through a confusion, to give rise to skepticism about propositions.) One may, e.g., reasonably posit structured abstract entities – propositions – that represent the features on which the truth-values of sentences depend. Then there is a good sense in which a sentence is true in virtue of the proposition it expresses. But how does the use of words in a certain context associate them with a particular proposition? Lacking an answer, we still cannot explain why a given sentence is true. Similarly, one cannot *explain* belief as the acceptance of a proposition, since only a substantive theory of thought would reveal how the mind "accepts" a proposition and what it does to accept one proposition rather than another. So a satisfactory doctrine of propositions remains elusive.

See also ABSTRACT ENTITY, INDEXICAL, INTENTIONALITY, MEANING, PROPERTY.

S.J.W.

proposition, maximal. See TOPICS.

propositional act. See PROPOSITION.

propositional attitude. See PHILOSOPHY OF MIND, PROPOSITION.

propositional calculus. See FORMAL LOGIC.

propositional connective. See SENTENTIAL CONNECTIVE.

propositional content. See CIRCULAR REASONING.

propositional function, an operation that, when applied to something as argument (or to more than one thing in a given order as arguments), yields a truth-value as the value of that function for that argument (or those arguments). This usage presupposes that truth-values are objects.

A function may be singular, binary, ternary, etc. A singular propositional function is applicable to one thing and yields, when so applied, a truth-value. For example, *being a prime number*, when applied to the number 2, yields truth; negation, when applied to truth, yields falsehood. A binary propositional function is applicable to two things in a certain order and yields, when so applied, a truth-value. For example, *being north of* when applied to New York and Boston in that order yields falsehood. Material implication when applied to falsehood and truth in that order yields truth.

The term 'propositional function' has a second use, to refer to an operation that, when applied to something as argument (or to more than one thing in a given order as arguments), yields a proposition as the value of the function for that argument (or those arguments). For example, *being a prime number* when applied to 2 yields the proposition that 2 is a prime number. *Being north of,* when applied to New York and Boston in that order, yields the proposition that New York is north of Boston. This usage presupposes that propositions are objects.

In a third use, 'propositional function' designates a sentence with free occurrences of variables. Thus, '*x* is a prime number', 'It is not the case that *p*', '*x* is north of *y*' and 'if *p* then *q*' are propositional functions in this sense.   C.S.

propositional justification. See EPISTEMOLOGY.

propositional knowledge. See EPISTEMOLOGY.

propositional object. See PROPOSITION.

propositional opacity, failure of a clause to express any particular proposition (especially due to the occurrence of pronouns or demonstratives). If having a belief about an individual involves a relation to a proposition, and if a part of the proposition is a way of representing the individual, then belief characterizations that do not indicate the believer's way of representing the individual could be called *propositionally opaque.* They do not show all of the propositional elements. For example, 'My son's clarinet teacher believes that he should try the bass drum' would be propositionally opaque because 'he' does not indicate how my son John's teacher represents John, e.g. as his student, as my son, as the boy now playing, etc. This characterization of the example is not appropriate if propositions are as Russell conceived them, sometimes containing the individuals themselves as constituents, because then the propositional constituent (John) has been referred to.

Generally, a characterization of a propositional

attitude is propositionally opaque if the expressions in the embedded clause do not refer to the propositional constituents. It is propositionally transparent if the expressions in the embedded clause do so refer. As a rule, referentially opaque contexts are used in propositionally transparent attributions if the referent of a term is distinct from the corresponding propositional constituent.

See also DE DICTO, KNOWLEDGE DE RE, PROPOSITION, REFERENTIALLY TRANSPARENT.   T.M.

propositional operator. See SENTENTIAL CONNECTIVE.

propositional representation. See COGNITIVE SCIENCE.

propositional theory of meaning. See MEANING.

propositional verb. See PROPOSITION.

proprietates terminorum (Latin, 'properties of terms'), in medieval logic from the twelfth century on, a cluster of semantic properties possessed by categorematic terms. For most authors, these properties apply only when the terms occur in the context of a proposition. The list of such properties and the theory governing them vary from author to author, but always include (1) *suppositio*. Some authors add (2) *appellatio* ('appellating', 'naming', 'calling', often not sharply distinguishing from *suppositio*), the property whereby a term in a certain proposition names or is truly predicable of things, or (in some authors) of presently existing things. Thus 'philosophers' in 'Some philosophers are wise' appellates philosophers alive today. (3) *Ampliatio* ('ampliation', 'broadening'), whereby a term refers to past or future or merely possible things. The reference of 'philosophers' is ampliated in 'Some philosophers were wise'. (4) *Restrictio* ('restriction', 'narrowing'), whereby the reference of a term is restricted to presently existing things ('philosophers' is so restricted in 'Some philosophers are wise'), or otherwise narrowed from its normal range ('philosophers' in 'Some Greek philosophers were wise'). (5) *Copulatio* ('copulation', 'coupling'), which is the type of reference adjectives have ('wise' in 'Some philosophers are wise'), or alternatively the semantic function of the copula. Other meanings too are sometimes given to these terms, depending on the author. *Appellatio* especially was given a wide variety of interpretations. In particular,

for Buridan and other fourteenth-century Continental authors, *appellatio* means 'connotation'. *Restrictio* and *copulatio* tended to drop out of the literature, or be treated only perfunctorily, after the thirteenth century. **See also** SUPPOSITIO.
                                                         P.V.S.

proprioception. See PERCEPTION.

proprium, one of Porphyry's five predicables, often translated as 'property' or 'attribute'; but this should not be confused with the broad modern sense in which any feature of a thing may be said to be a property of it. A *proprium* is a non-essential peculiarity of a species. (There are no *propria* of individuals or *genera generalissima*, although they may have other uniquely identifying features.) A *proprium* necessarily holds of all members of its species and of nothing else. It is not mentioned in a real definition of the species, and so is not essential to it. Yet it somehow follows from the essence or nature expressed in the real definition. The standard example is risibility (the ability to laugh) as a *proprium* of the species *man*. The real definition of 'man' is 'rational animal'. There is no mention of any ability to laugh. Nevertheless anything that can laugh has both the biological apparatus to produce the sounds (and so is an animal) and also a certain wit and insight into humor (and so is rational). Conversely, any rational animal will have both the vocal chords and diaphragm required for laughing (since it is an animal, although the inference may seem too quick) and also the mental wherewithal to see the point of a joke (since it is rational). Thus any rational animal has what it takes to laugh. In short, every man is risible, and conversely, but risibility is not an essential feature of man. **See also** ESSENTIALISM, PORPHYRY, PREDICABLES.   P.V.S.

prosyllogism. See POLYSYLLOGISM.

Protagoras. See SOPHISTS.

protasis. See COUNTERFACTUALS.

Protestant ethic. See WEBER.

Protestant principle. See TILLICH.

protocol statement, one of the statements that constitute the foundations of empirical knowledge. The term was introduced by proponents of foundationalism, who were convinced that in order to avoid the most radical skepticism, one must countenance beliefs that are justified but not as a result of an *inference*. If all justified beliefs are inferentially justified, then to be justified in believing one proposition *P* on the basis of another, *E*, one would have to be justified in believing both *E* and that *E* confirms *P*. But if all justification were inferential, then to be justified in believing *E* one would need to infer it from some other proposition one justifiably believes, and so on ad infinitum. The only way to avoid this regress is to find some statement knowable without inferring it from some other truth.

Philosophers who agree that empirical knowledge has foundations do not necessarily agree on what those foundations are. The British empiricists restrict the class of contingent protocol statements to propositions describing the contents of mind (sensations, beliefs, fears, desires, and the like). And even here a statement describing a mental state would be a protocol statement only for the person in that state. Other philosophers, however, would take protocol statements to include at least some assertions about the immediate physical environment. The plausibility of a given candidate for a protocol statement depends on how one analyzes non-inferential justification. Some philosophers rely on the idea of *acquaintance*. One is non-inferentially justified in believing something when one is directly acquainted with what makes it true. Other philosophers rely on the idea of a state that is in some sense self-presenting. Still others want to understand the notion in terms of the inconceivability of error.

The main difficulty in trying to defend a coherent conception of non-inferential justification is to find an account of protocol statements that gives them enough conceptual content to serve as the premises of arguments, while avoiding the charge that the application of concepts always brings with it the possibility of error and the necessity of inference.

See also EPISTEMOLOGY, FOUNDATIONALISM.   R.A.F.

protothetic. See LAWS OF THOUGHT, LEŚNIEWSKI.

prototype theory, a theory according to which human cognition involves the deployment of "categories" organized around stereotypical exemplars. Prototype theory differs from traditional theories that take the concepts with which we think to be individuated by means of boundary-specifying necessary and sufficient conditions. Advocates of prototypes hold that our concept of *bird*, for instance, consists in an indef-

initely bounded conceptual "space" in which robins and sparrows are central, and chickens and penguins are peripheral – though the category may be differently organized in different cultures or groups. Rather than being all-or-nothing, category membership is a matter of degree. This conception of categories was originally inspired by the notion, developed in a different context by Wittgenstein, of family resemblance. Prototypes were first discussed in detail and given empirical credibility in the work of Eleanor Rosch (see, e.g., "On the Internal Structure of Perceptual and Semantic Categories," 1973). **See also** ARTIFICIAL INTELLIGENCE, PHILOSOPHY OF MIND, WITTGENSTEIN.
                                                                                J.F.H.

Proudhon, Pierre-Joseph (1809–65), French socialist theorist and father of anarchism. He became well known following the publication of *What Is Property?* (1840), the work containing his main ideas.

He argued that the owner of the means of production deprives the workers of a part of their labor: "property is theft." In order to enable each worker to dispose of his labor, capital and large-scale property must be limited. The need to abolish large-scale private property surpassed the immediate need for a state as a controlling agent over chaotic social relationships. To this end he stressed the need for serious reforms in the exchange system. Since the economy and society largely depended on the credit system, Proudhon advocated establishing popular banks that would approve interest-free loans to the poor. Such a *mutualism* would start the transformation of the actual into a just and non-exploited society of free individuals. Without class antagonism and political authorities, such a society would tend toward an association of communal and industrial collectivities. It would move toward a flexible world federation based on self-management. The main task of social science, then, is to make manifest this immanent logic of social processes.

Proudhon's ideas influenced anarchists, populists (Bakunin, Herzen), and syndicalists (Jaurès). His conception of self-management was an important inspiration for the later concept of soviets (councils). He criticized the inequalities of the contemporary society from the viewpoint of small producers and peasants. Although eclectic and theoretically rather naive, his work attracted the serious attention of his contemporaries and led to a strong attack by Marx in *The Holy Family* and *The Poverty of Philosophy*.   G.Fl.

provability predicate. See GÖDEL'S INCOMPLETE-NESS THEOREMS.

prudence. See ETHICS.

pseudohallucination, a non-deceptive hallucination. An ordinary hallucination might be thought to comprise two components: (i) a sensory component, whereby one experiences an image or sensory episode similar in many respects to a veridical perceiving except in being non-veridical; and (ii) a cognitive component, whereby one takes (or is disposed to take) the image or sensory episode to be veridical. A pseudohallucination resembles a hallucination, but lacks this second component. In experiencing a pseudohallucination, one appreciates that one is not perceiving veridically. The source of the term seems to be the painter Wassily Kandinsky, who employed it (in 1885) to characterize a series of apparently drug-induced images experienced and pondered by a friend who recognized them, at the very time they were occurring, not to be veridical. Kandinsky's account is discussed by Jaspers (in his *General Psychopathology,* 1916), and thereby entered the clinical lore. Pseudohallucinations may be brought on by the sorts of pathological condition that give rise to hallucinations, or by simple fatigue, emotional adversity, or loneliness. Thus, a driver, late at night, may react to non-existent objects or figures on the road, and immediately recognize his error. **See also PERCEPTION.**   J.F.H.

pseudo-overdeterminism. See CAUSATION.

pseudorandomness. See COMPUTER THEORY.

psychoanalysis. See FREUD.

psycholinguistics, an interdisciplinary research area that uses theoretical descriptions of language taken from linguistics to investigate psychological processes underlying language production, perception, and learning. There is considerable disagreement as to the appropriate characterization of the field and the major problems. Philosophers discussed many of the problems now studied in psycholinguistics before either psychology or linguistics were spawned, but the self-consciously interdisciplinary field combining psychology and linguistics emerged not long after the birth of the two disciplines. (Meringer used the adjective '*psycholingisch-linguistische*' in an 1895 book.)

Various national traditions of psycholinguistics continued at a steady but fairly low level of activity through the 1920s and declined somewhat during the 1930s and 1940s because of the anti-mentalist attitudes in both linguistics and psychology. Psycholinguistic researchers in the USSR, mostly inspired by L. S. Vygotsky (*Thought and Language,* 1934), were more active during this period in spite of official suppression.

Numerous quasi-independent sources contributed to the rebirth of psycholinguistics in the 1950s; the most significant was a seminar held at Indiana University during the summer of 1953 that led to the publication of *Psycholinguistics: A Survey of Theory and Research Problems* (1954), edited by C. E. Osgood and T. A. Sebeok – a truly interdisciplinary book jointly written by more than a dozen authors. The contributors attempted to analyze and reconcile three disparate approaches: learning theory from psychology, descriptive linguistics, and information theory (which came mainly from engineering). The book had a wide impact and led to many further investigations, but the nature of the field changed rapidly soon after its publication with the Chomskyan revolution in linguistics and the cognitive turn in psychology. The two were not unrelated: Chomsky's positive contribution, *Syntactic Structures,* was less broadly influential than his negative review (*Language,* 1959) of B. F. Skinner's *Verbal Behavior.*

Against the empiricist-behaviorist view of language understanding and production, in which language is merely the exhibition of a more complex form of behavior, Chomsky argued the avowedly rationalist position that the ability to learn and use language is innate and unique to humans. He emphasized the creative aspect of language, that almost all sentences one hears or produces are novel. One of his premises was the alleged infinity of sentences in natural languages, but a less controversial argument can be given: there are tens of millions of five-word sentences in English, all of which are readily understood by speakers who have never heard them. Chomsky's work promised the possibility of uncovering a very special characteristic of the human mind. But the promise was qualified by the disclaimer that linguistic theory describes only the competence of the ideal speaker. Many psycholinguists spent countless hours during the 1960s and 1970s seeking the traces of underlying competence beneath the untidy performances of actual speakers.

During the 1970s, as Chomsky frequently revised his theories of syntax and semantics in significant ways, and numerous alternative linguistic models were under consideration, psychologists generated a range of productive research problems that are increasingly remote from the Chomskyan beginnings. Contemporary psycholinguistics addresses phonetic, phonological, syntactic, semantic, and pragmatic influences on language processing.

Few clear conclusions of philosophical import have been established. For example, several decades of animal research have shown that other species can use significant portions of human language, but controversy abounds over how central those portions are to language. Studies now clearly indicate the importance of word frequency and coarticulation, the dependency of a hearer's identification of a sound as a particular phoneme, or of a visual pattern as a particular letter, not only on the physical features of the pattern but on the properties of other patterns not necessarily adjacent. Physically identical patterns may be heard as a *d* in one context and a *t* in another. It is also accepted that at least some of the human lignuistic abilities, particularly those involved in reading and speech perception, are relatively isolated from other cognitive processes. Infant studies show that children as young as eight months learn statistically important patterns characteristic of their natural language – suggesting a complex set of mechanisms that are automatic and invisible to us.

See also CHOMSKY, COGNITIVE SCIENCE, GRAMMAR, PHILOSOPHY OF LANGUAGE.
R.E.G.

psychological behaviorism. See BEHAVIORISM.

psychological certainty. See CERTAINTY.

psychological continuity. See PERSONAL IDENTITY.

psychological egoism. See EGOISM.

psychological eudaimonism. See EUDAIMONISM.

psychological hedonism. See HEDONISM.

psychological immediacy. See IMMEDIACY.

psychological solipsism. See SOLIPSISM.

psychologism. See HUSSERL.

psychology, analytical. See JUNG.

psychology, autonomy of. See PHILOSOPHY OF PSYCHOLOGY.

psychology, philosophical. See PHILOSOPHY OF MIND.

psychology, philosophy of. See PHILOSOPHY OF PSYCHOLOGY.

psychophysical identity. See PHYSICALISM.

psychophysical parallelism. See PHILOSOPHY OF MIND.

psychophysics. See FECHNER.

psychosemantic theory. See PHILOSOPHY OF MIND.

public good. See COMMON GOOD, PHILOSOPHY OF ECONOMICS, SOCIAL CHOICE THEORY.

Pufendorf, Samuel (1632–94), German historian and theorist of natural law. Pufendorf was influenced by both Grotius and Hobbes. He portrayed people as contentious and quarrelsome, yet as needing one another's company and assistance. Natural law shows how people can live with one another while pursuing their own conflicting projects. To minimize religious disputes about morals, Pufendorf sought a way of deriving laws of nature from observable facts alone. Yet he thought divine activity essential to morality.

He opened his massive Latin treatise *On the Law of Nature and of Nations* (1672) with a voluntarist account of God's creation of the essence of mankind: given that we have the nature God gave us, certain laws must be valid for us, but only God's will determined our nature. As a result, our nature indicates God's will for us. Hence observable facts about ourselves show us what laws God commands us to obey. Because we so obviously need one another's assistance, the first law is to increase our sociability, i.e. our willingness to live together. All other laws indicate acts that would bring about this end.

In the course of expounding the laws he thought important for the development of social life to the high cultural level our complex nature points us toward, Pufendorf analyzed all the main points that a full legal system must cover. He presented the rudiments of laws of marriage, property, inheritance, contract, and international relations in both war and peace. He also developed the Grotian theory of personal rights, asserting for the first time that rights are pointless unless for each right there are correlative duties binding on others. Taking obligation as his fundamental concept, he developed an important distinction between perfect and imperfect duties and rights. And in working out a theory of property he suggested the first outlines of a historical sociology of wealth later developed by Adam Smith. Pufendorf's works on natural law were textbooks for all of Europe for over a century and were far more widely read than any other treatments of the subject.

See also DUTY, GROTIUS, HOBBES, NATURAL LAW.   J.B.S.

punishment, a distinctive form of legal sanction, distinguished first by its painful or unpleasant nature (to the offender), and second by the ground on which the sanction is imposed, which must be because the offender offended against the norms of a society. None of these three attributes is a strictly necessary condition for proper use of the word 'punishment'. There may be unpleasant consequences visited by nature upon an offender such that he might be said to have been "punished enough"; the consequences in a given case may not be unpleasant to a particular offender, as in the punishment of a masochist with his favorite form of self-abuse; and punishment may be imposed for reasons other than offense against society's norms, as is the case with punishment inflicted in order to deter others from like acts.

The "definitional stop" argument in discussions of punishment seeks to tie punishment analytically to retributivism. Retributivism is the theory that punishment is justified by the moral desert of the offender; on this view, a person who culpably does a wrongful action deserves punishment, and this desert is a sufficient as well as a necessary condition of just punishment. Punishment of the deserving, on this view, is an intrinsic good that does not need to be justified by any other good consequences such punishment may achieve, such as the prevention of crime. Retributivism is not to be confused with the view that punishment satisfies the feelings of vengeful citizens nor with the view that punishment preempts such citizens from taking the law into their own hands by vigilante action – these latter views being utilitarian. Retributivism is also not the view (sometimes called "weak" or "negative" retributivism) that *only* the deserving are to be punished, for desert on such a view typically operates only as a limiting and not as a justifying condition of punishment. The thesis known as the "definitional stop" says that punishment must be retributive in its justification if it is to be punishment at all. Bad treatment inflicted in order to prevent future crime is not punishment but deserves another name, usually 'telishment'.

The dominant justification of non-retributive punishment (or telishment) is deterrence. The good in whose name the bad of punishing is justified, on this view, is prevention of future criminal acts. If punishment is inflicted to prevent the offender from committing future criminal acts, it is styled "specific" or "special" deterrence; if punishment is inflicted to prevent others from committing future criminal acts, it is styled "general" deterrence. In either case, punishment of an action is justified by the future effect of that punishment in deterring future actors from committing crimes. There is some vagueness in the notion of deterrence because of the different mechanisms by which potential criminals are influenced not to be criminals by the example of punishment: such punishment may achieve its effects through fear or by more benignly educating those would-be criminals out of their criminal desires.

See also ETHICS, JUSTICE, PHILOSOPHY OF LAW, TELISHMENT.   M.S.M.

pure concept. See KANT.

pure reason. See KANT.

purpose. See INTENTION.

purposive explanation. See PHILOSOPHY OF SCIENCE.

Pūrva Mīmāmsā. SEE MĪMĀMSĀ.

Putnam, Hilary (b.1926), American philosopher who has made significant contributions to the philosophies of language, science, and mind, and to mathematical logic and metaphysics. He completed his Ph.D. in 1951 at the University of California (Los Angeles) and has taught at Northwestern, Princeton, MIT, and Harvard. In the late 1950s he contributed (with Martin Davis and Julia Robinson) to a proof of the unsolvability of Hilbert's tenth problem (completed in 1970 by Yuri Matiyasevich). Rejecting both Platonism and conventionalism in mathematics, he explored the concepts of mathematical truth and logical necessity on the assumption that logic is not entirely immune from empirical revision – e.g., quantum mechanics may require a rejection of classical logic.

In the 1950s and 1960s he advanced functionalism, an original theory of mind in which human beings are conceived as Turing machines (computers) and mental states are functional (or computational) states. While this theory is presupposed by much contemporary research in cognitive science, Putnam himself (in *Representation and Reality,* 1988) abandoned the view, arguing that genuine intentionality cannot be reduced to computational states because the content of beliefs is (a) determined by facts external to the individual and (b) individuatable only by interpreting our belief system as a whole (meaning holism).

Putnam's criticism of functionalism relies on the "new theory of reference" – sometimes called the "causal" or "direct" theory – that he and Kripke (working independently) developed during the late 1960s and early 1970s and that is today embraced by many philosophers and scientists. In "The Meaning of 'Meaning' " (1975) Putnam claims that the reference of natural kind terms like 'water' is determined by facts about the world – the microphysical structure of water (H_2O) and the linguistic practices of speakers – and not by the internal mental states of speakers.

Early in his career, Putnam championed scientific realism, rejecting conventionalism and arguing that without a realist commitment to theoretical entities (e.g., electrons) the success of science would be a "miracle." In 1976 he famously abandoned metaphysical realism in favor of "internal realism," which gives up commitment to mind-independent objects and relativizes ontology to conceptual schemes. In a series of model-theoretic arguments, Putnam challenged the metaphysical realist assumption that an epistemically ideal theory might be false, claiming that it requires an implausibly "magical" theory of reference. To the same end, he sought to demonstrate that we are not "brains in a vat" and that radical skepticism is incoherent (*Reason, Truth and History,* 1981). More recently, he has emphasized conceptual relativity in his attack on metaphysical realism's commitment to "one true theory" and, in his Dewey Lectures (1994), has defended direct perceptual realism, showing his allegiance to everyday "realism."

There is growing appreciation of the underlying unity in Putnam's work that helps correct his reputation for "changing his mind." He has consistently sought to do justice both to the "real world" of common sense and science and to distinctly human ways of representing that world. In the 1990s his energies were increasingly directed to our "moral image of the world." Leading a revival of American pragmatism, he has attacked the fact–value dichotomy, articulating a moral view that resists both relativism and

authoritarianism. Putnam's influence now extends beyond philosophers and scientists, to literary theorists, cognitive linguists, and theologians.

See also CAUSAL THEORY OF PROPER NAMES, FUNCTIONALISM, MEANING, PHILOSOPHY OF LANGUAGE, PHILOSOPHY OF SCIENCE.
D.L.A.

Pyrrhonian Skepticism. See SKEPTICISM, SKEPTICS.

Pyrrho of Elis (c.365–c.270 B.C.), Greek philosopher, regarded as the founder of Skepticism. Like Socrates, he wrote nothing, but impressed many with provocative ideas and calm demeanor. His equanimity was admired by Epicurus; his attitude of indifference influenced early Stoicism; his attack on knowledge was taken over by the skeptical Academy; and two centuries later, a revival of Skepticism adopted his name. Many of his ideas were anticipated by earlier thinkers, notably Democritus. But in denying the veracity of all sensations and beliefs, Pyrrho carried doubt to new and radical extremes. According to ancient anecdote, which presents him as highly eccentric, he paid so little heed to normal sensibilities that friends often had to rescue him from grave danger; some nonetheless insisted he lived into his nineties. He is also said to have emulated the "naked teachers" (as the Hindu Brahmans were called by Greeks) whom he met while traveling in the entourage of Alexander the Great.

Pyrrho's chief exponent and publicist was Timon of Phlius (c.325–c.235 B.C.). His best-preserved work, the *Silloi* ("Lampoons"), is a parody in Homeric epic verse that mocks the pretensions of numerous philosophers on an imaginary visit to the underworld. According to Timon, Pyrrho was a "negative dogmatist" who affirmed that knowledge is impossible, not because our cognitive apparatus is flawed, but because the world is fundamentally indeterminate: things themselves are "no more" cold than hot, or good than bad. But Timon makes clear that the key to Pyrrho's Skepticism, and a major source of his impact, was the ethical goal he sought to achieve: by training himself to disregard all perception and values, he hoped to attain mental tranquility.

See also ACADEMY, DEMOCRITUS, EPICUREANISM, SKEPTICS, STOICISM.   S.A.W.

Pythagoras (570?–495? B.C.), the most famous of the pre-Socratic Greek philosophers. He emigrated from the island of Samos (off Asia Minor) to Croton (southern Italy) in 530. There he founded societies based on a strict way of life. They had great political impact in southern Italy and aroused opposition that resulted in the burning of their meeting houses and, ultimately, in the societies' disappearance in the fourth century B.C.

Pythagoras's fame grew exponentially with the pasage of time. Plato's immediate successors in the Academy saw true philosophy as an unfolding of the original insight of Pythagoras. By the time of Iamblichus (late third century A.D.), Pythagoreanism and Platonism had become virtually identified. Spurious writings ascribed both to Pythagoras and to other Pythagoreans arose beginning in the third century B.C. Eventually any thinker who saw the natural world as ordered according to pleasing mathematical relations (e.g., Kepler) came to be called a Pythagorean.

Modern scholarship has shown that Pythagoras was not a scientist, mathematician, or systematic philosopher. He apparently wrote nothing. The early evidence shows that he was famous for introducing the doctrine of *metempsychosis*, according to which the soul is immortal and is reborn in both human and animal incarnations. Rules were established to purify the soul (including the prohibition against eating beans and the emphasis on training of the memory). General reflections on the natural world such as "number is the wisest thing" and "the most beautiful, harmony" were preserved orally. A belief in the mystical power of number is also visible in the veneration for the *tetractys* (*tetrad:* the numbers 1–4, which add up to the sacred number 10). The doctrine of the harmony of the spheres – that the heavens move in accord with number and produce music – may go back to Pythagoras.

It is often assumed that there must be more to Pythagoras's thought than this, given his fame in the later tradition. However, Plato refers to him only as the founder of a way of life (*Republic* 600a9). In his account of pre-Socratic philosophy, Aristotle refers not to Pythagoras himself, but to the "so-called Pythagoreans" whom he dates in the fifth century.

See also ARCHYTAS, PHILOLAUS.   C.A.H.

Pythagoreanism. See PYTHAGORAS.

quale. See QUALIA.

qualia (singular: quale), those properties of mental states or events, in particular of sensations and perceptual states, which determine "what it is like" to have them. Sometimes 'phenomenal properties' and 'qualitative features' are used with the same meaning. The felt difference between pains and itches is said to reside in differences in their "qualitative character," i.e., their qualia. For those who accept an "act-object" conception of perceptual experience, qualia may include such properties as "phenomenal redness" and "phenomenal roundness," thought of as properties of sense-data, "phenomenal objects," or portions of the visual field. But those who reject this conception do not thereby reject qualia; a proponent of the adverbial analysis of perceptual experience can hold that an experience of "sensing redly" is so in virtue of, in part, what qualia it has, while denying that there is any sense in which the experience itself is red. Qualia are thought of as non-intentional, i.e., non-representational, features of the states that have them. So in a case of "spectrum inversion," where one person's experiences of green are "qualitatively" just like another person's experiences of red, and vice versa, the visual experiences the two have when viewing a ripe tomato would be alike in their intentional features (both would be *of* a red, round, bulgy surface), but would have different qualia.

Critics of physicalist and functionalist accounts of mind have argued from the possibility of spectrum inversion and other kinds of "qualia inversion," and from such facts as that no physical or functional description will tell one "what it is like" to smell coffee, that such accounts cannot accommodate qualia. Defenders of such accounts are divided between those who claim that their accounts can accommodate qualia and those who claim that qualia are a philosophical myth and thus that there are none to accommodate.

See also PHILOSOPHY OF MIND, QUALITIES.

S.Sho.

qualisign. See PEIRCE.

qualitative identity. See IDENTITY.

qualitative predicate, a kind of predicate postulated in some attempts to solve the grue paradox. (1) On the *syntactic* view, a qualitative predicate is a syntactically more or less simple predicate. Such simplicity, however, is relative to the choice of primitives in a language. In English, 'green' and 'blue' are primitive, while 'grue' and 'bleen' must be introduced by definitions ('green and first examined before *T*, or blue otherwise', 'blue and first examined before *T*, or green otherwise', respectively). In other languages, 'grue' and 'bleen' may be primitive and hence "simple," while 'green' and 'blue' must be introduced by definitions ('grue and first examined before *T*, or bleen otherwise', 'bleen and first examined before *T*, or grue otherwise', respectively). (2) On the *semantic* view, a qualitative predicate is a predicate to which there corresponds a property that is "natural" (to us) or of easy semantic access. The quality of greenness is easy and natural; the quality of grueness is strained. (3) On the *ontological* view, a qualitative predicate is a predicate to which there corresponds a property that is woven into the causal or modal structure of reality in a way that gruesome properties are not. **See also** GRUE PARADOX, PROPERTY.

D.A.J.

qualities, properties or characteristics. There are three specific philosophical senses.

(1) Qualities are physical properties, logical constructions of physical properties, or dispositions. Physical properties, such as mass, shape, and electrical charge, are properties in virtue of which objects can enter into causal relations. Logical constructions of physical properties include conjunctions and disjunctions of them; being $10 \pm .02$ cm long is a disjunctive property. A disposition of an object is a potential for the object to enter into a causal interaction of some specific kind under some specific condition; e.g., an object is soluble in water if and only if it would dissolve were it in enough pure water. (Locke held a very complex theory of powers. On Locke's theory, the dispositions of objects are a kind of power and the human will is a kind of power. However, the human will is not part of

the modern notion of disposition.) So, predicating a disposition of an object implies a subjunctive conditional of the form: if such-and-such were to happen to the object, then so-and-so would happen to it; that my vase is fragile implies that if my vase were to be hit sufficiently hard then it would break. (Whether physical properties are distinct from dispositions is disputed.) Three sorts of qualities are often distinguished. *Primary qualities* are physical properties or logical constructions from physical properties. *Secondary qualities* are dispositions to produce sensory experiences of certain phenomenal sorts under appropriate conditions. The predication of a secondary quality, Q, to an object implies that if the object were to be perceived under normal conditions then the object would appear to be Q to the perceivers: if redness is a secondary quality, then that your coat is red implies that if your coat were to be seen under normal conditions, it would look red. Locke held that the following are secondary qualities: colors, tastes, smells, sounds, and warmth or cold. *Tertiary qualities* are dispositions that are not secondary qualities, e.g. fragility. (Contrary to Locke, the *color realist* holds that colors are either primary or tertiary qualities; so that x is yellow is logically independent of the fact that x looks yellow under normal conditions. Since different spectral reflectances appear to be the same shade of yellow, some color realists hold that any shade of yellow is a disjunctive property whose components are spectral reflectances.)

(2) Assuming a representative theory of perception, as Locke did, qualities have two characteristics: qualities are powers (or dispositions) of objects to produce sensory experiences (sense-data on some theories) in humans; and, in sensory experience, qualities are represented as intrinsic properties of objects. Instrinsic properties of objects are properties that objects have independently of their environment. Hence an exact duplicate of an object has all the intrinsic properties of the original, and an intrinsic property of x never has the form, x-stands-in-such-and-such-a-relation-to-y. Locke held that the primary qualities are extension (size), figure (shape), motion or rest, solidity (impenetrability), and number; the primary qualities are correctly represented in perception as intrinsic features of objects, and the secondary qualities (listed in (1)) are incorrectly represented in perception as intrinsic features of objects. (Locke seems to have been mistaken in holding that number is a quality of objects.) *Positional qualities* are qualities defined in terms of the relative posi-

tions of points in objects and their surrounding: shape, size, and motion and rest. Since most of Locke's primary qualities are positional, some non-positional quality is needed to occupy positions. On Locke's account, solidity fulfills this role, although some have argued (Hume) that solidity is not a primary quality.

(3) Primary qualities are properties common to and inseparable from all matter; secondary qualities are not really qualities in objects, but only powers of objects to produce sensory effects in us by means of their primary qualities. (This is another use of 'quality' by Locke, where 'primary' functions much like 'real' and real properties are given by the metaphysical assumptions of the science of Locke's time.)

Qualities are distinct from representations of them in predications. Sometimes the same quality is represented in different ways by different predications: 'That is water' and 'That is H_2O'. The distinction between qualities and the way they are represented in predications opens up the Lockean possibility that some qualities are incorrectly represented in some predications. Features of predications are sometimes used to define a quality; dispositions are sometimes defined in terms of subjunctive conditionals (see definition of 'secondary qualities' in (1)), and disjunctive properties are defined in terms of disjunctive predications. Features of predications are also used in the following definition of 'independent qualities': two qualities, P and Q, are independent if and only if, for any object x, the predication of P and of Q to x are logically independent (i.e., that x is P and that x is Q are logically independent); circularity and redness are independent, circularity and triangularity are dependent. (If two determinate qualities, e.g., circularity and triangularity, belong to the same determinable, say shape, then they are dependent, but if two determinate qualities, e.g., squareness and redness, belong to different determinables, say shape and color, they are independent.)

See also DISPOSITION, PROPERTY, QUALIA.

E.W.A.

quality. See SYLLOGISM.

quantification, the application of one or more quantifiers (e.g., 'for all x', 'for some y') to an open formula. A quantification (or quantified) sentence results from first forming an open formula from a sentence by replacing expressions belonging to a certain class of expressions in the sentences by variables (whose substituends are the expressions of that class) and then prefixing the formula with quantifiers using those variables. For example, from 'Bill hates Mary' we form 'x hates y', to which we prefix the quantifiers 'for all x' and 'for some y', getting the quantification sentence 'for all x, for some y, x hates y' ('Everyone hates someone').

In *referential quantification* only terms of reference may be replaced by variables. The replaceable terms of reference are the substituends of the variables. The values of the variables are all those objects to which reference could be made by a term of reference of the type that the variables may replace. Thus the previous example 'for all x, for some y, x hates y' is a referential quantification. Terms standing for people ('Bill', 'Mary', e.g.) are the substituends of the variables 'x' and 'y'. And people are the values of the variables.

In *substitutional quantification* any type of term may be replaced by variables. A variable replacing a term has as its substituends all terms of the type of the replaced term. For example, from 'Bill married Mary' we may form 'Bill R Mary', to which we prefix the quantifier 'for some R', getting the substitutional quantification 'for some R, Bill R Mary'. This is not a referential quantification, since the substituends of 'R' are binary predicates (such as 'marries'), which are not terms of reference.

Referential quantification is a species of objectual quantification. The truth conditions of quantification sentences objectually construed are understood in terms of the values of the variable bound by the quantifier. Thus, 'for all v, ϕv' is true provided 'ϕv' is true for all values of the variable 'v'; 'for some v, ϕv' is true provided 'ϕv' is true for some value of the variable 'v'. The truth or falsity of a substitutional quantification turns instead on the truth or falsity of the sentences that result from the quantified formula by replacing variables by their substituends. For example, 'for some R, Bill R Mary' is true provided some sentence of the form 'Bill R Mary' is true.

In classical logic the universal quantifier 'for all' is definable in terms of negation and the existential quantifier 'for some': 'for all x' is short for 'not for some x not'. The existential quantifier is similarly definable in terms of negation and the universal quantifier. In intuitionistic logic, this does not hold. Both quantifiers are regarded as primitive.

See also FORMAL LOGIC, PHILOSOPHY OF LOGIC.   C.S.

quantificational shift fallacy. See FORMAL FALLACY.

quantification theory, elementary. See FORMAL LOGIC.

quantifier. See FORMAL LOGIC, PLURALITIVE LOGIC.

quantifier elimination. See UNIVERSAL INSTANTIATION.

quantifier shift fallacy. See FORMAL FALLACY.

quantifying in, use of a quantifier outside of an opaque construction to attempt to bind a variable within it, a procedure whose legitimacy was first questioned by Quine. An opaque construction is one that resists substitutivity of identity. Among others, the constructions of quotation, the verbs of propositional attitude, and the logical modalities can give rise to opacity. For example, the position of 'six' in:

(1) 'six' contains exactly three letters

is opaque, since the substitution for 'six' by its codesignate 'immediate successor of five' renders a truth into a falsehood:

(1′) 'the immediate successor of five' contains exactly three letters.

Similarly, the position of 'the earth' in:

(2) Tom believes that the earth is habitable

is opaque, if the substitution of 'the earth' by its codesignate 'the third planet from the sun' renders a sentence that Tom would affirm into one that he would deny:

(2′) Tom believes that the third planet from the sun is habitable.

Finally, the position of '9' (and of '7') in:

(3) Necessarily (9 > 7)

is opaque, since the substitution of 'the number of major planets' for its codesignate '9' renders a truth into a falsehood:

(3′) Necessarily (the number of major planets > 7).

Quine argues that since the positions within opaque constructions resist substitutivity of identity, they cannot meaningfully be quantified. Accordingly, the following three quantified sentences are meaningless:

(1″) (Ex) ('x' > 7),
(2″) (Ex) (Tom believes that x is habitable),

(3″) (Ex) necessarily $(x > 7)$.

(1″), (2″), and (3″) are meaningless, since the second occurrence of 'x' in each of them does not function as a variable in the ordinary (non-essentialist) quantificational way. The second occurrence of 'x' in (1″) functions as a name that names the twenty-fourth letter of the alphabet. The second occurrences of 'x' in (2″) and in (3″) do not function as variables, since they do not allow all codesignative terms as substituends without change of truth-value. Thus, they may take objects as values but only objects designated in certain ways, e.g., in terms of their intensional or essential properties. So, short of acquiescing in an intensionalist or essentialist metaphysics, Quine argues, we cannot in general quantify into opaque contexts.

See also INTENSIONALITY, MEANING, SUBSTITUTIVITY SALVA VERITATE.   R.F.G.

quantity. See MAGNITUDE, SYLLOGISM.

quantum logic, the logic of which the models are certain non-Boolean algebras derived from the mathematical representation of quantum mechanical systems. (The models of classical logic are, formally, Boolean algebras.) This is the central notion of quantum logic in the literature, although the term covers a variety of modal logics, dialogics, and operational logics proposed to elucidate the structure of quantum mechanics and its relation to classical mechanics. The dynamical quantities of a classical mechanical system (position, momentum, energy, etc.) form a commutative algebra, and the dynamical properties of the system (e.g., the property that the position lies in a specified range, or the property that the momentum is greater than zero, etc.) form a Boolean algebra. The transition from classical to quantum mechanics involves the transition from a commutative algebra of dynamical quantities to a noncommutative algebra of so-called observables. One way of understanding the conceptual revolution from classical to quantum mechanics is in terms of a shift from the class of Boolean algebras to a class of non-Boolean algebras as the appropriate relational structures for the dynamical properties of mechanical systems, hence from a Boolean classical logic to a non-Boolean quantum logic as the logic applicable to the fundamental physical processes of our universe. This conception of quantum logic was developed formally in a classic 1936 paper by G. Birkhoff and J. von Neu-

mann (although von Neumann first proposed the idea in 1927).

The features that distinguish quantum logic from classical logic vary with the formulation. In the Birkhoff–von Neumann logic, the distributive law of classical logic fails, but this is by no means a feature of all versions of quantum logic. It follows from Gleason's theorem (1957) that the non-Boolean models do not admit two-valued homomorphisms in the general case, i.e., there is no partition of the dynamical properties of a quantum mechanical system into those possessed by the system and those not possessed by the system that preserves algebraic structure, and equivalently no assignment of values to the observables of the system that preserves algebraic structure. This result was proved independently for finite sets of observables by S. Kochen and E. P. Specker (1967). It follows that the probabilities specified by the Born interpretation of the state function of a quantum mechanical system for the results of measurements of observables cannot be derived from a probability distribution over the different possible sets of dynamical properties of the system, or the different possible sets of values assignable to the observables (of which one set is presumed to be actual), determined by hidden variables in addition to the state function, if these sets of properties or values are required to preserve algebraic structure. While Bell's theorem (1964) excludes hidden variables satisfying a certain locality condition, the Kochen-Specker theorem relates the non-Booleanity of quantum logic to the impossibility of hidden variable extensions of quantum mechanics, in which value assignments to the observables satisfy constraints imposed by the algebraic structure of the observables.

See also BOOLEAN ALGEBRA, PHILOSOPHY OF SCIENCE, QUANTUM MECHANICS.   J.Bub

quantum mechanics, also called quantum theory, the science governing objects of atomic and subatomic dimensions. Developed independently by Werner Heisenberg (as matrix mechanics, 1925) and Erwin Schrödinger (as wave mechanics, 1926), quantum mechanics breaks with classical treatments of the motions and interactions of bodies by introducing probability and acts of measurement in seemingly irreducible ways. In the widely used Schrödinger version, quantum mechanics associates with each physical system a time-dependent function, called the *state function* (alternatively, the state vector or Ψ function). The evolution of the system is represented by the temporal transformation of the state function in accord with a master equation, known as the Schrödinger equation. Also associated with a system are "observables": (in principle) measurable quantities, such as position, momentum, and energy, including some with no good classical analogue, such as spin. According to the Born interpretation (1926), the state function is understood instrumentally: it enables one to calculate, for any possible value of an observable, the probability that a measurement of that observable would find that particular value.

The formal properties of observables and state functions imply that certain pairs of observables (such as linear momentum in a given direction, and position in the same direction) are incompatible in the sense that no state function assigns probability 1 to the simultaneous determination of exact values for both observables. This is a qualitative statement of the Heisenberg uncertainty principle (alternatively, the indeterminacy principle, or just the uncertainty principle). Quantitatively, that principle places a precise limit on the accuracy with which one may simultaneously measure a pair of incompatible observables. There is no corresponding limit, however, on the accuracy with which a single observable (say, position alone, or momentum alone) may be measured. The uncertainty principle is sometimes understood in terms of complementarity, a general perspective proposed by Niels Bohr according to which the connection between quantum phenomena and observation forces our classical concepts to split into mutually exclusive packages, both of which are required for a complete understanding but only one of which is applicable under any particular experimental conditions. Some take this to imply an ontology in which quantum objects do not actually possess simultaneous values for incompatible observables; e.g., do not have simultaneous position and momentum. Others would hold, e.g., that measuring the position of an object causes an uncontrollable change in its momentum, in accord with the limits on simultaneous accuracy built into the uncertainty principle. These ways of treating the principle are not uncontroversial.

Philosophical interest arises in part from where the quantum theory breaks with classical physics: namely, from the apparent breakdown of determinism (or causality) that seems to result from the irreducibly statistical nature of the theory, and from the apparent breakdown of observer-independence or realism that seems to result from the fundamental role of measurement in the theory. Both features relate to the interpretation of the state function as providing only a summary of the probabilities for various measurement outcomes. Einstein, in particular, criticized the theory on these grounds, and in 1935 suggested a striking thought experiment to show that, assuming no action-at-a-distance, one would have to consider the state function as an incomplete description of the real physical state for an individual system, and therefore quantum mechanics as merely a provisional theory. Einstein's example involved a pair of systems that interact briefly and then separate, but in such a way that the outcomes of various measurements performed on each system, separately, show an uncanny correlation. In 1951 the physicist David Bohm simplified Einstein's example, and later (1957) indicated that it may be realizable experimentally. The physicist John S. Bell then formulated a locality assumption (1964), similar to Einstein's, that constrains factors which might be used in describing the state of an individual system, so-called hidden variables. Locality requires that in the Einstein-Bohm experiment hidden variables not allow the measurement performed on one system in a correlated pair immediately to influence the outcome obtained in measuring the other, spatially separated system. Bell demonstrated that locality (in conjunction with other assumptions about hidden variables) restricts the probabilities for measurement outcomes according to a system of inequalities known as the Bell inequalities, and that the probabilities of certain quantum systems violate these inequalities. This is Bell's theorem. Subsequently several experiments of the Einstein-Bohm type have been performed to test the Bell inequalities. Although the results have not been univocal, the consensus is that the experimental data support the quantum theory and violate the inequalities. Current research is trying to evaluate the implications of these results, including the extent to which they rule out local hidden variables. (See J. Cushing and E. McMullin, eds., *Philosophical Consequences of Quantum Theory*, 1989.)

The descriptive incompleteness with which Einstein charged the theory suggests other problems. A particularly dramatic one arose in correspondence between Schrödinger and Einstein; namely, the "gruesome" Schrödinger cat paradox. Here a cat is confined in a closed chamber containing a radioactive atom with a fifty-fifty chance of decaying in the next hour. If the atom decays it triggers a relay that causes a hammer to fall and smash a glass vial holding a quantity of prussic acid sufficient to kill the cat. According to the Schrödinger equation, after an hour the state function for the entire atom + relay + hammer + glass vial + cat system is such that if we observe the cat the probability for finding it alive (dead) is 50 percent. However, this evolved state function is one for which there is no definite result; according to it, the cat is neither alive nor dead. How then does any definite fact of the matter arise, and when? Is the act of observation itself instrumental in bringing about the observed result, does that result come about by virtue of some special random process, or is there some other account compatible with definite results of measurements? This is the so-called quantum measurement problem and it too is an active area of research.

See also DETERMINISM, EINSTEIN, FIELD THEORY, PHILOSOPHY OF SCIENCE, RELATIVITY.   A.F.

quasi-indicator, Castañeda's term for an expression used to ascribe indexical reference to a speaker or thinker. If John says "I am hungry" it is incorrect to report what he said with 'John claims that I am hungry', since 'I', being an indexical, expresses speaker's reference, not John's. However, 'John claims that John is hungry' fails to represent the indexical element of his assertion. Instead, we use 'John claims that he himself is hungry', where 'he himself' is a quasi-indicator depicting John's reference to himself *qua* self. Because of its subjective and perspectival character, we cannot grasp the exact content of another's indexical reference, yet quasi-indexical representations are possible since we confront the world through generically the same indexical *modes of presentation*. If these modes are irreducible, then quasi-indicators are indispensable for describing the thoughts and experiences of others. As such, they are not equivalent to or replaceable by any antecedents occurring outside the scope of psychological verbs to which they are subordinated. **See also** CASTAÑEDA, GUISE THEORY, INDEXICAL, SCOPE.   T.K.

quasi-quotes. See CORNERS.

quaternio terminorum. See SYLLOGISM.

quiddity. See AVICENNA, ESSENTIALISM.

Quine, W(illard) V(an) O(rman) (b.1908), American philosopher and logician, renowned for his rejection of the analytic–synthetic distinction and for his advocacy of extensionalism, natural-

ism, physicalism, empiricism, and holism. Quine took his doctorate in philosophy at Harvard in 1932. After four years of postdoctoral fellowships, he was appointed to the philosophy faculty at Harvard in 1936. There he remained until he retired from teaching in 1978.

During six decades Quine published scores of journal articles and more than twenty books. His writings touch a number of areas, including logic, philosophy of logic, set theory, philosophy of language, philosophy of mind, philosophy of science, metaphysics, epistemology, and ethics. Among his most influential articles and books are "New Foundations for Mathematical Logic" (1936), "Two Dogmas of Empiricism" (1951), "Epistemology Naturalized" (1969), and *Word and Object* (1960). In "New Foundations" he develops a set theory that avoids Russell's paradox without relying on Russell's theory of types. Rather, following Ernst Zermelo, Quine drops the presumption that every membership condition determines a set. The system of "New Foundations" continues to be widely discussed by mathematicians.

"Two Dogmas" sets out to repudiate what he sees as two dogmas of logical empiricism. The first is the so-called analytic–synthetic distinction; the second is a weak form of reductionism to the effect that each synthetic statement has associated with it a unique set of confirming experiences and a unique set of infirming experiences. Against the first dogma, Quine argues that none of the then-current attempts to characterize analyticity (e.g., "a statement is analytic if and only if it is true solely in virtue of its meaning") do so with sufficient clarity, and that any similar characterization is likewise doomed to fail. Against the second dogma, Quine argues that a more accurate account of the relation between the statements of a theory and experience is holistic rather than reductionistic, that is, only as a corporate body do the statements of a theory face the tribunal of experience. Quine concludes that the effects of rejecting these two dogmas of empiricism are (1) a blurring of the supposed boundary between speculative metaphysics and natural science and (2) a shift toward pragmatism.

In "Epistemology Naturalized" Quine argues in favor of naturalizing epistemology: old-time epistemology (first philosophy) has failed in its attempt to ground science on something firmer than science and should, therefore, be replaced by a scientific account of how we acquire our overall theory of the world and why it works so well.

In *Word and Object,* Quine's most famous book, he argues in favor of (1) naturalizing epistemology, (2) physicalism as against phenomenalism and mind–body dualism, and (3) extensionality as against intensionality. He also (4) develops a behavioristic conception of sentence-meaning, (5) theorizes about language learning, (6) speculates on the ontogenesis of reference, (7) explains various forms of ambiguity and vagueness, (8) recommends measures for regimenting language so as to eliminate ambiguity and vagueness as well as to make a theory's logic and ontic commitments perspicuous ("to be is to be the value of a bound variable"), (9) argues against quantified modal logic and the essentialism it presupposes, (10) argues for Platonic realism in mathematics, (11) argues for scientific realism and against instrumentalism, (12) develops a view of philosophical analysis as explication, (13) argues against analyticity and for holism, (14) argues against countenancing propositions, and (15) argues that the meanings of theoretical sentences are indeterminate and that the reference of terms is inscrutable. Quine's subsequent writings have largely been devoted to summing up, clarifying, and expanding on themes found in *Word and Object.*

See also ANALYTIC–SYNTHETIC DISTINCTION, EMPIRICISM, EXTENSIONALISM, HOLISM, NATURALISM, NATURALISTIC EPISTEMOLOGY, PHYSICALISM.   R.F.G.

quinque voces. See PREDICABLES.

R

Rabad. See IBN DAUD.

racetrack paradox. See ZENO'S PARADOXES.

racism, hostility, contempt, condescension, or prejudice, on the basis of social practices of racial classification, and the wider phenomena of social, economic, and political mistreatment that often accompany such classification. The most salient instances of racism include the Nazi ideology of the "Aryan master race," American chattel slavery, South African *apartheid* in the late twentieth century, and the "Jim Crow" laws and traditions of segregation that subjugated African descendants in the Southern United States during the century after the American Civil War.

Social theorists dispute whether, in its essence, racism is a belief or an ideology of racial inferiority, a system of social oppression on the basis of race, a form of discourse, discriminatory conduct, or an attitude of contempt or heartlessness (and its expression in individual or collective behavior). The case for any of these as the essence of racism has its drawbacks, and a proponent must show how the others can also come to be racist in virtue of that essence. Some deny that racism has any nature or essence, insisting it is nothing more than changing historical realities. However, these thinkers must explain what makes each reality an instance of racism. Theorists differ over who and what can be racist and under what circumstances, some restricting racism to the powerful, others finding it also in some reactions by the oppressed. Here, the former owe an explanation of why power is necessary for racism, what sort (economic or political? general or contextual?), and in whom or what (racist individuals? their racial groups?). Although virtually everyone thinks racism objectionable, people disagree over whether its central defect is cognitive (irrationality, prejudice), economic/prudential (inefficiency), or moral (unnecessary suffering, unequal treatment). Finally, racism's connection with the ambiguous and controversial concept of race itself is complex. Plainly, racism presupposes the legitimacy of racial classifications, and perhaps the metaphysical reality of races. Nevertheless, some hold that racism is also prior to race, with racial classifications invented chiefly to explain and help justify the oppression of some peoples by others.

The term originated to designate the pseudo-scientific theories of racial essence and inferiority that arose in Europe in the nineteenth century and were endorsed by Germany's Third Reich. Since the civil rights movement in the United States after World War II, the term has come to cover a much broader range of beliefs, attitudes, institutions, and practices. Today one hears charges of unconscious, covert, institutional, paternalistic, benign, anti-racist, liberal, and even reverse racism. Racism is widely regarded as involving ignorance, irrationality, unreasonableness, injustice, and other intellectual and moral vices, to such an extent that today virtually no one is willing to accept the classification of oneself, one's beliefs, and so on, as racist, except in contexts of self-reproach. As a result, classifying anything as racist, beyond the most egregious cases, is a serious charge and is often hotly disputed.

See also JUSTICE, POLITICAL PHILOSOPHY, SOCIAL PHILOSOPHY. J.L.A.G.

radical translation. See INDETERMINACY OF TRANSLATION.

Rāmānuja (1017?–1137?), Indian philosopher who founded the Viśistadvaita tradition. His theistic system provides the theoretical basis for Bhakti devotional Hinduism. His most important writings are the *Sribhāṣya* (a commentary on the *Brahma-Sūtras* of Badarayana that presents an interpretation competitive to Shaṅkara's), the *Gītā-Bhāṣya* (a commentary on the Bhagavad Gita), and the *Vedārthasamgraha* (a commentary on the Upanishads). He rejects natural theology, offers a powerful criticism of Advaita Vedanta, and presents a systematic articulation of devotional theism. **See also VIŚISTADVAITA VEDANTA.** K.E.Y.

ramified type theory. See TYPE THEORY.

Ramist movement. See RAMUS.

Ramsey, Frank Plumpton (1903–30), influential

British philosopher of logic and mathematics. His primary interests were in logic and philosophy, but decades after his untimely death two of his publications sparked new branches of economics, and in pure mathematics his combinatorial theorems gave rise to "Ramsey theory" (*Economic Journal* 1927, 1928; *Proc. London Math. Soc.*, 1928). During his lifetime Ramsey's philosophical reputation outside Cambridge was based largely on his architectural reparation of Whitehead and Russell's *Principia Mathematica*, strengthening its claim to reduce mathematics to the new logic formulated in Volume 1 – a reduction rounded out by Wittgenstein's assessment of logical truths as tautologous. Ramsey clarified this logicist picture of mathematics by radically simplifying Russell's ramified theory of types, eliminating the need for the unarguable axiom of reducibility (*Proc. London Math. Soc.*, 1925). His philosophical work was published mostly after his death. The canon, established by Richard Braithwaite (*The Foundations of Mathematics . . .*, 1931), remains generally intact in D. H. Mellor's edition (*Philosophical Papers*, 1990). Further writings of varying importance appear in his *Notes on Philosophy, Probability and Mathematics* (M. C. Galavotti, ed., 1991) and *On Truth* (Nicholas Rescher and Ulrich Majer, eds., 1991).

As an undergraduate Ramsey observed that the redundancy account of truth "enables us to rule out at once some theories of truth such as that 'to be true' means 'to work' or 'to cohere' since clearly '*p* works' and '*p* coheres' are not equivalent to '*p*'." Later, in the canonical "Truth and Probability" (1926), he readdressed to knowledge and belief the main questions ordinarily associated with truth, analyzing probability as a mode of judgment in the framework of a theory of choice under uncertainty. Reinvented and acknowledged by L. J. Savage (*Foundations of Statistics*, 1954), this forms the theoretical basis of the currently dominant "Bayesian" view of rational decision making. Ramsey cut his philosophical teeth on Wittgenstein's *Tractatus Logico-Philosophicus*. His translation appeared in 1922; a long critical notice of the work (1923) was his first substantial philosophical publication. His later role in Wittgenstein's rejection of the *Tractatus* is acknowledged in the foreword to *Philosophical Investigations* (1953).

The posthumous canon has been a gold mine. An example: "Propositions" (1929), reading the theoretical terms (*T, U*, etc.) of an axiomatized scientific theory as variables, sees the theory's content as conveyed by a "Ramsey sentence" saying that for some *T, U*, etc., the theory's axioms are true, a sentence in which all extralogical terms are observational. Another example: "General Propositions and Causality" (1929), offering in a footnote the "Ramsey test" for acceptability of conditionals, i.e., add the if-clause to your ambient beliefs (minimally modified to make the enlarged set self-consistent), and accept the conditional if the then-clause follows.

See also BAYESIAN RATIONALITY, PROBABILITY, TRUTH.   R.J.

Ramsey-eliminability. See BETH'S DEFINABILITY THEOREM.

Ramsey sentence. See PHILOSOPHY OF MIND, PHILOSOPHY OF SCIENCE.

Ramsey test. See RAMSEY.

Ramus, Petrus, in French, Pierre de La Ramée (1515–72), French philosopher who questioned the authority of Aristotle and influenced the methods and teaching of logic through the seventeenth century. In 1543 he published his *Dialecticae institutiones libri XV*, and in 1555 reworked it as *Dialectique* – the first philosophical work in French. He was appointed by François I as the first Regius Professor of the University of Paris, where he taught until he was killed in the St. Bartholomew's Day Massacre in 1572.

Ramus doubted that we can apodictically intuit the major premises required for Aristotle's rational syllogism. Turning instead to Plato, Ramus proposed that a "Socratizing" of logic would produce a more workable and fruitful result. As had Agricola and Sturm, he reworked the rhetorical and liberal arts traditions' concepts of "invention, judgment, and practice," placing "method" in the center of judgment. Proceeding in these stages, we can "read" nature's "arguments," because they are modeled on natural reasoning, which in turn can emulate the reasoning by which God creates. Often his results were depicted graphically in tables (as in chapter IX of Hobbes's *Leviathan*). When carefully done they would show both what is known and where gaps require further investigation; the process from invention to judgment is continuous.

Ramus's works saw some 750 editions in one century, fostering the "Ramist" movement in emerging Protestant universities and the American colonies. He influenced Bacon, Hobbes, Milton, Methodism, Cambridge Platonism, and Alsted in Europe, and Hooker and Congregationalism in Puritan America. Inconsistencies make him less than a major figure in the history of logic, but his many works and their rapid popularity led to philosophical and educational efforts to bring the world of learning to the "plain man" by using the vernacular, and by more closely correlating the rigor of philosophy with the memorable and persuasive powers of rhetoric; he saw this goal as Socratic. C.Wa.

randomness. See PHILOSOPHY OF SCIENCE.

range. See RELATION.

Rashdall, Hastings (1858–1924), English historian, theologian, and personal idealist. While acknowledging that Berkeley needed to be corrected by Kant, Rashdall defended Berkeley's thesis that objects only exist for minds. From this he concluded that there is a divine mind that guarantees the existence of nature and the objectivity of morality. In his most important philosophical work, *The Theory of Good and Evil* (1907), Rashdall argued that actions are right or wrong according to whether they produce well-being, in which pleasure as well as a virtuous disposition are constituents. Rashdall coined the name 'ideal utilitarianism' for this view. **See also UTILITARIANISM.** J.W.A.

rational choice theory. See DECISION THEORY.

rationalism, the position that reason has precedence over other ways of acquiring knowledge, or, more strongly, that it is the unique path to knowledge. It is most often encountered as a view in epistemology, where it is traditionally contrasted with empiricism, the view that the senses are primary with respect to knowledge. (It is important here to distinguish empiricism with respect to knowledge from empiricism with respect to ideas or concepts; whereas the former is opposed to rationalism, the latter is opposed to the doctrine of innate ideas.) The term is also encountered in the philosophy of religion, where it may designate those who oppose the view that revelation is central to religious knowledge; and in ethics, where it may designate those who oppose the view that ethical principles are grounded in or derive from emotion, empathy, or some other non-rational foundation.

The term 'rationalism' does not generally designate a single precise philosophical position; there are several ways in which reason can have precedence, and several accounts of knowledge to which it may be opposed. Furthermore, the very term 'reason' is not altogether clear. Often it designates a faculty of the soul, distinct from sensation, imagination, and memory, which is the ground of a priori knowledge. But there are other conceptions of reason, such as the narrower conception in which Pascal opposes reason to "knowledge of the heart" (*Pensées*, section 110), or the computational conception of reason Hobbes advances in *Leviathan* I.5.

The term might thus be applied to a number of philosophical positions from the ancients down to the present. Among the ancients, 'rationalism' and 'empiricism' especially denote two schools of medicine, the former relying primarily on a theoretical knowledge of the hidden workings of the human body, the latter relying on direct clinical experience. The term might also be used to characterize the views of Plato and later Neoplatonists, who argued that we have pure intellectual access to the Forms and general principles that govern reality, and rejected sensory knowledge of the imperfect realization of those Forms in the material world.

In recent philosophical writing, the term 'rationalism' is most closely associated with the positions of a group of seventeenth-century philosophers, Descartes, Spinoza, Leibniz, and sometimes Malebranche. These thinkers are often referred to collectively as the Continental rationalists, and are generally opposed to the so-called British empiricists, Locke, Berkeley, and Hume. All of the former share the view that we have a non-empirical and rational access to the truth about the way the world is, and all privilege reason over knowledge derived from the senses. These philosophers are also attracted to mathematics as a model for knowledge in general. But these common views are developed in quite different ways.

Descartes claims to take his inspiration from mathematics – not mathematics as commonly understood, but the analysis of the ancients. According to Descartes, we start from first principles known directly by reason (the *cogito ergo sum* of the *Meditations*), what he calls intuition in his *Rules for the Direction of the Mind;* all other knowledge is deduced from there. A central aim of his *Meditations* is to show that this faculty of reason is trustworthy. The senses, on the other hand, are generally deceptive, leading us to mistake sensory qualities for real qualities of extended bodies, and leading us to the false philosophy of Aristotle and to Scholasticism. Descartes does not reject the senses altogether; in Meditation VI he argues that the senses are most often correct in circumstances concerning the preservation of life. Perhaps paradoxically, experiment is important to Descartes's scientific work. However, his primary interest is in the theoretical account of the phenomena experiment reveals, and while his position is unclear, he may have considered experiment as an auxiliary to intuition and deduction, or as a second-best method that can be used with problems too complex for pure reason. Malebranche, following Descartes, takes similar views in his *Search after Truth*, though unlike Descartes, he emphasizes original sin as the cause of our tendency to trust the senses.

Spinoza's model for knowledge is Euclidean geometry, as realized in the geometrical form of the *Ethics*. Spinoza explicitly argues that we cannot have adequate ideas of the world through sensation (*Ethics* II, propositions 16–31). In the *Ethics* he does see a role for the senses in what he calls knowledge of the first and knowledge of the second kinds, and in the earlier *Emendation of the Intellect*, he suggests that the senses may be auxiliary aids to genuine knowledge. But the senses are imperfect and far less valuable, according to Spinoza, than intuition, i.e., knowledge of the third kind, from which sensory experience is excluded. Spinoza's rationalism is implicit in a central proposition of the *Ethics*, in accordance with which "the order and connection of ideas is the same as the order and connection of things" (*Ethics* II, proposition 7), allowing one to infer causal connections between bodies and states of the material world directly from the logical connections between ideas.

Leibniz, too, emphasizes reason over the senses in a number of ways. In his youth he believed that it would be possible to calculate the truth-value of every sentence by constructing a logical language whose structure mirrors the structure of relations between concepts in the world. This view is reflected in his mature thought in the doctrine that in every truth, the concept of the predicate is contained in the concept of the subject, so that if one could take the God's-eye view (which, he concedes, we cannot), one could determine the truth or falsity of any proposition without appeal to experience (*Discourse on Metaphysics*, section 8). Leibniz also argues that all truths are based on two basic principles, the law of non-contradiction (for necessary truths), and the principle of sufficient reason (for contingent truths) (*Monadology*, section 31), both of which can be known a priori. And so, at least in principle, the truth-values of all propositions can be determined a priori. This reflects his practice in physics, where he derives a number of laws of motion from the principle of the equality of cause and effect, which can be known a priori on the basis of the principle of sufficient reason. But, at the same time, referring to the empirical school of ancient medicine, Leibniz concedes that "we are all mere Empirics in three fourths of our actions" (*Monadology*, section 28).

Each of the so-called Continental rationalists does, in his own way, privilege reason over the senses. But the common designation 'Continental rationalism' arose only much later, probably in the nineteenth century. For their contemporaries, more impressed with their differences than their common doctrines, the Continental rationalists did not form a single homogeneous school of thought.

See also A PRIORI, EMPIRICISM, INTUITION.
D.Garb.

rationalism, Continental. See RATIONALISM.

rationalism, moral. See MORAL SENSE THEORY.

rationality. In its primary sense, rationality is a normative concept that philosophers have generally tried to characterize in such a way that, for any action, belief, or desire, if it is rational we ought to choose it. No such positive characterization has achieved anything close to universal assent because, often, several competing actions, beliefs, or desires count as rational. Equating what is rational with what is rationally required eliminates the category of what is rationally allowed. Irrationality seems to be the more fundamental normative category; for although there are conflicting substantive accounts of irrationality, all agree that to say of an action, belief, or desire that it is irrational is to claim that it should always be avoided.

Rationality is also a descriptive concept that refers to those intellectual capacities, usually involving the ability to use language, that distinguish persons from plants and most other animals. There is some dispute about whether some non-human animals, e.g., dolphins and chimpanzees, are rational in this sense.

Theoretical rationality applies to beliefs. An irrational belief is one that obviously conflicts with what one should know. This characterization of an irrational belief is identical with the psychiatric characterization of a delusion. It is a person-relative concept, because what obviously conflicts with what should be known by one person need not obviously conflict with what should be known by another. On this account, any belief that is not irrational counts as rational. Many positive characterizations of rational beliefs have been proposed, e.g., (1) beliefs that are either self-evident or derived from self-evident beliefs by a reliable procedure and (2) beliefs that are consistent with the overwhelming majority of one's beliefs; but all of these positive characterizations have encountered serious objections.

Practical rationality applies to actions. For some philosophers it is identical to *instrumental rationality*. On this view, commonly called *instrumentalism*, acting rationally simply means acting in a way that is maximally efficient in achieving one's goals. However, most philosophers realize that achieving one goal may conflict with achieving another, and therefore require that a rational action be one that best achieves one's goals only when these goals are considered as forming a system. Others have added that all of these goals must be ones that would be chosen given complete knowledge and understanding of what it would be like to achieve these goals. On the latter account of rational action, the system of goals is chosen by all persons for themselves, and apart from consistency there is no external standpoint from which to evaluate rationally any such system. Thus, for a person with a certain system of goals it will be irrational to act morally. Another account of rational action is not at all person-relative. On this account, to act rationally is to act on universalizable principles, so that what is a reason for one person must be a reason for everyone. One point of such an account is to make it rationally required to act morally, thus making all immoral action irrational.

However, if to call an action irrational is to claim that everyone would hold that it is always to be avoided, then it is neither irrational to act immorally in order to benefit oneself or one's friends, nor irrational to act morally even when that goes against one's system of goals. Only a negative characterization of what is rational as what is not irrational, which makes it rationally permissible to act either morally or in accordance with one's own system of goals, as long as these goals meet some minimal objective standard, seems likely to be adequate.

See also EPISTEMOLOGY, ETHICS, PRACTICAL REASONING, THEORETICAL REASON.

B.Ge.

rationality, epistemic. See IRRATIONALITY.

rationality, instrumental. See RATIONALITY.

rationality, practical. See RATIONALITY.

rationality, theoretical. See RATIONALITY.

rationalization, (1) an apparent explanation of a person's action or attitude by appeal to reasons that would justify or exculpate the person for it – if, contrary to fact, those reasons were to explain it; (2) an explanation or interpretation made from a rational perspective. In sense (1), rationalizations are *pseudo*-explanations, often motivated by a desire to exhibit an item in a favorable light. Such rationalizations sometimes involve self-deception. Depending on one's view of justification, a rationalization might justify an action – by adducing excellent reasons for its performance – even if the agent, not having acted for those reasons, deserves no credit for so acting. In sense (2) (a sense popularized in philosophy by Donald Davidson), rationalizations of intentional actions are genuine explanations in terms of agents' reasons. In this sense, we provide a rationalization for – or "rationalize" – Robert's shopping at Zed's by identifying the reason(s) for which he does so: e.g., he wants to buy an excellent kitchen knife and believes that Zed's sells the best cutlery in town. (Also, the reasons for which an agent acts may themselves be said to rationalize the action.) Beliefs, desires, and intentions may be similarly rationalized. In each case, a rationalization exhibits the rationalized item as, to some degree, rational from the standpoint of the person to whom it is attributed. **See also RATIONALITY, REASONS FOR ACTION, SELF-DECEPTION.**   A.R.M.

rational number. See MATHEMATICAL ANALYSIS.

rational psychology, the a priori study of the mind. This was a large component of eighteenth- and nineteenth-century psychology, and was contrasted by its exponents with empirical psychology, which is rooted in contingent experience. The term 'rational psychology' may also designate a mind, or form of mind, having the property of rationality. Current philosophy of mind includes much discussion of rational psychologies, but the notion is apparently ambiguous. On one hand, there is rationality as intelligibility. This is a minimal coherence, say of desires or inferences, that a mind must possess to be a mind. For instance, Donald Davidson, many functionalists, and some decision theorists believe there are principles of rationality of this sort that constrain the appropriate attribution of beliefs and desires to a person, so that a mind must meet such constraints if it is to have beliefs and desires. On another pole, there is rationality as justification. For someone's psychology to have this property is for that psychology to be as reason requires it to be, say for that person's inferences and desires to be supported by proper reasons given their proper weight, and hence to be justified. Rationality as justification is a normative property, which it would seem some minds lack. But despite the apparent differences between these two sorts of rationality, some important work in philosophy of mind implies either that these two senses in fact collapse, or at least that there are intervening and significant senses, so that things at least a lot like normative principles constrain what our psychologies are. **See also PHILOSOPHY OF MIND.**   J.R.M.

rational reconstruction, also called logical reconstruction, translation of a discourse of a certain conceptual type into a discourse of another conceptual type with the aim of making it possible to say everything (or everything important) that is expressible in the former more clearly (or perspicuously) in the latter. The best-known example is one in Carnap's *Der Logische Aufbau der Welt.* Carnap attempted to translate discourse concerning physical objects (e.g., 'There is a round brown table') into discourse concerning immediate objects of sense experience ('Color patches of such-and-such chromatic characteristics and shape appear in such-and-such a way'). He was motivated by the empiricist doctrine that immediate sense experience is conceptually prior to everything else, including our notion of a physical object. In addition to talk of immediate sense experience, Carnap relied on logic and set theory. Since their use is difficult to reconcile with strict empiricism, his translation would not have fully vindicated empiricism even if it had succeeded. **See also DEFINITION, LOGICAL POSITIVISM, PHENOMENALISM.**   T.Y.

ratio recta. See INDIRECT DISCOURSE.

ratio scale. See MAGNITUDE.

ravens paradox. See CONFIRMATION.

Rawls, John (b.1921), American philosopher widely recognized as one of the leading political philosophers of the twentieth century. His *A Theory of Justice* (1971) is one of the primary texts in political philosophy. *Political Liberalism* (1993) revises Rawls's theory to make his conception of justice compatible with liberal pluralism, but leaves the core of his conception intact.

Drawing on the liberal and democratic social contract traditions of Locke, Rousseau, and Kant,

Rawls argues that the most reasonable principles of justice are those everyone would accept and agree to from a fair position. Since these principles determine the justice of society's political constitution, economy, and property rules (its "basic structure"), Rawls takes a fair agreement situation to be one where everyone is impartially situated as equals. In this so-called original position everyone is equally situated by a hypothetical "veil of ignorance." This veil requires individuals to set aside their knowledge of their particular differences, including knowledge of their talents, wealth, social position, religious and philosophical views, and particular conceptions of value.

Rawls argues that in the hypothetical original position everyone would reject utilitarianism, perfectionism, and intuitionist views. Instead they would unanimously accept justice as fairness. This conception of justice consists mainly of two principles. The first principle says that certain liberties are basic and are to be equally provided to all: liberty of conscience, freedom of thought, freedom of association, equal political liberties, freedom and integrity of the person, and the liberties that maintain the rule of law. These are basic liberties, because they are necessary to exercise one's "moral powers." The two moral powers are, first, the capacity to be rational, to have a rational conception of one's good; and second, the capacity for a sense of justice, to understand, apply, and act from requirements of justice. These powers constitute essential interests of free and equal moral persons since they enable each person to be a free and responsible agent taking part in social cooperation.

Rawls's second principle of justice, the difference principle, regulates permissible differences in rights, powers, and privileges. It defines the limits of inequalities in wealth, income, powers, and positions that may exist in a just society. It says, first, that social positions are to be open to all to compete for on terms of fair equality of opportunity. Second, inequalities in wealth, income, and social powers and positions are permissible only if they maximally benefit the least advantaged class in society.

The difference principle implies that a just economic system distributes income and wealth so as to make the class of least advantaged persons better off than they would be under any alternative economic system. This principle is to be consistent with the "priority" of the first principle, which requires that equal basic liberties cannot be traded for other benefits. The least advantaged's right to vote, for example, cannot be limited for the sake of improving their relative economic position. Instead, a basic liberty can be limited only for the sake of maintaining other basic liberties.

Rawls contends that, taking the two principles of justice together, a just society maximizes the worth to the least advantaged of the basic liberties shared by all (*Theory*, p. 205). The priority of basic liberty implies a liberal egalitarian society in which each person is ensured adequate resources to effectively exercise her basic liberties and become independent and self-governing. A just society is then governed by a liberal-democratic constitution that protects the basic liberties and provides citizens with equally effective rights to participate in electoral processes and influence legislation. Economically a just society incorporates a modified market system that extensively distributes income and wealth – either a "property-owning democracy" with widespread ownership of means of production, or liberal socialism.

See also CONTRACTARIANISM, JUSTICE, KANT, LIBERALISM, RIGHTS, UTILITARIANISM.
S.Fr.

Ray, John (1627–1705), English naturalist whose work on the structure and habits of plants and animals led to important conclusions on the methodology of classification and gave a strong impetus to the design argument in natural theology. In an early paper he argued that the determining characteristics of a species are those transmitted by seed, since color, scent, size, etc., vary with climate and nutriment. Parallels from the animal kingdom suggested the correct basis for classification would be structural. But we have no knowledge of real essences. Our experience of nature is of a continuum, and for practical purposes kinships are best identified by a plurality of criteria. His mature theory is set out in *Dissertatio Brevis* (1696) and *Methodus Emendata* (1703). *The Wisdom of God Manifested in the Works of the Creation* (1691 and three revisions) was a best-selling compendium of Ray's own scientific learning and was imitated and quarried by many later exponents of the design argument. Philosophically, he relied on others, from Cicero to Cudworth, and was superseded by Paley.
M.A.St.

Rāzī, al. See AL-RĀZĪ.

reactive attitude. See STRAWSON.

real assent. See NEWMAN.

real definition. See DEFINITION.

real distinction. See FUNDAMENTUM DIVISIONIS.

real essence. See ESSENTIALISM.

realism, direct. See DIRECT REALISM.

realism, internal. See PHILOSOPHY OF SCIENCE.

realism, metaphysical. See ARMSTRONG, METAPHYSICAL REALISM.

realism, modal. See LEWIS, DAVID.

realism, moral. See MORAL REALISM.

realism, naive. See PERCEPTION.

realism, perceptual. See PERCEPTION.

realism, scientific. See PHILOSOPHY OF SCIENCE; SELLARS, WILFRID.

realism, Scotistic. See DUNS SCOTUS.

realism *ante rem*. See PROPERTY.

realism *in rebus*. See PROPERTY.

reality, in standard philosophical usage, how things actually are, in contrast with their mere appearance. Appearance has to do with how things seem to a particular perceiver or group of perceivers. Reality is sometimes said to be two-way-independent of appearance. This means that appearance does not determine reality. First, no matter how much agreement there is, based on appearance, about the nature of reality, it is always conceivable that reality differs from appearance. Secondly, appearances are in no way required for reality: reality can outstrip the range of all investigations that we are in a position to make. It may be that reality always brings with it the possibility of appearances, in the counterfactual sense that if there were observers suitably situated, then if conditions were not conducive to error, they would have experiences of such-and-such a kind. But the truth of such a counterfactual seems to be grounded in the facts of reality. Phenomenalism holds, to the contrary, that the facts of reality can be explained by such counterfactuals, but phenomenalists have failed to produce adequate non-circular analyses.

The concept of reality on which it is two-way-independent of experience is sometimes called *objective reality*. However, Descartes used this phrase differently, to effect a contrast with formal or actual reality. He held that there must be at least as much reality in the efficient and total cause of an effect as in the effect itself, and applied this principle as follows: "There must be at least as much actual or formal reality in the efficient and total cause of an idea as objective reality in the idea itself." The objective reality of an idea seems to have to do with its having representational content, while actual or formal reality has to do with existence independent of the mind. Thus the quoted principle relates features of the cause of an idea to the representational content of the idea. Descartes's main intended applications were to God and material objects.

See also DESCARTES.   G.Fo.

reality principle. See FREUD.

realizability, multiple. See FUNCTIONALISM.

realization. See PHILOSOPHY OF MIND.

realization, physical. See REDUCTION.

real mathematics. See HILBERT'S PROGRAM.

real number. See MATHEMATICAL ANALYSIS.

real proposition. See HILBERT'S PROGRAM.

reason. See PRACTICAL REASON, THEORETICAL REASON.

reason, all-things-considered. See REASONS FOR ACTION.

reason, evidential. See EPISTEMOLOGY.

reason, exciting. See HUTCHESON.

reason, explaining. See REASONS FOR ACTION.

reason, justifying. See HUTCHESON.

reason, normative. See REASONS FOR ACTION.

reason, objective. See REASONS FOR ACTION.

reason, overriding. See REASONS FOR ACTION.

reason, practical. See KANT, PRACTICAL REASON.

reason, principle of sufficient. See LEIBNIZ.

reason, productive. See THEORETICAL REASON.

reason, pure. See KANT.

reason, subjective. See REASONS FOR ACTION.

reason, theoretical. See THEORETICAL REASON.

reasoning. See CIRCULAR REASONING, KANT, PRACTICAL REASONING.

reasoning, circular. See CIRCULAR REASONING.

reasoning, demonstrative. See INFERENCE.

reasons externalism. See EXTERNALISM.

reasons for action, considerations that call for or justify action. They may be subjective or objective. A *subjective reason* is a consideration an agent understands to support a course of action, whether or not it actually does. An *objective reason* is one that does support a course of action, regardless of whether the agent realizes it. What are cited as reasons may be matters either of fact or of value, but when facts are cited values are also relevant. Thus the fact that cigarette smoke contains nicotine is a reason for not smoking only because nicotine has undesirable effects. The most important evaluative reasons are *normative reasons* – i.e., considerations having (e.g.) ethical force. Facts become *obligating reasons* when, in conjunction with normative considerations, they give rise to an obligation. Thus in view of the obligation to help the needy, the fact that others are hungry is an obligating reason to see they are fed.

Reasons for action enter practical thinking as the contents of beliefs, desires, and other mental states. But not all the reasons one has need motivate the corresponding behavior. Thus I may recognize an obligation to pay taxes, yet do so only for fear of punishment. If so, then only my fear is an *explaining reason* for my action. An *overriding reason* is one that takes precedence over all others. It is often claimed that moral reasons override all others objectively, and should do so subjectively as well. Finally, one may speak of an *all-things-considered reason* – one that after due consideration is taken as finally determinative of what shall be done.

See also PRACTICAL REASON, REASONS FOR BELIEF.   H.J.M.

reasons for belief, roughly, bases of belief. The word 'belief' is commonly used to designate both a particular sort of psychological state, a state of believing, and a particular intentional content or proposition believed. Reasons for belief exhibit an analogous duality. A proposition, p, might be said to provide a *normative reason to believe* a proposition, q, for instance, when p bears some appropriate warranting relation to q. And p might afford a perfectly good reason to believe q, even though no one, as a matter of fact, believes either p or q. In contrast, p is a *reason that I have* for believing q, if I believe p and p counts as a reason (in the sense above) to believe q. Undoubtedly, I have reason to believe countless propositions that I shall never, as it happens, come to believe. Suppose, however, that p is a *reason for which* I believe q. In that case, I must believe both p and q, and p must be a reason to believe q – or, at any rate, I must regard it as such. It may be that I must, in addition, believe q at least in part *because* I believe p.

Reasons in these senses are inevitably epistemic; they turn on considerations of evidence, truth-conduciveness, and the like. But not all reasons for belief are of this sort. An explanatory reason, a *reason why* I believe p, may simply be an explanation for my having or coming to have this belief. Perhaps I believe p because I was brainwashed, or struck on the head, or because I have strong non-epistemic motives for this belief. (I might, of course, hold the belief on the basis of unexceptionable epistemic grounds. When this is so, my believing p may both warrant *and* explain my believing q.) Reflections of this sort can lead to questions concerning the overall or "all-things-considered" reasonableness of a given belief. Some philosophers (e.g., Clifford) argue that a belief's reasonableness depends exclusively on its epistemic standing: my believing p is reasonable for me provided it is epistemically reasonable for me; where belief is concerned, epistemic reasons are *overriding*. Others, siding with James, have focused on the role of belief in our psychological economy, arguing that the reasonableness of my holding a given belief can be affected by a variety of non-epistemic considerations. Suppose I have some evidence that p is false, but that I stand to benefit in a significant way from coming to believe p. If that is so, and if the practical advantages of my holding p considerably outweigh the practical disadvantages, it might seem obvious that my holding p is reasonable for me in some all-embracing sense.

See also PASCAL, REASONS FOR ACTION.
J.F.H.

reasons internalism. See EXTERNALISM.

rebirth, wheel of. See BUDDHISM, SAṀSĀRA.

recognition, rule of. See JURISPRUDENCE.

recollection. See PLATO, SURVIVAL.

reconstruction. See RATIONAL RECONSTRUCTION.

reconstruction, logical. See RATIONAL RECONSTRUCTION.

reconstruction, rational. See RATIONAL RECONSTRUCTION.

Rectification of Names. See CHENG MING.

recurrence, eternal. See ETERNAL RETURN.

recursion, definition by. See DEFINITION.

recursion, proof by. See PROOF BY RECURSION.

recursive function theory, a relatively recent area of mathematics that takes as its point of departure the study of an extremely limited class of arithmetic functions called the recursive functions. Strictly speaking, recursive function theory is a branch of higher arithmetic (number theory, or the theory of natural numbers) whose universe of discourse is restricted to the non-negative integers: 0, 1, 2, etc. However, the techniques and results of the newer area do not resemble those traditionally associated with number theory. The class of recursive functions is defined in a way that makes evident that every recursive function can be computed or calculated. The hypothesis that every calculable function is recursive, which is known as Church's thesis, is often taken as a kind of axiom in recursive function theory. This theory has played an important role in modern philosophy of mathematics, especially when epistemological issues are studied. See also CHURCH'S THESIS, COMPUTABILITY, PHILOSOPHY OF MATHEMATICS, PROOF BY RECURSION.   J.Cor.

redintegration, a psychological process, similar to

or involving classical conditioning, in which one feature of a situation causes a person to recall, visualize, or recompose an entire original situation. On opening a pack of cigarettes, a person may visualize the entire process, including striking the match, lighting the cigarette, and puffing. Redintegration is used as a technique in behavior therapy, e.g. when someone trying to refrain from smoking is exposed to unpleasant odors and vivid pictures of lungs caked with cancer, and then permitted to smoke. If the unpleasantness of the odors and visualization outweighs the reinforcement of smoking, the person may resist smoking.

Philosophically, redintegration is of interest for two reasons. First, the process may be critical in *prudence*. By bringing long-range consequences of behavior into focus in present deliberation, redintegration may help to protect long-range interests. Second, redintegration offers a role for visual images in producing behavior. Images figure in paradigmatic cases of redintegration. In recollecting pictures of cancerous lungs, the person may refrain from smoking.

See also COGNITIVE PSYCHOTHERAPY, CONDITIONING.   G.A.G.

reducibility, axiom of. See TYPE THEORY.

reduct, Craig. See CRAIG'S INTERPOLATION THEOREM.

reductio ad absurdum. (1) The principles $(A \supset \sim A) \supset \sim A$ and $(\sim A \supset A) \supset A$. (2) The argument forms 'If A then B and not-B; therefore, not-A' and 'If not-A then B and not-B; therefore, A' and arguments of these forms. Reasoning via such arguments is known as the *method of indirect proof.* (3) The rules of inference that permit (i) inferring not-A having derived a contradiction from A and (ii) inferring A having derived a contradiction from not-A. Both rules hold in classical logic and come to the same thing in any logic with the law of double negation. In intuitionist logic, however, (i) holds but (ii) does not. **See also DOUBLE NEGATION, MATHEMATICAL INTUITIONISM.**   G.F.S.

reduction, the replacement of one expression by a second expression that differs from the first in prima facie reference. So-called reductions have been meant in the sense of uniformly applicable explicit definitions, contextual definitions, or replacements suitable only in a limited range of contexts. Thus, authors have spoken of reductive

conceptual analyses, especially in the early days of analytic philosophy. In particular, in the sense-datum theory (talk of) physical objects was supposed to be reduced to (talk of) sense-data by explicit definitions or other forms of conceptual analysis.

Logical positivists talked of the reduction of theoretical vocabulary to an observational vocabulary, first by explicit definitions, and later by other devices, such as Carnap's *reduction sentences*. These appealed to a test condition predicate, T (e.g., 'is placed in water'), and a display predicate, D (e.g., 'dissolves'), to introduce a dispositional or other "non-observational" term, S (e.g., 'is water-soluble'): $(\forall x) [Tx \supset (Dx \supset Sx)]$, with '$\supset$' representing the material conditional. Negative reduction sentences for non-occurrence of S took the form $(\forall x) [NTx \supset (NDx \supset \sim Sx)]$. For coinciding predicate pairs T and TD and $\sim D$ and ND Carnap referred to bilateral reduction sentences: $(\forall x) [Tx \supset (Dx \equiv Sx)]$. Like so many other attempted reductions, reduction sentences did not achieve replacement of the "reduced" term, S, since they do not fix application of S when the test condition, T, fails to apply.

In the philosophy of mathematics, *logicism* claimed that all of mathematics could be reduced to logic, i.e., all mathematical terms could be defined with the vocabulary of logic and all theorems of mathematics could be derived from the laws of logic supplemented by these definitions. Russell's *Principia Mathematica* carried out much of such a program with a reductive base of something much more like what we now call set theory rather than logic, strictly conceived. Many now accept the reducibility of mathematics to set theory, but only in a sense in which reductions are not unique. For example, the natural numbers can equally well be modeled as classes of equinumerous sets or as von Neumann ordinals. This non-uniqueness creates serious difficulties, with suggestions that set-theoretic reductions can throw light on what numbers and other mathematical objects "really are."

In contrast, we take scientific theories to tell us, unequivocally, that water is H_2O and that temperature is mean translational kinetic energy. Accounts of theory reduction in science attempt to analyze the circumstance in which a "reducing theory" appears to tell us the composition of objects or properties described by a "reduced theory." The simplest accounts follow the general pattern of reduction: one provides "identity statements" or "bridge laws," with at least the form of explicit definitions, for all terms in the reduced theory not already appearing in the reducing theory; and then one argues that the reduced theory can be deduced from the reducing theory augmented by the definitions. For example, the laws of thermodynamics are said to be deducible from those of statistical mechanics, together with statements such as 'temperature is mean translational kinetic energy' and 'pressure is mean momentum transfer'.

How should the identity statements or bridge laws be understood? It takes empirical investigation to confirm statements such as that temperature is mean translational kinetic energy. Consequently, some have argued, such statements at best constitute contingent correlations rather than strict identities. On the other hand, if the relevant terms and their extensions are not mediated by analytic definitions, the identity statements may be analogized to identities involving two names, such as 'Cicero is Tully', where it takes empirical investigation to establish that the two names happen to have the same referent.

One can generalize the idea of theory reduction in a variety of ways. One may require the bridge laws to suffice for the deduction of the reduced from the reducing theory without requiring that the bridge laws take the form of explicit identity statements or biconditional correlations. Some authors have also focused on the fact that in practice a reducing theory T_2 corrects or refines the reduced theory T_1, so that it is really only a correction or refinement, T_1^*, that is deducible from T_2 and the bridge laws. Some have consequently applied the term 'reduction' to any pair of theories where the second corrects and extends the first in ways that explain both why the first theory was as accurate as it was and why it made the errors that it did. In this extended sense, relativity is said to reduce Newtonian mechanics.

Do the social sciences, especially psychology, in principle reduce to physics? This prospect would support the so-called identity theory (of mind and body), in particular resolving important problems in the philosophy of mind, such as the mind–body problem and the problem of other minds. Many (though by no means all) are now skeptical about the prospects for identifying mental properties, and the properties of other special sciences, with complex physical properties. To illustrate with an example from economics (adapted from Fodor), in the right circumstances just about any physical object could count as a piece of money. Thus prospects seem

dim for finding a closed and finite statement of the form 'being a piece of money is . . .', with only predicates from physics appearing on the right (though some would want to admit infinite definitions in providing reductions). Similarly, one suspects that attributes, such as pain, are at best functional properties with indefinitely many possible physical realizations. Believing that reductions by finitely stable definitions are thus out of reach, many authors have tried to express the view that mental properties are still somehow physical by saying that they nonetheless supervene on the physical properties of the organisms that have them.

In fact, these same difficulties that affect mental properties affect the paradigm case of temperature, and probably all putative examples of theoretical reduction. Temperature is mean translational temperature only in gases, and only idealized ones at that. In other substances, quite different physical mechanisms realize temperature. Temperature is more accurately described as a functional property, having to do with the mechanism of heat transfer between bodies, where, in principle, the required mechanism could be physically realized in indefinitely many ways.

In most and quite possibly all cases of putative theory reduction by strict identities, we have instead a relation of *physical realization*, constitution, or instantiation, nicely illustrated by the property of being a calculator (example taken from Cummins). The property of being a calculator can be physically realized by an abacus, by devices with gears and levers, by ones with vacuum tubes or silicon chips, and, in the right circumstances, by indefinitely many other physical arrangements. Perhaps many who have used 'reduction', particularly in the sciences, have intended the term in this sense of physical realization rather than one of strict identity.

Let us restrict attention to properties that reduce in the sense of having a physical realization, as in the cases of being a calculator, having a certain temperature, and being a piece of money. Whether or not an object counts as having properties such as these will depend, not only on the physical properties of that object, but on various circumstances of the context. Intensions of relevant language users constitute a plausible candidate for relevant circumstances. In at least many cases, dependence on context arises because the property constitutes a functional property, where the relevant functional system (calculational practices, heat transfer, monetary systems) are much larger than the property-bearing object in question. These examples raise the question of whether many and perhaps all mental properties depend ineliminably on relations to things outside the organisms that have the mental properties.

See also EXPLANATION, PHILOSOPHY OF SCIENCE, SUPERVENIENCE, UNITY OF SCIENCE.
P.Te.

reduction, phenomenological. See HUSSERL.

reduction base. See REDUCTION.

reductionism. See REDUCTION.

reductionism, explanatory. See METHODOLOGICAL HOLISM.

reduction sentence, for a given predicate Q_3 of space-time points in a first-order language, any universal sentence S_1 of the form: (x) $[Q_1 x \supset (Q_2 x \supset Q_3 x)]$, provided that the predicates Q_1 and Q_2 are consistently applicable to the same space-time points. If S_1 has the form given above and S_2 is of the form (x) $[Q_4 x \supset (Q_5 \supset \sim Q_6)]$ and either S_1 is a reduction sentence for Q_3 or S_2 is a reduction sentence for $\sim Q_3$, the pair $\{S_1, S_2\}$ is a reduction pair for Q_3. If $Q_1 = Q_4$ and $Q_2 = \sim Q_5$, the conjunction of S_1 and S_2 is equivalent to a bilateral reduction sentence for Q_3 of the form (x) $[Q_1 \supset (Q_3 \equiv Q_2)]$.

These concepts were introduced by Carnap in "Testability and Meaning," *Philosophy of Science* (1936–37), to modify the verifiability criterion of meaning to a confirmability condition where terms can be introduced into meaningful scientific discourse by chains of reduction pairs rather than by definitions. The incentive for this modification seems to have been to accommodate the use of disposition predicates in scientific discourse. Carnap proposed explicating a disposition predicate Q_3 by bilateral reduction sentences for Q_3. An important but controversial feature of Carnap's approach is that it avoids appeal to non-extensional conditionals in explicating disposition predicates.

See also CARNAP, REDUCTION, VERIFICATIONISM.
I.L.

reductive naturalism. See NATURALISM.

redundancy theory of truth. See TRUTH.

reference. See MEANING, PHILOSOPHY OF LANGUAGE, THEORY OF DESCRIPTIONS.

reference, causal-historical theory of. See PHILOSOPHY OF LANGUAGE.

reference, description theory of. See PHILOSOPHY OF LANGUAGE.

reference, direct. See CAUSAL THEORY OF PROPER NAMES.

reference, historical theory of. See PHILOSOPHY OF LANGUAGE.

reference, inscrutability of. See INDETERMINACY OF TRANSLATION.

reference, new theory of. See PUTNAM.

reference class. See PROBABILITY.

referential. See REFERENTIALLY TRANSPARENT.

referentially transparent. An occurrence of a singular term t in a sentence '. . . t . . .' is referentially transparent (or purely referential) if and only if the truth-value of '. . . t . . .' depends on whether the referent of t satisfies the open sentence '. . . x . . .'; the satisfaction of '. . . x . . .' by the referent of t would guarantee the truth of '. . . t . . .', and failure of this individual to satisfy '. . . x . . .' would guarantee that '. . . t . . .' was not true. 'Boston is a city' is true if and only if the referent of 'Boston' satisfies the open sentence 'x is a city', so the occurrence of 'Boston' is referentially transparent. But in 'The expression "Boston" has six letters', the length of the word within the quotes, not the features of the city Boston, determines the truth-value of the sentence, so the occurrence is not referentially transparent.

According to a Fregean theory of meaning, the reference of any complex expression (that is a meaningful unit) is a function of the referents of its parts. Within this context, an occurrence of a referential term t in a meaningful expression '. . . t . . .' is referentially transparent (or purely referential) if and only if t contributes its referent to the reference of '. . . t . . .'. The expression 'the area around Boston' refers to the particular area it does because of the referent of 'Boston' (and the reference or extension of the function expressed by 'the area around x').

An occurrence of a referential term t in a meaningful expression '. . . t . . .' is *referentially opaque* if and only if it is not referentially transparent. Thus, if t has a referentially opaque occurrence in a sentence '. . . t . . .', then the truth-value of '. . . t . . .' depends on something other than whether the referent of t satisfies '. . . x . . .'.

Although these definitions apply to occurrences of referential terms, the terms 'referentially opaque' and 'referentially transparent' are used primarily to classify linguistic contexts for terms as referentially opaque contexts. If t occurs purely referentially in S but not in C(S), then C( ) is a referentially opaque context. But we must qualify this: C( ) is a referentially opaque context *for that occurrence of t in S*. It would not follow (without further argument) that C( ) is a referentially opaque context for other occurrences of terms in sentences that could be placed into C( ).

Contexts of quotation, propositional attitude, and modality have been widely noted for their potential to produce referential opacity. Consider:

(1) John believes that the number of planets is less than eight.
(2) John believes that nine is less than eight.

If (1) is true but (2) is not, then either 'the number of planets' or 'nine' has an occurrence that is not purely referential, because the sentences would differ in truth-value even though the expressions are co-referential. But within the sentences:

(3) The number of planets is less than eight.
(4) Nine is less than eight.

the expressions appear to have purely referential occurrence. In (3) and (4), the truth-value of the sentence as a whole depends on whether the referent of 'The number of planets' and 'Nine' satisfies 'x is less than eight'. Because the occurrences in (3) and (4) are purely referential but those in (1) and (2) are not, the context 'John believes that ( )' is a referentially opaque context for the relevant occurrence of at least one of the two singular terms. Some argue that the occurrence of 'nine' in (2) is purely referential because the truth-value of the sentence as a whole depends on whether the referent, nine, satisfies the open sentence 'John believes that x is less than eight'. Saying so requires that we make sense of the concept of satisfaction for such sentences (belief sentences and others) and that we show that the concept of satisfaction applies in this way in the case at hand (sentence (2)). There is controversy about whether these things can be done. In (1), on the other hand, the truth-value is not determined by whether nine (the referent of 'the number of planets') satisfies the open sen-

tence, so that occurrence is not purely referential.

Modal contexts raise similar questions.

(5) Necessarily, nine is odd.
(6) Necessarily, the number of planets is odd.

If (5) is true but (6) is not, then at least one of the expressions does not have a purely referential occurrence, even though both appear to be purely referential in the non-modal sentence that appears in the context 'Necessarily, _____'. Thus the context is referentially opaque for the occurrence of at least one of these terms.

On an alternative approach, genuinely singular terms always occur referentially, and 'the number of planets' is not a genuinely singular term. Russell's theory of definite descriptions, e.g., provides an alternative semantic analysis for sentences involving definite descriptions. This would enable us to say that even simple sentences like (3) and (4) differ considerably in syntactic and semantic structure, so that the similarity that suggests the problem, the seemingly similar occurrences of co-referential terms, is merely apparent.

See also DE DICTO, QUANTIFYING IN, SUBSTITUTIVITY SALVA VERITATE.   T.M.

referential occurrence. See QUANTIFYING IN.

referential opacity. See REFERENTIALLY TRANSPARENT.

referential quantification. See QUANTIFICATION.

referential theory of meaning. See MEANING, PHILOSOPHY OF LANGUAGE.

reflection principles, two varieties of internal statements related to correctness in formal axiomatic systems.

(1) *Proof-theoretic reflection principles* are formulated for effectively presented systems S that contain a modicum of elementary number theory sufficient to arithmetize their own syntactic notions, as done by Kurt Gödel in his 1931 work on incompleteness. Let $Prov_S(x)$ express that x is the Gödel number of a statement provable in S, and let n_A be the number of A, for any statement A of S. The weakest reflection principle considered for S is the collection $Rfn(S)$ of all statements of the form $Prov_S(n_A) \to A$, which express that if A is provable from S then A (is true). The proposition Con_S expressing the consistency of S is a consequence of $Rfn(S)$ (obtained by taking A to be a disprovable statement). Thus, by Gödel's second

incompleteness theorem, $Rfn(S)$ is stronger than S if S is consistent. Reflection principles are used in the construction of ordinal logics as a systematic means of overcoming incompleteness.

(2) *Set-theoretic reflection principles* are formulated for systems S of axiomatic set theory, such as ZF (Zermelo-Fraenkel). In the simplest form they express that any property A in the language of S that holds of the universe of "all" sets, already holds of a portion of that universe coextensive with some set x. This takes the form $A \rightarrow (\exists x)A^{(x)}$ where in $A^{(x)}$ all quantifiers of A are relativized to x. In contrast to proof-theoretic reflection principles, these may be established as theorems of ZF.

See also GÖDEL'S INCOMPLETENESS THEOREMS, ORDINAL LOGIC, SET THEORY.   S.Fe.

reflective equilibrium, as usually conceived, a coherence method for justifying evaluative principles and theories. The method was first described by Goodman, who proposed it be used to justify deductive and inductive principles. According to Goodman (*Fact, Fiction and Forecast,* 1965), a particular deductive inference is justified by its conforming with deductive principles, but these principles are justified in their turn by conforming with accepted deductive practice. The idea, then, is that justified inferences and principles are those that emerge from a process of mutual adjustment, with principles being revised when they sanction inferences we cannot bring ourselves to accept, and particular inferences being rejected when they conflict with rules we are unwilling to revise. Thus, neither principles nor particular inferences are epistemically privileged. At least in principle, everything is liable to revision.

Rawls further articulated the method of reflective equilibrium and applied it in ethics. According to Rawls (*A Theory of Justice,* 1971), inquiry begins with considered moral judgments, i.e., judgments about which we are confident and which are free from common sources of error, e.g., ignorance of facts, insufficient reflection, or emotional agitation. According to *narrow reflective equilibrium,* ethical principles are justified by bringing them into coherence with our considered moral judgments through a process of mutual adjustment. Rawls, however, pursues a *wide reflective equilibrium.* Wide equilibrium is attained by proceeding to consider alternatives to the moral conception accepted in narrow equilibrium, along with philosophical arguments that might decide among these conceptions. The principles and considered judgments accepted in narrow equilibrium are then adjusted as seems appropriate. One way to conceive of wide reflective equilibrium is as an effort to construct a coherent system of belief by a process of mutual adjustment to considered moral judgments and moral principles (as in narrow equilibrium) along with the background philosophical, social scientific, and any other relevant beliefs that might figure in the arguments for and against alternative moral conceptions, e.g., metaphysical views regarding the nature of persons. As in Goodman's original proposal, none of the judgments, principles, or theories involved is privileged: all are open to revision.

See also COHERENTISM, RAWLS.   M.R.D.

reflexive. See RELATION.

reformed epistemology. See EXISTENTIALISM, PLANTINGA.

regional supervenience. See SUPERVENIENCE.

regress. See INFINITE REGRESS ARGUMENT, VICIOUS REGRESS.

regress argument. See EPISTEMIC REGRESS ARGUMENT, INFINITE REGRESS ARGUMENT.

regression analysis, a part of statistical theory concerned with the analysis of data with the aim of inferring a linear functional relationship between assumed independent ("regressor") variables and a dependent ("response") variable. A typical example involves the dependence of crop yield on the application of fertilizer. For the most part, higher amounts of fertilizer are associated with higher yields. But typically, if crop yield is plotted vertically on a graph with the horizontal axis representing amount of fertilizer applied, the resulting points will not fall in a straight line. This can be due either to random ("stochastic") fluctuations (involving measurement errors, irreproducible conditions, or physical indeterminism) or to failure to take into account other relevant independent variables (such as amount of rainfall). In any case, from any resulting "scatter diagram," it is possible mathematically to infer a "best-fitting" line. One method is, roughly, to find the line that minimizes the average absolute distance between a line and the data points collected. More commonly, the average of the squares of these distances is minimized (this is the "least squares" method). If more than one independent variable is suspected, the theory of *multiple regression,* which takes into account multiple regressors, can be applied: this can help to minimize an "error term" involved in regression. Computers must be used for the complex computations typically encountered. Care must be taken in connection with the possibility that a lawlike, causal dependence is not really linear (even approximately) over all ranges of the regressor variables (e.g., in certain ranges of amounts of application, more fertilizer is good for a plant, but too much is bad). **See also** CURVE-FITTING PROBLEM.   E.Ee.

regressor variable. See REGRESSION ANALYSIS.

regularity theory of causation. See CAUSATION.

regulative principle. See KANT.

Reichenbach, Hans (1891–1953), German philosopher of science and a major leader of the movement known as logical empiricism. Born in Hamburg, he studied engineering for a brief time, then turned to mathematics, philosophy, and physics, which he pursued at the universities of Berlin, Munich, and Göttingen. He took his doctorate in philosophy at Erlangen (1915) with a dissertation on mathematical and philosophical aspects of probability, and a degree in mathematics and physics by state examination at Göttingen (1916). In 1933, with Hitler's rise to power, he fled to Istanbul, then to the University of California at Los Angeles, where he remained until his death. Prior to his departure from Germany he was professor of philosophy of science at the University of Berlin, leader of the Berlin Group of logical empiricists, and a close associate of Einstein. With Carnap he founded *Erkenntnis*, the major journal of scientific philosophy before World War II.

After a short period early in his career as a follower of Kant, Reichenbach rejected the synthetic a priori, chiefly because of considerations arising out of Einstein's general theory of relativity. He remained thereafter champion of empiricism, adhering to a probabilistic version of the verifiability theory of cognitive meaning. Never, however, did he embrace the logical positivism of the Vienna Circle; indeed, he explicitly described his principal epistemological work, *Experience and Prediction* (1938), as his refutation of logical positivism. In particular, his *logical empiricism* consisted in rejecting phenomenalism in favor of physicalism; he rejected phenomenalism both in embracing scientific realism and in insisting on a thoroughgoing probabilistic analysis of scientific meaning and scientific knowledge.

His main works span a wide range. In *Probability and Induction* he advocated the frequency interpretation of probability and offered a pragmatic justification of induction. In his philosophy of space and time he defended conventionality of geometry and of simultaneity. In foundations of quantum mechanics he adopted a three-valued logic to deal with causal anomalies. He wrote major works on epistemology, logic, laws of nature, counterfactuals, and modalities. At the time of his death he had almost completed *The Direction of Time*, which was published posthumously (1956).

See also CARNAP, LOGICAL POSITIVISM, PHILOSOPHY OF SCIENCE, PROBLEM OF INDUCTION, VIENNA CIRCLE.   W.C.S.

Reid, Thomas (1710–96), Scottish philosopher, a defender of common sense and critic of the theory of impressions and ideas articulated by Hume. Reid was born exactly one year before Hume, in Strachan, Scotland. A bright lad, he went to Marischal College in Aberdeen at the age of twelve, studying there with Thomas Blackwell and George Turnbull. The latter apparently had great influence on Reid. Turnbull contended that knowledge of the facts of sense and introspection may not be overturned by reasoning and that volition is the only active power known from experience. Turnbull defended common sense under the cloak of Berkeley. Reid threw off that cloak with considerable panache, but he took over the defense of common sense from Turnbull.

Reid moved to a position of regent and lecturer at King's College in Aberdeen in 1751. There he formed, with John Gregory, the Aberdeen Philosophical Society, which met fortnightly, often to discuss Hume. Reid published his *Inquiry into the Human Mind on the Principles of Common Sense* in 1764, and, in the same year, succeeded Adam Smith in the chair of moral philosophy at Old College in Glasgow. After 1780 he no longer lectured but devoted himself to his later works, *Essays on the Intellectual Powers* (1785) and *Essays on the Active Powers* (1788). He was highly influential in Scotland and on the Continent in the eighteenth century and, from time to time, in England and the United States thereafter.

Reid thought that one of his major contributions was the refutation of Hume's theory of impressions and ideas. Reid probably was convinced in his teens of the truth of Berkeley's doctrine that what the mind is immediately aware of is always some idea, but his later study of Hume's *Treatise* convinced him that, contrary to

Berkeley, it was impossible to reconcile this doctrine, the theory of ideas, with common sense. Hume had rigorously developed the theory, Reid said, and drew forth the conclusions. These, Reid averred, were absurd. They included the denial of our knowledge of body and mind, and, even more strikingly, of our conceptions of these things.

The reason Reid thought that Hume's theory of ideas led to these conclusions was that for Hume, ideas were faded impressions of sense, hence, sensations. No sensation is like a quality of a material thing, let alone like the object that has the quality. Consider movement. Movement is a quality of an object wherein the object changes from one place to another, but the visual sensation that arises in us is not the change of place of an object, it is an activity of mind. No two things could, in fact, be more unalike. If what is before the mind is always some sensation, whether vivacious or faded, we should never obtain the conception of something other than a sensation. Hence, we could never even conceive of material objects and their qualities. Even worse, we could not conceive of our own minds, for they are not sensations either, and only sensations are immediately before the mind, according to the theory of ideas. Finally, and even more absurdly, we could not conceive of past sensations or anything that does not now exist. For all that is immediately before the mind is sensations that exist presently. Thus, we could not even conceive of qualities, bodies, minds, and things that do not now exist. But this is absurd, since it is obvious that we do think of all these things and even of things that have never existed. The solution, Reid suggested, is to abandon the theory of ideas and seek a better one.

Many have thought Reid was unfair to Hume and misinterpreted him. Reid's *Inquiry* was presented to Hume by Dr. Blair in manuscript form, however, and in reply Hume does not at all suggest that he has been misinterpreted or handled unfairly. Whatever the merits of Reid's criticism of Hume, it was the study of the consequences of Hume's philosophy that accounts for Reid's central doctrine of the human faculties and their first principles. Faculties are innate powers, among them the powers of conception and conviction. Reid's strategy in reply to Hume is to build a *nativist theory of conception* on the failure of Hume's theory of ideas. Where the theory of ideas, the doctrine of impressions and ideas, fails to account for our conception of something, of qualities, bodies, minds, past things, nonexistent things, Reid hypothesizes that our conceptions

originate from a *faculty* of the mind, i.e., from an innate power of conception.

This line of argument reflects Reid's respect for Hume, whom he calls the greatest metaphysician of the age, because Hume drew forth the consequences of a theory of conception, which we might call *associationism*, according to which all our conceptions result from associating sensations. Where the associationism of Hume failed, Reid hypothesized that conceptions arise from innate powers of conception that manifest themselves in accordance with original *first principles* of the mind. The resulting hypotheses were not treated as a priori necessities but as empirical hypotheses. Reid notes, therefore, that there are marks by which we can discern the operation of an innate first principle, which include the early appearance of the operation, its universality in mankind, and its irresistibility. The operations of the mind that yield our conceptions of qualities, bodies, and minds all bear these marks, Reid contends, and that warrants the conclusion that they manifest first principles. It should be noted that Reid conjectured that nature would be frugal in the implantation of innate powers, supplying us with no more than necessary to produce the conceptions we manifest. Reid is, consequently, a parsimonious empiricist in the development of his nativist psychology.

Reid developed his theory of perception in great detail and his development led, surprisingly, to his articulation of non-Euclidean geometry. Indeed, while Kant was erroneously postulating the a priori necessity of Euclidean space, Reid was developing non-Euclidean geometry to account for the empirical features of visual space. Reid's theory of perception is an example of his empiricism. In the *Inquiry*, he says that sensations, which are operations of the mind, and impressions on the organs of sense, which are material, produce our conceptions of primary and secondary qualities. Sensations produce our original conceptions of secondary qualities as the causes of those sensations. They are signs that suggest the existence of the qualities. A sensation of smell suggests the existence of a quality in the object that causes the sensation, though the character of the cause is otherwise unknown. Thus, our original conception of secondary qualities is a relative conception of some unknown cause of a sensation. Our conception of primary qualities differs not, as Locke suggested, because of some resemblance between the sensation and the quality (for, as Berkeley noted, there is no resemblance between a sensation and quality), but because our original conceptions of primary qualities are clear and distinct. The sensation is a sign that suggests a definite conception of the primary quality, e.g. a definite conception of the movement of the object, rather than a mere conception of something, we know not what, that gives rise to the sensation.

These conceptions of qualities signified by sensations result from the operations of principles of our natural constitution. These signs, which suggest the conception of qualities, also suggest a conception of some object that has them. This conception of the object is also relative, in that it is simply a conception of a subject of the qualities. In the case of physical qualities, the conception of the object is a conception of a material object. Though sensations, which are activities of the mind, suggest the existence of qualities, they are not the only signs of sense perception. Some impressions on the organs of sense, the latter being material, also give rise to conceptions of qualities, especially to our conception of visual figure, the seen shape of the object. But Reid can discern no sensation of shape. There are, of course, sensations of color, but he is convinced from the experience of those who have cataracts and see color but not shape that the sensations of color are insufficient to suggest our conceptions of visual figure.

His detailed account of vision and especially of the seeing of visual figure leads him to one of his most brilliant moments. He asks what sort of data do we receive upon the eye and answers that the data must be received at the round surface of the eyeball and processed within. Thus, visual space is a projection in three dimensions of the information received on the round surface of the eye, and the geometry of this space is a non-Euclidean geometry of curved space. Reid goes on to derive the properties of the space quite correctly, e.g., in concluding that the angles of a triangle will sum to a figure greater than 180 degrees and thereby violate the parallels postulate. Thus Reid discovered that a non-Euclidean geometry was satisfiable and, indeed, insisted that it accurately described the space of vision (not, however, the space of touch, which he thought was Euclidean). From the standpoint of his theory of perceptual signs, the example of visual figure helps to clarify his doctrine of the signs of perception. We do not perceive signs and infer what they signify. This inference, Reid was convinced by Hume, would lack the support of reasoning, and Reid concluded that reasoning was, in this case, superfluous. The information received on the surface of the eye produces our conceptions of visual figure immediately. Indeed, these signs pass unnoticed as they give rise to the conception of visual figure in the mind. The relation of sensory signs to the external things they signify originally is effected by a first principle of the mind without the use of reason.

The first principles that yield our conceptions of qualities and objects yield convictions of the existence of these things at the same time. A question naturally arises as to the evidence of these convictions. First principles yield the convictions along with the conceptions, but do we have evidence of the existence of the qualities and objects we are convinced exist? We have the evidence of our senses, of our natural faculties, and that is all the evidence possible here. Reid's point is that the convictions in questions resulting from the original principles of our faculties are immediately justified. Our faculties are, however, all fallible, so the justification that our original convictions possess may be refuted.

We can now better understand Reid's reply to Hume. To account for our convictions of the existence of body, we must abandon Hume's theory of ideas, which cannot supply even the conception of body. We must discover both the original first principles that yield the conception and conviction of objects and their qualities, and first principles to account for our convictions of the past, of other thinking beings, and of morals. Just as there are first principles of perception that yield convictions of the existence of presently existing objects, so there are first principles of memory that yield the convictions of the existence of past things, principles of testimony that yield the convictions of the thoughts of others, and principles of morals that yield convictions of our obligations.

Reid's defense of a moral faculty alongside the faculties of perception and memory is striking. The moral faculty yields conceptions of the justice and injustice of an action in response to our conception of that action. Reid shrewdly notes that different people may conceive of the same action in different ways. I may conceive of giving some money as an action of gratitude, while you may consider it squandering money. How we conceive of an action depends on our moral education, but the response of our moral faculty to an action conceived in a specific way is original and the same in all who have the faculty. Hence differences in moral judgment are due, not to principles of the moral faculty, but to differences in how we conceive of our actions. This doctrine of a moral faculty again provides a counterpoint to the moral philosophy of Hume, for, according to Reid, judgments of justice and injustice pertaining to all matters, including promises, contracts, and property, arise from our natural faculties and do not depend on anything artificial.

Reid's strategy for defending common sense is clear enough. He thinks that Hume showed that we cannot arrive at our convictions of external objects, of past events, of the thoughts of others, of morals, or, for that matter, of our own minds, from reasoning about impressions and ideas. Since those convictions are a fact, philosophy must account for them in the only way that remains, by the hypothesis of innate faculties that yield them. But do we have any evidence for these convictions? Evidence, Reid says, is the ground of belief, and our evidence is that of our faculties. Might our faculties deceive us? Reid answers that it is a first principle of our faculties that they are not fallacious. Why should we assume that our faculties are not fallacious? First, the belief is irresistible. However we wage war with first principles, the principles of common sense, they prevail in daily life. There we trust our faculties whether we choose to or not. Second, all philosophy depends on the assumption that our faculties are not fallacious. Here Reid employs an ad hominem argument against Hume, but one with philosophical force. Reid says that, in response to a total skeptic who decides to trust none of his faculties, he puts his hand over his mouth in silence. But Hume trusted reason and consciousness, and therefore is guilty of pragmatic inconsistency in calling the other faculties into doubt. They come from the same shop, Reid says, and he who calls one into doubt has no right to trust the others. All our faculties are fallible, and, therefore, we must, to avoid arbitrary favoritism, trust them all at the outset or trust none. The first principles of our faculties are trustworthy. They not only account for our convictions, but are the ground and evidence of those convictions. This *nativism* is the original engine of justification.

Reid's theory of original perceptions is supplemented by a theory of *acquired perceptions*, those which incorporate the effects of habit and association, such as the perception of a passing coach. He distinguishes acquired perceptions from effects of reasoning. The most important way our original perceptions must be supplemented is by general conceptions. These result from a process whereby our attention is directed to some individual quality, e.g., the whiteness of a piece of paper, which he calls *abstraction*, and a further process of generalizing from the individual quality to the general conception of the universal whiteness shared by many individuals.

Reid is a sophisticated *nominalist;* he says that the only things that exist are individual, but he includes individual qualities as well as individual objects. The reason is that individual qualities obviously exist and are needed as the basis of generalization. To generalize from an individual we must have some conception of what it is like, and this conception cannot be general, on pain of circularity or regress, but must be a conception of an individual quality, e.g., the whiteness of this paper, which it uniquely possesses. Universals, though predicated of objects to articulate our knowledge, do not exist. We can think of universals, just as we can think of centaurs, but though they are the objects of thought and predicated of individuals that exist, they do not themselves exist. Generalization is not driven by ontology but by utility. It is we and not nature that sort things into kinds in ways that are useful to us. This leads to a division-of-labor theory of meaning because general conceptions are the meanings of general words. Thus, in those domains in which there are experts, in science or the law, we defer to the experts concerning the general conceptions that are the most useful in the area in question.

Reid's theory of the *intellectual powers,* summarized briefly above, is supplemented by his theory of our *active powers,* those that lead to actions. His theory of the active powers includes a theory of the principles of actions. These include animal principles that operate without understanding, but the most salient and philosophically important part of Reid's theory of the active powers is his theory of the rational principles of action, which involve understanding and the will. These rational principles are those in which we have a conception of the action to be performed and will its performance. Action thus involves an act of will or volition, but volitions as Reid conceived of them are not the esoteric inventions of philosophy but, instead, the commonplace activities of deciding and resolving to act.

Reid is a *libertarian* and maintains that our liberty or freedom refutes the principle of necessity or determinism. Freedom requires the power to will the action and also the power not to will it. The principle of necessity tells us that our action was necessitated and, therefore, that it was not in our power not to have willed as we did. It is not sufficient for freedom, as Hume suggested, that we act as we will. We must also have the power to determine what we will. The reason is that willing is the means to the end of action, and he who lacks power over the means lacks power over the end.

This doctrine of the active power over the determinations of our will is founded on the central principle of Reid's theory of the active powers, the principle of agent causation. The doctrine of acts of the will or volitions does not lead to a regress, as critics allege, because my act of will is an exercise of the most basic kind of causality, the efficient causality of an agent. I am the efficient cause of my acts of will. My act of will need not be caused by an antecedent act of will because my act of will is the result of my exercise of my causal power. This fact also refutes an objection to the doctrine of liberty – that if my action is not necessitated, then it is fortuitous. My free actions are *caused,* not fortuitous, though they are not necessitated, because they are caused *by me.*

How, one might inquire, do we know that we are free? The doubt that we are free is like other skeptical doubts, and receives a similar reply, namely, that the conviction of our freedom is a natural and original conviction arising from our faculties. It occurs prior to instruction and it is irresistible in practical life. Any person with two identical coins usable to pay for some item must be convinced that she can pay with the one or the other; and, unlike the ass of Buridan, she readily exercises her power to will the one or the other. The conviction of freedom is an original one, not the invention of philosophy, and it arises from the first principles of our natural faculties, which are trustworthy and not fallacious. The first principles of our faculties hang together like links in a chain, and one must either raise up the whole or the links prove useless. Together, they are the foundation of true philosophy, science, and practical life, and without them we shall lead ourselves into the coalpit of skepticism and despair.

See also AGENT CAUSATION, EMPIRICISM, HUME, IMMEDIACY, PERCEPTION, SCOTTISH COMMON SENSE PHILOSOPHY.   K.L.

reify. See HYPOSTASIS.

Reimarus, Hermann Samuel (1694–1768), German philosopher, born in Hamburg and educated in philosophy and theology at Jena. For most of his life he taught Oriental languages at a high school in Hamburg. The most important writings he published were a treatise on natural

religion, *Abhandlungen von den vornehmsten Wahrheiten der natürlichen Religion* (1754); a textbook on logic, *Vernunftlehre* (1756); and an interesting work on instincts in animals, *Allgemeine Betrachtungen über die Triebe der Tiere* (1760). However, he is today best known for his *Apologie oder Schutzschrift für die vernünftigen Verehrer Gottes* ("Apology for or Defense of the Rational Worshipers of God"), posthumously published in 1774–77. In it, Reimarus reversed his stance on natural theology and openly advocated a deism in the British tradition. The controversy created by its publication had a profound impact on the further development of German theology. Though Reimarus always remained basically a follower of Wolff, he was often quite critical of Wolffian rationalism in his discussion of logic and psychology. **See also** WOLFF.   M.K.

Reinhold, Karl Leonhard (1743–1819), Austrian philosopher who was both a popularizer and a critic of Kant. He was the first occupant of the chair of critical philosophy established at the University of Jena in 1787. His *Briefe über die Kantische Philosophie* (1786/87) helped to popularize Kantianism. Reinhold also proclaimed the need for a more "scientific" presentation of the critical philosophy, in the form of a rigorously deductive system in which everything is derivable from a single first principle ("the principle of consciousness"). He tried to satisfy this need with *Elementarphilosophie* ("Elementary Philosophy" or "Philosophy of the Elements"), expounded in his *Versuch einer neuen Theorie des menschlichen Vorstellungsvermögens* ("Attempt at a New Theory of the Human Faculty of Representation," 1789), *Beyträge zur Berichtigung bisheriger Missverständnisse der Philosophen* I ("Contributions to the Correction of the Prevailing Misunderstandings of Philosophers," 1790), and *Ueber das Fundament des philosophischen Wissens* ("On the Foundation of Philosophical Knowledge," 1791). His criticism of the duality of Kant's starting point and of the ad hoc character of his deductions contributed to the demand for a more coherent exposition of transcendental idealism, while his strategy for accomplishing this task stimulated others (above all, Fichte) to seek an even more "fundamental" first principle for philosophy. Reinhold later became an enthusiastic adherent, first of Fichte's *Wissenschaftslehre* and then of Bardili's "rational realism," before finally adopting a novel "linguistic" approach to philosophical problems. **See also** FICHTE, KANT, NEO-KANTIANISM.   D.Br.

reism, also called concretism, the theory that the basic entities are concrete objects. Reism differs from nominalism in that the problem of universals is not its only motivation and often not the principal motivation for the theory. Three types of reism can be distinguished.

(1) Brentano held that every object is a concrete or individual thing. He said that substances, aggregates of substances, parts of substances, and individual properties of substances are the only things that exist. There is no such thing as the *existence* or *being* of an object; and there are no non-existent objects. One consequence of this doctrine is that the object of thought (what the thought is about) is always an individual object and not a proposition. For example, the thought that this paper is white is about this paper and not about the proposition that this paper is white. Meinong attacked Brentano's concretism and argued that thoughts are about "objectives," not objects.

(2) Kotarbiński, who coined the term 'reism', holds as a basic principle that only concrete objects exist. Although things may be hard or soft, red or blue, there is no such thing as hardness, softness, redness, or blueness. Sentences that contain abstract words are either strictly meaningless or can be paraphrased into sentences that do not contain any abstract words. Kotarbinski is both a nominalist and a materialist. (Brentano was a nominalist and a dualist.)

(3) Thomas Garrigue Masaryk's concretism is quite different from the first two. For him, concretism is the theory that all of a person's cognitive faculties participate in every instance of knowing: reason, senses, emotion, and will.

See also BRENTANO, KOTARBIŃSKI, MEINONG.   A.P.M.

relation, a two-or-more-place property (e.g., *loves* or *between*), or the extension of such a property. In set theory, a relation is any set of ordered pairs (or triplets, etc., but these are reducible to pairs). For simplicity, the formal exposition here uses the language of set theory, although an intensional (property-theoretic) view is later assumed.

The *terms* of a relation R are the members of the pairs constituting R, the items that R relates. The collection D of all first terms of pairs in R is the *domain* of R; any collection with D as a subcollection may also be so called. Similarly, the second terms of these pairs make up (or are a subcollection of) the *range* (*counterdomain* or *converse domain*) of R. One usually works within a set

U such that R is a subset of the *Cartesian product* U×U (the set of all ordered pairs on U).

Relations can be:

(1) *reflexive* (or exhibit *reflexivity*): for all *a*, *aRa*. That is, a reflexive relation is one that, like identity, each thing bears to itself. Examples: *a* weighs as much as *b*; or the *universal relation*, i.e., the relation R such that for all *a* and *b*, *aRb*.

(2) *symmetrical* (or exhibit *symmetry*): for all *a* and *b*, *aRb* → *bRa*. In a symmetrical relation, the order of the terms is reversible. Examples: *a* is a sibling of *b*; *a* and *b* have a common divisor. Also symmetrical is the *null relation*, under which no object is related to anything.

(3) *transitive* (or exhibit *transitivity*): for all *a*, *b*, and *c*, (*aRb* & *bRc*) → *aRc*. Transitive relations carry across a middle term. Examples: *a* is less than *b*; *a* is an ancestor of *b*. Thus, if *a* is less than *b* and *b* is less than *c*, *a* is less than *c*: *less than* has carried across the middle term, *b*.

(4) *antisymmetrical*: for all *a* and *b*, (*aRb* & *bRa*) → *a* = *b*.

(5) *trichotomous, connected,* or *total* (*trichotomy*): for all *a* and *b*, *aRb* ∨ *bRa* ∨ *a* = *b*.

(6) *asymmetrical*: *aRb* & *bRa* holds for no *a* and *b*.

(7) *functional: for all *a*, *b*, and *c*, (*aRb* & *aRc*) → *b* = *c*. In a functional relation (which may also be called a function), each first term uniquely determines a second term.

R is *non-reflexive* if it is not reflexive, i.e., if the condition (1) fails for at least one object *a*. R is *non-symmetric* if (2) fails for at least one pair of objects (*a*, *b*). Analogously for *non-transitive*. R is *irreflexive* (aliorelative) if (1) holds for no object *a* and intransitive if (3) holds for no objects *a*, *b*, and *c*. Thus *understands* is non-reflexive since some things do not understand themselves, but not irreflexive, since some things do; *loves* is non-symmetric but not asymmetrical; and *being a cousin of* is non-transitive but not intransitive, as *being mother of* is.

(1)–(3) define an *equivalence relation* (e.g., the identity relation among numbers or the relation of being the same age as among people). A class of objects bearing an equivalence relation R to each other is an *equivalence class* under R. (1), (3), and (4) define a *partial order*; (3), (5), and (6) a *linear order*. Similar properties define other important classifications, such as lattice and Boolean algebra. The *converse* of a relation R is the set of all pairs (*b*, *a*) such that *aRb*; the com-

plement of R is the set of all pairs (a, b) such that $-aRb$ (i.e. aRb does not hold).

A more complex example will show the power of a relational vocabulary. The *ancestral* of R is the set of all (a, b) such that either aRb or there are finitely many $c_1, c_2, c_3, \ldots, c_n$ such that aRc_1 and c_1Rc_2 and c_2Rc_3 and $\ldots$ and c_nRb. Frege introduced the ancestral in his theory of number: the natural numbers are exactly those objects bearing the ancestral of the *successor-of* relation to zero. Equivalently, they are the intersection of all sets that contain zero and are closed under the successor relation. (This is formalizable in second-order logic.) Frege's idea has many applications. E.g., assume a set U, relation R on U, and property F. An element a of U is *hereditarily* F (with respect to R) if a is F and any object b which bears the ancestral of R to a is also F. Hence F is here said to be a hereditary property, and the set a is hereditarily finite (with respect to the membership relation) if a is finite, its members are, as are the members of its members, etc. The hereditarily finite sets (or the sets hereditarily of cardinality $< k$ for any inaccessible k) are an important subuniverse of the universe of sets.

Philosophical discussions of relations typically involve relations as special cases of properties (or sets). Thus nominalists and Platonists disagree over the reality of relations, since they disagree about properties in general. Similarly, one important connection is to formal semantics, where relations are customarily taken as the denotations of (relational) predicates. Disputes about the notion of essence are also pertinent. One says that a bears an *internal relation*, R, to b provided a's standing in R to b is an essential property of a; otherwise a bears an *external relation* to b. If the essential–accidental distinction is accepted, then a thing's essential properties will seem to include certain of its relations to other things, so that we must admit internal relations. Consider a point in space, which has no identity apart from its place in a certain system. Similarly for a number. Or consider my hand, which would perhaps not be the same object if it had not developed as part of my body. If it is true that I could not have had other parents – that possible persons similar to me but with distinct parents would not really be me – then I, too, am internally related to other things, namely my parents. Similar arguments would generate numerous internal relations for organisms, artifacts, and natural objects in general. Internal relations will also seem to exist among properties and relations themselves. Roundness is essentially a kind of shape, and the relation *larger than*

is essentially the converse of the relation *smaller than*.

In like usage, a relation between a and b is intrinsic if it depends just on how a and b are; extrinsic if they have it in virtue of their relation to other things. Thus, *higher-than* intrinsically relates the Alps to the Appalachians. That I prefer viewing the former to the latter establishes an extrinsic relation between the mountain ranges. Note that this distinction is obscure (as is internal-external). One could argue that the Alps are higher than the Appalachians only in virtue of the relation of each to something further, such as space, light rays, or measuring rods.

Another issue specific to the theory of relations is whether relations are real, given that properties do exist. That is, someone might reject nominalism only to the extent of admitting one-place properties. Although such doctrines have some historical importance (in, e.g., Plato and Bradley), they have disappeared. Since relations are indispensable to modern logic and semantics, their inferiority to one-place properties can no longer be seriously entertained. Hence relations now have little independent significance in philosophy.

See also ESSENTIALISM, IDENTITY, METAPHYSICS, POSSIBLE WORLDS, SET THEORY, SPACE.   S.J.W.

relationalism. See FIELD THEORY.

relational logic, the formal study of the properties of and operations on (binary) relations that was initiated by Peirce between 1870 and 1882. Thus, in relational logic, one might examine the formal properties of special kinds of relations, such as transitive relations, or asymmetrical ones, or orderings of certain types. Or the focus might be on various operations, such as that of forming the converse or relative product. Formal deductive systems used in such studies are generally known as *calculi of relations*. **See also** RELATION.   G.F.S.

relational semantics. See KRIPKE SEMANTICS.

relationism. See PHILOSOPHY OF SCIENCE.

relative identity. See IDENTITY.

relative threshold. See FECHNER.

relative time. See TIME.

relational value. See VALUE.

relativism, the denial that there are certain kinds of universal truths. There are two main types, *cognitive* and *ethical.* Cognitive relativism holds that there are no universal truths about the world: the world has no intrinsic characteristics, there are just different ways of interpreting it. The Greek Sophist Protagoras, the first person on record to hold such a view, said, "Man is the measure of all things; of things that are that they are, and of things that are not that they are not." Goodman, Putnam, and Rorty are contemporary philosophers who have held versions of relativism. Rorty says, e.g., that " 'objective truth' is no more and no less than the best idea we currently have about how to explain what is going on." Critics of cognitive relativism contend that it is self-referentially incoherent, since it presents its statements as universally true, rather than simply relatively so. Ethical relativism is the theory that there are no universally valid moral principles: all moral principles are valid relative to culture or individual choice. There are two subtypes: *conventionalism,* which holds that moral principles are valid relative to the conventions of a given culture or society; and *subjectivism,* which maintains that individual choices are what determine the validity of a moral principle. Its motto is, Morality lies in the eyes of the beholder. As Ernest Hemingway wrote, "So far, about morals, I know only that what is moral is what you feel good after and what is immoral is what you feel bad after."

Conventionalist ethical relativism consists of two theses: *a diversity thesis,* which specifies that what is considered morally right and wrong varies from society to society, so that there are no moral principles accepted by all societies; and a *dependency thesis,* which specifies that all moral principles derive their validity from cultural acceptance. From these two ideas relativists conclude that there are no universally valid moral principles applying everywhere and at all times. The first thesis, the diversity thesis, or what may simply be called *cultural relativism,* is anthropological; it registers the fact that moral rules differ from society to society. Although both ethical relativists and non-relativists typically accept cultural relativism, it is often confused with the normative thesis of ethical relativism.

The opposite of ethical relativism is *ethical objectivism,* which asserts that although cultures may differ in their moral principles, some moral principles have universal validity. Even if, e.g., a culture does not recognize a duty to refrain from gratuitous harm, that principle is valid and the culture should adhere to it. There are two types of ethical objectivism, strong and weak. Strong objectivism, sometimes called *absolutism,* holds that there is one true moral system with specific moral rules. The ethics of ancient Israel in the Old Testament with its hundreds of laws exemplifies absolutism. Weak objectivism holds that there is a *core morality,* a determinate set of principles that are universally valid (usually including prohibitions against killing the innocent, stealing, breaking of promises, and lying). But weak objectivism accepts an indeterminate area where relativism is legitimate, e.g., rules regarding sexual mores and regulations of property. Both types of objectivism recognize what might be called *application relativism,* the endeavor to apply moral rules where there is a conflict between rules or where rules can be applied in different ways. For example, the ancient Callactians ate their deceased parents but eschewed the impersonal practice of burying them as disrespectful, whereas contemporary society has the opposite attitudes about the care of dead relatives; but both practices exemplify the same principle of the respect for the dead.

According to objectivism, cultures or forms of life can fail to exemplify an adequate moral community in at least three ways: (1) the people are insufficiently intelligent to put constitutive principles in order; (2) they are under considerable stress so that it becomes too burdensome to live by moral principles; and (3) a combination of (1) and (2).

Ethical relativism is sometimes confused with *ethical skepticism,* the view that we cannot know whether there are any valid moral principles. *Ethical nihilism* holds that there are no valid moral principles. J. L. Mackie's *error theory* is a version of this view. Mackie held that while we all believe some moral principles to be true, there are compelling arguments to the contrary.

Ethical objectivism must be distinguished from *moral realism,* the view that valid moral principles are true, independently of human choice. Objectivism may be a form of *ethical constructivism,* typified by Rawls, whereby objective principles are simply those that impartial human beings would choose behind the veil of ignorance. That is, the principles are not truly independent of hypothetical human choices, but are constructs from those choices.

See also ETHICAL OBJECTIVISM, ETHICS, MORAL EPISTEMOLOGY, MORAL REALISM, SKEPTICISM.   L.P.P.

relativism, cultural. See RELATIVISM.

relativism, ethical. See RELATIVISM.

relativism, scientific. See THEORY-LADEN.

relativity, a term applied to Einstein's theories of electrodynamics (special relativity, 1905) and gravitation (general relativity, 1916) because both hold that certain physical quantities, formerly considered objective, are actually "relative to" the state of motion of the observer. They are called "special" and "general" because, in special relativity, electrodynamical laws determine a restricted class of kinematical reference frames, the "inertial frames"; in general relativity, the very distinction between inertial frames and others becomes a relative distinction.

Special relativity. Classical mechanics makes no distinction between uniform motion and rest: not velocity, but acceleration is physically detectable, and so different states of uniform motion are physically equivalent. But classical electrodynamics describes light as wave motion with a constant velocity through a medium, the "ether." It follows that the measured velocity of light should depend on the motion of the observer relative to the medium. When interferometer experiments suggested that the velocity of light is independent of the motion of the source, H. A. Lorentz proposed that objects in motion contract in the direction of motion through the ether (while their local time "dilates"), and that this effect masks the difference in the velocity of light. Einstein, however, associated the interferometry results with many other indications that the theoretical distinction between uniform motion and rest in the ether lacks empirical content. He therefore postulated that, in electrodynamics as in mechanics, all states of uniform motion are equivalent. To explain the apparent paradox that observers with different velocities can agree on the velocity of light, he criticized the idea of an "absolute" or frame-independent measure of simultaneity: simultaneity of distant events can only be established by some kind of signaling, but experiment suggested that light is the only signal with an invariant velocity, and observers in relative motion who determine simultaneity with light signals obtain different results. Furthermore, since objective measurement of time and length presupposes absolute simultaneity, observers in relative motion will also disagree on time and length. So Lorentz's contraction and dilatation are not physical effects, but consequences of the relativity of simultaneity, length, and time, to the motion of the observer. But this relativity follows from the invariance of the laws of electrodynam-

ics, and the invariant content of the theory is expressed geometrically in Minkowski space-time. Logical empiricists took the theory as an illustration of how epistemological analysis of a concept (time) could eliminate empirically superfluous notions (absolute simultaneity).

General relativity. Special relativity made the velocity of light a limit for all causal processes and required revision of Newton's theory of gravity as an instantaneous action at a distance. General relativity incorporates gravity into the geometry of space-time: instead of acting directly on one another, masses induce curvature in space-time. Thus the paths of falling bodies represent not forced deviations from the straight paths of a flat space-time, but "straightest" paths in a curved space-time. While space-time is "locally" Minkowskian, its global structure depends on mass-energy distribution. The insight behind this theory is the equivalence of gravitational and inertial mass: since a given gravitational field affects all bodies equally, weight is indistinguishable from the inertial force of acceleration; free-fall motion is indistinguishable from inertial motion. This suggests that the Newtonian decomposition of free fall into inertial and accelerated components is arbitrary, and that the free-fall path itself is the invariant basis for the structure of space-time.

A philosophical motive for the general theory was to extend the relativity of motion. Einstein saw special relativity's restricted class of equivalent reference frames as an "epistemological defect," and he sought laws that would apply to *any* frame. His inspiration was Mach's criticism of the Newtonian distinction between "absolute" rotation and rotation relative to observable bodies like the "fixed stars." Einstein formulated Mach's criticism as a fundamental principle: since only relative motions are observable, local inertial effects should be explained by the cosmic distribution of masses and by motion relative to them. Thus not only velocity and rest, but motion in general would be relative.

Einstein hoped to effect this generalization by eliminating the distinction between inertial frames and freely falling frames. Because free fall remains a privileged state of motion, however, non-gravitational acceleration remains detectable, and absolute rotation remains distinct from relative rotation. Einstein also thought that relativity of motion would result from the general covariance (coordinate-independence) of his theory – i.e., that general equivalence of coordinate systems meant general equivalence of states of motion. It is now clear, however, that general covariance is a mathematical property of physical theories without direct implications about motion. So general relativity does not "generalize" the relativity of motion as Einstein intended. Its great accomplishments are the unification of gravity and geometry and the generalization of special relativity to space-times of arbitrary curvature, which has made possible the modern investigation of cosmological structure.

See also EINSTEIN, FIELD THEORY, PHILOSOPHY OF SCIENCE, SPACE-TIME.   R.D.

relativity, general. See RELATIVITY.

relativity, perceptual. See PERCEPTION.

relativity, special. See RELATIVITY.

relativity, theory of. See RELATIVITY.

relativity of knowledge. See MANNHEIM.

relevance logic, any of a range of logics and philosophies of logic united by their insistence that the premises of a valid inference must be relevant to the conclusion. Standard, or classical, logic contains inferences that break this requirement, e.g., the *spread law,* that from a contradiction any proposition whatsoever follows. Relevance logic had its genesis in a system of *strenge Implikation* published by Wilhelm Ackermann in 1956. Ackermann's idea for rejecting irrelevance was taken up and developed by Alan Anderson and Nuel Belnap in a series of papers between 1959 and Anderson's death in 1974. The first main summaries of these researches appeared under their names, and those of many collaborators, in *Entailment: The Logic of Relevance and Necessity* (vol. 1, 1975; vol. 2, 1992).

By the time of Anderson's death, a substantial research effort into relevance logic was under way, and it has continued. Besides the rather vague unity of the idea of relevance between premises and conclusion, there is a technical criterion often used to mark out relevance logic, introduced by Belnap in 1960, and applicable really only to propositional logics (the main focus of concern to date): a necessary condition of relevance is that premises and conclusion should share a (propositional) variable.

Early attention was focused on systems E of *entailment* and T of *ticket entailment*. Both are subsystems of C. I. Lewis's system S4 of strict implication and of classical truth-functional logic (i.e., consequences in E and T in '→' are consequences

in S4 in '→' and in classical logic in '⊃'). Besides rejection of the spread law, probably the most notorious inference that is rejected is disjunctive syllogism (DS) for extensional disjunction (which is equivalent to detachment for material implication): $A \lor B, \neg A \therefore B$. The reason is immediate, given acceptance of Simplification and Addition: Simplification takes us from $A \,\&\, \neg A$ to each conjunct, and Addition turns the first conjunct into $A \lor B$. Unless DS were rejected, the spread law would follow.

Since the late 1960s, attention has shifted to the system R of *relevant implication*, which adds permutation to E, to mingle systems which extend E and R by the *mingle law* $A \to (A \to A)$, and to contraction-free logics, which additionally reject contraction, in one form reading $(A \to (A \to B)) \to (A \to B)$. R minus contraction (RW) differs from linear logic, much studied recently in computer science, only by accepting the distribution of '&' over '∨', which the latter rejects.

Like linear logic, relevance logic contains both truth-functional and non-truth-functional connectives. Unlike linear logic, however, R, E, and T are undecidable (unusual among propositional logics). This result was obtained only in 1984. In the early 1970s, relevance logics were given possible-worlds semantics by several authors working independently. They also have axiomatic, natural deduction, and sequent (or consecution) formulations. One technical result that has attracted attention has been the demonstration that, although relevance logics reject DS, they all accept *Ackermann's rule Gamma:* that if $A \lor B$ and $\neg A$ are theses, so is B. A recent result occasioning much surprise was that relevant arithmetic (consisting of Peano's postulates on the base of quantified R) does not admit Gamma.

See also IMPLICATION, MODAL LOGIC.
                                S.L.R.

relevant alternative. See CONTEXTUALISM.

reliabilism, a type of theory in epistemology that holds that what qualifies a belief as knowledge or as epistemically justified is its reliable linkage to the truth. David Armstrong motivates reliabilism with an analogy between a thermometer that reliably indicates the temperature and a belief that reliably indicates the truth. A belief qualifies as knowledge, he says, if there is a lawlike connection in nature that guarantees that the belief is true. A cousin of the nomic sufficiency account is the counterfactual approach, proposed by Dretske, Goldman, and Nozick. A typical formulation of this approach says that a belief qualifies as knowledge if the belief is true and the cognizer has reasons for believing it that would not obtain unless it were true. For example, someone knows that the telephone is ringing if he believes this, it is true, and he has a specific auditory experience that would not occur unless the telephone were ringing. In a slightly different formulation, someone knows a proposition if he believes it, it is true, and if it were not true he would not believe it. In the example, if the telephone were not ringing, he would not believe that it is, because he would not have the same auditory experience. These accounts are guided by the idea that to know a proposition it is not sufficient that the belief be "accidentally" true. Rather, the belief, or its mode of acquisition, must "track," "hook up with," or "indicate" the truth.

Unlike knowledge, justified belief need not guarantee or be "hooked up" with the truth, for a justified belief need not itself be true. Nonetheless, reliabilists insist that the concept of justified belief also has a connection with truth acquisition. According to Goldman's reliable process account, a belief's justificational status depends on the psychological processes that produce or sustain it. Justified beliefs are produced by appropriate psychological processes, unjustified beliefs by inappropriate processes. For example, beliefs produced or preserved by perception, memory, introspection, and "good" reasoning are justified, whereas beliefs produced by hunch, wishful thinking, or "bad" reasoning are unjustified. Why are the first group of processes appropriate and the second inappropriate? The difference appears to lie in their reliability. Among the beliefs produced by perception, introspection, or "good" reasoning, a high proportion are true; but only a low proportion of beliefs produced by hunch, wishful thinking, or "bad" reasoning are true. Thus, what qualifies a belief as justified is its being the outcome of a sequence of reliable belief-forming processes.

Reliabilism is a species of epistemological externalism, because it makes knowledge or justification depend on factors such as truth connections or truth ratios that are outside the cognizer's mind and not necessarily accessible to him. Yet reliabilism typically emphasizes internal factors as well, e.g., the cognitive processes responsible for a belief. Process reliabilism is a form of naturalistic epistemology because it centers on cognitive operations and thereby paves the way for cognitive psychology to play a role in epistemology.

See also EPISTEMOLOGY, NATURALISTIC EPISTEMOLOGY, PERCEPTION.   A.I.G.

religion, natural. See NATURAL RELIGION, PHILOSOPHY OF RELIGION.

religion, philosophy of. See NATURAL RELIGION, PHILOSOPHY OF RELIGION.

reminiscence. See PLATO.

Renouvier, Charles (1815–1903), French philosopher influenced by Kant and Comte, the latter being one of his teachers. Renouvier rejected many of the views of both these philosophers, however, charting his own course. He emphasized the irreducible plurality and individuality of all things against the contemporary tendencies toward absolute idealism. Human individuality he associated with indeterminism and freedom. To the extent that agents are undetermined by other things and self-determining, they are unique individuals. Indeterminism also extends to the physical world and to knowledge. He rejected absolute certitude, but defended the universality of the laws of logic and mathematics. In politics and religion, he emphasized individual freedom and freedom of conscience. His emphasis on plurality, indeterminism, freedom, novelty, and process influenced James and, through James, American pragmatism. **See also** FREE WILL PROBLEM.   R.H.K.

replacement, axiom of. See SET THEORY.

representation, mental. See COGNITIVE SCIENCE.

representationalism. See RORTY.

representational scheme. See GÖDEL'S INCOMPLETENESS THEOREMS.

representational theory of art. See MIMESIS.

representational theory of memory. See MEMORY.

representation theorem. See MAGNITUDE.

representative realism. See PERCEPTION.

repression. See FREUD.

republicanism, classical. See CLASSICAL REPUBLICANISM.

rerum natura (Latin, 'the nature of things'), metaphysics. The phrase can also be used more narrowly to mean the nature of physical reality, and often it presupposes a naturalistic view of all reality. Lucretius's epic poem *De rerum natura* is an Epicurean physics, designed to underpin the Epicurean morality.   A.P.M.

res cogitans. See DESCARTES.

res extensa. See DESCARTES.

residues, method of. See MILL'S METHODS.

respondent conditioning. See BEHAVIORISM.

response variable. See REGRESSION ANALYSIS.

responsibility, a condition that relates an agent to actions of, and consequences connected to, that agent, and is always necessary and sometimes sufficient for the appropriateness of certain kinds of appraisals of that agent. Responsibility has no single definition, but is several closely connected specific concepts.

Role responsibility. Agents are identified by social roles that they occupy, say parent or professor. Typically duties are associated with such roles – to care for the needs of their children, to attend classes and publish research papers. A person in a social role is "responsible for" the execution of those duties. One who carries out such duties is "a responsible person" or "is behaving responsibly."

Causal responsibility. Events, including but not limited to human actions, cause other events. The cause is "responsible" for the effect. Causal responsibility does not imply consciousness; objects and natural phenomena may have causal responsibility.

Liability responsibility. Practices of praise and blame include constraints on the mental stance that an agent must have toward an action or a consequence of action, in order for praise or blame to be appropriate. To meet such constraints is to meet a fundamental necessary condition for liability for praise or blame – hence the expression 'liability responsibility'. These constraints include such factors as intention, knowledge, recklessness toward consequences, absence of mistake, accident, inevitability of choice. An agent with the capability for liability responsibility may lack it on some occasion – when mistaken, for example.

Capacity responsibility. Practices of praise and blame assume a level of intellectual and emotional capability. The severely mentally disadvantaged or the very young, for example, do not have the capacity to meet the conditions for lia-

bility responsibility. They are not "responsible" in that they lack capacity responsibility.

Both morality and law embody and respect these distinctions, though law institutionalizes and formalizes them. Final or "bottom-line" assignment of responsibility equivalent to indeed deserving praise or blame standardly requires each of the latter three specific kinds of responsibility. The first kind supplies some normative standards for praise or blame.

See also CAUSATION, DIMINISHED CAPACITY, FREE WILL, HART, INTENTION, MENS REA.   R.A.Sh.

responsibility, diminished. See DIMINISHED CAPACITY.

restricted quantification. See FORMAL LOGIC.

restrictio. See PROPRIETATES TERMINORUM.

resultance, a relation according to which one property (the resultant property, sometimes called the consequential property) is possessed by some object or event in virtue of (and hence as a result of) that object or event possessing some other property or set of properties. The idea is that properties of things can be ordered into connected levels, some being more basic than and giving rise to others, the latter resulting from the former. For instance, a figure possesses the property of being a triangle in virtue of its possessing a collection of properties, including being a plane figure, having three sides, and so on; the former resulting from the latter. An object is brittle (has the property of being brittle) in virtue of having a certain molecular structure.

It is often claimed that moral properties like rightness and goodness are resultant properties: an action is right in virtue of its possessing other properties. These examples make it clear that the nature of the necessary connection holding between a resultant property and those base properties that ground it may differ from case to case. In the geometrical example, the very concept of being a triangle grounds the resultance relation in question, and while brittleness is nomologically related to the base properties from which it results, in the moral case, the resultance relation is arguably neither conceptual nor causal.

See also CONSTITUTION, NATURALISM, SUPERVENIENCE.   M.C.T.

resultant attribute. See SUPERVENIENCE.

retributive justice. See JUSTICE, PUNISHMENT.

retributivism. See PUNISHMENT.

retrocausation. See CAUSATION.

return, eternal. See ETERNAL RETURN.

revelation. See PHILOSOPHY OF RELIGION.

revisionary metaphysics. See METAPHYSICS.

Rhazes. See AL-RĀZĪ.

Richard Kilvington. See KILVINGTON.

Richard Rufus, also called Richard of Cornwall (d. c.1260), English philosopher-theologian who wrote some of the earliest commentaries on Aristotle in the Latin West. His commentaries were not cursory summaries; they included sustained philosophical discussions. Richard was a master of arts at Paris, where he studied with Alexander of Hales; he was also deeply influenced by Robert Grosseteste. He left Paris and joined the Franciscan order in 1238; he was ordained in England. In 1256, he became regent master of the Franciscan studium at Oxford; according to Roger Bacon, he was the most influential philosophical theologian at Oxford in the second half of the thirteenth century.

In addition to his Aristotle commentaries, Richard wrote two commentaries on Peter Lombard's *Sentences* (c.1250, c.1254). In the first of these he borrowed freely from Robert Grosseteste, Alexander of Hales, and Richard Fishacre; the second commentary was a critical condensation of the lectures of his younger contemporary, St. Bonaventure, presented in Paris. Richard Rufus was the first medieval proponent of the theory of impetus; his views on projectile motion were cited by Franciscus Meyronnes. He also advocated other arguments first presented by Johannes Philoponus. Against the eternity of the world, he argued: (1) past time is necessarily finite, since it has been traversed, and (2) the world is not eternal, since if the world had no beginning, no more time would transpire before tomorrow than before today. He also argued that if the world had not been created *ex nihilo*, the first cause would be mutable. Robert Grosseteste cited one of Richard's arguments against the eternity of the world in his notes on Aristotle's *Physics*.

In theology, Richard denied the validity of Anselm's ontological argument, but, anticipating Duns Scotus, he argued that the existence of an independent being could be inferred from its possibility. Like Duns Scotus, he employs the formal distinction as an explanatory tool; in presenting his own views, Duns Scotus cited Richard's definition of the formal distinction.

Richard stated his philosophical views briefly, even cryptically; his Latin prose style is sometimes eccentric, characterized by interjections in which he addresses questions to God, himself, and his readers. He was hesitant about the value of systematic theology for the theologian, deferring to biblical exposition as the primary forum for theological discussion. In systematic theology, he emphasized Aristotelian philosophy and logic. He was a well-known logician; some scholars believe he is the famous logician known as the Magister Abstractionum. Though he borrowed freely from his contemporaries, he was a profoundly original philosopher.

See also ALEXANDER OF HALES, BONAVENTURE, GROSSETESTE, PETER LOMBARD.   R.W.

Richard's paradox. See SEMANTIC PARADOXES.

Rickert, Heinrich. See NEO-KANTIANISM.

Ricoeur, Paul (b.1913), French hermeneuticist and phenomenologist who has been a professor at several French universities as well as the University of Naples, Yale University, and the University of Chicago. He has received major prizes from France, Germany, and Italy. He is the author of twenty-some volumes translated in a variety of languages. Among his best-known books are *Freedom and Nature: The Voluntary and the Involuntary; Freud and Philosophy: An Essay of Interpretation; The Conflict of Interpretations: Essay in Hermeneutics; The Role of the Metaphor: Multi-Disciplinary Studies of the Creation of Meaning in Language, Time and Narrative;* and *Oneself as Another.* His early studies with the French existentialist Marcel resulted in a book-length study of Marcel's work and later a series of published dialogues with him.

Ricoeur's philosophical enterprise is colored by a continuing tension between faith and reason. His long-standing commitments to both the significance of the individual and the Christian faith are reflected in his hermeneutical voyage, his commitment to the Esprit movement, and his interest in the writings of Emmanuel Mounier. This latter point is also seen in his claim of the inseparability of action and discourse in our quest for meaning. In our comprehension of both history and fiction one must turn to the text to understand its plot as guideline if we are to comprehend experience of any reflective sort. In the end there are no metaphysical or epistemological grounds by which meaning can be verified, and yet our nature is such that possibility must be present before us. Ricoeur attempts his explanation through a hermeneutic phenomenology. The very hermeneutics of existence that follows is itself limited by reason's questioning of experience and its attempts to transcend the limit through the language of symbols and metaphors. Freedom and meaning come to be realized in the actualization of an ethics that arises out of the very act of existing and thus transcends the mere natural voluntary distinction of a formal ethic. It is clear from his later work that he rejects any form of foundationalism including phenomenology as well as nihilism and easy skepticism. Through a sort of interdependent dialectic that goes beyond the more mechanical models of Hegelianism or Marxism, the self understands itself and is understood by the other in terms of its suffering and its moral actions.

See also HEGEL, HERMENEUTICS, HUSSERL, MARCEL, PHENOMENOLOGY.   J.Bi.

Riemann, G. F. B. See NON-EUCLIDEAN GEOMETRY.

right, absolute. See RIGHTS.

right, prima facie. See RIGHTS.

right action. See ETHICS.

rightness, objective. See OBJECTIVE RIGHTNESS.

rightness, subjective. See OBJECTIVE RIGHTNESS.

right of nature. See HOBBES.

rights, advantageous positions conferred on some possessor by law, morals, rules, or other norms. There is no agreement on the sense in which rights are advantages. *Will theories* hold that rights favor the will of the possessor over the conflicting will of some other party; *interest theories* maintain that rights serve to protect or promote the interests of the right-holder. Hohfeld identified four legal advantages: liberties, claims, powers, and immunities.

The concept of a right arose in Roman jurisprudence and was extended to ethics via natural law theory. Just as positive law, the law posited by human lawmakers, confers legal rights, so the natural law confers natural rights. Rights are classified by their specific sources in different sorts of rules. Legal rights are advantageous positions under the law of a society. Other species of institutional rights are conferred by the rules of private organizations, of the moral code of a society, or even of some game. Those who identify natural law with the moral law often identify natural rights with moral rights, but some limit natural rights to our most fundamental rights and contrast them with ordinary moral rights. Others deny that moral rights are natural because they believe that they are conferred by the mores or positive morality of one's society.

One always possesses any specific right by virtue of possessing some status. Thus, rights are also classified by status. Civil rights are those one possesses as a citizen; human rights are possessed by virtue of being human. Presumably women's rights, children's rights, patients' rights, and the rights of blacks as such are analogous.

Human rights play very much the same role in ethics once played by natural rights. This is partly because ontological doubts about the existence of God undermine the acceptance of any natural law taken to consist in divine commands, and epistemological doubts about self-evident moral truths lead many to reject any natural law conceived of as the dictates of reason. Although the Thomistic view that natural rights are grounded on the nature of man is often advocated, most moral philosophers reject its teleological conception of human nature defined by essential human purposes. It seems simpler to appeal instead to fundamental rights that must be universal among human beings because they are possessed merely by virtue of one's status *as* a human being. Human rights are still thought of as natural in the very broad sense of existing independently of any human action or institution. This explains how they can be used as an independent standard in terms of which to criticize the laws and policies of governments and other organizations. Since human rights are classified by status rather than source, there is another species of human rights that are institutional rather than natural. These are the human rights that have been incorporated into legal systems by international agreements such as the European Convention on Human Rights.

It is sometimes said that while natural rights were conceived as purely negative rights, such as the right not to be arbitrarily imprisoned, human rights are conceived more broadly to include positive social and economic rights, such as the right to social security or to an adequate standard of living. But this is surely not true by definition. Traditional natural law theorists such as Grotius and Locke spoke of natural rights as powers and associated them with liberties, rather than with claims against interference. And while modern declarations of human rights typically include social and economic rights, they assume that these are rights in the same sense that traditional political rights are.

Rights are often classified by their formal properties. For example, the right not to be battered is a negative right because it imposes a negative duty *not* to batter, while the creditor's right to be repaid is a positive right because it imposes a positive duty to repay. The right to be repaid is also a passive right because its content is properly formulated in the passive voice, while the right to defend oneself is an active right because its content is best stated in the active voice. Again, a right *in rem* is a right that holds against all second parties; a right *in personam* is a right that holds against one or a few others. This is not quite Hart's distinction between general and special rights, rights of everyone against everyone, such as the right to free speech, and rights arising from special relations, such as that between creditor and debtor or husband and wife.

Rights are conceptually contrasted with duties because rights are advantages while duties are disadvantages. Still, many jurists and philosophers have held that rights and duties are logical correlatives. This does seem to be true of claim rights; thus, the creditor's right to be repaid implies the debtor's duty to repay and vice versa. But the logical correlative of a liberty right, such as one's right to park in front of one's house, is the absence of any duty for one not to do so. This contrast is indicated by D. D. Raphael's distinction between rights of recipience and rights of action.

Sometimes to say that one has a right to do something is to say merely that it is not wrong for one to act in this way. This has been called the weak sense of 'a right'. More often to assert that one has a right to do something does not imply that exercising this right is right. Thus, I might have a right to refuse to do a favor for a friend even though it would be wrong for me to do so.

Finally, many philosophers distinguish between absolute and prima facie rights. An absolute right always holds, i.e., disadvantages some second party, within its scope; a prima facie right is one that holds unless the ground of the right is outweighed by some stronger contrary reason.

See also DUTY, HOHFELD, NATURAL LAW, PHILOSOPHY OF LAW, POLITICAL PHILOSOPHY.
C.We.

rights, Hohfeldian. See HOHFELD.

rights, imperfect. See GROTIUS.

rights, legal. See RIGHTS.

rights, natural. See RIGHTS.

rights, perfect. See RIGHTS.

rigid designator. See MEANING.

rigorism, the view that morality consists in that single set of simple or unqualified moral rules, discoverable by reason, which applies to all human beings at all times. It is often said that Kant's doctrine of the categorical imperative is rigoristic. Two main objections to rigorism are (1) some moral rules do not apply universally – e.g., 'Promises should be kept' applies only where there is an institution of promising; and (2) some rules that could be universally kept are absurd – e.g., that everyone should stand on one leg while the sun rises. Recent interpreters of Kant defend him against these objections by arguing, e.g., that the "rules" he had in mind are general guidelines for living well, which are in fact universal and practically relevant, or that he was not a rigorist at all, seeing moral worth as issuing primarily from the agent's character rather than adherence to rules. R.C.

rigorous duty. See DUTY.

ring of Gyges, a ring that gives its wearer invisibility, discussed in Plato's *Republic* (II, 359b–360d). Glaucon tells the story of a man who discovered the ring and used it to usurp the throne to defend the claim that those who behave justly do so only because they lack the power to act unjustly. If they could avoid paying the penalty of injustice, Glaucon argues, everyone would be unjust. **See also** PLATO, SOCRATES. W.J.P.

robot. See COMPUTER THEORY.

role responsibility. See RESPONSIBILITY.

Rorty, Richard (b.1931), American philosopher, notable for the breadth of his philosophical and cultural interests. He was educated at the University of Chicago and Yale and has taught at

Wellesley, Princeton, the University of Virginia, and Stanford. His early work was primarily in standard areas of analytic philosophy such as the philosophy of mind, where, for example, he developed an important defense of eliminative materialism. In 1979, however, he published *Philosophy and the Mirror of Nature*, which was both hailed and denounced as a fundamental critique of analytic philosophy. Both the praise and the abuse were often based on misconceptions, but there is no doubt that Rorty questioned fundamental presuppositions of many Anglo-American philosophers and showed affinities for Continental alternatives to analytic philosophy.

At root, however, Rorty's position is neither analytic (except in its stylistic clarity) nor Continental (except in its cultural breadth). His view is, rather, pragmatic, a contemporary incarnation of the distinctively American philosophizing of James, Peirce, and Dewey. On Rorty's reading, pragmatism involves a rejection of the representationalism that has dominated modern philosophy from Descartes through logical positivism. According to representationalism, we have direct access only to ideas that represent the world, not to the world itself. Philosophy has the privileged role of determining the criteria for judging that our representations are adequate to reality.

A main thrust of *Philosophy and the Mirror of Nature* is to discredit representationalism, first by showing how it has functioned as an unjustified presupposition in classical modern philosophers such as Descartes, Locke, and Kant, and second by showing how analytic philosophers such as Wilfrid Sellars and Quine have revealed the incoherence of representationalist assumptions in contemporary epistemology. Since, on Rorty's view, representationalism defines the epistemological project of modern philosophy, its failure requires that we abandon this project and, with it, traditional pretensions to a privileged cognitive role for philosophy. Rorty sees no point in seeking a non-representationalist basis for the justification or the truth of our knowledge claims. It is enough to accept as justified beliefs those on which our epistemic community agrees and to use 'true' as an honorific term for beliefs that we see as "justified to the hilt."

Rorty characterizes his positive position as "liberal ironism." His liberalism is of a standard sort, taking as its basic value the freedom of all individuals: first, their freedom from suffering, but then also freedom to form their lives with whatever values they find most compelling. Rorty distinguishes the "public sphere" in which we all share the liberal commitment to universal freedom from the "private spheres" in which we all work out our own specific conception of the good. His ironism reflects his realization that there is no grounding for public or private values other than our deep (but contingent) commitment to them and his appreciation of the multitude of private values that he does not himself happen to share. Rorty has emphasized the importance of literature and literary criticism – as opposed to traditional philosophy – for providing the citizens of a liberal society with appropriate sensitivities to the needs and values of others.

See also ANALYTIC PHILOSOPHY; CONTINENTAL PHILOSOPHY; PRAGMATISM; QUINE; SELLARS, WILFRID.   G.G.

Roscelin de Compiègne (c.1050–c.1125), French philosopher and logician who became embroiled in theological controversy when he applied his logical teachings to the doctrine of the Trinity. Since almost nothing survives of his written work, we must rely on hostile accounts of his views by Anselm of Canterbury and Peter Abelard, both of whom openly opposed his positions.

Perhaps the most notorious view Roscelin is said to have held is that universals are merely the puffs of air produced when a word is pronounced. On this point he opposed views current among many theologians that a universal has an existence independent of language, and somehow is what many different particulars are. Roscelin's aversion to any proposal that different things can be some one thing is probably what led him in his thinking about the three persons of God to a position that sounded suspiciously like the heresy of tritheism. Roscelin also evidently held that the qualities of things are not entities distinct from the subjects that possess them. This indicates that Roscelin probably denied that terms in the Aristotelian categories other than substance signified anything distinct from substances.

Abelard, the foremost logician of the twelfth century, studied under Roscelin around 1095 and was undoubtedly influenced by him on the question of universals. Roscelin's view that universals are linguistic entities remained an important option in medieval thought. Otherwise his positions do not appear to have had much currency in the ensuing decades.

See also ABSTRACT ENTITY, METAPHYSICS.
                                                           M.M.T.

Rosenzweig, Franz (1886–1929), German philosopher and Jewish theologian known as one of the founders of religious existentialism. His early relation to Judaism was tenuous, and at one point he came close to converting to Christianity. A religious experience in a synagogue made him change his mind and return to Judaism. His chief philosophic works are a two-volume study, *Hegel and the State* (1920), and his masterpiece, *The Star of Redemption* (1921).

Rosenzweig's experience in World War I caused him to reject absolute idealism on the ground that it cannot account for the privacy and finality of death. Instead of looking for a unifying principle behind existence, Rosenzweig starts with three independent realities "given" in experience: God, the self, and the world. Calling his method "radical empiricism," he explains how God, the self, and the world are connected by three primary relations: creation, revelation, and redemption. In revelation, God does not communicate verbal statements but merely a presence that calls for love and devotion from worshipers.

See also EXISTENTIALISM, JEWISH PHILOSO-PHY.   K.See.

Rosmini-Serbati, Antonio (1797–1855), Italian philosopher, Catholic priest, counselor to Pope Pius IX, and supporter of the supremacy of the church over civil government (Neo-Guelphism). Rosmini had two major concerns: the objectivity of human knowledge and the synthesis of philosophical thought within the tradition of Catholic thought. In his *Nuovo saggio sull'origine delle idee* ("New Essay on the Origin of Ideas," 1830), he identifies the universal a priori intuitive component of all human knowledge with the idea of being that gives us the notion of a possible or ideal being. Everything in the world is known by intellectual perception, which is the synthesis of sensation and the idea of being. Except for the idea of being, which is directly given by God, all ideas derive from abstraction. The objectivity of human knowledge rests on its universal origin in the idea of being. The harmony between philosophy and religion comes from the fact that all human knowledge is the result of divine revelation. Rosmini's thought was influenced by Augustine and Aquinas, and stimulated by the attempt to find a solution to the contrasting needs of rationalism and empiricism.   P.Gar.

Ross, W(illiam) D(avid) (1877–1971), British Aristotelian scholar and moral philosopher. Born in Edinburgh and educated at the University of Edinburgh and at Balliol College, Oxford, he became a fellow of Merton College, then a fellow, tutor, and eventually provost at Oriel College. He was vice-chancellor of Oxford University (1941–44) and president of the British Academy (1936–40). He was knighted in 1938 in view of national service.

Ross was a distinguished classical scholar: he edited the Oxford translations of Aristotle (1908–31) and translated the *Metaphysics* and the *Ethics* himself. His *Aristotle* (1923) is a judicious exposition of Aristotle's work as a whole. *Kant's Ethical Theory* (1954) is a commentary on Kant's *The Groundwork of Ethics*.

His major contribution to philosophy was in ethics: *The Right and the Good* (1930) and *Foundations of Ethics* (1939). The view he expressed there was controversial in English-speaking countries for ten years or so. He held that 'right' and 'good' are empirically indefinable terms that name objective properties the presence of which is known intuitively by persons who are mature and educated. We first cognize them in particular instances, then arrive at general principles involving them by "intuitive induction." (He thought every ethical theory must admit at least one intuition.) The knowledge of moral principles is thus rather like knowledge of the principles of geometry. 'Right' ('dutiful') applies to acts, in the sense of what an agent brings about (and there is no duty to act from a good motive, and a right act can have a bad motive); 'morally good' applies primarily to the desires that bring about action. He castigated utilitarianism as absorbing all duties into enhancing the well-being of everyone affected, whereas in fact we have strong special obligations to keep promises, make reparation for injuries, repay services done, distribute happiness in accord with merit, benefit individuals generally (and he concedes this is a weighty matter) and ourselves (only in respect of knowledge and virtue), and not injure others (normally a stronger obligation than that to benefit). That we have these "prima facie" duties is self-evident, but they are only prima facie in the sense that they are actual duties only if there is no stronger conflicting prima facie duty; and when prima facie duties conflict, what one ought to do is what satisfies all of them best – although which this is is a matter of judgment, not self-evidence. (He conceded, however, in contrast to his general critique of utilitarianism, that public support of these prima facie principles with their intuitive strength can be justified on utilitarian grounds.) To meet various counterexamples Ross introduced complications, such as that a promise is not binding if discharge of it will not benefit the promisee (providing this was an implicit understanding), and it is less binding if made long ago or in a casual manner.

Only four states of affairs are good in themselves: desire to do one's duty (virtue), knowledge, pleasure, and the distribution of happiness in accordance with desert. Of these, virtue is more valuable than any amount of knowledge or pleasure. In *Foundations of Ethics* he held that virtue and pleasure are not good in the same sense: virtue is "admirable" but pleasure only a "worthy object of satisfaction" (so 'good' does not name just one property).

See also DUTY, ETHICS, MORAL EPISTEMOLOGY, SELF-EVIDENCE.   R.B.B.

Rousseau, Jean-Jacques (1712–78), Swiss-born French philosopher, essayist, novelist, and musician, best known for his theories on social freedom and societal rights, education, and religion. Born in Geneva, he was largely self-educated and moved to France as a teenager. Throughout much of his life he moved between Paris and the provinces with several trips abroad (including a Scottish stay with Hume) and a return visit to Geneva, where he reconverted to Protestantism from his earlier conversion to Catholicism. For a time he was a friend of Diderot and other *philosophes* and was asked to contribute articles on music for the *Encyclopedia*.

Rousseau's work can be seen from at least three perspectives. As social contract theorist, he attempts to construct a hypothetical state of nature to explain the current human situation. This evolves a form of philosophical anthropology that gives us both a theory of human nature and a series of pragmatic claims concerning social organization. As a social commentator, he speaks of both practical and ideal forms of education and social organization. As a moralist, he continually attempts to unite the individual and the citizen through some form of universal political action or consent.

In *Discourse on the Origin and Foundation of Inequality Among Mankind* (1755), Rousseau presents us with an almost idyllic view of humanity. In nature humans are first seen as little more than animals except for their special species sympathy. Later, through an explanation of the development of reason and language, he is able to suggest how humans, while retaining this sympathy, can, by distancing themselves from nature, understand their individual selves. This leads to natural community and the closest thing to what Rousseau considers humanity's perfect moment. Private property quickly follows on the division of labor, and humans find themselves alienated from each other by the class divisions engendered by private property. Thus man, who was born in freedom, now finds himself in chains. *The Social Contract or Principles of Political Right* (1762) has a more ambitious goal. With an account of the practical role of the legislator and the introduction of the concept of the general will, Rousseau attempts to give us a foundation for good government by presenting a solution to the conflicts between the particular and the universal, the individual and the citizen, and the actual and the moral. Individuals, freely agreeing to a social pact and giving up their rights to the community, are assured of the liberties and equality of political citizenship found in the contract. It is only through being a citizen that the individual can fully realize his freedom and exercise his moral rights and duties. While the individual is naturally good, he must always guard against being dominated or dominating.

Rousseau finds a solution to the problems of individual freedoms and interests in a superior form of moral/political action that he calls the general will. The individual as citizen substitutes "I must" for "I will," which is also an "I shall" when it expresses assent to the general will. The general will is a universal force or statement and thus is more noble than any particular will. In willing his own interest, the citizen is at the same time willing what is communally good. The particular and the universal are united. The individual human participant realizes himself in realizing the good of all.

As a practical political commentator Rousseau knew that the universal and the particular do not always coincide. For this he introduced the idea of the legislator, which allows the individual citizen to realize his fulfillment as social being and to exercise his individual rights through universal consent. In moments of difference between the majority will and the general will the legislator will instill the correct moral/political understanding. This will be represented in the laws. While sovereignty rests with the citizens, Rousseau does not require that political action be direct. Although all government should be democratic, various forms of government from representative democracy (preferable in small societies) to strong monarchies (preferable in large nation-states) may be acceptable. To shore up the unity and stability of individual societies, Rousseau suggests a sort of civic religion to which all citizens subscribe and in which all members participate. His earlier writings on education and his later practical treatises on the governments of Poland and Corsica reflect related concerns with natural and moral development and with historical and geographical considerations.

See also SOCIAL CONTRACT.   J.Bi.

Royce, Josiah (1855–1916), American philosopher best known for his pragmatic idealism, his ethics of loyalty, and his theory of community. Educated at Berkeley, at Johns Hopkins, and in Germany, he taught philosophy at Harvard from 1882.

Royce held that a concept of the absolute or eternal was needed to account for truth, ultimate meaning, and reality in the face of very real evil in human experience. Seeking to reconcile individuals with the Absolute, he postulated, in *The World and the Individual* (1899,1901), Absolute Will and Thought as an expression of the concrete and differentiated individuality of the world.

Royce saw the individual self as both moral and sinful, developing through social interaction, community experience, and communal and self-interpretation. Self is constituted by a life plan, by loyalty to an ultimate goal. Yet self-limitation and egoism, two human sins, work against achievement of individual goals, perhaps rendering life a senseless failure. The self needs saving and this is the message of religion, argues Royce (*The Religious Aspects of Philosophy*, 1885; *The Sources of Religious Insight*, 1912).

For Royce, the instrument of salvation is the community. In *The Philosophy of Loyalty* (1908), he develops an ethics of loyalty to loyalty, i.e., the extension of loyalty throughout the human community. In *The Problem of Christianity* (1913), Royce presents a doctrine of community that overcomes the individualism–collectivism dilemma and allows a genuine blending of individual and social will.

Community is built through interpretation, a mediative process that reconciles two ideas, goals, and persons, bringing common meaning and understanding. Interpretation involves respect for selves as dynamos of ideas and purposes, the will to interpret, dissatisfaction with partial meanings and narrowness of view, reciprocity, and mutuality. In this work, the Absolute is a "Community of Interpretation and Hope," in which there is an endlessly accumulating series of interpretations and significant deeds. An individual contribution thus is not lost but becomes an indispensable element in the divine life.

Among Royce's influential students were C. I. Lewis, William Ernest Hocking, Norbert Wiener, Santayana, and T. S. Eliot.   J.A.K.K.

Rufus, Richard. See RICHARD RUFUS.

rule, primary. See HART.

rule, secondary. See HART.

rule of addition. See DISJUNCTION INTRODUCTION.

rule of conjunction. See CONJUNCTION INTRODUCTION.

rule of detachment. See LOTTERY PARADOX.

rule of double negation. See DOUBLE NEGATION.

rule of inference. See LOGISTIC SYSTEM.

rule of law, the largely formal or procedural properties of a well-ordered legal system. Commonly, these properties are thought to include: a prohibition of arbitrary power (the lawgiver is also subject to the laws); laws that are general, prospective, clear, and consistent (capable of guiding conduct); and tribunals (courts) that are reasonably accessible and fairly structured to hear and determine legal claims. Contemporary discussions of the rule of law focus on two major questions: (1) to what extent is conformity to the rule of law essential to the very idea of a legal system; and (2) what is the connection between the rule of law and the substantive moral value of a legal system? **See also PHILOSOPHY OF LAW, POLITICAL PHILOSOPHY.**   P.S.

rule of recognition. See HART, JURISPRUDENCE.

rule of simplification. See CONJUNCTION ELIMINATION.

rule of total evidence. See INDUCTION.

rule utilitarianism. See UTILITARIANISM.

Ruling Argument. See MEGARIANS.

Russell, Bertrand (Arthur William) (1872–1970), British philosopher, logician, social reformer, and man of letters, one of the founders of analytic philosophy. Born into an aristocratic political family, Russell always divided his interests between politics and philosophy. Orphaned at four, he was brought up by his grandmother, who educated him at home with the help of tutors. He studied mathematics at Cambridge from 1890 to 1893, when he turned to philosophy.

At home he had absorbed J. S. Mill's liberalism, but not his empiricism. At Cambridge he came under the influence of neo-Hegelianism, especially the idealism of McTaggart, Ward (his tutor), and Bradley. His earliest logical views were influenced most by Bradley, especially Bradley's rejection of psychologism. But, like Ward and McTaggart, he rejected Bradley's metaphysical monism in favor of pluralism (or monadism). Even as an idealist, he held that scientific knowledge was the best available and that philosophy should be built around it. Through many subsequent changes, this belief about science, his pluralism, and his anti-psychologism remained constant.

In 1895, he conceived the idea of an idealist encyclopedia of the sciences to be developed by the use of transcendental arguments to establish the conditions under which the special sciences are possible. Russell's first philosophical book, *An Essay on the Foundations of Geometry* (1897), was part of this project, as were other (mostly unfinished and unpublished) pieces on physics and arithmetic written at this time (see his *Collected Papers*, vols. 1–2). Russell claimed, in contrast to Kant, to use transcendental arguments in a purely logical way compatible with his anti-psychologism. In this case, however, it should be both possible and preferable to replace them by purely deductive arguments. Another problem arose in connection with asymmetrical relations, which led to contradictions if treated as internal relations, but which were essential for any treatment of mathematics. Russell resolved both problems in 1898 by abandoning idealism (including internal relations and his Kantian methodology). He called this the one real revolution in his philosophy. With his Cambridge contemporary Moore, he adopted an extreme Platonic realism, fully stated in *The Principles of Mathematics* (1903) though anticipated in *A Critical Exposition of the Philosophy of Leibniz* (1900).

Russell's work on the sciences was by then concentrated on pure mathematics, but the new philosophy yielded little progress until, in 1900, he discovered Peano's symbolic logic, which offered hope that pure mathematics could be treated without Kantian intuitions or transcendental arguments. On this basis Russell propounded *logicism*, the claim that the whole of pure mathematics could be derived deductively from logical principles, a position he came to

independently of Frege, who held a similar but more restricted view but whose work Russell discovered only later. Logicism was announced in *The Principles of Mathematics*; its development occupied Russell, in collaboration with Whitehead, for the next ten years. Their results were published in *Principia Mathematica* (1910–13, 3 vols.), in which detailed derivations were given for Cantor's set theory, finite and transfinite arithmetic, and elementary parts of measure theory. As a demonstration of Russell's logicism, *Principia* depends upon much prior arithmetization of mathematics, e.g. of analysis, which is not explicitly treated. Even with these allowances much is still left out: e.g., abstract algebra and statistics. Russell's unpublished papers (*Papers*, vols. 4–5), however, contain logical innovations not included in *Principia*, e.g., anticipations of Church's lambda-calculus.

On Russell's extreme realism, everything that can be referred to is a *term* that has being (though not necessarily existence). The combination of terms by means of a relation results in a complex term, which is a proposition. Terms are neither linguistic nor psychological. The first task of philosophy is the theoretical analysis of propositions into their constituents. The propositions of logic are unique in that they remain true when any of their terms (apart from logical constants) are replaced by *any* other terms.

In 1901 Russell discovered that this position fell prey to self-referential paradoxes. For example, if the combination of any number of terms is a new term, the combination of *all* terms is a term distinct from any term. The most famous such paradox is called Russell's paradox. Russell's solution was the *theory of types*, which banned self-reference by stratifying terms and expressions into complex hierarchies of disjoint subclasses. The expression 'all terms', e.g., is then meaningless unless restricted to terms of specified type(s), and the combination of terms of a given type is a term of different type. A simple version of the theory appeared in *Principles of Mathematics* (appendix A), but did not eliminate all the paradoxes. Russell developed a more elaborate version that did, in "Mathematical Logic as Based on the Theory of Types" (1908) and in *Principia*. From 1903 to 1908 Russell sought to preserve his earlier account of logic by finding other ways to avoid the paradoxes – including a well-developed substitutional theory of classes and relations (posthumously published in *Essays in Analysis*, 1974, and *Papers*, vol. 5). Other costs of type theory for Russell's logicism included the vastly increased complexity of the resulting system and the admission of the problematic axiom of reducibility.

Two other difficulties with Russell's extreme realism had important consequences: (1) 'I met Quine' and 'I met a man' are different propositions, even when Quine is the man I met. In the *Principles,* the first proposition contains a man, while the second contains a *denoting concept* that denotes the man. Denoting concepts are like Fregean senses; they are meanings and have denotations. When one occurs in a proposition the proposition is not about the concept but its denotation. This theory requires that there be some way in which a denoting concept, rather than its denotation, can be denoted. After much effort, Russell concluded in "On Denoting" (1905) that this was impossible and eliminated denoting concepts as intermediaries between denoting phrases and their denotations by means of his theory of descriptions. Using first-order predicate logic, Russell showed (in a broad, though not comprehensive range of cases) how denoting phrases could be eliminated in favor of predicates and quantified variables, for which *logically proper names* could be substituted. (These were names of objects of acquaintance – represented in ordinary language by 'this' and 'that'. Most names, he thought, were disguised definite descriptions.) Similar techniques were applied elsewhere to other kinds of expression (e.g. class names) resulting in the more general *theory of incomplete symbols.* One important consequence of this was that the ontological commitments of a theory could be reduced by reformulating the theory to remove expressions that apparently denoted problematic entities. (2) The theory of incomplete symbols also helped solve extreme realism's epistemic problems, namely how to account for knowledge of terms that do not exist, and for the distinction between true and false propositions. First, the theory explained how knowledge of a wide range of items could be achieved by knowledge by acquaintance of a much narrower range. Second, propositional expressions were treated as incomplete symbols and eliminated in favor of their constituents and a propositional attitude by Russell's multiple relation theory of judgment.

These innovations marked the end of Russell's extreme realism, though he remained a Platonist in that he included universals among the objects of acquaintance. Russell referred to all his philosophy after 1898 as *logical atomism,* indicating thereby that certain categories of items were taken as basic and items in other categories were constructed from them by rigorous logical means. It depends therefore upon reduction, which became a key concept in early analytic philosophy. Logical atomism changed as Russell's logic developed and as more philosophical consequences were drawn from its application, but the label is now most often applied to the modified realism Russell held from 1905 to 1919. Logic was central to Russell's philosophy from 1900 onward, and much of his fertility and importance as a philosopher came from his application of the new logic to old problems.

In 1910 Russell became a lecturer at Cambridge. There his interests turned to epistemology. In writing a popular book, *Problems of Philosophy* (1912), he first came to appreciate the work of the British empiricists, especially Hume and Berkeley. He held that empirical knowledge is based on direct acquaintance with sense-data, and that matter itself, of which we have only knowledge by description, is postulated as the best explanation of sense-data. He soon became dissatisfied with this idea and proposed instead that matter be logically constructed out of sense-data and unsensed sensibilia, thereby obviating dubious inferences to material objects as the causes of sensations. This proposal was inspired by the successful constructions of mathematical concepts in *Principia.* He planned a large work, "Theory of Knowledge," which was to use the multiple relation theory to extend his account from acquaintance to belief and inference (*Papers,* vol. 7). However, the project was abandoned as incomplete in the face of Wittgenstein's attacks on the multiple relation theory, and Russell published only those portions dealing with acquaintance. The construction of matter, however, went ahead, at least in outline, in *Our Knowledge of the External World* (1914), though the only detailed constructions were undertaken later by Carnap. On Russell's account, material objects are those series of sensibilia that obey the laws of physics. Sensibilia of which a mind is aware (sense-data) provide the experiential basis for that mind's knowledge of the physical world. This theory is similar, though not identical, to phenomenalism. Russell saw the theory as an application of Ockham's razor, by which postulated entities were replaced by logical constructions. He devoted much time to understanding modern physics, including relativity and quantum theory, and in *The Analysis of Matter* (1927) he incorporated the fundamental ideas of those theories into his construction of the physical world. In this book he abandoned sensibilia as fundamental constituents of the world in favor of events, which were "neutral" because intrinsically neither physical nor mental.

In 1916 Russell was dismissed from Cambridge on political grounds and from that time on had to earn his living by writing and public lecturing. His popular lectures, "The Philosophy of Logical Atomism" (1918), were a result of this. These lectures form an interim work, looking back on the logical achievements of 1905–10 and emphasizing their importance for philosophy, while taking stock of the problems raised by Wittgenstein's criticisms of the multiple relation theory. In 1919 Russell's philosophy of mind underwent substantial changes, partly in response to those criticisms. The changes appeared in "On Propositions: What They Are and How They Mean" (1919) and *The Analysis of Mind* (1921), where the influence of contemporary trends in psychology, especially behaviorism, is evident. Russell gave up the view that minds are among the fundamental constituents of the world, and adopted neutral monism, already advocated by Mach, James, and the American New Realists. On Russell's neutral monism, a mind is constituted by a set of events related by subjective temporal relations (simultaneity, successiveness) and by certain special ("mnemic") causal laws. In this way he was able to explain the apparent fact that "Hume's inability to perceive himself was not peculiar." In place of the multiple relation theory Russell identified the contents of beliefs with images ("image-propositions") and words ("word-propositions"), understood as certain sorts of events, and analyzed truth (*qua* correspondence) in terms of resemblance and causal relations.

From 1938 to 1944 Russell lived in the United States, where he wrote *An Inquiry into Meaning and Truth* (1940) and his popular *A History of Western Philosophy* (1945). His philosophical attention turned from metaphysics to epistemology and he continued to work in this field after he returned in 1944 to Cambridge, where he completed his last major philosophical work, *Human Knowledge: Its Scope and Limits* (1948). The framework of Russell's early epistemology consisted of an analysis of knowledge in terms of justified true belief (though it has been suggested that he unintentionally anticipated Edmund Gettier's objection to this analysis), and an analysis of epistemic justification that combined fallibilism with a weak empiricism and with a foundationalism that made room for coherence. This framework was retained in *An Inquiry* and *Human Knowledge*, but there were two sorts of changes that attenuated the foundationalist and

empiricist elements and accentuated the fallibilist element. First, the scope of human knowledge was reduced. Russell had already replaced his earlier Moorean consequentialism about values with subjectivism. (Contrast "The Elements of Ethics," 1910, with, e.g., *Religion and Science*, 1935, or *Human Society in Ethics and Politics*, 1954.) Consequently, what had been construed as self-evident judgments of intrinsic value came to be regarded as non-cognitive expressions of desire. In addition, Russell now reversed his earlier belief that deductive inference can yield new knowledge. Second, the degree of justification attainable in human knowledge was reduced at all levels. Regarding the foundation of perceptual beliefs, Russell came to admit that the object-knowledge ("acquaintance with a sense-datum" was replaced by "noticing a perceptive occurrence" in *An Inquiry*) that provides the non-inferential justification for a perceptual belief is buried under layers of "interpretation" and unconscious inference in even the earliest stages of perceptual processes. Regarding the superstructure of inferentially justified beliefs, Russell concluded in *Human Knowledge* that unrestricted induction is not generally truth-preserving (anticipating Goodman's "new riddle of induction"). Consideration of the work of Reichenbach and Keynes on probability led him to the conclusion that certain "postulates" are needed "to provide the antecedent probabilities required to justify inductions," and that the only possible justification for believing these postulates lies, not in their self-evidence, but in the resultant increase in the overall coherence of one's total belief system. In the end, Russell's desire for certainty went unsatisfied, as he felt himself forced to the conclusion that "all human knowledge is uncertain, inexact, and partial. To this doctrine we have not found any limitation whatever."

Russell's strictly philosophical writings of 1919 and later have generally been less influential than his earlier writings. His influence was eclipsed by that of logical positivism and ordinary language philosophy. He approved of the logical positivists' respect for logic and science, though he disagreed with their metaphysical agnosticism. But his dislike of ordinary language philosophy was visceral. In *My Philosophical Development* (1959), he accused its practitioners of abandoning the attempt to understand the world, "that grave and important task which philosophy throughout the ages has hitherto pursued."

See also FREGE, LOGICAL CONSTRUCTION,

LOGICISM, PERCEPTION, SET-THEORETIC PARADOXES, SET THEORY, THEORY OF DESCRIPTIONS, TYPE THEORY, WHITEHEAD.

N.G. & D.B.M.

Russell's paradox. See SET-THEORETIC PARADOXES.

Russian nihilism, a form of nihilism, a phenomenon mainly of Russia in the 1860s, which, in contrast to the general cultural nihilism that Nietzsche later criticized (in the 1880s) as a "dead-end" devaluing of *all* values, was future-oriented and "instrumental," exalting possibility over actuality. Russian nihilists urged the "annihilation" – figurative and literal – of the *past* and *present*, i.e., of realized social and cultural values and of such values in process of realization, in the name of the *future*, i.e., for the sake of social and cultural values yet to be realized. Bakunin, as early as 1842, had stated the basic nihilist theme: "the negation of what exists . . . for the benefit of the future which does not yet exist." The best-known literary exemplar of nihilism in Russia is the character Bazarov in Turgenev's novel *Fathers and Sons* (1862). Its most articulate spokesman was Dmitri Pisarev (1840–68), who shared Bazarov's cultural anti-Romanticism, philosophical anti-idealism, and unquestioned trust in the power of natural science to solve social and moral problems. Pisarev proclaimed, "It is precisely in the [spread-eagled, laboratory] frog that the salvation . . . of the Russian people is to be found." And he formulated what may serve as the manifesto of Russian nihilism: "What can be broken should be broken; what will stand the blow is fit to live; what breaks into smithereens is rubbish; in any case, strike right and left, it will not and cannot do any harm." **See also** RUSSIAN PHILOSOPHY.   G.L.K.

Russian philosophy, the philosophy produced by Russian thinkers, both in Russia and in the countries to which they emigrated, from the mid-eighteenth century to the present. There was no Renaissance in Russia, but in the early eighteenth century Peter the Great, in opening a "window to the West," opened Russia up to Western philosophical influences. The beginnings of Russian speculation date from that period, in the dialogues, fables, and poems of the anti-Enlightenment thinker Gregory Skovoroda (1722–94) and in the social tracts, metaphysical treatises, and poems of the Enlightenment thinker Alexander Radishchev (1749–1802).

Until the last quarter of the nineteenth century the most original and forceful Russian thinkers stood outside the academy. Since then, both in Russia and in Western exile, a number of the most important Russian philosophers – including Berdyaev and Lev Shestov (1866–1938) – have been university professors. The nineteenth-century thinkers, though university-educated, lacked advanced degrees. The only university professor among them, Peter Lavrov (1823–1900), taught mathematics and science rather than philosophy (during the 1850s). If we compare Russian philosophy to German philosophy of this period, with its galaxy of university professors – Wolff, Kant, Fichte, Schelling, Hegel, Dilthey – the contrast is sharp. However, if we compare Russian philosophy to English or French philosophy, the contrast fades. No professors of philosophy appear in the line from Francis Bacon through Hobbes, Locke, Berkeley, Hume, Bentham, and J. S. Mill, to Spencer. And in France Montaigne, Descartes, Pascal, Rousseau, and Comte were all non-professors.

True to their non-professional, even "amateur" status, Russian philosophers until the late nineteenth century paid little attention to the more technical disciplines: logic, epistemology, philosophy of language, and philosophy of science. They focused instead on philosophical anthropology, ethics, social and political philosophy, philosophy of history, and philosophy of religion.

In Russia, more than in any other Western cultural tradition, speculation, fiction, and poetry have been linked. On the one hand, major novelists such as Tolstoy and Dostoevsky, and major poets such as Pasternak and Brodsky, have engaged in wide-ranging philosophical reflection. On the other hand, philosophers such as Skovoroda, Alexei Khomyakov (1804–60), and Vladimir Solovyov (1853–1900) were gifted poets, while thinkers such as Herzen, Konstantin Leontyev (1831–91), and the anti-Leninist Marxist Alexander Bogdanov (1873–1928) made their literary mark with novels, short stories, and memoirs. Such Russian thinkers as Vasily Rozanov (1856–1919) and Shestov, although they wrote no *belles lettres*, were celebrated in literary circles for their sparkling essayistic and aphoristic styles.

Certain preoccupations of nineteenth-century Russian thinkers – especially Pyotr Chaadaev (1794–1856) during the 1820s and 1830s, the Slavophiles and Westernizers during the 1840s and 1850s, and the Populists during the 1860s and 1870s – might appear to be distinctive but in fact were not. The controversial questions of Russia's relation to Western Europe and of

Russia's "special path" to modernity have their counterparts in the reflections of thinkers in Spain ("Spain and Europe"), Germany (the *Sonderweg* – a term of which the Russian *osobyi put'* is a translation), and Poland ("the Polish Question").

The content of Russian philosophy may be characterized in general terms as tending toward utopianism, maximalism, moralism, and soteriology. To take the last point first: Hegelianism was received in Russia in the 1830s not only as an all-embracing philosophical system but also as a vehicle of secular salvation. In the 1860s Darwinism was similarly received, as was Marxism in the 1890s. Utopianism appears at the historical and sociopolitical level in two of Solovyov's characteristic doctrines: his early "free theocracy," in which the spiritual authority of the Roman pope was to be united with the secular authority of the Russian tsar; and his later ecumenical project of reuniting the Eastern (Russian Orthodox) and Western (Roman Catholic) churches in a single "universal [*vselenskaia*] church" that would also incorporate the "Protestant principle" of free philosophical and theological inquiry. Maximalism appears at the individual and religious level in Shestov's claim that God, for whom alone "all things are possible," can cause what has happened *not* to have happened and, in particular, can restore irrecoverable human loss, such as that associated with disease, deformity, madness, and death. Maximalism and moralism are united at the cosmic and "scientific-technological" level in Nikolai Fyodorov's (1829–1903) insistence on the overriding moral obligation of all men ("the sons") to join the common cause of restoring life to "the fathers," those who gave them life rather than, as sanctioned by the "theory of progress," pushing them, figuratively if not literally, into the grave.

Certain doctrinal emphases and assumptions link Russian thinkers from widely separated points on the political and ideological spectrum:

(1) Russian philosophers were nearly unanimous in dismissing the notorious Cartesian-Humean "problem of other minds" as a non-problem. Their convictions about human community and conciliarity (*sobornost'*), whether religious or secular, were too powerful to permit Russian thinkers to raise serious doubts as to whether their moaning and bleeding neighbor was "really" in pain.

(2) Most Russian thinkers – the Westernizers were a partial exception – viewed key Western philosophical positions and formulations, from the Socratic "know thyself" to the Cartesian *cog-ito*, as overly individualistic and overly intellectualistic, as failing to take into account the *wholeness* of the human person.

(3) Both such anti-Marxists as Herzen (with his "philosophy of the act") and Fyodorov (with his "projective" common task) and the early Russian Marxists were in agreement about the unacceptability of the "Western" dichotomy between thought and action. But when they stressed the unity of theory and practice, a key question remained: Who is to shape this unity? And what is its form? The threadbare Marxist-Leninist "philosophy" of the Stalin years paid lip service to the freedom involved in forging such a unity. Stalin in fact imposed crushing restraints upon both thought and action.

Since 1982, works by and about the previously abused or neglected religious and speculative thinkers of Russia's past have been widely republished and eagerly discussed. This applies to Fyodorov, Solovyov, Leontyev, Rozanov, Berdyaev, Shestov, and the Husserlian Shpet, among others.

See also BAKUNIN, BERDYAEV, HERZEN, LENIN, PLEKHANOV, RUSSIAN NIHILISM, SOLOVYOV.   G.L.K.

Ryle, Gilbert (1900–76), English analytic philosopher known especially for his contributions to the philosophy of mind and his attacks on Cartesianism.

His best-known work is the masterpiece *The Concept of Mind* (1949), an attack on what he calls "Cartesian dualism" and a defense of a type of logical behaviorism. This dualism he dubs "the dogma of the Ghost in the Machine," the Machine being the body, which is physical and publicly observable, and the Ghost being the mind conceived as a private or secret arena in which episodes of sense perception, consciousness, and inner perception take place. A person, then, is a combination of such a mind and a body, with the mind operating the body through exercises of will called "volitions." Ryle's attack on this doctrine is both sharply focused and multifarious. He finds that it rests on a category mistake, namely, assimilating statements about mental processes to the same category as statements about physical processes. This is a mistake in the logic of mental statements and mental concepts and leads to the mistaken metaphysical theory that a person is composed of two separate and distinct (though somehow related) entities, a mind and a body. It is true that statements about the physical are statements about things and their changes. But statements about the mental are not, and in particular are not about a thing called "the mind." These two types of statements do not belong to the same category. To show this, Ryle deploys a variety of arguments, including arguments alleging the impossibility of causal relations between mind and body and arguments alleging vicious infinite regresses. To develop his positive view on the nature of mind, Ryle studies the uses (and hence the logic) of mental terms and finds that mental statements tell us that the person performs observable actions in certain ways and has a disposition to perform other observable actions in specifiable circumstances. For example, to do something intelligently is to do something physical in a certain way and to adjust one's behavior to the circumstances, not, as the dogma of the Ghost in the Machine would have it, to perform two actions, one of which is a mental action of thinking that eventually causes a separate physical action. Ryle buttresses this position with many acute and subtle analyses of the uses of mental terms.

Much of Ryle's other work concerns philosophical methodology, sustaining the thesis (which is the backbone of *The Concept of Mind*) that philosophical problems and doctrines often arise from conceptual confusion, i.e., from mistakes about the logic of language. Important writings in this vein include the influential article "Systematically Misleading Expressions" and the book *Dilemmas* (1954). Ryle was also interested in Greek philosophy throughout his life, and his last major work, *Plato's Progress*, puts forward novel hypotheses about changes in Plato's views, the role of the Academy, the purposes and uses of Plato's dialogues, and Plato's relations with the rulers of Syracuse.

See also BEHAVIORISM, CATEGORY, PHILOSOPHY OF MIND, WITTGENSTEIN.   J.W.M.

S

S5. See MODAL LOGIC.

Saadiah Gaon (882–942), Jewish exegete, philosopher, liturgist, grammarian, and lexicographer. Born in the Fayyūm in Egypt, Saadiah wrote his first Hebrew dictionary by age twenty. He removed to Tiberias, probably fleeing the backlash of his polemic against the Karaite (biblicist, anti-Talmudic) sect. There he mastered the inductive techniques of semantic analysis pioneered by Muslim Mu'tazilites in defending their rationalistic monotheism and voluntaristic theodicy. He learned philologically from the Masoretes and liturgical poets, and philosophically from the Mu'tazilite-influenced Jewish metaphysician Daūd al-Muqammiṣ of Raqqa in Iraq, and Isaac Israeli of Qayrawan in Tunisia, a Neoplatonizing physician, with whom the young philosopher attempted a correspondence. But his sense of system, evidenced in his pioneering chronology, prayerbook, and scheme of tropes, and nurtured by Arabic versions of Plato (but seemingly not much Aristotle), allowed him to outgrow and outshine his mentors. He came to prominence by successfully defending the traditional Hebrew calendar, using astronomical, mathematical, and rabbinic arguments. Called to Baghdad, he became *Gaon* (Hebrew, 'Eminence') or head of the ancient Talmudic academy of Pumpedita, then nearly defunct. His commentaries on rabbinic property law and his letters to Jewish communities as far away as Spain refurbished the authority of the academy, but a controversy with the Exilarch, secular head of Mesopotamian Jewry, led to his deposition and six years in limbo, deprived of his judicial authority. He delved into scientific cosmology, translated many biblical books into Arabic with philosophic commentaries and thematic introductions, and around 933 completed *The Book of Critically Chosen Beliefs and Convictions,* the first Jewish philosophical summa. Unusual among medieval works for a lengthy epistemological introduction, its ten Arabic treatises defend and define creation, monotheism, human obligation and virtue, theodicy, natural retribution, resurrection, immortality and recompense, Israel's redemption, and the good life.

Saadiah argues that no single good suffices for human happiness; each in isolation is destructive. The Torah prepares the optimal blend of the appetitive and erotic, procreative, civilizational, ascetic, political, intellectual, pious, and tranquil. Following al-Rhāzī (d. 925 or 932), Saadiah argues that since destruction always overcomes organization in this world, sufferings will always outweigh pleasures; therefore (as in rabbinic and Mu'tazilite theodicy) God must be assumed to right the balances in the hereafter. Indeed, justice is the object of creation – not simply that the righteous be rewarded but that all should *earn* their deserved requital: the very light that is sown for the righteous is the fire that torments the wicked. But if requital and even recompense must be earned, this life is much more than an anteroom. Authenticity becomes a value in itself: the innocent are not told directly that their sufferings are a trial, or their testing would be invalid. Only by enduring their sufferings without interference can they demonstrate the qualities that make them worthy of the highest reward. Movingly reconciled with the Exilarch, Saadiah ended his life as *Gaon.* His voluntarism, naturalism, and rationalism laid philosophical foundations for Maimonides, and his inductive exegesis became a cornerstone of critical hermeneutics.

See also JEWISH PHILOSOPHY.   L.E.G.

sage. See SHENG.

Saint Petersburg paradox, a puzzle about gambling that motivated the distinction between expected return and expected utility. Daniel Bernoulli published it in a St. Petersburg journal in 1738. It concerns a gamble like this: it pays $2 if heads appears on the first toss of a coin, $4 if heads does not appear until the second toss, $8 if heads does not appear until the third toss, and so on. The expected return from the gamble is $(\frac{1}{2})2 + (\frac{1}{4})4 + (\frac{1}{8})8 + \ldots$, or $1 + 1 + 1 + \ldots$, i.e., it is infinite. But no one would pay much for the gamble. So it seems that expected returns do not govern rational preferences. Bernoulli argued that *expected utilities* govern rational preferences. He also held that the utility of wealth is proportional to the log of the amount of wealth. Given his assumptions, the gamble has finite expected utility, and should not be preferred to large sums of money. However, a twentieth-century version of the paradox, attributed to Karl Menger, reconstructs the gamble, putting utility payoffs in place of monetary payoffs, so that the new gamble has infinite expected utility. Since no one would trade much utility for the new gamble, it also seems that expected utilities do not govern rational preferences. The resolution of the paradox is under debate. **See also** DECISION THEORY, EMPIRICAL DECISION THEORY.

                                                                                P.We.

Saint-Simon, Comte de, title of Claude-Henri de Rouvroy (1760–1825), French social reformer. An aristocrat by birth, he initially joined the ranks of the enlightened and liberal bourgeoisie. His Newtonian *Letters to an Inhabitant of Geneva* (1803) and *Introduction to Scientific Works of the Nineteenth Century* (1808) championed Condorcet's vision of scientific and technological progress. With Auguste Comte, he shared a positivistic philosophy of history: the triumph of science over metaphysics. Written in wartime, *The Reorganization of European Society* (1814) urged the creation of a European parliamentary system to secure peace and unity. Having moved from scientism to pacifism, Saint-Simon moved further to industrialism.

In 1817, under the influence of two theocratic thinkers, de Maistre and Bonald, Saint-Simon turned away from classical economic liberalism and repudiated laissez-faire capitalism. *The Industrial System* (1820) drafts the program for a hierarchical state, a technocratic society, and a planned economy. The industrial society of the future is based on the principles of productivity and cooperation and led by a rational and efficient class, the industrialists (artists, scientists, and technicians). He argued that the association of positivism with unselfishness, of techniques of rational production with social solidarity and interdependency, would remedy the plight of the poor. Industrialism prefigures socialism, and socialism paves the way for the rule of the law of love, the eschatological age of *The New Christianity* (1825). This utopian treatise, which reveals Saint-Simon's alternative to reactionary Catholicism and Protestant individualism, became the Bible of the Saint-Simonians, a sectarian school of utopian socialists.   J.-L.S.

Sakti, in Hindu thought, force, power, or energy, personified as the divine consort of the god Siva. Sakti is viewed as the feminine active divine aspect (as contrasted with the masculine passive divine aspect), which affects the creation, maintenance, and dissolution of the universe, and possesses intelligence, will, knowledge, and action as modes.   K.E.Y.

Saktism. See SAKTI.

salva veritate. See SUBSTITUTIVITY SALVA VERITATE.

sāmādhi, Sanskrit term meaning 'concentration', 'absorption', 'superconscious state', 'altered state of consciousness'. In India's philosophical tradition this term was made famous by its use in the Yoga system of Patañjali (second century B.C.). In this system the goal was to attain the self's freedom, so that the self, conceived as pure consciousness in its true nature, would not be limited by the material modes of existence. It was believed that through a series of yogic techniques the self is freed from its karmic fetters and liberated to its original state of self-luminous consciousness, known as *samādhi*. The Indian philosophical systems had raised and debated many epistemological and metaphysical questions regarding the nature of consciousness, the concept of mind, and the idea of the self. They also wondered whether a yogi who has attained *samādhi* is within the confines of the conventional moral realm. This issue is similar to Nietzsche's idea of the transvaluation of values. **See also** NIETZSCHE.   D.K.C.

samanantara-pratyaya, in Buddhism, a causal term meaning 'immediately antecedent (*anantara*) and similar (*sama*) condition'. According to Buddhist causal theory, every existent is a continuum of momentary events of various kinds. These momentary events may be causally connected to one another in a variety of ways; one of these is denoted by the term *samanantara-pratyaya*. This kind of causal connection requires that every momentary event have, as a necessary condition for its existence, an immediately preceding event of the same kind. So, e.g., among the necessary conditions for the occurrence of a moment of sensation in some continuum must be the occurrence of an immediately preceding moment of sensation in that same continuum.
                                                                                P.J.G.

samatha, in Buddhism, tranquillity or calm. The term is used to describe both one kind of meditational practice and the states of consciousness produced by it. To cultivate tranquillity or calmness is to reduce the mind's level of affect and, finally, to produce a state of consciousness in which emotion is altogether absent. This condition is taken to have salvific significance because emotional disturbance of all kinds is thought to hinder clear perception and understanding of the way things are; reduction of affect therefore aids accurate cognition. The techniques designed to foster this reduction are essentially concentrative. **See also** JHĀNA, VIPASSANĀ.   P.J.G.

Samhita. See VEDAS.

Śaṁkara. See SHAṄKARA.

saṁsāra (Sanskrit, 'going around'), in Hindu thought, the ceaseless rounds of rebirth that constitute the human predicament. *Saṁsāra* speaks of the relentless cycle of coming and going in transmigration of the soul from body to body in this and other worlds. It is the manifestation of karma, for one's deeds bear fruition in the timing, status, form, and nature of the phenomenal person in future lives. Ordinary individuals have little prospect of release and in some systems the relationship among karma, rebirth, and *saṁsāra* is a highly mechanical cosmic law of debt and credit which affirms that human deeds produce their own reward or punishment. For theists the Deity is the ultimate controller of *saṁsāra* and can break the cycle, adjust it, or, by the god's kindness or grace, save one from future births regardless of one's actions. **See also** AVATAR.
R.N.Mi.

Sanches, Francisco (c.1551–1623), Portuguese-born philosopher and physician. Raised in southern France, he took his medical degree at the University of Montpellier. After a decade of medical practice he was professor of philosophy at the University of Toulouse and later professor of medicine there.

His most important work, *Quod nihil scitur* (*That Nothing Is Known*, 1581), is a classic of skeptical argumentation. Written at the same time that his cousin, Montaigne, wrote the "Apology for Raimund Sebond," it devastatingly criticized the Aristotelian theory of knowledge. He began by declaring that he did not even know if he knew nothing. Then he examined the Aristotelian view that science consists of certain knowledge gained by demonstrations from true definitions. First of all, we do not possess such definitions, since all our definitions are just arbitrary names of things. The Aristotelian theory of demonstration is useless, since in syllogistic reasoning the conclusion has to be part of the evidence for the premises.

E.g., how can one know that all men are mortal unless one knows that Socrates is mortal? Also, anything can be proven by syllogistic reasoning if one chooses the right premises. This does not produce real knowledge. Further we cannot know anything through its causes, since one would have to know the causes of the causes, and the causes of these, ad infinitum.

Sanches also attacked the Platonic theory of knowledge, since mathematical knowledge is about ideal rather than real objects. Mathematics is only hypothetical. Its relevance to experience is not known. True science would consist of perfect knowledge of a thing. Each particular would be understood in and by itself. Such knowledge can be attained only by God. We cannot study objects one by one, since they are all interrelated and interconnected. Our faculties are also not reliable enough. Hence genuine knowledge cannot be attained by humans. What we can do, using "scientific method" (a term first used by Sanches), is gather careful empirical information and make cautious judgments about it. His views were well known in the seventeenth century, and may have inspired the "mitigated skepticism" of Gassendi and others.
See also SKEPTICISM.   R.H.P.

sanction, anything whose function is to penalize or reward. It is useful to distinguish between social sanctions, legal sanctions, internal sanctions, and religious sanctions. Social sanctions are extralegal pressures exerted upon the agent by others. For example, others might distrust us, ostracize us, or even physically attack us, if we behave in certain ways. Legal sanctions include corporal punishment, imprisonment, fines, withdrawal of the legal rights to run a business or to leave the area, and other penalties. Internal sanctions may include not only guilt feelings but also the sympathetic pleasures of helping others or the gratified conscience of doing right. Divine sanctions, if there are any, are rewards or punishments given to us by a god while we are alive or after we die.

There are important philosophical questions concerning sanctions. Should law be defined as the rules the breaking of which elicits punishment by the state? Could there be a moral duty to behave in a given way if there were no social sanctions concerning such behavior? If not, then a conventionalist account of moral duty seems unavoidable. And, to what extent does the combined effect of external and internal sanctions make rational egoism (or prudence or self-interest) coincide with morality?   B.W.H.

Śaṅkara. See SHAṄKARA.

Sankhya-Yoga, a system of Hindu thought that posits two sorts of reality, immaterial (*purusha*) and material (*prakṛti*). *Prakṛti*, a physical stuff composed of what is lightweight and fine-grained (*sattva*), what is heavy and coarse (*tamas*), and what is active (*rajas*), is in some sense the source of matter, force, space, and time. Sankhya physical theory explains the complex by reference to the properties of its components.

The physical universe everlastingly oscillates between states in which the three elements exist unmixed and states in which they mingle; when they mingle, they compose physical bodies some of which incarnate bits of *purusha*. When the basic elements mingle, transmigration occurs. *Pursha* is inherently passive, and mental properties belong only to the composite of *prakṛti* and *purusha*, leading critics to ask what, when the physical elements are separated, individuates one mind from another. The answer is that one bit of *purusha* has one transmigratory history and another bit has another history. Critics (e.g., Nyāya-Vaishesika philosophers) were not satisfied with this answer, which allowed no intrinsic distinctions between bits of non-incarnate *purusha*. The dialectic of criticism led to Advaita Vedanta (for which all *purusha* distinctions are illusory) and other varieties of Vedanta (Dvaita and Viśistadvaita) for which minds have inherent, not merely embodied, consciousness. Sankhya claims that there can be no emergent properties (properties not somehow a reshuffling of prior properties), so the effect must in some sense preexist in the cause.

See also HINDUISM.   K.E.Y.

Santayana, George (1863–1952), Spanish-American philosopher and writer. Born in Spain, he arrived in the United States as a child, received his education at Harvard, and rose to professor of philosophy there. He first came to prominence for his view, developed in *The Sense of Beauty* (1896), that beauty is objectified pleasure. His *The Life of Reason* (5 vols., 1905), a celebrated expression of his naturalistic vision, traces human creativity in ordinary life, society, art, religion, and science. He denied that his philosophy ever changed, but the mature expression of his thought, in *Skepticism and Animal Faith* (1923) and *The Realms of Being* (4 vols., 1927–40), is deliberately ontological and lacks the phenomenological emphasis of the earlier work.

Human beings, according to Santayana, are animals in a material world contingent to the core. Reflection must take as its primary datum human action aimed at eating and fleeing. The philosophy of animal faith consists of disentangling the beliefs tacit in such actions and yields a realism concerning both the objects of immediate consciousness and the objects of belief. Knowledge is true belief rendered in symbolic terms. As symbolism, it constitutes the hauntingly beautiful worlds of the senses, poetry, and religion; as knowledge, it guides and is tested by successful action.

Santayana had been taught by William James, and his insistence on the primacy of action suggests a close similarity to the views of Dewey. He is, nevertheless, not a pragmatist in any ordinary sense: he views nature as the fully formed arena of human activity and experience as a flow of isolated, private sentience in this alien world. His deepest sympathy is with Aristotle, though he agrees with Plato about the mind-independent existence of Forms and with Schopenhauer about the dimness of human prospects.

His mature four-realm ontology turns on the distinction between *essence* and *matter*. Essences are forms of definiteness. They are infinite in number and encompass everything possible. Their eternity makes them causally inefficacious: as possibilities, they cannot accomplish their own actualization. Matter, a surd and formless force, generates the physical universe by selecting essences for embodiment. Truth is the realm of being created by the intersection of matter and form: it is the eternal record of essences that have been, are being, and will be given actuality in the history of the world. Spirit or consciousness cannot be reduced to the motions of the physical organism that give rise to it. It is constituted by a sequence of acts or intuitions whose objects are essences but whose time-spanning, synthetic nature renders them impotent.

Organic selectivity is the source of values. Accordingly, the good of each organism is a function of its nature. Santayana simply accepts the fact that some of these goods are incommensurable and the tragic reality that they may be incompatible, as well. Under favorable circumstances, a life of reason or of maximal harmonized satisfactions is possible for a while. The finest achievement of human beings, however, is the spiritual life in which we overcome animal partiality and thus all valuation in order to enjoy the intuition of eternal essences. Santayana identifies such spirituality with the best that religion and sound philosophy can offer. It does not help us escape finitude and death, but enables us in this short life to transcend care and to intuit the eternal.

Santayana's exquisite vision has gained him many admirers but few followers. His system is a self-consistent and sophisticated synthesis of elements, such as materialism and Platonism, that have hitherto been thought impossible to reconcile. His masterful writing makes his books instructive and pleasurable, even if many of his characteristic views engender resistance among philosophers.   J.La.

Sapir-Whorf hypothesis, broadly, the claim that one's perception, thought, and behavior are influenced by one's language. The hypothesis was named after Benjamin Lee Whorf (1897–1941) and his teacher Edward Sapir (1884–1939). We may discern different versions of this claim by distinguishing degrees of linguistic influence, the highest of which is complete and unalterable determination of the fundamental structures of perception, thought, and behavior. In the most radical form, the hypothesis says that one's reality is constructed by one's language and that differently structured languages give rise to different realities, which are incommensurable. **See also** LINGUISTIC RELATIVITY, PHILOSOPHY OF LANGUAGE, SOCIAL CONSTRUCTIVISM.

T.Y.

Sartre, Jean-Paul (1905–80), French philosopher and writer, the leading advocate of existentialism during the years following World War II. The heart of his philosophy was the precious notion of freedom and its concomitant sense of personal responsibility. He insisted, in an interview a few years before his death, that he never ceased to believe that "in the end one is always responsible for what is made of one," only a slight revision of his earlier, bolder slogan, "man makes himself." To be sure, as a student of Hegel, Marx, Husserl, and Heidegger – and because of his own physical frailty and the tragedies of the war – Sartre had to be well aware of the many constraints and obstacles to human freedom, but as a Cartesian, he never deviated from Descartes's classical portrait of human consciousness as free and distinct from the physical universe it inhabits. One is never free of one's "situation," Sartre tells us, though one is always free to deny ("negate") that situation and to try to change it. To be human, to be conscious, is to be free to imagine, free to choose, and responsible for one's lot in life.

As a student, Sartre was fascinated by Husserl's new philosophical method, phenomenology. His first essays were direct responses to Husserl and applications of the phenomenological method. His essay on *The Imagination* in 1936 established the groundwork for much of what was to follow: the celebration of our remarkable freedom to imagine the world other than it is and (following Kant) the way that this ability informs all of our experience. In *The Transcendence of the Ego* (1937) he reconsidered Husserl's central idea of a "phenomenological reduction" (the idea of examining the essential structures of consciousness as such) and argued (following Heidegger) that one cannot examine consciousness without at the same time recognizing the reality of actual objects in the world. In other words, there can be no such "reduction." In his novel *Nausea* (1938), Sartre made this point in a protracted example: his bored and often nauseated narrator confronts a gnarled chestnut tree in the park and recognizes with a visceral shock that its presence is simply given and utterly irreducible. In *The Transcendence of the Ego* Sartre also reconsiders the notion of the self, which Husserl (and so many earlier philosophers) had identified with consciousness. But the self, Sartre argues, is not "in" consciousness, much less identical to it. The self is out there "in the world, like the self of another." In other words, the self is an ongoing project in the world with other people; it is not simply self-awareness or self-consciousness as such ("I think, therefore I am").

This separation of self and consciousness and the rejection of the self as simply self-consciousness provide the framework for Sartre's greatest philosophical treatise, *L'être et le néant* (*Being and Nothingness*, 1943). Its structure is unabashedly Cartesian, consciousness ("being-for-itself" or *pour soi*) on the one side, the existence of mere things ("being-in-itself" or *en soi*) on the other. (The phraseology comes from Hegel.) But Sartre does not fall into the Cartesian trap of designating these two types of being as separate "substances." Instead, Sartre describes consciousness as "nothing' – "not a thing" but an activity, "a wind blowing from nowhere toward the world." Sartre often resorts to visceral metaphors when developing this theme (e.g., "a worm coiled in the heart of being"), but much of what he is arguing is familiar to philosophical readers in the more metaphor-free work of Kant, who also warned against the follies ("paralogisms") of understanding consciousness as itself a (possible) object of consciousness rather than as the activity of constituting the objects of consciousness. (As the lens of a camera can never see itself – and in a mirror only sees a reflection of itself – consciousness can never view itself as consciousness and is only aware of itself – "for itself" – through its experience of objects.) Ontologically, one might think of "nothingness" as "no-thing-ness," a much less outrageous suggestion than those that would make it an odd sort of a thing.

It is through the nothingness of consciousness and its activities that negation comes into the world, our ability to imagine the world other than it is and the inescapable necessity of imagining ourselves other than we seem to be. And because consciousness is nothingness, it is not subject to the rules of causality. Central to the argument of *L'être et le néant* and Sartre's insistence on the primacy of human freedom is his insistence that consciousness cannot be understood in causal terms. It is always self-determining and, as such, "it always is what it is not, and is not what it is" – a playful paradox that refers to the fact that we are always in the process of choosing.

Consciousness is "nothing," but the self is always on its way to being something. Throughout our lives we accumulate a body of facts that are true of us – our "facticity" – but during our lives we remain free to envision new possibilities, to reform ourselves and to reinterpret our facticity in the light of new projects and ambitions – our "transcendence." This indeterminacy means that we can never *be* anything, and when we try to establish ourselves as something particular – whether a social role (policeman, waiter) or a certain character (shy, intellectual, cowardly) – we are in "bad faith." Bad faith is erroneously viewing ourselves as something fixed and settled (Sartre utterly rejects Freud and his theory of the unconscious determination of our personalities and behavior), but it is also bad faith to view oneself as a being of infinite possibilities and ignore the always restrictive facts and circumstances within which all choices must be made. On the one hand, we are always trying to define ourselves; on the other hand we are always free to break away from what we are, and always responsible for what we have made of ourselves. But there is no easy resolution or "balance" between facticity and freedom, rather a kind of dialectic or tension. The result is our frustrated desire to be God, to be both in-itself and for-itself. But this is not so much blasphemy as an expression of despair, a form of ontological original sin, the impossibility of being both free and what we want to be.

Life for Sartre is yet more complicated. There is a third basic ontological category, on a par with the being-in-itself and being-for-itself and not derivative of them. He calls it "being-for-others." To say that it is not derivative is to insist that our knowledge of others is not inferred, e.g. by some argument by analogy, from the behavior of others, and we ourselves are not wholly constituted by our self-determinations and the facts about us. Sartre gives us a brutal but familiar everyday example of our experience of being-for-others in what he calls "the look" (*le regard*). Someone catches us "in the act" of doing something humiliating, and we find ourselves defining ourselves (probably also resisting that definition) in their terms. In his *Saint Genet* (1953), Sartre describes such a conversion of the ten-year-old Jean Genet into a thief. So, too, we tend to "catch" one another in the judgments we make and define one another in terms that are often unflattering. But these judgments become an essential and ineluctible ingredient in our sense of ourselves, and they too lead to conflicts indeed, conflicts so basic and so frustrating that in his play *Huis clos* (*No Exit,* 1943) Sartre has one of his characters utter the famous line, "Hell is other people."

In his later works, notably his *Critique of Dialectical Reason* (1958–59), Sartre turned increasingly to politics and, in particular, toward a defense of Marxism on existentialist principles. This entailed rejecting materialist determinism, but it also required a new sense of solidarity (or what Sartre had wistfully called, following Heidegger, *Mitsein* or "being with others"). Thus in his later work he struggled to find a way of overcoming the conflict and insularity or the rather "bourgeois" consciousness he had described in *Being and Nothingness*. Not surprisingly (given his constant political activities) he found it in revolutionary engagement. Consonant with his rejection of bourgeois selfhood, Sartre turned down the 1964 Nobel prize for literature.

See also CONTINENTAL PHILOSOPHY, EXISTENTIALISM, MARXISM, PHENOMENOLOGY.

R.C.So.

sat/chit/ānanda, also *saccidānanda*, three Sanskrit terms combined to refer to the Highest Reality as 'existence, intelligence, bliss'. The later thinkers of Advaita Vedanta, such as Shankara, used the term to denote the Absolute, Brahman, a state of oneness of being, of pure consciousness and of absolute value or freedom. These are not to be taken as attributes or accidents that qualify Brahman but terms that express its essential nature as experienced by human beings. *Sat* (being, existence) is also *satyam* (truth), affirming that Brahman is experienced as being itself, not a being over against another. *Chit* is pure consciousness,

consciousness without object, and *ānanda* is the experience of unlimited freedom and universal potentiality as well as satisfaction and the bliss that transcends both all that is pleasurable in the world and release from the bondage of *saṁsāra*. Hindu theists understand *sat/chit/ānanda* as the qualities of the supreme god. **See also** ADVAITA, BRAHMAN, VEDANTA.   R.N.Mi.

satisfaction, an auxiliary semantic notion introduced by Tarski in order to give a recursive definition of truth for languages containing quantifiers. Intuitively, the satisfaction relation holds between formulas containing free variables (such as 'Building(x) & Tall(x)') and objects or sequences of objects (such as the Empire State Building) if and only if the formula "holds of" or "applies to" the objects. Thus, 'Building(x) & Tall(x)', is satisfied by all and only tall buildings, and '~Tall(x_1) & Taller(x_1, x_2)' is satisfied by any pair of objects in which the first object (corresponding to 'x_1') is not tall, but nonetheless taller than the second (corresponding to 'x_2').

Satisfaction is needed when defining truth for languages with sentences built from formulas containing free variables, because the notions of truth and falsity do not apply to these "open" formulas. Thus, we cannot characterize the truth of the sentences '$\exists x$ (Building(x) & Tall(x))' ('Some building is tall') in terms of the truth or falsity of the open formula 'Building(x) & Tall(x)', since the latter is neither true nor false. But note that the sentence is true if and only if the formula is satisfied by some object. Since we can give a recursive definition of the notion of satisfaction for (possibly open) formulas, this enables us to use this auxiliary notion in defining truth.

See also SEMANTIC PARADOXES, TARSKI, TRUTH.   J.Et.

satisfaction conditions. See SEARLE.

satisfiable, having a common model, a structure in which all the sentences in the set are true; said of a set of sentences. In modern logic, satisfiability is the semantic analogue of the syntactic, proof-theoretic notion of consistency, the unprovability of any explicit contradiction. The completeness theorem for first-order logic, that all valid sentences are provable, can be formulated in terms of satisfiability: syntactic consistency implies satisfiability. This theorem does not necessarily hold for extensions of first-order logic. For any sound proof system for second-order logic there will be an unsatisfiable set of sentences without there being a formal deriva-

tion of a contradiction from the set. This follows from Gödel's incompleteness theorem. One of the central results of model theory for first-order logic concerns satisfiability: the compactness theorem, due to Gödel in 1936, says that if every finite subset of a set of sentences is satisfiable the set itself is satisfiable. It follows immediately from his completeness theorem for first-order logic, and gives a powerful method to prove the consistency of a set of sentences. **See also** COMPACTNESS THEOREM, COMPLETENESS, GÖDEL'S INCOMPLETENESS THEOREMS, MODEL THEORY, PROOF THEORY.   Z.G.S.

satisfice, to choose or do the good enough rather than the most or the best. 'Satisfice', an obsolete variant of 'satisfy', has been adopted by economist Herbert Simon and others to designate non-optimizing choice or action. According to some economists, limitations of time or information may make it impossible or inadvisable for an individual, firm, or state body to attempt to maximize pleasure, profits, market share, revenues, or some other desired result, and satisficing with respect to such results is then said to be rational, albeit less than ideally rational. Although many orthodox economists think that choice can and always should be conceived in maximizing or optimizing terms, satisficing models have been proposed in economics, evolutionary biology, and philosophy.

Biologists have sometimes conceived evolutionary change as largely consisting of "good enough" or satisficing adaptations to environmental pressures rather than as proceeding through optimal adjustments to such pressures, but in philosophy, the most frequent recent use of the idea of satisficing has been in ethics and rational choice theory. Economists typically regard satisficing as acceptable only where there are unwanted constraints on decision making; but it is also possible to see satisficing as entirely acceptable in itself, and in the field of ethics, it has recently been argued that there may be nothing remiss about *moral satisficing*, e.g., giving a good amount to charity, but less than one could give. It is possible to formulate satisficing forms of utilitarianism on which actions are morally right (even) if they contribute merely positively and/or in some large way, rather than maximally, to overall net human happiness. Bentham's original formulation of the *principle of utility* and Popper's *negative utilitarianism* are both examples of satisficing utilitarianism in this sense – and it should be noted that satisficing utilitarianism has the putative advantage over optimizing forms of allowing for supererogatory degrees of moral excellence. Moreover, any moral view that treats moral satisficing as permissible makes room for moral *supererogation* in cases where one optimally goes beyond the merely acceptable. But since moral satisficing is less than optimal moral behavior, but may be more meritorious than certain behavior that (in the same circumstances) would be merely permissible, some moral satisficing may actually count as supererogatory.

In recent work on rational individual choice, some philosophers have argued that satisficing may often be acceptable in itself, rather than merely second-best. Even Simon allows that an entrepreneur may simply seek a satisfactory return on investment or share of the market, rather than a maximum under one of these headings. But a number of philosophers have made the further claim that we may sometimes, without irrationality, turn down the readily available better in the light of the goodness and sufficiency of what we already have or are enjoying. Independently of the costs of taking a second dessert, a person may be entirely satisfied with what she has eaten and, though willing to admit she would enjoy that extra dessert, turn it down, saying "I'm just fine as I am." Whether such examples really involve an acceptable rejection of the (momentarily) better for the good enough has been disputed. However, some philosophers have gone on to say, even more strongly, that satisficing can sometimes be rationally required and optimizing rationally unacceptable. To keep on seeking pleasure from food or sex without ever being thoroughly satisfied with what one has enjoyed can seem compulsive and as such less than rational. If one is truly rational about such goods, one isn't insatiable: at some point one has had enough and doesn't want more, even though one *could* obtain further pleasure.

The idea that satisficing is sometimes a requirement of practical reason is reminiscent of Aristotle's view that moderation is inherently reasonable – rather than just a necessary means to later enjoyments and the avoidance of later pain or illness, which is the way the Epicureans conceived moderation. But perhaps the greatest advocate of satisficing is Plato, who argues in the *Philebus* that there must be measure or limit to our (desire for) pleasure in order for pleasure to count as a good thing for us. Insatiably to seek and obtain pleasure from a given source is to gain nothing good from it. And according to such a view, satisficing moderation is a necessary precondition of human good and flourishing, rather than merely being a rational restraint on the accumulation of independently conceived personal good or well-being.

See also DECISION THEORY, HEDONISM, RATIONALITY, UTILITARIANISM.   M.A.Sl.

saturated. See FREGE.

Saussure, Ferdinand de (1857–1913), Swiss linguist and founder of the school of structural linguistics. His work in linguistics was a major influence on the later development of French structuralist philosophy, as well as structural anthropology, structuralist literary criticism, and modern semiology. He pursued studies in linguistics largely under Georg Curtius at the University of Leipzig, along with such future *Junggrammatiker* (neogrammarians) as Leskien and Brugmann. Following the publication of his important *Mémoire sur le système primitif des voyelles dans les langues indo-européenes* (1879), Saussure left for Paris, where he associated himself with the Société Linguistique and taught comparative grammar. In 1891, he returned to Switzerland to teach Sanskrit, comparative grammar, and general linguistics at the University of Geneva. His major work, the *Course in General Linguistics* (1916), was assembled from students' notes and his original lecture outlines after his death.

The *Course in General Linguistics* argued against the prevalent historical and comparative philological approaches to language by advancing what Saussure termed a scientific model for linguistics, one borrowed in part from Durkheim. Such a model would take the "social fact" of language (*la langue*) as its object, and distinguish this from the variety of individual speech events (*la parole*), as well as from the collectivity of speech events and grammatical rules that form the general historical body of language as such (*le langage*). Thus, by separating out the unique and accidental elements of practiced speech, Saussure distinguished language (*la langue*) as the objective set of linguistic elements and rules that, taken as a system, governs the language use specific to a given community.

It was the systematic coherency and generality of language, so conceived, that inclined Saussure to approach linguistics principally in terms of its static or synchronic dimension, rather than its historical or diachronic dimension. For Saussure, the system of language is a "treasury" or "depository" of signs, and the basic unit of the linguistic sign is itself two-sided, having both a phonemic component ("the signifier") and a semantic component ("the signified"). He terms the former the "acoustical" or "sound" image – which may, in turn, be represented graphically, in writing – and the latter the "concept" or "meaning." Saussure construes the signifier to be a representation of linguistic sounds in the imagination or memory, i.e., a "psychological phenomenon," one that corresponds to a specifiable range of material phonetic sounds. Its distinctive property consists in its being readily differentiated from other signifiers in the particular language. It is the function of each signifier, as a distinct entity, to convey a particular meaning – or "signified" concept – and this is fixed purely by conventional association.

While the relation between the signifier and signified results in what Saussure terms the "positive" fact of the sign, the sign ultimately derives its linguistic value (its precise descriptive determination) from its position in the system of language as a whole, i.e., within the paradigmatic and syntagmatic relations that structurally and functionally differentiate it. Signifiers are differentially identified; signifiers are arbitrarily associated with their respective signified concepts; and signs assume the determination they do only through their configuration within the system of language as a whole: these facts enabled Saussure to claim that language is largely to be understood as a closed formal system of differences, and that the study of language would be principally governed by its autonomous structural determinations.

So conceived, linguistics would be but a part of the study of social sign systems in general, namely, the broader science of what Saussure termed semiology. Saussure's insights would be taken up by the subsequent Geneva, Prague, and Copenhagen schools of linguistics and by the Russian formalists, and would be further developed by the structuralists in France and elsewhere, as well as by recent semiological approaches to literary criticism, social anthropology, and psychoanalysis.

See also MEANING, PHILOSOPHY OF LANGUAGE, STRUCTURALISM, THEORY OF SIGNS.
                      D.Al.

scalar implicature. See IMPLICATURE.

scepticism. See SKEPTICISM.

Schadenfreude. See VALUE.

Scheler, Max (1874–1928), German phenomenologist, social philosopher, and sociologist of knowledge. Born in Munich, he studied in Jena; when he returned to Munich in 1907 he came in contact with phenomenology, especially the realist version of the early Husserl and his Munich School followers. Scheler's first works were phenomenological studies in ethics leading to his ultimate theory of value: he described the moral feelings of sympathy and resentment and wrote a criticism of Kantian formalism and rationalism, *Formalism in Ethics and a Non-Formal Ethics of Value* (1913). During the war, he was an ardent nationalist and wrote essays in support of the war that were also philosophical criticisms of modern culture, opposed to "Anglo-Saxon" naturalism and rational calculation. Although he later embraced a broader notion of community, such criticisms of modernity remained constant themes of his writings. His conversion to Catholicism after the war led him to apply phenomenological description to religious phenomena and feelings, and he later turned to themes of anthropology and natural science.

The core of Scheler's phenomenological method is his conception of the objectivity of essences, which, though contained in experience, are a priori and independent of the knower. For Scheler, values are such objective, though non-Platonic, essences. Their objectivity is intuitively accessible in immediate experience and feelings, as when we experience beauty in music and do not merely hear certain sounds. Scheler distinguished between valuations or value perspectives on the one hand, which are historically relative and variable, and values on the other, which are independent and invariant. There are four such values, the hierarchical organization of which could be both immediately intuited and established by various public criteria like duration and independence: pleasure, vitality, spirit, and religion. Corresponding to these values are various personalities who are not creators of value but their discoverers, historical disclosers, and exemplars: the "artist of consumption," the hero, the genius, and the saint. A similar hierarchy of values applies to forms of society, the highest of which is the church, or a Christian community of solidarity and love. Scheler criticizes the leveling tendencies of liberalism for violating this hierarchy, leading to forms of resentment, individualism, and nationalism, all of which represent the false ordering of values.

See also HUSSERL, KANT, NATURALISM, PHENOMENOLOGY.   J.Bo.

Schelling, Friedrich Wilhelm Joseph (1775–1854), German philosopher whose metamorphoses encompass the entire history of German idealism. A Schwabian, Schelling first studied at Tübingen, where he befriended Hölderlin and Hegel. The young Schelling was an enthusiastic exponent of Fichte's *Wissenschaftslehre* and devoted several early essays to its exposition. After studying science and mathematics at Leipzig, he joined Fichte at Jena in 1798. Meanwhile, in such writings as *Philosophische Briefe über Dogmatismus und Kritizismus* ("Philosophical Letters on Dogmatism and Criticism," 1795), Schelling betrayed growing doubts concerning Fichte's philosophy (above all, its treatment of nature) and a lively interest in Spinoza. He then turned to constructing a systematic *Naturphilosophie* (philosophy of nature) within the context of which nature would be treated more holistically than by either Newtonian science or transcendental idealism. Of his many publications on this topic, two of the more important are *Ideen zu einer Philosophie der Natur* ("Ideas concerning a Philosophy of Nature," 1797) and *Von der Weltseele* ("On the World-Soul," 1798).

Whereas transcendental idealism attempts to derive objective experience from an initial act of free self-positing, Schelling's philosophy of nature attempts to derive consciousness from objects. Beginning with "pure objectivity," the *Naturphilosophie* purports to show how nature undergoes a process of unconscious self-development, culminating in the conditions for its own self-representation. The method of *Naturphilosophie* is fundamentally a priori: it begins with the concept of the *unity* of nature and accounts for its *diversity* by interpreting nature as a *system* of opposed forces or "polarities," which manifest themselves in ever more complex levels of organization (*Potenzen*).

At Jena, Schelling came into contact with Tieck, Novalis, and the Schlegel brothers and became interested in art. This new interest is evident in his *System des transzendentalen Idealismus* (1800), which describes the path from pure subjectivity (self-consciousness) to objectivity (the necessary positing of the Not-I, or of nature). The most innovative and influential portion of this treatise, which is otherwise closely modeled on Fichte's *Wissenschaftslehre*, is its conclusion, which presents art as the concrete accomplishment of the philosophical task. In aesthetic experience the identity between the subjective and the objective, the ideal and the real, becomes an *object* to the experiencing I itself.

For Schelling, transcendental idealism and *Naturphilosophie* are two complementary sides or subdivisions of a larger, more encompassing sys-

tem, which he dubbed the System of Identity or Absolute Idealism and expounded in a series of publications, including the *Darstellung meines Systems der Philosophie* ("Presentation of My System of Philosophy," 1801), *Bruno* (1802), and *Vorlesungen über die Methode des akademischen Studiums* ("Lectures on the Method of Academic Study," 1803). The most distinctive feature of this system is that it *begins* with a bald assertion of the unity of thought and being, i.e., with the bare idea of the self-identical "Absolute," which is described as the first presupposition of all knowledge. Since the identity with which this system commences transcends every conceivable difference, it is also described as the "point of indifference." From this undifferentiated or "indifferent" starting point, Schelling proceeds to a description of reality as a whole, considered as a differentiated system within which unity is maintained by various synthetic relationships, such as substance and attribute, cause and effect, attraction and repulsion. Like his philosophy of nature, Schelling's System of Identity utilizes the notion of various hierarchically related *Potenzen* as its basic organizing principle. The obvious question concerns the precise relationship between the "indifferent" Absolute and the real system of differentiated elements, a question that may be said to have set the agenda for Schelling's subsequent philosophizing.

From 1803 to 1841 Schelling was in Bavaria, where he continued to expound his System of Identity and to explore the philosophies of art and nature. The most distinctive feature of his thought during this period, however, was a new interest in religion and in the theosophical writings of Boehme, whose influence is prominent in the *Philosophische Untersuchungen über das Wesen der menschlichen Freiheit* ("Philosophical Investigations concerning the Nature of Human Freedom," 1809), a work often interpreted as anticipating existentialism. He also worked on a speculative interpretation of human history, *Die Weltalter*, which remained unpublished, and lectured regularly on the history of philosophy.

In 1841 Schelling moved to Berlin, where he lectured on his new philosophy of revelation and mythology, which he now characterized as "positive philosophy," in contradistinction to the purely "negative" philosophy of Kant, Fichte, and Hegel. Some scholars have interpreted these posthumously published lectures as representing the culmination both of Schelling's own protracted philosophical development and of German idealism as a whole.

See also FICHTE, HEGEL, KANT.   D.Br.

schema. See THEMA.

schemata. See KANT.

schematic form. See LOGICAL FORM.

scheme, also schema (plural: schemata), a metalinguistic frame or template used to specify an infinite set of sentences, its instances, by finite means, often taken with a side condition on how its blanks or placeholders are to be filled. The sentence 'Either Abe argues or it is not the case that Abe argues' is an instance of the *excluded middle scheme* for English: 'Either . . . or it is not the case that . . .', where the two blanks are to be filled with one and the same (well-formed declarative) English sentence. Since first-order number theory cannot be finitely axiomatized, the *mathematical induction scheme* is used to effectively specify an infinite set of axioms: 'If zero is such that . . . and the successor of every number such that . . . is also such that . . . , then every number is such that . . .', where the four blanks are to be filled with one and the same arithmetic open sentence, such as 'it precedes its own successor' or 'it is finite'. Among the best-known is Tarski's *scheme T*: '. . . is a true sentence if and only if . . .', where the second blank is filled with a sentence and the first blank by a name of the sentence. **See also** CONVENTION T, LOGICAL FORM, METALANGUAGE, OPEN FORMULA, PHILOSO-PHY OF MATHEMATICS, TARSKI.   J.Cor.

Schiller, Johann Christoph Friedrich von (1759–1805), German poet, dramatist, and philosopher. Along with his colleagues Reinhold and Fichte, he participated in systematically revising Kant's transcendental idealism. Though Schiller's best-known theoretical contributions were to aesthetics, his philosophical ambitions were more general, and he proposed a novel solution to the problem of the *systematic unity,* not merely of the critical philosophy, but of human nature. His most substantial philosophical work, *Briefe über die ästhetische Erziehung des Menschen* ("Letters on the Aesthetic Education of Man," 1794/95), examines the relationship between natural necessity and practical freedom and addresses two problems raised by Kant: How can a creature governed by natural necessity and desire ever become aware of its own freedom and thus capable of autonomous moral action? And how can these two sides of human nature – the natural, sensuous side and the rational, supersensuous one – be reconciled? In contradistinction both to those who subordinate principles to feelings

("savages") and to those who insist that one should strive to subordinate feelings to principles ("barbarians"), Schiller posited an intermediary realm between the sphere of nature and that of freedom, as well as a third basic human drive capable of mediating between sensuous and rational impulses. This third impulse is dubbed the "play impulse," and the intermediary sphere to which it pertains is that of art and beauty. By cultivating the play impulse (i.e., via "aesthetic education") one is not only freed from bondage to sensuality and granted a first glimpse of one's practical freedom, but one also becomes capable of reconciling the rational and sensuous sides of one's own nature. This idea of a condition in which opposites are simultaneously cancelled and preserved, as well as the specific project of reconciling freedom and necessity, profoundly influenced subsequent thinkers such as Schelling and Hegel and contributed to the development of German idealism. **See also** FICHTE, IDEALISM, KANT, NEO-KANTIANISM, SCHELLING.   D.Br.

Schlegel, Friedrich von (1772–1829), German literary critic and philosopher, one of the principal representatives of German Romanticism. In *On the Study of Greek Poetry* (1795), Schlegel laid the foundations for the distinction of classical and Romantic literature and a pronounced consciousness of literary modernity. Together with his brother August Wilhelm, he edited the *Athenaeum* (1798–1800), the main theoretical organ of German Romanticism, famous for its collection of fragments as a new means of critical communication. Schlegel is the originator of the Romantic theory of irony, a non-dialectical form of philosophizing and literary writing that takes its inspiration from Socratic irony and combines it with Fichte's thought process of affirmation and negation, "self-creation" and "self-annihilation." Closely connected wih Schlegel's theory of irony is his theory of language and understanding (hermeneutics). Critical reflection on language promotes an ironic awareness of the "necessity and impossibility of complete communication" (*Critical Fragments,* No. 108); critical reflection on understanding reveals the amount of incomprehensibility, of "positive not-understanding" involved in every act of understanding (*On Incomprehensibility,* 1800). Schlegel's writings were essential for the rise of historical consciousness in German Romanticism. His *On Ancient and Modern Literature* (1812) is reputed to represent the first literary history in a modern and broadly comparative fashion. His *Philosophy of History* (1828), together with his *Philosophy of Life* (1828) and *Philosophy of Language* (1829), confront Hegel's philosophy from the point of view of a Christian and personalistic type of philosophizing. Schlegel converted to Catholicism in 1808. **See also** FICHTE.   E.Beh.

Schleiermacher, Friedrich (1768–1834), German philosopher, a "critical realist" working among post-Kantian idealists. In philosophy and science he presupposed transcendental features, noted in his dialectic lectures, and advocated integrative but historically contingent, empirical functions. Both develop, but, contra Hegel, not logically. Schleiermacher was a creator of modern general hermeneutics; a father of modern theological and religious studies; an advocate of women's rights; the cofounder, with Humboldt, of the University at Berlin (1808–10), where he taught until 1834; and the classic translator of Plato into German.

Schleiermacher has had an undeservedly minor place in histories of philosophy. Appointed chiefly to theology, he published less philosophy, though he regularly lectured, in tightly argued discourse, in Greek philosophy, history of philosophy, dialectic, hermeneutics and criticism, philosophy of mind ("psychology"), ethics, politics, aesthetics, and philosophy of education. From the 1980s, his collected writings and large correspondence began to appear in a forty-volume critical edition and in the larger Schleiermacher Studies and Translations series. Brilliant, newly available pieces from his twenties on freedom, the highest good, and values, previously known only in fragments but essential for understanding his views fully, were among the first to appear. Much of his outlook was formed before he became prominent in the early Romantic circle (1796–1806), distinguishable by his markedly religious, consistently liberal views.

See also HERMENEUTICS.   T.N.T.

Schlick, Moritz. See VIENNA CIRCLE.

Scholasticism, a set of scholarly and instructional techniques developed in Western European schools of the late medieval period, including the use of commentary and disputed question. 'Scholasticism' is derived from Latin *scholasticus*, which in the twelfth century meant the master of a school. The *Scholastic method* is usually presented as beginning in the law schools – notably at Bologna – and as being then transported into theology and philosophy by a series of masters including Abelard and Peter Lombard. Within

the new universities of the thirteenth century the standardization of the curriculum and the enormous prestige of Aristotle's work (despite the suspicion with which it was initially greeted) contributed to the entrenchment of the method and it was not until the educational reforms of the beginning of the sixteenth century that it ceased to be dominant.

There is, strictly speaking, no such thing as Scholasticism. As the term was originally used it presupposed that a single philosophy was taught in the universities of late medieval Europe, but there was no such philosophy. The philosophical movements working outside the universities in the late sixteenth and early seventeenth centuries and the "neo-Scholastics" of the late nineteenth and early twentieth centuries all found such a presupposition useful, and their influence led scholars to assume it. At first this generated efforts to find a common core in the philosophies taught in the late medieval schools. More recently it has led to efforts to find methods characteristic of their teaching, and to an extension of the term to the schools of late antiquity and of Byzantium.

Both among the opponents of the schools in the seventeenth century and among the "neo-Scholastics," 'Scholasticism' was supposed to designate a doctrine whose core was the doctrine of substance and accidents. As portrayed by Descartes and Locke, the Scholastics accepted the view that among the components of a thing were a substantial form and a number of real accidental forms, many of which corresponded to perceptible properties of the thing – its color, shape, temperature. They were also supposed to have accepted a sharp distinction between natural and unnatural motion.

See also NEO-SCHOLASTICISM.   C.G.Norm.

Scholastic method. See SCHOLASTICISM.

School of Laws. See CHINESE LEGALISM.

School of Names, also called, in Chinese, *ming chia*, a loosely associated group of Chinese philosophers of the Warring States period (403–221 B.C.), also known as *pien che* (Dialecticians or Sophists). The most famous were Hui Shih and Kung-sun Lung Tzu. Though interested in the relation between names and reality, the Sophists addressed such issues as relativity, perspectivism, space, time, causality, essentialism, universalism, and particularism. Perhaps more important than their subject matter, however, was their methodology. As their name suggests, the Sophists delighted in language games and logical puzzles. They used logic and rational argument not only as a weapon to defeat their philosophical opponents but as a tool to sharpen rational argumentation itself. Paradoxes such as 'I go to Yüeh today but arrive yesterday' and 'A white horse is not a horse' continue to stimulate philosophical discussion today. Yet frustrated Confucian, Taoist, and Legalist contemporaries chided Sophists for wasting their time on abstractions and puzzles, and for succumbing to intellectualism for its own sake. As Confucianism emerged to become the state ideology, the School of Names disappeared sometime in the early Han dynasty (206 B.C.–A.D. 220); having been in important measure co-opted by the leading interpreter of Confucianism of the period, Hsün Tzu. **See also CHINESE PHILOSOPHY, HSÜN TZU, KUNG-SUN LUNG TZU.**   R.P.P. & R.T.A.

Schopenhauer, Arthur (1788–1860), German philosopher. Born in Danzig and schooled in Germany, France, and England during a well-traveled childhood, he became acquainted through his novelist mother with Goethe, Schlegel, and the brothers Grimm. He studied medicine at the University of Göttingen and philosophy at the University of Berlin; received the doctorate from the University of Jena in 1813; and lived much of his adult life in Frankfurt, where he died.

Schopenhauer's dissertation, *On the Fourfold Root of the Principle of Sufficient Reason* (1813), lays the groundwork for all of his later philosophical work. The world of representation (equivalent to Kant's phenomenal world) is governed by "the principle of sufficient reason": "every possible object . . . stands in a necessary relation to other objects, on the one hand as determined, on the other as determining" (*The World as Will and Representation*). Thus, each object of consciousness can be explained in terms of its relations with other objects.

The systematic statement of Schopenhauer's philosophy appeared in *The World as Will and Representation* (1818). His other works are *On Vision and Colors* (1815), "On the Will in Nature" (1836), conjoined with "On the Foundation of Morality" in *The Two Fundamental Problems of Ethics* (1841); the second edition of *The World as Will and Representation*, which included a second volume of essays (1844); an enlarged and revised edition of *On the Fourfold Root of the Principle of Sufficient Reason* (1847); and *Parerga and Paralipomena*, a series of essays (1851). These are all consistent with the principal statement

of his thought in *The World as Will and Representation*.

The central postulate of Schopenhauer's system is that the fundamental reality is will, which he equates with the Kantian thing-in-itself. Unlike Kant, Schopenhauer contends that one can immediately know the thing-in-itself through the experience of an inner, volitional reality within one's own body. Every phenomenon, according to Schopenhauer, has a comparable inner reality. Consequently, the term 'will' can extend to the inner nature of all things. Moreover, because number pertains exclusively to the phenomenal world, the will, as thing-in-itself, is one. Nevertheless, different types of things manifest the will to different degrees. Schopenhauer accounts for these differences by invoking Plato's Ideas (or Forms). The Ideas are the universal prototypes for the various kinds of objects in the phenomenal world. Taken collectively, the Ideas constitute a hierarchy. We usually overlook them in everyday experience, focusing instead on particulars and their practical relationships to us. However, during aesthetic experience, we recognize the universal Idea within the particular; simultaneously, as aesthetic beholders, we become "the universal subject of knowledge."

Aesthetic experience also quiets the will within us. The complete silencing of the will is, for Schopenhauer, the ideal for human beings, though it is rarely attained. Because will is the fundamental metaphysical principle, our lives are dominated by willing – and, consequently, filled with struggle, conflict, and dissatisfaction. Inspired by Buddhism, Schopenhauer contends that all of life is suffering, which only an end to desire can permanently eliminate (as opposed to the respite of aesthetic experience). This is achieved only by the saint, who rejects desire in an inner act termed "denial of the will to live." The saint fully grasps that the same will motivates all phenomena and, recognizing that nothing is gained through struggle and competition, achieves "resignation." Such a person achieves the ethical ideal of all religions – compassion toward all beings, resulting from the insight that all are, fundamentally, one.

See also KANT, PLATO.   K.M.H.

Schröder-Bernstein theorem, the theorem that mutually dominant sets are equinumerous. A set *A* is said to be dominated by a set *B* if and only if each element of *A* can be mapped to a unique element of *B* in such a way that no two elements of *A* are mapped to the same element of *B* (possibly with some elements of B left over). Intuitively, if A is dominated by B, then B has at least as many members as A. Given this intuition, one would expect that if A is dominated by B and B is dominated by A, then A and B are equinumerous (i.e., A can be mapped to B as described above with no elements of B left over). This is the Schröder-Bernstein theorem. Stated in terms of cardinal numbers, the theorem says that if $\kappa \leq \lambda$ and $\lambda \leq \kappa$, then $\kappa = \lambda$. Despite the simplicity of the theorem's statement, its proof is non-trivial. **See also** SET THEORY.   P.Mad.

Schrödinger, Erwin (1887–1961), Austrian physicist best known for five papers published in 1926, in which he discovered the Schrödinger wave equation and created modern wave mechanics. For this achievement, he was awarded the Nobel prize in physics (shared with Paul Dirac) in 1933. Like Einstein, Schrödinger was a resolute but ultimately unsuccessful critic of the Copenhagen interpretation of quantum mechanics. Schrödinger defended the view (which he derived from Boltzmann) that theories should give a picture, continuous in space and time, of the real processes that produce observable phenomena. Schrödinger's realistic philosophy of science played an important role in his discovery of wave mechanics. Although his physical interpretation of the psi function was soon abandoned, his approach to quantum mechanics survives in the theories of Louis de Broglie and David Bohm. **See also** QUANTUM MECHANICS.   M.C.

Schrödinger cat paradox. See QUANTUM MECHANICS.

Schrödinger equation. See QUANTUM MECHANICS.

Schulze, Gottlob Ernst (1761–1833), German philosopher today known mainly as an acute and influential early critic of Kant and Reinhold. He taught at Wittenberg, Helmstedt, and Göttingen; one of his most important students was Schopenhauer, whose view of Kant was definitely influenced by Schulze's interpretation. Schulze's most important work was his *Aenesidemus,* or "On the Elementary Philosophy Put Forward by Mr. Reinhold in Jena. Together with a Defense of Skepticism" (1792). It fundamentally changed the discussion of Kantian philosophy. Kant's earliest critics had accused him of being a skeptic like Hume. Kantians, like Reinhold, had argued that critical philosophy was not only opposed to skepticism, but also contained the

only possible refutation of skepticism. Schulze tried to show that Kantianism could not refute skepticism, construed as the doctrine that doubts the possibility of any knowledge concerning the existence or non-existence of "things-in-themselves," and he argued that Kant and his followers begged the skeptic's question by presupposing that such things exist and causally interact with us. Schulze's *Aenesidemus* had a great impact on Fichte and Hegel, and it also influenced neo-Kantianism.   M.K.

science, philosophy of. See PHILOSOPHY OF SCIENCE.

scientia media. See MIDDLE KNOWLEDGE.

scientia universalis. See LEIBNIZ.

scientific behaviorism. See BEHAVIORISM.

scientific determinism. See DETERMINISM.

scientific realism, the view that the subject matter of scientific research and scientific theories exists independently of our knowledge of it, and that the goal of science is the description and explanation of both observable and unobservable aspects of the world. Scientific realism is contrasted with logical empiricism and social constructivism.

Early arguments for scientific realism simply stated that, in light of the impressive products and methods of science, realism is the only philosophy that does not make the success of science a miracle. Formulations of scientific realism focus on the objects of theoretical knowledge: theories, laws, and entities. One especially robust argument for scientific realism (due to Putnam and Richard Boyd) is that the instrumental reliability of scientific methodology in the mature sciences (such as physics, chemistry, and some areas of biology) can be explained adequately only if we suppose that theories in the mature sciences are at least approximately true and their central theoretical terms are at least partially referential (Putnam no longer holds this view).

More timid versions of scientific realism do not infer approximate truth of mature theories. For example, Ian Hacking's "entity realism" (1983) asserts that the instrumental manipulation of postulated entities to produce further effects gives us legitimate grounds for ontological commitment to theoretical entities, but not to laws or theories. Paul Humphreys's "austere realism" (1989) states that only theoretical commitment to unobserved structures or dispositions could explain the stability of observed outcomes of scientific inquiry. Distinctive versions of scientific realism can be found in works by Richard Boyd (1983), Philip Kitcher (1993), Richard Miller (1987), William Newton-Smith (1981), and J. D. Trout (1998). Despite their differences, all of these versions of realism are distinguished – against logical empiricism – by their commitment that knowledge of unobservable phenomena is not only possible but actual. As well, all of the arguments for scientific realism are *abductive*; they argue that either the approximate truth of background theories or the existence of theoretical entities and laws provides the best explanation for some significant fact about the scientific theory or practice.

Scientific realists address the difference between real entities and merely useful constructs, arguing that realism offers a better explanation for the success of science. In addition, scientific realism recruits evidence from the history and practice of science, and offers explanations for the success of science that are designed to honor the dynamic and uneven character of that evidence. Most arguments for scientific realism cohabit with versions of naturalism. Anti-realist opponents argue that the realist move from instrumental reliability to truth is question-begging. However, realists reply that such formal criticisms are irrelevant; the structure of explanationist arguments is inductive and their principles are a posteriori.

See also EXPLANATION, METAPHYSICS, PHILOSOPHY OF SCIENCE, SOCIAL CONSTRUCTIVISM.   J.D.T.

scientific relativism. See THEORY-LADEN.

scope, the "part" of the sentence (or proposition) to which a given term "applies" under a given interpretation of the sentence. If the sentence 'Abe does not believe Ben died' is interpreted as expressing the proposition that Abe believes that it is not the case that Ben died, the scope of 'not' is 'Ben died'; interpreted as "It is not the case that Abe believes that Ben died," the scope is the rest of the sentence, i.e., 'Abe believes Ben died'. In the first case we have narrow scope, in the second wide scope. If 'Every number is not even' is interpreted with narrow scope, it expresses the false proposition that every number is non-even, which is logically equivalent to the proposition that no number is even. Taken with wide scope it expresses the truth that not every number is even, which is equivalent to the truth that some number is non-even. Under normal interpreta-

tions of the sentences, 'hardened' has narrow scope in 'Carl is a hardened recidivist', whereas 'alleged' has wide scope in 'Dan is an alleged criminal'. Accordingly, 'Carl is a hardened recidivist' logically implies 'Carl is a recidivist', whereas 'Dan is an alleged criminal', being equivalent to 'Allegedly, Dan is a criminal', does not imply 'Dan is a criminal'. Scope considerations are useful in analyzing structural ambiguity and in understanding the difference between the grammatical form of a sentence and the logical form of a proposition it expresses. In a logically perfect language grammatical form mirrors logical form, there is no scope ambiguity, and the scope of a given term is uniquely determined by its context. See also AMBIGUITY; CONVERSE; CONVERSE, OUTER AND INNER; RELATION; STRUCTURAL AMBIGUITY.   J.Cor.

scope ambiguity. See AMBIGUITY.

scope of operators. See AMBIGUITY, SCOPE.

Scotistic realism. See DUNS SCOTUS.

Scottigena. See ERIGENA.

Scottish common sense philosophy, a comprehensive philosophical position developed by Reid in the latter part of the eighteenth century. Reid's views were propagated by a succession of Scottish popularizers, of whom the most successful was Dugald Stewart. Through them common sense doctrine became nearly a philosophical orthodoxy in Great Britain during the first half of the nineteenth century. Brought to the United States through the colleges in Princeton and Philadelphia, common sensism continued to be widely taught until the later nineteenth century. The early Reidians Beattie and Oswald were, like Reid himself, read in Germany by Kant and others; and Reid's views were widely taught in post-Napoleonic France.

The archenemy for the common sense theorists was Hume. Reid saw in his skepticism the inevitable outcome of Descartes's thesis, accepted by Locke, that we do not perceive external objects directly, but that the immediate object of perception is something in the mind. Against this he argued that perception involves both sensation and certain intuitively known general truths or principles that together yield knowledge of external objects. He also argued that there are many other intuitively known general principles, including moral principles, available to all normal humans. As a result he thought that whenever philosophical argument results in conclusions that run counter to common sense, the philosophy must be wrong.

Stewart made some changes in Reid's acute and original theory, but his main achievement was to propagate it through eloquent classes and widely used textbooks. Common sensism, defending the considered views of the ordinary man, was taken by many to provide a defense of the Christian religious and moral status quo. Reid had argued for free will, and presented a long list of self-evident moral axioms. If this might be plausibly presented as part of the common sense of his time, the same could not be said for some of the religious doctrines that Oswald thought equally self-evident. Reid had not given any rigorous tests for what might count as self-evident. The easy intuitionism of later common sensists was a natural target for those who, like J. S. Mill, thought that any appeal to self-evidence was simply a way of justifying vested interest. Whewell, in both his philosophy of science and his ethics, and Sidgwick, in his moral theory, acknowledged debts to Reid and tried to eliminate the abuses to which his method was open. But in doing so they transformed common sensism beyond the limits within which Reid and those shaped by him operated.

See also HUME, MOORE, REID, SIDGWICK.

J.B.S.

Scotus, John Duns. See DUNS SCOTUS.

script. See COGNITIVE SCIENCE.

sea battle. See ARISTOTLE.

Searle, John R. (b.1932), American philosopher of language and mind (D. Phil., Oxford) influenced by Frege, Wittgenstein, and J. L. Austin; a founder of speech act theory and an important contributor to debates on intentionality, consciousness, and institutional facts.

Language. In *Speech Acts: An Essay in the Philosophy of Language* (1969), Searle brings together modified versions of Frege's distinctions between the force (F) and content (P) of a sentence, and between singular reference and predication, Austin's analysis of speech acts, and Grice's analysis of speaker meaning. Searle explores the hypothesis that the semantics of a natural language can be regarded as a conventional realization of underlying constitutive rules and that illocutionary acts are acts performed in accordance with these rules. *Expression and Meaning*

(1979) extends this analysis to non-literal and indirect illocutionary acts, and attempts to explain Donnellan's referential-attributive distinction in these terms and proposes an influential taxonomy of five basic types of illocutionary acts based on the illocutionary point or purpose of the act, and word-to-world versus world-to-word direction of fit.

Language and mind. *Intentionality: An Essay in the Philosophy of Mind* (1983) forms the foundation for the earlier work on speech acts. Now the semantics of a natural language is seen as the result of the mind (intrinsic intentionality) imposing conditions of satisfaction or aboutness on objects (expressions in a language), which have intentionality only derivatively. Perception and action rather than belief are taken as fundamental. Satisfaction conditions are essentially Fregean (i.e. general versus singular) and internal – meaning is in the head, relative to a background of non-intentional states, and relative to a network of other intentional states. The philosophy of language becomes a branch of the philosophy of mind.

Mind. "Minds, Brains and Programs" (1980) introduced the famous "Chinese room" argument against strong artificial intelligence – the view that appropriately programming a machine is sufficient for giving it intentional states. Suppose a monolingual English-speaker is working in a room producing Chinese answers to Chinese questions well enough to mimic a Chinese-speaker, but by following an algorithm written in English. Such a person does not understand Chinese nor would a computer computing the same algorithm. This is true for any such algorithms because they are syntactically individuated and intentional states are semantically individuated. *The Rediscovery of the Mind* (1992) continues the attack on the thesis that the brain is a digital computer, and develops a non-reductive "biological naturalism" on which intentionality, like the liquidity of water, is a high-level feature, which is caused by and realized in the brain.

Society. *The Construction of Social Reality* (1995) develops his realistic worldview, starting with an independent world of particles and forces, up through evolutionary biological systems capable of consciousness and intentionality, to institutions and social facts, which are created when persons impose status-features on things, which are collectively recognized and accepted.

See also DIRECTION OF FIT, INTENTIONAL-

ITY, MEANING, PHILOSOPHY OF LANGUAGE, SPEECH ACT THEORY.   R.M.H.

second actualization. See ARISTOTLE.

secondarily evaluative word. See PRESCRIPTIVISM.

secondary process. See FREUD.

secondary qualities. See QUALITIES.

secondary rule. See HART.

secondary substance. See ARISTOTLE.

second imposition. See IMPOSITION.

second intention. See IMPOSITION.

second law of thermodynamics. See ENTROPY.

secondness. See PEIRCE.

second-order. See ORDER.

second-order logic, the logic of languages that contain, in addition to variables ranging over objects, variables ranging over properties, relations, functions, or classes of those objects. A model, or interpretation, of a formal language usually contains a domain of discourse. This domain is what the language is about, in the model in question. Variables that range over this domain are called *first-order variables*. If the language contains only first-order variables, it is called a *first-order language,* and it is within the purview of *first-order logic.* Some languages also contain variables that range over properties, relations, functions, or classes of members of the domain of discourse. These are *second-order variables*. A language that contains first-order and second-order variables, and no others, is a *second-order language.* The sentence 'There is a property shared by all and only prime numbers' is straightforwardly rendered in a second-order language, because of the (bound) variable ranging over properties.

There are also properties of properties, relations of properties, and the like. Consider, e.g., the property of properties expressed by '*P* has an infinite extension' or the relation expressed by '*P* has a smaller extension than *Q*'. A language with variables ranging over such items is called *third-order.* This construction can be continued, producing fourth-order languages, etc. A language is called *higher-order* if it is at least second-order.

Deductive systems for second-order languages are obtained from those for first-order languages by adding straightforward extensions of the axioms and rules concerning quantifiers that bind first-order variables. There may also be an axiom scheme of *comprehension:* $\exists P \forall x (Px \equiv \Phi(x))$, one instance for each formula Φ that does not contain P free. The scheme "asserts" that every formula determines the extension of a property. If the language has variables ranging over functions, there may also be a version of the *axiom of choice:* $\forall R(\forall x \exists y Rxy \to \exists f \forall x Rxfx)$. In *standard semantics* for second-order logic, a model of a given language is the same as a model for the corresponding first-order language. The relation variables range over *every* relation over the domain-of-discourse, the function variables range over every function from the domain to the domain, etc. In *non-standard,* or *Henkin semantics,* each model consists of a domain-of-discourse and a specified collection of relations, functions, etc., on the domain. The latter may not include every relation or function. The specified collections are the range of the second-order variables in the model in question. In effect, Henkin semantics regards second-order languages as multi-sorted, first-order languages.

  See also FORMAL LOGIC, FORMAL SEMANTICS, PHILOSOPHY OF LOGIC.   S.Sha.

second potentiality. See ARISTOTLE.

second Thomism. See THOMISM.

secundum quid, in a certain respect, or with a qualification. Fallacies can arise from confusing what is true only *secundum quid* with what is true *simpliciter* ('without qualification', 'absolutely', 'on the whole'), or conversely. Thus a strawberry is red *simpliciter* (on the whole). But it is black, not red, with respect to its seeds, *secundum quid.* By ignoring the distinction, one might mistakenly infer that the strawberry is both red and not red. Again, a certain thief is a good cook, *secundum quid;* but it does not follow that he is good *simpliciter* (without qualification). Aristotle was the first to recognize the fallacy *secundum quid et simpliciter* explicitly, in his *Sophistical Refutations.* On the basis of some exceptionally enigmatic remarks in the same work, the liar paradox was often regarded in the Middle Ages as an instance of this fallacy. **See also** PARADOX.   P.V.S.

security strategy. See MAXIMIN STRATEGY.

seeing, epistemic. See DRETSKE.

seeing, non-epistemic. See DRETSKE.

selection. See PHILOSOPHY OF BIOLOGY.

self, bundle theory of. See BUNDLE THEORY.

self-consciousness. See DE DICTO, KNOWLEDGE BY ACQUAINTANCE, PHILOSOPHY OF MIND.

self-control. See AKRASIA.

self-deception, (1) purposeful action to avoid unpleasant truths and painful topics (about oneself or the world); (2) unintentional processes of denial, avoidance, or biased perception; (3) mental states resulting from such action or processes, such as ignorance, false belief, wishful thinking, unjustified opinions, or lack of clear awareness. Thus, parents tend to exaggerate the virtues of their children; lovers disregard clear signs of unreciprocated affection; overeaters rationalize away the need to diet; patients dying of cancer pretend to themselves that their health is improving.

In some contexts 'self-deception' is neutral and implies no criticism. Deceiving oneself can even be desirable, generating a vital lie that promotes happiness or the ability to cope with difficulties. In other contexts 'self-deception' has negative connotations, suggesting bad faith, false consciousness, or what Joseph Butler called "inner hypocrisy" – the refusal to acknowledge our wrongdoing, character flaws, or onerous responsibilities. Existentialist philosophers, like Kierkegaard, Heidegger, and most notably Sartre (*Being and Nothingness,* 1943), denounced self-deception as an inauthentic (dishonest, cowardly) refusal to confront painful though significant truths, especially about freedom, responsibility, and death. Herbert Fingarette, however, argued that self-deception is morally ambiguous – neither clearly blameworthy nor clearly faultless – because of how it erodes capacities for acting rationally (*Self-Deception,* 1969).

The idea of intentionally deceiving oneself seems paradoxical. In deceiving other people I usually know a truth that guides me as I state the opposite falsehood, intending thereby to mislead them into believing the falsehood. Five difficulties seem to prevent me from doing anything like that to myself.

(1) With interpersonal deception, one person knows something that another person does not. Yet self-deceivers know the truth all along, and so it seems they cannot use it to make themselves ignorant. One solution is that self-deception occurs over time, with the initial knowledge becoming gradually eroded. Or perhaps self-deceivers only suspect rather than know the truth, and then disregard relevant evidence.

(2) If consciousness implies awareness of one's own conscious acts, then a conscious intention to deceive myself would be self-defeating, for I would remain conscious of the truth I wish to flee. Sartre's solution was to view self-deception as spontaneous and not explicitly reflected upon. Freud's solution was to conceive of self-deception as unconscious repression.

(3) It seems that self-deceivers believe a truth that they simultaneously get themselves not to believe, but how is that possible? Perhaps they keep one of two conflicting beliefs unconscious or not fully conscious.

(4) Self-deception suggests willfully creating beliefs, but that seems impossible since beliefs cannot voluntarily be chosen. Perhaps beliefs can be indirectly manipulated by selectively ignoring and attending to evidence.

(5) It seems that one part of a person (the deceiver) manipulates another part (the victim), but such extreme splits suggest multiple personality disorders rather than self-deception. Perhaps we are composed of "subselves" – relatively unified clusters of elements in the personality. Or perhaps at this point we should jettison interpersonal deception as a model for understanding self-deception.

    See also AKRASIA, FREUD, PHILOSOPHY OF MIND.   M.W.M.

self-determination, the autonomy possessed by a community when it is politically independent; in a strict sense, territorial sovereignty. Within international law, the *principle of self-determination* appears to grant every people a right to be self-determining, but there is controversy over its interpretation. Applied to established states, the principle calls for recognition of state sovereignty and non-intervention in internal affairs. By providing for the self-determination of subordinate communities, however, it can generate demands for secession that conflict with existing claims of sovereignty. Also, what non-self-governing groups qualify as beneficiaries? The *national* interpretation of the principle treats cultural or national units as the proper claimants, whereas the *regional* interpretation confers the right of self-determination upon the populations of well-defined regions regardless of cultural or national affiliations. This difference reflects the roots of the principle in the doctrines of *nationalism* and *popular sovereignty,* respectively, but com-

plicates its application. **See also** POLITICAL PHI-
LOSOPHY.   T.K.

self-evidence, the property of being self-evident.
Only true propositions (or truths) are self-evident, though false propositions can appear to be
self-evident. It is widely held that a true proposition is self-evident if and only if one would be
justified in believing it if one adequately understood it. Some would also require that self-evident propositions are known if believed on the
basis of such an understanding. Some self-evident propositions are obvious, such as the proposition that all stags are male, but others are not,
since it may take considerable reflection to
achieve an adequate understanding of them.
That slavery is wrong and that there is no knowledge of falsehoods are perhaps examples of the
latter. Not all obvious propositions are self-evident, e.g., it is obvious that a stone will fall if
dropped, but adequate understanding of that
claim does not by itself justify one in believing it.
An obvious proposition is one that immediately
seems true for anyone who adequately understands it, but its obviousness may rest on well-
known and commonly accepted empirical facts,
not on understanding.

All analytic propositions are self-evident but
not all self-evident propositions are analytic. The
propositions that if *A* is older than *B*, then *B* is
younger than *A*, and that no object can be red
and green all over at the same time and in the
same respects, are arguably self-evident but not
analytic. All self-evident propositions are necessary, for one could not be justified in believing a
contingent proposition simply in virtue of understanding it. However, not all necessary propositions are self-evident, e.g., that water is H_2O and
that temperature is the measure of the molecular activity in substances are necessary but not
self-evident. A proposition can appear to be self-
evident even though it is not. For instance, the
proposition that all unmarried adult males are
bachelors will appear self-evident to many until
they consider that the pope is such a male. A
proposition may appear self-evident to some but
not to others, even though it must either have or
lack the property of being self-evident. Self-evident propositions are knowable non-empirically,
or a priori, but some propositions knowable a
priori are not self-evident, e.g., certain conclusions of long and difficult chains of mathematical
reasoning.

See also ANALYTIC–SYNTHETIC DISTINC-
TION, A PRIORI, KANT, NECESSITY, RATIONAL-
ISM.   B.R.

self-interest theory. See PARFIT.

self-justification. See EPISTEMOLOGY.

self-love. See BUTLER, EGOISM.

self-organizing system. See COMPUTER THEORY.

self-presenting, in the philosophy of Meinong,
having the ability – common to all mental
states – to be immediately present to our
thought. In Meinong's view, no mental state can
be presented to our thought in any other
way – e.g., indirectly, via a Lockean "idea of
reflection." The only way to apprehend a mental
state is to experience or "live through" it. The
experience involved in the apprehension of an
external object has thus a double presentational
function: (1) via its "content" it presents the
object to our thought; (2) as its own "quasi-con-
tent" it presents itself immediately to our
thought. In the contemporary era, Roderick
Chisholm has based his account of empirical
knowledge in part on a related concept of the
self-presenting. (In Chisholm's sense – the definition of which we omit here – all self-presenting
states are mental, but not conversely; for
instance, being depressed because of the death of
one's spouse would not be self-presenting.) In
Chisholm's epistemology, self-presenting states
are a source of certainty in the following way: if
F is a self-presenting state, then to be certain that
one is in state *F* it is sufficient that one is, and
believes oneself to be in state *F*. **See also**
BRENTANO, MEINONG, PHILOSOPHY OF MIND.
R.Ke.

self-reference, paradoxes of. See RUSSELL, TYPE
THEORY.

self-referential incoherence, an internal defect of
an assertion or theory, which it possesses provided that (a) it establishes some requirement
that must be met by assertions or theories, (b) it
is itself subject to this requirement, and (c) it fails
to meet the requirement. The most famous
example is logical positivism's meaning criterion,
which requires that all meaningful assertions be
either tautological or empirically verifiable, yet is
itself neither. A possible early example is found
in Hume, whose own writings might have been
consigned to the flames had librarians followed
his counsel to do so with volumes that contain
neither "abstract reasoning concerning quantity
or number" nor "experimental reasoning concerning matter of fact and existence." Bold defi-

ance was shown by Wittgenstein, who, realizing that the propositions of the *Tractatus* did not "picture" the world, advised the reader to "throw away the ladder after he has climbed up it." An epistemological example is furnished by any foundationalist theory that establishes criteria for rational acceptability that the theory itself cannot meet. **See also** HUME, LOGICAL POSITIVISM.   W.Has.

self-reproducing automaton, a formal model of self-reproduction of a kind introduced by von Neumann. He worked with an intuitive robot model and then with a well-defined cellular automaton model. Imagine a class of robotic automata made of robot parts and operating in an environment of such parts. There are computer parts (switches, memory elements, wires), input-output parts (sensing elements, display elements), action parts (grasping and moving elements, joining and cutting elements), and straight bars (to maintain structure and to employ in a storage tape). There are also energy sources that enable the robots to operate and move around. These five categories of parts are sufficient for the construction of robots that can make objects of various kinds, including other robots.

These parts also clearly suffice for making a robot version of any *finite automaton*. Sensing and acting parts can then be added to this robot so that it can make an indefinitely expandable storage tape from straight bars. (A "blank tape" consists of bars joined in sequence, and the robot stores information on this tape by attaching bars or not at the junctions.) If its finite automaton part can execute programs and is sufficiently powerful, such a robot is a *universal computing robot* (cf. a universal Turing machine).

A universal computing robot can be augmented to form a universal constructing robot – a robot that can construct any robot, given its description. Let r be any robot with an indefinitely expandable tape, let $F(r)$ be the description of its finite part, and let $T(r)$ be the information on its tape. Now take a universal computing robot and augment it with sensing and acting devices and with programs so that when $F(r)$ followed by $T(r)$ is written on its tape, this augmented universal computer performs as follows. First, it reads the description $F(r)$, finds the needed parts, and constructs the finite part of r. Second, it makes a blank tape, attaches it to the finite part of r, and then copies the information $T(r)$ from its own tape onto the new tape. This augmentation of a universal computing robot is

a *universal constructor*. For when it starts with the information $F(r), T(r)$ written on its tape, it will construct a copy of r with $T(r)$ on its tape.

Robot self-reproduction results from applying the universal constructor to itself. Modify the universal constructor slightly so that when only a description $F(r)$ is written on its tape, it constructs the finite part of r and then attaches a tape with $F(r)$ written on it. Call this version of the universal constructor C_u. Now place C_u's description $F(C_u)$ on its own tape and start it up. C_u first reads this description and constructs a copy of the finite part of itself in an empty region of the cellular space. Then it adds a blank tape to the new construction and copies $F(C_u)$ onto it. Hence C_u with $F(C_u)$ on its tape has produced another copy of C_u with $F(C_u)$ on its tape. This is automaton self-reproduction.

This robot model of self-reproduction is very general. To develop the logic of self-reproduction further, von Neumann first extended the concept of a finite automaton to that of an infinite *cellular automaton* consisting of an array or "space" of *cells*, each cell containing the same finite automaton. He chose an infinite checkerboard array for modeling self-reproduction, and he specified a particular twenty-nine-state automaton for each square (cell). Each automaton is connected directly to its four contiguous neighbors, and communication between neighbors takes one or two time-steps.

The twenty-nine states of a cell fall into three categories. There is a blank state to represent the passivity of an empty area. There are twelve states for switching, storage, and communication, from which any finite automaton can be constructed in a sufficiently large region of cells. And there are sixteen states for simulating the activities of construction and destruction. Von Neumann chose these twenty-nine states in such a way that an area of non-blank cells could compute and grow, i.e., activate a path of cells out to a blank region and convert the cells of that region into a cellular automaton. A specific cellular automaton is embedded in this space by the selection of the initial states of a finite area of cells, all other cells being left blank. A *universal computer* consists of a sufficiently powerful finite automaton with a tape. The tape is an indefinitely long row of cells in which bits are represented by two different cell states. The finite automaton accesses these cells by means of a *construction arm* that it extends back and forth in rows of cells contiguous to the tape. When activated, this finite automaton will execute programs stored on its tape.

A *universal constructor* results from augmenting the universal computer (cf. the robot model). Another construction arm is added, together with a finite automaton controller to operate it. The controller sends signals into the arm to extend it out to a blank region of the cellular space, to move around that region, and to change the states of cells in that region. After the universal constructor has converted the region into a cellular automaton, it directs the construction arm to activate the new automaton and then withdraw from it. Cellular automaton self-reproduction results from applying the universal constructor to itself, as in the robot model.

Cellular automata are now studied extensively by humans working interactively with computers as abstract models of both physical and organic systems. (See Arthur W. Burks, "Von Neumann's Self-Reproducing Automata," in *Papers of John von Neumann on Computers and Computer Theory,* edited by William Aspray and Arthur Burks, 1987.) The study of artificial life is an outgrowth of computer simulations of cellular automata and related automata. Cellular automata organizations are sometimes used in highly parallel computers.

See also ARTIFICIAL INTELLIGENCE, ARTIFICIAL LIFE, COMPUTER THEORY, TURING MACHINE.   A.W.B.

Sellars, Roy Wood. See NEW REALISM.

Sellars, Wilfrid (1912–89), American philosopher, son of Roy Wood Sellars, and one of the great systematic philosophers of the century. His most influential and representative works are "Empiricism and the Philosophy of Mind" (1956) and "Philosophy and the Scientific Image of Man" (1960). The Sellarsian system may be outlined as follows.

The myth of the given. Thesis (1): Classical empiricism (foundationalism) maintains that our belief in the commonsense, objective world of physical objects is ultimately justified only by the way that world presents itself in sense experience. Thesis (2): It also typically maintains that sense experience (a) is not part of that world and (b) is not a form of conceptual cognition like thinking or believing. Thesis (3): From (1) and (2a) classical empiricism concludes that our knowledge of the physical world is inferred from sense experience. Thesis (4): Since inferences derive knowledge from knowledge, sense experience itself must be a form of knowledge. Theses (1)–(4) collectively are the doctrine of the

given. Each thesis taken individually is plausible. However, Sellars argues that (2b) and (4) are incompatible if, as he thinks, knowledge is a kind of conceptual cognition. Concluding that the doctrine of the given is false, he maintains that classical empiricism is a myth.

The positive system. From an analysis of theoretical explanation in the physical sciences, Sellars concludes that postulating theoretical entities is justified only if theoretical laws – nomological generalizations referring to theoretical entities – are needed to explain particular observable phenomena for which explanation in terms of exceptionless observation laws is unavailable. While rejecting any classical empiricist interpretation of observation, Sellars agrees that some account of non-inferential knowledge is required to make sense of theoretical explanation thus conceived. He thinks that utterances made in direct response to sensory stimuli (observational reports) count as non-inferential knowledge when (a) they possess authority, i.e., occur in conditions ensuring that they reliably indicate some physical property (say, shape) in the environment and are accepted by the linguistic community as possessing this quality; and (b) the utterer has justified belief that they possess this authority.

Sellars claims that some perceptual conditions induce ordinary people to make observation reports inconsistent with established explanatory principles of the commonsense framework. We thus might tend to report spontaneously that an object is green seen in daylight and blue seen indoors, and yet think it has not undergone any process that could change its color. Sellars sees in such conflicting tendencies vestiges of a primitive conceptual framework whose tensions have been partially resolved by introducing the concept of sense experiences. These experiences count as theoretical entities, since they are postulated to account for observational phenomena for which no exceptionless observation laws exist. This example may serve as a paradigm for a process of theoretical explanation occurring in the framework of commonsense beliefs that Sellars calls the *manifest image*, a process that itself is a model for his theory of the rational dynamics of conceptual change in both the manifest image and in science – the *scientific image*. Because the actual process of conceptual evolution in *Homo sapiens* may not fit this pattern of rational dynamics, Sellars treats these dynamics as occurring within certain hypothetical ideal histories (myths) of the way in which, from certain conceptually primitive beginnings, one might have come to postulate the requisite theoretical explanations.

The manifest image, like the proto-theories from which it arose, is itself subject to various tensions ultimately resolved in the scientific image. Because this latter image contains a metaphysical theory of material objects and persons that is inconsistent with that of its predecessor framework, Sellars regards the manifest image as replaced by its successor. In terms of the Peircean conception of truth that Sellars endorses, the scientific image is the only true image. In this sense Sellars is a scientific realist.

There is, however, also an important sense in which Sellars is not a scientific realist: despite discrediting classical empiricism, he thinks that the intrinsic nature of sense experience gives to conceptualization more than simply sensory stimulus yet less than the content of knowledge claims. Inspired by Kant, Sellars treats the manifest image as a Kantian *phenomenal world,* a world that exists as a cognitive construction which, though lacking ideal factual truth, is guided in part by intrinsic features of sense experience. This is not (analytic) phenomenalism, which Sellars rejects. Moreover, the special methodological role for sense experience has effects even within the scientific image itself.

Theories of mind, perception, and semantics.
Mind: In the manifest image thoughts are private episodes endowed with intentionality. Called inner speech, they are theoretical entities whose causal and intentional properties are modeled, respectively, on inferential and semantic properties of overt speech. They are introduced within a behaviorist proto-theory, the Rylean framework, to provide a theoretical explanation for behavior normally accompanied by linguistically overt reasons.

Perception: In the manifest image sense experiences are sense impressions – states of persons modeled on two-dimensional, colored physical replicas and introduced in the theoretical language of the adverbial theory of perception to explain why it can look as if some perceptible quality is present when it is not.

Semantics: The meaning of a simple predicate p in a language L is the role played in L by p defined in terms of three sets of linguistic rules: *language entry rules, intralinguistic rules,* and *language departure rules.* This account also supports a nominalist treatment of abstract entities. Identification of a role for a token of p in L can be effected demonstratively in the speaker's language by saying

that p in L is a member of the class of predicates playing the same role as a demonstrated predicate. Thus a speaker of English might say that '*rot*' in German plays the semantic role 'red' has in English.

Sellars sees science and metaphysics as autonomous strands in a single web of philosophical inquiry. Sellarsianism thus presents an important alternative to the view that what is fundamentally real is determined by the logical structure of scientific language alone. Sellars also sees ordinary language as expressing a common-sense framework of beliefs constituting a kind of proto-theory with its own methods, metaphysics, and theoretical entities. Thus, he also presents an important alternative to the view that philosophy concerns not what is ultimately real, but what words like 'real' ultimately mean in ordinary language.

See also EPISTEMOLOGY, METAPHYSICAL REALISM, ORDINARY LANGUAGE PHILOSOPHY.
T.V.

semantic atomism. See SEMANTIC HOLISM.

semantic completeness. See COMPLETENESS.

semantic compositionality. See MEANING.

semantic consequence. See MODAL LOGIC.

semantic consistency. See CONSISTENCY.

semantic holism, a metaphysical thesis about the nature of representation on which the meaning of a symbol is relative to the entire system of representations containing it. Thus, a linguistic expression can have meaning only in the context of a language; a hypothesis can have significance only in the context of a theory; a concept can have intentionality only in the context of the belief system. Holism about content has profoundly influenced virtually every aspect of contemporary theorizing about language and mind, not only in philosophy, but in linguistics, literary theory, artificial intelligence, psychology, and cognitive science. Contemporary semantic holists include Davidson, Quine, Gilbert Harman, Hartry Field, and Searle.

Because semantic holism is a metaphysical and not a semantic thesis, two theorists might agree about the semantic facts but disagree about semantic holism. So, e.g., nothing in Tarski's writings determines whether the semantic facts expressed by the theorems of an absolute truth theory are holistic or not. Yet Davidson, a semantic holist, argued that the correct form for a semantic theory for a natural language L is an absolute truth theory for L. Semantic theories, like other theories, need not wear their metaphysical commitments on their sleeves.

Holism has some startling consequences. Consider this. Franklin D. Roosevelt (who died when the United States still had just forty-eight states) did not believe there were fifty states, but I do; semantic holism says that what 'state' means in our mouths depends on the totality of our beliefs about states, including, therefore, our beliefs about how many states there are. It seems to follow that he and I must mean different things by 'state'; hence, if he says "Alaska is not a state" and I say "Alaska is a state" we are not disagreeing. This line of argument leads to such surprising declarations as that natural langauges are not, in general, intertranslatable (Quine, Saussure); that there may be no fact of the matter about the meanings of texts (Putnam, Derrida); and that scientific theories that differ in their basic postulates are "empirically incommensurable" (Paul Feyerabend, Kuhn).

For those who find these consequences of semantic holism unpalatable, there are three mutually exclusive responses: semantic atomism, semantic molecularism, or semantic nihilism.

Semantic atomists hold that the meaning of any representation (linguistic, mental, or otherwise) is not determined by the meaning of any other representation. Historically, Anglo-American philosophers in the eighteenth and nineteenth centuries thought that an idea of an X was about X's in virtue of this idea's physically resembling X's. Resemblance theories are no longer thought viable, but a number of contemporary semantic atomists still believe that the basic semantic relation is between a concept and the things to which it applies, and not one among concepts themselves. Thcsc philosophers include Dretske, Dennis Stampe, Fodor, and Ruth Millikan.

Semantic molecularism, like semantic holism, holds that the meaning of a representation in a language L is determined by its relationships to the meanings of other expressions in L, but, unlike holism, not by its relationships to every other expression in L. Semantic molecularists are committed to the view, contrary to Quine, that for any expression e in a language L there is an in-principle way of distinguishing between those representations in L the meanings of which determine the meaning of e and those represen-

tations in L the meanings of which do not determine the meaning of e. Traditionally, this in-principle delimitation is supported by an analytic/synthetic distinction. Those representations in L that are meaning-constituting of e are analytically connected to e and those that are not meaning-constituting are synthetically connected to e. Meaning molecularism seems to be the most common position among those philosophers who reject holism. Contemporary meaning molecularists include Michael Devitt, Dummett, Ned Block, and John Perry.

Semantic nihilism is perhaps the most radical response to the consequences of holism. It is the view that, strictly speaking, there are no semantic properties. Strictly speaking, there are no mental states; words lack meanings. At least for scientific purposes (and perhaps for other purposes as well) we must abandon the notion that people are moral or rational agents and that they act out of their beliefs and desires. Semantic nihilists include among their ranks Patricia and Paul Churchland, Stephen Stich, Dennett, and, sometimes, Quine.

See also ANALYTIC–SYNTHETIC DISTINCTION, MEANING, PHILOSOPHY OF MIND.   E.L.

semantic molecularism. See SEMANTIC HOLISM.

semantic nihilism. See SEMANTIC HOLISM.

semantic paradoxes, a collection of paradoxes involving the semantic notions of truth, predication, and definability. The liar paradox is the oldest and most widely known of these, having been formulated by Eubulides as an objection to Aristotle's correspondence theory of truth. In its simplest form, the liar paradox arises when we try to assess the truth of a sentence or proposition that asserts its own falsity, e.g.:

(A) Sentence (A) is not true.

It would seem that sentence (A) cannot be true, since it can be true only if what it says is the case, i.e., if it is not true. Thus sentence (A) is not true. But then, since this is precisely what it claims, it would seem to be true.

Several alternative forms of the liar paradox have been given their own names. The postcard paradox, also known as a liar cycle, envisions a postcard with sentence (B) on one side and sentence (C) on the other:

(B) The sentence on the other side of this card is true.

(C) The sentence on the other side of this card is false.

Here, no consistent assignment of truth-values to the pair of sentences is possible. In the preface paradox, it is imagined that a book begins with the claim that at least one sentence in the book is false. This claim is unproblematically true if some later sentence is false, but if the remainder of the book contains only truths, the initial sentence appears to be true if and only if false. The preface paradox is one of many examples of contingent liars, claims that can either have an unproblematic truth-value or be paradoxical, depending on the truth-values of various other claims (in this case, the remaining sentences in the book). Related to the preface paradox is Epimenedes' paradox: Epimenedes, himself from Crete, is said to have claimed that all Cretans are liars. This claim is paradoxical if interpreted to mean that Cretans always lie, or if interpreted to mean they sometimes lie and if no other claim made by Epimenedes was a lie. On the former interpretation, this is a simple variation of the liar paradox; on the latter, it is a form of contingent liar.

Other semantic paradoxes include Berry's paradox, Richard's paradox, and Grelling's paradox. The first two involve the notion of definability of numbers. Berry's paradox begins by noting that names (or descriptions) of integers consist of finite sequences of syllables. Thus the three-syllable sequence 'twenty-five' names 25, and the seven-syllable sequence 'the sum of three and seven' names ten. Now consider the collection of all sequences of (English) syllables that are less than nineteen syllables long. Of these, many are nonsensical ('bababa') and some make sense but do not name integers ('artichoke'), but some do ('the sum of three and seven'). Since there are only finitely many English syllables, there are only finitely many of these sequences, and only finitely many integers named by them. Berry's paradox arises when we consider the eighteen-syllable sequence 'the smallest integer not nameable in less than nineteen syllables'. This phrase appears to be a perfectly well-defined description of an integer. But if the phrase names an integer n, then n is nameable in less than nineteen syllables, and hence is not described by the phrase.

Richard's paradox constructs a similarly paradoxical description using what is known as a diagonal construction. Imagine a list of all finite sequences of letters of the alphabet (plus spaces and punctuation), ordered as in a dictionary.

Prune this list so that it contains only English definitions of real numbers between 0 and 1. Then consider the definition: "Let r be the real number between 0 and 1 whose kth decimal place is) if the kth decimal place of the number named by the kth member of this list is 1, and 0 otherwise'. This description seems to define a real number that must be different from any number defined on the list. For example, r cannot be defined by the 237th member of the list, because r will differ from that number in at least its 237th decimal place. But if it indeed defines a real number between 0 and 1, then this description should itself be on the list. Yet clearly, it cannot define a number different from the number defined by itself. Apparently, the definition defines a real number between 0 and 1 if and only if it does not appear on the list of such definitions.

Grelling's paradox, also known as the paradox of heterologicality, involves two predicates defined as follows. Say that a predicate is "autological" if it applies to itself. Thus 'polysyllabic' and 'short' are autological, since 'polysyllabic' is polysyllabic, and 'short' is short. In contrast, a predicate is "heterological" if and only if it is not autological. The question is whether the predicate 'heterological' is heterological. If our answer is yes, then 'heterological' applies to itself – and so is autological, not heterological. But if our answer is no, then it does not apply to itself – and so is heterological, once again contradicting our answer.

The semantic paradoxes have led to important work in both logic and the philosophy of language, most notably by Russell and Tarski. Russell developed the ramified theory of types as a unified treatment of all the semantic paradoxes. Russell's theory of types avoids the paradoxes by introducing complex syntactic conditions on formulas and on the definition of new predicates. In the resulting language, definitions like those used in formulating Berry's and Richard's paradoxes turn out to be ill-formed, since they quantify over collections of expressions that include themselves, violating what Russell called the vicious circle principle. The theory of types also rules out, on syntactic grounds, predicates that apply to themselves, or to larger expressions containing those very same predicates. In this way, the liar paradox and Grelling's paradox cannot be constructed within a language conforming to the theory of types.

Tarski's attention to the liar paradox made two fundamental contributions to logic: his development of semantic techniques for defining the truth predicate for formalized languages and his proof of Tarski's theorem. Tarskian semantics avoids the liar paradox by starting with a formal language, call it L, in which no semantic notions are expressible, and hence in which the liar paradox cannot be formulated. Then using another language, known as the metalanguage, Tarski applies recursive techniques to define the predicate *true-in-L*, which applies to exactly the true sentences of the original language L. The liar paradox does not arise in the metalanguage, because the sentence

(D) Sentence (D) is not *true-in-L*.

is, if expressible in the metalanguage, simply true. (It is true because (D) is not a sentence of L, and so *a fortiori* not a true sentence of L.) A *truth predicate* for the metalanguage can then be defined in yet another language, the metametalanguage, and so forth, resulting in a sequence of consistent truth predicates.

Tarski's theorem uses the liar paradox to prove a significant result in logic. The theorem states that the truth predicate for the first-order language of arithmetic is not definable in arithmetic. That is, if we devise a systematic way of representing sentences of arithmetic by numbers, then it is impossible to define an arithmetical predicate that applies to all and only those numbers that represent true sentences of arithmetic. The theorem is proven by showing that if such a predicate were definable, we could construct a sentence of arithmetic that is true if and only if it is not true: an arithmetical version of sentence (A), the liar paradox.

Both Russell's and Tarski's solutions to the semantic paradoxes have left many philosophers dissatisfied, since the solutions are basically prescriptions for constructing languages in which the paradoxes do not arise. But the fact that paradoxes can be avoided in artificially constructed languages does not itself give a satisfying explanation of what is going wrong when the paradoxes are encountered in natural language, or in an artificial language in which they can be formulated. Most recent work on the liar paradox, following Kripke's "Outline of a Theory of Truth" (1975), looks at languages in which the paradox can be formulated, and tries to provide a consistent account of truth that preserves as much as possible of the intuitive notion.

See also SET-THEORETIC PARADOXES, TRUTH, TYPE THEORY.   J.Et.

semantics. See FORMAL SEMANTICS, PHILOSOPHY OF LANGUAGE.

semantics, conceptual role. See MEANING, PHILOSOPHY OF MIND.

semantics, extensionalist. See EXTENSIONALISM.

semantics, Kripke. See KRIPKE SEMANTICS.

semantics, linguistic. See PHILOSOPHY OF LANGUAGE.

semantics, non-standard. See SECOND-ORDER LOGIC.

semantics, outer domain. See FREE LOGIC.

semantics, possible worlds. See KRIPKE SEMANTICS, POSSIBLE WORLDS.

semantics, situation. See POSSIBLE WORLDS.

semantics, standard. See SECOND-ORDER LOGIC.

semantics, supervaluation. See FREE LOGIC.

semantics, Tarskian. See FORMAL SEMANTICS.

semantics, truth-conditional. See MEANING.

semantic solipsism. See SOLIPSISM.

semantic tableaux. See PHILOSOPHY OF LOGIC.

semantic theory of truth. See TRUTH.

semantic truth. See TRUTH.

semi-order. See ORDERING.

semiosis (from Greek *sēmeiōsis*, 'observation of signs'), the relation of signification involving the three relata of sign, object, and mind. Semiotic is the science or study of semiosis. The semiotic of John of Saint Thomas and of Peirce includes two distinct components: the relation of signification and the classification of signs. The relation of signification is genuinely triadic and cannot be reduced to the sum of its three subordinate dyads: sign-object, sign-mind, object-mind. A sign represents an object to a mind just as A gives a gift to B. Semiosis is not, as it is often taken to be, a mere compound of a sign-object dyad and a sign-mind dyad because these dyads lack the essential intentionality that unites mind with object; similarly, the gift relation involves not just A giving and B receiving but, crucially, the intention uniting A and B.

In the Scholastic logic of John of Saint Thomas, the sign-object dyad is a categorial relation (*secundum esse*), that is, an essential relation, falling in Aristotle's category of relation, while the sign-mind dyad is a transcendental relation (*secundum dici*), that is, a relation only in an analogical sense, in a manner of speaking; thus the formal rationale of semiosis is constituted by the sign-object dyad. By contrast, in Peirce's logic, the sign-object dyad and the sign-mind dyad are each only potential semiosis: thus, the hieroglyphs of ancient Egypt were merely potential signs until the discovery of the Rosetta Stone, just as a road-marking was a merely potential sign to the driver who overlooked it.

Classifications of signs typically follow from the logic of semiosis. Thus John of Saint Thomas divides signs according to their relations to their objects into natural signs (smoke as a sign of fire), customary signs (napkins on the table as a sign that dinner is imminent), and stipulated signs (as when a neologism is coined); he also divides signs according to their relations to a mind. An *instrumental sign* must first be cognized as an object before it can signify (e.g., a written word or a symptom); a *formal sign*, by contrast, directs the mind to its object without having first been cognized (e.g., percepts and concepts). Formal signs are not that which we cognize but that by which we cognize. All instrumental signs presuppose the action of formal signs in the semiosis of cognition. Peirce similarly classified signs into three trichotomies according to their relations with (1) themselves, (2) their objects, and (3) their interpretants (usually minds); and Charles Morris, who followed Peirce closely, called the relationship of signs to one another the syntactical dimension of semiosis, the relationship of signs to their objects the semantical dimension of semiosis, and the relationship of signs to their interpreters the pragmatic dimension of semiosis.

See also JOHN OF SAINT THOMAS, PEIRCE, THEORY OF SIGNS.   J.B.M.

semiotic. See THEORY OF SIGNS.

Seneca, Lucius Annaeus. See STOICISM.

sensa. See PERCEPTION.

sensationalism, the belief that all mental states – particularly cognitive states – are derived, by composition or association, from sensation. It is often joined to the view that sensations provide the only evidence for our beliefs, or (more rarely) to the view that statements about the world can be reduced, without loss, to statements about sensation.

Hobbes was the first important sensationalist in modern times. "There is no conception in man's mind," he wrote, "which hath not at first, totally, or by parts, been begotten upon the organs of sense. The rest are derived from that original." But the belief gained prominence in the eighteenth century, due largely to the influence of Locke. Locke himself was not a sensationalist, because he took the mind's reflection on its own operations to be an independent source of ideas. But his distinction between simple and complex ideas was used by eighteenth-century sensationalists such as Condillac and Hartley to explain how conceptions that seem distant from sense might nonetheless be derived from it. And to account for the particular ways in which simple ideas are in fact combined, Condillac and Hartley appealed to a second device described by Locke: the association of ideas.

"Elementary" sensations – the building blocks of our mental life – were held by the sensationalists to be non-voluntary, independent of judgment, free of interpretation, discrete or atomic, and infallibly known. Nineteenth-century sensationalists tried to account for perception in terms of such building blocks; they struggled particularly with the perception of space and time. Late nineteenth-century critics such as Ward and James advanced powerful arguments against the reduction of perception to sensation. Perception, they claimed, involves more than the passive reception (or recombination and association) of discrete pellets of incorrigible information. They urged a change in perspective – to a functionalist viewpoint more closely allied with prevailing trends in biology – from which sensationalism never fully recovered.

See also EMPIRICISM, HOBBES, PERCEPTION.
K.P.W.

sense. See MEANING.

sense, direct. See OBLIQUE CONTEXT.

sense, indirect. See OBLIQUE CONTEXT.

sense-data. See PERCEPTION.

sense-datum theory. See PHENOMENALISM.

sense qualia. See QUALIA.

senses, special. See FACULTY PSYCHOLOGY.

sensibilia (singular: sensibile), as used by Russell, those entities that no one is (at the moment) perceptually aware of, but that are, in every other respect, just like the objects of perceptual awareness.

If one is a direct realist and believes that the objects one is aware of in sense perception are ordinary physical objects, then sensibilia are, of course, just physical objects of which no one is (at the moment) aware. Assuming (with common sense) that ordinary objects continue to exist when no one is aware of them, it follows that sensibilia exist. If, however, one believes (as Russell did) that what one is aware of in ordinary sense perception is some kind of idea in the mind, a so-called sense-datum, then sensibilia have a problematic status. A sensibile then turns out to be an unsensed sense-datum. On some (the usual) conceptions of sense-data, this is like an unfelt pain, since a sense-datum's existence (not *as* a sense-datum, but as anything at all) depends on our (someone's) perception of it. To exist (for such things) *is* to be perceived (see Berkeley's *"esse est percipii"*). If, however, one extends the notion of sense-datum (as Moore was inclined to do) to *whatever* it is of which one is (directly) aware in sense perception, then sensibilia may or may not exist. It depends on what – physical objects or ideas in the mind – we are directly aware of in sense perception (and, of course, on the empirical facts about whether objects continue to exist when they are not being perceived). If direct realists are right, horses and trees, when unobserved, are sensibilia. So are the front surfaces of horses and trees (things Moore once considered to be sense-data). If the direct realists are wrong, and what we are perceptually aware of are "ideas in the mind," then whether or not sensibilia exist depends on whether or not such ideas can exist *apart* from any mind.

See also PERCEPTION, RUSSELL.   F.D.

sensible intuition. See KANT.

sensibles, common. See ARISTOTLE, SENSUS COMMUNIS.

sensibles, proper. See ARISTOTLE.

sensibles, special. See ARISTOTLE, FACULTY PSYCHOLOGY.

sensorium, the seat and cause of sensation in the brain of humans and other animals. The term is not part of contemporary psychological parlance; it belongs to prebehavioral, prescientific psychology, especially of the seventeenth and eighteenth centuries. Only creatures possessed of a sensorium were thought capable of bodily and perceptual sensations. Some thinkers believed that the sensorium, when excited, also produced muscular activity and motion.   G.A.G.

sensum. See PERCEPTION.

sensus communis, a cognitive faculty to which the five senses report. It was first argued for in Aristotle's *On the Soul* II.1–2, though the term 'common sense' was first introduced in Scholastic thought. Aristotle refers to properties such as magnitude that are perceived by more than one sense as common sensibles. To recognize common sensibles, he claims, we must possess a single cognitive power to compare such qualities, received from the different senses, to one another. Augustine says the "inner sense" judges whether the senses are working properly, and perceives whether the animal perceives (*De libero arbitrio* II.3–5). Aquinas (*In De anima* II, 13.370) held that it is also by the common sense that we perceive we live. He says the common sense uses the external senses to know sensible forms, preparing the sensible species it receives for the operation of the cognitive power, which recognizes the real thing causing the sensible species. **See also** AQUINAS, ARISTOTLE.   J.Lo.

sentence, basic. See FOUNDATIONALISM.

sentential calculus. See FORMAL LOGIC.

sentential connective, also called sentential operator, propositional connective, propositional operator, a word or phrase, such as 'and', 'or', or 'if . . . then', that is used to construct compound sentences from atomic – i.e., non-compound – sentences. A sentential connective can be defined formally as an expression containing blanks, such that when the blanks are replaced with sentences the result is a compound sentence. Thus, 'if ——— then ——— ' and '——— or ——— ' are sentential connectives, since we can replace the blanks with sentences to get the compound sentences 'If the sky is clear then we can go swimming' and 'We can go swimming or we can stay home'.

Classical logic makes use of truth-functional connectives only, for which the truth-value of the compound sentence can be determined uniquely by the truth-value of the sentences that replace the blanks. The standard truth-functional connectives are 'and', 'or', 'not', 'if . . . then', and 'if and only if'. There are many non-truth-functional connectives as well, such as 'it is possible that ———' and '——— because ———'.

See also FORMAL LOGIC, OPERATOR, TRUTH TABLE.   V.K.

sentential operator. See SENTENTIAL CONNECTIVE.

sentiment. See SENTIMENTALISM.

sentimentalism, the theory, prominent in the eighteenth century, that epistemological or moral relations are derived from feelings. Although sentimentalism and sensationalism are both empiricist positions, the latter view has all knowledge built up from sensations, experiences impinging on the senses. Sentimentalists may allow that ideas derive from sensations, but hold that some relations between them are derived internally, that is, from sentiments arising upon reflection. Moral sentimentalists, such as Shaftesbury, Hutcheson, and Hume, argued that the virtue or vice of a character trait is established by approving or disapproving sentiments.

Hume, the most thoroughgoing sentimentalist, also argued that all beliefs about the world depend on sentiments. On his analysis, when we form a belief, we rely on the mind's causally connecting two experiences, e.g., fire and heat. But, he notes, such causal connections depend on the notion of necessity – that the two perceptions will always be so conjoined – and there is nothing in the perceptions themselves that supplies that notion. The idea of necessary connection is instead derived from a sentiment: our feeling of expectation of the one experience upon the other. Likewise, our notions of substance (the unity of experiences in an object) and of self (the unity of experiences in a subject) are sentiment-based. But whereas moral sentiments do not purport to represent the external world, these metaphysical notions of necessity, substance, and self are "fictions," creations of the imagination purporting to represent something in the outside world.

See also HUME, HUTCHESON, MORAL SENSE THEORY, SENSATIONALISM, SHAFTESBURY.
                                                E.S.R.

separation, axiom of. See AXIOM OF COMPREHENSION, SET THEORY.

separation of law and morals. See HART.

sequent calculus. See CUT-ELIMINATION THEOREM.

set. See SET THEORY.

set, singleton. See SET THEORY.

set, well-ordered. See SET-THEORETIC PARADOXES.

set-theoretic paradoxes, a collection of paradoxes that reveal difficulties in certain central notions of set theory. The best-known of these are Russell's paradox, Burali-Forti's paradox, and Cantor's paradox.

Russell's paradox, discovered in 1901 by Bertrand Russell, is the simplest (and so most problematic) of the set-theoretic paradoxes. Using it, we can derive a contradiction directly from Cantor's unrestricted comprehension schema. This schema asserts that for any formula $P(x)$ containing x as a free variable, there is a set $\{x \mid P(x)\}$ whose members are exactly those objects that satisfy $P(x)$. To derive the contradiction, take $P(x)$ to be the formula $x \in x$, and let z be the set $\{x \mid x \notin x\}$ whose existence is guaranteed by the comprehension schema. Thus z is the set whose members are exactly those objects that are not members of themselves. We now ask whether z is, itself, a member of z. If the answer is yes, then we can conclude that z must satisfy the criterion of membership in z, i.e., z must *not* be a member of z. But if the answer is no, then since z is not a member of itself, it satisfies the criterion for membership in z, and so z *is* a member of z.

All modern axiomatizations of set theory avoid Russell's paradox by restricting the principles that assert the existence of sets. The simplest restriction replaces unrestricted comprehension with the separation schema. *Separation* asserts that, given any set A and formula $P(x)$, there is a set $\{x \in A \mid P(x)\}$, whose members are exactly those members of A that satisfy $P(x)$. If we now take $P(x)$ to be the formula $x \notin x$, then separation guarantees the existence of a set $z_A = \{x \notin A \mid x \notin x\}$. We can then use Russell's reasoning to prove the result that z_A cannot be a member of the original set A. (If it were a member of A, then we could prove that it is a member of itself if and only if it is not a member of itself. Hence it is not a member of A.) But this result is not problematic, and so the paradox is avoided.

The Burali-Forti paradox and Cantor's paradox are sometimes known as paradoxes of size, since they show that some collections are too large to be considered sets. The Burali-Forti paradox, discovered by Cesare Burali-Forti, is concerned with the set of all ordinal numbers. In Cantor's set theory, an ordinal number can be assigned to any well-ordered set. (A set is well-ordered if every subset of the set has a least element.) But Cantor's set theory also guarantees the existence of the set of all ordinals, again due to the unrestricted comprehension schema. This set of ordinals is well-ordered, and so can be associated with an ordinal number. But it can be shown that the associated ordinal is greater than any ordinal in the set, hence greater than any ordinal number.

Cantor's paradox involves the cardinality of the set of all sets. *Cardinality* is another notion of size used in set theory: a set A is said to have greater cardinality than a set B if and only if B can be mapped one-to-one onto a subset of A but A cannot be so mapped onto B or any of its subsets. One of Cantor's fundamental results was that the set of all subsets of a set A (known as the power set of A) has greater cardinality than the set A. Applying this result to the set V of all sets, we can conclude that the power set of V has greater cardinality than V. But every set in the power set of V is also in V (since V contains all sets), and so the power set of V cannot have greater cardinality than V. We thus have a contradiction.

Like Russell's paradox, both of these paradoxes result from the unrestricted comprehension schema, and are avoided by replacing it with weaker set-existence principles. Various principles stronger than the separation schema are needed to get a reasonable set theory, and many alternative axiomatizations have been proposed. But the lesson of these paradoxes is that no set-existence principle can entail the existence of the Russell set, the set of all ordinals, or the set of all sets, on pain of contradiction.

See also SEMANTIC PARADOXES, SET THEORY.   J.Et.

set-theoretic reflection principles. See REFLECTION PRINCIPLES.

set theory, the study of collections, ranging from familiar examples like a set of encyclopedias or a deck of cards to mathematical examples like the set of natural numbers or the set of points on a line or the set of functions from a set A to another set B. Sets can be specified in two basic ways: by a list (e.g., {0, 2, 4, 6, 8}) and as the extension of a property (e.g., {x / x is an even natural number less than 10}, where this is read 'the set of all x such that x is an even natural number less than 10'). The most fundamental relation in set theory is *membership*, as in '2 is a member of the set of even natural numbers' (in symbols: $2 \in \{x \mid x$ is an even natural number}). Membership is

determinate, i.e., any candidate for membership in a given set is either in the set or not in the set, with no room for vagueness or ambiguity. A set's identity is completely determined by its *members* or *elements* (i.e., sets are extensional rather than intensional). Thus {$x \mid x$ is human} is the same set as {$x \mid x$ is a featherless biped} because they have the same members.

The smallest set possible is the *empty* or *null set*, the set with no members. (There cannot be more than one empty set, by extensionality.) It can be specified, e.g., as {$x \mid x \neq x$}, but it is most often symbolized as $\emptyset$ or { }. A set A is called a *subset* of a set B and B a *superset* of A if every member of A is also a member of B; in symbols, $A \subseteq B$. So, the set of even natural numbers is a subset of the set of all natural numbers, and any set is a superset of the empty set. The *union* of two sets A and B is the set whose members are the members of A and the members of B – in symbols, $A \cup B = \{x \mid x \in A$ or $x \in B\}$ – so the union of the set of even natural numbers and the set of odd natural numbers is the set of all natural numbers. The *intersection* of two sets A and B is the set whose members are common to both A and B – in symbols, $A \cap B = \{x \mid x \in A$ and $x \in B\}$ – so the intersection of the set of even natural numbers and the set of prime natural numbers is the *singleton* set {2}, whose only member is the number 2. Two sets whose intersection is empty are called *disjoint*, e.g., the set of even natural numbers and the set of odd natural numbers. Finally, the *difference* between a set A and a set B is the set whose members are members of A but not members of B – in symbols, $A - B = \{x \mid x \in A$ and $x \notin B\}$ – so the set of odd numbers between 5 and 20 minus the set of prime natural numbers is {9, 15}.

By extensionality, the order in which the members of a set are listed is unimportant, i.e., {1, 2, 3} = {2, 3, 1}. To introduce the concept of ordering, we need the notion of the *ordered pair* of a and b – in symbols, (a, b) or $<a, b>$. All that is essential to ordered pairs is that two of them are equal only when their first entries are equal and their second entries are equal. Various sets can be used to simulate this behavior, but the version most commonly used is the Kuratowski ordered pair: (a, b) is defined to be {{a}, {a, b}}. On this definition, it can indeed be proved that

$$(a, b) = (c, d) \text{ if and only if } a = c \text{ and } b = d.$$

The *Cartesian product* of two sets A and B is the set of all ordered pairs whose first entry is in A and whose second entry is B – in symbols, $A \times B = \{x \mid x = (a, b)$ for some $a \in A$ and some $b \in B\}$. This same technique can be used to form ordered triples – $(a, b, c) = ((a, b), c)$; ordered four-tuples – $(a, b, c, d) = ((a, b, c), d)$; and by extension, ordered n-tuples for all finite n.

Using only these simple building blocks, (substitutes for) all the objects of classical mathematics can be constructed inside set theory. For example, a relation is defined as a set of ordered pairs – so the successor relation among natural numbers becomes $\{(0, 1), (1, 2), (2, 3) \ldots \}$ – and a function is a relation containing no distinct ordered pairs of the form (a, b) and (a, c) – so the successor relation is a function. The natural numbers themselves can be identified with various sequences of sets, the most common of which are finite von Neumann *ordinal numbers*: $\emptyset, \{\emptyset\}, \{\emptyset, \{\emptyset\}\}, \{\emptyset, \{\emptyset\}, \{\emptyset, \{\emptyset\}\}\}, \ldots$ (On this definition, $0 = \emptyset$, $1 = \{\emptyset\}$, $2 = \{\emptyset, \{\emptyset\}\}$, etc., each number n has n members, the successor of n is $n \cup \{n\}$, and $n < m$ if and only if $n \in m$.) Addition and multiplication can be defined for these numbers, and the Peano axioms proved (from the axioms of set theory; see below). Negative, rational, real, and complex numbers, geometric spaces, and more esoteric mathematical objects can all be identified with sets, and the standard theorems about them proved. In this sense, set theory provides a foundation for mathematics.

Historically, the theory of sets arose in the late nineteenth century. In his work on the foundations of arithmetic, Frege identified the natural numbers with the extensions of certain concepts; e.g., the number two is the set of all concepts C under which two things fall – in symbols, $2 = \{x \mid x$ is a concept, and there are distinct things a and b which fall under x, and anything that falls under x is either a or $b\}$. Cantor was led to consider complex sets of points in the pursuit of a question in the theory of trigonometric series. To describe the properties of these sets, Cantor introduced infinite ordinal numbers after the finite ordinals described above. The first of these, ω, is $\{0, 1, 2, \ldots\}$, now understood in von Neumann's terms as the set of all finite ordinals. After ω, the successor function yields $\omega + 1 = \omega \cup \{\omega\} = \{0, 1, 2, \ldots n, n+1, \ldots, \omega\}$, then $\omega + 2 = (\omega + 1) + 1 = \{0, 1, 2, \ldots, \omega, \omega + 1\}$, $\omega + 3 = (\omega + 2) + 1 = \{0, 1, 2, \ldots, \omega, \omega + 1, \omega + 2\}$, and so on; after all these comes $\omega + \omega = \{0, 1, 2, \ldots, \omega, \omega + 1, \omega + 2, \ldots, (\omega + n), (\omega + n) + 1, \ldots\}$, and the process begins again.

The ordinal numbers are designed to label the positions in an ordering. Consider, e.g., a reordering of the natural numbers in which the odd numbers are placed after the evens: 0, 2, 4, 6, ... 1, 3, 5, 7, ... The number 4 is in the third

position of this sequence, and the number 5 is in the $(\omega + 2\text{nd})$. But finite numbers also perform a cardinal function; they tell us how many so-and-so's there are. Here the infinite ordinals are less effective. The natural numbers in their usual order have the same structure as ω, but when they are ordered as above, with the evens before the odds, they take on the structure of a much larger ordinal, $\omega + \omega$. But the answer to the question, How many natural numbers are there? should be the same no matter how they are arranged. Thus, the transfinite ordinals do not provide a stable measure of the size of an infinite set.

When are two infinite sets of the same size? On the one hand, the infinite set of even natural numbers seems clearly smaller than the set of all natural numbers; on the other hand, these two sets can be brought into one-to-one correspondence via the mapping that matches 0 to 0, 1 to 2, 2 to 4, 3 to 6, and in general, n to $2n$. This puzzle had troubled mathematicians as far back as Galileo, but Cantor took the existence of a one-to-one correspondence between two sets A and B as the definition of 'A is the same size as B'. This coincides with our usual understanding for finite sets, and it implies that the set of even natural numbers and the set of all natural numbers and $\omega + 1$ and $\omega + 2$ and $\omega + \omega$ and $\omega + \omega$ and many more all have the same size. Such infinite sets are called *countable*, and the number of their elements, the first infinite cardinal number, is $\aleph_0$. Cantor also showed that the set of all subsets of a set A has a size larger than A itself, so there are infinite cardinals greater than $\aleph_0$, namely $\aleph_1$, $\aleph_2$, and so on.

Unfortunately, the early set theories were prone to paradoxes. The most famous of these, Russell's paradox, arises from consideration of the set R of all sets that are not members of themselves: is $R \in R$? If it is, it isn't, and if it isn't, it is. The *Burali-Forti paradox* involves the set Ω of all ordinals: Ω itself qualifies as an ordinal, so $\Omega \in \Omega$, i.e., $\Omega < \Omega$. Similar difficulties surface with the set of all cardinal numbers and the set of all sets. At fault in all these cases is a seemingly innocuous principle of *unlimited comprehension*: for any property P, there is a set $\{x \mid x$ has $P\}$.

Just after the turn of the century, Zermelo undertook to systematize set theory by codifying its practice in a series of axioms from which the known derivations of the paradoxes could not be carried out. He proposed the axioms of *extensionality* (two sets with the same members are the same); *pairing* (for any a and b, there is a set $\{a, b\}$); *separation* (for any set A and property P, there is a set $\{x \mid x \in A$ and x has $P\}$); *power set* (for any set A, there is a set $\{x \mid x \subseteq A\}$); *union* (for any set of sets F, there is a set $\{x \mid x \in A$ for some $A \in F\}$ – this yields $A \cup B$, when $F = \{A, B\}$ and $\{A, B\}$ comes from A and B by pairing); *infinity* (ω exists); and *choice* (for any set of non-empty sets, there is a set that contains exactly one member from each). (The axiom of choice has a vast number of equivalents, including the well-ordering theorem – every set can be well-ordered – and Zorn's lemma – if every chain in a partially ordered set has an upper bound, then the set has a maximal element.) The axiom of separation limits that of unlimited comprehension by requiring a previously given set A from which members are separated by the property P; thus troublesome sets like Russell's that attempt to collect absolutely all things with P cannot be formed. The most controversial of Zermelo's axioms at the time was that of choice, because it posits the existence of a choice set – a set that "chooses" one from each of (possibly infinitely many) non-empty sets – without giving any rule for making the choices. For various philosophical and practical reasons, it is now accepted without much debate.

Fraenkel and Skolem later formalized the axiom of *replacement* (if A is a set, and every member a of A is replaced by some b, then there is a set containing all the b's), and Skolem made both replacement and separation more precise by expressing them as schemata of first-order logic. The final axiom of the contemporary theory is *foundation*, which guarantees that sets are formed in a series of stages called the *iterative hierarchy* (begin with some non-sets, then form all possible sets of these, then form all possible sets of the things formed so far, then form all possible sets of these, and so on). This iterative picture of sets built up in stages contrasts with the older notion of the extension of a concept; these are sometimes called the mathematical and the logical notions of collection, respectively. The early controversy over the paradoxes and the axiom of choice can be traced to the lack of a clear distinction between these at the time.

Zermelo's first five axioms (all but choice) plus foundation form a system usually called Z; ZC is Z with choice added. Z plus replacement is ZF, for Zermelo-Fraenkel, and adding choice makes ZFC, the theory of sets in most widespread use today. The consistency of ZFC cannot be proved by standard mathematical means, but decades of experience with the system and the strong intuitive picture provided by the iterative conception suggest that it is. Though ZFC is strong enough

for all standard mathematics, it is not enough to answer some natural set-theoretic questions (e.g., the continuum problem). This has led to a search for new axioms, such as large cardinal assumptions, but no consensus on these additional principles has yet been reached.

See also CANTOR, CLASS, CONTINUUM PROBLEM, GÖDEL'S INCOMPLETENESS THEOREMS, PHILOSOPHY OF MATHEMATICS, SET-THEORETIC PARADOXES.   P.Mad.

seven emotions (the). See KOREAN PHILOSOPHY.

Seven Worthies of the Bamboo Grove. See NEO-TAOISM.

Sextus Empiricus (third century A.D.), Greek Skeptic philosopher whose writings are the chief source of our knowledge about the extreme Skeptic view, Pyrrhonism. Practically nothing is known about him as a person. He was apparently a medical doctor and a teacher in a Skeptical school, probably in Alexandria. What has survived are his *Hypotoposes, Outlines of Pyrrhonism,* and a series of Skeptical critiques, *Against the Dogmatists*, questioning the premises and conclusions in many disciplines, such as physics, mathematics, rhetoric, and ethics. In these works, Sextus summarized and organized the views of Skeptical arguers before him.

The *Outlines* starts with an attempt to indicate what Skepticism is, to explain the terminology employed by the Skeptics, how Pyrrhonian Skepticism differs from other so-called Skeptical views, and how the usual answers to Skepticism are rebutted. Sextus points out that the main Hellenistic philosophies, Stoicism, Epicureanism, and Academic Skepticism (which is presented as a negative dogmatism), claimed that they would bring the adherent peace of mind, *ataraxia*. Unfortunately the dogmatic adherent would only become more perturbed by seeing the Skeptical objections that could be brought against his or her view. Then, by suspending judgment, *epoche*, one would find the tranquillity being sought. Pyrrhonian Skepticism is a kind of mental hygiene or therapy that cures one of dogmatism or rashness. It is like a purge that cleans out foul matter as well as itself. To bring about this state of affairs there are sets of Skeptical arguments that should bring one to suspense of judgment. The first set are the ten tropes of the earlier Skeptic, Anesidemus. The next are the five tropes about causality. And lastly are the tropes about the criterion of knowledge. The ten tropes stress the variability of sense experience among men and animals, among men, and within one individual. The varying and conflicting experiences present conflicts about what the perceived object is like. Any attempt to judge beyond appearances, to ascertain that which is non-evident, requires some way of choosing what data to accept. This requires a criterion. Since there is disagreement about what criterion to employ, we need a criterion of a criterion, and so on. Either we accept an arbitrary criterion or we get into an infinite regress. Similarly if we try to prove anything, we need a criterion of what constitutes a proof. If we offer a proof of a theory of proof, this will be circular reasoning, or end up in another infinite regress.

Sextus devotes most of his discussion to challenging Stoic logic, which claimed that evident signs could reveal what is non-evident. There might be signs that suggested what is temporarily non-evident, such as smoke indicating that there is a fire, but any supposed linkage between evident signs and what is non-evident can be challenged and questioned. Sextus then applies the groups of Skeptical arguments to various specific subjects – physics, mathematics, music, grammar, ethics – showing that one should suspend judgment on any knowledge claims in these areas. Sextus denies that he is saying any of this dogmatically: he is just stating how he feels at given moments. He hopes that dogmatists sick with a disease, rashness, will be cured and led to tranquillity no matter how good or bad the Skeptical arguments might be.

See also SKEPTICISM, SKEPTICS, STOICISM.
R.H.P.

Shaftesbury, Lord, in full, Third Earl of Shaftesbury, title of Anthony Ashley Cooper (1671–1713), English philosopher and politician who originated the moral sense theory. He was born at Wimborne St. Giles, Dorsetshire. As a Country Whig he served in the House of Commons for three years and later, as earl, monitored meetings of the House of Lords. Shaftesbury introduced into British moral philosophy the notion of a moral sense, a mental faculty unique to human beings, involving reflection and feeling and constituting their ability to discern right and wrong. He sometimes represents the moral sense as analogous to a purported aesthetic sense, a special capacity by which we perceive, through our emotions, the proportions and harmonies of which, on his Platonic view, beauty is composed.

For Shaftesbury, every creature has a "private good or interest," an end to which it is naturally disposed by its constitution. But there are other goods as well – notably, the public good and the good (without qualification) of a sentient being. An individual creature's goodness is defined by the tendency of its "natural affections" to contribute to the "universal system" of nature of which it is a part – i.e., their tendency to promote the public good. Because human beings can reflect on actions and affections, including their own and others', they experience emotional responses not only to physical stimuli but to these mental objects as well (e.g., to the thought of one's compassion or kindness). Thus, they are capable of perceiving – and acquiring through their actions – a particular species of goodness, namely, virtue. In the virtuous person, the person of integrity, natural appetites and affections are in harmony with each other (wherein lies her private good) and in harmony with the public interest.

Shaftesbury's attempted reconciliation of self-love and benevolence is in part a response to the egoism of Hobbes, who argued that everyone is in fact motivated by self-interest. His defining morality in terms of psychological and public harmony is also a reaction to the divine voluntarism of his former tutor, Locke, who held that the laws of nature and morality issue from the will of God. On Shaftesbury's view, morality exists independently of religion, but belief in God serves to produce the highest degree of virtue by nurturing a love for the universal system. Shaftesbury's theory led to a general refinement of eighteenth-century ideas about moral feelings; a theory of the moral sense emerged, whereby sentiments are – under certain conditions – perceptions of, or constitutive of, right and wrong.

In addition to several essays collected in three volumes under the title *Characteristics of Men, Manners, Opinions, Times* (second edition, 1714), Shaftesbury also wrote stoical moral and religious meditations reminiscent of Epictetus and Marcus Aurelius. His ideas on moral sentiments exercised considerable influence on the ethical theories of Hutcheson and Hume, who later worked out in detail their own accounts of the moral sense.

See also HOBBES, HUME, HUTCHESON, MORAL SENSE THEORY.   E.S.R.

shamanism. See KOREAN PHILOSOPHY.

shan, o, Chinese terms for 'good' and 'evil', respectively. These are primary concerns for Chinese philosophers: the Confucianists wanted to do good and get rid of evil, while the Taoists wanted to go beyond good and evil. In fact the

Taoists presupposed that man has the ability to reach a higher level of spirituality. Chinese philosophers often discussed *shan* and *o* in relation to human nature. Mencius believed that nature is good; his opponent Kao Tzu, nature is neither good nor evil; Hsün Tzu, nature is evil; and Yang Hsiung, nature is both good and evil. Most Chinese philosophers believed that man is able to do good; they also accepted evil as something natural that needed no explanation. **See also** CONFUCIANISM, HSÜN TZU, MENCIUS, TAOISM, YANG HSIUNG.   S.-h.L.

shang ti, Chinese term meaning 'high ancestor', 'God'. *Shang ti* – synonymous with *t'ien,* in the sense of a powerful anthropomorphic entity – is responsible for such things as the political fortunes of the state. Some speculate that *shang ti* was originally only a Shang deity, later identified by the Chou conquerors with their *t'ien*. The term *shang ti* is also used as a translation of 'God'. **See also** T'IEN.   B.W.V.N.

Shang Yang, also called Lord Shang (d. 338 B.C.), Chinese statesman. A prime minister of Ch'in and prominent Legalist, he emphasized the importance of *fa* (law, or more broadly, impartial standards for punishment and reward) to the sociopolitical order. Shang Yang maintained that agriculture and war were the keys to a strong state. However, humans are self-interested rational actors. Their interest to avoid hard work and the risk of death in battle is at odds with the ruler's desire for a strong state. Accordingly, the ruler must rely on harsh punishments and positive rewards to ensure the cooperation of the people. **See also** CHINESE LEGALISM.
     R.P.P. & R.T.A.

Shankara, also transliterated Śankara and Śaṁkara (A.D. 788–820), Indian philosopher who founded Advaita Vedanta Hinduism. His major works are the *Brahma-Sūtra-Bhāṣya* (a commentary on Badarayana's *Brahma Sūtras*) and his *Gītā-Bhāṣa* (a commentary on the Bhagavad Gita). He provides a vigorous defense of mind–body dualism, of the existence of a plurality of minds and mind-independent physical objects, and of monotheism. Then, on the basis of appeal to *sruti* (scripture) – i.e., the Vedas and Upanishads – and an esoteric enlightenment experience (*moksha*), he relegates dualism, realism, and theism to illusion (the level of appearance) in favor of a monism that holds that only *nirguna* or qualityless Brahman exists (the level of reality). Some interpreters read this distinc-

tion between levels metaphysically rather than epistemologically, but this is inconsistent with Shankara's monism. **See also** ADVAITA, VEDANTA.   K.E.Y.

Shao Yung (1011–77), Chinese philosopher, a controversial Neo-Confucian figure. His *Huang-chi ching-shih* ("Ultimate Principles Governing the World") advances a numerological interpretation of the *I-Ching*. Shao noticed that the *I-Ching* expresses certain cosmological features in numerical terms. He concluded that the cosmos itself must be based on numerical relationships and that the *I-Ching* is its cipher, which is why the text can be used to predict the future. One of Shao's charts of the *I-Ching*'s hexagrams came to the attention of Leibniz, who noticed that, so arranged, they can be construed as describing the numbers 0–63 in binary expression. Shao probably was not aware of this, and Leibniz interpreted Shao's arrangement in reverse order, but they shared the belief that certain numerical sequences revealed the structure of the cosmos.   P.J.I.

Sheffer stroke, also called alternative denial, a binary truth-functor represented by the symbol '$|$', the logical force of which can be expressed contextually in terms of '$\sim$' and '&' by the following definition: $p|q = \mathrm{Df} \sim(p\,\&\,q)$. The importance of the Sheffer stroke lies in the fact that it by itself can express any well-formed expression of truth-functional logic. Thus, since $\{\sim, \vee\}$ forms an expressively complete set, defining $\sim p$ as $p|p$ and $p \vee q$ as $(p|p)\,|\,(q|q)$ provides for the possibility of a further reduction of primitive functors to one. This system of symbols is commonly called the stroke notation.   I.Bo.

shen, Chinese term meaning 'spirit', 'spiritual', 'numinous', 'demonic'. In early texts, *shen* is used to mean various nature spirits, with emphasis on the efficacy of spirits to both know and accomplish (hence one seeks their advice and aid). *Shen* came to describe the operations of nature, which accomplishes its ends with "spiritual" efficacy. In texts like the *Chuang Tzu, Hsün Tzu,* and *I-Ching, shen* no longer refers to an entity but to a state of resonance with the cosmos. In such a state, the sage can tap into the "spiritual" nature of an event, situation, person, or text and successfully read, react to, and guide the course of events.   P.J.I.

sheng, Chinese term meaning 'the sage', 'sagehood'. This is the Chinese concept of extraordinary human attainment or perfection. Philosophical Taoism focuses primarily on *sheng* as complete attunement or adaptability to the natural order of events as well as irregular occurrences and phenomena. Classical Confucianism focuses, on the other hand, on the ideal unity of Heaven (*t'ien*) and human beings as having an ethical significance in resolving human problems. Neo-Confucianism tends to focus on *sheng* as a realizable ideal of the universe as a moral community. In Chang Tsai's words, "Heaven is my father and Earth is my mother, and even such a small creature as I finds an intimate place in their midst. . . . All people are my brothers and sisters, and all things are my companions." In Confucianism, *sheng* (the sage) is often viewed as one who possesses comprehensive knowledge and insights into the ethical significance of things, events, and human affairs. This ideal of *sheng* contrasts with *chün-tzu*, the paradigmatic individual who embodies basic ethical virtues (*jen, li, i,* and *chih*), but is always liable to error, especially in responding to changing circumstances of human life. For Confucius, *sheng* (sagehood) is more like an abstract, supreme ideal of a perfect moral personality, an imagined vision rather than a possible objective of the moral life. He once remarked that he could not ever hope to meet a *sheng-jen* (a sage), but only a *chün-tzu*. For his eminent followers, on the other hand, e.g., Mencius, Hsün Tzu, and the Neo-Confucians, *sheng* is a humanly attainable ideal. **See also** CONFUCIANISM, MENCIUS.

A.S.C.

Shen Pu-hai (d.337 B.C.), Chinese Legalist philosopher who emphasized *shu*, pragmatic methods or techniques of bureaucratic control whereby the ruler checked the power of officials and ensured their subordination. These techniques included impartial application of publicly promulgated positive law, appointment based on merit, mutual surveillance by officials, and most importantly *hsing ming* – the assignment of punishment and reward based on the correspondence between one's official title or stipulated duties (*ming*) and one's performance (*hsing*). Law for Shen Pu-hai was one more pragmatic means to ensure social and bureaucratic order. **See also** HSING, MING.

R.P.P. & R.T.A.

Shen Tao, also called Shen Tzu (350?–275? B.C.), Chinese philosopher associated with Legalism, Taoism, and the Huang–Lao school. Depicted in the *Chuang Tzu* as a simple-minded naturalist who believed that one only had to abandon

knowledge to follow *tao* (the Way), Shen Tao advocated rule by law where laws were to be impartial, publicly promulgated, and changed only if necessary and then in accordance with *tao*. His main contribution to Legalist theory is the notion that the ruler must rely on *shih* (political purchase, or the power held by virtue of his position). Shen's law is the pragmatic positive law of the Legalists rather than the natural law of Huang–Lao. **See also** HUANG–LAO, TAOISM.

R.P.P. & R.T.A.

Shepherd, Mary (d.1847), Scottish philosopher whose main philosophical works are *An Essay on the Relation of Cause and Effect* (1824) and *Essays on the Perception of an External Universe* (1827). The first addresses what she takes to be the skeptical consequences of Hume's account of causation, but a second target is the use William Lawrence (1783–1867) made of Hume's associative account of causation to argue that mental functions are reducible to physiological ones. The second work focuses on Hume's alleged skepticism with regard to the existence of the external world, but she is also concerned to distinguish her position from Berkeley's. Shepherd was drawn into a public controversy with John Fearn, who published some remarks she had sent him on a book of his, together with his extensive reply. Shepherd replied in an article in *Fraser's* magazine (1832), "Lady Mary Shepherd's Metaphysics," which deftly refuted Fearn's rather condescending attack. **See also** BERKELEY, HUME.

M.At.

Sherwood, William, also called William Shyreswood (1200/10–1266/71), English logician who taught logic at Oxford and at Paris between 1235 and 1250. He was the earliest of the three great "summulist" writers, the other two (whom he influenced strongly) being Peter of Spain and Lambert of Auxerre (fl. 1250).

His main works are *Introductiones in Logicam, Syncategoremata, De insolubilibus,* and *Obligationes* (some serious doubts have recently arisen about the authorship of the latter work). Since M. Grabmann published Sherwood's *Introductiones* in 1937, historians of logic have paid considerable attention to this seminal medieval logician. While the first four chapters of *Introductiones* offer the basic ideas of Aristotle's *Organon*, and the last chapter neatly lays out the *Sophistical Refutations,* the fifth tract expounds the famous doctrine of the properties of terms: signification, supposition, conjunction, and appellation – hence the label 'terminist' for this sort of logic. These logico-semantic discussions, together with the discussions of syncategorematic words, constitute the *logica moderna,* as opposed to the more strictly Aristotelian contents of the earlier *logica vetus* and *logica nova.*

The doctrine of properties of terms and the analysis of syncategorematic terms, especially those of 'all', 'no' and 'nothing', 'only', 'not', 'begins' and 'ceases', 'necessarily', 'if', 'and', and 'or', may be said to constitute Sherwood's philosophy of logic. He not only distinguishes categorematic (descriptive) and syncategorematic (logical) words but also shows how some terms are used categorematically in some contexts and syncategorematically in others. He recognizes the importance of the order of words and of the scope of logical functors; he also anticipates the variety of composite and divided senses of propositions. *Obligationes,* if indeed his, attempts to state conditions under which a formal disputation may take place. *De Insolubilibus* deals with paradoxes of self-reference and with ways of solving them. Understanding Sherwood's logic is important for understanding the later medieval developments of *logica moderna* down to Ockham.   I.Bo.

shih¹, Chinese term meaning 'strategic advantage'. *Shih* was the key and defining idea in the Militarist philosophers, later appropriated by some of the other classical schools, including the Legalists (Han Fei Tzu) and the Confucians (Hsün Tzu). Like ritual practices (*li*) and speaking (*yen*), *shih* is a level of discourse through which one actively cultivates the leverage and influence of one's particular place. In the Military texts, the most familiar metaphor for *shih* is the taut trigger on the drawn crossbow, emphasizing advantageous position, timing, and precision. *Shih* (like immanental order generally) begins from the full consideration of the concrete detail. The business of war or effective government does not occur as some independent and isolated event, but unfolds within a broad field of unique natural, social, and political conditions proceeding according to a general pattern that can not only be anticipated but manipulated to one's advantage. It is the changing configuration of these specific conditions that determines one's place and one's influence at any point in time, and gives one a defining disposition. *Shih* includes intangible forces such as morale, opportunity, timing, psychology, and logistics. **See also CHINESE LEGALISM, CONFUCIANISM.**
R.P.P. & R.T.A.

shih², Chinese term meaning 'scholar-knight' and 'service'. In the service of the rulers of the "central states" of preimperial China, *shih* were a lower echelon of the official nobility responsible for both warfare and matters at court, including official documentation, ritual protocol, and law. Most of the early philosophers, trained in the "six arts" of rites, music, archery, charioteering, writing, and counting, belonged to this stratum. Without hereditary position, they lived by their wits and their professional skills, and were responsible for both the intellectual vigor and the enormous social mobility of Warring States China (403–221 B.C.). **See also SHEN PU-HAI.**
R.P.P. & R.T.A.

ship of Theseus, the ship of the Greek hero Theseus, which, according to Plutarch ("Life of Theseus," 23), the Athenians preserved by gradually replacing its timbers. A classic debate ensued concerning identity over time. Suppose a ship's timbers are replaced one by one over a period of time; at what point, if any, does it cease to be the same ship? What if the ship's timbers, on removal, are used to build a new ship, identical in structure with the first: which ship has the best claim to be the original ship? **See also IDENTITY, INDIVIDUATION, PERSONAL IDENTITY.** W.J.P.

Shpet, Gustav Gustavovich (1879–1937), leading Russian phenomenologist and highly regarded student and friend of Husserl. He played a major role in the development of phenomenology in Russia prior to the revolution. Graduating from Kiev University in 1906, Shpet accompanied his mentor Chelpanov to Moscow in 1907, commencing graduate studies at Moscow University (M.A., 1910; Ph.D., 1916). He attended Husserl's seminars at Göttingen during 1912–13, out of which developed a continuing friendship between the two, recorded in correspondence extending through 1918. In 1914 Shpet published a meditation, *Iavlenie i smysl* (*Appearance and Sense*), inspired by Husserl's *Logical Investigations* and, especially, *Ideas I,* which had appeared in 1913. Between 1914 and 1927 he published six additional books on such disparate topics as the concept of history, Herzen, Russian philosophy, aesthetics, ethnic psychology, and language. He founded and edited the philosophical yearbook *Mysl' i slovo* (*Thought and Word*) between 1918 and 1921, publishing an important article on skepticism in it. He was arrested in 1935 and sentenced to internal exile. Under these conditions he completed a fine new translation of Hegel's *Phenomenology* into Russian, which was published in 1959. He was executed in November 1937. **See also** HUSSERL, RUSSIAN PHILOSOPHY.   P.T.G.

shriek operator. See APPENDIX OF SPECIAL SYMBOLS.

shu[1]*,* Chinese term for 'technique of statecraft'. Such techniques were advocated by Shen Pu-hai and the other Legalist philosophers as instruments of the ruler in power that would guarantee the stable and efficient operations of government. The best-known *shu* include (1) "accountability" (*hsing-ming*): the duties and obligations of office are clearly articulated, and at intervals a comparison is made between stipulated responsibilities (*ming*) and performance (*hsing*); (2) "doing nothing" (*wu-wei*): the engine of state is constructed so that the ministers are integral, functioning components guided by clearly promulgated laws (*fa*), while the ruler stands aloof as the embodiment of the authority of government, thereby receiving credit for successes and deflecting blame back to the officials; (3) "showing nothing" (*wu-hsien*): by secreting the royal person, concealing all likes and dislikes, and proffering no opinion, the ruler not only shields his limitations from public scrutiny, but further encourages a personal mystique as an ideal invested with a superlative degree of all things worthwhile.   R.P.P. & R.T.A.

shu[2]*.* See CHUNG, SHU.

Shyreswood, William. See SHERWOOD.

Sidgwick, Henry (1838–1900), English philosopher, economist, and educator. Best known for *The Methods of Ethics* (1874), he also wrote the still valuable *Outlines of the History of Ethics* (1886), as well as studies of economics, politics, literature, and alleged psychic phenomena. He was deeply involved in the founding of the first college for women at Cambridge University, where he was a professor.

In the *Methods* Sidgwick tried to assess the rationality of the main ways in which ordinary people go about making moral decisions. He thought that our common "methods of ethics" fall into three main patterns. One is articulated by the philosophical theory known as intuitionism. This is the view that we can just see straight off either what particular act is right or what binding rule or general principle we ought to follow. Another common method is spelled out by philosophical egoism, the view that we ought in each act to get as much good as we can for ourselves. The third widely used method is represented by utilitarianism, the view that we ought in each case to bring about as much good as possible for everyone affected. Can any or all of the methods prescribed by these views be rationally defended? And how are they related to one another?

By framing his philosophical questions in these terms, Sidgwick made it centrally important to examine the chief philosophical theories of morality in the light of the commonsense morals of his time. He thought that no theory wildly at odds with commonsense morality would be acceptable. Intuitionism, a theory originating with Butler, transmitted by Reid, and most systematically expounded during the Victorian era by Whewell, was widely held to be the best available defense of Christian morals. Egoism was thought by many to be the clearest pattern of practical rationality and was frequently said to be compatible with Christianity. And J. S. Mill had argued that utilitarianism was both rational and in accord with common sense. But whatever their relation to ordinary morality, the theories seemed to be seriously at odds with one another.

Examining all the chief commonsense precepts and rules of morality, such as that promises ought to be kept, Sidgwick argued that none is truly self-evident or intuitively certain. Each fails to guide us at certain points where we expect it to answer our practical questions. Utilitarianism, he found, could provide a complicated method for filling these gaps. But what ultimately justifies utilitarianism is certain very general axioms seen intuitively to be true. Among them are the principles that what is right in one case must be right in any similar case, and that we ought to aim at good generally, not just at some particular part of it. Thus intuitionism and utilitarianism can be reconciled. When taken together they yield a complete and justifiable method of ethics that is in accord with common sense.

What then of egoism? It can provide as complete a method as utilitarianism, and it also involves a self-evident axiom. But its results often contradict those of utilitarianism. Hence there is a serious problem. The method that instructs us to act always for the good generally and the method that tells one to act solely for one's own good are equally rational. Since the two methods give contradictory directions, while each method rests on self-evident axioms, it seems that practical reason is fundamentally incoherent. Sidgwick could see no way to solve the problem.

Sidgwick's bleak conclusion has not been generally accepted, but his *Methods* is widely viewed as one of the best works of moral philosophy ever written. His account of classical utilitarianism is unsurpassed. His discussions of the general status of morality and of particular moral concepts are enduring models of clarity and acumen. His insights about the relations between egoism and utilitarianism have stimulated much valuable research. And his way of framing moral problems, by asking about the relations between commonsense beliefs and the best available theories, has set much of the agenda for twentieth-century ethics.

See also BUTLER, EGOISM, INTUITION, UTILITARIANISM.   J.B.S.

Siger of Brabant (c.1240–84), French philosopher, an activist in the philosophical and political struggles both within the arts faculty and between arts and theology at Paris during the 1260s and 1270s. He is usually regarded as a leader of a "radical Aristotelianism" that owed much to *Liber de causis,* to Avicenna, and to Averroes. He taught that everything originates through a series of emanations from a first cause. The world and each species (including the human species) are eternal. Human beings share a single active intellect.

There is no good reason to think that Siger advanced the view that there was a double truth, one in theology and another in natural philosophy. It is difficult to distinguish Siger's own views from those he attributes to "the Philosophers" and thus to know the extent to which he held the heterodox views he taught as the best interpretation of the prescribed texts in the arts curriculum. In any case, Siger was summoned before the French Inquisition in 1276, but fled Paris. He was never convicted of heresy, but it seems that the condemnations at Paris in 1277 were partially directed at his teaching. He was stabbed to death by his clerk in Orvieto (then the papal seat) in 1284.   C.G.Norm.

sign. See THEORY OF SIGNS.

sign, conventional. See THEORY OF SIGNS.

sign, formal. See SEMIOSIS.

sign, instrumental. See SEMIOSIS.

sign, natural. See THEORY OF SIGNS.

signified. See SIGNIFIER.

signifier, a vocal sound or a written symbol. The concept owes its modern formulation to the Swiss linguist Saussure. Rather than using the older conception of sign and referent, he divided the sign itself into two interrelated parts, a signifier and a signified. The signified is the concept and the signifier is either a vocal sound or writing. The relation between the two, according to Saussure, is entirely arbitrary, in that signifiers tend to vary with different languages. We can utter or write '*vache*', 'cow', or '*vaca*', depending on our native language, and still come up with the same signified (i.e., concept). **See also** SAUSSURE, SEMIOSIS.   M.Ro.

signs, theory of. See THEORY OF SIGNS.

silhak. See KOREAN PHILOSOPHY.

similarity, exact. See IDENTITY.

Simmel, Georg (1858–1918), German philosopher and one of the founders of sociology as a distinct discipline. Born and educated in Berlin, he was a popular lecturer at its university. But the unorthodoxy of his interests and unprofessional writing style probably kept him from being offered a regular professorship until 1914, and then only at the provincial university of Strasbourg. He died four years later.

His writings ranged from conventional philosophical topics – with books on ethics, philosophy of history, education, religion, and the philosophers Kant, Schopenhauer, and Nietzsche – to books on Rembrandt, Goethe, and the philosophy of money. He wrote numerous essays on various artists and poets, on different cities, and on such themes as love, adventure, shame, and on being a stranger, as well as on many specifically sociological topics. Simmel was regarded as a *Kulturphilosoph* who meditated on his themes in an insightful and digressive rather than scholarly and systematic style. Though late in life he sketched a unifying *Lebensphilosophie* (philosophy of life) that considers all works and structures of culture as products of different forms of human experience, Simmel has remained of interest primarily for a multiplicity of insights into specific topics.   R.H.W.

simple ordering. See ORDERING.

simple supposition. See SUPPOSITIO.

simple theory of types. See TYPE THEORY.

simplicity. See CURVE-FITTING PROBLEM, DIVINE ATTRIBUTES, PHILOSOPHY OF SCIENCE.

Simplicius (sixth century A.D.), Greek Neoplatonist philosopher born in Cilicia on the southeast coast of modern Turkey. His surviving works are extensive commentaries on Aristotle's *On the Heavens, Physics,* and *Categories,* and on the *Encheiridion* of Epictetus. The authenticity of the commentary on Aristotle's *On the Soul* attributed to Simplicius has been disputed. He studied with Ammonius in Alexandria, and with Damascius, the last known head of the Platonist school in Athens. Justinian closed the school in 529. Two or three years later a group of philosophers, including Damascius and Simplicius, visited the court of the Sassanian king Khosrow I (Chosroes) but soon returned to the Byzantine Empire under a guarantee of their right to maintain their own beliefs. It is generally agreed that most, if not all, of Simplicius's extant works date from the period after his stay with Khosrow. But there is no consensus about where Simplicius spent his last years (both Athens and Harran have been proposed recently), or whether he resumed teaching philosophy; his commentaries, unlike most of the others that survive from that period, are scholarly treatises rather than classroom expositions.

Simplicius's Aristotle commentaries are the most valuable extant works in the genre. He is our source for many of the fragments of the pre-Socratic philosophers, and he frequently invokes material from now-lost commentaries and philosophical works. He is a deeply committed Neoplatonist, convinced that there is no serious conflict between the philosophies of Plato and Aristotle. The view of earlier scholars that his *Encheiridion* commentary embodies a more moderate Platonism associated with Alexandria is now generally rejected. Simplicius's virulent defense of the eternity of the world in response to the attack of the Christian John Philoponus illustrates the intellectual vitality of paganism at a time when the Mediterranean world had been officially Christian for about three centuries.

See also COMMENTARIES ON ARISTOTLE.

I.M.

simplification, rule of. See CONJUNCTION ELIMINATION.

simulation theory, the view that one represents the mental activities and processes of others by mentally simulating them, i.e., generating similar activities and processes in oneself. By simulating them, one can anticipate their product or outcome; or, where this is already known, test hypotheses about their starting point. For example, one anticipates the product of another's theoretical or practical inferences from given premises by making inferences from the same premises oneself; or, knowing what the product is, one retroduces the premises. In the case of practical reasoning, to reason from the same premises would typically require indexical adjustments, such as shifts in spatial, temporal, and personal "point of view," to place oneself in the other's physical and epistemic situation insofar as it differs from one's own. One may also compensate for the other's reasoning capacity and level of expertise, if possible, or modify one's character and outlook as an actor might, to fit the other's background. Such adjustments, even when insufficient for making decisions in the role of the other, allow one to discriminate between action options likely to be attractive or unattractive to the agent. One would be prepared for the former actions and surprised by the latter.

The simulation theory is usually considered an alternative to an assumption (sometimes called the "theory theory") that underlies much recent philosophy of mind: that our commonsense understanding of people rests on a speculative theory, a "folk psychology" that posits mental states, events, and processes as unobservables that explain behavior. Some hold that the simulation theory undercuts the debate between philosophers who consider folk psychology a respectable theory and those (the eliminative materialists) who reject it.

Unlike earlier writing on empathic understanding and historical reenactment, discussions of the simulation theory often appeal to empirical findings, particularly experimental results in developmental psychology. They also theorize about the mechanism that would accomplish simulation: presumably one that calls up computational resources ordinarily used for engagement with the world, but runs them off-line, so that their output is not "endorsed" or acted upon and their inputs are not limited to those that would regulate one's own behavior.

Although simulation theorists agree that the ascription of mental states to others relies chiefly on simulation, they differ on the nature of self-ascription. Some (especially Robert Gordon and

Jane Heal, who independently proposed the theory) give a non-introspectionist account, while others (especially Goldman) lean toward a more traditional introspectionist account.

The simulation theory has affected developmental psychology as well as branches of philosophy outside the philosophy of mind, especially aesthetics and philosophy of the social sciences. Some philosophers believe it sheds light on traditional topics such as the problem of other minds, referential opacity, broad and narrow content, and the peculiarities of self-knowledge. **See also** EMPATHY, FOLK PSYCHOLOGY, GOLDMAN, PHILOSOPHY OF MIND, PROBLEM OF OTHER MINDS, VERSTEHEN.   R.M.G.

simulator, universal. See COMPUTER THEORY.

simultaneity. See RELATIVITY.

sin. See PHILOSOPHY OF RELIGION.

sine qua non. See CONDITIO SINE QUA NON.

single case, problem of the. See PROBABILITY, PROPENSITY.

singleton set. See SET THEORY.

singular causal relation. See PHILOSOPHY OF MIND.

singular causal statement. See CAUSATION, COVERING LAW MODEL.

singular term, an expression, such as 'Zeus', 'the President', or 'my favorite chair', that can be the grammatical subject of what is semantically a subject-predicate sentence. By contrast, a *general term,* such as 'table' or 'swam' is one that can serve in predicative position. It is also often said that a singular term is a word or phrase that could refer or ostensibly refer, on a given occasion of use, only to a single object, whereas a general term is predicable of more than one object. Singular terms are thus the expressions that replace, or are replaced by, individual variables in applications of such quantifier rules as universal instantiation and existential generalization or flank '=' in identity statements. **See also** THEORY OF DESCRIPTIONS.   G.F.S.

Sinn. See FREGE.

sinsign. See PEIRCE.

Sittlichkeit. See HEGEL.

situation ethics, a kind of anti-theoretical, case-by-case applied ethics in vogue largely in some European and American religious circles for twenty years or so following World War II. It is characterized by the insistence that each moral choice must be determined by one's particular context or situation – i.e., by a consideration of the outcomes that various possible courses of action might have, given one's situation. To that degree, situation ethics has affinities to both act utilitarianism and traditional casuistry. But in contrast to utilitarianism, situation ethics rejects the idea that there are universal or even fixed moral principles beyond various indeterminate commitments or ideals (e.g., to Christian love or humanism). In contrast to traditional casuistry, it rejects the effort to construct general guidelines from a case or to classify the salient features of a case so that it can be used as a precedent. The anti-theoretical stance of situation ethics is so thoroughgoing that writers identified with the position have not carefully described its connections to consequentialism, existentialism, intuitionism, personalism, pragmatism, relativism, or any other developed philosophical view to which it appears to have some affinity. **See also** CASUISTRY, ETHICS, UTILITARIANISM, VIRTUE ETHICS.   L.C.B.

situation semantics. See POSSIBLE WORLDS.

situation theory. See MODEL THEORY.

Siva, one of the great gods of Hinduism (with Vishnu and Brahman), auspicious controller of karma and *saṁsāra,* destroyer but also giver of life. He is worshiped in Saivism with his consort Sakti. A variety of deities are regarded in Saivism as forms of Siva, with the consequence that polytheism is moved substantially toward monotheism.   K.E.Y.

six emotions (the). See CH'ING.

skepticism, in the most common sense, the refusal to grant that there is any knowledge or justification. Skepticism can be either partial or total, either practical or theoretical, and, if theoretical, either moderate or radical, and either of knowledge or of justification.

Skepticism is *partial* iff (if and only if) it is restricted to particular fields of beliefs or propositions, and *total* iff not thus restricted. And if partial, it may be highly restricted, as is the skepticism for which religion is only opium, or much more general, as when not only is religion called opium, but also history bunk and metaphysics meaningless.

Skepticism is *practical* iff it is an attitude of deliberately withholding both belief and disbelief, accompanied perhaps (but not necessarily) by commitment to a recommendation for people generally, that they do likewise. (Practical skepticism can of course be either total or partial, and if partial it can be more or less general.)

Skepticism is *theoretical* iff it is a commitment to the belief that there is no knowledge (justified belief) of a certain kind or of certain kinds. Such theoretical skepticism comes in several varieties. It is *moderate and total* iff it holds that there is no certain superknowledge (superjustified belief) whatsoever, not even in logic or mathematics, nor through introspection of one's present experience. It is *radical and total* iff it holds that there isn't even any ordinary knowledge (justified belief) at all. It is *moderate and partial,* on the other hand, iff it holds that there is no certain superknowledge (superjustified belief) of a certain specific kind K or of certain specific kinds $K_1, \ldots,$ K_n (less than the totality of such kinds). It is *radical and partial,* finally, iff it holds that there isn't even any ordinary knowledge (justified belief) at all of that kind K or of those kinds $K_1, \ldots, K_n$.

Greek skepticism can be traced back to Socrates' epistemic modesty. Suppressed by the prolific theoretical virtuosity of Plato and Aristotle, such modesty reasserted itself in the skepticism of the Academy led by Arcesilaus and later by Carneades. In this period began a long controversy pitting Academic Skeptics against the Stoics Zeno and (later) Chrysippus, and their followers. Prolonged controversy, sometimes heated, softened the competing views, but before agreement congealed Anesidemus broke with the Academy and reclaimed the arguments and tradition of Pyrrho, who wrote nothing, but whose Skeptic teachings had been preserved by a student, Timon (in the third century B.C.). After enduring more than two centuries, neo-Pyrrhonism was summarized, c.200 A.D., by Sextus Empiricus (*Outlines of Pyrrhonism* and *Adversus mathematicos*). Skepticism thus ended as a school, but as a philosophical tradition it has been influential long after that, and is so even now. It has influenced strongly not only Cicero (*Academica* and *De natura deorum*), St. Augustine (*Contra academicos*), and Montaigne ("Apology for Raimund Sebond"), but also the great historical philosophers of the Western tradition, from Descartes through Hegel. Both on the Continent and in the Anglophone sphere a new wave of skepticism has built for decades, with logical positivism,

deconstructionism, historicism, neopragmatism, and relativism, and the writings of Foucault (knowledge as a mask of power), Derrida (deconstruction), Quine (indeterminacy and eliminativism), Kuhn (incommensurability), and Rorty (solidarity over objectivity, edification over inquiry). At the same time a rising tide of books and articles continues other philosophical traditions in metaphysics, epistemology, ethics, etc.

It is interesting to compare the cognitive disengagement recommended by practical skepticism with the affective disengagement dear to stoicism (especially in light of the epistemological controversies that long divided Academic Skepticism from the Stoa, giving rise to a rivalry dominant in Hellenistic philosophy). If believing and favoring are positive, with disbelieving and disfavoring their respective negative counterparts, then the magnitude of our happiness (positive) or unhappiness (negative) over a given matter is determined by the product of our belief/disbelief and our favoring/disfavoring with regard to that same matter. The fear of unhappiness may lead one stoically to disengage from affective engagement, on either side of any matter that escapes one's total control. And this is a kind of practical affective "skepticism." Similarly, if believing and truth are positive, with disbelieving and falsity their respective negative counterparts, then the magnitude of our correctness (positive) or error (negative) over a given matter is determined by the product of our belief/disbelief and the truth/falsity with regard to that same matter (where the positive or negative magnitude of the truth or falsity at issue may be determined by some measure of "theoretical importance," though alternatively one could just assign all truths a value of $+1$ and all falsehoods a value of -1). The fear of error may lead one skeptically to disengage from cognitive engagement, on either side of any matter that involves risk of error. And this is "practical cognitive skepticism."

We wish to attain happiness and avoid unhappiness. This leads to the disengagement of the stoic. We wish to attain the truth and avoid error. This leads to the disengagement of the skeptic, the practical skeptic. Each opts for a conservative policy, but one that is surely optional, given just the reasoning indicated. For in avoiding unhappiness the stoic also forfeits a corresponding possibility of happiness. And in avoiding error the skeptic also forfeits a corresponding possibility to grasp a truth. These twin policies appeal to conservatism in our nature, and will reasonably prevail in the lives of those committed to avoiding risk as a paramount objective. For this very desire must then be given its due, if we judge it rational.

Skepticism is instrumental in the birth of modern epistemology, and modern philosophy, at the hands of Descartes, whose skepticism is methodological but sophisticated and well informed by that of the ancients. Skepticism is also a main force, perhaps *the* main force, in the broad sweep of Western philosophy from Descartes through Hegel. Though preeminent in the history of our subject, skepticism since then has suffered decades of neglect, and only in recent years has reclaimed much attention and even applause. Some recent influential discussions go so far as to grant that we do not know we are not dreaming. But they also insist one can still know when there is a fire before one. The key is to analyze knowledge as a kind of appropriate responsiveness to its object truth: what is required is that the subject "track" through his belief the truth of what he believes. (S *tracks* the truth of P iff: S would not believe P if P were false.) Such an analysis of tracking, when conjoined with the view of knowledge as tracking, enables one to explain how one can know about the fire even if for all one knows it is just a dream. The crucial fact here is that even if P logically entails Q, one may still be able to track the truth of P though unable to track the truth of Q. (Nozick, *Philosophical Explanations*, 1981.)

Many problems arise in the literature on this approach. One that seems especially troubling is that though it enables us to understand how contingent knowledge of our surroundings is *possible,* the tracking account falls short of enabling an explanation of how such knowledge on our part is *actual.* To explain how one knows that there is a fire before one (F), according to the tracking account one presumably would invoke one's tracking the truth of F. But this leads deductively almost immediately to the claim that one is not dreaming: Not D. And this is not something one can know, according to the tracking account. So how is one to explain one's justification for making that claim? Most troubling of all here is the fact that one is now cornered by the tracking account into making combinations of claims of the following form: I am quite sure that p, but I have no knowledge at all as to whether p. And this seems incoherent.

A Cartesian dream argument that has had much play in recent discussions of skepticism is made explicit (by Barry Stroud, *The Significance of Philosophical Scepticism*, 1984) as follows. One

knows that if one knows F then one is not dreaming, in which case if one really knows F then one must know one is not dreaming. However, one does not know one is not dreaming. So one does not know F. *Q.E.D.* And why does one fail to know one is not dreaming? Because in order to know it one would need to know that one has passed some test, some empirical procedure to determine whether one is dreaming. But any such supposed test – say, pinching oneself – could just be part of a dream, and dreaming one passes the test would not suffice to show one was not dreaming. However, might one not actually be witnessing the fire, and passing the test – and be doing this in wakeful life, not in a dream – and would that not be compatible with one's knowing of the fire and of one's wakefulness? Not so, according to the argument, since in order to know of the fire one needs *prior* knowledge of one's wakefulness. But in order to know of one's wakefulness one needs *prior* knowledge of the results of the test procedure. But this in turn requires prior knowledge that one is awake and not dreaming. And we have a vicious circle.

We might well hold that it is possible to know one is not dreaming even in the absence of any positive test result, or at most in conjunction with coordinate (not prior) knowledge of such a positive indication. How in that case would one know of one's wakefulness? Perhaps one would know it by believing it through the exercise of a reliable faculty. Perhaps one would know it through its coherence with the rest of one's comprehensive and coherent body of beliefs. Perhaps both. But, it may be urged, if these are the ways one might know of one's wakefulness, does not this answer commit us to a theory of the form of A below?

(A) The proposition that p is something one knows (believes justifiably) if and only if one satisfies conditions C with respect to it.

And if so, are we not caught in a vicious circle by the question as to how we know – what justifies us in believing – (A) itself? This is far from obvious, since the requirement that we must submit to some test procedure for wakefulness and know ourselves to test positively, before we can know ourselves to be awake, is itself a requirement that seems to lead equally to a principle such as (A). At least it is not evident why the proposal of the externalist or of the coherentist as to how we know we are awake should be any more closely related to a general principle like (A) than is the (foundationalist?) notion that in order to know we are awake we need epistemically prior knowledge that we test positive in a way that does not presuppose already acquired knowledge of the external world. The problem of how to justify the likes of (A) is a descendant of the (in)famous "problem of the criterion," reclaimed in the sixteenth century and again in this century (by Chisholm, *Theory of Knowledge,* 1966, 1977, and 1988) but much used already by the Skeptics of antiquity under the title of the *diallelus.*

About explanations of our knowledge or justification in general of the form indicated by (A), we are told that they are inadequate in a way revealed by examples like the following. Suppose we want to know how we know anything at all about the external world, and part of the answer is that we know the location of our neighbor by knowing the location of her car (in her driveway). Surely this would be at best the beginning of an answer that might be satisfactory in the end (if recursive, e.g.), but as it stands it cannot be satisfactory without supplementation. The objection here is based on a comparison between two appeals: the appeal of a theorist of knowledge to a principle like (A) in the course of explaining our knowledge or justification in general, on one side; and the appeal to the car's location in explaining our knowledge of facts about the external world, on the other side. This comparison is said to be fatal to the ambition to explain our knowledge or justification in general. But are the appeals relevantly analogous? One important difference is this. In the example of the car, we explain the presence, in some subject S, of a piece of knowledge of a certain kind (of the external world) by appeal to the presence in S of some other piece of knowledge of the very same kind. So there is an immediate problem if it is our aim to explain how *any* knowledge of the sort in question *ever* comes to be (unless the explication is just beginning, and is to turn recursive in due course). Now of course (A) is theoretically ambitious, and in that respect the theorist who gives an answer of the form of (A) is doing something similar to what must be done by the protagonist in our car example, someone who is attempting to provide a general explanation of how any knowledge of a certain kind comes about. Nevertheless, there is also an important difference, namely that the theorist whose aim it is to give a general account of the form of (A) need not attribute any knowledge whatsoever to a subject S in explaining how that subject comes to have a piece of knowledge (or justified belief). For there is no need to require

that the conditions *C* appealed to by principle (A) must be conditions that include attribution of any knowledge at all to the subject in question. It is true that in claiming that (A) itself meets conditions *C*, and that it is this which explains how one knows (A), we do perhaps take ourselves to know (A) or at least to be justified in believing it. But if so, this is the inevitable lot of anyone who seriously puts forward any explanation of anything. And it is quite different from a proposal that part of what explains how something is known or justifiably believed includes a claim to knowledge or justified belief of the very same sort. In sum, as in the case of one's belief that one is awake, the belief in something of the form of (A) may be said to be known, and in so saying one does not commit oneself to adducing an ulterior reason in favor of (A), or even to having such a reason in reserve. One is of course committed to being justified in believing (A), perhaps even to having knowledge that (A). But it is not at all clear that the only way to be justified in believing (A) is by way of adduced reasons in favor of (A), or that one knows (A) only if one adduces strong enough reasons in its favor. For we often know things in the absence of such adduced reasons. Thus consider one's knowledge through memory of which door one used to come into a room that has more than one open door. Returning finally to (A), in its case the explanation of how one knows it may, once again, take the form of an appeal to the justifying power of intellectual virtues or of coherence – or both.

Recent accounts of the nature of thought and representation undermine a tradition of wholesale doubt about nature, whose momentum is hard to stop, and threatens to leave the subject alone and restricted to a solipsism of the present moment. But there may be a way to stop skepticism early – by questioning the possibility of its being sensibly held, given what is required for meaningful language and thought. Consider our grasp of observable shape and color properties that objects around us might have. Such grasp seems partly constituted by our discriminatory abilities. When we discern a shape or a color we do so presumably in terms of a distinctive impact that such a shape or color has on us. We are put systematically into a certain distinctive state X when we are appropriately related, in good light, with our eyes open, etc., to the presence in our environment of that shape or color. What makes one's distinctive state one of thinking of sphericity rather than something else, is said to be that it is a state tied by systematic causal relations to the presence of sphericity in one's normal environment.

A light now flickers at the end of the skeptic's tunnel. In doubt now is the coherence of traditional skeptical reflection. Indeed, our predecessors in earlier centuries may have moved in the wrong direction when they attempted a reduction of nature to the mind. For there is no way to make sense of one's mind without its contents, and there is no way to make sense of how one's mind can have such contents except by appeal to how one is causally related to one's environment. If the very existence of that environment is put in doubt, that cuts the ground from under one's ability reasonably to characterize one's own mind, or to feel any confidence about its contents. Perhaps, then, one could not be a "brain in a vat." Much contemporary thought about language and the requirements for meaningful language thus suggests that a lot of knowledge must already be in place for us to be able to think meaningfully about a surrounding reality, so as to be able to question its very existence. If so, then radical skepticism answers itself. For if we can so much as understand a radical skepticism about the existence of our surrounding reality, then we must already know a great deal about that reality.

See also ACADEMY, CLOSURE, DESCARTES, EPISTEMOLOGY, FOUNDATIONALISM, JUSTIFICATION, SKEPTICS.   E.S.

skepticism, moral. See MORAL SKEPTICISM.

Skeptics, those ancient thinkers who developed sets of arguments to show either that no knowledge is possible (Academic Skepticism) or that there is not sufficient or adequate evidence to tell if any knowledge is possible. If the latter is the case then these thinkers advocated suspending judgment on all question concerning knowledge (Pyrrhonian Skepticism).

Academic Skepticism gets its name from the fact that it was formulated in Plato's Academy in the third century B.C., starting from Socrates' statement, "All I know is that I know nothing." It was developed by Arcesilaus (c.268–241) and Carneades (c.213–129), into a series of arguments, directed principally against the Stoics, purporting to show that nothing can be known. The Academics posed a series of problems to show that what we think we know by our senses may be unreliable, and that we cannot be sure about the reliability of our reasoning. We do not possess a guaranteed standard or criterion for ascertaining which of our judgments is true or false. Any purported knowledge claim contains some element that goes beyond immediate experience. If this claim constituted knowledge we would have to know something that could not possibly be false. The evidence for the claim would have to be based on our senses and our reason, both of which are to some degree unreliable. So the knowledge claim may be false or doubtful, and hence cannot constitute genuine knowledge. So, the Academics said that nothing is certain. The best we can attain is probable information.

Carneades is supposed to have developed a form of verification theory and a kind of probabilism, similar in some ways to that of modern pragmatists and positivists.

Academic Skepticism dominated the philosophizing of Plato's Academy until the first century B.C. While Cicero was a student there, the Academy turned from Skepticism to a kind of eclectic philosophy. Its Skeptical arguments have been preserved in Cicero's works, *Academia* and *De natura deorum*, in Augustine's refutation in his *Contra academicos*, as well as in the summary presented by Diogenes Laertius in his lives of the Greek philosophers.

Skeptical thinking found another home in the school of the Pyrrhonian Skeptics, probably connected with the Methodic school of medicine in Alexandria. The Pyrrhonian movement traces its origins to Pyrrho of Elis (c.360–275 B.C.) and his student Timon (c.315–225 B.C.). The stories about Pyrrho indicate that he was not a theoretician but a practical doubter who would not make any judgments that went beyond immediate experience. He is supposed to have refused to judge if what appeared to be chariots might strike him, and he was often rescued by his students because he would not make any commitments. His concerns were apparently ethical. He sought to avoid unhappiness that might result from accepting any value theory. If the theory was at all doubtful, accepting it might lead to mental anguish.

The theoretical formulation of Pyrrhonian Skepticism is attributed to Aenesidemus (c.100–40 B.C.). Pyrrhonists regarded dogmatic philosophers and Academic Skeptics as asserting too much, the former saying that something can be known and the latter that nothing can be known. The Pyrrhonists suspended judgments on all questions on which there was any conflicting evidence, including whether or not anything could be known.

The Pyrrhonists used some of the same kinds of arguments developed by Arcesilaus and

Carneades. Aenesidemus and those who followed after him organized the arguments into sets of "tropes" or ways of leading to suspense of judgment on various questions. Sets of ten, eight, five, and two tropes appear in the only surviving writing of the Pyrrhonists, the works of Sextus Empiricus, a third-century A.D. teacher of Pyrrhonism. Each set of tropes offers suggestions for suspending judgment about any knowledge claims that go beyond appearances. The tropes seek to show that for any claim, evidence for and evidence against it can be offered. The disagreements among human beings, the variety of human experiences, the fluctuation of human judgments under differing conditions, illness, drunkenness, etc., all point to the opposition of evidence for and against each knowledge claim. Any criterion we employ to sift and weigh the evidence can also be opposed by countercriterion claims.

Given this situation, the Pyrrhonian Skeptics sought to avoid committing themselves concerning any kind of question. They would not even commit themselves as to whether the arguments they put forth were sound or not. For them Skepticism was not a statable theory, but rather an ability or mental attitude for opposing evidence for and against any knowledge claim that went beyond what was apparent, that dealt with the non-evident. This opposing produced an equipollence, a balancing of the opposing evidences, that would lead to suspending judgment on any question. Suspending judgment led to a state of mind called "ataraxia," quietude, peace of mind, or unperturbedness. In such a state the Skeptic was no longer concerned or worried or disturbed about matters beyond appearances. The Pyrrhonians averred that Skepticism was a cure for a disease called "dogmatism" or rashness. The dogmatists made assertions about the non-evident, and then became disturbed about whether these assertions were true. The disturbance became a mental disease or disorder. The Pyrrhonians, who apparently were medical doctors, offered relief by showing the patient how and why he should suspend judgment instead of dogmatizing. Then the disease would disappear and the patient would be in a state of tranquility, the peace of mind sought by Hellenistic dogmatic philosophers.

The Pyrrhonists, unlike the Academic Skeptics, were not negative dogmatists. The Pyrrhonists said neither that knowledge is possible nor that it is impossible. They remained seekers, while allowing the Skeptical arguments and the equipollence of evidences to act as a purge of dogmatic assertions. The purge eliminates all dogmas as well as itself. After this the Pyrrhonist lives undogmatically, following natural inclinations, immediate experience, and the laws and customs of his society, without ever judging or committing himself to any view about them. In this state the Pyrrhonist would have no worries, and yet be able to function naturally and according to law and custom.

The Pyrrhonian movement disappeared during the third century A.D., possibly because it was not considered an alternative to the powerful religious movements of the time. Only scant traces of it appear before the Renaissance, when the texts of Sextus and Cicero were rediscovered and used to formulate a modern skeptical view by such thinkers as Montaigne and Charron.

See also SEXTUS EMPIRICUS, SKEPTICISM.

R.H.P.

Skolem, Thoralf (1887–1963), Norwegian mathematician. A pioneer of mathematical logic, he made fundamental contributions to recursion theory, set theory (in particular, the proposal and formulation in 1922 of the axiom of replacement), and model theory. His most important results for the philosophy of mathematics are the (Downward) Löwenheim-Skolem theorem (1919, 1922), whose first proof involved putting formulas into Skolem normal form; and a demonstration (1933–34) of the existence of models of (first-order) arithmetic not isomorphic to the standard model. Both results exhibit the extreme non-categoricity that can occur with formulations of mathematical theories in first-order logic, and caused Skolem to be skeptical about the use of formal systems, particularly for set theory, as a foundation for mathematics. The existence of non-standard models is actually a consequence of the completeness and first incompleteness theorems (Gödel, 1930, 1931), for these together show that there must be sentences of arithmetic (if consistent) that are true in the standard model, but false in some other, non-isomorphic model. However, Skolem's result describes a general technique for constructing such models. Skolem's theorem is now more easily proved using the compactness theorem, an easy consequence of the completeness theorem.

The Löwenheim-Skolem theorem produces a similar problem of characterization, the *Skolem paradox*, pointed out by Skolem in 1922. Roughly, this says that if first-order set theory has a model, it must also have a countable model whose continuum is a countable set, and thus apparently non-standard. This does not contradict *Cantor's theorem*, which merely demands that the countable model contain as an element no function that maps its natural numbers one-to-one onto its continuum, although there must be such a function *outside* the model. Although usually seen as limiting first-order logic, this result is extremely fruitful technically, providing one basis of the proof of the independence of the *continuum hypothesis* from the usual axioms of set theory given by Gödel in 1938 and Cohen in 1963. This connection between independence results and the existence of countable models was partially foreseen by Skolem in 1922.

See also CANTOR, COMPACTNESS THEOREM, GÖDEL'S INCOMPLETENESS THEOREMS, LÖWENHEIM-SKOLEM THEOREM, MODEL THEORY.

M.H.

Skolem-Löwenheim theorem. See LÖWENHEIM-SKOLEM THEOREM.

Skolem normal form. See NORMAL FORM.

Skolem's paradox. See LÖWENHEIM-SKOLEM THEOREM, SKOLEM.

slave morality. See NIETZSCHE.

slippery slope argument, an argument that an action apparently unobjectionable in itself would set in motion a train of events leading ultimately to an undesirable outcome. The metaphor portrays one on the edge of a slippery slope, where taking the first step down will inevitably cause sliding to the bottom. For example, it is sometimes argued that voluntary euthanasia should not be legalized because this will lead to killing unwanted people, e.g. the handicapped or elderly, against their will. In some versions the argument aims to show that one should intervene to stop an ongoing train of events; e.g., it has been argued that suppressing a Communist revolution in one country was necessary to prevent the spread of Communism throughout a whole region via the so-called domino effect. Slippery slope arguments with dubious causal assumptions are often classed as fallacies under the general heading of the fallacy of the false cause. This argument is also sometimes called the *wedge argument*. There is some disagreement concerning the breadth of the category of slippery slope arguments. Some would restrict the term to arguments with evaluative conclusions, while others construe it more broadly so as to include other sorites arguments. See also SORITES PARADOX, VAGUENESS.

W.T.

Smart, J(ohn) J(amieson) C(arswell) (b.1920), British-born Australian philosopher whose name is associated with three doctrines in particular: the mind–body identity theory, scientific realism, and utilitarianism. A student of Ryle's at Oxford, he rejected logical behaviorism in favor of what came to be known as Australian materialism. This is the view that mental processes – and, as Armstrong brought Smart to see, mental states – cannot be explained simply in terms of behavioristic dispositions. In order to make good sense of how the ordinary person talks of them we have to see them as brain processes – and states – under other names. Smart developed this identity theory of mind and brain, under the stimulus of his colleague, U. T. Place, in "Sensations and Brain Processes" (*Philosophical Review*, 1959). It became a mainstay of twentieth-century philosophy.

Smart endorsed the materialist analysis of mind on the grounds that it gave a simple picture that was consistent with the findings of science. He took a realist view of the claims of science, rejecting phenomenalism, instrumentalism, and the like, and he argued that commonsense beliefs should be maintained only so far as they are plausible in the light of total science. *Philosophy and Scientific Realism* (1963) gave forceful expression to this physicalist picture of the world, as did some later works. He attracted attention in particular for his argument that if we take science seriously then we have to endorse the four-dimensional picture of the universe and recognize as an illusion the experience of the passing of time.

He published a number of defenses of utilitarianism, the best known being his contribution to J. J. C. Smart and Bernard Williams, *Utilitarianism, For and Against* (1973). He gave new life to act utilitarianism at a time when utilitarians were few and most were attached to rule utilitarianism or other restricted forms of the doctrine.

See also PHILOSOPHY OF MIND, SCIENTIFIC REALISM, UTILITARIANISM.

P.P.

Smith, Adam (1723–90), Scottish economist and philosopher, a founder of modern political economy and a major contributor to ethics and the psychology of morals. His first published work was *The Theory of Moral Sentiments* (1759). This book immediately made him famous, and earned the praise of thinkers of the stature of Hume, Burke, and Kant. It sought to answer two questions: Wherein does virtue consist, and by means of what psychological principles do we determine this or that to be virtuous or the contrary? His answer to the first combined ancient Stoic and Aristotelian views of virtue with modern views derived from Hutcheson and others. His answer to the second built on Hume's theory of sympathy – our ability to put ourselves imaginatively in the situation of another – as well as on the notion of the "impartial spectator." Smith throughout is skeptical about metaphysical and theological views of virtue and of the psychology of morals. The self-understanding of reasonable moral actors ought to serve as the moral philosopher's guide. Smith's discussion ranges from the motivation of wealth to the psychological causes of religious and political fanaticism.

Smith's second published work, the immensely influential *An Inquiry into the Nature and Causes of the Wealth of Nations* (1776), attempts to explain why free economic, political, and religious markets are not only more efficient, when properly regulated, but also more in keeping with nature, more likely to win the approval of an impartial spectator, than monopolistic alternatives. Taken together, Smith's two books attempt to show how virtue and liberty can complement each other. He shows full awareness of the potentially dehumanizing force of what was later called "capitalism," and sought remedies in schemes for liberal education and properly organized religion.

Smith did not live to complete his system, which was to include an analysis of "natural jurisprudence." We possess student notes of his lectures on jurisprudence and on rhetoric, as well as several impressive essays on the evolution of the history of science and on the fine arts.

See also HUME, IDEAL OBSERVER, LIBERALISM, PHILOSOPHY OF ECONOMICS, SENTIMENTALISM, VIRTUE ETHICS.   C.L.G.

social action, a subclass of human action involving the interaction among agents and their mutual orientation, or the action of groups. While all intelligible actions are in some sense social, social actions must be directed to others. Talcott Parsons (1902–79) captured what is distinctive about social action in his concept of "double contingency," and similar concepts have been developed by other philosophers and sociologists, including Weber, Mead, and Wittgenstein. Whereas in monological action the agents' fulfilling their purposes depends only on contingent facts about the world, the success of social action is also contingent on how other agents react to what the agent does and how that agent reacts to other agents, and so on. An agent successfully communicates, e.g., not merely by finding some appropriate expression in an existing symbol system, but also by understanding how other agents will understand him.

Game theory describes and explains another type of double contingency in its analysis of the interdependency of choices and strategies among rational agents. Games are also significant in two other respects. First, they exemplify the cognitive requirements for social interaction, as in Mead's analysis of agents' perspective taking: as a subject ("I"), I am an object for others ("me"), and can take a third-person perspective along with others on the interaction itself ("the generalized other"). Second, games are regulated by shared rules and mediated through symbolic meanings; Wittgenstein's private language argument establishes that rules cannot be followed "privately." Some philosophers, such as Peter Winch, conclude from this argument that rule-following is a basic feature of distinctively social action.

Some actions are social in the sense that they can only be done in groups. Individualists (such as Weber, Jon Elster, and Raimo Tuomela) believe that these can be analyzed as the sum of the actions of each individual. But holists (such as Marx, Durkheim, and Margaret Gilbert) reject this reduction and argue that in social actions agents must see themselves as members of a collective agent. Holism has stronger or weaker versions: strong holists, such as Durkheim and Hegel, see the collective subject as singular, the collective consciousness of a society. Weak holists, such as Gilbert and Habermas, believe that social actions have plural, rather than singular, collective subjects. Holists generally establish the plausibility of their view by referring to larger contexts and sequences of action, such as shared symbol systems or social institutions. Explanations of social actions thus refer not only to the mutual expectations of agents, but also to these larger causal contexts, shared meanings, and mechanisms of coordination. Theories of social action must then explain the emergence of social order, and proposals range from Hobbes's coercive authority to Talcott Parsons's value consensus about shared goals among the members of groups.

See also ACTION THEORY, HOLISM, PHILOSOPHY OF THE SOCIAL SCIENCES, WEBER.
                                                              J.Bo.

social biology, the understanding of social behavior, especially human social behavior, from a biological perspective; often connected with the political philosophy of social Darwinism.

Charles Darwin's *Origin of Species* highlighted the significance of *social* behavior in organic evolution, and in the *Descent of Man*, he showed how significant such behavior is for humans. He argued that it is a product of natural selection; but it was not until 1964 that the English biologist William Hamilton showed precisely how such behavior could evolve, namely through "kin selection" as an aid to the biological well-being of close relatives. Since then, other models of explanation have been proposed, extending the theory to non-relatives. Best known is the self-describing "reciprocal altruism."

Social biology became notorious in 1975 when Edward O. Wilson published a major treatise on the subject: *Sociobiology: The New Synthesis*. Accusations of sexism and racism were leveled because Wilson suggested that Western social systems are biologically innate, and that in some respects males are stronger, more aggressive, more naturally promiscuous than females. Critics argued that all social biology is in fact a manifestation of social Darwinism, a nineteenth-century philosophy owing more to Herbert Spencer than to Charles Darwin, supposedly legitimating extreme laissez-faire economics and an unbridled societal struggle for existence. Such a charge is extremely serious, for as Moore pointed out in his *Principia Ethica* (1903), Spencer surely commits the naturalistic fallacy, inasmuch as he is attempting to derive the way that the world *ought* to be from the way that it *is*. Naturally enough, defenders of social biology, or "sociobiology" as it is now better known, denied vehemently that their science is mere right-wing ideology by another name. They pointed to many who have drawn very different social conclusions on the basis of biology. Best known is the Russian anarchist Kropotkin, who argued that societies are properly based on a biological propensity to mutual aid.

With respect to contemporary debate, it is perhaps fairest to say that sociobiology, particularly that pertaining to humans, did not always show sufficient sensitivity toward all societal groups – although certainly there was never the crude racism of the fascist regimes of the 1930s. However, recent work is far more careful in these respects. Now, indeed, the study of social behavior from a biological perspective is one of the most exciting and forward-moving branches of the life sciences.

See also DARWINISM, EVOLUTIONARY EPISTEMOLOGY, PHILOSOPHY OF BIOLOGY, POLITICAL PHILOSOPHY.   M.Ru.

social choice theory, the theory of the rational action of a group of agents. Important social choices are typically made over alternative means of collectively providing goods. These might be goods for individual members of the group, or more characteristically, *public goods*, goods such that no one can be excluded from enjoying their benefits once they are available. Perhaps the most central aspect of social choice theory concerns rational individual choice in a social context. Since what is rational for one agent to do will often depend on what is rational for another to do and vice versa, these choices take on a *strategic* dimension. The prisoner's dilemma illustrates how it can be very difficult to reconcile individual and collectively rational decisions, especially in non-dynamic contexts. There are many situations, particularly in the provision of public goods, however, where simple prisoner's dilemmas can be avoided and more manageable *coordination problems* remain. In these cases, individuals may find it rational to *contractually* or *conventionally* bind themselves to courses of action that lead to the greater good of all even though they are not straightforwardly utility-maximizing for particular individuals. Establishing the rationality of these contracts or conventions is one of the leading problems of social choice theory, because coordination can collapse if a rational agent first agrees to cooperate and then reneges and becomes a *free rider* on the collective efforts of others. Other forms of uncooperative behaviors such as violating rules established by society or being deceptive about one's preferences pose similar difficulties. Hobbes attempted to solve these problems by proposing that people would agree to submit to the authority of a sovereign whose punitive powers would make uncooperative behavior an unattractive option. It has also been argued that cooperation is rational if the concept of rationality is extended beyond utility-maximizing in the right way. Other arguments stress benefits beyond self-interest that accrue to cooperators.

Another major aspect of social choice theory concerns the rational action of a powerful central authority, or social planner, whose mission is to optimize the social good. Although the central planner may be instituted by rational individual choice, this part of the theory simply assumes the institution. The planner's task of making a one-time allocation of resources to the production of various commodities is tractable if social good or social utility is known as a function of various commodities. When the planner must take into account dynamical considerations, the technical problems are more difficult. This economic *growth theory* raises important ethical questions about intergenerational conflict.

The assumption of a social analogue of the individual utility functions is particularly worrisome. It can be shown formally that taking the results of majority votes can lead to intransitive social orderings of possible choices and it is, therefore, a generally unsuitable procedure for the planner to follow. Moreover, under very general conditions there is no way of aggregating individual preferences into a consistent social choice function of the kind needed by the planner.

See also ARROW'S PARADOX, GAME THEORY, PHILOSOPHY OF ECONOMICS, PRISONER'S DILEMMA.   A.N.

social constructivism, also called social constructionism, any of a variety of views which claim that knowledge in some area is the product of our social practices and institutions, or of the interactions and negotiations between relevant social groups. Mild versions hold that social factors shape interpretations of the world. Stronger versions maintain that the world, or some significant portion of it, is somehow constituted by theories, practices, and institutions. Defenders often move from mild to stronger versions by insisting that the world is accessible to us only through our interpretations, and that the idea of an independent reality is at best an irrelevant abstraction and at worst incoherent. (This philosophical position is distinct from, though distantly related to, a view of the same name in social and developmental psychology, associated with such figures as Piaget and Lev Vygotsky, which sees learning as a process in which subjects actively construct knowledge.)

Social constructivism has roots in Kant's idealism, which claims that we cannot know things in themselves and that knowledge of the world is possible only by imposing pre-given categories of thought on otherwise inchoate experience. But where Kant believed that the categories with which we interpret and thus construct the world are given a priori, contemporary constructivists believe that the relevant concepts and associated practices vary from one group or historical period to another. Since there are no independent standards for evaluating conceptual schemes, social constructivism leads naturally to relativism.

These views are generally thought to be present in Kuhn's *The Structure of Scientific Revolutions*, which argues that observation and methods in science are deeply theory-dependent and that scientists with fundamentally different assumptions (or paradigms) effectively live in different worlds. Kuhn thus offers a view of science in opposition to both scientific realism (which holds that theory-dependent methods can give us knowledge of a theory-independent world) and empiricism (which draws a sharp line between theory and observation).

Kuhn was reluctant to accept the apparently radical consequences of his views, but his work has influenced recent social studies of science, whose proponents frequently embrace both relativism and strong constructivism. Another influence is the principle of symmetry advocated by David Bloor and Barry Barnes, which holds that sociologists should explain the acceptance of scientific views in the same way whether they believe those views to be true or to be false. This approach is elaborated in the work of Harry Collins, Steve Woolgar, and others. Constructivist themes are also prominent in the work of feminist critics of science such as Sandra Harding and Donna Haraway, and in the complex views of Bruno Latour.

Critics, such as Richard Boyd and Philip Kitcher, while applauding the detailed case studies produced by constructivists, claim that the positive arguments for constructivism are fallacious, that it fails to account satisfactorily for actual scientific practice, and that like other versions of idealism and relativism it is only dubiously coherent.

See also ANTI-REALISM, ETHICAL CONSTRUCTIVISM, FEMINIST EPISTEMOLOGY, KANT, KUHN, MATHEMATICAL CONSTRUCTIVISM, RELATIVISM.   P.Gas.

social contract, an agreement either between the people and their ruler, or among the people in a community. The idea of a social contract has been used in arguments that differ in what they aim to justify or explain (e.g., the state, conceptions of justice, morality), what they take the problem of justification to be, and whether or not they presuppose a moral theory or purport to *be* a moral theory.

Traditionally the term has been used in arguments that attempt to explain the nature of political obligation and/or the kind of responsibility that rulers have to their subjects. Philosophers such as Plato, Hobbes, Locke, Rousseau, and Kant argue that human beings would find life in a prepolitical "state of nature" (a state that some argue is also presocietal) so difficult that they would agree – either with one another or with a prospective ruler – to the creation of political institutions that each believes would improve his or her lot. Note that because the argument explains political or social cohesion as the product of an agreement among individuals, it makes these individuals conceptually prior to political or social units. Marx and other socialist and communitarian thinkers have argued against conceptualizing an individual's relationship to her political and social community in this way.

Have social contracts in political societies actually taken place? Hume ridicules the idea that they are real, and questions what value make-believe agreements can have as explanations of actual political obligations. Although many social contract theorists admit that there is almost never an explicit act of agreement in a community, nonetheless they maintain that such an agreement is implicitly made when members of the society engage in certain acts through which they give their *tacit consent* to the ruling regime. It is controversial what actions constitute giving tacit consent: Plato and Locke maintain that the acceptance of benefits is sufficient to give such consent, but some have argued that it is wrong to feel obliged to those who foist upon us benefits for which we have not asked. It is also unclear how much of an obligation a person can be under if he gives only tacit consent to a regime.

How are we to understand the terms of a social contract establishing a state? When the people agree to obey the ruler, do they surrender their own power to him, as Hobbes tried to argue? Or do they merely lend him that power, reserving the right to take it from him if and when they see fit, as Locke maintained? If power is merely on loan to the ruler, rebellion against him could be condoned if he violates the conditions of that loan. But if the people's grant of power is a surrender, there are no such conditions, and the people could never be justified in taking back that power via revolution.

Despite controversies surrounding their interpretation, social contract arguments have been important to the development of modern democratic states: the idea of the government as the creation of the people, which they can and should judge and which they have the right to overthrow if they find it wanting, contributed to the development of democratic forms of polity in the eighteenth and nineteenth centuries. American and French revolutionaries explicitly acknowledged their debts to social contract theorists such as Locke and Rousseau.

In the twentieth century, the social contract idea has been used as a device for defining vari-

ous moral conceptions (e.g. theories of justice) by those who find its focus on individuals useful in the development of theories that argue against views (e.g. utilitarianism) that allow individuals to be sacrificed for the benefit of the group.

See also CONTRACTARIANISM, HOBBES, POLITICAL PHILOSOPHY, ROUSSEAU.   J.Ham.

social Darwinism. See DARWINISM, SOCIAL PHILOSOPHY.

social epistemology, the study of the social dimensions or determinants of knowledge, or the ways in which social factors promote or perturb the quest for knowledge. Some writers use the term 'knowledge' loosely, as designating mere belief. On their view social epistemology should simply describe how social factors influence beliefs, without concern for the rationality or truth of these beliefs. Many historians and sociologists of science, e.g., study scientific practices in the same spirit that anthropologists study native cultures, remaining neutral about the referential status of scientists' constructs or the truth-values of their beliefs. Others try to show that social factors like political or professional interests are causally operative, and take such findings to debunk any objectivist pretensions of science. Still other writers retain a normative, critical dimension in social epistemology, but do not presume that social practices necessarily undermine objectivity. Even if knowledge is construed as true or rational belief, social practices might enhance knowledge acquisition. One social practice is trusting the opinions of authorities, a practice that can produce truth if the trusted authorities are genuinely authoritative. Such trust may also be perfectly rational in a complex world, where division of epistemic labor is required. Even a scientist's pursuit of extra-epistemic interests such as professional rewards may not be antithetical to truth in favorable circumstances. Institutional provisions, e.g., judicial rules of evidence, provide another example of social factors. Exclusionary rules might actually serve the cause of truth or accuracy in judgment if the excluded evidence would tend to mislead or prejudice jurors. **See also** EPISTEMOLOGY, MANNHEIM, RELIABILISM.   A.I.G.

social ethics. See SOCIAL PHILOSOPHY.

socialism. See POLITICAL PHILOSOPHY.

social philosophy, broadly the philosophy of society, including the philosophy of social science (and many of its components, e.g., economics and history), political philosophy, most of what we now think of as ethics, and philosophy of law. But we may distinguish two narrower senses. In one, it is the conceptual theory of society, including the theory of the study of society – the common part of all the philosophical studies mentioned. In the other, it is a normative study, the part of moral philosophy that concerns social action and individual involvement with society in general.

The central job of social philosophy in the first of these narrower senses is to articulate the correct notion or concept of society. This would include formulating a suitable definition of 'society'; the question is then which concepts are better for which purposes, and how they are related. Thus we may distinguish "thin" and "thick" conceptions of society. The former would identify the least that can be said before we cease talking about society at all – say, a number of people who interact, whose actions affect the behavior of their fellows. Thicker conceptions would then add such things as community rules, goals, customs, and ideals. An important empirical question is whether any interacting groups ever do lack such things and what if anything is common to the rules, etc., that actual societies have.

Descriptive social philosophy will obviously border on, if not merge into, social science itself, e.g. into sociology, social psychology, or economics. And some outlooks in social philosophy will tend to ally with one social science as more distinctively typical than others – e.g., the individualist view looks to economics, the holist to sociology.

A major methodological controversy concerns *holism* versus *individualism*. Holism maintains that (at least some) social groups must be studied as units, irreducible to their members: we cannot understand a society merely by understanding the actions and motivations of its members. Individualism denies that societies are "organisms," and holds that we can understand society *only* in that way.

Classic German sociologists (e.g., Weber) distinguished between *Gesellschaft*, whose paradigm is the voluntary association, such as a chess club, whose activities are the coordinated actions of a number of people who intentionally join that group in order to pursue the purposes that identify it; and *Gemeinschaft*, whose members find their identities in that group. Thus, the French are not a group whose members teamed up with like-minded people to form French society. They

were French before they had separate individual purposes. The holist views society as essentially a *Gemeinschaft*. Individualists agree that there are such groupings but deny that they require a separate kind of irreducibly collective explanation: to understand the French we must understand how typical French individuals behave – compared, say, with the Germans, and so on. The methods of Western economics typify the analytical tendencies of methodological individualism, showing how we can understand large-scale economic phenomena in terms of the rational actions of particular economic agents. (Cf. Adam Smith's invisible hand thesis: each economic agent seeks only his own good, yet the result is the macrophenomenal good of the whole.)

Another pervasive issue concerns the role of intentional characterizations and explanations in these fields. Ordinary people explain behavior by reference to its purposes, and they formulate these in terms that rely on public rules of language and doubtless many other rules. To understand society, we must hook onto the self-understanding of the people *in* that society (this view is termed *Verstehen*).

Recent work in philosophy of science raises the question whether intentional concepts can really be fundamental in explaining anything, and whether we must ultimately conceive people as in some sense material systems, e.g. as computer-like. Major questions for the program of replicating human intelligence in data-processing terms (cf. artificial intelligence) are raised by the symbolic aspects of interaction. Additionally, we should note the emergence of sociobiology as a potent source of explanations of social phenomena.

Normative social philosophy, in turn, tends inevitably to merge into either politics or ethics, especially the part of ethics dealing with how people ought to treat others, especially in large groups, in relation to social institutions or social structures. This contrasts with ethics in the sense concerned with how individual people may attain the good life for themselves. All such theories allot major importance to social relations; but if one's theory leaves the individual wide freedom of choice, then a theory of individually chosen goods will still have a distinctive subject matter.

The normative involvements of social philosophy have paralleled the foregoing in important ways. Individualists have held that the good of a society must be analyzed in terms of the goods of its individual members. Of special importance has been the view that society must respect individual rights, blocking certain actions alleged to promote social good as a whole. Organicist philosophers such as Hegel hold that it is the other way around: the state or nation is higher than the individual, who is rightly subordinated to it, and individuals have fundamental duties toward the groups of which they are members. Outrightly fascist versions of such views are unpopular today, but more benign versions continue in modified form, notably by *communitarians*. Socialism and especially communism, though focused originally on economic aspects of society, have characteristically been identified with the organicist outlook.

Their extreme opposite is to be found in the *libertarians*, who hold that the right to individual liberty is fundamental in society, and that no institutions may override that right. Libertarians hold that society ought to be treated strictly as an association, a *Gesellschaft*, even though they might not deny that it is ontogenetically *Gemeinschaft*. They might agree that religious groups, e.g., cannot be wholly understood as separate individuals. Nevertheless, the libertarian holds that religious and cultural practices may not be interfered with or even supported by society. Libertarians are strong supporters of free-market economic methods, and opponents of any sort of state intervention into the affairs of individuals. *Social Darwinism*, advocating the "survival of the socially fittest," has sometimes been associated with the libertarian view.

Insofar as there is any kind of standard view on these matters, it combines elements of both individualism and holism. Typical social philosophers today accept that society has duties, not voluntary for individual members, to support education, health, and some degree of welfare for all. But they also agree that individual rights are to be respected, especially civil rights, such as freedom of speech and religion. How to combine these two apparently disparate sets of ideas into a coherent whole is the problem. (John Rawls's celebrated *Theory of Justice*, 1971, is a contemporary classic that attempts to do just that.)

See also ETHICS, METHODOLOGICAL HOLISM, PHILOSOPHY OF THE SOCIAL SCIENCES, POLITICAL PHILOSOPHY.   J.Na.

social sciences, philosophy of the. See PHILOSOPHY OF THE SOCIAL SCIENCES.

Socinianism, an unorthodox Christian religious movement originating in the sixteenth century from the work of Italian reformer Laelius Socinus ("Sozzini" in Italian; 1525–62) and his nephew Faustus Socinus (1539–1603). Born in Siena of a patrician family, Laelius was widely read in theology. Influenced by the evangelical movement in Italy, he made contact with noted Protestant reformers, including Calvin and Melanchthon, some of whom questioned his orthodoxy. In response, he wrote a confession of faith (one of a small number of his writings to have survived). After Laelius's death, his work was carried on by his nephew, Faustus, whose writings (including *On the Authority of Scripture*, 1570; *On the Savior Jesus Christ*, 1578; and *On Predestination*, 1578) expressed heterodox views. Faustus believed that Christ's nature was entirely human, that souls did not possess immortality by nature (though there would be selective resurrection for believers), that invocation of Christ in prayer was permissible but not required, and he argued against predestination. After publication of his 1578 writings, Faustus was invited to Transylvania and Poland to engage in a dispute within the Reformed churches there. He decided to make his permanent residence in Poland, which, through his tireless efforts, became the center of the Socinian movement. The most important document of this movement was the *Racovian Catechism*, published in 1605 (shortly after Faustus's death). The Minor church of Poland, centered at Racov, became the focal point of the movement. Its academy attracted hundreds of students and its publishing house produced books in many languages defending Socinian ideas.

Socinianism, as represented by the *Racovian Catechism* and other writings collected by Faustus's Polish disciples, involves the views of Laelius and especially Faustus Socinus, aligned with the anti-Trinitarian views of the Polish Minor church (founded in 1556). It accepts Christ's message as the definitive revelation of God, but regards Christ as human, not divine; rejects the natural immortality of the soul, but argues for the selective resurrection of the faithful; rejects the doctrine of the Trinity; emphasizes human free will against predestinationism; defends pacifism and the separation of church and state; and argues that reason – not creeds, dogmatic tradition, or church authority – must be the final interpreter of Scripture. Its view of God is temporalistic: God's eternity is existence at all times, not timelessness, and God knows future free actions only when they occur. (In these respects, the Socinian view of God anticipates aspects of modern process theology.) Socinianism was suppressed in Poland in 1658, but it had already spread to other European countries, including Holland (where it appealed to followers of Arminius) and England, where it influenced the Cambridge Platonists, Locke, and other philosophers, as well as scientists like Newton. In England, it also influenced and was closely associated with the development of Unitarianism.

See also TRINITARIANISM.   R.H.K.

Socinus, Faustus. See SOCINIANISM.

Socinus, Laelus. See SOCINIANISM.

sociobiology. See SOCIAL BIOLOGY.

sociological jurisprudence. See JURISPRUDENCE.

sociology of knowledge. See MANNHEIM.

Socrates (469–399 B.C.), Greek philosopher, the exemplar of the examined life, best known for his dictum that only such a life is worth living. Although he wrote nothing, his thoughts and way of life had a profound impact on many of his contemporaries, and, through Plato's portrayal of him in his early writings, he became a major source of inspiration and ideas for later generations of philosophers. His daily occupation was adversarial public conversation with anyone willing to argue with him. A man of great intellectual brilliance, moral integrity, personal magnetism, and physical self-command, he challenged the moral complacency of his fellow citizens, and embarrassed them with their inability to answer such questions as What is virtue? – questions that he thought we must answer, if we are to know how best to live our lives. His ideas and personality won him a devoted following among the young, but he was far from universally admired. Formal charges were made against him for refusing to recognize the gods of the city, introducing other new divinities, and corrupting the youth. Tried on a single day before a large jury (500 was a typical size), he was found guilty by a small margin: had thirty jurors voted differently, he would have been acquitted. The punishment selected by the jury was death and was administered by means of poison, probably hemlock.

Why was he brought to trial and convicted? Part of the answer lies in Plato's Apology, which purports to be the defense Socrates gave at his trial. Here he says that he has for many years been falsely portrayed as someone whose scientific theories dethrone the traditional gods and put natural forces in their place, and as someone who charges a fee for offering private instruction on how to make a weak argument seem strong in the courtroom. This is the picture of Socrates drawn in a play of Aristophanes, the Clouds, first presented in 423. It is unlikely that Aristophanes intended his play as an accurate depiction of Socrates, and the unscrupulous buffoon found in the Clouds would never have won the devotion of so serious a moralist as Plato. Aristophanes drew together the assorted characteristics of various fifth-century thinkers and named this amalgam "Socrates" because the real Socrates was one of several controversial intellectuals of the period.

Nonetheless, it is unlikely that the charges against Socrates or Aristophanes' caricature were entirely without foundation. Both Xenophon's Memorabilia and Plato's Euthyphro say that Socrates aroused suspicion because he thought a certain divine sign or voice appeared to him and gave him useful instruction about how to act. By claiming a unique and private source of divine inspiration, Socrates may have been thought to challenge the city's exclusive control over religious matters. His willingness to disobey the city is admitted in Plato's Apology, where he says that he would have to disobey a hypothetical order to stop asking his philosophical questions, since he regards them as serving a religious purpose. In the Euthyphro he seeks a rational basis for making sacrifices and performing other services to the gods; but he finds none, and implies that no one else has one. Such a challenge to traditional religious practice could easily have aroused a suspicion of atheism and lent credibility to the formal charges against him.

Furthermore, Socrates makes statements in Plato's early dialogues (and in Xenophon's Memorabilia) that could easily have offended the political sensibilities of his contemporaries. He holds that only those who have given special study to political matters should make decisions. For politics is a kind of craft, and in all other crafts only those who have shown their mastery are entrusted with public responsibilities. Athens was a democracy in which each citizen had an equal legal right to shape policy, and Socrates' analogy between the role of an expert in politics and in other crafts may have been seen as a threat to this egalitarianism. Doubts about his political allegiance, though not mentioned in the formal charges against him, could easily have swayed some jurors to vote against him.

Socrates is the subject not only of Plato's early dialogues but also of Xenophon's Memorabilia, and in many respects their portraits are consistent with each other. But there are also some important differences. In the *Memorabilia,* Socrates teaches whatever a gentleman needs to know for civic purposes. He is filled with platitudinous advice, and is never perplexed by the questions he raises; e.g., he knows what the virtues are, equating them with obedience to the law. His views are not threatening or controversial, and always receive the assent of his interlocutors. By contrast, Plato's Socrates presents himself as a perplexed inquirer who knows only that he knows nothing about moral matters. His interlocutors are sometimes annoyed by his questions and threatened by their inability to answer them. And he is sometimes led by force of argument to controversial conclusions. Such a Socrates could easily have made enemies, whereas Xenophon's Socrates is sometimes too "good" to be true.

But it is important to bear in mind that it is only the early works of Plato that should be read as an accurate depiction of the historical Socrates. Plato's own theories, as presented in his middle and late dialogues, enter into philosophical terrain that had not been explored by the historical Socrates – even though in the middle (and some of the late) dialogues a figure called Socrates remains the principal speaker. We are told by Aristotle that Socrates confined himself to ethical questions, and that he did not postulate a separate realm of imperceptible and eternal abstract objects called "Forms" or "Ideas." Although the figure called Socrates affirms the existence of these objects in such Platonic dialogues as the *Phaedo* and the *Republic,* Aristotle takes this interlocutor to be a vehicle for Platonic philosophy, and attributes to Socrates only those positions that we find in Plato's earlier writing, e.g. in the *Apology, Charmides, Crito, Euthyphro, Hippias Minor, Hippias Major, Ion, Laches, Lysis,* and *Protagoras.* Socrates focused on moral philosophy almost exclusively; Plato's attention was also devoted to the study of metaphysics, epistemology, physical theory, mathematics, language, and political philosophy.

When we distinguish the philosophies of Socrates and Plato in this way, we find continuities in their thought – for instance, the questions posed in the early dialogues receive answers in the *Republic* – but there are important differences. For Socrates, being virtuous is a purely intellectual matter: it simply involves knowing what is good for human beings; once we master this subject, we will act as we should. Because he equates virtue with knowledge, Socrates frequently draws analogies between being virtuous and having mastered any ordinary subject – cooking, building, or geometry, e.g. For mastery of these subjects does not involve a training of the emotions. By contrast, Plato affirms the existence of powerful emotional drives that can deflect us from our own good, if they are not disciplined by reason. He denies Socrates' assumption that the emotions will not resist reason, once one comes to understand where one's own good lies.

Socrates says in Plato's *Apology* that the only knowledge he has is that he knows nothing, but it would be a mistake to infer that he has no convictions about moral matters – convictions arrived at through a difficult process of reasoning. He holds that the unexamined life is not worth living, that it is better to be treated unjustly than to do injustice, that understanding of moral matters is the only unconditional good, that the virtues are all forms of knowledge and cannot be separated from each other, that death is not an evil, that a good person cannot be harmed, that the gods possess the wisdom human beings lack and never act immorally, and so on. He does not accept these propositions as articles of faith, but is prepared to defend any of them; for he can show his interlocutors that their beliefs ought to lead them to accept these conclusions, paradoxical though they may be.

Since Socrates can defend his beliefs and has subjected them to intellectual scrutiny, why does he present himself as someone who has no knowledge – excepting the knowledge of his own ignorance? The answer lies in his assumption that it is only a fully accomplished expert in any field who can claim knowledge or wisdom of that field; someone has knowledge of navigational matters, e.g., only if he has mastered the art of sailing, can answer all inquiries about this subject, and can train others to do the same. Judged by this high epistemic standard, Socrates can hardly claim to be a moral expert, for he lacks answers to the questions he raises, and cannot teach others to be virtuous. Though he has examined his moral beliefs and can offer reasons for them – an accomplishment that gives him an overbearing sense of superiority to his contemporaries – he takes himself to be quite distant from the ideal of moral perfection, which would involve a thorough understanding of all moral matters. This keen sense of the moral and intellectual deficiency of all human beings accounts for a great deal of Socrates' appeal, just as his arrogant disdain for his fellow citizens no doubt contributed to his demise.

See also ARISTOTLE, PLATO, SOCRATIC INTELLECTUALISM.   R.Kr.

Socratic intellectualism, the claim that moral goodness or virtue consists exclusively in a kind of knowledge, with the implication that if one knows what is good and evil, one cannot fail to be a good person and to act in a morally upright way. The claim and the term derive from Socrates; a corollary is another claim of Socrates: there is no moral weakness or *akrasia* – all wrong action is due to the agent's ignorance. Socrates defends this view in Plato's dialogue *Protagoras*.

There are two ways to understand Socrates' view that knowledge of the good is sufficient for right action. (1) All desires are rational, being focused on what is believed to be good; thus, an agent who knows what is good will have no desire to act contrary to that knowledge. (2) There are non-rational desires, but knowledge of the good has sufficient motivational power to overcome them. Socratic intellectualism was abandoned by Plato and Aristotle, both of whom held that emotional makeup is an essential part of moral character. However, they retained the Socratic idea that there is a kind of knowledge or wisdom that ensures right action – but this knowledge presupposes antecedent training and molding of the passions. Socratic intellectualism was later revived and enjoyed a long life as a key doctrine of the Stoics.

See also MOTIVATIONAL INTERNALISM, SOCRATES, STOICISM.   D.T.D.

Socratic irony, a form of indirect communication frequently employed by Socrates in Plato's early dialogues, chiefly to praise insincerely the abilities of his interlocutors while revealing their ignorance; or, to disparage his own abilities, e.g. by denying that he has knowledge. Interpreters disagree whether Socrates' self-disparagement is insincere. See also PLATO, SOCRATES.   W.J.P.

Socratic method. See SOCRATES.

Socratic paradoxes, a collection of theses associated with Socrates that contradict opinions about moral or practical matters shared by most people. Although there is no consensus on the precise number of Socratic paradoxes, each of the following theses has been identified as one. (1) Because no one desires evil things, anyone who pursues evil things does so involuntarily. (2) Because virtue is knowledge, anyone who does

something morally wrong does so involuntarily. (3) It is better to be unjustly treated than to do what is unjust. The first two theses are associated with weakness of will or *akrasia*. It is sometimes claimed that the topic of the first thesis is prudential weakness, whereas that of the second is moral weakness; the reference to "evil things" in (1) is not limited to things that are morally evil. Naturally, various competing interpretations of these theses have been offered. See also AKRASIA, PLATO, SOCRATES.   A.R.M.

soft determinism. See FREE WILL PROBLEM.

software. See COMPUTER THEORY.

solipsism, the doctrine that there exists a first-person perspective possessing privileged and irreducible characteristics, in virtue of which we stand in various kinds of isolation from any other persons or external things that may exist. This doctrine is associated with but distinct from *egocentricism*.

On one variant of solipsism (Thomas Nagel's) we are isolated from other sentient beings because we can never adequately understand their experience (*empathic solipsism*). Another variant depends on the thesis that the meanings or referents of all words are mental entities uniquely accessible only to the language user (*semantic solipsism*). A restricted variant, due to Wittgenstein, asserts that first-person ascriptions of psychological states have a meaning fundamentally different from that of second- or third-person ascriptions (*psychological solipsism*). In extreme forms semantic solipsism can lead to the view that the only things that can be meaningfully said to exist are ourselves or our mental states (*ontological solipsism*). Skepticism about the existence of the world external to our minds is sometimes considered a form of epistemological solipsism, since it asserts that we stand in epistemological isolation from that world, partly as a result of the epistemic priority possessed by first-person access to mental states.

In addition to these substantive versions of solipsism, several variants go under the rubric *methodological solipsism*. The idea is that when we seek to explain why sentient beings behave in certain ways by looking to what they believe, desire, hope, and fear, we should identify these psychological states only with events that occur inside the mind or brain, not with external events, since the former alone are the proximate and sufficient causal explanations of bodily behavior.

See also DESCARTES, EGOCENTRIC PRE-DICAMENT, PHILOSOPHY OF MIND, PRIVATE LANGUAGE ARGUMENT, SKEPTICISM.   T.V.

Solovyov, Vladimir (1853–1900), Russian philosopher, theologian, essayist, and poet. In addition to major treatises and dialogues in speculative philosophy, Solovyov wrote sensitive literary criticism and influential essays on current social, political, and ecclesiastical questions. His serious verse is subtle and delicate; his light verse is rich in comic invention.

The mystical image of the "Divine Sophia," which Solovyov articulated in theoretical concepts as well as poetic symbols, powerfully influenced the Russian symbolist poets of the early twentieth century. His stress on the *human* role in the "divine-human process" that creates both cosmic and historical being led to charges of heresy from Russian Orthodox traditionalists. Solovyov's rationalistic "justification of the good" in history, society, and individual life was inspired by Plato, Spinoza, and especially Hegel. However, at the end of his life Solovyov offered (in *Three Conversations on War, Progress, and the End of History,* 1900) a contrasting apocalyptic vision of historical and cosmic disaster, including the appearance, in the twenty-first century, of the Antichrist.

In ethics, social philosophy, philosophy of history, and theory of culture, Solovyov was both a vigorous ecumenist and a "good European" who affirmed the intrinsic value of both the "individual human person" (Russian *lichnost'*) and the "individual nation or people" (*narodnost'*), but he decisively repudiated the perversions of these values in egoism and nationalism, respectively. He contrasted the fruits of English *narodnost'* – the works of Shakespeare and Byron, Berkeley and Newton – with the fruits of English nationalism – the repressive and destructive expansion of the British Empire. In opposing ethnic, national, and religious exclusiveness and self-centeredness, Solovyov also, and quite consistently, opposed the growing xenophobia and anti-Semitism of his own time.

Since 1988 long-suppressed works by and about Solovyov have been widely republished in Russia, and fresh interpretations of his philosophy and theology have begun to appear.

See also RUSSIAN PHILOSOPHY.   G.L.K.

Son Buddhism. See KOREAN PHILOSOPHY.

sophia. See ARISTOTLE.

sophismata (singular: *sophisma*), sentences illustrating semantic or logical issues associated with the analysis of syncategorematic terms, or terms lacking independent signification. Typically a *sophisma* was used from the thirteenth century into the sixteenth century to analyze relations holding between logic or semantics and broader philosophical issues. For example, the syncategorematic term 'besides' (*praeter*) in 'Socrates twice sees every man besides Plato' is ambiguous, because it could mean 'On two occasions Socrates sees every-man-but-Plato' and also 'Except for overlooking Plato once, on two occasions Socrates sees every man'. Roger Bacon used this *sophisma* to discuss the ambiguity of distribution, in this case, of the scope of the reference of 'twice' and 'besides'. Sherwood used the *sophisma* to illustrate the applicability of his rule of the distribution of ambiguous syncategoremata, while Pseudo-Peter of Spain uses it to establish the truth of the rule, 'If a proposition is in part false, it can be made true by means of an exception, but not if it is completely false'. In each case, the philosopher uses the ambiguous signification of the syncategorematic term to analyze broader logical problems. The *sophisma* 'Every man is of necessity an animal' has ambiguity through the syncategorematic 'every' that leads to broader philosophical problems. In the 1270s, Boethius of Dacia analyzed this *sophisma* in terms of its applicability when no man exists. Is the knowledge derived from understanding the proposition destroyed when the object known is destroyed? Does 'man' signify anything when there are no men? If we can correctly predicate a genus of a species, is the nature of the genus in that species something other than, or distinct from, what finally differentiates the species? In this case, the *sophisma* proves a useful approach to addressing metaphysical and epistemological problems central to Scholastic discourse. See also BACON, ROGER; SHERWOOD; SYNCATEGOREMATA.   S.E.L.

Sophists, any of a number of ancient Greeks, roughly contemporaneous with Socrates, who professed to teach, for a fee, rhetoric, philosophy, and how to succeed in life. They typically were itinerants, visiting much of the Greek world, and gave public exhibitions at Olympia and Delphi. They were part of the general expansion of Greek learning and of the changing culture in which the previous informal educational methods were inadequate. For example, the growing litigiousness of Athenian society demanded instruction in the art of speaking well, which the Sophists helped fulfill. The Sophists have been portrayed as intellectual charlatans (hence the pejorative use of 'sophism'), teaching their sophistical reasoning for money, and (at the other extreme) as Victorian moralists and educators. The truth is more complex. They were not a school, and shared no body of opinions. They were typically concerned with ethics (unlike many earlier philosophers, who emphasized physical inquiries) and about the relationship between laws and customs (*nomos*) and nature (*phusis*).

Protagoras of Abdera (c.490–c.420 B.C.) was the most famous and perhaps the first Sophist. He visited Athens frequently, and became a friend of its leader, Pericles; he therefore was invited to draw up a legal code for the colony of Thurii (444). According to some late reports, he died in a shipwreck as he was leaving Athens, having been tried for and found guilty of impiety. (He claimed that he knew nothing about the gods, because of human limitations and the difficulty of the question.) We have only a few short quotations from his works. His "Truth" (also known as the "Throws," i.e., how to overthrow an opponent's arguments) begins with his most famous claim: "Humans are the measure of all things – of things that are, that they are, of things that are not, that they are not." That is, there is no objective truth; the world is for each person as it appears to that person. Of what use, then, are skills? Skilled people can change others' perceptions in useful ways. For example, a doctor can change a sick person's perceptions so that she is healthy. Protagoras taught his students to "make the weaker argument the stronger," i.e., to alter people's perceptions about the value of arguments. (Aristophanes satirizes Protagoras as one who would make unjust arguments defeat just arguments.) This is true for ethical judgments, too: laws and customs are simply products of human agreement. But because laws and customs result from experiences of what is most useful, they should be followed rather than nature. No perception or judgment is more true than another, but some are more useful, and those that are more useful should be followed.

Gorgias (c.483–376) was a student of Empedocles. His town, Leontini in Sicily, sent him as an ambassador to Athens in 427; his visit was a great success, and the Athenians were amazed at his rhetorical ability. Like other Sophists, he charged for instruction and gave speeches at religious festivals. Gorgias denied that he taught virtue; instead, he produced clever speakers. He insisted that different people have different virtues: for example, women's virtue differs from men's. Since there is no truth (and if there were we couldn't know it), we must rely on opinion, and so speakers who can change people's opinions have great power – greater than the power produced by any other skill. (In his "Encomium on Helen" he argues that if she left Menelaus and went with Paris because she was convinced by speech, she wasn't responsible for her actions.) Two paraphrases of Gorgias's "About What Doesn't Exist" survive; in this he argues that nothing exists, that even if something did, we couldn't know it, and that even if we could know anything we couldn't explain it to anyone. We can't know anything, because some things we think of do not exist, and so we have no way of judging whether the things we think of exist. And we can't express any knowledge we may have, because no two people can think of the same thing, since the same thing can't be in two places, and because we use words in speech, not colors or shapes or objects. (This may be merely a parody of Parmenides' argument that only one thing exists.)

Antiphon the Sophist (fifth century) is probably (although not certainly) to be distinguished from Antiphon the orator (d. 411), some of whose speeches we possess. We know nothing about his life (if he is distinct from the orator). In addition to brief quotations in later authors, we have two papyrus fragments of his "On Truth." In these he argues that we should follow laws and customs only if there are witnesses and so our action will affect our reputation; otherwise, we should follow nature, which is often inconsistent with following custom. Custom is established by human agreement, and so disobeying it is detrimental only if others know it is disobeyed, whereas nature's demands (unlike those of custom) can't be ignored with impunity. Antiphon assumes that rational actions are self-interested, and that justice demands actions contrary to self-interest – a position Plato attacks in the *Republic*. Antiphon was also a materialist: the nature of a bed is wood, since if a buried bed could grow it would grow wood, not a bed. His view is one of Aristotle's main concerns in the *Physics*, since Aristotle admits in the *Categories* that persistence through change is the best test for substance, but won't admit that matter is substance.

Hippias (fifth century) was from Elis, in the Peloponnesus, which used him as an ambassador. He competed at the festival of Olympus with both prepared and extemporaneous speeches. He had a phenomenal memory. Since Plato repeatedly makes fun of him in the two dialogues that bear his name, he probably was self-important and serious. He was a polymath who claimed he could do anything, including making speeches and clothes; he wrote a work collecting what he regarded as the best things said by others. According to one report, he made a mathematical discovery (the quadratrix, the first curve other than the circle known to the Greeks). In the *Protagoras,* Plato has Hippias contrast nature and custom, which often does violence to nature.

Prodicus (fifth century) was from Ceos, in the Cyclades, which frequently employed him on diplomatic missions. He apparently demanded high fees, but had two versions of his lecture – one cost fifty drachmas, the other one drachma. (Socrates jokes that if he could have afforded the fifty-drachma lecture, he would have learned the truth about the correctness of words, and Aristotle says that when Prodicus added something exciting to keep his audience's attention he called it "slipping in the fifty-drachma lecture for them.") We have at least the content of one lecture of his, the "Choice of Heracles," which consists of banal moralizing. Prodicus was praised by Socrates for his emphasis on the right use of words and on distinguishing between synonyms. He also had a naturalistic view of the origin of theology: useful things were regarded as gods.

H.A.I.

Sorel, Georges (1847–1922), French socialist activist and philosopher best known for his *Reflections on Violence* (1906), which develops the notion of revolutionary syndicalism as seen through proletarian violence and the interpretation of myth. An early proponent of the quasi-Marxist position of gradual democratic reformism, Sorel eventually developed a highly subjective interpretation of historical materialism that, while retaining a conception of proletarian revolution, now understood it through myth rather than reason. He was in large part reacting to the empiricism of the French Enlightenment and the statistical structuring of sociological studies.

In contrast to Marx and Engels, who held that revolution would occur when the proletariat attained its own class consciousness through an understanding of its true relationship to the means of production in capitalist society, Sorel introduced myth rather than reason as the cor-

rect way to interpret social totality. Myth allows for the necessary reaction to bourgeois rationalism and permits the social theorist to negate the status quo through the authenticity of revolutionary violence. By acknowledging the irrationality of the status quo, myth permits the possibility of social understanding and its necessary reaction, human emancipation through proletarian revolution. Marxism is myth because it juxtaposes the irreducibility of capitalist organization to its negation – violent proletarian revolution. The intermediary stage in this development is radical syndicalism, which organizes workers into groups opposed to bourgeois authority, instills the myth of proletarian revolution in the workers, and allows them in postrevolutionary times to work toward a social arrangement of worker and peasant governance and collaboration. The vehicle through which all this is accomplished is the general strike, whose aim, through the justified violence of its ends, is to facilitate the downfall and ultimate elimination of the bourgeoisie. In doing so the proletariat will lead society to a classless and harmonious stage in history. By stressing the notion of spontaneity Sorel thought he had solved the vexing problems of party and future bureaucracy found in much of the revolutionary literature of his day. In his later years he was interested in the writings of both Lenin and Mussolini.

See also MARXISM, POLITICAL PHILOSOPHY.

J.Bi.

sorites, an argument consisting of categorical propositions that can be represented as (or decomposed into) a sequence of categorical syllogisms such that the conclusion of each syllogism except the last one in the sequence is a premise of the next syllogism in the sequence. An example is 'All cats are felines; all felines are mammals; all mammals are warm-blooded animals; therefore, all cats are warm-blooded animals'. This sorites may be viewed as composed of the two syllogisms 'All cats are felines; all felines are mammals; therefore, all cats are mammals' and 'All cats are mammals; all mammals are warm-blooded animals; therefore, all cats are warm-blooded animals'. A sorites is valid if and only if each categorical syllogism into which it decomposes is valid. In the example, the sorites decomposes into two syllogisms in (the mood) Barbara; since any syllogism in Barbara is valid, the sorites is valid. **See also** SYLLOGISM.   R.W.B.

sorites paradox (from Greek *soros,* 'heap'), any of a number of paradoxes about heaps and their elements, and more broadly about gradations. A single grain of sand cannot be arranged so as to form a heap. Moreover, it seems that given a number of grains insufficient to form a heap, adding just one more grain still does not make a heap. (If a heap cannot be formed with one grain, it cannot be formed with two; if a heap cannot be formed with two, it cannot be formed with three; and so on.) But this seems to lead to the absurdity that however large the number of grains, it is not large enough to form a heap.

A similar paradox can be developed in the opposite direction. A million grains of sand can certainly be arranged so as to form a heap, and it is always possible to remove a grain from a heap in such a way that what is left is also a heap. This seems to lead to the absurdity that a heap can be formed even from just a single grain.

These paradoxes about heaps were known in antiquity (they are associated with Eubulides of Miletus, fourth century B.C.), and have since given their name to a number of similar paradoxes. The loss of a single hair does not make a man bald, and a man with a million hairs is certainly not bald. This seems to lead to the absurd conclusion that even a man with no hairs at all is not bald. Or consider a long painted wall (hundreds of yards or hundreds of miles long). The left-hand region is clearly painted red, but there is a subtle gradation of shades and the right-hand region is clearly yellow. A small double window exposes a small section of the wall at any one time. It is moved progressively rightward, in such a way that at each move after the initial position the left-hand segment of the window exposes just the area that was in the previous position exposed by the right-hand segment. The window is so small relative to the wall that in no position can you tell any difference in color between the exposed areas. When the window is at the extreme left, both exposed areas are certainly red. But as the window moves to the right, the area in the right segment looks just the same color as the area in the left, which you have already pronounced to be red. So it seems that one must call it red too. But then one is led to the absurdity of calling a clearly yellow area red.

As some of these cases suggest, there is a connection with dynamic processes. A tadpole turns gradually into a frog. Yet if you analyze a motion picture of the process, it seems that there are no two adjacent frames of which you can say the earlier shows a tadpole, the later a frog. So it seems that you could argue: if something is a tadpole at a given moment, it must also be a tadpole (and not a frog) a millionth of a second later, and

this seems to lead to the absurd conclusion that a tadpole can never turn into a frog.

Most responses to this paradox attempt to deny the "major premise," the one corresponding to the claim that if you cannot make a heap with n grains of sand then you cannot make a heap with $n + 1$. The difficulty is that the negation of this premise is equivalent, in classical logic, to the proposition that there is a sharp cutoff: that, e.g., there is some number n of grains that are not enough to make a heap, where $n + 1$ are enough to make a heap. The claim of a sharp cutoff may not be so very implausible for heaps (perhaps for things like grains of sand, four is the smallest number which can be formed into a heap) but is very implausible for colors and tadpoles.

There are two main kinds of response to sorites paradoxes. One is to accept that there is in every such case a sharp cutoff, though typically we do not, and perhaps cannot, know where it is. Another kind of response is to evolve a non-classical logic within which one can refuse to accept the major premise without being committed to a sharp cutoff. At present, no such non-classical logic is entirely free of difficulties. So sorites paradoxes are still taken very seriously by contemporary philosophers.

See also MANY-VALUED LOGIC, VAGUENESS.

R.M.S.

sortal. See NATURAL KIND, SORTAL PREDICATE.

sortal predicate, roughly, a predicate whose application to an object says what kind of object it is and implies conditions for objects of that kind to be identical. *Person, green apple, regular hexagon,* and *pile of coal* would generally be regarded as sortal predicates, whereas *tall, green thing,* and *coal* would generally be regarded as non-sortal predicates. An explicit and precise definition of the distinction is hard to come by. Sortal predicates are sometimes said to be distinguished by the fact that they provide a criterion of counting or that they do not apply to the parts of the objects to which they apply, but there are difficulties with each of these characterizations.

The notion figures in recent philosophical discussions on various topics. Robert Ackermann and others have suggested that any scientific law confirmable by observation might require the use of sortal predicates. Thus 'all non-black things are non-ravens', while logically equivalent to the putative scientific law 'all ravens are black', is not itself confirmable by observation because 'non-black' is not a sortal predicate. David Wiggins and others have discussed the idea that all identity claims are sortal-relative in the sense that an appropriate response to the claim $a = b$ is always "the same *what* as *b*?" John Wallace has argued that there would be advantages in relativizing the quantifiers of predicate logic to sortals. 'All humans are mortal' would be rendered $\forall x[m]Dx$, rather than $\forall x(Mx \rightarrow Dx)$. Crispin Wright has suggested that the view that *natural number* is a sortal concept is central to Frege's (or any other) number-theoretic platonism. The word 'sortal' as a technical term in philosophy apparently first occurs in Locke's *Essay Concerning Human Understanding*. Locke argues that the so-called essence of a genus or sort (unlike the real essence of a thing) is merely the abstract idea that the general or sortal name stands for. But 'sortal' has only one occurrence in Locke's *Essay*. Its currency in contemporary philosophical idiom probably should be credited to P. F. Strawson's *Individuals*. The general idea may be traced at least to the notion of *second substance* in Aristotle's *Categories*.

See also ARISTOTLE, CAUSAL LAW, ESSENTIALISM, PHILOSOPHY OF LANGUAGE.   S.T.K.

Soto, Domingo de (1494–1560), Spanish Dominican theologian and philosopher. Born in Segovia, he studied in Alcalá de Henares and Paris, taught at Segovia and Salamanca, and was named official representative of the Holy Roman Empire at the Council of Trent by Charles V. Among Soto's many works, his commentaries on Aristotle's *Physics* and *On the Soul* stand out. He also wrote a book on the nature of grace and an important treatise on law.

Soto was one of the early members of the school of Spanish Thomism, but he did not always follow Aquinas. He rejected the doctrine of the real distinction between essence and existence and adopted Duns Scotus's position that the primary object of human understanding is indeterminate being in general. Apart from metaphysics and theology, Soto's philosophy of law and political theory are historically important. He maintained, contrary to his teacher Vitoria, that law originates in the understanding rather than in the will of the legislator. He also distinguished natural from positive law: the latter arises from the decision of legislators, whereas the former is based on nature. Soto was a founder of the general theory of international law.

See also AQUINAS, PHILOSOPHY OF LAW.
                                                    J.J.E.G.

soul, also called spirit, an entity supposed to be present only in living things, corresponding to the Greek *psyche* and Latin *anima*. Since there seems to be no material difference between an organism in the last moments of its life and the organism's newly dead body, many philosophers since the time of Plato have claimed that the soul is an immaterial component of an organism. Because only material things are observed to be subject to dissolution, Plato took the soul's immateriality as grounds for its immortality. Neither Plato nor Aristotle thought that only persons had souls: Aristotle ascribed souls to animals and plants since they all exhibited some living functions. Unlike Plato, Aristotle denied the transmigration of souls from one species to another or from one body to another after death; he was also more skeptical about the soul's capacity for disembodiment – roughly, survival and functioning without a body. Descartes argued that only persons had souls and that the soul's immaterial nature made freedom possible even if the human body is subject to deterministic physical laws. As the subject of thought, memory, emotion, desire, and action, the soul has been supposed to be an entity that makes self-consciousness possible, that differentiates simultaneous experiences into experiences either of the same person or of different persons, and that accounts for personal identity or a person's continued identity through time. Dualists argue that soul and body must be distinct in order to explain consciousness and the possibility of immortality. Materialists argue that consciousness is entirely the result of complex physical processes. See also DESCARTES, PERSONAL IDENTITY, PLATO, SURVIVAL.   W.E.M.

soundness, (1) (of an argument) the property of being valid and having all true premises; (2) (of a logic) the property of being not too strong in a certain respect. A logic L has *weak soundness* provided every theorem of L is valid. And L has *strong soundness* if for every set Γ of sentences, every sentence deducible from Γ using L is a logical consequence of Γ. See also COMPLETENESS, LOGICAL CONSEQUENCE, LOGICAL FORM, VALID.   G.F.S.

soundness, strong. See SOUNDNESS.

soundness, weak. See SOUNDNESS.

sovereignty, divine. See DIVINE ATTRIBUTES.

space, an extended manifold of several dimensions, where the number of dimensions corresponds to the number of variable magnitudes needed to specify a location in the manifold; in particular, the three-dimensional manifold in which physical objects are situated and with respect to which their mutual positions and distances are defined.

Ancient Greek atomism defined space as the infinite void in which atoms move; but whether space is finite or infinite, and whether void spaces exist, have remained in question. Aristotle described the universe as a finite plenum and reduced space to the aggregate of all places of physical things. His view was preeminent until Renaissance Neoplatonism, the Copernican revolution, and the revival of atomism reintroduced infinite, homogeneous space as a fundamental cosmological assumption.

Further controversy concerned whether the space assumed by early modern astronomy should be thought of as an independently existing thing or as an abstraction from the spatial relations of physical bodies. Interest in the relativity of motion encouraged the latter view, but Newton pointed out that mechanics presupposes absolute distinctions among motions, and he concluded that absolute space must be postulated along with the basic laws of motion (*Principia*, 1687). Leibniz argued for the relational view from the identity of indiscernibles: the parts of space are indistinguishable from one another and therefore cannot be independently existing things. Relativistic physics has defused the original controversy by revealing both space and spatial relations as merely observer-dependent manifestations of the structure of space-time.

Meanwhile, Kant shifted the metaphysical controversy to epistemological grounds by claiming that space, with its Euclidean structure, is neither a "thing-in-itself" nor a relation of things-in-themselves, but the a priori form of outer intuition. His view was challenged by the elaboration of non-Euclidean geometries in the nineteenth century, by Helmholtz's arguments that both intuitive and physical space are known through empirical investigation, and finally by the use of non-Euclidean geometry in the theory of relativity. Precisely what geometrical presuppositions are inherent in human spatial perception, and what must be learned from experience, remain subjects of psychological investigation.

See also RELATIVITY, SPACE-TIME, TIME.
R.D.

space, absolute. See SPACE.

space, life. See LEWIN.

space, mathematical. See SPACE.

space, phase. See STATE.

space, state. See STATE.

space-time, a four-dimensional continuum combining the three dimensions of space with time in order to represent motion geometrically. Each point is the location of an event, all of which together represent "the world" through time; paths in the continuum (worldlines) represent the dynamical histories of moving particles, so that straight worldlines correspond to uniform motions; three-dimensional sections of constant time value ("spacelike hypersurfaces" or "simultaneity slices") represent all of space at a given time.

The idea was foreshadowed when Kant represented "the phenomenal world" as a plane defined by space and time as perpendicular axes (*Inaugural Dissertation*, 1770), and when Joseph Louis Lagrange (1736–1814) referred to mechanics as "the analytic geometry of four dimensions." But classical mechanics assumes a universal standard of simultaneity, and so it can treat space and time separately. The concept of space-time was explicitly developed only when Einstein criticized absolute simultaneity and made the velocity of light a universal constant. The mathematician Hermann Minkowski showed in 1908 that the observer-independent structure of special relativity could be represented by a metric space of four dimensions: observers in relative motion would disagree on intervals of length and time, but agree on a four-dimensional interval combining spatial and temporal measurements. Minkowski's model then made possible the general theory of relativity, which describes gravity as a curvature of space-time in the presence of mass and the paths of falling bodies as the straightest worldlines in curved space-time.

See also EINSTEIN, RELATIVITY, SPACE, TIME.
R.D.

spatiotemporal continuity, a property of the careers, or space-time paths, of well-behaved objects. Let a space-time path be a series of possible spatiotemporal positions, each represented (in a selected coordinate system) by an ordered pair consisting of a time (its temporal component) and a volume of space (its spatial component). Such a path will be spatiotemporally continuous provided it is such that, relative to any inertial frame selected as coordinate system,

(1) for every segment of the series, the temporal components of the members of that segment form a continuous temporal interval; and (2) for any two members $<ti, Vi>$ and $<tj, Vj>$ of the series that differ in their temporal components (ti and tj), if Vi and Vj (the spatial components) differ in either shape, size, or location, then between these members of the series there will be a member whose spatial component is more similar to Vi and Vj in these respects than these are to each other.

This notion is of philosophical interest partly because of its connections with the notions of identity over time and causality. Putting aside such qualifications as quantum considerations may require, material objects (at least macroscopic objects of familiar kinds) apparently cannot undergo discontinuous change of place, and cannot have temporal gaps in their histories, and therefore the path through space-time traced by such an object must apparently be spatiotemporally continuous. More controversial is the claim that spatiotemporal continuity, together with some continuity with respect to other properties, is sufficient as well as necessary for the identity of such objects – e.g., that if a spatiotemporally continuous path is such that the spatial component of each member of the series is occupied by a table of a certain description at the time that is the temporal component of that member, then there is a single table of that description that traces that path. Those who deny this claim sometimes maintain that it is further required for the identity of material objects that there be causal and counterfactual dependence of later states on earlier ones (*ceteris paribus*, if the table had been different yesterday, it would be correspondingly different now). Since it appears that chains of causality must trace spatiotemporally continuous paths, it may be that insofar as spatiotemporal continuity is required for transtemporal identity, this is because it is required for transtemporal causality.

See also PERSONAL IDENTITY, TIME SLICE.
                                                              S.Sho.

speaker's meaning. See MEANING.

special relativity. See RELATIVITY.

special senses. See ARISTOTLE, FACULTY PSYCHOLOGY.

special sensibles. See ARISTOTLE, FACULTY PSYCHOLOGY.

species. See DEFINITION.

species, intentional. See AQUINAS, ARISTOTLE.

speciesism. See MORAL STATUS.

species problem. See PHILOSOPHY OF BIOLOGY.

specious present, the supposed time between past and future. The term was first offered by E. R. Clay in *The Alternative: A Study in Psychology* (1882), and was cited by James in Chapter XV of his *Principles of Psychology* (1890). Clay challenges the assumption that the "present" as a "datum" is given as "present" to us in our experience. "The present to which the datum refers is really a part of the past – a recent past – delusively given as benign time that intervenes between the past and the future. Let it be named the specious present, and let the past that is given as being the past be known as the obvious past."

For James, this position is supportive of his contention that consciousness is a stream and can be divided into parts only by conceptual addition, i.e., only by our ascribing past, present, and future to what is, in our actual experience, a seamless flow. James holds that the "practically cognized present is no knife-edge but a saddleback," a sort of "ducatum" which we experience as a whole, and only upon reflective attention do we "distinguish its beginning from its end."

Whereas Clay refers to the datum of the present as "delusive," one might rather say that it is perpetually elusive, for as we have our experience, now, it is always bathed retrospectively and prospectively. Contrary to common wisdom, no single experience ever is had by our consciousness utterly alone, single and without relations, fore and aft.

See also TIME.   J.J.M.

speckled hen. See PROBLEM OF THE SPECKLED HEN.

spectrum inversion. See QUALIA.

speculative philosophy, a form of theorizing that goes beyond verifiable observation; specifically, a philosophical approach informed by the impulse to construct a grand narrative of a worldview that encompasses the whole of reality. Speculative philosophy purports to bind together reflections on the existence and nature of the cosmos, the psyche, and God. It sets for its goal a unifying matrix and an overarching system wherewith to comprehend the considered judgments of cosmology, psychology, and theology.

Hegel's absolute idealism, particularly as developed in his later thought, paradigmatically illustrates the requirements for speculative philosophizing. His system of idealism offered a vision of the unity of the categories of human thought as they come to realization in and through their opposition to each other. Speculative thought tends to place a premium on universality, totality, and unity; and it tends to marginalize the concrete particularities of the natural and social world. In its aggressive use of the systematic principle, geared to a unification of human experience, speculative philosophy aspires to a comprehensive understanding and ˙ structural interrelations of the ˙ience, morality, art, and reli-

C.O.S.

PRACTICAL REASONING.

˙eory of language use, ˙s, as opposed to the theory of meaning, or semantics. Based on the meaning–use distinction, it categorizes systematically the sorts of things that can be done with words and explicates the ways these are determined, underdetermined, or undetermined by the meanings of the words used. Relying further on the distinction between *speaker meaning* and *linguistic meaning*, it aims to characterize the nature of communicative intentions and how they are expressed and recognized.

Speech acts are a species of intentional action. In general, one and the same utterance may comprise a number of distinct though related acts, each corresponding to a different intention on the part of the speaker. Beyond intending to produce a certain sequence of sounds forming a sentence in English, a person who utters the sentence 'The door is open', e.g., is likely to be intending to perform, in the terminology of J. L. Austin (*How to Do Things with Words*, 1962), (1) the *locutionary act* of saying (expressing the proposition) that a certain door is open, (2) the *illocutionary act* of making the statement (expressing the belief) that it is open, and (3) the *perlocutionary act* of getting his listener to believe that it is open. In so doing, he may be performing the indirect speech act of requesting (illocutionary) the listener to close the door and of getting (perlocutionary) the hearer to close the door.

The primary focus of speech act theory is on illocutionary acts, which may be classified in a variety of ways. Statements, predictions, and answers exemplify *constatives;* requests, commands and permissions are *directives;* promises, offers, and bets are *commissives;* greetings, apologies, and congratulations are *acknowledgments*. These are all *communicative* illocutionary acts, each distinguished by the type of psychological state expressed by the speaker. Successful communication consists in the audience's recognition of the speaker's intention to be expressing a certain psychological state with a certain content. *Conventional* illocutionary acts, on the other hand, effect or officially affect institutional states of affairs. Examples of the former are appointing, resigning, sentencing, and adjourning; examples of the latter are assessing, acquitting, certifying, and grading. (See Kent Bach and Robert M. Harnish, *Linguistic Communication and Speech Acts*, 1979.)

The type of act an utterance exemplifies determines its *illocutionary force*. In the example 'The door is open', the utterance has the force of both a statement and a request. The *illocutionary force potential* of a sentence is the force or forces with which it can be used literally, e.g., in the case of the sentence 'The door is open', as a statement but not as a request. The *felicity conditions* on an illocutionary act pertain not only to its communicative or institutional success but also to its sincerity, appropriateness, and effectiveness.

An explicit *performative utterance* is an illocutionary act performed by uttering an indicative sentence in the simple present tense with a verb naming the type of act being performed, e.g., 'I apologize for everything I did' and 'You are requested not to smoke'. The adverb 'hereby' may be used before the *performative verb* ('apologize' and 'request' in these examples) to indicate that the very utterance being made is the vehicle of the performance of the illocutionary act in question. A good test for distinguishing illocutionary from perlocutionary acts is to determine whether a verb naming the act can be used performatively. Austin exploited the phenomenon of performative utterances to expose the common philosophical error of assuming that the primary use of language is to make statements.

See also AUSTIN, J. L.; PHILOSOPHY OF LANGUAGE.   K.B.

Spencer, Herbert (1820–1903), English philosopher, social reformer, and editor of *The Economist*. In epistemology, Spencer adopted the nineteenth-century trend toward positivism: the only reliable knowledge of the universe is to be found in the sciences. His ethics were utilitarian, following Bentham and J. S. Mill: pleasure and pain are the criteria of value as signs of happiness or unhappiness in the individual. His Synthetic Philosophy, expounded in books written over many years, assumed (both in biology and psychology) the existence of Lamarckian evolution: given a characteristic environment, every animal possesses a disposition to make itself into what it will, failing maladaptive interventions, eventually become. The dispositions gain expression as inherited acquired habits. Spencer could not accept that species originate by chance variations and natural selection alone: direct adaptation to environmental constraints is mainly responsible for biological changes. Evolution also includes the progression of societies in the direction of a dynamical equilibrium of individuals: the human condition is perfectible because human faculties are completely adapted to life in society, implying that evil and immorality will eventually disappear. His ideas on evolution predated publication of the major works of Darwin; A. R. Wallace was influenced by his writings.   R.E.B.

Speusippus. See ACADEMY.

Spinoza, Baruch (1632–77), Dutch metaphysician, epistemologist, psychologist, moral philosopher, political theorist, and philosopher of religion, generally regarded as one of the most important figures of seventeenth-century rationalism.

Life and works. Born and educated in the Jewish community of Amsterdam, he forsook his given name 'Baruch' in favor of the Latin 'Benedict' at the age of twenty-two. Between 1652 and 1656 he studied the philosophy of Descartes in the school of Francis van den Enden. Having developed unorthodox views of the divine nature (and having ceased to be fully observant of Jewish practice), he was excommunicated by the Jewish community in 1656. He spent his entire life in Holland; after leaving Amsterdam in 1660, he resided successively in Rijnsburg, Voorburg, and the Hague. He supported himself at least partly through grinding lenses, and his knowledge of optics involved him in an area of inquiry of great importance to seventeenth-century science. Acquainted with such leading intellectual figures as Leibniz, Huygens, and Henry Oldenberg, he declined a professorship at the University of Heidelberg partly on the grounds that it might interfere with his intellectual freedom. His premature death at the age of forty-four was due to consumption.

The only work published under Spinoza's name during his lifetime was his *Principles of Descartes's Philosophy* (*Renati Des Cartes Principiorum Philosophiae, Pars I et II*, 1663), an attempt to recast and present Parts I and II of Descartes's *Principles of Philosophy* in the manner that Spinoza called *geometrical order* or *geometrical method*. Modeled on the *Elements* of Euclid and on what Descartes called the method of synthesis, Spinoza's "geometrical order" involves an initial set of definitions and axioms, from which various propositions are demonstrated, with notes or scholia attached where necessary. This work, which established his credentials as an expositor of Cartesian philosophy, had its origins in his endeavor to teach Descartes's *Principles of Philosophy* to a private student. Spinoza's *Theological-Political Treatise* (*Tractatus Theologico-Politicus*) was published anonymously in 1670. After his death, his close circle of friends published his *Posthumous Works* (*Opera Postuma*, 1677), which included his masterpieces, *Ethic, Demonstrated in Geometrical Order* (*Ethica, Ordine Geometrico Demonstrata*). The *Posthumous Works* also included his early unfinished *Treatise on the Emendation of the Intellect* (*Tractatus de Intellectus Emendatione*), his later unfinished *Political Treatise* (*Tractatus Politicus*), a *Hebrew Grammar*, and *Correspondence*. An unpublished early work entitled *Short Treatise on God, Man, and His Well-Being* (*Korte Vorhandelung van God, de Mensch en deszelvs Welstand*), in many ways a forerunner of the *Ethics*, was rediscovered (in copied manuscript) and published in the nineteenth century. Spinoza's authorship of two brief scientific treatises, *On the Rainbow* and *On the Calculation of Chances*, is still disputed.

Metaphysics. Spinoza often uses the term 'God, or Nature' (*"Deus, sive Natura"*), and this identification of God with Nature is at the heart of his metaphysics. Because of this identification, his philosophy is often regarded as a version of pantheism and/or naturalism. But although philosophy begins with metaphysics for Spinoza, his metaphysics is ultimately in the service of his ethics. Because his naturalized God has no desires or purposes, human ethics cannot properly be derived from divine command. Rather, Spinozistic ethics seeks to demonstrate, from an adequate understanding of the divine nature and its expression in human nature, the way in which human beings can maximize their advantage. Central to the successful pursuit of this advantage is adequate knowledge, which leads to increasing control of the passions and to cooperative action.

Spinoza's ontology, like that of Descartes, consists of substances, their attributes (which Descartes called *principal attributes*), and their modes. In the *Ethics*, Spinoza defines 'substance' as what is "in itself, and is conceived through itself"; 'attribute' as that which "the intellect perceives of a substance as constituting its essence"; and 'mode' as "the affections of a substance, or that which is in another through which also it is conceived." While Descartes had recognized a strict sense in which only God is a substance, he also recognized a second sense in which there are two kinds of created substances, each with its own principal attribute: extended substances, whose only principal attribute is extension; and minds, whose only principal attribute is thought. Spinoza, in contrast, consistently maintains that there is only one substance. His metaphysics is thus a form of substantial monism. This one substance is God, which Spinoza defines as "a being absolutely infinite, i.e., a substance consisting of an infinity of attributes, of which each expresses an eternal and infinite essence." Thus, whereas Descartes limited each created substance to one principal attribute, Spinoza claims that the one substance has infinite attributes, each expressing the divine nature without limitation in its own way. Of these infinite attributes, however, humans can comprehend only two: extension and thought. Within each attribute, the modes of God are of two kinds: infinite modes, which are pervasive features of each attribute, such as the laws of nature; and finite modes, which are local and limited modifications of substance. There is an infinite sequence of finite modes.

Descartes regarded a human being as a substantial union of two different substances, the thinking soul and the extended body, in causal interaction with each other. Spinoza, in contrast, regards a human being as a finite mode of God, existing simultaneously in God as a mode of thought *and* as a mode of extension. He holds that every mode of extension is literally identical with the mode of thought that is the "idea of" that mode of extension. Since the human mind is the idea of the human body, it follows that the human mind and the human body are literally the same thing, conceived under two different attributes. Because they are actually identical, there is no causal interaction between the mind and the body; but there is a complete *parallelism* between what occurs in the mind and what occurs in the body. Since every mode of exten-

sion has a corresponding and identical mode of thought (however rudimentary that might be), Spinoza allows that every mode of extension is "animated to some degree"; his view is thus a form of *panpsychism*.

Another central feature of Spinoza's metaphysics is his necessitarianism, expressed in his claim that "things could have been produced . . . in no other way, and in no other order" than that in which they have been produced. He derives this necessitarianism from his doctrine that God exists necessarily (for which he offers several arguments, including a version of the ontological argument) and his doctrine that everything that can follow from the divine nature must necessarily do so. Thus, although he does not use the term, he accepts a very strong version of the principle of sufficient reason. At the outset of the *Ethics*, he defines a thing as free when its actions are determined by its own nature alone. Only God – whose actions are determined entirely by the necessity of his own nature, and for whom nothing is external – is completely free in this sense. Nevertheless, human beings can achieve a relative freedom to the extent that they live the kind of life described in the later parts of the *Ethics*. Hence, Spinoza is a compatibilist concerning the relation between freedom and determinism. "Freedom of the will" in any sense that implies a *lack* of causal determination, however, is simply an illusion based on ignorance of the true causes of a being's actions. The recognition that all occurrences are causally determined, Spinoza holds, has a positive consolatory power that aids one in controlling the passions.

Epistemology and psychology. Like other rationalists, Spinoza distinguishes two representational faculties: the imagination and the intellect. The imagination is a faculty of forming imagistic representations of things, derived ultimately from the mechanisms of the senses; the intellect is a faculty of forming adequate, nonimagistic conceptions of things. He also distinguishes three "kinds of knowledge." The first or lowest kind he calls opinion or imagination (*opinio, imaginatio*). It includes "random or indeterminate experience" (*experientia vaga*) and also "hearsay, or knowledge from mere signs"; it thus depends on the confused and mutilated deliverances of the senses, and is inadequate. The second kind of knowledge he calls reason (*ratio*); it depends on *common notions* (i.e., features of things that are "common to all, and equally in the part and in the whole") or on adequate knowledge of the properties (as opposed to the essences) of things. The third kind of knowledge he calls intuitive knowledge (*scientia intuitiva*); it proceeds from adequate knowledge of the essence or attributes of God to knowledge of the essence of things, and hence proceeds in the proper order, from causes to effects. Both the second and third kinds of knowledge are adequate. The third kind is preferable, however, as involving not only certain knowledge *that* something is so, but also knowledge of *how* and *why* it is so.

Because there is only one substance – God – the individual things of the world are not distinguished from one another by any difference of substance. Rather, among the internal qualitative modifications and differentiations of each divine attribute, there are patterns that have a tendency to endure; these constitute individual things. (As they occur within the attribute of extension, Spinoza calls these patterns *fixed proportions of motion and rest*.) Although these individual things are thus modes of the one substance, rather than substances in their own right, each has a nature or essence describable in terms of the thing's particular pattern and its mechanisms for the preservation of its own being. This tendency toward self-preservation Spinoza calls *conatus* (sometimes translated as 'endeavor'). Every individual thing has some *conatus*. An individual thing acts, or is active, to the extent that what occurs can be explained or understood through its own nature (i.e., its self-preservatory mechanism) alone; it is passive to the extent that what happens must be explained through the nature of other forces impinging on it. Thus, every thing, to whatever extent it can, actively strives to persevere in its existence; and whatever aids this self-preservation constitutes that individual's advantage.

Spinoza's specifically human psychology is an application of this more general doctrine of *conatus*. That application is made through appeal to several specific characteristics of human beings: they form imagistic representations of other individuals by means of their senses; they are sufficiently complex to undergo increases and decreases in their capacity for action; and they are capable of engaging in reason. The fundamental concepts of his psychology are desire, which is *conatus* itself, especially as one is conscious of it as directed toward attaining a particular object; pleasure, which is an increase in capacity for action; and pain, which is a decrease in capacity for action. He defines other emotions in terms of these basic emotions, as they occur in particular combinations, in particular kinds of circumstances, with particular kinds of causes,

and/or with particular kinds of objects. When a person is the adequate cause of his or her own emotions, these emotions are active emotions; otherwise, they are passions. Desire and pleasure can be either active emotions or passions, depending on the circumstances; pain, however, can only be a passion. Spinoza does not deny the phenomenon of altruism: one's self-preservatory mechanism, and hence one's desire, can become focused on a wide variety of objects, including the well-being of a loved person or object – even to one's own detriment. However, because he reduces all human motivation, including altruistic motivation, to permutations of the endeavor to seek one's own advantage, his theory is arguably a form of psychological egoism.

Ethics. Spinoza's ethical theory does not take the form of a set of moral commands. Rather, he seeks to demonstrate, by considering human actions and appetites objectively – "just as if it were a Question of lines, planes, and bodies" – wherein a person's true advantage lies. Readers who genuinely grasp the demonstrated truths will, he holds, *ipso facto* be motivated, to at least some extent, to live their lives accordingly. Thus, Spinozistic ethics seeks to show how a person acts when "guided by *reason*"; to act in this way is at the same time to act with virtue, or power. All actions that result from understanding – i.e., all virtuous actions – may be attributed to strength of character (*fortitudo*). Such virtuous actions may be further divided into two classes: those due to tenacity (*animositas*), or "the Desire by which each one strives, solely from the dictate of reason, to preserve his being"; and those due to nobility (*generositas*), or "the Desire by which each one strives, solely from the dictate of reason, to aid other men and join them to him in friendship." Thus, the virtuous person does not merely pursue private advantage, but seeks to cooperate with others; returns love for hatred; always acts honestly, not deceptively; and seeks to join himself with others in a political state. Nevertheless, the ultimate reason for aiding others and joining them to oneself in friendship is that "nothing is more useful to man than man" – i.e., because doing so is conducive to one's own advantage, and particularly to one's pursuit of knowledge, which is a good that can be shared without loss. Although Spinoza holds that we generally use the terms 'good' and 'evil' simply to report subjective appearances – so that we call "good" whatever we desire, and "evil" whatever we seek to avoid – he proposes that we define 'good' philosophically as 'what we certainly know to be useful to us', and 'evil' as 'what we certainly know prevents us from being masters of some good'. Since God is perfect and has no needs, it follows that nothing is either good or evil for God. Spinoza's ultimate appeal to the agent's advantage arguably renders his ethical theory a form of ethical egoism, even though he emphasizes the existence of common shareable goods and the (instrumental) ethical importance of cooperation with others. However, it is not a form of hedonism; for despite the prominence he gives to pleasure, the ultimate aim of human action is a higher state of perfection or capacity for action, of whose increasing attainment pleasure is only an indicator.

A human being whose self-preservatory mechanism is driven or distorted by external forces is said to be in bondage to the passions; in contrast, one who successfully pursues only what is truly advantageous, in consequence of genuine understanding of where that advantage properly lies, is free. Accordingly, Spinoza also expresses his conception of a virtuous life guided by reason in terms of an ideal "free man." Above all, the free man seeks understanding of himself and of Nature. Adequate knowledge, and particularly knowledge of the third kind, leads to blessedness, to peace of mind, and to the intellectual love of God. Blessedness is not a reward for virtue, however, but rather an integral aspect of the virtuous life. The human mind is itself a part of the infinite intellect of God, and adequate knowledge is an eternal aspect of that infinite intellect. Hence, as one gains knowledge, a greater part of one's own mind comes to be identified with something that is eternal, and one becomes less dependent on – and less disturbed by – the local forces of one's immediate environment. Accordingly, the free man "thinks of nothing less than of death, and his wisdom is a meditation on life, not on death." Moreover, just as one's adequate knowledge is literally an eternal part of the infinite intellect of God, the resulting blessedness, peace of mind, and intellectual love are literally aspects of what might be considered God's own eternal "emotional" life. Although this endows the free man with a kind of blessed immortality, it is not a personal immortality, since the sensation and memory that are essential to personal individuality are not eternal. Rather, the free man achieves during his lifetime an increasing participation in a body of adequate knowledge that has itself always been eternal, so that, at death, a large part of the free man's mind has become identified with the eternal. It is thus a kind of "immortality" in which one can participate while one lives, not merely when one dies.

Politics and philosophical theology. Spinoza's political theory, like that of Hobbes, treats rights and power as equivalent. Citizens give up rights to the state for the sake of the protection that the state can provide. Hobbes, however, regards this social contract as nearly absolute, one in which citizens give up all of their rights except the right to resist death. Spinoza, in contrast, emphasizes that citizens cannot give up the right to pursue their own advantage as they see it, in its full generality; and hence that the power, and right, of any actual state is always limited by the state's practical ability to enforce its dictates so as to alter the citizens' continuing perception of their own advantage. Furthermore, he has a more extensive conception of the nature of an individual's own advantage than Hobbes, since for him one's own true advantage lies not merely in fending off death and pursuing pleasure, but in achieving the adequate knowledge that brings blessedness and allows one to participate in that which is eternal. In consequence, Spinoza, unlike Hobbes, recommends a limited, constitutional state that encourages freedom of expression and religious toleration. Such a state – itself a kind of individual – best preserves its own being, and provides both the most stable and the most beneficial form of government for its citizens.

In his *Theological-Political Treatise*, Spinoza also takes up popular religion, the interpretation of Scripture, and their bearing on the well-being of the state. He characterizes the Old Testament prophets as individuals whose vivid imaginations produced messages of political value for the ancient Hebrew state. Using a naturalistic outlook and historical hermeneutic methods that anticipate the later "higher criticism" of the Bible, he seeks to show that Scriptural writers themselves consistently treat only justice and charity as essential to salvation, and hence that dogmatic doxastic requirements are not justified by Scripture. Popular religion should thus propound only these two requirements, which it may imaginatively represent, to the minds of the many, as the requirements for rewards granted by a divine Lawgiver. The few, who are more philosophical, and who thus rely on intellect, will recognize that the natural laws of human psychology require charity and justice as conditions of happiness, and that what the vulgar construe as rewards granted by personal divine intervention are in fact the natural consequences of a virtuous life.

Because of his identificaton of God with Nature and his treatment of popular religion, Spinoza's contemporaries often regarded his philosophy as a thinly disguised atheism. Paradoxically, however, nineteenth-century Romanticism embraced him for his pantheism; Novalis, e.g., famously characterized him as "the God-intoxicated man." In fact, Spinoza ascribes to Nature most of the characteristics that Western theologians have ascribed to God: Spinozistic Nature is infinite, eternal, necessarily existing, the object of an ontological argument, the first cause of all things, all-knowing, and the being whose contemplation produces blessedness, intellectual love, and participation in a kind of immortality or eternal life. Spinoza's claim to affirm the existence of God is therefore no mere evasion. However, he emphatically denies that God is a person or acts for purposes; that anything is good or evil from the divine perspective; or that there is a personal immortality involving memory.

In addition to his influence on the history of biblical criticism and on literature (including not only Novalis but such writers as Wordsworth, Coleridge, Heine, Shelley, George Eliot, George Sand, Somerset Maugham, Jorge Luis Borges, and Bernard Malamud), Spinoza has affected the philosophical outlooks of such diverse twentieth-century thinkers as Freud and Einstein. Contemporary physicists have seen in his monistic metaphysics an anticipation of twentieth-century field metaphysics. More generally, he is a leading intellectual forebear of twentieth-century determinism and naturalism, and of the mind–body identity theory.

See also DESCARTES, LEIBNIZ, RATIONALISM.   D.Garr.

Spir, Afrikan (1837–90), German philosopher. He served in the Crimean War as a Russian officer. A non-academic, he published books in German and French. His major works are *Forschung nach der Gewissheit in der Erkenntnis der Wirklichkeit* (*Inquiry concerning Certainty in the Knowledge of Actuality,* 1869) and the two-volume *Denken und Wirklichkeit: Versuch einer Erneuerung der kritischen Philosophie* (*Thought and Actuality: Attempt at a Revival of Critical Philosophy,* 1873).

Thought and Actuality presents a metaphysics based on the radical separation of the apparent world and an absolute reality. All we can know about the "unconditioned" is that it must conform with the principle of identity. While retaining the unknowable thing-in-itself of Kant, Spir argued for the empirical reality of time, which is given to us in immediate experience and depends on our experience of a succession of differential states. The aim of philosophy is to reach fundamental and immediate certainties. Of the works included in his *Gesammelte Schriften* (1883–84), only a relatively minor study, *Right and Wrong,* was translated into English (in 1954).

There are a number of references to Spir in the writings of Nietzsche, which indicate that some of Nietzsche's central notions were influenced, both positively and negatively, by Spir's analyses of becoming and temporality, as well as by his concept of the separation of the world of appearance and the "true world."   G.J.S.

spirit. See SOUL.

spirit, Absolute. See HEGEL.

spissitude. See MORE, HENRY.

split brain effects, a wide array of behavioral effects consequent upon the severing of the cerebral commisures, and generally interpreted as indicating asymmetry in cerebral functions. The human brain has considerable left–right functional differentiation, or asymmetry, that affects behavior. The most obvious example is handedness. By the 1860s Bouillaud, Dax, and Broca had observed that the effects of unilateral damage indicated that the left hemisphere was preferentially involved in language. Since the 1960s, this commitment to functional asymmetry has been reinforced by studies of patients in whom communication between the hemispheres has been surgically disrupted.

Split brain effects depend on severing the cerebral commisures, and especially the corpus callosum, which are neural structures mediating communication between the cerebral hemispheres. Commisurotomies have been performed since the 1940s to control severe epilepsy. This is intended to leave both hemispheres intact and functioning independently. Beginning in the 1960s, J. E. Bogen, M. S. Gazzaniga, and R. W. Sperry conducted an array of psychological tests to evaluate the distinctive abilities of the different hemispheres. Ascertaining the degree of cerebral asymmetry depends on a carefully controlled experimental design in which access of the disassociated hemispheres to peripheral cues is limited. The result has been a wide array of striking results. For example, patients are unable to match an object such as a key felt in one hand with a similar object felt in the other; patients are unable to name an object held in the left hand, though they can name an object held in the right.

Researchers have concluded that these results confirm a clear lateralization of speech, writing, and calculation in the left hemisphere (for right-handed patients), leaving the right hemisphere largely unable to respond in speech or writing, and typically unable to perform even simple calculations. It is often concluded that the left hemisphere is specialized for verbal and analytic modes of thinking, while the right hemisphere is specialized for more spatial and synthetic modes of thinking. The precise character and extent of these differences in normal subjects are less clear.

R.C.R.

spontaneity, liberty of. See FREE WILL PROBLEM, HUME.

spread law. See RELEVANCE LOGIC.

square of opposition, a graphic representation of various logical relations among categorical propositions. (Relations among modal and even among hypothetical propositions have also been represented on the square.) Two propositions are said to be each other's (1) *contradictories* if exactly one of them must be true and exactly one false; (2) *contraries* if they could not both be true although they could both be false; and (3) *subcontraries* if at least one of them must be true although both of them may be true. There is a relation of (4) *subalternation* of one proposition, called *subaltern,* to another called *superaltern,* if the truth of the latter implies the truth of the former, but not conversely.

Applying these definitions to the four types of categorical propositions, we find that *SaP* and *SoP* are contradictories, and so are *SeP* and *SiP. SaP* and *SeP* are contraries. *SiP* and *SoP* are subcontraries. *SiP* is subaltern to *SaP,* and *SoP* is subaltern to *SeP.* These relations can be represented graphically in a square of opposition:

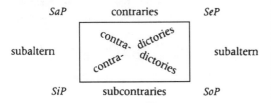

The four relations on the traditional square are expressed in the following theses:

Contradictories: $SaP \equiv \sim SoP, SeP \equiv \sim SiP$
Contraries: $\sim(SaP \text{ & } SeP) \text{ or } SaP \rightarrow \sim SeP$

Subcontraries: $SiP \lor SoP$
Subalterns: $SaP \rightarrow SiP, SeP \rightarrow SoP$

For these relations to hold, an underlying existential assumption must be satisfied: the terms serving as subjects of propositions must be satisfied, not empty (e.g., 'man' is satisfied and 'elf' empty). Only the contradictory opposition remains without that assumption. Modern interpretations of categorical propositions exclude the existential assumption; thus, only the contradictory opposition remains in the square.

See also SYLLOGISM.   I.Bo.

square of opposition, modal. See CONTINGENT.

stadium paradox. See ZENO'S PARADOXES.

Stagirite. See ARISTOTLE.

standard analysis. See MATHEMATICAL ANALYSIS.

standard interpretation. See FORMAL SEMANTICS.

standard model, a term that, like 'non-standard model', is used with regard to theories that systematize (part of) our knowledge of some mathematical structure, for instance the structure of natural numbers with addition, multiplication, and the successor function, or the structure of real numbers with ordering, addition, and multiplication. Models isomorphic to this intended mathematical structure are the "standard models" of the theory, while any other, non-isomorphic, model of the theory is a 'non-standard' model. Since Peano arithmetic is incomplete, it has consistent extensions that have no standard model. But there are also non-standard, countable models of complete number theory, the set of all true first-order sentences about natural numbers, as was first shown by Skolem in 1934.

Categorical theories do not have a non-standard model. It is less clear whether there is a standard model of set theory, although a countable model would certainly count as non-standard. The Skolem paradox is that any first-order formulation of set theory, like ZF, due to Zermelo and Fraenkel, has a countable model, while it seems to assert the existence of non-countable sets. Many other important mathematical structures cannot be characterized by a categorical set of first-order axioms, and thus allow non-standard models. The American philosopher Putnam has argued that this fact has important implications for the debate about realism in the philosophy of language. If axioms cannot capture the "intuitive" notion of a set, what could? Some of his detractors have pointed out that within second-order logic categorical characterizations are often possible. But Putnam has objected that the intended interpretation of second-order logic itself is not fixed by the use of the formalism of second-order logic, where "use" is determined by the rules of inference for second-order logic we know about. Moreover, categorical theories are sometimes uninformative.

See also CATEGORICAL THEORY, GÖDEL'S INCOMPLETENESS THEOREMS, SET THEORY.
Z.G.S.

standard semantics. See SECOND-ORDER LOGIC.

state, the way an object or system basically *is;* the fundamental, intrinsic properties of an object or system, and the basis of its other properties. An *instantaneous state* is a state at a given time. *State variables* are constituents of a state whose values may vary with time. In classical or Newtonian mechanics the instantaneous state of an n-particle system consists of the positions and momenta (masses multiplied by velocities) of the n particles at a given time. Other mechanical properties are functions of those in states. Fundamental and derived properties are often, though possibly misleadingly, called *observables*. The set of a system's possible states can be represented as an abstract phase space or state space, with dimensions or coordinates for (the components of) each state variable.

In quantum theory, states do not fix the particular values of observables, only the probabilities of observables assuming particular values in particular measurement situations. For positivism or instrumentalism, specifying a quantum state does nothing more than provide a means for calculating such probabilities. For realism, it does more – e.g., it refers to the basis of a quantum system's probabilistic dispositions or propensities. Vectors in Hilbert spaces represent possible states, and Hermitian operators on vectors represent observables.

See also DISPOSITION, INSTRUMENTALISM, PROBABILITY, PROPENSITY, QUANTUM MECHANICS, STATE OF AFFAIRS.   D.S.

state, liberal theory of the. See LOCKE, POLITICAL PHILOSOPHY.

state, political. See POLITICAL PHILOSOPHY.

state description. See CARNAP.

state function. See QUANTUM MECHANICS.

statement, basic. See FOUNDATIONALISM.

statement form. See LOGICAL FORM.

state of affairs, a possibility, actuality, or impossibility of the kind expressed by a nominalization of a declarative sentence. (The declarative sentence 'This die comes up six' can be nominalized either through the construction 'that this die comes up six' or through the likes of 'this die's coming up six'. The resulting nominalizations might be interpreted as naming corresponding propositions or states of affairs.)

States of affairs come in several varieties. Some are *possible* states of affairs, or possibilities. Consider the possibility of a certain die coming up six when rolled next. This possibility is a state of affairs, as is its "complement" – the die's *not* coming up six when rolled next. There is in addition the state of affairs which *conjoins* that die's coming up six with its *not* coming up six. And *this* (contradictory) state of affairs is of course *not* a possibility, not a possible state of affairs. Moreover, for every actual state of affairs there is a non-actual one, its complement.

For every proposition there is hence a state of affairs: possible or impossible, actual or not. Indeed some consider propositions to *be* states of affairs. Some take facts to be actual states of affairs, while others prefer to define them as true propositions. If propositions *are* states of affairs, then facts are of course *both* actual states of affairs and true propositions.

In a very broad sense, events are just possible states of affairs; in a narrower sense they are contingent states of affairs; and in a still narrower sense they are contingent *and* particular states of affairs, involving just the exemplification of an n-adic property by a sequence of individuals of length n. In a yet narrower sense events are only those particular and contingent states of affairs that entail *change*. A baseball's remaining round throughout a certain period does not count as an event in this narrower sense but only as a *state* of that baseball, unlike the event of its being hit by a certain bat.

See also CONDITION, PROPOSITION.   E.S.

state of nature. See HOBBES, LOCKE.

state space. See STATE.

state table. See TURING MACHINE.

state variable. See STATE.

state verb. See ACTION VERB.

statistical explanation, an explanation expressed in an explanatory argument containing premises and conclusions making claims about statistical probabilities. These arguments include deductions of less general from more general laws and differ from other such explanations only insofar as the contents of the laws imply claims about statistical probability.

Most philosophical discussion in the latter half of the twentieth century has focused on statistical explanation of events rather than laws. This type of argument was discussed by Ernest Nagel (*The Structure of Science,* 1961) under the rubric "probabilistic explanation," and by Hempel (*Aspects of Scientific Explanation,* 1965) as "inductive statistical" explanation. The explanans contains a statement asserting that a given system responds in one of several ways specified by a sample space of possible outcomes on a trial or experiment of some type, and that the statistical probability of an event (represented by a set of points in the sample space) on the given kind of trial is also given for each such event. Thus, the statement might assert that the statistical probability is near 1 of the relative frequency r/n of heads in n tosses being close to the statistical probability p of heads on a single toss, where the sample space consists of the 2^n possible sequences of heads and tails in n tosses. Nagel and Hempel understood such statistical probability statements to be covering laws, so that inductive-statistical explanation and deductive-nomological explanation of events are two species of covering law explanation.

The explanans also contains a claim that an experiment of the kind mentioned in the statistical assumption has taken place (e.g., the coin has been tossed n times). The explanandum asserts that an event of some kind has occurred (e.g., the coin has landed heads approximately r times in the n tosses).

In many cases, the kind of experiment can be described equivalently as an n-fold repetition of some other kind of experiment (as a thousand-fold repetition of the tossing of a given coin) or as the implementation of the kind of trial (thousand-fold tossing of the coin) one time. Hence, statistical explanation of events can always be construed as deriving conclusions about "single cases" from assumptions about statistical probabilities even when the concern is to explain mass phenomena. Yet, many authors controversially

contrast statistical explanation in quantum mechanics, which is alleged to require a single-case propensity interpretation of statistical probability, with statistical explanation in statistical mechanics, genetics, and the social sciences, which allegedly calls for a frequency interpretation.

The structure of the explanatory argument of such statistical explanation has the form of a direct inference from assumptions about statistical probabilities and the kind of experiment trial which has taken place to the outcome. One controversial aspect of direct inference is the problem of the reference class. Since the early nineteenth century, statistical probability has been understood to be relative to the way the experiment or trial is described. Authors like J. Venn, Peirce, R. A. Fisher, and Reichenbach, among many others, have been concerned with how to decide on which kind of trial to base a direct inference when the trial under investigation is correctly describable in several ways and the statistical probabilities of possible outcomes may differ relative to the different sorts of descriptions. The most comprehensive discussion of this problem of the reference class is found in the work of H. E. Kyburg (e.g., *Probability and the Logic of Rational Belief,* 1961). Hempel acknowledged its importance as an "epistemic ambiguity" in inductive statistical explanation.

Controversy also arises concerning inductive acceptance. May the conclusion of an explanatory direct inference be a judgment as to the subjective probability that the outcome event occurred? May a judgment that the outcome event occurred is inductively "accepted" be made? Is some other mode of assessing the claim about the outcome appropriate? Hempel's discussion of the "nonconjunctiveness of inductive-statistical" explanation derives from Kyburg's earlier account of direct inference where high probability is assumed to be sufficient for acceptance. Non-conjunctiveness has been avoided by abandoning the sufficiency of high probability (I. Levi, *Gambling with Truth,* 1967) or by denying that direct inference in inductive-statistical explanation involves inductive acceptance at all (R. C. Jeffrey, "Statistical Explanation vs. Statistical Inference," in *Essays in Honor of C. G. Hempel,* 1969).

See also CAUSATION, EXPLANATION.   I.L.

statistical independence. See PROBABILITY.

statistical law. See CAUSAL LAW.

statistical probability. See PROBABILITY.

Steiner, Rudolf (1861–1925), Austrian spiritualist and founder of anthroposophy. Trained as a scientist, he edited Goethe's scientific writings and prepared the standard edition of his complete works from 1889 to 1896. Steiner's major work, *Die Philosophie der Freiheit*, was published in 1894. His *Friedrich Nietzsche: Ein Kämpfer gegen seine Zeit* (1895) was translated in 1960 by Margaret deRis as *Friedrich Nietzsche: Fighter for Freedom*.

Steiner taught at a workingmen's college and edited a literary journal, *Magazin für Literatur*, in Berlin. In 1901 he embraced a spiritualism which emphasized a form of knowledge that transcended sensory experience and was attained by the "higher self." He held that man had previously been attuned to spiritual processes by virtue of a dreamlike state of consciousness, but was diverted from this consciousness by preoccupation with material entities. Through training, individuals could retrieve their innate capacity to perceive a spiritual realm. Steiner's writings on this theme are *The Philosophy of Spiritual Activity* (1894), *Occult Science: An Outline* (1913), *On the Riddle of Man* (1916), and *On the Riddles of the Soul* (1917). His last work was his autobiography (1924).

To advance his teachings, he founded the Anthroposophical Society (1912) and a school of "spiritual science" called the Goetheanum near Basel, Switzerland. His work inspired the Waldorf School movement, which comprises some eighty schools for children. The anthroposophy movement he established remains active in Europe and the United States.   G.J.S.

Stephen, Sir Leslie (1832–1904), English literary critic, editor, intellectual historian, and philosopher. He was the first chief editor of the great *Dictionary of National Biography*, writing hundreds of the entries himself. Brought up in an intensely religious household, he lost his faith and spent much of his time trying to construct a moral and intellectual outlook to replace it. His main works in intellectual history, the two-volume *History of English Thought in the Eighteenth Century* (1876) and the three-volume *English Utilitarians* (1900), were undertaken as part of this project. So was his one purely philosophical work, the *Science of Ethics* (1882), in which he tried to develop an evolutionary theory of morality. Stephen was impatient of philosophical technicalities. Hence his treatise on ethics does very little to resolve the problems – some of them pointed out to him by his friend Henry Sidgwick – with evolutionary ethics, and does not get beyond the several other works on the subject published during this period. His histories of thought are sometimes superficial, and their focus of interest is not ours; but they are still useful because of their scope and the massive scholarship they put to use. **See also** DARWINISM.   J.B.S.

Stewart, Dugald. See SCOTTISH COMMON SENSE PHILOSOPHY.

Stillingfleet, Edward (1635–99), English divine and controversialist who first made his name with *Irenicum* (1659), using natural-law doctrines to oppose religious sectarianism. His *Origines Sacrae* (1662), ostensibly on the superiority of the Scriptural record over other forms of ancient history, was for its day a learned study in the moral certainty of historical evidence, the authority of testimony, and the credibility of miracles. In drawing eclectically on philosophy from antiquity to the Cambridge Platonists, he was much influenced by the Cartesian theory of ideas, but later repudiated Cartesianism for its mechanist tendency. For three decades he pamphleteered on behalf of the moral certainty of orthodox Protestant belief against what he considered the beliefs "contrary to reason" of Roman Catholicism. This led to controversy with Unitarian and deist writers who argued that mysteries like the Trinity were equally contrary to "clear and distinct" ideas. He was alarmed at the use made of Locke's "new," i.e. non-Cartesian, way of ideas by John Toland in *Christianity not Mysterious* (1696), and devoted his last years to challenging Locke to prove his orthodoxy. The debate was largely over the concepts of substance, essence, and person, and of faith and certainty. Locke gave no quarter in the public controversy, but in the fourth edition of his *Essay* (1700) he silently amended some passages that had provoked Stillingfleet. **See also** CAMBRIDGE PLATONISTS, DEISM, DESCARTES, LOCKE.   M.A.St.

stipulative definition. See DEFINITION.

Stirner, Max, pseudonym of Kasper Schmidt (1805–56), German philosopher who proposed a theory of radical individualism. Born in Bayreuth, he taught in Gymnasiums and later at a Berlin academy for women. He translated what became a standard German version of Smith's *Wealth of Nations* and contributed articles to the *Rheinische Zeitung*. His most important work was

Der Einzige und sein Eigenthum (1845), translated by Steven T. Byington as *The Ego and His Own* (1907). His second book was *Die Geschichte der Reaktion* (1852).

Stirner was in reaction to Hegel and was for a time associated with the left Hegelians. He stressed the priority of will and instinct over reason and proposed a radical anarchic individualism. Each individual is unique, and the independent ego is the fundamental value and reality. Stirner attacked the state, religious ideas, and abstractions such as "humanity" as "spectres" that are deceptive illusions, remnants of erroneous hypostatizations. His defense of egoism is such that the individual is considered to have no obligations or duties, and especially not to the state. Encouraging an individual "rebellion" against state domination and control, Stirner attracted a following among nineteenth- and twentieth-century anarchists. The sole goal of life is the cultivation of "uniqueness" or "ownness." Engels and Marx attacked his ideas at length (under the rubric "Saint Marx") in *The German Ideology.* Insofar as his theory of radical individualism offers no clearly stated ethical requirements, it has been characterized as a form of nihilistic egoism.

See also HEGEL.   G.J.S.

stochastic process, a process that evolves, as time goes by, according to a probabilistic principle rather than a deterministic principle. Such processes are also called random processes, but 'stochastic' does not imply complete disorderliness. The principle of evolution governing a stochastic or random process is precise, though probabilistic, in form. For example, suppose some process unfolds in discrete successive stages. And suppose that given any initial sequence of stages, $S_1, S_2, \ldots, S_n$, there is a precise probability that the next stage S_{n+1} will be state S, a precise probability that it will be S', and so on for all possible continuations of the sequence of states. These probabilities are called transition probabilities. An evolving sequence of this kind is called a discrete-time stochastic process, or discrete-time random process.

A theoretically important special case occurs when transition probabilities depend only on the latest stage in the sequence of stages. When an evolving process has this property it is called a discrete-time *Markov process*. A simple example of a discrete-time Markov process is the behavior of a person who keeps taking either a step forward or a step back according to whether a coin falls heads or tails; the probabilistic principle of move-

ment is always applied to the person's most recent position.

The successive stages of a stochastic process need not be discrete. If they are continuous, they constitute a "continuous-time" stochastic or random process.

The mathematical theory of stochastic processes has many applications in science and technology. The evolution of epidemics, the process of soil erosion, and the spread of cracks in metals have all been given plausible models as stochastic processes, to mention just a few areas of research.

See also DETERMINISM, PROBABILITY, REGRESSION ANALYSIS.   T.H.

Stoicism, one of the three leading movements constituting Hellenistic philosophy. Its founder was Zeno of Citium (334–262 B.C.), who was succeeded as school head by Cleanthes (331–232). But the third head, Chrysippus (c.280–c.206), was its greatest exponent and most voluminous writer. These three are the leading representatives of *Early Stoicism.* No work by any early Stoic survives intact, except Cleanthes' short "Hymn to Zeus." Otherwise we are dependent on doxography, on isolated quotations, and on secondary sources, most of them hostile. Nevertheless, a remarkably coherent account of the system can be assembled.

The Stoic world is an ideally good organism, all of whose parts interact for the benefit of the whole. It is imbued with divine reason (*logos*), its entire development providentially ordained by fate and repeated identically from one world phase to the next in a never-ending cycle, each phase ending with a conflagration (*ekpyrosis*). Only bodies strictly "exist" and can interact. Body is infinitely divisible, and contains no void. At the lowest level, the world is analyzed into an active principle, god, and a passive principle, matter, both probably corporeal. Out of these are generated, at a higher level, the four elements air, fire, earth, and water, whose own interaction is analogous to that of god and matter: air and fire, severally or conjointly, are an active rational force called breath (Greek *pneuma*, Latin *spiritus*), while earth and water constitute the passive substrate on which these act, totally interpenetrating each other thanks to the non-particulate structure of body and its capacity to be mixed "through and through." Most physical analysis is conducted at this higher level, and *pneuma* becomes a key concept in physics and biology. A thing's qualities are constituted by its *pneuma*, which has the additional role of giving it cohesion and thus an essential identity. In inanimate objects this unifying *pneuma* is called a *hexis* (state); in plants it is called *physis* (nature); and in animals "soul." Even qualities of soul, e.g. justice, are portions of *pneuma*, and they too are therefore bodies: only thus could they have their evident causal efficacy. Four incorporeals are admitted: place, void (which surrounds the world), time, and *lekta* (see below); these do not strictly "exist" – they lack the corporeal power of interaction – but as items with some objective standing in the world they are, at least, "somethings." Universals, identified with Plato's Forms, are treated as concepts (*ennoemata*), convenient fictions that do not even earn the status of "somethings."

Stoic ethics is founded on the principle that only virtue is good, only vice bad. Other things conventionally assigned a value are "indifferent" (*adiaphora*), although some, e.g., health, wealth, and honor, are naturally "preferred" (*proegmena*), while their opposites are "dispreferred" (*apoproegmena*). Even though their possession is irrelevant to happiness, from birth these indifferents serve as the appropriate subject matter of our choices, each correct choice being a "proper function" (*kathekon*) – not yet a morally good act, but a step toward our eventual end (*telos*) of "living in accordance with nature." As we develop our rationality, the appropriate choices become more complex, less intuitive. For example, it may sometimes be more in accordance with nature's plan to sacrifice your wealth or health, in which case it becomes your "proper function" to do so. You have a specific role to play in the world plan, and moral progress (*prokope*) consists in learning it. This progress involves widening your natural "affinity" (*oikeiosis*): an initial concern for yourself and your parts is later extended to those close to you, and eventually to all mankind. That is the Stoic route toward justice. However, justice and the other virtues are actually found only in the sage, an idealized perfectly rational person totally in tune with the divine cosmic plan. The Stoics doubted whether any sages existed, although there was a tendency to treat at least Socrates as having been one. The sage is totally good, everyone else totally bad, on the paradoxical Stoic principle that all sins are equal. The sage's actions, however similar externally to mere "proper functions," have an entirely distinct character: they are renamed 'right actions' (*katorthomata*). Acting purely from "right reason," he is distinguished by his "freedom from passion" (*apatheia*): morally wrong impulses, or passions, are at root intellectual errors of mistak-

ing what is indifferent for good or bad, whereas the sage's evaluations are always correct. The sage alone is happy and truly free, living in perfect harmony with the divine plan. All human lives are predetermined by the providentially designed, all-embracing causal nexus of fate; yet being the principal causes of their actions, the good and the bad alike are responsible for them: determinism and morality are fully compatible.

Stoic epistemology defends the existence of cognitive certainty against the attacks of the New Academy. Belief is described as assent (*synkatathesis*) to an impression (*phantasia*), i.e. taking as true the propositional content of some perceptual or reflective impression. Certainty comes through the "cognitive impression" (*phantasia kataleptike*), a self-certifying perceptual representation of external fact, claimed to be commonplace. Out of sets of such impressions we acquire generic conceptions (*prolepseis*) and become rational. The highest intellectual state, knowledge (*episteme*), in which all cognitions become mutually supporting and hence "unshakable by reason," is the prerogative of the wise. Everyone else is in a state of mere opinion (*doxa*) or of ignorance. Nevertheless, the cognitive impression serves as a "criterion of truth" for all. A further important criterion is *prolepseis*, also called common conceptions and common notions (*koinai ennoiai*), often appealed to in philosophical argument. Although officially dependent on experience, they often sound more like innate intuitions, purportedly indubitable.

Stoic logic is propositional, by contrast with Aristotle's logic of terms. The basic unit is the simple proposition (*axioma*), the primary bearer of truth and falsehood. Syllogistic also employs complex propositions – conditional, conjunctive, and disjunctive – and rests on five "indemonstrable" inference schemata (to which others can be reduced with the aid of four rules called *themata*). All these items belong to the class of *lekta* – "sayables" or "expressibles." Words are bodies (vibrating portions of air), as are external objects, but predicates like that expressed by ' . . . walks', and the meanings of whole sentences, e.g., 'Socrates walks', are incorporeal *lekta*. The structure and content of both thoughts and sentences are analyzed by mapping them onto *lekta*, but the *lekta* are themselves causally inert.

Conventionally, a second phase of the school is distinguished as *Middle Stoicism*. It developed largely at Rhodes under Panaetius and Posidonius, both of whom influenced the presentation of Stoicism in Cicero's influential philosophical treatises (mid-first century B.C.). Panaetius (c.185–c.110) softened some classical Stoic positions, his ethics being more pragmatic and less concerned with the idealized sage. Posidonius (c.135–c.50) made Stoicism more open to Platonic and Aristotelian ideas, reviving Plato's inclusion of irrational components in the soul.

A third phase, *Roman Stoicism,* is the only Stoic era whose writings have survived in quantity. It is represented especially by the younger Seneca (A.D. c.1–65), Epictetus (A.D. c.55–c.135), and Marcus Aurelius (A.D. 121–80). It continued the trend set by Panaetius, with a strong primary focus on practical and personal ethics. Many prominent Roman political figures were Stoics.

After the second century A.D. Stoicism as a system fell from prominence, but its terminology and concepts had by then become an ineradicable part of ancient thought. Through the writings of Cicero and Seneca, its impact on the moral and political thought of the Renaissance was immense.

See also CICERO, DOXOGRAPHERS, HELLENISTIC PHILOSOPHY.   D.N.S.

Stoicism, Middle. See STOICISM.

stone paradox. See PARADOXES OF OMNIPOTENCE.

Stout, George Frederick (1860–1944), British psychologist and philosopher. A student of Ward, he was influenced by Herbart and especially Brentano. He was editor of *Mind* (1892–1920). He followed Ward in rejecting associationism and sensationism, and proposing analysis of mind as activity rather than passivity, consisting of acts of cognition, feeling, and conation. Stout stressed attention as the essential function of mind, and argued for the goal-directedness of all mental activity and behavior, greatly influencing McDougall's hormic psychology. He reinterpreted traditional associationist ideas to emphasize primacy of mental activity; e.g., association by contiguity – a passive mechanical process imposed on mind – became association by continuity of attentional interest. With Brentano, he argued that mental representation involves "thought reference" to a real object known through the representation that is itself the object of thought, like Locke's "idea." In philosophy he was influenced by Moore and Russell. His major works are *Analytic Psychology* (1896) and *Manual of Psychology* (1899). **See also** ASSOCIATIONISM, BRENTANO, SENSATIONALISM.   T.H.L.

St. Petersburg paradox. See SAINT PETERSBURG PARADOX.

strategy. See GAME THEORY.

Straton. See PERIPATETIC SCHOOL.

Strato of Lampsacus (c.335–c.267 B.C.), Greek philosopher and polymath nicknamed "the Physicist" for his innovative ideas in natural science. He succeeded Theophrastus as head of the Lyceum. Earlier he served as royal tutor in Alexandria, where his students included Aristarchus, who devised the first heliocentric model. Of Strato's many writings only fragments and summaries survive. These show him criticizing the abstract conceptual analysis of earlier theorists and paying closer attention to empirical evidence. Among his targets were atomist arguments that motion is impossible unless there is void, and also Aristotle's thesis that matter is fully continuous. Strato argued that no large void occurs in nature, but that matter is naturally porous, laced with tiny pockets of void. His investigations of compression and suction were influential in ancient physiology. In dynamics, he proposed that bodies have no property of lightness but only more or less weight. **See also** HELLENISTIC PHILOSOPHY, LYCEUM.   S.A.W.

Strawson, Sir **Peter** (b.1919), British philosopher who has made major contributions to logic, metaphysics, and the study of Kant. His career has been at Oxford, where he was the leading philosopher of his generation.

His first important work, "On Referring" (1950), argues that Russell's theory of descriptions fails to deal properly with the role of descriptions as "referring expressions" because Russell assumed the "bogus trichotomy" that sentences are true, false, or meaningless: for Strawson, sentences with empty descriptions are meaningful but "neither true nor false" because the general presuppositions governing the use of referring expressions are not fulfilled. One aspect of this argument was Russell's alleged insensitivity to the ordinary use of definite descriptions. The contrast between the abstract schemata of formal logic and the manifold richness of the inferences inherent in ordinary language is the central theme of Strawson's first book, *Introduction to Logical Theory* (1952).

In *Individuals* (1959) Strawson reintroduced metaphysics as a respectable philosophical discipline after decades of positivist rhetoric. But his project is only "descriptive" metaphysics – elucidation of the basic features of our own conceptual scheme – and his arguments are based on the philosophy of language: "basic" particulars are those which are basic objects of reference, and it is the spatiotemporal and sortal conditions for their identification and reidentification by speakers that constitute the basic categories. Three arguments are especially famous: (1) even in a purely auditory world objective reference on the basis of experience requires at least an analogue of space; (2) because self-reference presupposes reference to others, persons, conceived as bearers of both physical and psychological properties, are a type of basic particular; and (3) "feature-placing" discourse, such as 'it is snowing here now', is "the ultimate propositional level" through which reference to particulars enters discourse.

Strawson's next book, *The Bounds of Sense* (1966), provides a critical reading of Kant's theoretical philosophy. His aim is to extricate what he sees as the profound truths concerning the presuppositions of objective experience and judgment that Kant's transcendental arguments establish from the mysterious metaphysics of Kant's transcendental idealism. Strawson's critics have argued, however, that the resulting position is unstable: transcendental arguments can tell us only what we must suppose to be the case. So if Kant's idealism, which restricts such suppositions to things as they appear to us, is abandoned, we can draw conclusions concerning the way the world itself must be only if we add the verificationist thesis that ability to make sense of such suppositions requires ability to verify them. In his next book, *Skepticism and Naturalism: Some Varieties* (1985), Strawson conceded this: transcendental arguments belong within descriptive metaphysics and should not be regarded as attempts to provide an external justification of our conceptual scheme. In truth no such external justification is either possible or needed: instead – and here Strawson invokes Hume rather than Kant – our reasonings come to an end in natural propensities for belief that are beyond question because they alone make it possible to raise questions. In a famous earlier paper Strawson had urged much the same point concerning the free will debate: defenders of our ordinary attitudes of reproach and gratitude should not seek to ground them in the "panicky metaphysics" of a supra-causal free will; instead they can and need do no more than point to our unshakable commitment to these "reactive" attitudes through which we manifest our attachment to that fundamental category of our conceptual scheme – persons.

See also FREE WILL PROBLEM, KANT, ORDI-NARY LANGUAGE PHILOSOPHY, PARADIGM

CASE ARGUMENT, PRESUPPOSITION, RUSSELL, THEORY OF DESCRIPTIONS, TRANSCENDENTAL ARGUMENT.   T.R.B.

strict conditional. See COUNTERFACTUALS, IMPLICATION.

strict duty. See KANT.

strict identity. See IDENTITY.

strict implication. See IMPLICATION.

strict partial order. See ORDERING.

stroke notation. See SHEFFER STROKE.

strong semantic completeness. See COMPLETENESS.

strong soundness. See SOUNDNESS.

strong supervenience. See SUPERVENIENCE.

structural ambiguity. See AMBIGUITY.

structuralism, a distinctive yet extremely wide range of productive research conducted in the social and human sciences from the 1950s through the 1970s, principally in France. It is difficult to describe structuralism as a movement, because of the methodological constraints exercised by the various disciplines that came to be influenced by structuralism – e.g., anthropology, philosophy, literary theory, psychoanalysis, political theory, even mathematics. Nonetheless, structuralism is generally held to derive its organizing principles from the early twentieth-century work of Saussure, the founder of structural linguistics. Arguing against the prevailing historicist and philological approaches to linguistics, he proposed a "scientific" model of language, one understood as a closed system of elements and rules that account for the production and the social communication of meaning. Inspired by Durkheim's notion of a "social fact" – that domain of objectivity wherein the psychological and the social orders converge – Saussure viewed language as the repository of discursive signs shared by a given linguistic community. The particular sign is composed of two elements, a phonemic signifier, or distinctive sound element, and a corresponding meaning, or signified element. The defining relation between the sign's sound and meaning components is held to be arbitrary, i.e., based on conventional association, and not due to any function of the speaking subject's personal inclination, or to any external consideration of reference. What lends specificity or identity to each particular signifier is its differential relation to the other signifiers in the greater set; hence, each basic unit of language is itself the product of differences between other elements within the system. This principle of differential – and structural – relation was extended by Troubetzkoy to the order of phonemes, whereby a defining set of vocalic differences underlies the constitution of all linguistic phonemes. Finally, for Saussure, the closed set of signs is governed by a system of grammatical, phonemic, and syntactic rules. Language thus derives its significance from its own autonomous organization, and this serves to guarantee its communicative function.

Since language is the foremost instance of social sign systems in general, the structural account might serve as an exemplary model for understanding the very intelligibility of social systems as such – hence, its obvious relevance to the broader concerns of the social and human sciences. This implication was raised by Saussure himself, in his *Course on General Linguistics* (1916), but it was advanced dramatically by the French anthropologist Claude Lévi-Strauss – who is generally acknowledged to be the founder of modern structuralism – in his extensive analyses in the area of social anthropology, beginning with his *Elementary Structures of Kinship* (1949). Lévi-Strauss argued that society is itself organized according to one form or another of significant communication and exchange – whether this be of information, knowledge, or myths, or even of its members themselves. The organization of social phenomena could thus be clarified through a detailed elaboration of their subtending structures, which, collectively, testify to a deeper and all-inclusive, social rationality. As with the analysis of language, these social structures would be disclosed, not by direct observation, but by inference and deduction from the observed empirical data. Furthermore, since these structures are models of specific relations, which in turn express the differential properties of the component elements under investigation, the structural analysis is both readily formalizable and susceptible to a broad variety of applications. In Britain, e.g., Edmund Leach pursued these analyses in the domain of social anthropology; in the United States, Chomsky applied insights of structuralism to linguistic theory and philosophy of mind; in Italy, Eco conducted extensive structuralist analyses in the fields of social and literary semiotics.

With its acknowledgment that language is a rule-governed social system of signs, and that effective communication depends on the resources available to the speaker from within the codes of language itself, the structuralist approach tends to be less preoccupied with the more traditional considerations of "subjectivity" and "history" in its treatment of meaningful discourse. In the post-structuralism that grew out of this approach, the French philosopher Foucault, e.g., focused on the generation of the "subject" by the various epistemic discourses of imitation and representation, as well as on the institutional roles of knowledge and power in producing and conserving particular "disciplines" in the natural and social sciences. These disciplines, Foucault suggested, in turn govern our theoretical and practical notions of madness, criminality, punishment, sexuality, etc., notions that collectively serve to "normalize" the individual subject to their determinations. Likewise, in the domain of psychoanalysis, Lacan drew on the work of Saussure and Lévi-Strauss to emphasize Freud's concern with language and to argue that, as a set of determining codes, language serves to structure the subject's very unconscious. Problematically, however, it is the very dynamism of language, including metaphor, metonymy, condensation, displacement, etc., that introduces the social symbolic into the constitution of the subject. Althusser applied the principles of structuralist methodology to his analysis of Marxism, especially the role played by contradiction in understanding infrastructural and superstructural formation, i.e., for the constitution of the historical dialectic. His account followed Marx's rejection of Feuerbach, at once denying the role of traditional subjectivity and humanism, and presenting a "scientific" analysis of "historical materialism," one that would be anti-historicist in principle but attentive to the actual political state of affairs. For Althusser, such a philosophical analysis helped provide an "objective" discernment to the historical transformation of social reality.

The restraint the structuralists extended toward the traditional views of subjectivity and history dramatically colored their treatment both of the individuals who are agents of meaningful discourse and of the linguistically articulable object field in general. This redirection of research interests (particularly in France, due to the influential work of Barthes and Michel Serres in the fields of poetics, cultural semiotics, and communication theory) has resulted in a series of original analyses and also provoked lively debates between the adherents of structuralist methodology and the more conventionally oriented schools of thought (e.g., phenomenology, existentialism, Marxism, and empiricist and positivist philosophies of science). These debates served as an agency to open up subsequent discussions on deconstruction and postmodernist theory for the philosophical generation of the 1980s and later.

These post-structuralist thinkers were perhaps less concerned with the organization of social phenomena than with their initial constitution and subsequent dynamics. Hence, the problematics of the subject and history – or, in broader terms, temporality itself – were again engaged. The new discussions were abetted by a more critical appraisal of language and tended to be anti-Hegelian in their rejection of the totalizing tendency of systematic metaphysics. Heidegger's critique of traditional metaphysics was one of the major influences in the discussions following structuralism, as was the reexamination of Nietzsche's earlier accounts of "genealogy," his anti-essentialism, and his teaching of a dynamic "will to power." Additionally, many poststructuralist philosophers stressed the Freudian notions of the libido and the unconscious as determining factors in understanding not only the subject, but the deep rhetorical and affective components of language use. An astonishing variety of philosophers and critics engaged in the debates initially framed by the structuralist thinkers of the period, and their extended responses and critical reappraisals formed the vibrant, poststructuralist period of French intellectual life. Such figures as Ricoeur, Emmanuel Levinas, Kristeva, Maurice Blanchot, Derrida, Gilles Deleuze, Félix Guattari, Lyotard, Jean Baudrillard, Philippe Lacoue-Labarthe, Jean-Luc Nancy, and Irigaray inaugurated a series of contemporary reflections that have become international in scope.

See also CONTINENTAL PHILOSOPHY, DECONSTRUCTION, FOUCAULT, HEIDEGGER, LACAN, LYOTARD, POSTMODERN, SAUSSURE.

D.Al.

structuralism, mathematical. See MATHEMATICAL STRUCTURALISM.

structure. See GRAMMAR, PHILOSOPHY OF LANGUAGE, TRANSFORMATION RULE.

structure, deep. See GRAMMAR, PHILOSOPHY OF LANGUAGE, TRANSFORMATION RULE.

structure, surface. See GRAMMAR, PHILOSOPHY OF LANGUAGE, TRANSFORMATION RULE.

structure description. See CARNAP.

stuff. See METAPHYSICS.

Sturm und Drang. See GOETHE.

Suárez, Francisco, also known as Doctor Eximius (1548–1617), Spanish Jesuit philosopher and theologian. Born in Granada, he studied at Salamanca and taught there and at Rome, Coimbra, and other leading universities. Suárez's most important works are *De legibus* ("On Law," 1612), *De Deo uno et trino* ("On the Trinity," 1606), *De anima* ("On the Soul," 1621), and the monumental *Disputationes metaphysicae* ("Metaphysical Disputations," 1597). The *Disputationes* has a unique place in philosophy, being the first systematic and comprehensive work of metaphysics written in the West that is not a commentary on Aristotle's *Metaphysics*. Divided into fifty-four disputations, it discusses every metaphysical issue known at the time. Its influence was immediate and lasting and can be seen in the work of Scholastics in both Europe and Latin America, and of modern philosophers such as Descartes, Leibniz, Wolff, and Schopenhauer.

Suárez's main contributions to philosophy occurred in metaphysics, epistemology, and the philosophy of law. In all three areas he was influenced by Aristotle and Aquinas, although he also drew inspiration from Ockham, Duns Scotus, and others. In metaphysics, Suárez is known for his views on the nature of metaphysics, being, and individuation. Metaphysics is the science of "being insofar as it is real being" (*ens in quantum ens reale*), and its proper object of study is the object concept of being. This understanding of the object of metaphysics is often seen as paving the way for early modern metaphysical theory, in which the object of metaphysics is mental. For Suárez the concept of being is derived by analogy from the similarity existing among things. Existing reality for Suárez is composed of individuals: everything that exists is individual, including substances and their properties, accidents, principles, and components. He understands individuality as incommunicability, namely, the inability of individuals to be divided into entities of the same specific kind as themselves. The principle of individuation is "entity," which he identifies with "essence as it exists." This principle applies both to substances and their properties, accidents, principles, and components.

In epistemology, two of Suárez's views stand out: that the intellect knows the individual through a proper and separate concept without having to turn to reflection, a position that supports an empiricist epistemology in which, contrary to Thomism, knowledge of the individual is not mediated through universals; and (2) his view of middle knowledge (*scientia media*), the knowledge God has of what every free creature would freely do in every possible situation. This notion was used by Suárez and Molina to explain how God can control human actions without violating free will.

In philosophy of law, Suárez was an innovative thinker whose ideas influenced Grotius. For him law is fundamentally an act of the will rather than a result of an ordinance of reason, as Aquinas held. Law is divided into eternal, divine, natural, and human. Human law is based on natural or divine law and is not the result of human creation.

See also INDIVIDUATION, METAPHYSICS.

J.J.E.G.

subaltern. See SQUARE OF OPPOSITION.

subcontrary. See SQUARE OF OPPOSITION.

subdoxastic, pertaining to states of mind postulated to account for the production and character of certain apparently non-inferential beliefs. These were first discussed by Stephen P. Stich in "Beliefs and Subdoxastic States" (1978). I may form the belief that you are depressed, e.g., on the basis of subtle cues that I am unable to articulate. The psychological mechanism responsible for this belief might be thought to harbor information concerning these cues subdoxastically. Although subdoxastic states resemble beliefs in certain respects – they incorporate intentional content, they guide behavior, they can bestow justification on beliefs – they differ from fully-fledged doxastic states or beliefs in at least two respects. First, as noted above, subdoxastic states may be largely inaccessible to introspection; I may be unable to describe, even on reflection, the basis of my belief that you are depressed. Second, subdoxastic states seem cut off inferentially from an agent's corpus of beliefs; my subdoxastic appreciation that your forehead is creased may contribute to my believing that you are depressed, but, unlike the belief that your forehead is creased, it need not, in the presence of other beliefs, lead to further beliefs about your visage. See also BELIEF.   J.F.H.

subject. See GRAMMAR, LOGICAL SUBJECT.

subjective probability. See PROBABILITY.

subjective reason. See REASONS FOR ACTION.

subjective rightness. See OBJECTIVE RIGHTNESS.

subjectivism, any philosophical view that attempts to understand in a subjective manner what at first glance would seem to be a class of judgments that are objectively either true or false – i.e., true or false independently of what we believe, want, or hope. There are two ways of being a subjectivist. In the first way, one can say that the judgments in question, despite first appearances, are really judgments about our own attitudes, beliefs, emotions, etc. In the second way, one can deny that the judgments are true or false at all, arguing instead that they are disguised commands or expressions of attitudes. In ethics, for example, a subjective view of the second sort is that moral judgments are simply expressions of our positive and negative attitudes. This is emotivism. Prescriptivism is also a subjective view of the second sort; it is the view that moral judgments are really commands – to say "*X* is good" is to say, details aside, "Do *X.*" Views that make morality ultimately a matter of conventions (or what we or most people agree to) can also be construed as subjective theories, albeit of the first type. Subjectivism is not limited to ethics, however. According to a subjective view of epistemic rationality, the standards of rational belief are the standards that the individual (or perhaps most members in the individual's community) would approve of insofar as they are interested in believing those propositions that are true and not believing those propositions that are false. Similarly, phenomenalists can be regarded as proposing a subjective account of material object statements, since according to them, such statements are best understood as complex statements about the course of our experiences. See also EMOTIVISM, EPISTEMOLOGY, ETHICAL OBJECTIVISM, IDEAL OBSERVER.   R.Fo.

subjectivism, moral. See ETHICS.

subject–object dichotomy, the distinction between thinkers and what they think about. The distinction is not exclusive, since subjects can also be objects, as in reflexive self-conscious thought, which takes the subject as its intended object. The dichotomy also need not be an exhaustive distinction in the strong sense that everything is either a subject or an object, since in a logically possible world in which there are no thinkers, there may yet be mind-independent things that are neither subjects nor objects. Whether there are non-thinking things that are not objects of thought in the actual world depends on whether or not it is sufficient in logic to intend every individual thing by such thoughts and expressions as 'We can think of *everything* that exists'. The dichotomy is an inter-implicative distinction between thinkers and what they think about, in which each presupposes the other. If there are no subjects, then neither are there objects in the true sense, and conversely.

A subject–object dichotomy is acknowledged in most Western philosophical traditions, but emphasized especially in Continental philosophy, beginning with Kant, and carrying through idealist thought in Fichte, Schelling, Hegel, and Schopenhauer. It is also prominent in intentionalist philosophy, in the empirical psychology of Brentano, the object theory of Meinong, Ernst Mally (1879–1944), and Twardowski, and the transcendental phenomenology of Husserl. Subject–object dichotomy is denied by certain mysticisms, renounced as the philosophical fiction of duality, of which Cartesian mind–body dualism is a particular instance, and criticized by mystics as a confusion that prevents mind from recognizing its essential oneness with the world, thereby contributing to unnecessary intellectual and moral dilemmas.

See also BRENTANO, CONTINENTAL PHILOSOPHY, HUSSERL, INTENTIONALITY, PHENOMENOLOGY.   D.J.

subjunctive conditional. See COUNTERFACTUALS.

sublation. See HEGEL.

sublime, a feeling brought about by objects that are infinitely large or vast (such as the heavens or the ocean) or overwhelmingly powerful (such as a raging torrent, huge mountains, or precipices). The former (in Kant's terminology) is the *mathematically sublime* and the latter the *dynamically sublime*. Though the experience of the sublime is to an important extent unpleasant, it is also accompanied by a certain pleasure: we enjoy the feeling of being overwhelmed. On Kant's view, this pleasure results from an awareness that we have powers of reason that are not dependent on sensation, but that legislate over sense. The sublime thus displays both the limitations of sense experience (and hence our feeling of displeasure) and the power of our own mind (and hence the feeling of pleasure).

The sublime was an especially important concept in the aesthetic theory of the eighteenth and nineteenth centuries. Reflection on it was stimulated by the appearance of a translation of Longinus's *Peri hypsous* (*On the Sublime*) in 1674. The "postmodern sublime" has in addition emerged in late twentieth century thought as a basis for raising questions about art. Whereas beauty is associated with that whose form can be apprehended, the sublime is associated with the formless, that which is "unpresentable" in sensation. Thus, it is connected with critiques of "the aesthetic" – understood as that which is sensuously present – as a way of understanding what is important about art. It has also been given a political reading, where the sublime connects with resistance to rule, and beauty connects with conservative acceptance of existing forms or structures of society.

See also AESTHETIC PROPERTY, AESTHETICS, BEAUTY.   S.L.F.

subset. See SET THEORY.

subsidiarity, a basic principle of social order and the common good governing the relations between the higher and lower associations in a political community. Positively, the principle of subsidiarity holds that the common good, i.e., the ensemble of social resources and institutions that facilitate human self-realization, depends on fostering the free, creative initiatives of individuals and of their voluntary associations; thus, the state, in addition to its direct role in maintaining public good (which comprises justice, public peace, and public morality) also has an indirect role in promoting other aspects of the common good by rendering assistance (*subsidium*) to those individuals and associations whose activities facilitate cooperative human self-realization in work, play, the arts, sciences, and religion. Negatively, the principle of subsidiarity holds that higher-level (i.e., more comprehensive) associations – while they must monitor, regulate, and coordinate – ought not to absorb, replace, or undermine the free initiatives and activities of lower-level associations and individuals insofar as these are not contrary to the common good.

This presumption favoring free individual and social initiative has been defended on various grounds, such as the inefficiency of burdening the state with myriad local concerns, as well as the corresponding efficiency of unleashing the free, creative potential of subordinate groups and individuals who build up the shared economic, scientific, and artistic resources of society. But the deeper ground for this presumption is the view that human flourishing depends crucially on freedom for individual self-direction and for the self-government of voluntary associations and that human beings flourish best through their own personal and cooperative initiatives rather than as the passive consumers or beneficiaries of the initiatives of others.

See also COMMON GOOD, JUSTICE, LIBER-ALISM, POLITICAL PHILOSOPHY.   J.B.M.

subsistence (translation of German *Bestand*), in current philosophy, especially Meinong's system, the kind of being that belongs to "ideal" objects (such as mathematical objects, states of affairs, and abstractions like similarity and difference). By contrast, the kind of being that belongs to "real" (*wirklich*) objects, things of the sorts investigated by the sciences other than psychology and pure mathematics, is called *existence* (*Existenz*). Existence and subsistence together exhaust the realm of being (*Sein*). So, e.g., the subsistent ideal figures whose properties are investigated by geometers do not exist – they are nowhere to be found in the real world – but it is no less true of them that they have being than it is of an existent physical object: there *are* such figures.

Being does not, however, exhaust the realm of objects or things. The psychological phenomenon of intentionality shows that there are (in some sense of 'there are') objects that neither exist nor subsist. Every intentional state is directed toward an object. Although one may covet the Hope Diamond or desire the unification of Europe, one may also covet a non-existent material object or desire a non-subsistent state of affairs. If one covets a non-existent diamond, there is (in some sense of 'there is') something that one covets – one's state of mind has an object – and it has certain properties: it is, e.g., a diamond. It may therefore be said to inhabit the realm of *Sosein* ('being thus' or 'predication' or 'having properties'), which is the category comprising the totality of objects. Objects that do not have any sort of being, either existence or subsistence, belong to non-being (*Nichtsein*). In general, the properties of an object do not determine whether it has being or non-being. (But there are special cases: the round square, by its very nature, cannot subsist.) Meinong thus maintains that objecthood is *ausserseiend*, i.e., independent of both existence and subsistence.

See also ABSTRACT ENTITY, MEINONG, METAPHYSICS.   P.v.I.

sub specie aeternitatis. See SPINOZA.

substance, as defined by Aristotle in the *Categories,* that which is neither predicable ("sayable") of anything nor present in anything as an aspect or property of it. The examples he gives are an individual man and an individual horse. We can predicate *being a horse* of something but not a horse; nor is a horse *in* something else. He also held that only substances can remain self-identical through change. All other things are accidents of substances and exist only as aspects, properties, or relations of substances, or kinds of substances, which Aristotle called secondary substances. An example of an accident would be the color of an individual man, and an example of a secondary substance would be his being a man.

For Locke, a substance is that part of an individual thing in which its properties inhere. Since we can observe, indeed know, only a thing's properties, its substance is unknowable. Locke's sense is obviously rooted in Aristotle's but the latter carries no skeptical implications. In fact, Locke's sense is closer in meaning to what Aristotle calls matter, and would be better regarded as a synonym of 'substratum', as indeed it is by Locke. Substance may also be conceived as that which is capable of existing independently of anything else. This sense is also rooted in Aristotle's, but, understood quite strictly, leads to Spinoza's view that there can be only one substance, namely, the totality of reality or God.

A fourth sense of 'substance' is the common, ordinary sense, 'what a thing is made of'. This sense is related to Locke's, but lacks the latter's skeptical implications. It also corresponds to what Aristotle meant by matter, at least proximate matter, e.g., the bronze of a bronze statue (Aristotle analyzes individual things as composites of matter and form). This notion of matter, or stuff, has great philosophical importance, because it expresses an idea crucial to both our ordinary and our scientific understandings of the world. Philosophers such as Hume who deny the existence of substances hold that individual things are mere bundles of properties, namely, the properties ordinarily attributed to them, and usually hold that they are incapable of change; they are series of momentary events, rather than things enduring through time.

See also BUNDLE THEORY, PROPERTY.   P.Bu.

substance, primary. See ARISTOTLE.

substance, secondary. See ARISTOTLE.

substance causation. See AGENT CAUSATION.

substance-function. See T'I, YUNG.

substantial form. See FORM, HYLOMORPHISM.

substantialism, the view that the primary, most fundamental entities are substances, everything else being dependent for its existence on them, either as a property of them or a relation between them. Different versions of the view would correspond to the different senses of the word 'substance'. **See also SUBSTANCE.**   P.Bu.

substantival causation. See CAUSATION.

substantivalism. See PHILOSOPHY OF SCIENCE.

substantive pluralism. See PLURALISM.

substitutability *salva veritate.* See SUBSTITUTIVITY SALVA VERITATE.

substitutional quantification. See QUANTIFICATION.

substitutivity *salva veritate,* a condition met by two expressions when one is substitutable for the other at a certain occurrence in a sentence and the truth-value (truth or falsity) of the sentence is necessarily unchanged when the substitution is made. In such a case the two expressions are said to exhibit substitutivity or substitutability *salva veritate* (literally, 'with truth saved') with respect to one another in that context. The expressions are also said to be interchangeable or intersubstitutable *salva veritate* in that context. Where it is obvious from a given discussion that it is the truth-value that is to be preserved, it may be said that the one expression is substitutable for the other or exhibits substitutability with respect to the other at that place.

Leibniz proposed to use the universal interchangeability *salva veritate* of two terms in every "proposition" in which they occur as a necessary and sufficient condition for identity – presumably for the identity of the things denoted by the terms. There are apparent exceptions to this criterion, as Leibniz himself noted. If a sentence occurs in a context governed by a psychological verb such as 'believe' or 'desire', by an expression conveying modality (e.g., 'necessarily', 'possibly'), or by certain temporal expressions (such as 'it will soon be the case that'), then two terms may denote the same thing but not be interchangeable within such a sentence. Occurrences of expressions within quotation marks or where the expressions are both mentioned and used (cf. Quine's example, "Giorgione was so-called be-

cause of his size") also exhibit failure of substitutivity.

Frege urged that such failures are to be explained by the fact that within such contexts an expression does not have its ordinary denotation but denotes instead either its usual sense or the expression itself.

See also QUANTIFYING IN, REFERENTIALLY TRANSPARENT.   C.A.A.

substrate. See SUBSTANCE.

substratum. See BERKELEY, SUBSTANCE.

subsumption theory of explanation. See COVERING LAW MODEL.

sufficient condition. See CONDITION.

sufficient reason, principle of. See LEIBNIZ.

Sufism (from Arabic *ṣūfī,* 'mystic'), Islamic mysticism. The Arabic word is *taṣawwuf.* The philosophically significant aspects of Sufism are its psychology in its early phase and its epistemology and ontology in its later phase.

The early practices of asceticism, introspection, and meditation on God and the hereafter as depicted in the Koran eventually developed in classical Sufism (eighth–eleventh centuries) into the spiritual journey of the mystic, the successive stages of which were described with a sophisticated psychological terminology. Sufis differentiated two levels of spiritual attainment: the first was that of "stations" (*maqāmāt*) that were reached through individual effort, abnegation, and spiritual exercises (e.g., *tawakkul,* 'selfless trust in God', *ṣabr,* 'patience', etc.). The characteristic they all shared was that the Sufi, through an act of the will and deliberate deeds, suppressed his individual ego and its concomitant attachment to worldly things and emotions in order to become receptive to the following level of "states" (*aḥwāl*), which were vouchsafed to him through God's grace. These culminated in the goal of the mystical quest, the final states of bliss, which were variously identified by Sufis, according to their proclivities, as love (*maḥabba,* later *'ishq*), mystical knowledge (*ma'rifa*), and the total loss of ego consciousness and the concomitant absorption and subsistence in and through God (*fanā'* and *baqā'*). The language describing these stages and states was allusive and symbolical rather than descriptive.

Sufism, which was viewed initially with suspicion by the authorities and the orthodox, was integrated into mainstream belief in the eleventh century, primarily through the work of al-Gha-zālī (d.1111). After al-Ghazālī, the theoretical and practical aspects of Sufism, which had previously gone hand in hand, developed in different ways. At the popular level, Sufi practices and instruction were institutionalized in fraternities and orders that, ever since, have played a vital role in all Islamic societies, especially among the disenfranchised. Life in the orders revolved around the regimented initiation of the novices to the Sufi path by the master. Although theoretical instruction was also given, the goal of the mystic was primarily achieved by spiritual practices, chiefly the repetition of religious formulas (*dhikr*). Among the intellectuals, Sufism acquired a philosophical gloss and terminology. All the currents of earlier Sufism, as well as elements of Neoplatonic emanationism drawn from Arabic philosophy, were integrated into a complex and multifaceted system of "theosophy" in the monumental work of Ibn 'Arabī (d.1240). This system rests on the pivotal concept of "unity of being" (*waḥdat al-wujūd*), according to which God is the only being and the only reality, while the entire creation constitutes a series of his dynamic and continuous self-manifestations. The individual who combines in himself the totality of these manifestations to become the prototype of creation, as well as the medium through which God can be known, is the Perfect Man, identified with the Prophet Muhammad. The mystic's quest consists of an experiential (epistemological) retracing of the levels of manifestations back to their origin and culminates in the closest possible approximation to the level of the Perfect Man. Ibn 'Arabī's mystical thought, which completely dominated Sufism, found expression in later times primarily in the poetry of the various Islamic languages, while certain aspects of it were reintroduced into Arabic philosophy in Safavid times.

See also AL-GHAZĀLĪ, ARABIC PHILOSOPHY.

D.Gu.

suicide, assisted. See BIOETHICS.

summum bonum (Latin, 'highest good'), that in relation to which all other things have at most instrumental value (value only insofar as they are productive of what is the highest good).

Philosophical conceptions of the *summum bonum* have for the most part been teleological in character. That is, they have identified the highest good in terms of some goal or goals that human beings, it is supposed, pursue by their very nature. These natural goals or ends have differed considerably. For the theist, this end is God; for the rationalist, it is the rational comprehension of what is real; for hedonism, it is pleasure; etc. The highest good, however, need not be teleologically construed. It may simply be posited, or supposed, that it is known, through some intuitive process, that a certain type of thing is "intrinsically good." On such a view, the relevant contrast is not so much between what is good as an end and what is good as a means to this end, as between what is good purely in itself and what is good only in combination with certain other elements (the "extrinsically good"). Perhaps the best example of such a view of the highest good would be the position of Moore.

Must the *summum bonum* be just one thing, or one kind of thing? Yes, to this extent: although one could certainly combine pluralism (the view that there are many, irreducibly different goods) with an assertion that the *summum bonum* is "complex," the notion of the highest good has typically been the province of monists (believers in a single good), not pluralists.   J.A.M.

summum genus. See GENUS GENERALISSIMUM.

Sung Hsing, also called Sung Tzu (c.360–290 B.C.), Chinese philosopher associated with Mohism and the Huang–Lao school. He was a member of the Chi-hsia Academy of Ch'i, a late Warring States center that attracted intellectuals of every persuasion. His Mohist ideas include an emphasis on utility, thrift, meritocracy, and a reluctance to wage war. He is praised by the Taoist Chuang Tzu for his beliefs that one's essential desires and needs are few and that one should heed internal cultivation rather than social judgments. The combination of internal tranquillity and political activism is characteristic of Huang–Lao thought. **See also** MOHISM.

R.P.P. & R.T.A.

śūnyatā (Sanskrit, 'emptiness'), a property said by some Indian Buddhist philosophers to be possessed necessarily by everything that exists. If something is empty it possesses no essential or inherent nature (*svabhāva*), which is to say that both its existence and its nature are dependent on things or events other than itself. The thesis 'everything is empty' is therefore approximately equivalent to 'everything is causally dependent'; the contradictories of these theses were typically argued by defenders of emptiness to be incoherent and thus not worthy of assent. To deny emptiness was also taken to require the affirmation of permanence and non-contingency: if something is non-empty in any respect, it is in just that respect permanent and non-contingent. **See also** BUDDHISM, MĀDHYAMIKA, NĀGĀR-JUNA.   P.J.G.

Sun Yat-sen (1866–1925), Chinese statesman, founder of the Republic of China in 1911. Educated as a medical doctor in England, he became a revolutionary to end the reign of the last dynasty in China. He founded the Nationalist Party and developed the so-called Three People's Principles: the nationalist, democratic, and socialist principles. He claimed to be transmitting the Confucian Way. Sun adopted a policy of cooperation with the Communists, but his successor Chiang Kai-shek (1887–1975) broke with them. He is now also honored on the mainland as a bourgeois social democrat paving the way for the Communist Revolution. **See also** CHINESE PHILOSOPHY.   S.-h.L.

superaltern. See SQUARE OF OPPOSITION.

superego. See FREUD.

supererogation, the property of going beyond the call of duty. Supererogatory actions are sometimes equated with actions that are morally good in the sense that they are encouraged by morality but not required by it. Sometimes they are equated with morally commendable actions, i.e., actions that indicate a superior moral character. It is quite common for morally good actions to be morally commendable and vice versa, so that it is not surprising that these two kinds of supererogatory actions are not clearly distinguished even though they are quite distinct.

Certain kinds of actions are not normally considered to be morally required, e.g., giving to charity, though morality certainly encourages doing them. However, if one is wealthy and gives only a small amount to charity, then, although one's act is supererogatory in the sense of being morally good, it is not supererogatory in the sense of being morally commendable, for it does not indicate a superior moral character. Certain kinds of actions are normally morally required, e.g., keeping one's promises. However, when the harm or risk of harm of keeping one's promise is sufficiently great compared to the harm caused by breaking the promise to excuse breaking the promise, then keeping one's promise counts as a supererogatory act in the sense of being morally commendable.

Some versions of *consequentialism* claim that

everyone is always morally required to act so as to bring about the best consequences. On such a theory there are no actions that are morally encouraged but not required; thus, for those holding such theories, if there are supererogatory acts, they must be morally commendable. Many versions of non-consequentialism also fail to provide for acts that are morally encouraged but not morally required; thus, if they allow for supererogatory acts, they must regard them as morally required acts done at such significant personal cost that one might be excused for not doing them.

The view that all actions are either morally required, morally prohibited, or morally indifferent makes it impossible to secure a place for supererogatory acts in the sense of morally good acts. This view that there are no acts that are morally encouraged but not morally required may be the result of misleading terminology. Both Kant and Mill distinguish between duties of perfect obligation and duties of imperfect obligation, acknowledging that a duty of imperfect obligation does not specify any particular act that one is morally required to do. However, since they use the term 'duty' it is very easy to view all acts falling under these "duties" as being morally required.

One way of avoiding the view that all morally encouraged acts are morally required is to avoid the common philosophical misuse of the term 'duty'. One can replace 'duties of perfect obligation' with 'actions required by moral rules' and 'duties of imperfect obligation' with 'actions encouraged by moral ideals'. However, a theory that includes the kinds of acts that are supererogatory in the sense of being morally good has to distinguish between that sense of 'supererogatory' and the sense meaning 'morally commendable', i.e., indicating a superior moral character in the agent. For as pointed out above, not all morally good acts are morally commendable, nor are all morally commendable acts morally good, even though a particular act may be supererogatory in both senses.

See also DUTY, ETHICS, UTILITARIANISM.
                                        B.Ge.

superman. See NIETZSCHE.

supernaturalism. See MIRACLE, NATURALISM, THEOLOGICAL NATURALISM.

supernatural theology. See THEOLOGIA NATURALIS.

superseding cause. See CAUSATION.

superset. See SET THEORY.

supervaluation. See SET THEORY, VAGUENESS.

supervaluations, method of. See VAGUENESS.

supervaluation semantics. See FREE LOGIC.

supervenience, a dependence relation between properties or facts of one type, and properties or facts of another type. Moore, for instance, held that the property *intrinsic value* is dependent in the relevant way on certain non-moral properties (although he did not employ the word 'supervenience'). As he put it, "if a given thing possesses any kind of intrinsic value in a certain degree, then not only must that same thing possess it, under all circumstances, in the same degree, but also anything *exactly like it*, must, under all circumstances, possess it in exactly the same degree" (*Philosophical Studies*, 1922). The concept of supervenience, as a relation between properties, is essentially this: Properties of type A are supervenient on properties of type B if and only if two objects cannot differ with respect to their A-properties without also differing with respect to their B-properties. Properties that allegedly are supervenient on others are often called consequential properties, especially in ethics; the idea is that if something instantiates a moral property, then it does so *in virtue of*, i.e., as a (non-causal) *consequence of*, instantiating some lower-level property on which the moral property supervenes.

In another, related sense, supervenience is a feature of discourse of one type, vis-à-vis discourse of another type. The term was so used, again in connection with morals, by Hare, who wrote:

> First, let us take that characteristic of "good" which has been called its supervenience. Suppose that we say, "St. Francis was a good man." It is logically impossible to say this and to maintain at the same time that there might have been another man placed exactly in the same circumstances as St. Francis, and who behaved in exactly the same way, but who differed from St. Francis in this respect only, that he was not a good man. (*The Language of Morals*, 1952)

Here the idea is that it would be a misuse of moral language, a violation of the "logic of moral discourse," to apply 'good' to one thing but not to something else exactly similar in all pertinent non-moral respects. Hare is a metaethical irreal-

ist: he denies that there are moral properties or facts. So for him, moral supervenience is a feature of moral discourse and judgment, not a relation between properties or facts of two types.

The notion of supervenience has come to be used quite widely in metaphysics and philosophy of mind, usually in the first sense explained above. This use was heralded by Davidson in articulating a position about the relation between physical and mental properties, or state-types, that eschews the reducibility of mental properties to physical ones. He wrote:

> Although the position I describe denies there are psychophysical laws, it is consistent with the view that mental characteristics are in some sense dependent, or supervenient, on physical characteristics. Such supervenience might be taken to mean that there cannot be two events alike in all physical respects but differing in some mental respects, or that an object cannot alter in some mental respects without altering in some physical respects. Dependence or supervenience of this kind does not entail reducibility through law or definition. ("Mental Events," 1970)

A variety of supervenience theses have been propounded in metaphysics and philosophy of mind, usually (although not always) in conjunction with attempts to formulate metaphysical positions that are naturalistic, in some sense, without being strongly reductionistic. For instance, it is often asserted that mental properties and facts are supervenient on neurobiological properties, and/or on physicochemical properties and facts. And it is often claimed, more generally, that *all* properties and facts are supervenient on the properties and facts of the kind described by physics.

Much attention has been directed at how to formulate the desired supervenience theses, and thus how to characterize supervenience itself. A distinction has been drawn between *weak supervenience*, asserting that in any *single* possible world w, any two individuals in w that differ in their A-properties also differ in their B-properties; and *strong supervenience*, asserting that for any two individuals i and j, either within a single possible world *or in two distinct ones*, if i and j differ in A-properties then they also differ in B-properties. It is sometimes alleged that traditional formulations of supervenience, like Moore's or Hare's, articulate only weak supervenience, whereas strong supervenience is needed to express the relevant kind of determination or dependence. It is sometimes replied, however, that the traditional natural-language formulations do in fact express strong supervenience – and that formalizations expressing mere weak supervenience are mistranslations.

Questions about how best to formulate supervenience theses also arise in connection with intrinsic and non-intrinsic properties. For instance, the property *being a bank,* instantiated by the brick building on Main Street, is not supervenient on intrinsic physical properties of the building itself; rather, the building's having this social-institutional property depends on a considerably broader range of facts and features, some of which are involved in subserving the social practice of banking. The term 'supervenience base' is frequently used to denote the range of entities and happenings whose lower-level properties and relations jointly underlie the instantiation of some higher-level property (like *being a bank*) by some individual (like the brick building on Main Street).

Supervenience theses are sometimes formulated so as to smoothly accommodate properties and facts with broad supervenience bases. For instance, the idea that the physical facts determine all the facts is sometimes expressed as *global supervenience,* which asserts that any two physically possible worlds differing in some respect also differ in some physical respect. Or, sometimes this idea is expressed as the stronger thesis of *regional supervenience,* which asserts that for any two spatiotemporal regions *r* and *s,* either within a single physically possible world or in two distinct ones, if *r* and *s* differ in some intrinsic respect then they also differ in some intrinsic physical respect.

See also NATURALISM, PHILOSOPHY OF MIND, RESULTANCE.   T.E.H.

supervenient behaviorism. See PHILOSOPHY OF MIND.

suppositio (Latin, 'supposition'), in the Middle Ages, reference. The theory of supposition, the central notion in the theory of *proprietates terminorum,* was developed in the twelfth century, and was refined and discussed into early modern times. It has two parts (their names are a modern convenience).

(1) The theory of supposition proper. This typically divided *suppositio* into "personal" reference to individuals (not necessarily to persons, despite the name), "simple" reference to species or genera, and "material" reference to spoken or written expressions. Thus 'man' in 'Every man is an

animal' has personal supposition, in 'Man is a species' simple supposition, and in 'Man is a monosyllable' material supposition. The theory also included an account of how the range of a term's reference is affected by tense and by modal factors.

(2) The theory of "modes" of personal supposition. This part of supposition theory divided personal supposition typically into "discrete" ('Socrates' in 'Socrates is a man'), "determinate" ('man' in 'Some man is a Greek'), "confused and distributive" ('man' in 'Every man is an animal'), and "merely confused" ('animal' in 'Every man is an animal'). The purpose of this second part of the theory is a matter of some dispute. By the late fourteenth century, it had in some authors become a theory of quantification. The term *'suppositio'* was also used in the Middle Ages in the ordinary sense, to mean 'assumption', 'hypothesis'.   P.V.S.

supposition, material. See SUPPOSITIO.

supposition, personal. See SUPPOSITIO.

supposition, simple. See SUPPOSITIO.

sure-thing principle. See ALLAIS'S PARADOX, DECISION THEORY.

surface grammar. See GRAMMAR.

surface structure. See GRAMMAR, PHILOSOPHY OF LANGUAGE.

surplus value. See MARX.

survival, continued existence after one's biological death. So understood, survival can pertain only to beings that are organisms at some time or other, not to beings that are disembodied at all times (as angels are said to be) or to beings that are embodied but never as organisms (as might be said of computers). Theories that maintain that one's individual consciousness is absorbed into a universal consciousness after death or that one continues to exist only through one's descendants, insofar as they deny one's own continued existence as an individual, are not theories of survival. Although survival does not entail immortality or anything about reward or punishment in an afterlife, many theories of survival incorporate these features.

Theories about survival have expressed differing attitudes about the importance of the body.

Some philosophers have maintained that persons cannot survive without their own bodies, typically espousing a doctrine of resurrection; such a view was held by Aquinas. Others, including the Pythagoreans, have believed that one can survive in other bodies, allowing for reincarnation into a body of the same species or even for transmigration into a body of another species. Some, including Plato and perhaps the Pythagoreans, have claimed that no body is necessary, and that survival is fully achieved by one's escaping embodiment. There is a similar spectrum of opinion about the importance of one's mental life. Some, such as Locke, have supposed that survival of the same person would require memory of one's having experienced specific past events. Plato's doctrine of recollection, in contrast, supposes that one can survive without any experiential memory; all that one typically is capable of recollecting are impersonal necessary truths.

Philosophers have tested the relative importance of bodily versus mental factors by means of various thought experiments, of which the following is typical. Suppose that a person's whole mental life – memories, skills, and character traits – were somehow duplicated into a data bank and erased from the person, leaving a living radical amnesiac. Suppose further that the person's mental life were transcribed into another radically amnesiac body. Has the person survived, and if so, as whom?

See also PERSONAL IDENTITY, SOUL.

W.E.M.

sustaining cause. See CAUSATION.

sutra (from Sanskrit *sūtra*, 'thread', 'precept'), a single verse or aphorism of Hindu or Buddhist teaching, or a collection of them. Written to be memorized, they provide a means of encoding and transmitting laws and rules of grammar, ritual, poetic meter, and philosophical disputation. Typically using technical terms and written so as to be mnemonic, they serve well for passing on information in an oral tradition. What makes them serviceable for this purpose also makes them largely unintelligible without commentary.

The sutra style is typical in philosophical traditions. The *Brahma-Sūtras* of Badharana are an example of a set of sutras regarded as authoritative by Vedanta but interpreted in vastly different ways by Shaṅkara, Rāmānuja, and Madhva. The sutras associated with Buddhism typically are more expansive than those associated with

Hinduism, and thus more intelligible on their own. The *Tripiṭaka* ("Basket of the Teachings") is a collection of sutras that Buddhist tradition ascribes to Ananda, who is said to have recited them from memory at the first Buddhist council; each sutra is introduced by the words 'Thus have I heard'. Sutras are associated with Theravada as well as Mahayana Buddhism and deal with both religious and philosophical topics.   K.E.Y.

Swedenborgianism, the theosophy professed by a worldwide movement established as the New Jerusalem Church in London in 1788 by the followers of Emanuel Swedenborg (1688–1772), a Swedish natural philosopher, visionary, and biblical exegete. Author of geological and cosmological works, he fused the rationalist (Cartesian) and empiricist (Lockean) legacies into a natural philosophy (*Principia Rerum Naturalium,* 1734) that propounded the harmony of the mechanistic universe with biblical revelation. Inspired by Liebniz, Malebranche, Platonism, and Neoplatonism, he unfolded a doctrine of correspondence (*A Hieroglyphic Key,* 1741) to account for the relation between body and soul and between the natural and spiritual worlds, and applied it to biblical exegesis. What attracted the wide following of the "Spirit-Seer" were his theosophic speculations in the line of Boehme and the mystical, prophetic tradition in which he excelled (*Heavenly Arcana,* 1749–56).   J.-L.S.

Swinburne, Richard (b.1934), British philosopher of religion and of science. In philosophy of science, he has contributed to confirmation theory and to the philosophy of space and time. His work in philosophy of religion is the most ambitious project in philosophical theology undertaken by a British philosopher in the twentieth century. Its first part is a trilogy on the coherence and justification of theistic belief and the rationality of living by that belief: *The Coherence of Theism* (1977), *The Existence of God* (1979), and *Faith and Reason* (1981). Since 1985, when Swinburne became Nolloth Professor of the Philosophy of the Christian Religion at the University of Oxford, he has written a tetralogy about some of the most central of the distinctively Christian religious doctrines: *Responsibility and Atonement* (1989), *Revelation* (1992), *The Christian God* (1994), and *Providence and the Problem of Evil* (1998).

The most interesting feature of the trilogy is its contribution to natural theology. Using Bayesian reasoning, Swinburne builds a cumulative case for theism by arguing that its probability is raised by such things as the existence of the universe, its order, the existence of consciousness, human opportunities to do good, the pattern of history, evidence of miracles, and religious experience. The existence of evil does not count against the existence of God. On our total evidence theism is more probable than not. In the tetralogy he explicates and defends such Christian doctrines as original sin, the Atonement, Heaven, Hell, the Trinity, the Incarnation, and Providence. He also analyzes the grounds for supposing that some Christian doctrines are revealed truths, and argues for a Christian theodicy in response to the problem of evil.

See also BAYESIAN RATIONALITY, PHILOSO-PHY OF RELIGION, TRINITARIANISM.   P.L.Q.

syllogism, in Aristotle's words, "a discourse in which, a certain thing being stated, something other than what is stated follows of necessity from being so" (*Prior Analytics*, 24b 18). Three types of syllogism were usually distinguished: categorical, hypothetical, and disjunctive. Each will be treated in that order.

The categorical syllogism. This is an argument consisting of three categorical propositions, two serving as premises and one serving as conclusion. E.g., 'Some college students are happy; all college students are high school graduates; therefore, some high school graduates are happy'. If a syllogism is valid, the premises must be so related to the conclusion that it is impossible for both premises to be true and the conclusion false. There are four types of categorical propositions: universal affirmative or A-propositions – 'All S are P', or 'SaP'; universal negative or E-propositions – 'No S are P', or 'SeP'; particular affirmative or I-propositions – 'Some S are P', or 'SiP'; and particular negative or O-propositions: 'Some S are not P', or 'SoP'. The mediate basic components of categorical syllogism are terms serving as subjects or predicates in the premises and the conclusion. *There must be three and only three terms in any categorical syllogism,* the major term, the minor term, and the middle term. Violation of this basic rule of structure is called the fallacy of four terms (*quaternio termi-norum*); e.g., 'Whatever is right is useful; only one of my hands is right; therefore only one of my hands is useful'. Here 'right' does not have the same meaning in its two occurrences; we therefore have more than three terms and hence no genuine categorical syllogism.

The syllogistic terms are identifiable and defin-able with reference to the position they have in a given syllogism. The predicate of the conclusion is the *major term;* the subject of the conclusion is the *minor term;* the term that appears once in each premise but not in the conclusion is the *middle term.* As it is used in various types of categorical propositions, a term is either distributed (stands for each and every member of its extension) or undistributed. There is a simple rule regarding the distribution: *universal propositions (SaP and SeP) distribute their subject terms; negative propositions (SeP and SoP) distribute their predicate terms.* No terms are distributed in an I-proposition.

Various sets of rules governing validity of categorical syllogisms have been offered. The following is a "traditional" set from the popular *Port-Royal Logic* (1662).

R1: *The middle term must be distributed at least once.* Violation: 'All cats are animals; some animals do not eat liver; therefore some cats do not eat liver'. The middle term 'animals' is not distributed either in the first or minor premise, being the predicate of an affirmative proposition, nor in the second or major premise, being the subject of a particular proposition; hence, the *fallacy of undistributed middle.*

R2: *A term cannot be distributed in the conclusion if it is undistributed in the premises.* Violation: 'All dogs are carnivorous; no flowers are dogs; therefore, no flowers are carnivorous'. Here the major, 'carnivorous', is distributed in the conclusion, being the predicate of a negative proposition, but not in the premise, serving there as predicate of an affirmative proposition; hence, the *fallacy of illicit major term.* Another violation of R2: 'All students are happy individuals; no criminals are students; therefore, no happy individuals are criminals'. Here the minor, 'happy individuals', is distributed in the conclusion, but not distributed in the minor premise; hence the *fallacy of illicit minor term.*

R3: *No conclusion may be drawn from two negative premises.* Violation: 'No dogs are cats; some dogs do not like liver; therefore, some cats do not like liver'. Here R1 is satisfied, since the middle term 'dogs' is distributed in the minor premise; R2 is satisfied, since both the minor term 'cats' as well as the major term 'things that like liver' are distributed in the premises and thus no violation of distribution of terms occurs. It is only by virtue of R3 that we can proclaim this syllogism to be invalid.

R4: *A negative conclusion cannot be drawn where both premises are affirmative.* Violation: 'All educated people take good care of their children; all who take good care of their children are poor; therefore, some poor people are not educated'. Here, it is only by virtue of the rule of quality, R4, that we can proclaim this syllogism invalid.

R5: *The conclusion must follow the weaker premise; i.e., if one of the premises is negative, the conclusion must be negative, and if one of them is particular, the conclusion must be particular.*

R6: *From two particular premises nothing follows.* Let us offer an indirect proof for this rule. If both particular premises are affirmative, no term is distributed and therefore the fallacy of undistributed middle is inevitable. To avoid it, we have to make one of the premises negative, which will result in a distributed predicate as middle term. But by R5, the conclusion must then be negative; thus, the major term will be distributed in the conclusion. To avoid violating R2, we must distribute that term in the major premise. It could not be in the position of subject term, since only universal propositions distribute their subject term and, by hypothesis, both premises are particular. But we could not use the same negative premise used to distribute the middle term; we must make the other particular premise negative. But then we violate R3. Thus, any attempt to make a syllogism with two particular premises valid will violate one or more basic rules of syllogism. (This set of rules assumes that A- and E-propositions have existential import and hence that an I- or an O-proposition may legitimately be drawn from a set of exclusively universal premises.)

Categorical syllogisms are classified according to figure and mood. The *figure* of a categorical syllogism refers to the schema determined by the possible position of the middle term in relation to the major and minor terms. In "modern logic," four syllogistic figures are recognized. Using '*M*' for middle term, '*P*' for major term, and '*S*' for minor term, they can be depicted as follows:

Fig. 1	Fig. 2	Fig. 3	Fig. 4
M is *P*	*P* is *M*	*M* is *P*	*P* is *M*
S is *M*	*S* is *M*	*M* is *S*	*M* is *S*
∴ *S* is *P*	∴ *S* is *P*	∴ *S* is *P*	∴ *S* is *P*

Aristotle recognized only three syllogistic figures. He seems to have taken into account just the two premises and the extension of the three terms occurring in them, and then asked what conclusion, if any, can be derived from those premises. It turns out, then, that his procedure leaves room for three figures only: one in which

the *M* term is the subject of one and predicate of the other premise; another in which the *M* term is predicated in both premises; and a third one in which the *M* term is the subject in both premises. Medievals followed him, although all considered the so-called inverted first (i.e., moods of the first figure with their conclusion converted either simply or *per accidens*) to be legitimate also. Some medievals (e.g., Albalag) and most moderns since Leibniz recognize a fourth figure as a distinct figure, considering syllogistic terms on the basis not of their extension but of their position in the conclusion, the *S* term of the conclusion being defined as the minor term and the *P* term being defined as the major term.

The *mood* of a categorical syllogism refers to the configuration of types of categorical propositions determined on the basis of the quality and quantity of the propositions serving as premises and conclusion of any given syllogism; e.g., 'No animals are plants; all cats are animals; therefore no cats are plants', '(MeP, SaM /∴ SeP)', is a syllogism in the mood EAE in the first figure. 'All metals conduct electricity; no stones conduct electricity; therefore no stones are metals', '(PaM, SeM /∴ SeP)', is the mood AEE in the second figure. In the four syllogistic figures there are 256 possible moods, but only 24 are valid (only 19 in modern logic, on the ground of a non-existential treatment of A- and E-propositions). As a mnemonic device and to facilitate reference, names have been assigned to the valid moods, with each vowel representing the type of categorical proposition. William Sherwood and Peter of Spain offered the famous list designed to help students to remember which moods in any given figure are valid and how the "inevident" moods in the second and third figures are provable by reduction to those in the first figure: barbara, celarent, darii, ferio (direct Fig. 1); baralipton, celantes, dabitis, fapesmo, frisesomorum (indirect Fig. 1); cesare, camestres, festino, baroco (Fig. 2); darapti, felapton, disamis, datisi, bocardo, ferison (Fig. 3).

The hypothetical syllogism. The pure hypothetical syllogism is an argument in which both the premises and the conclusion are hypothetical, i.e. conditional, propositions; e.g., 'If the sun is shining, it is warm; if it is warm, the plants will grow; therefore if the sun is shining, the plants will grow'. Symbolically, this argument form can be represented by '$A \rightarrow B, B \rightarrow C /\therefore A \rightarrow C$'. It was not recognized as such by Aristotle, but Aristotle's pupil Theophrastus foreshadowed it, even though it is not clear from his example of it – 'If man is, animal is; if animal is, then substance is; if therefore man is, substance is' – whether this was seen to be a principle of term logic or a principle of propositional logic. It was the Megaric-Stoic philosophers and Boethius who fully recognized hypothetical propositions and syllogisms as principles of the most general theory of deduction.

Mixed hypothetical syllogisms are arguments consisting of a hypothetical premise and a categorical premise, and inferring a categorical proposition; e.g., 'If the sun is shining, the plants will grow; the sun is shining; therefore the plants will grow'. Symbolically, this is represented by '$P \rightarrow Q, P \mathbin{/} \therefore Q$'. This argument form was explicitly formulated in ancient times by the Stoics as one of the "indemonstrables" and is now known as *modus ponens*. Another equally basic form of mixed hypothetical syllogism is '$P \rightarrow Q, \sim Q \mathbin{/} \therefore \sim P$', known as *modus tollens*.

The disjunctive syllogism. This is an argument in which the leading premise is a disjunction, the other premise being a denial of one of the alternatives, concluding to the remaining alternative; e.g., 'It is raining or I will go for a walk; but it is not raining; therefore I will go for a walk'. It is not always clear whether the 'or' of the disjunctive premise is inclusive or exclusive. Symbolic logic removes the ambiguity by using two different symbols and thus clearly distinguishes between *inclusive* or *weak disjunction*, '$P \lor Q$', which is true provided not both alternatives are false, and *exclusive* or *strong disjunction*, '$P \veebar Q$', which is true provided exactly one alternative is true and exactly one false. The definition of 'disjunctive syllogism' presupposes that the lead premise is an inclusive or weak disjunction, on the basis of which two forms are valid: '$P \lor Q, \sim P \mathbin{/} \therefore Q$' and '$P \lor Q, \sim Q \mathbin{/} \therefore P$'. If the disjunctive premise is exclusive, we have four valid argument forms, and we should speak here of an exclusive disjunctive syllogism. This is defined as an argument in which either from an exclusive disjunction and the denial of one of its disjuncts we infer the remaining disjunct – '$P \veebar Q, \sim P \mathbin{/} \therefore Q$', and '$P \veebar Q, \sim Q \mathbin{/} \therefore P$' (*modus tollendo ponens*); or else, from an exclusive disjunction and one of its disjuncts we infer the denial of the remaining disjunct – '$P \veebar Q, P \mathbin{/} \therefore \sim Q$', and '$P \veebar Q, Q \mathbin{/} \therefore \sim P$' (*modus ponendo tollens*).   I.Bo.

syllogism, demonstrative. See ARISTOTLE.

syllogism, practical. See PRACTICAL REASONING.

symbol. See PEIRCE, SYNCATEGOREMATA.

symbol, complete. See SYNCATEGOREMATA.

symbol, improper. See SYNCATEGOREMATA.

symbol, incomplete. See SYNCATEGOREMATA.

symbol, primitive. See LOGISTIC SYSTEM.

symbol, proper. See SYNCATEGOREMATA.

symbolic logic. See FORMAL LOGIC.

symmetrical. See RELATION.

symmetry. See PHILOSOPHY OF SCIENCE.

symmetry thesis. See COVERING LAW MODEL, PHILOSOPHY OF SCIENCE.

symptom. See CRITERION.

synaesthesia, a conscious experience in which qualities normally associated with one sensory modality are or seem to be sensed in another. Examples include auditory and tactile visions such as "loud sunlight" and "soft moonlight" as well as visual bodily sensations such as "dark thoughts" and "bright smiles." Two features of synaesthesia are of philosophic interest. First, the experience may be used to judge the appropriateness of sensory metaphors and similes, such as Baudelaire's "sweet as oboes." The metaphor is appropriate just when oboes sound sweet. Second, synaesthesia challenges the manner in which common sense distinguishes among the external senses. It is commonly acknowledged that taste, e.g., is not only unlike hearing, smell, or any other sense, but differs from them because taste involves gustatory rather than auditory experiences. In synaesthesia, however, one might taste sounds (sweet-sounding oboes).
                                                            G.A.G.

syncategoremata, (1) in grammar, words that cannot serve by themselves as subjects or predicates of categorical propositions. The opposite is *categoremata*, words that can do this. For example, 'and', 'if', 'every', 'because', 'insofar', and 'under' are syncategorematic terms, whereas 'dog', 'smooth', and 'sings' are categorematic ones. This usage comes from the fifth-century Latin grammarian Priscian. It seems to have been the original way of drawing the distinction, and to have persisted through later periods along with other usages described below. (2) In medieval logic from the twelfth century on, the distinction was drawn semantically. Categoremata are words that have a (definite) independent signification. Syncategoremata do not have any independent signification (or, according to some authors, not a definite one anyway), but acquire a signification only when used in a proposition together with categoremata. The examples used above work here as well. (3) Medieval logic distinguished not only categorematic and syncategorematic words, but also categorematic and syncategorematic uses of a single word. The most important is the word 'is', which can be used both categorematically to make an existence claim ('Socrates is' in the sense 'Socrates exists') or syncategorematically as a copula ('Socrates is a philosopher'). But other words were treated this way too. Thus 'whole' was said to be used syncategorematically as a kind of quantifier in 'The whole surface is white' (from which it follows that each part of the surface is white), but categorematically in 'The whole surface is two square feet in area' (from which it does not follow that each part of the surface is two square feet in area). (4) In medieval logic, again, syncategoremata were sometimes taken to include words that can serve by themselves as subjects or predicates of categorical propositions, but may interfere with standard logical inference patterns when they do.

The most notorious example is the word 'nothing'. If nothing is better than eternal bliss and tepid tea is better than nothing, still it does not follow (by the transitivity of 'better than') that tepid tea is better than eternal bliss. Again, consider the verb 'begins'. Everything red is colored, but not everything that begins to be red begins to be colored (it might have been some other color earlier). Such words were classified as syncategorematic because an analysis (called an *expositio*) of propositions containing them reveals implicit *syncategoremata* in sense (1) or perhaps (2). Thus an analysis of 'The apple begins to be red' would include the claim that it was not red earlier, and 'not' is syncategorematic in both senses (1) and (2). (5) In modern logic, sense (2) is extended to apply to all logical symbols, not just to words in natural languages. In this usage, categoremata are also called "proper symbols" or "complete symbols," while syncategoremata are called "improper symbols" or "incomplete symbols." In the terminology of modern formal semantics, the meaning of categoremata is fixed by the models for the language, whereas the meaning of syncategoremata is fixed by specify-

ing truth conditions for the various formulas of the language in terms of the models.

See also FORMAL SEMANTICS, QUANTIFICATION, SYLLOGISM.   P.V.S.

syncategorematic. See LOGICAL FORM, SYNCATEGOREMATA.

synderesis, in medieval moral theology, conscience. St. Jerome used the term, and it became a fixture because of Peter Lombard's inclusion of it in his *Sentences*. Despite this origin, 'synderesis' is distinguished from 'conscience' by Aquinas, for whom synderesis is the quasi-habitual grasp of the most common principles of the moral order (i.e., natural law), whereas conscience is the application of such knowledge to fleeting and unrepeatable circumstances.

'Conscience' is ambiguous in the way in which 'knowledge' is: knowledge can be the mental state of the knower or what the knower knows. But 'conscience', like 'synderesis', is typically used for the mental state. Sometimes, however, conscience is taken to include general moral knowledge as well as its application here and now; but the content of synderesis is the most general precepts, whereas the content of conscience, if general knowledge, will be less general precepts. Since conscience can be erroneous, the question arises as to whether synderesis and its object, natural law precepts, can be obscured and forgotten because of bad behavior or upbringing. Aquinas held that while great attrition can take place, such common moral knowledge cannot be wholly expunged from the human mind. This is a version of the Aristotelian doctrine that there are starting points of knowledge so easily grasped that the grasping of them is a defining mark of the human being. However perversely the human agent behaves there will remain not only the comprehensive realization that good is to be done and evil avoided, but also the recognition of some substantive human goods.

See also AQUINAS, ARISTOTLE, ETHICS.
                                                                                                  R.M.

syndicalism. See SOREL.

synechism. See PEIRCE, TYCHISM.

synergism, in Christian soteriology, the cooperation within human consciousness of free will and divine grace in the processes of conversion and regeneration. Synergism became an issue in sixteenth-century Lutheranism during a controversy prompted by Philip Melanchthon (1497–

1569). Under the influence of Erasmus, Melanchthon mentioned, in the 1533 edition of his *Common Places,* three causes of good actions: "the Word, the Holy Spirit, and the will." Advocated by Pfeffinger, a Philipist, synergism was attacked by the orthodox, predestinarian, and monergist party, Amsdorf and Flacius, who retorted with Gnesio-Lutheranism. The ensuing *Formula of Concord* (1577) officialized monergism. Synergism occupies a middle position between uncritical trust in human noetic and salvific capacity (Pelagianism and deism) and exclusive trust in divine agency (Calvinist and Lutheran fideism). Catholicism, Arminianism, Anglicanism, Methodism, and nineteenth- and twentieth-century liberal Protestantism have professed versions of synergism. **See also ERASMUS, FIDEISM, JUSTIFICATION BY FAITH.** J.-L.S.

synergy. See SYNERGISM.

synonymous definition. See DEFINITION.

synonymy. See MEANING.

syntactic ambiguity. See AMBIGUITY.

syntactic consistency. See CONSISTENCY.

syntactic term. See GRAMMAR.

syntax. See GRAMMAR.

syntax, logical. See LOGICAL SYNTAX.

synthesis. See HEGEL.

synthetic. See ANALYTIC–SYNTHETIC DISTINCTION.

synthetic a priori. See A PRIORI, KANT.

Syrian school. See MIDDLE PLATONISM.

Syrianus. See COMMENTARIES ON ARISTOTLE, MIDDLE PLATONISM.

system, axiomatic. See AXIOMATIC METHOD.

system, interpretive. See OPERATIONALISM.

system, logical. See FORMAL SEMANTICS, LOGISTIC SYSTEM.

systems analysis. See COGNITIVE SCIENCE, COMPUTER THEORY, SYSTEMS THEORY.

systems theory, the transdisciplinary study of the abstract organization of phenomena, independent of their substance, type, or spatial or temporal scale of existence. It investigates both the principles common to all complex entities and the (usually mathematical) models that can be used to describe them.

Systems theory was proposed in the 1940s by the biologist Ludwig von Bertalanffy and furthered by Ross Ashby (*Introduction to Cybernetics,* 1956). Von Bertalanffy was both reacting against reductionism and attempting to revive the unity of science. He emphasized that real systems are open to, and interact with, their environments, and that they can acquire qualitatively new properties through emergence, resulting in continual evolution. Rather than reduce an entity (e.g. the human body) to the properties of its parts or elements (e.g. organs or cells), systems theory focuses on the arrangement of and relations among the parts that connect them into a whole (cf. holism). This particular organization determines a system, which is independent of the concrete substance of the elements (e.g. particles, cells, transistors, people). Thus, the same concepts and principles of organization underlie the different disciplines (physics, biology, technology, sociology, etc.), providing a basis for their unification. Systems concepts include: system–environment boundary, input, output, process, state, hierarchy, goal-directedness, and information.

The developments of systems theory are diverse (Klir, *Facets of Systems Science,* 1991), including conceptual foundations and philosophy (e.g. the philosophies of Bunge, Bahm, and Laszlo); mathematical modeling and information theory (e.g. the work of Mesarovic and Klir); and practical applications. Mathematical systems theory arose from the development of isomorphies between the models of electrical circuits and other systems. Applications include engineering, computing, ecology, management, and family psychotherapy.

Systems analysis, developed independently of systems theory, applies systems principles to aid a decision maker with problems of identifying, reconstructing, optimizing, and controlling a system (usually a socio-technical organization), while taking into account multiple objectives, constraints, and resources. It aims to specify possible courses of action, together with their risks, costs, and benefits. Systems theory is closely connected to cybernetics, and also to system dynamics, which models changes in a network of coupled variables (e.g. the "world dynamics" models of Jay Forrester and the Club of Rome). Related ideas are used in the emerging "sciences of complexity," studying self-organization and heterogeneous networks of interacting actors, and associated domains such as far-from-equilibrium thermodynamics, chaotic dynamics, arti-ficial life, artificial intelligence, neural networks, and computer modeling and simulation.

See also ARTIFICIAL INTELLIGENCE, COMPUTER THEORY, INFORMATION THEORY.

F.H. & C.J.

szu. See KUNG, SZU.

T

table of categories. See KANT.

table of judgments. See KANT.

tabula rasa. See LEIBNIZ, LOCKE.

tacit consent. See SOCIAL CONTRACT.

tacit knowledge. See EPISTEMOLOGY.

Ta-hsüeh, a part of the Chinese Confucian classic *Book of Rites* whose title is standardly translated as *Great Learning.* Chu Hsi significantly amended the text (composed in the third or second century B.C.) and elevated it to the status of an independent classic as one of the Four Books. He regarded it as a quotation from Confucius and a commentary by Confucius's disciple Tseng-tzu, but neither his emendations nor his interpretation of the text is beyond dispute.

The *Ta-hsüeh* instructs a ruler in how to bring order to his state by self-cultivation. Much discussion of the text revolves around the phrase *ko wu,* which describes the first step in self-cultivation but is left undefined. The *Ta-hsüeh* claims that one's virtuousness or viciousness is necessarily evident to others, and that virtue manifests itself first in one's familial relationships, which then serve as an exemplar of order in both families and the state.

See also CONFUCIANISM. B.W.V.N.

Tai Chen (1724–77), Chinese philologist, philosopher, mathematician, and astronomer. A prominent member of the *K'ao-cheng* (evidential research) School, Tai attacked the Neo-Confucian dualism of *li* (pattern) and *ch'i* (ether), insisting that *li* is simply the orderly structure of *ch'i.* In terms of ethics, *li* consists of "feelings that do not err." In his *Meng-tzu tzu-yi shu-cheng* ("Meanings of Terms in the *Mencius* Explained and Attested"), Tai argues for the need to move from mere *yi-chien* (opinions) to *pu-te chih-yi* (undeviating standards) by applying the Confucian golden rule – not as a formal principle determining right action but as a winnowing procedure that culls out improper desires and allows only proper ones to inform one's actions. Beginning with *tzu jan* (natural) desires, one tests their

universalizability with the golden rule, thereby identifying those that accord with what is *pi-jan* (necessary). One spontaneously *k'o* (approves of) the "necessary," and Tai claims this is what Mencius describes as the "joy" of moral action. See also MENCIUS. P.J.I.

t'ai-chi, Chinese term meaning 'Great Ultimate', an idea first developed in the "Appended Remarks" of the *I-Ching,* where it is said that in the system of Change there is the Great Ultimate. It generates the Two Modes (yin and yang); the Two Modes generate the Four Forms (major and minor yin and yang); and the Four Forms generate the Eight Trigrams. In his "Explanation of the Diagram of the Great Ultimate," Chou Tun-yi (1017–73) spoke of "Non-ultimate (*wu-chi*) and also the Great Ultimate!" He generated controversies. Chu Hsi (1130–1200) approved Chou's formulation and interpreted *t'ai-chi* as *li* (principle), which is formless on the one hand and has principle on the other hand. See also CH'IEN, K'UN; CHOU TUN-YI; CHU HSI. S.-h.L.

T'ang Chün-i (1909–78), Chinese philosopher, a leading contemporary New Confucian and cofounder, with Ch'ien Mu, of New Asia College in Hong Kong in 1949. He acknowledged that it was through the influence of Hsiung Shih-li that he could see the true insights in Chinese philosophy. He drafted a manifesto published in 1958 and signed by Carsun Chang (1887–1969), Hsü Fu-kuan, and Mou Tsung-san. They criticized current sinological studies as superficial and inadequate, and maintained that China must learn science and democracy from the West, but the West must also learn human-heartedness and love of harmony and peace from Chinese culture. See also CH'IEN MU, CHINESE PHILOSOPHY, HSIUNG SHIH-LI, HSÜ FU-KUAN. S.-h.L.

T'an Ssu-t'ung (1864–98), Chinese philosopher of the late Ching dynasty, a close associate of K'ang Yu-wei and Liang Ch'i-ch'ao. He was a syncretist who lumped together Confucianism, Mohism, Taoism, Buddhism, Christianity, and Western science. His book on *Jen-hsüeh* (philosophy of humanity) identified humanity with ether, a cosmic force, and gave a new interpretation to the unity between nature and humanity. *Jen* for him is the source of all existence and creatures; it is none other than reality itself. He participated in the Hundred Days Reform in 1898 and died a martyr. His personal example inspired many revolutionaries afterward. **See also** KANG YU-WEI, LIANG CH'I-CH'AO.   S.-h.L.

tao, Chinese term meaning 'path', 'way', 'account'. From the sense of a literal path, road, or way, the term comes to mean a way of doing something (e.g., living one's life or organizing society), especially the way advocated by a particular individual or school of thought ("the way of the Master," "the way of the Mohists," etc.). Frequently, it refers to *the* way of doing something, the right way (e.g., "The Way has not been put into practice for a long time"). *Tao* also came to refer to the linguistic account that embodies or describes a way. Finally, in some texts the *tao* is a metaphysical entity. For example, in Neo-Confucianism, *tao* is identified with *li* (principle). In some contexts it is difficult to tell what sense is intended. **See also** LI¹, NEO-CONFUCIANISM.

B.W.V.N.

tao-hsin, jen-hsin, Chinese terms used by Neo-Confucian philosophers to contrast the mind according to the Way (*tao-hsin*) and the mind according to man's artificial, selfish desires (*jen-hsin*). When one responds spontaneously without making discrimination, one is acting according to the Way. One is naturally happy, sad, angry, and joyful as circumstances require. But when one's self is alienated from the Way, one works only for self-interest, and the emotions and desires are excessive and deviate from the Mean. In the Confucian tradition sages and worthies take Heaven as their model, while common people are urged to take *chün-tzu* (the superior men) as their model. **See also** NEO-CONFUCIANISM; T'IEN LI, JEN-YÜ.

S.-h.L.

Taoism, a Chinese philosophy identified with the *Tao-chia* (School of the Way), represented by Chuang Tzu and Lao Tzu. The term may also refer to the Huang–Lao School; Neo-Taoists, such as Wang Pi and Kuo Hsiang; and *Tao-chiao*, a diverse religious movement. Only the *Tao-chia* is discussed here.

The school derives its name from the word *tao* (Way), a term used by Chinese thinkers of almost every persuasion. Taoists were the first to use the term to describe the comprehensive structure and dynamic of the cosmos. Taoists believe that (1) there is a way the world should be, a way that, in some deep sense, it is; (2) human beings can understand this and need to have and follow such knowledge if they and the world are to exist in harmony; and (3) the world was once in such a state. Most early Chinese thinkers shared similar beliefs, but Taoists are distinct in claiming that the Way is not codifiable, indeed is ineffable. Taoists thus are metaphysical and ethical realists, but epistemological skeptics of an unusual sort, being language skeptics. Taoists further deny that one can strive successfully to attain the Way; Taoist self-cultivation is a process not of accumulation but of paring away. One must unweave the social fabric, forsake one's cultural conditioning, and abandon rational thought, to be led instead by one's *tzu jan* (spontaneous) inclinations. With a *hsü* (tenuous) mind, one then will perceive the *li* (pattern) of the cosmos and live by *wu wei* (non-action).

Though sharing a strong family resemblance, the Taoisms of Lao Tzu and Chuang Tzu are distinct. Lao Tzu advocates a primitive utopianism in which people enjoy the simple life of small agrarian communities, indifferent to what is happening in the neighboring village. Having abandoned cultural achievements such as writing, they keep accounts by knotting cords. Lao Tzu blames human "cleverness," which imposes the "human" on the "Heavenly," for most of what is bad in the world. For him, a notion like beauty gives rise to its opposite and only serves to increase anxiety and dissatisfaction; extolling a virtue, such as benevolence, only encourages people to affect it hypocritically. Lao Tzu advocates "turning back" to the time when intellect was young and still obedient to intuition and instinct. To accomplish this, the Taoist sage must rule and enforce this view upon the clever, if they should "dare to act."

Chuang Tzu emphasizes changing oneself more than changing society. He too is a kind of anti-rationalist and sees wisdom as a "knowing how" rather than a "knowing that." He invokes a repertoire of skillful individuals as exemplars of the Way. Such individuals engage the world through a knack that eludes definitive description and display all the Taoist virtues. Their minds are *hsü* (empty) of preconceptions, and so they perceive the *li* (pattern) in each situation. They respond spontaneously and so are *tzu jan*; they don't force things and so practice *wu wei*. In accord with the *tao*, they lead a frictionless existence; they "walk without touching the ground."

See also NEO-TAOISM, TAO.   P.J.I.

Tao Te Ching. See LAO TZU.

tao-t'ung, Chinese term meaning 'the orthodox line of transmission of the Way'. According to Chu Hsi (1130–1200), the first to use this term, the line of transmission can be traced back to ancient sage-emperors, Confucius and Mencius. The line was broken since Mencius and was only revived by the Ch'eng brothers in the Sung dynasty. The interesting feature is that the line has excluded important Confucian scholars such as Hsün Tzu (fl. 298–238 B.C.) and Tung Chung-shu (c.179–c.104 B.C.). The idea of *tao-t'ung* can be traced back to Han Yü (768–824) and Mencius. **See also** CHU HSI, CONFUCIANISM, CONFUCIUS, HAN YÜ, HSÜN TZU, MENCIUS, NEO-CONFUCIANISM, TUNG CHUNG-SHU.

S.-h.L.

Tarski, Alfred (1901–83), Polish-born American mathematician, logician, and philosopher of logic famous for his investigations of the concepts of truth and consequence conducted in the 1930s. His analysis of the concept of truth in syntactically precise, fully interpreted languages resulted in a definition of truth and an articulate defense of the correspondence theory of truth. Sentences of the following kind are now known as Tarskian biconditionals: 'The sentence "Every perfect number is even" is true if and only if every perfect number is even.' One of Tarski's major philosophical insights is that each Tarskian biconditional is, in his words, a partial definition of truth and, consequently, all Tarskian biconditionals whose right-hand sides exhaust the sentences of a given formal language together constitute an implicit definition of 'true' as applicable to sentences of that given formal language. This insight, because of its penetrating depth and disarming simplicity, has become a staple of modern analytic philosophy. Moreover, it in effect reduced the philosophical problem of defining truth to the logical problem of constructing a single sentence having the form of a definition and having as consequences each of the Tarskian biconditionals. Tarski's solution to this problem is the famous Tarski truth definition, versions of which appear in virtually every mathematical logic text.

Tarski's second most widely recognized philosophical achievement was his analysis and explication of the concept of consequence. Consequence is interdefinable with validity as applied to arguments: a given conclusion is a consequence of a given premise-set if and only if the argument composed of the given conclusion and the given premise-set is valid; conversely, a given argument is valid if and only if its conclusion is a consequence of its premise-set. Shortly after discovering the truth definition, Tarski presented his "no-countermodels" definition of consequence: a given sentence is a consequence of a given set of sentences if and only if every model of the set is a model of the sentence (in other words, if and only if there is no way to reinterpret the non-logical terms in such a way as to render the sentence false while rendering all sentences in the set true). As Quine has emphasized, this definition reduces the modal notion of logical necessity to a combination of syntactic and semantic concepts, thus avoiding reference to modalities and/or to "possible worlds."

After Tarski's definitive work on truth and on consequence he devoted his energies largely to more purely mathematical work. For example, in answer to Gödel's proof that arithmetic is incomplete and undecidable, Tarski showed that algebra and geometry are both complete and decidable. Tarski's truth definition and his consequence definition are found in his 1956 collection *Logic, Semantics, Metamathematics* (2d ed., 1983): article VIII, pp. 152–278, contains the truth definition; article XVI, pp. 409–20, contains the consequence definition. His published articles, nearly 3,000 pages in all, have been available together since 1986 in the four-volume *Alfred Tarski, Collected Papers*, edited by S. Givant and R. McKenzie.

See also GÖDEL'S INCOMPLETENESS THEOREMS, LOGICAL CONSEQUENCE, TRUTH. J.Cor.

Tarskian biconditional. See CONVENTION T, TARSKI.

Tarskian satisfaction. See SATISFACTION.

Tarskian semantics. See FORMAL SEMANTICS.

Tarski's theorem. See SEMANTIC PARADOXES.

Tarski's (T) schema. See TRUTH.

task verb. See ACTION VERB.

tautology, a proposition whose negation is inconsistent, or (self-) contradictory, e.g. 'Socrates is Socrates', 'Every human is either male or non-male', 'No human is both male and non-male', 'Every human is identical to itself', 'If Socrates is human then Socrates is human'. A proposition that is (or is logically equivalent to) the negation of a tautology is called a (self-)contradiction. According to classical logic, the property of being implied by its own negation is a necessary and sufficient condition for being a tautology and the property of implying its own negation is a necessary and sufficient condition for being a contradiction. Tautologies are logically necessary and contradictions are logically impossible.

Epistemically, every proposition that can be known to be true by purely logical reasoning is a tautology and every proposition that can be known to be false by purely logical reasoning is a contradiction. The converses of these two statements are both controversial among classical logicians. Every proposition in the same logical form as a tautology is a tautology and every proposition in the same logical form as a contradiction is a contradiction. For this reason sometimes a tautology is said to be *true in virtue of form* and a contradiction is said to be *false in virtue of form;* being a tautology and being a contradiction (tautologousness and contradictoriness) are formal properties. Since the logical form of a proposition is determined by its logical terms ('every', 'some', 'is', etc.), a tautology is sometimes said to be true in virtue of its logical terms and likewise *mutatis mutandis* for a contradiction.

Since tautologies do not exclude any logical possibilities they are sometimes said to be "empty" or "uninformative"; and there is a tendency even to deny that they are genuine propositions and that knowledge of them is genuine knowledge. Since each contradiction "includes" (implies) all logical possibilities (which of course are jointly inconsistent), contradictions are sometimes said to be "overinformative." Tautologies and contradictions are sometimes said to be "useless," but for opposite reasons. More precisely, according to classical logic, being implied by each and every proposition is necessary and sufficient for being a tautology and, coordinately, implying each and every proposition is necessary and sufficient for being a contradiction.

Certain developments in mathematical logic, especially model theory and modal logic, seem to support use of Leibniz's expression 'true in all possible worlds' in connection with tautologies. There is a special subclass of tautologies called *truth-functional tautologies* that are true in virtue of a special subclass of logical terms called *truth-functional connectives* ('and', 'or', 'not', 'if', etc.). Some logical writings use 'tautology' exclusively for truth-functional tautologies and thus replace "tautology" in its broad sense by another expression, e.g. 'logical truth'. Tarski, Gödel, Russell, and many other logicians have used the word in its broad sense, but use of it in its narrow sense is widespread and entirely acceptable.

Propositions known to be tautologies are often given as examples of a priori knowledge. In philosophy of mathematics, the logistic hypothesis of logicism is the proposition that every true proposition of pure mathematics is a tautology. Some writers make a sharp distinction between the formal property of being a tautology and the non-formal metalogical property of being a law of logic. For example, 'One is one' is not metalogical but it is a tautology, whereas 'No tautology is a contradiction' is metalogical but is not a tautology.

See also LAWS OF THOUGHT, LOGICAL FORM, LOGICISM.   J.Cor.

Taylor, Charles (b.1931), Canadian philosopher and historian of modernity. Taylor was educated at McGill and Oxford and has taught primarily at these universities. His work has a broadly analytic character, although he has consistently opposed the naturalistic and reductionist tendencies that were associated with the positivist domination of analytic philosophy during the 1950s and 1960s. He was, for example, a strong opponent of behaviorism and defended the essentially interpretive nature of the social sciences against efforts to reduce their methodology to that of the natural sciences. Taylor has also done important work on the histiory of philosophy, particularly on Hegel, and has connected his work with that of Continental philosophers such as Heidegger and Merleau-Ponty. He has contributed to political theory and written on contemporary political issues such as multiculturalism (in, e.g., *The Ethics of Authenticity,* 1991), often with specific reference to Canadian politics. He has also taken an active political role in Quebec.

Taylor's most important work, *Sources of the Self* (1989), is a historical and critical study of the emergence of the modern concept of the self. Like many other critics of modernity, Taylor rejects modern tendencies to construe personal identity in entirely scientific or naturalistic terms, arguing that these construals lead to a view of the self that can make no sense of our undeniable experience of ourselves as moral agents. He develops this critique in a historical mode through discussion of the radical Enlightenment's (e.g., Locke's) reduction of the self to an atomic individual, essentially disengaged from everything except its own ideas and desires.

But unlike many critics, Taylor also finds in modernity other, richer sources for a conception of the self. These include the idea of the self's inwardness, traceable as far back as Augustine but developed in a distinctively modern way by Montaigne and Descartes; the affirmation of ordinary life (and of ourselves as participants in it), particularly associated with the Reformation; and the expressivism (of, e.g., the Romantics) for which the self fulfills itself by embracing and articulating the voice of nature present in its depths. Taylor thinks that these sources constitute a modern self that, unlike the "punctual self" of the radical Enlightenment, is a meaningful ethical agent. He suggests, nonetheless, that an adequate conception of the modern self will further require a relation of human inwardness to God. This suggestion so far remains undeveloped.

See also ENLIGHTENMENT, PERSONAL IDENTITY, PHILOSOPHY OF MIND.   G.G.

Taylor, Harriet (1807–58), English feminist and writer. She was the wife of J. S. Mill, who called her the "most admirable person" he had ever met; but according to her critics, Taylor was "a stupid woman" with "a knack for repeating prettily what J.S.M. said." Although Mill may have exaggerated her moral and intellectual virtues, her writings on marriage, the enfranchisement of women, and toleration did influence his *Subjection of Women* and *On Liberty*. In *The Enfranchisement of Women*, Taylor rejected the reigning "angel in the house" ideal of woman. She argued that confining women to the house impeded both sexes' development. Taylor was a feminist philosopher in her own right, who argued even more strongly than Mill that women are entitled to the same educational, legal, and economic opportunities that men enjoy.   R.T.

te, Chinese term meaning 'moral charisma' or 'virtue'. In its earliest use, *te* is the quality bestowed on a ruler by Heaven (*t'ien*) which makes his subjects willingly follow him. Rule by *te* is traditionally thought to be not just ethically preferable to rule by force but also more effective instrumentally. It is a necessary condition for having *te* that one be ethically exemplary, but traditional thinkers differ over whether being virtuous is also sufficient for the bestowal of *te*, and whether the bestowal of *te* makes one even more virtuous. *Te* soon came also to refer to virtue, in the sense of either a disposition that contributes to human flourishing (benevolence, courage, etc.) or the specific excellence of any kind of thing.   B.W.V.N.

techne (Greek, 'art', 'craft'), a human skill based on general principles and capable of being taught. In this sense, a manual craft such as carpentry is a *techne*, but so are sciences such as medicine and arithmetic. According to Plato (*Gorgias* 501a), a genuine *techne* understands its subject matter and can give a rational account of its activity. Aristotle (*Metaphysics* I.1) distinguishes *techne* from experience on the grounds that *techne* involves knowledge of universals and causes, and can be taught. Sometimes '*techne*' is restricted to the productive (as opposed to theoretical and practical) arts, as at *Nicomachean Ethics* VI.4. *Techne* and its products are often contrasted with *physis,* nature (*Physics* II.1). **See also** ARISTOTLE, PHYSIS, PLATO.   W.J.P.

Teichmüller, Gustav (1832–88), German philosopher who contributed to the history of philosophy and developed a theory of knowledge and a metaphysical conception based on these historical studies. Born in Braunschweig, he taught at Göttingen and Basel and was influenced by Lotze and Leibniz. His major works are *Aristotelische Forschungen* (*Aristotelian Investigations,* 1867–73) and *Die wirkliche und scheinbare Welt* (*The Actual and the Apparent World,* 1882). His other works are *Ueber die Unsterblichkeit der Seele* (1874), *Studien zur Geschichte der Begriffe* (1874), *Darwinismus und Philosophie* (1877), *Ueber das Wesen der Liebe* (1879), *Religionsphilosophie* (1886), and the posthumously published *Neue Grundlegung der Psychologie und Logik* (1889).

Teichmüller maintained that the self of immediate experience, the "I," is the most fundamental reality and that the conceptual world is a projection of its constituting activity. On the basis of his studies in the history of metaphysics and his sympathies with Leibniz's monadology, he held that each metaphysical system contained partial truths and construed each metaphysical standpoint as a perspective on a complex reality. Thinking of both metaphysical interpretations of reality and the subjectivity of individual immediate experience, Teichmüller christened his own philosophical position "perspectivism." His work influenced later European thought through its impact on the philosophical reflections of Nietzsche, who was probably influenced by him in the development of his perspectival theory of knowledge.

See also LEIBNIZ, LOTZE.   G.J.S.

Teilhard de Chardin, Pierre (1881–1955), French paleontologist, Jesuit priest, and philosopher. His philosophical work, while published only post-humously, was vigorously discussed throughout his career. His writings generated considerable controversy within the church, since one of his principal concerns was to bring about a forceful yet generous reconciliation between the traditional Christian dogma and the dramatic advances yielded by modern science. His philosophy consisted of systematic reflections on cosmology, biology, physics, anthropology, social theory, and theology – reflections guided, he maintained, by his fascination with the nature of life, energy, and matter, and by his profound respect for human spirituality.

Teilhard was educated in philosophy and mathematics at the Jesuit college of Mongré, near Lyons. He entered the Jesuit order at the age of eighteen and was ordained a priest in 1911. He went on to study at Aix-en-Provence, Laval, and Caen, as well as on the Isle of Jersey and at Hastings, England.

Returning to Paris after the war, he studied biology, geology, and paleontology at the Museum of Natural History and at the Institut Catholique, receiving a doctoral degree in geology in 1922. In 1923, shortly after appointment to the faculty of geology at the Institut Catholique, he took leave to pursue field research in China. His research resulted in the discovery, in 1929, of Peking man (*Sinanthropus pekinensis*) – which he saw as "perhaps the next to the last step traceable between the anthropoids and man." It was during this period that Teilhard began to compose one of his major theoretical works, *The Phenomenon of Man* (1955), in which he stressed the deep continuity of evolutionary development and the emergence of humanity from the animal realm. He argued that received evolutionary theory was fully compatible with Christian doctrine. Indeed, it is the synthesis of evolutionary theory with his own Christian theology that perhaps best characterizes the broad tenor of his thought.

Starting with the very inception of the evolutionary trajectory, i.e., with what he termed the "Alpha point" of creation, Teilhard's general theory resists any absolute disjunction between the inorganic and organic. Indeed, matter and spirit are two "stages" or "aspects" of the same cosmic stuff. These transitions from one state to another may be said to correspond to those between the somatic and psychic, the exterior and interior, according to the state of relative development, organization, and complexity. Hence, for Teilhard, much as for Bergson (whose work greatly influenced him), evolutionary development is characterized by a progression from the simplest components of matter and energy (what he termed the lithosphere), through the organization of flora and fauna (the biosphere), to the complex formations of sentient and cognitive human life (the noosphere). In this sense, evolution is a "progressive spiritualization of matter." He held this to be an orthogenetic process, one of "directed evolution" or "Genesis," by which matter would irreversibly metamorphose itself, in a process of involution and complexification, toward the psychic.

Specifically, Teilhard's account sought to overcome what he saw as a prescientific worldview, one based on a largely antiquated and indefensible metaphysical dualism. By accomplishing this, he hoped to realize a productive convergence of science and religion. The end of evolution, what he termed "the Omega point," would be the full presence of Christ, embodied in a universal human society. Many have tended to see a Christian pantheism expressed in such views. Teilhard himself stressed a profoundly personalist, spiritual perspective, drawn not only from the theological tradition of Thomism, but from that of Pauline Neoplatonism and Christian mysticism as well – especially that tradition extending from Meister Eckhart through Cardinal Bérulle and Malebranche.   D.Al.

telekinesis. See PARAPSYCHOLOGY.

teleofunctionalism. See FODOR.

teleological argument. See PHILOSOPHY OF RELIGION.

teleological ethics. See ETHICS.

teleological explanation. See TELEOLOGY.

teleological law. See CAUSAL LAW.

teleological suspension of the ethical. See KIERKEGAARD.

teleology, the philosophical doctrine that all of nature, or at least intentional agents, are goal-directed or functionally organized. Plato first suggested that the organization of the natural world can be understood by comparing it to the behavior of an intentional agent – *external teleology.* For example, human beings can anticipate the future and behave in ways calculated to realize their intentions. Aristotle invested nature itself with goals – *internal teleology*. Each kind has its own final cause, and entities are so constructed that they tend to realize this goal. Heavenly bodies travel as nearly as they are able in perfect circles because that is their nature, while horses give rise to other horses because that is their nature. Natural theologians combined these two teleological perspectives to explain all phenomena by reference to the intentions of a beneficent, omniscient, all-powerful God. God so constructed the world that each entity is invested with the tendency to fulfill its own God-given nature. Darwin explained the teleological character of the living world non-teleologically. The evolutionary process is not itself teleological, but it gives rise to functionally organized systems and intentional agents.

Present-day philosophers acknowledge intentional behavior and functional organization but attempt to explain both without reference to a supernatural agent or internal natures of the more metaphysical sort. Instead, they define 'function' cybernetically, in terms of persistence toward a goal state under varying conditions, or etiologically, in terms of the contribution that a structure or action makes to the realization of a goal state. These definitions confront a battery of counterexamples designed to show that the condition mentioned is either not necessary, not sufficient, or both; e.g., missing goal objects, too many goals, or functional equivalents. The trend has been to decrease the scope of teleological explanations from all of nature, to the organization of those entities that arise through natural selection, to their final refuge in the behavior of human beings. Behaviorists have attempted to eliminate this last vestige of teleology. Just as natural selection makes the attribution of goals for biological species redundant, the selection of behavior in terms of its consequences is designed to make any reference to intentions on the part of human beings unnecessary.

See also MECHANISTIC EXPLANATION.

D.L.H.

telepathy. See PARAPSYCHOLOGY.

Telesio, Bernardino (1509–88), Italian philosopher whose early scientific empiricism influenced Francis Bacon and Galileo. He studied in Padua, where he completed his doctorate in 1535, and practiced philosophy in Naples and Cosenza without holding any academic position. His major work, the nine volumes of *De rerum natura iuxta propria principia* ("On the Nature of

Things According to Their Principles," 1586), contains an attempt to interpret nature on the basis of its own principles, which Telesio identifies with the two incorporeal active forces of heat and cold, and the corporeal and passive physical substratum. As the two active forces permeate all of nature and are endowed with sensation, Telesio argues that all of nature possesses some degree of sensation. Human beings share with animals a material substance produced by heat and coming into existence with the body, called spirit. They are also given a mind by God. Telesio knew both the Averroistic and the Alexandrist interpretations of Aristotle. However, he broke with both, criticizing Aristotle's *Physics* and claiming that nature is investigated better by the senses than by the intellect. P.Gar.

telishment, punishment of one suspected of wrongdoing, but whom the authorities know to be innocent, imposed as a deterrent to future wrongdoers. Telishment is thus not punishment insofar as punishment requires that the recipient's harsh treatment be deserved. Telishment is classically given as one of the thought experiments challenging utilitarianism (and more broadly, consequentialism) as a theory of ethics, for such a theory seems to justify telishment on some occasions. **See also** PUNISHMENT.

M.S.M.

telos, ancient Greek term meaning 'end' or 'purpose'. *Telos* is a key concept not only in Greek ethics but also in Greek science. The purpose of a human being is a good life, and human activities are evaluated according to whether they lead to or manifest this *telos*. Plants, animals, and even inanimate objects were also thought to have a *telos* through which their activities and relations could be understood and evaluated. Though a *telos* could be something that transcends human activities and sensible things, as Plato thought, it need not be anything apart from nature. Aristotle, e.g., identified the *telos* of a sensible thing with its immanent form. It follows that the purpose of the thing is simply to be what it is and that, in general, a thing pursues its purpose when it endeavors to preserve itself. Aristotle's view shows that 'purpose in nature' need not mean a *higher* purpose beyond nature. Yet, his immanent purpose does not exclude "higher" purposes, and Aristotelian teleology was pressed into service by medieval thinkers as a framework for understanding God's agency through nature. Thinkers in the modern period argued against the prominent role accorded to *telos* by ancient and medieval thinkers, and they replaced it with analyses in terms of mechanism and law.

E.C.H.

temperance. See CARDINAL VIRTUES.

template. See COGNITIVE SCIENCE.

temporal becoming. See TIME.

tensed identity. See IDENTITY.

tense logic, an extension of classical logic introduced by Arthur Prior (*Past, Present, and Future,* 1967), involving operators P and F for the past and future tenses, or 'it was the case that . . .' and 'it will be the case that . . .'. Classical or mathematical logic was developed as a logic of unchanging mathematical truth, and can be applied to tensed discourse only by artificial regimentation inspired by mathematical physics, introducing quantification over "times" or "instants." Thus 'It will have been the case that p,' which Prior represents simply as FPp, classical logic represents as 'There [exists] an instant t and there [exists] an instant t' such that t [is] later than the present and t' [is] earlier than t, and at t' it [is] the case that p', or $\exists t \exists t'$ ($t_0 < t \wedge t' < t \wedge p(t'))$, where the brackets indicate that the verbs are to be understood as tenseless. Prior's motives were in part linguistic (to produce a formalization less removed from natural language than the classical) and in part metaphysical (to avoid ontological commitment to such entities as instants). Much effort was devoted to finding tense-logical principles equivalent to various classical assertions about the structure of the earlier–later order among instants; e.g., 'Between any two instants there is another instant' corresponds to the validity of the axioms P$p \rightarrow$ PPp and F$p \rightarrow$ FFp. Less is expressible using P and F than is expressible with explicit quantification over instants, and further operators for 'since' and 'until' or 'now' and 'then' have been introduced by Hans Kamp and others. These are especially important in combination with quantification, as in 'When he was in power, all who *now* condemn him *then* praised him.'

As tense is closely related to mood, so tense logic is closely related to modal logic. (As Kripke models for modal logic consist each of a set X of "worlds" and a relation R of 'x is an *alternative* to y', so for tense logic they consist each of a set X of "instants" and a relation R of 'x is *earlier* than y': Thus instants, banished from the syntax or proof theory, reappear in the semantics or model the-

ory.) Modality and tense are both involved in the issue of future contingents, and one of Prior's motives was a desire to produce a formalism in which the views on this topic of ancient, medieval, and early modern logicians (from Aristotle with his "sea fight tomorrow" and Diodorus Cronos with his "Master Argument" through Ockham to Peirce) could be represented.

The most important precursor to Prior's work on tense logic was that on many-valued logics by Łukasiewicz, which was motivated largely by the problem of future contingents. Also related to tense and mood is aspect, and modifications to represent this grammatical category (evaluating formulas at periods rather than instants of time) have also been introduced. Like modal logic, tense logic has been the object of intensive study in theoretical computer science, especially in connection with attempts to develop languages in which properties of programs can be expressed and proved; variants of tense logic (under such labels as "dynamic logic" or "process logic") have thus been extensively developed for technological rather than philosophical motives.

See also FUTURE CONTINGENTS, MANY-VALUED LOGIC.

J.Bur.

Teresa of Ávila, Saint (1515–82), Spanish religious, mystic, and author of spiritual treatises. Having entered the Carmelite order at Ávila at twenty-two, Teresa spent the next twenty-five years seeking guidance in the practice of prayer. Despite variously inept spiritual advisers, she seems to have undergone a number of mystical experiences and to have made increasingly important discoveries about interior life. After 1560 Teresa took on a public role by attaching herself to the reforming party within the Spanish Carmelites. Her remaining years were occupied with the reform, in which she was associated most famously with John of the Cross. She also composed several works, including a spiritual autobiography (the *Vida*) and two masterpieces of spirituality, the *Way of Perfection* and the *Interior Castle*. The latter two, but especially the *Castle*, offer philosophical suggestions about the soul's passions, activities, faculties, and ground. Their principal motive is to teach the reader how to progress, by successive surrender, toward the divine Trinity dwelling at the soul's center.

M.D.J.

term. See RELATION, RUSSELL, SYLLOGISM.

term, major. See SYLLOGISM.

term, minor. See SYLLOGISM.

term, observation. See PHILOSOPHY OF SCIENCE.

term, transcendental. See TRANSCENDENTALS.

terminist logic, a school of logic originating in twelfth-century Europe and dominant in the universities until its demise in the humanistic reforms. Its chief goal was the elucidation of the logical form (the "exposition") of propositions advanced in the context of Scholastic disputation. Its central theory concerned the properties of terms, especially supposition, and did the work of modern quantification theory. Important logicians in the school include Peter of Spain, William Sherwood, Walter Burley, William Heytesbury, and Paul of Venice. **See also BURLEY, HEYTESBURY, PAUL OF VENICE, PETER OF SPAIN, SHERWOOD.**   J.Lo.

terminus ad quem. See TERMINUS A QUO.

terminus a quo (Latin, 'term from which'), the starting point of some process. The *terminus ad quem* is the ending point. For example, change is a process that begins from some state (the *terminus a quo*) and proceeds to some state at which it ends (the *terminus ad quem*). In particular, in the ripening of an apple, the green apple is the *terminus a quo* and the red apple is the *terminus ad quem*.   A.P.M.

tertiary qualities. See QUALITIES.

Tertullian (A.D. c.155–c.240), Latin theologian, an early father of the Christian church. A layman from Carthage, he laid the conceptual and linguistic basis for the doctrine of the Trinity. Though appearing hostile to philosophy ("What has Athens to do with Jerusalem?") and to rationality ("It is certain because it is impossible"), Tertullian was steeped in Stoicism. He denounced all eclecticism not governed by the normative tradition of Christian doctrine, yet commonly used philosophical argument and Stoic concepts (e.g., the corporeality of God and the soul). Despite insisting on the sole authority of the New Testament apostles, he joined with Montanism, which taught that the Holy Spirit was still inspiring prophecy concerning moral discipline. Reflecting this interest in the Spirit, Tertullian pondered the distinctions (to which he gave the neologism *trinitas*) within God. God is one "substance" but three "persons": a plurality without division. The Father, Son, and Spirit are distinct, but share equally in the one Godhead. This threeness is manifest only in the "economy" of God's temporal action toward the world; later orthodoxy (e.g. Athanasius, Basil the Great, Augustine), would postulate a Trinity that is eternal and "immanent," i.e., internal to God's being. **See also MONTANISM, STOICISM, TRINITARIANISM.**   A.E.L.

testability, in the sciences, capacity of a theory to undergo experimental testing. Theories in the natural sciences are regularly subjected to experimental tests involving detailed and rigorous control of variable factors. Not naive observation of the workings of nature, but disciplined, designed intervention in such workings, is the hallmark of testability. Logically regarded, testing takes the form of seeking confirmation of theories by obtaining positive test results. We can represent a theory as a conjunction of a hypothesis and a statement of initial conditions, $(H \cdot A)$. This conjunction deductively entails testable or observational consequences O. Hence, $(H \cdot A) \rightarrow O$. If O obtains, $(H \cdot A)$ is said to be confirmed, or rendered probable. But such confirmation is not decisive; O may be entailed by, and hence explained by, many other theories. For this reason, Popper insisted that the testability of theories should seek disconfirmations or falsifications. The logical schema

$$(H \cdot A) \rightarrow O$$
$$\underline{\text{not-}O}$$
$$\text{not-}(H \cdot A)$$

is deductively valid, hence apparently decisive.

On this view, science progresses, not by finding the truth, but by discarding the false. Testability becomes *falsifiability*. This deductive schema (*modus tollens*) is also employed in the analysis of crucial tests. Consider two hypotheses H_1 and H_2, both introduced to explain some phenomenon. H_1 predicts that for some test condition C, we have the test result 'if C then e_1', and H_2, the result 'if C then e_2', where e_1 and e_2 are logically incompatible. If experiment falsifies 'if C then e_1' (e_1 does not actually occur as a test result), the hypothesis H_1 is false, which implies that H_2 is true. It was originally supposed that the experiments of J. B. L. Foucault constituted a decisive falsification of the corpuscular theory of the nature of light, and thus provided a decisive establishment of the truth of its rival, the wave theory of light.

This account of crucial experiments neglects certain points in logic and also the role of auxiliary hypotheses in science. As Duhem pointed out, rarely, if ever, does a hypothesis face the facts in isolation from other supporting assumptions. Furthermore, it is a fact of logic that the falsification of a conjunction of a hypothesis and its auxiliary assumptions and initial conditions (not-$(H \cdot A)$) is logically equivalent to (not-H or not-A), and the test result itself provides no warrant for choosing which alternative to reject. Duhem further suggested that rejection of any component part of a complex theory is based on extra-evidential considerations (factors like simplicity and fruitfulness) and cannot be forced by negative test results. Acceptance of Duhem's view led Quine to suggest that a theory must face the tribunal of experience *en bloc*; no single hypothesis can be tested in isolation. Original conceptions of testability and falsifiability construed scientific method as hypothetico-deductive. Difficulties with these reconstructions of the logic of experiment have led philosophers of science to favor an explication of empirical support based on the logic of probability.

See also CRUCIAL EXPERIMENT, DUHEM, HYPOTHETICO-DEDUCTIVE METHOD, PROBABILITY.   R.E.B.

testimony, an act of telling, including all assertions apparently intended to impart information, regardless of social setting. In an extended sense personal letters and messages, books, and other published material purporting to contain factual information also constitute testimony. Testimony may be sincere or insincere, and may express knowledge or baseless prejudice. When it expresses knowledge, and it is rightly believed, this knowledge is disseminated to its recipients, near or remote. Secondhand knowledge can be passed on further, producing long chains of testimony; but these chains always begin with the report of an eyewitness or expert.

In any social group with a common language there is potential for the sharing, through testimony, of the fruits of individuals' idiosyncratic acquisition of knowledge through perception and inference. In advanced societies specialization in the gathering and production of knowledge and its wider dissemination through spoken and written testimony is a fundamental socio-epistemic fact, and a very large part of each person's body of knowledge and belief stems from testimony.

Thus the question when a person may properly believe what another tells her, and what grounds her epistemic entitlement to do so, is a crucial one in epistemology. Reductionists about testimony insist that this entitlement must derive from our entitlement to believe what we perceive to be so, and to draw inferences from this according to familiar general principles. (See e.g., Hume's classic discussion, in his *Enquiry into Human Understanding,* section X.) On this view, I can perceive that someone has told me that p, but can thereby come to know that p only by means of an inference – one that goes via additional, empirically grounded knowledge of the trustworthiness of that person. Anti-reductionists insist, by contrast, that there is a general entitlement to believe what one is told just as such – defeated by knowledge of one's informant's lack of trustworthiness (her mendacity or incompetence), but not needing to be bolstered positively by empirically based knowledge of her trustworthiness. Anti-reductionists thus see testimony as an autonomous source of knowledge on a par with perception, inference, and memory. One argument adduced for anti-reductionism is transcendental: We have many beliefs acquired from testimony, and these beliefs are knowledge; their status as knowledge cannot be accounted for in the way required by the reductionist – that is, the reliability of testimony cannot be independently confirmed; therefore the reductionist's insistence on this is mistaken. However, while it is perhaps true that the reliability of *all* the beliefs one has that depend on past testimony cannot be simultaneously confirmed, one can certainly sometimes ascertain, without circularity, that a specific assertion by a particular person is likely to be correct – if, e.g.,one's own experience has established that that person has a good track record of reliability about that kind of thing.

See also EPISTEMOLOGY, HUME, INFERENTIAL KNOWLEDGE.   E.F.

Tetens, Johann Nicolas (1736–1807), German philosopher and psychologist, sometimes called the German Locke. After his studies in Rostock and Copenhagen, he taught at Bützow and Kiel (until 1789). He had a second successful career as a public servant in Denmark (1790–1807) that did not leave him time for philosophical work.

Tetens was one of the most important German philosophers between Wolff and Kant. Like Kant, whom he significantly influenced, Tetens attempted to find a middle way between empiricism and rationalism. His most important work, the *Philosophische Versuche über die menschliche Natur und ihre Entwicklung* ("Philosophical Essays on Human Nature and its Development," 1777), is indicative of the state of philosophical discussion in Germany before Kant's *Critique of Pure Reason*. Tetens, who followed the "psychological method" of Locke, tended toward a naturalism, like that of Hume. However, Tetens made a more radical distinction between reason and sensation than Hume allowed and attempted to show how basic rational principles guarantee the objectivity of human knowledge.   M.K.

Tetractys. See PYTHAGORAS.

Thales of Miletus (fl. c.585 B.C.), Greek philosopher who was regarded as one of the Seven Sages of Greece. He was also considered the first philosopher, founder of the Milesians. Thales is also reputed to have been an engineer, astronomer, mathematician, and statesman. His doctrines even early Greek sources know only by hearsay: he said that water is the *archē*, and that the earth floats on water like a raft. The magnet has a soul, and all things are full of the gods. Thales' attempt to explain natural phenomena in natural rather than exclusively supernatural terms bore fruit in his follower Anaximander. **See also** PRE-SOCRATICS.   D.W.G.

thema (plural: themata), in Stoic logic, a ground rule used to reduce argument forms to basic forms. The Stoics analyzed arguments by their form (*schēma*, or *tropos*). They represented forms using numbers to represent claims; for example, 'if the first, the second; but the first; therefore the second'. Some forms were undemonstrable; others were reduced to the undemonstrable argument forms by ground rules (themata); e.g., if *R* follows from *P & Q*, ~*Q* follows from *P & ~R*. The five undemonstrable arguments are: (1) *modus ponens*; (2) *modus tollens*; (3) not both (*P* and *Q*), *P*, so not-*Q*; (4) *P* or *Q* but not both, *P*, so not-*Q*; and (5) disjunctive syllogism. The evidence about the four ground rules is incomplete, but a sound and consistent system for propositional logic can be developed that is consistent with the evidence we have. (See Diogenes Laertius, *Lives of the Philosophers*, 776–81, for an introduction to the Stoic theory of arguments; other evidence is more scattered.) **See also** DOXOGRAPHERS, FORMAL LOGIC, LOGICAL FORM, STOICISM.   H.A.I.

Themistius. See COMMENTARIES ON ARISTOTLE.

theodicy (from Greek *theos*, 'God', and *dikē*, 'justice'), a defense of the justice or goodness of God in the face of doubts or objections arising from the phenomena of evil in the world ('evil' refers here to bad states of affairs of any sort). Many types of theodicy have been proposed and vigorously debated; only a few can be sketched here.

(1) It has been argued that evils are logically necessary for greater goods (e.g., hardships for the full exemplification of certain virtues), so that even an omnipotent being (roughly, one whose power has no logically contingent limits) would have a morally sufficient reason to cause or permit the evils in order to obtain the goods. Leibniz, in his *Theodicy* (1710), proposed a particularly comprehensive theodicy of this type. On his view, God had adequate reason to bring into existence the actual world, despite all its evils, because it is the best of all possible worlds, and all actual evils are essential ingredients in it, so that omitting any of them would spoil the design of the whole. Aside from issues about whether actual evils are in fact necessary for greater goods, this approach faces the question whether it assumes wrongly that the end justifies the means.

(2) An important type of theodicy traces some or all evils to sinful free actions of humans or other beings (such as angels) created by God. Proponents of this approach assume that free action in creatures is of great value and is logically incompatible with divine causal control of the creatures' actions. It follows that God's not intervening to prevent sins is necessary, though the sins themselves are not, to the good of created freedom. This is proposed as a morally sufficient reason for God's not preventing them. It is a major task for this type of theodicy to explain why God would permit those evils that are not themselves free choices of creatures but are at most consequences of such choices.

(3) Another type of theodicy, both ancient and currently influential among theologians, though less congenial to orthodox traditions in the major theistic religions, proposes to defend God's goodness by abandoning the doctrine that God is omnipotent. On this view, God is causally, rather than logically, unable to prevent many evils while pursuing sufficiently great goods. A principal sponsor of this approach at present is the movement known as process theology, inspired by Whitehead; it depends on a complex metaphysical theory about the nature of causal relationships.

(4) Other theodicies focus more on outcomes than on origins. Some religious beliefs suggest that God will turn out to have been very good to created persons by virtue of gifts (especially religious gifts, such as communion with God as supreme Good) that may be bestowed in a life after death or in religious experience in the present life. This approach may be combined with one of the other types of theodicy, or adopted by people who think that God's reasons for permitting evils are beyond our finding out.

See also DIVINE ATTRIBUTES, FREE WILL PROBLEM, PHILOSOPHY OF RELIGION, PROCESS THEOLOGY.					R.M.A.

Theodorus. See CYRENAICS.

theologia naturalis (Latin, 'natural theology'), theology that uses the methods of investigation and standards of rationality of any other area of philosophy. Traditionally, the central problems of natural theology are proofs for the existence of God and the problem of evil. In contrast with natural theology, supernatural theology uses methods that are supposedly revealed by God and accepts as fact beliefs that are similarly outside the realm of rational acceptability. Relying on a prophet or a pope to settle factual questions would be acceptable to supernatural, but not to natural, theology. Nothing prevents a natural theologian from analyzing concepts that can be used sanguinely by supernatural theologians, e.g., revelation, miracles, infallibility, and the doctrine of the Trinity.

Theologians often work in both areas, as did, e.g., Anselm and Aquinas. For his brilliant critiques of traditional theology, Hume deserves the title of "natural anti-theologian."

See also PHILOSOPHY OF RELIGION. A.P.M.

theological creationism. See PREEXISTENCE.

theological naturalism, the attempt to develop a naturalistic conception of God. As a philosophical position, naturalism holds (1) that the only reliable methods of knowing what there is are methods continuous with those of the developed sciences, and (2) that the application of those methods supports the view that the constituents of reality are either physical or are causally dependent on physical things and their modifications. Since *supernaturalism* affirms that God is purely spiritual and causally independent of physical things, naturalists hold that either belief in God must be abandoned as rationally unsupported or the concept of God must be reconstituted consistently with naturalism. Earlier attempts to do the latter include the work of Feuerbach and Comte. In twentieth-century American naturalism the most significant attempts to develop a naturalistic conception of God are due to Dewey and Henry Nelson Wieman (1884–1975). In *A Common Faith* Dewey proposed a view of God as the unity of ideal ends resulting from human imagination, ends arousing us to desire and action. Supernaturalism, he argued, was the product of a primitive need to convert the objects of desire, the greatest ideals, into an already existing reality.

In contrast to Dewey, Wieman insisted on viewing God as a process in the natural world that leads to the best that humans can achieve if they but submit to its working in their lives. In his earlier work he viewed God as a cosmic process that not only works for human good but is what actually produced human life. Later he identified God with creative interchange, a process that occurs only within already existing human communities. While Wieman's God is not a human creation, as are Dewey's ideal ends, it is difficult to see how love and devotion are appropriate to a natural process that works as it does without thought or purpose. Thus, while Dewey's God (ideal ends) lacks creative power but may well qualify as an object of love and devotion, Wieman's God (a process in nature) is capable of creative power but, while worthy of our care and attention, does not seem to qualify as an object of love and devotion. Neither view, then, satisfies the two fundamental features associated with the traditional idea of God: possessing creative power and being an appropriate object of supreme love and devotion.

See also NATURALISM, PHILOSOPHY OF RELIGION, PROCESS THEOLOGY.				W.L.R.

theological virtues. See AQUINAS.

theological voluntarism. See VOLUNTARISM.

theology, natural. See PHILOSOPHY OF RELIGION, THEOLOGIA NATURALIS.

theology, philosophical. See METAPHYSICS.

theology, supernatural. See THEOLOGIA NATURALIS.

theology of liberation. See LATIN AMERICAN PHILOSOPHY.

Theophrastus. See HELLENISTIC PHILOSOPHY, PERIPATETIC SCHOOL.

theorem. See AXIOMATIC METHOD, DEDUCTION.

theoretical concept. See THEORETICAL TERM.

theoretical construct. See THEORETICAL TERM.

theoretical entity. See THEORETICAL TERM.

theoretical identity. See PHILOSOPHY OF MIND.

theoretical judgment. See THEORETICAL REASON.

theoretical rationality. See RATIONALITY.

theoretical reason, in its traditional sense, a faculty or capacity whose province is theoretical knowledge or inquiry; more broadly, the faculty concerned with ascertaining truth of any kind (also sometimes called speculative reason). In Book 6 of his *Metaphysics,* Aristotle identifies mathematics, physics, and theology as the subject matter of theoretical reason. Theoretical reason is traditionally distinguished from *practical reason,* a faculty exercised in determining guides to good conduct and in deliberating about proper courses of action. Aristotle contrasts it, as well, with *productive reason,* which is concerned with "making": shipbuilding, sculpting, healing, and the like.

Kant distinguishes theoretical reason not only from practical reason but also (sometimes) from the faculty of understanding, in which the categories originate. Theoretical reason, possessed of its own a priori concepts ("ideas of reason"), regulates the activities of the understanding. It presupposes a systematic unity in nature, sets the goal for scientific inquiry, and determines the "criterion of empirical truth" (*Critique of Pure Reason*). Theoretical reason, on Kant's conception, seeks an explanatory "completeness" and an "unconditionedness" of being that transcend what is possible in experience.

Reason, as a faculty or capacity, may be regarded as a hybrid composed of theoretical and practical reason (broadly construed) or as a unity having both theoretical and practical functions. Some commentators take Aristotle to embrace the former conception and Kant the latter. Reason is contrasted sometimes with experience, sometimes with emotion and desire, sometimes with faith. Its presence in human beings has often been regarded as constituting the primary difference between human and non-human animals; and reason is sometimes represented as a divine element in human nature. Socrates, in Plato's *Philebus,* portrays reason as "the king of heaven and earth." Hobbes, in his *Leviathan,* paints a more sobering picture, contending that reason, "when we reckon it among the faculties of the mind, . . . is nothing but *reckoning* – that is, adding and subtracting – of the consequences of

general names agreed upon for the *marking* and *signifying* of our thoughts."
    See also PRACTICAL REASON, RATIONALITY.
                                     A.R.M.

theoretical reasoning. See PRACTICAL REASONING.

theoretical term, a term occurring in a scientific theory that purports to make reference to an unobservable entity (e.g., 'electron'), property (e.g., 'the monatomicity of a molecule'), or relation ('greater electrical resistance'). The qualification 'purports to' is required because *instrumentalists* deny that any such unobservables exist; nevertheless, they acknowledge that a scientific theory, such as the atomic theory of matter, may be a useful tool for organizing our knowledge of observables and predicting future experiences. *Scientific realists,* in contrast, maintain that at least some of the theoretical terms (e.g., 'quark' or 'neutrino') actually denote entities that are not directly observable – they hold, i.e., that such things exist. For either group, theoretical terms are contrasted with such observational terms as 'rope', 'smooth', and 'louder than', which refer to observable entities, properties, or relations.

Much philosophical controversy has centered on how to draw the distinction between the observable and the unobservable. Did Galileo observe the moons of Jupiter with his telescope? Do we observe bacteria under a microscope? Do physicists observe electrons in bubble chambers? Do astronomers observe the supernova explosions with neutrino counters? Do we observe ordinary material objects, or are sense-data the only observables? Are there any observational terms at all, or are all terms theory-laden?

Another important meaning of 'theoretical term' occurs if one regards a scientific theory as a semiformal axiomatic system. It is then natural to think of its vocabulary as divided into three parts, (i) terms of logic and mathematics, (ii) terms drawn from ordinary language or from other theories, and (iii) theoretical terms that constitute the special vocabulary of that particular theory. Thermodynamics, e.g., employs (i) terms for numbers and mathematical operations, (ii) such terms as 'pressure' and 'volume' that are common to many branches of physics, and (iii) such special thermodynamical terms as 'temperature', 'heat', and 'entropy'. In this second sense, a theoretical term need not even purport to refer to unobservables. For example, although special equipment is necessary for its precise quantitative measurement, temperature is an observable property.

Even if theories are not regarded as axiomatic systems, their technical terms can be considered theoretical. Such terms need not purport to refer to unobservables, nor be the exclusive property of one particular theory. In some cases, e.g., 'work' in physics, an ordinary word is used in the theory with a meaning that departs significantly from its ordinary use.

Serious questions have been raised about the meaning of theoretical terms. Some philosophers have insisted that, to be meaningful, they must be given operational definitions. Others have appealed to coordinative definitions to secure at least partial interpretation of axiomatic theories. The verifiability criterion has been invoked to secure the meaningfulness of scientific theories containing such terms.

A *theoretical concept* (or *construct*) is a concept expressed by a theoretical term in any of the foregoing senses. The term 'theoretical entity' has often been used to refer to unobservables, but this usage is confusing, in part because, without introducing any special vocabulary, we can talk about objects too small to be perceived directly – e.g., spheres of gamboge (a yellow resin) less than 10^{-6} meters in diameter, which figured in a historically important experiment by Jean Perrin.

See also OPERATIONALISM, PHILOSOPHY OF SCIENCE. W.C.S.

theoretical underdetermination. See OPERATIONALISM, THEORY-LADEN.

theoria. See ARISTOTLE.

theory, scientific. See PHILOSOPHY OF SCIENCE.

theory-laden, dependent on theory; specifically, involving a theoretical interpretation of what is perceived or recorded. In the heyday of logical empiricism it was thought, by Carnap and others, that a rigid distinction could be drawn between observational and theoretical terms. Later, N. R. Hanson, Paul Feyerabend, and others questioned this distinction, arguing that perhaps all observations are theory-laden either because our perception of the world is colored by perceptual, linguistic, and cultural differences or because no attempt to distinguish sharply between observation and theory has been successful. This shift brings a host of philosophical problems. If we accept the idea of radical theory-

ladenness, relativism of theory choice becomes possible, for, given rival theories each of which conditions its own observational evidence, the choice between them would seem to have to be made on extra-evidential grounds, since no theory-neutral observations are available. In its most perplexing form, relativism holds that, theory-ladenness being granted, one theory is as good as any other, so far as the relationship of theory to evidence is concerned. Relativists couple the thesis of theory-ladenness with the alleged fact of the underdetermination of a theory by its observational evidence, which yields the idea that any number of alternative theories can be supported by the same evidence. The question becomes one of what it is that constrains choices between theories. If theory-laden observations cannot constrain such choices, the individual subjective preferences of scientists, or rules of fraternal behavior agreed upon by groups of scientists, become the operative constraints. The logic of confirmation seems to be intrinsically contaminated by both idiosyncratic and social factors, posing a threat to the very idea of scientific rationality. See also CONFIRMATION, EPISTEMOLOGY, HYPOTHETICO-DEDUCTIVE METHOD, INCOMMENSURABILITY, TESTABILITY. R.E.B.

theory of appearing, the theory that to perceive an object is simply for that object to appear (present itself) to one as being a certain way, e.g., looking round or like a rock, smelling vinegary, sounding raucous, or tasting bitter. Nearly everyone would accept this formulation on some interpretation. But the theory takes this to be a rock-bottom characterization of perception, and not further analyzable. It takes "appearing to subject S as so-and-so" as a basic, irreducible relation, one readily identifiable in experience but not subject to definition in other terms. The theory preserves the idea that in normal perception we are directly aware of objects in the physical environment, not aware of them through non-physical sense-data, sensory impressions, or other intermediaries. When a tree looks to me a certain way, it is the tree and nothing else of which I am directly aware. That involves "having" a sensory experience, but that experience just consists of the tree's looking a certain way to me.

After enjoying a certain currency early in this century the theory was largely abandoned under the impact of criticisms by Price, Broad, and Chisholm. The most widely advertised difficulty is this. What is it that appears to the subject in completely hallucinatory experience? Perhaps the greatest strength of the theory is its fidelity to what perceptual experience seems to be.

See also PERCEPTION.   W.P.A.

theory of descriptions, an analysis, initially developed by Russell, of sentences containing descriptions. Descriptions include indefinite descriptions such as 'an elephant' and definite descriptions such as 'the positive square root of four'. On Russell's analysis, descriptions are "incomplete symbols" that are meaningful only in the context of other symbols, i.e., only in the context of the sentences containing them. Although the words 'the first president of the United States' appear to constitute a singular term that picks out a particular individual, much as the name 'George Washington' does, Russell held that descriptions are not referring expressions, and that they are "analyzed out" in a proper specification of the logical form of the sentences in which they occur. The grammatical form of 'The first president of the United States is tall' is simply misleading as to its logical form.

According to Russell's analysis of indefinite descriptions, the sentence 'I saw a man' asserts that there is at least one thing that is a man, and I saw that thing – symbolically, $(Ex) (Mx \ \& \ Sx)$. The role of the apparent singular term 'a man' is taken over by the existential quantifier '(Ex)' and the variables it binds, and the apparent singular term disappears on analysis. A sentence containing a definite description, such as 'The present king of France is bald', is taken to make three claims: that at least one thing is a present king of France, that at most one thing is a present king of France, and that that thing is bald – symbolically, $(Ex) \ \{[Fx \ \& \ (y) \ (Fy \supset y = x)] \ \& \ Bx\}$. Again, the apparent referring expression 'the present king of France' is analyzed away, with its role carried out by the quantifiers and variables in the symbolic representation of the logical form of the sentence in which it occurs. No element in that representation is a singular referring expression.

Russell held that this analysis solves at least three difficult puzzles posed by descriptions. The first is how it could be true that George IV wished to know whether Scott was the author of *Waverly*, but false that George IV wished to know whether Scott was Scott. Since Scott *is* the author of *Waverly*, we should apparently be able to substitute 'Scott' for 'the author of *Waverly*' and infer the second sentence from the first, but we cannot. On Russell's analysis, 'George IV wished to know whether Scott was the author of *Waverly*'

does not, when properly understood, contain an expression 'the author of *Waverly*' for which the name 'Scott' can be substituted. The second puzzle concerns the law of excluded middle, which rules that either 'The present king of France is bald' or 'The present king of France is not bald' must be true; the problem is that neither the list of bald men nor that of non-bald men contains an entry for the present king of France. Russell's solution is that 'The present king of France is not bald' is indeed true if it is understood as 'It is not the case that there is exactly one thing that is now King of France and is bald', i.e., as $\sim (Ex) \ \{Fx \ \& \ (y) \ \{[Fy \supset y = x)] \ \& \ Bx\}$. The final puzzle is how 'There is no present king of France' or 'The present king of France does not exist' can be true – if 'the present king of France' is a referring expression that picks out something, how can we truly deny that *that thing* exists? Since descriptions are not referring expressions on Russell's theory, it is easy for him to show that the negation of the claim that there is at least and at most (i.e., exactly) one present king of France, $\sim (Ex) \ [Fx \ \& \ (y) \ (Fy \supset y = x)]$, is true.

Strawson offered the first real challenge to Russell's theory, arguing that 'The present king of France is bald' does not *entail* but instead *presupposes* 'There is a present king of France', so that the former is not falsified by the falsity of the latter, but is instead deprived of a truth-value. Strawson argued for the natural view that definite descriptions are indeed referring expressions, used to single something out for predication. More recently, Keith Donnellan argued that both Russell and Strawson ignored the fact that definite descriptions have two uses. Used *attributively,* a definite description is intended to say something about whatever it is true of, and when a sentence is so used it conforms to Russell's analysis. Used *referentially,* a definite description is intended to single something out, but may not correctly describe it. For example, seeing an inebriated man in a policeman's uniform, one might say, "The cop on the corner is drunk!" Donnellan would say that even if the person were a drunken actor dressed as a policeman, the speaker would have referred to him and truly said of him that he was drunk. If it is for some reason crucial that the description be correct, as it might be if one said, "The cop on the corner has the authority to issue speeding tickets," the use is attributive; and because 'the cop on the corner' does not describe anyone correctly, no one has been said to have the authority to issue speeding tickets. Donnellan criticized Russell for overlooking referential uses of descriptions, and Strawson for both failing to acknowledge attributive uses and maintaining that with referential uses one can refer to something with a definite description only if the description is true of it. Discussion of Strawson's and Donnellan's criticisms is ongoing, and has provoked very useful work in both semantics and speech act theory, and on the distinctions between semantics and pragmatics and between semantic reference and speaker's reference, among others.

See also CAUSAL THEORY OF PROPER NAMES, PRESUPPOSITION, RUSSELL.   R.B.

theory of effluxes. See DEMOCRITUS.

theory of Forms. See PLATO.

theory of frequency. See PROBABILITY.

theory of relativity. See RELATIVITY.

theory of signs, the philosophical and scientific theory of information-carrying entities, communication, and information transmission. The term 'semiotic' was introduced by Locke for the science of signs and signification. The term became more widely used as a result of the influential work of Peirce and Charles Morris. With regard to linguistic signs, three areas of semiotic were distinguished: pragmatics – the study of the way people, animals, or machines such as computers use signs; semantics – the study of the relations between signs and their meanings, abstracting from their use; and syntax – the study of the relations among signs themselves, abstracting both from use and from meaning. In Europe, the near-equivalent term 'semiology' was introduced by Ferdinand de Saussure, the Swiss linguist.

Broadly, a *sign* is any information-carrying entity, including linguistic and animal signaling tokens, maps, road signs, diagrams, pictures, models, etc. Examples include smoke as a sign of fire, and a red light at a highway intersection as a sign to stop. Linguistically, vocal aspects of speech such as prosodic features (intonation, stress) and paralinguistic features (loudness and tone, gestures, facial expressions, etc.), as well as words and sentences, are signs in the most general sense. Peirce defined a sign as "something that stands for something in some respect or capacity." Among signs, he distinguished *symbols, icons,* and *indices.*

A symbol, or *conventional sign,* is a sign, typical of natural language forms, that lacks any signifi-

cant relevant physical correspondence with or resemblance to the entities to which the form refers (manifested by the fact that quite different forms may refer to the same class of objects), and for which there is no correlation between the occurrence of the sign and its referent.

An index, or *natural sign,* is a sign whose occurrence is causally or statistically correlated with occurrences of its referent, and whose production is not intentional. Thus, yawning is a natural sign of sleepiness; a bird call may be a natural sign of alarm. Linguistically, loudness with a rising pitch is a sign of anger.

An icon is a sign whose form corresponds to or resembles its referent or a characteristic of its referent. For instance, a tailor's swatch is an icon by being a sign that resembles a fabric in color, pattern, and texture. A linguistic example is onomatopoeia – as with 'buzz'. In general, there are conventional and cultural aspects to a sign being an icon.

See also GRAMMAR, MEANING, PHILOSOPHY OF LANGUAGE, SEMIOSIS.   W.K.W.

theory of types. See TYPE THEORY.

theory theory. See SIMULATION THEORY.

theosophy, any philosophical mysticism, especially those that purport to be mathematically or scientifically based, such as Pythagoreanism, Neoplatonism, or gnosticism. Vedic Hinduism, and certain aspects of Buddhism, Taoism, and Islamic Sufism, can also be considered theosophical.

In narrower senses, 'theosophy' may refer to the philosophy of Swedenborg, Steiner, or Madame Helena Petrovna Blavatsky (1831–91). Swedenborg's theosophy originally consisted of a rationalistic cosmology, inspired by certain elements of Cartesian and Leibnizian philosophy, and a Christian mysticism. Swedenborg labored to explain the interconnections between soul and body. Steiner's theosophy is a reaction to standard scientific theory. It purports to be as rigorous as ordinary science, but superior to it by incorporating spiritual truths about reality. According to his theosophy, reality is organic and evolving by its own resource. Genuine knowledge is intuitive, not discursive. Madame Blavatsky founded the Theosophical Society in 1875. Her views were eclectic, but were strongly influenced by mystical elements of Indian philosophy.

See also MYSTICISM, STEINER, SWEDENBORGIANISM.   A.P.M.

Theravada Buddhism. See BUDDHISM.

thermodynamics, first law of. See ENTROPY.

thermodynamics, second law of. See ENTROPY.

thesis. See HEGEL.

theurgy. See NEOPLATONISM.

thing. See METAPHYSICS.

thing-in-itself. See KANT.

Third Man argument. See PLATO.

thirdness. See PEIRCE.

thisness. See HAECCEITY.

Thomas Aquinas. See AQUINAS.

Thomism, the theology and philosophy of Thomas Aquinas. The term is applied broadly to various thinkers from different periods who were heavily influenced by Aquinas's thought in their own philosophizing and theologizing. Here three different eras and three different groups of thinkers will be distinguished: those who supported Aquinas's thought in the fifty years or so following his death in 1274; certain highly skilled interpreters and commentators who flourished during the period of "Second Thomism" (sixteenth–seventeenth centuries); and various late nineteenth- and twentieth-century thinkers who have been deeply influenced in their own work by Aquinas.

Thirteenth- and fourteenth-century Thomism. Although Aquinas's genius was recognized by many during his own lifetime, a number of his views were immediately contested by other Scholastic thinkers. Controversies ranged, e.g., over his defense of only one substantial form in human beings; his claim that prime matter is purely potential and cannot, therefore, be kept in existence without some substantial form, even by divine power; his emphasis on the role of the human intellect in the act of choice; his espousal of a real distinction betweeen the soul and its powers; and his defense of some kind of objective or "real" rather than a merely mind-dependent composition of essence and act of existing (*esse*) in creatures.

Some of Aquinas's positions were included directly or indirectly in the 219 propositions condemned by Bishop Stephen Tempier of Paris in 1277, and his defense of one single substantial form in man was condemned by Archbishop Robert Kilwardby at Oxford in 1277, with renewed prohibitions by his successor as archbishop of Canterbury, John Peckham, in 1284 and 1286. Only after Aquinas's canonization in 1323 were the Paris prohibitions revoked insofar as they touched on his teaching (in 1325). Even within his own Dominican order, disagreement about some of his views developed within the first decades after his death, notwithstanding the order's highly sympathetic espousal of his cause. Early English Dominican defenders of his general views included William Hothum (d.1298), Richard Knapwell (d.c.1288), Robert Orford (b. after 1250, fl.1290–95), Thomas Sutton (d. c.1315?), and William Macclesfield (d.1303). French Dominican Thomists included Bernard of Trilia (d.1292), Giles of Lessines in present-day Belgium (d.c.1304?), John Quidort of Paris (d. 1306), Bernard of Auvergne (d. after 1307), Hervé Nédélec (d.1323), Armand of Bellevue (fl. 1316–34), and William Peter Godin (d.1336). The secular master at Paris, Peter of Auvergne (d. 1304), while remaining very independent in his own views, knew Aquinas's thought well and completed some of his commentaries on Aristotle.

Sixteenth- and seventeenth-century Thomism. Sometimes known as the period of Second Thomism, this revival gained impetus from the early fifteenth-century writer John Capreolus (1380–1444) in his *Defenses of Thomas's Theology* (*Defensiones theologiae Divi Thomae*), a commentary on the *Sentences*. A number of fifteenth-century Dominican and secular teachers in German universities also contributed: Kaspar Grunwald (Freiburg); Cornelius Sneek and John Stoppe (in Rostock); Leonard of Brixental (Vienna); Gerard of Heerenberg, Lambert of Heerenberg, and John Versor (all at Cologne); Gerhard of Elten; and in Belgium Denis the Carthusian. Outstanding among various sixteenth-century commentators on Thomas were Tommaso de Vio (Cardinal) Cajetan, Francis Sylvester of Ferrara, Francisco de Vitoria (Salamanca), and Francisco's disciples Domingo de Soto and Melchior Cano. Most important among early seventeenth-century Thomists was John of St. Thomas, who lectured at Piacenza, Madrid, and Alcalá, and is best known for his *Cursus philosophicus* and his *Cursus theologicus*.

The nineteenth- and twentieth-century revival.
By the early to mid-nineteenth century the study of Aquinas had been largely abandoned outside Dominican circles, and in most Roman Catholic colleges and seminaries a kind of Cartesian and Suarezian Scholasticism was taught. Long before he became Pope Leo XIII, Joachim Pecci and his brother Joseph had taken steps to introduce the teaching of Thomistic philosophy at the diocesan seminary at Perugia in 1846. Earlier efforts in this direction had been made by Vincenzo Buzzetti (1778–1824), by Buzzetti's students Serafino and Domenico Sordi, and by Taparelli d'Aglezio, who became director of the Collegio Romano (Gregorian University) in 1824.

Leo's encyclical *Aeterni Patris* (1879) marked an official effort on the part of the Roman Catholic church to foster the study of the philosophy and theology of Thomas Aquinas. The intent was to draw upon Aquinas's original writings in order to prepare students of philosophy and theology to deal with problems raised by contemporary thought. The Leonine Commission was established to publish a critical edition of all of Aquinas's writings; this effort continues today. Important centers of Thomistic studies developed, such as the Higher Institute of Philosophy at Louvain (founded by Cardinal Mercier), the Dominican School of Saulchoir in France, and the Pontifical Institute of Mediaeval Studies in Toronto. Different groups of Roman, Belgian, and French Jesuits acknowledged a deep indebtedness to Aquinas for their personal philosophical reflections. There was also a concentration of effort in the United States at universities such as The Catholic University of America, St. Louis University, Notre Dame, Fordham, Marquette, and Boston College, to mention but a few, and by the Dominicans at River Forest.

A great weakness of many of the nineteenth- and twentieth-century Latin manuals produced during this effort was a lack of historical sensitivity and expertise, which resulted in an unreal and highly abstract presentation of an "Aristotelian-Thomistic" philosophy. This weakness was largely offset by the development of solid historical research both in the thought of Aquinas and in medieval philosophy and theology in general, championed by scholars such as H. Denifle, M. De Wulf, M. Grabmann, P. Mandonnet, F. Van Steenberghen, E. Gilson and many of his students at Toronto, and by a host of more recent and contemporary scholars. Much of this historical work continues today both within and without Catholic scholarly circles.

At the same time, remarkable diversity in interpreting Aquinas's thought has emerged on the part of many twentieth-century scholars. Witness, e.g., the heavy influence of Cajetan and John of St. Thomas on the Thomism of Maritain; the much more historically grounded approaches developed in quite different ways by Gilson and F. Van Steenberghen; the emphasis on the metaphysics of participation in Aquinas in the very different presentations by L. Geiger and C. Fabro; the emphasis on existence (*esse*) promoted by Gilson and many others but resisted by still other interpreters; the movement known as Transcendental Thomism, originally inspired by P. Rousselot and by J. Marechal (in dialogue with Kant); and the long controversy about the appropriateness of describing Thomas's philosophy (and that of other medievals) as a Christian philosophy. An increasing number of non-Catholic thinkers are currently directing considerable attention to Aquinas, and the varying backgrounds they bring to his texts will undoubtedly result in still other interesting interpretations and applications of his thought to contemporary concerns.

See also AQUINAS, GILSON, JOHN OF SAINT THOMAS, MARITAIN, NEO-THOMISM.   J.F.W.

Thomson, Judith Jarvis (b.1929), American analytic philosopher best known for her contribution to moral philosophy and for her paper "A Defense of Abortion" (1971). Thomson has taught at M.I.T. since 1964. Her work is centrally concerned with issues in moral philosophy, most notably questions regarding rights, and with issues in metaphysics such as the identity across time of people and the ontology of events. Her *Acts and Other Events* (1977) is a study of human action and provides an analysis of the part–whole relation among events.

"A Defense of Abortion" has not only influenced much later work on this topic but is one of the most widely discussed papers in contemporary philosophy. By appeal to imaginative scenarios analogous to pregnancy, Thomson argues that even if the fetus is assumed to be a person, its rights are in many circumstances outweighed by the rights of the pregnant woman. Thus the paper advances an argument for a right to abortion that does not turn upon the question of whether the fetus is a person. Several of Thomson's essays, including "Preferential Hiring" (1973), "The Right to Privacy" (1975), and "Killing, Letting Die, and the Trolley Problem" (1976), address the questions of what constitutes an infringement of rights and when it is morally permissible to infringe a right. These are collected in *Rights, Restitution, and Risk: Essays in Moral Theory* (1986). Thomson's *The Realm of Rights* (1990) offers a systematic account of human rights, addressing first what it is to have a right and second which rights we have.

Thomson's work is distinguished by its exceptionally lucid style and its reliance on highly inventive examples. The centrality of examples to her work reflects a methodological conviction that our views about actual and imagined cases provide the data for moral theorizing.

See also ACTION THEORY, ETHICS, RIGHTS.

A.E.B.

Thoreau, Henry David (1817–62), American naturalist and writer. Born in Concord, Massachusetts, he attended Harvard (1833–37) and then returned to Concord to study nature and write, making a frugal living as a schoolteacher, land surveyor, and pencil maker. Commentators have emphasized three aspects of his life: his love and penetrating study of the flora and fauna of the Concord area, recorded with philosophical reflections in *Walden* (1854); his continuous pursuit of simplicity in the externals of life, thus avoiding a life of "quiet desperation"; and his acts of civil disobedience. The last item has been somewhat overemphasized; not paying a poll tax by way of protest was not original with Thoreau. However, his essay "Resistance to Civil Government" immortalized his protest and influenced people like Gandhi and Martin Luther King, Jr., in later years. Thoreau eventually helped runaway slaves at considerable risk; still, he considered himself a student of nature and not a reformer. **See also** TRANSCENDENTALISM.

E.H.M.

thought, language of. See MEANING, MENTALESE, PHILOSOPHY OF LANGUAGE.

thought experiment, a technique for testing a hypothesis by imagining a situation and what would be said about it (or more rarely, happen in it). This technique is often used by philosophers to argue for (or against) a hypothesis about the meaning or applicability of a concept. For example, Locke imagined a switch of minds between a prince and a cobbler as a way to argue that personal identity is based on continuity of memory, not continuity of the body. To argue for the relativity of simultaneity, Einstein imagined two observers – one on a train, the other beside it – who observed lightning bolts. And according

to some scholars, Galileo only imagined the experiment of tying two five-pound weights together with a fine string in order to argue that heavier bodies do not fall faster. Thought experiments of this last type are rare because they can be used only when one is thoroughly familiar with the outcome of the imagined situation.

J.A.K.

Thrasymachus (fl. 427 B.C.), Greek Sophist from Bithynia who is known mainly as a character in Book I of Plato's *Republic*. He traveled and taught extensively throughout the Greek world, and was well known in Athens as a teacher and as the author of treatises on rhetoric. Innovative in his style, he was credited with inventing the "middle style" of rhetoric. The only surviving fragment of a speech by Thrasymachus was written for delivery by an Athenian citizen in the assembly, at a time when Athens was not faring well in the Peloponnesian War; it shows him concerned with the efficiency of government, pleading with the Athenians to recognize their common interests and give up their factionalism. Our only other source for his views on political matters is Plato's *Republic*, which most scholars accept as presenting at least a half-truth about Thrasymachus. There, Thrasymachus is represented as a foil to Socrates, claiming that justice is only what benefits the stronger, i.e., the rulers. From the point of view of those who are ruled, then, justice always serves the interest of someone else, and rulers who seek their own advantage are unjust. **See also** SOPHISTS.   P.Wo.

Three Profound Treatises. See NEO-TAOISM.

three-valued logic. See MANY-VALUED LOGIC.

Three Ways. See BONAVENTURE.

threshold, absolute. See FECHNER.

threshold, relative. See FECHNER.

t'i, yung, Chinese terms often rendered into English as 'substance' and 'function', respectively. Ch'eng Yi (1033–1107), in the preface to his *Commentary to the Book of Changes,* says: "Substance (*t'i*) and function (*yung*) come from the same source, and there is no gap between the manifest and the hidden." Such thought is characteristic of the Chinese way of thinking. Chu Hsi (1130–1200) applied the pair of concepts to his theory of human nature; he maintained that *jen* (humanity) is nature, substance, while love is feeling, function. In the late Ch'ing dynasty (1644–1912) Chang Chih-tung (1837–1909) advocated Chinese learning for *t'i* and Western learning for *yung*. **See also** CHINESE PHILOSOPHY, CHU HSI.   S.-h.L.

t'ien, Chinese term meaning 'heaven', 'sky'. *T'ien* has a range of uses running from the most to the least anthropomorphic. At one extreme, *t'ien* is identified with *shang ti*. *T'ien* can be spoken of as having desires and engaging in purposive actions, such as bestowing the Mandate of Heaven (*t'ien ming*). *T'ien ming* has a political and an ethical use. It can be the mandate to rule given to a virtuous individual. It can also be the moral requirements that apply to each individual, especially as these are embodied in one's nature. At the other extreme, thinkers such as Hsün-Tzu identify *t'ien* with the natural order. Even in texts where *t'ien* is sometimes used anthropomorphically, it can also be used as synonymous with *ming* (in the sense of fate), or simply refer to the sky. After the introduction of Buddhism into China, the phrase 'Hall of Heaven' (*t'ien t'ang*) is used to refer to the paradise awaiting some souls after death. **See also** CHUNG-YUNG, HSING, MING, SHANG TI.
B.W.V.N.

t'ien-jen ho-i, Chinese term for the relationship between *t'ien* (Heaven) and human beings. Most ancient Chinese philosophers agreed on the ideal *t'ien-jen ho-i*: the unity and harmony of Heaven or the natural order of events and human affairs. They differed on the means of achieving this ideal vision. The Taoists, Lao Tzu and Chuang Tzu, focused on adaptability to all natural occurrences without human intervention. The Confucians stressed the cultivation of virtues such as *jen* (benevolence), *i* (rightness), and *li* (propriety), both in the rulers and the people. Some later Confucians, along with Mo Tzu, emphasized the mutual influence and response or interaction of Heaven and humans. Perhaps the most distinctive Confucian conception is Hsün Tzu's thesis that Heaven provides resources for completion by human efforts.   A.S.C.

t'ien li, jen-yü, Chinese terms literally meaning 'heavenly principles' and 'human desires', respectively. Sung–Ming Neo-Confucian philosophers believed that Heaven enables us to understand principles and to act according to them. Therefore we must try our best to preserve heavenly principles and eliminate human desires. When hungry, one must eat; this is act-ing according to *t'ien li*. But when one craves gourmet food, the only thing one cares about is gratification of desire; this is *jen-yü*. Neo-Confucian philosophers were not teaching asceticism; they only urged us not to be slaves of our excessive, unnatural, artificial, "human" desires.

See also NEO-CONFUCIANISM; TAO-HSIN, JEN-HSIN.   S.-h.L.

t'ien ming. See MING.

Tillers. See HSÜ HSING.

Tillich, Paul (1886–1965), German-born American philosopher and theologian. Born in Starzeddel, eastern Germany, he was educated in philosophy and theology and ordained in the Prussian Evangelical Church in 1912. He served as an army chaplain during World War I and later taught at Berlin, Marburg, Dresden, Leipzig, and Frankfurt. In November 1933, following suspension from his teaching post by the Nazis, he emigrated to the United States, where he taught at Columbia and Union Theological Seminary until 1955, and then at Harvard and Chicago until his death. A popular preacher and speaker, he developed a wide audience in the United States through such writings as *The Protestant Era* (1948), *Systematic Theology* (three volumes: 1951, 1957, 1963), *The Courage to Be* (1952), and *Dynamics of Faith* (1957). His sometimes unconventional lifestyle, as well as his syncretic yet original thought, moved "on the boundary" between theology and other elements of culture – especially art, literature, political thought, and depth psychology – in the belief that religion should relate to the whole extent, and the very depths, of human existence.

Tillich's thought, despite its distinctive "ontological" vocabulary, was greatly influenced by the voluntaristic tradition from Augustine through Schelling, Schopenhauer, Marx, Nietzsche, and Freud. It was a systematic theology that sought to state fresh Christian answers to deep existential questions raised by individuals and cultures – his *method of correlation*. Every age has its distinctive *kairos*, "crisis" or "fullness of time," the right time for creative thought and action. In Weimar Germany, Tillich found the times ripe for religious socialism. In post–World War II America, he focused more on psychological themes: in the midst of anxiety over death, meaninglessness, and guilt, everyone seeks the courage to be, which comes only by avoiding the abyss of non-being (welling up in the demonic) and by placing one's unconditional faith – *ulti-*

mate concern – not in any particular being (e.g. God) but in Being-Itself ("the God above God," the ground of being). This is essentially the *Protestant principle*, which prohibits lodging ultimate concern in any finite and limited reality (including state, race, and religious institutions and symbols).

Tillich was especially influential after World War II. He represented for many a welcome critical openness to the spiritual depths of modern culture, opposing both demonic idolatry of this world (as in National Socialism) and sectarian denial of cultural resources for faith (as in Barthian neo-orthodoxy).

See also AUGUSTINE, EXISTENTIALISM, FREUD, NIETZSCHE.   W.L.S.

time, "a moving image of eternity" (Plato); "the number of movements in respect of the before and after" (Aristotle); "the Life of the Soul in movement as it passes from one stage of act or experience to another" (Plotinus); "a present of things past, memory, a present of things present, sight, and a present of things future, expectation" (Augustine). These definitions, like all attempts to encapsulate the essence of time in some neat formula, are unhelpfully circular because they employ temporal notions. Although time might be too basic to admit of definition, there still are many questions about time that philosophers have made some progress in answering by analysis both of how we ordinarily experience and talk about time, and of the deliverances of science, thereby clarifying and deepening our understanding of what time is. What follows gives a sample of some of the more important of these issues.

Temporal becoming and the A- and B-theories of time. According to the B-theory, time consists in nothing but a fixed "B-series" of events running from earlier to later. The A-theory requires that these events also form an "A-series" going from the future through the present into the past and, moreover, shift in respect to these determinations. The latter sort of change, commonly referred to as "temporal becoming," gives rise to well-known perplexities concerning both what does the shifting and the sort of shift involved. Often it is said that it is the present or now that shifts to ever-later times. This quickly leads to absurdity. 'The present' and 'now', like 'this time', are used to refer to a moment of time. Thus, to say that the present shifts to later times entails that this very moment of time – the pre-

sent – will become some other moment of time and thus cease to be identical with itself! Sometimes the entity that shifts is the property of nowness or presentness. The problem is that every event has this property at some time, namely when it occurs. Thus, what must qualify some event as being now *simpliciter* is its having the property of nowness now; and this is the start of an infinite regress that is vicious because at each stage we are left with an unexpurgated use of 'now', the very term that was supposed to be analyzed in terms of the property of nowness. If events are to change from being future to present and from present to past, as is required by temporal becoming, they must do so in relation to some mysterious transcendent entity, since temporal relations between events and/or times cannot change. The nature of the shift is equally perplexing, for it must occur at a particular rate; but a rate of change involves a comparison between one kind of change and a change of time. Herein, it is change of time that is compared to change of time, resulting in the seeming tautology that time passes or shifts at the rate of one second per second, surely an absurdity since this is not a rate of change at all. Broad attempted to skirt these perplexities by saying that becoming is *sui generis* and thereby defies analysis, which puts him on the side of the mystically inclined Bergson who thought that it could be known only through an act of ineffable intuition.

To escape the clutches of both perplexity and mysticism, as well as to satisfy the demand of science to view the world non-perspectivally, the B-theory attempted to reduce the A-series to the B-series via a linguistic reduction in which a temporal indexical proposition reporting an event as past, present, or future is shown to be identical with a non-indexical proposition reporting a relation of precedence or simultaneity between it and another event or time. It is generally conceded that such a reduction fails, since, in general, no indexical proposition is identical with any non-indexical one, this being due to the fact that one can have a propositional attitude toward one of them that is not had to the other; e.g., I can believe that it is now raining without believing that it rains (tenselessly) at t_7. The friends of becoming have drawn the wrong moral from this failure – that there is a mysterious Mr. X out there doing "The Shift." They have overlooked the fact that two sentences can express different propositions and yet report one and the same event or state of affairs; e.g., 'This is water' and 'this is a collection of H_2O molecules', though differing in sense, report the same state of affairs – this being water is nothing but this being a collection of H_2O molecules.

It could be claimed that the same holds for the appropriate use of indexical and non-indexical sentences; the tokening at t_7 of 'Georgie flies at this time (at present)' is coreporting with the non-synonymous 'Georgie flies (tenselessly) at t_7', since Georgie's flying at this time is the same event as Georgie's flying at t_7, given that this time is t_7. This effects the same ontological reduction of the becoming of events to their bearing temporal relations to each other as does the linguistic reduction. The "coreporting reduction" also shows the absurdity of the "psychological reduction" according to which an event's being present, etc., requires a relation to a perceiver, whereas an event's having a temporal relation to another event or time does not require a relation to a perceiver. Given that Georgie's flying at this time is identical with Georgie's flying at t_7, it follows that one and the same event both does and does not have the property of requiring relation to a perceiver, thereby violating Leibniz's law that identicals are indiscernible.

Continuous versus discrete time. Assume that the instants of time are linearly ordered by the relation R of 'earlier than'. To say that this order is continuous is, first, to imply the property of density or infinite divisibility: for any instants i_1 and i_2 such that Ri_1i_2, there is a third instant i_3, such that Ri_1i_3 and Ri_3i_2. But continuity implies something more since density allows for "gaps" between the instants, as with the rational numbers. (Think of R as the 'less than' relation and the i_n as rationals.) To rule out gaps and thereby assure genuine continuity it is necessary to require in addition to density that every convergent sequence of instants has a limit. To make this precise one needs a distance measure $d(\ ,\ )$ on pairs of instants, where $d(i_m, i_n)$ is interpreted as the lapse of time between i_m and i_n. The requirement of continuity proper is then that for any sequence $i_1, i_2, i_3, \ldots$, of instants, if $d(i_m\ i_n) \to 0$ as $m, n \to \infty$, there is a limit instant i_ℓ such that $d(i_n, i_\ell) \to 0$ as $n \to \infty$. The analogous property obviously fails for the rationals. But taking the completion of the rationals by adding in the limit points of convergent sequences yields the real number line, a genuine continuum.

Numerous objections have been raised to the idea of time as a continuum and to the very notion of the continuum itself. Thus, it was objected that time cannot be composed of durationless instants since a stack of such instants cannot produce a non-zero duration. Modern measure theory resolves this objection. Leibniz held that a continuum cannot be composed of points since the points in any (finite closed) interval can be put in one-to-one correspondence with a smaller subinterval, contradicting the axiom that the whole is greater than any proper part. What Leibniz took to be a contradictory feature is now taken to be a defining feature of infinite collections or totalities.

Modern-day Zenoians, while granting the viability of the mathematical doctrine of the continuum and even the usefulness of its employment in physical theory, will deny the possibility of its applying to real-life changes. Whitehead gave an analogue of Zeno's paradox of the dichotomy to show that a thing cannot endure in a continuous manner. For if (i_1, i_2) is the interval over which the thing is supposed to endure, then the thing would first have to endure until the instant i_3, halfway between i_1 and i_2; but before it can endure until i_3, it must first endure until the instant i_4 halfway between i_1 and i_3, etc. The seductiveness of this paradox rests upon an implicit anthropomorphic demand that the operations of nature must be understood in terms of concepts of human agency. Herein it is the demand that the physicist's description of a continuous change, such as a runner traversing a unit spatial distance by performing an infinity of runs of ever-decreasing distance, could be used as an action-guiding recipe for performing this feat, which, of course, is impossible since it does not specify any initial or final doing, as recipes that guide human actions must. But to make this anthropomorphic demand explicit renders this deployment of the dichotomy, as well as the arguments against the possibility of performing a "supertask," dubious. Anti-realists might deny that we are committed to real-life change being continuous by our acceptance of a physical theory that employs principles of mathematical continuity, but this is quite different from the Zenoian claim that it is impossible for such change to be continuous.

To maintain that time is discrete would require not only abandoning the continuum but also the density property as well. Giving up either conflicts with the intuition that time is one-dimensional. (For an explanation of how the topological analysis of dimensionality entails that the dimension of a discrete space is 0, see W. Hurewicz, *Dimension Theory*, 1941.) The philosophical and physics literatures contain speculations about a discrete time built of "chronons" or temporal atoms, but thus far such hypothetical entities have not been incorporated into a satisfactory theory.

Absolute versus relative and relational time. In a scholium to the *Principia*, Newton declared that "Absolute, true and mathematical time, of itself and from its own nature, flows equably without relation to anything external." There are at least five interrelated senses in which time was absolute for Newton. First, he thought that there was a frame-independent relation of simultaneity for events. Second, he thought that there was a frame-independent measure of duration for non-simultaneous events. He used 'flows equably' not to refer to the above sort of mysterious "temporal becoming," but instead to connote the second sense of absoluteness and partly to indicate two further kinds of absoluteness. To appreciate the latter, note that 'flows equably' is modified by 'without relation to anything external'. Here Newton was asserting (third sense of 'absolute') that the lapse of time between two events would be what it is even if the distribution and motions of material bodies were different. He was also presupposing a related form of absoluteness (fourth sense) according to which the metric of time is intrinsic to the temporal interval.

Leibniz's philosophy of time placed him in agreement with Newton as regards the first two senses of 'absolute', which assert the non-relative or frame-independent nature of time. However, Leibniz was very much opposed to Newton on the fourth sense of 'absolute'. According to Leibniz's relational conception of time, any talk about the length of a temporal interval must be unpacked in terms of talk about the relation of the interval to an extrinsic metric standard. Furthermore, Leibniz used his principles of sufficient reason and identity of indiscernibles to argue against a fifth sense of 'absolute', implicit in Newton's philosophy of time, according to which time is a substratum in which physical events are situated. On the contrary, the relational view holds that time is nothing over and above the structure of relations of events.

Einstein's special and general theories of relativity have direct bearing on parts of these controversies. The special theory necessitates the abandonment of frame-independent notions of simultaneity and duration. For any pair of spacelike related events in Minkowski space-time there is an inertial frame in which the events are

simultaneous, another frame in which the first event is temporally prior, and still a third in which the second event is temporally prior. And the temporal interval between two timelike related events depends on the worldline connecting them. In fact, for any $\varepsilon > 0$, no matter how small, there is a worldline connecting the events whose proper length is less than ε. (This is the essence of the so-called twin paradox.) The general theory of relativity abandons the third sense of absoluteness since it entails that the metrical structure of space-time covaries with the distribution of mass-energy in a manner specified by Einstein's field equations. But the heart of the absolute–relational controversy – as focused by the fourth and fifth senses of 'absolute' – is not settled by relativistic considerations. Indeed, opponents from both sides of the debate claim to find support for their positions in the special and general theories.

See also EINSTEIN, METAPHYSICS, RELATIVITY, SPACE, SPACE-TIME.   J.Ea. & R.M.Ga.

time lag argument. See PERCEPTION.

time slice, a temporal part or stage of any concrete particular that exists for some interval of time; a three-dimensional cross section of a four-dimensional object. To think of an object as consisting of time slices or temporal stages is to think of it as related to time in much the way that it is related to space: as *extending* through time as well as space, rather than as *enduring* through it. Just as an object made up of spatial parts is thought of as a whole made up of parts that exist at different locations, so an object made up of time slices is thought of as a whole made up of parts or stages that exist at successive times; hence, just as a spatial whole is only partly present in any space that does not include all its spatial parts, so a whole made up of time slices is only partly present in any stretch of time that does not include all its temporal parts.

A *continuant*, by contrast, is most commonly understood to be a particular that *endures* through time, i.e., that is wholly present at each moment at which it exists. To conceive of an object as a continuant is to conceive of it as related to time in a very different way from that in which it is related to space. A continuant does not *extend* through time as well as space; it does not exist at different times by virtue of the existence of successive parts of it at those times; it is the continuant itself that is wholly present at each such time. To conceive an object as a continuant, therefore, is to conceive it as not made up of temporal stages, or time slices, at all. There is another, less common, use of 'continuant' in which a continuant is understood to be any particular that exists for some stretch of time, regardless of whether it is the whole of the particular or only some part of it that is present at each moment of the particular's existence. According to this usage, an entity that is made up of time slices would be a kind of continuant rather than some other kind of particular.

Philosophers have disputed whether ordinary objects such as cabbages and kings endure through time (are continuants) or only extend through time (are sequences of time slices). Some argue that to understand the possibility of change one must think of such objects as sequences of time slices; others argue that for the same reason one must think of such objects as continuants. If an object changes, it comes to be different from itself. Some argue that this would be possible only if an object consisted of distinct, successive stages; so that change would simply consist in the differences among the successive temporal parts of an object. Others argue that this view would make change impossible; that differences among the successive temporal parts of a thing would no more imply the thing had changed than differences among its spatial parts would.

See also METAPHYSICS, WHITEHEAD.   P.F.

Timon of Philius. See SKEPTICS.

Tindal, Matthew. See DEISM.

Tisberi, William. See HEYTESBURY.

token. See ACTION THEORY, TYPE–TOKEN DISTINCTION.

token epiphenomenalism. See PHILOSOPHY OF MIND.

token physicalism. See PHILOSOPHY OF MIND.

token-reflexive, an expression that refers to itself in an act of speech or writing, such as 'this token'. The term was coined by Reichenbach, who conjectured that all indexicals, all expressions whose semantic value depends partly on features of the context of utterance, are token-reflexive and definable in terms of the phrase 'this token'. He suggested that 'I' means the same as 'the person who utters this token', 'now' means the same as 'the time at which this token is uttered', 'this table' means the same as

'the table pointed to by a gesture accompanying this token', and so forth. (Russell made a somewhat similar suggestion in his discussion of egocentric particulars.) Reichenbach's conjecture is widely regarded as false; although 'I' does pick out the person using it, it is not synonymous with 'the person who utters this token'. If it were, as David Kaplan observes, 'If no one were to utter this token, I would not exist' would be true. **See also** EGOCENTRIC PARTICULAR, INDEXICAL.   R.B.

token-token identity. See PHILOSOPHY OF MIND.

Toletus, Francisco (1532–96), Spanish Jesuit theologian and philosopher. Born in Córdoba, he studied at Valencia, Salamanca, and Rome, and became the first Jesuit cardinal in 1594. He composed commentaries on several of Aristotle's works and a commentary on Aquinas's *Summa theologiae*.

Toletus followed a Thomistic line, but departed from Thomism in some details. He held that individuals are directly apprehended by the intellect and that the agent intellect is the same power as the possible intellect. He rejected the Thomistic doctrines of the real distinction between essence and existence and of individuation by designated matter; for Toletus individuation results from form.

See also AQUINAS.   J.J.E.G.

tonk, a sentential connective whose meaning and logic are completely characterized by the two rules (or axioms)

(1) $[P \rightarrow (P \text{ tonk } Q)]$ and
(2) $[(P \text{ tonk } Q) \rightarrow Q]$.

If (1) and (2) are added to any normal system, then every Q can be derived from any P. Arthur Prior invented 'tonk' to show that deductive validity must not be conceived as depending solely on arbitrary syntactically defined rules or axioms. We may prohibit 'tonk' on the ground that it is not a natural, independently meaningful notion, but we may also prohibit it on purely syntactical grounds. E.g., we may require that, for every connective C, the C-introduction rule

$[(xxx) \rightarrow (\ldots C \ldots)]$

and the C-elimination rule

$[(\text{- - -} C \text{ - - -}) \rightarrow (yyy)]$

be such that the (yyy) is part of (xxx) or is related to (xxx) in some other syntactical way. **See also** RELEVANCE LOGIC.   D.H.

top-down. See COGNITIVE SCIENCE.

topic-neutral, noncommittal between two or more ontological interpretations of a term. J. J. C. Smart (in 1959) suggested that introspective reports can be taken as topic-neutral: composed of terms neutral between "dualistic metaphysics" and "materialistic metaphysics." When one asserts, e.g., that one has a yellowish-orange afterimage, this is tantamount to saying '*There is something going on that is like what is going on when* I have my eyes open, am awake, and there is an orange illuminated in good light in front of me, i.e., when I really see an orange'. The italicized phrase is, in Smart's terms, topic-neutral; it refers to an event, while remaining noncommittal about whether it is material or immaterial. The term has not always been restricted to neutrality regarding dualism and materialism. Smart suggests that topic-neutral descriptions are composed of "quasi-logical" words, and hence would be suitable for any occasion where a relatively noncommittal expression of a view is required. **See also** PHILOSOPHY OF MIND.   D.C.D.

topics, the analysis of common strategies of argumentation, later a genre of literature analyzing syllogistic reasoning. Aristotle considered the analysis of types of argument, or "topics," the best means of describing the art of dialectical reasoning; he also used the term to refer to the principle underlying the strategy's production of an argument. Later classical commentators on Aristotle, particularly Latin rhetoricians like Cicero, developed Aristotle's discussions of the theory of dialectical reasoning into a philosophical form. Boethius's work on topics exemplifies the later classical expansion of the scope of topics literature. For him, a topic is either a self-evidently true universal generalization, also called a "maximal proposition," or a *differentia,* a member of the set of a maximal proposition's characteristics that determine its genus and species. *Man is a rational animal* is a maximal proposition, and like *from genus,* the differentia that characterizes the maximal proposition as concerning genera, it is a topic. Because he believed dialectical reasoning leads to categorical, not conditional, conclusions, Boethius felt that the discovery of an argument entailed discovering a middle term uniting the two, previously unjoined terms of the conclusion. Differentiae are the genera of these middle terms, and one constructs arguments by choosing differentiae, thereby determining the middle term leading to the conclusion.

In the eleventh century, Boethius's logical structure of maximal propositions and differentiae was used to study hypothetical syllogisms, while twelfth-century theorists like Abelard extended the applicability of topics structure to the categorical syllogism. By the thirteenth century, Peter of Spain, Robert Kilwardby, and Boethius of Dacia applied topics structure exclusively to the categorical syllogism, principally those with non-necessary, probable premises. Within a century, discussion of topics structure to evaluate syllogistic reasoning was subsumed by consequences literature, which described implication, entailment, and inference relations between propositions. While the theory of consequences as an approach to understanding relations between propositions is grounded in Boethian, and perhaps Stoic, logic, it became prominent only in the later thirteenth century with Burley's recognition of the logical significance of propositional logic.

See also ABELARD, ARISTOTLE, BOETHIUS, BURLEY, CICERO, KILWARDBY, PETER OF SPAIN, SYLLOGISM.   S.E.L.

total. See RELATION.

total evidence, rule of. See INDUCTION.

total ordering. See ORDERING.

toxin puzzle, a puzzle about intention and practical rationality posed by Gregory Kavka. A trustworthy billionaire offers you a million dollars for intending tonight to drink a certain toxin tomorrow. You are convinced that he can tell what you intend independently of what you do. The toxin would make you painfully ill for a day, but you need to drink it to get the money. Constraints on the formation of a prize-winning intention include prohibitions against "gimmicks," "external incentives," and forgetting relevant details. For example, you will not receive the money if you have a hypnotist "implant the intention" or hire a hit man to kill you should you not drink the toxin. If, by midnight tonight, without violating any rules, you form an intention to drink the toxin tomorrow, you will find a million dollars in your bank account when you awake tomorrow morning. You probably would drink the toxin for a million dollars. But can you, without violating the rules, intend tonight to drink it tomorrow? Apparently, you have no reason to drink it and an excellent reason not to drink it. Seemingly, you will infer from this that you will eschew drinking the toxin, and believing that you will eschew drinking it seems inconsistent with intending to drink it. Even so, there are several reports in the philosophical literature of (possible) people who struck it rich when offered the toxin deal! **See also** ACTION THEORY, INTENTION, PRACTICAL REASONING.   A.R.M.

Toynbee, Arnold. See PHILOSOPHY OF HISTORY.

tracking. See NOZICK, RELIABILISM, SKEPTICISM.

Tractarian. See ANALYTIC PHILOSOPHY, WITTGENSTEIN.

traducianism. See CREATION EX NIHILO, PREEXISTENCE.

transcendence, broadly, the property of rising out of or above other things (virtually always understood figuratively); in philosophy, the property of being, in some way, of a higher order. A being, such as God, may be said to be transcendent in the sense of being not merely superior, but incomparably superior, to other things, in any sort of perfection. God's transcendence, or being outside or beyond the world, is also contrasted, and by some thinkers combined, with God's immanence, or existence within the world.

In medieval philosophy of logic, terms such as 'being' and 'one', which did not belong uniquely to any one of the Aristotelian categories or types of predication (such as substance, quality, and relation), but could be predicated of things belonging to any (or to none) of them, were called *transcendental*. In Kant's *Critique of Pure Reason*, principles that profess (wrongly) to take us beyond the limits of any possible experience are called *transcendent;* whereas anything belonging to non-empirical thought that establishes, and draws consequences from, the possibility and limits of experience may be called *transcendental*. Thus a transcendental argument (in a sense still current) is one that proceeds from premises about the way in which experience is possible to conclusions about what must be true of any experienced world.

Transcendentalism was a philosophical or religious movement in mid-nineteenth-century New England, characterized, in the thought of its leading representative, Ralph Waldo Emerson, by belief in a transcendent (spiritual and divine) principle in human nature.
See also EMERSON, IMMANENCE, KANT, PHILOSOPHY OF RELIGION, TRANSCENDENTAL ARGUMENT, TRANSCENDENTALISM.   R.M.A.

transcendental. See KANT, TRANSCENDENCE.

transcendental analytic. See KANT.

transcendental argument, an argument that elucidates the conditions for the possibility of some fundamental phenomenon whose existence is unchallenged or uncontroversial in the philosophical context in which the argument is propounded. Such an argument proceeds deductively, from a premise asserting the existence of some basic phenomenon (such as meaningful discourse, conceptualization of objective states of affairs, or the practice of making promises), to a conclusion asserting the existence of some interesting, substantive enabling conditions for that phenomenon. The term derives from Kant's *Critique of Pure Reason*, which gives several such arguments.

The paradigmatic Kantian transcendental argument is the "Transcendental Deduction of the Pure Concepts of Understanding." Kant argued there that the *objective validity* of certain pure, or a priori, concepts (the "categories") is a condition for the possibility of experience. Among the concepts allegedly required for having experience are those of substance and cause. Their apriority consists in the fact that instances of these concepts are not directly given in sense experience in the manner of instances of empirical concepts such as *red*. This fact gave rise to the skepticism of Hume concerning the very coherence of such alleged a priori concepts. Now if these concepts do have objective validity, as Kant endeavored to prove in opposition to Hume, then the world contains genuine instances of the concepts. In a transcendental argument concerning the conditions for the possibility of experience, it is crucial that some feature entailed by the having of experience is identified. Then it is argued that experience could not have this feature without satisfying some substantive conditions. In the Transcendental Deduction, the feature of experience on which Kant concentrates is the ability of a subject of experience to be aware of several distinct inner states as all belonging to a single consciousness. There is no general agreement on how Kant's argument actually unfolded, though it seems clear to most that he focused on the role of the categories in the synthesis or combination of one's inner states in judgments, where such synthesis is said to be required for one's awareness of the states as being all equally one's own states.

Another famous Kantian transcendental argument – the "Refutation of Idealism" in the *Cri-*

tique of Pure Reason – shares a noteworthy trait with the Transcendental Deduction. The Refutation proceeds from the premise that one is conscious of one's own existence as determined in time, i.e., knows the temporal order of some of one's inner states. According to the Refutation, a condition for the possibility of such knowledge is one's consciousness of the existence of objects located outside oneself in space. If one is indeed so conscious, that would refute the skeptical view, formulated by Descartes, that one lacks knowledge of the existence of a spatial world distinct from one's mind and its inner states.

Both of the Kantian transcendental arguments we have considered, then, conclude that the falsity of some skeptical view is a condition for the possibility of some phenomenon whose existence is acknowledged even by the skeptic (the having of experience; knowledge of temporal facts about one's own inner states). Thus, we can isolate an interesting subclass of transcendental arguments: those which are anti-skeptical in nature. Barry Stroud has raised the question whether such arguments depend on some sort of suppressed verificationism according to which the existence of language or conceptualization requires the availability of the knowledge that the skeptic questions (since verificationism has it that meaningful sentences expressing coherent concepts, e.g., 'There are tables', must be verifiable by what is given in sense experience). Dependence on a highly controversial premise is undesirable in itself. Further, Stroud argued, such a dependence would render superfluous whatever other content the anti-skeptical transcendental argument might embody (since the suppressed premise alone would refute the skeptic). There is no general agreement on whether Stroud's doubts about anti-skeptical transcendental arguments are well founded. It is not obvious whether the doubts apply to arguments that do not proceed from a premise asserting the existence of language or conceptualization, but instead conform more closely to the Kantian model. Even so, no anti-skeptical transcendental argument has been widely accepted. This is evidently due to the difficulty of uncovering substantive enabling conditions for phenomena that even a skeptic will countenance.

See also KANT, SKEPTICISM.   A.B.

transcendental deduction. See KANT.

transcendental dialectic. See DIALECTIC.

transcendental ego. See KANT.

transcendentalia. See TRANSCENDENTALS.

transcendental idealism. See KANT.

transcendentalism, a religious-philosophical viewpoint held by a group of New England intellectuals, of whom Emerson, Thoreau, and Theodore Parker were the most important. A distinction taken over from Samuel Taylor Coleridge was the only bond that universally united the members of the Transcendental Club, founded in 1836: the distinction between the understanding and reason, the former providing uncertain knowledge of appearances, the latter a priori knowledge of necessary truths gained through intuition. The transcendentalists insisted that philosophical truth could be reached only by reason, a capacity common to all people unless destroyed by living a life of externals and accepting as true only secondhand traditional beliefs. On almost every other point there were disagreements. Emerson was an idealist, while Parker was a natural realist – they simply had conflicting a priori intuitions. Emerson, Thoreau, and Parker rejected the supernatural aspects of Christianity, pointing out its unmistakable parochial nature and sociological development; while James Marsh, Frederick Henry Hedge, and Caleb Henry remained in the Christian fold. The influences on the transcendentalists differed widely and explain the diversity of opinion. For example, Emerson was influenced by the Platonic tradition, German Romanticism, Eastern religions, and nature poets, while Parker was influenced by modern science, the Scottish realism of Reid and Cousin (which also emphasized a priori intuitions), and the German Higher Critics.

Emerson, Thoreau, and Parker were also bonded by negative beliefs. They not only rejected Calvinism but Unitarianism as well; they rejected the ordinary concept of material success and put in its place an Aristotelian type of self-realization that emphasized the rational and moral self as the essence of humanity and decried idiosyncratic self-realization that admires what is *unique* in people as constituting their real value.

See also EMERSON, THOREAU.   E.H.M.

transcendental number. See MATHEMATICAL ANALYSIS.

transcendentals, also called *transcendentalia,* terms or concepts that apply to all things regardless of the things' ontological kind or category.

Terms or concepts of this sort are transcendental in the sense that they transcend or are superordinate to all classificatory categories. The classical doctrine of the transcendentals, developed in detail in the later Middle Ages, presupposes an Aristotelian ontology according to which all beings are substances or accidents classifiable within one of the ten highest genera, the ten Aristotelian categories. In this scheme *being* (Greek *on,* Latin *ens*) is not itself one of the categories since all categories mark out kinds of being. But neither is it a category above the ten categories of substance and accidents, an ultimate genus of which the ten categories are species. This is because *being* is homonymous or equivocal, i.e., there is no single generic property or nature shared by members of each category in virtue of which they are beings. The ten categories identify ten irreducible, most basic ways of being. *Being,* then, transcends the categorial structure of the world: anything at all that is ontologically classifiable is a being, and to say of anything that it is a being is not to identify it as a member of some kind distinct from other kinds of things.

According to this classical doctrine, *being* is the primary transcendental, but there are other terms or concepts that transcend the categories in a similar way. The most commonly recognized transcendentals other than *being* are *one* (*unum*), *true* (*verum*), and *good* (*bonum*), though some medieval philosophers also recognized *thing* (*res*), *something* (*aliquid*), and *beautiful* (*pulchrum*). These other terms or concepts are transcendental because the ontological ground of their application to a given thing is precisely the same as the ontological ground in virtue of which that thing can be called a being. For example, for a thing with a certain nature to be good is for it to perform well the activity that specifies it as a thing of that nature, and to perform this activity well is to have actualized that nature to a certain extent. But for a thing to have actualized its nature to some extent is just what it is for the thing to have being. So the actualities or properties in virtue of which a thing is good are precisely those in virtue of which it has being. Given this account, medieval philosophers held that transcendental terms are convertible (*convertuntur*) or extensionally equivalent (*idem secundum supposita*). They are not synonymous, however, since they are intensionally distinct (*differunt secundum rationem*). These secondary transcendentals are sometimes characterized as attributes (*passiones*) of being that are necessarily concomitant with it.

In the modern period, the notion of the transcendental is associated primarily with Kant, who made 'transcendental' a central technical term in his philosophy. For Kant the term no longer signifies that which transcends categorial classification but that which transcends our experience in the sense of providing its ground or structure. Kant allows, e.g., that the pure forms of intuition (space and time) and the pure concepts of understanding (categories such as substance and cause) are transcendental in this sense. Forms and concepts of this sort constitute the conditions of the possibility of experience. **See also** ARISTOTLE, KANT.   S.Ma.

transcendental subjectivity. See MERLEAU-PONTY.

transcendental terms. See TRANSCENDENTALS.

transeunt causation. See AGENT CAUSATION.

transferable utility. See GAME THEORY.

transfinite induction. See MATHEMATICAL INDUCTION.

transfinite number, in set theory, an infinite cardinal or ordinal number. **See also** CONTINUUM PROBLEM, SET THEORY.   P.Mad.

transformational grammar. See GRAMMAR.

transformation rule, an axiom-schema or rule of inference. A transformation rule is thus a rule for transforming a (possibly empty) set of well-formed formulas into a formula, where that rule operates only upon syntactic information. It was this conception of an axiom-schema and rule of inference that was one of the keys to creating a genuinely rigorous science of deductive reasoning. In the 1950s, the idea was imported into linguistics, giving rise to the notion of a *transformational rule.* Such a rule transforms tree structures into tree structures, taking one from the *deep structure* of a sentence, which determines its semantic interpretation, to the *surface structure* of that sentence, which determines its phonetic interpretation. **See also** GRAMMAR, LOGISTIC SYSTEM.   G.F.S.

transitive. See RELATION.

transitive closure. See ANCESTRAL.

translation, radical. See INDETERMINACY OF TRANSLATION.

transparent. See REFERENTIALLY TRANSPARENT.

transparent context. See REFERENTIALLY TRANSPARENT.

transubstantiation, change of one substance into another. Aristotelian metaphysics distinguishes between substances and the accidents that inhere in them; thus, Socrates is a substance and being snub-nosed is one of his accidents. The Roman Catholic and Eastern Orthodox churches appeal to transubstantiation to explain how Jesus Christ becomes really present in the Eucharist when the consecration takes place: the whole substances of the bread and wine are transformed into the body and blood of Christ, but the accidents of the bread and wine such as their shape, color, and taste persist after the transformation. This seems to commit its adherents to holding that these persisting accidents subsequently either inhere in Christ or do not inhere in any substance. Luther proposed an alternative explanation in terms of *consubstantiation* that avoids this hard choice: the substances of the bread and wine coexist in the Eucharist with the body and blood of Christ after the consecration; they are united but each remains unchanged.   P.L.Q.

transvaluation of values. See NIETZSCHE.

transversality, transcendence of the sovereignty of identity or self-sameness by recognizing the alterity of the Other as *Unterschied* – to use Heidegger's term – which signifies the sense of relatedness by way of difference. An innovative idea employed and appropriated by such diverse philosophers as Merleau-Ponty, Sartre, Gilles Deleuze, and Félix Guattari, transversality is meant to replace the Eurocentric formulation of truth as universal in an age when the world is said to be rushing toward the global village. Universality has been a Eurocentric idea because what is particular in the West is universalized, whereas what is particular elsewhere remains particularized. Since its center is everywhere and its circumference nowhere, truth is polycentric and correlative. Particularly noteworthy is the American phenomenologist Calvin O. Schrag's attempt to appropriate transversality by splitting the difference between the two extremes of absolutism and relativism on the one hand and modernity's totalizing practices and postmodernity's fragmentary tendencies on the other. **See also HEIDEGGER, MERLEAU-PONTY, PHENOMENOLOGY, SARTRE.**   H.Y.J.

tree of Porphyry, a structure generated from the logical and metaphysical apparatus of Aristotle's *Categories,* as systematized by Porphyry and later writers. A tree in the category of substance begins with substance as its highest genus and divides that genus into mutually exclusive and collectively exhaustive subordinate genera by means of a pair of opposites, called differentiae, yielding, e.g., corporeal substance and incorporeal substance. The process of division by differentiae continues until a lowest species is reached, a species that cannot be divided further. The species "human being" is said to be a lowest species whose derivation can be recaptured from the formula "mortal, rational, sensitive, animate, corporeal substance." **See also ARISTOTLE, INFIMA SPECIES, PORPHYRY.**   W.E.M.

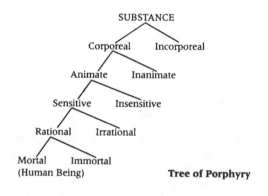

Tree of Porphyry

trichotomous. See RELATION.

trichotomy, law of. See CHOICE SEQUENCE, RELATION.

Trinitarianism, the theological doctrine that God consists of three persons. The persons who constitute the Holy Trinity are the Father; the Son, who is Jesus Christ; and the Holy Spirit (or Holy Ghost). The doctrine states that each of these three persons is God and yet they are not three Gods but one God. According to a traditional formulation, the three persons are but one substance. In the opinion of Aquinas, the existence of God can be proved by human reason, but the existence of the three persons cannot be proved and is known only by revelation. According to Christian tradition, revelation contains information about the relations among the three persons, and these relations ground proper attributes of each that distinguish them from one another. Thus, since the Father begets the Son, a proper attribute of the Father is paternity and a proper attribute of the Son is filiation. Procession (or spiration) is a proper attribute of the Holy Spirit. A disagreement about procession has contributed to dividing Eastern and Western Christianity. The Eastern Orthodox church teaches that the Holy Spirit proceeds from the Father *through* the Son. A theory of double procession according to which the Holy Spirit proceeds from the Father *and* the Son has been widely accepted in the West. This disagreement is known as the *filioque* ('and the Son') controversy because it arose from the fact that adding this Latin phrase to the Nicene Creed became acceptable in the West but not in the East. *Unitarianism* denies that God consists of three persons and so is committed to denying the divinity of Jesus. The monotheistic faiths of Judaism and Islam are unitarian, but there are unitarians who consider themselves Christians.

See also PHILOSOPHY OF RELIGION.   P.L.Q.

Trinity. See TRINITARIANISM.

Troeltsch, Ernst (1865–1923), German philosopher and historian whose primary aim was to provide a scientific foundation for theology. Educated at Erlangen, Göttingen (under Ritschl and Lagarde), and Berlin, he initially taught theology at Heidelberg and later philosophy in Berlin. He launched the school of history of religion with his epoch-making "On Historical and Dogmatical Method in Theology" (1896). His contributions to theology (*The Religious Apriori,* 1904), philosophy, sociology, and history (*Historicism and Its Problems,* 1922) were vastly influential. Troeltsch claimed that only a philosophy of religion drawn from the history and development of religious consciousness could strengthen the standing of the science of religion among the sciences and advance the Christian strategy against materialism, naturalism, skepticism, aestheticism, and pantheism.

His historical masterpiece, *Protestantism and Progress* (1906), argues that early Protestantism was a modified medieval Catholicism that delayed the development of modern culture. As a sociologist, he addressed, in *The Social Teachings of the Christian Churches* (1912), the twofold issue of whether religious beliefs and movements are conditioned by external factors and whether, in turn, they affect society and culture. From Christian social history he inferred three types of "sociological self-formation of the Christian idea": the church, the sect, and the mystic.

                                                            J.-L.S.

trope, in recent philosophical usage, an "abstract particular"; an instance of a property occurring at a particular place and time, such as the color of the cover of this book or this page. The whiteness of this page and the whiteness of the previous page are two distinct tropes, identical neither with the universal whiteness that is instantiated in both pages, nor with the page itself; although the whiteness of this page cannot exist independently of this page, this page could be dyed some other color. A number of writers, perhaps beginning with D. C. Williams, have argued that tropes must be included in our ontology if we are to achieve an adequate metaphysics.

More generally, a trope is a figure of speech, or the use of an expression in a figurative or non-literal sense. Metaphor and irony, e.g., fall under the category of tropes. If you are helping someone move a glass table but drop your end, and your companion says, "Well, you've certainly been a *big help,*" her utterance is probably ironical, with the intended meaning that you have been no help. One important question is whether, in order to account for the ironical use of this sentence, we must suppose that it has an ironical meaning in addition to its literal meaning. Quite generally, does a sentence usable to express two different metaphors have, in addition to its literal meaning, two metaphorical meanings – and another if it can be hyperbolic, and so forth? Many philosophers and other theorists from Aristotle on have answered yes, and postulated such figurative meanings in addition to literal sentence meaning. Recently, philosophers loath to multiply sentence meanings have denied that sentences have any non-literal meanings; their burden is to explain how, e.g., a sentence can be used ironically if it does not have an ironical sense or meaning. Such philosophers disagree on whether tropes are to be explained semantically or pragmatically. A semantic account might hypothesize that tropes are generated by violations of semantical rules. An important pragmatic approach is Grice's suggestion that tropes can be subsumed under the more general phenomenon of conversational implicature.

See also IMPLICATURE, METAPHOR, META-PHYSICS, SKEPTICS.   R.B.

Trotter, Catherine. See COCKBURN.

truth, the quality of those propositions that accord with reality, specifying what is in fact the case. Whereas the aim of a science is to discover which of the propositions in its domain are true i.e., which propositions possess the property of truth – the central philosophical concern with truth is to discover the nature of that property. Thus the philosophical question is not What is true? but rather, What is truth? – What is one saying about a proposition in saying that it is true? The importance of this question stems from the variety and depth of the principles in which the concept of truth is deployed. We are tempted to think, e.g., that truth is the proper aim and natural result of scientific inquiry, that true beliefs are useful, that the meaning of a sentence is given by the conditions that would render it true, and that valid reasoning preserves truth. Therefore insofar as we wish to understand, assess, and refine these epistemological, ethical, semantic, and logical views, some account of the nature of truth would seem to be required. Such a thing, however, has been notoriously elusive.

The belief that snow is white owes its truth to a certain feature of the external world: the fact that snow is white. Similarly, the belief that dogs bark is true because of the fact that dogs bark. Such trivial observations lead to what is perhaps the most natural and widely held account of truth, the *correspondence theory*, according to which a belief (statement, sentence, proposition, etc.) is true provided there exists a fact corresponding to it. This Aristotelian thesis is unexceptionable in itself. However, if it is to provide a complete theory of truth – and if it is to be more than merely a picturesque way of asserting all instances of 'the belief that *p* is true if and only if *p*' – then it must be supplemented with accounts of what *facts* are, and what it is for a belief to *correspond* to a fact; and these are the problems on which the correspondence theory of truth has foundered.

A popular alternative to the correspondence theory has been to identify truth with verifiability. This idea can take on various forms. One version involves the further assumption that verification is holistic – i.e., that a belief is verified when it is part of an entire system of beliefs that is consistent and "harmonious." This is known as the *coherence theory* of truth and was developed by Bradley and Brand Blanchard. Another version, due to Dummett and Putnam, involves the assumption that there is, for each proposition, some specific procedure for finding out whether one should believe it or not. On this account, to say that a proposition is true is to say that it would be verified by the appropriate procedure. In mathematics this amounts to the identification of truth with provability and is sometimes referred to as *intuitionistic truth*. Such

theories aim to avoid obscure metaphysical notions and explain the close relation between knowability and truth. They appear, however, to overstate the intimacy of that link: for we can easily imagine a statement that, though true, is beyond our power to establish as true.

A third major account of truth is James's *pragmatic theory*. As we have just seen, the verificationist selects a prominent property of truth and considers it to be the essence of truth. Similarly the pragmatist focuses on another important characteristic – namely, that true beliefs are a good basis for action – and takes this to be the very nature of truth. True assumptions are said to be, by definition, those that provoke actions with desirable results. Again we have an account with a single attractive explanatory feature. But again the central objection is that the relationship it postulates between truth and its alleged analysans – in this case, utility – is implausibly close. Granted, true beliefs tend to foster success. But often actions based on true beliefs lead to disaster, while false assumptions, by pure chance, produce wonderful results.

One of the few fairly uncontroversial facts about truth is that the proposition that snow is white is true if and only if snow is white, the proposition that lying is wrong is true if and only if lying is wrong, and so on. Traditional theories of truth acknowledge this fact but regard it as insufficient and, as we have seen, inflate it with some further principle of the form '*X* is true if and only if *X* has property *P*' (such as corresponding to reality, verifiability, or being suitable as a basis for action), which is supposed to specify what truth is. A collection of radical alternatives to the traditional theories results from denying the need for any such further specification. For example, one might suppose (with Ramsey, Ayer, and Strawson) that the basic theory of truth contains nothing more than equivalences of the form, 'The proposition that *p* is true if and only if *p*' (excluding instantiation by sentences such as 'This proposition is not true' that generate contradiction).

This so-called *deflationary theory* is best presented (following Quine) in conjunction with an account of the raison d'être of our notion of truth: namely, that its function is not to describe propositions, as one might naively infer from its syntactic form, but rather to enable us to construct a certain type of generalization. For example, 'What Einstein said is true' is intuitively equivalent to the infinite conjunction 'If Einstein said that nothing goes faster than light, then nothing goes faster than light; and if Einstein said that nuclear weapons should never be built, then nuclear weapons should never be built; . . . and so on.' But without a truth predicate we could not capture this statement. The deflationist argues, moreover, that all legitimate uses of the truth predicate – including those in science, logic, semantics, and metaphysics – are simply displays of this generalizing function, and that the equivalence schema is just what is needed to explain that function.

Within the deflationary camp there are various competing proposals. According to Frege's so-called *redundancy theory*, corresponding instances of 'It is true that *p*' and '*p*' have exactly the same meaning, whereas the *minimalist theory* assumes merely that such propositions are necessarily equivalent. Other deflationists are skeptical about the existence of propositions and therefore take sentences to be the basic vehicles of truth. Thus the *disquotation theory* supposes that truth is captured by the disquotation principle, '*p*' is true if and only if *p*'. More ambitiously, Tarski does not regard the disquotation principle, also known as *Tarski's (T) schema*, as an adequate theory in itself, but as a specification of what any adequate definition must imply. His own account shows how to give an explicit definition of truth for all the sentences of certain formal languages in terms of the referents of their primitive names and predicates. This is known as the *semantic theory* of truth.

   See also EPISTEMOLOGY, METAPHYSICAL REALISM, SEMANTIC HOLISM, SET-THEORETIC PARADOXES.   P.Hor.

truth, coherence theory of. See TRUTH.

truth, correspondence theory of. See TRUTH.

truth, disquotation theory of. See TRUTH.

truth, pragmatic theory of. See PRAGMATISM, TRUTH.

truth, redundancy theory of. See TRUTH.

truth, semantic theory of. See TRUTH.

truth-conditional semantics. See MEANING.

truth-conditional theory of meaning. See MEANING.

truth conditions. See TRUTH.

truth definition. See TRUTH.

truth-functions. See TRUTH TABLE.

truthlikeness, a term introduced by Karl Popper in 1960 to explicate the idea that one theory may have a better correspondence with reality, or be closer to the truth, or have more verisimilitude, than another theory. Truthlikeness, which combines truth with information content, has to be distinguished from probability, which increases with lack of content. Let *T* and *F* be the classes of all true and false sentences, respectively, and *A* and *B* deductively closed sets of sentences. According to Popper's qualitative definition, *A* is more truthlike than *B* if and only if $B \cap T \subseteq A \cap T$ and $A \cap F \subseteq B \cap F$, where one of these set-inclusions is strict. In particular, when *A* and *B* are non-equivalent and both true, *A* is more truthlike than *B* if and only if *A* logically entails *B*. David Miller and Pavel Tichý proved in 1974 that Popper's definition is not applicable to the comparison of false theories: if *A* is more truthlike than *B*, then *A* must be true.

   Since the mid-1970s, a new approach to truthlikeness has been based upon the concept of similarity: the degree of truthlikeness of a statement *A* depends on the distances from the states of affairs allowed by *A* to the true state. In Graham Oddie's *Likeness to Truth* (1986), this dependence is expressed by the average function; in Ilkka Niiniluoto's *Truthlikeness* (1987), by the weighted average of the minimum distance and the sum of all distances. The concept of verisimilitude is also used in the epistemic sense to express a rational evaluation of how close to the truth a theory appears to be on available evidence.

   See also CONFIRMATION, INFORMATION THEORY, INSTRUMENTALISM, PROBABILITY.
                                                      I.N.

truthmaker principle. See ARMSTRONG.

truth predicate. See SEMANTIC PARADOXES.

truth table, a tabular display of one or more truth-functions, truth-functional operators, or representatives of truth-functions or truth-functional operators (such as well-formed formulas of propositional logic). In the tabular display, each row displays a possible assignment of truth-values to the arguments of the truth-functions or truth-functional operators. Thus, the collection of all rows in the table displays all possible assignments of truth-values to these arguments. The following simple truth table represents the truth-functional operators negation and conjunction:

P	Q	Not-P	P-and-Q
T	T	F	T
T	F	F	F
F	T	T	F
F	F	T	F

Because a truth table displays all possible assignments of truth-values to the arguments of a truth-function, truth tables are useful devices for quickly ascertaining logical properties of propositions. If, e.g., all entries in the column of a truth table representing a proposition are T, then the proposition is true for all possible assignments of truth-values to its ultimate constituent propositions; in this sort of case, the proposition is said to be logically or tautologically true: a *tautology*. If all entries in the column of a truth table representing a proposition are F, then the proposition is false for all possible assignments of truth-values to its ultimate constituent propositions, and the proposition is said to be logically or tautologically false: a *contradiction*. If a proposition is neither a tautology nor a contradiction, then it is said to be a *contingency*. The truth table above shows that both Not-P and P-and-Q are contingencies.

For the same reason that truth tables are useful devices for ascertaining the logical qualities of single propositions, truth tables are also useful for ascertaining whether arguments are valid or invalid. A valid argument is one such that there is no possibility (no row in the relevant truth table) in which all its premises are true and its conclusion false. Thus the above truth table shows that the argument 'P-and-Q; therefore, P' is valid.

    See also CONTINGENT, FORMAL LOGIC, TAU-TOLOGY.   R.W.B.

truth-table method. See TRUTH TABLE.

truth-value, most narrowly, one of the values T (for 'true') or F (for 'false') that a proposition may be considered to have or take on when it is regarded as true or false, respectively. More broadly, a truth-value is any one of a range of values that a proposition may be considered to have when taken to have one of a range of different cognitive or epistemic statuses. For example, some philosophers speak of the truth-value I (for 'indeterminate') and regard a proposition as having the value I when it is indeterminate whether the proposition is true or false. Logical systems employing a specific number n of truth-values are said to be n-valued logical systems; the

simplest sort of useful logical system has two truth-values, T and F, and accordingly is said to be two-valued. Truth-functions are functions that take truth-values as arguments and that yield truth-values as resultant values. The truth-table method in propositional logic exploits the idea of truth-functions by using tabular displays. **See also TRUTH TABLE.**   R.W.B.

truth-value gaps. See MANY-VALUED LOGIC, PRESUP-POSITION.

truth-value semantics, interpretations of formal systems in which the truth-value of a formula rests ultimately only on truth-values that are assigned to its atomic subformulas (where 'subformula' is suitably defined). The label is due to Hugues Leblanc. On a truth-value interpretation for first-order predicate logic, for example, the formula atomic $\forall xFx$ is true in a model if and only if all its *instances Fm, Fn, . . .* are true, where the truth-value of these formulas is simply assigned by the model. On the standard Tarskian or objectual interpretation, by contrast, $\forall xFx$ is true in a model if and only if every object in the domain of the model is an element of the set that interprets F in the model. Thus a truth-value semantics for predicate logic comprises a substitutional interpretation of the quantifiers and a "non-denotational" interpretation of terms and predicates. If $t_1, t_2, . . .$ are all the terms of some first-order language, then there are objectual models that satisfy the set $\{\exists x\text{-}Fx, Ft_1, Ft_2 . . . .\}$, but no truth-value interpretations that do. One can ensure that truth-value semantics delivers the standard logic, however, by suitable modifications in the definitions of consistency and consequence. A set Γ of formulas of language L is said to be consistent, for example, if there is some Γ' obtained from Γ by relettering terms such that Γ' is satisfied by some truth-value assignment, or, alternatively, if there is some language L^+ obtained by adding terms to L such that Γ is satisfied by some truth-value assignment to the atoms of L^+.

Truth-value semantics is of both technical and philosophical interest. Technically, it allows the completeness of first-order predicate logic and a variety of other formal systems to be obtained in a natural way from that of propositional logic. Philosophically, it dramatizes the fact that the formulas in one's theories about the world do not, in themselves, determine one's ontological commitments. It is at least possible to interpret first-order formulas without reference to special domains of objects, and higher-order formulas without reference to special domains of relations and properties.

The idea of truth-value semantics dates at least to the writings of E. W. Beth on first-order predicate logic in 1959 and of K. Schütte on simple type theory in 1960. In more recent years similar semantics have been suggested for second-order logics, modal and tense logics, intuitionistic logic, and set theory.

See also FORMAL SEMANTICS, MEANING, QUANTIFICATION, TRUTH TABLE.   S.T.K.

Tsou Yen (350?–270? B.C.), Chinese cosmologist, a member of the Chi-hsia Academy and influential political figure who applied yin–yang five-phases thinking to dynastic cycles. Tsou Yen believed that the natural order, the human order, and the relation between the two were all governed and made intelligible by the dynamic interplay among yin–yang and the five phases (*wu-hsing:* earth, wood, metal, fire, and water). He gained political fame for his idea that the rise and fall of dynasties are correlated with the five phases and accord with the same cyclical pattern: earth, wood, metal, fire, and water. Thus, the reign of the Yellow Emperor, correlated with the earth phase, was followed by the Hsia (wood), the Shang (metal), and the Chou (fire) dynasties. Tsou Yen predicted that the ascendancy of the water phase would signal the end of the Chou and the beginning of a new dynasty. **See also** CHINESE PHILOSOPHY.   R.P.P. & R.T.A.

Tung Chung-shu (c.179–c.104 B.C.), Chinese philosopher, a Han scholar famous for his answers to questions by Emperor Wu, which were instrumental in making Confucianism the state doctrine in 136 B.C. He wrote *Ch'un-ch'iu fan-lu* ("Luxuriant Gems of the Spring and Autumn Annals"), in which he read moral messages from historical events recorded in the classic in such a way that they could be applied to future history. Tung's teachings were actually quite different from those of Confucius and Mencius. He believed that Heaven and the Way do not change, and he taught the so-called Three Bonds, according to which the ruler, the father, and the husband are to be the standards of the ruled, the son, and the wife. These added a conservative ring to Confucianism, so that the rulers were happy to use it in combination with Legalist practice to create a state Confucianism. He also incorporated many ideas from the yin–yang school in his philosophy. He believed that history

goes in cycles, the five powers (wood, fire, earth, metal, water) succeed each other, and there is a strict correlation between natural affairs and human affairs. He saw natural disasters as warning signs for the rulers to cultivate virtues and not to abuse their powers. **See also** CONFUCIANISM, CONFUCIUS, MENCIUS.   S.-h.L.

tu quoque. See INFORMAL FALLACY.

Turing degree. See DEGREE OF UNSOLVABILITY.

Turing machine, an abstract automaton or imagined computer consisting of a finite automaton operating an indefinitely long storage tape. The finite automaton provides the computing power of the machine. The tape is used for input, output, and calculation workspace; in the case of the universal Turing machine, it also specifies another Turing machine.

Initially, only a finite number of squares of the tape are marked with symbols, while the rest are blank. The finite automaton part of the machine has a finite number of internal states and operates discretely, at times $t = 0, 1, 2, \ldots$. At each time-step the automaton examines the tape square under its tape head, possibly changes what is there, moves the tape left or right, and then changes its internal state.

The law governing this sequence of actions is deterministic and is defined in a *state table*. For each internal state and each tape symbol (or blank) under the tape head, the state table describes the tape action performed by the machine and gives the next internal state of the machine.

Since a machine has only a finite number of internal states and of tape symbols, the state table of a machine is finite in length and can be stored on a tape. There is a *universal Turing machine* M_u that can simulate every Turing machine (including itself): when the state table of any machine M is written on the tape of M_u, the universal machine M_u will perform the same input-output computation that M performs. M_u does this by using the state table of M to calculate M's complete history for any given input.

Turing machines may be thought of as conceptual devices for enumerating the elements of an infinite set (e.g., the theorems of a formal language), or as decision machines (e.g., deciding of any truth-functional formula whether it is a tautology). A. M. Turing showed that there are well-defined logical tasks that cannot be carried out by any machine; in particular, no machine can solve the halting problem.

Turing's definition of a machine was theoretical; it was not a practical specification for a machine. After the modern electronic computer was invented, he proposed a test for judging whether there is a computer that is *behaviorally equivalent* to a human in reasoning and intellectual creative power.

The *Turing test* is a "black box" type of experiment that Turing proposed as a way of deciding whether a computer can think. Two rooms are fitted with the same input-output equipment going to an outside experimenter. A person is placed in one room and a programmed electronic computer in the other, each in communication with the experimenter. By issuing instructions and asking questions, the experimenter tries to decide which room has the computer and which the human. If the experimenter cannot tell, that outcome is strong evidence that the computer can think as well as the person. More directly, it shows that the computer and the human are equivalent for all the behaviors tested. Since the computer is a finite automaton, perhaps the most significant test task is that of doing creative mathematics about the non-enumerable infinite.

See also BEHAVIORISM, COMPUTER THEORY, GÖDEL'S INCOMPLETENESS THEOREMS, INFINITY, LÖWENHEIM-SKOLEM THEOREM.   A.W.B.

Turing machine functionalism. See FUNCTIONALISM.

Turing test. See TURING MACHINE.

Turnbull, George (1698–1748), Scottish moral sense philosopher and educational theorist. He was briefly a philosophy regent at Aberdeen (1721–27) and a teacher of Reid. His *Principles of Moral and Christian Philosophy* (1740) and *Discourse upon the Nature and Origin of Moral and Civil Laws* (1741) show him as the most systematic of those who aimed to recast moral philosophy on a Newtonian model, deriving moral laws "experimentally" from human psychology. In *A Treatise on Ancient Painting* (1740), *Observations Upon Liberal Education* (1742), and some smaller works, he extolled history and the arts as propaedeutic to the teaching of virtue and natural religion. See also MORAL SENSE THEORY.   M.A.St.

Twardowski. See ACT-OBJECT PSYCHOLOGY, POLISH LOGIC.

Twin-Earth, a fictitious planet first visited by Hilary Putnam in a thought experiment designed to show, among other things, that " 'meanings' just ain't in the head" ("The Meaning of 'Mean-ing'," 1975). Twin-Earth is exactly like Earth with one notable exception: ponds, rivers, and ice trays on Twin-Earth contain, not H_2O, but XYZ, a liquid superficially indistinguishable from water but with a different chemical constitution. According to Putnam, although some inhabitants of Twin-Earth closely resemble inhabitants of Earth, 'water', when uttered by a Twin-Earthling, does not mean *water*. Water is H_2O, and, on Twin-Earth, the word 'water' designates a different substance, XYZ, *Twin*-water. The moral drawn by Putnam is that the meanings of at least some of our words, and the significance of some of our thoughts, depend, in part, on how things stand outside our heads. Two "molecular duplicates," two agents with qualitatively similar mental lives, might mean very different things by their utterances and think very different thoughts. Although Twin-Earth has become a popular stopping-off place for philosophers en route to theories of meaning and mental content, others regard Twin-Earth as hopelessly remote, doubting that useful conclusions can be drawn about our Earthly circumstances from research conducted there. See also MEANING, PHILOSOPHY OF LANGUAGE.   J.F.H.

tychism (from Greek *tyche*, 'chance'), Peirce's doctrine that there is absolute chance in the universe and its fundamental laws are probabilistic and inexact. Peirce's tychism is part of his evolutionary cosmology, according to which all regularities of nature are products of growth and development, i.e., results of evolution. The laws of nature develop over time and become increasingly rigid and exact; the apparently deterministic laws of physics are limiting cases of the basic, probabilistic laws. Underlying all other laws is "the tendency of all things to take habits"; Peirce calls this the Law of Habit. In his cosmology his tychism is associated with *synechism*, the doctrine of the continuity of nature. His synechism involves the doctrine of the continuity of mind and matter; Peirce sometimes expressed this view by saying that "matter is effete mind."   R.Hi.

type. See ACTION THEORY, DARWINISM, DETERMINISM, TYPE THEORY, TYPE–TOKEN DISTINCTION.

type epiphenomenalism. See PHILOSOPHY OF MIND.

type physicalism. See PHYSICALISM.

types, simple theory of. See TYPE THEORY.

types, theory of. See TYPE THEORY.

type theory, broadly, any theory according to which the things that exist fall into natural, perhaps mutually exclusive, categories or *types*. In most modern discussions, 'type theory' refers to the theory of logical types first sketched by Russell in *The Principles of Mathematics* (1903). It is a theory of *logical* types insofar as it purports only to classify things into the most general categories that must be presupposed by an adequate logical theory. Russell proposed his theory in response to his discovery of the now-famous paradox that bears his name. The paradox is this. Common sense suggests that some classes are members of themselves (e.g., the class of all classes), while others are not (e.g., the class of philosophers). Let *R* be the class whose membership consists of exactly those classes of the latter sort, i.e., those that are not members of themselves. Is *R* a member of itself? If so, then it is a member of the class of all classes that are *not* members of themselves, and hence is not a member of itself. If, on the other hand, it is not a member of itself, then it satisfies its own membership conditions, and hence is a member of itself after all. Either way there is a contradiction.

The source of the paradox, Russell suggested, is the assumption that classes and their members form a single, homogeneous logical type. To the contrary, he proposed that the logical universe is stratified into a regimented *hierarchy* of types. *Individuals* constitute the lowest type in the hierarchy, type 0. (For purposes of exposition, individuals can be taken to be ordinary objects like chairs and persons.) Type 1 consists of classes of individuals, type 2 of classes of classes of individuals, type 3 classes of classes of classes of individuals, and so on. Unlike the homogeneous universe, then, in the type hierarchy the members of a given class must all be drawn from a single logical type n, and the class itself must reside in the next higher type $n + 1$. (Russell's sketch in the *Principles* differs from this account in certain details.)

Russell's paradox cannot arise in this conception of the universe of classes. Because the members of a class must all be of the same logical type, there is no such class as *R*, whose definition cuts across *all* types. Rather, there is only, for each type n, the class R_n of all non-self-membered classes *of that type*. Since R_n itself is of type $n + 1$, the paradox breaks down: from the assumption that R_n is not a member of itself (as in fact it is not in the type hierarchy), it no longer follows that it satisfies its own membership conditions, since those conditions apply only to objects of type n.

Most formal type theories, including Russell's

own, enforce the class membership restrictions of simple type theory syntactically such that a can be asserted to be a member of b only if b is of the next higher type than a. In such theories, the definition of *R*, hence the paradox itself, cannot even be expressed.

Numerous paradoxes remain unscathed by the simple type hierarchy. Of these, the most prominent are the *semantic* paradoxes, so called because they explicitly involve semantic notions like *truth*, as in the following version of the liar paradox. Suppose Epimenides asserts that all the propositions he asserts today are false; suppose also that that is the only proposition he asserts today. It follows immediately that, under those conditions, the proposition he asserts is true if and only if it is false. To address such paradoxes, Russell was led to the more refined and substantially more complicated system known as *ramified type theory*, developed in detail in his 1908 paper "Mathematical Logic as Based on the Theory of Types." In the ramified theory, *propositions* and *properties* (or *propositional functions*, in Russell's jargon) come to play the central roles in the type-theoretic universe. Propositions are best construed as the metaphysical and semantical counterparts of sentences – what sentences *express* – and properties as the counterparts of "open sentences" like '*x* is a philosopher' that contain a variable '*x*' in place of a noun phrase. To distinguish linguistic expressions from their semantic counterparts, the property expressed by, say, '*x* is a philosopher', will be denoted by '$\hat{x}$ *is a philosopher*', and the proposition expressed by 'Aristotle is a philosopher' will be denoted by '*Aristotle is a philosopher*'. A property $\ldots \hat{x} \ldots$ is said to be *true of* an individual a if $\ldots a \ldots$ is a true proposition, and *false of a* if $\ldots a \ldots$ is a false proposition (where '$\ldots a \ldots$' is the result of replacing '$\hat{x}$' with 'a' in '$\ldots \hat{x} \ldots$'). So, e.g., $\hat{x}$ *is a philosopher* is true of Aristotle. The *range of significance* of a property P is the collection of objects of which P is true or false. a is a *possible argument* for P if it is in P's range of significance.

In the ramified theory, the hierarchy of classes is supplanted by a hierarchy of properties: first, properties of individuals (i.e., properties whose range of significance is restricted to individuals), then properties of properties of individuals, and so on. Parallel to the simple theory, then, the type of a property must exceed the type of its possible arguments by one. Thus, Russell's paradox with *R* now in the guise of the property $\hat{x}$ *is a property that is not true of itself* – is avoided along analogous lines. Following the French mathematician Henri Poincaré, Russell traced the source of the semantic paradoxes to a kind of illicit *self-reference*. So, for example, in the liar paradox, Epimenides ostensibly asserts a proposition *p* about *all* propositions, *p* itself among them, namely that they are false if asserted by him today. *p* thus refers to itself in the sense that it – or more exactly, the sentence that expresses it – *quantifies over* (i.e., refers generally to *all* or *some* of the elements of) a collection of entities among which *p* itself is included. The source of semantic paradox thus isolated, Russell formulated the *vicious circle principle* (VCP), which proscribes all such self-reference in properties and propositions generally. The liar proposition *p* and its ilk were thus effectively banished from the realm of legitimate propositions and so the semantic paradoxes could not arise.

Wedded to the restrictions of simple type theory, the VCP generates a *ramified* hierarchy based on a more complicated form of typing. The key notion is that of an object's *order*. The order of an individual, like its type, is 0. However, the order of a property must exceed the order not only of its possible arguments, as in simple type theory, but also the orders of the things it quantifies over. Thus, type 1 properties like *x̂ is a philosopher* and *x̂ is as wise as all other philosophers* are *first-order* properties, since they are true of and, in the second instance, quantify over, individuals only. Properties like these whose order exceeds the order of their possible arguments by one are called *predicative,* and are of the lowest possible order relative to their range of significance. Consider, by contrast, the property (call it *Q*) *x̂ has all the (first-order) properties of a great philosopher.* Like those above, *Q* also is a property of individuals. However, since *Q* quantifies over first-order properties, by the VDP, it cannot be counted among them. Accordingly, in the ramified hierarchy, *Q* is a *second-order* property of individuals, and hence *non*-predicative (or impredicative). Like *Q*, the property *x̂ is a (first-order) property of all great philosophers* is also second-order, since its range of significance consists of objects of order 1 (and it quantifies only over objects of order 0); but since it is a property of first-order properties, it is predicative. In like manner it is possible to define third-order properties of individuals, third-order properties of first-order properties, third-order properties of second-order properties of individuals, third-order properties of second-order properties of first-order properties, and then, in the same fashion, fourth-order properties, fifth-order properties, and so on ad infinitum.

A serious shortcoming of ramified type theory,

from Russell's perspective, is that it is an inadequate foundation for classical mathematics. The most prominent difficulty is that many classical theorems appeal to definitions that, though consistent, violate the VCP. For instance, a well-known theorem of real analysis asserts that every bounded set of real numbers has a least upper bound. In the ramified theory, real numbers are identified with certain predicative properties of rationals. Under such an identification, the usual procedure is to define the least upper bound of a bounded set *S* of reals to be the property (call it *b*) *some real number in S is true of x̂,* and then prove that this property is itself a real number with the requisite characteristics. However, *b* quantifies over the real numbers. Hence, by the VCP, *b* cannot itself be taken to be a real number: although of the same *type* as the reals, and although true of the right things, *b* must be assigned a higher *order* than the reals. So, contrary to the classical theorem, *S* fails to have a least upper bound. Russell introduced a special axiom to obviate this difficulty: the *axiom of reducibility*. Reducibility says, in effect, that for any property *P*, there is a *predicative* property *Q* that is true of exactly the same things as *P*. Reducibility thus assures that there is a predicative property *b'* true of the same rational numbers as *b*. Since the reals are predicative, hence of the same order as *b'*, it turns out that *b'* is a real number, and hence that *S* has a least upper bound after all, as required by the classical theorem. The general role of reducibility is thus to undo the draconian mathematical effects of ramification without undermining its capacity to fend off the semantic paradoxes.

See also HIERARCHY, PARADOX, RUSSELL.

C.M.

type theory, ramified. See TYPE THEORY.

type–token distinction, as drawn by Peirce, the contrast between a category and a member of that category. An individual or token is said to exemplify a type; it possesses the property that characterizes that type. In philosophy this distinction is often applied to linguistic expressions and to mental states, but it can be applied also to objects, events, properties, and states of affairs. Related to it are the distinctions between type and token individuation and between qualitative and numerical identity. Distinct tokens of the same type, such as two ants, may be qualitatively identical but cannot be numerically identical. Irrespective of the controversial metaphysical view that every individual has an essence, a type to which it belongs essentially, every individual belongs to many types, although for a certain theoretical or practical purpose it may belong to one particularly salient type (e.g., the entomologist's Formicidae or the picnicker's buttinsky).

The type–token distinction as applied in the philosophy of language marks the difference between linguistic expressions, such as words and sentences, which are the subject of linguistics, and the products of acts of writing or speaking (the subject of speech act theory). Confusing the two can lead to conflating matters of speaker meaning with matters of word or sentence meaning (as noted by Grice). An expression is a linguistic type and can be used over and over, whereas a token of a type can be produced only once, though of course it may be *re*produced (copied). A writer composes an essay (a type) and produces a manuscript (a token), of which there might be many copies (more tokens). A token of a type is not the same as an *occurrence* of a type. In the previous sentence there are two occurrences of the word 'type'; in each inscription of that sentence, there are two tokens of that word.

In philosophy of mind the type–token distinc-tion underlies the contrast between two forms of physicalism, the type–type identity theory or *type physicalism* and the token–token identity theory or *token physicalism*.

See also ACTION THEORY, PEIRCE, PHILOSOPHY OF MIND. K.B.

type-type identity. See PHILOSOPHY OF MIND.

tzu jan, Chinese term meaning 'naturally', 'spontaneity', or 'so-of-itself'. It is a Taoist term of art describing the ideal state of agents and quality of actions. A coordinate concept is *wu wei* (non-action), particularly in the *Tao Te Ching*. Taoists seek to eliminate the rational "human" perspective and return to spontaneous "Heavenly" inclinations. Actions then will be unself-conscious, and we and what we do will be *tzu jan* (spontaneous). Wang Ch'ung presents an early critique of this Taoist notion in chapter 54 of his *Lun Heng*. Later thinkers appropriate the term to support their own positions. For example, Neo-Confucians regard particular familial and social obligations as *tzu jan*, as are certain virtuous inclinations. **See also** NEO-TAOISM, TAOISM.

P.J.I.

U

Übermensch. See NIETZSCHE.

Udana. See NYĀYA-VAISHESIKA.

Unamuno, Miguel de (1864–1936), Spanish philosopher, scholar, and writer. Born in Bilbao, he studied in Bilbao and Madrid and taught Greek and philosophy in Salamanca. His open criticism of the Spanish government led to dismissal from the university and exile (1924–30) and, again, to dismissal from the rectorship in 1936.

Unamuno is an important figure in Spanish letters. Like Ortega y Gasset, his aim was to capture life in its complex emotional and intellectual dimensions rather than to describe the world scientifically. Thus, he favored fiction as a medium for his ideas and may be considered a precursor of existentialism. He wrote several philosophically significant novels, a commentary on *Don Quijote* (1905), and some poetry and drama; his philosophical ideas are most explicitly stated in *Del sentimiento trágico de la vida* ("The Tragic Sense of Life," 1913).

Unamuno perceived a *tragic sense* permeating human life, a sense arising from our desire for immortality and from the certainty of death. In this predicament man must abandon all pretense of rationalism and embrace faith. Faith characterizes the *authentic life*, while reason leads to despair, but faith can never completely displace reason. Torn between the two, we can find hope only in faith; for reason deals only with abstractions, while we are "flesh and bones" and can find fulfillment only through commitment to an ideal.   J.J.E.G.

unary quantifier. See PLURALITIVE LOGIC.

uncertainty principle. See PHILOSOPHY OF SCIENCE, QUANTUM MECHANICS.

unconscious. See FREUD, JUNG.

uncountable. See CANTOR.

undecidable. See CONVENTIONALISM.

undefeated. See EPISTEMOLOGY.

undemonstrable argument. See THEMA.

underdetermination, perceptual. See FIGURE–GROUND.

underdetermination, theoretical. See OPERATIONALISM, THEORY-LADEN.

underdetermination thesis. See PHILOSOPHY OF SCIENCE.

understanding. See DILTHEY, EXPLANATION, VERSTEHEN.

understanding, categories of the. See KANT.

unexpected examination paradox, a paradox about belief and prediction. One version is as follows: It seems that a teacher could both make, and act on, the following announcement to his class: "Sometime during the next week I will set you an examination, but at breakfast time on the day it will occur, you will have no good reason to expect that it will occur on that day." If he announces this on Friday, could he not do what he said he would by, say, setting the examination on the following Wednesday? The paradox is that there is an argument purporting to show that there could not be an unexpected examination of this kind. For let us suppose that the teacher will carry out his threat, in both its parts; i.e., he will set an examination, and it will be unexpected. Then he cannot set the examination on Friday (assuming this to be the last possible day of the week). For, by the time Friday breakfast arrives, and we know that all the previous days have been examination-free, we would have every reason to expect the examination to occur on Friday. So leaving the examination until Friday is inconsistent with setting an *unexpected* examination. For similar reasons, the examination cannot be held on Thursday. Given our previous conclusion that it cannot be delayed until Friday, we would know, when Thursday morning came, and the previous days had been examination-free, that it would have to be held on Thursday. So if it were held on Thursday it would not be unexpected. So it cannot be held on Thursday. Similar reasoning supposedly shows that there is no day of the week on which it can be held, and so supposedly shows that the supposition that the teacher can carry out his threat must be rejected. This is paradoxical, for it seems plain that the teacher *can* carry out his threat. **See also PARADOX.**   R.M.S.

unified science. See UNITY OF SCIENCE.

uniformity of nature, a state of affairs thought to be required if induction is to be justified. For example, inductively strong arguments, such as 'The sun has risen every day in the past; therefore, the sun will rise tomorrow', are thought to presuppose that nature is uniform in the sense that the future will resemble the past, in this case with respect to the diurnal cycle.

The Scottish empiricist Hume was the first to make explicit that the uniformity of nature is a substantial assumption in inductive reasoning. Hume argued that, because the belief that the future will resemble the past cannot be grounded in experience – for the future is as yet unobserved – induction cannot be rationally justified; appeal to it in defense of induction is either question-begging or illicitly metaphysical. Francis Bacon's "induction by enumeration" and J. S. Mill's "five methods of experimental inquiry" presuppose that nature is uniform. Whewell appealed to the uniformity of nature in order to account for the "consilience of inductions," the tendency of a hypothesis to explain data different from those it was originally introduced to explain. For reasons similar to Hume's, Popper holds that our belief in the uniformity of nature is a matter of faith. Reichenbach held that although this belief cannot be justified in advance of any instance of inductive reasoning, its presupposition is vindicated by successful inductions.

It has proved difficult to formulate a philosophical statement of the uniformity of nature that is both coherent and informative. It appears contradictory to say that nature is uniform in *all* respects, because inductive inferences always mark differences of some sort (e.g., from present to future, from observed to unobserved, etc.), and it seems trivial to say that nature is uniform in *some* respects, because any two states of nature, no matter how different, will be similar in some respect.

Not all observed regularities in the world (or in data) are taken to support successful inductive reasoning; not all uniformities are, to use Goodman's term, "projectible." Philosophers of science have therefore proposed various rules of

projectibility, involving such notions as simplicity and explanatory power, in an attempt to distinguish those observed patterns that support successful inductions (and thus are taken to represent genuine causal relations) from those that are accidental or spurious.

See also CAUSATION, GRUE PARADOX, LAW-LIKE GENERALIZATION, PROBLEM OF INDUCTION.   J.D.T.

union. See SET THEORY.

unitarianism. See TRINITARIANISM.

unity, organic. See ORGANIC.

unity in diversity, in aesthetics, the principle that the parts of the aesthetic object must cohere or hang together while at the same time being different enough to allow for the object to be complex. This principle defines an important formal requirement used in judging aesthetic objects. If an object has insufficient unity (e.g., a collection of color patches with no recognizable patterns of any sort), it is chaotic or lacks harmony; it is more a collection than one object. But if it has insufficient diversity (e.g., a canvas consisting entirely of one color with no internal differentiations), it is monotonous. Thus, the formal pattern desired in an aesthetic object is that of complex parts that differ significantly from each other but fit together to form one interdependent whole such that the character or meaning of the whole would be changed by the change of any part. **See also AESTHETICS, ORGANIC.**   J.A.K.

unity of science, a situation in which all branches of empirical science form a coherent system called *unified science*. Unified science is sometimes extended to include formal sciences (e.g., branches of logic and mathematics). 'Unity of science' is also used to refer to a research program aimed at unified science.

Interest in the unity of science has a long history with many roots, including ancient atomism and the work of the French Encyclopedists. In the twentieth century this interest was prominent in logical empiricism (see Otto Neurath et al., *International Encyclopedia of Unified Science*, vol. I, 1938). Logical empiricists originally conceived of unified science in terms of a unified language of science, in particular, a universal observation language. All laws and theoretical statements in any branch of science were to be translatable into such an observation language, or else be appropriately related to sentences of this language. In addition to encountering technical difficulties with the observational–theoretical distinction, this conception of unified science also leaves open the possibility that phenomena of one branch may require special concepts and hypotheses that are explanatorily independent of other branches.

Another concept of unity of science requires that all branches of science be combined by the intertheoretic reduction of the theories of all non-basic branches to one basic theory (usually assumed to be some future physics). These reductions may proceed stepwise; an oversimplified example would be reduction of psychology to biology, together with reductions of biology to chemistry and chemistry to physics. The conditions for reducing theory T_2 to theory T_1 are complex, but include identification of the ontology of T_2 with that of T_1, along with explanation of the laws of T_2 by laws of T_1 together with appropriate connecting sentences. These conditions for reduction can be supplemented with conditions for the unity of the basic theory, to produce a general research program for the unification of science (see Robert L. Causey, *Unity of Science*, 1977).

Adopting this research program does not commit one to the proposition that complete unification will ever be achieved; the latter is primarily an empirical proposition. This program has been criticized, and some have argued that reductions are impossible for particular pairs of theories, or that some branches of science are autonomous. For example, some writers have defended a view of *autonomous biology*, according to which biological science is not reducible to the physical sciences. Vitalism postulated non-physical attributes or vital forces that were supposed to be present in living organisms. More recent neo-vitalistic positions avoid these postulates, but attempt to give empirical reasons against the feasibility of reducing biology. Other, sometimes a priori, arguments have been given against the reducibility of psychology to physiology and of the social sciences to psychology. These disputes indicate the continuing intellectual significance of the idea of unity of science and the broad range of issues it encompasses.

See also EXPLANATION, PHILOSOPHY OF SCIENCE, PHILOSOPHY OF THE SOCIAL SCIENCES, REDUCTION.   R.L.C.

universal. See METAPHYSICS.

universal, concrete. See HEGEL.

universal characteristic. See LEIBNIZ.

universal constructor. See SELF-REPRODUCING AUTOMATON.

universal disposition. See DISPOSITION.

universal generalization. See UNIVERSAL INSTANTIATION.

universal grammar. See CHOMSKY, GRAMMAR.

universal instantiation, also called *universal quantifier elimination*. (1) The argument form 'Everything is ϕ; therefore *a* is ϕ', and arguments of this form. (2) The rule of inference that permits one to infer that any given thing is ϕ from the premise that everything is ϕ. In classical logic, where all terms are taken to denote things in the domain of discourse, the rule says simply that from $(v)A[v]$ one may infer $A[t]$, the result of replacing all free occurrences of v in $A[v]$ by the term t. If non-denoting terms are allowed, however, as in free logic, then the rule would require an auxiliary premise of the form $(\exists u)u = t$ to ensure that t denotes something in the range of the variable v. Likewise in modal logic, which is sometimes held to contain terms that do not denote "genuine individuals" (the things over which variables range), an auxiliary premise may be required. (3) In higher-order logic, the rule of inference that says that from $(X)A[X]$ one may infer $A[F]$, where F is any expression of the grammatical category (e.g., *n*-ary predicate) appropriate to that of X (e.g., *n*-ary predicate variable).   G.F.S.

universality, principle of. See UNIVERSALIZABILITY.

universalizability. (1) Since the 1920s, the moral criterion implicit in Kant's first formulation of the categorical imperative: "Act only on that maxim that you can at the same time will to be a universal law," often called the *principle of universality*. A maxim or principle of action that satisfies this test is said to be universalizable, hence morally acceptable; one that does not is said to be not universalizable, hence contrary to duty. (2) A second sense developed in connection with the work of Hare in the 1950s. For Hare, universalizability is "common to all judgments which carry descriptive meaning"; so not only normative claims (moral and evaluative judgments) but also empirical statements are universalizable. Although Hare describes how such universalizability can figure in moral argument, for Hare "offenses against ... universalizability are logical, not moral." Consequently, whereas for Kant not all maxims are universalizable, on Hare's view they all are, since they all have descriptive meaning. (3) In a third sense, one that also appears in Hare, 'universalizability' refers to the principle of universalizability: "What is right (or wrong) for one person is right (or wrong) for any similar person in similar circumstances." This principle is identical with what Sidgwick (*The Methods of Ethics*) called the Principle of Justice. In *Generalization in Ethics* (1961) by M. G. Singer (b.1926), it is called the Generalization Principle and is said to be the formal principle presupposed in all moral reasoning and consequently the explanation for the feature alleged to hold of all moral judgments, that of being generalizable. A particular judgment of the form '*A* is right in doing *x*' is said to imply that anyone relevantly similar to *A* would be right in doing any act of the kind *x* in relevantly similar circumstances. The characteristic of generalizability, of presupposing a general rule, was said to be true of normative claims, but not of all empirical or descriptive statements. The Generalization Principle (GP) was said to be involved in the Generalization *Argument* (GA): "If the consequences of everyone's doing *x* would be undesirable, while the consequences of no one's doing *x* would not be, then no one ought to do *x* without a justifying reason," a form of moral reasoning resembling, though not identical with, the categorical imperative (CI). One alleged resemblance is that if the GP is involved in the GA, then it is involved in the CI, and this would help explain the moral relevance of Kant's universalizability test. (4) A further extension of the term 'universalizability' appears in Alan Gewirth's *Reason and Morality* (1978). Gewirth formulates "the logical principle of universalizability": "if some predicate *P* belongs to some subject *S* because *S* has the property *Q* ... then *P* must also belong to all other subjects *S*1, *S*2, . . . , *Sn* that have *Q*." The principle of universalizability "in its moral application" is then deduced from the logical principle of universalizability, and is presupposed in Gewirth's Principle of Generic Consistency, "Act in accord with the generic rights of your recipients as well as yourself," which is taken to provide an a priori determinate way of determining relevant similarities and differences, hence of applying the principle of universalizability.

The principle of universalizability is a formal principle; universalizability in sense (1), however, is intended to be a substantive principle of morality.

See also ETHICS, KANT.   M.G.S.

universalizability, principle of. See UNIVERSALIZABILITY.

universal quantifier. See FORMAL LOGIC.

universal relation. See RELATION.

universal simulator. See COMPUTER THEORY.

universe of discourse, the usually limited class of individuals under discussion, whose existence is presupposed by the discussants, and which in some sense constitutes the ultimate subject matter of the discussion. Once the universe of a discourse has been established, expressions such as 'every object' and 'some object' refer respectively to every object or to some object in the universe of discourse. The concept of universe of discourse is due to De Morgan in 1846, but the expression was coined by Boole eight years later. When a discussion is formalized in an interpreted standard first-order language, the universe of discourse is taken as the "universe" of the interpretation, i.e., as the range of values of the variables. Quine and others have emphasized that the universe of discourse represents an ontological commitment of the discussants. In a discussion in a particular science, the universe of discourse is often wider than the domain of the science, although economies of expression can be achieved by limiting the universe of discourse to the domain. **See also** DOMAIN, FORMAL LOGIC, MODEL THEORY, ONTOLOGICAL COMMITMENT, VARIABLE.   J.Cor.

unmoved mover. See PRIME MOVER.

unsaturated. See FREGE.

unsolvability, degree of. See DEGREE OF UNSOLVABILITY.

Upanishads, a group of ancient Hindu philosophical texts, or the esoteric sacred doctrines contained in them. 'Upanishad' includes the notion of the student "sitting near" the guru. In the eighth century A.D., Shankara identified certain Upanishads as the official source of Vedanta teachings: *Aitreya, Brhadāranyaka, Chāndogya, Īśa, Katha, Kauṣitāki, Kena, Maitrī, Muṇḍaka, Praśna, Svetāśvatara,* and *Taittirīya.* These are the classic

Upanishads; together with the *Vedānta Sūtras,* they constitute the doctrinally authoritative sources for Vedanta. The *Vedānta Sūtras* are a series of aphorisms, composed somewhere between 200 B.C. and A.D. 200, attributed to Bādarāyana. Practically unintelligible without commentary, these sutras are interpreted in one way by Shaṅkara, in another by Rāmānuja, and in a third way by Madhva (though Madhva's reading is closer to Rāmānuja's than to Shaṅkara's).

For Vedanta, the Upanishads are "the end of the Vedas," both in the sense of completing the transcript of the immutable source of truth and articulating the foundational wisdom that the Vedas presuppose. While the Upanishads agree on the importance of religious knowledge, on the priority of religious over other sorts of well-being, and on the necessity of religious discipline, they contain radically disparate cosmologies that differ regarding agent, modality, and product of the creative process and offer various notions of Brahman and *Ātman.*

See also BRAHMAN, RĀMĀNUJA, SHAṄKARA, VEDANTA.   K.E.Y.

use–mention distinction, two ways in which terms enter into discourse – *used* when they refer to or assert something, *mentioned* when they are exhibited for consideration of their properties as terms. If I say, "Mary is sad," I use the name 'Mary' to refer to Mary so that I can predicate of her the property of being sad. But if I say, " 'Mary' contains four letters," I am mentioning Mary's name, exhibiting it in writing or speech to predicate of that term the property of being spelled with four letters. In the first case, the sentence occurs in what Carnap refers to as the material mode; in the second, it occurs in the formal mode, and hence in a metalanguage (a language used to talk about another language). Single quotation marks or similar orthographic devices are conventionally used to disambiguate mentioned from used terms.

The distinction is important because there are fallacies of reasoning based on use–mention confusions in the failure to observe the use–mention distinction, especially when the referents of terms are themselves linguistic entities. Consider the inference:

(1) Some sentences are written in English.
(2) Some sentences are written in English.

Here it looks as though the argument offers a counterexample to the claim that all arguments of the form '*P,* therefore *P*' are circular. But either

(1) *asserts* that some sentences are written in English, or it *provides evidence* in support of the conclusion in (2) by *exhibiting* a sentence written in English. In the first case, the sentence is used to assert the same truth in the premise as expressed in the conclusion, so that the argument remains circular. In the second case, the sentence is mentioned, and although the argument so interpreted is not circular, it is no longer strictly of the form '*P,* therefore *P*', but has the significantly different form, ' "*P*" is a sentence written in English, therefore *P*'.

See also CIRCULAR REASONING, METALANGUAGE, PHILOSOPHY OF LANGUAGE, TYPE–TOKEN DISTINCTION.   D.J.

use theory of meaning. See MEANING, PHILOSOPHY OF LANGUAGE.

utilitarianism, the moral theory that an action is morally right if and only if it produces at least as much good (utility) for all people affected by the action as any alternative action the person could do instead. Its best-known proponent is J. S. Mill, who formulated the greatest happiness principle (also called the principle of utility): always act so as to produce the greatest happiness. Two kinds of issues have been central in debates about whether utilitarianism is an adequate or true moral theory: first, whether and how utilitarianism can be clearly and precisely formulated and applied; second, whether the moral implications of utilitarianism in particular cases are acceptable, or instead constitute objections to it.

Issues of formulation. A central issue of formulation is how utility is to be defined and whether it can be measured in the way utilitarianism requires. Early utilitarians often held some form of hedonism, according to which only pleasure and the absence of pain have utility or intrinsic value. For something to have intrinsic value is for it to be valuable for its own sake and apart from its consequences or its relations to other things. Something has instrumental value, on the other hand, provided it brings about what has intrinsic value. Most utilitarians have held that hedonism is too narrow an account of utility because there are many things that people value intrinsically besides pleasure. Some non-hedonists define utility as happiness, and among them there is considerable debate about the proper account of happiness. Happiness has also been criticized as too narrow to exhaust utility or intrinsic value; e.g., many people value accomplishments, not just the happiness that may accompany them. Sometimes utilitarianism is understood as the view that either pleasure or happiness has utility, while *consequentialism* is understood as the broader view that morally right action is action that maximizes the good, however the good is understood. Here, we take utilitarianism in this broader interpretation that some philosophers reserve for consequentialism. Most utilitarians who believe hedonism gives too narrow an account of utility have held that utility is the satisfaction of people's informed preferences or desires. This view is neutral about what people desire, and so can account for the full variety of things and experiences that different people in fact desire or value. Finally, *ideal utilitarians* have held that some things or experiences, e.g. knowledge or being autonomous, are intrinsically valuable or good whether or not people value or prefer them or are happier with them.

Whatever account of utility a utilitarian adopts, it must be possible to quantify or measure the good effects or consequences of actions in order to apply the utilitarian standard of moral rightness. Happiness utilitarianism, e.g., must calculate whether a particular action, or instead some possible alternative, would produce more happiness for a given person; this is called the *intrapersonal utility comparison*. The method of measurement may allow cardinal utility measurements, in which numerical units of happiness may be assigned to different actions (e.g., 30 units for Jones expected from action *a*, 25 units for Jones from alternative action *b*), or only ordinal utility measurements may be possible, in which actions are ranked only as producing more or less happiness than alternative actions. Since nearly all interesting and difficult moral problems involve the happiness of more than one person, utilitarianism requires calculating which among alternative actions produces the greatest happiness for all people affected; this is called the *interpersonal utility comparison*. Many ordinary judgments about personal action or public policy implicitly rely on interpersonal utility comparisons; e.g., would a family whose members disagree be happiest overall taking its vacation at the seashore or in the mountains? Some critics of utilitarianism doubt that it is possible to make interpersonal utility comparisons.

Another issue of formulation is whether the utilitarian principle should be applied to individual actions or to some form of moral rule. According to *act utilitarianism*, each action's rightness or wrongness depends on the utility *it* produces in comparison with possible alternatives.

Even act utilitarians agree, however, that rules of thumb like 'keep your promises' can be used for the most part in practice because following them tends to maximize utility. According to *rule utilitarianism*, on the other hand, individual actions are evaluated, in theory not just in practice, by whether they conform to a justified moral rule, and the utilitarian standard is applied only to general rules. Some rule utilitarians hold that actions are right provided they are permitted by rules the general acceptance of which would maximize utility in the agent's society, and wrong only if they would be prohibited by such rules. There are a number of forms of rule utilitarianism, and utilitarians disagree about whether act or rule utilitarianism is correct.

Moral implications. Most debate about utilitarianism has focused on its moral implications. Critics have argued that its implications sharply conflict with most people's considered moral judgments, and that this is a strong reason to reject utilitarianism. Proponents have argued both that many of these conflicts disappear on a proper understanding of utilitarianism and that the remaining conflicts should throw the particular judgments, not utilitarianism, into doubt. One important controversy concerns utilitarianism's implications for distributive justice. Utilitarianism requires, in individual actions and in public policy, maximizing utility without regard to its distribution between different persons. Thus, it seems to ignore individual rights, whether specific individuals morally deserve particular benefits or burdens, and potentially to endorse great inequalities between persons; e.g., some critics have charged that according to utilitarianism slavery would be morally justified if its benefits to the slaveowners sufficiently outweighed the burdens to the slaves and if it produced more overall utility than alternative practices possible in that society. Defenders of utilitarianism typically argue that in the real world there is virtually always a better alternative than the action or practice that the critic charges utilitarianism wrongly supports; e.g., no system of slavery that has ever existed is plausibly thought to have maximized utility for the society in question. Defenders of utilitarianism also typically try to show that it does take account of the moral consideration the critic claims it wrongly ignores; for instance, utilitarians commonly appeal to the *declining marginal utility* of money – equal marginal increments of money tend to produce less utility (e.g. happiness) for persons, the more money they already have – as giving some support to equality in income distribution.

Another source of controversy concerns whether moral principles should be *agent-neutral* or, in at least some cases, *agent-relative*. Utilitarianism is agent-neutral in that it gives all people the same moral aim – act so as to maximize utility for everyone – whereas agent-relative principles give different moral aims to different individuals. Defenders of agent-relative principles note that a commonly accepted moral rule like the prohibition of killing the innocent is understood as telling each agent that *he or she* must not kill, even if doing so is the only way to prevent a still greater number of killings by others. In this way, a non-utilitarian, agent-relative prohibition reflects the common moral view that each person bears special moral responsibility for what he or she does, which is greater than his or her responsibility to prevent similar wrong actions by others. Common moral beliefs also permit people to give special weight to their own projects and commitments and, e.g., to favor to some extent their own children at the expense of other children in greater need; agent-relative responsibilities to one's own family reflect these moral views in a way that agent-neutral utilitarian responsibilities apparently do not.

The debate over neutrality and relativity is related to a final area of controversy about utilitarianism. Critics charge that utilitarianism makes morality far too demanding by requiring that one always act to maximize utility. If, e.g., one reads a book or goes to a movie, one could nearly always be using one's time and resources to do more good by aiding famine relief. The critics believe that this wrongly makes morally required what should be only *supererogatory* – action that is good, but goes beyond "the call of duty" and is not morally required. Here, utilitarians have often argued that ordinary moral views are seriously mistaken and that morality can demand greater sacrifices of one's own interests for the benefit of others than is commonly believed. There is little doubt that here, and in many other cases, utilitarianism's moral implications significantly conflict with commonsense moral beliefs – the dispute is whether this should count against commonsense moral beliefs or against utilitarianism.

See also ETHICS, HEDONISM, JUSTICE, KANT, MOORE.   D.W.B.

utility. See UTILITARIANISM.

utility, cardinal. See UTILITARIANISM.

utility, ordinal. See UTILITARIANISM.

utility, transferable. See GAME THEORY, UTILITARIANISM.

utility function. See UTILITARIANISM.

Uttara Mīmamsā. See ADVAITA, VEDANTA.

utterer's meaning. See MEANING.

V

vacuous truth. See IMPLICATION.

vagueness, a property of an expression in virtue of which it can give rise to a "borderline case." A borderline case is a situation in which the application of a particular expression to a (name of) a particular object does not generate an expression with a definite truth-value; i.e., the piece of language in question neither unequivocally applies to the object nor fails to apply.

Although such a formulation leaves it open what the pieces of language might be (whole sentences, individual words, names or singular terms, predicates or general terms), most discussions have focused on vague general terms and have considered other types of terms to be non-vague. (Exceptions to this have called attention to the possibility of vague objects, thereby rendering vague the designation relation for singular terms.) The formulation also leaves open the possible causes for the expression's lacking a definite truth-value. If this indeterminacy is due to there being insufficient information available to determine applicability or non-applicability of the term (i.e., we are convinced the term either does or does not apply, but we just do not have enough information to determine which), then this is sometimes called *epistemic vagueness*. It is somewhat misleading to call this vagueness, for unlike true vagueness, this epistemic vagueness disappears if more information is brought into the situation. ('There are between 1.89×10^6 and 1.9×10^6 stars in the sky' is epistemically vague but is not vague in the generally accepted sense of the term.)

'Vagueness' may also be used to characterize non-linguistic items such as concepts, memories, and objects, as well as such semilinguistic items as statements and propositions. Many of the issues involved in discussing the topic of vagueness impinge upon other philosophical topics, such as the existence of truth-value *gaps* – (declarative sentences that are neither true nor false) – and the plausibility of many-valued logic. There are other related issues such as the nature of propositions and whether they must be either true or false. We focus here on linguistic vagueness, as it manifests itself with general terms; for it is this sort of indeterminacy that defines what

most researchers call vagueness, and which has led the push in some schools of thought to "eliminate vagueness" or to construct languages that do not manifest vagueness.

Linguistic vagueness is sometimes confused with other linguistic phenomena: generality, ambiguity, and open texture. Statements can be general ('Some wheelbarrows are red', 'All insects have antennae') and if there is no other vagueness infecting them, they are true or false – and not borderline or vague. Terms can be general ('person', 'dog') without being vague. Those general terms apply to many different objects but are not therefore vague; and furthermore, the fact that they apply to different *kinds* of objects ('person' applies to both men and women) also does not show them to be vague or ambiguous. A vague term admits of borderline cases – a completely determinate situation in which there just is no correct answer as to whether the term applies to a certain object or not – and this is not the case with generality. Ambiguous linguistic items, including structurally ambiguous sentences, also do not have this feature (unless they also contain vague terms). Rather, an ambiguous sentence allows there to be a completely determinate situation in which one can simultaneously correctly affirm the sentence and also deny the sentence, depending on which of the claims allowed by the ambiguities is being affirmed or denied. Terms are considered open-textured if they are precise along some dimensions of their meaning but where other possible dimensions simply have not been considered. It would therefore not be clear what the applicability of the term would be were objects to vary along these other dimensions. Although related to vagueness, open texture is a different notion. Friedrich Waismann, who coined the term, put it this way: "Open texture . . . is something like the possibility of vagueness."

Vagueness has long been an irritant to philosophers of logic and language. Among the oldest of the puzzles associated with vagueness is the sorites ('heap') paradox reported by Cicero (*Academica* 93): One grain of sand does not make a heap, and adding a grain of sand to something that is not a heap will not create a heap; therefore there are no heaps. This type of paradox is traditionally attributed to Zeno of Elea, who said that a single millet seed makes no sound when it falls, so a basket of millet seeds cannot make a sound when it is dumped. The term 'sorites' is also applied to the entire series of paradoxes that have this form, such as the *falakros* ('bald man', Diogenes Laertius, *Grammatica* II, 1, 45): A man with no hairs is bald, and adding one hair to a bald man results in a bald man; therefore all men are bald. The original version of these sorites paradoxes is attributed to Eubulides (Diogenes Laertius II, 108): "Isn't it true that two are few? and also three, and also four, and so on until ten? But since two are few, ten are also few." The linchpin in all these paradoxes is the analysis of vagueness in terms of some underlying continuum along which an imperceptible or unimportant change occurs. Almost all modern accounts of the logic of vagueness have assumed this to be the correct analysis of vagueness, and have geared their logics to deal with such vagueness. But we will see below that there are other kinds of vagueness too.

The search for a solution to the sorites-type paradoxes has been the stimulus for much research into alternative semantics. Some philosophers, e.g. Frege, view vagueness as a pervasive defect of natural language and urge the adoption of an artificial language in which each predicate is completely precise, without borderline cases. Russell too thought vagueness thoroughly infected natural language, but thought it unavoidable – and indeed beneficial – for ordinary usage and discourse. Despite the occasional argument that vagueness is pragmatic rather than a semantic phenomenon, the attitude that vagueness is inextricably bound to natural language (together with the philosophical logician's self-ascribed task of formalizing natural language semantics) has led modern writers to the exploration of alternative logics that might adequately characterize vagueness – i.e., that would account for our pretheoretic beliefs concerning truth, falsity, necessary truth, validity, etc., of sentences containing vague predicates. Some recent writers have also argued that vague language undermines realism, and that it shows our concepts to be "incoherent."

Long ago it was seen that the attempt to introduce a third truth-value, *indeterminate*, solved nothing – replacing, as it were, the sharp cutoff between a predicate's applying and not applying with two sharp cutoffs. Similar remarks could be made against the adoption of *any* finitely many-valued logic as a characterization of vagueness.

In the late 1960s and early 1970s, fuzzy logic was introduced into the philosophic world. Actually a restatement of the Tarski-Łukasiewicz infinite-valued logics of the 1930s, one of the side benefits of fuzzy logics was claimed to be an adequate logic for vagueness. In contrast to classical logic, in which there are two truth-values (*true* and *false*), in fuzzy logic a sentence is allowed to take any real number between 0 and 1 as a truth-value. Intuitively, the closer to 1 the value is, the "more true" the sentence is. The value of a negated sentence is 1 minus the value of the unnegated sentence; conjunction is viewed as a minimum function and disjunction as a maximum function. (Thus, a conjunction takes the value of the "least true" conjunct, while a disjunction takes the value of the "most true" disjunct.) Since vague sentences are maximally neither true nor false, they will be valued at approximately 0.5. It follows that if Φ is maximally vague, so is the negation $\sim\Phi$; and so are the conjunction (Φ & $\sim\Phi$) and the disjunction ($\sim\Phi$ ∨ $\sim\Phi$). Some theorists object to these results, but defenders of fuzzy logic have argued in favor of them.

Other theorists have attempted to capture the elusive logic of vagueness by employing modal logic, having the operators $\Box\Phi$ (meaning 'Φ is definite') and $\Diamond\Phi$ (meaning 'Φ is vague'). The logic generated in this way is peculiar in that $\Box(\Phi$ & $\Psi)\rightarrow(\Box\Phi$ & $\Box\Psi)$ is not a theorem. E.g., (p & $\sim p$) is definitely false, hence definite; hence $\Box(p$ & $\sim p)$. Yet neither p nor $\sim p$ need be definite. (Technically, it is a non-Kripke-normal modal logic.) Some other peculiarities are that ($\Box\Phi \leftrightarrow \Box\sim\Phi$) is a theorem, and that ($\Box\Phi\rightarrow\Diamond\Phi$) is not. There are also puzzles about whether (($\Diamond\Phi\rightarrow\Box\Diamond\Phi$) should be a theorem, and about iterated modalities in general. Modal logic treatments of vagueness have not attracted many advocates, except as a portion of a general epistemic logic (i.e., modal logics might be seen as an account of so-called epistemic vagueness).

A third direction that has been advocated as a logical account of vagueness has been the method of supervaluations (sometimes called "supertruth"). The underlying idea here is to allow the vague predicate in a sentence to be "precisified" in an arbitrary manner. Thus, for the sentence 'Friar Tuck is bald', we arbitrarily choose a precise number of hairs on the head that will demarcate the bald/not-bald border. In this valuation Friar Tuck is either definitely bald or definitely not bald, and the sentence either is true or is false. Next, we alter the valuation so that there is some other bald/not-bald borderline, etc. A sentence true in all such valuations is deemed "really true" or "supertrue"; one false in all such valuations is "really false" or "super-false." All others are vague. Note that, in this conception of vagueness, if Φ is vague, so is $\sim\Phi$. However, unlike fuzzy logic '$\Phi \& \sim\Phi$' is not evaluated as vague – it is false in every valuation and hence is superfalse. And '$\Phi \lor \sim\Phi$' is supertrue. These are seen by some as positive features of the method of supervaluations, and as an argument against the whole fuzzy logic enterprise.

In fact there seem to be at least two distinct types of (linguistic) vagueness, and it is not at all clear that any of the previously mentioned logic approaches can deal with both. Without going into the details, we can just point out that the "sorites vagueness" discussed above presumes an ordering on a continuous underlying scale; and it is the indistinguishability of adjacent points on this scale that gives rise to borderline cases. But there are examples of vague terms for which there is no such scale. A classic example is 'religion': there are a number of factors relevant to determining whether a social practice is a religion. Having none of these properties guarantees failing to be a religion, and having all of them guarantees being one. However, there is no continuum of the sorites variety here; for example, it is easy to distinguish possessing four from possessing five of the properties, unlike the sorites case where such a change is imperceptible. In the present type of vagueness, although we can tell these different cases apart, we just do not know whether to call the practice a religion or not. Furthermore, some of the properties (or combinations of properties) are more important or salient in determining whether the practice is a religion than are other properties or combinations. We might call this *family resemblance vagueness*: there are a number of clearly distinguishable conditions of varying degrees of importance, and family resemblance vagueness is attributed to there being no definite answer to the question, How many of which conditions are necessary for the term to apply? Other examples of family resemblance vagueness are 'schizophrenia sufferer', 'sexual perversion', and the venerable 'game'.

A special subclass of family resemblance vagueness occurs when there are pairs of underlying properties that normally co-occur, but occasionally apply to different objects. Consider, e.g., 'tributary'. When two rivers meet, one is usually considered a tributary of the other. Among the properties relevant to being a tributary rather than the main river are: relative vol-

ume of water and relative length. Normally, the shorter of the two rivers has a lesser volume, and in that case it is the tributary of the other. But occasionally the two properties do not co-occur and then there is a conflict, giving rise to a kind of vagueness we might call *conflict vagueness*. The term 'tributary' is vague because its background conditions admit of such conflicts: there are borderline cases when these two properties apply to different objects.

To conclude: the fundamental philosophical problems involving vagueness are (1) to give an adequate characterization of what the phenomenon is, and (2) to characterize our ability to reason with these terms. These were the problems for the ancient philosophers, and they remain the problems for modern philosophers.

See also DEFINITION, MEANING, PHILOSOPHY OF LANGUAGE, TRUTH.   F.J.P. & I.Be.

Vaihinger, Hans (1852–1933), German philosopher best known for *Die Philosophie des Als Ob* (1911; translated by C. K. Ogden as *The Philosophy of "As If"* in 1924). A neo-Kantian, he was also influenced by Schopenhauer and Nietzsche. His commentary on Kant's *Critique of Pure Reason* (2 vols., 1881) is still a standard work. Vaihinger was a cofounder of both the Kant Society and *Kant-Studien*. The "philosophy of the as if" involves the claim that values and ideals amount only to "fictions" that serve "life" even if they are irrational. We must act "as if" they were true because they have biological utility.   M.K.

Vair, Guillaume du. See DU VAIR.

Valentinianism, a form of Christian gnosticism of Alexandrian origin, founded by Valentinus in the second century and propagated by Theodotus in Eastern, and Heracleon in Western, Christianity. To every gnostic, pagan or Christian, knowledge leads to salvation from the perishable, material world. Valentinianism therefore prompted famous refutations by Tertullian (*Adversus Valentinianos*) and Irenaeus (*Adversus haereses*). The latter accused the Valentinians of maintaining "*creatio ex nihilo*." Valentinus is believed to have authored the *Peri trion phuseon,* the *Evangelium veritatis,* and the *Treatise on the Resurrection.* Since only a few fragments of these remain, his Neoplatonic cosmogony is accessible mainly through his opponents and critics (Hippolytus, Clement of Alexandria) and in the Nag Hammadi codices. To explain the origins of creation and of evil, Valentinus separated God (primal Father) from the Creator (Demiurge) and attributed the crucial role in the processes of emanation and redemption to Sophia.

See also CREATION EX NIHILO, GNOSTICISM.

J.-L.S.

Valentinus (A.D. 100–65), Christian gnostic teacher. He was born in Alexandria, where he taught until he moved to Rome in 135. A dualist, he constructed an elaborate cosmology in which God the Father (Bythos, or Deep Unknown) unites the the feminine Silence (Sige) and in the overflow of love produces thirty successive divine emanations (or aeons) constituting the Pleroma (fullness of the Godhead). Each emanation is arranged hierarchically with a graded existence, becoming progressively further removed from the Father and hence less divine. The lowest emanation, Sophia (wisdom), yields to passion and seeks to reach, beyond her ability, to the Father, which causes her fall. In the process, she causes the creation of the material universe (wherein resides evil) and the loss of divine sparks from the Pleroma. The divine elements are embodied in those humans who are the elect. Jesus Christ is an aeon close to the Father and is sent to retrieve the souls into the heavenly Pleroma. Valentinus wrote a gospel. His sect stood out in the early church for ordaining women priests and prophetesses. **See also** BASILIDES, GNOSTICISM.

L.P.P.

valid, having the property that a well-formed formula, argument, argument form, or rule of inference has when it is logically correct in a certain respect. A well-formed formula is valid if it is true under every admissible reinterpretation of its non-logical symbols. (If *truth-value gaps* or multiple truth-values are allowed, 'true' here might be replaced by 'non-false' or takes a "designated" truth-value.) An argument is valid if it is impossible for the premises all to be true and, at the same time, the conclusion false. An argument form (schema) is valid if every argument of that form is valid. A rule of inference is valid if it cannot lead from all true premises to a false conclusion. **See also** FREE LOGIC, MANY-VALUED LOGIC.

G.F.S.

Valla, Lorenzo (c.1407–57), Italian humanist and historian who taught rhetoric in Pavia and was later secretary of King Alfonso I of Aragona in Naples, and apostolic secretary in Rome under Pope Nicholas V. In his dialogue *On Pleasure* or *On the True Good* (1431–34), Stoic and Epicurean interlocutors present their ethical views, which Valla proceeds to criticize from a Christian point of view. This work is often regarded as a defense of Epicurean hedonism, because Valla equates the good with pleasure; but he claims that Christians can find pleasure only in heaven. His description of the Christian pleasures reflects the contemporary Renaissance attitude toward the joys of life and might have contributed to Valla's reputation for hedonism. In the later work, *On Free Will* (between 1435 and 1448), Valla discusses the conflict between divine foreknowledge and human freedom and rejects Boethius's then predominantly accepted solution. Valla distinguishes between God's knowledge and God's will, but denies that there is a rational solution of the apparent conflict between God's will and human freedom. As a historian, he is famous for *The Donation of Constantine* (1440), which denounces as spurious the famous document on which medieval jurists and theologians based the papal rights to secular power.

P.Ga.

value, the worth of something. Philosophers have discerned these main forms: intrinsic, instrumental, inherent, and relational value. Intrinsic value may be taken as basic and many of the others defined in terms of it. Among the many attempts to explicate the concept of intrinsic value, some deal primarily with the source of value, while others employ the concept of the "fittingness" or "appropriateness" to it of certain kinds of emotions and desires. The first is favored by Moore and the second by Brentano. Proponents of the first view hold that the intrinsic value of X is the value that X has solely in virtue of its intrinsic nature. Thus, the state of affairs, Smith's experiencing pleasure, has intrinsic value provided it has value solely in virtue of its intrinsic nature. Followers of the second approach explicate intrinsic value in terms of the sorts of emotions and desires appropriate to a thing "in and for itself" (or "for its own sake"). Thus, one might say X has intrinsic value (or is intrinsically good) if and only if X is worthy of desire in and for itself, or, alternatively, it is fitting or appropriate for anyone to favor X in and for itself. Thus, the state of affairs of Smith's experiencing pleasure is intrinsically valuable provided that state of affairs is worthy of desire for its own sake, or it is fitting for anyone to favor that state of affairs in and for itself.

Concerning the other forms of value, we may say that X has *instrumental value* if and only if it is a means to, or causally contributes to, something that is intrinsically valuable. If Smith's experiencing pleasure is intrinsically valuable and his taking a warm bath is a means to, or causally contributes to, his being pleased, then his taking a warm bath is instrumentally valuable or "valuable as a means." Similarly, if health is intrinsically valuable and exercise is a means to health, then exercise is instrumentally valuable. *X* has *inherent value* if and only if the experience, awareness, or contemplation of *X* is intrinsically valuable. If the experience of a beautiful sunset is intrinsically valuable, then the beautiful sunset has inherent value. *X* has *contributory value* if and only if *X* contributes to the value of some whole, *W*, of which it is a part. If *W* is a whole that consists of the facts that Smith is pleased and Brown is pleased, then the fact that Smith is pleased contributes to the value of *W*, and Smith's being pleased has contributory value. Our example illustrates that something can have contributory value without having instrumental value, for the fact that Smith is pleased is not a means to *W* and, strictly speaking, it does not bring about or causally contribute to *W*. Given the distinction between instrumental and contributory value, we may say that certain sorts of experiences and activities can have contributory value if they are part of an intrinsically valuable life and contribute to its value, even though they are not means to it. Finally, we may say that *X* has *relational value* if and only if *X* has value in virtue of bearing some relation to something else. Instrumental, inherent, and contributory value may be construed as forms of relational value. But there are other forms of relational value one might accept, e.g. one might hold that *X* is valuable for *S* in virtue of being desired by *S* or being such that *S* would desire *X* were *S* "fully informed" and "rational."

Some philosophers defend the organicity of intrinsic value. Moore, for example, held that the intrinsic value of a whole is not necessarily equal to the sum of the intrinsic values of its parts. According to this view, the presence of an intrinsically good part might lower the intrinsic value of a whole of which it is a part and the presence of an intrinsically bad part might raise the intrinsic value of a whole to which it belongs. Defenders of organicity sometimes point to examples of *Mitfreude* (taking joy or pleasure in another's joy) and *Schadenfreude* (taking joy or pleasure in another's suffering) to illustrate their view. Suppose Jones believes incorrectly that Smith is happy and Brown believes incorrectly that Gray is suffering, but Jones is pleased that Smith is happy and Brown is pleased that Gray is suffering. The former instance of *Mitfreude* seems intrinsically better than the latter instance of *Schadenfreude* even though they are both instances of pleasure and neither whole has an intrinsically bad part. The value of each whole is not a "mere sum" of the values of its parts.

See also ETHICS, HEDONISM, MOORE, PROPERTY, UTILITARIANISM, VALUE THEORY.

N.M.L.

value, cognitive. See FREGE.

value, contributive. See VALUE.

value, inherent. See VALUE.

value, instrumental. See VALUE.

value, intrinsic. See VALUE.

value, surplus. See MARX.

value of a variable. See ONTOLOGICAL COMMITMENT, VARIABLE.

value theory, also called axiology, the branch of philosophy concerned with the nature of value and with what kinds of things have value. Construed very broadly, value theory is concerned with all forms of value, such as the aesthetic values of beauty and ugliness, the ethical values of right, wrong, obligation, virtue, and vice, and the epistemic values of justification and lack of justification. Understood more narrowly, value theory is concerned with what is intrinsically valuable or ultimately worthwhile and desirable for its own sake and with the related concepts of instrumental, inherent, and contributive value. When construed very broadly, the study of ethics may be taken as a branch of value theory, but understood more narrowly value theory may be taken as a branch of ethics.

In its more narrow form, one of the chief questions of the theory of value is, What is desirable for its own sake? One traditional sort of answer is hedonism. Hedonism is roughly the view that (i) the only intrinsically good experiences or states of affairs are those containing pleasure, and the only instrinsically bad experiences or states of affairs are those containing pain; (ii) all experiences or states of affairs that contain more pleasure than pain are intrinsically good and all experiences or states of affairs that contain more pain than pleasure are intrinsically bad; and (iii) any experience or state of affairs that is intrinsically good is so in virtue of being pleasant or containing pleasure and any experience or state of affairs that is intrinsically bad is so in virtue of being painful or involving pain. Hedonism has been defended by philosophers such as Epicurus, Bentham, Sidgwick, and, with significant qualifications, J. S. Mill. Other philosophers, such as C. I. Lewis, and, perhaps, Brand Blanshard, have held that what is intrinsically or ultimately desirable are experiences that exhibit "satisfactoriness," where being pleasant is but one form of being satisfying. Other philosophers have recognized a plurality of things other than pleasure or satisfaction as having intrinsic value. Among the value pluralists are Moore, Rashdall, Ross, Brentano, Hartmann, and Scheler. In addition to certain kinds of pleasures, these thinkers count some or all of the following as intrinsically good: consciousness and the flourishing of life, knowledge and insight, moral virtue and virtuous actions, friendship and mutual affection, beauty and aesthetic experience, a just distribution of goods, and self-expression.

Many, if not all, of the philosophers mentioned above distinguish between what has value or is desirable for its own sake and what is instrumentally valuable. Furthermore, they hold that what is desirable for its own sake or intrinsically good has a value not dependent on anyone's having an interest in it. Both of these claims have been challenged by other value theorists. Dewey, for example, criticizes any sharp distinction between what is intrinsically good or good as an end and what is good as a means on the ground that we adopt and abandon ends to the extent that they serve as means to the resolution of conflicting impulses and desires. Perry denies that anything can have value without being an object of interest. Indeed, Perry claims that 'X is valuable' means 'Interest is taken in X' and that it is a subject's interest in a thing that confers value on it. Insofar as he holds that the value of a thing is dependent upon a subject's interest in that thing, Perry's value theory is a subjective theory and contrasts sharply with objective theories holding that some things have value not dependent on a subject's interests or attitudes. Some philosophers, dissatisfied with the view that value depends on a subject's actual interests and theories, have proposed various alternatives, including theories holding that the value of a thing depends on what a subject *would* desire or have an interest in if he were fully rational or if desires were based on full information. Such theories may be called "counterfactual" desire theories since they take value to be dependent, not upon a subject's actual interests, but upon what a subject would desire if certain conditions, which do not obtain, were to obtain.

Value theory is also concerned with the nature of value. Some philosophers have denied that sentences of the forms 'X is good' or 'X is intrinsically good' are, strictly speaking, either true or false. As with other forms of ethical discourse, they claim that anyone who utters these sentences is either expressing his emotional attitudes or else prescribing or commending something. Other philosophers hold that such sentences can express what is true or false, but disagree about the nature of value and the meaning of value terms like 'good', 'bad', and 'better'. Some philosophers, such as Moore, hold that in a truth of the form 'X is intrinsically good', 'good' refers to a simple, unanalyzable, non-natural property, a property not identical with or analyzable by any "natural" property such as being pleasant or being desired. Moore's view is one form of non-naturalism. Other philosophers, such as Brentano, hold that 'good' is a syncategorematic expression; as such it does not refer to a property or relation at all, though it contributes to the meaning of the sentence. Still other philosophers have held that 'X is good' and 'X is intrinsically good' can be analyzed in natural or non-ethical terms. This sort of naturalism about value is illustrated by Perry, who holds that 'X is valuable' means 'X is an object of interest'. The history of value theory is full of other attempted naturalistic analyses, some of which identify or analyze 'good' in terms of pleasure or being the object of rational desire. Many philosophers argue that naturalism is preferable on epistemic grounds. If, e.g., 'X is valuable' just means 'X is an object of interest', then in order to know whether something is valuable, one need only know whether it is the object of someone's interest. Our knowledge of value is fundamentally no different in kind from our knowledge of any other empirical fact. This argument, however, is not decisive against non-naturalism, since it is not obvious that there is no synthetic a priori knowledge of the sort Moore takes as the fundamental value cognition. Furthermore, it is not clear that one cannot combine non-naturalism about value with a broadly empirical epistemology, one that takes certain kinds of experience as epistemic grounds for beliefs about value.

See also ETHICS, EUDAIMONISM, HEDONISM, MOORE, VALUE.   N.M.L.

Vanini, Giulio Cesare (c.1584–1619), Italian philosopher, a Renaissance Aristotelian who studied law and theology. He became a monk and traveled all over Europe. After abjuring, he taught and practiced medicine. He was burned at the stake by the Inquisition. His major work is four volumes of dialogues, *De admirandis naturae reginae deaeque mortalium arcanis* ("On the Secrets of Nature, Queen and Goddess of Mortal Beings," 1616). He was influenced by Averroes and Pietro Pomponazzi, whom he regarded as his teacher.

Vanini rejects revealed religion and claims that God is immanent in nature. The world is ruled by a necessary natural order and is eternal. Like Averroes, he denies the immortality and the immateriality of the human soul. Like Pomponazzi, he denies the existence of miracles and claims that all apparently extraordinary phenomena can be shown to have natural causes and to be predetermined. Despite the absence of any original contribution, from the second half of the seventeenth century Vanini was popular as a symbol of free and atheist thought.   P.Gar.

Vardhamāna Jnātrputra. See MAHĀVĪRA.

variable, in logic and mathematics, a symbol interpreted so as to be associated with a *range of values,* a set of entities any one of which may be temporarily assigned as a *value of the variable.* An occurrence of a variable in a mathematical or logical expression is a *free occurrence* if assigning a value is necessary in order for the containing expression to acquire a semantic value – a denotation, truth-value, or other meaning. Suppose a semantic value is assigned to a variable and the same value is attached to a constant as meaning of the same kind; if an expression contains free occurrences of just that variable, the value of the expression for that assignment of value to the variable is standardly taken to be the same as the value of the expression obtained by substituting the constant for all the free occurrences of the variable. A *bound occurrence* of a variable is one that is not free. **See also FORMAL LOGIC, LOGICAL SYNTAX, QUANTIFICATION, WELL-FORMED FORMULA.**   C.A.A.

variable, bound. See ONTOLOGICAL COMMITMENT, VARIABLE.

variable, free. See VARIABLE.

variable, regressor. See REGRESSION ANALYSIS.

variable, response. See REGRESSION ANALYSIS.

variable, state. See STATE.

variable, value of. See ONTOLOGICAL COMMITMENT, VARIABLE.

variable sum game. See GAME THEORY.

vāsanā, Buddhist philosophical term meaning 'tendency'. It is an explanatory category, designed to show how it is possible to talk of tendencies or capacities in persons on the basis of a metaphysic that denies that there are any enduring existents in the continua of events conventionally called "persons." According to this metaphysic, when we speak of the tendency of persons understood in this way to do this or that – to be jealous, lustful, angry – we are speaking of the presence of karmic seeds in continua of events, seeds that may mature at different times and so produce tendencies to engage in this or that action. **See also ĀLAYA-VIJÑĀNA.**   P.J.G.

Vasubandhu (fourth–fifth century A.D.), Indian philosopher, a Mahayana Buddhist of the Yogācāra or Sarvāstivāda school. He wrote the *Abhidharmakosá* ("Treasure Chamber of the *Abhidharma,*" the *Abhidharma* being a compilation of Buddhist philosophy and psychology) and the *Vimśatikā* ("Proof in Twenty Verses That Everything Is Only Conception"). He held that the mind is only a stream of ideas and that there is nothing non-mental. In contrast to Buddhist direct and representational realists, he argued that dream experience seems to be of objects located in space and existing independent of the dreamer without their actually doing so. **See also BUDDHISM.**   K.E.Y.

Vauvenargues, Luc de Clapiers de (1715–47), French army officer and secular moralist. Discovering Plutarch at an early age, he critically adopted Stoic idealism. Poverty-stricken, obscure, and solitary, he was ambitious for glory. Though eventful, his military career brought little reward. In poor health, he resigned in 1744 to write. In 1747, he published *Introduction to the Knowledge of the Human Mind,* followed by *Reflections and Maxims.* Voltaire and Mirabeau praised his vigorous and eclectic thought, which aimed at teaching people how to live. Vauvenargues was a deist and an optimist who equally rejected Bossuet's Christian pessimism and La Rochefoucauld's secular pessimism. He asserted human freedom and natural goodness, but denied social and political equality. A lover of martial virtues and noble passions, Vauvenargues crafted memorable maxims and excelled in character depiction. His complete works were published in 1862. **See also** DEISM.   J.-L.S.

Vázquez, Gabriel (1549–1604), Spanish Jesuit theologian and philosopher. Born in Villaescusa de Haro, he studied at Alcalá de Henares and taught at Ocaña, Madrid, Alcalá, and Rome. He was a prolific writer; his philosophically most important work is a commentary on Aquinas's *Summa theologiae.*

Vázquez was strongly influenced by Aquinas, but he differed from him in important ways and showed marked leanings toward Augustine. He rejected the Thomistic doctrine of the real distinction between essence and existence and the position that matter designated by quantity (*materia signata quantitate*) is the principle of individuation. Instead of Aquinas's five ways for proving the existence of God, he favored a version of the moral argument similar to the one later used by Kant and also favored the teleological argument. Following Augustine, he described the union of body and soul as a union of two parts. Finally, Vázquez modified the doctrine of formal and objective concepts present in Toletus and Suárez in a way that facilitated the development of idealism in early modern philosophy. He accomplished this by identifying the actual being (*esse*) of the thing that is known (*conceptus objectivus*) with the act (*conceptus formalis*) whereby it is known.

See also AQUINAS, AUGUSTINE, ESSENTIALISM, IDEALISM, SUÁREZ, TOLETUS.   J.J.E.G.

Vedanta, also called Uttara Mīmāmsā ('the end of the Vedas'), the most influential of the six orthodox schools of Hinduism. Much of the philosophical content of other schools has been taken up into it. It claims to present the correct interpretation of the Vedas and Upanishads, along with the Bhagavad Gita, sacred texts within Indian culture. Much of the dispute over these texts is religious as well as philosophical in nature; it concerns whether or not they are best read theistically or monistically. To read these texts theistically is to see them as teaching the existence of an omnipotent and omniscient personal Brahman, who in sport (not out of need, but not without moral seriousness) everlastingly sustains the material world and conscious selves in existence; the ultimate good of the conscious selves then consists in being rightly related to Brahman. To read these texts monistically is to see them as teaching the existence of a qualityless ineffable Brahman who appears to the unen-

lightened to be manifested in a multiplicity of bodies and minds and in a personal deity; critics naturally ask to whom such an appearance appears.

Two great thinkers in the theistic Vedantic tradition are Rāmānuja (traditional dates: 1017–1137) and Madhva (b.1238). Shankara (788–820?) represents Advaita Vedanta ('Advaita' meaning 'non-dual') and defends the view that the sacred texts ought to be read monistically; his view is often compared to the absolute idealism embraced by Bradley; for Shankara what appears as a pluralistic world is really a seamless unity. Madhva is a leading proponent of Dvaita Vedanta, an uncompromisingly theistic reading of the same texts; for him, what appears as a pluralistic world is a pluralistic world that exists distinct from, though dependent on, Brahman. Rāmānuja is a leading exponent of Viśistadvaita Vedanta, often called "qualified non-dualism" because Rāmānuja, in contrast to Madhva, views the pluralistic world that appears as the body of Brahman but, in contrast to Shankara, views that body as real and distinct from Brahman conceived as an omnicompetent person.

See also BRADLEY, BRAHMAN, HINDUISM.

K.E.Y.

Vedas, the earliest Hindu sacred texts. 'Veda' literally means a text that contains knowledge, in particular sacred knowledge concerning the nature of ultimate reality and the proper human ways of relating thereto. Passed down orally and then composed over a millennium beginning around 1400 B.C., there are four collections of Vedas: the *Rg Veda* (1,028 sacred songs of praise with some cosmological speculations), the *Sāma Veda* (chants to accompany sacrifices), *Yajur Veda* (sacrificial formulas and mantras), and *Atharva Veda* (magical formulas, myths, and legends). The term 'Veda' also applies to the *Brāhmanas* (ritual and theological commentaries on the prior Vedas); the *Āranyakas* (mainly composed by men who have passed through their householder stage of life and retired to the forest to meditate), and the Upanishads, which more fully reflect the idea of theoretical sacred knowledge, while the early Vedas are more practice-oriented, concerned with ritual and sacrifice.

All these texts are regarded as scripture (*śruti*), "heard" in an oral tradition believed to be handed down by sages by whom their content was "seen." The content is held to express a timeless and uncreated wisdom produced by neither God nor human. It contains material ranging from instructions concerning the proper sacrifices to make and how to make them properly, through hymns and mantras, to accounts of the nature of Brahman, humankind, and the cosmos. *Śruti* contrasts with *smṛti* (tradition), which is humanly produced commentary on scripture. The Bhagavad Gita, perhaps strictly *smṛti*, typically has the de facto status of *śruti*.   K.E.Y.

veil of ignorance. See RAWLS.

velleity. See VOLITION.

Venn diagram, a logic diagram invented by the logician John Venn in which standard form statements (the four kinds listed below) are represented by two appropriately marked overlapping circles, as follows:

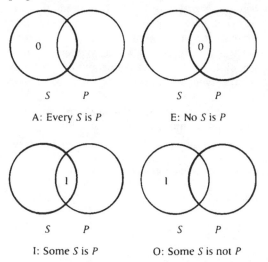

A: Every *S* is *P*   E: No *S* is *P*

I: Some *S* is *P*   O: Some *S* is not *P*

Syllogisms are represented by three overlapping circles, as in the examples below.

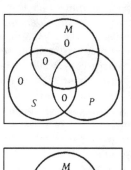

Every *M* is *P*
Every *S* is *M*
Every *S* is *P*

No *M* is *P*
Every *S* is *M*
No *S* is *P*

If a few simple rules are followed, e.g. "diagram universal premises first," then in a valid syllogism diagramming the premises automatically gives a diagram in which the conclusion is represented. In an invalid syllogism diagramming the premises does not automatically give a diagram in which the conclusion is represented, as below.

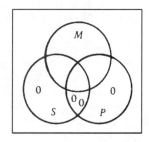

Every *P* is *M*
Every *S* is *M*
Every *S* is *P*

Venn diagrams are less perspicuous for the beginner than Euler diagrams. **See also EULER DIAGRAM, SYLLOGISM.**   R.P.

verifiability, principle of. See PRINCIPLE OF VERIFIABILITY.

verifiability theory of meaning. See MEANING, PHILOSOPHY OF LANGUAGE, VERIFICATIONISM.

verificationism, a metaphysical theory about what determines meaning: the meaning of a statement consists in its method(s) of verification. Verificationism thus differs radically from the account that identifies meaning with truth conditions, as is implicit in Frege's work and explicit in Wittgenstein's *Tractatus* and throughout the writings of Davidson. On Davidson's theory, e.g., the crucial notions for a theory of meaning are truth and falsity.

Contemporary verificationists, under the influence of the Oxford philosopher Michael Dummett, propose what they see as a constraint on the concept of truth rather than a criterion of meaningfulness. No foundational place is generally assigned in modern verificationist semantics to corroboration by observation statements; and modern verificationism is not reductionist. Thus, many philosophers read Quine's "Two Dogmas of Empiricism" as rejecting verificationism. This is because they fail to notice an important distinction. What Quine rejects is not verificationism but "reductionism," namely, the theory that there is, for each statement, a corresponding range of verifying conditions determinable a priori. Reductionism is inherently localist with regard to verification; whereas verificationism, as such, is neutral on whether verification is holistic. And, lastly, modern verificationism is, whereas traditional verificationism never was, connected with revisionism in the philosophy of logic and mathematics (e.g., rejecting the principle of bivalence).

See also LOGICAL POSITIVISM, MEANING, PRINCIPLE OF VERIFIABILITY, VIENNA CIRCLE.
E.L.

verisimilitude. See TRUTHLIKENESS.

Verstehen (German, 'understanding', 'interpretation'), a method in the human sciences that aims at reconstructing meanings from the "agent's point of view." Such a method makes primary how agents understand themselves, as, e.g., when cultural anthropologists try to understand symbols and practices from the "native's point of view." Understanding in this sense is often contrasted with explanation, or *Erklärung*. Whereas explanations discover causes in light of general laws and take an external perspective, understanding aims at explicating the meaning that, from an internal perspective, an action or expression has for the actor. This distinction often is the basis for a further methodological and ontological distinction between the natural and the human sciences, the *Natur-* and the *Geisteswissenschaften*. Whereas the data of the natural sciences may be theory-dependent and in that sense interpretive, the human sciences are "doubly" interpretive; they try to interpret the interpretations that human subjects give to their actions and practices. The human sciences do not aim at explaining events but at understanding meanings, texts, and text analogues. Actions, artifacts, and social relations are all like texts in that they have a significance for and by human subjects. The method of *Verstehen* thus denies the "unity of science" thesis typical of accounts of explanation given by empiricists and positivists. However, other philosophers such as Weber argue against such a dichotomy and assert that the social sciences in particular must incorporate features of both explanation and understanding, and psychoanalysis and theories of ideology unify both approaches.

Even among proponents of this method, the precise nature of interpretation remains controversial. While Dilthey and other neo-Kantians proposed that *Verstehen* is the imaginative reexperiencing of the subjective point of view of the actor, Wittgenstein and his following propose a sharp distinction between reasons and causes and understand reasons in terms of relating an action to the relevant rules or norms that it fol-

lows. In both cases, the aim of the human sciences is to understand what the text or text analogue really means for the agent. Following Heidegger, recent German hermeneutics argues that *Verstehen* does not refer to special disciplinary techniques nor to merely cognitive and theoretical achievements, but to the practical mode of all human existence, its situatedness in a world that projects various possibilities. All understanding then becomes interpretation, itself a universal feature of all human activity, including the natural sciences. The criteria of success in *Verstehen* also remain disputed, particularly since many philosophers deny that it constitutes a method. If all understanding is interpretation, then there are no presuppositionless, neutral data that can put them to an empirical test. *Verstehen* is therefore not a method but an event, in which there is a "fusion of horizons" between text and interpreter. Whether criteria such as coherence, the capacity to engage in a tradition, or increasing dialogue apply depends on the type, purpose, and context of various interpretations.

See also DILTHEY, EXPLANATION, HEIDEGGER, HERMENEUTICS, UNITY OF SCIENCE.
J.Bo.

verum. See Appendix of Special Symbols.

vibratinuncle. See HARTLEY.

vice. See VIRTUE ETHICS.

vicious circle principle. See TYPE THEORY.

vicious regress, regress that is in some way unacceptable, where a regress is an infinite series of items each of which is in some sense dependent on a prior item of a similar sort, e.g. an infinite series of events each of which is caused by the next prior event in the series. Reasons for holding a regress to be vicious might be that it is either impossible or that its existence is inconsistent with things known to be true. The claim that something would lead to a vicious regress is often made as part of a *reductio ad absurdum* argument strategy. An example of this can be found in Aquinas's argument for the existence of an uncaused cause on the ground that an infinite regress of causes is vicious. Those responding to the argument have sometimes contended that this regress is not in fact vicious and hence that the argument fails.

A more convincing example of a vicious

regress is generated by the principle that one's coming to know the meaning of a word must always be based on a prior understanding of other words. If this principle is correct, then one can know the meaning of a word w_1 only on the basis of previously understanding the meanings of other words (w_2 and w_3). But a further application of the principle yields the result that one can understand these words (w_2 and w_3) only on the basis of understanding still other words. This leads to an infinite regress. Since no one understands any words at birth, the regress implies that no one ever comes to understand any words. But this is clearly false. Since the existence of this regress is inconsistent with an obvious truth, we may conclude that the regress is vicious and consequently that the principle that generates it is false.

See also EPISTEMIC REGRESS ARGUMENT, REDUCTIO AD ABSURDUM.   W.T.

Vico, Giambattista (1668–1744), Italian philosopher who founded modern philosophy of history, philosophy of culture, and philosophy of mythology. He was born and lived all his life in or near Naples, where he taught Latin eloquence at the university (1699–1741). The Inquisition was a force in Naples throughout Vico's lifetime. A turning point in his career was his loss of the concourse for a chair of civil law (1723). Although a disappointment and an injustice, it enabled him to produce his major philosophical work. He was appointed royal historiographer by Charles of Bourbon in 1735.

Vico's major work is the *New Science* (*La scienza nuova*, 1725), completely revised in a second, definitive version in 1730. In the 1720s, he published three connected works in Latin on jurisprudence, under the title *Universal Law*; one contains a sketch of his conception of a "new science" of the historical life of nations. Vico's principal works preceding this are *On the Study Methods of Our Time* (1709), comparing the ancients with the moderns regarding human education, and *On the Most Ancient Wisdom of the Italians* (1710), attacking the Cartesian conception of metaphysics. His *Autobiography* (1728–31) inaugurates the conception of modern intellectual autobiography.

Basic to Vico's philosophy is his principle that "the true is the made" (*verum ipsum factum*), that what is true is convertible with what is made. This principle is central in his conception of "science" (*scientia, scienza*). A science is possible only for those subjects in which such a conversion is possible. There can be a science of mathematics, since mathematical truths are such because we make them. Analogously, there can be a science of the civil world of the historical life of nations. Since we make the things of the civil world, it is possible for us to have a science of them. As the makers of our own world, like God as the maker who makes by knowing and knows by making, we can have knowledge *per caussas* (through causes, from within). In the natural sciences we can have only *conscientia* (a kind of "consciousness"), not *scientia*, because things in nature are not made by the knower.

Vico's "new science" is a science of the principles whereby "men make history"; it is also a demonstration of "what providence has wrought in history." All nations rise and fall in cycles within history (*corsi e ricorsi*) in a pattern governed by providence. The world of nations or, in the Augustinian phrase Vico uses, "the great city of the human race," exhibits a pattern of three ages of "ideal eternal history" (*storia ideale eterna*). Every nation passes through an age of gods (when people think in terms of gods), an age of heroes (when all virtues and institutions are formed through the personalities of heroes), and an age of humans (when all sense of the divine is lost, life becomes luxurious and false, and thought becomes abstract and ineffective); then the cycle must begin again. In the first two ages all life and thought are governed by the primordial power of "imagination" (*fantasia*) and the world is ordered through the power of humans to form experience in terms of "imaginative universals" (*universali fantastici*). These two ages are governed by "poetic wisdom" (*sapienza poetica*). At the basis of Vico's conception of history, society, and knowledge is a conception of mythical thought as the origin of the human world. *Fantasia* is the original power of the human mind through which the true and the made are converted to create the myths and gods that are at the basis of any cycle of history.

Michelet was the primary supporter of Vico's ideas in the nineteenth century; he made them the basis of his own philosophy of history. Coleridge was the principal disseminator of Vichian views in England. James Joyce used the *New Science* as a substructure for *Finnegans Wake*, making plays on Vico's name, beginning with one in Latin in the first sentence: "by a commodius vicus of recirculation." Croce revived Vico's philosophical thought in the twentieth century, wishing to conceive Vico as the Italian Hegel. Vico's ideas have been the subject of analysis by such prominent philosophical thinkers as Horkheimer and Berlin, by anthropologists such as Edmund Leach, and by literary critics such as René Wellek and Herbert Read.

See also CROCE, PHILOSOPHY OF HISTORY.

D.P.V.

Vienna Circle, a group of philosophers and scientists who met periodically for discussions in Vienna from 1922 to 1938 and who proposed a self-consciously revolutionary conception of scientific knowledge. The Circle was initiated by the mathematician Hans Hahn to continue a prewar forum with the physicist Philip Frank and the social scientist Otto Neurath after the arrival in Vienna of Moritz Schlick, a philosopher who had studied with Max Planck. Carnap joined in 1926 (from 1931 in Prague); other members included Herbert Feigl (from 1930 in Iowa), Friedrich Waismann, Bergmann, Viktor Kraft, and Bela von Juhos. Viennese associates of the Circle included Kurt Gödel, Karl Menger, Felix Kaufmann, and Edgar Zilsel. (Popper was not a member or associate.) During its formative period the Circle's activities were confined to discussion meetings (many on Wittgenstein's *Tractatus*). In 1929 the Circle entered its public period with the formation of the Verein Ernst Mach, the publication of its manifesto *Wissenschaftliche Weltauffassung: Der Wiener Kreis* by Carnap, Hahn, and Neurath (translated in Neurath, *Empiricism and Sociology,* 1973), and the first of a series of philosophical monographs edited by Frank and Schlick. It also began collaboration with the independent but broadly like-minded Berlin "Society of Empirical Philosophy," including Reichenbach, Kurt Grelling, Kurt Lewin, Friedrich Kraus, Walter Dubislav, Hempel, and Richard von Mises: the groups together organized their first public conferences in Prague and Königsberg, acquired editorship of a philosophical journal renamed *Erkenntnis,* and later organized the international Unity of Science congresses. The death and dispersion of key members from 1934 onward (Hahn died in 1934, Neurath left for Holland in 1934, Carnap left for the United States in 1935, Schlick died in 1936) did not mean the extinction of Vienna Circle philosophy. Through the subsequent work of earlier visitors (Ayer, Ernest Nagel, Quine) and members and collaborators who emigrated to the United States (Carnap, Feigl, Frank, Hempel, and Reichenbach), the logical positivism of the Circle (Reichenbach and Neurath independently preferred "logical empiricism") strongly influenced the development of analytic philosophy.

The Circle's discussions concerned the philosophy of formal and physical science, and even though their individual publications ranged much wider, it is the attitude toward science that defines the Circle within the philosophical movements of central Europe at the time. The Circle rejected the need for a specifically philosophical epistemology that bestowed justification on knowledge claims from beyond science itself. In this, the Circle may also have drawn on a distinct Austrian tradition (a thesis of its historian Neurath): in most of Germany, science and philosophy had parted ways during the nineteenth century. Starting with Helmholtz, of course, there also arose a movement that sought to distinguish the scientific respectability of the Kantian tradition from the speculations of German idealism, yet after 1880 neo-Kantians insisted on the autonomy of epistemology, disparaging earlier fellow travelers as "positivist." Yet the program of reducing the knowledge claim of science and providing legitimations to what's left found wide favor with the more empirical-minded like Mach. Comprehensive description, not explanation, of natural phenomena became the task for theorists who no longer looked to philosophy for foundations, but found them in the utility of their preferred empirical procedures. Along with the positivists, the Vienna Circle thought uneconomical the Kantian answer to the question of the possibility of objectivity, the *synthetic a priori.* Moreover, the Vienna Circle and its conventionalist precursors Poincaré and Duhem saw them contradicted by the results of formal science. Riemann's geometries showed that questions about the geometry of physical space were open to more than one answer: Was physical space Euclidean or non-Euclidean? It fell to Einstein and the pre-Circle Schlick (*Space and Time in Contemporary Physics,* 1917) to argue that relativity theory showed the untenability of Kant's conception of space and time as forever fixed synthetic a priori forms of intuition. Yet Frege's anti-psychologistic critique had also shown empiricism unable to account for knowledge of arithmetic and the conventionalists had ended the positivist dream of a theory of experiential elements that bridged the gap between descriptions of fact and general principles of science. How, then, could the Vienna Circle defend the claim – under attack as just one worldview among others – that science provides knowledge?

The Circle confronted the problem of constitutive conventions. As befitted their self-image beyond Kant and Mach, they found their paradigmatic answer in the theory of relativity: they thought that irreducible conventions of measurement with wide-ranging implications were sharply separable from pure facts like point coincidences. Empirical theories were viewed as logical structures of statements freely created, yet accountable to experiential input via their predictive consequences identifiable by observation. The Vienna Circle defended empiricism by the reconceptualization of the relation between a priori and a posteriori inquiries. First, in a manner sympathetic to Frege's and Russell's doctrine of logicism and guided by Wittgenstein's notion of tautology, arithmetic was considered a part of logic and treated as entirely analytical, without any empirical content; its truth was held to be exhausted by what is provable from the premises and rules of a formal symbolic system. (Carnap's *Logical Syntax of Language*, 1934, assimilated Gödel's incompleteness result by claiming that not every such proof could be demonstrated in those systems themselves which are powerful enough to represent classical arithmetic.) The synthetic a priori was not needed for formal science because all of its results were non-synthetic. Second, the Circle adopted verificationism: supposedly empirical concepts whose applicability was indiscernible were excluded from science. The terms for unobservables were to be reconstructed by logical operations from the observational terms. Only if such reconstructions were provided did the more theoretical parts of science retain their empirical character. (Just what kind of reduction was aimed for was not always clear and earlier radical positions were gradually weakened; Reichenbach instead considered the relation between observational and theoretical statements to be probabilistic.) Empirical science needed no synthetic a priori either; all of its statements were a posteriori.

Combined with the view that the analysis of the logical form of expressions allowed for the exact determination of their combinatorial value, verificationism was to exhibit the knowledge claims of science and eliminate metaphysics. Whatever meaning did not survive identification with the scientific was deemed irrelevant to knowledge claims (Reichenbach did not share this view either). Since the Circle also observed the then long-discussed ban on issuing unconditional value statements in science, its metaethical positions may be broadly characterized as endorsing noncognitivism. Its members were not simply emotivists, however, holding that value judgments were *mere* expressions of feeling, but sought to distinguish the factual and

evaluative contents of value judgments. Those who, like Schlick (*Questions of Ethics*, 1930), engaged in metaethics, distinguished the expressive component (*x* desires *y*) of value judgments from their implied descriptive component (doing *z* furthers aim *y*) and held that the demand inherent in moral principles possessed validity if the implied description was true and the expressed desire was endorsed. This analysis of normative concepts did not render them meaningless but allowed for psychological and sociological studies of ethical systems; Menger's formal variant (*Morality, Decision and Social Organization*, 1934) proved influential for decision theory.

The semiotic view that knowledge required structured representations was developed in close contact with foundational research in mathematics and depended on the "new" logic of Frege, Russell, and Wittgenstein, out of which quantification theory was emerging. Major new results were quickly integrated (albeit controversially) and Carnap's works reflect the development of the conception of logic itself. In his *Logical Syntax* he adopted the "Principle of Tolerance" vis-à-vis the question of the foundation of the formal sciences: the choice of logics (and languages) was conventional and constrained, apart from the demand for consistency, only by pragmatic considerations. The proposed language form and its difference from alternatives simply had to be stated as exactly as possible: whether a logico-linguistic framework as a whole correctly represented reality was a cognitively meaningless question. Yet what was the status of the verifiability principle? Carnap's suggestion that it represents not a discovery but a *proposal* for future scientific language use deserves to be taken seriously, for it not only characterizes his own conventionalism, but also amplifies the Circle's *linguistic turn*, according to which all philosophy concerned ways of representing, rather than the nature of the represented. What the Vienna Circle "discovered" was how much of science was conventional: its verificationism was a proposal for accommodating the creativity of scientific theorizing without accommodating idealism.

Whether an empirical claim in order to be meaningful needed to be actually verified or only potentially verifiable, or fallible or only potentially testable, and whether so by current or only by future means, became matters of discussion during the 1930s. Equally important for the question whether the Circle's conventionalism avoided idealism and metaphysics were the issues of the status of theoretical discourse about unobservables and the nature of science's empirical foundation. The view suggested in Schlick's early *General Theory of Knowledge* (1918, 2d. ed. 1925) and Frank's *The Causal Law and its Limitations* (1932) and elaborated in Carnap's "Logical Foundations of the Unity of Science" (in *Foundations of the Unity of Science* I.1, 1938) characterized the theoretical language as an uninterpreted calculus that is related to the fully interpreted observational language only by partial definitions. Did such an instrumentalism require for its empirical anchor the sharp separation of observational from theoretical terms? Could such a separation even be maintained?

Consider the *unity of science thesis*. According to the methodological version, endorsed by all members, all of science abides by the same criteria: no basic methodological differences separate the natural from the social or cultural sciences (*Geisteswissenschaften*) as claimed by those who distinguish between 'explanation' and 'understanding'. According to the metalinguistic version, all objects of scientific knowledge could in principle be comprehended by the same "universal" language. *Physicalism* asserts that this is the language that speaks of physical objects. While everybody in the Circle endorsed physicalism in this sense, the understanding of its importance varied, as became clear in the so-called protocol sentence debate. (The nomological version of the unity thesis was only later clearly distinguished: whether all scientific laws could be reduced to those of physics was another matter on which Neurath came to differ.) Ostensively, this debate concerned the question of the form, content, and epistemological status of scientific evidence statements. Schlick's unrevisable "affirmations" talked about phenomenal states in statements not themselves part of the language of science ("The Foundation of Knowledge," 1934, translated in Ayer, ed., *Logical Positivism*). Carnap's preference changed from unrevisable statements in a primitive methodologically solipsistic protocol language that were fallibly translatable into the physicalistic system language (1931; see *Unity of Science*, 1934), via arbitrary revisable statements of that system language that are taken as temporary resting points in testing (1932), to revisable statements in the scientific observation language (1935; see "Testability and Meaning," *Philosophy of Science*, 1936–37). These changes were partly prompted by Neurath, whose own revisable "protocol statements" spoke, amongst other matters, of the relation between observers and the observed in a "universal slang" that mixed expressions of the phys-

icalistically cleansed colloquial and the high scientific languages ("Protocol Statements," 1932, translated in Ayer, ed., *Logical Positivism*). Ultimately, these proposals answered to different projects. Since all agreed that all statements of science were hypothetical, the questions of their "foundation" concerned rather the very nature of Vienna Circle philosophy. For Schlick philosophy became the activity of meaning determination (inspired by Wittgenstein); Carnap pursued it as the rational reconstruction of knowledge claims concerned only with what Reichenbach called the "context of justification" (its logical aspects, not the "context of discovery"); and Neurath replaced philosophy altogether with a naturalistic, interdisciplinary, empirical inquiry into science as a distinctive discursive practice, precluding the orthodox conception of the unity of science.

The Vienna Circle was neither a monolithic nor a necessarily reductionist philosophical movement, and quick assimilation to the tradition of British empiricism mistakes its struggles with the form–content dichotomy for foundationalism, when instead sophisticated responses to the question of the presuppositions of their own theories of knowledge were being developed. In its time and place, the Circle was a minority voice; the sociopolitical dimension of its theories – stressed more by some (Neurath) than others (Schlick) – as a renewal of Enlightenment thought, ultimately against the rising tide of *Blut-und-Boden* metaphysics, is gaining recognition. After the celebrated "death" of reductionist logical positivism in the 1960s the historical Vienna Circle is reemerging as a multifaceted object of the history of analytical philosophy itself, revealing *in nuce* different strands of reasoning still significant for postpositivist theory of science.

See also MEANING, OPERATIONALISM, PHILOSOPHY OF SCIENCE, REDUCTION, UNITY OF SCIENCE.   T.U.

Vijñānavāda, an idealist school of Buddhist thought in India in the fourth century A.D. It engaged in lively debates on important epistemological and metaphysical issues with the Buddhist Mādhyamika school (known for its relativistic and nihilistic views), with Buddhist realist schools, and with various Hindu philosophical systems of its time. Mādhyamika philosophy used effective dialectic to show the contradictions in our everyday philosophical notions such as cause, substance, self, etc., but the Vijñānavāda school, while agreeing with the Mādhyamikas on this point, went further and gave innovative explanations regarding the origin and the status of our mental constructions and of the mind itself. Unlike the Mādhyamikas, who held that reality is "emptiness" (*śūnyatā*), the Vijñānavādins held that the reality is consciousness or the mind (*vijñāna*). The Vijñānavāda school is also known as Yogācāra. Its idealism is remarkably similar to the subjective idealism of Berkeley. Consistent with the process ontology of all the Buddhist schools in India, Vijñānavādins held that consciousness or the mind is not a substance but an ever-changing stream of ideas or impressions. **See also BUD-DHISM.**   D.K.C.

vijñapti, Indian Buddhist term meaning 'representation', used by some philosophers as a label for a mental event that appears, phenomenally, to have an intentional object and to represent or communicate to its possessor some information about extramental reality. The term was used mostly by Buddhists with idealist tendencies who claimed that there is nothing but representation, nothing but communicative mental events, and that a complete account of human experience can be given without postulating the existence of anything extramental. This view was not uncontroversial, and in defending it Indian Buddhists developed arguments that are in important ways analogous to those constructed by Western idealists.   P.J.G.

Vio, Tommaso de. See CAJETAN.

violence, (1) the use of force to cause physical harm, death, or destruction (physical violence); (2) the causing of severe mental or emotional harm, as through humiliation, deprivation, or brainwashing, whether using force or not (psychological violence); (3) more broadly, profaning, desecrating, defiling, or showing disrespect for (i.e., "doing violence" to) something valued, sacred, or cherished; (4) extreme physical force in the natural world, as in tornados, hurricanes, and earthquakes.

Physical violence may be directed against persons, animals, or property. In the first two cases, harm, pain, suffering, and death figure prominently; in the third, illegality or illegitimacy (the forceful destruction of property is typically considered violence when it lacks authorization). Psychological violence applies principally to persons. It may be understood as the violation of beings worthy of respect. But it can apply to higher animals as well (as in the damaging mental effects of some experimentation, e.g., involv-

ing isolation and deprivation). Environmentalists sometimes speak of violence against the environment, implying both destruction and disrespect for the natural world.

Sometimes the concept of violence is used to characterize acts or practices of which one morally disapproves. To this extent it has a normative force. But this prejudges whether violence is wrong. One may, on the other hand, regard inflicting harm or death as only prima facie wrong (i.e., wrong all other things being equal). This gives violence a normative character, establishing its prima facie wrongness. But it leaves open the ultimate moral justifiability of its use. Established practices of physical or psychological violence – e.g., war, capital punishment – constitute institutionalized violence. So do illegal or extralegal practices like vigilantism, torture, and state terrorism (e.g., death squads). Anarchists sometimes regard the courts, prisons, and police essential to maintaining the state as violence. Racism and sexism may be considered institutional violence owing to their associated psychological as well as physical violence. **See also NONVIOLENCE.**   R.L.H.

vipassanā (Pali, 'insight', 'discernment'), Indian Buddhist term used to describe both a particular kind of meditational practice and the states of consciousness produced by it. The meditational practice is aimed at getting the practitioner to perceive and cognize in accord with the major categories of Buddhist metaphysics. Since that metaphysics is constitutively deconstructive, being concerned with parts rather than wholes, the method too is analytic and deconstructive. The practitioner is encouraged to analyze the perceived solidities and continuities of her everyday experience into transitory events, and so to cultivate the perception of such events until she experiences the world no longer in terms of medium-sized physical objects that endure through time, but solely in terms of transitory events. Arriving at such a condition is called the attainment of *vipassanā*.   P.J.G.

virtù. See CLASSICAL REPUBLICANISM, MACHIAVELLI.

virtue, epistemic. See VIRTUE EPISTEMOLOGY.

virtue epistemology, the subfield of epistemology that takes epistemic virtue to be central to understanding justification or knowledge or both. An epistemic virtue is a personal quality conducive to the discovery of truth, the avoidance of error, or some other intellectually valuable goal. Following Aristotle, we should distinguish these virtues from such qualities as wisdom or good judgment, which are the intellectual basis of practical – but not necessarily intellectual – success.

The importance, and to an extent, the very definition, of this notion depends, however, on larger issues of epistemology. For those who favor a naturalist conception of knowledge (say, as belief formed in a "reliable" way), there is reason to call any truth-conducive quality or properly working cognitive mechanism an epistemic virtue. There is no particular reason to limit the epistemic virtues to recognizable personal qualities: a high mathematical aptitude may count as an epistemic virtue. For those who favor a more "normative" conception of knowledge, the corresponding notion of an epistemic virtue (or vice) will be narrower: it will be tied to personal qualities (like impartiality or carelessness) whose exercise one would associate with an ethics of belief.

See also RELIABILISM, VIRTUE ETHICS.

J.A.M.

virtue ethics, also called virtue-based ethics and agent-based ethics, conceptions or theories of morality in which virtues play a central or independent role. Thus, it is more than simply the account of the virtues offered by a given theory. Some take the principal claim of virtue ethics to be about the *moral subject* – that, in living her life, she should focus her attention on the cultivation of her (or others') virtues. Others take the principal claim to be about the *moral theorist* – that, in mapping the structure of our moral thought, she should concentrate on the virtues. This latter view can be construed weakly as holding that the moral virtues are no less basic than other moral concepts. In this type of virtue ethics, virtues are independent of other moral concepts in that claims about morally virtuous character or action are, in the main, neither reducible to nor justified on the basis of underlying claims about moral duty or rights, or about what is impersonally valuable. It can also be construed strongly as holding that the moral virtues are more basic than other moral concepts. In such a virtue ethics, virtues are fundamental, i.e., claims about other moral concepts are either reducible to underlying claims about moral virtues or justified on their basis.

Forms of virtue ethics predominated in Western philosophy before the Renaissance, most notably in Aristotle, but also in Plato and Aquinas. Several ancient and medieval philoso-

phers endorsed strong versions of virtue ethics. These views focused on character rather than on discrete behavior, identifying illicit behavior with vicious behavior, i.e., conduct that would be seriously out of character for a virtuous person. A virtuous person, in turn, was defined as one with dispositions relevantly linked to human flourishing. On these views, while a person of good character, or someone who carefully observes her, may be able to articulate certain principles or rules by which she guides her conduct (or to which, at least, it outwardly conforms), the principles are not an ultimate source of moral justification. On the contrary, they are justified only insofar as the conduct they endorse would be in character for a virtuous person.

For Aristotle, the connection between flourishing and virtue seems conceptual. (He conceived moral virtues as dispositions to choose under the proper guidance of reason, and defined a flourishing life as one lived in accordance with these virtues.) While most accounts of the virtues link them to the flourishing of the virtuous person, there are other possibilities. In principle, the flourishing to which virtue is tied (whether causally or conceptually) may be either that of the virtuous subject herself, or that of some patient who is a recipient of her virtuous behavior, or that of some larger affected group – the agent's community, perhaps, or all humanity, or even sentient life in general.

For the philosophers of ancient Greece, it was human nature, usually conceived teleologically, that fixed the content of this flourishing. Medieval Christian writers reinterpreted this, stipulating both that the flourishing life to which the virtues lead extends past death, and that human flourishing is not merely the fulfillment of capacities and tendencies inherent in human nature, but is the realization of a divine plan. In late twentieth-century versions of virtue ethics, some theorists have suggested that it is neither to a teleology inherent in human nature nor to the divine will that we should look in determining the content of that flourishing to which the virtues lead. They understand flourishing more as a matter of a person's living a life that meets the standards of her cultural, historical tradition.

In his most general characterization, Aristotle called a thing's virtues those features of it that made it and its operation good. The moral virtues were what made people live well. This use of 'making' is ambiguous. Where he and other premodern thinkers thought the connection between virtues and living well to be conceptual, moral theorists of the modernist era have usually understood it causally. They commonly maintain that a virtue is a character trait that disposes a person to do what can be independently identified as morally required or to effect what is best (best for herself, according to some theories; best for others, according to different ones). Benjamin Franklin, e.g., deemed it virtuous for a person to be frugal, because he thought frugality was likely to result in her having a less troubled life. On views of this sort, a lively concern for the welfare of others has moral importance only inasmuch as it tends to motivate people actually to perform helpful actions. In short, benevolence is a virtue because it conduces to beneficent conduct; veracity, because it conduces to truth telling; fidelity, because it conduces to promise keeping; and so on. Reacting to this aspect of modernist philosophy, recent proponents of virtue ethics deny that moral virtues derive from prior determinations of what actions are right or of what states of affairs are best. Some, especially certain theorists of liberalism, assign virtues to what they see as one compartment of moral thought and duties to a separate, and only loosely connected compartment. For them, the life (and theory) of virtue is autonomous. They hold that virtues and duties have independent sources of justification, with virtues chiefly concerned with the individual's personal "ideals," self-image, or conception of her life goals, while duties and rights are thought to derive from social rules regulating interpersonal dealings.

Proponents of virtue ethics maintain that it has certain advantages over more modern alternatives. They argue that virtue ethics is properly concrete, because it grounds morality in facts about human nature or about the concrete development of particular cultural traditions, in contrast with modernist attempts to ground morality in subjective preference or in abstract principles of reason. They also claim that virtue ethics is truer to human psychology in concentrating on the less conscious aspects of motivation – on relatively stable dispositions, habits, and long-term goals, for example – where modern ethics focuses on decision making directed by principles and rules. Virtue ethics, some say, offers a more unified and comprehensive conception of moral life, one that extends beyond actions to comprise wants, goals, likes and dislikes, and, in general, what sort of person one is and aims to be. Proponents of virtue ethics also contend that, without the sensitivity and appreciation of their situation and its opportunities that only virtues consistently make available, agents cannot properly apply the rules that mod-

ernist ethical theories offer to guide their actions. Nor, in their view, will the agent follow those rules unless her virtues offer her sufficient clarity of purpose and perseverance against temptation.

Several objections have been raised against virtue ethics in its most recent forms. Critics contend that it is antiquarian, because it relies on conceptions of human nature whose teleology renders them obsolete; circular, because it allegedly defines right action in terms of virtues while defining virtues in terms of right action; arbitrary and irrelevant to modern society, since there is today no accepted standard either of what constitutes human flourishing or of which dispositions lead to it; of no practical use, because it offers no guidance when virtues seem to conflict; egoistic, in that it ultimately directs the subject's moral attention to herself rather than to others; and fatalistic, in allowing the morality of one's behavior to hinge finally on luck in one's constitution, upbringing, and opportunities. There may be versions of virtue ethics that escape the force of all or most of the objections, but not every form of virtue ethics can claim for itself all the advantages mentioned above.

See also AQUINAS, ARISTOTLE, ETHICS, PLATO.   J.L.A.G.

virtues, cardinal. See CARDINAL VIRTUES.

virtues, theological. See AQUINAS.

virtue theory. See VIRTUE ETHICS.

Vishnu (from Sanskrit *Viṣṇu*), major Hindu god and Supreme Lord for his devotees, the Vaishnavites. Vaishnavite philosophers regard Vishnu as the referent of the term 'Brahman' in the Vedic texts. Later texts attempt a synthesis of Vishnu with two other deities into a *trimūrti* ('three forms' of the Absolute), with Brahma as Creator, Vishnu as Preserver, and Siva as Destroyer. This relatively unpopular idea is used by modern thinkers to speak of these gods as three forms of the formless Absolute. Madhva and Rāmānuja regard Vishnu as the Highest Lord, possessed of infinite good qualities and superior to the qualityless Absolute of the nondualist thinkers. Vaishnavite thinkers identify Vishnu with the Puruśa, the primeval, cosmic person, and Prājapati, Creator god, of the Vedas, and give him epithets that identify Vishnu with other representatives of a Supreme Being. He is Creator, Preserver, and Destroyer of the Universe. Vishnu is best known for the doctrine of avatar, his "descents" into the world in various forms to promote righteousness. Through this and the concept of *vyūhas*, aspects or fragments, Vaishnavites incorporated other deities, hero cults, and savior myths into their fold. He was a minor deity in the early Vedic literature, known for his "three strides" across the universe, which indicate that he pervades all. During the epic period (400 B.C.–A.D. 400), Vishnu became one of the most popular gods in India, represented iconographically as dark-complexioned and holding a conch and discus. His consort is usually Laksmī and his vehicle the bird Garuda. **See also** AVATAR, BRAHMAN.   R.N.Mi.

Viśistadvaita Vedanta, a form of Hinduism for which Brahman is an independently existing, omnipotent, omniscient personal deity. In creative, morally serious sport, Brahman everlastingly sustains in existence a world of both minds and physical things, these together being the body of Brahman in the sense that Brahman can act on any part of the world without first acting on some other part and that the world manifests (though in some ways it also hides) Brahman's nature. In response to repentance and trust, Brahman will forgive one's sins and bring one into a gracious relationship that ends the cycle of rebirths. **See also** HINDUISM.   K.E.Y.

vitalism. See PHILOSOPHY OF BIOLOGY.

vital lie, (1) an instance of self-deception (or lying to oneself) when it fosters hope, confidence, self-esteem, mental health, or creativity; (2) any false belief or unjustified attitude that helps people cope with difficulties; (3) a lie to other people designed to promote their well-being. For example, self-deceiving optimism about one's prospects for success in work or personal relationships may generate hope, mobilize energy, enrich life's meaning, and increase chances for success. Henrik Ibsen dramatized "life-lies" as essential for happiness (*The Wild Duck*, 1884), and Eugene O'Neill portrayed "pipe dreams" as necessary crutches (*The Iceman Cometh*, 1939). Nietzsche endorsed "pious illusions" or "holy fictions" about the past that liberate individuals and societies from shame and guilt (*On the Advantage and Disadvantage of History for Life*, 1874). Schiller praised normal degrees of vanity and self-conceit because they support self-esteem (*Problems of Belief*, 1924). **See also** BAD FAITH, FALSE CONSCIOUSNESS.   M.W.M.

Vitoria, Francisco de (1492/93–1546), Spanish Dominican jurist, political philosopher, and the-

ologian who is regarded as the founder of modern international law. Born in Vitoria or Burgos, he studied and taught at the College of Saint-Jacques in Paris, where he met Erasmus and Vives. He also taught at the College of San Gregorio in Valladolid and at Salamanca.

His most famous works are the notes (*relectiones*) for twelve public addresses he delivered at Salamanca, published posthumously in 1557. Two *relectiones* stand out: *De Indis* and *De jure belli*. They were responses to the legal and political issues raised by the discovery and colonization of America. In contrast with Mariana's contract Arianism, Vitoria held that political society is our natural state. The aim of the state is to promote the common good and preserve the rights of citizens. Citizenship is the result of birthplace (*jus solis*) rather than blood (*jus sanguini*). The authority of the state resides in the body politic but is transferred to rulers for its proper exercise. The best form of government is monarchy because it preserves the unity necessary for social action while safeguarding individual freedoms. Apart from the societies of individual states, humans belong to an international society. This society has its own authority and laws that establish the rights and duties of the states. These laws constitute the law of nations (*jus gentium*).

J.J.E.G.

Vives, Juan Luis (1492?–1540), Spanish humanist and teacher. Born in Valencia, he attended the University of Paris (1509–14) and lived most of his life in Flanders. With his friend Erasmus he prepared a widely used commentary (1522) of Augustine's *De civitate Dei*. From 1523 to 1528 Vives visited England, taught at Oxford, befriended More, and became Catherine of Aragon's confidant. While in Paris, Vives repudiated medieval logic as useless (*Adversus pseudodialecticos*, 1520) and proposed instead a dialectic emphasizing resourceful reasoning and clear and persuasive exposition (*De tradendis disciplinis*, 1532). His method was partially inspired by Rudolph Agricola and probably influential upon Peter Ramus.

Less interested in theology than Erasmus or More, he surpassed both in philosophical depth. As one of the great pedagogues of his age, Vives proposed a plan of education that substituted the Aristotelian ideal of speculative certainty for a pragmatic probability capable of guiding action. Vives enlarged the scope of women's education (*De institutione feminae Christianae*, 1524) and contributed to the teaching of classical Latin (*Exercitatio linguae latinae*, 1538). A champion of European unity against the Turks, he professed the belief that international order (*De concordia,* 1526) depended upon the control of passion (*De anima et vita,* 1538). As a social reformer, Vives pioneered the secularization of welfare (*De subventione pauperum,* 1526) and opposed the abuse of legal jargon (*Aedes legum,* 1520). Although his Jewish parents were victimized by the Inquisition, Vives remained a Catholic and managed to write an apology of Christianity without taking sides in controversial theological matters (*De veritate fidei,* 1543).   C.G.Nore.

volition, a mental event involved with the initiation of action. 'To will' is sometimes taken to be the corresponding verb form of 'volition'. The concept of volition is rooted in modern philosophy; contemporary philosophers have transformed it by identifying volitions with ordinary mental events, such as intentions, or beliefs plus desires. Volitions, especially in contemporary guises, are often taken to be complex mental events consisting of cognitive, affective, and *conative* elements. The conative element is the impetus – the underlying motivation – for the action. A *velleity* is a conative element insufficient by itself to initiate action. The *will* is a faculty, or set of abilities, that yields the mental events involved in initiating action.

There are three primary theories about the role of volitions in action. The first is a reductive account in which action is identified with the entire causal sequence of the mental event (the volition) causing the bodily behavior. J. S. Mill, for example, says: "Now what is action? Not one thing, but a series of two things: the state of mind called a volition, followed by an effect. . . . [T]he two together constitute the action" (*Logic*). Mary's raising her arm *is* Mary's mental state causing her arm to rise. Neither Mary's volitional state nor her arm's rising are themselves actions; rather, the entire causal sequence (the "causing") is the action. The primary difficulty for this account is maintaining its reductive status. There is no way to delineate volition and the resultant bodily behavior without referring to action.

There are two non-reductive accounts, one that identifies the action with the initiating volition and another that identifies the action with the effect of the volition. In the former, a volition *is* the action, and bodily movements are mere causal consequences. Berkeley advocates this view: "The Mind . . . is to be accounted *active* in . . . so far forth as *volition* is included. . . . In plucking this flower I am active, because I do it by the motion of my hand, which was conse-

quent upon my volition" (*Three Dialogues*). In this century, Prichard is associated with this theory: "to act is really to will something" (*Moral Obligation,* 1949), where willing is *sui generis* (though at other places Prichard equates willing with the action of mentally setting oneself to do something). In this sense, a volition is an act of will. This account has come under attack by Ryle (*Concept of Mind,* 1949). Ryle argues that it leads to a vicious regress, in that to will to do something, one must will to will to do it, and so on. It has been countered that the regress collapses; there is nothing beyond willing that one must do in order to will. Another criticism of Ryle's, which is more telling, is that 'volition' is an obscurantic term of art; "[volition] is an artificial concept. We have to study certain specialist theories in order to find out how it is to be manipulated. . . . [It is like] 'phlogiston' and 'animal spirits' . . . [which] have now no utility" (*Concept of Mind*).

Another approach, the causal theory of action, identifies an action with the causal consequences of volition. Locke, e.g., says: "*Volition* or *willing* is an act of the mind directing its thought to the production of any action, and thereby exerting its power to produce it. . . . [V]olition is nothing but that particular determination of the mind, whereby . . . the mind endeavors to give rise, continuation, or stop, to any action which it takes to be in its power" (*Essay concerning Human Understanding*). This is a functional account, since an event is an action in virtue of its causal role. Mary's arm rising *is* Mary's action of raising her arm in virtue of being caused by her willing to raise it. If her arm's rising had been caused by a nervous twitch, it would not be action, even if the bodily movements were photographically the same.

In response to Ryle's charge of obscurantism, contemporary causal theorists tend to identify volitions with ordinary mental events. For example, Davidson takes the cause of actions to be beliefs plus desires and Wilfrid Sellars takes volitions to be intentions to do something here and now. Despite its plausibility, however, the causal theory faces two difficult problems: the first is purported counterexamples based on wayward causal chains connecting the antecedent mental event and the bodily movements; the second is provision of an enlightening account of these mental events, e.g. intending, that does justice to the conative element.

See also ACTION THEORY, FREE WILL PROBLEM, PRACTICAL REASONING, WAYWARD CAUSAL CHAIN.   M.B.

Voltaire, pen name of François-Marie Arouet (1694–1778), French philosopher and writer who won early fame as a playwright and poet and later was an influential popularizer of Newtonian natural philosophy. His enduring reputation rests on his acerbically witty essays on religious and moral topics (especially the *Philosophical Letters*, 1734, and the *Philosophical Dictionary*, 1764), his brilliant stories, and his passionate polemics against the injustices of the *ancien régime*. In Whitehead's phrase, he was more "a *philosophe* than a philosopher" in the current specialized disciplinary sense. He borrowed most of his views on metaphysics and epistemology from Locke, whose work, along with Newton's, he came to know and extravagantly admire during his stay (1726–28) in England. His is best placed in the line of great French literary moralists that includes Montaigne, Pascal, Diderot, and Camus.

Voltaire's position is skeptical, empirical, and humanistic. His skepticism is not of the radical sort that concerned Descartes. But he denies that we can find adequate support for the grand metaphysical claims of systematic philosophers, such as Leibniz, or for the dogmatic theology of institutional religions. Voltaire's empiricism urges us to be content with the limited and fallible knowledge of our everyday experience and its development through the methods of empirical science. His humanism makes a plea, based on his empiricist skepticism, for religious and social tolerance: none of us can know enough to be justified in persecuting those who disagree with us on fundamental philosophical and theological matters. Voltaire's positive view is that our human condition, for all its flaws and perils, is meaningful and livable strictly in its own terms, quite apart from any connection to the threats and promises of dubious transcendental realms.

Voltaire's position is well illustrated by his views on religion. Although complex doctrines about the Trinity or the Incarnation strike him as gratuitous nonsense, he nonetheless is firmly convinced of the reality of a good God who enjoins us through our moral sense to love one another as brothers and sisters. Indeed, it is precisely this moral sense that he finds outraged by the intolerance of institutional Christianity. His deepest religious thinking concerns the problem of evil, which he treated in his "Poem of the Lisbon Earthquake" and the classic tales *Zadig* (1747) and *Candide* (1759). He rejects the Panglossian view (held by *Candide*'s Dr. Pangloss, a caricature of Leibniz) that we can see the hand of providence in our daily life but is prepared to acknowledge that an all-good God does not (as an extreme deism would hold) let his universe just blindly run. Whatever metaphysical truth there may be in the thought that "all is for the best in the best of all possible worlds," Voltaire insists that this idea is ludicrous as a practical response to evil and recommends instead concrete action to solve specific local problems: "We must cultivate our garden."

Voltaire was and remains an immensely controversial figure. Will Durant regarded him as "the greatest man who ever lived," while Joseph de Maistre maintained that "admiration for Voltaire is an infallible sign of a corrupt soul." Perhaps it is enough to say that he wrote with unequaled charm and wit and stood for values that are essential to, if perhaps not the very core of, our humanity.

See also ENCYCLOPEDIA, LEIBNIZ.				G.G.

voluntarism, any philosophical view that makes our ability to control the phenomena in question an essential part of the correct understanding of those phenomena. Thus, ethical voluntarism is the doctrine that the standards that define right and wrong conduct are in some sense chosen by us. Doxastic voluntarism is the doctrine that we have extensive control over what we believe; we choose what to believe. A special case of doxastic voluntarism is theological voluntarism, which implies that religious belief requires a substantial element of choice; the evidence alone cannot decide the issue. This is a view that is closely associated with Pascal, Kierkegaard, and James. Historical voluntarism is the doctrine that the human will is a major factor in history. Such views contrast with Marxist views of history. Metaphysical voluntarism is the doctrine, linked with Schopenhauer, that the fundamental organizing principle of the world is not the incarnation of a rational or a moral order but rather the will, which for Schopenhauer is an ultimately meaningless striving for survival, to be found in all of nature. **See also** EPISTEMOLOGY.		R.Fo.

voluntarism, doxastic. See VOLUNTARISM.

voluntarism, ethical. See NATURAL LAW.

voluntarism, metaphysical. See VOLUNTARISM.

voluntarism, theological. See VOLUNTARISM.

voluntary act. See ACTION THEORY.

voluntary euthanasia. See EUTHANASIA.

von Neumann, John (1903–57), Hungarian-born American mathematician, physicist, logician, economist, engineer, and computer scientist. Born in Budapest and trained in Hungary, Switzerland, and Germany, he visited Princeton University in 1930 and became a professor at the Institute for Advanced Study at Princeton in 1933. His most outstanding work in pure mathematics was on rings of operators in Hilbert spaces. In quantum mechanics he showed the equivalence of matrix mechanics to wave mechanics, and argued that quantum mechanics could not be embedded in an underlying deterministic system. He established important results in set theory and mathematical logic, and worked on Hilbert's Program to prove the consistency of mathematics within mathematics until he was shocked by Gödel's incompleteness theorems. He established the mathematical theory of games and later showed its application to economics.

In these many different areas, von Neumann demonstrated a remarkable ability to analyze a subject matter and develop a mathematical formalism that answered basic questions about that subject matter; formalization in logic is the special case of this process where the subject matter is language and reasoning. With the advent of World War II von Neumann turned his great analytical ability to more applied areas of hydrodynamics, ballistics, and nuclear explosives. In 1945 he began to work on the design, use, and theory of electronic computers. He later became a leading scientist in government.

Von Neumann contributed to the hardware architecture of the modern electronic computer, and he invented the first modern program language. A program in this language could change the addresses of its own instructions, so that it became possible to use the same subroutine on different data structures and to write programs to process programs. Von Neumann proposed to use a computer as a research tool for exploring very complex phenomena, such as the discontinuous nature of shock waves. He began the development of a theory of automata that would cover computing, communication, and control systems, as well as natural organisms, biological evolution, and societies. To this end, he initiated the study of probabilistic automata and of self-reproducing and cellular automata.

See also COGNITIVE SCIENCE, COMPUTER THEORY, CYBERNETICS, PHILOSOPHY OF MIND, SELF-REPRODUCING AUTOMATON.   A.W.B.

von Wright, G. H. (b.1916), Finnish philosopher, one of the most influential analytic philosophers of the twentieth century. His early work, influenced by logical empiricism, is on logic, probability, and induction, including contributions in modal and deontic logic, the logic of norms and action, preference logic, tense logic, causality, and determinism. In the 1970s his ideas about the explanation of action helped to link the analytic tradition to Continental hermeneutics. His most important contribution is *A Treatise on Induction and Probability* (1951), which develops a system of eliminative induction using the concepts of necessary and sufficient condition.

In 1939 von Wright went to Cambridge to meet Broad, and he attended Wittgenstein's lectures. Regular discussions with Moore also had an impact on him. In 1948 von Wright succeeded Wittgenstein as professor at Cambridge University. After Wittgenstein's death in 1951, von Wright returned to Helsinki. Together with Anscombe and Rush Rhees, he became executor and editor of Wittgenstein's *Nachlass*. The study, organization, systematization, and publication of this exceptionally rich work became a lifelong task for him.

In his Cambridge years von Wright became interested in the logical properties of various modalities: alethic, deontic, epistemic. *An Essay in Modal Logic* (1951) studies, syntactically, various deductive systems of modal logic. That year he published his famous article "Deontic Logic" in *Mind*. It made him the founder of modern deontic logic. These logical works profoundly influenced analytic philosophy, especially action theory. Von Wright distinguishes technical oughts (means-ends relationships) from norms issued by a norm-authority. His *Norm and Action* (1963) discusses philosophical problems concerning the existence of norms and the truth of normative statements. His main work on metaethics is *The Varieties of Goodness* (1963).

In *Explanation and Understanding* (1971) he turned to philosophical problems concerning the human sciences. He defends a manipulation view of causality, where the concept of action is basic for that of cause: human action cannot be explained causally by laws, but must be understood intentionally. The basic model of intentionality is the practical syllogism, which explains action by a logical connection with wants and beliefs. This work, sometimes characterized as anti-positivist analytical hermeneutics, bridges analytic and Continental philosophy. His studies in truth, knowledge, modality, lawlikeness, causality, determinism, norms, and practical inference were published in 1983–84 in his *Philosophical Papers*.

In 1961 von Wright became a member of the Academy of Finland, the highest honor Finland gives to its scientists. Over many years he has written, in Swedish and Finnish, eloquent essays in the history of ideas and the philosophy of culture. He has become increasingly critical of the modern scientific-technological civilization, its narrowly instrumental concept of rationality, and its myth of progress. His public pleas for peace, human rights, and a more harmonious coexistence of human beings and nature have made him the most esteemed intellectual in the Scandinavian countries.

See also ACTION THEORY, DEONTIC LOGIC, EPISTEMIC LOGIC, PRACTICAL REASONING, PROBLEM OF INDUCTION, WITTGENSTEIN.

I.N.

Vorstellung. See PERCEPTION.

vortex theory. See DESCARTES.

voting paradox, the possibility that if there are three candidates, A, B, and C, for democratic choice, with at least three choosers, and the choosers are asked to make sequential choices among pairs of candidates, A could defeat B by a majority vote, B could defeat C, and C could defeat A. (This would be the outcome if the choosers' preferences were ABC, BCA, and CAB.) Hence, although each individual voter may have a clear preference ordering over the candidates, the collective may have cyclic preferences, so that individual and majoritarian collective preference orderings are not analogous. While this fact is not a logical paradox, it is perplexing to many analysts of social choice. It may also be morally perplexing in that it suggests majority rule can be quite capricious. For exam-

ple, suppose we vote sequentially over various pairs of candidates, with the winner at each step facing a new candidate. If the candidates are favored by cyclic majorities, the last candidate to enter the fray will win the final vote. Hence, control over the sequence of votes may determine the outcome.

It is easy to find cyclic preferences over such candidates as movies and other matters of taste. Hence, the problem of the voting paradox is clearly real and not merely a logical contrivance. But is it important? Institutions may block the generation of evidence for cyclic majorities by making choices pairwise and sequentially, as above. And some issues over which we vote provoke preference patterns that cannot produce cycles. For example, if our issue is one of unidimensional liberalism versus conservatism on some major political issue such as welfare programs, there may be no one who would prefer to spend both more and less money than what is spent in the status quo. Hence, everyone may display single-peaked preferences with preferences falling as we move in either direction (toward more money or toward less) from the peak. If all important issues and combinations of issues had this preference structure, the voting paradox would be unimportant. It is widely supposed by many public choice scholars that collective preferences are not single-peaked for many issues or, therefore, for combinations of issues. Hence, collective choices may be quite chaotic. What order they display may result from institutional manipulation. If this is correct, we may wonder whether democracy in the sense of the sovereignty of the electorate is a coherent notion.

See also ARROW'S PARADOX, DECISION THEORY, SOCIAL CHOICE THEORY.   R.Ha.

wang, pa, Chinese political titles meaning 'king' and 'hegemon', respectively. A true *wang* has the Mandate of Heaven and rules by *te* rather than by force. The institution of the *pa* developed during a period in which the kings of China lacked any real power. In order to bring an end to political chaos, the most powerful of the nobles was appointed *pa*, and effectively ruled while the *wang* reigned. During the Warring States period in China (403–221 B.C.), rulers began to assume the title of *wang* regardless of whether they had either the power of a *pa* or the right to rule of a *wang*. After this period, the title of Emperor (*ti* or *huang-ti*) replaced *wang*.   B.W.V.N.

Wang Ch'ung (A.D. 27–100?), Chinese philosopher, commonly regarded as the most independent-minded thinker in the Later Han period (25–220). He wrote the *Lun-heng* ("Balanced Inquiries"). Since Tung Chung-shu, Confucian doctrine of the unity of man and nature had degenerated into one of mutual influence, with talk of strange phenomena and calamities abounding. Wang Ch'ung cast serious doubts on such superstitions. He even dared to challenge the authority of Confucius and Mencius. His outlook was naturalistic. According to him, things in the world are produced by the interaction of material forces (*ch'i*). He rejected the teleological point of view and was fatalistic. **See also** TUNG CHUNG-SHU.   S.-h.L.

Wang Fu-chih (1619–92), Chinese philosopher and innovative Confucian thinker. Wang attacked the Neo-Confucian dualism of *li* (pattern) and *ch'i* (ether), arguing that *li* is the orderly structure of individual *ch'i* (implements/things and events), which are composed of *ch'i* (ether). Wang rejected all transcendental ontology and believed society evolves and improves over time. He is touted as a "materialist" by Marxist thinkers in contemporary China, though the term is hardly applicable, as is clear from his criticisms of Shao Yung. Wang attacked Shao's overly "objective" account of the world, arguing that all such formal descriptions fail because they disregard intuition, our only access to the lively, *shen* (spiritual) nature of the universe. **See also** CONFUCIANISM.   P.J.I.

Wang Pi (A.D. 226–49), Chinese philosopher of the *Hsüan hsüeh* (Mysterious Learning) School. He is described, along with thinkers like Kuo Hsiang, as a Neo-Taoist. Unlike Kuo, who believed the world to be self-generated, Wang claimed it arose from a mysterious unified state called *wu* (non-being). But like Kuo, Wang regarded Confucius as the one true sage, arguing that Lao Tzu and Chuang Tzu only "talked about" non-being, whereas Confucius embodied it. Wang is important for his development of the notion *li* (pattern) and his pioneering use of the paired concepts *t'i* (substance) and *yung* (function). His commentary on the *Tao Te Ching*, the oldest known, has had a profound and persistent influence on later Chinese thought. **See also** NEO-TAOISM, TAOISM.   P.J.I.

Wang Yang-ming (1472–1529), Chinese philosopher known for his doctrines of the unity of knowledge and action (*chih-hsing ho-i*) and *liang-chih* (innate knowledge of the good). Wang was also known as a sort of metaphysical idealist, anticipated by Lu Hsiang-shan, for his insistence on the quasi-identity of mind and *li* (principle, reason). The basic concern of Wang's philosophy is the question, How can one become a Confucian sage (*sheng*)? This is a question intelligible only in the light of understanding and commitment to the Confucian vision of *jen* or ideal of the universe as a moral community. Wang reminded his students that the concrete significance of such a vision in human life cannot be exhausted with any claim to finality. He stressed that one must get rid of any selfish desires in the pursuit of *jen*. Unlike Chu Hsi, Wang showed little interest in empirical inquiry concerning the rationales of existing things. For him, "things" are the objectives of moral will. To investigate things is to rectify one's mind, to get rid of evil thoughts and to do good. Rectification of the mind involves, in particular, an acknowledgment of the unity of moral knowledge and action (*chih-hsing ho-i*), an enlargement of the scope of moral concern in the light of the vision of *jen*, rather than extensive acquisition of factual knowledge. **See also** CHIH-HSING HO-I, CONFUCIANISM, LIANG-CHIH.   A.S.C.

want-belief model. See INTENTION.

Ward, James (1843–1925), English philosopher and psychologist. Influenced by Lotze, Herbart, and Brentano, Ward sharply criticized Bain's associationism and its allied nineteenth-century reductive naturalism. His psychology rejected the associationists' sensationism, which regarded mind as passive, capable only of sensory receptivity and composed solely of cognitive presentations. Ward emphasized the mind's inherent activity, asserting, like Kant, the prior existence of an inferred but necessarily existing ego or subject capable of feeling and, most importantly, of conation, shaping both experience and behavior by the willful exercise of attention. By its stress on attention and will, Ward's psychology resembles that of his contemporary, James. In his metaphysics, Ward resisted the naturalists' mechanistic materialism, proposing instead a teleological spiritualistic monism. While his criticisms of associationism and naturalism were telling, Ward was a transitional figure whose positive influence was limited. Although sympathetic to scientific psychology – he founded scientific psychology in Britain by establishing a psychology laboratory at Cambridge in 1891 – he, with his student Stout, represented the end of armchair psychology in Britain; through Stout he influenced the hormic psychology of McDougall. Ward's major work is "Psychology" (*Encyclopedia Britannica*, 9th ed., 1886), reworked as *Psychological Principles* (1918). **See also ASSO-CIATIONISM, JAMES, KANT.**   T.H.L.

warranted assertability. See DEWEY.

Warsaw School. See POLISH LOGIC.

wave mechanics. See QUANTUM MECHANICS.

wayward causal chain, a causal chain, referred to in a proposed causal analysis of a key concept, that goes awry. Causal analyses have been proposed for key concepts – e.g., reference, action, explanation, knowledge, artwork. There are two main cases of wayward (or deviant) causal chains that defeat a causal analysis: (1) those in which the prescribed causal route is followed, but the expected event does not occur; and (2) those in which the expected event occurs, but the prescribed causal route is not followed. Consider action. One proposed analysis is that a person's doing something is an action if and only if what he does is caused by his beliefs and desires. The possibility of wayward causal chains defeats

this analysis. For case (1), suppose, while climbing, John finds he is supporting another man on a rope. John wants to rid himself of this danger, and he believes that he can do so by loosening his grip. His belief and desire unnerve him, causing him to loosen his hold. The prescribed causal route was followed, but the ensuing event, his grip loosening, is not an action. For case (2), suppose Harry wants to kill his rich uncle, and he believes that he can find him at home. His beliefs and desires so agitate him that he drives recklessly. He hits and kills a pedestrian, who, by chance, is his uncle. The killing occurs, but without following the prescribed causal route; the killing was an accidental consequence of what Harry did. **See also ACTION THEORY.**   M.B.

weak law of large numbers. See BERNOULLI'S THEOREM, PROBABILITY.

weakness of will. See AKRASIA.

weak semantic completeness. See COMPLETENESS.

weak soundness. See SOUNDNESS.

weak supervenience. See SUPERVENIENCE.

Weber, Max (1864–1920), German social theorist and sociologist. Born in Berlin in a liberal and intellectual household, he taught economics in Heidelberg, where his circle included leading sociologists and philosophers such as Simmel and Lukacs. Although Weber gave up his professorship after a nervous breakdown in 1889, he remained important in public life, an adviser to the commissions that drafted the peace treaty at Versailles and the Weimar constitution.

Weber's social theory was influenced philosophically by both neo-Kantianism and Nietzsche, creating tensions in a theorist who focused much of his attention on Occidental rationalism and yet was a noncognitivist in ethics. He wrote many comparative studies on topics such as law and urbanization and a celebrated study of the cultural factors responsible for the rise of capitalism, *The Protestant Ethic and the Spirit of Capitalism* (1904). But his major, synthetic work in social theory is *Economy and Society* (1914); it includes a methodological introduction to the basic concepts of sociology that has been treated by many philosophers of social science.

One of the main theoretical goals of Weber's work is to understand how social processes become "rationalized," taking up certain themes of the German philosophy of history since Hegel as part of social theory. Culture, e.g., became rationalized in the process of the "disenchantment of worldviews" in the West, a process that Weber thought had "universal significance." But because of his goal-oriented theory of action and his noncognitivism in ethics, Weber saw rationalization exclusively in terms of the spread of purposive, or means–ends rationality (*Zweckrationalität*). Rational action means choosing the most effective means of achieving one's goals and implies judging the consequences of one's actions and choices. In contrast, value rationality (*Wertrationalität*) consists of actions oriented to ultimate ends, where considerations of consequences are irrelevant. Although such action is rational insofar as it directs and organizes human conduct, the choice of such ends or values themselves cannot be a matter for rational or scientific judgment. Indeed, for Weber this meant that politics was the sphere for the struggle between irreducibly competing ultimate ends, where "gods and demons fight it out" and charismatic leaders invent new gods and values. Professional politicians, however, should act according to an "ethics of responsibility" (*Verantwortungsethik*) aimed at consequences, and not an "ethics of conviction" (*Gesinnungsethik*) aimed at abstract principles or ultimate ends. Weber also believed that rationalization brought the separation of "value spheres" that can never again be unified by reason: art, science, and morality have their own "logics."

Weber's influential methodological writings reject positivist philosophy of science, yet call for "value neutrality." He accepts the neo-Kantian distinction, common in his day under the influence of Rickert, between the natural and the human sciences, between the *Natur-* and the *Geisteswissenschaften*. Because human social action is purposive and meaningful, the explanations of social sciences must be related to the values (*Wertbezogen*) and ideals of the actors it studies. Against positivism, Weber saw an ineliminable element of *Verstehen*, or understanding of meanings, in the methodology of the human sciences. For example, he criticized the legal positivist notion of behavioral conformity for failing to refer to actors' beliefs in legitimacy. But for Weber *Verstehen* is not intuition or empathy and does not exclude causal analysis; reasons can be causes. Thus, explanations in social science must have both causal and subjective adequacy. Weber also thought that adequate explanations of large-scale, macrosocial phenomena require the construction of *ideal types*, which abstract and

summarize the common features of complex, empirical phenomena such as "sects," "authority," or even "the Protestant ethic." Weberian ideal types are neither merely descriptive nor simply heuristic, but come at the end of inquiry through the successful theoretical analysis of diverse phenomena in various historical and cultural contexts.

Weber's analysis of rationality as the disenchantment of the world and the spread of purposive reason led him to argue that reason and progress could turn into their opposites, a notion that enormously influenced critical theory. Weber had a critical "diagnosis of the times" and a pessimistic philosophy of history. At the end of *The Protestant Ethic* Weber warns that rationalism is desiccating sources of value and constructing an "iron cage" of increasing bureaucratization, resulting in a loss of meaning and freedom in social life. According to Weber, these basic tensions of modern rationality cannot be resolved.

See also CRITICAL THEORY, DILTHEY, EXPLANATION, PHILOSOPHY OF THE SOCIAL SCIENCES.   J.Bo.

Weber's law. See FECHNER.

wedge argument. See SLIPPERY SLOPE ARGUMENT.

Weil, Simone (1909–43), French religious philosopher and writer. Born in Paris, Weil was one of the first women to graduate from the École Normale Supérieure, having earlier studied under the philosopher Alain. While teaching in various French *lycées* Weil became involved in radical leftist politics, and her early works concern social problems and labor. They also show an attempt to work out a theory of action as fundamental to human knowing. This is seen first in her diploma essay, "Science and Perception in Descartes," and later in her critique of Marx, capitalism, and technocracy in "Reflections concerning the Causes of Social Oppression and Liberty." Believing that humans cannot escape certain basic harsh necessities of embodied life, Weil sought to find a way by which freedom and dignity could be achieved by organizing labor in such a way that the mind could understand that necessity and thereby come to consent to it.

After a year of testing her theories by working in three factories in 1934–35, Weil's early optimism was shattered by the discovery of what she called "affliction" (*malheur*), a destruction of the human person to which one cannot consent. Three important religious experiences, however, caused her to attempt to put the problem into a larger context. By arguing that necessity obeys a transcendent goodness and then by using a kenotic model of Christ's incarnation and crucifixion, she tried to show that affliction can have a purpose and be morally enlightening. The key is the renunciation of any ultimate possession of power as well as the social personality constituted by that power. This is a process of "attention" and "decreation" by which one sheds the veil that otherwise separates one from appreciating goodness in anything but oneself, but most especially from God. She understands God as a goodness that is revealed in self-emptying and in incarnation, and creation as an act of renunciation and not power.

During her last months, while working for the Free French in London, Weil's social and religious interests came together, especially in *The Need for Roots*. Beginning with a critique of social rights and replacing it with obligations, Weil sought to show, on the one hand, how modern societies had illegitimately become the focus of value, and on the other hand, how cultures could be reconstructed so that they would root humans in something more ultimate than themselves. Returning to her earlier themes, Weil argued that in order for this rootedness to occur, physical labor must become the spiritual core of culture. Weil died of tuberculosis while this book was in progress.

Often regarded as mystical and syncretistic, Weil's philosophy owes much to an original reading of Plato (e.g., in *Intimations of Christianity Among the Ancient Greeks*) as well as to Marx, Alain, and Christianity. Recent studies, however, have also seen her as significantly contributing to social, moral, and religious philosophy. Her concern with problems of action and persons is not dissimilar to Wittgenstein's.

See also MARX, PHILOSOPHY OF RELIGION.
E.O.S.

welfare economics. See PHILOSOPHY OF ECONOMICS.

welfare liberalism. See POLITICAL PHILOSOPHY.

well-formed formula, a grammatically well-formed sentence or (structured) predicate of an artificial language of the sort studied by logicians. A well-formed formula is sometimes known as a *wff* (pronounced 'woof') or simply a *formula*. Delineating the formulas of a language involves providing it with a *syntax* or *grammar,* composed of both a vocabulary (a specification of the symbols from which the language is to be built,

sorted into grammatical categories) and *formation rules* (a purely formal or syntactical specification of which strings of symbols are grammatically well-formed and which are not). Formulas are classified as either *open* or *closed,* depending on whether or not they contain *free variables* (variables not bound by quantifiers). Closed formulas, such as (x) $(Fx \supset Gx)$, are sentences, the potential bearers of truth-values. Open formulas, such as $Fx \supset Gx$, are handled in any of three ways. On some accounts, these formulas are on a par with closed ones, the free variables being treated as names. On others, open formulas are (structured) predicates, the free variables being treated as place holders for terms. And on still other accounts, the free variables are regarded as implicitly bound by universal quantifiers, again making open formulas sentences. **See also** FORMAL LOGIC, LOGICAL CONSTANT, LOGICAL SYNTAX, QUANTIFICATION.   G.F.S.

well-ordered set. See MATHEMATICAL INDUCTION, SET-THEORETIC PARADOXES.

well ordering. See ORDERING.

Weltanschauung. See DILTHEY.

Wertrationalität. See WEBER.

Westermarck, Edward (1862–1939), Finnish anthropologist and philosopher who spent his life studying the mores and morals of cultures. His main works, *The Origin and Development of Moral Ideas* (1906–08) and *Ethical Relativity* (1932), attack the idea that moral principles express objective value. In defending ethical relativism, he argued that moral judgments are based not on intellectual but on emotional grounds. He admitted that cultural variability in itself does not prove ethical relativism, but contended that the fundamental differences are so comprehensive and deep as to constitute a strong presumption in favor of relativism. **See also** ETHICAL OBJECTIVISM, RELATIVISM.   L.P.P.

wff. See WELL-FORMED FORMULA.

wheel of rebirth. See BUDDHISM, SAṂSĀRA.

Whewell, William (1794–1866), English historian, astronomer, and philosopher of science. He was a master of Trinity College, Cambridge (1841–66). Francis Bacon's early work on induction was furthered by Whewell, J. F. W. Herschel, and J. S. Mill, who attempted to create a logic of induction, a methodology that can both discover generalizations about experience and prove them to be necessary.

Whewell's theory of scientific method is based on his reading of the history of the inductive sciences. He thought that induction began with a non-inferential act, the superimposition of an idea on data, a "colligation," a way of seeing facts in a "new light." Colligations generalize over data, and must satisfy three "tests of truth." First, colligations must be empirically adequate; they must account for the given data. Any number of ideas may be adequate to explain given data, so a more severe test is required. Second, because colligations introduce generalizations, they must apply to events or properties of objects not yet given: they must provide successful predictions, thereby enlarging the evidence in favor of the colligation. Third, the best inductions are those where evidence for various hypotheses originally thought to cover unrelated kinds of data "jumps together," providing a *consilience* of inductions. Consilience characterizes those theories achieving large measures of simplicity, generality, unification, and deductive strength. Furthermore, consilience is a test of the necessary truth of theories, which implies that what many regard as merely pragmatic virtues of theories like simplicity and unifying force have an epistemic status. Whewell thus provides a strong argument for scientific realism. Whewell's examples of consilient theories are Newton's theory of universal gravitation, which covers phenomena as seemingly diverse as the motions of the heavenly bodies and the motions of the tides, and the undulatory theory of light, which explains both the polarization of light by crystals and the colors of fringes. There is evidence that Whewell's methodology was employed by Maxwell, who designed the influential Cavendish Laboratories at Cambridge. Peirce and Mach favored Whewell's account of method over Mill's empiricist theory of induction.

See also EXPLANATION, PHILOSOPHY OF SCIENCE.   R.E.B.

Whichcote, Benjamin. See CAMBRIDGE PLATONISTS.

Whitehead, Alfred North (1861–1947), English mathematician, logician, philosopher of science, and metaphysician. Educated first at the Sherborne School in Dorsetshire and then at Trinity College, Cambridge, Whitehead emerged as a first-class mathematician with a rich general background. In 1885 he became a fellow of Trinity College and remained there in a teaching role until 1910. In the early 1890s Bertrand Russell entered Trinity College as a student in mathematics; by the beginning of the new century Russell had become not only a student and friend but a colleague of Whitehead's at Trinity College. Each had written a first book on algebra (Whitehead's *A Treatise on Universal Algebra* won him election to the Royal Society in 1903). When they discovered that their projected second books largely overlapped, they undertook a collaboration on a volume that they estimated would take about a year to write; in fact, it was a decade later that the three volumes of their ground-breaking *Principia Mathematica* appeared, launching symbolic logic in its modern form.

In the second decade of this century Whitehead and Russell drifted apart; their responses to World War I differed radically, and their intellectual interests and orientations diverged. Whitehead's London period (1910–24) is often viewed as the second phase of a three-phase career. His association with the University of London involved him in practical issues affecting the character of working-class education. For a decade (1914–24) Whitehead held a professorship at the Imperial College of Science and Technology and also served as dean of the Faculty of Science in the University, chair of the Academic Council (which managed educational affairs in London), and chair of the council that managed Goldsmith's College. His book *The Aims of Education* (1928) is a collection of essays largely growing out of reflections on the experiences of these years. Intellectually, Whitehead's interests were moving toward issues in the philosophy of science. In the years 1919–22 he published *An Enquiry Concerning the Principles of Natural Knowledge, The Concept of Nature,* and *The Principle of Relativity* – the third led to his later (1931) election as a fellow of the British Academy.

In 1924, at the age of sixty-three, Whitehead made a dramatic move, both geographically and intellectually, to launch phase three of his career: never having formally studied philosophy in his life, he agreed to become professor of philosophy at Harvard University, a position he held until retirement in 1937. The accompanying intellectual shift was a move from philosophy of science to metaphysics. The earlier investigations had assumed the self-containedness of nature: "nature is closed to mind." The philosophy of nature examined nature at the level of abstraction entailed by this assumption. Whitehead had come to regard philosophy as "the critic of abstractions," a notion introduced in *Science and the Modern World* (1925). This book traced the intertwined emergence of Newtonian science and its philosophical presuppositions. It noted that with the development of the theory of relativity in the twentieth century, scientific understanding had left behind the Newtonian conceptuality that had generated the still-dominant philosophical assumptions, and that those philosophical assumptions considered in themselves had become inadequate to explicate our full concrete experience. Philosophy as the critic of abstractions must recognize the limitations of a stance that assumes that nature is closed to mind, and must push deeper, beyond such an abstraction, to create a scheme of ideas more in harmony with scientific developments and able to do justice to human beings as part of nature. *Science and the Modern World* merely outlines what such a philosophy might be; in 1929 Whitehead published his magnum opus, titled *Process and Reality.* In this volume, subtitled "An Essay in Cosmology," his metaphysical understanding is given its final form. It is customary to regard this book as the central document of what has become known as *process philosophy,* though Whitehead himself frequently spoke of his system of ideas as the *philosophy of organism.*

Process and Reality begins with a sentence that sheds a great deal of light upon Whitehead's metaphysical orientation: "These lectures are based upon a recurrence to that phase of philosophic thought which began with Descartes and ended with Hume." Descartes, adapting the classical notion of substance to his own purposes, begins a "phase of philosophic thought" by assuming there are two distinct, utterly different kinds of substance, mind and matter, each requiring nothing but itself in order to exist. This assumption launches the reign of epistemology within philosophy: if knowing begins with the experiencing of a mental substance capable of existing by itself and cut off from everything external to it, then the philosophical challenge is to try to justify the claim to establish contact with a reality external to it. The phrase "and ended with Hume" expresses Whitehead's conviction that Hume (and more elegantly, he notes, Santayana) showed that if one begins with Descartes's metaphysical assumptions, skepticism is inevitable. Contemporary philosophers have talked about the end of philosophy. From Whitehead's perspective such talk presupposes a far too narrow view of the nature of philosophy. It is true that a phase of philosophy has ended, a phase dominated by epistemology. Whitehead's response is to offer the dictum that all epistemological difficulties are at bottom only camou-

flaged metaphysical difficulties. One must return to that moment of Cartesian beginning and replace the substance metaphysics with an orientation that avoids the epistemological trap, meshes harmoniously with the scientific understandings that have displaced the much simpler physics of Descartes's day, and is consonant with the facts of evolution. These are the considerations that generate Whitehead's fundamental metaphysical category, the category of an *actual occasion.*

An actual occasion is not an enduring, substantial entity. Rather, it is a process of becoming, a process of weaving together the "prehensions" (a primitive form of 'apprehension' meant to indicate a "taking account of," or "feeling," devoid of conscious awareness) of the actual occasions that are in the immediate past. Whitehead calls this process of weaving together the inheritances of the past "concrescence." An actual entity *is* its process of concrescence, its process of growing together into a unified perspective on its immediate past. (The seeds of Whitehead's epistemological realism are planted in these fundamental first moves: "The philosophy of organism is the inversion of Kant's philosophy. . . . For Kant, the world emerges from the subject; for the philosophy of organism, the subject emerges from the world.") It is customary to compare an actual occasion with a Leibnizian monad, with the caveat that whereas a monad is windowless, an actual occasion is "all window." It is as though one were to take Aristotle's system of categories and ask what would result if the category of substance were displaced from its position of preeminence by the category of relation – the result would, *mutatis mutandis,* be an understanding of being somewhat on the model of a Whiteheadian actual occasion.

In moving from Descartes's dualism of mental substance and material substance to his own notion of an actual entity, Whitehead has been doing philosophy conceived of as the critique of abstractions. He holds that both mind and matter are abstractions from the concretely real. They are important abstractions, necessary for everyday thought and, of supreme importance, absolutely essential in enabling the seventeenth through nineteenth centuries to accomplish their magnificent advances in scientific thinking. Indeed, Whitehead, in his philosophy of science phase, by proceeding as though "nature is closed to mind," was operating with those selfsame abstractions. He came to see that while these abstractions were indispensable for certain kinds of investigations, they were, at the philosophical level, as Hume had demonstrated, a disaster. In considering mind and matter to be ontological ultimates, Descartes had committed what Whitehead termed the *fallacy of misplaced concreteness*. The category of an actual occasion designates the fully real, the fully concrete. The challenge for such an orientation, the challenge that *Process and Reality* is designed to meet, is so to describe actual occasions that it is intelligible how collections of actual occasions, termed "nexūs" or societies, emerge, exhibiting the characteristics we find associated with "minds" and "material structures." Perhaps most significantly, if this challenge is met successfully, biology will be placed, in the eyes of philosophy, on an even footing with physics; metaphysics will do justice both to human beings and to human beings as a part of nature; and such vexing contemporary problem areas as animal rights and environmental ethics will appear in a new light.

Whitehead's last two books, *Adventures of Ideas* (1933) and *Modes of Thought* (1938), are less technical and more lyrical than is *Process and Reality*. *Adventures of Ideas* is clearly the more significant of these two. It presents a philosophical study of the notion of civilization. It holds that the social changes in a civilization are driven by two sorts of forces: brute, senseless agencies of compulsion on the one hand, and formulated aspirations and articulated beliefs on the other. (These two sorts of forces are epitomized by barbarians and Christianity in the ancient Roman world and by steam and democracy in the world of the industrial revolution.) Whitehead's focal point in *Adventures of Ideas* is aspirations, beliefs, and ideals as instruments of change. In particular, he is concerned to articulate the ideals and aspirations appropriate to our own era. The character of such ideals and aspirations at any moment is limited by the philosophical understandings available at that moment, because in their struggle for release and efficacy such ideals and aspirations can appear only in the forms permitted by the available philosophical discourse. In the final section of *Adventures of Ideas* Whitehead presents a statement of ideals and aspirations fit for our era as his own philosophy of organism allows them to take shape and be articulated. The notions of beauty, truth, adventure, zest, Eros, and peace are given a content drawn from the technical understandings elaborated in *Process and Reality*. But in *Adventures of Ideas* a less technical language is used, a language reminiscent of the poetic imagery found in the style of Plato's *Republic*, a language making the ideas accessible to readers who have not mas-

tered *Process and Reality*, but at the same time far richer and more meaningful to those who have. Whitehead notes in *Adventures of Ideas* that Plato's later thought "circles round the interweaving of seven main notions, namely, The Ideas, The Physical Elements, The Psyche, The Eros, The Harmony, The Mathematical Relations, The Receptacle. These notions are as important for us now, as they were then at the dawn of the modern world, when civilizations of the old type were dying." Whitehead uses these notions in quite novel and modern ways; one who is unfamiliar with his metaphysics can get something of what he means as he speaks of the Eros of the Universe, but if one is familiar from *Process and Reality* with the notions of the Primordial Nature of God and the Consequent Nature of God then one sees much deeper into the meanings present in *Adventures of Ideas*.

Whitehead was not religious in any narrow, doctrinal, sectarian sense. He explicitly likened his stance to that of Aristotle, dispassionately considering the requirements of his metaphysical system as they refer to the question of the existence and nature of God. Whitehead's thoughts on these matters are most fully developed in Chapter 11 of *Science and the Modern World*, in the final chapter of *Process and Reality*, and in *Religion in the Making* (1926). These thoughts are expressed at a high level of generality. Perhaps because of this, a large part of the interest generated by Whitehead's thought has been within the community of theologians. His ideas fairly beg for elaboration and development in the context of particular modes of religious understanding. It is as though many modern theologians, recalling the relation between the theology of Aquinas and the metaphysics of Aristotle, cannot resist the temptation to play Aquinas to Whitehead's Aristotle. Process theology, or Neo-Classical Theology as it is referred to by Hartshorne, one of its leading practitioners, has been the arena within which a great deal of clarification and development of Whitehead's ideas has occurred.

Whitehead was a gentle man, soft-spoken, never overbearing or threatening. He constantly encouraged students to step out on their own, to develop their creative capacities. His concern not to inhibit students made him a notoriously easy grader; it was said that an A-minus in one of his courses was equivalent to failure. Lucien Price's *Dialogues of Alfred North Whitehead* chronicles many evenings of discussion in the Whitehead household. He there described Whitehead as follows:

his face, serene, luminous, often smiling, the complexion pink and white, the eyes brilliant blue, clear and candid as a child's yet with the depth of the sage, often laughing or twinkling with humour. And there was his figure, slender, frail, and bent with its lifetime of a scholar's toil. Always benign, there was not a grain of ill will anywhere in him; for all his formidable armament, never a wounding word.

See also LEIBNIZ, METAPHYSICS, PROCESS THEOLOGY, RUSSELL.   D.W.S.

white horse paradox. See KUNG-SUN LUNG TZU.

wide content. See PHILOSOPHY OF MIND.

wide reflective equilibrium. See REFLECTIVE EQUILIBRIUM.

will. See VOLITION.

will, general. See ROUSSEAU.

will, weakness of. See AKRASIA.

Wille. See KANT.

William Ockham. See OCKHAM.

William of Alnwick (d. 1333), English Franciscan theologian. William studied under Duns Scotus at Paris, and wrote the *Reportatio Parisiensia*, a central source for Duns Scotus's teaching. In his own works, William opposed Scotus on the univocity of being and *haecceitas*. Some of his views were attacked by Ockham. **See also** DUNS SCOTUS, HAECCEITY.   J.Lo.

William of Auvergne (c.1190–1249), French philosopher who was born in Aurillac, taught at Paris, and became bishop of Paris in 1228. Critical of the new Aristotelianism of his time, he insisted that the soul is an individual, immortal form of intellectual activity alone, so that a second form was needed for the body and sensation. Though he rejected the notion of an agent intellect, he described the soul as a mirror that reflects both exemplary ideas in God's mind and sensible singulars. He conceived being as something common to everything that is, after the manner of Duns Scotus, but rejected the Avicennan doctrine that God necessarily produces the universe, arguing that His creative activity is free of all determination. He is the first example of the

complex of ideas we call Augustinianism, which would pass on through Alexander of Hales to Bonaventure and other Franciscans, forming a point of departure for the philosophy of Duns Scotus. **See also** AUGUSTINE, DUNS SCOTUS.   J.Lo.

William of Auxerre (c.1140–1231), French theologian and renowned teacher of grammar, arts, and theology at the University of Paris. In 1231 he was appointed by Pope Gregory IX to a commission charged with editing Aristotle's writings for doctrinal purity. The commission never submitted a report, perhaps partly due to William's death later that same year.

William's major work, the *Summa aurea* (1215–20), represents one of the earliest systematic attempts to reconcile the Augustinian and Aristotelian traditions in medieval philosophy. William tempers, e.g., the Aristotelian concession that human cognition begins with the reception in the material intellect of a species or sensible representation from a corporeal thing, with the Augustinian idea that it is not possible to understand the principles of any discipline without an interior, supernatural illumination. He also originated the theological distinction between perfect happiness, which is uncreated and proper to God, and imperfect happiness, which pertains to human beings. William was also one of the first to express what became, in later centuries, the important distinction between God's absolute and ordained powers, taking, with Gilbert of Poitiers, the view that God could, absolutely speaking, change the past.

The *Summa aurea* helped shape the thought of several important philosophers and theologians who were active later in the century, including Albertus Magnus, Bonaventure, and Aquinas. William remained an authority in theological discussions throughout the fourteenth and fifteenth centuries.

See also ARISTOTLE, AUGUSTINE.   J.A.Z.

William of Heytesbury. See HEYTESBURY.

William of Moerbeke (c.1215–1286), French scholar who was the most important thirteenth-century translator from Greek into Latin of works in philosophy and natural science. Having joined the Dominicans and spent some time in Greek-speaking territories, William served at the papal court and then as (Catholic) archbishop of Corinth (1278–c.1286). But he worked from the 1260s on as a careful and literal-minded translator. William was the first to render into Latin some of the most important works by Aristotle, including the *Politics, Poetics,* and *History of Animals.* He retranslated or revised earlier translations of several other Aristotelian works. William also provided the first Latin versions of commentaries on Aristotle by Alexander of Aphrodisias, Themistius, Ammonius, John Philoponus, and Simplicius, not to mention his efforts on behalf of Greek optics, mathematics, and medicine. When William provided the first Latin translation of Proclus's *Elements of Theology,* Western readers could at last recognize the *Liber de causis* as an Arabic compilation from Proclus rather than as a work by Aristotle.   M.D.J.

William of Sherwood. See SHERWOOD.

Williams, Bernard (b.1929), English philosopher who has made major contributions to many fields but is primarily known as a moral philosopher. His approach to ethics, set out in *Ethics and the Limits of Philosophy* (1985), is characterized by a wide-ranging skepticism, directed mainly at the capacity of academic moral philosophy to further the aim of reflectively living an ethical life.

One line of skeptical argument attacks the very idea of practical reason. Attributions of practical reasons to a particular agent must, in Williams's view, be attributions of states that can potentially explain the agent's action. Therefore such reasons must be either within the agent's existing set of motivations or within the revised set of motivations that the agent would acquire upon sound reasoning. Williams argues from these minimal assumptions that this view of reasons as internal reasons undermines the idea of reason itself being a source of authority over practice.

Williams's connected skepticism about the claims of moral realism is based both on his general stance toward realism and on his view of the nature of modern societies. In opposition to internal realism, Williams has consistently argued that reflection on our conception of the world allows one to develop a conception of the world maximally independent of our peculiar ways of conceptualizing reality – an absolute conception of the world. Such absoluteness is, he argues, an inappropriate aspiration for ethical thought. Our ethical thinking is better viewed as one way of structuring a form of ethical life than as the ethical truth about how life is best lived. The pervasive reflectiveness and radical pluralism of modern societies makes them inhospitable contexts for viewing ethical concepts as making knowledge available to groups of concept users.

Modernity has produced at the level of theory a distortion of our ethical practice, namely a conception of the morality system. This view is reductionist, is focused centrally on obligations, and rests on various fictions about responsibility and blame that Williams challenges in such works as *Shame and Necessity* (1993). Much academic moral philosophy, in his view, is shaped by the covert influence of the morality system, and such distinctively modern outlooks as Kantianism and utilitarianism monopolize the terms of contemporary debate with insufficient attention to their origin in a distorted view of the ethical.

Williams's views are not skeptical through and through; he retains a commitment to the values of truth, truthfulness in a life, and individualism. His most recent work, which thematizes the long-implicit influence of Nietzsche on his ethical philosophy, explicitly offers a vindicatory "genealogical" narrative for these ideals.

See also EXTERNALISM, MORALITY, MORAL REALISM, NIETZSCHE, PRACTICAL REASON.
                                                                 A.T.

Willkür. See KANT.

will to believe. See JAMES.

will to power. See NIETZSCHE.

Wilson, John Cook (1849–1915), English logician, an Oxford realist. Cook Wilson studied with T. H. Green before becoming Wykeham Professor of Logic at Oxford and leading the Oxford reaction against the then entrenched absolute idealism. More influential as a teacher than as a writer, his major work, *Statement and Inference,* was posthumously reconstructed from drafts of papers, philosophical correspondence, and an extensive set of often inconsistent lectures for his logic courses. A staunch critic of mathematical logic, Cook Wilson conceived of logic as the study of thinking, an activity unified by the fact that thinking either is knowledge or depends on knowledge. He claimed that knowledge involves apprehending an object that in most cases is independent of the act of apprehension and that knowledge is indefinable without circularity, views he defended by appealing to common usage. Many of Cook Wilson's ideas were disseminated by H. W. B. Joseph (1867–1944), especially in his *Introduction to Logic* (1906). Rejecting "symbolic logic," Joseph attempted to reinvigorate traditional logic conceived along Cook Wilsonian lines. To do so he combined a careful exposition of Aristotle with insights drawn from idealistic logicians. Besides Joseph, Cook Wilson decisively influenced a generation of Oxford philosophers including Prichard and Ross. J.W.A.

Windelband, Wilhelm (1848–1915), German philosopher and originator of Baden neo-Kantianism. He studied under Kuno Fischer (1824–1907) and Lotze, and was professor at Zürich, Freiburg, Strasbourg, and Heidelberg. Windelband gave Baden neo-Kantianism its distinctive mark of Kantian axiology as the core of critical philosophy. He is widely recognized for innovative work in the history of philosophy, in which problems rather than individual philosophers are the focus and organizing principle of exposition. He is also known for his distinction, first drawn in "Geschichte und Naturwissenschaft" ("History and Natural Science," 1894), between the nomothetic knowledge that most natural sciences seek (the discovery of general laws in order to master nature) and the idiographic knowledge that the historical sciences pursue (description of individual and unique aspects of reality with the aim of self-affirmation). His most important student, and successor at Heidelberg, was Heinrich Rickert (1863–1936), who made lasting contributions to the methodology of the historical sciences. **See also** NEO-KANTIANISM. H.v.d.L.

wisdom, an understanding of the highest principles of things that functions as a guide for living a truly exemplary human life. From the pre-Socratics through Plato this was a unified notion. But Aristotle introduced a distinction between theoretical wisdom (*sophia*) and practical wisdom (*phronesis*), the former being the intellectual virtue that disposed one to grasp the nature of reality in terms of its ultimate causes (metaphysics), the latter being the ultimate practical virtue that disposed one to make sound judgments bearing on the conduct of life. The former invoked a contrast between deep understanding versus wide information, whereas the latter invoked a contrast between sound judgment and mere technical facility. This distinction between theoretical and practical wisdom persisted through the Middle Ages and continues to our own day, as is evident in our use of the term 'wisdom' to designate both knowledge of the highest kind and the capacity for sound judgment in matters of conduct. **See also** ARISTOTLE, PRACTICAL REASON, THEORETICAL REASON. C.F.D.

Wittgenstein, Ludwig (1889–1951), Austrian-born British philosopher, one of the most original and challenging philosophical writers of the twentieth century. Born in Vienna into an assimilated family of Jewish extraction, he went to England as a student and eventually became a protégé of Russell's at Cambridge. He returned to Austria at the beginning of World War I, but went back to Cambridge in 1928 and taught there as a fellow and professor. Despite spending much of his professional life in England, Wittgenstein never lost contact with his Austrian background, and his writings combine in a unique way ideas derived from both the Anglo-Saxon and the Continental European tradition. His thought is strongly marked by a deep skepticism about philosophy, but he retained the conviction that there was something important to be rescued from the traditional enterprise. In his *Blue Book* (1958) he referred to his own work as "one of the heirs of the subject that used to be called philosophy."

What strikes readers first when they look at Wittgenstein's writings is the peculiar form of their composition. They are generally made up of short individual notes that are most often numbered in sequence and, in the more finished writings, evidently selected and arranged with the greatest care. Those notes range from fairly technical discussions on matters of logic, the mind, meaning, understanding, acting, seeing, mathematics, and knowledge, to aphoristic observations about ethics, culture, art, and the meaning of life. Because of their wide-ranging character, their unusual perspective on things, and their often intriguing style, Wittgenstein's writings have proved to appeal to both professional philosophers and those interested in philosophy in a more general way. The writings as well as his unusual life and personality have already produced a large body of interpretive literature. But given his uncompromising stand, it is questionable whether his thought will ever be fully integrated into academic philosophy. It is more likely that, like Pascal and Nietzsche, he will remain an uneasy presence in philosophy.

From an early date onward Wittgenstein was greatly influenced by the idea that philosophical problems can be resolved by paying attention to the working of language – a thought he may have gained from Fritz Mauthner's *Beiträge zu einer Kritik der Sprache* (1901–02). Wittgenstein's affinity to Mauthner is, indeed, evident in all phases of his philosophical development, though it is particularly noticeable in his later thinking.

Until recently it has been common to divide Wittgenstein's work into two sharply distinct phases, separated by a prolonged period of dormancy. According to this schema the early ("Tractarian") period is that of the *Tractatus Logico-Philosophicus* (1921), which Wittgenstein wrote in the trenches of World War I, and the later period that of the *Philosophical Investigations* (1953), which he composed between 1936 and 1948. But the division of his work into these two periods has proved misleading. First, in spite of obvious changes in his thinking, Wittgenstein remained throughout skeptical toward traditional philosophy and persisted in channeling philosophical questioning in a new direction. Second, the common view fails to account for the fact that even between 1920 and 1928, when Wittgenstein abstained from actual work in philosophy, he read widely in philosophical and semiphilosophical authors, and between 1928 and 1936 he renewed his interest in philosophical work and wrote copiously on philosophical matters. The posthumous publication of texts such as *The Blue and Brown Books, Philosophical Grammar, Philosophical Remarks,* and *Conversations with the Vienna Circle* has led to acknowledgment of a middle period in Wittgenstein's development, in which he explored a large number of philosophical issues and viewpoints – a period that served as a transition between the early and the late work.

Early period. As the son of a greatly successful industrialist and engineer, Wittgenstein first studied engineering in Berlin and Manchester, and traces of that early training are evident throughout his writing. But his interest shifted soon to pure mathematics and the foundations of mathematics, and in pursuing questions about them he became acquainted with Russell and Frege and their work. The two men had a profound and lasting effect on Wittgenstein even when he later came to criticize and reject their ideas. That influence is particularly noticeable in the *Tractatus,* which can be read as an attempt to reconcile Russell's atomism with Frege's apriorism. But the book is at the same time moved by quite different and non-technical concerns. For even before turning to systematic philosophy Wittgenstein had been profoundly moved by Schopenhauer's thought as it is spelled out in *The World as Will and Representation,* and while he was serving as a soldier in World War I, he renewed his interest in Schopenhauer's metaphysical, ethical, aesthetic, and mystical outlook. The resulting confluence of ideas is evident in the *Tractatus Logico-Philosophicus* and gives the book its peculiar character.

Composed in a dauntingly severe and compressed style, the book attempts to show that traditional philosophy rests entirely on a misunderstanding of "the logic of our language." Following in Frege's and Russell's footsteps, Wittgenstein argued that every meaningful sentence must have a precise logical structure. That structure may, however, be hidden beneath the clothing of the grammatical appearance of the sentence and may therefore require the most detailed analysis in order to be made evident. Such analysis, Wittgenstein was convinced, would establish that every meaningful sentence is either a truth-functional composite of another simpler sentence or an atomic sentence consisting of a concatenation of simple names. He argued further that every atomic sentence is a logical picture of a possible state of affairs, which must, as a result, have exactly the same formal structure as the atomic sentence that depicts it. He employed this "picture theory of meaning" – as it is usually called – to derive conclusions about the nature of the world from his observations about the structure of the atomic sentences. He postulated, in particular, that the world must itself have a precise logical structure, even though we may not be able to determine it completely. He also held that the world consists primarily of facts, corresponding to the true atomic sentences, rather than of things, and that those facts, in turn, are concatenations of simple objects, corresponding to the simple names of which the atomic sentences are composed. Because he derived these metaphysical conclusions from his view of the nature of language, Wittgenstein did not consider it essential to describe what those simple objects, their concatenations, and the facts consisting of them are actually like. As a result, there has been a great deal of uncertainty and disagreement among interpreters about their character.

The propositions of the *Tractatus* are for the most part concerned with spelling out Wittgenstein's account of the logical structure of language and the world and these parts of the book have understandably been of most interest to philosophers who are primarily concerned with questions of symbolic logic and its applications. But for Wittgenstein himself the most important part of the book consisted of the negative conclusions about philosophy that he reaches at the end of his text: in particular, that all sentences that are not atomic pictures of concatenations of objects or truth-functional composites of such are strictly speaking meaningless. Among these he included all the propositions of ethics and aesthetics, all propositions dealing with the meaning of life, all propositions of logic, indeed all philosophical propositions, and finally all the propositions of the *Tractatus* itself. These are all strictly meaningless; they aim at saying something important, but what they try to express in words can only show itself.

As a result Wittgenstein concluded that anyone who understood what the *Tractatus* was saying would finally discard its propositions as senseless, that she would throw away the ladder after climbing up on it. Someone who reached such a state would have no more temptation to pronounce philosophical propositions. She would see the world rightly and would then also recognize that the only strictly meaningful propositions are those of natural science; but those could never touch what was really important in human life, the mystical. That would have to be contemplated in silence. For "whereof one cannot speak, thereof one must be silent," as the last proposition of the *Tractatus* declared.

Middle period. It was only natural that Wittgenstein should not embark on an academic career after he had completed that work. Instead he trained to be a school teacher and taught primary school for a number of years in the mountains of lower Austria. In the mid-1920s he also built a house for his sister; this can be seen as an attempt to give visual expression to the logical, aesthetic, and ethical ideas of the *Tractatus*. In those years he developed a number of interests seminal for his later development. His school experience drew his attention to the way in which children learn language and to the whole process of enculturation. He also developed an interest in psychology and read Freud and others. Though he remained hostile to Freud's theoretical explanations of his psychoanalytic work, he was fascinated with the analytic practice itself and later came to speak of his own work as therapeutic in character. In this period of dormancy Wittgenstein also became acquainted with the members of the Vienna Circle, who had adopted his *Tractatus* as one of their key texts. For a while he even accepted the positivist principle of meaning advocated by the members of that Circle, according to which the meaning of a sentence is the method of its verification. This he would later modify into the more generous claim that the meaning of a sentence is its use.

Wittgenstein's most decisive step in his middle period was to abandon the belief of the *Tractatus* that meaningful sentences must have a precise (hidden) logical structure and the accompanying belief that this structure corresponds to the logical structure of the facts depicted by those sentences. The *Tractatus* had, indeed, proceeded on the assumption that all the different symbolic devices that can describe the world must be constructed according to the same underlying logic. In a sense, there was then only one meaningful language in the *Tractatus*, and from it one was supposed to be able to read off the logical structure of the world. In the middle period Wittgenstein concluded that this doctrine constituted a piece of unwarranted metaphysics and that the *Tractatus* was itself flawed by what it had tried to combat, i.e., the misunderstanding of the logic of language. Where he had previously held it possible to ground metaphysics on logic, he now argued that metaphysics leads the philosopher into complete darkness. Turning his attention back to language he concluded that almost everything he had said about it in the *Tractatus* had been in error. There were, in fact, many different languages with many different structures that could meet quite different specific needs. Language was not strictly held together by logical structure, but consisted, in fact, of a multiplicity of simpler substructures or *language games*. Sentences could not be taken to be logical pictures of facts and the simple components of sentences did not all function as names of simple objects.

These new reflections on language served Wittgenstein, in the first place, as an aid to thinking about the nature of the human mind, and specifically about the relation between private experience and the physical world. Against the existence of a Cartesian mental substance, he argued that the word 'I' did not serve as a name of anything, but occurred in expressions meant to draw attention to a particular body. For a while, at least, he also thought he could explain the difference between private experience and the physical world in terms of the existence of two languages, a primary language of experience and a secondary language of physics. This dual-language view, which is evident in both the *Philosophical Remarks* and *The Blue Book*, Wittgenstein was to give up later in favor of the assumption that our grasp of inner phenomena is dependent on the existence of outer *criteria*. From the mid-1930s onward he also renewed his interest in the philosophy of mathematics. In contrast to Frege and Russell, he argued strenuously that no part of mathematics is reducible purely to logic. Instead he set out to describe mathematics as part of our natural history and as consisting of a number of diverse language games. He also insisted that the meaning of those games depended on the uses to which the mathematical formulas were put. Applying the principle of verification to mathematics, he held that the meaning of a mathematical formula lies in its proof. These remarks on the philosophy of mathematics have remained among Wittgenstein's most controversial and least explored writings.

Later period. Wittgenstein's middle period was characterized by intensive philosophical work on a broad but quickly changing front. By 1936, however, his thinking was finally ready to settle down once again into a steadier pattern, and he now began to elaborate the views for which he became most famous. Where he had constructed his earlier work around the logic devised by Frege and Russell, he now concerned himself mainly with the actual working of ordinary language. This brought him close to the tradition of British common sense philosophy that Moore had revived and made him one of the godfathers of the ordinary language philosophy that was to flourish in Oxford in the 1950s. In the *Philosophical Investigations* Wittgenstein emphasized that there are countless different uses of what we call "symbols," "words," and "sentences." The task of philosophy is to gain a perspicuous view of those multiple uses and thereby to dissolve philosophical and metaphysical puzzles. These puzzles were the result of insufficient attention to the working of language and could be resolved only by carefully retracing the linguistic steps by which they had been reached.

Wittgenstein thus came to think of philosophy as a descriptive, analytic, and ultimately *therapeutic* practice. In the *Investigations* he set out to show how common philosophical views about meaning (including the logical atomism of the *Tractatus*), about the nature of concepts, about logical necessity, about rule-following, and about the mind–body problem were all the product of an insufficient grasp of how language works. In one of the most influential passages of the book he argued that concept words do not denote sharply circumscribed concepts, but are meant to mark *family resemblances* between the things labeled with the concept. He also held that logical necessity results from linguistic convention and that rules cannot determine their own applications, that rule-following presupposes the existence of regular practices. Furthermore, the words of our language have meaning only insofar as there exist public criteria for their correct application. As a consequence, he argued, there cannot be a completely private language, i.e., a language that in principle can be used only to speak about one's own inner experience.

This private language argument has caused much discussion. Interpreters have disagreed not only over the structure of the argument and where it occurs in Wittgenstein's text, but also over the question whether he meant to say that language is necessarily social. Because he said that to speak of inner experiences there must be external and publicly available criteria, he has often been taken to be advocating a logical behaviorism, but nowhere does he, in fact, deny the existence of inner states. What he says is merely that our understanding of someone's pain is connected to the existence of natural and linguistic expressions of pain.

In the *Philosophical Investigations* Wittgenstein repeatedly draws attention to the fact that language must be learned. This learning, he says, is fundamentally a process of inculcation and drill. In learning a language the child is initiated in a form of life. In Wittgenstein's later work the notion of form of life serves to identify the whole complex of natural and cultural circumstances presupposed by our language and by a particular understanding of the world. He elaborated those ideas in notes on which he worked between 1948 and his death in 1951 and which are now published under the title *On Certainty.* He insisted in them that every belief is always part of a system of beliefs that together constitute a worldview. All confirmation and disconfirmation of a belief presuppose such a system and are internal to the system. For all this he was not advocating a relativism, but a *naturalism* that assumes that the world ultimately determines which language games can be played.

Wittgenstein's final notes vividly illustrate the continuity of his basic concerns throughout all the changes his thinking went through. For they reveal once more how he remained skeptical about all philosophical theories and how he understood his own undertaking as the attempt to undermine the need for any such theorizing. The considerations of *On Certainty* are evidently directed against both philosophical skeptics and those philosophers who want to refute skepticism. Against the philosophical skeptics Wittgenstein insisted that there is real knowledge, but this knowledge is always dispersed and not necessarily reliable; it consists of things we have heard and read, of what has been drilled into us, and of our modifications of this inheritance. We have no general reason to doubt this inherited body of knowledge, we do not generally doubt it, and we are, in fact, not in a position to do so. But *On Certainty* also argues that it is impossible to refute skepticism by pointing to propositions that are absolutely certain, as Descartes did when he declared 'I think, therefore I am' indubitable, or as Moore did when he said, "I know for certain that this is a hand here." The fact that such propositions are considered certain, Wittgenstein argued, indicates only that they play an indispensable, normative role in our language game; they are the riverbed through which the thought of our language game flows. Such propositions cannot be taken to express metaphysical truths. Here, too, the conclusion is that all philosophical argumentation must come to an end, but that the end of such argumentation is not an absolute, self-evident truth, but a certain kind of natural human practice.

See also FREGE, MEANING, ORDINARY LANGUAGE PHILOSOPHY, PRIVATE LANGUAGE ARGUMENT, RUSSELL, VIENNA CIRCLE.   H.S.

Wodeham, Adam de (c. 1295–1358), English Franciscan philosopher-theologian who lectured on Peter Lombard's *Sentences* at London, Norwich, and Oxford. His published works include the *Tractatus de indivisibilibus*; his *Lectura secunda* (Norwich lectures); and an abbreviation of his Oxford lectures by Henry Totting of Oyta, published by John Major in 1512. Wodeham's main work, the Oxford lectures, themselves remain unpublished.

A brilliant interpreter of Duns Scotus, whose original manuscripts he consulted, Wodeham deemed Duns Scotus the greatest Franciscan doctor. William Ockham, Wodeham's teacher, was the other great influence on Wodeham's philosophical theology. Wodeham defended Ockham's views against attacks mounted by Walter Chatton; he also wrote the prologue to Ockham's *Summa logicae*. Wodeham's own influence rivaled that of Ockham. Among the authors he strongly influenced are Gregory of Rimini, John of Mirecourt, Nicholas of Autrecourt, Pierre d'Ailly, Peter Ceffons, Alfonso Vargas, Peter of Candia (Alexander V), Henry Totting of Oyta, and John Major.

Wodeham's theological works were written for an audience with a very sophisticated understanding of current issues in semantics, logic, and medieval mathematical physics. Contrary to Duns Scotus and Ockham, Wodeham argued that the sensitive and intellective souls were not distinct. He further develops the theory of intuitive cognition, distinguishing intellectual intu-

ition of our own acts of intellect, will, and memory from sensory intuition of external objects. Scientific knowledge based on experience can be based on intuition, according to Wodeham. He distinguishes different grades of evidence, and allows that sensory perceptions may be mistaken. Nonetheless, they can form the basis for scientific knowledge, since they are reliable; mistakes can be corrected by reason and experience. In semantic theory, Wodeham defends the view that the immediate object of scientific knowledge is the *complexe significabile,* that which the conclusion is designed to signify.

See also DUNS SCOTUS, OCKHAM, PETER LOMBARD.   R.W.

Wolff, Christian (1679–1754), German philosopher and the most powerful advocate for secular rationalism in early eighteenth-century Germany. Although he was a Lutheran, his early education in Catholic Breslau made him familiar with both the Scholasticism of Aquinas and Suárez and more modern sources. His later studies at Leipzig were completed with a dissertation on the application of mathematical methods to ethics (1703), which brought him to the attention of Leibniz. He remained in correspondence with Leibniz until the latter's death (1716), and became known as the popularizer of Leibniz's philosophy, although his views did not derive from that source alone. Appointed to teach mathematics in Halle in 1706 (he published mathematical textbooks and compendia that dominated German universities for decades), Wolff began lecturing on philosophy as well by 1709. His rectoral address *On the Practical Philosophy of the Chinese* (1721) argued that revelation and even belief in God were unnecessary for arriving at sound principles of moral and political reasoning; this brought his uneasy relations with the Halle Pietists to a head, and in 1723 they secured his dismissal and indeed banishment. Wolff was immediately welcomed in Marburg, where he became a hero for freedom of thought, and did not return to Prussia until the ascension of Frederick the Great in 1740, when he resumed his post at Halle.

Wolff published an immense series of texts on logic, metaphysics, ethics, politics, natural theology, and teleology (1713–24), in which he created the philosophical terminology of modern German; he then published an even more extensive series of works in Latin for the rest of his life, expanding and modifying his German works but also adding works on natural and positive law and economics (1723–55). He accepted the traditional division of logic into the doctrines of concepts, judgment, and inference, which influenced the organization of Kant's *Critique of Pure Reason* (1781–87) and even Hegel's *Science of Logic* (1816). In metaphysics, he included general ontology and then the special disciplines of rational cosmology, rational psychology, and rational theology (Kant replaced Wolff's general ontology with his transcendental aesthetic and analytic, and then demolished Wolff's special metaphysics in his transcendental dialectic).

Wolff's metaphysics drew heavily on Leibniz, but also on Descartes and even empiricists like Locke. Methodologically, he attempted to derive the principle of sufficient reason from the logical law of identity (like the unpublished Leibniz of the 1680s rather than the published Leibniz of the 1700s); substantively, he began his German metaphysics with a reconstruction of Descartes's *cogito* argument, then argued for a simple, immaterial soul, all of its faculties reducible to forms of representation and related to body by preestablished harmony. Although rejected by Crusius and then Kant, Wolff's attempt to found philosophy on a single principle continued to influence German idealism as late as Reinhold, Fichte, and Hegel, and his example of beginning metaphysics from the unique representative power of the soul continued to influence not only later writers such as Reinhold and Fichte but also Kant's own conception of the transcendental unity of apperception.

In spite of the academic influence of his metaphysics, Wolff's importance for German culture lay in his rationalist rather than theological ethics. He argued that moral worth lies in the perfection of the objective essence of mankind; as the essence of a human is to be an intellect and a will (with the latter dependent on the former), which are physically embodied and dependent for their well-being on the well-being of their physical body, morality requires perfection of the intellect and will, physical body, and external conditions for the well-being of that combination. Each person is obliged to perfect all instantiations of this essence, but in practice does so most effectively in his own case; duties to oneself therefore precede duties to others and to God. Because pleasure is the sensible sign of perfection, Wolff's perfectionism resembles contemporary utilitarianism. Since he held that human perfection can be understood by human reason independently of any revelation, Wolff joined contemporary British enlighteners such as Shaftesbury and Hutcheson in arguing that morality does not depend on divine commands,

indeed the recognition of divine commands depends on an antecedent comprehension of morality (although morality does require respect for God, and thus the atheistic morality of the Chinese, even though sound as far as it went, was not complete). This was the doctrine that put Wolff's life in danger, but it had tremendous repercussions for the remainder of his century, and certainly in Kant.

See also KANT, LEIBNIZ.   P.Gu.

Wollaston, William (1659–1724), English moralist notorious for arguing that the immorality of actions lies in their implying false propositions. An assistant headmaster who later took priestly orders, Wollaston maintains in his one published work, *The Religion of Nature Delineated* (1722), that the foundations of religion and morality are mutually dependent. God has preestablished a harmony between reason (or truth) and happiness, so that actions that contradict truth through misrepresentation thereby frustrate human happiness and are thus evil. For instance, if a person steals another's watch, her falsely representing the watch as her own makes the act wrong. Wollaston's views, particularly his taking morality to consist in universal and necessary truths, were influenced by the rationalists Ralph Cudworth and Clarke. Among his many critics the most famous was Hume, who contends that Wollaston's theory implies an absurdity: any action concealed from public view (e.g., adultery) conveys no false proposition and therefore is not immoral.   E.S.R.

Wollstonecraft, Mary (1759–97), English author and feminist whose *A Vindication of the Rights of Women* (1792) is a central text of feminist philosophy. Her chief target is Rousseau: her goal is to argue against the separate and different education Rousseau provided for girls and to extend his recommendations to girls as well as boys. Wollstonecraft saw such an improved education for women as necessary to their asserting their right as "human creatures" to develop their faculties in a way conducive to human virtue. She also wrote *A Vindication of the Rights of Men* (1790), an attack on Edmund Burke's pamphlet on the French Revolution, as well as novels, essays, an account of her travels, and books for children. **See also FEMINIST PHILOSOPHY.**

                                                           M.At.

woof. See WELL-FORMED FORMULA.

works, justification by. See JUSTIFICATION BY FAITH.

worldline. See SPACE-TIME.

worldview. See DILTHEY.

Wright, Chauncey (1830–75), American philosopher and mathematician. He graduated from Harvard in 1852 and until 1872 was employed by the periodical *American Ephemeris*. His philosophical discussions were stimulating and attracted many, including Peirce, James, and Oliver Wendell Holmes, Jr., who thought of him as their "intellectual boxing master." Wright eventually accepted British empiricism, especially that of J. S. Mill, though under Darwinian influence he modified Mill's view considerably by rejecting the empiricist claim that general propositions merely summarize particulars. Wright claimed instead that scientific theories are hypotheses to be further developed, and insisted that moral rules are irreducible and need no utilitarian "proof." Though he denied the "summary" view of universals, he was not strictly a pragmatist, since for him a low-level empirical proposition like Peirce's 'this diamond is hard' is not a hypothesis but a self-contained irreducible statement. **See also PEIRCE, PRAGMATISM.**

E.H.M.

Wright, G. H. von. See VON WRIGHT.

wu. See YU, WU.

wu-hsing, Chinese term meaning 'five phases, processes, or elements'. The five phases – earth, wood, metal, fire, and water – along with yin and yang, were the basis of Chinese correlative cosmologies developed in the Warring States period (403–221 B.C.) and early Han dynasty (206 B.C.–A.D. 220). These cosmologies posited a relation between the human world and the natural order. Thus the five phases were correlated to patterns in human history such as the cyclical rise and fall of dynasties, to sociopolitical order and the monthly rituals of rulers, to musical notes and tastes, even to organs of the body. Whereas the goal of early cosmologists such as Tsou Yen was to bring the human order into harmony with the natural order via the five phases, Han dynasty cosmologists and immortality seekers sought to control nature and prolong life by manipulating the five phases, particularly within the body.

R.P.P. & R.T.A.

Wundt, Wilhelm Maximilien (1832–1920), German philosopher and psychologist, a founder of scientific psychology. Although trained as a physician, he turned to philosophy and in 1879, at the University of Leipzig, established the first recognized psychology laboratory. For Wundt, psychology was the science of conscious experience, a definition soon overtaken by behaviorism. Wundt's psychology had two departments: the so-called physiological psychology (*Grundzuge der physiologischen Psychologie,* 3 vols., 1873–74; only vol. 1 of the fifth edition, 1910, was translated into English), primarily the experimental study of immediate experience broadly modeled on Fechner's psychophysics; and the *Volkerpsychologie* (*Volkerpsychologie,* 10 vols., 1900–20; fragment translated as *The Language of Gestures,* 1973), the non-experimental study of the higher mental processes via their products, language, myth, and custom. Although Wundt was a prodigious investigator and author, and was revered as psychology's founder, his theories, unlike his methods, exerted little influence. A typical German scholar of his time, he also wrote across the whole of philosophy, including logic and ethics.

T.H.L.

wu wei, Chinese philosophical term often translated as 'non-action' and associated with Taoism. It is actually used in both Taoist and non-Taoist texts to describe an ideal state of existence or ideal form of government, interpreted differently in different texts. In the *Chuang Tzu,* it describes a state of existence in which one is not guided by preconceived goals or projects, including moral ideals; in the *Lao Tzu,* it refers to the absence of striving toward worldly goals, and also describes the ideal form of government, which does not teach or impose on the people standards of behavior, including those of conventional morality. In other texts, it is sometimes used to describe the effortlessness of moral action, and sometimes used to refer to the absence of any need for active participation in government by the ruler, resulting either from the appointment of worthy and able officials inspired by the moral example of the ruler, or from the establishment of an effective machinery of government presided over by a ruler with prestige. **See also TAOISM.** K.-l.S.

Wyclif, John (c.1330–84), English theologian and religious reformer. He worked for most of his life in Oxford as a secular clerk, teaching philosophy and later theology and writing extensively in both fields. The mode of thought expressed in his surviving works is one of extreme realism, and in this his thought fostered the split of Bohemian, later Hussite, philosophy from that of the German masters teaching in Prague. His philosophical summa was most influential for his teaching on universals, but also dealt extensively with the question of determinism; these issues underlay his later handling of the questions of the Eucharist and of the identity of the church respectively. His influence on English philosophy was severely curtailed by the growing hostility of the church to his ideas, the condemnation of many of his tenets, the persecution of his followers, and the destruction of his writings.

A.Hu.

X

Xenocrates. See ACADEMY.

Xenophanes (c.570–c.475 B.C.), Greek philosopher, a proponent of an idealized conception of the divine, and the first of the pre-Socratics to propound epistemological views. Born in Colophon, an Ionian Greek city on the coast of Asia Minor, he emigrated as a young man to the Greek West (Sicily and southern Italy). The formative influence of the Milesians is evident in his rationalism. He is the first of the pre-Socratics for whom we have not only ancient reports but also quite a few verbatim quotations – fragments from his "Lampoons" (*Silloi*) and from other didactic poetry.

Xenophanes attacks the worldview of Homer, Hesiod, and traditional Greek piety: it is an outrage that the poets attribute moral failings to the gods. Traditional religion reflects regional biases (blond gods for the Northerners; black gods for the Africans). Indeed, anthropomorphic gods reflect the ultimate bias, that of the human viewpoint ("If cattle, or horses, or lions . . . could draw pictures of the gods . . . ," frg. 15). There is a single "greatest" god, who is not at all like a human being, either in body or in mind; he perceives without the aid of organs, he effects changes without "moving," through the sheer power of his thought. The rainbow is no sign from Zeus; it is simply a special cloud formation. Nor are the sun or the moon gods. All phenomena in the skies, from the elusive "Twin Sons of Zeus" (St. Elmo's fire) to sun, moon, and stars, are varieties of cloud formation. There are no mysterious infernal regions; the familiar strata of earth stretch down ad infinitum. The only cosmic limit is the one visible at our feet: the horizontal border between earth and air. Remarkably, Xenophanes tempers his theological and cosmological pronouncements with an epistemological caveat: what he offers is only a "conjecture."

In later antiquity Xenophanes came to be regarded as the founder of the Eleatic School, and his teachings were assimilated to those of Parmenides and Melissus. This appears to be based on nothing more than Xenophanes' emphasis on the oneness and utter immobility of God.

See also ELEATIC SCHOOL, PRE-SOCRATICS.

A.P.D.M.

Xenophon (c.430–c.350 B.C.), Greek soldier and historian, author of several Socratic dialogues, along with important works on history, education, political theory, and other topics. He was interested in philosophy, and he was a penetrating and intelligent "social thinker" whose views on morality and society have been influential over many centuries. His perspective on Socrates' character and moral significance provides a valuable supplement and corrective to the better-known views of Plato.

Xenophon's Socratic dialogues, the only ones besides Plato's to survive intact, help us obtain a broader picture of the Socratic dialogue as a literary genre. They also provide precious evidence concerning the thoughts and personalities of other followers of Socrates, such as Antisthenes and Alcibiades. Xenophon's longest and richest Socratic work is the *Memorabilia,* or "Memoirs of Socrates," which stresses Socrates' self-sufficiency and his beneficial effect on his companions. Xenophon's *Apology of Socrates* and his *Symposium* were probably intended as responses to Plato's *Apology* and *Symposium.* Xenophon's Socratic dialogue on estate management, the *Oeconomicus,* is valuable for its underlying social theory and its evidence concerning the role and status of women in classical Athens.

See also SOCRATES.

D.R.M.

Y

yang. See YIN, YANG.

Yang Chu, also called Yang Tzu (c.370–319 B.C.), Chinese philosopher most famous for the assertion, attributed to him by Mencius, that one ought not sacrifice even a single hair to save the whole world. Widely criticized as a selfish egotist and hedonist, Yang Chu was a private person who valued bodily integrity, health, and longevity over fame, fortune, and power. He believed that because one's body and lifespan were bestowed by Heaven (*t'ien*), one has a duty (and natural inclination) to maintain bodily health and live out one's years. Far from sanctioning hedonistic indulgence, this Heaven-imposed duty requires discipline.   R.P.P. & R.T.A.

Yang Hsiung (53 B.C.–A.D. 18), Chinese philosopher who wrote two books: *Tai-hsüan ching* ("Classic of the Supremely Profound Principle"), an imitation of the *I-Ching,* and *Fa-yen* ("Model Sayings"), an imitation of the *Analects.* The former was ignored by his contemporaries, but the latter was quite popular in his time. His thoughts were eclectic. He was the first in the history of Chinese thought to advance the doctrine of human nature as a mixture of good and evil in order to avoid the extremes of Mencius and Hsün Tzu. **See also** HSÜN TZU, MENCIUS.   S.-h.L.

Yen Yuan (1635–1704), Chinese traditionalist and social critic. Like Wang Fu-chih, he attacked Neo-Confucian metaphysical dualism, regarding the Neo-Confucians' views as wild speculations obscuring the true nature of Confucianism. Chu Hsi interpreted *ko wu* (investigating things) as discovering some transcendent "thing" called *li* (pattern), and Wang Yang-ming understood *ko wu* as rectifying one's thoughts, but Yen argued it meant a kind of knowledge by acquaintance: the "hands-on" practice of traditional rituals and disciplines. As "proof" that Sung–Ming Confucians were wrong, Yen pointed to their social and political failures. Like many, he believed Confucianism was not only true but efficacious as well; failure to reform the world could be understood only as a personal failure to grasp and implement

the Way. **See also** CONFUCIANISM, WANG FU-CHIH.   P.J.I.

yi, Chinese term probably with an earlier meaning of 'sense of honor', subsequently used to refer to the fitting or right way of conducting oneself (when so used, it is often translated as 'rightness' or 'duty'), as well as to a commitment to doing what is fitting or right (when so used, it is often translated as 'righteousness' or 'dutifulness'). For Mohists, *yi* is determined by what benefits (*li*) the public, where benefit is understood in terms of such things as order and increased resources in society. For Confucians, while *yi* behavior is often behavior in accordance with traditional norms, it may also call for departure from such norms. *Yi* is determined not by specific rules of conduct, but by the proper weighing (*chüan*) of relevant considerations in a given context of action. *Yi* in the sense of a firm commitment to doing what is fitting or right, even in adverse circumstances, is an important component of the Confucian ethical ideal. **See also** CONFUCIANISM, MO TZU.   K.-l.S.

Yi Ching. See I-CHING.

yin, yang, metaphors used in the classical tradition of Chinese philosophy to express contrast and difference. Originally they designated the shady side and the sunny side of a hill, and gradually came to suggest the way in which one thing "overshadows" another in some particular aspect of their relationship. Yin and yang are not "principles" or "essences" that help classify things; rather, they are ad hoc explanatory categories that report on relationships and interactions among immediate concrete things of the world. Yin and yang always describe the relationships that are constitutive of unique particulars, and provide a vocabulary for "reading" the distinctions that obtain among them. The complementary nature of the opposition captured in this pairing expresses the mutuality, interdependence, diversity, and creative efficacy of the dynamic *relationships* that are deemed immanent in and valorize the world. The full range of difference in the world is deemed explicable

through this pairing. **See also** CHINESE PHILOS-
OPHY.   R.P.P. & R.T.A.

Yoga. See SANKHYA-YOGA.

Yogācārā Buddhism. See BUDDHISM.

Young Hegelians. See HEGEL.

yü, Chinese term meaning 'desire'. One can feel
yü toward sex objects or food, but one can also
yü to be a more virtuous person. *Yü* is paired con-
trastively with *wu* (aversion), which has a similarly broad range of objects. After the introduction of Buddhism into China, some
thinkers contended that the absence of *yü* and *wu*
was the goal of self-cultivation. Generally, however, the presence of at least some *yü* and *wu* has
been thought to be essential to moral perfection.
                                                      B.W.V.N.

yu, wu, Chinese terms literally meaning 'having'
and 'nothing', respectively; they are often rendered into English as 'being' and 'non-being'.
But the Chinese never developed the mutually
contradictory concepts of Being and Non-Being
in Parmenides' sense. In chapter 2 of *Tao Te Ching,*
Lao Tzu says that "being (*yu*) and non-being (*wu*)
produce each other." They appear to be a pair of
interdependent concepts. But in chapter 40 Lao
Tzu also says that "being comes from non-being."
It seems that for Taoism non-being is more fundamental than being, while for Confucianism
the opposite is true. The two traditions were seen
to be complementary by later scholars. **See also**
CHINESE PHILOSOPHY, CONFUCIANISM, LAO
TZU, PARMENIDES, TAOISM.   S.-h.L.

yung, Chinese term usually translated as
'courage' or 'bravery'. Different forms of *yung* are
described in Chinese philosophical texts, such as
a readiness to avenge an insult or to compete
with others, or an absence of fear. Confucians
advocate an ideal form of *yung* guided by rightness (*yi*). A person with *yung* of the ideal kind is
fully committed to rightness, and will abide by
rightness even at the risk of death. Also, realizing upon self-examination that there is no fault
in oneself, the person will be without fear or
uncertainty.   K.-l.S.

Z

Z. See SET THEORY.

Zabarella, Jacopo (1532–89), Italian Aristotelian philosopher who taught at the University of Padua. He wrote extensive commentaries on Aristotle's *Physics* and *On the Soul* and also discussed other interpreters such as Averroes. However, his most original contribution was his work in logic, *Opera logica* (1578). Zabarella regards logic as a preliminary study that provides the tools necessary for philosophical analysis. Two such tools are order and method: order teaches us how to organize the content of a discipline to apprehend it more easily; method teaches us how to draw syllogistic inferences. Zabarella reduces the varieties of orders and methods classified by other interpreters to compositive and resolutive orders and methods. The compositive order from first principles to their consequences applies to theoretical disciplines. The resolutive order from a desired end to means appropriate to its achievement applies to practical disciplines. This much was already in Aristotle. Zabarella offers an original analysis of method. The compositive method infers particular consequences from general principles. The resolutive method infers originating principles from particular consequences, as in inductive reasoning or in reasoning from effect to cause. It has been suggested that Zabarella's terminology might have influenced Galileo's mechanics.   P.Gar.

Zarathustra. See NIETZSCHE, ZOROASTRIANISM.

ZC. See SET THEORY.

Zeigarnik effect, the selective recall of uncompleted tasks in comparison to completed tasks. The effect was named for Bluma Zeigarnik, a student of K. Lewin, who discovered it and described it in a paper published in the *Psychologische Forschung* in 1927. Subjects received an array of short tasks, such as counting backward and stringing beads, for rapid completion. Performance on half of these was interrupted. Subsequent recall for the tasks favored the interrupted tasks. Zeigarnik concluded that recall is influenced by motivation and not merely associational strength.

The effect was thought relevant to Freud's claim that unfulfilled wishes are persistent. Lewin attempted to derive the effect from field theory, suggesting that an attempt to reach a goal creates a tension released only when that goal is reached; interruption of the attempt produces a tension favoring recall. Conditions affecting the Zeigarnik effect are incompletely understood, as is its significance.   R.C.R.

Zen. See BUDDHISM.

Zeno of Citium. See STOICISM.

Zeno of Elea. See PRE-SOCRATICS.

Zeno's paradoxes, four paradoxes relating to space and motion attributed to Zeno of Elea (fifth century B.C.): the racetrack, Achilles and the tortoise, the stadium, and the arrow. Zeno's work is known to us through secondary sources, in particular Aristotle.

The racetrack paradox. If a runner is to reach the end of the track, he must first complete an infinite number of different journeys: getting to the midpoint, then to the point midway between the midpoint and the end, then to the point midway between this one and the end, and so on. But it is logically impossible for someone to complete an infinite series of journeys. Therefore the runner cannot reach the end of the track. Since it is irrelevant to the argument how far the end of the track is – it could be a foot or an inch or a micron away – this argument, if sound, shows that all motion is impossible. Moving to any point will involve an infinite number of journeys, and an infinite number of journeys cannot be completed.

The paradox of Achilles and the tortoise. Achilles can run much faster than the tortoise, so when a race is arranged between them the tortoise is given a lead. Zeno argued that Achilles can never catch up with the tortoise no matter how fast he runs and no matter how long the race goes on. For the first thing Achilles has to do is to get to the place from which the tortoise started. But the tortoise, though slow, is unflag-

987

ging: while Achilles was occupied in making up his handicap, the tortoise has advanced a little farther. So the next thing Achilles has to do is to get to the new place the tortoise occupies. While he is doing this, the tortoise will have gone a little farther still. However small the gap that remains, it will take Achilles some time to cross it, and in that time the tortoise will have created another gap. So however fast Achilles runs, all that the tortoise has to do, in order not to be beaten, is not to stop.

The stadium paradox. Imagine three equal cubes, A, B, and C, with sides all of length l, arranged in a line stretching away from one. A is moved perpendicularly out of line to the right by a distance equal to l. At the same time, and at the same rate, C is moved perpendicularly out of line to the left by a distance equal to l. The time it takes A to travel $l/2$ (relative to B) equals the time it takes A to travel to l (relative to C). So, in Aristotle's words, "it follows, he [Zeno] thinks, that half the time equals its double" (*Physics* 259b35).

The arrow paradox. At any instant of time, the flying arrow "occupies a space equal to itself." That is, the arrow at an instant cannot be moving, for motion takes a period of time, and a temporal instant is conceived as a point, not itself having duration. It follows that the arrow is at rest at every instant, and so does not move. What goes for arrows goes for everything: nothing moves.

Scholars disagree about what Zeno himself took his paradoxes to show. There is no evidence that he offered any "solutions" to them. One view is that they were part of a program to establish that multiplicity is an illusion, and that reality is a seamless whole. The argument could be reconstructed like this: if you allow that reality can be successively divided into parts, you find yourself with these insupportable paradoxes; so you must think of reality as a single indivisible One.

See also PARADOX, PRE-SOCRATICS, TIME.
R.M.S.

Zeno the Stoic. See STOICISM.

Zermelo. See QUINE, SET THEORY.

zero-sum game. See GAME THEORY.

ZF. See SET THEORY.

ZFC. See INDEPENDENCE RESULTS.

Zohar. See CABALA.

Zorn's lemma. See SET THEORY.

Zoroaster. See ZOROASTRIANISM.

Zoroastrianism, the national religion of ancient Iran. Zoroastrianism suffered a steep decline after the seventh century A.D. because of conversion to Islam. Of a remnant of roughly 100,000 adherents today, three-fourths are Parsis ("Persians") in or from western India; the others are Iranian Zoroastrians. The tradition is identified with its prophet; his name in Persian, Zarathushtra, is preserved in German, but the ancient Greek rendering of that name, Zoroaster, is the form used in most other modern European languages.

Zoroaster's hymns to Ahura Mazda ("the Wise Lord"), called the Gathas, are interspersed among ritual hymns to other divine powers in the collection known as the Avesta. In them, Zoroaster seeks reassurance that good will ultimately triumph over evil and that Ahura Mazda will be a protector to him in his prophetic mission. The Gathas expect that humans, by aligning themselves with the force of righteousness and against evil, will receive bliss and benefit in the next existence.

The dating of the texts and of the prophet himself is an elusive matter for scholars, but it is clear that Zoroaster lived somewhere in Iran sometime prior to the emergence of the Achaemenid empire in the sixth century B.C. His own faith in Ahura Mazda, reflected in the Gathas, came to be integrated with other strains of old Indo-Iranian religion. We see these in the Avesta's hymns and the religion's ritual practices. They venerate an array of Iranian divine powers that resemble in function the deities found in the Vedas of India. A common Indo-Iranian heritage is indicated conclusively by similarities of language and of content between the Avesta and the Vedas. Classical Zoroastrian orthodoxy does not replace the Indo-Iranian divinities with Ahura Mazda, but instead incorporates them into its thinking more or less as Ahura Mazda's agents.

The Achaemenid kings from the sixth through the fourth centuries B.C. mention Ahura Mazda in their inscriptions, but not Zoroaster. The Parthians, from the third century B.C. to the third century A.D., highlighted Mithra among the Indo-Iranian pantheon. But it was under the

Sasanians, who ruled Iran from the third to the seventh centuries, that Zoroastrianism became the established religion.

A salient doctrine is the teaching concerning the struggle between good and evil. The time frame from the world's creation to the final resolution or judgment finds the Wise Lord, Ahura Mazda (or Ohrmazd, in the Pahlavi language of Sasanian times), locked in a struggle with the evil spirit, Angra Mainyu (in Pahlavi, Ahriman). The teaching expands on an implication in the text of the Gathas, particularly Yasna 30, that the good and evil spirits, coming together in the beginning and establishing the living and inanimate realms, determined that at the end benefit would accrue to the righteous but not the wicked.

In Sasanian times, there was speculative concern to assert Ahura Mazda's infinity, omnipotence, and omniscience, qualities that may indicate an impact of Mediterranean philosophy. For example, the *Bundahishn*, a Pahlavi cosmological and eschatological narrative, portrays Ahura Mazda as infinite in all four compass directions but the evil spirit as limited in one and therefore doomed to ultimate defeat.

Such doctrine has been termed by some *dualistic*, in that it has (at least in Sasanian times) seen the power of God rivaled by that of an evil spirit. Zoroastrians today assert that they are monotheists, and do not worship the evil spirit. But to the extent that the characterization may hold historically, Zoroastrianism has manifested an "ethical" dualism, of good and evil forces. Although capable of ritual pollution through waste products and decay, the physical world, God's creation, remains potentially morally good. Contrast "ontological" dualism, as in gnostic and Manichaean teaching, where the physical world itself is the result of the fall or entrapment of spirit in matter.

In the nineteenth century, Zoroastrian texts newly accessible to Europe produced an awareness of the prophet's concern for ethical matters. Nietzsche's values in his work *Thus Spake Zarathustra*, however, are his own, not those of the ancient prophet. The title is arresting, but the connection of Nietzsche with historical Zoroastrianism is a connection in theme only, in that the work advances ideas about good and evil in an oracular style.   W.G.O.

Zweckrationalität. See WEBER.

APPENDIX OF SPECIAL SYMBOLS AND LOGICAL NOTATION

The following are the most common uses, though others are encountered. Some of these symbols might also appear in different fonts (e.g., 'P', 'P', or '**P**' for 'P').

$$
\left.
\begin{array}{l}
- \\
\sim \\
\neg \\
N \\
\& \\
\wedge \\
\cdot \\
K \\
\vee \\
\underline{\vee} \\
\dot{\vee} \\
\dagger \\
A \\
\supset \\
\rightarrow \\
\Rightarrow \\
C \\
\equiv \\
\leftrightarrow \\
\Leftrightarrow \\
E \\
\forall \\
\Pi \\
\exists \\
\Sigma \\
M \\
\Diamond \\
L \\
\Box \\
\dashv
\end{array}
\right\}
$$

For these and other logical symbols, **see** LOGICAL NOTATION.

$\mid$ **See** SHEFFER STROKE.

$$
\left.
\begin{array}{l}
\& \\
\wedge \\
\bigwedge
\end{array}
\right\}
$$
Used to express conjunction of a (possibly infinite) set of formulas.

$$
\left.
\begin{array}{l}
\vee \\
\bigvee
\end{array}
\right\}
$$
Used to express the disjunction of a (possibly infinite) set of formulas.

⊤   (1) Shorthand for an arbitrarily chosen tautology. (2) A logical constant (the *verum*) that takes the truth-value *true* under every valuation. (3) Name of the truth-value *true*.

⊥   (1) Shorthand for an arbitrarily chosen contradiction. (2) A logical constant (the *falsum*) that takes the truth-value *false* under every valuation. (3) Name of the truth-value *false*.

$$
\left.
\begin{array}{l}
E! \\
\exists !
\end{array}
\right\}
$$
Shorthand for 'there exists a unique' (pronounced 'E shriek', with '!' known as the *shriek operator*).

$$
\left.
\begin{array}{l}
P \\
F
\end{array}
\right\}
$$
See TENSE LOGIC.

G   Shorthand for 'it always will be that'.

H   Shorthand for 'it always was that'.

K_a **See** EPISTEMIC LOGIC, KK-THESIS.

B_a Shorthand for '*a* believes that'.

$$
\left.
\begin{array}{l}
O \\
O(\ /\ )
\end{array}
\right\}
$$
See DEONTIC LOGIC.

P   Shorthand for 'it is permissible that' and frequently defined as '~O~'

P(/)   Frequently defined as '~O(~ /)' and expressing conditional permission.

$$
\left.
\begin{array}{l}
> \\
\Box\!\!\rightarrow
\end{array}
\right\}
$$
Used to express subjunctive conditionals, in some cases counterfactual or causal conditionals in particular.

A(*t*/*x*)   Name of the result of replacing all occurrences of variable *x* in formula *A* by the term *t*.

⌐   Name of an operator on open sentences (known as the *definite description operator* or *iota operator*) used to form definite descriptions. '$(\imath x)\phi x$' is thus read as 'the ϕ'. **See** THEORY OF DESCRIPTIONS.

^   Name of an operator on open sentences used to form names (known as *abstracts*) of sets or properties. '$\hat{x}\phi x$' names the set of all ϕs or the property of being a ϕ.

ϵ (1) Variant of '$\in$'. (2) Name of an operator on open sentences used to form *epsilon terms*. '$\epsilon x\phi x$' names a ϕ if there is one and some arbitrary individual if there is not.

λ **See** COMBINATORY LOGIC.

PC   **See** FORMAL LOGIC.

I, IC }   Names of the intuitionist propositional calculus. **See** INTUITIONISM.

S4, S5 }   **See** MODAL LOGIC.

MP, $\supset$E }   **See** MODUS PONENS.

MT   **See** MODUS TOLLENS.

&I, $\wedge$I }   **See** CONJUNCTION INTRODUCTION.

$\vee$I   **See** DISJUNCTION INTRODUCTION.

&E, $\wedge$E }   **See** CONJUNCTION ELIMINATION.

$\vee$E   **See** DISJUNCTION ELIMINATION.

DN   **See** DOUBLE NEGATION.

DS   Disjunctive syllogism. **See** SYLLOGISM.

CP, $\supset$I }   **See** CONDITIONAL PROOF.

RAA   **See** REDUCTIO AD ABSURDUM.

UG, $\forall$G }   Universal generalization.

EG, $\exists$G }   **See** EXISTENTIAL GENERALIZATION.

UI, $\forall$I }   **See** UNIVERSAL INSTANTIATION.

EI, $\exists$I }   **See** EXISTENTIAL INSTANTIATION.

PM   Abbreviation for *Principia Mathematica*, by Whitehead and Russell. **See** RUSSELL, TYPE THEORY.

$\vdash$ Name of the deducibility relation. '$\Gamma \vdash A$' is thus shorthand for 'A is deducible from the set Γ of formulas'. (2) Used to express theoremhood. '$\vdash A$' is thus shorthand for 'A is a theorem'. (3) Frege's assertion sign, used to indicate that a proposition is being judged to be true.

$\vdash_L$ Used to express theoremhood, or sometimes deducibility, in the logic L.

$\vdash_T$ Used to express truth (provability) in the theory T.

$\vDash$ **See** LOGICAL CONSEQUENCE.

$\| \ \|$ Used to form a name of the semantic value of a linguistic item. Thus, depending on the grammatical category of α, $\|\alpha\|$ might be an individual, a truth-value, an intension, a proposition, or a set of possible worlds.

$\in$, { }, $\subseteq$, $\cup$, $\cap$, $\emptyset$, < >, $\aleph_0$ }   **See** SET THEORY.

Λ, O }   Variants of '$\emptyset$'.

$\subset$ Used to express the fact that one set is a proper subset of another. Thus $X \subset Y$ if and only if $X \subseteq Y$ and $X \neq Y$.

$\mathcal{P}$ Used to form a name of the *power set* (set of all subsets) of a set.

$\cup$ Used to form a name of the union of a collection of sets. Thus $\cup_{i \in I} X_i$ is the set that contains a if and only if a is in X_i for some i in I.

$\cap$ Used to form a name of the intersection of a collection of sets. Thus $\cap_{i \in I} X_i$ is the set that contains a if and only if a is in X_i for all i in I.

ω **See** OMEGA, SET THEORY.

$\times$ Used to form a name of the *Cartesian product* of two sets. Thus $X \times Y$ is the set of all ordered pairs, the first entry of which comes from X and the second of which comes from Y. **See** SET THEORY.

D^n Name of the set of all ordered n-tuples of members of the set D.

$\sim$ Used to express sameness of size (or *cardinality*) of sets.

$\leq$ Used to express the fact that one set is smaller than or the same size as another set.

$<$ Used to express the fact that one set is smaller in size than another set.

$\left.\begin{array}{l} \text{ZF} \\ \text{ZFC} \end{array}\right\}$ **See** SET THEORY.

AC   Name of the *axiom of choice*, which says that for any set X of non-empty pairwise disjoint sets, there exists a set (a *choice set* for X) containing as members one and only one member of each member of X.

CH   **See** CONTINUUM PROBLEM.

GCH   Name of the *generalized continuum hypothesis*, which says that for every infinite set X there is no set intermediate in cardinality between X and the power set of X.

$\left.\begin{array}{l} \Sigma_1^0 \\ \Sigma_1 \end{array}\right\}$ Used to refer to sentences of arithmetic obtained by prefixing zero or more existential quantifiers to a formula built up from atomic formulas by means of truth-functional connectives and bounded universal quantifiers. **See** HIERARCHY.

$\left.\begin{array}{l} \Pi_1^0 \\ \Pi_1 \end{array}\right\}$ Used to refer to sentences of arithmetic obtained by prefixing zero or more universal quantifiers to a formula built up from atomic formulas by means of truth-functional connectives and bounded existential quantifiers. **See** HIERARCHY.

PA   Name of *Peano arithmetic*, the arithmetical theory based upon the Peano postulates. **See** PEANO POSTULATES.

$\mathcal{N}$ Name of the *intended model of arithmetic*, with the set of natural numbers as its domain and the symbols for zero, addition, multiplication, and successor assigned zero and the addition, multiplication, and successor functions, respectively. **See** MODEL THEORY.

$\left.\begin{array}{l} T_n \\ M_n \end{array}\right\}$ Names of the nth Turing machine in a given enumeration of all such machines.

CT   **See** CHURCH'S THESIS.

$\left.\begin{array}{l} Pr \\ Pr(\mid) \end{array}\right\}$ **See** PROBABILITY.

$\ulcorner \urcorner$ **See** CORNERS.

$\therefore$ Shorthand for 'therefore'.

@   Name of the actual world. (Pronounced 'A round', as in "A round here" – D. Lewis.)

G.F.S.

INDEX OF SELECTED NAMES

Most thinkers cited in the Dictionary are themselves the subjects of entries. The following is a list of selected names cited by contributors but not separately entered.